BLOOD, SWEAT AND VALOUR

BLOOD, SWEAT AND VALOUR

41 SQUADRON RAF 1942-1945

STEVE BREW

FONTHILL

Fonthill Media Limited
Fonthill Media LLC
www.fonthillmedia.com
office@fonthillmedia.com

First published in the United Kingdom 2012

British Library Cataloguing in Publication Data:
A catalogue record for this book is available from the British Library

Copyright © Steve Brew 2012

ISBN 978-1-78155-193-6

The right of Steve Brew to be identified as the author of this work has been asserted by him in accordance with the Copyright, Designs and Patents Act 1988.

All rights reserved. No part of this publication may be reproduced, stored in a retrieval system or transmitted in any form or by any means, electronic, mechanical, photocopying, recording or otherwise, without prior permission in writing from Fonthill Media Limited

Typeset in Adobe Garamond Pro 10/12

Printed and bound in England

For Mum

You bore, nursed, and raised me;
you loved me unconditionally.
You gave me a happy home to grow up in,
have only ever wanted the best for me,
and have always been there for me.
Words are barely sufficient to express
my appreciation and love for you.
Thank you.

Jacket Illustrations

FRONT COVER

On 12 April 1944, RAF photographer B. J. Daventry took a series of photographs of 41 Squadron's Spitfire XIIs, and in particular MB882, EB-B, the personal mount of OC A Flight, Flt Lt Don Smith RAAF. Some of these images appeared in the national newspapers soon afterwards, as news of the Spitfire XII was broken to the public – approximately 14 months after the Mark entered service. This image is one of the better known of that series. © By permission of The Imperial War Museum, IWM Image CH 12754

BACK COVER FROM TOP

Spitfire XII, MB801, EB-X, was flown by Flt Lt Arthur A. 'Pinkie' Glen on 24 September 1943 when he shot down two FW190s north of Beauvais, France, thereby earning a Bar to his DFC. © Gaëtan Marie

Flt Lt Terry Spencer was flying Spitfire XII, MB882, EB-B, on 3 September 1944, when he shot down 173-victory Luftwaffe Ace Hptm Emil 'Bully' Lang over Overhespen, Belgium. © Gaëtan Marie

Spitfire XIV, RM791, EB-V, was being flown by Sqn Ldr Doug Benham when he claimed two destroyed FW190Ds near Münster, Germany, on 23 January 1945. © Gaëtan Marie

Flt Lt Derek Rake claimed 41 Squadron's last victory of the War, a Junkers Ju188 in the Norderstapel-Husum area, in Spitfire XIV, NH915, EB-H, on 3 May 1945. © Gaëtan Marie

BACK FLAP FROM TOP

Author Steve Brew, right, with Gp Capt Rich Davies MA, Officer Commanding 41 Squadron 2009–2012, at RAF Coningsby. © UK MOD Crown Copyright (2010), licensed under the terms of the Open Government Licence (www.nationalarchives.gov.uk/doc/open-government-licence)

Fg Off Tom Slack was shot down 15 miles southwest of Abbeville in Spitfire XII, EN233, EB-G, on 18 July 1943. He evaded capture and returned to the United Kingdom on 24 August 1943, via Spain and Gibraltar. © Gaëtan Marie

Plt Off Peter Gibbs shot down 41 Squadron's first V1 flying bomb, north of Eastbourne, in Spitfire XII, MB875, EB-G, on 20 June 1944. © Gaëtan Marie

Plt Off Patrick Coleman was flying Spitfire XIV, SM823, EB-E, on 1 May 1945 when he destroyed three FW190s, one southwest of Plau and two over Lake Schwerin. © Gaëtan Marie

Sqn Ldr John Shepherd DFC shot down an Me110 towing an Me163 over Nordholz, Germany, destroying both, whilst flying Spitfire XIV, SM825, EB-B, on 14 April 1945. © Gaëtan Marie

Contents

Acknowledgements	8
Preface	10
Foreword	11
Introduction	12
1 Operation *Jubilee* 1 Aug 1942 – 22 Aug 1942	15
2 Llanbedr 23 Aug 1942 – 24 Feb 1943	40
3 Griffon Power 25 Feb 1943 – 20 Jun 1943	97
4 The Spitfire XII Wing 21 Jun 1943 – 29 Feb 1944	153
5 Preparing for *Overlord* 1 Mar 1944 – 19 Jun 1944	401
6 Repelling the V1 19 Jun 1944 – 27 Aug 1944	488
7 Big Ben, *Market Garden* & the Oil Campaign 28 Aug 1944 – 3 Dec 1944	546
8 Continental Operations 4 Dec 1944 – 7 Mar 1945	621
9 Crossing the Rhine 8 Mar 1945 – 15 Apr 1945	673
10 Victory in Their Sights 16 Apr 1945 – 31 May 1945	713
APPENDICES	
I The Pilots	776
II Officers Commanding	838
III Flight Commanders	839
IV Ground Staff	840
V Casualties, Accidents and Incidents	842
VI Roll of Honour	855
VII Prisoners of War	856
VIII Aerial Victories	857
IX Ground Victories	862
X Decorations	868
XI Aircraft in Service	869
XII Base Locations	870
XIII Extant Combat Films	871
XIV Index to TNA Combat Reports	875
REFERENCES AND INDICES	
Styles and Terminology	894
Glossary of Terms and Equivalent Ranks	895
Abbreviations	898
Further Reading	908
Notes to the Text	909
Bibliography	984

Acknowledgements

Histories such as this are impossible to produce without the assistance and support of many individuals and sources. I would therefore like to express my sincere thanks to the following people, many of them ex-41 Squadron pilots, for their generous help and kind permission to reproduce their personal accounts and papers, their logbooks, research and photographs.

These include: John C. Adams, Rich Allenby, Sarah Batchelor, Wg Cdr (Ret) Douglas I. Benham OBE DFC* AFC†, Alexandre Bonnet, Serge Bonge, Steve Bracey, Flt Sgt (Ret) John T. 'Jack' Bradshaw, Mike Brampton, Steve Brooking, Raymond Brown, Terry Brown, Terry Carter, Peter Celis, WO (Ret) John A. Chalmers†, Mike Chattin, Patricia Clanzy-Hodge, Arthur Cooper, Jeremy and Tim Cowell, Brian Cull, Sqn Ldr (Ret) Keith R. Curtis†, Cynrik de Decker, Régis Decobeck†, Richard Downing, David Duxbury, T. Ryle Dwyer, Peter East, John Engelsted, Philip Farfan, Tom Finucane, Doug Fishburn†, John Foreman, Sqn Ldr (Ret) F. A. O. 'Tony' Gaze OAM DFC** & Diana Gaze, Michael Gibbs, Lord Gisborough, Martin Gleeson, Ian and Mike Glen, Flt Lt (Ret) Peter B. Graham†, Lyndon Griffith, WO (Ret) Peter H. Hale, Hugh Halliday, Tom Harvey, Allan Hillman, Alan & Patricia Hodgson, Jan Horn, Andy Ingham, George Irvine, Phill Jones, Tony Kearns, Chris van Kerckhoven, Max Lambert, Joss Leclercq, Gareth Lewis, Henry Lewis, John and Kay Livingston, Dr P. Erwin van Loo, Maj (Ret) C. J. 'Jack' Malone CD, Errol Martyn, Sqn Ldr (Ret) Ian G. S. Matthew DFC†, Colin May, John McCormick, John McGill, Stein Meum, Wg Cdr (Ret) Rupert W. 'Lew' Munson and John Munson, Vic Murphy, Karen Neale, Andrew Pairman, David Park, Flt Lt (Ret) Hugh L. Parry & Dale Parry, Flt Lt (Ret) Jim C. J. 'Jimmy' Payne†, Rob Philips†, Kerry Porter, Gp Capt (Ret) Derek S. V. Rake OBE AFC*, Gideon Remez, James Schauer, Martin Sheppard, Christopher Shores, Grzegorz Sliżewski, Cara and Raina Spencer, Sqn Ldr (Ret) Terence 'Terry' Spencer DFC TEM†, Nan Spurr, Neil & Joyce Stevenson, Wg Cdr (Ret) William N. 'Bill' Stowe DFC†, Sqn Ldr Keith F. Thiele DSO DFC**, Jennie Tocock, Mike and Nick Underwood, Pavel Vančata, Laurent Viton, Flt Lt (Ret) Herbert A. 'Wag' Wagner† & Brooke Wagner, Flt Lt (Ret) Ken Warren† & Wendy Warren, Alan Wells, Henk Welting†, and Deb Whale, and my many fellow researchers on the RAF Commands Forum, who kindly answered my numerous queries.

A special thanks also to Dan Johnson, who kindly provided me access to his significant collection of letters and personal papers, and copies of logbooks, from pilots of the Spitfire XII era that have helped provide many of the personal comments on events, people and places that have been included in the text, and photographs that have helped illustrate this work.

Particular thanks also to Ray Brown, Terry Brown, Hugh Halliday, and Allan Hillman for proof-reading, correcting and trimming.

I would also like to expressly thank 41 (R) Squadron RAF, who have supported this History throughout and opened their archives to me in order that as accurate a record as possible could be documented. Thank you to the Officers Commanding whilst I was researching and writing, Wg Cdr (Ret) Dick MacCormac MA MRAeS (2004-2006), Air Cdre Gary Waterfall CBE (2006-2007), Gp Capt (Ret) Andy Myers MBE MA (2007-2009), and particularly Gp Capt Rich Davies MA (2009-2012), as well as Flt Sgt Chris Walster, who arranged permissions, access, transport and escorts on RAF Coningsby, provided advice on terminology and format, and assisted with proof-reading and editing.

Thank you especially to Jacqui for her love and encouragement, for her support of this project, for becoming involved and understanding my passion for 41 Squadron's history and the men who made it, and for helping make this work a reality.

Quotes from documents of 41 Squadron's archives and The National Archives (TNA) that have been reproduced in this work have been licensed under the terms of the Open Government Licence. See http://www.nationalarchives.gov.uk/doc/open-government-licence for further details.

The author has sought to establish and acknowledge the copyright holders of all photographs and material used in this work. Should you become aware of any material that you believe has not been correctly acknowledged, the author welcomes contact via the publisher, and all reasonable endeavours will be used to correct the error.

Preface

This work had its humble beginnings as research into my great uncle Bill Brew's service with 41 Squadron, which was his only operational posting during World War II. By natural progression this research covered the pilots serving with him on the Squadron at that time. In due course, my interest grew to encompass all of the Squadron's World War II pilots, and resulted in a website about them.

As I researched, I found that no definitive History of the Squadron existed. However, my subsequent discovery that detailed, unpublished, and previously inaccessible information from the World War II era lay within 41 Squadron's own archives became the catalyst for a growing belief that it was perhaps possible for me to produce a History of the unit encompassing this period. After several years work, and the support of many people – the Squadron itself, ex-pilots and ground crew, their families, and fellow researchers – my dream has been realised.

What has resulted is a day-to-day account of the unit's activity between the outbreak of War in September 1939 and the cessation of hostilities in May 1945. This particular volume covers the period 1 August 1942–31 May 1945.

My sources have been many, and include files from Britain's National Archives, RAF Museum and Imperial War Museum, archived collections in Australia, Belgium, Canada, New Zealand and the Netherlands, published English and German works and periodicals, and numerous unpublished and previously inaccessible documents, thereunder pilots' logbooks, diaries, letters, personal accounts and photographs, and, most significantly, 41 Squadron's own archive of original World War II material, much of it hand-written and most of it unavailable in British repositories.

I believe that the drawing together of all these files in one work, particularly those previously unpublished, ensures that this History is a thorough, true account of a Squadron that deserves greater recognition than has often been bestowed upon it in the past. Indeed, it is hoped this work should be sufficiently compelling for historians and authors to review their research insofar as 41 Squadron's role in particular campaigns is concerned.

I have consciously not retold the story of World War II or its origins, except to set the scene, as innumerable works already cover this subject. Nor indeed have I sought to cover all aspects of particular battles during the War, as these, too, are covered in depth by various works. Rather, I have recounted 41 Squadron's role within battles, operations, offensives and larger strategies, and detailed experiences of the pilots and ground crews participating in them. In fact, I have consciously included as much information on individuals as possible, regardless of the length of a man's tenure: it has been important to me throughout this project to give every man his place in history.

Lastly, I would like to share three things in particular that have struck me whilst researching 41 Squadron's role in World War II: (i) the human cost to the unit of the victory achieved in May 1945, (ii) the physical exertion and sheer hard work by every man on the Squadron, whether pilot or ground crew, and (iii) the raw courage shown by every one of them in the face of a determined adversary. It is from these three elements that I have drawn my choice of title.

I hope that *Blood, Sweat and Valour* will become a valuable and informative reference work, not only for aviation historians, but also for those wishing to trace a family member's service with this famous Squadron between August 1942 and May 1945.

Steve Brew
December 2012

Foreword

As an ex-Commanding Officer of No 41(F) Squadron, and a current serving senior Royal Air Force officer, I am pleased to be associated with the publication of the first History of No 41(F) Squadron that covers the War Years of August 1942 – May 1945.

To me, the feelings evoked by Steve Brew in his choice of title are a poignant reminder of our forbears' sacrifices, altruism and gallantry. The title certainly underscores the components of all the great traditions of the youngest of our three Services. It is indisputable that through their *Blood, Sweat and Valour,* the men of No 41(F) Squadron played a significant part in a period of history that the men and women of today's Royal Air Force can be immensely and justifiably proud.

As the generation of those who participated in World War II inevitably dwindles, Steve has clearly written a biographical account of No 41 Squadron with the express intention of giving many men their rightful place in history. He has beautifully captured living memories and has thus held for posterity numerous selfless and valiant acts that have already become the stuff of legend.

Having first served on No 41 Squadron as a young officer, I later returned to command the Squadron and to participate on active service in the air over the Balkans. In those years, and indeed since, I was constantly aware that No 41 Squadron enjoyed something very special indeed. There has always been a family spirit associated with No 41 Squadron; this was reflected not only in the quality and attitudes of the young men and women with whom I had the honour to serve but also in the reflected pride of their loved ones and all those former members and their families that I had the privilege to meet.

During No 41 Squadron's 95th anniversary celebrations in 2011, I had the pleasure of talking to a number of the Squadron's World War II pilots and ground personnel, as well as to the family members of Servicemen from the same era. Underscored on every occasion was that same feeling of pride and wider family sentiment.

Steve Brew has masterfully ensured that every possible member of No 41 Squadron during the period covered by his book has been properly remembered for his role and deeds. It seems to me that there can be no more fitting tribute to those who fought so hard to protect all the freedoms and liberties that we value and cherish today. This is a book to treasure and to enjoy; to read, to re-read and to dip into. I hope that you will appreciate it as much as I have.

Air Marshal Sir Christopher Harper KBE MA FCMI RAF
Officer Commanding No 41 (F) Squadron, October 1994 – January 1997

Introduction

A few brief months after its formation, 41 Squadron was deployed to France equipped with the F.E.8 pusher in October 1916, in the dying days of the First Battle of the Somme. Over the remaining 24 months of the Great War, the Squadron participated in the Battles of Arras, Messines, and Cambrai, the German 1918 Spring Offensive, and the Battle of Amiens.

By the time of its return to the United Kingdom in early 1919, the Squadron boasted a well-earned reputation with a respectable record of victories and accolades. The pilots were credited with destroying 111 aircraft and 14 balloons, sending down 112 aircraft out of control, and driving down a further 25 aircraft and five balloons. They were awarded no less than four DSOs, six MCs, nine DFCs, four Mentions in Despatches, and two French and two Belgian Croix de Guerre; two of the ground crew also received Military Medals.

At least 185 pilots from Britain, the Commonwealth, and the United States served with the Squadron during World War I. Of these, 39 were killed in action or died on active service, 48 were wounded or injured, and 20 became Prisoners of War. Their Battle Honours are 'Western Front 1916-1918', 'Somme 1916', 'Arras and Cambrai 1917', and 'Somme 1918'.

41 Squadron was formally disbanded on 31 December 1919, but re-formed again at RAF Northolt on 1 April 1923, under an Air Ministry scheme to expand the RAF by fifteen squadrons for home defence, increase the size of the Reserve, and purchase 500 aircraft.

Upon its re-birth, the Squadron consisted of just one flight of six World War I vintage aircraft, but would grow significantly in size and fly seven different aircraft types before the outbreak of World War II: the Sopwith Snipe, the Armstrong Whitworth Siskin III and IIIA, the Bristol Bulldog IIa, the two-seat Hawker Demon I, the Hawker Fury II and finally the Squadron's first monoplane, the famous Spitfire I.

The inter-war years were an exciting and colourful time for 41 Squadron, during which approximately 200 pilots served with the unit. This generation of pilots and ground crew experienced all manner of activity in addition to their training, such as competitions, air displays and aerobatics, a deployment to the Aden Protectorate on air policing duties, and the development, growth and maturity of the Royal Air Force.

In 1929, eleven of the Squadron's pilots flew their aircraft to Calais to rendezvous with the French aviation pioneer, Louis Blériot, and escort him back to Dover in a re-enactment of the first aerial crossing of the English Channel 20 years earlier. During 1929-1930, the Squadron trained their Royal Highnesses, the Prince of Wales (later King Edward VIII) and Prince George (later the Duke of Kent), to fly and, between 1930 and 1935, they played host to a myriad of other British and foreign royal, government and military dignitaries. These included an official visit by the French Armée de l'Air, when the Squadron's pilots rendezvoused with four twin-engined monoplane Marcel Bloch 200 bombers – then the cutting edge of technology – over the English Channel in June 1935 and escorted them back to Northolt. One particularly noteworthy visitor was Japanese General Matsui Iwane who, after World War II, would be held accountable and executed for the 1937 'Rape of Nanjing', in which his armies murdered an estimated 300,000 Chinese civilians.

British dignitaries included their Royal Highnesses the Duke and Duchess of York, who were escorted to Brussels, the Prime Minister, J. Ramsay MacDonald, the Chief of Air Staff, Marshal of the RAF Hugh Trenchard, the AOC-in-C ADGB, Air Marshal Sir Edward Ellington, and the AOC Fighting Area, ADGB, Air Vice-Marshal Hugh Dowding. They also hosted literally hundreds of students of the country's Army and Navy colleges, all of whom visited the Squadron for familiarisations, lectures and flying demonstrations.

In 1930, following the R.101 Airship disaster in Beauvais, France, 41 Squadron pilots and ground crew formed a part of the Guard of Honour for the Lying-in-State of the 48 victims in the Palace of Westminster. Amongst the dead were the Secretary of State for Air, Brigadier General Lord Christopher Thomson, and the Director of Civil Aviation, Air Vice-Marshal Sir Sefton Branker.

However the Squadron had also suffered its own setbacks and losses during the inter-war period, recording no less than 55 accidents in the air or on the ground. Eleven men were killed and three injured in flying accidents, three injured in airscrew accidents on the ground, and one pilot killed and a second injured in automobile accidents. Although no Battle Honours were granted nor any decorations awarded during this time, the era produced ten Air Commodores, nine Air Vice-Marshals, two Air Marshals and two Air Chief Marshals.

On 30 December 1938, the Squadron was issued with its first Spitfires, thereby becoming the third RAF squadron in history to receive them. By early February 1939, the unit had received a full complement of twenty Mark I Spitfires, which cost the Government the princely sum of £129,130 for the lot! The pilots and crews then spent much of 1939 familiarising themselves with the new aircraft and its new technology, handling and procedures.

Throughout the inter-war period, but most intensively following the 1938 European Crisis which saw the German annexation of the Sudetenland, the Squadron busied itself with a demanding regimen of flying training. This included Home Defence exercises, dog fights, practice attacks, low level attacks, firing exercises, bomber affiliation exercises, turns, dives, formation flying, battle flying, battle climbs, oxygen climbs to 30,000 feet, 'breaking formation by rate of turn', cross-country navigation exercises, night flying, cloud flying, reconnaissance patrols, beam approach landings, air exercises, group operations, R/T range tests, Pip-squeak practice, and host of other activities. The darkening clouds over the Continent, and a foreboding of what was to come, leant an urgency to the task.

The Declaration of War on 3 September 1939 meant that all their training would now be put to the ultimate test. However, the Squadron did not play any significant role in the fighting until the evacuation of Dunkirk in May-June 1940. Although the pilots were involved in minor skirmishes with the Luftwaffe over northern England and the North Sea prior to this, it was the Dunkirk campaign that constituted the Squadron's real baptism of fire.

The experience stood them in good stead for the ensuing Battle of Britain. Based at Hornchurch throughout the Battle and beyond, the Squadron was not rested until February 1941. The cost was great, but so was the damage inflicted on the Luftwaffe. By early 1941, the pilots had claimed over 110 aircraft destroyed, over 40 probable and almost 60 damaged. Their courage was also recognised, and they were awarded one DSO, eight DFCs and one Mention in Despatches.

The battle-weary pilots were rested and all were replaced with fresh young pilots from Britain and the Commonwealth; by June 1941, not one pilot that had arrived in Hornchurch the previous September was still with the Squadron. Inexperienced pilots once again formed the backbone of the Squadron, and much of the summer of 1941 was spent in intensive training in the north of England, readying the men for the unit's return to operations.

This occurred in late July 1941, when 41 Squadron was deployed to the Tangmere Wing under Wg Cdr Douglas Bader and took the War back across the Channel to occupied France in offensive sweeps and bomber escorts. August 1941, in particular, was a costly month for the unit, but the Squadron once again grew in strength and experience, and was soon claiming more victories and being awarded more decorations.

In February 1942, the Squadron participated in operations against the German warships *Scharnhorst*, *Gneisenau* and *Prinz Eugen*, after their escape from Brest, but took a very hard knock in April when five pilots were shot down on a single operation. One pilot made it back across the Channel to crash-land at Dover, injured, whilst three were taken Prisoners of War, and one killed in action. Once again, more fresh pilots were brought on board and the Squadron rebuilt.

The ensuing summer of 1942 was spent in an intensive combination of offensive operations across the Channel, and defending the southern coast against the Luftwaffe's 'tip and run' raids on coastal towns. In the space of three months, these operations cost the Squadron four pilots killed and two wounded in action, for counter-claims of four Luftwaffe aircraft destroyed, one probably destroyed and five damaged.

By this time, however, the British were holding the line in North Africa, and Allied forces had grown in strength with reinforcements from the Commonwealth. Their confidence was further bolstered by the entry of the United States into the War the previous December, and by the promise of American troops for the European theatre. It was time, Churchill's advisers felt, to attempt a first large scale raid on occupied territory. Dieppe was chosen and the operation code-named *Jubilee*.

We now join 41 Squadron, approximately three years into the War, a battle-hardened fighting unit equipped with their third Spitfire version, the Mark Vb, as planning for the Dieppe raid is in its final stages. What fate awaited them on this intensive day? And at what price? They would soon find out.

Operation Jubilee

1 – 22 August 1942

August 1942 – This month would see 41 Squadron involved in its first major offensive of the War, and provided many of the pilots their first experience of action.

Operation *Jubilee*, the Allied landings at Dieppe, in the Upper Normandy Region of France, on 19 August, constituted the unit's most intensive action since the Battle of Britain, some two years before. Although the landings and withdrawals were over in less than a day, the Squadron's involvement lasted almost a week from preparations for their deployment to RAF Tangmere on 15 August until the ground crew's return to RAF Llanbedr on 22 August. During that time, the unit suffered two deaths, one of which was the Commanding Officer, whilst two aircraft were destroyed and seven damaged.

Poor weather prevented flying on 1-3, 7-8, 15 and 22 August, but there was also no operational flying on 9-10 August on account of the Squadron's move from RAF Longtown to RAF Llanbedr, on 13 August as the Squadron was not called upon all day, on 16 August owing to the Squadron's repositioning to RAF Tangmere to participate in Operation *Jubilee*, and on 20-21 August, whilst the Squadron returned to RAF Llanbedr from RAF Tangmere and re-settled into their quarters.

Exercise Dryshod

On the morning of 31 July 1942, an advance party of ground personnel left RAF Debden by road for RAF Longtown in Cumberland. Led by Plt Off Ron Harrison, the group planned to arrive at the airfield, a satellite of RAF Annan located around seven miles north of Carlisle, ahead of the rest of the Squadron for a week-long Army cooperation exercise named 'Dryshod'.

Unbeknown to the men, the exercise was being undertaken in preparation for the pending raid on Dieppe. However, the weather wrought havoc and it took days to get there and hindered the Squadron's participation after their delayed arrival. A lot of effort in packing and moving was invested for very little reward, and this would set an unfortunate pattern for the rest of the year's exercises!

1 August 1942 – The Squadron was released from operational duties at RAF Debden to allow them to pack equipment, and there was no flying all day.

2 August 1942 – The pilots departed for RAF Longtown by air on schedule, but were forced to return when poor weather prevented them from reaching their destination.

3 August 1942 – The poor weather conditions continued today and the pilots remained at RAF Debden another 24 hours. Not allowing themselves to be beaten by the weather, however, Sqn Ldr Geoffrey Hyde and the Squadron Adjutant, Fg Off Harry Smith, left for RAF Longtown by rail instead.

4 August 1942 – Finally, by this morning, the weather had cleared sufficiently for the pilots to make the 246-mile journey to RAF Longtown, where they landed at 12:25. Sqn Ldr Hyde then flew to RAF Dumfries for instructions and, on his return, the pilots began the exercise by attacking road transport. Airborne for an hour from 15:45, followed by further instruction, it had been a long day by the time of their release at 22:30. The pilots involved in the exercise during the afternoon were:

Pilots, 4 August 1942	Serial	Section	Up	Down
Poynton, T. Rex	W3843	Blue	15:45	16:45
Warren, Kenneth G.	BL518			
Robinson, Kenneth B.	AD562			
Schou, Kenneth V. J.	AB809	Yellow		
Coombes, William M.	AD271			
Harrison, Ronald	BL674			
Lloyd, J. Max W.	EN836	Red		
King, Jeffrey C.	AB378			
Knight, Harold C.	EN828			

5 August 1942 – A full day of flying and 'attacking' troops commenced at 10:00 and concluded at 18:50. Practically every pilot on the Squadron flew today, and Plt Off Robert Wood was the Squadron's only 'casualty'.

Pilots, 5 August 1942	Serial	Section	Up	Down
Imbert, André	AR392	NR	10:05	11:05
Hyde, Geoffrey C.	BL777	Red	10:30	11:20
Warren, Kenneth G.	BL518			
Schou, Kenneth V. J.	BM573	Yellow		
Scott, Thomas R.	W3843			
Goodall, Bernard B.	AB809	White		
East, Walter R.	BL304			
King, Jeffrey C.	AB378	Blue	15:05	15:45
Robinson, Kenneth B.	EN780			
Hone, Douglas H.	EN827	Green		
Wood, Robert L.	BM533			
Imbert, André	EN836	Black		
Benjamin, Sydney H.	AR392			
King, Jeffrey C.	AB378	Blue	16:20	17:20
Robinson, Kenneth B.	EN780			
Hone, Douglas H.	EN827	Green		
Imbert, André	EN836	Black		
Atkinson, Thomas G.	AB809			
Hyde, Geoffrey C.	BL777	Red	18:00	18:50
Harrison, Ronald	BL304			
Wood, Robert L.	BM533			
Hone, Douglas H.	EN827			
Stepp, Malta L.	BM573	Yellow		
East, Walter R.	AD271			
Prickett, Leslie A.	EN836			
Stonier, Jack	AB378			
Goodall, Bernard B.	W3843	Blue		
Warren, Kenneth G.	BL518			
Vine, Edward E.	EN780			
Scott, Thomas R.	EN828			

6 August 1942 – The exercise continued in earnest from 07:35 this morning, but the Squadron was fighting a losing battle as 'aggressor' in attacks against troops, transports and tanks.

Flt Lt Lord Gisborough, Intelligence Officer, displayed a large map explaining progress of the exercise in which 41 [Squadron] *acted as hostile A/C and results showed that they were being repulsed by the ground troops.*[1]

Pilots, 6 August 1942	Serial	Section	Up	Down
Hyde, Geoffrey C.	BL777	Red	07:35	08:20
East, Walter R.	AD271	Red		
Stepp, Malta L.	BM573	Yellow		
Prickett, Leslie A.	W3843	Yellow		
Schou, Kenneth V. J.	AB809	White		
Harrison, Ronald	BL304	White		
Hyde, Geoffrey C.	BL777	Red	09:35	10:10
East, Walter R.	AD271	Red		
Schou, Kenneth V. J.	AB809	Blue		
Harrison, Ronald	BL304	Blue		
Stepp, Malta L.	BM573	Yellow		
Prickett, Leslie A.	BL518	Yellow		
Hyde, Geoffrey C.	BL777	Red	11:05	11:40
East, Walter R.	AD271	Red		
Stepp, Malta L.	BM573	Yellow		
Prickett, Leslie A.	BL518	Yellow		
Hyde, Geoffrey C.	BL777	Red	12:55	13:45
East, Walter R.	AD271	Red		
Stepp, Malta L.	BM573	Yellow		
Prickett, Leslie A.	BL518	Yellow		
Schou, Kenneth V. J.	AB809	White		
Harrison, Ronald	BL304	White		
Hyde, Geoffrey C.	BL304	Red	17:55	18:40
East, Walter R.	AD271	Red		
Hone, Douglas H.	EN827	Red		
Hogarth, Rycherde H.	AB378	Red		
Stepp, Malta L.	BM573	Blue		
Prickett, Leslie A.	BL518	Blue		
Knight, Harold C.	EN828	Blue		
Wood, Robert L.	BM533	Blue		
Schou, Kenneth V. J.	AB809	Yellow		
Scott, Thomas R.	AR331	Yellow		
Slack, Thomas A. H.	EN780	Yellow		
Lloyd, J. Max W.	EN836	Yellow		

7 August 1942 – Considering the Squadron was losing ground in the exercise, the poor weather this morning was perhaps a welcome relief! Despite coming to readiness at 07:00, the weather prevented any flying whatsoever and the Squadron was released for the day.

8 August 1942 – Unsuitable weather conditions continued all day today, and once again the Squadron was grounded and unable to participate in the exercise.

9 August 1942 – After a two-day break, the weather had improved sufficiently by this morning to allow B Flight to get airborne again and attack troops and transports on the Dumfries road, between 08:35 and 09:00. However, all activity on the exercise ceased at 10:15, when the order was received to pack up and head home.

Pilots, 9 August 1942	Serial	Section	Up	Down
Hone, Douglas H.	EN827	Green		
Lloyd, J. Max W.	EN836			
Knight, Harold C.	BM533	Black	08:35	09:00
Robinson, Kenneth B.	AD562			
Slack, Thomas A. H.	EN780	Blue		
Atkinson, Thomas G.	AB378			

Prior to their departure, the Squadron participated in what the ORB refers to as a 'very interesting ceremony' before the Lord Mayor of Carlisle, who visited them at RAF Longtown. He addressed the men and explained that Carlisle had sponsored the Squadron in 1939. In honour of this, American Flt Lt Malta Stepp "gave a display of aerobatics showing the capabilities of a Spitfire."[2]

Instead of returning to their base of the last month, RAF Debden, as they might have expected, the Squadron was informed they were instead to head immediately for a new base, RAF Llanbedr, in Merionethshire, on the northwest Welsh coast. Following a busy summer of frontline operations at RAF Hawkinge and RAF Debden, the Squadron was now being sent to Wales for a period of rest.

Seventeen pilots therefore took off from RAF Longtown for the 159-mile flight to RAF Llanbedr at 17:35 and arrived at 18:30. Putting on a good show for their new hosts, all 17 aircraft were on the ground within 13 minutes. The ground crews followed them by road and rail the next day, the last men finally reaching their new base on 11 August, and spent the ensuing days unpacking and getting settled in.

RAF Llanbedr

Located less than half a mile southwest of the village of Llanbedr, the airfield is protected by a stretch of farmland and sand dunes lining the coast of Cardigan Bay and the Irish Sea, and is around three miles south-southwest of the ruins of historic Harlech Castle.

When it opened in June 1941, the airfield was initially home to No. 6 Air Observer Navigation School, and subsequently 74 and 131 Squadrons. Most recently, RAF Llanbedr had been occupied by 232 Squadron, whilst re-forming and building up strength following a mauling of the original 232 Squadron by Japanese forces in Singapore and Malaya, which had led to the unit's disbandment in that theatre in February 1942.

One of 41 Squadron's pilots, Plt Off Tom Slack, recalls the 'peace and quiet of Llanbedr' in his autobiography, recalling,

> *Llanbedr was very much in Welsh Wales, where many people spoke Welsh and there was no drinking in pubs on Sundays, at least officially. A deputation even came from Barmouth to ask us not to fly on the Sabbath [...]. Now and again the Squadron would return south for a few days to carry out sweeps and rhubarb[s] to brush away the cobwebs. But apart from this we just practiced formation and night flying, high and low level navigation across country, and firing at air to ground targets. The only real excitement was when we were sometimes scrambled to intercept JU88s flying low over the Irish Sea....*[3]

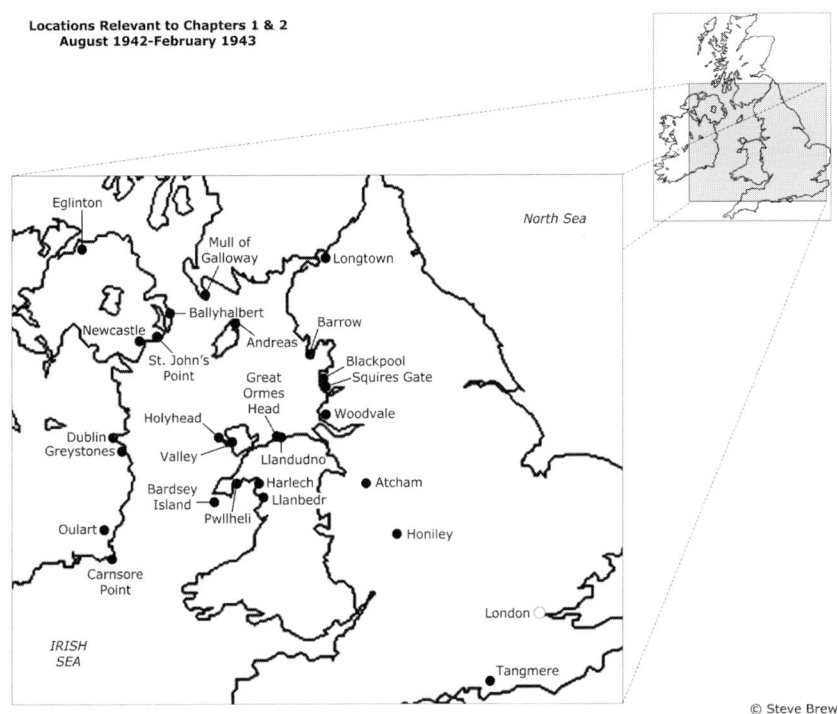

Locations Relevant to Chapters 1 & 2
August 1942-February 1943

© Steve Brew

RAF Llanbedr was a Station within 9 Group, which was created in October 1940 to defend Manchester, Liverpool, Birmingham, Wales, the Isle of Man and the Western Approaches. The area encompassed the main airfields of Andreas, Atcham, High Ercall, Honiley, Woodvale, Wrexham, and Llanbedr.

Sector Headquarters was located at RAF Valley, and 9 Group's own headquarters were based at Barton Hall, around three miles north of Preston, Lancashire. At this time, the Group was responsible for the following squadrons, equipped with quite a variety of aircraft:

Squadron	Location	Aircraft	State
41	Llanbedr	Spitfire Vb	Operational
48 (USAAF)	Atcham	Lightning	Non-Operational
49 (USAAF)	Atcham	Lightning	Non-Operational
93	Andreas	Spitfire Vb	Operational
96	Wrexham	Beaufighter II	Operational
255	Honiley	Beaufighter VI	Operational
256	Woodvale	Beaufighter I	Operational
257	High Ercall	Hurricane IIa/b/c & Typhoon I	Operational
315 (Polish)	Woodvale	Spitfire Vb	Operational
456 (Aust)	Valley	Beaufighter VI	Operational
1456 Flight[4]	High Ercall	Havoc I & II, & Boston III	Operational

11 August 1942 – The Squadron spent most of the day settling in, and it was not until late in the day that a number of pilots were airborne to conduct sector familiarisation reconnaissances. Eight sorties were flown between 15:25 and 19:55, when flying ceased, and by the end of the day 9 Group Headquarters had changed 41 Squadron's status to 'fully operational'.

12 August 1942 – A Flight's Red Section was placed at dawn readiness, and the rest of the Squadron at 15 minutes; B Flight took over readiness at 13:00. Sector familiarisation reconnaissances continued today, with seven sorties flown between 10:25 and 13:55. Plt Off Rycherde Hogarth (AR392) and Sgt Plt Thomas Atkinson (EN780) were scrambled at 15:30, but returned at 16:35 with nothing to report.

14 August 1942 – A Flight at dawn readiness. At 08:10, Red Section (Prickett AD271, Warren BL304) was ordered to scramble base, but returned 20 minutes later with nothing to report. Blue Section (Poynton BL304 & Scott AD271) was then scrambled at 11:13 and White Section at 12:11. Both sections, the ORB's F540 records, returned at 13:45, with nothing to report. However, this is erroneous as one of 41 Squadron's few contacts with the Luftwaffe during their stay at RAF Llanbedr occurred today.[5]

An Interception off Dublin

At 12:10, A Flight's Sgt Plts Ken Warren (BM573) and Leslie Prickett (AR331) were scrambled from RAF Llanbedr as Yellow Section and ordered to orbit off the coast from Penrhos, a short distance northwest of Llanbedr, whilst Sector Control obtained a fix on an unidentified 'bogey'. Within a short time, they were vectored by the Controller, Plt Off Pearson, to intercept an aircraft just east of the Irish coast.

The two pilots headed northwest to the vicinity of Dublin at an altitude of 3,000 feet, and received several vectors whilst underway. As they reached a point approximately 72 miles from Penrhos, just off the coast from the Irish capital, they bore to starboard and headed north up the coast. Just north of the Kish Light Ship, Sector Control informed them they should descend to 2,000 feet and expect a bandit at the same altitude at two o'clock.

As predicted, an aircraft was soon sighted below and to starboard only half a mile away at sea level – Warren later stated it was flying no higher than about 20 feet above the waves – heading southwest towards Dublin. Identifying it as a Junkers Ju88 reconnaissance aircraft, Warren tally-hoed and Prickett followed him down on his rear starboard quarter.

Contemporary research today suggests this was a Ju88D from 1.(F)/123[6], based at Toussus-le-Buc [Toussus-le-Noble], France, around 11 miles southwest of Paris, and about two miles south of Versailles. The crew had re-positioned their aircraft to Brest for a photo-reconnaissance sortie to Barrow-in-Furness. Having entered St. George's Channel via the Western Approaches, they had flown northwards up the Channel and into the Irish Sea, as far as Barrow-in-Furness, before encountering RAF aircraft.

By the time Prickett and Warren were scrambled, the Ju88 was on its return journey having already been intercepted by another squadron. 9 Group had originally plotted the aircraft when it entered the sector shortly before 11:30. At that time, it was six miles northeast of Arklow flying northeast. Altogether four squadrons were sent up to find and intercept it: 41, 93, 257 and 315.

The Ju88 was first sighted southeast of the Calf of Man, but dived to zero feet in a north-easterly direction and was next seen off Barrow-in-Furness by pilots of RAF Woodvale based 315 (Polish) Squadron. That unit's Green Section, comprising Flt Lt Wlodzimierz Miksa and Sgt Plt Jerzy Malec, had been scrambled by Sector Control and were airborne at 11:20. Initially vectored west towards Amlwch, on the Isle of Anglesey, they were subsequently ordered north towards Clay Head on the eastern coast of the Isle of Man, before being sent east, in the direction of Barrow-in-Furness.

The two pilots were orbiting off Barrow-in-Furness at 29,000 feet, when Malec caught sight of the aircraft flying at 22,000 feet, heading straight for the town. They confirmed the 'bogey' to be an enemy reconnaissance aircraft and made an initial attack northwest of Barrow-in-Furness at 12:05.

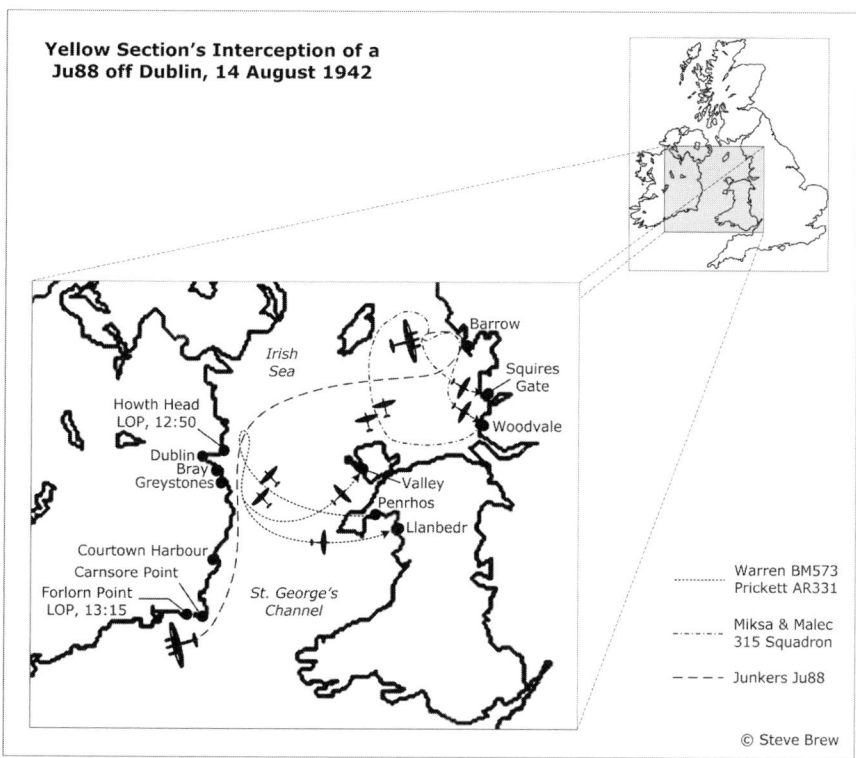

LEFT Sgt Plt Kenneth Warren served with 41 Squadron from 1 April 1942 to 2 September 1942, during which time he claimed a shared damaged Junkers Ju88 off neutral Éire on 14 August 1942 with Sgt Plt Leslie Prickett and two pilots from 315 Squadron. © KG Warren family

RIGHT Sgt Plt (later Fg Off) Leslie Prickett, shown here writing a letter home, served with 41 Squadron from 2 July 1942 to 27 August 1943. He claimed a shared damaged Junkers Ju88 off neutral Éire on 14 August 1942 with Sgt Plt Ken Warren and two pilots from 315 Squadron. © Cowell family

A Junkers Ju88 similar to this was intercepted and attacked off neutral Eire by Sgt Plts Kenneth Warren and Leslie Prickett on 14 August 1942. © Deutsches Bundesarchiv Bild 101I-363-2258-11

Malec attacked first, diving to 22,000 feet where he fired off several bursts of machine gun and cannon fire from a range of 350 yards and less. When his windscreen was sprayed with oil, he took this as a sign he had damaged the Ju88 and pulled up and away. However, he had in fact been hit by return fire from the Ju88's dorsal gunner. Unable to make the 40 miles back to base, he force-landed at RAF Squires Gate, just south of Blackpool, at 12:18.

Miksa took over and delivered his own attack, as the Ju88 continued towards Barrow-in-Furness all the while taking evasive action by weaving erratically and diving to 4,000 feet. He followed it as far as Barrow-in-Furness but when it entered the balloon barrage area, he was called back to RAF Woodvale, where he landed at 12:40.

After Miksa and Malec's withdrawal, the Ju88's pilot turned his aircraft back southwards for the return journey down St. George's Channel and back to Brest. Sector Control plotted the aircraft's movements during the entire episode, and it clearly shows some forward thinking that they scrambled 41 Squadron at 12:10, only five minutes after Malec had begun his attack on the enemy aircraft northwest of Barrow-in-Furness.

It was during this return flight that Warren and Prickett intercepted the Ju88 just northeast of Dublin at 12:41.[7] Camouflaged in a drab "greeny black"[8], they noted that the colour scheme made the 46-foot-long aircraft discernible from above against the Irish Sea, but almost invisible against the coast, despite cloudless skies and good visibility.

Warren turned about and attacked the Ju88 from its port rear quarter, firing all his ammunition in about six to seven bursts from a range of no more than 250 yards. He saw his tracers striking the port wing and fuselage, and the engine began to emit smoke. Despite his attack, however, he noted the Ju88's pilot took little evasive action, and he only experienced a small amount of return fire from the dorsal gunner, positioned in the rear of the cockpit.

The two Spitfires and the Ju88 were tracked down the coast by Irish Coastwatchers in their Look-Out Posts, between 12:50 and 13:15, both inside and outside the territorial limit off Dublin, Wicklow and Wexford. The Daily Report Summaries of the LOPs at Howth, Dalkey, Sandycove and Bullwall record observing and hearing three aircraft between three to seven miles to the east, moving south. The Ju88 was specifically identified by the LOPs between Bray and Carnsore, and the LOPs at Greystones and Courtown Harbour added that the aircraft was flying one to six miles east of the coast, heading south.[9]

This fits comfortably with Warren's report which states he broke off his attack around 10 miles south of Dublin, off Greystones, and allowed his No. 2 to take over the attack. Having already fired two or three bursts from his position on Warren's rear starboard quarter, Prickett now pulled in behind the Ju88, in an effort to line up his attack from dead astern. The Luftwaffe pilot began evasive action by weaving, but by now he was picking up speed and pulling away. Despite his efforts, with his throttle wide open, Prickett could not close on the bomber and was forced to fire all his ammunition from a range of around 600 yards, but noted his "bullets falling around the tail".[10]

With his ammunition expended, and the Ju88 now some distance ahead, Prickett was forced to break off his attack and head home with Warren. Between them, they had expended 240 rounds of 20mm cannon ammunition and 2,720 rounds of .303 inch machine gun.

Prickett, however, suffered a similar fate to 315 Squadron's Sgt Plt Malec, as he was hit by return fire. It is possible that he did not know this at the time, as he appears to have only thought that his engine had started playing up. Whilst Warren continued on to RAF Llanbedr, Prickett landed at RAF Valley where he found a shell had struck his radiator. Considering Warren had noted a lack of return fire from the Ju88's dorsal gunner, but Prickett had subsequently been hit by the same gun, the gunner may have suffered a jam during Warren's engagement but then successfully cleared it by the time Prickett attacked.

The Ju88 was last observed by Irish Coastwatchers at Forlorn Point at low altitude, eight miles off the coast moving west. It is believed the crew made it back to Brest, and they can be considered fortunate indeed to have survived two separate attacks from four aircraft.

Ju88D, 14 August 1942	Serial	Section	Target	Location
Warren, Kenneth G.	BM573	Yellow	Ju88D, 1.(F)/123	St. George's Channel, 10-20 miles SSE of Dublin
Prickett, Leslie A.	AR331			
Miksa, Wlodzimierz	BL751	Green		NW of Barrow-in-Furness (315 Sqn pilots)
Malec, Jerzy	AA929			

Operation Jubilee

The original idea of Allied landings at Dieppe was conceived in April 1942 in response to Russian Premier, Joseph Stalin's, insistence that British Prime Minister, Winston Churchill, open a new Western Front to alleviate German pressure on Russian forces on the Eastern Front.

Whilst Allied Command were only too aware of their inability at this time to launch a full-scale invasion of the Continent, on the scale of what would be seen in June 1944, they felt they could, in the least, cause trouble and achieve the ultimate aim of drawing the Wehrmacht and Luftwaffe off the Russian Front.

An initial plan, code-named *Rutter*, was therefore tabled in May 1942, which foresaw landings taking place in France in late June or early July. The plan was approved by the Chiefs of Staff but

Canadian Prisoners of War being led through Dieppe by German soldiers, following the ill-fated landings on 19 August 1942. © Library and Archives Canada / C-014171

Dieppe's flint covered beach and cliff following Operation *Jubilee* on 19 August 1942.
© Deutsches Bundesarchiv Bild 101I-362-2211-04

several issues, thereunder poor weather, led to the originally chosen date of 7 July being abandoned and the troops, which had been prepared, being dispersed again.

An alternative plan, code-named *Jubilee*, was subsequently approved, which foresaw amphibious landings by 6,100 troops of the 2nd Canadian Infantry Division and a Canadian tank regiment, supported by British Commandos and a platoon of U.S. Rangers. Hoping for the element of surprise, it was also decided to launch the attack without the precursor of naval or aerial bombardment, nor the utilisation of airborne troops. Air support would be provided in the form of Hurricane bombers to destroy gun batteries that may endanger the landings, with close support provided by fighters.

Their main aim was to attack and destroy local defences, power stations, airfields and invasion barges, to capture German troops and to briefly occupy Dieppe; it was not intended that Allied troops should stay permanently. The landings and combined operations would provide the Chiefs of Staff vital information and lessons for future landings in North Africa, Italy and the Continent, most notably at Normandy in June 1944's Operation *Overlord*.

The RAF's operations for *Jubilee* were commanded by the AOC of 11 Group, AVM Trafford Leigh-Mallory CB DSO. He had at his disposal, gathered at southern English airfields, the aircraft of no less than 75 squadrons: 48 equipped with Spitfire Vb's, Vc's, VI's and IX's, of which three were USAAF squadrons, eight Hurricane II squadrons, three Typhoon squadrons, four Mustang squadrons, five Boston squadrons, two Blenheim squadrons, one Beaufighter squadron, and four USAAF B17 Flying Fortress squadrons. ASR units were also placed in readiness. In fact, Leigh-Mallory,

> ...*had a far greater fighter force available* [to him] *than Air Chief Marshal Hugh Dowding had at any one time when he commanded Fighter Command during the Battle of Britain in 1940.*[11]

Opposing the Allied onslaught were the Wehrmacht's resident garrison in Dieppe, the 302nd Infantry Division, reinforced by Artillery. They were supported in the air by the fighters of JG26 *Schlageter* and JG2 *Richthofen* Wings. Together, they could muster a formidable force of 190 Focke-Wulf FW190s and 16 Messerschmitt Me109s. The Luftwaffe also had several bomber units available to them, thereunder Kampfgeschwader 2, 40, and 77 and Küstenfliegergruppe 106, boasting a combined 109 aircraft, consisting mostly of Dornier Do217s, Heinkel He111s and Junkers Ju88s.

It would prove to be quite a show.

15 August 1942 – It was intended that 41 Squadron should fly to RAF Tangmere today to reposition itself for the Dieppe landings, but the move was hindered by cloud. The day was instead marred by the unfortunate death of one of the Squadron's young pilots in a flying accident.

Sgt Plt Bernard Goodall RNZAF, in a photograph believed to have been taken at 3 EFTS Harewood in May 1941, was killed in a flying accident on 15 August 1942. © Smith family

When the unit was sent to RAF Longtown at the beginning of August for an Army cooperation exercise, it was only intended to be a temporary move, and most kit and some aircraft were left behind at RAF Debden. However, whilst at Longtown, the Squadron was informed they would not be returning to Essex, but rather moving to their new base at RAF Llanbedr. It is apparent the Squadron took some time to get fully established at Llanbedr, and this is likely the result of the amount of equipment which required retrieval from RAF Debden.

As such, 23-year-old Sgt Plt Bernard Goodall RNZAF was sent to Debden to fetch Spitfire Vb, P8607, EB-C, and fly it to RAF Tangmere, where it would be deployed in the pending Dieppe landings, before bringing it on to RAF Llanbedr. A presentation aircraft named 'Palembang Oeloe II', P8607 had been transferred to 41 Squadron from 124 Squadron on 25 July 1942, around the time the latter squadron commenced equipping with Spitfire VI's. By the time of its arrival on the Squadron, the aircraft had served with three previous squadrons, and was a little under 14 months old. It also appears to have been the only P series Spitfire Vb to have served with 41 Squadron.

Goodall arrived in Debden, probably after a prolonged rail journey from Llanbedr, and took possession on the aircraft. He departed the airfield during the late afternoon, and headed for RAF Tangmere. However, at about 17:45, when approximately 77 miles from RAF Debden, he inexplicably dived out of low cloud and into the ground near Blounce Farm, around two-and-a-half miles south-southwest of RAF Odiham in Hampshire. He was killed instantly.[12]

16 August 1942 – The Squadron was reduced to non-operational status today as it departed RAF Llanbedr at 11:00 on its 200 mile ferry flight to RAF Tangmere, where they were to be based for the duration of Operation *Jubilee*. Seventeen aircraft were sent, which were followed by air in two HP54 Harrow transports full of equipment, by road in the form of two lorries and Sqn Ldr Hyde's car, and by rail for the remaining personnel.

RAF Tangmere's 412 (Canadian) Squadron found their airfield was about to become home to several squadrons for the length of Operation *Jubilee*. In addition to 41 Squadron, they were required to make room for the pilots and crews of RAF Charmy Down based 87 Squadron, and RAF Ibsley based 66, 118 and 501 Spitfire Squadrons, as well. In fact, 412 Squadron had not been forewarned of the imminent battle, but their unexpected premature recall from an Air Firing Exercise at nearby RAF Merston, the presence at Tangmere of the Head of Combined Operations, Lord Louis Mountbatten, and the sudden arrival of five additional Squadrons were all obvious give-aways that something big was on the cards.

17 August 1942 – 41 Squadron's A Flight was placed at readiness at 13:00 for Station defence. Three patrols were undertaken during the afternoon, the first pair in the Selsey and Shoreham areas; the third is not recorded.

Patrols, 17 August 1942	Serial	Section	Up	Down
Knight, Harold C.	EN780	Blue	14:55	16:30
Hogarth, Rycherde H. W.	AR392			
Hone, Douglas H.	EN836	Yellow	16:00	17:00
King, Jeffrey C.	AB378			
Warren, Kenneth G.	EN836	Black	17:30	18:45
Imbert, André	AD562			

The day was spent settling in, which was a challenging task as the Squadron was only provided two small rooms in which they needed to accommodate an Orderly Room, an operational Armoury, a pilots' rest room, and the Intelligence and Engineer Officers. Clearly inadequate, the Squadron were soon able to obtain two round canvas Bell Tents with furniture, into the first of which they moved the Armoury. The second was taken over as an Orderly Room and working space for Lord Gisborough in his role as Intelligence Officer.

The remaining staff and ground crew were accommodated on the Station with 87 Squadron, but those of 66, 118 and 501 Squadrons were put up in a makeshift tent camp on the Station's Sports Field. 41's Flight Commanders were still unhappy, though, as they would have preferred two additional Bell Tents for their respective flights, complaining that conditions were "Rather too Crowded and noisy to allow [the] Pilots to get a good rest before the show…".[13] However, five of the pilots were fortunate enough to be subsequently billeted in Woodfield House, a schoolhouse around a mile from the airfield, which left a little more room for the remaining pilots.

A less-than-satisfactory communication system was also provided for the Squadron, which consisted of a single telephone for all communication with Operations and the Station Intelligence and Engineer Officers. Not surprisingly, heavy usage of the line resulted in delays for outside calls, and although there were no communication breakdowns per se, "an extra Phone would have been desireable [sic]".[14]

The telephone also proved impractical at times, particularly when the deafening roar of nearby Spitfire engines being run up made it impossible to hear the person on the other end of the line. In fact, one report later suggested this was the reason Sqn Ldr Hyde did not understand the briefing for one of the operations on 19 August and was forced to take off without actually knowing what the target was.

The single telephone line also meant that only one person – the Commanding Officer – could receive briefs on what the Squadron was required to do, leaving the Intelligence Officer, to some extent, in the dark and unable to assist him. This did not bode well for the coming battle.

18 August 1942 – It was quite clear to the men that something big was about to happen. Lord Mountbatten had already been seen on the base and today the AOC, 11 Group, AVM Leigh-Mallory, and his SASO, Air Cdre Gilbert Harcourt-Smith CBE MVO, also arrived.

During the afternoon, a briefing was held in RAF Tangmere's intelligence hut to explain to squadron commanders the battle that lay ahead of them. It was chaired by Leigh-Mallory and

Harcourt-Smith, and attended by the Sector Commander, ex-41 Squadron pilot Gp Capt Charles H. Appleton DSO DFC, the RAF Tangmere Wing Commander Flying, Wg Cdr Peter R. 'Johnnie' Walker DFC, and the Commanding Officers and Flight Commanders of all the squadrons based in the Tangmere Sector for the operation: 3, 32, 41, 43, 66, 87, 88, 107, 118, 129, 130, 131, 174, 175, 245, 253, 309, 412 and 501.

This was the first time the squadrons had been informed of their participation in a combined operation over Dieppe named *Jubilee*. At the meeting's conclusion, Gp Capt Appleton took the Commanding Officer and Flight Commanders of the eight Hurricane and 'Hurri-Bomber' squadrons aside for a separate briefing on their roles, followed by another for the same officers of the nine Spitfire squadrons, thereunder 41 Squadron's Sqn Ldr Hyde and Flt Lts Douglas Hone and Malta Stepp.

Separately, as soon as A Flight was placed at readiness at 13:00, two pilots were sent up for the Squadron's first patrol of the day. The unit's role today was to ensure no enemy aircraft observed Allied preparations for the next morning's landings. Red Section was up at 13:00 to patrol St. Catherine's Point and escort a convoy in the Channel, followed by Yellow Section at 13:20. At 14:10[15], White Section commenced a patrol of Selsey Bill[16], after which Red and Yellow Sections undertook patrols of St. Catherine's Point and the Channel, at 15:00 and 15:50 respectively. At no time were any enemy aircraft seen.

Patrols, 18 August 1942	Serial	Section	Up	Down
Poynton, Thomas R.	W3843	Red	13:00	14:25
Coombes, William M.	BM573			
Schou, Kenneth V. J.	AB809	Yellow	13:20	14:35
East, Walter R.	AD271			
Hoare, Reginald M.	BL304	White	14:10	15:35
Stonier, Jack	BL518			
Poynton, Thomas R.	W3843	Red	15:00	16:15
Coombes, William M.	BM573			
Schou, Kenneth V. J.	AB809	Yellow	15:50	17:20
Harrison, Ronald	AD562			

During the night, almost 240 ships left southern English ports, bound for France, to be in place for the commencement of pre-dawn landings by ground forces. Amongst them were eight destroyers for protection, one of which – HMS *Calpe* – was designated Forward Headquarters for the operation. Aboard this vessel, to control movements and communications, were Canadian Maj-Gen John H. Roberts MC, commanding the ground forces, the Royal Navy's Capt John Hughes-Hallett, commanding naval operations, and Air Cdre Adrian Cole CBE MC DFC, coordinating the battle in the air.

HMS *Calpe* left Portsmouth at 20:00 and was followed out by the rest of the armada of ships. Passing through a gap in a German minefield that had been cleared and marked by minesweepers in advance, the ships were all in place off Dieppe at 03:00 on 19 August.

Five minutes later, the first landing craft were lowered into the darkness of the Channel and headed for the beaches. At around the same time, the first orders were issued to the RAF, and 107, 418 and 605 Squadrons, all equipped with Bostons, were ordered into the air to bomb the four-gun *Hitler* and *Göring* Batteries. They were closely followed by 88 Squadron, also equipped with Bostons, ordered to bomb *Rommel* Battery. The major gun emplacements had been given codenames for the operation, each wryly named after a German Commander. Their aim was to take out any heavy guns threatening the landings.

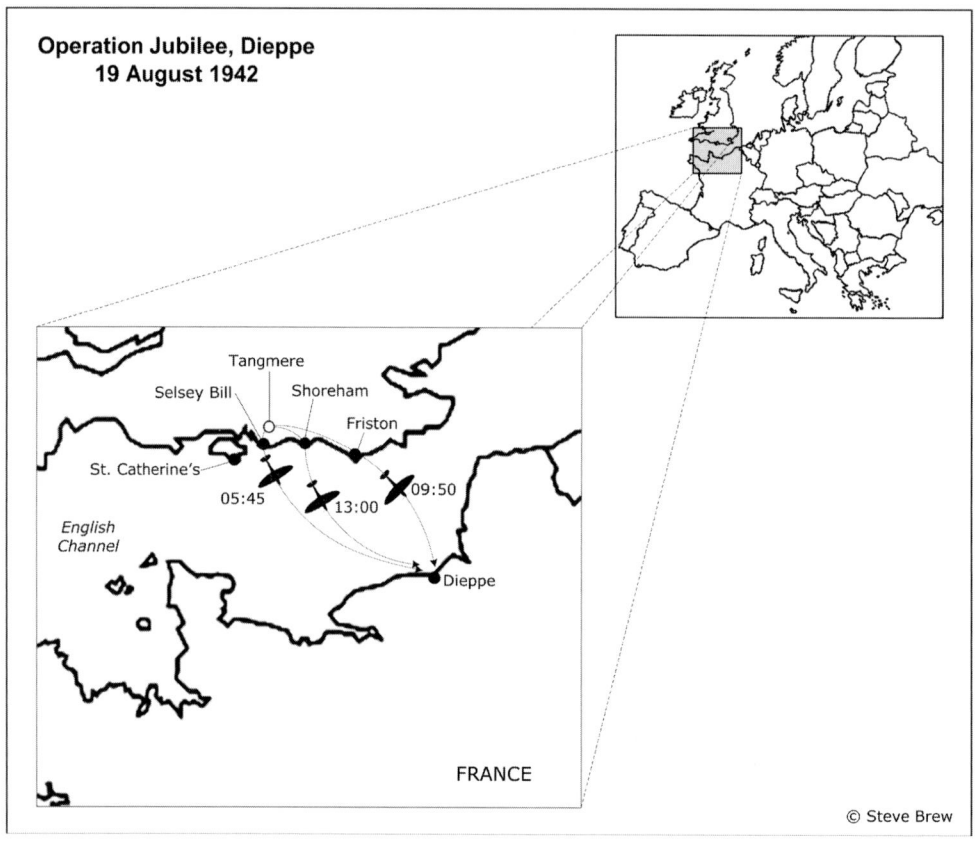

19 August 1942 – 41 Squadron was brought to readiness at 04:30 in preparation for their own role in the operation. Throughout the day, the pilots would participate in eight operations and fly a total of 47 sorties.

Summary of 41 Squadron's Operations, 19 August 1942

Operation	Up	Down	Aircraft	Duty
1	05:45	07:26	12	Cover for Hurricane Bombers, Dieppe
2	08:30	09:55	2	Air-Sea Rescue patrol, off Brighton
3	08:35	09:55	2	Base area patrol, RAF Tangmere
4	09:35	10:10	2	Air-Sea Rescue patrol, off Brighton
5	09:50	11:20	11	Escort for Hurricane bombers, Dieppe
6	13:00	14:05	12	Escort for Hurricane bombers, Dieppe
7	15:35	16:15	4	Scramble, Selsey Bill
8	16:00	16:25	2	Base area patrol, RAF Tangmere

By the time 41 Squadron took to the air for their first operation, however, several dozen squadrons had already been in action, the landings were in full swing, aircraft had been brought down and men had lost their lives. Even at this early stage, it was proving to be a formidable battle.

Operation 1 – Bomber Cover, Dieppe

Twenty-four Spitfires took off from RAF Tangmere at 05:45, twelve from 41 Squadron and twelve from 412. They flew to Dieppe together as a Wing, under the command of Wg Cdr 'Johnnie' Walker, and crossed out over Selsey Bill.

The pilots traversed the Channel on the deck, with 41 Squadron stepped up and back, and reached Dieppe at 06:05. Upon arrival, the two squadrons patrolled the French coast in 2/10ths cloud between 4,000 and 8,000 feet for 30 minutes to act as cover for 107 Squadron's Bostons, which were sent in to bomb *Hitler* Battery, a few miles inland, south of Dieppe. This was already 107's second operation of the day, their earlier sorties to this same battery having failed to silence it.

As the Squadrons orbited over the ships off the coast from Dieppe, both light and heavy inaccurate Flak were encountered from the cliffs west of the town. Although 412 (Canadian) Squadron had a brief skirmish with six FW190s, 41 Squadron had no opportunity to join the attack. The ORB reported that "…a good time was had by all…[but] …the Squ[adron] did not get a chance of having a crack at the Huns".[17] They landed back at Tangmere at 07:26, and 412 Squadron landed ten minutes behind them.

Many of the pilots saw the bombers hit their targets, but these are unlikely to have been 107 Squadron's Bostons hitting *Hitler* Battery as they did not leave their base at RAF Ford until 06:15, a full ten minutes after 41 and 412 arrived off Dieppe. By the time they reached the French coast at 06:47, the two Spitfire squadrons had completed their 30-minute patrol and appear to have already left for home. Moreover, considering the Spitfires remained off the coast, and 107's target was a few miles inland behind a shroud of cloud and smoke, it is debatable whether they would have seen them even if they were present at the same time. In fact, 107's Bostons overshot their target as a result of visibility problems. It is more likely the Squadron observed *Hess* Battery being destroyed by Commandos on the ground, an event also observed and reported by 611 Squadron.

Operation 2 – ASR Patrol

At 08:30, Sgt Plts Thomas Atkinson and Max Lloyd were sent to a location approximately six miles off the eastern side of Brighton as Pink Section to confirm an observation made by a Walrus of a "light greenish part of [an] a/c".[18] Arriving over the debris at 09:15, Pink section confirmed its existence and reported it to Flight Control. They returned to RAF Tangmere at 09:55.

Operation 3 – Patrol Base

Little mention is made of this patrol outside of the ORB's F541. Flt Lt Malta Stepp and Plt Off Reg Hoare departed RAF Tangmere as Red Section to patrol the base area at 08:35 and landed again at 09:55, with nothing to report.

Operation 4 – ASR Patrol

Purple Section, consisting of Sgt Plts Edward Vine and Kenneth Warren, took off at 09:35 to escort a Walrus to a location only described as east of Brighton. They arrived back at RAF Tangmere at 10:10, reporting having sighted 15 destroyers 20 miles out to sea, and a line of boats east of Beachy Head.[19]

Operation 5 – Escort Cover, Dieppe

Whilst the ground forces attacking Dieppe's western headland had been successful and had achieved their objectives, the operation on the eastern headland had not gone so well. Tanks were held up on the beaches and the Engineers had been unable to blast a gap in the promenade wall to assist the advance. Ground forces had put *Hess* Battery out of action, but aerial attacks had failed to silence *Göring*, *Hitler* and *Rommel*; these emplacements continued to shell the landing beaches, wreaking a horrific toll on both men and machines.

More Bostons were sent in to attack *Hitler* Battery, and the last few available light bombers, from 88 Squadron, were sent to hit *Rommel* again. When no more Bostons were available to halt their deadly fire, Hurricane bombers were ordered in to take over, and 41 Squadron's Spitfires were called upon to provide them an escort.

At 09:50 therefore, the Squadron was in the air again, once more accompanied by 412 (Canadian) Squadron. The two units rendezvoused over Friston at an altitude of just 1,000 feet where they orbited, and waited for the arrival of the ten Hurricane IIb's from RAF Warmwell based 175 Squadron.[20]

The operation was carried out under the command of Sqn Ldr John 'Knobby' Fee, leading 412 Squadron. Until recently, he had been 41 Squadron's Commanding Officer, having only been replaced by Sqn Ldr Geoffrey Hyde three weeks before. 41 Squadron's formation for this mission comprised the following pilots and sections:

Red Section	Yellow Section[21]	Blue Section
Hyde	Stepp	Hone
Schou	Coombes	King
Slack	Poynton	Knight
Robinson		Imbert

It is clear from several accounts, most notably AVM Leigh-Mallory's formal post-Operation report [TNA AIR 25/204], that it was already apparent by this time to those in higher echelons that the attack was not proceeding as had been intended and that their plans were in disarray. There was confusion both on the ground and in the air, and Allied Forces on the beaches were being successfully repelled by the Wehrmacht.

Orders were given and cancelled, and opposition in the air and on the ground were growing as the Luftwaffe and Wehrmacht organised their counter-attacks, having regained clarity and order after their initial recoil and surprise. The situation on the beaches began to grow critical and batteries of guns continued to pound the shoreline unabated. A call was made for a smoke screen to be laid down to assist them and, at RAF Thruxton, every aircraft that could be fitted with smoke-laying equipment was prepared and sent off. With the Luftwaffe now sending in bombers of their own to attack ships off Dieppe, the Allied situation was steadily deteriorating. Indeed, when Leigh-Mallory demanded an update on the situation, he received a sobering reply from HMS *Calpe*: "Situation too obscure to give [a] useful report."[22]

The disarray was soon creeping into other areas of the battle plan and as 41 Squadron took off for Dieppe this time they were not even fully aware of their target! A startling discovery in 41 Squadron's Archives is an Intelligence Report that states,

S/L HYSE [sic] RECEIVED INSTRUCTIONS BY TELEPHONE TO RENDEZVOUS AT FRISTON WITH 412 SQDN S/L FEE LEADING. FOR SOME REASON HE WAS UNABLE TO GRASP FULLY WHAT THE TARGET WAS, AND OWING TO THE SHORTAGE OF TIME WAS ORDERED TO TAKE OFF IMMEDIATELY. AT 0950 HRS HE PROCEEDED TO FRISTON WITH 412 SQDN. WHEN NEAR FRISTON THEY WERE TOLD TO WAIT FOR OUR FRIENDS "QUITE A CONSIDERABLE TIME". [THE] 8 HURRICANES WERE ENQUIRING WHAT THEIR TARGET WAS ON THEIR WAY TO DIEPPE.[23]

The Squadrons orbited Friston five times before they received orders to proceed, whereupon they escorted the Hurricanes 70 miles across the Channel at zero feet, whose pilots "were nattering all [the] way over trying to find out what their target was".[24]

Finally, their objective became clear: they were to attack the four-gun *Rommel* Battery behind Blue Beach, just east of Dieppe. They arrived a short while later over the western end of Dieppe and 412 Squadron accompanied the Hurricanes into the attack as they swept across Dieppe to reach *Rommel*. 41 Squadron was ordered to port and into a holding pattern off the coast at 2,000-5,000 feet to await and cover their withdrawal.

Each of the 'Hurribombers' carried two 250 lb. bombs, which were seen to land in the target area, some considered direct hits. In doing so, however, they came under intense Flak fire and several aircraft were hit. They also came across various enemy aircraft and attacked them too, making subsequent claims for damaged and probably destroyed FW190s and He111s. Despite everything being thrown against them, however, they suffered no losses and all the aircraft returned to RAF Warmwell at 11:20, their crews "very pleased with themselves".[25] 412 Squadron had suffered more severely under the onslaught of anti-aircraft fire, however: two aircraft were shot down, and one pilot lost.[26]

Some distance from the action around *Rommel* Battery, 41 Squadron continued orbiting off the coast in fine weather, noting 7/10ths cloud over the coast, 9/10ths over land, and heavy smoke over Dieppe. Below them, landing craft were approaching the beaches to commence the planned withdrawal. The final phase of the Operation had commenced. They observed "dozens of other squadrons… milling above"[27], but their relative peace was about to be shattered.

Just before 11:00, they were bounced from the rear by two pairs of FW190s and the air exploded as aircraft broke in every direction. However, "the boys were ready for the attack"[28], and successful evasive action avoided any casualties. The Squadron turned on their attackers and drove them off, with two pilots claiming Focke-Wulfs damaged before they withdrew into France.

The first pair, taking advantage of Yellow Section's reduced numbers, attacked Flt Lt Malta Stepp, Plt Off Rex Poynton and Sgt Plt Bill Coombes RAAF, but wasted their opportunity and Stepp managed to get behind one of them. As his Spitfire was equipped with a cine camera gun, he recorded his part of the action.

Coming up from below and to the port of a FW190, he hit the aircraft with a good burst and saw black smoke emanating from the starboard side of the engine before it made off inland. His Combat Report provides very little detail, and his *Pilot Service Record* only serves to confirm, "19.8.42 SFVB 1100 hrs Dieppe C.C. [cine camera] used 1 FW 190 DAMAGED".[29]

Whilst Yellow Section was busy, the second pair of FW190s attacked but overshot Blue Section at 5,000 feet, and had the misfortune of having all four aircraft turn on them. Flt Lt Douglas Hone, leading the section, Plt Off Harold Knight, and Sgt Plts Jeffrey King RAAF and André Imbert FAFL gave chase and each "had a squirt".[30] Hone's assault consisted of a single eight-second burst at 480 yards. Although his angle of attack closed from 55° to 9°, his opponent pulled away and took wild evasive action, including flipping on his back, leaving Hone unable to submit a claim.

However, the fourth pilot of the quartet, André Imbert, flying Blue 4, fired at the port aircraft of the pair and was able to claim it damaged. He later reported his action thus:

> *While being No. 4 on the Port section I was attacked by two F.W.190, I saw them come in and I went into a skiding [sic] turn in order to escape them. They undershut [sic] me and while they were pulling off after firing at some other aircraft, I gave a long burst to the one flying on the Port side. I fired a burst of 5 seconds using all my cannon ammunition [and] half ¾ of the machine gun, using 15° deflection and I saw white smoke pouring out of the cockpit and the aircraft break formation towards the land.*[31]

The Squadron then broke off to cover the Hurricanes back to the English coast, and flew on to RAF Tangmere, where they landed again at 11:25. Upon inspection by the ground crews, it was found that several of the aircraft bore the scars of the fight, and were peppered with bullet holes.

The ammunition expended by the pilots on this operation was as follows:

Pilot, 09:50-11:20	20mm Cannon	.303 inch MG
Stepp, Malta L.	120	1360
Imbert, André	116	800
Coombes, William M.	60	240
Hone, Douglas H.	20	650
Knight, Harold C.	17	200
Poynton, Thomas R.	15	200
King, Jeffrey C.	0	200

However, the patrol had an unexpected subsequent twist. Despite the fact that Hone had made no claim against the FW190 he had fired upon that morning, he had actually hit and damaged it. This fact did not emerge until some three weeks later when the day's cine camera film (No. K2264) was analysed.[32] Realising his failure to claim a legitimate victory, he belatedly submitted a claim via the formal channels and was granted his FW190 damaged several weeks later.

In support of Hone's claim, the Squadron's Intelligence Officer, Flt Lt Lord Gisborough, sent a telex to 11 Group, RAF Tangmere and RAF Valley on 9 September 1942 stating,

> PLEASE AMEND MY CLAIM FOR 41 SQUADRON 19/8/42 1045 HRS. "TWO FW190 DAMAGED" TO "THREE DAMAGED". F/LT HONE CLAIMS ONE FW190 DAMAGED FROM CINE FILM EVIDENCE IN AN ATTACK HE MADE WHILE ESCORTING HURRI BOMBERS. COMBAT REPORT FOLLOWING.[33]

Hone's ensuing Combat Report states that the attack took place two miles west of Dieppe at 2,000 feet at 10:45, in 7/10ths cloud and smoke haze. He wrote,

> As [the] bombers were on [their] way out, Blue 4 was bounced by two FW.190's from cloud – I turned towards them and managed to get on the tail of one of the FW.190's and opened fire at approx. 350-400 yards, judging by [the cine-gun] film. Owing to the necessity to cover the Bombers, and the fact that there were many more FW.190's above us, I turned back with the Bombers and was unable to notice the effect of my firing. On seeing my film on 8/9/'42, I wish to claim this machine (FW.190) as damaged.[34]

On the reverse of his Combat Report, an additional paragraph has been added and signed by Lord Gisborough, stating,

> Cine Film shows a cannon burst on the Port tail plane in direct line with [the] cockpit on two consecutive exposures.[35]

This is additionally supported by Hone's *Pilot Service Record*, which confirms,

> 19.8.42 Battle of Dieppe <u>1 FW190 Damaged</u>. Leading B Flight on three Patrols and Escort Duties. Whilst escorting Hurribombers Drove off several F.W 190 including one at which he fired & made no claim on landing. However Cine Film showed hit with cannon shell in Port Tail plane with cockpit in direct line beyond. Claimed as F.W.190 Damaged.[36]

Hone's victory is neither recorded in the Squadron ORB nor in any contemporary works as his claim was not submitted until 9 September 1942, a full three weeks after the event occurred.

Operation 6 – Escort Cover, Dieppe

By the time of 41 Squadron's third mission to Dieppe, the evacuation of the beachhead was virtually over. German fire had concentrated on the withdrawing landing craft and ships throughout and the RAF had been continuously called on to provide cover, attack gun emplacements and lay smoke screens.

During the late morning, twenty-four B-17 Flying Fortresses were sent to pound Abbeville-Drucat Airfield, home to JG26, in an attempt to limit the Luftwaffe's airborne assault on the Allied armada. This brought some relief as the bombs hit runways and dispersals, and put the airfield out of service for several hours, during which time pilots were forced to land and refuel elsewhere.

A diversionary attack by the RAF's Typhoon Wing, comprising 56, 266, and 609 Squadrons, was also made at Ostend [Oostende], Belgium, in an effort to draw the Luftwaffe off their onslaught over the evacuation beaches, whilst Bostons from 88 and 107 Squadrons were sent in again to bomb batteries located just behind the beaches.

As the final withdrawals were being made, Fighter Command increased the intensity of its air cover, and it is during this time that 41 Squadron was called upon once again to cover Hurricane bombers attacking batteries that were still laying down concentrated fire on the evacuation efforts.

At 12:50, 175 Squadron took off from RAF Warmwell and five minutes later, RAF Shoreham based 245 Squadron was also airborne. At 13:00, 253 Squadron also took off from RAF Friston and, at the same time, 41 Squadron took to the air to escort the latter two units, codenamed 'Wireworm' and 'Linseed', to Dieppe. The first formation consisted of seven aircraft and the second of eight.

Although ordered not to engage enemy aircraft, this trip across the Channel and back would prove much more intensive than 41 Squadron's previous. Rendezvousing over Shoreham, roughly 19 miles east of Tangmere, they crossed the coast at zero feet and made a bearing for the headland just southwest of Dieppe.

Cloud and heavy smoke obscured their vision as they crossed the French coast with the Hurribombers at zero feet over the cliffs just west of Dieppe. As they did so, they turned to port and headed for an area just beyond the harbour. At this point, the two formations separated, with the leading eight Hurricanes from 253 Squadron veering inland over the railway yards to strafe and bomb batteries firing on the ships. They then turned back towards the coast and came back out right over the centre of Dieppe. 41 Squadron did their best to cover them but, as they arrived over the area target at 13:30, they came under "considerable machine gun [fire] and light flak… and damage was caused to five of our Spitfires".[37]

The formation of seven Hurricanes from 245 Squadron did not turn over the rail yards, but continued further on into Dieppe, over the Arques River and came back out east of the river again to bomb gun positions on the eastern headland. 41 Squadron's Yellow 3 and 4, believed to have been Plt Off Rex Poynton and Sgt Plt Bill Coombes RAAF, broke away from the main formation to escort them.

As they moved through the Dieppe area, the Squadron noted the Luftwaffe was flying a range of aircraft, including FW190s seen below them, Ju88s seen 1,000 feet above them, and an Me210 or FW187, which was spotted in a gap between the clouds higher still. Many fierce dogfights were witnessed but the pilots took no part as they had been ordered not to engage.

Once the bombers had dropped their payloads, it was time to get out again through the smoke and hail of anti-aircraft fire. There was "considerable M.G. fire from [the] ground and 7 out of 12 [aircraft were] hit by bullets".[38] Several of 253 Squadron's Hurricanes suffered similarly and one pilot was forced to bale out.[39]

However, as 41 Squadron crossed the coastal cliffs on their way out again, the pilots realised that the concentrated Flak, smoke and general excitement had caused some confusion: they had unwittingly broken formation and lost sight of each other, and this also resulted in several Hurribombers coming out unescorted, ahead of 41 Squadron.

OC B Flight Flt Lt Douglas Hone was granted a damaged FW190 on the basis of combat film analysis 20 days after Operation *Jubilee*. © Cowell family

One of 41 Squadron's Intelligence Reports from the operation records a staccato of short snippets of information, clearly pieced together from the reports of several different men, of events they had caught sight of in the confusion and their efforts to get back out of the fire storm over Dieppe unscathed.

THE SHIPS OFF DIEPPE WERE NOW BEING BOMBED BY JU 88[s] FROM 1000 FEET IN CLOUD. BOMBS MOSTLY WIDE OF MARK. SGT LLOYD FIRED AT A GUN POST.... A PARACCHUTIST [sic] SEEN FALLING IN FRONT OF A DESTROYER HALF [WAY] ACROSS CHANNEL. ONE BOMB WAS SEEN TO BLOW UP A HOUSE ON CLIFF TOP, EAST OF DIEPPE.[40]

As they headed back across the Channel, it then became apparent that Sqn Ldr Hyde was not with them. When they landed at RAF Tangmere again at 14:08, this fact was confirmed, and when someone recalled seeing that "as we came out the C.O. disappeared over the cliff"[41], it was assumed he had fallen victim to the intense Flak. Sadly, despite ORBs existing at Squadron, Station, Wing and Group level, Intelligence Reports, and a substantial amount of writing on Operation *Jubilee* since 1942, this single, unobtrusive little sentence buried in the middle of an Intelligence Report, that has been hidden away unnoticed in 41 Squadron's Archives for over 60 years, appears to be the only concrete evidence we have of Sqn Ldr Hyde's fate.

Yet another Squadron Intelligence Report suggests it was nonetheless initially hoped that Hyde had survived, stating "S L Hyde NYR [Not Yet Returned]. May have Baled out near a Destroyer"[42], in the vain hope that the man mentioned in Intelligence Escort Report No. 8 (see above) was actually him. However, when no further news was received, he was formally posted missing. It was a tragic and sobering blow for the Squadron. RAF Llanbedr was signalled from RAF Tangmere that same afternoon to inform them of the situation and the Squadron ORB recorded,

On coming out we lost sight of our Commanding Officer S/Ldr. G. C. Hyde and unfortunately he did not return, now reported as missing. He had not been with the Squadron very long but during the short time he

was he was recognised as an efficient Commanding Officer with a charming personality and his loss is very much felt by all his new friends of the Squadron.[43]

It transpired some time later that Sqn Ldr Geoffrey Hyde had indeed been killed by Flak. Just 27 years old at the time, he was a career pilot who had joined the RAF on a Short Service Commission in October 1935. Prior to being posted to command 41 Squadron on 28 July 1942, he had served as a Test Pilot for Vickers-Armstrong at Castle Bromwich, as a flying instructor at 58 OTU at RAF Grangemouth, and most recently as a senior officer with both 65 and 64 Squadrons. His *Pilot Service Record* simply states,

Dieppe. Led 41 Squadron on the three Sorties.
Cover over Dieppe.
Escort to Hurribombers.
Escort to Hurribombers.
SHOT DOWN IN BATTLE OF DIEPPE 3rd SORTIE[44]

Sqn Ldr Hyde's body was recovered and he was buried in the Dieppe Canadian War Cemetery.

The Squadron's third mission over Dieppe would also be their last to France in Operation *Jubilee*. Although it had been the first frightening and frenzied experience of combat for several of the men, only three pilots actually recorded having expended ammunition on this final mission, having been "snap shots at gun posts etc. with unobserved results".[45] They were:

Pilot, 13:00-14:05	20mm Cannon	.303 MG
Atkinson, Thomas G.	10	40
Harrison, Ronald	60	300
Lloyd, J. Max W.	20	100

The RAF Llanbedr ORB reports in a stiff-upper-lip manner that five of the Squadron's pilots returned to their Welsh base during the afternoon, "tired but cheerful"[46], with many stories to relate of events over France. The day was, however, not yet over and six of the pilots remaining at RAF Tangmere – Hone, Hogarth, Poynton, King, Robinson and Warren – were to each fly another sortie before their day drew to a close.

Operation 7 – Scramble

The Luftwaffe followed the withdrawing convoy of ships back across the Channel, compelling Fighter Command to keep up vigilant air cover all afternoon. The weather also deteriorated as the day wore on and, as the convoy made its back towards the English coast, rain began to fall. The 1,000-foot cloud base gave the Luftwaffe a distinct advantage by enabling their pilots to hide in cloud until they pounced on unsuspecting escort fighters and ships, and then disappear back into it to cover their escape.

As such, it came as no surprise when reports were received of a sighting of enemy aircraft off Selsey Bill and, at 15:35, two sections from 41 Squadron were scrambled to intercept them. Yellow Section, comprising Plt Off Rex Poynton and Sgt Plt Ken Warren, and Blue Section, comprising Flt Lt Doug Hone and Sgt Plt Jeffrey King RAAF, made the nine-mile distance within minutes, but nothing was seen and no contact was made. The quartet returned to RAF Tangmere at 16:15.

Operation 8 – Patrol Base

At 16:00, White Section was ordered to patrol the Tangmere area as a precautionary measure. Plt Off Rycherde Hogarth and Sgt Plt Ken Robinson spent 25 uneventful minutes in the air in what would be the Squadron's final operation of the day.[47]

This concluded the Squadron's operational flying on 19 August 1942. The pilots' sorties from RAF Tangmere during Operation *Jubilee* are summarised in the table below:

Pilot / Time	05:45	08:30	08:35	09:35	09:50	13:00	15:35	16:00
Atkinson	-	AB809	-	-	-	BL518	-	-
Coombes	EN781	-	-	-	BL304	EN781	-	-
Harrison	-	-	-	-	-	BL304	-	-
Hoare	BL304	-	BL304	-	-	-	-	-
Hogarth	AR392	-	-	-	-	-	-	W3457
Hone	EN828	-	-	-	EN828	-	EN828	-
Hyde	BL777	-	-	-	BL777	BL777	-	-
Imbert	-	-	-	-	AR392	EN836	-	-
King	BL850	-	-	-	BL850	BL850	BL850	-
Knight	BM533	-	-	-	BM533	AB378	-	-
Lloyd	EN836	BL674	-	-	-	AR392	-	-
Poynton	W3843	-	-	-	BL513[48]	W3843	W3843	-
Robinson	-	-	-	-	EN836	-	-	AD562
Schou	AD271	-	-	-	AD271	AB809	-	-
Slack	AD562	-	-	-	AD562	AD562	-	-
Stepp	BM573	-	BM573	-	BM573	BM573	-	-
Vine	-	-	-	EN781	-	-	-	-
Warren	-	-	-	AB378	-	-	AR392	-
Total Sorties	12	2	2	2	11	12	4	2

Although the information in the above table has been sourced from the ORB's F541 and shows 47 sorties, one Intelligence Report states there were 49 sorties flown: twelve at 05:45, two each at 08:30, 08:35 and 09:35, eleven at 09:50, twelve at 13:00, all in agreement with the F541, but then three at 15:45 and five at 16:00, instead of four and two.[49]

The day's claims against the Luftwaffe were as follows:

Claims, 19 August 1942	Damaged	Location
Hone, Douglas H.	FW190	2 miles west of Dieppe, France
Imbert, André	FW190	Off Dieppe, France
Stepp, Malta L.	FW190	Off Dieppe, France

Whilst it is not clear what the serials of all the damaged aircraft were – by some accounts, there were at least seven – the following casualties are known:

Operation Jubilee

Casualties, 19 August 1942	Serial	Circumstances
Harrison, Ronald	BL304	CD, Cat AC, Dieppe, NI
Hyde, Geoffrey C.	BL777	AA, Dieppe, KIA
Imbert, André	EN836	CD, Cat A, Dieppe, NI
Benjamin, Sydney H.	EN836	Wheels-up landing, Hamble, NI

Additionally, although it did not occur on 19 August 1942, one post-*Jubilee* Intelligence Report lists Sgt Plt Bernard Goodall's death alongside Sqn Ldr Hyde's as an Operation *Jubilee* casualty. Indeed, Goodall's loss was certainly *Jubilee*-related as he was bringing one of the Squadron's aircraft to RAF Tangmere for the operation.

Whilst all of the pilots would have been physically exhausted, some must have been particularly so. Plt Off Rex Poynton and Sgt Plt Jeffrey King RAAF had flown four operational sorties that day and Plt Off Hogarth had been up for the first operation and had participated in the last.

At the conclusion of the day's operational sorties, a number of pilots also made an additional 40-minute non-operational flight back to RAF Llanbedr. It had been a long, intensive day for all involved, and they must have been absolutely worn out.

The Squadron's return to RAF Llanbedr continued the following day, when a further six pilots flew up that afternoon, and a final two on 21 August. The rest of the men undertook the return journey to Llanbedr by train, in two lorries and a car.

As *Jubilee* drew to a close, RAF Commanders sought to assess the damage inflicted on the Luftwaffe and to ascertain what they had themselves sustained. The Tangmere Wing, from which 41 Squadron had operated, recorded the following statistics:[50]

LEFT A plaque commemorating Sgt Plt Bernard Goodall was erected in Weston Patrick churchyard cemetery in March 1994. © Frank Sutton

RIGHT Initially buried at Weston Patrick, Sgt Plt Bernard Goodall was later re-interred in Brookwood Military Cemetery in Woking, Surrey. © Frank Sutton

LEFT Sgt Plt J. M. W. 'Max' Lloyd served with 41 Squadron from 24 September 1941 to 20 August 1942, departing the Squadron only a day after flying three sorties over Dieppe in Operation *Jubilee*. This photograph was taken some time after he was commissioned at the end of 1942. © Lloyd family

RIGHT The man who kept 41 Squadron's aircraft flying from August 1942 until July 1943: Plt Off (later Fg Off) Roger Whipp. He was awarded an OBE for his services in January 1958 and retired in October 1959. © Cowell family

Victories Claimed	Six aircraft destroyed, five probable, 13 damaged, and a number of heavy and light gun posts destroyed
Casualties to Pilots	12 missing, five picked up safe, two killed in accidents, and one slightly wounded
Casualties to Aircraft	12 Spitfires and five Hurricanes missing, three Spitfires Cat E, one Spitfire Cat B, and three Hurricanes Cat Bt
Sorties Flown	744 by single-engined aircraft

It soon became clear that the RAF as a whole had lost around 100 aircraft but after tallying Squadron claims it was felt the Luftwaffe had suffered similarly that day. After the War, however, it was discovered that the Luftwaffe had actually lost just half that number, although many more had been damaged to some extent. In fact, in his work *The Greatest Air Battle*, Norman Franks states that on the day following *Jubilee*, JGs 2 and 26 could only muster 70 serviceable aircraft from a force of 206 the previous morning.

Conversely, however, the Luftwaffe claimed it had shot down 100 aircraft, but later analysis of records suggests around 70 had fallen victim to aerial attack and the rest to ground based Flak, such as was the case with Sqn Ldr Hyde.

Whilst recognising that most 'official' RAF casualty lists differ to some extent, author Norman Franks estimates that 62 pilots and aircrew lost their lives in action, while another two died in accidents. It is not clear whether Sgt Plt Goodall is included in this figure. A further 17 pilots were shot down and captured an estimated 29 were wounded in action or injured. In addition to the 100 aircraft lost, it is believed at least another 66 aircraft were damaged, either in action or in accidents. It had been an expensive day for the RAF.

However, despite these casualties and estimated Allied losses on the ground of 1,000 men killed, 600 wounded, and 1,900 captured, the British media heralded the operation as the greatest victory since the Battle of Britain. So too in Canada, until the casualty figures started appearing in their newspapers, at which time the full scale of the 'cost' of the operation began to become apparent, and some shock set in.

However, none of this should detract from the courage shown by all participants, and the blood, sweat and tears that were shed at Dieppe during the operation. Though not all objectives were realised, *Jubilee* taught Allied Commanders and tacticians valuable lessons that were to benefit them in their future landings, such as those in North Africa, Sicily, Italy and, ultimately, D-Day itself.

In appreciation of their role in *Jubilee*, 41 Squadron received a telex from the Chief of Air Staff, Air Marshal Sir Charles Portal GCB DSO MC, via Headquarters Fighter Command, 9 Group, and finally RAF Llanbedr, stating,

WARMEST CONGRATULATIONS TO ALL SQUADRONS WHO TOOK PART IN TODAYS[51] GREAT BATTLE AND TO ALL THOSE WHOSE WORK ON THE GROUND CONTRIBUTED TO THEIR SUCCESS. YOUR SQUADRONS HAVE THE SATISFACTION OF HAVING SCORED A STRIKING VICTORY OVER THE GERMAN AIR FORCE ON ITS HOME GROUND BUT MORE IMPORTANT STILL OF HAVING EARNED THE CONFIDENCE OF THE ARMY AND NAVY WITH WHOM FOR THE FIRST TIME THEY HAVE HAD THE CHANCE TO CO-OPERATE IN THEIR FULL STRENGTH. PLEASE CONVEY TO ALL CONCERNED MY APPRECIATION AND THANKS FOR A GREAT DAYS WORK.[52]

20 August 1942 – Most of the personnel of 66, 87, 118 and 501 Squadrons left RAF Tangmere for their home bases, as did six pilots from 41 Squadron. Led by Flt Lt Malta Stepp, they were airborne at 15:25 and landed back at RAF Llanbedr at 17:40. During the day, the RAF Valley Sector Commander, Wg Cdr Henry Ramsbottom-Isherwood, visited the pilots who had already returned to Llanbedr. Pending a replacement for Sqn Ldr Hyde, Flt Lt Douglas Hone was appointed Acting Officer Commanding.

Sgt Plt Max Lloyd also left the Squadron around this date, having made his final operational flight with 41 Squadron during Operation *Jubilee*. He became another of the many 41 Squadron pilots who would be posted to Malta, and was commissioned at the end of the year. Lloyd was awarded the DFC in 1945 and retired from the Air Force in 1955 as a Flight Lieutenant.[53]

21 August 1942 – The last of the Squadron's pilots, Plt Off Reg Hoare and Sgt Plt Ken Schou departed for RAF Llanbedr at 10:00, but their trip was delayed by poor weather and they were forced to land at RAF Atcham. The ground crews also left RAF Tangmere for Llanbedr by train this morning, thereby ending 41 Squadron's participation in Operation *Jubilee*.

Llanbedr
23 August 1942 – 24 February 1943

2

August 1942 – During the remaining days of the month, the Squadron spent much of its time conducting flying training, with intermittent scrambles or routine patrols. Weather prevented any flying on 25 August, and the Squadron was not called upon operationally on 23 and 27 August.

23 August 1942 – Dull weather with low clouds welcomed the Squadron back to its previous routine. The pilots were on readiness all day and released at dusk, but no operational flying was undertaken. EB-W arrived in Llanbedr from Hamble at 13:40, flown in by 1st Officer Shuurman of the ATA.[1] This is thought to have been one of the two aircraft that had been flown to Hamble on 19 and 20 August, which had now been repaired.

Plt Off Rycherde Hogarth and Sgt Plt Jeffrey King flew to RAF Woodvale in the Magister, and the AOC 12 Group, Air Cdre Charles Steele DFC, visited dispersals. Several men participated in a Station cricket match between the Officers' Mess and the Sergeants' Mess in which the latter team won by over 100 runs.

24 August 1942 – B Flight at dawn readiness; A Flight at 30 minutes. Flying training was undertaken all day until 20:00, and included practice dogfights and formation flying. Fg Off Thomas Scott (BL518) undertook a local reconnaissance flight between 10:30-11:30, and Red Section (Scott AD271 & Schou AB809) was airborne on a patrol between 16:45 and 18:10.

Around this time, 19-year-old Sgt Plt Anthony Beard and 21-year-old Sgt Plt Clifford Monk joined the Squadron on their first operational postings. Having both joined the RAFVR in January 1941, they had completed EFTS in the United Kingdom and SFTS in Canada, before returning to the United Kingdom with their Wings to complete AFU and OTU courses. Beard arrived with 265 non-operational flying hours in his logbook and would remain with the Squadron for four months; by the time of his arrival, Monk had logged 260 non-operational hours and would remain with the unit approximately five months.

26 August 1942 – B Flight at dawn readiness; A Flight at 15 minutes. Good weather allowed flying training to be undertaken throughout the day, and several local reconnaissance flights were also made. These took place at 11:35, 14:10, 15:45, and 17:40, and concluded with a patrol between 19:35 and 21:00, which was undertaken by Plt Off Rex Poynton and Sgt Plt Leslie Prickett. All were uneventful.

The Inspector-General of the Air Training Corps, ACM Sir Robert Brooke-Popham GCVO KCB CMG DSO AFC, also visited the Station today, accompanied by Gp Capt George Bailey DSO, and stayed overnight.

27 August 1942 – A Flight at dawn readiness; B Flight at 30 minutes. Flying training today included a practice interception on two Lockheed Hudson bombers of No. 1 (Coastal) OTU, as they departed Silloth in Cumberland. At 15:50, the entire Squadron was airborne to practice Wing formation flying with Andreas based 93 Squadron. Despite extremely poor visibility, the two units rendezvoused over Llandudno and followed the coast to Blackpool via Preston, before returning to their respective bases. 41 Squadron was released at dusk.

Separately, Plt Off Reg Hoare was sent to Tangmere to retrieve Spitfire Vb, W3457, which had remained in Sussex since the Squadron's recent deployment to the station for Operation *Jubilee*.

Fg Off (later Flt Lt) Tom Slack served with 41 Squadron from 14 April 1942 until he was shot down over France on 18 July 1943. He evaded, escaped over the Pyrenees and was flown back to the United Kingdom from Gibraltar approximately six weeks later. In an exception to the general rule, he was then posted back to 41 Squadron. © Tom Slack, via Dan Johnson

On his return flight, he put down at Brize Norton in Oxfordshire at 15:40 but, being unfamiliar with the airfield, overshot the runway, swung to avoid the boundary, and crash-landed when the undercarriage collapsed. Fortunately he was not injured, but his logbook was endorsed 'Carelessness'.

28 August 1942 – B Flight at dawn readiness; A Flight at 30 minutes. No entry appears on the Squadron ORB's F540 for this date, and it appears to have been erroneously omitted: the F541 shows that at least one operational patrol was undertaken when White Section (Coombes W3935 & Warren BL518) were airborne between 14:50 and 15:40.

An Intelligence Report in 41 Squadron's Archives shows a Squadron-strength exercise with 93 Squadron was held in the evening today. 41 Squadron was off the deck at 17:00 led by Flt Lt Doug Hone and rendezvoused with 93 Squadron over Amlwch, Anglesey, at 7,000 feet at 17:15. The goal was to sweep Squires Gate and seek out aircraft of 315 (Polish) Squadron which were designated the role of 'the enemy'.

With 41 Squadron leading and 93 on their starboard quarter, the two units set a heading of 080° for Squires Gate. They crossed the coast a short while later and climbed to 15,000 feet. However, weather conditions made the exercise difficult, and Hone soon realised that despite clear skies, thick haze between 10,000 and 15,000 feet hindered his downwards vision and he was unable to see land or pinpoint his position, even though the Controller informed him he was over Squires Gate.

Realising the exercise was therefore futile, Hone obtained a second objective: Preston. Heading on an easterly course for a few minutes, Hone turned the Wing south. The Controller informed him he was four miles north of Preston but the haze still hindered his vision. He turned the Wing southeast and headed in that direction for a few minutes, then swung back west towards the Irish Sea. As he was about to reach the coast and head home, he finally spotted Preston through the haze.

At this time, 93 Squadron turned northwest for Andreas, whilst 41 Squadron turned southwest for Llanbedr where they landed at 18:20. As not one single 'hostile' aircraft of 315 Squadron had been sighted or attacked during the exercise, there was little solace in the fact there were therefore no 'casualties' to report in the Wing.

Sgt Plt Walter 'Wingco' East served with 41 Squadron from 18 June 1942 until 3 May 1943, when he was killed in action. He is seen here reading, waiting in readiness with his Mae West on.
© Cowell family

29 August 1942 – A Flight at dawn readiness; B Flight at 15 minutes. Practice flying was undertaken all day and the routine was only broken by a scramble at 13:45 by Plt Off Harold Knight (AB378) and Sgt Plt Sydney Benjamin (W3848), who returned at 14:30, reporting having seen nothing.

30 August 1942 – B Flight at dawn readiness; A Flight at 15 minutes. Practice interceptions and formation flying practice were undertaken all day. Flt Lt Doug Hone (EN827) and Plt Off Robert Wood (AB378) conducted an offensive patrol along the Irish coast between 18:54 and 20:00, but returned with nothing to report.

31 August 1942 – B Flight placed at readiness at 13:00; A Flight at 30 minutes. Once again, practice flying was undertaken throughout the day. The F540 states that no operational flying took place, but the F541 indicates that offensive patrols were undertaken by Black Section (Hogarth BL562 & Roberts BL674) at 14:25 and by Black again (Hone EN827 & Hogarth AR392) at 19:10.

September 1942 – As summer turned to autumn this month, the weather deteriorated with it, thereby reducing operational flying during September to a total of just 13 convoy patrols, 12 area patrols, four scrambles and one ASR search on 12 days. No contact was made with the Luftwaffe.

Nonetheless, the Squadron was able to complete much of their planned flying programme, which consisted of practice Rhubarbs, formation drill, dusk circuits and landings, low level sweeps, night flying, and practice interceptions on Hudson aircraft from No. 1 (Coastal) OTU.

The Squadron also participated in an exercise in Northern Ireland late in the month, but it was hampered by weather and it took the pilots over two days just to get there. Whilst three of the ensuing days were fit for flying, weather conditions caused a reduction in flying on another three, and an overnight stop on the Isle of Man on the way home.

The month also saw the arrival of a new Commanding Officer, replacing Sqn Ldr Hyde, who had been killed at Dieppe, whilst one pilot was killed in a flying accident. Three pilots were also posted overseas, and two new pilots joined the unit.

1 September 1942 – Poor weather with light rain. B Flight went at dawn readiness at 05:30, and remained at this state until sunset; the rest of the Squadron were set at 30 minutes readiness.

Weather improvement permitted Yellow Section to get airborne at 14:30 to practice camera attacks and do a Sector Reconnaissance. Flt Lt Stepp practiced attacks by himself whilst Plt Off Hoare and Sgt Plts Coombes, Stonier, Vine and Warren practiced camera attacks and formation flying. An offensive patrol was also undertaken by Blue Section (Imbert BL674 & Underwood AB378) between 14:50 and 16:00). The AOC of 25 (Armament) Group, AVM Edward Davis OBE, visited the Station, and the Squadron was released at 20:38.

2 September 1942 – Poor weather with rain, cloud base at 1,000 feet, visibility 2-4 miles. A Flight at dawn readiness until 13:00 when B Flight took over. From 09:00, four pilots spent an hour on the Link Trainer[2] whilst two pilots practiced camera attacks.

At 11:45, Flt Sgt Jack Stonier (AR331) & Sgt Plt Kenneth Warren (BL518) were scrambled but returned within 35 minutes with nothing to report. This was followed at 14:20 by a patrol of the Irish coast by Flt Lt Stepp (BM573) and Sgt Plts Atkinson (BL850), Coombes (W3935) and Imbert (BL674) until 15:25.[3] At 14:25, two sections took off to practice formation flying and returned at 15:55 and, between 16:10 and 17:40, one section practice direction findings. Formation and local flying practice continued until 19:19 and the Squadron was released shortly after 20:30.

Separately, 26-year-old Australian Sgt Plt Frederick White joined the Squadron today, replacing Sgt Plt Ken Warren who was posted overseas.[4]

3 September 1942 – B Flight at dawn readiness; the rest of the Squadron at 30 minutes. Day of Prayer; the ten Officers and 350 Airmen on the Station attended Church Parades. As poor weather with low cloud and rain hindered all flying until midday, the pilots attended a lecture to assess combat film footage instead. During the afternoon, formation flying and break-away practice were commenced, which continued until 19:10. Plt Off Ronald Green re-joined the unit from is attachment to Merston.

Separately, Sqn Ldr Thomas F. Neil DFC* joined the Squadron today as its new Commanding Officer. The ORB records, "We understand that he has been having a rest from operations and he seems keen to get 'Cracking' again."[5]

A Replacement for Sqn Ldr Hyde

It had taken a full two weeks to replace Sqn Ldr Geoffrey Hyde, who had been killed over Dieppe during Operation *Jubilee* on 19 August. During this time, Flt Lt Douglas Hone had fulfilled the role of Commanding Officer in an interim, acting capacity.

The new Commanding Officer was 22-year-old Liverpudlian, Sqn Ldr Thomas Francis 'Ginger' Neil DFC and Bar, who had joined the RAFVR as an NCO pilot in October 1938 at the age of just 18. He had attended 17 E&RFTS at Barton prior to his mobilisation on 2 September 1939 and completing his training at 8 FTS at Montrose. His first operational posting came in May 1940, when he joined 249 Squadron at Church Fenton flying Hurricanes.

Commissioned just two days after his arrival, he claimed his first victory on 7 September, followed by several more in quick succession: one on 11 September, three-and-a-half on 15 September, one on 18 September, another three-and-a-half on 27 September, and one shared on 6 October. Quickly gaining a reputation as a good marksman, he was awarded the DFC on 8 October 1940. Not resting on his laurels, he claimed another five victories within the following month. This resulted in him being awarded a Bar to his DFC on 26 November.

His closest shave came on 7 November when the North Weald Wing Leader, Wg Cdr Victor Beamish, collided with his aircraft in mid-air, which cut off his Hurricane's tail. Fortunately, however, he was able to bale out uninjured. Undaunted by the incident, he was appointed Flight Commander in mid-December 1940, despite the fact he was still a Pilot Officer. His promotion

Sgt W. M. 'Bill' Coombes RAAF flew with 41 Squadron from 9 June 1942 to 18 September 1942, during which time he was commissioned. He remained in the Air Force after the War, serving as Air Attaché in Saigon early in the Vietnam War and retired as an Honorary Group Captain in February 1968. © The Spitfire Association, Australia

to Probationary Flying Officer came through in early March 1941, followed by Flying Officer (WS) in May.

That same month, he embarked for Malta with 249 Squadron aboard HMS *Ark Royal*, where the unit arrived on 21 May, and moved into quarters at Ta Kali. He claimed one victory the following month and left the island on Boxing Day 1941, his tour expired. He returned to the United Kingdom via the Middle East, South Africa, West Africa and Canada, and finally docked at Liverpool in early March 1942. Upon arrival, he was posted to 81 Group as a Flight Lieutenant, and rested in the role of Tactics Officer until June 1942.

He spent the months of June to September 1942 at 56 OTU at Tealing, where he fulfilled the role of Chief Flying Instructor, after which he returned to operations as 41 Squadron's new Commanding Officer, with a promotion to Squadron Leader.

4 September 1942 – A Flight at dawn readiness. The day's training commenced shortly after 09:00, when the first pilots were in the air, and aerobatics, formation flying and local reconnaissance continued until 17:15. One section was sent up on a patrol between 09:05 and 09:55 (Stepp AR393 & Poynton BM573), and a second between 09:50 and 10:45 (Benjamin EN827 & Wood EN780). Both were uneventful.

6 September 1942 – A Flight at dawn readiness from 05:30. At around 09:00, a message was received that a Hudson bomber had been reported missing and Plt Off Reg Hoare (AB809) and Sgt Plt Bill Coombes (W3935) were sent up ten minutes later to conduct a search. A Beaufighter of Valley based 456 Squadron had also been airborne between 06:25 and 07:50 to search for the same aircraft north of The Skerries.

The aircraft in question was Lockheed Hudson I, N7325, B59, of Silloth based No. 1 (Coastal) OTU, which had been on a night navigation exercise from its base to South Rock, to the Kish Light Vessel off Dublin, to The Skerries, and back to base. The last radio contact with the crew was at 00:30 on 6 September when they were about 20 miles south of South Rock. The 1 OTU ORB records,

At 0515 hrs Air Sea Rescue was instituted through 15 Group, who arranged for aircraft from Valley and Andreas to search the Irish Sea, and for a broadcast to be made to all shipping in the area. At 0817 and 0823 Anson aircraft left Silloth to fly over the course. Returning at 1127 and 1150 these aircraft had nothing to report. Aircraft from Valley and Andreas and 82 Group also had nothing to report. At 1234 hrs Hudson aircraft B69 left to carry out search of Cardigan Bay, but returned at 1800 hrs, having located nothing.[6]

It was a similar story for Hoare and Coombes who returned at 10:00, having seen nothing.[7]

At 09:50, all pilots and the Station Commander attended a lecture on Enemy Flak in the A Flight dispersals area. It was felt the lecture was of, "inestimable value to the pilots, especially in view of their possible operations which would include ground targets."[8]

Sgt Plts André Imbert (W3848) and Peter Roberts (BM533) received the order to 'scramble base' at 15:55, but returned 50 minutes later with nothing to report. This was Imbert's last operational flight with 41 Squadron. He was commissioned the following year but was killed in action with 165 Squadron in late July 1943.

Finally, Flt Lt Charles Chappell (EN827) and Sgt Plt Russel Oxenham (EN780) were sent up on an uneventful patrol between 19.25 and 20:30, and this concluded the day's flying.

7 September 1942 – There is little available information on the day's activity, with the exception of the fact that the Squadron placed at readiness at 13:00, whilst an uneventful offensive patrol was undertaken by Green Section (Wood BM533 & King W3848) between 17:25 and 19:25.

8 September 1942 – A Flight at dawn readiness. The Squadron occupied itself during the day with low flying practice, but two operational patrols were also conducted to southern Éire. The first of these, by Black Section (Roberts BL674 & Robinson BM533), appears to have been abortive, and was only airborne between 18:05 and 18:25. The second, Pink Section (Benjamin AR392, Chappell W3848, Hone EN827), was airborne at 18:35 and returned at 19:40 with nothing to report.

9 September 1942 – B Flight at dawn readiness. The afternoon was taken up with patrols over convoy 'Wheel'[9], in cooperation with Beaufighters from Valley's 456 Squadron. Patrols commenced at 13:45 and continued until 20:35.

Convoy Patrols, 9 September 1942	Section	Up	Down
Green BL518, Vine AR331	Red	13:45	15:15
Harrison AR393, Poynton BM573	Yellow	14:30	15:55
Hone EN827, Wood BM533	Blue	15:15	16:55
Knight EN780, Oxenham W3848	Green	16:10	17:30
Imbert AD562, Roberts BL674	Black	16:50	18:25
Green BL518, White R6919	White	17:45	19:10
Hoare AR331, Prickett W3935	Red	18:40	20:10
Benjamin W3848, Robinson EN780	Blue	19:35	20:35

10 September 1942 – A Flight at dawn readiness. The morning was spent on convoy patrols, and Sqn Ldr Neil took the entire Squadron up to conduct formation practice during the afternoon. It was the first time the whole Squadron had been airborne together under Neil's leadership, and they spent 65 minutes in the air from 14:55. At 18:05, Blue Section (Atkinson AR392 & King BL850) were ordered on an offensive patrol and returned at 19:40 with nothing to report.

Convoy Patrols, 10 September 1942	Section	Up	Down
Green AR331, Harrison R6919	Red	06:40	08:35
Poynton AB809, Stonier W3935	Yellow	07:45	09:20
Atkinson BL674, King AD562	Blue	08:30	10:05
Roberts AR392, Robinson EN780	Green	09:05	11:05
Coombes W3935, Scott AB809	White	10:00	11:25

11 September 1942 – B Flight at dawn readiness; A Flight at 30 minutes. Four pilots, designated Red Section, practiced formation flying between 11:30 and 12:10 despite the cloudy conditions, and individual practice flying was conducted during the afternoon. Plt Off Ronald Green (BL518) & Flt Sgt Jack Stonier (W3935) were sent on an operational patrol between 18:50 and 20:10, and the Squadron was released at 20:20.

12 September 1942 – A Flight at dawn readiness; B Flight at 30 minutes. Practice flying was carried out throughout the day, which included formation flying and dogfights. At 12:40, Yellow Section (Poynton W3378 & Stonier W3935) was scrambled, but returned an hour later with nothing to report. Sqn Ldr Neil led four pilots, similarly designated Yellow Section, on formation practice between 15:20 and 16:15, and the Squadron was released at 20:15.

15 September 1942 – B Flight at dawn readiness; A Flight at 30 minutes. Red Section made a practice Rhubarb of the Isle of Man between 11:10 and 12:15, and another section with the same designation performed a local patrol between 15:10 and 16:05. White section was then sent up to practice camera attacks whilst Sgt Plt Frederick White RAAF practiced individual aerobatics, and Red Section was sent on a patrol of Carnsore Point between 18:10 and 19:05. Unfortunately, neither the participants of this operational patrol nor those of the 15:10 patrol are recorded.

16 September 1942 – A Flight at dawn readiness; B Flight at 30 minutes. Local flying practice was carried out throughout the day and in the evening six pilots participated in a night flying exercise from RAF Valley, around 35 miles northeast of Llanbedr, commencing at 19:15. The participants were Sqn Ldr Neil, Flt Lts Douglas Hone and Malta Stepp, and Plt Offs Rycherde Hogarth, Thomas Scott and Tom Slack.

17 September 1942 – B Flight at dawn readiness; A Flight at 30 minutes. Five of the pilots who participated in the previous evening's night flying exercise at RAF Valley returned during the morning, whilst the rest of the Squadron were occupied with practice flying and camera attacks. Yellow Section was sent up on an operational patrol at 18:35, but nothing was seen and the participants are not recorded.

18 September 1942 – A Flight at dawn readiness under cloudy skies; B Flight at 30 minutes. Local reconnaissance flights and camera tests were carried out by the pilots, after which they all reported to A Flight dispersals for a lecture by Wg Cdr Desmond Sheen on the subjects of 'action on meeting enemy aircraft', 'tactics during convoy patrols when enemy aircraft approach', and 'landing without flaps'.

Separately, there were also a number of personnel movements today. These included the arrival of 29-year-old Londoner, Fg Off Douglas Haywood, who would be nicknamed 'Haybag', and the departure of two of the Squadron's Australian pilots, 22-year-old Plt Off Bill Coombes and 20-year-old Sgt Plt Jeffrey King.[10]

Having joined the RAF as an NCO pilot trainee in late summer 1936, Douglas Haywood was by now quite an experienced pilot. Initially seeing service flying Fairey Battles with 88 Squadron during the Battle of France, he was shot down in mid-June 1940, shortly after the fall of France,

Fg Off Harry W. Smith was the Squadron Adjutant from August 1942 until early 1944. © Ron Johnson, via Dan Johnson

but was rescued and returned to his unit. He then spent a year with 504 Squadron and was commissioned in July 1941. Now a Flying Officer, 41 Squadron became his third operational unit.

19 September 1942 – B Flight at dawn readiness; A Flight at 30 minutes. Poor weather with low mist and visibility of approximately three miles. A Flight's pilots practiced on the Link Trainer from 09:05, followed by three pilots undertaking air tests. Sgt Plt Jack Stonier subsequently gave a lecture on dismantling a machine gun, and this was followed by a briefing by the Sqn Ldr Neil. He informed the pilots that they would be heading to RAF Eglinton, in County Londonderry, Northern Ireland, for a week-long Army, Transport and Shipping cooperation exercise codenamed 'Punch'.

20 September 1942 – Very poor weather, low mist, and no flying as the pilots prepared to fly to Eglinton. However, there was a large attendance during the day at a Church of England Parade for the National Day of Thanksgiving recognition of "the deliverance wrought in the Battle of Britain".[11]

Exercise Punch

The Squadron prepared to fly to Northern Ireland and waited in readiness for weather conditions to improve. However, their wait was in vain and at 15:30 it was decided not to proceed today after all. At 11:30 the following morning, when the weather had still not lifted sufficiently, it was decided to wait yet another day at Llanbedr.

It was not until 16:15 on 22 September, that conditions finally allowed 14 aircraft to take off for Ballyhalbert in County Down, where they landed at 17:15. An hour later, twelve aircraft took off for the remaining 30-minute flight to Eglinton, leaving two pilots behind, although no reason is given. The ground personnel followed in a pair of HP54 Harrow transport aircraft and arrived later in the evening.[12]

The ORB records the Squadron's mood at this time. Whilst taking the weather-forced delays with some humour, at the same time a little cynicism also crept into the report. It states,

> *The Squadron, it appears, has become the "Wandering 41st" of the Royal Air Force, in fact it has been suggested that the title be changed to "The Forty First (Nomad) Squadron" and St. Christopher be adopted as the Squadron Crest. Rumour has it that all ground crews are being issued with Parachutes and Dinghies,*

Flt Lt Douglas Hone served with 41 Squadron from 23 May 1942 to 30 August 1943, serving as OC B Flight from 10 June 1942 until his departure. His also acted as interim OC 41 Squadron, between Sqn Ldr Geoffrey Hyde's loss at Dieppe on 19 August 1942 and Sqn Ldr Tom Neil's arrival on 3 September 1942. © Tom Harvey

as they are so frequently airborne in Handley Page Harrows, that it is becoming positively dangerous to fly so much without the chance of baling out with safety. Flying 'hours'?:- 15th June Merston to Martlesham, 30th June Martlesham to Hawkinge, 1st July Hawkinge to Debden, 31st July Debden to Longtown (Carlisle), 11th August Longtown to Llanbedr, 17th August Llanbedr to Tangmere (Dieppe Show), 23rd September Llanbedr to Eglinton, 30th September Eglinton to Llanbedr, so we certainly do get around![13]

Despite the humour, it would become a memorable posting, but not for the right reasons, as it was dogged by inclement weather and flying accidents that left one pilot dead, one aircraft destroyed and a second damaged. Although the Squadron attempted to take part in the exercise between the 23 and 29 September, much of their time was spent on the ground waiting for conditions to improve sufficiently to allow them to fly.

23 September 1942 – Continuous rain with low cloud. The Squadron formally commenced the exercise today, following a briefing at dispersals at 08:00. The first six aircraft were airborne at 10:00 and spent 45 minutes attacking troops and vehicles, despite unremitting rain, and one pilot later recorded his successful 'destruction' of an 'enemy' Defiant. Six aircraft were kept at readiness from dawn until dusk and the movements were followed by Flt Lt Lord Gisborough and an Army Captain on a large "fully detailed map, using marking flags."[14]

24 September 1942 – A Flight at dawn readiness; B Flight took over at 08:00. In significantly improved weather, B Flight was tasked with attacking shipping and landing craft at Newcastle, County Down, between 09:20 and 10:25. During this exercise, however, Sgt Plt Russel Oxenham made a low level turn over Dundrum Bay in Spitfire Vb, AD574, EB-H, to attack the 'enemy'. In doing so, his wing clipped the swell and he plunged straight into shallow water about 1¼ miles off the beach. He was killed instantly.

Though trained and authorised to carry out such a manoeuvre, a Court of Enquiry found that Oxenham had misjudged his height. The ORB recorded, "It is very sad to lose a young and promising pilot in such a manner. He was a keen pilot and without exception was liked by all the pilots."[15,16]

25 September 1942 – B Flight at dawn readiness; A Flight took over at 08:30. Heavy rain with low cloud hindered flying until 15:20, when Red Section was sent to attack lorries and troops for 45

minutes. Unexpectedly, Green Section (Slack EN780 & Chappell AR392) was scrambled at 15:35 to intercept an unidentified aircraft in the area, but it proved to be the Squadron's own Sgt Plt Ken Robinson, who was conducting an R/T test, and they landed again at 16:15.[17] The exercise was continued into the evening and at 19:10 Red and Yellow Sections were sent up to attack armoured cars. They returned at 19:50, and the Squadron was released at ten minutes later.

26 September 1942 – A Flight at dawn readiness; B Flight at 15 minutes. Today proved to be one of the few good days for flying, and the exercise proceeded in earnest. B Flight's Diary recorded that the,

> …*weather [was] pretty good today for flying; at 07.38 two sections from 'A' Flight took off on Army Co-op and landed at 08.20; today turned out to be very active for the Squadron as the enemy were making progress […] After very many sorties shooting up convoys, troop concentrations and pontoon bridges the Squadron was released at 18.45.*[18]

Attacks were made throughout the day on troops, on a pontoon bridge, and on transport, and another Defiant was claimed 'destroyed'.

Flt Lt Malta Stepp arrived in Eglinton during the afternoon, having flown from Llanbedr in one of the Squadron's Spitfires. He was wearing a brand new USAAF uniform, which he had just taken delivery of, upon his transfer to that service with the rank of Captain. This was clearly reason enough for a big night on the town and the ORB reports it in unusually candid detail,

> *The Squadron took Londonderry by storm in the evening with the redoubtable assistance of our two army liaison officers. The only place of amusement in 'Derry is the Northern Counties Club – and we turned up in force to consume a few firkins of the native brew i.e. Guiness* [sic] *and glance with approving eye upon the Colleens. However as the Navy were there we didn't have all our own way, nevertheless the Squadron had many pleasant dances to the music of an excellent R.A.F. band.*[19]

Flt Lt Stepp was posted to 121 (Eagle) Squadron at Rochford, in time for the unit's transfer to the USAAF as the 335th Fighter Squadron on 29 September. He transferred to the 336th Fighter Squadron in 1943, but was posted to the 2906th Observation Training Group USAAF at Atcham

Sqn Ldr Thomas F. 'Ginger' Neil DFC* was OC 41 Squadron from 3 September 1942 to 25 July 1943. © Cowell family

as a flying instructor later in the year. Whilst flying with a student pilot on 30 September 1943, both men flew into the side of the mountain Cats Tor in Cheshire and were killed.

27 September 1942 – B Flight at readiness at 07:30; A Flight at 30 minutes. The weather cooperated again today and the Squadron had another busy day on the exercise.

> *Weather today ideal for flying and the Squadron was very active again today* [sic] *as the enemy were quite near to base in parts, and the A/C were attacking the enemy at there* [sic] *most advanced points near base; in red & yellow's second sortie at 13.25 P/O Green, P/O Scott & Sgt Schou claimed a Hurricane each while Sgt Vine*['s] *claim was one Defiant* [...] *All sorties today were in Co-op with the Army Exercise, released at 18.00 hrs.*[20]

However, the Squadron also sustained a minor casualty, which could have ended disastrously for the pilot. A Flight's Plt Off Thomas Scott was flying one of four aircraft that took off from Eglinton at 10:35 for a 20-minute 'attack' on troops. As he took off, he "...hit a tree but landed okay."[21] Fortunately, Scott was uninjured and he was able to carry on with the exercise later, no doubt a little shaken for the experience.[22]

28 September 1942 – A Flight at dawn readiness; B Flight at 30 minutes. Activities were again curtailed by low cloud, rain, mist and poor visibility today. Nonetheless, the pilots continued the exercise, flying attacks against ground targets until it was formally concluded at 16:45. Red Section was placed on readiness for Station defence until dusk, and the Squadron was released at 19:45.

29 September 1942 – B Flight on dawn readiness for Station defences, whilst the unit prepared for their return to Llanbedr. However, continuing poor weather hindered their departure until 14:50. On their way, however, they received the message that the weather at Llanbedr was unsuitable for them to land, and were instead diverted to Andreas, on the Isle of Man.

When the weather at Llanbedr failed to improve, the decision was made to remain in Andreas overnight. Their initial disappointment at the postponement of their return 'home', soon changed when,

> *The Station people 'looked us over'* [and] *suggested that a dance be arranged to welcome us. With Beer at 8d per pint and a number of very charming W.A.A.F.'s, a good time was enjoyed by all. Naturally the "Specialist Officers" – "Engineering Officer and Adjutant" went along with the boys to keep them out of mischief.*
> *After our successful night at Andreas, the Squadron plus Harrows took off enroute for Llanbedr and Home Sweet Home. Incidentally, the charming W.A.A.F. Officers turned out in force to bid the Squadron a fond farewell.*[23]

The Squadron departed Andreas at 09:20 the following morning, and arrived back in Llanbedr an hour later to find the weather had improved little.

30 September 1942 – Despite bad weather, heavy rain, and low visibility, three sections were airborne during the day. Yellow Section (Schou BM573 & Vine W3935) was ordered to scramble base at 12:05, and returned 65 minutes later with nothing to report. Blue Section was ordered up at 16:50 to escort a ship, and Green Section was sent up at 18:10 to escort a destroyer. Both convoy patrols were uneventful and the sections landed at 18:15 and 18:30, respectively.

Separately today, Plt Off Ken Schou RNZAF, who had been with the Squadron since April 1942, was posted away, destined for Malta. He returned to the United Kingdom as a Flying Officer in late May 1943, and then appears to have fulfilled non-flying postings in Northern Ireland until late 1944. Schou was repatriated home in mid-December 1944 as a Flight Lieutenant, and arrived in New Zealand in February 1945. He remained in the RNZAF Reserve after the War and retired in 1964.

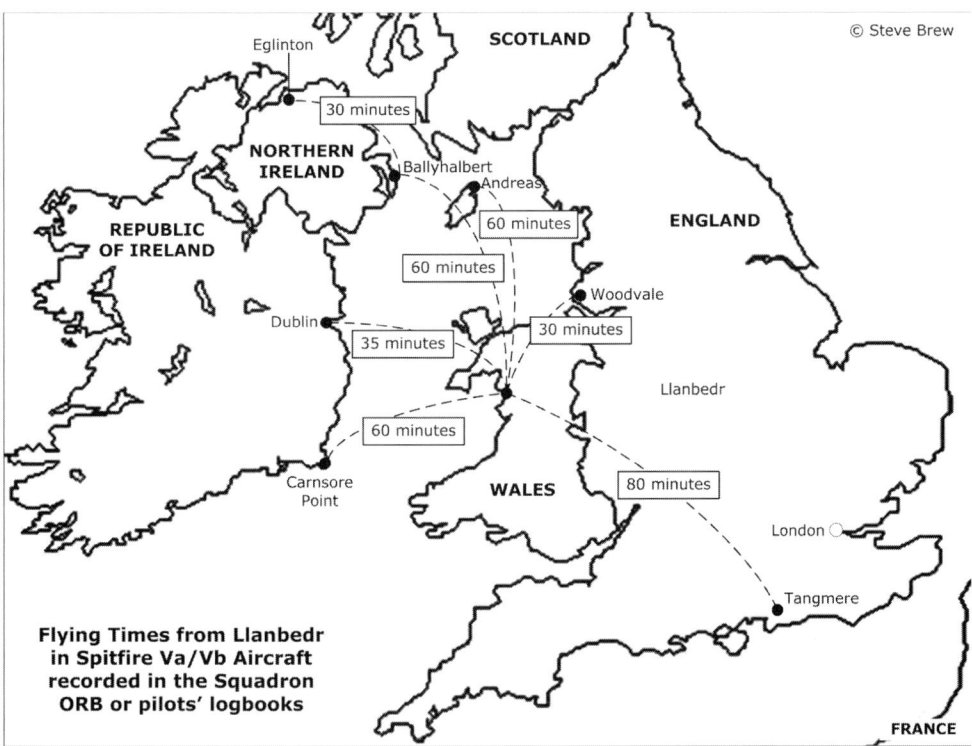

October 1942 – It was a messy month, plagued by poor weather, that proved memorable for all the wrong reasons. During the last ten days of October, the Squadron lost eight pilots – approximately one third of its Establishment – to death, posting and internment. The deaths were a particularly hard blow for the unit, as three pilots were killed in a single flying accident; they had nothing to do with enemy action.

Weather severely restricted flying throughout the month, which was particularly evident during the Squadron's attempts to participate in an exercise at Tangmere: it took five days to get to there, and one day to prepare the aircraft for one day's flying, before the exercise was cancelled. It then took two days to get back to Llanbedr again!

Operational flying was undertaken on only nine days – 1-2, 9, 11, 15, 22, 26, 28 and 31 October – and the month's total flying amounted to 27 operations (55 sorties). These included nine operations (18 sorties) on the one day flown in defence of an exercise at Tangmere, but only six operations (12 sorties) of those remaining took place during the second half of the month.

2 October 1942 – There was no flying all day today as the Squadron prepared to move to Tangmere for another exercise the following morning. As 18 aircraft were required to be serviceable, ground crews worked through the night. The Squadron paraded at 19:00 for instructions to prepare for the move. After their release, the men attended a concert and show given in No. 2 Dining Hall by the No. 3 MT School at Pwllheli.

At this time, Flt Sgt 'Barney' Underwood was posted away, having suffered sinus issues for some time. After medical treatment, he was posted to a refresher course and commissioned before being posted to 748 Squadron FAA as a ferry pilot, where he remained until the cessation of hostilities. Demobbed as a Flying Officer in March 1946, he re-joined the RAFVR General Duties Branch in 1952 and retired in 1962.

Sgt Pilot Frederick C. White RAAF flew with 41 Squadron from 2 September 1942 to 15 October 1942, when he was posted back to Australia and continued to serve until retiring in 1946 as a Flying Officer. © The Spitfire Association, Australia

Exercise Aflame

3-4 October 1942 – Poor weather with heavy rain prevailed all day, which hindered the Squadron's move to Tangmere for a new exercise, named 'Aflame', and they were released until 07:30 on 5 October. In a repeat of the havoc wrought by the weather during Exercise 'Punch' not a week earlier, it took five full days before the entire unit was there.

5 October 1942 – Poor weather this morning hindered an early start, but when conditions improved around midday, 18 aircraft took off for Tangmere. However, the weather came down again enroute and they were forced down at Honiley, seven miles southwest of Coventry, where they were compelled to stay the night. Three HP54 Harrow transport aircraft with ground crew and equipment did, however, manage to make the full journey and arrived in Tangmere just before 14:30, whereupon the men were released.

6 October 1942 – The ground crews assembled at the dispersals at Tangmere at 08:00, in expectation of the arrival of their aircraft. However, abysmal weather at Honiley kept the pilots on the ground all day, and they had no choice but to remain there another night.

7 October 1942 – The day dawned to a frustrating repetition of the previous day's weather. Thick fog reduced visibility to nil, thereby grounding the pilots yet another full day.

8 October 1942 – Conditions finally improved sufficiently today to allow the pilots to fly the final leg of the journey from Honiley to Tangmere, where they arrived at 14:25. During the afternoon, the Squadron's Tiger Moth and Magister also arrived, having made the direct trip from Llanbedr.

Upon their arrival, the ground crews set about modifying the Spitfires' hoods and radio sets and, as such, there was no operational flying during the rest of the day. The Squadron was also issued the call-sign 'Slumber'.

9 October 1942 – As the Squadron had arrived at Tangmere several days too late for Exercise 'Aflame', they did not take part in it at all. The pilots were instead tasked with spotting and defensive patrols in protection of those participating in it, and provided Station defence for Tangmere, whilst the Station's squadrons were participating in the exercise.

At 06:25 this morning, therefore, 41 Squadron was ordered to readiness and maintained Station defence throughout the day. The weather had finally improved sufficiently to permit the pilots to get airborne and the first patrol, of St. Catherine's Point at 3,000-4,000 feet, was undertaken by Blue Section from 07:00. Standing patrols were then kept up in the area on an hourly basis until

Fg Off (later Flt Lt) Douglas 'Haybag' Haywood served with 41 Squadron from 18 September 1942 to 27 August 1943, when he came down near Hardelot and was captured. Rejoining the RAF in 1947, he retired as Squadron Leader in 1955. © Ron Johnson, via Dan Johnson

12:45, with "each relieving section […] in position before the returning section returned to base."[24]

In addition to this, one section was also tasked with spotting, five miles northeast of Beachy Head between 09:30 and 10:55. Between 13:00 and 15:00, the entire Squadron was placed on 30 minutes readiness, which was followed by some individual local flying. The day constituted the Squadron's best day flying for the entire month, and consisted of the following flights:

Patrols, 9 October 1942	Section	Up	Down	Locality
Neil BL406, Gillitt BM573	Red	07:05		
Green BL518, Scott W3935	Blue	07:35	08:00	
Wood BM533, Slack EN780	Yellow	07:45		St. Catherine's Point
Knight BL850, Atkinson AD580	Black	08:00	08:30	
Schou AB809, Vine W3378	Green	08:25	09:50	
Haywood AD580, Robinson EN780	Black	09:30	10:50	Beachy Head
Hone EN827, Hogarth AR392	Blue		11:10	
Chappell W3848, Wood BM533	Green	10:20	11:50	St. Catherine's Point
Knight BL850, Atkinson AD580	Black	11:25	12:45	

Flt Lt Hone and Fg Off Haywood also flew the Squadron's Tiger Moth to RAF Croydon in Surrey, whilst Sgt Plt Robinson and the Squadron's Engineer Officer, Fg Off Roger Whipp flew the unit's Magister to RAF Harrowbeer, Devon.

10 October 1942 – Having only spent one full day at Tangmere, Exercise 'Aflame' was cancelled today, and the Squadron packed up once again for their return to Llanbedr. Preparations commenced immediately, but poor weather restricted their departure to the majority of the ground crew only, as they were able to return by rail; the rest of the men were forced to remain in Tangmere until conditions improved enough to allow passage by air.

11 October 1942 – The weather had improved sufficiently by 10:00 to allow the pilots to return to Llanbedr in their Spitfires, where they arrived at 11:30. They were joined 30 minutes later by the rest of the ground crew, who arrived in HP54 Harrow transports.

Only 90 minutes after the pilots' arrival back in Llanbedr, B Flight was placed at readiness, as they swung back into their regular routine. Less than an hour later, a section was scrambled to intercept an enemy aircraft reported to be bombing shipping off the Welsh coast. Blue Section (Hone EN827 & Hogarth AR850), were vectored to Holyhead at 25,000 feet, where they spotted an aircraft and tally-hoed. Green Section (Slack BL392 & Atkinson W3848), were also scrambled and vectored to the area. Spotting vapour trails, they also gave chase. Despite their efforts, however, none of the four made contact and they returned to Llanbedr at 14:50 and 14:40 respectively.

Hone (EN827) and Hogarth (BL392) were scrambled again at 16:10 and sent to Carnsore Point, but nothing was seen and they landed again at 16:55. This concluded the day's flying.

12 October 1943 – B Flight at dawn readiness. Poor weather limited activity to a little local flying during the afternoon and the Squadron was released at dusk. However, a new pilot arrived today and another was posted away.

The departing pilot was Plt Off Ron Green, who had joined 41 Squadron as a Sergeant Pilot in August 1941 and had been commissioned in April 1942. He was posted to Malta today where he joined 126 Squadron and was awarded the DFC in August 1943. In March 1945, Green was posted to command 64 Squadron and remained with the RAFVR until May 1949.

The new arrival was 24-year-old Australian Fg Off Benjamin 'Barney' Newman. Having joined the RAAF from the Australian Infantry in June 1941, he had undertaken initial training in Australia, and was awarded his Wings and granted a commission on completion of SFTS at Camp Borden, Canada, in March 1942. After his arrival in the United Kingdom in May 1942, Newman undertook advanced training at AFU and OTU, and was posted to 41 Squadron today on his first operational posting as a Flying Officer with 252 flying hours in his logbook. He would remain with the Squadron for a full year.

15 October 1942 – A Flight at dawn readiness. Following three days of poor weather which hindered operational flying and only permitted a little practice flying, the weather improved sufficiently today to allow flying training to be undertaken throughout the day. This included air-to-sea firing and camera gun practice, and a scramble was also made by Blue Section (Hone BM533 & Knight EN780), between 13:35 and 14:50.

The ORB also makes reference to former Sgt Plt George Beurling today. The 21-year-old Canadian had departed the Squadron for Malta approximately five months prior to this entry, and the diary notes with some pride,

> ...Sgt. Beurling, now Pilot Officer, [...] has made quite a name for himself as an 'ace pilot', his score now standing at 29 enemy A/C destroyed.[25]

Separately today, Australian Sgt Plt Frederick White departed the unit on a posting home to Australia where he served with 457 Squadron in the Northern Territory until the end of his tour. He was commissioned in November 1944 and spent the remainder of the War as a ferry pilot.

16 October 1942 – B Flight at dawn readiness. Poor weather prevented flying until 15:00 when an improvement allowed four aircraft to patrol Carnsore Point, 105 miles to the southwest, on the south-eastern most point of Éire. They returned an hour and 20 minutes later, after which the weather closed down again, accompanied by heavy rain, and all flying ceased. The participants are not recorded in the ORB. A Sergeants' dance was held in the evening.

18 October 1942 – B Flight at dawn readiness. When the poor weather looked to continue, the Squadron was set back to 30 minutes readiness all day, but no flying was undertaken. At 14:00, all pilots were assembled at A Flight's dispersal for a lecture by the 9 Group Controller, Sqn Ldr John Chatham, on encountering enemy aircraft during night flying. In the evening, some 'excellent entertainment' was enjoyed by the men in No. 2 Dining Hall, provided by Ralph Reader's Gang Show.

19 October 1942 – A Flight at dawn readiness; B Flight at 30 minutes. Ground mist hindered local practice flying until the afternoon. In the evening, Flt Lt Doug Hone (EB-W), Fg Off Harold

The funeral procession at Plymouth for 20-year-old Sgt Plt Russel E. G. Oxenham, who was killed in a flying accident off Newcastle, County Down, on 24 September 1942. © Unknown English newspaper

Knight (EB-X), Plt Off Tom Slack (EB-T), and Sgt Plt Thomas Atkinson (EB-Y) flew to Valley for a night flying exercise and returned later that same night. The ORB suggests that Sqn Ldr Anthony Robinson, believed to have been a flying instructor attached to RAF Llanbedr, Flt Lt Frank Gillitt and Plt Off Rex Poynton also flew to Valley for the exercise.

21 October 1942 – A Flight at dawn readiness; B Flight at 30 minutes. Dull weather prevented most flying and only two aircraft were able to participate in air-to-air firing practice before the weather closed down once again.

Separately today, 27-year-old Fg Off Harold Knight, 20-year-old Plt Off Robert Wood, and 19-year-old Sgt Plt Thomas Atkinson were all posted to Malta. The trio completed their Mediterranean tours and returned to Europe, where all three were killed with separate units in May 1944.[26]

Twenty-year-old Sgt Plt Kenneth 'Robbie' Robinson was also posted overseas today. Although his posting was initially cancelled, it is understood he did go overseas shortly afterwards after all. Nothing is known of his postings, although it he was commissioned in mid-January 1943 and promoted to Flying Officer six months later. As an exception from general practice, he was posted back to 41 Squadron in January 1944, but was no more fortunate than his three colleagues, losing his own life in June 1944 [see Chapter 5].

22 October 1942 – B Flight at dawn readiness; A Flight at 30 minutes. B Flight's Blue Section (Hone BL299 & Hogarth W3848) took off at 09:20 for formation practice, but returned at 09:55 reporting weather conditions too poor to continue.[27] In fact, the weather conditions today would play a major role in one of the Squadron's greatest tragedies.

Tragedy Strikes

At 11:20, 23-year-old Flt Lt Frank 'Gilly' Gillitt (BM573), and 22-year-old Fg Offs Ronald Harrison (R7296) and Thomas Scott (BL518) took off to practice cloud flying in cover that consisted of four layers, between a base of 800 feet and a ceiling of 18,000 feet.

Heading out over Cardigan Bay, the trio flew south along the Welsh coast, and were last seen in formation at sea off Aberdovey [Aberdyfi], approximately 20 miles south of Llanbedr. A short time later, radio contact was lost and after a tense wait they were reported overdue.

Flt Sgt B. W. 'Barney' Underwood served with 41 Squadron from 23 October 1941 to 19 November 1941 and 12 August 1942 to 1 October 1942. He was commissioned in August 1944 and retired from the Air Force in October 1962. © Underwood family

A search was mounted at 14:30 by two sections, consisting of Flt Lt Charles Chappell and Fg Off Douglas Haywood in the first, and Plt Offs Rex Poynton and Tom Slack in the second. Chappell, flying EB-U, almost became a casualty himself when he was forced to return early with an internal glycol leak, "which gave him some very worrying moments".[28] Poynton and Slack, searching out to sea, sighted a floating mine which they attempted but failed to destroy with 20mm cannon and .303 inch machine gun fire.

9 Group also sent up three Lysanders from 275 Squadron and a Beaufighter from 456 Squadron between 14:50 and 16:25 to assist them. All aircraft returned to their respective airfields reporting having seen no sign of the three missing pilots or their Spitfires.

The following day, there was still no sign of the pilots or their aircraft, but the weather was so unfavourable – 8/10ths-10/10ths cloud with a base of 600 feet – search aircraft were prevented from taking off at all. During the day, however, a Court of Enquiry was convened to enquire into the disappearance of the three aircraft, led by the Station Commander of RAF Wrexham (and temporary Commander of Sector Headquarters), Wg Cdr George Tomlinson OBE DFC, and 9 Group's Flying Control Officer, Sqn Ldr Frederick Thompson. In the light of the tragic loss of the three pilots, Wg Cdr Rev John Appleyard, the RAF's OD Staff Chaplain, also arrived in Llanbedr.[29]

On 24 October, the weather lifted sufficiently to permit the search to be resumed. The three aircraft were finally sighted at 13:00, burnt out on the side of the 2,077-foot [634-metre] mountain Tarrenhendre, approximately seven miles northeast of the coastal town of Towyn [Tywyn], Merionethshire.[30] The pilots had apparently flown straight into the side of the mountain and had been killed instantly. Their remains were carried down the mountainside and transported to Barmouth, and the following day, a party was sent to retrieve the remains of the aircraft for inspection.

At 12:30 on 26 October[31], all SHQ Officers paraded at Llanbedr's Victoria Bridge "to salute [Plt Off Thomas Scott's] cortege as it passed enroute for Portmadoc".[32] His funeral took place at Portmadoc [Porthmadog] Public Cemetery, in Caernarvonshire at 14:00, with Sqn Ldr Neil leading the funeral party and the Chaplain, Sqn Ldr Rev Reginald Parkes, leading the ceremony. Following flying training, Plt Off Scott had joined 41 Squadron in early July 1942 as his first operational unit. His funeral was attended by his parents and sister, and the Squadron ORB states, "The ceremony was quite impressive, Mr. Scott expressing his appreciation for the tribute and sympathy of his son's co-pilots".³³ His *Pilot Service Record* simply states, "Killed in formation of 3 cloud flying from LLANBEDR".³⁴

Flt Lt Frank Gillitt had been with 41 Squadron a mere three weeks, having previously served ten months with 91 Squadron. His funeral was held privately at Wellingborough Cemetery, Northamptonshire, on 28 October, and the Squadron was represented by Flt Lt Charles Chappell. Plt Off Ronald Harrison, who had been with the Squadron four months, was also buried privately the same day. His funeral took place at Slough, Buckinghamshire, and the Squadron was represented by the Adjutant, Fg Off Harry Smith. 41 Squadron was his first operational posting.

Although the findings of the Court of Enquiry are not recorded, a later entry in the Squadron ORB hints at the cause, stating the three men died "…when 'Gilly', misjudging his position, led the section into the hills."³⁵

24 October 1942 – B Flight at dawn readiness; A Flight at 30 minutes. Fair weather, becoming cloudy with showers and high wind. Operational flying was cancelled at 12:35 and the only flying to take place was when Fg Off Douglas Haywood flew to Northolt in the Magister during the afternoon. An ENSA Classical Concert was held in the evening.

25 October 1942 – Poor weather and bad visibility; entire Squadron at 30 minutes readiness. Green and Blue Sections, comprising of four aircraft, flew to Portmadoc and back, which constituted the only flying all day. In the evening, a film was shown in No. 2 Dining Hall.

During the day, Australian Fg Off Robert Hollow joined the Squadron. The 28-year-old school teacher joined the RAAF in October 1940 and undertook his elementary flying training in Australia, before shipping to Canada to undertake his SFTS course. Graduating from that course with his Wings and a commission, Hollow arrived in the United Kingdom in May 1942 and attended AFU and OTU courses until October 1942, during which time he was promoted to Flying Officer. 41 Squadron was his first operational unit, and he arrived today with 265.5 non-operational flying hours in his logbook.

Fg Off Benjamin B. 'Barney' Newman RAAF, pictured here with Squadron mascot 'Perkin' during 1943, served with 41 Squadron from 12 October 1942 to 25 October 1943, during that time claiming one destroyed Me109, one probable Me109 and one probable FW190. © Cowell family

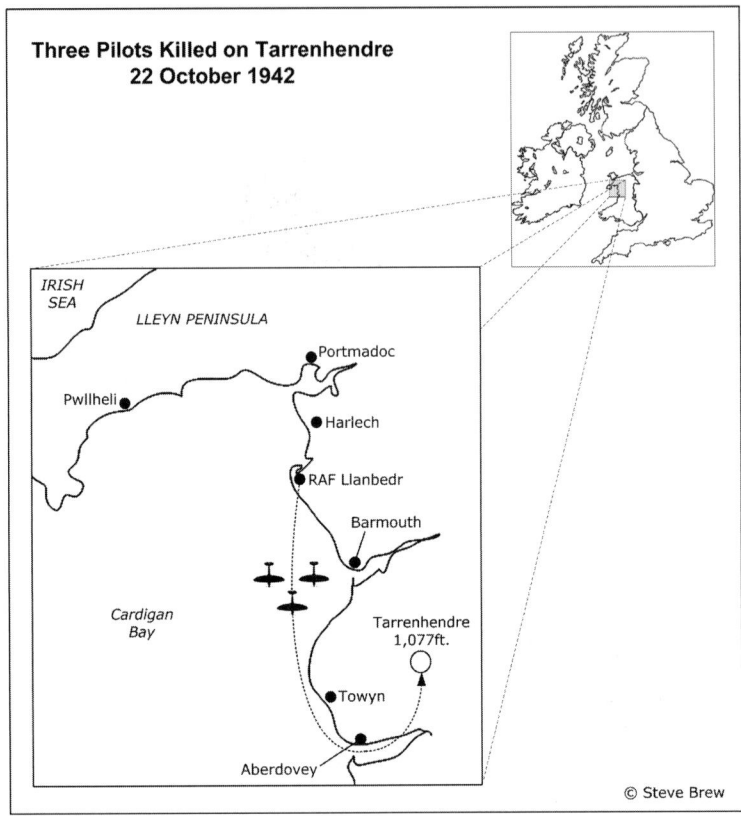

26 October 1942 – A Flight at dawn readiness; B Flight at 30 minutes. Fair weather allowed a good amount of flying to be undertaken during the morning. This included an operational patrol from 10:10 by Blue Section (Hone EN827, Benjamin EN780, Quine AR392) to counter Luftwaffe activity both south and northeast of the Sector. This also generated patrols being flown by 96 and 317 Squadrons, but no interceptions were made. 41 squadron's trio returned at 11:00 with nothing to report.

Separately, three sections from 41 Squadron participated in practice flying, but Sgt Plt Clifford Monk's sortie ended early when he crash-landed Spitfire Vb, R6919, on the Penrhos Aerodrome boundary at 11:50, after suffering engine failure during aerobatics. He was fortunate enough to have only been slightly injured.

A later examination of the engine revealed the pressure filter was choked with a "non-metallic substance including sand"[36], which indicated the cause lay with poor maintenance rather than pilot error. The damage to the aircraft, however, was so serious that it was written off and disciplinary action recommended against the NCO in charge of the Flight. This incident provides an indication of the issues the Squadron's ground crews dealt with on this coastal airfield, protected as it was by the sand dunes of Cardigan Bay.

In the afternoon, three more sections patrolled, and Blue Section performed a practice Rhubarb on Andreas, on the Isle of Man. Plt Off Rycherde Hogarth (EB-S) and Sgt Plt Sydney Benjamin (EB-T) also practiced dusk landings before the day's flying drew to a close.

Separately today, 23-year-old Polish Sgt Plt Jan Zimek arrived on the Squadron on posting from 317 (Polish) Squadron at Woodvale. Having fled occupied Poland in January 1940, he undertook flying training in the United Kingdom, which was completed in March 1942. Zimek was posted to his first operational unit, 315 (Polish) Squadron, in May 1942, and was moved to 317 (Polish) Squadron four months later. He was now arriving on his third operational posting but was not

Flt Lt Frank 'Gilly' Gillitt (pictured), and Fg Offs Ronald Harrison and Thomas Scott did not return from practice flying on 22 October 1942. They were later found dead, evidence strongly suggesting they had flown into the side of the 2,077-foot mountain Tarrenhendre, in zero visibility.
© Mr A. S. Gillitt, via Derek Inskeep

destined to stay long; within days he would be embroiled in an international incident he had not reckoned with.

27 October 1942 – Poor weather kept the Squadron on the ground all day, but another Polish pilot arrived at Llanbedr to join the unit today: 23-year-old Plt Off Wladislaw Banach. Having been an Officer Cadet at the Polish Air Force College near Warsaw at the outbreak of War, he had fled Poland via the Romanian border and arrived safely in France before that country capitulated. When France fell, Banach was evacuated to the United Kingdom, where he completed his flying training and was commissioned in December 1941. Following OTU, which was completed in early September 1942, he was posted to 317 (Polish) Squadron at Woodvale, and arrived on 41 Squadron today having logged 500 flying hours, but none operational.

28 October 1942 – B Flight at dawn readiness; A Flight at 30 minutes. Practice flying was carried out during the morning and Sgt Plt Peter Roberts flew to Hawarden in the Tiger Moth. At 15:20, B Flight's Red Section (Stonier EN780 & Vine AB809) was ordered to scramble base but returned at 16:00 with nothing to report.

A lecture on night flying was given at A Flight dispersal by Sqn Ldrs Neil and Anthony Robinson and, as a result of good weather, a full moon and excellent visibility, a dusk and night-flying programme was subsequently undertaken. Three aircraft from B Flight participated between 18:20 and 19:00, followed by another three between 23:00 and 00:10.

29 October 1942 – The weather deteriorated at dawn, making practice flying virtually impossible. The only two aircraft in the air all day were Fg Off 'Haybag' Haywood (EB-X), who towed the drogue so that Sgt Plt Peter Roberts (EB-Y) could practice air-to-air firing for 50 minutes.

30 October 1942 – The weather was good enough to allow practice flying to be undertaken all day. Two new pilots were sent on a one-hour sector reconnaissance to familiarise themselves with the region.[37] Flt Lt Douglas Hone and Aircraftsman Griffin flew to Croydon in the Squadron's Magister, and the Squadron was released at 18:05.

31 October 1942 – A Flight at dawn readiness; B Flight at 30 minutes. Fair weather permitted practice flying all day, which included flight formation practice in the morning and air to air firing in the afternoon. Flt Lt Charles Chappell towed the drogue in EB-X and three pilots took turns to fire on it. Blind take-offs were also practiced, as were dusk landings and night flying practice by four pilots, between 18:15 and 19:10.

At 16:15, A Flight's Blue Section, consisting of Sgt Plts Peter H. P. Roberts (BL850) and Jan Zimek (BM533), was ordered to scramble to 22,000 feet over Bardsey Island, around 28 miles west-southwest of Llanbedr. This was in response to a raid plotted by 9 Group heading northeast from Dundalk (ca 60 miles northeast of Dublin), and over the Isle of Man. 41 Squadron was also joined in the hunt for the unidentified aircraft by 317 and 456 Squadrons. None of the patrols made any interceptions, but 41 Squadron's section became separated in cloud and Sgt Plt Jan Zimek failed to return to base.[38]

A Pilot is Interned in Éire

When Zimek failed to return from his patrol with Sgt Plt Roberts, it was not immediately clear what had occurred, beyond the basic facts. It later transpired that after his separation from Roberts, the 23-year-old Pole had become lost, suffered radio failure, run out of fuel, and force-landed two miles north of Wells, near Oulart, in County Wexford, Éire, around 95 miles west-southwest of Llanbedr.

Zimek was injured when he crashed his aircraft on landing, and was hospitalised for several weeks. However, instead of being handed across the border to Northern Ireland as, in practice, most pilots were, upon his release from hospital he was interned at The Curragh Military Camp, southwest of Dublin. In fact, Zimek's detention was so unusual that he was the only Allied pilot interned in the whole of 1942, from some 35 Allied landings in the neutral state during the year. More than just for this reason alone, however, Zimek's case is an extraordinary one.

As there are no apparent findings of a Court of Enquiry to explain the exact circumstances of Zimek's loss and internment, contemporary study of his story required scrutiny of Squadron, Station, Sector and Group ORBs, the Flying Accident Card for his aircraft, files from the Defence Forces Military Archives in Dublin and The National Archives in London, reports located within 41 Squadron's own archives, and information provided by Irish historian and author T. Ryle Dwyer in his work *Guests of the State* (Brandon, 1994).

An initial review of available ORBs indicates that Zimek receives no further mention in the Squadron ORB after 31 October 1942. The RAF Llanbedr and 9 Group ORBs afford the incident barely more than one line and offer no new information, and the ORB of Sector Headquarters at RAF Valley makes no mention of the incident whatsoever. Zimek's *Pilot Service Record* merely states, "Missing from Shipping [sic] Patrol off Anglesea [sic]. Landed Ireland & interned."[39]

For many years, therefore, details of the story remained vague. However, an account of the incident is held in within a file at The National Archives, which was initially closed to the public until 2020, but opened in 1972, and appears to have been written after Zimek's release. A few files are also now available in the Irish Defence Forces Military Archives, but even today these are still not particularly easy to access.

Dwyer's *Guests of the State*, written in 1994 is most notable for the part of Zimek's story that concerns his internment, particularly as it often deviates from officialdom and relates the story from the aspect of men who were there. Dwyer's sources for his account of Zimek come chiefly from papers in the Defence Forces Military Archives that, at the time of writing, are still not 100% within the public domain. The exclusive access Dwyer had to these files, which required special permission from the Minister of Defence, along with the lengths he went to, to trace and interview internees held in Éire during the War, or their families, therefore offers quite an insight into this extraordinary story.

The amalgamation of all of these sources exposes quite an unusual tale. On face value, it is a simple open and shut case. Closer investigation, however, reveals that there is much more to this story than meets the eye…

The basic facts surrounding his initial failure to return to base on 31 October 1942 are laid out on the Flying Accident Card for his aircraft, BM533, which states:

> *A/C landed in neutral territory after becoming lost. Pilot lost leader during descent thro' thin layer of cloud and it is considered that* [he] *landed due to petrol shortage not knowing he was in Éire.*[40]

Having joined 41 Squadron on 26 October 1942, Polish Sgt Plt Jan Zimek came down in neutral Eire five days later. A pawn in higher political wrangling, he was interned, and only released eight months later after sustaining serious injuries at the hands of a German internee; via Peter Sikora

Whilst it is understood that Zimek became separated from Sgt Plt Roberts and got lost, it is harder to comprehend his ensuing actions. To have come down in Éire, Zimek must have continued flying in a more-or-less westerly direction for a distance of some 70 miles beyond Bardsey Island. This may be put down to inexperience, but Zimek had been flying operationally in 9 Group, on the west coast of the United Kingdom, for five months. As such, it remains unexplained why there no apparent application of basic navigation skills to head back due east to the Welsh coast; flight in any remotely easterly direction would have put him back on British soil.

Subsequent reports made by Zimek to the Irish authorities also suggest that he either lost radio contact or suffered radio failure; it is not clear which. However, statements recorded on his Flying Accident Card are critical of this claim and question the suggestion of radio malfunction:

> *Leader reports poor R/T communication [...], bad a*[ir]*manship coupled* [?] *with language difficulties. Insufficient evidence to show R/T faulty, probably a/c too low for R/T. Remains unresolved.*[41]

In any case, this would go some way towards explaining why there was neither radio contact with Roberts seeking assistance, nor radio direction finding attempted with Sector Headquarters at RAF Valley, for example, which could have assisted Zimek to find Llanbedr again.

Irish records indicate that, upon reaching the coast low on fuel, Zimek brought his aircraft down in a field. As his aircraft came to a halt in the soft farmland, it flipped over and was damaged beyond repair. Dazed from a resulting injury to his forehead and both his arms, Zimek was helped from the upturned aircraft by two local farmers, Timothy Carr and Edward Gordon, who were working in the same field.

The pair took him to the local post office, where his head injury was dressed by the District Medical Officer, Dr John Devlin, and he was visited by the local priest.[42] The Oulart Garda arrived on the scene a short while later and, in accordance with Irish neutrality law, took Zimek into custody and placed a guard on the aircraft.

In the evening, Zimek was taken to see one Dr Michael Dunphy where he still was when the military arrived at 19:30. Lt. Gavin, in command of the military party, took charge of him from the Garda and placed his own armed guard on the aircraft. He then took the young Pole to see a third doctor, a Dr Furlong, in Wexford at 22:15 and, the following evening, escorted him to the General Military Hospital at The Curragh in County Kildare. Upon arrival, he was asked to sign a parole form, then hospitalised for five weeks.

Considering Zimek had been a pilot within 9 Group for several months, he should have been aware of an amendment to Clause 6A 'Aircraft Forced to Land in Eire' of Standing Operational Instruction No. 71(A), 'Destruction of Aircraft Forced to Land in Enemy or Neutral Territory', dated 12 September 1942. The one-page document instructed pilots on how they should act in the event they are compelled to land in Éire.

> (i) *Aircraft forced to land in Eire may expect assistance both at aerodromes and elsewhere to enable them to return to the United Kingdom or Northern Ireland, provided aircrews state in a convincing manner that they have been involved on a training flight, on ferrying, or on air/sea rescue work. As this assistance can be afforded most easily and with the least embarrassment to the Eire authorities if aircraft land at aerodromes, pilots should subject to proviso at (ii) and (iii) below, endeavour to land at aerodromes whenever possible.*
>
> (ii) *Aircraft equipped with A.I. or c.m. type A.S.V. or wired for c.m. type A.I. or A.S.V. or other c.m. radio equipment, even if the apparatus itself is not on board, are not to be landed on aerodromes in any circumstances, but are to be put down in open county and destroyed. Alternatively the crew are to bale out and the aircraft allowed to crash.*[43]
>
> (iii) *In the case of experimental aircraft or an aircraft fitted with secret experimental equipment, destruction of the aircraft is to be carried out irrespective of the circumstances.*
>
> (iv) *In the case of an aircraft which carries types of secret equipment not entailing destruction of the aircraft under Paras. 6A (ii) and 6A (iii) above, the Eire authorities are to be informed that the aircraft has secret equipment on board and that the captain of the aircraft has orders to stay with it until the arrival of the British Air Attache, Dublin, with whom a member of the aircrew should communicate. Permission for this communication will be granted on request.*[44]

It has been suggested that Zimek may not have known he was in Éire when he crash-landed, so it is unlikely he knew where the nearest airfield was; perhaps his fuel shortage was so acute that staying airborne long enough to find an aerodrome was not even possible. Whilst the aircraft was neither experimental, nor is it believed to have been carrying any secret or experimental devices or radio equipment, Zimek's case was quite unusual in that, despite the above instruction, he was still interned at The Curragh.

The reason he was 'chosen' to be interned appears to be twofold. On the one hand, it seems that Zimek may not have been as cautious with the information he gave the Irish authorities during his interrogation as he perhaps should have been. For instance, a report on his case in The National Archives clearly shows the Irish were well aware that Zimek was on an operational sortie; there seems to have been no initial attempt on Zimek's behalf to 'state in a convincing manner that they have been involved on a training flight, on ferrying, or on air/sea rescue work' [see above]. In fact, a file in the Irish military archives even states that whilst still being treated immediately after his crash-landing, he dictated a message to be sent by telegram to 41 Squadron's Commanding Officer, Sqn Ldr Tom Neil, at the address as '41 Fighter Squadron, Llanbedr Aerodrome, Wales'.

Whether Zimek asked to be taken to the Post Office in order to deliver his message, or whether he took the opportunity to send his telegram whilst being treated at the Post Office, is unknown. Either way, it is understood the telegram was never sent as it was halted by the Irish censors. Any wonder: a pilot freely contacting his OC from a neutral country whilst on an operational flight was precisely the type of embarrassment the amendment to 9 Group's Standing Order was intended to avoid!

Other documents in the Irish military archives suggest that Zimek finally stated he was on a training mission, but when ammunition was also found on the aircraft, the claim could no longer be accepted.

In subsequent interviews, he also told the Irish authorities that he had been born in southern Poland and that both his parents were dead, and gave his interviewers contact information for two 'next of kin' to be informed of his predicament. One was an Aunt named Radochonski of South Laflin Street, Chicago, and the other a Miss Dorothy Foster of Stamford Street, Blackpool. Despite the fact that he had already nominated these two next of kin, Zimek then named his 'deceased' father Wiktor as his next of kin, giving yet another address in Chicago.

In spite of the messy situation with Zimek, however, the main reason for his internment appears to be none other than bad timing! He was unfortunate enough to have come down immediately after a series of both successful and unsuccessful escapes from the Allied Camp at The Curragh. These were assisted by a British MI9-backed escape organisation called 'The Escape Club', which had recently been broken up by the Irish intelligence organisation, G2. The whole issue caused the Irish Government significant embarrassment, particularly as some of the Club members were Irish nationals, and therefore seen as quasi 'Fifth Column' agents.

These escape activities had led to soured relations between the internees and their Irish guards. One attempt in particular[45] had been thwarted with bloody force – batons, boots and fists – which resulted in a heated exchange of words between the internees' national representations in Dublin and the Irish Government on the correct handling of their servicemen. A draft letter from Downing Street in one National Archives file, for example, shows that the British Representative to Dublin, Sir John Maffey, was asked to approach the Irish Taoiseach, Eamon de Valera, to…

> …press for an undertaking that methods of brutality will not be used towards our internees in future. The best guarantee would be a change in… the Guard who were most deeply involved in the recent incident and against whom the feeling of our officers and N.C.O.'s is naturally considerably inflamed.[46]

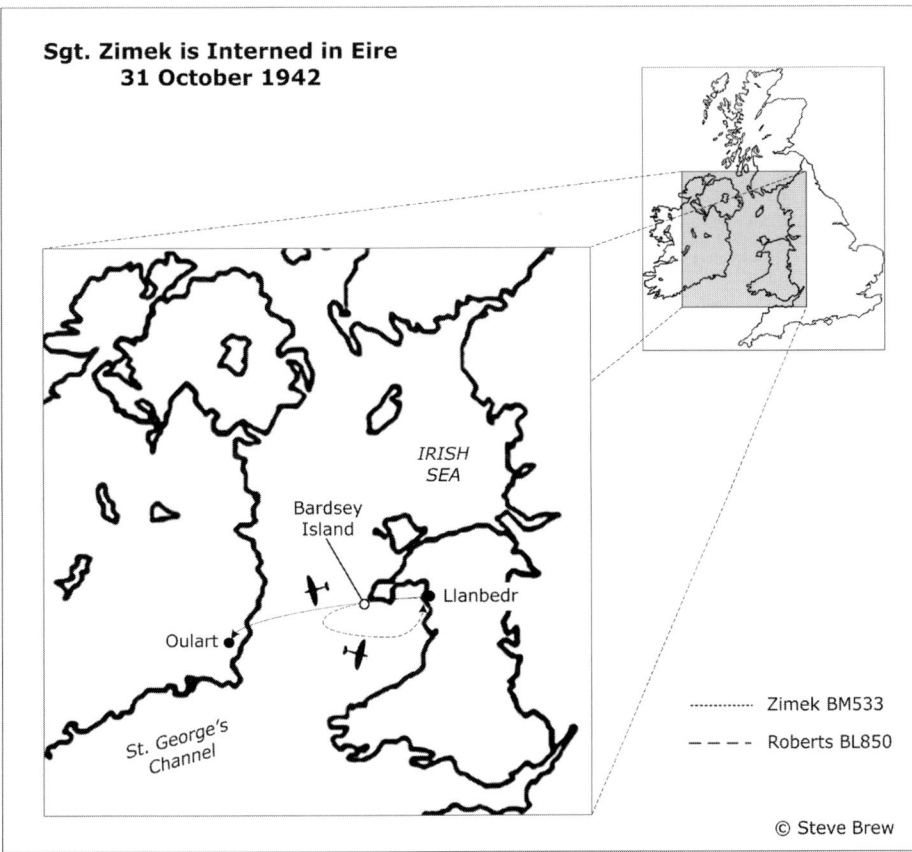

De Valera agreed to the resumption of parole, which had been suspended immediately following the incident, but would not consent to the suggestion that the guards be removed, deciding instead to strengthen security, including fencing, to help avoid such incidents in future.

Undaunted by the efforts to improve security, however, a further nine Allied airmen escaped in August 1942. Three made it across the border to Northern Ireland, whilst another stayed at large for five days before capture, in both cases with the assistance of members of The Escape Club. The latter man's eventual capture could have come straight out of one of the gangster movies of the day with a car chase followed by an escape on foot through the slums of Dublin! Considering the efforts that MI9 went to, to assist Allied airmen to escape from The Curragh, and the lengths that the Irish Government went to, to stop them doing so, it is no surprise emotions were riding so high between the Irish and British Governments in 1942, just prior to Zimek coming down in Wexford.

Sir John Maffey pressed for Zimek's release, playing the 'training flight' card, but as Zimek appears to have already given away the fact that he was on an operational sortie and ammunition was found loaded in his aircraft's guns, his efforts were in vain. Moreover, however, Prime Minister de Valera decided personally that he should be interned. Although his order was clearly in retaliation for recent events, the British were also eager that they should be smoothed over and not be made public – which would be an embarrassment for Downing Street – and felt compelled to allow Zimek to be interned as "something of a peace offering to the Irish army".[47]

Zimek's internment, therefore, was a direct result of recent events, particularly considering not one single Allied airman had yet been interned in 1942. De Valera believed he had clearly demonstrated a more-than-sympathetic attitude towards Allied service personnel finding themselves involuntarily in Éire: Despite the tightrope he was walking in the face of Irish neutrality law, de Valera had quietly repatriated every single one of the 45 Allied airmen that had come down in Éire thus far in 1942, but at the same time interned all eight German airmen – a fact he could not risk becoming public.

He felt that all his covert efforts, rather than being recognised, were instead thanked with a series of British-backed escapes. Thus, poor Zimek had simply been in the wrong place at the wrong time and become a sacrificial lamb in a political feud he knew nothing about and could not influence. He was merely a pawn in a snub to Downing Street, and a firm statement to the British Government that de Valera could only be pushed so far!

Oblivious to the political squabbles between London and Dublin, however, Allied internees at The Curragh continued their efforts to escape, though no longer assisted by The Escape Club. Indeed, Zimek himself was also soon involved in such activities and, in January 1943, planned an escape with a fellow Polish pilot, Flt Lt Kazimierz Baranowski, who had been interned since May 1941. The idea was to feign illness to gain access to the hospital, then overpower, gag and tie up the sole Irish guard, walk out of the hospital as if on parole, and simply ride away on two bicycles which were strategically positioned by two collaborating British internees. Unfortunately for the pair, however, the presence of Irish political internees – likely IRA operatives – and their additional guards on the intended day of escape put paid to the plan.

Available records suggest that Zimek quite resented being interned at The Curragh alongside German airmen – the very people who had occupied his homeland. B [British] and G [German] Camps were separated by wire, but the two groups often saw each other whilst on parole in nearby towns, at dances or the cinema. Although Allied and Axis aircrews did not socialise, they could often not avoid one another, as they would independently decide to attend the same events or visit the same locales in nearby towns.

It was a series, and indeed an escalation, of events during a few of these local encounters that led to Zimek being released by the Irish authorities, despite the prevailing mood, and he was returned to the United Kingdom on 'compassionate grounds' less than nine months after his internment.

The truth behind the euphemism was that he had been seriously beaten by a German internee, Obfw Karl Hund, whilst on parole in late May 1943.[48]

The trouble started in early April 1943 when the senior German officer in G Camp, Oblt Kurt Mollenhauer, complained to the officer in charge of The Curragh, Col Thomas McNally, that one of his men had been assaulted by Zimek outside the Grand Hotel in Newbridge, about a mile or two northeast of The Curragh. The senior Allied officer, Fg Off Leslie Ward, countered that it was the other way around and that Zimek had actually been tripped by some of the German internees.

On 16 May, however, another incident occurred at the same hotel, where Zimek appears to have been the instigator. Versions vary slightly depending on the source but the following appears to be the gist of what occurred: Whilst at a dance attended by several men of both B and G Camps, Zimek spotted one of his fellow countrymen, Stanley Kerniewski, at the back of the hall chatting with one of the German internees, Willi Krupp. Kerniewski's behaviour irritated Zimek as he felt his conduct caused British internees, who never associated with the Germans, to become suspicious of the Polish internees. One source alleges that, incensed by this apparent fraternisation with the enemy, Zimek approached Kerniewski and rebuked him for speaking to a 'f***ing German', whilst a National Archives file states that,

> Zimek remarked to one of the Germans that [Kerniewski] was behaving in a peculiar way "for a member of the Herrenvolk". On leaving the building Zimek was struck from behind by an unknown person.[49,50]

As Zimek left the dance hall, Krupp and four other German airmen followed him and one of them struck him from behind. He tried to retaliate but was restrained.

Then, on 1 June, a final event brought Zimek's clashes with the Germans to a head, but to his detriment. Once again attending a dance in the Grand Hotel at Newbridge, Zimek spent the evening dancing with a local girl, Theresa Birchill. After one of the dances, a German internee, Otto Jäger, approached Theresa and asked her to dance with him. Much to Zimek's delight, she declined.

They got on well and Zimek agreed to walk her home. However, on leaving the hall, they became separated and when Zimek caught up, she was walking along Naas Road with another local girl, Maureen Gibbons, and two German airmen, Obfw Karl Hund and Uffz Josef Reiser, who were chatting together. The pair were part of the four-man crew of Ju88D, 4U+KH of 1.(F)/123, that was shot down at Tramore, Waterford, by a pilot of one of Zimek's previous units, 315 (Polish) Squadron, on 23 August 1942.

Angered at being 'dumped' for a German, Zimek started cycling around the quartet, and tempers began to rise. When Zimek collided with the front wheel of Hund's bicycle, he called them 'f***ing Germans'. At this, the three men became quite aggressive with one another and the two girls hurried off home alone. In retaliation, Hund struck Zimek with such force that he fell to the ground, struck his head and was knocked unconscious. Hund and Reiser then dragged him to the side of the road and left him there.

This was where some of the Allied internees found him a short while later. They called the Garda and took him to The Curragh Military Hospital where he was diagnosed with a fractured skull. Immediately transferred to Sir Patrick Dun's Hospital in Dublin, he did not regain consciousness until over three weeks later, on 26 June.

As his memory began to return, he painted a slightly different picture of the evening's events. A National Archives file reports that whilst the initial exchange of words between Zimek and the German airmen took place at the dance, another occurred on the way back to the Camp at its conclusion. Zimek then went to a house in the town "occupied by three young women"[51] to collect his bicycle and rode back through the town at around 23:45, stopping by a bridge "to admire the scenery".[52] The next thing he knew, he was lying in hospital in Dublin.

At this time, Zimek also realised that his money was missing and estimated he had had between £3 and £4 on his person as he cycled home, as that particular day had been payday. He then explained that some German internees had spread a story around The Curragh Camp that he had insulted one of them and "interfered with some girl in their company"[53], both of which allegations he vehemently denied. As a result, he contended, a party of German airmen took him "unawares and knocked [him] unconscious".[54]

Whilst recuperating, Zimek was visited in hospital by the British Air Attaché, Wg Cdr Malcolm Begg MC, and the only two employees of the Polish Legation in Dublin, the Consul, Waclaw Dobrzynski, and Press Bureau Chief, Xavier Zaleski. Zimek later explained that the trio told him to act as if he were crazed "to enhance his opportunity of securing repatriation".[55] As such, when subsequently examined by the hospital's Consulting Psychiatrist, Dr Henry J. Eustace, Zimek…

> …contrived to weep copiously. Euston [sic] *asked him if he wished to go back to England, and he said, "No", but that he hoped to go back to The Curragh. When Euston [sic] asked him if he liked the Curragh, Zimek said that he had a very special reason for returning there, because he intended to kill every one of the German internees.*[56]

Colonel McNally, the Camp Commander, was naturally concerned about the trouble Zimek might cause if he were to be returned to the camp. There was also reason enough to be afraid for Hund's safety, if the Allied airmen got hold of him, and concern it might end in mass brawl. He therefore amended the parole system, and only let Allied and Axis internees out on separate days. He also felt it prudent to have an additional camp built some distance from The Curragh, to separate the two groups altogether. This did in fact eventuate, and although the idea had already been suggested prior to Zimek's confrontation with Hund, the incident certainly swung opinion in favour of taking such a step and hastened its construction.

Ever seeking to have the Allied airmen freed, Sir John Maffey stepped in on Zimek's behalf once again and pleaded for his release on compassionate grounds, playing up the potential for trouble and further bloodshed if Zimek were returned to Camp upon his release from hospital. Prime Minister de Valera concurred and when Zimek was released from hospital on 6 July 1943, he was immediately taken across the border into Northern Ireland. From there, he travelled to Heysham, Lancashire, then transported to the RAF Hospital in Halton, Cheshire, where he was admitted on 10 July to continue his recuperation. One of Zimek's fellow internees was under the impression he was finally transferred to an asylum.

This is where this rather intriguing and quite extraordinary story presently concludes, as Zimek's subsequent movements and fate are unknown. However, his case set a precedent for releasing internees on compassionate grounds. As such, several other Allied pilots were subsequently released on the same grounds, as was one German airman, who had been hospitalised for over two years as a result of the injuries he had sustained when landing in Éire, and who it was felt could not return to military service.

November 1942 – The Squadron conducted only five operational flights (ten sorties) all month and made no contacts with enemy aircraft. Weather prevented flying on two days – 5 and 19 November – and restricted it on another five – 3, 10, 18, 20 and 25 November. However, a significant amount of practice flying was undertaken, thereunder no less than 123 night-flying hours, which earned particular mention in the Sector Headquarters ORB in its monthly summary:

> *No. 41 Squadron… carried out a record number of night training sorties under Sector Control and flew in an area bounded by the ISLE OF MAN, FLEETWOOD, GLOUCESTER AND CARDIGAN. It is worthy of note that on one night alone approximately 35 practice sorties were made.*[57]

Unfortunately, however, detail on the Squadron's activity during this period is relatively scant, and most entries in the Squadron ORB are limited to one to two lines per day.

Polish Plt Off Wladislaw Banach served with 41 Squadron from 27 October 1942 to 9 December 1942; via Peter Sikora

1 November 1942 – B Flight at dawn readiness; A Flight at 30 minutes. Practice flying was undertaken all day, only interrupted by a search patrol by Blue Section between 08:30 and 09:30, but the ORB does not record the participants. Dusk landing practice was also undertaken by Sgt Plt Peter Roberts for 45 minutes from 18:25. During the evening, the pilots enjoyed a film show in No. 2 Dining Hall.

Around this time, 24-year-old Plt Off Robert 'Bob' Boyd joined the Squadron. Considerably more experienced than many of the pilots currently on the Squadron, he had joined the RAFVR in June 1939 and served through the Battle of Britain with 234 Squadron as an NCO pilot. Moving to 609 Squadron in November 1940, Boyd claimed two destroyed, one probable and one damaged Me109s in summer 1941, but was himself shot down into the Channel and rescued at the end of July. Rested as a flying instructor at two different OTUs from September 1941, during which time he was commissioned, he was now returning to operations with 41 Squadron, with 650 flying hours logged, of which 200 were operational.[58]

2 November 1942 – A Flight at dawn readiness; B Flight at 30 minutes. Cine camera gun practice was carried out during the morning by two sections from B Flight. At 15:55, Blue and Green Sections, consisting of Fg Off Douglas Haywood (EB-Q), Sgt Plt Sydney Benjamin (EB-L), Plt Off Bob Boyd (EB-U), and Sgt Plt Peter Roberts (EB-R) practiced interceptions for 50 minutes, whilst Sgt Plts Robert Quine RAAF and Fraser Clark RNZAF practiced blind take-offs in the Master for 70 minutes with Flt Lt Charles Chappell. At 17:00, Flt Lt Douglas Hone returned from Birmingham in the Magister.

Flt Lt Chappell and Fg Off Haywood undertook a successful session of night-flying practice at 19:00. However, as Chappell landed Spitfire Vb, BL850, twenty-two minutes later[59], his undercarriage collapsed. He was not injured in the incident but as the aircraft blocked the runway, Haywood was compelled to fly on to RAF Valley, where he spent the night, and returned the following morning.

Chappell later explained that he had switched to 'undercarriage down', but that he was unable to check whether the wheels were actually in place as the green light on the left of the dashboard, which usually indicated this, was not working. The Engineering Officer put the accident down to a technical fault, but the Station Commander disagreed and felt it was caused instead by carelessness.

The Squadron's mascot throughout this period was a black French Poodle named 'Perkin' which belonged to Fg Off Reg Hoare. Perkin is shown here with a stone balanced on his nose. © Cowell family

Unfortunately, the AOC concurred and, citing faulty cockpit drill, insisted that Chappell's logbook be endorsed 'Carelessness'.

During the day, 22-year-old Sgt Plt Malcolm Rowe joined the Squadron. He had joined the RAFVR in May 1940 and undertaken EFTS and SFTS in Rhodesia, prior to returning to the United Kingdom to complete AFU and OTU courses. 41 Squadron was his first operational posting and he arrived at Llanbedr today with 310 non-operational flying hours in his logbook.

4 November 1942 – Practice flying was undertaken all day, thereunder two pilots who practiced air-to-air firing with the drogue from 10:45. Between 12:35 and 13:45, an operational patrol was undertaken by Red Section, comprising Flt Sgt Jack Stonier (AR393) and Sgt Plt Edward Vine (AD562), but they returned with nothing to report.

Separately, Sgt Plt Edward Vine was posted away today, as yet another pilot destined for Malta. He was served with 1435 Squadron from January 1943, but was shot down, wounded and captured just south of the Italian coast approximately six weeks later. Following hospitalisation in Italy and Germany, Vine was sent to Stalag VII-A at Moosburg, from where he escaped a few weeks later. Captured anew, he spent the rest of the War behind wire.

6 November 1942 – A Flight at dawn readiness; B Flight at 30 minutes. Good weather allowed a fair amount of flying to be undertaken today, and one section of four aircraft participated in practice flying whilst another section practiced fours drills. Sgt Plts Robert Quine RAAF and Fraser Clark RNZAF also practiced air-to-air firing. During the day, Llanbedr was visited by the AOC 12 Group, Air Cdre Charles Steele DFC, accompanied by Wg Cdr Edward Wolfe DFC. The Squadron was released at 18:00.

7 November 1942 – B Flight at dawn readiness; A Flight at 30 minutes. At dawn, the Readiness Section, Flt Lt Charles Chappell (EB-X) and Sgt Plt Bill Downing (EB-L), spent approximately 30 minutes in the air undertaking local flying, possibly Downing's first flying and area familiarisation since joining the Squadron four days before. This was repeated by a section from B Flight at 11:15. Red Section (Poynton W3378 & Banach AB809) was scrambled at 15:05 and returned at 16:00 with nothing to report. A cinema show was held in the evening in No. 2 Dining Hall.

8 November 1942 – Remembrance Sunday. The entire Squadron attended a Church Parade in the morning, led by Sqn Ldr Rev Reginald Parkes. Good weather all day allowed a good amount of flying practice to be undertaken, including B Flight's Blue and Green Sections which practiced dogfights for 55 minutes in the morning and formation flying in the afternoon. Four more aircraft participated in a fighter-versus-bomber interception exercise.

Flt Lt Douglas Hone and Fg Off Douglas Haywood flew the Squadron's Miles Master to RAF Ringway in Cheshire, around eight miles south of Manchester, where they took possession of a new Spitfire for the Squadron, possibly a replacement for the aircraft Flt Lt Chappell had crash-landed on 2 November. Hone returned to Llanbedr in the Master and Haywood in the Spitfire. 'The Private Life of Henry VIII', starring Charles Laughton, was shown in a cinema show in No. 2 Dining Hall in the evening, but was a disappointment due to a number of stoppages.

11 November 1942 – B Flight at dawn readiness; A Flight at 30 minutes. Plt Off Bob Boyd and Sgt Plt Bill Downing were sent up on dawn flying, whilst Blue Section, comprising Plt Off Rycherde Hogarth and Sgt Plt Peter Roberts, performed a weather test and practiced homings on base. Later, Flt Lt Charles Chappell and Sgt Plt Robert Quine RAAF practiced scrambles, and a dummy sweep of Andreas was undertaken by a section of four aircraft piloted by Fg Off Douglas Haywood, Plt Off Bob Boyd, and Sgt Plts Sydney Benjamin and Bill Downing. An all ranks dance was held in No. 2 Dining Hall in the evening.

12 November 1942 – A Flight at dawn readiness; B Flight at 30 minutes. Good weather allowed several hours of practice flying to be logged. This included a dummy Rhubarb on Great Ormes Head, air-to-air firing with the drogue, practice interceptions, and dusk landing practice, the latter of which was undertaken by Sgt Plts Robert Quine and Bill Downing. A dusk patrol was also performed by Blue and Green Sections, which consisted of Plt Off Douglas Hogarth and Sgt Plt Sydney Benjamin, and Fg Off Douglas Haywood and Plt Off Bob Boyd, respectively.

13 November 1942 – B Flight at dawn readiness; A Flight at 30 minutes. Good weather today resulted in a very busy flying schedule. Blue section, comprising Fg Off Douglas Haywood and Sgt Plt Sydney Benjamin, started the morning with a dawn patrol, which was followed by formation

Plt Off R. J. 'Bob' Boyd joined 41 Squadron in November 1942 and was killed in action over France as Flying Officer on 6 September 1943. © Steve Bracey

practice by six aircraft, three from each Flight. Later, Green Section, consisting of Sgt Plts Benjamin and Fraser Clark RNZAF, undertook dog-fighting practice using cine-gun cameras, after which Benjamin was employed towing the drogue whilst others practiced air-to-air firing.

In the early afternoon, Sgt Plt Peter Roberts was flown to Valley in the Tiger Moth by Sgt Plt Bill Downing and, on his return, Fg Off Rycherde Hogarth was flown to Valley by Flt Lt Charles Chappell. Finally, in the late afternoon, Sgt Plts Downing and Clark practiced dusk landings, whilst Blue Section, made up of Fg Off Haywood and Plt Off Bob Boyd, undertook a dusk patrol. A Sergeants' Mess Dance was held in No. 2 Dining Hall in the evening.

15 November 1942 – B Flight at dawn readiness; A Flight at 30 minutes. The day dawned at 07:50 to fair weather. Sgt Plts Sydney Benjamin and Fraser Clark RNZAF started the day with a dawn patrol, which was followed by practice flying all morning. In the afternoon, the entire Squadron practiced formation flying between 15:50 and 16:45. B Flight's diary notes, "This was the first time 12 A/C of 41 Sqdn have been airbourne [sic] for some time…."[60] In the evening, the musical drama 'Sailing Along', starring Jessie Matthews, was shown in a cinema show in No. 2 Dining Hall.

16 November 1942 – A Flight at dawn readiness; B Flight at 30 minutes. Favourable weather conditions allowed Flt Lt Douglas Hone, Fg Off Douglas Haywood and Sgt Plt Sydney Benjamin to take off at 09:00 to search for a balloon. They were airborne for 55 minutes, but there is no indication of their success. Air-to-sea firing practice was undertaken in the afternoon, followed at 14:55 by a 40-minute practice Rhubarb against HMS *Glendower*, a Royal Navy recruit assessment camp based at the Butlins holiday camp at Pwllheli. The participants in the exercise were Sqn Ldr Anthony E. Robinson (EB-Y), Flt Lt Hone (EB-Q), Sgt Plt Benjamin (EB-U) and Sgt Plt Fraser Clark (EB-L). Finally, Flt Lt Hone and Plt Off Rycherde Hogarth, in EB-Q and EB-S respectively, practiced night flying for 45 minutes.

During the day, 22-year-old Welshman, Sgt Plt John Thomas joined the Squadron. The young school master had joined the RAFVR in July 1940 and undertaken his flying training in the United States. Returning to the United Kingdom with his Wings, he completed OTU and arrived at RAF Llanbedr today on his first operational posting, having logged 295 non-operational flying hours.

17 November 1942 – B Flight at dawn readiness; A Flight at 30 minutes. A dawn patrol was undertaken by Fg Off Douglas Haywood and Plt Off Bob Boyd, and good weather today resulted in a significant amount of practice flying being logged, thereunder twelve pilots that participated in an hour and 40 minutes' formation practice from 15:00.

Owing to a perfectly moonlit night, an intensive night-flying exercise was also undertaken that evening, which ran until 03:00 the following morning. A total of 40 hours night flying were recorded, and the only mishap was a less-than-elegant end to the exercise at 19:40 for Australian Flt Sgt Robert Quine, who overshot the runway onto rough ground in the darkness in Spitfire Vb, AD536.

The accident caused Cat B damage to the aircraft and Cat A damage to the engine. Fortunately, however, apart from bruised pride, he was uninjured. Having flown 78 hours in Spitfires, of which barely four were at night, the accident was put down to inexperience.

Separately today, a young pilot joined the Squadron who would, in time, become the longest serving of all of the unit's World War II pilots: 20-year-old Plt Off Peter Cowell. Having joined the RAFVR in February 1941, he undertook a six-month course with Manchester University Air Squadron before being shipped to the United States for his elementary flying training. Graduating with his Wings and a commission in June 1942, Cowell returned to the United Kingdom to undertake AFU and OTU courses, the latter of which was completed in early November 1942. Following two weeks' leave, Cowell arrived at RAF Llanbedr today on his first operational posting, with 300 flying hours in his logbook but none operational. He would ultimately complete two tours with 41 Squadron, from November 1942 to July 1944, and from January 1945 to March 1946.

18 November 1942 – Following the previous night's good flying conditions, the weather closed down at dawn and no practice flying was undertaken all day. Despite conditions, however, Blue Section, comprising Fg Off Haywood (EN827/Q) and Plt Off Boyd (BL299/L), were scrambled to Bardsey Island at 13:50. The pilots spent an hour and 25 minutes in the air and returned with nothing to report, and there was no further flying.

Another new pilot joined the Squadron today: 22-year-old Welsh Fg Off David 'Daibach' Davies. He had joined the RAFVR in January 1941 and undertaken his flying training in the United States, where he earned his Wings and was commissioned. He returned to the United Kingdom to undertake his AFU and OTU courses and arrived on 41 Squadron today on his first operational posting with 270 non-operational flying hours in his logbook.

20 November 1942 – A Flight at dawn readiness; B Flight at 30 minutes. Following a day on the ground as a result of poor weather, Flt Lt Douglas Hone undertook a weather test this morning, and concluded it was not suitable for flying. By 14:00, however, the weather had improved sufficiently to permit twelve aircraft to participate in Balbo 'Big Wing' formation practice, during which the "formation was notably good"[61]. This was followed by a party in the evening, the "alleged reason, Dakar taken!"[62]

21 November 1942 – B Flight at dawn readiness; A Flight at 30 minutes. The weather was suitable for formation flying this morning and twelve aircraft were soon up, practicing new configurations. Another night-flying exercise was commenced in the early evening with dusk landings, but was prematurely ended when the weather closed in at 20:00. No doubt, the men would have been pleased with this eventuality, as they were on the ground again in time to participate in an all-ranks dance in No. 2 Dining Hall. "It was voted the best dance – so far this season. Trust '41' to produce the right spirit!"[63]

22 November 1942 – A Flight at dawn readiness; B Flight at 30 minutes. Good weather enabled practice flying to be undertaken all day. Following the previous evening's early cancellation of night flying practice, a new night flying programme was scheduled for this evening, commencing with dusk landings. However, flying had to be suspended at 18:00 due to mist, but this proved to be only a temporary hindrance as the fog lifted a few hours later. At 23:00, therefore, the pilots were ordered up again and continued flying exercises until 04:00 the following morning, logging a total of 40 hours night flying.

23 November 1942 – B Flight at dawn readiness; A Flight at 30 minutes. Little flying was undertaken today as a result of the pilots' and ground crews' participation in night flying exercises until 04:00. Only four aircraft were up in the afternoon to do a little formation practice.

24 November 1942 – A Flight at dawn readiness; B Flight at 30 minutes. The weather was not the best for flying but a 'beat-up' of a lorry was undertaken by Sqn Ldr Neil, Flt Lt Charles Chappell and Plt Off Bob Boyd. The new pilots practiced formation flying and Morse communication with pip-squeaks[64], and a section from A Flight conducted a 55 minute patrol. The day's flying concluded at dusk.

25 November 1942 – B Flight at dawn readiness; A Flight at 30 minutes. The weather was not ideal for flying and visibility considered poor, but a practice scramble was conducted by the readiness section. A Squadron parade was held at 14:00, which was inspected by the Llanbedr Station Commander, Sqn Ldr Eynon Bullimore. He addressed the parade and "expressed his compliments on the smartness of the airmen"[65], after which proceedings were concluded with a march past. Shortly thereafter, the Squadron had a group photograph taken.

As this was in progress, however, two pilots were scrambled. Plt Off Wladislaw Banach (AB809) and Sgt Plt Malcolm Rowe (AR393), constituting Red Section, were in the air at 14:35, but the

B Flight Diary considered their timing not particularly good as it took them four minutes and 20 seconds to get airborne. Moreover, states the ORB,

> *The scramble ended at 30,000 feet when they were told by Ops' that they had 'No Customers'. 30,000 feet and then no customers was a blow but still there might be next time.*[66]

They landed again at 15:40 and this constituted the only operational flying all day.

26 November 1942 – A Flight at dawn readiness; B Flight at 30 minutes. B Flight spent the morning on the Link trainer and practiced aircraft recognition skills. Flying training was carried out during the afternoon, which included B Flight's Black and Green Sections practicing formation flying for 60 minutes. The Squadron was released at 17:30, after which Sqn Ldr Neil and a number of Officers travelled to RAF Valley to attend an 'All Star Variety Concert' hosted by BBC artists, then participated in a party in the RAF Valley mess. The B Flight Diary adds that "…needless to say a good time was had by all!"[67]

During the day, another new pilot arrived on the Squadron in the form of 20-year-old Australian Flt Sgt John Davidson. Having joined the RAAF in March 1941, he had undertaken his elementary training in Australia and Southern Rhodesia, before shipping to the United Kingdom with his Wings in May 1942. Following AFU and OTU courses, Davidson was promoted to Flight Sergeant and posted to his first operational unit, 285 (Anti-Aircraft Co-Operation and Target Towing) Squadron at RAF Honiley on 24 October 1942. Now, just a month later, he was posted to 41 Squadron, having logged 380 flying hours, but none operational.

28 November 1942 – A Flight at dawn readiness; B Flight at 30 minutes. Fair but cloudy weather permitted flying practice to continue throughout the day. Four pilots, comprising Blue and Green Sections, were sent up on formation practice at 09:25 and returned at 10:50. Sgt Plt Fraser Clark RNZAF and Flt Sgt Robert Quine RAAF were sent to RAF Valley for a four-day air-firing course, Clark flying over in EB-U and Quine following by train.

At 16:25 that afternoon, seven pilots – three from A Flight and four from B – flew to RAF Woodvale, 12 miles northwest of Liverpool, to participate in a night flying operation, called a 'Fighter Night'. The pilots arrived at 17:05, and remained there overnight.

Sqn Ldr Tom Neil dedicates an entire chapter to this event in his book *From the Cockpit; Spitfire*, and recalls therein that another night-time attack was expected on Liverpool, which resulted in local fighter numbers being increased. During the evening, the pilots were airborne, tasked with patrolling the area and layered at intervals of 1,000 feet throughout altitudes it was thought bombers were most likely to attack.

Neil felt that without airborne radar, there was little chance of the pilots intercepting anything in the darkness, and in fact two unidentified aircraft did appear over Liverpool that night. Neil dived to intercept one of these, but by the time he had descended from 24,000 feet to 15,000, the 'bogey' had disappeared into the darkness. Frustrated, he was compelled to return to RAF Woodvale empty-handed.

During the day, Fg Off Robert Hollow RAAF was posted away, having only been with the Squadron a little over a month. He was shipped to Australia in December 1942 and was discharged as a Flight Lieutenant in October 1945.[68]

It was also around this time that Flt Lt Charles Chappell left the Squadron, at which time Fg Off Rex Poynton assumed his role of OC A Flight. Chappell was posted to Malta, where he served with both 229 and 185 Squadrons prior to becoming a Flight Commander with 152 Squadron in Sicily at the end of August 1943. However, his tenure was cut short when he broke an ankle in a football match two months later and was repatriated home. Chappell remained in the RAF after the War and retired as a Flight Lieutenant in April 1965.

Plt Off (later Flt Lt) Peter Cowell served two tours with 41 Squadron, from 17 November 1942 to 23 July 1944 and from 31 January 1945 to 31 March 1946. © 41 Squadron RAF

29 November 1942 – B Flight at dawn readiness; A Flight at 30 minutes. Poor weather. The seven aircraft sent to Woodvale the previous afternoon returned to Llanbedr at 11:45. Firing practice was held during the afternoon, and Blue and Green sections spent an hour in the air practicing fours drill. In the evening, a cinema show was screened in No. 2 Dining Hall.

30 November 1942 – A Flight at dawn readiness; B Flight at 30 minutes. Cloudy weather with light rain prevailed throughout the day, and the first pilots were not airborne until just after lunch. At 13:00, B Flight's Fg Off Douglas Haywood and Plt Off Bob Boyd were placed at readiness, whilst two of the Squadron's newest pilots, Flt Sgt John Davidson and Sgt Plt John Thomas, were sent on a one-hour sector reconnaissance. On completion, the pair undertook 35 minutes' air-to-ground firing practice with live ammunition on a target behind Harlech, around three miles northeast of Llanbedr, accompanied by Sgt Plt Sydney Benjamin.

Blue and Black Sections also calibrated their guns and practiced dogfights for 40 minutes, and the day ended with a 75-minute dusk patrol to Dublin and back by Flt Lt Doug Hone and Fg Off 'Haybag' Haywood, departing Llanbedr at 16:50.[69] The Squadron was released at 17:30.

The Days Since Dieppe

In a summary of events seldom seen in the 41 Squadron ORB – at least not at this length – the writer[70] spent quite a bit of time at the end of November 1942 reviewing the unit's activities since their last air battle, over Dieppe in August. The wealth of general information and biographical detail is rare in the ORB, which makes it that much more invaluable, and gives the contemporary reader a good indication of the pilots' frustration at being away from the front line for so long.

> The following resume of our 'Fortune' – or perhaps it should be said 'Misfortune' for the last three months is worthy of note. :- When originally the motto SEEK AND <u>DESTROY</u> was decided upon, it was indeed a cruel jest. Or would anyone have visualised in those far off days the tearing asunder of the great 41st. Seldom has there been a more poignant instance of the 'Biter' being 'Bitten'. On September 20th, 11 pilots were posted.[71] It is said that the best are first to go. Words are but mockers of the truth. Two days later our gallant Engineer Officer P/O. Whipp fell to the 'Poster's Pen'; will our aircraft ever be the same? And then, the most

cruel cut of all. Our diminutive F/Lt. F. N. Gillitt, together with P/O T. R. Scott and P/O. R. Harrison, died on active service, when 'Gilly' misjudging his position, led the Section into the hills. '41' will miss and remember them. Misfortune followed tragedy – taxying accidents, engine failures – it was inconceivable that any one squadron could suffer so much – aircraft, pilots, personnel, posted, lost, injured.

The spirit was low, only a nucleus remained. Let all tribute be paid to 'Adj' (F/O. Smith) and the indomitable 'Gizzy' (F/Lt. Lord Gisborough). Their efforts and the combined response of F/Lt. Hone F/Lt. Poynton, and the rest, not excluding the remaining Sgt. Pilots, who, although lacking in experience, were full of spirit, tided the squadron over an unhappy period. F/O. Slack's humour, F/Lt. Poynton's thoroughness, coupled with the energy of F/Lt. Hone and the soundness of our binding F/O. Haywood, has set the squadron on its feet again. From the depths of O.T.U. came the new blood, with a sprinkling of experience in the shape of P/O. Boyd, P/O. Newman and P/O. Hollow from Australia, P/O. Banach, our Polish ally, Sgts. Downing and Rowe, staff pilots, Sgt. Clarke [sic] N. Zealand, succeeding Sgt. Schou (posted) and the rest. In one month and less these boys have done more than respond; in one month the Squadron is living again, not shooting down 'Huns' admittedly, but putting up a good show.

A total of 120 hours night flying were completed in 4 weeks with one excusable accident – plus 100 hours Link trainer exercise. THAT IS PROOF ENOUGH. Above all, there is the harbinger of a SPIRIT, that something which makes all good squadrons what they are. It is not indefineable [sic]. It is keenness, together with team work. The squadron plays well – it is a good sign. Given a month '41' will do more than well. Everything is here, the guts, the energy and the will. It only remains for us to try just a fraction more, and we shall be at the only worthwhile position – 'The Top'.[72]

December 1942 – There was no enemy activity recorded in the Valley Sector during the month, but the weather was so poor that it even hindered the completion of flying training programmes. Weather conditions prevented flying on nine days – 1, 7-8, 10, 13, 16, and 27-29 December – whilst it restricted or prematurely ended flying on another seven – 5, 9, 11, 20-21, 24 and 26 December. Flying was additionally reduced on Christmas Day, and on 30-31 December on account of a number of pilots flying to and from attachments at RAF Westhampnett.

Despite conditions and other hindrances, however, the Squadron flew 51 operational hours, two hours of convoy patrols, 289 day non-operational hours, and 22 night non-operational hours. The day hours included several practice interceptions on 1 (Coastal) OTU's Silloth based Hudsons, under Trewan Sands Control, and in cooperation with Andreas Control. Practice sweeps were also conducted as far northwest as St. John's Point in County Down, Northern Ireland, and as far southwest as Carnsore Point in County Wexford, Éire.

Several pilots were attached to RAF Westhampnett between 13 and 31 December as a part of an operational training programme, which generally consisted of defensive patrols of Selsey, Shoreham, Beachy Head and St. Catherine's Point. Four pilots also took part in an offensive Rhubarb to France on 22 December. In total, ten pilots participated in 18 operations from Tangmere during this time.

2 December 1942 – A Flight at dawn readiness; B Flight at 30 minutes. Following a day on the ground, the weather improved considerably overnight allowing practice flying to be undertaken throughout the day. This included four sections of two aircraft practicing fours drill. The first four aircraft, Blue and Green Sections, were up between 10:30 and 11:30, and the next four, also designated Blue and Green, but with different pilots, between 13:45 and 14:15.

Fg Off David Davies and Plt Off Bob Boyd were sent up on a practice scramble at 15:00 and were airborne within two minutes of the order being given, "This being very good indeed," noted the B Flight Diary, "taking into account the widely dispersed A/C."[73] Later that afternoon, air firing practice was undertaken, and dusk landings were practiced between 17:20 and 18:35.

Fg Off Roger Whipp returned to the Squadron today to resume control of the unit's Engineering Section after a brief sojourn with 72 Squadron at Ouston. When the Squadron was posted to Gibraltar on 8 November 1942, Whipp was left behind, considered unfit for overseas service.

3 December 1942 – B Flight at dawn readiness; A Flight at 30 minutes. The day dawned at 08:20 to initially very poor weather. However, when conditions improved as midday approached, it turned out to be a busy day for flying and personnel movements after all. Flt Lt Douglas Hone and Sgt Plt John Thomas drew the first shift and did some local flying, after which Flt Sgt John Davidson RAAF went up to practice aerobatics for an hour. An air firing programme with the drogue was launched in the afternoon and carried on until dusk, with B Flight's EB-Q, EB-T, and EB-U loaded with ball ammunition for the exercise. The Squadron was released at 17:20.

Sgt Plt Fraser Clark RNZAF returned from his four-day course at Valley in EB-U at 11:20, and Flt Sgt Robert Quine RAAF followed a while later by train. Sgt Plt Bill Downing was sent on seven days' privilege leave and Sgt Plt Peter Roberts was sent on seven days embarkation leave, in advance of a posting to Malta.

4 December 1942 – A Flight at dawn readiness; B Flight at 30 minutes. Similar to the previous morning, initial cloudy weather with heavy haze improved considerably as the morning progressed, allowing a successful training programme to be conducted. This included four pilots who went up to practice formation flying, two to practice using their cine-gun cameras, and six on general flying practice.

5 December 1942 – Very bad weather at dawn which deteriorated to a gale with 60-mile-an-hour winds. Prior to the weather closing in, B Flight's Fg Off Haywood made an early morning weather test, and four aircraft from A Flight completed some cine-gun camera exercises. Thereafter, the Squadron was grounded for the rest of the day.

6 December 1942 – The weather improved again today, allowing a good training programme to be conducted. In all, eleven sorties were recorded, which included local and formation flying, cannon tests, and R/T tests. However, the weather closed down again in the afternoon, hindering further flying, and the Squadron was released at dusk.

9 December 1942 – Following two days grounded by poor weather, conditions had not greatly improved by this morning, but two sorties were conducted before the weather deteriorated again, accompanied by high winds, when all flying ceased. B Flight remained on readiness from dawn to dusk, but the rest of the Squadron spent the afternoon playing rugby.

11 December 1942 – The day commenced with poor weather with gale force winds, including low cloud and continuous rain. Unable to fly, the pilots attended a lecture on the Lewis Gun instead, but when conditions improved around 15:00, six aircraft ventured up for limited practice flying.

12 December 1942 – A Flight at dawn readiness. Weather much improved from recent days, allowing flying training to be restarted. At 10:55, B Flight's Fg Off Rycherde Hogarth and Flt Sgt Robert Quine RAAF practiced formation flying to St. John's Point in County Down, followed by formation landings at RAF Squires Gate, before returning to Llanbedr at 12:35. Fg Off Douglas Haywood and Sgt Plt Peter Roberts also made a practice sweep on Barrow and landed briefly at Andreas on the Isle of Man. At 15:15, three pilots practiced interceptions and, at 16:00, two more practiced dog-fighting. A Flight, meanwhile, was busied with practice patrols and interceptions, and finally practiced dusk landings, until the weather closed down and flying ceased.

13 December 1942 – B Flight on readiness from dawn to dusk. The poor weather continued and during the day a gale blew up with winds of 40 to 60 mph. As a result, no flying was undertaken all day, but the Squadron did receive a visit from the new 9 Group AOC, AVM John Whitworth-Jones CB, to whom all the pilots were introduced. The AOC made an inspection of the aircraft and dispersals area, viewed a combat film, and stayed the night.

ABOVE Sgt Plt Bill Downing in the cockpit of a Spitfire V, possibly at Llanbedr, late 1942-early 1943. © Downing family

LEFT Sgt Plt William Downing, right, with his younger brother during his leave in early December 1942. He served with 41 Squadron from 3 November 1942 to 7 June 1943, and retired as a Squadron Leader in July 1968. © Downing family

14 December 1942 – A Flight at dawn readiness. The weather had improved sufficiently to permit flying practice to be undertaken again today. At 10:10, four pilots participated in an air firing programme whilst two pilots practiced flying individually. At 10:40, Fg Off Douglas Haywood flew to Croydon in the Master to collect Flt Lt Douglas Hone, who flew the aircraft back with Haywood as passenger.

A HP54 Harrow transport aircraft arrived at Llanbedr during the day to take a number of the ground crew to Westhampnett, in the Tangmere Wing, where a month's operational training had been arranged for the pilots, with a rotating change of men planned for each week. The programme would allow them to build up operational flying hours in preparation for their yet-to-be-announced return to the front line in late February. The Squadron was released at dusk.

15 December 1942 – B Flight on readiness from dawn to dusk. At 08:55, Fg Off Douglas Haywood and Sgt Plt Fraser Clark RNZAF were airborne in fair weather on a practice patrol and at 09:40 Black Section, comprising three aircraft, was sent up to practice formation attacks with their cine-gun cameras. At 14:10, an order to scramble was received from Valley and Blue Section, Fg Off Rycherde Hogarth (AA944) and Sgt Plt Peter Roberts (EN827), were vectored to Llandudno at 15,000 feet. Nothing was seen and the pair returned to Llanbedr at 14:50. Practice flying continued in the afternoon, which included a Rhubarb on Andreas by Black Section, consisting of Sgt Plts Sydney Benjamin and Bill Downing.

At 14:45, the first four pilots scheduled for operational training at Westhampnett – Fg Offs Rex Poynton and 'Barney' Newman, and Sgt Plts Anthony Beard and Jack Stonier – departed Llanbedr by air. Inclement weather, however, delayed their arrival, forcing them to put down in Honiley on the way until the worst of the weather passed.

16 December 1942 – A Flight on readiness from dawn to dusk. A gale warning was received and very poor weather all day kept the pilots grounded. B Flight's pilots were involved in ground training instead, thereunder a lecture on armament.

During the day, Sgt Plt Peter Roberts was posted away to Malta. He arrived at Hal Far at the beginning of March 1943 and was posted to 185 Squadron. Commissioned in November 1943, he remained in the RAF after the War. Rising to the rank of Squadron Leader, Roberts co-incidentally returned to 185 Squadron at Hal Far in 1952 as the unit's Commanding Officer. He was awarded a Kings Commendation for Valuable Services in the Air that same year and retired from the RAF in November 1960.

In the evening a "very successful Squadron supper"[74] was held in the Airmen's Dining Hall attended by the Station Commander, Sqn Ldr Eynon R. Bullimore, and all of the Squadron's personnel, and was hosted by Sqn Ldr Tom Neil. The ORB records that,

The arrangements were in the capable hands of F/O Smith, Adjutant, who proved his versatility as compere [sic], toast master, interlocutor and entertainer. A varied programme was very much enjoyed by all, with the addition of excellent fare and a satisfactory 'flow' of refreshments.[75]

The Station ORB adds that the Supper was "much appreciated, thanks to the Padre who was responsible for obtaining the hampers."[76]

17 December 1942 – B Flight on readiness from dawn until dusk. The weather had improved sufficiently from the previous day for flying practice to be undertaken for a few hours today. During the morning, the readiness section, comprising Fg Offs Rycherde Hogarth and David Davies, logged 30 minutes local flying, whilst Green and Black Sections both undertook an hour's practice flying, commencing with a practice scramble that took four minutes to get off the deck. When the weather closed in late in the afternoon, flying ceased and the Squadron's Medical Officer, Flt Lt Richard Armin, gave the pilots a First Aid lecture.

Separately today, 22-year-old Polish Sgt Plt Josef Bednarz joined the unit. He had undertaken first level aviation training prior to fleeing Poland in the wake of the German occupation and arrived safely in France, only to be evacuated from that country in 1940 when it also fell. On arrival in the United Kingdom, Bednarz joined the RAFVR at Blackpool and subsequently undertook EFTS, SFTS and OTU courses, and was posted to his first operational unit, 317 (Polish) Squadron, on 10 September 1942. Six weeks later, he was transferred to 403 (Canadian) Squadron, and was posted to 41 Squadron today, his operational flying hours thus far amounting to a single convoy patrol.

18 December 1942 – A Flight on readiness all day; B Flight at 30 minutes. The weather was initially poor with bad visibility, but improved as the morning progressed. B Flight's Blue, Green and Black Sections took off at 10:25 for formation flying training for 85 minutes and practice flying then continued into the afternoon. This included air-to-air firing, interceptions and local flying. At 14:00, Fg Offs Rycherde Hogarth and David Davies, and Sgt Plt Fraser Clark RNZAF and Flt Sgt Robert Quine RAAF practiced air firing on the drogue, which was towed by Fg Off Douglas Haywood in EB-W.

A night-flying programme commenced at 17:00 and six B Flight pilots – Flt Lt Douglas Hone, Fg Offs Haywood and Hogarth, Plt Off Bob Boyd and Flt Sgt Quine and Sgt Plt Clark – logged several night-flying hours. However, the weather closed down late in the evening and all flying ceased at 23:00. A Sergeants' Dance was held in the evening for those not on flying duties.

19 December 1942 – B Flight on readiness all day; A Flight at 30 minutes. Good weather allowed flying training to be carried out throughout the day. The readiness section, comprising Fg Off Bob Boyd and Sgt Plt Fraser Clark RNZAF, logged 30 minutes local flying, whilst Blue, Green and Black Sections practiced dogfights and cine-gun camera handling. Fg Off Rycherde Hogarth and Flt Sgt Robert Quine RAAF also practiced dusk landings for 20 minutes, and a 'successful' Officers' Dance was held in the evening.

Separately, 24-year-old Polish Plt Off Jerzy Polak arrived on the Squadron today and was posted to B Flight. Having attended the Polish Air Force Officer Cadet School prior to the War, he had initially fled to France on the occupation of Poland, and then to the United Kingdom upon France's capitulation in 1940. Initially joining 308 (Polish) Squadron in early March 1942, Polak was commissioned ten days later and posted to 306 (Polish) Squadron on 29 March. He remained with that unit until 18 December 1942 but during that time attended an Officers' course at Cosford. He arrived on 41 Squadron today, having logged 800 flying hours, of which 35 were operational. These hours included 12 sweeps, one Rhubarb, and a number of convoy and sea patrols.

20 December 1942 – B Flight at dawn readiness; A Flight at 30 minutes. Poor weather all day only allowed two sorties to be flown, when Fg Off David Davies and Sgt Plt Bill Downing completed 50 minutes local flying. As no further flying could be undertaken, the pilots attended lectures instead.

21 December 1942 – Although there was no real improvement in the weather, six B Flight pilots were sent up at 09:00 to practice formation flying. However, four returned after just 20 minutes reporting the conditions unsuitable for the exercise and the remaining two, Flt Lt Douglas Hone and Fg Off David Davies, set down at Valley and stayed the night.[77] The weather deteriorated further during the afternoon and no further flying was undertaken all day. The Squadron was released at dusk.

22 December 1942 – A Flight at dawn readiness; B Flight at 30 minutes. There was considerable weather improvement overnight and dawn brought an "excellent day for flying, weather perfect"[78]. As such, a considerable amount of flying was undertaken throughout the day, with B Flight alone flying 29 sorties. Flt Lt Douglas Hone and Fg Off David Davies returned from Valley, departing that airfield at 09:40, and arriving at Llanbedr at 10:05. Not long after his return, Hone was in the air again, flying the Master to Ternhill and back, bringing tools for the Squadron's Engineer Officer, Fg Off Roger Whipp.

At 10:45, Blue Section, comprising four aircraft, and Green Section, comprising two, commenced 90 minutes practice flying. At 11:20, six more pilots were airborne, as Black, Blue, and Green sections, in an hour-long interception exercise on six Wellington bombers.

During the afternoon, six pilots participated in a low flying exercise, two flying to Llandow, a few miles west of Cardiff, and the remaining four to Blackpool, where they practiced low level attacks. The latter four continued on a route that led them to the Mull of Galloway, Andreas and Ballyhalbert, where they refuelled, and then returned to Llanbedr, via Andreas once again, and landed back at base 15 minutes after dusk. As a result, the last leg was logged by the pilots as night flying.

Local flying exercises were also undertaken by other pilots throughout the day, and the Squadron was released at dusk. It proved to be one of the most successful days of practice flying in some time.

Separately, 22-year-old Australian Sgt Plt Arthur Cope was posted to the Squadron today. Having joined the RAAF in July 1941, he completed EFTS and SFTS courses and earned his Wings in Australia, before embarking for the United Kingdom in July 1942. After his arrival and a period of leave, Cope undertook AFU and OTU courses and was now being sent to 41 Squadron for his first operational posting, with 247 non-operational flying hours in his logbook. He would only remain with the unit for approximately five weeks before being posted to North Africa.

23 December 1942 – Fair weather today meant that a significant amount of flying practice was undertaken, although the programme was not as intensive as the previous day. At 09:45, four aircraft participated in an interception exercise and, at 12:20, three sections of two aircraft were sent on search patrols to locate a raft reported to be southeast of Bardsey Island, containing eight survivors of a mined vessel.

The vessel in question was the Danish cargo ship *Knut*, which was chartered by the Ministry of War Transport, and had been enroute between Belfast and The Mumbles, in South Wales, when it hit a mine around nine miles south-southeast of Bardsey Island. There were in fact 15 crew members, and all abandoned the ship in its own lifeboat, as the 18-year-old, 1,274-ton steamer sank beneath them.

Extensive searches were made of the area by 41 Squadron in cooperation with 275 (ASR) and 456 (Australian) Squadrons between 10:15 and 15:45. The RNLI was also called out from the Porthdinllaen Lifeboat Station to locate the crew, but as they were given an incorrect position, they found nothing.

Only some debris and a floating mine were sighted by various pilots from the air, until 15:10 when 41 Squadron's Blue Section, consisting of Flt Lt Douglas Hone and Flt Sgt John Davidson RAAF, sighted an empty raft off the Lleyn [Llŷn] Peninsula and radioed its location to Valley Control. It later transpired, however, that the seamen had already been picked up by a Coaster and landed at Holyhead.

Meanwhile, back in Llanbedr, local flying was carried out throughout the afternoon by the rest of the Squadron's pilots until their dusk release.

24 December 1942 – A Flight at dawn readiness; B Flight at 30 minutes. The weather started to close down in the morning, but Fg Off Bob Boyd was sent up for a 20-minute weather test. He reported the Squadron could potentially squeeze in an hour's flying if required, at which point Blue Section of four aircraft was sent up for fours drill. Within 40 minutes, however, they were forced to conclude that the weather had deteriorated to such an extent which prohibited them continuing. They returned to Llanbedr and the Squadron was grounded for the rest of the day.

A successful Christmas Eve all-ranks Dance and Cabaret was held in the Dining Hall that evening, "which was cheerfully decorated for Christmas Festivities"[79] and "enjoyed by everyone."[80]

25 December 1942 – Christmas Day. No flying was undertaken all day, although one section was kept at readiness for Station and Sector defence in case.

Christmas festivities began with a friendly game of 'Rugsoc', which was followed by Senior Station and 41 Squadron NCOs visiting the Officers' Mess for a toast. At its conclusion, the Station Commander paraded and marched both Officers and Senior NCOs from the Officers' Mess to the Airmen's Dining Hall, where they served Christmas Dinner to the airmen at 13:00, as was custom, "much to the enjoyment of the personnel".[81]

The celebrations continued through the evening when a Station Concert Party and variety show was held for all ranks between 18:00 and 23:59, which was attended by a great number of WAAFs. The Squadron ORB recorded,

> *The Dining Hall was very tastily decorated, and an excellent dinner was served. There was also plenty of beer, cigarettes and fruit on service. Officers and Senior N.C.O.s were compelled to give short speeches, each speaker was met with loud acclamations, finally the dinner ended at 14.30 hrs. In the evening a very good concert was given by the Station Concert Party, which contained a good sprinkling of Squadron Men. The show continued until 1 a.m. on Boxing Day.*[82,83]

26 December 1942 – Boxing Day. A Flight at dawn readiness; B Flight at 30 minutes. The weather was not particularly suitable for flying training, but one section of four was sent up for some limited formation flying. On their return, they reported the weather too poor to continue, but when it cleared a little in the early evening, another section was sent up for 55 minutes local flying.

The Squadron won a rather convincing 17:0 in a rugby match against Station Headquarters in the afternoon and ENSA gave a concert in the Dining Hall in the evening. This was followed by a cabaret and dance, which continued until 01:00 the following morning. The Station ORB almost expresses some surprise that "personnel still had 'pep' for dancing"[84] but added it was now time to get back to routine: "Tomorrow we give up dancing and face realities – work as never before."[85]

27 December 1942 – As the weather was extremely poor today, with zero visibility, the Squadron was released on base. Even though their release was conditional on 30-minute availability, the break was welcome as the men were "dead beat after Xmas activities".[86] The day also saw the departure of Sgt Plt Sydney Benjamin, who was posted overseas.[87]

December Tangmere Operations

Meanwhile, at Westhampnett [see 15 December 1942], the Squadron's detached pilots were busy logging operational flying hours in cooperation with other Westhampnett based and Tangmere Wing squadrons, which mostly consisted of patrols over Selsey, Shoreham, Beachy Head and St. Catherine's Point.

However, one of the more notable operations they participated in was a Rhubarb to the French coast on 22 December 1942. On that occasion, Fg Offs Rex Poynton and 'Barney' Newman, Flt Sgt Jack Stonier and Sgt Plt Anthony Beard flew across the Channel at zero feet to Quiberville, approximately 12km southwest of Dieppe, to seek out railway targets between Bolbec and Yvetot.

However, when they reached the coast, they found no cloud cover to hide their approach. They banked to starboard and flew southwest, slightly off-shore and on past St. Valery, Fécamp and Étretat on their port side, until they reached Le Havre.

No reaction was experienced from the shoreline until light Flak opened up on them from Octeville-sur-Mer, a few miles north of Le Havre. Anti-aircraft fire then continued the rest of the way to Le Havre Harbour, where intense heavy calibre Flak joined in. This was the first time the Squadron's pilots had come under fire since Dieppe, some four months previously.

As they approached Le Havre, they sighted a "small ship of coast guard cutter type painted green with one funnel"[88] just outside the harbour. The initial reaction was to attack the vessel, but almost immediately any "idea of attacking this ship was given up"[89] owing to the intensity of the anti-aircraft fire they were experiencing. Left little choice, the men reluctantly turned for home, where they landed at 16:20, reporting 1/10th high cloud and excellent visibility.

The sorties flown from Westhampnett between 17 and 29 December 1942 by the Squadron's detached pilots are shown in the table below.

Date	Pilots, Westhampnett	Timings	Patrol
17	Poynton W3378, Newman AD562	14:45-16:00	St. Catherine's Pt. & Shoreham
18	Poynton W3378, Beard AB809	10:35-12:00	St. Catherine's Point
19	Poynton W3378, Stonier AD562	15:40-16:30	Convoy Patrol
20	Poynton W3378, Beard AD562, Stonier AB809	12:40-14:15	Sweep
22	Poynton W3378, Newman AD562, Stonier BL966, Beard AB809	14:55-16:20	Rhubarb, Quiberville-Le Havre
23	Clark EN828, Quine AB849	12:20-13:35	Air-Sea Search Formation
23	Hogarth AA944, Boyd AD185	12:25-13:25	Air-Sea Search Formation
23	Poynton W3378, Newman AD562	12:35-13:40	Selsey and St. Catherine's Pt.
23	Stonier BL966, Beard AB809	13:20-14:15	Selsey and Shoreham
23	Poynton W3378, Newman AD562	14:15-15:20	Selsey and Shoreham
23	Hone EN828, Davidson BL299	13:50-14:20	Search Patrol
23	Hone EN828, Davidson BL299	14:35-16:05	Search Patrol
23	Neil BL406, Stonier BL966	15:50-17:25	Selsey and St. Catherine's Pt.
23	Poynton W3378, Newman AD562	15:50-17:25	Selsey and Shoreham
24	Stonier BL966, Beard AB562	13:30-14:45	Selsey and St. Catherine's Pt.
24	Poynton W3378, Stonier BL966, Newman AB809	15:35-17:00	Selsey and St. Catherine's Pt.
29	Poynton W3378, Newman AD562	10:05-11:20	Selsey and St. Catherine's Pt.
29	Newman AD562, Stonier BL966	13:00-13:45	Selsey and Shoreham

Polish Sgt Plt Josef Bednarz served with 41 Squadron from 17 December 1942 to 1 February 1943, when he was killed in a flying accident on a beach west of Pwllheli, Wales; via Peter Sikora

28 December 1942 – Poor weather prohibited any flying taking place today, and the Squadron remained at 30 minutes readiness until dusk. The main event of the day was the arrival of two new pilots, 21-year-old Scottish Sgt Plt Walter Brown, and 22-year-old Polish Flt Sgt Jan Rogowski.

Having joined the RAFVR in Edinburgh in March 1941, Brown had undertaken his flying training in the United States, where he graduated with his Wings as an NCO pilot in May 1942. Brown returned to the United Kingdom to complete his AFU and OTU courses, and was posted to 41 Squadron today with 330 non-operational hours in his logbook. However, he was only destined to remain with the unit less than two weeks.

Rogowski had joined the Polish Air Force in late 1939, but soon fled to the United Kingdom, where he joined the RAFVR in February 1940. Attending EFTS, SFTS and OTU in England and Scotland, he was posted to his first operational unit, 306 (Polish) Squadron, in June 1942. Four months later, he was posted to 403 (Canadian) Squadron, but returned to 306 (Polish) Squadron again in late December for one week. He arrived on 41 Squadron today with significantly more active experience than many of the unit's current NCO pilots. This included four sweeps, four convoy patrols, three circuses, one Rhubarb to St. Omer Airfield, and two indecisive combats with enemy aircraft.

30 December 1942 – A Flight at dawn readiness, B Flight at 30 minutes. When the weather improved towards midday, Fg Off David Davies performed a one-hour weather test from 13:30 to ascertain whether conditions would allow flying training to recommence. Reporting things acceptable, the readiness section, comprising Fg Off Rycherde Hogarth and Flt Sgt John Davidson RAAF, took off for 30 minutes local flying. Fg Off Bob Boyd and Sgt Plt Arthur Cope RAAF were also cleared for their own trip, but the weather closed down again before they could get airborne, and this put an end to their plans.

Six more pilots and aircraft were also sent to Westhampnett for operational training today. They were Flt Lt Douglas Hone, Fg Offs Douglas Haywood and Rycherde Hogarth, Plt Off Jerzy Polak, and Sgt Plts Fraser Clark RNZAF and John Thomas, who remained in Sussex until mid-January.

31 December 1942 – B Flight at dawn readiness; A Flight at 30 minutes. Owing to the number of aircraft detached to Westhampnett, B Flight could only muster three aircraft and three pilots

(Boyd, Brown and Davies), leaving Fg Off Bob Boyd and Sgt Plt Walter Brown at readiness for most of the day. As such, although A Flight was set at 30 minutes, the Flight's pilots relieved Boyd and Brown when necessary.

New Year's Eve was celebrated with a cabaret and dance in No. 2 Dining Hall, where the Station welcomed in the New Year, "leaving behind a road of disappointments and triumphs".[90] The Squadron ORB adds that "41 Squadron is again looking forward to a very successful new year in 1943."[91]

January 1943 – 41 Squadron's operational flying was limited to 3, 14, 21 and 29 January, and weather prevented flying altogether on 1-2, 5, 9, 16 and 28 January. Nonetheless, the pilots flew 56 operational hours, 404 day non-operational hours and 35 night non-operational hours during the month.

Although Control at Valley scrambled the Sector's squadrons nine times during the month, "not a single Hun has crossed the Group boundaries and once more the Squadrons operated by this Sector have had to content themselves with extensive training programmes".[92]

Aside from practice interceptions on Wellington bombers, practice sweeps took the pilots over a wide area, bounded by Carnsore Point in southern Éire, Ballyhalbert in Northern Ireland, and the Scottish coast, due north of the Isle of Man.

Separately, seven more pilots were detached to RAF Westhampnett until 13 January to gain experience on a total of 19 operational patrols. These were generally confined to defensive sorties of Beachy Head, Selsey, Shoreham and St. Catherine's Point, but on 9 January four pilots also participated in an offensive Circus to Le Touquet and Berck-sur-Mer, France.

3 January 1943 – A Flight at dawn readiness; B Flight at 30 minutes. Improved weather conditions allowed the pilots to commence flying practice at 10:00, and Fg Off David Davies and Fg Off Bob Boyd spent the day training B Flight's new NCO pilots, Walter Brown and Arthur Cope RAAF. A scramble of the base area was ordered just after 11:00 and A Flight's Sgt Plts Clifford Monk (X4279) and Leslie Prickett (EN780) were sent up as Yellow Section in response. They returned at 12:30 with nothing to report. In the afternoon, Fg Off Boyd flew to Woodvale and Atcham in the Squadron's Miles Master, but became stranded at the latter airfield as a result of starter failure on the aircraft, and remained the night. Flying training ceased at Llanbedr at 17:40.

4 January 1943 – B Flight at dawn readiness; A Flight at 30 minutes. As a result of most of B Flight being at Westhampnett, of Fg Off Bob Boyd being stranded at Atcham, and of Sgt Plts Walter Brown and Arthur Cope's not-yet-operational status, the readiness section this morning comprised B Flight's Fg Off David Davies and A Flight's Fg Off Peter Cowell. Suitable weather allowed flying practice to be undertaken throughout the day, and this included formation flying and aerobatics. Fg Off Bob Boyd also had the Master's starter problem fixed and returned to Llanbedr.

6 January 1943 – B Flight at dawn readiness; A Flight at 30 minutes. Fg Off David Davies and Fg Off Bob Boyd formed the readiness section. Flying training was undertaken throughout the day, and included formation flying and practice interceptions on Pershore based 23 (Bomber) OTU's Wellingtons. Owing to B Flight's readiness status, only limited practice flying was also carried out with the Flight's Sgt Plts Walter Brown and Arthur Cope.

7 January 1943 – A Flight at dawn readiness; B Flight at 30 minutes. The day's weather is described in B Flight's Diary as 'dull', and no flying was undertaken all day. In the afternoon, the pilots and ground crews – in all roughly 70% of the entire Station staff – were given a 'Fighter Command Demonstration Flight' displaying aerodrome defence by "a capable Section of the R.A.F. Regiment."[93]

8 January 1943 – B Flight at dawn readiness; A Flight at 30 minutes. The readiness section, comprising Fg Off David Davies and Fg Off Bob Boyd, completed 30 minutes local flying. At 10:00, six A Flight pilots took off for a patrol to Carnsore Point, Éire, led by Flt Lt Rex Poynton, and later another three of A Flight's pilots participated in a search for a missing aircraft. Fg Off Rycherde Hogarth arrived at Llanbedr from Tangmere in EB-L at 13:30, but flew back again in EB-W at 15:00. Practice flying continued throughout the afternoon, but when all three of B Flight's remaining aircraft became unserviceable as the day progressed, A Flight was obliged to take over readiness until dusk.

A Circus Operation from Tangmere

The Squadron's Westhampnett detachment was due back at Llanbedr on 7 January 1943, but their return was postponed until 13 January. Although the reason for the delay remains unexplained, it may have partially been to give four of B Flight's pilots the opportunity to participate in Circus 248 on 9 January.

Date	9 January 1943
Operation	Circus 248
Target Area	Le Touquet & Berck-sur-Mer, Pas-de-Calais
Bouncing Wing	Tangmere: 165 Squadron (12 Spitfire Vb) Westhampnett: 485 Squadron (12 Spitfire Vb) Westhampnett (attached): 41 Squadron (4 Spitfire Vb)

The Tangmere Wing was led by Wg Cdr Peter Brothers DFC, who flew with 485 (NZ) Squadron, under Appledore Control. The pilots were airborne from 12:40 and crossed the French coast over Merlimont Plage, approximately half way between Berck and Le Touquet, stepped up and back with 485 (NZ) Squadron at a base of 19,000 feet. As the formation swept in over Hesdin, they climbed to 20,000 feet, whereupon they were given a vector of 180°.

Turning back for the coast, six enemy aircraft were seen flying north at 10,000 feet in the Abbeville area, which were believed to have been FW190s. Elements of the Wing turned to intercept them, but the aircraft soon disappeared into haze and could not be engaged.

The Wing re-crossed the French coast six miles south of Berck-sur-Mer, farewelled by a brief but ineffective barrage of heavy Flak. Moments later, however, they were vectored south to intercept what were believed to have been more enemy aircraft, but they turned out to be Spitfires. More formations were spotted during the return journey over the Channel, but these were also all friendly.

The formation returned to Tangmere and Westhampnett, landing again around 14:25. Uneventful as it was, the Tangmere Wing ORB barely affords it a mention, merely reporting that a detachment from 41 Squadron cooperated with 165 and 485 Squadrons acting as 'bouncing wing' under Appledore control on Circus 248 to Berck.

41 Squadron's contingent on the operation was airborne between 12:50 and 14:10 and consisted of Fg Off Douglas Haywood (EN827), Fg Off Rycherde Hogarth (EN828), Plt Off Jerzy Polak (W3348) and Sgt Plt Fraser Clark RNZAF (AD185).

13 January 1943 – A Flight at dawn readiness; B Flight at 30 minutes. Fair weather permitted flying practice to commence at 10:45, and five of the detached pilots returned from Westhampnett during the morning. The rest of the pilots spent the day working on cine-gun attacks, air firing, local flying, and a practice interception on a Wellington from 23 (Bomber) OTU, the latter of which was undertaken by Fg Off Bob Boyd and Flt Sgt John Davidson RAAF. At 22:45, a night

flying programme was launched, during which four aircraft conducted patrols until 01:00 the following morning.

January's Operational Flights from Tangmere

The operational flights undertaken by 41 Squadron's pilots between New Year's Day 1943 and their return to Llanbedr on 13 January are shown in the below table.

Date	Pilot, Westhampnett	Timings	Patrol
2	Hone BL905, Haywood EN828	15:40-16:15	Needles to St. Catherine's Pt.
3	Hogarth AD185, Thomas EN828	09:25-10:40	Selsey to Beachy Head
3	Hogarth AD185, Thomas EN828	11:30-12:30	Selsey to Beachy Head
3	Polak AD185, Clark BL299	14:05-15:35	Selsey to Shoreham
3	Hone AD185, Thomas BL299	15:55-17:25	Selsey to Shoreham
4	Hone AD185, Haywood EN828	08:50-10:10	Selsey to Shoreham
4	Polak AD185, Thomas EN828	10:50-12:05	Selsey to Shoreham
4	Hogarth EN827, Clark BL299	14:05-15:40	Selsey to St. Catherine's Pt.
4	Robinson AD185, Thomas EN828	15:00-16:30	Convoy Patrol
4	Hone EN827, Haywood EN828	16:45-17:35	Selsey to Shoreham
8	Haywood EN828, Clark AD185	15:10-16:40	Selsey to Beachy Head
9	Polak W3348, Thomas EN828	10:45-12:25	Selsey to Shoreham
9	Haywood EN827, Polak W3348, Hogarth EN828, Clark AD185	12:50-14:10	Le Touquet-Berck area
9	Hogarth AD125, Thomas AD185	15:45-17:25	Shoreham to Selsey
11	Hogarth AD185, Polak W3348	11:25-12:35	Selsey to Shoreham
11	Hone EN827, Haywood EN828	12:20-14:10	Selsey to Beachy Head
11	Clark AD185, Thomas AD125	14:30-15:40	Selsey to Beachy Head
11	Haywood EN828, Polak AD185	16:15-17:30	Selsey to St. Catherine's Pt.
12	Haywood EN828, Polak AD185	11:55-12:10	Selsey to Shoreham

14 January 1943 – B Flight at dawn readiness; A Flight at 30 minutes. Just after midday a practice interception was undertaken by two pilots on a Wellington bomber from 23 (Bomber) OTU, 20 miles northwest of Bardsey Island.

The exercise was run as if it were real, and a dummy Combat Report shows that Fg Off David Davies and his No. 2 were scrambled at 12:15 and airborne at 12:19. The pair flew a vector of 340° in battle formation and spotted the Wellington ten minutes into their flight off their starboard quarter, flying in an easterly direction.

They climbed into the sun and carried out six attacks before the bomber gave any sign of noticing them. Surprised by this, Davies checked with control that they were actually 'attacking' the right aircraft, and it was confirmed they were. As such, Davies carried out eight more attacks, from port beam and below starboard, using a total of 25 feet of film, before the Wellington took evasive action "in the form of a corkscrew motion, which was not effective and not sufficiently vigorous".[94]

Davies' No. 2, unfortunately unnamed in the report, also 'fired' upon the Wellington out of the sun, from above the bomber, from astern, and from its port beam, using 24 feet of cine-gun film. Subsequent analysis of the film showed they it would likely have been destroyed.

During their return to base on completion of the exercise, the pair were vectored 225° onto "a real bogey"[95], whilst at 13:05 an order was received back at Llanbedr for a section to 'scramble

Polish Plt Off Jerzy Polak served with 41 Squadron from 19 December 1942 to 29 April 1943. He remained in the United Kingdom after the War; via Peter Sikora

base' at 10,000 feet. Although there is no evidence that the interception exercise's 'real bogey' and the object of the scramble from Llanbedr are the same event, the timings appear to correspond circumstantially.

The readiness section, consisting of Plt Off Jerzy Polak (AD185) and Sgt Plt Fraser Clark RNZAF (AA718), were quickly airborne from Llanbedr as Green Section. However, they returned within ten minutes owing to engine trouble with Polak's aircraft, and were replaced by another two pilots, who were airborne at 13:15. This section, designated Red, comprised Flt Lt Rex Poynton (AB809) and Plt Off Wladislaw Banach (BL905).

Meanwhile, Davies and his No. 2 were also searching for the 'bogey', but due to bright sunlight on the vector they were given, they were unable to see the aircraft even though it was supposed to have been only three miles away from them. Poynton and Banach were more successful, and returned at 13:45 reporting the aircraft friendly. Davies and his No. 2 landed five minutes later.

The rest of the day was spent on flying training in fair weather and the afternoon's activities included air firing and local flying. Fg Off Douglas Haywood also returned from Westhampnett in EB-S.

15 January 1943 – A Flight at dawn readiness; B Flight at 30 minutes. The pilots flew to Valley in fair weather at 10:10 for a lecture. They arrived at 10:50 and returned to Llanbedr again at 15:45. There was little further flying activity, and "the Officers had a very enjoyable party in the Mess in the evening."[96] The Station ORB called it "a night beyond description"[97], whilst the Squadron's B Flight diary, records a little more candidly, "Opening night for [the] Officers' Mess, drinks all night until 6 AM. Flt Lt Hone tipped W/C Dwyer out of bed in mistake for F/O Hogarth."[98] One can only hope 456 Squadron's Commanding Officer, Wg Cdr Michael Dwyer, had a sense of humour; no doubt Douglas Hone was just as shocked as Dwyer when he realised his error!

17 January 1943 – A Flight at dawn readiness; B Flight at 30 minutes. Formation practice was undertaken by the entire Squadron, which departed Llanbedr in fair weather at 14:10 led by Sqn Ldr Neil, and landed at Andreas at 15:10. Departing Andreas again at 17:00, they arrived back at Llanbedr at 18:00, with the exception of Sgt Plt John Thomas, who landed at Valley low on fuel.

Nominal Roll, January 1943

This nominal roll has been extracted from the Squadron's B Flight diary, which is held in 41 Squadron's Archive. Names are listed in the order they appear in the diary, which is headed, "Monday, Jan. 18th 1943. List of Present Pilots to Date. 41 Squadron."

A Flight	B Flight
S/Ldr Neil	F/Lt Hone
F/O Poynton	F/O Haywood
F/O Slack	F/O Hogarth
F/O Hoare	F/O Davies
P/O Cowell	P/O Boyd
P/O Banach	P/O Polak
Sgt Prickett	Sgt Clark
Sgt Stonier	Sgt Downing
Sgt Monk	Sgt Thomas
Sgt Rowe	-
Sgt Bednarz	-
P/O Newman	-
F/O Whipp – Engineering Officer	
F/O Smith – Squadron Adjutant	

18 January 1943 – A Flight at dawn readiness; B Flight at 30 minutes. Flt Lt Douglas Hone flew Plt Off Jerzy Polak to Valley in fair weather in the Master for an air-firing course, and Fg Off Bob Boyd followed later in EB-M. Air-to-air firing was also carried out from Llanbedr by several pilots of both Flights, the drogue being towed by the unit's Miles Martinet. In the early evening, dusk landing practice was carried out by Sgt Plts Fraser Clark RNZAF and John Thomas, led by Flt Lt Hone, and flying ceased at 18:35.

19 January 1943 – A Flight at dawn readiness; B Flight at 30 minutes. An air-to-air firing programme was run during the morning in fair weather with the drogue towed by Fg Off Douglas Haywood in the Martinet, and the drogue itself operated by Aircraftman Sanderson. Squadron formation practice was carried out between 14:50 and 15:35, led by Flt Lt Douglas Hone, after which air-to-air firing and interception practice were continued until flying ceased at 17:45.

A new pilot also joined the Squadron today in the form of 22-year-old Sgt Plt Robert Duckworth. He arrived on 41 Squadron today for his first operational posting with 292 non-operational flying hours in his logbook, but his tenure must have been extremely brief, as he is not mentioned again after this date.

20 January 1943 – B Flight at dawn readiness; A Flight at 30 minutes. The readiness section comprised Flt Lt Douglas Hone and Sgt Plt Fraser Clark RNZAF, and fair weather allowed for a considerable amount of flying training to be undertaken throughout the day. Activity included local flying, practice scrambles and dusk landings, and the Squadron was released at dusk, in time for an evening dance.

21 January 1943 – A Flight at dawn readiness; B Flight at 30 minutes. Fair weather enabled three pilots to be sent on an air-to-sea firing programme at 10:00. At 12:05, Polish Sgt Plt Josef Bednarz (EN780) was scrambled and vectored onto a hostile plot. However, nothing was seen and he returned within five minutes. Blue and Black Sections took off for an hour's dog-fighting practice from 13:25, but Blue 2, Sgt Plt John Thomas, returned early with a glycol leak. He landed not a moment too soon as the aircraft overheated, seized and ground to a halt in the middle of the runway. A scheduled night flying exercise was postponed when the weather deteriorated, and the pilots were released at dusk.

22 January 1943 – B Flight at dawn readiness; A Flight at 30 minutes. In conditions of poor weather with low cloud and rain, B Flight's Fg Off Douglas Haywood (EB-U) and Plt Off Bob Boyd (EB-M) practiced ZZ Landings for two hours from 10:00, followed by two pilots from A Flight. At 14:30, the pilots were given a lecture in the Intelligence Office on the subject of tanks, which concluded the day's activity. The Squadron was released at dusk, and this enabled them to attend a mobile cinema show and dance during the evening.

23 January 1943 – A Flight at dawn readiness; B Flight at 30 minutes. ZZ landing practice was carried out during the morning, but by midday the weather had improved sufficiently to allow formation flying, direction finding homing practice, and aerobatics to be undertaken throughout the afternoon. At 14:50, Fg Off Douglas Haywood (EB-U), Fg Off Bob Boyd (EB-L) and Plt Off Jerzy Polak (EB-P) conducted a practice sweep of Andreas, then refuelled at Ballyhalbert in Northern Ireland and returned to Llanbedr at 17:45.

A dusk landing and night flying programme was commenced in the late afternoon, which included Fg Off David Davies and Plt Off Jerzy Polak practicing landings for 45 minutes, whilst Flt Lt Douglas Hone, Fg Offs Douglas Haywood and Bob Boyd and Sgt Plt John Thomas undertook an hour's night flying practice from 22:20. Upon landing, Thomas crashed his aircraft, EB-M, but was fortunately not injured. Those not involved in the night exercise attended an all-ranks dance.

24 January 1943 – B Flight at dawn readiness; A Flight at 30 minutes. As the weather was "not too bad,"[99] some local flying was carried out during the day, as was direction-finding homing practice by Fg Offs Douglas Haywood and Bob Boyd and Sgt Plt John Thomas. The Squadron was released at dusk and saw the comedy 'My Favourite Wife', starring Cary Grant, at the evening's cinema show.

26 January 1943 – B Flight at dawn readiness; A Flight at 30 minutes. The weather was initially misty, but this lifted as the morning progressed. The readiness section, comprising Fg Off Douglas Haywood and Sgt Plt John Thomas, undertook some local flying from 08:50-09:25 followed by a practice scramble at 11:05. They were airborne in just 2½ minutes, and returned to Llanbedr at 12:00. B Flight's Fg Off David Davies carried out an air test in EB-X, whilst Plt Offs Bob Boyd and Jerzy Polak undertook some local formation flying. A Flight was busied meanwhile with air firing and cine-gun camera practice.

27 January 1943 – A Flight at dawn readiness; B Flight at 30 minutes. Fair weather allowed an air-to-air firing programme to be undertaken by B Flight, with Fg Off Bob Boyd towing the drogue in the Martinet. Fg Offs Douglas Haywood, Rycherde Hogarth and David Davies and Sgt Plt John Thomas all took turns firing at the drogue, and it was reported that shooting had clearly "improved with quite a lot of hits by the Pilots".[100]

Fg Off Haywood then took over drogue towing in the Martinet, allowing Fg Off Bob Boyd to also do some firing. However, Haywood was obliged to return after just 15 minutes in the air in order to obtain more drogues. Whilst taxiing around the airfield's perimeter, he moved off the strip to allow A Flight's Flight Commander, Flt Lt Rex Poynton, to pass him in his own aircraft. Unfortunately, the Martinet's wheels became bogged in the soft sand and Haywood was unable to proceed any further. The weather closed down in the afternoon and this put an end to the day's flying, but allowed the men to attend a film show in the evening.

29 January 1943 – A Flight at dawn readiness; B Flight at 30 minutes. Fair weather with a strong south-westerly wind and occasional showers. At 09:10, Red Section, comprising Fg Off 'Barney' Newman RAAF (BL905) and Plt Off Leslie Prickett (AB809), conducted a 50-minute patrol of a small northbound convoy of three ships and a sloop.

When the RNLI base at Barmouth sighted red flares in Cardigan Bay shortly after midday, it was felt they were likely from a dinghy from a missing Blackburn Skua. They sent out a boat and, at 12:42, 41 Squadron was also sent up for a search but nothing was found.[101]

Range estimation and cine-gun camera practice was carried out by B Flight during the afternoon and, at 14:35, Fg Off Haywood flew to Northolt in the Tiger Moth, arriving at 16:00. Squadron formation practice was undertaken from 15:00, led by Flt Lt Rex Poynton, but all flying ceased when the weather closed in at 16:30.

A new pilot joined the Squadron today: 22-year-old Sgt Plt Peter Cross, who had joined the RAFVR in February 1940. He undertook his elementary flying training in the United States, where he had earned his Wings, and returned to the United Kingdom to complete his AFU and OTU courses. Cross was posted to B Flight upon his arrival and would remain with the Squadron just one month.

30 January 1943 – B Flight at dawn readiness; A Flight at 30 minutes. Flying practice was undertaken throughout the day, which included cine-gun attacks and local flying. The Squadron was released at 18:25 and, in the evening, the RAF Llanbedr Rugby Team went to dinner near Dolgelley [Dolgellau], 11 miles southeast of Llanbedr, whilst the remaining airmen attended a dance.

Separately today, two of the Squadron's Australian pilots, Sgt Plt Arthur Cope and Flt Sgt Robert Quine, were posted away. Having already taken a few days embarkation leave, they were sent to 1 Personnel Despatch Centre at West Kirby, where they subsequently parted company on separate postings to the Mediterranean. Sadly, however, in less than six months, both young men would be dead.

Cope, who had only been with 41 Squadron six weeks, was sent to Gibraltar to ferry an aircraft to North Africa. Unfortunately, he never made it across the Alboran Sea and is presumed to have lost his life enroute, just five weeks after his departure from 41 Squadron. He is remembered today on the Malta Memorial.[102]

Quine remained at West Kirby until late March when he, too, was sent to Gibraltar, and subsequently joined 152 Squadron in Tunisia. However, he was lost as a result of enemy action in the Comiso-Gela region of Sicily on 12 July 1943. One of eight aircraft attacked by enemy fighters, he was not seen or heard from again and is also remembered today on the Malta Memorial.[103]

31 January 1943 – A Flight at dawn readiness; B Flight at 30 minutes. The dawn broke to very bad weather with cloud down to 800 feet, heavy rain, a south-westerly gale and poor visibility. As a result, the entire Squadron was set back to 30 minutes readiness, and as even practice flying was out of the question, the pilots attended a lecture in the Intelligence Office instead.

However, when conditions improved late in the afternoon, flying could be commenced and Fg Offs Rycherde Hogarth and David Davies were the first pilots in the air, at 16:00. They were followed by several more sections, which were sent to beat up a road convoy of 75 Army lorries,

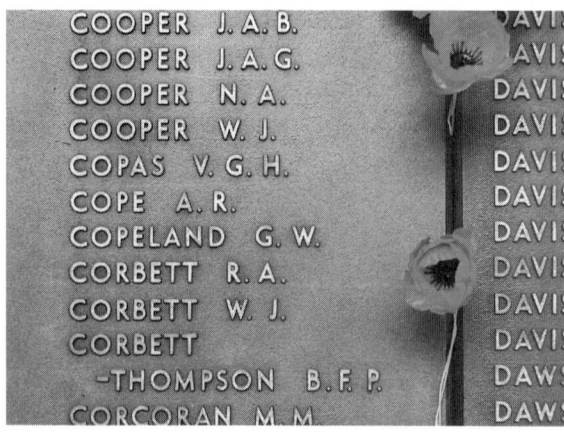

Sgt Plt Arthur Cope RAAF served with 41 Squadron from 22 December 1942 to 30 January 1943. Subsequently posted to the Mediterranean, he disappeared on 9 March 1943 whilst ferrying a Spitfire to North Africa. His name appears on the Roll of Honour on the walls of the Australian War Memorial in Canberra (pictured) and on the Malta Memorial. © Steve Brew

in cooperation with No. 10 (Inter-Allied) Commando. Undergoing training in Aberdovey, 20 miles south of Llanbedr, the Commando unit was quite unique as it consisted of free forces from German-occupied territories, which included Belgian, Dutch, French, Norwegian and other European nationals, as well as one entirely Jewish troop, made up of exiled and escaped German-speaking Jews from Germany and Austria.

The Sector Headquarters ORB states that this was 41 Squadron's first exercise in Army cooperation under a newly introduced procedure for Army Air Support. The new regulations were clearly no issue for the pilots who reported that "a jolly good time was had by all".[104] The pilots concluded the afternoon with some air-to-sea firing.

In their absence, dancing lessons were held in the B Flight dispersals office by LAC Booth for the benefit of Flt Lt Douglas Hone and Fg Off Roger Whipp, apparently with "refreshments being served"![105] The Squadron was released at 17:15.

February 1943 – There was no enemy activity in the Valley Sector during the month, although sections from 41 Squadron and aircraft from 456 (Australian) Squadron were scrambled for precautionary patrols against raids in the Bristol Channel and Midlands areas, and 41 Squadron also participated in ASR searches.

Operational flying was limited to just five days – 4, 8, 13, 16 and 19 February – even though weather only prevented flying on 9-10, 14-15 and 17 February. The Squadron otherwise carried out a significant amount of flying training, thereunder several Army Air Support sorties in cooperation with infantry and mobile artillery, and low altitude sweeps over the Irish Sea as far south as Carnsore Point, Éire, and St. David's Head, on the southern-most extremity of Cardigan Bay. However, in the scope of this activity, one pilot was killed in a flying accident.

1 February 1943 – B Flight at dawn readiness; A Flight at 30 minutes. Poor weather with 10/10ths cloud at 1,500 feet dominated the morning, reducing visibility to less than two miles. A Flight therefore reported to the Service Echelon for a demonstration of inspections, but when the weather improved in the afternoon they were able to undertake a fair amount of practice flying, which included cine-gun attacks and local flying. However, one sortie ended on a beach in Tremadog Bay with fatal results.

For their part, B Flight did little flying all day with the exception of the readiness section, consisting of Flt Lt Douglas Hone and Fg Off Rycherde Hogarth, doing some local flying between 12:00 and 12:35, and Fg Off Douglas Haywood returning from Northolt in the Tiger Moth at 16:55.

A Fatal Flying Accident

On 1 February 1943, Polish Sgt Plt Jozef Bednarz was sent up on a low-level flying test in Spitfire Vb, X4279, EB-C, but was killed when he crashed on the beach west of Pwllheli, around 14 miles northwest of Llanbedr. The 22-year-old had only been with the Squadron a little over six weeks.

Despite his brief tenure, the ORB records that Bednarz was "very popular with the Squadron".[106] Six of the Squadron's NCO Pilots acted as pallbearers at his funeral on 5 February, accompanied by an escort and rifle party. He was buried Portmadoc [Porthmadog] Public Cemetery, in Caernarvonshire [today Gwynedd], 13 miles east of where was killed.

Unfortunately, it appears his death was a result of pilot error. On 3 February, an inquiry into the accident, conducted by Flt Lt Peter McGregor, the OC of Valley based 1486 Fighter Gunnery Flight, officially found that Bednarz died as a result of "Unauthorised Low Flying".[107]

The aircraft he was flying at the time, X4279, was an ex-Battle of Britain Spitfire I, that had been converted to a Vb in February 1941. It had been received from 129 Squadron on 3 March 1942, and was destroyed beyond repair in the accident.

Sgt Plt Josef Bednarz's grave in Portmadoc Public Cemetery, Caernarvonshire, Wales. © Author's collection

2 February 1943 – A Flight at dawn readiness; B Flight at 30 minutes. Better weather enabled five of B Flight's pilots to undertake formation practice, range estimation and cine-gun camera practice. Airborne at 13:15, they were back at Llanbedr at 15:05. A section from A Flight also practiced interceptions on a Mustang and cine-gun attacks at 30,000 feet. During the afternoon, the Squadron's newest pilot, Sgt Plt Peter Cross, also flew a sector reconnaissance, which constituted his first flight with the unit.

Another new pilot arrived at Llanbedr today: 21-year-old Australian Flt Sgt Stanley May. Having joined the RAAF in July 1941, he had undertaken his EFTS and SFTS courses in Australia, where he was awarded his Wings, then shipped to the United Kingdom in June 1942, where he completed AFU and OTU courses. He arrived today on his first operational posting with 243 non-operational flying hours in his logbook.

3 February 1943 – B Flight at dawn readiness; A Flight at 30 minutes. Good weather allowed for a significant amount of flying training to be undertaken today. The first flight of the day was undertaken by the readiness section's Sgt Plts Fraser Clark RNZAF and John Thomas, who did some local flying between 09:15 and 10:00. A while later, five aircraft took part in an Army cooperation exercise, shooting up a road convoy near Menai Bridge, Anglesey, with 'very successful' results. Several pilots practiced cine-gun attacks or undertook local flying, whilst Fg Off Douglas Haywood flew the Engineer Officer, Fg Off Roger Whipp, to RAF Harrowbeer in the Master, returning at 17:05. The Squadron was released at dusk.

4 February 1943 – A Flight at dawn readiness; B Flight at 30 minutes. At 09:20, A Flight's Red Section was airborne to do some local flying in good weather but were informed that a Wellington bomber was missing in Cardigan Bay, and ordered to search for it.[108] They scoured a 23-mile stretch of Cardigan Bay on the longitude 4°30'W from latitude 52°50'N, southwards to 52°30'N, but saw nothing besides a lone buoy, and returned to base at 10:00.

The pilots are believed to have been searching for 547 Squadron's Wellington VIII, HX596, that had departed Chivenor, Devonshire, at 13:05 the previous day on a ferry flight to RAF Tain, on the Moray Firth in Scotland. At 14:30, the pilot, Sgt Plt Ayley, radioed that he was experiencing engine trouble, and then issued an SOS. Nothing more was heard from the aircraft, and it was believed to have ditched in Cardigan Bay, approximately 20 miles south of Penrhos. The following morning, 41 Squadron was tasked with locating it.

At 10:30, Yellow Section took over the search and they, in turn, were replaced at 12:00 by Red Section again, accompanied by White Section. These four aircraft returned at 12:41, all patrols having been unsuccessful in their search.[109] They did, however, spot a floating mine adrift six miles from Bardsey Light and reported it to the Controller at Valley.

Yellow Section, consisting of Flt Sgts Jack Stonier (BL966) and Jan Rogowski (AR393), was scrambled to 10,000 feet at 13:02 on the report of enemy aircraft in the area. Sector Headquarters at Valley then ordered them to 30,000 feet, followed by a new order to 25,000 feet. The Squadron ORB also records the pilots at 22,000 feet, but they returned at 13:50, "not having contacted the Hun."[110]

Meanwhile, the day's good weather provided the right conditions for B Flight to carry out an air-to-air firing programme in the morning, in which Sgt Plt Fraser Clark RNZAF was allocated the job of towing the drogue in EB-P. Another air-to-air firing programme was held in the afternoon.

Five pilots, constituting Blue Section, also took part in an Army cooperation exercise between 12:40 and 13:30. An Intelligence Report from the day explains the pilots' attack on eight vehicles and numerous men. It states,

> …GEORGE SURPRISED AT FIRST BUT TOO[K] GOOD COVER AFTER ATTAC[K]. SAW ONE SOLDIER WAL[K]ING DOWN STREET AFTER EVERY OTHER PERSON HAD TA[K]EN COVER. ON ARRIVAL OVER TARGET 5 SPITFIRES VB, BLUE SECTION LED BY F/LT HONE WENT IN TO ATTAC[K] AT 1300 HOURS ACROSS SUN TA[K]ING ADVANTAGE OF HILL AT NEWBOROUGH. ATTAC[K]ED FROM WEST TO EAST TURNING IN A RIGHT HAND ORBIT SO THAT TARGET WAS BEING ATTAC[K]ED CONTINUOUSLY. TURNED INTO SUN AFTER ATTAC[K]. TURNED LEFT HAND CIRCUIT TO SURPRISE OBJECTIVE AND FINALLY BRO[K]E AWAY INTO SUN….[111]

Fg Off Douglas Haywood sustained a bird strike during the exercise and, although unhurt, returned early with feathers from a number of wild ducks in his radiator. The day's training concluded with some night flying practice for Fg Offs Haywood and Rycherde Hogarth, and Fg Off Bob Boyd, between 18:00 and 19:25.

5 February 1943 – B Flight at dawn readiness; A Flight at 30 minutes. Sgt Plts Fraser Clark RNZAF and John Thomas were rostered as the morning's readiness section. Despite the poor weather, Flt Lt Douglas Hone and Fg Off Douglas Haywood took off at 08:35 to participate in an Army cooperation exercise at Pwllheli. However, when they were informed their mission was to attack individual commandos on the side of a hill, they ruled the exercise too dangerous under the prevailing conditions and returned to Llanbedr, where they landed at 09:05. No further flying was undertaken all day, and a dance was held in the evening in support of the Red Cross, which 300 men from the entire Station attended.

6 February 1943 – A Flight at dawn readiness; B Flight at 30 minutes. Good weather allowed flying training to resume, with the day's emphasis on dogfights and cine-gun camera attacks. An Army cooperation exercise was also held between 11:35 and 12:25, in which Red Section attacked anti-aircraft emplacements at Newtown, around 40 miles southeast of Llanbedr. An Intelligence Report records,

> OVER TARGET 10 MINS AFTER TA[K]E OFF. APPROACHED LOW ALONG RAILWAY AS CLOUDS WERE LOW OVER HILLS. BEFORE ARRIVING AT NEWTOWN RED SECTION TURNED SOUTH OF TOWN TO APPROACH FROM THE SUN. TOO[K] THE OBJECTIVE BY SURPRISE INITIALLY. WE PROCEEDED TO DO LOW LEVEL BOMBING AND DIVE BOMBING ATTAC[K]S FOR 15 MINS. HAVING COMPLETED OUR EXERCISE WE CLIMBED THROUGH

THE CLOUDS AND SET COURSE FOR BASE. REMAR[K]S:- BRIG GENERAL PHONED THROUGH TO SQUADRON TO CONGRATULATE PILOTS ON A VERY GOOD SHOW.[112]

Fg Off Douglas Haywood flew Fg Off Rycherde Hogarth to Pershore in Worcester, in the Master on his way to pick up Fg Off Roger Whipp from RAF Harrowbeer in Devon, having taken him there on 3 February. They returned to Llanbedr at 16:10.

A practice interception on a 23 (Bomber) OTU Wellington was also undertaken and the day's activity concluded at 18:20. An Airmen's Dance was held in the evening.

7 February 1943 – B Flight at dawn readiness; A Flight at 30 minutes. The readiness section, comprising Sgt Plts Fraser Clark RNZAF and John Thomas, took off at 09:00 for 30 minutes local flying. Three aircraft, designated Green Section, participated in an Army cooperation exercise from 10:10, this time held near Welshpool, about 42 miles east-southeast of Llanbedr. Tasked with attacking Bofors gun positions, they were back at Llanbedr within 25 minutes of their departure, but no reason is given for the brevity of the exercise. It was long enough, however, for the trio to earn the congratulations of the OC, Welsh Border Sub-Area, for their "excellent air co-operation".[113] Flying training continued until 18:20 and the Squadron was released at dusk.

8 February 1943 – A Flight at dawn readiness; B Flight at 30 minutes. Initial fair weather allowed B Flight to undertake some air-to-air firing practice, with Sgt Plt John Thomas chosen to tow the drogue in EB-X. However, conditions deteriorated before they could achieve much and they were forced to return to base early. Later improvement in the weather permitted Fg Off Douglas Haywood to fly to Valley and back in the Master, and subsequently five aircraft participated in a beat-up of six Bofors guns at Ruabon, about 45 miles east-northeast of Llanbedr, using their cine-gun cameras.

At 15:26, Red Section was ordered to scramble base at 15,000 feet. Plt Off Wladislaw Banach (W3771) and Flt Sgt Jan Rogowski (BL905) were off the deck within three minutes and ascended through 10/10ths cloud at 10,000 feet. Horizontal visibility was 10-15 miles, but the thick cloud layer hid the intruder and aided its escape, making any further search pointless. Nonetheless, the Squadron ORB boasted with false bravado that the pair returned less than 20 minutes later "as the Hun had turned back"![114]

A new pilot was posted to the Squadron today in the form of Fg Off Clive Birbeck, the youngest son of Brigadier John H. B. Birbeck, who was commanding the Royal Artillery with the 19th Indian Division in India. Having enlisted as an 18-year-old in August 1940, Birbeck completed his flying training in the United Kingdom, and was commissioned on graduation from SFTS in October 1941. Following his OTU course, he was posted to his first operational unit, 610 Squadron, in early December 1941. Subsequently volunteering for the Merchant Ship Fighter Unit, he was posted to that unit in April 1942, where he remained until his posting to 41 Squadron today. Birbeck now arrived with 390 flying hours in his logbook, of which 30 were operational and included an "engagement with a Do 217 and a Ju 88".[115] Birbeck would remain with 41 Squadron almost one-and-a-half years and would have a number of victories to his credit by the time of his departure.

News of past pilots was also received by the Squadron today, and the ORB records the 'good news' that Wg Cdr 'Dutch' Hugo, who had commanded the unit between November 1941 and April 1942, had recently been promoted to Group Captain, whilst Harold Knight, who had left the Squadron in late October 1942, had been promoted to Flight Lieutenant in Malta.

9 February 1943 – B Flight at dawn readiness; A Flight at 30 minutes. The readiness section, comprising Fg Off Douglas Haywood and Sgt Plt Stan May RAAF, took off at 08:35 for some local flying and returned 45 minutes later. However, poor weather limited the amount of flying practice that could be undertaken today, and plans for an Army cooperation exercise were

Sgt Plt Stanley May RAAF served with 41 Squadron from 2 February 1943 to 19 September 1943. He was discharged from the RAAF as a Flying Officer in August 1945. © May family

cancelled. Although the Squadron was released at sunset, the evening was concluded with dusk landing practice and night flying, which continued until 19:30.

11 February 1943 – B Flight at dawn readiness; A Flight at 30 minutes. Fg Off David Davies and Sgt Plt Stan May RAAF were designated the day's readiness section. Good weather permitted four pilots to practice formation flying between 13:50 and 15:00, which was followed by a Squadron scramble, in which six B Flight aircraft and four A Flight aircraft were airborne within 2½ minutes of the order being given. A "very good formation was observed,"[116] and all aircraft landed back at Llanbedr at 14:45.[117] Flt Lt Douglas Hone and Fg Off Douglas Haywood later undertook 20 minutes night flying, and the Squadron was released at dusk.

The third and fourth new pilots to join the Squadron this month arrived at Llanbedr today: 22-year-old Sgt Plt Stanley Biggs and 24-year-old Sgt Plt Douglas Fisher. Both arrived from 535 Squadron, which had just been disbanded at High Ercall.

Biggs had enlisted in the RAFVR in August 1940 and undertaken his entire flying training in the United Kingdom. He was posted to his first operational unit, 257 Squadron, in October 1941, followed by 535 Squadron in September 1942.

Having enlisted in the RAFVR in May 1941, Fisher had undertaken EFTS in the United Kingdom and SFTS in Canada, and then returned home to complete his AFU and OTU courses. He was posted to 535 Squadron as his first operational unit on 16 October 1942, thereby joining Biggs at High Ercall.

When 535 Squadron was disbanded on 25 January 1943, both pilots were initially posted to Station Headquarters as supernumeraries, whilst new units were sought for all of the Squadron's pilots. This search resulted in Biggs and Fisher being posted together to 41 Squadron today.

By this time, Biggs had logged almost 408 flying hours, but only two were considered operational, comprising a pair of interception scrambles over Birmingham. He would remain with the Squadron for approximately four months. Fisher had logged almost 312 flying hours by the time of his arrival, but all were non-operational. He was destined to remain with 41 Squadron until September 1944.

Fg Off Clive 'Joe' Birbeck served with 41 Squadron from 8 February 1943 to 23 July 1944, during that time claiming one destroyed FW190, two probable FW190s, one damaged FW190, one damaged Me109, and half a destroyed V1. © Cowell family

13 February 1943 – B Flight at dawn readiness; A Flight at 30 minutes. The readiness section comprised Fg Off Jerzy Polak (EN827) and Sgt Plt Peter Cross (BL299). Flying commenced at 08:15 when four aircraft were airborne in fine weather to practice formation flying, which was followed by two aircraft practicing cine-gun attacks and another pair on a sector reconnaissance. At 11:35, 9 Group ordered a section to 'scramble base' to 15,000 feet to intercept a 'bogey' inbound from the Isle of Wight. The readiness section was airborne within 2½ minutes, but their efforts were in vain as they returned 50 minutes later having seen nothing.[118] Practice flying continued until dusk, when the Squadron was released.

16 February 1943 – A Flight at dawn readiness; B Flight at 30 minutes. Considerable improvement in the weather allowed an extensive flying programme to be undertaken today. Twenty-four hours and 35 minutes flying time were logged by B Flight's pilots alone, which included five hours of night flying.[119] This consisted of two Flight formations of six aircraft, three sections of two aircraft, and a section of four aircraft on formation practice, cine-gun attacks and local flying. The night flying hours consisted of 40 minutes dusk landing practice by Fg Off Jerzy Polak and Sgt Plt Bill Downing, and 75 minutes night flying by Fg Offs Clive Birbeck and Bob Boyd and Sgt Plts Fraser Clark RNZAF and John Thomas. It was generally considered that a "very successful training programme"[120] had been carried out that day.

The ORB also records that two pilots flew to Hawkinge, but their names, the aircraft serials, their timings and the reason for the flights is not disclosed. Finally, a scramble of the base area to 30,000 feet was ordered at 11:43, for which A Flight's Fg Off Peter Cowell (AD562) and Sgt Plt Douglas Fisher (W3771) were off the deck within two minutes as Red Section. They returned at 12:47[121] with nothing to report, but this scramble is believed to have constituted both Cowell's and Fisher's first operational flying of their careers.

17 February 1943 – B Flight at dawn readiness; A Flight at 30 minutes. As the weather had deteriorated overnight, no flying could be undertaken in the morning and B Flight was soon set back to 30 minutes readiness. The pilots spent their time on the Link trainer and on aircraft recognition revision instead. An improvement in conditions in the afternoon subsequently allowed for some local flying and cine-gun practice to be logged by A Flight. The Squadron was released at dusk, and B Flight's Sgt Plt Fraser Clark RNZAF was posted to 485 (NZ) Squadron at Westhampnett, in the Tangmere Wing.[122]

Yet another new pilot arrived at Llanbedr today to join the Squadron: 23-year-old Uruguayan Flt Sgt Herbert Coates. The only Uruguayan to join the Squadron during World War II, he had enlisted in the RAFVR in Montevideo in May 1940 and embarked for the United Kingdom the following month. Coates completed his EFTS course in England before being sent to Canada to attend SFTS. Returning to the United Kingdom, he then undertook his OTU course, from which he graduated in early January 1942.

His first operational posting, to 81 Squadron, ensued that same month, but he was moved to 289 (Anti-Aircraft Co-Operation) Squadron two months later, where he then remained until August 1942. At that time, he was posted to 222 Squadron, and was now posted to 41 Squadron. However, his tenure was only brief and he is last mentioned on 4 March 1943. His subsequent movements are unknown.

18 February 1943 – A Flight at dawn readiness; B Flight at 30 minutes. Fine weather allowed an air-to-air firing programme, local flying, cine-gun attacks and a shipping reconnaissance flight to be carried out today. Flying training was concluded with 40 minutes dusk landing practice by Fg Off Jerzy Polak and Sgt Plt Bill Downing.

Although not mentioned in Squadron documentation, the Sector ORB states than an exercise was also conducted by two Mosquitos of Valley based 456 (Australian) Squadron and a section from 41 Squadron, in cooperation with the submarine chaser HMS *PC74*, commanded by Cdr Charles Hughes-White DSO. RAF Valley's Fg Off Parkin was also aboard *PC74* to attempt an interception under ship-borne control, but the experiment was not as successful as a previous trial. Another attempt was made in collaboration with the destroyer HMS *Carlisle*, but it also failed as the aircraft were unable to establish R/T contact with the ship.[123]

19 February 1943 – B Flight at dawn readiness; A Flight at 30 minutes. Despite dull to fair weather, B Flight's Black and Blue Sections each made a 45-minute sector reconnaissance flight, and an operational scramble of the Exeter area was ordered at 15:12.[124] The latter Section, comprising Fg Offs Clive Birbeck (W3848) and Rycherde Hogarth (AA944), returned 45 minutes later, having seen nothing.

The great event of the day, however, which had the Squadron abuzz with excitement, was a lecture was given by Sqn Ldr Thomas Neil during the afternoon. He made the long awaited announcement that the Squadron would immediately begin preparing to leave Llanbedr. They would be moving to RAF High Ercall, where they would be the first Squadron in the RAF to be issued the latest model Spitfire, the Mark XII. This re-equipment also brought "prospects of ACTION [which was] welcome news for everyone."[125]

22 February 1943 – No flying was undertaken by the Squadron all day, as they were busied with preparations for their move to RAF High Ercall, outside a village of the same name in Shropshire. With a return to the front line pending, Fg Off Hatton of RAF Penrhos visited the Squadron at RAF Llanbedr today to give the pilots a vital lecture on 'Experiences in a Prisoner of War Camp'. It was "most interesting… and well attended"[126].

It was important advice: no fewer than five of the pilots attending the lecture today would be behind wire before the end of the War, and one of them within six weeks. In fact, on their 1945 Prisoner of War Repatriation Forms [ref. TNA WO 344], pilots Downing, Haywood, Hoare, Prickett and Slack all refer to being briefed whilst with 41 Squadron on how to behave in the event of capture, on escape and on evasion.

23 February 1943 – B Flight at dawn readiness; A Flight at 30 minutes. Weather improvement allowed a successful practice interception to be carried out by Fg Off David Davies and Sgt Plts Stan May and Peter Cross, whilst Fg Off Douglas Haywood flew to Croydon in the Tiger Moth. On the ground, preparations for the move to High Ercall continued.

Fg Off Ronald Johnson served with 41 Squadron from 24 February 1943 to 28 April 1944, subsequently becoming a test pilot with Vickers Armstrong at Castle Bromwich. © Ron Johnson, via Dan Johnson

24 February 1943 – Misty weather. One aircraft flew to Speke, whilst an Advance Party, supplies and equipment were transported to Pensarn Station for despatch to High Ercall, where they arrived late in the day. The pilots would follow the next day, and farewelled Llanbedr that evening with a dining-in night and dance.

In the midst of all the preparations to leave, yet another new pilot arrived – the sixth in twenty-four days – 28-year-old Durham school teacher Fg Off Ronald Johnson. Having trained in the United Kingdom and Canada, he had been posted to 64 Squadron in September 1941, logging 80 hours operational flying. In June 1942, Johnson was posted to 57 OTU as a flying instructor, during which time he was commissioned, and remained with this unit until February 1943. Initially earmarked for a squadron in Malta, his posting was cancelled within hours of his embarkation and he was posted instead to 41 Squadron. He was destined to remain with the unit for 14 months.

When the Squadron moved from Llanbedr on 25 February 1943, they left the Welsh airfield for the final time. In some respects, 41 Squadron's stay at Llanbedr between early August 1942 and late February 1943 had been a sobering one, as it had been marred by fatal accidents, by an almost complete turnover of pilots and, according to some reports, also by low morale.

During the Squadron's 6½ month residence in this relatively quiet 'support trench', the unit had lost six pilots to fatal flying accidents, and the Commanding Officer in combat, whilst one pilot was interned in Éire after he ran out of fuel. Having been rested for a little over half a year, the Squadron was now ready for some action, and they would not have to wait long to see it.

Valley's 456 Squadron, although equipped with Mosquitoes, took over readiness from 41 Squadron on their departure. The unit's B Flight also took over 41 Squadron's call sign until the next single seat fighter squadron arrived to take over from them. This is believed to have been 302 (Polish) Squadron, who arrived at Llanbedr the following month.

GRIFFON POWER
25 February – 20 June 1943

3

High Ercall

"A hearty farewell to Llanbedr, where the Squadron had been recuperating since arrival on 3rd August 1942".[1]

25 February 1943 – The pilots took off for High Ercall at 12:15 with the exception of Sqn Ldr Tom Neil, who "killed his engine whilst taxying to take off. Station personnel thought this a jolly good show".[2]

As the pilots landed at their new base at 13:30 in showery conditions, the ground personnel were still on their way to Crudgington, having entrained at Talwrn Halt[3] with the personnel of 3016 Servicing Echelon. They subsequently marched the rest of the way to High Ercall, about 2¼ miles to the west of the Station, apparently "raring to GO."[4]

Lying approximately 8½ miles northeast of Shrewsbury, Shropshire, the village of High Ercall is located in the borough of Telford and Wrekin. The airfield itself was situated just northeast of the village (52°45'45" N 2°35'15" W), at an elevation of only 220 feet above sea level, and boasted three concrete runways of 1,612 yards, 1,377 yards and 1,251 yards, each of which was 50 yards wide.

RAF High Ercall had been opened in 1941 and was equipped with a number of permanent buildings, including blister hangars and Nissen Huts for accommodation. There were sufficient quarters for 40 Officers, 80 Senior NCOs and 1384 Other Ranks.

The Spitfire Mark XII Arrives

On 24 February 1943, the day the Squadron commenced its move to High Ercall, the unit received its initial Spitfires LF Mark XII, the first operational Spitfire version with the Rolls Royce Griffon engine.

Whilst the first Spitfire to be fitted with Griffon engine was a Spitfire IV, this airframe only proceeded to prototype stage, and it was not until the Spitfire XII that the Griffon actually went into service with the RAF.

Whilst the Mk V had proven itself successful against successive Messerschmitt Me109 versions, it was considerably inferior to the Focke-Wulf FW190, which was first seen in action in late 1941. The Luftwaffe was soon using this aircraft successfully in small groups in low-level 'hit and run' raids to southern England and, by early 1942, the RAF realised that a successor to the Mark V was urgently required. This requirement was exacerbated by the fact that the Mark IX, expected to be the next major version, was still a few months away from its entry into service.

An alternative was found in the original Mark IV airframe fitted with 1,735 hp Rolls-Royce Griffon III engine. This model was developed further and became the prototype for the Mark XII. It was a very different aircraft to the Spitfires seen thus far, particularly recognisable for its clipped wings and retractable tail wheel.

Although only 100 were built, of which 41 Squadron received 73, its two Hispano 20mm cannon and four Browning .303 inch machine guns, and its greater manoeuvrability at low altitude, made it an ideal adversary for the FW190. Other characteristics included an improved broad chord rudder, and a strengthened fuselage that was approximately two feet longer than the Mark V, allowing the engine to be mounted ten inches further forward. The Mark XII was also fitted with a four-blade wood composite Rotol propeller that rotated clockwise, that is, in the opposite direction to previous models.

The only other unit to be equipped with the Mark was 91 Squadron, which went operational with theirs when they moved to Hawkinge in May 1943, and subsequently joined 41 Squadron at Westhampnett in late June 1943 to become a Spitfire XII bomber support wing.

However, 91 Squadron converted to Spitfire XIVs in March 1944, and this left 41 Squadron as the only RAF unit flying the Mk. XII in action until mid-September 1944. During this time, however, the aircraft proved successful against the Germans' newest weapon, the V1 flying bomb, of which 53 were destroyed by the Squadron in a ten-week period.

Spitfire Variants Flown by 41 Squadron between 1939 and 1944[5]

Mark	I	IIa	Va	Vb	XII
Wing Span	36' 10"	36' 10"	36' 10"	36' 10"	32' 7"
Length	29' 11"	29' 11"	29' 11"	29' 11"	31' 10"
Height	11' 5"	11' 5"	11' 5"	11' 5"	11' 0"
Min Weight	4,810 lb	4,900 lb	4,981 lb	5,065 lb	5,600 lb
Max Weight	6,200 lb	6,317 lb	6,700 lb	6,700 lb	7,400 lb
Armament	8 x .303	8 x .303	8 x .303	4 x .303 2 x 20mm	4 x .303 2 x 20mm
Max Speed	363 mph	357 mph	371 mph	371 mph	393 mph
Ceiling	31,900 ft	33,900 ft	37,000 ft	37,000 ft	40,000 ft
Max Range	575 miles	500 miles	470 miles	470 miles	493 miles*

* with jettison tank

41 Squadron took an immediate liking to their new aircraft, the ORB at one stage reporting, "The pilots are very enthusiastic about the new Spitfire XII's…. other than one or two minor faults they are the finest planes yet".[6] They did, however, make several observations on its performance and maintenance:

> Upon receipt of these aircraft the pilots complained of "cutting", under conditions of positive and negative G at low revs. Investigations carried out in co-operation with Rolls Royce representatives proved of no avail, but an anti G crib was fitted and after a trial was found to function perfectly under positive G only. At normal cruising and combat conditions the engine functions perfectly and although it is desirable that the engine behaves normally at all settings it is not thought to be vitally important to continue further experiments. The Squadron has the greatest confidence in the engine and are anxious to fly these aircraft operationally and prove that "41" have not lost the knack of keeping the Hun down.
>
> One matter of importance that should be kept in mind when new aircraft are allotted to Squadrons, is that of servicing equipment. We have received no tools or equipment as laid down in the Air Ministry Initial Orders.[7]

26 February 1943 – Fine and hazy, with cloud increasing from 3/10ths to 6/10ths at 2,000-4,000 feet, and visibility of 2,000-4,000 yards. A Flight kept one section at readiness and one at 30 minutes from dawn until 13:00, when B Flight took over both sections until dusk. The pilots conducted several local non-operational sector reconnaissance flights during the day and, following their dusk release, headed into the village where "the major interest was the attraction of local amenities."[8]

Known 41 Squadron Spitfire XII Serials and Codes February 1943–September 1944

EN221	EB-Z	EN607	EB-U	MB804	EB-T	MB850	EB-K
EN224	EB-L	EN609	EB-K/Y	MB829	EB-W	MB853	EB-P
EN226	EB-J/X	EN611	EB-P	MB830	EB-Q	MB854	EB-T/Z
EN227	EB-S	EN615	EB-W	MB831	EB-R	MB856	EB-N/X
EN228	EB-N	EN620	EB-F	MB833	EB-G	MB857	EB-L/X
EN229	EB-K	EN622	EB-J	MB834	EB-P	MB858	EB-D
EN231	EB-M	EN625	EB-L	MB836	EB-V	MB861	EB-T
EN233	EB-G	MB794	EB-H	MB837	EB-P	MB862	EB-E
EN234	EB-Q	MB795	EB-A	MB838	EB-L	MB875	EB-G
EN236	EB-D	MB796	EB-U	MB840	EB-J	MB876	EB-V
EN237	EB-V	MB797	EB-Y	MB841	EB-R	MB878	EB-L
EN238	EB-Q/Y	MB798	EB-U	MB842	EB-Y	MB880	EB-X
EN602	EB-H/T	MB800	EB-B	MB843	EB-V	MB881	EB-S
EN603	EB-B	MB801	EB-X	MB845	EB-G	MB882	EB-B
EN604	EB-F/U	MB802	EB-K/Z	MB846	EB-S	–	–
EN605	EB-R/D	MB803	EB-X	MB847	EB-N	–	–

© Steve Brew

27 February 1943 – Cloudy with 7/10ths-10/10ths cloud at 2,500-3,500 feet and visibility of 4-8 miles. B Flight was ordered to have one section at readiness and one at 30 minutes until 13:00, when A Flight took over. Fg Offs 'Joe' Birbeck and Bob Boyd were scheduled as Readiness Section and took off at 07:40 for 40 minutes local flying. Four further pilots also did an hour's sector reconnaissance each to familiarise themselves with the area and their new aircraft.

The day also saw a few personnel movements when Sgt Plt Malcolm Rowe transferred from A Flight to B Flight, and Sgt Plt Peter Cross was posted away to RAF Valley.[9]

28 February 1943 – Cloudy with 8/10ths-10/10ths cloud at 2,000-3,000 feet and visibility of 3-6 miles. A Flight at dawn readiness; B Flight on training until 13:00, when the Flights swapped duties. Most of the pilots spent the day familiarising themselves with their new Spitfire XIIs.

At 10:05, Blue Section, comprising of Fg Off 'Daibach' Davies and Sgt Plt Malcolm Rowe, took off for a sector reconnaissance in two Spitfire Vb's. Davies landed an hour later without Rowe, who had crashed his aircraft, BL299, after engine failure had obliged him to make a forced landing. Coming to an abrupt stop in a ploughed field at Whitchurch Heath, 1½ miles from Malpas, near Wrexham, Rowe sustained concussion, "luckily escaping," states the ORB, "with superficial wounds."[10]

The RAF Atcham ORB also records that "Filtrate 44, 41 Squadron aircraft crashed near Whitchurch Heath, pilot badly bruised and machine more or less a write off."[11] Now in the process of re-equipping with the Spitfire XII, Rowe's flying accident constituted 41 Squadron's last ever Spitfire V write off, although there would be one more Mark V casualty on one of the Squadron hacks in mid-April.

After lunch, B Flight Officers, acting as enemy pilots, "…abley [sic] led by F/LT Hone… succeeded breaking into camp but were seen and reported by a F/LT from M.U."[12] Another Spitfire XII was delivered to B Flight at 14:30 by a ferry pilot by the name of First Officer Anna Leska. It is not clear why this ferry pilot's name is noted; perhaps it was the source of a bit of a joke that afternoon, as Flt Lt Hone is also recorded in B Flight's Diary as having remarked that the pilot was "not a bad bit of Polish Tookey."[13] The Squadron was released at 19:15.

Sgt Plt Bill Downing drew this sketch of his 'kite', Spitfire XII, EB-M, in 1944, which he named for his wife Joan.
© Downing family

March 1943 – As a result of the Squadron's re-equipping with the Mark XII, operational flying was only undertaken on 4, 7 and 8 March 1943, accounting for four scrambles and a total of eight sorties. The unit was made officially non-operational on 12 March, with a total strength of just three Spitfire XIIs and two Spitfire Vbs, and remained in this state until their move to Hawkinge on 13 April.[14]

Although weather restricted or stopped flying altogether on 3-4, 13, 18-21, and 23-25 March, the rest of the month was taken up with non-operational training flights and aircraft familiarisation, which included routine daily aircraft inspections, Link simulator training, dog fights, local flying, formation flying, cross country flying, cannon tests and air firing, camera exercises, height climbs to 25,000 feet, long range drop tank tests, mock shipping reconnaissances, an army co-operation exercise, aircraft recognition tests, French language lessons, and Intelligence lectures.

1 March 1943 – Fair to cloudy weather with 8/10ths to 10/10ths cloud at 1,000-2,000 feet, and visibility of 3-6 miles. A Flight at dawn readiness. Flying activity was confined to local reconnaissance and area familiarisation flights by sections from both A and B Flights in the new Spitfire XIIs.

2 March 1943 – Fair weather with 8/10ths to 10/10ths cloud at 1,000-2,000 feet, and visibility of 3-6 miles. A Flight at dawn readiness. Local flying continued on the new aircraft, which included formation flying and camera attacks. The pilots were also demonstrated the daily inspection they were now required to carry out on the Spitfire XII. After they were released for the day, the pilots and a number of other men travelled down to Shrewsbury for a night out.

3 March 1943 – Poor weather, with 8/10ths to 10/10ths cloud at 1,500-2,500 feet, kept the Squadron on the ground nearly all day, and only two sorties were flown. However, the aircrafts' guns were tested in the range during the afternoon, and the men spent another enjoyable night in Shrewsbury.

4 March 1943 – Although initially poor weather and low mist kept the planned flying training programme on the ground today, Fg Off Reg Hoare (W3935) and Flt Sgt Herbert Coates (AD809) were scrambled to patrol the base area at 09:00 on the report of an enemy aircraft approaching the area from the south at 3,000 feet. They found no sign of the aircraft, which was later said to have turned back, and returned to High Ercall at 10:00 with nothing to report. The pair was, however, praised by the Controller, for having been airborne within two minutes and 45 seconds of receiving the order to scramble. The rest of the day was uneventful and ground training was undertaken instead of flying, which included an Intelligence lecture and time on the Link Trainer.

5 March 1943 – Initially poor weather with low mist kept the Squadron on the ground all morning, despite being kept at 30 minutes readiness all day. During the afternoon, improved weather and visibility allowed some practice flying to be carried out, which included local and area reconnaissances, and, for one section, an Army co-operation exercise.

6 March 1943 – Fair weather with 6/10ths to 9/10ths cloud at 2,000-3,000 feet, deteriorating to foggy conditions after sunset. All of the Squadron's Spitfire Vb's were now grounded with the exception of B Flight's EB-Q and EB-Y (believed to have been AB809 and BL406). To date, a total of five Spitfire XIIs had been delivered to 41 Squadron, and a training programme continued on the new aircraft, limited only by the number of aircraft available for flying.

7 March 1943 – Flying practice continued today, despite initially poor weather, with Flt Lt Douglas Hone and Fg Off Bob Boyd making short flights in the morning, and Sgt Plts John Thomas and William Downing undertaken formation flying and cine-gun practice during the afternoon. At 16:25, Fg Off Tom Slack (AB809) and Peter Cowell (BL406) were ordered to scramble base at 15,000 feet. Finding nothing, however, they were quickly recalled and were back on the ground within ten minutes.

8 March 1943 – Early rain with visibility of 1,000-4,000 yards, clearing later to visibility of 5-10 miles. Training and familiarisations continued today, only broken by two scrambles around midday. Polish Fg Offs Wladislaw Banach (AB809) and Jerzy Polak (BL905) were airborne at 12:00, followed by Plt Off Leslie Prickett (BL406) and Fg Off 'Barney' Newman (AD185) at 12:10. These were in response to Raid 337 plotted over the Wirral Peninsula at 11:54. Initially reported as one aircraft at 12,000 feet, the plot was updated to two aircraft at 20,000 feet.

However, the two sections found absolutely nothing to report, and the plot faded at 12:20 over Prestatyn. The former pair was back at 13:05 and the latter at 13:25. It was believed the plots were likely friendly aircraft, but Control felt it best to send up 41 Squadron and a section from 195 Squadron. 41 Squadron's patrols also constituted 41 Squadron's final operational sorties on the Spitfire Mk V.

9 March 1943 – Fine becoming fair, with increasing amounts of cloud. Improved weather resulted in an increased flying programme, which included dog fights and, during the afternoon, instrument training for B Flight's pilots in the Squadron's Tiger Moth. The training was conducted by Fg Off Clive Birbeck and Sgt Plt William Downing.

10 March 1943 – Fair weather with varying cloud continued, and the pilots made longer forays with their Spitfire XIIs, Fg Offs Birbeck and Boyd flying to Liverpool Bay, and Sqn Ldr Neil and Fg Off Haywood to Hawkinge. Cannon tests were also carried out by other pilots.

The Squadron was paid a visit today by Capt. Malta Stepp, who had been OC, A Flight, between late May 1942 and late September 1942, before transferring to the USAAF. He was now a flying instructor with the 2906th Observation Group, USAAF, an operational training unit based at nearby Atcham, Shropshire.

11 March 1943 – Fair weather, with 8/10ths-10/10ths cloud at 1,000 feet, with 4-8 miles visibility above the ceiling, provided some good flying weather. B Flight was kept at readiness all day whilst flying practice continued for the pilots and ground crews. The men were released shortly after 19:30.

12 March 1943 – Continuing good flying weather; A Flight at dawn readiness. The Squadron's status was officially changed today to non-operational pending re-equipping with the Spitfire XII. Local practice flying continued throughout the day, although there is no detail available on what this included.

14 March 1943 – Fair to fine weather with small amounts of cloud at 2,500-3,500 feet, and visibility of 2,000-4,000 yards over land and 10-15 miles over sea. The improved weather allowed practice flying to recommence after a day's break resulting from inclement weather. This included local reconnaissance flights and a mock shipping reconnaissance.

15 March 1943 – Practice flying continued throughout the day in good weather with little cloud and visibility of 3-6 miles. No other detail of the day's activity is available.

16 March 1943 – Mainly cloudy with 8/10ths-10/10ths cover at 1,000-2,000 feet, improving throughout the day. The weather permitted the flying training programme on the Mark XIIs to continue as planned, and included local flying and cross-country flying to Liverpool Bay.

17 March 1943 – Excellent local flying weather all day resulted in an 'active' flying programme being carried out, thereunder local reconnaissances, long range tank tests, mock shipping reconnaissances in visibility of 5-10 miles, and height climbs to 25,000 feet.

19 March 1943 – As local drizzle and 8/10ths-10/10ths cloud down to 800 feet stopped all flying, the pilots were taken by lorry to a point eight miles from the Station and given the task, as 'enemy pilots', to reach the Airfield undetected. Seven succeeded!

20 March 1943 – A limited flying programme was undertaken in poor, though improved, weather conditions of light to variable wind and 8/10ths-10/10ths cloud between 1,500 and 2,500 feet. No further detail is available for the day's activity.

22 March 1943 – After several days of poor weather, significantly improved conditions with little cloud and 2,000-4,000 yards visibility, enabled an active flying training programme to be undertaken today, until 18:00 when the weather deteriorated anew. B Flight managed to log 15 flying hours in this time.

During the day, a new pilot joined the Squadron in the form of 20-year-old Sgt Plt Norman Heale of Somerset. Having enlisted in the RAFVR soon after his 19th birthday, Heale had undertaken most of his flying training in Canada, rounding off his training at 58 OTU at Grangemouth. Although he had logged some 370 flying hours to date, 41 Squadron was his first operational posting.

23 March 1943 – Poor weather with rain and cloud down to 1,000 feet limited the day's flying to just six non-operational sorties, which included a cross-country flight by Sqn Ldr Neil, back to their previous Sector Headquarters, RAF Valley, whilst Fg Offs Peter Cowell and David Davies were detached to Hawkinge to gain operational experience with 91 Squadron.

24 March 1943 – There was only limited flying today as a result of low cloud and intermittent rain, so the pilots attended French language lectures instead. No further detail on the day's activity is available.

Flt Sgt George Wilson of Trinidad served with 41 Squadron from 11 March 1943 to ca 20 May 1943, during which time he was promoted to Warrant Officer. © Cowell family

25 March 1943 – Heavy rain all day kept the pilots firmly on the ground today. They attended an Intelligence lecture and undertook Link Trainer practice instead.

26 March 1943 – Following several more days of inclement weather, the Squadron was back in the air today and almost all pilots participated in mock shipping reconnaissance flights. During the afternoon, the pilots also participated in further French lessons.

Fg Offs Reg Hoare and Clive Birbeck left High Ercall for Hawkinge today for attachment to the Station. Two days later, they were attached to 91 Squadron, whose ORB recorded their activity with the unit: "F/O Hoare and F/O Birbeck of 41 Squadron joined the Squadron for a few days and were taken on the reconnaissances to Ostend and Dieppe."[15]

27 March 1943 – Generally fine with scattered showers and visibility of 5-10 miles in a north-easterly wind at 10-15 mph. Local flying practice was carried out throughout the day, only breaking for a visit to the Station during the afternoon by the AOC 9 Group, AVM John Whitworth-Jones CB. He visited A Flight dispersals at around 17:00 and inspected their new Spitfire XIIs.

28 March 1943 – Good weather continued today, allowing flying training to proceed unhindered, and a total of 44 flying hours was logged before the weather deteriorated to rain during the night. Activity included formation flying, cross-country flights, local reconnaissance, cannon tests, and camera exercises.

29 March 1943 – Flying training continued today in fair conditions, with cloud of 6-10ths-10/10ths, reducing to 3/10ths, and moderate to good visibility. The Squadron's activity included formation flying, local reconnaissances, air-to-sea firing and cine-gun practice. Separately, Fg Offs Peter Cowell and David Davies returned from attachment to Hawkinge.[16]

30 March 1943 – Fair weather today with occasional rain in gusty winds allowed the first pair of pilots, Plt Offs 'Johnnie' Johnson and 'Barney' Newman, to fly to RAF Valley for a new air firing practice programme the Squadron was to participate in. Fg Off Wladislaw Banach flew a practice shipping reconnaissance of Liverpool Bay, and Plt Off Leslie Prickett and Sgt Plt Jan Rogowski flew local reconnaissance flights.

Hugh Parry was posted to 41 Squadron as a Supernumerary Flight Lieutenant from Vickers Armstrong for the Squadron's conversion to the Spitfire XII on 25 March 1943. He assumed the role of OC A Flight upon Flt Lt Richard Inness' departure on 1 May 1943. © Hugh Parry

Aside from the usual training activity today, Fg Off Douglas Haywood and Sgt Plt John Thomas participated in the "Wings for Victory" parade at Shrewsbury during the afternoon. Separately, two more Mk. XIIs were delivered during the day, bringing 41 Squadron up to its full establishment of Spitfire Mk. XII aircraft for the first time.

31 March 1943 – Fair weather with 3/10ths cloud increasing later to 10/10ths with light rainfall and decreased visibility. The second pair of pilots departed for RAF Valley this morning for air firing practice. On this occasion, the participants were Fg Off David Davies and Sgt Plt Jack Stonier, who returned at 17:20, having been delayed by poor weather over northern Wales.

A notable event also took place today when "for the first time in history, a Squadron formation was carried out with Spitfire XII aircraft"[17], the twelve pilots being led by Flt Lt Douglas Hone.

April 1943 – Training on the new aircraft continued during the first half of the month, until the Squadron was posted to Hawkinge. As such, there was no operational flying until 15 April, with the exception of one scramble on 3 April. However, as a result of temperamental spring weather, no flying was undertaken at all on 6, 12, 25 and 30 April, whilst 9-11 April were spent packing for the move to Hawkinge and 14 April was taken up with unpacking again.

Training activity until the move included air firing at RAF Valley, cross-country flying, formation flying, an Army Co-operation beat-up, time on the Link Trainer, and Intelligence lectures.

However, the Squadron's return to the front line this month for the first time since Operation *Jubilee* the previous August took its toll. Although the last two weeks of the month saw the first victories fall to the Spitfire XII, it also claimed five pilots in quick succession: one killed in action, one killed in a flying accident, one lost as a Prisoner of War, and two wounded in action. In addition to these losses, five new pilots were posted in and six departed for other units.

1 April 1943 – The day dawned to rain, cloud down to 600 feet, and visibility at times as low as 200 yards. Conditions were less than ideal for a number of events planned for the 25th Anniversary of the RAF today. However, before breakfast, some news came in that dampened spirits even more.

Hoare is Lost

Having been attached to 91 Squadron at Hawkinge for operational training since 28 March, 41 Squadron's Fg Offs Hoare and Clive Birbeck had undertaken a number of operational patrols across the Channel in accompaniment with other 91 Squadron pilots.

Pilots, 28 March 1943	Spit. Vb	Unit	Up	Down	Recce
Kynaston, Norman A.	EN905	91 Sqn	18:20	19:00	Dieppe
Hoare, Reginald M.	AA836	41 Sqn			
Matthew, Ian G. S.	EP500	91 Sqn	18:15	19:00	Ostend
Birbeck, Clive R.	BL697	41 Sqn			

Pilots, 29 March 1943	Spit. Vb	Unit	Up	Down	Recce
Davy, Dennis H.	AD198	91 Sqn	06:25	07:25	Dieppe
Hoare, Reginald M.	AA836	41 Sqn			
Hoonaert, Roger C.	EN905	91 Sqn	06:25	07:15	Ostend
Birbeck, Clive R.	AR331	41 Sqn			
Hoonaert, Roger C.	EN905	91 Sqn	07:40	08:45	Dungeness
Birbeck, Clive R.	EP500	41 Sqn			
Davy, Dennis H.	AD198	91 Sqn	08:00	09:10	Dungeness
Hoare, Reginald M.	AA836	41 Sqn			

However, during the next patrol, an early morning shipping reconnaissance to Ostend [Oostende] on 1 April with 91 Squadron's Fg Off Barrass Todd, Hoare went missing. He was one of 41 Squadron's longest serving pilots.

Pilots, 1 April 1943	Spit. Vb	Unit	Up	Down	Recce
Todd, Barrass J.	AD124	91 Sqn	06:25	07:10	Ostend
Hoare, Reginald M.	BL423	41 Sqn		FTR	
Nash, Raymond S.	BL697	91 Sqn	06:25	07:25	Dieppe
Birbeck, Clive R.	BL714	41 Sqn			

Todd was leading as the pair flew across the Channel towards France at zero feet at an IAS of 240 mph, approximately 200 yards apart. At Gris Nez, they climbed to 1,500 feet to stay just below the cloud base at 2,000 feet. Four miles east of Nieuport [Nieuwpoort], Belgium, however, they entered rain and 10/10ths cloud, which reached down to ground level.

Todd looked back to see Hoare forming up with him as they turned about, and this was the last time he saw him. It was two to three minutes before Todd re-emerged from the cloud, but when he did so, there was no sign of Hoare. Despite Todd's repeated calls to him over the R/T, and attempts by the Controller to raise him, he did not respond.

When Flt Lt Hugh Parry arrived on the Squadron on 25 March 1943, he brought with him his dog, a white Bull Terrier named 'Monty'. © Cowell family

A veteran of the Battle of Britain, Flt Lt Roy 'Lulu' Lane served with 41 Squadron from 6 April 1943 to ca 27 September 1943. He was sent to Burma in late 1943 and is believed to have worked as an Air Liaison Officer with the Chindits, but was executed by the Japanese on 26 April 1944. © Cowell family

Though the cause of Hoare's loss was initially unknown, it later transpired that he had fallen victim to Flak and baled out, and was subsequently captured. 41 Squadron's ORB lamented his loss, noting,

Hoare had been with the squadron since April 1942, a charming boy and a keen pilot. We will miss him very much and 'Perkin' his dog, a French poodle, seems lost without him.[18]

Fg Off Birbeck returned from his own patrol to Dieppe with Fg Off Raymond Nash, the pair having turned back southwest of Le Tréport as a result of low cloud. Birbeck made no more flights with 91 Squadron and was promptly returned to 41.

Files still in existence today show that a German recovery unit was sent to the village of Leffinge, south of Ostend, on 4 April 1943 to investigate an Allied aircraft that had come down there on 1 April. However, there was little for them to find. Almost the entire aircraft had buried itself into the marshy ground, and they could not even recover a serial plate. Nonetheless, as Hoare had been shot down and captured that day, they were sure the aircraft was his, and closed their investigation.

It was not until 8 May, however, that news was received on the Squadron that Hoare had been captured:

The Squadron are delighted to hear that F/O R.M. Hoare missing on 1.4.43 is alive and well and his mother has already had a letter from him from the P.O.W. Camp at Dulag Luft which is the interrogation Camp of the Luftwaffe. It cannot be imagined that Hoare is likely to give away any secrets.[19]

The Squadron's Intelligence Officer, Flt Lt Lord Gisborough, wrote to Hoare's mother, offering the Squadron's sympathy and speaking highly of the young pilot. Mrs Hoare replied to Lord Gisborough on 22 May 1943, stating,

Thank you for what you say about my son Regie. I can't be too grateful that he is safe. I haven't heard any more particulars since he arrived at Dulag Luft.[20]

Hoare was held for the next 22 months in Stalag Luft III, where he was involved in work on the tunnel 'Harry' in the North Compound for what we know today as 'The Great Escape', which took place on 24 March 1944. Following repatriation at the conclusion of hostilities in Europe, he reported that he had, "worked in connection with the tunnel in the North Camp at Luft III Sagan [but] failed to draw a ticket in the lottery."[21] He was repatriated home at the end of April 1945, and died in 2005.[22]

Returning now to 1 April, the events surrounding the RAF's Silver Jubilee that day were not halted, despite Hoare's loss. A Wing parade took place at 10:00 before a number of invited dignitaries and local residents. As the weather had improved little by this time, the planned Squadron flypast was reduced to just two sections from B Flight, led by OC B Flight, Flt Lt Douglas Hone.

In the evening the entire Squadron was treated to dinner and a dance in the Officers' Mess. It was, however, preceded by a visit a rather comical event that almost left egg on one Flight Commander's face.

> *We had had a fairly busy day with various 'spit and polish' parades and services and a squadron fly past and display. In the evening there was the formal Mess Dinner which all officers were required to attend. Most of us (pilots) mounted our bikes and hared off down to the local about two miles away in time for opening time in order to fortify ourselves for the coming ordeal. On the way back to camp we were all a trifle wobbly on our bikes and I remember seeing Duggie [sic] Hone in the ditch with his bike round his neck looking a bit under the weather. When we got back to our quarters we washed, dressed up in our best blues and assembled dutifully in the Mess. Duggie's [sic] place at the top table was empty and I don't think any of [us] expected him to make it and we were, by this time, feeling a bit guilty about leaving him in the ditch. However, to our astonishment, just as we were being called to order to receive grace before the meal, in he walked, rather pale but otherwise immaculate and seemingly as sober as anyone else in the room.*
>
> *After the meal and the formal speeches etc., the evening developed into a traditional R.A.F. Mess party with mock fights between flights, or pilots and penguins, or other improvised teams, and phenomenal acrobatic feats which did not always come off – and the inevitable consequences – ginormous hangovers and 'damages' on the next mess bills.*[23]

2 April 1943 – Early intermittent drizzle and 8/10ths to 10/10ths cloud at 800-1,500 feet, clearing after midday, which allowed the Squadron to re-commence flying training. The pilots also spent several hours on the Link Trainer, whilst some flew to Valley for air firing.

3 April 1943 – A routine day on which training continued on the Spitfire XIIs. Fg Off Clive Birbeck (EN601) and Sgt Plt Jack Stonier (EN609) were sent to RAF Valley for air firing and whilst there were scrambled to 27,000 feet on the report of two enemy aircraft in the vicinity. The pair was off the deck at 16:00 and returned 35 minutes later having seen nothing. Although uneventful, this scramble constituted the first operation hours ever flown on a Mk. XII.

4 April 1943 – Fair weather with small amounts of cloud and 4-8 miles visibility allowed the Squadron to complete a full flying training programme today. This included cross-country and formation flying, whilst another pair of pilots flew to Valley for air firing practice. The Squadron had now received its full allotment of Spitfire XIIs.

5 April 1943 – Cloudy with rain periods, 8/10ths-10/10ths cloud at 2,000-4,000 feet, and visibility of 2,000-4,000 yards. Training continued according to plan, which included four pilots on air firing at Valley. However, a gale blew up in the evening that continued for the next two days and kept the Squadron almost entirely on the ground.

Separately today, a message was received on 41 Squadron from HQ Fighter Command that the unit was to move to Hawkinge on 12 April 1943, together with 3016 Servicing Echelon, to relieve 91 Squadron. They were to take over their 'unique' work consisting "entirely of spotting & reccos and the odd scramble when the Hun comes too near".[24]

6 April 1943 – Terrible weather conditions, which included a 60 mph gale and squally showers, halted all flying today, were instead occupied on the Link Trainer and in Intelligence lectures.

7 April 1943 – Although there was only a little flying today on account of the weather, three new pilots arrived at RAF High Ercall on posting to 41 Squadron: 27-year-old Flt Lt Hugh L. Parry who came from Vickers, and 23-year-old Flt Lt Roy Lane and 26-year-old Canadian Fg Off H. Bruce Moffett from the Merchant Ship Fighter Unit at Speke.

Parry had a distinct advantage over Lane and Moffett as he was one of the few pilots outside 41 Squadron already versed in the performance of the Spitfire XII. He had most recently been a Test Pilot with Vickers Armstrong Ltd. at Southampton and had been involved in the pre-issue trials of the Mark XII. He recalled the reason for his posting today was that "as a Test Pilot, I had more hours on Spitfire XIIs than anyone else and 41 were being equipped with them."[25]

Born in Dartford, Kent, Parry had spent several years in South Africa and Rhodesia in his civil occupation as a mining surveyor and is therefore erroneously referred to in many texts today as Rhodesian. He returned to the United Kingdom in September 1939 to enlist and was commissioned in December 1940. Having spent 1941 with 260 and 266 (Rhodesia) Squadrons, Parry sailed to Malta as a Flight Commander with 601 Squadron in April 1942. He returned to the United Kingdom for leave in July 1942 and was subsequently posted to Supermarine as a Test Pilot. Promoted to Flight Lieutenant in December 1942, Parry was now returning to operations as a Supernumerary Flight Lieutenant with 41 Squadron, to assist with its re-equipping to the Spitfire XII.[26]

Flt Lt Roy Lane, whose nickname was, or became, 'Lulu', haled from Southsea, Hampshire, and was granted a Short Service Commission in August 1938. His first operational posting was to 43 Squadron, where he enjoyed some success before being shot down and wounded in August 1940, which resulted in eight months sick leave. In June 1941, Lane returned to operations with the Merchant Ship Fighting Unit, and with the exception of a brief attachment to 602 Squadron, remained with the MSFU until his posting to 41 Squadron today.[27]

Fg Off Bruce Moffett, an accountant from Viceroy, Saskatchewan, joined the RCAF in Regina in October 1940, and completed his flying training in Canada, at the conclusion of which he was commissioned. He was subsequently shipped to the United Kingdom where he attended OTU and was then posted to his first operational unit, 416 (RCAF) Squadron, upon its formation at Peterhead, Scotland, in mid-November 1941. Moffett was posted to the MSFU at Speke in March 1942, and spent time with this unit in Gibraltar and Algiers, and aboard CAM ships. He remained with this unit until early April 1943, and now joined 41 Squadron with Lane.

Fg Off (later Flt Lt) H. Bruce Moffett RCAF served with 41 Squadron from 7 April 1943 to 26 February 1944. He shot down the RAF's first V1 in daylight on 16 June 1944, his first of eight destroyed with 91 Squadron during summer 1944. © May Moffett, via Dan Johnson

8 April 1943 – Today the Squadron received the official order to move to Hawkinge by 12 April, to finally take their Spitfire XII's onto the front line in 11 Group and introduce them to the Luftwaffe. The weather was fair all day, but flying nonetheless restricted to enable the crews to attain maximum serviceability of the aircraft by the twelfth of the month, the day upon which they were scheduled to move.

9 April 1943 – No flying was undertaken all day whilst the Squadron packed and prepared for their move. Another new pilot joined the unit during the day in the form of 33-year-old Pole, Flt Lt Jerzy J. Solak. Born in Przecław, near Krakow, Solak had been with the Polish Air Force since 1930. He was evacuated to the United Kingdom in early 1940, where he joined the RAFVR, and was initially posted to British squadrons. In February 1941, he was posted to 317 (Polish) Squadron and was commissioned with this unit a month later, but was posted away again the following June. In November 1942, Solak was posted to the AFDU at Duxford as a Test Pilot, and it is from this unit that he was posted to 41 Squadron today.[28]

10-11 April 1943 – There was no operational flying during both days, despite fair flying conditions, as they were spent instead packing and preparing for the move to Hawkinge. Everything was loaded into seven goods wagons, but sufficient equipment was left at High Ercall to service the aircraft between the train's departure for Folkestone Station and the aircrafts' departure for Hawkinge.

The Squadron moves to Hawkinge

On Monday, 12 April 1943, Squadron's ground personnel, and that of 3016 Servicing Echelon, departed High Ercall in cloudy and damp conditions for their new base at Hawkinge, thereby moving from 9 Group back to 11 Group. As the Squadron had spent a week at this airfield the previous year (30 June-8 July 1942), this move would constitute their second, but also final stay at Hawkinge and on this occasion would last just under six weeks.

A movement order for the relocation shows an advance party of NCOs had already departed for Hawkinge by train from Crudgington Station at 07:25 on 10 April. However, the main party proceeded to Hawkinge by rail on Monday, 12 April, dressed in best blue. Having formed up for a final parade in the Echelon Hangar at High Ercall at 07:30, they then marched to the station, accompanied by a van with the day's remaining rations. The train departed Crudgington at 08:20 and the men arrived at Hawkinge that evening at 19:00.

The pilots should have followed them over in their aircraft during the morning and have arrived before them, but "as usual when a Squadron is scheduled to move the weather clamps down and this day was no exception".[29] They were compelled to stay another night, and only left late the next morning.

Ground Crew Nominal Roll

The Movement Order for the Squadron today[30] provides us an informal roll of ground staff, whilst also listing some of the aircrew.

Advance Party.	Rear Party (Technical Trades).		
F/Sgt Luscombe – NCO i/c	Sgt Robertson	(Echelon) – NCO i/c	
Sgt Kingerley	Sgt Howells	"	
Cpl White	Cpl Gibbons	"	
LAC Temple	Cpl Elliott	"	
LAC Mitchell (927)	Cpl Sallnow	"	

Advance Party. [cont.]
LAC Williams (801)
LAC Anderson
LAC Pate
LAC Cooke
AC1 Beaton
AC1 Mackin
Cpl Raymond
AC1 Simister
LAC King
LAC Field (Echelon)
LAC Plows
Cpl Couch

Air Party.
F/Sgt Juggins – NCO i/c
F/Sgt Armer – NCO i/c
Sgt Jones
Sgt Palmer
Cpl Fulham
Cpl Canter
Cpl Rogers
Cpl Parcell
Cpl Roylance
Cpl Drew
LAC Hardiman
AC1 Sanderson (678)
LAC Milner
LAC Botwood
LAC Parfitt
LAC Bennison
LAC Brown (189)
LAC Parrish
LAC Powell (489)
LAC Bowel
LAC Cadman
LAC Blower
LAC Clements
AC2 Gregory
AC2 Batho
LAC Price (871)

Rail Party.
F/Lt Lane – Officer i/c
F/O Moffett
Sgt Nicholas
AC2 Savage
AC2 Melough
AC2 Botterill
Cpl/LAC Harmer
LAC Moffatt
AC1 Smith (573)
AC1 Newman
AC2 Terry

Rear Party (Technical Trades). [cont.]
Cpl Holden   "
AC2 Lockitt
AC2 Quinn
AC1 Evans (775)
AC1 Maggs
LAC Lovely
LAC Charlesworth
LAC Clarke (841)
LAC Cook (560) (Echelon)

                "
                "

Air Party (cont).
AC1 Creigh
LAC Groome
LAC Booth
Sgt Prout (Echelon)
Cpl Sparrow   "
AC Taylor   "

Road Party (2 – 5/10 cwt vans).
F/O Whipp
LAC Holloway (Echelon)
LAC Salt   "
LAC Beckwith   "
LAC Higgerty   "

Rear Party (Cleaning up).
F/Sgt Shuter – NCO i/c
LAC Foulger
Cpl Naylor
AC1 Lake (Echelon)

Rail Party. [cont.]
LAC Bents
Cpl Murrin
LAC Benedict
LAC Holt
LAC Bathgate
LAC Shaw
LAC Bla[?]a
AC1 Sanderson (973)
AC1 Griffin
LAC Wootten
Cpl Hayden

Rail Party. [cont.]
AC2 Goodbody (Echelon)
LAC Glanfield   "
LAC Haynes   "
LAC Hartley   "
AC2 Hutchins   "
Cpl Irving   "
AC2 Jones   "
LAC Lomberg   "
AC2 Mooney   "
LAC Mair   "
AC1 Moore   "

Rail Party. [cont.]	Rail Party. [cont.]	Rail Party. [cont.]	
LAC Powell (209)	LAC Moss	AC1 Marjoram	"
AC2 Moore	AC2 Jardine	AC2 Magford	"
AC2 Read	Cpl MacLean	LAC Penny	"
Cpl Armstrong	LAC Mackinnon	LAC Parsons	"
AC2 Matcher	AC1 Best	LAC Platts	"
Cpl Russell	AC1 Keene	Cpl Presser	"
LAC Polley	Cpl Herbert	AC2 Payne	"
AC1 Jones (722)	AC1 Emmerson	AC2 Speakman	"
F/Sgt Rodman	Sgt Heal	Cpl Shields	"
AC2 Bryant	LAC Alder (Echelon)	AC1 Sitch	"
AC1 Pinnock	LAC Brown (197) "	AC1 Tanner	"
AC1 Grosfield	Cpl Brownlee "	LAC Topping	"
AC2 Roberts	AC2 Basford "	Cpl Woodward	"
LAC Isaacson	LAC Cook (702) "	Sgt Ingram	"
AC1 McCouloch	LAC Clark "	Sgt McHolm	"
LAC Deakin	Cpl Dyson "	F/Sgt Wilcox	"
LAC Allen	AC1 Firth "	Cpl Troakes	"
AC1 Mitchell (222)	AC2 Forrest "	LAC Gaff	"
AC1 Williams (543)	AC1 Girt "	LAC Botting	"

13 April 1943 – Fair, though cloudy, weather today allowed the pilots to leave High Ercall by air just before midday. They arrived at Hawkinge in 19 Spitfire XIIs and two Vbs at 12:40, followed closely by two Harrow transport aircraft loaded with the remaining thirty ground crew and servicing equipment.

Following their departure, two vans followed by road, conveying the last of the servicing equipment, but still left behind a rear party, consisting of technical tradesmen, under Sgt Robertson of 3016 Echelon, and a detail assigned to cleaning duties, led by Flt Sgt Shuter, who headed for Hawkinge a day later.

14 April 1943 – There was no operational flying all day, whilst 41 Squadron unpacked and, as such, 91 Squadron continued to be operational whilst they settled in. Flt Lt Hugh Parry later remembered Hawkinge as a "peacetime air station [which was] very well maintained. It had plenty of fresh fish to eat, which was donated by the local fishermen, who we kept an eye on while they fished."[31]

During the day, one of the Squadron's Polish pilots, Sgt Plt Jan Rogowski, departed on posting to 315 (Dęblinski) Squadron at Northolt. Unfortunately, however, he was shot down by Me109s over Bergues during a Circus operation only six weeks later. He is buried today Pihen-les-Guines Cemetery in Calais, France.

Tom Slack's Gen

41 Squadron's Archives holds a three-page hand-written document in point form, which was penned by Fg Off Tom Slack and is titled *The GEN*. Although undated, the information contained within it suggests it was written around the time of the Squadron's move to Hawkinge, or perhaps in preparation for it, as it outlines their duties. It is not clear whether the list was made as advice for inexperienced pilots or whether they are his own notes made during a briefing in preparation for going back into operations with the Spitfire XII. It states,

1. *Know your Coast*
2. *Know the french* [sic] *Ports.*
3. *Know your ships, tonnage, variety, etc.*

4. Know the wrecks on the French Coast.
5. Study oblique photography – which is fitted to 2 of the a/c at the moment.
6. Practice cloud flying & coming out when you think you have reached your objective. i.e. see your objective 2 miles ahead – pop into cloud and practice coming out over the place.
7. Leave before the 'flak' starts over the objective. Don't wait until it bursts – it may be on the way up. watch for flashes on the shore & take the necessary avoiding action.
8. If no clouds – get your height over England [and] gain more on the way over. Then dive all the way and go like hell.
9. If you hear the Gerry Beam on your radio alter your height quickly [and] you will lose it – it is a bit disconcerting & one is fixed on the 'drome so as soon as you take off they have you taped. I believe the gen is that they have 2 different beams – one for height – one for direction – they have to coordinate so if you climb or dive you spoil the whole issue (this can be checked.)
10. Any report given by a Jim Crow receives immediate action. So your gen must be accurate.
11. <u>Your Job.</u>
 a. Each Dawn & Dusk –
 One Shipping Recco – Gris Nez to Ostend
 One Shipping Recco – Gris Nez to Dieppe
 b. Spotting for Sweeps
 c. Individual Reccos of damage down after bombing raids on the French Coast or to see if ships have moved from one birth to another. These sort of things happen all day.
 d. Weather tests over France to see if certain places can be bombed.
 e. Usual patrols on the South Coast.
 f. Air Sea Rescue
 You travel alone & can do the job in any way you like as long as [you] <u>do</u> the job.
 On patrols on the English Coast you travel in pairs.
 One Flight is on from 1pm [on one day] to 1pm [on the next], the other is either released or on 30 minutes. The 91 Chaps love it & that's on clipped Spit V.B's – if they are bounced they have to come back: even if they only see the big guns in the distance, which often happens. To think how wizard it will be for us with our new Secret aircraft.
12. Recommended that Gizzy processes large photos of each port on the coat, photos of all landmarks, special maps of French Coast, Chart showing the wrecks, Models & the latest gen on ships & shipping, Flak positions. All of the above are available.

Tom Slack F/O[32]

Further explaining their new line of work, called 'Jim Crow' patrols, Flt Lt Douglas Hone later explained,

It was normal procedure at first light and at last light to fly from Cape Gris Nez to Le Havre and from Cape Gris to Flushing reporting on enemy shipping in the various harbours / ports. One aircraft went one way & the other in the opposite direction. Tactics were left to the pilots concerned & ships were reported to HQ Naval Ops. Dover. They often did not believe us so we took oblique photos. […] We also shot up ground targets, spotted for mines, did air sea rescue work and gave weather reports.[33]

15 April 1943 – The good weather provided ideal conditions for OC A Flight, Flt Lt Rex Poynton (EN601), to undertake a patrol between Dieppe and Gris Nez with 91 Squadron's Commanding Officer, Sqn Ldr Raymond Harries (EN236), who flew one of 41 Squadron's Spitfire XIIs. Departing Hawkinge at 10:45, the pair returned again at 11:35, reporting having sighted a ship of 1,000 tons in the entrance of Calais Harbour and three smaller vessels off Boulogne.

This constituted the day's total operational flying, but the pilots made several non-operational flights to other stations within 11 Group, to introduce them to the Spitfire XII. It was not, however, a mere public relations exercise, as the ORB testifies: "We certainly do not like the idea of being fired at by friendly aircraft"![34]

Flt Lt Roy Lane, Sgt Plt Peter Wall, Sgt Plt Alan Hope and Fg Off Peter Cowell watching aircraft flying above them, ca April-August 1943. © Cowell family

16 April 1943 – Good weather all day gave the Squadron the opportunity to take over duties from 91 Squadron, and introduce the Spitfire XII to the Luftwaffe for the first time. Having been out of the action since the previous August, the Squadron was raring to go, but most men lacked any frontline experience. That was about to change.

The day started with dawn reconnaissance flights to Dieppe-Le Havre, France, and Ostend [Oostende], Belgium, by B Flight. These were undertaken by Fg Off Douglas Haywood (EN602) from 06:25, and Flt Lt Douglas Hone (EN234) from 06:30. Hone was back first, at 07:00, with nothing to report but the weather conditions, but Haywood, who pancaked at 07:20, had sighted several ships up to ca. 5,000 tons and come under inaccurate Flak fire from land and sea. A typical report on return from such a sortie is shown in the following example of Haywood's patrol:

…BOULOGNE FOUR E/R BOATS 1 MILE SOUTH OF BOULOGNE MOLE GOING NORTH. TWO SMALL SHIPS IN OUTER HARBOUR… LE TOUQUET NIL MISTY LE TREPORT NIL HAZY DIEPPE FOUR SHIPS 4,000 TO 6,000 TONS 1 TO 2 MILES OFF DIEPPE GOING IN. IN POOR LIGHT LOOK LIKE TANKERS, THIN AND LONG BRIDGE IN MIDDLE ENGINES AFT ALL FOUR IDENTICAL. THESE FOUR FIRED RED TRACERS FROM ASTERN ALSO SHORE BATTERIES FIRED HEAVY AND LIGHT. SEEN AT 0655 FROM 500 FT CLIMBED TO 15,000 FT WESTWARD FOR LE HAVRE WEATHER….[35]

Similar patrols in followed throughout the day and continued until just after 20:00, with little to report but the several ships in port or off the coast; all were uneventful. In total, 20 sorties were undertaken, which made a good day's flying.

17 April 1943 – The day commenced with shipping reconnaissances to Boulogne and Calais by Flt Lt Rex Poynton (EN601), and a second to Ostend by Australian Fg Off 'Barney' Newman (EN236), both taking off at 06:40. Newman was back first, at 07:25, reporting a 300-ton vessel

Fg Off Jerzy 'George' Solak served with 41 Squadron from 9 April 1943 to 12 October 1943, during that time claiming one FW190 destroyed. Posted to the 492nd Fighter Squadron USAAF in June 1944, he was shot down over Normandy and captured in August 1944. He escaped and returned to his unit, and emigrated to the United States in 1948. © Stanislaw Bochniak Collection, via Peter Sikora

off Ostend, and Poynton landed five minutes later reporting E or R Boats two miles off the French coast, approaching Boulogne from the south. He also experienced an amount Flak, which was accurate in altitude but wide of the mark.

Similar to the previous day, several patrols were then undertaken to Dieppe, Ostend and Boulogne, intermingled with a scramble to Dungeness on the report of enemy aircraft, and spotting patrols of the same area. All of these were uneventful and concluded at 17:45 in time for dinner. Following the evening meal, however, the Squadron was airborne yet again, but this time there was somewhat more to report.

The First Spitfire XII Victory and Casualties

At 20:20, Fg Off Rycherde Hogarth (EN235) was airborne for a patrol from Calais to Ostend, whilst Fg Off Clive Birbeck (EN604) was sent on a patrol to Dieppe. Approximately 20 minutes into Hogarth's sortie, around two miles north of Ostend, he descended to take a closer look at a tug when a Junkers Ju88, painted completely black, passed across his path from port to starboard at an altitude of just 200 feet above sea level.

Hogarth whipped around onto its tail and quickly closed from 500 to 100 feet, as he fired a full ten-second burst. He hit the tail and rear fuselage, which resulted in the fuselage 'crumpling up'. Breaking to starboard, Hogarth renewed his attack from a quarter to full astern, allowing a quarter ring deflection, and fired another two-to-three second burst of machine gun fire, thereby using up the last of his ammunition.[36]

The Ju88 was now well alight on the port side of the fuselage and glided down to crash land on the beach at Bredene.[37] Hogarth had captured the combat in eight feet of cine-gun film and was awarded his first victory, one destroyed Ju88. However, he did not come away completely unscathed, as his aircraft had been hit in the starboard wing by return fire from the Junkers' gunner. The damage was not serious enough to affect the aircraft's handling, though, and Hogarth landed at Hawkinge again at 21:00.

This was the first enemy aircraft destroyed by the Squadron since June 1942, and the ORB notes they were "highly delighted at this early success"[38] of the Spitfire XII.

Meanwhile, however, Fg Off Birbeck was having a more difficult time of it. It started well, as he had spotted a 400-ton coaster six miles north of Dieppe at 21:00, accompanied by a Flak ship. They were easy to see in the sunny and clear conditions; visibility still extended 10-15 miles despite the late hour.

Coming under immediate heavy fire from the Flak ship, Birbeck decided to take a closer look. He orbited briefly at 3,000 feet, deciding his strategy, and then made a beam attack on the coaster. Coming in fast at an altitude from 1,000 feet down to just 50, he opened fire from ranges of 1,200 feet down to 100, expending 100 rounds of cannon and 562 of .303.[39]

He saw strikes on the vessel and subsequently claimed it damaged to Cat. 3 status, but presently had more immediate problems. Birbeck's Spitfire had been hit by a 40mm high explosive round and by two 7.9mm machine gun bullets, but was himself uninjured. He broke off the attack and returned home with Cat. B damage, thereby sustaining the first combat damage to the Mark.

On his way back to Hawkinge, at an altitude of 1,500 feet, Birbeck sighted a red Verey light, which was fired from a dinghy approximately six miles off Berck-sur-Mer. This was followed by a second, and Birbeck descended and orbited the dinghy for ten minutes. He observed three occupants and, whilst he was unable to determine whether they were friendly or hostile, notified Control. The Royal Navy subsequently located the dinghy and picked up *four* occupants, but their identity is unknown.

Despite assisting these downed airmen, Birbeck's own troubles were still on-going. Although he was able to fly his aircraft without any trouble, the Flak damage had rendered his air speed indicator useless. He radioed Hawkinge for assistance, and Flt Lt Douglas Hone (EN234) took off at 21:10 to rendezvous with Birbeck and help him land.

The operation was executed perfectly and Hone accompanied Birbeck down during his landing, then went around again and made his own landing five minutes later. "Both pilots made successful landings in the fast approaching darkness, Birbeck at 21.20 led by Hone, and Hone at 21.25."[40] This concluded the day's flying.

Ammunition Expenditure Report for 17 April 1943[41]

Pilot	Aircraft	20mm S A P/1	20mm H E/1	.303 MK VI.Z	.303 Arm. Piercing
F/O Birbeck	EN604	50	50	252	310
F/O Hogarth	EN235	54	54	240	250

That evening, a large party was held in the Officers' Mess to farewell 91 Squadron, attended by 41 Squadron, by 1 Squadron, who came over from Lympne, and by the local Chief Police Constable, amongst others. The unit was leaving for Honiley to re-equip with the Mark XII, and would be joining 41 Squadron again in two months' time, to form a combined Spitfire XII Wing.

18 April 1943 – The day commenced at 06:25 when Flt Lt Hugh Parry (EN238) and Sgt Plt Malcolm Rowe (EN231) took off for shipping and weather reconnaissances of the Ostend and Dieppe areas, respectively. Parry was back on the ground within 30 minutes, and Rowe 55 minutes later, both reporting minor shipping movements, but little else of consequence.

There was then no flying until 12:10, when Parry was airborne again in the same aircraft for a reconnaissance sortie to Boulogne. Besides light Flak, which was inaccurate, he sighted three E or R Boats heading north at speed, approximately seven miles off Hardelot, but did not attack them. He was back at Hawkinge at 12:40.

Similar patrols continued throughout the afternoon and evening, and included an ASR escort to a 277 Squadron Lysander at 14:40 by Flt Lt Jerzy Solak (EN609) and Fg Off Jerzy Polak (EN603). However, nothing was seen and the pair returned at 15:50. Four pilots were also scrambled at 18:22 on suspicion of inbound Luftwaffe aircraft, but again nothing was seen. All of the day's operations were uneventful.

19 April 1943 – Initially fine, becoming cloudy with rain. Fg Off Tom Slack (EN233) was the first airborne today on a shipping reconnaissance to Ostend at 06:30, followed five minutes later by Sgt Plt Walter 'Wingco' East (EN603) who flew a reconnaissance sortie to Dieppe. At the same time, Red Section, Fg Off Peter Cowell (EN236) and Trinidadian Sgt Plt George Wilson (EN609), took off to patrol the Dungeness area.

Slack and East returned with nothing to report at 07:20 and 07:30, respectively, and Red Section, likewise, at 07:35. Cowell and Wilson were airborne again at 09:12 for another patrol, on this occasion to the south of Dungeness, but were back just 23 minutes later, once again with nothing to report.

There was no more flying until 18:10, when Fg Offs Hogarth and Birbeck were sent on a patrol – the ORB does not share the destination or area – but they returned after a similarly uneventful 35 minutes.

This concluded the day's operational flying, but some non-operational was also undertaken by the pilots. Two of these sorties, however, had unfortunate ends. Flt Lt Jerzy Solak landed correctly on the east-west runway at North Weald in one of the Squadron's two remaining Spitfire Vb's, believed to have been BL406. At the intersection with the second strip, he collided with a Miles M.11 Whitney Straight communications aircraft, which had landed on the wrong runway. Fortunately, he was not hurt but the aircraft was damaged to Cat. B status.[42] This was 41 Squadron's last ever Spitfire Mk V casualty.

Then, at 17:00, Fg Off 'Haybag' Haywood belly landed one of the new Spitfire XIIs at Hawkinge, causing significant damage to the aircraft: the propeller was smashed, and fuselage, oil cooler, and radiator bath all crushed. "We can repair the aircraft here b[u]t it will take some considerable time before it is again serviceable."[43,44]

The other event of note this day was the departure of 91 Squadron, leaving 41 Squadron in complete control of the Station's shipping and weather reconnaissance duties. Having been based at Hawkinge almost since their formation in October 1940, 91 Squadron left during the morning in 19 Spitfire Vbs, a Tiger Moth and two Harrow transports.

20 April 1943 – Fine and cloudless but cool. This morning's Dieppe reconnaissance was undertaken by Sgt Plt John Thomas, whilst the Ostend patrol was flown by Sgt Plt William Downing. They were airborne at 06:25 and returned simultaneously at 07:05, reporting that nothing of interest had been seen.

There was then no flying until 12:05, when Fg Off Douglas Haywood, and Sgt Plts William Downing, Douglas Fisher and John Thomas were scrambled on the report of inbound enemy aircraft off Calais. However, nothing was seen and they returned at 12:50. Further patrols followed at 15:30, 20:20 and 20:35.

There was little to report besides inaccurate Flak, but the pilots were getting the impression the German military was now well aware of their new aircraft:

> *The pilots are settling down to this new work, but we are beginning to think the Hun is now aware of our new machines as the reccos are being carried out very much quicker on Spitfire XII's and he has probably noticed it.*[45]

21 April 1943 – Mainly dull weather during the morning and afternoon. Today's Dieppe reconnaissance was undertaken by Plt Off 'Barney' Newman (EN236), whilst the Ostend reconnaissance was flown by Flt Lts Rex Poynton (EN601) and Roy Lane (EN604) as Red Section. All three took off at 06:35 and returned at 07:20 and 07:30 respectively, reporting dredgers in harbour at Boulogne and Calais, and otherwise a few scattered vessels.

A scramble was made by two pilots at 10:25 on the report of incoming enemy aircraft, but this proved to be unfounded. Uneventful spotting patrols of Hastings and Dungeness were undertaken at 11:15, 14:35, 15:15, 16:05, 16:50, 17:25, 18:05, 18:25, 18:30, 19:05 and 19:25. All were uneventful.

A Flight pilots at Hawkinge in April 1943. From left to right Fg Off Tom Slack, Sgt Plt 'Wingco' East, Fg Off Harry Smith (Adjt), Plt Off Leslie Prickett, Fg Off Jerzy Polak (Poland), Fg Off 'Barney' Newman RAAF with 'Perkin', Sgt Plt Norman Heale, Flt Lt 'Lulu' Lane, WO Arthur 'Junior' Appleton, WO George Wilson (Trinidad), and Flt Lt Rex Poynton. © Cowell family

At 14:05, Fg Off Haywood (EN602) was sent on a shipping reconnaissance of the Dieppe area, but saw nothing of consequence. However, on his return, he sighted a 300-ton motor barge heading south, approximately five miles south of Boulogne. Diving to sea level, he fired two short bursts at it, expending 38 rounds of 20mm and 60 of .303. He saw hits on the vessel but no particular damage was recognised.

During the day, however, the Squadron were advised of intelligence that had been received from the Royal Navy suggesting a Kriegsmarine cruiser was expected off the Dutch islands, which would "attempt to run the gauntlet through the Straits".[46] As a result, their patrol area was extended northwards from Ostend to Flushing [Vlissingen] and the Walcheren Islands.

At 14:10, Australian Sgt Plt Stan May (EN611) was sent on the first extended patrol, but on his return at 15:10, reported haze and industrial smoke over the entire area, rendering it impossible to see Flushing at all. At 16:35, the exercise was repeated by Flt Lt Hone (EN234), who found thick black smoke rising from the harbour area. He also noted two motor boats between Flushing and Ostend, but there was otherwise nothing of note, and certainly no cruiser.

Another patrol each to Ostend and Dieppe followed at 20:00, and the last aircraft was on the ground again at 21:25. Both were uneventful and this concluded the day's flying, which had consisted of no less than 30 sorties.

22 April 1943 – Low cloud and rainy storms, which did not clear until the evening, limited the day's flying to two specific blocks: 06:55-11:45 and 18:55-21:35. The day commenced with the usual morning Ostend and Dieppe reconnaissance flights, with today's undertaken by Fg Offs Ron Johnson (EN607) and Bruce Moffett (EN611), respectively.

Johnson returned at 07:40 having sighted a small coaster entering the channel at Calais and come under heavy, accurate Flak at Dunkirk, and heavy, inaccurate Flak at Ostend. Moffett, however, had an experience that was enough to put the wind up any pilot. Whilst observing shipping from 1,200 feet in the Gris Nez area, he came under attack from three unidentified aircraft at a range of

Fg Off (Actg Flt Lt) T. Rex Poynton served with 41 Squadron from 16 April 1942 to 23 April 1943, and was OC A Flight from 22 October 1942 until killed in action north of Dieppe on 23 April 1943. This was the first ever loss of a Spitfire XII in action. © Cowell family

just 1,000 yards. He managed to evade them with superior speed: "No use hanging about so he… just left them standing. These new XII's have certainly [sic] all the speed that is necessary"![47] He landed at Hawkinge at 07:40, shaken but uninjured.

There followed five patrols (eight sorties) of the Dungeness area at 07:00, 08:00, 08:55, 09:17 and 10:55. The penultimate of these began as a scramble, but when nothing was seen the pilots were diverted to Dungeness to patrol instead. The last pair was on the ground again at 11:45 in rapidly deteriorating conditions, and the Squadron then remained earth-bound until after dinner, when conditions allowed a resumption of work.

Dungeness patrols recommenced at 18:55, and were also flown at 20:15 and 20:50. These were intermingled with two brief scrambles, at 19:40 and 20:35, during which nothing was seen, and a patrol from Dieppe to Boulogne, and a final to Ostend, both departing at 20:35. During the latter patrols, vessels of 300, 400 and 600 tons were sighted, and some Flak experienced, but were otherwise uneventful. They landed again an hour later and this concluded the day's flying.

23 April 1943 – Initially fine weather, deteriorating to rain and low cloud, but with bright periods during the evening. Flt Lt Tom Slack (EN233) undertook the morning's Gris Nez-Ostend patrol between 06:30 and 07:20, whilst Fg Off Peter Cowell (EN236) flew the Dieppe-Boulogne patrol between 06:50 and 07:25. In both cases, there was little to report.

Six Dungeness patrols were undertaken throughout the morning in pairs, at 06:40, 07:30, 08:25, 09:20, 10:10 and 11:10, with the last of these returning at 11:55. All were uneventful, but this was not the case for the day's remaining two sorties.

At 10:55, Plt Off 'Barney' Newman (EN236) and Flt Lt Rex Poynton (EN601) were sent to Ostend and Dieppe, respectively. Newman sighted several vessels off Gravelines and Nieuport [Nieuwpoort], and particularly off Ostend, where he took a closer look at both a 500-ton and a 1,000-ton ship. The larger of the two opened up on Newman with heavy, accurate Flak and his Spitfire was damaged. He made it home without any problem, though, and landed at Hawkinge at 11:40 with Cat. A damage.

Poynton was not so fortunate. At 11:30, when ten miles north of Dieppe, he was advised of the presence of eight enemy aircraft, approximately 20 miles to the north of his position. He acknowledged the message and was given a course for home, but was not heard from again. His plot was seen to turn sharply towards the French coast, but then disappeared. He made no further contact, and is believed to have fallen victim to Obfw Paul Fritsch in a FW190 of 5/JG26 who claimed a Mustang at this time, 25km west of the Somme Estuary.

23-year-old Fg Off (Actg Flt Lt) T. Rex Poynton of Zululand is remembered today on the Runnymede Memorial. © Steve Brew

This event signalled the end of operational flying for the day, and although ASR was unable to deploy any aircraft owing to the deteriorating weather conditions, several pilots from A Flight are reported to have flown over the area to search for him during the evening. They were forced to call off the search after a short time, however, forced back by heavy rain and cloud down to zero feet.

The 23-year-old Flight Commander would be sorely missed. Poynton was eulogised thus in the Squadron ORB:

> *It is with the deepest regret that we have to record him as missing. He was with 41 for twelve months and came to us from 52 O.T.U. having previously been an instructor at No. 19 E.F.T.S. A brilliant leader and most enthusiastic pilot who was respected and liked by all the Squadron. He was promoted to A/F/Lt. in November 1942 and his keenness robbed him of leave during this time. We [have] the most affectionate memories of him, a brave and fearless boy.*[48]

The son of Thomas and Gladys Poynton of Eshowe, Zululand, he is remembered today on Panel 120 of the Runnymede Memorial.

24 April 1943 – Mainly fine, though cold, with occasional rain and low cloud. The day started as had every other since the Squadron's arrival at Hawkinge, and the Ostend patrol was commenced at 06:25 by Sgt Plt Stanley Biggs (EN238), followed at five minutes later by Sgt Plt Douglas Fisher (EN607), who flew the Dieppe patrol.

Biggs only sighted two small vessels of no importance and was back at 07:05. Fisher, however, whilst finding no shipping worthy of reporting, did make a more sobering discovery, seeing a body floating in the Channel approximately 20 miles north of Dieppe. He descended for closer observation, but owing to poor weather and rough seas, was unable to locate it again. He landed again at 07:40 to report his sighting. Was it Poynton? Given the location, it is possible, but we shall never know.

A Tragic Loss

At 11:25, Sgt Plts Douglas Fisher (EN607) and John Thomas (EN610) took off for a patrol from Ostend to Flushing. The operation ran smoothly, with unlimited visibility above 4,000 feet, but no shipping was seen and they returned to Hawkinge at 11:55 with nothing to report.[49]

However, as they prepared to land, Thomas made a tight left hand turn on approach – not unusual in itself – but the aircraft suddenly lost speed, stalled, and fell to the ground. The aircraft came down in a field near the White Horse Inn on Canterbury Road, just short of the runway.[50] Thomas was killed instantly and the aircraft was written off.

Although an immediate cause was unknown, preliminary investigations pointed to engine trouble, rather than pilot error. The Air Investigation Branch was requested, as was a representative

Sgt Plt John I. Thomas served with 41 Squadron from 16 November 1942 to 24 April 1943, when he was killed in a flying accident at Hawkinge, the result of engine failure during a final tight turn in preparation for landing. © Kerry Thomas

from Rolls Royce, in order to conduct a proper enquiry. Initial examination of the wreckage appeared to show that "five big ends had gone in the engine".[51]

The subsequent formal investigation included a complete strip of the engine by Rolls Royce at Derby. This resulted in the conclusion that the most probable cause of the accident was "a broken oil pipe or connection in the installation causing either oil starvation or excessive oil aeration".[52]

Regardless of the cause, however, there was no comfort for the 22-year-old's father, who had already lost his wife. Thomas was sent home for a private funeral and subsequently buried in the Hengoed Welsh Baptist Chapelyard in Glamorgan.

Returning to 24 April 1943 now, Plt Off 'Barney' Newman (EN236) was airborne at 16:50 for another shipping reconnaissance to Ostend. He sighted a dredger at work off Dunkirk and an 800-ton hopper entering the harbour at Ostend, but little else. However, he came under accurate Flak fire at Dunkirk, and was again hit, in the same aircraft and with the same severity as the previous morning's brush with the German anti-aircraft defences.

Ten minutes after Newman took off, Fg Off Tom Slack was airborne on his own patrol of Dieppe. He returned at 17:40 with nothing to report but weather conditions. This concluded the day's flying.

26 April 1943 – Generally fine, but gale force winds limited the day's flying to just four patrols, consisting of two to Dieppe and two to Ostend. Blue Section to Dieppe was airborne at 06:25 (Hogarth EN235 & Johnson EN238), as were Green Section to Ostend (Birbeck EN234 & Fisher EN231). They returned at 07:10, respectively 07:25, with nothing to report.

This concluded flying until 16:05 when Yellow (Solak EN603 & Wilson EN609) and Red Sections (Cowell EN238 & Prickett EN604) took off for the same respective patrols. Both sections returned early without completing the task, Yellow at 16:35 as a result of engine trouble on EN603, and Red five minutes before them due to poor weather. There were no further operations today.

Separately, ex-41 Squadron Flight Commander, Capt Malta Stepp of the 336th Squadron USAAF, visited Hawkinge today to show the pilots the newest American fighter, the P-47 Thunderbolt, and displayed its abilities.

27 April 1943 – Mainly fine with broken cloud. Despite the weather, only five patrols (ten sorties) were undertaken between 06:20 and 13:45. The early morning Ostend and Dieppe reconnaissances were off the deck together at 06:25, these consisting of Red Section (Slack EN612 & Lane NR) to the former location and Yellow Section (Solak EN236 & Heale EN604) to the latter. The sections returned at 07:05, respectively 07:00, with nothing to report.

At 09:05, a second Dieppe reconnaissance was launched, this time flown by Plt Off Leslie Prickett and WO George Wilson as White Section. They returned 35 minutes later, also with nothing to report. A second uneventful Ostend reconnaissance was also airborne at 11:55, consisting of Flt Lt Roy Lane and Fg Off Peter Cowell, who returned at 13:10.

Fifteen minutes before this latter patrol's return, Fg Offs Douglas Haywood (EN607) and Clive Birbeck (EN608) took off as Blue Section on a weather reconnaissance to Calais and the Somme Estuary. They flew to Calais at zero feet, and then turned south down the coast towards the estuary. As they did so, they climbed gradually to approximately 1,500 feet, and had only just passed the mouth of the river, when the Controller gave them a vector of 330° for home.

Whilst turning onto this bearing, Birbeck spotted a pair of FW190s coming straight towards them from three o'clock at the same altitude, flying line abreast approximately 75 feet apart, around 2,000 yards away. He warned Haywood, who immediately turned to face them. Birbeck adopted a different tactic, diving to sea level with the intent of coming up from below the enemy aircraft.

Birbeck's strategy had merit. He singled out one of the Focke-Wulfs and made a steep climbing turn towards it. Seeing the pilot climb with his counterpart towards Haywood, two against one, Birbeck opened his throttle and soon made a beam attack upon it with full deflection, opening at 700 yards and closing to 300, firing a full six seconds of cannon and machine gun fire.

Around this time, Haywood, in an effort to shake his attackers, accidently stalled his aircraft. He pointed the nose down to keep the speed up and avoid the wings stalling, and after a moment the Griffon kicked into life again. It was only about two seconds, estimated Haywood, but it was sufficient for the aggressors to pepper his tail with both cannon shells and machine gun bullets. Spiralling down to sea level to shake the 190's, Haywood then applied full boost and headed for Dungeness.

Birbeck's aim had been straight, and his FW190 caught fire on the port side of the fuselage, just forward of the cockpit. The aircraft turned for France, but Birbeck had no opportunity to pursue it: the other aircraft, having lost interest in Haywood, now came after him.

This pilot pursued Birbeck back up the French coast for approximately five minutes, periodically firing at him from around 600 yards range, each time missing down his port side, except for a single round, which left no more than a graze on his fuselage. Two more FW190s subsequently attempted to join the chase, but they were too far off to play any role in the combat, and gave up a short while later.

Birbeck took all sorts of evasive action, including skidding turns at sea level, and was surprised the Luftwaffe pilot was matching his 340 mph IAS. Strangely, the Luftwaffe pilot actually flew abreast of Birbeck for a few minutes, keeping himself a good 200 yards away and sizing him up. Apparently satisfied, this pilot eventually gave up, peeled away, and headed for the French coast.

Rear to front: Plt Off Leslie Prickett, Fg Off Jerzy Solak (Polish), Fg Off 'Barney' Newman RAAF, and Squadron mascot 'Perkin', Hawkinge, April-May 1943. © Herb Wagner, via Dan Johnson

Birbeck had had enough, too, and turned for England. One wonders what the Luftwaffe pilot might have thought had he known his opponent was just 19 years old?!

Haywood, meanwhile, was almost home, but just off Dungeness his aircraft began to vibrate violently and started emitting glycol. Then he began to hear a loud 'clanging' sound, too. Realising his aircraft was about to give up the ghost, he made landfall and belly-landed the limping Spitfire on Littlestone Golf Course, near New Romney, at 13:40.

Clambering safely out of the aircraft, though exhausted by the experience, Haywood found he had received a slight splinter wound in the foot and was taken to Canterbury Hospital, following initial treatment in the Station Sick Quarters. His aircraft had fared much worse, however, having sustained no less than 33 hits by machine gun and cannon shells, three of which had hit the engine.

For his part, Birbeck put down at Hawkinge at 13:45, and claimed his first victory, one destroyed FW190. He had expended 130 rounds of cannon and 400 rounds of machine gun ammunition in doing so. His claim was initially granted based on the fact that a German radio message had been intercepted stating an aircraft had been shot down. However, subsequent investigation by the RAF reduced his victory to 'Probable'.

A memo concerning Birbeck's claim from Headquarters, 11 Group, to RAF Station Hawkinge, dated 3 May 1943, states

> *Headquarters, Fighter Command regret that they cannot agree* [with] *this pilot's claim to one FW.190 destroyed as the evidence in his personal combat report is only sufficient to warrant a probable and the additional evidence referred to by you at the end of the Intelligence Form "F"*[53] *does not carry the matter any further. Therefore, the Form "F" rendered by you has been altered.*[54]
>
> *2. Please amend your and the squadron's records accordingly.*
>
> *3. Please explain to F/O. Birbeck that the rejection or stepping down of claims does not imply that the pilot's story is doubted: it simply means that the evidence is not considered sufficient.*[55]

Despite his age, and perhaps his disappointment at this decision, Birbeck was a man with promise and had much before him yet.

Returning to 27 April 1943, three personnel movements also took place today. Most notably, 25-year-old Flt Lt Richard F. Inness arrived to take over duties as OC, A Flight, but Flt Sgts Jack Stonier and Malcolm Rowe were also sent on embarkation leave.

Inness had joined the RAF on a Short Service Commission in October 1938, and served throughout the Battle of Britain with 152 Squadron. By the completion of his tour, he had accumulated significant combat experience, with 2⅓ destroyed and one damaged enemy aircraft to his credit. He was rested as a Flying Instructor with 53 OTU between February and September

Flt Lt Richard Inness was briefly posted to 41 Squadron as OC A Flight, on 27 April 1943, but departed again on 1 May 1943. © Rosemary Inness & Jennie Tocock

Fg Off Jerzy Polak was posted away from 41 Squadron on 29 April 1943 and spent the ensuing 20 months with 315 (Polish) Squadron. He claimed two destroyed Messerschmitt Me109s, one shared destroyed Arado Ar96, and one shared destroyed V1, and remained in the United Kingdom after the cessation of hostilities.
© Cowell family

1941, and returned to operations as a Flight Lieutenant with 611 Squadron, before being rested again prior to joining 41 Squadron today. His tenure with this unit, however, would only last a few days.

22-year-old Stonier had much before him as he left 41 Squadron today. He was commissioned in late September 1943, and subsequently served with the RAF's meteorological services in Cyprus, for which he was awarded an AFC in June 1945. He remained in the post-War RAF and retired in June 1955.

It is unfortunate, however, that at the time of writing [November 2011], nothing is known of Rowe's subsequent RAF career. That said, he does not appear to have been commissioned, become a Prisoner of War, or to have died on active service. On their departure, the ORB noted,

> *Two of our Sgt. Pilots – Sgt. Stonier & Sgt. Rowe* [were] *sent on embarkation leave* [today], *their target date is 5th May. Best of luck to these two lads. If they go to Malta they will probably see at least a dozen ex-41 Squadron pilots there.*[56]

Flt Lt Hugh Parry travelled to Dungeness today, where he gave a talk to local fishermen in the evening in relation to "Wings for Victory" Week[57], at a meeting hosted by the Mayor of Lydd, Alderman Gordon Paine. The following day, the Mayor wrote to Parry to thank him for his time, stating,

> *I feel I must send you a line to thank you for so kindly coming down to our meeting at Dungeness last night – it was extremely kind of you and although you must have thought it a somewhat unusual gathering – your very stirring address and appeal made a tremendous impression on us all.*
>
> *After you left, I chatted informally with the fishermen, and I am sure you would have felt that your time had been well spent if you had heard all the good things they said of you. They all had profound admiration for you and the moving address you gave and many remarked on your modesty in making no mention of your own deeds.* [...]
>
> *With many many thanks to you and wishing you the best of luck always.*[58]

Whilst Parry was away that evening, the rest of the Squadron was entertained by a snooker match between the unit and Station Headquarters in the Officers Mess. Teams were nine a side, and were captained by the respective Commanding Officers, Sqn Ldr Neil and Wg Cdr Frederick F. Barrett. SHQ beat 41 by 336 to 289 points, mainly due to Hawkinge's Fg Off Falkner beating Fg Off Polak in their round by 58 points!

LEFT Sgt Plt Walter 'Wingco' East was killed in action off Dieppe on 3 May 1943, when he was shot down by pilots of 4./JG26 during a routine shipping reconnaissance. © East family

ABOVE 21-year-old Sgt Plt Walter East is remembered today on the Runnymede Memorial. © Steve Brew

28 April 1943 – Although fine and hazy, only six patrols (12 sorties) were undertaken between 06:10 and 13:30, when the day's flying ceased. The usual morning reconnaissance flights were flown to Dieppe and Ostend, the former by Flt Lt Hone (EN234) and Flt Sgt May (EN611) from 06:10 as Blue Section, and the latter by Fg Offs Johnson (EN602) and Moffett (EN238) from 06:15 as Green.

Both sections were back on the ground at 07:05, and whilst Johnson and Moffett had seen nothing but a dredger, Hone and May had had a close shave with the Luftwaffe. On their way back from Dieppe at zero feet, they sighted four enemy aircraft ahead of them at 1,000 feet off Le Touquet. Being at a disadvantage in both numbers and altitude, the pair quickly altered course unseen, and were able to elude them.

Ten minutes before their return, Fg Offs Birbeck and Hogarth were scrambled towards Boulogne, but returned within 15 minutes with nothing to report. At 09:55, Flt Lt Hone was airborne again, on this occasion with Fg Off Davies, for a weather reconnaissance to the French coast. In a situation not dissimilar to Hone's earlier flight, they managed to avoid six enemy aircraft that had been sent up to intercept them. The pair returned to Hawkinge at 10:25, and the ORB noted with some bravado, "The enemy appear to be troubled by 41 and their new aircraft".[59] At 11:20, Fg Offs Birbeck and Hogarth were also sent on a reconnaissance patrol to the Somme Estuary, and returned 25 minutes later with nothing to report.

In the day's final operation, two of the Squadron's Spitfire XII's cooperated with six of another squadron's Spitfire IX's in an attempt to entice the Luftwaffe into the air. The Squadron ORB called it a "Bait Patrol" as Flt Lt Hone and Fg Off Birbeck clearly put themselves in some danger by making their presence known off Gris Nez, and then turned south down the coast. The Spitfire IX's lay in waiting, and although the Luftwaffe scrambled several aircraft, it appears they smelt a rat as, "after a lot of conversation was heard on the R.T., apparently all enemy aircraft were ordered to land".[60]

29 April 1943 – Early fair weather deteriorating to haze and medium cloud. It was a busy day with twice the number of sorties flown as the day before, in a total of eleven operations.

Flt Lt Parry (EN612) and Fg Off Polak (EN603) were sent on the morning's Dieppe reconnaissance as Red Section at 06:25, whilst Fg Offs Hogarth (EN235) and Davies (EN611)

carried out the Ostend reconnaissance as Blue Section five minutes later. Parry and Polak returned at 07:15 reporting a trawler and a dredger one mile off the entrance to Dieppe Harbour, but nothing else of consequence. This patrol constituted Polak's final sortie with the Squadron as he was posted away today to 315 (Polish) Squadron at Northolt. He had been with the unit some five months and was a popular man, the ORB considering his posting represented "…the loss of a friend to all."[61,62]

Hogarth and Davies saw no shipping on their patrol but on their return at 07:25 reported having encountered considerable accurate Flak. One burst exploded between their aircraft and Davies' Spitfire was hit and damaged in five places. One piece of shrapnel penetrated the hood and missed Davies' head 'by inches'; he was unhurt but shaken.

At 06:40, Sqn Ldr Tom Neil led Yellow Section of four pilots (Neil EN237, Slack EN236, Solak EN609, Prickett EN604) on the Squadron's first offensive patrol in the Spitfire XII. Apparently "expecting trouble as a result of Birbeck's success"[63], Neil led the Rodeo on a triangular path defined by the towns of Dungeness, Le Touquet, and Berck, making two full rotations of this route at 8,000 feet. Despite hopes of sighting enemy aircraft, none were seen and they returned at 07:20 with nothing to report.

At 12:15, two pilots were sent on a spotting patrol of the Dungeness area and returned at 13:30 with nothing to report. At 13:20, two pilots were sent on an ASR spotting patrol in the Channel and reported an object that appeared to be an adrift barrage balloon, floating just below the surface with only its end showing. Two more pilots were sent on a similar patrol at 14:15, but returned to report they had seen nothing. At 14:35, another Jim Crow shipping reconnaissance was flown by a pair of pilots to Dieppe; they, too, returned to report the trip uneventful.

There was then a two-hour pause in operations, before Fg Offs Clive Birbeck (EN608) and David Davies (EN231) were airborne on a special mission to see if they could sight sea mines, which were thought to have been laid over recent nights. The pair returned just 30 minutes later reporting having successfully spotted objects in the Channel around seven miles off the coast from Le Touquet, spaced around 200 yards apart. The Royal Navy was very interested in the observation and obtained a full report from the men. They were subsequently congratulated by the Chief of Dover Naval Staff "for bringing back [such] useful information".[64]

Three further patrols were dispatched in pairs shortly before 20:00 that evening: one to Dieppe, the second to Calais and Ostend and a third to an unnamed location. However, all three were uneventful and returned with little of significance to report. The last pair was down at 20:55 and this concluded the day's, and indeed the month's, flying.

May 1943 – A busy month that saw two airfield moves, a visit by Lord Trenchard, and seven new pilots joining the Squadron. One pilot was posted away, another killed in action and one of the ground crew killed in a cycling accident; there was also a change in Medical Officers. The weather was generally good and there was no flying on only three days of the month, and limited

Sketches of Fg Off Reg Hoare, Fg Off Rex Poynton, Flt Sgt Jan Rogowski (Polish), and Sgt Plt Walter East in early 1943. © Tom Slack, via Dan Johnson

or postponed operations on another three, as a result of adverse weather conditions. There was no operational flying on 22-24 May on account of the Squadron's move to Biggin Hill, limited operational flying on 27 May, and none at all on 28 May, due to their move to Friston.

1 May 1943 – Mainly cloudy, with rainy intervals that forced the usual morning reconnaissances across the Channel to be cancelled. It was therefore not until 10:15 that Flt Lt Hugh Parry and Sgt Plt Walter 'Wingco' East were airborne for the day's first of only three patrols, on this occasion to Ostend and Flushing [Vlissingen]. They returned 50 minutes later reporting no shipping but significant amounts of cloud from 800 up to 20,000 feet.

There was no more flying until 17:45, when Fg Offs Clive Birbeck and Bruce Moffett were airborne as Blue Section, and Fg Offs Rycherde Hogarth and David Davies as Green Section for reconnaissance flights to Dieppe and Ostend, respectively. Both sections returned at 18:30, with Blue reporting having sighted a dredger at Boulogne, and Green having seen three to four small barges in the canal at Gravelines and a dredger at Ostend. Both patrols were otherwise uneventful, and this concluded the day's flying.

There were, however, a number of personnel movements of note today. Most significantly, barely three days with 41 Squadron, Flt Lt Richard Inness was posted away from the unit today and sent to Biggin Hill as a Supernumerary; he had not flown a single operational flight. There is no explanation for his departure and it is not mentioned in the Squadron ORB. However, a single line at the end of the day's entries in the Station ORB states, "F/Lt. INNES [sic] has been posted supernumerary to Biggin Hill".[65] His role as OC A Flight, was taken over by Flt Lt Hugh Parry.

Sqn Ldr Neil returned from a conference at Biggin Hill during the day reporting that German wireless propaganda had stated that Fg Off Reg Hoare, lost on 1 April, was now a Prisoner of War. Plt Off Bob Boyd returned from sick leave today after three weeks away, and there was a change in Medical Officers when Flt Lt Armin, who had been with the Squadron around six months, was posted to 17 ITW at Scarborough. He was replaced by Fg Off Walter Burnett, who would remain with 41 for approximately one year, and become known as 'Doc Burnett'.

2 May 1943 – Initially cloudy with a little rain, clearing by midday to a mainly fine afternoon. The morning's Ostend reconnaissance was carried out by Flt Lt Douglas Hone and Fg Off Rycherde Hogarth from 08:35, whilst the Dieppe reconnaissance was undertaken by Fg Offs Ron Johnson and Bruce Moffett from 08:45. The former section had nothing to report owing to weather conditions and poor visibility, and the latter reported a dredger at Boulogne, a fishing boat at Dieppe, and a fishing fleet off the Somme Estuary.

After their return, fog dropped at Hawkinge, and there was no more flying until 19:35 when Flt Lt Hugh Parry (EN609) was airborne with WO George Wilson (EN612) to escort a 277 Squadron Lysander on an ASR patrol. The patrol resulted from a report by a civilian that he had seen a parachute fall into the Channel around 1½ miles off Folkestone. Locating the object four miles southeast of Dymchurch, it was soon identified as two small balloons attached to each other, one of which was trailing in the water.

Shortly thereafter, however, Parry and Wilson were scrambled to 15,000 feet to intercept three fast incoming bogies plotted 15 miles from Folkestone. Climbing quickly to this altitude, they saw absolutely nothing, and returned to base. Finding his flaps stuck up, Wilson made a premature safe landing at Manston, whilst Parry continued on to Hawkinge where he landed at 20:20. Having fixed the problem, Wilson returned to base in his aircraft at 21:50.

The final patrols of the day were reconnaissances to Dieppe at 20:45 by Fg Offs 'Barney' Newman and Peter Cowell, and to Ostend at 20:50 by Plt Off Leslie Prickett and Sgt Plt Bill Downing. Whilst no shipping movements worthy of reporting were seen on the either patrol, Prickett and Downing attempted an interception of the Luftwaffe six miles north of Dunkirk, but saw nothing. Both sections arrived back at Hawkinge in the growing darkness and were compelled to land using a flare path, "rather a test for a Spitfire XII".[66]

Sgt Plt Peter Graham served with 41 Squadron from 5 May 1943 to 1 September 1944, when he was shot down and captured. He was commissioned in December 1943 and ordained in the Church of England in May 1953. © Peter Graham

A new pilot joined the Squadron during the day: 22-year-old American Plt Off Herbert 'Wag' Wagner, the second of only three Americans to serve on the Squadron during World War II. Having enlisted in the RAFVR in Washington DC in October 1941, prior Pearl Harbour, Wagner had undergone flying training in the United States where he earned his Wings, and was commissioned in August 1942. Shipping to Glasgow on the *Queen Mary* the following month, Wagner completed OTU at Rhoose, Glamorgan, and was then retained as a staff pilot until May 1943. Wagner would remain with 41 Squadron for 13 months, and it would be his first and only operational unit.

3 May 1943 – Cold easterly winds reaching gale force in gusts, but otherwise mainly fine. The normal early morning shipping and weather reconnaissance flights to the Continental coast resumed at 06:15 this morning, with the Dieppe patrol undertaken by Flt Lt Hugh Parry (EN236) and Sgt Plt Walter East (EN612) as Red Section, and the Ostend patrol by Plt Off Leslie Prickett (EN609) and WO George Wilson (EN239) as Yellow.

There was nothing to report on the Ostend patrol, but Parry and East were intercepted by the Luftwaffe on the run to Dieppe. Flying down the French coast at zero feet, the pair turned onto a bearing of 30° when five miles west of Dieppe, and five minutes later onto a bearing of 60°. Barely had they done so, they were bounced by six FW190s from JG26 on their starboard side, at an altitude of only 500 feet. Behind them, two more enemy aircraft were also seen approaching from Dieppe.

Parry immediately turned to face the Focke-Wulfs and approached them head on, firing a short burst of cannon and machine gun at point blank range at one of them. He believed he hit the aircraft, but made no subsequent claim. He and East jostled for position with the fighters, but the 190s managed to get astern of the pair and broke them up. Three Focke-Wulfs went after Parry, and the remainder after East.

Parry jettisoned his auxiliary tank and opened up to 347 mph IAS, and was able to out-distance his opponents, which were emitting considerable boost smoke. They gave up the chase after around three minutes and Parry returned to Hawkinge at sea level at 07:10.

East was less fortunate. He was last seen by Parry about a mile to his starboard side at sea level, being fired upon from astern. He was subsequently heard over the R/T to issue a brief mayday, but he did not return and was not seen again. A German radio message was intercepted at 06:49, which sealed his fate: it stated that they had shot down a Spitfire. The claimant was Lt Walter Radener of 4./JG26, who thereby recorded his first victory, 20km west of the Somme Estuary.

OC A Flight, Flt Lt Hugh Parry, Station Commander RAF Hawkinge, Wg Cdr Frederick F. Barrett, OC 41 Squadron, Sqn Ldr 'Ginger' Neil, and Patriarch of the RAF, MRAF Viscount Trenchard GCB GCVO DSO on a visit to 41 Squadron at RAF Hawkinge on 14 May 1943. © Cowell family

Almost immediately, Sgt Plts William Downing and Stanley Biggs were despatched to search for East, followed a while later by Flt Lt Douglas Hone and Fg Off Clive Birbeck. It was, however, all in vain:

SEARCH[ED] *POSITION 30 MILES ON 190* [DEGREES] *FROM DUNGENESS FOR PILOT MISSING ON DIEPPE RECCO. WIDE SEARCH MADE ROUND POSITION GIVEN. NOTHING SEEN.*[67]

By the time of his loss, 21-year-old East had been with 41 Squadron almost eleven months. "Sgt. East will be a loss to the Squadron. He was known as the 'Wing Commander' for some obscure reason".[68] East is still missing today and is remembered on the Runnymede Memorial.

Returning to 3 May 1943, all this had transpired, and yet the day had barely begun. Following East's loss, there was a short lull in operations, but these resumed briefly at 11:45, when Fg Off David Davies and Sgt Plt William Downing were sent on a weather reconnaissance to Flushing [Vlissingen]. The weather had by now deteriorated to such an extent that the pair abandoned the patrol and returned to Hawkinge within 20 minutes.

At 13:25, another attempt was made, this time by Flt Lt Hone and Flt Sgt Stan May. On this occasion, they succeeded in getting through to the coast and returned at 14:10 with a full weather report. A final patrol was airborne at 18:05, when two pilots were sent on a spotting patrol over Deal. They returned an hour later with nothing to report, and this concluded the day's flying.

4 May 1943 – Fine, but cold and windy, with wind speeds reaching gale force at times. Nonetheless, eight patrols (18 sorties) were flown today between 06:45 and 21:05, several of which were in relation to offensive Allied bomber operations.

The day commenced with a convoy patrol by Fg Off Rycherde Hogarth and Sgt Plt 'Jackie' Fisher, who returned at 07:05 with nothing to report. This was followed by a reconnaissance patrol from Dunkirk to Ostend, which was carried out by Fg Offs Birbeck and Johnson between 10:55 and 11:35. Beside one ship of 200-300 tons seen at Dunkirk, the pair could only report being fired at by heavy Flak, albeit inaccurate, from Ostend. No further flying was undertaken until 18:35, when Sqn Ldr Neil and Fg Off 'Barney' Newman took off for an uneventful spotting patrol off Foulness; they landed again at 19:10.

As a result of Allied bombers and their crews coming down in the Channel on their return from the day's operations, the Squadron's next five patrols were all flown in support of ASR operations. Sections of pilots took off from Hawkinge at 18:40 (two), 19:25, 19:40, and 20:20, but all were uneventful. Nothing was seen, and the last pilots were on the deck again at 21:05.

5 May 1943 – Initially poor, clearing to a fine and warm day, during which seven patrols (16 sorties) were undertaken between 10:15 and 18:05. Operations commenced today with an escort to a 277 ASR Squadron Spitfire II, by Sqn Ldr Neil (EN237) and Plt Off Leslie Prickett (EN233). The search area was given as 20-30 miles south of Dungeness on a bearing of 195°, and 41's pilots maintained an altitude of 4,000 feet, whilst the ASR aircraft, flown by 277 Squadron's Sgt Plt Moir, flew at zero feet. They arrived over the area ten minutes later, but when Moir turned into low lying mist, he disappeared and they lost contact. As this could not be re-established, Neil and Prickett returned to Hawkinge alone at 10:55, with otherwise nothing to report. Moir returned safely by himself, but reported having been fired upon by Flak from Gris Nez.

A patrol to Ostend followed at 10:25, which was undertaken by Flt Lt 'Lulu' Lane and Sgt Plt Norman Heale. They sighted a fishing fleet, a dredger and a motor barge, but had little else to report on their return at 11:15. A patrol to Dieppe was undertaken by Fg Off 'Barney' Newman and WO George Wilson between 12:20 and 13:15 but they saw nothing of note and the trip was uneventful; it was a similar story on a patrol of Dungeness between 13:35 and 14:05 by Fg Off Rycherde Hogarth and Sgt Plt 'Jackie' Fisher.

However, a more interesting operation was on the cards for eight pilots just after 17:00. Briefed by the Duty Staff Commander at the Naval Operations room at Dover Castle, they were asked to re-locate the sea minefield already reported by Fg Offs Birbeck and Davies. Given an area to sweep, from seven miles west of Le Touquet to 12 miles west-northwest of the Somme Estuary, they were to be led by Birbeck and Davies as Green Section, with close cover provided at 4,000 feet by Flt Lt Hone and Fg Off Hogarth as Blue Section. They, in turn, would receive top cover from Red Section of four pilots: Sqn Ldr Neil, Flt Lt Parry, and Fg Offs Newman and Cowell. All eight men were then to be covered by six aircraft from Biggin Hill's 611 Squadron.

Flt Lt David Fearon served with 41 Squadron from 20 May 1943 to ca 23 April 1944. He retired from the RAF as a Wing Commander in May 1966. © Ron Johnson, via Dan Johnson

41 Squadron was based at RAF Biggin Hill between 21 and 28 May 1943. This photo shows, left to right, Plt Off Leslie Prickett, Flt Lt Doug Hone, and Fg Offs Ron Johnson, Bob Boyd, and Clive Birbeck at Biggin Hill during that week. © Cowell family

The octet took off at 17:10, and before long Birbeck and Davies quickly located the buoy they had previously seen near the minefield. However, searches in the area failed to find any further sign of mines. The weather was clear and water calm, but the tide slightly above low water, which may have obscured their vision. However, the assumption was that the mines had all been 'swept up', and they returned to Hawkinge between 18:00 and 18:05 reporting they had seen nothing. Likely, this is exactly what the Royal Navy wanted to hear. This concluded the day's flying.

Separately today, two Sergeant Pilots joined the Squadron, 20-year-old Peter Graham and 21 year-old Peter Wall. Little is known of the latter pilot's prior career, but Graham had joined the RAFVR in April 1941 and completed his flying training in the United States. Shipping to the U.S. in October that year, it was not until the following August that he arrived back in the United Kingdom with his Wings, and was posted to OTU at Rednal in September 1942. Much to his disappointment, however, on completion of the course, he was retained as a staff pilot and used for drogue towing until May 1943. His posting to 41 Squadron today constituted his first to an operational unit, and it is believed to have been the same case for Wall.

6 May 1943 – The day started bright, but deteriorated as it progressed to heavy rain, hail, easterly gales and low temperatures. The weather significantly hindered operations today and only six pilots were airborne on three patrols, but there were no forays across the Channel at all. They consisted of one defensive patrol of Dungeness at 08:35 and two scrambles over the Station at 12:05 and 19:30, but in each case the pilots were back on the ground within 10-20 minutes, having seen nothing worthy of reporting.

The only real cause for excitement all day was when a fire broke out at 03:00 in a small hut used by the Squadron's B Flight dispersals ground crew. The hut was destroyed, but fortunately no-one was hurt.

Later that day, another new pilot joined the Squadron in the form of 20-year-old Sgt Plt Alan Hope. He had joined the RAFVR six months after his 18th birthday and completed his initial training in the United Kingdom. In January 1942, however, Hope was sent to the United States to undertake the SFTS portion of his training, which he completed in August that year and graduated with Wings as an NCO pilot. Returning to the United Kingdom in September 1942, Hope attended (P)AFU, followed by a Flying Instructors Course. Being found unsuitable as a flying instructor, he was instead posted to 58 OTU in Grangemouth in February 1943, and arrived on 41 Squadron today for his first operational posting.

7 May 1943 – The poor weather continued to hamper operations, and although four separate patrols were airborne between 08:30 and 17:00, this constituted the final flying for four days.

The day commenced with a patrol to Dieppe by Red Section, consisting of Flt Lt Hugh Parry and Sgt Plt Norman Heale, who were off the deck at 08:30. They were followed ten minutes later by Sqn Ldr Neil, Fg Off Peter Cowell and WO George Wilson as Yellow Section and, five minutes after them, by Flt Lt Roy Lane and Plt Off Leslie Prickett as White Section. The latter five pilots were all to act as cover for Parry and Heale, who were to look for shipping at Dieppe.

Finding nothing worth reporting, however, Sqn Ldr Neil decided to undertake a patrol of Le Touquet, Berck-sur-Mer and Boulogne instead, orbiting the area at altitudes of between 5,000 and 10,000 feet. Despite their efforts, the patrol was uneventful and all the sections landed back at Hawkinge between 09:10 and 09:15.

At 09:50, Fg Off Clive Birbeck and Sgt Plt William Downing flew a reconnaissance to Ostend, passing over the town at 7,000 feet. They sighted a 600-ton tanker approximately two miles off the port, which they described as very long and narrow with no masts. They returned to base at 10:30, with nothing further to report.

Only two more patrols were airborne today, a 15-minute shipping and weather reconnaissance to Boulogne by two pilots at 13:10 and a spotting patrol off Dungeness by another pair, between 15:55 and 17:00. Both were uneventful, and this concluded the day's flying.

11 May 1943 – Following several days of poor weather that had kept the Squadron firmly on the ground, the day commenced warm and sunny, and routine patrols were recommenced.

Flt Lt Parry and Fg Off Cowell undertook the morning's reconnaissance to Ostend between 07:20 and 07:50, but saw nothing worthy of reporting. At 08:15, Fg Off Jerzy Solak and Flt Sgt Stan Biggs took off for the Dieppe patrol, exiting England over Hastings and flying mid-Channel towards Dieppe. They sighted four small vessels of an undeterminable tonnage heading south, but had little else to report on their return at 09:05.

As a subsequently planned reconnaissance to Calais and Boulogne, and a spotting patrol off North Foreland, were cancelled, the next pilots airborne were Flt Lt Roy Lane (EN603) and Fg Off Tom Slack (EN233), who were sent on spotting south of Dungeness at 12:40. At 13:00, the pair was dived upon by a section of Typhoons from a Squadron returning from an aborted bomber escort to the Belgian coast. The pilots opened up their throttles and managed to escape unharmed.

Fifteen minutes later, whilst they were still airborne, Control advised them of 'bogeys' off Deal and ordered them to intercept. No enemy aircraft were seen but Lane and Slack witnessed the German coastal batteries open up on Allied shipping off Folkestone and promptly pinpointed and reported their locations on their return to Hawkinge at 13:50.

It was several hours before the Squadron was airborne again, at which time two pilots were scrambled to Gris Nez at 18:25. A little over an hour later, two more pilots were ordered to 'scramble base'. On both occasions, however, nothing was seen. At 20:30, another pair was sent on a shipping reconnaissance to Ostend. A ship was seen at Dunkirk, but otherwise nothing of consequence.

The final operation of the day was, however, some cause for excitement, when Sqn Ldr Neil (EN237) and Sgt Plt 'Jackie' Fisher (EN602) were ordered to 'scramble base' at 20:40 on the report of enemy aircraft five miles off Hastings. These were sighted two miles off and chased across the Channel, but could not be engaged. "As the Huns got away, the C.O. and Fisher carried out a shipping recco to Boulogne but nothing was seen"[69], and the pair returned to Hawkinge at 21:15.

12 May 1943 – A cloudy day, improving later, which delayed the usual early start to the day's operations. Fg Offs 'Daibach' Davies and Bob Boyd were scrambled over the base at 09:30 but this amounted to nothing and it was not until after midday that the first reconnaissance was airborne across the Channel.

Flt Lt Douglas Hone (EN234) and Sgt Plt Douglas Fisher (EN238) were airborne at 12:30 for the Ostend reconnaissance, but Fisher was compelled to return early with engine trouble, putting down at Hawkinge again at 12:55. Hone continued on to Ostend and returned at 13:10 reporting only that the fishing fleet was out in rough seas.

Two patrols from Dungeness to Beachy Head ensued in sections of two between 14:25 and 15:35, and from 15:25 to 16:15, but both were uneventful. There was then no more flying until just after 18:00 when reconnaissances of Boulogne and Dunkirk-Ostend were launched. Flt Lt Lane and Fg Off Slack were sent on the former of the two at 18:05 and sighted a ship of 900-1,000 tons with steam up making for Boulogne Harbour. When Control warned them that four enemy aircraft were waiting for them at Calais, they avoided the area and returned at 18:50 with nothing further to report.

Fg Off Solak and Plt Off Prickett were sent on the Dunkirk-Ostend reconnaissance at the same time as Lane and Slack and saw barges inland from Ostend, and a barge at Nieuport, but nothing at all at Dunkirk. They also returned at 18:50.

Slack and Lane were airborne again at 20:10, with the intention of relocating the ship they had seen earlier in the afternoon making for Boulogne Harbour. It was to be pinpointed for a bombing attack but, to their disappointment, the ship was nowhere to be seen. Initially tempted to hunt for it, Control warned them of 14 enemy aircraft in the area, which were acting strangely. Instead of attacking the two Spitfires, however, "they were being vectored away from our patrol. Strange. They probably thought we were trying to intercept."[70] The pair decided to keep their distance anyway, and returned home at 20:45.

Whilst they were absent, however, four aircraft were scrambled to Dungeness on the report of enemy aircraft were approaching Ramsgate (Neil EN237, Wilson EN236, Parry EN239, Prickett EN604). As the quartet reached Deal, the enemy aircraft were reported to be now four miles off Ramsgate. They approached at 1,000 feet but no interception was made and it was later revealed that they were flying a few thousand feet higher. The enemy aircraft were not sighted, and the ORB bemoans the fact that "control gave the wrong height of the Huns"[71], the pilots upset, perhaps, by the danger that information had potentially put them in.

They returned to base at 21:15, but as they did so, Red Section (Parry and Prickett) were bounced by two Typhoons. This was the second such occurrence in two days but fortunately they were recognised as friendly before being fired upon. This concluded the day's flying.

13 May 1943 – Fine and warm with excellent visibility, which resulted in an extremely busy day, during which 42 operational sorties were flown in 22 patrols between 06:05 and 22:10.

The morning started early following the report of a bomber having come down in the Channel around 35 miles southeast of North Foreland. An ASR Walrus from 277 Squadron was airborne from 06:00 and five successive sections of Spitfires were sent to escort it between 06:05 and 09:35. The last pair was, however, recalled after only ten minutes in the air as there was no sign of a dinghy anywhere.

An uneventful reconnaissance to Dieppe was undertaken by Flt Lt Parry and Plt Off Prickett between 08:00 and 08:55, and this was followed by two equally uneventful spotting patrols of the Hawkinge-Dungeness areas at 11:40 and 12:35.

A 277 Squadron Walrus resumed the ASR search during the afternoon for the same bomber reported in the Channel southeast of North Foreland that morning, and was escorted by sections of 41 Squadron's pilots from 14:20, 16:45, 17:15, 17:55, 18:05, and 18:45. Unfortunately, however, nothing was seen on any of these operations.

A similar patrol was sent to look for a bomber crew believed to be east of Manston, at 16:40, and another to the Hastings area at 17:35, but they, too, were unfruitful. The day concluded

Flt Lt Donald H. Smith RAAF flew with 41 Squadron from 23 May 1943 to 2 May 1944, serving as OC A Flight from 25 September 1943 until his departure, when he was given his own command. During that time he claimed one destroyed and one damaged FW190, and ended the War as a Wing Commander. © Ron Johnson, via Dan Johnson

with reconnaissances to Ostend and Dieppe, the former at 19:55 and the latter at 21:25. Fg Offs Hogarth and Boyd returned from the Ostend patrol at 20:40, reporting only a dredger at Calais, whilst Fg Off Davies and Flt Sgt May returned from their Dieppe sorties at 22:10, reporting having seen four E Boats leaving the harbour, but little else of consequence.

14 May 1943 – A fine and very warm day, and the usual Ostend and Dieppe reconnaissances were airborne between 07:30 and 07:35. Except for good weather on both sides of the Channel, nothing else was seen that was considered worthy of reporting. At 10:55, Fg Offs Bruce Moffett and David Davies were scrambled over the base on the report of enemy aircraft in the area. They returned an hour later, also with nothing to report, having seen no sign of enemy aircraft.

At 11:00, Sgt Plt Alan Hope took off for a non-operational flight, but hit a ridge on the runway just before becoming airborne, and on climbing found he could not raise the undercarriage. The selector lever would not move from the 'Down' position, but the indicator lights in the cockpit suggested his wheels were not locked. Unable to establish what was correct by himself, another pilot was sent up to assist and from his observation considered the wheels were indeed locked down. Hope therefore brought his aircraft in for a landing, but had only run 200 yards down the strip when the starboard oleo leg collapsed. He was not hurt, but the aircraft sustained Cat. B damage.[72]

A section was airborne at 12:35 for a spotting patrol off Dover but the trip was uneventful. This was followed by an ASR patrol at 13:25 by Flt Lt Hugh Parry (MB802) and Fg Off Peter Cowell. They aborted after just ten minutes as Parry's R/T system was u/s, and were replaced in the air at 13:40 by Fg Off Jerzy Solak and Plt Off Herb Wagner. The latter pair returned at 14:25 with nothing to report, and this concluded flying until after dinner, as the Squadron was preparing to host a VIP.

A Visit from Lord Trenchard

At 15:00, the patriarch of the RAF, MRAF Viscount Trenchard GCB GCVO DSO visited RAF Hawkinge, landing in a Lockheed 12 Electra passenger aircraft. He toured the station accompanied by Wg Cdr Barrett and Sqn Ldr Neil, and took time to chat with the pilots at dispersals.

> Lord Trenchard, the founder and father of the RAF, came to my flight and we sat around him and chatted for about half an hour. Marvellous luck.[73]

Trenchard stayed for tea in the Officers Mess and departed again by air at 17:30.

Belgian Fg Off Roger 'Chat' Duchateau served with 41 Squadron from 25 May 1943 to 9 June 1943 and from 3August1943 to 24 November 1943. He commanded 350 Squadron of the Belgian Air Force 1947-1948 and retired from the BAF in 1950. © Terry Spencer, via Cara and Raina Spencer

After that, it was back to business again and three more reconnaissances were flown across the Channel before the day concluded. The first two were off simultaneously at 19:20, with Fg Off Solak and Plt Off Wagner heading to Dieppe and the Somme Estuary as Yellow Section, and Fg Off Newman and WO Wilson flying to Ostend as White Section. The former pair returned at 20:00 with nothing to report but clear skies. The latter returned five minutes before them, having turned back between Dunkirk and Ostend, as Wilson's aircraft, EN609, was having engine trouble.

The final section was airborne at 21:25, when Fg Off Peter Cowell and Plt Off Leslie Prickett were sent on a shipping reconnaissance to the Calais and Boulogne areas. The uneventful patrol was completed without trouble, but on preparing to land at Hawkinge again, Plt Off Prickett found he could not lower MB802's undercarriage. However, it ended well:

> The Engineer Officer F/O R. H. Whipp was rushed to the Flying Control room and gave him advice over R/T and eventually after Prickett had turned the machine on its back the wheels came down and he landed safely at 22:15. We had visions of a belly landing taking place.[74]

Thus ended the day's flying.

Separately, another new pilot joined the Squadron today, who was someone quite special: he was a Prince and the great-great-grandson of Catherine the Great! Fg Off Prince Emanuel Vladimirovitch Galitzine, of Russian royal descent had fled the Stalinist State in the wake of the October Revolution and emigrated to the United Kingdom with his parents.

Galitzine initially joined the RAFVR as a 20-year-old on a Short Service Commission in December 1938. However, still bitter about his family's exile, he left the Air Force and travelled to Helsinki in March 1940 to join the Finnish Air Force, then in a bitter struggle with the Soviets. This he did until February 1941, when he returned to the United Kingdom and re-joined the RAFVR.

Following flying training, he was re-commissioned into the RAFVR in September and posted to his first operational unit, 504 Squadron two months later. Galitzine subsequently served with 222 and 611 Squadrons, and was with 124 Squadron until posted to 41 Squadron today. He would remain with the unit until December.

15 May 1943 – Fine weather with a chilly wind made for another busy day upon which 26 sorties were flown in 13 patrols between 06:40 and 22:25. It was, nonetheless, a very routine day and the ORB sums the Squadron's entire activity up in just three lines, concluding that there was "nothing of importance to report".[75]

The morning's Ostend patrol was flown between 06:40 and 07:05, and a reconnaissance to Dieppe and Fécamp from 08:45 to 09:50. Both were uneventful. Flt Lt Parry and Fg Off Solak flew out to rendezvous with a lone bomber at 10:25 and escorted it home, and were back on the ground at 10:50. Fifty-five minutes later Solak was airborne again, this time in unison with Fg Off Cowell, for a spotting patrol southeast of Dungeness. They landed again at 12:45 with nothing to report.

The next operation saw Fg Off Tom Slack and Plt Off Herb Wagner scrambled at 12:50. Five minutes after their departure, Fg Off David Davies and Flt Sgt Stan May were sent on a weather reconnaissance of the Fécamp area. The former pair returned at 13:25 having seen nothing, and the latter at 13:50 reporting the trip uneventful.

It was another hour before the next section was airborne, when two pilots undertook a spotting patrol along the coast from Beachy Head to Hastings. Four similar patrols followed at 15:50, 16:55 (two) and 17:50, but all returned with nothing to report. The last of these was down again at 19:00.

After dinner, a reconnaissance was flown to Dieppe by Sgt Plt William Downing and Flt Sgt Stan May. They were airborne between 20:55 and 21:40, and returned to report seeing a convoy of 25 ships, 'presumably ours', moving up the Channel. The day concluded with a spotting patrol of Dungeness between 21:35 and 22:25, which was also reported uneventful.

16 May 1943 – Fine and warm, but a day considered "very quiet… just the usual routine patrols and reconnaissances plus a few scrambles when enemy aircraft came too near".[76] Nonetheless, 28 sorties were flown in 14 patrols between 06:55 and 21:40.

The day commenced with a scramble by four pilots, but they returned at 07:15 having seen nothing. A weather and shipping reconnaissance of Dieppe was then airborne at 07:05, flown by Fg Offs Hogarth and Boyd, who returned at 08:00 with nothing to report. Two uneventful convoy patrols were flown off North Foreland 07:50-08:30 and 08:05-09:15, which were followed by a weather and shipping reconnaissance of the Somme Estuary between 10:55 and 11:25. Five small vessels of no consequence were seen, but there was otherwise nothing to report.

At 11:55, Fg Offs Hogarth and Davies were scrambled to patrol the base area at 10,000 feet to intercept incoming plots, however nothing was seen and the pair landed 65 minutes later. During

The Officers Mess at RAF Friston, to where the Squadron moved on 28 May 1943. Although their stay would last less than a month, this would be the first of three occasions during the War that they would call this airfield home. © Cowell family

The A Flight dispersal area at RAF Friston between 28 May 1943 and 21 June 1943. © Herb Wagner, via Dan Johnson

the afternoon, three spotting patrols were undertaken ten miles south of Beachy Head. These took place at 15:30, 17:25, and 18:10, but all were uneventful.

The evening kept the men occupied on scrambles, with four aircraft airborne between 19:00 and 19:55, and another four at 21:20. Of the latter quartet, two pilots were recalled almost immediately and were back on the ground within ten minutes. The other pair, Fg Off 'Barney' Newman (EN236) and Plt Off Herb Wagner (EN603), was vectored to incoming plots off the coast from Rye. However, the "E/A turned back [and were] not seen by Yellow Section".[77] They were back at Hawkinge again at 21:40, and this concluded the day's flying.

The Squadron did not, however, have a peaceful night's sleep. The air raid siren sounded at midnight, and the local coastal guns put up a noisy barrage against inbound enemy bombers. This occurred again in the early hours of the following morning, but they were not the target on either occasion; the bombers were passing over towards targets in the London area instead.

17 May 1943 – Another fine and warm day, which entailed much less flying than the past few days, as there was still "no sign of the Huns".[78] The Squadron only undertook 13 sorties on seven patrols, but one ended less than gloriously for one pilot.

The first operation of the day was airborne at 06:35 when Flt Lt Hugh Parry (MB802) and Sgt Plt Norman Heale (EN229) were scrambled to patrol the base area. Nothing was seen and the pair returned to base at 07:30. However, whilst Parry made a good landing, Heale landed with his airspeed too high and overshot the runway. The accident wrote off the machine, but he was fortunately not injured.

The verdict was scathing and the Air Accident Card records "Pilot through sheer stupidity failed to go round again" and recommended an "example be made of this man".[79] The AOC concurred, recommending severe disciplinary action and that Heale's logbook be endorsed 'Carelessness'. No disciplinary action is recorded, however, this is the last occasion upon which Heale is mentioned in the Squadron ORB; he does not appear to have flown again operationally with the unit. By the time of his accident, he had logged at total of 291 flying hours, of which 11 were on Spitfires.

Perhaps showing some understanding for Heale's plight, the Squadron ORB commented on the difficulty of landing at Hawkinge, noting, "These Spitfire XII's need to be put down directly the aerodrome is reached, otherwise they run too far."[80]

Heale is known to have joined 130 Squadron in August 1943, and was commissioned in May 1944. He was shot down and wounded in action in early March 1945 and spent the rest of the War as a Prisoner of War. Heale remained in the RAF after his repatriation and was granted a Short Service Commission in October 1947 and posted to 72 Squadron flying Vampires. Awarded a KCVSA in 1949, he was promoted to Squadron Leader in 1955 and retired from the RAF in August 1971.

Returning now to 17 May 1943, the day had barely begun when Heale had had his flying accident. During the morning, two spotting patrols were undertaken ten miles south of Brighton, one at 10:20, constituting Prince Galitzine's first operational sortie with the Squadron (in EN604), and the other at 11:05. Both sections returned with nothing to report.

Whilst they were away, Fg Off David Davies was scrambled on reports of an incoming plot. Airborne at 11:35, he was back on the ground again within ten minutes having seen nothing. There was then no more operational flying until after dinner that evening.

From 19:15, three successive, but slightly overlapping patrols of the Dungeness area were undertaken. The first was back at 20:25, by which time the second had been airborne for 20 minutes. The second landed at 21:20, fifteen minutes after the third took off, and the third and last was back home at 22:00, thereby ending the day's flying.

18 May 1943 – Continued fine and warm weather, but little flying activity. Only 12 sorties were flown all day in six patrols, but the day ended in tragedy, marred by the accidental death of one of the Squadron's ground crew.

The day began with a scramble at 07:05, but it proved uneventful despite the section being airborne a full hour. An Air-Sea Rescue escort was undertaken between 10:15 and 11:15, but it was not until 14:40 that the next section was airborne to conduct a spotting patrol of the Dungeness area. Both sections returned with nothing to report.

At 19:20, Flt Lt Parry and Plt Off Prickett were scrambled to Dungeness at 5,000 feet, but nothing was seen, and the flying day ended with uneventful reconnaissances to Dieppe and Ostend between 21:15 and 21:55.

A Tragic Accident

At 20:30 that evening, A Flight's 549592 Cpl Wilfred Murrin was cycling downhill near Folkestone when the lighting dynamo attached to the front forks of the bicycle became loose and jammed the front wheel. The sudden stop threw Murrin over the handle bars and he hit the ground hard, fracturing his skull.

He was admitted to Royal Victoria Hospital in Folkestone, but died of his injuries at 22:30. He was subsequently buried in St. Bartholomew's Churchyard Extension, in Bow, Devon. The ORB eulogised, "The Squadron will miss him very much as he was an excellent N.C.O. and an enthusiastic workman".[81]

The Squadron collected money for his widow, and the Adjutant, Fg Off Harry Smith, wrote her a letter, offering the Squadron's condolences. In early July, Mrs Murrin responded to his note, penning,

> *Please accept my most sincere and grateful thanks for the Money Order for £19.3.0. and cheque for £5, which I received this morning.*
>
> *Your kind words have greatly touched me. It is a great comfort to me to know that my dear husband was held in such high regard.*
>
> *I shall use the Squadron's most generous gift for the erection of a headstone on my husband's grave, and shall arrange for the stone to bear the name of the Squadron.*
>
> *I should be grateful if you will kindly convey my heartfelt thanks to the members of the Squadron who have shown me such sympathy and generosity in my overwhelming sorrow.*
>
> *May God bless you all.*[82]

19 May 1943 – Fine and very warm weather saw the Squadron on routine flying again, with nine patrols (18 sorties) flown between 05:15 and 22:30.

The day's flying commenced with a patrol to the south of Dungeness by Flt Lt Parry and Plt Off Prickett, who returned at 06:25 with nothing to report. A weather and shipping reconnaissance to Ostend followed at 07:00, flown by Fg Off Jerzy Solak and WO George Wilson. They returned at the conclusion of an uneventful patrol at 07:40 and there was no further flying until 11:10.

Between this time and 19:35, five sections undertook spotting and ASR patrols between Dungeness and South Foreland, but all returned with nothing to report. In the late evening, a shipping reconnaissance was sent to Ostend and Flushing. Fg Offs Moffett and Boyd were airborne at 21:25 and returned at 22:15 reporting four small craft and one ship at Zeebrugge. A final section was airborne at 21:45 on an uneventful convoy patrol and returned at 22:30 with nothing to report.

During the evening, a dance and cabaret were held at the Leas Cliff Hall at Folkestone in aid of Wings for Victory week, attended by the Station Commander and a number of Officers and men. The cabaret was reported to be 'first class' and a significant amount of money was raised, bringing the Station total to £2,888 thus far.

20 May 1943 – Continuing fine and very warm weather, which resulted in a busy, though again uneventful, day of flying for the Squadron. They flew 12 patrols (24 sorties) between 09:10 and 22:25, consisting of three spotting patrols off Deal, three patrols of the Dungeness area, two weather and shipping reconnaissances to the Somme area, and Dunkirk-Cap Gris Nez, three scrambles, and, concluding the day's flying, a weather reconnaissance of Calais and Boulogne. Every patrol returned with nothing to report.

The day's main focus, however, came after 16:30 when news was received that the Squadron was to move to Biggin Hill the very next day.

> *This was very short notice and at once the whole Squadron turned to packing equipment. A tremendous amount of work was completed by the ground crews and they worked until midnight.*[83]

In the midst of it all, a new pilot, 23-year-old Flt Lt David Fearon, arrived at Hawkinge on posting to 41 Squadron. Having been granted a Short Service Commission in the RAF in December 1938, Fearon had previously logged considerable flying time with 64 Squadron – some 2,188 hours – but had only recorded a total of 75 minutes operational flying. Though already a Flight Lieutenant, 41 Squadron effectively represented his first operational unit. He was destined to remain with the unit for a good 12 months.

The Squadron also received a visitor today, when Captain Malta Stepp USAAF, who had served with the unit from May to September of the previous year, flew into Hawkinge in a Thunderbolt. He was on his return from an offensive operation over France.

21 May 1943 – Fine and warm with thick haze up to 4,000 feet. Despite the continued packing, the Squadron still undertook their usual morning patrols, which commenced with a weather and shipping reconnaissance to Calais and Boulogne at 08:25 by Fg Off Jerzy Solak and Plt Off Leslie Prickett. They returned 25 minutes later with nothing to report.

At 09:50, a patrol of Dungeness was undertaken by another section, followed by a weather reconnaissance to Gris Nez and Le Touquet at 10:15, and finally a similar patrol to Ostend at 10:40. All returned within five minutes of each other, the second section down at 10:55 and the first at 11:00, both with nothing to report, and the third at 11:05, forced home early by unsuitable weather conditions in the Ostend area. This concluded the day's flying and, as a result of the pending move to Biggin Hill, was also the last operational flying for another three days.

Ten minutes after the last section's return, 91 Squadron landed at Hawkinge now equipped with Spitfire XIIs, thereby becoming the second and only other unit besides 41 Squadron to use

A post-operation debrief at RAF Friston in May-June 1943; left to right: Sqn Ldr Tom 'Ginger' Neil DFC, Flt Lt Lord Gisborough (IO), Flt Sgt Stan May RAAF, Fg Off Tom Slack, Plt Off Leslie Prickett, Flt Lt Hugh Parry, and Fg Off Clive Birbeck (behind Parry). © Cowell family

Another image of the same post-operation debrief at RAF Friston in May-June 1943; left to right: Sqn Ldr Tom 'Ginger' Neil DFC, Plt Off Leslie Prickett, and Flt Lt Hugh Parry. Flt Sgt Stan May RAAF and Fg Off Ross Harding can be seen in the background. © Cowell family

Left to right; Flt Lt Hugh Parry, Fg Off Herb Wagner (USA), Plt Off Leslie Prickett and Sqn Ldr Tom 'Ginger' Neil at RAF Friston, ca May-June 1943. © Herb Wagner, via Dan Johnson

this Mark operationally. They were back at Hawkinge after to training up on their new aircraft, to relieve 41 Squadron and take over their old Jim Crow duties again.

Whilst 91 Squadron settled back in, 41 Squadron's pilots maintained readiness, and the ground crews continued transporting equipment to Folkestone Junction Railway Station, where it was packed into a total of nine goods wagons. Packing of the train was completed at 15:00 and the designated rail party left Hawkinge to entrain at Folkestone for Bromley South Railway Station.

The Squadron's pilots were airborne in their Spitfires at 17:15, and were closely followed by two Handley Page Harrow transports with thirty ground crew and essential servicing equipment. They arrived at Biggin without incident.

The rest of the Squadron was still some distance away as the pilots landed, and did not arrive at Bromley until 19:00. They were immediately taken to Biggin Hill to have dinner, and then returned to the railway station to start unpacking. Activity continued all night and everything was at Biggin Hill by 04:00 the following morning.

Biggin Hill

Situated on a plateau atop the North Downs, RAF Biggin Hill had been established during World War I, and was used for early wireless experiments. Between the Wars, the Station hosted a number of units in addition to regular squadrons, thereunder the Instrument Design Establishment, the Army School of Anti-Aircraft Defence and the Searchlight Experimental Establishment and the Night Flying Flight.

New buildings were added between 1929 and 1932, after which the Anti-Aircraft Co-operation Flight was formed there, and the Station was opened to the public every Empire Day during the 1930s for displays of aircraft and aerobatics.

Now a part of the London air defences, the Station grew in importance and was therefore constantly in action after the outbreak of the World War II. A Biggin Hill-based squadron claimed its first victory early in the War, bringing down a Do17 bomber just two months after the declaration of War.

The Station was in constant action throughout Dunkirk and the Battle of Britain, and was attacked by the Luftwaffe no less than 12 times between August 1940 and January 1941. Some of these attacks caused considerable damage and resulted in a significant number of fatalities. Despite these attacks, Biggin Hill remained operational throughout the period. Perfectly positioned for August 1942's Dieppe attack, Operation *Jubilee*, Biggin Hill continued to be involved in the mounting number of offensive operations across the Channel.

RAF Biggin Hill became the main station in its sector, and maintained satellites at Gravesend, Hawkinge, Lympne and West Malling, three of which 41 Squadron was based at during the War. This would, however, be the Squadron's first and only posting during the War to Biggin Hill itself, but it only lasted a few days.[84]

As Biggin was already home to 341 (French) and 611 Squadron, 41 was allocated dispersals and offices some distance from the Mess. Consequently, the pilots spent a lot of time on bicycles at meal times, but the ride was considered "very pleasant on fine days".[85] The Wing Commander Flying was New Zealander Alan Deere, who was awarded the DSO two days after 41's arrival.

The Squadron's OC A Flight, Flt Lt Hugh Parry, later recalled his time at Biggin Hill…

I suppose [it was] the No. 1 station in the metropolitan sector for the defence of London. Very comfortable indeed and the only station that permitted ladies in the ante-room. The Chief Intelligence Officer was the owner/boss/manager of the Windmill Club ('we never close') and I guess he was responsible for the girls coming there! They were pretty smart pieces of pulchritude and much admired. Several married pilots from Biggin Hill.[86]

Sgt Plt Peter Graham had less complimentary memories, writing many years later,

I cannot for the life of me think why we were sent to Biggin Hill, unless perhaps it was so that some bigwigs could assess our competence. Anyway we only stayed there for a week, during which we did no operational flying. Indeed the only time I went up was to take part in some formation flying practice.[87]

23 May 1943 – Some flight formation practice took place during the day, but otherwise the ORB had nothing of consequence to report. The only other event of the day was the arrival of 27-year-old Flt Lt Donald H. Smith RAAF on his first posting in over ten months following recuperation from wounds received in combat over Malta. Smith was destined to spend almost a year with 41 Squadron and would play a significant role, becoming OC A Flight, in late September 1943.[88]

Squadron Adjutant, Fg Off Harry Smith, left, and the Medical Officer, Fg Off Walter 'Jock' Burnett at Hawkinge, May 1943. © Cowell family

Fg Off Tom Slack, Fg Off Peter Cowell, Squadron mascot 'Perkin', and Fg Off 'Barney' Newman RAAF, at Hawkinge April-May 1943. © Cowell family

24 May 1943 – The Squadron was now ready to fly, but heavy rain kept the pilots on the ground and they were released at lunchtime. A number of men therefore took the opportunity to travel into London.

25 May 1943 – The Squadron was placed at readiness today, and finally took to the air when six pilots were scrambled on report of 14+ enemy aircraft off Brighton. Led by OC B Flight, Flt Lt Douglas Hone, they were airborne at 12:30 and headed to the area, only to find the bogies had not made landfall and instead turned back for France. They returned to Biggin between 13:20 and 13:25 with nothing to report, and this concluded the day's operational flying. Another new pilot joined the Squadron today in the form of 28-year-old Belgian Flying Officer, Roger A. J. 'Chat' Duchateau.[89]

26 May 1943 – Whilst the rest of the Biggin Hill Wing operated over France on an uneventful Rodeo today, 41 Squadron remained at home and only undertook an early morning patrol of Dungeness. Four pilots were airborne at 06:50 as Blue and Green Sections, led by Flt Lt Douglas Hone. They returned again at 08:05 with nothing to report, and this concluded the day's operational flying.

Barely five days at Biggin Hill, there were already "definite signs of another move"[90] for the Squadron. They had not been used on any of the Wing's cross-Channel operations yet and the men were beginning to wonder what they were doing here.

27 May 1943 – At last, today, the Squadron was allocated its first operation over France, an offensive Rhubarb to Ault, Beauchamps and Tocqueville-sur-Eu. Four pilots were airborne at 12:50 as Blue (Birbeck EN608 & Fisher EN602) and Red Sections (Lane EN603 & Slack EN622) and made their way across the Channel in anticipation. However, the weather, which had not been ideal at the outset, deteriorated further and the quartet was forced to abandon the operation and return home.

Sgt Plt Bill Downing with his wife Joan on his wedding day, 8 June 1943, one day after leaving 41 Squadron. He embarked for Malta two weeks later and was shot down and captured on 19 July 1943. © Downing family

They put down at Biggin again at 13:20, and this concluded the Squadron's operational flying that day. With the exception of a few defensive patrols, all other Wing operations were also cancelled.

However, it was now official; the Squadron was moving again, on this occasion to Friston, near Eastbourne, "presumably to protect the coastal towns against tip and run raiders".[91] They presumed correctly. As the move was scheduled for the following day, packing was hastily undertaken, although it cannot have been pleasant in the inclement weather. The trek back to Bromley South Railway Station with all the equipment began in earnest, and would continue until shortly before midday on 28 May.

28 May 1943 – No operational flying was undertaken today, whilst the Squadron moved from Biggin Hill to Friston. An Advance Party left for the new airfield at 10:45, and freight wagons at Bromley South were filled and closed by 11:30. The pilots took off in their Spitfires at 12:50, and the Rail Party departed Bromley South at 14:35. The latter party arrived at Friston at 17:05, when unpacking commenced, and continued until midnight.

However, the move was marred by a flying accident, when Flt Sgt Stan Biggs made a bad landing at Friston in EN232. The airscrew touched the ground and the aircraft crashed and was written off. By this time, Biggs had logged a total of 286 flying hours, of which 23 were on Spitfires, and his logbook was endorsed 'carelessness' and disciplinary action was recommended. Both the Station Commander and AOC concurred. Biggs undertook no further operational flying with the Squadron and was posted away on 7 June.[92]

Friston

A small Wartime fighter satellite airfield of RAF Kenley, Friston was situated above the Seven Sisters cliffs, between Seaford and Eastbourne, and boasted a 5,020-foot southwest-northeast grass strip. Its location made it a perfect emergency landing ground, which was used by all manner of damaged aircraft on their return from operations over the Channel and Continent. However, its obvious position also drew significant unwanted attention from the Luftwaffe, and it remained a very busy station throughout the War.

The Friston ORB recorded the unit's arrival on 28 May 1943,

> No. 41 Squadron moved from R.A.F. BIGGIN HILL to R.A.F. FRISTON with 23 Officers, 22 Senior N.C.O.'s, 102 airmen (20 SPITFIRES, MK.12's) by rail and air. S/L. T. F. NEIL, Officer Commanding.[93]

NCO pilot Peter Graham recalled, "…on 28 May, we were transferred to Friston, a wartime fighter station without runways or any permanent accommodation. I loved this place, which was perched on the edge of the cliffs just to the west of Beachy Head."[94] OC, A Flight, Flt Lt Hugh

Parry, also remembered that the Officers were "billeted in Friston Village at a fairly substantial house – very comfortable for the short stay there."⁹⁵

Although the Squadron's stay at Friston would only last less than a month, it would be the first of three occasions during the War that they would call this airfield home.

29 May 1943 – Fine weather meant an early start for the Squadron today, and B Flight was placed at 'cockpit readiness' from 04:20. Fg Offs Birbeck and Davies flew a patrol south of Beachy Head between 05:55 and 06:20, and Fg Off Boyd and Sgt Plt Wall patrolled the same area from 06:00 to 07:15, but nothing was seen by either party.

Whilst they were patrolling, Plt Off Johnson and Sgt Plt Graham were ordered to 'scramble base'. Airborne at 06:15, they returned at 07:15, with nothing to report. Another scramble took place at 13:35, when Flt Lt Parry and Plt Off Wagner were sent south of Beachy Head. However, they also saw nothing, and landed again at 14:35 with nothing to report.

This concluded the day's operational flying, but the Friston ORB indicates the entire Squadron was airborne during the afternoon, likely on non-operational practice flying.

30 May 1943 – Despite fine and hot weather, the Squadron undertook very little operational flying all day, and only four pilots were airborne on two operational patrols. In the first of these, Flt Lt 'Lulu' Lane and Fg Off 'George' Solak were sent on a weather reconnaissance of the Le Havre and Cherbourg areas at 13:40. They returned 30 minutes later, reporting the trip uneventful. The second operation was not until after dinner when Fg Offs 'Johnnie' Johnson and 'Daibach' Davies were scrambled. They were in the air at 19:15, but already back on the ground within 20 minutes having seen nothing. This concluded the day's operational flying.

31 May 1943 – Another day of little activity, that consisted of just two scrambles and a single patrol. The first scramble took place at 09:35, but the pilots, Flt Lt Hugh Parry and Plt Off Herb Wagner, were back in just ten minutes, having seen nothing.

There was no further operational flying until 14:00 when Flt Sgt Stan May and Sgt Plt Peter Graham undertook an uneventful hour-and-twenty-minute patrol south of Brighton. At 15:30, five minutes after May and Graham's return, the day's second scramble was airborne, when Fg Off David Davies and Sgt Plt Peter Wall took off for the Brighton area. They returned 50 minutes later with nothing to report. This concluded the day's operational flying.

The compiler of the Squadron ORB paused to reflect on the past year on this last day of May 1943, and recorded for posterity,

> *The Squadron are now beginning to settle down again. It is worthy of note that since leaving Merston in June 1942 we have been to the following Stations:- Martlesham, Hawkinge, Debden, Longtown, Llanbedr, Tangmere, Eglinton, Tangmere again, High Ercall, Hawkinge, Biggin Hill and Friston. All these moves have not been for the whole Squadron, but in each case all aircraft have been sent and approximately half of the ground crews. It is now hoped that we are able to stay at Friston for a few months as it is a delightful place. The airfield is not too good, grass runways and rather bumpy and incidentally the short runway is only 950 yards in length with a sheer drop at the southern end. During fine weather the airfield and conditions are fair, but with the slightest rain the ground becomes very sticky as the surface is covered with about 6 inches of clay. The dispersals have no permanent buildings and the pilots and crews are using large marquees, but nevertheless the surroundings are pleasant and generally the Squadron like the place.*⁹⁶

June 1943 – On nine days of the month – 8, 18, 21-25, 27 and 30 June – no operational flying was undertaken as a result of a number of factors, including weather and the Squadron's move to Westhampnett. Most other days were long and busy, and it would prove to be an intensive month of flying, with no less than 524 sorties recorded in the ORB, nearly all in sections of two.

During the first three weeks of May, the Squadron flew a monotonous litany of 248 patrols and scrambles, in which the Luftwaffe was sighted just three times and engaged once. However, their role changed completely in the last week of the month, when they were joined by 91 Squadron at RAF Westhampnett to become a Spitfire XII Wing, and were deployed on 'Ramrod' (bomber escort) operations. This then became their chief duty for the ensuing nine months.

1 June 1943 – Fair weather. After days of little flying, the Squadron stepped up their activity from the beginning of the month in response to the Luftwaffe's 'tip and run' raids on the south and south-eastern English coast. This resulted in two to four pilots sitting in their cockpits in readiness for immediate take-off, should they be called upon. The ORB noted that this tactic "…is very tiring but it is hoped to knock off minutes on Scrambles".[97] During the day, several scrambles took place, as did standing patrols of the wider area, but the Luftwaffe was not seen.

Separately, another new pilot joined the Squadron today, 28-year-old Plt Off Maurice 'Momo' Balasse, the second Belgian to be posted to the unit in the space of a week.[98]

2 June 1943 – Slight wind with low cloud, and a day of little action. Operational flying consisted of ten patrols and scrambles, totalling 20 sorties, between 07:05 and 22:40, all of which were uneventful. The ORB summarises the entire day's activity in just two brief sentences: "A small number of Scrambles but no enemy aircraft seen. Many patrols off Beachy Head."[99]

3 June 1943 – Low cloud with slight rain during the morning limited operations to 18 patrols and scrambles. "Another day similar to yesterday"[100], begins the day's entry in the ORB, which totals three brief sentences. It concludes with "Nothing seen".[101]

4 June 1943 – Overcast but otherwise fair weather resulted in one of the Squadron's busiest days in a long time, and 21 patrols (40 sorties) were flown between 04:45 and 20:40. It was also the first time the Squadron had encountered the Luftwaffe in over five weeks.

The day commenced routinely enough, albeit very early, and four uneventful patrols were flown ten miles south of Beachy Head between 04:45 and 06:40. There followed a break in flying for a few hours, but between 09:00 and midday, a series of scrambles kept the pilots busy. Nothing was seen on the first two scrambles, but as the second pair of pilots switched off their engines at 11:20, the alarm was sounded again and Polish Fg Off Jerzy Solak and Australian Flt Lt Don Smith roared off in the direction of Eastbourne.

They immediately sighted FW190s over Eastbourne, counted 18 of them[102], and called for back-up. The enemy aircraft were FW190A-5 Jabos [Jagdbomber = Fighter Bombers] from Cognac based IV/SKG 10 [Schnellkampfgeschwader = Fast Bomber Wing], which caused considerable damage in the Eastbourne area with bombs and machine gun fire, resulting in six fatalities and 43 injuries. Bombs landed in Meads Street, killing the occupants of Nos. 24a, 26a and 28, in Channel View Road, near Beach Laundry and the Beach Hotel, and hit and set fire to Caffrey's Garage in Lushington Road.

As 41 Squadron sent up three more sections to assist Solak and Smith, the pair went straight in to attack a force considerably greater than theirs.

As Solak and Smith approached Beachy Head, they were given an initial vector of 150°, and subsequently a second of 100°, being informed at the same time that 'Bandits' were now over Beachy Head. As they neared the area, they saw a red flare rise over Beachy Head and noted columns of smoke rising from Eastbourne. They then sighted "a huge formation of aircraft going south at sea level"[103] that were "painted dark khaki grey as ours [with] white and black crosses"[104], which were in an ideal beam attack position.

Solak immediately fired several bursts at the aircraft as they passed him, at ranges of 600 down to 200 yards, and caught the second last aircraft in the formation with a solid burst of fire in full beam deflection at just 100 yards' range.

Smith had already fired a full beam shot at one of the leading aircraft without noticeable result, and now swung around behind the last in the formation. Solak also turned hard and pulled in behind the aircraft he had fired at, with the intention of continuing his attack. As he did so, however, he saw that "hehit [sic] the water with his propeller, wentup [sic] a little and hit the water and exploded in a huge column of black smoke"[105] about three miles south of Eastbourne.

With his target gone, Solak now followed Smith as he closed to attack his own aircraft. They could not communicate with one another, however, as Smith's R/T system was malfunctioning. The Australian pilot tried to press home his own attack but was not as successful as his counterpart:

> *Then I turned into* [the] *rear of* [the] *formation and attacked one enemy aircraft on the portside of* [the] *formation. Ifired* [sic] *several intermittent bursts atthis* [sic] *aircraft fro*[m] *line astern, one causing the aircraft the fl*[l]*ick its starboardwing* [sic] *down owing to a cannon strike. The aircraft recovered and flew on, gradually drawing away from me.*[106]

The FW190s pulled away, even though the two Spitfires were flying at approximately 330 mph IAS, and headed for home. Solak fired a parting burst out of range, at 600-1,000 yards distance, to obtain cine-gun film of the retreating enemy formation of sixteen aircraft, and the pair turned back for Friston. The Squadron's other six aircraft arrived too late to be of any real support and only saw the enemy aircraft pulling away and heading south across the Channel.

The entire action was over in less than twenty minutes, and White Section's pilots landed at 11:40 claiming one FW190 destroyed and a second damaged. Smith had seen Solak's victory and subsequently confirmed at the bottom of Solak's Combat Report: "I saw the enemy aircraft crash into the sea followed by [a] cloud of black smoke 20-30 ft. high approximately 3-5 miles from land. (Eastbourne.)".[107] Flt Lt Roy Lane, by that time also in the air as Yellow 2, later attested that he, too, had seen the FW190 crash into the sea.

Smith supported his own claim by stating,

> *I observed two cannon bursts to fall around the enemy aircraft which was flying just above the sea. With the cannon strike on the starboard wing, I claim to have damaged the enemy aircraft about 10 miles from Beachy Head.*[108]

Solak in turn reinforced Smith's claim, by adding to the bottom of the Australian pilot's Combat Report that he saw…

> *…several very close bursts and flashes over the water where* [W]*hite 2 was firing, I also saw the flicking of the enemy aircraft, after one of the bursts which looked to me like the beginning of a quick evasive action which was abandoned for no apparent reason.*[109]

Pilot	Dest	Dam	Cine Camera Gun Film[110]		Cannon	Machine Gun
Solak	FW190	-	5 feet	No. 9609	120 Rounds	656 Rounds
Smith	-	FW190	7 feet	No. 57717	280 Rounds	1040 Rounds

Smith's damaged FW190 constituted 41 Squadron's first damaged aircraft since the Dieppe landings on 19 August 1942. Meanwhile, the anti-aircraft batteries around Eastbourne submitted their own claims for three FW190s destroyed.[111]

As the Eastbourne attack was underway, and unrelated to it, 11 Group had launched Rodeo 226 at 11:30, in which four Spitfire IX squadrons from Hornchurch and North Weald were ordered to sweep an area bounded by Gravelines, Aire-sur-la-Lys, and Berck. However, on the report of the FW190 Jabos heading back towards France from the Eastbourne attack, the Rodeo was diverted and the pilots instead ordered to sweep the Dieppe and Somme Estuary areas in an effort to intercept the returning aircraft.

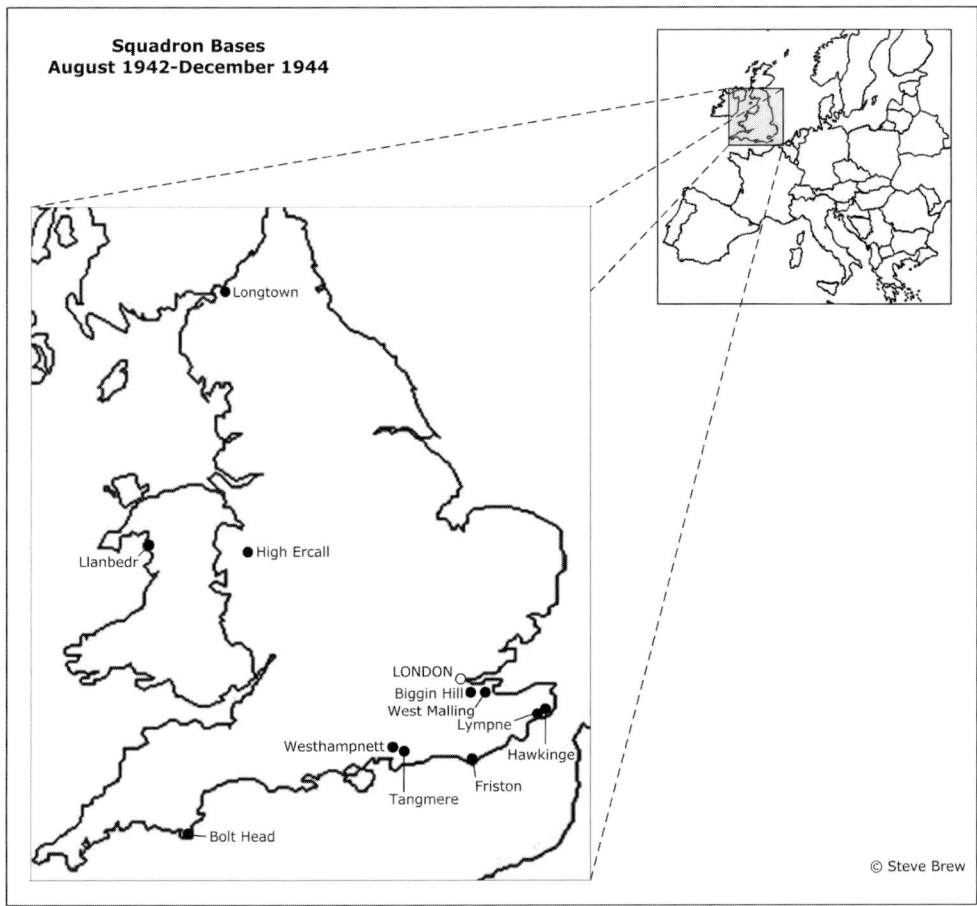

Whilst the North Weald squadrons saw nothing, those from Hornchurch, and in particular 453 (Australian) Squadron, found and engaged a formation of FW190s believed to be those returning from Eastbourne. In the ensuing combats, Sqn Ldr Kevin Barclay damaged one FW190 over the Somme Estuary and Wg Cdr John Ratten DFC, leading the Hornchurch Wing, claimed one destroyed. They suffered no casualties.

During the rest of the day, the Squadron maintained patrols of Brighton, Shoreham, Beachy Head and Selsey Bill, "but the Hun did not try again"[112], boasts the ORB. Solak's FW190 today brought 41 Squadron's victory score to 149 enemy aircraft destroyed, and the pilots ended the day "hoping that very shortly we will celebrate our one and half century".[113]

5 June 1943 – Low cloud for most of the day delayed the start of operational flying until after 11:00. The day consisted of ten patrols of the Beachy Head area and a handful of scrambles, but all returned with nothing to report; there was "no joy"[114] for the pilots, who the ORB reported were "looking forward to another brush with the Hun"[115] after the previous day's successes.

6 June 1943 – Despite poor weather conditions prevailing for the most part of the day, it proved to be long one and encompassed 19 patrols (38 sorties) between 05:30 and 21:55. After an initial early morning patrol of Beachy, standing patrols were maintained over the Channel some distance south of the Head from 10:15 to 13:00, but all were uneventful.

At 13:00, two pilots were scrambled in the base area, but returned within ten minutes as nothing was seen. At 13:30, however, fighter bombers were reported over Eastbourne and B Flight's Blue (Moffett EN611 & Graham EN631) and Green Sections (Hone EN234 & May EN238) were scrambled to intercept them. In conditions of low rain clouds and poor visibility, six FW190 Jabos had managed to come in over East Dean and bomb the Eastbourne area once again.

The two sections searched for them in vain. The Luftwaffe was able to escape under cloud cover, though not completely unscathed. Although 41 Squadron was unable to find them, the local anti-aircraft batteries did, and one FW190 was hit and damaged by Brownings from 2793 Squadron RAF Regiment. This aircraft was last seen crossing back out over Birling Gap, just west of Beachy Head, trailing smoke from under its fuselage.

The excitement over, 41 Squadron returned to routine patrols at 14:30, combing the coast between Shoreham and Beachy Head until almost 22:00. The Luftwaffe was not seen again, but on the last patrol of the day Flt Lt Douglas Hone (EN234) and Flt Sgt Stan May (MB801), sighted a barrage balloon floating in the Channel off Beachy Head. Its location was reported and the balloon was subsequently retrieved by the Royal Navy.

7 June 1943 – Thick fog, clearing later in the day. Operations started early, but there was a pause in flying between 12:00 and 16:00 when conditions deteriorated and Fg Off Bruce Moffett was forced to land at Redhill after only ten minutes in the air.

Attesting to the monotony of their current work, the ORB recorded the day's activity in two sentences: "Mainly patrols today of the usual places, Beach[y] Head, Brighton and Newhaven. Several operational scrambles, but nothing of note to report."[116]

9 June 1943 – Poor weather with bad visibility, though warm. Weather hampered most operational flying today and only one patrol was undertaken all day, in addition to four scrambles in the space of nine hours.

The day's first operation did not take place until 11:10, when Fg Off Ron Johnson and Flt Sgt Stan May were scrambled out to sea on the report of a German bomber operating in the area. South of Beachy Head, in conditions of half to one mile visibility and a cloud base of just 300 feet, they were vectored onto a Do217, which they soon spotted ahead of them. Closing rapidly, Johnson opened fire but the Do217 immediately climbed into cloud cover and was not seen again. Left little choice, the pair returned to Friston, and Johnson was unable to make a claim.[117] The rest of the day's operational flights were uneventful.

Waiting in Readiness

Fg Off Ron Johnson later recalled how the Squadron operated during this time, explaining that…

> *Much of the pilots' duty time was spent on readiness at dispersal – a hut on the perimeter of the aerodrome near which the aircraft were parked. Parachutes, helmets, etc. would all be in situ in the aircraft while pilots on readiness would be wearing flying clothes and "Mae West's" and reading, listening to worn out gramophone records or more likely, playing cards – poker or pontoon. If there was a scramble the table, cards and stakes would be left. These were never touched until we returned.*[118]

Johnson also vividly recalled…

> *Sitting in readiness at Friston waiting to be scrambled to intercept FW 190 tip and run raiders. Strapped tightly in the cockpit, radio on, engine warmed and primed ready for pressing the tit on signal for scramble – radio "Scramble Blue 1" and Red Very* [sic] *Signal. Could be airborne in a matter of seconds… dip below* [the] *cliff to pick up air speed and hope to be vectored onto* [a] *target.*

41 Squadron's main adversary from April 1942 until May 1945 was the Luftwaffe's Focke-Wulf FW190. © Public domain, U.S. Air Force Photo, via the National Museum of the US Air Force

[…]
[One] *time two of the Women's Voluntary Service ladies had brought me a cup of tea. While I was drinking it the red Very* [sic] *went up – so did my tea. I started the engine, opened the throttle and had a fleeting glimpse in the mirror of 2 ladies in some disarray.*[119]

10 June 1943 – Fog and low cloud prevailed all day, limiting flying to one 25-minute patrol at 19:45 and a scramble by six aircraft at 20:55. In the latter of the two, three sections were scrambled to intercept four aircraft reported over Hastings, but these proved to be friendly and the six pilots returned to base within ten minutes. This concluded a very brief day's flying.

11 June 1943 – Fine and fair weather all day resulted in a very busy day of flying with 19 patrols and scrambles (38 sorties) flown between 10:40 and 22:05. However, all were uneventful, and the Luftwaffe was not seen.
 Sqn Ldr Neil returned from leave today, and on arriving at the airfield saw Flt Lt 'Lulu' Lane taxi his aircraft, EN603, into another during an operational scramble. No-one was hurt, but the aircraft suffered considerable damage. "This was a very unhappy ending after a days [sic] excellent flying."[120]

12 June 1943 – Poor weather in the morning, clearing later to cloudless skies and a light wind. Red and Yellow Sections were both airborne at 10:25, but recalled within 30 minutes as a result of the foggy conditions. However, Flt Lt Don Smith (EN609) and Plt Off Leslie Prickett (MB800) had already been forced down at Ford at 10:45. Leaving again five minutes later in an attempt to reach Friston, they were compelled to land again, this time at Tangmere, where they touched down at 11:05. They made another attempt a full hour later, and finally returned to Friston again at 12:35. For their part, Flt Lt Roy Lane (EN233) and Sgt Plt Peter Wall (EN226) were also forced to make a brief landing at Tangmere, but made it home long before Smith and Prickett.

The weather then cleared sufficiently and another very busy day's flying ensued in which 20 patrols (40 sorties) were flown between 05:10 and 21:55, totalling some 37 operational flying hours. All patrols were, however, uneventful.

13 June 1943 – High cloud with good visibility, which resulted in one of the Squadron's busiest day's in a long time. Altogether, 27 patrols (54 sorties) were flown between 06:10 and 22:50, for a total of 43.5 hours operational flying, "which is a high figure, when it is considered that the Squadron is not on sweeps".[121]

All sorties were uneventful, however, with the exception Flt Lt Roy Lane and Sgt Plt Peter Wall's 11:40 Shoreham to Brighton patrol, when Lane (EN233) found his R/T system would not function and returned to base within 15 minutes. Wall continued on without him, and landed at 12:45 after an uneventful sortie. There was nothing else of consequence worthy of being reported in the ORB.

14 June 1943 – Fine weather with high cloud and good visibility resulted in another long day's flying, which totalled 19 patrols (37 sorties), and included four scrambles and one ASR patrol. Nothing was seen all day, but just after 21:30 three sections were scrambled as the RDF had plotted a large formation of aircraft in the Channel. However, "nothing materialized and it is thought that the plot must have been a cloud. It must have had an unusually high metal contact."[122] In all, 29 operational flying hours were completed during the day, which were recently becoming longer as dawn was breaking just after 03:30 and dusk not occurring until 23:00.

15 June 1943 – High cloud with good visibility; another long day's flying, totalling 18 patrols (36 sorties) and one scramble (2 sorties). Commencing at 05:10, the Squadron maintained continuous patrols off Beachy, with only one hour break mid-morning. The monotony of the patrols is apparent in the ORB, which sums up the morning's work, "Nine hours of just stooging off Beachy and nothing to report".[123]

The only break in the routine all day was a scramble by Fg Off Solak and Sgt Plt Hope, who were sent to Eastbourne on the report of an incoming raid. However, nothing was seen and the pair was back on the ground within ten minutes. Standing patrols of Beachy resumed again after dinner and concluded just before 23:00. All were uneventful.

16 June 1943 – Overcast conditions with some rain limited operations today, but the standing patrols undertaken between 09:05 and 12:40 moved from Beachy Head to the coastal stretch between Shoreham and Brighton. There followed a patrol of the area between Eastbourne and Hastings and, several hours later, another south of Beachy Head, but all were uneventful. In the evening, Fg Offs Solak and Cowell were scrambled over Friston, but once again nothing was seen and they returned within 20 minutes. This concluded the day's flying, which ended much earlier than on recent days.

17 June 1943 – Medium cloud with good visibility. The day consisted of eight patrols and seven scrambles between 09:40 and 21:30, which gave the impression it was, "a day full of alarms".[124] However, their efforts were in vain as there was…

> …not a Hun sighted. Numerous patrols off Beachy Head and Brighton but nothing to report. The Hun seems to have become rather cautious and rarely do we have contact with them these days.[125]

News also came through today that the Squadron would be moving again, this time to Westhampnett, Sussex, in the Tangmere Wing, in order to form a Spitfire XII Wing with 91 Squadron. The ORB hints at grumbles amongst the men about yet another move, complaining that "we could say with certainty that 41 Squadron are the most moved Squadron in the Royal Air Force"[126], but placates

The Squadron also met the Messerschmitt Me109 on a regular basis over the skies of occupied Europe. © Deutsches Bundesarchiv Bild 101I-487-3066-04

them with the reminder that many on the Squadron already knew the airfield from their time at this base and in the Tangmere Wing between July 1941 and June 1942.[127]

18 June 1943 – Cloudy all day, with visibility down to the deck, hindering all operational flying. However, this gave the Squadron the opportunity to start packing for Westhampnett, whilst arrangements were made with Movement Control for transportation of equipment to Chichester. A number of necessary repairs were also carried out on aircraft that had been hampered by the amount of flying recently undertaken.

19 June 1943 – Poor weather in the morning, which lifted in the afternoon. Aside from an uneventful weather and shipping reconnaissance to Fécamp, undertaken by Fg Off 'Joe' Birbeck mid-morning, no scheduled flying was undertaken all day. This allowed the Squadron to forge ahead with packing, an activity only set aside for five scrambles between 11:55 and 22:30. No contact was made with the Luftwaffe, however, and all returned with nothing to report.

20 June 1943 – No cloud and good visibility, but a total of only seven patrols and scrambles were undertaken all day, as the Squadron completed packing for their move. There was one small incident to report, on the last patrol of the day, when Fg Off Bruce Moffett (EN611) returned within five minutes of departure with a loose hood. Flt Sgt Stan May continued on without him and returned at 22:00, having completed the patrol alone. There was otherwise "nothing else of importance"[128] to report from the day's flying.

Whilst packing continued, an advance party left Friston for Westhampnett via Chichester at 12:50. The Squadron's equipment and men's personal kit were meanwhile loaded into nine railway trucks, to be ready for the unit's move the following morning, and the job was completed by early evening. However, it had not been a simple task:

Had the information regarding our move been received with only 24 hours' notice it would have been almost an impossibility to pack and transport equipment to the railway station. It is suggested that when a movement takes place that at least five three ton lorries are provided for the transport of equipment to the Station. The transport at Friston was inadequate to deal with the move and fortunately we were able to acquire a "Queen Mary" low loader and two 3 tonners from Kenley. The Squadron ground crews worked extremely hard and everything was aboard the railway wagons by 19.00 hours.[129,130]

The Spitfire XII Wing
21 June 1943 – 29 February 1944

4

Late June 1943 saw the creation of a Wing of Spitfire XII squadrons. Only 100 of the Mark were ever built, which were enough aircraft two equip just two units: 41 and 91 Squadrons. They were therefore brought together at RAF Westhampnett to form the Wing, moving later in the year to Tangmere, and remained together in an odd two-squadron entity lasting exactly eight months, from 29 June 1943 to 28 February 1944.

The creation of the Wing brought a distinct change in operational deployment for both units. 91 Squadron had been employed on Jim Crow reconnaissance operations for some time, whilst 41 Squadron, having been rested practically since the beginning of the previous August, had relieved 91 Squadron on Jim Crows since mid-April, whilst 91 had re-equipped with the Spitfire XII.

Their duties now chiefly consisted of Ramrod bomber escorts of USAAF Flying Fortresses, Marauders and Bostons, and RAF Mitchells, Bostons, Mosquitos and Bomphoons to targets in France, Belgium and the Netherlands, paving the way for the launch of the 'Second Front' in June 1944. Their main objective were airfields, but V1 facilities were also visited on a regular basis, particularly during winter 1943/1944.

A summary of each month's Ramrods is listed in a table at the beginning of every month throughout this chapter. The first of these operations, in late June 1943, are shown below:

▦ Marshalling Yards   ▥ Industrial Target

Date	Operation	Role	Type	Destination / Target
26	Ramrod 108	Withdrawal Support	▦	Le Mans, France
29	Ramrod 114	Rear Withdrawal Support	▥	Le Mans, France

21 June 1943 – The rail party, mainly consisting of personnel of 3016 Servicing Echelon, left Friston at 07:30, under the charge of Flt Lt Lord Gisborough and Fg Off 'Jock' Burnett, and boarded a train bound for Chichester at 08:52. On arrival at their destination, they were met by a number of buses and conveyed to Westhampnett in time for lunch. Following their meal, the rail party returned to Chichester Station and began unpacking the Squadron's equipment and personal kit. This was completed by 01:00 the following morning.

Meanwhile, three Harrow transport aircraft arrived at Friston carrying aircrew and freight from 412 Squadron, two of which were then used to transport 41 Squadron's remaining kit and air party to Westhampnett. However, poor weather at Westhampnett meant that the Harrows and the Squadron's pilots and Spitfires could not leave Friston until 19:00, even though the transfer then only took 30 minutes.

Westhampnett

Built on the Goodwood Estate, 1½ miles northeast of Chichester, Sussex, RAF Westhampnett was opened in July 1940, originally intended as an emergency landing ground for fighter aircraft. Designated a satellite airfield within the Tangmere Wing, facilities by mid-1943 included eight blister hangars and a permanent watch office, and four grass strips laid with Sommerfeld Tracking[1], one measuring 1,500 yards, two measuring 1,130 yards, and the last 920 yards. Sgt Plt Peter Graham recalled,

> On 21 June, we moved to Westhampnett, a satellite aerodrome of Tangmere, which was one of the busiest of our fighter stations and which also housed the top secret Lysander squadron, whose intrepid pilots flew by night to land agents in France and bring them back after their jobs were completed.[2]

Accommodation was provided for airmen at nearby Westerton, for senior NCOs in Fishers Cottage, just outside the airfield perimeter, and for officers in the historical Georgian manor, Shopwyke Hall, in Oving, approximately 2½ miles south of the airfield. Flt Lt Hugh Parry also remembered,

> Westhampnett airfield is now the Goodwood racing circuit and was a grass field with no runways. We were billeted in a large country house nearby, with a swimming pool, tennis court, billiard room, etc. and it was extremely comfortable. It is now a Preparatory School.[3]

41 Squadron replaced 501 Squadron and 3037 Servicing Echelon, who had moved to Hawkinge this same day. As 167 Squadron had already left Westhampnett ten days earlier, this left 41 Squadron as the only resident unit at the time of their arrival. Within days, however, they would be joined by 91 Squadron.

23 June 1943 – Following a day of unpacking and getting settled, the Squadron undertook some practice flying today, "but as we have been accustomed to defensive patrols and reccos during the last few months, it is not expected to be perfect".[4]

During the afternoon, the pilots were briefed for their first bomber escort, Ramrod 100/B, to provide withdrawal support to 65 Flying Fortresses returning from an attack on Le Mans Marshalling Yards. However, after consultation with the USAAF, it was decided to cancel the operation. The bombers and their close escorts were already airborne but were recalled shortly after they crossed the English coast.

As 41 Squadron was one of three units assigned to withdrawal support, they were not yet airborne when the show was cancelled, and consequently undertook no operational flying at all today.

26 June 1943 – The Squadron's pilots spent the morning practice flying, but in the early afternoon Fg Offs Clive Birbeck and Rycherde Hogarth undertook a weather reconnaissance to the Cherbourg area. Airborne at 14:15 on the unit's first operational flying since leaving Friston on 20 June, the pair returned 65 minutes later reporting good weather.

During the late afternoon, the pilots were briefed for their first ever Ramrod operation, as Withdrawal Support for USAAF Flying Fortresses attacking Le Mans Marshalling Yards. OC B Flight, Flt Lt Douglas Hone, recorded the event in his logbook, "1st Sweep comprising Spit XII's".[5]

Date	26 June 1943
Operation	Ramrod 108
Targets	Part IA: Ford SAF Vehicle Factory, Poissy, Île-de-France Part IB: Marshalling Yards, Le Mans, Pays de la Loire Part II: Triqueville Airfield, Haute-Normandie Part III: Abbeville Airfield, Picardie
Bombers[6]	Part IA: 124 Flying Fortresses; 22 bombed (weather) Part IB: 81 Flying Fortresses; aborted (weather) Part II: 41 Flying Fortresses; 39 bombed Part III: 2 Group RAF: 12 Bostons
Casualties	384 BG/544 BS: B-17F, 42-30031, CD/CL Bernouville; B-17F, 42-30037, SD/CL Gouchaupre; B-17F, 42-30048, 'Flak Dancer' SD/CL Laon Airfield[7]; B-17F, 42-30058, SD/CL Guillerval; & B-17F, 42-3188, 'Miss Carriage' SD/CL nr Paris

Withdrawal Part IA	USAAF 4 FG (Debden) & 56 FG (Horsham St. Faith): 8 Thunderbolt Squadrons (96 aircraft)
Withdrawal Part IB	Ibsley: 129 & 616 Squadrons (Spitfire Vb)
	Perranporth: 302 & 317 Squadrons (Spitfire Vb)
	Digby 402 & 416 Squadrons (Spitfire Vb)
	Coltishall: 118 Squadron (Spitfire Vb)
Withdrawal Support	Bognor Regis: 19 & 122 Squadrons (Spitfire Vb)
	Westhampnett: 41 Squadron (Spitfire XII)
Fighter Cover Part II	North Weald: 331 & 332 Squadrons (Spitfire IX)
	Kenley: 403 & 421 Squadrons (Spitfire IXb)
	Northolt: 303 & 316 Squadrons (Spitfire IXc)
Close Escort Part III	Redhill: 401 & 411 Squadrons (Spitfire Vb)
Escort Cover	Church Fenton: 308 Squadron (Spitfire Vb)
	Heston: 315 Squadron (Spitfire Vb)
High Cover	Biggin Hill: 341 & 611 Squadrons (Spitfire IX)
Casualties USAAF[8]	56 FG/61 FS: Capts Roger B. Dyar, Merle C. Eby & Robert H. Wetherbee & 2 Lt Louis T. Barron KIA, Forges-les-Eaux; 1 Lt Ralph A. Johnson, CD Forges-les-Eaux, ditched Channel; 1 Lt Justus D. Foster, CD Forges-les-Eaux, CL base (All P-47 Thunderbolts)
Casualties RAF	118 Sqn: Plt Off Stanley A. Jones, SD in Spit Vb, EP413, RR; 316 Sqn: Sgt Plt Feliks Grzywacz, SD/KIA in Spit IX, EN128; 403 Sqn: Sqn Ldr Hugh C. Godefroy Spit IX, MA467, MAC with Fg Off Robert D. Bowen in Spit IX, MA564, IFA

Part's I bombers all passed over their Beachy Head rendezvous at 17:50 and flew to a point five miles north of Fécamp, where they turned northwest until 15 miles south of Selsey Bill. At this time, they turned again and set a course for a point 20 miles north of Pointe de Barfleur, then crossed in and arrived over Lisieux at 18:10. The force then split into two, with 124 Fortresses heading for Poissy, in Paris' western outskirts, and 81 for the marshalling yards at Le Mans.

However, as the Part I/A bombers found 9/10ths cloud over the target area, only 22 bombed. It was even worse at Le Mans, where 10/10ths cloud was encountered and every Part I/B bomber turned back with its payload intact.

The Withdrawal Cover squadrons for the Poissy attack met the outbound Fortresses according to plan and escorted them back to the English coast. However, they were attacked by between 25 and 40 FW190s at Forges-les-Eaux and multiple combats ensued until ten miles off the French

A Spitfire at RAF Westhampnett Airfield by Fishers Cottage on the east boundary, looking north towards the Downs in the background. © Mark Hillier

coast. The USAAF Thunderbolts fought hard to keep the Focke-Wulfs from the bombers, but five Fortresses and five Thunderbolts were lost for the claim of six enemy aircraft.[9]

The Withdrawal Cover for the Le Mans bombers crossed in just before 19:00 and set course for Argentan, which they reached less than ten minutes later at altitudes of between 17,000 and 22,000 feet. They did not see the bombers, and swept the Argentan-Caen-Lisieux area instead, crossing out again at 19:30 having seen no other Allied or enemy aircraft.

41 Squadron was airborne at 19:05 in three sections of four pilots, led by Wg Cdr Rhys Thomas, Sqn Ldr Neil, and Flt Lt Douglas Hone. They rendezvoused with Bognor's 19 and 122 Squadrons, and patrolled off the French coast behind the Fortresses' return path at altitudes of 2,000-10,000 feet between 19:20 and 19:50. They also saw neither the bombers nor any enemy aircraft and returned to base with nothing to report. 41 Squadron landed again at 20:10.

Part II to Triqueville Airfield was more successful and 39 of the 42 Fortresses bombed with fair results. However, they were also engaged by the Luftwaffe, and although no bombers were lost, one pilot of 316 Squadron was shot down and killed. Part III to Abbeville Airfield was similarly successful and nine of the 12 bombers attacked, whilst their escorting fighters reported the operation uneventful.

28 June 1943 – The day's operational flying was confined to two weather and shipping reconnaissances, two scrambles, and two spotting patrols. The day commenced at 08:35, when Fg Off Clive Birbeck and Sgt Plt 'Jackie' Fisher took off on a reconnaissance to Fécamp and Le Havre. Crossing the Channel at zero feet, they passed a fishing fleet as they approached Fécamp and continued on to Le Havre, but found nothing else to report. They returned to base at 09:45.

Ten minutes later, Fg Offs Jerzy Solak and Peter Cowell took off for a similar reconnaissance, this time heading for the Baie de la Seine. They maintained a height of 17,000 feet throughout and returned at 10:35 reporting a thin layer of 10/10ths cloud 20 miles off the French coast between 1,900 and 2,000 feet.

Red and Yellow Sections were scrambled at 10:50 and 10:55, respectively, when enemy aircraft were reported just five miles off St. Catherine's Point. However, they turned back towards the Cotentin [Cherbourg] Peninsula, and none were intercepted. The two sections landed again 11:20 with nothing to report.

It was then another six hours before the Squadron was called on again, to undertake spotting patrols approximately 15 miles east of Selsey Bill, at 17:15-18:20 and 18:10-19:00, to keep an eye out for any bombers in distress returning from an operation in France. They saw nothing worthy of reporting, but Fg Off Prince Galitzine recorded in his logbook that he, "Saw lots of smoke trails milling around over France".[10] This concluded the day's operational flying.

Separately today, 91 Squadron and 3028 Servicing Echelon arrived at Westhampnett on posting from Hawkinge. Now fully equipped and au fait with their Spitfire XIIs, they would form a Spitfire XII Wing with 41 Squadron, led by initially by Wg Cdr Rhys Thomas DSO DFC, that would now serve together on Ramrod operations through to the end of February 1944.

Nominal Roll, 28 June 1943

The following data has been extracted from a memo from Squadron Intelligence Officer, Flt Lt Lord Gisborough, to the Sector Intelligence Officer, RAF Tangmere, dated 28 June 1943. Titled "41st. Squadron of the Line" and held in 41 Squadron's Archives, the memo is laid out below as close to the original format as possible, with some minor correction made by the author.
The document also notes the Squadron's Call Sign was *Bumper* at the time, and that 13 boxes and 13 purses for escape kits were being held with no losses to report. Numbers next to pilots' names are understood to be their individual call signs.

S/Ldr T. F. Neil, DFC and Bar (Squadron Commander)

'A' Flight	'B' Flight
F/Lt H. L. Parry (Rhodesia)	F/Lt D. H. Hone
F/O T. A. H. Slack	F/O D. Haywood (wounded)
F/Lt R. Lane (detached)	F/O H. B. Moffett (Canadian)
F/O B. B. Newman (Australian)	F/O C. R. Birbeck
F/O P. Cowell	F/O R. H. W. Hogarth
P/O H. A. Wagner (USA)	F/O D. D. Davies
F/O J. Solak ((Polish)	F/O R. J. Boyd
P/O L. A. Prickett	F/O R. Johnson
Sgt A. Hope	Sgt P. B. Graham
F/O (Prince) Galitzine (Russian)	Sgt D. P. Fisher
F/O D. H. Smith (Australian)	F/Sgt S. H. May
Sgt P. R. Wall	F/Lt D. N. Fearon (detached)

29 June 1943 – 41 Squadron was not called on operationally today until mid-afternoon, allowing Wg Cdr Rhys Thomas to take up 41 and 91 Squadrons together for the first time, for Wing Formation Practice. There was one minor issue, however, when Plt Off Herb Wagner was compelled to return early with a malfunctioning jettison tank.[11]

At 16:35, 41 Squadron's Fg Offs Rycherde Hogarth and Bruce Moffett were sent on a weather reconnaissance to Cherbourg and Le Havre, and returned 65 minutes later reporting all quiet and weather conditions good.

With 91 Squadron now settled in to their new quarters, they were deployed on their first Ramrod operation with 41 Squadron as the newly formed Spitfire XII Wing during the evening. These two squadrons would end up being the only two front line RAF units ever to be equipped with the Spitfire XII, and their inaugural collaboration today would be the first of many between now and the eventual break-up of the Wing in February 1944, when 91 Squadron was re-equipped with the Spitfire XIV.

They were assigned to Rear Withdrawal Support for USAAF Flying Fortresses returning from an attack on the Gnome-Rhône factory at Le Mans.

Date	29 June 1943
Operation	Ramrod 114
Targets	Part I/A: Villacoublay Airfield, Île-de-France Part I/B: Gnome-Rhône Aircraft Engine Factory, Le Mans, Pays de la Loire Part II : Triqueville Airfield, Haute-Normandie
Bombers	Part I/A: 108 Flying Fortresses; aborted (weather) Part I/B: 84 Flying Fortresses; 75 bombed Part II: 40 Flying Fortresses; aborted (weather)
Fighter Escort Part I	Kenley: 403 & 421 Squadrons (Spitfire IXb) Hornchurch: 222 Squadron (Spitfire IX)
Withdrawal Part I/A	8 USAAF Thunderbolt Squadrons
Withdrawal Part I/B	Perranporth: 302, 317 & 610 Squadrons (Spitfire Vb) Ibsley: 504 & 616 Squadrons (Spitfire Vb) Coltishall: 118 Squadron (Spitfire Vb) Digby 402 & 416 Squadrons (Spitfire Vb) Redhill: 401 & 411 Squadrons (Spitfire Vb)
Rear Withdrawal Support Fighter Cover Part II	Selsey: 65 & 602 Squadrons (Spitfire Vb) Westhampnett: 41 & 91 Squadrons (Spitfire XII) Northolt: 303 & 316 Squadrons (Spitfire IX) Biggin Hill: 341 & 611 Squadrons (Spitfire IX) North Weald: 331 & 332 Squadrons (Spitfire IX)

Part I's Flying Fortresses passed over Beachy Head at 19:15 and set course for Bolbec, northeast of Le Havre, where the armada split into forces of 108, for the attack on Villacoublay Airfield, and 84, targeting the Gnome-Rhône factory at Le Mans.

ABOVE AND OPPOSITE PAGE The Spitfire XII Wing routinely escorted B-17 Flying Fortresses, B-24 Liberators, and B-26 Marauders, such as these, on Ramrod operations between June 1943 and February 1944 from Westhampnett and Tangmere. © Public domain, U.S. Air Force Photo, National Museum of the US Air Force

However, the cloud cover was so thick over the former target that the bombers were unable to locate the airfield, and returned home with their payloads. Conditions were better over Le Mans, and 75 of the Fortresses dropped a total of 187 tons of bombs with fair to poor results.

The Thunderbolt squadrons assigned to cover the withdrawal of the bombers returning from Villacoublay rendezvoused with their Fortresses between Rouen and the coast of France at altitudes of between 26,000 and 29,000 feet. Almost immediately, Me109s were seen to attack the bomber force head on, and these were chased by the Thunderbolt pilots, who claimed two destroyed.

The 10, 11 and 12 Group Squadrons assigned to the withdrawal of the Fortresses returning from Le Mans made their rendezvous with the bombers between Caen and Le Havre. Some accurate heavy and light Flak was experienced but no aircraft were hit. Aside from the sighting of four enemy aircraft some distance to starboard and below the aircraft off the French coast, which did not attempt to interfere, the escort was uneventful.

The four Rear Withdrawal Support units, thereunder 41 and 91 Squadrons, also rendezvoused as planned, in the Cabourg area. The Spitfire XII Wing had taken off from Westhampnett at 20:25, led by Wg Cdr Thomas, who flew with 41 Squadron. Thomas led one section of four, whilst Sqn Ldr Neil and Flt Lt Doug Hone led the other two. After forming up, the Wing crossed out over Selsey Bill at 1,500 feet, and reached the Cabourg area at 20:45.

On arrival, the Wing broke up into loose fours between 6,000 and 10,000 feet, with 65 and 602 Squadrons above them at around 12,000 feet. However, almost immediately, the outbound Le Mans force was seen, accompanied by their Withdrawal Cover squadrons, flying at altitudes of 8,000 to 12,000 feet. The Selsey and Westhampnett Wings made way for them, and then wheeled around, positioning themselves on the flanks and behind the bombers to accompany them home, with a particular eye to protecting any stragglers.

Five miles off Le Havre, 65 Squadron spotted about sixteen FW190s approaching from the west, intent on attacking the bombers. Whilst 602 Squadron remained above as high cover, 65 dived on the aircraft and subsequently claimed one probably destroyed for no loss of their own.

Meanwhile, the Fortresses were escorted across the Channel to Beachy Head by 41, 91 and 602 Squadrons in what was an otherwise uneventful operation. Although 41 Squadron had previously been assigned to operations involving Flying Fortresses, they had not actually seen them and, as such, today's Ramrod was their first actual encounter with these impressive bombers.

OC B Flight, Flt Lt Douglas Hone, noted the event in his logbook today, "Saw about 70 Fortresses. No Bandits"[12], whilst Fg Off Prince Galitzine, flying No. 2 to Sqn Ldr Neil, was a little more candid when he recorded in his own logbook, "Misty over Channel. Saw lots of forts in wizard formation. Did a few orbits and saw the forts back to Beachy. No enemy opposition."[13] The Spitfire XII Wing landed back at Westhampnett at 21:35, concluding their first successful collaborative Ramrod; there would be many more.

Part II's heavy bomber diversionary attack on Triqueville Airfield had also come up against unsuitable weather, and could not locate the target. Their fighter cover rendezvoused with them over Beachy Head as planned, escorted them to the target area, then turned with them and headed home again, with their payloads intact. No enemy aircraft were encountered and all 40 Flying Fortresses and six squadrons of fighters returned to base without incident.

Thus commenced a new routine that saw 41 and 91 Squadrons airborne as the Spitfire XII Wing at least once every two days for the next eight months, to provide escorts to bombers attacking strategic targets in France and the Netherlands.

During the summer of 1943, these consisted largely of airfields, in an effort to achieve air superiority and drive the Luftwaffe back from the coast. During winter 1943/1944, however, the priority changed and the predominant objective became the destruction of 'Noball' targets, which were construction sites for the development and launch of the V1 flying bomb. The weapon itself, however, would not be physically seen by either squadron until June 1944, particularly as bombing by the RAF and USAAF, in which the Spitfire XII Wing was involved, seriously delayed the operational launch of the German rocket programme.

With some exceptions, the pilots generally found these operations rather monotonous and repetitive – the ORB contains several comments to this effect – but it is also likely the pilots had no idea at the time of the significance of the sites that were being attacked, and were not told.

30 June 1943 – A new system of readiness came into force at Westhampnett today, whereby one Squadron was allocated to dawn readiness, whilst the other remained at 30 minutes. This changed at 13:00 when the readiness squadron was rolled back to 30 minutes, and the squadron on 30 minutes was brought to immediate readiness.

41 Squadron was assigned the dawn shift today, but were not called upon operationally. Instead, practice flying was undertaken by several pilots and beat-ups were conducted by two sections on Ford and Tangmere airfields. 91 Squadron took over at 13:00, but the weather deteriorated during the afternoon and evening, "which probably prevented another show".[14] As such, there was no operational flying by either squadron all day.

Dogs and Dogfights

41 Squadron had two dogs during the summer of 1943, a black French Poodle named Perkin, and a white Bull Terrier by the name of Monty.

Perkin was the Squadron's mascot, and is visible in a number of photographs from around this time, most famously perched on the hood of a Spitfire XII, with Fg Off 'Barney' Newman in the cockpit. He had belonged to Fg Off Reg Hoare but was adopted by the Squadron when Hoare was shot down in April 1943. Monty belonged to Flt Lt Hugh Parry, who had obtained him during his time as a Test Pilot with Vickers, and had brought him with him when he was posted to 41 Squadron in March 1943.

91 Squadron had their own dog, too: a large Alsatian, named Boris, who was their mascot. However Boris did not see eye-to-eye with 41 Squadron's pooches, and Monty and Boris had a bad falling out this summer. Hugh Parry recalled that they…

> …got into a terrible fight because Boris, a jumped-up 'Wing Commander', tried to eat Monty's food. Despite everyone doing everything to separate them – blazing newspaper, soda-water siphons, buckets of water, etc. – it was to no avail. Ultimately one of Boris' legs was removed at the knee and he was taken to the local vet and put down. Monty had a badly skinned head but otherwise was okay.[15]

When Parry was shot down in September 1943, Monty was sent to live in Southampton. Not understanding the circumstances, however, he was often seen at the railway station trying to board a train back to Tangmere.

July 1943 – The Squadron undertook no operational flying on twelve days of the month, 3, 5-6, 8, 11-12, 19-22, 24, 28 July, as a result of poor weather conditions or operational allocations, but otherwise flew thirteen Ramrod operations, and participated in numerous Rhubarbs to France. A total of 318 operational and 279 non-operational hours were flown by the Squadron's pilots during the month.

It was also an expensive month, which saw one pilot killed in action, two wounded in action, and one shot down who managed to evade and return to the United Kingdom. However, seven pilots also joined the Squadron and the Commanding Officer was also replaced. Following is a summary of the month's Ramrods.

△ Airfield   ▥ Marshalling Yards   ▬ Industrial Target

Date	Operation	Role	Type	Destination / Target
1	Ramrod 117	Target Support	△	Abbeville, France
4	Ramrod 124	Fighter Sweep	▥	Amiens, France
9	Ramrod 127	Fighter Sweep	▥	St. Omer, France
10	Ramrod 130	Fighter Sweep	△	Triqueville, France
14	Ramrod 133	Withdrawal Cover	△	Villacoublay & Le Bourget, France
16	Ramrod 144	Fighter Sweep	▥	Abbeville, France
18	Ramrod 148	Fighter Sweep	△	Abbeville, France

26	Ramrod 159	Fighter Sweep	△	St. Omer, France
27	Ramrod 164	Fighter Sweep	△	Triqueville, France
29	Ramrod 171	Fighter Sweep	⬛	Yainville, France
30	Ramrod 176	Escort Cover	⬛	Yainville, France
31	Ramrod 180	Escort Cover	△	St. Omer-Fort Rouge, France
31	Ramrod 181	Escort Cover	△	Abbeville, France

1 July 1943 – With the exception of a late afternoon scramble, 41 Squadron's only operational flying consisted of an early afternoon Ramrod, supporting Bomphoons attacking Abbeville Airfield.

Date	1 July 1943
Operation	Ramrod 117
Targets	Part I: Abbeville-Drucat Airfield, Picardie, France Part II: Courtrai [Kortrijk] Airfield, West-Vlaanderen, Belgium Part III: Poix Airfield, Picardie, France
Bombers	Part I: 8 Bomphoons; 175 & 182 Squadrons (Typhoon Ib) – CXLD Part II: 8 Bomphoons; 3 Squadron (Typhoon Ib) – Recalled Part III: 8 Bomphoons; 175 & 182 Squadrons (Typhoon Ib)
Escort Part I Target Support Escort Part II 1st Fighter Sweep 2nd Fighter Sweep Escort Part III	Tangmere: 197 Squadron (12 Typhoon Ib) – CXLD Westhampnett: 41 & 91 Squadrons (12 Spitfire XII) Biggin Hill: 1 Squadron (12 Typhoon Ib) – Recalled Kenley: 403 & 421 Squadrons (Spitfire IX) Hornchurch: 129 & 222 Squadrons (Spitfire IX) North Weald: 331 & 332 Squadrons (Spitfire IX) Northolt: 303 & 316 Squadrons (Spitfire IX) Tangmere: 197 Squadron (9 Typhoon Ib)
Casualties	197 Sqn: Sqn Ldr Allan H. Corkett, CO of 197 Sqn, EF/glycol leak in Typhoon Ib, DN357, baled out Poix area, POW; 175 Sqn: Plt Off Osmond R. Kelsick, EF, ditched off Beachy Head in Typhoon Ib, DN408, RR

The Spitfire XII Wing was detailed to arrive over Courtrai Airfield ahead of the Bomphoons to engage any Luftwaffe aircraft taking off to escape the attack. The pilots were airborne at 14:35 led by Wg Cdr Thomas, with 41 Squadron in three sections of four pilots, led by Sqn Ldr Neil, Flt Lt Hugh Parry and Flt Lt Douglas Hone.

Hone had a slight mishap on take-off from Westhampnett, when his aircraft (EN234) struck a wireless mast. He was not hurt and the damage did not affect flying, but the incident removed approximately five feet of the mast, and the wireless post "looked rather a wreck".[16]

The Wing set its course from Newhaven to a point ten miles northwest of Ault and crossed the Channel at zero feet. The pilots then climbed, crossed in over Ault at 7,000 feet, and flew to ten miles southeast of Abbeville where they banked to port and flew to Abbeville-Drucat Airfield. Crossing the area at 10,000 feet, medium accurate Flak was encountered and Flt Lt Parry's aircraft

(MB802) sustained slight damage from shell fragments. However, they did not hinder stability and he was not aware of the damage until after landing again.

The Wing made an orbit of the area and, finding no enemy aircraft movement in the air or on the ground, crossed out at Berck-sur-Mer, made another quick orbit at 8,000 feet and returned to England. They landed at Westhampnett at 16:00, unaware that the Bomphoons of 175 and 182 Squadrons had been cancelled before take-off.

Part II's Bomphoons and Typhoons fared similarly. Although they were airborne and crossed the Channel, they were recalled when still ten miles north of Dunkirk. The first and second Fighter Sweeps did, however, fly according to plan and both Wings encountered the Luftwaffe in the air. Kenley's 403 Squadron claimed three Me109s destroyed whilst North Weald's 331 Squadron claimed one FW190 destroyed, a second probably destroyed and a third damaged for no casualty of their own.

Part III had not existed when the Ramrod was originally planned and only put on after Part I's Bomphoons and Typhoons were cancelled. 175 and 182 Squadrons were sent to Poix Airfield with 197 Squadron as escort, but were unable to locate it owing to 8/10ths cloud in the target area. They jettisoned their bombs on Fécamp Harbour, in woods, and over the sea, but two aircraft were lost when they developed engine trouble.

Meanwhile, 41 Squadron also completed its last operational flights of the day, when Fg Offs Prince Emanuel Galitzine and Peter Cowell were scrambled to Beachy Head at 16:35 on reports of enemy aircraft in the area. However, they returned an hour and ten minutes later have seen nothing, and with just as much to report.

2 July 1943 – It was a generally quiet day upon which an operation was planned but eventually cancelled. 65 and 602 Squadrons had flown over to Westhampnett at 11:00 in anticipation, but when the weather was deemed too unsuitable, they lunched and returned to Selsey.

When the weather improved during the early evening, however, Wg Cdr Thomas took the opportunity to take the Spitfire XII Wing on a fighter sweep to Le Havre. The two Squadrons were airborne at 18:55, with Thomas leading both the Wing and 41 Squadron and 91 Squadron above, covering them.

Eight minutes into the operation, however, Sqn Ldr Neil (EN237), who was flying No. 2 to Wg Cdr Thomas, developed engine trouble and returned to base. The rest of the Wing returned to Westhampnett at 20:05 after an uneventful sweep, during which neither Flak nor enemy aircraft were encountered. This concluded operational flying until mid-afternoon on 4 July as a result of continuing hazy conditions.

4 July 1943 – Again today, weather impeded operations, frustrating the pilots.

> *During the morning a large number of Flying Fortresses flew over the airfield going towards the Channel. The Wing should have been on the show but* [the] *weather was still hazy and much to our disappointment the "Powers that be" left us out.*[17]

The Wing was brought to readiness at midday in case any of the returning Fortresses required assistance, but they were not called upon, and the state was relaxed again at 13:30. It was not until three hours later that the Wing was finally airborne on its first and only operation of the day, when it was assigned a fighter sweep as an element of Ramrod 124 targeting Amiens Marshalling Yards.

Date	4 July 1943
Operation	Ramrod 124
Target	Amiens Marshalling Yards, Picardie
Bombers	2 Group: 12 Mitchells; 12 dispatched, 12 bombed

Close Escort	Redhill: 401 & 411 Squadrons (Spitfire Vb)
Escort Cover	Kingsnorth: 65, 122 & 602 Squadrons (Spitfire Vb)
High Cover	Hornchurch: 129 & 222 Squadrons (Spitfire IX)
Target Withdrawal	Northolt: 303 & 316 Squadrons (Spitfire IX)
1st Fighter Sweep	Westhampnett: 41 & 91 Squadrons (12 Spitfire XII) – to Poix
2nd Fighter Sweep	Kenley: 403 & 421 Squadrons (Spitfire IX) – to Pointe D'Ailly
3rd Fighter Sweep	North Weald: 331 & 332 Squadrons (Spitfire IX) – to Ambleteuse
Casualties	122 Sqn: Sgt Plt W. M. Whittaker, SD in Spit Vb, AD416, Amiens, POW, & Flt Sgt Robert S. Williams (RAAF), SD/WIA in Spit Vb, BM634, Amiens, POW; 129 Sqn: Flt Sgt Cyril Woodall, SD/KIA in Spit IX, BS273, Amiens; 411 Sqn: Fg Off John R. Spaetzel (RCAF), SD/KIA in Spit Vb, AB802, Amiens, & Sgt Plt H. D. Stewart, CD/WIA in Spit Vb, BM422, Amiens.

The Spitfire XII Wing was briefed on the operation after lunch, assigned to a fighter sweep in the Poix area, and was airborne at 16:40. The pilots were led by Wg Cdr Thomas, who also flew with 41 Squadron, leading one of the three sections. The other two were led by Sqn Ldr Neil and Flt Lt Hugh Parry.

Setting course for Poix, the Wing crossed the Channel at 500 feet until 15 miles off the French coast, where they climbed at 17:05 to 6,500 feet. Five miles off Berck-sur-Mer, the pilots dropped their jettison tanks and crossed in, in sections line abreast. They experienced no Flak, and climbed to 10,000 feet in 'perfect' visibility, arriving over Poix at 17:15.

On doing so, they sighted between fifteen and thirty FW190s a mile ahead of them between 8,000 and 11,000 feet.[18] The enemy aircraft were still climbing, the foremost aircraft above the Wing and the rearmost still below and 90° to the Wing's bearing. Wg Cdr Thomas turned sharply to starboard to intercept them and the Wing followed him around. However, they were spotted almost immediately and the Focke-Wulfs turned to the south and opened their throttles, climbed rapidly, and out-paced the Wing; in a very short time, the enemy aircraft were 5,000-6,000 feet above them.

The Wing was now in a dangerous position to be bounced, and turned north, immediately followed by the Focke-Wulfs. Although several half-rolled in mock dives, they did not actually attack and continued on their way, gradually pulling away from the Wing.

Now left behind, Wg Cdr Thomas gave up the chase and had the Wing make an orbit approximately ten miles inland from the coast. Seeing the outbound bombers approaching at 11,000 feet from the direction of Le Touquet, the Wing dived gradually and passed underneath them.

Thomas then led 41 and 91 Squadrons back to the coast and they crossed out north of Le Tréport, at a speed of approximately 400 mph IAS as enemy aircraft were still in the area. The Wing made a final orbit off the French coast, but the Luftwaffe was no longer visible.

They then headed home and landed in Westhampnett at 18:00, with the exception of 41 Squadron's Fg Off Bob Boyd (MB796), who had developed flap trouble and put down at Tangmere instead. Clearly disappointed at having just missed out on some action, the Squadron ORB recorded that day,

> The object of the Wing was to bounce the enemy fighters coming from Poix, before they could intercept the bomber force of Mitchells. Had the timing of the approach to Poix aerodrome been one minute earlier, the wing would have been in a perfect position to bounce the enemy aircraft taking off from the drome, as the enemy aircraft when first spotted were strung out and climbing loosely.[19]

The bombers had meanwhile successfully bombed Amiens Marshalling Yards from 12,500 feet and bursts were seen on the sidings and repair shops. Their Close Escort, Escort Cover, and High Cover shielded the bombers from attack; however the Escort Cover was bounced by almost 30 Me109s whilst returning to the French coast. The High Cover was also heavily engaged by numbers of FW190s and Me109s. These squadrons claimed two FW190s destroyed and three

Me109s damaged, but also lost four pilots of their own. The remaining fighter sweeps operated largely uneventfully.

5 July 1943 – There was no operational flying today, but four new pilots arrived at Westhampnett on posting to the Squadron, Fg Off Ross Harding, Flt Sgt James Still and Sgt Plt Jim Payne from 53 OTU, all aged 22, and Fg Off Ron Loweth from 56 OTU, aged 27.

Harding had joined the RAFVR from Oxford University in March 1941 and was commissioned in December that year. He completed EFTS at Derby and SFTS at Little Rissington, and was posted to 53 OTU at Kirton-in-Lindsey in April 1943 for the completion of his operational training. He arrived on 41 Squadron today, by now a Flying Officer, with 950 flying hours logged, but none operational. Assigned to A Flight, he would advance to Flight Commander and remain on the Squadron until mid-February 1945.

Edinburgh born Still had joined the RAFVR on transfer from the Royal Corps of Signals in April 1941, completed EFTS at Reading and SFTS at Ternhill, graduating as an NCO pilot. He was also posted to Kirton-in-Lindsey for the same OTU course as Harding, and arrived on 41 Squadron today with 660 non-operational flying hours in his logbook.

Payne had joined the RAFVR in May 1941 and was sent to the United States to undertake his flying training. Graduating as an NCO pilot, he returned to the United Kingdom to attend the same OTU course as Harding and Still, and arrived today with 543 flying hours in this logbook, however none operational. Assigned to B Flight, Payne would be commissioned with 41 Squadron and remain with the unit until early March 1945.

Loweth had joined the RAFVR in May 1940, and was similarly sent to the United States for his flying training, which was completed in the southern states of Florida, Georgia and Alabama. He was commissioned in May 1942, and returned to the United Kingdom as a Flying Officer, where he completed his operational training at 56 OTU in Tealing. Loweth arrived with 504 non-operational flying hours logged and would remain with the Squadron approximately six months.

7 July 1943 – Improved weather saw the Squadron participating in two operations today: a Roadstead to Le Havre at 12:35 and a shipping reconnaissance to the same port at 21:00.

In the first of these, the Spitfire XII Wing was called upon to provide top cover, and Tangmere's 486 Squadron to provide close escort to Bomphoons attacking two Kriegsmarine destroyers in Le Havre harbour. The pilots were airborne at 12:35, with the exception of Flt Lt Tom Slack (EN226), who was having engine trouble and did not get off until ten minutes later. He attempted to catch up, but was unable to and returned to base at 13:00.

The rest of the Wing had meanwhile crossed the Channel at zero feet, but was quite upset by 486 Squadron, which flew straight through the middle of 41 Squadron's formation at 270 mph. The Operational Instructions for the Roadstead had stipulated their speed across the Channel should have been 250 mph, and consequently the Spitfires had to open their throttles to chase after them and keep up.

Five miles off the coast, to the north of Le Havre, 91 Squadron climbed to 12,000 feet and 41 Squadron to 14,000 feet, but found significant cloud cover over the harbour. They saw the Bomphoons go in, but they were unable to locate their targets and dropped their bombs blind. These were seen to fall harmlessly into the water just off the harbour.

The Wing then continued on to Cherbourg where they crossed back out at 9,000-12,000 feet and headed home. They landed again at 13:50, but as there was no Flak and no sign of the Luftwaffe, the pilots considered it a "most uneventful trip".[20]

Just over seven hours later, four pilots were airborne as Blue and Black Sections for a shipping reconnaissance back to Le Havre. Although records do not elaborate, the main aim was likely to establish whether the two destroyers were still in the harbour. The quartet was airborne at 21:00 and flew along the coast between Cap d'Antifer and the Somme Estuary.

No shipping was seen, but the pilots did sight two FW190s flying some distance above them at 10,000 feet. However, on seeing 41 Squadron's four Spitfires, they banked and flew off, making no attempt to engage them. They could not be enticed down, and the Squadron returned to Westhampnett at 22:15 with nothing further to report.

9 July 1943 – The Wing participated in a single operation today, as a fighter sweep supporting RAF Mitchells bombing St. Omer Marshalling Yards in Ramrod 127. Although the operation had its own legitimate target, it was actually only a diversion for a larger bomber raid south of Paris.

Date	9 July 1943
Operation	Ramrod 127
Target	St. Omer Marshalling Yards, Pas-de-Calais
Bombers	2 Group: 12 Mitchells; 12 dispatched, 12 bombed
Close Escort	Newchurch: 19 & 132 Squadrons (Spitfire Vb)
Escort Cover	Kingsnorth: 65, 122 & 602 Squadrons (Spitfire Vb)
High Cover	Biggin Hill: 341 & 485 Squadrons (Spitfire IX)
1st Fighter Sweep	Hornchurch: 129 & 222 Squadrons (Spitfire IX)
	North Weald: 331 & 332 Squadrons (Spitfire IX)
2nd Fighter Sweep	Northolt: 303 & 316 Squadrons (Spitfire IX)
3rd Fighter Sweep	Westhampnett: 41 & 91 Squadrons (12 Spitfire XII)
	Tangmere: 197 & 486 Squadrons (Typhoon Ib)

It was an early start to the day and the Wing was airborne at 07:10, led by Wg Cdr Thomas, who flew with 41 Squadron. Just after take-off, however, Thomas (MB849) realised that his jettison tank had become adrift in its fittings, whilst 41's Fg Off 'Barney' Newman (EN236) also discovered he had jettison tank trouble. Newman turned around immediately and landed again within ten minutes, but Wg Cdr Thomas led the Wing as far as the French coast, where he handed over the reins to Flt Lt Hugh Parry, and turned for home.

Having crossed the Channel on the deck, the Wing climbed 20 miles off France and crossed in over Le Tréport. 41 Squadron led the way, with 91 Squadron stepped up to port and Tangmere's 197 and 486 Typhoon Squadrons stepped up to starboard.

As the Westhampnett and Tangmere Wings swept to just short of Poix Airfield, the 12 Mitchells successfully bombed St. Omer's Marshalling Yards from 11,000 feet at 07:55, dropping forty-eight 1,000 lb. bombs on both the yards and assembly shop. The escort and cover squadrons escorted them all the way and neither saw enemy aircraft nor experienced any Flak.

The first and second fighter sweeps did, however, meet the Luftwaffe. The Hornchurch Wing dived on 15-20 aircraft, which avoided the interception, but one of the Northolt Wing's Polish squadrons was bounced by four FW190s out of the sun. Several combats ensued in which the Poles sustained no casualties but returned claiming one FW190 destroyed, one probable, and one damaged.

The Spitfires and Typhoons of the third sweep carried out their sweep unopposed, passed over the Somme River at Longpré-les-Corps-Saints, then crossed out at Berck-sur-Mer at 8,000-9,000 feet. They gradually reduced their altitude over the Channel in order to keep an eye out for any dinghies. This was a precaution in case any bomber crews from the mission to the south of Paris, for which they had provided the diversion, had been forced to ditch.

However, the Spitfire XII Wing saw nothing and, crossing the English coast at 2,000 feet, proceeded to Westhampnett where they landed at 08:25. Although 91 Squadron later undertook a shipping reconnaissance, there was no further operational flying by 41 Squadron all day.

10 July 1943 – In a day similar to the previous, the Spitfire XII Wing had a relatively early start and only participated in a single operation all day. On this occasion, they provided a fighter sweep as an element of a Ramrod, in which several Bomphoons targeted Triqueville Airfield. Once again, the Ramrod acted as a diversion for Flying Fortresses attacking targets south of Paris.

Date	10 July 1943
Operation	Ramrod 130
Target	Triqueville Airfield, Haute-Normandie
Bombers	8 Bomphoons; 181 Squadron (Typhoon Ib)
Escort	New Romney: 6 Bomphoons; 182 Squadron (Typhoon Ib)
	Selsey: 3 Bomphoons; 245 Squadron (Typhoon Ib)
Fighter Sweep	Westhampnett: 41 & 91 Squadrons (Spitfire XII)
	Tangmere: 486 Squadron (Typhoon Ib)

The Wing took off at 08:10, led by Wg Cdr Thomas, who flew with 41 Squadron. As the fighter sweep was being undertaken in cooperation with Tangmere's 486 Squadron, the three squadrons rendezvoused over Selsey Bill, and then crossed the Channel together at zero feet. They climbed as they approached Trouville, crossed in at 7,000 feet, and flew towards Triqueville but made a turn to port just west of the town.

181 Squadron's Bomphoons crossed the coast near Fécamp at 7,000 feet, however 10/10ths cloud with rain was experienced over Triqueville Airfield and, as such, the target could not be attacked. Returning to the coast, they jettisoned their bombs two to three miles northeast of Fécamp instead. Results were unobserved, and they returned to base with nothing further to report.

The Tangmere and Westhampnett Wings had meanwhile enjoyed more success. With the exception of two sections from 91 Squadron who returned early with technical issues with their aircraft, the rest of the pilots flew on towards Bernay Airfield. Approaching from the northwest with 41 and 91 Squadrons at 8,000 feet, and 486 Squadron 2,000 feet below them, the Typhoons then banked to port to line up for a strafing run. Their targets were enemy aircraft parked in the dispersals area in the south-eastern corner of the airfield.

Three of 486's pilots fired three to four second bursts at the aircraft from 3,000 feet. Although it was unclear whether they had actually struck any from this altitude, strikes were seen on the ground around the aircraft. The three pilots climbed again to join the rest of their Squadron, which then formed up with 41 and 91 Squadrons again.

They then flew together towards the coast to head home. On the way, two pilots from 91 Squadron attacked a goods train near Pont-l'Évêque, and strikes were seen on the engine. A number of high altitude vapour trails were also seen, which they assumed were Flying Fortresses returning from the operation for which they had acted as a diversion.

The three squadrons made an orbit of Cabourg, and then headed back across the Channel to Tangmere and Westhampnett, where 41 Squadron landed at 09:25. The weather dropped during the afternoon, which hindered any further operational flying, and did not improve for the next three days.

Time for Reflection

Having returned to the southeast on 13 April 1943, the scribe tasked with writing daily entries in the Squadron ORB felt the break in operations a suitable time to contemplate the state of affairs:

The Squadron have now been back in No: 11 Group for three months and it is perhaps opportune to make a few observations regarding the Squadron in general. The first, is that a different spirit is observed amongst the ground crews, as they know that the Squadron is again in action. Even with the long periods of readiness the ground crews are keen and enthusiastic and always willing and happy to carry on working. The health of all members of the Squadron has not suffered with the strain of operational work, in fact there are now fewer on sick parades. There is fierce competition amongst the pilots for a place in the Squadron when an operational flight is planned and in two cases pilots have foregone leave to be in on

LEFT Although not 41 Squadron's mascot, Bull Terrier 'Monty' defended 41 Squadron's honour as if he were, and did not see eye-to-eye with 91 Squadron's mascot, Alsatian 'Boris'. Boris made the fatal error in summer 1943 of trying to steal some of Monty's food. © Hugh Parry

RIGHT 'Monty' belonged to OC A Flight Flt Lt Hugh Parry, who had obtained him during his time as a Test Pilot with Vickers, and had brought him with him when he was posted to 41 Squadron in March 1943. © Hugh Parry

a few extra shows. As the Squadron were out of the line for nearly nine months, they feel that it is about time they did something worthwhile.

A big celebration is being planned for the day we shoot down our 150th Hun and as we are now on the 149th mark we expect this to be any day! Altogether there is crowds of enthusiasm [sic] in the Squadron and we are all expecting to have our former luck and success now that we are once more in the line.

Few of our present pilots were with the Squadron when we were in the Tangmere Sector during 1941-42 and Flt Lt D. H. Hone "B" Flight Commander and F/O T. A. H. Slack are the only two who operated with the Squadron during those days.[21]

14 July 1943 – Following a period of inclement weather that had prevented the Wing's participation in operations for three days, conditions had improved sufficiently by this morning to allow them to take part in a single, albeit large, Ramrod in two parts and a diversion, targeting the airfields at Villacoublay, Le Bourget and Amiens.

It was a major operation consisting of 267 USAAF Flying Fortresses, 23 RAF Spitfire squadrons, and eight USAAF Thunderbolt squadrons. The Spitfire XII Wing's role was to provide the Fortresses Rear Withdrawal Cover.

At the time the Wing was scheduled to meet the withdrawing B-17s, seventeen Bostons were to bomb Abbeville-Drucat Airfield in Ramrod 134, and simultaneously two formations of eight Bomphoons each, were to attack Triqueville and Poix Airfields in Ramrods 135 and 136. With so many Allied aircraft in the air over northern France and the Channel at the same time, it had to be intricately timed.

Date	14 July 1943
Operation	Ramrod 133
Targets	Target I: Villacoublay Airfield, Île-de-France Target II: Le Bourget Airfield, Île-de-France Diversion: Amiens-Glisy Airfield, Picardie

Bombers	Target I: 118 Flying Fortresses; 96 bombed Target II: 84 Flying Fortresses; 55 bombed Diversion: 65 Flying Fortresses; 53 bombed
Casualties	94 BG/331 BS: (1) B-17F 42-3190, 'Nip'n'Tuck', SD/CL Bérengeville-la-Campagne, (2) B-17F 42-3331, 'Naturals/7-11', SD Saint-Germain-des-Angles & (3) B-17F 42-3071, SD Le Bourget; 303 BG/358 BS: B-17F 42-29781, 'Memphis Blues', CD/AA, ditched 40m S of Shoreham; 381 BG/535 BS: B-17F 42-30011, 'Widget', SD Merlimont-Plage, & (2) B-17F 42-3211, 'T.S.' [abbreviation for 'Tough Sh#t'], CL Manston after MAC with FW190; 384 BG/544 BS: B-17F 42-3330, SD Les Essarts-le-Roi
Fighter Cover, Target I Withdrawal Cover Fighter Cover, Target II Withdrawal Cover Rear Withdrawal Cover Fighter Cover Diversion	Kenley: 403 & 421 Squadrons (Spitfire IX) Hornchurch: 19 & 132 Squadrons (Spitfire Vb) Exeter: 66, 131 & 504 Squadrons (Spitfire Vb) Coltishall: 118 Squadron (Spitfire Vb) Digby: 402 Squadron (Spitfire Vb) Matlaske: 611 Squadron (Spitfire Vb) Biggin Hill: 341 & 485 Squadrons (Spitfire IX) North Weald: 331 & 332 Squadrons (Spitfire IX) Northolt: 303 & 316 Squadrons (Spitfire IX) Ibsley: 165, 453 & 616 Squadrons (Spitfire Vb) Portreath: 302 & 317 Squadrons (Spitfire Vb) Westhampnett: 41 & 91 Squadrons (Spitfire XII) 4th FG, 56th FG & 78th FG USAAF; 8 Sqns Thunderbolts
USAAF Casualties	4 FG, 335 FS: Lt. Ward K. Woortman, P-47 Thunderbolt 42-7939, SD/KIA Toutencourt
RAF Casualties	317 Sqn: Fg Off Czesław Mroczyk, CD/WIA (elbow) in Spit Vb nr Bernay; 485 Sqn: Capt John R. Walker (USAAF), SD/KIA in Spit IX, EN564, nr Bernay

Ninety-six of the 118 Flying Fortresses attacking Villacoublay bombed the target with 240 U.S. tons achieving very good results, whilst 55 of the 84 attacking Le Bourget dropped 130 U.S. tons with fair to good results. In both cases, strong opposition from the Luftwaffe was met, along with moderate to intense Flak, which cost the USAAF seven bombers.

The Fighter Cover squadrons for the Villacoublay attack intercepted three formations of enemy fighters, which were driven off, but nonetheless succeeded in shooting down one of the Fortresses, for the loss of one Me109 by return fire from another B-17, and one FW190 claimed probably destroyed by 129 Squadron.

The 12 Group squadrons in the Withdrawal Cover Wings encountered three small formations of enemy aircraft, one of which was claimed destroyed and another damaged by 403 Squadron for no casualty of their own. The Biggin Hill Wing then sighted 40 and 50 enemy fighters, which attempted to attack the withdrawing bomber force from the rear. Numerous combats ensued in which one enemy aircraft was claimed probably destroyed and another damaged by the fighters, and one shot down by a Flying Fortress. However, 485 Squadron lost one pilot, and two Fortresses were seen to be shot down, one near Trouville and the other near Bernay.

The Fighter Cover squadrons on the Le Bourget attack did not sight any enemy aircraft on the way in, but escorted two Fortresses back to the English coast that aborted early. Their Withdrawal Cover Wings intercepted eight FW190s near Bernay, of which three were claimed destroyed by 317 Squadron at the cost of one of their own pilots wounded and his aircraft damaged. The Wing also reported back fixes on one fighter dinghy and two Flying Fortress dinghies, and escorted a straggling Fortress back to Brighton.

In the Diversionary attack on Amiens-Glisy Airfield, 53 of the 65 Flying Fortresses dropped fifty-five U.S. tons of bombs with good results. Both fighter opposition and Flak were met and two B-17s were lost. Their Thunderbolt escorts engaged four separate formations of FW190s east of Amiens, totalling approximately 40 aircraft. A number of combats ensued in which three Focke-Wulfs were claimed destroyed and nine damaged. However, the fighters also sustained a loss of their own. The bombers' gunners also claimed three FW190s destroyed, and a fourth destroyed itself when it collided with a B-17.

As the last of the Fortresses were crossing out again, the Spitfire XII Wing arrived on the scene to commence their Rear Withdrawal Cover duties. Having taken off at 08:20 with Wg Cdr Thomas leading both the Wing and 41 Squadron, the pilots crossed out over Selsey at just 1,000 feet. They climbed before the French coast, and made landfall over Trouville at 11,000 feet.

As the Wing approached Lisieux, several outbound boxes of Fortresses and their fighter escorts were met, and two FW190s were also seen at the same altitude as the Wing. Several pilots turned to engage them, but the enemy aircraft beat a hasty retreat, and dived away. Returning their attention to the bombers, the Wing noticed one box returning without an escort. They wheeled around and escorted them back to the English coast. However, as the Wing crossed out, a Spitfire was seen to crash into a wood at Forêt de Saint-Gatien, between Trouville and Honfleur. This is believed to have been 485 Squadron's Capt John Walker.

Three Fortresses dropped out of the formation in distress, and were given particular attention. One of the aircraft "appeared to have a large white stripe down its tail but on closer inspection it was seen that a large piece had been shot away."[22] A photograph of this aircraft later appeared in the newspaper with the caption, "When Fortresses returning from operations over France were attacked by F.W. 190s one of them was hit in the tail and had to fall out of formation. Spitfires flew to the rescue and drove off the attackers…"[23] Fg Off Ron Johnson also remarked on this aircraft in his logbook that day: "Escort for 'Forts' returning from Paris. Escorted straggler home […] Saw Fort that had head on collision with 190."[24]

This and one other B-17 were escorted safely back to the English coast, but the third was forced to ditch around 40 miles south of Shoreham. The crew were seen to climb into two dinghies and a fix was radioed to shore. The Spitfire XII Wing landed back at Westhampnett at 09:55, ending the day's operational flying.

Separately, Ramrod 134 had proceeded according to plan and all 17 Bostons bombed Abbeville-Drucat Airfield from 11,000 feet, with good results, scoring hits on a hangar and the north and south dispersal areas. Their fighter escorts operated uneventfully. Ramrod 135 was similarly successful, and fourteen 500 lb. bombs were dropped on the north dispersals area. Flak was experienced but no casualties recorded. However, Ramrod 136's Typhoons found weather conditions over Poix Airfield unsuitable and bombed a railway near Eu instead, with unknown results.

On 17 July, 41 Squadron received a copy of a signal from the Commanding Officer of the 8th U.S. Bomber Command, Brigadier General Frederick L. Anderson, recognising the efforts of the RAF fighter squadrons on Ramrod 133. It read,

> *American Bomber Crews are enthusiastically grateful for the splendid fighter cover provided to-day by the Spitfire Pilots of your Command. Following are typical comments of our crews "As we were leaving the Target area a heavy formation of enemy fighters flew in to attack but almost immediately they were chased off by [a] particularly strong formation of Spitfires, On the way home about mid-Channel one of our ships with half its tail blown off dropped out of formation. A couple of Spits went to the aid of the crippled bomber immediately, circled the ship and brought her home safely". "The Spit cover was perfect" exclaimed Capt. Carrol [sic] D. Briscoa [sic].*[25] *"I'd like to thank them personally". May I add my grateful appreciation to that of our crew members for the splendid co-operation of your command.*[26]

It was a nice piece of recognition for the role the Spitfire XII Wing had played today.

15 July 1943 – It was a quieter day for 41 Squadron today, and although 24 operational sorties were flown, all were ASR operations flown between 13:10 and 20:35. 91 Squadron was airborne before 41 this morning, tasked with escorting a Hudson bomber that was to drop a lifeboat to the crew of a Flying Fortress that had come down in the Channel after an operation the previous evening, which was located approximately 15-20 miles northwest of Le Havre.

The bomber crew transferred from their dinghies to the lifeboat and at 13:15, twelve of 41

Fg Off Ron Loweth served with 41 Squadron from 5 July 1943 to ca 10 January 1944. He ended the War as a test pilot. © Ron Johnson, via Dan Johnson

Squadron's pilots took off in three sections, led by Flt Lts Hugh Parry, Fg Off Tom Slack, and Fg Off Jerzy Solak, to locate them again, and escort them home. Tangmere's 197 and 486 Squadrons were also airborne on the same duty, the latter of which were bounced by several enemy aircraft. They subsequently claimed two FW190s destroyed and two damaged for no loss.

41 Squadron saw these combats but were not themselves engaged. Fg Off Prince Galitzine later recorded in his logbook, "As we came up we saw the Tiffy's & 190s milling around, there was a terrific splash as a 190 went in. When we got onto the scene amongst them all the Huns were nowhere to be seen."[27]

The Squadron then continued to search, albeit unsuccessfully, for the Fortress crew in their lifeboat. However, the Typhoon pilots were still clearly jumpy after having been bounced and "appeared about to attack us one time from the head on position but veered off just in time".[28] The rest of the operation continued uneventfully and the Squadron returned to England with the Typhoons, putting down at Westhampnett again at 14:35.

Approximately two hours later, Wg Cdr Thomas led another three pilots from 41 Squadron in an attempt to find the lifeboat that the earlier operation had been unable to do. They set a course of 175° from Selsey, and passed over a number of British High Speed Launches that were also searching for the lifeboat.

The quartet flew on this bearing for 17 minutes, and succeeded in finding the boat, which was at the time travelling at approximately five knots towards the British coast. Whilst Thomas (MB849) and Fg Off Bruce Moffett (EN611) circled the boat, Fg Off Rycherde Hogarth (EN235) and Sgt Plt 'Jackie Fisher (EN602) were sent back to find the HSLs and guide them to the downed airmen.

The four pilots then provided cover to the sea craft until relieved by Blue Section of four pilots at 17:30. This section then monitored the area until 18:40, and was replaced at 19:00 by a section of two, who were joined by another two pilots at 19:55. The last section was on the ground at 20:25, reporting the task successful but otherwise uneventful. This concluded the day's operations.

16 July 1943 – The Wing was only assigned to a single Ramrod during the evening today. In fact, it was the only offensive operation undertaken by 11 Group all day, aside from a Rodeo by Hornchurch and North Weald based Spitfire IX squadrons. Although only a small operation in comparison to others recently, the Ramrod was notable for the fact that it was the first time that 11 Group had operated with USAAF Marauders.

Date	16 July 1943
Operation	Ramrod 144
Targets	Primary: Abbeville Marshalling Yards, Picardie Diversion: Off Gravelines
Bombers	Primary: 16 Marauders; 16 dispatched, 14 bombed Diversion: 18 Marauders
Escort Wings[29] Fighter Sweep	83 Group, Kenley, Biggin Hill, Hornchurch, North Weald & Northolt Westhampnett: 41 & 91 Squadrons (Spitfire XII)

The Ramrod proceeded generally according to plan and 14 of the 19 Marauders attacked Abbeville Marshalling Yards, dropping a total of 15 tons of bombs, with fair results. However, the Luftwaffe came up to meet them in the target area and most Wings were engaged. In the ensuing combats, the escorts claimed three FW190s destroyed and one probably destroyed, and four FW190s and one Me109 damaged for no loss of their own.

For their part, the Spitfire XII Wing, which was assigned a fighter sweep to Poix Airfield, was airborne at 19:10 with 41 Squadron providing twelve aircraft, led by Sqn Ldr Neil. They crossed out over Selsey and made landfall 10,000 feet over Le Tréport at 19:40. As they approached Poix Airfield, heavy Flak opened up and enemy aircraft were seen taking off.

91 Squadron's Commanding Officer, Sqn Ldr Raymond Harries, led a section down to attack them. Taking one FW190 by surprise, the pilot, who had just become airborne, took evasive action but over-corrected and spun in to crash in flames on the airfield. The section re-joined the rest of 91 Squadron, but just they were doing so, they were bounced by another group of enemy aircraft. Combats ensued, but none were successful and no casualties sustained. 41 Squadron would have assisted but were busy keeping an eye on a number of Spitfire IXs, "who appeared likely to attack us".[30]

These Spitfire IXs apparently belonged to the Hornchurch and Kenley Wings, which had already been sighted by the Spitfire XII Wing, above them at 17,000 feet. A number of their pilots dived on 41 Squadron just as 91 Squadron were themselves being attacked by the Luftwaffe, the squared off wings of their Spitfire XIIs possibly being mistaken for those of Me109s. Although there was no friendly fire incident in the end, 41 Squadron felt that the early arrival of these wings over the target area "caused unnecessary confusion".[31]

After some time, 91 Squadron formed up with 41 Squadron again, and they crossed out together three miles west of Dieppe at 8,000 feet, landing back at Westhampnett at 20:35.

17 July 1943 – Today's operational flying was also confined to the evening, and included a Rodeo, a spotting patrol and a shipping reconnaissance. The Rodeo was flown in cooperation with 91 Squadron and Tangmere's 486 Squadron, and targeted the Triqueville area.

The Spitfire XII Wing was airborne at 18:30, with the Wing and 41 Squadron led by Wg Cdr Thomas. The Sector Gunnery Officer, Sqn Ldr Hubert R. Allen DFC, flew as Thomas' No. 2, but the reason for his participation is unknown. Shortly after take-off, Flt Lt Tom Slack (MB802), who was leading another of the Squadron's three sections, turned for home with jettison tank problems, whilst Sgt Plt Peter Graham (EN231) returned home with engine trouble. Fg Off Prince Galitzine (EN266) then found his R/T system malfunctioning, but continued on regardless.

It was, however, a thoroughly uneventful operation, and neither the Luftwaffe nor Flak was seen. The pilots landed again at 19:45 reporting the job "most uninteresting".[32] In their absence, Flt Lt 'Lulu' Lane and Fg Off 'Barney' Newman were sent up at 18:50 to search for a sea mine that had been reported off Selsey. They were unsuccessful and landed again at 20:10 with nothing to report.

An hour and ten minutes later, four more pilots were airborne in two sections for a shipping reconnaissance to Dieppe Harbour. They crossed the Channel to within ten miles west of Fécamp, then swept line abreast on the deck to Dieppe. The only shipping seen was a medium sized vessel in the last dock of the inner harbour. Heavy Flak was directed towards them, but none was accurate and they returned to Westhampnett at 22:25.

18 July 1943 – Although it started innocuously enough with an uneventful ASR patrol, the day would prove to be one of the Squadron's most intensive and memorable for some time.

Sections from both 41 and 91 Squadrons were airborne early this morning on ASR searches for the crew of a Defiant off the Isle of Wight. 41 Squadron deployed four pilots between 06:10 and 07:30 but none were successful.

It was then another ten hours before 41 Squadron was airborne operationally again, when they were detailed to provide a fighter sweep in cooperation with 91 and 197 Squadrons, as an element of Ramrod 148, in which Bomphoons targeted Abbeville-Drucat Airfield.

197 Squadron would go in low in their Typhoons, with 91 Squadron above them and 41 Squadron in turn covering 91 Squadron. The object of the sweep was to catch any enemy aircraft that may be taking off from Poix Airfield with the intention of intercepting the Bomphoons.

Date	18 July 1943
Operation	Ramrod 148
Target	Abbeville-Drucat Airfield, Picardie
Bombers	7 Bomphoons; 175 Squadron (Typhoon Ib); 5 bombed 8 Bomphoons; 182 Squadron (Typhoon Ib); 6 bombed
Escort Fighter Sweep	New Romney: 9 Bomphoons; 181 Squadron (Typhoon Ib) Westhampnett: 41 & 91 Squadrons (Spitfire XII) Tangmere: 197 Squadron (Typhoon Ib)
Casualties	41 Sqn: Flt Sgt Douglas P. Fisher, CD/WIA nr Abbeville in Spit XII, EN231; Fg Off Rycherde H. W. Hogarth, SD/KIA nr Abbeville in Spit XII, EN235; & Fg Off Thomas A. H. Slack, SD/WIA Foucaucourt in Spit XII, EN233, RR; 197 Sqn: Sgt Plt Leonard S. Clark, SD in Typhoon Ib, DN371, ditched 4 miles S of Newhaven, RR

The Spitfire XII Wing deployed 24 aircraft, with Wg Cdr Thomas leading the Wing and 91 Squadron. The pilots took off at 17:45, and rendezvoused with 197 Squadron over Tangmere then crossed the Channel on the deck above very rough seas and through haze rising to between 5,000 and 6,000 feet. Around ten miles off the French coast, they commenced a climb to between 8,000 and 11,000 feet, and then crossed in just southwest of Le Tréport finding 8/10ths cloud at 13,000-14,000 feet. Around this time, Sqn Ldr Neil realised he had jettison tank trouble, and returned to base with his No. 2, Sgt Plt Peter Wall.

The Bomphoons had meanwhile rendezvoused with their escort over Rye and traversed the Channel at 500 feet. They commenced their climb 12 miles off the coast and flew directly to Abbeville-Drucat Airfield. 175 Squadron's Bomphoons made the first bombing run on the target, from north to south at altitudes of 6,000 to 11,000 feet. The bombs of two aircraft overshot and hit a factory outside the airfield's perimeter, two aircraft bombed the nearby marshalling yards and one bombed the airfield.

182 Squadron then went in from south to north at 5,000 to 9,000 feet, and their bombs were seen to burst at the intersection of the southwest-northeast and east-west runways and southern dispersals area. Between the two Bomphoon squadrons, a total of twenty-two 500 lb. bombs were dropped, and although moderate heavy accurate Flak was experienced over the airfield, the Luftwaffe was not seen and the Typhoons returned uneventfully.

However, it was a very different story for the Spitfire XII Wing and 197 Squadron. The Controller had reported enemy aircraft to their east, and as they continued inland towards Poix, they spotted 15 aircraft five miles ahead of them and 1,000 feet below. The Wing turned 45° to the northeast to give chase, and had flown almost as far as Abbeville when it was realised the aircraft were friendly, as local anti-aircraft batteries had "opened up a lively fire on them".[33]

It was now that they realised that these aircraft were 175 and 182 Squadrons' Bomphoons heading inbound for Abbeville-Drucat Airfield. They were not expected them in this location as Wg Cdr Thomas had been told that they were to be crossing in north of the Somme and that they would be late.

Returning to the initial task, Wg Cdr Thomas turned the Wing towards Poix. Having observed the airfield from 10,000 feet, they were in the process of banking to starboard when they were bounced by 25-30 Me109s and a number of FW190s, believed to be from JG2, which dived on them from the south and out of the sun, appearing out of the cloud base at 13,000 feet.[34] The Me109s had yellow noses and blue under-surfaces, and were identified as 109G's by their underslung cannon.

Numerous combats ensued during which two Me109Gs were claimed destroyed and one damaged by 91 Squadron's Sqn Ldr Raymond Harries. However casualties were also sustained. One of 197 Squadron's pilots was shot up and was eventually forced to bale out over the Channel four miles south of Newhaven. A fix was given and he was eventually picked up by HSL 145. Worst of all, however, two of 41 Squadron's longest-serving pilots failed to return.

Ramrod 148, 18 July 1943	Serial	Section	Time Up	Time Down
Neil, Thomas F.	EN237	Red		Unkn[35]
Wall, Peter R.	EN603			
Birbeck, Clive R.	EN234			19:10
Moffett, H. Bruce	EN611			19:05
Parry, Hugh L.	MB802	Yellow	17:45	18:55
Wagner, Herbert A.	EN609			
Slack, Thomas A. H.	EN233			FTR
Hope, Alan	EN226			18:55
Hogarth, Rycherde H. W.	EN235	Blue		FTR
Fisher, Douglas P.	EN231			19:05
Johnson, Ronald	EN238			19:10
Davies, David D.	MB796			19:05

Blue Section was bounced first and Fg Off Rycherde Hogarth, leading the quartet, turned to port to face the enemy aircraft. His No. 2, Sgt Plt 'Jackie' Fisher followed him around and dived after an enemy aircraft at 420 mph IAS. He fired two bursts with full deflection, but could not make a claim. Blue 3, Fg Off Ron Johnson tried to cover him, but was attacked by another aircraft. Fisher was then chased and badly shot up, and his aircraft was "riddled with bullet holes".[36] His R/T system was rendered inoperable and "he was lucky to get home."[37] Hogarth was never seen again.

Yellow Section, positioned on the starboard side of the Squadron, closest to the inbound enemy formations, was keeping an eye on about a dozen enemy aircraft when they were also bounced. Parry turned the section to face them but was immediately attacked head-on by two FW190s. He took swift evasive action to avoid their fire, but was unable to open fire himself. Yellow 3, Fg Off Tom Slack meanwhile dived after another aircraft and was last seen on its tail. He was also not seen again.

Sgt Plt Alan Hope, who was experiencing his first major air battle, counted some 20 enemy aircraft diving from the sun right past him at over 500 mph, he estimated. Due to their speed, he was "unable to open fire in time [even] though he had his finger on the trigger".[38] He was also attacked by an enemy aircraft from a range of 400 yards or less, and at least 20 cannon rounds were fired at him.

Red Section also saw action, and Fg Off 'Joe' Birbeck chased an Me109, "diving and skidding"[39] after it. He fired two bursts at the Messerschmitt but owing to its pilot's evasive action, he was

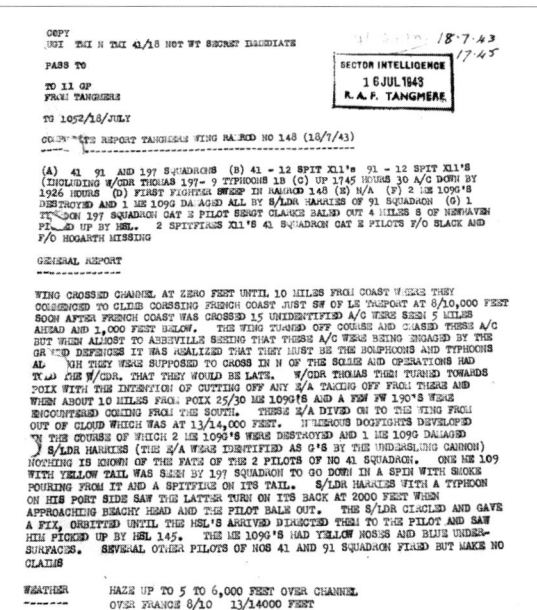

Intelligence Report for the Tangmere Wing's participation in the first fighter sweep of Ramrod 148 on 18 July 1943, during which 41 Squadron lost Fg Offs Rycherde Hogarth and Tom Slack. © 41 Squadron Archives

unable to establish the effectiveness of his attack. Fg Off Bruce Moffett also fired at enemy aircraft but was unable to make any claim.

Suddenly it was all over, and the Wing regrouped and headed back across the Channel, badly shaken. Fg Off Bruce Moffett landed early at Friston, presumably a result of petrol shortage, and the rest of the Wing put down at Westhampnett at 18:55 to count the cost.

> The Squadron are very upset by the loss of F/O T.A.H. Slack and F/O R.H.W. Hogarth, as they had been with the Squadron a very long time and were two of our most experienced pilots. Slack with his lively wit and friendly nature was a great favourite with pilots and ground crews, and Hogarth with his shy but efficient manner will be greatly missed.[40]

Fg Off Ron Johnson also reminisced that Slack was, "…about the most senior pilot in the squadron and the most popular. He was a born humorist [sic] and practical joker (always in good taste), unfairly handsome and a good pilot."[41]

South African Hogarth, aged just 21, was killed in the incident, and subsequently buried in Abbeville. It is believed he fell victim to Obfw Kurt Goltzsch of 4./JG2. Slack, on the other hand, baled out slightly wounded, but unhurt and went on the run. More fortunate than many, he managed to evade capture and made it back to England via Spain and Gibraltar in just five weeks and three days.

The ground crews later recorded the following ammunition expenditure by the Squadron's pilots after they returned to base:[42]

Aircraft	Pilot	SAP/I 20mm	HE/I 20mm	B.VI.Z .303	A.P. .303
M	Sgt Fisher	18	18	68	68
Q	F/O Birbeck	10	10	60	60
P	F/O Moffett	18	18	68	68

The report also noted that Fg Off Birbeck's aircraft suffered a stoppage in its starboard cannon. These pilots also produced five feet of cine-gun film.

An Evader

Slack later recalled his loss and evasion in his autobiography, explaining what had happened:

> Before I could press the firing button a series of explosions shook my aircraft, in the excitement I had forgotten to watch my tail and another Messerschmidt [sic] was firing at me from dead astern. By this time I was separated from the Squadron so I skidded and weaved all over the sky to make the German's aim more difficult. I was gradually losing height, and when smoke or glycol started pouring from the engine, I ripped off my helmet, released the safety straps, turned the aircraft onto its back and tried to bale out. My parachute got caught in the cockpit hood so I started kicking frantically. My foot must have pushed the stick forward because I was suddenly thrown clear to tumble head over heels towards France and a continental holiday.[43]

Slack was fired upon by ground troops, but was fortunately not hit, and landed near Foucaucourt-Hors-Nesle, approximately 15 miles southwest of Abbeville. He did not see where his aircraft came down but learned later that it had been completely destroyed.

A couple of enemy aircraft circled him as he landed, and he came to rest on his back. Before he could stand up and disentangle himself, two Frenchmen grabbed him and indicated to the circling Luftwaffe pilots that they had him in their custody. When the pilots flew off, apparently satisfied, his 'captors' told him that German troops would be here shortly. Having some understanding of French, Slack grasped the message and ran off in the opposite direction to that from which German soldiers were expected to arrive, leaving behind his Mae West and parachute.

He ran for approximately one mile through some woods, where he paused and took the opportunity to open his escape kit and purse. They contained a silk map of France, French Francs, four passport photographs, a black tie, a sports coat, a black thread with magnetic button and a fluorescent dot always pointing to north, a short fishing line, a rubber worm on a hook, some concentrated chocolate and a number of Benzedrine stimulant tablets.

He continued on and a little while later met a shepherd who directed him to a small shooting chalet nearby. Once there, he was given some bread and goats milk and told to stay until dark. Soon afterwards, however, he heard some commotion in the surrounding woods and felt it would be safer to move on.

Having walked southwards for some time, Slack had reached a point by dusk just east of Senarpont, approximately 39km west of Amiens. Whilst crossing a road in this vicinity around 22:00, he was seen by a German soldier, who was armed with a revolver. Still wearing his RAF uniform and badges, Slack felt an obvious target. However, he kept his cool and stopped long enough to readjust his scarf as calmly as he could to cover his pilots' Wings. To his surprise, the soldier walked past Slack, dismissing him with a nonchalant 'Bonsoir Monsieur", to which Slack responded with his own polite, "Bonsoir". No doubt assisted by the dull light and the soldier's apparent intoxication, Slack made a quick exit and did not stop to look around for another mile.

Having walked all night, Slack rested at dawn the following morning, but hunger drove him on and during the afternoon he approached some farmers, who gave him food and advised him which villages he should avoid. By late afternoon on 19 July, Slack had reached village of Le Quesne, a few kilometres southeast of Senarpont, when he was seen by a Frenchman on a bicycle.

Slack became suspicious when he looked directly at him, then turned and cycled back past him again. He decided it best to hide, and did so behind some nearby bushes. However, the man returned a little while later with some colleagues and proceeded to look for him.

> They seemed good types, and were obviously looking for me, so I showed myself. When they learned that I was an R.A.F. pilot, they brought me wine and some civilian clothes, and one of them told me that he would come and fetch me after dark. From this point on my subsequent journey was arranged for me.[44]

Slack had apparently stumbled upon the Angot brothers, who assisted on an escape line run by Joseph Balfe, an Englishman who had been awarded a Military Medal in World War I and had remained in France after the Armistice. He became naturalised, married a French national, and now owned and ran the 'Hotel de France' in nearby Hornoy-le-Bourg. Over the course of the War, Balfe, and his two sons, two daughters, and friends, helped over 250 pilots home.

Slack remained in hiding in the hotel until 24 July, when he was moved to the attic of a house behind the local hairdresser. Locals prepared false papers for him, and on 5 August a woman belonging to the Belgian Comete organisation came to meet Slack and Balfe at Amiens, from where Slack was taken across the Pyrenees into Spain on 11 August. The final leg of Slack's journey was in the coal hold of a Norwegian ship that took him from Seville to Gibraltar on 20 August 1943.

His sister was a WREN stationed in Gibraltar, and he managed to find her – much to her surprise – and they spent a few days together before he was flown back to England by Dakota on 23 August. Slack arrived in Bristol the following morning, where he was interviewed by MI9.

Before going home on leave, he visited the Squadron briefly, and they were overjoyed to see him and hear about his escape. However, having not expected this outcome, a few precautions had been taken before his personal effects were sent home to his parents. His Flight Commander, Flt Lt Hugh Parry, recalled,

Our adjutant, named Smith, and I destroyed Tom's address book etc., as it contained notes which he would not have wished for his parents to see. Imagine how we were cursed on his return![45]

Many years later, Slack recalled,

After escaping and being interrogated by British Intelligence I was told to prepare a talk on 'Escaping' and give it to a group of people in some sort of secret place outside (or just inside?) London. This I did & they must have been happy with it because I was sent to give it to every fighter station in England, Wales, Scotland and Northern Ireland – and also to some Radar Stations in the outer Scottish Islands – presumably to give the latter a bit of fun & some contact with people from the mainland![46]

Following a period of leave, Slack was promoted to Flight Lieutenant and then, quite unusually, returned to 41 Squadron in late September. His first flight back with the unit, a non-operational refresher, took place on 27 September, and the lecture tour of RAF stations referred to by Slack, above, took place between 3 October and 18 December 1943.[47]

There was no operational flying from 19-22 July 1943, but two pilots joined the Squadron on 20 July, Fg Off Arthur A. 'Pinkie' Glen DFC and Plt Off Arthur C. Cook, and one on 21 July, Flt Sgt William H. Vann.

25-year-old Glen was no stranger to 41 Squadron, as he had already completed a tour with the unit between March 1941 and May 1942, initially as an NCO pilot, and subsequently as a junior officer. During that tour, Glen had distinguished himself over 59 operational sorties, claiming a shared damaged He111 within days of joining the unit, a destroyed Me109 in August 1941, two destroyed Me109s in March 1942 and a damaged FW190 in April 1942. He was commissioned in January 1942, and awarded a DFC in May 1942.

Posted to Malta in May 1942, Glen was still enroute, flying from the carrier HMS *Eagle* on 3 June, when his section was bounced by a formation of Me109s off Pantellaria. As the other pilots had little combat experience and were running short of fuel, he told them to go on to Malta but turned back himself to face the enemy fighters. Despite inoperable guns, he managed to drive off the attackers and land uninjured at Ta Kali after 3½ hours airborne. On arrival, he was posted to 603 Squadron and within a short time claimed a number of further victories: one damaged Me109 on 23 June, one destroyed and one damaged Me109 and a damaged Z1007 on 26 June, two destroyed Ju88s, one destroyed Me109 and a shared damaged Z1007 on 6 July.

However, he was injured by a bomb blast on the ground in early July and taken off operations. Evacuated from Malta and repatriated to the United Kingdom as a result, he was hospitalised for several weeks before being posted to ground duties. He remained in such roles until today, when he returned to operations for the first time since being injured.

Nicknamed 'Pinkie', a moniker believed to have originated in Malta[48], he would now remain with 41 Squadron until late May 1944, during which time he would distinguish himself yet again. Promoted to OC, B Flight, in September 1943, he destroyed two FW190s that same month, was awarded a Bar to his DFC in November, and was promoted to command the Squadron in early 1944.

The second pilot to join the Squadron on 20 July was 26-year-old Plt Off Arthur Charles Cook. Having joined the RAFVR in February 1942, he completed his entire flying training in the United Kingdom and was commissioned on graduation in April 1943. 41 Squadron was his first operational unit, and he arrived today with 290 non-operational flying hours logged.

The third pilot to join the unit during this period was Flt Sgt William H. Vann, who had joined the RAFVR in October and similarly completed his flying training in the United Kingdom. However, Vann already had approximately nine months operational experience, with 243 Squadron in the United Kingdom and North Africa, during which time he undertook a number of sweeps and destroyed a truck from the air. He arrived on the Squadron on 21 July with 30 operational and 360 non-operational flying hours in his logbook.

23 July 1943 – It was rather ironic that an exercise codenamed 'Downpour' was to have taken place today but was cancelled on account of poor weather. As such, the day's operational activity for 41 Squadron was limited to a single Rhubarb to the Le Havre area during the afternoon. Carried out by Fg Off 'Joe' Birbeck (EN608) and Sgt Plt Peter Graham (EN238), it was the Squadron's first operation since their bruising on 18 July, and would result in yet another casualty.

The pair was airborne at 14:45 and crossed the Channel at zero feet. No Flak was experienced when they made landfall at Cap d'Antifer on the deck, but they were kept low owing to 10/10ths cloud cover between 2,000 and 2,300 feet. They turned to port and headed north, and soon found a hutted camp at Épreville, just south of Fécamp. This was duly shot up by Fg Off Birbeck, with 520 rounds of each 20mm cannon and .303 inch machine gun. This was the unit's first claim against a ground target in just over three months.

The pair then crossed out five miles east of St. Valéry-en-Caux at 15:20 at an IAS of 280 mph. They were flying at an altitude of just 50 feet when Graham's aircraft was hit by light Flak and a 20mm high explosive shell entered his cockpit. He recalled later,

> …as we crossed the coast there was an almighty bang and everything changed. After the roar and racket of the past quarter of an hour there was suddenly total silence. There was glass everywhere except in the instrument panel where it belonged. My right arm wouldn't obey my commands but hung loose at my side. Almost every dial, indicator and gauge in front of me had gone haywire. Not a squeak from the radio; not a murmur from the engine; no wind noise; total silence; and around me total chaos. I was stone deaf.[49]

However, as his Spitfire's engine was still running, and as his other arm and both legs and feet were uninjured, he was able to keep flying. The only instrument in the panel that still appeared to be working was his air speed indicator, and with Birbeck still just ahead to his starboard side, he could be guided home.

The return journey back across the Channel to Westhampnett was without problem, but landing presented a new challenge. Birbeck landed first, putting down at 15:40, whilst Graham made an additional circuit. He did not know whether he could get the undercarriage down or, if he could, how he would even know the wheels were down and locked. Seeing no crash wagon or ambulance, and as Birbeck landed first, Graham thinks it possible that Birbeck was not even aware of the trouble he was in.

He flew over Westhampnett a few times waggling his wings to try to give those on the ground the message that he was trouble, then climbed to 3,000 feet to give himself enough room to let the aircraft fly by itself for a few seconds whilst he attempted to lower the undercarriage with his good left hand, via a lever located on the right-hand side of the cockpit.

Unable to apply the brake, as it was physically impossible, he decided instead to come in low over the airfield boundary hedge at stalling speed, and then drop the aircraft onto the runway early to allow enough time for the aircraft to run to a stop without brakes. This he did quite successfully, landing without any incident at 15:45, and was able to taxi quite normally to dispersals.

The ground crew jumped up on the wing and opened the canopy with some effort. Seeing the state Graham was in, they called for an ambulance whereupon he fainted. He was taken to hospital where the surgeons operated on his right elbow and removed several pieces of shrapnel, the largest of which he kept all his life as a souvenir. He spent 17 days in hospital, after which he was sent on 14 days sick leave. His full hearing returned within a short time.

Graham's aircraft was damaged to Category B status. The shell had detonated on striking the Spitfire's skin, causing the following recorded damage:

- Penetration at junction of No. 11 Frame datum longeron on the starboard side
- Flak splinters penetrated starboard mainplane
- Flak splinters penetrated port side of fuselage, damaging sliding hood runner
- Leads to IFF starting switch, detonating switch and remote contactor severed
- Blast effect on rear of armour plate behind pilot seat
- R/T system rendered inoperable
- IFF detonated

Graham's saving grace was that the aircraft's engine, fuel tank and propeller remained undamaged. His logbook for the day states, "Rhubarb, 1:00, wounded slightly by Flak A/C EN238 Cat. B. 17 days in hospital, H.E. shell from St. Valery".[50]

Separately today, the Squadron received the news that their Commanding Officer, Sqn Ldr Tom Neil, would be rested and posted to a fighter OTU in Lincolnshire. His replacement was Flt Lt Bernard Ingham, who would be posted from 129 Squadron within two days.

A New Commanding Officer

Command of the Squadron changed hands on 25 July 1943 when 23-year-old Sqn Ldr Bernard Ingham DFC arrived to take over from Sqn Ldr Thomas 'Ginger' Neil DFC*.

Ingham had joined the RAFVR in July 1935 and re-mustered to become an NCO pilot by August 1939. He was posted to his first operational unit, 234 Squadron, at St. Eval in November 1940, and moved to 72 Squadron at Gravesend in mid-July 1941.

Commissioned in November 1941, Ingham claimed his first victories, two shared destroyed aircraft, only five days later. He claimed another victory, a destroyed FW190 in February 1942, and days later was promoted to Acting Flight Lieutenant and Flight Commander on posting to 129 Squadron at Westhampnett. Promoted to Flying Officer (WS) in May 1942, Ingham was awarded a DFC in July and claimed another enemy aircraft destroyed during Operation *Jubilee* a month later.

He was now promoted to Acting Squadron Leader and Commanding Officer of 41 Squadron, a position he would hold until November 1943, when a further promotion awaited him.

Neil had commanded 41 Squadron since early September 1942, and was now rested as a flying instructor with 53 OTU at Kirton-in-Lindsey.

Sqn Ldr Bernard Ingham DFC was OC 41 Squadron from 25 July 1943 to 20 November 1943. Sadly, he died of tuberculosis in August 1947, aged just 27. © Sheppard Family

S/Ldr. T. F. Neil came to us on 3rd of September 1942 and during the time he has been with us the Squadron has kept a fine record of training during our long "rest" in No. 9 Group. The Squadron under his command reequipped with the latest Spitfire XII's and the training on these machines was carried out without an accident – a very successful accomplishment. We all wish him the best of luck in his new post – not exciting work, but a very useful job.[51]

Neil remained with 53 OTU until January 1944 when he was posted to the 9th U.S. Air Force as a Liaison Officer. He managed to fly several sorties during May and June 1944, during which he claimed several ground targets and the distinction of being the first English pilot to land on French soil after D-Day.

Neil was sent to Burma in March 1945 and served briefly with 1 Squadron, Indian Air Force, before returning to the United Kingdom to end the War as an instructor with the School of Land/Air Warfare at Old Sarum. He remained in the RAF after the War and spent some time in the United States involved in high altitude pressure suit experiments, for which he was awarded the Bronze Star.

Neil subsequently served in the United Kingdom, Egypt, and the British Embassy in Washington DC. Following a posting to the Ministry of Defence, he retired in 1964, retaining Wing Commander, and spent the ensuing years in the private sector. At the time of writing, he was residing in Suffolk.

26 July 1943 – Following two days of whether that did not allow any operational flying, the Squadron was in the air again today on another Ramrod with 91 Squadron, which provided Sqn Ldr Ingham his first opportunity to fly operationally with his new Squadron.

On this occasion, the Spitfire XII Wing was assigned to a fighter sweep with Tangmere's 486 Squadron, as an element of Ramrod 159. In the event, weather forced an alteration of Parts III and IV to the Luftwaffe airfields at Merville and Poix, and Abbeville Airfield was attacked instead. The Spitfire XII Wing ended up providing them withdrawal support after their sweep.

Date	26 July 1943
Operation	Ramrod 159
Targets	Part I: St. Omer Airfield, Pas-de-Calais, France Part II: Courtrai [Kortrijk] Airfield, West-Vlaanderen, Belgium
Bombers	Part I: USAAF: 18 Marauders Part II: 2 Group: 88 & 107 Sqns: 12 Bostons
Casualties	Part II: 88 Sqn Boston IIIA, BZ399, SD/WUL Lille-Vendeville Airfield, crew unhurt but POW[52]
Fighter Sweep Close Escort Part I Escort Cover High Cover Fwd Target Support Fighter Sweep Close Escort Part II Escort Cover High Cover Fwd Target Support Withdrawal Support	4 FG USAAF: 334, 335 & 336 FS (Thunderbolt) Newchurch: 19, 65 & 132 Squadrons (Spitfire Vb) Ibsley: 165 & 453 Squadrons (Spitfire Vb) Biggin Hill: 341 & 485 Squadrons (Spitfire IX) Kenley: 403 & 421 Squadrons (Spitfire IX) Tangmere: 486 Squadron (Typhoon Ib) Westhampnett: 41 & 91 Squadrons (Spitfire XII) Portreath: 302 & 317 Squadrons (Spitfire Vb) Exeter: 66 & 504 Squadrons (Spitfire Vb) Hornchurch: 129 & 222 Squadrons (Spitfire IX) North Weald: 331 & 332 Squadrons (Spitfire IX) Northolt: 303 & 316 Squadrons (Spitfire IX)
Casualties	317 Sqn: Fg Off Tadeusz Felc SD/POW in Spit Vb, EP328, & Flt Sgt Piotr Bartys SD/POW in Spit Vb, AD137; 504 Sqn: Flt Lt Christopher C. McCarthy-Jones, SD/POW in Spit Vb, BM145

As cover for the Ramrod, three squadrons of Thunderbolts of the USAAF's 4th Fighter Group were assigned a sweep from Schouwen Island to the north of Numansdorp, then to the east of Rotterdam and back out over The Hague. They bounced four FW190s, claiming one probably destroyed, and sighted fifteen more FW190s that were not engaged, but the operation was otherwise uneventful.

Part I's eighteen Marauders carried out an initial feint attack from Clacton to Mardyck, then returned to North Foreland, where they rendezvoused with the escort fighters at 12,000 feet. They crossed the Channel together and made landfall between Mardyck and Dunkirk, and then proceeded to St. Omer Airfield.

Fifteen of the 18 Marauders attacked the target, dropping fifty-six 300 lb. GP bombs and one hundred and twenty-eight 100 lb. incendiaries from 24,000 feet. Results were considered good as reports were received of bursts amongst buildings and dispersals areas on the northern and western sides of the airfield.

The Luftwaffe was not sighted and the bombers crossed out again between Berck-sur-Mer and Le Touquet, escorted by the Close Escort, Escort Cover and High Cover wings. The Forward Support Wing swept from Bergues to Berck without incident when they, too, returned across the Channel.

For their part, the Spitfire XII Wing was airborne at 11:15, with Wg Cdr Thomas leading the Wing and 41 Squadron, and Sqn Ldr Ingham as his No. 2. They crossed the Channel at zero feet until within five miles of Le Tréport, and then climbed to between 5,000 and 6,000 feet to cross in.

Sweeping the area towards Poix uneventfully, the Wing then headed for Abbeville where they observed Ramrod 160's Bomphoons attacking the airfield, noting bursts in the western dispersals area. They then joined up with their Typhoon escort and accompanied them back across the Channel, landing at Westhampnett at 12:30.

The operation had proved a "most uneventful trip"[53], felt 41 Squadron, as no contact had been made with enemy aircraft. The Wing had little to report, and this concluded the day's operational flying.[54]

Separately, Part II of the Ramrod began in a similar fashion, when twelve 2 Group Bostons undertook an initial feint attack towards Ostend [Oostende], and then returned to Clacton to rendezvous with their escort wings.

Returning across the Channel to Belgium, they proceeded to Courtrai [Kortrijk] Airfield unhindered where 11 Bostons dropped forty-four 500 lb. bombs from 10,500 feet at 11:17. Results were initially considered poor as many bursts were seen to have overshot the target. However, the Forward Support Wing later reported to have seen many bursts amongst buildings and ensuing fires.

On the way out, however, the bombers were attacked by thirty to forty FW190s and Me109s, all the way from the target to the coast. The Close Escort, Escort Cover and High Cover Wings all attempted to fend off the enemy fighters, and in the ensuing combats claimed two FW190s and two Me109s destroyed, and one FW190 and two Me109s damaged. However, 317 Squadron lost two pilots, and 504 Squadron one pilot, who were shot down and all captured. Additionally, one Boston failed to return, also falling victim to the Luftwaffe.

The Forward Target Support Wing operated uneventfully and the Withdrawal Support Wing, which dived upon at least ten enemy aircraft over Lille, was unable to make any claims. Although these aircraft were not definitively identified, it was confirmed that they were not FW190s or Me109s, and thought instead to have possibly been Koolhoven 58's. Their unexpected low speed caused the Northolt Wing to overshoot the aircraft and although a few shots were fired, no results were observed.

27 July 1943 – Several Rhubarbs and a Ramrod were planned for the morning, but all were cancelled as a result of fog. However, when conditions improved throughout the day and the first pilots were airborne operationally just after lunch.

On that occasion, Fg Off Ron Johnson and Flt Sgt Stan May were scrambled to Selsey Bill at 13:45. However, nothing was seen and the section landed again 25 minutes later with nothing to report. During the early afternoon, the unit participated in a gas exercise with tear gas. However, it "was spoilt by a rapid change of wind, just after the gas was released".⁵⁵

At 17:30, the Wing was finally called upon to participate in a Ramrod, providing a fighter sweep for Marauders bombing Triqueville Airfield. The intention of the Wing's operation was to bounce any enemy fighters taking off from Bernay or Triqueville Airfields.

Date	27 July 1943
Operation	Ramrod 164
Target	Triqueville Airfield, Haute-Normandie
Bombers	USAAF: 18 Marauders, 18 bombed
Close Escort Escort Cover High Cover Forward Target Support 1st Fighter Sweep 2nd Fighter Sweep	Kingsnorth: 65, 122 & 602 Squadrons (Spitfire Vb) Exeter: 66 & 131 Squadrons (Spitfire Vb) Biggin Hill: 341 & 485 Squadrons (Spitfire IX) Kenley: 403 & 421 Squadrons (Spitfire IX) Redhill: 411 & 412 Squadrons (Spitfire Vb) Westhampnett: 41 & 91 Squadrons (Spitfire XII)
Casualties	65 Sqn: Flt Sgt Ian R. Pittock, EF in Spit Vb, BM373, baled out into Channel, RR; 412 Sqn: Sqn Ldr George C. Keefer DFC, EF in Spit Vb, baled out into Channel, RR

The escort wings all made rendezvous with the bombers over Rye at 18:00 and reached Triqueville Airfield at 18:25, whereupon approximately 14 tons of bombs were dropped. One box of six Marauders dropped their payload near the target, but the second and third boxes' aim was more accurate, and their bombs were seen to burst inside the target area. The Luftwaffe was not seen, but one pilot suffered engine failure and baled out into the Channel and was subsequently rescued up by ASR.

The High Cover Wing was informed enemy fighters were in the vicinity and turned to intercept them. A formation of fourteen FW190s was sighted, which attempted to bounce 485 Squadron. Both Biggin Hill squadrons climbed to meet them and frenzied combats took place for approximately eight minutes at 21,000 feet, in which a total of nine FW190s were claimed destroyed and one damaged for no casualty of their own.

The Forward Target Support squadrons operated uneventfully but for the fact that 412 Squadron's Commanding Officer also suffered engine failure and was compelled to bale out into the Channel from where he was subsequently picked up by ASR services. The first fighter sweep also operated uneventfully.

For their part, the Spitfire XII Wing was airborne at 17:30, with 41 Squadron in three sections of four led by Sqn Ldr Ingham, Flt Lt Hugh Parry, and Fg Off Ron Johnson. The pilots crossed in west of Trouville at 9,000 feet, then fly towards Bernay, turning five miles west of the town to keep up-sun of the airfield. Fg Off Glen (MB846) realised he could not jettison his long range fuel tank and returned home early, landing back at Westhampnett at 18:30.

Seeing no sign of the Luftwaffe, the rest of the Wing continued to Triqueville, made a single orbit and then crossed back out at Trouville again. Having neither sighted enemy aircraft on the ground and in the air, nor experienced any Flak, there was little to report when the Wing landed again at 18:45.

Whilst they were absent, Flt Lt Dave Fearon and Plt Off Arthur Cook were sent on a spotting patrol ten miles south of Ford. They took off at 18:20, saw nothing worthy of reporting, and returned at 19:50, concluding the day's operational flying.

29 July 1943 – There was no operational flying until after 17:30 today when 14 sorties were flown, encompassing a fighter sweep of Bernay and Triqueville with 91 and 197 Squadrons in support of a Ramrod to Yainville Power Station, and an evening shipping reconnaissance to Le Havre.

Date	29 July 1943
Operation	Ramrod 171
Target	Yainville Power Station, Haute-Normandie
Bombers	2 Group: 12 Bostons; 12 bombed
Close Escort Escort Cover High Cover Forward Target Support Fighter Sweep	Kingsnorth: 65, 122 & 602 Squadrons (Spitfire Vb) Newchurch: 19 & 132 Squadrons (Spitfire Vb) Hornchurch: 129 & 222 Squadrons (Spitfire IX) Kenley: 403 & 421 Squadrons (Spitfire IX) Westhampnett: 41 & 91 Squadrons (Spitfire XII) Tangmere: 197 Squadron (Typhoon Ib)

The Close Escort, Escort Cover and High Cover squadrons rendezvoused with the Bostons at low altitude over Rye at 11:03, and then proceeded across the Channel on the deck for 13 minutes. At this time, they climbed steeply, crossed in at Fécamp and were stepped up to 19,000 feet by the time they reached the target.

The bombers went in at 9,000 feet unhindered, and dropped forty-four 500 lb. bombs on the power station with 25 second delay fuses at 11:27. Results were not seen as a result of the amount of smoke billowing from the area, but it is believed that bursts straddled the target. There was no opposition and the bombers and their escorts all returned to base without incident.

The Forward Target Support squadrons crossed the Channel independently of the main force and arrived over the target area as the bombing commenced at an altitude of 22,000 feet. Continuing on to Dieppe, 403 and 421 Squadrons climbed to 29,000 feet to Neufchâtel-en-Bray, then descended to 20,000 feet again to cross out again over the Somme Estuary, returning without incident.

The Spitfire XII Wing and Tangmere's 197 Squadron were airborne at 11:40, 41 Squadron deploying three sections of four led by Sqn Ldr Ingham, Flt Lt Hugh Parry, and Fg Off Ron Johnson. The pilots traversed the Channel at sea level until 12 miles northwest of Trouville, when they climbed to between 9,000 and 10,000 feet to cross in.

With the exception of Sgt Plt Peter Wall (MB800) who returned early with jettison tank trouble, the three squadrons flew directly to Bernay Airfield, and then on to Triqueville. However, both airfields appeared to be deserted: the Luftwaffe was not seen and they did not encounter any Flak whatsoever.

From left to right: Fg Off Bruce Moffett RCAF, Fg Off David Davies, Fg Off 'Barney' Newman RAAF, Flt Lt David Fearon, Flt Lt Lord Gisborough (in chair), Fg Off Ron Johnson (foreground, looking towards Newman), Fg Off Clive Birbeck, Fg Off Ross Harding, Fg Off Ron Loweth (behind Harding), and Fg Off Leslie Prickett at Westhampnett, late July 1943. © Ron Johnson, via Dan Johnson

The squadrons crossed out again and made an orbit off Le Havre, but still "the enemy did not play".[56] One of the pilots sighted a merchant vessel of about 400 tons lying half a mile off Le Havre harbour, but there was otherwise little else to report when the Wing landed again at 19:00.

Capping off the day's flying, Flt Lt Hugh Parry and Fg Off Peter Cowell undertook an uneventful shipping reconnaissance to Le Havre after dinner. Airborne at 21:05, they returned 55 minutes later with "Nothing to report. No joy!".[57]

30 July 1943 – The Squadron's total operational flying today was confined to the provision of Escort Cover with 91 Squadron in a single Ramrod, in which RAF Venturas targeted Yainville Power Station once again.

Date	30 July 1943
Operation	Ramrod 176
Target	Yainville Power Station, Haute-Normandie
Bombers	2 Group: 12 Venturas; 12 bombed
Close Escort Escort Cover High Cover Target Withdrawal Support Bouncing Wing	Redhill: 411 & 412 Squadrons (Spitfire Vb) Westhampnett: 41 & 91 Squadrons (Spitfire XII) Biggin Hill: 341 & 485 Squadrons (Spitfire IX) Northolt: 303 & 316 Squadrons (Spitfire IX) North Weald: 331 & 332 Squadrons (Spitfire IX)

The Spitfire XII Wing was airborne at 14:20 with Wg Cdr Thomas leading, and 41 Squadron's twelve pilots led by Sqn Ldr Ingham. They rendezvoused with the bombers and fellow escort squadrons at just 500 feet over Newhaven and crossed the Channel on the deck before climbing to cross in.

The formations made landfall five miles east of St. Valéry[58], the Redhill squadrons at 7,000 feet with the bombers, the Spitfire XII Wing at 9,000 feet on either side of the bombers, and the Biggin Hill squadrons at 14,000 feet. They headed straight for Yainville and were over the target area at 15:00, where the Venturas released thirty-six 500 lb. and forty-six 250 lb. bombs. Some of these were seen northwest of the target but the majority fell in the target area. 41 Squadron felt the bombing was quite effective, recording in their ORB that the target, "appeared to be well pranged".[59]

The Luftwaffe was not seen by the Wing, although other squadrons reported seeing six enemy aircraft east of Rouen that did not interfere, and the formations drew no Flak. On the way out, however, 41 Squadron sighted three ships on stocks in Le Trait shipyards, one of which was estimated to have been of 1,000 tons, and several gun emplacements were seen under construction in the Dieppe area.

The bombers and escort squadrons all returned uneventfully, and the Spitfire XII Wing landed at Westhampnett at 15:45. It was a similar situation for the Target Withdrawal Support and Bouncing Wings. Although the Northolt Wing was warned of enemy aircraft nearby, none were seen and they returned to base with nothing of significance to report.

31 July 1943 – The last day of the Squadron's first full month in the Spitfire XII Wing saw their participation in two Ramrod operations and one spotting patrol, totalling 26 sorties. The first Ramrod took the Squadron to St. Omer-Fort Rouge Airfield and the second to Abbeville Airfield.

Date	31 July 1943
Operation	Ramrod 180
Targets	Part I: St. Omer-Fort Rouge Airfield, Pas-de-Calais Part II: Amiens Airfield, Picardie Part III: Lille-Vendeville Airfield, Pas-de-Calais
Bombers	Part I: 2 Group: 12 Mitchells; 12 bombed Part II: 83 Group: 8 Bomphoons Part III: 181 Squadron: 8 Bomphoons
Close Escort Part I Escort Cover High Cover Close Escort Part II Close Escort Part III	Kenley: 411 & 412 Squadrons (Spitfire Vb) Westhampnett: 41 & 91 Squadrons (Spitfire XII) North Weald: 331 & 332 Squadrons (Spitfire IX) Lydd: 175 Squadron (8 Typhoon Ib) New Romney: 247 Squadron (8 Typhoon Ib)
Casualties	247 Sqn: WO1 Charles D. Macintosh RCAF, AA/KIA, Gravelines, in Typhoon Ib, JP545

The Spitfire XII Wing was airborne at 11:35, led by Wg Cdr Thomas, and rendezvoused with the Mitchells and Close Escort and High Cover Wings 20 minutes later over Pevensey, Sussex, at 500 feet. They proceeded across the Channel below this altitude until 11:59, when they climbed and crossed in at Hardelot, stepped up and back to 21,000 feet.

Reaching St. Omer-Fort Rouge Airfield at 12:20, the bombers released ninety-three 500 lb. bombs from 12,000 feet. Results were considered good and bursts were seen on the northeast and southeast dispersals.

On the way back out, 91 Squadron sighted four enemy aircraft, which they attempted to attack, but they dived away and headed east, further into France. 332 Squadron also attacked two FW190s, and claim one of them destroyed. 41 Squadron, however, found it "a most unexciting flight".[60] Whilst Fg Off David Davies (MB829) and Flt Sgt Stan May (EN611) landed early at Friston to refuel, the rest of the Squadron continued to Westhampnett, where they put down at 13:05 with nothing to report.[61]

Parts II and III also operated successfully and although the Luftwaffe interfered with the withdrawal of the Part III, their attacks were without result. However, accurate Flak was experienced from Merville Airfield and St. Omer and one of the escorting Typhoons was shot down, and its pilot killed.

During the afternoon, the Spitfire XII Wing was airborne again, on its second Ramrod of the day, on this occasion providing Escort Cover to 21 Marauders targeting Abbeville Airfield.[62]

Date	31 July 1943
Operation	Ramrod 181
Targets	Part I: Abbeville Airfield, Picardie Part II: Triqueville Airfield, Haute-Normandie
Bombers	Part I: 21 Marauders; 21 bombed Part II: 21 Marauders; 18 bombed

The Spitfire XII Wing was airborne at 15:35 with Wg Cdr Thomas leading the Wing and Sqn Ldr Ingham leading 41 Squadron. They rendezvoused with the Part I's Marauders and the other escort squadrons at 12,000 feet over Hastings, then crossed the Channel to make landfall at Cayeux.

Continuing to Abbeville, the bombers dropped seventy-two 300 lb. bombs and two hundred and nine 100 lb. bombs, with reportedly fair to good results. 41 Squadron, however, had a different opinion, considering their aim poor. Fg Off Ron Johnson recorded this sentiment in his logbook that day, "21 Marauders missed Abbeville – hit village about 2 miles away – plenty of accurate Flak".[63] There was, at least, no sign of the Luftwaffe.

The Wing returned to the French coast via Ault, and then re-crossed the Channel to Beachy Head. On landing at Westhampnett again at 16:55, the pilots felt there was "nothing of importance to report".[64]

Part II's bombing proceeded according to plan and fifty-six 300 lb. and one hundred and sixty-seven 100 lb. bombs were dropped on Triqueville Airfield with fair results. However, after leaving the target, significant Luftwaffe resistance was met, and the Close Escort, Escort Cover and High Cover Wings were all engaged by a mixed group of about twenty FW190s and Me109s. The Hornchurch Wing claimed one enemy aircraft destroyed and one damaged, whilst two were claimed as damaged by other wings, for no Allied loss. The Marauders themselves also claimed one enemy aircraft destroyed and one probable for no loss.

Shortly before the Spitfire XII Wing returned to Westhampnett, Flt Lt Dave Fearon and Fg Off Ron Loweth were sent on a spotting patrol off Selsey. Airborne at 16:40, they returned at 17:40 with nothing to report, thereby ending both the day's and the month's operational flying.

Nominal Roll, 31 July 1943

On 31 July 1943, the Squadron's Officers and Airman pilots were Sqn Ldr Bernard Ingham DFC, Commanding Officer, Flt Lts Hugh L. Parry (OC A Flight), Douglas H. Hone (OC B Flight), David N. Fearon, Roy Lane, Donald H. Smith (Australian), Fg Offs Clive R. Birbeck, Robert J. Boyd, Peter Cowell, David D. Davies, Emanuel V. Galitzine (Russian), Arthur A. Glen, Ross P. Harding, H. Bruce Moffett (Canadian), Benjamin B. Newman (Australian), Jerzy J. Solak (Polish) and Herbert A. Wagner (American), Plt Offs Arthur C. Cook, Ronald Johnson, Ronald A. Loweth and Leslie A. Prickett, Flt Sgts Douglas P. Fisher, James A. B. Gray, Stanley H. May (Australian), Jim C. J. Payne, James W. Still and William H. Vann, and Sgt Plts Alan Hope and Peter R. Wall. The chief ground staff positions were held by Flt Lt Lord Gisborough (Intelligence Officer), Fg Off Walter 'Jock' Burnett (Medical Officer), Fg Off Harry W. Smith (Adjutant), and Fg Off Richard H. Norman (Engineering Officer).[65]

August 1943 – August was an intensive month that saw the Squadron flying 22 Ramrod operations and several sweeps and Rhubarbs, the main focus of which were the destruction of Luftwaffe airfields in France. Over 700 hours were flown during the month, of which 500 were operational, and no operational flying was undertaken on only four days – 3, 10, 15 and 21 August. The month also saw the loss of two pilots who came down in enemy territory and were captured.

Airfield   Marshalling Yards   Big Ben Target

Date	Operation	Role	Type	Destination / Target
2	Ramrod 184	Escort Cover	Airfield	St. Omer-Fort Rouge, France
8	Ramrod 190	Escort Cover	Airfield	Poix, France
9	Ramrod 191	Escort Cover	Airfield	St. Omer-Fort Rouge, France
12	Ramrod 196	Escort Cover	Airfield	Poix, France
12	Ramrod 197	Escort Cover	Airfield	Poix, France
16	Ramrod 203	Top Cover	Airfield	Triqueville, France
17	Ramrod 206	Escort Cover	Airfield	Bryas Sud [Brias], France
17	Ramrod 207	Escort Cover	Airfield	Poix, France
18	Ramrod 208	Escort Cover	Airfield	Lille-Vendeville, France
19	Ramrod 209	Escort Cover	Airfield	Poix, France
19	Ramrod 210	Escort Cover	Airfield	Bryas Sud [Brias], France
20	Ramrod 211	Escort Cover	Marshalling Yards	Abbeville, France
22	Ramrod 213	Escort Cover	Airfield	Poix, France
23	Ramrod 214	Escort Cover	Airfield	Poix, France
24	Ramrod 215	Fighter Sweep	Airfield	Trouville, Bernay & Beaumont, Fr.
25	Ramrod S.2	Escort	Airfield	Bernay, France
26	Ramrod S.4	Fighter Sweep	Airfield	Beauvais, France
26	Ramrod S.5	Fighter Sweep	Airfield	Bernay & Beaumont, France
27	Ramrod S.6	Escort Cover	Airfield	Bernay, France
27	Ramrod S.8	Fighter Cover	Big Ben Target	Fôret d'Éperleques, France
30	Ramrod S.14	High Cover	Big Ben Target	Fôret d'Éperleques, France
31	Ramrod S.16	Escort Cover	Airfield	Monchy-Breton, France

1 August 1943 – The first day of the month saw the Squadron given a brief respite from Ramrod operations, employed instead on something completely different: the provision of fighter cover to a cable-laying ship between Beachy Head and the Isle of Wight, which was accompanied by two Royal Navy corvettes and a destroyer.

Sections of pilots conducted convoy patrols over the vessels from 07:55-09:10, 08:45-10:00, 09:25-10:25, 09:55-11:25 and 10:55-11:40. Fg Off Ron Johnson (MB801) and Flt Lt Dave Fearon (MB847) should have also conducted a patrol and were in fact airborne at 10:40. However, when Johnson found his R/T set malfunctioning, both men returned to base and landed ten minutes later. They were replaced in the air at 10:55 by a section consisting of Fg Off Clive Birbeck and Flt Lt Dave Fearon again.

During the afternoon, Birbeck and Flt Sgt Stan May were sent across the Channel for a Rhubarb to attack ground targets of opportunity in the St. Valéry-Fécamp area. When they arrived off the coast from St. Valéry, however, they found the cloud so low that they did not attempt to venture inland. Instead, they followed the coastline south-westwards to Fécamp, where they sighted eight barges. These were not attacked and the pair decided instead to abort the operation and head home, landing back at Westhampnett at 16:00.

Whilst this was the entire operational flying for the day, a large amount of non-operational practice flying was also undertaken, which included air-to-air and air-to-ground firing exercises.

2 August 1943 – It was back to Ramrods again for the Spitfire XII Wing today and the pilots participated in a single operation, providing an early morning Escort Cover to Marauders attacking St. Omer-Fort Rouge Airfield once again.

Date	2 August 1943
Operation	Ramrod 184
Targets	Part I: Merville Airfield, Pas-de-Calais
	Part II: St. Omer-Fort Rouge Airfield, Pas-de-Calais
Bombers	Part I: 36 Marauders USAAF; 34 dispatched, 31 bombed
	Part II: 21 Marauders USAAF; 21 dispatched, 18 bombed
Close Escort Part I	Kingsnorth: 65, 122 & 602 Squadrons (Spitfire Vb)
Escort Cover	Newchurch: 19 & 132 Squadrons (Spitfire Vb)
High Cover	Biggin Hill: 341 & 485 Squadrons (Spitfire IX)
Forward Target Support	Northolt: 303 & 316 Squadrons (Spitfire IX)
Fighter Sweep	Kenley: 403 & 421 Squadrons (Spitfire IX)
Close Escort Part II	Redhill: 401, 411 & 412 Squadrons (Spitfire Vb)
Escort Cover	Westhampnett: 41 & 91 Squadrons (Spitfire XII)
High Cover	Hornchurch: 129 & 222 Squadrons (Spitfire IX)
Fighter Sweep	North Weald: 331 & 332 Squadrons (Spitfire IX)
Additional Fighter Sweep	Tangmere: 486 Squadron (Typhoon Ib)

Part I operated according to plan and 31 of the dispatched bombers dropped two hundred and forty-five 300 lb. bombs on Merville Airfield with fair results. All the Marauders returned to base but 15 were damaged by Flak and two crew members wounded. Their escort fighters all completed the task without incident and the Luftwaffe was not sighted.

The Spitfire XII Wing was airborne at 08:15 with Wg Cdr Thomas leading 41 Squadron and the Wing. The pilots rendezvoused with Part II's Marauders and fellow escort wings 15,000 feet over North Foreland at 08:45 and crossed the Channel at the same altitude.

The formations made landfall just east of Gravelines and continued on to the target without opposition, where 18 Marauders dropped sixty-four 300 lb. bombs and one hundred and thirty-seven 100 lb. bombs at 09:00. 41 Squadron felt the bombing was accurate as they saw sticks falling across the north and northeast dispersal areas.

Although moderate heavy Flak was experienced from the airfield and from the Boulogne area on

Left to right: Fg Off Ross Harding, Fg Off Leslie Prickett, Fg Off Ron Loweth, Fg Off 'Barney' Newman RAAF, Flt Lt Roy Lane, Fg Off Peter Cowell, Fg Off Jerzy Solak PAF (with tennis racket), Flt Lt David Fearon, Fg Off Bruce Moffett RCAF, and Fg Off Clive Birbeck at Westhampnett, ca late July 1943. © Ron Johnson, via Dan Johnson

the way out, it was inaccurate and all aircraft returned to base unscathed. The fighter sweeps also operated uneventfully, and whilst a dozen enemy aircraft were seen on the ground at Poix Airfield, the Luftwaffe was not seen in the air. The Spitfire XII Wing landed at Westhampnett at 09:45 and undertook no further operational flying all day.

4 August 1943 – Following a day of poor weather upon which there was no operational flying, the Squadron's operations today comprised six sections flying ASR patrols during the morning and a Wing fighter sweep during the early evening.

Sections of both 41 and 91 Squadrons were airborne from 09:30 to support an ASR Walrus, which had been sent to pick up the crew of an Albacore that had ditched the night before. Having attacked an enemy vessel of 4,000 tons and twelve E-Boats 3½ miles from Pointe Barfleur, a Tangmere based Fairey Albacore torpedo bomber (BF777) of 841 Squadron FAA had been hit by Flak at 01:01 and ditched in the Channel nearby.

A Walrus was sent out to retrieve the crew, escorted by sections of fighters from Westhampnett and the Albacore's Observer, Sub-Lt F. R. Schofield, was found and picked up injured after 10½ hours in his dinghy. There was, however, no trace of the pilot, Sub-Lt (A) Francis W. E. Dixon.

The Walrus was then escorted home by again by additional sections of fighters. 41 Squadron provided three sections between 09:30 and 10:50 and another three between 10:20 and 11:20, throughout which time 91 Squadron also provided several sections. The Luftwaffe did not show itself, and Plt Off Ross Harding noted in his logbook, "Successful rescue by Walrus off French Coast. No opposition".[66]

During the early evening, a Wing fighter sweep of Bernay and Triqueville Airfields was undertaken, led by Wg Cdr Thomas. The two squadrons were airborne at 18:25, but 41 Squadron's Sgt Plt Peter Wall (MB800) switched over to his jettison tank to find it empty and promptly returned to base.

The rest of the Wing continued on but unfortunately "did not succeed in bringing out the enemy fighters. [It was] a most uninteresting sweep".[67] The pilots returned to Westhampnett at 19:50, and this concluded the day's operational flying.

5 August 1943 – It was a quiet day for the Squadron operationally, and just three sections were airborne all day, undertaking a convoy patrol, a Rhubarb and a shipping reconnaissance.

At 09:55, Fg Offs 'Joe' Birbeck (EN608) and Ron Loweth (MB801) were sent on a convoy patrol off St. Catherine's Point. However, it was uneventful and the pair returned at 11:10 with nothing to report. Clearly not content with the monotony of recent work, Birbeck was airborne again at 12:40 with Fg Off Ross Harding, to go "looking for trouble along the railway line running south from Dieppe".[68]

From left to right: Fg Offs 'Barney' Newman RAAF, Bob Boyd, Bruce Moffett RCAF, David Davies, and Clive Birbeck with Perkin at Westhampnett, ca late July 1943. © Ron Johnson, via Dan Johnson

The pair crossed in 3,000 feet over Ste. Marguerite-sur-Mer, a few miles west of Dieppe, at 13:00 and did not encounter any Flak. They flew east to the railway line running out of Dieppe and followed it southwards using 6/10ths cloud at 1,500 feet as cover until they found a stationary locomotive and a number of goods wagons in the station at Vassonville at 13:10.

Birbeck made a head-on attack on the goods train with a three-second burst aimed at both the engine and wagons. White flashes were seen on the engine, confirming it had been hit and damaged. Birbeck and Harding continued on to Clères, but as no further rolling stock was seen, they turned about and ran back up the line.

Reaching Vassonville again and finding the goods train still there, Birbeck had "another squirt"[69] at it, and Harding also fired upon it for the first time. They headed out the same way they had crossed in, but before crossing the coast again Birbeck also dived to ground level six miles from Dieppe to shoot up a blue motor car, and claimed it damaged, too.

The pilots attracted a little Flak as they headed out, but it was inaccurate and they returned home unscathed, landing at Westhampnett again at 13:45. Birbeck had expended 133 rounds of 20mm cannon and 820 rounds of .303 inch machine gun, whilst Harding fired 54 rounds of cannon and 50 rounds of .303.

It was another five hours before the third and last section of the day was airborne, when Flt Lt Don Smith and Sgt Plt Alan Hope were airborne to conduct a shipping reconnaissance to Trouville. They took off at 19:00 "with the hope of spotting something interesting"[70] but returned 55 minutes later with nothing to report.

6 August 1943 – On this very quiet day as a result of poor weather conditions, 41 Squadron was only called upon once operationally. At 16:10, Flt Lt Don Smith and Sgt Plt Alan Hope were scrambled to 15,000 feet south of St. Catherine's Point, but "as usual nothing was seen"[71], and they landed again 35 minutes later.

7 August 1943 – Weather continued to hamper operations, and most of those planned were cancelled. As such, the only pilots airborne all day were Fg Offs Clive Birbeck (EN608) and Ross Harding (MB829) who were eager to repeat their success of two days before. Up for an early morning Rhubarb to Dieppe again, the pair were airborne at 07:20 and crossed the Channel on the deck. They made landfall at Ste. Marguerite but had only flown a few minutes inland when they encountered thick fog, which reduced visibility to just 200 yards. Left little choice, they abandoned the operation and returned to base where they landed at 08:20. There was no further operational flying all day.

8 August 1943 – Improved weather saw the Squadron back in the air today and they participated in a Ramrod to Poix Airfield and a Rhubarb to Lisieux before lunch, when operational flying ceased.

Date	8 August 1943
Operation	Ramrod 190
Target	Poix Airfield, Picardie
Bombers	36 Marauders USAAF; 36 dispatched – recalled (weather)
Close Escort Part I	Newchurch: 19 & 132 Squadrons (Spitfire Vb) – recalled Redhill: 401, 411 & 412 Squadrons (Spitfire Vb) – recalled Kingsnorth: 602 Squadron (Spitfire Vb) – recalled
Escort Cover	Westhampnett: 41 & 91 Squadrons (Spitfire XII) – recalled
High Cover	Biggin Hill: 341 & 485 Squadrons (Spitfire IX) – recalled
Forward Target Support	Northolt: 303 & 316 Squadrons (Spitfire IX)
1st Fighter Sweep	Hornchurch: 129 & 222 Squadrons (Spitfire IX)
2nd Fighter Sweep	Lashenden: 403 & 421 Squadrons (Spitfire IX)

It was a relatively early start for the Ramrod, and the Spitfire XII Wing was airborne at 09:05 led by Wg Cdr Thomas. They rendezvoused with the Marauders, and the Close Escort and High Cover Wings 12,000 feet over Hastings at 09:30, but Fg Off Herb Wagner (EN609) returned home soon afterwards when his jettison tank fell off.

The rest of the formation crossed the Channel together above 5/10ths cloud at 7,000 feet, and made landfall at Ault at 09:42. However, the cloud thickened over France and within minutes they were flying above a layer of 8/10ths-10/10ths between 6,000 and 7,000 feet. The conditions clearly not suitable for the attack they had come to deliver, the fighters and bombers were recalled at 09:50 when still south of Abbeville.

The aircraft turned about and headed back out again without incident; the Luftwaffe was not seen and they did not encounter any Flak. Although the Forward Target Support and Fighter Sweep Wings continued as planned and completed their assigned tasks, they also returned without incident. The Spitfire XII Wing put down again at 10:20 with nothing to report.

At 11:45, Fg Off Clive Birbeck (EN608) went up again "with his usual offensive spirit"[72] to continue his recent private war on rolling stock in France. On this occasion, he took Fg Off 'Barney' Newman (EN236) with him and headed for the Lisieux area. They crossed the Channel at sea level and climbed before reaching the French coast to make landfall 3,000 feet over Cabourg.

Birbeck and Newman then followed the railway line south to Lisieux using 6/10ths cloud between 3,000 and 4,000 feet as cover. In due course, they found a number of goods wagons in a siding southeast of Caen, and dived down to shoot them up. Each man fired a three-second burst, and strikes were seen.

They found nothing else worth attacking, so headed home again the way they came in without experiencing any Flak. They landed back at Westhampnett at 12:45 for a late lunch, and there was no further operational flying by the Squadron all day.

9 August 1943 – Fg Off 'Joe' Birbeck was in the air again this morning furthering his recent personal mission against enemy rolling stock in France. However, another section got in on the act this morning, too, and beat him across the Channel.

Fg Off 'Barney' Newman, who had already accompanied Birbeck on one of his Rhubarbs, took off at 10:15 with Flt Lt 'Lulu' Lane for a beat-up of the Caen area. They crossed the Channel on the deck and made landfall at Arromanches-les-Bains, just northeast of Bayeux in the Baie de la Seine. However, they were faced with rain and low visibility inland, and decided to abort the operation and head home again, landing at 11:25.

Before their return, Birbeck (EN602) had taken off with Flt Sgt Stan May (MB847) at 10:50, and had headed across the Channel for their own show. Making landfall two miles west of Dieppe, they quickly found a small locomotive in a cutting just one mile south of the town on the Dieppe-Rouen railway line.

Both pilots made an attack on the engine and saw strikes, leaving it issuing smoke and stream and considering it had suffered Cat. B damage. They continued along the Dieppe to Fécamp railway line, but then sighted a large blue staff car approximately a quarter mile east of Le Bourg, heading towards Dieppe.

Both pilots attacked the vehicle and watched as four Wehrmacht officers "scuttled out and took refuge in a near-by ditch".[73] One of these men was dragging his leg as he ran, indicating that he had probably been hit. With the officers now in the ditch, Birbeck and May continued their attack on both the car and the ditch, the former of which was left in flames. Both pilots made three attacks each.

Satisfied their work was done, Birbeck and May crossed out at St. Aubin-sur-Mer and landed at Westhampnett again at 11:55 in time for lunch. The Tangmere Wing ORB made light of the attack, although their account appears to have fallen victim to a case of 'Chinese whispers". It reported,

> *A section of 41 Squadron during a Rhubarb shot up an engine and followed that up by two attacks on a silver staff car. The occupants, identified as five fat Germans, were reported to have "had it."*[74]

During the late afternoon, whilst being briefed for a Ramrod that they would be participating in that evening, the Foreign Secretary and Leader of the House of Commons, Anthony Eden, made an unofficial visit to the Spitfire XII Wing with his wife and son. He listened to the briefing, after which he visited the pilots' rooms and both 41 and 91 Squadrons' dispersal areas.

Eden took the time to chat with a number of the pilots, and stayed long enough to see the Wing take off for the Ramrod, in which they provided escort cover for Marauders attacking St. Omer-Fort Rouge Airfield.

Date	9 August 1943
Operation	Ramrod 191
Targets	Part I: St. Omer-Fort Rouge Airfield, Pas-de-Calais Part II: St. Omer-Fort Rouge Airfield, Pas-de-Calais Part III: Merville Airfield, Pas-de-Calais – cancelled Part IV: Poix Airfield, Picardie
Bombers	Part I: 36 Marauders USAAF; 38 dispatched, all aborted Part II: 36 Marauders USAAF; 36 dispatched, 1 bombed Part III: Bomphoons – cancelled Part IV: 8 Bomphoons, 182 Sqn; 8 dispatched, all aborted
Casualties	Part I: 386 BG/555 BS: B-26 Marauder 41-31634, mis-ID'd in cloud & SD by Spitfire (6 crew †); Part II: 1 Marauder CD/AA but escorted home safely
Close Escort Part I Escort Cover High Cover Forward Target Support Close Escort Part II Escort Cover High Cover Forward Target Support Escort Part IV Fighter Sweep	Redhill: 401, 411 & 412 Squadrons (Spitfire Vb) Portreath (10 Group): 302 & 317 Squadrons (Spitfire Vb) Lashenden: 403 & 421 Squadrons (Spitfire IX) Northolt: 303 & 316 Squadrons (Spitfire IX) Newchurch: 19, 132 & 602 Squadrons (Spitfire Vb) Westhampnett: 41 & 91 Squadrons (Spitfire XII) Biggin Hill: 341 & 485 Squadrons (Spitfire IX) North Weald: 331 & 332 Squadrons (Spitfire IX) Lydd: 174 Squadron (Typhoon Ib) Hornchurch: 129 & 222 Squadrons (Spitfire IX)
Casualties	316 Sqn: Fg Off Michael M. Maciejowski DFC DFM (POW), MAC in Spit IX, BS302, with Fg Off Lech A. Kondracki (†) in Spit IX, BS457; 421 Sqn: Fg Off Robert T. Heeney (†), EF/baled out of Spit IX, BS290

Part I's bombers and escorts rendezvoused 12,000 feet over North Foreland at 18:00 and proceeded across the Channel to make landfall at Gravelines. On reaching the target area, however, 10/10ths cloud was encountered and the bombers were unable to locate the airfield. The bombers were recalled and the fighters escorted them home again.

One Marauder was, however, lost. It was seen entering cloud at 10,000 feet with a dead engine, and next seen splashing into the sea off Gravelines. This is believed to have been Marauder 41-31634, which was misidentified in cloud and shot down by one of the escorting Spitfires. Sadly, all six crew were killed.

One of the escorting fighters was also lost when the pilot suffered engine failure and baled out but was killed. The Forward Target Support Wing operated as planned but lost two pilots when they had a mid-air collision in a turn. One man was killed and the other captured.

The Spitfire XII Wing was airborne at 18:25 led by Wg Cdr Thomas, who flew with 41 Squadron. They rendezvoused with Part II's bombers and the other escort squadrons 12,000 feet over North Foreland at 18:50, and a report in 41 Squadron's Archives records the exact timings provided for the Spitfire XII Wing[75]:

ZERO = 1800 hrs.   <u>RAMROD 191</u>   9.8.43

Squadrons 41 and 91 (Spit XII)

RENDEZVOUS – N. FORELAND at 12,000'

WESTHAMPNETT TO N. FORELAND
Course   069   CLIMBING TO 12,000' at
I.A.S.   190   800' per min.
Time   15 mins.

Course   068
I.A.S.   240   AT HEIGHT.
Time   9 mins.

N. FORELAND TO GRAVELINES
Course   139
I.A.S.   210
Time   8 mins.

GRAVELINES TO ST. OMER
Course   189
I.A.S.   310
Time   4 mins.

ST. OMER TO GRAVELINES
Course   349
I.A.S.   210
Time   5½ mins.

GRAVELINES TO N. FORELAND
Course   315
I.A.S.   210   (Probably landing at Hawkinge)
Time   13 mins.

TIMINGS			WINDS		
SET COURSE WESTHAMPNETT.	1826				
N. FORELAND............	1850	SURFACE	N.W.	10/20	
GRAVELINES............	1858	2000'	330	30	
ST. OMER..............	1902	5000'	310	40	
GRAVELINES............	1907½	10,000'	310	50	
N. FORELAND...........	1920½	15,000'	-	-	

Flt Sgts Jim Payne, 'Jackie' Fisher and Peter Wall standing behind a Spitfire XII at Westhampnett in summer 1943. Payne joined 41 Squadron on 5 July 1943, Fisher on 12 February 1943, and Wall on 5 May 1943. © Jim Payne, via Dan Johnson

After crossing in at Gravelines, the bombers also found 10/10ths cloud south of Calais at 5,000-6,000 feet, and flew to a point approximately 15 miles east of the airfield. They then split up and turned south, but reformed on the return to the target area. Although the Spitfire XII Wing did not see any bombs drop, one Marauder did in fact drop five 500 lb. bombs. Light Flak was also experienced in the St. Omer area and one bomber was hit.

Fg Offs Peter Cowell (MB834) and 'Barney' Newman (EN236) both returned early when they found they could not jettison their long range tanks, but they were followed closely by everyone else, when the bombers were recalled and returned home with their escort, jettisoning their payloads into the Channel as they went. Finding himself short of fuel, 41 Squadron's Plt Off Arthur Cook (EN226) landed early at Hawkinge, and the rest of the Spitfire XII Wing landed again at 19:35.

Whilst most squadrons had operated uneventfully, the High Cover Wing's 485 Squadron was bounced by eight Me109s, but returned claiming six of their assailants destroyed and one probably destroyed for no casualty of their own. The Forward Target Support Wing was also bounced by ten enemy aircraft, but these were similarly repelled for no casualty but the claim of one FW190 destroyed.

Part IV's Bomphoons and their escorts rendezvoused over Rye and traversed the Channel together, crossing in 12 miles west of Cayeux-sur-Mer. On reaching the Poix area, however, they also encountered 10/10ths cloud and promptly aborted the mission. They returned to England with the Hornchurch Wing, the Bomphoons jettisoning their bombs into the Channel as they went.

11 August 1943 – As weather conditions were not congenial to large scale bomber operations today, the Squadron's pilots were instead occupied on four ASR patrols, two Rhubarbs and a shipping reconnaissance between 06:10 and 15:45, totalling 14 sorties.

It was an early start for Fg Offs Douglas Haywood and Ross Harding, who were on dawn readiness, and scrambled to the Cherbourg area to locate an Allied bomber that had become lost on its return journey from Germany. Airborne at 06:10, they were joined by a section from 277 (ASR) Squadron, who together found the bomber orbiting off Cherbourg, "completely lost".[76]

On sighting the Spitfires, the bomber's pilot immediately pulled out of his orbit and approached them. They then flew back to England together, but as a result of poor visibility the bomber landed at Merston instead of Tangmere. Haywood and Harding were back on the ground again at 07:15, the latter pilot noting the successful conclusion to the job in his logbook that day, "Lancaster from Nuremberg lost off Cherbourg, found and guided home".[77]

Between 08:20 and 09:30, 09:25 and 10:35, and finally briefly between 11:10 and 11:30, ASR patrols were flown by sections of two, eight miles south of Selsey Bill, looking for a bomber crew that had baled out on their way home from an operation. Nothing was seen by the pilots, and when their allocated three hours of searching was complete, the task was taken over by another squadron.

Whilst the ASR searches were on-going, Flt Lt Douglas Hone and Sgt Plt Alan Hope took off for a weather reconnaissance to Dieppe. Airborne at 09:25, the patrol was uneventful and the pair returned at 10:05 with nothing to report.[78]

Intent in continuing his recent private campaign against rolling stock in France, Fg Off Clive Birbeck (EN608) flew back to the Dieppe area today to try his luck once again. On this occasion, he was accompanied by Australian pilot, Flt Sgt Stan May (EN611). Having taken off at 11:40, the two pilots crossed in over Ste. Marguerite-sur-Mer at 12:05 under 6/10ths cloud at 3,000 feet.

On turning to port, they almost immediately spotted a goods train in a siding on the Dieppe-Rouen line, around eight miles south of Dieppe, near Crosville. Both pilots made attacks on the engine, observed strikes, and left it in clouds of steam and smoke. Continuing along the line towards Dieppe, they soon sighted another train near St. Aubin, travelling into the town, and May attacked it, too. Strikes were seen on the locomotive, but mainly only from machine gun fire. However, as the train was defended by a Flak wagon positioned at the rear, which opened up intense light calibre fire upon them, they made a brisk exit.

Soon afterwards, Birbeck spotted two unidentified aircraft approximately 2,000 yards south of them, which they presumed to be hostile. They were flying on the deck perpendicular to their route. As both aircraft were now getting short on ammunition, they decided that "it was a case of discretion being the better part of valour"[79], and decided it was time to head home. By the time the hostile aircraft had turned towards them, Birbeck and May had already opened their throttles and put some distance between them. The pursuers quickly gave up and 41 Squadron's section left France at Ste. Marguerite and crossed the Channel without interference.

On landing back at Westhampnett at 12:40, the two men claimed both locomotives damaged to Cat. B status, half a locomotive credited to Birbeck and one-and-a-half to May. The former pilot had expended 70 rounds of 20mm cannon and 200 rounds of .303 inch machine gun, whilst the latter had fired 112, respectively 600, of each. However, May (EN611) had actually had a close shave, as a single machine gun bullet was found to have struck his engine during the Rhubarb. The appearance of a Flak wagon and enemy aircraft in the area for the first time also suggests that the Germans may have noticed a pattern in Birbeck's recent actions against the railways south of Dieppe and been ready for him this time.

Unperturbed, however, Flt Lt 'Lulu' Lane and Fg Off 'Barney' Newman[80] took off at 14:35, and crossed the Channel for their own Rhubarb. Making landfall at Ouistreham, they "tried their luck"[81] on the coastal railway line between Lion-sur-Mer and Saint-Côme-de-Fresné. Finding nothing, they continued on to the main line between Bayeux and Caen. Again luckless, they moved on to the branch line between Caen and Desvres, but still found no suitable target.

Finally, giving up, the pair crossed back out at Longues-sur-Mer, and flew back across the Channel uneventfully, to land at base again at 15:45, ending the day's operational flying for the Squadron.

12 August 1943 – It proved to be a busy day for the Squadron's pilots today. They participated in two Ramrods, a bomber interception exercise, and a shipping reconnaissance, totalling 32 sorties between 10:05 and 22:15.

In the first of these, the Spitfire XII Wing flew as Escort Cover to 36 Marauders bombing Poix Airfield, in an operation in itself considerably smaller than others recently, but operating in connection with two other Ramrods. These were Ramrod 194, in which a fighter escort was provided to Flying Fortresses withdrawing from bombing targets in the Ruhr, and Ramrod 195, in which attacks were made by Bomphoons on the airfields at Courtrai [Kortrijk] and Lille-Vendeville.

Date	12 August 1943
Operation	Ramrod 196
Target	Poix Airfield, Picardie
Bombers	36 Marauders USAAF; 36 dispatched, 33 bombed
Casualties	12 Marauders CD/AA
Escort	Coltishall: 118 & 611 Squadrons (Spitfire Vb)
	Merston: 402 & 416 Squadrons (Spitfire Vb)
Escort Cover	Westhampnett: 41 & 91 Squadrons (Spitfire XII)
High Cover	Biggin Hill: 341 & 485 Squadrons (Spitfire IX)
Forward Target Support	North Weald: 331 & 332 Squadrons (Spitfire IX)

The Spitfire XII Wing was airborne at 10:05, 41 Squadron deploying 12 aircraft for the operation, led by Sqn Ldr Ingham. However, within minutes, Ingham (EN237) was forced to return, when he was unable to lock his hood in place.

The rest of the pilots rendezvoused with the Marauders and fellow escort squadrons 12,000 feet over Rye at 10:30, and proceeded across the Channel to make landfall two miles south of Cayeux. Proceeding to the target area via Hamel, Flt Lt Don Smith (MB845) was also forced to return when he found he was unable to jettison his long range tank. He landed again at 11:15.

Poix Airfield was reached at 10:56 where the bombers dropped one hundred and sixty-one 500 lb. GP bombs with good results. Although bursts were seen to fall in the northern dispersal area, some were also seen in the fields to the southwest, and six aircraft, seen on hard standing on the western side of the airfield, were also not hit. However, accurate Flak was experienced and a third of the bombers sustained some form of damage.

The fighters escorted the bombers back to the coast via Triqueville with the Forward Target Support Wing, and returned across the Channel uneventfully. The Spitfire XII Wing landed at Westhampnett at 11:40.

After lunch, four pilots were sent up on a bomber interception exercise.[82] Scrambled at 14:35, they were given a vector of 310° and an altitude of 10,000 feet, told to orbit south of Winchester and to attack any targets they could see. Within a short time, three Wellingtons were spotted flying south, 2,000 feet above them, and the quartet climbed to intercept them. Quarter and stern attacks were made on the bombers, after which the four pilots split up and made a number of attacks on other bombers in the vicinity. When the pilots landed again at 15:25, they reported that evasive action by two Stirlings in particular was very good, and also felt they had obtained some valuable practice.

At 17:45, the whole wing was back in the air again for another Ramrod, on this occasion providing Escort Cover for a dozen Venturas bombing Poix Airfield again, perhaps as a result of the fact that aircraft seen on the ground during the morning's trip to the airfield, indicated it was still in use. This Ramrod was followed by yet another to Poix, less than an hour later, by 36 Marauders.

Date	12 August 1943
Operation	Ramrod 197
Targets	Part I: Amiens-Longueau Marshalling Yards, Picardie
	Part II: Poix Airfield, Picardie
Bombers	Part I: 24 Mitchells, 2 Group; 24 dispatched, all aborted
	Part II: 12 Venturas, 2 Group; 12 dispatched, all aborted
Close Escort Part I	Staplehurst: 401, 411 & 412 Squadrons (Spit Vb) – aborted
Escort Cover	Kenley: 66 & 165 Squadrons (Spitfire Vb) – aborted
High Cover	Biggin Hill: 341 & 485 Squadrons (Spitfire IX) – aborted
Forward Target Support	North Weald: 331 & 332 Squadrons (Spitfire IX)
Close Escort Part II	Newchurch: 19, 132 & 602 Squadrons (Spit Vb) – aborted
Escort Cover	Westhampnett: 41 & 91 Squadrons (Spitfire XII) – aborted
High Cover	Northolt: 303 & 316 Squadrons (Spitfire IX) – aborted
Fighter Sweep	Lashenden: 403 & 421 Squadrons (Spitfire IX)

Led by Sqn Ldr Harries, the Spitfire XII Wing rendezvoused with Part II's escorts and bombers at low altitude over Pevensey Bay at 18:00. They crossed the Channel together on the deck until 18:06, when they commenced their climb towards the French coast. As they did, however, Flt Lt Don Smith (MB845) realised he had the same problem as during the morning's Ramrod when his long range tank would not jettison. He returned to base and landed at 18:50.

The rest of the formation continued to the French coast, but encountered 7/10ths cloud and heavy haze at 7,000 feet as they crossed in at Criel-sur-Mer. The entire operation was scuttled as a result, and the aircraft turned 180° and headed home again without having fired a shot or dropped a bomb. The Spitfire XII Wing landed only 15 minutes after Flt Lt Smith.

The Fighter Sweep operated nonetheless according to plan and swept the Amiens area at 25,000 feet. They sighted twenty Me109s 5,000 feet below them, but they dived to ground level and scattered, and the Wing was unable to engage a single aircraft. There was nothing further of consequence and 403 and 421 Squadrons returned to base uneventfully.

The Ramrod's Part I aircraft fared similarly and aborted the mission on account of weather conditions on reaching the French coast. Their Forward Target Support wing also operated as planned but swept uneventfully and returned to base with nothing to report.

After dinner that evening, four of 41 Squadron's pilots went up for one last operation when they undertook a shipping patrol to the Cherbourg area. The pilots were airborne at 21:15 led by Flt Lt Dave Fearon, but within a few minutes Flt Sgt 'Jackie' Fisher (MB829) started to have R/T trouble and returned to base, where he landed within ten minutes of his departure.

The remaining trio crossed the Channel on the deck until four miles off Cherbourg, where they briefly climbed to 1,000 feet. Dropping again to sea level, they flew along the coastline between Le Havre and Fécamp, but saw nothing of interest and returned to base at 22:15, concluding the day's flying.

13 August 1943 – As the weather today was unsuitable for Ramrod operations, the Squadron spent the day flying a number of Air-Sea Rescue patrols south of Fécamp. The searches were the result of reports that a bomber returning from overnight operations over enemy territory had ditched just off the French coast. The search was begun by Albacores of 841 Squadron FAA at 01:00 and continued by Spitfires after first light. For their part, 41 Squadron mounted four searches, each consisting of four aircraft, at 06:25-07:45, 09:05-10:20, 12:35-13:15, and 16:55-18:15. Unfortunately, nothing was seen by any of them.

14 August 1943 – The weather was still poor today, and the only operational flying undertaken was a scramble by three sections during the evening when enemy aircraft were reported in the vicinity. At 20:25, Red, Yellow and White Sections of each two pilots took off and were ordered to patrol Selsey at 10,000 feet. However, nothing was seen and the six pilots were back on the ground at 20:50 with nothing to report.

15 August 1943 – Once again, weather hindered large scale Ramrod operations and the only operational flying conducted by the Squadron all day was when Fg Off Clive Birbeck and Flt Sgt Stan May returned to the south of Dieppe for a Rhubarb against rolling stock at 14:50. However, on reaching their chosen target area, visibility was found to be too poor for an effective operation to be undertaken, and both aircraft returned to base without firing. They landed again at 15:45.[83]

Separately, a new pilot arrived on the Squadron in the form of 23-year-old Londoner, Flt Lt Ronald T. H. Collis. Having enlisted in the RAFVR in June 1940, he completed his entire flying training in the United Kingdom, and was commissioned 13 months later. Having spent the ensuing two years as a flying instructor, Collis was finally released to operational training at Rednal in July 1943, and posted to 41 Squadron today as his first front line unit. Although he had logged a significant 1,130 flying hours, none were operational.

16 August 1943 – The weather much improved today, the Spitfire XII Wing was called on once again to provide support for an element of a large Ramrod in four parts, targeting five airfields. The Wing's role was to afford Top Cover to a dozen RAF Venturas attacking Triqueville Airfield.

Date	16 August 1943
Operation	Ramrod 203
Targets	Part I: Le Bourget Airfield, Île-de-France Part II: Poix & Abbeville-Drucat Airfields, Picardie Part III: Triqueville Airfield, Haute-Normandie Part IV: Amiens-Glisy Airfield, Picardie
Bombers	Part I: 180 USAAF Flying Fortresses; 170 bombed Part II: 60 USAAF Flying Fortresses; 64 dispatched, 64 bombed Part III: 2 Group RAF: 12 Venturas; 12 dispatched Part IV: 36 USAAF Marauders; 31 bombed
Casualties	91 BG/323 BS: B-17F 42-3213 'All American', AA/ditched 4m off English coast, crew RR; 384 BG/546 BS: B-17F 42-5797, SD/AA Rambouillet (1 KIA, 6 POW, 3 ER); 379 BG/524 BS: B-17F 42-29866, 'Judy Bea' SD/AA Le Bourget (1 KIA, 5 POW, 4 ER); 379 BG/526 BS: B-17F 42-30001 'Mary Ann' SD Le Coudray-Montceaux (5 KIA, 4 POW, 1 ER)
Support Part I High Cover High Cover Part II Close Escort Part III Escort Cover Top Cover Close Escort Part IV Escort Cover High Cover	4th, 56th, 78th & 353rd Fighter Groups USAAF (Thunderbolt) Lashenden: 403 & 421 Squadrons (Spitfire IX) Northolt: 303 & 316 Squadrons (Spitfire IX) Hornchurch: 129 & 222 Squadrons (Spitfire IX) Kingsnorth: 65 & 122 Squadrons (Spitfire IX) North Weald: 331 & 332 Squadrons (Spitfire IX) Staplehurst: 401 & 412 Squadrons (Spit Vb) Ibsley: 453 & 616 Squadrons (Spitfire Vb) Westhampnett: 41 & 91 Squadrons (Spitfire XII) Merston: 402 & 416 Squadrons (Spitfire Vb) Coltishall: 611 Squadron (Spitfire Vb) Hutton Cranswick: 308 Squadron (Spitfire Vb) Kenley: 66 & 165 Squadrons (Spitfire Vb) Biggin Hill: 341 & 485 Squadrons (Spitfire IX)
USAAF Casualties	4 FG/336 FS: Lt. Joseph Matthews SD/ER nr Paris in Thunderbolt 42-7949; 56 FG/63 FS: 1 Lt George R. Spaleny EF/CL/POW Gournay-en-Bray in Thunderbolt 42-7865; 353 FG/351 FS: Lt. Col. Joseph A. Morris (OC, 353 FG) SD/KIA Elbeuf in Thunderbolt 42-7990
RAF Casualties	308 Sqn: Fg Off Olgierd Ilinkski, SD/KIA nr Maulévrier in Spit Vb, R7161; Flt Sgt Waclaw Korwel, CD/WIA (legs), CL N of Brighton in Spit Vb, BM137; Fg Off Wieslaw Mejer, SD/POW Bernay area in Spit Vb, AB803; Flt Sgt Wladyslaw Sznapka, SD nr Bernay in Spit Vb, W3404, ER; 616 Sqn: Fg Off Michael H. F. Cooper, EF/ER, baled out of Spit Vc, BR987

The U.S. 8th Bomber Command dispatched 180 Flying Fortresses in Part I to attack Le Bourget Airfield, just north of Paris. They were escorted to and from the French coast by RAF Spitfire squadrons, whilst Thunderbolts with long range tanks of the U.S. 4th, 56th, 78th & 353rd Fighter Groups provided them an escort from Fécamp to Le Bourget and back to Bernay.

The B17s were attacked by the Luftwaffe almost immediately after reaching Fécamp and combats with USAAF Thunderbolts resulted in the 353rd Fighter Group claiming of one FW190 destroyed, one Me109 probably destroyed and one FW190 damaged for the loss of one pilot. The 4th Fighter Group was also heavily engaged and although they sustained the loss of one pilot, they made claims of no less than 17 enemy aircraft destroyed, one probably destroyed and five damaged. The 78th Fighter Group did not sight any enemy aircraft, and the 56th Fighter Group only had minor skirmishes which resulted in no claims but the loss of one pilot who suffered engine failure.

Fg Off Leslie Prickett force-landed his aircraft 60-70 miles south of St Omer, France, as a result of engine failure on 27 August 1943. Initially hidden by the Resistance, he was captured by the Gestapo in Paris on 17 December 1943. Whilst held in Stalag Luft III, he was the chief utensil maker of items made from cocoa cans. © Ron Johnson, via Dan Johnson

One hundred and seventy Flying Fortresses dropped a total of 408 tons of bombs on Le Bourget and heavy smoke and flames engulfed the target. Despite this, five enemy aircraft were seen taking off from the airfield in the middle of the attack. However, anti-aircraft fire was also heavy and three bombers failed to return as a result.

Another 64 Flying Fortresses were dispatched to Poix and Abbeville-Drucat Airfields in Part II, which were met by escorting Spitfire squadrons at the French coast. The Luftwaffe was not seen on the way to the targets and the bombers dropped a total of 79.2 tons of bombs, approximately half of this tonnage falling on each airfield. Results were considered good as bursts were seen in the dispersals areas of both.

On the way home, eight FW190s made an attack on the rear of the bomber formation, but these were repelled by 331 Squadron, who claimed one enemy aircraft destroyed for no loss. The pilots also made an unexpected observation, that a number of the FW190s, including the one destroyed bore Italian markings on both the wings and tail fins.

In Part III, 12 Venturas were sent to Triqueville Airfield, escorted by several Spitfire squadrons, thereunder those of the Spitfire XII Wing. The Wing was airborne at 10:45, led by Wg Cdr Thomas, who also led 41 Squadron. His number two was the Sector Gunnery Officer, Sqn Ldr Hubert Allen. Flt Lt Hugh Parry led 41 Squadron's second section, whilst Sqn Ldr Ingham led the third. Fg Off Bruce Moffett (EN608), assigned to Wg Cdr Thomas' section, sustained a puncture to a tyre whilst taxiing for take-off and did not become airborne.

The rest of the Wing rendezvoused according to plan and the target area was reached without any interference from the Luftwaffe. Flak was only light and the bombers' payloads were seen to land near headquarters buildings, on the dispersal area, and on the fuel dump, which resulted in large explosions and fire. The resulting smoke plume could still be seen from 50 miles away on the return journey.

The fighter escorts operated generally without incident, and no contact was made with enemy aircraft. The Spitfire XII Wing sighted eight FW190s above and behind them, but these dived away when the Wing turned to engage them. They continued toward the French coast, but when west of Le Havre, the Wing left the homeward-bound bombers to go to the assistance of RAF fighters to their east, which were escorting Part IV's bombers home from Bernay. No enemy aircraft were seen but the Wing swung in behind the Marauders and escorted them back across the Channel.

Part IV's operation had otherwise gone well and 31 Marauders had dropped a total of two hundred and forty-eight 300 lb. bombs on Bernay-St. Martin Airfield from 11,000 feet with good results. On the way out, the Close Escort squadrons were bounced by 20+ Me109s, which resulted in the Spitfire XII Wing turning back to assist. 308 Squadron was hit hard and sustained four casualties: three pilots were shot down, of which one was killed, one captured, and one evaded,

OC B Flight Flt Lt Douglas Hone left 41 Squadron on 30 August 1943 and retired as a Flight Lieutenant in September 1975. It is believed he was the last man to retire from the RAF who had flown in the Battle of Britain. © Tom Harvey

whilst the fourth was wounded in action but managed to make it back to England where he crash-landed his damaged aircraft north of Brighton. Claims were also submitted for one FW190 destroyed and two damaged.

The Spitfire XII Wing returned to Westhampnett where they put down at 12:10. However, Fg Off Douglas Haywood (EN602) found his undercarriage was jammed in the 'up' position and could not lower it, despite several attempts to do so. Finally, left little choice, he continued a short distance to Tangmere, where he made a safe wheels-up landing and was not injured.

Back at Westhampnett, the pilots were advised that another Ramrod was planned for the afternoon, but it was cancelled and the men were released. Intent on enjoying the night, however, they were disappointed to find that…

> *During the evening the Mess ran out of liquid refreshment as they often do, and a number of pilots visited a charming old "pub", the Angel at Bosham, where a few quiet beers were consumed.*[84]

17 August 1943 – 41 Squadron participated in three bomber escorts to France today. The first was abandoned ten minutes into the flight, but the remaining two were carried out to St. Pol and Poix, respectively.

In the first (aborted) escort, twelve aircraft took off at 09:05 with 91 Squadron to escort Marauders to Bryas Sud Airfield, but they did not make rendezvous with the bombers, which had not become airborne, and were recalled at 09:15.[85]

Unbeknown to the Squadron, the second operation saw their participation in a minor piece of history. Known today as the 'Schweinfurt-Regensburg Mission', the operation was conceived as a part of a larger strategy designed to cripple the German aircraft industry at home. The crux of the attack was a so-called 'double strike' as it entailed the deployment of two separate large formations of Flying Fortresses to different targets, which was intended to dilute any Luftwaffe counter strikes by fighters. Moreover, it was also the first 'shuttle' mission, as it became known, in which the bomber force landed in another country, refuelled, rearmed, and bombed another target before returning home. Especially equipped with long range fuel tanks called 'Tokyo Tanks', they would continue on to bases in North Africa on completion of their attacks.

The attack foresaw the utilisation of 376 bombers from sixteen Bomb Groups against the ball bearing factories at Schweinfurt, and the Messerschmitt factory at Regensburg, Bavaria, supported by six diversionary attacks to airfields and marshalling yards in Northern France and the Netherlands.

Date	17 August 1943
Operation	Ramrod 206
Targets Part I	Ball bearing factories, Schweinfurt, & Messerschmitt factory, Regensburg, Bavaria [Bayern], Germany
Part II	Return from Schweinfurt & Regensburg, Germany
Part III	Diversion A: Bryas Sud [Brias] Airfield, Pas-de-Calais, F.
	Diversion B: Calais Marshalling Yards, Pas-de-Calais, F.
	Diversion C: Dunkirk Marshalling Yards, Pas-de-Cal., F.
Part IV	1st Attack: Poix Airfield, Picardie, France
	2nd Attack: Lille-Vendeville Airfield, Pas-de-Calais, F.
	3rd Attack: Woensdrecht Airfield, Noord-Brabant, NL
Bombers Part I	376 USAAF Flying Fortresses in 3 Outbound Forces
Part II	USAAF Flying Fortresses; in 3 Outbound Forces
Part III	Diversion A: 36 USAAF Marauders; 29 bombed
	Diversion B: 6 Mitchells, 2 Group; 5 bombed
	Diversion C: 6 Mitchells, 2 Group; all aborted
Part IV	1st Attack: Tangmere: 183 Sqn Bomphoons
	2nd Attack: New Romney: 182 Sqn Bomphoons
	3rd Attack: Hornchurch: 3 & 175 Sqn Bomphoons
Casualties	Parts I & II: 60 B-17F Flying Fortresses lost & dozens more damaged: Regensburg: 94 BG: 1 lost; 95 BG: 4 lost; 100 BG: 9 lost; 385 BG: 3 lost; 388 BG: 1 lost; 390 BG: 6 lost; Schweinfurt: 91 BG: 7 lost; 92 BG: 2 lost; 101 BG: 6 lost; 103 BG: 4 lost; 305 BG: 2 lost; 351 BG: 1 lost; 381 BG: 9 lost; 384 BG: 5 lost; Part III, Diversion A: 2 Marauders CD/AA; Part IV, 1st Attack: 3 Bomphoons CD/AA; Part IV, 2nd Attack: 182 Sqn: Flt Lt Walter H. Bewg SD/KIA nr Lille in Typhoon Ib, DN553
Escort Part I, Force I	USAAF: 56 FG & 353 FG (P-47 Thunderbolt)
Escort Part I, Force II	Hornchurch: 129 & 222 Squadrons (Spitfire IX)
	North Weald: 331 & 332 Squadrons (Spitfire IX)
Escort Part I, Force III	Lashenden: 403 & 421 Squadrons (Spitfire IX)
	Northolt: 303 & 316 Squadrons (Spitfire IX)
Escort Part II	USAAF: 56 FG & 353 FG (P-47 Thunderbolt)
	Hornchurch: 129 & 222 Squadrons (Spitfire IX)
	North Weald: 331 & 332 Squadrons (Spitfire IX)
	Lashenden: 403 & 421 Squadrons (Spitfire IX)
	Northolt: 303 & 316 Squadrons (Spitfire IX)
Close Escort Pt III Div A	Merston: 402 & 416 Squadrons (Spitfire Vb)
Escort Cover	Westhampnett: 41 & 91 Squadrons (Spitfire XII)
High Cover	Biggin Hill: 341 & 485 Squadrons (Spitfire IX)
Forward Target Support	Kingsnorth: 65 & 122 Squadrons (Spitfire IX)
Close Escort Pt III Div B	Newchurch: 19, 132 & 602 Squadrons (Spitfire Vb)
Close Escort Pt III Div C	Staplehurst: 401, 411 & 412 Squadrons (Spitfire Vb)
Fighters Pt IV 1st Attack	Tangmere: 486 Squadron (Typhoon Ib)
Fighters Pt IV 2nd Attack	New Romney: 181 & 247 Squadrons (Typhoon Ib)
Fighters Pt IV 3rd Attack	Hornchurch: 56, 174 & 245 Squadrons (Typhoon Ib)
USAAF Casualties	56 FG/62 FS: 1 Lt Voorhis H. Day SD/KIA in Thunderbolt 42-7891 & 1 Lt Robert M. Stultz SD/KIA in Thunderbolt 41-6398; 56 FG/63 FS: 1 Lt Arthur Sugas SD/KIA NL, in Thunderbolt, 41-6372
RAF Casualties	341 Sqn: Sgt Plt André Poirier SD in Spit IX, initially evaded, captured 17 Dec 1943; 403 Sqn: Flt Lt Walter A. C. Conrad DFC (ER), MAC nr Gent in Spit IX, LZ997, with Flt Sgt Graham M. Shouldice (†) in Spit IX, MA615

The Flying Fortresses, forming Force I of Part I, made landfall at Haamstede, in the Netherlands, at 10:05 and were escorted by USAAF Thunderbolts to a point five miles south of Diest. Force II made landfall over Walcheren and were escorted to a point ten miles northeast of Antwerp. Their escorts made contact with the Luftwaffe, bouncing 12 aircraft with the result of four Me109s and a FW190 claimed destroyed for no loss of their own. Force III crossed in north of Walcheren and were escorted as far as Antwerp. Their escorts also engaged the Luftwaffe, claiming another four FW190s destroyed for no loss. The escorts then headed home and left the bombers unescorted for the next two hours, whilst they continued into Germany towards their Bavarian targets.

The Fortresses' bombing caused significant damage to the Messerschmitt factory at Regensburg, and resulted in the destruction of or substantial damage to all six main workshops, the final assembly shop and supporting buildings. Whilst the attack on Schweinfurt was not considered as successful, it nonetheless resulted in 80 direct hits on the two largest ball bearing factories, Kugelfischer Georg Schäfer & Co. and Vereinigte Kugellager Fabriken AG. Incendiaries also ignited machine oil storage, which resulted in extensive additional fire damage. Damage was spread over an area estimated to have been approximately $100,000m^2$.

However, the toll on the bombers was horrendous. No less than 60 Fortresses were lost to Flak or the Luftwaffe, and dozens more were damaged. This figure was more than double the previous highest loss record for a single mission. At the end of the day, 55 crews, totalling over 550 men, were listed as missing. The majority had come down in German-held territory, whilst the remainder came down in Switzerland or the Channel, the latter of which enabled five crews to be rescued. Seven dead crew members and 21 wounded were also brought home in those aircraft that did return to base. Whilst the attacks were successful, the mission was a hard lesson for the USAAF in the consequences of sending unescorted bombers into Germany.

Reichsminister for Armament and War Production, Albert Speer, considered the attack had caused an immediate 34% reduction in ball bearing production, but as a result of the day's bomber losses, the 8th Air Force was unable to follow up with attacks on other ball bearing factories. Speer was therefore able to fill the immediate gap with surplus ball bearing storages elsewhere in Germany, and it was soon evident that whilst the aircraft industry could have been crippled through a sustained bombing campaign, a single attack was insufficient to halt production.

The homeward bound bombers were met again from 16:45 in Part II, by the same units as had escorted them on the way out. Once again, the Luftwaffe was engaged and claims were made for four Me110s and one FW190 destroyed, this time for the loss of two pilots from 403 Squadron. Their losses were not, however, a result of enemy action, rather they collided with each other, with the result that one was killed, whilst the other managed to evade.

Whilst the Spitfire XII Wing was not involved with the Flying Fortresses, they were deployed on one of the diversionary attacks, providing Escort Cover in Diversion A of Part III, to Bryas Sud Airfield in Pas-de-Calais. Delays in Part I, however, meant that each of the Diversions operated a few hours before the Flying Fortresses, thereby eliminating any value in the strategy at all.

The Wing was airborne at 10:10, led by Wg Cdr Thomas, and rendezvoused with the Close Escort and High Cover wings 12,000 feet over Dungeness at 10:30. The Marauders were, however, 15 minutes late and then approached the French coast too near to Boulogne, which attracted some unwelcome heavy Flak.

Crossing in at Le Touquet, stepped up and back between 12,000 and 18.000 feet, the formation proceeded the target via Fruges, where the High Cover Wing was bounced by approximately 25 Me109s and FW190s. In the ensuing combats, 341 and 485 Squadrons claimed one Me109 and one FW190 destroyed, and one FW190 probable, for the loss of one pilot, who initially evaded, but was captured in December 1943.

The Marauders reached the target area without further interference, where 29 dropped a total of two hundred and thirty-two 300 lb. GP bombs with reportedly fair results, although escorting fighters also reported seeing bursts in the centre of the airfield.

The return journey was without incident and all the bombers returned safely; two sustained damage from 'weak' Flak over the airfield. 41 Squadron's Flt Sgt Jimmy Payne (EN234) had returned early as his long range fuel tank would not jettison and landed again at 11:00, and the rest of the Spitfire XII Wing put down at Westhampnett at 11:40.

In Part III, Diversion B, five of the six dispatched Mitchells dropped thirty-two 500 lb. bombs onto Calais Marshalling Yards, but they missed their target and fell in open country west of the rail yards instead. The operation was otherwise uneventful for both the bombers and their escorts. Diversion C was aborted half way across the Channel, when it was realised the bombers would not have sufficient distance to gain the right bombing altitude.

Part IV foresaw attacks on the airfields at Poix and Lille in France, and Woensdrecht in the Netherlands. In the first of these, sixteen 500 lb. bombs were dropped, of which two were seen to make direct hits on the east-west runway. Three Typhoons were slightly damaged by Flak, but the operation was otherwise uneventful.

Sixteen 500 lb-ers were also dropped on Lille-Vendeville of which several bursts were seen across the airfield, and close to hangars and the northern dispersals area. Whilst Flak was only light over the airfield itself, heavier accurate Flak was experienced on the way out one Typhoon was hit, with the result that the pilot was killed.

Woensdrecht was also attacked with sixteen 500 lb. bombs by 3 Squadron, which were seen to explode on the airfield and in the north-eastern dispersals area. 175 Squadron abandoned the operation on account of the amount of Flak they were experiencing on their way to the target and found alternative targets instead. Four miles east of Flushing [Vlissingen], they attacked a 3,000-ton tanker, protected by two Flak ships, with eight 500 lb. bombs, scoring near misses. The Typhoons all returned without incident.

The third Ramrod that 41 Squadron participated in today entailed the provision of Escort Cover with 91 Squadron for 36 Marauders. "This time the familiar Poix Airfield was due for another of our numerous visits. There will not be much left o[f] this place if it is bombed much more!"[86] This was their fourth visit to Poix this month, and they would make another three before the end of August.

Date	17 August 1943
Operation	Ramrod 207
Targets	Part I: Poix Airfield, Picardie
	Part II: Poix Airfield, Picardie
Bombers	Part I: 36 USAAF Marauders; 35 bombed
	Part II: 36 USAAF Marauders – recalled (weather)
Casualties	Part I: 20 Marauders CD/AA
Close Escort Part I	Merston: 402 & 416 Squadrons (Spitfire Vb)
	Coltishall: 118 & 611 Squadrons (Spitfire Vb)
Escort Cover	Westhampnett: 41 & 91 Squadrons (Spitfire XII)
High Cover	Kingsnorth: 65 & 122 Squadrons (Spitfire IX)
Fighter Sweep	Tangmere: 183, 197 & 486 Squadrons (Typhoon Ib)
Close Escort Part II	Newchurch: 19, 132 & 602 Squadrons (Spitfire Vb) – recalled
Escort Cover	Kenley: 66, 131, 165 & 504 Sqns (Spitfire Vb) – recalled
High Cover	Biggin Hill: 341 & 485 Squadrons (Spitfire IX) – recalled

The Spitfire XII Wing was airborne at 15:15, led by Wg Cdr Thomas once again, who also flew with 41 Squadron, leading Red Section. Yellow was led by Flt Lt Hugh Parry and Blue by Sqn Ldr Ingham. They rendezvoused with the Marauders and fellow escort wings 12,000 feet over Rye at 15:30, and crossed in between Ault and Cayeux.

The formation proceeded to Poix via Hornoy stepped up and back between 12,000 and 15,000 feet, despite 8/10ths-10/10ths cloud between 11,000 and 14,000 feet. However, around this time, Wg Cdr Thomas (MB849) exited early and headed home with jettison tank trouble.

Thirty-five of the 36 Marauders bombed the airfield, dropping a total of two hundred and seventy-nine 300 lb. GP bombs with good results. Bursts were seen in the north-eastern dispersals area, among six stationary single-engined aircraft, and on one building. Flak was moderate but accurate over the airfield and 20 bombers were hit.

The first fighter sweep operated independently, sweeping Beaumont-le-Roger, Bernay and Triqueville at 8,000 feet, finding nothing worthy of attacking. 41 Squadron considered the Ramrod "very tame from our angle"[87] and the pilots returned at 16:35, with nothing to report.

Part II was aborted as a result of weather conditions and all bombers and fighters were recalled.

18 August 1943 – A much quieter day today, the Squadron was only involved in a single, abortive five-part Ramrod during the morning, escorting Marauders to Lille-Vendeville Airfield.

Date	18 August 1943
Operation	Ramrod 208
Targets	Part I: Lille-Vendeville Airfield, Pas-de-Calais, France
	Part II: Woensdrecht Airfield, Noord-Brabant, Netherlands
	Part III: Flushing [Vlissingen] Petrol Stores, Walcheren, Netherlands
	Part IV: Poix Airfield, Picardie, France – cancelled
	Part V: Merville Airfield, Pas-de-Calais, France – cancelled
Bombers	Part I: 36 USAAF Marauders; 36 dispatched, 22 bombed
	Part II: 36 USAAF Marauders; 36 dispatched, 28 bombed
	Part III: 7 Mitchells, 2 Group – recalled
Casualties	Part I: 23 Marauders CD/AA & Part II: 8 Marauders CD/AA
Close Escort Part I	Staplehurst: 401, 411 & 412 Squadrons (Spitfire Vb) – aborted
	Newchurch: 19 & 602 Squadrons (Spitfire Vb) – aborted
Escort Cover	Westhampnett: 41 & 91 Squadrons (Spitfire XII) – aborted
High Cover	Lashenden: 403 & 421 Squadrons (Spitfire IX) – aborted
Fwd Target Support	Kingsnorth: 65 & 122 Squadrons (Spitfire IX)
Close Escort Part II	Merston: 118, 402 & 416 Squadrons (Spitfire Vb)
	Kenley: 66 & 165 Squadrons (Spitfire Vb)
Escort Cover	Kenley: 131 & 504 Squadrons (Spitfire Vb)
High Cover	Biggin Hill: 341 & 485 Squadrons (Spitfire IX)
Fwd Target Support	Hornchurch: 129 & 222 Squadrons (Spitfire IX)
Close Escort Part III	West Malling: 130 & 234 Squadrons (Spitfire Vb) – recalled
Escort Cover	Friston: 64 Squadron (Spitfire Vb) – recalled
High Cover	Northolt: 303 & 316 Squadrons (Spitfire IX) – recalled
Fwd Target Support	North Weald: 331 & 332 Squadrons (Spitfire IX) – recalled
Casualties	131 Sqn: Fg Off Cyril B. Smith RAAF, EF nr Woensdrecht in Spit Vc, AR506, POW

The Spitfire XII Wing was airborne at 09:40, led by Wg Cdr Thomas, and rendezvoused with the bombers and escort wings 12,000 feet over North Foreland at 10:00. The formation set course for Fort-Mardyck but encountered 6/10ths to 9/10ths cloud layers between 6,000 and 15,000 feet with haze five miles off the French coast.

As a result of the conditions, the fighters and bombers were split up – 41 Squadron's ORB even suggests they were lost – and Wg Cdr Thomas advised Control that "the weather was hopeless".[88] As such, the Close Escort, Escort Cover and High Cover Wings were recalled; turning back at Merville, they returned to base.

The Spitfire XII Wing landed at Westhampnett at 10:30, but Fg Off Ron Johnson (MB801) stuck two birds on landing. He was uninjured and recorded a tongue in cheek comment in his logbook that day, "Hit 2 seagulls, bust mirror and bent spinner – 2 seagulls confirmed"![89]

Despite the loss of their escorts, however, Part I's bombers carried on to the target. They were unable to locate it, but 22 found an alternative target, and dropped two hundred and six 300 lb. bombs in the Armentières-Bailleul area instead. The Forward Target Support Wing also operated, but fortunately changed their role to High Cover; 15-20 Me109s and FW190s were sighted in the St. Omer area at 15,000 feet, whilst the Wing was 3,000 feet above them. Bouncing the enemy aircraft, 65 Squadron claimed one Me109G destroyed for no loss.

Part II operated as planned, despite weather conditions making escort duties difficult for the

Spitfire squadrons. Twenty-eight Marauders bombed Woensdrecht Airfield with two hundred and fifty 300 lb. GP bombs with fair results, and bursts were seen on the runways and edge of the airfield. Moderate to intense Flak was also experienced over the target area and eight bombers sustained damage, whilst one fighter was lost when it suffered engine failure, and its pilot was forced to bale out.

Part III was aborted, and whilst the bombers departed for their target with their escorts, they were all recalled before reaching the Continent. Parts IV and V were also subsequently cancelled and did not become airborne.

Separately today, Flt Sgt James Still made a heavy, tail-first landing at Hawkinge at 10:45, causing the oleo leg of Spitfire XII, EN226 to collapse.[90] It was felt that he had landed with too low an airspeed at an airfield with which he was unfamiliar. The error was put down to inexperience as, although Still had logged 682 flying hours, only 21 of them were on Spitfires by the time of his accident.

19 August 1943 – The Spitfire XII Wing was assigned to two escorts today, the first just after midday to Poix Airfield again, in Part III of Ramrod 209, and the second during the late afternoon to Bryas Sud Airfield, in Part B of Ramrod 210.

Date	19 August 1943
Operation	Ramrod 209
Targets	Parts I: Amiens-Glisy Airfield, Picardie Parts II & III: Poix Airfield, Picardie
Bombers	Part I: 323BG: 36 USAAF Marauders; 36 bombed Part II: 387BG: 36 USAAF Marauders; 35 bombed Part III: 12 Mitchells, 2 Group; 12 bombed
Casualties	Part I: 9 Marauders CD/AA Cat. AC, 1 Marauder CL Cat. E Part II: 1 Marauder CD/AA Cat. AC
Close Escort Part I	Newchurch: 132 & 602 Squadrons (Spitfire Vb) Biggin Hill: 130 & 234 Squadrons (Spitfire Vb)
Escort Cover	Redhill: 131 & 504 Squadrons (Spitfire Vb)
High Cover	Biggin Hill: 341 & 485 Squadrons (Spitfire IX)
Target Cover	Northolt: 303 & 316 Squadrons (Spitfire IX)
1st Fighter Sweep	Tangmere: 183, 197 & 245 Squadrons (Typhoon Ib)
2nd Fighter Sweep	Lydd: 174, 175 & 245 Squadrons (Typhoon Ib)
3rd Fighter Sweep	New Romney: 181, 182 & 247 Squadrons (Typhoon Ib)
Close Escort Part II	Merston: 118, 402 & 416 Squadrons (Spitfire Vb)
Escort Cover	Kenley: 66 & 165 Squadrons (Spitfire Vb)
High Cover	Hornchurch: 129 & 222 Squadrons (Spitfire IX)
Target Cover	Kingsnorth: 65 & 122 Squadrons (Spitfire IX)
Close Escort Part III	Staplehurst: 401, 411 & 412 Squadrons (Spitfire Vb)
Escort Cover	Westhampnett: 41 & 91 Squadrons (Spitfire XII)
High Cover	North Weald: 331 & 332 Squadrons (Spitfire IX)
Fighter Sweep	Lashenden: 403 & 421 Squadrons (Spitfire IX)
Casualties	182 Sqn: Flt Lt Geoffrey F. Ball, SD nr Amiens in Typhoon Ib, JP400, POW; Fg Off Manley I. Fraleigh RCAF, SD/KIA nr Amiens in Typhoon Ib, R8927; & Flt Sgt Ronald L. H. Dench, SD nr Amiens in Typhoon Ib, JP552, ER; 316 Sqn: Fg Off Andrzej F. M. Prochnicki, SD/KIA in Spit IX, EN179; 421 Sqn: J/18047 Plt Off F. C. Joyce RCAF, SD in Spit IX, MA543, POW

Part I's bombers and escorts rendezvoused at 11:00, made landfall at Cayeux, and proceeded to Amiens-Glisy Airfield according to plan. The Marauders dropped a total of three hundred and forty-one 300 lb. incendiary bombs with good results, but moderate accurate Flak caused damage to nine bombers.

During a visit to the Tangmere Wing on 3 September 1943, Lord Trenchard held an informal talk with many of the men at RAF Merston (pictured), and had lunch with 41 Squadron in the RAF Westhampnett Officers Mess, Shopwyke House. © Cowell family

Immediately after the bombing, the formation was attacked by the Luftwaffe and all wings and the Marauders were engaged. The High Cover Wing was attacked by fifteen to twenty Me109s and FW190s and multiple engagements ensued in which the bombers claimed one enemy aircraft destroyed and two damaged, whilst the fighters claimed one Me109 destroyed, one FW190 probably destroyed and one Me109 and eight FW190s damaged for no casualty of their own.

The Target Cover Wing also engaged five to six FW190s near Amiens, but was then attacked by another 20 enemy aircraft north of Amiens. This resulted in the loss of one pilot from 316 Squadron, but subsequent claims for four FW190s destroyed, one probably destroyed and five damaged. The Wing also reported sighting "at least 15 unusual aircraft identified as Koolhoven 58's with French roundels on the wings".[91,92]

The first and second Fighter Sweeps both operated without incident, but the third engaged enemy aircraft near Amiens, which were initially sighted 4,000-5,000 feet below them. The New Romney Wing was unable to make any claims of its own, but 182 Squadron lost three pilots, who were shot down. Of these, one was killed and one captured, but the third successfully evaded.

Part II's bombers and escorts rendezvoused at 11:50 and crossed in at Trouville stepped up between 12,000 and 14,000 feet. There was no opposition on the way to Poix and 35 bombers dropped three hundred and thirty-five 500 lb. GP bombs with good results. Bursts were seen on the north-eastern dispersals area and Flak was only weak, lightly damaging one bomber; the escorts operated uneventfully.

The Spitfire XII Wing was airborne at 12:25, led by Wg Cdr Thomas, and rendezvoused with the Marauders and escort wings over Rye at 12:40. Landfall was made at Cayeux and 14,000 feet, after which the formation climbed away from the bombers to reach Poix stepped up to 23,000-25,000 feet.

The Mitchells completed their bombing run at 12,000 feet, dropping ninety-six 500 lb. GP bombs at 13:14, and bursts were seen in the middle of the airfield, on a hangar and dispersal area on the western side of the airfield, and just off the airfield to the north. Approximately 20 bursts were also seen in the north-eastern dispersals area.

No enemy aircraft were seen and no Flak was experienced. On the way out, the Wing made an orbit off Cayeux to tempt the Luftwaffe, but there was no reaction and the pilots returned to Westhampnett at 14:00 with nothing to report.
It was not the same case for the Lashenden Wing, operating a fighter sweep from their landfall at Hardelot. They spotted a dozen Me109s south of Abbeville, which split up and dived away on being sighted. Two were however, engaged, with the result that one was claimed destroyed and one damaged, but at the cost of one pilot from 421 Squadron who was shot down and captured.

The Spitfire XII Wing was airborne again 16:40 to participate in a larger operation, supporting both Flying Fortresses and Marauders, whose targets were once again enemy airfields.

Date	19 August 1943
Operation	Ramrod 210
Targets	Part A: Brussels Evere Airfield, Belgium Part B: Bryas Sud [Brias] Airfield, Pas-de-Calais, France
Bombers	Part A: 60 USAAF Flying Fortresses; 58 dispatched, 55 bombed Part B: 36 USAAF Marauders; 36 dispatched, all aborted
Casualties	Part A: 305 BG/364 BS: B-17F Flying Fortress, 42-29807, SD/AA; Part B: 9 Marauders CD/AA
1st Escort Part A	North Weald: 331 & 332 Squadrons (Spitfire IX) Northolt: 303 & 316 Squadrons (Spitfire IX)
2nd Escort	Biggin Hill: 341 & 485 Squadrons (Spitfire IX) Hornchurch: 129 & 222 Squadrons (Spitfire IX) Lashenden: 403 & 421 Squadrons (Spitfire IX)
Close Escort Part B	Kenley: 66 & 165 Squadrons (Spitfire Vb) Redhill: 131 & 504 Squadrons (Spitfire Vb)
Escort Cover	Westhampnett: 41 & 91 Squadrons (Spitfire XII)
High Cover	Kingsnorth: 65 & 122 Squadrons (Spitfire IX)
Casualties RAF	131 Sqn: Flt Sgt R. K. Parry, EF after CD from FW190, baled out of Spit Vb, AR371, off Dungeness, RR by ASR HSL

Part A's Fortresses and the First Escort rendezvoused five miles northeast of Ostend [Oostende] at 17:43, the Fortresses at 22,000 feet and the escorts at 24,000. They continued on towards Brussels but found the area covered by 10/10ths cloud at 8,000 feet. The primary target was therefore aborted and Flushing [Vlissingen] chosen as a secondary, instead.

Now accompanied by the Biggin Hill Wing of Second Escort, which had joined up at Lokeren, Belgium, the combined force continued to Sas van Gent, then turned north towards Goes, where a new west-south-westerly course was adopted to take them over Flushing. Arriving over the area, 55 of the 58 dispatched Fortresses dropped 118 tons of GP bombs on the target with reportedly fair results, and although the Luftwaffe was not seen, Flak was moderate and one Fortress was shot down.

Crossing back out at Knokke, however, the First Escort wings sighted fifteen Me109s at 28,000 feet, approximately four miles away, heading straight for the bombers. 331 Squadron bounced these aircraft, with the result that four were claimed destroyed for no loss. Three FW190s were also sighted, but they did not approach.

The Hornchurch Wing, in the Second Escort, also sighted six Me109s at 14,000 feet in the Knokke area, which they bounced out of the sun. The Lashenden Wing (127 Airfield) also engaged twelve Me109s coming out of Flushing. Engagements ensued in which two enemy aircraft were claimed destroyed and one damaged by 222 Squadron and two destroyed by 403 Squadron, for no loss of their own. The fighters then formed up again and escorted the Fortresses uneventfully back to Clacton.

The Spitfire XII Wing was airborne at 16:40 led by Wg Cdr Thomas, and rendezvoused with Part B's Marauders and Close Escort Wings off Hastings at 13,000 feet. The formation made landfall between Le Touquet and Camiers, but 41 Squadron's Fg Off Ron Johnson (MB801) found both his R/T system and flap indicator malfunctioning, and returned to Westhampnett, where he landed at 17:35.[93]

The rest of the formation continued towards Bryas Sud, but on approaching the target area encountered 10/10ths cloud at 6,000-7,000 feet.[94] The Close Escort's Wing Leader attempted to raise the bombers on the R/T to recall them but was unable to. As such, he flew in front of them, "wiggled his wings and the bombers turned back".[95] The formations then turned south for five minutes, where they turned 180° and headed north again as far as St. Omer. The formations exited cloud near Fruges, then turned west for England again and crossed out again near Le Touquet. About one hundred rounds of Flak were fired at the bombers from the Boulogne area, but these all burst behind them.

On the way back to the coast, however, six FW190s were seen above at 12,000 feet, behind the Close Escort Wings. These then attacked and one pilot from 131 Squadron sustained sufficient damage to his aircraft to force him to bale out into the Channel off Dungeness. He was subsequently rescued by an ASR high speed launch.

The Spitfire XII Wing made a similar experience to the Close Escorts when six FW190s were also seen, of which two dived onto the rear of 41 Squadron, but did not open fire. Flt Sgt Jimmy Payne recorded the event in his logbook, "FW 190's dived past. Saw 4 of them!!"[96]

Two FW190s were then seen to be bounced by Spitfire IXs below them, and "shortly after[ward]s a cloud of smoke was seen rising from the Canche Estuary – so probably one of them "bought it".[97] These possibly belonged to a group of thirty plus FW190s led by Me109s seen by the High Cover Wing in the Boulogne area. These aircraft attempted to attack the bombers but were engaged by 65 and 122 Squadrons' Spitfire IXs, which subsequently claimed one FW190 destroyed and one damaged for no casualty.

The escort was uneventful after leaving the French coast, and made landfall on the English coast at Dungeness. Flt Sgt Payne (EN231) landed at Ford low on fuel, but the rest of the Wing continued on to Westhampnett, where they landed at 18:00. This concluded the day's flying.

20 August 1943 – During the morning, the Wing was informed that Wg Cdr Thomas was being posted to Staff College and that his successor would be 91 Squadron's Raymond Harries, who was promoted to take over the post. The Squadron ORB recorded the changeover,

> *The Squadron will miss [Wg Cdr Thomas] very much as he is a first class leader and has the confidence of the whole wing. We wish him the best of luck. The new wing [sic] Commander is W/C Harries D.F.C., until lately C.O. of 91 Squadron, and in him we have a pilot who knows how to handle Spitfire X11s to the best advantage. At the same time the news has come through that he has just received the second bar to his D.F.C. – Congratulations.*[98]

The handover took immediate effect, as Thomas did not lead the Wing again, and when the Spitfire XII Wing headed across the Channel this afternoon for their only Ramrod of the day, it was under the command of freshly promoted Wg Cdr Harries. The new Commanding Officer of 91 Squadron was Sqn Ldr Norman A. Kynaston.

Date	20 August 1943
Operation	Ramrod 211
Targets	Part I: Dornier Airframe Factory, Flushing [Vlissingen], Netherlands
	Part II: Abbeville Marshalling Yards, Pas-de-Calais, France
Bombers	Part I: 12 Mitchells, 2 Group; 12 dispatched, 12 bombed
	Part II: 11 Bostons, 2 Group; 11 dispatched, 11 bombed

Casualties	320 Sqn: Mitchell II, FR147 (ex-USAAF 42-32280), NO-C, AA/ditched North Sea 50m E of Southwold, Sflk, crew RR
Close Escort Part I	Newchurch: 132 & 602 Squadrons (Spitfire Vb)
Escort Cover	Gravesend: 64 Squadron (Spitfire Vb)
High Cover	Hornchurch: 129 & 222 Squadrons (Spitfire IX)
Forward Target Support	Northolt: 303 & 316 Squadrons (Spitfire IX)
Close Escort Part II	West Malling: 130 & 234 Squadrons (Spitfire Vb)
Escort Cover	Westhampnett: 41 & 91 Squadrons (Spitfire XII)
High Cover	Kingsnorth: 65 & 122 Squadrons (Spitfire IX)
Forward Target Support	Lashenden: 403 & 421 Squadrons (Spitfire IX)

Part I's bombers and escorts rendezvoused at Margate and were joined by the High Cover Wing whilst underway. The formation approached the target unhindered, where the Mitchells dropped a total of ninety-six 500 lb. bombs. There was, however, intense Flak and one bomber was forced to ditch in the Channel as a result of the damage it sustained. The escorts operated otherwise uneventfully.

The Spitfire XII Wing was airborne at 14:45, led by Wg Cdr Harries, who flew with 91 Squadron. 41 Squadron deployed twelve aircraft in three sections, led by Flt Lt Hugh Parry, Sqn Ldr Ingham and Fg Off Bob Boyd, respectively. They made the rendezvous point, over Rye, on time but found that the bombers had passed over early, as had the Close Escort.

The Spitfire XII and High Cover Wings hurried to catch up with the bombers, which they managed to do over the Channel, and continued the escort otherwise as planned. They crossed in 13,000 feet over Berck-sur-Mer, and proceeded to Abbeville, where the Bostons dropped forty-four 500 lb. bombs on the marshalling yards.[99] Bursts were seen slightly to the west of the target and although Flak was "moderate heavy, fairly accurate"[100], all bombers returned to base safely.

The only sighting of the Luftwaffe consisted of four FW190s seen 500 feet above 130 Squadron, approaching head-on. These were driven off by several Spitfires but no claims could be made. The formation crossed out at Cayeux, where the Spitfire XII Wing made two orbits, "but the Hun was not seen".[101] The pilots then headed across the Channel and landed at Westhampnett again at 16:05.

Approximately two-and-a-half hours later, 41 Squadron was called on briefly again, when Flt Lt Roy Lane (MB844) and Fg Off Roger Duchateau (MB845) were scrambled to 12,000 feet off St. Catherine's Point on the report of enemy aircraft in the area. However, they saw nothing and returned to base 20 minutes later, concluding the day's operational flying.

21 August 1943 – There was no operational flying all day as a result of inclement weather. However, the Wing was visited by the Under Secretary of State for Air, Sir Archibald Sinclair KT CMG PC, accompanied by Gp Capt Sir Louis Greig KBE CVO of the Air Ministry. Sinclair gave the pilots a,

> ...short but effective "pep" talk which contained a hint of future hotting up of Air Operations. May be [sic] we interpreted his words in the wrong manner, but he certainly gave all of us the impression that things were likely to happen in the near future. This coupled with the fact that all leave is stopped from the 24th onwards rather suggests we shall be right in our assumption!¹⁰²

The men would indeed be busy over the coming months, but the 'hotting up' that Sinclair was likely referring to was probably not quite what 41 Squadron was expecting [see 25 August 1943].

22 August 1943 – The Squadron was back in the air today, although only deployed on a single, abortive, Ramrod to Poix Airfield, and an ASR patrol in the evening.

Date	22 August 1943
Operation	Ramrod 213
Target	Poix Airfield, Picardie
Bombers	36 USAAF Marauders; 36 dispatched, all aborted
Close Escort	Staplehurst: 401, 411 & 412 Squadrons (Spitfire Vb) – recalled
Escort Cover	Westhampnett: 41 & 91 Squadrons (Spitfire XII) – recalled
High Cover	Hornchurch: 129 & 222 Squadrons (Spitfire IX)
Target Cover	Kingsnorth: 65 & 122 Squadrons (Spitfire IX)
Fighter Sweep	Headcorn: 403 & 421 Squadrons (Spitfire IX)
Rear Support	Kingsnorth: 19 Squadron (Spitfire IX)

The Spitfire XII Wing was airborne at 18:15 and arrived at the rendezvous over Rye on time to find the Close Escort Wing, but no bombers. It transpired that the Marauders had arrived over Rye 30 minutes too early, and headed across the Channel independently. The upshot was that the bombers, and both Close Escort and Escort Cover Wings were recalled, according to 41 Squadron's ORB, "as we would have been too late to help them… if they had run into any trouble".[103]

41 and 91 Squadrons returned to base, where they landed again at 19:05. The High Cover, Target Cover, Fighter Sweep and Rear Support Wings nonetheless operated, using the opportunity to sweep an area of France, looking for targets of opportunity. The Hornchurch Wing encountered eight FW190s four miles northeast of Abbeville and returned home claiming one destroyed and one probable for no loss; the Headcorn Wing engaged 20+ FW190s near Lille and claimed one damaged for no loss, and the remaining two Wings operated uneventfully.

An hour after 41 Squadron had landed, Fg Offs Bruce Moffett and Ron Johnson were both scrambled to undertake an ASR search. Although their patrol, and another by 486 Squadron, are mentioned in the Squadron and Wing ORB, neither records the patrol area, nor the aircraft they were seeking. The patrol proved to be uneventful and when darkness started setting in, 41 Squadron's pilots were recalled to base, where they landed at 20:45.

During the day, news finally reached the Squadron of Flt Lt Tom Slack's evasion and safe arrival in Gibraltar. Fg Off Herb Wagner recorded the news in his logbook that day, "Tom Slack safe at Gib. Good show!"[104]

23 August 1943 – The Squadron was only involved in a Ramrod during the morning but it was abortive once again, this time on account of the weather rather than human error. The only other operational flying was an uneventful 55-minute weather reconnaissance to the French coast.

Fg Off Bob Boyd was killed near Fauville-en-Caux, France, on 6 September 1943, aged 24. He baled out of his aircraft but his parachute caught on the tailplane. © Ron Johnson, via Dan Johnson

Date	23 August 1943
Operation	Ramrod 214
Targets	Part I: St. Omer Marshalling Yards, Pas-de-Calais Part II: Poix Airfield, Picardie Part III: Gosnay Power Station, Pas-de-Calais
Bombers	Part I: 98 & 180 Sqns: 24 Mitchells; 24 dispatched, 24 bombed Part II: 36 USAAF Marauders; 36 dispatched, all aborted Part III: 36 USAAF Marauders; 36 dispatched, all aborted
Close Escort Part I	Newchurch: 132 & 602 Squadrons (Spitfire Vb) West Malling: 130 & 234 Squadrons (Spitfire Vb)
Escort Cover	Fairlop: 302 & 317 Squadrons (Spitfire Vb)
High Cover	Hornchurch: 129 & 222 Squadrons (Spitfire IX)
Target Cover	North Weald: 331 & 332 Squadrons (Spitfire IX)
Close Escort Part II	Staplehurst: 401, 411 & 412 Sqns (Spitfire Vb) – recalled
Escort Cover	Westhampnett: 41 & 91 Squadrons (Spitfire XII) – recalled
High Cover	Biggin Hill: 341 & 485 Squadrons (Spitfire IX) – recalled
Target Cover	Kingsnorth: 65 & 122 Squadrons (Spitfire IX) – recalled
Close Escort Part III	Merston: 118, 402 & 416 Squadrons (Spitfire Vb) – recalled
Escort Cover	Kenley: 66 & 165 Squadrons (Spitfire Vb) – recalled Redhill: 131 & 504 Squadrons (Spitfire Vb) – recalled
High Cover	Northolt: 303 & 316 Squadrons (Spitfire IX)
Target Cover	Headcorn: 403 & 421 Squadrons (Spitfire IX)

Part I operated according to plan, and 24 Mitchells bombed St. Omer Marshalling Yards, dropping one hundred and ninety-two 500 lb. bombs. The Luftwaffe was not seen and aside from moderate heavy inaccurate Flak, the operation was uneventful for both bombers and their escorts.

The Spitfire XII Wing was airborne at 08:35, led by Wg Cdr Harries, who flew with 41 Squadron. They rendezvoused with Part II's Marauders and escorts on time and proceeded across the Channel, but Plt Off Leslie Prickett (MB862) started having oxygen trouble and returned to base, where he landed again at 09:00.

However, the rest of the formation were only half way over when weather reports of 9/10ths to 10/10ths cloud at 16,000 feet from the French coast onwards resulted in the recall of the bombers. At this, all the escorts turned 180° and headed home again, too, the Spitfire XII Wing landing at Westhampnett at 09:35.

Part III fared similarly. The Marauders and escorts made it a little further and were not recalled until they reached Berck-sur-Mer. The bombers, Close Escort and Escort Cover Wings all headed home, but the High Cover Wing made an uneventful sweep of the Berck-St. Pol-St. Omer-Desvres-Hardelot areas before returning home. The Target Cover Wing decided to continue on to Gosnay anyway. They intercepted 15+ Me109s in the Gosnay area flying west at 24,000 feet and engaged them, with the result that they claimed one destroyed and one damaged without casualty.

At 11:45, Fg Off 'Barney' Newman and Flt Sgt James Still took off to undertake a weather reconnaissance. They returned at 12:40 with nothing to report and there was no further operational flying by the Squadron for the next almost 30 hours.

24 August 1943 – The Squadron participated in a single Ramrod today, as an element a large operation involving 188 Flying Fortresses and 72 Marauders, targeting five airfields. This operation was particularly unusual for the Spitfire XII Wing as they were not deployed to provide a sweep in support of bombers in Part IV of the operation, rather they were Part IV, which was purely a fighter sweep.

Date	24 August 1943
Operation	Ramrod 215
Targets	Part I: Villacoublay Airfield, Île-de-France
	Part II: Évreux-Fauville & Conches-en-Ouche Airfields, Haute-Normandie
	Diversion: Over North Sea
	Part III: Over North Sea
	Part IV: Trouville, Bernay & Beaumont-le-Roger, Haute-Normandie
Bombers	Part I: 110 Flying Fortresses; 110 dispatched, 88 bombed
	Part II: 42 Flying Fortresses; 42 dispatched, 22 bombed
	Diversion: 36 Flying Fortresses; 36 dispatched, 0 bombed
	Part III: 72 Marauders; 73 dispatched, 0 bombed
	Part IV: None[105]
Casualties	Part I: 64 Flying Fortresses CD/AA, 10 crew WIA; Part II: 562BS/388BG: B-17F, 42-30230, RF/FL 1m E of Stanton, UK; otherwise 15 Flying Fortresses CD/AA, 1 crew KIA & 10 WIA
Escort Part I	192 USAAF P-47 Thunderbolts from four Groups
First Escort Part II	Biggin Hill: 341 & 485 Squadrons (Spitfire IX)
	Headcorn: 403 & 421 Squadrons (Spitfire IX)
	Kingsnorth: 19, 65 & 122 Squadrons (Spitfire IX)
Second Escort	Hornchurch: 129 & 222 Squadrons (Spitfire IX)
	Northolt: 303 & 316 Squadrons (Spitfire IX)
	North Weald: 331 & 332 Squadrons (Spitfire IX)
First Escort Divers'n	Lydd: 174, 175 & 245 Squadrons (Typhoon Ib)
Second Escort	Gravesend: 64 Squadron (Spitfire Vb)
	Hawkinge: 313 Squadron (Spitfire Vb)
Escort Part III	Fairlop: 302 & 317 Squadrons (Spitfire Vb)
	Redhill: 131 & 504 Squadrons (Spitfire Vb)
Fighter Sweep Pt IV	Westhampnett: 41 & 91 Squadrons (Spitfire XII)

Part I operated according to plan and 88 Flying Fortresses dropped 264 tons of bombs on Villacoublay Airfield with fair to good results. Although they were intercepted by the Luftwaffe, all the bombers returned, and one enemy aircraft was claimed destroyed by an air gunner. Flak was, however, intense and a large percentage of Fortresses were damaged. The escort Thunderbolts also engaged the Luftwaffe and subsequently claimed four FW190s and two Me109s destroyed, one FW190 probable and six FW190s damaged.

Owing to cloud cover, Part II was less successful and only 14 Fortresses bombed Conches-en-Ouche Airfield, and eight bombed Évreux-Fauville Airfield, dropping a total of 31 tons with poor results. The First Escort operated uneventfully and, despite sighting approximately 18 enemy aircraft, were not engaged. The Second Escort was also uneventful but for a lone FW190 sighted at Lisieux, which was shared destroyed by two pilots of 303 Squadron.

Part III was completely uneventful and did not make landfall. The Luftwaffe was not seen and the formation did not approach the coast close enough for Flak to be an issue.

The Spitfire XII Wing took off at 18:15 and crossed the Channel at low altitude to within 12 miles of the French coast. The pilots then climbed and made landfall 9,000 feet over Cabourg, then followed a straight and level course to Bernay at 280 mph IAS.

Continuing on to Beaumont-le-Roger, they made an orbit and were south of the town when two FW190s dived on 91 Squadron from above and behind. Fg Off Gray Stenborg RNZAF and Flt Sgt Bernard Mulcahy RAAF both turned to meet them and fired at the leading aircraft. The aircraft was hit and the pilot baled out. The Focke-Wulf fell to the ground and exploded, and Stenborg and Mulcahy shared the victory – the Tangmere Wing's 700th of the War.

Another pair of FW190s also attempted to attack 91 Squadron, but the whole unit went after them, whilst 41 Squadron remained above on guard. No claims could be made on either side, but it had been prudent for 41 Squadron to keep out of it, as around thirty more FW190s were soon seen above them at 15,000 feet.

41 Squadron pilots and ground staff at Westhampnett, ca. 10-18 September 1943. Front row: Fg Off Ron Johnson, Flt Lt 'Pinkie' Glen DFC, Sqn Ldr Bernard Ingham DFC, Flt Lt Hugh Parry with 'Monty', Fg Off Jerzy Solak (Poland), Flt Lt David Fearon, Fg Off 'Barney' Newman RAAF with Perkin, and Fg Off Harry Smith; 2nd row: Fg Off Ron Loweth, Fg Off Peter Cowell, Flt Lt Roy Lane, Flt Sgt 'Jackie' Fisher, Fg Off Herb Wagner (USA), Fg Off Clive Birbeck, Fg Off Bruce Moffett RCAF, Flt Lt Don Smith RAAF, Fg Off Richard 'Monty' Norman (Eng Off), Flt Lt 'Jock' Burnett (MO); 3rd row: Flt Lt John Smith, Fg Off Ross Harding (behind Smith), Flt Sgt John Still, Flt Sgt James Gray, Flt Sgt Peter Graham, Flt Sgt Alan Hope, Flt Sgt Jimmy Payne, Flt Sgt William Vann, Flt Sgt Stan May RAAF, Fg Off Roger Duchateau (Belgian), Flt Lt Lord Gisborough (IO). © May family

However, these made no attempt to attack and the Wing withdrew to the coast. After crossing out at Trouville, the pilots made two orbits off Le Havre. No further enemy aircraft were seen, but four vessels were sighted approximately two miles west of Le Havre, which were believed to have been Flak ships. The Wing then returned to Westhampnett, where they landed at 19:35, reporting no presence of enemy aircraft on either Bernay or Beaumont-le-Roger Airfields.

25 August 1943 – The day saw the commencement of Operation *Starkey*, a combined operation in which it was sought to gain air superiority over the Luftwaffe to ensure the success of future planned operations on the Continent.

The object was to destroy the greatest number of enemy aircraft possible both in the air and on the ground over a prolonged period. This would be achieved through an increasingly intensive programme of attacks on enemy airfields, particularly in Pas-de-Calais, between 25 August and 9 September, supported by increased reconnaissance activity and heavy night-time bombing of coastal batteries.

Large scale deception activity was also played out in England for several weeks building up to 8 September, during which large troop movements were undertaken and ground forces concentrated in the southeast of the country. Motorised transport was moved about and troops embarked.

This was very likely what Sir Archibald Sinclair was alluding to during his visit on 21 August and why leave was cancelled from 24 August. As much as it was merely an exercise for Allied servicemen, it had to achieve and maintain the guise of an imminent invasion for the German High Command.

All *Starkey* operations were numbered with an 'S' prefix and, as such, the usual chronological numbering of the Spitfire XII Wing's Ramrods ceased between today and the end of the operation. The Wing instead participated in Ramrods S.2, S.5, S.6, S.8, S.14 and S.16 during August, and Ramrods S.24, S.26, S.29, S.31, S.33, S.35, S.36, S.38, S.41, S.42 and S.43, and Circus S.1, during September. The regular numbering system was resumed again afterwards. Having ended with Ramrod 215 on 24 August, the Wing resumed 'normal' operations again with Ramrod 216 on 11 September 1943.

During this first day of Operation *Starkey* today, 41 Squadron was only involved in a single Ramrod in the evening, in cooperation with other Tangmere Wing squadrons. On this occasion, they provided escort cover to Mitchells targeting Bernay Airfield.

Date	25 August 1943
Operation[106]	Ramrod S.2
Targets	Part I: Triqueville Airfield, Haute-Normandie Part II: Le Grand-Quevilly Power Station, Haute-Normandie Part III: Bernay Airfield, Haute-Normandie Part IV: Beaumont-le-Roger Airfield, Haute-Normandie Part V: Poix Airfield, Picardie
Bombers	Part I: 36 Marauders, USAAF; 36 dispatched, 31 bombed Part II: 21 Marauders, USAAF; 21 dispatched, 21 bombed Part III: 18 Mitchells, 2 Group; 18 dispatched, 18 bombed Part IV: 18 Bostons, 2 Group; 18 dispatched, 18 bombed Part V: Bomphoons – Cancelled (weather)
Escort Part I[107] Escort Part II Close Escort Part III Escort Cover High Cover Close Escort Part IV Escort Cover High Cover Escort Part V Sweep	10 Spitfire Squadrons 10 Spitfire Squadrons Merston: 118, 402 & 416 Squadrons (Spitfire Vb) 2 Spitfire Squadrons Westhampnett: 41 & 91 Squadrons (Spitfire XII) 2 Spitfire Squadrons Ibsley & Kenley (4 Spitfire Vb Squadrons) Fairlop: 302 & 317 Squadrons (Spitfire Vb) Headcorn: 403 & 421 Squadrons (Spitfire IX) New Romney: Typhoon Ib – Cancelled (weather) Attlebridge: Typhoon Ib
Casualties	Ibsley: One Spitfire CD

Ramrod S.2 was planned is such a way that Parts I and II were to take place simultaneously, followed 50 minutes later by Parts III and IV, also to be effected simultaneously. Finally, Part V was to take place between the first two and latter two operations, in which a squadron of Bomphoons would attack Poix Airfield. This Part was, however, cancelled, although its subsidiary fighter sweep operated in spite of this, both according to plan and uneventfully.

Part I operated as planned and 31 of the dispatched bombers dropped a total of two hundred and ninety-five 300 lb. bombs on Triqueville Airfield from 10,000 feet with good results. Three hangars were hit, 100 bursts were seen on the landing ground, and 22 bursts were seen in the oil storage area. No enemy aircraft were seen by the bombers, although the escort fighters did sight seven at 24,000 feet that did not attempt to attack. Part II was completely uneventful and the 21 Marauders dropped sixty-three 1,000 lb. bombs on the power station uninterrupted at 18:30 from 10,000 feet. Fair results were achieved and bursts were seen to hit the transformer.

In order to participate in Part III, the Spitfire XII Wing was airborne at 18:40 and rendezvoused with the Merston Wing and bombers over Selsey Bill. Proceeding across the Channel to Cap d'Antifer and then directly to Bernay, the airfield was bombed without any interference from the Luftwaffe, the Mitchells dropping a total of one hundred and thirty-seven 300 lb. bombs from 11,000 feet at 19:20. Bursts were seen on the airfield, southern dispersals, and main hangar.

Four FW190s were sighted after leaving the target but they did not attempt to engage the formation, and the operation was otherwise uneventful. All aircraft returned safely, the Spitfire XII Wing landing at Westhampnett again at 20:10.

Finally, Part IV's bombers dropped twenty-four 500 lb. bombs and three hundred and eighty-four 40 lb. bombs on Beaumont-le-Roger Airfield from 12,000 feet at 19:20, which resulted in bursts in dispersal areas and amongst huts in the southwest corner of the airfield.

On the way out, the Ibsley Wing was attacked by a single FW190, and one Spitfire was damaged.

The Fairlop Wing also sighted four FW190s at 20,000 feet in the target area, but these were attacking 421 Squadron and were not engaged. In fact, 421 Squadron was actually attacked by an estimated 10-15 enemy aircraft, and in the ensuing combats one FW190 was destroyed for no loss.

26 August 1943 – The Spitfire XII Wing participated in two Ramrods today, providing an abortive fighter sweep to Beauvais in the first and a sweep of Bernay and Beaumont-le-Roger Airfields in the second. A 50-minute weather reconnaissance was also undertaken by a section between the two larger operations.

Date	26 August 1943
Operation	Ramrod S.4
Targets	Part I: Bryas Sud [Brias] Airfield, Pas-de-Calais Part II: St. Omer Repair Factory, Pas-de-Calais Part III: Poix Airfield, Picardie
Bombers	Part I: Mitchells – Cancelled Part II: 8 Bomphoons – aborted (weather) Part III: 8 Bomphoons – aborted (weather)
Escort Part I Escort Part II Fighter Sweep	Attlebridge: 2 Squadrons (Typhoon Ib) – aborted (weather) Tangmere: 2 Squadrons (Typhoon Ib) – aborted (weather) Westhampnett: 41 & 91 Squadrons (Spitfire XII) – aborted (weather)

Despite the cancellation of Part I, the aircraft of Parts II and III still attempted to undertake their missions. However, the former aborted on finding 10/10ths cloud at the French coast, whilst the latter aborted at Blangy-sur-Ternoise for the same reason.

The Spitfire XII Wing also attempted to undertake their sweep in spite of conditions, and was airborne at 11:20, led by Wg Cdr Harries. They proceeded across the Channel to the French coast where 10/10ths cloud was also encountered at 7,000 feet, and seen to extend a considerable distance inland.

Harries decided not to cross in and opted instead to take the Wing on a coastal sweep from Le Tréport to the Somme Estuary and back to Dieppe at 6,000 feet. When, on reaching Dieppe, nothing of interest had been seen, the Wing returned home, landing again at 12:30.

At 15:10, Fg Off 'Barney' Newman and Sgt Plt Peter Wall took off to conduct a weather reconnaissance to Cherbourg. No enemy aircraft were seen and the pair returned at 16:00 reporting the trip uneventful.

The Wing was up again at 17:45 to participate in their second Ramrod, providing a fighter sweep of Bernay and Beaumont-le-Roger Airfields in support of an attack on Caen-Carpiquet Airfield.

Date	26 August 1943
Operation	Ramrod S.5
Target	Caen-Carpiquet Airfield, Basse-Normandie
Bombers	36 Marauders; 36 dispatched, 36 bombed
Casualties	B-26 Marauder, 41-34703, CD/AA, WUL S Downs, whilst attempting emergency landing at Shoreham, Ssx
Close Escort[108] Escort Cover High Cover Forward Target Support 1st Fighter Sweep 2nd Fighter Sweep 3rd Fighter Sweep 4th Fighter Sweep 5th Fighter Sweep	Newchurch & Staplehurst (Spitfire Vb) Redhill Biggin Hill Kingsnorth Westhampnett: 41 & 91 Squadrons (Spitfire XII) Northolt North Weald Headcorn Hornchurch

Ramrod S.5 foresaw an attack by 36 USAAF Marauders on Caen-Carpiquet Airfield, with rendezvous 12,000 feet over Selsey Bill at 18:15. Significant numbers of squadrons were assigned to escort them, and five separate fighter sweeps to keep the Luftwaffe at a distance.

Caen was approached without event and the Marauders dropped a total of three hundred and seven 300 lb. GP bombs with good results. Bursts were seen to destroy a hangar on the eastern side of the airfield and damage five other buildings, and a large number of explosions were otherwise observed within the airfield perimeter.

The escort squadrons operated without incident and the Luftwaffe was not seen, however one Marauder was damaged by Flak. Although it safely re-crossed the Channel to England, the pilot was compelled to make a wheels-up landing near Shoreham.

The Spitfire XII Wing was assigned to the 1st Fighter Sweep, which operated independently of the main attack and escort. Airborne at 17:45 and led by Wg Cdr Harries, the pilots undertook their sweep at 11,000 feet as instructed, but found the cloud cover too great to be effective. On the way out, a goods train was sighted through a gap in the clouds southeast of Trouville and a section of four pilots from 91 Squadron received permission to leave the formation to attack it.

Strikes were seen and the locomotive drew to a quick halt in clouds of steam. It was claimed damaged 'Cat. B'. Nothing else of interest was seen and the Wing returned to Westhampnett where they landed at 19:15, concluding the day's flying.

The 2nd, 3rd and 5th Fighter Sweeps operated uneventfully, but the fourth, consisting of Hornchurch based squadrons under the command of Wg Cdr J. E. 'Johnnie' Johnson, sighted 15-20 FW190s and Me190s flying west below them, near Rouen. These aircraft were bounced with limited success, and one was claimed destroyed by Johnson. An Me109 was also shot down, but not by the RAF – a FW190 was reported to have shot it down in error.

27 August 1943 – A busy day awaited the Squadron today, in which the pilots participated in two large Ramrods. In the first of these, the Spitfire XII Wing provided escort cover to Mitchells targeting Bernay Airfield, and in the second they provided fighter cover to 240 Flying Fortresses targeting a V2 site for the first time. However, two of the Squadron's pilots failed to return from the latter operation.

Date	27 August 1943
Operation	Ramrod S.6
Targets	Part I: Poix Airfield, Picardie Part II: Le Grand-Quevilly Power Station, Haute-Normandie Part III: Bernay Airfield, Haute-Normandie Part IV: Beaumont le Roger Airfield, Haute-Normandie Part V: Poix Airfield, Picardie
Bombers	Part I: 36 Marauders; 36 dispatched, 35 bombed Part II: 21 Marauders; 21 dispatched, all aborted (weather) Part III: 18 Mitchells; 18 dispatched, all aborted (weather) Part IV: 18 Bostons; 18 dispatched, all aborted (weather) Part V: Bomphoons – cancelled (weather)
Casualties	Part I: 1 Marauder CD/AA Part II: 322 BG: Marauder 41-18299 FTR

Close Escort Part I	Staplehurst: 401, 411 & 412 Squadrons (Spitfire Vb)
Escort Cover	Gravesend: 64 Squadron (Spitfire Vb)
	Hawkinge: 313 Squadron (Spitfire Vb)
High Cover	Biggin Hill: 341 & 485 Squadrons (Spitfire IX)
Target Cover	Northolt: 303 & 316 Squadrons (Spitfire IX)
Close Escort Part II	Newchurch: 132 & 602 Squadrons (Spitfire Vb)
	West Malling: 130 & 234 Squadrons (Spitfire Vb)
Escort Cover	Redhill: 131 & 504 Squadrons (Spitfire Vb)
High Cover	Hornchurch: 129 & 222 Squadrons (Spitfire IX)
Target Cover	North Weald: 331 & 332 Squadrons (Spitfire IX)
Close Escort Part III	Merston: 118, 402 & 416 Squadrons (Spitfire Vb) – aborted
Escort Cover	Westhampnett: 41 & 91 Squadrons (Spitfire XII) – aborted
High Cover	Kingsnorth: 19, 65 & 122 Squadrons (Spitfire IX)
Close Escort Part IV	Kenley: 66 & 165 Squadrons (Spitfire Vb) – aborted
	Ibsley: 616 Squadron (Spitfire VI) – aborted
Escort Cover	Fairlop: 302 & 317 Squadrons (Spitfire Vb) – aborted
High Cover	Headcorn: 403 & 421 Squadrons (Spitfire IX)
Casualties	131 Sqn: Plt Off Francis W. Bateman, SD/KIA W of Queville in Spit Vb, EE768 & Flt Sgt Guy F. Andrew SD/WIA/POW, W of Queville in Spit Vb, EP547; 504 Sqn: Sgt Plt Clarence H. Jacotine, SD/KIA in Spit Vb, BM302

Part I's bombers and escorts rendezvoused as planned over Dungeness at 08:00 and proceeded to Poix, where 35 Marauders dropped a total of three hundred and forty-four 300 lb. GP bombs on the airfield from 11,000 feet with fair to good results. The Luftwaffe was not encountered and just one bomber sustained Flak damage. The escorts operated uneventfully and all aircraft returned to base.

Part II's bombers and escorts rendezvoused over Hastings at the same time as Part I rendezvoused over Dungeness. However, when cloud cover was found to be too thick in the target area to facilitate effective bombing, the operation was aborted and the Marauders returned home without bombing. One bomber failed to return, and the Close Escort and Escort Cover Wings were engaged by about 17 enemy aircraft from JG2. Combats ensued and one FW190 was claimed destroyed, but at the cost of three of the Redhill Wing's pilots, two of whom were killed and the other captured.

The Spitfire XII Wing was airborne at 08:40 and rendezvoused with the Merston Wing and Part III's bombers at Selsey Bill at sea level a few minutes later.[109] They proceeded across the Channel and made landfall at Cap d'Antifer, but then encountered a blanket of 9/10ths-10/10ths cloud between 3,000 and 7,000 feet and abandoned the operation. The fighters and bombers returned to England, and the Spitfire XII Wing landed at Westhampnett again at 09:35. The High Cover Wing used the opportunity for an independent sweep of the Le Trait area at 24,000 feet, but it was uneventful and they returned home with nothing to report.

Part IV fared similarly. Rendezvous was made at 08:45 as planned and the bombers and their escorts crossed the Channel to find 9/10ths cloud at 2,500 feet. The operation was also aborted and the bombers and fighters returned home, with the exception of the High Cover Wing, which undertook an uneventful sweep of Rouen, Le Havre and the Somme Estuary, before re-crossing the Channel.

Rocket Development in the Fôret d'Éperleques

During the early evening, the Squadron participated in a piece of history. Following the raid against the rocket development facility at Peenemünde in Germany on the night of 17-18 August, the Spitfire XII Wing supported the second Allied attack on Germany's new generation of rocket-powered weapons this evening. It was, however, the first of many daylight raids on such sites, which would continue until the cessation of hostilities.

11 Group told their pilots that the attack was on St. Omer Marshalling Yards, but this was a conscious deception by commanders.[110] The USAAF told their bomber crews that they were targeting 'aeronautical facilities' and bombing freshly-poured concrete. The Germans also ran their own subterfuge, calling the site *Kraftwerk Nord West* or 'Power Station Northwest'. The target was in actual fact an underground bunker complex in the in Fôret d'Éperleques [Eperleques Forest], seven miles north-northwest of St. Omer that was intended to become a storage, final assembly and launching facility for the A-4 rocket, which would become known in time as the V2.

Having commenced construction in March 1943, the facility was originally designed to store up to 100 rockets and launch them against England at a rate of up to 36 per day. It would also have included a liquid oxygen manufacturing facility and an underground railway station to accept trainloads of rockets from factories in Germany.

Germany's development of rocket technology was still top secret to the general public, and Allied intentions were to destroy the threat before the new weapons could be launched. In due course, attacks on the V-Weapons programme would become known as 'Crossbow' operations, whilst attacks on V2 programme were code-named 'Big Ben' and on the V1 programme 'Noball'.

Date	27 August 1943
Operation	Ramrod S.8
Target	"Target near St. Omer Marshalling Yards"; ruse for bunker complex under construction in the Fôret d'Éperleques, 7m NNW of St. Omer, Pas-de-Calais
Bombers	240 USAAF Flying Fortresses in 4 forces of 60 aircraft from 91, 92, 94, 95, 100, 303, 305, 306, 351, 379, 381, 384, 385 & 388 BGs, of 1st & 4th Bomber Wings; 185 bombed
Casualties	303 BG/360 BS: B-17F 42-29754, SD/AA Morbecque (3 KIA, 7 POW); 305 BG/365 BS: B-17F 42-29530, SD/AA Saint-Martin-au-Laërt; 351 BG/508 BS: B-17F 42-29716, SD by Me109s, Villers-Sir-Simon; 92 BG/326 BS: B-17F 42-29698, CD/AA, CL Alconbury, UK (1 †, 2 inj.); 66 B17s CD/AA, 11 CD/cannon fire, 11 CD/MG fire, 10 CD/small calibre fire, & 13 damage other causes
Fighter Cover 1st Force	Biggin Hill: 341 & 485 Squadrons (Spitfire IX) North Weald: 331 & 332 Squadrons (Spitfire IX)
Top Cover	8th USAAF: 1 Group of Thunderbolts
Fighter Cover 2nd Force	Redhill: 131 & 504 Squadrons (Spitfire Vb) Headcorn: 403 & 421 Squadrons (Spitfire IX) Northolt: 303 & 316 Squadrons (Spitfire IX) Gravesend: 64 Squadron (Spitfire Vb) Hawkinge: 313 Squadron (Spitfire Vb)
Top Cover	8th USAAF: 2 Groups of Thunderbolts
Fighter Cover 3rd Force	Westhampnett: 41 & 91 Squadrons (Spitfire XII) Fairlop: 302 & 317 Squadrons (Spitfire Vb) Hornchurch: 129 & 222 Squadrons (Spitfire IX)
Fighter Cover 4th Force	Kenley: 66 & 165 Squadrons (Spitfire Vb) Kingsnorth: 19, 65 & 122 Squadrons (Spitfire IX)
USAAF Casualty	1st Wave: One P-47 Thunderbolt FTR
RAF Casualties	41 Sqn: Fg Off Douglas Haywood SD or EF, POW, 10m ENE of Hardelot, in Spit XII, EN236, & Plt Off Leslie A. Prickett EF/POW, 60-70m S. of St. Omer in Spit XII, EN611; 341 Sqn: Cmdt (Sqn Ldr) René G. O. J. Mouchotte DFC SD/KIA in Spit IX, MH417, & Sgt Plt Pierre Magrot, SD/KIA in Spit IX.

A total of 185 Flying Fortresses of the 8th U.S. Air Force attacked the target in four waves at 20-minute intervals from 18:46, and dropped 368 tons of bombs from altitudes of between 14,000 and 17,000 feet with considered fair to good results.

The escorts to the first formation operated according to plan, and whilst the North Weald Wing sighted no enemy aircraft, the Biggin Hill Wing was continually engaged by Me109s and

FW190s from St. Omer to Mardyck. These combats resulted in claims for two FW190s destroyed, one probably destroyed and two damaged by 341 Squadron, and one FW190 destroyed by 485 Squadron, for the loss of two pilots from 341 Squadron, one of whom was their Commanding Officer. The USAAF also lost one Thunderbolt.

The escorts for the second wave failed to rendezvous with the bombers as the USAAF arrived too early and continued across the Channel without them. However, the fighters hurried to catch up and ultimately engaged 12 enemy aircraft. The ensuing combats resulted in the claim of one FW190 destroyed by 313 Squadron for no loss, whilst the USAAF Thunderbolts operated uneventfully.

The Spitfire XII Wing was airborne at 18:35, under the command of Wg Cdr Harries, with 41 Squadron deploying three sections of four led by Sqn Ldr Ingham, and Flt Lts Don Smith and Douglas Hone. The Wing rendezvoused with the Fairlop and Hornchurch Wings, and the third wave of Flying Fortresses, according to plan.

Soon after crossing the French coast, however, Plt Off Leslie Prickett (EN611) broke away from the formation and was not seen again. It is believed he suffered engine failure approximately 60-70 miles south of St. Omer and force-landed his aircraft. A while later, Flt Lt Hone (MB796) could not jettison his long range tank, and turned for home alone, leaving Fg Off Douglas Haywood to take over command of the section. However, whilst still inbound to the target, approximately ten miles east-northeast of Hardelot, Haywood (EN236) was also seen to break away from the formation and bale out. The Squadron assumed that he, too, had suffered from some form of engine failure, but Flak may have played a role.[111]

The bombers penetrated as far as Béthune, 23 miles southeast of St. Omer, but flew above their allocated altitude, forcing the Spitfire XII Wing to alter theirs as well. Just before reaching St. Omer, intense accurate Flak opened up and one of the Fortresses was shot down. 41 Squadron saw several of the crew bale out safely, but then sighted eighteen FW190s over St. Omer, below and approximately five miles ahead of them. These aircraft climbed in front of the Wing but did not attack; presumably, their eyes were on the bigger prey they were escorting.

However, six Me109s were then sighted by the Fairlop Wing and nine FW190s by the Hornchurch Wing, possibly from the same group seen by 41 Squadron. Hornchurch engaged these aircraft and ultimately claimed three FW190s destroyed and one damaged for no loss.

The formations returned to England without further event and the Spitfire XII Wing landed back at Westhampnett at 20:05, 41 Squadron however doing so with only half the pilots that had departed 90 minutes earlier. Aside from Hone, who had returned early with jettison tank trouble, and Haywood and Prickett, who had come down in France, Sgt Plt Peter Graham (MB829) and Flt Sgt James Still (EN609) both landed at Ford low on fuel, whilst Fg Off Ron Loweth (MB846) landed at Hawkinge for the same reason.

Meanwhile, the fourth wave was well underway, the Fortresses and their escorts having rendezvoused according to plan and proceeded together towards St. Omer. As they approached, the Kenley Wing was engaged by approximately ten FW190s, one of which was claimed destroyed by 66 Squadron for no loss.

When the operation was over and analysed, it was estimated that some 130 enemy aircraft had been in action in around 180 sorties against the combined force of 185 bombers, three Groups of USAAF fighters and 23 squadrons of RAF fighters. Four Fortresses and five fighters were lost, but the bombers' gunners had claimed seven enemy aircraft destroyed and six damaged, whilst the fighters claimed another eight destroyed, one probably destroyed and two damaged.

The attack caused substantial damage to the complex, particularly in its northern section, which contained the railway station and ancillary buildings, where large quantities of fresh concrete had recently been poured and had not yet set. This, and subsequent attacks, the next occurring only three days later, compelled the German High Command to abandon their plans and construction was never completed on the site. The main bunker was subsequently converted to a liquid oxygen factory, but Germany was forced to re-think its strategy for the V2, and ultimately opted for mobile launch vehicles instead. In time, 41 Squadron would also be involved in the hunt for, and destruction of, these sites [See Chapter 7].

This afternoon's operation had cost 41 Squadron two experienced pilots. Plt Off Prickett had been with 41 Squadron since June 1942, having joined the unit as an NCO pilot fresh from flying training. The Squadron ORB recorded that, "after excellent work he was recommended and received his commission in February of this year".[112]

He had force-landed his Spitfire in a field near Campagne-lès-Boulonnais, where he spent the next 15 minutes trying to destroy it. Walking all night to put distance between him and his aircraft, Prickett met a French girl at 09:30 the following morning, who took him to a mill owned by her uncle in Riotte (Reclinghem). He was hidden here for a week, whilst the Underground was contacted to arrange for him to be moved on.

On 4 September, Prickett was driven to the village of Renty, where he was provided with civilian clothes and an identity card, and hidden for a further six weeks in the house of Norbert Fillerin. During this time, the Underground made further arrangements to move him down the escape line, and he was taken to briefly to Auxi-le-Chateau in late October, where he spent three days in a milliners shop in the main town square.

He was then driven to Amiens in the back of a truck, and took the train from there to Paris, where he was hidden for nine weeks in the house of Monsieur and Madame Marecheaux in Rue de la Chapelle, close to the *Gare du Nord* Railway Station. A neighbour in the same street, Madame Camblin, also assisted with food, and during this time Prickett received more civilian clothing and a new identity card.

Whilst in Paris, various arrangements were made to move Prickett again, but it all fell through. Finally, a rendezvous was arranged with another underground organisation for Prickett be picked up at Place de la Porte de Pantin in Paris at 17:00 on 17 December 1943. He arrived five minutes early for the pick-up but instead of *La Résistance*, the Gestapo turned up and arrested him.

Prickett was taken to Fresnes Prison along with 25 others and subjected to interrogation for the ensuing 11 days, which included "the usual threats"[113] and shouting. He was subsequently sent to Dulag Luft outside Frankfurt, then briefly to Stalag Luft III at Sagan, before being moved in February 1944 to the Officers Camp, Oflag III-A at Luckenwalde in Germany, where he became the 'chief utensil maker' of plates, pots, etc., from cocoa cans, and remained here until liberated by the Russians on 27 April 1945.

'Haybag', as Haywood was affectionately known on the Squadron, had headed back towards the coast, and made it out over the Channel before being forced to bale out of his aircraft. A number of pilots from the Biggin Hill Wing reported seeing him in his dinghy whilst returning from the Ramrod and reported his location.

Aircraft were sent out later to find him again but failed to do so; HSLs were sent out to find him, too, but gave up as darkness fell. ASR searches were recommenced at first light, but were again unsuccessful. In fact, by this time, the Germans had already found Haywood and taken him into captivity.

The Squadron ORB recorded that Haywood was "a very experienced pilot [who] had been through the Battle of France and was one of the few remaining pilots who had flown 'Battles' during the period. He had seen plenty of action and had been twice wounded".[114] In summing up the loss of Haywood and Prickett, the ORB added, "Both these pilots will be greatly missed by all Squadron members".[115]

One man felt the loss perhaps more than others: Flt Lt Douglas Hone, who recalled many years later,

> On 27 AUG 1943 we were escorting Flying Forts to bomb St. Pol & St. Omer. I was flying "U" for Uncle. The centre drop tank would not jettison, so under orders I had to return to base (Westhampnett). My 2nd in

Command & personal friend, F/O Haywood, took over the Flight. I later heard [he] had failed to return. F/O Haywood became a prisoner. I wrote to him until the end of the War but all my letters were returned to me in 1945 undelivered. I met Haybag on his release after the War & gave him all the undelivered letters.[116]

Haywood was captured and sent to Stalag Luft III, Sagan, in early September, where he remained until January 1945. Prickett had passed through briefly in January 1944, but it is unknown whether the two men met. However, in February 1945, Haywood was moved to Oflag III-A at Luckenwalde, where Prickett had been held the past year, and remained there with him until liberated by the Russians on 27 April 1945.

Prickett joined the Auxiliary Air Force in February 1947, and transferred to the Secretarial Branch as a Flying Officer in 1947. Promoted to Flight Lieutenant in 1951, he transferred to the RAFO in February 1958 and left the Service. Haywood also re-joined the RAFVR and was commissioned a Flight Lieutenant in April 1947. He extended his service until mid-1955, when he retired as a Squadron Leader. Nothing is known of both men's ensuing lives.

28 August 1943 – Activity today for the Squadron was limited to a sole, independent, Rhubarb to Woensdrecht in the Netherlands during the early evening. The pilots flew over to Manston during the morning in preparation, and departed from this airfield in three sections of four at 18:25.

The operation was, however, unsuccessful as poor weather impeded visibility and the target could not be found. The Squadron flew low to keep under the cloud base and as heavy Flak was experienced, it was "surprising that no hits were received".[117] Under these conditions, fuel became low and the Squadron was split up. Fg Off Ron Johnson also had some 'tank trouble' and all the pilots headed home individually or in sections, with the following results:

Pilot	Serial	Section	Circumstances	Time
Ingham, Bernard	MB845	Red	Landed Ipswich, Suffolk	20:10
Loweth, Ronald A.	MB846		Landed Westhampnett, Sussex	19:55
Cowell, Peter	MB834			20:10
Wall, Peter R.	MB838	Yellow	Landed Manston, Kent	
Parry, Hugh L.	MB802			
Wagner, Herbert A.	EN609			20:15
Newman, Benjamin B.	MB800			
Hope, Alan	MB844			
Boyd, Robert J.	MB796	Blue	Landed Westhampnett, Sussex	19:50
Harding, Ross P.	EN231			
Johnson, Ronald	MB829			
Moffett, H. Bruce	EN608			

29 August 1943 – With five of the twelve pilots at Manston and the Commanding Officer at Ipswich, all of whom remained at these airfields overnight, the Squadron was unable to participate in any large scale operations on 29 August. The pilots returned to Westhampnett during the day to have their aircraft serviced, and the only operational flying undertaken was a weather reconnaissance to the Dieppe area by Fg Off Clive Birbeck and Flt Sgt Stan May at 11:40. The patrol proved uneventful and the pair returned at 12:30 reporting unsuitable weather on the other side of the Channel. Following their report, the ORB noted,

The weather still continues to be rather poor for mass operations, and everyone is keyed up expecting that something big is about to happen. This assumption is merely conjecture – so the least recorded the better.[118]

30 August 1943 – Following a slight weather improvement overnight, the Squadron was back onto Ramrod operations today, and was sent on another visit to the bunker complex in the Eperleques Forest. This time, however, the jumping off point was Manston, to where the pilots flew during the morning.

This Ramrod was on a significantly smaller scale than the previous, but nonetheless involved 78 RAF and USAAF bombers in three parts, supported by 34 Spitfire squadrons. The Spitfire XII Wing was assigned to the provision of High Cover to 18 RAF Venturas in Part II.

Date	30 August 1943
Operation	Ramrod S.14
Target	Bunkers under construction, Fôret d'Éperleques, 7m NNW of St. Omer, Pas-de-Calais
Bombers	Part I: 98 & 180 Sqns: 24 Mitchells; 24 dispatched, 24 bombed
	Part II: 21 Sqn: 18 Venturas; 18 dispatched, 17 bombed
	Part III: USAAF: 36 Marauders; 36 dispatched, 34 bombed
Casualties	Part I: 180 Sqn: Mitchell II, FL190, SD/AA, crashed into house, Watten, 2 ER & 2 KIA[119]; Part III: 14 Marauders CD/AA
Close Escort Part I	Newchurch: 132 & 602 Squadrons (Spitfire Vb)
	West Malling: 130 & 234 Squadrons (Spitfire Vb)
Escort Cover	Kenley: 66 & 165 Squadrons (Spitfire Vb)
	Redhill: 131 & 504 Squadrons (Spitfire Vb)
High Cover	Hornchurch: 129 & 222 Squadrons (Spitfire IX)
Close Escort Part II	Merston: 118, 402 & 416 Squadrons (Spitfire Vb)
Escort Cover	Gravesend: 64 Squadron (Spitfire Vb)
	Hawkinge: 313 Squadron (Spitfire Vb)
High Cover	Westhampnett: 41 & 91 Squadrons (Spitfire XII)
Close Escort Part III	Staplehurst: 401, 411 & 412 Squadrons (Spitfire Vb)
Escort Cover	Fairlop: 302 & 317 Squadrons (Spitfire Vb)
High Cover	Biggin Hill: 341 & 485 Squadrons (Spitfire IX)
Fighter Cover	North Weald: 331 & 332 Squadrons (Spitfire IX)
	Northolt: 124, 303 & 316 Squadrons (Spitfire IX)
	Kingsnorth: 19, 65 & 122 Squadrons (Spitfire IX)
	Headcorn: 403 & 421 Squadrons (Spitfire IX)

Part I's bombers and escorts rendezvoused at 12,000 feet over North Foreland at 18:30 and proceeded to the target where a total of one hundred and ninety 500 lb. GP bombs were dropped. However, the results were extremely poor and a mere four bursts were seen in the target area, the rest overshooting into the surrounding land. The Luftwaffe was not seen, but Flak claimed one bomber, which ultimately crashed into a house in Watten, killing two of the crew.

The Spitfire XII Wing was airborne at 18:25, led by Wg Cdr Harries, and rendezvoused with Part II's bombers and escorts 12,000 feet over Deal at 18:40. They proceeded to the target where thirty-three 250 lb. GP bombs, five hundred and eighty-four 30 lb. incendiaries, and five cans of incendiaries were dropped, and bursts seen in the forest and along its western edge.

Although the Spitfire XII Wing sighted a group of seven and a section of three enemy aircraft well above their own altitude of 20,000 feet, they did not attempt to attack. Flak was also of no consequence, and no damage was recorded.

41 Squadron's Fg Off Ron Loweth (EN234) experienced some difficulty with his fuel tank and returned early, but the rest of the Wing returned to Westhampnett only 25 minutes behind him. On the way, however, Plt Off Arthur Cook (MB862) decided to land early at Tangmere, short of fuel, but the aircraft stalled and crashed, injuring himself in the process. Although kept in the Station Sick Quarters overnight, his injuries were fortunately only light and he returned to the Squadron soon afterwards.

Meanwhile, Part III's bombers and escorts had rendezvoused 12,000 feet over Herne Bay at 18:45, although the Close escort initially missed the bombers and had to catch up. The Marauders dropped a total of one hundred and thirty-five 300 lb. GP and fifty-seven 1,000 lb. bombs, with good results but Flak was intense and 14 of the bombers returned with damage. Their escorts operated uneventfully.

All the Fighter Cover squadrons operated according to plan, and enemy aircraft were only sighted by the Northolt Wing, which unsuccessfully attempted to engage four FW190s at 20,000 feet, and the Kingsnorth Wing, which saw at least 30 enemy aircraft at 15,000 feet east of St. Omer. 65 Squadron dived down to bounce them, but they disappeared into cloud and were not seen again. These Wings all returned to base without further event, and ultimately no casualties were recorded by any of the fighter squadrons on the Ramrod.

Separately today, it was announced that OC B Flight, Flt Lt Douglas H. Hone, who had been with the Squadron since April 1942, would be posted to 501 Squadron at Hawkinge. He was replaced as OC B Flight, by Flt Lt Arthur 'Pinkie' Glen DFC on 5 September.

Hone made his first flight with his new unit on 3 September and was promoted to Flight Commander on 7 October. He remained in the RAFVR after the cessation of hostilities and relinquished his commission in May 1949 on appointment to a commission as Flying Officer in the Aircraft Control Branch of the reconstituted RAFVR that same day. Relinquishing his commission anew in July 1950, he was granted a permanent commission as a Flying Officer in the Fighter Control Branch, again on the same day. Hone extended his service until September 1975, when he retired, retaining the rank of Flight Lieutenant, apparently the last man to retire from the RAF who had flown in the Battle of Britain.

31 August 1943 – It was an early start to the day for the Squadron, which began with a weather reconnaissance before 06:00, followed by a Ramrod at 07:30.

The weather reconnaissance was carried out by Fg Off Bruce Moffett and Flt Sgt 'Jackie' Fisher between 05:55 and 06:50, and proved uneventful. It was a quick turnaround for Moffett, however, as he was also assigned to the morning's Ramrod. Just 40 minutes after his return from the weather reconnaissance, he was airborne again to participate in the Spitfire XII Wing's provision of Escort Cover to 18 Mitchells targeting Monchy-Breton Airfield in Part III of Ramrod S.16. Lying a few miles northeast of St. Pol, the airfield has been established by the RAF during World War I, but was only used by the Luftwaffe during in World War II.

Date	31 August 1943
Operation	Ramrod S.16
Targets	Part I: Lille-Vendeville Airfield, Pas-de-Calais Part II: Mazingarbe Power Station, Pas-de-Calais Part III: Monchy-Breton Airfield, Pas-de-Calais Part IV: Merville Airfield, Pas-de-Calais Part V: Bryas Sud [Brias] Airfield, Pas-de-Calais Part VI: Ursel Airfield, Oost-Vlaanderen, Belgium
Bombers	Part I: 36 Marauders; 36 dispatched, 36 bombed Part II: 36 Marauders; 36 dispatched, 31 bombed Part III: 2 Group: 18 Mitchells; 18 dispatched, 18 bombed Part IV: 2 Group: 12 Bostons – aborted (failed to rendezvous) Part V: Tangmere: 8 Bomphoons – one squadron Part VI: Tangmere: 8 Bomphoons – aborted (weather)
Casualties	Part I: 387 BG/558 BS: Marauder 41-31653, 'King Bee', KX-M, SD Lille/Vendeville by 88mm Flak, breaking a/c in two

Close Escort Part I	Staplehurst: 401, 411 & 412 Squadrons (Spitfire Vb)
Escort Cover	Redhill: 131 & 504 Squadrons (Spitfire Vb)
High Cover	Hornchurch: 129 & 222 Squadrons (Spitfire IX)
Top Cover	Kingsnorth: 19, 65 & 122 Squadrons (Spitfire IX)
Close Escort Part II	Newchurch: 132 & 602 Squadrons (Spitfire Vb)
Escort Cover	Fairlop: 302 & 317 Squadrons (Spitfire Vb)
High Cover	Biggin Hill: 341 & 485 Squadrons (Spitfire IX)
Top Cover	Headcorn: 403 & 421 Squadrons (Spitfire IX)
Close Escort Part III	Merston: 118, 402 & 416 Squadrons (Spitfire Vb)
Escort Cover	Westhampnett: 41 & 91 Squadrons (Spitfire XII)
High Cover	Northolt: 303 & 316 Squadrons (Spitfire IX)
Close Escort Part IV	West Malling: 130 & 234 Squadrons (Spitfire Vb) – recalled
Escort Cover	Gravesend: 64 Squadron (Spitfire Vb) – recalled
	Hawkinge: 313 Squadron (Spitfire Vb) – recalled
High Cover	North Weald: 331 & 332 Squadrons (Spitfire IX)
RAF Casualties	129 Sqn: Sgt Plt Norman Roggenkamp, CD Lille area, CL nr Dover, inj, in Spit IX, MH385; 222 Sqn: Flt Sgt John M. V. Thompson SD nr Lens in Spit IX, MH429, POW

Part I's Marauders and their escorts proceeded to Lille where the Hornchurch Wing sighted ten to twelve FW190s flying west at 15,000 feet. Engagements ensued in which 129 Squadron claimed three destroyed and three damaged, and 222 Squadron one probable, for the loss of one pilot from 222 Squadron shot down and captured, and an aircraft from 129 Squadron damaged, resulting in it crash-landing near Dover.

The Top Cover Wing was also engaged but no claims could be made. Meanwhile, the Marauders dropped 48 tons of bombs on Lille-Vendeville Airfield with good results, but heavy Flak was also experienced and one bomber was shot down.

Part II's bombers managed to drop 43 tons of bombs on Mazingarbe Power Station with fair to poor results, despite a very active Luftwaffe. The Close Escort Wing sighted twelve Me109s in the Lens area on the way in, which fired at the bombers from 1,000 yards but were unable press their attack home. They also saw an additional 30+ enemy aircraft in the target area, which did not attempt to attack. The Escort Cover Wing fought off ten FW190s that attempted to attack the second box of bombers, but were unable to make any claims.

The High Cover Wing also sighted 16 enemy aircraft in the target area that they were unable to engage, although they were followed all the way to Le Touquet. The only incident occurred when two Me109s tried to attack four Spitfires, but were fought off, without result on either side. Finally, the Top Cover Wing sighted twelve Me109s some distance away, but they were too far off to engage.

The Spitfire XII Wing was airborne at 07:30, rendezvoused with the Merston and Northolt Wings and Part III's Mitchells, and proceeded to Monchy-Breton Airfield without event. Eighteen of the bombers dropped eight 500 lb. bombs each, totalling 144 bombs, of which 40 were seen to burst on the airfield, and a number short of the dispersals area in the village itself.

Very little information on Part III is available in the 41 Squadron, Tangmere Wing or 11 Group ORBs, except that the first source records the trip was uneventful and the last that the operation ran according to plan. The Luftwaffe was not seen and there were no claims or casualties. Running short on fuel, Flt Lt David Fearon (MB834) and Sgt Plt Peter Wall (MB845) landed at Friston, and Fg Off Ross Harding (MB829) landed at Tangmere, whilst the rest of the Spitfire XII Wing landed at Westhampnett at 09:05.

Part IV was aborted when the Bostons failed to make the rendezvous. The Close Escort and Escort Cover Wings were recalled, but the High Cover Wing, from North Weald decided to sweep the St. Pol area anyway, which they did uneventfully.

Part VI operated according to plan and a total of sixteen 500 lb. bombs were dropped on Bryas Sud airfield with fair to good results. Bursts were seen on dispersal huts and on the woods on the north-eastern airfield boundary; the Luftwaffe was not seen. Part VI was subsequently abandoned as a result of 10/10ths cloud between 2,500 and 5,000 feet in the target area.

The Squadron was airborne again at 17:05 when they conducted an independent sweep in the Abbeville area. Fg Off Clive Birbeck (EN234) and Flt Sgt James Still (MB801) both returned to based early owing to jettison tank trouble, whilst Sgt Plt Peter Graham (MB829) at Friston on the way home as a result of low fuel. Little further information is otherwise available on the operation, which was reported to have been uneventful.

At the end of the month, the ORB recorded the big news that had recently been received on the Squadron:

> We are happy to report that Fg Off T. A. H. Slack who was posted as missing on 18 July 1943 evaded capture after he had baled out over France. After numerous adventures of which he will not divulge, he reached Gibraltar and is now back in England. He was missing five weeks and his squadron heartily congratulate him on his escape. A Posting Notice has been received from A. M. today and he is to rejoin us on 30 September. We look forward to seeing him again.[120]

It was a good way to end the month.

Nominal Roll, 31 August 1943

On 31 August 1943, the ORB recorded that the Squadron's officers and pilots were Sqn Ldr Bernard Ingham DFC, Flt Lts Hugh L. Parry (OC A Flight), David N. Fearon, Roy Lane, Donald H. Smith (RAAF) and Jerzy J. Solak (Polish), Fg Offs Clive R. Birbeck, Robert J. Boyd, Ronald T. H. Collis, Peter Cowell, Roger Duchateau (Belgian), Emanuel V. Galitzine (Russian), Arthur A. Glen, Ross P. Harding, Ronald Johnson, Ronald A. Loweth, Hubert B. Moffett (RCAF), Benjamin B. Newman (RAAF) and Herbert A. Wagner (USA), Plt Off Arthur C. Cook, Flt Sgt James A. B. Gray, and Sgt Plts Alan Hope, Peter B. Graham, Jim C. J. Payne, William H. Vann and Peter R. Wall, Flt Lt Lord Gisborough, Intelligence Officer, Fg Off Walter 'Jock' Burnett, Medical Officer, and Fg Off Harry W. Smith, Adjutant.[121]

September 1943 – There was no operational flying on seven days of the month as a result of poor autumn weather conditions: 1, 12, 17, 20, and 28-30 September. However, it was nonetheless another very intensive month, which encompassed 29 Ramrods, one Circus and a Rodeo, and cost the Squadron the life of one pilot, a second pilot shot down, wounded and captured, a third shot down, who evaded and returned to the United Kingdom several weeks later, and a fourth who baled out into the Channel but was rescued.

This article appeared in an unknown Australian newspaper after Flt Sgt Stan May was shot down on 19 September 1943; via Colin May

Airfield   Marshalling Yards

 Gun Emplacement   Tactical Target

Date	Operation	Role	Type	Destination / Target
2	Ramrod S.24	High Cover	▲	Fôret d'Hesdin, France
3	Ramrod S.26	Escort Cover	Airfield	Beaumont-le-Roger, France
4	Ramrod S.29	High Cover	Marshalling Yards	Abbeville, France
4	Ramrod S.31	Escort Cover	Marshalling Yards	St. Pol, France
5	Ramrod S.33	Escort	Airfield	Woensdrecht, Netherlands
6	Ramrod S.35	Escort Cover	Marshalling Yards	Rouen-Sotteville, France
6	Ramrod S.36	Escort Cover	Marshalling Yards	Abbeville, France
7	Ramrod S.38	Escort Cover	Marshalling Yards	St. Omer, France
8	Ramrod S.41	Escort	Airfield	Vitry-en-Artois, France
8	Circus S.1	High Cover	Marshalling Yards	Abbeville, France
8	Ramrod S.42	Medium Cover	Gun Emplacement	Wimereux-Boulogne, France
9	Ramrod S.43	High Cover	Airfield	Monchy-Breton, France
11	Ramrod 216	Escort Cover	Airfield	Beaumont-le-Roger, France
14	Ramrod 218	Escort Cover	Airfield	Woensdrecht, Netherlands
15	Ramrod 220	High Cover	Airfield	Lille-Nord, France
16	Ramrod 223	Escort Cover	Airfield	Beaumont-le-Roger, France
18	Ramrod 228	Escort Cover	Airfield	Beauvais-Tillé, France
18	Ramrod 230	Escort Cover	Airfield	Beaumont-le-Roger, France
19	Ramrod 232	Escort Cover	Airfield	Lille-Nord, France
19	Ramrod 233	Escort Cover	Airfield	Merville, France

21	Ramrod 235	Close Escort	⊼	Beauvais-Tillé, France
22	Ramrod 237	Close Escort	⊼	Évreux-Fauville, France
23	Ramrod 239	Escort Cover	⊼	Conches-en-Ouche, France
23	Ramrod 240	Escort Cover	⊼	Beauvais-Tillé, France
24	Ramrod 242	Escort Cover	⊼	Évreux-Fauville, France
24	Ramrod 243	Escort Cover	⊼	Beauvais, France
25	Ramrod 246	Escort Cover	⊼	St. Omer-Longuenesse, France
26	Ramrod 247	Escort Cover	⊼	Conches-en-Ouche, France
27	Ramrod 250	Escort Cover	⊼	Beauvais, France
27	Ramrod 251	Escort Cover	⊼	Conches-en-Ouche, France

2 September 1943 – The Wing flew to Lympne just after breakfast today to position themselves for the morning's activity. From 10:50, 41 Squadron provided twelve aircraft to patrol above several minesweepers and protective craft busy in the Channel, and returned at 12:15, with the exception of Fg Off Ross Harding (EN608), who had already returned early with jettison tank trouble. During their patrol, which was otherwise uneventful, a number of Bostons lay down a smoke screen between the naval vessels and the French coast.

It was then quiet until 16:15, when the whole Squadron was scrambled to the French coast at 15,000 feet. There appears to have been some confusion about the whole point of the exercise, the ORB noting that the pilots "…assumed that a number of bombers were returning from extensive operations over France and we were there to provide cover and escort for any stragglers."[122] Fg Off Prince Galitzine also recorded in his logbook: "Bogeys turned out to be friends. Bags of activity in the Channel."[123] They returned at 17:20 with otherwise nothing to report.

Less than an hour-and-a-half after their return, the entire Squadron was airborne for the third time today, this time an operation "of a more interesting nature"[124], when they were detailed to provide High Cover to Marauders bombing a fuel dump in the Hesdin Forest in Part III of Ramrod S.24. The operation was designed as support and diversion for attacks by USAAF B-17 Flying Fortresses on the Luftwaffe airfields at Évreux, Beauvais and Brussels-Evere, escorted by USAAF Thunderbolts.

Date	2 September 1943
Operation	Ramrod S.24
Targets	Part I: Lille-Nord Airfield, Pas-de-Calais Part II: Mazingarbe Power Station, Pas-de-Calais Parts III-V: Fuel dump, Fôret d'Hesdin, Pas-de-Calais
Bombers	Part I: 36 Marauders; 36 dispatched – aborted Part II: 36 Marauders; 36 dispatched, 35 bombed Part III: 72 Marauders; 72 dispatched, 70 bombed Part IV: 21 Sqn: 18 Venturas; 18 dispatched, 16 bombed Part V: 98 & 180 Sqns: 18 Mitchells; 18 dispatched, 18 bombed

Casualties	Part I: 387th BG: 1 B-26 Marauder FTR
Close Escort Part I	Staplehurst: 401, 411 & 412 Squadrons (Spitfire Vb) – aborted
Escort Cover	Fairlop: 302 & 317 Squadrons (Spitfire Vb) – aborted
High Cover	Hornchurch: 129 & 222 Squadrons (Spitfire IX) – aborted
Top Cover	North Weald: 331 & 332 Squadrons (Spitfire IX)
Close Escort Part II	Merston: 118, 402 & 416 Squadrons (Spitfire Vb)
Escort Cover	Kenley: 66 & 165 Squadrons (Spitfire IX)
High Cover	Biggin Hill: 341 & 485 Squadrons (Spitfire IX)
Top Cover	Northolt: 303 & 316 Squadrons (Spitfire IX)
Close Escort Part III	West Malling: 130 & 234 Squadrons (Spitfire Vb)
	Friston: 306 Squadron (Spitfire Vb)
Escort Cover	Redhill: 131 & 504 Squadrons (Spitfire Vb)
High Cover	Kingsnorth: 19, 65 & 122 Squadrons (Spitfire IX)
Extra High Cover	Westhampnett: 41 & 91 Squadrons (Spitfire XII)
Top Cover	Headcorn: 403 & 421 Squadrons (Spitfire IX)
Close Escort Part IV	Newchurch: 132 & 602 Squadrons (Spitfire Vb)
Close Escort Part V	Gravesend: 64 Squadron (Spitfire Vb)
	Hawkinge: 313 Squadron (Spitfire Vb)
Casualties	66 Sqn: Flt Sgt John S. Harries SD/AA/KIA, Dunkirk-Gravelines, in Spit Vc, EN892

Although the USAAF attack on Évreux was cancelled as a result of poor weather, 83 Flying Fortresses were dispatched to Beauvais and Brussels. Of these, just 15 bombed Beauvais, and another 18 bombed Mardyck as a secondary target to Brussels. Nonetheless, bombing results were considered good.

Part I of the support operations rendezvoused as planned but the bombers aborted in the St. Omer are when the weather was found unsuitable. Nonetheless, one Marauder was hit by Flak and came down near the town. The Close Escort, Escort Cover and High Cover Wings aborted the operation with the bombers, but the Top Cover Wing undertook an uneventful sweep of the Lille area instead.

Part II's bombers and escorts rendezvoused according to plan but encountered the Luftwaffe soon after crossing in. The Escort Cover and Top Cover Wings engaged approximately twenty-five FW190s which dived on the bombers from the east, and one of 66 Squadron's pilots was hit by Flak and killed. Another twenty Me109s attempted to attack the bombers in the Béthune area, but these were engaged by the High Cover Wing. A mixed group of twelve FW190s and Me109s also attacked the formation in the St. Pol area, but they were also intercepted by the High Cover Wing, which claimed one FW190 destroyed.

The bombers meanwhile managed to get through to the target safely, and 35 of the bombers dropped a total of three hundred and eleven 100 lb. incendiary bombs and fifty-one 1,000 lb. bombs. Results were considered good and Mazingarbe Power Station received several direct hits.

Part III operated according to plan and was able to approach the target without any interference from the Luftwaffe. For their part, the Spitfire XII Wing was airborne at 18:45, and whilst 41 Squadron did not see the Luftwaffe, two pilots from 91 Squadron "had rather an extraordinary piece of luck".[125] That unit's Flt Lt Ian Matthew [and future OC 41 Squadron] had returned early as his engine was running roughly, accompanied by Fg Off Geoffrey Bond, when they were attacked by four Me109s, from 1,000 feet above them, approximately four miles from the French coast at Le Touquet.

Two of these aircraft attacked Matthew and Bond, one making an unsuccessful beam attack and the other approaching head-on. When still 700 yards from the latter, Matthew opened fire on the aircraft, which he hit, achieving strikes on the cowling. It immediately broke away, turned on its back and dived down to crash on the beach.

Bond, meanwhile, was attacked from astern by the second pair, but shook them off only to see Matthew about to be attacked by the aircraft that had made the original beam attack. Being in a favourable position, Bond opened fire and observed strikes all along the starboard side of the fuselage. He followed the Me109 down, continuously firing until it crashed into the sea. Both

Matthew and Bond's aircraft received combat damage, and Matthew noted that his opponent bore Italian markings.

Whilst this was on-going, Part III's Marauders and escorts reached the Fôret d'Hesdin, where one hundred and thirty-six 1,000 lb. GP bombs, one hundred and seventy-seven 300 lb. GP bombs, and two hundred and eighty-four 100 lb. incendiary bombs were dropped Results were reported to have been good, and the operation was otherwise uneventful. The Spitfire XII Wing landed again at 19:50 to conclude a long day's operational flying.

Both Parts IV and V also operated according to plan and uneventfully. In the former of these, 16 Venturas dropped thirty-two 250 lb. GP bombs and six hundred and twenty-four 30 lb. incendiaries on the fuel dump, causing an explosion and large fires. In the latter operation, 18 Mitchells dropped seventy-two 1,000 lb. GP bombs on the same target with similarly good results. There were no casualties to report from either.

3 September 1943 – Britain had now been at War four years. Operational flying started at 09:15 today for the Spitfire XII Wing when they provided Escort Cover for 36 Marauders attacking Beaumont-le-Roger Airfield. It was, however, only a small element of a much larger operation in which B-17 Flying Fortresses attacked Romilly Air Depot (168 aircraft), Mureaux Airfield (65 aircraft) and industrial works at Caudron-Renault near Paris (65 aircraft), escorted by 160 USAAF Thunderbolts.

These attacks enjoyed varying levels of success, with primary, secondary, and targets of opportunity bombed between 08:45 and 09:55. The Luftwaffe was up in force to meet them and claims were made by the bombers' air gunners for 26 destroyed enemy aircraft, 5 probable, and 18 damaged for the loss of nine Flying Fortresses, 75 damaged, six airmen wounded and 90 missing. The Thunderbolt pilots claimed an additional four enemy aircraft destroyed and one probable for the loss of one Thunderbolt and two damaged.

Ramrod S.26 operated simultaneously as a diversion, and consisted of the following targets, bombers and escorts:

Date	3 September 1943
Operation	Ramrod S.26
Targets	Part I: Lille-Nord Airfield, Pas-de-Calais Part II: Beauvais-Tillé Airfield, Picardie Part III: Beaumont-le-Roger Airfield, Haute-Normandie
Bombers	Part I: 36 Marauders; 36 dispatched, 34 bombed Part II: 36 Marauders; 36 dispatched, 36 bombed Part III: 36 Marauders; 36 dispatched, 31 bombed
Casualties	20 Marauders CD/AA; 1 man WIA
Close Escort Part I	Staplehurst: 401, 411 & 412 Squadrons (Spitfire Vb) West Malling: 130 & 234 Squadrons (Spitfire Vb)
Escort Cover	Gravesend: 64 Squadron (Spitfire Vb) Hawkinge: 313 Squadron (Spitfire Vb)
High Cover	Hornchurch: 129 & 222 Squadrons (Spitfire IX)
Top Cover	North Weald: 331 & 332 Squadrons (Spitfire IX)
Close Escort Part II	Redhill: 131 & 504 Squadrons (Spitfire Vb) Kenley: 66 & 165 Squadrons (Spitfire IX)
Escort Cover	Fairlop: 302 & 317 Squadrons (Spitfire Vb)
High Cover	Biggin Hill: 341 & 485 Squadrons (Spitfire IX)
Top Cover	Kingsnorth: 19, 65 & 122 Squadrons (Spitfire IX)
Withdrawal Support	Newchurch: 132 & 602 Squadrons (Spitfire Vb)
Close Escort Part III	Merston: 118, 402 & 416 Squadrons (Spitfire Vb)
Escort Cover	Westhampnett: 41 & 91 Squadrons (Spitfire XII)
High Cover	Northolt: 303 & 316 Squadrons (Spitfire IX)
Top Cover	Headcorn: 403 & 421 Squadrons (Spitfire IX)
Casualties	421 Sqn: Fg Off M. C. Love, SD Beaumont-Bernay in Spit IX, MA334, POW

Part I's bombers and escorts rendezvoused five miles northwest of Furnes [Veurne] and proceeded to Lille-Nord Airfield without incident. Thirty-four Marauders dropped three hundred and nine 300 lb. bombs with good results, as bursts were seen on the western, northern and north-eastern dispersals areas.

Part II's Marauders and Spitfire escorts rendezvoused over Hastings and were also able to complete the task without event. Three hundred and fifty-seven 300 lb. bombs were dropped on Beauvais-Tillé Airfield with good results, both the north-eastern and south-western dispersals areas observed to have been hit. The Withdrawal Support Wing swept behind the returning formation, and escorted the bombers back across the Channel without incident.

For their part, the Spitfire XII Wing was airborne at 09:15, led by Wg Cdr Harries, who flew with 41 Squadron. The pilots rendezvoused with Part III's bombers and fellow escort wings over Shoreham, and proceeded to Beaumont-le-Roger Airfield unhindered where the Marauders dropped three hundred and five 300 lb. bombs with good results. 41 Squadron's pilots reported seeing bursts on the airfield's eastern dispersals area.

Twelve FW190s were seen in the target area, but did not attack, and another four were also seen in the Trouville area that were not engaged. However, the Top Cover Wing, which did not rendezvous with the formation until four miles northeast of Fécamp, saw an additional four Me109s in the target area that they attacked. Two of these enemy aircraft were claimed destroyed by 421 Squadron, but they also lost one pilot, who was shot down and captured.

The Spitfire XII Wing landed safely again at 10:45, but 41 Squadron felt it was "a most uninteresting operation from our point of view, as the pilots are keen to get the Squadron's 150th Hun destroyed."[126]

During the morning, the Tangmere Wing was visited by MRAF Viscount Trenchard GCB GCVO DSO. He had an informal chat with many of the men at Merston, lunched in the Westhampnett Officers Mess, Shopwyke House, and left again during the afternoon.

At 15:35, Fg Offs 'Pinkie' Glen and Ron Loweth were sent across the Channel to an area approximately ten miles northwest of Le Havre, to search for a Flying Fortress crew believed to have come down in the area. However, they were unsuccessful, and returned to base at 16:40 with nothing to report.

At 17:30, another four pilots were sent up to provide cover to 91 Squadron, who were detailed to escort a Hudson carrying an airborne lifeboat, in search of bomber crews. The pilots and Hudson crew searched unsuccessfully for over an hour and returned to base at 18:50. This concluded the day's operational flying.

4 September 1943 – The day's operational flying for 41 Squadron encompassed two Ramrod operations in cooperation with 91 Squadron, the first at 08:40 as High Cover to 18 Mitchells attacking Abbeville Marshalling Yards, and the second at 17:50 as Escort Cover to 36 Marauders targeting St. Pol Marshalling Yards.

In the former of these, a similar programme was foreseen as in the previous day's Ramrod S.26, in which four combat wings Flying Fortresses were to attack Romilly Airfield and the Citroën factory in Paris. However, despite the fact that the USAAF attacks were cancelled, the support operations – Parts III, IV and V – were nonetheless flown by the RAF, and consisted of the following elements:

Date	4 September 1943
Operation	Ramrod S.29
Targets	Part I: Romilly Airfield, Champagne-Ardenne
	Part II: Citroën Works, Billancourt, Île-de-France
	Part III: Rouen-Sotteville Marshalling Yards, Haute-Normandie
	Part IV: Amiens-Longueau Marshalling Yards, Picardie
	Part V: Abbeville Marshalling Yards, Picardie
Bombers	Part I: Flying Fortresses – cancelled
	Part II: Flying Fortresses – cancelled
	Part III: 98 & 180 Sqns: 18 Mitchells; 18 bombed
	Part IV: 88 & 107 Sqns: 24 Bostons; 24 bombed
	Part V: 18 Venturas; 15 bombed
Escort Parts I & II	USAAF Thunderbolts – Cancelled
Close Escort Part III	Fairlop: 302 & 317 Squadrons (Spitfire Vb)
	Friston: 306 Squadron (Spitfire Vb)
Escort Cover	Redhill: 131 & 504 Squadrons (Spitfire Vb)
High Cover	Biggin Hill: 341 & 485 Squadrons (Spitfire IX)
Fwd Target Support	Northolt: 303 & 316 Squadrons (Spitfire IX)
Close Escort Part IV	Staplehurst: 401, 411 & 412 Squadrons (Spitfire Vb)
Escort Cover	Kenley: 66 & 165 Squadrons (Spitfire IX)
High Cover	Hornchurch: 129 & 222 Squadrons (Spitfire IX)
Fwd Target Support	North Weald: 331 & 332 Squadrons (Spitfire IX)
Close Escort Part V	West Malling: 130 & 234 Squadrons (Spitfire Vb)
Escort Cover	Gravesend: 64 Squadron (Spitfire Vb)
	Hawkinge: 313 Squadron (Spitfire Vb)
High Cover	Westhampnett: 41 & 91 Squadrons (Spitfire XII)
1st Fighter Sweep	Headcorn: 403 & 421 Squadrons (Spitfire IX)
2nd Fighter Sweep	Kingsnorth: 19, 65 & 122 Squadrons (Spitfire IX)
Casualties	66 Sqn: Flt Lt F. A. O. 'Tony' Gaze DFC, SD Ault in Spit Vb, AR281, ER

Part III's escorts and bombers rendezvoused over Beachy Head and proceeded to Rouen-Sotteville Marshalling Yards without incident. The Mitchells dropped one hundred and thirty 500 lb. bombs, but their aim was poor and bursts were seen both in the town quarter west of the marshalling yards, as well as to the north. The operation was otherwise uneventful and the Luftwaffe was not seen.

Part IV rendezvoused over Hastings and proceeded to the target, but numbers of enemy aircraft were seen and engaged by the Escort Cover and Forward Target Support Wings. 66 Squadron intercepted a dozen FW190s near Ault and the subsequent combats resulted in one FW190 claimed damaged for the loss of Flt Lt Tony Gaze, who was shot down but evaded, and within 18 months would become a Flight Commander on 41 Squadron.

North Weald's Norwegian squadrons sighted fifteen Me109s flying southwest at 20,000 feet, approximately ten miles northeast of the target area. These aircraft tried to avoid an engagement, but were caught by 331 Squadron, whose pilots claimed one Me109 destroyed and one probable for no loss.

Meanwhile, Part IV's Bostons dropped ninety-six 500 lb. bombs from 11,500-12,000 feet with good results. Bursts were seen on the wagon repair shops, on railway trucks on the eastern side of the marshalling yards, and on buildings on the south-eastern side.

The Spitfire XII Wing was airborne at 08:40 and rendezvoused with Part V's bombers and escorts over Rye, although the Venturas arrived two minutes late. The Wing proceeded across the Channel towards Cayeux on the deck, then climbed to 14,000 feet to cross in, and made a direct course for Abbeville Marshalling Yards.

The operation was undertaken according to plan and the Luftwaffe was not seen. This enabled the Venturas to drop one hundred and five 500 lb. bombs unhindered, with fair results. Bursts were seen near the yards, and near engine sheds and workshops, but two bursts were also seen to straddle the southern edge of the yards.

On the way back out, the Spitfire XII Wing turned back at Berck-sur-Mer and swept back into France almost as far as Abbeville, however nothing of consequence was seen and the Wing then returned home. 41 Squadron's Fg Off Ron Johnson (EN608) and Flt Sgt 'Jackie' Fisher (MB829) both returned early as their drop tanks would not jettison, and Flt Lt Jerzy Solak (EN609) landed at Friston short of fuel, but the rest of the Squadron continued on to Westhampnett, where they landed between 10:00 and 10:15.

During this time, the first and second fighter sweeps had also been flown, both being completed without incident.

There was no further operational flying for the Spitfire XII Wing until early evening, when the pilots were called upon to provide Escort Cover for 36 Marauders bombing St. Pol Marshalling Yards in Part III of Ramrod S.31.

Date	4 September 1943
Operation	Ramrod S.31
Targets	Part I: Lille-Deliverance Marshalling Yards, Pas-de-Calais, France Part II: Courtrai Marshalling Yards, West-Vlaanderen, Belgium Part III: St. Pol Marshalling Yards, Pas-de-Calais, France Part IV: Hazebrouck Marshalling Yards, Pas-de-Calais, France
Bombers	Part I: 36 Marauders, 386 BG; 33 bombed Part II: 36 Marauders, 387 BG; 35 bombed Part III: 36 Marauders, 322 BG; 24 bombed Part IV: 36 Marauders, 323 BG; 33 bombed
Close Escort Part I Escort Cover High Cover Top Cover Close Escort Part II Escort Cover High Cover Top Cover Close Escort Part III Escort Cover High Cover	Staplehurst: 401, 411 & 412 Squadrons (Spitfire Vb) Redhill: 131 & 504 Squadrons (Spitfire Vb) Headcorn: 403 & 421 Squadrons (Spitfire IX) Northolt: 303 & 316 Squadrons (Spitfire IX) Newchurch: 132 & 602 Squadrons (Spitfire Vb) Gravesend: 64 Squadron (Spitfire Vb) Kenley: 66 & 165 Squadrons (Spitfire IX) Biggin Hill: 341 & 485 Squadrons (Spitfire IX) North Weald: 331 & 332 Squadrons (Spitfire IX) Merston: 402 & 416 Squadrons (Spitfire Vb) Friston: 306 Squadron (Spitfire Vb) Westhampnett: 41 & 91 Squadrons (Spitfire XII) Kingsnorth: 19, 65 & 122 Squadrons (Spitfire IX)
Casualties	41 Sqn: Sgt Plt Peter B. Graham, damaged radiator in Spit XII, MB829; 131 Sqn: 1 Lt Franklin D. Burt USAAF, SD/KIA nr Dunkirk in Spit Vc, EE746; 403 Sqn: Sqn Ldr Frank E. Grant, SD/KIA nr Roubaix in Spit IX, MA838; 416 Sqn: Fg Off David F. Prentice, SD off Le Touquet in Spit Vb, BL532, RR

Part I's bombers and escorts rendezvoused near Deal according to plan but encountered the Luftwaffe soon after crossing in. Four FW190s attacked a section of 401 Squadron without result, whilst another four attacked a section from 131 Squadron, resulting in the loss of one pilot.[127]

A further nine FW190s were engaged in the target area by the Headcorn and Northolt Wings, resulting in claims of three FW190s destroyed and one probably destroyed for the loss of 403 Squadron's Commanding Officer. Whilst this was on-going, 33 Marauders dropped a total of 44 tons on Lille-Deliverance Marshalling Yards with good results.

Part II rendezvoused over North Foreland and the Luftwaffe was encountered once again soon after crossing in. The Biggin Hill Wing attempted to engage a group of up to twenty Me109s in the target area, but they avoided the fight and could not be enticed into combat. The Marauders then proceeded to drop 40 tons of bombs on Courtrai [Kortrijk] Marshalling Yards unhindered, with fair results. On the way out, the Close Escort squadrons engaged around twenty-five FW190s near Nieuport [Nieuwpoort] and returned home claiming two destroyed for no loss.

Part III rendezvoused at Dungeness at 18:15, the Spitfire XII Wing having taken off from Westhampnett at 17:50, with 41 Squadron's three sections led by Sqn Ldr Ingham, and Flt Lt Hugh Parry and Fg Off 'Pinkie' Glen.[128] The Spitfire XII Wing crossed in 12,000 feet over Berck-sur-Mer at 18:35 where Sqn Ldr Ingham (MB838) was compelled to return with an oxygen leak, and handed over command of the Squadron to Flt Lt Parry. Not long afterwards, Fg Off Ron Loweth (MB837) followed him home as his drop tank would not jettison.

The rest of the formation continued on, approaching St. Pol unhindered, and 24 Marauders dropped 31 tons of bombs on the marshalling yards with fair results. After dropping their payloads, the bombers continued on their course, penetrating deeper into France until reaching a point northwest Valenciennes, where they turned north about. Following them around, 41 Squadron's pilots saw that "many bombing operations were in progress and huge columns of smoke were seen rising in the direction of Lille."[129]

The return journey, however, stood in stark contrast to the quiet, ordered approach to St. Pol. The Wing became involved in a major air battle when the Close Escort Wings were attacked by twenty FW190s at 6,000 feet between St. Pol and Le Touquet. Seeing the engagements taking place 6,000 feet below them, the Spitfire XII Wing dived down to assist them. "As the result of this scrap the Tangmere and Merston wings destroyed 9 enemy aircraft and damaged 3."[130]

122 Squadron claimed one FW190 damaged, 402 Squadron claimed three FW190s and one Me109 destroyed and one FW190 damaged, 416 Squadron claimed one Me109 destroyed, and the Merston Wing Leader, Wg Cdr Lloyd Chadburn, claimed one FW190 destroyed and one Me109 damaged, for the loss of one pilot of 416 Squadron, who was shot down and ditched off Le Touquet. 41 Squadron's Fg Off 'Pinkie' Glen saw him go in and issued a mayday, and in due course he was rescued by ASR.

91 Squadron wasted no time getting in amongst them but Sqn Ldr Kynaston soon found two FW190s on his tail. Taking evasive action, he out-turned them, losing one and forcing the other into a steep climb. Closing on this aircraft, Kynaston opened fire from 200 yards and hit his mark, causing it to burst into fire. The pilot baled out and the FW190 dived straight into the sea.

91's Fg Off Gray Stenborg DFC came in behind another pair of FW190s that were diving. On seeing him, they pulled up steeply, but Stenborg followed them and when they turned to starboard, he opened fire from 350 yards, hitting the tail of one. Its pilot half-rolled and exited the combat and Stenborg moved his attention to the second Focke-Wulf. Closing rapidly, Stenborg fired at it from just 50 yards, obtaining strikes along its fuselage, and it dived straight into the sea.

41 Squadron also enjoyed some success, and Fg Off Clive Birbeck (EN608) claimed one FW190 destroyed at Le Touquet. Approaching the mêlée with his No. 2, Sgt Plt Peter Graham (MB829), Birbeck initially orbited, seeking a suitable target. In time, he sighted a FW190 at 5,000 feet and dived onto its tail, closely followed by Graham.

On sighting the pair, the German pilot climbed steeply to port, but Birbeck had already closed sufficiently to open fire, and expended bursts at suitable intervals. After steering his Focke-Wulf in a full orbit of Le Touquet with Birbeck and Graham following him, the pilot half-rolled and dived inland, pulling away from the pair as he descended at speed.

At this point, Graham dived away, believing his radiator was hit by Flak, and consequently headed back across the Channel alone. After inspection, however, the damage proved to be more innocuous than initially thought. Graham recalled many years later,

Joe Birbeck and I were lucky enough to be able to engage a pair of FW190s that were attacking some Spit Vs below us. He shot one down and almost at the same moment I was hit, I thought, by flak. My engine temperature gauge began to climb; so I headed straight for home – or rather for Ford, where I landed without trouble, though the temperature of the engine was now dangerously high. As I'd suspected there was a hole in the radiator, which I put down to flak but learned later that in fact the damage had been caused by bullet clips – presumably emanating from the successful guns of my Number One.[131]

Meanwhile, Birbeck had opened his throttle to close on the FW190 that had dived away inland. Increasing to 355mph IAS, he closed anew, firing three bursts from 300-400 yards as he did. Now dangerously close to ground level, the Focke-Wulf clipped some trees, cart-wheeled and crashed at Beussent. Birbeck had expended 189 rounds of 20mm cannon and 1,000 rounds of .303 inch machine gun in achieving the victory – the Squadron's 150th aircraft destroyed of the War – and used nine feet on cine-gun film.[132]

Looking about, Birbeck "then made a pass at a F.W. 190 which had been flying straight and level alongside him, without interfering in the combat".[133] However, finding he had no ammunition left, he decided it was prudent to head home as quickly as possible, and headed towards the Channel on the deck, chased by light Flak as he went. Running short of fuel, Birbeck put down early at Shoreham to top up, before continuing on to Westhampnett.

Other pilots also fired but were unable to make claims, and the Wing landed back at Westhampnett at 19:25, concluding the day's flying.

In Part IV, 33 Marauders dropped 49 tons on Hazebrouck Marshalling Yards, with good results; at least ten bursts were sighted on lines, one on the depot, at least one on tank wagons, and all lines were considered cut.[134]

5 September 1943 – 41 Squadron participated in a single operation today, when the Spitfire XII Wing was called upon to provide Escort Cover to 24 Bostons targeting Woensdrecht Airfield in the Netherlands. In order to do so, the Wing was required to reposition itself to Bradwell Bay, Essex, and as the operation was to commence at 08:30, they flew over at first light.

Date	5 September 1943
Operation	Ramrod S.33
Targets	Part I: Ghent [Gent] Marshalling Yards, Oost-Vlaanderen, Belgium Part II: Courtrai [Kortrijk] Marshalling Yards, West-Vlaanderen, Belgium Part III: Woensdrecht Airfield, Noord-Brabant, Netherlands
Bombers	Part I: 72 Marauders; 72 dispatched, 63 bombed Part II: 36 Marauders; 36 dispatched, all aborted Part III: 88 & 107 Sqns; 24 Bostons; 24 dispatched, 20 bombed
Close Escort Part I	Staplehurst: 401, 411 & 412 Squadrons (Spitfire Vb) Fairlop: 302 & 317 Squadrons (Spitfire Vb)
Escort Cover	Kenley: 66 & 165 Squadrons (Spitfire IX) Redhill: 131 & 504 Squadrons (Spitfire Vb)
High Cover	Hornchurch: 129 & 222 Squadrons (Spitfire IX) Headcorn: 403 & 421 Squadrons (Spitfire IX)
Top Cover	North Weald: 331 & 332 Squadrons (Spitfire IX)
Close Escort Part II	Newchurch: 132 & 602 Squadrons (Spitfire Vb) West Malling: 130 & 234 Squadrons (Spitfire Vb)
Escort Cover	Gravesend: 64 Squadron (Spitfire Vb) Friston: 306 Squadron (Spitfire Vb)
High Cover	Biggin Hill: 341 & 485 Squadrons (Spitfire IX)
Top Cover	Northolt: 303 & 316 Squadrons (Spitfire IX)
Close Escort Part III	Merston: 118, 402 & 416 Squadrons (Spitfire Vb)
Escort Cover	Westhampnett: 41 & 91 Squadrons (Spitfire XII)
High Cover	Kingsnorth: 19, 65 & 122 Squadrons (Spitfire IX)
Casualties	129 Sqn: Sgt Plt John S. Carmichael, SD/KIA Nieuport in Spit IX, MH471; 130 Sqn: Flt Sgt G. Jones, CD/AA/WIA nr Courtrai in Spit Vb, AD329; 222 Sqn: Fg Off H. L. Stuart, CD/FL Manston in Spit IX, MH506

Part I operated generally according to plan and the Marauders dropped 83 tons of bombs on Ghent Marshalling Yards, the first box achieving poor results but the second doing better. The bombers also made some important sightings, the first box reporting on their return have seen what appeared to be a concentration of tanks in the Aalter-Thielt [Tielt] area, and the second recognising that the centre of woods west of Thourout [Torhout] had been cleared and now contained barracks.

Whilst the Luftwaffe was not seen by the Marauders and most of the escort wings, several enemy aircraft were intercepted by the Headcorn Wing. Five Me109s were sighted in the Deinze area, of which four were engaged and two damaged, and 421 Squadron also attacked two FW190s south of Gravelines without result.

Additionally, the Hornchurch Wing was bounced by a dozen FW190s eight miles southeast of Nieuport [Nieuwpoort]. In the ensuing combats, Wg Cdr William Crawford-Compton claimed one FW190 destroyed and 222 Squadron claimed two FW190s destroyed and one probably destroyed, for the loss of one pilot of 129 Squadron who was shot down and killed.

Part II rendezvoused as planned but owing to poor visibility, the Marauders aborted before reaching Courtrai Marshalling Yards and jettisoned their bombs into the sea during the return journey. However, whilst still trying to locate the target, five FW190s approached them, but the bombers' air gunners repelled the attack, claiming three of the enemy aircraft destroyed. Two of 130 Squadron's aircraft were damaged when they attempted to fend off the fighters and one of the Squadron's pilots was also injured. Other enemy aircraft were seen but no further engagements ensued.

The Spitfire XII Wing was airborne from Bradwell Bay at 08:30 and rendezvoused with Part III's bombers and fellow escort squadrons according to plan. The weather was poor over the Netherlands and visibility less than ideal, but the bombing went ahead and six hundred 40 lb. bombs were dropped on Woensdrecht Airfield without interference from the Luftwaffe.

Several bursts were seen within the airfield perimeter, as were "large flashes followed by volumes of dark smoke"[135] in the eastern dispersals area and woods in the north-eastern corner of the airfield. An enemy aircraft was seen to take off through bursts as they exploded around it in one dispersals area.

Despite significant amounts of Flak over the Dutch coast, the entire operation was carried out without event, and 41 Squadron landed back at Bradwell Bay at 10:05 with nothing of significance to report. During the afternoon, the Wing returned to Westhampnett but there was no further operational flying.

Separately today, Fg Off Arthur 'Pinkie' Glen was promoted to Flight Lieutenant, and appointed OC B Flight, a position he retained until 26 January 1944, when he was promoted again.

6 September 1943 – The Spitfire XII Wing participated in two Ramrods today, the first as Escort Cover to Marauders targeting Rouen-Sotteville Marshalling Yards in Part V of Ramrod S.35, and the second in a similar role for Mitchells attacking Abbeville Marshalling Yards.

The first of these was a significant operation, in which over 300 Flying Fortresses were sent to bomb the Bosch factory in Stuttgart in two parts. Part III consisted of a diversionary approach to the Dutch coast by Liberators, and the remaining five parts were supporting and diversionary operations.

Date	6 September 1943
Operation	Ramrod S.35
Targets	Part I: Robert Bosch GmbH, Stuttgart, Baden-Württemberg, Germany
	Part II: Robert Bosch GmbH, Stuttgart, Baden-Württemberg, Germany
	Part III: Diversion, Knokke-Den Helder area, North Sea
	Part IV: Ghent [Gent] Marshalling Yards, Oost-Vlaanderen, Belgium
	Part V: Rouen-Sotteville Marshalling Yards, Haute-Normandie, France
	Part VI: Bassin Loubet, Boulogne Harbour, Pas-de-Calais, France
	Part VII: Bassin Loubet, Boulogne Harbour, Pas-de-Calais, France
	Part VIII: Serqueux Marshalling Yards, Haute-Normandie, France

Bombers	Part I: 157 Flying Fortresses, 111 bombed
	Part II: 181 Flying Fortresses, 151 bombed
	Part III: 40 Liberators; 40 dispatched, 0 bombed
	Part IV: 72 Marauders – cancelled
	Part V: 72 Marauders; 72 dispatched, 66 bombed
	Part VI: 18 Mitchells; 18 dispatched, 18 bombed
	Part VII: 18 Venturas, 18 dispatched, 12 bombed
	Part VIII: 183 Sqn: 8 Bomphoons; 8 dispatched, 8 bombed
Casualties	Part I: 18 Flying Fortresses SD & 1 Cat. E; Part II: 27 Flying Fortresses SD & 9 Cat. E; Part VI: 98 Sqn: Mitchell III, FV921, AA Boulogne, CL nr Brenzett, 4 crew injured; Part VII: 21 Sqn: Ventura II, AE918, AA/CL nr Rye, crew safe
Escort Outbound Part I	56 FG & 353 FG USAAF (Thunderbolt)
Withdrawal Cover	4 FG & 78 FG USAAF (Thunderbolt)
	North Weald: 331 & 332 Squadrons (Spitfire IX)
	Hornchurch: 129 & 222 Squadrons (Spitfire IX)
Escort Outbound Part II	None
Withdrawal Cover	One Group of USAAF Thunderbolts
	Biggin Hill: 341 & 485 Squadrons (Spitfire IX)
	Northolt: 303 & 316 Sqns (Spit IX) & 124 Sqn (Spit Vb)
	Kingsnorth: 19, 65 & 122 Squadrons (Spitfire IX)
	Headcorn: 403 & 421 Squadrons (Spitfire IX)
Escort Part III	None
Escort Part IV	Cancelled
Close Escort Part V	Newchurch: 132 & 602 Squadrons (Spitfire Vb)
	Merston: 118, 402 & 416 Squadrons (Spitfire Vb)
Escort Cover	Redhill: 131 & 504 Squadrons (Spitfire Vb)
	Westhampnett: 41 & 91 Squadrons (Spitfire XII)
High Cover	Biggin Hill: 341 & 485 Squadrons (Spitfire IX)
Top Cover	Kingsnorth: 19, 65 & 122 Squadrons (Spitfire IX)
1st Fighter Sweep	Northolt: 303 & 316 Sqns (Spit IX) & 124 Sqn (Spit Vb)
2nd Fighter Sweep	Headcorn: 403 & 421 Squadrons (Spitfire IX)
Close Escort Part VI	Gravesend: 193 & 257 Squadrons (Typhoon Ib)
Close Escort Part VII	West Malling: 130 & 234 Squadrons (Spitfire Vb)
Fighter Sweep	Hornchurch: 129 & 222 Squadrons (Spitfire IX)
Close Escort Part VIII	Tangmere: 197 & 486 Squadrons (Typhoon Ib)
USAAF Casualties	353 FG/352 FS: Lt Earl W. Perry, SD/KIA in P-47 Thunderbolt 42-7901, nr Ligny, B.
RAF Casualties	41 Sqn: Fg Off Robert J. Boyd, KIA/AA nr Fauville in Spit XII, MB796; 486 Sqn: Plt Off Roderick H. Fitzgibbon RNZAF, SD/AA/KIA off Berneval in Typhoon Ib, EK119.

Thunderbolts escorted Part I's Flying Fortresses to the region of Rheims, where they left them to continue their journey unescorted to Stuttgart. Before parting company, approximately 14 enemy aircraft attacked the bombers and in fending them off one Thunderbolt pilot was shot down and killed.

The Withdrawal Cover Wings met the returning Fortresses near Épernay, seeing another fifteen FW190s attacking the bombers as they arrived. However, as the Thunderbolts entered the affray, the FW190s quickly withdrew. Near Châlons-en-Champagne, another thirty to forty FW190s approached the formation, and in the ensuing combats one enemy aircraft was claimed destroyed for no loss. The North Weald and Hornchurch Wings also met the returning Fortresses, and whilst the former wing operated uneventfully, the latter engaged several FW190s, of which two were claimed damaged.

Part II was provided no escort to the target, but was met on the return journey by a Group of Thunderbolts and four Spitfire Wings, the latter of which intercepted the bombers in the Bernay area. The Wings operated uneventfully, with the exception of 421 Squadron, which saw one FW190 and claimed it destroyed for no loss.

The bombing in Parts I and II was considered successful, despite the fact that 45 Flying Fortresses failed to return. However, ten of these ditched in the Channel and 98 men were rescued by Dover,

Newhaven and Portsmouth ASR vessels, by fishing boats and by a mine sweeper. A lifeboat was also dropped to a crew that had failed to deploy its dinghy.

The double feint diversion operated according to plan, the Liberators flying a route from Orford Ness to Knokke to Den Helder and back to Cromer. They successfully drew up a significant number of Luftwaffe aircraft that included the Luftwaffe's Brussels and Antwerp Wings, as well as fighters from Schipol and Leeuwarden.

Part IV was cancelled, but Part V, in which 41 Squadron participated, operated as planned. The Spitfire XII Wing was airborne at 07:05, with 41 Squadron led by Sqn Ldr Ingham and the other sections led by Flt Lt Hugh Parry and Fg Off Bob Boyd. The Wing arrived at the rendezvous point to find the Marauders had arrived early, and hurried across the Channel to catch up. The Wing crossed in at 07:30 at an altitude of 15,000 feet but did not catch up with the bombers until they were over Rouen-Sotteville Marshalling Yards.

The target was bombed at 07:37, instead of 07:47, as had been scheduled, and the Marauders dropped three 1,000 lb. GP bombs and three hundred and eighty-four 500 lb. GP bombs with fair to good results. Most bursts were observed at the northern end of the marshalling yards.

The Luftwaffe did not interfere and was not seen by any of the escorting fighters. Sparse heavy Flak was, however, experienced and when leaving the target area, Blue 1, Fg Off Bob Boyd (MB796), is believed to have been hit. Some doubt surrounds the circumstances of his loss, but a hand-written report in 41 Squadron's Archives offers some clues:

Soon after leaving Target area at 14,000 [feet] S.L. Ingham warned Blue 1 F.O. Boyd that he was leaving a white trail & ordered him home. Very shortly afterwards Blue 1's engine almost cut and Blue 2 F.O. Harding advised him to try his Kigas[s]. He replied it was not petrol trouble & was heard by Blue 3 F.O. Moffett to say that it was his constant speed unit. Blue 1 glided down gently for several thousand feet. Blue 2 followed to 8500 [feet] & Blue 3 & 4 to 10,000 where he was lost sight of for 30 secs. but [was] seen again in a medium dive, streaming white smoke & crashed into the ground & burst into flames AT FAUVILLE. Blue section did several orbits but saw no parachute. At about 9 000 ft F.O. Moffett warned him against fire. He replied 'say again'. After repeating the warning no reply was received. F.Lt Drew of 118 Sqdn reports seeing a white object flapping about not far from the crashed aircraft. He was not prepared to say what it was.[136,137]

The ORB also recorded that Fg Off Bruce Moffett (MB837) "saw the machine burst into flames just before crashing. Boyd was not seen to bale out and it is feared that he was killed."[138] As it is apparent from the hand-written report that 24-year-old Boyd was quite coherent until minutes before the aircraft crashed, the Squadron was in shock at his inexplicable loss.

However, a civilian eyewitness on the ground later reported having seen Boyd's parachute caught on his aircraft's tailplane, and subsequently saw his body close by the crash-site. If Boyd had indeed baled out, this may account for him having not replied to Moffett's R/T message. It would also explain why Flt Lt Tony Drew of 118 Squadron believed he saw a white object flapping about near the crash-site.

The German military wrapped Boyd in his parachute and buried him in St. Riquier Cemetery. Following the War, he was reinterred in Grandcourt War Cemetery. Although the exact cause of Boyd's initial issue is unknown, damage to hydraulics as a result of a Flak burst is a possible cause. The aircraft crashed in farmland in the village of Cliponville, approximately 5km northeast of Fauville-en-Caux, where it still lies buried today.

At approximately the same time of Boyd's loss, 91 Squadron was dealing with a problem of their own, when one of their pilots blacked out as a result of oxygen trouble. He spun down a significant distance with his section following him, but recovered at about 5,000 feet. This section headed straight for home but took the opportunity to attack and damage a locomotive and wagons in the Yvetot area, and a large limousine, which was forced off the road and burst into flames.

The rest of the Spitfire XII Wing returned to Westhampnett at 08:15, one man down. 41 Squadron's Adjutant, Fg Off Harry Smith then had the unenviable task of sending a telegram to Boyd's father, to inform him of his son's loss. Smith wrote again the following day in a more personal letter:

> Dear Mr Boyd,
> Following my telegram of yesterday, I very much regret to confirm that Bob is still missing as the result of air operations.
> It is impossible to convey in a few words how his colleagues and friends feel about his loss.
> You will wish to know how it all happened and I will tell you what I can from the scanty information that has been received. He was seen to dive down from a considerable height and in fact was followed down as far as possible by another of our pilots and a machine was seen to crash. Another of the pilots reports that he saw a parachute canopy on the ground near the scene of the crash, so we are all rather hopeful that he is at the very worst a prisoner of War. I regret there will be a period of at least three to five weeks before any news is received through the British Red Cross, who will inform you at the same time as the Squadron.
> During the time Bob was with us I came to know him well and I believe it will give you a little comfort to know that he became a most valued member of our squadron and his quiet dry humour endeared him to us all. [...]
> May I express the great sympathy which all of us feel with you and Mrs Boyd during this time of great anxiety. We have very affectionate memories of Bob, a gallant pilot and a real man.[139]

41 Squadron also eulogised Boyd in the ORB thus:

> He joined the Squadron on the 18th November, 1942 and proved himself a very efficient pilot. During the early part of the war he destroyed two Huns and had one probable and one damaged. He was also shot down twice, but on each occasion he managed to bale out without injury. He will be missed very much by all ranks, as his keen North Country humour was appreciated by all of us.[140]

Returning briefly to Ramrod S.35, 18 Mitchells and 18 Venturas were meanwhile sent to bomb Bassin Loubet in Boulogne Harbour in Parts VI and VII. The Mitchells bombed from an altitude of just 1,400 feet at 08:09, dropping a total of one hundred and twenty-six 500 lb. bombs. Bursts were seen across the entrance to the basin and the quay by the E Boat shelter.

The Venturas made their own attack only five minutes later, twelve aircraft dropping thirty-six 500 lb. bombs and forty-seven 250 lb. bombs with good results. Although the Luftwaffe was not seen, both attacks had to contend with significant Flak and one aircraft from each attack was damaged so severely that they crash-landed on return to England.

The two Close Escort wings operated uneventfully, as did the Fighter Sweep, with the exception that the latter wing sighted two FW190s near Dunkirk. These were, however, not attacked as they were thought to have been decoys.

Lastly, 183 Squadron Bomphoons attacked Serquex Marshalling Yards, dropping sixteen 500 lb. bombs with good results. However, a pilot of the Close Escort was hit by Flak and killed off Berneval during an attack on an R Boat on the way home.

That evening, the Spitfire XII Wing was called upon again, to provide Escort Cover to 18 Mitchells attacking Abbeville Marshalling Yards, in Part III of Ramrod S.36.

The Spitfire XII Wing

[Left to right, line by line] Sketches of Fg Off Tom Slack (self portrait), Sgt Plts Peter Wall and Alan Hope, Fg Off Tommy Burne, Fg Off 'Barney' Newman RAAF, Fg Off Prince Emanuel Galitzine, Fg Off Peter Cowell, Plt Off Leslie Prickett, Flt Lt Jerzy Solak (Poland), Flt Sgt 'Jackie' Fisher, Sqn Ldr Ian Matthew, Flt Lt Hugh Parry, Fg Off Herb Wagner, WO Arthur 'Junior' Appleton, Flt Lt Don Smith RAAF, Fg Off Ron Johnson, Flt Lt Lord Gisborough (IO), Fg Off Harry Smith (Adjt), and Fg Off 'Jock' Burnett (MO) during mid to late 1943. © Tom Slack, via Dan Johnson

Date	6 September 1943
Operation	Ramrod S.36
Targets	Part I: Serqueux Marshalling Yards, Haute-Normandie Part II: Amiens-Longeau Marshalling Yards, Picardie Part III: Abbeville Marshalling Yards, Picardie
Bombers	Part I: 72 Marauders; 72 dispatched, 70 bombed Part II: 72 Marauders; 72 dispatched, 65 bombed Part III: 98 & 180 Sqns: 18 Mitchells; 18 dispatched, 18 bombed
Close Escort Part I	Merston: 118, 402 & 416 Squadrons (Spitfire Vb) Newchurch: 132 & 602 Squadrons (Spitfire Vb)
Escort Cover	Redhill: 131 & 504 Squadrons (Spitfire Vb)
High Cover	Biggin Hill: 341 & 485 Squadrons (Spitfire IX)
Top Cover	Kingsnorth: 19, 65 & 122 Squadrons (Spitfire IX)
Close Escort Part II	Staplehurst: 401, 411 & 412 Squadrons (Spitfire Vb) Kenley: 66 & 165 Squadrons (Spitfire IX)
Escort Cover	Fairlop: 302 & 317 Squadrons (Spitfire Vb) Gravesend: 64 Squadron (Spitfire Vb) Hawkinge: 313 Squadron (Spitfire Vb)
High Cover	Hornchurch: 129 & 222 Squadrons (Spitfire IX)
Top Cover	Northolt: 303 & 316 Sqns (Spit IX) & 124 Sqn (Spit Vb)
Fighter Sweep	North Weald: 331 & 332 Squadrons (Spitfire IX)
Close Escort Part III	West Malling: 130 & 234 Squadrons (Spitfire Vb)
Escort Cover	Westhampnett: 41 & 91 Squadrons (Spitfire XII)
High Cover	Headcorn: 403 & 421 Squadrons (Spitfire IX)
Casualties	129 Sqn: Fg Off John D. Mackay RAAF, MAC/KIA in Spit IX, MH422; 485 Sqn: Sqn Ldr John M. Checketts DFC, SD/WIA nr Cayeux in Spit IX, EN572, ER.

Part I saw a return to Serqueux Marshalling Yards, which had been attacked that same morning in Ramrod S.35. On this occasion, 72 Marauders were sent to bomb the railway yards, dropping four hundred and eighteen 500 lb. bombs, over twenty-five times more than that morning's attack. Results were considered fair to good and all Marauders returned safely.

The Close Escort, Escort Cover and Top Cover Wings all operated according to plan, but a significant number of enemy aircraft bounced the High Cover Wing as they banked away from the target area. 485 Squadron reported approximately twenty FW190s diving upon them, whilst 341 Squadron was bounced by a like number of Me109s. In the ensuing combats, 485 Squadron claimed one Me109 destroyed and one FW190 damaged for the loss of 485 Squadron's Commanding Officer, who baled out and subsequently evaded.

The Luftwaffe was all over Part II to Amiens-Longeau Marshalling Yards, and the Close Escort encountered at least fifteen enemy aircraft south of the target area. The Escort Cover Wing reported seeing fifteen to twenty FW190s in the target area, of which 317 Squadron claimed an Me109F destroyed for no loss. The High Cover Wing engaged nine to twelve Me109s over the target area, and a section from 129 Squadron was bounced by a small group of FW190s. One of the Focke-Wulfs rammed one of the Spitfire IXs in this section, destroying both aircraft and killing the two pilots. The Top Cover Wing also sighted a dozen Me109s in the target area, but subsequently engaged a formation of FW190s. 303 Squadron also claimed four FW190s and one Me109 destroyed for no loss. The Fighter Sweep operated uneventfully.

Whilst this was on-going, 65 of the Marauders attacked Amiens-Longeau Marshalling Yards, dropping three hundred and eighty-four 500 lb. bombs with good results. The Luftwaffe did not break through the fighter protection and all Marauders returned safely.

The Spitfire XII Wing was airborne at 17:20 for Part III and rendezvoused with the Mitchells and fellow escort wings according to plan. Prior to making landfall in France, the Close Escort Wing reported seeing three enemy aircraft at 16,000 feet, but they did not interfere. Soon after crossing in, the Spitfire XII Wing sighted a large explosion at Amiens, likely a result of Part II's attack.

At 18:00, the Mitchells attacked Abbeville Marshalling Yards unhindered, dropping one hundred and forty-four 500 lb. bombs with good results. Bursts were seen on the southern convergence of lines and in the centre of the yards, and the only resistance met was when six FW190s were bounced by the High Cover Wing in the Amiens area. Catching the Luftwaffe at a disadvantage, the Wing came away 403 Squadron claiming two destroyed and one damaged, and 421 Squadron claiming one damaged.

The Spitfire XII Wing was not engaged and all pilots returned to Westhampnett safely at 18:40 with nothing to report. This concluded the day's operational flying.

7 September 1943 – The Spitfire XII Wing participated in just one Ramrod today, in which Escort Cover was provided for Mitchells attacking St. Omer Marshalling Yards, in an element of a large operation, involving 430 bombers.[141]

Date	7 September 1943
Operation	Ramrod S.38
Targets	Part I: Evere Airfield, Brussels, Belgium
	Part IIA: Forêt d'Éperleques, Pas-de-Calais, France
	Part IIB: Forêt d'Éperleques, Pas-de-Calais, France
	Part III: St. Omer Marshalling Yards, Pas-de-Calais, France
	Part IV: Lille-Deliverance Marshalling Yards, Pas-de-Calais, France
	Part V: St. Pol Airfield, Pas-de-Calais, France
	Part VI: Abbeville Airfield, Picardie, France
Bombers	Part I: 114 Flying Fortresses dispatched, 104 bombed
	Part II: 147 Flying Fortresses dispatched, 58 bombed, 81 aborted
	Part III: 98 & 180 Sqns: 18 Mitchells; 18 dispatched, 18 bombed
	Part IV: 72 Marauders: 72 dispatched, 12 bombed, 60 aborted
	Part V: 72 Marauders; 72 dispatched, 70 bombed
	Part VI: 174 Sqn: 8 Bomphoons; 8 dispatched, 8 bombed
Escort Part I	USAAF Thunderbolts
Escort Part IIA	Headcorn: 403 & 421 Squadrons (Spitfire IX)
Escort Part IIB	Kingsnorth: 19, 65 & 122 Squadrons (Spitfire IX)
Close Escort Part III	Gravesend: 64 Squadron (Spitfire Vb)
	Friston: 306 Squadron (Spitfire Vb)
	Hawkinge: 313 Squadron (Spitfire Vb)
Escort Cover	Westhampnett: 41 & 91 Squadrons (Spitfire XII)
Close Escort Part IV	Staplehurst: 401, 411 & 412 Squadrons (Spitfire Vb)
	Newchurch: 132 & 602 Squadrons (Spitfire Vb)
Escort Cover	Redhill: 131 & 504 Squadrons (Spitfire Vb)
	Fairlop: 302 & 317 Squadrons (Spitfire Vb)
High Cover	Hornchurch: 129 & 222 Squadrons (Spitfire IX)
Top Cover	North Weald: 331 & 332 Squadrons (Spitfire IX)
Close Escort Part V	West Malling: 130 & 234 Squadrons (Spitfire Vb)
	Merston: 118, 402 & 416 Squadrons (Spitfire Vb)
Escort Cover	Kenley: 66 & 165 Squadrons (Spitfire IX)
High Cover	Biggin Hill: 341 & 485 Squadrons (Spitfire IX)
Top Cover	Northolt: 303 & 316 Squadrons (Spitfire IX)
Escort Part VI	Lydd: 175 & 245 Squadrons (Typhoon Ib)
USAAF Casualties	Part I: 1 Thunderbolt pilot FTR

Part I operated generally according to plan and 104 Flying Fortresses attacked Brussels' Evere Airfield, dropping 315 tons with fair to good results, sustaining no losses of their own. The escorting USAAF Thunderbolts claimed two Me109s destroyed and three damaged, for the loss of one pilot.

Parts IIA and IIB was much less successful as a result of poor weather conditions. Eighty-one of the 147 dispatched Fortresses aborted the operation and only 58 attacked the Big Ben target in the Fôret d'Éperleques, with fair to good results. The escorting Spitfires from the Headcorn and Kingsnorth Wings operated according to plan, and the only enemy aircraft seen were four taking off from Mardyck Airfield.

The Spitfire XII Wing was airborne at 07:35 to participate in Part III and rendezvoused with the Mitchells and Close Escort Squadrons 12,000 feet over Sandwich. The formation crossed in three miles northeast of Gravelines and proceeded to St. Omer.

The Luftwaffe did not interfere and a total of twenty-four 1,000 lb. bombs and eighty-six 500 lb. bombs were dropped on St. Omer Marshalling Yards. However, the results were not observed owing to cloud cover. The operation was completed without incident and all aircraft returned safely.

The Spitfire XII Wing landed back at Westhampnett at 08:55 with nothing to report, and there was no more operational flying all day. Having seen "nothing at all", 41 Squadron considered it, "a most uninteresting Sweep".[142]

Meanwhile, Part IV had also operated. The Close Escort's Staplehurst Wing arrived at the rendezvous, where they orbited until joined by 72 Marauders and escorted them across the Channel. It later transpired these were actually Part V's bombers, an error caused by Part IV's Marauders arriving at the rendezvous almost 15 minutes late. The Wing accompanied the Marauders to St. Pol Airfield and home again.

Part IV's other Close Escort Wing, Newchurch, and the Escort Cover, High Cover and Top Cover Wings all rendezvoused with the Marauders despite their late arrival and crossed into France where the weather was found less than ideal. Sixty bombers aborted the operation south of Lens, and the Newchurch and Escort Cover Wings returned with them to England.

The High Cover Wing continued to escort the remaining 12 Marauders, who found themselves unable to attack the primary target, Lille-Deliverance Marshalling Yards, but upon sighting Part V's Marauders attacking St. Pol Airfield, attached themselves to that formation and bombed this target, too. The Top Cover Wing operated uneventfully.

Part V operated according to plan with the exception that 12 of Part IV's Marauders and the Staplehurst Wing attached themselves to the operation. Seventy of Part V's Marauders, and Part IV's twelve, attacked St. Pol Airfield dropping a total of four hundred and eighty-four 500 lb. bombs with fair to poor results.

Lastly, in Part VI, eight Bomphoons attacked Abbeville Airfield with sixteen 500 lb. bombs achieving good results, and several bursts were seen on the northern dispersals area. The Bomphoons and their escort squadrons all operated uneventfully.

8 September 1943 – In contrast to the previous day, where there was no operational flying after 09:00, today's programme saw the Spitfire XII Wing deployed on three separate Ramrod operations between 09:25 and 18:55. The first of these took the Wing to Vitry-en-Artois Airfield, the second to Abbeville Marshalling Yards, and the third to the Wimereux-Boulogne Coastal Batteries.

In order to participate in the initial attack, it was necessary for the Wing to fly to their designated jumping off point, Lympne, at first light.

Date	8 September 1943
Operation	Ramrod S.41
Targets	Part I: Lille-Nord Airfield, Pas-de-Calais Part II: Lille-Vendeville Airfield, Pas-de-Calais Part III: Vitry-en-Artois Airfield, Pas-de-Calais
Bombers	Part I: 72 Marauders; 72 dispatched, 68 bombed Part II: 72 Marauders; 72 dispatched, 68 bombed Part III: 98 & 180 Sqns: 18 Mitchells; 18 dispatched, 18 bombed
Casualties	Part II: 386 BG/552 BS: B-26 Marauder, 41-34970, RG-L, 'Margie', CD/AA/SD, ditched English Channel (4 RR & 1 KIA)

Close Escort Part I	Staplehurst: 401, 411 & 412 Squadrons (Spitfire Vb)
	West Malling: 130 & 234 Squadrons (Spitfire Vb)
Escort Cover	Redhill: 131 & 504 Squadrons (Spitfire Vb)
	Fairlop: 302 & 317 Squadrons (Spitfire Vb)
High Cover	Hornchurch: 129 & 222 Squadrons (Spitfire IX)
Top Cover	Kingsnorth: 19, 65 & 122 Squadrons (Spitfire IX)
Fighter Sweep	Northolt: 303 & 316 Squadrons (Spitfire IX)
Close Escort Part II	Newchurch: 132 & 602 Squadrons (Spitfire Vb)
	Southend: 610 & 611 Squadrons (Spitfire Vb)
Escort Cover	Kenley: 66, 165 & 453 Squadrons (Spitfire IX)
High Cover	Biggin Hill: 341 & 485 Squadrons (Spitfire IX)
Top Cover	North Weald: 331 & 332 Squadrons (Spitfire IX)
Close Escort Part III	Merston: 118, 402 & 416 Squadrons (Spitfire Vb)
Escort Cover	Hawkinge: 313 Squadron (Spitfire Vb)
	West Malling: 64 & 350 Squadrons (Spitfire Vb)
High Cover	Westhampnett: 41 & 91 Squadrons (Spitfire XII)
Top Cover	Headcorn: 403 & 421 Squadrons (Spitfire IX)
Casualties	91 Sqn: Plt Off Charles R. Fraser, SD nr Vitry-en-Artois, in Spit XII, MB852, POW; 222 Sqn: Sgt Plt A. E. Townsend, SD Lille in Spit IX, MH389, POW; 302 Sqn: WO Bronislaw Malinowski, SD Lille in Spit Vb, AA928, ER, & Fg Off Czeslaw Sniec, SD Lille in Spit Vb, AA909, ER

Part I rendezvoused and operated according to plan, but the Fairlop Wing engaged a mixed group of approximately twenty FW190s and Me109s that tried to break through to the bombers shortly before reaching the target. In the resulting combats, 302 Squadron claimed two Me109s and a FW190 destroyed, and a second FW190 probable, whilst 317 Squadron claimed three Me109s destroyed and one damaged. Two pilots of 302 Squadron were also shot down, but both were able to evade and return to England.

The High Cover Wing also met ten to twelve enemy aircraft over Lille, and were unable to make any claims but lost one pilot who was shot down and captured. The Top Cover Wing also engaged significant numbers of Luftwaffe aircraft but made no claims and reported no losses.

Despite the presence of the Luftwaffe, the bombing proceeded to plan and sixty-eight Marauders dropped four hundred and seven 500 lb. bombs on Lille-Nord Airfield with fair to good results. All returned safely.

Part II took place 50 minutes after Part I. Whilst their destination was in the same area, their target was Lille-Vendeville Airfield. Although the Luftwaffe was met once again, their numbers were significantly fewer. The Top Cover Wing arrived over the target area ahead of the bombers, where they sighted two formations of eight FW190s. These were engaged and in the ensuing combats, one FW190 was claimed destroyed and three damaged for no loss.

Arriving over Lille, sixty-eight Marauders attacked dropped six hundred and sixty-four 300 lb. bombs with fair to good results, but one was hit and seriously damaged by Flak. The Southend Wing escorted this aircraft back to England, but they were attacked by six FW190s south of Dunkirk as they were about to cross out. One Spitfire was damaged, and the Marauder ended up ditching in the Channel. One of the crew was killed but four were rescued.

Having repositioned to Lympne at first light, the Spitfire XII Wing took off from that airfield again at 09:25 to rendezvous with Part III's Mitchells and the Merston, Hawkinge, West Malling and Headcorn Wings. The High Cover and Top Cover Wings were intercepted over Vitry-en-Artois Airfield by approximately fifteen FW190s, and 91 and 403 Squadrons were engaged.

91 Squadron's Sgt Plt Richmond Blumer claimed one FW190 destroyed and 403 Squadron claimed another damaged, but 91 Squadron also lost one pilot, who was shot down and captured. 41 Squadron was not involved.

The Mitchells meanwhile dropped forty-eight 1,000 lb. bombs and a like number of 500 lb. bombs with good results. Bursts were observed in the centre of the airfield and across the east-west runway. They did not experience any Flak and did not see the Luftwaffe. On the way home, however, the Close Escort Wing sighted seven Me109s, which were attacked and one was claimed destroyed for no loss.

The Spitfire XII Wing landed back at Lympne at 11:00, then refuelled and took off again for Westhampnett. However...

> *On approaching the airfield the first two sections were about to land when operations called up and told the Squadron to proceed to Hawkinge and after one circuit the Squadron shot off much to the surprise of the waiting ground crews and disappeared. We learned later that they had arrived at Hawkinge.*[143]

The pilots soon discovered that they were assigned to a Circus, the first in a very long time, the jumping off point of which would be Hawkinge. Following lunch and a briefing, the Wing was airborne again at 13:45 to provide High Cover for RAF Venturas attacking Abbeville Marshalling Yards.

Date	8 September 1943
Operation	Circus S.1
Target	Abbeville Marshalling Yards, Picardie
Bombers	21 Sqn: 18 Ventura II, 18 dispatched, 17 bombed
Close Escort	West Malling: 64, 130 & 234 Squadrons (Spitfire Vb)
Escort Cover	Redhill: 131 & 504 Squadrons (Spitfire Vb)
High Cover	Westhampnett: 41 & 91 Squadrons (Spitfire XII)
1st Fighter Sweep	Biggin Hill: 341 & 485 Squadrons (Spitfire IX) – Poix
2nd Fighter Sweep	Northolt: 124, 303 & 316 Squadrons (Spitfire IX) – St. Valéry
3rd Fighter Sweep	Hornchurch: 129 & 222 Squadrons (Spitfire IX) – Doullens
4th Fighter Sweep	North Weald: 331 & 332 Squadrons (Spitfire IX) – Aire
5th Fighter Sweep	Headcorn: 403 & 421 Squadrons (Spitfire IX) – St. Pol
6th Fighter Sweep	Kingsnorth: 19, 65 & 122 Squadrons (Spitfire IX) – Neufchâtel

The Spitfire XII Wing rendezvoused with the Venturas and fellow escort wings 12,000 feet over Dungeness at 14:00 and proceeded across the Channel together, whilst the six fighter sweeps operated independently under Beachy and Appledore Control.

41 Squadron's Sgt Plt Peter Wall (MB846) returned at around the same time of the rendezvous for unexplained reasons, possibly the result of jettison tank issues. The rest of the formation continued to Abbeville, where the Venturas dropped fifty 500 lb. bombs and sixty-eight 250 lb. bombs on the Marshalling Yards from an altitude of 12,000 feet. Results were, however, not as accurate as planned. Whilst bursts were seen in the centre and on the western and south-western edges of the yards, some were also seen in the town itself. However, no movement was observed on the rails, Flak was not experienced and the Luftwaffe was not seen.

Disappointed with the lack of action, the Spitfire XII Wing turned back into France after seeing the bombers out, in the hope of "enticing the Hun up to fight".[144] They swept Abbeville without success and returned directly to Westhampnett, landing again at 15:05, "very disappointed".[145]

Meanwhile, the second, fifth and sixth Fighter Sweeps were all completed uneventfully. The first dived on six FW190s, but these evaded by heading for cloud cover and avoided a fight. As the third climbed to 27,000 feet towards Montdidier, they sighted ten to twelve FW190s ahead of them. These were attacked and one damaged.

The fourth Fighter Sweep was only a little more successful. The North Weald Wing bounced ten to twelve Me109s at 10,000 feet in the Merville area from 24,000 feet, and one was damaged, but the enemy aircraft dived into cloud cover and were lost before any further damage could be done. The Wing climbed again to the same altitude, when the Messerschmitts appeared anew, climbing out of the cloud ceiling. 331 & 332 Squadrons dived once again, but could only succeed in damaging a second Me109.

The Spitfire XII Wing had already participated in two operations today, but would be called on to take part in yet another before operational flying concluded for the day. This time, they were tasked with providing Medium Cover to Mitchells, Whirlwind bombers, Marauders and Bomphoons attacking the coastal batteries between Boulogne and Wimereux in seven waves, as an element of Ramrod S.42.

> *A huge air umbrella was put up over Boulogne, whilst approximately 100 bombers blitzed gun positions and other targets in that area.*[146]

Date	8 September 1943
Operation	Ramrod S.42
Targets	Wimereux-Boulogne Coastal Batteries, Pas-de-Calais
	Part IA: N. and S. of Wimereux
	Part IB: N. of Wimereux
	Part IIA: E. of Wimereux
	Part IIB: S. of Boulogne
	Part IIC: Hardelot
	Part IIIA: E. of Wimereux
	Part IIIB: S. of Boulogne
Bombers	Part IA: 19 Mitchells; 19 dispatched, 18 bombed
	Part IB: 263 Sqn: 12 Whirlibombers; 12 dispatched, 7 bombed
	Part IIA: 18 Marauders; 18 dispatched, 14 bombed
	Part IIB: 18 Marauders; 18 dispatched, 18 bombed
	Part IIC: 181 Sqn: 8 Bomphoons; 8 dispatched, 8 bombed
	Part IIIA: 18 Marauders; 18 dispatched, 18 bombed
	Part IIIB: 18 Marauders; 18 dispatched, 18 bombed
Close Escort Part IA	Southend: 610 & 611 Squadrons (Spitfire Vb)
Close Escort Part IB	Lympne: 1 & 609 Squadrons (Typhoon Ib)
Close Escort Part IIA	Staplehurst: 401, 411 & 412 Squadrons (Spitfire Vb)
Close Escort Part IIB	Newchurch: 132 & 602 Squadrons (Spitfire Vb)
Close Escort Part IIC	New Romney: 247 Squadron (Typhoon Ib)
Close Escort Part IIIA	West Malling: 130 & 234 Squadrons (Spitfire Vb)
	Friston: 306 & 308 Squadrons (Spitfire Vb)
Close Escort Part IIIB	Merston: 118, 402 & 416 Squadrons (Spitfire Vb)
Medium Cover	Fairlop: 302 & 317 Squadrons (Spitfire Vb)
	Kenley: 66, 165 & 453 Squadrons (Spitfire IX)
	Redhill: 131 & 504 Squadrons (Spitfire Vb)
	Hawkinge: 313 Squadron (Spitfire Vb)
	West Malling: 64 & 350 Squadrons (Spitfire Vb)
	Westhampnett: 41 & 91 Squadrons (Spitfire XII)
High Cover	Hornchurch: 129 & 222 Squadrons (Spitfire IX)
	Biggin Hill: 341 & 485 Squadrons (Spitfire IX)
	Northolt: 303 & 316 Squadrons (Spitfire IX)
1st Fighter Sweep	Cancelled
2nd Fighter Sweep	North Weald: 331 & 332 Squadrons (Spitfire IX)
3rd Fighter Sweep	Kingsnorth: 19, 65 & 122 Squadrons (Spitfire IX)

Part IA operated successfully and twelve Mitchells dropped forty-five 1,000 lb. bombs south of Wimereux, whilst six Mitchells dropped a further twenty-four 1,000 lb. bombs north of the town. Results were believed to have been good, as bursts were seen in the target area during the former attack but unobserved during the latter as a result of smoke obscuring the view. Part IB enjoyed similar success and seven Whirlibombers attacked their target from altitudes of between 7,000 and 14,000 feet. Six bursts were seen within the target area.

In Part II, fourteen of the eighteen Marauders attacked target A to the east of Wimereux, dropping seventy-nine 500 lb. bombs with fair results. Eighteen Marauders also dropped one hundred and eight 500 lb. bombs on target B with good results, whilst eight Bomphoons bombed target C, observing all bursts inside the target area.

OC A Flight, Flt Lt Hugh Parry was shot down near Crillon, France, on 24 September 1943. He was hidden by the Resistance until 7 February 1944, when he was betrayed and arrested by the Gestapo. © Ron Johnson, via Dan Johnson

Eighteen Marauders succeeded in dropping one hundred and eight 500 lb. bombs with fair results in Part IIIA, whilst a like number of Marauders dropped one hundred and seven 500 lb. bombs with fair results in Part IIIB.

All Parts reported heavy Flak, but the Luftwaffe only made an appearance during Part IIIA. The Medium and High Cover Wings also reported significant Flak, but only the Hornchurch Wing actually engaged the Luftwaffe, and returned claiming one Me109 destroyed for no loss.

For their part, the Spitfire XII Wing was airborne from Westhampnett at 17:15, and proceeded across the Channel to patrol the Boulogne area at 13,000-16,000 feet. They found the Flak very intense but no-one was hit. On the way home, Flt Sgt James Still (EN609) and Sgt Plt Alan Hope (MB838) landed at Friston to refuel, whilst Flt Sgt Stan May (EN231) landed at Ford for the same reason.

The rest of 41 Squadron's pilots continued on to Westhampnett where they landed at 18:55, concluding an intensive and tiring day's flying. They did, however, arrive home to some good news:

> *The greatest news of the day was given on* [the] *wireless at 18.00 hours, when we learned that Italy had capitulated, but the evening could not be spent in celebration, as a big day was expected on the morrow. At 21.00 the Westhampnett and Merston Wings were briefed for the following days* [sic] *show and there was great excitement and expectation.*[147]

9 September 1943 – Today saw the final Ramrod of Operation *Starkey*, which officially ended at 23:59. Two Ramrods were planned for the day, but the second was cancelled as a result of poor weather conditions, leaving just S.43, in which the Spitfire XII Wing participated. Following Italy's capitulation and the previous night's briefing, great things were expected today.

41 Squadron was airborne for the first time today at 08:05, when they provided twelve aircraft to cover shipping in the Channel. They landed at 09:40 with nothing to report, but were airborne again at 10:20 with the same task, led by Wg Cdr Harries. The second convoy patrol was just as uneventful as the first and they returned to Westhampnett again 90 minutes later.

After landing, the pilots were surprised to find tea, ham and tomato sandwiches and fresh oranges awaiting them. Having enjoyed this welcome break, the pilots were briefed anew and were called upon again just after 14:00, to undertake offensive operations into France.

Date	9 September 1943
Operation	Ramrod S.43
Targets	Part I: Monchy-Breton Airfield, Pas-de-Calais, France Part II: Bryas Sud [Brias] Airfield, Pas-de-Calais, France Part III: Merville Airfield, Pas-de-Calais, France Part IV: Coxyde [Koksijde] Airfield, West-Vlaanderen, Belgium
Bombers	Part I: 107 & 342 Sqn: 24 Bostons; 23 dispatched, 20 bombed Part II: 98 & 189 Sqn: 12 Mitchells; 18 dispatched, 12 bombed Part III: 21 Sqn: 18 Venturas; 12 dispatched, 8 bombed Part IV: 181 Sqn: 12 Bomphoons; 12 dispatched, 12 bombed

Close Escort Part I	Merston: 118, 402 & 416 Squadrons (Spitfire Vb)
Escort Cover	Redhill: 131 & 504 Squadrons (Spitfire Vb)
High Cover	Westhampnett: 41 & 91 Squadrons (Spitfire XII)
Top Cover	Biggin Hill: 341 & 485 Squadrons (Spitfire IX)
Fighter Sweep	Northolt: 303 & 316 Squadrons (Spitfire IX)
Close Escort Part II	Staplehurst: 401, 411 & 412 Squadrons (Spitfire Vb)
Escort Cover	Kenley: 66, 165 & 453 Squadrons (Spitfire IX)
High Cover	Headcorn: 403 & 421 Squadrons (Spitfire IX)
Fighter Sweep	Kingsnorth: 19, 65 & 122 Squadrons (Spitfire IX)
Close Escort Part III	West Malling: 130 & 234 Squadrons (Spitfire Vb)
	Southend: 610 & 611 Squadrons (Spitfire Vb)
Escort Cover	West Malling: 64 & 350 Squadrons (Spitfire Vb)
	Hawkinge: 313 Squadron (Spitfire Vb)
High Cover	Hornchurch: 129 & 222 Squadrons (Spitfire IX)
Fighter Sweep	North Weald: 331 & 332 Squadrons (Spitfire IX)
Escort Part IV	New Romney: 247 Squadron (Typhoon Ib)
Casualties	122 Sqn: Flt Sgt R. Furness, SD Amiens-Desvres in Spit IX, MA839, POW; 331 Sqn: Sgt Plt Håkon A. Horg, SD/AA/KIA off Dunkirk in Spit IX, MA748

The Spitfire XII Wing was airborne at 14:05 and rendezvoused with Part I's bombers and other escort squadrons 12,000 feet over Beachy Head at 14:20. They proceeded to Monchy-Breton Airfield unhindered, where the Bostons dropped seventy-six 500 lb. bombs with very good accuracy at 14:44. The only enemy aircraft seen were ten Me109s that were too far away to be engaged. The Fighter Sweep also operated uneventfully, and all aircraft returned safely to base, 41 Squadron landing at 15:25.

Part II rendezvoused over Dungeness at the same altitude and time as Part I and approached Bryas Sud Airfield just as uneventfully. The Mitchells dropped twenty-four 1,000 lb. and forty-four 500 lb. bombs at 14:45 with results that were considered good. These aircraft all returned unhindered, but the Part's Fighter Sweep encountered significant numbers of enemy aircraft.

The first of these were seen in the Lille-Béthune area, when eight Me109s were engaged without result. A short while later, a lone FW190 was sighted and shot down by 65 Squadron, followed by the sighting of twenty Me109s near Amiens, of which one was claimed probably destroyed by 122 Squadron. Finally, the Kingsnorth Wing was attacked by a mixed group of FW190s and Me109s over the Somme Estuary, three miles from the French coast. Another Me109 was claimed probably destroyed by 122 Squadron, but at the cost of one pilot who was shot down between Amiens and Desvres and captured.

Part III rendezvoused 12,000 feet over North Foreland at 14:40 and around ten enemy aircraft were seen at 20,000 feet by the Close Escort Wing between the coast and Merville Airfield. The Venturas attacked the target from 11,000 feet at 14:59, dropping twenty-three 500 lb. and thirty-two 250 lb. bombs with good results. On the way out, seven enemy aircraft were seen by the Close Escort Wing, whilst twelve FW190s were engaged by the Hornchurch Wing without result.

Part III's Fighter Sweep by the North Weald Wing operated generally uneventfully, but one man was lost when he was seen to dive into the Channel off Dunkirk, presumably having fallen victim to Flak.

Finally, in Part IV, twelve Bomphoons attacked Coxyde Airfield with an escort of Typhoons, dropping twenty-four 500 lb. bombs with good results.

Thus ended Operation *Starkey* for the Spitfire XII Wing, going out with somewhat of a whimper instead of a bang. For all the hype and expectation, 41 Squadron was thoroughly underwhelmed. Underscoring this point, the following was recorded in the ORB today with great sarcasm,

> *Since August 24th all leave has been stopped and numbers of Squadrons have come to reinforce the present Tangmere Sector Squadrons. Feeling has been tense and the local censors have been prying into most of the private mail going from this district.*

The big day dawns and the crews, pilots, medic, intelligence officer and Adjutant are turned out of bed at 04.30 hours. Breakfast proceeds amongst the hum and chatter of pilots speculating how many Huns they will shoot down during the day and away we go to dispersal.

Then we sit and chat and make things ready for the big offensive or whatever this day will eventually be called – and incidentally it was called all sorts of names when darkness eventually came!

[…] By this time the pilots felt that the terrific build up for the day had somehow been wasted, but we read in the evening papers that a big amphibious exercise had taken place in the Channel and the success was stupendous! One can't disbelieve the papers. The day gradually draws to a close and not one Hun has been seen and the tension of the last few weeks lapses.

The pilots are now looking forward to the normal escort covers of an ordinary days [sic] *operations and the chance of seeing a few Huns. So ends the great day!*[148]

Separately today, a new pilot arrived on the Squadron in the form of 22-year-old Fg Off John B. Smith. Having joined the RAFVR in January 1941, he was commissioned eight months later and completed OTU at Aston Down before being posted to 29 EFTS as a flying instructor. He joined 41 Squadron today on his first operational posting, with 893 non-operational flying hours in his logbook.

10 September 1943 – Following their busy schedule during Operation *Starkey*, the Squadron was able to rest today, and the only operational flying undertaken was a shipping reconnaissance to France by Flt Lt 'George' Solak and Sgt Plt Peter Graham as Red Section. Airborne at 10:40, the pair swept the coast past Cherbourg, Le Havre and Étretat but no shipping was seen and they landed again at 11:35.

11 September 1943 – Returning to the previous routine today, the Spitfire XII Wing was assigned to a single Ramrod, the first since the end of *Starkey*. The normal chronology of Ramrod numbers picked up again from where they were left on 24 August, and the Wing provided Escort Cover to Marauders attacking Beaumont-le-Roger Airfield in Part II of Ramrod 216.

Date	11 September 1943
Operation	Ramrod 216
Targets	Part I: Le Grand-Quevilly Power Station, Haute-Normandie Part II: Beaumont-le-Roger Airfield, Haute-Normandie Part III: Beaumont-le-Roger Airfield, Haute-Normandie Part IV: Beauvais-Tillé Airfield, Picardie
Bombers	Part I: 21 Marauders; 20 dispatched, 18 bombed Part II: 323 BG: 36 Marauders; 36 dispatched, 32 bombed Part III: 320 Sqn: 12 Mitchells; 12 dispatched, 11 bombed Part IV: 181 Sqn: 8 Typhoon Ib; 8 dispatched, 8 bombed
Casualties	Part II: 1 Marauder CL on return, 4 crew †
Close Escort Part I	Newchurch: 132 & 602 Squadrons (Spitfire Vb) Staplehurst: 401, 411 & 412 Squadrons (Spitfire Vb)
Escort Cover	Fairlop: 302 & 317 Squadrons (Spitfire Vb)
High Cover	Hornchurch: 129 & 222 Squadrons (Spitfire IX)
Top Cover	North Weald: 331 & 332 Squadrons (Spitfire IX)
Close Escort Part II	Merston: 118, 402 & 416 Squadrons (Spitfire Vb)
Escort Cover	Westhampnett: 41 & 91 Squadrons (Spitfire XII)
High Cover	Kingsnorth: 19, 65 & 122 Squadrons (Spitfire IX)
Top Cover	Headcorn: 403 & 421 Squadrons (Spitfire IX)
Close Escort Part III	Kenley: 66 & 165 Squadrons (Spitfire IX)
Escort Cover	Redhill: 131 & 504 Squadrons (Spitfire Vb)
High Cover	Biggin Hill: 341 & 485 Squadrons (Spitfire IX)
Top Cover	Northolt: 303 & 316 Squadrons (Spitfire IX)
Close Escort Part IV	New Romney: 182 & 247 Squadrons (Typhoon Ib)
Escort Cover	Lydd: 175 & 245 Squadrons (Typhoon Ib)

Casualties	16 Wing: Wg Cdr Alec Ingle DFC AFC, SD Beauvais in Typhoon Ib, JP436, POW; 182 Sqn: Flt Sgt Robin O'Hara-Murray, SD/KIA Quincampoix in Typhoon Ib, JP536; 317 Sqn: Fg Off S. Kurowicki, SD/KIA Le Havre-Rouen in Spit Vb, BL406; 332 Sqn: 2 Lt Sigmund J. M. Sandvik, SD nr Rouen in Spit IX, LZ898, ER

In Part I, the Marauders were unable to attack the primary target, Le Grand-Quevilly Power Station, owing to thick cumulus cloud, and dropped one hundred and five 500 lb. bombs on the secondary target, Le Trait Shipping Yards, at 17:05 instead. Results were considered good and bursts were seen on the north side of the river and on buildings in the yards.

Estimates of between 30 and 70 FW190s and Me109s were engaged in the target area by the escort wings. Strangely, considering Italy's capitulation, some of these aircraft bore Italian markings. Intensive combats ensued and the following victories were claimed: Wg Cdr Henry Woodhouse, one FW190 damaged; 129 Squadron, one Me109 destroyed and one damaged; 302 Squadron, one FW190 damaged; 317 Squadron, four FW190 destroyed and one damaged; 331 Squadron, two FW190 destroyed; and 332 Squadron, one FW190 destroyed. However, 317 Squadron lost one pilot, who was shot down and killed, whilst 331 Squadron lost another, who was shot down but evaded and returned to the United Kingdom.

The Spitfire XII Wing took off at 17:00 and rendezvoused with Part II's bombers and fellow escort wings before crossing the Channel. However, 41 Squadron's Flt Lt Roy Lane (MB844), leading Yellow Section, developed R/T trouble and returned to base within 15 minutes. Flt Sgt Jimmy Payne (MB804), in Blue Section, found his fuel cock leaking, and also returned to Westhampnett early.[149] Lastly, Flt Lt Hugh Parry (MB802), leading the Squadron, also headed home early, landing again 50 minutes after his departure, although the reason is not recorded.

A much depleted 41 Squadron continued on, now just three sections of three, and the operation was carried out otherwise according to plan. The Marauders dropped both 500 lb. and 100 lb. bombs on Beaumont-le-Roger Airfield at 18:00 with good results, and bursts were seen in the dispersals area on the western side of the airfield and on buildings south of the airfield.

On the way out, 15 miles from Fécamp, around twelve Me109s approached from the northeast and dived from 17,000 feet to 10,000 feet, passing under the formation. The Close Escort Wing dived after them, prompting the Spitfire XII Wing to take over Close Escort of the bombers in case any other enemy aircraft should attack, but this did not eventuate. The Me109s escaped an engagement by diving to the deck and dispersing, and the Close Escort Wing was unable to make any claims.

The Top Cover Wing also encountered twelve enemy aircraft in the Barentin area, northwest of Rouen, and in the ensuing combats 403 Squadron claimed one Me109 destroyed. There was no further interference for the returning formation, but one Marauder crash-landed on return to its base, killing four of the crew.

Part III's destination was the same as Part II's and ran according to plan without any sign of the Luftwaffe. Eleven Mitchells dropped eighty-eight 500 lb. bombs with good results and bursts were reported on the landing ground, on the western and north-western dispersals areas, and on buildings on the western and south-western sides of the airfield.

Part IV's Bomphoons also attacked Beauvais-Tillé Airfield as planned and bursts and fires were seen in the northern and western dispersals areas. Both escort wings were engaged by the Luftwaffe, the Close Escort attacked by six to eight FW190s south-southwest of Poix, and the Escort Cover by twenty FW190s whilst approaching the target area. 175 and 182 Squadrons claimed a FW190 damaged each, but 16 Wing's Commanding Officer was shot down and captured whilst a pilot of 182 Squadron was shot down and killed.

13 September 1943 – The Spitfire XII Wing's operational flying today was limited to a fighter sweep in Rodeo 253, in co-operation with Merston-based 118, 402 and 416 Squadrons. Both Wings swept the Cap d'Antifer and Beaumont-le-Roger areas, the Spitfire XII Wing following the

Merston Wing at 18:10. Although the Flak was aggressive, and Fg Off Peter Cowell (MB834) was hit ("Bags of very accurate flak – I was hit twice!!")[150], nothing of interest was seen by the Wing and their guns were not fired. Returning at 19:45 with nothing to report, the ORB bemoaned the lack of action,

> *A fighter sweep was carried out by the wing – but as usual the Hun did not play. Fighter sweeps do not appear to draw up the Hun these days and it usually gives the less operational pilots a chance to gain further experience and confidence. Only two enemy aircraft were seen and these were at some distance over Evreux.*[151]

14 September 1943 – The Wing was involved in one abortive Ramrod today, in which it was intended they provide Escort Cover to Marauders bombing Woensdrecht Airfield in the Netherlands, in Part II of Ramrod 218. Although airborne, weather conditions resulted in Parts I and II being recalled.[152]

Date	14 September 1943
Operation	Ramrod 218
Targets	Part I: Lille-Nord Airfield, Pas-de-Calais, France Part II: Woensdrecht Airfield, Noord-Brabant, Netherlands Part III: Merville Airfield, Pas-de-Calais, France
Bombers	Part I: 72 Marauders; 79 dispatched – recalled (weather) Part II: 36 Marauders; 36 dispatched – recalled (weather) Part III: 175 Sqn: 8 Bomphoons; 8 disp., 8 bombed secondary
Close Escort Part I	Newchurch: 132 & 602 Squadrons (Spitfire Vb) – recalled Staplehurst: 401, 411 & 412 Squadrons (Spitfire Vb) – recalled
Escort Cover	Redhill: 131 & 504 Squadrons (Spitfire Vb) – recalled West Malling: 64 Squadron (Spitfire Vb) – recalled Hawkinge: 313 Squadron (Spitfire Vb) – recalled
High Cover	Biggin Hill: 341 & 485 Squadrons (Spitfire IX) – recalled
Top Cover	Kingsnorth: 19, 65 & 122 Squadrons (Spitfire IX)
Fighter Sweep	Northolt: 303 & 316 Squadrons (Spitfire IX)
Close Escort Part II	Merston: 118, 402 & 416 Squadrons (Spitfire Vb) – recalled Fairlop: 302 & 317 Squadrons (Spitfire Vb) – recalled
Escort Cover	Westhampnett: 41 & 91 Squadrons (Spitfire XII) – recalled Kenley: 66 & 165 Squadrons (Spitfire IX) – recalled
High Cover	Hornchurch: 129 & 222 Squadrons (Spitfire IX)
Top Cover	North Weald: 331 & 332 Squadrons (Spitfire IX)
Fighter Sweep	Headcorn: 403 & 421 Squadrons (Spitfire IX)
Escort Part III	Lydd: 174 & 245 Squadrons (Typhoon Ib)
Casualties	303 Sqn: Fg Off Tadeusz Kolecki EF/KIFA Moor Park Golf Course, Herts, in Spit IX, MA574

Part I was airborne according to plan but after making landfall in France, 9/10ths cloud was encountered between 10,000 and 23,000 feet. As a result, the bombers were recalled, and the Close Escort, Escort Cover and High Cover Wings returned with them. The latter Wing sighted seven Me109s in the Dunkirk area, but they were not engaged. The Top Cover and Fighter Sweep Wings operated uneventfully, but 303 Squadron lost a pilot who was killed in a crash-landing on return to Northolt when his engine failed.

The Spitfire XII Wing was airborne at 16:55 at rendezvoused with Part II's bombers and fellow escort wings as planned. However, this Part fared similarly to the previous, encountering 10/10ths cloud up to 12,000 feet. The bombers, Close Escort and Escort Cover Wings were recalled 20 minutes after rendezvous, whilst still approximately ten miles off Walcheren. 41 and 91 Squadrons were therefore back on the ground at 18:10 with nothing to report.

Part II's remaining escort wings took the opportunity to make free-range sweeps of France, and the High Cover Wing swept the Bruges-Ypres [Ieper]-St. Omer area uneventfully. The Top Cover

Wing swept Blankenberge, Dixmude [Diksmuide] and Calais, encountering seven FW190s and a short while later nine Me109Gs, of which 332 Squadron claimed one destroyed and one damaged. The Fighter Sweep operated uneventfully, with the exception of sighting two Me109s off Ostend that were not engaged.

Finally, Part III operated in spite of the recall of Parts I and II. Weather also hindered their operation, however, and an attack on the primary target, Merville Airfield, proved impossible despite efforts. Instead, the Bomphoons attacked locks located approximately eight miles northwest of Ypres with sixteen 500 lb. bombs, although with poor results. Their escorts operated uneventfully, and the Luftwaffe was not seen; all aircraft returned safely.

15 September 1943 – The Spitfire XII Wing was involved in a single, large operation today as a part of three diversions, supporting four task forces of B-17 Flying Fortresses and one of B-24 Liberators attacking targets in France. In order to participate, the Wing repositioned to Manston during the morning, where they were given lunch, but were not required to take off until around 17:00.

Date	15 September 1943
Operation	Ramrod 220
Targets	1st Task Force: Airpark Romilly-sur-Seine, Champagne-Ardenne 2nd Task Force: Rheims Airfield, Champagne-Ardenne 3rd Task Force: Citroën Works, Billancourt, Île-de-France 4th Task Force: Hispano-Suiza Works, Ivry, Île-de-France 5th Task Force: Conches-en-Ouche & St. André Airfields, Eure 1st Diversion: Lille-Nord Airfield, Pas-de-Calais 2nd Diversion: Merville Airfield, Pas-de-Calais 3rd Diversion: Bryas Sud [Brias] Airfield, Pas-de-Calais
Bombers	1st Task Force: 100 Flying Fortresses 2nd Task Force: 60 Flying Fortresses – cancelled 3rd Task Force: 60 Flying Fortresses 4th Task Force: 80 Flying Fortresses 5th Task Force: 80 Liberators; 63 dispatched; 47 bombed 1st Diversion: Unknown – recalled 2nd Diversion: 72 Marauders; 72 dispatched, 70 bombed 3rd Diversion: 12 Mitchells; 12 dispatched, 12 bombed
Casualties	5 Flying Fortresses & 1 Liberator FTR
Escorts to Task Force	4 FG, 56 FG, 78 FG, 352 FG & 353 FG USAAF
High Cover 3rd & 4th Task Forces	Northolt: 303 & 316 Squadrons (Spitfire IX) North Weald: 331 & 332 Squadrons (Spitfire IX)
Withdrawal Cover 5th Task Force	Kingsnorth: 19, 65 & 122 Squadrons (Spitfire IX) Headcorn: 403 & 421 Squadrons (Spitfire IX)
Close Escort 1st Dvsn	Staplehurst: 401, 411 & 412 Squadrons (Spitfire Vb) – recalled West Malling: 130 & 234 Squadrons (Spitfire Vb) – recalled
Escort Cover	Kenley: 66 & 165 Squadrons (Spitfire IX) – recalled Redhill: 131 & 504 Squadrons (Spitfire Vb) – recalled
High Cover	Westhampnett: 41 & 91 Squadrons (Spitfire XII) – recalled
Top Cover	Biggin Hill: 341 & 485 Squadrons (Spitfire IX)
Close Escort 2nd Dvsn	Merston: 118, 402 & 416 Squadrons (Spitfire Vb) Friston: 306 Squadron (Spitfire Vb)
Escort Cover	Fairlop: 302 & 317 Squadrons (Spitfire Vb) West Malling: 64 Squadron (Spitfire Vb) Hawkinge: 313 Squadron (Spitfire Vb)
High Cover	Hornchurch: 129 & 222 Squadrons (Spitfire IX)
Close Escort 3rd Dvsn	Lympne: 1 & 609 Squadrons (Typhoon Ib)
Escort Cover	Tangmere: 197, 183 & 486 Squadrons (Typhoon Ib)

USAAF Casualties	353FG/352FS: 2 Lt Walter J. Donovan RF & ditched off Portland Bill in Thunderbolt 42-8494 †; & Capt. Robert C. Durlin RF in Thunderbolt 42-8420, baled out Bude, Cornwall, but inj landing as too low for parachute to fully deploy
RAF Casualty	118 Sqn: Plt Off Roy J. Flight, EF Merville in Spit Vb, AR433, POW

The Second Task Force, to Rheims Airfield, was cancelled, but the remaining four operated as planned. Bombing results at Romilly Airpark were considered good, at the Citroën Works at Billancourt fair to good, and at the Hispano-Suiza Works at Ivry also good.

The RAF squadrons assigned to High Cover for the 3rd & 4th Task Forces operated according to plan, rendezvousing at 22,000 feet at 18:17, and escorting the bombers from 50°00'N 01°15'E (off Tocqueville-sur-Eu) to eight miles east of Les Andelys, Haute-Normandie (approximately 35km northeast of Évreux). On the way home, eight to nine enemy aircraft were seen southwest of Rouen but were too far away to engage. The operation ran otherwise uneventfully.

Withdrawal Cover was also provided by the RAF for the Fifth Task Force, from Les Andelys back to the English coast. The Kingsnorth Wing rendezvoused with the first box at 22,000 feet at 18:48, whilst the Headcorn Wing was scheduled to rendezvous with the second box at the same altitude five minutes later. Headcorn's Canadian squadrons arrived on time but there was no sign of the Liberators. They orbited for 17 minutes and then gave up and headed back to the French coast. Shortly after crossing out, however, they looked back to see the bombers "proceeding out unmolested".[153]

In the meantime, the three diversions had also been completed, although the first was aborted soon after crossing out, owing to both timing and weather issues. The Spitfire XII Wing had taken off at 16:50 to meet them, with 41 Squadron deploying ten aircraft plus Wg Cdr Harries, who was leading the unit, as Sqn Ldr Ingham had contracted a severe cold and was grounded for at least 48 hours. However,

> As the bombers were 15 minutes early at the rendezvous the [Spitfire XII] wing was scrambled before the correct take-off time, and at 1,700 [sic] they were picked up over N. Foreland. Owing to weather the bombers turned back after proceeding over the coast for 5 miles.[154]

When the bombers were recalled, the Spitfire XII Wing returned with the Close Escort and Escort Cover Wings, but orbited over Manston until they received new orders.

These came at 17:20, when they were given a vector of 145° back to France. The Wing crossed the French coast at 15,000 feet, then swept behind St. Omer, where they experienced very accurate heavy Flak, but did not see the Luftwaffe or anything else of significance.

Flt Lt 'Pinkie' Glen (MB846) returned 30 minutes earlier than everyone else as his engine was playing up, and put down at Manston at 18:00. He returned to Westhampnett after he had the engine seen to, recording in his logbook that day, "Engine cutting so landed Manston. Accurate flak, again! No Huns".[155] Sgt Plt Peter Graham (MB829) also landed safely at Manston without flaps, but the rest of the Wing continued on home to Westhampnett, where they landed at 18:30.

The Top Cover Wing, also initially recalled, landed back at Biggin Hill at 17:15, but were ordered off again at 17:50 and assigned to a sweep of the St. Pol, Arras and Merville areas. It was, however, also uneventful.

The Second Diversion proceeded as planned, but the Merston Wing did not make the rendezvous and caught up with the bombers half way across the Channel. Four to six FW190s attempted to attack the bombers in the target area but were driven off by 118 Squadron, which claimed one enemy aircraft probably destroyed for the loss of one pilot of their own, who was shot down and captured. 118 Squadron also shot up a gun post "and scattered soldiers".[156]

Seventy Marauders successfully attacked Merville Airfield, dropping six hundred and sixty-one 300 lb. bombs with fair to good results. The Escort Cover Wing operated uneventfully, but the High Cover Wing engaged twelve Me109s in the target area, claiming one probably destroyed for no loss.

The Third Diversion also operated as planned, and quite uneventfully. The Mitchells dropped ninety-six 500 lb. bombs on Bryas Sud Airfield unhindered, with good results, and bursts were reported on the airfield and north-eastern dispersals area.

16 September 1943 – It was quite a day for the Wing, which provided Escort Cover for 36 Marauders attacking Beaumont-le-Roger Airfield in Part I of Ramrod 223. It was the first time in almost two weeks that they had come face to face with the Luftwaffe, and returned home victorious, 91 Squadron claiming four destroyed and one damaged, and 41 Squadron one probably destroyed.

Date	16 September 1943
Operation	Ramrod 223
Targets	Part I: Beaumont-le-Roger Airfield, Haute-Normandie Part II: Triqueville Airfield, Haute-Normandie Part III: Serqueux Marshalling Yards, Haute-Normandie Part IV: Le Grand-Quevilly Power Station, Haute-Normandie
Bombers	Part I: 36 Marauders; 36 dispatched, 36 bombed Part II: 36 Marauders; 36 dispatched, 34 bombed Part III: 18 Mitchells; 18 dispatched, 17 bombed Part IV: 12 Mitchells; 12 dispatched, 12 bombed
Close Escort Part I	Merston: 118, 402 & 416 Squadrons (Spitfire Vb) Redhill: 131 & 504 Squadrons (Spitfire Vb)
Escort Cover	Westhampnett: 41 & 91 Squadrons (Spitfire XII)
High Cover	Biggin Hill: 341 & 485 Squadrons (Spitfire IX)
Top Cover	Kingsnorth: 19 & 122 Squadrons (Spitfire IX)
Close Escort Part II	Staplehurst: 401, 411 & 412 Squadrons (Spitfire Vb) West Malling: 130 Squadron (Spitfire Vb)
Escort Cover	Kenley: 66 & 165 Squadrons (Spitfire IX)
High Cover	Hornchurch: 129 & 222 Squadrons (Spitfire IX)
Close Escort Part III	West Malling: 64 Squadron (Spitfire Vb) Friston: 306 Squadron (Spitfire Vb) Hawkinge: 313 Squadron (Spitfire Vb)
Escort Cover	Fairlop: 302 & 317 Squadrons (Spitfire Vb)
High Cover	North Weald: 331 & 332 Squadrons (Spitfire IX)
Top Cover	Headcorn: 403 & 421 Squadrons (Spitfire IX)
Close Escort Part IV	Lympne: 1 & 609 Squadrons (Typhoon Ib)
Escort Cover	Tangmere: 197, 183 & 486 Squadrons (Typhoon Ib)
Fighter Sweep	Northolt: 303 & 316 Squadrons (Spitfire IX)
Casualties	91 Sqn: Flt Sgt Bernard G. Mulcahy RAAF, EF, baled out 8m W of Le Havre in Spit XII, EN617, POW; 485 Sqn: Fg Off Murray Metcalfe RNZAF, KIA 12m W of Le Havre in Spit IX, EN529

The Spitfire XII Wing was airborne at 16:55, with 41 Squadron led by Wg Cdr Harries, and the unit's Yellow and Blue Sections led by Flt Lts Hugh Parry and 'Pinkie' Glen, respectively. The planned route, altitude, speeds and timings were as follows[157]:

From	To	Altitude	IAS mph	Bearing	Time
Tangmere	Rendezvous	Climbing to 12,000	160	150°	15
at height			200	148°	7
Rendezvous	St. Valéry		200	193°	5½
St. Valéry	Beaumont-le-Roger			193°	14
Target	4m SW Trouville		200	295°	10½
4m SW Trouville	Selsey			340°	26
					78

The Wing rendezvoused with Part I's Marauders and escort squadrons 20 miles north of St. Valéry-en-Caux at 12,000 feet at 17:15, but the Luftwaffe knew the formation was inbound.

The Cambrai, Courtrai [Kortrijk], Évreux and Beauvais Wings were ordered to the Beauvais area as the formation was crossing in at Fécamp, and Allied radar started picking up plots in the area at 17:20, numbering initially three aircraft, then twelve, followed by two more plots of six to ten aircraft.

The first of these were sighted by Part I just before the formation reached Beaumont-le-Roger Airfield, when at least twelve aircraft dived behind 118 Squadron out of the sun. 416 Squadron broke formation to follow them, but they dived away too quickly in an easterly direction, below the bombers, and avoided an engagement.

The bombers completed their bombing run according to plan, dropping three hundred and forty-eight 300 lb. bombs with good results. Bursts were seen across the airfield, on the western side of the runway, and on the airfield perimeter. Around this time, the Redhill Wing sighted twenty FW190s approaching from the direction of Rouen, and on leaving the target, four FW190s were seen to dive towards the bombers from 11 o'clock, but continue past them.

However, as the formation turned to starboard immediately following the bombing, ten more FW190s were seen to dive towards the bombers from the south by the Spitfire XII Wing. Wg Cdr Harries turned towards them with 41 Squadron following, but when he saw he would not be able to bring the Wing into a position to engage them, he returned to the previous course.

Yellow 2, Fg Off 'Barney' Newman (MB857), was "too hard over"[158] to see Harries' turn back to port, and continued down after them. Having turned sharply to starboard, the rest of the Squadron was lost from sight behind his wing. Realising after some time that he had lost his section, he looked around and joined up with the nearest section of friendly aircraft, which turned out to be 91 Squadron's Red Section.

Whilst this was happening, Harries noticed another group of ten FW190s and Me109s above and to port of them at 16,000 feet, approaching at great speed from the southwest. Harries kept 41 Squadron with the bombers and sent 91 Squadron in a climbing turn into the sun to attack them. They then "became embroiled in a general dogfight with excellent results".[159]

Now climbing as No. 5, Red Section of 91 Squadron, Newman saw Sqn Ldr Kynaston dive on six to eight Me109Gs, and took his lead, attaching himself to the last Me109 in the group. Newman followed the aircraft down from 15,000 feet to only 2,000-3,000 feet, but had difficulty closing and finally opened fire with two bursts at a range of 1,000 yards.

He saw no strikes, and it was apparent the Me109 had also not seen him, as it turned and presented Newman the opportunity to make a deflection attack. He fired again, but still saw no result. Due to the Messerschmitt's turn, however, Newman was at last able to close rapidly and quickly reduced his range to just 200 yards, where he opened fire anew. This time, he saw strikes along the fuselage and "a puff of white smoke which almost completely enveloped the A/C".[160]

Seeing flashes on the Me109 and pieces flying off, Newman broke off his attack, considering it "unlikely this A/C could go much further".[161] Climbing to 500 feet, he sighted the coast at Trouville, approximately three miles west of him, and headed towards it. In time, he joined up with 91 Squadron again, and came out with them, eventually landing back at Westhampnett at 18:20. He initially claimed the Messerschmitt damaged, but this was raised to probably destroyed, a fact noted both on his Combat Report and in the Squadron ORB. In achieving his victory, Newman had fired just 116 rounds of 20mm cannon and no .303 inch machine gun, and had exposed three feet of cine-gun film. His combat film is held today in the Imperial War Museum.

Meanwhile, 91 Squadron's Sqn Ldr Kynaston, Flt Lt Gray Stenborg, Fg Off Jacques Andrieux (FAFL), and Flt Sgt Richmond Blumer (RAAF) had also been in action and claimed their own victories. Leading 91 Squadron in their climbing turn into the sun after the group of ten enemy aircraft that Wg Cdr Harries had ordered them onto, Kynaston found they scattered as soon as they started closing. Picking out individual aircraft, Kynaston succeeded in claiming one FW190 destroyed and one damaged, whilst Stenborg and Andrieux each claimed one Me109G destroyed.

Kynaston chased his opponent inland some distance before closing to 300 yards before firing, resulting in the FW190 clipping trees, then flying into the ground and exploding. Turning after another Focke-Wulf, he damaged it, too, before running out of ammunition and being forced to disengage.

Whilst Stenborg was chasing an Me109G at some distance, another passed him close by in the opposite direction. Immediately losing interest in his initial target, he made a steep climb to port, and came in behind it. Closing from 500 feet to 200 dead astern, he fired hard into the aircraft, seeing strikes all over the fuselage. It dived straight into a field and burst into flames. Andrieux chased his own Me109G on the deck, closing from 600 feet to 400 as he fired, and observed strikes on the starboard wing. This aircraft then flew into some trees and crashed in flames.

In the middle of it all, Flt Sgt Bernard Mulcahy (RAAF), developed engine trouble and headed home, covered by Flt Sgt Blumer. On the way out, they were attacked by six FW190s, and Blumer turned to meet them, leaving Mulcahy heading for the coast. Finally getting onto one Focke-Wulf's tail, Blumer fired at close range, sending the aircraft onto its back and straight into the ground where it exploded. Escaping the remaining enemy aircraft with wild evasive action, as well as another eight that soon appeared on the scene, Blumer retreated at speed and the 190s gave up as he crossed out.

Mulcahy managed to cross out unmolested but his engine refused to take him home all the way, and only made it as far as eight miles off Le Havre. He issued a mayday before baling out, and was subsequently seen in his dinghy. However, he was retrieved by the Germans before Allied ASR could reach him and spent the rest of the War behind wire.

The Biggin Hill Wing, flying High Cover, was also occupied with the Luftwaffe, and 341 Squadron was bounced by six FW190s at 18,000 feet just after leaving the target area. A section of 485 Squadron also dived on a dozen FW190s and Me109Gs, which were flying at 10,000 feet, around 25 miles southwest of Beaumont-le-Roger Airfield. In the ensuing combats, two Me109Gs and a FW190 were destroyed and one FW190 damaged, but 485 Squadron lost one pilot who was killed. The remaining two sections of 485 Squadron climbed to 24,000 feet to attack another twelve FW190s, but these dived away inland and avoided engagement.

The Spitfire XII Wing returned to Westhampnett at 18:20, quite pleased with themselves. The ORB summed up the day,

> *Altogether it was a successful day and as well as knocking down the Hun, the bombing was reported to have been good and many fires were observed on the target area. All aircraft of the squadron returned to base.*[162]

By this time, Parts II, III and IV had also been undertaken. For all the action of Part I, Part II was, although successful, completely uneventful. The Luftwaffe was not seen and the bombers dropped one hundred and sixty-seven 300 lb. GP bombs and two hundred and ninety-five 100 lb. fragmentation bombs on Triqueville Airfield with fair results. Bursts were seen in the wooded dispersal area, along the south-eastern side of the airfield, and outside the airfield by the Close Escort squadrons, in the north-eastern corner and on the western side of the airfield by the Escort Cover Wing, and on buildings south-west of the airfield by the High Cover Wing.

Part III was similarly uneventful for all participants, although less successful as far as the bombing was concerned. Seventeen Mitchells dropped sixty-eight 1,000 lb. bombs, although the leading box was unable to identify Serqueux Marshalling Yards and released their payload at a point three to four miles from Formerie on a bearing of 80°. The remaining two boxes attacked the primary target, although bursts were seen to overshoot slightly into fields just east of the yards. The Close Escort Wing reported only seeing a single stick of bombs actually land in the target area.

Part IV saw little more action, and only a few Luftwaffe aircraft were seen by the Close Escort Wing in the target area, which were not engaged. Six unidentified aircraft were also seen with one black and one white wing. Though the Mitchells were unhindered in their attack on Le Grand-Quevilly Power Station, they dropped eighty-six 500 lb. bombs with only poor results. Bursts were seen to the south of the target, and some on the target, with only one possible hit on a transformer station itself.

18 September 1943 – Following a day on the ground as a result of unsuitable weather, the Spitfire XII Wing participated in two operations today. In the first of these, the Wing provided Escort Cover for 72 Marauders attacking Beauvais-Tillé Airfield as an element of Ramrod 228. In the second, they were tasked with providing Escort Cover for 72 Marauders bombing Beaumont-le-Roger Airfield in Ramrod 230, but it was aborted after becoming airborne owing to poor weather.

Date	18 September 1943
Operation	Ramrod 228
Targets	Part I: Rouen Marshalling Yards, Haute-Normandie Part II: Beauvais-Tillé Airfield, Picardie
Bombers	Part I: 320 Sqn: 12 Mitchells, 12 dispatched, 12 bombed Part II: 72 Marauders; 72 dispatched, 25 bombed (poor visibility)
Casualties	Part II: 1 Marauder EF; escorted to Beachy Head by 402 Sqn
Close Escort Part I	Newchurch: 132 & 602 Squadrons (Spitfire Vb)
Escort Cover	Staplehurst: 401, 411 & 412 Squadrons (Spitfire Vb)
High Cover	Hornchurch: 129 & 222 Squadrons (Spitfire IX)
Top Cover	Kingsnorth: 19, 65 & 122 Squadrons (Spitfire IX)
Fighter Sweep	North Weald: 331 & 332 Squadrons (Spitfire IX)
Close Escort Part II	Merston: 118, 402 & 416 Squadrons (34 Spitfire Vb) Fairlop: 302 & 317 Squadrons (Spitfire Vb)
Escort Cover	Westhampnett: 41 & 91 Squadrons (25 Spitfire XII)
High Cover	Biggin Hill: 341 & 485 Squadrons (Spitfire IX)
Top Cover	Headcorn: 403 & 421 Squadrons (Spitfire IX)
Fighter Sweep	Northolt: 303 & 316 Squadrons (Spitfire IX)
Casualties	401 Sqn: Fg Off James W. Fiander, glycol leak, baled out of Spit Vb, BM199, N of Dieppe, RR

Part I rendezvoused at Rye at 09:30 and operated according to plan. Twelve Mitchells dropped a total of forty 1,000 lb. bombs on Rouen Marshalling Yards from altitudes of 10,800-11,500 feet at 10:04 with good results. Bursts were seen across the northern side of the yards, in a built-up area west of the yards, and alongside a viaduct leading to the engine sheds. The Close escort Wing also reported seeing bursts on railway trucks, which resulted in "large red explosions".[163]

The operation proved uneventful for most of the participating squadrons, but the Top Cover Wing bounced fifty FW190s north of Rouen, during which 129 Squadron claimed one destroyed and one damaged for no loss of their own. A short while later, the same wing sighted another thirty FW190s and Me109s, but did not engage them. On the way home, a pilot of 401 Squadron developed a glycol leak and was forced to bale out north of Dieppe. He was later picked up by a 277 (ASR) Squadron Walrus and returned to Staplehurst.

The Spitfire XII Wing was airborne at 10:00, with 41 Squadron led by Wg Cdr Harries, and joined Part II's bombers and escorts 12,000 feet over Beachy Head at 10:18. With the exception of the sighting of six enemy aircraft 10-15 miles south of the target, and three climbing near Rouen, all of which were not engaged, the operation was uneventful for all participants. The Wing landed at Westhampnett again at 11:40 with little to report.

Seventy-two Marauders were dispatched but owing to 5/10ths scattered cumulus cloud at 4,000-8,000 feet over Beauvais-Tillé Airfield, only twenty-five attacked, dropping two hundred and fifty-six 300 lb. bombs with fair to poor results. The remaining bombers jettisoned their payloads into the Channel during their return flight.

The Wing was airborne again at 16:40, to participate in their second Ramrod, supporting Part II to Beaumont-le-Roger Airfield.

Date	18 September 1943
Operation	Ramrod 230
Targets	Part I: Yainville Power Station, Haute-Normandie
	Part II: Beaumont-le-Roger Airfield, Haute-Normandie
	Part III: Rouen Marshalling Yards, Haute-Normandie
Bombers	Part I: 8 Bostons – cancelled
	Part II: 72 Marauders – aborted (weather)
	Part III: 18 Marauders – aborted (weather)
Withdrawal Part I	2 Typhoon squadrons – cancelled
Close Escort Part II	Merston: 118, 402 & 416 Squadrons (Spitfire Vb) – aborted
	Fairlop: 302 & 317 Squadrons (Spitfire Vb) – aborted
Escort Cover	Westhampnett: 41 & 91 Squadrons (Spitfire XII) – aborted
High Cover	Biggin Hill: 341 & 485 Squadrons (Spitfire IX)
Top Cover	Headcorn: 403 & 421 Squadrons (Spitfire IX)
Fighter Sweep	Kingsnorth: 19, 65 & 122 Squadrons (Spitfire IX)
Close Escort Part III	Staplehurst: 401, 411 & 412 Squadrons (Spitfire Vb) – aborted
	Friston: 306 Squadron (Spitfire Vb) – aborted
Escort Cover	Newchurch: 132 & 602 Squadrons (Spitfire Vb) – aborted
High Cover	Hornchurch: 129 & 222 Squadrons (Spitfire IX)
Top Cover	North Weald: 331 & 332 Squadrons (Spitfire IX)

Part II's bombers and escorts rendezvoused 12,000 feet over Shoreham at 16:55 and proceeded across the Channel as planned. However, the bombers were recalled approximately 13 miles off the French coast when they encountered 10/10ths cloud between 9,000 and 14,000 feet, and received reports of a cloud base of just 6,000 feet over land. They turned about and returned home accompanied by the Close Escort and Escort Cover Wings.

The Spitfire XII Wing obtained permission to make a shallow, free-range sweep into France, which was undertaken without event. 41 Squadron was led again by Wg Cdr Harries, and landed with nothing to report at 17:50 to conclude the day's operational flying. The High Cover, Top Cover and Fighter Sweep Wings also undertook sweeps into France, but they were similarly uneventful.

In a practical repetition of Part II, Part III's bombers also aborted before reaching the French coast on account of weather conditions. Whilst the Close Escort and Escort Cover Wings returned with the bombers, the High Cover and Top Cover Wings undertook sweeps, but both were uneventful.

Separately today, a new pilot joined 41 Squadron in the form of 21-year-old Scot, Flt Sgt Thomas Garrie. Having enlisted in August 1941, Garrie had undertaken his flying training in the United States and arrived today with 405 flying hours in his logbook. 41 Squadron was his first operational posting and he remained with the unit for six months.

19 September 1943 – The Squadron's operational activity today consisted of two Ramrods, the first at 10:45 and the second at 17:00. In stark contrast to the latter operation, the former, an escort to Marauders targeting Lille-Nord Airfield with 91 Squadron, was an intense affair, which cost both 41 and 91 Squadrons a pilot.

Date	19 September 1943
Operation	Ramrod 232
Targets	Part I: Lille-Nord Airfield, Pas-de-Calais, France
	Part II: Gent-Merelbeke Marshalling Yards, Oost-Vlaanderen, Belgium
	Part III: Merville Airfield, Pas-de-Calais, France
	Part IV: Woensdrecht Airfield, Noord-Brabant, Netherlands

Bombers	Part I: 72 Marauders; 78 dispatched, 18 bombed
	Part II: 24 Mitchells – cancelled
	Part III: 181 Squadron: 8 Bomphoons
	Part IV: 3 Squadron: 8 Bomphoons
Casualties	Part I: 14 bombers CD/AA
Close Escort Part I	Staplehurst: 401, 411 & 412 Squadrons (Spitfire Vb)
	Friston: 306 Squadron (Spitfire Vb)
Escort Cover	Westhampnett: 41 & 91 Squadrons (Spitfire XII)
High Cover	North Weald: 331 & 332 Squadrons (Spitfire IX)
Top Cover	Kingsnorth: 65 & 122 Squadrons (Spitfire IX)
Fighter Sweep	Hornchurch: 129 & 222 Squadrons (Spitfire IX)
Escort Part III	New Romney: 245 & 247 Squadrons (Typhoon Ib)
Escort Part IV	Manston: 1 & 198 Squadrons (Typhoon Ib)
Casualties	41 Sqn: Flt Sgt Stanley H. May RAAF, SD bet. Ypres & Dunkirk in Spit XII, MB800, ER; 91 Sqn: Fg Off Geoffrey W. Bond SD/KIA nr Lille in Spit XII, MB799; Flt Sgt Richmond A. B. Blumer RAAF, EF in Spit XII, ditched off Deal, RR by HSL; 411 Sqn: Fg Off Victor A. Haw AFM RCAF, SD NW of Courtrai in Spit Vb, BL422, POW

The Spitfire XII Wing flew over to Manston after breakfast and, following a briefing, were airborne again at 10:45 to make the rendezvous over Ashford on time. The Wing was led by Wg Cdr Harries and the Squadron by Flt Lt 'Pinkie' Glen, in the absence of Sqn Ldr Ingham who was off for a few days with a head cold.

The Marauders were seven minutes late but nonetheless rendezvoused successfully with their escorts, and crossed at Furnes [Veurne], Belgium. They immediately encountered 10/10ths cloud at 13,000 feet, which stretched some distance inland, but continued on, in spite of it.

Approximately 15 miles northwest of the target, the Close Escort encountered at least nine FW190s, whilst another four attacked 411 Squadron. No claims could be made from the ensuing combats, but 411 Squadron lost one pilot, who was last seen diving with two enemy aircraft on his tail.

Arriving in the target area, another 10+ FW190s from JG26 attempted to attack the bombers but Flt Lt Glen felt these were likely a decoy. He held 41 Squadron above, "refus[ing] to be enticed"[164], whilst 91 Squadron followed the enemy aircraft down and drove them off. Glen's suspicions were justified: no sooner had 91 Squadron done so than another ten enemy aircraft dived on the Wing. Glen turned the Squadron to intercept them, but this caused the enemy aircraft to bank away, directly towards 91 Squadron. Soon afterwards, yet another group of enemy aircraft arrived on the scene.

A series of combats ensued between 91 Squadron and a mixture of FW190s and Me109s, and 41 Squadron lost sight of 91 in the mêlée. When Glen realised that the Close Escort squadrons had also broken away, he ordered 41 Squadron to hold formation just above and behind the bombers, to their port side, having found them with "practically no escort".[165] The Squadron's pilots subsequently fended off a number of attacks on the bombers by quartets and quintets of enemy aircraft, and Fg Off Clive Birbeck expended 60 rounds of 20mm cannon and 160 of .303 inch machine gun ammunition, but could make no claims.

11 Group reports estimate that twelve enemy aircraft attacked the formation at 18,000 feet in the Douai area between 11:23 and 11:29, twenty-five at the same altitude in the Arras area between 11:23 and 11:30, twelve at 25,000 feet east of Béthune between 11:30 and 11:40, three at 20,000 feet in the Lille-Courtrai [Kortrijk] area between 11:32 and 11:45, and six at 9,000 feet in the Brussels-Courtrai area between 11:39 and 11:50, totalling almost 60 aircraft. 41 Squadron's Fg Off Herb Wagner was therefore not exaggerating when he recorded in his logbook that day, "LOTS of Huns about".[166]

Meanwhile, as a result of the cloud cover, only 18 of the 78 Marauders managed to bomb the target through 10/10ths cloud at 11:30. They dropped a total of one hundred and seventy-one 300 lb. bombs, but also ran the gauntlet of heavy calibre anti-aircraft defences and swarming enemy aircraft, which resulted in Flak and combat damage to 14 of the bombers. However, their air gunners also claimed two FW190s destroyed and one damaged for no loss of their own.

Whereas the Close Escort and Escort Cover Wings were fully occupied from making landfall, the High Cover Wing and Fighter Sweep had operated uneventfully. The Top Cover Wing was, however, intercepted by 15 enemy aircraft over Merville and claimed one Me109 damaged for no loss.

After escorting the bombers back to the Channel at Dunkirk, 41 Squadron turned back inland to support 91 Squadron, but found nothing to do; it was all over. Wg Cdr Harries, who had remained with 91 Squadron, had claimed one FW190 destroyed, whilst the unit's Flt Lt John Doll claimed another FW190 destroyed and one damaged.[167]

91 Squadron was split up, and two pilots landed at Manston, three at Westhampnett and five at Hawkinge. Unfortunately, their victories had come at the cost of one pilot, 20-year-old Fg Off Geoffrey Bond, who was shot down and killed, and was believed to have gone into the sea between Furnes and Dunkirk on the return journey. Returning bombers reported seeing an aircraft go into the sea at this location, and German rescue launches heading towards it. A second pilot from 91 Squadron, Flt Sgt Richmond Blumer, suffered engine failure on the way home and ditched off Deal. He was subsequently rescued by high speed launch and brought ashore uninjured.

41 Squadron returned home without any further incident and landed at Manston at 12:05. However, as the operation had been so intense, it was not until they were on the ground again that it was realised that Flt Sgt Stan May (MB800) was absent. He was last seen on the way home "to peel off as if to attack"[168,169] half way between Lille and Dunkirk on the way out, but no-one recalled seeing any enemy aircraft at their altitude [11,000 ft.], and nobody heard anything from him on the R/T system; he was not seen again.[170]

Elsewhere on the Ramrod, Part II was cancelled as some of the fighter escorts were unable to get airborne on account of poor visibility. In contrast, Parts III and IV operated as planned and their respective airfields successfully bombed. Bursts were seen in the northeast corner of Merville Airfield, on runways and on the northern and southern dispersals areas. The airfield was otherwise observed to be "deserted and covered with craters".[171] Sixteen 500 lb. bombs were also dropped on Woensdrecht Airfield, which was attacked from east to west and bursts were seen on both the north-eastern and north-western dispersals areas. Nineteen enemy aircraft were plotted during the two Ramrods but none seen; no engagements, claims or casualties were recorded.

Another Evader

41 Squadron's Flt Sgt Jimmy Payne recorded May's loss today in his logbook, "My "Cobber" Stan May didn't return – a grand chap and a real friend. I hope he is O.K.".[172] Two days later, having no further intelligence on May's fate, Sqn Ldr Ingham wrote to his mother,

> *It is with deep regret that I have to confirm our message of the 19th September, to the R.A.A.F. Headquarters regarding the loss of Stanley.*
>
> *[…] There is of course a good chance that he managed to bale out or crash land, and I regret that we have now the distressing job of waiting in hope that news comes through the Red Cross.*
>
> *I will not attempt to convey the feelings of the Squadron about the loss of Stanley, but think you will understand when I say that he was a fine man, and we have only the most affectionate memories of him. His happy tolerant nature made him a favourite with his fellow pilots, and he was considered to be the leader of the Squadron N.C.Os.*
>
> *It is more than unfortunate that this should have happened, just at the time he had been recommended for a commission, but it will give you a little comfort to know that the Squadron thought him well worthy of this recommendation. […]*[173]

Hopes for May's survival were, in fact, realised. Having been shot down over Belgian territory by FW190s of JG26, he successfully evaded capture and returned to the United Kingdom via Spain and Gibraltar in November 1943. Upon his return, he submitted the following report of events:

On the return journey from the target, the unit was followed by a number of enemy aircraft, which remained approximately 2,000 feet above them. He kept his eye on one aircraft in particular, which soon disappeared into cloud. He searched for it and soon saw an aircraft below his No. 2, Sgt Plt Peter Wall. Unable to identify it, but assuming it was an Me109, he broke to port. Half way through his downward turn, he recognised it as one of the Squadron's aircraft that had been trailing the formation but was now catching up.

Realising it was not the 'missing' enemy aircraft, May began searching above him again for enemy fighters, and hurried to catch up with the rest of the Squadron. Barely had he begun to do so, however, than an explosive cannon shell hit his aircraft between the dashboard and fuel tank, both of which were damaged, and his ignition switches were also destroyed. The explosion also resulted in an injury to his left hand, which received three splinters from the cannon shell.

Left little choice, May baled out of his aircraft approximately half way between Ypres [Ieper] and the Belgian coast at around 11:30. On the way down, he watched his Spitfire crash. He landed northwest of Ypres on the Furnes-Ypres road, just outside Hoogstade, Belgium, unhurt but for his left hand, but had lost one of his shoes whilst escaping from his aircraft. Even before he was able to remove his parachute, several locals appeared on the scene, but he ran off nonetheless, leaving behind his Mae West and parachute. It was only later that he realised he had left his money purse in the Mae West.

May headed away from the coast and towards the Yser River, but as he went a man indicated to him where his aircraft lay. He went to the aircraft with the intention of destroying it, as the Spitfire XII was still considered secret, but found it on its back, a complete wreck, which had buried itself about eight feet into the ground. A crowd of people had already gathered around it, and he abandoned any idea of destroying it further.[174]

May pressed on again to the east, turning his battle dress jacket inside out so he was not too conspicuous at a distance. Reaching the Yser, he walked along the bank looking for a suitable place to cross but being a Sunday, numbers of people were fishing. As this made it impossible to cross inconspicuously, he continued walking along the northern bank until a Belgian youth passed him on a bicycle and beckoned to him.

May approached the cyclist and stated who he was. The young man subsequently took him across the river in a small boat and gave him a coat, then took him to a farm, which May felt was his home, and hid him in the barn. He subsequently provided May a complete change of clothes, then took him in the direction of Oostvleteren. Before reaching the village, however, they were met by three men on bicycles, who escorted May the rest of the way, tended his wounds and fed him.

May stated in his report, "My subsequent journey was arranged for me"[175], and does not divulge any further information on the route he took to Spain, nor those who helped him. However, his RAAF Casualty File[176] indicates that he arrived at the Spanish border at around midnight of 31 October, accompanied by other British airmen. They slept until midday on 1 November in a house on the Spanish side of the border and were then moved to San Sebastian, where they remained until 4 November. At this time, they were picked up by a car that had been sent for them by the British Embassy in Madrid.

May remained at the Embassy three days, during which time he was given a vest, a shirt, some shoes and handkerchiefs, and 35 Pesetas. Then, on 8 November, he was taken across the border to Gibraltar by a member of the Military Attaché staff. He departed Gibraltar by air on 10 November, and arrived back in the United Kingdom, landing in Bristol, the following morning.[177]

Returning now to 19 September, 41 Squadron was involved in another Ramrod during the afternoon, when the Spitfire XII Wing provided Escort Cover to Marauders targeting Merville Airfield in Part II of Ramrod 233. The jumping off point on this occasion was West Malling.[178]

Date	19 September 1943
Operation	Ramrod 233
Targets	Part I: Petrol Plant & Coking Ovens, Liéven, Pas-de-Calais Part II: Merville Airfield, Pas-de-Calais
Bombers	Part I: 226 Sqn: 12 Mitchells; bombed alternate targets Part II: 72 Marauders – aborted 10m N of Dunkirk
Close Escort Part I Escort Cover High Cover Top Cover Fighter Sweep Close Escort Part II Escort Cover High Cover Top Cover Fighter Sweep	Newchurch: 132 & 602 Squadrons (Spitfire Vb) Fairlop: 302 & 317 Squadrons (Spitfire Vb) Biggin Hill: 341 & 485 Squadrons (Spitfire IX) Headcorn: 403 & 421 Squadrons (Spitfire IX) Northolt: 303 & 316 Squadrons (Spitfire IX) Staplehurst: 401, 411 & 412 Squadrons (Spitfire Vb) – aborted Westhampnett: 41 & 91 Squadrons (Spitfire XII) – aborted Hornchurch: 129 & 222 Squadrons (Spitfire IX) Kingsnorth: 19 & 65 Squadrons (Spitfire IX) – aborted North Weald: 331 & 332 Squadrons (Spitfire IX)
Casualties	302 Sqn: WO Jerzy J. Krzysztofiński, AA Béthune, ditched 10m SE of Dover in Spit Vb, W3631, RR by ASR Walrus[179]

Part I operated generally according to plan, except that the first box of Mitchells bombed Gosnay Power Station, whilst the second bombed crossroads at Vendin-lès-Béthune at 17:40. All the escorts were dogged by the Luftwaffe, the Close Escort and Top Cover Wings encountering 50+ FW190s and Me109s at Bruay-la-Buissière, the Escort Cover Wing intercepting another 15 enemy aircraft on their way to the target, and the High Cover Wing engaging eight Me109s north of the target area.

During these engagements, Allied fighters claimed one FW190 and one Me109 destroyed, and two FW190s and one Me109 damaged. The sole casualty was a pilot of 302 Squadron who was hit by Flak in the Béthune area but managed to limp his aircraft back to within ten miles of Dover, where he was obliged to ditch. He was subsequently rescued by a 277 (ASR) Squadron Walrus, which was forced to taxi back to Dover in rough conditions, escorted by four aircraft from 501 Squadron.

Part II commenced as planned, and the bombers and escorts rendezvoused 12,000 feet over North Foreland at 17:20. The formation approached the French coast but the weather was found to be unsuitable and the bombers were recalled when still ten miles north of Dunkirk.

The Close Escort, Escort Cover and Top Cover Wings all turned for home with the bombers, and the Spitfire XII Wing landed at Westhampnett again at 18:10 with nothing to report. The High Cover Wing decided to undertake a sweep of the Hazebrouck area, where they intercepted twenty FW190s head on. Engagements ensued but the only claim that could be made was one damaged FW190 for no casualty. The Fighter Sweep Wing completed their operation as planned, and bounced at least a dozen FW190s in the Béthune area, of which they also claimed one damaged.

21 September 1943 – Following a day where operations were cancelled on account of unsuitable weather conditions, 41 Squadron was back in the air today for a single operation, in which the Spitfire XII Wing provided Escort Cover to Marauders bombing Beauvais-Tillé Airfield in Part III of Ramrod 235.

It was a large operation, which foresaw the deployment of 480 Flying Fortresses against airfields and a power station in France, with a large diversion planned over the North Sea. However, with poor weather from the previous day still lingering, both Parts I and II were cancelled, and only Parts III and IV operated according to plan.

Date	21 September 1943
Operation	Ramrod 235
Targets	Part I-A: Rheims Airfield, Champagne-Ardenne Part I-B: Meulan Airfield, Île-de-France Part I-C: Ivry-sur-Seine Power Station, Île-de-France Part I-D: Chartres Airfield, Eure-et-Loir Part II: Diversion over North Sea Part III: Beauvais-Tillé Airfield, Picardie Part IV: Liévin Synthetic Oil Plant & Coking Ovens, Pas-de-Calais
Bombers	Part I: 480 Fortresses in 4 forces of 120 – cancelled (weather) Part II: 60 Liberators – cancelled (weather) Part III: 72 Marauders; 43 bombed Part IV: 18 Mitchells; 20 bombed
Casualties	Part III: 387 BG/559 BS: Marauder 41-31721, SD/AA Beauvais; Part IV: 98 Sqn Mitchell II, FL683, SD Hesdin (crew KIA)[180], & Mitchell II, FV944, SD/AA Hesdin, ditched Channel (crew RR)
Penetration Part I	Northolt: 303 & 316 Squadrons (Spitfire IX) – cancelled
	North Weald: 331 & 332 Squadrons (Spitfire IX) – cancelled
Withdrawal	USAAF Thunderbolts – cancelled
Escort Part II	Two Typhoon Squadrons – cancelled
Escort Part III	Newchurch: 132 & 602 Squadrons (Spitfire Vb)
	Digby: 402 & 416 Squadrons (Spitfire Vb)
Escort Cover	Westhampnett: 41 & 91 Squadrons (Spitfire XII)
High Cover	Biggin Hill: 341 & 485 Squadrons (Spitfire IX)
Top Cover	Headcorn: 403 & 421 Squadrons (Spitfire IX)
Escort Part IV	Staplehurst: 401, 411 & 412 Squadrons (Spitfire Vb)
Escort Cover	West Malling: 64 Squadron (Spitfire Vb)
High Cover	Hornchurch: 129 & 222 Squadrons (Spitfire IX)
Top Cover	Kingsnorth: 19 & 122 Squadrons (Spitfire IX)
1st Fighter Sweep	Northolt: 303 & 316 Squadrons (Spitfire IX)
2nd Fighter Sweep	North Weald: 331 & 332 Squadrons (Spitfire IX)

The Spitfire XII Wing was airborne at 08:55 and as Sqn Ldr Ingham was still off flying, 41 Squadron was led by Flt Lt Parry, who also led one of three sections. The remaining two were led by Flt Lts Don Smith and 'Pinkie' Glen. Rendezvous was made on time, but the Wing was informed that the route had changed and the bombers would now be crossing in at Dieppe, instead of Le Tréport. Hurrying to catch up with them, the bombers were not met until just before reaching the target area.

Meanwhile the bomber formation had also caused problems for the Close Escort Wing, as many Marauders straggled, making it difficult to provide adequate cover. The Digby Wing saw three FW190s south of Dieppe, who did not attempt to interfere, whilst the Newchurch Wing sighted a few in the target area and a dozen who followed the formation at a distance, but these were driven off.

The High Cover Wing saw three FW190s below them and another four above whilst south of St. Omer area, and thought they saw one of those below them shoot down a Spitfire. However, there were none missing at the conclusion of the operation. The Top Cover Wing also saw three FW190s on the way in, which only made a half-hearted attack on 403 Squadron but were not engaged.

The Marauders reached Beauvais-Tillé Airfield at 09:40, whereupon 43 of the 72 aircraft dropped twenty-seven 1,000 lb. bombs and three hundred and thirty-four 300 lb. bombs, with 'fairly satisfactory' results. Having caught up with the bombers just before reaching the target area, the Spitfire XII Wing arrived in time to see one stick of bombs hit a hangar, causing a large explosion and creating a pillar of black smoke that reached high into the air. Bombs were also seen by the High Cover Wing to land on the dispersals area and runway, and saw one bomber shot down by Flak.

On leaving the target area, the bombers turned to port, instead of starboard as anticipated by the escort wings. This once again created problems for the fighters, who found the Marauders "too scattered to escort satisfactorily".[181] The return journey was, however, otherwise uneventful, and the Spitfire XII Wing landed back at Westhampnett at 10:35, with the exception of Sgt Plt William Vann (EN231), who landed at Friston at 10:20 short of fuel.

Part IV to Liévin Synthetic Oil Plant and Coking Ovens operated according to plan and 20 Mitchells attacked the target at 09:35, dropping ninety-six 500 lb. and thirty-two 100 lb. bombs. The first box missed the target by several hundred yards but the second box was more accurate and bursts were seen on the ammonia plant and railway sidings.

However, the Luftwaffe was very active and two Mitchells were shot down in an attack by eight FW190s over Hesdin. Another ten FW190s attacked the Close Escort, resulting in one FW190 claimed damaged by 401 Squadron for no loss. The Escort Cover Wing attempted to engage the enemy aircraft attacking the bombers but were unsuccessful, whilst the High Cover and Top Cover Wings saw enemy aircraft in the distance but only one engagement took place, resulting in 19 Squadron claiming one FW190 damaged.

Operating independently, the first Fighter Sweep made a wide circuit to Paris and back, which was uneventful, but the second Fighter Sweep, sweeping towards Lille, encountered twelve FW190s flying west near Cambrai, 4,000 feet below them. Shortly, another 30-40 enemy aircraft were also seen heading west. 331 Squadron dived on the first group of aircraft, leaving 332 Squadron above for cover, and subsequently returned home claiming two FW190s destroyed and one probable.

22 September 1943 – It was not until mid-afternoon that 41 Squadron was airborne operationally today, on this occasion providing Escort Cover with 91 Squadron to Marauders bombing Évreux-Fauville Airfield in Part II of Ramrod 237. It proved to be one of the Squadron's most exciting and successful operations in some time.

Date	22 September 1943
Operation	Ramrod 237
Targets	Part I: Beauvais-Tillé Airfield, Picardie Part II: Évreux-Fauville Airfield, Haute-Normandie
Bombers	Part I: 72 Marauders; 72 dispatched – recalled (weather) Part II: 72 Marauders; 72 dispatched, 71 bombed
Escort Part I	Staplehurst: 401, 411 & 412 Squadrons (Spitfire Vb) – recalled West Malling: 64 Squadron (Spitfire Vb) – recalled
Escort Cover	Newchurch: 132 & 602 Squadrons (Spitfire Vb)
High Cover	Hornchurch: 129 & 222 Squadrons (Spitfire IX)
Top Cover	North Weald: 331 & 332 Squadrons (Spitfire IX)
Fighter Sweep	Northolt: 303 & 316 Squadrons (Spitfire IX)
Escort Part II	Digby: 402 & 416 Squadrons (Spitfire Vb) Heston: 306 & 308 Squadrons (Spitfire Vb)
Escort Cover	Westhampnett: 41 & 91 Squadrons (Spitfire XII)
High Cover	Biggin Hill: 341 & 485 Squadrons (Spitfire IX)
Top Cover	Headcorn: 403 & 421 Squadrons (Spitfire IX)
Fighter Sweep	Kingsnorth: 19 & 65 Squadrons (Spitfire IX)
Casualties	41 Sqn: Fg Off Clive R. Birbeck, EF in Spit XII, EN608, ditched 20m S of Ford, RR; 308 Sqn: Sgt Plt Jan Trnobranski, SD nr Évreux in Spit Vb, EN916, ER; & Fg Off Henryk Jurewicz, SD/KIA nr Évreux in Spit Vb, W3440

Part I's bombers and escorts rendezvoused according to plan, 36 miles south of Dungeness at 12,000 feet at 15:10, and proceeded across the Channel together. However, upon reaching the French coast at 15:15, the bombers were recalled as a result of a report of bad weather over the target area. The Close Escort returned with the Marauders, who jettisoned their payloads into the Channel on the way home.

The remaining escort squadrons continued into France on free-range patrols, the Escort Cover Wing sweeping Le Tréport, the High Cover Wing sweeping Poix, Amiens, Douai and Lille, the Top Cover Wing sweeping Aumale, Rouen, Beauvais and the Somme Estuary, and the First Fighter Sweep Wing sweeping Berck-sur-Mer, Amiens and Le Tréport, all ending uneventfully.

Part II stood in stark contrast to Part I. The Spitfire XII Wing, led by Wg Cdr Harries, who also led 41 Squadron, made rendezvous according to plan, 36 miles south of Beachy Head at 12,000 feet at 15:50. The Wing then proceeded to escort the Marauders to Évreux in textbook formation, but the Luftwaffe was up in force.

The Close Escort Wings intercepted 50+ FW190s and Me109s head-on in the target area. Strangely, however, they made no attempt to attack the bombers, and only made "half-hearted attacks"[182] on the fighters. The ensuing combats resulted in two FW190s damaged by the Digby Wing Commander, one Me109G damaged by 416 Squadron and another damaged by Heston's 308 Squadron. However, two pilots from 308 Squadron were shot down, one of whom was killed; the other evaded.

The Marauders nonetheless attacked Évreux-Fauville Airfield as planned, dropping a total of seven hundred and one 300 lb. bombs. Thirty-five Marauders bombed with good results, whilst 36 achieved fair to good results, and the airfield was observed to be covered with a significant amount of smoke. Flak was unexpectedly weak and no casualties were recorded, although the air gunners did claim one enemy aircraft destroyed.

Immediately after the bombing, as the formation turned for home, Wg Cdr Harries sighted five to six FW190s below and approaching the bombers head on.[183] Pilots of 41 Squadron also saw another four to the south. Harries turned his section towards the first group of aircraft, which immediately half rolled and dived south.

Harries and Fg Off Peter Cowell immediately dived after three FW190s, and followed them down, but were unable to close. Harries then spotted another four FW190s flying line astern approximately 2,000 feet below him to starboard. However, no sooner had he seen them, than they saw Red Section, too, and "all half rolled, one after the other".[184]

Nonetheless, having the advantages of height and greater speed, Harries quickly closed on the No. 2 and opened fire with and one-and-a-half-second burst as he reduced his range from 300 yards to 250. He saw strikes on the fuselage and one wing, and the aircraft continued down in a dive and was later seen by Fg Off Cowell on the ground.

Harries now turned his attention to the leading FW190, and made a deflection shot from around 300 yards astern, holding in the firing button for one-and-a-half seconds until he saw strikes close to the cockpit, which were also confirmed by Cowell. This aircraft immediately rolled onto its back but soon disappeared into a 300-foot-thick cloud layer at 5,000 feet.

Harries was intent on following him down but was forced to break of his attack on account of other enemy aircraft nearby. Pulling out of a turn, however, he found himself below the cloud base and was able to see the FW190 at around 2,500 feet, spinning down with black smoke pouring from it. Harries subsequently claimed his first FW190 destroyed and his second probable.

Meanwhile, Fg Off 'Joe' Birbeck and Sgt Plt William Vann had gone after three Me109Gs that were seen to be climbing behind the rear-most box of Marauders, west of Évreux. Diving down in a 90-degree turn to starboard, Birbeck opened fire on the starboard aircraft with a short burst but missed him and the aircraft broke away. Vann followed this aircraft down whilst Birbeck's attention was drawn to the leading aircraft, as it had only made a gentle turn to port.

Closing to just 100 yards, line astern, Birbeck fired a full three seconds, "during which time [the pilot] took no evasive action".[185] Birbeck saw large flashes around the cockpit area and pieces fly off the aircraft, before it flipped onto its back and dived to earth, emitting a long plume of white smoke. Breaking off his attack to avoid an approaching enemy aircraft, Birbeck did not see the aircraft crash, but last observed it in a vertical position at 2,500 feet. His statement was verified by 91 Squadron's Fg Off John Round, but despite his claim of one destroyed Me109G, he was only granted a probable victory.[186]

Sgt Plt Vann had continued after the Me109G that Birbeck had given up on, and had made two bursts of fire at 500 yards, expending 260 rounds of 20mm cannon and 810 rounds of .303 inch machine gun. He saw "2 large flashes"[187] on the aircraft, but it then entered cloud and was lost from sight. He subsequently claimed this Messerschmitt damaged.

Harries, Cowell, Birbeck and Vann all re-joined the Squadron, reforming into their original Red Section, but within five minutes four more FW190s attempted to attack the Marauders. This time, Blue Section took the initiative and drove the attackers off. Two of these were attacked by Flt Lt 'Pinkie' Glen and Fg Off Ron Collis, the former pilot firing a short burst at them without observed result.

Yellow Section also saw action. Six to eight miles west of Évreux, Flt Lt Don Smith saw two FW190s passing across the path of his section, approximately 1,000 feet below them, at around 15,500 feet. Smith broke formation and half-rolled down after them with his No. 2, Fg Off Roger Duchateau. Still in a steep dive, he opened fire on one of the Focke-Wulfs with three short bursts from the port quarter and ranges of 400 down to 350 yards. Smith observed…

> …one strike on [the] *port side of his cock pit* [sic] *and one in the centre of his starboard wing. The latter produced a series of small explosions in the starboard wing which eventually caused the outer end of the wing to break off. The E/A continued to dive towards the ground, yawing violently from side to side.*[188]

Having received a direct hit on the ammunition magazine inside his aircraft's wing, the German pilot stood little chance. He was not seen to leave the cockpit and Smith claimed the FW190 destroyed. He had only expended 80 rounds of 20mm cannon, and no .303 inch machine gun, but used 1.6 feet of cine-gun camera film, which has survived to this day.[189]

Whilst all this was on-going, the High Cover Wing had sighted six FW190s in the target area that were not engaged, but bounced another three, ten miles north of St. Valéry. One of these was claimed as damaged for no loss. The Top Cover Wing did not see the Luftwaffe, but reported excellent bombing by the Marauders and a large explosion just northwest of the airfield. Lastly, the Fighter Sweep Wing saw nothing of consequence with the exception of seven aircraft, which were seen at a distance but not engaged.

The return journey across the Channel, which was uneventful for most participants, proved a challenge for 41 Squadron's Fg Off Clive Birbeck, who had started having engine trouble after his combat. The ORB narrates in a jovial tone,

> *The days* [sic] *events even after a terrific show were not yet over as F/O Birbeck began having engine trouble after shooting down his Hun. He was chased by enemy aircraft and crossing the Seine near Quilleboef* [sic]*, began to think he was not going to get home. He then turned west in the hopes* [sic] *of getting to the sea and ditching as near* [to] *the English coast as possible. Much to Birbeck's relief, the enemy aircraft gave up the chase and he started to follow the coast and came out at Trouville. He then made for home but had to bale out about 20 miles South of Ford. Two Typhoons saw him get out and immediatley* [sic] *orbitted* [sic] *him. On hitting the sea --- he must have made a terrific splash as he weighs 16½ stone --- he gained his dinghy but in his efforts to bale it out he got up and immediately fell into the water again! However, he did eventually g*[o]*t back and thanks to the A.S.R. launch and the Typhoons was picked up none the worse for his two hours in the sea. Any way* [sic] *the pilots are now saying a trip to France is worthwhile.*[190]

Following his rescue, Birbeck filled in an Air/Sea Rescue Questionnaire, the original hand-written version of which is held in 41 Squadron's Archives. He recorded that he issued a distress signal from 7,000 feet and gave his position before baling out by 'bunting' out of the cockpit of his Spitfire. Birbeck released his parachute harness on hitting the water at 16:30, and noted that his Spitfire sank immediately and did not remain on the surface at all.

Two Typhoons from 197 Squadron and two Spitfires from 277 (ASR) Squadron were sent out to find him, and subsequently did so, 20-25 miles south of Ford, Sussex.[191] A High Speed Launch was sent out to retrieve him and he was brought ashore at Newhaven. The participants on the Ramrod were as follows:

Pilot	Serial	Section	Up	Down
Harries, Raymond H.	MB836	Red		17:00
Cowell, Peter	MB834			17:00
Birbeck, Clive R.	EN608			Baled 16:30
Vann, William H.	MB804	Yellow	15:30	17:00
Parry, Hugh L.	MB802			
Galitzine, Emanuel V.	MB838			
Smith, Donald H.	MB845			
Duchateau, Roger	EN609			
Glen, Arthur A.	MB846	Blue		
Collis, Ronald T. H.	EN231			
Moffett, H. Bruce	MB839			
Harding, Ross P.	MB797			

23 September 1943 – Following yesterday's excitement, the Squadron was involved in a much quieter operation this morning. In the first of two Ramrods today, the Spitfire XII Wing provided Escort Cover to 70 Marauders targeting Conches-en-Ouche Airfield, 60 miles west of Paris, in Part II of Ramrod 239.

Date	23 September 1943
Operation	Ramrod 239
Targets	Part I: Le Grand-Quevilly Power Station, Haute-Normandie Part II: Conches-en-Ouche Airfield, Haute-Normandie
Bombers	Part I: 226 Sqn: 18 Mitchells; 12 dispatched, 12 bombed Part II: 322 BG/451 BS: 72 Marauders; 72 dispatched, 70 bombed
Close Escort Part I Escort Cover High Cover Top Cover Close Escort Part II Escort Cover High Cover Top Cover 1st Fighter Sweep 2nd Fighter Sweep 3rd Fighter Sweep	Newchurch: 132 & 602 Squadrons (Spitfire Vb) West Malling: 64 Squadron (Spitfire Vb) Hornchurch: 129 & 222 Squadrons (Spitfire IX) North Weald: 331 & 332 Squadrons (Spitfire IX) Digby: 402 & 416 Squadrons (Spitfire Vb) Westhampnett: 41 & 91 Squadrons (Spitfire XII) Perranporth: 66 & 453 Squadrons (Spitfire Vb) Biggin Hill: 341 & 485 Squadrons (Spitfire IX) Kingsnorth: 19 & 65 Squadrons (Spitfire IX) Northolt: 302 & 303 Squadrons (Spitfire IX) Headcorn: 403 & 421 Squadrons (Spitfire IX) Tangmere: 197 & 486 Squadrons (Typhoon Ib)
Casualties	222 Sqn: Fg Off Daniel Thiriez EF in Spit IX, MH987, ditched in Channel, S of Beachy Head, not recovered †

Part I operated generally according to plan and the bombers were over the target at 08:18, where they dropped forty-eight 1,000 lb. bombs from 11,000 feet. However, as visibility of the power station was obscured by ground mist, the bombing was inaccurate and bursts were seen to land in a wood in a bend in the river southwest of Rouen.

The Close Escort and Escort Cover Wings operated without interference from the Luftwaffe, and the High Cover and Top Cover Wings even had time to loop back and make sweeps, the former Wing claiming two destroyed locomotives, but losing one pilot who suffered engine failure and ditched, but did not escape from his aircraft.

The Spitfire XII Wing was airborne at 08:25, both the Wing and the Squadron led by Wg Cdr Harries. They rendezvoused with Part II's Marauders and fellow escort wings on schedule and proceeded to France, but Harries (MB836) was compelled to return early suffering engine trouble, and did not cross the Channel.

Arriving over Conches-en-Ouche Airfield at 09:05, seventy of the bombers dropped a total of six hundred and ninety-four 300 lb. bombs with good results. Bursts were seen on the north-eastern and south-western dispersals areas, and on buildings and runways in the southeast corner of the airfield. However, one stick was also seen to land in the village.

Once again, the Luftwaffe did not make a show, and all the escorting and Fighter Sweep squadrons operated uneventfully. However, the Spitfire XII Wing did make an unusual sighting, reporting on their return having seen "a round cream coloured free balloon with basket at 12,000 feet about five minutes out from Trouville."[192] No suggestion was made as to its source or use. The Wing landed at 09:55 with nothing further to report.

The Squadron was airborne with 91 Squadron again at 15:00, and this "second Show of the day proved more producti[ve]"[193] than the first. On this occasion, the Wing was tasked with providing Escort Cover for Marauders attacking Beauvais-Tillé Airfield once again, in Part I of Ramrod 240.

Date	23 September 1943
Operation	Ramrod 240
Targets	Part I: Beauvais-Tillé Airfield, Picardie Part II: Lille-Nord Airfield, Pas-de-Calais Part III: Abbeville Airfield, Picardie
Bombers	Part I: 323 & 386 BGs: 72 Marauders; 72 dispatched, 70 bombed Part II: 175 Sqn: 8 Bomphoons Part III: 181 Sqn: 6 Bomphoons
Casualties	Part I: 20 Marauders CD/AA
Close Escort Part I	Digby: 402 & 416 Squadrons (Spitfire Vb) Heston: 306 & 308 Squadrons (Spitfire Vb)
Escort Cover	Westhampnett: 41 & 91 Squadrons (Spitfire XII)
High Cover	Hornchurch: 129 & 222 Squadrons (Spitfire IX) Biggin Hill: 341 & 485 Squadrons (Spitfire IX)
Top Cover	Kingsnorth: 19 & 65 Squadrons (Spitfire IX)
1st Fighter Sweep	Northolt: 302 & 303 Squadrons (Spitfire IX)
2nd Fighter Sweep	North Weald: 331 & 332 Squadrons (Spitfire IX)
3rd Fighter Sweep	Headcorn: 403 & 421 Squadrons (Spitfire IX)
4th Fighter Sweep	Newchurch: 132 & 602 Squadrons (Spitfire Vb)
5th Fighter Sweep	Staplehurst: 401, 411 & 412 Squadrons (Spitfire Vb)
6th Fighter Sweep	Tangmere: 197 & 486 Squadrons (Typhoon Ib)
Escort Part II	New Romney: 247 Squadrons (Typhoon Ib) Lydd: 174 & 245 Squadrons (Typhoon Ib)
Escort Part III	New Romney: 182 Squadron (Typhoon Ib)
Casualties	308 Sqn: Plt Off Andrzej J. W. Czerwiński, SD in Spit Vb, AA935, ER; & Flt Sgt Kazimierz Lipiec, SD/KIA Saint-Pierre-en-Val in Spit Vb, AA912

The Spitfire XII Wing took off at 15:00, led by Wg Cdr Harries, who led 41 Squadron again. They made rendezvous with Part I's bombers and other escort wings according to plan, 40 miles north of Fécamp at 12,000 feet at 15:40, and proceeded to Beauvais.

As the formation approached the target area, the Digby Wing sighted approximately 70 enemy aircraft comprising both Me109s and FW190s. These aircraft made multiple attempts to attack the bombers but were successfully driven off, 416 claiming one Me109 damaged in the process. The Heston Wing was attacked by ten to fifteen Me 109s and FW190s as they approached the target and lost two pilots, one killed but the other evading.

The Spitfire XII Wing was ordered to keep close to the bombers as the Close Escort Wings were fully occupied with enemy aircraft. As the formation made its final bank to approach the target, several enemy aircraft attempted to dive on the bombers, and the Wing turned to meet them. However, the enemy aircraft turned and "hurried off not attempting to fight."[194]

The High Cover Wings also encountered the Luftwaffe between the coast and the target area, which attempted to reach the bombers in groups of three, six and twelve. Several engagements ensued in which 341 Squadron claimed two FW190s and one Me109 destroyed for no loss. The Top Cover Wing also saw 20-25 enemy aircraft on the way in, but no engagements ensued.

The bombing proceeded otherwise according to plan and 70 of the 72 Marauders attacked Beauvais-Tillé Airfield with a total of five hundred and thirty 300 lb. bombs and two hundred and ninety-one 100 lb. bombs. Bombing results were reported by the fighter pilots to have been excellent, especially on the eastern and western dispersal areas, and in the north-western corner of the airfield. However, Flak was intense and almost a third of the entire bomber force sustained some form of damage. Nonetheless, all the bombers returned to base and claims were registered by their air gunners for one enemy aircraft probably destroyed and five damaged.

On the way home, several enemy aircraft dived on the bombers again, and whilst 41 Squadron stayed with them, 91 Squadron dived on six FW190s and two Me109s seen below the bombers. Combats between 91 Squadron and these eight aircraft resulted in the pilots claiming two FW190s and one Me109 destroyed and one Me109 damaged for no loss.

Flt Lt Glen (MB846), meanwhile, was likely quite relieved that the Squadron had stayed out of the fight this time, as he had started having engine trouble in the target area. Had he been compelled to combat the Luftwaffe, the handicap created by his engine may have ended his sortie prematurely. He recorded in his logbook that day, "My engine nearly fell out over target but I staggered home. Ropey kite. Shaky do!"[195] 41 Squadron landed again at 16:35, reporting the Ramrod "a most successful operation".[196]

In the meantime, the six Fighter Sweeps had all operated according to plan, but only the fourth and fifth did not sight the Luftwaffe. The first was the most heavily engaged when it was vectored onto eight to ten Me109s and FW190s southeast of Le Tréport and came out of the fight claiming two FW190s and one Me109 destroyed and three FW190s probably destroyed for no loss.

The second Fighter Sweep encountered a similar number of Me109s at the same altitude near Arras, two miles ahead. Giving chase, there were short engagements south of Cambrai, during which one Me109 was claimed damaged, but the rest escaped, diving away further inland, where they knew they could not be followed indefinitely.

In the third and sixth Fighter Sweeps, significant numbers of enemy aircraft were sighted, but engagements did not take place when the wings could either not close or the Luftwaffe avoided the fight and dived away.

As the Spitfire XII Wing was landing, the Bomphoons of Parts II and III were arriving over their respective targets. Both operations ran according to plan and bombing results were good in both cases, bursts being seen in the eastern dispersals area in the former attack and on the dispersals area and landing ground in the latter.

24 September 1943 – A fine day with high cloud meant that another intense and exhausting day lay in store for the Wing today. They were assigned to two Ramrod escorts, the first "another big bombing operation"[197] in which they provided Escort Cover to Marauders attacking Évreux-Fauville Airfield in Part III of Ramrod 242. In the second, the Wing provided Escort Cover to another 72 Marauders, this time targeting Beauvais-Tillé Airfield in Part II of Ramrod 243.

However, it also proved an expensive day. During the latter of these operations, 41 Squadron claimed two enemy aircraft destroyed and two probable, but lost a Flight Commander. 91 Squadron were also heavily engaged and returned claiming three destroyed and two damaged, but also at the cost of one man.

Date	24 September 1943
Operation	Ramrod 242
Targets	Part I: Amiens-Longueau Marshalling Yards, Picardie Part II: St. Omer-Longuenesse Airfield, Pas-de-Calais Part III: Évreux-Fauville Airfield, Haute-Normandie
Bombers	Part I: 180 Sqn: 12 Mitchells; 12 dispatched, 12 bombed Part II: 16 Wing: 8 Bomphoons Part III: 72 Marauders; 72 dispatched, 71 bombed
Casualties	Part I: All 12 Mitchells CD/AA
Close Escort Part I Escort Cover High Cover Top Cover 1st Fighter Sweep 2nd Fighter Sweep Escort Part II Close Escort Part III Escort Cover High Cover Top Cover 1st Fighter Sweep	Staplehurst: 401, 411 & 412 Squadrons (Spitfire Vb) Newchurch: 132 & 602 Squadrons (Spitfire Vb) Hornchurch: 129 & 222 Squadrons (Spitfire IX) North Weald: 331 & 332 Squadrons (Spitfire IX) Northolt: 302 & 303 Squadrons (Spitfire IX) Tangmere: 197 & 486 Squadrons (Typhoon Ib) 16 Wing: 16 Typhoons Digby: 402 & 416 Squadrons (Spitfire Vb) Heston: 306 & 308 Squadrons (Spitfire Vb) West Malling: 64 Squadron (Spitfire Vb) Westhampnett: 41 & 91 Squadrons (Spitfire XII) Biggin Hill: 341 & 485 Squadrons (Spitfire IX) Kingsnorth: 65 & 122 Squadrons (Spitfire IX) Headcorn: 403 & 421 Squadrons (Spitfire IX)
Casualties	129 Sqn: Flt Lt George A. Mason, SD NW of Amiens in Spit IX, MH472, POW; 303 Sqn: Flt Sgt Tadeusz Szymkowiak, SD/KIA Tilloy-lès-Conty in Spit IX, EN173; 485 Sqn: Fg Off John A. Ainge RNZAF, KIA in Spit IX, MH470; 486 Sqn: Flt Sgt Howard C. Saward RNZAF, SD nr Trouville in Typhoon Ib, EJ915, POW

Part I operated according to plan and the Mitchells dropped a total of ninety-one 500 lb. bombs with reportedly good results, and bursts were seen both on trains and tracks. Some bombs overshot, but these were seen to land on Amiens-Glisy Airfield. Flak was, however, intense and every single Mitchell returned with some degree of damage.

The Luftwaffe was active throughout and the Close Escort engaged four FW190s and five Me109s, although without conclusive result. Although the Escort Cover sighted 12 enemy aircraft that were not engaged, the High Cover Wing was attacked northwest of Amiens at 19,000-20,000 feet by twelve to fifteen Me109s that dived on them from 3,000-4,000 feet above. In the ensuing combats, the Wing claimed one FW190 destroyed and one damaged, but lost one pilot who was shot down and captured.

The Top Cover Wing sighted only three FW190s, which approached head on at 22,000 feet when crossing out over the Somme Estuary, and one was claimed damaged for no casualty. The first Fighter Sweep, flown by Northolt's Polish Wing attacked four FW190s, followed a short while later by another one. They claimed two of these probably destroyed and one damaged, but lost one pilot who was shot down and killed.

Finally, the second Fighter Sweep, operated by Tangmere based Typhoons, shot up the dispersals area at Beaumont Airfield and fired at six Me109s parked on the airfield, but with no visible results. However, they also engaged seven enemy aircraft comprising both Me109s and FW190s, and came away claiming three FW190s damaged for the loss of one pilot shot down and captured.

Part II also operated as planned, with no claims and no losses. Eight Bomphoons attacked St. Omer-Longuenesse Airfield from altitudes of 6,000 and 10,000 feet, with good results, and bursts were seen on the south-eastern dispersals area and on the landing ground.

The Spitfire XII Wing was airborne at 11:05, with the Wing and 41 Squadron led by Wg Cdr Harries, and 41 Squadron's other two sections led by Flt Lts Hugh Parry and 'Pinkie' Glen. They rendezvoused with Part III's bombers and escorts 40 miles south of Beachy Head and proceeded across the Channel without interference.

Landfall was made four miles south of Fécamp, and Évreux-Fauville Airfield was reached via Quittebeuf, where the Marauders dropped three hundred and fifty-eight 300 lb. GP bombs and four hundred and eighty-four 100 lb. bombs. Results were considered good, and both dispersals areas and headquarters buildings were seen to be hit. Weak to moderate Flak was experienced, but none of the bombers were damaged.

On the way out, the Close Escort was attacked by a number of FW190s five miles southwest of Rouen, but these dived away when a section turned towards them. A lone unidentified enemy aircraft was also sighted below, and a section from 64 Squadron dived on it, claiming it as "1 believed Me.109 destroyed".[198] A few enemy aircraft also made it through to the bombers, but they defended themselves, and one of the Marauders' air gunners claimed an enemy aircraft probably destroyed.

The operation was completely uneventful for the Spitfire XII Wing on Escort Cover duties, and they had nothing to report when they landed at 12:35 in time for lunch. Whilst 41 Squadron was happy that "we are being kept busy now, much to the delight of the pilots"[199], they were nonetheless disappointed that "there was no joy for any of our Squadron, as the enemy did not play".[200]

The High Cover Wing saw two small formations of enemy aircraft in the Seine area, but they were not engaged. Nonetheless, 485 Squadron lost one pilot, who was seen diving away from the Squadron and is thought to have suffered oxygen failure. The Top Cover Wing had a brief engagement with three FW190s soon after leaving the target area, but their combats ended inconclusively.

Finally, the Fighter Sweep Wing encountered a dozen FW190s at 24,000 feet over Fleury, but the pilots were unable to engage them. However, two of 421 Squadron's pilots, who returned early on the deck owing to oxygen problems, sighted a locomotive at St. Valéry, which they shot up and claimed damaged.

After lunch, the Wing was briefed for its second operation of the day, which would take them back to Beauvais, escorting 72 Marauders. They were accompanied by eight other squadrons, and four assigned to fighter sweeps. Whilst Part I operated uneventfully, Part II was heavily engaged by the Luftwaffe resulting in claims of no less than twelve enemy aircraft destroyed, three probable, and seven damaged. It would be a day the Spitfire XII Wing would not forget.

Date	24 September 1943
Operation	Ramrod 243
Targets	Part I: St. Omer Airfield, Pas-de-Calais
	Part II: Beauvais-Tillé Airfield, Picardie
Bombers	Part I: 12 Mitchells; 4 bombed primary, 6 bombed secondary
	Part II: 72 Marauders; 71 bombed
Casualties	Part II: 17 BG/432 BS: Marauder 41-18320, 'Wild Kitty', severe CD/AA; returned safely but not repaired
Close Escort Part I	Staplehurst: 401, 411 & 412 Squadrons (Spitfire Vb)
Escort Cover	Newchurch: 132 & 602 Squadrons (Spitfire Vb)
High Cover	Hornchurch: 129 & 222 Squadrons (Spitfire IX)
Top Cover	Northolt: 302 & 303 Squadrons (Spitfire IX)
Close Escort Part II	Digby: 402 & 416 Squadrons (Spitfire Vb)
	Heston: 306 & 308 Squadrons (Spitfire Vb)
Escort Cover	Westhampnett: 41 & 91 Squadrons (Spitfire XII)
High Cover	Biggin Hill: 341 & 485 Squadrons (Spitfire IX)
Top Cover	Headcorn: 403 & 421 Squadrons (Spitfire IX)
1st Fighter Sweep	North Weald: 331 & 332 Squadrons (Spitfire IX)
2nd Fighter Sweep	Kingsnorth: 65 & 122 Squadrons (Spitfire IX)
Casualties	41 Sqn: Flt Lt Hugh L. Parry SD/WIA Poix-Beauvais area in Spit XII, MB802, POW; 91 Sqn: Flt Lt Gray Stenborg DFC RNZAF, SD/KIA Beauvais in Spit XII, MB805

Part I operated according to plan and the Luftwaffe was not seen. The only opposition was Flak, which was intense and heavy but caused no damage. However, despite no cloud and excellent visibility, only four Mitchells bombed the primary target, St. Omer Airfield, with poor results. They dropped a total of thirty-two 500 lb. bombs, but sixteen were seen to fall 1,000-1,500 yards northeast of the target. Six aircraft dropped another forty-eight 500 lb. bombs on a secondary target, Samer/Wierre-au-Bois Airfield, but all overshot.

The Spitfire XII Wing was airborne at 15:20, led by Wg Cdr Harries. He also led 41 Squadron once again, with the remaining two sections led by Flt Lts Hugh Parry and 'Pinkie' Glen. However, within minutes, Harries (MB836) turned for home again with R/T trouble, and handed the Wing over to Glen.[201] He then led the two Squadrons to the appointed rendezvous point, and arrived at the allocated time, but found that Part II's bombers were already out over the Channel, ten miles ahead of them. Opening their throttles, the pilots raced to catch up, and only did so as the bombers were crossing in southwest of Le Tréport.

The Wing took up position at 16,000 feet, to the port side and 3,000 feet above the bombers. They proceeded with them to Beauvais, accompanied by the Close Escort Squadrons, but Glen's No. 4, Fg Off Ross Harding (MB837), also then pulled out and returned home with engine trouble, reducing 41 Squadron to two sections of three and one of four.[202]

When still two miles from the target, heavy Flak opened up on the bombers and one Marauder was hit; it was seen to go down issuing clouds of black smoke. The rest of bombers carried on and reached Beauvais-Tillé at around 16:00. As they went in for their bombing run, the Spitfire XII Wing banked 90° to starboard across their path, but whilst in this turn, ten FW190s dived between them, heading straight for the bombers. Then it all happened at once:

F/Lt A.A. Glen D.F.C. led 41 into a turn behind them causing the enemy aircraft to pull away to the right, and the attack on the bombers was foiled. Spitfires V, IX and XII closed in from every direction, and a most glorious dog fight ensued....[203]

The sky exploded into umpteen combats. At 12,000 feet, the Digby Wing counted 40 enemy aircraft inbound over the target area, diving on them from 6,000 feet above, whilst the Heston Wing was attacked by a mixture of ten to fifteen Me109s and FW190s over Beauvais. The ensuing combats resulted in one FW190 destroyed and one probable, and four FW190s and one Me109 damaged.

As soon as 41 Squadron had turned the ten FW190s that dived through the Spitfire XII Wing[204], twenty Me109s attempted to bounce the two units. However, as 41 Squadron was already chasing the original group of FW190s, 91 Squadron fended off the 109s alone.

'Pinkie' Glen (MB801) was the first to strike. With his own R/T now malfunctioning, he had heard no warnings of enemy aircraft until he saw the original ten FW190s streak past in their dive towards the bombers. Acting instinctively, he broke to port and quickly closed on them. They pulled up steeply to starboard just north of Beauvais but,

Two of the E/A were lagging slightly and I took a quick squirt at the leader from about 300 yds. at 45° deflection using cannon and m/g. I saw a large flash in the cockpit and he flicked over and collided with the E/A following him. Both A/E [sic] disintegrated.[205]

The Squadron ORB adds more drama, recounting the incident, "[Flt Lt Glen] took a shot at a FW. 190 and blew the Cock pit [sic] to pieces and the enemy's No. 2 flew into the leader and both aircraft disintegrated with a tremendous flash."[206] He had only fired 30 rounds of 20mm cannon and 120 rounds of .303 inch machine gun, and used 1½ feet of cine-gun film to record the victory.

Fg Off Prince Galitzine (MB838) also chased the original group of FW190s. When one broke upwards, he followed it and gradually closed. As he did so, he opened fire at 500 yards, making a two-second burst, which resulted in the FW190 breaking downwards. Galitzine kept on its tail, and made another three-second burst of fire from 300 yards. The aircraft was hit and it continued its downward path, now streaming 'greyish black' smoke.

Following it down further still, now southwest of Beauvais, Galitzine then "saw a large portion break off which I think was the tail unit".[207] However, he was then attacked by another FW190 and forced to break away. Therefore unable to witness the definitive destruction of the aircraft, Galitzine was compelled to claim the victory as one FW190 probably destroyed. He secured the victory with 62 rounds of 20mm cannon and 208 rounds of .303 inch machine gun.

Having not had an opportunity with the FW190s, Fg Off 'Barney' Newman (MB845) went after the Me109s that had followed them down. Coming in behind one, he fired a short burst with no result, but had no opportunity to press home his attack as he spotted two FW190s diving in his direction. Breaking away, he wheeled around to find himself now in a suitable position to attack the two Focke-Wulfs.

I turned behind the second of these two and gave one burst as E/A was rolling on its back to dive down. I followed in to about 600 yds seeing strikes on the fuselage. I gave a third burst as we were leveling [sic] *out but had to break* [off my] *attack when my aircraft became very difficult to handle.*[208]

Newman had fired 80 rounds of cannon and 240 of machine gun and claimed his FW190 damaged. However, his Combat Report states "Raised to probably destroyed" and a hand-written note adds, "admitted probably destroyed on further evidence".[209] An Intelligence Report for the Ramrod indicates that this evidence was provided by 91 Squadron's Commanding Officer, Sqn Ldr Norman Kynaston:

F/O Newman followed E/A down to 1,000 ft and claims to have damaged a F.W.190 seen to be very hard hit by S/L Kynaston who saw hits on E/A cockpit, who considered this 'Damaged' as unlikely to have recovered. Consequently his claim was raised to probably destroyed.[210]

91 Squadron had meanwhile also been very busy. Following his combat, Newman had found another FW190 and was lining up to make an attack, when a Spitfire XII from 91 Squadron intercepted it and shot it down with a single burst. He watched as the Focke-Wulf crashed next to a building and burst into flames.

This had been the work of Sqn Ldr Kynaston, who had ordered 91 Squadron to attack the Me109s that had followed the FW190s down. Kynaston chased one of these aircraft down to ground level, but pulled out when he realised it was leading him straight to Beauvais-Tillé Airfield. Climbing again, he saw two pairs of FW190s below him and dived on one of them.

I was then joined by another Spitfire XII and I took the right hand FW. 190 and after a short chase closed to about 250 yards. After about 3 seconds burst I saw numerous strikes on the engine and cockpit of the FW. 190 and it began to break up into tiny pieces and then flew into the ground, where it exploded and burnt.[211]

The other pilot was, of course, Fg Off 'Barney' Newman, who subsequently confirmed Kynaston's victory: one FW190 destroyed.

91 Squadron's Flt Lt John Doll, who was flying as Kynaston's No. 2, had followed his Squadron Commander down and was concentrating on staying with him when he saw a flash go past his port wing and another bright flash about two yards from his cockpit on his port side. Craning his neck, he saw an Me109 was on his tail, approximately 800 yards to his rear. Taking immediate evasive action, he half rolled and dived towards the ground from 9,000 feet, losing Kynaston in the process.

Looking about again at 3,000 feet, Doll saw numerous Spitfires, FW190s and Me109s at various heights between 4,000 feet and ground level. His gaze settled on two FW190s flying south at just 300 feet, line abreast, about four miles away. Dropping to just 200 feet, he rapidly closed on them from behind, "apparently quite unnoticed as they both continued straight and level abreast 50 yards apart".[212]

When within four hundred yards of them, he climbed to 500 feet, the altitude at which they were now flying. As he did so, the starboard Focke-Wulf made a gentle climb to starboard, thereby presenting Doll a larger target. Taking his opportunity, now closed to 250-300 yards, he fired a short burst, which resulted in the FW190 "straighten[ing] out as though hit".[213] Closure then became more rapid, and Doll made another burst from 150 down to 50 yards, but had to break away over the aircraft to avoid colliding with it.

As he did so, the engine and cockpit area burst into flames, pieces flew off the aircraft, and white smoke billowed from it. Banking around again, Doll saw it make a turn to starboard and crash into a wood, where it exploded on impact. Looking about again, he saw the second FW190 a mile away on the other side of the wood, coming straight towards him. Feeling a strategic retreat was the prudent thing to do, Doll turned onto a course of 220° and headed for home on the deck.

Not to be outdone, however, the FW190 chased him a full 40 miles, although he was unable to close any nearer than approximately one mile to his rear. Doll was eager to avoid an engagement as his engine was now running roughly with occasional puffs of smoke issuing from his port exhaust. Trying an evasive tactic to shake the FW190, Doll made a full 360° turn around the base of a hill and succeeded in losing him. He then throttled back and crossed out in the general direction of Westhampnett.

Another 91 Squadron pilot had also been in action during this time. When the Me109s had bounced the unit, French Flt Lt Jean Maridor dived after an Me109 but was unable to catch him. Seeing four FW190s diving on his port side, Maridor gave up on the Messerschmitt and went after this quartet instead. Picking out one of these, he followed it down to ground level, where he fired just a two-second burst from its starboard beam. This was sufficient, however, and the Focke-Wulf dived straight into a wood and exploded.

He then sighted two more FW190s flying line abreast just ahead of him, and fired for a full five seconds at the No. 1 aircraft from 400 yards, closing to 300. Seeing no result, he switched to its No. 2, firing another five-second burst from 250 down to 150 yards. The pilot took immediate evasive action, but Maridor saw strikes on the aircraft and a significant amount of black smoke issued from its engine cowlings. Unable to press home the attack any further, however, he claimed this aircraft damaged.

In the meantime, the Marauders had attacked Beauvais-Tillé Airfield, dropping three hundred and nineteen 300 lb. bombs and five hundred and fifty-three 100 lb. bombs with fair results. Not surprisingly, the Spitfire XII Wing was too occupied to have observed the bombing, but the 322nd Bomb Group bombers praised the fighter support they received, which prevented enemy aircraft causing any casualties. The remaining escort squadrons and the Fighter Sweep squadrons all operated according to plan and without incident.

As the Spitfire XII Wing came out of their combats, they started heading towards the coast, eventually sighting the bombers above them on their homeward leg. The pilots climbed and crossed out on the starboard flank of the last box of Marauders, and landed back at base at 16:40, making the following claims[214]:

Victories, 24 Sep 1943	Unit	Dest.	Prob.	Dam.	Location
Doll, John C. S.	91 Sqn	FW190	-	-	Beauvais
Galitzine, Emanuel V.	41 Sqn	-	FW190	-	SW of Beauvais
Glen, Arthur A.	41 Sqn	2 FW190	-	-	N of Beauvais
Kynaston, Norman A.	91 Sqn	FW190	-	-	Beauvais
Maridor, Jean P.	91 Sqn	FW190	-	FW190	Beauvais
Newman, Benjamin B.	41 Sqn	-	FW190	-	Beauvais

However, soon after landing at Westhampnett, it was realised that Flt Lt Hugh Parry had not returned. As time passed, it also became apparent that he would not be, but no-one had seen anything to indicate why. "In Parry we have lost a fine leader and we shall miss him very much."[215]

Flying MB802 on the operation, Parry had been shot down. Although he initially succeeded in evading capture, he was ultimately captured and spent the rest of the War behind wire. However, 91 Squadron had also lost a pilot, 21-year-old New Zealander, Flt Lt Gray Stenborg DFC, who was killed in action.

No-one had seen exactly what had happened to the two pilots, and the only sighting of any relevance was made by 41 Squadron's Fg Off Roger Duchateau, who thought he had seen "a Spitfire XII go down, streaming glycol, just before reaching the Target".[216] Once the engagements began, everyone was too busy with their own attacks or defence, and no R/T communication was heard over the excited hubbub that began when the first group of FW190s dived on the Wing.

The New Zealand Fighter Pilots Museum website states that "Stenborg's aircraft was hit and he headed for home. He was last heard on the radio, saying that he was going to get as close to the French coast as possible and then bale out. His ultimate fate is still unknown."[217] He cannot, however, have made it far, as he is buried today in Marissel French National Cemetery, 1km north of Beauvais.

41 Squadron's Fg Off Prince Galitzine recorded in his logbook that day that the Squadron was "heavily engaged", having been…

> …bounced by about 20 190's over the target. Hugh was shot down! I was Yellow 1, attacked a 190 and while following it down a large bit fell off the tail & it was streaming black smoke. A 190 got on my tail & [I] had to break away.[218]

Flt Lt 'Pinkie' Glen's recorded in his own logbook,

> Escort cover 72 marauders Beauvais. Wizard dogfight over target with 40+ Huns. I hit one in cockpit and he crashed into his no. 2. Both blew up. 2 FW190's destroyed. Unfortunately we lost Hugh Parry A Flt.[219]

As a result of his victories, Glen was awarded a Bar to his DFC on 5 November 1943. The citation read,

> This officer has led his flight with exceptional skill and keenness. He is a most determined fighter, whose efforts to destroy the enemy at every opportunity have been highly commendable. Since being awarded the Distinguished Flying Cross, Flight Lieutenant Glenn [sic] has destroyed 6 enemy aircraft and damaged several more.[220]

Many years later, Fg Off Ron Johnson broadly reflected on the Squadron's activity during summer 1943, recalling that the unit…

> …lost several pilots some of whom had been with the squadron a long time – Dickie Hogarth, Bob Boyd, Haybag (F/O Haywood), F/O [sic] Parry, F/Sgt May. Although their loss was felt very deeply I think, by this time, we had come to accept it as inevitable and we did not even think who might be next or indeed that there would be a next.[221]

Hidden by La Résistance

Although wounded when he was shot down, Parry managed to remain hidden by the French for over four months, until betrayed to the Gestapo in February 1944. Following interrogation, he arrived in Stalag Luft III immediately prior to 'The Great Escape' but was not able to participate in the escape itself. He therefore remained a Prisoner of War until liberated in late April 1945.

Following his release, he filled in his obligatory Liberation Report and went back to civilian life, much of the past put away until interviewed broadly about his RAF career by the Imperial War Museum in September 1985. It was then another 20 years before this author interviewed him in more depth about the events surrounding his being shot down on 24 September 1943, and the following story was revealed:

> *I was hit in the right shoulder by a piece of nose cap of a 20mm cannon shell which must have penetrated the armour-plating behind the cockpit – size about 2.5cms. My plane was on fire so I baled out, delayed the drop from 12,000 feet to about 3,000 feet when I pulled the tit. I landed on the edge of a wood 'guesstimating' I was about 5-10 miles N.W. of Beauvais.*[222]

Just after Parry pulled his ripcord, a FW190 approached and circled him. He waved and the aircraft turned towards him. As he was afraid that he was going to be shot at, Parry pulled one side of his parachute to drop faster and shot down into trees and the aircraft passed over without firing a shot. In hindsight, he felt the Luftwaffe pilot may not have wanted to shoot him, but may have rather been trying to identify him and communicate his location.

On landing, Parry hit a tree and damaged his watch, a 21st birthday gift, which he still wears today. Extricating himself from his harness, he pulled in his parachute and hid it, and moved away from the area as quickly as he could. He soon reached the edge of a wood with a six to eight-foot high fence and climbed over it. On the other side was a sunken lane, lined with hedges. Checking it was safe he crossed the lane in time to hide himself again atop the other side, as a German troop carrier passed full of soldiers, likely sent to look for him.

Parry knew he needed to head for Spain but realised he would need help to do so. There was a main road nearby, but as German vehicles were regularly passing along it, he decided to avoid it and head in the direction of the coast instead. He felt that as everyone knew there was no way a pilot could get back across the Channel, they would not expect a pilot to go in that direction.

Darkness came but Parry kept moving to put as much distance between him and where he had landed. He eventually found refuge in a dry ditch, covered by a hedge beside a meadow, where he caught a few hours restless sleep. However, he was awoken the following morning to noise in the meadow. Peering out from his hiding place, he saw German soldiers in the field excavating an aircraft that had crashed there. He remained hidden until dusk, then moved on, soon coming to a small lake at Lyons-la-Fôret with many little weekend shacks around it.

Waiting until darkness fell, he tried to break into one of the huts but was unable to. Then he noticed the door of a hut 50-60 yards away was slightly ajar, as light shone from the opening, and carefully approached it. Assuming the occupiers would be locals, he knocked and a Frenchman came to the door. His wife and two small children were also with him but his wife was terrified. Parry explained he was a pilot who had been shot down and was taken inside. The man had a look at his injured shoulder, but couldn't do much more than clean it with some schnapps. Then he was offered a drink and some bread, and hidden for a few hours in a nearby storeroom.

Woken by the man at 03:00, Parry was given a beret, a raincoat and half a bottle of wine and told to move on. He was informed a German camp was located on the other side of the lake, and that it would therefore be prudent to be gone before sunrise. He left as requested, under the cover of darkness, thanking the man for his hospitality.

During the day, Parry came to a field where a farmer was ploughing. He watched for a while to be sure it was safe, then approached him to ask if there were any Germans around, and if he may have something to eat. The man told him to wait, went off for some time, and then returned with some bread and meat, but told him to move on.

Having walked all day, Parry came to a farmhouse after dark that evening and knocked on the door. He was given food and shown to a place in the barn where he had a few hours' sleep but, once again, was woken before sunrise and urged to leave.

During that day, Parry found himself on the northern bank of the Seine near Vernon, but was presented with a new challenge when he saw that the bridge was guarded at both ends. However, he soon came across a farmer with a cart of hay who was travelling in the direction of the bridge and agreed to help him across. Parry walked over the bridge with him, pretending to be a farm labourer, and passed the guards without problem. On the other side, Parry stopped at a café briefly for a drink, paying for two beers with money from his escape kit. The proprietor realised he was an Allied pilot from his broken French, but served him and said nothing. Parry then continued towards Évreux.

He was walking through open countryside when it started to rain. Quickly wet and cold, he decided to stop at the next farmhouse and seek assistance. In time, he came to a large farmhouse where some men were standing at the far corner of the yard, and approached them, explaining who he was. They fetched the owner, a lady who came to see if he really was English. She asked him about London, and tested his knowledge of Fortnum & Masons, Swan & Edgars, and Regent Street. Suitably convinced, he was taken for a hot bath and fed, and it was then arranged for him to be picked up by the Resistance.

Parry was taken back into Vernon, where he was hidden in the house of one Madam Fournier, who brought a doctor to look at his shoulder wound. Whilst there, he met two Americans and they were all told they would be taken to a rendezvous with the French Underground. In due course, they were taken to a Chateau owned by the Rothschilds where they were hidden in the gardener's shed.

During this time, however, Parry became extremely ill, he assumes from the water he had been drinking, and was eventually taken by ambulance to a pharmacy in Évreux, where he was hidden upstairs in a bed to recuperate. He was soon taken from the pharmacy again to another farmhouse where the housewife was a former hospital theatre sister and put to bed in a room, which was also housing an American, Lt. Paul Pascal.[223] A short while later, Pascal was taken down the escape lines, over the Pyrenees into Spain, and subsequently made it back to the United Kingdom.

When he departed, Parry asked him to make contact with his parents and tell them he was alive and safe, which he did. However, this was not before his parents posted a Missing notice in *The Times* on 3 December 1943, which read,

PARRY.–Missing in Sept., 1943, while leading his Squadron over enemy occupied country. FLT LT HUGH LAWRENCE PARRY, N. Rhodesia, second son of Mr. and Mrs. W. L. Parry, 27, Watling Street, Dartford, Kent, aged 27.[224]

Meanwhile being hidden in the house in Évreux, Parry found the owner had a little dog called Ahmed that he had brought back from North Africa, and had taught a trick. On the command, 'Heil Hitler', the dog would sit and lift one front paw in the air. The locals found this as amusing as the Germans did, and in fact several German soldiers made offers to buy the dog from him. The dog would also fetch his master's pipe when commanded to do so.

Whilst recuperating, his host, who was a salt and yeast distributor, took him for a brief tour of the town in his van. Once, they were stopped by the Gendarmerie and asked to show their papers. Parry also showed his papers, which identified him falsely as 'Jean Piccard', born in Dunkirk. The Gendarme checking the papers realised he was an Allied pilot but was a sympathiser, and part of the joke, so let them through.

Now well enough to travel again, Parry was moved to Paris by train early in the New Year and hidden in an apartment in the Latin Quarter, which he shared with an American pilot. The two Allied airmen spent their days playing Gin Rummy until Parry was moved to a new hiding place, in a block of 14-16 apartments at 48 Avenue President Wilson, Trocadéro, owned by a Madame Jeanette Huet, who had been working for the Resistance since June 1943. She was reputed to have been one of the richest people in Paris, and her husband was an engineer that the Americans had picked up in a submarine.

Parry recalls that he has almost never lived better than during his time here from the beginning of January to the beginning of February. He was given cigars and, together with Madame Huet drank a bottle of Brandy every day and a bottle of Champagne on Sundays, "all black market stuff, of course!"[225] He was even able to do some sightseeing and go to the cinema, and began to speak French rather well.

However, it was all over in early February. At 03:00 on 7 February 1944, the Gestapo arrived and knocked down the door. Hearing them coming, Parry jumped out of bed and quickly dressed before they reached him. He was arrested at gun-point and slapped around a bit, then taken to Fresnes Prison.

Parry last saw Madame Huet in Fresnes Prison when they passed each other in the hallway and had no idea what had happened to her after that.[226] He remembered,

> *I was captured by the Gestapo and, after initial questioning at their headquarters, spent a month in Fresnes Prison with almost daily visits from them. They wanted information on any French contacts I had made, but I could not have given them anything as I never knew names or addresses, except Mme Huet who was arrested at the same time.*[227]

Parry received dreadful treatment from the Gestapo to intimidate and coerce him into talking. He was struck and threatened numerous times, had the chain tightened around his wrist, was refused food, told he was a spy and would be shot, shown a torture chamber, and also brought to see several captured French Resistance workers "in [a] pitiful condition as a result of questioning [and] semi-starved".[228] However, having gained nothing of assistance from Parry, the Gestapo eventually gave up and sent him to Germany, where he was received at Dulag Luft outside Frankfurt, for the usual interrogation of airmen.

Initially placed in a cell that had standing room only and had no windows, Parry was sent for on his first evening there, and found himself in before an Officer who introduced himself in an English accent, calling himself 'Black'. Taken aback, Parry asked if he was a traitor, but the man laughed and said, "No, my name is actually Schwarz," and added that he had attended Manchester University.

He then asked Parry if he would like to hear the news from London, and the radio was turned on in time for him to catch the BBC news. They talked for some time, but no questions were asked. After a while, Schwarz finally pulled out a folder marked, '41 Squadron' and looked down a list of the pilots that had been shot down, until he reached Parry's name, which had an annotation next to it, 'Escaped'. Schwarz remarked, "But he didn't, did he?"

He then went on to astonish Parry with his knowledge of him, asking if he missed his dog Monty, but assured him not to worry as he was being looked after by Flt Lt 'Barney' Newman. He also knew about his history in the RAF, including his time in Malta and his previous life in South Africa and Rhodesia. Parry remarked how astonished he was at their incredible intelligence. Schwarz responded, "Yes, it isn't bad but not nearly as good as yours; you see, we can't buy Cabinet Ministers."

To this day, Parry does not know how Schwarz could have obtained this information. They did, however, have one gap in his RAF career, which was the time during which he was a test pilot at Vickers. Knowing that, had he told them that this was where he was, the interrogation would have been endless, Parry told them instead that he had been an instructor at an OTU.

After approximately a week at Dulag Luft, Parry was sent to Stalag Luft III at Sagan in a railway truck marked '8 horses or 40 men', on which he caught the flu and was taken straight to the camp sick quarters on arrival. On his recuperation and release into the North Compound, he was questioned by French prisoners on the state of Paris and France in general then taken to see 'Big X'.

He had no idea who this was, but soon found it was Sqn Ldr Roger Bushell, in charge of the escape committee. Bushell asked who he was and what he'd done before the War, and Parry told him he was a surveyor at a mine in South Africa. In one of those coincidences in life that would not be believed if it were in a movie, it turned out that Bushell's father had been the Mine Manager at West Springs Mine in South Africa and Parry's boss. Parry told Bushell that he played tennis with his sisters Rosemary and Elizabeth, and that his father always wore white socks, convincingly proving that he was not a German 'plant'.[229]

Having arrived in Stalag Luft III shortly before 'The Great Escape', Parry was enrolled in the tunnel project on a modest scale to assist with security. A system was in operation to observe any entry into the North Compound by the Germans, which enabled tunnel workers to cease work so no noise would be made until the coast was clear again. Parry sat beside a window and watched one in the next hut, where another observer sat. This continued throughout various huts in the camp, where a signal had been instituted in which the observer was to open or shut the window, and in this way pass the message down the line that German guards were on their way.

After the execution of 50 of the escapees, very real anger was felt by the men still in camp. They held a service in which the uncivilised behaviour of the Germans was condemned and, far from breaking their spirit, another tunnel was soon under construction under the theatre. However, they had just cleared the surrounding wire when the men were unceremoniously removed from the compound by the SS and marched to Bad Muskau on the German-Polish border.

I remained [in Stalag Luft III] *until February 1945 when we evacuated the camp and marched/walked west to Bad Muskau and on to Spremberg (5 days & nights), then entrained for Marlag Nord, outside Bremen (3 days & nights). A short stay and we were off on foot towards Hamburg. We crossed the Elbe downstream from Hamburg, which had been obliterated by fire apparently shortly beforehand, and finished up at a huge farm called Trenthorst at Lübeck, in the stables. On VE Day eve, I flew home from Deepholst where Monty had just accepted the German surrender.*[230,231]

Returning now to 24 September 1943, it was also around this time that Flt Lt Prince Emanuel Galitzine left the Squadron. The exact date is unclear, but he is last mentioned in the ORB on 24 September 1943, the day he claimed a probably destroyed FW190 southwest of Beauvais, and the same day upon which Hugh Parry was shot down. Although his immediate subsequent movements are unknown, it is understood that Galitzine was posted to 83 (Composite) Group Headquarters, where he became the Personal Assistant of AVM Sir William F. Dickson CB OBE DSO AFC, OC 83 Group, in December 1943. He returned to operations with 72 Squadron in Italy in September 1944, and remained with this unit until after the cessation of hostilities in Europe.[232]

25 September 1943 – As a result of Parry's loss the day before, Flt Lt Donald Smith RAAF was appointed OC A Flight today, and would remain in this role until his departure from 41 Squadron on 2 May 1944, when he was given his own squadron.

Following their previous exhausting day, cloudy conditions with mist gave the Wing some respite today and they were not called upon until mid-afternoon, when the pilots participated in an uneventful operation, in which they provided Escort Cover to 72 Marauders targeting St. Omer-Longuenesse Airfield.

Date	25 September 1943
Operation	Ramrod 246
Target	St. Omer-Longuenesse Airfield, Pas-de-Calais
Bombers	72 Marauders in two boxes; 72 dispatched, 68 bombed
Casualties	2 Marauders CD/AA
Close Escort	Newchurch: 132 & 602 Squadrons (Spitfire Vb)
	Staplehurst: 401, 411 & 412 Squadrons (Spitfire Vb)
Escort Cover	Westhampnett: 41 & 91 Squadrons (Spitfire XII)
High Cover	Hornchurch: 129 & 222 Squadrons (Spitfire IX)
Top Cover	Northolt: 302 & 303 Squadrons (Spitfire IX)
1st Fighter Sweep	Headcorn: 403 & 421 Squadrons (Spitfire IX)
2nd Fighter Sweep	Kingsnorth: 19 & 65 Squadrons (Spitfire IX)
3rd Fighter Sweep	Biggin Hill: 341 & 485 Squadrons (Spitfire IX)

The Spitfire XII Wing was airborne at 16:40, with both the Wing and 41 Squadron led by Wg Cdr Harries. The pilots rendezvoused with the Marauders, which were three minutes early, and with their fellow escort wings, 12,000 feet over Hastings, above a 9/10ths cloud layer between 7,000 and 9,000 feet.

Flt Lt Glen (MB801), leading 41 Squadron's Blue Section was compelled to return with rudder problems after a short time in the air, and landed again within 25 minutes of having departed. The rest of the formation proceeded across the Channel and on to the target without incident.

Arriving over St. Omer at 17:17, 5/10ths cloud was encountered, which did not hinder the bombing itself but made both aiming and observation of results difficult. The Marauders dropped a total of four hundred and one 500 lb. bombs from 11,000 feet, the results of which were considered fair to poor. Bursts were seen to land to the north and northeast of the airfield, whilst some were also seen in the city itself.

However, very intense Flak was experienced and whilst this did not cause any human casualties, two bombers were damaged, but all returned to base. The Luftwaffe was not sighted at all, and the escorting squadrons operated according to plan, with nothing to report except Flak and weather conditions.

The Spitfire Wing XII landed again at 18:10 and this concluded the day's operational flying.

26 September 1943 – The Wing was only involved in a single operation during the morning. The intention was to escort Marauders targeting Conches-en-Ouche Airfield in Part II of Ramrod 247, but the operation was cancelled soon after take-off, when reports were received of poor weather over France.

Date	26 September 1943
Operation	Ramrod 247
Targets	Part I: Rouen-Sotteville Marshalling Yards, Haute-Normandie Part II: Conches-en-Ouche Airfield, Haute-Normandie
Bombers	Part I: 98 & 180 Squadrons: 18 Mitchells – aborted (weather) Part II: 72 Marauders; 72 dispatched – aborted (weather)
Close Escort Part I Escort Cover High Cover Top Cover Fighter Sweep Close Escort Part II Escort Cover High & Top Cover Fighter Sweep	Newchurch: 132 & 602 Squadrons (Spitfire Vb) – aborted Staplehurst: 401, 411 & 412 Squadrons (Spitfire Vb) – aborted Tangmere: 197 & 486 Squadrons (Typhoon Ib) – aborted Hornchurch: 129 & 222 Squadrons (Spitfire IX) – aborted Northolt: 302 & 303 Squadrons (Spitfire IX) North Weald: 331 & 332 Squadrons (Spitfire IX) Heston: 306 & 308 Squadrons (Spitfire Vb) – recalled Westhampnett: 41 & 91 Squadrons (Spitfire XII) – recalled Headcorn: 403 & 421 Squadrons (Spitfire IX) – recalled Kingsnorth: 19 & 165 Squadrons (Spitfire IX)
Casualties	401 Sqn: Sqn Ldr Ian C. Ormston EF, baled out of Spit Vb, BM627, 10m N of Le Crotoy, RR.

Part I's bombers and escorts had reached as far as a point seven miles east of Dieppe when the operation was cancelled at 09:21, on account of 10/10ths cloud in layers between 6,000 and 20,000 feet. The Close Escort, Escort Cover and High Cover Wings all returned with the bombers, although 401 Squadron's Commanding Officer was obliged to bale out into the Channel after his aircraft developed engine trouble. The Top Cover and Fighter Sweep Wings both continued on, undertaking uneventful sweeps.

The Spitfire XII Wing was airborne at 09:30, led by Wg Cdr Harries to rendezvous with Part II's bombers and fellow escort wings. However, shortly after take-off, the operation was cancelled on account of the weather, presumably a result of reports from Part I. The Close Escort and Escort Cover Wings were recalled prior to rendezvousing with the bombers, whilst the High Cover and

Top Cover Wings were recalled 20 miles off the English coast. Only the Fighter Sweep operated as planned, but their operation was uneventful.

The Spitfire XII Wing was back on the ground within 15 minutes of their departure, and as the weather remained unsuitable for the rest of the day, the Wing was not called upon again. However, being Battle of Britain Sunday, the men attended a service in Chichester Cathedral, led by the Bishop of Chichester. It was,

> ...preceded by a Parade through Chichester in which members of the Civil Defence, Army and Royal Air Force took part. The salute was taken by the Commanding Officer of R.A.F. Tangmere, together with the Mayor of Chichester.[233]

27 September 1943 – Following two relatively quiet days, the Wing was back in the air today on two Ramrods, No. 250 to Beauvais-Tillé Airfield as Escort Cover, and No. 251 to Conches-en-Ouche Airfield, again as Escort Cover, and likely a re-run of the previous day's cancelled Ramrod to the same destination.

In the former of these, the Luftwaffe was encountered in force and every escort squadron engaged. Both 41 and 91 Squadron claimed victories, as did Wg Cdr Harries, but on this occasion there were no casualties to report.

Date	27 September 1943
Operation	Ramrod 250
Targets	Part I: Rouen-Sotteville Marshalling Yards, Haute-Normandie Part II: Beauvais-Tillé Airfield, Picardie
Bombers	Part I: 18 Mitchells; 19 dispatched, 18 bombed Part II: 72 Marauders; 72 dispatched, 64 bombed
Casualties	Part II: 30 Marauders CD/AA
Close Escort Part I	Newchurch: 132 & 602 Squadrons (Spitfire Vb) Staplehurst: 401, 411 & 412 Squadrons (Spitfire Vb)
Escort Cover	Tangmere: 197 & 486 Squadrons (Typhoon Ib)
High Cover	Headcorn: 403 & 421 Squadrons (Spitfire IX)
Top Cover	Kingsnorth: 19 & 122 Squadrons (Spitfire IX)
Close Escort Part II	Heston: 306 & 308 Squadrons (Spitfire Vb) Ibsley: 310, 312 & 313 Squadrons (Spitfire Vb)
Escort Cover	Westhampnett: 41 & 91 Squadrons (Spitfire XII)
High Cover	Hornchurch: 129 & 222 Squadrons (Spitfire IX)
Top Cover	North Weald: 331 & 332 Squadrons (Spitfire IX)
Fighter Sweep	Northolt: 302 & 303 Squadrons (Spitfire IX)
Casualties	306 Sqn: Flt Sgt Arkadiusz Bondarczuk SD/KIA in Spit Vb, EE683; 313 Sqn: Flt Sgt Tomáš Zrnik SD/KIA Beauvais in Spit Vb, BM293

Part I's bombers and escorts rendezvoused according to plan and proceeded to Rouen-Sotteville Marshalling Yards without interference from the Luftwaffe. Eighteen Mitchells bombed the target, dropping a total of forty-eight 1,000 lb. bombs and a similar number of 500 lb. bombs from 12,000 feet at 10:00. Results were considered good and bursts were reported on the northern side of the rail yards and by the locomotive repair shop. No casualties were reported and all squadrons returned with little else to report.

Part II was a very different operation. The Spitfire XII Wing was airborne at 10:00 and rendezvoused with the Marauders and escort squadrons 15 miles west of Berck-sur-Mer at 12,000 feet at 10:25. The target was approached without issue but in scenes reminiscent of the attack on Beauvais-Tillé Airfield on 24 September, the Luftwaffe intercepted them in force in the target area.

The Close Escort Wing's Polish squadrons first sighted six to eight FW190s over Beauvais, which were engaged with the result that one was shot down by 306 Squadron for the loss of one of their own. The Close Escort's Czech squadrons engaged twenty FW190s, which approached them head-on in the same area. In the ensuing engagements, one enemy aircraft was claimed destroyed by 310 Squadron, and three damaged by 313 Squadron, but at the cost of one pilot from the latter unit.

As the bombers banked to starboard for their final bombing run, two full Luftwaffe squadrons dived onto the Spitfire XII Wing from the north. From this point onward, all the way back to the French coast, the Wing was constantly in combat with formations of 10 to 15 enemy aircraft, as numerous attacks on the bombers were driven off.

Fg Off Clive Birbeck broke with his No. 2, Sgt Plt Peter Graham, as the initial attack was made approaching the target. Birbeck fired at a FW190 in a group of four at extreme range, but was unable to hit it and gave up the chase. Looking about, the two pilots saw approximately fifteen enemy aircraft[234] above them above them, and climbed.

Picking out an Me109G, Birbeck opened fire with his cannon and hit its starboard wing. He was then himself attacked and forced to break away, unable to finish the job. As this was going on, Graham spotted three FW190s approximately 15 miles northwest of Beauvais climbing from below them, in a steep climbing turn to starboard. Being in an advantageous position, he fired a three-second burst of both cannon and machine gun fire, and saw several strikes on its hood causing a piece to fly off.

Graham broke off without pressing the attack home, to re-join Birbeck, but immediately sighted two more FW190s diving on them from 7 o'clock. He called out to Birbeck on the R/T to break, which both he and Birbeck did. They dived to 5,000 feet, then looked back to see the FW190s had given up. Deciding it was time to head home, the pair flew in and out of the cover of broken 4/10th cloud at 6,000 feet towards the coast.

When approximately ten FW190s climbed in front of them near Dieppe, Birbeck and Graham climbed to engage them. Picking one out, Birbeck fired three bursts at the aircraft, which soon emitted thick black smoke. Graham, covering Birbeck's tail, then spotted another two FW190s coming in behind them. He shouted a warning to Birbeck and both pilots broke away, "forced to make a strategic retreat"[235], and dived again. The two enemy pilots soon gave up the chase and the pair returned to base "without further molestation".[236]

The two pilots landed at base at 11:30, where Birbeck claimed one FW190 and one Me109G damaged, having expended 156 rounds of cannon and 528 rounds of machine gun in doing so. Graham also claimed one FW190 damaged for the expenditure of 60 rounds of cannon and 260 rounds of machine gun ammunition.[237] Graham's *Pilot Service Record* adds,

> 27.9.43 – 10:40 Beauvais Damaged a F.W. 190 with 60 Rds cannon & 260 S.A.A. F.O. Birbeck & Sgt Graham made [a] determined attack to prevent attacks on bombers damaging three e/a between them & driving enemy off successfully. The large number of e/a prevented further observation of results to e/a in each case.[238]

In the meantime, Wg Cdr Harries had also been in action. When the original large group of Luftwaffe fighters dived, he ordered 91 Squadron to attack them. He then saw one Marauder lagging approximately four miles behind the rest of the formation. When some fifteen Me109s proceeded to attack the lone aircraft, Harries "quickly brought 41 Squadron on the scene and several dog fights ensued".[239]

One of these Messerschmitts sighted Harries and banked around to make a head-on attack upon him. One step ahead of his aggressor, Harries turned into him, forcing the dull grey camouflaged Me109G to dive away. Jumping on his tail, Harries turned the tables and chased him down to ground level with his No. 2, 41 Squadron's Flt Lt Dave Fearon, close behind.

Closing rapidly, Harries opened fire from dead astern, with a one-and-a-half second burst from 300 yards range, and saw immediate strikes on the Messerschmitt's fuselage. Following it down through a thin layer of cloud, he saw it enter a spin, emit thick black smoke, followed by fire, and finally hit the ground in a wood. Fearon had also opened fire on an Me109 in the mêlée but had observed no results.[240]

91 Squadron's Yellow Section, Flt Lt Richard Easby and Fg Off Albert O'Shaughnessy, also had successful combats. Initially unsuccessful in an attack on the first group of enemy aircraft to dive on the bombers, the pair headed home on the deck when they sighted an aircraft off to starboard. Approaching to investigate, it proved to be an Me109, which O'Shaughnessy then attacked. He closed to 150 yards before opening fire, and obtaining many strikes, which resulted in the Messerschmitt bursting into flames and crashing in a field.[241]

Continuing on towards the coast, Easby sighted another Me109, this one flying across their path on the deck. Turning onto its tail, he made a quarter attack from its starboard side, closing in to full astern, firing as he did. Pieces began to fly off the Messerschmitt, which suddenly climbed steeply to 500 feet. Easby continued to fire at the now much larger target presented him, until the Me109 started to disintegrate. Bursting into flames, it fell to earth and crashed in flames. Each man claimed an Me109 destroyed.

Hornchurch's High Cover Wing was also in action. Having initially sighted fifteen FW190s that had dived on the bombers from the northeast, they ended up engaged with an estimated 50+ enemy aircraft for a full fifteen minutes at altitudes down to 6,000 feet. The net result was that Wg Cdr William Crawford-Compton claimed one FW190 damaged, 129 Squadron claimed two damaged Me109s, and 222 Squadron claimed three FW190s destroyed and three damaged for no casualty.

North Weald's Top Cover Wing arrived over the target approximately two minutes ahead of the rest of the formation and immediately headed off twelve FW190s and two Me109Gs heading for the bombers. 331 Squadron claimed one Me109G destroyed, but no other victories could be claimed, despite further engagements with six to eight enemy aircraft on the way back to the coast.

Finally, the Fighter Sweep was undertaken by Northolt's Polish squadrons, which swept the Dieppe-Neufchatel-Mantes-Abbeville area. Two of 302 Squadron's pilots who returned early from the sweep encountered two FW190s in the Le Tréport and destroyed one of them.

The Spitfire XII Wing returned to base without any damage but did so individually, in pairs, or in sections, most of 41 Squadron's pilots opting to land at forward bases to refuel before continuing to Westhampnett:

Pilots, 27 Sep 1943	Serial	Section	Up	Down	Location
Harries, Raymond H.	MB836	Red		11:35	Friston
Fearon, David N.	EN234	Red		11:35	Friston
Lane, Roy	MB844	Red		11:40	Lympne
Gray, James A. B.	EN237	Red		11:40	Lympne
Smith, Donald H.	MB845	Yellow	10:00	11:35	Friston
Hope, Alan	MB838	Yellow	10:00	11:35	Friston
Newman, Bernard B.	MB857	Yellow	10:00	11:35	Friston
Wall, Peter R.	MB834	Yellow	10:00	11:40	Westhampnett
Moffett, H. Bruce	MB837	Blue		11:40	Friston
Vann, William H.	EN231	Blue		11:35	Friston
Birbeck, Clive R.	EN608	Blue		11:30	Friston
Graham, Peter B.	MB798	Blue		11:30	Friston

Today's victories for the Spitfire XII Wing were as shown in the following table. 41 Squadron's damaged enemy aircraft were the last such victories claimed for almost another year, whilst 91 Squadron's victories brought their total number of enemy aircraft destroyed during the War to exactly 100. Moreover, they also made 91 Squadron the top-scoring unit in 11 Group this month, having claimed no less than 18 enemy aircraft destroyed.

Victories, 27 Sep 1943	Unit	Dest	Dam	Location
Birbeck, Clive R.	41 Sqn	-	Me109G	Beauvais-Dieppe
			FW190	
Graham, Peter B.	41 Sqn	-	FW190	15 miles NW of Beauvais
Harries, Raymond H.	Wg Ldr	Me109G	-	Beauvais area
Easby, Richard S.	91 Sqn	Me109	-	
O'Shaughnessy, Albert G.	91 Sqn	Me109	-	

In all, the Ramrod's claims amounted to nine destroyed, one probable and 14 damaged for the loss of two pilots. Throughout all this, 64 of the 72 dispatched Marauders had managed to drop a total of six hundred and twenty 300 lb. bombs through 6/10ths-8/10ths alto stratus cloud, with considered fair results. It was just as intensive for the bombers and the fighters and 30 Marauders suffered battle damage from Flak and enemy aircraft. They also repulsed their own fair share of enemy fighters and whilst all the bombers returned, they claimed four aircraft destroyed, five probable and three damaged.

11 Group plotted a total of 63 enemy fighters that engaged the RAF and USAAF in Part II of Ramrod 250. It was felt that 30 each were from the Luftwaffe's Cambrai and Courtrai [Kortrijk] Wings, which had been airborne to attack Part I, but had not engaged them. The RAF clearly did a good job of protecting the bombers as a Luftwaffe radio message was intercepted and translated stating, "the Spitfires were protecting the bombers very well".[242]

The Spitfire XII Wing was given a five-hour respite before it was called upon again. On this occasion, the Wing participated in a repeat of the previous day's cancelled attack on Conches-en-Ouche Airfield, providing Escort Cover to 72 Marauders. The Ramrod had only one objective, but considering the morning's encounter with significant numbers of Luftwaffe fighters, the RAF was up in force to cover the bombers. A full 26 squadrons of fighters were deployed, providing in addition to the usual escort format an additional two squadrons for Escort Cover, and an additional two for High Cover, two for Forward Target Cover, four for Rear Withdrawal Support and two fighter sweeps of each two squadrons.

Date	27 September 1943
Operation	Ramrod 251
Target	Conches-en-Ouche Airfield, Haute-Normandie
Bombers	72 Marauders; 72 dispatched, 68 attacked
Casualties	386 BG/552 BS: Marauder 41-34987, AA Yvetot, ditched Channel, 10m SSW of Dieppe (4 KIA, 2 RR); 387 BG/558 BS: Marauder 41-31666, CD nr Conches, crash-landed UK
Close Escort	Digby: 402 & 416 Squadrons (Spitfire Vb)
	Heston: 306 & 308 Squadrons (Spitfire Vb)
Escort Cover	Westhampnett: 41 & 91 Squadrons (Spitfire XII)
	Ibsley: 310, 312 & 313 Squadrons (Spitfire Vb)
High Cover	Biggin Hill: 341 & 485 Squadrons (Spitfire IX)
	Hornchurch: 129 & 222 Squadrons (Spitfire IX)
Top Cover	Northolt: 302 & 303 Squadrons (Spitfire IX)
Forward Target Cover	Kingsnorth: 65 & 122 Squadrons (Spitfire IX)
Rear Withdrawal Support	Newchurch: 132 & 602 Squadrons (Spitfire Vb)
	Staplehurst: 401, 411 & 412 Squadrons (Spitfire Vb)
1st Fighter Sweep	Headcorn: 403 & 421 Squadrons (Spitfire IX)
2nd Fighter Sweep	North Weald: 331 & 332 Squadrons (Spitfire IX)
Casualties	129 Sqn: Fg Off Rowland D. Rosser SD/KIA in Spit IX, MH440; 222 Sqn: Flt Sgt Thomas B. Hannam SD in Spit IX, MH390, ER; 331 Sqn: Sgt Plt Arlid Hellan, poss. oxygen failure, into Channel in Spit IX, MA305 †; 402 Sqn: Plt Off Robert E. Crewe RCAF, SD/KIA in Spit Vb, BM152

At 16:50, the Spitfire XII Wing took off "with great expectation"[243] to rendezvous with the Ramrod's bombers and escorts at 17:10 at 12,000 feet, 20 miles north-northwest of Fécamp. Finding the bombers had arrived four minutes early, the wing had to increase speed to catch up but crossed in and proceeded to the target as planned.

Before reaching the target area, two enemy aircraft dived past the Close Escort squadrons, followed by ten Me109s, which dived out of the sun. There were no engagements with these aircraft but two Me109Gs were attacked between Triqueville and Conches, of which Wg Cdr Lloyd Chadburn destroyed one and damaged the other.

Ten FW190s then bounced 402 Squadron in the Bolbec area. In the subsequent engagements, 402 Squadron claimed one probably destroyed and two damaged, and Wg Cdr Chadburn claimed another probably destroyed. However, it came at the cost of one pilot from 402 Squadron who was shot down and killed.

The Escort Cover Wing sighted two groups of enemy aircraft in the target area, one of at least 15 and the other of around four, but both were too far away to engage. On leaving the Conches area, however, four Me109s, and an FW190 operating individually, attempted to bounce the Ibsley Wing, but the FW190 was destroyed instead for no loss to the Wing.

The High Cover Wing sighted three formations of enemy aircraft in the target area, and four Me109s and four FW190s also dived past them, which could not be engaged. However, the Hornchurch Wing was bounced by 20+ mixed Me109s and FW190s out of the sun at 20,000-22,000 feet near Bernay at 17:25. When multiple combats ensued, more enemy aircraft joined in the pitched battle, which continued for almost 15 minutes.

129 Squadron returned home claiming two FW190s destroyed and one FW190 and one Me109 damaged, whilst 222 Squadron claimed one Me109 destroyed. However, the victories came at the cost of a pilot from each squadron, one of whom was killed and the other who evaded and returned to England to fly again.

The remaining elements of the Ramrod, the Forward Target Cover, Rear Withdrawal Support and Fighter Sweep wings all otherwise operated according to plan and did not sight the Luftwaffe. 331 Squadron did, however, lose one pilot not due to enemy action. He dived into the Channel and was killed, believed to have been the result of oxygen failure.

Meanwhile, 68 of the 72 dispatched Marauders attacked Conches-en-Ouche Airfield in hazy conditions at 17:26, dropping a total of three hundred and seventy-five 300 lb. bombs and five hundred and twenty-three 100 lb. bombs, which were seen to land "dead on target".[244] The Luftwaffe failed to reach the bombers, but Flak claimed one aircraft, which ditched in the Channel ten miles south-southwest of Dieppe, killing four of the six crew.

The Spitfire XII Wing landed at Westhampnett again at 18:20, with the exception of 41 Squadron's Sgt Plt Peter Wall (EN237) who landed at Friston short of fuel. This concluded the day's operational flying.

Separately, Flt Lt Roy 'Lulu' Lane was posted away around this time, having spent almost six months with 41 Squadron. He is last mentioned in the Squadron ORB flying operationally on 27 September 1943, but the exact date of his departure is unknown. Little is also documented of his exact subsequent movements, but it is known that he was promoted to Squadron Leader and sent to Southeast Asia, where he is understood to have worked closely with the Chindits on the ground in Burma, likely as an air liaison officer. It appears he was captured by the Japanese in April 1944, and died – some reports suggest he was beheaded – on 26 April 1944, aged just 24. It was a sad end for a young man who had been in the RAF since 1938 and seen significant action during the Battle of Britain. He is buried today in Taukkyan War Cemetery, Myanmar (Burma).

28-30 September 1943 – There was no operational flying by the Wing during the last three days of the month on account of "very rough, cloudy and cold"[245] weather conditions, with the exception of a single, uneventful shipping reconnaissance to Le Havre by 91 Squadron on 29 September.

41 Squadron's programme was wound back significantly during these days. Although some synthetic training was carried out, the three days were generally spent relaxing, which included a hockey game against the Operations Room staff. "One game turned out an "all in" affair, and a few casualties were sustained on both sides".[246]

During these few days of the month, two pieces of news reached the Wing that are worthy of note. Firstly, the Wing received a congratulatory message to the AOC 11 Group, AVM Hugh Saunders, from the Under Secretary of State for Air, Sir Archibald Sinclair, who had visited Westhampnett in late August, stating,

> *I have followed with admiration in recent weeks the remarkable exploits of your Spitfire XII Wing. I should be grateful if you would convey my congratulations to Wing Commander Harries and to the officers and men both of 41 and 91 Squadron. The destruction of 16 German aircraft in the last four weeks by No. 91 Squadron is an outstanding achievement.*[247,248]

The message was well received and "cheered the boys up tremendously"[249], particularly as the other piece of news they received was not so welcome. The Wing was advised they would be moving from Westhampnett to Tangmere on 4 October, and packing began immediately. However, "knowing Tangmere and the usual R.A.F. Station surroundings"[250], it was felt that the Wing would miss Westhampnett's Officers Mess in Shopwyke House and its 'delightful' gardens.

October 1943 – It was a much quieter month for the Squadron than the previous, and the progression into winter particularly obvious. Weather hampered operations during October to such an extent that there was no operational flying by the Squadron on fourteen days: 1, 5-7, 10-12, 16, 19, 21, 27, and 29-31 October 1943, and limited flying on another four: 13-15 and 28 October. It was still a busy month, however, and 14 Ramrods and two Rodeos were flown on the remaining 12 days, and one pilot was killed in action.

△ Airfield   🏭 Industrial Target   ▲ Tactical Target

Date	Operation	Role	Type	Destination / Target
2	Ramrod 256	Escort Cover	△	St. Omer-Longuenesse, France
3	Ramrod 257	Escort Cover	△	Lille-Vendeville, France – CXLD
3	Ramrod 257	Escort Cover	△	Woensdrecht, Netherlands
3	Ramrod 258	Withdrawal Cover	🏭	Chevilly-Larue, France
3	Ramrod 259	Escort Cover	△	Beauvais-Tillé, France
8	Ramrod 264	Escort Cover	△	Lille-Vendeville, France
9	Ramrod 266	Fighter Sweep	△	Woensdrecht, Netherlands
18	Ramrod 272	Escort Cover	△	Évreux, France

18	Ramrod 273	Fighter Sweep	▲	Ault-Abbeville-Poix-Amiens, Fr.
18	Ramrod 274	Fighter Sweep	⟁	St. Omer, France
20	Ramrod 277	Fighter Sweep	▲	Le Tréport, France
22	Ramrod 280	Fighter Sweep	⟁	Évreux-Fauville, France
22	Ramrod 282	Escort Cover	⛫	Le Grand-Quevilly, France – CXLD
24	Ramrod 283	Escort Cover	⟁	Beauvais-Tillé, France

2 October 1943 – Following four days of poor weather that had prevented the Wing from flying operationally, the two Squadrons were back in the air today, participating in a single Ramrod 256, in which they provided Escort Cover to 72 Marauders attacking St. Omer-Longuenesse Airfield.

Date	2 October 1943
Operation	Ramrod 256
Targets	Part I: St. Omer-Longuenesse Airfield, Pas-de-Calais Part II: Calais-Fontinettes Marshalling Yards, Pas-de-Calais
Bombers	Part I: 72 Marauders; 72 dispatched, 6 bombed Part II: 98 & 180 Sqns: 24 Mitchells; 24 dispatched – aborted
Casualties	Part I: 11 Marauders CD/AA, 1 crew KIA
Close Escort Part I Escort Cover High Cover Top Cover Fighter Sweep Close Escort Part II	Staplehurst: 401, 411 & 412 Squadrons (Spitfire Vb) Westhampnett: 41 & 91 Squadrons (Spitfire XII) Biggin Hill: 341 & 485 Squadrons (Spitfire IX) Northolt: 302 & 303 Squadrons (Spitfire IX) North Weald: 331 & 332 Squadrons (Spitfire IX) Coltishall: 64 & 611 Squadrons (Spitfire Vb) Digby: 350 Squadron (Spitfire Vb)

The Spitfire XII Wing was airborne at 16:40, led by Sqn Ldr Ingham in the absence of Wg Cdr Harries, and rendezvoused with the bombers and fellow escort squadrons 12,000 feet over Dungeness at 17:00. This was Flt Lt Tom Slack's first operational sortie since being shot down on 18 July. However, he only participated in this one operation before being detached on a lecture tour of RAF stations on the subject of evasion, which continued until 18 December 1943.

The formation crossed in between Boulogne and Hardelot but as the weather was still not ideal and cloud obscured St. Omer, only six Marauders were able to find the target and drop their payloads. These consisted of a total of thirty-six 500 lb. GP bombs, but the results were unobserved. Whilst the Luftwaffe was not seen, moderate heavy Flak was experienced that caused damage to 11 Marauders and killed one of the aircrew.

The bombers and escorts crossed out again between Knokke and Zeebrugge, Belgium, shortly after which the Spitfire XII Wing left the bombers and flew straight for South Foreland. On making landfall, they made a new course for Westhampnett where they landed at 18:20, with the exception of WO James Still (EN237) who landed at Friston at 18:10, presumably a result of fuel shortage.

Part II was scheduled to rendezvous 12,000 feet over North Foreland at 17:05 but the bombers headed out without waiting for the escort wings to join them. The Coltishall Wing struggled to catch up and followed them across the Channel, but were ordered back to base when the bombers aborted the operation at 17:10, approximately three minutes from the French coast. All aircraft returned to their respective bases and there were no casualties.

3 October 1943 – In one of their busiest days in some time, the Squadron participated in three Ramrods today, one target of which lay in the Netherlands, and two in France. The Spitfire XII Wing actually participated in two Parts of the first Ramrod, which was designed as a diversion and withdrawal cover for attacks by USAAF Bomber Command heavy bombers on targets in Western Germany.

Little information is available on the participants of Part I of Ramrod 257 to Lille-Vendeville Airfield and the 11 Group ORB only states that it was cancelled. However, 41 Squadron's ORB indicates that the Spitfire XII Wing was airborne at 07:10 to provide Escort Cover, but were recalled and landed again at Manston at 08:15.

The Wing was then airborne again from Manston at a few hours later, this time assigned to Part II of the same Ramrod, to provide Escort Cover to 72 Marauders targeting Woensdrecht Airfield in the Netherlands.

Date	3 October 1943
Operation	Ramrod 257
Targets	Part I: Lille-Vendeville Airfield, Pas-de-Calais, France Part II: Woensdrecht Airfield, Noord-Brabant, Netherlands Part III: Schipol Airfield, Noord-Holland, Netherlands Part IV: Withdrawal Support – cancelled
Bombers	Part I: 72 Marauders – cancelled Part II: 72 Marauders; 72 dispatched, 60 bombed Part III: 72 Marauders; 72 dispatched, 72 bombed Part IV: Withdrawal Support – cancelled
Casualties	Part II: 14 Marauders CD/AA Part III: 38 Marauders CD/AA
Close Escort Part II	Perranporth: 66 & 453 Squadrons (Spitfire Vb) Heston: 306 & 308 Squadrons (Spitfire Vb)
Escort Cover	Westhampnett: 41 & 91 Squadrons (Spitfire XII)
High Cover	Biggin Hill: 341 & 485 Squadrons (Spitfire IX)
Top Cover	Headcorn: 403 & 421 Squadrons (Spitfire IX)
1st Fighter Sweep	Northolt: 302 & 303 Squadrons (Spitfire IX)
2nd Fighter Sweep	Kingsnorth: 65 & 122 Squadrons (Spitfire IX)
Close Escort Part III	Digby: 402 & 416 Squadrons (Spitfire Vb) Coltishall: 64 (Spit Vb) & 611 Squadrons (Spit IX)
Escort Cover	Ibsley: 310, 312 & 313 Squadrons (Spitfire Vb)
High Cover	Hornchurch: 129 & 222 Squadrons (Spitfire IX)
Top Cover	North Weald: 331 & 332 Squadrons (Spitfire IX)

The Wing took off from Manston at 10:40 with the exception of 41 Squadron's Sgt Plt William Vann (MB798) whose "flight [was] cancelled".[251] The pilots rendezvoused with the bombers and other escort wings 25 miles north of Knokke at 11:00 and proceeded to the target unopposed.

The Marauders arrived over Woensdrecht Airfield at 11,000 feet at 11:25 but 8/10ths cloud hindered bombing by two boxes. As such, only 34 Marauders bombed the primary target, dropping a total of two hundred and ninety-eight 300 lb. bombs on the target. However, 26 Marauders also attacked a secondary target, Haamstede, on which they dropped another two hundred and fifty-nine 300 lb. bombs between 11:28 and 11:36.

The bombing was initially considered fair by the bombers, but the Close Escort Wing later reported they considered the results good, as several bursts were seen in the dispersals area at Woensdrecht. The Luftwaffe was not seen by the bombers and whilst no Flak was encountered at Haamstede, moderate accurate Flak was experienced at Woensdrecht and 14 Marauders suffered a degree of damage.

The Escort Wings and Fighter Sweeps operated generally according to plan and uneventfully, with the exception of the Canadian squadrons of the Top Cover Wing. Encountering twenty-five FW190s in the target area, they returned home claiming one destroyed for no loss. The Spitfire XII Wing landed at Manston again at 12:15, in time for lunch.

In the meantime, the Ramrod's Part III, to Amsterdam's Schipol Airfield, had also taken place. The target was approached unhindered, but the High Cover Wing engaged a group of approximately twenty Me109s that attempted to reach the bombers, diving out of the sun from above and behind. These were engaged by 129 Squadron, whose pilots claimed three enemy aircraft destroyed for no loss.

The attack by the Me109s having been repelled, the 72 Marauders made their attack on Schipol according to plan, dropping three hundred and forty-nine 300 lb. bombs and two hundred and eleven 500 lb. bombs at 11:20. The USAAF felt the results were fair to good, whilst the Close Escort Wing considered results excellent, having observed bursts among airfield buildings and the dispersals area. Flak was, however, moderate to intense and 38 Marauders were damaged.

The Luftwaffe made its presence felt on the return journey, and before reaching the Channel coast to cross out, the Close Escort Wing had engaged a number of Me109s, claiming two Me109s destroyed and three damaged. The High Cover Wing also engaged three Me109s, of which one was claimed destroyed. The Top Cover Wing also sighted six Me109s and two FW190s and attempted to engage them, but were unable to. All aircraft on Part III returned and no casualties reported beyond the Flak damage sustained by the Marauders.

Following lunch, the Spitfire XII Wing was briefed for their next operation, a significantly smaller Ramrod, in which they were required to provide Withdrawal Cover for 12 RAF Bostons conducting a low-level attack on Chevilly-Larue Power Station, outside Paris.

The three Parts of the Ramrod only called for the combined deployment of six wings of aircraft – 13 squadrons – but proved costly. Four bombers were shot down, and six Spitfires were lost. Three fighter pilots evaded and returned, two pilots ditched in the Channel and were rescued, and 41 Squadron lost one pilot killed in action.

Date	3 October 1943
Operation	Ramrod 258
Targets	Part I: Distré Power Station, Maine-et-Loire Part II: Chaingy Transformer & Switching Station, Loiret Part III: Chevilly-Larue Power Station, Île-de-France
Bombers	Part I: 88 Sqn: 12 Boston III; 12 dispatched, 8 bombed Part II: 107 Sqn: 12 Boston III; 12 dispatched, 12 bombed Part III: 342 Sqn: 12 Boston III; 12 dispatched, 11 bombed
Casualties	Part I: 88 Sqn Bostons BZ316 & BZ322, AA Distré, both ditched in Channel[252]; Part III: 342 Sqn: Boston BZ319, AA Chevilly-Larue, crashed Paris, & Boston BZ388, AA Chevilly-Larue, crashed Crépy-en-Valois, NE of Paris[253]
Withdrawal Cover Pt I Withdrawal Cover Pt II Withdrawal Cover Pt III	Tangmere: 197 & 486 Squadrons (Typhoon Ib) Newchurch: 132 & 602 Squadrons (Spitfire Vb) Headcorn: 403 & 421 Squadrons (Spitfire IX) Staplehurst: 401, 411 & 412 Squadrons (Spitfire Vb) Westhampnett: 41 & 91 Squadrons (Spitfire XII) Biggin Hill: 341 & 485 Squadrons (Spitfire IX)
Casualties	41 Sqn: Flt Sgt James A. B. Gray, SD/KIA in Spit XII, MB834, Crèvecœur-le-Grand; 341 Sqn: Lt George R. Lents, SD Somme Est in Spit IX, JL347, ER; 485 Sqn: WO Bert S. Wipiti, SD/KIA Somme Est in Spit IX, JK769; Fg Off James E. Mortimer DFC, SD Somme Est in Spit IX, MH490, ER; & Flt Sgt Neville E. Frehner, CD from Me109s in Spit IX, MH351, baled out 10m S of Dungeness, RR; 486 Sqn: Flt Sgt C. James Sheddan SD/AA in Typhoon Ib, EK272, ditched 35m NNE Pte Barfleur, RR

Flt Sgt James A. B. Gray served with 41 Squadron from 11 July 1943 to 3 October 1943, when he was killed at Crèvecœur-le-Grand, France. The reason for his loss is unknown; he was not seen to go down and no mayday was heard. Aged 22 at the time, he is buried today in Abbeville.
© Livingston Family

Part I's withdrawal cover Wing reached the rendezvous point, ten miles north of Vire in Lower Normandy, at 3,000 feet at 14:46. When no bombers were seen after orbiting for 10-15 minutes, the Tangmere Wing returned home without them. The Luftwaffe did not interfere, but one of 486 Squadron's pilots was hit by Flak and ditched in the Channel.

In the meantime, eight Bostons completed the attack on Distré Power Station in two boxes at 500 feet and 1,500 feet. Thirty 500 lb. bombs were dropped at 14:20, eight of which were fitted with 11-second delay fuses, achieving good results. However, two Bostons were shot down by Flak, and ditched in the Channel, resulting in the deaths of two men and the rescue of four.[254]

Part II's Spitfire Vb and IX squadrons reached the rendezvous point, 12 miles northeast of Falaise, Normandy, at 14:39, the Newchurch Wing at 3,000 feet and the Headcorn Wing at 9,000 feet. In a repetition of Part I, when the Spitfires orbited for ten minutes but saw no bombers, they gave up and headed home, the failure to rendezvous with them assumed to be a result of cloud conditions. However, the bombers were sighted on the way home, a significant distance ahead of them, out over the Channel.

The 12 Bostons had attacked Chaingy Transformer & Switching Station in two boxes at 50 feet and 1,500 feet, at 14:12. They dropped forty-five 500 lb. bombs, twenty-three of which contained 11-second delay fuses. Results of the bombing were considered good and all aircraft returned safely.

The Spitfire XII Wing took off from Manston at 13:40 in order to rendezvous with Part III's other two escort wings at Crèvecœur-le-Grand at 14:16, the Staplehurst Wing to arrive at 3,000 feet, the Westhampnett (Spitfire XII) Wing at 6,000 feet, and the Biggin Hill Wing at 10,000 feet.

The Spitfire XII Wing was led by Wg Cdr Harries and 41 and 91 Squadrons by their respective Commanding Officers. 41 Squadron deployed eleven aircraft, Sgt Plt Vann's MB798 notably missing again. However, barely airborne, three pilots returned owing to the failure of their jettison tanks – Flt Lt Don Smith (MB845), WO James Still (MB837), and Flt Sgt Jimmy Payne (MB797) – and only eight of the Squadron's pilots crossed the Channel.

After crossing in, the Staplehurst Wing sighted fifteen FW190s flying southwest at 6,000-8,000 feet between the French coast and Abbeville, which were believed to be elements of JG2 and JG26. These were engaged by 412 Squadron and in the ensuing combats the unit's pilots claimed two destroyed and one damaged for no loss.

Both the Spitfire XII and Biggin Hill Wings reached the rendezvous point on time where several orbits were made but the bombers were once again not seen. After waiting 15 minutes, the two Wings turned for home, but the latter wing finally caught sight of the bombers on their way home over the Somme Estuary. However, they also intercepted around 20 enemy aircraft which were engaged with the results of one Me109 and two FW190s destroyed and one FW190 damaged, at the cost of three of the Wing's pilots shot down, and one pilot sustaining combat damage serious enough to necessitate him baling out off Dungeness. Fortunately, the first three pilots all evaded and returned to the United Kingdom, and the latter pilot was rescued by ASR.

Although the Spitfire XII Wing had no engagements with the Luftwaffe, Flt Sgt James Gray (MB834) was lost on the return journey. He was "seen to be lagging behind the squadron and was told to catch up"[255] and was last seen by fellow pilots orbiting with the Squadron at the rendezvous point. However, he did not return. Nothing was seen or heard, and no-one had any information to add after the pilots landed back at Westhampnett at 15:10.

His disappearance was a complete mystery at the time. Fellow pilot Fg Off Ron Johnson noted in his logbook, "F/Sgt Gray missing for no apparent reason"[256], whilst his *Pilot Service Record* states, "Missing 3.10.43 [blank] hrs. Not seen to go down and no R.T. heard. No Mayday."[257] The 22-year-old Glaswegian is thought to have been shot down by the Luftwaffe over Crèvecœur-le-Grand and is buried today in Abbeville Communal Cemetery Extension. The Squadron ORB eulogised him thus: "Gray had not been with the Squadron very long, but showed himself to be a keen quiet boy. He was well liked by his fellow pilots."[258]

Meanwhile, Part III's twelve Bostons had attacked Chevilly-Larue Power Station, outside Paris, in two boxes, the first at 500 feet and the second at 1,500 feet. They dropped forty-six 500 lb. bombs, twenty-three of which had 11-second delay fuses, with good results. However, the Flak was accurate in the Crépy-en-Valois area and two of the twelve bombers failed to return.

In an unusual move, several enemy aircraft followed the Ramrod's bombers back across the Channel and made landfall between Brighton and Hastings. They strafed RAF Ford, and dropped anti-personnel butterfly bombs on the airfield, which resulted in it being closed and rendered unserviceable for the rest of the day. Aircraft already airborne from the Station were compelled to land at Tangmere instead.

There was no rest for the weary, however, and the Spitfire XII Wing had barely landed from the above operation when they were called to a briefing for the next: Ramrod 259, as escort cover to 72 Marauders bombing Beauvais-Tillé.

Date	3 October 1943
Operation	Ramrod 259
Targets	Part I: Beauvais-Tillé Airfield, Picardie Part II: Le Grand-Quevilly Power Station, Haute-Normandie
Bombers	Part I: 72 Marauders; 72 dispatched, 64 bombed Part II: 12 Mitchells; 12 dispatched, 12 bombed
Casualties	Part I: 9 Marauders missing, 30 Marauders CD/AA
Close Escort Part I	Staplehurst: 401, 411 & 412 Squadrons (Spitfire Vb) Perranporth: 66 & 453 Squadrons (Spitfire Vb)
Escort Cover	Westhampnett: 41 & 91 Squadrons (Spitfire XII)
High Cover	Hornchurch: 129 & 222 Squadrons (Spitfire IX)
Top Cover	North Weald: 331 & 332 Squadrons (Spitfire IX)
1st Fighter Sweep	Northolt: 302 & 303 Squadrons (Spitfire IX)
2nd Fighter Sweep	Headcorn: 403 & 421 Squadrons (Spitfire IX)
Close Escort Part II	Newchurch: 132 & 602 Squadrons (Spitfire Vb)
Escort Cover	Heston: 306 & 308 Squadrons (Spitfire Vb)
High Cover	Biggin Hill: 341 & 485 Squadrons (Spitfire IX)
Top Cover	Kingsnorth: 65 & 122 Squadrons (Spitfire IX)

Casualties	66 Sqn: Flt Sgt A. J. Edwards SD/WIA in Spit Vb, BL762, POW; 222 Sqn: Flt Lt Raymond B. Hesselyn DFC DFM, SD/WIA in Spit IX, MH783, POW; 403 Sqn: Sgt Plt S. Barnes SD nr Roye in Spit IX, MA648, POW; 421 Sqn: Fg Off William F. Cook RCAF, SD in Spit IX, BS532, ER.

The Wing took off again at 16:40 led by Wg Cdr Harries, whilst 41 Squadron was led by Sqn Ldr Ingham. Ten minutes into the operation, Fg Off Ron Johnson (MB801) pulled out with engine trouble, and landed again at 17:00. In fact, Johnson had not had a good day at all, recording in his logbook, "Everything went wrong for me – S [MB846] had flat tyre – oil filter cap of X [MB801] blew off on take-off, landed and took off again but engine cut on jet tank."[259]

The rest of the Wing continued on and rendezvoused on time with Part I's bombers and escort wings, 30 miles south of Dungeness at 12,000 feet at 17:03. The formation traversed the Channel and approached Beauvais without problem, with the exception of the Top Cover Wing, which was bounced just after they crossed in at Dieppe. The Luftwaffe was otherwise not seen until leaving the area, following the bombing.

The Top Cover Wing never made it to the target area, as they were attacked by two formations of FW190s and Me109s in the Rouen area. In the ensuing combats, one FW190 and two Me109s were claimed destroyed and one FW190 and one Me109 damaged by 331 Squadron, one FW190 was claimed destroyed by 332 Squadron, one FW190 claimed destroyed by the Wing Leader, Maj Kaj Birksted, and one additional, unidentified aircraft claimed destroyed by the Wing, all for no loss.

Sixty-four of the 72 dispatched Marauders attacked Beauvais-Tillé Airfield, dropping two hundred and fourteen 500 lb. bombs and two hundred and eighty-five 300 lb. bombs at 17:25 from 11,000 feet. Results were considered good, and in fact 41 Squadron felt they were excellent as they observed bombs falling on the dispersals area. However, intense accurate heavy Flak was met at Beauvais and light Flak on the coast, and nine Marauders were shot down. The Spitfire XII Wing saw one of these aircraft ditch, reporting to the Tangmere Controller having observed "a large splash… in the sea just after crossing out over the coast".[260]

On the way out, the Close Escort Wings sighted large numbers of FW190s and Me109s climbing towards the bombers from the southwest. More enemy aircraft approached the Marauders in the Poix area. These were engaged, but the various combats only resulted in one claim for a damaged FW190 by 453 Squadron at the cost of one pilot of 66 Squadron shot down, wounded and captured.

The Spitfire XII Wing operated generally uneventfully and only saw five enemy aircraft, which did not attempt to engage them. They landed again at 18:20, concluding a long day's flying, but with little to report on this operation.

It was a very different story for the High Cover Wing, which was bounced out of the sun by approximately thirty FW190s and Me109s. One Me109 was destroyed by 222 Squadron, but the pilot responsible for the victory was himself subsequently shot down and captured. Incidentally, that pilot, Flt Lt Raymond B. Hesselyn DFC DFM, RNZAF, would become 41 Squadron's Commanding Officer for a brief period in 1951.

The two Fighter Sweeps also saw action, the Northolt Wing claiming two of four engaged FW190s damaged in the first of these. The Canadian squadrons of the Headcorn Wing swept the Hardelot-Béthune-Amiens-Roye area in the second, and engaged an estimated 60 enemy aircraft. Each squadron claimed two FW190s destroyed, but also each lost a pilot, 403 Squadron's pilot being captured and 421 Squadron's successfully evading.

Part II had meanwhile also taken place, and operated according to plan, with no interference from the Luftwaffe whatsoever. Twelve Mitchells dropped a total of forty-eight 1,000 lb. bombs from 10,300 feet with fair results. Flak did not cause any issues, and all aircraft returned from the operation safely.

Tangmere

4 October 1943 – The Spitfire XII Wing moved from Westhampnett to Tangmere during the morning. Located three miles east of Chichester, Sussex, the airfield was opened in 1917 for use by the RFC, but was mainly utilised during World War I as a training base by American air services.

Closed after the Armistice in 1918, the station was re-opened in 1925 with the intention of serving the Royal Navy's Fleet Air Arm. When Tangmere was declared operational in 1926, however, its first residents were 43 Squadron RAF, and the airfield then remained in RAF service. With war looming, Tangmere was enlarged in 1939, which entailed demolishing several houses and the local pub. The RAF subsequently commandeered the majority of houses in the village and built a large number of additional buildings as the airfield grew in importance.

The Luftwaffe recognised the significance of Tangmere early in the War and sent one hundred Stukas and escort fighters to make a first attack on 16 August 1940. Extensive damage was caused to both aircraft and infrastructure, and 20 people killed, but the airfield was rebuilt and brought back to full operational status again as soon as possible.

In time, Tangmere also become the hub of SOE activity, and dozens of agents were flown to and from France in Lysanders under the cover of darkness. By the time of the Spitfire XII Wing's arrival, the airfield's facilities included two concrete runways, one Type T2 hangar, two Bessonneau hangars, ten Blister hangars, and six others.

This would be 41 Squadron's only real stay at Tangmere of any significance during the War. The unit had served in the Tangmere Wing previously – at Merston and Westhampnett from July 1941 to April 1942, and of course at Westhampnett from June to October 1943 – but they had only been based at RAF Tangmere itself on two previous occasions. The first of these was a brief attachment for Operation *Jubilee*, the ill-fated Dieppe landings in August 1942, and the second an even shorter stay for an aborted exercise in October that same year.

During the early afternoon, the pilots were in the dispersals area still organising furniture and personal belongings when, "above the general hubbub"[261], they were surprised to hear they were being scrambled. Having only just received a new call sign a few hours earlier, many did not even recognise that they had been called. Suddenly, all…

> …*the pilots on readiness hurled themselves at the nearest exit (in some cases the window) in a mad rush to be 'first off'. The whole Squadron had scrambled in some four minutes and had set course – a very creditable effort considering they were taken somewhat unawares.*[262]

The Squadron was scrambled to Pointe Barfleur to provide air cover for an ASR operation then in progress. This is believed to have been for fellow Tangmere-based 486 Squadron's Flt Sgt 'Jim' Sheddan who had ditched 35 miles north-northeast of Barfleur during Ramrod 258 to Chevilly-Larue Power Station the previous afternoon.

Sheddan was quickly located but the operation began having difficulties when a Walrus sent out to retrieve him damaged a float landing on the sea, which was extremely choppy. Left little choice, High Speed Launches were sent out to retrieve Sheddan instead, and to bring home the Walrus crew, too, as a take-off was now out of the question.

41 Squadron only provided cover between 13:25 and 14:10, when it is assumed another squadron took over from them. In due course, Sheddan and the crew were transferred to the launches and the Walrus was "sunk on the spot".[263] Sheddan survived the ordeal and was admitted to Portsmouth Hospital to recover.

8 October 1943 – Following three days of weather that was unsuitable for operations, and only allowed limited practice flying, the Wing was back in the air again today on a Ramrod to Lille.

Fg Off Keith Curtis RCAF served with 41 Squadron from 8 October 1943 to 26 August 1944. He joined the RAF post-War and retired as a Squadron Leader in 1975. © Karen Neale

They provided Escort Cover to 72 Marauders attacking Vendeville Airfield, but the weather was still not ideal and all three parts of the Ramrod were aborted as a result.

Date	8 October 1943
Operation	Ramrod 264
Targets	Part I: Lille-Vendeville Airfield, Pas-de-Calais, France
	Part II: St. Omer-Longuenesse Airfield, Pas-de-Calais, France
	Part III: Chièvres Airfield, Hainaut, Belgium
Bombers	Part I: 72 Marauders; 72 dispatched – recalled (weather)
	Part II: 24 Mitchells; 25 dispatched – aborted (weather)
	Part III: 72 Marauders; 72 dispatched – aborted (weather)
Casualties	Part III: 6 Marauders CD/AA
Close Escort Part I	Staplehurst: 401 & 411 Squadrons (Spitfire Vb) – recalled
Escort Cover	Tangmere: 41 & 91 Squadrons (Spitfire XII)
High Cover	Hornchurch: 129 & 222 Squadrons (Spitfire IX)
Top Cover	North Weald: 331 & 332 Squadrons (Spitfire IX)
Close Escort Part II	Biggin Hill: 1 & 609 Squadrons (Typhoon Ib)
Escort Cover	Tangmere: 197 & 486 Squadrons (Typhoon Ib)
High Cover	Hornchurch: 198 Squadron (Typhoon Ib)
Close Escort Part III	Coltishall: 64 & 611 Squadrons (Spitfire Vb)
	Northolt: 306 & 308 Squadrons (Spitfire Vb)
Escort Cover	Newchurch: 132 & 602 Squadrons (Spitfire Vb)
High Cover	Northolt: 302, 303 & 317 Squadrons (Spitfire IX)
Top Cover	Ashford: 65 & 122 Squadrons (Spitfire IX)
Fighter Sweep	Headcorn: 403 & 421 Squadrons (Spitfire IX)

The Spitfire XII Wing took off from Tangmere at 15:15, with 41 Squadron deploying ten aircraft in sections of four, four and two, led by Sqn Ldr Ingham. The pilots rendezvoused with Part I's bombers and their fellow escort squadrons 12,000 feet over Dungeness at 15:30 and proceeded across the Channel as planned. However, prior to reaching the French coast, the Marauders were recalled on reports of 10/10ths cloud over France, and returned home accompanied by the Close Escort Wing.

41 and 91 Squadrons took the opportunity to continue on despite the weather, crossed in at Hardelot, and made a sweep as far as St. Omer and back, but the trip was uneventful. Very accurate Flak was experienced in an area believed to have been around St. Omer and some bursts occurred uncomfortably close to some of 91 Squadron's aircraft. The Wing crossed out in the Boulogne area, where more Flak was encountered, but returned to Tangmere without casualty, putting down at 16:35. Similarly, the High Cover and Top Cover Wings continued to France and made sweeps to Lille, respectively of the Boulogne area, but they, too, were uneventful.

Part II rendezvoused over Deal and initially proceeded across the Channel. However, at 15:40, whilst still 12 miles north of Calais, the operation was aborted on account of 10/10ths cloud with a ceiling of 4,000 feet. The Close Escort and High Cover Wings escorted the bombers back to the English coast, and then turned back for France to make independent sweeps. The former wing swept the St. Omer area and the latter the Gravelines-St. Omer-Berck area, both uneventfully. The Escort Cover Wing did not return with the bombers, but instead patrolled north of the Straits of Dover for 40 minutes, without making landfall in France. It, too, was uneventful.

Part III rendezvoused as planned, 12,000 feet over North Foreland at 16:20. Although the formation proceeded as far as the target area, the operation was no more successful than Parts I and II, as the Marauders were unable to locate Chièvres Airfield as a result of heavy ground haze and returned without bombing. Flak was nonetheless experienced and although the gunners must have been firing more-or-less blind, six Marauders were hit and damaged.

The escort wings operated uneventfully, and only the Close Escort Wing saw the Luftwaffe. This consisted of six aircraft sighted southwest of Chièvres, flying north, but no engagements ensued. Part III's Fighter Sweep, operating independently of the escorts, experienced accurate Flak from the Dunkirk and Mardyck areas, but reported the job otherwise uneventful.

Separately today, two Canadian pilots joined 41 Squadron, 21-year-old Plt Off Keith Curtis and 22-year-old Flt Sgt Bruce Adams.

Having joined the RCAF in July 1941, Curtis completed his flying training in Canada and was then retained as a Staff Pilot at No. 1 Wireless School at St. Hubert, Quebec. He was commissioned in November 1942, and released for operations in March 1943, when he embarked for the United Kingdom. Curtis completed advanced and operational flying training between May and September 1943, and was now posted to 41 Squadron with 583 flying hours in his logbook, but none operational.

Adams joined the RCAF in October 1941 and also completed his flying training in Canada, but was shipped to the United Kingdom on Christmas Eve 1942. He attended advanced and operational flying training schools between April and September 1943, and arrived on 41 Squadron today, as his first operational unit, having previously logged 350 non-operational flying hours.

9 October 1943 – The Spitfire XII Wing participated in a single Ramrod today, providing a fighter sweep in support of an attack by Marauders on Woensdrecht Airfield in the Netherlands. The jumping off point was Hawkinge, to which airfield they flew at 12:30.

Date	9 October 1943
Operation	Ramrod 266
Target	Woensdrecht Airfield, Noord-Brabant, Netherlands
Bombers	72 Marauders; 75 dispatched, 67 bombed
Casualties	16 Marauders CD/AA

Close Escort	Coltishall: 64 (Spit Vb) & 611 Squadrons (Spit IX)
Escort Cover	Newchurch: 132 & 602 Squadrons (Spitfire Vb)
High Cover	Hornchurch: 129 & 222 Squadrons (Spitfire IX)
Top Cover	North Weald: 331 & 332 Squadrons (Spitfire IX)
1st Fighter Sweep	Tangmere: 41 & 91 Squadrons (Spitfire XII)
2nd Fighter Sweep	Northolt: 302, 303 & 317 Squadrons (Spitfire IX)
3rd Fighter Sweep	Headcorn: 403 & 421 Squadrons (Spitfire IX)
4th Fighter Sweep	Kingsnorth: 65 & 122 Squadrons (Spitfire IX)
5th Fighter Sweep	8th USAAF: 1 Group of Thunderbolts

The Spitfire XII Wing was airborne from Hawkinge at 14:35, 41 Squadron deploying ten aircraft and 91 Squadron twelve. The pilots rendezvoused with the bombers and escort wings 23 miles north of Zeebrugge at 8,000 feet at 15:00, then proceeded at Wg Cdr Harries' discretion.

The Wing crossed in at Flushing [Vlissingen] whereupon medium heavy Flak opened up on the bombers. Several received superficial damage, but all were able to continue. After crossing in at 11,000 feet, 41 and 91 Squadrons dived to 7,500 feet, then performed a wide sweep to port 10-15 miles behind the target area.

Meanwhile, 67 of the 75 Marauders attacked Woensdrecht Airfield without interference from the Luftwaffe. As a result of poor visibility created by haze up to 5,000 feet, one of the two boxes of Marauders made a second run over the target, but the lack of opposition in the air meant this could be done successfully. The Marauders dropped a total of two hundred and three 500 lb. and three hundred and six 300 lb. GP bombs with fair to good results. The Close Escort was more confident, reporting the centre of the airfield and dispersals area were "well and truly bombed".[264]

The Spitfire XII Wing completed their sweep uneventfully, in time to follow the box of bombers making their second run over the target. They then escorted them out to the coast and left them shortly afterwards, making directly for Manston, likely a result of petrol shortage. Fg Off Peter Cowell was certainly getting nervous about fuel, noting in his logbook after his return, "Awful bind. No 2 landed with 7 galls!".[265] 41 Squadron put down at Manston at 16:05 after 90 minutes in the air, and refuelled before returning to Tangmere at 18:00.

Many years later, Fg Off Ronald Johnson related the difficulties of such long distance operations. Although his comments cannot be correlated with any specific event or operation, it does give a good indication of the types of issues the pilots experienced:

> *I do remember that we had some difficulty with drop tanks. We were supposed to use the petrol from them first and then on a signal drop them before we crossed the enemy coast because there would be danger from the petrol vapour left in them if hit by flak or bullets. Once on a long trip to Woensdrecht in Holland my tank would not come off in spite of all sorts of violent manoeuvres to try and release it. I hated coming back because so often when this happened to others (by the way it was an instruction to do so if the tank would not release) and they, or the fitter, had pulled the release after landing the tank fell gently on the ground to the accompaniment of knowing looks, winks and nods amongst the ground crews. I was certainly relieved when they had to get a hammer and hacksaw to get my tank off.*[266]

The remaining fighter sweeps on the Ramrod also operated uneventfully, and returned to their respective bases with little to report and no casualties to record.

12 October 1943 – There was no operational flying on 10, 11 and 12 October, but Flt Lt Jerzy 'George' Solak was posted away from the Squadron during this period. He had served with 41 Squadron since early April 1943 and, following a six-month tenure, was now rested on a posting to Headquarters, Fighter Command, as Polish Liaison Officer. Solak returned to operations in June 1944 when he joined the USAAF's 492nd Fighter Squadron, but was shot down over Normandy and captured two months later. Solak managed to escape, however, returning to his unit within ten

days, and continued to fly until December 1944, when he was posted to Headquarters, Polish Air Force. He emigrated to the United States in 1946, and died there in 2002, aged 92.

13 October 1943 – The weather was not conducive to large scale operations today, but it did suit Rhubarbs, and sections from 41 and 91 Squadrons were given permission to undertake such an operation.

41 Squadron's Fg Off Herb Wagner (MB850) and WO James Still (MB838), were airborne at 14:35 as Red Section and were assigned an area bounded by Cabourg, Mézidon-Canon, Lisieux and Trouville-sur-Mer. Making landfall three miles west of Trouville, and finding 10/10ths cloud between 600 and 1,000 feet, the pair headed southwest until they came across a stationary locomotive with four coal trucks just south of Saint-Julien-le-Faucon. Both men attacked the engine, leaving it in smoke and steam.

Continuing on towards Falaise, they found two more locomotives on minor lines just south of Villy-lez-Falaise. The two men attacked one engine each, seeing numerous strikes on both and steam emanating from the damage. Subsequently reaching Falaise Marshalling Yards, Wagner made an attack on another locomotive and a number of freight wagons, observing strikes on all of them. Still was about to do the same when heavy Flak opened up and he swerved to port to avoid it.

Deciding it was now time to head home, they headed towards the coast. As they did, they passed over a group of six or seven farmhouses approximately one and a half miles west of Falaise, where Flak guns were hiding and now opened up upon them. Still's Spitfire was hit in its port wing but the damage did not cause him any problems flying or handling the aircraft.[267]

The pair crossed out three miles west of Cabourg where they experienced yet more Flak, albeit light and inaccurate. However, approximately two miles off the coast, they were intercepted by six FW190s, with bright yellow fins and rudders, that approached them in pairs from the direction of Le Havre or Trouville. Wagner and Still turned into them, but "after approximately 10 minutes […] managed to shake them off"[268], then opened their throttles and made a beeline for England. They were chased at a range of 500-600 yards, to approximately mid-Channel, when the Luftwaffe gave up and let them go.

The two pilots made landfall over Brighton, and landed five minutes later, at 15:45, concluding the only operational flying undertaken by 41 Squadron all day. In achieving their ground victories, Wagner had expended 132 rounds of 20mm cannon and 400 rounds of .303 inch machine gun, and exposed seven feet of cine-gun film, whilst Still had expended 60 rounds of 20mm cannon and 200 rounds of .303 inch machine gun, and exposed five feet of film.[269]

14 October 1943 – A generally quiet day again today on account of weather, the first operational flying did not take place until 15:10, when Fg Offs Herb Wagner (MB850) and Ross Harding (EN603) took off as White Section to undertake a weather reconnaissance to Fécamp. They returned just 40 minutes later reporting conditions too poor for large operations.

The only other operational flying undertaken today was at 17:50 when Flt Lt Don Smith (MB845) and Flt Sgt Alan Hope (EN237) were sent out to find a Flying Fortress around 40 miles south of Selsey Bill that had lost its way on the return journey from a large daylight raid to Schweinfurt, Germany. They were intent on escorting the bomber back to England, but encountered conditions of very thick haze up to 3,000 feet with visibility of only half a mile. In addition, a cloud layer of 5/10ths-6/10ths lay between 3,000 and 4,000 feet.

Under these conditions, it comes as no surprise that they were unable to find it and returned at 18:40 in very poor visibility with nothing to report. Smith's comment on the operation in his logbook was simply, "Shaky do".[270]

Another Flying Fortress did, however, find its way to Tangmere on return from the same operation to Germany whilst Smith and Hope were absent:

> …members of the Squadron were greatly interested in another Fortress from the same raid that landed at Tangmere. The pilot had been severely wounded and later died in sick quarters – the copilot [sic] landed the machine which had a burst tyre and more holes than a colander. One engine caught fire just as the machine had stopped rolling. This incident did more to promote our good feeling and admiration for the Fortress crews than a hundred articles in the newspaper or talks on the radio.[271,272]

15 October 1943 – Today was an unusual one by recent standards, as the only operational flying undertaken was by six sections, who were ordered to patrol ten miles south of Ford, Sussex.[273] Three sections were airborne between 14:05 and 15:25 and another three from 16:00 to 17:15, but they were not sent out to intercept enemy fighters or shipping, rather their mission was a precautionary measure, which was…

> …presumably to protect Ford from any enemy air attack as there [were] many important people present at that station then, among them being P.M. Winston Churchill.[274]

The participants were as follows:

Name	Serial	Section	Up	Down
Smith, Donald H.	MB845	Red	14:05	15:25
Hope, Alan	EN237			
Cowell, Peter	MB837	Yellow		
Collis, Ronald T. H.	MB858			
Wagner, Herbert A.	MB850	White		
Still, James W.	MB794			
Glen, Arthur A.	MB846	Blue	16:00	17:15
Fisher, Douglas P.	MB847			
Johnson, Ronald	MB801			
Payne, Jim C. J.	MB804			
Birbeck, Clive R.	EN231			
Graham, Peter B.	MB798			

The task was uneventful, and the only issue was when Flt Sgt Jimmy Payne was compelled to land at Tangmere without flaps, but he did so safely. Clearly chuffed about the job, however, Wagner proudly noted in his logbook that day, "Protected Winston C. at Ford".[275]

Exercise Pirate

17 October 1943 – The Spitfire XII Wing was taken off offensive operations for a day in order to participate in Exercise 'Pirate', in which units of the 3rd Canadian Infantry Division and 83 Group were detailed to take part in an amphibious landing exercise. This took place on 'Charlie Green' and 'Charlie Amber' beaches in Studland Bay, southwest of Bournemouth, with the day prior referred to as 'D minus one Day' and the day of the exercise itself referred to as 'D Day'. It was clearly preparation for the assault on Normandy in June 1944 that we know today by the same name.

The assault convoy was to leave the Solent by Spithead in successive groups to a point 15 miles south of St. Catherine's Point on D-1, and make an assault on a 900 yard stretch of each of the two nominated beaches at 10:30 on D Day, 17 October.

Fighter squadrons from RAF Tangmere were assigned to provide air cover for the assault convoy during D-1. Night-fighters were assigned overnight and at dawn on D Day, cover was to be provided by a squadron of fighters on standing patrol until the assault was completed. Aircraft providing cover handed over VHF R/T control to the Controller of the Divisional Headquarters Ship and remain under their control until relieving squadrons arrived over the assault convoy. Any squadrons arriving over the assault whilst it was taking place were also to advise the Controller, on call sign 'Barnboy', of their approach.

For added protection for the exercise, anti-aircraft guns were given freedom to fire up to 2,000 feet, except where the identity of an aircraft was in doubt. They were also given permission to fire on any enemy aircraft above 2,000 feet, provided no Allied aircraft were in the vicinity. In order for this to operate safely, Allied aircraft were forbidden to fly under 3,000 feet at any time, unless pursuing enemy aircraft in the immediate vicinity of the assault ships. As such, any aircraft below this altitude, or seen to fly directly towards ships or landing craft were to be regarded as hostile.

41 Squadron was not required to participate in 'Pirate' on D-1, but was airborne at 07:10 on D Day, 17 October, to provide air cover. It is understood that sections from other squadrons were also airborne at this time on similar duties. 41 Squadron's first patrol consisted of Red Section (Smith MB845 & Still EN603), who arrived over the assault convoy on time and advised Barnboy of their arrival. They then proceeded to patrol one to three miles south of the assault, between St. Catherine's Point and The Needles, and later reported sighting three destroyers, six small transports and numerous landing craft.

The exercise did in fact draw some attention from the Luftwaffe, and at 07:35 the first plot was picked up five miles south of St. Pol, which was tracked to Bembridge, Southampton, west of Winchester and back to Bembridge at a height of 5,000 feet. Two sections from 197 Squadron, a section from 609 Squadron and another two from 198 Squadron were scrambled to intercept it.

A Messerschmitt Me210 was also sighted at 12,000 feet in the Beachy Head area between 07:43 and 08:21, and an unknown aircraft was also plotted at 8,000 feet in the Newhaven area between 07:51 and 08:07, which one of the airborne sections from 197 Squadron was sent to intercept. Another unidentified aircraft was plotted at 3,000 feet around Brighton and to the town's north between 08:11 and 08:19, and a further aircraft was plotted at 5,000 feet between 08:16 and 08:32, southwest of Mayfield, and in the Pevensey and Hastings areas.

Although not stated, it was likely the result of one of these plots that 41 Squadron's White Section (Harding MB795 & Collis MB844) was scrambled to the south of the Needles at 08:10. It was, however, particularly difficult to find the hostile plots as the weather in the area consisted of 10/10ths cloud with a base of 2,000 feet, and steady rain.

Red Section (Smith and Still) were therefore very much on the lookout and perhaps not at all surprised when they, too, were vectored by Barnboy onto a 'bandit' soon after 08:00. However, when investigated, it eventuated the plots were actually 41 Squadron's Yellow Section (Smith MB858 & Hope MB850), which were just arriving in the area to take over the patrol from Red Section. It was soon evident that reception of messages between aircraft and Barnboy was too poor and an alternative solution was required. Within a short time the issue was resolved when messages were given to Tangmere Control to pass on to Barnboy.

White and Yellow Sections then relieved Red Section, which returned to Tangmere at 08:30. The two sections patrolled two to three miles south of the assault convoy but had little to report when they landed again at 08:50 and 09:00, respectively. B Flight's Blue, Green and Black Sections were sent up to relieve Yellow and White from 08:20 to 10:10, but were ordered to patrol south of Selsey Bill "owing to [the] presence of E/A in the Channel".[276]

When nothing eventuated, Green Section was recalled, and Blue and Black took over the air cover of the assault convoy as originally planned.[277] They landed again at 10:10 and were replaced in the air by five aircraft from B Flight, 91 Squadron, between 09:55 and 10:55, and by six aircraft from A Flight, 41 Squadron, between 10:20 and 11:50. 41 Squadron's six aircraft comprised the morning's original Red, Yellow and White Sections.

Both 91 and 41 Squadrons' pilots managed to make contact with Barnboy, although barely audible, and 91 Squadron was soon vectored onto two 'bogies', which turned out to be Spitfires.

By this time, however, visibility had improved significantly, and the weather had lifted to just 3/10ths cloud with a base of 3,000 feet, gradually clearing from the west.

Many landing craft were now seen by the two units, thereunder several three to four miles east of the invasion beaches, and another fifty approximately half a mile off the beaches, escorted by three destroyers, which were shelling the landing area. Six troop transports were sighted four to five miles off Handfast Point and three vessels were also seen laying a smoke screen off Bournemouth. Attesting to the size of the exercise, 100-150 invasion craft were then seen between Studland Bay and north of The Needles, escorted by motor gun boats and destroyers, whilst a small stationary convoy was sighted off Durleston Head.

41 Squadron's final participation in the exercise came at 12:15, when another six aircraft from B Flight took off to patrol over the exercise. Contact was made with Barnboy once again and orders were received to patrol at 11 o'clock from Barnboy's position. However, as Barnboy's location could not be identified, the six pilots patrolled south of the exercise instead, sighting on the way landing craft on the invasion beaches, troop transports lying off the beaches, and three groups of 50 landing craft four miles off Handfast Point. Minesweepers were also sighted operating to the south of the assault in improving weather. The pilots landed again at 13:20, and this concluded the Squadron's operational flying for the day.[278]

18 October 1943 – Back to normal operations today, the Spitfire XII Wing was assigned roles in three separate Ramrods, the first as Escort Cover to 72 Marauders attacking Évreux Airfield in Ramrod 272, the second as a Fighter Sweep in the Ault-Abbeville-Poix-Amiens areas in Ramrod 273, and the third as a Fighter Sweep to St. Omer in Ramrod 274.

Date	18 October 1943
Operation	Ramrod 272
Targets	Part I: Évreux Airfield, Haute-Normandie
	Part II: Beauvais Airfield, Picardie
Bombers	Part I: 72 Marauders; 36 dispatched – aborted (weather)
	Part II: 72 Marauders; 36 dispatched – aborted (weather)
Close Escort Part I	Coltishall: 64 (Spit Vb) & 611 Squadrons (Spit IX)
Escort Cover	Tangmere: 41 & 91 Squadrons (Spitfire XII)
High Cover	Northolt: 303 & 317 Squadrons (Spitfire IX)
Top Cover	Gatwick: 19 & 65 Squadrons (Spitfire IX)
Close Escort Part II	Biggin Hill: 401 & 412 Squadrons (Spitfire Vb) – recalled
	Heston: 306 & 308 Squadrons (Spitfire Vb) – recalled
Escort Cover	Detling: 132 & 602 Squadrons (Spitfire IX)
High Cover	Hornchurch: 129, 222 & 485 Squadrons (Spitfire IX)
Top Cover	Kenley: 403 & 421 Squadrons (Spitfire IX)
1st Fighter Sweep	North Weald: 331 & 332 Squadrons (Spitfire IX)

The Spitfire XII Wing was airborne at 08:40 and made rendezvous with the Marauders and escorts 15 miles west of the Somme Estuary at 12,000 feet at 09:00. On reaching the French coast, however, 10/10ths cloud at 5,000 feet was encountered, which stretched a considerable distance inland, beyond the target area.

Initially continuing inland, the Marauders aborted the operation over Évreux Airfield and returned home with their payloads intact. The Close Escort, Escort Cover and High Cover Wings accompanied the bombers to and from the target and reported the operation uneventful. The Luftwaffe was not seen and only slight heavy Flak was experienced 15-20 miles inland, which did not cause any casualties.

The Top Cover Wing failed to make rendezvous but hurried to catch up with the rest of the formation and set a direct course for Évreux. The wing flew to ten miles east of Dreux, then swept Triqueville and found and attached themselves to the withdrawing formation.

It was a similar story for Part II. Once again, the bombers aborted on finding 10/10ths cloud and all bombs were brought back. The two Close Escort Wings were recalled when still ten miles west of Beauvais Airfield, whilst the Escort Cover operated uneventfully. After the bombers aborted the operation, the High Cover Wing left the formation near Poix to investigate some aircraft in the area. Four FW190s were subsequently attacked by 485 Squadron, of which two were damaged, whilst another two were engaged by 222 Squadron 20 miles south of Le Tréport with no result. The Top Cover wing also encountered the Luftwaffe, when at least 50 enemy aircraft were sighted flying west at 22,000 feet, south of Abbeville. Five of these were attacked without result south of Forges, whilst the Fighter sweep operated uneventfully.

The Spitfire XII Wing landed at Tangmere again at 10:15, and had a little over three hours break before their next operation, which was designed to support USAAF heavy bombers attacking industrial targets at Düren, Germany.

Date	18 October 1943
Operation	Ramrod 273
Targets	Part I: Industrial targets, Düren, Nordrhein-Westphalen, Germany Part II: Diversion over North Sea
Bombers	Part I: 329 Flying Fortresses in 2 formations – recalled Part II: Liberators – recalled
Casualties	Part I: 3 Flying Fortresses FTR, 4 crew baled out of one Part II: 1 Liberator FTR
Penetration Sup 1st Frmtn Target Support Withdrawal Support Fighter Cover 1st Frmtn Penetration Sup 2nd Frmtn Target Support Withdrawal Support Fighter Cover 2nd Frmtn 1st Fighter Sweep 2nd Fighter Sweep 3rd Fighter Sweep	USAAF 66 FW/78 FG: 49 Thunderbolts – aborted USAAF 65 FW/4 FG: 48 Thunderbolts – aborted USAAF 67 FW/352 FG: 54 Thunderbolts – recalled USAAF 67 FW/356 FG: 52 Thunderbolts – recalled North Weald: 331 & 332 Squadrons (Spitfire IX) Northolt: 302, 303 & 317 Squadrons (Spitfire IX) USAAF 65 FW/355 FG: 55 Thunderbolts – aborted USAAF 65 FW/56 FG: 49 Thunderbolts – aborted USAAF 66 FW/353 FG: 52 Thunderbolts – recalled USAAF 66 FW/55 FG: 37 P-38 Lightnings – aborted Kenley: 403 & 421 Squadrons (Spitfire IX) Gatwick: 19 & 65 Squadrons (Spitfire IX) – aborted West Malling: 124 Squadron (Spitfire VII) Hornchurch: 129, 222 & 485 Squadrons (Spitfire IX) Detling: 132 & 602 Squadrons (Spitfire IX) Tangmere: 41 & 91 Squadrons (Spitfire XII)
USAAF Casualties	78 FG/84 FS: 2 Lt Franklin B. Resseguie, EF Lens-St. Omer in Thunderbolt 41-6240, ER; 355 FG/358 FS: 2 Lt Eugene W. Maben Jr, SD/KIA E of Cambrai in Thunderbolt 42-22533; 55 FG/38 FS: 2 Lt Hugh E. Gillette SD/KIA in Lightning 42-66519, into Channel
RAF Casualties	132 Sqn: Fg Off Ernest B. Overton, SD Berck-sur-Mer in Spit IX, MH481, POW; 602 Sqn: Plt Off Alister M. Finnie RAAF, SD/KIA Berck-sur-Mer in Spit IX, MH730

Part of the first formation of Part I's Flying Fortresses made landfall on the Continent with their escorts but cloud conditions – 6/10ths at 6,000 feet and 10/10ths between 23,000 and 28,000 feet – caused the operation to be aborted. The rest of the first formation aborted before crossing in, and the entire second formation were still over England when they were ordered to abort. Part II's diversion by Liberators was also abandoned as a result, and the bombers recalled early.

Those USAAF fighter squadrons that had not yet reached their rendezvous point were recalled, whilst those that had orbited for some time until compelled to return. Their presence attracted the Luftwaffe in significant numbers and approximately 100 enemy aircraft were plotted by Allied radar. One Me210 was claimed destroyed by the 56th Fighter Group northeast of Maastricht, but two Thunderbolts and a Lightning were also lost.

The RAF Fighter Cover wings for the first formation, from North Weald and Northolt, both operated uneventfully whereas the Fighter Cover for the second was a mixed bag. The Kenley Wing continued into France after the Fortresses were recalled, sweeping from Abbeville to Lille and back to St. Omer. 421 Squadron engaged a group of approximately eight FW190s at 16,000 feet near Lille, claiming one destroyed for two of their own aircraft damaged.

The Gatwick Wing saw the Fortresses forming up but little more, owing to cloud. They flew as far as Arras before giving up and returning to base. West Malling's 124 Squadron encountered severe icing as a result of 10/10ths cloud between 23,000 and 28,000 feet, and three aircraft returned early. The rest of the unit climbed above the cloud ceiling and flew as far as Berck, but saw no other aircraft and returned with nothing to report.

All three Fighter Sweeps carried out the operation as ordered, detailed to cover the Furnes [Veurne]-Ypres [Ieper]-Lille-Dunkirk area, Berck-sur-Mer area, and the Ault-Abbeville-Poix-Amiens area, respectively. The Spitfire XII Wing was assigned to the third of these.

The Hornchurch Wing, consisting of a total of 39 aircraft, carried out their sweep between 25,000 and 28,000 feet, sighting three FW190s near Lille, which were not attacked, and another 20 were later bounced by 485 Squadron near Dunkirk. Seeing the RAF coming, the Luftwaffe avoided the attack and 485 Squadron was unable to close.

The Detling Wing encountered a mixed group of twenty FW190s and Me109s at 28,000 feet in the Berck area. A number of engagements ensued during which two Me109Gs were claimed destroyed and one probably destroyed by 132 Squadron, and another probably destroyed by 602 Squadron, for the loss of a pilot from each squadron.

The Spitfire XII Wing also saw some action. Airborne at 13:30, 41 Squadron deployed ten aircraft led by Sqn Ldr Ingham, with the remaining two positions in Red Section filled by Tangmere Sector Commander, Gp Capt William J. Crisham and Wg Cdr Harries, the former flying as No. 2 to the latter.

The Wing operated generally according to plan and generally uneventfully, the exception being a minor engagement by 91 Squadron. Crossing in at Ault, the pilots met considerable cloud between 11,000 and 16,000 feet, and swept over Abbeville, Poix and Amiens.

In October 1943, the Air Ministry seriously considered re-equipping 41 and 91 Squadrons with the Mustang III. The plan did not, however, eventuate and 41 Squadron retained their Spitfire XIIs for another eleven months. © Public domain, U.S. Air Force Photo, National Museum of the US Air Force

Arriving over the latter town, ten Luftwaffe aircraft were seen approximately ten miles away, flying northeast at 18,000 feet. Clearly unaware of the Wing's presence, two Me109Gs detached themselves from the group and flew southwards. 91 Squadron's Fg Off Jacques Andrieux, flying as Blue 1, closed on one of the aircraft and opened fire, and it was subsequently seen to crash northwest of Amiens. He claimed it destroyed.

The Wing returned to Tangmere at 15:05 without further event. There was little rest, however, as the pilots were briefed for another operation straight after they landed. Once again a fighter sweep was on the cards and little more than an hour later they were airborne again, destined for St. Omer.

Date	18 October 1943
Operation	Ramrod 274
Targets	Part I: St. Omer-Longuenesse Airfield, Pas-de-Calais
	Part II: St. Omer-Fort Rouge Airfield, Pas-de-Calais
Bombers	Part I: 72 Marauders – recalled (weather)
	Part II: 72 Marauders – recalled (weather)
Close Escort Part I	Digby: 402 & 416 Squadrons (Spitfire Vb) – recalled
	Coltishall: 64 (Spit Vb) & 616 Squadrons (Spit IX) – recalled
Escort Cover	Detling: 132 & 602 Squadrons (Spitfire IX)
High Cover	Kenley: 403 & 421 Squadrons (Spitfire IX)
Close Escort Part II	Biggin Hill: 401 & 412 Squadrons (Spitfire Vb) – recalled
	Heston: 306 & 308 Squadrons (Spitfire Vb) – recalled
Escort Cover	Hornchurch: 129, 222 & 485 Squadrons (Spitfire IX)
High Cover	Northolt: 302, 303 & 317 Squadrons (Spitfire IX)
1st Fighter Sweep	North Weald: 331 & 332 Squadrons (Spitfire IX)
2nd Fighter Sweep	Tangmere: 41 & 91 Squadrons (Spitfire XII)
3rd Fighter Sweep	Gatwick: 19 & 65 Squadrons (Spitfire IX)
4th Fighter Sweep	Lympne: 56 & 609 Squadrons (Typhoon Ib)
5th Fighter Sweep	Tangmere: 197 & 486 Squadrons (Typhoon Ib)

In a repetition of the day's earlier operations, the bombers in both Parts I and II were recalled on account of weather conditions, accompanied by their Close Escorts.

Part I's bombers and escorts rendezvoused 12,000 feet over Dungeness at 16:35 and had only reached mid-Channel when the bombers turned for home. The Escort Cover Wing continued on to sweep the St. Omer area, and fired at four or five FW190s without result, whilst the High Cover Wing swept Lille and St. Omer uneventfully.

Part II's bombers and close escorts rendezvoused 12,000 feet over Beachy Head at 16:35 and also turned back mid-Channel. The remaining two escort wings continued to France and swept the Somme estuary to St. Omer, and 60 miles south of Beachy Head, respectively. The Escort Cover Wing engaged three Me109s, but these escaped into cloud and no conclusive claims could be made.

The five Fighter Sweeps all operated according to plan, the first to Nieuport [Nieuwpoort]-Walcheren-Nieuport-St. Omer at 16,000-23,000 feet, the second to St. Omer and Cap Gris Nez at 22,000 feet, the third to St. Pol and St. Omer, the fourth from Furnes [Veurne] to the Dutch Islands and back again at 11,000 feet, and the fifth to the Poix area at 6,000-8,000 feet. All but the second – the Spitfire XII Wing's part in the operation – were uneventful.

The Wing was airborne at 16:10, led by Wg Cdr Harries and made landfall at Berck-sur-Mer under Beachy Head Control. The pilots were then vectored southwards towards Abbeville at 18,000 feet and on reaching the town were informed that enemy aircraft were passing underneath them at 12,000 feet. Looking down, the pilots sighted ten FW190s and 91 Squadron immediately dived after them. The Luftwaffe saw them coming, however, and dived into thick haze at 8,000 feet, and successfully evaded.

Left little choice, 91 Squadron gave up the chase and climbed again to join 41 Squadron at 22,000 feet. The Wing then uneventfully swept St. Omer to Gris Nez together, where they crossed out at 10,000 feet, and landed again at 17:40, concluding the day's flying.

20 October 1943 – After a day on the ground as a result of inclement weather, it was another busy day for the Wing today, upon which they participated in a Rodeo and a Ramrod. It was, however, "the best day the squadron in particular, and the wing in general, has enjoyed for a very long time".²⁷⁹ The day's first operation provided significant action, and the Wing returned home claiming a total of ten enemy aircraft destroyed for no loss.

Date	20 October 1943
Operation	Rodeo 263
Targets	Part I: Bernay-Beaumont-Triqueville, Haute-Normandie Part II: Le Tréport-Beauvais Airfield-Abbeville, Picardie Part III: Furnes-Vitry en Artois Airfield-St. Omer, Pas-de-Calais
1st Fighter Sweep Pt I 2nd Fighter Sweep 3rd Fighter Sweep 1st Fighter Sweep Pt II 2nd Fighter Sweep 1st Fighter Sweep Pt III 2nd Fighter Sweep	Tangmere: 41 & 91 Squadrons (Spitfire XII) Northolt: 302, 303 & 317 Squadrons (Spitfire IX) Gatwick:19 & 65 Squadrons (Spitfire IX) Detling: 132 & 602 Squadrons (Spitfire IX) Kenley: 403 & 421 Squadrons (Spitfire IX) Hornchurch: 129, 222 & 485 Squadrons (Spitfire IX) North Weald: 331 & 332 Squadrons (Spitfire IX)
Casualties	485 Sqn: Fg Off Ronald L. Baker in Spit IX, JK762, believed MAC w. Fg Off John Thomson in Spit IX, EN559, Ostend, both pilots †; Plt Off Frank Transom, CD Ostend in Spit IX, MH364, baled out Margate, RR

Allocated the first Fighter Sweep of Part I, the Spitfire XII Wing was airborne at 09:10, 41 Squadron once again deploying ten aircraft, with Wg Cdr Harries leading as eleventh man and Gp Capt Crisham as his No. 2, and twelfth man in the formation. 91 Squadron was led by Sqn Ldr Kynaston.

The Wing crossed the Channel at zero feet until 15 miles west of Trouville-sur-Mer, where they commenced a climb to 8,000 feet, but upon doing so were informed by Control, "Enemy A/C travelling very fast, vector [010°] flat out".²⁸⁰ Harries turned the Wing northeast and led them towards Cap de la Hève, but the reported aircraft were not seen. Around Le Havre area, however, accurate Flak was encountered and Fg Off Clive Birbeck's aircraft was hit, although he was unhurt himself. He was forced to return home early, accompanied by his No. 2, Flt Sgt Peter Graham, and the pair landed safely at Tangmere at 10:05.

The rest of the Wing carried on northwards along the coast, made landfall between Cap d'Antifer and Étretat, and then swept back to Trouville under a band of 3/10ths cloud at 15,000 feet to re-join their originally planned route. Heading inland from Trouville in a south-easterly direction, they passed over Bernay, and continued on to Beaumont-le-Roger. Seven aircraft were seen on the eastern perimeter of the airfield of the latter town, which were presumed to be dummies, and cows were observed grazing on the western side of the airfield.

Continuing inland towards the north of Évreux, with the intent of sweeping around behind the town, Wg Cdr Harries caught sight of twenty-five to thirty FW190s and Me109s around ten miles north of the town, diving towards them from the west out of the sun and from 5,000 feet above them. Simultaneously, another Luftwaffe squadron climbed from below the Wing's starboard quarter and bounced 41 Squadron. 41 broke hard and split up "under heavy cannon and M.G. fire"²⁸¹ whilst those diving from above opened fire on 91 Squadron when still at extreme range. 91 Squadron banked to port and climbed to engage them, but the enemy aircraft turned and dived away steeply, and 91 gave chase. "It was in fact a badly timed bounce by the Hun and he paid for it."²⁸²

Within a short time, the entire Wing was split up and involved in a number of frenzied combats. Leading the Wing into the attack, Harries spotted an Me109G approximately 1,000 feet below him, at 7,000 feet, diving towards the ground. Opening his throttle, he followed it down and opened fire with a five-second burst when he was within 400 yards range. Striking his opponent when it was at just 500 feet above the ground, the Me109G flipped over and dived straight into the ground near Bernay and exploded. Gp Capt Crisham, who had followed remained by him throughout, confirmed the victory.

Now on the deck, he and Crisham headed in the direction of the French coast, when four Me109Gs dived from their starboard quarter to attack them near Rouen. Breaking into them, Harries managed to pull around behind one of the Messerschmitts, and fired a short burst with 2½ rings deflection. The aircraft immediately "whipped on its side and exploded on hitting the ground".[283]

One of the other Me109Gs fired at Harries and hit his aircraft with machine gun ammunition behind the cockpit, however it did not cause him any trouble and the two pilots quickly climbed into the cover of cloud. Evading the remaining three Messerschmitts, they crossed out near Fécamp and returned to Tangmere to claim two Me109Gs destroyed.

After the Wing was split up, 91 Squadron's Commanding Officer, Sqn Ldr Norman Kynaston was unable to successfully close on any enemy aircraft, but on the way back out to the coast on the deck sighted two FW190s ahead of him at 1,000 feet, just below the cloud base. He drew in behind them behind them and was joined by 91 Squadron's Fg Off Dennis Davy just as he was sighted by the Luftwaffe pilots. Opening their throttles, the pair gave chase and Kynaston was finally able to close on one, firing a short burst from 200 yards with about a half ring deflection. He hit the cockpit and engine, and the Focke-Wulf "dived gently into the bank of the River Seine".[284]

He and Davy headed home together, where Kynaston claimed the aircraft destroyed and Davy claimed a damaged locomotive on the Rouen-Le Havre line, which Kynaston had allowed him to attack on the way out. The locomotive, a "large Canadian type"[285], was pulling carriages with a Flak battery to its rear when Davy attacked. He was not hit by return fire and instead inflicted serious damage of his own.

91 Squadron's Yellow Section, led by Flt Lt John Doll, was attacked by three Me109Gs from head-on. They passed underneath the section and Doll pulled up sharply to port. On doing so, he was attacked by another two Me109Gs, which fired at him from his port quarter. Pulling further to port, Doll sighted yet another two Me109s, to his port and below. Turning the tables, Doll dived on the latter pair, splitting them apart, one banking to starboard and the other to port.

Pulling to starboard now, he chased the former of the two Messerschmitts and quickly closed to 300 yards, where he opened fire with a two second burst. However, he had not allowed for enough deflection, and missed his mark. In an effort to evade Doll, the Me109G's pilot pulled tightly to port but in doing so showed his wings. Doll fired another two-second burst and saw strikes, but then noticed another Me109G on his tail. Pulling around tighter to port, Doll kept firing at the Messerschmitt ahead of him, and reduced his deflection until "my cannon shells caught up to the correct deflection and removed the tail unit of the 109".[286] The aircraft flipped onto its back and went straight down.

Doll soon shook off the Me109 on his tail, then descended to tree-top height and made a beeline for the coast. On his way out, he fired randomly at a lorry and a barge, but saw no strikes on them, on both occasions "badly overshooting".[287] He arrived back in Tangmere safely, claiming one Me109G destroyed.

Also a part of 91 Squadron's Yellow Section, Fg Off Ray Nash became separated from the rest of the section when they were attacked head-on by the three Me109Gs. Climbing alone towards six aircraft at 10,000 feet, he soon recognised them as yellow-nosed FW190s and Me109s. Splitting up the sextet, Nash and his No. 2, Flt Sgt Richmond 'Red' Blumer, chased a pair of Me109Gs down to ground level, where they broke in different directions.

Nash chose the one that broke to starboard, and closed to just 300 yards at tree-top height, where he opened fire from dead astern. Buffeted by the Messerschmitt's turbulence, he was unable to reduce his range any further, but continued to fire, whereupon the Me109G "eventually crashed into a field, after receiving many hits, all over it".[288]

Blumer had meanwhile gone after the other, holding his fire until he had closed to within 300 yards range. He fired a one-second burst, and saw immediate strikes on its fuselage. Continuing to follow the Me109 around in its bank to port, he fired another one-second burst from 200 yards and saw pieces fly off it, and immediately afterwards the petrol tank, located beneath and behind the pilot, caught fire. The aircraft stalled, flipped onto its back and dived into the ground where it exploded. Deciding it was time to get out of the area, he headed for the coast, firing upon and damaging a tug on the Seine west of Rouen on the way.

Meanwhile, 41 Squadron had also been in action. With Harries and Crisham forming a part of the Squadron's formation of 12 aircraft, and Birbeck and Graham having returned early, the unit had been reduced to just eight of its own, but half of them claimed definitive victories today. These fell to Fg Offs Ron Collis, Peter Cowell and Benjamin Newman, and to Flt Sgt Douglas Fisher, although Fisher did not claim the victory until a year later, when it was granted.

After the Wing broke, Yellow 3, Fg Off 'Barney' Newman, was keeping an eye on the enemy aircraft coming down from above when he sighted an Me109G below him and dived on it, following it down from about 5,000 feet to just 500. He closed from 600 yards to just 100, and fired five bursts of machine gun and cannon as he did. He saw no strikes until he was closed to 100 yards, when he recognised,

> …*flashes on the wings and fuselage and pieces breaking off the A/C, some of which stuck my A/C damaging the air[s]crew. As I broke off the attack, I saw this A/C strike the ground and burst into flames.*[289]

Heading home, Newman saw another of 41 Squadron's Spitfires, which turned out to be Blue 3, Fg Off Peter Cowell, attacking an enemy aircraft. When the Squadron first broke, Cowell had banked hard to port and in doing so sighted an FW190 diving away on his port side.

Following this aircraft down, Cowell initially opened fire at 600 yards, making several bursts as he closed to 200-150 yards. Then reducing his range to just 50 yards, he fired another long burst from his machine guns. This had the desired affect and the starboard oleo leg dropped and the engine caught fire. Realising his Focke-Wulf was beyond saving, the Luftwaffe pilot baled out at between 1,000 and 500 feet, and the unmanned aircraft crashed in flames in a field. This was Cowell's first engagement.

Newman now joined up with Cowell and headed for the coast. They were attacked by another enemy aircraft that caused some minor damage to Cowell's aircraft, "which broke off its attack when we turned [towards it]".[290] They continued home, passing two FW190s on the way, but there was no further incident.

Cowell recorded in his logbook that day, "Squadron bounced by 20+ E/A. Wing destroyed 9. Got my first Hun, a 190 – Pilot baled out!"[291] Many years later, he recalled his first victory, commenting on his youthful exuberance with the benefit of hindsight, "I remember getting on his tail and firing like mad…".[292]

Fg Off Ron Collis, flying as Yellow 4, initially opened fire on an FW190 at 8,000 feet from a range of 400 yards whilst in a turn after the Squadron broke. The Focke-Wulf rolled onto its back and dived away, but Collis gave chase, firing several short bursts at suitable intervals, until the aircraft made a vertical turn, and white smoke issued from it.

Collis then saw his cannon fire strike the aircraft, which resulted in "a large flash about the cockpit".[293] Realising he had struck the FW190 a significant blow, he immediately pulled out of his descent, however, "owing to the speed of his dive, had to pull out at 3,000 ft. so violently as to split the back of the Spitfire".[294] As a result of the 'G Forces',

> *I blacked out badly and saw nothing until I was just clear of the ground doing about 500 M.P.H. In this recovering from the dive my A/C was damaged. The back being broken and the IFF set coming adrift into the rear of the fuselage.*[295]

Collis limped his Spitfire back to Tangmere, where he landed safely and noted in his logbook, "Broke back of my a/c pulling out of a dive. Cat B. Landed safely without further dam."[296] Believing his FW190 could not have recovered from its vertical dive at 2,000 feet, when he last saw it, Collis claimed the aircraft destroyed. However, it was denied and only "admitted probably destroyed on evidence in Form F. [Intelligence Report]".[297]

Feeling strongly about the victory, the Squadron disputed the ruling and wrote to 11 Group on 12 November 1943. A reply was received Wg Cdr Morris S. Whitehouse MBE, on behalf of the AOC 11 Group, AVM Hugh Saunders, on 20 December stating,

ASSESSMENT OF COMBAT CLAIMS

Reference is made to your TS/71/1/Int. date 12th November 1943, on the above subject, and it is notified for your information that Headquarters, A.D.G.B., after having given careful consideration to the case, have agreed that F/Lt. Collis' claim should be allowed as 1 FW. 190 destroyed.

2. It is requested that the pilot be notified accordingly and the Squadron records amended.[298,299]

Perhaps the most interesting victory of the day was that of Flt Sgt 'Jackie' Fisher, who did not claim his victory until 30 September 1944 as he was leaving the Squadron. A note on his Pilot Service Record states, "1 Me 109 forced down & destroyed without firing guns. Manoeuvred into the ground. Claimed a year later! & granted."[300]

Flying as Blue 2, Fisher attempted to keep an eye on the enemy aircraft coming down out of the sun, but had difficulty doing so for that reason.

A minute later from the excited remarks on the R/T I knew that 91 Squadron were being engaged. My leader Blue 1, went into a turn to port – I followed him and kept a lookout behind. As we turned port I saw 2 F.W. 190's coming in fast 300 yards away, slightly above from an angle of approximately 60°. I warned Blue 1 and he immediately pulled up and headed into sun, whilst I tightened my turn to port as hard as I could, and I saw the 190's roll on their backs and flash underneath me upside down.[301]

Fisher then started to reverse his bank, back to starboard, to keep the pair in view with the intention of following them down. However, as he rolled back to a straight position, he sighted a number of Me109s climbing steeply from below and firing at 41 Squadron's aircraft as they did. Now turning hard to starboard, a full 180°, he straightened out again just as an Me109 shot up almost vertically a mere ten yards in front of his spinner.

Pulling up quickly to follow him, Fisher found his speed was too low to close and the Messerschmitt quickly drew away. However, this aircraft was then attacked by another Spitfire, and Fisher followed them both down, watching from 1,000 yards behind as pieces flew off the Me109, after which it burst into flames and crashed.

As this occurred, Fisher was travelling south at 1,500 feet, doing 450 mph in a shallow dive. Looking around him, he then saw another Me109 slightly below and right in front of him. Setting up his attack,

I closed very rapidly and was about to open fire, when he suddenly turned hard starboard, flicked on to his back and flicked again into a vertical position, as I overshot him. He appeared to hang motionless for a second, and I turned right and kept him in sight. I saw him trying to pull out, but he hit the corner of a field and blew up.[302]

Making a half orbit around the burning wreck, Fisher turned for home at tree-top height and headed for the coast at a fast cruising speed of 300 mph. Within five or six minutes, he reached the Seine and spotted a large steam tug to his left. Deciding to take a shot at it, he turned towards it but suddenly "felt and heard a loud bang and my machine went almost on its back".[303]

He successfully recovered the aircraft from the direct Flak hit, but saw his port aileron was seriously holed. His first thought was to get out of the area and head home as quickly as possible, but found he was unable to keep the Spitfire level at any speed higher than 220 mph. Crossing out east of Fécamp, he maintained this speed across the Channel and landed safely back at Tangmere approximately ten minutes after the rest of the Squadron. In his Combat Report, he claimed the Me109 "forced down and destroyed".[304]

Almost 40 years later, Fg Off Ron Johnson, who was flying as Fisher's No. 1, leading Blue Section on the operation, recalled his own participation in the day's combats:

> *Huns were sighted well above us when we were just about to turn for home. The longest and most nerve wracking part of the affair was waiting for the Wing Leader's order to break. After the break I tried to get on to a 109 when another one flashed down past my nose seemingly only feet away. I have a vivid memory of the underside of a 109 – black crosses and all. I don't know if he had been firing at me but I wasn't hit. I sort of instinctively fired my guns but there could not have been a hope of hitting him. Eventually I found myself apparently alone and set course for home, head swivelling all the time until I spotted another Spit and joined up with him.*[305]

The pilots had all returned individually or in pairs, but the whole Wing was back on the ground between 10:40 and 10:50, "Everyone… feeling very pleased with themselves and eager to have another crack at the Hun".[306] There were no casualties at all, although several aircraft sustained Flak or combat damage to varying degrees. Including Fisher's Me109, which was only claimed a year later, the Wing's victories for the operation were as follows:[307]

Victories, Rodeo 263	Unit	Dest	Location	Cannon	SAA	Film (ft)
Blumer, Richmond A.	91 Sqn	Me109G	Bernay-Évreux	220	620	2
Blumer, Richmond A.	91 Sqn	Tug	Seine			
Collis, Ronald T. H.	41 Sqn	FW190	N of Rouen	173	704	5
Cowell, Peter	41 Sqn	FW190	Nr Bmnt-le-R.	280	1,280	7
Davy, Dennis H.	91 Sqn	Loco	Bmnt-le-Roger	120	560	yes
Doll, John C. S.	91 Sqn	Me109G	25m S Rouen	120	560	5
Fisher, Douglas P.	41 Sqn	Me109	Évreux	NR	NR	NR
Harries, Raymond H.	Wg Ldr	2 Me109G	Rouen	-	-	-
Kynaston, Norman A.	91 Sqn	FW190	Rouen	40	80	1
Nash, Raymond S.	91 Sqn	Me109G	Évreux	280	1,200	8
Newman, Benjamin B.	41 Sqn	Me109G	Nr Bmnt-le-R.	176	712	6

41 Squadron's participants in the Rodeo were as follows:

Name	Serial	Section	Up	Down
Ingham, Bernard	MB843	Yellow	09:10	10:40
Smith, Donald H.	MB838	Yellow	09:10	10:40
Newman, Benjamin B.	MB858	Yellow	09:10	10:40
Collis, Ronald T. H.	MB850	Yellow	09:10	10:40
Harries, Raymond H.	NR	Red	09:10	10:40
Crisham, William J.	NR	Red	09:10	10:40
Fearon, David N.	MB847	Red	09:10	10:40
Cowell, Peter	MB795	Red	09:10	10:40
Johnson, Ronald	MB801	Blue	09:10	10:40
Fisher, Douglas P.	MB804	Blue	09:10	10:50
Birbeck, Clive R.	EN605	Blue	09:10	10:40
Graham, Peter B.	MB798	Blue	09:10	10:40

All this had occurred, and yet the day had only begun. For all the action of the Spitfire XII Wing's first sweep of Part I, the second and third Sweeps were completely uneventful and no enemy aircraft were seen.

Part II's two sweeps to Le Tréport, Beauvais Airfield, and Abbeville were almost as uneventful, the only exception being the sighting of approximately half a dozen enemy aircraft seen on the ground near Crécy by the Kenley Wing on the Second Fighter Sweep. It was not until Part III that the Luftwaffe was encountered again, when the Hornchurch Wing was vectored onto enemy aircraft at 30,000 feet near Ostend [Oostende].

Climbing towards the area, 485 Squadron was surprised when they were attacked from below and behind by four FW190s. Two of the unit's pilots were killed, although they are believed to have collided with each other in the ensuing confusion, and one pilot's aircraft was hit by fire from the enemy aircraft, resulting in loss of glycol and his eventual abandonment of the Spitfire off Margate. The Squadron did, however, also claim one of the FW190s damaged. Meanwhile, the second sweep of Part III operated uneventfully.

After lunch, the Spitfire XII Wing was called upon again to participate in a Ramrod, this time providing a diversionary fighter sweep in the Le Tréport-Beauvais area. It was a small part in a large USAAF operation to Düren, Germany, supported by three USAAF Fighter Wings and four RAF Wings for penetration and withdrawal support, and three RAF Wings as fighter sweeps.

Date	20 October 1943
Operation	Ramrod 277
Targets	Rail Junction, Düren, Nordrhein-Westfalen, Germany Diversion: 25m N of Trouville to 40m N of Isigny, France
Bombers	1st Formation: 120 Flying Fortresses; 109 dispatched, 92 bombed 2nd Formation: 120 Flying Fortresses; 103 dispatched, 18 bombed Diversion: 2 Combat Wings, Liberators
Casualties	1st Formation: 7 Flying Fortresses lost & 1 ditched in Channel 2nd Formation: 2 Flying Fortresses lost
Penetration, 1st Formation	RAF: Kenley: 403 & 421 Squadrons (Spitfire IX) RAF: Gatwick:19 & 65 Squadrons (Spitfire IX)
Penetration Support	USAAF: 66 FW/78 FG: 50x P-47 Thunderbolt USAAF: 65 FW/56 FG: 50x P-47 Thunderbolt
Target Support	USAAF: 67 FW/352 FG: 50x P-47 Thunderbolt
Withdrawal Support	USAAF: 66 FW/55 FG: 41x P-38 Lightning
Penetration, 2nd Formation	RAF: North Weald: 331 & 332 Squadrons (Spitfire IX) RAF: Northolt: 302, 303 & 317 Squadrons (Spitfire IX)
Penetration Support	USAAF: 65 FW/355 FG: 51x P-47 Thunderbolt USAAF: 65 FW/4 FG: 49x P-47 Thunderbolt
Target Support	USAAF: 66 FW/353 FG: 54x P-47 Thunderbolt
Withdrawal Support	USAAF: 67 FW/356 FG: 54x P-47 Thunderbolt
1st Fighter Sweep 2nd Fighter Sweep 3rd Fighter Sweep	Hornchurch: 129, 222 & 485 Squadrons (Spitfire IX) – Gravelines Detling: 132 & 602 Squadrons (Spitfire IX) – Abbeville Tangmere: 41 & 91 Squadrons (Spitfire XII) – Le Tréport

The attack by the bombers of the first formation was completed generally according to plan, with 92 Fortresses attacking the primary target and dropping 194 tons of high explosive and incendiary bombs with unobserved results. The second formation changed plans when poor weather was encountered, and 17 bombed Gilze-Rijen Airfield, and one Woensdrecht Airfield, with fair results. The others returned without bombing, although a total of nine Fortresses were shot down by Flak, and one ditched in the Channel on its return journey.

The crew of the ditched bomber was later discovered in two dinghies approximately 25 miles east of Aldeburgh, Suffolk, by two Spitfires of 277 (ASR) Squadron. A Walrus was subsequently sent out but when it was unable to alight, it dropped flares to guide HSLs to the location and all ten men were rescued.

USAAF and RAF fighter cover for the first formation operated mainly uneventfully, but the second formation attracted approximately 65 enemy fighters from the Lille-Cambrai area, according to Allied radar plots. Thirty of these were sighted by the North Weald Wing at 25,000-27,000 feet diving out of the sun near Douai. Whilst the Northolt Wing operated uneventfully, 331 Squadron came away claiming three FW190s destroyed and one damaged for no loss, but also noted that one FW190 was probably destroyed by German Flak. The USAAF was also in action and claimed four enemy aircraft destroyed, two probably destroyed and six damaged for no loss of their own.

Supporting the operation, the First and Second Fighter Sweeps operated as planned, although uneventfully, and no enemy aircraft were seen. For their part in the operation, the Spitfire XII Wing was airborne at 12:55, led by Wg Cdr Harries, and crossed in at Le Tréport at 17,000 feet under Beachy Head Control.

The Wing was given a number of vectors, taking them over the Beauvais and Poix areas at the same altitude, although heavy Flak was experienced at Beauvais, which caused no damage. When over Gournay-en-Bray, contrails from unidentified aircraft were seen high above them, travelling northeast. These were presumably some of the Fortresses on their way to Düren.

A short time later, more aircraft were seen high over Poix to the north, followed by a sighting of formations of six and twelve aircraft at the same altitude as the Wing, but some distance to the north, and considered all too far off to engage. The French coast was re-crossed at Ault and the pilots landed back at Tangmere at 14:25, with the exception of 41 Squadron's Fg Off Ross Harding (EN231) and WO James Still (MB838), who landed at Friston at 14:15 short of fuel.

This concluded the day's operational flying, and during the evening "There was great celebration… in view of the day's success."[308] It did not take long for the Wing's exploits today to reach the highest echelons, and that same day a telegram was received from AOC 11 Group, AVM Hugh Saunders, congratulating them on their successful operation. It read,

> *MY HEARTFELT CONGRATULATIONS ON YOUR WONDERFUL RECORD THIS MORNING. THE FACT THAT HAVING BEEN BOUNCED BY THE HUN YOU WHIPPED AROUND ON HIM AND DESTROYED NINE WITHOUT LOSS REFLECTS THE GREATEST CREDIT ON ALL CONCERNED.*[309,310]

22 October 1943 – Following a day on the ground on account of unsuitable weather, the Wing was airborne again today on two Ramrod operations. In the first of these, the pilots provided a fighter sweep in advance of the bombing of Évreux-Fauville Airfield by 72 Marauders, in Part I of Ramrod 280. In the second, they were assigned to an abortive Escort Cover of 24 Mitchells attacking Le Grand-Quevilly Power Station, in Part I of Ramrod 282.

Date	22 October 1943
Operation	Ramrod 280
Targets	Part I: Évreux-Fauville Airfield, Haute-Normandie
	Part II: Triqueville Airfield, Haute-Normandie
	Part III: Abbeville Airfield, Picardie
Bombers	Part I: 72 Marauders; 71 dispatched, 65 bombed
	Part II: 174 Sqn: 8 Bomphoons; 8 dispatched, 8 bombed
	Part III: 3 Sqn: 8 Bomphoons; 8 dispatched, 8 bombed

Close Escort Part I	Heston: 306 & 308 Squadrons (Spitfire Vb)
	Ibsley: 310 & 312 Squadrons (Spitfire Vb)
Escort Cover	Detling: 132 & 602 Squadrons (Spitfire IX)
High Cover	Northolt: 302, 303 & 317 Squadrons (Spitfire IX)
Top Cover	Gatwick:19 & 65 Squadrons (Spitfire IX)
1st Fighter Sweep	Tangmere: 41 & 91 Squadrons (Spitfire XII)
2nd Fighter Sweep	Kenley: 403 & 421 Squadrons (Spitfire IX)
3rd Fighter Sweep	Hornchurch: 129, 222 & 485 Squadrons (Spitfire IX)
4th Fighter Sweep	North Weald: 331 & 332 Squadrons (Spitfire IX)
Escort Part II	Attlebridge: 175 & 245 Squadrons (Typhoon Ib)
Escort Part III	Manston: 198 Squadron (Typhoon Ib)
Casualties	421 Sqn: Plt Off Ivor R. Forster RCAF, SD/KIA, Beauvais

Part I's bombers and escorts rendezvoused at 12,000 feet, five miles north of Fécamp at 10:00 and proceeded to Évreux-Fauville Airfield according to plan. The Close Escort Wings did not see any enemy aircraft, and the bombers were able to attack the target without interference, dropping three hundred and eighty-seven 500 lb. bombs. The bombing was considered fair to excellent and fires were seen in the south-eastern dispersals area. Flak had been experienced on the way in over Rouen, but none in the target area and all aircraft returned without casualty.

The Escort Cover Wing sighted six enemy aircraft heading north in the Rouen area at 21,000 feet, but were not engaged. However, the High Cover Wing were approached from behind by five Me109s at 15,000 feet, south of Rouen, but dived away when the Wing turned to attack them. The Top Cover Wing sighted no enemy aircraft at all, and the entire bombing and escort operation was completed according to plan, with neither claim nor casualty.

For their part, the Spitfire XII Wing was airborne at 09:50 to conduct a fighter sweep, with Sqn Ldr Ingham leading both the Squadron and the Wing. Fg Off Clive Birbeck (EN605) returned to Tangmere within ten minutes of his departure with 'petrol trouble', presumably unable to switch over to his jettison tank. Fg Off Ross Harding (EN603) followed him just five minutes later with what the ORB simply refers to as 'hood trouble'.

The rest of the Wing swept from Rouen to Conches at 8,000-10,000 feet uneventfully, above a 5/10ths cloud layer at 5,000 feet, then sighted and joined up with the bombers and their escorts over Vernon. The Wing made three orbits on the way out, then headed across the French coast between Fécamp and St. Valéry. As they crossed out, a formation of aircraft was seen orbiting at a significant altitude above them, but they were not engaged and the Wing landed again at 11:20.

The Second, Third and Fourth Fighter Sweeps all encountered and engaged significant numbers of Luftwaffe aircraft, claiming several victories for the loss of one pilot killed in action. The Kenley Wing met at least fifty FW190 northeast of Beauvais, which turned towards the Wing, then broke, leading to a number of individual combats over a wide area. 421 Squadron returned home, claiming two FW190s destroyed and one damaged for the loss of one pilot.

The Hornchurch Wing crossed in at Dieppe and were vectored onto ten FW190s and Me109s, which were successfully bounced. 129 Squadron damaged two FW190s and an Me109, whilst 222 Squadron claimed one Me109 destroyed, all for no loss.

The North Weald Wing swept Arras at 27,000 feet where they encountered thirty FW190s. These were successfully attacked by the Wing Leader, Maj Kaj Birksted, who claimed one FW190 destroyed, by 331 Squadron, which claimed two FW190s and one Me109 destroyed and one FW190 probable, and by 332 Squadron, which claimed one FW190 destroyed.

Part II to Triqueville operated according to plan, all Bomphoons attacking the Airfield, dropping a total of sixteen 500 lb. bombs with good results. Bursts were seen on the western dispersals area and airfield buildings. Part III was just as successful, the Bomphoons dropping the same amount of ordnance on Abbeville Airfield. Bursts were seen in the northern dispersals area, two of which exploded close to a large hangar. All the aircraft returned safely from both attacks.

After lunch, Flt Lt 'Pinkie' Glen (MB846) and Fg Off Patrick Hood (EN605) were sent on a weather reconnaissance flight to Rouen. Airborne at 13:25, the pair returned 65 minutes later reporting unfavourable conditions.

It must have come as a surprise, therefore, when the Wing was called upon again for another Ramrod, taking off just twenty minutes after Glen and Hood landed.

Date	22 October 1943
Operation	Ramrod 282
Targets	Part I: Le Grand-Quevilly Power Station, Haute-Normandie Part II: Saint-André-de-l'Eure Airfield, Haute-Normandie Part III: Cambrai Airfield, Pas-de-Calais
Bombers	Part I: 226 & 320 Sqns: 24 Mitchells; 24 dispatched – aborted (weather) Part II: 72 Marauders; 72 dispatched – aborted (weather) Part III: 72 Marauders; 72 dispatched – aborted (weather)
Close Escort Part I Escort Cover High Cover Top Cover Close Escort Part II Escort Cover High Cover Top Cover 1st Fighter Sweep 2nd Fighter Sweep Escort Part III	Biggin Hill: 401, 411 & 412 Squadrons (Spitfire Vb) – recalled Tangmere: 41 & 91 Squadrons (Spitfire XII) – recalled Northolt: 302, 303 & 317 Squadrons (Spitfire IX) – recalled North Weald: 331 & 332 Squadrons (Spitfire IX) – recalled Digby: 402 & 416 Squadrons (Spitfire Vb) – recalled Heston: 306 & 308 Squadrons (Spitfire IX) – recalled Detling: 132 & 602 Squadrons (Spitfire IX) – recalled Hornchurch: 129, 222 & 485 Squadrons (Spitfire IX) – recalled Gatwick:19 & 65 Squadrons (Spitfire IX) – recalled Kenley: 403 & 421 Squadrons (Spitfire IX) – cancelled Attlebridge: 175, 245 & 247 Sqns (Typhoon Ib) – cancelled USAAF P-47 Thunderbolts and P-38 Lightnings – recalled
Casualties	416 Sqn: 1 A/C Cat E, pilot NI

The Spitfire XII Wing was airborne at 14:50 and rendezvoused with Part I's bombers and escorts 12,000 feet over Beachy Head at 15:00, just below 10/10ths cloud. The formation proceeded across the Channel towards Le Grand-Quevilly Power Station in spite of conditions, but the weather only deteriorated the further they flew, the cloud base dropping to 6,000 feet before they reached the French coast.

Not surprisingly, approximately five miles from St. Valéry, the bombers aborted the mission and returned home. All the escort wings followed them back, the Spitfire XII Wing landing at Tangmere again at 15:50 with nothing to report. This concluded their operational flying for the day in quite an anti-climax after the morning's events.

It was a similar story for Part II: the bombers were recalled before making rendezvous and their escorts were recalled before reaching the French coast. Part III was also recalled, but not before one box of Marauders had made a shallow penetration of the French coast and were intercepted by the Luftwaffe. Their USAAF escort returned with them, and whilst there were no losses to report, claims were submitted for four probable and four damaged enemy aircraft.

23 October 1943 – The Wing's activity today was confined to a weather reconnaissance and an uneventful fighter sweep to Triqueville and Beaumont-le-Roger in Haute-Normandie.

Fg Offs Herb Wagner (EN237) and Ron Collis (MB794) were airborne as Red Section at 12:20 and flew to Triqueville, where they encountered favourable weather. They returned to Tangmere at 13:20 and reported the weather suitable for operations.

Suitably encouraged, Wg Cdr Harries took the Wing on a sweep to Triqueville and Beaumont-le-Roger at 14:10. Crossing the Channel on the deck until 15 miles north of Trouville-sur-Mer, the pilots then climbed rapidly as they approached the coast, and crossed in at between 9,000 and 10,000 feet.

However, in spite of hopes, "It was a very uneventful operation – no enemy aircraft were sighted and no flak experience[d], and no shipping seen."[311] The Wing swept as planned and returned to base at 15:35 with nothing to report.

New Aircraft for the Squadron?

Unbeknown to the Spitfire XII Wing at the time, a potential replacement for the Spitfire XII was being discussed a significant distance up the chain of command. The North American (P-51B) Mustang III had been ordered by the Air Ministry, foreseen in an armed reconnaissance role under 2 TAF, and as an eventual replacement for the Typhoon.

However, there was some indecision around to whom the aircraft should be issued, which had still had not been resolved after their arrival in the United Kingdom. On 18 October, a letter from the Director-General of Organisation at the Air Ministry, AVM George C. Pirie CB CBE MC DFC, to the AOC-in-C, Headquarters Fighter Command, AM Sir Trafford Leigh-Mallory KCB DSO, indicated that the first Mustang IIIs were already in country but that the only decision made thus far was that four Spitfire squadrons should be re-equipped with the aircraft as soon as possible.

The AOC-in-C was asked to nominate which they should be, but it was stipulated that, "two of these should be Spitfire XII Squadrons, as all Spitfire XII are urgently required for a special overseas operation".[312] Five days later, Fighter Command SASO, AVM William B. Callaway CBE AFC, reiterated this point, stating that "two Squadrons are automatically selected, i.e. Nos. 91 and 41 as they are the only ones equipped with Spitfire XIIs", but added that "the remaining two Squadrons selected are Nos. 349 and 350"[313], both of which were Belgian squadrons equipped with the Spitfire Vb at the time.

Despite all indications of a clear decision to re-equip 41 and 91 Squadrons with the Mustang III, operational requirements changed once again within a few days of this, and by 26 October the decision had been reversed. A telex was then received by Headquarters Fighter Command from the Air Ministry that stated,

> REFERENCE PARA 5 OF AIR MINISTRY LETTER S41556/DGO DATED OCTOBER 18TH DECIDED THAT THE SPITFIRE XIIS ARE NOT REPEAT NOT TO BE WITHDRAWN FROM YOUR COMMAND AND RE-EQUIPMENT OF NOS 41 AND 91 SQUADRONS TO MUSTANG III NO LONGER NECESSARY.[314]

Unfortunately, there is no indication of why the decision was made, or what 'special overseas operation' had been foreseen for the Spitfire XIIs. Ultimately, 91 Squadron kept their Spitfire XIIs until the end of February 1944, when the unit was re-equipped with the Spitfire XIV, and 41 Squadron continued flying theirs until mid-September 1944, when they also exchanged them for Mark XIVs.

350 Squadron was also not equipped with the Mustang III, and instead received the Spitfire IX in January 1944, followed by the Mark XIV in August 1944, which they continued to fly for the rest of the War. Similarly, 349 Squadron continued to fly Mark Vb's until February 1944 when they, too received Mark IX's, but converted to the Hawker Tempest V temporarily in February 1945 before reverting to the Spitfire IX again two months later.

The Mustang IIIs went instead to three squadrons based at 122 Airfield [Gravesend], which was at that time equipped with the Spitfire IX. Re-equipping started in December 1943 with 65 Squadron receiving theirs first and 19 and 122 Squadrons following in January 1944. These units were soon heavily involved in Ranger operations, and flew long-range escorts and dive bombing attacks, particularly in connection with Operation *Overlord*. These three squadrons were also amongst the first to be based on the Continent from 25 June 1944.

Would this have been 41 Squadron's history, too, had they been re-equipped with the Mustang III at this time? Retaining their Spitfire XIIs until September 1944, when they re-equipped with the Spitfire XIV, it was not until early December 1944 that 41 Squadron finally moved across the Channel to Belgium, the front by that time having already reached well beyond Brussels, and into the Netherlands.

24 October 1943 – The Wing's operational activity today consisted of a single mission, in which they provided Escort Cover to 72 Marauders attacking Beauvais Airfield in Part II of Ramrod 283.

Date	24 October 1943
Operation	Ramrod 283
Targets	Part I: Montdidier Airfield, Picardie Part II: Beauvais-Tillé Airfield, Picardie Part III: Saint-André-de-l'Eure Airfield, Haute-Normandie
Bombers	Part I: 72 Marauders; 72 dispatched, 64 bombed Part II: 72 Marauders; 72 dispatched, 67 bombed Part III: 72 Marauders; 72 dispatched, 70 bombed
Casualties	Part I: 24 Marauders CD/AA & Part III: 1 Marauder CD/AA
Close Escort Part I Escort Cover High Cover Top Cover 1st Fighter Sweep 2nd Fighter Sweep 3rd Fighter Sweep	Digby: 402 & 416 Squadrons (Spitfire Vb) Heston: 306 & 308 Squadrons (Spitfire Vb) Detling: 132 & 602 Squadrons (Spitfire IX) Hornchurch: 129, 222 & 485 Squadrons (Spitfire IX) North Weald: 331 & 332 Squadrons (Spitfire IX) Kenley: 403 & 421 Squadrons (Spitfire IX) Manston: 3 & 198 Squadrons (Typhoon Ib) Lympne: 1 & 609 Squadrons (Typhoon Ib)
Close Escort Part II Escort Cover Top Cover 1st Fighter Sweep 2nd Fighter Sweep	Biggin Hill: 401, 411 (Spit Vb) & 412 Sqns (Spitfire IX) Friston: 349 Squadron (Spitfire Vb) Tangmere: 41 & 91 Squadrons (Spitfire XII) Gatwick: 19 & 65 Squadrons (Spitfire IX) Tangmere: 197 & 486 Squadrons (Typhoon Ib) Attlebridge: 175, 245 & 247 Squadrons (Typhoon Ib)
Close Escort Part III Medium Cover Top Cover Diversionary Sweep	USAAF: One Fighter Wing P-38 Lightnings USAAF: One Fighter Wing P-47 Thunderbolts USAAF: One Fighter Wing P-47 Thunderbolts USAAF: One Fighter Wing P-47 Thunderbolts USAAF: One Fighter Wing P-47 Thunderbolts
Casualties	421 Sqn: Flt Lt Herbert J. Southwood RCAF, SD/KIA nr Doullens in Spit IX, MH665

Part I's bombers and escorts rendezvoused 12,000 feet over Rye at 11:53 and proceeded across the Channel as planned. The Luftwaffe was active and the Close Escort Wings were attacked by seven to eight FW190s south of Amiens, and another 20 in the target area. 402 Squadron claimed one of these aircraft destroyed and another damaged for no loss.

The Escort Cover Wing was attacked several times out of 10/10ths cloud at 20,000 feet, but did not suffer any casualties, whilst the High Cover Wing dived on FW190s seen attacking the bombers, which evaded and no combats ensued. More successful, the Top Cover Wing sighted two formations of enemy aircraft immediately below them when east of Abbeville, and bounced them, 331 Squadron claiming three Me109s and one FW190 destroyed, and a like number of each damaged, whilst 332 Squadron claimed one FW190 destroyed.

Meanwhile, 64 of the 72 dispatched Marauders attacked Montdidier Airfield, dropping one hundred and fifteen 1,000 lb. bombs and two hundred and one 500 lb. bombs with good results. Twenty-four Marauders sustained combat damage from fighters or Flak, but the bombers' air gunners also claimed a total of three enemy aircraft destroyed, three probably destroyed and six damaged.

The Part's three Fighter Sweeps operated according to plan, and only the first engaged the Luftwaffe. This occurred near Doullens, where twenty Me109s were encountered, and also near Amiens, where twenty FW190s were seen. 403 Squadron returned home claiming one Me109 destroyed and one damaged, whilst 421 Squadron claimed two FW190s damaged, but lost one pilot who was killed in action.

The Spitfire XII wing was airborne at 11:45, 41 Squadron deploying only eleven pilots, of which one was the Sector Gunnery Officer, Sqn Ldr Hubert R. Allen DFC, flying Red 1. The Wing rendezvoused with Part II's Marauders and their fellow escort squadrons at 12,000 feet at midday, 20 miles south of Bexhill and approached the Beauvais area without interference.

Two FW190s were seen over Beauvais-Tillé Airfield by the Close Escort Wing, and two more were seen "dodging in and out of cloud"[315] over the target area by the Spitfire XII Wing, attempting to bounce another Spitfire squadron. They were possibly the same pair seen by the Close Escort squadrons.

Meanwhile, 67 Marauders attacked the airfield from 11,000 feet, dropping one hundred and twenty-eight 1,000 lb. bombs and two hundred and ten 500 lb. bombs with good results. The Spitfire XII Wing observed sticks falling right across the airfield as well as several in the woods to its east. The Marauders did not see any enemy aircraft or sustain Flak damage, and all returned safely.

Before banking for the return journey, pilots of 41 and 91 Squadrons sighted something burning on the ground emitting heavy smoke, approximately one mile east of Beauvais-Tillé Airfield. As no claims were made or casualties sustained, its identity remained a mystery. On the way out, the Top Cover Wing also made an unusual sighting, reporting on their return what they described as unusual rail activity, observing no less than ten trains heading out from Rouen towards the coast.

After crossing out, the Spitfire XII Wing also saw something drop into the sea about one mile of Le Tréport, and 349 Squadron reported seeing an unidentified aircraft go in six miles west of Cayeux. 41 Squadron dived down for a closer look, but saw nothing further of the object. The Spitfire XII Wing continued home and landed at Tangmere at 13:35 in time for a late lunch. There was no further operational flying for the remainder of the day.

Part II's two fighter sweeps were uneventful. The first was vectored onto two enemy aircraft near Lisieux, but nothing was seen of them. A while later, they also saw two unidentified aircraft on Beaumont Airfield. The second sweep followed the same route five minutes behind them and saw nothing worthy of reporting. There were no engagements and no casualties.

Meanwhile, Part III's Marauders had undertaken their attack on Saint-André-de-l'Eure Airfield, with an escort of Thunderbolts and Lightnings. Having made landfall at Fécamp at 12:38, the bombers were over the target at 13:00 where they dropped four hundred and eighteen 500 lb. bombs with good results. One Marauder sustained Flak damage and one Me109 was claimed probably destroyed by the escorts, but the operation otherwise ran according to plan.

25 October 1943 – The Wing was only called upon once today, to undertake Rodeo 268 to the Poix-Abbeville area. Airborne at 15:45, the pilots crossed the Channel at zero feet under Beachy Head Control, led by Sqn Ldr Ingham, and commenced their climb ten miles off the coast. Around this time, Flt Lt 'Pinkie' Glen (MB837) started having R/T trouble and returned to base, where he landed again at 16:15.

Crossing in at Pointe D'Ailly, the rest of the Wing made a shallow penetration at 8,000 feet on reports of enemy aircraft in the vicinity, but none were seen. Continuing eastwards towards Poix under 6/10ths cloud at 7,000 feet, a long goods train was seen at Envermeu. It immediately braked to a halt and emitted large clouds of steam, but was avoided in case it was a Flak trap. Their suspicions were soon confirmed when intensive light Flak opened up at them from a nearby wood.

Shortly thereafter, Beachy Head Control ordered the Wing to return early as a result of deteriorating weather conditions in the Tangmere area. The pilots broke off the operation before reaching Poix, and crossed out at Criel-sur-Mer. Arriving over Tangmere and finding conditions difficult for landing, the entire Wing climbed to 6,000 feet, then sent down sections of four to land in turns, one after the other. Everyone had landed safely by 17:05, and this concluded the day's flying.

26 October 1943 – It was a relatively quiet day for the Wing today, and only a handful of Rhubarbs were undertaken. One of these was flown by 41 Squadron and three by 91.

41 Squadron's Rhubarb was carried out in the Dieppe area by Fg Off Clive Birbeck (EN605) and Flt Lt Dave Fearon (MB847), who were airborne at 11:05 as Green Section. Crossing in between Ste. Marguerite-sur-Mer and Quiberville at 11:30, under 8/10ths cloud at 300 feet, they found a stationary goods train at Ouville-la-Rivière within five minutes. Birbeck made a head on attack on the large engine and observed a number of strikes.

Continuing on to Crosville-sur-Scie, they found another stationary goods train, which Birbeck attacked from 90°, observing strikes on the locomotive and first two trucks. A Flak wagon mounted at the rear of the train opened up on the two pilots, but their fire was inaccurate and neither was hit. The locomotive was left steaming and smoking.

Birbeck and Fearon then flew on to Vassonville, where a third locomotive was attacked whilst in motion, once again from a head-on position. The train drew to a halt and was left issuing steam and smoke. Trying their luck once more, the pair spotted four locomotives in Longueville Marshalling Yards and dived to make an attack on one. However, they were forced to break off due to the intensity of light Flak being directed towards them.

Nonetheless, Birbeck's aircraft was hit by a 20mm round and a hole was blown in the elevator of his tailplane. He was not hurt and the damage did not hinder flying, but the two men decided it was time to head home. They made a bearing for the coast and crossed out at Berneval at 11:50.

In the meantime, Red, Yellow and Blue Sections had taken off from Tangmere at 11:15, led by Flt Lt Glen, and patrolled off the coast from Dieppe, awaiting Birbeck and Fearon's withdrawal. The withdrawal support was provided in case the Rhubarb section was intercepted by alerted Luftwaffe aircraft, as was the case with Fg Off Herb Wagner and WO James Still two weeks before [see 13 October 1943].

The Luftwaffe did not appear but as a result of poor visibility Birbeck and Fearon did not make contact with Glen's withdrawal party. The two groups returned independently of each other, Green Section landing at Tangmere at 12:20, and Red, Yellow and Blue five minutes later.

Birbeck submitted a Combat Report for the Rhubarb, claiming three locomotives and wagons damaged between Dieppe and Clères, during which he expended 143 rounds of 20mm cannon and 351 rounds of .303 machine gun ammunition, and exposed four feet of cine-gun film. Fearon does not appear to have fired at all. There was no further operational flying all day.

28 October 1943 – Following a day on the ground as a result of inclement weather, today dawned to continued poor conditions, which continued throughout the day. As such, "everybody was surprised to hear the Tannoy calling "Viceroy 'A' Flight Scramble!"[316] just before 15:30.

Within three minutes, Red, Yellow and White Sections were airborne and vectored towards St. Catherine's Point on reports of inbound enemy aircraft. However, "the panic was unfounded"[317], nothing was seen, and the pilots were recalled. Fg Offs Herb Wagner, Jack Sabourin, Ross Harding, Ron Collis, Bruce Moffett and Keith Curtis were all back on the ground within 15 minutes. Owing to further poor weather, this concluded the Squadron's operational flying for the month of October, and the pilots did not fly again operationally until 3 November.

Around this time, 27-year-old Fg Off Jack Sabourin joined the unit, and is first mentioned in Squadron records on 28 October 1943. Having joined the RAFVR in August 1939, he undertook his flying training in the United Kingdom before being posted to his first operational unit, 258 Squadron, on 26 January 1941. He was posted to 615 Squadron the following month, and remained with this until late December 1941, when he was commissioned and transferred to the MSFU at Speke. Sabourin was posted to 610 Squadron in April 1943 but stayed with the unit less than three weeks before moving to 501 Squadron in early May, and subsequently to the Coast Artillery Co-Operation Unit at Detling in early August. Remaining with this latter unit until its disbandment on 11 October 1943, he was now posted to 41 Squadron with 670 flying hours in his logbook, of which 87 were operational.

November 1943 – There was no operational flying on thirteen days of the month as a result of poor weather conditions – 1-2, 6, 9, 12-14, 17, 21-22, 27-28 and 30 November – whilst weather significantly restricted operational flying on another five – 4, 15, 16, 18 and 24 November. The Squadron otherwise participated in 15 Ramrod operations, two Rodeos and a Circus, replaced the Commanding Officer, and acquired three new senior officer pilots.

Date	Operation	Role	Type	Destination / Target
3	Ramrod 289	Escort Cover	⟁	Triqueville, France
5	Ramrod 291	Fighter Umbrella	▮	Mimoyecques, France
5	Ramrod 292	Fighter Umbrella	▮	Mimoyecques, France
7	Ramrod 297	Escort Cover	⟁	Bernay St. Martin, France
7	Circus 315	Fighter Sweep	⟁	Bernay St. Martin, France
8	Ramrod 300	Close Escort	▮	Mimoyecques, France
10	Ramrod 307	Escort Cover	⟁	Lille-Vendeville, France
10	Ramrod 308	Close Escort	▬	Cap Gris Nez, France
11	Ramrod 311	Fighter Umbrella	↑	Martinvast, France
11	Ramrod 312	Fighter Sweep	▬	Audinghen, France
19	Ramrod 316	Withdrawal Support	⟁	St. André-de-l'Eure, France
23	Ramrod 326	Close Escort	⟁	St. Omer-Longuenesse, France
25	Ramrod 330	Fighter Sweep	▬	Audinghen, France
25	Ramrod 333	Fighter Sweep	▬	Audinghen, France
26	Ramrod 336	Escort Cover	⟁	Cambrai, France
29	Ramrod 339	Escort Cover	⟁	Cambrai-Epinoy, France

2 November 1943 – For the fifth day in a row, weather hindered operational flying, and once again "the Hun had a days [sic] respite".³¹⁸ Some practice flying was undertaken, but the day also saw the arrival of a new pilot, 21-year-old New Zealander Flt Lt Lyndon P. Griffith DFC.

Having joined the RNZAF in April 1940, Griffith attended EFTS and SFTS in New Zealand, prior to embarking for the United Kingdom with his Wings at the end of October that year. He was posted to his first operational unit, 616 Squadron at Tangmere, at the beginning of the following March, but was moved to 485 Squadron upon its formation a few days later. Commissioned in November 1941, and clearly a leader with promise, he was posted to 122 Squadron as a Flight Commander in May 1942 and awarded a DFC the following month. Several victories followed during summer 1942, as did his promotion to Flying Officer that August. Completing his tour in December 1942, Griffith spent five months as a Sector Gunnery Officer with 9 Group, followed by four months at the Fighter Command School of Air Tactics. He returned to operations in August 1943 when he was posted back to 485 Squadron as a Flight Lieutenant, and now arrived on 41 Squadron from that unit with nine victories to his credit: three destroyed, one probable and five damaged enemy aircraft.

3 November 1943 – Following five days of inclement weather, conditions had improved sufficiently by today to allow the Squadron to undertake operational flying again. However, operations were confined to a single Ramrod to escort Marauders to Triqueville Airfield. The operation was the second part of a three-part Ramrod, the first of which was targeting St. André-de-l'Eure Airfield, and the third Beaumont-le-Roger.

Date	3 November 1943
Operation	Ramrod 289
Targets	Part I: St. André-de-l'Eure Airfield, Haute-Normandie
	Part II: Triqueville Airfield, Haute-Normandie
	Part IIIA: Beaumont-le-Roger Airfield, Haute-Normandie
	Part IIIB: Bernay-St. Martin Airfield, Haute-Normandie
Bombers	Part I: 72 Marauders; 72 dispatched, 72 bombed
	Part II: 72 Marauders; 72 dispatched, 71 bombed
	Part IIIA: Westhampnett: 174 Sqn (Typhoon Ib) – cancelled
	Part IIIB: Merston: 181 Sqn (Typhoon Ib) – cancelled
Casualties	Part I: 1 Marauder FTR, 5 CD/AA
Close Escort Part I	Ibsley: 310, 312 & 313 Squadrons (Spitfire Vb)
	Heston: 306 & 308 Squadrons (Spitfire Vb)
Escort Cover	Detling: 132 & 602 Squadrons (Spitfire IXb)
High Cover	Gravesend: 19 & 65 Squadrons (Spitfire IX)
Top Cover	Kenley: 403 & 421 Squadrons (Spitfire IXb)
1st Fighter Sweep	North Weald: 331 & 332 Squadrons (Spitfire IX)
2nd Fighter Sweep	Hornchurch: 129, 222 & 485 Squadrons (Spitfire IXb)
Close Escort Part II	Biggin Hill: 401, 411 & 412 Squadrons (Spitfire IX)
Escort Cover	Tangmere: 41 & 91 Squadrons (Spitfire XII)
High Cover	Northolt: 302, 303, 317 Squadrons (Spitfire IX)
Close Escort Part IIIA	Westhampnett: 175 & 245 Squadrons (Typhoon Ib) – cancelled
Close Escort Part IIIB	Merston: 182 & 247 Squadrons (Typhoon Ib) – cancelled

Part I's bombers and escorts rendezvoused 15 miles west of the Somme Estuary at 12,000 feet at 10:30, and proceeded to the target according to plan. A single FW190 was engaged by the Close Escort's 306 Squadron for no claim, but the High Cover Wing sighted 45 enemy aircraft in the Évreux area at 26,000 feet. However, these were engaged by the Top Cover Wing, which reported only 30 aircraft at 26,000 feet over the Seine, and returned home claiming two FW190s destroyed, one Me109 probably destroyed and one Me109 damaged for no loss. None of other escort squadrons saw or engaged the Luftwaffe.

Flt Lt Lyndon Griffith DFC RNZAF, was with 41 Squadron from 2 November 1943 to 26 January 1944. © Ron Johnson, via Dan Johnson

Meanwhile, all 72 Marauders attacked St. André Airfield, dropping two hundred and eighty 1,000 lb. bombs with good to excellent results. One Marauder was lost to Flak and five sustained damage, but the bombers' air gunners also claimed one enemy aircraft destroyed and one damaged. Part II's rendezvous was 20 miles west of the Somme Estuary at 12,000 feet at 10:45, five miles further west and fifteen minutes after Part I. However, some confusion resulted when Part II's bombers arrived five minutes late. As a consequence, Part II's Close Escort Wing escorted Part I's seventy-two Marauders to their target instead.

The Spitfire XII Wing was airborne at 10:20, 41 Squadron providing twelve aircraft for the operation, which were led by Wg Cdr Harries. As a result of the Close Escort Wing's absence, one of the Wing's squadrons therefore acted as Close Escort and the other as Escort Cover.

The bombers arrived over Triqueville Airfield at 10:57 in conditions of 6/10ths-8/10ths cloud, and two hundred and eighty-two 1,000lb. GP bombs were dropped on the target with fair to good results. 41 Squadron felt the bombing was 'excellent' and reported seeing 'mass bursts' on the airfield and north dispersals.

There was no sign of the Luftwaffe and there was no Flak, and the operation was carried out otherwise according to plan. A planned sweep on the way back was scuttled when the bombers took a different route back, but after the bombers had crossed out again, the High Cover Wing returned to the coast and uneventfully swept the Le Havre area. The Spitfire XII Wing was back on the ground at Tangmere at 11:45, and 41 Squadron undertook no further flying today.

4 November 1943 – Weather was an issue again today, and the only operational flying undertaken by the Squadron was a weather reconnaissance to the Hardelot area between 08:40 and 09:45. Blue Section, comprising Fg Offs Ron Johnson and Ron Loweth, found thick haze up to 1,000 feet as they crossed the Channel, then made landfall at zero feet, finding low cloud on the coast, and layers of cloud at 1,000, 2,000 and 5,000 feet up to 15-20 miles inland. Visibility was considered three to five miles through ground haze.

On the way back out, the two men encountered a little light Flak from Hardelot, but it was sufficient to hit Johnson's aircraft (MB801) both in the rudder and tail plane. It did not, however, have any undue effect on flying, and he returned to Tangmere without a problem, where he and Loweth landed at 09:45.

The weather was considered too poor for further operations over France and the Squadron had instead "to content itself with some practice flying and synthetic training".[319]

The V3 Long Range Gun

5 November 1943 – Continued poor weather kept the Squadron on the ground until after midday, but improved conditions resulted in the pilots completing two Ramrods and two scrambles within the space of four hours. Both Ramrods saw the Squadron providing a fighter umbrella for bombers attacking field works in the Mimoyecques area, around eight miles east of Gris Nez.

The Germany military began the development of a long range artillery piece, dubbed the V3, during 1943 that would be capable of firing 140kg shells across the Channel to London. The range was achieved by adding velocity to the projectile through the detonation of multiple charges along the length of the barrel. In order to discharge the necessary amount of propellant, however, a barrel measuring some 150 metres [492 feet] was necessitated. This created additional problems of ensuring stability along its length but avoiding visibility from the air, but it was felt these problems would be resolved by burying the barrels inside shafts in hills and quarries.

Mimoyecques was chosen as one of several for up to 50 such guns, and excavation began in September 1943. However, it did not take long for Allied reconnaissance to recognise suspicious activity in the area. Today's bombing attacks by 9th US Air Force on what were referred to merely as 'field works' were the first on the site, and three separate attacks by were made in Ramrods 291, 292 and 294. 41 Squadron participated in two of these.

Date	5 November 1943
Operation	Ramrod 291
Target	'Field works', Mimoyecques, Pas-de-Calais
Bombers	216 Marauders in 6 formations of 36 aircraft; 203 dispatched, 181 bombed
Casualties	322 BG/451 BS: Marauder 41-18075, SD/AA; & 386 BG/553 BS: Marauder 41-31889, SD/AA[320]
1st Fighter Umbrella	Heston: 306 & 308 Squadrons (Spitfire Vb) Biggin Hill: 401 & 411 Sqns (Spit IX), & 412 Sqn (Spit Vb) Detling: 132 & 602 Squadrons (Spitfire IX) Northolt: 302, 303, 317 Squadrons (Spitfire IX) West Malling: 124 Squadron (Spitfire VII)
2nd Fighter Umbrella	Coltishall: 64 & 611 Squadrons (Spitfire Vb) Digby: 402 & 416 Squadrons (Spitfire Vb) Hawkinge: 350 Squadron (Spitfire Vb) Tangmere: 41 & 91 Squadrons (Spitfire XII) Hornchurch: 129, 222 & 485 Squadrons (Spitfire IX) Gravesend: 19, 65 & 122 Squadrons (Spitfire IX)
1st Fighter Sweep	North Weald: 331 & 332 Squadrons (Spitfire IX)
2nd Fighter Sweep	Kenley: 403 & 421 Squadrons (Spitfire IX)
3rd Fighter Sweep	Lympne: 1 & 609 Squadrons (Typhoon Ib)
4th Fighter Sweep	Tangmere: 197 & 486 Squadrons (Typhoon Ib)

The bombers' route took them to a point nine miles southwest of Boulogne (50°40' N 1°25' E) at 12,000 feet, then on a south-easterly course to a point four miles south of Hardelot, then east-northeast to a point three miles north of Desvres, then nine-and-a-half miles north-northwest to Mimoyecques, and cross back out over Wissant. The first formation was to arrive over the initial coordinates, nine miles southwest of Boulogne, at 13:00 and expected over the target area at 13:10. The subsequent five formations were to follow them at ten minute intervals.

For their part, the Spitfire XII wing was airborne at 13:05 led by Wg Cdr Harries, who flew with 91 Squadron, to participate in the second fighter umbrella. 41 Squadron flew in three sections of four pilots, designated Red, Yellow and Blue, led by Sqn Ldr Ingham. However, Fg Off Bruce Moffett (MB858), leading Yellow soon found his R/T malfunctioning and returned to base 25 minutes after departure.

The Spitfire XII Wing arrived over their designated area, east of Boulogne, at 13:30 and proceeded to patrol the Berck-sur-Mer and Cap Gris Nez areas at 15,000 feet, above a 4/10ths cloud layer at 4,000 feet, until 13:55. The Luftwaffe was not seen by the entire second fighter umbrella and the Squadron ORB boasted that, "no enemy fighters were intrepid enough to engage them".[321] The first umbrella sighted five FW190s but they prudently kept their distance and were not engaged.

Although heavy Flak was directed at the bombers in the target area, it did not hinder their task and 171 bombers dropped a total of three hundred and thirty-one 2,000lb. GP bombs. The Spitfire XII Wing was too far away to observe the effects of the bombing, but the bomber crews considered they had achieved fair to good results. This was later confirmed by photographic analysis.

The Wing waited until the bombers had crossed out again, and then set course for Tangmere. They felt the operation had been carried out according to plan and landed at 14:30 without further ado.

Whilst they were absent, Flt Lt Terence Welsh and Flt Sgt Bruce Adams were scrambled and vectored 30 miles south of base to assist a friendly fighter reported to be in difficulty. Airborne at 13:10, they saw nothing and were returning to base when they spotted a Mustang just as they re-crossed the English coast. They then escorted the pilot to land at Tangmere, where all three landed at 13:40.[322]

An hour and five minutes after the Squadron's return from Ramrod 291, they were airborne on the second Ramrod, which was on a slightly smaller scale than the previous. Once again, the target was the 'field works' at Mimoyecques, this being the third of the day's three operations against the site.

Date	5 November 1943
Operation	Ramrod 292
Target	'Field works', Mimoyecques, Pas-de-Calais
Bombers	1st Wave: 24 Mitchells; 25 dispatched, 24 bombed 2nd Wave: 24 Bostons; 24 dispatched – aborted 3rd Wave: 24 Mitchells; 24 dispatched, 24 bombed
Fighter Umbrella	Heston: 306 & 308 Squadrons (Spitfire Vb) Hawkinge: 350 Squadron (Spitfire Vb) Coltishall: 64 & 611 Squadrons (Spitfire Vb) Digby: 402 & 416 Squadrons (Spitfire Vb) Biggin Hill: 401 & 411 Sqns (Spit IX), & 412 Sqn (Spit Vb) Tangmere: 41 & 91 Squadrons (Spitfire XII) Detling: 132 & 602 Squadrons (Spitfire IX) Northolt: 302, 303, 317 Squadrons (Spitfire IX) West Malling: 124 Squadron (Spitfire VII)
1st Fighter Sweep	Hornchurch: 129, 222 & 485 Squadrons (Spitfire IX)
2nd Fighter Sweep	Lympne: 1 & 609 Squadrons (Typhoon Ib)
3rd Fighter Sweep	Tangmere: 197 & 486 Squadrons (Typhoon Ib)

On this occasion, the bombers took a slightly different route, initially flying via Dungeness in a south-easterly direction approximately 38 miles to a point three miles south of Hardelot, then northeast 11 miles to Desvres, north-northwest 21.5 miles to Mimoyecques at 10,000 feet at 16:15, then crossing back out three miles southwest of Sangatte, around eight miles beyond the target area, on almost the same bearing. Once again, the ensuing formations were to follow them at ten minute intervals.

The Spitfire XII Wing was airborne at 15:35 to participate in the fighter umbrella, with 41 Squadron in three sections of four comprising the same pilots as the previous Ramrod. The Squadron was led by Sqn Ldr Ingham, and the Wing by Wg Cdr Harries. Fg Off John Smith (EN603) returned within 15 minutes with R/T trouble, but the rest of the Squadron continued on to their patrol area.

Initially finding 10/10ths cloud at 2,000 feet to within five miles of the French coast, it began thinning out from this point and there was only a light 1/10ths cloud at 3,000 feet over the target area. However, haze up to the cloud base made downwards visibility very poor. The pilots patrolled in the Cap Gris Nez area between 16:05 and 16:30, and were able to see bursts in the target area. However, they could not say from their perspective whether they were accurate or not.

The second formation of bombers, comprising 24 Bostons, had aborted the mission prior to leaving the English coast as a result of thick haze and only the 48 Mitchells bombed, dropping three hundred and seventy-nine 500lb. bombs. Although the Luftwaffe was not seen, Flak was experienced, but no bombers were hit.

12 Group's fighter squadrons, who were to escort the second formation, were ordered instead to undertake a fighter sweep. As they crossed in, Digby's two squadrons met outbound Mitchells, and escorted them back to the English coast, whilst Coltishall's units swept on a general north-easterly direction over Hardelot, Desvres and Audruicq at 12,000 feet, before heading home. They sighted 15 enemy aircraft in the St. Omer area and another eight over Calais as they crossed out, but none were engaged.

As far as the Spitfire XII Wing was concerned, the operation was carried out according to plan and they landed at Tangmere again at 17:05, reporting the job uneventful.

Whilst they were away, Flt Lt Welsh and Flt Sgt Adams were scrambled on another patrol, similar to their previous, to find and escort a Typhoon that was lost over the Channel south of Selsey Bill. They pair were airborne at 15:55, but landed again just ten minutes later when they were informed the Typhoon had landed at Merston. This ended the day's flying.

6 November 1943 – Weather severely hampered operations today and the Squadron was only airborne on a single operation all day, when Blue (Johnson MB847 & Fisher MB829) and Green (Loweth MB830 & Adams EN231) Sections were sent on an ASR patrol to find a dinghy of crew from a Flying Fortress.[323]

Led by Fg Off Ron Johnson, the pilots were given a vector of 201° for 19 minutes at an IAS of 260 mph, to a point ten miles southeast of Barfleur, in the Baie de la Seine. They then searched the area for ten minutes as far as Le Havre, but approached the coast no closer than five miles at any time.

Despite good visibility below a 5/10ths cloud at 1,200 feet, which increased to 10/10ths at 3,000 feet, the quartet saw no sign of the crew and returned to base at 14:05 with nothing to report.

7 November 1943 – Today's operational flying consisted of two operations, a Ramrod to Bernay-St. Martin Airfield at 09:00 and a Circus to the same area at 16:00. The first of these was a particularly large operation in five parts with 168 bombers, 16 Bomphoons, 26 escort squadrons, and four squadrons on fighter sweeps. The Spitfire XII Wing's part was to provide escort cover to two dozen Bostons in Part I.

	7 November 1943
Operation	Ramrod 297
Targets	Part I: Bernay-St. Martin Airfield, Haute-Normandie Part II: Montdidier Airfield, Picardie Part III: Montdidier Airfield, Picardie Part IV: Triqueville Airfield, Haute-Normandie Part V: Beaumont-le-Roger Airfield, Haute-Normandie
Bombers	Part I: 24 Bostons; 24 dispatched, 24 bombed Part II: 72 Marauders; 72 dispatched – aborted Part III: 72 Marauders; 72 dispatched – aborted Part IV: 8 Bomphoons; 8 dispatched, 8 bombed Part V: 8 Bomphoons; 8 dispatched, 8 bombed

Close Escort Part I	Ibsley: 310, 312 & 313 Squadrons (Spitfire Vb)
Escort Cover	Tangmere: 41 & 91 Squadrons (Spitfire XII)
High Cover	Church Stanton: 131 & 165 Squadrons (Spitfire IX)
Close Escort Part II	Biggin Hill: 401 & 412 Squadrons (Spitfire Vb) – aborted
	Heston: 306 & 308 Squadrons (Spitfire Vb) – aborted
Escort Cover	Detling: 132 & 602 Squadrons (Spitfire IX) – aborted
High Cover	Hornchurch: 129, 222 & 485 Squadrons (Spitfire IX)
Top Cover	North Weald: 331 & 332 Squadrons (Spitfire IX)
Additional Top Cover	West Malling: 124 Squadron (9 Spitfire VII)
Fighter Sweep	Kenley: 403 & 421 Squadrons (Spitfire IX)
Close Escort Part III	Digby: 402 & 416 Squadrons (Spit Vb) – aborted
	Hawkinge: 350 Squadron (Spitfire Vb) – aborted
Escort Cover	Northolt: 317 Squadron (Spitfire IX) – aborted
	Biggin Hill: 411 Squadron (Spitfire IX) – aborted
High Cover	Northolt: 302 & 303 Squadrons (Spitfire IX)
Top Cover	Gravesend: 19, 65 & 122 Squadrons (Spitfire IX) – aborted
Escort Part IV	Westhampnett: 175 & 245 Squadrons (8 Typhoon Ib)
Escort Part V	Merston: 181 & 247 Squadrons (8 Typhoon Ib)
Fighter Sweep	Tangmere: 197 & 486 Squadrons (Typhoon Ib)
Casualties	19 Sqn: Flt Sgt Francis J. D. Prebble, EF & ditched MJ215, KAS; 175 Sqn: Fg Off Dickens CD/NI from 165 Sqn A/C, mistaken for FW190, WUL Tangmere, A/C Cat. B.

Twenty-three aircraft of the Spitfire XII Wing were airborne at 09:00 with Wg Cdr Harries leading as Red 1 of 41 Squadron. 41 Squadron's Yellow Section was led by Sqn Ldr Ingham and Blue Section by Fg Off Ron Johnson.

The Wing made rendezvous with the bombers as planned, 25 miles south of Beachy Head at 09:10, but the close escort from Ibsley failed to find them, possibly owing to 10/10ths cloud at 8,000-10,000 feet. In fact, Ibsley's three squadrons located Marauders from Part II and escorted them to France instead.

The Spitfire XII and Church Stanton Wings escorted the Bostons to Bernay-St. Martin Airfield and were over the target on time at 09:33 (zero + 23), in clear conditions with good visibility. Ninety-three 500lb. bombs were dropped and bursts were seen on dispersals, hangars and station headquarters, despite accurate heavy Flak over the target area.

41 Squadron reported seeing three enemy aircraft and giving chase but they were too far away to engage them. One of 165 Squadron's pilots fired at what he thought was an FW190 three miles northwest of Trouville, but it was actually a Typhoon of one of Part IV's escorts, 175 Squadron. This aircraft was damaged and made a belly landing at Tangmere, but the pilot was unhurt.

As far as the Spitfire XII Wing was concerned, however, the operation ran according to plan and they returned to Tangmere at 10:20. It eventuated that this Part of the Ramrod was the only success of the main bombing operation. Part II's and III's bombers, both targeting Montdidier, found 10/10ths cloud between 6,000 and 11,000 feet over the target area and returned home with their payloads intact. Most of their escort fighters also aborted but one pilot was lost when he suffered engine trouble and ditched, but could not be rescued.

The Bomphoons of Parts IV and V also reached their targets and dropped sixteen 500lb. bombs each on Triqueville and Beaumont-le-Roger Airfields, achieving hits on dispersal areas and landing grounds.

41 Squadron undertook no further flying until 16:00 when the Wing was called upon to participate in an abortive Circus operation back to Bernay-St. Martin Airfield. Their role on this occasion was to provide a fighter sweep of the St. Valery-Montfort area.

The Spitfire XII Wing

Date	7 November 1943
Operation	Circus 315
Targets	Part I: Bernay-St. Martin Airfield, Haute-Normandie
	Part II: Moorsele Airfield, Wevelgem, Belgium
Bombers	Part I: 2 Bomphoon Squadrons (16 Wing) – aborted
	Part II: 8 Bomphoons (3 Squadron) – aborted
Escort Part I	16 Wing, three Typhoon squadrons – aborted
1st Fighter Sweep	Tangmere: 197 & 486 Squadrons (Typhoon Ib)
2nd Fighter Sweep	Tangmere: 41 & 91 Squadrons (Spitfire XII)
3rd Fighter Sweep	Gravesend: 19, 65 & 122 Squadrons (Spitfire IX)
Escort Part II	Typhoons – aborted
1st Fighter Sweep	Lympne: 1 & 609 Squadrons (Typhoon Ib)
2nd Fighter Sweep	Hornchurch: 129, 222 & 485 Squadrons (Spitfire IXb)
3rd Fighter Sweep	Kenley: 403 & 421 Squadrons (Spitfire IXb)
Casualties	65 Sqn: 1 A/C Cat. B, NDEA

The Wing was airborne at 16:00 led by Wg Cdr Harries once again, who flew with 91 Squadron; 41 Squadron's three sections were led by Sqn Ldr Ingham, Fg Off Bruce Moffett and Fg Off Ron Johnson.

The Wing crossed in west of St. Valéry-en-Caux at 12,000 feet and flew southwards 40 miles to Montfort-sur-Risle in fair visibility, where Beachy Head Control gave them a new vector to Argentan, 49 miles to the southwest. The Luftwaffe was not seen and the Wing crossed back out near Cabourg, approximately 39 miles due north of Argentan, returning to Tangmere at 17:30 with nothing to report.

Unbeknown to them at the time, the Bomphoon and Escort squadrons of both Parts had aborted the operation due to unsuitable weather, which had likely stemmed from the 10/10ths cloud at 6,000 feet off the French coast encountered by the Spitfire XII Wing. The remaining squadrons operated their fighter sweeps according to plan, but returned to their respective bases with nothing to report.

8 November 1943 – The Spitfire XII Wing participated in a single Ramrod today, in which the V3 site at Mimoyecques was once again the target. On this occasion, three waves of RAF bombers were sent to the target, each protected by its own fighter escort and fighter umbrella.

Date	8 November 1943
Operation	Ramrod 300
Target	Mimoyecques, Pas-de-Calais
Bombers 1st Attack	88 & 342 Sqns: 24 Bostons; 24 dispatched, 24 bombed
	320 Sqn: 6 Mitchells; 6 dispatched, 6 bombed
Bombers 2nd Attack	98 & 180 Sqns: 24 Mitchells; 24 dispatched, 24 bombed
Bombers 3rd Attack	226 & 305 Sqns: 24 Mitchells; 19 dispatched, 18 bombed
Casualties	Part III: 226 Sqn: Mitchell II, FV927, MQ-R, SD/AA, crew †[324]; Mitchell II, FV939, MQ-B, AA/CL Manston, one crew inj; 11 bombers CD/AA
Close Escort 1st Attack	Hawkinge: 350 Squadron (Spitfire Vb)
	Biggin Hill: 401 Squadron (Spitfire IX)
Fighter Umbrella	Detling: 132 & 602 Squadrons (Spitfire IX)
Close Escort 2nd Attack	Gravesend: 19 Squadron (Spitfire IX)
Fighter Umbrella	Gravesend: 65 & 122 Squadrons (Spitfire IX)
Close Escort 3rd Attack	Tangmere: 41 & 91 Squadrons (Spitfire XII)
Fighter Umbrella	Kenley: 403 & 421 Squadrons (Spitfire IX)
Casualties	41 Sqn: 1 A/C CD/AA, pilot unhurt; 350 or 412 Sqn: 1 A/C CD/AA Cat A, pilot unhurt; Kenley: 1 A/C CD/AA Cat B, pilot unhurt.

Twenty-four aircraft of the Spitfire XII Wing were airborne at 09:00, led by 41 Squadron's Sqn Ldr Ingham to provide close escort to the third wave of Mitchells.

The first wave was to rendezvous over Dungeness at 09:00, with the subsequent formations at 09:10 and 09:20 respectively. The Wing rendezvoused with the bombers according to plan, but 41 Squadron's Flt Sgt Alan Hope (MB830) started having trouble with his electrical system and returned alone, putting down at Tangmere again at 09:30. Meanwhile, the rest of the Wing crossed in just south of Boulogne and were over the target area at 09:28.

From crossing in to leaving the coast again, the entire formation was accompanied by very accurate heavy Flak and one of the bombers received a direct hit in the centre of the fuselage, which set it on fire and sent it spiralling to the ground to crash near Sangatte. Three of the crew were seen to bale out, but none survived. Nineteen other bombers also received Flak damage, and one of these also force-landed near Manston. One of 41 Squadron's aircraft also received Flak damage but it was only slight and the pilot was unhurt; stability and handling were not affected.[325]

The remaining 18 bombers attacked the target with four 1,000 lb. bombs each, and bursts were seen near the northern aiming point. The Spitfire XII Wing also reported seeing a single large explosion in the target area. There was no reaction from the Luftwaffe, and the operation was otherwise carried out according to plan.

The bombers of the first two attacks had also successfully dropped four 500 lb. or four 1000 lb. bombs each and numerous bursts were seen in the target area, on tunnel entrances and railway lines. All, however, came under accurate and intense heavy Flak, which hindered effective observation of the results. The escorting fighters operated according to plan, as did those of the fighter umbrellas, although two were damaged by Flak to Cat A and Cat B status. The Kenley Wing also made an attack on three locomotives and shot up a military parade.

The Spitfire XII Wing crossed out again at Sangatte and landed back at Tangmere at 10:20. The Wing was not called upon again today, and when poor weather set in, 41 Squadron was not airborne operationally for the next 50 hours.

Separately today, a new pilot joined the Squadron in the form of 24-year-old New Zealander and supernumerary Squadron Leader John Clouston. Having joined the RNZAF in January 1940, Clouston had gained his Wings as an NCO pilot in New Zealand before shipping to the United Kingdom. He completed OTU in the United Kingdom and was posted to his first operational unit, 258 Squadron at Leconfield, at the beginning of December, just after its formation. Clouston was commissioned in May 1941, and subsequently served in 403 and 111 Squadrons at Debden prior to his promotion to Flying Officer in mid-December 1941. In March 1942, he was posted to 486 Squadron and attained the rank of Flight Lieutenant with this unit in December 1942. In January 1943, Clouston was rested as Sector Gunnery Officer at Biggin Hill and returned to operations with 41 Squadron today.

10 November 1943 – The Spitfire Wing was back in the air today after two days' break, and participated in two Ramrods between 12:55 and 16:45, one to Lille and the other to Cap Gris Nez; both operated from Manston.

In the first of these, the Wing acted as escort cover in Part I of Ramrod 307, an attack by 72 Marauders of the 9th USAAF on Lille-Vendeville Airfield. Twenty-four aircraft from 41 and 91 Squadrons departed Tangmere at 11:40, led by Sqn Ldr Ingham, and landed at Manston at 12:10, forty-five minutes ahead of the Ramrod's commencement.

Date	10 November 1943
Operation	Ramrod 307
Targets	Part I: Lille-Vendeville Airfield, Pas-de-Calais, France
	Part II: Chièvres Airfield, Hainaut, Belgium
	Secondary Target: Mimoyecques V3 Site
Bombers	Part I: 72 Marauders; 72 dispatched, 3 bombed
	Part II: 72 Marauders; 72 dispatched, 59 bombed

Casualties	Part I: 29 Marauders CD/AA
	Part II: 13 Marauders CD/AA
Close Escort Part I	Biggin Hill: 411 (Spitfire IX) & 412 Squadrons (Spitfire Vb)
	Heston: 306 & 308 Squadrons (Spitfire Vb)
	Hawkinge: 350 Squadron (Spitfire Vb)
Escort Cover	Tangmere: 41 & 91 Squadrons (Spitfire XII)
High Cover	Northolt: 302, 303 & 317 Squadrons (Spitfire IX)
Top Cover	Kenley: 403 & 421 Squadrons (Spitfire IX)
Fighter Sweep	Gravesend: 19, 65 & 122 Squadrons (Spitfire IX)
Close Escort Part II	Digby: 402 & 416 Squadrons (Spit Vb)
	Coltishall: 64 & 611 Squadrons (Spitfire Vb)
Escort Cover	Hornchurch: 129 & 222 Squadrons (Spitfire IX)
High Cover	Detling: 132 & 602 Squadrons (Spitfire IX)
Top Cover	North Weald: 331 & 332 Squadrons (Spitfire IX)

The Wing was airborne from Manston at 12:55 and made rendezvous as planned, forming up above and behind the bombers and close escorts, which had assembled over North Foreland at 13:00, with the bombers at 12,000 feet.

The Marauders crossed in at Gravelines at zero+8 minutes at 24,000 feet under Hythe Control, and were scheduled to be over Lille-Vendeville Airfield at an altitude of 11,000 feet at zero+27. However, most of the bombers turned away before reaching the target, when 10/10ths cloud was encountered at 5,000 feet, and only three Marauders actually bombed, dropping eighteen 500 lb. bombs through gaps in the cloud.

Intense heavy Flak, including red marker and phosphorous, were directed at the bombers throughout and no less than 29 sustained damage, although none were lost. The rest of the bombers turned back and headed for the Cap Gris Nez area, where they bombed the secondary target, Mimoyecques, instead.

Part II's bombers were more successful on their primary target, and 59 bombers dropped three hundred and forty-seven 500 lb. bombs on Chièvres Airfield; bursts were seen in the centre of the target. The secondary target was not attacked, but 13 bombers were also damaged by Flak.

The operations were uneventful for all the escorting fighter squadrons; the Luftwaffe was not seen and there were no claims or casualties. As far as the Spitfire XII Wing was concerned, their escort cover was carried out according to plan and they returned with little to report. Whilst one aircraft headed straight back to Tangmere, the remaining 23 aircraft landed at Manston at 14:10.

It was from here, therefore, that 22 aircraft, including Wg Cdr Harries leading, took off at 15:45 to act as close escort to the third wave of bombers in Part IV of Ramrod 308 to Audinghen, Pas-de-Calais.

Although only a small town, Audinghen was of interest to the Allies due to its gun emplacements, which formed a part of the German coastal defences, the Atlantic Wall ['Atlantikwall'].

Date	10 November 1943
Operation	Ramrod 308
Targets	Parts I-IV: Audinghen, Pas-de-Calais
	Secondary target: Cap Gris Nez, Pas-de-Calais
Bombers	Part I: 174 & 245 Sqn, 8 Bomphoons; 16 dispatched, 16 bombed
	Part II: 247 Sqn, 8 Bomphoons; 15 dispatched, 13 bombed
	Part III: 3 Sqn, 8 Bomphoons; 12 dispatched – aborted
	Part IV-A: 24 Mitchells; 25 dispatched, 17 bombed
	Part IV-B: 24 Bostons; 12 dispatched – aborted
	Part IV-C: 24 Mitchells; 24 dispatched, 5 bombed primary, 6 bombed secondary
Casualties	247 Sqn: Fg Off Herbert L. van Zuilecom RAAF † nr Ford in Typhoon Ib, JP544, ZY-D, 500 lb. bomb dropped from cradle on TO & exploded, bringing down A/C

Escort Part I	Westhampnett: 175 Squadron (Typhoon Ib)
Escort Part II	Unknown (NR)
Escort Part III	Fairlop: 195 Sqn, & Manston: 198 Sqn (Typhoon Ib)
Escort Part IV-A	Hawkinge: 350 Sqn, & Biggin Hill: 401 & 412 Sqns (Spitfire Vb)
Escort Part IV-B	Heston: 306 & 308 Squadrons (Spitfire Vb)
Escort Part IV-C	Tangmere: 41 & 91 Squadrons (Spitfire XII)
Fighter Umbrella	Detling: 132 & 602 Squadrons (Spitfire IX)
	Northolt: 302, 303 & 317 Squadrons (Spitfire IX)
1st Fighter Sweep	Lympne: 1 & 605 Squadrons (Typhoon Ib)
2nd Fighter Sweep	Tangmere: 197 & 486 Squadrons (Typhoon Ib)
3rd Fighter Sweep	North Weald: 331 & 332 Squadrons (Spitfire IX)
4th Fighter Sweep	Hornchurch: 129 & 222 Squadrons (Spitfire IX)
5th Fighter Sweep	Gravesend: 19, 65 & 122 Squadrons (Spitfire IX)
6th Fighter Sweep	Kenley: 403 & 421 Squadrons (Spitfire IX)

The first three parts of the Ramrod foresaw attacks by Bomphoons with Typhoon escorts at ten-minute intervals from 15:00. Two fighter sweeps of each two Typhoon squadrons were to operate in the Blankenberge-Courtrai [Kortrijk] area of Belgium, and Ault-Poix area of France throughout the three parts, from 15:20.

Parts I to III were only priming the target as Part IV followed the Bomphoons on a much larger scale with 72 bombers in three waves of 24, attacking Audinghen from 13,000 feet at ten minute intervals from 15:52. They were accompanied by seven fighter squadrons, a fighter umbrella of four squadrons in the Hardelot, St. Omer and Gravelines areas, and four fighter sweeps in the Blankenberge-Courtrai [Kortrijk], Furnes [Veurne]-Lille, Hardelot-Béthune, and Le Touquet areas, involving nine fighter squadrons from 15:50.

The Spitfire XII Wing was assigned to a close escort of the third and last wave of bombers and was airborne from Manston between 15:45 and 15:50. 41 Squadron deployed twelve aircraft in three sections, with Wg Cdr Harries leading Red Section, Sqn Ldr Ingham leading Yellow, and Flt Lt 'Pinkie' Glen leading Blue. They rendezvoused with the bombers as planned and set course for France.

Ahead of them, 17 bombers of the first wave attacked Audinghen through almost 10/10ths cloud at 4,000 feet, with the result that the bombs fell approximately one mile from the target. On finding such thick cloud cover, the second formation did not bomb at all and aborted the attack. The third formation, escorted by 41 and 91 Squadron, had differing opinions on what should be done about the cloud cover and only five of the 24 bombers attacked Audinghen. Six made for the secondary target, gun emplacements half a mile east of Cap Gris Nez, instead, and the rest turned back before reaching the French coast.

In all, eighty-five 1,000 lb. bombs were dropped on Audinghen and twenty-four on Cap Gris Nez's coastal guns. The escorts were all completed uneventfully, as were the first, second, third, and fifth fighter sweeps. Fighters of the fourth sweep attacked a train near Dunkirk, whilst elements of the sixth damaged a locomotive near Le Tréport.

The Spitfire XII Wing landed at Tangmere again between 16:45 and 16:50 with nothing further to report and this concluded the day's flying.

11 November 1943 – Good weather today saw the Wing airborne on two operations, the first at 11:45 to Martinvast and the second at 15:15 back to Audinghen.

The former of these was to another construction site close to Cherbourg, which was thought to be a Crossbow target related to the development of rocket technology. The site, known as Brécourt, was originally a French Navy [Marine Nationale] underground oil storage facility that comprised eight concrete tanks with a steel lining, measuring 240 feet in length, 50 feet wide and 50 feet deep, linked by a series of inter-connecting tunnels.

The Germans took an initial interest in the storage facility in 1941, when they drained the tanks and converted four to barracks and workshops on three levels. However, as the War progressed, the Germans recognised its potential for conversion to a V2 rocket assembly and launching base, and new building works were undertaken from August 1943. The site was considered particularly suitable as all activity could be undertaken underground and would therefore remain virtually undetectable from the air.

It was nonetheless discovered by Allied reconnaissance, recognised by unusual activity around it, and attacked in the first operation against the site today with the deployment of 162 Marauders of the 9th US Air Force in five waves.[326]

Date	11 November 1943
Operation	Ramrod 311
Target	Martinvast, Basse-Normandie
Bombers	387th BG: 162 Marauders in formations of 36, 36, 36, 36 & 18; 162 dispatched, 157 bombed
Casualties	1 Marauder EF/RTB, 1 Marauder AA/CL at base
Escort 1st Formation	Coltishall: 64 & 611 Squadrons (Spitfire Vb)
Escort 2nd Formation	Digby: 402 & 416 Squadrons (Spitfire Vb)
Escort 3rd Formation	Ibsley: 310 & 312 Squadrons (Spitfire Vb)
Escort 4th Formation	Ibsley: 313 Sqn, & Hawkinge: 350 Sqn (Spitfire Vb)
Escort 5th Formation	Perranporth: 341 Sqn, & Heston: 306 Sqn (Spitfire Vb)
1st Fighter Umbrella	Tangmere: 41 & 91 Squadrons (Spitfire XII)
	Hornchurch: 129 & 222 Squadrons (Spitfire IXb)
	Kenley: 403 & 421 Squadrons (Spitfire IXb)
2nd Fighter Umbrella	Biggin Hill: 411 Squadron (Spitfire IX)
	Detling: 132 & 602 Squadrons (Spitfire IXb)
	Northolt: 302 & 317 Squadrons (Spitfire IXc)
	Church Stanton: 131 & 165 Squadrons (Spitfire IX)
1st Fighter Sweep	North Weald: 331 & 332 Squadrons (Spitfire IX)
2nd Fighter Sweep	Gravesend: 19, 65 & 122 Squadrons (Spitfire IX)

The first bomber formation rendezvoused 30 miles south of Portsmouth at 12,000 feet at 12:00, and was scheduled to be over the target 20 minutes later. The subsequent formations were to follow at five minute intervals, each escorted by two fighter squadrons. All five formations were further supported by 13 Spitfire squadrons providing a fighter umbrella in two parts, and five Spitfire squadrons providing fighter sweeps in two parts in the St. Valéry-en-Caux area.

The Spitfire XII Wing participated in the first fighter umbrella and was airborne at 11:45, led by Wg Cdr Harries. 41 Squadron deployed three sections of four pilots, led by Sqn Ldr Ingham, Fg Off Bruce Moffett, and Flt Lt 'Pinkie' Glen, respectively. As the Wing neared the French coast, a Marauder approached them, heading home with black smoke emitting from an engine. Two pilots from 91 Squadron were ordered to provide it an escort, whilst the remaining aircraft crossed in west of the Îles St.-Marcouf.

The Wing then proceeded to patrol the Valognes-Bricquebec-Flamanville areas on the Cotentin [Cherbourg] Peninsula, only a short distance south of the bombers' target. They flew at 12,000 feet under Beachy Head Control in good visibility above 6/10ths cloud at 6,000 feet, but the Luftwaffe was not seen and the job proved uneventful. They crossed back out and passed between Cap de la Hague and the Channel island of Alderney, coming under heavy but inaccurate Flak from both locations as they did.

The Wing landed at Tangmere again at 13:15, where 41 Squadron's Flt Sgt Jimmy Payne (MB797) found he had to bring his aircraft down without flaps. He succeeded and the aircraft was not damaged. There was otherwise nothing further to report.

The bombing, meanwhile, had gone ahead according to plan, and 157 of the 162 bombers attacked the target, dropping three hundred and seven 2,000 lb. bombs and six 500 lb. bombs with fair to good results. Flak was moderate but accurate and at least one bomber sustained damage, and subsequently crash-landed on return to its home base.

The fighter operations were all uneventful, with the exception of the second fighter sweep, which intercepted eight FW190s near St. Pol. Two were claimed destroyed by pilots of 19 and 122 Squadrons, and the former squadron's victory constituted its 100th destroyed during the War.

Two hours after their return, the Spitfire XII Wing was airborne again on a Ramrod to Audinghen, France. Although the village itself was of no strategic importance, a section of Germany's Atlantic Wall defences lay nearby that was the actual target of the attack by Bomphoons and RAF 2 Group bombers.

Date	11 November 1943
Operation	Ramrod 312
Targets	Parts I-IV: Audinghen, Pas-de-Calais
Bombers	Part I: 486 Sqn, 8 Bomphoons; 8 dispatched, 8 bombed
	Part II: 3 Sqn, 8 Bomphoons; 8 dispatched, 8 bombed
	Part III-A: 24 Bostons; 24 dispatched, 24 bombed
	Part III-B: 24 Mitchells; 24 dispatched, 24 bombed
	Part III-C: 24 Mitchells; 24 dispatched, 24 bombed
Close Escort Part I	Tangmere: 197 Squadron (16 Typhoon Ib)
Close Escort Part II	Fairlop: 195 Sqn, & Manston: 198 Sqn (17 Typhoon Ib)
Close Escort Part III-A	Coltishall: 64 & 611 Squadrons (Spit Vb)
Close Escort Part III-B	Digby: 402 & 416 Squadrons (Spit Vb)
Close Escort Part III-C	Hawkinge: 350 Sqn, & Friston: 349 Sqn (Spit Vb)
Fighter Umbrella	Detling: 132 & 602 Squadrons (Spitfire IXb)
	Northolt: 302 & 317 Squadrons (Spitfire IXc)
	West Malling: 124 Squadron (Spitfire VII)
1st Fighter Sweep	Tangmere: 41 & 91 Squadrons (Spitfire XII)
2nd Fighter Sweep	Gravesend: 19, 65 & 122 Squadrons (Spitfire IX)
3rd Fighter Sweep	Kenley: 403 & 421 Squadrons (Spitfire IXb)
4th Fighter Sweep	Hornchurch: 129 & 222 Squadrons (Spitfire IXb)
5th Fighter Sweep	North Weald: 331 & 332 Squadrons (Spitfire IX)

The Bomphoons were intended only as a primer and marker, and their times over target were assigned at zero minus 30 minutes and zero minus 20, zero hour being 15:30. Eight Bomphoons participated in Part I, each dropping two 500 lb. bombs on the coastal gun emplacements from altitudes of between 6,000 and 10,000 feet, obtaining direct hits on buildings belonging to the positions.

Part II similarly comprised eight Bomphoons, which dropped two 500 lb. bombs each from between 6,000 and 10,000 feet, although they fell wide and some were seen to burst in the centre of the village. Immediately afterwards, 198 Squadron was vectored to the Le Touquet area on reports of enemy aircraft in the vicinity. They sighted four and chased them a significant distance inland before being recalled, but no claims were made.

The first wave of bombers rendezvoused 12,000 feet over Dungeness at 15:30, and was over the target just seven minutes later, dropping eighty-eight 500 lb. bombs with fair results; bursts were seen on buildings on the outskirts of Audinghen village.

The second and third waves arrived over Dungeness at subsequent ten minute intervals, and were over the target seven minutes later, dropping ninety-six, respectively ninety-eight, 1,000 lb. bombs with good results. Their escorts and fighter umbrella all operated according to plan and without incident.

The Spitfire XII Wing was airborne at zero-15, and 22 aircraft crossed the Channel on the deck under Beachy Head Control, both the Squadron and the Wing led by Wg Cdr Harries. Underway, 41 Squadron's Fg Off Jack Sabourin (EN237) found his R/T malfunctioning, and returned to base alone, putting down at 15:40.

The rest of the Wing climbed steeply to 11,000-12,000 feet as they approached the French coast, and crossed in west of Dieppe. They then flew south towards Yerville at the same altitude, above a 2/10ths cloud layer at 5,000 feet, where they received a new vector northeast to Amiens. Before reaching the town, they turned north and flew between Abbeville and Amiens, and subsequently west, and crossed out again over Le Touquet, noting thick haze up to 5,000 feet on the way.

As no enemy aircraft were seen, the Squadron considered the operation, "altogether an uneventful show from our point of view".[327]

12 November 1943 – Another attack was planned on Mimoyecques in Ramrod 313 today, in which the Spitfire XII Wing was to participate. However, unsuitable weather caused it to be cancelled before it commenced. The poor weather then continued for the next few days and the Squadron did not fly operationally again until 15 November. In the meantime, however, some practice flying was undertaken, which included air firing, and time was also spent on the Link trainer.

Separately today, news reached the Squadron that Flt Sgt Stan May RAAF, who had been shot down in Belgium on 19 September, had evaded capture and arrived safely in Gibraltar. Flt Sgt Jimmy Payne recorded in his logbook today, "Heard Stan was safe at Gib. – Good old Stan".[328] He arrived back in the United Kingdom this same day but, unlike Flt Lt Tom Slack, was not destined to return to 41 Squadron.

15 November 1943 – As the past few days' poor weather conditions continued today, operational flying was limited to a single weather reconnaissance to France, which was flown after lunch. At 13:15, Fg Off Clive Birbeck and Flt Sgt Peter Graham took off for Le Havre and then flew to Cherbourg, returning 55 minutes later reporting 8-9/10ths cloud under 2,000 feet at the former location and 10/10ths at 2,000 feet at the latter. As the cloud cover was similar inland, and visibility extended no more than four miles, it was considered that the conditions were too poor for any further operational flying.

During the day, the pilots otherwise undertook local practice flying, but Fg Off Herb Wagner (MB838) had a lucky escape when he lost power on take-off for such a sortie. A wing clipped the ground and he cartwheeled off the end of the runway.[329] Surprisingly, Wagner was not hurt; less surprisingly, the aircraft was written off.

Separately today, the 2nd Tactical Air Force ('2 TAF') was formed as an element of the Allied Expeditionary Air Force (AEAF), commanded by ACM Sir Trafford Leigh-Mallory KCB DSO, in preparation for the invasion of mainland Europe. It would be almost another year before this event would have any relevance to 41 Squadron, but 2 TAF would then play a significant role in the unit's activity until the cessation of hostilities.

16 November 1943 – In a day not dissimilar to the previous, the Squadron's operational activity only consisted of three weather reconnaissances to France today. Flying commenced at 10:10, when Flt Lts Bruce Moffett and Terence Welsh reconnoitred the Bernay area, followed at 11:15 by Sqn Ldr John Clouston and Flt Sgt Peter Wall, who flew to Cherbourg. However, the pair returned early for unexplained reasons and was replaced on the job by Fg Offs Peter Cowell and Ross Harding at 12:15. The first section returned at 12:15, the second at 12:05 and the third at 13:05, all three reporting unsuitable conditions in France.

18 November 1943 – Following yet another day of no operational flying as a result of adverse weather conditions, the Squadron was in the air again today, but only to fly a single weather reconnaissance.[330] Flt Sgt Peter Wall and Plt Off Keith Curtis were airborne at 08:25 to Cherbourg, but Curtis (EN237) was compelled to return early with 'petrol trouble' and Wall continued alone. He returned at 09:30 with another discouraging report and the ORB lamented, "It would seem that this spell of bad weather must break soon and give our pilots an opportunity of continuing in their active operations against the Hun."[331]

Separately today, a captured FW190 arrived at Tangmere to participate in practice dog fights, which enabled many men a close-up investigation of an aircraft most had only seen at distance

Flt Lt (Actg Sqn Ldr) Bernard Ingham DFC was posted as Wing Commander Flying of the Spitfire XII Wing at RAF Tangmere on 16 November 1943. He married Joan Stringer in late 1944, and retired as a Wing Commander in December 1945. © Sheppard Family

and at high speed. Flt Sgt Stan May also visited 41 Squadron today, having returned to the United Kingdom following almost two months on the run through Belgium, France and Spain to Gibraltar.

19 November 1943 – The weather had finally improved sufficiently for the Spitfire XII Wing to participate in another Ramrod today, the targets of which were German airfields in France. Despite best intentions, however, weather hampered the operation once again and all 110 bombers all aborted.

Date	19 November 1943
Operation	Ramrod 316
Targets	Part I: St. André-de-l'Eure Airfield, Haute-Normandie Part II: Évreux Airfield, Picardie
Bombers	Part I: 72 Marauders; 72 dispatched – aborted Part II: 38 Marauders; 38 dispatched – recalled
Close Escort Part I	Heston: 306 & 315 Squadrons (Spitfire Vb) – aborted Friston: 349 & 350 Squadron (Spitfire Vb) – aborted
Escort Cover	Hornchurch: 129 & 222 Squadrons (Spitfire IX)
High Cover	North Weald: 331 & 332 Squadrons (Spitfire IX)
Withdrawal Cover	Tangmere: 41 & 91 Squadrons (Spitfire XII)
Close Escort Part II	Digby & Coltishall – cancelled, DNTO
Escort Cover	Detling: 132 & 602 Squadrons (Spitfire IX)
High Cover	Gravesend: 19, 65 & 122 Squadrons (Spitfire IX)
Top Cover	West Malling: 124 Squadron (Spitfire VII)
Withdrawal Cover	Northolt: 302, 308 & 317 Squadrons (Spitfire IX)
Casualties	308 Sqn: Fg Off Zbigniew Frackiewicz EF in Spit IX, BS411, FL nr Lisieux, POW

The Spitfire XII Wing was assigned to withdrawal support for Part I, and although the bombers aborted over the French coast as a result of cloud cover, the Wing continued inbound on an independent sweep.

The pilots crossed the Channel at zero feet, then climbed rapidly to make landfall at Fécamp at 15,000 feet, before descending to 10,000 feet over Le Trait. Meanwhile, the High Cover squadrons had been engaged by the Luftwaffe south of Saint-Clair-d'Arcey, when eight to ten FW190s dived vertically through their formation at 28,000 feet without result. The two squadrons followed them down to 15,000 feet and both the Escort Cover squadrons and Spitfire XII Wing were vectored to the vicinity to give chase.

41 and 91 Squadrons flew to Beaumont-le-Roger, where they sighted nine aircraft, believed to have been FW190s, flying northwest at 17,000 feet, and another eight further west at an altitude of 21,000 feet. The Wing turned in their general direction but the enemy aircraft were lost sight of near Triqueville. After orbiting a short while, the Wing was given a new vector to Caen, but no more enemy aircraft were seen and they crossed out again at Trouville. The pilots landed again between 15:15 and 15:20 with little to report.

Although Part I's High Cover squadrons were also unable to make any interceptions, the Escort Cover squadrons enjoyed some success when they climbed to 27,000 feet over Bernay and engaged several enemy aircraft. 129 Squadron claimed one FW190 destroyed and one Me109 damaged.

Part II's Escort Cover, High Cover, Top Cover and Withdrawal Cover squadrons also swept uneventfully without the bombers, but one of 308 Squadron's pilots suffered engine failure and came down in France. He was captured and spent the rest of the War behind wire.

There was no further flying today for the Spitfire XII Wing, but there was considerable excitement late in the evening when an RAF Halifax crashed into the servicing hangar at Tangmere at 21:35. The aircraft was returning from a raid to Leverkusen, Germany, and attempting to land at Tangmere when it crashed, killing the entire crew.[332]

The crash also destroyed two Lysanders, three Spitfires and six Typhoons[333] that were in the hangar at the time. The resulting large fire caused ammunition to explode and the station personnel were warned to take cover; airborne aircraft were diverted to Ford, and when inbound enemy aircraft were plotted, all off duty personnel were ordered to evacuate the airfield.

A Change of Command

Sqn Ldr Bernard Ingham DFC had been promoted to Wing Commander Flying of the Spitfire Wing, at RAF Tangmere on 16 November 1943, to replace Wg Cdr Raymond Harries who was posted to Headquarters, 11 Group. Ingham's replacement, Sqn Ldr Ian Matthew DFC of 91 Squadron, took over command of 41 Squadron three days later.

Matthew had joined the RAFVR in April 1939 and was awarded his flying badge in July 1940. His first operational posting came in early November 1940 when he joined 611 Squadron, and shortly thereafter moved to 66 Squadron at Biggin Hill. In July 1941, Matthew was posted to 58 OTU as a flying instructor and remained in this post until May 1942, by which time he had been commissioned. He then returned to operations with 91 Squadron and remained with this unit until his posting to 41 Squadron today, having been awarded a DFC in July 1943. He would only remain with the unit for a brief two months and summed up his tenure many years later as "10 close escorts to USAAF bombers & 7 fighter sweeps with little action".[334]

Flt Lt (Actg Wg Cdr) Ingham was promoted to Squadron Leader (WS) in February 1944 and relinquished his commission as 'medically unfit' at the beginning of December 1945, retaining Wing Commander. Sadly, he died of tuberculosis in August 1947, aged just 27 years old.

20 November 1943 – The Squadron flew three operations today, the first of which was a weather reconnaissance to the Cherbourg area by Fg Off Birbeck and Flt Sgt Peter Graham. They were airborne at 09:10 and reached Cherbourg 20 minutes later, where they found 9/10ths cloud between 2,500 and 9,000 feet. They landed again at 10:05, reporting visibility below the cloud base of four miles owing to haze.

It was almost another four hours before the Squadron was airborne again, and on that occasion flew with 91 Squadron to undertake Rodeo 271 to the Abbeville area. Twenty-four aircraft were airborne at 14:00 led by Wg Cdr Ingham, with Sqn Ldr Matthew as his No. 2 on his first operation with the Squadron, and flew across the Channel at zero feet. Fifteen minutes later they climbed to 11,000 feet and crossed the French coast east of Dieppe.

The Wing was then vectored southwards by Beachy Head Control, after which they received several more vectors that took them over Poix and back to Aumale, where enemy aircraft were reported below them. None were seen, but Flt Lt Don Smith, who was on his first operational flight after a month away on a course and leave, started having trouble with his jettison tank, and returned home alone, landing at 14:50.

The rest of the Wing flew on to Abbeville and stationary and moving trains were seen in the vicinity of Rue, but these were not attacked. The pilots crossed out again at Cayeux-sur-Mer at 8,000 feet and headed back to Tangmere, above 6/10ths to 9/10ths cloud at 3,000 feet, where they landed at 15:20.

41 Squadron was in the air one more time today, but only for a brief ASR patrol. Flt Sgt Peter Wall and Fg Off Jack Sabourin took off at 16:07 to conduct a search but had only reached a point 15 miles south of Selsey Bill when they were recalled owing to deteriorating weather conditions at Tangmere. They put down at 16:32, having seen nothing, and there was no more flying until after midday three days later.

23 November 1943 – Following a few days of poor weather, the Squadron was airborne again today on a single Ramrod operation to St. Omer-Longuenesse Airfield in support of the 9th U.S. Air Force. The Spitfire XII Wing provided close escort to Part II, which proved successful despite five fighter squadrons not getting airborne on account of fog.

Date	23 November 1943
Operation	Ramrod 326
Targets	Part I: Lille-Vendeville Airfield, Pas-de-Calais Part II: St. Omer-Longuenesse Airfield, Pas-de-Calais
Bombers	Part I: 72 Marauders; 72 dispatched, 19 bombed alternative target, believed Berck-sur-Mer Airfield Part II: 72 Marauders; 72 dispatched, 62 bombed
Casualties	322 BG/452 BS: B-26 Marauder, 41-31817, SD/AA, 6 crew †; 323 BG/454 BS: B-26 Marauder, 41-34713, hit by falling bomb & crashed
Close Escort Part I	Heston: 306 & 315 Squadrons (Spitfire Vb) – DNTO Friston: 349 & 350 Squadrons (Spitfire Vb)
Escort Cover	Biggin Hill: 401, 411 & 412 Squadrons (Spitfire IX)
High Cover	Gravesend: 19, 65 & 122 Squadrons (Spitfire IX)
Fighter Sweep	North Weald: 331 & 332 Squadrons (Spitfire IX) – DNTO
Close Escort Part II	Ibsley: 310, 312 & 313 Squadrons (Spitfire Vb) – DNTO Hawkinge: 501 Squadron (Spitfire Vb)
Escort Cover [Clse Escort]	Tangmere: 41 & 91 Squadrons (Spitfire XII)
Esc't Cover [Replacement]	Detling: 132 & 602 Squadrons (Spitfire IXb)
High Cover	Hornchurch: 129 & 222 Squadrons (Spitfire IX) – DNTO
High Cover [Replacement]	Northolt: 302, 303 & 317 Squadrons (Spitfire IX)
1st Fighter Sweep	Detling: 132 & 602 Squadrons (Spitfire IXb) – cancelled
2nd Fighter Sweep	Northolt: 302, 303 & 317 Sqns (Spitfire IXc) – cancelled
Casualties	411 Sqn: Plt Off Stanley M. Kent RCAF, EF into Channel in Spit IX, MA312, †

Part I was marred by weather and when Lille-Vendeville Airfield was found obscured by 10/10ths cloud, 19 bombers attacked an alternative target, believed to have been Berck-sur-Mer Airfield. Four of the twelve escort squadrons did not participate on account of the conditions, but of those that joined one pilot was lost when he suffered engine failure and ditched in the Channel.

The Spitfire XII Wing was airborne at 12:25 led by 91 Squadron's Commanding Officer, Sqn Ldr Norman Kynaston, and 41 Squadron was led by Sqn Ldr Matthew for the first time. Within

Sqn Ldr Ian G. S. Matthew DFC was OC 41 Squadron from 20 November 1943 to 25 January 1944. He retired from the RAF in late 1946 and emigrated to Canada in 1957. © 41 Squadron RAF

minutes, Flt Sgt Bruce Adams (MB798), who was No. 2 to Sqn Ldr Matthew, found his jettison tank malfunctioning and was compelled to return. He landed again at 12:35. The rest of the Wing crossed the Channel as planned.

However, when Ibsley's Close Escort squadrons and Hornchurch's High Cover squadrons were unable to take off owing to fog, Part II was compelled to operate with eight instead of 13 escort squadrons. As this left only one squadron for the close escort of 72 Marauders, 41 and 91 Squadrons were moved into Ibsley's place and assumed the role of Close Escort wing. To cover their move, the first fighter sweep was cancelled and 132 and 602 became the new Escort Cover wing. It then followed that when Hornchurch's High Cover wing failed to join, the second fighter sweep was also cancelled and 302, 303 and 317 Squadrons became the new High Cover wing.

The bombers otherwise operated according to plan and attacked St. Omer-Longuenesse Airfield with fair results. However, Flak was heavy, intense and accurate and two Marauders were brought down in the target area, but only one parachute was seen. Attesting to this, 41 Squadron's Fg Off Ron Johnson recorded in his logbook, "Most flak I have seen this season"[335], whilst Flt Sgt Jimmy Payne wrote, "Bags of Flak – one Marauder down in flames".[336]

The Spitfire XII Wing completed the job otherwise without incident, although 41 Squadron landed at Hawkinge at 13:45 on the way home to refuel, before returning to Tangmere, reporting the operation ran according to plan.

Separately today, Fg Off 'Momo' Balasse re-joined 41 Squadron, having been detached to 611 Squadron between 6 and 23 November 1943. He would now remain with the unit until January 1945.

24 November 1943 – Owing to weather still being less than ideal for operations, the Squadron's flying today was limited to two weather reconnaissances, at 08:25-09:35 and 10:05-10:55.

The first of these was flown by Fg Off Ron Loweth and Flt Sgt William Vann, who flew across the Channel at zero feet to just off Cherbourg, where they made a new vector for a point five miles north of Pointe de Barfleur. They then aimed for 15 miles north of Caen where they climbed to 4,000 feet and verified the altitude of the cloud base. The pair returned across the Channel at zero feet again and landed back at Tangmere reporting 10/10ths cloud over France with a base of 4,000 feet and visibility of ten miles, similar cloud off the coast, but with severe rain squalls in places, cloud down to 500 feet, and visibility of only 300-400 yards.

Just 30 minutes after their return, Fg Off Ron Johnson and Flt Sgt Jimmy Payne were sent on another weather reconnaissance to Cherbourg, which confirmed Loweth and Vann's report. They returned at 10:55 stating they had encountered 10/10ths cloud from 2,000 feet with rain squalls over the Channel in the Cherbourg area, and 6/10ths-7/10ths cloud from 2,000 feet, and a second cloud layer of 10/10ths at 6,000 feet over France.

25 November 1943 – The Spitfire XII Wing participated in two fighter sweeps in support of Ramrod operations today, both targeting Audinghen once again.

Following the first, failed, raid of 10 November, and the second, more successful, raid of 11 November, which targeted the military site and tried to avoid the village, the Germans took shelter in the village. The French Résistance took advantage of this fact and two of its operatives broke into a few requisitioned houses in the hope of finding German documents and maps. They were successful and a series of documents were appropriated and subsequently forwarded to London.

To cover the theft, however, the village was attacked today by RAF bombers and Typhoons in three Ramrod operations, Nos. 330, 331, and 333. The Spitfire XII Wing participated in the first and last of these, which eventually forced the Germans to withdraw to nearby Hardinghen.

Date	25 November 1943
Operation	Ramrod 330
Target	Audinghen, Pas-de-Calais
Bombers	Part I: 2 Group RAF: 24 Bostons; 24 dispatched, 21 bombed Part II: 2 Group RAF: 24 Mitchells; 24 dispatched, 24 bombed Part III: 2 Group RAF: 24 Mitchells; 24 dispatched, 21 bombed
Casualties	226 Sqn: Mitchell II, FL196, MQ-J, crashed in flames, Dover, crew †[337]; 88 Sqn: Boston IIIA, BZ217, RH-Q, CL Hawkinge, & Boston IIIA, BZ278, RH-G, AA/CL nr Hartford Bridge, crew inj.
Close Escort Part I	Friston: 349 & 350 Squadrons (Spitfire Vb)
Close Escort Part II	Heston: 306 & 315 Squadrons (Spitfire Vb)
Close Escort Part III	Friston: 349 & 350 Squadrons (Spitfire Vb) [i.e. Parts I *and* III]
Fighter Umbrella	Detling: 132 & 602 Squadrons (Spitfire IX)
1st Fighter Sweep	North Weald: 331 & 332 Squadrons (Spitfire IX)
2nd Fighter Sweep	Hornchurch: 129 & 222 Squadrons (Spitfire IX)
3rd Fighter Sweep	Kenley: 403 & 421 Squadrons (Spitfire IX)
4th Fighter Sweep	Tangmere: 41 & 91 Squadrons (Spitfire XII)

The Ramrod foresaw Part I's bombers rendezvousing over Dungeness at 10,000 feet at 09:30 (zero), with time over target scheduled seven minutes later. Parts II and III were to follow at ten-minute intervals. The Fighter Umbrella arrived over the target at zero plus five minutes and patrolled the area until Part III's bombers had dropped their payloads. During this time, the Fighter Sweeps operated in the Furnes [Veurne]-Cambrai, Sangatte-Boulogne, Hardelot-Courtrai [Kortrijk] and Cayeux-Le Touquet areas with altitudes and return times at their respective wing leaders' discretion.

The Spitfire XII Wing was airborne before the bombers, at 09:05, with 91 Squadron and the Wing led by Wg Cdr Ingham and 41 Squadron led by Sqn Ldr Matthew. They crossed the Channel at zero feet, but before reaching the French coast Sqn Ldr Clouston (MB794) pulled out and returned home with jettison tank trouble. The rest of the pilots climbed to 13,000 feet as they approached the coast and crossed in north of Ault under Beachy Head Control.

As the Wing flew towards Abbeville in generally clear skies, they were warned that enemy aircraft had been plotted just ahead of them. However, none could be seen. The pilots then flew toward Montdidier at high speed at an altitude of 9,000 feet in the hope of an interception there, but still nothing was seen. They subsequently flew northwards to a point west of Albert, and crossed out again at Le Touquet, landing again at 10:35 with nothing to report.

The bombers had meanwhile operated successfully. Part I's Bostons attacked the target from altitudes of between 9,700 and 10,700 feet, dropping eighty-three 500 lb. bombs, of which many were seen to burst in the target area. Part II's Mitchells attacked the target from between 10,000 and 11,000 feet, dropping ninety-two 1,000 lb. bombs, from which four sticks were seen to land in the centre of the village. Part III's bombers attacked from 9,200 to 10,300 feet, dropping eighty-four 1,000 lb. bombs, which were "seen to cover the target".[338]

All the other escorting, fighter umbrella and fighter sweep squadrons also operated without incident, but barely had they cleared the area, than Ramrod 331 arrived. Six waves of Typhoon bombers attacked Audinghen village from altitudes of between 6,000 and 12,000 feet with 500 lb. bombs. These commenced at 10:15 (zero+45) and subsequent attacks followed at five to ten minute intervals until 10:45.

The first wave, consisting of 56 and 195 Squadrons, dropped 40 bombs; the second, Tangmere's 197 and 486 Squadrons, dropped 48; the third, 181, 182 and 247 Squadrons, dropped 32; the fourth, 174, 175, and 245 Squadrons, dropped 29; the fifth, 3 and 198 Squadrons, dropped 15; and the sixth, 1 and 609 Squadrons, dropped 20. All experienced Flak, but no casualties were recorded, and bombing results were considered fair to good.

Audinghen village was then left to burn and smoulder for almost five hours before the next attack was made, once again by three waves of 2 Group bombers, one of 24 Bostons and two of each 24 Mitchells. They were covered by fighter squadrons in a similar manner to the morning's operation, with the exception that seven fighter sweeps were laid on instead of four.

Date	25 November 1943
Operation	Ramrod 333
Target	Audinghen, Pas-de-Calais
Bombers	Part I: 24 Bostons; 24 dispatched, 18 bombed Part II: 24 Mitchells; 24 dispatched, 24 bombed Part III: 24 Mitchells; 24 dispatched, 24 bombed
Close Escort Part I	Friston: 349 & 350 Squadrons (Spitfire Vb)
Close Escort Part II	Heston: 306 & 315 Squadrons (Spitfire Vb)
Close Escort Part III	Friston: 349 & 350 Squadrons (Spitfire Vb) [i.e. Parts I *and* III]
Fighter Umbrella	Hornchurch: 129 & 222 Squadrons (Spitfire IXb)
1st Fighter Sweep	North Weald: 331 & 332 Squadrons (Spitfire IX)
2nd Fighter Sweep	Gravesend: 19, 65 & 122 Squadrons (Spitfire IX)
3rd Fighter Sweep	Biggin Hill: 401, 411 & 412 Squadrons (Spitfire IX)
4th Fighter Sweep	Tangmere: 41 & 91 Squadrons (Spitfire XII)
5th Fighter Sweep	Detling: 132 & 602 Squadrons (Spitfire IXb)
6th Fighter Sweep	Northolt: 302, 308 & 317 Squadrons (Spitfire IXc)
7th Fighter Sweep	Kenley: 403 & 421 Squadrons (Spitfire IXb)
Casualties	122 Sqn: Flt Sgt Donald Bostock, glycol leak, baled out of Spit IX, MA764, SW of Béthune, ER

This Ramrod foresaw Part I's bombers rendezvousing over Dungeness at 12,000 feet at 15:30 (zero), with time over target scheduled seven minutes later at the same altitude. Parts II and III were to follow at ten-minute intervals. Once again, the Fighter Umbrella arrived over the target at zero+5 and patrolled the target area until Part III's bombers had dropped their payloads. The Fighter Sweeps operated in the Blankenberge-Deynze [Deinze], Gravelines-Lille, Hardelot-Béthune, and Ault-Amiens areas.

In a similar pattern to the morning's operation, the Spitfire XII Wing was airborne at 15:05, twenty-five minutes before Part I's bombers rendezvoused, with Wg Cdr Ingham leading the Wing and 41 Squadron. The pilots crossed in 12,000 feet over Quend-Plage-les-Pins, Picardie, under Beachy Head Control and swept from Abbeville to Poix.

A pilot, possibly Fg Off Maurice 'Momo' Balasse, sitting in the cockpit of Spitfire XII, RM797, EB-Y, being prepared for take-off in late 1943. © Jean-Louis Roba

When nearing Amiens, Control warned them that enemy aircraft were flying at low altitude near St. Pol. As a result, they descended to 5,000 feet, and after several vectors and climbing again to 8,000 feet, then sweeping Doullens, Hesdin and Hucqueliers, they gave up, having seen no sign of the reported aircraft despite clear weather. They crossed out again over Le Touquet at 8,000 feet, where they came under light, inaccurate Flak fire and sighted three trains, which were not attacked.

Returning across the Channel once again, they landed at Tangmere at 16:35, thereby concluding the day's flying. The Squadron ORB summed up the day's flying by stating that, "both of today's shows proved uneventful in spite of a lot of Huns being reported. We all hope to be more fortunate in the near future."[339] In fact, they would have to wait some time yet.

The bombers had meanwhile completed their tasks, Part I dropping seventy-two 500 lb. bombs from 13,100 feet, resulting in bursts in the centre of the village, and some to the northwest, northeast, and southeast of the target. Part II's bombers dropped ninety-two 1,000 lb. bombs from between 11,500 and 12,800 feet, which achieved a fair concentration of bursts in the village and along the northern boundary of the target area. Part III attacked the target from 11,500 to 12,500 feet, dropping ninety-five 1,000 lb. bombs, many of which were seen to fall in the target area.

The escorting fighter squadrons operated generally according to plan and uneventfully, with two exceptions. The first fighter sweep encountered six enemy aircraft 15 miles southeast of Lille, which were bounced by 332 Squadron. They claimed one Me109G destroyed, and subsequently a FW190 and another Me109G, both of which were seen by several pilots to be fired upon, but "not by our own a/c"[340], and as such were credited to the North Weald Wing as a whole.

The second fighter sweep also intercepted two Me109s southwest of Béthune, one of which was damaged by 122 Squadron. However, the unit also lost one pilot, who suffered a glycol leak, possibly from combat damage, southwest of Béthune but would ultimately avoid capture and return to England.

26 November 1943 – The day's operational flying for the Spitfire XII Wing consisted of escort cover for a single Ramrod operation to Rosières-en-Santerre Airfield in Picardie, which operated from Hawkinge. As such, they flew to the station at 09:05, and arrived 30 minutes later, where they were briefed and fed prior to the commencement of the Ramrod's Part III, at 12:55.

Date	26 November 1943
Operation	Ramrod 336
Targets	Part I: Audinghen, Pas-de-Calais
	Part II: Cambrai Airfield, Pas-de-Calais
	Part III: Rosières-en-Santerre Airfield, Picardie
	Part III Alternative Targets: Poix or Amiens-Glisy Airfields
Bombers	Part I: 72 Marauders; 51 dispatched, 50 bombed
	Part II: 72 Marauders; 69 dispatched, 34 bombed
	Part III: 72 Marauders; 69 dispatched, 32 bombed unknown target & 23 bombed unidentified airfield, possibly Roye-Amy
Casualties	Part I: 22 Marauders CD/AA
	Part III: 2 crew WIA/AA
Close Escort Part I	Lympne: 1 & 609 Squadrons (Typhoon Ib)
	Manston: 3 & 198 Squadrons (Typhoon Ib)
	Fairlop: 56 & 195 Squadrons (Typhoon Ib) – 195 Sqn DNTO
Close Escort Part II	Digby: 402 & 416 Squadrons (Spit Vb)
Escort Cover	Detling: 132 & 602 Squadrons (Spitfire IX)
High Cover	Biggin Hill: 401, 411 & 412 Squadrons (Spitfire IX)
Top Cover	West Malling: 124 Squadron (Spitfire VII)
Close Escort Part III	Friston: 349 & 350 Squadrons (Spitfire Vb)
	Heston: 306 & 315 Squadrons (Spitfire Vb)
Escort Cover	Tangmere: 41 & 91 Squadrons (Spitfire XII)
	Gravesend: 19, 65 & 122 Squadrons (Spitfire IX)
High Cover	Northolt: 302, 308 & 317 Squadrons (Spitfire IX)
1st Fighter Sweep	Kenley: 403 & 421 Squadrons (Spitfire IX)
2nd Fighter Sweep	North Weald: 331 & 332 Squadrons (Spitfire IX)
3rd Fighter Sweep	Merston: 181 & 245 Squadrons (8 Typhoon Ib)
Casualties	401 Sqn: Flt Lt T. Koch CD/AA, FL Spit IX, MH886, nr Hawkinge, IFA, A/C Cat E;
	416 Sqn: WO2 Harry Dubnick, EF/FL Spit Vb, EN908, nr Doullens †

Part I delivered yet another attack on Audinghen by Marauders and Typhoons, which dropped one hundred and eighty-eight 1,000 lb. bombs with fair to good results. However, the Flak was intense and whilst all the bombers returned, almost half of them sustained damage of some degree.

Part II to Cambrai Airfield was also considered successful, even though only 34 of the 69 dispatched bombers attacked the target. A total of four hundred and eighty-five 100 lb. bombs and one hundred and fifty-eight 300 lb. bombs were dropped with fair to good results, the escort squadrons considering the bombing 'very accurate and effective'.

Their Close Escort spotted four FW190s taking off from an airfield, believed to have been Grevillers, and one was claimed destroyed by 416 Squadron near Epinoy. However, another aircraft of the same squadron force-landed near Doullens with engine failure, killing the pilot. The High Cover squadrons also caught five FW190s taking off from Achiet-le-Grand, one of which was claimed destroyed by 401 Squadron.

Part III's target, Rosières-en-Santerre Airfield, proved a more difficult objective. The bombers were scheduled to rendezvous 15 miles southwest of Le Touquet at 12,000 feet at 12:10 (zero+10), and to be over the target at zero+32. However, the bombers arrived at the rendezvous four to five minutes early and missed their Close Escort, half of which did not catch them up until reaching the French coast, and half not until 15 miles inland.

The Escort Cover wings also had issues rendezvousing. 19, 65 & 122 Squadrons arrived at the rendezvous four minutes late but caught up with the bombers over the target area. The Spitfire XII Wing was airborne from Hawkinge at 12:55, led by Wg Cdr Ingham, with 41 Squadron led by Sqn Ldr Matthew. They also missed the rendezvous, when alterations were made to the plan, and the "necessary information [was] received too late to make the R/V on time".[341] They caught up with the bombers over the target area, but not before Fg Off Herb Wagner (EN603) had turned for home with engine trouble, landing again at 13:50.

Part III's bombers, now accompanied by all their escort squadrons, encountered 5/10ths cloud at 5,000-6,000 feet, with another thin cloud layer at 20,000 feet. However, 32 of the 69 Marauders attacked an unidentified target with one hundred and sixty-nine 300 lb. bombs and eighty-six 500 lb. bombs, whilst another 23 Marauders attacked an unidentified airfield with three hundred and forty-nine 100 lb. bombs and ninety 300 lb. bombs. 41 Squadron later reported they believed the airfield was Roye-Amy, and saw bursts on the intersection of the runways, on dispersals, and in fields south-southwest of the airfield. The remaining 14 Marauders returned home without bombing.

The Spitfire XII Wing escorted the bombers home again, and reported heavy Flak directed at them from Rosières-en-Santerre. All the aircraft returned but fragments of exploding AA shells wounded two members of the bomber crews. No enemy aircraft were seen, and all escorting squadrons reported the trip otherwise uneventful. 41 and 91 Squadrons landed at Tangmere again at 14:35, thereby concluding the day's operational flying.

29 November 1943 – Following two days of inclement weather, which had kept Tangmere's squadrons on the ground, 41 Squadron was airborne three times today, for a Ramrod, a weather reconnaissance and a Rodeo.

In the first of these, the Spitfire XII Wing took off at 09:50 to participate in Ramrod 339, as Escort Cover to 72 Marauders attacking Cambrai-Epinoy Airfield in the Pas-de-Calais. However, the attack was cancelled on account of unsuitable weather and the Wing recalled when ten miles south of Hastings. They landed again at 10:30.

Much to their surprise, however, after landing Fg Off Ron Johnson's aircraft (MB837) was found to have a single .303 inch round in the engine, "time and place unknown"[342], which caused slight damage. Johnson took the incident in his stride, recording nonchalantly in his logbook, "Weather duff – came back – hit in engine by .303 from our own side".[343]

Fg Off Clive Birbeck (EN605) and Flt Sgt Bruce Adams (MB846) were airborne after lunch to conduct a weather reconnaissance of the Caen area and the Baie de la Seine. Birbeck was off the deck at 13:00, but Adams was delayed five minutes with engine trouble. He finally became airborne, but was unable to locate Birbeck and returned at 13:15.

Birbeck had continued on to complete the reconnaissance alone, and returned to base at 13:55, reporting a front stretching north-south just west of the Caen Canal, rising from 2,000 feet to 20,000. To the east of the front, a bank of 6/10ths cloud hung between 4,000 and 8,000 feet, with six miles vertical visibility. Conditions and visibility over the Channel were considerably better with only 1/10th cloud on the English side.

The Squadron was airborne again at 15:15 with 91 Squadron for a Wing operation, Rodeo 272, involving 24 aircraft led by Wg Cdr Ingham. The pilots made landfall at Cabourg and swept to Lisieux, Bernay, and Montreuil, then back to Lisieux, and crossed out over the Caen Canal. The weather was clear over France, but neither Flak nor enemy aircraft were encountered. The Wing returned back across the Channel, finding thick cumulus cloud from 2,000 to 15,000 feet 40 miles off the coast, with storms and rain, and landed safely back at Tangmere at 16:50. This concluded the day's operational flying.

30 November 1943 – The Squadron was airborne at 08:50 and flew to Hawkinge, where they landed at 09:15, to position themselves for another Ramrod today. However, the briefing for the operation was continually postponed and finally the entire operation was scrubbed on account of unsuitable weather. The pilots took off again at 14:40 and returned to Tangmere, where they landed at 15:20, considering it "a disappointing day".[344] There was no more operational flying.

December 1943 – As a result of poor winter flying conditions in December 1943, very little flying was done. No operational flying was undertaken on eighteen days of the month – 7-12, 14-19, 23, and 25-29 December – and was otherwise significantly reduced on a further two days – 3 and 6 December.

The Squadron nonetheless managed to participate in 15 Ramrods on the remaining days of the month, many of the objectives of which were 'Noball' targets for the first time. It is doubtful whether the pilots even knew the significance of these sites at this point in time.

Separately, one pilot was seriously injured in a flying accident, and four pilots were posted away, but were replaced by a like number of arrivals.

△ Airfield ✝ Noball Target ▮ Big Ben Target

Date	Operation	Role	Type	Destination / Target
1	Ramrod 343	Escort Cover	△	Lille-Vendeville, France
2	Ramrod 111	Fighter Sweep	▮	Martinvast, France
4	Ramrod 348	Escort Cover	△	Chièvres, Belgium
5	Ramrod 351	Close Escort	✝	St. Josse-au-Bois & Ligescourt, Fr
13	Ramrod 363	Fighter Sweep	△	Schipol, Netherlands
20	Ramrod 375	Close Escort	✝	Agenvillers, Vacqueriette, Le Meillard & Bonnières, France
20	Ramrod 377	Close Escort	✝	Drionville, France
21	Ramrod 381	Close Escort	✝	Le Mesnil-Allard, France
22	Ramrod 383	Close Escort	✝	Le Mesnil-Allard, France
22	Ramrod 386	Fighter Sweep	✝	Arras, France
24	Ramrod 393	Fighter Umbrella	✝	Le Mesnil-au-Val & La Glacerie, France
30	Ramrod 399	Fighter Cover	✝	East of Hesdin, France
31	Ramrod 401	Close Escort	✝	Yvrench/Bois de Waripel, France

1 December 1943 – The Wing participated in a single Ramrod today, but it ended up quite a shambles. It was a relatively early start to the day and the pilots were airborne at 09:00 to provide escort cover to 9th U.S. Air Force Marauders attacking Lille-Vendeville Airfield in Part I of Ramrod 343.

Spitfire XII, RM850, EB-K, taxiing for take-off on a long distance operation, with an auxiliary fuel tank slung underneath. © Jean-Louis Roba

Date	1 December 1943
Operation	Ramrod 343
Targets	Part I: Lille-Vendeville Airfield, Pas-de-Calais
	Part II: Cambrai-Epinoy Airfield, Pas-de-Calais
	Part III: Aircraft Component Factory, Albert, Picardie
	Part IV: Cambrai-Niergnies Airfield, Pas-de-Calais
Bombers	Part I: 72 Marauders; 73 dispatched, 63 bombed
	Part II: 72 Marauders; 68 dispatched, 61 bombed
	Part III: 24 Mitchells; 24 dispatched, 20 bombed
	Part IV: 54 Marauders; 55 dispatched, 52 bombed
Casualties	1 Marauder, SD/AA, E. of Lille, France
Close Escort Part I	Heston: 306 & 315 Squadrons (Spitfire Vb)
Escort Cover	Tangmere: 41 & 91 Squadrons (Spitfire XII)
High Cover	Detling: 132 & 602 Squadrons (Spitfire IX)
Top Cover	West Malling: 124 Squadron (Spitfire VII)
Close Escort Part II	Friston: 349 & 350 Squadrons (Spitfire Vb)
Escort Cover	Biggin Hill: 401, 411 & 412 Squadrons (Spitfire IX)
High Cover	Kenley: 403 & 421 Squadrons (Spitfire IX)
Close Escort Part III	Tangmere: 197 & 486 Squadrons (Typhoon Ib)
Escort Cover	Manston: 3 Squadron; & Fairlop: 195 Squadron (Typhoon Ib)
High Cover	Merston: 181 & 247 Squadrons (Typhoon Ib)
Close Escort Part IV	Digby: 402 & 416 Squadrons (Spitfire Vb)
Escort Cover	Ibsley: 310, 312 & 313 Squadrons (Spitfire Vb)
High Cover	Church Stanton: 131 & 165 Squadrons (Spitfire IX)
Casualties	411 Sqn: Flt Lt Douglas R. Matheson SD/AA in Spit IX, MJ236, POW; & Plt Off John A. St. Denis SD/AA/KIA in Spit IX, MJ288

Part I's bombers were scheduled to rendezvous 12,000 feet over Dungeness at 09:30 (zero) and to be over the target at zero+26. However, they were three minutes late at the rendezvous, and Heston's Close Escort squadrons arrived five minutes late. The Spitfire XII Wing was on time, but not at full strength.

The Wing was to be off the deck at 16:00, comprising 24 aircraft, led by 91 Squadron's Sqn Ldr Norman Kynaston, with 41 Squadron providing three sections of four, led by Sqn Ldr Matthew, Flt Lt Don Smith and Flt Lt 'Pinkie' Glen. However, Glen (MB837) failed to get airborne, likely a result of engine trouble, and whilst the rest of the pilots made rendezvous, one by one, the pilots of Smith's Yellow Section pulled out and returned home, Smith (MB845) with jettison tank trouble, Flt Lt Terence Welsh (MB844) with engine trouble, Sqn Ldr John Clouston (EN237) with a 'u/s hood', and Fg Off Keith Curtis (EN603) with a malfunctioning R/T system.

Before long, Sqn Ldr Kynaston also found his own R/T system malfunctioning, and he, too, pulled out, handing over command of the Wing to Fg Off Jacques Andrieux. This left 91 Squadron with eleven aircraft and 41 Squadron with just seven to fulfil their assigned task. From here on, however, things went smoothly, and Lille-Vendeville Airfield was located in good visibility and scattered cloud on a route that took them via Hardelot and Béthune at 15,000-17,000 feet.

Sixty-three of the 73 bombers from the 322nd and 386th Bomb Groups attacked the target, dropping six hundred and twenty-seven 300 lb. M-31 GP bombs from an altitude of 11,500 feet with good results. Bursts were seen on dispersals and runways, and on an ammunition dump which caused a "violent conflagration 3,000 feet high with yellow flames".[345] A Luftwaffe fighter was seen to take off in the middle of it all, but a bomb blast caused it to crash, and bursts were also seen to land near a line of seven to nine aircraft lined up along the east-west runway.

Moderate heavy Flak was concentrated on the bombers and Close Escort, and one bomber was seen to be hit and go down just east of Lille. Their job done, the bombers and escorts headed for home, and the Spitfire XII Wing maintained their escort until ten miles off Hardelot, when they made a vector for Tangmere.

Almost home, Flt Sgt Jimmy Payne (MB804) found he was running short of fuel. Deciding not to take the risk, he landed at Hawkinge to refuel at 10:45, before completing his journey to Tangmere. The remaining six pilots, Sqn Ldr Matthew's intact Red Section and Flt Sgts Bruce Adams and 'Jackie' Fisher, the last two pilots of Blue Section, continued to base.

Adams (MB846) was also short of fuel, but he had felt he had enough left to get him back to Tangmere. It is believed that, independent of this fact, he then found he had trouble lowering his undercarriage, as he advised over R/T that he would need to make a belly landing. He made a half orbit of the airfield and planned to land next to the runway, but stalled during banking at around 50-75 feet, dug a wingtip into the ground and cartwheeled the aircraft. He was seriously injured and lucky to have survived, and did not wake up until three weeks later in St. Richard's Hospital in Chichester.

Many years later, Adams recalled that it was his day off but that he was taking the place of another pilot who was unfit to fly. So serious were his injuries that he spent several months in hospital in the United Kingdom before being repatriated home to Canada in May 1944. Adams did not fly a Spitfire again, and it was poor consolation that he was commissioned the day before his accident.[346]

Returning now to 1 December 1943, as a consequence of the morning's casualties and technical issues, only five of the Squadron's 12 aircraft and pilots deployed on Ramrod 343 actually completed it without a problem.

Pay Parade at RAF Tangmere, winter 1943-1944. © Jean-Louis Roba

So much had occurred and it was not even lunchtime; the flying day would not be over for several hours. However, 41 Squadron was only called on once more all day, to participate in an ASR patrol. Sqn Ldr John Clouston and Fg Off Keith Curtis were airborne at 14:05 and found a Flying Fortress floating six miles east of Ventnor, on the south-eastern coast of the Isle of Wight; the crew were nearby in dinghies.

Clouston and Curtis orbited the site until two Walruses arrived, followed soon after by Naval Launch No. 44, and subsequently by an RAF launch. The crews were retrieved and 41 Squadron's pilots returned to Tangmere, where they landed again at 15:45. This ended the day's operational flying for the unit.

2 December 1943 – The day started with a scramble to intercept inbound enemy aircraft, when Flt Lts Glen and Griffith, and Flt Sgts Payne, Fisher and Graham, were ordered into the air at 10:35. Enemy aircraft were reported over Shoreham and St. Catherine's Point, but the pilots were unable to catch them, despite a chase out to sea. One aircraft was, however, claimed destroyed by the coastal anti-aircraft guns. The quintet returned to base at 11:20 with nothing further to report.

An hour and a half later, Fg Offs Peter Cowell and Ross Harding were scrambled as White Section on an ASR patrol to search for six light naval craft that were overdue. The pair was ordered onto a course of 175° for 15 minutes, but were recalled soon after they crossed the coast and landed again at 12:15.

During the early afternoon, the Spitfire XII Wing was once again called upon to participate in a Ramrod. On this occasion they were to provide escort cover to RAF Bostons and Mitchells in a 10 Group operation to a Big Ben site at Martinvast on the Cotentin Peninsula.

Date	2 December 1943
Operation	Ramrod 111 (10 Group)
Target	Martinvast, Basse-Normandie
Bombers	Force A: 24 Bostons in 4 boxes of 6, 25 dispatched, 23 bombed Force B: 18 Mitchells in 3 boxes of 6, 18 dispatched – aborted
Casualties	Force A: 17 Bostons CD/AA, 1 pilot WIA
Close Escort Force A	Harrowbeer: 193 & 266 Squadrons (15 Typhoon Ib)
Escort Cover	Warmwell: 257 Squadron (12 Typhoon Ib)
Close Escort Force B	Exeter: 340 & 341 Squadrons (21 Spitfire Vb)
Escort Cover	Exeter: 616 Squadron (5 Spitfire VII)
Fighter Cover	Tangmere: 41 and 91 Squadrons (23 Spitfire XII)

Force A's bombers and escorts rendezvoused 12,000 feet over Portland Bill at 12:15 and set course for Cap de Flamanville, then on to Martinvast at 210 mph IAS, with a scheduled time over target of 12:36, at 12,000 feet.

The target area was reached according to plan and 23 of the Bostons bombed from 12,000-13,200 feet with good results. A concentration of bursts was observed from east to west along the southern end of the site and a large flash was seen in the area. Another concentration of bursts was observed in the north-eastern corner of the site, and at least two direct hits were seen on the railway line from Cherbourg. However, not all were so accurate and several sticks overshot by up to 800 yards to the east and northeast.

Intense accurate Flak was experienced in the Martinvast area and the majority of bombers received some form of damage, with one pilot wounded as a result. However, the Luftwaffe was not seen and the operation was carried out otherwise according to plan. The escorts accompanied the bombers back across the Channel, keeping an eye on one bomber in particular, which was trailing smoke from an engine and lost significant altitude, but succeeded in reaching the English coast safely.

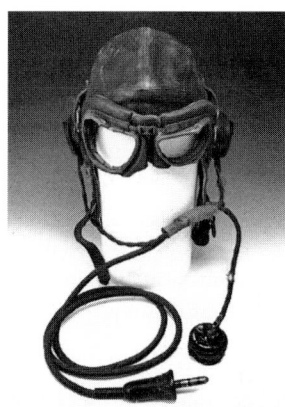

LEFT Canadian Bruce Adams was commissioned on 1 December 1943, but had a serious flying accident the same day and was subsequently repatriated to Canada, following a significant hospital stay. © John C. Adams

RIGHT The crushed flying helmet and goggles worn by Plt Off Bruce Adams during his flying accident on 1 December 1943 are still in his family's possession. © John C. Adams

Force B was scheduled to rendezvous at the same altitude and location as Force A, but five minutes later, and then to follow them on the same route to Martinvast at the same speed. However, it ended up being anything but straight forward.

The Close Escort Wing had been briefed late and took off in a hurry. As a result, three of 340 Squadron's pilots were unable to rendezvous with the rest of the Squadron and returned early. Another developed engine trouble and landed at Perranporth. The remaining eight pilots did not wait to rendezvous with 341 Squadron, and set course directly for Portland Bill, arriving just in time to see the bombers from Force A heading out. They then orbited at 12,000 feet to await the arrival of Force B's bombers.

341 Squadron was off the deck just after 340 Squadron, nine aircraft taking off at 12:09, from which three soon returned as a result of engine trouble. As 340 Squadron had already gone on ahead of them, the remaining six aircraft also made their own way to Portland Bill, similarly arriving in time to see Force A heading out. However, mistaking them for Force B, the six pilots hurried to catch up, which they did approximately ten miles off the French coast. They followed through with the first attack, and returned to Exeter at 13:25.

616 Squadron was airborne at 12:05 and flew directly to Pointe de Barfleur at 24,000 feet, where they arrived at 12:34. Seeing the Force A's Bostons heading in, with no sign of Force's B's Mitchells, the Squadron swept in behind and south of the target until 12:50, when they were given permission to withdraw. They landed back at Exeter at 13:25.

The Spitfire XII Wing was airborne at 12:05 to provide Force B's Fighter Cover, led by Wg Cdr Ingham who flew with 91 Squadron. 41 Squadron deployed eleven aircraft, whose sections were led by Sqn Ldr Matthew, and Flt Lts Don Smith and 'Pinkie' Glen. Heading straight for Pointe de Barfleur, where they made landfall, they then patrolled the Martinvast area at 15,000-16,000 feet. Around this time, 41 Squadron's Flt Lt Ron Collis (MB795) developed engine trouble and returned to Tangmere, whilst Flt Sgt Peter Graham (EN605) started having R/T trouble and also headed home.[347]

The Wing was asked to stay in the area until the second formation had completed their bombing. However, when they did not appear, they headed home at 13:15, crossing out at Cap de la Hague. No enemy aircraft were seen, but the Wing saw intense heavy Flak aimed at the bombers from the target area. They landed back at Tangmere at 13:40.[348]

Meanwhile, as 341 had attached itself to Force A, and 616, 41 and 91 Squadrons all flew directly to Pointe de Barfleur as planned, Force B's 18 Mitchells were only escorted across the Channel by eight aircraft from 340 Squadron. However, the bombers made a navigational error, which was also attributed to cloudy conditions, and flew too far southwards, before turning towards the French coast. They therefore crossed in over Guernsey and Jersey where they were greeted by slight heavy Flak. Sighting 9/10ths to 10/10ths cloud to the east, the bombers decided to abandon the operation, and returned home with their payloads intact, accompanied by the eight aircraft from 340 Squadron.

3 December 1943 – The Squadron flew 20 minutes to Friston for an operation at 11:50, but it was cancelled on account of weather conditions and they returned to Tangmere later in the day. There was no further operational flying.

4 December 1943 – The day commenced with a weather reconnaissance to the Le Havre area by Flt Lt Don Smith and Fg Off Jack Sabourin. Airborne at 08:45, the two pilots first sighted the French coast at Octeville-sur-Mer through thick haze in visibility of just one mile. The pair turned southwest and climbed through two layers of 10/10th cloud, one between 500 and 2,000 feet and the other between 5,500 and 6,500 feet, finding excellent vision in all directions above the upper ceiling. They returned at 09:47 to report their observations.

It was not until after lunch today that the Wing was called upon as a whole, to provide Escort Cover to 72 Marauders attacking Chièvres Airfield in Belgium in Ramrod 348, for which the jumping off point was Manston.

Date	4 December 1943
Operation	Ramrod 348
Target	Chièvres Airfield, Hainaut, Belgium
Bombers	72 Marauders; 72 dispatched – aborted (weather)
Close Escort	Friston: 349 Squadron (Spitfire Vb)
	Hawkinge: 350 & 501 Squadrons (Spitfire Vb)
Escort Cover	Tangmere: 41 & 91 Squadrons (Spitfire XII)
High Cover	Detling: 132 & 602 Squadrons (Spitfire IX)
1st Fighter Sweep	Manston: 198 & 609 Squadrons (Typhoon Ib)
2nd Fighter Sweep	Gravesend: 19 & 65 Squadrons (Spitfire IX)

The Spitfire XII Wing was airborne at 13:45, and rendezvoused with the bombers and their fellow escorts at 12,000 feet, 20 miles east of Ramsgate at 14:00. The formation proceeded to Belgium according to plan, experiencing slight heavy Flak from Ostend [Oostende] on making landfall, but on approaching the target area found 10/10ths cloud at 2,000 feet.

Realising they could not bomb in these conditions, the Marauders turned back south of Courtrai [Kortrijk] and returned home accompanied by the escorts, with their payloads intact. The Spitfire XII Wing landed at Manston at 15:05, and continued on to Tangmere after refuelling.

As straightforward as the operation had been, there were a few mishaps at its conclusion. Flt Sgt Jim Payne (MB804) took a bird strike in his radiator but was unhurt. More seriously, soon after Fg Off Jack Sabourin landed in EN603, Flt Sgt Peter Wall landed MB844 behind him without flaps and collided with him. Wall's aircraft was damaged to Cat B status, but Sabourin's was written off. Both men were uninjured, but this was the last time that Wall flew with 41 Squadron. It is not clear whether the accident was the catalyst for Wall's departure.[349]

The fighter sweeps operated according to plan, and whilst the second was completed without incident, the first encountered the Luftwaffe near Eindhoven and enjoyed significant success for no loss. Following a delayed rendezvous over North Foreland at 14:05, the Manston Wing made landfall over Schouwen Island between 8,000 and 10,000 feet. Approaching Eindhoven, they sighted fourteen Do217 bombers flying southeast at 8,000 feet in three formations of four and one of two. As they saw each other, the Luftwaffe formations broke up and scattered, chased by individual pilots of both squadrons.

A large number of combats ensued that were all one-sided, as no return fire was experienced from any of the German bombers. 198 Squadron claimed four destroyed near Eindhoven, whilst 609 Squadron claimed six destroyed in the same area, followed by a seventh south of Gilze Rijen, making a total of 11 destroyed for the operation. The pilots reported seeing many parachutes and crashed aircraft.

5 December 1943 – The Wing participated in a single Ramrod today, which constituted the first ever Noball target not only by the Wing but also by Allied forces in general. 'Noball' was a code-name for targets related to the V1 flying bomb.

Allied intelligence of German rocket-propelled technology had been building for some months and significant data had been gathered by agents in Germany, Denmark and France, including photographs and sketches.

By late October 1943, sufficient concern had been raised to justify a decision to have RAF Photographic Reconnaissance squadrons photograph all of northern France. During the following month, the first photographs were obtained of 'ski ramps' and of 'midget aircraft' on one such ramp. By the end of November, 72 ski ramps had been photographed and, as a result, the British-American Combined Chiefs of Staff gave the order to launch "Crossbow Operations against Ski Sites" on 2 December.[350]

The first attacks were planned for 5 December at St. Josse-au-Bois in the Pas-de-Calais and at Ligescourt in Picardie, which were the targets that the Spitfire XII Wing supported today. The Wing would support another eight such attacks during December 1943 (totalling nine out of 13 operations by the Wing that month), twenty-one in January 1944 (constituting every operation by the Wing that month) and another eight attacks during February (80% of the Wing's operations).

By early 1944, the damage wrought by Allied attacks on Noball sites had compelled the Germans to move to mobile launch ramps, the first of which was complete by 25 February. At this time, however, the Spitfire XII Wing had been split up and although 41 Squadron supported another eleven attacks on Noball targets during March and April 1944, the unit was withdrawn from Ramrod operations altogether from 28 April. They were then deployed instead on ground attack operations in preparation for the launch of Operation *Overlord*.

It should be emphasised that, all this time, not a single V1 was launched against the United Kingdom and all the attacks that 41 Squadron, and indeed the Spitfire XII Wing, were involved in during late 1943 and early 1944 were of a purely precautionary and preventative nature.

However, whilst 41 Squadron was relieved of operations against Noball sites at the end of April 1944, it would only be a brief respite; less than two months later the Squadron was called upon again against the V1 – this time, however, in a defensive role against aerial targets rather than stationary ground targets [see Chapter 5].

Date	5 December 1943
Operation	Ramrod 351
Targets – Parts I to V	1st Box: St. Josse-au-Bois, Pas-de-Calais
	2nd Box: Ligescourt, Picardie
Target – Part VI	Ligescourt, Picardie
Bombers	Parts I to V: 36 Marauders in each, in 2 boxes of 18
	Part VI: 18 Marauders
Close Escort Parts I & III	Friston: 349 Sqn & Hawkinge: 350 Sqn (Spitfire Vb)
Close Escort Parts II & V	Heston: 306 & 315 Squadrons (Spitfire Vb)
Close Escort Parts IV & VI	Coltishall: 64 & 611 Squadrons (Spitfire Vb)
	Tangmere: 41 & 91 Squadrons (Spitfire Vb)
1st Fighter Umbrella	Detling: 132 & 602 Squadrons (Spitfire IX)
	Gravesend: 19, 65 & 122 Squadrons (Spitfire IX)
	West Malling: 124 Squadron (Spitfire VII)
2nd Fighter Umbrella	Hornchurch: 66, 129 & 222 Squadrons (Spitfire IX)
	Kenley: 403 & 421 Squadrons (Spitfire IX)

Despite high hopes, poor weather interfered with the operation, and 10/10ths cloud with a base of 4,000 feet was encountered in the target areas, with thick ground haze to the south and southeast. As a result, of the 90 Marauders dispatched to St. Josse only 18 (one box) actually attacked, dropping seventy 1,000 lb. bombs with fair results. Similarly, of the 108 Marauders dispatched to Ligescourt, only 34 attacked, dropping one hundred and thirty 1,000 lb. bombs with fair results. Flak in both cases was only negligible.

The four Close Escort Wings and five Fighter Umbrella Wings all operated uneventfully. For their part, the Spitfire XII Wing was airborne at 13:10, with both 41 Squadron and the Wing led by Wg Cdr Ingham. Flt Lts Terence Welsh (MB840) and 'Pinkie' Glen (MB847) both returned early with jettison tank trouble, landing back at Tangmere at 13:20, respectively 13:30.

The rest of the Wing continued on and rendezvoused with their allotted boxes, 91 Squadron meeting the first 15 miles west-northwest of Étaples at 12,000 feet, and 41 Squadron meeting the second at the same location and altitude ten minutes later. The Wing escorted the fourth attack over the target and ten miles back out to sea, then swept back to catch up with the sixth attack, it escorted it, too, over the targets.

Neither the bombing, nor the Luftwaffe were seen, 41 Squadron's ORB complaining that "the Hun refused to come up".[351] The Spitfire XII Wing returned to Tangmere at 15:05, with the exception of Flt Sgt Peter Graham (MB798), who was running short of fuel and landed at Friston before continuing back to base. There was no further operational flying today.

6 December 1943 – Owing to poor weather conditions, the only operational flying undertaken by all the Tangmere based squadrons today was a weather reconnaissance by 41 Squadron's Flt Sgts 'Jackie' Fisher and William Vann. Airborne at 08:50, they returned at 10:05 with an adverse weather report and no further operational flying was made all day.[352]

13 December 1943 – Following six days on the ground as a result of unsuitable weather, the Spitfire XII Wing was airborne again today, providing a fighter sweep in support of an attack on Schipol Airfield in the Netherlands by 216 USAAF Marauders. The Wing's jumping off point was Bradwell Bay, Essex. Poor weather continued to dominate operations, however, and following this one operation, the Wing remained on the ground for yet another week before conditions improved sufficiently to allow them to participate in operations once again.

Date	13 December 1943
Operation	Ramrod 363
Target	Schipol Airfield, Noord-Holland, Netherlands
Bombers	216 Marauders in 3 waves of 72; 212 dispatched, 192 bombed
Casualties	386 BG/555 BS: Marauder 41-31625, SD/AA Aalsmer NL; 323 BG/455 BS: Marauder 41-34785 SD/AA Schipol NL, & Marauder 41-34940, CD/AA, ditched North Sea off NL; 145 other Marauders CD/AA
Close Escort 1st Wave Escort Cover Close Escort 2nd Wave Escort Cover Close Escort 3rd Wave Escort Cover 1st Fighter Sweep 2nd Fighter Sweep 3rd Fighter Sweep	Heston: 306 & 315 Squadrons (Spitfire Vb) Hornchurch: 66 & 222 Squadrons (Spitfire IX) Biggin Hill: 401, 411 & 412 Squadrons (Spitfire Vb) Kenley: 403 & 421 Squadrons (Spitfire IX) Coltishall: 64 & 611 Squadrons (Spit Vb) Detling: 132 & 602 Squadrons (Spitfire IX) Tangmere: 41 & 91 Squadrons (Spitfire XII) North Weald: 331 & 332 Squadrons (Spitfire IX) Gravesend: 65 & 122 Squadrons (Spitfire IX)
Casualties	306 Sqn: 1 A/C CD from FW190s; 315 Sqn: Fg Off Roman Wal, EF/FL in Spit Vb, AA968, POW

The bombing attack by USAAF Marauders on Schipol Airfield ran according to plan, the three waves dropping a total of six hundred and sixty-seven 1,000 lb. bombs with good results. Bursts were seen in the centre of the airfield and in the western dispersals area but the Flak was intense: three Marauders were shot down and 145 received Flak damage of varying degrees, therefore affecting approximately 70% of the dispatched bombers.

The Escort Wing for the first wave swept the target area, and were attacked by a dozen FW190s between Zandvoort and Noordwijkerhout, which caused damaged to one aircraft of 306 Squadron, whilst an aircraft of 315 Squadron suffered engine failure and force-landed, its pilot unhurt but captured. The Escort Cover Wing operated uneventfully.

The Escort and Escort Cover Wings for the second wave also operated as planned and generally uneventfully, with the only exception being the sighting of two FW190s over the target area that were chased and damaged by 411 Squadron. It was a similar story for the Escort and Escort Cover Wings for the third wave, which completed their task uneventfully. Six Me109s were sighted by the Coltishall Wing, but no engagements ensued.

Detailed to provide the first Fighter Sweep, the Spitfire XII Wing was airborne from Bradwell Bay at 13:55, led by Wg Cdr Ingham, who flew with 41 Squadron. The pilots crossed in, in the Furnes [Veurne]-Dunkirk area between 13,000 and 14,000 feet above a 10/10ths cloud layer at 1,500 feet, experiencing moderate heavy Flak as they did.

The Wing swept the Gravelines-Lille area above the cloud ceiling for 25 minutes, then crossed out again over what was believed to have been Calais, experiencing intense heavy, though inaccurate, Flak as they did. As with the second and third Fighter Sweeps, no enemy aircraft were seen by the Wing and the operation was completely uneventful.

Fuel consumption was, however, significant, and two pilots from each squadron were compelled to land early on the return journey. Flt Lt Ron Collis (MB795) landed at Ford and Fg Off Jack Sabourin (EN237) landed at Lympne along with two of 91 Squadron's pilots. The rest of the Wing landed at Tangmere at 15:15, and this concluded the day's operational flying.

During the ensuing week, there was no operational flying on account of weather conditions, but three new pilots joined 41 Squadron: 23-year-old Flt Lt Thomas R. 'Tommy' Burne AFC[353] and 23-year-old Fg Off Harry Cook[354] on 16 December 1943, and 22-year-old Flt Sgt Frederick G. 'Freddie' Woollard[355] on 18 December.

20 December 1943 – "At last the weather broke and we were allowed to continue the offensive against enemy occupied Europe."[356] Today was the busiest day in some weeks for the Spitfire XII Wing, and they flew two Ramrod operations, both to Noball targets.

In the first of these, the Wing provided Close Escort to 72 Marauders attacking Vacqueriette-Erquières and Bonnières in the Pas-de-Calais, and Agenvillers and Le Meillard in Picardie, in Part II of Ramrod 375. In the second, they provided Close Escort to thirty 2 Group RAF Mitchells attacking Drionville, Pas-de-Calais, in Part II of Ramrod 377.

Date	20 December 1943
Operation	Ramrod 375
Targets	Parts I & II: Vacqueriette-Erquières & Bonnières, Pas-de-Calais, & Agenvillers & Le Meillard, Picardie Part III: Audincthun & Bois de Cocove (Recques-sur-Hem), Pas-de-Calais
Bombers	Part I: 72 Marauders; 4 boxes of 18, one to each target Part II: 72 Marauders; 4 boxes of 18, one to each target – aborted Part III: 72 Marauders; 2 boxes of 36, one to each target – aborted
Close Escort Pt I	Friston: 349 Sqn & Hawkinge: 350 Sqn (Spitfire Vb) Northolt: 317 Squadron (Spitfire Vb)
Close Escort Pt II	Tangmere: 41 & 91 Squadrons (Spitfire XII) Hawkinge: 501 Squadron (Spitfire Vb)
Fighter Cover	Hornchurch: 66, 129 & 222 Squadrons (Spitfire IX) West Malling: 124 Squadron (Spitfire VII)
Close Escort Pt III	Manston: 3 Squadron (Typhoon Ib) Martlesham Heath: 56 Squadron (Typhoon Ib) Tangmere: 197 & 486 Squadrons (Typhoon Ib)
Fighter Cover	Detling: 132 & 602 Squadrons (Spitfire IX)
1st Fighter Sweep	Kenley: 403 & 421 Squadrons (Spitfire IX)
2nd Fighter Sweep	Gravesend: 19, 65 & 122 Squadrons (Spitfire IX)
3rd Fighter Sweep	North Weald: 331 & 332 Squadrons (Spitfire IX)
Casualties	421 Sqn: Sqn Ldr James F. Lambert RCAF, SD/KIA nr Merville in Spit IX, MH903

Part I's bombers and escorts rendezvoused 12,000 feet over Hastings at 10:30 and proceeded together to a point eight miles southeast of Abbeville, where the 72 Marauders split into four boxes of 18, and made bearings for their respective targets.

Owing to cloud cover of 5/10ths to 10/10ths, however, Vacqueriette-Erquières, Bonnières and Le Meillard were not attacked. Thirty-five Marauders attacked Agenvillers instead, with fair to good results. A few bursts were seen by the escorting fighters to fall in the target area, but several were also seen to the north and to the east. The Close Escort operated uneventfully and there were no claims or casualties.

The Spitfire XII Wing was airborne at 10:25, 41 Squadron deploying twelve aircraft and 91 Squadron eleven. The pilots rendezvoused with Part II's bombers and fellow escort wings in the same location and altitude as Part I, but ten minutes later, and proceeded as before to a point southeast of Abbeville, where the bomber formation split in four, destined for their assigned targets.

Flying between 14,000 and 16,000 feet, the Spitfire XII Wing escorted the third and fourth boxes. Although visibility was good above cloud, both targets were obscured by 8/10ths to 10/10ths cloud in several layers, the thickest at 8,000 feet, and none of the four targets could be located. The Marauders aborted the operation and returned without bombing, escorted by the fighters, which operated uneventfully. The Spitfire XII Wing landed again at 11:55 with nothing to report.

It was a similar story for Part III, whose bombers and fighters rendezvoused at Dungeness at 12,000 feet at 10:40. The formation proceeded to a point four miles north of Le Touquet, where it split in two and made bearings for their individual targets. On account of the prevailing cloud conditions, neither target could be located, and the Marauders returned home with their escorts, and their payloads intact.

All three Fighter Sweeps, however, were anything but uneventful. Whilst sweeping from Douai

B Flight pilots at Tangmere in late 1943-early 1944 'being religious for the Press', in a scene staged for the camera for a story about the Padre, Rev Sqn Ldr John H. Storr. From left to right: Storr, Fg Off Keith Curtis, Plt Off Jimmy Payne, Fg Off Ron Loweth (mostly hidden), Flt Sgt 'Jackie' Fisher, Flt Sgt Freddie Woollard, Flt Lt Tommy Burne, Flt Lt Dave Fearon, Flt Sgt Ian Stevenson, Flt Sgt Peter Graham, Fg Off Herb Wagner, Fg Off Harry Cook, Flt Lt Tom Slack and Flt Lt Patrick Hood. © Peter Graham

Another view of the same event with B Flight pilots at Tangmere in late 1943-early 1944. Left to right: the Padre, Rev Sqn Ldr John H. Storr, Fg Off Keith Curtis, Flt Sgt 'Jackie' Fisher, Plt Off Jimmy Payne, Fg Off Ron Loweth, Flt Lt Dave Fearon, Flt Lt Tommy Burne, Flt Sgt Freddie Woollard, Flt Sgt Ian Stevenson, Flt Lt Patrick Hood, Flt Sgt Peter Graham.

to Lille, the Kenley Wing engaged eighteen Me109s and at least twenty FW190s in the Merville area. They returned home claiming four FW190s destroyed and one damaged, and one Me109 probable and three damaged, but lost the OC, 421 Squadron, who was shot down and killed.

The second Fighter Sweep sighted at least 45 enemy aircraft in the Cambrai area, but they disappeared into cloud. One section fired, but no claims could be made. The third Fighter Sweep also sighted thirty to forty FW190s in the same area, flying in three formations at 18,000, 24,000 and 28,000 feet. These were attacked by North Weald's Norwegian squadrons, who claimed three FW190s destroyed for no loss.

The Spitfire XII Wing's pilots were back in the air again only 55 minutes after landing from Ramrod 375, allowing for only a very brief lunch break, and likely ate whilst they were briefed. This operation was much smaller than the morning's, but it was also affected by the weather.

Date	20 December 1943
Operation	Ramrod 377
Targets	Part I: Audincthun, Pas-de-Calais Part II: Drionville, Pas-de-Calais Part III: Heuringhem, Pas-de-Calais
Bombers	Part I: 2 Grp: 30 Mitchells II; 11 bombed Part II: 2 Grp: 30 Mitchells II; 18 dispatched – aborted (weather) Part III: 2 Grp: 36 Bostons III, 23 dispatched, 23 bombed
Close Escort Part I Close Escort Part II Close Escort Part III 1st Fighter Cover 2nd Fighter Cover 3rd Fighter Cover	Friston: 349 Sqn & Hawkinge: 350 Sqn (Spitfire Vb) Tangmere: 41 & 91 Squadrons (Spitfire XII) Detling: 132 & 602 Squadrons (Spitfire IX) Hornchurch: 66, 129 & 222 Squadrons (Spitfire IX) West Malling: 124 Squadron (Spitfire VII) Kenley: 403 & 421 Squadrons (Spitfire IX) Biggin Hill: 401, 411 & 412 Squadrons (Spitfire IX)
Casualties	350 Sqn: Flt Sgt Leon J. G. Harmel, SD nr Abbeville in Spit Vb, AD314, ER

Part I's bombers and fighter escort rendezvoused 10,000 feet over Hastings at 13:00 and proceeded to Audincthun as planned. However, on reaching the area, 9/10ths cloud was encountered at 7,000 feet and as a result only eleven Mitchells attacked, dropping eighty-eight 500 lb. bombs with fair to poor results. Bursts were seen at the edge of a wood inside the target area, whilst a number overshot, but no Flak was encountered.

350 Squadron was intercepted by a very fast unidentified aircraft at 25,000 feet whilst northeast of Abbeville, which was likely the cause of the loss of one of the Squadron's pilots. No other enemy aircraft were seen.

The Spitfire XII Wing was airborne at 12:50, led by Wg Cdr Ingham, who flew with 91 Squadron, and rendezvoused with Part II's Mitchells 10,000 feet over Hastings at 13:05. However only 18 of the 30 planned Mitchells were dispatched, and when the bombers found 9/10ths to 10/10ths cloud over Drionville, they aborted the attack and returned without bombing. Slight heavy Flak intensified when they were over the target area, but no casualties were recorded and the Spitfire XII Wing returned at 14:10 with little more to report than weather conditions.

Part III was more successful than Parts I and II, and following a rendezvous 13,000 feet over Hastings at 13:10, approached Heuringhem according to plan. Although 9/10ths cloud covered the area at 7,000 feet, a gap over the target allowed all 23 Bostons to attack, dropping a total of ninety-two 500 lb. bombs with largely unobserved results. The escorts operated uneventfully, despite medium light Flak over Heuringhem.

All three Fighter Cover wings operated uneventfully, sweeping their designated areas without sighting the Luftwaffe. Both 401 and 403 Squadron suffered casualties and one pilot was injured, but not due to enemy action.

Later that afternoon, a section from 41 Squadron was scrambled from Tangmere on reports of incoming bogies. Flt Lt Lyndon Griffith and Fg Off 'Momo' Balasse took off at 16:45, ordered to patrol base. However, they saw nothing and landed again within 15 minutes, thereby concluding the day's operational flying.

21 December 1943 – In the air again today against a Noball target, the Spitfire XII Wing participated in a single Ramrod operation, providing Close Escort to 2 Group Bostons attacking Le Mesnil-Allard in Part IV of Ramrod 381.[357]

Date	21 December 1943
Operation	Ramrod 381
Targets	Part I: Sainte-Agathe-d'Aliermont, Haute-Normandie Part II: Saint-Pierre-des-Jonquières, Haute-Normandie Part III: Puchervin, Haute-Normandie Part IV: Le Mesnil-Allard, Haute-Normandie
Bombers	Part I: 40 Mosquitos; 40 dispatched – aborted (weather) Part II: 24 Mitchells; 24 dispatched, 6 bombed Part III: 18 Mitchells; 18 dispatched – aborted (weather) Part IV: 36 Bostons; 36 dispatched – aborted (weather)
Close Escort Part I	None
Close Escort Part II	Ibsley: 310 & 313 Squadrons (Spitfire Vb)
Close Escort Part III	Friston: 349 Squadron & Hawkinge: 350 Squadron (Spitfire Vb)
Close Escort Part IV	Tangmere: 41 & 91 Squadrons (Spitfire XII)
Fighter Cover	Biggin Hill: 401, 411 & 412 Squadrons (Spitfire IX)
1st Fighter Sweep	North Weald: 331 & 332 Squadrons (Spitfire IX)
Casualties	411 Sqn: Sqn Ldr Ian C. Ormston IFA, EF on TO in Spit IX, MJ287, Cat E

Part I was unescorted but the Mosquitos abandoned the task in the target area as visibility was too poor. The weather continued to wreak havoc with the Ramrod. Part II was dispatched as planned and rendezvoused 6,000 feet over Beachy Head at 9:25. However, 9/10ths cloud in the target area resulted in only a quarter of the Mitchells bombing Saint-Pierre-des-Jonquières with unobserved results, whilst their escort operated uneventfully.

Part III's Mitchells rendezvoused at the same location and altitude as Part II, at 09:30. On this occasion, 10/10ths cloud was encountered at 4,000 feet over Puchervin, which forced a completed abandonment of the attack. 349 Squadron operated uneventfully, but 350 Squadron was informed of a dozen enemy aircraft in the Berck-sur-Mer area. Investigating, they sighted and destroyed a single FW190.

The Spitfire XII Wing was airborne at 09:25 and rendezvoused with Part IV's Bostons at the same location and altitude as Parts II and III, but at 09:35, and proceeded to Le Mesnil-Allard where they, too, found 10/10ths cloud, with a ceiling of just 2,000 feet. The operation was also abandoned and the Bostons returned without bombing, escorted by 41 and 91 Squadrons for whom the operation was uneventful.

The Wing landed at Tangmere again at 10:50, with the exception of Fg Off Herb Wagner (MB795) who landed early at Ford without the benefit of any flaps at all, as only one could be lowered. He brought the aircraft down safely and returned to Tangmere later in the day. The Wing undertook no further operational flying that day.

The Fighter Cover and Fighter Sweep Wings both operated as planned, although uneventfully. However, 411 Squadron's Officer Commanding crashed on take-off for the operation and was injured.

Separately today, another new pilot joined 41 Squadron in the form of 21-year-old Scot Flt Sgt Ian T. 'Steve' Stevenson. Having joined the RAFVR in May 1941, Stevenson had earned his Wings in the United States and returned to the United Kingdom to complete AFU, OTU and TEU in

Sgt Plt (later WO) Ian 'Steve' Stevenson served with 41 Squadron from 21 December 1943 to 6 August 1945, during that time claiming four destroyed FW90s and 2½ destroyed V1s. He was awarded the DFC in July 1945. © Neil Stevenson

1943. Having logged 337 flying hours, none of which were operational, 41 Squadron became his first and only operational posting of the War, as he was destined to remain with the unit until beyond the cessation of hostilities.

22 December 1943 – Following the failed attempt to attack Sainte-Agathe-d'Aliermont, St.-Pierre-des-Jonquières, Puchervin and Le Mesnil-Allard Noball sites on 21 December as result of poor weather conditions, a new attempt was made today in Ramrod 383, which was a virtual repetition of Ramrod 381; nearly every participating squadron was the same.

Once again, the Spitfire XII Wing provided Close Escort to 36 Bostons tasked with attacking Le Mesnil-Allard in Part IV of the operation.

Date	22 December 1943
Operation	Ramrod 383
Targets	Part I: Sainte-Agathe-d'Aliermont, Haute-Normandie
	Part II: St.-Pierre-des-Jonquières, Haute-Normandie
	Part III: Puchervin, Haute-Normandie
	Part IV: Le Mesnil-Allard, Haute-Normandie
Bombers	Part I: 40 Mosquitos; 27 bombed
	Part II: 24 Mitchells – aborted (weather)
	Part III: 24 Mitchells – aborted (weather)
	Part IV: 36 Bostons; 6 bombed
Escort Part I	No escort
Close Escort Part II	Ibsley: 312 & 313 Squadrons (Spitfire Vb)
Close Escort Part III	Friston: 349 Squadron & Hawkinge: 350 Squadron (Spitfire Vb)
Close Escort Part IV	Tangmere: 41 & 91 Squadrons (Spitfire XII)
Fighter Cover	Biggin Hill: 401, 411 & 412 Squadrons (Spitfire Vb)
1st Fighter Sweep	North Weald: 331 & 332 Squadrons (Spitfire IX)
2nd Fighter Sweep	Culmhead: 131 & 165 Squadrons (Spitfire IX)

Part I's Mosquitos enjoyed a more successful attack on Sainte-Agathe-d'Aliermont today, and dropped a total of one hundred and six 500 lb. bombs and one 250 lb. bomb at 11:47. Results were considered good and bursts were observed throughout the target area, and on a large square building, which resulted in red and green flashes.

Part II and III rendezvoused over Beachy Head according to plan, but suffered similar problems to the previous day when 10/10ths cloud was encountered over both targets. The Mitchells returned without bombing, no Flak was experienced and the escorts reported their operations uneventful.

The Spitfire XII Wing was airborne at 11:30 and rendezvoused with Part IV's Bostons 6,000 feet over Beachy Head at 11:40. Proceeding to Le Mesnil-Allard as planned, the formation found thick cloud, which permitted only six Bostons to attack the target through brief gaps. Twenty-three 500 lb. bombs were dropped, which fell wide and bursts were seen 300-400 yards southeast of the target.

There was no reaction whatsoever from the Luftwaffe, not even radar plots, prompting 41 Squadron to record in their ORB, "It seems as though the Hun has decided never to engage us".[358] The Wing landed again at 12:50 with nothing to report.

Meanwhile the Fighter Cover and two Fighter Sweep Wings had completed their own operations, which were just as uneventful.

Following lunch, the Wing was called upon to provide a Fighter Sweep to Arras in support of Typhoons and RP Hurricanes attacking eight Noball targets in nine parts of Ramrod 386.

Date	22 December 1943
Operation	Ramrod 386
Targets	Part I: Vacquerie-le-Boucq, Pas-de-Calais Part II: Pommeréval, Haute-Normandie Part III: Preuseville, Haute-Normandie Part IV: Beauvoir, Pas-de-Calais Part V: Heuringhem, Pas-de-Calais Part VI: Eclimeux, Pas-de-Calais Part VII: Campagne-lès-Hesdin, Pas-de-Calais Part VIII: Campagne-lès-Hesdin, Pas-de-Calais Part IX: Le Plouy Ferme, Pas-de-Calais
Bomphoons & RP Aircraft	Part I: Tangmere: 197 & 486 Squadrons (Typhoon Ib) Part II: Merston: 182 & 247 Squadrons (Typhoon Ib) Part III: Westhampnett: 175 & 245 Squadrons (Typhoon Ib) Part IV: Manston: 3 Squadron (Typhoon Ib) Part V: Martlesham Heath: 56 Squadron (Typhoon Ib) Part VI: Lympne: 1 Squadron (Typhoon Ib) Part VII: Odiham: 181 Squadron (RP Typhoon Ib) Part VIII: Manston: 137 Squadron (RP Hurricane IV) Part IX: Fairlop: 164 Squadron (RP Hurricane IV)
Casualties	1 Sqn: 1 A/C damaged by bomb fragments from own bomb
Fighter Sweeps	1st: Manston: 198 & 609 Squadrons (Typhoon Ib) 2nd: Tangmere: 41 & 91 Squadrons (Spitfire XII) 3rd: North Weald: 331 & 332 Squadrons (Spitfire IX) 4th: Biggin Hill: 401, 411 & 412 Squadrons (Spitfire Vb)

Weather continued to cause trouble for Noball attacks in northern France, and Part I found Vacquerie-le-Boucq obscured by cloud. Unable to locate it, the Tangmere Wing's Bomphoons continued in search of another Noball target and found Beauvoir – Part IV's target – which ten pilots attacked, and Agenvillers, which three pilots bombed and subsequently strafed.

Part II similarly failed to locate their target, attacking instead a gun emplacement between Ault and Le Tréport with sixteen 500 lb. bombs. Gaps in the cloud cover enabled the Westhampnett Wing to drop thirty-two 500 lb. bombs on Preuseville in Part III, although some bursts were also seen to land in the village. Part IV operated according to plan and sixteen 500 lb. bombs were dropped on Beauvoir with excellent results, bursts being seen on buildings in the centre of the

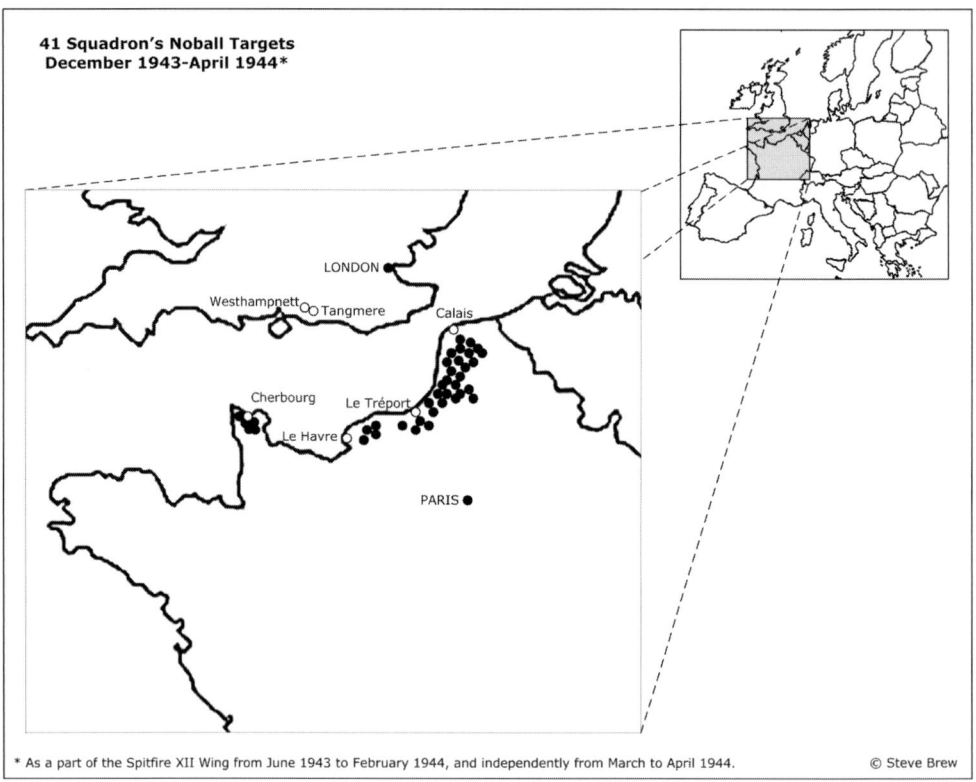

*As a part of the Spitfire XII Wing from June 1943 to February 1944, and independently from March to April 1944.   © Steve Brew

target area resulting in a large cloud of black smoke rising to 7,000 feet. Intense accurate Flak was experienced in the area but no casualties were reported. Part V also operated as planned, and sixteen 500 lb. bombs were dropped on Heuringhem with good results.

In contrast, Part VI had a more difficult time, resulting partially from one aircraft's engine cutting and the entire section of four – half the aircraft dispatched – returning early. These aircraft jettisoned their 500 lb. bombs on the coast near Le Touquet as they crossed out, with unobserved results. The remaining four aircraft attacked Eclimeux as planned, but as one bomb would not release, only seven 500 lb. bombs were dropped of which two were seen to burst just inside the southeast corner of the target; the rest fell short. On the way out, the pilot whose bomb hung, fired at a gun emplacement from 500 feet. The vibration on the wing was sufficient to cause his 500 lb. bomb to release but the explosion caused Cat. B damage to his aircraft when it was struck by bomb fragments.

Part VII operated according to plan and thirty-two rockets with 60 lb. heads were fired at Campagne-les-Hesdin in a shallow dive from 10,000 to 2,000 feet. Within five minutes, cloud closed over the area and caused Part VIII to abort their attack and return without firing. It was a similar story for Part IX, whose attack on Le Plouy Ferme was also thwarted by 10/10ths cloud.

All four Fighter Sweeps operated uneventfully and the Luftwaffe was not seen. For their part, the Spitfire XII Wing was airborne at 14:50, and proceeded to the Arras area. The sweep was undertaken according to plan, but Blue 3, Fg Off Clive Birbeck (EN605), developed engine trouble and was escorted back by the rest of Blue Section, (Hood MB847, Johnson MB880, Payne EN231) all four pilots landing at Hawkinge at 16 :05. The rest of the Squadron returned to Tangmere at 16:15 with nothing to report.

24 December 1943 – Following another day on the ground as a result of inclement weather, the day commenced with a weather reconnaissance to the Cherbourg-Le Havre area by Fg Offs Herb Wagner (MB843) and Keith Curtis (MB862) at 08:50.

The result of attacks on the Beauvoir Noball site in the Pas-de-Calais, the destination of attacks supported by the Spitfire XII Wing on 22 December 1943 and 28 February 1944. U.S. Air Force Photo, via the National Museum of the US Air Force

They returned an hour later with a favourable report and the Wing was initially planned to provide a Fighter Sweep to St. Valéry-Beauvais at 09:55, as an element of Ramrod 389 to four Noball sites. It was, however, cancelled for unrecorded reasons and the Wing was not called upon again until the early afternoon. At that time, they were tasked with providing a Fighter Sweep for 24 Bostons and 18 Mitchells to Le Mesnil-au-Val and La Glacerie Noball sites, instead, as an element of Ramrod 393.

Date	24 December 1943
Operation	Ramrod 393
Targets	Part I: Le Mesnil-au-Val, Basse-Normandie
	Parts II & III: La Glacerie, Basse-Normandie
Bombers	Part I: 24 Mitchells; 24 bombed
	Part II: 24 Mitchells; 12 bombed
	Part III: 18 Bostons; 12 bombed
Close Escort Part I	Ibsley: 310 & 312 Squadrons (Spitfire Vb)
Close Escort Part II	Friston: 349 Squadron & Hawkinge: 350 Squadron (Spitfire Vb)
Close Escort Part III	Ibsley: 313 Squadron (Spitfire Vb)
Fighter Umbrella	Tangmere: 41 & 91 Squadrons (Spitfire XII)
	West Malling: 124 Squadron (Spitfire VII)
1st Fighter Sweep	Culmhead: 131 & 165 Squadrons (Spitfire IX)
Casualties	312 Sqn: 1 A/C EF/FL Isle of Wight

Part I's Mitchells and their Close Escort Wing approached Le Mesnil-au-Val according to plan and dropped one hundred and eighty-two 500 lb. bombs from an altitude of 13,000 feet at 14:12. Bursts were seen inside the northern and eastern boundaries of the target area resulting in explosions with reddish-brown smoke. The escorts encountered accurate heavy Flak from Cherbourg and Le Mesnil-au-Val, but no casualties were recorded. One pilot from 312 Squadron force-landed on the Isle of Wight upon his return from the operation, but it was not the result of enemy action.

Part II's and III's bombers and escorts approached La Glacerie without problem but found 6/10ths cloud between 7,000 and 8,000 feet, which hindered both attacks. As a result, only half of Part II's Mitchells were able to attack the target, dropping forty-four 500 lb. bombs from 14,000 feet at 14:17. They were followed five minutes later by twelve of Part III's eighteen Bostons, which dropped another ninety-six 500 lb. bombs on the target from 13,000 feet at 14:22.

Bursts from the former attack were largely unseen, although some were sighted on the boundary of the target area. Those from the latter were considered more accurate as they were observed to land in the centre of the target area.

Their escorts became mixed up and although Part II's bombers were escorted to and from the target generally as planned, when crossing out, 350 Squadron sighted Part III's eighteen Bostons heading in towards the target apparently unprotected. Swinging around behind them, 350 Squadron escorted them to La Glacerie and back out again without incident, and followed them home.

Part III's escort, 313 Squadron, did not rendezvous with the Bostons and headed to France alone. On the way in, they caught up with Part II's Mitchells and escorted them to the target instead. On the way out, four of the Squadron's fighters also saw Part III's bombers inbound towards the target, and turned to escort them to La Glacerie with 350 Squadron. A single FW190 appeared and fired on the bombers from long range, however it dived away before anyone could give chase.

The Spitfire XII Wing took off at 13:45, 41 Squadron deploying twelve aircraft led by Sqn Ldr Matthew. The pilots provided fighter cover 15,000 feet over the target area, in co-operation with 124 Squadron at 22,000 feet, from 14:10 until Part III's bombers had crossed out again. The operation was uneventful, with the exception of the sighting of a single aircraft diving steeply away from an altitude of 15,000 feet west of Barfleur. The Spitfire XII Wing was back on the ground at Tangmere at 15:10 with nothing to report, except that, "the Hun still did not attempt to engage us".[359]

The Fighter Sweep also operated according to plan and uneventfully.

30 December 1943 – "Refreshed after the enforced rest"[360] of a combination of Christmas festivities and poor weather, the Wing was airborne again today for the first time in six days. They were initially planned to provide a fighter sweep of the Évreux-Guyancourt area at 14:20 as an element of Ramrod 396, in which Flying Fortresses and Liberators were sent to bomb Ludwigshafen, but their part was cancelled, although no reason is recorded.

However, they were called upon in the early afternoon as an element of Ramrod 399 instead, tasked with providing Fighter Cover for three 2 Group RAF attacks on Noball sites in Northern France.

Date	30 December 1943
Operation	Ramrod 399
Targets	Part I: Fruges/Bois de Coupelle, Pas-de-Calais Part II: Le Plouy Ferme, Pas-de-Calais Part III: Fôret d'Hesdin, Pas-de-Calais
Bombers	Part I: 24 Mitchells; 18 bombed Part II: 24 Mitchells – aborted (weather) Part III: 24 Bostons; 22 bombed
Close Escort Part I Close Escort Part II Close Escort Part III Fighter Cover	Coltishall: 64 & 611 Squadrons (Spit Vb) Northolt: 317 Squadron (Spitfire IX) Friston: 349 Squadron (Spitfire Vb) Hornchurch: 66 & 129 Squadrons (Spitfire IX) Tangmere: 41 & 91 Squadrons (Spitfire XII)

Part I's bombers and escorts rendezvoused 8,000 feet over Dungeness and approached Fruges/Bois de Coupelle without trouble. Eighteen Mitchells dropped eighty-five 500 lb. bombs from 8,000 feet at 13:46 with good results. Their escorts operated uneventfully.

Part II rendezvoused at the same location and altitude as Part I, but ten minutes later, and similarly proceeded to their target according to plan. However, cloud cover was encountered over Le Plouy Ferme, which prevented the Mitchells from bombing and they returned with their payloads intact. Their escort fighters also operated uneventfully.

Part III's Bostons and Close Escort also rendezvoused over Dungeness, however at 10,000 feet, eleven minutes after Part II. The formation approached the Fôret d'Hesdin as planned and all but two of the Bostons attacked, dropping ninety-five 500 lb. bombs from 11,500 feet at 14:23 with mixed results. One concentration was observed inside the target area, but another was seen to its south. Once again, the fighter escort reported the operation uneventful.

In order to provide fighter cover, the Spitfire XII Wing was airborne at 13:05, 41 Squadron deploying twelve aircraft in sections of three led by Flt Lts 'Pinkie' Glen and Don Smith, and Fg Off Clive Birbeck. However, Plt Off Peter Graham (MB847) could not get airborne, presumably the result of engine trouble, and remained behind. The Wing crossed the Channel without him, but approximately 30 minutes into the operation, Flt Sgt Jimmy Payne (MB797) developed R/T trouble and returned to Tangmere too, putting down at 14:00.

The rest of the Wing completed the job uneventfully, sweeping east of Hesdin in good visibility above 8/10ths cloud between 5,000 and 7,000 feet, and no enemy aircraft were seen. They returned to base at 14:50.

Forty minutes later, seven of 41 Squadron's pilots were scrambled on ASR patrols to assist American bombers returning from Ludwigshafen, and searched a large area south and southwest of the Isle of Wight.

During the search, Flt Lt Don Smith (MB882) spotted a Flying Fortress ditched in the Channel approximately six miles south of St. Catherine's Point, along with a dinghy containing some of the crew members. A few of the pilots circled the dinghy until rescue boats reached the area, while others searched for more aircraft. Flt Lt 'Pinkie' Glen and Fg Off Jack Sabourin were also sent up at 16:45 to continue the search, with mixed success.

Tom Slack was pleased to note in his logbook that day, "F/LT. SMITH, my No. 1, found Fortress in Drink. 6 crew subsequently rescued".[361] However, Fg Off Keith Curtis (EN237) had an altogether different experience. He recalled many years later that he was declared shot down that afternoon, when he and another [unnamed] pilot found a badly damaged Liberator and its American crew and attempted to escort it back to the English coast in case it ditched.

When they reached the Liberator, the bomber's crew opened fire on them. The two pilots peeled away, keeping clear of the guns and eventually headed home. Upon returning to base, Curtis informed the Squadron's Intelligence Officer, Lord Gisborough, who contacted the Liberator's Squadron only to find out the Spitfires had been claimed destroyed![362]

The last section was on the ground at 17:20, and this concluded the day's operational flying.

31 December 1943 – On the final day of the year, the Wing was airborne on a Ramrod during the morning and a Rodeo during the afternoon. The morning's operational orders called for the Wing to provide a Close Escort to 24 Mitchells attacking the Noball target at Yvrench/Bois de Waripel in Picardie, as an element of Ramrod 401.

Date	31 December 1943
Operation	Ramrod 401
Targets	Parts I & II: Le Plouy Ferme, Pas-de-Calais Part III: Ligescourt, Picardie Part IV: Yvrench/Bois de Waripel, Picardie Part V: Gueschart, Picardie
Bombers	Part I: 20 Mosquitos; 21 dispatched; 21 bombed Part II: 20 Mosquitos; 20 dispatched; 20 bombed Part III: 24 Bostons, 25 dispatched; 25 bombed Part IV: 24 Mitchells; 20 bombed Part V: 24 Mitchells; 12 bombed
Close Escort Parts I & II	None
Close Escort Part III	Friston: 349 Squadron (Spitfire Vb) Hawkinge: 501 Squadron (Spitfire Vb)
Close Escort Part IV	Tangmere: 41 & 91 Squadrons (Spitfire XII)
Close Escort Part V	Detling: 132 & 602 Squadrons (Spitfire IX)
Fighter Umbrella	Northolt: 302 & 317 Squadrons (Spitfire Vb) North Weald: 331 & 332 Squadrons (Spitfire IX)

Having no escort to rendezvous with, the Mosquitos of Parts I and II headed straight for Le Plouy Ferme, where they dropped a total of one hundred and sixty-three 500 lb. bombs with a good concentration of bursts seen in the target area. The Luftwaffe did not hinder the attack and all aircraft returned safely.

Part III's bombers and escorts rendezvoused 9,000 feet over Hastings at 10:00 and approached Ligescourt according to plan. Twenty-five Bostons attacked the target from 9,000 feet at 10:18, dropping ninety-five 500 lb. bombs with good results. Their escort Wing operated as planned and when the Luftwaffe did not appear, four of the fighters dived down to attack a rectangular concrete building inside the target area, achieving several cannon strikes with unknown result, except for return fire from a single machine gun on the ground.

The Spitfire XII Wing was airborne at 09:50, with 91 Squadron's Sqn Ldr Norman Kynaston leading, and rendezvoused with Part IV's Mitchells at an altitude of 8,000 feet over Hastings at 10:10. Approximately 30 minutes into the trip, 41 Squadron's Flt Lt 'Pinkie' Glen (MB881) and Fg Off 'Momo' Balasse (MB797) developed R/T trouble and returned to base.

The rest of the Wing continued on to Yvrench/Bois de Waripel where the Mitchells dropped one hundred and forty-seven 500 lb. bombs with poor results, the crews observing bursts northwest, southeast and south of the target. Despite clear weather over the target and good visibility, the Spitfire XII Wing did not actually see the target itself, but did observe bursts over a wide area, attesting to the scattered nature of the bombing.

Once again, the Luftwaffe did not react and the formation crossed back out without interference and returned home safely. The Spitfire XII Wing was back on the ground at Tangmere between 11:20 and 11:30.

In the meantime, Part V had also rendezvoused at the same location and altitude as Part IV, but ten minutes behind them. Here, too, the operation ran according to plan without any reaction by the Luftwaffe. Twelve of the 24 Mitchells dropped ninety-four 500 lb. bombs on Gueschart, one stick being seen to fall close to a building, but most others falling to the south and west of the target. Another two of Part V's Mitchells dropped sixteen 500 lb. bombs on Part IV's target, Yvrench/Bois de Waripel, with unobserved results. Their escort wing operated uneventfully, as did both Fighter Umbrella Wings.

During the afternoon, all the Tangmere based fighter squadrons participated in Rodeo 274, "being the last offensive operation in December and also in 1943".[363] The Spitfire XII Wing's Spitfires were fitted with 45 gallon drop tanks for the first time operationally and twenty aircraft, thereunder seven from 41 Squadron, took off at 14:25 for a sweep as far as Évreux.

The Wing crossed in 8,000 feet over Cabourg and flew in good visibility above a 9/10ths cloud layer at 4,000-6,000 feet. The pilots dropped below the cloud base near Lisieux, but attracted light Flak from the area. Climbing again to 9,000 feet, the Wing swept uneventfully southeast as far as the estimated position of Évreux. The Luftwaffe was not seen but on the way home they sighted a fully inflated balloon in the Channel 30 miles northwest of Le Havre.

On their return to Tangmere at 15:55, the scribe of 41 Squadron's ORB noted the uneventful nature of the Rodeo, recording, "Once again the enemy did not attempt to intercept. And thus ended the month in which, despite many chances offered to him, the Hun did not attack the Squadron once."[364]

197 and 486 Squadrons followed the Spitfire XII Wing into the air ten minutes later, deploying eight and nine Typhoons Ib, respectively. Crossing in at St. André at 15:15, the operation was carried out according to plan, initially above 10/10ths cloud at 5,000 feet. Dipping below the cloud base for a period, the Wing attracted accurate heavy Flak from Conches, but otherwise nothing of interest was seen. They returned to base at 16:00, concluding the year's flying for the Station.

A New Year

January 1944 – The first month of the new year was an extremely busy one, considering the season and that freezing weather conditions stopped operational flying on ten days – 11-13, 15-19, 22, 27 and 30 January – and limited operations on five more – 1, 3, 9, 20 and 31 January. The rest of the month was taken up with a total of 21 Ramrod operations to French targets, plus sweeps and ASR operations. Despite the volume of work, however, operations were on a considerably smaller scale than during recent months. January also saw a change in Officer Commanding and a new Flight Commander. The following table shows the month's Ramrod operations.

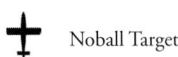 Noball Target

Date	Operation	Role	Type	Destination / Target
2	Ramrod 412	Fighter Cover	✝	Ruisseauville, France
4	Ramrod 418	Fighter Umbrella	✝	Ruisseauville, Ligescourt, Gueschart, & Noyelles-en-Chaussée, France
4	Ramrod 419	Fighter Sweep	✝	Fécamp-Évreux, France
5	Ramrod 423	Fighter Umbrella	✝	Campneuseville, Vaux-Marquenneville, & Le Mesnil-Allard France
6	Ramrod 428	Fighter Umbrella	✝	Dieppe-Rouen, France
7	Ramrod 431	Escort Cover	✝✝	La Glacerie & La Sorellerie I & II, Fr.
7	Ramrod 435	Fighter Cover	✝	Embry/Bois de Pottier, France
8	Ramrod 440	Close Escort	✝	Belmesnil, France

10	Ramrod 444	Close Escort	✝	Belmesnil, France
14	Ramrod 452	Fighter Umbrella	✝	Gorenflos & Petit Bois Tillencourt, Fr.
14	Ramrod 456	Close Escort	✝	Flottemanville-Hague, France
21	Ramrod 468	Fighter Umbrella	✝	Le Grismont, Bois d'Enfer & Bois d'Esquerdes, France
21	Ramrod 470	Fighter Sweep	✝	Fécamp-Évreux, France
23	Ramrod 472	Close Escort	✝	Zudausques, Bois d'Esquerdes & Bois de Renty, France
24	Ramrod 474	Close Escort	✝	Marquenneville, France
25	Ramrod 479	Close Escort	✝	Bois Rempre, Bois de Créquy & Ruisseauville, France
26	Ramrod 486	Target Cover	✝	Bailly-en-Campagne, France
28	Ramrod 489	Fighter Sweep	✝	Fécamp-Beauvais, France
29	Ramrod 492	Fighter Cover	✝	Heudiere, France
29	Ramrod 493	Fighter Umbrella	✝	SE of Dieppe, France
31	Ramrod 500	Fighter Cover	✝	Bois Megle, France

1 January 1944 – Operational flying for 41 Squadron commenced at 10:45 today when Red Section (Moffett MB882, Slack MB845, Wagner MB843 & Curtis EN237) were sent on an ASR patrol to find missing Naval and Commando units in the Channel. In due course, they located three motor torpedo boats and two landing craft, which were escorted back to England. The four pilots returned to Tangmere at 11:45, reporting the operation uneventful.

Flt Lt Ron Collis and Fg Off Jack Sabourin then took off at 11:55 to undertake a weather reconnaissance to France. Crossing in eight miles east of Fécamp, the pair flew as far as Elbeuf between 4,500 and 5,000 feet, and returned to base at 12:50 with an unfavourable weather report. There was no further operational flying all day.

2 January 1944 – Having been grounded for over 24 hours on account of unsuitable weather conditions, 41 Squadron was airborne during the afternoon today for their first Ramrod of the year. They were tasked with providing Fighter Cover to Mosquitos attacking a Noball target at Ruisseauville in the Pas-de-Calais.

The Spitfire XII Wing often escorted RAF de Havilland Mosquitos to Noball targets during Winter 1943-1944.
© Crown copyright expired

Date	2 January 1944
Operation	Ramrod 412
Target	Ruisseauville, Pas-de-Calais
Bombers	25 Mosquitos; 19 dispatched, 17 bombed
Casualties	3 Mosquitos CD/AA
Fighter Cover	Tangmere: 41 & 91 Squadrons (Spitfire XII)

Six fewer Mosquitos were dispatched as planned, but these made their way to Ruisseauville unaccompanied, arriving over the target at low level at 15:30. The Spitfire XII Wing was airborne at 14:50, led by Sqn Ldr Norman Kynaston, and traversed the Channel on the deck. Crossing in just south of Cayeux, the pilots approached Ruisseauville just below the 10/10ths cloud layer, with a base of 2,000-2,500 feet, and arrived in the area at the same time as the Mosquitos.

The Wing then proceeded to patrol the area below the cloud base whilst the Mosquitos made their bombing runs at 1,200-1,800 feet. Seventeen Mosquitos attacked, dropping sixty-eight 500 lb. bombs, and achieved good results, with bursts covering the target area; only a few overshoots were observed. Flak was light but accurate and three Mosquitos were hit and sustained minor damage.

41 and 91 Squadrons confirmed that concentrated bombing was achieved, but also attracted the attention of anti-aircraft gunners: "Considerable light flak experienced with green and white tracers, especially west of Hesdin".[365] On the way out, a stationary train with four Flak wagons was seen in a station at Hesdin, which the Wing steered clear of.

Owing to excessive fuel consumption, nine aircraft from 41 Squadron and four from 91 Squadron landed early at Friston to refuel, whilst the rest of the pilots continued to Tangmere, where they landed at 16:30 and reported the operation otherwise uneventful. Although the Luftwaffe was not seen, the amount of anti-aircraft fire experienced by the pilots prompted Fg Off Herb Wagner to record in his logbook that day, "In France at 1500 feet for 30 minutes. Intense flak all the way. Very shakey"[sic].[366]

3 January 1944 – Weather again hindered operations today, and the only operational flying undertaken all day were two "Anti-Enemy Anti-Rhubarb patrols".[367] A section from each 41 and 91 Squadrons took off at 11:05, and patrolled together at zero feet off the French coast between Le Touquet and Cayeux. 41 Squadron's pilots were Flt Lts Bruce Moffett and Ron Collis. No enemy aircraft were seen but they did note that Berck-sur-Mer Airfield was clear of any obstructions.

The pilots returned at 12:30 after an uneventful trip, reporting the weather to be 10/10ths stratocumulus inland of the French coast between 2,000 and 3,000 feet, with another band of 8/10ths cloud at 10,000 feet, and rain storms further west. There was no further operational flying all day.

4 January 1944 – In its first full day of operations in some time, the Spitfire XII Wing was airborne today on two Ramrod operations to Noball targets. In the first of these, they provided a Fighter Umbrella, in unison with the Biggin Hill Wing, for attacks by Mosquitos, Bostons and Mitchells on Noball targets at Ruisseauville, Ligescourt, Gueschart, and Noyelles-en-Chaussée in Ramrod 418. In the second, the Wing flew a Fighter Sweep of the Étretat-Rouen-Évreux area, supporting attacks by Marauders on 'Longuemont' & Béhen, 'Bois Coquerel' and Gorenflos, in Picardie.

Date	4 January 1944
Operation	Ramrod 418
Targets	Part I: Ruisseauville, Pas-de-Calais Part II: Ligescourt, Picardie Part III: Gueschart, Picardie Part IV: Noyelles-en-Chaussée, Picardie
Bombers	Part I: 25 Mosquitos; 17 dispatched, 4 bombed Part II: 24 Bostons; 24 dispatched, 24 bombed Part III: 24 Mitchells; 26 dispatched, 24 bombed Part IV: 24 Mitchells; 24 dispatched, 23 bombed
Casualties	Part I: 21 Sqn Mosq VI, HX954, hit sand on beach whilst crossing French coast, turned back for coast but forced down, crew POW; & 487 Sqn: Mosq VI, LR331, believed ditched in North Sea, cause unknown, crew†368
Close Escort Part I	None
Close Escort Part II	Heston: 306 Squadron (Spitfire Vb)
Close Escort Part III	Heston: 315 Squadron (Spitfire Vb)
Close Escort Part IV	Hawkinge: 322 Squadron (Spitfire Vb)
Fighter Umbrella	Tangmere: 41 & 91 Squadrons (Spitfire XII) Biggin Hill: 401 Squadron (Spitfire IX)
Fighter Sweep	North Weald: 331 & 332 Squadrons (Spitfire IX)

Part I's Mosquitos approached Ruisseauville independently at low altitude, but only four attacked the target from 11:35, dropping sixteen 500 lb. bombs with good results. One Mosquito was damaged and force-landed on the way in, and another failed to return for unknown reasons.

Part II's bombers and escorts rendezvoused at 6,000 feet over Beachy Head at 11:15, and reached Ligescourt as planned at 11:35. All 24 Bostons attacked the target from 8,000 feet, dropping a total of ninety-four 500 lb. bombs with good results, and near misses on a large rectangular building and a 'pyramidal pit'. Thirty-two new craters were created inside the target area, but the operation was otherwise uneventful for both the bombers and their fighter escort.

Part III rendezvoused at the same location and altitude as Part II, five minutes later, and reached Gueschart without trouble. Twenty-four Mitchells dropped ninety-six 500 lb. bombs at 11:40, most of which were seen to fall inside the target area. Their escort operated uneventfully.

Part IV's bombers and their escorts arrived over Beachy Head at 6,000 feet, rendezvousing on time at 11:25. Eighteen Mitchells attacked Noyelles-en-Chaussée from 7,000 feet at 11:45, dropping one hundred and forty-four 500 lb. bombs with good results. A quarter of the main square concrete building was seen to have been demolished by the attack, and a crater caused at the end of a platform. Another five Mitchells dropped an additional forty 500 lb. bombs onto a small wood just short of the target area. Their close escort also operated according to plan and uneventfully.

Tasked with providing a Fighter Umbrella over the target area from zero+20 to zero+35 (11:35-11:50), the Spitfire XII Wing was airborne at 11:00 led by 91 Squadron's Commanding Officer, Sqn Ldr Norman Kynaston. The pilots caught up with the bombers – considering the timings, presumably those of Parts III and/or IV – as they reached at the French coast, off Berck-sur-Mer. Around this time, Flt Lt Ron Collis (MB858) developed jettison tank trouble and returned to Tangmere, landing at 11:50.

As the rest of the Wing was about to cross in, Beachy Head Control informed them that enemy aircraft were south of their location and ordered them to the Somme Estuary. Banking inland over Abbeville, the Wing sighted a squadron of enemy aircraft orbiting the target area at 11,000 feet. As the pilots approached, however, they were spotted and the enemy aircraft "suddenly dived and were lost sight of".[369]

The Wing was then given various vectors and patrolled the target area as far as northwest of Amiens in clear weather with visibility of up to 25 miles. The Luftwaffe was not seen again, and no Flak was encountered. The pilots crossed out at Berck again and landed at Tangmere at 12:30, with the exception of Plt Off Peter Graham (MB798), who had developed a fuel leak and landed early at Friston.

Biggin Hill's 401 Squadron operated uneventfully, as did North Weald's Fighter Sweep.

The Spitfire XII Wing was airborne again at 15:00 for their second operation of the day, supporting an attack on four Noball sites in Picardie.

Date	4 January 1944
Operation	Ramrod 419
Targets, Parts I & II	1st Box: 'Longuemont'[370] & Béhen, Picardie 2nd Box: 'Bois Coquerel' & Gorenflos, Picardie
Bombers	Part I: 72 Marauders in two boxes of 36; 18 bombed secondary Part II: 72 Marauders in two boxes of 36; 18 bombed secondary
Close Escort Part I	Hornchurch: 66 & 129 Squadrons (Spitfire IX)
Escort Cover	Kenley: 403 & 421 Squadrons (Spitfire IX)
Close Escort Part II	Detling: 132 & 602 Squadrons (Spitfire IX)
Escort Cover	Gravesend: 19 & 122 Squadrons (Spitfire IX)
1st Fighter Sweep	Northolt: 302, 308 & 317 Squadrons (Spitfire IX)
2nd Fighter Sweep	Biggin Hill: 401, 411 & 412 Squadrons (Spitfire Vb)
3rd Fighter Sweep	Tangmere: 41 & 91 Squadrons (Spitfire XII)

Having rendezvoused with their escort fighters 12,000 feet over Beachy Head at 15:00, Part I's bombers arrived over the target area at 15:25 at 11,000 feet, as planned. However, weather conditions prevented the Marauders attacking the primary targets. One formation of 18 attacked Noyelles-en-Chaussée instead, dropping one hundred and eight 500 lb. bombs with fair results, but the remainder returned with their payloads intact. Both Close Escort and Escort Cover Wings operated uneventfully.

It was a similar situation for Part II, which rendezvoused at the same location and altitude, but 20 minutes behind Part I. Weather conditions prevented their targets being attacked and 18 Marauders bombed Longuemont instead, dropping one hundred and one 500 lb. bombs with poor results. Whilst the Close Escort Wing operated uneventfully, the Escort Cover Wing engaged two FW190s on the way in, which attempted to attack the bombers, and 122 Squadron claimed both probably destroyed.

The first Fighter Sweep was uneventful, but the second was attacked by eight to ten FW190s and Me109s from 1,000 feet above them when south of Bernay at 18,000 feet. 411 Squadron followed them down and was able to claim one Me109 damaged for no casualty of their own.

The Spitfire XII Wing was airborne at 15:00 led by Sqn Ldr Kynaston to provide the Ramrod's third Fighter Sweep. Crossing in at Étretat at 8,000 feet, above a bank of 10/10ths cloud at 4,000 feet, the Wing set a course for Rouen, where they experienced slight heavy Flak through 3/10ths cloud. On reaching the area, however, Beachy Head Control gave them a new vector to the Évreux-Bernay area where they sighted six unidentified aircraft five miles away at the same altitude.

Two of these aircraft broke away from the others, one diving under 91 Squadron, which was chased by 41 Squadron's, Flt Lt Don Smith RAAF (MB882). Smith was able to close sufficiently to identify it as a FW190 but insufficiently to engage it. The second aircraft made a wide orbit of the Wing and was identified as an Me109, but neither this aircraft, nor the remaining four, could be drawn into an engagement either.

The Wing crossed back out at Étretat again at 5,000 feet, and proceeded to Tangmere, where they landed at 16:25, concluding the day's operational flying.

5 January 1944 – The day's operational flying for 41 Squadron commenced with three separate weather reconnaissances, undertaken by A Flight's White Section (Slack MB845 & Sabourin MB862), Red Section (Smith MB882 & Cook MB794), and Yellow Section (Wagner MB843 & Curtis EN237).

White Section was airborne at 09:25 and Red and Yellow at 09:30, each heading for their respective patrol areas: Beauvais, Évreux and the Calais. All three reconnaissances proved uneventful and returned in that same order, at 10:30, 10:25 and 10:40.

As their reports were favourable, the Wing spent the rest of the day employed on two Wing operations. The first of these entailed the provision of Fighter Cover for attacks on Vaux-Marquenneville, Campneuseville and Le Mesnil-Allard Noball sites in Northern France in Ramrod 423, and the second saw the Wing flying a Rodeo in a triangular area bordered by Dreux, northwest Paris and Rouen.

Date	5 January 1944
Operation	Ramrod 423
Targets	Part I: Vaux-Marquenneville, Picardie Part II: Campneuseville, Haute-Normandie Part III: Le Mesnil-Allard, Haute-Normandie
Bombers	Part I: 24 Bostons; 15 bombed Part II: 24 Mitchells; 23 bombed Part III: 24 Mitchells; 24 bombed
Close Escort Part I Close Escort Part II Close Escort Part III Fighter Umbrella	Friston: 349 Squadron & Hawkinge: 501 Squadron (Spitfire Vb) Hawkinge: 322 Squadron (Spitfire Vb) Ibsley: 310 & 312 Squadrons (Spitfire Vb) Tangmere: 41 & 91 Squadrons (Spitfire XII)

Even though weather interfered with Part I's bombing, Ramrod 423 operated as close to a textbook operation as possible under the circumstances. Part I rendezvoused 6,000 feet over Beachy Head at 11:30, and dropped sixty-three 500 lb. bombs on Vaux-Marquenneville from 9,000 feet at 12:05 with fair to poor results. Part II rendezvoused at the same location and altitude at 11:35, and dropped one hundred and eighty-two 500 lb. bombs on Campneuseville from 7,000 feet at 12:06, achieving a good concentration inside the target area. Part III rendezvoused 7,000 feet over Beachy Head at 11:40, and dropped one hundred and ninety-one 500 lb. bombs on Le Mesnil-Allard at 12:11 with good results. All three Close Escort wings operated uneventfully; the Luftwaffe was not seen, and no casualties or claims were recorded by any of the participants.

For their part, the Spitfire XII Wing was airborne at 11:20 and reached the area on time, intending to patrol east of the target area from 12:00 to 12:15 at 14,000 feet. 41 Squadron deployed 11 aircraft in sections of four, three and four, led by Sqn Ldr Matthew. The bombers were sighted and kept an eye on throughout the operation, however a thin 10/10ths cloud layer at 14,000 feet forced the Wing slightly lower than planned and they were compelled to patrol below the cloud base at 13,000 feet instead.

Slight inaccurate heavy Flak was experienced, but the pilots could not determine from where it was coming owing to haze that rose to 4,000 feet. Where the ground could be seen, it was observed to have been covered in frost or a light layer of snow. The Luftwaffe did not attempt to interfere and operation proved uneventful. There was little to report when the Wing landed again at 12:55 for a late lunch.

The Wing was scheduled to take off again at 15:00, led by Sqn Ldr Kynaston, for Rodeo 275 to Dreux, northwest Paris and Rouen. However, as a result of unnamed issues, only eight aircraft from 41 Squadron and nine from 91 Squadron actually got airborne. Plt Off Jimmy Payne was not impressed, recording in his logbook, "Shambles. Wing became only 1 Squadron".[371,372]

The Wing therefore flew all the way to Dreux in a single formation at between 4,000 and 5,000 feet, above 1/10th scattered cloud at 2,000 feet. Turning northeast towards northwest Paris, the pilots flew almost as far as Mantes-Gassicourt [today Mantes-la-Jolie] before turning northwest towards Rouen. Seeing nothing of interest, they continued westwards towards the mouth of the Seine, pausing briefly to orbit Quillebeuf to take a closer look at an unidentified sunken vessel at the mouth of the Canal de Tancarville.

The Wing crossed out at Étretat and landed back at Tangmere between 16:30 and 16:40, with the exception of one (unnamed) pilot of 41 Squadron who landed at Friston, presumably short of fuel. The operation proved completely uneventful, and pilots did not see the Luftwaffe or experience any Flak. There was no further operational flying today.

6 January 1944 – The Wing was airborne on a single operation today, providing a Fighter Umbrella for attacks on Noball sites in Northern France, as an element of Ramrod 428.

Date	6 January 1944
Operation	Ramrod 428
Targets	Part I: Le Petit Bois-Robert, Esclavelles, Haute-Normandie
	Part II: Pommeréval, Haute-Normandie
	Part III: Écalles sur Buchy, Haute-Normandie
	Part IV: Belleville-en-Caux, Haute-Normandie
Bombers	Part I: 12 Mosquitos; 11 bombed
	Part II: 24 Mitchells – aborted (weather)
	Part III: 24 Bostons – aborted (weather)
	Part IV: 24 Mitchells; 15 bombed
Close Escort Part I	None
Close Escort Part II	Friston: 349 Squadron (Spitfire Vb)
Close Escort Part III	Hawkinge: 322 & 501 Squadrons (Spitfire Vb)
Close Escort Part IV	Ibsley: 310 & 312 Squadrons (Spitfire Vb)
Fighter Umbrella	Tangmere: 41 & 91 Squadrons (Spitfire XII)
	Gravesend: 19 & 122 Squadrons (Spitfire IX)
1st Fighter Sweep	Detling: 132 & 602 Squadrons (Spitfire IX)
2nd Fighter Sweep	Biggin Hill: 401 & 411 Squadrons (Spitfire Vb)
Casualties	91 Sqn: Fg Off Harold F. Heninger RCAF, EF in Spit XII, EN223, baled out nr St. Valéry, parachute caught on tailplane †; Hawkinge Wing: 1 A/C CL/UC failure Hawkinge, NDEA

Part I's Mosquitos made their way to Le Petit Bois-Robert without fighter escort and attacked through 6/10ths to 8/10ths cloud between 3,000 and 5,000 feet. Forty-four 500 lb. bombs were dropped from 11:55 with generally unobserved results.

Parts II and III both aborted their attacks upon finding 9/10ths to 10/10ths cloud at 4,000 feet over their respective target areas, and returned with their payloads intact. Part IV also partially aborted their attack as a result of weather conditions, and only 15 of the 24 dispatched Mitchells actually bombed. Even these aircraft had difficulty locating the target, eventually dropping one hundred and twenty 500 lb. bombs on Belleville-en-Caux with only 'fair' results. The Close Escorts for Parts II, III and IV all operated uneventfully.

They stood in stark contrast to the Fighter Umbrella provided by the Gravesend Wing (122 Airfield) and the Spitfire XII Wing. 41 and 91 Squadrons took off at 11:30, in order to patrol the target area from 11:55 to 12:15, with 41 Squadron's three sections led by Flt Lts 'Pinkie' Glen, Don Smith RAAF and Lyndon Griffith RNZAF.

The Wing crossed into France in time to see Bostons and Mitchells inbound to their targets, and was then vectored to the Beauvais area, and subsequently toward Rouen. When east of the latter city, the pilots were informed of enemy aircraft flying in a westerly direction from Paris to Beauvais. The...

> *Wing attempted to head them off at Rouen, but although informed* [by Beachy Head Control] *e/a first above and later below the wing, no e/a sighted. High cover* [presumably implying 19 and 122 Squadrons] *not seen.*[373]

Around this time, 91 Squadron's Fg Off Patrick Schade DFM broke away with engine trouble, and headed for home, accompanied by Fg Off Harold Heninger (EN223, DL-B). Approximately seven miles east of the French coast, Heninger informed Schade that he would have to bale out. Looking back, Schade saw smoke coming from Heninger's aircraft, and spotted two unidentified aircraft approximately 2,000 yards to his rear, which he believed were FW190s.

Heninger did indeed bale out, but his parachute caught on his Spitfire's tailplane, and he was dragged to his death. EN223 crashed at Le Mesnil-Durdent, just south St Valéry-en-Caux, and he was buried at St. Riquier, but subsequently reinterred at Grandcourt War Cemetery.[374]

Having seen nothing, the rest of the Wing returned to Tangmere none the wiser at 13:00, and was surprised to find that Fg Off Heninger had not returned. There was no further operational flying by the Wing for the rest of the day.

Meanwhile, Gravesend's 19 and 122 Squadrons had been vectored onto the same plots at Rouen as the Spitfire XII Wing, and intercepted some thirty FW190s north of Rouen at 21,000 feet. The Wing orbited at 17,000 feet to draw them down, with the desired effect. The enemy aircraft dived and several combats ensued in which 19 Squadron claimed one FW190 destroyed and two damaged, and 122 Squadron claimed a further FW190 damaged, all for no casualties of their own.

Separately, the first Fighter Sweep operated uneventfully, but the second sighted six enemy aircraft whilst crossing in at Pointe D'Ailly and chased them inland. In the resulting combats, two FW190s were claimed destroyed, one each by 401 and 411 Squadrons, for no loss.

7 January 1944 – The day commenced with a weather reconnaissance by Fg Off Ron Johnson and Plt Off Peter Graham, who took off at 09:00 for the Cherbourg area. The pair returned 55 minutes later reporting the first half of the Channel clear and the second half covered in a 10/10ths cloud layer between 1,000 and 4,000 feet. The cloud cleared completely over Barfleur but increased again to 5/10ths with a ceiling of 4,000 feet over the northwest of the Cherbourg [Cotentin] Peninsula. They also reported visibility of six to eight miles at sea level and unlimited at 6,000 feet.

Their report cleared the way for the first of the day's two Ramrod operations, in which the Spitfire XII Wing provided Escort Cover to Marauders attacking Noball sites ('construction works and a ski sites') in three Parts at 'La Glacerie', 'La Sorellerie I' and 'La Sorellerie II' located a short distance from Cherbourg.[375]

Date	7 January 1944
Operation	Ramrod 431
Targets	Part I: La Glacerie (3 boxes) & Le Mesnil-au-Val (1 box), Basse-Normandie Part II: La Glacerie (2 boxes) La Sorellerie II (1 box) & La Sorellerie I (1 box), Basse-Normandie Part III: La Glacerie (2 boxes) La Sorellerie II (1 box) & La Sorellerie I (1 box), Basse-Normandie

Bombers	Part I: 72 Marauders in 4 boxes – aborted
	Part II: 72 Marauders in 4 boxes; 36 bombed alternate target
	Part III: 72 Marauders in 4 boxes – aborted
Close Escort Part I	Heston: 306 & 315 Squadrons (Spitfire Vb)
Escort Cover	Biggin Hill: 401 & 411 Squadrons (Spitfire Vb)
Close Escort Part II	Hawkinge: 322 & 501 Squadrons (Spitfire Vb)
Escort Cover	Hornchurch: 66, 129 & 350 Squadrons (Spitfire IX)
Close Escort Part III	Digby: 402 & 416 Squadrons (Spitfire IX)
Escort Cover	Tangmere: 41 & 91 Squadrons (Spitfire XII)

By the time the bombers reached the Cotentin Peninsula, the weather had closed in again and they were unable to identify and attack any of the primary targets. Thirty-six Marauders dropped one hundred and ninety-six 500 lb. bombs on Cherbourg-Maupertus Airfield with fair results instead but this was the total bombing for the Ramrod as the rest of the Marauders returned home with their payloads intact.

The Close Escort and Escort Cover Wings all operated uneventfully, with the only exception being a sighting of two FW190s by the Heston Wing, approximately five miles south of Cherbourg-Maupertus Airfield. On sighting the RAF, however, they banked away and avoided any engagement.

For their part, the Spitfire XII Wing was airborne at 11:25 and rendezvoused with Part III's Marauders 12,000 feet over St. Valéry-en-Caux at 11:45. The formation set a westerly course for the Cotentin Peninsula three minutes early and, as a result, Digby's Close Escort Wing arrived at the rendezvous but did not see the bombers. 41 and 91 Squadrons escorted the Marauders all the way to the target area alone, where heavy Flak was directed towards the bombers.

However, the Digby Wing joined up with them on the way back out, at which time the Spitfire XII Wing took the opportunity to turn back for France and conduct a free-range sweep. Flying down the length of the Cotentin Peninsula at 10,000 feet, the Wing turned eastwards towards the south of Caen, and then crossed out again, but saw no sign of the Luftwaffe. The pilots landed back at Tangmere at 12:50.

Less than two hours later, the Wing had been lunched and briefed for another show, and was airborne at 14:45 to provide Fighter Cover to Mosquitos bombing construction works and a ski site in Bois de Pottier, a woodland approximately 1.5km west of the village of Embry, in Ramrod 435.[376]

Date	7 January 1944
Operation	Ramrod 435
Target	Embry/Bois de Pottier, Pas-de-Calais
Bombers	2 Group RAF: 6 Mosquitos; 5 bombed
Fighter Cover	Tangmere: 41 & 91 Squadrons (Spitfire XII)
Fighter Sweep	Biggin Hill: 401 & 411 Squadrons (Spitfire Vb)

The Spitfire XII Wing was airborne at 14:45 and made their own way to the Berck-sur-Mer area, arriving at zero-5 (15:10). 41 Squadron deployed eleven aircraft, in sections of three, four and four, with the smaller section, the Squadron, and the Wing led by Wg Cdr Ingham.

After barely five minutes in the air, however, Fg Off Keith Curtis (EN237) turned back with a malfunctioning hood and landed again at 15:55. The rest of the Wing crossed the Channel on the deck, then climbed to 3,000 feet to cross in, and proceeded to patrol up sun of the Mosquitos and south of the target area, below a 9/10ths cloud base between 4,000 and 5,000 feet. Around this time, Flt Lt 'Pinkie' Glen (MB881) also pulled out and returned home with jettison tank trouble.

The Mosquitos flew directly to Embry and five attacked Bois de Pottier from altitudes of just 400-500 feet, dropping a total of sixteen 500 lb. bombs with good results. Nearly all the bombs fell in the target area and no Flak was experienced.

Meanwhile, Fg Off Ron Loweth (MB830) sighted two unidentified aircraft above the Wing at about 4,000 feet, through breaks in the cloud. Aware the Luftwaffe was likely lurking, the Wing kept an eye out and about 15 minutes later, 91 Squadron's Fg Off Jacques Andrieux (FAFL) saw two aircraft banking away. He gave chase, diving after them from 4,000 feet down to 400 feet and soon identified them as FW190s.

Closing on the pair at a speed of 340 mph IAS to a range of just 250 yards, he fired at the starboard aircraft, striking its underside. The pilot tried to evade by banking to starboard, but Andrieux followed him around and fired again, hitting the Focke-Wulf in the tail, fuselage and both wings. The aircraft flick-rolled to starboard three times at an altitude of just 50 feet, then hit the ground and burst into flames, and was seen by many of the Wing's pilots.

41 Squadron's Flt Lt Dave Fearon had initially tried to follow the other FW190, but lost it owing to its dark camouflage. Flying over to where Andrieux had shot the starboard FW190, he took two feet on cinegun film of the wreckage burning on the ground, then re-joined the Wing.

The Wing experienced light Flak in the Montreuil and Berck areas, and more intense light Flak from Berck's airfield. A Flak train also opened up on the Wing, but no casualties were sustained. The pilots returned to Tangmere at 16:20, concluding the day's operational flying.

Whilst the Wing had been occupied over the Berck area, the Biggin Hill Wing undertook an uneventful Fighter Sweep of the Amiens area. They returned with little to report but for the observance of repairs being undertaken to Amiens-Glisy Airfield.

8 January 1944 – Today's operational flying was limited to a single operation in which the Wing provided a Close Escort to Mosquitos attacking a Noball site at Belmesnil, supported by an Escort Cover Wing and seven Fighter Sweeps, in Ramrod 440.

Date	8 January 1944
Operation	Ramrod 440
Target	Belmesnil, Haute-Normandie
Bombers	2 Group: 7 Mosquitos – aborted (navigational error)
Close Escort	Tangmere: 41 & 91 Squadrons (Spitfire XII)
Escort Cover	Biggin Hill: 401 & 411 Squadrons (Spitfire Vb)
1st Fighter Sweep	Westhampnett: 174 & 245 Squadrons (Typhoon Ib)
2nd Fighter Sweep	Manston: 198 & 609 Squadrons (Typhoon Ib) – aborted (weather)
3rd Fighter Sweep	Detling: 132 & 602 Squadrons (Spitfire IX)
4th Fighter Sweep	Kenley: 403 Squadron, & Tangmere: 421 Squadron (Spitfire IX)
5th Fighter Sweep	Gravesend: 19 & 122 Squadrons (Spitfire IX)
6th Fighter Sweep	Hornchurch: 66 & 129 Squadrons (Spitfire IX)
7th Fighter Sweep	Northolt: 302, 308 & 317 Squadrons (Spitfire IX)
Casualties	245 Sqn: Flt Sgt William N. Waudby SD nr Évreux in Typhoon Ib, JP971, ER

The Spitfire XII Wing was airborne at 13:30, with the Squadron and Wing again led by Wg Cdr Ingham, and rendezvoused with the Mosquitos on time. The Wing followed the Mosquitos across the Channel in order to cover their bombing and withdrawal, but they aborted the operation off Le Tréport, due to a navigational error.

It is doubtful whether the attack would have gone ahead anyway, as a band of 9/10ths cloud lay between a base of 500-1,000 feet and a ceiling of 2,000 feet. A further band of 10/10ths cloud lay between 4,000 and 5,000 feet, and yet another between 8,000 and 9,000 feet.

Turning back for England, the Wing followed the Mosquitos in the direction of Beachy Head for 20 miles, by which time they had obtained permission to head back to France to undertake a free-range sweep. Climbing through cloud to 9,500 feet over the Somme Estuary, the pilots turned south and descended to 4,000 feet to orbit the Abbeville area. Seeing nothing of interest, they crossed out again at Ault, encountering considerable light Flak from just south of Saint-Valéry-sur-Somme and from southeast of Ault.

The Wing landed back at Tangmere at 15:00 without Fg Off Herb Wagner (EN237), who landed at Friston at 14:50, presumably low on fuel. There was no further operational flying today.

Meanwhile the seven Fighter Sweeps had also operated, all of them uneventful except for the first. Westhampnett's 174 and 245 Squadrons were sent on a sweep around Paris, from Compiègne to Villaroche and on to Chartres. They sighted a twin-engined transport aircraft at Compiègne that was attacked and destroyed and, shortly before reaching Chartres, five Junkers Ju88s were seen around the airfield at Brétigny-sur-Orge.

One of these aircraft, making its final run in to land, was damaged by Wg Cdr Robert Davidson and a pilot of 245 Squadron, whilst another in the circuit was attacked by 174 Squadron and went down at Guyancourt spewing black smoke, which was claimed probably destroyed. 245 Squadron attacked a third Ju88, but observed no strikes, however return fire was also experienced from the aircraft which shot down one of 245 Squadron's Typhoons; the pilot subsequently evaded. Not over yet, four pilots from 245 Squadron attacked and destroyed six motorised transports and Wg Cdr Henry Woodhouse fired head-on at an Arado 96B, but made no claim.

9 January 1944 – Dreadful weather dominated the day, and the only operational flying carried out by the entire Tangmere Wing was a weather reconnaissance to Beauvais by two pilots of 41 Squadron, which almost had a bad outcome.

Fg Offs Peter Cowell (MB862) and Ross Harding (MB794) took off at 09:00 in order to fly the route Tangmere-Beachy Head-Dieppe-Beauvais-Le Havre-Tangmere, but became separated in the poor weather and carried out the reconnaissance independent of one another.

On his return, Harding became disoriented, lost his bearings, and landed near Portsmouth at 10:35, whilst Cowell made it back to Tangmere safely, but only had three gallons of fuel left in his tank. Owing to the dangerous conditions, no further operational flying was undertaken by the Squadron for another 29 hours.

10 January 1944 – Following a day on the ground, the Spitfire XII Wing was in the air today for a single Ramrod, in another attempt to attack a Noball site at Belmesnil, which had been aborted on 8 January. On this occasion, however, it was just the Mosquitos and the Wing acting as Close Escort; no-one else participated.

Date	10 January 1944
Operation	Ramrod 444
Target	Belmesnil, Haute-Normandie
Bombers	2 Group RAF: 7 Mosquitos; 7 dispatched, 6 bombed
Close Escort	Tangmere: 41 & 91 Squadrons (Spitfire XII)

The Wing was airborne at 15:20, led by Wg Cdr Ingham, who flew with 91 Squadron, with Wg Cdr Crisham as his No. 2. 41 Squadron provided twelve aircraft in three sections, led by Flt Lts 'Pinkie' Glen and Don Smith, and Fg Off Ron Johnson. After forming up, a bearing was made for Brighton where rendezvous was made with the seven Mosquitos at an altitude of just 500 feet at 15:30.

They proceeded across the Channel together at zero feet, but shortly before reaching the French coast, one of the Mosquitos pulled out and returned home. The remaining six crossed in between Dieppe and Le Tréport, whilst the Spitfire XII Wing orbited just off the coast at around 500 feet, on account of 10/10ths cloud with a base of 2,300 feet, and rain squalls and poor visibility below it.

Slight heavy Flak was experienced from Dieppe, but it was inaccurate and caused no damage. Their low altitude, however, allowed them to sight several individual sea mines floating approximately one to two miles off the coast from Dieppe, and these were reported on their return.

Whilst the Wing orbited, the Mosquitos attacked Belmesnil from 500 feet, dropping twenty-four 500 lb. bombs with generally good results. Fourteen bursts were seen inside the target area, the majority in close proximity to a number of rectangular buildings, but some were also seen to the northeast and northwest of the target area. As no Flak was encountered, two of the Mosquitos also strafed the target with cannon fire.

The Wing met the Mosquitos on the way out, and although 41 Squadron only saw five come out, all of them made it home safely. The formation returned as they came, and the Luftwaffe was not seen and there were no claims or casualties. The Spitfire XII Wing landed back at Tangmere between 16:45 and 16:50, and this concluded flying for the day.

There was no further operational flying until 14 January on account of poor weather conditions, but three pilots were posted away during this period: Plt Off James Still, Fg Off Ron Loweth, and Sqn Ldr John Clouston. The actual departure dates of the former two pilots are unknown, but both men are last mentioned in the ORB on 10 January 1944; Clouston ended his tenure on 12 January.

Still was rested as a flying instructor at 57 OTU before returning to operations in September 1944 with 1 Squadron. Awarded a Mention in Despatches in June 1945, he served with the Auxiliary Air Force until relinquishing his commission in August 1960. Little is known of Loweth's subsequent postings and life, although he is believed have served as a test pilot for the rest of the War.

Clouston was posted to 165 Squadron at Culmhead on 13 January 1944 and remained with this unit until he was shot down on D-Day. He baled out into the Channel 3km west of Trégastel, France, and was captured. However, he was fatally wounded whilst being transported from Tours with six other POWs when the vehicle was strafed by Allied aircraft. He died of his wounds two weeks later.

14 January 1944 – Following several days on the ground as a result of unsuitable conditions, the weather had improved sufficiently by today to allow the Spitfire XII Wing to participate in two Ramrod operations to Noball targets. In the first of these, the Wing provided a Fighter Umbrella to 2 Group Bostons and Mitchells attacking Gorenflos and Petit Bois Tillencourt, in Ramrod 452.[377]

Date	14 January 1944
Operation	Ramrod 452
Targets	Part I: Gorenflos, Picardie Part II: Petit Bois Tillencourt, Picardie
Bombers	Part I: 2 Group: 18 Bostons; 18 dispatched, 18 bombed Part II: 2 Group: 24 Mitchells; 24 dispatched, 24 bombed
Casualties	Part II: 9 Mitchells CD/AA
Close Escort Part I Close Escort Part II Fighter Umbrella	Friston: 349 Squadron (Spitfire Vb) Digby: 402 & 416 Squadrons (Spitfire IX) Tangmere: 41 & 91 Squadrons (Spitfire XII) Biggin Hill: 401 & 411 Squadrons (Spitfire Vb)

Parts I and II rendezvoused 6,000 feet over Beachy Head at 11:00 (zero) and 11:10 (zero+10), respectively, and proceeded to France according to plan. However, intense heavy Flak hampered the attack on Gorenflos, and only six of the Bostons were able to complete their attacks, dropping twenty-four 500 lb. bombs with good results and a few near misses. The remaining twelve Bostons attacked the Flixecourt/Domart-en-Ponthieu Noball site, instead, dropping forty-eight 500 lb. bombs with good results. Subsequent reconnaissance photography showed damage to buildings inside the target area.

In contrast, although intense heavy Flak was also experienced over Petit Bois Tillencourt, all 24 Mitchells attacked the primary, dropping one hundred and eighty 500 lb. bombs. Most were seen to fall inside the target area, but nine bombers sustained Flak damage of varying degrees. In both Parts, the Close Escorts operated according to plan and uneventfully.

For their part, the Spitfire XII Wing was tasked with providing a Fighter Umbrella in the target area from zero+24 to zero+35 at 10,000 feet, in unison with the Biggin Hill Wing. Airborne at 10:50, with Wg Cdr Ingham leading 41 Squadron and the Wing, the pilots crossed in at Le Crotoy at 10,000 feet.

The Wing initially flew due east to Conteville, then turned southwest and flew to the south of Abbeville, where they turned west for Cayeux. On reaching Cayeux, the Wing turned inland again, heading northeast to Hesdin, then southeast again to Doullens, where intense heavy Flak was experienced. Unimpressed with the unwanted attention, Plt Off Peter Graham (MB798) later penned in his logbook, "Very accurate heavy flak. No Joke".[378]

Sighting a homeward-bound bomber formation heading south from the St. Omer area, the Wing then swung in behind them and withdrew with them. The Luftwaffe was not seen and the Wing returned to Tangmere without event, landing again at 12:25.

The Biggin Hill Wing encountered the Luftwaffe in small numbers on their own operation, sighting three FW190s west of Arras, and one Me109 near Hesdin. Two of the trio of FW190s made a head-on attack on the Wing, but no damage was done, and they could not be overhauled in a chase.

Following lunch, the pilots were briefed for their second operation of the day, in which the Wing was split up in separate parts, and detailed to provide Close Escorts to Bostons and Mitchells attacking the Noball site at Flottemanville-Hague in Lower Normandy.

Date	14 January 1944
Operation	Ramrod 456
Targets	Parts I-III: Flottemanville-Hague, Basse-Normandie
Bombers	Part I: 24 Mitchells; 23 bombed Part II: 18 Bostons; 14 bombed Part III: 12 Mitchells; 12 bombed
Close Escort Part I Close Escort Part II Close Escort Part III 1st Fighter Sweep 2nd Fighter Sweep 3rd Fighter Sweep	Ibsley: 310 & 312 Squadrons (Spitfire Vb) Tangmere: 41 Squadron (Spitfire XII) Tangmere: 91 Squadron (Spitfire XII) Unknown[379] Unknown Culmhead: 165 Squadron (Spitfire IX)

Part I rendezvoused 10,000 feet over St. Albans Head, Dorset, at 15:15 and proceeded directly to Flottemanville-Hague where 23 Mitchells dropped one hundred and eighty-two 500 lb. bombs from 12,000 feet at 15:40. Bursts were seen inside the target area and also to the south and southwest. Intense heavy Flak was experienced from Flottemanville-Hague and from between Querqueville and Cherbourg, but the Close Escort Wing operated otherwise uneventfully.

41 Squadron was airborne at 14:55, led by Flt Lt 'Pinkie' Glen, and rendezvoused with Part II's Bostons 10,000 feet over St. Albans Head, five minutes behind Part I. However, the bombers headed for France in formations of five, five, and six at 14,000 to 16,000 feet, and were therefore spread too far apart be to effectively escorted by a single squadron. Left little choice, Glen allocated one section to each box.

Intense, accurate heavy Flak was experienced from both the Octeville and Cherbourg areas, but 14 Bostons were still able to attack Flottemanville-Hague, dropping fifty-five 500 lb. bombs from 13,000 feet at 15:44. Good results were achieved and bursts were seen in the northern part of the target, although some overshot.

Led by Wg Cdr Ingham, eleven aircraft of 91 Squadron rendezvoused with Part III's Mitchells at the same location and altitude as Parts I and II, but five minutes after the latter. Presented the same problem as 41 Squadron, Ingham also found Part III's two boxes of six Mitchells much too far apart to provide an effective close escort.

He therefore detailed one section to each box as they approached Flottemanville-Hague and all twelve Mitchells attacked the target, dropping ninety-six 500 lb. bombs with good results. Intense Flak was experienced once again from the Cherbourg area, but no casualties were recorded.

41 and 91 Squadrons landed back at Tangmere between 16:20 and 16:25, reporting their respective escorts, whilst frustrating, uneventful. There was one minor exception, however. 41 Squadron's Flt Lt Dave Fearon (MB847) reported seeing,

> …*a large splash in the sea about 10 miles from* [the] *French Coast on bearing of 350 degrees from Raz du Cap Levy* [Lévi] *NE of Cherbourg at 1547 hours. F/Lt. Fearon states that on going down it looked like a large black object in the sea but he did not go right down. This has been* [r]*eported to Tangmere Ops B by the Squadron I.O. soon after the Sqdn landed.*[380]

It is not clear what the object was, and subsequent reports do not make any further mention of the sighting. It may have been an aircraft or potentially a German weapons test, but this is, of course, only speculation.

This was the last operational flying for several days on account of poor weather conditions. During this period, limited practice flying and synthetic training was carried out, and three new pilots arrived, presumably to replace those posted away within the past week.

On 17 January 1944, Kenneth 'Robbie' Robinson re-joined the Squadron, having previously served with the unit as an NCO pilot between 1 July and 21 October 1942. Although nothing is known of his postings in the interim, he had been commissioned in January 1943, and returned to the Squadron today as a Flying Officer.

Two days later, 29-year-old Dutch Fg Off Rijklof 'Charlie' van Goens and 20-year-old Canadian Fg Off David Shea also joined the Squadron. Having joined the Dutch National Flight School in February 1937, van Goens had fled occupied Holland in January 1942, and reached England, where he joined the RAFVR that June. Awarded his Wings almost immediately, he was commissioned in early July 1942, and attended EFTS, RAF College Cranwell, OTU and TEU prior to being posted to his first operational unit today with 510 flying hours in his logbook, but none operational.

Shea had joined the RCAF in January 1942 and completed EFTS and SFTS in Canada, passing out with a commission from the latter, prior to shipping to the United Kingdom in early February 1943. Initially attached to 50 Group, he was posted to AFU in May, OTU in June and TEU in late December 1943. He was now joining 41 Squadron on his first operational posting, having logged 360 non-operational flying hours.

20 January 1944 – Following five days on the ground, the Squadron was airborne today at 09:00, led by Wg Cdr Ingham, on a Roadstead to Cap Gris Nez to cover the Tangmere Typhoon Wing – 197 and 486 Squadrons.

During the night a ship had been reported hit off the French coast by coastal guns that was believed to be the blockade runner MV *Münsterland*. This morning, nineteen Typhoons from 198 and 609 Squadrons were sent across the Channel to attack it at 09:10, and found the vessel approximately one mile west of Sangatte, but with only the funnel and superstructure still visible above the surface. Realising there was therefore no point attacking it, it was decided instead that it would a good object for target practice.

197 and 486 Squadrons were then also called upon for the same reason and were sent up soon afterwards, with 41 Squadron as cover. 41 Squadron's pilots took off from Tangmere at 09:00 and flew in the direction of Worthing at an altitude of just 300 feet. Fog then forced them to climb

through cloud to 1,500 feet, but at this time they received an order to return to base; they had not even crossed out. 41 Squadron landed again at 09:30, and were not called upon again all day.

21 January 1944 – With conditions considerably improved today, a long and busy day in wintry conditions awaited 41 Squadron. At 08:50, Fg Offs Herb Wagner and Ross Harding were sent up to conduct a weather reconnaissance in the Cherbourg area, and returned 50 minutes later, after an uneventful patrol.

Approximately ten minutes after their departure, Red (Matthew MB880 & Slack MB840) and Yellow (Smith MB882 & Cowell MB795) Sections were also airborne to conduct an ASR search for a naval dinghy in the Baie de la Seine area, between Le Havre and Cherbourg. Flying initially to Pointe de la Percée, the quartet then flew line abreast in a north-easterly direction for 14 minutes in cloudless skies with good visibility. Seeing nothing, they returned to Tangmere, where they put down at 10:10 with nothing to report.

The Spitfire XII Wing was also called upon today to participate in two Ramrod operations. In the first of these, the Wing provided a Fighter Umbrella for Mitchells and Bostons attacking construction works and a ski sites at 'Le Grismont'[381], 'Bois d'Enfer'[382] and Bois d'Esquerdes in the Pas-de-Calais from 12:10. In the second, they provided a Fighter Sweep for Mosquitos attacking a Noball site at Ardouval from 15:55.

Date	21 January 1944
Operation	Ramrod 468
Targets	Part I: 'Le Grismont' Pas-de-Calais Part II: 'Bois d'Enfer', Pas-de-Calais Part III: Bois d'Esquerdes, Pas-de-Calais
Bombers	Part I: 2 Group: 24 Mitchells; 24 dispatched, 11 bombed Part II: 2 Group: 18 Bostons; 18 dispatched, 16 bombed Part III: 2 Group: 24 Mitchells; 24 dispatched, 15 bombed
Casualties	Part III: One Mitchell CD/AA
Close Escort Part I	Ibsley: 310 & 312 Squadrons (Spitfire Vb)
Close Escort Part II	Digby: 402 & 416 Squadrons (Spitfire Vb)
Close Escort Part III	Perranporth: 341 Squadron (Spitfire Vb)
Fighter Umbrella	Tangmere: 41 & 91 Squadrons (Spitfire XII) Hornchurch: 66 & 350 Squadrons (Spitfire IX)
Fighter Sweep	Gravesend: 19 & 122 Squadrons (Spitfire IX)

Part I rendezvoused 10,000 feet over Hastings at 12:00 (zero), and proceeded to the target area where five Mitchells attacked 'Le Grismont', dropping twenty-four 500 lb. long delay fused bombs and sixteen 500 lb. GP bombs with poor results. Nineteen Mitchells failed to locate the target, but six of these attacked Le Plouy Ferme Noball site instead, dropping another twelve 500 lb. long delay fused bombs and thirty-six 500 lb. GP bombs with unobserved results. Two sections of three FW190s dived past the Close Escort towards the Mitchells just after the bombing, but were not seen to attack. The bombers, however, claimed one of them as probably destroyed.

Part II also rendezvoused 10,000 feet over Hastings, five minutes after Part I, and operated uneventfully. Two Bostons failed to locate the target, but the remaining sixteen attacked 'Bois d'Enfer', dropping a total of sixteen 500 lb. long delay fused bombs and forty-six 500 lb. GP bombs with fair to good results.

Part III rendezvoused at the same altitude and location as Parts I and II, five minutes after the latter, and proceeded to Bois d'Esquerdes where fifteen Mitchells dropped sixteen 500 lb. long delay fused bombs and one hundred and three 500 lb. GP bombs with fair results. Six Mitchells failed to bomb when the box leader was hit by Flak on the run-up and swung off course, followed by the rest of the box. The remaining three did not bomb on account of 'technical difficulties'.

Meanwhile, a Fighter Umbrella had been provided by the Spitfire XII and Hornchurch Wings, who patrolled the target area from zero+20 to zero+35. Whilst the latter Wing operated uneventfully, the Spitfire XII Wing encountered a number of Luftwaffe aircraft that were chased for some distance.

41 and 91 Squadrons were airborne at 15:55, led by Wg Cdr Ingham. They arrived in the St. Omer area two minutes ahead of the bombers and were immediately informed that the Luftwaffe was off St. Pol, to their north. As a formation of bombers was turning west after bombing, the Wing saw them being attacked out of the sun by eight FW190s and one Me109.

The pilots dived after the enemy aircraft, straight through the Close Escort, which did not appear to have seen them. 91 Squadron immediately split up, chasing individual aircraft, as did 41 Squadron's Blue Section (Johnson MB880, Fearon MB847, Birbeck EN605, Fisher MB829), whilst 41 Squadron's remaining two sections, Red, led by Sqn Ldr Matthew, and Yellow, led by Flt Lt Don Smith, covered them.

Wg Cdr Ingham chased one FW190 from 10,000 feet almost down to ground level, but despite a five-minute pursuit at speeds of 375 mph IAS, the Focke-Wulf gradually pulled away, streaming black smoke from its boost. One of 91 Squadron's pilots continued to pursue this aircraft almost all the way to Amiens, gaining slightly, but was only able to fire a single burst at 800 yards and could make no claim. Another FW190 was also chased by 91 Squadron in the same general direction, but also could not be overhauled.

Unable to find suitable opponents, 41 Squadron's Blue Section formed up with the rest of the Squadron and continued to provide the Fighter Umbrella they had been ordered to provide. Meanwhile, 91 Squadron continued to patrol the target area in pairs. No more enemy aircraft were seen and the Wing headed home, noting a large number of trucks, troops and other vehicles, and large block-houses amongst the dunes, on the tip of the Berck-sur-Mer peninsula as they crossed out at 9,000 feet.

Eighteen pilots landed back at Tangmere between 13:35 and 13:40 for a late lunch, whilst five landed early at Friston and one at Hawkinge, presumably short of fuel. Their identities and aircraft serials are not recorded.

The Ramrod's Fighter Sweep had also operated during this time between Cayeux and Cambrai. They sighted twenty FW190s that dived away east of Douai when approached, and could not be engaged. However, the Wing Leader, Wg Cdr Reg Grant, then spotted a Messerschmitt Me210 in the Somme area at 12,000 feet, which he attacked with a pilot of 122 Squadron. One man baled out and the aircraft crashed in flames and was claimed destroyed.

A little over two hours after they landed from Ramrod 468, the Spitfire XII Wing was airborne again, on this occasion tasked with providing a Fighter Sweep in support of an attack by RAF 2 Group Mosquitos on a Noball target at Ardouval, a small farming and forestry village in the Pays de Bray, situated approximately 26 km southeast of Dieppe.

Date	21 January 1944
Operation	Ramrod 470
Targets	Ardouval, Haute-Normandie
Bombers	2 Group RAF: 16 Mosquitos; 16 dispatched, 14 bombed
Fighter Cover	Hawkinge: 322 Squadron, & Friston: 349 Squadron (Spitfire Vb)
Fighter Sweep	Tangmere: 41 & 91 Squadrons (Spitfire XII)

The Mosquitos made their own way to Ardouval, taking a route via six miles southwest of Le Tréport to Senarpont to Serqueux, and finally to Ardouval, arriving over the target at 16:30. The Fighter Cover Wing patrolled the target area from 16:15 until the Mosquitos' arrival, and then returned home reporting the trip uneventful.

Meanwhile, fourteen of the sixteen Mosquitos had attacked Ardouval with forty-two 400 lb. GP bombs and fourteen 500 lb. long delay bombs, with fair to good results. Two Mosquitos did not attack on account of technical issues, but the Luftwaffe did not appear and there were no claims or casualties.

For their part, the Spitfire XII Wing was airborne at 15:55, led by Wg Cdr Ingham with Gp Capt Crisham as his No.2, who both flew with 41 Squadron. Their task was to provide a Fighter Sweep from Fécamp at 16:15, to Évreux, and back to Fécamp. However, Fg Off Ross Harding (EN237) developed jettison tank trouble shortly after take-off and was compelled to return to Tangmere at 16:15. Fg Off Harry Cook (MB795) also returned early and landed at the same time, owing to a problem that is not clearly specified in the ORB but was probably related to the fuel system.

The rest of the Wing crossed in at Fécamp at 7,000 feet, swept west of Bernay and descended to 6,000 feet over Conches. Sweeping around Évreux above a 7/10ths cloud band between 3,000 and 4,000 feet, they headed north again and crossed back out at Fécamp. The pilots attracted only a little light Flak from Triqueville, and saw nothing of the Luftwaffe, but did make one sighting of note that they reported on their return:

> …just S. of Fecamp behind the cemetery a large excavation seen in [the] shape of an arrow with freshly turned earth. the whole surrounded by barbed wire.[383]

The Wing landed back at Tangmere at 17:15, and this concluded the day's flying.

Separately, another two new pilots joined the Squadron today: 25-year-old Scotsman Flt Sgt Robert 'Bob' Fleming and 22-year-old Plt Off Peter Gibbs. Having joined the RAFVR from the Army in May 1941, Fleming undertook his elementary flying training in the United States, and similarly arrived today on his first operational posting, with 672 flying hours in his logbook, but none operational.

Gibbs joined the RAFVR in April 1941 and also undertook his elementary flying training in the United States. Returning to the United Kingdom in May 1942, he completed OTU at Balado Bridge and Llandow before shipping to North Africa for a brief posting to RAF Maison Blanche, Algiers, in late July. Remaining with this unit until September 1943, he completed a course at TEU at Balado Bridge in December, and was commissioned with effect from the day before his arrival on 41 Squadron. He arrived at Tangmere today to join the unit with 600 flying hours in his logbook, but none operational.

23 January 1944 – Following a day on the ground as a result of poor weather, 41 Squadron was airborne with 91 Squadron today on another Ramrod, on this occasion providing a Close Escort to Marauders attacking the Noball sites at Zudausques, Bois d'Esquerdes and Bois de Renty.

Date	23 January 1944
Operation	Ramrod 472
Targets	Part I: 'Le Nieppe' (2 boxes) & 'Bois d'Enfer' (1 box) , Pas-de-Calais Part II: 'Le Grismont', Pas-de-Calais (1 box), 'Bois d'Enfer' (1 box) & Bois de Renty, Pas-de-Calais Part III: Zudausques (1 box), Bois d'Esquerdes (1 box), & Bois de Renty (1 box), Pas-de-Calais Part IV: Zudausques (1 box), 'Le Grismont' (1 box), Zudausques (1 box), Pas-de-Calais
Bombers	Part I: 54 Marauders in 3 boxes Part II: 54 Marauders in 3 boxes Part III: 54 Marauders in 3 boxes Part IV: ; 54 Marauders in 3 boxes
Casualties	Part I: 386 BG/555 BS: Marauder 41-31618, SD by FW190, North Sea nr Gravelines[384]

Close Escort Part I	Heston: 306 & 315 Squadrons (Spitfire Vb)
Escort Cover	Biggin Hill: 401 & 412 Squadrons (Spitfire IX)
Close Escort Part II	Hawkinge: 322 Squadron, & Friston: 349 Squadron (Spitfire Vb)
Escort Cover	Hornchurch: 66 & 350 Squadrons (Spitfire IX)
Close Escort Part III	Tangmere: 41 & 91 Squadrons (Spitfire XII)
Escort Cover	Northolt: 302, 308 & 317 Squadrons (Spitfire IX)
Close Escort Part IV	Ibsley: 310 & 312 Squadrons (Spitfire Vb)
Escort Cover	Gravesend: 19 & 122 Squadrons (Spitfire IX)
1st Fighter Sweep	Kenley: 403 & 421 Squadrons (Spitfire IX)
2nd Fighter Sweep	North Weald: 331 & 332 Squadrons (Spitfire IX)
Casualties	91 Sqn: Flt Sgt John H. Hymas, SD/WIA in Spit XII, MB832, POW

Part I rendezvoused 12,000 feet over Hastings at 15:00 and proceeded to their targets, where they bombed at 15:20 from 11,000 feet despite intense heavy Flak. On the way out, the first box of Marauders was attacked by five FW190s, which attacked from below, having climbed out of 4/10ths cloud between 5,000 and 7,000 feet. One Marauder was shot down but the crew was able to bale out, and one of the FW190s was attacked and damaged by 306 Squadron. The Escort Cover operated uneventfully.

Part II rendezvoused at the same location and altitude, ten minutes behind Part I. The operation was completed uneventfully and the Luftwaffe was not seen. The bombers delivered their attacks from 11,000 feet at 15:30.

The Spitfire XII Wing was airborne at 15:05, with both the Wing and 41 Squadron led by Wg Cdr Ingham. The pilots rendezvoused with the Marauders 12,000 over Hastings at 15:20, but by this time had Fg Off Ross Harding (MB79) had already returned to base with jettison tank trouble, landing ten minutes after take-off.

The formation crossed in at Le Touquet, where the bombers split up into three boxes destined for their respective targets. Six of the 18 Marauders of the third box appeared to be missing and did not join up until later. Intense accurate Flak opened up on the bombers in the target area, where the bombing was undertaken from 11,000 feet at 15:40. The pilots observed the bombing but did not see the results.

The Wing swung around to starboard with the Marauders and crossed back out at Berck-sur-Mer, where another twenty-four Marauders, plus the six missing from the third box on the way in, joined up with them.

As they crossed out, 91 Squadron's Sqn Ldr Norman Kynaston noticed that one of his NCO pilots, Yellow 4, Flt Sgt John Hymas, was missing. He called him on the R/T but received no reply. No-one had even seen him leave the formation or go down. The Wing returned to Tangmere between 16:25 and 16:35, with the exception of two unnamed pilots who landed at Ford at 16:40.

Hymas was reported missing in action and it later transpired that he had been shot down, wounded and captured. He was admitted to Lille Hospital in early February and remained there until June 1944, when he was sent to Stalag IX-C. Contemporary research suggests that Hymas may have fallen victim to Fw Schwarz of 4./JG26, who claimed a Spitfire north of Fort Philippe at 15:37.

Separately, Part IV of the Ramrod had also rendezvoused at the same location and altitude as Parts I, II and III, but ten minutes behind the latter. It ran uneventfully and the bombers attacked their targets from 12,000 feet at 15:50.

The first Fighter Sweep, which was undertaken from Cayeux to Cambrai and Lille, operated uneventfully but the second, operating on generally the same route as the first but 15 minutes behind it, encountered a small number of Luftwaffe aircraft, which were engaged. The North Weald Wing was flying towards Beauvais at 26,000 feet, when four FW190s passed 4,000 feet below them, flying north. Being in a perfect position for an attack, the Wing dived upon them, claiming three of the quartet destroyed.

A total of 208 Marauders had been dispatched for the operation and, of these, 191 bombed. The results of their attacks were as follows:

Primary Targets	Bombers	Tons of Bombs	Result
'Le Grismont'	17	25	Poor
'Bois d'Enfer'	32	49	Good
Bois de Renty	34	50	Good
Bois d'Esquerdes	27	46	Poor
Zudausques	18	25	Poor
'Le Nieppe'	32	47	Good
Alternative Targets			
Constructional works, Crécy	16	22	Poor
Gun Emplacement, nr St. Omer	15	22	Poor

24 January 1944 – Operational flying for 41 Squadron commenced at 08:35 today when Flt Lt Dave Fearon (MB847) and Fg Off Harry Cook (MB840) undertook a weather reconnaissance to Cherbourg.

They returned at 09:50 with a mixed report, but it was of little immediate relevance to the Wing, which had already taken off 30 minutes before their return on a Ramrod to northern France. In that operation, the pilots provided a Close Escort to 24 Mitchells attacking a Noball site at Marquenneville in Part IV of Ramrod 474.

Date	24 January 1944
Operation	Ramrod 474
Targets	Part I: 'Longuemont', Picardie Part II: Béhen, Picardie Part III: 'Bois Coquerel', Picardie Part IV: Marquenneville, Picardie
Bombers	Part I: 2 Group: 24 Mosquitos; 21 bombed Part II: 2 Group: 24 Mitchells – aborted Part III: 2 Group: 18 Bostons; 4 bombed Part IV: 2 Group: 24 Mitchells; 23 bombed
Close Escort Part I Close Escort Part II Close Escort Part III Close Escort Part IV Fighter Umbrella	None Friston: 349 Squadron (Spitfire Vb) – aborted Hawkinge: 322 Squadron (Spitfire Vb) Tangmere: 41 & 91 Squadrons (Spitfire XII) Gravesend: 19 & 122 Squadrons (Spitfire IX) West Malling: 124 Squadron (Spitfire VII)

Part I's Mosquitos proceeded to 'Longuemont' unescorted where 21 of the 24 Mosquitos attacked the target between 09:55 and 10:10, dropping eighty-six 500 lb. bombs. They achieved good results, including a building in the southwest corner of the target that was seen to have been holed.

Part II's bombers and escorts rendezvoused 6,000 feet over Rye at 09:30 and proceeded across the Channel, but aborted the operation, turning back mid-way on account of weather conditions.

Part III rendezvoused at the same location and altitude at 09:35, but weather also hampered the operation and only four bombers attacked 'Bois Coquerel', dropping sixteen 500 lb. bombs. None were seen to hit their target. One bomber dropped its payload on an unidentified target southwest of Abbeville, and the remainder jettisoned their bombs into the Channel on the return journey.

Eleven aircraft from each of 41 and 91 Squadrons, plus Wg Cdr Ingham who flew with 91

Squadron, were airborne at 09:20 and rendezvoused with Part IV's Mitchells 6,000 feet over Rye at 09:40. The formation crossed into French territory at 10,000 feet, then descended to 7,000 feet as they moved inland.

Twenty-three Marauders attacked Marquenneville at 10:06 from 7,000 feet, dropping a total of one hundred and eight-four 500 lb. bombs. One stick was seen to burst right across the target but the rest overshot, scattering to the northwest of the target area. A large burst was also observed at approximately 6,000 feet, and was thought to have been a bomb prematurely detonating on the way down.

A cloud band of 8/10ths to 9/10ths lay between 12,000 and 13,000 feet, well above the formation, and a little scattered cumulus below them at 3,000 feet, which did not hinder bombing. The Luftwaffe was not seen and no Flak was experienced. The Wing crossed out at Ault at 10,000 feet and landed back at Tangmere at 10:50. They were not called upon again operationally for the rest of the day.

Similar to the other fighter squadrons on the operation, Gravesend and West Malling's Fighter Umbrella also operated according to plan and uneventfully.

25 January 1944 – Today's operational flying was confined to the Wing's involvement in a single Ramrod, providing an abortive Close Escort to Marauders attacking the Bois Rempre, Bois de Créquy and Ruisseauville Noball sites.

Date	25 January 1944
Operation	Ramrod 479
Targets	Part I: 'Le Grismont' (2 boxes) & Ruisseauville (1 box), Pas-de-Calais Part II: Bois Rempre (1 box), Bois de Créquy (1 box) & Ruisseauville (1 box), Pas-de-Calais Part III: Bois Rempre (1 box), Bois de Créquy (1 box) & Ruisseauville (1 box), Pas-de-Calais
Bombers	Part I: 54 Marauders in 3 boxes – recalled Part II: 54 Marauders in 3 boxes – recalled Part III: 54 Marauders in 3 boxes – recalled
Close Escort Part I Close Escort Part II Close Escort Part III Fighter Umbrella	Biggin Hill: 401 & 411 Squadrons (Spitfire IX) – aborted Tangmere: 41 & 91 Squadrons (Spitfire XII) – aborted Hornchurch: 66 & 350 Squadrons (Spitfire IX) North Weald: 331 & 332 Squadrons (Spitfire IX) Kenley: 403 & 421 Squadrons (Spitfire IX)
Casualties	66 Sqn: Fg Off Henry Furness-Roe EF/FL in Spit IX, EN575, 5m S of St. Omer, ER

Part I's rendezvoused 12,000 feet over Hastings at 09:45 and proceeded towards the target but were recalled when approximately half way across the Channel on account of weather conditions. Their Close Escort swept briefly inland to investigate some contrails, but saw nothing and returned early.

The Spitfire XII Wing was off the deck at 09:45, led by Wg Cdr Ingham, with Sqn Ldr Matthew leading 41 Squadron on his last operational flight with the unit. The pilots rendezvoused with Part II's Marauders at 10:00, at the same location and altitude as Part I, but had already lost Fg Off Harry Cook (MB862), who found his instruments malfunctioning and returned to base within ten minutes of his departure.

The rest of the formation proceeded across the Channel on a bearing of 183° for a distance of approximately 50 miles where they were confronted by a bank of storm clouds that rose from 1,000 to 20,000 feet. The Marauders attempted to find a way through the cloud but were forced to turn back, accompanied by the Spitfire XII Wing, which landed back at Tangmere between 10:45 and 10:50. They were not called upon operationally again today.

It was a similar story for Part III. Having rendezvoused 12,000 over Hastings at 10:10, they, too, were recalled half way across the Channel. The Hornchurch Wing escorted the Marauders

On his departure from 41 Squadron on 25 January 1944, Sqn Ldr Ian Matthew was rested as Tactics Officer with 12 Group, but returned to operations as OC 33 Squadron, based at Marville, France, in September 1944. He left the RAF two years later, his final role being Chief Fighter Control Officer at RAF Gatow in Berlin. © Ron Johnson, via Dan Johnson

back to Dungeness, then flew back to France to undertake independent free ranging sweeps of the Hardelot-Desvres area. 66 Squadron, however, lost one pilot who was forced to land in France as a result of engine failure.

During this time, the Fighter Umbrella operations were also carried out. With the exception of six enemy aircraft seen diving away inland by the North Weald Wing in the Béthune area, their patrol was uneventful. In contrast, whilst flying at an altitude of just 2,000 feet west of St. Omer, the Kenley Wing sighted fifteen FW190s 2,000 feet above them, and another fifteen long-nosed FW190s 1,500 feet below them, all travelling in the opposite direction. The Wing attempted to attack them, but every one evaded and made for the cover of cloud, and could not be engaged.

A Change in Command

26 January 1944 – 41 Squadron saw a change in command today when OC A Flight, 25-year-old Flt Lt Arthur A. 'Pinkie' Glen was promoted to Acting Squadron Leader and assumed command. The appointment had been announced on 21 January, and he took over today on Ian Matthew's departure.

Having joined 41 Squadron in early 1941 as an NCO pilot, Glen was commissioned ten months later and was awarded a DFC in early May 1942. Posted to Malta that same month, he was injured in a bomb blast in July 1942 and evacuated back to the United Kingdom the following month. Following a period of recuperation, Glen was posted to ground duties, where he remained until July 1943.

At that time, he was posted back to operations as a Flying Officer, coincidentally returning to 41 Squadron. He was promoted to Acting Flight Lieutenant and OC B Flight in early September 1943 and, following two further victories, was awarded a Bar to his DFC two months later. A promotion to War Substantive Flight Lieutenant followed in early January 1944.

Glen's promotion to Acting Squadron Leader and OC 41 Squadron today meant that he had now held practically every flying rank on the Squadron. He was a popular and respected pilot and Fg Off (later Flt Lt) Peter Cowell recalled that Glen was, "a first class C.O. and an excellent leader with a lot of operational experience."[385] Flt Lt Tom Slack was appointed OC B Flight upon Glen's promotion.

He replaced outgoing OC 41 Squadron, Sqn Ldr Ian Matthew, who rested in a posting to 12 Group as Tactics Officer. Matthew returned to operations in September 1944 as OC 33 Squadron, and saw significant action in France and the Low Countries. After attending Flying Control School in late 1945, he became Chief Flying Control Officer at RAF Gatow in Berlin and retired from the RAF in September 1946. Matthew emigrated to Canada in July 1957 and is believed to have passed away around 2005.

Sqn Ldr Arthur Allan 'Pinkie' Glen DFC* was OC 41 Squadron from 26 January to 28 May 1944. He ended the War as Staff with the Fighter Leaders' School and was released from the RAF in February 1946. © Peter Graham

Aside from these personnel movements today, the Wing was involved in one Ramrod operation in which they provided Target Cover to 24 Mosquitos attacking Bailly-en-Campagne Noball site. This was the first occasion that 'Pinkie' Glen formally led 41 Squadron as its Commanding Officer.

Date	26 January 1944
Operation	Ramrod 486
Targets	Part I: Bailly-en-Campagne, Haute-Normandie Part II: Marquenneville, Picardie Part III: 'Bois Coquerel', Picardie Part IV: Béhen, Picardie
Bombers	Part I: 2 Group: 24 Mosquitos; 22 bombed Part II: 2 Group: 24 Mitchells; 17 bombed Part III: 2 Group: 12 Bostons; 11 bombed Part IV: 2 Group: 24 Mitchells; 17 bombed
Target Cover Part I Close Escort Part II Close Escort Part III Close Escort Part IV	Tangmere: 41 & 91 Squadrons (Spitfire XII) Heston: 306 & 315 Squadrons (Spitfire Vb) Friston: 349 Squadron (Spitfire Vb) Digby: 402 & 416 Squadrons (Spitfire Vb)

The Spitfire XII Wing was airborne at 09:05 led by Wg Cdr Ingham, who flew with 91 Squadron. The Wing crossed the Channel independently of the Mosquitos to patrol at 7,000 feet east of Bailly-en-Campagne until the last Mosquitos had withdrawn.

The Mosquitos arrived over the target at 09:35 and twenty-two attacked, dropping eighty-eight 500 lb. bombs from altitudes of between 400 feet and 1,000 feet, until 09:50, achieving good results. The Luftwaffe did not appear and there was no Flak whatsoever.

After the last of the Mosquitos had left the area, the Wing set a course to sweep Montdidier, but was recalled ten miles east of Amiens. Crossing out over Ault, the Wing sighted a formation of Bostons – likely those of Part III – ahead of them on their homeward journey. The pilots landed back at Tangmere at 10:10, and this concluded the day's operational flying.

Part II rendezvoused 6,000 feet over Beachy Head at 09:15 and attacked Marquenneville according to plan at 09:41, seventeen of the twenty-four Mitchells dropping seventy-six 500 lb. GP bombs and thirty-six 500 lb. bombs with long delay fuses, achieving only poor results.

Part III rendezvoused at the same location and altitude as Part I, but five minutes later, and proceeded to the target area, where none of the Bostons attacked the primary target, 'Bois Coquerel'. Six of the twelve Bostons attacked instead Part IV's target, Béhen, dropping twenty-two 500 lb. bombs with fair results. Another five Bostons attacked the Noball site at Moyenneville, dropping twenty 500 lb. bombs with fair results, and one Boston did not attack at all.

Part IV rendezvoused at the same place and location as Parts II and III, but five minutes behind Part III, and proceeded to Béhen where six Mitchells attacked the target, dropping thirty-two 500 lb. GP bombs and sixteen 500 lb. bombs with long delay fuses. The remainder were unable to attack the primary, but eleven bombed Part III's target, 'Bois Coquerel', instead, dropping sixty-four 500 lb. GP bombs and twenty-four 500 lb. bombs with long delay fuses, achieving good results.

In all cases, the escorts operated uneventfully and the Luftwaffe was not seen. There were no claims or casualties and there was little to report.

28 January 1944 – Following a day on the ground as a result of unsuitable weather, the Wing was in the air again today, tasked with providing a Fighter Sweep in the Fécamp-Beauvais area, in support of six attacks on Noball sites by Bomphoons in Ramrod 489.

Date	28 January 1944
Operation	Ramrod 489
Targets	Part I: Saint-Pierre-des-Jonquières, Haute-Normandie Part II: Moyenneville, Pas-de-Calais Part III: 'Heudiere', Haute-Normandie Part IV: Zudausques, Pas-de-Calais Part V: 'Le Grismont', Pas-de-Calais Part VI: Bois d'Esquerdes, Pas-de-Calais
Bombers	Part I: 16 Wing: 247 Sqn: 12 Bomphoons; 11 bombed Part II: 16 Wing: 175 Sqn: 12 Bomphoons – aborted Part III: Tangmere: 197 & 486 Sqns: 16 Bomphoons; 16 bombed Part IV: Martlesham: 56 Sqn: 8 Bomphoons – aborted Part V: Lympne: 1 Sqn: 8 Bomphoons; 8 bombed Part VI: Fairlop: 195 Sqn: 8 Bomphoons – cancelled
Close Escort Part V 1st Fighter Sweep 2nd Fighter Sweep	Lympne: 3 Typhoon Ib Biggin Hill: 401, 411 & 412 Squadrons (Spitfire IX) Tangmere: 41 & 91 Squadrons (Spitfire XII)
Casualties	412 Sqn: Flt Lt D. G. McKay, EF baled out of Spit IX, MJ302, S of Dungeness, RR

Eleven of the twelve Bomphoons attacked Saint-Pierre-des-Jonquières in Part I, dropping twenty-two 500 lb. bombs from altitudes of 1,500 to 3,000 feet, with good results. No Flak was experienced.

Part II was aborted owing to 10/10ths cloud with a base of 800 feet east of Cayeux and Part IV also aborted their attack, turning back before crossing the French coast as a result of 9/10ths cloud down to 1,000 feet. In both case, the pilots jettisoned their bombs into the Channel on the way home.

The Bomphoons in Part III prepared to make attacks on 'Heudiere' but became separated when descending through 10/10ths cloud, which resulted in the primary target not being located. Two Bomphoons attacked an unidentified target, dropping four 500 lb. bombs, and the remaining fourteen attacked the Noball site at 'Bois Megle', dropping twenty-eight 500 lb. bombs, all of which fell inside the target area.

Part VI was cancelled before take-off, but Part V still operated, despite weather hampering the mission. The pilots were unable to find 'Le Grismont' as a result of 10/10ths cloud between 3,000 and 6,000 feet, but located the Noball site at 'Bois d'Enfer' and attacked it instead. They dropped fourteen 500 lb. bombs and bursts were seen on the western edge of the target area. Two bombs hung up and could not be released, but both aircraft landed safely in their return.

The first Fighter Sweep was carried out by the Biggin Hill Wing in the Furnes [Veurne]-Arras area from 10:50. The Luftwaffe was not encountered and the operation was completed according to plan, with the exception of a pilot of 412 Squadron having to bale out over the Channel as a result of engine trouble, who was rescued by 277 (ASR) Squadron.

The Spitfire XII Wing was airborne at 10:25 to provide the Ramrod's second Fighter Sweep, led by Wg Cdr Ingham, who flew with 41 Squadron. Crossing the Channel on the deck, the Wing climbed ten miles from the French coast and crossed in at Fécamp at 7,000 feet at 10:50. The pilots made a deep penetration to Beauvais above 10/10ths cloud, but nothing was seen of the Luftwaffe and no Flak was experienced.

Shortly after crossing in, however, Fg Off Clive Birbeck's aircraft (EN605) started displaying an extreme radiator temperature and pulled out of the operation. He returned home early with his No. 2, Plt Off Peter Graham (MB798), and both pilots landed safely back at Tangmere at 11:25.

The rest of the Wing carried on to complete the operation and returned to base at 12:00 in time for lunch. There was no further operational flying for the rest of the day.

29 January 1944 – The Wing was called upon to participate in two operations today. In the first, they provided Fighter Cover for Mosquitos attacking construction works and a ski site at 'Heudiere'[386] in Ramrod 492. In the second, they were assigned to a Fighter Umbrella southwest of Dieppe, whilst 144 Marauders attacked several Noball targets in Ramrod 493.

Date	29 January 1944
Operation	Ramrod 492
Targets	'Heudiere', Haute-Normandie
Bombers	2 Group RAF: 24 Mosquitos; 23 dispatched, 15 bombed
Fighter Cover	Tangmere: 41 & 91 Squadrons (Spitfire XII)

The Spitfire XII Wing was airborne at 10:25, each Squadron led by its respective Officer Commanding, and set a course for France of 153° at 250 mph IAS. Approximately 15 minutes into the flight, 91 Squadron's Sqn Ldr Norman Kynaston sighted an empty raft of about ten square feet, made of casks and wicker tied together.

Continuing on, the Wing arrived over the target area at 10:55, five minutes ahead of the Mosquitos, and proceeded to patrol the area at 7,000 feet. Shortly thereafter, the 23 Mosquitos arrived over 'Heudiere', tasked with bombing the area from zero to zero+15 (11:00-11:15) from below 500 feet.

However, a band of 10/10ths cloud between 1,200 and 3,500 feet from the French coast to approximately 12 miles inland hindered the attack and only 15 Mosquitos bombed the target, dropping sixty 500 lb. bombs. Nonetheless, a good concentration of bursts was achieved in the vicinity of buildings and in woods in the target area.

The Spitfire XII Wing completed their Fighter Cover according to plan, but noted six balloons at 2,000 feet, west of Rouen. The operation was otherwise uneventful, and the Wing withdrew after the last of the Mosquitos had completed their bombing runs. The pilots landed back at 11:55 in time for lunch.

The Wing was airborne again just before 14:00 to provide a Fighter Umbrella southeast of Dieppe.

An amateur cartoonist of some talent who illustrated many of the pilots' logbooks and drew caricatures of them, Flt Lt Tom Slack was promoted to OC B Flight in January 1944 when Flt Lt 'Pinkie' Glen vacated the role on assuming command of the Squadron. On 23 August 1944, Slack was forced to land in France as a result of fuel cock failure, and spent the rest of the War behind wire. © Cowell family

Date	29 January 1944
Operation	Ramrod 493
Targets	Part I: 'Beaulieu Ferme' & Preuseville, Haute-Normandie
	Part II: Le Mesnil-Allard & 'Beaulieu Ferme', Haute-Normandie
	Part III: Les Petits Moraux & Pommeréval, Haute-Normandie
	Part IV: Pommeréval & Les Hayons, Haute-Normandie
Bombers	Part I: 36 Marauders in 2 boxes of 18; 18 dispatched, 17 bombed
	Part II: 36 Marauders in 2 boxes of 18 – aborted
	Part III: 36 Marauders in 2 boxes of 18; 30 bombed
	Part IV: 36 Marauders in 2 boxes of 18; 34 bombed
Close Escort Part I	Heston: 306 & 315 Squadrons (Spitfire Vb)
Close Escort Part II	Hawkinge: 322 Sqn, & Friston: 349 Sqn (Spitfire Vb)
Close Escort Part III	Ibsley: 310 & 312 Squadrons (Spitfire Vb)
Close Escort Part IV	Digby: 402 & 416 Squadrons (Spitfire Vb)
Fighter Umbrella	Tangmere: 41 & 91 Squadrons (Spitfire XII)
	West Malling: 124 Squadron (Spitfire VII)
	Perranporth: 340 & 341 Squadrons (Spitfire Vb)
1st Fighter Sweep	Merston: 181 & 247 Squadrons (Typhoon Ib)
2nd Fighter Sweep	Harrowbeer: 193 & 266 Squadrons (Typhoon Ib)
3rd Fighter Sweep	Culmhead: 131 & 165 Squadron (Spitfire IX)
4th Fighter Sweep	Gravesend: 122 Squadron (Spitfire IX)

One box of Marauders and Part I's escorts rendezvoused at 12,000 feet approximately 15 miles north of Dieppe at 13:15 and proceeded to 'Beaulieu Ferme'. However, they were unable to locate the target on account of 10/10ths cloud over the area, and 11 Marauders attacked Les Petits Moraux instead, dropping sixty-six 500 lb. bombs with poor results. Another six bombed the village of Saint-Maulvis, 19km south of Abbeville, in mistaken identity, whilst one did not bomb at all.

Part II's bombers and escorts rendezvoused in the same location as Part I, ten minutes behind them, and proceeded to Le Mesnil-Allard and 'Beaulieu Ferme'. However, once again, the Marauders were unable to locate the targets owing to cloud cover, and they returned to base without bombing.

Part III arrived at the same rendezvous point at 14:15, and was also hindered by weather conditions. Unable to locate their target, the first box attacked what they thought to be the Noball site at Preuseville, dropping one hundred and eight 500 lb. bombs. However, photographic evidence later suggested their bombs had in fact fallen close to Puchervin. The second box managed to locate Pommeréval, but only 12 of the 18 Marauders attacked, dropping seventy-eight 500 lb. bombs with poor results.

Part IV rendezvoused in the same location as the first three attacks, 15 minutes behind Part III, and also had trouble locating their targets as a result of the weather. The first box was unable find Pommeréval and attacked 'Beaulieu Ferme' instead, dropping one hundred and eight 500 lb. bombs with fair results, whilst 16 of 18 Marauders in the second box attacked Les Hayons, as planned, dropping ninety-two 500 lb. bombs with poor results. The escorts in all four attacks operated uneventfully.

The Spitfire XII Wing took off at 13:55 led by Wg Cdr Ingham to provide a Fighter Umbrella in the target area from zero+70 (14:25) in unison with the West Malling and Perranporth Wings. 41 and 91 Squadrons patrolled in clear skies at 15,000 feet southeast of Dieppe (south of the target area), above a 10/10ths cloud band between 1,500 and 3,000 feet.

One box of Marauders was seen to bomb but the cloud cover made it impossible to assess their accuracy. As the Luftwaffe was not seen and no Flak was experienced, the operation ran uneventfully, and it was a similar situation for the West Malling and Perranporth Wings.

One observation was, however, made by the Spitfire XII Wing, when work in progress was noticed on the southwest end of the northeast/southwest runway at Poix Airfield. This was reported on their return at 15:35, all pilots landing at Tangmere with the exception of 41 Squadron's Plt Off Peter Graham (MB847) who landed at Friston low on fuel. Finding just seven gallons left in his tank, he topped up and completed his journey to Tangmere a short while later.

Meanwhile, four Fighter Sweeps had also been undertaken. The second, third and fourth were uneventful, but the Merston Wing, flying the first sweep, sighted a four-engined FW200 Kondor transport at an altitude of only 1,000 feet, just south of Châteaudun Airfield. The aircraft was attacked by four pilots and was seen to subsequently crash and explode. The Wing also spotted a hutted camp west of Châteaudun, approximately five miles northeast of Le Mans, which was also shot up. All pilots and aircraft returned safely.

31 January 1944 – On this last day of the month, the Wing participated in a single operation, in which they escorted Mosquitos attacking construction works and a ski site at 'Bois Megle'[387] in Ramrod 500. Conditions were, however, atrocious and cost the lives of two of 91 Squadron's pilots and the crew of one of the Mosquitos.

Date	31 January 1944
Operation	Ramrod 500
Targets	'Bois Megle', Haute-Normandie
Bombers	2 Group RAF: 16 Mosquitos – aborted
Casualties	487 Sqn: Mosq VI, HX951, crashed in fog at Priors Leas Farm, Poling, Worthing, Sussex, both crew †
Fighter Cover	Tangmere: 41 & 91 Squadrons (Spitfire XII) – aborted
Casualties	91 Sqn: Fg Off Derek R. Inskip MAC off French coast in Spit XII, EN613, with Flt Sgt Robert K. Y. Fairbairn in Spit XII, EN618, both pilots †

Sixteen Mosquitos took off but the conditions were so poor that they all aborted the operation and turned for home shortly after crossing the English coast. On the way home, however, one of the Mosquitos crashed and both crew were killed.[388]

The Spitfire XII Wing was airborne at 13:20 led by 91 Squadron's Sqn Ldr Norman Kynaston, with the intention of patrolling the target area from zero-5 to zero+15 (13:55-14:15). The pilots flew at sea level on a course of 150° at 250 mph IAS but with haze down to sea level, the sea dead calm, and visibility of less than one mile, Kynaston decided to abort the operation only 15 minutes after take-off. He ordered the Wing home and led them in a gentle turn to port to return to base.

However, as they did so, Sqn Ldr 'Pinkie' Glen saw 91 Squadron's Yellow 3 and 4, Fg Off Derek Inskip and Flt Sgt Robert Fairbairn, collide. One aircraft dived straight into the sea approximately 10-15 miles north of Fécamp. The other climbed into cloud, the unidentified pilot reporting over his R/T that he would have to bale out. However, within seven to ten seconds, the aircraft reappeared and dived straight into the Channel, with no sign of its pilot or a parachute.

The Wing orbited the area but nothing was seen except patches of oil, and as a result an international SOS message was broadcast. In some shock, the pilots returned to Tangmere at 14:55, from where several ASR searches were launched during the afternoon.[389] However, despite efforts, neither man was found and they are both remembered today on the Runnymede Memorial in Surrey.

Attesting to the horrendous conditions and lack of visibility, Flt Sgt Jimmy Payne penned in his logbook that afternoon,

Very poor visibility. 2 of 91 aircraft collided off French coast. My No. 1 – F/L. Slack & I went through cloud – came back on homings above 10/10. Let down over sea and broke cloud at 400' off Selsey = complete bloody shambles.[390]

February 1944 – In a stark change from the previous month's busy schedule, there was no operational flying on 19 days of this month – 1-2, 23 and 26-27 February, as a result of weather conditions, and 7-20 February, as a result of the Squadron's participation in an air firing course at 17 APC, Southend. This therefore left just ten days of operational flying out of this leap year's 29 days of February, upon which the unit took part in ten Ramrod operations.

✝ Noball Target △ Airfield

Date	Operation	Role	Type	Destination / Target
3	Ramrod 505	Close Escort	✝	'Le Grismont' & Bois d'Esquerdes, Fr.
4	Ramrod 508	Fighter Cover	✝	Beaulieu Ferme, France
5	Ramrod 517	Close Escort	✝	'Le Grismont' & Linghem, France
6	Ramrod 520	Fighter Umbrella	✝	Dieppe area, France
21	Ramrod 573	Escort Cover	△	Beaumont-le-Roger, France
24	Ramrod 587	Close Escort	✝	Bois Rempre, France
25	Ramrod 591	Close Escort	△	Cambrai-Epinoy, France
25	Ramrod 593	Close Escort	✝	'Bois d'Enfer', France
28	Ramrod 597	Close Escort	✝	Beauvoir, Bonnières & Gorenflos, Fr.
29	Ramrod 600	Fighter Cover	✝	Belleville-en-Caux, France

3 February 1944 – Following two days of inclement weather, the Squadron was back in the air today in significantly improved visibility, and a number of practice flights were undertaken below at 7/10ths cloud base at 8,000 feet during the morning.

Immediately after lunch, the Spitfire XII Wing participated in a Ramrod to Noball sites in northern France, on this occasion assigned to the close escort of Marauders attacking 'Le Grismont' and Bois d'Esquerdes in Part III of Ramrod 505.

Date	3 February 1944
Operation	Ramrod 505
Targets	Part I: Bois de Huit Rues, Pas-de-Calais
	Parts II & IV: La Longueville, Embry/Bois de Pottier & Ruisseauville, Pas-de-Calais
	Part III: 'Le Grismont' & Bois d'Esquerdes, Pas-de-Calais
Bombers	Part I: 42 Marauders; 42 dispatched, 16 bombed secndry target
	Part II: 54 Marauders; 20 dispatched – aborted (weather)
	Part III: 54 Marauders; 54 dispatched, 36 bombed secndry target
	Part IV: 54 Marauders; 54 dispatched – aborted (weather)
Close Escort Part I	Hawkinge: 322 Squadron, & Friston: 349 Squadron (Spitfire Vb)
Fighter Umbrella	Biggin Hill: 401, 411 & 412 Squadrons (Spitfire IX)
	West Malling: 124 Squadron (Spitfire VII)
Close Escort Part II	Heston: 306 & 315 Squadrons (Spitfire Vb)
Fighter Umbrella	Northolt: 302, 308 & 317 Squadrons (Spitfire IX)
Close Escort Part III	Tangmere: 41 & 91 Squadrons (Spitfire XII)
Fighter Umbrella	As per Part I
Escort Part IV	Hornchurch: 66 & 350 Squadrons (Spitfire IX)
Fighter Umbrella	As per Part II
Fighter Sweep	Kenley: 403 & 421 Squadrons (Spitfire IX)

The Marauders' four parts were scheduled to rendezvous over Dungeness at 12:30 (zero), over Beachy Head at 12:40, over Dungeness at 12:45, and over Beachy Head at 12:50, respectively, all at 12,000 feet. Their times over target were scheduled for zero+23, zero+40, zero+31, and zero+50, in that order, all at an altitude of 11,000 feet.

The Spitfire XII Wing was airborne at 12:30, led by 91 Squadron's Sqn Ldr Norman Kynaston, with Tangmere's Sector Commander, Gp Capt William Crisham, as his No. 2. 41 Squadron comprised twelve aircraft in sections of four, led by Sqn Ldr Glen, and Flt Lts Bruce Moffett and Tom Slack.

The Wing made rendezvous on schedule with Part III's 54 Marauders, which subsequently parted and headed for their respective destinations, 'Le Grismont' & Bois d'Esquerdes. However, 9/10ths cloud was found over the target areas at 10,000-12,000 feet, and the targets could not be attacked. Whilst the 18 bombers targeting Bois d'Esquerdes returned home with their payloads intact, the remaining 36, whose target was 'Le Grismont', found a secondary target, Dannes, which they bombed instead.

Although no enemy aircraft were seen, moderate, though ineffective heavy Flak was experienced from the St. Omer and Boulogne areas. The operation was otherwise uneventful for the Spitfire XII Wing, and the pilots landed back at Tangmere between 13:45 and 13:50, with the exception of two who landed at Hawkinge ten minutes earlier, presumably low on fuel.[391] This concluded the day's flying for 41 Squadron.

Similar experiences were made on Parts I, II and IV. Part I's bombers were recalled as a result of weather conditions, but 16 aircraft bombed Merville Airfield with good results. However, Parts II's and IV's bombers were prevented from attacking at all owing to unsuitable poor visibility and returned home without bombing. In all cases, no enemy aircraft were seen, and there were no claims or casualties; the escorting fighter squadrons all reported their trips were uneventful.

Separately today, there was one minor aircraft accident, when a pilot of 91 Squadron taxied his aircraft into that of 41 Squadron's Plt Off Jim Payne, possibly MB804. Quite put out, though

Following his departure from 41 Squadron in January 1944, Flt Lt Lyndon Griffith DFC RNZAF served with a number of units, thereunder 1426 (Enemy Aircraft) Flight at Duxford in late 1944, where he flew the Junkers Ju88 and Messerschmitt Me109. © Griffith family

unhurt, Payne recorded in his logbook that day, "One of 91 Sqdn taxied into my aircraft & damaged pitot head!"[392]

4 February 1944 – The Spitfire XII Wing was sent up for a relatively early start today when it was called upon to provide Close Escort to 24 Mosquitos attacking the Noball site 'Beaulieu Ferme'[393] in Part IV of Ramrod 508. The first three attacks were cancelled before the fourth was airborne, which initially proceeded as planned. The Wing was airborne at 09:15, and the Mosquitoes were also already airborne when all were recalled and the operation cancelled in its entirety.

Taking the opportunity, as the Squadron was already in the air, Sqn Ldr Glen decided to undertake some squadron formation flying below to 10/10ths cloud base at 4,000, and they returned to Tangmere at 10:45.

During the afternoon, the Wing was ordered to repeat Ramrod 508 – it was not renumbered – but once more the first three attacks, by 2 Group bombers, were cancelled. This again left Part IV the sole participant, but this time the operation was carried out as planned.[394]

Date	4 February 1944
Operation	Ramrod 508
Targets	Part I: Bois de la Justice, Pas-de-Calais Part II: Bonnières, Pas-de-Calais Part III: Beauvoir, Pas-de-Calais Part IV: 'Beaulieu Ferme', Haute-Normandie
Bombers	Part I: 24 Mitchells – cancelled Part II: 18 Bostons – cancelled Part III: 24 Mitchells – cancelled Part IV: 24 Mosquitos; 22 dispatched, 19 bombed
Close Escorts	Parts I-III: NR; cancelled Part IV: Tangmere: 41 & 91 Squadrons (Spitfire XII)

The Mosquitos were scheduled to make a low-level attack Part III's target, 'Beaulieu Ferme', between 16:00 and 16:15, whilst the Spitfire XII Wing was tasked with making a low-level patrol to the south and east of the target from 15:55 until the Mosquitos were clear of the area.

Of the 22 Mosquitos dispatched, 19 made successful attacks on construction works and a ski site, dropping a total of seventy-six 500 lb. bombs, and bursts were observed very close to three buildings, designated 'Q', 'R1', and 'R2'. Meanwhile, twelve aircraft of 41 Squadron and eleven of 91 Squadron patrolled at 4,000 feet, and although they came under "fairly intense light and heavy flak"[395] from the area, they remained unscathed, and the Luftwaffe was not seen.

The Spitfire XII Wing left the area at 16:15, having not seen the bombing at all, and landed back at base at 17:00, reporting good visibility below the 8-9/10ths cloud base at 4,000 feet, and an otherwise uneventful operation. This concluded the day's flying for 41 Squadron's pilots.

5 February 1944 – As a result of clear conditions, with only a little scattered cloud at 3,000-4,000 feet, and good visibility, the Squadron spent some time in the air during the morning on practice flying. They also received the news that they were to move the following day to RAF Southend to attend 17 Armament Practice Camp.

However, another two Ramrods were on the cards before any move could take place. The first of these took place during the early afternoon today, when the Spitfire XII Wing was required to provide a Close Escort for Marauders attacking Noball targets in northern France in Ramrod 517.

Date	5 February 1944
Operation	Ramrod 517
Targets	Part I: Embry/Bois de Pottier, La Longueville, & Bois de Créquy, Pas-de-Calais Part II: 'Le Grismont' & Linghem, Pas-de-Calais Part III: Bois Rempre, Embry/Bois de Pottier, & Ruisseauville, Pas-de-Calais Part IV: Bois Rempre, La Longueville, & Ruisseauville, Pas-de-Calais
Bombers	Part I: 54 Marauders; 18 bombed Embry/Bois de Pottier Part II: 54 Marauders; aborted, bombed secondary targets Part III: 54 Marauders; 18 bombed Embry/Bois de Pottier Part IV: 54 Marauders; aborted, bombed secondary targets
Casualties	323 BG/455 BS: Marauder 41-31884, SD/AA, Frévent area, & Marauder 41-35000, SD/AA; 323 BG: Marauder 41-31825, SD/AA, crew baled out; 386 BG/555 BS Marauder 41-31947, SD/AA, St. Pol; 387 BG/558 BS: Marauder 41-31879, SD/AA in flames; 387 BG, Marauder 41-31703, CD/AA, CL Friston, crew safe; ca 30 Marauders from all parts damaged by AA
Close Escort Part I Close Escort Part II Close Escort Part III Close Escort Part IV Fighter Umbrella	Heston: 306 & 315 Squadrons (Spitfire Vb) Tangmere: 41 & 91 Squadrons (Spitfire XII) Hawkinge: 322 Squadron, & Friston: 349 Squadron (Spitfire Vb) Perranporth: 340 & 341 Squadrons (Spitfire Vb) Northolt: 302, 308 & 317 Squadrons (Spitfire IX) West Malling: 124 Squadron (Spitfire VII)

Part II's bombers arrived over Beachy Head at 13:25 at 10,500 feet, whilst the Spitfire XII Wing was airborne at 13:15 and rendezvoused with them at 12,000 feet. 41 Squadron consisted of eleven aircraft in sections of three, four and four, led by Sqn Ldr Glen, Flt Lt Bruce Moffett and Flt Lt Tom Slack, respectively.

A notable participant in the unit's numbers today was Sqn Ldr John Mackenzie DFC RNZAF, who had served with 41 Squadron as a young officer between September 1938 and March 1941. He had achieved a significant number of victories with the unit during the Battle of Britain, for which he was awarded his DFC, and served as OC, A Flight, between mid-January and mid-March 1941. Mackenzie was posted back to 41 Squadron for a brief sojourn as a Supernumerary Squadron Leader between 1 and 9 February 1944 and his sortie with the Squadron during Ramrod 517 today appears to have been his only operational flight.[396]

The bombers and fighters entered France at 13:45, three miles south of Berck, and one of 41 Squadron's pilots reported seeing "an enormous red explosion"[397] on the ground east-southeast of Berck as they crossed in. The formation proceeded to the target area via Auxi-le-Chateau and Frévent, and was over the target at 14:00. However, weather prevented 'Le Grismont' and Linghem, being located and alternative targets south of Boulogne were bombed instead. This did not hinder the ferocity of the Flak directed towards Part II's bombers and no less than three Marauders were shot down.

> One Marauder burst into flames and crashed, another severely hit turned south and seven parachutes were seen to descend from it; a third was also hit and headed inland until lost from view.[398]

Nonetheless, 41 Squadron considered the bombing excellent. The Luftwaffe was not seen, and the Wing returned to Tangmere at 14:40. This concluded the day's flying for the unit, who spent the rest of the day packing, and threw a farewell party during the evening.

6 February 1944 – As the Squadron spent the morning completing their packing for the day's move to RAF Southend, "it was surprised to find itself detailed to provide a fighter umbrella in the Dieppe area for 24 Mosquito bombers".[399] The Spitfire XII Wing had been assigned to a Fighter Umbrella for attacks on Noball targets in Ramrod 520.

Date	6 February 1944
Operation	Ramrod 520
Targets	Part I: 'Bois Coquerel', Picardie Part II: Marquenneville, Picardie Part III: Béhen, Picardie Part IV: Moyenneville, Pas-de-Calais
Bombers	Part I: 24 Mosquitos; 18 bombed Part II: 24 Mitchells; all aborted (weather) Part III: 12 Bostons; all aborted (weather) Part IV: 24 Mitchells; all aborted (weather)
Close Escort Part I Close Escort Part II Close Escort Part III Close Escort Part IV Fighter Umbrella	None Friston: 349 Squadron (Spitfire Vb) Hawkinge: 322 Squadron (Spitfire Vb) Hawkinge: 501 Squadron (Spitfire IX) Tangmere: 41 & 91 Squadrons (Spitfire XII)

Part I's Mosquitos were scheduled fly directly to their target without fighter cover and to bomb the construction works and ski site 'Bois Coquerel'[400] between 12:55 and 13:10. Parts II's, III's and IV's bombers were planned to rendezvous with their fighter escorts 6,000 feet over Beachy Head at five-minute intervals from 12:30 (zero), and to be over their targets at similar intervals from zero+24.

The Spitfire XII Wing was tasked with providing a fighter umbrella independent of the bombers and their escorts, by patrolling the Dieppe area at 12,000 feet under Hythe Control, between zero+24 and zero+40. The Wing was led by 91 Squadron's Sqn Ldr Norman Kynaston, whilst 41 Squadron, which detailed 12 aircraft for the job, was led by Sqn Ldr Glen.

At the last minute, however, Glen's aircraft (MB881) would not start and he was compelled to hand over command to Flt Lt Tom Slack. Eleven aircraft took off at 12:25, but within ten minutes, Plt Off 'Jackie' Fisher (MB794) developed engine trouble and was forced to return.

This left ten aircraft to fly with 91 Squadron's twelve, who continued to France. Half way over the Channel, the pilots passed between 50 and 60 Flying Fortresses returning from another bombing mission, who were stepped up and back between 11,000 and 13,000 feet. Crossing in, the Wing found 10/10ths cloud with a ceiling of 5,000 feet, but proceeded to patrol, and returned to Tangmere at 13:50, reporting the operation uneventful; no Flak was experienced, and the Luftwaffe was not seen.

Whilst Part I's Mosquitos bombed according to plan, dropping forty-five 500 lb. GP bombs and fifteen 500 lb. LD bombs, and additionally attacked a heavy gun emplacement, a fuel dump and gun position, all the bombers in Parts II, III and IV aborted owing to cloud cover and poor visibility, and returned home without attacking. The Luftwaffe was not seen and the escorting fighter squadrons all reported the operation uneventful.

During the afternoon, 41 Squadron finally moved to RAF Southend, in Essex, flying 13 Spitfires and the Tiger Moth there, where they arrived at 16:05. They replaced 501 Squadron, which had departed two days before.

Southend

Likely unknown to almost all of the Squadron's pilots and ground crew, RAF Southend – or rather RAF Rochford, as it was known until late October 1940 – was an important forward base for 41 Squadron during the Battle of Britain. As the Squadron arrived there today, Sqn Ldr John Noble DFC and Flt Lt Lord Gisborough were probably the only ones left from that era who would have been able to remember it.

41 Squadron were frequent visitors to Rochford throughout most of September and the beginning of October 1940, and based several aircraft there during daylight hours to effect a timely reaction to the inbound armada of attacking Luftwaffe bombers and fighters. At that time they were based at Hornchurch, and Rochford was a satellite.

The history of the airfield reaches back to the earliest days of the RFC when the site was acquired for training in late 1914. It lay 25 feet above sea level, approximately 2½ miles north of Southend Pier, between Westbarrow Hall and the railway line at Warners Bridge. RFC activity continued until May 1915 when the RNAS took over the site as a Night Flying Station to combat the Zeppelin menace.

After the threat had passed, the RFC re-occupied the airfield and whilst night flying continued, the main focus was home defence of London and eastern counties, which role the station continued to fulfil until the cessation of hostilities in November 1918. Air Force activity then gradually wound down to be replaced by limited civil flying, but even this ceased in 1920 when the airfield was closed and the site resumed for farming.

Despite its reversion to farmland, the site was purchased anew in 1933 by Southend Council in order to build a civil airport. This was opened in September 1935 as the Southend Municipal Airport. In 1939, however, with war looming, the airport was requisitioned by the Air Ministry and became RAF Rochford, as a satellite airfield of RAF Hornchurch, an advanced landing ground within 11 Group. It came into its own during the Battle of Britain when flying units such as 41 Squadron were based there, and became an airfield in its own right in late October 1940, when it was re-named RAF Southend.

Throughout the War, the airfield used grass runways and was equipped with a number of Bellman and Blister hangars, which were defended by several Pickett Hamilton Fort retractable pillboxes. In October 1943, RAF Southend became home to 17 Armament Practice Camp, and in early 1944 to 24 Balloon Centre. At the time of 41 Squadron's arrival in February 1944, Southend was also home to 2766 Squadron RAF Regiment's Bofors and Hispano Flights and a detachment of 287 (AAC) Squadron.

Games rooms offered billiards, snooker, darts, and table tennis, and at the end of February 1944, Station strength stood at 85 Officers RAF and four WAAF, 112 senior NCOs RAF and seven WAAF, and 868 Other Ranks RAF and 150 WAAF. The Station Commander was Sqn Ldr Donald E. Kingaby DSO DFM**.

7 February 1944 – 41 Squadron commenced Air Firing Course No. 6 this morning with instruction on the activity to be expected during the ensuing two weeks. It was intended to get the pilots airborne during the afternoon but as the weather conditions proved too poor, there was no

flying all day. In the meantime, the pilots were allocated instructors and told "they would return to Tangmere as ace shots".[401]

8 February 1944 – When the day dawned to improved conditions with scattered cloud at 3,000 feet, dual instruction commenced and the first in the air were Flt Lt Ron Collis and Plt Off Peter Gibbs. Air firing and cine-gun practice were carried out until 16:25, when the weather stopped flying. The last pilot down was Plt Off 'Jackie' Fisher, who had just flown over from Tangmere with another of the Squadron's aircraft under thick haze at 1,000 feet. In all, 20 air firing sorties were undertaken during the day.

9 February 1944 – Although the previous day's haze had cleared by this morning, it was back with a vengeance in the early afternoon, and flying was halted at 15:15. Prior to that time, however, the Squadron was able to enjoy a full morning's flying programme and at least 25 air firing sorties were undertaken.[402] Not everything went to plan, however, and Fg Off Peter Cowell had a problem with one of his guns jamming.

Sqn Ldr Glen and Plt Off Peter Graham flew over to Southend from Tangmere in the early afternoon, and found flying conditions difficult. Graham felt safe flying almost impossible, having flown over the Thames at an altitude of just 500 feet in visibility of barely 300 yards, with his undercarriage lowered.

10 February 1944 – Industrial haze and low cloud allowed the Squadron no more than two hours flying today, during which time just three air firing sorties could be completed. During the last of these, Flt Sgt Ian Stevenson had barely fired 40 rounds at the drogue when he was recalled, and flying ceased at 11:45.

Despite conditions, however, Tangmere's Sector Commander, Gp Capt William Crisham, landed at 12:05 to pay the Squadron a quick visit. He left again at 12:25. Four hours later, Fg Off Ross Harding also arrived at Southend, after "a difficult flight"[403] from Tangmere. This concluded the day's flying.

11 February 1944 – Conditions today were similar to the previous, although the weather did not stop flying until 15:00. Prior to that time, the pilots managed to fly 17 air firing sorties, during which Fg Off Peter Cowell had more trouble firing freely, noting in his logbook, "One gun jammed again!".[404]

12 February 1944 – Weather continued to plague the course and limited flying to under ten air firing sorties today.[405] There was little else to report except that Flt Lt Bruce Moffett departed Southend for Tangmere at 10:55, and returned again at 13:30.

13 February 1944 – At last, the weather cleared sufficiently today for a full flying programme to be undertaken by the Squadron. Over 30 air firing sorties were completed by the pilots[406], although Fg Off Cowell was frustrated as "one gun jammed yet again!".[407] During the day, RAF Southend's Station Commander, Sqn Ldr Kingaby took the opportunity to make an air firing sortie in one of the Squadron's Spitfire XIIs, which likely constituted his first experience on the type.

14 February 1944 – Another good day for flying, despite low cloud and haze, in which about 25 air firing sorties and a number of cine-gun exercises were undertaken.[408] Fg Off Peter Cowell had a better day and fired accurately, recording his pleasure in his logbook, "Shot drogue away – wizzo!".[409] It was Fg Off Ron Johnson's turn today to have aircraft trouble, and though he was uninjured and the aircraft (MB880) undamaged, he experienced some unnerving moments when his engine cut on take-off.

During the afternoon, Fg Off Cowell flew back to Tangmere to have a reflector sight bracket repaired on his aircraft, and Flt Lt Bruce Moffett also flew back so that his aircraft could be given its 40 flying hours inspection.

15 February 1944 – Improved weather with scattered cloud at 4,000 feet and light haze made for a solid day's flying, allowing the pilots to complete 19 air firing sorties and 12 cine-gun sorties.[410] Visibility declined during the afternoon, but did not stop flying. Flt Lt Bruce Moffett returned from Tangmere at 12:40, and Fg Off Peter Cowell arrived back at Southend at 16:10.

16 February 1944 – The weather was so poor today that no air firing could be undertaken at all. The pilots spent the morning reviewing the previous day's cine-gun films, and were released in the afternoon.

17 February 1944 – The weather today was just as bad as the day before and, once again, there was no flying. During the morning, the pilots were given a lecture on the new mark Gyro Gunsight reflector sight, and to test it on a model that had been set up in dispersals. "All were greatly impressed by the results already obtained with this sight and hoped to have the chance of using in action, as soon as possible."[411] During the evening, the Squadron held an enjoyable farewell dance at Southend, which was also attended by about 50 National Fire Service girls.

18 February 1944 – The Squadron spent this very cold day packing and preparing for their return to Tangmere the following day, and there was no flying. During the evening, the Squadron attended a WAAF fancy dress dance, which was "very lively entertainment".[412] Getting in on the act, Fg Off Ross Harding apparently give "an excellent exhibition".[413]

19 February 1944 – The Squadron had intended to return to Tangmere this morning, but low cloud and poor visibility stopped them doing so. The men were asked to remain available all day in case the weather should sufficiently improve, but when this failed to materialise, the move was postponed until the following day.

20 February 1944 – The day dawned to fine and clear weather, allowing the Squadron to return to Tangmere. The pilots took off at 10:45, followed by the Squadron's Tiger Moth (DE374). However, the latter aircraft was airborne too early and flipped over on its back on take-off. The damage was extensive, and all four mainplanes, starboard front interplane strut, propeller, fin, rudder and fuel tank were all affected. The aircraft was categorised AC, and eventually repaired and flew again. The pilot and passenger were fortunately not injured.[414]

The Squadron was back at Tangmere in time for lunch, and Flt Lt Dave Fearon, who had remained behind at Southend to complete paperwork, also arrived back soon after midday. The men spent the afternoon unpacking and settling in again, and in the evening were treated to entertainment in the Station theatre in the form of a play. "It was an excellent show and a very good welcome back to the parent station."[415]

21 February 1944 – It was back to business this morning and A Flight was assigned to dawn readiness. B Flight relieved them at 08:45, and during the morning the pilots were informed the Spitfire XII Wing would be participating in a bomber escort that afternoon. The jumping off point, however, would be Friston, which necessitated the pilots flying over to the airfield at midday. They arrived at 12:20 and, after lunching in the Mess, were briefed for an operation to Beaumont-le-Roger Airfield as an element of Ramrod 573, which operated in conjunction with separate attacks on German targets by Flying Fortresses and Liberators.

Date	21 February 1944
Operation	Ramrod 573
Targets	Part I: Soesterberg Airfield, Utrecht, Netherlands Part II: Gilze-Rijen Airfield, Noord-Brabant, Netherlands Part III: Beaumont-le-Roger Airfield, Haute-Normandie, France
Bombers	Part I: 72 Marauders – aborted (weather) Part II: 72 Marauders – aborted (weather) Part III: 36 Marauders – aborted (weather)
Close Escort Part I	Detling: 118 & 453 Squadrons (Spitfire IX)
Escort Cover	Biggin Hill: 401, 411 & 412 Squadrons (Spitfire IX)
High Cover	Kenley: 403, 416 & 421 Squadrons (Spitfire IX)
Close Escort Part II	Hornchurch: 66 & 504 Squadrons (Spitfire IX)
Escort Cover	North Weald: 331 & 332 Squadrons (Spitfire IX)
High Cover	Northolt: 302, 308 & 317 Squadrons (Spitfire IX)
Close Escort Part III	Friston: 349 Squadron, & Hawkinge: 501 Squadron (Spitfire IX)
Escort Cover	Tangmere: 41 & 91 Squadrons (Spitfire XII)
High Cover	West Malling: 124 Squadron (Spitfire VII)
1st Fighter Sweep	Gravesend: 19 & 65 Squadrons (Mustang III)
2nd Fighter Sweep	Manston: 198 Squadron (Typhoon Ib) – aborted
Casualties	453 Sqn: 2 A/C COG, pilots not inj., aircraft Cat B

The Wing took off from Friston at 15:20 through a 10/10ths layer of cloud between 1,500 and 3,000 feet, led by Wg Cdr Ingham. Ingham also led 41 Squadron as Sqn Ldr Glen had left for RAF Milfield in Northumberland today, to attend a Ground Attack Course until 11 March. The Squadron's other two sections were led by Flt Lts Don Smith and Tom Slack.

The Wing formed up above the cloud layer, then climbed to 14,000 feet and hurried to catch up with the bombers, which had arrived at the rendezvous three minutes early. The Marauders had been scheduled to arrive over Beachy Head at 12,000 feet at 15:30 (zero+15) and to be over the target at zero+59 at the same altitude.

However, all the way across the Channel, the bombers and fighters flew above a 10/10ths cloud blanket, which had an upper level of 6,000 feet that stretched as far as the eye could see. It came as no surprise, therefore, that when still west of Le Havre the bombers aborted, and returned home.

The Wing followed them back some distance, but then made a bearing for Tangmere, where they landed at 16:30 with nothing to report. This constituted 41 Squadron's total operational flying for the day.

Parts I and II of the Ramrod had fared similarly, and returned home without bombing, unable to attack their targets owing to cloud cover. Though some Flak was experienced, the Luftwaffe was not seen and the escorting fighters operated otherwise uneventfully.

22 February 1944 – It was an early start for the Wing today, and they were up and breakfasted before dawn in order to fly to Manston at first light to participate in a Ramrod. However, 'very threatening' weather and snow storms delayed their departure until 08:00, but they nonetheless arrived at Manston "in time for a second breakfast, which included a second egg, which was most welcome".[416]

After some time relaxing in the Mess, the pilots were finally briefed for participation in Ramrod 577, in which they were to provide a fighter sweep in the Antwerp area, supporting attacks by 144 Marauders on the Dutch airfields at Soesterberg and Gilze-Rijen, accompanied by close escort and escort cover squadrons.

However, the weather continued to worsen during the morning, and as the Wing's pilots climbed into their cockpits to commence the operation, it began to snow. When the snowfall had not abated after some time, the pilots were ordered to dismount and return to dispersals, where they were informed their sweep was cancelled. The men then lunched, and waited for the chance to return to Tangmere, but were hindered by further snowfall, despite once more climbing into their cockpits, and dismounting anew.

It was therefore not until 15:50 that the Wing was finally able to take off again, without Fg Off David Shea, however, who could not start his aircraft. They flew back to Tangmere under low cloud, where they arrived just before solid snowfall commenced to blanket the airfield.

Fg Off Shea was finally able to depart Manston at 16:45, but had only made it as far as Ford, where he was forced to land again on account of the conditions, and was ultimately compelled to stay the night. He returned to Tangmere at 15:50 the following day.[417]

24 February 1944 – Following a day on the ground on account of unsuitable weather, today dawned to cloudless skies, although there was thick haze to the north of Tangmere. Several pilots undertook practice flying during the morning, which included a section of four led by Flt Lt Tom Slack which undertook a low altitude navigation exercise to Cuddeson, near Oxford.

Then, at 15:50, the Wing was called upon to provide a Close Escort to Marauders bombing construction works on a ski site at 'Bois Rempre'.[418]

Date	24 February 1944
Operation	Ramrod 587
Targets	Part I: Lottinghen-Les Grands Bois, Pas-de-Calais Part II: Bois Rempre, Pas-de-Calais Part III: Vacqueriette-Erquières, Pas-de-Calais Part IV: Raye-sur-Authie & St. Josse-au-Bois, Pas-de-Calais
Bombers	Part I: 36 Marauders; 40 dispatched, 40 bombed Part II: 36 Marauders; 36 dispatched, 35 bombed Part III: 36 Marauders; 35 dispatched, 35 bombed Part IV: 36 Marauders; 36 dispatched, 35 bombed
Close Escort Part I Close Escort Part II Close Escort Part III Close Escort Part IV Fighter Umbrella	Coltishall: 64 & 611 Squadrons (Spitfire Vb) Tangmere: 41 & 91 Squadrons (Spitfire XII) North Weald: 331 & 332 Squadrons (Spitfire IX) Northolt: 302 & 308 Squadrons (Spitfire IX) Colerne: 165 Squadron (Spitfire IX) Exeter: 616 Squadron (Spitfire VII) West Malling: 124 Squadron (Spitfire VII)

'Bois Rempre' was one of four Noball sites successfully attacked this afternoon, the first and third attacks of which rendezvoused 12,000 feet over Dungeness, and the second and fourth at the same altitude over Beachy Head.

The Spitfire XII Wing was airborne at 15:30 and rendezvoused with Part II's bombers not quite to schedule as the bombers were three minutes late. However, from here on in, the operation ran according to plan, and the formation was over the target at 16:23 in clear skies with 20 miles visibility. The Marauders dropped 68 tons of bombs from 12,000 feet with fair results, although the Spitfire XII Wing was less optimistic, reporting the bombs were "seen to burst but impossible to say where".[419]

The Luftwaffe was not seen and only three meagre bursts of Flak were directed towards them as the aircraft crossed back out again south of Berck-sur-Mer. The Wing landed back at Tangmere between 17:05 and 17:10, however "without much petrol to spare"[420], and this concluded the day's operational flying.[421]

Parts I, III and IV also operated without interference, respectively dropping 83 tons with good results, 69 tons with fair results, and 47 tons with fair results. There were no casualties and the escorting fighters reported the operation uneventful and according to plan.

Separately today, two new experienced pilots joined the Squadron: Flt Lt Keith F. 'Jimmy' Thiele DSO, DFC* RNZAF, who was a day off his 23rd birthday, and 21-year-old Fg Off William 'Bill' N. Stowe RCAF.

A pre-War journalist from Christchurch, Thiele had joined the RNZAF in December 1940 and earned his Wings in New Zealand, where he was also commissioned in late May 1941. He embarked for Europe in June 1941 and travelled to the United Kingdom via Canada, arriving at his final destination at the end of July. Assigned to Bomber Command, Thiele attended OTU until early October, when he was posted to his first operational unit, 405 (Canadian) Squadron, in Pocklington, Yorkshire, flying Wellingtons and subsequently Halifaxes.

He was quickly recognised for his natural leadership ability and promoted to Acting Squadron Leader with this unit, prior to a promotion to Flying Officer, in May 1942. Only three months later, he was promoted to Flight Lieutenant and awarded the DFC. Following attendance at various courses in conversion, beam approach, and flying instruction, Thiele was posted to 467 (Australian) Squadron at Bottesford on Christmas Eve 1942, flying Lancasters.

It was a significant posting. Although only with this unit until his tour expired on 12 May 1943, Thiele was appointed OC C Flight, promoted to Acting Squadron Leader again, and awarded both the DSO and a Bar to his DFC in that time.

He was subsequently rested with 24 Squadron at RAF Hendon and as a Ferry Pilot with 45 Group at Dorval in Canada, but requested conversion to fighters, which was granted in late 1943. Thiele returned to the United Kingdom where he attended 57 OTU, and was now being posted to 41 Squadron directly from this course, as his first operational fighter unit. Assigned to B Flight, Thiele would remain with the unit until mid-August, and was destined to command his own squadron before the year was out.

Fg Off Bill Stowe had joined the RCAF in May 1941 and completed his flying training in Canada, where he was commissioned in March 1942. Posted to his first operational unit, 118 Squadron RCAF, at Dartmouth, Nova Scotia, that same month, he served with this unit 17 months, which included a period in Alaska.

Stowe shipped to the United Kingdom aboard HMTS *Queen Mary* in October 1943, and was subsequently posted to 57 OTU, attending the same course as Flt Lt 'Jimmy' Thiele. He was assigned to A Flight on arrival on the Squadron today, and would remain with 41 Squadron until April 1945, returning for a second brief tour after the cessation of hostilities.

25 February 1944 – The Wing was involved in two Ramrods today and pilots were up at 06:30 for the first, which was to commence at Hawkinge. Following breakfast, the Wing took off for Hawkinge at 07:40, but Fg Off Clive Birbeck (MB881) had engine trouble on the way and landed at Friston at 08:00.

The rest of the Wing landed at Hawkinge at 08:15, and breakfasted for a second time before they were briefed for the operation, on this occasion a close escort to Marauders attacking Cambrai-Epinoy Airfield in Part II of Ramrod 591.

Date	25 February 1944
Operation	Ramrod 591
Targets	Part I: Venlo Airfield, Limburg, Netherlands Part II: Cambrai-Epinoy Airfield, Pas-de-Calais, France Part III: St. Truiden-Brustem Airfield, Limburg, Belgium
Bombers	Part I: 108 Marauders; 103 dispatched, 98 bombed Part II: 36 Marauders; 36 dispatched – aborted Part III: 108 Marauders; 100 dispatched, 98 bombed
Casualties	Part I: 387 BG/558 BS: Marauders 41-31648, 41-31660 & 41-31671, SD by FW190s, NW Knokke, Belgium

Close Escort Part I	Manston: 3, 198 & 609 Squadrons (Typhoon Ib)
	Merston: 181 Sqn, & Westhampnett: 245 Sqn (Typhoon Ib)
Escort Cover	Gravesend: 19 & 65 Squadrons (Mustang III)
Withdrawal Support	Biggin Hill: 401 & 412 Squadrons (Spitfire IX)
	Kenley: 416 & 421 Squadrons (Spitfire IX)
Close Escort Part II	Tangmere: 41 & 91 Squadrons (Spitfire XII)
Escort Cover	West Malling: 124 Squadron (Spitfire VII)
Rear Support	Tangmere: 183 Squadron (Typhoon Ib)
Close Escort Part III	North Weald: 331 & 332 Squadrons (Spitfire IX)
	Colerne: 165 Squadron (Spitfire IX)
	Exeter: 616 Squadron (Spitfire VII)
Escort Cover	Northolt: 302 & 308 Squadrons (Spitfire IX)
	Hornchurch: 350 Squadron (Spitfire IX)
1st Fighter Sweep	Perranporth: 340 & 341 Squadrons (Spitfire Vb) – cancelled
2nd Fighter Sweep	Detling: 118 & 453 Squadrons (Spitfire IX)
Casualties	331 Sqn: Lt Fredrik A. S. Fearnley DFC, SD/AA/KIA in Spit IX, MJ534

The Spitfire XII Wing was airborne again at 09:55, consisting of eleven aircraft from 41 Squadron, led by Flt Lt Don Smith, and eleven from 91 Squadron, plus Wg Cdr Ingham leading the Wing, flying with 91 Squadron. They climbed through 10/10ths cloud between 2,000 and 3,000 feet, and formed up above the cloud layer. Climbing to 12,000 feet, they passed over Dungeness at 10:07, and headed for the rendezvous.

Part II's Marauders were scheduled to rendezvous with the Wing 15 miles southwest of Berck-sur-Mer, at 10:20 (zero+10), but 41 and 91 Squadrons arrived on time to find that the bombers were running up to seven minutes ahead of schedule. The Wing quickly caught up with them and crossed in over Criel-sur-Mer, with the bombers at an altitude of 12,000 feet and the Wing 1,000 feet above them.

From this point on, however, the escort deteriorated into a comedy of errors. The Marauders split into two boxes, and the Wing split down Squadron lines to stay with them. The box escorted by 91 Squadron erroneously turned southwest, and then south, crossing over Neufchâtel-en-Bray, and continuing to a few miles east of Vernon, Eure, where Wg Cdr Ingham could finally head off the leader.

However, even then, only six bombers returned with 91 Squadron and the others still continued on their way. Ingham sent 91 Squadron's Blue Section home with these six bombers, which crossed out west of Abbeville and made a bearing for Hastings. Meanwhile, the box escorted by 41 Squadron initially headed southeast, and then northeast over Gisors, and into the Beauvais area. From this point, they turned southwest and reached Les Andelys, 25 miles southeast of Rouen.

It proved an impossible task for the Wing to escort the Marauders, and multiple attempts were made to raise them by radio and head them off in the same manner that Ingham had done with limited success with the first box. With no sign of the target, fuel began to be a problem for the Wing and, before much longer, Ingham recalled the pilots and headed home. The bombers were last seen in the Évreux area still heading inland.

The Wing had encountered "no opposition of any sort"[422] despite cloudless skies and visibility of 20 miles. They crossed out at St. Valéry-en-Caux, and made a bearing for Beachy Head, from where they made their way to Tangmere and landed at 11:30. The 11 Group ORB blamed the fiasco on a navigational error and reported in its usual official tone:

> Both boxes of bombers appeared to get lost, and our fighters were only partially successful in repeated efforts to head off and recall them, fighters having to withdraw owing to petrol shortage whilst a number of the Marauders were still over France.[423]

The Squadron's pilots were more candid, and called it as they saw it. Plt Off Jimmy Payne recorded in his logbook that day, "Most complete shambles ever! Bombers wandered all over France &

finished up at Paris!!"⁴²⁴, whilst Plt Off Peter Graham recorded "Marauders packed off S.W. of Paris! We left them to it."⁴²⁵

The Squadron was back in time for lunch and was airborne again at 16:15 to provide a Close Escort to another 36 Marauders targeting a Noball site in Part IV of Ramrod 593. Unfortunately, this operation was as unsuccessful as the morning's, although it was weather that hindered the bombers this time, rather than navigational issues.

Date	25 February 1944
Operation	Ramrod 593
Targets	Part I: Lottinghen-Les Grands Bois, Pas-de-Calais Part II: La Longueville & Bois Rempre & La Groseillier, Pas-de-Calais Part III: 'Le Grismont', Pas-de-Calais Part IV: 'Bois d'Enfer', Pas-de-Calais
Bombers	Part I: 36 Marauders – recalled (weather) Part II: 54 Marauders – recalled (weather) Part III: 36 Marauders – recalled (weather) Part IV: 36 Marauders – recalled (weather)
Close Escort Part I Escort Cover Close Escort Part II Close Escort Part III Close Escort Part IV	Heston: 306 & 315 Squadrons (Spitfire Vb) West Malling: 124 Squadron (Spitfire VII) Friston: 349 Sqn, & Hornchurch: 350 Sqn (Spitfire IX) North Weald: 331 & 332 Squadrons (Spitfire IX) – recalled Tangmere: 41 & 91 Squadrons (Spitfire XII) – recalled

The entire Ramrod fell apart soon after it had begun. Part I's bombers rendezvoused with their escorts 12,000 feet over Beachy Head at 16:00, whilst Part II's rendezvoused with their own escorts at the same altitude and location at 16:10. The two formations proceeded to France, but when 10/10ths cloud cover was encountered, the bombers were recalled. Their escorts nonetheless continued on to orbit their respective target areas, then returned home with nothing to report.

Part III commenced similarly, bombers and escorts rendezvousing at 12,000 feet over Beachy Head at 16:20. Once again, they continued across the Channel, but when 10/10ths cloud was encountered, the bombers turned for home. On this occasion, however, their escort fighters returned with them.

The Spitfire XII Wing deployed 24 aircraft for Part IV, led by Wg Cdr Ingham, who flew with 41 Squadron. Ingham led one section and the other two were led by Flt Lts Don Smith and Tom Slack. The pilots were airborne in sufficient time to reach the rendezvous punctually, however found that the bombers had arrived three minutes early.

The Wing quickly caught up but found 10/10ths cloud at 2,000-3,000 feet north of its southern extremity, running east to west through the Somme Estuary. The bombers decided their attack would not be possible under these conditions and they, too, aborted the operation, at Berck-sur-Mer.

The 36 Marauders and 24 Spitfires turned for home, and the Spitfire XII Wing landed at Tangmere again at 17:15. On landing, the pilots reported that "thousands [of] all types of A/C were over [the] coast of France, making flying very dangerous".⁴²⁶

26 February 1944 – There was no operational flying all day as a result of unsuitable weather and the Squadron was released during the afternoon. However, Flt Lt Bruce Moffett left the Squadron today after a ten-month tenure, and was posted across the airfield to 91 Squadron as a Flight Commander. He remained with the unit until mid-August 1944, during this time becoming a V1 Ace by shooting down eight flying bombs, one of which was the first ever claimed by any RAF pilot during daylight. Although discharged in March 1945, Moffett re-joined the post-War RCAF and served another ten years.⁴²⁷

28 February 1944 – The Spitfire XII Wing was called upon today to participate in a single Ramrod, once again as Close Escort to Marauders attacking Noball sites in northern France. However, as 91 Squadron had received orders to leave Tangmere and move to Castle Camps to convert to the Spitfire XIV, it also proved to be the very last conducted as a joint 41 Squadron/91 Squadron, Spitfire XII Wing operation.

Date	28 February 1944
Operation	Ramrod 597
Targets	Part I: Rosières-en-Santerre Airfield, Picardie
	Part II: Beauvoir, Bonnières & Gorenflos, Pas-de-Calais
	Part III: Lottinghen-Les Grands Bois, La Longueville & Bois Rempre, Pas-de-Calais
	Part IV: Raye-sur-Authie & Bois de Créquy, Pas-de-Calais
	Part V: Beauvoir, Bonnières & Gorenflos, Pas-de-Calais
Bombers	Part I: 36 Marauders; 36 dispatched, 18 bombed
	Part II: 54 Marauders; 54 dispatched, 18 bombed
	Part III: 54 Marauders; 51 dispatched, 49 bombed
	Part IV: 42 Marauders; 36 dispatched, 17 bombed
	Part V: 54 Marauders; 56 dispatched, 37 bombed
Close Escort Part I	Biggin Hill: 401 & 412 Squadrons (Spitfire IX)
Escort Cover	Detling: 118 & 453 Squadrons (Spitfire IX)
Close Escort Part II	Tangmere: 41 & 91 Squadrons (Spitfire XII)
Close Escort Part III	Heston: 306 & 315 Squadrons (Spitfire Vb)
Close Escort Part IV	Hornchurch: 350 & 504 Squadrons (Spitfire IX)
Close Escort Part V	North Weald: 331 & 332 Squadrons (Spitfire IX)
Fighter Umbrella	Gravesend: 19, 65 & 122 Squadrons (Mustang III)
	West Malling: 124 Squadron (Spitfire VII) – cancelled
1st Fighter Sweep	Northolt: 302 & 308 Squadrons (Spitfire IX)
2nd Fighter Sweep	Kenley: 416 & 421 Squadrons (Spitfire IX)
Casualties	Gravesend: Wg Cdr Reginald J. C. Grant DFC* DFM RNZAF, EF, baled out of Mstg III, FX996, NE Gravesend, parachute failed to open†

The bombers of the first attack were scheduled to rendezvous 12,000 feet over Beachy Head at 13:00 (zero), whilst the bombers of the second, third, fourth and fifth attacks were to rendezvous over Dungeness at the same altitude at zero, zero+10, zero+20 and zero+30 minutes. The five parts' times over target were planned for zero+30, zero+20, zero+30, zero+40 minutes, and zero+50, respectively.

The Spitfire XII Wing was airborne in fine but cold weather at 12:35[428] and made a "perfect rendezvous"[429] with Part II's bombers over Dungeness. They proceeded to France together and crossed in over Cayeux, where the Marauders split into three boxes of eighteen. 91 Squadron escorted the third box, whilst 41 Squadron, led by Wg Cdr Ingham, escorted the first and second boxes.[430]

Intense heavy Flak was experienced by all aircraft from southwest of Abbeville to the respective target areas, particularly west of Doullens, but ultimately Beauvoir and Bonnières could not be attacked owing to cloud cover and the bombers returned with their payloads intact. The remaining 18 Marauders to Gorenflos could also not locate their target, but attacked an alternative instead, which was believed to be Raye-sur-Authie, with 22 tons of bombs. The Spitfire XII Wing reported seeing bursts, but was unable to assess the results, but the bombers considered them fair.

Parts I, III, IV and V also reported varying results as a result of weather issues. In Part I, only half the bombers attacked the target with 12 tons of bombs, achieving poor results. Part III's bombers were the most successful of the day, 49 bombers dropping a total of 89 tons on their three targets with fair to poor results. In Part IV, 17 bombers dropped 21 tons on Raye-sur-Authie, but could not locate Bois de Créquy owing to cloud over the target area. Finally, only approximately 60% of Part V's bombers could successfully bomb their three targets with fair to poor results.

Although Flak was also experienced by other escorting squadrons, the Luftwaffe was not seen and the Spitfire XII Wing reported the operation uneventful and according to plan. When the they landed for a final time at Tangmere at 14:10, they had little to report.

That evening, a farewell party was thrown for 91 Squadron, "with whom we have had 8 months successful cooperation in all our major operations."[431]

29 February 1944 – For the first time in eight months today, 41 Squadron participated in a Ramrod without 91 Squadron as the Spitfire XII Wing, to provide cover for 20 Mosquitos bombing a Noball target south at Belleville-en-Caux.

Date	29 February 1944
Operation	Ramrod 600
Targets	Belleville-en-Caux, Haute-Normandie
Bombers	2 Group RAF: 20 Mosquitos
Casualties	464 (RAAF) Sqn: Mosq VI, LR389, & 21 Sqn: Mosq VI, LR403, FTR, both crews †
Fighter Cover	Tangmere: 41 Squadron (12 Spitfire XII)

41 Squadron was airborne in a cloudless sky at 10:00 in three sections of four, led by Flt Lt Don Smith. They crossed the Channel at sea level, but were forced to climb 20 miles out from the coast when the weather deteriorated to 10/10ths cloud at between 200 and 1,000 feet, with six additional layers of 5/10ths to 10/10ths cloud up to 8,000 feet, and intermittent snowfall.

In these conditions, it was impossible for the pilots to patrol over France and afford the Mosquitos cover. As such, they turned back out to sea slightly and patrolled off the coast instead, flying between Dieppe and Fécamp at 800-1,000 feet, where the weather was clear up to 1,500 feet. From this location, they were able to see two of the Mosquitos make their bombing run between patches of cloud at 2,000 feet, but did not see any of the others, or observe the results of their bombing.

Unseen by the pilots, however, eleven of the Mosquitos attacked and several bursts were seen in the target area. There was no reaction from the Luftwaffe but two Mosquitos failed to return, although the actual cause is unknown. It is likely, however, that weather caused the losses of both aircraft, as they experienced snow storms and heavy icing on crossing into France. 464 Squadron's missing aircraft was last seen in cloud near the coast on the way out, whilst 21 Squadron's was last seen in a snowstorm at 3,000 feet.[432]

The operation was otherwise uneventful for 41 Squadron, who returned at 11:25 to find 91 Squadron had already left. After landing, it was also discovered that Fg Off Herb Wagner's aircraft, MB843, had been hit by a small calibre bullet, time and location unknown. Another pilot's logbook records this was caused by a .303 round. A similar event had occurred the previous 29 November, when Fg Off Ron Johnson's aircraft had also been hit by such a round.

Separately today, a new pilot arrived at Tangmere on posting to 41 Squadron to replace Flt Lt Bruce Moffett: 20-year-old compatriot Plt Off Charles J. 'Jack' Malone RCAF. Having joined the RCAF in March 1941, Malone undertook his flying training in Canada prior to the award of his Wings that December. He shipped to the United Kingdom in January 1942, attended Flying Instructors School and was posted to Peterborough as a Flying Instructor in June 1942. Just the following month, however, Malone was shipped back across the Atlantic and sent to Moose Jaw on a posting to 32 SFTS as a Flying Instructor. Subsequent postings in this role ensued in November 1942 to 34 SFTS at Medicine Hat, in December 1942 to 13 SFTS at St. Hubert, and in May 1943 to 1 OTU at Bagotville. He was commissioned in August 1943 and shipped back to the United Kingdom that same month aboard HMTS *Queen Mary*. Malone was then posted to 57 OTU, where he joined Flt Lt 'Jimmy' Thiele and Fg Off Bill Stowe, and arrived on 41 Squadron today to be assigned to A Flight.

91 Squadron's departure today did not leave 41 Squadron alone at Tangmere, but they were the only Spitfire squadron, the others all being equipped with Typhoons. On departure from the

airfield today, 91 made a flypast in formation, then headed for Castle Camps, where they landed at 12:25 to find half a dozen Spitfire XIVs awaiting them.

41 Squadron would have to wait until September before they could convert to the Spitfire XIV, but would then fly the Mark for a full year. Between now and then, however, 41 Squadron was the only frontline Allied squadron flying the Spitfire XII.

The Spitfire XII Wing had been in existence for eight intensive and exhausting months, from 29 June 1943 to 28 February 1944. In that time, they had participated in a total of 139 Ramrod operations together.

Spitfire XII Wing Operational Targets June 1943–February 1944

	Airfield	Nobell (V1) Target	Marshalling Yards	Industrial Target	Gun Enhancement	Big Ben (V2) Target	Long Range Gun (V3)	Tactical Target	Total Targets
Jun 43	–	–	1	1	–	–	–	–	2
Jul 43	8	–	3	2	–	–	–	–	13
Aug 43	19	–	1	–	–	2	–	–	22
Sep 43	22	–	5	–	1	–	–	1	29
Oct 43	10	–	–	–	–	–	–	2	14
Nov 43	7	–	–	2	4	1	3	–	15
Dec 43	3	9	–	–	–	1	–	–	13
Jan 44	–	21	–	–	–	–	–	–	21
Feb 44	2	8	–	–	–	–	–	–	10
Totals	71	38	10	5	5	4	3	3	139

© Steve Brew

Preparing for Overlord
1 March – 19 June 1944

5

41 Squadron continued to be chiefly occupied on Ramrod operations during March and April 1944 in the ramp up towards the launch of the invasion of Western Europe. These operations ceased for the Squadron on 27 April and did not resume until the end of August 1944, following the conclusion of D-Day operations and the peak of the V1 offensive. During March and April, these operations involved the Squadron in attacks on a range of strategic targets in France and Belgium, which encompassed Noball sites, airfields, gun emplacements and marshalling yards.

March 1944 – This first month that the Squadron operated independently again after eight months as a part of the Spitfire XII Wing was a disastrous one for the unit as weather played havoc with operations.

Whilst conditions completely stopped operational flying on seven days: 6-9, 12 and 29-30 March, the weather also reduced operations to a minimum on another ten: 1, 10, 13-14, 18-19, 21, 24, 27 and 31 March. As if this did not restrict flying enough, there was also no operational flying on 11 March on account of the Squadron's move to Friston, and on 15 and 17 March as they were not allocated any operational duties despite suitable weather. This left only eleven days of 'normal' flying out of 31, which included only a handful of Ramrod operations, marking a stark reduction from previous months.

When the pilots did fly, however, the conditions took their toll on both men and machines. Fourteen pilots were forced to land at other bases during operational flights, unable to return to their own airfield as a result of low visibility caused by haze, cloud or fog, whilst wind resulted in one pilot being tipped on his nose as he began to taxi for take-off, and another almost hit his wingtip on the ground as he took off. Most tragic, however, was the loss of one man's life whose engine failed as he attempted to land in windy conditions.

On other matters, Sqn Ldr Glen was away for the first three weeks of the month at a course and on leave, during time which he was relieved by Flt Lt Don Smith, and three new pilots joined the Squadron. Lastly, as mentioned above, in this unsettled month, the Squadron also moved to Friston, following their five-month stay at Tangmere.

✈ Aircraft Recognition   ✢ Noball Target   △ Airfield

Date	Operation	Role	Type	Destination / Target
1	Ramrod 605	Close Escort	✈	Dieppe, France – cancelled
2	Ramrod 613	Close Escort	✢	Maisoncelle, France
3	Ramrod 616	Withdrawal Support	△	Rosières-en-Santerre, France
4	Ramrod 622	Close Escort	△	Bernay-St. Martin, France
5	Ramrod 628	Fighter Umbrella	✢	Abbeville-Hesdin area, France

20	Ramrod 672	Close Escort		Somme Est. & Hardelot, France
23	Ramrod 680	Close Escort		Flixecourt/Domart-en-Ponthieu, Fr.
26	Ramrod 689	Close Escort		Vacqueriette-Erquières, France

1 March 1944 – The month commenced with a reduced state of readiness, with foresaw just one section kept at readiness, with another two or more at 15 minutes. In 'very bad weather', B Flight took the first such shift at dawn but there was no flying until twelve pilots in three sections took off at 12:50 to provide close escort for Ramrod 605.

The operation called for the Squadron to escort 18 Bostons on a feint attack towards Dieppe, with a rendezvous over Beachy Head at 12,000 feet at 13:00. The pilots took off on time led by Flt Lt Don Smith, but they did so in extremely poor conditions of heavy rain squalls, a cloud base of 1,000 feet, and visibility of around 1,000 yards.

They made two circuits of Tangmere whilst forming up, but within ten minutes the operation was cancelled and they were recalled. A Flight took over readiness from B Flight at 13:00, and although the weather cleared sufficiently during the afternoon for two aircraft to do some practice flying, there was no more operational flying all day.

2 March 1944 – The new day dawned to clear skies, and A Flight was placed at dawn readiness. Throughout the day 16 pilots conducted flying practice, during which 12 men conducted air-to-ground firing training; others busied themselves on the Link Trainer.

The day's first operational flights came at 09:33, when Yellow Section (Wagner MB843 & Cook MB845) was ordered to conduct an ASR search for a missing bomber crew, believed to be in a dinghy approximately 20 miles off the French coast between Le Havre and the Cotentin [Cherbourg] Peninsula. However, Cook began to have engine trouble, and returned with Wagner at 10:55, whereupon White Section (Collis MB863 & Robinson MB840) took over. The latter section returned at 10:45, having found no sign of downed airmen, but otherwise seeing a "partially deflated ship type baloon[sic]".[1]

There was no further operational flying until after 17:00, when the Squadron was briefed for participation in Ramrod 613, in which they were to act as Close Escort for one of four attacks made by 2 Group bombers on Noball targets in north-western France.

Date	2 March 1944
Operation	Ramrod 613
Targets	1st Attack: Bois Rempre, Pas-de-Calais 2nd Attack: Bois de la Justice, Pas-de-Calais 3rd Attack: Maisoncelle, Pas-de-Calais 4th Attack: Écalles & Grand Parc, Haute-Normandie
Bombers	1st Attack: 22 Mitchells; 18 dispatched, 17 bombed 2nd Attack: 12 Bostons; 12 dispatched, 11 bombed 3rd Attack: 18 Mitchells; 18 dispatched, 7 bombed 4th Attack: 19 Mosquitos; 19 dispatched, 14 bombed
Casualties	2nd attack: 342 Sqn: Boston IIIA, BZ308, OA-V, SD/AA (2 KIA, 1 DOW, 1 POW)[2]
Fighter Umbrella	Detling: 118 & 453 Squadrons (Spitfire IX)
Close Escort 1st Attack	North Weald: 331 Squadron (Spitfire IX)
Close Escort 2nd Attack	North Weald: 332 Squadron (Spitfire IX)
Close Escort 3rd Attack	Tangmere: 41 Squadron (Spitfire XII)
Fighter Cover 4th Attack	Tangmere: 197, 183 & 257 Squadrons (Bomphoons)

41 Squadron was airborne at 17:25 and rendezvoused with their bombers at 12,000 feet over Dungeness, just above a 9/10ths cloud ceiling. However, as the 18 Mitchells were spread well apart in three boxes of six aircraft, Flt Lt Don Smith, leading the Squadron, had little choice but to split the pilots up, allocating Red Section to the first box, Yellow to the second and Blue to the third.

The 30 aircraft crossed in at Le Tréport in 3/10ths cloud at 7,000-8,000 feet, turned east, and then north towards Hesdin, where heavy Flak was encountered. However, it was inaccurate as the aircraft were flying at 12,000 feet and the Flak was bursting at 15,000. The bombing was undertaken according to plan, and the Squadron escorted the bombers home again in what an Intelligence Report for the Ramrod called a "perfect operation according to plan".[3]

The pilots were unable to see the results of the bombing, although bursts were later stated to have been seen northeast of the target. On the way out, however, they saw two things they felt were worthy of reporting, the first of which was that Flt Lt Tom Slack, leading Blue Section, saw a "terrific red flash"[4] and flames 200 feet into the air following an explosion south of Hucqueliers. As the pilots crossed out over the French coast again, they also saw part of a force of 1,000 heavy American bombers and fighters, that they felt was "a most inspiring sight".[5] They landed back at Tangmere at 18:50 and this concluded the day's flying.

The other attacks of the Ramrod also went according to plan and were generally uneventful. In some cases, the bombing results were either unseen or thought to have fallen slightly short of their targets, but in the fourth attack 90% of the bombs were observed to have landed in the target area. None of the fighters on the Ramrod saw the Luftwaffe, and the Tangmere based Bomphoon Wing, supporting the fourth attack, strafed the target areas with cannon after the Mosquitos had departed.

Nominal Roll, Tangmere, March 1944

This information has been extracted from a document titled, *Nominal Roll of Officers and Airmen*, dated 2 March 1944, and referenced *41S/521/P.2*, which is held in 41 Squadron's archives. Although names are listed in the order they appear on the original document, minor corrections have been made where errors have been recognised.

Name	Rank	Number	Nationality
Glen, A. A.	Actg Sqn Ldr	115332	
Smith, D. H.	Flt Lt	407256	Australian
Collis, R. T.	Flt Lt	111107	
Fearon, D. N.	Flt Lt	41389	
Slack, T. A. H.	Flt Lt	112428	
Burne, T. R.	Flt Lt	33457	
Thiele, K. F.	Flt Lt	404966	New Zealand
Cowell, P.	Fg Off	124530	
Birbeck, C. R.	Fg Off	108990	
Wagner, H. A.	Fg Off	130242	American
Johnson, R.	Fg Off	129667	
Harding, R. P.	Flt Lt	113876	
Curtis, K. R.	Fg Off	J.22759	Canadian
Cook, H.	Fg Off	126096	
Robinson, K. B.	Fg Off	139816	
Balasse, M. A. L.	Fg Off	135895	Belgian
Van Goens, R.	Fg Off	124239	Netherlands

Shea, D. J.	Fg Off	J.22158	Canadian
Stowe, W. N.	Fg Off	J.10643	Canadian
Graham, P. B.	Plt Off	161780	
Fisher, D. P.	Plt Off	169435	
Payne, J. C. J.	Plt Off	170730	
Malone, C. J.	Fg Off	J.29235	Canadian
Woollard, F. G.	Flt Sgt	1312058	
Garrie, T. A.	Flt Sgt	1348819	
Stevenson, I. T.	Flt Sgt	1348985	
Fleming, R.	Flt Sgt	656285	
Gibbs, N. P.	Flt Sgt	1317449	

3 March 1944 – At 08:30, the Squadron was briefed for a close escort to 18 Bostons to Poix Airfield in the third attack of Ramrod 616. The Ramrod foresaw three attacks on airfields by U.S. 9th Air Force Marauders in the Picardie region of north-western France, the other being Laon-Couvron and Montdidier.

For reasons unexplained, however, the third attack was cancelled at last minute, when 41 Squadron's pilots were already in their cockpits, preparing for take-off. They dismounted and returned to the briefing room, where they were immediately briefed for a new operation. A fourth attack for Ramrod 616 had quickly been created by Bomber Command, on this occasion targeting Rosières Airfield, which foresaw the deployment of 108 Marauders, four escort Spitfire IX squadrons, and 41 Squadron who were to undertake a fighter sweep of the Dieppe and Poix areas as withdrawal support for the attack.

Date	3 March 1944
Operation	Ramrod 616
Targets	1st Attack: Laon-Couvron Airfield, Picardie 2nd Attack: Montdidier Airfield, Picardie 3rd Attack: Poix-de-Picardie Airfield, Picardie 4th Attack: Rosières-en-Santerre Airfield, Picardie
Bombers	1st Attack: 108 Marauders; 98 dispatched, 84 bombed 2nd Attack: 54 Marauders; 54 dispatched, 54 bombed 3rd Attack: 18 Bostons; 0 dispatched – cancelled 4th Attack: 108 Marauders; 99 dispatched, 80 bombed
Close Escort 1st Attack Escort Cover Close Escort 2nd Attack Escort Cover Close Escort 3rd Attack Close Escort 4th Attack Escort Cover Withdrawal Fighter Sweep	Detling: 118 & 453 Squadrons (Spitfire IX) Biggin Hill: 401 & 412 Squadrons (Spitfire IX) Kenley: 403 & 416 Squadrons (Spitfire IX) Mendlesham: 310 & 313 Squadron (Spitfire IX) Northolt: 308 & 317 Squadrons (Spitfire IX) Tangmere: 41 Squadron (Spitfire XII) – cancelled North Weald: 331 & 332 Squadrons (Spitfire IX) Hornchurch: 350 & 504 Squadrons (Spitfire IX) – cancelled Tangmere: 41 Squadron (Spitfire XII)

It was a very short briefing and the pilots had to hurry back to their aircraft to take off in time to be in position for the withdrawal. This was particularly urgent as the escort cover squadrons from Hornchurch were cancelled, leaving only two escort squadrons besides 41 Squadron to cover around 100 aircraft– "a very inadequate fighter support"[6], felt the ORB scribe. By comparison, the first attack, which comprised of approximately the same number of bombers, was escorted by six Spitfire squadrons!

41 Squadron was off the ground at 09:25 and crossed in just east of Dieppe. At this time, they

were ordered to drop the sweep and just provide withdrawal support instead. The pilots penetrated approximately 15 miles into France, where they intercepted the last box Marauders, then wheeled around behind them and escorted them back across the Channel.

The operation was uneventful and all 12 pilots were back on the ground at 11:00. However, the patrol was not in vain. Upon their arrival at Tangmere, Flt Lt Smith received a congratulatory message from Headquarters, 11 Group, as "it appeared that we had arrived in time to make a large number of Huns return just after they had come up from Beauvais to attack the bombers."[7]

The other attacks in the Ramrod had also gone well and had no casualties to report. However, the results of the bombing were broader than originally intended. Attack 1, whose target was Laon-Couvron Airfield, returned to report that 18 Marauders dropped 22 tons on bombs on Juvincourt-et-Damary Airfield with 'good results', 16 bombed coastal positions near Berneval-le-Grand, and 50 had bombed an unidentified airfield with unobserved results.

In Attack 2, whose target was Montdidier Airfield, 54 Marauders dropped 49 tons on Beauvais-Tillé Airfield with 'poor results', whilst in Attack 3, whose target was Rosières Airfield, 33 Marauders dropped 33 tons on Rosières Airfield, six Marauders dropped 8 tons on Roye-Amy Airfield, and 41 Marauders dropped 60 tons on Attack 2's target, Montdidier Airfield, with 'fair results'.

41 Squadron's participation in the 3rd Attack of the Ramrod constituted their total operational flying today. During the afternoon, conditions became hazy, and only limited practice flying was undertaken.

4 March 1944 – The morning dawned to a clear day, and the Squadron was briefed by Flt Lt Don Smith at 08:15 for a close escort to 18 bombers to Bernay-St. Martin Airfield, west-northwest of Paris, in one of four attacks of Ramrod 622. The operation foresaw three attacks by U.S. 9th Air Force Marauders on Malines Marshalling Yards and a fourth on Bernay, escorted by 17 fighter squadrons, as follows:

Date	4 March 1944
Operation	Ramrod 622
Targets	1st-3rd Attacks: Malines Marshalling Yards, Belgium[8] 4th Attack: Bernay-St. Martin Airfield, Haute-Normandie, France
Bombers	1st Attack: 108 Marauders; 6 boxes of 18 – recalled 2nd Attack: 54 Marauders; 3 boxes of 18 – recalled 3rd Attack: 108 Marauders; 6 boxes of 18 – recalled 4th Attack: 18 Bostons; 1 box of 18 – recalled
Close Escort 1st, Boxes 1-3 Close Escort 1st, Boxes 4-6	Hornchurch: 350, 485 & 504 Squadrons (Spitfire IX) North Weald: 66, 331 & 332 Squadrons (Spitfire IX)
Close Escort 2nd, Boxes 1-2 Close Escort 2nd, Box 3	Manston: 198 & 609 Squadrons (Typhoon Ib) Manston: 1 (DNTO) & 3 Squadrons (Typhoon Ib)
Close Escort 3rd, Boxes 1-3 Close Escort 3rd, Boxes 4-6 Withdrawal Sup, 3rd Attack	Kenley: 403 & 416 Squadrons (Spitfire IX) Detling: 118 & 453 Squadrons (Spitfire IX) Biggin Hill: 401 & 412 Squadrons (Spitfire IX)
Close Escort 4th Attack	Tangmere: 41 Squadron (Spitfire XII)
Casualties	198 Sqn: Fg Off R. Armstrong, EF/FL, Greatstone-on-Sea nr Dungeness, Kent

41 Squadron had 12 pilots airborne at 09:10, once again led by OC, A Flight, Flt Lt Don Smith, in Sqn Ldr 'Pinkie' Glen's absence. They rendezvoused with the bombers over the Channel, slightly east of the planned coordinates, but from this point onwards, the sky was covered in a 10/10ths cloud layer at 8,000 feet. Nonetheless, they escorted the bombers over the French coast at 14,000 feet, and saw through rare small breaks in the cloud that the ground was covered in snow.

A Battle of Britain veteran, Fg Off (later Flt Lt) Harry Cook served with 41 Squadron from 16 December 1943 to 11 February 1945. © Jack Malone

The weather was not on the RAF's side today, and despite the fact that visibility above the cloud was excellent, targets could not be located and bombing results would not be seen. As such, the bombers from all four attacks were recalled, but the Bostons of the fourth would not give up so easily. Apparently,

> ...the bombers were determined to find a clear patch and continued to fly southward. When they finally turned back, we were plotted at Nogent Le Rotrou 75 miles west-southwest of Chart[r]es and 220 miles from Tangmere, and 100 miles inside France, our deepest penetration so far.
> After flying a course of of [sic] 010° for about 25 minutes after leaving Nogent, we were considerably perturbed by encountering flak from Rouen as we, most of us, imagined we were over the Channel. However, slightly afterwards we reached the edge of the cloud layers and crossed out of France at St. Valery-en-Caux under a clear sky and with good visibility.[9]

Within ten further minutes, Beachy Head was sighted, and the Squadron set course for Tangmere, finally landing at 10:55 in perfect weather, with the exception of Fg Off Clive Birbeck (MB830), who landed in Friston, likely a result of low fuel. The Squadron had been airborne an hour and 45 minutes.

Owing to weather conditions on the Continent, the pilots undertook no further operational flying today, but spent the afternoon instead practicing air to ground firing.

5 March 1944 – Poor weather with thick fog and ground haze. Despite conditions, the Squadron was airborne on two operations today, the first as an escort to 36 Marauders in a feint attack over the Channel, and the second as a part of the five-squadron-strong fighter umbrella for the first, second and third attacks of Ramrod 628.

There is no discussion in the ORB of any non-operational activity during the morning, and the F541 also suggests there was no other operational flying until 13:45, when 12 pilots took off for the feint attack. Rendezvous was made with the Marauders mid-Channel and the Squadron then proceeded to fly to "very close to the bombers as we were required to make their crews well acquainted with the appearance of the Spitfire XII".[10]

The pilots escorted the bombers to a point approximately 15 miles northwest of Le Tréport, and then turned back for England, making landfall at Hastings. This concluded the exercise and the Squadron landed at Tangmere again at 14:50.

There was, however, no immediate break; as soon as the pilots landed and were gathered in the briefing room again, they were briefed for the next operation. They would now be providing cover for 246 Marauders of the U.S. 9th Air Force, which were conducting five attacks on No Ball targets.

N. Peter Gibbs, a violinist of some talent, joined 41 Squadron as an NCO pilot on 21 January 1944 and was commissioned shortly afterward (effective 20 January 1944). He remained with the unit until 7 March 1945, having claimed four V1s destroyed in that time, including the Squadron's first ever, on 20 June 1944. © Jim Payne, via Dan Johnson

Date	5 March 1944
Operation	Ramrod 628
Targets	1st Attack: Raye-sur-Authie & Vacqueriette-Erquières, Pas-de-Calais 2nd & 3rd Attacks: Moyenneville, Béhen and Vaux-Marquenneville, Picardie 4th & 5th Attacks: Lottinghen/Les Grands Bois and Fôret de Tournehem, Pas-de-Calais
Bombers	1st Attack: 48 Marauders; 2 boxes of 12, 43 bombed 2nd & 3rd Attacks: 108 Marauders; 54 aircraft in 3 boxes of 18 each per attack, total 87 bombed 4th & 5th Attacks: 90 Marauders; 54 in 3 boxes of 18 in 4th & 36 in 2 boxes of 18, total of 53 bombed
Casualties	386 BG/552 BS: B-26 Marauder 41-31586, 'Shadrack', RG-U, SD/AA at Buigny-lès-Gamaches, approx. 12km SE of Le Tréport
Fighter Umbrella, 1st, 2nd & 3rd Attacks	Heston: 306 Squadron (Spitfire Vb) Hawkinge: 322 Squadron (Spitfire Vb) Tangmere: 41 Squadron (Spitfire XII) Hornchurch: 504 Squadron (Spitfire IX) Kenley: 416 Squadron (Spitfire IX)
Fighter Umbrella, 4th & 5th Attacks	Tangmere: 197 & 183 Squadrons (Bomphoons) Manston: 609 Squadrons (Typhoon Ib)

The same 12 pilots were back in the air at 16:35, all flying the same aircraft as they did in the earlier operation, with the exception of Fg Off Herb Wagner, who changed his Spitfire for another.

They crossed the Channel well above a 10/10ths cloud layer at 2,000 feet, and made landfall on the French coast just south of Berck-sur-Mer. The Squadron then proceeded to patrol the Abbeville-Hesdin area for 45 minutes in hazy conditions with 1/10th cloud at 6,000 feet. During this time, Flt Lt Ron Collis (MB863) began to have engine trouble and returned to base independently, where he put down at 17:10. Within 30 minutes, Fg Off Peter Cowell's aircraft (MB795) also developed engine trouble, perhaps of a more serious nature, as he was escorted home by Fg Off Ken Robinson (MB840). Both men landed back at Tangmere at 17:40.

Nine pilots completed the Ramrod, which was otherwise uneventful, although they observed moderate density Flak of heavy calibre around the bombers, one of which was hit. Flt Lt Dave Fearon reported this bomber to be in trouble and soon afterwards saw one of the crew bale out.

At approximately 17:45, Flt Lt Don Smith decided the objective had been fulfilled, and called everyone home. Upon arriving back in the region of Tangmere, however, they found that visibility had considerably deteriorated, with haze now rising from zero to 6,000 feet. Unable to navigate for a safe landing, they were ordered to West Malling where they landed without trouble at 18:20.

The pilots had been airborne around an hour and 45 minutes by now, and both the pilots and the Squadron's ground crew at Tangmere were becoming concerned about the fuel situation. This was exacerbated by initially erroneous reports that reached Tangmere to the effect that only five pilots had landed.

They were, however, all safe, but the weather conditions would not permit a completion of their journey to Tangmere today. The pilots therefore stayed the night at West Malling, compelling the rest of the Squadron at Tangmere to cancel readiness, due to the resulting shortage of serviceable aircraft.

6 March 1944 – Despite the fact that nine pilots were still at West Malling at dawn, the Squadron's only two serviceable aircraft were placed at dawn readiness. The pilots at West Malling were given an order to return to Tangmere as soon as possible, but it was not until 10:50 that they could finally get airborne, owing to thick haze in the area. When they did take-off, however, it was without Fg Off Herb Wagner, who was not well enough to fly. The other eight pilots arrived back at base at 11:05.

There was no operational flying throughout the rest of the day, but aircraft tests were conducted on a 'new' tail unit, which was received with the latest Spitfire XII to be delivered. It failed poorly, making the aircraft 'very dangerous' to fly, and it was quickly grounded. It was soon revealed, however, that this modification had been designed for the Spitfire Vc, had not been approved for the Mk. XII, and was actually fitted erroneously by the Maintenance Unit, apparently a result of a lack of the approved spares!

Fg Off Perkin DOCT

The Squadron's mascot, a black French Poodle by the name of Perkin, had belonged to Fg Off Reg Hoare until he was shot down on 1 April 1943. The Squadron kept the dog following Hoare's loss, but he ran around their bases more-or-less wild at times, until he was adopted by Plt Off Peter Gibbs after he joined the unit in January 1944.

Finding Perkin in a poor state with rashes all over his body, Gibbs, an animal-lover at heart, caught him, treated the inflammations, and bound his paws so he couldn't scratch himself. In time, the rashes healed and, in apparent thanks, Perkin became devoted to Gibbs and would follow him wherever he went.

They became such good friends that when taxiing out for flights, Perkin would jump up onto the port wingtip of Gibbs' aircraft to escort him to the runway. At this point, he would jump down and wait for his return. On landing again, Perkin would reverse the process, jumping back up onto Gibbs' wing to escort him on the taxi back to dispersals. When Gibbs stopped the engine and dropped the cockpit's side flap, Perkin would run down the wing and jump into the cockpit to greet his best friend.

When the Squadron moved base, Perkin would also ride with Gibbs in the cockpit, sitting on his lap, with his paws on either side of the gun sight, but with his head down, almost like a child too afraid to look, so that Gibbs could see to fly.

He was clearly quite a bright dog, but he had a penchant for cows milk. This was not unusual in itself, but Perkin would cheekily take a drink directly from any suitably located cow's udder whenever he wished! This earned Perkin, whose rank by this time was Flying Officer, his own unique decoration, the DOCT, or *Distinguished Order of the Cow Tits*, and he would appear on the pilot rota as "F/O Perkin DOCT".

When the Squadron moved to the Continent in December 1944, Gibbs was forced to leave Perkin behind, but placed him in the care of his father. At the end of the War, however, Perkin was returned to Reg Hoare following his repatriation, much to the sadness of both Gibbs and his father.[11]

The Squadron's mascot, a black French Poodle by the name of 'Perkin', had belonged to Fg Off Reg Hoare until he was shot down on 1 April 1943. The unit kept the dog following Hoare's loss and he was adopted by Plt Off Peter Gibbs after he joined the unit in January 1944.
© Jack Malone

9 March 1944 – For three days, the weather had been too poor for operational flying, even though the Squadron had been brought to a state of readiness on a few occasions. There was, however, a limited amount of practice flying.

Following rumours that had been circulating for a week, it was announced today that the Squadron would be moving back to Friston on 11 March, where they had spent three weeks the previous summer. Flt Lt Don Smith and Fg Off Peter Cowell flew over to the airfield during the day to prepare for their arrival, whilst Fg Off 'Charlie' van Goens was detached from the Squadron to tour several RAF stations to demonstrate the Spitfire XII's features to facilitate recognition. Although obviously deemed necessary, it seems an unusual activity to undertake when one considers the Mark was already over a year in operation.

10 March 1944 – Poor weather conditions continued today, and 10/10ths cloud at 3,000 feet and haze below that limited the day's operational flying to two weather reconnaissances performed by Plt Offs 'Jackie' Fisher and Jimmy Payne. Airborne together from 13:45 to 14:35 and from 16:35 to 17:05 as Blue Section, the pair undertook their flights around Studland Bay, Dorset, where mock landings were taking place "in connection with invasion practices by the Army and Navy"[12] The village and beach at Studland were used as a training area for the D-Day invasion of France, and were well fortified. Their patrols were uneventful.

During the evening, the Squadron held a farewell party at the King's Head Hotel at Pagham, which was also attended by the Tangmere Sector Commander, Gp Capt William J. Crisham.

The Squadron moves back to Friston

11 March 1944 – Having had the dispersals area cleaned up for a handover by 10:00, the pilots took off for Friston at 11:15. They left in style, the pilots flying over Tangmere once in the form of the unit's badge, the Cross of St. Omer, after which they orbited, re-formed, and made a low level flypast of the airfield, before heading off to their new base.

Thus ended a five-month stay at Tangmere, excluding a week at Southend in February 1944 for an air firing course. Although the Squadron would return to the Tangmere Wing, this would be the last time that the unit would call RAF Tangmere home.

Fg Off C. J. 'Jack' Malone RCAF served with 41 Squadron from 29 February 1944 to 15 August 1944. © Jack Malone

The pilots landed at Friston at 11:40, but found the strip "even rougher than it had been when we were there in June 1943".[13] The ground crews and remaining aircrew arrived at Friston by road near dusk, and the rest of the day was spent settling in; there was no operational flying.

The unit would spend seven weeks at Friston on this occasion, deployed on operations in support of preparations for the pending invasion of the Continent. The Squadron's Plt Off Peter Graham recalls this change-over in his autobiography:

It was at this time that the Allied air assault on German targets in France was stepped up.... Our own squadron now began penetrating up to one hundred miles inland escorting medium bombers or just engaged in fighter sweeps. We sighted very few enemy aircraft, though there was often quite a lot of flak about.[14]

12 March 1944 – Being back at Friston meant a return to two impracticalities and inconveniences, namely that the Messes were located some distance from the airfield, and the Station had no parachute section. In response to the former issue, the Squadron decided to leave two sections at 15 minutes readiness in dispersals with another section scheduled on immediate readiness in their aircraft. As a consequence of the latter, Fg Off Clive Birbeck made a flight to Biggin Hill today, to "find out how our parachutes were going to be looked after".[15] Flt Lt Don Smith, still commanding 41 Squadron in Sqn Ldr 'Pinkie' Glen's absence, also made a flight back to Tangmere, but the Squadron was not called upon to undertake any operational flying all day.

A Fatal Flying Accident

13 March 1944 – When the day dawned to poor flying weather, with strong winds and intermittent gale force gusts, Flt Lt Don Smith called Sector Headquarters in Biggin Hill and expressly asked them not to call on 41 Squadron unless unavoidable. Nonetheless, Red Section (Wagner NR[16] & Shea EN237) was scrambled at 11:50 on an ASR patrol to relieve Thunderbolts circling a dinghy south of Dungeness.

Despite the conditions, the order was carried out and the men taxied to the runway. However, Fg Off Herb Wagner had barely moved ten yards when a gust of wind tipped his Spitfire on its nose, abruptly ending his sortie before it began. Fg Off Shea only just managed to get off the ground himself, his port wingtip seen to nearly hit the ground as he did so, but was soon joined by White Section (Cook MB862 & Harding MB794) at 11:55, who were sent up to replace Wagner.

Fg Off Ross Harding was recalled soon afterwards and landed safely at Friston again at 12:13, leaving Fg Off Harry Cook to form a section, re-designated Yellow, with Fg Off David Shea to complete the assigned ASR patrol.

The pair was vectored 120° for six minutes, then 010° for one minute, and orbited the area at 1,000 feet, but saw nothing owing to thick cloud cover. They were then ordered to land, but to do so at Lympne, instead of Friston, owing to the blustery conditions. Reaching Lympne without trouble, the pilots found the conditions were indeed better and prepared to land.

In doing so, however, Shea was killed. An Intelligence Report telexed that afternoon from Lympne to 11 Group with copy to Biggin Hill, Hawkinge and Friston explained,

> ON COMING IN TO CIRCUIT F/O COOK GAVE ORDER TO PREPARE FOR LANDING. ON HIS LAST APPROACH F/O COOK HEARD UNINTELLIGABLE SHRIEK ON R/T AND ON ASKING FOR REPEAT HEARD NOTHING MORE. F/O SHEA CRASHED INTO TREES S.E. OF AERODROME AND WAS KILLED.[17]

The Duty Flying Control Officer at Lympne later stated that he had noticed Shea's aircraft markedly lose speed and become unsteady as he came in to land. It suddenly lost height and then rolled over onto its side and dived into the ground: the aircraft had stalled on approach at 13:06, immediately before putting down on the strip.

Sadly, subsequent investigation of the wreckage suggested the cause was likely pilot error, probably an issue of inexperience. It appears that Shea had omitted to switch over from his main tank to his jettison tank after take-off. He then ran out of fuel in the main tank and the resultant cut in power came at a fatal moment, when he was at low speed and minimal height on final approach.[18] Two days later, Flt Lt Don Smith reported,

> *On the morning of 13th March 1944, as Acting Commanding Officer, 41 Squadron, I notified Biggin Hill operations room that conditions for taking off and landing at Friston were very unsafe. I requested that aircraft should only be scrambled from this aerodrome in cases of extreme emergency, owing to a gale force wind, which was blowing across both runways.*
>
> *F/O Shea, flying Spitfire XII, EN237, was scrambled at 1150 hours from Friston as Red 2, on an ASR mission. His No.1's aircraft was blown over on to its nose while endeavouring to taxi to a take-off position, but F/O Shea managed to become airborne after a very dangerous take-off, during which his port wing tip appeared to nearly hit the ground....*
>
> *I consider that the appalling weather conditions under which this pilot was expected to scramble may have contributed in some measure to his forgetting to use his jettison tank soon after take-off.*
>
> *From the evidence supplied by eyewitnesses and the position of the pilot's engine and ancillary controls after the crash, it appears that his engine cut while approaching to land. Instinctively he opened the throttle wide, shouted some unintelligible words over the R/T, and while endeavouring to maintain height, stalled and crashed.*[19]

Smith's second last paragraph was a thinly veiled criticism of whoever had issued the order to fly in spite of his advice against doing so. Twenty-year-old Shea was only in the second month of his first operational posting, and was 11 Group's only loss all day. He was subsequently buried in Brookwood Military Cemetery in Surrey.

Not surprisingly, the mood on the Squadron was rather subdued during that afternoon and the weather, if anything, grew worse. Therefore, when B Flight received an order to undertake a calibration exercise at 15,000 feet over Beachy Head and to send a section to Newhaven for a bomber cooperation exercise, it was greeted with considerable disbelief. OC B Flight, Flt Lt Tom

Slack, otherwise known for his jovial nature, "did not think much of this idea"[20] and the Powers That Be were eventually persuaded to cancel both operations before take-off.

The 'Powers' therefore decided the Squadron could be released for practice flying instead! Incredulous, the Flight Commanders ensured the Squadron undertook none whatsoever. "So ended a black day for the Squadron."[21]

14 March 1944 – The winds had calmed considerably by the next morning, and several pilots were sent up to undertake flying practice. It was not until 16:05 that the Squadron was called on operationally for the first time today, to scramble a section to investigate an unidentified aircraft approaching the coast. On intercepting the bogey, it was recognised as a Mosquito, and the section returned to base, landing only ten minutes after take-off. This concluded the day's flying.[22]

16 March 1944 – The Squadron was back in the air today in improved weather conditions and undertook two patrols off Bognor Regis in the morning escorting shipping heading west towards Portsmouth. These were flown by Red Section between 07:55 and 09:25, and by Blue Section between 09:05 and 09:50, and both were uneventful.

The Squadron was busier during the afternoon and two ASR patrols were undertaken with six aircraft allocated to each, A Flight providing the pilots for the first, and B Flight those for the second.

The earlier of the two was airborne at 14:35, with Fg Off Herb Wagner leading, to escort an amphibious Supermarine Sea Otter on an ASR mission to retrieve a pilot of a Canadian Squadron who was in a dinghy in the Somme Estuary. The pilots were ordered to rendezvous with the Otter over Beachy Head, then given a vector of 130° and told to follow the ASR aircraft. Twenty-five minutes later, they reached Point de la Dune Blanche, where they orbited just off the coast.

It then appeared that the Sea Otter had given up finding the pilot, as it headed back out to sea, towards England. Just at that time, however, Fg Off Peter Cowell (MB795) caught sight of the dinghy's sail and reported it to Fg Off Wagner (MB843), who then flew after the Sea Otter with Flt Lt Ross Harding (MB794). Apparently unable to communicate with the aircraft directly, they made several dives in front of it, and eventually headed the captain towards the dinghy, which was floating approximately 400 yards off shore, and slightly north of Point de St. Quentin.

The Sea Otter landed nearby and proceeded to rescue the airman in his K Type dinghy but came under fairly accurate heavy fire from German shore batteries at Fort-Mahon-Plage and St. Quentin-en-Tourmont. 41 Squadron's six pilots orbited the area in an attempt to draw off fire but there were still "many near misses"[23] on the Sea Otter. 41 Squadron also received some assistance from another Allied aircraft:

A FLIGHT THROUGHOUT THE RESCUE RECEIVED INVALUABLE HELP FROM UNKNOWN PILOT (HUMBUG RED 3) [and] SMOKE BOMBS WERE OBSERVED N. OF DINGHY.[24]

When the Sea Otter had successfully completed its task, it took off again with the pilot safely on board, and 41 Squadron provided it cover for their return flight, to a point east of Eastbourne. The pilots had been airborne an hour and 50 minutes by the time they put down at Friston again at 16:25, all agreeing it had been a long patrol but "a very useful one".[25] Wagner later recorded in his logbook, "Probably the closest rescue on record"![26,27]

At 17:40, B Flight was up on their own ASR patrol, the two readiness pilots and the four pilots at 15 minutes, all airborne within four minutes. Once up, they were given a vector of 160° and told to look for a Walrus just off the French coast between Dieppe and the Somme Estuary. Within ten minutes, however, Flt Sgt Freddie Woollard (MB798) developed engine trouble and returned to Friston, where he put down again at 18:00.

Meanwhile, the remaining five pilots reached the coast, and made a square search of the area until they spotted the Walrus taxiing along in calm waters approximately 3-6 miles northeast of Dieppe. It was unable to take off due to the weight of ten crew members of a USAAF Flying Fortress it had rescued, and had therefore begun to taxi back across the Channel towards England.

The pilots orbited the aircraft, affording it cover in case of trouble, until an ASR Sea Otter arrived on the scene and relieved the Walrus of half its wet passengers. Both aircraft then took off and returned to England safely with 41 Squadron escorting them in thick haze. At one stage, they were forced to fly at sea level for several minutes as there was zero visibility at 3,000-4,000 feet, but the Squadron landed back at Friston without further trouble at 19:15, thereby concluding the day's operational flying.

18 March 1944 – The day was hazy and, as a result, A Flight undertook no flying whatsoever whilst on morning readiness. B Flight took over from them at 13:00 and during the late afternoon/early evening, three sections were scrambled, despite the prevailing conditions, to search for survivors of a USAAF Flying Fortress that was reported to have ditched in the Channel, approximately 35 miles southeast of Beachy Head.

Blue Section (Payne MB804 & Balasse MB842) was airborne at 17:15, followed just ten minutes later by Green Section (Fearon MB847 & Woollard MB798). They were also joined, at 18:05, by Black Section (Slack MB830 & Thiele MB837), however their searches were all in vain and they all returned empty-handed.

Blue Section returned to Friston at 18:30 and landed in very poor visibility. Although their landing was without mishap, it was decided that, in the interests of safety, the remaining four pilots should land at Lympne instead. Green Section landed at that airfield at 18:45 and Black followed them down at 19:30. The conditions remained so poor at Friston that the four pilots were compelled to stay the night at Lympne. It was not until mid-afternoon of the following day that conditions had improved sufficiently to allow them to complete their journey to Friston.

Separately, a new pilot joined the Squadron on 18 March 1944, 23-year-old Australian Flying Officer Robert E. 'Andy' Anderson. Having joined in the RAAF in August 1940, he completed EFTS in Australia before shipping to Canada to undertake SFTS at Camp Borden in late December. Graduating as an NCO pilot in mid-March 1941, Anderson shipped to the United

Fg Off Robert Anderson RAAF served with 41 Squadron RAF from 18 March 1944 to 18 December 1944, during which time he shared in the destruction of two V1s.
© Doug Fishburn

Kingdom in April and attended 57 OTU until June. His first operational posting came in July 1941, when he was sent to 457 (Australian) Squadron, and claimed his first victory, a share in a destroyed He114 the following February, by this time with 452 Squadron. Commissioned in April 1942, Anderson married an English girl that September, but within six weeks was posted to North Africa, where he was to remain until July 1943. There followed a quick succession of short postings between September 1943 and March 1944, to the 84 Group Communications Flight, 1530 BAT Flight, 31 Base and 84 GSU, after which he was posted to 41 Squadron today. Although arriving as a Flying Officer, his promotion to Flight Lieutenant was announced soon afterwards, and took affect from the day of his arrival on 41 Squadron. He would remain with the unit exactly nine months.

Nominal Roll

A Nominal Roll is held in 41 Squadron's Archives titled *Nominal Roll of No. 41 Squadron. 18.3.44.*, which is almost identical to the one shown above (see 2 March 1944). The only exception is that Fg Off David Shea has been replaced by Fg Off (Flt Lt) Robert Anderson, who had joined the Squadron the day the nominal roll was compiled.

In addition, two new pilots were hand-written on the list after it was completed: WO Archie Appleton and Flt Sgt Ronald Stephens, who arrived on the Squadron on 21 March 1944. Ground staff are also included, and listed in typed print under the sub-title, 'Non-Flying' as follows:

73814	F/Lt.	Lord	Gisborough	Int.
140841	F/O.	F. G.	Herman	Med
11978881	Sgt	E.	Fulham	F2E
1629100	LAC	J.	Matcher	CLK/GD

19 March 1944 – Dense fog persisted all morning and did not begin to clear until midday, keeping A Flight firmly on the ground. Very little flying was undertaken all day, and the first flights appear to have been by Flt Lts Fearon, Slack and Thiele, and Flt Sgt Woollard, who returned to Friston from Lympne at 17:10.[28] During the afternoon, Fg Off 'Charlie' van Goens also arrived back at Friston, returning from his ten-day tour of airfields displaying the Spitfire XII.

The only operational flying the Squadron was called on to do all day came at 17:30, when Flt Lt Ron Collis and Fg Off Ken Robinson took off to conduct a convoy patrol off Deal. The patrol was uneventful and they returned at 19:10 with nothing to report.[29]

20 March 1944 – With the weather cooperating once again, the Squadron was off to an early start today, and two of A Flight's readiness sections were airborne at 06:40. Red Section was sent to Cherbourg on a weather reconnaissance, whilst Yellow was detailed to carry out a convoy patrol in the Channel. The former section was back at Friston at 07:45, and the latter at 08:10, both patrols being uneventful. At 08:00, White Section was airborne to relieve Yellow, but their convoy patrol was equally as uneventful and they landed again at 09:35.

Just after breakfast, A Flight was briefed for an escort to 36 Marauders in Ramrod 672, which would be a feint attack across the Channel in an exercise similar to that, which they had carried out on 5 March, "so Yank bombers can get familiar with [the] Spitfire XII".[30] Twelve pilots were airborne at 10:45 in three sections of four pilots designated 'Red Attack', 'Yellow Attack' and 'Blue Attack', and rendezvoused with the bombers 20,000 feet above Beachy Head.

They flew together in a south-easterly direction towards the Somme Estuary, but turned north about ten miles out, and made a vector for a point off Hardelot. Upon reaching this location, they turned back toward England again, making an initial vector for Dungeness. The pilots landed back at Friston at 11:30 after an uneventful trip.

Left to right: B Flight pilots Plt Off Jimmy Payne, unknown, Flt Lts Tommy Burne AFC, Clive Birbeck, Dave Fearon, and Tom Slack, Plt Off Peter Graham, and Fg Offs Rijklof van Goens and Maurice Balasse at Tangmere, ca early 1944.
© Jean-Louis Roba

At 16:00, Fg Off 'Charlie' van Goens took off for Holmsley South, in Hampshire, once again detached for another tour of RAF stations to display the Spitfire XII and, during the afternoon, Flt Lt Dave Fearon made a non-operational flight to Tangmere and back. This concluded the day's flying.

21 March 1944 – Thick haze with a ceiling of 1,000 feet dominated the day's weather, and the only operational flight made all day was to locate a Flying Fortress reported to be in distress off Beachy Head. Fg Offs Clive Birbeck and Ron Johnson were assigned the duty and were off the deck at 15:25 in EN605 and MB880 respectively.

After a short search, they found the aircraft south of the Thames Estuary, but all efforts to lead the aircraft to West Malling were in vain, and they "could not persuade it to following them".[31] Eventually, the pair gave up and returned to Friston where they put down again at 16:00.

During the day, two new pilots joined the Squadron: 22-year-old Englishman, WO Arthur S. 'Archie' Appleton, and 23-year-old Australian Flt Sgt Ronald Vincent Stephens. Little is known of Appleton's previous postings, although it is known he had trained at 57 OTU and 2 TEU. He arrived on the Squadron today having logged 680 flying hours, of which 96 were operational. He would remain with the Squadron until mid-December 1944.

Stephens, on the other hand, was arriving on his first operational posting, with 339 flying hours in his logbook, but none operational. He had completed EFTS and SFTS in Australia in 1942 before shipping directly to the United Kingdom, where he arrived in mid-March 1943. Stephens then undertook courses at AFU, OTU, GFS and TEU, the last of which he completed only the day before arriving on the Squadron.

During the evening, a party was held by B Flight at the Junction Hotel at Polegate, although the object of celebration is not recorded. Most of A Flight attended, too, as did several WAAFs and the YMCA workers "who provide us so much comfort on the airfield".[32] Music was provided by members of the Squadron and everyone enjoyed a dance.

22 March 1944 – Good weather allowed the Squadron to get airborne early today and a total of eight patrols were undertaken by 16:00 when operational flying ceased. They were, however, quite routine and uneventful, and the ORB sums up the entire day in just two sentences.

The first pilots airborne were Fg Offs Peter Cowell and Ken Robinson, who were sent to Cherbourg on a weather reconnaissance at 06:45. They returned at 07:50 with nothing to report. The remaining flights were all convoy patrols, the first of which took off only ten minutes after the Cherbourg patrol had departed. There followed another six such patrols at 07:55, 09:05, 09:45,

12:45, 13:30 and 14:40. The last of these was back at Friston at 15:40, all having been uneventful.

23 March 1944 – Most of the day was spent in practice flying, broken only by a brief and uneventful ASR patrol between 12:00 and 12:15. The Squadron was otherwise not called upon until 17:15, when they participated in a Ramrod, their first penetration of France in force in almost three weeks.

The Squadron was one of two units providing close support for two formations of RAF 2 Group Mitchells and Bostons tasked with attacking Noball targets southeast, and east, of Abbeville in northern France. It was also the first time that Sqn Ldr Glen had led the Squadron since 6 February, mainly on account of course attendance and leave.

Date	23 March 1944
Operation	Ramrod 680
Targets	1st Attack: Flixecourt-Domart-en-Ponthieu, Picardie 2nd Attack: Gorenflos, Picardie
Bombers	1st Attack: 24 Mitchells; 19 bombed 2nd Attack: 12 Bostons; 12 bombed
Close Escort, 1st Attack Close Escort, 2nd Attack	Friston: 41 Squadron (Spitfire XII) Hawkinge: 501 Squadron (6 Spitfire Vb & 3 Spitfire IX)

41 Squadron's twelve pilots were airborne at 17:15 and rendezvoused with the bombers at 10,000 feet over Beachy Head. The pilots provided an escort to the first of the two attacks, and reported heavy accurate Flak in the target area. In good weather and clear visibility, they were able to observe the bombing, which consisted of a total of one hundred and fifty-two 500 lb. bombs dropped from 12,000 feet. Many bursts were seen in the target area, and as the Luftwaffe did not interfere, the entire operation was otherwise uneventful. The Squadron landed back at Friston between 18:30 and 18:35, and this concluded the day's flying.

The second attack, escorted by 501 Squadron's Spitfires, took place approximately five minutes after the first, and was equally uneventful. However, the bombing was less accurate and many of the forty-eight 500 lb. bombs were seen to fall in fields southwest of the target area.

Flt Lts Tommy Burne AFC and Dave Fearon at Tangmere, ca. early 1944. © Ron Johnson, via Dan Johnson

24 March 1944 – The ORB's F540 offers very little detail on today's activity, confining a summary of the day's events to just two sentences. A Flight's Readiness Section and its two sections at 15 minutes flew a total of four ASR patrols between 07:10 and 09:40, and Fg Off Bill Stowe's logbook adds the detail that these were escorts to high-speed Motor Torpedo Boats returning from the French coast. All were uneventful. The only other flight undertaken today was an air test, flown by B Flight's Flt Sgt Freddie Woollard.

25 March 1944 – The day commenced at 08:00 with a scramble by B Flight's Plt Off Peter Graham and Fg Off 'Momo' Balasse, who were sent up to intercept a Luftwaffe aircraft at 10,000 feet over Beachy Head. On reaching this location, there was nothing to be seen, so the pair were given a new vector of 190° and told to climb to 18,000 feet and conduct a weather reconnaissance of Dieppe.[33] They returned to Friston at 08:50 reporting 10/10ths cloud at 6,000 feet with thick haze below this altitude.

Whilst they were airborne, another section, consisting of Fg Off Ron Johnson and Flt Sgt Freddie Woollard, was airborne at 08:15 and sent to St. Omer on a similar patrol. They were back at 09:20 to report the same conditions in that area, too.

There was no more operational flying until 15:50, when eleven pilots in three sections took off on a Rodeo to Évreux, led by Sqn Ldr Glen. However, Fg Off Peter Cowell, leading Yellow Section, returned within 15 minutes, after a near disaster. He recalled forty years later…

> *I was leading a section of the Squadron with Peter Gibbs as my No 2 on a Fighter Sweep. We were to cross the Channel at 0 feet & then climb rapidly just before reaching the French coast to avoid enemy radar in the usual way.*
> *The sea was like a mill pond – flat calm & there was no horizon because of the haze & it was therefore difficult to gauge ones height accurately with nobody in front of you.*
> *I realised that I was a bit too close to the sea & was just easing back slightly on the stick when the prop hit & I was enveloped in a cloud of spray. Peter Gibbs actually had his hand on the R/T button to warn me as I hit.*
> *I pulled up to about 1000 ft & headed back for Friston but the speed was only about 120 mph & the vibration was tremendous. I really thought I was going to have to jump out or ditch. Peter Gibbs came back with me & I told Friston that I was in trouble.*
> *Suddenly the vibration ceased & the speed built up to about 200 mph & I afterwards found that the blades had shattered systematically to balance the prop which looked like this* [hand-drawn diagram inserted] *when I landed at Friston. I was left with about 18" on each blade and subsequently a picture appeared in "Flight" or "The Aeroplane", I forget which, demonstrating what a small prop the Spit could cope with!!*
> *[…] Actually, as I recall, it only needed a prop change & the engine was not damaged.*[34]

With Cowell (MB882) and Gibbs (MB845) on their way home, the remaining nine pilots made landfall at Lion-sur-Mer, 5km north of Caen on the Normandy coast at 16:25, then…

> *…turned east diving to 5,000 feet and passing just north of Bernay and Beaumont-le-Roger, whence accurate light flak drove us up to 8,000 feet. Then we came down again to 6,000 feet and turned west again just beyond Évreux visiting Conches on our way out by the same way we came in.*[35]

The Luftwaffe was not seen at all, and the pilots all returned to Friston without any ado, putting down again between 17:30 and 17:35. Fg Off Herb Wagner summed up Cowell's experience in his logbook today, "Peter Cowell flew into sea but got away with it."[36]

There was one further operation before flying concluded for the day, and this consisted of Fg Off Peter Cowell and Flt Sgt Peter Gibbs who undertook an ASR patrol from 18:55.[37] The pair were scrambled to search for a Marauder reported in the sea off Tocqueville, under Beachy Control, and vectored to a point approximately five miles west of Dieppe. On reaching the area, nothing could be seen and they were ordered back to base, where they landed again at 19:35.

26 March 1944 – Good weather heralded an early start for the Squadron this morning and, being on dawn readiness, A Flight flew three ASR patrols, Red Section airborne 06:20-07:44, Yellow 07:33-08:21, and Red again 08:18-10:25, with mixed success. They were tasked with locating an aircraft reported ditched off Beachy Head, and a Marauder in the Channel off Dieppe. The aircraft themselves were not seen, however…

1 TO 2 MILES OFF THE COAST AT DIEPPE STRETCHING A DISTANCE OF 15 MLS. WERE SMALL AREAS OF WRECKAGE AND POSSIBLY BODIES FLOATING ON THE SEA.[38]

Red Section also sighted a 40-foot boat with two masts in the bow approximately 200 yards off shore from St. Valery. Initially tempted to attack it, they observed gun fire from shore batteries bouncing off the water and decided against it! All three sections returned to Friston after otherwise uneventful patrols. Whilst these were on-going, an uneventful weather reconnaissance was also flown to Cherbourg by White Section, between 07:40 and 08:30.

B Flight came on duty before 12:00, and two sections were similarly sent on ASR patrols, between 11:20 and 13:10. This time, they were sent to a point approximately 17-20 miles south of Beachy Head to locate a bomber reported to have ditched there. The first section returned having seen nothing, but the second, comprising of Fg Off Ron Johnson and Flt Lt Tommy Burne, reported having seen "a white bottle shaped object about the size of a 45 gallon drop tank"[39] at the location assumed to have been where the bomber ditched. An Intelligence Report for the same patrol adds a little more detail, describing it as a "large white object shaped like a petrol capsule 2/3 ft out of water and 14" in diam[etre]."[40,41]

After lunch, the Squadron was airborne on another Ramrod, on this occasion providing close escort to 36 Marauders bombing a Noball site at Vacqueriette-Erquières in the Pas-de-Calais region. Their role was a small part in a much larger operation consisting of a total of 378 Marauders and 54 Bostons of the U.S. 9th Air Force, and 30 Mitchells from the RAF's 2 Group tasked with attacking the torpedo boat pens in the port at IJmuiden, in the Netherlands. Zero hour was set at 13:00.

Date	26 March 1944
Operation	Ramrod 689
Targets	1st-6th Attacks: IJmuiden port area, NL, TOT zero + 30, zero + 35, zero + 60, zero + 70, zero + 85, & zero + 100 7th Attack: Vacqueriette-Erquières, France, TOT zero + 60
Bombers	1st Attack: 30 Mitchells; 27 bombed, 54 tons 2nd Attack: 18 Bostons; 16 bombed, 15 tons 3rd Attack: 108 Marauders; 93 bombed, 154 tons 4th Attack: 54 Marauders; 47 bombed, 86 tons 5th Attack: 108 Marauders; 96 bombed, 175 tons 6th Attack: 108 Marauders; 102 bombed, 175 tons 7th Attack: 36 Bostons, 35 bombed, 34 tons
Casualties	180 Sqn: Mitchell II, CD/AA, CL Bungay, Suffolk; 323 BG/453 BS: Marauder 41-34853, SD/AA, IJmuiden
Escort, 1st Attack Escort, 2nd Attack Escort, 3rd Attack Escort, 4th Attack: Escort, 5th Attack: Escort, 6th Attack: Escort, 7th Attack: Target Supp't IJmuiden	Coltishall: 64 & 611 Squadrons (Spitfire Vb) Digby: 402 Squadron (Spitfire Vb) Hornchurch: 222 & 349 Squadrons (Spitfire IX) North Weald: 66 & 331 Squadrons (Spitfire IX) Detling: 132, 453 & 602 Squadrons (Spitfire IX) Mendlesham: 310, 312 & 313 Squadron (Spitfire IX) Friston: 41 Squadron (Spitfire XII) Gravesend: 19, 65 & 122 Squadrons (Mustang III)
Casualties	65 Sqn: Fg Off Neville E. S. Mutter crashed on TO, fault with Mustang III, FZ117, YT-G, pilot unhurt, A/C Cat. E.

For their part, 41 Squadron had eleven pilots airborne at 13:45, led by Sqn Ldr Glen. They made rendezvous with the Bostons over Beachy Head at 10,000 feet, and could see Flak already in the air, though well ahead of them, as they crossed in over the Somme Estuary. None, however, was directed at the Squadron throughout the operation and it ran according to plan.

Although the first attack mainly undershot, they dropped one hundred and eight 1,000lb bombs, and the second attack, which dropped sixty-one 500lb bombs, was unable to see their results owing to smoke from the first. Otherwise, for all intents and purposes, the bombing went well, and the 11 Group ORB Appendix's report on the Ramrod records the bombing in the remaining attacks as 'good results', 'bombing excellent', 'fair results', 'fair to good results', and 'good results'.

41 Squadron concurred. In an Intelligence Report reporting their participation in the seventh attack, they noted, "Bombing Conc[entrated] and on target. Bomber formation excellent simplifying escort duties".[42] They landed again at 14:50, having seen no sign of the Luftwaffe.

The only other flight of note that took place today was when WO 'Archie' Appleton flew his first on the Spitfire XII, an undertaking known for the difficulty it presented a pilot as the propeller torque pulled in the opposite direction to all other production Spitfires to date.

27 March 1944 – Weather once again hampered operations and a cloud base of just 1,000 feet kept the Squadron on the ground almost all day. The only exceptions were two uneventful ASR patrols during the afternoon, the first of which conducted a search below the cloud base between 15:00 and 16:20 for a Flying Fortress lost ten miles south of Dungeness. The second, airborne at 17:32, was sent ten miles out on a vector of 260°, then another 50 miles on a vector of 240°, searching east and west. Seeing nothing, they were ordered back to base and landed at 18:16, concluding the day's flying.

28 March 1944 – With B Flight on readiness, A Flight was free to spend the morning on practice flying. Throughout this time, B Flight was only called on once operationally, to conduct a weather reconnaissance to Cherbourg. This was undertaken by Plt Off Peter Graham and Fg Off 'Momo' Balasse from 10:15, who reported 1/10th cloud at 18,000 feet and light haze up to 8,000 feet on their return at 11:00.

There was no further operational flying until mid-afternoon when the Squadron was assigned a Rodeo over northern France. Twelve pilots took off at 15:58, with Sqn Ldr Glen leading, but Fg Off Keith Curtis (MB845) returned within five minutes. This was likely the result of engine trouble, but the ORB provides no explanation.

The rest of the pilots crossed in at Lion-sur-Mer at 11,000 feet[43] and flew a similar route to their Rodeo of 25 March, sweeping the airfields at Bernay, Beaumont-le-Roger, Conches, St. André and Évreux. However, there was no sign of the Luftwaffe on the ground or in the air.

Attempting to entice a reaction, the Squadron orbited Conches at 8,000 feet[44], but they failed to draw a single burst of Flak. At Bernay Airfield, they sighted transport moving around the perimeter track, but as they were hunting for aircraft, left the vehicles alone and did not attack. Having found no trace of the Luftwaffe, and having elicited no reaction from anti-aircraft fire, the Squadron headed home empty-handed, via the route of the Seine to the Channel and landed at Friston between 17:20 and 17:30.

31 March 1944 – Following two days of poor weather, which had allowed no operational flying whatsoever, the Squadron was in the air again today, albeit in a reduced capacity. The pilots had been briefed for a Ramrod at 08:15, but weather initially postponed, and eventually cancelled, the operation.

The only operational flying all day therefore consisted of two ASR patrols[45], in a wide area approximately 30 miles south of Beachy Head, 10:55-12:05 and 13:15-14:40. The first section saw nothing but a stray buoy, and the second nothing at all, and could only report thick haze to 3,000 feet on their return.

At 13:40, Fg Off 'Charlie' van Goens took off again to continue his tour of RAF bases to display the Spitfire XII, having arrived late the previous afternoon, literally on a flying visit.

April 1944 – Once again, weather made a significant dent in the flying programme this month, and no operational flying was undertaken on nine days, 2, 4-5, 7, 10, 16-17, 24 and 28 April 1944, whilst operations were significantly reduced on another eight: 3, 8-9, 11, 13-15 and 22 April. The Squadron also moved to Bolt Head after seven weeks at Friston, and as the launch of the Second Front drew nearer, the Squadron's personnel found leave cancelled and mail censored.

Gun Emplacement   Noball Target   Marshalling Yard

Date	Operation	Role	Type	Destination / Target
18	Ramrod 742	Close Escort	Gun Emplacement	Fécamp, France
19	Ramrod 748	Close Escort	Noball	Linghem, France
19	Ramrod 753	Target Patrol	Noball	Abbeville area, France
20	Ramrod 756	Close Escort	Noball	Gorenflos, France
20	Ramrod 760	Close Escort	Noball	Vacqueriette-Erquières, France
21	Ramrod 762	Escort Cover	Noball	Le Plouy Ferme, France
23	Ramrod 778	Close Escort	Noball	Béhen, France
26	Ramrod 799	Close Escort	Noball	Belleville-en-Caux, France
27	Ramrod 800	Close Escort	Gun Emplacement	Ouistreham, France
27	Ramrod 802	Close Escort	Marshalling Yard	Béthune, France

1 April 1944 – The day commenced with hazy weather, which cleared around midday, allowing Fg Off Clive Birbeck and Flt Sgt Bob Fleming to get airborne as Blue Section at 12:40 on an ASR patrol for two American Thunderbolt pilots believed to have baled out five miles west of Boulogne. Soon after they were airborne, however, they were diverted instead to a point 20 miles south of Dungeness to intercept three inbound B-24 Liberators of the US 8th Air Force, one of which was in distress. As a result, Green Section, consisting of Plt Off Jimmy Payne and Flt Sgt Freddie Woollard, were sent up only ten minutes after the former section's departure to search for the Thunderbolt pilots.

Birbeck and Fleming found a lone bomber at 2,000 feet, and escorted her to the coast at Hastings, then returned towards the same location where they saw a second Liberator, this one flying at 9,000 feet with one feathered engine, slowly losing altitude. They escorted this bomber to Dungeness, and were then ordered back onto their original job, to find the Thunderbolt pilots.

Just before their return, Birbeck and Fleming sighted an object in the Channel around 40 miles east-southeast of Beachy Head, which they believed was a parachute, but it sank shortly afterwards.

Then, between one and two miles upwind of this location, they thought they saw "what might have been a dinghy"[46] but then lost sight of it, and could not locate it again. Nonetheless, the pair reported both positions via R/T, and then returned to Friston, putting down again at 13:55.

Meanwhile, Payne and Woollard had spent a good hour searching for the Thunderbolt pilots themselves in poor visibility with thick haze, but were unsuccessful. They did, however, spot a yellow mine with a black spot on top floating on the surface around 25 miles southeast of Hastings, which they reported, and then returned to base at 14:10.

Green Section were relieved by Red Section, consisting of Fg Offs Harry Cook and 'Jack' Malone, who were off the deck a 14:00, but they were compelled to return again within ten minutes when Cook's aircraft developed engine trouble.[47] As such, as Payne, Woollard, Cook and Malone were landing, Fg Off Keith Curtis and Flt Sgt Ian Stevenson took off as Yellow Section to take their place. However, it was to no avail, as nothing further was seen, and they returned empty-handed at 15:20.[48]

The last patrol of the day came at 17:25 when Fg Off Ron Johnson and Flt Lt Tommy Burne were sent on an ASR patrol of the Portland area during a glider exercise. However, the exercise was cancelled and the pair recalled to base, landing again at 17:40.

3 April 1944 – The only operational flight undertaken by the Squadron all day was a weather reconnaissance to Cherbourg and Abbeville by Plt Off Jimmy Payne and Flt Sgt Bob Fleming between 07:05 and 07:45. The Friston area was hazy, and they encountered 8/10ths cloud at 5,000 feet all the way across the Channel. They returned to report the weather in Cherbourg was clear to 3,000 feet with haze above this level. The Squadron was not called upon again all day, allowing for limited flying practice during the afternoon.

6 April 1944 – Following two days of poor weather, which had allowed no operational flying, the Squadron was airborne again today, to a limited extent, and flew two patrols during the morning. Although the cloud base lay at 1,500 feet at dawn, Plt Offs Payne and Fisher took off at 07:05 to conduct a weather reconnaissance to Amiens.

The low cloud over Friston thickened to 10/10th across the Channel and French coast, but the pair climbed above its ceiling to find clear skies from 4,000 feet. Amiens was completely free of cloud, as was the area south of the town, but the pilots could see nothing else worthy of reporting. They landed at Friston again at 07:50.

The morning's second patrol was airborne at 10:25 when Flt Lt Collis and Flt Sgt Stevenson flew a weather reconnaissance to Gravelines and St. Pol. They climbed through 10/10ths cloud after becoming airborne and returned at 11:45 reporting the same weather conditions at their destinations. There followed three non-operational flights, but when the weather came down at 14:00, all flying ceased.

The only other event worth of mention today, was an incident in the Officers Mess late that night that "considerably enlivened"[49] the evening. The ORB records,

> F/LT. LORD GISBOROUGH was endeavouring to run a hot bath and when turning on the hot tap, the whole fixture turned and came out. The resultant floods brought down the kitchen ceiling with a certain amount of damage, but no casualties. The only sufferer was LORD GISBOROUGH himself who was valiantly trying to stop the flood of boiling water with his thumb while yelling vainly for assistance.[50]

8 April 1944 – Following yet another day of inaction due to poor weather, conditions had barely improved today to a cloud base of 2,000 feet, which once again significantly hindered operations. As such, the only operational flying undertaken by the Squadron was a single weather reconnaissance to Gravelines and St. Pol by Flt Lt Don Smith (MB882) and Fg Off 'Jack' Malone (MB858).

The pair was airborne at 10:20 as Red Section and flew as far as St. Omer and Abbeville, sighting six small ships near the broken mole at Boulogne Harbour, which they thought were Flak or sea-going barges. On return from their otherwise uneventful trip, they also reported 10/10th cloud at St. Omer and Abbeville, haze but no cloud over Boulogne or the Channel.

If anyone was in any doubt as to the proximity of the launch of the long-rumoured 'Second Front', new security regulations introduced at Friston today confirmed the day was drawing near.

> *Censorship of Unit mail came into force at R.A.F. Station, Friston, and at the same time instructions were received regarding the suspension of privilege leave for all personnel.*[51]

As the month progressed, Friston, and its satellite airfield Deanland, were kept very busy building up stores reserves in preparation for what would become known as D-Day. Personnel strength was also increased to fill all establishment vacancies, including those of the WAAF.

9 April 1944 – Easter Sunday was a quiet day, upon which the weather across the Channel hindered activity. At 10:20, Blue Section (Fisher MB829 & Fearon MB847) was sent on a weather reconnaissance of Le Havre and Fécamp, but within minutes Fearon developed engine trouble and returned to base at 10:30. Fisher appears to have initially carried on alone but was then recalled, as he put down at 10:40.

As Fearon landed, Green Section (Slack MB837 & Woollard MB804) took off to relieve them, and was able to complete the job. They returned at 11:40 reporting 9/10ths cloud at 8,000 feet, but nothing else of consequence. Flt Lt Fearon was scheduled to fly again, this time in MB842 with Flt Sgt Bob Fleming in MB830, but the patrol was cancelled and there was no further operational flying all day.

11 April 1944 – "At last a really fine day!", begins the ORB today, adding "but only two operational sorties were flown."[52] Indeed, the Squadron was only called upon to undertaken two ASR patrols, and the first of these was not airborne until 12:05. At that time, Blue Section took off to search for a Marauder believed to have ditched off Dieppe. They returned at 13:05, having seen no sign of it, and were replaced in the air by Yellow Section five minutes later. This pair also searched to no avail, and landed again at 14:30 with nothing further to report.

During the day, however, several practice flights were undertaken by the pilots, but the most interesting event was the most unusual award of the Russian Medal for Valour to OC A Flight, Flt Lt Donald Smith RAAF. The recommendation read:

> *This officer is a daring and skilful fighter who has served both in this country* [i.e. the United Kingdom] *and in Malta. He has destroyed four enemy aircraft including two bombers. On one occasion, when flying alone over Malta, he attacked and shot down a bomber which was escorted by four fighters. In the combat his own aircraft was extensively damaged. In operations whilst serving in England he has continued to display great courage and fine fighting qualities.*[53]

Smith had never spent a day in a Russian battle or on a Russian front, but it appears the Soviet Government had offered the British a block of Russian honours, to be distributed as the British considered suitable. The majority were allocated to Royal Navy personnel, but a number went to RAF personnel if a Russian connection could be established. In Smith's case, this appears to have been 'personnel escorting Russian-bound convoys'. The Soviets had probably never heard of him, but the Air Ministry decided to award it to someone deserving and settled on Smith, who would shortly be promoted to lead his own squadron and would also be awarded the DFC before the year was out.[54]

12 April 1944 – Perfect weather from dawn to dusk with cloudless skies allowed the first solid day's flying in some time. Flying commenced at 07:40, continued through until 21:20, and included six operational patrols and 26 non-operational sorties.

The first operation of the day was a weather reconnaissance to Renaix and Brussels, in Belgium, flown by Flt Lt 'Joe' Birbeck (EN605) and Fg Off 'Momo' Balasse (MB842) as Blue Section. They found good weather on the Continent, and sighted a 1,000-ton ship with steam up outside the mole at Dunkirk, with several barges moored around it. The pair returned to Friston at 09:20, having put down at Manston first to refuel at 08:45.

Before their return, two more sections were airborne on weather reconnaissances, the first, Black Section (Thiele & Fleming) at 09:04 to Gravelines, St. Pol and Abbeville, and the second, Green Section (Payne & Woollard) only a minute later to Amiens and Dieppe.

As the former section flew between St. Pol and Abbeville at 12,000 feet, they were followed by an aircraft, approximately 10,000 feet above them, emitting vapour trails. They were also fired upon by heavy Flak from Calais and, although accurate in height, burst approximately four miles astern of them. Thiele & Fleming returned at 10:04, reporting 4-5/10ths cloud at 8,000 feet at Gravelines, 8-9/10ths at 8,000 feet over St. Pol, 8/10ths at 8,000 feet over Abbeville, and 4-5/10ths over the Channel.[55]

The latter section were back just six minutes later reporting only light cloud across the Channel, along the French coast and at Dieppe, but 9/10ths cloud with haze at Amiens. Their trip was otherwise uneventful.

There followed a 2½-hour break in operational flying, which ended at 14:35, when Flt Lt Tom Slack and Fg Off Balasse were sent on an ASR search for a bomber crew off Boulogne. The pair was vectored 120° to ten miles off the French coast at altitudes of between zero and 2,000 feet, and although the weather was fine with visibility of 15 miles, they were unable to locate the crew. However, they returned at 15:45 reporting having sighted a "barrel, two floating mines and a large shoal of porpoises"[56] in the search area!

There was then another almost four-hour break in operational flying, during which several non-operational flights were made in relation to a visit to the Squadron by one of the RAF's official photographers, B. J. Daventry[57], who had come to capture the Spitfire XII on film. Daventry took a series of photographs of the Squadron's aircraft, and in particular of OC, A Flight, Flt Lt Don Smith's Spitfire, MB882, EB-B. Some of these images appeared in the national newspapers just days later, thereunder the *Daily Mirror* on 20 April 1944, whilst others featured in *Flight* magazine's editions of 20 April and 4 May 1944. The images are still well known today.[58]

The fun over, it was back to work again at 19:30 when Fg Offs Ken Robinson and 'Jack' Malone were sent to an area ten miles south of Beachy Head for a defensive patrol, and to assist any bombers seen to be returning in distress. They landed again at 20:35, reporting having seen a "high vapour trail over Portsmouth making one orbit".[59] They were relieved by another section comprising Flt Lts Dave Fearon and 'Jimmy' Thiele, who patrolled uneventfully for one hour and returned on dusk at 21:20, reporting only 3/10ths cloud at 5,000 feet with visibility deteriorating. This concluded the day's flying.

13 April 1944 – The new day dawned to poor weather with 9/10ths cloud at 3,000 feet, which did not bode well for flying. Nonetheless, Fg Offs Herb Wagner and 'Andy' Anderson were airborne at 06:45 for a weather reconnaissance to Cherbourg. The pair returned at 07:30 reporting 10/10ths cloud over the peninsula at 8,000 feet, with haze below this altitude. There were a few practice flights throughout the day, but there was otherwise no operational flying, and nothing of importance worthy of reporting.

14 April 1944 – The day started clear and sunny, but varying levels of haze and visibility throughout the day limited operational flying to just two patrols. The first of these was airborne at 06:40 when Flt Lt 'Joe' Birbeck and Fg Off 'Momo' Balasse were sent on a weather reconnaissance to Dieppe and Amiens. They found enough low cloud in these areas to make bombing operations unsuitable and landed again at 07:45 in increasing haze at Friston.

For the ensuing three hours, haze dominated conditions and hindered operational flying, although Fg Off Ken Robinson was able to get airborne at 11:00 for a non-operational flight to Holmsley South, where he relieved Fg Off 'Charlie' van Goens, who was detached for display purposes to show the Spitfire XII to the RAF and other Allied air force units. Whilst Robinson flew to Holmsley without problem, the weather continued to deteriorate at Friston to low cloud and rain, and Van Goens was compelled to wait until 14:20 before he could return to the unit.

Later that afternoon, three non-operational sorties were flown, but it was not until 19:40 that the Squadron was airborne for its second and final patrol of the day. At that time, Flt Lt Don Smith and Flt Sgt 'Steve' Stevenson took off on an ASR patrol to mid-Channel. It was, however, uneventful, and the pair returned at 20:45 reporting having seen nothing.

Separately today, a new pilot joined the Squadron in the form of 24-year-old Australian Fg Off John G. H. Refshauge, who was assigned to A Flight. Having completed his flying training in Australia up to the point of earning his Wings and a commission, Refshauge shipped to the United Kingdom in August 1942, and was posted to the ATA at White Waltham in early February 1943 as a Flying Officer. He subsequently attended (P)AFU and OTU, before being posted to 1685 Bomber Defence Training Flight at RAF Ossington as a Staff Pilot in June 1943. He remained with this unit until January 1944 when he was posted to 453 (Australian) Squadron at Detling. However, he was ill during this time and unable to undertake any flying. Following sick leave and a refresher course, Refshauge was posted to 41 Squadron and arrived today.[60]

15 April 1944 – The weather today was similar to the previous in that conditions only allowed flying early in the morning and in the evening, and only three patrols were flown all day.

Fg Offs Peter Cowell and 'Andy' Anderson flew the first of these, a weather reconnaissance to Cherbourg, at 06:55. The pair landed at Friston again at 07:40 through cloud, but reported no low cloud in the Cherbourg area, although there was 10/10ths at 21,000 feet. Visibility up-sun was 70 miles and down-sun 30 miles, the skies were good up to 20,000 feet over the Channel, and the sea was calm.

Throughout the day, weather conditions improved sufficiently to allow A Flight to do some practice formation flying, but B Flight did not fly at all. The Squadron was otherwise not called upon again operationally until after 20:00 when, in the space of 30 minutes, two sections were scrambled to intercept incoming plots.

Yellow Section (Collis & Anderson) was airborne at 20:05 and Red Section (Smith & Stevenson) at 20:30 and sent to a point 30 miles southwest of Beachy Head. However, neither section sighted anything and they returned at 21:00 and 21:05, respectively, reporting 5/10ths to 10/10ths cloud between 1,500 and 20,000 feet, with visibility of 10-15 miles.

18 April 1944 – The day began foggy, but the mist lifted by midday to reveal a fine afternoon. Several practice flights were undertaken by A Flight after this time, as well as a number of non-operational flights, but the Squadron was not called on operationally until after 18:30, when the unit provided close escort to bombers for the first time in over three weeks. In that operation, a combination of U.S. 9th Air Force and RAF 2 TAF bombers attacked coastal batteries and a V-Weapon (Noball) target in Northern France, and a railway marshalling yard in Belgium, supported by USAAF Thunderbolt bombers, and escorted by RAF Spitfire squadrons.

Date	18 April 1944
Operation	Ramrod 742
Target, Parts A, B & C	Charleroi Marshalling Yards, Belgium
Target, Part D	Gun batteries, Fécamp, Haute-Normandie, France
Target, Part E	Noball site, Le Plouy Ferme, Pas-de-Calais, France
Target, Part F	Gun Battery, Varengeville-sur-Mer, Seine-Maritime, France
Target, Part G	Heavy Railway Battery, Sangatte, France
Target, Part H	Coastal Defences, Dunkirk & Calais, France
Bombers, Part A	US 9th AF: 36 Marauders — Total of 96 Marauders & 36 Bostons dropped 220½ tons of bombs
Bombers, Part B	US 9th AF: 72 Marauders
Bombers, Part C	US 9th AF: 72 Bostons
Bombers, Part D	RAF 2 TAF: 30 Mitchells; 24 dispatched, 22 bombed
Bombers, Part E	RAF 2 TAF: 24 Bostons; 24 dispatched, 23 bombed
Bombers, Part F	RAF 2 TAF: 12 Mosquitos; 12 dispatched, 10 bombed
Bombers, Part G	US 9th AF: 72 Marauders
Bombers, Part H	US 9th AF: 72 Marauders
Escort, Part A	32 USAAF Thunderbolt bombers (2x 250lb each)
Escort, Part B	32 USAAF Thunderbolt bombers (2x 250lb each)
Escort, Part C	Appledram: Spitfires[61]
Close Escort, Part D	Friston: 41 Squadron (12 Spitfire XII)
Close Escort, Part E	Hawkinge: 501 Squadron (11 Spitfire Vb)
Close Escort, Part F	None
Fighter Umbrella	Spitfires in target area[62]

For their part, 41 Squadron was airborne at 18:35 in Red, Blue and Yellow Sections and rendezvoused with the Part D bombers over Hastings at 12,000 feet at 18:50. Making a vector for Fécamp, they were over the target area at 19:21, where they observed the Mitchells bombing run in three boxes of eight aircraft in clear skies.

The bombers dropped a total of one hundred and seventy-six 500lb bombs from 10,000 feet, but the first box undershot the target and their payload landed on the cliff edge, the second dropped just inside the target area, and the third dropped well short, and into the sea. The Luftwaffe did not interfere, and "Flak was the only opposition".[63] However, it was both light and inaccurate in height, bursting approximately 1,500 feet below them.

501 Squadron was airborne to escort Part E at 18:45 and were over the target at Le Plouy Ferme at 19:16. They did not see the bombing results despite cloudless skies and good visibility, but the bombers themselves reported a good concentration of sixty-seven 500lb general purpose and twenty-four 50lb LD bombs in the target area, with the majority falling just south of the aiming point. 'Meagre' light inaccurate Flak was experienced from Berck airfield, but the Luftwaffe was not seen.

The Mosquitos in Part F attacked the medium gun battery at Varengeville with forty 500lb bombs from altitudes of 200-1,000 feet. Although some bursts undershot, and others overshot, many were seen on the target itself, which was well concealed with dark netting. Two of the Mosquitos also attacked a Flak position with unobserved results.

All the bombers and Mosquitos returned to base unscathed, and the trip was equally as uneventful for both 41 and 501 Squadrons, which returned to their bases at 19:55, respectively 19:45.

The bombing in Parts A, B, and C was considered to have ranged from poor to excellent, whilst that of Parts G and H was blind, but felt to have yielded poor to good results. All the bombers and escort fighters returned to their respective bases without any casualties.

19 April 1944 – The day began foggy, but it cleared around 10:00 and by the end of the day, the pilots had participated in two Ramrods and a scramble, totalling 26 sorties. The initial operation was a close escort to the first of three attacks on four Noball targets by Mitchells and Bostons in northern France.

Flt Lt Dave Fearon, in the cockpit, being assisted on return from an operation, early 1944. © Jean-Louis Roba

Date	19 April 1944
Operation	Ramrod 748
Targets	1st Attack: Linghem, Pas-de-Calais 2nd Attack: Bonnières & Beauvoir, Pas-de-Calais 3rd Attack: Vacqueriette-Erquières, Pas-de-Calais
Bombers	1st Attack: 12 Mitchells; 12 bombed 2nd Attack: 24 Bostons; 21 bombed 3rd Attack: 12 Mitchells; 12 bombed
Close Escort, 1st Attack Fighter Umbrella	Friston: 41 Squadron (12 Spitfire XII) Deanland: 302 & 308 Squadrons (22 Spitfire IX)

The Squadron was airborne at 11:45 fitted with 30 gallon tanks and rendezvoused with the bombers at 11,000 feet over Hastings 12:00. They crossed the Channel together between Beachy Head and Le Tréport, finding 10/10ths cloud at 1,000-1,500 feet, decreasing to 6/10ths at 1,800 feet as they approached France. By the time they arrived over the target area at 12:23, the skies were clear.

The bombers went in at 12,000 feet and 41 Squadron at 13,000, and bombs were seen to fall all across the target. The Luftwaffe was not seen but light, generally inaccurate, Flak was experienced in the Berck area. One bomber was, however, damaged and this aircraft was escorted back across the Channel by Flt Lts 'Jimmy' Thiele and Dave Fearon. The operation was otherwise uneventful and the Squadron returned to Friston at 13:15, having not fired a shot.

The bombing results were thought to have been 'moderate', whilst the results of the attacks on the remaining three targets were considered 'fair'. 302 and 308 Squadrons, which were airborne at 11:55, also saw no sign of the Luftwaffe, but reported heavy accurate and intense Flak directed at the bombers from Frévent, and from Auxi-le-Chateau to Doullens. No casualties are recorded and the fighters landed again at 13:05.

At 17.30, twelve of 41 Squadron's pilots were airborne on their second Ramrod, on this occasion as an element of a large operation, which foresaw three attacks on Malines [Mechelen] Marshalling Yards, and seven attacks on Noball targets in northern France, by the USAAF's 322nd, 386th, 387th, 391st, and 394th Bomber Groups.

Date	19 April 1944
Operation	Ramrod 753
Targets	1st-3rd Attacks: Malines Marshalling Yards, Antwerpen, Belgium 4th Attack: Fôret de Tournehem, Pas-de-Calais, France 5th Attack: Bois de Cocove (Recques-sur-Hem), Pas-de-Calais, France 6th Attack: Bois de Huit Rues, Pas-de-Calais, France 7th Attack: Béhen, Picardie, France 8th Attack: Yvrench/Bois Carré & Petit Bois Tillencourt, Picardie, France 9th Attack: Watten, Pas-de-Calais, France 10th Attack: Watten, Pas-de-Calais, France
Bombers	1st Attack: 72 Marauders; 76 dispatched, 74 bombed 2nd Attack: 72 Marauders; 75 dispatched, 74 bombed 3rd Attack: 36 Marauders; 37 dispatched, 34 bombed 4th Attack: 36 Bostons; 37 dispatched, 37 bombed 5th Attack: 36 Marauders; 40 dispatched, 38 bombed 6th Attack: 36 Bostons; 35 dispatched, 35 bombed 7th Attack: 18 Bostons – cancelled 8th Attack: 24 Mitchells – cancelled 9th Attack: 18 Liberators – cancelled 10th Attack: 27 Liberators; numbers not available
Casualties	10th Attack: 448 BG/715 BS: B-24H Liberator 41-29565, SD/AA, Dunkirk
Close Escort	Westhampnett: 442 & 443 Squadrons (24 Spitfire IX) Lympne: 130 Squadron (12 Spitfire Vb) Deanland: 302 & 308 Squadrons (19 Spitfire IX) Appledram: 310, 312 & 313 Squadrons (34 Spitfire IX) Selsey: Cancelled
Target Patrol	Hawkinge: 501 Squadron (12 Spitfire Vb) Friston: 41 Squadron (12 Spitfire XII)
Casualties	130 Sqn: 1 A/C, tyre burst on TO; 312 Sqn: Flt Lt Bohuslav Budil, MK248, SD nr Malines, POW; 313 Sqn: WO Arnošt Mrtvý, MJ558, SD/KIA over target area

41 Squadron was airborne at 17:30, once again fitted with 30 gallon tanks, with orders to provide fighter cover in the Abbeville area at 15,000 feet between 18:00 and 18:05, supporting 501 Squadron in the same area at 13,000 feet.

It was somewhat messy, however, as the Squadron arrived in the area on time at 16,000 feet, to find 501 Squadron slightly above them at 16,500 feet, instead of 2,000 feet below them. The bombers did not appear until 18:10, and then only just, through thick haze, causing 41 Squadron to stay in the target area longer than anticipated.

The bombing from one box was nonetheless observed, and a large dust cloud was seen rise directly over the target. Flak was scarce and only a few inaccurate bursts of heavy calibre were seen to explode over the target area, whilst the Luftwaffe was completely absent.

Their job done, the Squadron headed for home at 18:15, passing a number of inbound Thunderbolts as they crossed out over the French coast. However, "nothing else of interest was observed"[64], and the pilots landed back at Friston again at 18.45.

It had not as quiet in other sectors of the Ramrod, and claims were made and losses reported on both sides. Whilst bombing was considered fair to good, one Liberator was lost to Flak on the Watten attack. Local reports later indicated the bombing had indeed been effective as the locomotive repair shops at Malines had suffered structural or superficial damage to 94% of the buildings.

Earlier in the operation, as the escort formations were entering France, they were approached by a yellow-nosed Thunderbolt, which they felt was likely an enemy spotter. This is supported by the fact that two of the Czech squadrons were attacked by an estimated eight FW190s and twenty Me109s of I./JG26 and 4./JG26, whilst still approximately 15 miles west of Malines. These fighters made repeated attacks on 312 and 313 Squadrons, who returned to home without a pilot from each squadron.

Budil was shot down and captured near Malines and spent the rest of the War behind wire, but Mrtvý was killed in action and is buried today in Antwerp. The Czechs were unable to make any claims of their own against the Luftwaffe, but 443 Squadron's Sqn Ldr Henry W. McLeod DFC* claimed one destroyed Do217 in the Tirlemont [Tienen] area.

Meanwhile, back at Friston, 41 Squadron's operational flying was not quite over for the day. At 20:25, Red Section (Smith MB882 & Collis EN620) was scrambled to a position 20 miles into the Channel. Reaching the area within ten minutes, there was nothing to be seen, so they headed west for a short while, before heading home again. They landed at 20:45 with nothing to report but haze up to 5,000-6,000 feet and deteriorating visibility.

20 April 1944 – Similarly to the previous day, today also dawned to foggy conditions, which lifted during the morning. The Squadron's operational flying then began, and consisted solely of two Ramrod operations (24 sorties) to Noball targets in northern France, the first to Gorenflos and the second to Vacqueriette.

The former attack consisted of no less than ten attacks by 180 Marauders on coastal batteries, and four attacks on Noball targets, all provided with fighter cover. 41 Squadron supported the last of these.

Date	20 April 1944
Operation	Ramrod 756
Targets	1st-2nd Attacks: Medium battery, Trouville-sur-Mer, Haute-Normandie 3rd-4th Attacks: Medium battery, Fécamp, Haute-Normandie 5th-6th Attacks: Medium battery, Varengeville-sur-Mer, Haute-Normandie 7th-8th Attacks: Heavy railway battery, Marquise, Pas-de-Calais 9th-10th Attacks: Railway battery, Étaples, Pas-de-Calais 11th Attack: Noball, Le Plouy Ferme, Pas-de-Calais 12th Attack: Noball, Fôret de Tournehem, Pas-de-Calais 13th Attack: Noball, Flixecourt-Domart-en-Ponthieu, Picardie 14th Attack: Noball, Gorenflos, Picardie
Bombers	1st-2nd Attacks: 2x18 Marauders; 36 dispatched, 36 bombed 3rd-4th Attacks: 2x18 Marauders; 36 dispatched, 33 bombed 5th-6th Attacks: 2x18 Marauders; 38 dispatched, all abortive 7th-8th Attacks: 2x18 Marauders; 37 dispatched, 31 bombed 9th-10th Attacks: 2x18 Marauders; 38 dispatched, 26 bombed 11th Attack: 36 Marauders; 38 dispatched, 18 bombed 12th Attack: 36 Marauders; 40 dispatched, 36 bombed 13th Attack: 36 Marauders; 36 dispatched, all abortive 14th Attack: 36 Marauders; 38 dispatched, all abortive
Escort	1st-2nd Attacks: Selsey: 222 Squadron (12 Spitfire IX) 3rd-4th Attacks: Selsey: 485 Squadron (12 Spitfire IX) 5th-6th Attacks: Selsey: 349 Squadron (12 Spitfire IX) 7th-8th Attacks: Detling: 132 & 453 Sqns (24 Spitfire IX) 9th-12th Attacks: Appledram: 310, 312 & 313 Sqns (36 Spitfire IX) 13th Attack: Lympne: 130 Squadron (12 Spitfire Vb) 14th Attack: Friston: 41 Squadron (12 Spitfire XII)
Casualties	Detling: 2 A/C mechanical problems, RTB, 1 A/C escorted; Appledram: 2 A/C mechanical problems, RTB

For their part, 41 Squadron was airborne at 13:20, and climbed through 8/10ths cloud to rendezvous with the bombers over Friston. They crossed the French coast to find 6/10ths cloud at 10,000 feet, but continued on the Gorenflos, where they found 8-9/10ths cumulus from 5,000-8,000 feet, and 9-10/10ths stratus from 9,000-10,000 feet. It came as no surprise, therefore, that the bombers aborted the attack, considering visibility too poor to make an accurate attack.[65] 41

Squadron returned to base at 14:40, with nothing to report but weather conditions over France.

Although the attacks on the medium battery at Varengeville and the Noball target at Flixecourt were also aborted for 'technical reasons', respectively as a result of poor visibility due to cloud cover over the target area, the remaining attacks went ahead with varying degrees of success. Trouville received 70 tons of bombs with considered poor results, Fécamp 65 tons with excellent results, Marquise 48 tons with poor to fair results, Étaples 49 tons with fair results, and Le Plouy Ferme 35 tons with fair to good results. Only 17 aircraft attacked the primary target at Forêt de Tournehem with 32 tons, achieving poor results, but another 19 aircraft of the same formation attacked a radar station at Ostend [Oostende] instead, dropping 36 tons at this location, but once again only with poor results.

All the bombers and escort fighters returned home unscathed, having seen no sign of the Luftwaffe, and were otherwise unaffected by the minimal amounts of Flak encountered at Marquise and Poix.

At 19:30, twelve of 41 Squadron's pilots were airborne on the day's second Ramrod, this time escorting Bostons and Mitchells to a Noball target at Vacqueriette.[66]

Date	20 April 1944
Operation	Ramrod 760
Targets	1st Attack: Vacqueriette-Erquières, Pas-de-Calais 2nd Attack: Vacqueriette-Erquières, Pas-de-Calais
Bombers	1st Attack: 18 Bostons; 12 dispatched, all abortive 2nd Attack: 24 Mitchells; 24 dispatched, 18 abortive, 6 bombed secondary target at Ligescourt, Picardie
Close Escort	1st Attack: Lympne: 130 Squadron (12 Spitfire Vb) 2nd Attack: Friston: 41 Squadron (12 Spitfire XII)

Cloud and haze over the target area caused both attacks to be aborted, although six of the Mitchells in the second attack bombed Ligescourt, instead. Forty-eight 500lb bombs were dropped, and the results considered good. However, considerable heavy Flak was encountered around Arras and at least one Boston was hit, which Fg Off Herbert Wagner reported the Squadron escorted home again: "Came back with crippled Havoc".[67,68]

Although the escort was largely uneventful for 41 Squadron on account of the aborted attacks, Blue Section's pilots reported some unusual sightings after landing back at Friston at 20:50. Flt Lts Tom Slack and 'Jimmy' Thiele saw a number of "white small puffs 13000 ft. not flak"[69] whilst Flt Sgt Bob Fleming saw "quantities of small pieces of paper or cardboard"[70] at the same altitude in the Abbeville-Amiens area. What they saw was probably 'Window', which the USAAF called 'Chaff', and was likely aluminium foil which had been dropped by the bombers to jam German radar.

Separately today, news reached the Squadron that Flt Lt Hugh Parry, who had been shot down the previous September, had become a Prisoner of War. Parry had been in hiding with the Resistance since then, but was betrayed and arrested in Paris by the Gestapo just before dawn on 7 February 1944. By the time the Squadron received this news, Parry had been interrogated by the Gestapo in Fresnes Prison in Paris and by the Luftwaffe at Dulag Luft, outside Frankfurt. He was now sitting in Stalag Luft III, Sagan, enveloped in the pall of depression, anger and shock in the wake of the recently failed "Great Escape", as we know it today, of 24 March 1944.

21 April 1944 – Fine and clear weather all day allowed the Squadron to make an early start to the day's Ramrods. The pilots were briefed at 08:15 for a 09:05 take-off to escort 30 Bostons and Mitchells to the Noball site at Le Plouy Ferme with 130 Squadron.

Date	21 April 1944
Operation	Ramrod 762
Targets	1st & 2nd Attacks: Le Plouy Ferme, Pas-de-Calais
Bombers	1st Attack: 18 Bostons; 18 bombed 2nd Attack: 12 Mitchells; 12 bombed
Escort Cover	Lympne: 130 Squadron (12 Spitfire Vb) Friston: 41 Squadron (11 Spitfire XII)
Casualties	130 Sqn: 1 A/C aborted; 41 Sqn: Flt Lt Clive R. Birbeck, EF Friston, DNTO

Flt Lt Clive Birbeck (EN605) suffered engine failure as the Squadron prepared for take-off and could not get airborne. The remaining 11 pilots were compelled to leave without him and crossed the Channel in good weather with perfect visibility and arrived over the target area at 15,000 feet between 09:30 and 09:40. Whilst 41 Squadron did not see the results of the bombing, 130 Squadron did, and reported it appeared to be well concentrated.

Indeed, subsequent reconnaissance photos showed the first attack made direct hits or near misses with forty-six 500lb medium capacity bombs with .025 second delay fuses and eight 500lb long delay bombs, whilst the second straddled the target area from southwest to northeast, with eighty-eight medium capacity.025 second fuses and eight long delay bombs.

There was no opposition from the Luftwaffe and only slight, inaccurate Flak was encountered. The operation was otherwise uneventful for all the participants, who returned to base without any problems. 41 Squadron put down at Friston at 10:05 with nothing to report, whilst 130 Squadron landed back at Lympne five minutes before them, reporting having seen three small ships at Boulogne and trucks on the beach at Plage St. Cecile.

Despite the good weather, 41 Squadron was not airborne again until 14:20, when Flt Lt Don Smith and Plt Off Peter Gibbs were scrambled and ordered onto a vector of 210° as Kriegsmarine E-Boats had been sighted approximately 50 miles off the coast. They reached the area at 14:35, but saw nothing, and returned at 14:50 reporting 10/10ths cloud at 15,000-20,000 feet, hazy conditions below the cloud base, and moderate but roughening seas.

Just five minutes after their return, Fg Off Herb Wagner and Flt Lt Ron Collis took off to search for "a Boston in the drink".[71] Sent on a bearing of 140° until two miles off the French coast, the pair made a square search of the coast from Cayeux-sur-Mer. Finding nothing, they were then ordered to Berck-sur-Mer, Dieppe and Hardelot, to continue the search just one mile off the coast. Their efforts were fruitless and they returned to Friston at 16:20, reporting having seen nothing but a fishing fleet between Dieppe and Cayeux, which they had "examined closely without result".[72] This concluded the day's operational flying.

22 April 1944 – Despite the day's good weather, only two operational patrols (four sorties) were undertaken, the first of which was not airborne until 17:30. The pilots filled the rest of the day on air-to-air firing and other practice flights. Fg Off Harry Cook flew to Thorney Island, Sussex, and the readiness sections "spent their time in the now habitual game of bridge".[73]

At 17:30, Fg Offs Peter Cowell and Bill Stowe took off for an ASR search for a dinghy reportedly in the Channel 20 miles south of Dungeness. They did not find any sign of the dinghy, but they did sight two sea mines around 20 miles and 190° south of Dungeness. Perhaps one of the mines had resulted in a misidentification as a dinghy. Cowell and Stowe returned at 18:00, reporting no cloud, but haze at 2,000 feet and smooth seas.

The second and last operational patrol of the day was airborne at 20:55 when Flt Lts Tom Slack and 'Jimmy' Thiele were scrambled to intercept a dusk reconnaissance flight by the Luftwaffe. They flew 30-40 miles on a bearing of 210° from Beachy Head, but found nothing and returned to base at 21:30 reporting cloudless but hazy conditions.

Fg Off (later Flt Lt) Bill Stowe RCAF served with 41 Squadron from 24 February 1944 to 24 April 1945. Posted to 130 Squadron as a Flight Commander in late April 1945, he returned to 41 Squadron as a Flight Commander two weeks later but was posted to a Canadian squadron on 20 June 1945. © Jack Malone

23 April 1944 – Despite good weather, it was a quiet day for the Squadron and most of the day was spent practice flying. Operational flying was confined to a single Ramrod to a Noball target at Béhen in the Somme Department of the Picardie Region in northern France by twelve pilots from 15:00.

Date	23 April 1944
Operation	Ramrod 778
Targets	1st Attack: Béhen, Picardie 2nd Attack: Yvrench/Bois Carré, Picardie
Bombers	1st Attack: 24 Mitchells; 21 bombed 2nd Attack: 18 Bostons; 18 bombed
Escort Cover	1st Attack: Friston 41 Squadron (12 Spitfire XII) 2nd Attack: Funtington: 442 Squadron (12 Spitfire IX)

41 Squadron was airborne at 15:05 and arrived over the target area at 15:36 in clear skies with good visibility. The Luftwaffe did not interfere in the first attack and bombing by 21 Mitchells went ahead according to plan. However, their aim was off and the one hundred and fifty-two 500lb GP bombs and sixteen 500lb LD bombs landed with what were considered poor results.

In the second attack, 442 Squadron was airborne at 14:45 with twelve aircraft but two aborted with equipment trouble, and the remaining ten continued on without them. They escorted the Bostons, which dropped sixty 500lb GP bombs and twelve 500lb LD bombs with poor to fair results, although one stick was seen to fall right across the centre of the target.

Having completed the job, all the participants returned home as "opposition was non-existent".[74] 41 Squadron landed at Friston at 16:05, and reported having seen a ship of approximately 800 tons berthed in the North Quay of Le Tréport, and this concluded the day's operational flying for the unit.

24 April 1944 – Thick haze dominated weather conditions throughout the day and no operational flying was undertaken whatsoever. The only flight of the day was when Sqn Ldr Glen landed at Friston at 16:05, on return from a visit to Leconfield, and the rest of the day's activity is summed

up thus in the ORB: "Numerous rubbers of bridge occupied most of the pilots for most of the day except for those officers who had to do their share of censoring letters."[75]

25 April 1944 – Whilst some practice flying was undertaken today, only two operational patrols (four sorties) were flown all day. The first of these took place at 11:45, when Plt Offs 'Jackie' Fisher and Peter Graham took off on an ASR patrol as Blue Section, to search for both a B-17 Flying Fortress and a Mustang.

Thirty miles south of Dungeness, they located a large oil patch, but whilst investigating it closer witnessed a "huge splash" some distance away, and approached the area to find "another patch of oil with bits of wreckage".[76] Clearly another aircraft had come down, broken up on impact and sunk immediately. They radioed back coordinates, and orbited the area until relieved by aircraft from another squadron.

At this time, Fisher and Graham departed to continue their search for the Fortress and Mustang, commencing a 20 mile square search off Berck-sur-Mer. However, only ten minutes into the search, they received a new order, to escort Fortresses and Liberators in distress, limping home to the English coast. The two pilots then returned to base at 13:00.[77]

It was not until just after 20:00 that the next operational patrol was airborne, the task this time to find a missing fighter pilot approximately 20 miles north of Fécamp. Yellow Section, consisting of Fg Offs Ken Robinson and 'Jack' Malone, took off at 20:05 and flew on a vector 220° for 50 miles, then 070° for 20 miles, followed by 235° for 20 miles, but saw absolutely nothing. They landed again at 21:15.

26 April 1944 – Good weather allowed an early start to the day, and as soon as sufficient light permitted, B Flight sent up two sections of two pilots, "in the hope of catching the odd Hun recco".[78] Both sections were airborne at 06:30 and Blue (Birbeck MB804 & van Goens MB847) was given various vectors to the Isle of Wight where they orbited two MTBs and seven other sea craft moving out to sea. On investigation, however, these proved to be Allied.

Meanwhile, Green Section (Burne MB880 & Johnson MB837) was vectored 180° for ten minutes at 10,000 feet, then ordered to search east and west of this location. However, nothing was seen. Both sections returned to base at 07:45 with nothing but weather conditions to report. "As usual," scoffs the ORB, "the enemy declined our company."[79]

Three hours later, Flt Lt Don Smith (MB882) and Flt Sgt 'Steve' Stevenson (MB795) were scrambled to intercept plots over the Channel. They reached the area only to find four USAAF Mustangs orbiting smoke floats, and returned to base at 11:35, reporting this fact and 9/10ths cloud at 6,000 feet.

Mid-afternoon, the pilots were briefed for another Ramrod, once again to Noball targets, but this time on a much smaller scale than previously, with only twelve 2 Group bombers involved in two attacks, escorted by a total of 18 fighters.

Date	26 April 1944
Operation	Ramrod 799
Targets	1st Attack: Yvrench, Picardie 2nd Attack: Belleville-en-Caux, Haute-Normandie
Bombers 1st Attack Bombers 2nd Attack	21 Sqn: 5 Mosq & 487 Sqn: 1 Mosq – all aborted 226 Sqn: 6 Mitchells; 6 bombed
Escort Cover 1st Attack Escort Cover 2nd Attack	Bradwell Bay: 124 Squadron (6 Spitfire VII) Friston: 41 Squadron (12 Spitfire XII)

41 Squadron took off at 16:20 in Red, Blue and Yellow Sections of four aircraft each, led by Sqn Ldr Glen, and rendezvoused with the Mitchells over Selsey Bill. They crossed the Channel together and made landfall at Le Tréport, arriving over the target area at 17:00.

The Mitchells dropped their payloads from the west in a "close concentration dead on target",[80] straddling the area from west-southwest of the target to its centre, and orange-red explosions were seen. So accurate and successful was the bombing, felt 41 Squadron, the target area was "completely obliterated by bomb-bursts".[81] The pilots returned to base at 17:30 and this concluded the day's operational flying.

The first attack, however, was less successful and aborted whilst still 15 miles west of the French coast, as the PFF aircraft, a 21 Squadron Mosquito, developed engine trouble and had to return. Without their pathfinder, the remaining five aircraft were also compelled to return, and the attack was abandoned. Unable to contact their escort, 124 Squadron was oblivious to the Mosquitos' return, and the fighters continued on to the target, where they orbited briefly, then headed home again, putting down at 17:45.

27 April 1944 – Excellent weather meant a busy day for the Squadron, which involved two Ramrod operations and two scrambles, totalling 28 sorties. The day's operational activity began with an escort to Marauders attacking Ouistreham, as a part of a larger 2 Group operation, targeting eight coastal batteries and marshalling yards.

Date	27 April 1944
Operation	Ramrod 800
Targets	1st Attack: Marshalling yards, Monceau-sur-Sambre, Belgium 2nd Attack: Medium battery, Ste. Marie-au-Bosc, Haute-Normandie, France 3rd Attack: Medium coastal battery, Fort-Mardyck, Pas-de-Calais, France 4th Attack: Medium coastal battery, Gravelines, Pas-de-Calais, France 5th Attack: Heavy railway battery, Wimereux, Pas-de-Calais, France 6th Attack: Medium coastal battery, Hardelot, Pas-de-Calais, France 7th Attack: Medium coastal battery, St. Cécile, Pas-de-Calais, France 8th Attack: Coastal battery, Ouistreham, Basse-Normandie, France
Bombers	1st Attack: 72 Bostons; 37 bombed 2nd Attack: 30 Mitchells & 18 Bostons; 22 & 17 bombed 3rd Attack: 36 Marauders; 32 bombed 4th Attack: 36 Marauders; 37 bombed 5th Attack: 36 Marauders; 36 bombed 6th Attack: 36 Marauders; 36 bombed 7th Attack: 36 Marauders; 33 bombed 8th Attack: 36 Marauders; 37 bombed
Close Escort, 1st Attack	Selsey: 222, 349 & 485 Squadrons (34 Spitfire IX) Chailey: 302, 308 & 317 Squadrons (36 Spitfire IX)
Target Cover & Sweep, 2nd Attack	Tangmere: 403 Squadron (13 Spitfire IX)
Fighter Umbrella, 3rd & 4th Attacks	Detling: 132 & 602 Squadrons (24 Spitfire IX)
Fighter Umbrella, 5th, 6th & 7th Attacks	Funtington: 441 & 443 Squadrons (24 Spitfire IX)
Close Escort, 8th Attack	Friston: 41 Squadron (12 Spitfire XII)
Casualties:	Chailey: 1 A/C mechanical problems, RTB; 403 Sqn: 1 A/C EF, RTB; Detling, 1 A/C EF, RTB

41 Squadron was airborne at 10:10 in three sections of four pilots, led respectively by Sqn Ldr Glen and both Flight Commanders. They rendezvoused with 37 Marauders half way across the Channel, which were flying in formations of 19 and 18, and then in boxes of six, and one with seven. Landfall was made 13,000 feet over Fécamp where the formation turned southeast until the Seine was crossed. At this location, the fighters and bombers turned southwest and continued on this heading for 20 miles.

Now ten miles south of Ouistreham, the formation turned north and made a good bombing run over the target at 15,000 feet just before 11:00, despite thick haze and several bursts of heavy Flak, which were accurate in height but 50 yards wide of the mark. The Marauders dropped 72½ tons of bombs on the coastal batteries, all of which were seen to drop in the target area, with the exception of four, which fell in the town. There was no opposition from the Luftwaffe, and 41 Squadron was back on the ground at Friston at 11:45.

The other attacks in the Ramrod were made with results varying from unobserved, poor, fair and moderate to good. However, as the Luftwaffe was not seen by anyone, and the Flak was inaccurate, all aircraft returned to base with otherwise little to report.

There was no further flying for the Squadron until 14:30, when Red Section (Harding MB882 & Malone MB795) was scrambled to intercept a bogey off Beachy Head. Seeing nothing on various vectors, they were ordered to patrol Beachy Head and Brighton at 2,000 feet, then returned to base at 15:30 with nothing to report.

Mid-afternoon, the pilots were briefed for another Ramrod, on this occasion a much smaller operation, escorting Bostons to Béthune Marshalling Yards.

Date	27 April 1944
Operation	Ramrod 802
Target	1st & 2nd Attacks: Marshalling Yards, Béthune, Pas-de-Calais
Bombers	1st Attack: 12 Bostons; 12 bombed 2nd Attack: 30 Mitchells; 29 bombed
Close Escort, 1st Attack Close Escort, 2nd Attack	Friston: 41 Squadron (12 Spitfire XII) Funtington: 441 & 443 Squadrons (24 Spitfire IX)

Twelve of 41 Squadron's pilots were airborne at 16:35, led by Sqn Ldr Glen, and rendezvoused with the bombers 11,000 feet over South Foreland. The formation made landfall at 13,000 feet in cloudless skies with slight haze just east of Dunkirk, where a 1,000-ton ship was observed in the outer harbour.

The target area was reached at 17:26, and the bombers had a clear run, dropping thirty-nine 500lb GP and eight 500lb LD bombs. A good concentration was observed with bursts on the marshalling yards and workshops, with results considered moderate to good. No enemy aircraft were seen, but moderate heavy Flak was experienced just after leaving the target, which included "3 bursts giving out a shower of small particles at 13,000 feet".[82] 41 Squadron was unaffected and crossed out again over Berck, landing at Friston at 18:10 with otherwise nothing to report.

The second attack on Béthune Marshalling Yards followed less than ten minutes after 41 Squadron had passed through with their Bostons, and dropped significantly more on the target. A total of two hundred 500lb GP and thirty 500lb LD bombs achieved moderate to good results on the round house and the area south of the engine sheds, with possible direct hits also made. The escorting squadrons felt the bombing was good but experienced heavy, though inaccurate, Flak. 144 Airfield's squadrons were back at 18:42, reporting a similarly uneventful trip.

This operation constituted 41 Squadron's final Ramrod for four months, and marked another significant change in their deployment. Much lay in store for the men during the summer of 1944, and they would participate in both offensive ground attack missions in support of Operation *Overlord*, and defensive air-to-air operations against Germany's new generation of terror weapons, the V1 flying bomb.

By the time the Squadron recommenced bomber support operations in late August and rejoined the push toward Berlin, the second front had made significant headway and Paris had been liberated. Elsewhere in Europe, Allied landings had taken place in southern France, approximately three quarters of Italy was in Allied hands, and Romania had surrendered to the Russians.

From this time, 41 Squadron's pilots would find themselves penetrating deeper into the Continent than ever before. This was a result not only of the steadily advancing front but also as a result of new aircraft with a longer range. Only five weeks later, the pilots would fly their first sorties over Germany and 'the end', though still many months away, would finally be in sight.

Returning now to 27 April 1944, the day was not quite over for the pilots. Whilst the Squadron was still in France on Ramrod 802, Flt Lt Ron Collis returned from a five-hour round trip to Bolt Head, Devon, as news had come through that the Squadron was to move there as soon as possible. He gave the men an "excellent report on the aerodrome and accommodation in the officers mess".[83] The only negative he had to report was an apparent "total lack of hot water".[84]

There was brief operational flying again at 20:00, when Flt Lt Collis and Flt Sgt 'Steve' Stevenson were scrambled as Red Section. However, they were barely off the ground when they were recalled and put down again within five minutes. This, finally, concluded the day's flying.

28 April 1944 – It looked as though the Squadron would be sent on another Ramrod today. The men were briefed at 08:00 for a fighter umbrella in the Abbeville area, but just before they were due to take off, the operation was cancelled and the pilots dismounted again.

They were scheduled to participate in Ramrod 804, which foresaw six attacks by a total of 30 Mitchells, 18 Bostons and 216 Marauders on marshalling yards at Mantes-Gassicourt[85] and Creil, with close escorts provided by nine Spitfire squadrons and area sweeps undertaken by two Mustang Squadrons. In addition, an attack was also planned on Noball targets at 'Bois Coquerel'[86] and Marquenneville, both in the Picardie region, by two formations of 36 USAAF Bostons with area cover provided by 41 Squadron, plus dive-bombing attacks on Baupte, Marquenneville, and Bois Coquerel by three squadrons of Typhoons and two of Bomphoons.

The attacks on the Noball targets were cancelled before take-off, scuttling 41 Squadron's participation, and the bombers attacking the marshalling yards all aborted the mission due to cloud cover. They turned back before reaching their targets and jettisoned their LD bombs into the Channel on the way home, but returned with their GP bombs. Only the Mustangs performing area sweeps and the Bomphoons targeting Baupte completed their missions, the latter aircraft dropping fifteen 500lb bombs.

As a result of the cancellation of their participation in the Ramrod, and although they remained in readiness until their formal release at 13:00, 41 Squadron spent the rest of the day packing for their move to Bolt Head. The only flying undertaken all day, therefore, was when Flt Lt Tom Slack departed Friston by air at 10:25 in order to air test a Seafire XV. He returned just before 15:00 reporting "very favourably on it's [sic] performance".[87]

The day also saw the departure of Fg Off Ronald Johnson, who had been with 41 Squadron since late February 1943, and was now to be rested on completion of his tour. He was seconded to the Ministry of Aircraft Production and posted to Vickers Armstrong at Castle Bromwich as a Spitfire XIV and XVI Production Test Pilot. Promoted to Flight Lieutenant in July, he remained a test pilot until October 1945, when he was released, having in that time also assisted with the development of the Spitfire XXI. In 1946, Johnson returned to his pre-War occupation as a teacher, ascending to a secondary school Headmaster role by 1952. He continued in similar roles in Surrey high schools until his retirement in 1974. He passed away in 2003.

29 April 1944 – The road and rail parties departed Friston early in the morning, with Fg Offs Kenneth Robinson and Peter Cowell driving the distance in Flt Lt Ross Harding's motorcar. The journey proved more eventful and indeed frustrating than they had no doubt envisaged as the car broke down 50 miles into the journey. "…For the rest of the day and far into the night they proceeded by short laps, punctuated by breakdowns of the combustion."[88] Their time of arrival at Bolt Head is not recorded!

Meanwhile, 18 of the pilots departed Friston by air in their Spitfires at 15:10 and flew to Bolt Head via Winchester and Exeter, arriving at their final destination at 16:20. Upon landing, A Flight

The Officers Mess at RAF Friston, where the Squadron was based from 11 March to 29 April 1944, and 2 July to 11 July 1944.
© Jack Malone

was placed immediately on readiness, with one section kept on standby at the end of the strip.

Less than an hour and a half later, the first alarm was sounded, and at 17:45, Flt Lts Ross Harding (MB794) and Ron Collis (MB882) were scrambled to intercept a hostile aircraft. However, as a result of 'starting trouble', it took them five minutes to get airborne, and they "just failed to make an interception".[89,90] The pair landed again at 18:40.

Some two hours later, the next alarm sounded and Fg Offs Herb Wagner (MB795) and 'Ref' Refshauge (MB794) were scrambled to 12,000 feet to identify an unrecognised plot at 20:45. They climbed quickly to this altitude, intercepted the aircraft and found it to be friendly. Owing to a rough engine in one of the Spitfire XIIs, however, they returned to base immediately, landing within 20 minutes of their departure.[91,92]

Only ten minutes after their return, yet another section was scrambled, on this occasion Fg Off Keith Curtis and Plt Off Peter Gibbs as White Section, who were sent up after another hostile plot. However, they found nothing and returned within half an hour with nothing to report. This ended the day's flying.

Bolt Head

When 41 Squadron and 6041 Servicing Echelon moved to Bolt Head today, they replaced 234 Squadron and 6234 Servicing Echelon, who had moved to Deanland. 41 Squadron was in turn replaced at Friston by 501 Squadron, who moved from Hawkinge.

The Squadron's relocation also meant a move from 11 Group to 10 Group for the first time, where the AOC was AVM Charles R. Steele CB DFC. No. 10 Group lay in the west and southwest of England, and at the time covered the RAF Stations of Bolt Head, Colerne, Culmhead, Defford, Exeter (Sector Headquarters), Fairwood Common, Harrowbeer, Merryfield, Portreath, Predannack, Upottery, and Winkleigh.

RAF Bolt Head was a grass airfield that lay one-and-a-half miles southwest of Salcombe, Devon, on the southern English coast. The strip was built in 1941 as a satellite of RAF Exeter, with initially scant infrastructure and accommodation under canvas. Facilities improved with huts and hangars added as the War progressed and its two runways, initially both 2,700 feet in length, were extended and covered in Sommerfeld Tracking on coconut matting.[93]

At the time of 41 Squadron's arrival in late April 1944, Bolt Head was defended by 2704 Squadron RAF Regiment, which was armed with four Bofors 40mm anti-aircraft guns, twelve Hispano-Suiza 20mm cannons and four twin .50 calibre Browning machine guns. By the beginning of June, however, the Brownings had been replaced with four more Hispanos. RAF Hope Cove, a Ground Control Interceptor Station that had been established nearby in 1941, coordinated all flying operations in the sector.

By 1944, facilities had improved significantly for those posted to the airfield, and 41 Squadron's Peter Graham, who was promoted to Flying Officer on the day of the unit's move, recalled that,

> *The officers' mess was the Cottage Hotel at Hope Cove, some two miles from the airfield. The road between was a typical Devon country lane. […] The hotel was great. I had a room with a beautiful view over the cove. It was possible to walk down to a little beach but not to swim since the beach was covered in a barbed wire entanglement….*[94]

OC, B Flight, Flt Lt Tom Slack, remembered that the Cottage Hotel also included a pub called the Cabin Bar, and there was another bar in the area that the pilots frequented, called the Hope & Anchor. Both the Cottage Hotel and the Hope and Anchor still exist today.

The Squadron's arrival at Bolt Head marked a change in the Squadron's deployment that would see them conducting shipping reconnaissances and sweeps of the Brittany [Bretagne] region of France. The closest point of France now lay 97 miles to their south-southeast, but in a short time they were operating up to 80 miles [ca. 140km] inland, roaming the region seeking out targets of opportunity. The occupied British Channel Islands of Alderney, Guernsey, Jersey and Sark would also become frequent destinations, and visits to Guernsey in particular would cause the Squadron significant grief.

The Squadron was stationed at Bolt Head for six weeks, from 29 April to 16 May and from 24 May to 19 June 1944. The week-long break between stays was a result of the unit's attachment to 11 Armament Practice Camp at RAF Fairwood Common for an air firing course.

Between 29 April and the Squadron's ultimate departure from Bolt Head on 19 June, casualties amounted to one pilot killed, one wounded, one captured, and three rescued from the Channel otherwise uninjured. Six aircraft were destroyed, four damaged by Flak, and four damaged in flying accidents.

30 April 1944 – At dawn on the last day of the month and the Squadron's first full day at Bolt Head, B Flight took over readiness, with one section held in standby at the top of the strip and another in dispersals on 30 minutes. Nonetheless, the Squadron was not called upon all morning, and it was not until lunchtime that the men learned they would be required to maintain standing patrols ten miles south of the Isle of Portland, Dorset, between 13:00 and dusk.

Seven patrols in sections of two were flown at 13:15, 14:20, 15:00, 17:55, 18:40, 19:30 and 20:10, but all were uneventful. The routine was only broken by two scrambles, the first of which took place at 16:40, when Flt Lt Tommy Burne and WO 'Archie' Appleton were sent up to intercept an inbound plot coming from France.[95] Upon their approach, the aircraft turned 180° and flew back to France, and the pair were recalled once RDF indicated the aircraft had crossed the French coast again.

The second was airborne at 19:05, when Fg Offs Peter Cowell (MB795) and Kenneth Robinson (MB843) were scrambled to chase another inbound plot. A little after they took off, however, Cowell's machine developed engine trouble, and they were compelled to return, spending a total of just 15 minutes in the air. With mock bravado, the ORB boasts that despite such a short time airborne, "…their mission was successful as the enemy turned back and retreated at high speed to France"![96] This concluded the day's flying.

Nominal Roll, Bolt Head

The following list was extracted from a document held in 41 Squadron's Archives, which is undated but headed, *Nominal Roll Officers and Aircrew 41 Squadron Bolt Head*. The fact that Flt Sgt Ronald Stephens appears on the list places this Roll in the ten-day period between 29 April, when the Squadron arrived at Bolt Head, and 8 May, when Stephens was posted away. Names are listed in the order they appear on the original document, but minor corrections have been made by the author, where errors have been recognised.

Name	Rank	Number	Notes
Glen, A. A.	Actg Sqn Ldr	115332	
Slack, T. A. H.	Fg Off	112428	
Collis, R. T.	Flt Lt	111107	
Burne, T. R.	Flt Lt	33457	
Thiele, K. F.	Flt Lt	404966	New Zealand
Birbeck, C. R.	Flt Lt	108990	
Harding, R. P.	Flt Lt	113876	
Cowell, P.	Fg Off	124530	
Curtis, K. R.	Fg Off	J.22759	Canadian
Cook, H.	Fg Off	126096	
Wagner, H. A.	Fg Off	130242	American
Robinson, K. B.	Fg Off	139816	
Balasse, M. A. L.	Fg Off	135895	Belgian
Goens, R. van	Fg Off	124239	Netherlands
Anderson, R. E.	Fg Off	402337	Australian
Refshauge, J. G. H.	Fg Off	409447	Australian
Stowe, W. N.	Fg Off	J.10643	Canadian
Malone, C. J.	Fg Off	J.29235	Canadian
Graham, P. B.	Plt Off	161780	
Fisher, D. P.	Plt Off	169435	
Payne, J. C. J.	Plt Off	170730	
Gibbs, N. P.	Plt Off	173284	
Appleton, A. S.	WO	1576662	
Fleming, R.	Flt Sgt	656285	
Woollard, F. G.	Flt Sgt	1312058	
Stevenson, I. T.	Flt Sgt	1348985	
Stephens, R. V.	Flt Sgt	420631	Australian
Non-Flying Personnel			
Lord Gisborough	Flt Lt	73814	Intelligence
Herman, F. G.	Fg Off	140841	Medical
Fullam, E.	Sgt	1197888	Fitter IIE Grp (i)
Matcher, J. S.	LAC	1629100	Clerk/GD Grp (iv)

May 1944 – Not surprisingly, with the Allies in the final planning stages for Operation *Overlord*, 41 Squadron found most of their operations this month of two specific types: (i) of a defensive nature, to keep prying Luftwaffe eyes away from the English coast, and (ii) of an offensive nature, within support areas to the west and southwest of the planned landing beaches, between the western coast of the Cotentin [Cherbourg] Peninsula and the southern coast of the Brittany [Bretagne] Peninsula, on the Bay of Biscay, a region occupied by the German Seventh Army under General Friedrich Dollmann.

The Squadron's offensive operations themselves comprised of two distinct forms, one of which encompassed early morning shipping reconnaissances of coastal areas of mainland France and the Channel Islands, and the other wide-ranging sweeps over the whole Brittany region, seeking and attacking ground targets of opportunity on road, rail and river.

However, in the midst of this heightened activity, the Squadron found other events this month more difficult to comprehend: They were not assigned any operational duty on 10 May, and were taken off operations and sent on an air firing course at Fairwood Common between 17 and 24 May. Moreover, the Squadron's popular Commanding Officer, Sqn Ldr Arthur 'Pinkie' Glen, was removed for apparent political reasons, barely more than a week prior to D-Day.

Nevertheless, weather played a lesser role than in recent months, and inclement conditions only reduced operations on seven days – 4-5, 7, 26-27, and 29-30 May – but did not completely prevent flying on any day. The Squadron reported a total of 323 operational flying hours during the month, and undertook a significant amount of flying practice aside from the air firing course, which totalled 263 non-operational flying hours on Spitfires and 50 on the unit's Tiger Moth. Flying practice encompassed 477 sorties, which included 285 cine-gun exercises, 149 air firing exercises, and 43 air-to-sea and air-to-ground firing exercises, in which they exposed 3,275 feet of film and expended 59,300 rounds of .303 ammunition and 8,100 of 20mm cannon.

1 May 1944 – The day consisted chiefly of a continuation of the previous afternoon's standing patrols ten miles south of Portland, to keep the Luftwaffe at a distance whilst preparations were ramping up for the Normandy landings. Twelve patrols were flown in this area between 09:50 and 21:55 by sections of two aircraft, but all were uneventful.

Despite their presence off the coast, hostile aircraft still generated three scrambles, the first of which took place at 18:00, when Fg Offs 'Momo' Balasse and 'Charlie' van Goens were sent up to chase a plot that faded almost immediately; they were recalled and landed at 18:20. An hour and 15 minutes later, Flt Lt Tom Slack and WO 'Archie' Appleton were scrambled and chased an aircraft southwards until they sighted the French coast. Unable to close, they discontinued the pursuit and patrolled off Guernsey before returning to base at 20:40. In a similar scenario, Flt Lt Ross Harding and Fg Off Harry Cook were airborne at 20:45 and chased a plot that stayed 20 miles ahead of them and was never seen. They returned at 21:35, and the day's last standing patrol of Portland arrived back 20 minutes later, ending a long day's flying.

2 May 1944 – It was a very routine day for the Squadron, which is summed up in the ORB in just five short sentences. The core activity of the day was the maintenance of uneventful standing patrols ten miles south of Portland in sections of two, totalling 24 sorties, between 06:25 and 21:05.

Fg Off Peter Graham (MB798) returned early from his third such patrol – and the Squadron's last of the day – with his engine playing up, and both his R/T and compass malfunctioning. In a very dicey landing, he brought his aircraft down safely at Bolt Head just after 21:00, despite additionally breaking through 10/10ths cloud at just 100 feet; it could have been disastrous.[97]

The pattern of the day's standing patrols was only broken at 16:15, when Red (Cowell MB795 & Gibbs MB845) and Yellow (Wagner MB843 & Collis MB882) Sections were sent together on a shipping reconnaissance to St. Malo in Brittany [Bretagne], France. Neither Flak nor the Luftwaffe were encountered, but they did see a merchant vessel of 3,000-4,000 tons and a second vessel of 2,000-3,000 tons with a tug in Harbour.[98] They returned to base at 17:30.

Two personnel movements of note also took place today, when OC, A Flight, Flt Lt Donald Smith RAAF, was posted away and replaced in the role by Flt Lt Terry Spencer. Smith had been with the Squadron since May 1943 and had become a Flight Commander four months later, following

An ex-Great War pilot and Prisoner of War, Flt Lt Thomas W. P. L. Chaloner, The Right Honourable Lord Gisborough, 2nd Baron Gisborough of Cleveland, Yorkshire, was 41 Squadron's Intelligence Officer from 6 May 1940 to 19 June 1945. © Cowell family

Hugh Parry's loss. He had been an asset to the Squadron and, on his departure, Sqn Ldr Glen spoke highly of him, recording in his personnel file, "This officer has proved himself to be definitely above the average in every respect in the performance of his duties as Flight Commander".[99]

There was no rest for Smith, who was immediately promoted to Acting Squadron Leader and posted to 125 Airfield at Ford to take over command of 453 (Australian) Squadron, which was then flying Spitfire IXs. Remaining in this role until late September 1944, Smith claimed a number of aerial victories with the unit and was awarded a DFC shortly before his departure for rest. Following leave and ground duties, Smith was promoted to Wing Commander and given command of 11 PDRC at Charmy Down in mid-January 1945, which processed multitudes of repatriated Allied Prisoners of War. He held this position until his embarkation for Australia in September 1945, and was discharged from the RAAF on 4 December 1945.

26-year-old Terence 'Terry' Spencer, described by one pilot as "a good looking dapper Errol Flynn type"[100], had been a 2nd Lieutenant in the Royal Engineers prior to his transfer to, and commissioning in, the RAFVR in October 1941. He completed his entire flying training in the United Kingdom, and was already a Flying Officer by the time of his posting to his first operational unit, 26 Squadron at Gatwick, in November 1942. In June 1943, Spencer was promoted to Flight Commander of the unit, and four months later to Flight Lieutenant (WS). Having spent 15 months with 26 Squadron, he was posted to 165 (Ceylon) Squadron at Culmhead as a Flight Commander at the beginning of February 1944, flying Spitfire IXs. He was flown over to Bolt Head from Predannack today, where 165 Squadron was now based, in that unit's Oxford, to join 41 Squadron and take up his third Flight Commander post.

Spencer would remain with the unit until January 1945, when he was given command of his own Squadron. He was a very popular leader, known for his humour and bravery, and became somewhat of a legend in his own time. Anyone who had the honour of knowing him found him a complete gentleman, and everyone who mentioned him during the preparation of this work could not speak highly enough of him and expressed their deepest respect for him.

3 May 1944 – The Squadron was relieved from its previous days' task of maintaining standing patrols south of Portland, but still had eight sections airborne between 11:45 and 21:05, four allocated to patrols south of Bolt Head and four to scrambles.

The patrols were airborne at 11:45, 12:45, 13:30 and 14:45, and all were uneventful, each section returning with nothing to report. The first scramble, which was off the deck at 13:05, was apparently accidental, and the section was recalled as soon as it was airborne, putting down again within five minutes. Flt Lt 'Joe' Birbeck and Flt Sgt Freddie Woollard were the next section scrambled and "chased an elusive Hun"[101] unsuccessfully, between 18:40 and 19:40.

Only ten minutes after their return, Flt Lt 'Jimmy' Thiele and WO 'Archie' Appleton were scrambled after an unidentified plot. Intercepting the aircraft, it was found to be friendly, and they returned to base at 20:25. The last section airborne today comprised Flt Lts Ron Collis and Ross Harding, who were scrambled at 21:40, and closed to within five miles of the aircraft they were seeking, only to find it was a Mustang. They returned at 22:05 with nothing further to report.

Separately today, Fg Off Peter Graham suffered an unfortunate taxiing accident at the conclusion of a non-operational flight when he tipped his aircraft, MB829, on its nose. He had flown to RAF Ramsbury in Wiltshire to give a recognition display of the Spitfire XII to the Observer Corps, and upon landing was directed along the edge of the airfield to an assembly point. Finding the ground muddy and feeling the drag on his undercarriage, he opened his throttle to increase speed and avoid getting bogged. As soon as he did so, however, the aircraft tipped on its nose, promptly ending all hope of carrying out his recognition exercise.

> *I had to abandon my Spit and go home with my head hanging down. My own CO was sympathetic and would have taken no action against me. Later however I was to learn that higher powers thought I should be disciplined for carelessness.*[102]

Indeed, one report in the 10 Group Appendix is scathing in its criticism:.

> *Unable to turn corner, ran off perimeter track and aircraft tipped on nose. A frightful display in airmanship and lack of elementary common sense.... Gross carelessness.*[103]

In due course, Graham was informed he was to attend a three-week course at Aircrew Refresher School in Sheffield, and was given ten extra duties. Although disappointed he missed the launch of Operation *Overlord* in early June, he found the course quite enjoyable and a nice break from the usual Squadron routine. His fiancée even travelled up to Sheffield where they were able to spend time together when he was off duty. This, he felt, made the punishment as good as a period of leave!

4 May 1944 – The day dawned to poor weather, and although a section was scrambled at 06:20, they were recalled within minutes and were back on the ground at 06:35, unable to complete the task. A limited amount of practice flying was undertaken during the morning, but no operational flying until the weather improved in the late afternoon.

Between 17:45 and 21:55, four sections were employed on convoy patrols, but even these were hindered by 8/10ths cloud cover at 3,000 feet and periodic rain. All were uneventful and returned with nothing to report but weather conditions.

5 May 1944 – The new day brought initially improved weather, but another deterioration in the early afternoon stopped flying for around four hours and limited operational flying to only five convoy patrols south of Portland. These were flown at 09:10, 12:00, 17:20, 17:55, and 19:15, and all were uneventful. Five practice sorties were also flown, but this constituted the Squadron's total flying for the day.[104]

6 May 1944 – The weather had improved sufficiently by this morning to allow the Squadron's participation in an early morning offensive operation to France. Eight pilots were airborne at 06:50 as Red and Blue Sections, with Sqn Ldr Glen leading.[105] The pilots rendezvoused with four

Seafire IIIs of Culmhead based 887 Squadron FAA over Lamballe, Brittany [Bretagne], at 07:31 to provide them cover as a part of Rodeo 128.

The area was, however, blanketed in 9/10ths cloud and the Squadron was unable to see them when they dived down to sweep Rennes and Gaël. The Seafires shot up the airfield at Gaël, observing strikes on the control tower, a hangar and two gun posts. 41 Squadron returned to Bolt Head between 08:35 reporting that the Luftwaffe was not seen and no Flak experienced. A second sweep, as a part of the same Rodeo, was also made by six Spitfires of Predannack based 165 Squadron on Vannes and Kerlin Bastard, which was uneventful.

Although a large amount of practice flights were carried out during the day, the Squadron only flew once more operationally, when Flt Lt Terry Spencer and Fg Off Keith Curtis were scrambled to 25,000 feet at 18:20 on the report of Luftwaffe aircraft 30 miles south of Bolt Head. However, they saw nothing and, after several vectors, were recalled to base where they landed at 19:10.

7 May 1944 – Less than ideal weather kept the Squadron on the ground until just after midday, after which the day's entire operational flying activity was confined to the support of a rodeo to Brittany [Bretagne], one ASR patrol, and one scramble.

Eight pilots were airborne at 12:10 as Blue Section, led by Sqn Ldr Glen, and Red Section, led by Flt Lt Terry Spencer. They were assigned the provision of forward cover and withdrawal support to eight Seafire IIIs of Culmhead based 894 Squadron FAA in Rodeo 131, a low-level sweep of Brittany.

Whilst the operation was uneventful for 41 Squadron, who provided cover between Pointe de Minard and St.-Michel-en-Grève, 894 Squadron succeeded in shooting up pillboxes south of 'Lake Morbihan' and construction equipment in a railway siding south of Baud.[106] 41 Squadron escorted the Seafires back as far as Bolt Head, landing at 13:30.

During the afternoon, both Flights undertook cine-gun practice and sector reconnaissances until 16:50 when Red Section of four aircraft supported two Spitfires of 276 (ASR) Squadron to investigate a plot southwest of Start Point, Devon. They were led by Flt Lt Terry Spencer[107] and returned at 17:55 having seen nothing.

Finally, at 20:10, Flt Lt Ron Collis and Fg Off Ken Robinson were scrambled to intercept hostile plots. They succeeded in closing from a range of 23 miles to just ten, but at this time they were recalled and landed at Bolt Head again at 21:00, concluding the day's flying.

Fg Off Keith 'Curt' Curtis RCAF skeet shooting between operations at Lympne in summer 1944. © Jack Malone

8 May 1944 – Fine weather today had the Squadron off to an early start and provided a good day's flying. Just after 06:00, B Flight's readiness section was advised that four MTBs were inbound from a reconnaissance to Guernsey and requesting air cover. Plt Offs 'Jackie' Fisher (MB847) and Jimmy Payne (MB804) were off the deck at 06:15 to assist, but had to returned just 25 minutes later with engine trouble.[108] Fg Off Peter Graham and Flt Sgt Bob Fleming were airborne at 06:40 to replace them, located the MTBs 20 miles southwest of Start Point, Devon, and escorted them back to Dartmouth, before returning to Bolt Head at 07:50.

In the meantime, at 07:35, Sqn Ldr Glen and Plt Off 'Andy' Anderson were sent on a patrol of Dartmouth, but fifteen minutes later ordered instead to conduct an ASR search. Given a vector of 180° and a range of 30 miles, they were asked to look for a Lancaster believed ditched roughly mid-Channel. However, barely had they begun on this heading when they received yet another order, this time to intercept a hostile plot. They closed to within four miles of their target, but were then recalled and landed again at 08:35.

As they landed, Plt Offs Fisher and Payne took off again, both pilots in different aircraft, to continue the ASR search that Glen and Anderson were compelled to abandon. They searched for the Lancaster unsuccessfully and returned again at 09:40 with nothing to report.

It was a little over four hours before the Squadron was airborne operationally again, when Flt Lt Tommy Burne and WO 'Archie' Appleton were sent on a patrol. Airborne at 13:55, they carried out the patrol as ordered but were also vectored onto an unidentified plot, which they were unable to find, and landed again at 15:00.[109]

Twenty minutes after Burne and Appleton's return, eight pilots were airborne on what the ORB calls their "first real show since we came to Bolt Head"[110], a low level sweep to Dinard-Pleurtuit Airfield, 137 miles across the Channel from Bolt Head, as an element of 10 Group Circus 61. The operation was scheduled as a result of recent photo reconnaissance that had showed Focke-Wulf 190s parked on the airfield. The participants were as follows:

Date	8 May 1944
Operation	Circus 61
Target	Dinard-Pleurtuit Airfield, Brittany [Bretagne][111]
Bomphoons	Harrowbeer: 263 Squadron, 8 Typhoon Ib (15:19-16:45)
Fighter Sweep	Bolt Head: 41 Squadron, 8 Spitfire XII (15:25-16:42)
Fighter Cover	Culmhead: 610 Squadron, 9 Spitfire XIV (15:15-16:51)

Flying straight to Dinard, 41 Squadron arrived on time but found bombs from 263 Squadron's Typhoons bursting on the airfield as they were due to pass over. A number of bombs landed in the northwest dispersal area, two of which were close to hangars. However, no aircraft were seen.

After a quick orbit, 41 Squadron dashed across the airfield themselves at zero feet, several pilots firing on forts and guns without observed results. However, Flt Lt Terry Spencer and Fg Off Peter Cowell both claimed to have made strikes on a gun-post, thereby constituting the Squadron's first ground target since October 1943. Despite the lack of material success, the attacks caused considerable distress to those on the receiving end, and "Huns [were seen] dashing in all directions!"[112]

Although by this time, intense light Flak was being experienced from the area, it was of no consequence to the Squadron, who returned to Bolt Head and "landed very happy"[113] at 16:40. This ended the day's operational flying. The pilots participating in the attack were as follows:

Pilot	Serial	Section	Up	Down
Glen, Arthur A.	MB881	Red	15:20	16:40
Cowell, Peter	MB843	Red	15:20	16:40
Spencer, Terence	MB882	Red	15:20	16:40
Robinson, Kenneth B.	MB840	Red	15:20	16:40
Slack, Thomas A. H.	MB794	Blue	15:20	16:40
Fleming, Robert	MB682	Blue	15:20	16:40
Thiele, Keith F.	MB847	Blue	15:20	16:40
Woollard, Frederick G.	MB845	Blue	15:20	16:40

Separately today, Sgt Plt Ron Stephens left the Squadron after just six weeks with the unit. He was posted to 165 Squadron at Predannack, with which unit he remained until July 1945, and was commissioned in August 1944. Stephens was subsequently repatriated to Australia where he was discharged as a Flying Officer in November 1945 and awarded a Mention in Despatches in January 1946.

9 May 1944 – It was another early start for the pilots this morning, when two separate shipping reconnaissances of four pilots were sent to Brittany at 05:55 and 06:00. The former, led by Flt Lt Tom Slack, headed for Lézardrieux (104m SSE of Bolt Head) and St. Malo (135 miles SE), whilst the latter, led by Fg Off Peter Cowell, made for Morlaix (114 miles SSW) and L'Aber-Wrac'h (117 miles SW).

The light was barely sufficient, but Slack's Blue Section recognised a tug and a small cargo vessel at St. Malo. All was otherwise quiet and they were not fired upon by the anti-aircraft defences. At Lézardrieux, however, whilst no shipping was seen, 18 balloons were flying at 800 feet, and the foursome came under intense Flak fire. They remained unscathed and returned to Bolt Head at 07:30.

Cowell's Yellow Section had meanwhile reached Morlaix to find a sea-going tug off the coast, along with two 3,000-5,000-ton ships.[114] As a result of the section's IFF set malfunctioning, they headed home early, but were intercepted by Flt Lt Terry Spencer and Flt Sgt Ian Stevenson who had been scrambled as Red Section at 07:05, to intercept four 'inbound bogeys'. Spencer noted in his logbook, "Scramble – 8,000 ft. Intercepted Peter Cowell returning from a shipping recco."[115]

Cowell's section landed again at 07:10, but Spencer and Stevenson continued on their own brief shipping reconnaissance, returning to base at 07:25, a few minutes before Blue Section's return.

Most of the rest of the day was quiet. With the exception of a scramble by Flt Lt Tommy Burne and Fg Off 'Andy' Anderson between 09:30 and 10:15, in which they chased a plot as far as Jersey before turning back, B Flight remained on readiness, whilst A Flight made just three practice flights.

It was not until just before 18:00 that the Squadron was airborne again on a planned operation, when they provided cover for a composite unit, comprising four Seafire IIIs each from 887 and 894 Squadrons FAA, of Culmhead's 24 Naval Wing, in Rodeo 133. The FAA was tasked with undertaking a low-level sweep for targets of opportunity in the Kerlin-Bastard, Vannes, and Gaël areas of Brittany [Bretagne], and eight pilots of 41 Squadron were sent to afford them forward and withdrawal cover.

Red and Blue Sections, led by Flt Lts Terry Spencer and Tom Slack, respectively, were airborne at 17:55, and headed for the Pléneuf-Val-André area where they orbited. Meanwhile, the Seafires made attacks with cannon and machine gun fire on Kerlin-Bastard airfield, near Vannes, making strikes on dispersals, the control tower, and other buildings. They also fired on a Flak tower near St. Méen-le-Grand and a lorry near Merdrignac.

The Luftwaffe was not seen in the air or on the ground but the Seafires encountered intense light Flak at both Kerlin-Bastard and Vannes. Two aircraft suffered Cat. A damage as a result, but one aircraft was seriously hit in the Vannes area, and glided down to crash-land at Ploërmel, approximately 57km southwest of Rennes.[116]

As far as 41 Squadron was concerned, however, the operation was uneventful and "carried out exactly as planned".[117] No opposition was encountered, and withdrawal cover was provided to the Seafires as they came back out. The pilots noted that one aircraft was missing, and subsequently made various comments to this end in their logbooks. They landed back at Bolt Head at 19:45.

The flying day was, however, not quite over as the pilots were airborne two more times before they could stand down. In the first of these, Flt Lt 'Jimmy' Thiele and Fg Off 'Andy' Anderson were airborne at 20:10 and sent on a southward vector to intercept a hostile plot. However, nothing was seen and the plot faded; they landed again at 21:20. Meanwhile, at 21:05, Plt Off Peter Gibbs and Flt Sgt Ian Stevenson were sent up to conduct a patrol south of Portland. It was entirely uneventful and they were back on the ground at 22:15 to end the day's flying.

10 May 1944 – Despite good weather all day, the Squadron was not called on operationally. Flying practice was undertaken instead, which included cine-gun attacks on a Sunderland in sections of two, and a total of 26 sorties were flown. There was one minor mishap during the during these flights, when one of the Spitfires lost an oleo leg when landing.[118,119]

11 May 1944 – The Squadron's operational flying commenced at 08:50 this morning with a freelance fighter sweep for eight pilots to St. Brieuc and Morlaix, Brittany [Bretagne] in Rodeo 134.

Flying in two sections, designated Red and Blue, and led by Flt Lt Terry Spencer and Sqn Ldr Glen, respectively, the octet crossed into France at Pointe de Minard. They swept St. Brieuc and Morlaix airfields at 4,000 feet, but as no aircraft were seen, they decided to search for other targets of opportunity instead.

At Plougonver, southwest of Guingamp, Blue 3 and 4 fired on a large open staff car with a driver and six passengers, sending it into a ditch, after which the entire section shot up a three-ton truck at Plouaret, northwest of Guingamp; Red Section attacked a similar-sized lorry in Guingamp. The pilots encountered no opposition and turned for home, intending to cross out again over St.-Michel-en-Grève.

Just south of the town, however, they sighted a small convoy of eight camouflaged horse-drawn wagons heading east, and attacked it from astern. Under fire from cannon and machine gun, their target "almost disintegrated"[120], records the Squadron ORB. Continuing home, the pilots landed again at 10:25. The participants were:

Pilots, 11 May 1944	Serial	Section	Up	Down
Spencer, Terence	MB882	Red	8:55	10:25
Cook, Harry	MB795	Red	8:55	10:25
Wagner, Herbert A.	MB843	Red	8:55	10:25
Harding, Ross P.	MB794	Red	8:55	10:25
Glen, Arthur A.	MB881	Blue	8:55	10:25
Slack, Thomas A. H.	MB804	Blue	8:55	10:25
Thiele, Keith F.	MB847	Blue	8:55	10:25
Burne, Thomas R.	MB837	Blue	8:55	10:25

Whilst Red and Blue Sections were away, the remaining pilots were briefed on a new method of scrambling from Bolt Head. The procedure called for the pilots to set a bearing of 190° as soon as they were airborne, then to fly on the deck on this bearing for seven minutes at 300mph. At this point, they were to change course to starboard onto 200° for three minutes, then starboard again, onto 010° for five minutes, maintaining radio silence throughout.

The pilots would have to wait until later in the day to test the procedure operationally, but then had six uneventful scrambles varying from broad daylight through to dusk conditions that provided the perfect testing environment. These occurred at 15:55, 19:20, 19:40, 20:55, 21:50 and 22:30.

The 10 Group ORB reports that enemy fighter reconnaissances were 'unusually active' during the evening, which is evident in the number of sections from both 41 and 610 Squadrons being vectored from existing patrols or scrambled specifically during this time. Despite efforts, however, no interceptions were. 41's Blue Section, for example, which was airborne at 19:20 to intercept a single plot flying northwest 40 to 35 miles south of Bolt Head, "closed to within 5 miles of [the] Hun but couldn't get a visual".[121] White Section was also scrambled at 20:55 after a hostile plot 30 miles from Bolt Head, and chased and unseen bogey as far as Lorient, but saw nothing. The weather did not assist in the matter, as a heavy sea mist considerably reduced visibility.

12 May 1944 – Similar to the early morning operations of 9 May, two sections of four pilots were airborne again this morning for shipping reconnaissances to Morlaix and L'Aber-Wrac'h, and to St. Malo and Lézardrieux, Brittany [Bretagne].

Red and Blue Sections, led by Fg Off Peter Cowell and Flt Lt 'Jimmy' Thiele, respectively, were both off the deck at 06:05, and set their bearings for their individual destinations. Cowell's section found little to report except six barges at Morlaix, but Thiele's was more successful, sighting two large vessels at St. Malo, one of which was estimated at 5,000-6,000 tons, and had no smoke issuing from its funnel. However, their presence drew "bags of accurate light flak".[122] The two sections returned to Bolt Head to report their observations, Red Section landing at 07:30 and Blue Section five minutes later.

The reaction was swift and Roadstead 105 was mounted at 09:15 to attack the two ships that had been seen at St. Malo. Seven Bomphoons of 263 Squadron were sent to the port with eight Seafires of 887 and 894 Squadrons and attacked the larger of the two vessels, which they identified as the 'M Class' minesweeper *M65*. Unfortunately, the bombs all overshot their mark and 887 Squadron reported a loss, when Lt. Hawkins-King was shot down by Flak and ditched into the Channel ten miles northwest of St. Malo. 263 Squadron returned again at 15:15 in Roadstead 106 to make a fresh attack and succeeded this time in scoring two direct hits on *M65*. 41 Squadron was not involved in either attack, but was called upon to assist in an ASR search for Hawkins-King during the afternoon.

The Squadron was scrambled three times during the morning (07:10, 09:20 and 10:55), the first and last of which were uneventful, but the second provided something a little more unexpected.

At 09:20, Fg Offs Harry Cook (MB840) and 'Jack' Malone (MB843) were scrambled to investigate a hostile raid of three aircraft.[123] Initially, plotted at 09:09, the bogeys flew a zigzag course at an altitude 1,000 feet, and approached from 36 miles south of Portland to within ten miles east of Dartmouth. Cook and Malone were airborne within minutes and gave chase.

As they approached, the aircraft climbed to 10,000 feet and turned southeast towards France again. 41 Squadron drew close enough to recognise them as Spitfires, "which they definitely identified as such"[124], but no markings or cannon were visible. They watched as the middle aircraft half-rolled down and made a bearing for Morlaix, whilst the other two made a slow turn to port towards Alderney, giving Cook and Malone a clear dead-astern line of fire.

They informed Control that they were unable to identify them as friend or foe, and were given a new vector to Guernsey. Subsequently receiving a new bearing of 320° back to base, the pair landed again at 09:55 to report their strange sighting.[125] The 10 Group ORB later reported,

> *Subsequent investigation has failed to identify these aircraft although information was received that two aircraft took off from Dinard to fly over the Portland area at a time at a time which corresponds to the above.*[126]

At 14:20, six pilots took off as Red and Yellow Sections, led by Flt Lt Terry Spencer, to search for 887 Squadron's Lt. Hawkins-King, who had been shot down that morning during the attack

After leaving 41 Squadron on 28 April 1944, Fg Off Ronald Johnson was seconded to the Ministry of Aircraft Production and posted to Vickers Armstrong at Castle Bromwich as a Spitfire Production Test Pilot. Relinquishing his commission in October 1945, he devoted the rest of his life to teaching. © Cowell family

on shipping at St. Malo. Six Seafires of 894 Squadron and a number of Spitfires of 276 (ASR) Squadron also participated. 41 Squadron was of little assistance, however, as they were searching way off course, ending up at Ushant [Île d'Ouessant], an island 135 miles southwest of Bolt Head and 45km northwest of Brest, which marks France's most westerly point. They returned to base at 16:00, and Fg Off Herb Wagner subsequently noted in his logbook, "What a hell of a shambles."[127] However, Hawkins-King was not found by any of the aircraft sent out to find him today.[128]

It was then quiet for the Squadron until 21:10, when Flt Lt Tom Slack and Fg Off Peter Graham were scrambled after a hostile plot as Green Section. They chased the unidentified aircraft back to the French coast and then patrolled awhile off Morlaix. They returned to base at 22:10 with nothing to report and this concluded the day's flying.

13 May 1944 – At first light today, two separate shipping reconnaissances were sent to Brittany [Bretagne]. Red Section of three pilots, and Blue of four, were both off the deck at 06:10, led by Flt Lt Terry Spencer and Flt Lt Tom Slack, respectively.

Spencer's section flew to Morlaix and L'Aber-Wrac'h, but found the weather too poor to continue and returned early, putting down at 07:00 with nothing to report. Slack's section made for St. Malo and Lézardrieux, where the weather was more accommodating, and sighted a 1,000-2,000 ton ship outside the torpedo net at St. Malo, with small tenders at its bow and stern. They returned at 07:45 having encountered no opposition and only 'meagre' Flak.

One section was scrambled from Bolt Head whilst they were absent, but saw nothing, and the Squadron otherwise spent the morning and early afternoon on four convoy patrols south of Portland at 09:00, 10:10, 11:35, and 13:00. The ORB gives nothing away in regard to the convoy type or size, but Flt Lt Terry Spencer gives us a hint in his logbook, where he penned that day, "Masses of invasion craft".[129]

Little operational flying was undertaken during the afternoon, and only three more patrols were flown before an unusually early end to the flying day at 15:20. The first two of these were weather reconnaissances, 13:10-14:15 and 13:25-14:35, to the French islands of Île de Bréhat (ca. 102m SSE of Bolt Head), and Île Vierge (ca. 115m SW of Bolt Head). Both were uneventful, as was the final operation of the day, a scramble between 14:10 and 15:20.

14 May 1944 – In a day quieter than others recently, Red Section of four aircraft was airborne at 06:10, led by Flt Lt Tommy Burne, for a dawn shipping reconnaissance to Morlaix and L'Aber-Wrac'h. Likely preparing for their pending move to Bolt Head to take over from 41 Squadron whilst they attending Air Practice Camp in a few days' time, 610 Squadron sent up a section of four of its own pilots around the same time to undertake the usual morning St. Malo and Lézardrieux shipping reconnaissance.

41 Squadron's section flew as far as Morlaix, but could see nothing as a result of thick haze. With visibility not improving, they turned back soon after reaching the French coast and landed at Bolt Head at 07:15 with nothing to report. Although away longer, 610 Squadron fared no better and returned to report they had also seen nothing of consequence.

There was an uneventful scramble between 13:50 and 14:40, and the day's operational flying was completed with a Rodeo to Brittany for seven pilots from 15:40.[130] Theirs was one of five successive Rodeos during the afternoon, intended to sweep Brittany's airfields for signs of bombers believed to have moved into the area during the previous night.

Rodeo 141	Kerlin Bastard, Vannes, Gaël	1 Squadron	8 Spitfire IX
Rodeo 142	Kerlin Bastard, Vannes, Gaël	41 Squadron	7 Spitfire XII
Rodeo 143	Chartres-Orly (Paris)	263 Squadron	6 Typhoon Ib
Rodeo 144	Kerlin Bastard & Vannes	610 Squadron	8 Spitfire XIV
Rodeo 145	Kerlin Bastard & Vannes	165 Squadron	6 Spitfire IX

Taking a 200-mile route directly to Kerlin Bastard, then to Vannes, Gaël and back to Bolt Head, 41 Squadron's formation comprised two sections, designated Blue and Red, which were led by Flt Lts Tom Slack and Terry Spencer, respectively.

The pilots did not see the airfields or any enemy aircraft, and ground targets were few and far between. Blue Section's Flt Lt 'Joe' Birbeck (MB841) attacked a technical lorry at St. Méen-le-Grande and claimed it damaged, whilst Red Section's Fg Off Bill Stowe (MB845) sighted a motor car in "a sandy yellow desert camouflage"[131] scheme between St. Méen-le-Grande and Broons.

Obtaining permission from Flt Lt Spencer, Stowe dived on the vehicle from astern, firing a three-second burst which covered the car in a cloud of dust and sent it into a ditch. Orbiting once, Stowe attacked it a second time with a short burst, then re-joined Red Section, having expended 55 rounds of cannon and 160 of machine gun ammunition.

The two sections returned across the Channel and landed back at Bolt Head between 17:30 and 17:35, with little further to report. Unimpressed by the lack of action, Terry Spencer wrote in his logbook today, "200 miles of sweet F.A. Cruised at 240 & at 2,500ft. Not even any flak".[132] This concluded the day's flying.

15 May 1944 – Despite fair weather, it was a very quiet day for 41 Squadron, and the day's total operational flying was limited to just four scrambles.[133] These took place at 10:15, 12:40, 14:20 and 16:50. Flt Lt Terry Spencer and Plt Off Peter Gibbs intercepted a Mosquito in the first, and were back on the ground again with 15 minutes, but nothing was seen on the remaining sorties.

There was otherwise a little non-operational flying during the day, when Fg Off Peter Cowell flew to Friston and back to retrieve four parachutes that had been left there when the Squadron moved to Bolt Head at the end of April, whilst Flt Sgt 'Steve' Stevenson made his first solo in the Squadron's Tiger Moth. Finally, Flt Lts Spencer and Collis flew to Predannack and back, making a dusk landing at Bolt Head at 22:35.

16 May 1944 – The Squadron was scheduled to move to RAF Fairwood Common, in Glamorgan, today to attend Armament Practice Camp, but was required to maintain a state of readiness until 610 Squadron arrived at Bolt Head to take over from them.

This had the consequence that Fg Off Harry Cook and Flt Sgt Ian Stevenson were scrambled at 08:55 to intercept a plot. When they identified it as friendly, they were ordered to maintain a patrol south of Bolt Head, however returned early anyway, when one of the aircraft developed engine trouble.[134]

610 Squadron arrived at 10:00 and hurried to bring themselves to a state of readiness, which they achieved in just 30 minutes. 41 Squadron then completed the last of their packing, and thirteen pilots took off for Fairwood Common in their Spitfires at 11:30. Their departure completed a triangle of movements today, with 610 Squadron arriving from Culmhead, and 616 Squadron replacing them at Culmhead from Fairwood Common.

Landing at Fairwood Common only 30 minutes after departure from Bolt Head, the Squadron's pilots found much pleasure landing on a paved runway again for the first time since the Squadron had left Tangmere on 11 March. The afternoon was spent unpacking what they could as the rail party and most of the kit did not arrive until the evening. Time was set aside during the afternoon, however, for a lecture to the pilots on the coming week's course. During the talk,

…we were introduced to an intricate method of drogue shooting employing barrel roll attacks and two drogues on one cable. This latter scheme being so arranged that if the pilot aims at the front drogue he hits the back one and if he imagines the back drogue to be travelling at 300 m.p.h. instead of 150 m.p.h., and makes due deflection allowance, he will pepper the front drogue. We were very impressed.[135]

The last bus left the Mess at 21:00 and all the pilots were in their quarters by 21:15, planning on a good night's sleep in advance of an intensive week of air-to-air firing, air-to-ground firing and bombing practice.

Fairwood Common

Opened in June 1941 on the Gower Peninsula, west of Swansea, Glamorganshire, RAF Fairwood Common was originally planned only as a fighter station, but soon became a sector station, taking on responsibility for the air defence of southern Wales.[136]

Fifteen fighter pens were scattered around the airfield, reinforced with earth ramparts and designed with minimal entrances to provide maximum protection to aircraft and pilots within them. The station was equipped with two sealed runways of 4,100 feet and one of 4,800 feet and a triangular layout, which lay 272 feet above sea level.

Fairwood Common was home to several fighter squadrons and servicing echelons throughout the War, as well as the Swansea University Air Squadron, the Air-Sea Rescue Flight, and a number of Armament Practice Camps (APCs). At the time of 41 Squadron's arrival, the Station's Officer Commanding was Wg Cdr Alexander V. R. Johnstone DFC.

No. 11 APC, which 41 Squadron was now attending, had taken up residence at the station the previous October, and was currently equipped with six Martinets, four Masters and one Lysander. The Commanding Officer was fighter Ace, Sqn Ldr William 'Cherry' Vale DFC and Bar.

17 May 1944 – The Squadron's course commenced this morning with exhibits of German aircraft and lectures on deflection shooting and bombing by Sqn Ldr Vale. Now prepared to get flying, the pilots arrived at dispersals, but found an insufficient number of serviceable aircraft to allow them to do so before lunch.

They returned at 13:15 to find everything ready and took off straight away. The weather and light were sufficient to allow the pilots to complete 32 air-to-air and 25 air-to-ground firing sorties before the flying day ended at 18:05.[137,138] None of the initial scores achieved by the pilots were particularly notable, but these were used as a benchmark as the week progressed.

OC A Flight, Flt Lt Donald Smith RAAF was promoted to Squadron Leader and given command of 453 (Australian) Squadron on 2 May 1944. This photograph was taken at RAF Ford just before D-Day, approximately one month after leaving 41 Squadron. © Donald Smith, via Garry Cooper

18 May 1944 – Ideal weather enabled the Squadron to undertake a full day's flying, which commenced at 09:25 and ended at 18:50. The pilots flew a total of 95 sorties, which included 49 air-firing sorties and 27 air-to-ground and cine-gun exercises.[139] The day's best firing score was achieved by Flt Sgt Bob Fleming, who only flew once and fired just 60 rounds of cannon all day, but managed to score 55 strikes on the target. During the evening, the Station provided entertainment in the station theatre, playing "It's a Wow".

19 May 1944 – The day's flying commenced at 09:15 and continued through to 18:10, the pilots concentrating today on air-to-ground firing, bombing and cine-gun exercises. They completed a total of 23 sorties of air-to-ground and cine-gun exercises, 21 of low-level bombing, and 11 of dive bombing.[140] Today's top scorer was Sqn Ldr Glen who achieved an average error of just 18 yards in the low-level bombing exercises.

20 May 1944 – A total of 73 sorties were flown today between 09:40 and 17:55, which included 39 of air-to-air firing, and 33 of low-level dive bombing.[141] Bombing was performed in sections of four over the sea, in which they aimed for a line between the target and a 100-yard marker buoy. The day's top scoring section was led by Flt Lt 'Joe' Birbeck, which gained an average error of just 30 yards from the target.

21 May 1944 – Flying commenced at 09:40, but as low cloud hindered dive bombing until after 11:30, the initial two hours were spent only on air-to-air firing. Bombing then commenced, and by the cessation of flying at 18:10, the Squadron had completed 27 air firing sorties, 15 low-level bombing sorties, and 31 dive-bombing sorties in sections of four.[142]

22 May 1944 – The weather was less than ideal today and although flying began at 09:00, it was terminated at 15:00 for the day. In that time, however, the Squadron completed 23 air-to-air firing sorties and 31 dive-bombing sorties.[143]

The Squadron also suffered a minor flying accident today when Flt Sgt Freddie Woollard landed MB858 at 14:40, and the starboard oleo leg collapsed causing damage to the starboard wing, rudder and propeller. Woollard was unhurt and later explained that the rudder bar had jammed after landing causing him to skid, thus resulting in the oleo leg collapsing. When the controls were inspected after the accident and found to be 'completely free', his superiors were unimpressed and penalised him 14 extra duties.[144]

23 May 1944 – Flying on the final day of the course commenced at 08:30 and continued through until 17:00, by which time the pilots had flown 52 sorties of air-to-air firing, and 43 sorties of low-level bombing.[145] That afternoon, Sqn Ldr Glen returned to Bolt Head by motor car with Flt Lt Ron Collis, leaving the rest of the Squadron to return the following day. The Squadron achieved the following results during the course:[146]

Air-to-air firing sorties (average 10 per pilot)	218
Air-to-ground firing sorties (average three per pilot)	66
Cine-gun sorties	284
Feet of film footage reviewed and criticised	2,151
Sorties of high dive bombing	97
Sorties of low level bombing	85
Hours flying (average 9 hours per pilot)	183.55
Rounds of 20mm ammunition fired	8,265
Rounds of .303 ammunition fired	65,267
10lb practice bombs dropped	739
Rounds fired at clay pigeon targets	1,400
Days fit for flying	6½

No. 11 APC also flew 78 hours drogue towing, and 13.4 hours dual. The Squadron's over all averages were 78 yards for High Dive Bombing, 40 yards for Low Level Bombing, 1.9% for Air to Air Firing and 17% for Air to Ground Firing.

Whereas Fairwood Common's Commanding Officer, Wg Cdr Johnstone, felt it was only an "Average course [that I feel] would… have produced some very good results had if it had stayed a few days longer"[147], 11 APC's Commanding Officer, Sqn Ldr Vale, was more upbeat:

> *Each pilot carried out bombing, Air to Air and Air to Ground Firing, and also several attacks at Dive and Low Level Bombing. After a very poor start a great improvement was shown in all respects especially Air to Air Firing. The Final results obtained at the end of the Course being above average. The double drogue system was used for Air to Air and a vast improvement was obtained on the single drogue on the last day.*[148]

24 May 1944 – There was no operational flying today, as it was dedicated purely to packing up, returning to Bolt Head, and unpacking again. The pilots departed Fairwood Common at 13:00 and arrived back 30 minutes later, and their return also entailed the movement of 610 Squadron once again. This unit departed for Harrowbeer whilst 131 Squadron moved from Harrowbeer to Culmhead. During the day, Sqn Ldr Glen was summoned to Sector Headquarters at Exeter with some urgency and left immediately.

25 May 1944 – Although a limited amount of non-operational flying was undertaken today, poor weather conditions prevented almost all operational flying. This was no doubt a welcome respite for both the pilots and ground crews as they settled in to Bolt Head again, where they would remain until 19 June. The only job of the day took place at 05:55, when Flt Lt Tom Slack and Fg Off Peter Graham were sent up to search for five MTBs. They landed again at 06:45, the results of the search unrecorded, and there was no more operational flying for the next 34 hours.

26 May 1944 – Weather once again hindered flying and the only operational flight all day was a ten-minute scramble by Flt Lt Terry Spencer and Fg Off Keith Curtis at 15:55. The main event of the day however, was the arrival of crushing news that Sqn Ldr Glen was being posted to 10 Group

as a Supernumerary. It was not a promotion. So disgusted were the pilots, its announcement almost caused a mutiny.

The ORB explains that Glen was summoned to see the Group Captain at Exeter on the day the Squadron returned to Bolt Head from Fairwood Common to be told he was being relieved of his command. The Group Captain was…

> …undecided as to wether [sic] the Squadron or it's [sic] Commander lacked that vital spark, so posted our Leader. There was a great deal of resentment in the Squadron on the sudden and altogether incomprehensible move, for we had not been in 10 Group for more than three weeks.[149]

This was a most perplexing and unusual statement to make about Glen, and stands in stark contrast to the RAF's statement only six months before, when he was awarded a Bar to his DFC. His citation read,

> This officer has led his flight with exceptional skill and keenness. He is a most determined fighter, whose efforts to destroy the enemy at every opportunity have been highly commendable.[150]

Many years after the event, the pilots still spoke strongly of the event, every man resenting Glen's dismissal. Flt Lt Ron Collis recalled,

> I never knew why he was fired. One afternoon at Hope Cove, when we were at Bolt Head, he and I had been fishing, and when we got ashore an urgent message was awaiting, ordering him to report to Sector HQ at Exeter. I went along for the ride, and he certainly had no inkling what it was all about. Apparently the Sector Commander (? Sir Archie Hope) had blasted him about how he was running the squadron and told him he was being relieved. Personally I had thought he was running it pretty well. He was very surprised and upset.[151]

Fg Off Peter Cowell felt that Glen had possibly "…upset Group Capt. Morgan & Group Capt. Sir Archibald Hope. This was very unpopular with the Squadron and there was nearly a mutiny at the time!!"[152]

Having joined 41 Squadron as a Sergeant Pilot in March 1941, Glen had been commissioned in January 1942 whilst still with the unit. By the time he left on a posting to Malta in early May 1942, he had achieved 3-0-1½ victories to his credit over 59 operational sorties, and was awarded the DFC shortly after his departure.

His tenure in Malta only lasted three months as he was seriously injured in a bomb blast, but in that time had achieved another 4-0-4½ victories. Glen was evacuated home in August 1942 and spent six weeks in hospital before being assigned to ground duties for the following ten months.

By July 1943, Glen was considered fit enough to return to operations and found himself, much to his surprise, posted back to 41 Squadron as a Flying Officer. Subsequent promotions to Acting Flight Lieutenant and OC, B Flight, to Flight Lieutenant, and finally to Acting Squadron Leader to command 41 Squadron, in January 1944, meant that Glen had, in effect, filled every flying rank on the unit, and was indeed the only man to have done so throughout the entire War.

Having served in the RAF in the air and on the ground, and having been wounded and twice decorated – he was awarded a Bar to his DFC in November 1943 after achieving two more victories – he was a very experienced airman, well liked, and understandably very respected by the entire Squadron. He, if anyone, suggests one researcher, was the heart and soul of 41 Squadron. All the greater, therefore, was the shock amongst the men that he was removed for what were looking increasingly like political reasons. Some felt it was an effort to 'knock the 11 Group attitude' out of a Squadron now in 10 Group, and Glen was a mere pawn in the game; it has merit.

Even Flt Lt Terry Spencer, who in the end only served on the Squadron with Glen for one month, felt most upset by the entire affair. He kept detailed diaries throughout the War, and entries from the period reflect the level of anger on the Squadron:

Preparing for Overlord

Flt Lt Terry Spencer joined 41 Squadron on 2 May 1944 as OC A Flight, replacing Flt Lt Don Smith RAAF. Spencer remained with the Squadron until 3 January 1945, during which time he claimed one destroyed FW190 and seven destroyed V1s. © Terry Spencer, via Cara and Raina Spencer

26 May 1944   *Very heavy blow to the squadron – news that Pinky Glen is posted. A wizard bloke – liked by everyone. No one knows why. A ginormous piss-up and break up in the mess.*

27 May 1944   *Everyone really bolshy over Pinky leaving.*[153]

27 May 1944 – Regardless of the level of anger amongst the men, mutiny was not an option, and the show had to go on. The Squadron was back to routine business today, as they trod water, waiting to see who their new Commanding Officer would be. In the end, however, low cloud and mist kept the Squadron on the ground until lunchtime and the day's total operational flying was limited to just three uneventful scrambles. The first of these took place from 13:40 to 14:10, and the second from 16:30 to 17:05.[154]

Just before 20:20, Control plotted a fighter reconnaissance of two aircraft 45 miles south-southeast of The Lizard at 2,000 feet. The aircraft were tracked as they flew in a northerly direction for five miles at 3,000 feet, then changed course to the southeast as far as 30 miles north of Île Vierge, France, where the plot faded.

In reaction, 610 Squadron's Blue Section, then on routine patrol, was diverted to Morlaix, 1 Squadron's White Section, also already airborne, was ordered to intercept the plots, and 41 Squadron's Red Section (Robinson MB845 & Refshauge MB862) was scrambled with similar orders, and was airborne at 20:30.

Nine minutes into Red Section's patrol, a new hostile raid of at least three aircraft was plotted flying northwest at 2,000 feet, their path followed by Allied radar from 20 miles northwest of Alderney to 30 miles south-southwest of Portland. At this point, the aircraft climbed to 30,000 feet, turned south, and split into two separate formations, one of which faded 20 miles north of Guernsey, and the other 15 miles northwest of Alderney.

Red Section was diverted to attempt an interception of the aircraft, but Fg Offs Robinson and Refshauge were too far west to mount any effective chase. When the plots faded, they returned to base with nothing to report, putting down at 21:20.[155]

28 May 1944 – Fine weather allowed an early start to the day, and Flt Lt Terry Spencer and Fg Off 'Jack' Malone conducted a shipping reconnaissance to St. Malo and Guernsey at first light.

Airborne at 05:55, the pair flew a route that took them directly to St. Peter Port, then to St. Malo, Lézardrieux, and back to Bolt Head. They put down again at 07:00 with no shipping to report, but having been greeted by a little accurate Flak at Cap d'Erquy, northeast of St. Brieuc.[156]

Despite good conditions, there was no more operational flying until 17:00 when the unit participated in Rhubarb 259, which consisted of a sweep of Pontusval, Vannes and Cap d'Erquy by four Spitfire XIVs from 610 Squadron, and a sweep of Landivisiau, Lamballe and Cap d'Erquy by four Spitfire XIIs from 41 Squadron.

Both squadrons were airborne at 17:00, and 610 Squadron found and attacked locomotives and wagons west of Landivisiau and southeast of Lamballe. However, they lost one pilot, Fg Off Brian Colgan, who was hit by Flak, force-landed eight miles east-southeast of Lamballe and was captured. His aircraft, RB175, was the first Spitfire XIV to be lost over enemy territory.

41 Squadron's contingent was led by Flt Lt Tom Slack (MB847), and had only been in the air a few minutes when Fg Off Peter Cowell (EN224) realised he could switch over to his jettison tank but it would not feed, and he was forced to return. He landed unimpressed ten minutes after take-off, recording in his logbook that day, "Jet tank not feeding – had to return!!!"[157,158]

Slack and the remaining two pilots, Fg Offs Ken Robinson (MB794) and 'Momo' Balasse (MB841) continued on, determined to complete the sweep. Searching the roads and railways of the Brittany coast, they came across four motor cars on the road between Bourbriac and Morlaix, which were shot up and damaged.

Near Yffiniac, they also spotted a locomotive hauling 40 trucks. They all attacked and the locomotive received numerous strikes in the boiler, resulting in large clouds of steam and black smoke emanating from it. Satisfied, they returned to Bolt Head, where they landed at 18:45.

The day ended with an uneventful scramble between 20:10 and 20:55, but the main topic of conversation today was the arrival of the Squadron's new Commanding Officer and the departure of Sqn Ldr Glen.

Spitfire XII, MB882, EB-B, the aircraft of the OC A Flight. Initially flown by Flt Lt Don Smith RAAF, Flt Terry Spencer adopted the aircraft as his personal mount from 3 May 1944 onwards. © Terry Spencer, via Cara and Raina Spencer

'Pinkie' Glen is Replaced

The AOC 10 Group's substitute for Glen arrived on 28 May 1944 in the form of 25-year-old Squadron Leader Robert Hugh Chapman, an experienced career officer, but one who had relatively little combat experience.

Having joined the RAF in December 1937, Chapman was granted a Short Service Commission in February 1938 and posted to his first operational unit, 32 Squadron, in September that year. By May 1939, he had been posted to Egypt where he joined his second unit, 112 Squadron, flying Gladiators from Helwan.

He subsequently served briefly with 102 Maintenance Unit in Khartoum, but was posted to 250 Squadron flying Tomahawks in Palestine in May 1941, and was promoted to Flying Officer two months later. On completion of his tour in 1943, Chapman returned to the United Kingdom and was posted to 57 OTU as a flying instructor, but was sent to Coltishall to join 64 Squadron as a Supernumerary Squadron Leader in mid-December that year.

He now arrived from that unit, without victory or decoration. These are, of course, no qualification for becoming a Squadron Commander, but his experience stood in stark contrast to the man he was replacing, on the eve of the launch of the invasion of Europe, when a strong and experienced leader was required. If nothing else, changing the Commanding Officer at this pending watershed in the War for apparent political reasons was questionable to say the least.

Pilots from the time have lauded Chapman as a 'good type', but felt he did not have the experience required to lead the unit at this crucial time. This is not intended to criticise Chapman as he, too, was just a pawn in the AOC 10 Group's politics and, moreover, his job was all the more difficult because of the resentment the pilots felt – not at Chapman – but simply because 'Pinkie' Glen had been replaced. In reality, Chapman was little more than a victim himself; the upshot was that he never felt accepted by the men and was gone again within three months.

A deeply upset Sqn Ldr Glen was immediately sent on a week's leave, and joined the Fighter Leaders School at RAF Milfield as Staff on the day the invasion of Europe commenced. He remained with this unit until October 1945, seeing no more action, and was released from the RAFVR in early February 1946.

By the time of his departure from the RAF, Glen had served significant time with both the Fighter Leaders School and Central Fighter Establishment. He was asked to stay on as a Test Pilot, however he reluctantly declined the offer, despite his love for flying, as his wife considered he had put himself in enough danger for one lifetime.

He then forged a solid career with the Central Manufacturing & Trading Co. (Dudley) Ltd., rising to Board level, before being forced into early retirement after suffering a major heart attack. A second heart attack took his life in December 1979; he was aged just 61.

29 May 1944 – There was an early start to the day today, with a shipping and weather reconnaissance flown to Brest, L'Aber-Wrac'h, and Morlaix by two pilots between 05:40 and 07:05. The operation was uneventful and no shipping was seen.[159]

Despite fair weather persisting until a deterioration in conditions in the late afternoon and evening, the Squadron only flew once more operationally all day, which was another Rhubarb in conjunction with 610 Squadron late in the morning.

41 Squadron was airborne at 10:55 and 610 Squadron approximately ten minutes later, to participate in Rhubarb 261, the chief purpose of which was to find targets of opportunity, but also to locate the Spitfire XIV lost by 610 Squadron the day before and, if possible, destroy it. 41 Squadron was sent to Coutances, Avranches, Dol-de-Bretagne and Lamballe, led by Flt Lt Terry Spencer, whilst 610 was sent to Lamballe, Rennes, Redon and Vannes.

Commencing their sweep on the Cotentin Peninsula, east of Jersey, 41 Squadron's section found a train with a few dozen goods trucks at La Haye-du-Puits. They made three attacks, claiming the locomotive and all 40 trucks damaged. A short distance further south, in the Lessay area, Plt Off Peter Gibbs spotted three locomotives, and dived on them, followed by Flt Lt Terry Spencer and Fg Off 'Andy' Anderson, leaving Plt Off Jimmy Payne above to provide them cover. They were similarly claimed as damaged.

From there, they continued the search for the Spitfire XIV, passing over Dinan, Jugon-les-Lacs and Lamballe, but saw no sign of it. They concluded that it was likely "the Hun had moved it away during the night"[160], and returned to Bolt Head at 12:45. This concluded the day's operational flying. Spencer noted in his logbook that day, "We shot up four engines & about 40 goods trucks & searched unsuccessfully for a Spit XIV – the first to be shot down".[161] 610 Squadron made no claims on their sweep and their search for the Spitfire XIV was similarly fruitless.

Pilots, 29 May 1944	Serial	Section	Up	Down
Spencer, Terence	MB843	Red	10:55	12:45
Gibbs, N. Peter	MB845			
Payne, Jim C. J.	MB847	Blue		
Anderson, Robert E.	MB837			

30 May 1944 – The morning commenced with two shipping reconnaissances of two pilots each to Brittany and the Channel Islands. The first pair was airborne at 05:35 to St. Peter Port, St. Malo and Lézardrieux, and the second pair at 05:52 to Brest, L'Aber-Wrac'h, and Morlaix. They landed at 06:55 and 06:58, respectively, reporting uneventful patrols and no shipping.[162]

Despite less than ideal weather, four pilots were sent on Rodeo 152 to Gaël, Vannes and Kerlin Bastard at 11:35 in search of German bombers that were believed to have moved into the area overnight. However, deteriorating weather before reaching the French coast forced the operation to be aborted mid-Channel and the pilots returned to Bolt Head at 12:05. A second sweep as a part of the same Rodeo was planned for 12:30 but thunderstorms and poor visibility forced its cancellation before take-off, and it was another 9½ hours before the pilots would be airborne operationally again today.

A hostile raid of one aircraft was plotted just before 21:30 flying northwards at 4,000 feet around ten miles off Cap de la Hague, the most north-westerly point of the Cotentin Peninsula, and approximately 80 miles southeast of Bolt Head. Fg Off 'Andy' Anderson and Flt Sgt Freddie Woollard were scrambled as Green Section at 21:35 to intercept it, but the enemy aircraft turned south soon after they were airborne and lost height. The pair gave chase, but the plot faded and they saw no sign of it.

At 22:05, however, the two pilots were diverted to a new plot, this one moving in a southerly direction around 24 miles west-northwest of Guernsey, which was only around 60 miles from Bolt Head. Changing course to attempt an interception, the plot faded immediately and did not reappear on radar. Once again nothing was seen, and Anderson and Woollard returned to base at 22:35, with nothing to report.

31 May 1944 – The Squadron was relieved of their usual early morning shipping reconnaissances this morning, as the patrols to St. Peter Port, St. Malo and Lézardrieux, and to L'Aber-Wrac'h and Morlaix, were undertaken by 610 Squadron instead.

The only operational flying 41 Squadron undertook all day was Rodeo 152, an apparent repetition of the previous day's two aborted low-level sweeps of the Gaël, Vannes and Kerlin Bastard areas to find Ju188 bombers, thought to be in the region.

Blue Section of four pilots was airborne at 11:30, led by Flt Lt Tom Slack, and swept the aerodromes at Gaël and Vannes at zero feet, but found them devoid of any aircraft. They did, however, shoot up dispersal huts at Vannes Aerodrome as a parting gesture.

As they encountered heavy accurate Flak on reaching the Kerlin Bastard area, which split the section up, Slack ordered Blues 2, 3 and 4 to operate and return independently. Slack then swept

Kerlin Bastard airfield alone and found no aircraft again, but soon spotted a large German lorry, which he strafed, causing it to overturn and catch fire. On their way out, the rest of the section attacked a locomotive and goods wagons in the Carhaix area, which they claimed as damaged, and Slack followed them out, finding nothing more of note on the way.

By the time they were heading home, the second section, Red, which was led by Flt Lt Terry Spencer, was already in France, having taken off from Bolt Head at 12:25. Slack radioed Spencer, using a pre-arranged code, to inform him that his section had swept the aerodromes and found no aircraft, thereby allowing Spencer a free-range sweep for targets of opportunity.

His section spotted a passenger train at Landévant and, recognising the presence of civilians, made a warning beat up on it. Understanding what this meant, the passengers streamed out of the train with great haste, after which Terry Spencer dived down, attacked the locomotive and blew it up.

Continuing on, the section spotted a 400-ton merchant ship on the Blavet River between Hennebont and Lorient. All four pilots dived on the vessel and riddled it with cannon fire from bow to stern, then pulled up and headed for home, where they landed at 14:20, claiming it damaged. This concluded the day's operational flying. The participating pilots were:

Pilots, 31 May 1944	Serial	Section	Up	Down
Slack, Thomas A. H.	MB876	Blue	11:30	13:15
Balasse, Maurice A. L.	MB803			
Thiele, Keith F.	MB841			
Appleton, Arthur S.	MB837			
Spencer, Terence	MB882	Red	12:25	14:20
Malone, Charles J.	MB843			
Cowell, Peter	MB795			
Stevenson, Ian T.	EN620			

June 1944 – On the eve of the launch of Operation *Overlord*, the Squadron was busied all along the invasion front, and the ground crews painted black and white 'Invasion Stripes' on the fuselages and wings of the Squadron's Spitfires the day before D-Day. These were designed to enhance recognition of friendly aircraft in the air, on the ground and at sea in the nerves and confusion expected in the heat of battle during the Normandy landings.

There was no operational flying on only one day during this period as a result of weather conditions, 11 June, whilst flying was reduced on 1, 8, 9, 13 and 16 June for the same reason. The otherwise generally increased intensity of operations and long flying days as summer approached took their toll on the pilots and several men fell victim to Flak batteries on the Channel Islands; one pilot was killed, one captured and one wounded. Three more pilots ditched in the Channel and were rescued, and numerous other aircraft suffered damage from anti-aircraft fire, but were able to make it back to Bolt Head.

Mid-month, however, the German military released their newest weapon, the V1 flying bomb. As a result, the Squadron found itself hastily pulled off offensive invasion support on 19 June, with just half a day to pack, and thrust once again into defensive operations. This time, they were dealing with something completely new to them: trying to intercept and bring down rocket-powered flying bombs before they reached London and other civilian targets.

1 June 1944 – D-Day -5. Generally cloudy weather with widespread drizzle reduced the Squadron's operational flying today to just the usual morning shipping reconnaissances of the French coast, and an uneventful evening scramble.

Four pilots in two sections of two were airborne at 08:15, the first consisting of Fg Offs Herb Wagner and 'Jack' Refshauge, who swept westwards from the Sept-Îles to L'Aber-Wrac'h. They found nothing but cloudy conditions with poor visibility along the coastline and returned at 09:30 with nothing to report.

The second section, however, was much more successful. Comprising Fg Off Ken Robinson (MB881) and Plt Off Peter Gibbs (EN224), they were tasked with sweeping the coast in a general westerly direction from St. Malo to the Sept-Îles.

On the way in, they did a beat-up of Guernsey at zero feet, "as ordered by the Controller"[163], to provoke German troops on the ground. A Flak post swivelled its gun to aim at them, and Gibbs fired at it, scoring hits. However, the Flak post managed to get a shot in first – or they fired simultaneously – and was not far off the mark, as Gibbs received a hit in his tail fin. This did not cause him any trouble, and he was not aware of it until it was discovered by ground crews after his return.

Continuing towards the French coast at St. Malo, the two pilots climbed to 8,000 feet and commenced their shipping reconnaissance. Finding no sign of shipping between St. Malo and St. Brieuc, they ventured inland, and soon spotted a locomotive at Yffiniac, just southeast of the latter town. As the No. 1 in the section, Robinson took the lead and went in first, attacking with a long burst of cannon fire. Gibbs followed him down and made a similar attack, which resulted in a large explosion of steam and black smoke.

On climbing again, Gibbs sighted another locomotive on the same line, just a mile to the north. Diving again, he fired a burst of 20mm cannon, causing the boiler of this locomotive to explode, too. A short while later, yet another locomotive was spotted nearby, and both pilots attacked this engine with the same result.[164]

Satisfied with the morning's work, Robinson and Gibbs then returned to Bolt Head, where they touched down at 09:45 claiming three locomotives damaged to Cat. B status, and a hole was discovered in the tail of Gibbs' aircraft.[165] The weather was by now quite unsuitable for further operations and there was no more operational flying for the next eleven hours.

An alarm to scramble went off at 20:45, and Fg Off 'Momo' Balasse and WO 'Archie' Appleton were quickly airborne to make an interception of an inbound plot. However, they saw nothing and landed again 55 minutes later.

2 June 1944 – D-Day -4. Fair weather today provided good flying conditions, but the Squadron ending up spending a lot more time in the air than they had originally envisaged. They lost one of the 'old hands' today, which constituted the unit's first loss in action in eight months.

The day started early with a weather reconnaissance of the French coast between St. Malo and Brehat Island [Île-de-Bréhat], close to the most northerly point of the Brittany [Bretagne] Peninsula. Fg Off 'Momo' Balasse and WO 'Archie' Appleton, were airborne at 05:35, but the trip was uneventful and they returned at 07:00 with nothing to report.

As routine as this seemed, it was the proverbial lull before the storm, as the next patrol would be anything but uneventful. Around 10:00, the Squadron mounted two shipping reconnaissances. The first of these, Black Section, consisting of Flt Lts Ronald Collis (MB837) and William Stowe (EN620), was airborne at 10:00 but they returned immediately as Collis' aircraft was 'u/s'.

Collis swapped MB837 for MB795, and they were off the deck again at 10:15, flying directly to the Sept-Îles, and from there to Morlaix, Lannilis, and finally L'Aber-Wrac'h, where five sea-going barges were observed in the estuary, moored off Landéda. One of these opened fire on the section, but no damage is recorded. The pilots did not attack the barges and returned to base at 11:30.[166]

The second shipping reconnaissance was undertaken by Fg Off Herb Wagner (MB843) and Flt Sgt 'Steve' Stevenson (MB847), who were also airborne at 10:00, as White Section. Their task was to reconnoitre St. Peter Port on Guernsey on the way in, followed by St. Malo on the mainland; they did not make it past their first destination.

Sweeping down the Little Russel, the strait between Guernsey and Herm, they flew past Brehon Tower, a solid, round, 56-foot (19-metre) stone fortification built in 1856 on a small rocky outcrop between the islands, on top of which the German garrison had mounted an anti-aircraft gun.

Fg Off Herb Wagner, an American who joined the RAF prior to the United States' entry into the War, served with 41 Squadron from 2 May 1943 to 2 June 1944, when he was shot down by Flak from Guernsey and captured. © Cowell family

The gun opened up on the pair and Wagner's aircraft took a hit in the radiator. Immediately recognising he had a problem, Wagner climbed steeply and turned back for England. However, he had only covered a short distance when he engine seized and he was forced to bale out at 3,000 feet, approximately 4-6 miles northeast of Guernsey.

Flt Sgt Stevenson climbed higher and orbited Wagner whilst he issued maydays and reported the situation to Bolt Head. He continued to circle Wagner until he was relieved by two Spitfire Vb's from 276 (ASR) Squadron, and made a final departing dive over his counterpart, who he last saw "waving cheerfully"[167] from the water.

276 Squadron's Spitfires dropped Wagner a dinghy, which he clambered into, after which they maintained an orbit over him until they were themselves relieved. This relief came in the form of a 276 Squadron Vickers Warwick from Portreath, escorted by 41 Squadron's Red Section (Spencer MB882, Cowell MB804, Robinson MB881 & Gibbs MB837). Whilst Plt Off Gibbs returned early with tank trouble, the remaining pilots orbited the Warwick as it proceeded to drop a lifeboat to Wagner, coming under intense fire from Guernsey's anti-aircraft guns as it did. Although the boat landed in the water just 50 yards from him, its parachutes failed to collapse, and it was blown out of his reach. All the while, the current was drawing Wagner towards Guernsey and the Little Russel.

Left little choice, Spencer, Cowell and Robinson had to leave Wagner and escort the Warwick home, landing at Bolt Head again at 12:15. Soon thereafter, another Warwick headed out to Guernsey without 41 Squadron in a second attempt to rescue him. On this occasion, however, only one of the boat's parachutes deployed, which was insufficient for its weight, and it broke up on hitting the water. Unable to help further, they also returned to base, but left 276 Squadron Spitfires orbiting Wagner, at least reassuring him with their presence, even if they were unable to physically rescue him.

41 Squadron returned to Guernsey again during the afternoon, escorting an amphibious Supermarine Walrus on a third attempt to retrieve Wagner, which planned to effect a rescue by landing in the sea by his dinghy.[168] Red Section (Spencer MB882, Refshauge MB845, Robinson MB795 & Curtis EN620) and Black Section (Slack MB803 and Anderson MB876) were airborne at 15:10 to return to Guernsey anew, but only ten minutes later received advice over the R/T from 276 Squadron's Spitfires that a boat had been sent out from Guernsey to pick Wagner up.

> *At 15 20 hours a small white boat with red white and blue vertical stripes on its starboard bow came out from Guernsey, picked up F/O Wagner and returned to the island.*[169]

The Squadron's pilots were on the scene soon thereafter but there was little they could do but shoot up the dinghy and stray lifeboat and sink them. Disappointed, they returned to base and landed between 16:05 and 16:15. Some 40 aircraft had been involved in the ASR operation throughout the day. Although expressing the likely opinion of the whole Squadron that day, Fg Off Peter Cowell was perhaps a little less reserved in his choice of words when he recorded in is logbook, "[Wagner was] eventually picked up from GUERNSEY by the Huns!! Bastards."[170]

Wagner was taken under guard on coming ashore and moved to the mainland for processing. He found himself uncomfortably close to the front when the Operation *Overlord* was launched four days later, and moved further back. Whilst under way, he made a dash for freedom, by jumping a hedge and running when no-one was looking. Although initially successful, he was recaptured later the same day by the Panzer Corps in the Falaise area.

Wagner was then transported to Chartres, some 80 miles (130km) to the southeast, from where he was entrained for interrogation at Dulag Luft, outside Frankfurt. By late July, Wagner found himself in Stalag Luft I, in Barth, Germany, and this is where he remained until he was liberated in May 1945.

He had served exactly 13 months with 41 Squadron, even though, as an American, he could have left the RAFVR at any time and transferred to the USAAF. However, he chose to stay where he was, and this fact had earned him considerable kudos amongst his fellow pilots on the Squadron.[171] In September 2005, he recalled,

> *On June 2, 1944, I was leader on low level recco to Guernsey Harbour. I flew directly over a flak tower but was going fast enough to get out of the harbour and bale out. 41 Squadron had a flight over me all day to keep the Germans from picking me up. ASR dropped airborne life boats twice, but one broke up and one drifted away. At sunset, the Germans sent French fishermen out to pick me up. I was in Caen in Normandy on D Day – very dicey.*[172]

However, the day was not quite over for 41 Squadron, as, upon its return, the second Warwick had reported having seen a periscope six miles southeast of St. Peter Port, and just west of Sark, at 49°25' N 02°25' W, on a course of 190°, as well as two surfaced U-Boats in a Bay in south-eastern Guernsey, close to St. Peter Port at 14:00. As a result, Flt Lts Terry Spencer (MB882) and Ron Collis (MB845) took off again at 17:00 and returned to Guernsey, but "nothing was seen apart from intense flak".[173] They were back on the ground again at 17:50, unable to confirm the report, and this concluded the day's flying.

3 June 1944 – D-Day -3. The Squadron was off to an early start today, and Red Section was airborne on a shipping reconnaissance to Guernsey, St. Malo and Lézardrieux at 06:55. A section of four from 126 Squadron and two sections of two from 610 Squadron were also airborne around the same time on similar reconnaissance flights. However, weather conditions on the French coast hindered visibility, and all returned with nothing to report.

At 10:15, 41 Squadron's Green Section was sent on another shipping reconnaissance, to Guernsey, St. Malo, Lézardrieux, the Sept-Îles and L'Aber-Wrac'h, with special instructions to search for the U-Boats reported the previous afternoon near St. Peter Port. They, too, returned with nothing to report.[174]

Yellow Section was scrambled at 13:20, but saw nothing, and was subsequently ordered to search for a Liberator crew, which had ditched in the Channel. They returned with nothing to report, and were replaced in the air by Black Section at 15:10. They, too, searched unsuccessfully, and landed again at 16:15.

Yellow Section (Stevenson MB804 & Gibbs EN221) was scrambled at 18:20 when Raid H.926 of one aircraft was plotted 30 miles north of Morlaix, flying in a northerly direction. The pair patrolled south of Start Point, but when the plot faded and nothing was seen, they returned to base and landed at 18:55.

In the meantime, White Section had also been scrambled at 18:25. It was, however, a false alarm and the two pilots did one circuit and landed again within five minutes. As they did so, Red Section (Chapman MB881 & Stowe EN224) took off[175] on a convoy patrol, escorting ships around Lizard Point, Cornwall. This constituted the new Commanding Officer's first operational sortie with the Squadron.

White Section was also scrambled for an ASR patrol at 19:05, but returned 50 minutes later having seen nothing. They were followed down five minutes later by Red Section, who had been relieved by Blue Section (Slack MB876 & Balasse MB837). The latter pair had taken off at 19:25 and returned at 21:00 after an uneventful patrol, completing the last of 18 operational sorties for the day.

4 June 1944 – D-Day -2. Clearly underwhelmed by the day's activity, the author of the Squadron's ORB summed up the entire day in just one sentence: "From 05.30 to 17.35 the Squadron carried out a series of boring and uneventful Convoy Patrols."[176] Indeed, eight uneventful convoy patrols were flown throughout the day in sections of two to four pilots, but as mundane as these must patrols must have been for the Squadron, the fact that the launch of the Second Front was less than 48 hours away meant they were also imperative.

Had the German Military gotten wind of the movements and sent raiders in any force, SHAEF's intricately laid plans could have been significantly set back at a time it could ill-afford any obstructions. The launch of the Second Front was actually planned for tonight, and thousands of ships, hundreds of thousands of men and thousands of tons of equipment were jostling to reach their final embarkation points along England's south coast.

In the event, the launch was set back a day as weather conditions were not suitable, and seas were rough, but the RAF's presence over their heads was a security cordon that was necessary, even if mundane. The Squadron's contribution to this protective barrier today was as follows:

Convoy Patrols, 4 June 1944	Section	Up	Down
Chapman MB881, Curtis EN620, Spencer MB882, Refshauge MB845	Red	05:30	06:45
Cowell MB882, Collis EN224, Cook EN620	Yellow	07:20	09:00
Birbeck MB841, Woollard MB803, Thiele MB804, Fleming MB798	Blue	09:40	11:05
Slack MB876, Appleton MB847, Thiele MB804, Woollard MB803	Blue	11:40	13:10
Cowell MB881, Refshauge MB845, Cook MB862, Stowe EN224	White	13:40	14:55
Birbeck MB876, Fleming MB847, Payne MB804, Woollard MB803	Blue	14:40	15:55
Spencer MB882, Stevenson MB881, Robinson MB862, Curtis EN620	Red	15:40	17:00
Slack MB876, Anderson EN221	Black	16:45	17:35

5 June 1944 – D-Day -1. In a repetition of the previous day's activity, the Squadron once again spent the entire day on "special convoy patrols on fixed patrol lines"[177], which were only interrupted by scrambles at 12:50 and 18:30. Of greater significance today, perhaps, was that the Squadron's Spitfires were all painted with black and white invasion stripes in preparation for the overnight launch of the Operation *Overlord*.[178] Historically, the day was also significant in the Mediterranean Theatre where Rome was liberated by Allied forces.

With the Second Front just hours away, it was not surprising, based on the south coast as they were, that the pilots just saw today "Bags of invasion craft – That's all".[179] The day's nine convoy patrols today consisted of the following:

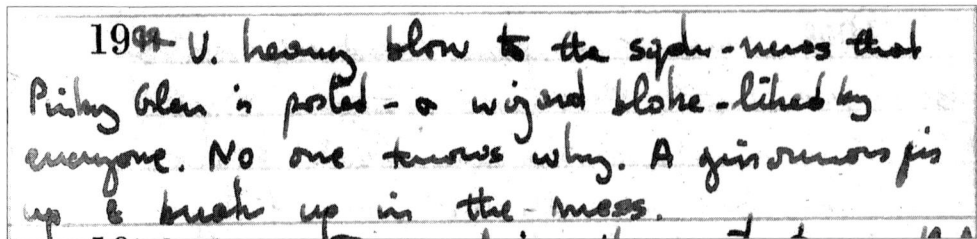

Entry for 26 May 1944 in Flt Lt Terry Spencer's personal diary, noting the outcry over the announcement of Sqn Ldr 'Pinkie' Glen's removal as OC 41 Squadron. © Terry Spencer, via Cara and Raina Spencer

Convoy Patrols, 5 June 1944	Section	Up	Down
Chapman MB881, Woollard MB803, Birbeck MB841, Thiele MB847	Blue	05:25	07:00
Chapman MB881, Woollard MB837, Birbeck MB841, Thiele MB847	Green	07:55	09:05
Spencer MB882, Stevenson MB862, Cowell EN224, Robinson MB845	Yellow	10:20	11:40
Collis EN224, Refshauge MB845, Curtis EN620, Stowe MB798	White	11:15	12:35
Payne MB804, Woollard MB837, Balasse MB842, Anderson EN221	Green	13:15	14:35
Birbeck MB841, Appleton EN221, Thiele MB841, Fleming MB803	Blue	15:20	16:55
Birbeck MB841, Appleton EN221, Thiele MB841, Fleming MB803	Blue	17:40	19:00
Chapman MB881, Stevenson EN224, Curtis EN620, Collis MB794	Red	19:45	21:10
Chapman MB881, Stevenson EN224, Collis MB795, Curtis EN620	Yellow	21:55	22:55

At 12:30, in the midst of the patrols, Blue Section (Slack MB876 & Fleming MB841) was scrambled but saw nothing, and landed again 55 minutes later. At 18:30, White Section (Spencer MB882 & Stowe MB794) was also scrambled, and was sent to 8,000 feet where they intercepted an Allied Mosquito. Identifying the plot as friendly, they turned for home and were back on the ground within 20 minutes. This concluded the day's flying.

By the time the last convoy patrol was on the ground that evening, Operation *Overlord* – the Second Front – had already begun, and the first five assault groups were on their way to Normandy. As the Squadron slept, bombers began dropping their payloads on coastal batteries between Cherbourg and Le Havre, and thousands of commandoes were landing behind the invasion beaches by parachute and glider. The Allied invasion of Europe had begun. Like a slingshot pulled taut and suddenly released, a mighty force had been set in motion that could now not be stopped.

The Second Front

British Prime Minister Winston Churchill's War Cabinet had long since realised that the only way to conquer Hitler would be to launch an assault on Europe, and the Russian Premier, Joseph Stalin, had begun demanding the British introduce a second front ever since the launch of Operation *Barbarossa*, the German invasion of Russia, in June 1941. Although long-term plans for an invasion of France had been drawn up by the British as early as September 1941 under the codename *Roundup*, these were indefinitely deferred when Japan and the United States entered the War two months later.

However, following consultation with the American government during 1942, *Roundup* was revived and scheduled for execution by 48 Allied Divisions in Spring 1943. Nonetheless, as preparations progressed, shortages became obvious in many resources, not the least of which were landing craft, which caused the plan to be shelved permanently. Although an attack was made at Dieppe in Operation *Jubilee* in August 1942, it was effectively little more than a test bed for an eventual invasion of France, and Churchill opted instead for Operation *Torch*, the invasion of North Africa, in November 1942.

Even though American Commanders favoured an earlier attack on mainland Europe under their own proposal, Operation *Sledgehammer*, which foresaw a landing at either Brest or Cherbourg, the Dieppe raid clearly demonstrated to the Allies that they were still some time away from an effective invasion. The logistics of such a combined operation – multi-national forces in the air, on the land and on the sea – still needed significant work. Moreover, one deciding factor had not yet been achieved: air superiority.

Whilst the British proposed an invasion of Europe from the south, which would follow a successful sweep across North Africa – and did in fact commence with the invasion of Sicily in July 1943 – it was not until the conclusion of the Tehran Conference on 1 December 1943 that the United States, United Kingdom and Russia finally reached mutual agreement for a full scale invasion of mainland Europe in 1944. Codenamed *Overlord*[180], it was tentatively planned for May and American General Dwight D. Eisenhower was named over all Commander, and given the title 'Supreme Allied Commander of the Allied Expeditionary Force'.

The original concept of Operation *Sledgehammer* was resurrected, and landings in force were planned along a heavily fortified 50-mile (80km) beachhead in the Bay of the Seine [Baie de la Seine] in France's Lower Normandy [Basse-Normandie] Region, supported by diversionary operations in the Pas-de-Calais and Brittany regions. The coastline between La Madeleine and Ouistreham was split into five code-named sectors from west to east, which are well-known even today: *Utah*, *Omaha*, *Gold*, *Juno* and *Sword*.

The strategy developed into the largest amphibious landing in history, with the battle plan on Day One alone calling for approximately 156,000 troops to be landed on the beaches, and the deployment of some 197,000 Navy personnel manning over 6,900 navy and merchant vessels drawn from eight countries, preceded by an airborne assault by 23,400 men by parachute from 2,395 aircraft and in 867 gliders.[181] Fighter cover was provided over the beaches by nine squadrons of Spitfires, supported just inland by Bomphoons and Mustang fighter-bombers.

Now that air superiority had been achieved, the new condition precedent for the launch of *Overlord* was sufficient moonlight. This provided Eisenhower a window of just a few days each month immediately preceding, during, and immediately following the full moon. This would allow navigational landmarks to be sufficiently visible for shipping and aircraft, and particularly for airborne troops, to enable them to all reach their initial, pre-dawn objectives.

For practical reasons, rather than meteorological, the operation was set back one month, and provisionally planned for 5 June, as a full moon was due the following night. However, when conditions deteriorated on 4 June to wind, high seas and cloudy skies, a launch that night for a landing on the following morning was ruled out. If the unsuitable weather continued, it meant that the operation would have to be set back yet another month.

On 5 June, though, Eisenhower's meteorologists advised him that a weather improvement was expected for the next day. Consulting with his staff and advisors, and weighing up the risks and advantages, Eisenhower decided to launch the operation, and formally gave the order to proceed.

Following his decision, he transmitted a message to the troops about to embark on this historic battle, and printed copies were also distributed to each man and woman involved. This included the personnel of 41 Squadron and Flt Lt Terry Spencer glued his copy into his logbook. It read,

SUPREME HEADQUARTERS
ALLIED EXPEDITIONARY FORCE

[SHAEF insignia]

Soldiers, Sailors and Airmen of the Allied Expeditionary Force!

You are about to embark upon the Great Crusade, toward which we have striven these many months. The eyes of the world are upon you. The hopes and prayers of liberty-loving people everywhere march with you. In company with our brave Allies and brothers-in-arms on other Fronts, you will bring about the destruction of the German war machine, the elimination of Nazi tyranny over the oppressed peoples of Europe, and security for ourselves in a free world.

Your task will not be an easy one. Your enemy is well trained, well equipped and battle-hardened. He will fight savagely.

But this is the year 1944! Much has happened since the Nazi triumphs of 1940-41. The United Nations have inflicted upon the Germans great defeats, in open battle, man-to-man. Our air offensive has seriously reduced their strength in the air and their capacity to wage war on the ground. Our Home Fronts have given us an overwhelming superiority in weapons and munitions of war, and placed at our disposal great reserved of trained fighting men. The tide has turned ! The free men of the world are marching together to Victory!

I have full confidence in your courage, devotion to duty and skill in battle. We will accept nothing less than full Victory !

Good luck! And let us all beseech the blessing of Almighty God upon this great and noble undertaking.

[signature *Dwight D. Eisenhower*][182]

6 June 1944 – D-Day. By the time 41 Squadron started operational flying today at 10:25, the battle in the Bay of the Seine was in full swing. Landings had begun on *Utah* and *Omaha* beaches at 06:30, on *Gold* and *Sword* at 07:25, and on *Juno* at 07:30. At 09:00, General Eisenhower released his first official communiqué to the press informing the world that the Second Front had begun. It was a simple, one sentence brief that concealed the enormity and ferocity of the battle in progress, and stated,

UNDER THE COMMAND OF GENERAL EISENHOWER, ALLIED NAVAL FORCES, SUPPORTED BY STRONG AIR FORCES, BEGAN LANDING ALLIED ARMIES THIS MORNING ON THE NORTHERN COAST OF FRANCE.[183]

Three hours later, Winston Churchill provided significantly more detail when he made the following formal announcement in the House of Commons, without any dramatic introduction:

> *I have also to announce to the House that during the night and the early hours of this morning the first of the series of landings in force upon the European Continent has taken place. In this case the liberating assault fell upon the coast of France. An immense armada of upwards of 4,000 ships, together with several thousand smaller craft, crossed the Channel. Massed airborne landings have been successfully effected behind the enemy lines and landings on the beaches are proceeding at various points at the present time. The fire of the shore batteries has been largely quelled. The obstacles that were constructed in the sea have not proved so difficult as was apprehended. The Anglo-American Allies are sustained by about 11,000 first line aircraft, which can be drawn upon as may be needed for the purposes of the battle. I cannot, of course, commit myself to any particular details. Reports are coming in in rapid succession. So far the Commanders who are engaged report that everything is proceeding according to plan. And what a plan! This vast operation is undoubtedly the most complicated and difficult that has ever occurred. It involves tides, wind, waves, visibility, both from the air and the sea standpoint, and the combined employment of land, air and sea forces in the highest degree of intimacy and in contact with conditions which could not and cannot be fully foreseen.*
>
> *There are already hopes that actual tactical surprise has been attained, and we hope to furnish the enemy with a succession of surprises during the course of the fighting. The battle that has now begun will grow constantly in scale and in intensity for many weeks to come and I shall not attempt to speculate upon its course. This I may say, however. Complete unity prevails throughout the Allied Armies. There is a brotherhood in arms between us and our friends of the United States. There is complete confidence in the supreme commander, General Eisenhower, and his lieutenants, and also in the commander of the Expeditionary Force, General Montgomery. The ardour and spirit of the troops, as I saw myself, embarking in these last few days was splendid to witness. Nothing that equipment, science or forethought could do has been neglected, and the whole process of opening this great new front will be pursued with the utmost resolution both by the commanders and by the United States and British Governments whom they serve.*[184]

Surprisingly perhaps, 41 Squadron was largely unaware of the events going on in Normandy. Nonetheless, despite their unusually late start to the day, it would prove to be a busy one for them and at least 14 operations (28 sorties) were flown in the ten-hour period between 10:25 and 22:40. These consisted of five ASR patrols, five convoy patrols, three shipping reconnaissances, and one scramble.

However, detail is frustratingly scant in the Squadron ORB, which summarises the day's activity in just four sentences over five lines. Additional detail is provided in the Bolt Head and 10 Group ORBs, but indications are that the lack of detail on the Squadron's operations illustrates the routine nature of their activity today, located ca. 125-175 miles (200-280km) from the landing beaches, as they were. Indeed, the Squadron ORB ends the day's entry with, "None of the Sections concerned had anything to report".[185]

The day commenced and ended with similar routine convoy patrols to the previous days, covering all shipping movements off 10 Group's coasts, and were undertaken as follows:

Convoy Patrols, 6 June 1944	Section	Up	Down
Payne MB804 & Woollard MB837186	Blue	10:25	11:45
Robinson MB881 & Stowe EN620	White	17:45	18:55
Cowell MB795 & Curtis MB862	Yellow	18:45	19:55
Fleming MB837 & Appleton MB803	Green	19:45	21:30
Payne MB876 & Appleton MB841	Black	21:15	22:40

In all, 10 Group's squadrons flew 47 convoy protection patrols today, totalling 107 sorties, of which 41 Squadron provided ten.

Accompanying Fg Off Herb Wagner on the reconnaissance when he was shot down on 2 June 1944, Flt Sgt Ian 'Steve' Stevenson issued maydays and orbited Wagner until relieved by other Allied aircraft. © Rossow family

At 11:55, Flt Lts Tom Slack (MB803) and 'Jimmy' Thiele (MB798) took off on a shipping reconnaissance of Guernsey, St. Malo and Lézardrieux, Brittany, followed by Fg Off 'Momo' Balasse (MB842) and Sqn Ldr Chapman (MB881) at 12:50. However, nothing of consequence was seen been either pair, and they returned at 13:35, respectively 13:20, with nothing to report.[187]

Uneventful ASR patrols were flown at 13:00, 13:35, 14:50, and two at 15:40. These were mounted to locate a pilot who baled out at Z.2050, in response to a collision reported at Y.8630, and to find an aircraft reported to have exploded in mid-air at 49°40' N 03°03' W. One of the two ASR patrols at 15:40 also involved an escort to a Warwick of 276 (ASR) Squadron over Guernsey. Considering Fg Off Herb Wagner's recent loss to the island's Flak defences, this patrol must have been particularly hair-raising. Flt Lt Terry Spencer (MB882), whose No. 2 was Flt Sgt Ian Stevenson (MB795), noted in his logbook, "Escorted a Warwick 500 ft over Guernsey A.S.I. 160".[188]

The most notable of the Squadron's patrols today, perhaps, was the last of the day: a shipping reconnaissance flown by Flt Lt 'Joe' Birbeck (EN221) and Flt Sgt Freddie Woollard (MB847) to Morlaix, Lézardrieux, Ushant [Île d'Ouessant] and Brest between 21:30 and 22:50. Between Ushant and the mainland, two miles offshore, they sighted six Kriegsmarine M Class minesweepers sailing in an easterly direction. Five miles to their northwest, they also saw six Allied destroyers "steaming towards them at great speed".[189,190]

By the end of the day, approximately 73,000 American and 83,000 British and Canadian troops had been landed in Normandy, supported by 14,700 sorties by Allied aircraft. Although American objectives on the ground had not been fully realised, the entire beachhead was being held and, in the British and Canadian sectors, it extended six miles (10km) into French territory. As tenuous as it had been at times, particularly in the American sectors, Eisenhower's armies had managed to establish a solid foothold in Normandy and would not be dislodged. The price had, however, been high, and over 4,400 Allied troops had been killed, and many more wounded, whilst the Allied Air Forces had also lost 127 aircraft.[191]

7 June 1944 – D-Day +1. It was an early start for the Squadron today, and they were airborne at 05:30 for two shipping reconnaissances. Red Section, consisting of Flt Lt Terry Spencer (MB882) and Fg Off Keith Curtis (EN620)[192] headed for St. Peter Port, St. Malo and Lézardrieux, whilst

General Dwight D. Eisenhower was appointed Supreme Allied Commander of the Allied Expeditionary Force for Operation *Overlord*, and formally gave the order on 5 June 1944 to proceed with Allied landings the following day, despite concerns about the weather. © Public domain; official U.S. Army photo 77-18-1442

Yellow, comprising Fg Off Harry Cook (MB795) and Flt Sgt 'Steve' Stevenson (MB845) were assigned Morlaix, L'Aber-Wrac'h and Ushant [Île d'Ouessant]. Whilst the latter pair found nothing of interest, and returned at 07:15 reporting an uneventful patrol, the former was more successful.

Arriving over St. Peter Port at 06:10, Spencer and Curtis were greeted by intense light Flak, but sighted at least a dozen Tank Landing Craft. Continuing on, they then saw five medium class minesweepers and a torpedo boat north of Cap Fréhel at 06:25, heading towards St. Malo at a speed of approximately 15 knots. The two pilots then headed for Harrowbeer to report their sightings, then continued on to Bolt Head, where they landed at 07:12.

The reaction was swift. Roadstead 126 was quickly laid on and an hour later eight Typhoon bombers of 263 Squadron were sent to attack the Minesweepers with an escort of eight Spitfires from 610 Squadron. They found a large, 1,500-ton motor vessel in the mouth of The Rance river [La Rance], at St. Malo, but could only straddle its stern with near misses. Unfortunately, no other shipping was seen.

The twelve vessels Spencer and Curtis had seen at St. Peter Port were the target of Roadstead 127, which was airborne 25 minutes after Roadstead 126. 263 Squadron was once again involved, this time deploying eight Typhoons fitted with RP-3 Rocket Projectiles. A close escort was provided by eight Spitfire XIIs from 41 Squadron, in two sections of four, led by Flt Lt Tom Slack and Fg Off Peter Cowell.

Roadstead 127, 7 June 1944	Serial	Section193	Up	Down194
Cowell, Peter	EN620	Red	08:40	09:40
Robinson, Kenneth B.	MB881	Red	08:40	FTR
Collis, Ronald T. H.	EN224	Red	08:40	10:30
Stowe, William N.	MB882	Red	08:40	09:40
Slack, Thomas A. H.	MB847	Blue	08:40	10:10
Thiele, Keith F.	MB803	Blue	08:40	10:10
Payne, Jim C. J.	MB841	Blue	08:40	10:10
Balasse, Maurice A. L.	EN221	Blue	08:40	10:10

The 16 aircraft came in low over St. Peter Port and recognised, "a group of long narrow barges in the centre of the harbour which were probably responsible for the previous reports of the presence of T.L.C's".[195] However, a small group of ships were also seen on the northern side of the harbour, and these were attacked instead. 263 Squadron's rockets were seen to burst amongst them, but the results were not observed owing to significant amounts of smoke.

The pilots encountered intense light and heavy calibre Flak, which broke up the sections, and in the furore of the battle three of the Squadron's eight aircraft were hit: Cowell in the wings, Collis in the tail and Robinson in the radiator. However, no-one was injured. Fg Off Robinson pulled out of the mêlée and headed northwards, but the damage to his aircraft was too serious, and he soon radioed Cowell that he would have to bale out. He climbed to 10,000 feet, issued maydays, inverted his aircraft, unstrapped and dropped to the sea below. It was 09:10.

Whilst the Squadron ORB refrains from recording the location that Robinson baled out, the Bolt Head ORB places him 20 miles north of Guernsey, the 10 Group ORB records the coordinate Y6300, and the 10 Group ORB Appendix states it was 40 miles south-southeast of Start Point.

Unfortunately, however, when he baled out, his dinghy became detached from his parachute, and he landed in the Channel with no floatation device but his Mae West. As the rest of the pilots were still tied up with the operation, it took some time for Collis to locate Robinson and drop him his own dinghy.[196] Whilst Cowell and Stowe escorted the Typhoons home, Collis stayed to orbit Robinson until help came.

Robinson attempted to get into the dinghy that Collis had dropped, but the seas were rough and he was thrown out again and lost hold of it. Thus began a significant rescue operation over several hours, and although the exact timings are unknown, several successive attempts were made to save Robinson, which involved at least two aircraft of 41 Squadron, and two Spitfires, two Walruses and a Warwick of 276 (ASR) Squadron. A number of dinghies and a boat were dropped to him down wind or too far away, and a Walrus landed on the sea, but the conditions were too rough to reach him. Finally an ASR High Speed Launch from Salcombe reached the area and took Robinson aboard, but he did not survive this 18th attempt to rescue him.[197] Artificial respiration was performed but without success, and he could not be revived. The launch returned to Salcombe with Robinson's body, towing the Walrus as it did, as the aircraft had been unable to take off again in the rough conditions. They arrived in port at 17:30.

The Squadron was dumfounded by his loss. Robinson had not been wounded by Flak, rather he either drowned or succumbed to the effects of hypothermia, likely the latter as was in the water at least six hours. His death affected everyone and the rest of his section and his Flight Commander all made remarks about it in their logbooks that day:

A landing craft from the U.S. Coast Guard-manned USS *Samuel Chase* disembarks troops of the U.S. Army's First Division on the morning of D-Day, 6 June 1944, at Omaha Beach. © Public domain; official U.S. Coast Guard photograph

Cowell:	*Red 1. 'Robby' Red 2, shot down by flak from Guernsey. Picked up drowned by Walrus. Damned bad luck. I was hit by flak in 4 places. Each wing.*[198]
Collis:	*Escort R/P Typhoons St Peter Port. Own a/c hit in tail – Landed with only 5-10 gallons. Threw dinghy to Robinson – who got into it.*[199]
Stowe:	*Roby hit by Flack [sic] (Guernsey) bails out but picked up dead – No dingy.*[200]
Spencer:	*Robbie shot down escorting Tiffies… He bailed into the drink – no dinghy – died of cold.*[201]

Many years later, Flt Lt Ron Collis recalled the day, writing,

I […] flew with him on 7 June 1944, his last flight. At that time, I was Squadron Adjutant, a system which was inaugurated for a brief time, and was therefore much involved with his loss – specifically in clearing up his things and meeting with his relations.

We had been supporting an attack by rocket firing Typhoons on St. Peter's Port and were returning to base at Bolt Head, when Robinson found he had been hit and had bale out…. Then followed an agonizing period in which he was struggling in a fairly rough sea and, although he got into his dinghy, he was unable to cope. I stayed with him, presumably calling for Air Sea Rescue help, but finally had to leave, as I only had enough gas for a short time.

Before leaving I was able to wriggle out of my dinghy pack and dropped it very nearly on him. On the way back I met the ASR aircraft and turned back to show them where they would find him. I then continued to return to base, where I landed for a total time of 1 hour 50 minutes, which was cutting it very fine; I landed with 5-10 gallons of gas.[202]

Similarly, Flt Lt 'Jimmy' Thiele remembered the incident, writing many years later,

Escort [of] Typhoons to Guernsey. Robby in the drink. Hit by flak, he had to bail out. Being Irish, he didn't have his liferaft [sic] attached and as a result in the rough seas it drifted beyond his reach. Circling over him, two of us managed to get our rafts from under our bums and chuck them out to him. No mean feat in the confined space of a Spit cockpit! He reached one, got into it, but was immediately thrown out by the rough water. He lost this one too and was left drifting around in his Mae West. At this stage, the ASR Walrus arrived on the scene. I've got to hand it to those chaps. Just landing in those seas was a feat in itself, especially as they were under intermittent gun fire from German forces on the shore! They made at least a dozen passes at Robbie before they finally managed to get him aboard. Unable to take off in the rough water they set off to taxi back to England until eventually a Navy Destroyer [sic] took them in tow. Unfortunately, we learned later, Robbie was dead when they finally got him aboard. No doubt he died from hypothermia.[203]

A summary of Robinson's loss was recorded at the time on his *Pilot Service Record*, which states,

7.6.44 Baled out N of Guernsey after being hit in Radiator by Flak. Lost his own dinghy & from others including A.S.R. Boat dropped down wind of him. Then F/L Collis dropped his after giving Maydays at 10000 [feet] & Robinson was seen to get in & was quite cheerful. Some hours later reports came in from A.S.R. that he was picked up dead by launch after many attempts by Walrus.[204]

By the time of his loss, 22-year-old Robinson was in his second tour with 41 Squadron, having originally joined the unit as an NCO pilot fresh from OTU in July 1942. He was posted overseas in October 1942 and returned as a Flying Officer in mid-January 1944. He is buried today in Buckland Monachorum Cemetery in Devon.

Whilst Robinson's rescue was on-going, two pilots were called on to undertake an ASR patrol in liaison with two Spitfires from 276 Squadron to locate a dinghy dropped by an aircraft of Coastal Command in the area of vY50. They were unsuccessful.[205]

At 12:00, Sqn Ldr Chapman and Flt Lt Terry Spencer took off for a shipping reconnaissance of St. Peter Port, St. Malo and Lézardrieux. They passed over St. Peter Port, but were unable to get close enough to confirm the results of Rodeo 127's rocket attack on the harbour. Cloud cover prevented productive observation of St. Malo, but 20 small vessels were seen at Granville. The patrol was otherwise uneventful and the pair returned to base at 13:20.

A convoy patrol was undertaken by a section between 12:35 and 13:45, and three routine patrols were conducted by sections of two ten miles south of Bolt Head at 13:35, 14:35, and 15:40. All were uneventful.

At 17:55, the Squadron was airborne again when four pilots were provided for the second sweep of Rhubarb 274. The first sweep was conducted by four pilots of Culmhead based 126 Squadron, who were airborne only five minutes before 41 Squadron and operated in a triangular area bounded by Dol, Rennes and Lamballe. They returned at 19:50 claiming a locomotive, a three-ton lorry, a limousine and a motorcar damaged.

41 Squadron's route took them from 126 Squadron's jumping off point, Lamballe, and along a generally westerly path through Guingamp, Morlaix and Landerneau to Brest, and the pilots returned claiming a bigger bag than 126 Squadron.

Rhubarb 274, 7 June 1944	Serial	Section	Up	Down[206]
Slack, Thomas A. H.	MB876	Blue	17:55	19:50
Balasse, Maurice A. L.	MB842			
Thiele, Keith F.	MB847			
Fleming, Robert	MB837			

Near Lamballe, the pilots spotted a car and dived on it. However, when they realised it contained civilians, they held their fire and pulled up again. Then they sighted a camouflaged lorry near St. Brieuc, which they made two attacks upon and left it smoking. Near Guingamp, they saw what appeared to be a large camouflaged MT tanker with two turrets mounted on top. Once again, two attacks were made and the vehicle was left in a cloud of smoke.

Continuing on to Morlaix, they found a lorry that they shot up. In a small shunting yard just east of Morlaix, three attacks were made by each pilot on a locomotive and four trucks, leaving the engine emitting plumes of black smoke, whilst in the same area twelve goods wagons were also strafed, the pilots aiming specifically at their wheels. Lastly, a lorry was observed south of Morlaix. Attacks were made and strikes seen, but the pilots were running out of ammunition and decided to return to base.

Climbing above a 5/10ths cloud layer between 2,000 and 6,000 feet, the quartet crossed the Channel without event and landed at Bolt Head at 19:50, having expended 896 rounds of 20mm cannon ammunition, 3,920 rounds of .303, and 34 feet of cine-gun film.

The day ended with a final ASR patrol southeast of base by Fg Off 'Andy' Anderson (MB841) and WO 'Archie' Appleton (EN221) between 21:00 and 22:45. They were supporting two Spitfires and a Warwick from 276 Squadron who were searching in aD45 for the crew of an American bomber[207], who were located in dinghies 70 miles from Bolt Head. A lifeboat was dropped to them by the Warwick and seven men clambered aboard. A 406 Squadron Mosquito took over orbiting the men until a High Speed Launch arrived on the scene from Salcombe, and they were taken in tow.

8 June 1944 – D-Day +2. Although 41 Squadron was the first unit airborne in 10 Group today, significant amounts of low cloud and scattered rain, deteriorating to continuous drizzle in the afternoon, made for a much quieter day than the previous. The flying day consisted of just four

shipping reconnaissances and four convoy patrols – a total of 16 sorties – between 05:25 and 17:40, when flying ceased for the day. It was "not a particularly active day for the opening of the second front".[208]

At 05:25, Flt Sgt Freddie Woollard and WO 'Archie' Appleton were airborne to conduct a convoy protection patrol ten miles south of base. The patrol was uneventful, and they returned at 06:45 with nothing to report. At 06:30 and 07:30, two more such patrols were flown in sections of two pilots. These were similarly uneventful, and returned at 07:45 and 09:10, respectively.

Meanwhile, Sqn Ldr Chapman (MB845) and Fg Off 'Jack' Refshauge (MB798) took off at 05:35 on a successful shipping reconnaissance to St. Peter Port, Granville, St. Malo and Lézardrieux. At 06:05, they sighted three medium class Kriegsmarine minesweepers ten miles south of Jersey, sailing in an easterly direction at 14-20 knots, which fired medium calibre Flak at them. Ten minutes later, they spotted another three minesweepers approximately ten miles north of Cap Fréhel, heading towards St. Malo at a speed of 15-20 knots. However, nothing was seen in the harbours of St. Peter Port, St. Malo or Lézardrieux. They landed at Harrowbeer to report their sightings at 07:10, then returned to Bolt Head at 07:20.

Five minutes after Chapman and Refshauge's departure on their shipping reconnaissance, Fg Off Peter Cowell and Flt Lt Bill Stowe were airborne on their own, although their destinations were Sept-Îles, Morlaix and the roadstead of Brest [Goulet de Brest]. In contrast to the previous shipping reconnaissance, theirs was uneventful and they returned at 07:05, having seen nothing to report.

Another two shipping reconnaissances were airborne at 11:40, consisting of Blue Section (Payne MB804 & Burne MB876) and Green Section (Woollard MB803 & Fleming MB842). The former section was sent to reconnoitre the harbours at St. Peter Port, St. Malo and Lézardrieux again, whilst the latter headed for Morlaix and Ushant [Île d'Ouessant].

Whilst Green Section's patrol was uneventful and returned at 13:05 with nothing to report but smoke from Ushant, Blue Section spotted a 1,500-ton vessel at St. Malo, but also came under fire from the harbour's anti-aircraft defences. Plt Off Jim Payne later recorded in his logbook,

Nothing in Guernsey or Granville – Found a 1500 ton merchantman in St. Malo – bags of accurate Flak – also plenty from Lizardrieux [sic]. Landed at Harrowbeer to report [the ship] – who sent out Typhoon bombers to prang it.[209]

They returned to base just after Green Section, and there was no more flying on account of the weather until 17:10. At this time, Flt Lts Ron Collis and Bill Stowe took off for another convoy patrol, however returned only 30 minutes later, driven back by deteriorating visibility and rain, which subsequently put an end to the day's flying.

An Influx of New Pilots

During the evening, five NCO pilots arrived at Bolt Head on posting to 41 Squadron, following a lengthy rail journey literally traversing the length and breadth of the United Kingdom. They had been posted from 1 TEU at Tealing, near Dundee, Scotland, and travelled out to Bolt Head via London. All Flight Sergeants, they were British pilots Patrick Coleman, Clifford Oddy and Roger Short, and Australians Colin Robertson and James Ware.

Clearly excited about his posting to the unit, Coleman penned in his diary,

We soon learn… that five of us F/Sgts., two Australians Ware & Robinson [sic] & three British Oddy, Short & self, are (marvel of marvels) posted to 41 Sqdn which is in 10 Group, Air Defence of Great Britain. On the face of it this seems the greatest luck I've ever had in the Air Force….

> *We all entrain for our destination R.A.F. BOLT HEAD, Devonshire, via London.... Long train journey, eventually arrive in the evening. First person I meet is P/O Peter Gibbs. who was a Sgt at O.T.U. with me, he's awfully pleased to see us, tells us the gen, again almost too good to be true – our kites are Spit XII's with Griffin III engines & four bladed props., clipped wings. This is the latest Spitfire known to the general public & 41 is the only Sqdn. using them. Low level '400 mph' fighters armed with 2 canon & 6 m[achine] guns. This squadron hasn't enough pilots (unheard of), we are very welcome.*[210]

Twenty-one year old Coleman had joined the RAFVR in March 1941, and undertaken his elementary flying training in the United States, where he was awarded his Wings in May 1942. Returning to the United Kingdom the following month, he undertook courses at AFU, signals school and OTU, before being posted to 83 Group Communications Squadron in July 1943. He remained with this unit until April 1944, when he was posted to TEU in Tealing and now arrived from that unit with 1,114 flying hours logged, of which none were operational. Although Coleman arrived today as a Flight Sergeant, he had actually been promoted to Warrant Officer in May. As such, it is presumed that he had not yet been advised.

Oddy, likewise 21 years old, joined the RAFVR in February 1941 and also undertook his flying training in the United States. Little is known about his subsequent training in the United Kingdom, but it is understood that he joined 610 Squadron, coincidentally also at Bolt Head, in October 1943. He was posted from the unit to TEU in Tealing in January 1944, by which time he had logged 20 operational flying hours. At the time of joining 41 Squadron today, he had logged a total of 410 flying hours.

Short, a year older than his compatriots, had also joined the RAFVR in February 1941 and undertaken his flying training in the United States. Back in the United Kingdom, he attended AFU and OTU before being posted to TEU around February 1944, and arrived at Bolt Head today with 549 flying hours, of which none were operational.

At 26 years of age, Robertson was several years older than all the others. He had joined up in February 1942 and had completed his elementary flying training in Australia, then shipped to Canada in October 1942, where he undertook SFTS and was awarded his Wings. Arriving in the United Kingdom in May 1943, Robertson was posted to AFU, a Merlin Engine Course, OTU and TEU, and arrived today with 360 non-operational flying hours in his logbook.

Ware, who was 22 years old, had joined the RAAF in October 1941 and undertaken his elementary training in Australia, receiving his Wings a year later. He shipped to the United Kingdom in March 1943 and attended AFU and OTU courses, before being posted TEU in February 1944. He joined the Squadron today with 348 flying hours, but none operational.

9 June 1944 – D-Day +3. Poor weather throughout 10 Group's area for most of the day kept 41 Squadron on the ground until almost 17:00. The remaining hours of the day only allowed enough time for four shipping protection patrols and a fighter sweep, however this latter operation took the entire Squadron over the Normandy beachhead for the first time.

The first of the convoy patrols, designated Blue Section, was airborne at 16:45, and the remaining three, Red, Green and Black Sections, all at 17:40. By now mundane and routine, the patrols were presumably uneventful as they barely warrant mention in the unit's ORB, and are only listed on the F541.

The main event of the day was 41 Squadron's participation in 10 Group's contingent of beachhead patrols. The Group sent 68 aircraft over the invasion front from 41, 126, 131 and 616 Squadrons, however the weather was generally poor throughout the area and the pilots were compelled to operate a various altitudes between 1,500 and 20,000 feet depending on cloud cover and visibility.

131 Squadron was the first of the Group's units to fly through the area during the late afternoon, seeking enemy aircraft following a report of twelve operating in the area. Passing over at an altitude of 20,000 feet, the four pilots saw nothing and returned to base at 18:15. At around the same time,

The type of scene observed by 41 Squadron's pilots flying over the Normandy beachhead for the first time on 9 June 1944, three days after the D-Day landings: masses of men, vehicles, barrage balloons, landing craft, and ships. © Public domain; official U.S. Army photograph

another eight Spitfire VIIs from 131 Squadron took off with twelve Spitfire VIIs from 616 Squadron took off to undertake a protective patrol of the coastline between Pointe de Barfleur and Trouville-sur-Mer at 2,000-3,000 feet. The operation was uneventful and they returned at 20:40. Meanwhile, twelve Spitfire IXs of 126 Squadron had taken off at 19:20 and conducted a patrol of the Bayeux area between 1,500 and 2,000 feet. It, too, was uneventful and the unit landed again at 21:10.

41 Squadron was the next of the Group's units to patrol the beachhead, and twelve aircraft were off the deck at 19:40 in three sections of four, led by Sqn Ldr Chapman.[211]

Patrols, 9 June 1944	Serial	Section	Up	Down
Chapman, Robert H.	EN227	Blue	19:40	21:10
Slack, Thomas A. H.	MB876			
Balasse, Maurice A. L.	MB842			
Payne, Jim C. J.	MB804	Red		
Thiele, Keith F.	MB847			
Fleming, Robert	EN221			
Appleton, Arthur S.	MB803			
Collis, Ronald T. H.	MB845			
Spencer, Terence	MB882	Yellow		21:15
Refshauge, John G. H.	MB794			FTR
Cowell, Peter	MB795			21:15
Stevenson, Ian T.	EN229			

Reaching the area, cloud up to 8,000 feet broke up the Squadron, and Blue Section went over the beachhead east of Bayeux, where they saw many crashed gliders, and large numbers of horses, carts and jeeps, but nothing of concern.

Spencer took his Yellow Section in over Bayeux, then turned southwest and flew as far as Saint-Lô. Rounding the town, they turned northwest, and flew to Carentan where they saw what they assumed was a German transport moving north in dappled camouflage. The pilots then flew over Sainte-Mère-Eglise and crossed out over the beachhead at zero feet, Cowell later noting in his logbook, "Bayeux – St. Mère en Eglise [sic]. 0 feet over beachhead!"[212]

On the way home, Spencer led his section back over the Cotentin Peninsula where they came under Flak fire from Cherbourg, and Fg Off 'Jack' Refshauge was hit. He notified Spencer over the R/T that he had to bale out, and Spencer replied but he heard nothing more from Refshauge. He was not seen to jump, but it was assumed he had baled out, although his initial fate was unknown.

FAR LEFT Fg Off Kenneth 'Robbie' Robinson was killed on active service on 7 June 1944, when he was hit by Flak from Guernsey. He baled out uninjured southeast of Sark, but by the time he was retrieved had died, lost either to drowning or hypothermia. © Keith Curtis, via Karen Neale

LEFT 22-year-old Fg Off Kenneth Robinson is buried today in Buckland Monachorum Cemetery in Devon. © Karen Neale

Spencer, Cowell and Stevenson had little choice but to continue home and passed over Alderney on the way, where three ships of approximately 1,000-1,500 tons were sighted. They landed back at Bolt Head at 21:15, to find the rest of the Squadron had arrived shortly before them, reporting their sorties somewhat less eventful than their own. Spencer recorded in his logbook that day,

> *Filthy weather – swept at 800 ft. Vast quantities of shipping all sizes lying off coast. LCs unloading on beach. Most towns & villages in smoke. Refshauge shot down by flak from Cherbourg. We were in cloud.*[213]

Approximately fifteen minutes after Spencer's Yellow Section landed, the Group's last beachhead patrols of the day were airborne, when twelve Spitfire VIIs of 131 Squadron and eight Spitfire VIIs of 616 Squadron took to the air. Their destinations were Bayeux and Caen, but they were recalled when still five miles off the French coast owing to 10/10ths cloud over their patrol areas. They were back on the ground at 22:40, thereby ending the Group's operational flying for the day.

Refshauge was initially posted 'Missing in Action' near Houtteville, on the Cotentin Peninsula. The following morning, a telex message was sent to RAAF Overseas Headquarters, Kingsway, London, stating,

> DEEPLY REGRET TO INFORM YOU THAT FLYING OFFICER JOHN GEORGE HAMILTON REFSHAUGE AUS 409447 REPORTED MISSING AS A RESULT OF AIR OPERATIONS INFORM NEXT OF KIN MOTHER....[214]

A message to this effect was then delivered to Refshauge's mother, but three days later, the Squadron received news of Refshauge. He had been rescued by the Americans, who found he had been wounded by bullet through his left hand causing a fracture of the third and fourth fingers, and a bullet in his left leg.

He had been rescued by the Americans and was hospitalised in the US Army 94th General Hospital in Falfield, Gloucester, where he had undergone surgery. As a result of the report, Sqn Ldr Chapman telexed RAAF Overseas Headquarters in London, stating,

> INFORMATION RECEIVED FROM RAF WARMWELL THAT F/O J G H REFSHAUGE AUS 409447 REPORTED MISSING FROM AIR OPERATIONS ON 9/6/44 NOW IN AMERICAN HOSPITAL IN THIS COUNTRY AND BELIEVED TO HAVE BEEN OPERATED ON STOP THIS UNIT AWAITS FURTHER INFORMATION TOO.[215]

Refshauge's mother soon received a new telegram containing the good news:

> PLEASED TO INFORM YOU THAT YOUR SON FLYING OFFICER GEORGE JOHN [sic] HAMILTON REFSHAUGE PREVIOUSLY REPORTED MISSING IS NOW RECLASSIFIED SAFE

STOP HE HAS BEEN ADMITTED TO AN AMERICAN HOSPITAL IN ENGLAND AND IS BELIEVED TO HAVE UNDERGONE AN OPERATION STOP FURTHER INFORMATION IS AWAITED AND WHEN RECEIVED WILL BE FORWARDED TO YOU IMMEDIATELY.[216]

Refshauge, who had been rescued by American forces, was transferred to the RAF Hospital at Wroughton in early July, and subsequently to the RAF Rehabilitation Unit at Loughborough, before being sent on extended sick leave. He was promoted to Flight Lieutenant during this period and returned to 41 Squadron in early September 1944.

Some reports today suggest that Refshauge had actually been shot down by friendly fire, possibly from a U.S. Merchant Navy ship, but no evidence for this lies within Refshauge's RAAF personnel or casualty files. That said, fellow pilot Fg Off Keith Curtis recalled many years later that he was indeed shot down accidentally by the Americans who picked him up but initially thought to be German! Curtis also remembered that as 41 Squadron originally assumed Refshauge had been captured or killed in action, he was given the task of returning Refshauge's kit to Australia, which duly he did. Days later, however, Refshauge turned up alive in an American hospital and had to be issued new kit.[217]

Perhaps alluding to Refshauge's loss on 9 June 1944, Flt Lt Tom Slack also recalled many years later that the Squadron was assigned operations over the beachhead…

…to give cover for the Normandy Landing. We had to fly low level & the whole scene was pretty chaotic & dangerous – with everyone firing at everyone else. The US Navy was particularly trigger happy…[218]

10 June 1944 – D-Day +4. Fair weather becoming cloudy with showers and rain by midday, but decreasing again during the afternoon. Though a busy day for the Squadron, it began routine with four sections patrolling ten miles south of base and two sections flying convoy patrols between 05:35 and 12:05.

At 10:45, Flt Lt Ron Collis (EN224) and Fg Off Keith Curtis (EN620) took off on a shipping reconnaissance to Lézardrieux and Ushant [Île d'Ouessant], and although the patrol was generally uneventful, they reported on their return at 12:05 having seen two Allied Corvettes in the Channel, and a stationary power-driven commercial barge in the outer estuary mouth at Morlaix.

Five minutes after their return, Fg Off 'Jack' Malone and Plt Off Peter Gibbs took off on an ASR scramble. They located a dinghy with a single occupant 30 miles southeast of Bolt Head, which already had a 276 Squadron Warwick orbiting above it. Two Spitfires of 276 Squadron also assisted and Flt Lt Michael Graves DFC of 616 Squadron was subsequently rescued by a Walrus. Malone and Gibbs returned at 13:25.

The main operation of the day, however, was an anti-shipping strike on Sark Harbour at 13:05, designated Fighter Roadstead 3, which consisted of eight pilots led by Sqn Ldr Chapman.[219] Barges had been reported there by pilots of 610 Squadron during an earlier Roadstead and 41 Squadron was detailed to attack them. Locating the vessels, Sqn Ldr Chapman went in first, firing a long burst at distance. However, as he grew nearer, he recognised them as fishing vessels, but it was "too late to warn off the remainder of the Squadron, who were firing into the general melee among the fishing craft".[220] The pilots beat a hasty retreat and landed back at Bolt Head at 13:55.

During the afternoon and into the evening, the Squadron undertook eight routine patrols, consisting of scrambles at 13:50 and 15:50, and shipping protection patrols ten miles south of Bolt Head at 17:00, 18:05, 19:00, 20:00, 20:45 and 22:00, but all were uneventful and the pilots returned with nothing to report.

There were also two shipping reconnaissances during the evening, the first at 18:45 and the second at 21:25. The former was conducted by Fg Off Peter Cowell (MB882) and Flt Lt Ron Collis (EN224), who flew to Cherbourg, Alderney and St. Peter Port on Guernsey. Inside the western inner mole of Cherbourg Harbour, they sighted a 4,000-5,000 ton merchant vessel with one funnel and two masts, a cruiser stern and a straight bow, and steam up. They returned to base at 19:55 to report it.

The second shipping reconnaissance was flown by Blue Section (Slack MB876, Thiele MB803, Birbeck MB841, Balasse EN221) to the same areas as Cowell and Collis and they saw the same vessel still in Cherbourg Harbour, but felt it was only of 3,000 tons, and noted it had torpedo nets slung out. Two small coasters were also seen in the harbour, and a 300-ton vessel was also seen at St. Peter Port with steam up. They landed on dusk at 22:45.

The last of the Squadron's routine patrols landed ten minutes later, and this concluded a long day's flying, which had encompassed 46 sorties on 19 separate operations between 05:35 and 22:55.

11 June 1944 – D-Day +5. By the end of the day, almost 327,000 troops, over 54,000 vehicles, and well over 104,000 tons of equipment and supplies had been landed on the beachhead at Normandy.

However, the weather left a lot to be desired for this time of the year and low cloud, rain and mist persisted throughout the day at Bolt Head and hindered all operational flying from the airfield. The Squadron ORB indicates that the only flying undertaken were air tests by Fg Off Robert Anderson and WO Arthur Appleton.

Separately, a new pilot joined the Squadron today in the form of 23-year-old Peter Chattin. Married, with two young children, Chattin may well have been on the other side of the Channel right now, had he followed the path the RAF appeared to have had mapped out for him. Having joined the RAFVR in August 1941, and completed ITW and EFTS in the United Kingdom, he shipped across the Atlantic to attend BFTS in Oklahoma between January and August 1942. On returning to England, Chattin was posted to Glider Instructors School, and from there to Glider Training School as a tug pilot, where he remained until August 1943.

It appears that around this time a request for a transfer to fighter pilot training was approved, as he was posted to OTU, and subsequently to TEU in Tealing. He arrived at Bolt Head today from the same location, and only two days after, his fellow students Coleman, Oddy, Short, Robertson and Ware. He had logged 560 flying hours, but 41 Squadron was his first operational unit.

12 June 1944 – Varying amounts of cumulus cloud throughout the day, ranging between 2/10ths and 4/10ths during the morning, and increasing to 5/10ths to 9/10ths during the afternoon and evening. It would prove a busy day for the Squadron that saw one aircraft lost and the pilot rescued from the Channel, and another crash-land and its pilot injured.

WO Pat Coleman served with 41 Squadron from 7 June 1944 to 6 August 1945, and was commissioned in December 1944. He claimed five destroyed FW190s, a shared destroyed Ju188, a shared destroyed He111, and three damaged aircraft on the ground, and was awarded the DFC in July 1945. © Coleman family

Operational flying started early when eight pilots were airborne at 05:20, led by Sqn Ldr Chapman, to join twelve pilots from 610 Squadron in the first sweep of Rodeo 168 on the Rennes-Gaël area, with a particular emphasis on Gaël Aerodrome. The second sweep of the Rodeo was undertaken simultaneously by eight pilots each from 1 Squadron and 165 Squadron on the Vannes-Kerlin Bastard area.

41 and 610 Squadrons were led by Harrowbeer-Perranporth's Wing Commander Flying, Wg Cdr Harold Bird-Wilson DFC, but he lost his way in the cloudy conditions and returned alone. In any case, the first sweep was abandoned by the rest of the pilots when 8/10ths cloud cover at 5,000 feet was encountered over France, and both units returned home having not fired a shot. 41 Squadron landed at 07:00. The second sweep was uneventful for similar reasons, although six escort vessels were sighted entering the basin at Lorient.

An uneventful shipping protection patrol was flown ten miles south of Bolt Head between 09:45 and 11:05, but between 10:50 and 10:55 another eight pilots in two sections took off on Rhubarb 280 to attack motor transport. The first section was led by Flt Lt 'Jimmy' Thiele and headed for the area between St. Brieuc and Coutances, whilst the second, led by Flt Lt Terry Spencer, headed for the road between Châteaulin, southeast of Brest, and Loudéac, due south of St. Brieuc, where motorised transport had previously been reported.

Rhubarb 280, 12 June 1944	Serial	Section	Up	Down
Thiele, Keith F.	MB803	Green	10:50	12:45
Goens, Rijklof van	MB841			
Payne, Jim C. J.	MB804			
Balasse, Maurice A. L.	MB842			
Spencer, Terence	MB882	Red	10:55	12:50
Gibbs, N. Peter	MB845			
Cowell, Peter	EN224			
Curtis, Keith R.	EN620			

It was a successful trip. Green Section sighted an armoured car with two guns south of Guingamp, which was attacked by Plt Off Jim Payne and Fg Off 'Momo' Balasse. The entire section fired upon and set fire to two cars near St. Gilles-Pligeaux, and Flt Lt 'Jimmy' Thiele and Fg Off 'Charlie' van Goens shot up an encampment north of Corlay. Between Loudéac & St. Méen- le-Grande, the section damaged four large motor lorries parked on the side of the road under camouflage netting, whilst Payne and Balasse also damaged a large vehicle carrying wireless aerials in the same area. Finally, a locomotive and four railway carriages were attacked near Broons, and Balasse's fire succeeded in blowing up the engine.

Spencer's section had less success but still managed to locate a balloon flying above an electrical station near Loudéac, which was shot down by Spencer and Plt Off Peter Gibbs. The section also attacked and damaged four lorries in the same area.

Although the operation had been uneventful as far as opposition was concerned, fuel burn had been significant, particularly as both sweeps ran almost two hours. The result was that two pilots ran out of fuel on the return journey, causing the loss of two aircraft. In the first case, Fg Off 'Momo' Balasse ran out of fuel still 15 miles from Bolt Head. He was compelled to bale out into the Channel, and was rescued from the sea at 12:54 by a 276 Squadron Walrus, having spent just ten minutes in the water; he was flown straight to Bolt Head.

The second case was a little more serious. Plt Off Peter Gibbs would have realised he was low on fuel, but had no doubt hoped he had enough left to get him home. Unfortunately, it was not quite sufficient and he crash-landed his aircraft on approach, just short of the runway. He was slightly injured and taken to Station Sick Quarters where he was soon met by Balasse, who arrived "smiling but wet"[221], and otherwise none the worse for wear for his dunking.

During the afternoon, there was an uneventful scramble, but at 17:00 and 17:05, two shipping reconnaissances were undertaken, the former to St. Malo and St. Peter Port by Green Section (Burne MB837 & Woollard MB803), and the latter to Ushant [Île d'Ouessant] and Île de Batz, Brittany, by Yellow Section (Cook EN227 & Stevenson EN229). Burne and Woollard sighted a 300-ton coaster in Alderney Harbour, a fishing boat off St. Peter Port, two barges at St. Helier, and eight barges and three ships under 1,000 tons at St. Malo, and returned to base at 18:30 to report them. Owing to poor weather and reduced visibility, Cook and Stevenson returned to Bolt Head at 18:35 with nothing to report but a dead body seen floating in the water on the French coast. This ended the day's flying.

13 June 1944 – It was a relatively quiet day for the Squadron on account of weather conditions, particularly in the morning during which there was low cloud, drizzle and thundery rain. As a result, only six operations were flown all day, consisting of three shipping reconnaissances and three shipping protection patrols. The first of these was airborne at 14:00 and the last landed at 22:45.

At 14:00, Flt Lts Terry Spencer and Bill Stowe took off for a shipping reconnaissance to St. Peter Port on Guernsey and St. Malo. They returned at 15:20 after an uneventful in patrol in which they could only report having sighted a four-masted schooner in the estuary at St. Malo.[222]

At 17:45, two more sections were sent on shipping reconnaissances, Blue Section (Birbeck MB841 & Oddy MB798) to Alderney and Cherbourg, and Yellow Section (Cowell MB795 & Malone EN620) to St. Helier on Jersey, and to St. Peter Port and St. Malo again. Blue Section returned to Bolt Head an hour later, reporting a 100-ton coaster at Alderney and two M Class minesweepers, a 4,000 vessel and a river boat at Cherbourg; Yellow Section arrived at base 20 minutes later with nothing to report.

During the day, 10 Group's squadrons undertook twelve shipping protection patrols involving 24 aircraft. 41 Squadron flew three of these patrols in sections of two pilots at 20:20, 21:15, and 22:20 to cover a convoy entering the Channel from the Atlantic Ocean. They were uneventful and the day's flying ended when the last aircraft landed at 22:45.

Separately today, news reached the Squadron that Fg Off 'Jack' Refshauge had been picked up by the Americans after he baled out and taken to a U.S. Army hospital. However, there was another event today that the Squadron would not become aware of for a few days, but one that would affect their deployment for the rest of summer. It was today that the first V1 Flying Bombs landed on London, having been launched from sites in and around Pas-de-Calais, France. These bombs would terrorise Britain from now until 5 September, when the last launch sites capable of attacking the United Kingdom were overrun by ground forces.

Nominal Roll, June 1944

The following list of pilots has been extracted from a document within 41 Squadron's Archives titled *Nominal Roll of Flying Personnel*. It is undated, but the inclusion of Flt Sgt Peter Chattin who joined the Squadron on 11 June 1944, and the exclusion of Flt Sgt Larry Spurr, who joined the Squadron on 14 June, suggests it was compiled in the brief day period between these dates.

It is unique amongst Nominal Rolls found within the Squadron's Archives as, in addition to including Flights and dates of posting to the Squadron (as opposed to dates of arrival), it also shows the Squadron's Authorised Establishment at the time.

The establishment constituted one Squadron Leader, two Flight Lieutenants (Flight Commanders), nine Officer Pilots and 11 Airman Pilots, but the list indicates the Squadron had an over-supply of eight men, which consisted of five supernumerary Flight Lieutenants and three supernumerary Pilot Officers.

Although it is laid out as close to the format of the original as possible, minor corrections have been made by the author where errors have been recognised.

Flt	Rank and Name			Number	Branch	Date Posted	Nationality
	S/Ldr	R. H.	Chapman	40510	GD	26.5.44	
	(Commanding 41 Sqdn)						
B	F/Lt	T.A.H.	Slack	112428	GD	25.1.44	
	(Flight Commander)						
A	F/Lt	T.	Spencer	47269	GD	1.5.44	
	(Flight Commander)						
A	F/O	P.	Cowell	124530	GD	10.11.42	
A	F/O	K.R.	Curtis	J.22759	GD	8.10.43	Canadian
B	F/O	M.A.L.	Balasse	135893	GD	2.11.43	Belgian
A	F/O	H.	Cook	126096	GD	16.12.43	
B	F/O	R.	Van Goens	124239	GD	17.1.44	Netherlands
A	F/Lt	W.N.	Stowe	J.10643	GD	24.2.44	Canadian
A	F/O	C.J.	Malone	J.29253	GD	24.2.44	Canadian
B	F/O	R.E.	Anderson	A.402337	GD	18.3.44	Australian
			(1 Vacant)				
B	F/Sgt	F.G.	Woollard	1312058	A.P.	16.12.43	
A	F/Sgt	I.T.	Stevenson	1348985	A.P.	16.12.43	
B	F/Sgt	R.	Fleming	656285	A.P.	19.1.44	
B	W/O	A.S.	Appleton	1576662	A.P.	21.3.44	
A	F/Sgt	P.T.	Coleman	1386814	A.P.	7.6.44	
A	F/Sgt	R.L.	Short	1333690	A.P.	7.6.44	
B	F/Sgt	C.	Oddy	1218157	A.P.	7.6.44	
B	F/Sgt	J.P.	Ware	A.420311	A.P.	7.6.44	Australian
	F/Sgt	C.S.	Robertson	A.421627	A.P.	7.6.44	Australian
A	F/Sgt	P.W.	Chattin	1239825	A.P.	9.6.44	
			(1 Vacant)				

Supernumerary.

Flt	Rank and Name			Number	Branch	Date Posted	Nationality
B	F/Lt	C.R.	Birbeck	108990	GD	8.2.43	
A	F/Lt	R.P.	Harding	113876	GD	1.7.43	
A	F/Lt	R.T.H.	Collis	111107	GD	14.8.43	
B	F/Lt	T.R.	Burne AFC	33457	GD	16.2.43	
B	F/Lt	K.F.	Thiele	NZ.404966	GD	25.2.44	New Zealand
			DSO, DFC & Bar				
B	P/O	P.B.	Graham	161780	GD	29.10.43	
B	P/O	J.C.J.	Payne	170730	GD	1.1.44	
A	P/O	N.P.	Gibbs	173284	GD	5.4.44	

WO James 'Jimmy' Ware RAAF served with 41 Squadron from 8 June 1944 to 1 November 1944. © James Ware, via Garry Cooper

14 June 1944 – Although the day's weather was intermingled with scattered showers, otherwise generally fair conditions allowed 41 Squadron to operate from dawn to after dusk. The day's flying consisted of nine shipping reconnaissances of the Channel Islands, the Cotentin Peninsula and Brittany, and three shipping protection patrols.

Fg Offs Harry Cook and 'Jack' Malone were airborne on the day's first shipping reconnaissance at 05:30 and flew along the Brittany coast in the Morlaix area. However, they saw nothing and returned at 07:00. Flt Lt Ron Collis and Flt Sgt 'Steve' Stevenson, who were airborne five minutes after Cook and Malone took off on their own reconnaissance, headed for the islands of Guernsey and Alderney. At 05:55, they sighted four trawler type auxiliaries in Little Russel strait off St. Peter Port, and returned at 06:40, beating Cook and Malone home by a full 20 minutes.

Whilst they were away, eight rocket-armed Typhoons of 263 Squadron flew their owned armed shipping reconnaissance to St. Helier, Granville and St. Malo, escorted by eight Spitfires from 610 Squadron. In the Rance estuary at St. Malo, they sighted a schooner, presumably the same one reported by Flt Lts Spencer and Stowe the previous afternoon, and attacked it, registering several direct hits with their rockets. On their way home, they also saw the trawler type auxiliaries off Guernsey that Flt Lt Collis and Flt Sgt Stevenson had seen, and these were attacked by 610 Squadron's Spitfires and left smoking.

Following 41 Squadron's two dawn shipping reconnaissances, the unit was not airborne again until 12:10, when Flt Lt Terry Spencer and Fg Off Keith Curtis took off on a shipping reconnaissance mirroring that of 263 and 610 Squadrons a few hours earlier, visiting St. Helier, Granville and St. Malo again. Ten minutes later, Flt Lt 'Jimmy' Thiele and WO 'Archie' Appleton took off for their own shipping reconnaissance, to Cherbourg, Alderney and St. Peter Port. Spencer and Curtis returned at 13:30 reporting four medium barges at St. Helier and another eight due east of Dinard Aerodrome, and Thiele and Appleton returned at more-or-less the same time reporting 'the usual' motor vessel alongside the centre pier in Cherbourg Harbour, a small minesweeper by the mole, and three other small vessels in the harbour, as well as a small coaster seen at St. Peter Port.

A section was next airborne at 16:55, followed just five minutes later by two more, all three undertaking shipping reconnaissances across the Channel. The first of these flew to Lézardrieux, Ushant [Île d'Ouessant], Cherbourg, Alderney and Guernsey, the second to St. Helier, Granville and St. Malo, and the third to Lézardrieux and Ushant.

Nothing worthy of reporting was seen on the earliest of the three, which returned at 18:10. On the second, the pilots (Cowell MB795 & Stowe EN229) sighted eight small barges on the

Flt Sgt Lawrence 'Larry' Spurr RCAF served with 41 Squadron briefly from 14 June 1944 to 4 August 1944, when he was commissioned and posted to a Canadian squadron. © Nan Spurr

eastern side of the harbour at St. Helier, and a white ship of around 1,000 tons by the mole at St. Malo, and returned to base at the same time as the first section. The last of these (Cook EN605 & Malone EN620) saw no shipping, but came under intense light calibre Flak fire on Île de Batz. They were not hit and landed again at 18:30.

Three shipping protection patrols were flown ten miles south of base at 19:40-20:55, 20:40-21:35 and 21:25-22:50, but all were uneventful. The last operation of the day was yet another shipping reconnaissance, this time carried out by Flt Lt Terry Spencer (EN227) and Flt Sgt Ian Stevenson (EN620) to St. Peter Port between 22:15 and 23:00. Spencer's logbook indicates they came under very intense Flak fire from the port, but still managed to sight a U-Boat and four minesweepers. They landed in the darkness, approximately 30 minutes after dusk.

During the day, Canadian Flt Sgt Lawrence 'Larry' Spurr arrived in Bolt Head to fill the Squadron's remaining NCO pilot vacancy. Having enlisted in the RCAF in June 1942, just after his 19th birthday, he completed his elementary and service flying training in Canada, where he earned his Wings. Arriving in the United Kingdom in late 1943, he attended an OTU course and TEU, and was posted to 41 Squadron today as his first operational unit with over 400 flying hours in his logbook. He turned 21 the day after his arrival.

15 June 1944 – Fair and fine weather provided for another long and busy day's flying between 06:00 and 22:05. The day commenced with an uneventful shipping protection patrol ten miles south of base between 06:30 and 07:55, but more interesting work was on the cards at 09:00. As a result of the previous evening's sighting of a U-Boat at St. Peter Port by Flt Lt Spencer and by 263 and 610 Squadrons, Roadstead 142 was laid on to destroy it.

The operation foresaw the deployment of eight rocket-equipped Typhoons from 263 Squadron and eight Spitfires from 41 Squadron[223] in a first sweep, and by 14 Spitfire bombers of 1 and 165 Squadrons, equipped with 500 lb. bombs, in a second sweep. Harrowbeer's 263 Squadron was airborne at 08:53 and rendezvoused with 41 Squadron, which was airborne at 09:02, led by Flt Lt Terry Spencer.

Despite "the usual enthusiastic heavy and light flak"[224] that greeted the 16 aircraft when they arrived over St. Peter Port, the Typhoons went in and fired their rockets at two vessels lying in the positions indicated by reports, making strikes upon them and on the mole. However, neither could be identified as a U-Boat as a result of obstructed visibility, but one of the Typhoons was hit by Flak and sustained Cat. B damage. 41 Squadron's escort was uneventful and it is believed they did not fire.

The second sweep arrived a few minutes later and dropped their bombs on the port, which were seen to hit the centre jetty, Castle Pier, and the outer jetty, whilst a few were seen to land in the water between the centre and outer jetties. Vessels were also noted on the seaward side of the northern and southern ends of the centre jetty.

All aircraft returned to base, and at 12:10 and 12:15, 41 Squadron sent two sections back to St. Peter Port to observe what damage the rocket and bombing strikes may have caused. Unfortunately, little was seen owing to the amount of smoke coming from the port, but one trawler type auxiliary was seen to have been sunk. They returned at 13:15 and 13:35, respectively.

The Squadron was next airborne at 14:35-14:40, when eight aircraft were airborne in two sections led by Flt Lt Tom Slack and Sqn Ldr Chapman, respectively, for an armed shipping reconnaissance to Granville, St. Helier and St. Peter Port. They sighted small sea craft and a wireless mast at Granville, and a small coaster of approximately 200 tons at St. Helier, but no shipping was seen at St. Peter Port, where smoke was still rising from the outer jetty. Although coming under intense light and heavy Flak from each location, the pilots were unable to find shipping of any significance, and returned to Bolt Head at 15:55, having not fired a shot.

Uneventful shipping protection patrols were flown ten miles south of base 17:55-19:10 and 18:35-19:50, and then eight pilots were airborne at 20:45 for the Squadron's last operation of the day, an armed shipping reconnaissance to St. Peter Port, Granville and St. Malo. The pilots flew in two sections, led by Fg Off Peter Cowell and Sqn Ldr Chapman, but once again were unable to locate any shipping of significance. Two pilots were sent down to take a closer look at St. Peter Port, still trying to establish the presence of a U-Boat identified in PRU images on the west side of the centre jetty. They were unable to confirm the report, and the pilots all returned to Bolt Head at 22:05, thus ending operational flying for the day.

16 June 1944 – Initially poor weather improved during the day, although the cloud base did not rise about 2,000 feet. The day therefore started later than usual, and the first operational flight was a scramble to intercept an unidentified plot at 07:45. The aircraft was approached and found to be friendly, and the pilots were back on the ground 15 minutes later.

Flt Sgts Bob Fleming and Jimmy Ware took off at 08:20 to conduct a shipping reconnaissance of St. Peter Port, but low cloud prevented any observations and they were back at Bolt Head within 60 minutes with nothing to report. Another shipping reconnaissance was airborne at 10:30, when Flt Lt Ross Harding and Fg Off 'Jack' Malone were sent back to St. Peter Port in another attempt to verify the presence of enemy shipping. Once again, nothing was seen, and they returned within 45 minutes.

The exercise was repeated yet again at 12:55 when Flt Lt Terry Spencer (EN224) and Plt Off Peter Gibbs (MB795) were sent back to the port in the hope of better visibility. On this occasion they had better luck and sighted a 4,000-ton, 250-foot ship alongside the centre jetty on the seaward side. Spencer noted in his logbook that he found St. Peter Port surprisingly 'very peaceful'. They returned at 13:45 to report their sighting.

Meanwhile, two uneventful shipping protection patrols had been flown ten miles south of Bolt Head, at 09:35-09:50 and 11:45-13:10. However, the main operation of the day took place from 16:30, when four pilots participated in Rhubarb 285 to Brittany, led by Flt Lt Terry Spencer. The operation consisted of four sweeps, as follows:

No.	Sqn	Aircraft	Destinations	Up	Down
1	610	4 Spit XIV	Guingamp, Morlaix & Landivisiau	15:35	17:10
2	41	4 Spit XII	Guingamp, Carhaix & Yffiniac	16:30	18:10
3	126	8 Spit IX	Folligny, Mortain, Virey & Pontaubault	18:00	20:05
4	616	8 Spit VII	Mont-St.-Michel, Pontorson, Pontaubault, Lessay	19:55	20:45

Senior ground crew, Chf Tech Redman, Sgt Roylance, Flt Lt Richard 'Monty' Norman, and Chf Tech Wilcox, ca summer 1943. Flt Lt Norman was 41 Squadron's Engineering Officer from July 1943 to June 1944, and was awarded an MBE for his servoces in January 1945. © Cowell family

As the main railway line was obscured by cloud, 610 Squadron was forced to fly further south than anticipated and sighted a 4,000 ton ship entering the roadstead at Brest.

41 Squadron flew off course, making landfall at Lannion, slightly west of where they should have been, instead of closer to Guingamp. However, as they flew past Lannion airfield they took the opportunity to dive down to attack its Flak posts, and then shot up a nearby radar station. Continuing on towards Yffiniac, the section sighted a lorry and staff car in the Lamballe-St. Brieuc area, which were also attacked.

Rhubarb 285, 16 June 1944	Serial	Section	Up	Down
Spencer, Terence	EN224	Red	16:30	18:10
Stowe, William N.	MB875			
Harding, Ross P.	MB795			
Curtis, Keith R.	EN229			

They returned to base at 18:10, ending the day's operational flying a good four hours earlier than usual.

126 Squadron was airborne just before 41 Squadron's return and found nothing of significance on the roads, returning at 20:05 with nothing to report. 616 Squadron's sweep was no more successful, but they returned to report they had come under rocket fire from a small island off St. Malo.

17 June 1944 – Cloudy conditions in the morning improved later to fair to fine weather, and the Squadron's flying today consisted of five operations between 05:35 and 21:30, comprising 26 sorties.

The day commenced with an all too familiar shipping reconnaissance to Lézardrieux and L'Aber-Wrac'h, on this occasion by Flt Lt Ross Harding and Plt Off Peter Gibbs. It was, however, uneventful and they returned at 06:50 reporting having seen nothing of consequence.

Chf Tech 'Chiefy' Redman and his cat 'Tookie'. © Cowell family

At 08:30-09:45 and 09:25-10:55, shipping protection patrols were flown ten miles south of base, but both were similarly uneventful. Just after lunch, however, the Squadron provided eight aircraft in two sections for sweeps seven and eight of Rhubarb 286, which had commenced at 05:15, and ended at 15:10 when 41 Squadron's last four pilots landed again.

No.	Sqn	Aircraft	Destinations	Up	Down
1	616	4 Spit VII	Kerlin Bastard, Vannes & Rennes	05:15	-
2	616	4 Spit VII	Kerlin Bastard, Vannes & Rennes	-	-
3	1	4 Spit IX	Kerlin Bastard, Vannes & Rennes	-	-
4	1	4 Spit IX	Kerlin Bastard, Vannes & Rennes	-	07:45
5	131	4 Spit VII	Pontorson, Antrain, Fougères, Mayenne, Domfront, Pontaubault & Folligny	-	-
6	131	4 Spit VII	Pontorson, Rennes, Ploërmel, Pontivy, Loudéac & Yffiniac	-	-
7	41	4 Spit XII	Lamballe, Loudéac & Dinan	13:25	15:10
8	41	4 Spitfires	Lamballe, Dinan & Dol	13:30	15:05

The first four sweeps of the Rhubarb were completely uneventful, and 616 and 1 Squadrons' 16 pilots all returned with nothing to report. 131 Squadron's (fifth and sixth) sweeps were somewhat more successful despite poor weather over Brittany and they returned from the first of the two claiming one lorry destroyed near Mortain, and from the second claiming a lorry and trailer of packing crates set on fire north of Rennes, and a motorcycle and sidecar "containing two Boches"[225] shot up.

41 Squadron's (seventh and eighth) sweeps were, however, the most successful of the entire Rhubarb, and consisted of the following pilots:

Rhubarb 286, 17 June 1944	Serial	Section	Up	Down
Cowell, Peter	MB795	Red	13:25	15:10
Malone, Charles J.	MB875			
Harding, Ross P.	EN602			
Collis, Ronald T. H.	EN229			
Bird-Wilson, Harold A. C.	Spit XIV	Blue	13:30	15:05
Slack, Thomas A. H.	MB880			
Payne, Jim C. J.	MB804			
Appleton, Arthur S.	EN221			

The first of the two sections, led by Fg Off Peter Cowell, attacked a camouflaged lorry near Plancoët, and left it damaged. Between Plestin-les-Grèves and Noyal-Pontivy, they also fired on a large camouflaged stationary open wagon, which they felt was likely a decoy for a nearby concealed Flak position, as it simultaneously open fire upon them. No-one was hit.

The second section was led by Wg Cdr Harold Bird-Wilson DFC, and succeeded in damaging a number of targets. These included a two-ton truck shot up between Lamballe and Plancoët, 24 railway trucks strafed in a station east of Plancoët, a staff car strafed and set on fire south of Plancoët, a lorry damaged south of Dinan, and finally another lorry damaged between Pleudihen-sur-Rance and Combourg.

All in all, they were two successful sweeps from which both sections returned safely just after 15:00. As a result of the Squadron's pending change in deployment as a result of the launch of the V1 offensive, these vehicles would also constitute 41 Squadron's final ground targets for over two months.

It was then almost five hours before the unit was airborne again, but then it was in Squadron strength on an armed anti-shipping reconnaissance. No. 10 Group launched six such operations to the Channel Islands and Brittany today between 12:30 and almost 23:00. The first consisted of seven RP Typhoons of 263 Squadron and eight Spitfires of 610 Squadron to St. Peter Port and St. Helier, the second of eight bomb-equipped Spitfires from 165 Squadron to the Goulet de Brest, the third by eight bomb-equipped Spitfires from 1 Squadron to the Goulet de Brest again, the fourth by 12 RP Typhoons of 263 Squadron and eight Spitfires of 610 Squadron to St. Malo, the fifth by 12 Spitfires of 41 Squadron to St. Brieuc, and the sixth by another eight bomb-equipped Spitfires from 165 Squadron back to the Goulet de Brest a final time.

41 Squadron was airborne at 19:55 in three sections. Blue, Red and Yellow, led by Sqn Ldr Chapman, Fg Off Peter Cowell and Flt Lt Terry Spencer, respectively. Flying the coast between Pointe de Minard and St. Brieuc Bay, all they could locate was a fishing fleet of approximately 20 small vessels off Saint-Quay-Portrieux, and returned to base disappointed between 21:20 and 21:30. Flt Lt Bill Stowe voiced exactly this opinion when he noted in his logbook that day, "No joy!".[226] This concluded the day's flying.

18 June 1944 – Mainly fair weather throughout the day got the Squadron off to an early start again, and the morning's usual shipping reconnaissance to Lézardrieux and L'Aber-Wrac'h was assigned to Flt Lt Tom Slack (MB876) and one of the Squadron's new Sergeant Pilots, Australian 'Jimmy' Ware (EN231).

The pair sighted three MTBs heading northeast approximately 15 miles north of Lézardrieux and encountered light Flak all along the French coast. Slack felt some of the shells strike his Spitfire but recognised no immediate reaction from the aircraft. Shortly after turning for home, however, he noticed the fuel gauge steadily dropping, and before long the engine spluttered and died. Left little choice, he gave a few quick maydays, turned the aircraft on its back, and baled out. It was a sad end to the aircraft, which was Slack's preferred mount and his most often flown.

Ware orbited, issued maydays of his own and reported the situation, giving a grid reference of aC07. The time was 06:40 and they were still close to Ushant [Île d'Ouessant]. Meanwhile, Slack's

LEFT Flt Lt Peter Cowell's Fitter, LAC 'Pop' Groome. © Cowell family

RIGHT Flt Lt Terry Spencer's Fitter and Rigger on 41 Squadron, Joe and 'Watty'. © Terry Spencer, via Cara and Raina Spencer

dinghy automatically inflated and he climbed into it waiting – hoping – to be rescued. After a while, Ware needed to return to base as he was getting short of fuel. On the way back, however, the Controller asked him to return to ensure Slack was in his dinghy. Unfortunately, he was unable to find him again, and turned for home again. At 07:00, Ware's aircraft ran out of fuel and he, too, baled out. He was able to radio his location beforehand, however, giving it as aC20.

A Warwick and a Walrus of 276 (ASR) Squadron and four Spitfires of 165 Squadron were all sent out to find Slack and Ware, and Slack was located by the Warwick, which dropped smoke floats and a large dinghy into the sea only feet from him. However, Ware was also soon spotted and the Walrus landed on the sea at 08:00 to pick him up first, then continued on to Slack and alighted on the sea near him at 08:45.

Although the seas were not rough where Slack was found, the swell was large enough to stop the Walrus taking off again. As such, it started for home on the surface, using its propeller for propulsion, but they were soon met by an ASR launch, to which Slack and Ware were transferred. The Walrus crew then jettisoned all unnecessary equipment and used the launch to zigzag in front of it to calm the seas, and finally managed to take off again.

The launch then returned to Slack's dinghies and sunk them with machine gun fire and salvaged his parachute, which Slack felt would likely have been taken home by the crew to "make lovely silk underwear for their wives and sweethearts on shore"![227] Slack and Ware were given warm dry clothing and tots of rum, then collapsed into the bunks of the launch, where they slept all the way back to Newlyn Harbour, Cornwall. The pair was then transported back to Bolt Head, where they celebrated their safe return, and pending Caterpillar Club and Gold Fish Club memberships.

It was quite a literal thrust into the deep end for Ware, having only joined the Squadron ten days before on his first operational posting. He noted in his logbook that day, "Both No. 1 & Myself baled out. F/LT. SLACK ran out of juice after 1 hr. 10 mins., something wrong somewhere, bags of fairly accurate flack [sic] over Morlaix. Picked up after 40 mins by Walrus & then M.T.B".[228]

Slack wrote about his experience in his autobiography, *Happy is the Day*, but added to the story in March 1983,

> ...*I had a very close girl friend WAAF Officer in the Control Room at Portreath & when she heard that I was in the sea she launched a veritable Armada of planes and boats to rescue me.... there were so many smoke floats dropped all around me that I could hardly breathe. When the Walrus landed, my No 2, Sergeant Wade* [sic], *was waving at me from the rear. He had run out of Petrol looking for me & it was his May Days* [sic] *which were received at Portreath because mine were given too low & too far away to give an accurate position.... The Walrus couldn't take off in the swell so an ASR launch came along & took us both on board & zigzagged in front of the plane to calm the waters & allow it to take off. We were landed at Newlyn Harbour... before being taken to Portreath & then back to Bolthead* [sic].[229]

As Slack and Ware were returning, Squadron business continued and three sections were airborne on uneventful shipping protection patrols ten miles south of base. These were flown at 11:25-12:45, 12:30-13:40, and 13:30-14:50. However, during this time the Squadron also received orders that it was to move to West Malling as soon as possible, and all further operations were ceased.

The last of the three shipping protection patrols was flown by Fg Off Keith Curtis and Flt Sgt Roger Short, and whilst the Squadron returned to 10 Group briefly for an air firing course in March 1945, this patrol constituted the unit's final operational sorties ever in 10 Group. The rest of the day was spent packing.

19 June 1944 – There was no operational flying today, as the Squadron was abruptly pulled off D-Day support operations and sent to West Malling in Kent to combat the new V1 threat. The pilots took off at 11:00, followed by the ground staff and 6041 Servicing Echelon in five C-47 Dakotas. They were joined at West Malling by fellow 10 Group units, 610 Squadron and 6610 Servicing Echelon from Harrowbeer.

Their moves created a great shuffling of the units remaining in 10 Group. 263 Squadron and 6263 Servicing Echelon moved from Harrowbeer to Bolt Head to fill 41 Squadron's place, both 1 and 165 Squadrons and their respective servicing echelons moved from Predannack to Harrowbeer to replace 610 and 263 Squadrons, and 234 Squadron moved from Deanland to Predannack to replace 1 and 165 Squadrons.

Today also marked the departure of one of 41 Squadron's supernumerary Flight Lieutenants, Ron Collis, who had been with the unit since August 1943, and now remained behind in 10 Group to be posted to 126 Squadron at Culmhead as a Flight Commander. Awarded a DFC with this unit in May 1945, and a Mention in Despatches the following month, he remained in the RAFVR until 1950, when he was appointed to a commission as a flying instructor in the Royal Navy. His tenure ended in 1955, after which he emigrated to the United States, and he authored *Contending Fighters of World War II* in 2003.[230]

There would be no more rest for 41 the Squadron, and they would now be in the firing line right through until the cessation of hostilities in May 1945. This day was the start of a new era that would see the unit battling V1s, V2s, V3s and jet aircraft, would include a move to the Continent and involve them in the push into Germany and the final victory. They had a long, intensive, exhausting and deadly eleven months ahead of them, and only three of the pilots with the Squadron today would still be with the unit on VE Day.

Repelling the V1
19 June – 27 August 1944

6

In Mid-June 1944, just after the Allied D-Day landings, Germany unleashed a new and deadly weapon on England: the V1 unmanned flying bomb. Although its official designation was the Fieseler Fi103, it was widely known as the 'V1' by the Germans, and codenamed 'Diver' by the Allies. The British press and public, on the other hand, preferred to call it the 'Doodlebug' or the 'Buzz Bomb' because of the sound the engine made.

The 'V' in the German name for the weapon was an abbreviation for the word *Vergeltungswaffe* which, in strict translation, means 'Vengeance Weapon'. Some writers have also used the terms 'Reprisal', 'Retaliation' and 'Revenge', each also aptly describing the weapon, so-named as its designers sought retribution for the Allied bombings of German territory.

Based on timer settings, and launched from ramps at numerous locations in France and Holland, the unmanned bomb suddenly stopped when the set time had elapsed, and simply fell to the ground where it was.

The Allies knew this weapon was coming in some form, several months before the first was launched. In February 1944, for example, Prime Minister Churchill foretold its arrival, announcing to the House of Commons that…

> …there is no doubt that the Germans are preparing on the French shore new means of attack on this country, either by pilotless aircraft or possibly rockets, or both, on a considerable scale. We have long been watching this with the utmost vigilance.[1]

However, the Allies were unable to stop the V1's arrival, and knowing it was coming did not make it any less dangerous. The Buzz Bomb was the precursor to today's guided 'smart bombs' in that range and direction could be set by compass, but at the time an exact grid reference could not yet be defined. In this fashion, the bomb was somewhat imprecise, but on the other hand, on the receiving end, it wrought horror as its victims were not necessarily military or strategic in nature. It fell where it fell, and the victims were more often civilian than not; there was nothing more frightening than hearing the V1 stop humming.

> …the dreaded doodle era …it was very scary hearing them rumbling through the sky waiting for the engine to cut out and then the explosion. So impersonal. Indiscriminate destruction.[2]

The V1 was of relatively cheap manufacture, and built of plywood and sheet steel to avoid the use of scarce aluminium.

Fieseler Fi103 'V1' Flying Bomb Vital Statistics	
Length	7.9 metres (25 ft. 11 in.)
Height	1.42 metres (4 ft. 8 in.)
Diameter	80cm (2 ft. 7 in.)
Wingspan	5.37 metres (17 ft. 7 in.)
Weight	2,150kg (4,750 lb.)
Engine	Argus As 109-014 pulse jet engine
Propellant	80 octane petrol

Fuel Capacity	568 litres (124.5 imperial gallons)
Max Flying Time	2 hours
Maximum Speed	625-655 kmph (390-410 mph)
Typical Altitude	760 metres (2,500 ft.)
Maximum Altitude	3,000 metres (10,000 ft.)
Range	240 km (150 miles) to 400 km (250 miles)
Warhead	830kg (1,832 lb.) Amatol

Initially, they were launched from static ramps, which the Germans attempted to hide in forests in the Pas-de-Calais region, but the long launch rails were easily detectable from the air and quickly become Allied bombing targets. In response to this, the Wehrmacht switched to mobile ramps, which were kept on the move. He111 bombers were also used to launch V1s over the North Sea at night-time, which proved effective for a period. However, the weight slowed the bombers significantly, which made them an easy target for Allied night fighters, and several fell before the strategy was abandoned.

These German weapons were also known as terror weapons, and with some justification. I vividly recall hearing one for the first time as it came in over the coast at Friston. It was flying at about two hundred feet making this weird and frightening thumping sound. We knew that if the noise stopped it would mean the bomb would come down. That didn't prevent the sound being highly alarming, though the silence that might follow would of course be worse.[3]

In reaction to this new threat, the RAF reorganised its defence of Britain, and set up a Diver defence belt in 11 Group's area, to stop the V1s reaching London. Only Tempests and late-model Spitfires were considered fast enough to counter the threat in the air and, as a result, many squadrons were rapidly moved to forward bases and placed on round-the-clock Diver patrols.

As the Spitfire XII was considered capable of combating the threat, 41 Squadron was one of those chosen to be deployed against this new menace, and their role was abruptly altered from offense to defence.

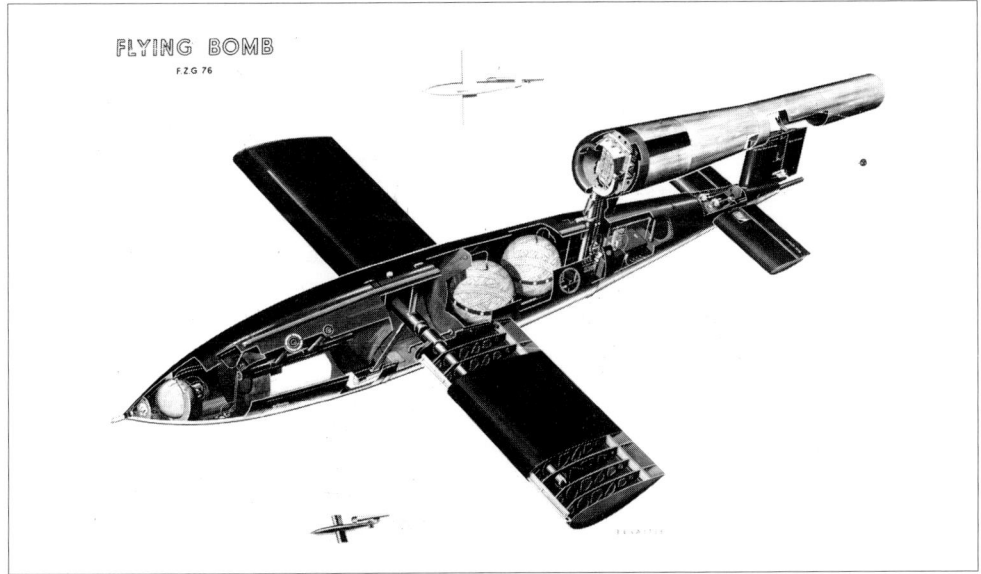

A cutaway drawing of a V1 flying bomb, showing fuel cells, warhead and other equipment. © Public domain, U.S. Air Force Photo, via the National Museum of the U.S. Air Force

A V1 flying bomb falls on London, close to St. Pauls, precisely the threat that 41 Squadron was deployed to hinder during the summer of 1944. © Public domain, U.S. Air Force Photo, via the National Museum of the U.S. Air Force

West Malling

19 June 1944 – The Squadron was moved to West Malling on the Kent coast with barely a day's notice, the swiftness of which is evident in an entry in the RAF West Malling Station ORB that day that states,

> *Great change-over in consequence of the German "Diver" effort. This station in one day ceased to be a night fighter station and turned into a day fighter one. 96 Squadron went to Ford – 148 Airfield with 29 and 409 to Hunsdon, leaving 91 Squadron here to be joined by 41 and 610 Squadrons from 10 Group Bolthead [sic] and Harrowbeer respectively. When the trouble is over – it is hoped West Malling will resume its proper role. 17 Spitfires of 41 Squadron arrived 1313 hours and 15 Spitfires of 610 Squadron arrived 1504 hours.*[4]

The Station, a grass strip located five miles west of Maidstone, and thus directly in the firing line as it were, recorded the arrival of yet another squadron only a day later, when 322 (Dutch) Squadron arrived with another 17 Spitfires. This meant that between 41, 91, 322 and 610 Squadrons, at least 67 Spitfires were now based at West Malling, under Station Commander Wg Cdr J. A. 'Tony' O'Neill DFC, for the sole purpose of preventing V1s from reaching London.

41 Squadron would now spend two solid months on anti-Diver patrols and ended this phase in their history having destroyed 12 V1s in the last ten days of June 1944, 23 in July and another 18 in August, making a total of 53 (45 + 8 shared) destroyed, and one damaged.

> *At the end of June a new phase in our work began: dealing with doodlebugs. […] Defending London from doodlebugs was done in three ways: first were the barrage balloons which were of course quite capable of downing the bombs but couldn't stop them from exploding on or near inhabited places; then there were the anti-aircraft guns, which were given special zones in which to operate and in which it was more likely the bombs would fall in open country; and finally came the fighters of ADGB (the Air Defence of Great Britain) of which 41 Squadron was a part. Our job was to patrol high up over the Channel and if possible to down the brutes into the sea. Often enough we had to follow our quarry a little inland but need to keep careful note of where the anti-aircraft gunners had exclusive rights.*[5]

20 June 1944 – Broken cloud with excellent visibility. Twenty-nine Buzz Bombs were plotted in 11 Group's area during the day, of which 23 crossed the coast and 21 were destroyed by fighters.[6]

In response to the threat, West Malling's resident Squadrons flew 144 anti-Diver sorties, during which 610 Squadron claimed four destroyed, 41 Squadron two, 91 Squadron one and one shared with Newchurch-based 486 Squadron, and 322 Squadron one.

41 Squadron's first ever Anti-Diver Patrol was airborne at 07:10 when Plt Off Jim Payne and Fg Off Maurice Balasse took off as Blue Section (Payne MB804 & Balasse EN609). This was then followed by another 22 overlapping patrols in pairs over the Channel until 22:35, when the last aircraft touched down again. With a measure of cynicism, 41 Squadron's ORB recorded that day,

> There were thirteen unsuccessful patrols from Beachy Head to Dungeness after the Jet-propelled bombs which had been worrying London for the past five days. The old XII was once more called on for its speed to deal with the Huns [sic] latest witticis[m].[7,8,9]

41 Squadron's two claims constituted the unit's first ever V1 victories, and these were credited to Plt Off Peter Gibbs and Canadian Fg Off Keith Curtis.

Flying as Number 2 to Flt Lt Peter Cowell in Yellow Section (Cowell MB795 & Gibbs MB875), Gibbs was airborne at 19:20 and intercepted his Buzz Bomb over Eastbourne, Sussex, at 19:55.[10] It was flying at an altitude of 3,000 feet, and on a course of 350° at an IAS of 270-280 mph. As the Combat Report gives little detail of the actual attack, it is otherwise only known that this V1 crashed and exploded north of Eastbourne. In a business-like manner, Gibbs merely noted in his logbook, "Patrol. Destroyed squadron's first 'Pilotless A/C'".[11]

Barely an hour later, Fg Off Keith Curtis was airborne with Flt Sgt Roger Short at 20:50 as White Section (Curtis EB229 & Short MB862) and intercepted his Buzz Bomb 40 minutes later at 4,000 feet south-southeast of Tunbridge Wells, Kent. The V1 was on a course of 345° and doing an IAS of 280 mph. He later recalled,

> I was vectored on to the V1 by ground radar. I initially fired a short burst with no result so I kept firing until the wing fell off. We were not given any instruction on how to destroy a V1.[12]

The flying bomb crashed and exploded nearby, and Curtis landed at 21:50 claiming the Squadron's second V1.

So new was this weapon that there appears to have been no consensus on the Squadron at the time about what they should be called! The ORB called them "J.P. [jet-propelled] bombs"; Peter Gibbs called them "Pilotless A/C"; and Jimmy Payne called them "Buzz Bombs"; and Flt Lt Bill Stowe referred to patrols in his logbook as "Robot Bomb patrol", "Anti-Divers Patrol" and "Doodlebug Patrol". Flt Lt Terry Spencer recorded in his own logbook today, "We start hunting the Pilotless Jet Aircraft. Alias "Doodlebug" or Buzz Bomb".[13]

Of the other 6½ V1s claimed by the West Malling Wing today, one of those destroyed by 610 Squadron was claimed by Flt Lt John Shepherd, who would become 41 Squadron's Commanding Officer within ten months, whilst that claimed by 322 Squadron was downed by Dutch Flt Lt 'Kees' van Eendenburg, who had served with 41 Squadron as a Pilot Officer from early December 1941 to mid-July 1942.

However, not everything on this first day of anti-Diver Patrols, as they would become known, went completely to plan. Flt Lt Ross Harding (EN229) states in his logbook that he "Landed [at] Redhill with disastrous results".[14] Unfortunately, however, neither the ORB nor his logbook indicate a reason or offer further detail on the incident.

21 June 1944 – Low cloud with fair visibility. Forty Buzz Bombs were plotted in 11 Group's area during the day, of which 35 crossed the coast but only eight were destroyed by fighters. Half of these were brought down by West Malling's squadrons.

41 Squadron's activity today comprised around 20 anti-Diver patrols in pairs, commencing at 06:45 and continuing until 23:05.[15] Only one V1 was claimed by the unit today, and this fell to Plt Off Peter Gibbs again, during his 07:45-08:45 patrol as Yellow Section (Cowell MB862 & Gibbs MB875). However, it was only through sheer luck that he could make the claim.

The Doodlebug was spotted by the pair just 15 minutes into their patrol above 10/10ths cloud at 4,500 feet, on a course of 350° and flying at an IAS of 300 mph. Fg Off Peter Cowell pulled in behind the Buzz Bomb but found himself in the frustrating position of being lined up for the kill but unable to fire. "200 yds behind 'Doodlebug' & cannon jammed! Told Gibby to go in & finish it off – he did!!"[16]

Gibbs got into position and made two attacks. His first caused pieces of the V1 to come away, but his second burst set it on fire and sent it down in a spin. Due to the thick cloud cover, they were unaware of their exact position at the time, but assumed it to be still near the coast, somewhere between Hastings and Beachy Head.

It was just the second day of anti-Diver patrols, and already Gibbs had claimed two. However, despite the good start to the day, no more were claimed by the Squadron throughout the day, and there was little success reported by the rest of the Wing either. 91 Squadron claimed two destroyed and 322 Squadron just one, whilst 610 Squadron were unable to make any claims at all.

Testifying to the difficulty in catching and bringing down V1s, Flt Lt 'Jimmy' Thiele later recalled:

> *Our Mk. XII Spitfires were equipped with the Griffon engine, more powerful than the Merlin. Despite this making them the fastest, they were still unable to catch the V1 in level flight. This meant that we had to patrol at about 8,000 ft. or more and carry out a full-powered dive at them. In this the Spitty was a very poor gun platform. It was impossible to trim our skid and one was jammed hard in one corner of the cockpit. The Tempest on the other hand, with its 3500 H.P. Napier Sabre engine, was able to catch them easily and became their principle destroyer.*[17]

22 June 1944 – A dull and cloudy day, which cleared from the west to good visibility. Sixty-four V1s were plotted in 11 Group's area during the day, of which 47 crossed the coast and 29 were destroyed by fighters.

For their part, 41 Squadron flew 24 anti-Diver patrols between 05:05 and 22:50[18], of which at least four – Red, Yellow, Blue and Green Sections – operated from Friston between 11:25 and 14:55, patrolling an area approximately ten miles south of Lympne.

The day's first success came on just the second patrol, falling to White Section (Malone EN605 & Robertson MB875). At 06:47, Australian Flt Sgt Colin Robertson intercepted a V1 3,500 feet above Pevensey, Sussex, on an almost reciprocal course. Robertson pulled his aircraft around and gave chase, closing to 250 yards before opening fire, and reduced his range to 150 yards as he fired. He hit the V1's port wing, which caused it to spiral down in flames and crash six miles north of Pevensey.

Although Robertson's Combat Report gives no indication of a disagreement, his claim appears to have been disputed by a Tempest from another squadron. The hint lies in an entry on his *Pilot Service Record*, which states he was finally awarded the full victory, "1 Flying Bomb Destroyed confirmed over Tempest claim by A.O.C."[19]

Not long afterwards, Flt Lt Terry Spencer almost got his first, too, but as he lined up to fire, a Spitfire XIV jumped in and beat him to it! "Closed to within 600' of one but a Spit XIV got him."[20]

In the evening, several sorties later, Green Section (Birbeck MB841 & Anderson MB837) finally intercepted another V1, 2,500 feet over Maidstone. Flt Lt 'Joe' Birbeck expended his entire ammunition trying to bring it down, but without success, then pulled away to allow Fg Off 'Andy' Anderson an opportunity. Anderson finished it off, sending the V1 down into a field north of Maidstone at 18:25. The pair returned to West Malling at 19:00, claiming half each. Today's two Diver victories constituted the Squadron's fourth and fifth V1s in just three days.

Flt Lt Clive 'Joe' Birbeck was posted away on 23 July 1944 after a tenure of over 17 months with 41 Squadron, having in that time enjoyed significant success: one destroyed, two probable and one damaged FW190s, one damaged Me109, and a shared destroyed V1. He was posted to 127 Squadron on 6 January 1945, but was shot down and captured only eleven days later and spent the remaining months of the War behind wire.
© Cowell family

41 Squadron had enjoyed little success for their 48 sorties today, but West Malling's other resident squadrons were more fortunate. 610 Squadron claimed four V1s destroyed, 91 Squadron claimed 3⅓ – the other two thirds believed to have been shared with aircraft from 3 and 486 Squadrons – and 322 Squadron claimed three. To help combat this new threat, the RAF also added a balloon barrage today, increasing the existing number of balloons from 480 to 1,400.

23 June 1944 – Cloudy with fair to good visibility. A massive 94 Doodlebugs were plotted in 11 Group's area during the day, of which 89 crossed the coast but only 20 were destroyed by fighters. However, nearly every one of these was downed by West Malling's squadrons.

41 Squadron flew 22 anti-Diver patrols between 04:45 and 23:20, but the lack of detail in the Squadron ORB – only one patrol is mentioned – conceals the fact that this was the Squadron's most successful and intensive day against the V1 onslaught yet. West Malling's ORB reveals that the unit claimed three and one shared destroyed, but it is only thanks to Combat Reports and entries in pilots' flying logbook's that we can gain a true picture of the day's activity.

On the morning's second patrol, Green Section (Slack MB880 & Thiele MB856) sighted the exhaust flame of a V1 at 04:55, flying at just 1,500 feet, at an IAS of 320 mph on a course of 330°. Flt Lt Tom Slack made two attacks on the Buzz Bomb over Hastings, but was frustrated by the intervention of two Tempests. The V1 was destroyed, but after his return to West Malling at 05:30, he was compelled to share the victory with them.[21]

At 08:00, Blue Section (Payne MB837 & Balasse MB830) was airborne on their second patrol; their first together had been between 04:45 and 05:55. On this successful patrol, Plt Off Jimmy Payne and Belgian Fg Off 'Momo' Balasse each brought down their first V1s. Balasse was the first of the pair to claim, sighting his ten miles north of Hastings at 3,000 feet, on a bearing of 340° and at a speed of 370 mph, at 08:30. His attack produced long flames from the fuselage and sent it down through 10/10ths cloud on an angle of 45°. Payne sighted another just ten minutes later, southwest of Rye, Sussex. This Buzz Bomb was flying at a similar altitude, though a little slower at 320 mph, and on a bearing of 350°. Payne's attack was perfect: a single one-second burst caused it to explode.

However, their excited chases had led to excessive fuel consumption, and Balasse did not make it back to West Malling. His engine cut and he crash-landed west of Farleigh, about three miles short of the airfield. Balasse was injured and the Spitfire was written off. Payne recorded the morning's events in his logbook,

Claimed a 'Buzz Bomb' confirmed destroyed. F/O Balasse also claimed one destroyed. F/O Balasse – my No. 2 – crash-landed owing to lack of fuel!![22]

Flt Lt Bill Stowe was airborne with Flt Sgt Roger Short as Purple Section at 17:00 and again, as Yellow Section, at 20:50. They, too, sighted V1s, but could not claim any victories. Stowe recorded in his logbook, "Chase[d] 3. No Luck."[23]

However, on the last patrol of the day, another V1 could be claimed for the Squadron. Flying a dusk patrol from 22:20, Red Section (Spencer MB856 & Coleman MB837) was vectored to a V1 coming in over Hastings at 3,000 feet on a course of 340° at an IAS of 380 mph, just on 23:00. Flt Lt Terry Spencer pulled around and lined himself up, but had to hurry as a couple of Tempests tried to cut in and steal his victory:

Patrolling at 6,000 feet [over] Beachy Head [and] ordered to Hastings. Saw gun fire from ships and flickering light from Jet Bomb over coast. Closed to 350 yds. astern [and] opened fire closing to 200 yds. Two Tempests came alongsode [sic] over taking, [so] I fired three long bursts of 5 Seconds each. Diver turned to Starboard and blew up on the ground 10/15 miles N.N.E. of Hastings.[24,25]

Spencer and Coleman returned to West Malling at 23:15, where Spencer claimed his first V1 destroyed. He recorded the event dryly in his logbook, "Destroyed 1 Pilotless J.P. Aircraft 2300 hrs."[26]

There had been so much action today and yet the Squadron's entire operations are summed up in the ORB in a single sentence, "22.30, Patrolling at dusk, F/Lt. Spencer destroyed a diver 10/15 miles NNE of Hastings."[27] In fact, it had been an intense day for the whole Wing. 91 Squadron had shot down seven V1s plus another four shared with aircraft from other squadrons, 322 Squadron shot down two of their own, and 610 Squadron two shared with other squadrons, plus one damaged. The Wing was the most successful in 11 Group today, their total bag amounting to 12 destroyed and one damaged, and seven shared destroyed with other squadrons.

24 June 1944 – The weather was fine and warm today with good visibility. In contrast to the previous day, however, there was little business for the West Malling Wing. Only 17 Buzz Bombs were plotted in 11 Group's area during the day, of which 15 crossed the coast and nine were destroyed by fighters.

41 Squadron flew 20 patrols, totalling 39 sorties[28], between 04:35 and 23:10 but could only claim a single Buzz Bomb destroyed. This fell to Plt Off Peter Gibbs, who claimed his third in just four days. The Wing's other squadrons fared a little better, however, with 91 and 610 Squadrons each claiming two destroyed, but 322 Squadron none at all.

Gibbs' success came on the morning's second patrol. Yellow Section (Harding EN602 & Gibbs MB875) was airborne at 05:40 and, at 06:15, was vectored onto an incoming V1 at an altitude of 3,000 feet. It was flying on a course of 340° and at an IAS of 350 mph. It is apparent that Flt Lt Ross Harding's engine was playing up, as once again Gibbs found himself in the fortunate position of having a No. 1 that could not bring a V1 down due to problems with his aircraft. This allowed Gibbs to slip into position and line up his attack.

Two bursts of fire struck the Doodlebug and upset its aerodynamics enough to perform continuous half rolls, but it remained on an almost straight path, only gradually losing height. Gibbs fired once more at the crippled V1 and this time succeeded in forcing it into the sea approximately 8-10 miles south of Hastings.[29]

Flt Lt Ross Harding, meanwhile, was experiencing some difficulty with his aircraft and made an emergency landing at Friston. His logbook suggests the pair were busier than otherwise reported but adds some confusion to the day's V1 claims, implying he also had a claim to make. Although this is not documented elsewhere, and no Combat Report exists to formalise the assertion, he penned, "Chased 3 Doodlebugs, clobbered last one (not confirmed) but engine quit and forced to land at Friston."³⁰ During the afternoon, he was flown back to West Malling by 501 Squadron's Fg Off James Grottick in that unit's Tiger Moth.

RAF West Malling's ORB records the Station's score between the start of the V1 onslaught and midnight on 24 June 1944 as 60 plus 15 shared destroyed, thereunder two brought down by the Bofors of 2769 Squadron RAF Regiment. The Squadron breakdown was recorded as follows:

Squadron[31]	Destroyed	Shared
91	29	11
610	10	2
41	8	2
322	7	0
96 (Night)	4	0
2769 RAF Regt.	2	0
Totals	60	15

25 June 1944 – Fine with southerly winds, but hazy. Twenty-four V1s were plotted in 11 Group's area during the day, all of which crossed the coast; ten of these were destroyed by fighters. The West Malling Wing sent up 130 anti-Diver sorties throughout the day, to which 41 Squadron contributed at least 42 sorties in 21 patrols.[32]

It was another long day of anti-Diver patrols for little reward. The first patrol was airborne at 04:40, but not a single success could be recorded until the final patrol of the day. On that patrol, Flt Lt Terry Spencer and Flt Sgt Roger Short were airborne as Yellow Section (Spencer EN229 & Short EN260) at 22:45.

A few minutes after 23:00, Spencer spotted a lone V1, which had not been seen or reported by ground control. It was coming in at 2,500 feet on a course of 360° and at a speed of 340 mph. Spencer's fire was accurate, striking the flying bomb's fuel tank and setting it alight. It hit the ground and blew up, at which time a fix was finally obtained, placing it at High Halden, approximately 7½ miles southwest of Ashford, Kent.[33]

As darkness was setting in, Spencer decided it was time to head home with his No. 2. However, just five minutes before landing, Short spotted a Buzz Bomb in his rear-view mirror, approaching him in the darkness at between 1,500 and 2,000 feet, and slowly overhauling at 330 IAS. He…

> …saw the flames of a J.P. Bomb behind him, pulled up, and gave a burst from above and to starboard, seeing strikes, as two other Spits were firing from below and behind, he claimed one half J.P. Bomb destroyed when it crashed North of Ashford.[34,35]

The Squadron had to wait a long time today to make a V1 claim, but their final score, as small as it was, was the highest for any other West Malling-based unit, but only just: 91 and 610 Squadrons each claimed one V1 and 322 Squadron could not make a claim at all.

26 June 1944 – Bad weather all day, and most of 11 Group was non-operational. The German military took full advantage of the conditions and sent over 54 Buzz Bombs, of which 34 crossed the coast, and just four were destroyed by fighters.

41 Squadron flew four uneventful patrols (eight sorties) between 05:25 and 08:30, and this was all their operational flying for the day as they had received orders to move to Tangmere with 610 Squadron. They reached the airfield before lunch, despite the continuing poor weather, and although another three anti-Diver patrols (six sorties) were flown from Tangmere during the afternoon, all were uneventful.

Westhampnett

27 June 1944 – Cloudy with some showers, but generally good visibility. Again the Germans sent over a massive number of V1s, with no less than 91 plotted in 11 Group's area. Sixty-seven crossed the coast, but as conditions were generally better than the previous day, forty-one were brought down by fighters. However, 41 Squadron only played a minor role and could make no claims all day.

Following a night at Tangmere waiting for the ground crews to reach them, the pilots moved to Tangmere's satellite airfield Westhampnett with 610 Squadron. The weather gave the pilots little chance against the V1s and although at least 19 uneventful anti-Diver patrols[36] were flown between 13:55 and 23:10, "Divers were seen but no contacts were made close enough for firing".[37]

Despite the lack of action in the air, however, the Squadron recorded two flying accidents, which left one man hurt. Although the exact circumstances are unknown, Plt Off Peter Gibbs crash-landed at Westhampnett in EN620, but was not injured. In the second accident, Australian Flt Sgt Colin Robertson overshot the runway at Westhampnett in EN221 on his first dusk landing and struck EN224, which was parked on the airfield. He was injured and both aircraft were damaged. To add insult to injury, his logbook was endorsed 'carelessness'.

28 June 1944 – Low cloud with rain and showers. Almost one hundred V1s were plotted in 11 Group's area during the day, of which 65 made landfall and 32 were destroyed by fighters.

However, 41 Squadron was not involved. Their brief stay at Westhampnett was dogged by poor weather and they undertook no operational flying all day today. The ORB records, therefore, that "the 'Doodle Bugs' sailed through low cloud with sublime immunity."[38] The only highlight of the day was apparently "a good session in the bar with F/Lt. Burne undisputed chairman and noggin-master."[39] This event was most likely related to an all-ranks dance held in the evening in the Station Cinema at Tangmere to celebrate the 5th anniversary of the founding of the WAAF.

By now, the anti-aircraft batteries ringing the coast attempting to defend London against the V1 onslaught numbered around 375 heavy guns, 575 light guns, another 560 light guns of the RAF Regiment, plus two US Army anti-aircraft batteries. Along with the balloon barrage and fighters, there was now a formidable line of defence between the coast and London.

29 June 1944 – Cloudy with occasional showers. Eighty-two Buzz Bombs were plotted in 11 Group's area during the day, of which 70 crossed the coast and 45 were destroyed by fighters. Although 41 Squadron was airborne on 20 anti-Diver patrols between 05:05 and 20:35 today, their efforts were in vain; all were unsuccessful.

However, behind the business-like façade of the ORB, discontent was brewing within the Squadron, which had been fermenting since Sqn Ldr 'Pinkie' Glen's unpopular removal in late May. One pilot recorded in his diary today, "We have lost 10 aircraft this month. Squadron is not what it was under Pinky. Chapman is a very decent bloke but completely clueless."[40]

30 June 1944 – Very cloudy with limited visibility. Not surprisingly, the German military made the most of it. No less than 122 Buzz Bombs were plotted by 11 Group during the day, of which 88 made landfall, and 37 were destroyed by fighters. However, 41 Squadron played no role whatsoever and undertook no operational flying all day.

During the month of June 1944, 41 Squadron had mounted 173 anti-Diver patrols, consisting of almost 350 sorties, for a score of 12 V1s destroyed (10 + 2 shared).

1 July 1944 – Low cloud and rain continued from the previous day, making 11 Group non-operational for most of the day. Another 122 Doodlebugs were plotted by the Group again today, of which 93 crossed the coast, but only 18 were brought down by fighters.

The poor conditions preventing operational flying by 41 Squadron until the evening "when the usual uneventful J.P. Bomb patrols were resumed in mid-channel".[41] However, only six patrols had been carried out between 16:45 and 20:45, when the weather came down again and flying was stopped once more.

Separately, on this date, the RAF reached its peak wartime strength of 1,185,833 personnel, consisting of 1,011,427 men and 174,406 women.

The Squadron Moves to Friston

2 July 1944 – The poor weather conditions, with drizzle and dense fog, were even worse than the day before. Despite the weather, only 47 V1s were plotted in 11 Group's area during the day. All but three of these crossed the coast but not a single one was brought down by fighters.

41 Squadron undertook no operational flying all day, but Fg Offs Peter Graham and 'Jack' Malone, and WO Jimmy Ware, were sent by road transport to collect three aircraft, one from Friston and two from West Malling.

At 15:00, the Squadron learnt they would be moving again today with 610 Squadron, this time to Friston, on the Sussex coast. At the same time, with equally short notice, 350 and 501 Squadrons were ordered to make the opposite move, from Friston to Westhampnett. 41 Squadron packed "in record time"[42] and were airborne for Friston at 17:05. The pilots landed 20 minutes later, after which B Flight was placed on readiness until dusk, but their services were not required and they were released without having undertaken any operational flying.

41 Squadron had been based at Friston twice previously during the War; in May-June 1943 and March-April 1944. One of the Squadron's pilots recalled that Friston was a "ghastly 'drome for flying but good for accommodation".[43]

3 July 1944 – The day commenced with thick cloud, fog and drizzle, which cleared later from the west. One hundred and ten Buzz Bombs were plotted by 11 Group today, of which 92 crossed the coast, and 24 were shot down by fighters.

41 and 610 Squadrons were organised at Friston in such a way that, between them, they were to maintain one stand-by section, two readiness sections and two patrols airborne at all times. As such, 41 Squadron's B Flight was placed on dawn readiness from 05:35, but had only carried out two patrols before the weather deteriorated and flying ceased. Nonetheless, both were successful. During the first of these, Fg Off Maurice 'Momo' Balasse claimed one V1 destroyed and, during the second, Sqn Ldr Chapman claimed one, too. These were the first V1s claimed in eight days.

Blue Section (Birbeck MB836 & Balasse EN609) was airborne at 05:35 and intercepted a V1 at 06:35 at an altitude of 3,000 feet northeast of Bexhill on a course of 340° and at an IAS of 340-350 mph.[44] Balasse made a stern attack, closing from 100 yards to just 50 as he fired, and sent the Buzz Bomb down into a field four miles north of Bexhill where it exploded on impact.

Sqn Ldr Chapman was airborne at 07:03 and intercepted a V1 in mid-Channel, southeast of Beachy Head, just 12 minutes later. It was flying at 2,000 feet on a heading of 340° at 340 mph. Chapman launched his attack from quarter astern at 400 yards, closing to dead astern at 300 yards, and sent the V1 down into the sea 30 miles southeast of Beachy Head in what the ORB describes as "very difficult conditions, with cloud right down to deck."[45] He returned at 07:34, claiming his first and only V1 destroyed, and his only victory during his tenure with 41 Squadron.[46]

Weather then kept the Squadron grounded until late in the evening, by which time the weather had improved a little, but only left enough time in the poor light for two patrols to be flown. The first operated between 20:45 and 21:40, and the second between 21:30 and 22:30, but both were uneventful.

4 July 1944 – Poor weather continued throughout the morning, with cloud and mist. The first wave of V1s did not come over until 08:30, but thereafter 108 were plotted by 11 Group. Of these, 84 crossed the coast and 52 were shot down by fighters.

Weather conditions prevented 41 Squadron from getting airborne until after lunch, but from 12:40 onwards twelve anti-Diver patrols were flown over the Channel, southeast of the Isle of Wight, and the last pair landed at Friston at 22:30.[47] However, despite their efforts, just one victory could be claimed by the Squadron, which was shared between Fg Off 'Momo' Balasse and Flt Sgt Freddie Woollard on the third patrol.[48]

Blue Section (Balasse EN229 & Woollard MB856) was airborne at 14:10 to patrol an area ten miles out to sea between Hastings and Rye. The pair were vectored onto a Diver by Wartling Control at 14:30, and soon spotted it approaching Dungeness at 3,000 feet on a course of 340° and at an IAS of 340-350 mph.

Balasse and Woollard took turns firing on the V1, attacking it from quarter astern to full astern, at ranges of 250-200 yards, and sent it down to explode on impact at a location they described as "approx. 1 Mile W. of Lydd. (actually N. of Rye.)".[49] They returned to base at 15:30, claiming the Squadron's fifteenth destroyed V1 (13 + 2 shared).

5 July 1944 – Although poor weather in the morning postponed the start of flying by several hours, 119 Doodlebugs were plotted by 11 Group during the day. Eighty-two of these made landfall and 36 were brought down by the Group's fighters.

41 Squadron's first aircraft airborne were Flt Lts Tom Slack and 'Jimmy' Thiele, who undertook a weather reconnaissance between 08:30 and 09:15. Although conditions were not ideal, the pair recommended that anti-Diver patrols should commence and the first patrol was airborne at 09:55. It was a good call; the weather continued to improve and the day ended up becoming fine and hot, allowing a full flying programme to be undertaken, with 15 patrols completed by 23:05.

One more V1 victory could be chalked up for the Squadron today, this time by Flt Lt Ross Harding, who claimed his first of three, but in a rather unconventional manner. Harding was airborne at 14:00 with Flt Sgt Roger Short as Yellow Section (Harding EN602 & Short EN620) to patrol between Dungeness and Hastings, and intercepted the V1 over Rye at 14:40 at an altitude of 3,000 feet and an IAS of 400 mph.

Harding dived on the Buzz Bomb from 12,000 feet – the only way to gain enough speed to catch it at the speed it was doing – and made a stern attack, firing off all his ammunition, however without success, and concluding his gun sight was malfunctioning. He then drew level with it, and used his wing tip to tilt it over and send it down to explode on the ground northwest of Rye.

Trial and error during summer 1944 had shown that whilst flying abreast of a V1, a pilot could place his wing tip under that of the V1, and lift it to tap the V1s wing up and send it off course. Although a successful method of destruction, it had an unfortunate side effect as it damaged the aircraft's wing tip, and many needed replacement after execution. It was therefore unpopular with the powers-that-be.

However, in time it was accidently discovered that the same method could be successfully applied without actually touching the V1s wing tip. At a distance of approximately six inches, the airflow between an aircraft's and a V1's wing tips was sufficient to unbalance its aerodynamics. Perfectly executed, the air movement between the wing tips was sufficient to raise the V1's wing and upset its gyroscopes, which sent it to the ground out of control.

This was the first time that one of 41 Squadron's pilots used the wing tip method, and was remembered vividly even 60 years after the event by fellow pilot Fg Off Keith Curtis, who recalled that Harding…

> …was on the tail of a V1 when he ran out of ammunition. He flew alongside it, put his wing tip under the wing tip of the V1 and tipped it over. He managed to land safely – only losing his wooden wing tip.[50]

Harding's victory today was the first of three occasions that 41 Squadron's pilots would bring down a V1 in this 'frowned-upon' manner. When Harding returned to base at 15:00, he claimed the Squadron's sixteenth V1 (14 + 2 shared) destroyed.

Unbeknown to Harding at the time, he had actually saved an anti-aircraft battery from destruction. On 1 August 1944, he received a memo from AOC, 11 Group, Air Cdre Cecil Bouchier CBE DFC, passing on a congratulatory message from the GOC-in-C, Anti-Aircraft Command, General Sir Frederick A. Pile KCB DSO MC, for causing the V1 to alter course away from a light anti-aircraft gun site near Hawkhurst, Kent. A report, naming Harding, also subsequently appeared in the newspaper.

6 July 1944 – Fine and hot weather but a quiet day for Doodlebugs. Only 36 were plotted by 11 Group all day, of which 25 crossed the coast and 11 were shot down by fighters. 41 Squadron flew a full programme of anti-Diver patrols between 07:25 and 23:00, but despite 18 patrols between Beachy Head and Dungeness, and between the Somme River and Dieppe, "few bombs came over and no interceptions were made".[51,52]

It was during the Squadron's brief stay at Friston that an embarrassing faux pas was made by Flt Lt Tom Slack. He does not give the date, but reveals in his autobiography that…

I returned from one scramble to report to Gizzy that I thought I had shot down a doodlebug in the Ashford area but I had not seen it hit the ground. He made a few phone calls and was told a doodlebug had exploded half an hour ago in the middle of the Ashford Railway Yards, causing considerable damage to railway property and military equipment destined for the Front in Europe. We both hurriedly agreed not to claim it shot down by me or anyone else in 41 Squadron.

After this unfortunate incident Gizzy said that if Hitler ever heard about all the British equipment I had been responsible for destroying, like the Audax in the desert [1941], the Spitfires in France [July 1943] and in the Channel [June 1944], and now the marshalling yards at Ashford, he would probably award me the Iron Cross First Class with diamonds and crossed swords.[53]

7 July 1944 – Cloud and rain, clearing to a fine day upon which 80 Buzz Bombs were plotted by 11 Group. Forty-six of these were shot down by fighters. For their part, 41 Squadron flew a total of 16 patrols between 05:40 and 23:30.[54]

Following the previous, uneventful day, the Squadron was off to a good start today, claiming success on the very first patrol. A share in a second victory came mid-afternoon, bringing the unit's score to 16½ V1s destroyed in 18 days.

Blue Section (Graham MB856 & Appleton EN609) was airborne at 05:40 and was barely in the air, when they spotted a V1 sailing in over Friston at 2,000 feet and gave chase. They caught up with it about six miles west of Hailsham, Sussex, on a heading of 320° and doing an IAS of 350 mph. However, two Tempests had also seen it, and were determined to make the victory theirs.

One Tempest got in first, but Fg Off Peter Graham was also determined to have the next shot. After he was done, the second Tempest also had a go, too, before the V1 finally went down. Graham subsequently staked a claimed for a part of the victory, but it was not as straightforward as it initially appeared. His Combat Report explains,

Claimed half share with second tempest [sic] to engage. Formating [sic] on 1st Tempest without results seen F/O. Graham opened fire ½ second burst obtaining hits on tail of J.P. Bomb, causing bright flash followed by J.P. Bomb climbing for 10 seconds then steep dive levelling out at 1,000 ft where 2 nd. [sic] Tempest finished it off to explode in a field 8 miles N.E. of Lewis [sic].[55]

On his return to base at 06:50, Graham claimed half a V1 destroyed but, in an unusual twist, Sector Headquarters at Biggin Hill received a telephone call from 11 Group at 18:00 that evening granting Graham the whole victory as no other claim had been received. His *Pilot Service Record* confirms, "1 J.P. Bomb claimed as ½ share with Tempest, granted in whole as Tempest did not claim."[56,57]

The day's second victory fell to WO 'Steve' Stevenson, who was airborne at 15:35 for an aircraft test when he spotted a V1 coming over Eastbourne at 2,000 feet at 16:15. He was eager to claim his first victory, but was beaten to the punch by Flt Lt Longin Majewski of 316 Squadron, who was flying a Mustang III. However, although Majewski attacked from 200 yards, he overshot, and thereby handed Stevenson his opportunity.[58]

Stevenson opened his own attack at a range of 250 yards and fired a two-second burst as he closed to 100 yards. He saw strikes on the Buzz Bomb, after which it spiralled down to explode seven miles north of Friston. He returned at 16:20 and was granted a half share with Majewski, who had initially claimed the entire victory for himself!

8 July 1944 – A fine and sunny day until just before dusk, when the cloud base came down to 3,000 feet, accompanied by heavy rain. Fifty-four V1s were plotted by 11 Group today, of which 42 crossed the coast, and 34 were shot down by fighters.

41 Squadron's pilots flew 22 anti-Diver patrols between 05:00 and 23:00, and added another two Doodlebugs to their tally. Once again, the day's first victory came on the very first patrol of the day.

Flt Lt Terry Spencer and Flt Sgt Peter Chattin were airborne at 05:00 as Yellow Section (Spencer MB875 & Chattin MB857 [sic]) and intercepted their V1 eight miles north of West Foreland 23 minutes later. It was flying at an altitude 3,500 feet, on a course of 270°, and at an IAS of 390 mph. Spencer attacked first, but unsuccessfully, so pulled away to allow Chattin an opportunity. He explained,

> *After Yellow 1 had attacked and reduced the J.P. Bomb speed* [to] *270 I.A.S. and made two unsuccessful attempts to tip the bomb over after whic*[h] *it recovered level flight at 2,500 and 1,500 ft. F/Sgt. Chattin fired 2 x 5 seconds bursts at 200 and 100 yds causing it to explode in the air in the Thames Estuary. Yellow 1 does not claim.*[59]

Unfortunately, however, debris from the V1's explosion hit Chattin's aircraft, which damaged the radiator, starboard wing and spinner, and shattered the propeller. Chattin was extremely lucky to have still been able to make a safe landing at Friston at 05.40. He must have been very shaken by the experience, and noted the event in his logbook, "My first D. Bug. Exploded – damaged prop, rad. & stb. mainpl.".[60]

During the evening, in a similar experience to that made by WO Ian Stevenson on the previous day, Plt Off Peter 'Gibby' Gibbs intercepted a Buzz Bomb whilst on a non-operational aircraft test.

Airborne at 21:30 with Fg Off Peter Cowell as Yellow Section (Gibbs EN227 & Cowell MB840), Gibbs spotted the V1 at an altitude of 2,000 feet, around two miles south of Eastbourne, on a heading of 350° and doing an IAS of 360 mph. He closed to within 300 yards range and fired a two-second burst, recording the time of his attack as 22:05, and sent it down to explode on the ground around about seven miles north of Eastbourne.

As the Squadron's present top scorer on V1s, Gibbs was lauded in the ORB that day as the "top-moving pilot of the Squadron, [who] destroyed his 4th bomb".[61] Unfortunately, however, his fourth Doodlebug would also be his last and two other pilots on the Squadron would soon surpass his tally and become V1 Aces.

Darkness fell that evening at 22:45, at which time Yellow Section, Black Section (Fleming & Appleton) and Green Section (Graham & van Goens) were all still airborne on anti-Diver patrols. They were back on the ground at Friston again by 23:00, but the ORB states there was "a certain amount of anxiety until we were all safely down."[62] Spitfires were not night-fighters and were infamous for night blindness caused by flames emitting from the exhaust. Fg Off Peter Graham vividly remembered both this issue and the day itself,

> *…just before dusk, I and my Number 2 were scrambled to try to deal with a doodlebug that had been spotted coming in while still some way out over the Channel. We didn't catch it and were then kept airborne for three-quarters of an hour and eventually were allowed to land only when it was raining and really dark. The Spitfire – and more particularly the Mk XII – was not designed for night flying. The Griffon engine emitted great plumes of flame from its exhaust manifolds right in front of the pilot's eyes when he was trying*

Flt Sgt Ian Stevenson destroyed 2½ V1s during the summer of 1944, one of which he brought down by tipping it off course with his Spitfire's wing. © 41 Squadron RAF

to look along the nose when landing. In the daytime these flames were not a hazard but at night their light was spectacular and well-nigh blinding. So it was with some relief that we both got down safely at Friston, which was quite a small airfield.[63]

Chattin and Gibbs' V1 victories today brought the Squadron's V1 tally to 20 (17 + 3 shared) destroyed.

9 July 1944 – The day dawned to fine weather, which continued to dusk, during which 76 Doodlebugs were plotted in 11 Group's area. Fifty-three made landfall, of which 27 were shot down by fighters, ten by anti-aircraft fire and one brought down by the balloon barrage.

Between 04:50 and 23:00, 41 Squadron completed 14 anti-Diver patrols and one weather reconnaissance. Although most flights were uneventful, one more V1 was claimed for the Squadron by Flt Lt 'Andy' Anderson and WO Archie Appleton on the day's ninth patrol.

Within 15 minutes of becoming airborne as Blue Section (Anderson EN228 & Appleton EN238) at 12:35, the pair intercepted a Buzz Bomb 12 miles southeast of Beachy Head, Sussex. It was flying on a course of 330° at 340 mph, and at an altitude of between 1,500 and 2,000 feet, when they attacked, opening fire at 600 yards and closing to just 50.

Their aim was accurate and they sent the Diver down into the Channel where it exploded on impact with the sea. Anderson and Appleton returned to Friston at 13:40 where they claimed the V1 shared destroyed.[64] This raised the Squadron's score to 21 (18 + 3 shared) V1s destroyed.

During the evening, the Squadron learned they would be moving to Lympne, in Kent, in two days' time. "We were glad we had sufficient warning this time, but not too happy over our 5th move in four weeks. Laundry, shoe repairs and mail were becoming real problems."[65,66] Unbeknown to the pilots, however, this would in fact be their last move before heading to the Continent in December, and Lympne would become their last operational base in the United Kingdom of the entire War.

10 July 1944 – The weather was not ideal during the morning, but a total of 56 Doodlebugs were plotted in 11 Group's area throughout the day. Forty made landfall, of which 17 were shot down by fighters and two were brought down by the balloon barrage.

41 Squadron sent up eight anti-Diver patrols between 04:45 and 12:25, but the low cloud closed in completely around midday and brought all operational flying to a halt. Under such conditions, it came as no surprise that the patrols that were flown were uneventful.

At 14:55, Flt Lt Ross Harding took off for Lympne, despite the conditions, "to make arrangements for our reception"[67] but the rest of the Squadron were released, allowing them good time to pack for their move. During the evening, they also took the opportunity to enjoy a last drink in their local, the "Sussex" in Eastbourne.

> *The blokes cram into odd types [of] cars & after a while hell is loose. Roy Short & I, who are well and truly out of practice, have to be very careful, we manage O.K. & end up more sober than most. Disgraceful scenes of Officers and NCO's misbehaving themselves in sedate snobbish Eastbourne, under the disapproving eyes of commissioned brown jobs – Who cares!*[68]

11 July 1944 – Cloudy with good visibility. A total of 99 Doodlebugs were plotted by 11 Group during the day, of which 75 crossed the coast. Thirty-four were shot down by fighters, and anti-aircraft fire and balloons brought down an additional six each.

However, 41 Squadron played no part and undertook no operational flying all day due to their pending move. However, despite being packed and ready in the morning, the Squadron did not receive permission to fly to Lympne until early afternoon. The pilots took off at 15:15 and arrived at their new base 25 minutes later, whereupon they were released for the rest of the day.

There was some excitement shortly after their arrival at Lympne, as four Doodlebugs sailed in straight over the airfield, one of which was shot down by the anti-aircraft guns. The men concluded, "It looked as though we might have plenty of fun in store."[69]

The Squadron was replaced at Friston by 316 (Polish) Squadron, who arrived from West Malling in their Mustangs, which were considered better aircraft for Diver Patrols due to their superior speed. An advance party of 1 (Spitfire IX) and 165 (Typhoon Ib) Squadrons also arrived at Lympne during the day, and the rest of their aircraft and their servicing echelons a day later.

Lympne[70]

RAF Lympne, a level grass airfield on the hills overlooking Romney Marsh, farmland and the English Channel, was established in 1916 as an RFC emergency landing ground. Six permanent hangars were erected during World War I, which were maintained until August 1920 when the RAF moved out and released the airfield for civilian use.

Limited mail and passenger flights operated from Lympne during the 1920s and 1930s, thereunder Imperial Airways who used the airfield as a refuelling stopover for cross-channel services. Fledgling Belgian airline SABENA also stopped at Lympne to bring newspapers from the Continent, but a highlight of the period was when the airfield hosted an international air rally in 1938.

In July 1939, however, as the storm clouds gathered over the Continent, the Fleet Air Arm requisitioned the airfield and named it HMS *Buzzard*. Nonetheless, RAF bomber and Army-cooperation squadrons were soon using Lympne and it was not long before its significance as an advanced landing ground was recognised by the Luftwaffe. Stukas were sent to bomb the airfield in August 1940, and major damage was done to the buildings and facilities.

Despite the attack, however, RAF fighter squadrons began to be stationed at Lympne from the following month, and continued to do so for the rest of the War. As such, the airfield played a significant role during the Operations *Jubilee* and *Overlord*, and was now perfectly located to combat the Flying Bomb onslaught.

By mid-July 1944, RAF Lympne supported a substantial infrastructure, which included a Station Headquarters, 1, 41 and 165 Squadrons, and 6001, 6041 and 6165 Servicing Echelons.

> *There were no runways; the surface was simply mown grass. In order to get safely airborne in the limited space, the Spit XII pilot had to rev up his engine, standing on the brakes, and let go as soon as full throttle was achieved. That way with the maximum possible acceleration it was reasonably easy to get airborne within the airfield boundaries.*[71]

There was an indoor tennis court, which was requisitioned for visiting bands and shows, and whilst the Sergeants' Mess was housed in a requisitioned property called French House, the Officers' Mess was extremely luxurious for Wartime Britain.

It was located in a large mansion on the hillside overlooking the sea, which had been commandeered from Sir Phillip Sassoon, and the grounds surrounding it were bounded by eight-foot-high hedges that hid a swimming pool. At the rear of the house was a large patio enclosed by a stone wall upon which the pilots would sometimes sit and watch the V1s fly over and the coastal batteries attempt to bring them down.[72] Flt Lt Tom Slack also remembered the Officers' Mess, recalling it had "sunken baths with gold taps, and all sorts of intriguing connecting doors between the bedrooms".[73]

12 July 1944 – 10/10ths cloud with fair visibility. A massive 145 Buzz Bombs were plotted by 11 Group during the day, of which 114 made landfall. Sixty-three of these were shot down by fighters and 11 by anti-aircraft fire, whilst balloons were responsible for another six.

41 Squadron's A Flight was brought to readiness at dawn, with one section in the air and one on standby. Sqn Ldr Chapman led the first of the day's 20 anti-Diver patrols, which was airborne at 04:50. Patrols continued throughout the day until 22:45, mostly in the Pas-de-Calais area.

Flt Sgt Peter Chattin chalked up the Squadron's only success today, at 08:40 on the day's fourth patrol. He was airborne with Flt Lt Terry Spencer at 08:05 as Yellow Section (Spencer MB840 & Chattin EN602) and vectored onto the V1 by Kingsley Control, which they intercepted over Dymchurch. The Buzz Bomb was sighted at 2,000 feet, on a course of 340°, and flying at a speed of 300mph.

Chattin opened up on the V1, firing a long six-second burst from dead astern, whilst closing to 100 yards. His accurate fire produced flames and the Buzz Bomb dived to earth, crashing four miles northwest of Ashford, Kent.

It was his second V1 in four days and the only one claimed by the entire Wing today. As 1 and 165 Squadrons were not yet fully operational, only their advance parties were available to undertake limited operations, the former squadron completing four patrols and the latter just three.

13 July 1944 – Poor weather throughout the day, which left 11 Group mostly non-operational. However, 47 Doodlebugs were plotted within the Group's area, of which 37 crossed the coast. Seventeen of these were brought down by fighters, five by anti-aircraft fire and two by balloons.

Weather conditions postponed the commencement of 41 Squadron's flying today by approximately 2½ hours and it was not until 07:25 that the first section was airborne on a patrol. Twelve anti-Diver patrols were then flown between that time and an early finish at 17:50, as a result of rain. Despite shortened operations, the Squadron was able to add another Buzz Bomb to its growing tally.

Fg Off Jim Payne and WO 'Jimmy' Ware were airborne at 09:50 as Blue Section (Payne MB804 & Ware MB841) and were vectored onto a Buzz Bomb at 10:20, when initially around 15 miles south of Hastings.

> *After various Vectors Diver seen 10 Miles S. of Hastings on course 340° [and at] 300 I.A.S. at 2,500 ft. After 4x2 seconds bursts [from] 200 yards dropping back to 250 correcting for excessive speed, diver peeled over and spun in through 5/10 cloud where I gave fix to Kingsley [Control] East of Battle [and] N. of Hastings, in a wood where Blue 2 saw cloud of smoke.*[74]

Blue Section returned to Lympne at 10:45, where Payne entered into his logbook, "Claimed 1 Diver destroyed 10 miles N of Hastings. Confirmed."[75] It was his second V1 victory, and the Squadron's twenty-third V1 (20 + 3 shared) destroyed.

The Wing's other squadrons were now fully operational and also laid on full flying programmes during the day. 1 Squadron completed 20 uneventful anti-Diver sorties whilst 165 undertook another 23, for one victory in the Ashford area.

In the evening, 41 Squadron received a visit from their ex-Commanding Officer, Sqn Ldr

'Pinkie' Glen DFC*, who was warmly welcomed. He was now on the staff of the Fighter Leaders School at Milfield, and would continue to fulfil non-combat roles until his release from the RAFVR in early 1946.

14 July 1944 – Poor weather continued in the morning, but improved later. During the day, 39 V1s were plotted by 11 Group, of which 30 made landfall. Twenty were shot down by fighters and one brought down by the balloon barrage.

As the remnants of the previous evening's weather hampered 41 Squadron's operations during the morning, the first section airborne today conducted a brief weather test from 08:20 to 08:35. The weather started to clear by late morning, and between 11:20 and 22:30, 14 anti-Diver patrols were undertaken, ten of which were flown by B Flight. Once again, a single V1 was claimed by the Squadron, this one falling to Flt Lt 'Jimmy' Thiele in the early evening.

Thiele was airborne at 17:25 with Fg Off Jim Payne as Black Section (Payne MB804 & Thiele MB856)[76] for an anti-Diver patrol off Dieppe. Just before 18:30, Upsett Control vectored the pair onto an incoming V1, which they soon spotted heading for Cliff End at 2,500 feet, on a course of 340°, doing a very fast IAS of 400 mph. Closing on the Buzz Bomb, Thiele opened fire.

> *A one second burst of C. & M.G. caused a large flash from the Jet unit, and a large piece flew off the Port Wing. Losing distance, 2 or 3 long shots were taken without result. Twenty seconds later, at approx. 1830 the Bomb blew up and fell into the sea at a point approx R.3515.*[77]

The pair returned to Lympne at 18:40, where Thiele claimed the V1 destroyed. Another five patrols were flown into the evening, but all were uneventful. Thiele's victory raised the Squadron's V1 tally to 24 (21 + 3 shared) destroyed.

In addition to 41 Squadron's patrols, 1 Squadron had sent up twenty-five aircraft on anti-Diver patrols today, and 165 Squadron another eighteen. 1 Squadron claimed its first two victories at Lympne, whilst 165 Squadron claimed their second in two days.

15 July 1944 – Poor weather all day kept 11 Group grounded for much of the day. However, similar weather also prevailed across the Channel, which minimised Diver activity and only 26 were plotted within the Group's area all day. Of these, 22 made landfall, but only six could be brought down by fighters.

As thick fog blanketed the Lympne area until around midday, 41 Squadron's readiness state was rolled back to three sections available at 15 minutes and the remainder of the Squadron at 60 minutes. When the fog began to lift, Flt Lt 'Jimmy' Thiele and Fg Off Leslie McKellar undertook an air test and returned at 13:55 recommending that operational flying should commence. The first anti-Diver patrol took off at 14:15 and nine were flown until 23:05, flying east to west in mid-Channel, between Le Tréport and Dieppe. All, however, were uneventful.

The weather also hindered 1 and 165 Squadrons' operational flying, and they were only able to send up eight patrols each throughout the day. However, whilst 41 and 165 Squadrons had no joy, 1 Squadron still managed to claim one Buzz Bomb to add to their growing tally.

Separately, 41 Squadron's Fg Off Douglas 'Jackie' Fisher re-joined the unit during the day, after an absence of six weeks due to illness.

By the middle of July 1944, Germany had launched approximately 4,000 V1s at England, of which only around 3,000 reached the air defence corridor. Of these, 1,192 were brought down by the anti-Diver defences, 924 falling to fighters, 261 to anti-aircraft guns and 55 to the balloon barrage.

16 July 1944 – Poor weather prevailed all along the coast, with low cloud but fair visibility. Thirty-eight Buzz Bombs were plotted by 11 Group during the day, of which 27 crossed the coast, and 18 were shot down by fighters.

A cloud base of 500-1,000 feet at Lympne postponed 41 Squadron's flying until shortly before 09:00, when it began to lift and allowed an otherwise full day of flying, with 14 anti-Diver patrols flown until 22:25.[78] Another Doodlebug fell to the Squadron today, this one being claimed by Fg Off 'Jackie' Fisher, who was on his first flight in six weeks. Having been absent due to illness, he had missed the entire V1 onslaught until now and had had no practice in the hunt for V1s at all.

Fisher had taken off as No. 2 to Fg Off Peter Graham as Green Section (Graham MB877 & Fisher MB798) at 18:15. They were about to head home at 19:20, when Upsett Control vectored them straight onto a V1, which they spotted 50 miles south-southwest of Dungeness at 3,000 feet, on a course of 340° and doing an IAS of 340 mph.

They were half a mile away, flying at 11,000 feet at the time, which gave them good altitude and distance for a dive onto the V1. However, Fisher came in too fast behind it, misjudged, and almost overshot. He had closed to 20 yards before he realised his error, and consciously dropped back to 200 yards, where he opened fire with a few half-second bursts of machine-gun fire. When these produced no results, Fisher tried his cannon instead.

This time, it only took a single half-second burst to produce the desired effect. Pieces flew off the V1 in flames, and it initially twisted upwards, then spiralled down through 10/10ths cloud to explode on impact with the sea, around 15 miles south of Beachy Head.

Fisher found a strange beauty in the resulting explosion, recording on his Combat Report that it "caused a mushroom effect followed by concentric cloud ripples."[79] His victory lifted the Squadron's tally to 25 (22 + 3 shared) destroyed V1s.

1 and 165 Squadrons also had victories to claim today, the former unit claiming one destroyed for 13 patrols and the latter two for 12 patrols.

17 July 1944 – Initial fog, mostly lifting by around midday. The German military used the fog to their advantage and limited their entire V1 activity during the daylight hours to between 05:00 and 10:40. During this time, 20 were plotted in 11 Group's area, of which 15 made landfall. Whilst anti-aircraft defences and balloon barrage brought down two apiece, the RAF's fighters were unable to claim any.

Fog kept 41 Squadron on the ground until it cleared just after lunch, and then three uneventful anti-Diver patrols were flown between 13:05 and 15:10. There would have been a fourth from 15:55, but it ended in tragedy just after take-off. As a result, all flying by the Squadron was suspended for the rest of the day.

A Fatal Error of Judgement

Flt Sgts 'Steve' Stevenson and Roger Short took off at 15:55 as Red Section (Stevenson EN226 & Short MB877) for a routine anti-Diver patrol, which ended abruptly only half a mile south of the airfield when Short collided in mid-air with the Squadron's Tiger Moth II (DV575), flown by 21-year-old Flt Sgt Cliff Oddy. Both pilots were killed. Oddy died immediately, but 22-year-old Short survived a few hours before succumbing to his injuries.[80]

The shock sat deep on the Squadron. OC, A Flight, Flt Lt Terry Spencer noted in his diary that day, "Oddy pranged Shorty with a Tiger Moth. Oddy was killed outright. Shorty gravely injured, his Spit being just a few fragments."[81] A few days later, Spencer added to his previous entry, "Poor Shorty died five hours after the crash. The CO and I attended his funeral at Hawkinge. Pretty grim affair..."[82]

WO Pat Coleman, who had struck up a good friendship with Short since their days together at 1 TEU Tealing, wrote in his own diary, "I see to Roy's kit, attend funeral and have a talk with Dorothy, his wife, whom I met in Arbroath. Wish I could comfort the poor soul".[83]

Subsequent investigations undertaken by Wg Cdr Thomas of the Air Ministry's Air Accidents Branch concluded that Oddy had turned across Red Section's take-off path whilst making an unauthorised low-altitude circuit over Lympne Aerodrome. Suddenly realising his mistake, he had turned away sharply, but his reaction came too late and he collided with Short at a height of 200 feet. Thomas found Oddy "wholly to blame"[84] for the tragedy.

Leeds-born Oddy, who had previously served three months with 610 Squadron, had logged 451 hours on Spitfires by the time of the accident. Short, from Sunderland, who had joined the Squadron as his first operational posting, had logged 573 hours. Oddy and Short joined 41 Squadron together on 8 June 1944 from 1 TEU, the former man attached to B Flight and the latter to A. It was a sad blow to the Squadron, and its worst flying accident since three pilots were killed simultaneously in September 1942 [see Chapter 2].[85]

Little was left of the Spitfire, which crashed straight to the ground, whilst the Tiger Moth spun in and crashed in the grounds of Lympne Castle. The Spitfire frame was written off, but its Griffon IV engine was only rated 'Cat. B', and could be salvaged. However, the Tiger Moth and its Gipsy Major engine were both declared beyond salvage and written off.

Whilst 41 Squadron remained grounded for the rest of the day on 17 July, 1 Squadron carried out 11 anti-Diver patrols and 165 Squadron carried out ten; all, however, were uneventful.

18 July 1944 – It was a fine, summery day, which was "…almost unbearably hot flying in the afternoon and the glare of the sun was terrific".[86] Forty-five V1s were plotted in 11 Group's area during the day, of which 37 crossed the coast. Fifteen were shot down by fighters and one by anti-aircraft fire, whilst another four were brought down by the balloon barrage.

A full flying programme was undertaken by all three Lympne Wing squadrons today and they flew a total of 107 sorties. 165 Squadron was able to claim three Buzz Bombs, but both 1 and 41 Squadrons came home empty-handed. For their part, 41 Squadron had flown 19 anti-Diver patrols between 06:25 and 22:20 but "no bombs came our way"[87], lamented the ORB.

There was, however, one mishap during the day, when 23-year-old Flt Sgt Freddie Woollard made a heavy landing in MB841 on return from his anti-Diver patrol with Fg Off 'Momo' Balasse at 18:45. Unfortunately, Woollard hit his face hard and suffered extensive facial injuries. He was sent to East Grinstead Hospital for plastic surgery to his nose, and thereby became one of Dr Sir Archibald McIndoe's famous 'Guinea Pigs'. Woollard had been posted to 41 Squadron on 18 December 1943 as his first operational unit, and did not return to the Squadron on recovery.

19 July 1944 – Another fine day with haze, upon which 82 V1s were plotted by 11 Group, of which 67 crossed the coast. Fighters shot down 30, anti-aircraft fire brought down nine, and the balloon barrage was responsible for another two.

A full flying programme was undertaken by the Lympne Wing again, and nineteen anti-Diver patrols were flown by 41 Squadron between 05:00 and 22:40. 1 Squadron flew sixteen patrols, and 165 flew seventeen. There was haze below 6,000 feet, blanketing the range of altitudes flown by the Buzz Bombs, but the pilots operated their patrols well above this height, and enjoyed good visibility.

41 and 165 Squadrons each claimed a V1 today, but 1 Squadron was unable to make any claim. 41's victory fell to Belgian Fg Off 'Momo' Balasse near Lamberhurst in Kent during the day's second anti-Diver patrol, when he shared the Doodlebug with a Tempest.[88]

Balasse was airborne from Newchurch at 08:30 as No. 2 to Flt Lt 'Jimmy' Thiele in Blue Section (Thiele EN228 & Balasse MB880). Approximately 40 minutes into the patrol, the pair was vectored onto a V1, which they intercepted off Dungeness at 2,000 feet. It was flying on a bearing of 340° and at 360 mph when Balasse opened his attack upon it, firing three bursts for a total of five seconds, and obtaining strikes on both wings.

Suddenly, an unidentified Tempest appeared beside him in the air and opened fire on Balasse's Buzz Bomb. The attack sent it into an initial climb, after which it turned over to port, and dived through 9/10ths cloud to explode in a wood near Lamberhurst.

Balasse and Thiele returned to Lympne at 09:35 where Balasse was granted a half share in the V1's destruction. It was Balasse's third such victory and the Squadron's twenty-sixth (22 + 4 shared) destroyed. The remainder of the day's anti-Diver patrols were uneventful.

20 July 1944 – Fine weather prevailed again today, although the haze had risen to 8,000 feet. Diver activity during the day was limited to 05:00 to 11:15, during which time 42 V1s were plotted by 11 Group. Thirty-one made landfall, 15 were shot down by fighters, five by anti-aircraft fire, and one brought down by the balloon barrage.

41 Squadron carried out at least 21 anti-Diver patrols and one reconnaissance flight – their first in weeks – between 05:10 and 22:25, whilst 1 Squadron carried out twenty-three anti-Diver patrols and 165 Squadron another twenty-six.[89] Two Buzz Bombs were claimed by the Wing today, one by 41 Squadron and one by 165. 41 Squadron's fell on the second anti-Diver patrol of the day.

Airborne at 05:55 as Yellow Section, Flt Sgts 'Steve' Stevenson and 'Robbie' Robertson (Stevenson MB878 & Robertson MB880) were vectored onto a V1 southeast of Dungeness at around 06:40. It was coming in at 3,000 feet at 320 mph, on a course of 340°, but the pair were flying on a reciprocal course until ordered to turn a full 180° by Cathy Control.

Stevenson closed to almost 50 yards and opened fire with a single three-second burst and immediately obtained strikes. He throttled back to 150 yards and opened fire again with another three-second burst, whilst he closed to 25 yards. His aim was accurate again, and the Doodlebug rolled over to port and dived into the sea.

Yellow Section returned to Lympne at 07:05, where Stevenson claimed his first full victory, bringing the Squadron's tally to twenty-seven (23 + 4 shared) destroyed. The rest of the day's patrols were uneventful, although…

…after dusk some flying bombs came in near Lympne and the succession of explosions all around us testified to the ever increasing efficiency of the anti-aircraft guns.[90]

21 July 1944 – The day dawned to poor weather, with a low cloud base and poor visibility over the Channel. It was, considered the 11 Group ORB, 'perfect Diver weather' and no less than 140 were plotted during the day. One hundred and two crossed the coast, but just ten were shot down by fighters, three by the anti-aircraft defences, and 13 brought down by the balloon barrage.

Despite conditions, 41 Squadron's first patrol was off the deck at 05:25, but the optimism was in vain. Although four patrols were airborne in succession, the weather soon dropped and within three hours all flying had ceased; the fourth patrol was abandoned immediately after take-off; the weather was no longer suitable for operations. Rain and fog prevailed for the rest of the day keeping the entire Wing grounded.

Considering the weather, 41 Squadron had done quite well, as 1 and 165 Squadrons only managed to get one anti-Diver patrol airborne each before halting operations. Attesting to the atrocious conditions, 41's Fg Off Jimmy Payne was forced to make a belly landing in MB861 with no flaps in a strong crosswind and collided with MB840, which was parked and stationary on the airfield. Payne recorded the event in his logbook that day,

Arrived back over base short of fuel – flaps in but U/S – had to land in a bad crosswind – couldn't get speed down so had to select wheels up – collided with EBJ – Two A/C cat A.C. – exonerated.[91]

There was, however, one highlight: despite the poor weather and only three full anti-Diver patrols being undertaken by the Squadron all day, WO 'Archie' Appleton still managed to bring down a V1.

Airborne at 05:25 with Fg Off Maurice Balasse as Blue Section (Balasse EN228 & Appleton EN602), the pair became separated in cloud and operated briefly independently of one other. At 06:10, Appleton intercepted a Buzz Bomb 20 miles south of Hastings, Sussex, at 2,000 feet, on a

Renowned for looking significantly younger than his age, Fg Off (later Flt Lt) 'Johnny' Wilkinson served with 41 Squadron from 21 July 1944 to 30 December 1945. He claimed his first aerial victory, a shared destroyed V1, on 11 August 1944, just three weeks after his arrival. © 41 Squadron RAF

course of 330° and doing 320 mph. He attacked with four two-second bursts at ranges of between 250 and 100 yards, resulting in the V1 exploding in mid-air and falling through 10/10ths cloud into the sea around eight miles south of Hastings. His victory raised the Squadron's tally to twenty-eight (24 + 4 shared) destroyed.

Separately, two new pilots joined the Squadron today, beginning an influx of seven new men in the space of approximately three weeks. The last major arrival was on 7 June, when four pilots arrived on the Squadron together from 1 TEU. Today, Fg Off John F. 'Johnny' Wilkinson and Plt Off Eric 'Ricky' Gray joined the unit, the former allocated to A Flight and the latter to B.

21-year-old Wilkinson, remembered even today for his very youthful appearance, joined the RAFVR in December 1941 and earned his Wings at 5 BFTS in Florida, where he was commissioned, before returning to the United Kingdom to complete OTU at Eshott. Upon graduation, he was posted to 2 TEU at Grangemouth, where he was promoted to Flying Officer prior to a two-month sojourn at 3501 GSU at Cranfield from May 1944. 41 Squadron was his first operational unit. He was later remembered by one of his fellow pilots on the Squadron for looking "at least 5 years younger than his age but blessed with marvellous eyesight. Picked things up well ahead of anyone else."[92]

22-year-old Queenslander 'Ricky' Gray had joined the RAAF in Brisbane in July 1941, and completed his entire flying training in Australia. He arrived in England with his Wings in early April 1943, and was promoted to Flight Sergeant less than two weeks later. He then has a succession of training postings, thereunder 17 (P)AFU at Watton and Calverley, 57 OTU at Eshott, GFS at Boulmer, and 2 TEU at Grangemouth, where he was commissioned in April 1944, exactly a year after his arrival in the United Kingdom. A final, brief stint followed at 3501 GSU at Cranfield from May to July 1944 and, like Wilkinson, his posting to 41 Squadron was also his first to an operational unit.

22 July 1944 – The poor weather and low cloud continued overnight and did not start clearing until the early afternoon. Diver activity consisted of 91 plots by 11 Group, of which 68 made landfall. Thirty-seven were shot down by fighters, nine by the anti-aircraft defences, and two brought down by balloons.

As a result of the weather, 41 Squadron's first anti-Diver patrol was not airborne until 15:25, but thereafter continued until 22:55. Altogether, the Squadron put nine patrols in the air – an excellent effort considering the late start – but all were in vain.

There was quite a lot of flying bomb activity, but they were all coming in in a belt of low cloud from 2,000-3,000 ft. and no interceptions were made.[93]

The luck today fell instead to the Wing's other two squadrons, who, although they flew less patrols than 41 Squadron – six apiece – still managed to bring down two V1s each.

23 July 1944 – Perfect weather all day meant a manic day for the Lympne Wing, but it ended disastrously for the airfield. Forty-seven V1s were plotted by 11 Group during the day, of which 30 crossed the coast. Fighters shot down 21, anti-aircraft fire brought down four, and balloons were responsible for yet another.

41 Squadron started operations very early at 05:05 and had a total of 44 aircraft airborne on anti-Diver duties until 23:00. 1 Squadron sent up forty-three aircraft and 165 Squadron another fifty-eight. The effort reaped its rewards, and the day's tally for the Wing would be 7½ Buzz Bombs destroyed, four falling victim to 1 Squadron, two to 41 Squadron, and 1½ to 165 Squadron.

However, it was not until 41 Squadron's twelfth patrol that they claimed their first victory. Fg Offs Jimmy Payne and 'Momo' Balasse were airborne at 13:45 as Green Section (Payne MB880 & Balasse MB798) and were flying at 8,000 feet when vectored onto a Buzz Bomb by Cathy Control just after 14:00. Dropping through cloud between 6,000 and 7,000 feet around 10-15 miles southeast of Hastings, they spotted it one mile to starboard at 2,500 feet, on a course of 340°, doing a speed of 320 mph.

Payne attacked first, opening fire at 300 yards and making four two-second bursts as he closed to 200 yards.[94] His fire hit the V1 on the port wing and caused it to bank 45°, but it returned to level flight, though now significantly slower. Further strikes caused it to emit grey smoke, but his ammunition soon ran out, so he moved aside and allowed 'Momo' Balasse to take over.

Balasse commenced his own attack at 200 yards, closing to 50, which resulted in the Diver slowing to just 220 mph with considerable weaving. By now, both wings were well holed and the rear of the end of the jet had broken away. Balasse wanted to finish it off but was ordered to break off his attack by Cathy Control as the pair was entering the anti-aircraft gun belt.

As such, they were unable to see whether the Diver was destroyed, however they had no cause for concern as the Police later confirmed seeing it fall into the sea at 14:15, ten miles south of Rye. Payne and Balasse landed back at Lympne at 14:50 and were granted one V1 shared destroyed.

Plt Off Eric 'Ricky' Gray RAAF served with 41 Squadron from 21 July 1944 to 3 September 1945 during which time he claimed two destroyed FW190s, one shared destroyed FW190, one shared destroyed Me110, two destroyed V1s, and one damaged Me262. © 41 Squadron RAF

At 14:30, shortly before they returned, Fg Off Peter Graham and WO 'Archie' Appleton were airborne to relieve them, designated Black Section (Graham MB882 & Appleton MB831).[95] Barely had they reached the patrol line at 14:45, the pair were vectored onto another incoming Doodlebug, which they spotted 160° south of Bexhill, Sussex, on a course of 340°, flying at 2,500 feet, but doing an IAS of just 250 mph.

Perfectly positioned for an attack, Appleton roared in from behind, but had to throttle back to avoid overshooting the unusually slow flying target. Appleton let his aircraft fall back to 150 yards range, where he opened fire with a single two-second burst. His aim was perfect, and the Diver "blew up with [a] sheet of Flame and then burst in [the] air"[96] eight miles south of Bexhill.

Appleton had little choice but to fly straight through the blast and debris, but unlike WO Peter Chattin's unlucky encounter on 8 July, came through it unscathed. Black Section landed at 15:35, whereupon Appleton claimed the Buzz Bomb destroyed. It was his third V1 (2 + 1 shared), but the Squadron's thirtieth, of which four were shared with pilots of other units (26 + 4 shared).

Just after Peter Graham and Archie Appleton's departure at 14:30 to commence their patrol, however, a V1 came straight over Lympne Airfield and was engaged by the RAF Regiment's anti-aircraft guns. It was well intended, but the gunners' efforts ended in disaster when several of their own were killed.

The Buzz Bomb was hit by the guns, but it fell onto the airfield, landing on and destroying a Nissen hut housing RAF Regiment personnel on the aerodrome's eastern boundary. Two nearby Nissens were also destroyed and the main small arms ammunition hut was severely damaged, the roof lifted off its pillars and several beams fractured. Seven other nearby accommodation buildings were also damaged, one beyond repair. Unfortunately, there were also several casualties, all RAF Regiment gunners. One man was killed outright, a second died in hospital less than two hours later; three gunners were seriously injured, and three gunners received minor injuries. All were admitted to Willesborough Hospital, but two of the seriously injured died the following day. The final toll: four dead and four injured.

Separately, business carried on as usual, and there were a few personnel movements for the Squadron today. Two long-serving pilots were posted away, their tours complete, and one new pilot arrived. Those departing were Flt Lts Peter Cowell and 'Joe' Birbeck, who had joined the Squadron in November 1942 and February 1943, respectively, and were now posted together to the Fighter Affiliation Unit with the Air Fighting Development Unit in Wittering.[97]

The new pilot who joined 41 Squadron today was Fg Off Donald Frank Jellicoe Tebbit, who turned 30 this very day. 'Tebby', as he became known, had joined the RAFVR just prior to the outbreak of War in 1939 and trained in the United Kingdom before being posted to 263 Squadron at Exeter in mid-February 1941, flying Whirlwinds. Following an attachment to 286 (Anti-Aircraft Cooperation) Squadron in late 1941, he returned to 263 Squadron in October 1942 and was commissioned in August 1943. On posting to 41 Squadron, he had logged 1,026 flying hours, of which 140 were operational. His combat experience thus far had included 35 bombing sorties to shipping, dock and aerodrome targets at Brest, Cherbourg, and in the Channel Islands. Upon arrival on the Squadron, he was assigned to A Flight.

24 July 1944 – It was a fine and warm summer day, with cloud and haze, but Diver activity did not commence until 14:55. After this time, 32 Buzz Bombs were plotted by 11 Group and 28 made landfall. Eight were brought down by fighters, two by anti-aircraft fire and one by the balloon barrage.

Despite 41 Squadron flying 18 patrols between 05:35 and 22:35, neither they, nor any of the Lympne Wing's other units, made any interceptions all day. At lunchtime the ceiling of the Officers' Mess anteroom collapsed, "causing a lot of mess and some temporary inconvenience".[98] It was not, however, the result of the previous day's V1 incident, rather plumbing issues instead.

25 July 1944 – Another fine day, with haze and broken cloud between 8,000 and 14,000 feet, and visibility improving towards the evening. Surprisingly, however, the German military did

Fg Off Donald 'Tebby' Tebbit served with 41 Squadron from 23 July 1944 to 22 February 1945 when he was shot down and captured. He remained in the RAF after the War and retired as a Wing Commander in 1965. © Don Tebbit, via Dan Johnson

not launch a single V1 during the daylight hours, and only commenced activity shortly before midnight.

As such, the 22 patrols (43 sorties) that 41 Squadron had airborne between 05:10 and 22:30 were in vain. Naturally, 1 and 165 Squadrons, who had sent up 28 and 30 patrols, respectively, fared similarly.

26 July 1944 – Fine and clear weather all day, but Diver activity was intermittent and unusual. An initial salvo of 15 was fired at 06:20, followed by sporadic V1s until 08:20, when they ceased again. The next Doodlebugs came over between 14:06 and 14:20, but then there were no more until 22:04, when a salvo of nine were fired together.

Altogether, 11 Group plotted 63 Doodlebugs throughout the daylight hours, of which 51 made landfall. The vast majority were destroyed before reaching their targets, 44 falling to fighters, eight to anti-aircraft fire, and five to the balloon barrage.

The good weather permitted 41 Squadron to send up 44 aircraft on 22 anti-Diver patrols between 05:15 and 23:00, whilst 1 Squadron completed forty-five sorties and 165 Squadron another fifty-six. It was a good day for the Wing, with the day's tally totalling 9½ V1s destroyed, consisting of five by 165 Squadron, three by 1 Squadron and 1½ by 41 Squadron.

Coming off worse than 1 and 165 Squadrons, 41 had to wait until the last two patrols of the entire day to claim their own victories, both of which came in the day's final salvo of nine. The first of these fell to Plt Off 'Ricky' Gray, who had only been with the Squadron five days. Gray was airborne at 21:05 as Black 2 to Fg Off Jimmy Payne (Payne MB860 & Gray MB853) and was patrolling at 8,000 feet off Boulogne when vectored onto a V1 by Cathy Control just after 22:00.

Payne and Gray dived through 5/10ths cloud with a base at 5,000 feet, and spotted the Diver off to port at 3,000 feet on a course of 340°. As they approached, a Mustang was breaking off his attack so Gray took over and closed on it, recording its speed as 360 mph. He fired three bursts at it, totalling six seconds, and observed at least three definite strikes on the fuselage. These caused the Buzz Bomb to emit enough smoke to obscure the jet flame, after which Gray broke away. However, in breaking away, he lost sight of his target, but was pleased to hear his No. 1 confirm it had fallen into the Channel, approximately six miles south of Hastings at 22:05.

They landed by at Lympne around 22:30, where Gray claimed his first of two V1s destroyed. At this time, Blue Section was still in the air, completing the day's last anti-Diver patrol. When they returned to base they, too, would claim a V1 destroyed to add to the Squadron's growing tally.

Fg Off 'Momo' Balasse and WO 'Archie' Appleton had taken off at 21:45 as Blue Section (Balasse EN609 & Appleton EN602) and were vectored onto a Doodlebug by Kingsley Control at 22:10 as they reached the patrol line. As they approached on the opposite heading, still outbound from Lympne, Balasse saw a Mustang on the V1's tail off to starboard, and did a full 180° turn to bring himself behind the target, now approximately 15 miles south of Hastings, at an altitude of 2,000 feet, on a course of 340°, and at an IAS of 350 mph.

Opening his attack from dead astern and slightly below it, Balasse fired a single two-second burst at a range of 200 yards, which resulted in bright flashes on the fuselage, after which it dived into the Channel five to eight miles south of Beachy Head, and exploded on impact.

Blue Section landed back at Lympne at 23:00 and Balasse claimed his V1 destroyed, which was shared with the Mustang. It was Balasse's sixth victory (2 + 4 shared), and the Squadron's thirty-second, of which five were shared with pilots of other units (27 + 5 shared).

27 July 1944 – Low cloud and rain dominated weather conditions today. However, despite this being perfect V1 weather, there was no activity until 15:00, "when an intensive bombardment commenced, a series of heavy salvoes being fired at intervals of approximately 1½ hours".[99]

In the space of about six-and-a-half hours, no fewer than 106 Buzz Bombs were plotted by 11 Group: an approximate average rate of one every three-and-a-half minutes; 89 made landfall. Struggling to keep up with this launch rate, Allied fighters only managed to shoot down 24 and anti-aircraft guns another six.

The weather hindered the start of 41 Squadron's operational flying today until mid-afternoon. When the pilots were finally airborne, they had to climb through two separate cloud layers, from 800-2,000 feet and from 6,000-8,000 feet, before they reached their patrol altitude. The Squadron flew at least eight anti-Diver patrols between 15:40 and 22:35, and although the cloud layers made V1 interceptions 'practically impossible', one of the pilots still managed to catch one.[100] For their part, 1 and 165 Squadrons each flew ten anti-Diver patrols, but only 165 Squadron was able to make a claim, for a single V1.

41 Squadron's Buzz Bomb fell to Flt Sgt Colin Robertson – his personal second – on the day's second last patrol. Airborne at 20:30 with Flt Sgt 'Steve' Stevenson as White Section (Stevenson EN229 & Robertson EN602), they were patrolling mid-Channel shortly before 21:15, when Cathy Control advised them of an approaching V1, which was on a course of 330° and ten miles distant. Before long, the pair sighted it just above the thin cloud ceiling at 3,000 feet, doing an IAS of 340 mph.

Robertson made a stern attack, opening fire at 300 yards, with three bursts of two seconds. He saw many strikes on the V1, which sent it 30° off course to port, rapidly losing height. He watched it disappear through 10/10ths cloud at 2,000 feet at 21:16, and initially did not know if he could claim a definitive victory.

However, subsequent enquiries revealed that three explosions were heard out to sea around this time, and only two were claimed by other squadrons. Cathy Control also confirmed that plots of Robertson's Buzz Bomb faded at the place and time of his attack, and it was therefore concluded that it had dived into the sea around 15 miles south of Dungeness. He was subsequently awarded the victory, which lifted the Squadron's tally to thirty-three (28 + 5 shared) destroyed.

28 July 1944 – Perfect flying weather prevailed all day, and Diver activity was once again designed to foil any type of organised defence. The first Doodlebugs came over at around 09:30, but then there were none until 13:21, when a salvo of 20 was fired, followed by a few individual V1s until 13:50. There was then another lull until 21:35, when another salvo of 27 was fired.

In total, 71 Buzz Bombs were plotted by 11 Group during the day, of which 50 crossed the coast. Fighters shot down 22, the anti-aircraft defences brought down a respectable 15, and the balloon barrage another.

The Lympne Wing sent up 145 aircraft on anti-Diver patrols today, thereunder forty-nine from 1 Squadron, forty-four from 41 Squadron, and fifty-two from 165 Squadron.[101] Despite their efforts, however, the Wing's bag for the day was a meagre 3⅓: two plus one shared by 1 Squadron, and one destroyed by 165 Squadron. 41 Squadron could claim none at all, despite being in the air virtually non-stop from 05:40 to 22:40. It had been a long and tiring day for no reward.

WO Pat Coleman recalled the sleepless nights of this period created by the anti-aircraft guns defending the coast against the V1 menace. He penned in his diary,

> Our rest hours are terribly noisy with the tremendous Ack-Ack barrage put up against these flying bombs. A.A. is confined to a 5 mile coastal belt (in which we live) & every available gun has been rushed to it. A new "radah" [sic] sighting predictor gives exceptionally good results to the guns. […] Bombs are shot down in great number[s], often to explode on the ground in our vicinity, its [sic] a bit unnerving at night sometimes. Our billet has windows blown in, our mess the ceiling down etc., however relatively few are hurt.[102]

29 July 1944 – Poor weather and low cloud dominated conditions from before dawn to mid-afternoon, and 10/10ths cloud blanketed the sky from a base of just 800 feet. Heavy rain also fell at around 16:00, but conditions improved considerably thereafter. Divers were active between 05:04 and 21:35, during which 65 V1s were plotted by 11 Group. Fifty-eight crossed the coast, but only 17 were brought down by fighters, eight by anti-aircraft fire, and one by the balloon barrage.

The weather kept 41 Squadron firmly on the ground until 16:30, when their first patrol of the day was airborne. The unit was able to complete seven patrols by 22:30, whilst 1 Squadron mounted ten and 165 Squadron another seven.[103] Neither 1 nor 165 Squadrons were able to make claims for Doodlebugs today, but 41 Squadron made two, both of them falling to Fg Off Maurice Balasse, who thereby became the Squadron's first V1 Ace.

Balasse undertook his first and only anti-Diver patrol of the day from 18:00 with Fg Off Jimmy Payne as Black Section (Payne EN238 & Balasse EN609), assigned to cover a north to south line in the Pas-de-Calais area. Soon after their arrival on the patrol line at 7,000 feet, Cathy Control vectored them onto a V1, which they spotted at 2,500 feet approximately 10-15 miles from Le Touquet, on a course of 310°.[104]

Balasse dived upon it, whilst Payne remained above, but his dive and closing speed were much too great and Balasse momentarily blacked-out as a result of the G Forces. In a brief brush with death, he narrowly missed colliding with the Buzz Bomb, which was estimated to be doing approximately 350 mph, and overshot it. Balasse regained consciousness as he passed underneath the V1 in very close proximity, and banked around for another attack.

However, his aircraft's slipstream had passed close enough to knock the V1 off its path. Both Balasse and Payne, still above, watched the bomb 'rock' and 'shudder', and did not correct itself. Before long, the V1 flipped over and dived into the Channel, where it exploded on impact. Payne had observed the entire encounter and confirmed the victory on account of Balasse's action, albeit accidental.[105]

Black Section returned to Lympne at 19:20, where Balasse claimed his fifth V1 destroyed (3 plus 4 shared, i.e. 3 + 4 halves) at 18:20, making him the Squadron's first V1 Ace. The ORB recorded of his victory that it was "…the first of these missiles to be destroyed by us without being touched by a shell, bullet or wing-tip"![106]

As if this were not enough for one day, however, Balasse was airborne again at 21:25 for an air test and claimed yet another Buzz Bomb.[107] Only airborne five minutes, he saw Flak in the Dungeness area and headed over to investigate. There, at somewhere between 2,500 and 3,000 feet was a Doodlebug, sailing through the anti-aircraft fire unscathed on a course of 330° and doing an IAS of 300 mph.

Balasse opened his throttle and intercepted it near Old Romney. He closed to just 100 yards and fired a single one-second burst from astern. He hit the V1 in exactly the right spot and it exploded in mid-air, the debris falling around three miles southeast of Woodchurch, Kent.[108]

The job done, Balasse then completed his air test and returned to Lympne at 22:10. He claimed his second Buzz Bomb destroyed within the space of just over three hours, "thus bringing his flying bomb score to six destroyed and making him top-scorer of the Squadron."[109]

41 Squadron Pilots at Lympne, 3 August 1944. Front row, seated: Fg Off Keith Curtis RCAF, Flt Sgt Bob Fleming, Plt Off Peter Gibbs, Fg Off F. G. 'Doc' Herman (MO), Flt Sgt Ian Stevenson, Fg Off Bob Anderson RAAF, Fg Off Charlie van Goens (Dutch), and Flt Sgt James Ware RAAF; Back row, standing: Flt Lt Ross Harding, Fg Off John Wilkinson, Plt Off Eric Gray RAAF, Flt Lt Daniel Reid RAAF, Sqn Ldr Robert Chapman, Flt Lt Tom Slack, Fg Off Douglas 'Jackie' Fisher, Plt Off Jimmy Payne, Flt Lt Tommy Burne, Flt Sgt Larry Spurr RCAF, and Fg Off Maurice Balasse (Belgian); on the propeller: Fg Off Harry Cook with Squadron mascot 'Perkin'. © Rossow family

41 Squadron's Ground Crew, 6041 Servicing Echelon, 3 August 1944. © Rossow family

His efforts today increased the Squadron's total tally of V1s since 20 June 1944 to thirty-five, of which five were shared (30 + 5 shared).

30 July 1944 – Cloudy with haze. Diver activity did not commence today until 13:30, when a salvo of 27 was fired towards England, followed by several further smaller salvoes. Although the day's Diver activity ceased altogether at 18:15, fifty-one V1s were plotted by 11 Group, of which 29 made landfall. Just eight of these were shot down by fighters, and another three by anti-aircraft guns.

A five-minute weather test preceded 41 Squadron's launch of anti-Diver patrols for the day, after which 20 were flown between 05:55 and 22:10. Whilst the weather around Lympne was fine, conditions over the Channel were less than ideal. By the evening, the cloud ceiling had climbed as high as 13,000 feet, above which the pilots were compelled to operate their patrols. With so much cloud to contend with, it comes as no surprise that not a single V1 was intercepted all day. It was a similar story for 1 and 165 Squadrons, who sent up 35 and 31 patrols, respectively, for no claim.[110]

31 July 1944 – Low cloud and mist again hindered 11 Group's operations during the morning, though it improved later. Diver activity was brief today, commencing at 14:47 with a salvo of 18, followed by a second salvo from 18:08, making a total of just 28 V1s plotted by 11 Group all day. Twenty-two crossed the coast, seven were shot down by fighters and two brought down by balloons.

41 Squadron's first anti-Diver patrol was not airborne until 12:45. Thereafter, nine patrols were flown until 22:00, but no interceptions were made and the Squadron came home empty-handed again.[111] For their parts, 1 and 165 Squadrons sent up 22 aircraft each on anti-Diver patrols but fared no better than 41 Squadron.

During the month of July 1944, despite poor weather often hindering operations, 41 Squadron had mounted at least 406 anti-Diver patrols, consisting of over 800 sorties, for a score of 23 V1s destroyed (20 + 3 shared). This implies an average of 13 patrols per day, or 26 sorties, for around 0.75 V1s destroyed per day. If nothing else, it must be recognised that the Germans certainly kept the RAF busy at home on 'wild goose chases' after V1 flying bombs, instead of over the growing foothold on the Continent, where they could no doubt have been better employed.

However, as the front advanced in France, V1 sites began to be over-run, whilst in southeastern England technological advances in radar-based automatic gun laying and proximity fuses led to more V1s being brought down than ever before. As the V1 threat began to wane during August 1944, 41 Squadron found themselves gradually moved off anti-Diver patrols and back onto offensive sweeps and attacks on ground targets in France, Belgium and the Netherlands.

1 August 1944 – Extremely poor weather dominated the day, with thick fog and low cloud keeping 11 Group's activity to a minimum. Fifty V1s were plotted during the day, of which 34 made landfall. Allied reaction was scant, with only one shot down by fighters, three by anti-aircraft fire, and one destroyed by the balloon barrage.

The conditions kept 41 Squadron operationally grounded all day. The only pilot airborne at all was Plt Off Peter Gibbs who made a 20-minute, non-operational flight from Friston to Lympne just after lunch under a cloud base of just 200 feet, "hedge-hopping all the way".[112] Despite the Squadron's inactivity, Lympne's other two resident units, 1 and 165 Squadrons, undertook limited operational flying, the former mounting five anti-Diver patrols and the latter six, but all came home empty-handed.

2 August 1944 – The poor weather continued overnight and into the afternoon today. Forty-six V1s were plotted by 11 Group between 05:30 and 22:30, of which 33 crossed the coast. Fighters shot down five, anti-aircraft fire brought down three, and balloons were responsible for another six.

As a result of the continuing inclement weather, 41 Squadron was not airborne on anti-Diver operations until conditions improved after lunch. The first patrol was up at 14:50, but only five had been completed by the time the weather dropped again at 19:40, and brought flying to a halt again. 1 and 165 Squadrons did a little better, sending up eight and seven patrols, respectively, but none of the three units were able to make any claims.

In the House of Commons today, The Prime Minister, Winston Churchill, addressed the V1 onslaught and tried to reassure the British public, announcing,

> …*We are sure that our defences are gaining in power. We press to the utmost our counter-offensive measures. The patience and courage of our people at a time when they might have thought that for London her trials were past have been wonderful. We are sure that the people will continue to the end. […] If the Germans imagine that the continuance of this present attack—which has cost them dear in many ways in other branches of production—will have the slightest effect upon the course of the war, or upon the resolve of the nation or the morale of the men, women and children who are under fire, they will only be making another of those psychological blunders for which they have so long been celebrated. The only result of the use of this indiscriminate weapon, so far as they are concerned, will be that the severity of the punishment which they will receive after their weapons have been struck from their hands by our fighting men will be appreciably increased. There is no question of diverting our strength from the extreme prosecution of the war, or of allowing this particular infliction to weaken in any way our energetic support of our Allies. Every effort in human power is being made to prevent and mitigate the effects of this bombardment. Hundreds of the best expert brains we have are constantly riveted upon the problem.*[113]

3 August 1944 – Although the weather was fine from dawn to dusk, Diver activity was limited to a seven-hour period today, between 05:30 and 12:40. During this time, however, activity was intense and the Germans launched V1s towards England at an average rate of 18 per hour, making a total of 128 for the day. Ninety of these crossed the coast, 32 were shot down by fighters, ten brought down by anti-aircraft fire, and seven by balloons.

41 Squadron undertook 19 anti-Diver patrols between 06:10 and 21:50, but very few V1s came through their patrol areas and they made no interceptions.[114] 1 and 165 Squadrons were slightly more successful on their 21, respectively 22, patrols, ending the day with one, and one-and-a-half V1s destroyed.

41 Squadron's Flt Sgt Peter Chattin (MB795) had a scare during his afternoon patrol with Fg Off Keith Curtis as Red Section. Having taken off from Lympne at 15:40, they were only about 20 minutes into the flight, cruising at an altitude of 8,000 feet, when Chattin's engine cut out without warning. He had the presence of mind to not bale out and instead attempted to restart the engine, but had fallen a full 4,000 feet before he succeeded. Chattin then made a hasty landing at Brenzett, where he touched down at 16:05, uninjured but shaken.

Separately, two new pilots, both Australian, were posted to 41 Squadron today. They were 24-year-old Victorian Flt Lt Daniel J. Reid, and 25-year-old Queenslander WO Vivian 'Bill' J. Rossow.

Reid had joined the RAAF in June 1940 and commenced his training in Australia, but had earned his Wings in Canada, graduating from SFTS at Borden with a commission in December 1941. Reid shipped to England in early January 1942 and attended AFU at Ternhill, OTU at Rednal, a cine-gun assessment course at Duxford and a parachute-packing course before being posted to his first operational unit, 453 (Australian) Squadron at Drem in June 1942. Six months later, he was posted to Tunisia to join 152 Squadron and was promoted to Flying Officer a few days before Christmas. Following extended sick leave for a collapsed lung, which necessitated evacuation back to the United Kingdom in March 1943, he was posted to non-operational duties in October 1943 and remained in such roles until his posting to 41 Squadron. This was therefore his first operational posting in almost 17 months.

Rossow had briefly served in the Australian 2nd Light Horse Regiment prior to enlisting in the RAAF in November 1941. He completed his entire flying training in Australia, earning his Wings as a Sergeant Pilot in December 1942. Rossow arrived in England in March 1943 and completed

Flt Lt Daniel J. Reid RAAF flew with 41 Squadron from 3 August 1944 to 25 March 1945, serving as OC B Flight from 10 February 1945 until his departure. © 41 Squadron RAF

courses at AFU, OTU, GFS and TEU prior to his posting to 41 Squadron as a Flight Sergeant. This was his first operational posting, and he arrived at the Squadron on 9 August.

4 August 1944 – The weather was fine with haze and late showers. Diver activity did not commence until 15:38 today, after which 128 were plotted by 11 Group until 20:35, when activity ceased again. Of these, 89 made landfall, 37 were destroyed by fighters, 20 by the anti-aircraft batteries, and three by balloons.

41 Squadron mounted 17 anti-Diver patrols between 05:15 and 21:45[115], and finally, after five days of poor weather and uneventful patrols, Flt Lt Tom Slack added another V1 to the unit's tally. 1 Squadron also flew twenty patrols and 165 another nineteen, and they, too, both ended the day victorious, claiming one, respectively three, Buzz Bombs.

41 Squadron's victory came mid-afternoon, during Black Section's patrol (Slack EN238 & Spurr EN228) from 15:10. Flt Lt Slack and Flt Sgt Larry Spurr were around an hour into the patrol, when they were vectored onto a Buzz Bomb near Dungeness by Kingsley Control. As they approached the area, they could see anti-aircraft fire trying to bring it down, but without success. The V1 was sailing through the defences at 2,000 feet, on a course of 330°, and at an IAS of 300 mph.

Slack gave chase and closed his range to 200 yards before firing a single 1½-second burst, which was enough to send the Doodlebug off course to port and fall into a field on the Isle of Oxney at 16:10. Slack initially landed at Friston at 16:40 – no reason is given, although it was presumably a fuel issue – but later returned to Lympne where he claimed his second and last V1 victory (1 + 1 shared), and the Squadron's thirty-sixth (31 + 5 shared) destroyed.

5 August 1944 – Although low cloud delayed the start to the day's flying, Diver activity commenced at 06:49 when a salvo of 12 was fired. Thereafter, nothing came over again until 16:23, after which intermittent launches continued until 19:29. There was then no more activity until after 01:00. During the day, some 58 Doodlebugs were plotted by 11 Group, of which 23 were shot down by fighters, eight brought down by anti-aircraft fire, and two destroyed by balloons.

As a result of a weather test flown by Flt Lt Terry Spencer at 06:05, 41 Squadron decided to delay their anti-Diver operations until the weather had cleared further. Within a few hours, conditions had improved sufficiently and the first patrol was airborne at 09:20. The weather continued to improve throughout the morning and, by the end of operations at 21:55, fourteen patrols had been flown.

It was a good day for the Wing. Although 1 Squadron flew fifteen patrols for no claim, 165 Squadron flew just eleven, but claimed four Buzz Bombs destroyed. For their part, 41 Squadron claimed one, this one falling, after much effort and frustration, to Flt Sgt 'Steve' Stevenson.

Stevenson was airborne at 18:40 as No. 2 to Flt Lt Ross Harding as White Section (Harding MB850 & Stevenson MB795) to patrol the Rye area. Shortly before 19:00, the pair was vectored onto a Buzz Bomb by Kingsley Control. Despite light stratus cloud at between 4,000 and 5,000 feet, visibility was still over 20 miles, and before long they intercepted it over Brede, Sussex, at 2,500 feet, flying on a course of 340° and at an IAS of 350-360 mph.

Stevenson positioned himself for a stern attack and fired several short bursts as he closed from 200 yards to 100. This had the effect of slowing the Diver down to 300 mph but it kept flying. Frustratingly, his ammunition also ran out earlier than expected when one cannon jammed, but he was determined not to lose this victory. Opening his throttle, Stevenson caught up with the V1 and flew alongside it until they had passed Maidstone. As soon as they were clear of the town, Stevenson tipped its wing with his, and though the Buzz Bomb continued on the same course, it was sufficient to send it into a dive to crash in a field five-six miles northeast of Maidstone.

When White Section returned to Lympne at 19:10, Stevenson claimed the Squadron's second V1 to be brought down by tipping it with a wing, his own personal third and last (2 + 1 shared), and the Squadron's thirty-seventh (32 + 5 shared) destroyed.

Separately, one of 41 Squadron's Canadian pilots, 21-year-old Flt Sgt Larry Spurr, left the unit today after a brief tenure of just seven weeks. He was commissioned and posted to a Canadian Squadron, where he saw out the end of the War.[116]

6 August 1944 – Poor weather with bad visibility until the early afternoon. Diver activity was limited to three brief periods during the day, 05:50-06:15, 13:18-14:00, and 16:56-17:30. The volume of V1s fired during these timeframes numbered 15, 33 and 33 respectively, making a total of 81 plotted by 11 Group during the day. Of these, 55 made landfall, 24 were destroyed by fighters, 11 by anti-aircraft fire, and six by balloons.

As a result of the weather conditions, 41 Squadron remained on the ground all morning, and the first anti-Diver patrol was not airborne until 12:10. However, only five patrols had been completed by 18:30 when the weather deteriorated again and flying ceased again.

Although two of the day's patrols were flown during the day's second wave of Divers, and three during the third, all were uneventful. The ORB lamented, "…though a few bombs came over in cloud it was quite impossible to make any interceptions".[117]

7 August 1944 – The day dawned to poor weather, which soon improved, but deteriorated to localised thunderstorms during the late afternoon. Diver activity during the day was limited to 05:55 to 10:49, during which 11 Group plotted 69 Doodlebugs. Thirty-five crossed the coast, 17 were destroyed by fighters, 12 by the anti-aircraft batteries, and two by the balloon barrage.

The morning's initial poor conditions improved sufficiently for 41 Squadron to have the first aircraft airborne on anti-Diver operations at 09:10. Fifteen patrols were then flown until 21:50, but it was "a quiet one"[118] today, and all were uneventful. It was a similar story for Lympne's other two resident units: 1 Squadron flew thirteen patrols and 165 Squadron twelve, but theirs were also all to no avail.

8 August 1944 – Morning fog lifted by midday, but it remained hazy over the Channel. Similarly to the previous day, Diver activity was limited to only between 05:50 and 09:13, during which time 48 Buzz Bombs were plotted in 11 Group's area. Thirty-one made landfall, but due to the foggy conditions, only three were destroyed by fighters, two by anti-aircraft fire, and four by balloons.

The fog kept 41 Squadron on the ground until almost 11:00, and although 13 anti-Diver patrols were flown between 10:55 and 22:05, all fell after the cessation of the day's only wave of V1s. As such, there were no interceptions and the ORB bemoaned, "the enemy again were not very active and nothing came our way".[119] Not surprisingly, 1 and 165 Squadrons, who flew thirteen

Flt Sgt 'Larry' Spurr RCAF was posted to a Canadian squadron on 4 August 1944, and remained in the RCAF after the War. He was seconded to the USAF during the Korean War and claimed one MiG-15 destroyed in July 1952 whilst flying Sabres with the 25th Fighter Squadron. He was subsequently awarded the U.S. DFC.
© Nan Spurr

and twelve patrols, respectively, also came home empty-handed. However, they both received word today that they would be departing Lympne for Detling on 10 August with their Servicing Echelons, to be replaced with 130 Squadron a day later.

Separately, another new pilot joined 41 Squadron today on his first operational posting: 22-year-old WO Peter Harold Hale. He had joined the RAFVR in January 1941 and completed ITW and EFTS in the United Kingdom before being shipped to Canada just before Christmas to attend 41 and 39 SFTSs in Saskatchewan. Hale graduated with his Wings as an NCO pilot in late April 1942 and was sent to CFS, then BGS, before being posted as staff to 31 SFTS at Kingston in early October 1942. The following July, he was posted to OTU at Bagotville and returned to the United Kingdom in October 1943. Following a month's leave, he was promoted to Flight Sergeant with seven months seniority, and posted to 53 OTU at Kirton-in-Lindsey. In late February 1944, Hale was posted to the TEU at Annan, and subsequently Tealing, where he was promoted to Warrant Officer. In late June, he was sent to GSU in Cranfield where he remained until joining 41 Squadron at Lympne today. He would remain with the unit until after the cessation of hostilities.

9 August 1944 – Early mist, lifting to a fine day with little cloud and good visibility. Diver activity was limited to a two-and-a-half hour period between 06:16 and 08:40, during which time 11 Group plotted 25 V1s. Twelve of these made landfall and 13 were shot down, six by fighters and seven by anti-aircraft fire.

It was a good start to the day for 41 Squadron, who brought down two of the day's six Doodlebugs within five minutes of each other on the morning's first two patrols.

> *For a welcome change we had a clear sky from dawn to dusk and quickly made use of it by destroying two flying bombs just after day break – the usual time for the first wave to arrive.*[120]

41 Squadron flew 22 anti-Diver patrols mid-Channel between Dieppe and the Somme Estuary, from 05:40 to 22:00, but after the morning's initial excitement the rest of the day was uneventful until late evening.

The Squadron's first victory of the day fell to Flt Lt Terry Spencer, who had taken off with Flt Sgt Colin Robertson as Yellow Section (Spencer MB875 & Robertson MB852) at 06:30. The pair was only minutes in the air, still outbound on their way to the patrol area, when Kingsley Control vectored them onto an inbound Buzz Bomb. In the cloudless three-quarter dawn light, their visibility was approximately eight miles, and they soon spotted the bomb, intercepting it around five miles north of Hastings.

It was flying at an altitude of 3,000 feet, on a course of 340°, and at an IAS of 320 mph when Spencer commenced a series of attacks. In a similar scenario to Flt Sgt 'Steve' Stevenson's victory only four days previously, Spencer fired several bursts at the Doodlebug, at ranges of between 600 yards and 300, swinging from quarter starboard to astern as he did so.

Before long, he had expended his entire ammunition and the only visible effect was that the V1 had slowed to 230 mph. However, as this gave Spencer the advantage of superior speed, he opened his throttle, flew alongside the bomb and tipped it up, causing it to stall and fall to the ground near Wadhurst, Sussex, at 06:41, where it exploded on impact.

Only four minutes later, over the Channel, Fg Off Harry Cook claimed his own victory. He had taken off with Flt Lt Bill Stowe at 05:40 as Red Section (Cook MB878 & Stowe MB850), a full fifty minutes prior to Spencer and Robertson, to patrol the Channel between Cayeux and Dieppe. They were approximately an hour into their flight when vectored onto a Buzz Bomb mid-Channel by Upsett and Fairlight Controls.

When they sighted it, it was flying at between 1,500 and 2,000 feet on a course of 340°, and Cook observed it was "larger than usual and [the] jet unit glowed red instead of white".[121] Cook made two attacks on the bomb from astern, but as it was only doing a relatively slow speed of 160 mph (half the speed of Spencer's V1), it comes as no surprise that he overshot on the first attempt. However, he still managed to get in a one-second burst at 200 yards, which hit the target.

Decreasing his speed, Cook dropped back for his second attack, firing a three-second burst at 300 yards. He hit the V1 again, and sent it straight down into the sea around 10-12 miles out from the Flak Belt, where it exploded on impact at 06:45.

Yellow Section was back in Lympne first, Spencer and Robertson, putting down at 06:55, having only been airborne 25 minutes. It was no use continuing the patrol as Spencer was out of ammunition. Red Section arrived back only minutes behind them, after a long 90-minute patrol, Cook and Stowe touching down at 07:10.

Spencer claimed his third full V1 victory, and the Squadron's third and last to be destroyed by tipping it off course, whilst Cook claimed his first and only V1. These victories raised the Squadron's Buzz Bomb tally to thirty-nine (34 + 5 shared). Spencer's victory was immortalised in a drawing in his logbook by the Squadron's amateur artist, Flt Lt Tom Slack, who titled his work, 'TIP 'EM UP TERRY'.

In the evening, Plt Off Jimmy Payne and Fg Off Maurice Balasse were airborne for an otherwise uneventful and quite routine anti-Diver patrol when they encountered some aerial activity of another type. Having taken off as Green Section (Payne EN228 & Balasse EN609) at 20:35, they were patrolling on a course of approximately 40°, around 15 miles west-northwest of the Somme at 21:10, when they sighted a large number of Allied bombers flying north, with one straggler to the rear.

They watched, too far away to assist, as an enemy fighter engaged the straggler, observing tracer fire followed by an explosion aboard the bomber. The fighter broke to starboard and headed for Abbeville and the bomber fell into the Channel in flames. Payne and Balasse saw five parachutes descend but only arrived on the scene after the action was over. They did what they could, Payne radioing a fix eight miles off Cayeux, and Balasse descending to circle the crew in the water.

Payne's logbook contains a note indicating his concern that despite their efforts to notify their location, it was too late in the evening for the ASR aircraft or launches to come out to find them, and they would therefore have to spend the night in the water.[122]

On their final day at Lympne, 1 Squadron flew sixteen patrols for a single victory and 165 flew seventeen for none. Whilst these were being flown, an advance party of 52 men from Nos. 6001 and 6165 Servicing Echelons left Lympne for Detling by road.

10 August 1944 – Cloudy with 10/10ths cloud at 2,000 feet. Diver activity did not commence until 17:40 but was then limited to a total of 25 plotted in 11 Group's area all day. Twelve crossed the coast and 16 were destroyed, six by fighters and ten by the coastal anti-aircraft batteries.

41 Squadron remained at Lympne alone today, whilst 1 and 165 Squadrons departed for Detling by air at 10:30, and 6001 and 6165 Servicing Echelons followed them by road. Although the weather was perfect for flying, and 41 Squadron flew 21 anti-diver patrols between 05:20 and 21:55, fifteen of them were completed before the day's only wave of Doodlebugs commenced. However, even after 17:30, no interceptions were made, and then Squadron came home empty-handed.

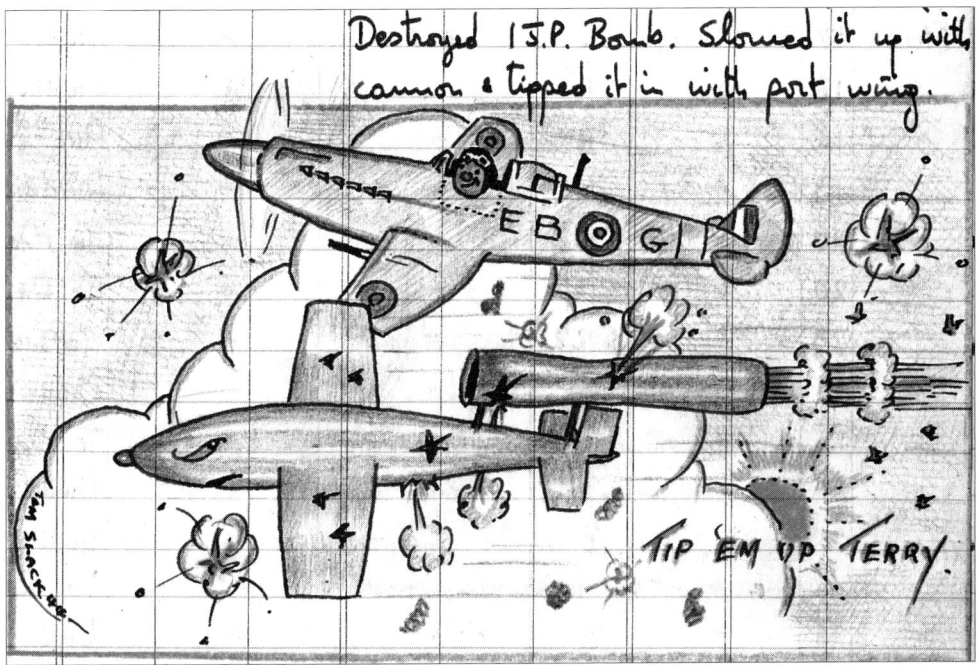

On 9 August 1944, Flt Lt Terry Spencer destroyed a V1 five miles north of Hastings. Having unsuccessfully expended his entire ammunition on the flying bomb, he flew alongside it and succeeded in tipping it up with his wing. The event was captured in his logbook in a sketch by fellow Flight Commander Flt Lt Tom Slack. © Terry Spencer & Thomas Slack, via Cara and Raina Spencer

> *To make up for this quiet day, the Germans gave us a noisy night, but today they again failed to present us with any targets. The flak had been steadily increasing in efficiency and was now accounting for 3 out of 4 bombs, that crossed our stretch of the coast. However we found it hard to increase our success as fewer bombs were crossing our patrol line, which was designed to catch them coming from the Somme-Dieppe area.*[123]

With opportunities waning as anti-aircraft batteries' efficiency steadily increased, it was clear that 41 Squadron's days in 'Doodlebug Alley' were numbered. The peak of the onslaught had passed, and the pilots were needed on more pressing work. It would not be long before their reversion to offensive sweeps would commence.

11 August 1944 – The day dawned to fog and low cloud in England's southeast, which cleared around lunchtime. Thirty-two Buzz Bombs were plotted by 11 Group today, of which 18 made landfall. Two of these were destroyed by fighters, five by anti-aircraft fire and two by the balloon barrage.

As a result of the weather conditions, 41 Squadron's first anti-Diver patrol was not airborne until 13:10, and 14 were completed by the time flying ceased for the day at 21:50.[124] The Squadron was able to claim a single victory today, but it was shared with another squadron.

Flt Lt Bill Stowe and Fg Off Johnny Wilkinson were off the deck at 13:10 as Red Section (Stowe EN229 & Wilkinson EN609) and headed to the Folkestone area where they maintained a patrol at 10,000 feet in a clear sky, with patches of cloud at 2,000 feet. Around an hour into the flight, the pair was vectored onto an inbound Buzz Bomb over the Channel.

They intercepted it east of Lympne, and recorded it coming in at 3,000 feet on a course of 320° and at an IAS of 360 mph. However, they were beaten to the mark by Flt Sgt Jakub Bargielowski of 315 Squadron[125], who intercepted the V1 over Folkestone, but recorded it was at an altitude of

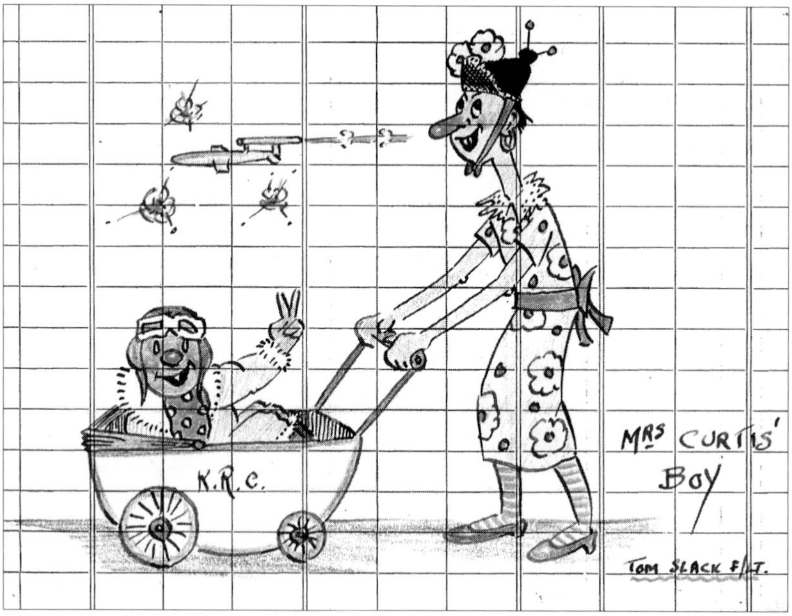

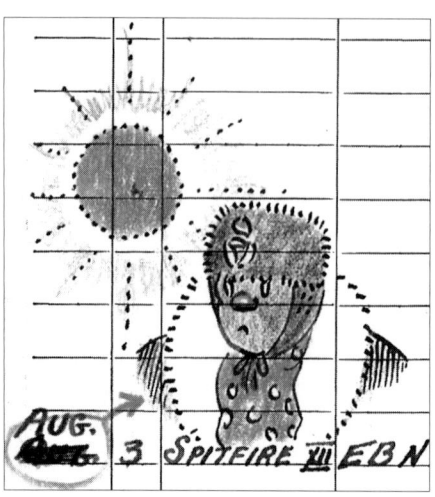

Three sketches by Flt Lt Tom Slack in the logbook of Fg Off Keith Curtis RCAF © Keith Curtis & Thomas Slack, via Karen Neale

Belgian Fg Off (later Flt Lt) Maurice 'Momo' Balasse served with 41 Squadron from 1 to 10 June 1943 and from 23 November 1943 to 23 January 1945. In summer 1944, he claimed four destroyed and four shared destroyed V1s, but was shot down and killed over Germany on 23 January 1945. © 41 Squadron RAF

2,000 feet, on a vector of 300° and doing a speed of 370 mph. Bargielowski delivered his attack at 14:15 from line astern at ranges of 100 to 70 yards.

When Bargielowski pulled away, Flt Lt Stowe urged Johnny Wilkinson to have a crack, which he then did, but he dived onto it with too great a speed. Initially drawing level with the Doodlebug and flying briefly alongside it, Wilkinson reduced his airspeed and dropped back behind it. Then, from ranges of 200 yards and less, he fired one long, ten-second burst of both cannon and machine gun from astern. The time was 14:18.

Wilkinson saw strikes on the V1, and then watched as it dropped its nose and dived into a field near Brabourne, four miles east of Ashford. Bargielowski also watched the V1 go down, but he recorded the location as eight miles southwest of Canterbury. Stowe and Wilkinson then returned to Lympne, where they put down at 14:30, whilst Bargielowski landed at Brenzett at 14:26.

As both men had attacked this V1, Wilkinson and Bargielowski were compelled to share the victory, taking half each. This was Wilkinson's first and only V1 victory and 41 Squadron's fortieth (34 + 6 shared).

During the afternoon, 130 Squadron arrived at Lympne, led by Sqn Ldr William Ireson, their aircraft all landing within a ten-minute period between 15:35 and 15:45. Their ground staff and the personnel of 6130 Servicing Echelon had been due to arrive by air before midday, in advance of their aircraft, but did not arrive in Lympne until 19:30 due to unsuitable weather. The Squadron had just come from a week's sojourn at Tangmere, for the sole purpose of converting from Spitfire Vs to Spitfire XIVs. The pilots and crews had undergone an "intensive training programme… at high pressure throughout these days in order that the Squadron should become operational [against the V1 onslaught] as soon as possible".[126]

Another personnel movement of note today was the arrival from Detling of Wg Cdr Colin Gray DSO DFC** who took over as Lympne's new Wing Commander Flying. A New Zealander on an RAF Short Service Commission, Gray had an interesting relationship with 41 Squadron. In August 1941, almost three years ago to the day, he had been attached to 41 Squadron from 1 Squadron as a Flight Lieutenant for a single sweep to Le Havre and Le Tréport, France. On that patrol, Gray destroyed an Me109E whilst flying a 41 Squadron Spitfire, and although the personal victory went to Gray, the claim was awarded to 41 Squadron.

One of the top ten Aces of the Battle of Britain, Gray was New Zealand's top-scoring fighter pilot, having been credited with no less than 27 aircraft destroyed, one shared destroyed, and 22

Jim C. J. 'Jimmy' Payne joined 41 Squadron as an NCO pilot on 5 July 1943 and was commissioned in January 1944. He claimed 2½ V1s destroyed during the summer of 1944 and departed as a Flying Officer on 7 March 1945. © 41 Squadron RAF

probably destroyed or damaged. He remained one of the highest-scoring Allied fighter pilots of World War II, becoming one of only 14 to score more than 25 confirmed victories.

However, discontent continued to rise inside 41 Squadron and within weeks of becoming Lympne's Wing Commander Flying, Gray would have another direct effect on the unit's history.

12 August 1944 – Low cloud in the morning with fair visibility. Although Diver activity was minimal – just 13 were plotted, of which ten crossed the coast – the weather kept the RAF's fighters at bay and the only Doodlebugs brought down were one by anti-aircraft fire and two by the balloon barrage.

The weather delayed the start of 41 Squadron's operational flying until 09:50 but thereafter continued through to 22:00, despite less than ideal visibility. By the day's end, the Squadron had flown 17 anti-Diver patrols and had "sought vainly for anything to destroy"[127], but nothing came their way. 130 Squadron was also airborne today on their first full day of anti-Diver operations, flying 29 sorties in roughly the same time-frame as 41 Squadron, but they too came home empty-handed.

41 had one minor incident to report today when Flt Sgt Peter Chattin's tyre burst on landing at Lympne, on return from his only anti-Diver patrol of the day. He had been airborne with Flt Lt Terry Spencer as White Section (Spencer MB831 & Chattin EN609) between 20:15 and 21:30 on an otherwise completely uneventful patrol but was not injured in the incident.

13 August 1944 – Thick ground mist delayed the commencement of operations for the second day in a row, after which conditions improved to a fair to fine day. Diver activity commenced at 06:05 and continued intermittently all day, a total of 34 being plotted in 11 Group's area. Fifteen made landfall, three were shot down by fighters and two by anti-aircraft fire.

The fog began to lift mid-morning and 130 Squadron was off the deck at 10:00, followed by 41 Squadron twenty minutes later. By the end of the day, both squadrons had flown 14 patrols each, with the last 41 Squadron aircraft putting down at Lympne at 21:45. However, every pilot came home empty-handed once again.

Apart from a wave just after dawn and another just before dusk, the enemy seemed lately to have rather given up sending his flying bombs over in daylight and concentrated on keeping us awake at nights, in which he was not altogether [un]successful, as when the guns opened up at night, we just had to watch the fantastic effects in the sky.[128]

14 August 1944 – A little cloud with haze, but generally good visibility. The day's Diver activity was limited to a single salvo of eleven V1s, which were plotted between 06:48 and 06:56. Of these, nine crossed the coast, one was shot down by a fighter, three by anti-aircraft batteries and one brought down by a balloon.

A full flying programme was undertaken by 41 Squadron during the day. Their first anti-Diver patrol was airborne at 05:35 and seventeen were flown by the time flying ended at 21:35. For their part, 130 Squadron flew 18 patrols, but neither unit was able to make any claim. One of 41 Squadron's pilots did, however, have a very close shave.

Fg Offs Peter Graham and 'Momo' Balasse were in the air at 05:35 as Blue Section (Graham MB831 & Balasse MB853) to intercept the usual dawn wave of Buzz Bombs. However, the only salvo of V1s came over later than expected, after the pair had given up and returned to Lympne. They were already in the circuit when Control informed them that V1s had just crossed the coast nearby.

The two pilots climbed again, spotted two separate Buzz Bombs and split up, each after his own. Unfortunately, they had both already lost the advantage of height and were unable to catch them; both V1s continued on their paths to London unhindered.

Meanwhile, Fg Off Graham had climbed back to 12,000 feet again and was returning to Lympne anew when he spotted yet another Doodlebug 9,000 feet below him. What happened next would be enough to put the wind up any man:

He dived almost vertically down and came in behind it at what he thought was about 250 yards range and was promptly thrown on to [sic] his back by the tremendous slip stream coming from the bomb. After recovery, he attempted a burst from astern, but accuracy was quite impossible. He dived and came up underneath it firing a short burst at one ring deflection, before getting in the slip stream again. [He closed] up to try tipping it over, but it reached the Balloon Barrage, before the attempt at tipping could be made.[129]

It appears there was more unusual about this particular V1 than what was reported in the Squadron's ORB. 11 Group ORB noted that:

A pilot of 41 Squadron reports attacking one missile from astern with cannon, and although strikes were seen the Diver seemed unaffected. He describes the missile as twice as large as normal with [a] fuselage of heavy barrel shape resembling a Thunderbolt.[130]

Graham and Balasse were back on the ground at 06:50 to tell their story, but neither could make a formal claim. Unfortunately, after this brief excitement on the day's first patrol, no further Doodlebugs came over for the rest of the day.

At 17:30, the AOCinC ADGB, Air Marshal Sir Roderic Hill KCB MC AFC, flew in to visit the Station. He addressed the Squadron, informing the men they were presently deployed in 'Doodlebug Alley' owing to the reputation they had gained in 1943 for quick interception.

15 August 1944 – Fine weather prevailed all day, with a little high cloud and visibility of 10-15 miles. Diver activity did not commence until a few minutes before 09:00 but then continued intermittently all day, with a total of 77 plotted by 11 Group during the day phase. Of these, 36 made landfall, fighters shot down 11, anti-aircraft batteries brought down 17, and balloons accounted for another four.

41 Squadron flew sixteen anti-Diver patrols between 05:50 and 21:35. After a number of quiet days, the Squadron was finally able to claim two more successes against the V1s. One fell to Canadian Fg Off 'Jack' Malone, who shared his with a pilot from 129 Squadron, and the second to Flt Lt Ross Harding. 130 Squadron was also airborne on seventeen patrols of their own but experienced yet "another unsuccessful day"[131], despite four days now on anti-Diver operations.

Malone was off the deck at 08:00 with WO Pat Coleman as White Section (Malone EN622 & Coleman MB875) and flew the patrol in mid-Channel between Gris Nez and Sangatte, France.

Having completed the job uneventfully, they returned to Lympne and were coming in to land, at an altitude of only 3,500 feet, when Kingsley Control informed them of a Doodlebug incoming towards Ashford, Kent, in a north-westerly direction.

Opening their throttles and climbing again, the pair headed for Ashford. Despite slight haze, visibility was still a good 20 miles, and they soon saw a Mustang attacking 'their' Buzz Bomb around three miles southwest of Ashford. It was flying at between 1,500 and 2,000 feet and doing an IAS of 300 mph. Malone closed and lined himself up for his own attack as soon as the Mustang broke away, delivering it from dead astern just after 09:30.

He made a single attack, opening up at 200 yards, and closing to 100 as he fired a two second burst. His aim was straight and the V1 "burst into flames and [its] wings flapped as if about to fall off."[132,133] Malone broke away and the Mustang pilot made his second attack, after which the Diver crashed, hitting the ground two miles northwest of Ashford.

White Section returned to Lympne at 09:35, where Malone claimed a half share in the V1's destruction. It later transpired that the Mustang pilot was Australian Flt Lt Robert 'Dutch' Kleimeyer (RNZAF), who had briefly flown with 41 Squadron in June 1942. He was now with 129 Squadron, and on this sortie had flown Mustang III, FB137.

It was then quiet for eight hours until Flt Lt Ross Harding's 17:20 mid-Channel patrol between Gris Nez and Sangatte, with WO Pat Coleman as Yellow Section (Harding MB795 & Coleman MB875). Unfortunately for poor Coleman, it would be the second time in one day that he would have to watch his No. 1 claim a V1 victory!

Similarly to the morning's patrol, the pair had finished their patrol and was on their way back to Lympne when Upsett Control vectored them onto a Doodlebug at 18:45. Harding intercepted it over Romney Marsh in clear weather with good visibility, judging its altitude at 3,000 feet and IAS at 320 mph.

He came in from line astern on a course of 330° and opened fire at 250 yards, making a single two-second burst. This was sufficient to send the V1 down to explode in a field north of Ivychurch. It was quick work, and Yellow Section was on the ground at Lympne again only five minutes after the Buzz Bomb was intercepted. This was Harding's second of three V1 victories.

Harding and Malone's victories today raised the Squadron's V1 tally to forty-two (35 + 7 shared) destroyed. Malone had claimed his victory in just a nick of time, as he was posted away today. He was sent to Italy where he joined a Canadian squadron and saw out the War. Although he left the Air Force in September 1945, he re-joined five years later and was finally discharged 18 years later as a Major.[134]

16 August 1944 – Fair to fine weather with thick haze. Diver activity was considerably greater than usual with no less than 148 Buzz Bombs plotted by 11 Group throughout the day. Eighty of these crossed the coast, but a significant number were destroyed by British defences, 36 falling to fighters, 29 to anti-aircraft fire, and three to the balloon barrage.

The good weather and heightened Diver activity brought more successes for 41 Squadron today and, finally, the first for 130. 41 Squadron was airborne on eighteen anti-Diver patrols, mostly inland, between 05:45 and 21:50, claiming two successes, whilst 130 was airborne on another fourteen, claiming three.

41 Squadron's first of the day fell to Flt Sgt 'Bill' Rossow, who was airborne at 15:50 to patrol the Ashford area with Fg Off 'Charlie' van Goens as Blue Section (van Goens MB880 & Rossow MB857). A full hour into the patrol, the pair were vectored onto a Buzz Bomb by Kingsley II Control, which they intercepted in clear skies, west of Ashford. It was flying at an altitude of 2,000 feet on a course of 310°, and doing an IAS of 350 mph.

Rossow positioned himself for an attack, and fired on the Doodlebug from astern in five bursts of three seconds at ranges of between 300 to 250 yards. This caused its starboard wing to tear away, at which it made a quick spin to earth five miles west-northwest of Ashford, where it exploded on impact.[135] Blue Section returned to Lympne at 17:10, where Rossow claimed the V1 destroyed.

Flt Sgt (later WO) Vivian Rossow RAAF served with 41 Squadron as his only operational unit of the War, from 9 August 1944 to 19 July 1945, and claimed a V1 destroyed only ten days after his arrival.
© Rossow family

At around the same time as they were landing, Fg Off Peter Graham and Plt Off 'Ricky' Gray took off as Green Section (Graham MB851 & Gray EN609) for their own anti-Diver patrol, between Ashford and Canterbury. At 18:10, the pair was vectored onto a wave of inbound Doodlebugs by Kingsley II Control, which resulted in a feeding frenzy by several squadrons. Both Graham and Gray chased their own Buzz Bombs; Gray came up empty-handed but Graham was more fortunate.

Intercepting his flying bomb ten miles west-northwest of Tenterden, Kent, in clear skies, Graham dived from 12,000 feet to reach it at an altitude of just 2,000 feet. He recorded its course as 320° and its IAS at 360 mph. As he did so, however, he saw three aircraft behind it – two Tempests and a jet-powered Meteor – all firing from ranges of 600-800 yards, but without success.

Using the speed from his dive, Graham flew underneath these aircraft and, as they broke away, came up in front of their position at a closer range. He opened fire from astern at 400 yards with just two one-second bursts, but succeeded in hitting the Doodlebug in the starboard wing, which folded up, and then broke off.

Graham watched the bomb spin once towards the earth near Wrotham, but was unable to watch its final demise as he had entered the balloon barrage boundary and was compelled to pull up sharply to avoid the balloons. Heading back to Lympne, however, he came across yet another Doodlebug, and took a shot. The ORB records it was "already a lame duck"[136], but Graham recorded it in his logbook as damaged.[137]

He returned to Lympne at 18:35, initially claiming a probable V1, but it was later confirmed destroyed – his third. Rossow and Graham's efforts today had brought the Squadron's tally to forty-four (37 + 7 shared) destroyed.

17 August 1944 – Poor weather, with low cloud but fair visibility. Diver activity continued on an increased scale today, with 116 plotted by 11 Group from 06:10 onwards. Sixty-one crossed the coast and 15 were brought down by fighters and one by the balloon barrage. However, attesting to the success of radar-based automatic gun laying and proximity fuses, a respectable 38 Doodlebugs were also destroyed by anti-aircraft fire – their greatest single day tally to date. In fact, only the day before, Fg Off Peter Graham had noted in his logbook that he had chased three V1s but anti-aircraft fire got them all before he could.

Dutch Fg Off Rijklof 'Charlie' van Goens served with 41 Squadron from 19 January 1944 to 17 August 1944 when he failed to return from an anti-Diver patrol. It is theorised that he inadvertently strayed into the no-fly zone along the English coast and was hit by Allied Flak. © Peter Graham

41 Squadron continued with inland patrols today, although the weather was not perfect for such operations, as two separate layers of 7/10ths cloud covered the patrol area, one at 800 feet and the other at 3,000 feet.[138] Nonetheless, the Squadron had 13 anti-Diver patrols in the air between 05:50 and 21:30, and claimed two more Divers destroyed. 130 Squadron also continued their success, claiming four V1s on 14 patrols, bringing them to a tally of seven in just two days. However, it would also be a sombre day for 41 Squadron, as they lost another pilot to a flying accident – the third in two months.

The first of the day's Buzz Bombs fell to Flt Lt Ross Harding, who was airborne at 06:45 with WO Pat Coleman as Yellow Section (Harding MB854 & Coleman MB850) to patrol the Ashford area. Almost an hour into the patrol, Kingsley II vectored them onto a Doodlebug, which they intercepted over Romney Marsh, Kent, at 2,000 feet. It was a course of 320° and doing a speed of 300 mph.

Harding attacked it from astern, firing three bursts of two seconds each at ranges of 80 to 200 yards. He scored strikes all over the Buzz Bomb, which lost fragments, then turned over and dived through the cloud cover towards the ground 1½ miles northeast of Brenzett, Kent. It was his third and last V1 victory.

However, Harding had little time to enjoy his success. Within five minutes, he suffered engine failure after being hit by Allied anti-aircraft fire and was forced to make a hasty landing, crash-landing at Brookland, around a mile southwest of Brenzett, at 07:50.

He was uninjured and soon returned to Lympne, but had not actually seen his Diver crash and was therefore unsure of the exact status of his victory. He had little to fear, though, as a searchlight battery near Ashford confirmed the V1 had indeed hit the ground.[139]

On August 17, 1944 I was on an 'Anti-Diver Patrol' on the English Channel with 8/8ths cloud below at 500/100 feet. I chased a Doodlebug towards the English Coast. As I hit it, the English Anti-Aircraft fire along the coast hit me. The V-1 went in and I descended through the clouds and made a forced landing in Romney Marsh, near Dungeness. The aircraft was later lifted and repaired. On the same day my recollection is that Charlie Van Goens was lost over the Channel – remarkable man.[140]

Van Goens Fails to Return

At 09:05, only an hour and 15 minutes after Harding's forced landing, Dutch Fg Off Rijklof 'Charlie' van Goens took off with Australian Flt Sgt 'Bill' Rossow, as Blue Section (van Goens

MB880 & Rossow MB857). It was an otherwise uneventful patrol but shortly after 10:00, van Goens fell from the sky without warning and was never seen again.

Strangely, however, neither the 41 Squadron ORB's F540 nor the Lympne Station ORB make any mention of van Goens' disappearance, although the Squadron F541 records next to his name that he was reported as missing on the 09:05 patrol, whilst his loss is recorded in the 11 Group ORB without any explanation as simply missing, "cause unknown".[141]

This has led to a range of theories on the cause of van Goens' disappearance, thereunder oxygen failure, lack of fuel, enemy action and accidental friendly fire. Contemporary researchers conclude that three of these four scenarios are highly unlikely.

Considering the nature of V1 operations, it is improbable that van Goens' fuel was consumed at such a rate that he was unable to make it safely to either the English or French coasts. Had van Goens indeed found himself in a position of lack of fuel, he had a number of options open to him, which were not exercised: He could have baled out and taken to his dingy; he could have glided to shore and, in particular, he could have used his R/T system to notify Control of his plight and position.

Enemy fighter action is unlikely at this period of the War, as the Luftwaffe was not seen over southeast England very often during 1944. Many aircraft were tied up on the Eastern Front, and fuel supply problems and retreating fronts meant that the Luftwaffe's ability to carry out offensive operations over England had been significantly curtailed.

Oxygen failure was a real issue, and had cost the lives of some of 41 Squadron's pilots throughout the War, but is felt not to have been the cause of van Goens' loss. He was heard over the radio by fellow pilots and although the message was garbled and not understood, oxygen failure would most likely have caused unconsciousness within a short space of time.

Fg Off Peter Graham, who took off with Plt Off 'Ricky' Gray at 10:05 as Green Section (Graham MB853 & Gray MB831) recalls hearing him shortly after becoming airborne:

> *He was a good pilot but alas when he got excited his English used to desert him. […] He radioed me in a very agitated voice and I told him to fly due North before descending and returning to base (Lympne). My fear, I know, was that he would find himself in the no-fly zone.*
>
> *His message to me was incoherent and he was clearly in one of his (rare) states of excitement and his English had vanished. We were very near a zone which was wholly given to our AA gunners, so I was trying to warn him of this and tell him what to do. He never replied to me in understandable English and his radio soon went dead. I never saw him or his aircraft again.*[142]

It is believed that Graham had heard van Goens cursing in Dutch, which implies he was not only conscious but knew he was in serious trouble. The most likely scenario, therefore, is that van Goens had been hit by Allied Flak. Even Flt Lt Bill Stowe, who was also airborne at the same time, recorded in his logbook at the time that the cause was Allied Flak. Considering the fortifications along the Channel coast in 1944, guarding against the V1 menace, this appears to be the most plausible cause of his loss.

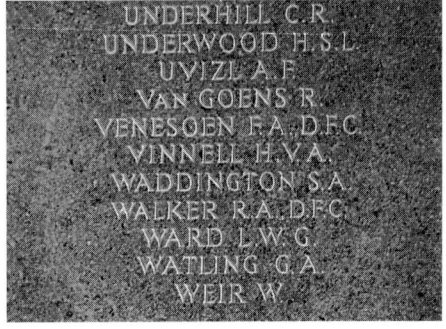

Thirty-year-old Fg Off Rijklof van Goens remains missing to this day and is remembered on the Runnymede Memorial.
© Steve Brew

By the end of August 1944, the British had positioned no less than 1,935 anti-aircraft guns in the anti-Diver gun belt along the southeast coast, consisting of approximately 500 heavy guns, and over 1,400 smaller calibre 20mm and 40mm weapons. In addition to these, another five U.S. anti-aircraft battalions were also dug in amongst them along the same front, armed with another eighty 90mm heavy guns.

These were then enhanced by the introduction of microwave radar-guided gun laying with shells equipped with proximity fuses. This technology allowed the Allies to aim at a target both before it was visible and before it came in range. It also allowed for 'firing blind', if a target was, for example, obscured by cloud cover. The radar's maximum range was up to 40 miles (64km), but it could track targets automatically from 18 miles (29km) out.

Accuracy was deemed to be within 25 yards (23 metres), from where the shells' proximity fuses took over. These reacted to the reflection of a radio signal and exploded automatically if within around 17 yards (15 metres), thereby often bringing down a target without even hitting it. This significantly increased the effectiveness of the guns to a point where one V1 was being shot down for every 100 shells fired, rather than one for every 2,500 as had been the case prior to the radar's introduction.

There was, however, a safeguard installed in Allied aircraft to ensure they were not shot at accidentally. In use since the beginning of the War, "Identification Friend or Foe", or "IFF", was designed to transmit code to ground-based radar that identified an aircraft as friendly. This produced a blinking dot on a radar's IFF screen, whereas an enemy aircraft would remain a constant dot.

As good as the system was, however, there was a major pitfall. The IFF appeared on one system, whereas the radar-based gun laying operated on another, with separate antennas and control systems. They were not inter-linked and information on the two systems could only be shared by human communication, over a radio or in person. This hindered effective and rapid communication, and it is therefore likely that many incidents occurred that resulted in Allied casualties.

This is particularly startling when one considers that the anti-aircraft guns were able to fire inland as well, and the gunners were allowed a degree of flexibility in following a target inland with their proximity fuses. In effect, this placed airfields such as Lympne both in the gun belt and in the firing line. Despite the fact that the guns' free fire ceiling was set at 6,000 feet, and Allied pilots were allowed to cross the gun belt at altitudes higher than 8,000 feet to ensure their safety, the proximity-fused shells travelled freely above their ceiling, so even aircraft in the '8,000-feet-plus safe zone' were still in very real danger.

As such, based on the information available today, although there is no proof per se, it is most probable that van Goens was a victim of friendly fire in the anti-Diver gun belt and crashed into the Channel off the coast. He was probably never seen by the anti-aircraft batteries, and he has not been found to this day; van Goens is still listed as missing, presumed dead. Aged 30 at the time of his loss, he was the son of Gustaaf and Willemine van Goens of Apeldoorn, in the Netherlands, and is remembered today on Panel 203 of the Runnymede Memorial in Surrey.

Despite the lack of hard evidence, Fg Off Graham always assumed that anti-aircraft fire was the cause of van Goens' loss, which stems, in particular, from a memory of a meeting with…

> …some Ack-Ack gunners at a pub that evening, who swore that that afternoon they had shot down a Spitfire that was trespassing in their airspace. They were, I suppose, entitled to think it could have been a captured one being flown by a German. They were very pleased with their achievement, while I was speechless with anger and grief, being sure it was our Charlie… whom they had killed.[143]

On the day van Goens was lost, however, Graham had no time to look for him immediately as his section was ordered to land within 15 minutes of becoming airborne as a result of deteriorating weather. He put down at Manston at 10:20 and it was then another three hours before operational flying resumed, commencing with Blue Section at 13:30. Graham and Gray found their way back to Lympne on non-operational flights, and the rest of the afternoon and evening were taken up with another eight anti-Diver patrols (16 sorties), and searches for van Goens.

At 15:30, Flt Sgt Bob Fleming and WO 'Jimmy' Ware took off as White Section (Fleming EN609 & Ware EN229) to search for a sign of van Goens, followed by Flt Lt Tom Slack (EN238, section colour not designated) five minutes later. Unfortunately, however, their searches proved fruitless and the former pair returned at 16:50, and Slack at 17:10, all with nothing to report.

Despite van Goens' loss, operations continued largely as normal during the rest of the day; his loss was, after all, still unexplained at that point, and there was no way of knowing whether he was alive or not.

On the last of the day's patrols, Fg Off Graham recorded the day's second V1 victory, flying this time with Flt Sgt 'Bill' Rossow as Green Section (Graham MB831 & Rossow EN228). Having taken off at 20:15 to orbit the Ashford and Canterbury areas, they were vectored onto an incoming V1 by Kingsley Control at 20:35.

In clear skies with visibility of around 30 miles, it did not take long before they spotted the Doodlebug, which they intercepted at 20:35 at 3,000 feet, half a mile southeast of Denge Wood, and a few miles southwest of Canterbury. They recorded its course as 320° and its IAS as 380 mph.

Graham came in from astern and made a single attack, firing a half-second burst from 200 yards. It was enough to cause the Buzz Bomb to burst into flames and send it spiralling to the ground, crashing in Denge Wood. By this time, the day's second last patrol, Blue Section (Slack EN238 & Gray MB853) had also arrived on the scene, and Flt Lt Tom Slack confirmed Peter Graham's victory, his fourth.

Shortly afterwards, Graham spotted yet another V1 and went after it, too. However, he had neither the speed nor the altitude required to catch it and had to satisfy himself with "a long burst at extreme range with no results".[144] However, he recorded in his logbook that he actually had damaged it, noting that "this one was probably finished off by another aircraft".[145]

Harding and Graham's victories today raised the Squadron's V1 tally to forty-six (39 + 7 shared) destroyed.

18 August 1944 – Cloudy with visibility of 6-15 miles. The only Diver activity today consisted of 17 Doodlebugs launched between 06:56 and 07:30. All but one were shot down by fighters or anti-aircraft guns.

41 Squadron flew a full programme today, with 14 anti-Diver patrols undertaken inland between 06:00 and 21:30 for one more victory.[146] For their part, 130 Squadron flew 29 anti-Diver sorties for no victories, but sustained one casualty when a Mustang collided with one of their aircraft.

41 Squadron's victory fell to Australian WO 'Jimmy' Ware on the day's first patrol – his first and only aerial victory with the unit. Ware was airborne at 06:00 with fellow Australian, Plt Off 'Ricky' Gray as Blue Section (Ware EN238 & Gray EN228) and reported 3-4/10ths cloud at 4,000 feet, but good visibility below this altitude.

Conditions therefore proved perfect when the pair were vectored onto an incoming Buzz Bomb by Kingsley II an hour into the patrol, at an altitude of 2,000 feet. They intercepted it northwest of Ashford on a course of 330°, but doing a relatively low IAS of 250 mph.

Ware dived onto the flying bomb and made a single attack from dead astern, firing a two-second burst from two hundred yards. His aim was good and it burst into flames and fell into a field north of Hollingbourne, Kent, exploding on impact. Two pilots from 130 Squadron were also in the vicinity at the time and confirmed his victory. Ware's V1 brought the Squadron's tally up a notch to forty-seven (40 + 7 shared) destroyed.

Separately, one pilot was posted away today, and three new NCO pilots joined the Squadron. Flt Lt 'Jimmy' Thiele DSO DFC*, who had been with the unit since February, left on a brief posting to 2 GSU, Swanton Morley, followed by five-week stint at 83 GSU at Bognor Regis and Thorney Island. In mid-October, Thiele was sent to Volkel, in the Netherlands, where he spent two months with 486 Squadron, before being posted to 3 Squadron as a Flight Commander.

Sgt Plt John Irvine served with 41 Squadron briefly from 18 August 1944 to ca 23 September 1944. He is seen here with an unidentified local girl at RAF Lympne during that period. © John Irvine, via Dan Johnson

On Boxing Day 1944, he became that unit's Commanding Officer, and experienced some success in this role until he was shot down by Flak, wounded and captured on 10 February 1945. Held captive until 31 March 1945, Thiele managed to escape with 41 Squadron's Flt Lt Terry Spencer – by this time Commanding Officer of 350 Squadron and himself shot down and captured – and they successfully returned to Allied lines to reclaim their roles as Commanding Officers of their respective squadrons![147]

The three new pilots all arrived from 26 Squadron at Lee-on-Solent, and consisted of 23-year-old American Flt Sgt John T. 'Jack' Bradshaw[148], 22-year-old New Zealander WO Brian Weeds[149], and 20-year-old Scotsman Sgt Plt John Irvine.[150] All three pilots were posted together to 41 Squadron today, but none of their tenures with the unit would last longer than three months.

19 August 1944 – The weather was not as good as the previous day, with intermittent rain, which worsened towards dusk. Diver activity consisted of three distinct phases: a wave of 18 Buzz Bombs commencing at 06:39, a wave of 22 between 14:32 and 15:02, and a final wave of 21 from 21:03 to 21:26, totalling 61 for the day. Of these, 32 made landfall, 24 were shot down by fighters and 18 by the anti-aircraft batteries, whilst balloons accounted for another two.

Despite the weather conditions, visibility was good on the whole, and 41 Squadron completed 17 anti-Diver patrols between 05:50 and 21:35 for one more victory.[151] 130 Squadron had a better day than their previous, coming home with one destroyed and two damaged over 15 patrols.

41 Squadron's V1 today fell once again on the first patrol of the day, this time to Flt Lt Terry Spencer – his fourth individual victory – who was airborne at 05:50 with WO Pat Coleman as White Section (Spencer MB878 & Coleman EN228). Orbiting the Ashford area for the morning's usual first wave of flying bombs, they were almost an hour into the patrol when Kingsley II vectored them onto an incoming Doodlebug.

They were experiencing 7/10ths cloud cover at 6,000 feet, but still managed to intercept the Doodlebug over Appledore, Kent, at 2,000 feet, on a course of 340° and doing an IAS of 320 mph. Spencer dived upon it from quarter astern. He fired a two-second burst from 350 yards, but did not see any strikes. Closing to 250 yards, he fired a second burst of just one second, and this had the desired effect. The petrol tank blew up and the Diver spun in, crashing into open ground two miles north-northwest of Appledore, near High Halden airfield.

A Mustang tried to take a piece of the action and Spencer reported that a "nearby Mustang overshot to port of [the] diver", but it was "not thought to have fired."[152] Indeed, Spencer was awarded the full victory, which was the Squadron's forty-eighth (41 + 7 shared) destroyed.

Back row: WO Peter Hale, Flt Sgt Bob Fleming, Flt Sgt Jack Bradshaw (USA), Flt Sgt Ian Stevenson, Flt Sgt Viv Rossow RAAF; front row: Flt Sgt John Irvine, Lympne, ca August-September 1944. The children were locals, who have not been identified. © Rossow family

Despite the final wave of V1s at sunset, and several chases by the Squadron, cloud cover at 800 feet and the glare of the setting sun "made interception well-nigh impossible and no successes were attained".[153] Nonetheless, Plt Off Pat Coleman recorded in his logbook that he "fired at and saw hits on [a] flying bomb" near Canterbury.[154]

20 August 1944 – The day started with very poor weather consisting of thick, low cloud and rain. Diver activity commenced at 06:05 and continued throughout the day, with a total of 90 being plotted by 11 Group. Of these, 48 made landfall but, as a result of the poor weather, fighters were only able to claim eight and the balloons none at all. Thankfully, however, the anti-aircraft batteries accounted for 19.

Despite conditions, the Squadron made an effort to get airborne and the first anti-Diver patrol (Slack EN238 & Gray EN228) was off the deck at 07:50 to belatedly meet the usual morning wave of Doodlebugs. However, conditions proved too poor, and the pair was forced to return after just 40 uneventful minutes in the air.

The Squadron then remained on the ground until the weather improved at lunchtime, and between 13:05 and 21:30 another eight anti-Diver patrols were mounted. The afternoon's operations also gave two of the Squadron's new NCO pilots – 'Jack' Bradshaw and Brian Weeds – the opportunity to make their first operational flights with the unit.

In the middle of the afternoon, the Squadron added another victory to their tally when Fg Off 'Ricky' Gray downed a V1 into the Channel. He had taken off at 15:15 as No. 2 to Flt Lt Tom Slack as Black Section (Slack EN238 & Gray EN228) and the pair were an hour and ten minutes into their patrol between Boulogne and Gris Nez at 6,000 feet when Gray spotted a Doodlebug 3,000 feet below him.

It was doing an IAS of 360 mph on a course of 320°, and it was with some luck that Gray saw it at all; conditions were hazy and visibility was limited to only five miles. Gray dived straight onto

Back row: Flt Sgt 'Jock' Stevenson (Batman), Flt Sgt Bob Fleming, Flt Sgt Jack Bradshaw (USA), and WO Brian Weeds RNZAF; front row: WO Arthur Appleton, WO Pete Hale, and Flt Sgt Viv Rossow RAAF, Lympne, ca August-September 1944. The children were locals, who have not been identified. © John Irvine, via Dan Johnson

it and delivered two attacks from astern at 250 yards, the first a burst of four seconds, and the second of two seconds.

The second burst had the desired effect and the Buzz Bomb dived into the Channel around seven miles off Folkestone, Kent. When Black Section returned to base at 16:45, Gray claimed his second full V1 victory, and the Squadron's forty-ninth (42 + 7 shared) destroyed. For their part, 130 Squadron undertook eleven patrols and claimed one Diver probable. It was, however, confirmed destroyed the following day by the Royal Observer Corps.

During the early evening, 41's Flt Lt Terry Spencer had a close shave whilst flying a Spitfire IXa of 33 Squadron[155], possibly MH790, when he suffered engine failure on approach to Lympne and made "a skilful crash landing"[156] in an orchard just outside the aerodrome. Although Spencer was not hurt, the aircraft was written off, and the orchard was badly damaged. As it was a non-operational flight, however, the serial is unfortunately not recorded.

21 August 1944 – As poor weather with rain and low cloud dominated the day, 11 Group was virtually non-operational. All offensive operations were cancelled and only a very few anti-Diver patrols were flown all day. Taking advantage of conditions, the German military launched 85 V1s, of which 38 crossed the coast. Although a fighter claimed just one of them, anti-aircraft batteries successfully brought down 28, and balloons another nine.

No operational flying was undertaken today by either of Lympne's squadrons. During the morning, 41 Squadron studied their own combat films instead. "Many were very good, and the clearest and most interesting film was F/O WILKINSON'S."[157,158] During the afternoon, however, two security films were shown, one of which was titled "Information Please" about what the men should expect, and how they were expected to behave, when being interrogated at *Dulag Luft*, the Luftwaffe's interrogation centre outside Frankfurt for all new Allied airmen Prisoners of War.

22 August 1944 – Bad weather with low cloud with drizzle, and poor to moderate visibility. 11 Group was non-operational again today, and whilst no offensive operations were undertaken, a few unsuccessful anti-Diver patrols were flown late in the afternoon. Twenty-five V1s were plotted during the day with 11 making landfall, and 44 were plotted during the night phase with 12 making landfall. Whilst the RAF could claim none of these, anti-aircraft fire destroyed 28 and balloons accounted for two more.

As the previous day's poor weather continued for most of the day today, 41 Squadron did not commence operational flying until 17:05. However, flying was halted again at 20:50 after only four patrols, when the weather deteriorated once again.

Fg Off Peter Graham (MB831) should have participated in the first patrol but was unable to when he found his R/T system unserviceable. Otherwise, all the patrols were uneventful. Frustratingly, a wave of V1s came in just 15 minutes after the last patrol touched down, but Lympne was unable to do anything do stop them.

It is believed that 130 Squadron was not airborne operationally all day[159] but 41 Squadron recorded a personnel movement when Australian Flight Sergeant Colin Robertson departed the unit for 83 GSU at Bognor Regis.[160]

23 August 1944 – The day dawned to thick cloud, which lifted and broke up as the day progressed. Seventy-six Divers were plotted by 11 Group between 07:45 and 21:00, and 41 of these made landfall. Fighters brought down 15 and the anti-aircraft batteries 22.

This was one of 41 Squadron's most intensive and successful days in some time, which saw not only the Squadron's first offensive operation in over two months, but also the destruction of two and a half V1s and the damaging of another, and the loss of one pilot. The Squadron's day consisted of 13 anti-Diver patrols and an offensive sweep to France, which commenced at 08:05, when Flt Lt Terry Spencer was airborne with Flt Sgt 'Steve' Stevenson as Red Section (Spencer MB882 & Stevenson EN229) for an anti-Diver patrol.[161]

The pair were barely 15 minutes into the patrol when Kingsley II vectored them onto an incoming Doodlebug, approaching from east of Folkestone in hazy conditions. Hurrying to the area, Spencer spotted Flak and dived from 9,000 feet to 2,000 to find it. He soon saw the V1 flying 1,000 feet above him at 10 o'clock, around two miles south of Mersham, Kent. It was flying on a course of 310° but doing a relatively low IAS of just 240 mph.

Attacking from astern and slightly below, Spencer made a single burst of two seconds, saw strikes, but overshot. Looking back, he saw his fire had nonetheless been accurate as the Buzz Bomb fell from the sky and crashed near the railway line about four miles southeast of Ashford.

Following this success, Spencer and Stevenson formed up again and climbed to 10,000 feet to continue their patrol. The next 40 minutes passed without event, but as they were returning to Lympne at around 09:05, Kingsley II advised that yet another Doodlebug was incoming, expected to pass four miles west of Ashford.

Looking about, Spencer spotted flares and dived towards them, sighting the V1 from 4,000 feet near Pluckley, west-northwest of Ashford, at 2 o'clock. It was flying at an altitude of 2,500 feet on a course of 340° and doing a speed of 360 mph. Coming in from astern, Spencer opened fire from 300 yards with a burst of four seconds.

Seeing no result, he closed to 250 yards and fired a second burst of two seconds. This time, the port side of the fuselage and port wing root were hit, and the fuel tank exploded. The Doodlebug flipped over to port and went down streaming black smoke, crashing north the railway line near Harrietsham, northwest of Ashford, at 09:07.

A NAAFI wagon serving the pilots and ground crew at Lympne in August-September 1944. The tail of Flt Lt Terry Spencer's Spit XII, MB882, EB-B, is showing to the right.
© John Irvine, via Dan Johnson

Fg Off 'Jack' Malone RCAF was posted to a Canadian squadron in the Mediterranean in August 1944. He ended the War as a Flight Lieutenant and retired from the RCAF as a Major in October 1968. © Jack Malone

At 09:20, Red Section landed back at Lympne where Spencer claimed the Squadron's fiftieth and fifty-first V1s (43 *and* 44 + 7 shared) destroyed.[162] He had brought them down with 1,200 rounds of .303 ammunition and 280 rounds of 20mm, completely expending his entire ammunition.

The Squadron had put together a reward for the pilot who scored the fiftieth, totalling £2 10s., which was consequently awarded to Spencer. As if this were not enough, though, these two victories made Spencer a V1 Ace; they were his personal fifth and sixth Buzz Bombs.

A Casualty on the First Sweep in Two Months

At 15:00, the pilots were briefed for Rodeo 392 to the World War I Somme battlefields, in an area bounded by the towns of Amiens, Rosières-en-Santerre, Roye, and Montdidier. It was their first Continental operation since being brought in to combat the V1 threat on 19 June, and the pilots were glad to be back in action: "We joyfully abandoned our patrols and… took off for France."[163]

41 Squadron was one of a total of 17 Spitfire squadrons from 10 and 11 Groups that participated in fighter sweeps over France during the day. One pilot's logbook suggests that 41 Squadron's role was to find Junkers Ju188 medium bombers reported to be operating out of the Amiens area.[164]

The Squadron was airborne at 16:00 and crossed the French coast near Dunkirk at 14,000 feet, whereupon they descended to 12,000 feet.[165] The patrol proved uneventful, despite 3,400 rounds of .303 and 820 rounds of 20mm being fired, and no ground victories were recorded.

However, the Squadron had only swept as far as Hesdin, around 30 minutes into the operation, when Flt Lt Tom Slack reported fuel cock failure, as he was unable to switch over from his 45-gallon jettison tank to his main tank. Without fuel, his engine died, and he gradually descended towards French soil as he "tried in vain to get it to work".[166]

> *I was losing height, with everyone telling me what to do over the RT, which I jolly well knew like the back of my hand, but none of the emergency drill seemed to work. As far as we knew, Rex* [Flt Lt Thomas Poynton], *Haybag* [Flt Lt Douglas Haywood] *and Leslie* [Fg Off Leslie Prickett] *had gone missing in our Squadron for the same reason, due to a fault in the cable or an airlock somewhere.*
>
> *By this time the aircraft was too low for me to bail out, so I crash-landed in a field near Hesdin, knocking myself out. When I came to, a few seconds later, there were two German soldiers with rifles standing on the wing of the Spitfire. One of them was screaming for me to get "Aus, Aus," so I asked him politely to jolly well help me 'Aus'.*[167]

Unfortunately, none of the Squadron's pilots had actually seen Slack land. He was last seen at just 200 feet, gliding towards a field between Hesdin and Fruges. The Squadron had little choice but to continue on without him, and exited France again between Berck sur Mer and Le Touquet, heading for Lympne, where they put down between 16:55 and 17:00.

Despite Slack's loss, it had been a quiet day for 41 Squadron, but they were not alone. Whilst numbers of ground targets were shot up by Rodeo 392's participating Spitfire squadrons, little was actually seen of German forces by anyone in the air, despite it being a day of great activity on the ground: a part of Paris was liberated, Evreux fell, and the advance along the coast reached Trouville, east-northeast of Le Havre. In fact, Slack's loss was the only one for 11 Group on the entire front all day.

Rodeo 392, 23 August 1944	Serial	Section	Time Up	Time Down
Chapman, Robert H.	EN226	Blue	16:00	16:55
Reid, Daniel J.	EN228			
Slack, Thomas A. H.	EN226	Green		FTR
Fleming, Robert	MB853			17:00
Graham, Peter B.	MB833	Black		16:55
Anderson, Robert E.	EN238			
Spencer, Terence	MB882	Yellow		17:00
Tebbit, Donald F. J.	MB795			
Harding, Ross P.	EN602	White		
Stevenson, Ian T.	EN229			
Coleman, Patrick T.	MB850	Red		

Unfortunately for Slack, however, though largely unhurt, he had come down behind the front line. Unlike his previous Continental adventure [See Chapter 4], he had no opportunity to evade this time, and spent the remainder of the War behind wire. News did not reach 41 Squadron of his survival, albeit as a POW, until 21 November 1944.

Of note, however, is that during his questioning in Dulag Luft, he was confronted by a German interrogator who had done his homework and surprised him with the knowledge he had of him:

"You escaped once, didn't you?"
This took me completely by surprise. "How on earth do you know that?"
"Someone put your name as missing in the personal columns of the Telegraph or Times or somewhere. It's lucky France has been overrun by your armies, or we would want to know how you got away." [168,169]

Slack was sent to Stalag Luft III at Sagan, Germany (Żagań, Poland) on 3 September 1944, where he remained until 27 January 1945. He was then force-marched to Stalag III-A, at Luckenwalde, where he remained from 5 February until 20 May 1945, when he was repatriated to England.[170]

The day was, however, still a long way from over, as the evening's usual second wave of Doodlebugs was expected any time. Only five minutes after the Squadron's return from their Rodeo, Australians Fg Off 'Ricky' Gray and Flt Sgt 'Bill' Rossow were airborne on another anti-Diver patrol, designated Black Section (Gray MB857 & Rossow EN609). When they returned at 18:25, Rossow reported he had attacked and damaged a V1 west of Gris Nez, France, from a range of 120 yards closing to 25 yards. He saw strikes upon it but it would not go down and he could not claim a definitive victory. It was possibly the Squadron's fourth damaged Doodlebug, but it was the only one officially recorded.[171]

Four anti-Diver patrols later, the Squadron claimed another success. Australian Flt Lts 'Andy' Anderson and 'Denny' Reid were airborne at 19:30 as Blue Section (Anderson EN238 & Reid

MB853) and were returning to Lympne around an hour and ten minutes into their patrol when advised by Kuvey Control of an incoming V1.

Conditions were hazy but visibility was still a good 15 miles when Reid sighted it around five miles southwest of Ashford at 2,000 feet on a heading of 340°, and doing an IAS of 380 mph. He climbed to 4,000 feet, then dived on the Buzz Bomb and made two attacks from astern of each five seconds duration, from a range of 250 yards.

He saw strikes and flames, when a Tempest cut in and finished it off, before Reid had the opportunity to do so himself. The Doodlebug crashed ten miles northwest of Ashford, and Reid had little choice but to claim only half with the Tempest pilot when he returned to Lympne at 21:00.[172]

It would prove to be Reid's only V1 victory of the War, but more success would come his way in Spring 1945. It did, however, raise the Squadron's V1 tally thus far to fifty-two (44 + 8 shared) destroyed and one damaged. 130 Squadron was also active on patrols throughout the day and matched 41 Squadron by downing 2½ of their own.

24 August 1944 – Cloudy with rain and thunder, made the perfect cover for significantly increased Diver activity today, and 136 were plotted by 11 Group. Sixty-one of these crossed the coast, and although fighters were able to claim eleven V1s, the anti-aircraft batteries claimed a massive 85 – by far their biggest haul to date.

All in all, however, it was an uneventful day for the Lympne-based squadrons. 41 Squadron was airborne on at least eight anti-Diver patrols, both inland and off Gris Nez, between 06:10 and 13:05 when the weather deteriorated and halted operations. Another was attempted between 17:45 and 19:00, but the weather proved still too poor to continue and no more flying was undertaken thereafter.[173]

Several chases occurred during the morning but no successes were recorded, and the rest of the day's flying was uneventful. 130 Squadron was airborne on eleven patrols of their own, and although they ceased flying when the weather deteriorated around midday, they were able to claim a small success, when one pilot claimed half a Doodlebug with a Tempest from another squadron.

Despite 41 Squadron's lack of success today, they did receive some welcome news:

We were today informed that we would definitely be coming off flying bomb work and taking up an offensive role in the near future. Another bit of news that was definitely confirmed was that the Squadron would shortly be re-equipped with Spitfire XIV's. We were very glad to get both these bits of news.[174]

The Squadron had been flying Griffon-powered Spitfire XIIs since late February 1943, and was one of only two RAF squadrons ever to be equipped with the aircraft. The other unit, 91 Squadron, had already re-equipped to Spitfire Mk. XIVs in March 1944, and 41 Squadron was now the only remaining unit in the RAF flying and servicing the type.

25 August 1944 – The weather played havoc with operations again today, but only 17 Divers were plotted by 11 Group during the day, of which just three made landfall. Fighters claimed just one destroyed, but the anti-aircraft defences accounted for another eight.

Although 41 Squadron completed 11 anti-Diver patrols inland between 08:25 and 21:35, low cloud halted flying on several occasions, and no successes were recorded. During the afternoon, the weather permitted some practice flying to be undertaken by B Flight and four sorties were made of air-to-air firing on the drogue. The top scorer was Australian WO 'Jimmy' Ware.

There were two incidents during the day, the first when Sqn Ldr Chapman returned from the day's third patrol within ten minutes of taking off in EN227, possibly with engine trouble, and secondly when New Zealander WO Brian Weeds suffered engine failure on take-off and crash-landed MB875, turning the aircraft over. Fortunately, he was barely hurt, but it could have been a lot more serious. Almost 40 years later, he recalled,

Fellow Canadians Flt Lt Bill Stowe and Fg Off Keith Curtis skeet shooting at Lympne in summer 1944, accompanied by Squadron mascot Perkin. © Jack Malone

My memory of that was [that the aircraft] started o.k. but seemed to lack all the power that was needed to get off. Belly tank was on it as well, which to me made it a bit [dicey] to pull the undercarriage up as I had seen one go up in flames which landed and the belly tank went up. I just trusted that the brakes would pull it up in time but didn't. Went between 2 parked aircraft, hit an embankment, flipped upside down and went backwards on its back for 75-100 yards. Naturally I passed out but luckily the canopy was still open. When I came to I released the parachute, forgetting about the Mae West clipped to it, and dropped the short distance onto my head, so I was cramped upside down and couldn't get out through the small opening – and I think it ran through my mind about it going on fire. However, some ground staff came running up and lifted the plane up and managed to drag me out.[175]

130 Squadron was also airborne on approximately 14 anti-diver patrols today, but they, too, came home empty-handed. The unit was pleased to be informed today that they would also be returning to offensive operations shortly, and coming off Diver patrols.

26 August 1944 – A fine day, after fog cleared, upon which not a single V1 was plotted by 11 Group. 41 Squadron conducted eleven anti-diver patrols off Gris Nez between 06:05 and 15:15 but, as a result of the lack of Diver activity, all were in vain. However, these were then followed by two low-level offensive sweeps to the Lille area of France.

Between 11:00 and 13:30, whilst the morning's patrols were on-going, five pilots from B Flight took to the air to practice formation flying in preparation for the afternoon's operation. These were followed by a briefing for the sweep – only one had been planned – "to destroy anything moving on the ground".[176] However, when it passed uneventfully a second was mounted in the evening.

41 Squadron's activity was part of a larger 11 Group operation, Ramrod 1234, in which 18 Squadrons, thereunder two each from 10 and 12 Groups, were deployed on attacks of road and rail targets in a triangle enclosed by the towns of Calais, Ghent and Aulnoye. Sweeps were continuously conducted within the area, which lay over the French-Belgian border, between 15:00 and 21:00.

The Squadron's first show, latterly designated Ramrod 1234A, was airborne at 16:50, when three sections of four – designated Red, Yellow and Blue – were led across the French coast over Gravelines at 13,000 feet by Sqn Ldr Chapman. They then descended to 6,000 feet and swept towards Lille, arriving over the target area at 17:27, but only saw "6 lorries of Refugees on road Poperinghe-Ypres, taking cover on roadside".[177] Having not fired a shot, they returned home again, crossing back out over Coxyde [Koksijde], Belgium, just southwest of Nieuport [Nieuwpoort], and landed at Lympne at 18:00.

130 Squadron had followed 41 Squadron out of Lympne half an hour later and swept the same general area. They, too, saw little and felt that "the enemy had gone to ground for the day"[178], but returned to Lympne around the same time as 41 Squadron, claiming eight stationary covered railway trucks left smoking around a mile south of Armentières, France.

Shortly after 41 Squadron's return, a briefing was given for a second sweep, designated Ramrod 1234B, which was intended as an exact repetition of the first. All but two of 1234A's twelve pilots took part in the second operation, but as one of those not participating was Sqn Ldr Chapman, it was led by Flt Lt Terry Spencer instead. On this occasion, however, there was some action for the pilots.

Ramrod 1234B, 26 Aug 1944	Serial	Section	Up	Down
Spencer, Terence	EN227	Red		
Anderson, Robert E.	MB857			
Appleton, Arthur S.	MB853			
Chattin, Peter W.	MB878			
Harding, Ross P.	EN602	Yellow	19:40	21:05
Stowe, William N.	MB850			
Tebbit, Donald F. J.	MB795			
Stevenson, Ian T.	EN229			
Fisher, Douglas P.	MB880	Blue		
Balasse, Maurice A. L.	EN609			
Graham, Peter B.	MB831			
Fleming, Robert	EN238			

They were airborne at 19:40 and crossed the French coast at Gravelines again, at the same altitude. The pilots took the opposite route, flying clockwise this time, and entered Belgian airspace. North of Ypres [Ieper], they attacked six barges on a canal between two railway lines and one burst into flames.

The Squadron continued on to Lille, then headed back towards Gravelines, where they damaged another barge at the junction of two canals around eight miles south of Bergues, northeast of St. Omer.

However, this attack fire drew 20mm and 40mm Flak and although no-one was wounded, three Spitfires suffered light damage. Flt Lt Terry Spencer (EN227) had the closest shave when a shell splinter passed through his canopy and grazed his flying helmet, and Flt Sgt Peter Chattin's (MB878) and WO 'Steve' Stevenson's (EN229) aircraft were also hit.

Peter Chattin on his first op.[179] is badly hit by flak & thinks it quite normal. Steve gets a 20mm shell through his wing. Terry Spencer has hood damaged.[180]

Flt Lt Bill Stowe RCAF trying his hand at motorcycling, Lympne, summer 1944.
© Jack Malone

The Squadron landed back at Lympne at 21:05, claiming their first ground victories in ten weeks, to find that 130 Squadron had returned 15 minutes before them, having been out on their own, uneventful, second sweep. All of the Wing's pilots had returned safely today, but it was not the same story everywhere. 64 Squadron lost two pilots, and 91 and 322 Squadrons one each.

27 August 1944 – A fine and cloudless day in England's southeast. Diver activity was mild, with a total of just 34 Doodlebugs plotted by 11 Group all day, of which 19 made landfall. Fighters shot down 13 and anti-aircraft batteries accounted for another 11.

For the first time in over two months, 41 Squadron's day did not commence with anti-Diver patrols. The pilots were briefed instead for two separate bomber escorts, one taking place mid-morning and the other in the evening. However, there was brief excitement early in the morning:

> We were definitely off the flying bomb patrols now. During the two months we had been on the job, we had accounted for 52, top-scorers being F/LT. SPENCER and F/O BALASSE with six each.
>
> Not conten[t] with being equal top-scorer against the flying bombs F/LT. SPENCER sought and destroyed another shortly after dawn this morning while carrying out an air test.[181]

Following the previous long day with operations into the evening, Flt Lt Terry Spencer was up early for an air test. He took off at 06:40 and around 25 minutes later, whilst at an altitude of 10,000 feet over Romney Marsh, sighted Flak at Dungeness.

He received no advice from Control, but hurried to the area where he sighted an inbound V1 that had come through the anti-aircraft defences unscathed. Spencer noted it was flying at 2,500 feet on a course of 340°, and at an IAS of 300 mph. Intercepting it approximately 15 miles north of Rye, Sussex, Spencer dived upon it and came up from astern and below, opening fire with a trio of bursts of two, three and one seconds consecutively at 100 yards, closing to 80 yards.

He had expended just 345 rounds of .303 and 95 rounds of 20mm when the Doodlebug blew up in mid-air at close proximity. Spencer returned to Lympne at 07:20 "somewhat shaken"[182] and claimed his seventh Buzz Bomb, thereby becoming the Squadron's highest scorer in the V1 onslaught. Moreover, this victory was the Squadron's last V1 of World War II, their final tally numbering fifty-three (45 + 8 shared) destroyed.[183]

At 10:30, the Squadron was briefed for the day's first bomber escort, Ramrod 1237, in which eight of the unit's pilots would provide area cover to four boxes of thirty-six U.S. 9th Air Force B-26 Marauders, in unison with nine aircraft from 130 Squadron. These would be followed by another three formations of thirty-six U.S. 9th Air Force B-7 Bostons, escorted by 24 Spitfires from Hawkinge-based 350 and 402 Squadrons. Their target was a large concentration of German troops and transport in a bend of the south bank of the River Seine at Rouen, which would be bombed in seven attacks at ten-minute intervals.

130 Squadron was off the deck first, followed by 41 Squadron fifteen minutes later, at 11:40, having been delayed by 90-gallon jettison tanks being fitted for the very first time; the crews clearly not yet au fait with their operation. Flt Lt Terry Spencer led 41 Squadron's pilots and crossed the French coast at Quiberville, just west of Dieppe, in clear weather with slight haze below 12,000 feet. Approaching Rouen from the north, they found the area already completely hidden by thick smoke rising to 10,000 feet.

The pilots patrolled to the south of Rouen for an hour whilst the first 144 bombers went to work, and observed "some absolutely shattering bombing".[184]

> [We] …gave area cover in the Rouen area, while medium bombers endeavoured to liquidate enemy forces trying to retreat across the Seine. A heavy pall of smoke prevented detailed observation, but reports indicate that the bombing was well concentrated….[185]

The remaining 108 Bostons followed them in and dropped their payloads, covered by 350 and 402 Squadrons. They also reported well-concentrated bombing and observed large fires in the target area. Like 41 and 130 Squadrons, and the first four boxes of Marauders, they were not hindered by Luftwaffe and not a shot was fired. Flak was only light and sporadic and no-one was hit.

130 Squadron landed back at Lympne 13:15, followed by 350 and 402 Squadrons, who landed at Hawkinge at 13:40. 41 Squadron was the last Spitfire squadron home, landing at Lympne at 13:50, after a long two hours and ten minutes in the air. It was the longest operation they had ever undertaken in the Spitfire XII.

The V3 Long Range Gun

At 18:30, the pilots were briefed for the day's second operation, Ramrod 1238, a close escort to 216 Halifaxes and 10 Pathfinder Mosquitos bombing a secret weapons launch site at Marquise/Mimoyecques, around 8km east of Gris Nez.

In 1943, the German military had begun development of a long range artillery piece, intended to fire shells at London across the Channel from Pas-de-Calais, known as the V3. The gun fired with multiple propelling charges along the 130-metre barrel's length, timed to fire as the 140kg projectile passed them to add additional velocity. These charges gave the shell a theoretical range of 165 kilometres. Trials in late May 1944 sent the 180cm shell a distance of 88km, whilst early July trials saw the range increased to 93km.

Adolf Hitler ordered that 50 launch sites should be built in the Pas-de-Calais region of France, but the design meant that the long barrels would need to be placed in shafts inside hills and quarries to support their length, keep them stable, and protect them from Allied attack. However, this also meant that the guns would be immovable, and therefore permanently within range of, and aimed at, London.

The site attacked in Ramrod 1238 was a launch site located in a limestone hill around 5km north of the Hydrequent quarries, near Mimoyecques, where V1 and V2 launch sites were already under construction. Excavation on the V3 site began in September 1943 but it did not take long for Allied reconnaissance to recognise suspicious activity going on.

Interpretation of aerial photography resulted in the site, which they referred to as 'Marquise/Mimoyecques', being bombed by the U.S. 9th Air Force in early November 1943. Unfortunately, it was largely a failure, as only light damage was done, so a follow-up attack was undertaken six days later. Although this second attack was more successful, additional attacks were made in April, May, June and July 1944.

The latter of these was undertaken by the RAF with a number of 12,000 lb. Tallboy earthquake bombs, which definitively put the site out of action, and construction was never completed. Unaware of this, however, the Allies made additional attacks on 6 and 12 August, and now in Ramrod 1238 on 27 August, in which 41 Squadron was involved.

216 heavy bombers – 176 Halifaxes and 40 Lancasters – plus 10 Pathfinder Mosquitos of the RAF's No. 6 and No. 8 Groups were assigned to the task, with target cover provided by 12 Spitfires each from Hawkinge-based 350 and 402 Squadrons, and target and rear cover provided by eight Spitfires from 41 Squadron and twelve from 130.[186] Another two squadrons were also assigned to sweep the Douai area in case of Luftwaffe activity.

The four target and rear cover squadrons were airborne from their respective airfields at 19:30, with 41 Squadron departing Lympne in Yellow, Blue and Red Sections fitted with 30-gallon jettison tanks and led by Flt Lt Terry Spencer. The Squadron met the Pathfinder Mosquitos in clear skies over Gris Nez at 19:50 and reached the target area six minutes later. Five bombers turned back before reaching the V3 site, and three aircraft from 130 Squadron and one each from 350 and 402 Squadrons turned back early due to mechanical problems, but 41 Squadron and the Mosquitos arrived at full strength.

Flt Lt Terry Spencer perched on the cockpit of his Spitfire XII, presumably MB882, EB-B, at Lympne, summer 1944. © Terry Spencer, via Cara and Raina Spencer

The unit then patrolled to the south of area for 30 minutes whilst the bombers dropped their payloads of high explosive and incendiary bombs. The attack drew some heavy calibre Flak, but no bombers were hit and the Luftwaffe was not encountered. The bombing was well concentrated and "the area was one blazing mass when we set course for home after the last bomber had dropped its load."[187]

Every Spitfire returned from the operation, 130 Squadron putting down at Lympne at 20:25, followed by 41 Squadron twenty minutes later, whilst 350 and 402 Squadrons landed at Hawkinge at 20:58.

One man was conspicuous in his absence from the day's two Ramrods: Sqn Ldr Chapman, who was posted away today, but his departure was just one of two. The second was Canadian Fg Off Keith Curtis, who was posted to 417 (RCAF) Squadron, based in Italy. Curtis was promoted to Flight Lieutenant in November 1944 and was discharged from the RCAF in October 1945.[188]

A New OC

Sqn Ldr Chapman's departure was not so straight forward. As 41 Squadron had been suffering discipline and morale problems for some time, 11 Group's Senior Air Staff Officer, Air Cdre Cecil Bouchier CBE DFC stepped in and asked RAF Lympne's Wing Commander Flying, Colin Gray, to recommend someone to replace Chapman. Gray's recommendation was an old colleague, 26-year-old Douglas Benham DFC.

They knew each other well, having crossed paths on several occasions during postings in the United Kingdom, and particularly in North Africa. Benham was given the job, but tasked with

Flt Lt Lord Gisborough, Flt Lt Ross Harding and Flt Lt Terry Spencer at Lympne in summer 1944 with Spencer's Singer Le Mans, 'The Blue Peril'Harding. © Terry Spencer, via Cara and Raina Spencer

cleaning up the Squadron and re-instilling discipline, under Bouchier's watchful eye. The SASO took a personal interest in the unit as he had served on 41 Squadron as a Flight Commander in the mid to late 1920s.

Though the exact details are unknown, it is apparent that Sqn Ldr Chapman left under a bit of a cloud; he had only been in command of the Squadron for three months. However, in all fairness it should be recognised that his unpopularity and lack of acceptance by the pilots were likely exacerbated by the fact that the previous Commanding Officer, Sqn Ldr Arthur A. 'Pinkie' Glen, who was very popular, was removed for political reasons and not because of performance issues. As his removal upset the Squadron, who did not want to see him go [see Chapter 5], his successor's arrival was therefore not greeted with the usual cordiality that a new OC would have been, through no fault of his own.

Indeed, asked many years later about how he was received by 41 Squadron, Chapman responded that he had no idea about Glen's removal, but felt it would explain why he never felt accepted and why the Squadron was cold towards him.[189]

Despite this underlying discontent, the Squadron took Chapman out for a farewell party at the Royal Oak the following evening. It was attended by Wg Cdr Ray Harries DSO DFC, who had led the Squadron on many operations to the Continent the previous summer.

OC, A Flight, Flt Lt Terry Spencer remarked on the arrival of the new Commanding Officer in his diary, "New C.O. S'Ldr Benham took over 41. Seems an excellent type."[190] He certainly had his work cut out for him.[191,192]

Big Ben, Market Garden & the Oil Campaign

7

28 August – 3 December 1944

Back on the Offensive

28 August 1944 – Initially cloudy with rain, clearing to fair weather during the afternoon. The day's Diver activity was confined to an eight hour period between 14:00 and 22:00, during which a massive 106 Buzz Bombs were plotted by 11 Group. Of these, however, just 36 crossed the coast. In excellent form, the anti-aircraft batteries shot down an astounding 65 V1s, whilst fighters destroyed 24, and balloons two more. Together, they accounted for almost 96.5% of the day's flying bombs. The Diver threat had at last been overcome.

Today, though, 41 Squadron was barely involved. During both the morning and afternoon, 17 pilots practiced air-to-ground firing on floating targets at Leysdown range, off the Isle of Sheppey, which had been the scene of much aerial warfare during the Battle of Britain. A total of 890 rounds of 20mm were fired over the space of nine hours and 40 minutes flying.

At 14:00, the Squadron as whole had its first opportunity to meet its new Commander, when Sqn Ldr Benham briefed the men on the latest gen.

> …S/L BENHAM *gave us a talk in which he was able to give us lots of good news. We were going to get very good aircraft very soon, and we were going to get offensive work only in the future.* [He] *foretold escort duties into the heart of Germany and a real chance of meeting the Hun in the air again. He said we should be doing plenty of rangers and when we could not get enemy aircraft we would use our ammunition on ground targets. We would have plenty of occasions to use the 90 gallon drop tanks for we should have to go far afield to find the elusive Hun. We broke up considerably encouraged by our future prospects.*[1]

There was a scramble at 15:40 by Red Section, but they returned at 17:00 with nothing to report. Ten minutes before they landed, however, Yellow Section (Spencer MB831 & Stevenson MB853) took off for an anti-Diver patrol. They also returned, at 17:05, with nothing to report. There was no fanfare and it is not even mentioned on the F540, but this brief flight constituted the Squadron's final anti-Diver patrol of the War.[2,3]

At 17:30, the pilots were briefed for an offensive operation, Ramrod 1243, in which they were to provide close escort with 130 Squadron to 60 Bostons bombing an oil dump near Doullens, France, around 30km north of Amiens.[4] On his first full day with the Squadron, Sqn Ldr Benham was eager to get into the thick of it and would lead the unit on the operation.

Ramrod 1243 replaced Ramrod 1241, which was to have taken place in the morning, but cancelled as a result of unsuitable weather conditions. This latter Ramrod consisted of separate attacks on three fuel dumps in the St. Quentin and Doullens areas, an ammunition dump at Compiègne, and an alcohol distillery and fuel storage depot at Hamm. The attacks were scheduled to be made between 19:05 and 19:25 by a total of 216 Marauder medium and Boston light bombers of the U.S. 9th Air Force, with close escort provided by 12 Spitfire Squadrons.[5] The following units participated in the operation.[6]

Date	28 August 1944
Operation	Ramrod 1243
Targets	Part I: Distillery and Fuel Storage Depot, Hamm, France Part II: Ammunition Dump, Compiègne, France Part III: Fuel Dump, Barisis-aux-Bois, France Part IV: Fuel Dump, Doullens, France
Bombers	Part I: 36 B-26 Marauders Part II: 65 B-26 Marauders (in 2 formations) Part III: 36 B-26 Marauders Part IV: 73 B-7 Bostons (in 2 formations)
Close Escort, Pt I Close Escort, Pt II Close Escort, Pt III Close Escort, Pt IV	Hawkinge: 350 & 402 Squadrons (22 Spitfire XIV) Detling: 1 & 165 Squadrons (24 Spitfire IX) Deanland: 91 & 322 Squadrons (24 Spitfire IX) Westhampnett: 124 & 303 Squadrons (24 Spitfire IX) 135 Wing: 33 & 349 Squadrons (24 Spitfire IX) Lympne: 130 Sqn (12 Spitfire XIV) & 41 Sqn (10 Spitfire XII)[7]

41 and 130 Squadrons were assigned to escort the second group of Bostons to Doullens. 41 Squadron was off the deck at 18:30 in Red, Yellow and Blue Sections, with 30-gallon jettison tanks fitted, and Sqn Ldr Benham leading the Squadron for the first time. They crossed the coast at Sandwich Bay, Kent, and rendezvoused with the bombers 12,000 feet over Furnes [Veurne], a few kilometres southwest of Nieuport [Nieuwpoort], Belgium, at 18:55.

There was 10/10ths cloud at 22,000 feet over the target area, but clear below this altitude, and 'no serious opposition' was encountered from the Luftwaffe.[8] As Flak was also light over the area, the bombers were able to complete their job with good to excellent results, and many fires were seen. 41 Squadron reported seeing "palls of black smoke demonstrating their accuracy of aim"[9] near the railway line northeast of Doullens.

However, whilst some heavy Flak was encountered by the bombers on the way out over the Lens area, no damage was done and 41 and 130 Squadrons left them as they crossed the Channel coast towards England. The fighters changed their bearing to home and put down at Lympne at 20:15.

Separately today, 28-year-old New Zealander Flt Lt David John Verdun 'Jack' Henry DFC, was posted from 130 Squadron to 41 Squadron to become the new OC, B Flight, replacing Flt Lt Tom Slack, who had been shot down and taken prisoner on 23 August.[10]

Another personnel movement of note at Lympne today was the departure of 130 Squadron's Commanding Officer, Sqn Ldr William H. Ireson, who had completed his tour and was posted to

11 Group SASO, Air Cdre Cecil Bouchier, asked Wg Cdr Colin Gray to recommend a suitable man to take over command of 41 Squadron in August 1944, to clean up the unit and re-instil discipline at a time when morale was low and discipline lax. He chose Sqn Ldr Douglas Benham. Crown copyright expired

ground duties. He was replaced this same day by 26-year-old Canadian Sqn Ldr Philip V. K. Tripe DFC, who was already with the Squadron, having joined as a Supernumerary on 6 June 1944. Thus, within the space of just two days, both resident squadrons at Lympne had replaced their Commanding Officers.

29 August 1944 – Poor weather with rain over the southeast of England, and even worse conditions over France, restricted 11 Group's operations all day. The German military took full advantage of the situation and fired 130 V1s towards the southeast of England from 06:00 onwards. Although 130 Squadron was airborne on seven uneventful anti-Diver patrols during the day, 41 Squadron was not airborne at all.

However, this made time for the two new Commanding Officers to settle in, whilst "…several of our tireless pilots accepted the invitation to a dance in Bexhill but arrived too late to get a drink".[11]

30 August 1944 – The previous day's poor weather continued until well into the afternoon, with cloud down to 500 feet, and it was not until 16:00 that 41 Squadron was briefed for its first operation of the day. Between 16:55 and 20:45, the unit flew two offensive sweeps as a part of a larger operation, titled Ramrod 1246.

The Ramrod foresaw 17 Squadron sorties flown independently by two Squadrons at a time, at roughly 30-minute intervals between 16:00 and nightfall, to strafe road, rail and canal movements by German forces in a triangular area formed by the towns of Calais and Aulnoye in France, and Ghent [Gent], Belgium.

Although operations started late in the day, the sweeps proved extremely successful for 41 Squadron and they claimed arguably their greatest ever haul of ground targets in a single day to date. Fellow Lympne based 130 Squadron was similarly involved, flying its own two sweeps practically simultaneously to 41's. The following units participated:

Ramrod 1246, 30 August 1944[12]				
No.	Unit	Aircraft	Up	Down
0	222 Squadron	2 Spitfire IX (weather recce)	14:05	15:15
1	485 Squadron	11 Spitfire IX (1 mech.)	15:48	17:20
2	349 Squadron	12 Spitfire IX (1 MIA)	16:00	17:30
3	33 Squadron	11 Spitfire IX	16:28	18:24
4	222 Squadron	12 Spitfire IX	16:48	18:30
5	41 Squadron	12 Spitfire XII	16:55	18:10
6	130 Squadron	12 Spitfire XIV	17:08	18:05
7	345 Squadron	12 Spitfire V	17:31	19:56
8	322 Squadron	12 Spitfire IX (1 mech.)	17:31	19:07
9	234 Squadron	12 Spitfire V	17:50	19:55
10	312 Squadron	12 Spitfire IX (1 mech.)	17:58	19:25
11	165 Squadron	12 Spitfire IX	18:30	19:40
12	1 Squadron	11 Spitfire IX	18:45	19:48
13	91 Squadron	12 Spitfire IX	19:11	20:42
14	504 Squadron	12 Spitfire IX	19:30	20:50
15	130 Squadron	11 Spitfire XIV (2 mech.)	19:45	20:45
16	41 Squadron	10 Spitfire XII	19:45	20:46
17	322 Squadron	12 Spitfire IX (1 MIA)	20:00	21:30

Sqn Ldr Douglas I. Benham DFC AFC was OC 41 Squadron from 28 August 1944 to 8 April 1945. He was awarded a Bar to his DFC in May 1945 and an OBE in June 1957, shortly before his retirement from the RAF. © Benham family

On the first operation, 41 Squadron was assigned to a low-level attack in the Roulers-Courtrai areas, "…to strafe anything moving on the ground, with the special intention of dealing with railway wagons that might contain flying bombs".[13]

The pilots were airborne at 16:55, carrying 30-gallon jettison tanks, and crossed the Belgian coast between Coxyde [Koksijde] and Furnes [Veurne] in three sections of four. Sqn Ldr Benham led the Squadron and each of the Flight Commanders led a section each; it was Flt Lt Henry's first operation with the Squadron.

1st Sweep, Ramrod 1246, 30 August 1944				
Pilot	Serial	Section	Up	Down
Benham, Douglas I.	MB850	Red	16:55	18:10
Harding, Ross P.	EN602			
Irvine, John	MB862			
Bradshaw, John T.	EN622			
Henry, David V. J.	EN238	Blue		
Ware, James P.	MB836			
Fisher, Douglas P.	MB857			
Fleming, Robert	MB831			
Spencer, Terence	MB882	Yellow		
Stevenson, Ian T.	EN229			
Balasse, Maurice A. L.	EN609			
Gray, Eric	EN228			

The Squadron headed southeast towards Roulers [Roeselare], with 130 Squadron close behind. Arriving over the town at 17:30, they dropped to 8,000 feet and attacked coaches and vans on railway lines in the area. Continuing southwards, towards Courtrai [Kortrijk], the pilots got down to their real business at 17:35, picking out targets of opportunity north of the city, taking turns to dive on them in pairs.

Turning for home, they headed back through Roulers again, but on this occasion the whole Squadron dived on the town's marshalling yards and shot them up, before heading back out to Lympne, where they landed at 18:10. They were beaten home by 130 Squadron, who had arrived just five minutes before them.

41 Squadron's haul for the operation was impressive. For 13,360 rounds of .303 and 3,440 of 20mm ammunition, they claimed three covered railway wagons in flames and 24 damaged at Roulers, one locomotive damaged at Thourout [Torhout], to the north of Roulers, seven lorries damaged between Roulers and Courtrai, and one light anti-tank gun and its carrier damaged.[14] For their part, 130 Squadron claimed strikes on 15 railway wagons, one 2-ton lorry in flames and one lorry damaged.

On landing, 41 Squadron "refuelled and rearmed and prepared to repeat the performance".[15] They were airborne again at 19:45, for the second sweep to the same area, this time only eleven pilots participating in three sections, as follows:[16]

2nd Sweep, Ramrod 1246, 30 August 1944				
Pilot	Serial	Section	Up	Down
Benham, Douglas I.	MB850	Red		
Stowe, William N.	MB862			
Balasse, Maurice A. L.	EN609			
Henry, David V. J.	EN226	Blue	19:45	20:46
Ware, James P.	EN228			
Fisher, Douglas P.	MB836			
Graham, Peter B.	MB831			
Spencer, Terence	MB882	Yellow		
Stevenson, Ian T.	EN229			
Harding, Ross P.	EN602			
Bradshaw, John T.	EN622			

The Squadron crossed in again over the Belgian coast at the same point, accompanied by 130 Squadron, but at an altitude of only 2,500-3,000 feet, due to a low 9/10ths cloud base. They were met by intense light Flak east of Roulers that had not been encountered on the first sweep, but fortunately it was inaccurate.

Once again, the pilots identified targets of opportunity and "everyone fired their guns".[17] A shorter trip this time, the pilots were back in Lympne just an hour later, but had expended 11,360 rounds of .303 and another 1,082 of 20mm ammunition for claims of five barges damaged north of Roulers, two tugs towing three barges each damaged east of Roulers, three large covered technical lorries damaged southeast of Roulers, two eight-ton Reichsbahn lorries and trailers destroyed in flames, one staff car damaged, and two railway wagons destroyed and 13 damaged (two smoking).[18]

130 Squadron arrived back just before 41, claiming for their part strikes on lock gates and six barges on a canal, and on 20 railway wagons, three of which emitted black smoke. It had been a busy afternoon and evening for the Lympne based squadrons' pilots and ground crews, but all the pilots had returned home safely, and only minor Flak damage was found on three of 41 Squadron's aircraft.[19] It had been a successful day.

31 August 1944 – The day started cloudy with frequent showers and thunderstorms, which restricted flying to non-operational air tests, and seven pilots who practiced air-to-air gunnery. These men flew a total of 30 minutes each and fired 1,200 rounds of .303 and 240 of 20mm.

By lunchtime, however, conditions had improved significantly and Flt Lt 'Jack' Henry and Flt Sgt Bob Fleming took off as Blue Section (Henry EN226 & Fleming MB880) at 12:20 for a Weather Reconnaissance flight that took them clockwise around the towns of Ghent [Gent] in Belgium, and Lille and Calais in France.

On their way out, travelling northwest towards Calais, the pair spotted a locomotive at St. Omer and dived down to attack it. Firing 273 rounds of .303 and 78 of 20mm, the pilots damaged it to what they considered Category B status.

Henry and Fleming landed back at Lympne at 13:15, reporting their victory, and 5/10th cumulus cloud between 3,000 and 7,000 feet. They considered visibility at 15 miles, though poorer to the south.

It was good enough for 11 Group and an operation similar to the previous day's sweeps was laid on in the afternoon and evening. Between 14:47 and 21:30, nine Spitfire squadrons were sent to strafe road, rail and canal movements in the area formed by the towns of Ghent, Calais and Aulnoye. The following squadrons participated:

11 Group Armed Reconnaissances, 31 August 1944					
No.	Area	Unit	Aircraft	Up	Down
1	East of Lille	41 Squadron[20]	12 Spitfire XII	14:45	16:05
2	West of Lille	130 Squadron	8 Spitfire XIV	14:47	15:50
3	Calais-Ghent	64 Squadron	31 Spitfire IX	18:14	20:01
4		126 Squadron			
5		611 Squadron			
6	Lens	124 Squadron	22 Spitfire IX	18:45	20:30
7		303 Squadron (1 MIA)			
8	Calais-Ghent	91 Squadron	25 Spitfire IX	19:29	21:06
9		322 Squadron			

41 Squadron was airborne at 14:45 in three sections, each aircraft fitted with a 30-gallon jettison tank. They climbed to 10,000 feet as they reached the French coast, and then dropped below the 6/10ths cloud base at 3,000 feet once they reached the target area, to commence their attacks.[21]

Armed Recce, 31 Aug 1944	Serial	Section	Up	Down
Spencer, Terence	MB850	Yellow		
Chattin, Peter W.	MB862			
Stowe, William N.	EN602			
Coleman, Patrick T.	EN625			
Fisher, Douglas P.	MB853	Blue	14:45	16:05
Gray, Eric	EN228			
Anderson, Robert E.	EN238			
Ware, James P.	MB831			
Gray, Colin F.	NR	Red		
Balasse, Maurice A. L.	EN609			
Rossow, Vivian J.	MB880			
Irvine, John	MB836			

Finding a stationary locomotive in the Lille area with its steam up, they attacked and damaged it to Cat. B status. Rounding Lille from the south and turning north-westward, the pilots destroyed a five-ton covered lorry, leaving it in flames, and shot up a car, three 3-ton lorries and a barge on a canal at Armentières, then crossed into Belgian airspace and turned north to head out, damaging nine covered railway wagons at Roulers [Roeselare], Menin [Menen] and Dixmude [Diksmuide], ten railway trucks at Dixmude, and six lorries at Menin, Roulers and Poperinghe [Poperinge].[22]

41 Squadron crossed back out safely and returned to Lympne at 16:05, beaten home by 130 Squadron by a few minutes, with their own list of claims. The squadrons' aircraft were refuelled and rearmed, and the pilots were then briefed for another show in the evening in unison with each other.

The units were ordered on an armed Crossbow Reconnaissance to locate long range rockets and associated railways in the Béthune-Hesdin-St. Omer area of France. This is the first time in over a year that 41 Squadron was involved in the hunt for the V2 Rocket, which the Allies knew about, but which had not yet been used in an attack on the United Kingdom.

Twelve aircraft from 41 Squadron were allocated the task of sweeping the perimeter of the area formed by the towns, whilst seven aircraft from 130 Squadron were tasked with sweeping inside this perimeter. They were airborne at 19:25, with 41 Squadron in three sections of four pilots led by Sqn Ldr Benham.

The two squadrons reached the target area without incident, swept and re-swept their designated zones, and returned to Lympne between 20:30 and 20:35. Conditions were not ideal for the operation and all they sighted was a lorry travelling northeast on the St. Pol-Béthune road at great speed, and eight or nine barges near the railway station at Watten at 20:00, but none of these was attacked.

> *Results were not good owing to cloud, and the position of the sun was a handicap. Apart from a quantity of flak, the trip was uneventful.*[23]

It was an anti-climactic end to a long, busy and intensive month. However, things were only beginning to warm up and much awaited them in the next three months. The first week of September would prove to be an expensive but exciting few days. And yet, they would be just a taste of things to come. The ensuing three months saw 41 Squadron heavily involved in a number of major operations on the Continent, most notably Big Ben/Crossbow operations, Operation *Market Garden*, Walcheren and the campaign against German oil targets.

September 1944 – No operational flying was undertaken on fourteen days – 2, 4-9, 13, 15, 21-22, 24-25, and 28 September. The weather was often unsuitable for operations, but a few days were also non-operational whilst the Squadron re-equipped with the Spitfire XIV. On each of the remaining 14 days, the Squadron participated in armed reconnaissance operations to Crossbow Targets, Operation *Market Garden*, operations over Walcheren, and the Squadron's first operations over German territory of the War. Following is a summary of 41 Squadron's operations this month:

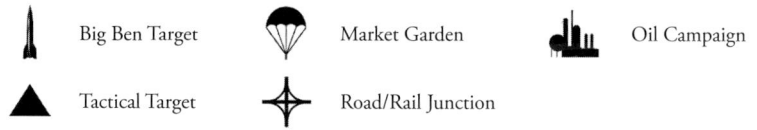

Date	Operation	Role	Type	Destination / Target
1	Armed Crossbow Recce.		🚀	St. Omer, France-Gent, Belgium area
1	Armed Crossbow Recce.		🚀	Lumbres-St. Omer-Béthune-Hesdin, Fr.
1	Armed Crossbow Recce.		🚀	St. Omer-Béthune-Hesdin area, France
3	Armed Crossbow Recce.		🚀	Ieper-Proven, Belgium
3	Ranger A10		▲	Koksijde-Liège-Knokke, Belgium
3	Ranger A17		▲	Koksijde-Liège-Knokke, Belgium

10	Armed Crossbow Recce.		🚀	Den Haag-Rotterdam-Walcheren, NL
10	Armed Crossbow Recce.		🚀	NW Belgium-Walcheren, NL area
11	Ramrod 1271	Target Cover	▲	Breskens-Vlissingen, Netherlands
11	Ramrod 1272	Reconnaissance	🚀	Noord & Zuid Beveland Islands, NL
12	Ramrod 1275	Reconnaissance	🚀	Den Haag-Katwijk area, Netherlands
12	Escort to B-17 Flying Fortress		🚀	Dutch coast
14	Escort to B-17 Flying Fortress		🚀	Dutch coast
16	Armed Crossbow Recce.		🚀	Haag-Leiden-Noordwijk, Netherlands
17	Withdrawal Escort		🪂	North Sea
18	Anti-Flak Patrol		🪂	s-Hertogenbosch, Netherlands
19	Escort and Anti-Flak Patrol		🪂	S of Geel, Belgium
20	Escort and Anti-Flak Patrol		🪂	Leopoldsburg, Belgium
23	Escort		🪂	Eindhoven, Netherlands
26	Escort and Target Cover		🪂	SW of Nijmegen, NL
27	Rodeo 404	Sweep	▲	Katwijk-Hengelo-Overflakkee, NL
29	Ramrod 1301	Escort	✦	Geldern, Germany
30	Ramrod 1302	Support & Sweep	🏭	Bottrop & Sterkrade, Germany
30	Ramrod 1304	Escort	✦	Goch, Germany

The V2 Rocket and Operation Big Ben

The German V2 Rocket was the world's first long-range ballistic missile, and the antecedent of all modern-day rockets. Serious rocket research had begun in Germany in the early 1930s, mostly based on the work of American physicist and scientist Robert Goddard. Their first physical tests took place in 1934 when projectiles were successfully fired to altitudes of 2,200 and 3,500 metres.

By 1936, the *Aggregat* series of rockets, also known as the 'A Series', had commenced construction. However, aerodynamic stability issues in earlier models led to a plan to build the A-4, a much larger rocket with a 25-tonne thrust, by the early 1940s. With the War now in full swing, the Nazi leadership invested heavily in the project and a research centre was established at Peenemünde to bring together Germany's greatest minds and overcome the issues in creating reliable gyroscopic guidance, liquid-fuel rocket engines, and supersonic aerodynamics.

Although the project was considered almost complete by September 1943, it would be another twelve months before sufficient launch facilities could be built, and adequate reserves of rockets stockpiled; by mid-September 1944, 1,900 had been constructed.

A-4 'V2' Rocket Vital Statistics

Height/Length	14 metres (45 ft 11 in)
Diameter	1.65 metres (5 ft 5 in)
Wingspan	3.56 metres (11 ft 8 in)
Weight	12,500kg (28,000 lb)
Maximum Speed	5,760 kmph (3,580 mph)
Maximum Altitude	206km (128 miles) vertically
Range	320km (200 miles)
Warhead	980kg (2,200 lb) Amatol
Propellant	3,810kg (8,400 lb) of 75% ethanol / 25% water, plus 4,910kg (10,800 lb) of liquid oxygen

As a result of the both the altitude and speeds attainable by the V2 – technically the A-4 – it was practically invulnerable to Allied aircraft or ground based weaponry at the time. It was therefore felt that the only way the V2 threat could be beaten would be to attack the launch sites along the Channel coast.

The Allies became aware of the V2 project as early as August 1943, when Bomber Command sent almost 600 Lancasters, Halifaxes, and Stirlings to attack the German rocket research centre at Peenemünde, thereby delaying the project by an estimated two months.

During 1943, the Germans began construction on a heavily fortified static launch pad at Éperlecques in the Pas-de-Calais region of France. However, the Allies spotted the site almost immediately and systematic bombing from August 1943 to August 1944 forced its abandonment. The Germans also commenced construction of another launch site, in a quarry at nearby La Coupole, but it, too, was bombed until it could no longer be utilised.

Construction was then started on a third site near Cherbourg, but the Allies found and destroyed it, too. This forced the Germans to devise a system of mobile launch pads, in which both rockets and launchers were towed by trucks, and transported by railway, that could be moved at will and hidden in sites such as forests, which became a favourite launch location. It became an Allied priority to destroy supply lines and launch sites, and whilst all operations against German flying bombs became known codenamed *Crossbow*, all events specifically dealing with the V2 menace earned the codename *Big Ben*.

These codenames also helped maintain security on the Home Front, and it was not until 10 November that Prime Minister Winston Churchill even announced to the House of Commons that the country was under attack by this 'new' weapon.[24] This was two months after the first launch, and after the German High Command had issued their own announcement, by which time about one hundred V2s had fallen in the United Kingdom.

41 Squadron participated in *Crossbow* and assisted in the search for V2 sites in France and the Netherlands during the first half of September 1944. As such, their involvement was over before the public even knew of the V2's existence.

1 September 1944 – Early rain, clearing to generally fine weather with broken cloud and good visibility. The Squadron was involved in three separate armed reconnaissances today.[25] It was an

early start for the first, and the men were briefed at 06:00 for a trip to the St. Omer-Ghent [Gent] area. However, it would be a messy start to the month.

Twelve pilots participated in the armed reconnaissance, but delays and jettison tank trouble caused "a ragged take-off",[26] which saw five aircraft from A Flight and one from B Flight airborne at 06:50, five from B Flight airborne at 07:10, and the final pilot from A Flight, Fg Off 'Jackie' Fisher, not airborne until 07:35.

Composite sections and pairs then formed for the operation, and the pilots headed across the Channel for the target area where they found 6/10ths cloud at 6,000 feet, but good visibility below this level. Despite the initial confusion, the Squadron enjoyed significant success against ground targets, however they lost Fg Off Peter Graham, who was shot down by Flak.

Red Section's Sqn Ldr Benham, Flt Lt Bill Stowe and Sgt Plt John Irvine attacked 13 railway wagons and a locomotive in sidings west of Menin [Menen], Belgium. The locomotive was left steaming from the front with what they considered Cat. B damage, whilst one of the wagons burst into flames and another was left smoking. They also damaged four open railway wagons and two passenger coaches in Menin Station. Stowe and Stevenson also sighted five railway wagons at Waergham (vH9765) which were hooped and covered with camouflaged canvas, but these were not attacked.

Flt Lt 'Jack' Henry, Plt Off 'Ricky' Gray and WO Peter Chattin were flying together near Cassel, just south of the French-Belgian border, when they spotted a pair of lorries. Chattin dived down and attacked them, leaving them with presumed Cat. B damage. Fg Off 'Jackie' Fisher and Flt Sgt Pat Coleman then spotted an 80-foot barge on a canal just north of Ypres [Ieper], which they attacked and damaged, and then damaged a locomotive on the line just northwest of Esquelbecq at vH2668 to Cat. B status. Fisher later reported having seen a house on fire at Winnezeele, France, and a whole train on fire a little further south at Cassel or Hazebrouck.

Blue Section's Fg Offs Peter Graham and 'Momo' Balasse also spotted three lorries. Flying up sun, Graham fired at the centre of the trio, and Balasse at the rear lorry. As they passed over the vehicles, however, they looked back to see that the centre lorry was actually a white vehicle with a large red cross, and it was on fire. They feared the worst, but then the lorry blew up with a large explosion. Realising by the size of the blast that its cargo therefore had nothing to do with medical supplies or evacuations, Balasse turned back and attacked the lead vehicle, too.

Moving on to find new targets, Graham and Balasse came upon a train on the Thielt [Tielt]-Deinze railway line.

> *In the train were eight of the flat trucks that had been described to us, each piled high with their 'telegraph poles'. Unfortunately there were not only trucks like these, but also an equal number of trucks which turned out to be flak wagons. I'm not sure of the numbers but my guess is that there were four anti-aircraft guns on each truck, making thirty-two guns in all. They were coupled in pairs: two V2 wagons followed by two flak wagons, with a guard's van at the rear.*[27]

They attacked the train at tree-top height from its flank, aiming at the driver's cabin and the engine. Their aim was straight, and the locomotive was damaged to Cat. B status, but Graham's aircraft was fatally hit by anti-aircraft fire.

> *I think my attack was effective for as I passed over the engine there was a great explosion. It was however quite impossible to say what hit my Spit because all the guns on the train were blazing away at me. Everything seemed to be OK as I roared away but in a very short time my engine temperature started to soar, so that I knew I was losing glycol fast. Without this coolant my engine would seize up in a matter of minutes.*
>
> *My Number Two was with me. I climbed steeply and headed northwest hoping I might be able to reach the sea, which I knew was swarming with the ships of the Royal Navy. It would, I thought, be easy enough to bale out over water and I'd soon be rescued. Stupidly, I made no attempt to report back by radio, giving the map reference of the stopped train. Instead, when my engine seized up, I simply said 'Give my love to my true*

love and say I'll be all right.' I put the nose down to ensure I wouldn't stall and had time to trim the aircraft so that I was descending straight ahead. Then I undid my safety harness, pulled back the cockpit hood, rolled the Spit over and fell out.[28]

The last fix on Graham was a broad one: north of St. Omer to south of Coxyde [Koksijde].

The rest of the pilots returned to Lympne independently, in pairs or in sections, the first putting down at 08:00 and the last at 08:45. They had expended 8,448 rounds of .303 calibre ammunition and 1,820 rounds of 20mm.

Pilots, 06:50 Armed Reconnaissance, 1 September 1944				
Pilot	Serial	Section	Up	Down
Benham, Douglas I.	MB850	Red	06:50	08:00
Irvine, John	EN625			
Stowe, William N.	MB862			
Stevenson, Ian T.	EN229			
Gray, Eric	EN228	Yellow	07:10	
Fisher, Douglas P.	EN615		07:35	08:45
Chattin, Peter W.	EN622		07:10	08:15
Coleman, Patrick T.	EN238		06:50	08:10
Henry, David J. V.	MB856	Blue	07:10	08:00
Ware, James P.	MB853		06:50	08:10
Graham, Peter B.	MB831		07:10	FTR
Balasse, Maurice A. L.	EN609			08:10

Peter Graham was immediately captured by two Wehrmacht soldiers riding a motorcycle and sidecar, and was marched to the village of Esquelbecq.[29] He was taken to the town hall, where he was briefly interrogated by a German Officer, then locked in an attic overnight. The following day, he was loaded onto a truck and driven to Düsseldorf via Bruges [Bruggen] in a convoy of four vehicles, and then put on a train to Dulag Luft in Frankfurt.

Graham's experience on being captured was likely to have been similar to that laid out below. It is a translation of a German document dated late August 1944, which explains instructions for dealing with downed Allied pilots immediately after their capture.

a) Immediately after capture, the prisoner's official and personal property (maps, letters, note books, cheque books, pay books, leave passes, railway tickets, mess bills, photographs, escape kits, money, both identity discs, etc.) with the exception of rings and watches must be removed. The confiscated articles must be kept as separate batches, according to their owners.

b) The enemy crew must immediately be taken away from their aircraft and any other equipment. All communication between prisoners must be prevented.

c) Any attempt on the part of the crew to destroy the captured equipment or documents must be countered by all possible means.

d) In order to determine the crashed aircraft to which individual P/W belong, it is permissible to question individual prisoners about their aircraft, colleagues, etc. If necessary, pressure may be brought to bear on prisoners, assumption of sabotage even, so as to force him to give information which can lead to the rapid capture of the other members of the crew.

e) *All personal conversation with P/W is forbidden. They must be treated in such a way that they are neither embittered by unnecessary severity, nor spoilt by excessive friendliness, and thus rendered unreceptive to small concessions during interrogation. Prisoners who are treated in too friendly a manner on capture and on the journey, lose the discipline inculcated by British propaganda and frequently become arrogant and "cocky".*

f) *If members of crews are taken prisoner near the scene of the crash, it is advisable to hand them over, with the articles confiscated from them, to the crash officer of the Fliegerhorst (station) who will take them to the Fliegerhorst.*

g) *The prisoners must be carefully watched until their arrival at Dulag Luft. Any peculiarities observed must be reported by the escort on handing over the prisoner at Dulag Luft.*[30]

Following his interrogation at Dulag Luft, Graham was sent to Stalag Luft I at Barth, where he was held until his liberation on 1 May 1945.[31] Though his capture was assumed by 41 Squadron, this fact was not actually confirmed until a telex was received at Lympne from the Air Ministry on 28 November, stating,

TELEGRAM FROM IRCC QUOTING GERMAN INFORMATION STATES 1SPE [sic] *161780 F/O PB GRAHAM CAPTURED. RECLASSIFIED PRISONER OF WAR KINFORMED.*[32]

Let us now return to 1 September 1944. At 09:30, the Squadron was briefed for the day's second operation, a sweep over rocket sites with orders to "shoot up any targets that presented themselves".[33] Eleven pilots were airborne at 10:00, led by Sqn Ldr Benham, but barely had they crossed in at Gravelines than the weather forced them to abort the sweep. Turning about 180°, they flew home again and put down at Lympne at 10:40, where they remained another nine hours.

At 19:30, eight pilots were briefed for an armed reconnaissance to the St. Omer-Béthune-Hesdin area. They were airborne at 19:56, led by Sqn Ldr Benham, and crossed in at Gravelines again. On this occasion, instead of poor weather, however, they were met by heavy Flak just north of St. Omer and Flt Lt Terry Spencer's aircraft was hit in the tail. Fortunately, it only caused light damage and he was able to continue flying.

Fg Off Peter Graham was shot down by Flak during an attack on a train-load of V2s and was captured near St. Omer, France, on 1 September 1944. He spent the remainder of the War behind wire and married his sweetheart ten days after being repatriated in May 1945.
© Peter Graham

Blue Section, led by Spencer, then attacked and damaged four barges south of St. Omer, after which all eight pilots attacked a goods train at Armentières, and six locomotives and six railway wagons south of Ypres. Flt Lt Harding then destroyed three ammunition trucks, which blew up a quarter mile southwest of Ypres, and fired at a railway engine shed, resulting in a bright flash inside, suggesting he had ignited petrol or oil.

The pilots also made some interesting observations during the reconnaissance, which they reported back as a potential Crossbow target. They very accurately described what they saw…

…in a ploughed and harrowed square field. Two large round haystacks and 6 to 8 cylindrical objects 40 to 50 ft. long lying haphazard about the field with lorry tracks between each. Light flak was fired at our aircraft while making observations. This field was S.E. of Ypres over one railway bridge and short of the second railway line at 50° 51 N 2° 54 E.[34]

They also noted large fires burning at Lille and Armentières.

The Squadron returned to Lympne without further ado, and Red Section touched down at 21:15. However, before Blue Section could pancake, ten aircraft from 127 Squadron cut in from operations on the Continent without R/T notification, and landed ahead of them. However, two of 127's pilot collided whilst doing so, resulting in the death of one and injury of the other, and blocked the runway with half of 41 Squadron still airborne.[35]

Terry Spencer, Bill Stowe, Pete Chattin & I are left airborne in the dark with practically no petrol. Those three are together, I am alone & thus ready to bale out at a moment's notice. We proceed to Manston & land (luck with us) all O.K. – a shaky evening, I feel whacked with this as [it was] *the third operation I've done today.*[36]

The quartet landed at Manston at 21:20, and subsequently stayed the night.

Armed Recce, 1 Sep 1944	Serial	Section	Up	Down
Benham, Douglas I.	EN238	Red	19:55	21:15
Bradshaw, John T.	EN609			
Stevenson, Ian T.	EN229			
Coleman, Patrick T.	MB857	Blue		21:20
Spencer, Terence	MB882			
Chattin, Peter W.	MB850			
Harding, Ross P.	EN602			21:15
Stowe, William N.	MB862			21:20

2 September 1944 – Having been stranded in Manston the night before, the remaining elements of the previous evening's armed reconnaissance, Flt Lts Terry Spencer and Bill Stowe, and WOs Peter Chattin, Pat Coleman and Peter Hale returned to Lympne at 10:00 this morning after a ten-minute flight.[37] Strong wind and storms stopped all other flying for the rest of the day.

3 September 1944 – Fine with high cloud, deteriorating during the afternoon to cloud below 1,000 feet with rain. There was similar weather to report on the Continent, providing a somewhat anti-climactic atmosphere in the Belgian capital Brussels, which was liberated by the advancing Allied armies today.

The day saw three operations carried out by 41 Squadron, although the first was almost abortive. Eight pilots were briefed at 11:00 with twelve from 130 Squadron for an armed Crossbow reconnaissance to the Ypres [Ieper] area. However, as a result of "various difficulties with tanks and one aircraft temporarily on fire"[38], only four aircraft became airborne with their 30-gallon jettison tanks for the operation at 11:35, approximately ten minutes behind 130 Squadron.

Pilots, Armed Crossbow Recce	Serial	Section	Up	Down
Henry, David J. V.	MB856	Blue	11:35	12:40
Rossow, Vivian J.	MB836			
Burne, Thomas R.	EN238			
Reid, Daniel J.	EN228			

130 had no luck locating Crossbow sites, but returned to Lympne at 12:25 claiming strikes on 20-30 mostly empty railway wagons west of Lumbres Station in the Pas-de-Calais region of northern France. 41 Squadron fared better. On their way in, at 11:45, the pilots observed a number of large explosions on the Mole on the eastern side of Calais Harbour, from 7,000 feet, which they assumed to be demolition work by the encircled German forces there.[39] Heading on into Belgium, they were unable to shoot up any Crossbow sites, but did identify one and reported that a "large pathway was seen for the first time through the forest East of Pruven [sic] with no signs of bombing".[40] It was later identified as a V1 storage and launch area, and taken care of.

However, not satisfied with returning home without any action, they damaged three out of ten barges seen north of Ypres, and damaged 20 covered railway wagons at Proven, west-northwest of Ypres, expending 2,512 rounds of .303 calibre and 610 of 20mm ammunition.

A Feisty Little Battle

Just before Blue section returned, however, a second operation was off the deck, under the command of Flt Lt Terry Spencer. The eight pilots were briefed at 11:30 for a deep penetration to the Liège area, titled Ranger A10, the object of which was simply "to clobber any Huns"[41] they encountered.

Pilots, Ranger A10	Serial	Section	Up	Down
Spencer, Terence	MB882	Black	12:30	14:45
Chattin, Peter W.	EN622			FTR
Stowe, William N.	EN602			14:45
Colman, Patrick T.	EN229			
Fisher, Douglas P.	EN615	White	12:35	
Fleming, Robert	MB857			
Balasse, Maurice A. L.	EN609			
Ware, James P.	MB853			

The pilots were airborne between 12:30 and 12:35, equipped with 90-gallon jettison tanks, and crossed the French coast over Gravelines at 12:50. They set their course for Liège at between 6,000 and 8,000 feet, and passed over Brussels on their way, where they observed large concentrations of enemy traffic heading towards the town. These were not attacked and the pilots continued to the Liège area, which they reached at 13:25 without incident.

Turning about, Spencer then intended to cross over Antwerp to the Dutch coast at Flushing [Vlissingen], then turn south and travel as far as Ostend [Oostende] searching for enemy transport, before crossing out and making a course for Ramsgate. At 13:30, Flt Lt Bill Stowe sighted some MET in the Louvain [Leuven] area, but as the cloud cover had by now built to 7/10ths cumulus between 4,500 and 6,000 feet, Spencer decided to leave White Section as top cover, and took

On 3 September 1944, Flt Lt Terry Spencer shot down 173-victory Luftwaffe Ace, Hptm Emil 'Bully' Lang, at Overhespen, Belgium.
© Terry Spencer, via Cara and Raina Spencer

Black Section down below the cloud base for a better look.[42] However, WO Pat Coleman then spotted a much more attractive target off to port: three FW190s flying east at just 1,000 feet.[43]

The aircraft were piloted by 173-victory Luftwaffe Ace Hptm. Emil 'Bully' Lang (No. 1), 52-victory Ace Lt. Alfred Gross (No. 2), and Uffz. Hans-Joachim Borreck (No. 3), all of Stab II./JG26, who had taken off from Brussels-Melsbroek at 13:20 on a transfer flight to Düsseldorf, in the next move of JG26's retreat. Most of the Geschwader's pilots had already departed, but Lang was held up by problems with his aircraft, and was last to take off with his two wingmen. Shortly after becoming airborne, however, Lang realised he also had undercarriage trouble, and it took him ten minutes to retract his wheels. The trio were therefore still at very low altitude and extremely vulnerable when spotted by 41 Squadron.

Being in the perfect position to bounce them, Spencer tally-hoed and the section dived with him onto their prey. Having the advantages of height and not having been seen, Spencer went straight in after Lang on the port side, ordering Black 2 – WO Peter Chattin – to attack the starboard aircraft, flown by Gross. The third Focke-Wulf broke to starboard, but things suddenly got messy. As Spencer attacked Lang, Gross got on his tail and immediately opened fire. Bullets struck Spencer's starboard wing and elevator, and he took abrupt evasive action, pulling hard to port.

Losing Gross in the process, Spencer looked around and saw that Lang had made the error of pulling away to port, too, and closed once again. He opened fire with 1½ rings deflection and scored strikes, which resulted in the 190's undercarriage dropping. Significantly slowed by this damage, Spencer took his opportunity and fired again. This time, flame spewed from the port side of the engine cowling and the aircraft dived straight in, exploding on impact. His ammunition expenditure on his target was 220 rounds of .303 and 840 rounds of 20mm.

Taking stock of the situation, Spencer looked around in time to see "a Spitfire XII go in nearby with a pilot descending by parachute close by".[44] In the mêlée, Spencer had heard Chattin over the R/T stating that "he had thought he got one"[45] but moments later was seen with smoke issuing from his own aircraft and was heard again, reporting he would have to bale out, but gave no reason. However, it appears he decided not to bale out after all, as he "made a good wheels up landing… and later caught fire"[46] near Tirlemont. It is now apparent that whilst Spencer was occupied with the Lang, Gross had broken away and attacked Chattin whilst he was attempting to

WO Peter Chattin damaged the FW190 of Uffz Hans-Joachim Borreck near Overhespen, Belgium, on 3 September 1944, but minutes later was shot down and killed by Lt Alfred Gross at Neerhespen. © Mike Chattin & Liz Irving

engage Borreck. This is also confirmed by WO Coleman, who recorded in his diary, "…the second in course of the dogfight shot down Pete and damaged Terry's tail unit."[47]

Flt Lt Bill Stowe and Coleman then went after Gross, executing wingover turns to attack him head on. Stowe fired a deflection shot but saw no strikes as the FW190 passed underneath him. Coleman then opened fire on the aircraft at a range of 500-600 feet, which resulted in Gross initially diving and then pulling up vertically before Coleman's nose. He later reported…

> *I kept firing, pulling back on the stick first with a ring & a half then pulling through him as he showed me his underside at less than 30 yards. The aircraft continued vertically* [then] *stalled.*[48]

Coleman lost sight of the FW190 for an instant, then looked back to see it dive vertically to the ground and explode on impact. He and Stowe also saw a pilot descending by parachute, but Borreck escaped to the north at tree-top level.

These three actions – Spencer's FW190, Chattin's loss, and Stowe and Coleman's FW190 – appear to have all occurred simultaneously, as Spencer reported seeing three aircraft burning on the ground and a pilot descending by parachute, which he assumed to have been Chattin. This is also supported by a Biggin Hill Sector Intelligence Report for the day[49], which states that Chattin's belly landing was seen to have taken place near the two crashed FW190s.

Seeing a nearby motorised convoy of approximately 40 vehicles travelling eastwards, and considering the amount of light Flak being fired at them from the area of the village, Spencer considered Chattin would soon be picked up. He therefore regrouped with White Section and headed home, arriving back in Lympne one man down at 14:45. Chattin was officially reported to have baled out but was believed safe.

However, whilst the claim of two FW190s for the loss of one pilot seems straight forward on face value, it is by no means so clear cut. First and foremost, WO Chattin did not survive, contrary to the belief at the time, but moreover, whilst Lang was killed, Gross survived, having baled out of his aircraft. This implies that Chattin did not bale out at all, and remained in his aircraft for the belly-landing that was observed. It is likely, therefore, that he was killed in doing so, particularly as his aircraft was later seen to on be fire: "The three aircraft were seen burning on the ground near Tirlemont"[50], states one Intelligence Report, and it is believed that all three came down within a kilometre of each other. As such, the pilot seen descending by parachute was clearly Gross, not Chattin, as had been believed and reported.

Flt Lt Spencer's opponent was Lang, who was flying FW190A-5, WkNr 150 1240, Green 1. His observation of Lang's undercarriage falling when he attacked makes more sense when one considers the trouble Lang was having with it only minutes before. The 35-year-old German Ace was killed instantly when his aircraft came down near the village of Overhespen, almost mid-way between Tirlemont [Tienen] and St. Trond [Sint Truiden], and around 40km east of Brussels. He is believed to be buried today amongst the unknowns in the German cemetery at Lommel.

Gross' aircraft, FW190A-8, WkNr 171 569, Green 4, was claimed destroyed by Coleman[51], but the German pilot's survival, although seriously wounded and unable to return to active service, meant that he was able to make a claim for one Spitfire destroyed 7km east of Tirlemont. This clearly fits with Chattin's loss. Gross survived the War but died of Tuberculosis on 19 August 1947.

It also appears that Borreck's aircraft had indeed been hit by Chattin (he claimed he had 'got one') as his canopy became covered in oil, and he made a forced landing at a nearby airfield.[52] Although he survived the incident unscathed, Borreck was subsequently killed in action on 6 November 1944.

Researchers in the Brabant area of Belgium have since sought to shed more light on 41 Squadron's encounter with Lang, Gross and Borreck. One interviewed a witness of the dogfight in Overhespen who recalled hearing machine gun fire and went outside to see the two FW190s hitting the ground. They were followed a short time later by a parachutist, and then a Spitfire circling slowly to a forced landing. He did not see the Spitfire pilot bale out.

The village was still occupied by the Germans at the time, and they also saw the combat. Another witness recalled that the German troops opened fire on the man descending by parachute, not realising it was actually Lt. Gross. It is believed they hit him and he landed, seriously wounded, near the village church; he never flew again.

Some of the folk from the village later saw German soldiers carrying WO Chattin to his first place of burial. He had apparently suffered a major injury to the head, which they assumed to have been his cause of death. He was wrapped in his parachute and buried near the village church at map reference K101476.

A week after the village's liberation, the townsfolk held a funeral service for Chattin, which was attended by the whole village. His grave was surrounded with a wooden railing, and a cross and flowers were added. They tended his grave until July 1947, when Allied authorities exhumed his body and reinterred him in Grave III.C.13 of Geel War Cemetery in Antwerp, where he rests today.

The last page of Peter Chattin's logbook was completed by Pat Coleman, who recorded that Chattin had been flying EN622, EB-J, "Offensive Sweep – Liège. Baled out Tirlemont 1.40pm".[53] The Squadron initially believed that Chattin had come down safely, and expected to hear soon that he had become a Prisoner of War. However, it was not until almost three months later, on 23 November, that word finally reached the Squadron of Chattin's fate; it was not the news that had been expecting to hear. Aged just 23, he left behind a young wife, a four-year-old son and a nine-month-old daughter.

WO Pat Coleman claimed his first of several victories against the Luftwaffe on 3 September 1944, when he shot down 52-victory Luftwaffe Ace, Lt Alfred Gross, at Overhespen, Belgium.
© Peter Cowell, via Dan Johnson

The two destroyed FW190s on 3 September 1944 constituted not only Spencer and Coleman's first air-to-air victories, but in fact the only aircraft destroyed by 41 Squadron all year. Moreover, they constituted the last air to air victories in a Spitfire XII. Coleman wrote proudly in his diary today,

> *Spencer & I are the only ones at present in the squadron who can claim to have shot down one of* [the Squadron's] *159* [destroyed enemy aircraft], *though some other members have scored with former squadrons.*[54]

The 11 Group ORB also hailed the operation as the Group's "most successful… Ranger"[55] of the day.

However, the pilots were unable to rest long. As a result of Spencer and Coleman's successes in Ranger A10, Wg Cdr Gray decided to put on a Wing operation during the early evening to Coxyde [Koksijde], Liège and Knokke, titled Ranger A17.

Eleven pilots from 41 Squadron and twelve from 130 Squadron were briefed at 16:45 and were airborne between 17:30 and 17:40 fitted with 30-gallon jettison tanks. However, they found 10/10ths cloud at 5,000 feet over the Continent, accompanied by drizzle, and decided to abandon the operation. They returned home, landing back at Lympne between 18:05 and 18:10, and this concluded the day's flying.

WO Coleman took a train to Redhill to see his wife that evening, and the train-ride gave him time to process the day's activity, though not necessarily for the better. He penned in his diary,

> *After thoughts:– Poor devil – God, his relations! – Think of the many you must have killed whilst ground-strafing. Doesn't bear much thinking about! Those Belgian houses – oh dear, this is a disease we've all contracted.*[56]

Sobering thoughts.

5 September 1944 – Cloudy with gusty winds and occasional showers. With the exception of an air test undertaken by Flt Lt Ross Harding, and two cross-country flights made by Flt Lt 'Tommy' Burne and Fg Off 'Momo' Balasse, no flying was undertaken by 41 Squadron today. There was also no operational flying for 130 Squadron. The reason for the inactivity, explains the ORB, was "…Allied Armies advancing so fast that the targets open to us were overrun by the time we could lay on a decent show."[57]

6 September 1944 – In similar conditions to the previous day, 41 Squadron undertook no operational flying, although 130 Squadron was airborne in squadron strength for a successful anti-Flak reconnaissance over the Overflakkee and Arnhem areas. 41 Squadron's flying for the day was limited to Flt Lt Terry Spencer and Flt Sgt 'Jack' Bradshaw from A Flight undertaking an air test and a cross-country flight, respectively, and Fg Off Jimmy Payne and 'Jackie' Fisher of B Flight doing a little local flying.

8 September 1944 – Once again, no operational flying was made by the Squadron, however "'A' Flight suddenly got a bit keen and organised some cross country flying in formation".[58] This was undertaken by Flt Lt Ross Harding and WO Peter Hale as Red Section, and Flt Lt Bill Stowe and Flt Sgt 'Jack' Bradshaw as Yellow Section. Separately, Sqn Ldr Benham flew to Manston and stayed overnight, and this constituted the day's total flying.

The long-awaited and much-feared V2 was launched against the Allies for the first time today when a rocket landed and exploded in Porte d'Italie, a suburb of Paris, causing minor damage. A few hours later, a second was fired from The Hague area, which hit Staveley Road in Chiswick, London, killing three and injuring 17. With the launch of the world's first long range ballistic missile today, mankind was thrust into a new era in science and technology.

A V2 rocket with a transportation trailer ('Meillerwagen'), preparing for a mobile launch. © Public domain, U.S. Air Force Photo, via the National Museum of the U.S. Air Force

9 September 1944 – Fair to fine with broken cloud and good visibility. Although no operational flying was undertaken by 41 Squadron today, Wg Cdr Gray, Flt Lt 'Jack' Henry, Flt Lt 'Denny' Reid and Fg Off 'Momo' Balasse flew to Brussels for the day, which was a one-way trip of approximately 45 minutes.

It was a special trip for Balasse, a Belgian from Brussels, who had not been home for several years as a result of the War. In the hope of finding his family, he brought with him several gifts, including soap and food, and other items in short supply. Whilst Gray and Reid did not land, Henry and Balasse did, however Henry suffered a mishap in doing so when one of the tyres of his aircraft, MB856, burst on landing. The aircraft stopped suddenly and tipped on its nose, which resulted in Henry hitting his head on the front of the cockpit and seriously lacerating his forehead.

Balasse, on the other hand, made a perfect landing and stepped out onto his home soil for the first time in almost two-and-a-half years. He raced to find his family and returned to Lympne again that evening "…having found his wife and daughter in fine fettle after being under Nazi occupation since 1940. 'Maurice' is now a very happy man."[49]

Separately, back at Lympne, A Flight carried out a full-day training programme, which included twelve sorties of formation flying, dive bombing and bouncing practice. Sqn Ldr Benham also returned from Manston.

10 September 1944 – Fine, with well broken cloud at 3,000 feet, and good visibility. Between 08:25 and 20:35, with the exception of a break between 12:00 and 13:00, eighteen 11 Group squadrons – totalling 172 Spitfires and 24 Tempests – undertook armed reconnaissance flights in the Netherlands, north of the front line, with a particular emphasis on seeking out and attacking Big Ben targets.

The Lympne Wing was involved in these and flew to RAF Coltishall at 12:20, led by Wg Cdr Gray, as this was to be the starting point for the operation. The pilots landed at 12:25 and whilst they ate lunch and were briefed, the aircraft were refuelled and readied.

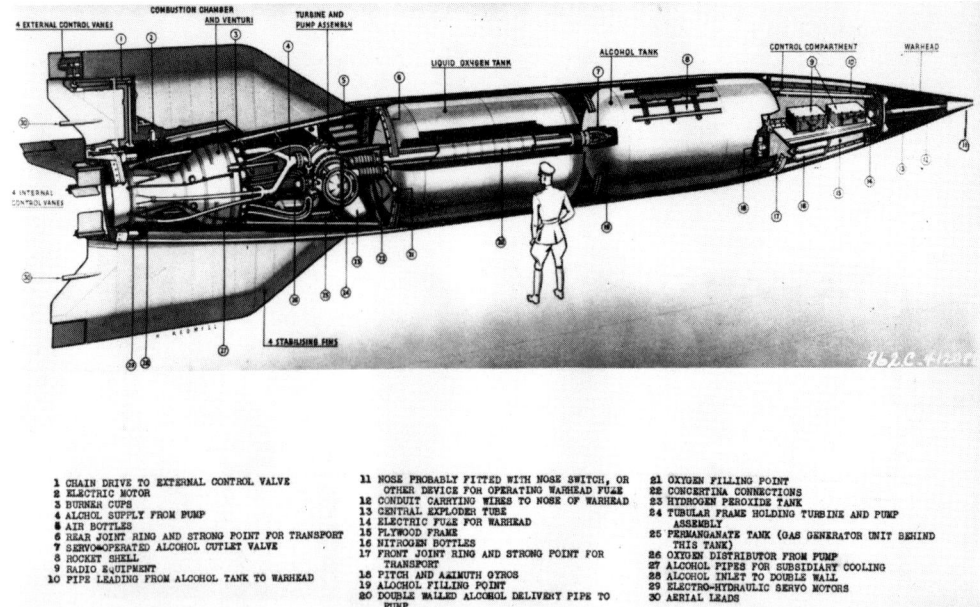

Cutaway drawing of a V2 rocket, showing engine, fuel cells, guidance units and warhead. © Public domain, U.S. Air Force Photo, via the National Museum of the U.S. Air Force

The Wing was airborne again at 15:15, with Wg Cdr Gray leading 11 aircraft of 41 Squadron and Sqn Ldr Tripe leading ten aircraft of 130 Squadron. The pilots flew across the Channel on the deck until within sight of the Dutch coast, at which point they climbed to 8,000 feet, and crossed in between Katwijk and Zandvoort.

The Wing then split in two, 41 Squadron turning south and flying a route which took them between The Hague [Den Haag] and Rotterdam. They spotted two holes approximately five feet in diameter in a wood on the western side of a road leading south from The Hague, and also noted two Kriegsmarine minesweepers travelling in a westerly direction down a canal west of Schiedam, one of which had a balloon tethered above it. The vessels were not attacked on account of the concentrated, though inaccurate, light Flak fired at them from the ships and batteries at Schiedam.

The pilots continued on a route that took them over Walcheren Island, and then set course for Lympne again, putting down at 16:55. The Squadron's American Sgt Plt 'Jack' Bradshaw recalled the operation many years later,

[We were sent on a] *secret mission from Coltishall where we were briefed to take off when notified, cross the channel on the deck, then climb to 500' when we hit the coast, fly three minutes, turn around and return to base. When we returned, we were told that we should never mention the operation. I learned a number of years later that it was to test the accuracy of the underground's information as to when the missile would be launched, so that they could send the Typhoons out to destroy them on the pad. The V-2 mission was on 10 September (1944) and was called Project Big Ben.*[60]

130 Squadron had more success that day. Soon after crossing in near Zandvoort and orbiting to starboard, Sqn Ldr Tripe spotted what he thought to be the type of Big Ben target they were seeking, approximately four miles south-southeast of Zandvoort. Descending for a better view, he observed…

…*tunnel entrances on the south side of the target which was of peculiar formation – a series of tunnel entrances to a hill, the concrete doorways from the tunnels facing onto a concrete road similar in shape to a horseshoe.*[61]

As there was almost no Flak to speak of, and no enemy aircraft around, the unit went down and attacked the site. Satisfied with their work, they headed directly for home and beat 41 Squadron in by ten minutes.

This ended 130 Squadron's flying for the day, but 41 Squadron was airborne again at 19:15 on a similar operation in the north-western Belgium and Walcheren, Netherlands, areas. The operation consisted of eight pilots, led by Sqn Ldr Benham, who headed across the Channel at zero feet again on a course for Ostend [Oostende]. On sighting the coast, they climbed to 8,000 feet again and crossed in straight over Ostend.

The pilots sighted many fires south of Bruges and headed inland straight for Ghent [Gent]. Once there, they turned north and flew up the canal towards Terneuzen, where they came under attack from light but inaccurate Flak. A Kriegsmarine destroyer or light cruiser and two Siebel ferries[62] were spotted docked in Terneuzen but these were not attacked; instead the pilots turned west and headed up the Scheldt River to Flushing.

Ten small ferries and twelve large fishing boats were seen on the river and two 1,000-ton merchant ships were observed in dock at Flushing. Once again, the pilots changed course, heading roughly north to Veere on the northern side of Walcheren Island, on the way coming under fire from rocket Flak just east of Middelburg. They were unaffected and reached Veere without trouble, where they sighted two 1,000-ton coasters.

Once again, the pilots changed course, this time heading west back across Walcheren Island. They came under heavy Flak as they did so but, reaching the coast again, set course for home, where they landed at 20:35. This concluded the day's flying.

Separately, Australian Flt Lt John 'Jack' Refshauge returned to the Squadron from sick leave and ground duties today, following his wounding in a friendly fire incident near Cherbourg on 9 June [See Chapter 5]. Having been absent for three months, Refshauge had missed the entire V1 onslaught, and returned to find a new Commanding Officer and several other personnel changes that had occurred in the meantime.

RAF Lympne also received advice from 11 Group Headquarters today that 610 Squadron and 6610 Servicing Echelon would be moving from Friston to Lympne on 12 September 1944.

11 September 1944 – Broken cloud at 3,000 feet, with initial poor visibility, improving later. 41 Squadron participated in two shows today, the first as a result of the Squadron's observations on the Scheldt on the previous evening, and the second another armed Crossbow reconnaissance.

The pilots were briefed for the former operation at 14:20, and found they were tasked with providing escort to Bostons and Marauders bombing the Breskens-Flushing [Vlissingen] ferry crossing on the Breskens side of the Scheldt, which the Squadron had seen during their flight up the river to Flushing last night. Designated Ramrod 1271, the operation foresaw the deployment of three formations of 18 Mitchells and two formations of 12 Bostons from 2 Group, escorted by 41 Squadron and Manston based 274 Squadron.

Date	11 September 1944
Operation	Ramrod 1271
Target	Ferry crossing at Breskens, NL
Bombers	54 Mitchells and 24 Bostons in five waves
Casualties	3 bombers Cat. A damage from Flak
Target Cover	Lympne: 41 Squadron (12 Spitfire XII) Manston: 274 Squadron (10 Tempest V)

41 Squadron was airborne at 14:45, consisting of twelve pilots led by Sqn Ldr Benham, and crossed in at Blankenberge, a few kilometres southwest of Zeebrugge on the Belgian coast. Banking

It was not until 10 November 1944 that Prime Minister Winston Churchill announced to the House of Commons that the United Kingdom was under attack by the V2. By this time about one hundred V2s had already fallen in the country. © Crown copyright expired

to port, the unit headed north towards Breskens and proceeded to patrol the target area for 30 minutes. For their part, 274 Squadron took off at 15:00, arrived over the target area at 15:25, and proceeded to patrol the area with 41 Squadron until 15:47, whilst the bomber formations came in and went to work.

A total of 46 Mitchells and 20 Bostons attacked the target between 15:32 and 15:45, from altitudes of between 12,000 and 15,000 feet. Good concentrations of bombs were seen to fall on the pier at Breskens and on its landward end. Other strikes were observed on a vehicle parking area just southeast of the pier. A large fire and a pall of black smoke rising to approximately 5,000 feet from the pier were observed and one ferry was seen on fire.

Two ships were also seen near the harbour and three moving down the river west-northwest of Terneuzen. Another two vessels, believed to be escorts, were also seen with smoking funnels, making for the safety of Breskens harbour as quickly as possible. When they saw the bombs fall on the harbour, however, they did an about face and headed further down the Scheldt to Hoofdplaat.

There was no opposition from the Luftwaffe, but heavy Flak of medium intensity was aimed at the bombers. Three suffered light damaged, but there were no casualties. The escort fighters also sustained no casualties and returned to base reporting an otherwise uneventful operation. 274 Squadron put down at Manston again at 16:15, whilst 41 Squadron landed at Lympne at 16:35.

Whilst landing, however, New Zealander WO Brian Weeds' aircraft (MB862) stalled and crash-landed. He injured his right knee and grazed his forehead, which resulted in him being hospitalised briefly in the Station Sick Quarters at Lympne. After recuperation, however, he did not return to the Squadron and was sent to PDC in Brighton instead, from where he was repatriated home.[63]

Soon after their return, the pilots were briefed for yet another operation: Ramrod 1272. Their task on this occasion was to hunt for Crossbow targets again, this time over the Dutch North [Noord] and South [Zuid] Beveland Islands. They shared the operation with 274 Squadron once again, who simultaneously patrolled an eight-mile-wide corridor north of 41 Squadron's target area, between The Hague and Vlaardingen.

41 Squadron was airborne at 18:25, led by Sqn Ldr Benham, in three pairs designated Red, Blue and Yellow Sections. They crossed the Channel at zero feet and then climbed to 8,000 feet to make landfall over Knokke, Belgium. As they did, they spotted, "two concrete cubes 30 feet high with a 90 ft. hole in the centre and 2 buildings nearby, one with a red tiled roof and the other camouflaged"[64] at Het Zoute.

They swept in behind the afternoon's earlier target, Breskens, turned north over Terneuzen and crossed out over the Scheldt at 10,000 feet towards South Beveland. They noted that the destroyer or light cruiser they had seen at Terneuzen the previous evening was no longer there, but the two Siebel ferries were. Underway, they came under inaccurate fire from four Flak barges on the Western Scheldt [Westerschelde] but were not affected.

Making landfall again, they descended to 3,000 feet and searched the island for signs of Big Ben activity. At one location, two avenues of trees were spotted running east-west, one south of the lake and one north, the latter with buildings at its western end, although they felt these were "nothing terribly suspicious".[65] The pilots came under intense light Flak from a battery hidden in a wood south of Goes, which forced them to climb to 9,000 feet again, but they were still able to note railway wagons in Goes and barges docked on the Goes-Goese Sas canal, with 40-foot tarpaulins covering the cargo on one.

One pilot reported that a light was flashed at him from a location amongst a group of 50 buildings west of Goes, possibly at Wissekerke, which was "neither helio nor reflection from the sun".[66] They continued on to search North Beveland, and saw a cleared strip running southwest in a wood on Schouwen Island, before returning to Lympne, where they landed at 20:00.

For their part, six aircraft from 274 Squadron were airborne at 18:30, and later reported having seen several zig-zagged trenches stemming from a central point between the railway line and canal just south of Delft. At the far end of one of the trenches was a large mound with a hole in the centre. A house on the western side of the railway line was also seen to have trenches running from it, but no personnel movement was seen at either point. However, they attacked and obtained strikes on a stationary northbound train, on the line next to the trench-system, which consisted of a locomotive and 30 trucks. Finding nothing else of interest, the pilots headed home and landed back at Manston at 20:05.

Separately today, 130 Squadron escorted bombers on an attack on oil installations at Gelsenkirchen, led by Wg Cdr Gray, and an advance party from 610 Squadron arrived at Lympne at 15:30, consisting of one senior NCO and seven ORs.

12 September 1944 – Fine with no cloud and good visibility, but some haze up to 5,000 feet. The Squadron had an early start today, when six pilots were woken at 05:00 for breakfast in the Sergeants' Mess and briefed at 05:30 for Ramrod 1275, in which they were to reconnoitre and destroy Big Ben targets between Katwijk and The Hague [Den Haag] in the Netherlands from first light. Three specific targets were allocated:[67]

LEFT Flt Lt Bill Stowe RCAF, Squadron mascot 'Perkin' and an unidentified pilot examine the wreck of Stowe's Spitfire XII, MB862, EB-E, after WO Brian Weeds RNZAF stalled the aircraft on landing and belly landed it on 11 September 1944. It was the Squadron's last Spitfire XII accident. © Bill Stowe, via Garry Cooper

RIGHT Flt Lt Bill Stowe RCAF, with his head in his hands in mock sorrow at the damage to his Spitfire XII, MB862, EB-E, which stalled on landing when being flown by WO Brian Weeds RNZAF on 11 September 1944. © Bill Stowe, via Garry Cooper

qD677953 near Waalsdorperlaan (52°06'31" N 4°20'46" E)
qD705995 near Wassenaar (52°08'50" N 4°23'04" E)
qY714028 near Valkenburg (52°10'38" N 4°23'43" E)

The pilots were airborne at 06:45, fitted with 60-gallon jettison tanks and led by Flt Lt Terry Spencer. They set a north-easterly course for The Hague, traversing the Channel on the deck. On sighting the city, they climbed to 10,000 feet and made landfall just north of it, noting the visibility was 15-20 miles.

Heading straight to the first location, at Waalsdorperlaan, just northeast of The Hague, they could only see mounds of earth and felled trees from their patrol altitude at 3,500 feet. Continuing northwards to the second location, just west of Wassenaar, they found nothing at all to arouse suspicion. At the third location, just a little further north again, between Wassenaar and Katwijk, and just west of Valkenburg, they only found a quarry. Within a short time, all three sites had been investigated but the results were disappointing.

They then headed to Katwijk, where they finally found what they suspected was just the type of secret weapons site they were seeking. Located in a duned coastal area approximately 2½km north of the town at qY731080 (52°13'29" N 4°25'00" E), the complex consisted of six concrete huts backing onto a large mound, an above-ground tunnel with two entrances running north-south, a derrick on the beach 300 feet to the southwest, and two railway lines running inland away from the site. There was also evidence of new excavations, and camouflage netting covered the entire site.

As there was no Flak to hinder them, all six pilots made four strafing attacks each on the whole area, and four pilots made an additional two attacks each on the buildings, camouflage and derrick. A total of 7,050 rounds of .303 and 1,500 rounds of 20mm ammunition were used in the attack, and a combined length of approximately 120 feet of cine-gun film of the site was also made.[68]

Climbing again, the Squadron set course for home, but found one aircraft suffering carburettor trouble. As such, they altered their course to make an earlier landing at Bradwell Bay, six miles northeast of Southminster, Essex, instead. All of the aircraft landed safely at Bradwell at 08:45, and the pilots continued on to Lympne at 11:05, pancaking at base again 20 minutes later.[69]

After lunch, the Squadron was assigned to escorts of a single B-17 Flying Fortress, which was maintaining continuous patrols up and down the Dutch coast, from The Hague northwards, on

Fg Off (later Flt Lt) Harry W. Charnock DFC DFM served with 41 Squadron from ca 12 September 1944 to 7 March 1945. In 1947, he was also awarded the Belgian Order of Leopold II and the Croix de Guerre with Palm. © 41 Squadron RAF

the look-out for V2 launch sites. Eleven sorties were flown between 13:20 and 17:25 in thick haze, but all were uneventful.[70]

During the day, eleven pilots undertook 14 hours and 30 minutes practice flying, and veteran pilot Fg Off Harry W. Charnock DFC DFM joined the Squadron. Born in June 1905, he was markedly older than all of his fellow pilots.[71]

Separately, 610 Squadron's pilots arrived in Lympne by air during the morning, followed by 6610 Servicing Echelon by road during the afternoon. They had little time to settle in as they joined 130 Squadron on two bomber escorts to oil targets during the afternoon. The first target, just after lunch, was Wanne-Eickel and the second, in the early evening, Dortmund.

However, the day's big news for 41 Squadron today was the delivery by the ATA of twelve Spitfire XIVs, so the unit could re-equip. The ORB reported,

> *Today our new Spitfire XIV's arrived. They have not all arrived yet, but the rest are expected in a couple of days. So we are getting ready to say goodbye to the XII's, our faithful steeds since April* [sic], *1943.*[72]

The last operational sorties flown on the Spitfire XII by the Squadron were by Fg Off Don Tebbit in MB850 and Flt Sgt Ian Stevenson in MB858 during this afternoon.

The Spitfire XIV Arrives

41 Squadron was now in line for the latest version of the Spitfire, the Mark XIV. This was the unit's first re-equipment since February 1943, and its final version before the cessation of hostilities; the next change would be year away. The Spitfire XIV was last Spitfire Mark to see full service in World War II, and provided significantly enhanced performance at higher altitudes than the Squadron's Mark XIIs.

Three versions were produced: the F.XIV with universal 'C' type wing and standard Spitfire canopy, the F.XIVE with 'E' wing, some of which were clipped for low-level operations and had a bubble or 'teardrop' canopy, and FR.XIVE for low-level operations and reconnaissance, all of which were equipped with clipped wings, bubble canopy, rear fuselage fuel tank and oblique camera in the rear of the fuselage. As far as can be established, 41 Squadron was equipped with only the first two of these, although the bubble canopies did not appear on the Squadron until March 1945 – another six months away.

The 2nd Tactical Air Force – or 2 TAF, of which we will see more later – was equipped with Spitfire XIVs from September 1944 onwards, and eventually re-equipped most of its Spitfire squadrons with the Mark by May 1945.

For 41 Squadron, the new aircraft's introduction was particularly significant: for the first time in its history it would have the range to fly to Germany from the United Kingdom. The aircraft would serve the Squadron well as it advanced with the Front into Germany over the ensuing months. The unit thereby became of only few RAF squadrons to fly the Spitfire throughout the entirety of the War [see also Appendix XI, Aircraft in Service].

Spitfire Variants Flown by 41 Squadron between 1939 and 1945[73]						
Mark	I	IIa	Va	Vb	XII	XIV
Wing Span	36' 10"	36' 10"	36' 10"	36' 10"	32' 7"	36' 10"
Length	29' 11"	29' 11"	29' 11"	29' 11"	31' 10"	32' 8"
Height	11' 5"	11' 5"	11' 5"	11' 5"	11' 0"	12' 8"
Min Weight	4,810 lb	4,900 lb	4,981 lb	5,065 lb	5,600 lb	6,600 lb
Max Weight	6,200 lb	6,317 lb	6,700 lb	6,700 lb	7,400 lb	10,280 lb
Armament	8 x .303	8 x .303	8 x .303	4 x .303 2 x 20mm	4 x .303 2 x 20mm	4 x .303 2 x 20mm

Max Speed	363 mph	357 mph	371 mph	371 mph	393 mph	448 mph
Ceiling	31,900 ft	33,900 ft	37,000 ft	37,000 ft	40,000 ft	44,500 ft
Max Range	575 miles	500 miles	470 miles	470 miles	493 miles*	850 miles*

* with jettison tank

Aircraft Arrivals and Departures

Initial Spitfire XIV Arrivals		Spitfire XII Disposals		
Serial	Date[74]	Serial	Date	To
RM759	12 Sep 1944	MB795	15 Sep 1944	4875M
RM698	12 Sep 1944	EN225	20 Sep 1944	FLS Milfield
RM699	12 Sep 1944	EN227	20 Sep 1944	FLS Milfield
RM705	12 Sep 1944	EN228	20 Sep 1944	FLS Milfield
RM707	12 Sep 1944	EN615	20 Sep 1944	FLS Milfield
RM710	12 Sep 1944	MB798	20 Sep 1944	AST
RM767	12 Sep 1944	MB840	20 Sep 1944	FLS Milfield
RM770	12 Sep 1944	MB850	20 Sep 1944	FLS Milfield
RM789	12 Sep 1944	MB853	20 Sep 1944	FLS Milfield
RM790	12 Sep 1944	MB882	20 Sep 1944	FLS Milfield
RM791	12 Sep 1944	EN602	22 Sep 1944	AST
RM796	12 Sep 1944	EN609	23 Sep 1944	FLS Milfield
RM797	12 Sep 1944	EN229	28 Sep 1944	FLS Milfield
RM793	18 Sep 1944	EN619	28 Sep 1944	FLS Milfield
RM799	18 Sep 1944	MB836	28 Sep 1944	FLS Milfield
RM765	20 Sep 1944	MB878	28 Sep 1944	FLS Milfield
RM787	20 Sep 1944			
RM788	20 Sep 1944			
RM769	26 Sep 1944			
RM680	12 Oct 1944			

13 September 1944 – Fair with early fog, which dispersed during the morning to good visibility. Nonetheless, no operational flying was undertaken today as the Squadron was released for conversion work to the Spitfire XIV. This gave the ground crews some time to familiarise themselves with their new aircraft, whilst the pilots were lectured on the features of the .5 calibre Browning.

14 September 1944 – Early mist and fog, clearing during the day, but deteriorating again towards the evening. The pilots spent most of the day testing and getting used to their new aircraft but during the afternoon, the Squadron was asked to provide two aircraft for a brief Fortress escort up and down the Dutch coast.

Fg Off Don Tebbit was airborne at 14:20 in RM767 for what should have been the Squadron's first ever offensive operation in new Spitfire XIVs, but he returned within just ten minutes with an unspecified issue. He was airborne again at 15:15 in RM698 with Flt Sgt 'Steve' Stevenson in RM797 but once again Tebbit was forced to return just 15 minutes later, this time with an 'oxygen deficiency'. These being the day's only recorded operational flights, it therefore appears that the allocated escort was never carried out.[75]

That afternoon, whilst the pilots were testing their aircraft, the weather dropped at Lympne and Flt Sgts Bob Fleming and 'Bill' Rossow were forced to land at Manston at 16:50 instead. With no improvement in sight, they ended up staying the night.

Meanwhile that day, 130 and 610 Squadrons had been much more active, both participating in squadron-strength armed reconnaissances to the Netherlands. Later in the afternoon, they also provided four sections between them to escort the Flying Fortress maintaining its patrol of the Dutch coast, which 41 Squadron was unable to support.

15 September 1944 – Poor weather with low cloud and mist continued throughout the day, which hindered any more activity than a few air tests and brief aircraft evaluations for pilots trying to gain some experience on the new aircraft. Opinions on the Spitfire XIV varied within the Squadron, "…but it seems to be generally accepted that they have a great sensitivity of control which demands good flying and concentration."[76]

Separately, Flt Sgts Fleming and Rossow returned to Lympne during a brief break in the weather during the morning, having landed in Manston on the previous afternoon as a result of poor weather conditions.

16 September 1944 – Local early mist cleared rapidly to a fine day with good visibility. 6/10ths to 8/10ths cloud built during the afternoon with a base of 2,000-3,000 feet and a ceiling of 5,000.

During the morning, A Flight practiced being bounced by Flt Lt Bill Stowe in their new aircraft, whilst B Flight undertook cine camera gun exercises. During the afternoon, however, 41, 130 and 610 Squadrons participated in a series of armed Crossbow reconnaissances in the Netherlands that the Lympne, Detling, Bradwell Bay, Hawkinge, Deanland and Friston Wings were assigned to, between 13:00 and 20:30.

Wing	Squadron	Timings	Target Area
Lympne	610	13:00-14:56	Den Haag-Leiden-Noordwijk area Storage Depots and Firing Points
	130	13:43-15:20	
	41	14:55-16:30	
Detling	1	13:00-14:50	Den Haag-Den Helder-Amsterdam-Utrecht
	165	13:40-15:50	
Bradwell Bay	64	14:00-16:15	Amsterdam-Zwolle-Apeldoorn-Utrecht-Leiden
	611	15:00-17:01	
Hawkinge	402	16:05-17:50	Den Haag-Leiden-Noordwijk area Storage Depots and Firing Points
	350	16:45-18:24	
Deanland	345	16:00-18:33	Den Haag-Den Helder-Amsterdam-Utrecht
	322	16:44-19:21	
Friston	131	18:00-20:30	Den Haag area

The Lympne Wing was assigned to attack storage depots at map references:
qD722960 southeast of Wassenaar (52°07'00" N 4°24'41" E),
qD712968 south of Wassenaar (52°07'24" N 4°23'47" E), and
qD714973 just south of Wassenaar (52°07'41" N 4°23'56" E),

…and firing points at:
qD723973 just southeast of Wassenaar (52°07'42" N 4°24'43" E), and
qD1435 on Walcheren Island (51°32'36" N 3°36'43" E).[77]

Eleven aircraft from 41 Squadron were airborne at 14:55, fitted with 90-gallon jettison tanks, and flew across the Channel at zero feet, towards Katwijk. When still approximately 20 miles out, they sighted the vapour trail of a V2 dead ahead of them, above 4/10ths cloud at about 5,000 feet, displaying a 'considerable wobble'.

As they reached Katwijk about five minutes later, the Squadron climbed to 9,000 feet and crossed in, the vapour trail still visible to them but its original source no longer discernible. As a search of the area revealed nothing obvious, the pilots moved northwards towards Amsterdam, looking for anything else of interest.

On reaching Amsterdam, they turned about and headed towards Katwijk again, and this time sighted a large fire at a factory located at the junction of the road and canal at qY7803, at Warmond, just north of Leiden. Two ambulances and a camouflaged 32-seat charabanc transporter were seen at the site, and Flt Lt Ross Harding fired at the latter, setting it on fire.[78]

The pilots also noted a wireless station, consisting of two huts and four masts on sand dunes at qY7715 (52°17'20" N 4°28'10" E), northeast of Katwijk, in the north-western corner of what is today the *Noordwijk Golfclub*, whilst long, empty barges were also seen on the canal at Warmond, but neither of these targets were attacked. Satisfied their job was done, the pilots returned to Lympne again, putting down at 16:30.

610 and 130 Squadrons had more success than 41 Squadron on their own missions. 610 Squadron returned at 15:00 claiming strikes on six barges they attacked near Leiden and seven near Katwijk, whilst 130 was back at base at 15:20 claiming attacks on several loaded barges, an electric train, two MET, a motorboat, and installations with hillside excavations on the coast a little further north of the wireless station seen by 41 Squadron. Both squadrons also reported other items of interest they had observed, including woods being cleared and construction work southeast of Wassenaar and on the outskirts of Noordwijk, five or six large concrete platforms pointing toward the sea at an angle of 260° between Katwijk and the Hague, and a long covered truck 'bigger than a tramcar' on the road just east of Wassenaar.

With all three of the Wing's squadrons home by 16:30, and no more business on the cards, Wg Cdr Gray granted them early release. The Officers therefore had plenty of time to prepare for a Mess Party that evening, which was considered a resounding success, and was also attended by Sqn Ldr Ireson, who flew over from Westhampnett.

41 Squadron recorded two statistics today. The day saw the unit's first offensive operation on the Spitfire XIV, but simultaneously its last armed Crossbow reconnaissance; they would never again be deployed against Germany's V-Weapons.

According to archived Home Office statistics, 7,532 civilians were killed and 19,495 injured by German aerial bombing in 1944 – a total of just over 27,000 casualties. One report, dated 12 April 1945, estimates that flying bombs alone caused 20,545 casualties, of which 5,376 were fatalities.[79]

Operation Market Garden

By September 1944 – three months after the invasion of Europe had begun – the second front was progressing well and nearly all of France and Belgium had been retaken. The front line in the north was now almost upon the Dutch border.

Attempting to exploit the disarray amongst the German forces created by the rapid Allied advance, Field-Marshal Sir Bernard Montgomery proposed an ambitious plan to land some 34,600 men of the British 2nd Army behind German lines in the Netherlands. His hope was to deal German forces a crushing blow that may bring the War to its conclusion by the end of the year.

Montgomery would deploy three Divisions by glider and parachute to capture six key bridges across the Rhine – Zon [Son], Veghel, Grave, Nijmegen, Oosterbeek and Arnhem – before the Germans could destroy them in their retreat. Their capture would remove the final major water obstacle into Germany and thereby pave the way for a rapid advance and end to the War. He

An image synonymous today with the failed attack, Arnhem Bridge could not taken by Allied paratroops in Operation *Market Garden*, for which 41 Squadron provided air support, in September 1944. © Unknown

named the operation, the largest airborne operation in history, *Market Garden*, and set its launch date at Sunday, 17 September 1944.

The bridges Zon and Veghel, northwest of Eindhoven, were allocated to the U.S. 101st Airborne Division, those at Grave and Nijmegen to the U.S. 82nd Airborne Division, and the rail bridge at Oosterbeek and road bridge at Arnhem to the British 1st Airborne Division. A total of 14,589 glider troops and 20,011 paratroopers, 1,736 vehicles, 263 artillery pieces, and 3,342 tons of ammunition and other supplies were to be dropped almost 100km behind German lines, whilst ground troops and tanks advanced towards them in a thrust that was expected to take three days to link up with the airborne troops on the Rhine.

The aircraft used to transport the men and equipment consisted of 1,438 C-47 Dakotas, 321 converted RAF Stirling and Halifax bombers, 2,160 CG-4A Waco gliders, 916 Airspeed Horsa gliders, and 64 GAL.49 Hamilcars. However, as this number of aircraft was insufficient to move all the troops on day one, successive drops were to be made over the ensuing days to reinforce the troops already on the ground.

As a result of Allied policy at the time that large airborne operations were prohibited in total darkness, and because there was no moon on 17 September, and the new moon set before dark on the ensuing days, it was determined that the operation would have to take place during the day. However, as the Allies now clearly held air superiority, it was felt the Luftwaffe could be held at bay, thereby minimising the operation's greatest threat. Flak was still considered a significant danger, particularly around Arnhem, but it was felt that recent Allied concentration on these batteries – and anti-Flak patrols during the operation – would reduce the danger and make a daylight airborne landing feasible.

Meanwhile, XXX Corps, spearheaded by the Guards Armoured Division, and subsequently the 43rd Wessex and 50th Northumbrian Infantry Divisions, would drive from the present front line to reach the Eindhoven area on the first day, the Grave and Nijmegen area by day two, and Oosterbeek and Arnhem by day four at the latest. Although four days was considered a long time for airborne troops to be fighting without support or reinforcements, it was felt that the time period would be no issue for the advancing ground troops as intelligence suggested that German resistance would be limited because the 15th Army was in disarray from its constant retreat and rear-guard actions.

The truth was very different.

17 September 1944 – Considerable fog at first in south-eastern England, becoming fine by 10:00 but deteriorating again towards the evening. "A second 'D' Day today. The hour for the liberation for Holland has come."[80]

Between 13:00 and 14:05, a 'Northern Force' of airborne RAF troops was flown to the Arnhem, Deelen and Nijmegen areas by 623 parachute aircraft, 334 tug aircraft and 334 glider aircraft of 38 (Airborne Force) and 46 (Transport) Groups. Escorts were provided by 18 Spitfire squadrons between 11:45 and 15:30, from 32 miles [51.5km] east of Aldeburgh, Suffolk, to 10 miles [16km] west of most the easterly point on Schouwen Island, whilst anti-Flak patrols were flown by five Tempest, three Mustang and two Spitfire squadrons between 11:45 and 16:00 along the parachute and tug aircraft route, from 10 miles [16km] west of the most easterly point on Schouwen Island to 10 miles [16km] south of Herzogenbusch [s-Hertogenbosch]. Another three Tempest squadrons were ordered to patrol the same line between 14:45 and 17:00 in case of homeward bound stragglers.

Between 13:00 and 13:40, the 'Southern Force' of airborne troops was landed north of Eindhoven via 432 parachute aircraft and 70 tugs and gliders. American airborne forces were also flown to their own target areas during this time, transported by 1,138 tugs, and 600 parachute aircraft provided by the IXth Troop Carrier Command. Escort and anti-Flak squadrons were provided throughout by the U.S. 8th Air Force, consisting of 503 P-38 Lightnings, P-47 Thunderbolts, and P-51 Mustangs.

Meanwhile, 2 Group supported the landings around the RAF target areas in three separate attacks. These included 16 Mosquitos detailed to attack German barracks at Nijmegen and 34 Mosquitos ordered to attack barracks at Arnhem at 12:20, and 48 Mitchells and 24 Bostons tasked with bombing barracks at Ede between 14:10 and 14:20. Additionally, 112 Lancasters and 20 Mosquitos of the RAF's 1 and 8 Groups were deployed to attack Flak batteries along the approach routes, in the Flushing [Vlissingen] area.

At 14:15, artillery from XXX Corps opened a barrage along a one mile [1.6 km] wide front, and to a depth of five miles [8 km]. This was supported by seven Typhoon squadrons tasked with attacking German positions along the road to Valkenswaard. Tanks started their advance towards the Dutch border 20 minutes after the barrage had begun and by 15:00 had already crossed into Dutch territory. Soon afterwards they were halted by flanking German forces but these were routed by additional artillery and aerial attacks, and by some solid ground fighting, and the advance could continue. Within three hours, however, they had only penetrated 11km, whereas the plan foresaw them reaching Eindhoven – 21km distant – in that time.

The Lympne Wing participated in this first day's escort to the airborne landings by providing anti-Flak patrols and an escort between 12:15 and 16:10. 130 Squadron was airborne at 12:15 with eleven aircraft plus Wg Cdr Gray, and patrolled along the invasion route. A little Flak was experienced but no enemy aircraft were seen, and although one aircraft was slightly damaged by Flak, the patrol was otherwise uneventful. The pilots took their aircraft to the limit of their endurance, and landed back at Lympne at 14:40. On their patrol, 610 Squadron saw more action, attacking two Flak ships, a tender and a barge. The two ships were left smoking and the barge was left on fire.

Twelve aircraft of 41 Squadron were airborne at 14:20 fitted with 90-gallon jettison tanks and headed across the North Sea.[81] They were tasked with providing an escort to the returning armada of parachute and tug aircraft:

> *Nothing in the way of hostile aircraft was seen, but several aircraft fuselages were seen floating on the water with A.S.R. boats in attendance. The great fleet of Stirlings, Halifaxes, Lancasters and Albermales, to say nothing of Dakotas in great numbers came streaming back from Holland, having encountered no serious opposition.*[82]

The sky was clear and water calm, and no opposition of any nature was experienced by the Squadron. It was, all in all, a completely uneventful operation, and the unit returned to Lympne between 16:05 and 16:10, having not fired a shot. They were not alone. Of the 18 squadrons allocated to escort the airborne force to and from the target area, only four saw any action when they attacked ground targets; the rest reported it uneventful.

The only casualties amongst the fighters were one aircraft with Cat. A damage and one with Cat. B damage from Flak, but no pilots were injured. The only event reported by 41 Squadron was the premature landing, at Manston, by Flt Lt Bill Stowe (RM797) who suffered serious engine vibration during the return flight. Fg Off Don Tebbit flew over to Manston in the Squadron's Tiger Moth to pick him up, and he arrived back during the evening.

At the end of the day, 38 and 46 Groups praised the fighter support as excellent, stating that "… whenever flak was seen, it was immediately 'silenced' by fighters".[83] There were no losses amongst the 334 tugs despatched, but 36 gliders failed to reach the designated dropping zones. Although, at 1,138 tugs, the USAAF force was larger, they only suffered the loss of 22, mainly a result of Flak. The vast majority of gliders reached their landing zones and the distribution of troops was considered excellent. The escorting U.S. fighter squadrons claimed seven enemy aircraft and 107 Flak batteries destroyed, but sustained casualties of 13 fighters lost and 52 damaged.

18 September 1944 – Cloud and haze above 3,000 feet over south-eastern England, deteriorating to rain and cloud below 1,000 feet in the evening. By first light, British troops in the Netherlands had begun their advance towards the road bridge at Arnhem, but become bogged down in several skirmishes after daybreak, which slowed their advance.

At Grave, the 82nd Airborne was also facing fierce resistance and was beaten back to the extent that one of the landing grounds earmarked for today's supply of fresh troops and equipment was retaken by German troops in the early morning. It was 14:00 before Allied troops could reoccupy the area.

The 101st Airborne was in more trouble. As the bridge at Zon could not be captured – and was subsequently destroyed by the Germans – they attempted to capture the bridge at Best instead, but it, too, proved impossible. At this point, several units attempted to move south to Eindhoven, instead.

The campaign was now clearly in disarray. The only good piece of news was that around midday reconnaissance parties from XXX Corps, which had continued its advance from day break, had made contact with airborne units. It would be another several hours, however, before they would arrive in any force.

Although all battle areas desperately required troop reinforcements and supplies, the day's scheduled uplift for *Market Garden* was delayed by three hours in the United Kingdom as a result of the morning's fog both there and over the Netherlands. It was therefore not until after midday that parachute and tug aircraft were at last airborne, at which time 260 parachute aircraft, 1,100 tugs, 1,100 gliders, and 250 Liberators carrying supplies took to the air.

Twenty-seven fighter squadrons, consisting of 19 Spitfire, five Tempest and three Mustang units, provided both escorts to and from the day's landing and dropping zones, and anti-Flak patrols, "to neutralize enemy flak ships and ground flak throughout the operation"[84], from 30 miles [48km] east of Aldeburgh as far as Herzogenbusch. The U.S. 8th Air Force took over from this point on, to the dropping zones.

The day's armada began crossing the Dutch coast at approximately 13:25 and the first drops began to be reported only six minutes later. These continued until 16:18, in the areas of Arnhem, Breda, Deelen, Eindhoven, Herzogenbusch, Hilversum and Utrecht.

All three Lympne Wing squadrons participated in the day's uplift by providing anti-Flak patrols. Each unit became airborne between 14:15 and 14:30, fitted with 90-gallon jettison tanks, and rendezvoused with the east-bound aircraft east of Aldeburgh, as planned, and continued with them to the Dutch mainland.

41 Squadron pilots at Lympne, ca. late September 1944. On the wing: Flt Sgt Peter Hale, Flt Sgt Arthur Appleton; Back row, standing: Flt Sgt Jack Bradshaw USA, Plt Off Peter Gibbs, Flt Lt John Refshauge RAAF, Fg Off John Wilkinson, Fg Off Don Tebbit, Fg Off Richard 'Monty' Norman (Eng Off), Flt Lt Lord Gisborough (Int Off), Flt Sgt Bob Fleming, Fg Off Harry Charnock, Flt Lt Bob Anderson RAAF, Plt Off Jimmy Payne, WO Jimmy Ware RAAF; Front row, seated: Flt Lt Bill Stowe RCAF, Fg Off Harry Cook, Flt Lt Ross Harding, Flt Lt Terry Spencer, Sqn Ldr Doug Benham, Flt Lt Jack Henry RNZAF, Fg Off 'Jackie' Fisher, Fg Off Daniel Reid RAAF, and Plt Off Eric Gray RAAF. © Rossow family

The operation proved uneventful for 130 Squadron, whose pilots found poor weather conditions in their patrol area, with 5/10ths cloud between 1,000 and 1,500 feet, and thick haze. One pilot returned early with engine trouble and the rest of the pilots were home at 16:30, reporting their patrol uneventful.

610 Squadron's patrol was quite the contrary. They sighted three large and two small ships entering the harbour at qD4845 (51°38'55" N 4°05'40" E) on the eastern side of Schouwen Island, which were attacked, and one of which was left smoking. They then attacked a Flak ship at Zijpe, just south of Bruinisse, on the island's most easterly point, which was set on fire and subsequently exploded. One aircraft suffered light Flak damage, and another crashed on landing back at Lympne, but on both occasions the pilots were not injured.

41 Squadron also saw action over the Netherlands today. Led by Flt Lt Terry Spencer, eleven aircraft were airborne at 14:25. Arriving over Schouwen Island, Spencer spotted a Flak ship almost at the same location as 610 Squadron's, just south of Bruinisse. He, Flt Lts Ross Harding and 'Jack' Refshauge, Fg Off Don Tebbit, WO Pat Coleman and Sgt Plt John Irvine all had shots at it, and it was in flames when the pilots pulled away in search of new targets.

However, as a result of weather conditions they were experiencing – 7/10ths cloud with a base of 10,000 feet and haze below this altitude – Spencer decided to split the Squadron into two separate sections for the rest of the operation.[85]

Shortly afterwards, he received an order from Control to find and destroy a C-47 Dakota that had force-landed on a German-held aerodrome on Schouwen Island, and led his section back to the west coast of the island. Locating it at qD2455 (51°43'39" N 3°44'26" E) just northeast of

Nieuw-Haamstede, he sent Flt Lts Harding and Refshauge, and WO Coleman, down to attack it. Refshauge and Coleman fired first, observing strikes and damaging the aircraft, however Harding, coming in last, "blew it up with a well aimed burst".[86] The pilots also noted near the aircraft a number of concrete buildings covered in camouflage netting, and slit trenches around them.[87]

Returning east towards the mainland once again, Spencer's section came under fire from Flak around Sint Annaland, a few miles south-southeast of Bruinisse, but was unable to pinpoint the source. However, they noted a tug and three barges heading northeast up the Mastgat from 5,000 feet, but did not attack.

By this time, the Squadron's other pilots had returned to Lympne and put down at 16:30; as Spencer's pilots had been out for longer than normal, he decided it was time to head home, too. On the way out, however, Spencer decided to have one last crack, and he and WO Coleman dived down to shoot up some empty anti-aircraft guns on the western coast of Schouwen Island; this would prove to be the Squadron's last ground victory – indeed victory of any kind – for a full three months.

A Flight pancaked at Lympne at 17:15. It had been a long mission, and one worthy of comment in the ORB: "…it was remarkable for the length of time 'A' Flight remained airborne – 2 hours 50 minutes!"[88] Between them, the pilots had expended 1,552 rounds of .303 calibre ammunition and 1,102 of 20mm.

Pilots, 18 September 1944	Serial	Section	Up	Down
Spencer, Terence	RM767	Red	14:25	17:15
Coleman, Patrick T.	RM789			
Harding. Ross P.	RM707			
Refshauge, John G. H.	RM799			
Tebbit, Donald F. J.	RM793	Yellow		
Irvine, John	RM705			
Fleming, Robert	RM698			
Fisher, Douglas P.	RM710			
Henry, David J. V.	RM788	Blue		16:30
Appleton, Arthur S.	RM699			
Payne, Jim C. J.	RM790			

The day's reinforcements and supplies were desperately needed on the Arnhem area. The uplift brought in troops of the 4th Parachute Brigade and 2nd South Staffordshire Regiment and by the end of the day, the British force had entered the town. They advanced to within 2km of the road bridge but the original force had been decimated: only approximately one-sixth, or 200 men, still stood from those dropped the day before; the rest had been killed, wounded or captured.

The RAF's 38 Group reported that out of 210 tugs and 210 gliders airborne, 188 were successful, 19 were aborted and three missing. 46 Group reported that 120 out of 122 Dakotas with paratroops made successful drops. One aircraft was reported missing and the pilot of another was killed by Flak. The fighter escort throughout was reported very successful. They were unable to claim any enemy fighters, but sustained losses of four Tempests, one Spitfire XIV and four Spitfire IXs.

For their part, the IXth Troop Carrying Command dropped paratroops from 136 Dakotas, whilst 904 tugs towed a like number of gliders. Of these, 26 were reported missing. The U.S. 8th Air Force also reported that of 252 Liberators despatched, 246 successfully dropped approximately 782 tons of supplies. Flak claimed seven of these and damaged another 160. The entire American force was escorted by over 500 Lightnings, Thunderbolts, and Mustangs, which were attacked by at least 100 enemy aircraft. The U.S. force claimed 29 of these destroyed and one damaged, but sustained casualties of 20 aircraft lost and 55 damaged.

19 September 1944 – Cloudy with local drizzle or occasional rain over south-eastern England, a variable cloud base sometimes below 1,000 feet, and initial poor visibility improving to moderate, but deteriorating again towards dusk.

Before daybreak in the Netherlands, the 1st Parachute Brigade broke out towards the bridge at Arnhem, supported by South Staffordshire Regiment. Initially making good progress, they were halted when it became light and came under withering fire from three sides. The troops were decimated and those left were forced to withdraw, just 500 remaining men moving westwards towards the main force in Oosterbeek, approximately 5km away. However, another 600 men of the 2nd Battalion had managed to seize the northern approach ramp to the bridge at Arnhem and could not be dislodged. The German Army spent the rest of the day shelling them with mortars, tanks and artillery, demolishing house after house in a vain effort to remove them.

The 4th Parachute Brigade then attempted to break through German lines to the north of Oosterbeek, but the attack was repelled with heavy losses through intensive German resistance and their own communication difficulties. Incapable of any further offensive operations, they withdrew to a defensive position in Oosterbeek.

During the morning, the 504th Parachute Infantry Regiment was reached by XXX Corps' Grenadier Guards, reinforcing their ranks and enabling them to make up delays, and finally move forward towards Arnhem. They made a concerted effort to take the bride at Nijmegen, but were repelled within 400 metres of their goal. Although skirmishes continued into the night, all were unsuccessful.

Units of the 101st Airborne, which had failed to take the bridges at Zon and Best on 18 September, and had attempted to move southwards towards Eindhoven, were forced to retreat under the pressure of German counterattacks during the morning. However, British tanks reached them later in the day and together they managed to push German troops back to Zon again. The bridge had been destroyed by the Germans but the British had managed to build a Bailey Bridge before being repelled. The afternoon's push resulted in the British being able to retake the river crossing.

The weather once again played havoc with the day's airborne operations for *Market Garden*, and it was not until just after 13:00 that the first of 435 tug and glider combinations and 163 supply aircraft were airborne to the Netherlands. However, these then continued until 18:00 along a route from Bradwell Bay to a point five miles [8km] south of Geel, Belgium, then on to their dropping zones, and back via North Foreland.

They were to be escorted and provided anti-Flak cover as far as Geel by 19 RAF squadrons – five Spitfire V units, eleven Spitfire IX units and three Spitfire XIV units – where the USAAF was to take over and escort them to the dropping and landing zones. However, the poor weather – down to 10/10ths cloud at 200 feet, with visibility at 300 feet – resulted in every RAF fighter squadron, bar No. 1 Squadron, aborting the operation, most turning back at the Belgian coast.

It was a disastrous day for the Lympne Wing. Rain had begun to fall around midday and continued into the afternoon, significantly reducing visibility. Nonetheless the operation was on and 41 Squadron was the first of the three squadrons to be ordered off. Despite "certain doubtful glances… cast skywards"[89], twelve pilots took off at 15:15, led by Flt Lt Terry Spencer, formed up in the circuit and headed out. It was, however, to no avail. Owing to poor visibility – a cloud base down to 400 feet – they put down at Manston again only 20 minutes later.

Before 41 Squadron could report back that they had had to land at Manston, six of 610 Squadron's aircraft had also taken off. They were consequently also ordered to return to Lympne but, on landing, three of the aircraft slid on the airfield's slippery surface and crashed. Within the space of two minutes three Spitfires finished up on a south-easterly slope of the strip with Category B damage. Fortunately, however, the pilots were uninjured.

An expensive sortie. The C.O. [*of 130 Squadron, Sqn Ldr Tripe*], *as acting Wing Commander Flying, felt pretty sick about this, but it was not the weather – the prangs were due to a mixture of conditions of the airfield and finger trouble.*[90]

130 Squadron was due to take off at 15:44, and the ten pilots assigned to the mission were already in their cockpits when news of 41 Squadron being forced down at Manston came in, and 610 Squadron's pilots crash-landed on the airfield on their return. The accidents forced a closure of Lympne and the operation was cancelled. 130 Squadron's pilots dismounted again and undertook no further flying for the rest of the day.

Nonetheless, over at Manston, 41 Squadron made another attempt to fulfil their mission. Although the poor conditions continued, "we decided to see what the prospects were after crossing out".[91] It was not to be; conditions gradually became worse, and by the time the Squadron reached the Belgian coast off Ostend, they were flying through heavy rain with visibility of only 600 feet. Flt Lt Spencer therefore decided it was time to abort and head home.

On contacting Lympne, however, he was informed that the airfield was obstructed – clearly they had received no information about 610 Squadron's misfortunes until now – and were asked to land at Manston instead. When the weather failed to clear for the rest of the day, it was decided they should stay the night.

Despite conditions, 38 Group despatched 144 aircraft, of which 41 were tug and glider combinations. Thirty-one of the gliders successfully delivered 106 troops, 36 jeeps, 26 trailers, 19 motorcycles and seven 6-pounder anti-tank guns to the Arnhem area. Of the remaining aircraft, 89 dropped 2,489 containers and 342 panniers. 46 Group also despatched 63 Dakotas with supplies, of which 54 made successful drops.

Both Groups reported Flak that was much more intensive than the previous days, and had escorted them on their direct route from Herentals in Belgium to Arnhem. 38 Group reported ten Stirlings missing and 46 Group seven Dakotas.

The U.S. IXth Troop Carrying Command despatched 445 aircraft, which suffered considerably in the weather conditions. Of these aircraft, 385 were tug and glider combinations. Tug pilots later reported having to fly on instruments as visibility was so poor, and that they could not even see their own gliders! A total of 177 aircraft (almost 40%) aborted, but of those that continued on, 27 aircraft failed to return, nine reported Cat. E, 41 Cat. B, and 76 Cat. AC damage.

The U.S. 8th Air Force sent up 172 Mustangs, whose pilots encountered greater opposition from the Luftwaffe than on either of the previous two days. They estimated at least 180 enemy aircraft airborne, thereunder over 30 Me109s and FW190s in the Wessel area, over 50 Me109s and FW190s in the Zwolle area, approximately 36 FW190s and 40 Me109s in the Arnhem area, and another 20-30 single-engined enemy aircraft at IJsselstein, just southwest of Utrecht. Of these, they made claims for 23 destroyed, one probable and four damaged, for losses of eight of their own.

Considering such conditions, it is perhaps no surprise that Air-Sea Rescue was busier than ever. By the end of the day, they had rescued 79 men, 75 by high-speed sea craft, and four by Walrus amphibian flying boats.

20 September 1944 – Fog and mist, which lifted around midday, although haze continued throughout, with broken cloud from 2,000 feet. In the Netherlands, Operation *Market Garden* was now into its fourth day and seriously faltering.

At Arnhem, the troops holding the northern approach ramp to the bridge had held on overnight but learnt during the late morning that XXX Corps had no chance of relieving them; they were still stalled south of the bridge at Nijmegen. Under constant heavy fire at close range, and their food, water, medical supplies and ammunition dwindling, casualties continued to mount, until their position was considered no longer tenable.

The British Commander therefore arranged a truce, in which the wounded, including himself, were evacuated from the front and taken into German captivity. Soon thereafter, the Wehrmacht overcame the remaining Allied resistance and recaptured the bridge, enabling them to send reinforcements south towards Nijmegen.

At Oosterbeek, a short distance to the west of Arnhem, the remaining troops of the 1st Airborne Division were holding on and organised themselves into defensive positions that held against a German attack later that day. The 4th Parachute Brigade, further west, was fighting towards them to reinforce their position, but they also came under heavy attack, and finally reached Oosterbeek with only 60 men. The 156th Parachute Battalion, to the south, also came under heavy attack and was reduced to just 150 men, who remained pinned down for eight hours. By the end of the day, just 75 men were able to break out and reach the dwindling Allied pocket at Oosterbeek.

At Nijmegen, the 82nd Airborne had wanted to make an assault across the Rhine by boat, but the canvas craft arrived over 24 hours late. Twenty-six finally arrived today and a hasty and daring daylight crossing was mounted at 15:00 by Paratroops, Sappers and Engineers into well-defended positions on the opposite bank. Despite a shortage of oars, compelling men to paddle with rifle butts, and only around a quarter of the craft surviving two crossings, the men managed to seize the northern end of the bridge. As German forces withdrew, the bridge was rushed by the Grenadier Guards and elements of the 505th Parachute Infantry Regiment, who declared it secure at 19:10.

Skirmishes continued around to the east and south of Nijmegen, and the series of advances and retreats throughout the day made it clear that the German strategy was to cut off the Airborne units in the north from advancing ground units of XXX Corps in the south. The situation on the ground was getting desperate.

Airborne reinforcements and supplies were delivered to the Netherlands in two separate phases today. In the first of these, 67 Stirling heavy bombers were sent in from 13:45 to drop supplies to the troops at Arnhem. They were escorted by three Mustang and three Spitfire squadrons from the Brenzett and Westhampnett Wings, respectively, who were also to attack German Flak batteries.

Some light Flak was experienced but none of the batteries could be pinpointed and attacked, as a result of haze and low cloud. Their inability to do so cost each Wing one pilot and aircraft, and ten Stirlings.

The second phase foresaw the despatch of 357 Dakotas carrying paratroops to various dropping zones in the Netherlands between 15:00 and 19:00. They were escorted from North Foreland to Bourg Leopold [Leopoldsburg], Belgium, by seven Spitfire squadrons, and from Bourg Leopold to Eindhoven by another nine. Every escort squadron was additionally to provide anti-Flak protection, but reported the operation uneventful, except for 234 Squadron, who aborted the mission at the Belgian coast on account of weather conditions.

The Lympne Wing was assigned to the first part of the second phase, escorting and providing anti-Flak defence to Dakotas as far as Bourg Leopold. 41 Squadron, having remained in Manston overnight, did not return to Lympne until 13:00, arriving in time to be briefed and have their aircraft serviced for the operation. Attesting perhaps to the short time available to the ground crews to prepare the aircraft, only ten of the Squadron's aircraft participated in the escort, whilst 130 and 610 Squadrons provided 12 aircraft each.

130 Squadron was first airborne at 15:15, and 41 Squadron last up, an hour later, all fitted with 90-gallon jettison tanks. The squadrons rendezvoused with the Dakotas at Margate and escorted them to Ostend where landfall was made, then on to Ghent [Gent] and finally Bourg Leopold, before returning home. 130 and 610 reported the mission uneventful, but 41 Squadron split up, and Blue Section, led by Flt Lt 'Jack' Henry, returned to Lympne again by 18:15.[92]

Instead of turning back at Bourg Leopold, however, Flt Lt Terry Spencer took Red and Yellow Sections on to Eindhoven, escorting the Dakotas to the maximum of their Spitfires' endurance. Nonetheless, they saw no action and arrived back at Lympne at 19:00, just in time for dinner. It was…

41 Squadron's Ground Crew, 6041 Servicing Echelon, at Lympne ca. late September 1944. © Rossow family

…another endurance test of two hours forty minutes… […] Nothing in the way of hostile aircraft was seen, and it is sincerely hoped that the fundamental parts of our anatomy would be given a break in future.[93]

Whilst this operation was on-going, 38 and 46 Groups despatched another 33 Stirlings and 63 Dakotas to the Arnhem area without escort. Seven of these aircraft failed to return. IXth Troop Carrying Command also reported a successful day with good drops and all Dakotas returning.

The U.S. 8th Air Force provided 634 Lightnings, Thunderbolts and Mustangs to escort and provide anti-Flak defence between Eindhoven and the dropping zones for the Stirlings and Dakotas, but no enemy aircraft were seen. They were unable to ground strafe owing to low cloud but dropped several fragmentation bombs near enemy gun positions, although with unobserved results. Two USAAF pilots failed to return, as did two pilots amongst the RAF force, but no claims for victories were made.

21 September 1944 – Thick fog and low cloud kept the Squadron grounded all day, despite a planned patrol over the Netherlands that was to take place should the weather improve sufficiently to permit it. In the end, the only person on the Squadron to fly was Flt Lt Terry Spencer, who made a brief flight in the Squadron's Tiger Moth.

The remaining 3,600 troops of the 1st Airborne Division established a defensive perimeter around Oosterbeek today, in the hope of holding their 700-metre-wide bridgehead of the northern bank of the Rhine until the arrival of XXX Corps. They came under constant heavy attacks all day, which were successfully repulsed, though with heavy losses. Radio contact was finally established with XXX Corps' medium artillery during the day, and they were able to provide considerable fire power to support the 1st Airborne.

38 Group sent in more Stirlings to deliver supplies to them today, but they were attacked by FW190s when the USAAF fighter cover failed to arrive in the area on time. The Luftwaffe shot down 15 of the bombers, but was caught during their departure when the 56th FG shot down 15 of the 22 FW190s that attacked the Stirlings.

At Nijmegen, despite the capture of the bridge the previous day, the tanks of the Guards Armoured Division did not advance towards Arnhem for another 18 hours, at around midday on 21 September. Other elements of the Division were meanwhile fighting at Groesbeek and Eindhoven, and otherwise scattered over a 64km² [25 sq. mile] area south of the Waal River.

The delay enabled the Germans to bring up reinforcements and replenish supplies, thereby strengthening their position at Ressen, south of Arnhem. As such, they were able to halt the advance of Allied troops from the south when they did arrive. Despite supplies being delivered that afternoon by 30 Dakotas and 350 gliders, which were desperately needed, it was now quite clear that German forces had gained the upper hand.

The Armoured Division's delay and failure to exploit their opportunity to advance to Arnhem after the capture of the bridge at Nijmegen is recognised today as one of the key failures of the Operation.

22 September 1944 – Another day firmly on the ground, despite the Squadron maintaining a state of readiness all day for an operation that did not eventuate… "and lo' there was a great cleaning of aircraft, and men did sweat the sweat of a mighty accumulation of idleness."[94]

The Germans brought over 100 heavy guns to Oosterbeek today, to attempt the same tactic as they applied with success at Arnhem. Although German forces in the area now out-numbered the remnants of the 1st Airborne Division by around four to one, German artillery attacks were made systematically against specific positions and buildings, rather than indiscriminately shelling the area.

The Polish 1st Parachute Brigade, that had been dropped the previous day, now made their presence felt for the first time, by advancing towards Arnhem. Fearing a recapture of the bridge there or an attack on the German forces blocking the troops of XXX Corps attempting to advance from the south, the Germans withdrew 2,400 troops from the Oosterbeek area and sent them to Driel to engage the Polish paratroops.

The Poles held on well, and were reached during the evening by the XXX Corps' 43rd Division. However, the Germans foiled their plans to advance towards Arnhem when they moved two armoured formations into the area and blocked the way northwards.

23 September 1944 – Initially cloudy with some rain, becoming mainly fine with fair visibility. On Day Seven of Operation *Market Garden*, German forces spent the day trying to cut off the bridgehead at Oosterbeek with Allied forces in the south. Although suffering heavy losses, the British held on, assisted by tanks from XXX Corps that had reached the area. To the south, the Germans still held the road, hindering reinforcement. The Guards Armoured Division was therefore sent 19km southwards to retake the road, which they managed to do successfully.

To resupply and alleviate the desperate situation around Oosterbeek, a force of approximately 600 Dakotas and Stirlings was sent to the area today by 38 and 46 Groups, and IXth Troop Carrying Command, to deliver much needed equipment between 16:00 and 17:30. A total of 18 Spitfire and three Mustang squadrons were deployed to protect them along the route.

Fourteen of these provided escort from North Foreland to Eindhoven and back, timed to arrive at Bourg Leopold in Flight strength at five-minute intervals between 15:35 and 17:50. The three Mustang squadrons were tasked with patrolling the Bourg Leopold-Volkel area between 16:00 and 17:30, whilst the remaining four Spitfire squadrons were assigned to patrol continuously between Bourg Leopold and Eindhoven in squadron strength from 15:30 to approximately 18:00. The escort was on the whole uneventful for the fighters, although two aircraft were forced down on the Continent with engine trouble.

The U.S. 8th Air Force also provided the Dakotas and Stirlings escort cover from Eindhoven to and from the respective dropping zones, which consisted of some 560 Lightnings, Thunderbolts and Mustangs. The Americans met approximately 180 enemy aircraft in the Arnhem area and came away claiming 27 destroyed, two probable, and six damaged for total losses of 12 Mustangs and 12 Thunderbolts.

The entire Lympne Wing was involved in the day's escorts, escorting the airborne forces to the Eindhoven area, led by Wg Cdr Gray. 130 Squadron was airborne at 14:56, 41 at 15:05, and 610 at 15:15, each providing twelve aircraft fitted with 90-gallon tanks. They split into Flights after take-off, then flew to North Foreland to rendezvous with the main force, and crossed in at Ostend. They found hazy conditions, with visibility at 4-5 miles, and 5/10ths cloud at varying heights.

For their part, 41 Squadron was led by Flt Lt Ross Harding, and reached Bourg Leopold at 15:55, losing Plt Off Peter Gibbs (RM789) before crossing in as he returned early with mechanical trouble. The escorts then continued to Eindhoven, but were uneventful; no enemy aircraft were seen and there was little Flak to contend with. Not a shot was fired. 130 Squadron arrived back at Lympne at 17:25 and 610 at 17:35, but 41 Squadron was not on the ground again until 17:45, after another long mission of two hours and forty minutes.

38 Group had despatched a total of 73 Stirlings to dropping zones west of Arnhem. Sixty-four of these were considered successful, but seven fell victim to Flak. 46 Group sent 50 Dakotas to the Arnhem area in a mission considered successful, but three Dakotas failed to return on account of Flak. IXth Troop Carrying Command despatched a total of 531 Dakotas, of which 490 were tug and glider combinations and the rest carrying parachute troops. They considered their landings and drops in the Nijmegen area to have been excellent, but reported eight Dakotas missing.

Separately today, 20-year-old Scottish Flt Sgt John Irvine left 41 Squadron, following just over two months with the unit. He was posted to a Typhoon conversion course at Aston Down and, upon its conclusion, to 84 GSU at Thruxton. In early November, Irvine was posted to 263 Squadron at B.70 Antwerp, flying the Typhoon. He was still with the unit at the cessation of hostilities in early May 1945, when he was promoted to Warrant Officer.

25 September 1944 – Although no operational flying was undertaken by the Wing today, orders were received at Lympne that 130 Squadron would be transferred from 11 Group to 125 Wing in 83 Group, and move to Antwerp within five days.

However, their aircraft would be serviced by 6132 Servicing Echelon; their present crew, 6130 Servicing Echelon, would remain behind and move to Hawkinge instead. The Squadron would also be joined on the Continent by 402 (RCAF) Squadron, also flying Spitfire XIVs.

Simultaneously, 130 Squadron would be replaced at Lympne by 350 (Belgian) Squadron, which was serviced by 6350 Servicing Echelon, and both squadrons were to exchange their aircraft before-hand.

However, this separation of 41, 130 and 610 Squadrons was only an interlude. 41 would be reunited with 130 as a part of 125 Wing on the Continent in a little over two months' time, and 350 and 610 Squadrons would join them, too, in a quasi re-formation of the Lympne Wing, around a month later, on the eve of the new year.

In the Netherlands, the German Army had succeeded in cutting the road south to Veghel, forcing the Allies to accept that the objectives of *Market Garden* were not going to be achieved. At this point, the Operation was affectively abandoned and a decision was made instead to make a defensive stand at Nijmegen instead.

At dawn on 25 September, the 1st Airborne Division received orders to withdraw across the Rhine in a new operation codenamed *Berlin*. However, as the withdrawal could not be put into effect until nightfall, the remnants of the Division spent the day holding German forces at bay, despite intensive attacks and at one time a break in their lines, which was repelled by Allied artillery.

The withdrawal began at 22:00, when British and Canadian engineers began ferrying troops back across the Rhine. By early morning on 26 September, almost 2,400 men had succeeded in withdrawing, but this still left 300 men at daybreak, who were forced to surrender when German fire halted the crossings.

Those who had succeeded in withdrawing joined the troops around Nijmegen, and these men succeeding in holding the pocket until they were relieved in early November by the 1st Canadian Army.

26 September 1944 – Fair with well broken cloud above 2,000 feet, and good visibility. Despite the failure of *Market Garden*, airborne operations were mounted today to resupply the troops still holding out around Grave and Nijmegen. These were delivered in two separate operations, the first of which took place from 14:00 when 30 Dakotas were sent to Grave, supported by Lightnings of the U.S. 8th Air Force.

Simultaneously, 320 Lightnings, Thunderbolts and Mustangs patrolled the front, and encountered enemy aircraft to the east and northeast of the front, in the Münster and Haltern areas. The USAAF came away claiming 32 enemy aircraft destroyed, one probably destroyed and eight damaged, for the loss of just one Lightning, and ten other aircraft damaged.

In the second operation, 180 Dakotas in five formations of 36 aircraft, delivered supplies to a landing strip located eight miles [ca. 13km] southwest of Nijmegen. Escort and target cover was provided from Antwerp to the landing strip and back by 20 Spitfire and three Mustang squadrons. No enemy aircraft were seen and all escorts proved uneventful. Although three Dakotas failed to return, they all landed at Belgian airfields.

The Lympne Wing participated the second operation, with 130 and 41 Squadrons flying together, and 610 Squadron following them ten minutes later. 130 Squadron was off first at 13:32, followed by Wg Cdr Gray, who led eleven aircraft from 41 Squadron into the air three minutes later. They were to meet the Dakotas over Antwerp, but arrived to find their Dakotas had passed over the area five minutes ahead of schedule. However, they caught up with them south-southeast of Herentals, and escorted them the rest of the way in clear skies, according to plan.

> *We accompanied* [the Dakotas] *to our destination,* [but] *it was a bewildering business to keep in flights of six, for Lightnings, Thunderbolts and long-range Mustangs were milling around the landing strip, where the Dakotas were depositing their supplies.*[95]

The pilots noted that the bridge over the river at Grave was still intact and recognised large movements of Allied transport moving northwards towards Nijmegen, whilst Wg Cdr Gray sighted the trail of what he believed was one of the new German jets east of Nijmegen. However, it was too far off to do anything about, so the Wing returned to Lympne, experiencing inaccurate light Flak over Zeebrugge, and put down between 16:15 and 16:35.

This was the Wing's final participation in Operation *Market Garden*, and 130 Squadron's final operation with the Lympne Wing. Within days the Squadron would cross the Channel to the Continent, and 350 Squadron would arrive from Hawkinge; the first rumours also filtered through to 41 Squadron today, too, that "we may be going over the Channel soon", too.[96]

27 September 1944 – Fair to cloudy with occasional showers, but generally good visibility. The day commenced for 41 Squadron with two weather reconnaissance flights being undertaken from 06:25. Red Section, consisting of Flt Lts Ross Harding and 'Jack' Refshauge headed for the Rotterdam-Antwerp area, whilst Blue Section, made up of Fg Off Jimmy Payne and Plt Off 'Ricky' Gray, headed to the Amiens, Rouen and Fécamp areas. Blue Section returned at 07:55 reporting 10/10ths cloud over France between 3,000 and 6,000 feet, and Red Section returned 08:05 reporting clear skies over the Netherlands.

This resulted in 41 and 610 Squadrons being assigned to a rodeo during the afternoon to sweep the Katwijk-Hengelo-Overflakkee areas, in unison with Deanland based 91 and 345 Squadrons, who were tasked with sweeping the Arnhem-Soesterberg areas. However, the operation proved to be a failure as the weather had changed markedly by the time of the Wings arrived over the Netherlands.

Date	27 September 1944
Operation	Rodeo 404
Targets	Katwijk-Hengelo-Overflakkee & Arnhem-Soesterberg, Netherlands
Sweep	Lympne: 41 & 610 Squadrons (24 Spitfire XIV) Deanland: 91 & 345 Squadrons (24 Spitfire IX)
Casualties	610 Sqn: All 12 A/C landed Antwerp as a result of weather

The Deanland Wing turned back southeast of Rotterdam as conditions were so poor, but did manage to shoot up six gun posts on the northern coast of Walcheren Island on their way out. The Lympne Wing fared worse. 610 Squadron was airborne first, led by Wg Cdr Gray, followed by twelve aircraft from 41 Squadron, led by Flt Lt Terry Spencer.

From 40 miles east of Manston, the Wing faced a wall of 10/10ths cloud between 5,000 and 16,000 feet and was forced to climb to 20,000 feet to stay above it all the way to the coast. Before crossing in over Walcheren Island, Fg Off Don Tebbit and WO 'Jimmy' Ware had to turn back due to engine trouble – Ware's aircraft was emitting smoke and flames at times – accompanied by Fg Off 'Jackie' Fisher and WO Peter Hale, reducing 41 Squadron to just eight pilots.

After making landfall, the Squadron turned north to Rotterdam but was still ten minutes from this destination, when Flt Lt Spencer decided conditions were too poor to continue and ordered they should abort and return home. However, his R/T system then failed, and he had to hand over control to Flt Lt 'Jack' Henry.[97]

The Squadron then made for Lympne, where they arrived at around 17:40 with nothing to report, except that they had lost contact with 610 Squadron. At first no word was received; the entire Squadron had simply failed to return. Their last fix was at 17:05 some ten miles east of Gilze-Rijen. However, it subsequently transpired that the pilots had landed at Antwerp on account of the poor weather, and they returned the following day.

28 September 1944 – Although the weather in 11 Group's area was considered good, weather over the Continent was considered too poor for 41 Squadron to undertake any operations. Several of the pilots busied themselves with local flying instead: Flt Lt Daniel Reid undertook an air test, Flt Lt Ross Harding and Johnnie Wilkinson did some practice flying, and Flt Lt Terry Spencer and Fg Off Donald Tebbit carried out cross-country flights, Spencer flying to Farnborough and back, and Tebbit to Ipswich and back.

29 September 1944 – Cloud below 1,000 feet at first, with moderate visibility, deteriorating later. It was a momentous day for 41 Squadron, in which they flew their first mission over German territory in their history, as an element of Ramrod 1301.

The operation consisted of an early morning attack by 48 B-25 Mitchell medium bombers and 24 B-7 Boston light bombers on road and rail junctions at Geldern, approximately 8km due east of the German border with the Netherlands, and around 20km north-northeast of Venlo.

Date	29 September 1944
Operation	Ramrod 1301
Target	Road and rail junctions, Geldern, Nordrhein-Westfalen
Bombers	1st Formation: 18 Mitchells 2nd Formation: 18 Mitchells 3rd Formation: 12 Mitchells 4th Formation: 24 Bostons

Escort, 1st Formation	Manston: 118 & 124 Squadrons (24 Spitfire IX)
Escort, 2nd Formation	Manston: 229 & 504 Squadrons (23 Spitfire IX)
Escort, 3rd Formation	Lympne: 41 & 610 Squadrons (24 Spitfire XIV)
Escort, 4th Formation	Bradwell Bay: 64 & 126 Squadrons (22 Spitfire IX)
Casualties	124 Sqn: 1 A/C landed at Brussels

The attack was made in four formations, and Lympne's 41 and 610 Squadrons were assigned to escort the third box, consisting of twelve Mitchells. 41 Squadron was airborne at 07:55 in three sections of four pilots and crossed the Belgian coast over Nieuport [Nieuwpoort]. Soon afterwards, however, WO Peter Hale started suffering engine problems and returned to base, whilst the remaining pilots continued on to rendezvous with the bombers over Antwerp [Antwerpen].

41 and 610 Squadrons escorted the twelve bombers at 18,000 feet above 10/10ths cloud, but found the target still obscured upon reaching the area. The Mitchells then continued on their path until they found a break in the cloud. Turning back, they pinpointed their position through the opening by making a line to the target and bombed through the cloud cover.

Not surprisingly, however, no results were observed by 41 Squadron, "though the C.O. swears they missed".[98] Nonetheless, some of the other formations claimed to have made some direct hits on railway tracks. The Luftwaffe was not seen at all and the operation proved uneventful for all participants; no losses were sustained by bombers or fighters, although one Spitfire from 124 Squadron landed at Brussels.

Having set course for Lympne, 41 Squadron descended through the cloud base to find atrocious weather all the way home. On hearing their airfield was closed as a result, the pilots all landed at Manston at 10:05 instead.[99] At 11:20, the eleven pilots took off again to try to reach Lympne, which was only about 23 miles away, but as the weather was still too poor, they returned to Manston yet again, landing anew at 12:00. Deciding it was better to wait until the weather cleared, the men had lunch at Manston and took off once again at 15:50. In significantly improved weather, they found Lympne in just 15 minutes, happy to be home after what had become quite a long day. However, the significance of the day did not pass them by:

Everybody is particularly pleased with the day's operations, as this is the first time the Squadron crossed the German frontier, and although the penetration was not very deep it is very satisfying.[100]

Pilots, Ramrod 1301	Serial	Section	Up	Down
Benham, Douglas I.	RM710	Red	07:55	10:00
Gray, Eric	RM770	Red	07:55	10:00
Stevenson, Ian T.	RM797	Red	07:55	10:00
Bradshaw, John T.	RM799	Red	07:55	10:00
Payne, Jim C. J.	RM790	Blue	07:55	10:00
Appleton, Arthur S.	RM699	Blue	07:55	10:00
Fisher, Douglas P.	RM769	Blue	07:55	10:00
Reid, Daniel J.	RM796	Blue	07:55	10:00
Spencer, Terence	RM767	Yellow	07:55	10:00
Hale, Peter H.	RM789	Yellow	07:55	RTB
Harding, Ross P.	RM707	Yellow	07:55	10:00
Wilkinson, John F.	RM698	Yellow	07:55	10:00

30 September 1944 – Generally fine with little cloud and good visibility. Today the Lympne Wing participated in two separate Ramrods, one into Germany again, and the second to a target in the Netherlands.

The first of these, Ramrod 1302, saw the Wing airborne at 11:20, to support an attack by 200 Bomber Command Halifaxes and Lancasters on the synthetic oil plants at Bottrop and Sterkrade, Germany, supported by ten Pathfinder Mosquitos, and escorted by 15 Spitfire and six Mustang squadrons. Bottrop is located approximately 14km northeast of Duisburg, and Sterkrade around 7½km northwest of Bottrop.

This operation constituted 41 Squadron's first participation in the on-going Allied Oil Campaign against Germany.

The Allied Oil Campaign

The objective of the Allied Oil Campaign was to bomb facilities throughout occupied Europe that supplied Axis forces with petroleum, oil, and lubrication products. Such targets included refineries, synthetic oil plants, storage depots, and related chemical works.

The Allied war effort considered such targets of vital importance, and although the first oil-specific attacks took place in May 1940, they continued only as a lower priority target, at varying degrees of intensity, throughout the ensuing four years. It was not until early 1944 that oil targets became the top bombing priority.

At that time, a plan was tabled by the British Ministry of Economic Warfare that foresaw the systematic bombing of German oil production facilities, which the report considered could reduce output by 50%. It also re-arranged the priorities of potential bombing targets to: (i) oil production, (ii) fighter and ball-bearing production, (iii) rubber production, and (iv) bomber production, in that order.

The bombing of oil production facilities therefore increased significantly from May 1944 onwards to a point where attacks were made on oil targets in some part of occupied Europe practically on a daily basis, and often several times a day. Aided by continuously updated reconnaissance photography, repeat attacks were also made on facilities, where damage was recognised to have been minimal or production had re-commenced.

Although production was significantly curtailed by the bombing campaign, and the frequency of attacks therefore reduced late in the War, the Oil Campaign continued almost until the cessation of hostilities, the final target being the Vallø Oil Refinery, near Tønsberg, Norway, on the night of 25-26 April 1945. However, 41 Squadron's involvement in the campaign was limited to 30 September to 30 November 1944.

On 30 September 1944, the Lympne Wing was tasked with supporting Ramrod 1302 to the synthetic oil plants at Bottrop and Sterkrade, by sweeping the area through which the bombers passed in their run-up to the targets. Today's attacks constituted the third on both sites since July, respectively August, and the second on each within three days.[101]

Date	30 September 1944
Operation	Ramrod 1302
Target	Synthetic Oil Plants at Bottrop and Sterkrade, Nordrhein-Westfalen.
Bombers	200 Halifaxes & Lancasters and 10 Mosquitos[102]
Casualties	109 Sqn Mosq. XVI, ML997, crashed on take-off, Little Staughton, both crew inj.; 426 Sqn Halifax VII, LW197, Flak nr Oberhausen, 5 crew KIA, 2 crew POW
Escort	Matlaske (12 Group): 19, 65 & 122 Squadron (31 Mustang III) Manston: 118, 124 & 229 Squadrons (36 Spitfire IX) North Weald: 310 & 312 Sqns (24 Spitfire IX) [w. 504 Sqn] Manston: 504 Squadron (12 Spitfire IX) [w. 310 & 312 Sqns] Brenzett: 129, 306 & 315 Squadrons (34 Mstg III) Bradwell Bay: 64, 126 & 611 Squadrons (36 Spitfire IX) Deanland: 91, 322 & 345 Squadrons (36 Spitfire IX)

| Support and Sweep | Lympne: 41, 350 & 610 Squadrons (33 Spitfire XIV) |

Both 41 Squadron and the Lympne Wing were led by Sqn Ldr Benham for the operation, with 41 Squadron providing nine aircraft, and 350 and 610 Squadrons twelve each. This was 350 Squadron's first outing as a part of the Lympne Wing. The thirty-three aircraft were airborne between 11:15 and 11:20[103] and made landfall on the Continent near Knokke, Belgium, where they climbed to 25,000 feet, before rendezvousing with the bombers north of Antwerp. They escorted them on a course via Peddenburg and Dorsten, some 15-20km north of the targets, after which the bombers turned south on their bombing run, a few minutes after midday.

However, 10/10ths cloud was found over the target area and in the end only 27 bombers dropped their payloads on the primary targets. Some of the others bombed secondary targets, such as Oberhausen and Gelsenkirchen instead. As such, results were largely unseen, however intense Flak was encountered up to 20,000 feet, and one bomber was lost to Flak.[104]

The Wing swept undisturbed around the area between Dorsten and Borken, approximately 20km north of Dorsten, as the bombers passed through, but the operation was uneventful, as it was for the other escorting Wings. Although the Luftwaffe was reported to have been seen some distance off, they made no attempt to attack the Allied force.

The Lympne Wing reported seeing a dozen vapour trails from what they believed were jet-propelled enemy aircraft heading south near Peddenburg at 30,000 feet, but they made no attempt to attack. 41 Squadron tried to climb to engage them but were unable to do so fast enough whilst carrying their 90-gallon jettison tanks.

Their job done, the Wing set a course for Lympne, flying above the 10/10ths cloud layer until passing over Walcheren, then descended and returned straight to base, where they landed between 13:15 and 13:30.

The Wing was airborne for a second operation during the afternoon to escort 48 Mitchell and 18 Boston bombers of the U.S. 9th Air Force attacking road and rail junctions at Goch, just inside the German border, and approximately 27km southeast of Nijmegen.

Date	30 September 1944
Operation	Ramrod 1304
Target	Road and rail junctions, Goch, Nordrhein-Westfalen
Bombers	USAAF: 48 Mitchells and 18 Bostons in waves of 24, 24 and 18
Escort, 1st Wave	North Weald: 310 & 312 Squadrons (24 Spitfire IX)
Escort, 2nd Wave	Lympne: 41, 350 & 610 Squadrons (31 Spitfire XIV)
Escort, 3rd Wave	Bradwell Bay: 64, 126 & 611 Squadrons (34 Spitfire IX)
Target Cover	Brenzett: 129, 306 & 315 Squadrons (32 Mustang III)
Casualties	64 Sqn: Flt Sgt Winston E. Recile, EF/FL SW of Eindhoven, NL, pilot safe but injured.

Lympne provided three of the operation's eleven supporting fighter squadrons, eight of which were equipped with Spitfires and three with Mustangs. The Wing was airborne at 15:45, with 41 Squadron led by Sqn Ldr Benham, and crossed the Belgian coast at Knokke. They were greeted by some heavy but ineffective Flak from nearby Flushing [Vlissingen], and continued on to make rendezvous with the third wave of bombers – 18 Bostons – northeast of Antwerp at 18,000 feet. The bombers were escorted to Goch, where they bombed through cloud just after 16:00, unhindered by the Luftwaffe.

As thick cloud covered the general target area, only around a third of the entire bomber force was able to attack the primary target with what were considered 'fair results'. The remaining bombers dropped their payloads on targets of opportunity with unobserved results.

The Lympne Wing returned home without opposition from the Luftwaffe or Flak batteries, but was…

...greatly perturbed by the unwelcome attention of a solitary Spitfire IX which persisted in approaching the rear end of the formation in a hostile manner, much to the alarm of all concerned.[105]

However, all the pilots arrived safely back to Lympne, where they landed at 17:45 after a trip of two hours.

Meanwhile, 130 Squadron left Lympne for the last time in the early afternoon, the pilots flying 18 aircraft to Antwerp, followed by five Dakotas carrying the remaining pilots, the Medical Officer, Continuity NCO and Clerk, personal kit and equipment.

October 1944 – The weather for most of the month proved to be unsuitable for operations, and on 23 days – 1, 3-4, 8-13, 15-24, 26-27, 29 and 31 October – no operational flying was undertaken. However, on each of the remaining eight days, the Squadron participated in escorts to bombers targeting the front around Arnhem, and German industrial centres.

Troop Concentration | Tactical Target | Gun Emplacement
Oil Campaign | Industrial Target | Marshalling Yards

Date	Operation	Role	Type	Destination / Target
2	Ramrod 1306	Target Cover		SE of Arnhem, Netherlands
5	Ramrod 1314	Formation Escort		N of Nijmegen, Netherlands
6	Ramrod 1318	Formation Escort		Sterkrade, Germany
7	Ramrod 1319	Withdrawal Cover		Emmerich, Germany
14	Ramrod 1332	Close Escort		Duisburg, Germany
25	Ramrod 1347	Target Cover		Essen, Germany
28	Ramrod 1349	Target Cover		Walcheren Island, Netherlands
28	Ramrod 1350	Formation Escort		Köln, Germany
30	Ramrod 1352	Target Cover		Wesseling, Germany

1 October 1944 – A cloudy day with scattered showers limited the day's entire flying for 41 Squadron to just three non-operational air tests conducted by WO 'Archie' Appleton at 10:35, Plt Off 'Ricky' Gray at 14:00, and Flt Lt Harry Cook at 14:05.

Whilst the movement from Lympne to Antwerp by 130 Squadron, and the arrival of 350 Squadron at Lympne from Hawkinge, were considered complete today, a major new piece of news was received at Lympne, which was cause for much excitement:

A warning order was received from Headquarters A.D.G.B. to the effect that Nos. 41, 350 (Belg) and 610 Sqdns., Nos. 6041, 6350, and 6610 S.E. will be required to move from Lympne to the Continent as soon as possible. These Squadrons & Echelons will be transferred from A.D.G.B. to T.A.F.[106]

Just a day later, this order was updated:

> *Notification received that the effective date by which the Wing and Echelons are to be transferred is the 5th, October. 1944. Squadrons to remain at Lympne under the operational control of No.11 Group A.D.G.B. until such time as T.A.F. orders their move to the Continent.*[107]

'T.A.F.' was a reference to 2 TAF – the Second Tactical Air Force – which was formed on 1 June 1943 in order to prepare for and support an Allied invasion of the Continent. Units were extracted from Fighter Command and Bomber Command and posted to 2 TAF with the express purpose of supporting Allied ground forces.

2 TAF comprised of four Groups, three of which were composites of both Commands – 83, 84, 85 Groups – and one – 2 Group – that had only bombers. 83 Group, under which command 41, 130, 350 and 610 Squadron would ultimately come, comprised of eight Wings of fighter, fighter bomber, and fighter reconnaissance squadrons, supporting the British 2nd Army. 84 Group comprised of seven Wings of similar squadrons supporting the Canadian 1st Army. 85 Group was specifically designed for base defence, whilst 2 Group comprised of medium bombers – mainly Mosquitos and Mitchells – which were transferred from Bomber Command.

As the Front grew on the Continent, RAF fighter units were brought across the Channel to support it, such as was the case with 130 Squadron's recent move. However, despite the fact that 41, 350 and 610 Squadrons joined 2 TAF on 5 October, weather-related issues meant it would be almost another two months before the three Squadrons would become effective units within 2 TAF. At that time, they joined separate Wings within 83 Group, under the command of AVM Harry Broadhurst CB DSO* DFC* AFC, a former 41 Squadron pilot, but were reunited within the same Wing again by the end of the year.

2 October 1944 – Fine with little cloud and good visibility. The Lympne Wing's only operational flying today was limited to Target Cover for one of three waves of bombers attacking enemy troop concentrations the Netherlands.

Ramrod 1306 consisted of two waves of 24 Mitchells and a wave of 24 Bostons, supported by nine Spitfire squadrons, targeting German troops along the Front, around four to five miles (ca. 6.5 to 8km) southeast of Arnhem.

Date	2 October 1944
Operation	Ramrod 1306
Target	Troop concentrations, southeast of Arnhem, Gelderland
Bombers	48 Mitchells and 24 Bostons, in three waves of 24 bombers
Escort, 1st Wave	Manston: 118 & 124 Squadrons (24 Spitfire IX)
Escort, 2nd Wave	Deanland: 322 & 345 Squadrons (24 Spitfire IX)
Escort, 3rd Wave	Detling: 1 & 65 Squadrons (24 Spitfire IX)
Target Cover	Lympne: 41, 350 & 610 Squadrons (35 Spitfire XIV)
Casualties	322 Sqn: Fg Off Pieter A. Cramerus landed S. of Eindhoven; Detling: 2 A/C landed Eindhoven

41, 350 and 610 Squadrons were airborne at 10.30 and crossed the English coast at Deal, where they climbed to 17,000 feet. They made landfall on the Dutch coast north of Walcheren Island, and "had an uneventful trip to the bombing area, where a few odd rounds of anti-aircraft fire failed to perturb anyone."[108]

All 72 bombers attacked the primary target through 7/10ths cloud with what were believed to have been good results. There was little Flak and no sign of the Luftwaffe, and every bomber returned home safely. Three fighters from other Wings landed in Eindhoven, but the Lympne Wing completed the operation without mishap.

On their return, 41 Squadron, led by Flt Lt Terry Spencer, encountered a little anti-aircraft fire south of Walcheren Island but it did no damage. The Wing landed again just after midday, reporting having sighted a possible V2 site on west Schouwen Island from 14,000 feet. They described it as "an overgrown avenue of trees… in a wood, and on the sandy edges of [the] wood, there were white patches, suggesting flashing…"[109]

3 October 1944 – Although no operational flying took place today, WOs Pat Coleman and 'Jimmy' Ware, and Flt Sgt 'Steve' Stevenson all undertook air tests, whilst Flt Lt Terry Spencer flew to Farnborough and Fg Off Johnnie Wilkinson to Derby, both returning the same day. Separately, a new pilot joined the Squadron today, 24-year-old Londoner Flt Lt Charles James 'Sammy' Samouelle DFC*.[110]

4 October 1944 – No operational flying was undertaken by the Squadron today, but Sqn Ldr Benham received a welcome letter from the 11 Group SASO, Air Cdre Cecil 'Boy' Bouchier.

As 41 Squadron had been suffering discipline and morale problems for some time, Bouchier had stepped in, in summer 1944, and asked RAF Lympne's Wg Cdr Colin Gray to recommend someone to replace Sqn Ldr Robert Chapman. Gray had recommended Sqn Ldr Douglas Benham DFC, who took over the role on 28 August.

Tasked with cleaning up the Squadron and re-instilling discipline, Benham had worked hard since then to re-mould the Squadron into a tight-knit and effective fighting unit. Feeling he had made significant progress, Benham sent Bouchier a photograph of the 'new' improved Squadron, and Bouchier replied on 4 October 1944, thanking him for his hard work.

My dear Benham

Thank you so much for your very kind thought in sending me a photo of No.41 Squadron. I am particularly glad to have this photo because a long time ago I had the honour of serving for three years in the great Squadron you now command, and I think they were the happiest years of my life.[111] Time cannot erase the affection for Squadrons one has served in for a long time, particularly when that Squadron, such as '41', has, over the years, always been just that little bit better than all the others.

Naturally I am sorry to lose '41', but glad for your sakes and because I know you and your lads will make rings around the Hun.[112]

I shall follow your fortunes and successes 'over there', as I have always done and my good wishes will always be with you.

Good luck to you all and my thanks for all the gallant and splendid work you have done in 11 Group.

P.S. Please give my special regards to Lord Gisborough. He came with the Squadron to HORNCHURCH during their long stay with me there in the Battle of Britain.[113] His affection, loyalty and service to your Squadron has been truly wonderful.[114]

It was a good boost for 26-year-old Benham; not only was it a confirmation that what he was doing was right, but it was also encouragement for the future.

Co-incidentally, however, although moving from 11 Group to 2 TAF meant that 41 Squadron would leave the watchful eye of Bouchier, a 41 Squadron pilot from 1926 to 1929, they would come under the watchful gaze of another, AVM Harry Broadhurst, who commanded 83 Group and had served on 41 Squadron from 1931 to 1933.

5 October 1944 – Scattered showers and local thunderstorms with 10/10ths cloud below 1,000 feet in the morning, followed by fair periods with variable cloud at 2,000-3,000 feet and good visibility during the afternoon and evening.

The Lympne Wing was tasked today with a similar operation to that of 2 October, by supporting 48 Mitchells and 24 Bostons bombing German troop concentrations just north of Nijmegen in the Netherlands in Ramrod 1314. The bombers were supported by nine Spitfire squadrons, of which two – 41 and 610 Squadrons – were provided by the Lympne Wing.

Date	5 October 1944
Operation	Ramrod 1314
Target	Troop concentrations, north of Nijmegen, Gelderland, NL
Bombers	48 Mitchells and 24 Bostons, in waves of 18, 18, & 12 Mitchells, and 24 Bostons
Casualties	342 Sqn Boston IIIA, BZ318, hit by AA Arnhem, CL Boort
Escort, 1st Wave Escort, 2nd Wave Escort, 3rd Wave Escort, 4th Wave Target Cover	Bradwell Bay: 64 & 126 Squadrons (23 Spitfire IX) Lympne: 41 & 610 Squadrons (13 Spitfire XIV) Detling: 1 & 165 Squadrons (24 Spitfire IX) Hawkinge: 132 & 441 Squadrons (25 Spitfire IX) Friston: 131 Squadron (11 Spitfire VII)
Casualties	41 Sqn: Fg Off D. F. J. Tebbit IFA, EF on TO & CL; 165 Sqn: Fg Off V. Porich, poor visibility, landed Antwerp

The pilots were woken at 07:15 on this very cold morning to be briefed for the operation, and were airborne between 08:20 and 08:25, led by Wg Cdr Gray, who also led 610 Squadron. 610 took off with eight aircraft, whilst 41 Squadron, led by Flt Lt Terry Spencer, prepared to take off with ten. More aircraft should have participated from both Squadrons, but a problem with the petrol bowser meant that the remaining aircrafts' 90-gallon jettison tanks could not be filled.

However, within minutes this reduced force was further diminished in a series of mishaps. Firstly, Australian WO 'Jimmy' Ware (RM788) collided with another aircraft on the ground (believed to have been RM705) and was unable to take off. Then Fg Off Don Tebbit (RM793) tried to get airborne, but…

> …could not develop enough power to take off, closed his throttle and had to retract his undercarriage to stop in time. Unfortunately his 90 gallon jet-tank caught fire, and in a moment the aircraft was well ablaze. F/O D.F.J. Tebbit was able to get out quickly, but not without receiving superficial facial burns and lacerations.[115]

As if this were not enough, within five minutes of take-off, 610 Squadron's WO 'Chalky' White turned back with his engine running roughly and landed at Lympne again at 08:35. Only minutes later, 41 Squadron's Fg Off Johnnie Wilkinson (RM769) started to have trouble with his R/T system and he, too, returned to base, putting down at 08:45. Not to be out-done, 610 Squadron's WO Pope then found that his R/T system was also not working and similarly returned, landing at Lympne five minutes after Wilkinson.

Thus, within the space of 30 minutes, three of 41 Squadron's pilots and two of 610's had dropped out of an already depleted Wing operation, and only 13 aircraft (seven from 41 Squadron and six from 610 Squadron, including Gray) actually completed the escort. In the end, Gray led no more than the strength a single squadron!

Gray and his 'composite squadron' made landfall between Ostend [Oostende] and Knokke, Belgium, at 12,000 feet and rendezvoused with the bombers over Eindhoven. However, 8/10ths-9/10ths cloud was found over the target area at 9,000-10,000 feet, and there was "a good deal of orbiting before the bombers were able to get into position for a good run-up to the target".[116]

In fact, only 27 bombers dropped their payloads in poor visibility, and although some bursts were seen in the target area, results were largely unobserved. Moderate heavy Flak was fired at the bombers, and one crash-landed in Belgium as a result. The fighter escorts were otherwise uneventful, except for a pilot of 165 Squadron, who landed in Antwerp as a result of poor visibility.

Gray then led the Wing home, but Fg Off Peter Gibbs (RM797) had a scare near Eindhoven when his engine cut out in mid-air. He was able to restart the machine, but lost the Wing in the

Fg Off Donald Tebbit wrote off Spitfire XIV, RM793, EB-A, at Lympne on 5 October 1944. The engine failed on take-off and as the undercarriage was retracted, the jettison tank exploded on hitting the ground and destroyed the aircraft. © Terry Spencer, via Cara and Raina Spencer

process and returned home alone. However, he made it back to Lympne in time to join A Flight in the circuit for landing at 10:45.

Separately today, 41, 350 and 610 Squadrons officially transferred from ADGB to 2 TAF, and had now only to await their orders to proceed from Lympne to the Continent. Unfortunately, they were to have a longer wait than anyone might have predicted – almost a two full months!

6 October 1944 – Fair weather with well broken cloud at a base of 2,000 feet and good visibility. Despite their transfer to 2 TAF, it was business as usual today for all three Lympne Wing squadrons, and they participated in an escort to a formation of bombers attacking German synthetic oil plants.

The escort was an element of Ramrod 1318, which had two separate targets: the Nordstern Synthetic Oil Plant[117], in the north-western districts of Gelsenkirchen, and the synthetic oil plant at Sterkrade. The operation consisted of a total of 300 Bomber Command Halifaxes and Lancasters led by 20 Pathfinder Mosquitos, which were supported by twelve Spitfire and seven Mustang Squadrons.

The bomber force consisted of 254 Halifaxes from 4 Group, and 46 Lancasters of 8 Group. Of these, 151 bombers were assigned to the attack on Gelsenkirchen and 149 to Sterkrade. Each force was led in by ten Oboe Mosquitos, which also belonged to 8 Group. The fighter escorts consisted of two squadrons of Mustangs and three squadrons of Spitfires, plus target cover of three Spitfire squadrons, to each target, whilst three Mustang squadrons were ordered to sweep the Gladbach [Bergisch Gladbach]-Cologne [Köln]-Bonn region to the south of the target area, and the Gütersloh-Hopsten region to the north and northeast of the target area.

Date	6 October 1944
Operation	Ramrod 1318
Target	Synthetic Oil Plants, Gelsenkirchen & Sterkrade, Nordrhein-Westfalen
Bombers	4 Group: 254 Halifaxes & 8 Group: 46 Lancasters & 20 Pathfinder Mosquitos; half of force to each target
Casualties	Gelsenkirchen: 7 Sqn Lancs III, PA964 & PB241, 78 Sqn Halifaxes III, LL588, LW511 & MZ310, and 346 Sqn Halifax III, NA555; Sterkrade: 51 Sqn Halifax III, MZ343, 466 Sqn Halifax III, LW372, & 640 Sqn Halifax III, MZ925.118
Escort Gelsenkirchen	Matlaske (12 Group): 19 & 122 Squadrons (24 Mustang III) Bradwell Bay: 64, 126 & 312 Squadrons (36 Spitfire IX)

Target Cover Glsnkchn.	Hawkinge: 131, 132 & 441 Sqns (12 Spitfire VII & 25 Spitfire IX)
Escort Sterkrade	Matlaske (12 Group): 65 Squadron (12 Mustang III) Coltishall (12 Group) : 316 Squadron (12 Mustang III) Lympne: 41, 350 & 610 Squadrons (34 Spitfire XIV)
Target Cover Sterkrade	Detling: 1, 165 & 229 Squadrons (34 Spitfire IX)
Sweep	Brenzett: 129, 306 & 315 Squadrons (36 Mustang III)

The Lympne Wing was tasked with escorting the bombers to Sterkrade in unison with two Mustang squadrons from 12 Group, and constituted their second trip to Sterkrade within a week. The Wing's contingent consisted of 34 aircraft from all three squadrons – eleven each from 41 and 610 Squadrons, and twelve from 350 Squadron – which were airborne just before 16:00. Within a few minutes, however, 41's WO 'Archie' Appleton (RM699) discovered an oxygen leak and returned to base, and 350 Squadron's Flt Lt Roger Hoornaert returned with engine trouble.

The Wing crossed in south of Walcheren Island at 25,000 feet, having already rendezvoused with the bombers prior to making landfall[119], but shortly thereafter 350 Squadron's contingent suffered a serious set-back. Flt Lt André Plisnier, leading Yellow Section, started suffering tank trouble, and his No. 3, Plt Off Robert Bladt, discovered he had R/T trouble. Both men, pulled out, accompanied by their wingmen, which reduced the unit's numbers from eleven to just seven.

The Wing's numbers had thereby fallen by almost 20% before even reaching the target. Nonetheless, they continued on, finding conditions clear all the way to the targets; "the Rhine Valley was easily distinguishable".[120] This made for accurate and well concentrated bombing, and large explosions were seen in the target areas, with black smoke soon obscuring the downwards visibility.[121]

Despite the good visibility, the number of bombers that actually attacked the targets was somewhat lower than despatched. Of the 151 bombers and ten Mosquitos sent to Gelsenkirchen, only 136 and three attacked, and of the 149 bombers and ten Mosquitos assigned to Sterkrade, only 137 and five attacked. However, the clear skies also meant that anti-aircraft fire from the target areas was accurate and deadly. 41 Squadron recalled that…

> …the bombers encountered exceedingly intense flak over the target. It could be easily as paramount [sic] to the anti-doodle bug barrage in the South Coast near Lympne, and along the Dungeness tip. The target was well and truly pounded, and three big boys were seen to go down in flames.[122]

In fact, no less than nine bombers and crews were lost – the three Halifaxes seen to go down at Sterkrade by 41 Squadron, and another four Halifaxes and two Lancasters at Gelsenkirchen.

On the completion of the bombing run over Sterkrade, the Lympne Wing headed for home via Peddenburg and West Schouwen. Whilst the Wing continued on to land at base between 18:05 and 18:20, Flt Lts Ross Harding (RM707) and Bill Stowe (RM769) discovered they were running low on fuel and decided not to risk the flight across the Channel. The pair put down at Antwerp instead and stayed the night, returning to Lympne at 09:20 the following morning.

7 October 1944 – Cloudy with a base below 1,000 feet, rain in the west, visibility moderate, 6-8 miles, deteriorating to poor.

Another escort was laid on today for the Lympne Wing, on this occasion providing withdrawal cover to 750 Lancasters sent to bomb Emmerich, 5km east of the Germany border to the Netherlands, and approximately 25km east of Nijmegen.

Once again, the Wing's role was just a component of a much larger operation, which foresaw attacks on Kleve by 90 Lancasters and 251 Halifaxes of 1 and 3 Groups, and on Emmerich by another 340 Lancasters, each led by ten Pathfinder Mosquitos of 8 Group, who were to mark the targets from 30,000 feet approximately five minutes prior to the main attack. The formations were escorted by 21 Spitfire and four Mustang squadrons. It was the largest attack on the area of the entire War thus far.

These targets were considered purely tactical, as the towns, 10km apart across the Rhine, lay on major routes to the Netherlands that Allied commanders felt German troops could use to threaten their right flank near Nijmegen that had been left exposed by the failure of *Market Garden*. Grave concerns were held for the possibility of a German counter-attack along the Nijmegen Salient, and the concentration German of artillery in the area was reported to have been the largest met by the Allied advance since the invasion began. It was also hoped to catch supplies and troops in the town destined for the front.[123]

Date	7 October 1944
Operation	Ramrod 1319
Target	Tactical targets, Kleve and Emmerich, Nordrhein-Westfalen
Bombers	3, 4 & 8 Groups: 251 Halifaxes, 90 Lancasters, 10 Mosquitos to Kleve; 1, 3 and 8 Groups: 340 Lancasters & 10 Mosquitos to Emmerich
Casualties	Kleve: 51 Sqn, Halifax III, NP933, & 78 Sqn Halifax III, LV796; Emmerich: 166 Sqn Lanc I, PD239, 460 Sqn Lanc III, PB407, & 514 Sqn Lanc III, LM735.[124]
Escort to Kleve, Front	Manston: 118, 124, 229 & 504 Squadrons (47 Spitfire IX)
Escort to Kleve, Rear	North Weald: 310 Squadron (11 Spitfire IX) Coltishall (12 Group): 303 & 602 Squadrons (18 Spitfire IX)
Withdrawal Cover	Deanland: 322 & 345 Squadrons (23 Spitfire IX)
Escort Emmerich, Front	Detling: 1 & 165 Squadrons (22 Spitfire IX) Hawkinge: 132 & 441 Squadrons (24 Spitfire IX)
Escort Emmerich, Rear	Bradwell Bay: 64, 126 & 312 Squadrons (36 Spitfire IX)
Withdrawal Cover	Lympne: 41 & 350 Squadrons (20 Spitfire XIV)
Target & Withdrawal Cover, both Targets	Matlaske (12 Group): 19, 65 & 122 Squadrons (26 Mustang III) Coltishall (12 Group): 316 Squadron (10 Mustang III)
Casualties	350 Sqn: Fg Off P. Delorme, landed in Belg

The Lympne Wing's component should have included 610 Squadron, but as the weather was so poor, the unit was stood down shortly before take-off and only 41 and 350 Squadrons participated, each providing ten aircraft for the operation.[125] The aircraft were airborne just before 13:30, but operated independently to and from Emmerich due to the poor conditions. In addition, Hawkinge based 132 and 441 Squadrons returned to base within 15 minutes of becoming airborne, and at least three other squadrons also abandoned the operation prior to take-off, as a result of the weather.

The trips to the target areas were uneventful for all participants, even though the visibility was clear. As such, both towns were heavily and accurately bombed, although it was reported that some bombers dropped too early, their payloads falling in the region of Nijmegen, instead.

Of the 700 bombers and Mosquitoes initially assigned to the Ramrod, 673 attacked "with results believed to be excellent".[126] The bombing was well concentrated and the escort squadrons all reported having seen many explosions and fires, and columns of black smoke rising to between 11,000 and 15,000 feet in the air over the target areas, particularly emanating from a large oil fire on the south bank of the Rhine. A large explosion was also seen around 10km west of Emmerich that sent smoke up to 12,000 feet.

Both Kleve and Emmerich were hit hard. Kleve had been bombed on a smaller scale on a number of occasions since the beginning of the War, but this attack constituted its largest to date. Approximately 1,728 tons of explosive shells and 4.5 tons of incendiary bombs were dropped on the centre of the town, destroying an area bounded by the streets Lindenallee, Römerstrasse, Gruftstrasse, Tiergartenstrasse and Kermisdahl.[127] Emmerich, however, was hit harder. Different sources place the level of destruction of the town from this single attack at between 91% and 97%, thereby achieving the unenviable statistic of being the most destroyed German town of the War.

41 Squadron spent seventeen minutes in the target area but reported no opposition except for intense heavy Flak. This caused no damage to any of the Ramrod's escort fighters but claimed two Halifaxes at Kleve and three Lancasters at Emmerich.

41 Squadron headed home escorting a box of 80 bombers away from Emmerich and landed 15:25, reporting an otherwise uneventful trip. 350 Squadron's experience was similar, but arrived home between 15:35 and 15:40 minus Fg Off Paul Delorme (RM158), who had landed in Belgium.

8 October 1944 – No operational flying was undertaken by 41 Squadron today, although air tests were flown by Flt Lt 'Sammy' Samouelle, Fg Off 'Momo' Balasse, WO Pat Coleman and Flt Sgt 'Steve' Stevenson. Separately, the Lympne Wing received a visit today from a trio of officers to help them prepare for packing for their pending move to the Continent: the 2 TAF Equipment Officer, Sqn Ldr Solley, the 83 Group Equipment Officer, Sqn Ldr Campbell, and the Equipment Officer for 125 Wing, Flt Lt Nicholas. Within days, the squadrons were also issued Belgian currency in exchange for Sterling.

9 October 1944 – Although no operational flying was undertaken by 41 Squadron today, air tests were flown by Flt Lts Ross Harding, 'Denny' Reid, 'Sammy' Samouelle, and Bill Stowe, Fg Off Johnnie Wilkinson, WO Pat Coleman and Flt Sgt 'Steve' Stevenson. Separately, both Sqn Ldr Benham and Wg Cdr Gray left Lympne for London to attend an investiture.

Operation Hurricane

14 October 1944 – Fair with broken cloud above 2,000 feet and scattered showers, but generally good visibility. The Lympne Wing was up early to participate in Operation *Hurricane*, the Allies' greatest airborne raid of the War, which was a 24-hour bombing campaign designed to…

> …demonstrate to the enemy in Germany generally the overwhelming superiority of the Allied Air Forces in this theatre… the intention is to apply within the shortest practical period the maximum effort of the Royal Air Force Bomber Command and the VIIIth United States Bomber Command against objectives in the densely populated Ruhr…[128]

…and, further, to…

> …cause mass panic and disorganization in the Ruhr, disrupt frontline communications and demonstrate the futility of resistance.[129]

To achieve this, Bomber Command sent 1,000 bombers to Duisburg during the morning of 14 October, whilst the U.S. 8th Air Force sent another 1,000 bombers to Cologne [Köln] soon after midday, both operations supported by escorts of several hundred fighters. *Hurricane* continued during the night, when yet another 1,000-strong raid was made on Duisburg by Bomber Command, whilst a separate attack was also made on Braunschweig by an additional 240 bombers.

The Lympne Wing participated in the first attack, providing three of the 20 Spitfire and eight Mustang squadrons assigned to escort the mission, officially named Ramrod 1332. The bomber force consisted of a total of 1,013 bombers, comprising of 519 Lancasters, 474 Halifaxes and 20 Pathfinder Mosquitos. Seven Spitfire squadrons were assigned to a close escort of the front of the formation, five to the centre – thereunder the three Lympne Wing squadrons and Coltishall based 306 and 602 Squadrons – and eight Spitfire squadrons to the rear. An additional seven Mustang squadrons were ordered to provide area patrols to cover the bombers, and one to cover the Mosquitos.

Date	14 October 1944
Operation	Ramrod 1332
Target	Tactical target, Duisburg, Germany (Operation Hurricane)
Bombers	519 Lancasters, 474 Halifaxes and 20 Mosquitos
Casualties[130]	12 Sqn Lancs I, LL909, ME788 & NF928, 115 Sqn Lanc I, HK599, & Lanc III, ND805, 153 Sqn Lanc I, NG190 & Lanc III, JB297, 166 Sqn Lanc I, PD224, 300 Sqn Lanc I, NF959, 419 Sqn Lanc X, KB800, 428 Sqn Lanc X, KB780, 550 Sqn Lancs I, NG133 & PD319, & 626 Sqn Lanc III, NE163, & 425 Sqn Halifax III, MZ674, & 429 Sqn Halifax III, MZ453.
Close Escort Front	Bradwell Bay: 64, 91, 126 & 312 Squadrons (45 Spitfire IX) Hawkinge: 132 & 441 Squadrons (24 Spitfire IX) Friston: 131 Squadron (12 Spitfire VII)
Close Escort Centre	Coltishall (12 Group): 303 & 602 Squadrons (23 Spitfire IX) Lympne: 41, 350 & 610 Squadrons (34 Spitfire XIV)
Close Escort Rear	Manston: 118, 124, 229 & 504 Squadrons (48 Spitfire IX) North Weald: 310 & 313 Squadrons (24 Spitfire IX) Detling: 1 & 165 Squadrons (24 Spitfire IX)
Area Patrol Bombers	Matlaske (12 Group): 19, 65 & 122 Squadrons (36 Mustang III) Coltishall (12 Group): 316 Squadron (12 Mustang III) Andrews Field: 129, 306 & 315 Squadrons (28 Mustang III)
Area Patrol Mosquitoes	North Weald: 234 Squadron (8 Mustang III)
Casualties	1 Sqn: 1 A/C landed St. Omer/Fort Rouge, France; 234 Sqn: Plt Off J. R. May, EF/CL Moerbeke, N of Ghent; 306 Sqn: Fg Off C. Gierycz CL, Andrews Fld; 312 Sqn: Flt Sgt J. Bílek, EF Wesel, CL Volkel; 350 Sqn: Sqn Ldr M. Donnet, EF landed B.61 Ghent/St. Denis-Westrem; 602 Sqn: Fg Off Robinson EF, CL on TO, Coltishall, seriously inj; Lympne Wing: Wg Cdr C. F. Gray, EF, landed Merville.

The Lympne Wing supported the operation with eleven aircraft from 41 Squadron, ten from 350 Squadron, and twelve from 610 Squadron, with Wg Cdr Gray leading the Wing, and the respective Squadron Leaders leading their own squadrons. All three units were airborne between 08:00 and 08:05, but Wg Cdr Gray had starter trouble and was airborne late. He hurried to catch up but then started having engine trouble, made a hasty landing in Merville, France, and did not participate further in the operation.

The rest of the Wing made rendezvous with the bombers south of Eindhoven, but at 08:45, 350 Squadron's Sqn Ldr Michel Donnet also bowed out with problems and landed at Ghent. The remaining pilots escorted the bombers to Duisburg according to plan, but found 9/10ths cloud between 10,000 and 12,000 feet.

Despite the cloud cover, the bombers went to work, and a total of 957 Lancasters and Halifaxes dropped 3,574 tons of high explosive and 820 tons of incendiary bombs on the target area between 08:45 and 09:15. The escorting fighters reported the bombing to be well concentrated, with many explosions and oil fires seen, and dense black smoke rising to around 3,000 feet. An ineffective smoke screen was also observed and reported by the Lympne Wing.

The only airborne opposition met by the entire force was a lone Me109, which attacked the bombers ten miles northwest of Duisburg. It was shot down by WO Aleksander Pietrzak of Coltishall's 316 (Polish) Squadron, and the pilot was seen to bale out. However, the bombers came under intense accurate heavy Flak and no less than 16 aircraft were lost: 14 Lancasters and two Halifaxes. Some of the Flak rose to 23,000-24,000 feet and made enormous explosions, which the pilots likened to that of a V1 exploding in mid-air. This appeared to be the cause of two or three bombers blowing up over the target area.

The task completed, 41, 350 and 610 Squadrons passed back out over the Netherlands, returning home to land at base again between 10:00 and 10:30, and reported the operation was otherwise uneventful. There was no more operational flying for the Wing for the rest of the day.

From the end of Operation *Market Garden*, through to the end of November 1944, 41 Squadron provided air support for the Allied Oil Campaign, the attempted destruction of all of Germany's remaining oil reserves, refineries and synthetic oil plants. © Public domain, U.S. Air Force Photo, via the National Museum of the U.S. Air Force

Playing their own role in Operation *Hurricane*, the U.S. 8th Air Force despatched 1,066 bombers to targets in the Cologne area in three waves between 12:15 and 12:45, the total force consisting of 748 B-17 Flying Fortresses and 318 B-24 Liberators, escorted by several hundred P-51 Mustangs and P-47 Thunderbolts. The first attack was made on the Gereon marshalling yards by 434 Flying Fortresses, of which two were lost and 93 damaged; the second was made on the Gremberg and Eifelter marshalling yards and the town of Euskirchen by 318 Liberators, of which three were lost and 138 damaged, and the third was made on the Gereon marshalling yards again by another 314 Flying Fortresses, of which none were lost but 125 damaged.

During the night, a second raid was made on Duisburg by the RAF, which saw another 1,005 bombers despatched in two waves about two hours apart. On this occasion, an additional 4,040 tons of high explosive and 500 tons of incendiary bombs were dropped on the city, for the loss of seven aircraft.

During the 24 hours encompassing Operation *Hurricane*, Bomber Command logged 2,589 sorties for the loss of 24 aircraft – less than one percent of the total force – and had dropped around 10,050 tons of high explosive and incendiary bombs. These records were not surpassed during the remaining months of the War.

The two raids on Duisburg today constituted the 240th and 241st attacks on the city since the beginning of the War.[131] By the end of the day, 100,000 houses had been destroyed, gas, water and electricity lines were cut, and river shipping facilities and rail infrastructure destroyed.[132]

According to the official count of the Air Defence Police, a total of 299 aerial attacks were made on Duisburg during the War. By the cessation of hostilities, 80% of the city's housing was destroyed or seriously damaged, and of the 131,000 houses and apartments that existed in 1939, only 3,000 remained completely undamaged at its conclusion.[133] It would take a full 15 years to rebuild the city.

15-24 October 1944 – 11 Group had no work for 41 Squadron except for a single shipping reconnaissance to Dunkirk on 17 October. The rest of the time was spent on "an occasional airtest [sic], and frequent beer-swills."[134]

17 October 1944 – Heavy rain during the afternoon. The only operational flying undertaken by 41 Squadron today was a shipping reconnaissance to Dunkirk by Australian Flt Lts Robert Anderson and Daniel Reid. Whilst the Squadron's F541 omits any detail on the operation, the RAF Lympne ORB indicates that these two sorties were the only operational flights that day for the entire Wing. However, the lack of information suggests the patrol was uneventful.

19 October 1944 – As there was no operational flying, 6041 Servicing Echelon used the opportunity to pack in preparation for their pending move to Belgium.

21 October 1944 – The Squadron organised a party at the Royal Oak Hotel and invited 610 Squadron "to settle various misunderstandings, which occurred during our stay in 10 Group."[135,136] It was a good evening, considered 610 Squadron, as 41 Squadron "suffered a defeat in a beer drinking contest"![137]

However, it appears that not all misunderstandings were settled at all: 41 Squadron's Australian WO 'Jimmy' Ware got himself into a brawl with two airmen. It had serious repercussions for the 23-year-old; he was immediately grounded, posted away on 1 November, and severely reprimanded in a General Court Martial three weeks later.[138]

23 October 1944 – No operational flying was undertaken by the Wing today as a result of the weather, but it did not stop 41 Squadron playing a game of Rugby against 610 Squadron in the rain, which they won 22:0! Separately, two new pilots joined the Squadron today: 21-year-old WO Alister Donald 'Andy' Miller[139] from Armadale, Victoria, and 22-year-old Flt Sgt Crawford Noal 'Micky' Moyle[140] of Port Pirie, South Australia. Both men arrived on the Squadron today from 83 GSU at Bognor Regis for their first operational postings.

24 October 1944 – No operational flying today for the ninth day in the last ten. However, becoming concerned that the men were beginning to suffer from a lack of exercise, Wg Cdr Colin Gray ordered all three squadrons to the indoor tennis courts to keep fit. Two softball teams were selected from 41 and 610 Squadrons, and whilst the rest of the men stayed for P.T. and games, 41 and 610 battled it out on the field once again.

> *The softball match took place on the airfield but* [610] *Squadron was defeated by the Wing Commander and 41 Squadron (also the umpire according to some opinions) by 23 to 5.*[141]

25 October 1944 – Widespread fog or low stratus cloud, improving during the afternoon to broken cloud at 2,000 feet. Visibility initially poor, improving to one to three miles. After several days of inactivity, the Lympne Wing was back in the air in force today, to provide an escort to 600 Lancasters and Halifaxes attacking Essen in Ramrod 1347.

The operation was a two-pronged attack which despatched 32 Lancasters, 199 Halifaxes and 12 Pathfinder Mosquitos to the Moers-Meerbeck Synthetic Oil Plant, and another 508 Lancasters, 251 Halifaxes and 12 Pathfinder Mosquitos to the Krupp Werke in Essen, approximately 20km due east of Homberg, escorted by 17 Spitfire and eight Mustang squadrons. The Mosquitos were tasked with marking the target areas at zero minus 25 minutes from a height of 30,000 feet.

WO Alister Miller RAAF served with 41 Squadron from 23 October 1944 to 21 January 1945. Subsequently posted to 130 Squadron, he was shot down and killed by return fire from the rear gunner of a Ju188 on 27 April 1945. © Shirley Keenan, via Garry Cooper

Date	25 October 1944
Operation	Ramrod 1347
Target	Krupp Werke, Essen, Nordrhein-Westfalen Synthetic Oil Plant, Moers, Nordrhein-Westfalen
Bombers	Essen: 508 Lancasters, 251 Halifaxes & 12 Mosquitos Homberg: 199 Halifaxes, 32 Lancasters & 12 Mosquitos
Casualties	Essen: 115 Sqn Lanc I, PD276, 428 Sqn Lanc X, KB737, & 158 Sqn Halifaxes III, MZ734 & MZ945
Essen: Escort Front	North Weald: 310 & 313 Squadrons (24 Spitfire IX)
Escort to Centre, Penetration & Withdrawal	Andrews Field: 19, 65 & 122 Squadrons (36 Mustang III)
Escort to Rear	Bradwell Bay: 64, 126 & 312 Squadrons (36 Spitfire IX)
Target Cover & Escort on Withdrawal to Front	Friston: 131 Squadron (12 Spitfire VII)
Target Cover & Escort on Withdrawal to Rear	Lympne: 41, 350 & 610 Squadrons (38 Spitfire XIV)
Withdrawal Cover	North Weald: 234 Squadron (12 Mustang III)
Homberg: Escort Front	Detling: 1 & 165 Squadrons (25 Spitfire IX)
Escort to Centre, Penetration & Withdrawal	Andrews Field: 129 & 306 Squadrons (24 Mustang III)
Escort to Rear	Hawkinge: 132 & 441 Squadrons (25 Spitfire IX)
Target Cover & Escort on Withdrawal to Front	Manston: 504 Squadron (13 Spitfire IX)
Target Cover & Escort on Withdrawal to Rear	Manston: 118 & 124 Squadrons (24 Spitfire IX)
Withdrawal Cover	Coltishall (12 Group): 315 Squadron (12 Mustang III)
Casualties	126 Sqn: Capt J. Clayton, EF, landed Continent; 312 Sqn: Flt Sgt J. Konvička, EF, landed Brussels; 313 Sqn: Flt Sgt W. H. Hallett, RF, baled out, inj, Bruges; 350 Sqn: Flt Lt A. Plisnier & Fg Off P. Pacco, landed Brussels, Flt Sgt L. Lambrechts CL Meslin L'Eveque, & Sgt Plts M. Morel & E. Pauwels landed Antwerp; 610 Sqn: Sgt Plt T. Higgs, RF, landed Antwerp

The Lympne Wing was assigned to target cover and an escort on withdrawal to the rear of the bomber formation on the Essen attack, and consisted of twelve aircraft from 41 Squadron, twelve from 350 Squadron and fourteen from 610 Squadron. The pilots were airborne between 14:35 and 14:55, crossed in at Blankenberge, Belgium, and flew directly to Essen, where they rendezvoused with the bombers and provided them cover over the city, at 25,000 feet.

The bombers relied solely on the markers dropped over Essen by the Pathfinders as the city was covered in 8/10ths to 10/10ths cloud up to 3,000 feet. A total of 736 bombers therefore dropped their payloads blind from 20,000 feet, and initial concerns were that the bombing had thus became scattered, despite reports of large explosions and smoke up to 7,000 feet.

However, subsequent reconnaissance photography – and documents from Essen accessed post-War – reveal that the damage was far greater than originally assumed. In all, 1,163 buildings were destroyed – a far greater number than during a larger attack on Essen 36 hours earlier – and the raid caused...

> *...severe damage to the remaining industrial concerns in Essen, particularly to the Krupps steelworks […] ...and there are references to the firm's archives to the 'almost complete breakdown of the electrical supply network' and to 'a complete paralysis'. The Borbeck pig-iron plant ceased work completely and there is no record of any further production from this important section of Krupps. Much of Essen's surviving industrial capacity was now dispersed and the city lost its role as one of Germany's most important centres of war production.*[142]

Although four unidentified aircraft acting in a hostile way were seen ten miles south of Emmerich on the way out, they did not attack and opposition was limited to anti-aircraft fire directed at the bombers over the target area. The Flak was intense and of heavy calibre, and four aircraft were lost – two Lancasters and two Halifaxes. Two of these were seen to explode in mid-air, whilst the remaining pair was seen to lose height over the target area.

On the way back out, the Lympne Wing fulfilled the rest of their mission, by providing a withdrawal escort to the rear of the bomber formation, and accompanied them as far as Antwerp before changing course for base. Whilst the vast majority of the Wing arrived back at Lympne between 16:30 and 16:50 without further event, five pilots from 350 Squadron and one from 610 Squadron landed in Belgium either short on fuel or with engine trouble, returning later.

Flt Sgt (later WO) Crawford N. 'Micky' Moyle RAAF served with 41 Squadron from 23 October 1944 to 29 October 1945, during which time he claimed one destroyed FW190D and one shared destroyed He111. © 41 Squadron RAF

On their return from the Ramrod, several Wings reported seeing V2 vapour trails during their escorts to Essen. The Friston Wing reported observing vertical vapour trails rising to 20,000-25,000 feet from Wesel and Düsseldorf at 15:11. Andrews Field, North Weald and Lympne all reported seeing a near-vertical vapour trail rising to a height of 20,000-40,000 feet approximately 20 miles south of Düren at 15:20, and the North Weald Wing also saw another approximately ten miles north of Essen at 15:30. Bradwell Bay also reported seeing two vapour trails, one 20 miles northeast of Koblenz, and the other 15-20 miles southwest of Dortmund at 15:40.

Meanwhile, 228 bombers of 6 and 8 Groups had also attacked the Synthetic Oil Plant at Homberg in similar conditions. Blind bombing was also undertaken, and although initially scattered, concentration improved as the attack progressed. No bombers were lost over this target. Fighter Wings supporting this attack also reported seeing up to half a dozen V2 vapour trails, but to what extent these were simultaneous sightings of those seen by fighters on the Essen attack cannot be established with certainty.

26 October 1944 – No operational flying. During the afternoon the Lympne Wing received a visit from the AOC 11 Group, AVM Hugh Saunders CB CBE MC DFC MM, who was on a farewell tour of his stations. He had been posted to the Air Ministry as Director-General of Personnel, his move likely a result of his lengthy illness, which necessitated Air Cdre Cecil Bouchier filling in for him for most of the last four months.

> He addressed the Officers Commanding, and the pilots of the three Squadrons at the Station Intelligence Section, thanking them for their work and co-operation. He also made special mention of the ground crews and the consistent good work they have done.[143]

Saunders was succeeded by AVM John Cole-Hamilton CB CBE on 1 November 1944.

Walcheren

28 October 1944 – Continuous rain in the morning, improving slightly to frequent showers and broken cloud with a base at 2,000 feet. Poor visibility during the showers; moderate to good visibility otherwise. Two operations were undertaken by the Lympne Wing today: Ramrod 1349 to Walcheren and Ramrod 1350 to Cologne [Köln].

The first of these foresaw an attack by 200 bombers on gun emplacements on Walcheren Island in the Netherlands. The destruction of these batteries had become crucial as they were hindering the forward movement of supplies to provision the Allied advance, and previous attempts to silence them had failed.

As the front line had pressed northwards and eastwards towards Germany, supply-lines became over-stretched, making provision logistically more and more difficult as time progressed. Trucking supplies to the front from the available ports in France was also unnecessarily using large amounts of valuable fuel.

When Antwerp was captured with its deep-water port more-or-less intact on 4 September 1944, it was felt the logistical issues might be resolved. The port facilities consisted of almost 26km^2 of docks, 32km of waterfront and 600 cranes capable of concurrently handling several hundred ships up to 19,000 grt. It was expected that the port could deliver approximately 40,000 tons of supplies per day to the Allied war effort.

However, Antwerp was located approximately 129km from the open sea down the Scheldt River, the mouth of which was guarded by solid coastal gun batteries on Walcheren Island and North [Noord] and South [Zuid] Beveland Islands. These islands were still held by the German military, which was therefore in a position to obstruct any attempt by the Allies to move supplies down the Scheldt to Antwerp.

The defences, particularly those on Walcheren, formed a part of the Atlantic Wall, built by the German military between 1942 and 1944 to defend against Allied invasion. The Wall was an extensive system of defences stretching from the Spanish border to the northern tip of Norway, consisting of coastal gun batteries and bunkers, underwater spikes and tank-traps, and barbed wire and minefields on the beaches and areas immediately behind them.

The Allied capture of Antwerp's dock was therefore of little use unless the garrisons occupying the defences on Walcheren Island could be destroyed. Hitler knew this and declared the island a bastion to be held to the last man. Walcheren's defences consisted of guns of different calibres, including 37mm Flak, 50mm machine guns, 88mm field guns, and large 150mm batteries built in six to eight foot thick reinforced concrete emplacements. The island also contained several V2 rocket launch sites, that the Allies were eager to silence.

The Allied strategy to resolve the problem was two-fold. Initially, the RAF would bomb the island, and then land forces would approach from North and South Beveland, once the islands were captured by Commandos. The aerial bombing strategy relied on the fact that, like many Dutch islands, Walcheren lay below sea level and was dyked. The RAF therefore set about attempting to blow the dykes and flood the island, hoping this would not only submerge and silence the gun batteries but also hinder any attempt to counter or reinforce the ensuing ground attack.

An initial attack was made on 3 October 1944, when eight waves of 30 Lancasters attacked the sea wall at Westkapelle on the western-most point of the island mostly with 1,000lb and 500lb high explosive bombs. Some 4,000lb bombs were also used and a breach was finally achieved in the fifth wave. The ensuing waves of bombers widened the breach to 100 yards, allowing sea water to flow in freely through the gap. Nonetheless, the gun emplacements were not put out of action.

A second attempt was made on 7 October when 120 Lancasters successfully breached the sea wall near Flushing [Vlissingen] and another on 17 October, when 47 Lancasters attacked the sea wall at Westkapelle again. Whilst the bombing was considered accurate, no major result was observed from either. Meanwhile, ground forces were experiencing considerable success in their advances on North and South Beveland, and it was felt an approach on Walcheren could soon be made from the east. However, if each gun position now needed to be silenced one at a time, it would be a drawn out and dangerous battle that would cost many lives.

On 28 October, the RAF made its fourth attempt to silence the gun emplacements by sending in 200 bombers in eight boxes of 25 aircraft in 15 minute intervals on eight batteries located between Flushing, Noorderhoofd, and the northern tip of Walcheren Island. The total force allocated to the operation consisted of 74 Lancasters and 155 Halifaxes of 4 and 8 Groups, led by 36 Pathfinder Mosquitos and twelve Pathfinder Lancasters, escorted by nine Spitfire squadrons. This time, 41 Squadron was involved.

Date	28 October 1944
Operation	Ramrod 1349
Target	Gun emplacements, Walcheren Island, Zeeland, Netherlands
Bombers	155 Halifaxes, 74 Lancasters, 36 Mosquitos & 12 Pathfinder Lancasters
Casualties	90 Sqn Lancaster I, HK602, & 76 Sqn Halifax III, MZ599
Target Cover & Withdrawal Escort	Lympne: 41, 350 & 610 Squadrons (34 Spitfire XIV) North Weald: 63, 310 & 313 Squadrons (36 Spitfire IX) Bradwell Bay: 312 Squadron (12 Spitfire IX) Biggin Hill: 91 Squadron (12 Spitfire IX) Detling: 1 Squadron (12 Spitfire IX)

The Lympne Wing was airborne this morning between 10:05 and 10:25 to provide target and withdrawal cover to three of the eight boxes of bombers. Consisting of twelve Spitfires each from 41 and 610 Squadrons and ten from 350, the Wing headed directly to the target area, reporting thick haze at between 2,000 and 8,000 feet on the way.

Four of 610 Squadron's pilots dropped out around 30 minutes into the operation and returned to base, one pair with engine problems and the other with R/T trouble. Whilst they landed back at Lympne between 11:20 and 11:25, the remaining pilots arrived over Walcheren to find clear conditions. They then patrolled the target area for 30 minutes at altitudes of between 10,000 and 12,000 feet whilst the bombers went to work.

The bombing was reported to be accurate and well concentrated on gun positions, and the results considered good. North Weald based 310 Squadron and Lympne's 350 Squadron both reported seeing a 'terrific explosion' between Noorderhoofd and Domberg, suggesting an ammunition dump had been hit, whilst 350 also observed "one gun site silenced by direct hits".[144] So impressed was 41 Squadron's Flt Lt 'Andy' Anderson, that he recorded in his logbook, "Area cover to Lancs Bombing gun emplacements – wizard bombing."[145]

Whilst the Luftwaffe was not seen, moderate to intense Flak of both light and heavy calibres was fired at the bombers, and one Lancaster and one Halifax were lost. One of these was seen to hit the sea ten miles southwest of Westkapelle at 10:25 by 310 Squadron, and 41 Squadron also reported a large black oil patch in the Scheldt, suggesting that a bomber had possibly gone in at that location.

The Wing then escorted their boxes of bombers back out on their withdrawal, and headed straight for home, where they landed without loss between 11:50 and 12:10. The operation proved uneventful for the Wing, but this one operation over Walcheren was sufficient to earn the Battle Honour 'Walcheren' for having participated in "operations in support of the capture of the island of Walcheren, 3 October to 9 November 1944".[146]

Two further attacks were made on Walcheren by the RAF, on 29 and 30 October, although without the Lympne Wing's participation. On the former of these, 358 Lancasters, Halifaxes and Mosquitos attacked eleven ground targets and gun emplacements, whilst on the latter 110 Lancasters and Mosquitos attacked gun batteries. The 30 October attack was also the last by Bomber Command in support of the Walcheren campaign.

By 31 October, the 2nd Canadian Infantry Division had successfully cleared South Beveland of all German forces, which paved the way for an attack on Walcheren from the east by Canadian and Scottish troops. The Island was connected to South Beveland by a narrow causeway measuring 1,600 metres in length but just 40 metres wide, and this would lend its name to the ensuing conflict: the Battle of Walcheren Causeway. Walcheren fell a week later, assisted by British Commandos who landed at Flushing and Westkapelle and drove their landing craft in through the breaches in the sea walls that had been created by the RAF.

Nonetheless, it took another three weeks to clear the Scheldt River of mines and other obstructions, to make it safe for shipping. As such, the first convoy of supply ships did not arrive in Antwerp until 28 November, almost three months after the port was captured.

Returning to 28 October, the Lympne Wing was airborne again after lunch on another escort assignment as a component of Ramrod 1350. This time the destination was Cologne and the target the goods yard and railway station.

733 aircraft – 428 Lancasters, 286 Halifaxes and 19 Pathfinder Mosquitos – were assigned to the task in two formations, accompanied by 17 Spitfire and eight Mustang squadrons. The Lympne Wing was assigned to an escort to the target of the rear of the second formation, and consisted of twelve Spitfires each from 41 and 610 Squadrons and eleven from 350 Squadron.

Date	28 October 1944
Operation	Ramrod 1350
Target	Goods Yard/Railway Station, Köln, Nordrhein-Westfalen
Bombers	428 Lancs, 286 Halifaxes & 19 Mosquitos in two formations
Casualties[147]	35 Sqn Lanc III, PB612, 115 Sqn Lanc I, NF960; 419 Sqn Lanc X, KB712, 10 Sqn Halifax III, MZ576, 347 Sqn Halifaxes III, NA512 & NA519, & 434 Sqn Halifax III, MZ420.

Escort to Front 1st Fmn	Detling: 1 & 165 Squadrons (26 Spitfire IX)
Escort to Rear 1st Fmn	Bradwell Bay: 64, 126 & 312 Squadrons (37 Spitfire IX)
Escort from Target to Front of 1st Formation	Biggin Hill: 91 Squadron (12 Spitfire IX) Friston: 131 Squadron (13 Spitfire VII)
Escort from Target to Rear of 1st Formation	Manston: 118, 124 & 504 Squadrons (34 Spitfire IX)
Escort to Front 2nd Fmn	North Weald: 310 & 313 Squadrons (24 Spitfire IX)
Escort to Rear 2nd Fmn	Lympne: 41, 350 & 610 Squadrons (35 Spitfire XIV)
Withdrawal Cover to Front of 2nd Formation	Hawkinge: 132 & 441 Squadrons (26 Spitfire IX)
Target & Withdrawal Cover to Rear 2nd Fmn	North Weald: 234 Squadron (12 Mustang III) Andrews Field: 129, 306 & 316 Squadrons (35 Mustang III) Andrews Field: 19, 65 & 122 Squadrons (37 Mustang III) Coltishall (12 Group): 315 Squadron (12 Mustang III)
Casualties148	65 Sqn: Flt Lt G. C. L. Watt, glycol leak, FL Douai; 91 Sqn: Sqn Ldr G. St. C. B. Reid KIFA; 126 Sqn: WO K. C. Loe landed Ghent, Flt Lt J. L. Flinterman & Fg Off G. Tunnadine landed Antwerp, Fg Off A. Tate, landed Continent; 310 Sqn: 1 A/C RF, landed Brussels to refuel; 350 Sqn: Flt Sgt W. Laloux, RF, landed Brussels, accompanied by Flt Sgt H. Boels; 441 Sqn: Fg Off A. J. McDonald & Plt Off V. A. G. Brochu both KIFA, in low cloud, S. of Brussels

The Lympne Wing was airborne at 14:45 and rendezvoused with the second formation of bombers over Aywaille, Belgium, around 20km south-southeast of Liège, above 10/10ths cloud at 5,000 feet. Two of 610 Squadron's pilots returned home early with engine trouble, but the remaining pilots escorted the bombers to Cologne via Manderfeld, Belgium, finding better conditions – 2/10ths could at 10,000-15,000 feet – and good visibility over the target area.

641 of the bombers attacked in waves of 257 aircraft at 15:25 and 384 at 15:40 from an altitude of 25,000 feet. Their payloads consisted of 120,000 incendiary stick bombs, 3,200 high explosive bombs (of which 96 failed to explode), 435 phosphor incendiary bombs, and 105 blockbusters, which mainly hit the Cologne districts of Deutz, Kalk, Klettenberg, Mülheim, Nippes, Sülz, and Zollstock, and parts of the city centre.[149] Considered accurate and concentrated, the bombing caused considerable damage to the city, with major damage done to railway and harbour infrastructures, power stations and housing. Fires and a large amount of smoke were seen rising up to 20,000 feet, and at least 630 were killed.

The bombers encountered medium heavy Flak inbound and outbound, and intense heavy Flak over the city, resulting in the loss three Lancasters and three Halifaxes. At least one of these was seen to explode and break up after a direct hit.

Six of 41 Squadron's aircraft suffered engine trouble over the target area but base was reached safely by all of them, particularly as, due to the potential issue of fuel shortage, the entire Lympne Wing headed straight for home from Cologne without escorting the bombers.

The Wing was back on the ground at Lympne between 16:50 and 17:05, with the exception of one pilot from 610 Squadron who returned half an hour early suffering jettison tank trouble, and two from 350 Squadron, who landed in Belgium as a result of mechanical trouble.

30 October 1944 – Variable cloud with a base of 1,500-2,500 feet, and occasional showers in the east and southeast. Early local mist improving to moderate visibility. Following a day of inactivity, the Lympne Wing was airborne today on an escort to bombers attacking another oil target in Germany.

Ramrod 1352 foresaw 100 Lancasters from 3 Group bombing the Synthetic Oil Plant at Wesseling, approximately 13km due south of Cologne [Köln], which was owned by the Union Rheinische Braunkohlen Kraftstoff AG. No Pathfinder Mosquitos were assigned to the operation, as was normally the case, but escort was to be provided by three Spitfire and eight Mustang squadrons. All eleven squadrons were to provide escort and target cover, and Lympne provided the three Spitfire squadrons.

Date	30 October 1944
Operation	Ramrod 1352
Target	Synthetic Oil Plant, Wesseling, Nordrhein-Westfalen
Bombers	102 Lancasters
Escort & Target Cover	Lympne: 41, 350 & 610 Squadrons (35 Spitfire XIV) North Weald: 234 Squadron (11 Mustang III) Coltishall (12 Group): 315 Squadron (12 Mustang III) Andrews Field: 129, 306 & 316 Squadrons (33 Mustang III) Andrews Field: 19, 65 & 122 Squadrons (37 Mustang III)

The Wing on this occasion consisted of twelve aircraft from both 41 and 610 Squadrons and eleven from 350 Squadron, which were airborne at 10:50. 610 Squadron's WO 'Chalky' White returned within ten minutes with engine trouble, but the rest of pilots flew directly to Wesseling. Arriving there at the same time as the bombers at 12:00, they found 9/10ths-10/10ths cloud over the target area up to an altitude of 8,000 feet.

The bombers, 102 in total, therefore dropped their payloads blind from an altitude of 17,000 feet, and although the bombing was believed to have been accurate, the results remained unseen. The escort pilots of Andrews Field were the only ones to report having seen any result, observing a mushroom cloud rising to 5,000 feet.

In fact, the bombs struck the target as planned, and the synthetic oil plant suffered considerable damage. Following an attack in July, production faltered, but today's raid put the Union Kraftstoff refinery out of action for the rest of the War. At its peak in 1943, the plant had produced an annual rate of 250,000 tons of synthetic oil, but as a result of this raid production did not recommence until after the cessation of hostilities.

Three or four salvoes of heavy Flak were fired at the escorting fighters, which was accurate in height but caused no damage. As usual, though, the bombers received the most attention, and medium to intense heavy Flak was directed at them over, and to the south of, the target area. None was successful, however, and every bomber returned safely.

They Lympne Wing circled the target area at 22,000-24,000 feet for just five minutes, then headed directly home again, and crossed out over Dunkirk, where they encountered Flak aimed directly at them. No damage was done and the pilots landed back at Lympne between 13:00 and 13:05. This concluded the day's, and indeed the month's, flying.

Several squadrons reported seeing V2 vapour trails during the operation. The Lympne Wing saw two on the way in, one rising vertically in a spiral to 30,000 feet at 11:20, and a second approximately 40 miles west of Cologne at 11:50; the North Weald Wing observed two separate vapour trails northwest of the target area at 11:45, one at 18,000 feet and another at 40,000; the Andrews Field Wing reported seeing two as well, rising from the Apeldoorn area at 11:40 and 11:50 respectively. On the way out, similar sightings were made, with Andrews Field reporting another two from the Hague [Den Haag]-Utrecht area at 12:20, and Lympne reporting two more, 20-30 miles east of Rotterdam at 12:35. Whilst it is difficult to assess how many of these were double sightings of the same V2s, it is known that six Big Ben incidents occurred within 11 Group's boundaries during the day.

November 1944 – The weather for most of the month once again proved most unsuitable for operations. On 22 days – 1, 3, 5, 7-8, 10-15, 17-20, 22-25, and 27-29 November – no operational flying was undertaken. On each of the remaining eight days, the Squadron participated in escorts or decoys for bomber operations targeting German industrial centres.

	Oil Campaign		Tactical Target
	Industrial Target		Marshalling Yards

Date	Operation	Role	Type	Bombers' Targets
2	Ramrod 1357	Target Cover	Oil	Moers, Germany
4	Ramrod 1359	Target Cover	Industrial	Solingen, Germany
6	Ramrod 1361	Escort to Target	Oil	Gelsenkirchen, Germany
9	Ramrod 1363	Target Cover	Oil	Wanne-Eickel, Germany
16	Ramrod 1372	Target Cover	Tactical	Düren, Jülich & Heinsberg, Germany
21	Ramrod 1375	Target Cover	Oil	Moers, Germany
26	Ramrod 1378	Sweep	Tactical	Bonn area, Germany
30	Ramrod 1384	Escort	Marshalling	Osterfeld, Germany

1 November 1944 – No operational flying all day due to poor weather, but Flt Lts Harry Cook, 'Sammy' Samouelle and Terry Spencer, and Plt Off Ricky Gray, flew to Biggin Hill in a Proctor communications aircraft, with Spencer piloting the aircraft, to be guests of the AOC for the evening.

Separately, the Squadron's sole American pilot, Flt Sgt 'Jack' Bradshaw, departed on transfer to the USAAF. He was posted to the 63rd Fighter Squadron in the 56th Fighter Group – the famed 'Zemke's Wolfpack' – flying P-47 Thunderbolts and P-51 Mustangs, where he continued to serve until the cessation of hostilities in Europe.[150]

2 November 1944 – 5/10ths to 10/10ths cloud at 3,000-4,000 feet, with visibility of just one to two miles. The Lympne Wing's only job today was to provide target support for 180 Lancasters from the Bomber Command's 3 Group bombing the Moers-Meerbeck Synthetic Oil Plant at Homberg, on the western outskirts of Duisburg, in Ramrod 1357. This was the first of five attacks on the same target within three weeks, a period which became known by the residents of the Homberg area as *Schwarzer November*.

Date	2 November 1944
Operation	Ramrod 1357
Target	Synthetic Oil Plant, Moers, Nordrhein-Westfalen
Bombers	184 Lancasters: 15 Sqn (14), 75 NZ Sqn (20), 90 Sqn (17), 115 Sqn (16), 149 Sqn (22), 186 Sqn (18), 195 Sqn (19), 218 Sqn (17), 514 Sqn (23), and 622 Sqn (18)
Casualties	15 Sqn Lancs HK612 & PB115, 186 Sqn Lanc LM618, 195 Sqn Lancs HK663 & LM473, and 622 Sqn Lanc LL803
Target Cover	Lympne: 41, 130 & 610 Squadrons (36 Spitfire XIV)
Target Cover & Escort on Withdrawal	Manston: 91 Squadron (12 Spitfire IX) Detling: 1 & 165 Squadron (25 Spitfire IX)

Escort to & from target, Front	Andrews Field: 129, 306 & 316 Squadrons (35 Mustang III) North Weald: 234 Squadron (10 Mustang III)
Escort to & from target, Rear	Bradwell Bay: 64 & 126 Squadrons (25 Spitfire IX) North Weald: 310 Squadron (11 Spitfire IX)
Casualties	64 Sqn: Fg Off Brook, EF/CL nr Erpe, Belg, safe; 91 Sqn: 1 Spit Cat. B; 350 Sqn: WO L. Verbeeck, u/s throttle, landed Evere accompanied by Sgt Plt G. Gigot

The Lympne Wing provided Target Cover for the operation, constituting three of the nine escorting Spitfire squadrons and four Mustang squadrons. Each of the Wing's squadrons contributed twelve aircraft, and were airborne at 12:55 with long-range 90-gallon jettison tanks fitted.

The target area was covered in 5/10ths cloud, but this was no hindrance and a total of 177 of bombers attacked the target. At the end of the raid, black clouds and smoke could be seen rising from the oil plant. However, accurate and intense heavy Flak was experienced and six bombers were lost.

The fighters, however, returned reporting the operation otherwise uneventful; the Luftwaffe was not sighted. The Lympne Wing landed again between 15:00 and 15:20, and this concluded the day's flying.

4 November 1944 – Fair with broken cloud at 2,000 feet and good visibility. The day saw another Wing operation, this time led by Sqn Ldr Benham, as target cover in Ramrod 1359 for 176 Lancasters of 3 Group bombing an aircraft component factory at Solingen, just south of the Ruhr, and around 20km east-southeast of Düsseldorf.

The bombers were covered by three Spitfire and six Mustang squadrons, whilst another seven Spitfire squadrons swept north and south of Cologne [Köln] and covered the withdrawal.

Date	4 November 1944
Operation	Ramrod 1359
Target	Aircraft Component Factory, Solingen, Nordrhein-Westfalen
Bombers	178 Lancasters: 15 Sqn (14), 75 NZ Sqn (21), 90 Sqn (18), 115 Sqn (16), 149 Sqn (17), 186 Sqn (18), 195 Sqn (19), 218 Sqn (17), 514 Sqn (20), and 622 Sqn (18)
Casualties	75 Sqn Lanc ND917, and 195 Sqn Lancs HK658, HK689 & NG219
Escort on Penetration & Withdrawal	Andrews Field: 129, 306 & 316 Squadrons (35 Mustang III) Andrews Field: 19 & 65 Squadrons (25 Mustang IIIA) North Weald: 234 Squadron (12 Mustang III)
Target Cover	Lympne: 41, 350 & 610 Squadrons (34 Spitfire XIV)
Sweep S Köln to Target	Manston: 91, 118, 124 & 504 Squadrons (49 Spitfire IX)
Sweep N Köln to Target	Bradwell Bay: 64, 126 & 312 Squadron (37 Spitfire IX)
Casualty	350 Sqn: Sqn Ldr L. C. Collignon u/s fuel cock, CL Aix-La-Chapelle

Cloud cover was experienced over the target area between 7/10ths and 10/10ths, but this was overcome by the use of Oboe targeting. 170 out of 176 bombers attacked the target, resulting in large palls of black smoke reaching to 25,000 feet. Four bombers were lost to light Flak, although some reports suggest casualties were also caused by aircraft being hit by 500lb and 1,000lb bombs dropped from Allied aircraft above them.

Airborne between 13:00 and 13:10, the Lympne Wing contributed 34 aircraft to the operation, of which twelve were provided by 41 Squadron. The pilots reported the operation uneventful and according to plan, there being just one casualty, 350 Squadron's Commanding Officer, Leopold Collignon, who was forced to land in Belgium with a problem with his fuel cock. He managed to reach Allied territory and returned home a short while later.

41 Squadron landed at base again at 15:30, in what was their longest Spitfire XIV mission to date, and in the evening attended an SHQ party at Hawkinge.

6 November 1944 – Broken cloud with a base of 2,000 feet, occasional showers but generally good visibility, and a strong south-westerly wind at ground level.

Yet another Lympne Wing escort to bombers was laid on today, this time to the Nordstern Synthetic Oil Plant, in north-western districts of Gelsenkirchen, in the Ruhr.[151] Ramrod 1361 consisted of 738 Bomber Command aircraft, consisting of 31 Oboe Mosquitos, 383 Halifaxes and 324 Lancasters. Escort and cover were provided by 16 Spitfire and seven Mustang squadrons.

Date	6 November 1944
Operation	Ramrod 1361
Target	Nordstern Synthetic Oil Plant, Gelsenkirchen, Nordrhein-Westfalen
Bombers	31 Mosquitos, 383 Halifaxes and 324 Lancasters
Casualties	408 Sqn Halifax NP761, 432 Sqn Halifax NP815, 101 Sqn Lanc PB692, 300 Sqn Lanc LM141, & 550 Sqn Lanc PB562
Escort to Target	Lympne: 41, 610 & 350 Squadrons (38 Spitfire XIV) North Weald: 310 & 313 Squadrons (22 Spitfire IX) Detling: 1 & 165 Squadrons (24 Spitfire IX) Biggin Hill: 340 Squadron (13 Spitfire IX)
Escort to & from Target, Front & Rear	Andrews Field: 129, 306 & 316 Squadrons (31 Mustang III) Andrews Field: 19, 65 & 122 Squadrons (37 Mustang III)
Withdrawal Escort	Bradwell Bay: 64, 126 & 312 Squadrons (37 Spitfire IX) Manston: 91, 118, 124 & 504 Squadrons (49 Spitfire IX) Hawkinge: 441 Squadron (12 Spitfire IX)
Patrol Route & Escort Withdrawal	North Weald: 234 Squadron (12 Mustang III)
Casualties	122 Sqn: Plt Off A. K. Thomas rtnd early CL/KIFA; 126 Sqn: Flt Lts G. Braidwood, J. Garden & M. Woods landed Continent; 310 Sqn: Sgt Plt M. Churáň, RF/CL Hunsdon; 350 Sqn: Fg Off F. Verpoorten, EF, landed Antwerp, accompanied by Flt Sgt R. Jaminé; 610 Sqn: Flt Lt B. M. Madden MAC with WO R. C. White, safe, A/C Cat. AC & Cat. A.

The Lympne Wing was ordered to escort the formation to the target area, and all three squadrons participated, providing a total of 38 aircraft. 41 Squadron contributed eleven pilots, who were off the deck at 13:05, led by Flt Lt Terry Spencer. However, Flt Lt 'Andy' Anderson (RM698) had technical problems that delayed his take-off by 20 minutes, and WO Peter Hale (RM704) had a similar experience. Having taken off with the main group, he did not get far before finding his

Following a posting with 274 Squadron, WO Keith Clanzy served with 41 Squadron from 6 November 1944 to mid-March 1945.
© 41 Squadron RAF

aircraft u/s. He turned back and landed at Manston, just fifteen minutes after getting airborne.

The rest of the Wing joined a group of 220 Lancasters just north of Eindhoven, and although the operation was otherwise uneventful, the pilots were "honoured by the solicitous attention of the Hun flak which was very accurate and unwelcome".[152] 513 bombers dropped their payloads in the area of the oil plant, but numerous bombs fell in and around the city, too, and just over 500 people were killed.

41 Squadron returned to base unscathed at 15:15, but it was not the same story for other participating units: Two Halifaxes and three Lancasters were lost to Flak, a Mustang of 122 Squadron crashed on take-off, killing the pilot, an aircraft of 350 Squadron landed in Belgium with engine trouble, and two from 610 Squadron collided in mid-air off Dover on the return journey, although the pilots were not injured.

Separately today, two new pilots joined 41 Squadron, 25-year-old Welshman WO Keith Clanzy and 21-year-old Londoner Flt Sgt Hubert Kelly.

Clanzy, of Bridgend, Glamorgan, had joined the RAFVR in January 1940, whilst Kelly joined in May 1941. Both men completed their flying training in the British Flying Training School at Riddle Field in Florida, and returned to the United Kingdom to complete separate OTUs, AFUs and TEUs, before being posted to 274 Squadron at West Malling on 20 June, respectively 30 July 1944. The pair was then posted together to 83 GSU at Westhampnett on 11 August, and now together to 41 Squadron.[153]

7 November 1944 – Although there was no operational flying for any of Lympne's squadrons today, Flt Lts Terry Spencer and 'Jack' Refshauge, Fg Off 'Ricky' Gray, and WO Keith Clanzy left Lympne for Tilbury with ground crew and 6041 Servicing Echelon bound for Belgium in advance of the pending Squadron move to the Continent. The men spent several days in temporary tent accommodation, and finally boarded a ship to cross the Channel on 13 November. It was another two days before they arrived at Ostend [Oostende], where they spent the night "in the local brewery with one Madam Fraye".[154] The men finally arrived at B.64 Diest-Schaffen Aerodrome on 17 November to start preparing for the arrival of the rest of the Squadron.

6350 and 6610 Servicing Echelons also received orders today to be prepared to move at six hours' notice from 00:01 on 10 November, their destination being B.56 Brussels-Evere Aerodrome.

Sgt Plt (later WO) Hubert 'Hugh' Kelly served with 41 Squadron from 6 November 1944 to 31 March 1946. He claimed four damaged Arado Ar196s on Lake Ratzeburg in April 1945 and was commissioned six months later.
© Rossow family

A day later, this order was later set back to 11 November, but on 13 November, the move still not having been made, it was set back formally yet again to 15 November.

8 November 1944 – The day's weather brought the season's first snowfall at Lympne, and there was no operational flying by any of the Wing's squadrons. A combined party for all three units was held in the Officers Mess in the evening with entertainment provided by 6610 Echelon's 'Fighter Follies'. However, the festivities were curbed after news was received of a Wing operation planned for the following morning.

9 November 1944 – A fresh north-westerly wind with light cloud and moderate visibility made suitable conditions for a Wing escort to 256 Lancasters and 21 Oboe Mosquitos attacking the Wanne-Eickel Synthetic Oil Plant, just southeast of Gelsenkirchen, in Ramrod 1363.[155] The escort was provided by a total of nine Spitfire and seven Mustang squadrons.

Date	9 November 1944
Operation	Ramrod 1363
Target	Wanne-Eickel Synthetic Oil Plant, Nordrhein-Westfalen
Bombers	20 Mosquitos and 256 Lancasters
Casualties	625 Sqn Lancs NG239 and LM731
Escort, Front Escort, Centre Escort, Rear Withdrawal Escort Front Target Cover Escort to & from Target	Bradwell Bay: 64, 126 & 312 Squadrons (31 Spitfire IX) Andrews Field: 129, 306 & 316 Squadrons (34 Mustang III) Andrews Field: 19, 65 & 122 Squadrons (37 Mustang IIIA) Manston: 91, 124 & 504 Squadrons (35 Spitfire IX) Lympne: 41, 610 & 350 Squadrons (37 Spitfire XIV) North Weald: 234 Squadron (11 Mustang III)
Casualties	41 Sqn: Fg Off H. W. Charnock, AA landed Ghent; 64 Sqn: Fg Off S. Brandt MIA, safe; 91 Sqn: Flt Lt W. C. Marshall landed Antwerp; 312 Sqn: Flt Sgt J. Kukucka & Sgt Plt K. Lamberton RF, landed Ghent; 504 Sqn: Fg Off Laws landed Antwerp; 610 Sqn: Fg Off S. A. Jones, lost glycol, FL, E. of Ghent; Bradwell Bay: Wg Cdr H. A. C. Bird-Wilson RF, landed Antwerp to refuel.

The Lympne Wing was allocated to target cover, and provided 37 aircraft for the operation. 41 Squadron was airborne with at least eleven aircraft[156] at 09:25, led by Sqn Ldr Benham, but similar to the previous escort, WO Peter Hale (RM797) once again suffered aircraft trouble shortly after take-off, and turned back to put down at Manston at 09:50. The rest of the Squadron continued to the target area without further issue.

However, conditions over the Continent proved less than favourable, and freezing conditions and thick cloud seriously hampered the operation. As the cloud cover over Wanne-Eickel reached 21,000 feet, the markers dropped by the Pathfinders disappeared soon after being released. As such, the town itself was bombed by 228 of the 256 bombers, which was severely damaged and ten people were killed. Two bombers were also lost to the Flak.

41 Squadron continued to the target but encountered heavy Flak over the area, and Fg Off Harry Charnock (RM767) had a lucky escape when he was flipped over by "a class burst".[157] He managed to regain control and made an initial landing in Ghent, whilst the Squadron continued to Lympne, putting down at 11:50. Charnock returned home later that day with his fuselage seriously damaged.

The operation also proved otherwise uneventful for 350 Squadron, although one of 610 Squadron's pilots force landed east of Ghent with a glycol leak. He belly-landed uninjured and returned to the unit two days later by Dakota. But it was the cold more than anything that stood out in everyone's mind. 610 Squadron reported that the Continent was…

...obscured by layers of cloud, the only outstanding feature of the trip being the intense cold. Operating up to 27,000ft. with [the] freezing level at 2000ft was rather too much of a good thing for the pilots all of whom came back half frozen.[158]

They were not the only ones have trouble with the temperature. The 11 Group ORB Appendix records that,

Great difficulty was experienced owing to very severe icing conditions which compelled 6 a/c 504 Squadron to return early and at least seven others to land in Belgium....[159]

16 November 1944 – Widespread fog and low cloud up to 600 feet, with cloud lifting to 2,000 feet during the afternoon and visibility increasing to one-to-two miles.

41 Squadron participated in Ramrod 1372 today, a combined daylight operation consisting of approximately 1,190 Lancasters, Halifaxes and Mosquitos of Bomber Command's Nos. 4, 6 and 8 Groups, tasked with attacking the towns of Düren, Jülich and Heinsberg, between Aachen and the Rhine. They were escorted by twelve Spitfire squadrons and seven Mustang squadrons. Simultaneously, another 1,438 U.S. 8th Air Force Flying Fortresses and Liberators were allocated their own targets in the Düren and Eschweiler areas, northeast of Aachen, escorted by 280 Mustangs.

The targets were all close to a front which was about to be attacked by troops of the U.S. 1st and 9th Armies, with the intention of cutting the lines of communication directly behind the front.

The RAF allocated 485 Lancasters and 13 Oboe Mosquitos to the Düren attack, 182 Lancasters to the Heinsberg attack, and 413 Halifaxes, 78 Lancasters and 17 Oboe Mosquitos to the Jülich attack.

Date	16 November 1944
Operation	Ramrod 1372
Target	Düren, Jülich and Heinsberg, Nordrhein-Westfalen
Bombers	30 Mosquitos, 413 Halifaxes & 745 Lancasters
Casualties	4 Lancasters shot down by Flak
Escort Heinsberg, Front	Biggin Hill: 340 Squadron (13 Spitfire IX)
Escort Heinsberg, Rear	North Weald: 310 & 313 Squadrons (26 Spitfire IX) & 234 Squadron (9 Mustang III)
Escort Jülich, Front	Manston: 91, 118, 124 & 504 Squadrons (48 Spitfire IX)
Escort Jülich, Rear	Andrews Field (133 Wing): 129, 306 & 316 Squadrons (36 Mustang III)
Escort Düren, Front	Hawkinge: 441 Squadron (12 Spitfire IX) Detling: 1 & 165 Squadrons (25 Spitfire IXb)
Escort Düren, Rear	Bradwell Bay: 64, 126 & 312 Squadrons (36 Spitfire IX)
Escort Cover	Andrews Field (150 Wing): 19, 65 & 122 Squadrons (37 Mustang III)
Target Cover, Mosquit-os to Jülich & Düren	Lympne: 41, 350 & 610 Squadron (32 Spitfire XIV)
Casualties	41 Sqn: Flt Lt J. F. Wilkinson EF/RF, landed Ghent with WO A. D. Miller; 65 Sqn: Flt Sgt O. H. Robison, EF/FL, WUL Ostend area; 306 Sqn: WO J. Rogowski, EF, landed Belg; 312 Sqn: Flt Sgts J. Konvička, RF/CL, Oordegem, & V. Liška, & Sgt Plt J. Zářecký, RF, landed Belg; 316 Sqn: 2 A/C collided on landing (Cat. B), one plt poss WO T. Jaskolski; 340 Sqn: Lt Revherlac, landed Belg; 350 Sqn: Plt Off R. Bladt, EF Antwerp-Ghent area; 441 Sqn: Fg Off A. B. Jewett, EF Düren, baled out Frelenberg, Germany, safe; 610 Sqn: 1 aircraft RF, Cat. B on landing, Manston

The Lympne Wing was tasked with escorting the Pathfinder Mosquitos to Jülich and Düren, which lie approximately 40km west of Cologne [Köln]. Consisting of a total of 32 aircraft, they were airborne at 14:30, led by Wg Cdr Colin Gray. 41 Squadron provided fourteen of these, and

The Squadron's WAAF Drivers at Lympne in early November 1944, just prior to the ground crew's move to the Continent. © Terry Spencer, via Cara and Raina Spencer

were led by Flt Lt Ross Harding. The Wing rendezvoused with the Mosquitos according to plan and escorted them from 35,000 feet, a full 10,000 feet above the Mosquitoes.

Of the 1,190 aircraft dispatched by Bomber Command, 1,108 attacked the targets in good visibility, causing considerable damage. The bombing appeared to be concentrated and smoke was seen to rise to several thousand feet, but Flak was heavy and three Lancasters were lost over Düren and one over Heinsberg. However, none were lost in the Jülich attack. Of those deployed by the 8th Air Force, 1,204 aircraft attacked their targets with unobserved results, but lost three bombers and sixteen sustained damage; although the Luftwaffe was not encountered, six Mustangs failed to return. The combined Allied force dropped at least 9,400 tons of high-explosive bombs.

The operation was largely uneventful for the Lympne Wing, so much so that 41 Squadron reported the entire operation in a just two-sentence entry in the ORB, summarising that it was "carried out according to plan with no incident".[160]

However, whilst most of the pilots returned to Lympne between 16:45 and 16:50, Fg Off Johnnie Wilkinson (RM765) landed in the Ghent [Gent] area short of fuel as a result of engine trouble, accompanied by WO Alister Miller (RM793), and returned later.[161] One of 350 Squadron's eight pilots also landed in Ghent with engine trouble, and one of 610 Squadron's twelve aircraft suffered Cat. B damage on landing back at Manston short of fuel.

Despite the massive attack, however, the U.S. 1st and 9th Armies' advance faltered, brought to a halt not by military opposition, but by weather. Wet terrain prevented tanks from moving forward, and limited the resupply of ammunition to artillery units at the front, which were soon short of shells. The conditions also slowed the advance of infantry.

19 November 1944 – Flt Lt Terry Spencer returned to Lympne from Diest today, in a Spitfire XIV he had borrowed from 130 Squadron (AP-G), to lecture the Squadron on conditions at their future base, which was suffering the effects of recent wet and bitterly cold conditions. He flew back to the Continent that same afternoon.

Back in Diest, 125 Wing recorded the status of 41 Squadron's move, thus: "All the ground personnel of 41 Sqn have now arrived and the aircraft are expected as soon as the weather and the strip combine to make that possible."[162] The following day, tracking for Diest's strip finally arrived, which would make landing and taking off easier, but unfortunately no-one was available to lay it. In fact, work did not start until 25 November, but was then expected to take another seven days to complete.

21 November 1944 – Fair to fine with little cloud and moderate to good visibility. Conditions were ideal for another Wing escort to bombers attacking targets in the on-going Oil Campaign in Germany.

On 7 November 1944, Flt Lts Terry Spencer and 'Jack' Refshauge RAAF, Fg Off 'Ricky' Gray RAAF, and WO Keith Clanzy left for Tilbury with ground crew of 6041 Servicing Echelon bound for Belgium in advance of the pending Squadron move to the Continent. This photo was taken at Lympne just prior to boarding buses to depart. © Terry Spencer, via Cara and Raina Spencer

Today's operation, Ramrod 1375, targeted the Moers-Meerbeck Synthetic Oil Plant at Homberg, near Duisburg, which was the same destination as the Wing's escort on 2 November. This was the fifth of five attacks on this target within three weeks. The operation foresaw the deployment of 180 of No. 3 Group's Lancasters escorted by 14 Spitfire squadrons and two Mustang squadrons. Simultaneously, two Mustang squadrons were detailed to sweep the areas of the airfields at Merzhausen, Nidda, Limberg and Wiesbaden in Hessen, a second pair to sweep the areas of the airfields at Gutersloh, Detmold, Paderborn and Lippstadt in Nordrhein-Westfalen, and a fifth Mustang squadron to sweep the areas of the airfields at Plantlünne and Rheine in Germany, and Twente in the Netherlands.

Only 162 of the planned 180 bombers were despatched, of which 150 attacked the Synthetic Oil Plant with good visual results from concentrated bombing, despite a smoke screen released as a decoy by the town. Intense and accurate heavy Flak was reported and three bombers and five fighters failed to return.

Date	21 November 1944
Operation	Ramrod 1375
Target	Synthetic Oil Plant, Moers, Nordrhein-Westfalen
Bombers	162 Lancasters: 115 Sqn (15), 514 Sqn (22), 75 NZ Sqn (20), 622 Sqn (17), 15 Sqn (16), 90 Sqn (14), 218 Sqn (12), 149 Sqn (17), 186 Sqn (17), and 195 Sqn (12)
Casualties	514 Sqn Lancs LM684, PD265 and NG121
Escort, Front	North Weald: 310 & 313 Squadrons (24 Spitfire IX) Biggin Hill: 340 Squadron (12 Spitfire IX)
Escort, Centre	Bradwell Bay: 126 & 312 Squadrons (25 Spitfire IX)
Escort, Rear	Manston: 91, 118, 124 & 504 Squadrons (48 Spitfire IX)
Top Cover	Andrews Field: 122 & 306 Squadrons (21 Mustang III)
Target Cover	Detling: 1 & 165 Squadrons (25 Spitfire IX) Hawkinge: 441 Squadron (14 Spitfire IX) Lympne: 41 & 610 Squadrons (23 Spitfire XIV)
Sweep Merzhausen, etc.	Andrews Field (150 Wing): 19 & 65 Sqns (24 Mustang III)
Sweep Gutersloh, etc.	Andrews Field (133 Wing): 129 & 316 Sqns (25 Mustang III)
Sweep Plantlünne, etc.	North Weald: 234 Squadron (12 Mustang III)
Casualties	118 Sqn: Fg Off C. C. Kingston & WO Bennett, NYR; 124 Sqn: 2 A/C landed Friston; 234 Sqn: Plt Off P. J. W. Bell IFA, EF on TO, CL, facial burns; 340 Sqn: Lt F. Hardi, glycol leak, CL safe; 504 Sqn: Flt Lt D. F. Chadwick, RF/WUL Deurne; 610 Sqn: Fg Off B. R. Scaman, RF landed Hawkinge

On this occasion, Sqn Ldr Benham led the Wing, which consisted of only 41 and 610 Squadrons, as two of five squadrons providing target cover to the Lancasters. Twelve pilots from 41 Squadron and eleven from 610 were airborne at 14:05. However, 41's Flt Sgt 'Micky' Moyle (RM707) exited the operation and landed at Manston with engine trouble within 20 minutes, escorted by a second pilot.[163] 610 Squadron had similar issues. Shortly after take-off, Flt Lt Tony Gaze and Fg Off Stephen Jones also turned back, one with engine trouble and the other unable to switch over to his jettison tank; they landed at Manston at 14:35.

The remaining 19 pilots continued on to Homberg, where they rendezvoused with the Lancasters. They swept around the city, and then escorted the bombers away from the area. Although they ran into bad weather on the way, the Homberg area was generally clear and the bombers returned triumphant, having succeeded in destroying their target this time.

The Luftwaffe was not encountered and 41 and 610 Squadrons returned to Lympne at 16:25 without further incident, with the exception of one 610's pilots who landed at Hawkinge short of fuel.

26 November 1944 – The day began fine with moderate to good visibility, but deteriorated to low cloud and rain during the afternoon, with visibility of only 500-1000 yards.

The morning's good weather made perfect conditions for a Wing sweep to the Bonn area at 23,000 feet, as a decoy element of Ramrod 1378. The ultimate target of the operation was the bombing of an ordnance depot at Fulda in Hessen, approximately 65km northeast of Frankfurt, by 75 Lancasters. They were directly supported by seven Mustang squadrons, an indirectly by another nine Spitfire squadrons, six of which swept the Koblenz area, and three of which swept the Bonn area.

Date	26 November 1944
Operation	Ramrod 1378
Target	Ordnance depot, Fulda, Hessen
Bombers	75 Lancasters
Escort to & from Target	Andrews Field: 19, 65, 122 & 129 Sqns (49 Mustang III) North Weald: 234 Squadron (10 Mustang III)
Target Cover & Escort on Withdrawal	Andrews Field: 306 & 316 Squadrons (20 Mustang III)
Sweep Koblenz area	Manston: 91, 118, 124 & 504 Squadrons (48 Spitfire IX) Bradwell Bay: 126 & 312 Squadrons (23 Spitfire IX)

Flt Lt Terry Spencer, Fg Off 'Ricky' Gray RAAF, Flt Sgt Collins (6041 Servicing Echelon) and Flt Lt 'Jack' Refshauge RAAF at Diest, Belgium, after their arrival with the advance party on 17 November 1944. © Terry Spencer, via Cara and Raina Spencer

Sweep Bonn area	Lympne: 41, 350 & 610 Squadrons (32 Spitfire XIV)
Casualties	65 Sqn: Flt Lt F. H. Bradford, AA, FL Continent; 118 Sqn: Flt Sgt Clark landed on Continent; 312 Sqn: Plt Off E. Smolka AA/WIA; Manston Wing: Wg Cdr Carter landed B.58 Brussels-Melsbroek

The sweep of the Bonn area was allocated to the Lympne Wing, which was led by Sqn Ldr Benham. 41 Squadron was airborne at 09:45 for a very long round trip of two hours and ten minutes, covering 266 miles in each direction as the crow flies, in which the pilots relied on heating within their boots and jackets for warmth.

Unfortunately, however, technical problems once again dogged the Wing and 41's Fg Off Johnnie Wilkinson (RM793) who was off the deck five minutes later than the rest of the unit, soon turned back again with engine trouble and landed at Manston 30 minutes after take-off.[164] Two of 350 Squadron pilots also suffered engine trouble and landed at Manston, as did 610 Squadron's Flt Lt Tony Gaze, who landed at Manston with engine trouble 25 minutes after take-off, and Fg Off Stephen Jones, who landed five minutes later with oxygen failure.

The remaining pilots completed the trip uneventfully. Although there was some accurate heavy Flak, the Luftwaffe was not encountered. Seventy-one of the 75 bombers allocated to the operation attacked the target, but with unobserved results due to 10/10ths cloud cover over Fulda at 12,000 feet. However, no casualties were recorded amongst the bomber force.

The Wing landed back at Lympne again between 11:55 and 12:10, much to their pleasure, "just in time for lunch".[165]

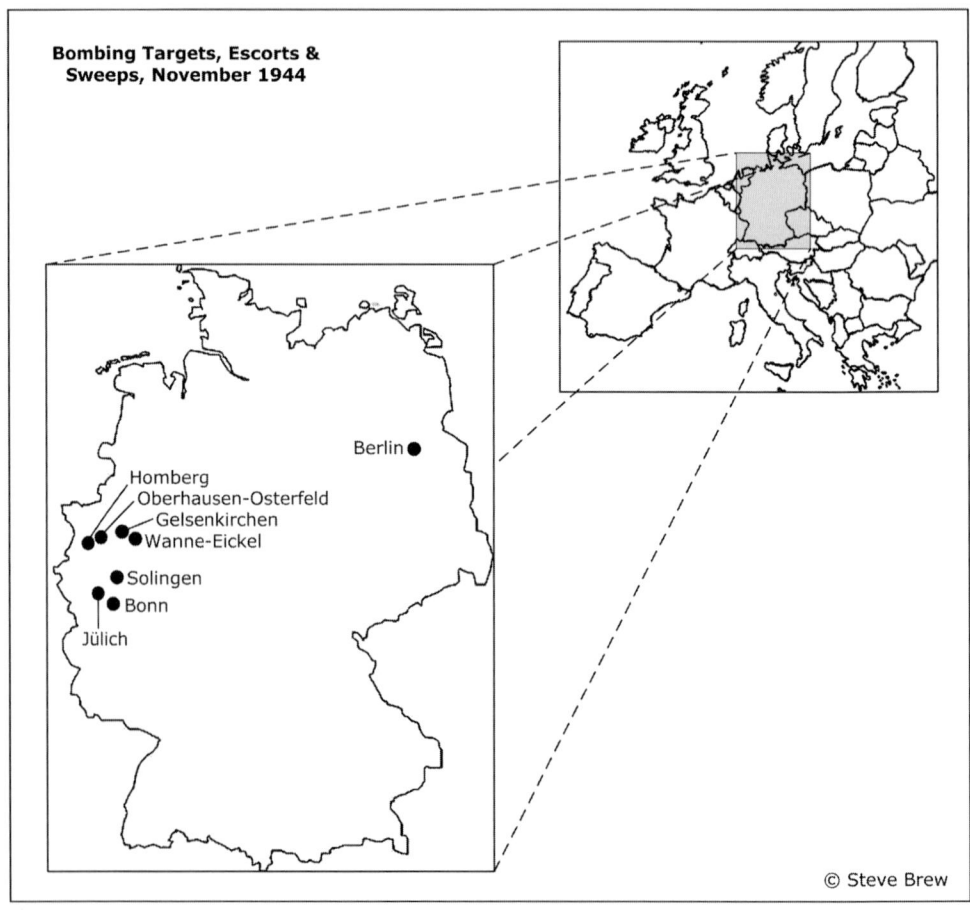

30 November 1944 – Partly cloudy between 2,000 and 5,000 feet, with moderate visibility of 1,000 to 1,500 yards. The Wing's last operation of the month – and indeed its last in its current composition (41, 350 and 610 Spitfire XIV Squadrons) from Lympne – consisted of an escort element of a two-part Ramrod to the Ruhr Valley, targeting the Synthetic Oil Plant at Bottrop, and the Marshalling Yards at Osterfeld, which was located approximately three kilometres southwest of Bottrop.

A total of 120 Lancasters were assigned to the operation, titled Ramrod 1384, escorted by 12 Spitfire and three Mustang squadrons from 11 Group, and one Spitfire squadron from 12 Group. Sixty bombers were allocated to each of the targets, with six escort squadrons assigned to Bottrop and seven to Osterfeld, whilst three Mustang squadrons were ordered to sweep from Hilversum, in the Netherlands, to Münster, Hannover and Paderborn in Germany, and back to Hilversum.

Date	30 November 1944
Operation	Ramrod 1384
Targets	Synthetic Oil Plant, Bottrop, Nordrhein-Westfalen Marshalling Yards, Osterfeld, nr Oberhausen, Nordrhein-Westfalen
Bombers	120 Lancasters: 115 Sqn (15), 514 Sqn (17), 75 NZ Sqn (18), 622 Sqn (16), 15 Sqn (16), 90 Sqn (15), 218 Sqn (4), 149 Sqn (10), and 186 Sqn (9)
Casualties	75 Sqn Lanc NF980 & 115 Sqn Lanc PD367
Escort Bottrop, Front	North Weald: 310 & 313 Squadrons (24 Spitfire IX)
Escort Bottrop, Rear	Coltishall (12 Group): 303 Squadron (13 Spitfire IX) Hawkinge: 441 Squadron (13 Spitfire IX)
Target Cover, Bottrop	Manston: 91 & 504 Squadrons (22 Spitfire IX)
Escort Osterfeld, Front	Lympne: 41, 350 & 610 Squadrons (34 Spitfire XIV)
Escort Osterfeld, Rear	Bradwell Bay: 126 & 312 Squadrons (25 Spitfire IX)
Target Cover, Osterfeld	Manston: 118 & 124 Squadrons (23 Spitfire IX)
Sweep Hilversum, etc.	Andrews Field: 19, 65 & 122 Squadrons (37 Mustang III)
Casualties	303 Sqn: Red Section landed Bradwell Bay & Sgt Plt J. P. Kukuc CL, seriously inj; 350 Sqn: Plt Off R. Bladt, EF landed Evere & Fg Off R. Vanderveken, AA, landed B.61 Ghent/St. Denis-Westrem; 504 Sqn: Flt Lt D. F. Chadwick, EF landed B.61 Ghent/St. Denis-Westrem; 610 Sqn: Fg Off F. M. McFarlane landed B.61 Ghent/St. Denis-Westrem

41, 350 and 610 Squadrons, led by Wg Cdr Colin Gray as the Lympne Wing for the last time, were ordered to escort the front of the bomber formation to and from Osterfeld. They were airborne at midday, with 41 Squadron led by Sqn Ldr Benham, but Fg Off Harry Charnock (RM789) and WO 'Archie' Appleton (RM699) were both compelled to turn back with engine trouble, landing at Manston at 12:20 and 12:45 respectively. One aircraft of 350 Squadron also turned back with similar issues.

The remaining pilots continued to the target with the bombers, but found 10/10ths cloud over the Bottrop-Osterfeld area to an altitude of 12,000 feet. Although the markers still had sufficient height to give the Lancasters a good point of reference, some of the bombers arrived late, and aircraft of the two separate attacks ended up intermingled due to the proximity of the targets. Despite this, and light Flak which brought down two Lancasters, the bombing was considered successful.[166]

The operation was largely uneventful for the Lympne Wing, which was perhaps somewhat of an anti-climax for what constituted the three squadrons' last bomber escort from the British Isles during World War II. The pilots were back on the ground at 14:30.

1 December 1944 – Cloudy with some drizzle; visibility three to five miles. No operational flying was undertaken all day by Lympne's squadrons. Films were shown and talks given instead, but otherwise no activity was considered of sufficient importance to record.

Spitfire XIV, EB-E, about to touch down, location unknown. Note the aircraft parked in the background. © Rossow family

Over on the Continent, the strip at Diest was still not ready for 41 Squadron, but the advance parties were kept occupied with intelligence films and talks.

> *Subsequently F/L. Herman (The Doc 41 Sqn) gave a chat on "Medical treatment up to date" especially detailing the vast strides that medical science had made since the last war and how modern treatment was saving the lives of thousands who a few years ago must have perished. Other subjects dealt with were the dreaded VD and burns and their treatment.*[167]

During the afternoon, 41 Squadron's advance party and ground crew formed teams with Intelligence and Operations, and played a soccer match against the two units already present at Diest, 130 and 402 Squadrons.

2 December 1944 – Cloudy to fine in England's southeast, with generally good visibility. Once again, however, no operational flying was undertaken all day by any of Lympne's squadrons. Some men played sport until an early release was given, but by now every man was "full of expectation of their long awaited move to the Continent… and everyone [was] on their toes awaiting the word 'Go'."[168]

3 December 1944 – Thick cloud with rain and visibility of only one to three miles at Lympne. For the third day in a row, 41 and 610 Squadrons undertook no operational flying, but twelve aircraft from 350 Squadron were deployed on Ramrod 1390. They were one of six Spitfire and four Mustang squadrons assigned to an escort of 180 Lancasters bombing the 58-metre-high and six-metre-wide Urft Dam near Heimbach, west of Euskirchen, Germany.

However, the operation was abandoned shortly before reaching the target owing to unsuitable weather, and all participants returned home with the exception of 350 Squadron. Flying conditions were certainly poor but it appears that, whilst still airborne, the pilots received the news the Lympne Wing had been waiting so long to hear:

ABOVE WO Viv Rossow RAAF climbing into the cockpit of his Spitfire XIV. © Rossow family

RIGHT Fg Off Rupert 'Lew' Munson RAAF served with 41 Squadron from 1 December 1944 to 14 March 1945. © Munson family

> *...authority was received to-day that aircraft and pilots were to be ready to proceed to the continent to-morrow, everyone is overjoyed at this news, and a dry day is expected for the "Great Day"....*[169]

As it therefore made sense for 350 Squadron to remain on the Continent rather than return across the Channel, the pilots landed at B.56 Brussels-Evere Aerodrome and joined 127 Wing.[170]

The Lympne Wing had now begun to be broken up definitively and leave England for new bases on the Continent. Although 41, 350 and 610 Squadrons – and indeed 130 Squadron – would be split up in the immediate term, they would be reunited as a Wing again by the end of the month.

4 December 1944 – A fine day with good visibility allowed the dispersal of the Lympne Wing to continue this morning when 17 pilots from 610 Squadron flew to Evere for allocation to 127 Wing, and were soon joined there by the remaining pilots from 350 Squadron. Close on their heels were 21 pilots from 41 Squadron, undertaking their first move to the Continent since the Great War.

In fact, these three squadrons' moves represent defining moments in their histories. Whilst 610 Squadron was arriving on the Continent for the first time, the occasion was particularly momentous for 350 Squadron. Formed in Wales in November 1941, the pilots and airmen were returning home to Belgium for the first time since fleeing the country in the wake of the German occupation.

Moreover, their moves to Belgium paved the way for an intensive and exhaustive period, but one that would ultimately result in victory over Germany. It came at a price, however, and the 41 Squadron that flew to Evere today was a very different Squadron to that, which ended the War on 8 May 1945. Of the 21 pilots that flew across the Channel today, only six would remain when the War came to an end in north-western Germany six months later. Six had been posted away, but the remainder were either killed, wounded, captured, or injured.

Continental Operations
4 December 1944 – 7 March 1945

8

The winter weather played havoc with operations during the month of December 1944. On seventeen days – 1-5, 9, 11-16, 20-21 and 28-30 December – there was no operational flying, although it should be noted that the Squadron was busied with its move from Lympne to the Continent on 4-5 December. The remaining days of the month were taken up with intensive days of patrols, sweeps and armed reconnaissance flights over Belgium, Germany and the Netherlands.

4 December 1944 – Following weeks of delay and several days of packing and preparing, 41 Squadron was finally airborne after lunch to move to the Continent. Twenty-one pilots made this historic flight to Brussels, where they landed at B.56 Evere Aerodrome. It was a mere 50-minute transfer, yet a significant milestone for the Squadron as it became their first base on the Continent since World War I.

Those making the flight in their own aircraft were Sqn Ldr Benham, Flt Lts Anderson (RAAF), Burne, Cook, Harding, Henry, Reid, Samouelle and Stowe (RCAF), Fg Offs Balasse (Belgian), Charnock, Payne and Wilkinson, WOs Appleton, Coleman, Hale, Miller (RAAF) and Rossow (RAAF), and Flt Sgts Fleming, Moyle (RAAF) and Stevenson.

The intention had been to fly to B.64 Diest, but due to poor reports of the condition of the runway, the decision was made to 'park' the aircraft at Evere first and travel to nearby Diest by road to check the conditions first hand. The pilots stayed at Diest for the night and returned to Evere the following morning to retrieve their aircraft, "having satisfied ourselves that the strip was serviceable."[1]

5 December 1944 – The pilots flew their aircraft to Diest, with the exception of Flt Lt Harry Cook, who couldn't get his aircraft airborne. There was no further flying today as the Squadron settled in to their new quarters.

Diest-Schaffen Aerodrome

Located two kilometres north-northeast of the town of Diest, and approximately 52km northeast of Brussels, Diest Aerodrome had originally been built by the German Air Force during the Great War.[2] The airfield was expanded by the air echelon of the Belgian Army – the *Aéronautique Militaire Belge* – to 700 metres x 800 metres in 1931, and four large hangars, brick auxiliary buildings and airfield defences were added during the ensuing years.

By the time of the German attack on Belgium on 10 May 1940, the airfield was occupied by four Belgian squadrons equipped with Fairey Foxes, Gloster Gladiators, and Hawker Hurricanes. When the Luftwaffe bombed the airfield that day, they destroyed most of the aircraft present. Those that survived, mainly Gladiators and Foxes, were decimated by Me109s in dogfights the following day.

Within four days of the launch of the German offensive, the airfield was occupied by the Luftwaffe, who subsequently expanded facilities and made improvements that included two additional hangars, barracks, camouflaged and reinforced aircraft bays, and repair shops. The Luftwaffe continued to use the airfield with impunity for almost four years, until sixty 8th Air Force Flying Fortresses bombed it on 10 April 1944, rendering the strip and facilities unserviceable, thereby ending the Luftwaffe's activity.

Diest was liberated by British troops on 6 September 1944, and repair and construction units were then sent in to make the airfield fully serviceable again. Despite their work, the fact the airfield was relatively short and had a slope at one end, caused many problems for pilots, who were compelled to land in one direction only, with the rise at the end of the run, regardless of wind direction. The strip would prove very difficult for Spitfire XIVs, particularly as the brakes were not sufficient to stop the aircraft with wind behind it before reaching the end of the strip.

The first fighter unit to arrive there was 130 Squadron on 1 November 1944, followed by 402 Squadron two days later. However, conditions continued to be quite hazardous for the pilots and many accidents were logged during both take-off and landing, despite Sommerfeld Track being laid down to help. These problems kept 41 Squadron's pilots at Lympne another month, champing at the bit, awaiting final permission to join 130 and 402 at Diest, which was not granted until 4 December. However, it did not take long for 41 Squadron to understand what all the fuss was about, the ORB wasting no time criticising Diest as an "exceptionally bumpy strip which was only 850 yards long".³

On arrival, 41 Squadron joined 125 Wing, consisting then of just 130 and 402 (RCAF) Squadrons, which was one of eight Wings within 83 Group, commanded by AVM Harry Broadhurst CB DSO* DFC* AFC. The others were 39 Recce (Spitfire IXc, PR XI, & XIVe), 121 (Typhoon Ib RP), 122 (Tempest V), 124 (Typhoon Ib RP), 126 RCAF (Spitfire IXb/e), 127 RCAF (Spitfire IXb) and 143 RCAF (Typhoon Bomber Ib) Wings. 125 Wing was commanded by Group Captain F. David S. Scott-Malden DSO DFC* and his Wing Commander Flying was Canadian Wg Cdr George C. 'Keefe' Keefer DSO DFC* RCAF, who had been in this role since mid-November, and was now on his third tour.

41 Squadron's pilots were accommodated in Diest's Beguine Convent, which was one of the largest convents in Belgium. Half of the facilities were requisitioned for the pilots, but the other half was still occupied by the nuns. WO Peter Hale recalls it was quite civilised with hot water available and good food served, which included plentiful helpings of asparagus. The ground crews were accommodated in the town's Citadel, built in the 1850s to defend against an expected Dutch attack.

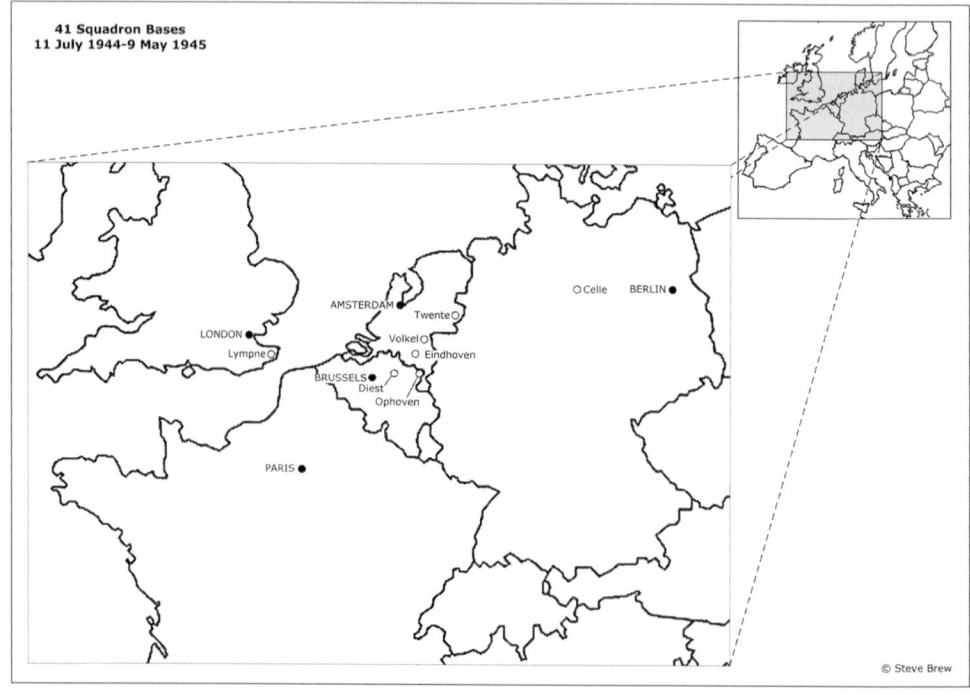

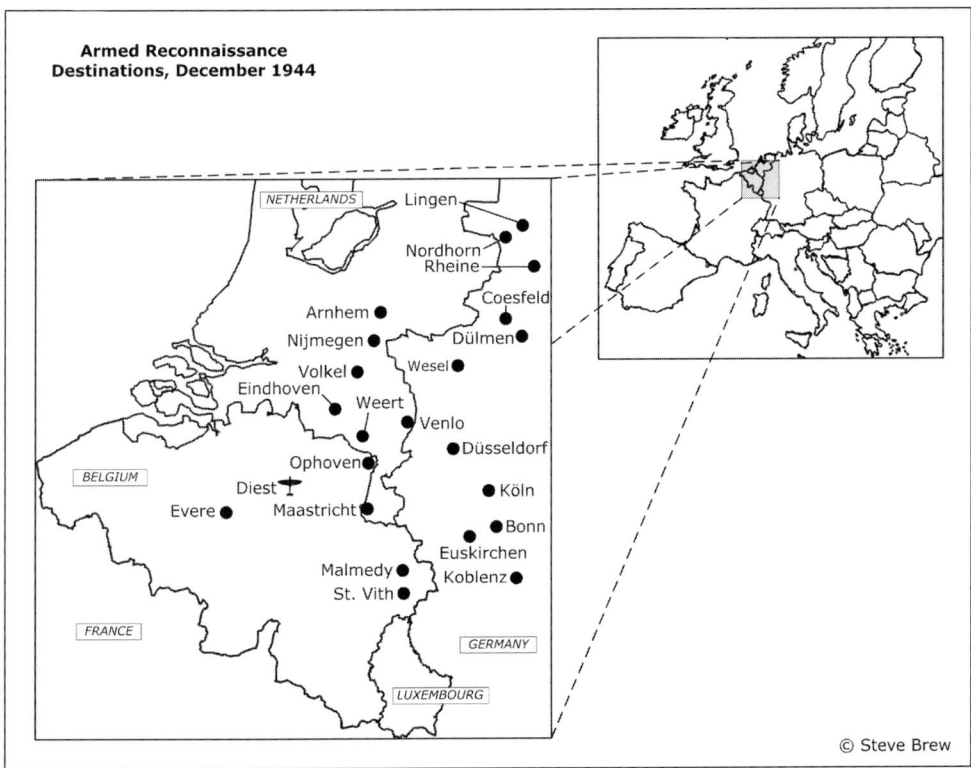

6 December 1944 – The strip at Diest continued to be a problem today, made worse by the weather conditions. 130 Squadron flew a brief weather recce, after which it was decided that no further flying would be possible. However, although 130 and 402 Squadrons were consequently released, 41 Squadron were placed at 30 minutes readiness and flew two brief sector reconnaissances between 15:30 and 16:45 to familiarise themselves with the area. These constituted the Squadron's first operational sorties from a Continental base since 11 November 1918.[4]

In the meantime, the rest of the pilots were shown a film on the gyro sight, followed by a briefing by Group Captain Scott-Malden.

> *Primarily his remarks were addressed to 41 Sqn as the newcomers to A/F conditions, but most of the chaps were present and learnt a lot. The G/C talked on the wing and its functional sections, and then detailed how a wing move was organised pointing out snags which always occur, and have to be overcome. To conclude he spoke of the ultimate move into Germany, and of the need for greater security and precaution that would be inevitable once amongst unfriendly people, and finally of the paramount importance of the members of the wing bearing themselves as conquerors and absolutely refusing to fraternize in any way.*[5]

Following the briefing, some entertainment was on the cards, and the men were treated to MGM's Comedy-Romance film *Andy Hardy's Blonde Trouble*, staring Mickey Rooney.

On 6 December 1944, 83 Group was spread over five airfields in Belgium and Holland, as shown in the following table.[6]

41 Squadron joined 125 Wing on 4 December 1944, one of eight Wings within 83 Group, which was commanded by AVM Harry Broadhurst CB DSO* DFC* AFC. Broadhurst had served as a young officer with 41 Squadron from 1931 to 1933; Crown copyright expired

Airfield	Runway	Occupied by
B.56 Evere	3,600 ft. partially tracked	127 (RCAF) Wing
B.64 Diest	3,000 ft. untracked	125 Wing
B.78 Eindhoven	5,000 ft. brick	39 (Recce), 124 & 143 (RCAF) Wings, & 83 GCS
B.80 Volkel	5,000 ft. brick	121 & 122 Wings, 419 RSU
B.88 Heesch	3,600 ft. PSP	126 (RCAF) Wing

7 December 1944 – The day's activity was limited to a single, uneventful 'anti-jet patrol' from Volkel to Nijmegen at 18,000 feet by Red Section (Henry RM710 & Appleton RM770) between 09:45 and 10:40. They were hunting for the Luftwaffe's newest weapon, the Messerschmitt Me262 *Schwalbe* [Swallow] jet-powered fighter. This aircraft was the latest in a series of new weapons in Hitler's arsenal, which had entered service this year employing jet and rocket technology. The V1 menace had been tackled by 41 Squadron in June, the V2 in September and now the Me262 in December. It was the world's first jet-powered fighter.

The ORB indicates the Wing's pilots were experiencing some difficulty taking off from and landing on Diest's strip, but still managed to boast,

> *With regard to the difficult conditions on the landing strip, it can now be told that the Squadron put up an exceptionally fine record of only two prangs, against the numerous other write-offs which fell to the other Squadrons (402 and 130 Squadrons) comprising 125 Wing at Diest.*[7,8]

The First Jet Encounter

8 December 1944 – A full day of anti-jet patrols for the Squadron, in which 16 pilots participated in nine patrols between 08:05 and 16:30. Most of these were uneventful, but Black Section, Australian Flt Lts Robert 'Andy' Anderson (RM769) and 'Ref' Refshauge (RM696), encountered a pair of Me262s north of Nijmegen in the early afternoon. Recognising them from lectures, the two pilots attacked them head-on, but observed no strikes. A short while later, they were almost bounced by another, but they managed to foil its attack by turning towards it. Anderson recorded in his logbook, "Chased 2 Me 262's. Bounced by another – turned into it, but all pulled away easily".[9] This was the first ever sighting and contact with such aircraft made by the Squadron.[10]

9 December 1944 – The Squadron's remaining pilots at Lympne flew across the Channel to join the unit at Diest today. There was otherwise no operational flying or activity of note.

10 December 1944 – At 11:50, twelve pilots were airborne on an armed reconnaissance via Arnhem, to an area within the triangle formed between the towns of Nordhorn, Lingen and Rheine. They returned early at 13:15 reporting 10/10ths cloud cover over the target area, but as the strip at Diest was rendered unserviceable by a slush of mud and snow under the Sommerfeld Track, further flying by the Wing was cancelled and this therefore constituted the Squadron's only operational flying for the day.

16 December 1944 – The Wehrmacht launched a surprise attack through the forested Ardennes region of Belgium and Luxembourg today, the significance of which was initially not appreciated by Allied commanders. The Ardennes Offensive, which Germany called *Unternehmen Wacht am Rhein* [Operation 'Guard on the Rhine'], but is widely known today as *The Battle of the Bulge*, was Germany's last great land offensive of the War. The object was to burst through the front line and capture Brussels on the way to Antwerp on the coast, thereby splitting the Allied armies in two, with the British to the north and Americans to the south. Having thus encircled four Allied armies to the north of the line, Hitler planned to sue for peace, using them as a bargaining chip to win a treaty on Axis terms and save Germany from a crushing defeat.

The offensive was launched under the cover of poor winter conditions, including snow, fog, low cloud and freezing temperatures, which gave the Wehrmacht an initial advantage as it hampered the Allied response, particularly from the air. The main offensive was supported by three further sub-operations: *Unternehmen Bodenplatte* ['Baseplate'], *Greif* ['Griffin'], and *Währung* ['Currency'], the former of which will be discussed in more detail in due course.

17 December 1944 – At 10:35, Sqn Ldr Benham led the Squadron on an armed reconnaissance within the triangle Wesel-Dülmen-Coesfeld, just inside the German border, but the operation was aborted early due to weather and the pilots were back in Diest by 11:10. Flt Sgt 'Micky' Moyle had already returned early in RM680 with engine trouble, but when the remaining men found 10/10ths cloud cover up to 14,000 feet over their patrol area, they returned to base, too. The destination and inactivity of this patrol suggests the Allies had not yet appreciated the significance of the German Ardennes offensive.

The Luftwaffe's jet-powered Messerschmitt Me262, similar to the one pictured here, was first sighted by pilots of 41 Squadron when a pair were seen north of Nijmegen by Australian Flt Lts 'Jack' Refshauge and 'Andy' Anderson on 8 December 1944. © Deutsches Bundesarchiv Bild 141-2497

WO Arthur 'Archie' Appleton served with 41 Squadron from 21 March 1944 to 18 December 1944, when he was shot down by Flak during an attack on a train ten miles northwest of Münster and captured. He was the Squadron's first casualty in Germany.
© 41 Squadron RAF

An Expensive Day

18 December 1944 – It proved to be intense and expensive day for the Squadron, with 23 sorties flown on two separate operations between 08:30 and 13:50. Blue, Yellow and Red Sections were airborne at 08:35 for an armed reconnaissance to the Coesfeld-Dülmen area, led by Flt Lt Terry Spencer. Once again, thick cloud was experienced up to 14,000 feet, and Yellow Section became separated when WO Peter Hale (RM790) started having oxygen trouble at this altitude. They were ordered to return to base and put down at 09:40.

Meanwhile, Red (Anderson RM770, Reid RM796, Spencer RM767, Refshauge RM799) and Blue (Henry RM710, Appleton RM699, Burne RM769, Rossow RM788) Sections completed their patrol and decided to make a sweep of Münster from around 09:45, moving anti-clockwise around the city from the southwest to the northeast, and found great activity on the railway lines. Taking the opportunity presented them, the eight pilots damaged a like number of locomotives: three on the Münster-Dülmen line, three on the Münster-Hamm line, and then two on the Münster-Osnabrück line, approximately 10km northeast of Münster.

During this latter attack, they came under accurate and concentrated anti-aircraft fire of both light and heavy calibres, which hit Flt Lt 'Andy' Anderson and WO Archie Appleton. The shot that hit Anderson passed straight through his fuselage just behind the cockpit and appeared not to have caused any internal damage; he maintained control of his machine and returned to base without any trouble. The damage to Appleton's aircraft, however, was more serious and he reported streaming glycol and other engine difficulties.

He was ordered to bale out, which he did at approximately 3,000 feet over Ostbevern. WO Viv Rossow saw his parachute open and watched his aircraft nose-dive into the ground and explode about 3km west of Lienen. Though he had cut his leg in his haste to bale out, Appleton was otherwise not wounded by the Flak, and soon captured.[11] "'Archie' was a sad loss to the Squadron and it was agreed that he was an outstanding N.C.O. pilot."[12]

The rest of the pilots returned to Diest, where they landed at 10:15 to tell the story. Rossow, however, damaged his aircraft on landing and had his logbook endorsed 'carelessness'. He was not hurt, but RM788 was damaged to Cat AC status and was not back in service until 13 January 1945.

Following an early lunch, the Squadron was airborne again at 12:30, on another armed reconnaissance of the Dülmen-Coesfeld area, led by Wg Cdr George Keefer as the twelfth pilot in

Flt Lt R. E. 'Andy' Anderson RAAF served with 41 Squadron from 18 March 1944 to 18 December 1944, when was hit by Flak over Münster, then stalled on landing at Diest and sustained serious injuries to his face. He did not return to the unit after medical treatment. © Doug Fishburn

three Sections of four. Flt Lt 'Jack' Henry (RM710) returned within 30 minutes with mechanical trouble, but the remaining pilots continued on, looking for suitable targets. As they did, they came under the increasingly aggressive attention of German Flak, some of which WO Hale felt was much too close for comfort.

Approximately 30 miles west of the town, they came upon a hutted camp, which they attacked with cannon. A lorry and a motor car were also damaged, and Flt Lt 'Momo' Balasse claimed four damaged armoured cars of his own.

Happy with the result, the Squadron returned to base at 13:50, but Australian Flt Lt 'Andy' Anderson stalled RM769 on landing on the troublesome strip at Diest and sustained seriously facial injuries. He was immediately hospitalised, then returned to England to recuperate, and did not return to the Squadron.[13] The aircraft sustained Cat B damage, and was salvaged by 409 RSU and sent back to Air Services Training at Hamble to undergo repairs.

Nominal Roll, December 1944

The following list has been extracted from an undated document, titled "R/T Call Signs", held in 41 Squadron's Archives. Although compiled as a record of radio call signs, it also serves as an effective nominal roll for late December 1944. The list must have been compiled in the two-week period between 18 December 1944, as WO Arthur Appleton is no longer on the list, and 4 January 1945, when Flt Lt Terry Spencer was posted away to command 350 Squadron. Names are listed in the order they appear on the document, and numbers refer to pilots' call signs.

Name	No.	Name	No.
Sqn Ldr Benham	14	WO Stevenson	27
Flt Lt Spencer	16	Flt Lt Henry	31
Flt Lt Harding	26	Flt Lt Burne	32
Flt Lt Cook	24	Flt Lt Anderson	34
Flt Lt Stowe	29	Flt Lt Reid	37
Fg Off Wilkinson	18	Flt Lt Samouelle	42
Flt Lt Refshauge	20	Fg Off Balasse	36
Fg Off Gibbs	25	Fg Off Gray	33
WO Hale	17	WO Rossow	45
WO Coleman	21	WO Fleming	43
Flt Sgt Moyle	22	Flt Sgt Kelly	39
Fg Off Charnock	23	Fg Off Munson	44
WO Miller	28	WO Clanzy	40
Fg Off Tebbit	19	Fg Off Payne	38

19 December 1944 – A quiet day upon which just two high patrols were undertaken in unidentified areas from 13:50 by Red and Blue Sections, each consisting of two pilots. Blue Section returned at 14:10 and Red at 14:50, both patrols being uneventful.[14] Fog came down in mid-afternoon, which cancelled all further flying by the Wing, and the afternoon was spent reviewing combat films in the Briefing Room instead.

22 December 1944 – Six patrols to Weert and Nijmegen, in the north-eastern Netherlands, were undertaken in sections of two between 10:20 and 13:00. All were uneventful, but half the pilots were forced to land early at B.78 Eindhoven. Flt Lts Harding (RM701) and Henry (RM710), Fg Off Gibbs (RM789) and WO Stevenson (RM863), were compelled to land due to poor weather, and WO Coleman (RM759) found his air speed indicator malfunctioning. In order to get him down safely, Flt Lt Spencer (RM767) landed at Eindhoven with him.

23 December 1944 – The Squadron made a single sweep of the Koblenz area from 13:05, in three sections of four, led by Sqn Ldr Benham. However, the weather played havoc once again, preventing an effective search for ground targets, and the patrol was uneventful. Moreover, on their return, all the pilots were compelled to land at Eindhoven "…owing to the weather at base making landing conditions impossible on an 850 yard strip with a tail wind".[15] Though they were on the deck at Eindhoven at 14:30, they ended up spending the night. Similarly, 130 and 402 Squadrons spent the night at Volkel.

Strange Objects in the Sky

24 December 1944 – Temporarily 'stranded' at Eindhoven, the Squadron operated from Eindhoven today. At least nine patrols involving 19 sorties were flown between 08:30 and 16:10 of the Düsseldorf, Geldern, Nijmegen, Roermond, Weert, Venlo, and Volkel areas.

Though no interceptions were made during these patrols, they did make a few noteworthy sightings. On one patrol, for example, three Me262s were seen in the Nijmegen area at approximately 5,000 feet, but were considered too far away to engage.[16] On another patrol, a sweep from Eindhoven to Venlo by a single aircraft, the pilot had a most unusual experience.[17]

> *At 1540 hrs at 10,000 ft south of Eindhoven whilst climbing through cloud* [the pilot] *passed through* [a] *large number of objects which appeared to be cardboard boxes with one side out. Size 9 x 4 x 2 ins.* [The] *pilot estimates* [the] *number at 100,000* [and] *says, flying at 180 m.p.h.* [it] *took him one minute to pass through. Later* [the] *same pilot whilst returning to base saw* [the] *same objects floating in* [the] *air at 7,000 ft. near Neerpelt (K.3896).*[18,19]

On a third patrol, a mid-afternoon sweep to the Venlo area by six aircraft[20], the pilots also made an unusual sighting. Just west of Eindhoven at 15:31, they saw sheets of paper floating through the air, which they felt "might have been conical or small parachutes".[21,22] Around 30 minutes later, they also sighted a lone Me109 near Emmerich on an easterly course at 20,000 feet, but it was not engaged.

By late afternoon, the conditions at Diest had improved sufficiently for the pilots to return, and they

> *…nipped smartly back to base, even with oil leaks and abnormal behaviour of aircraft in general, which would almost have led one to believe that Christmas was near….*[23]

25 December 1944 – A full programme was run throughout the day, which started with a Christmas Service by Rev. D. R. Green in the Casino at 09:30, followed by Officers vs. NCOs 'Comic Football' at 10:30.

The AOC 83 Group, AVM Harry Broadhurst, visited 125 Wing during the morning to address the men in the Briefing Room about the current state of the War and their expectations for the coming months. Having once been a pilot with 41 Squadron, Broadhurst took the opportunity to reacquaint himself with the unit and spent some time with Sqn Ldr Benham and Flt Lt Terry Spencer.

Then, as tradition has it, the Officers served the airmen Christmas Dinner in the Airmen's Mess at midday. The main course was roast pork with apple sauce and stuffing, roast potatoes, Brussels sprouts and peas, while dessert consisted of plum pudding with rum sauce, mince pies, cheese and biscuits. Apples, oranges, nuts, beer, cigarettes and cigars were available throughout.

Despite the fact it was Christmas Day, however, the pilots were airborne for a single Squadron-strength sweep of the Köln-Koblenz area between 13:45 and 15:20. 130 and 402 Squadrons were also airborne on similar operations. The Luftwaffe was also up to show a token presence and between Liege, Belgium, and Euskirchen, to the southwest of Bonn, several sightings were made of Me262s flying alone or in sections of four, but they were not engaged. One Me262 was seen by 41 Squadron at close quarters, when it cheekily dashed across the unit's path at an estimated 500 mph. Flt Lt Ross Harding gave it an ineffective "good-will burst".[24] The pilots also reported seeing a lone Mustang at 12,000 feet in the Euskirchen area bearing black crosses. On two occasions, enemy aircraft fired on the Squadron, but these, too, were ineffective.

For those not involved in the sweep, however, a film show was held in the Citadel at 14:00, closely followed by Ralph Reader's Christmas Show in the Casino at 14:30. Then, after the pilots' return from flying, the Officers were able to sit down and enjoy their own Christmas Dinner in the Officers' Mess. During the festivities, it was revealed that 402 Squadron would be leaving 125 Wing, but bigger changes were afoot that would see the Wing grow in size and move again in a matter of days.

At 19:30, Steeplechasing was held in the Airmen's Mess, and the day was rounded off by another presentation of Ralph Reader's Christmas Show in the Casino at 20:00 for those that had missed out earlier in the day.

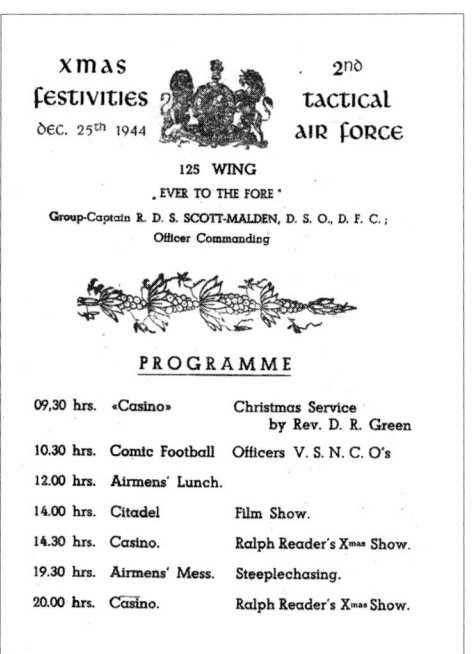

125 Wing Christmas Programme and Menu, Diest, 25 December 1944. © Terry Spencer, via Cara and Raina Spencer

26 December 1944 – The day saw a single sweep to the Malmedy area by eight pilots from 11:35, which was almost uneventful. Flt Lt Charles Samouelle (RM696) and Fg Off Harry Charnock (RM680) both returned to Diest early with mechanical trouble, but the pilots also experienced some anti-aircraft fire which hit Flt Lt 'Jack' Henry (RM698) in the tail. He was not injured, though, and the damage was only slight. The Squadron landed at 12:45 and this constituted the day's only operation as the weather conditions prevented further flying. 41 and 130 Squadrons would have provided area cover for Lancasters to the St. Vith area had flying continued, but as the operation was cancelled the pilots stayed on the ground.

The day also saw the Wehrmacht's Ardennes Offensive reach its furthest penetration into Belgium, before American and British ground forces drove them back. Meanwhile, to the north of the 'Bulge', the U.S. 9th Army, under the command of Montgomery's 21st Army Group, had already entered Germany and advanced to the Rur [Roer] River.

27 December 1944 – As weather prevented flying until after lunch, the day's total operational flying comprised two uneventful patrols of the Nijmegen-Weert areas by Blue and Yellow Sections between 14:20 and 15:55.

31 December 1944 – B Flight's Blue and Green Sections of each four aircraft flew uneventful patrols of the Maastricht-St. Vith area between 08:25 and 10:55. Returning to Diest early with undercarriage problems, Flt Lt 'Jack' Henry crash-landed his aircraft (RM842, according to the ORB) at 09:05, but was not injured. On the conclusion of the patrol, the remaining three pilots of Blue Section (Gibbs, Moyle & Reid) landed at the Squadron's new base at Y.32 Ophoven just after 10:00, and Green Section followed them in at 10:55.

At 10:15 and 10:55, respectively, Yellow and Red sections, also constituting four pilots each, took off from Diest to patrol the Malmedy-St. Vith area, and landed at Ophoven at 12:15 and 12:35, without event. Flt Lt Henry flew with Red Section, this time flying RM863.[25]

During the afternoon, several armed reconnaissance flights were made of the Malmedy-St. Vith and Liege areas, but not a single shot was fired. 41 Squadron's last aircraft was on the ground at 16:40.

Ophoven

The Squadron's new base near the village of Ophoven brought them closer to the German border and the front line, the latter of which was now barely ten minutes flying distance.[26] Located three kilometres west of Opglabbeek, in the province of Limburg, Ophoven lay in an area liberated by the U.S. 82nd Armored Reconnaissance Battalion, 2nd U.S. Armored Division, on 14-15 September 1944.

The main force of the German 21st and 24th Parachute Regiments had withdrawn to Kinrooi during 13-14 September, but had left a dug-in and well camouflaged rear guard of paratroops and Luftwaffe personnel, armed with machine guns and Panzerfausts. These were engaged by the 82nd's A Company and overcome through intense shelling from their 75mm guns, and hand grenades for close support. Around two dozen German troops were killed and 40 captured, but those able to withdraw retreated across the canal near Tongerloo and blew the bridge behind them. American casualties amounted to a single man seriously wounded.

With Allied troops now east of the area, RAF engineers visited and selected the site for an airfield shortly thereafter, but it was not until 24 November 1944 that the U.S. 829th Engineer Aviation Battalion arrived and commenced construction of the 5,000-foot strip. The RAF's 6610 Servicing Echelon provided airfield servicing and the aerodrome was declared operational on 10 December. Assigned to the RAF, 2 TAF's 125 Wing became the first official occupants, led by an advance party of 3206 Servicing Commando Unit who were declared operational in tented accommodation on

The 125 Wing Briefing Hut at Y.32 Ophoven, Belgium, where the Squadron was based from 31 December 1944. © Terry Spencer, via Cara and Raina Spencer

30 December. The following day, 125 Wing arrived and was formally established with the arrival of no less than four RAF squadrons: 41, 130, 350, and 610.

Their arrival at Ophoven today consolidated several of the RAF's latest-mark Spitfire Squadrons and simultaneously reunited old colleagues who had flown together throughout Summer and Autumn from West Malling, Westhampnett, Friston and Lympne during the V1 and V2 onslaughts, Walcheren, *Market Garden* and lastly as escorts for bombers attacking strategic German targets. The move also brought many men together that would soon become good friends and colleagues: the pilots were often moved between these four squadrons over the ensuing months, as they worked closely together and filled each other's manning requirements.

> *Quite an exciting end to the old year.... Our aircraft from Diest (41 and 130 Sqdns) and from Brussels (610 and 350 Sqdns) arrived at our new base, having operated from our old fields, landed at Y.32 and then continued to work for the remainder of the day. […] Most of the chaps were tired out by the end of the day, but a few remained up to bid farewell to 1944. "Fritz" tried to dampen our spirits with a few bombs and a shoot-up, but at midnight we sang in 1945 with Auld Lang Syne. A few of the windows in our new billet failed to live long enough to let in the light of the new year.*[27]

A lone Luftwaffe aircraft, who the Americans had nicknamed 'Bed-Check Charlie', had been regularly visiting Y.29 Asch around midnight, dropping a bomb or making a brief strafing run. The airmen at Y.29 were already familiar with this late-night visitor, and now Y.32 Ophoven would also receive a regular wake-up call.

However, the accommodation at Ophoven was less than satisfactory and a report made by 83 Group's Senior Medical Officer in early January 1945, recorded,

> *…the main camp, about 3 miles from the airfield, had been in German occupation. It had been a Russian Prisoner of War Camp, and latterly Belgian collaborationists had been incarcerated there. The camp was in a filthy condition when the Wing moved in. Quarters are widely dispersed and include civilian dwellings which have been vacated by the owners, and a large Convent school. There are good baths at a nearby colliery. Sick quarters are in a wooden block which was the womens' [sic] sick quarters of the P.O.W. Camp.*[28]

The men were fed U.S. rations and entertained with American films. There were trams nearby, and the pilots were sometimes invited to the homes of locals for meals.

WO Patrick Coleman missed out on the move as he was sent home on leave today. He flew as a passenger in a Dakota from Evere to Northolt, a trip of two hours and ten minutes. Little did he suspect the action he had just avoided. He returned by Dakota again on 9 January.

125 Wing's pilots were billeted in the large St. Albertus Convent School at Zwartberg whilst based at Ophoven during January 1945. © Terry Spencer, via Cara and Raina Spencer

During the month of December 1944, since arriving on the Continent, 41 Squadron flew 134 operational sorties, totalling 190 hours and 30 minutes, and 15 non-operational sorties, totalling 11 flying hours. The pilots had expended just 50 rounds of 20mm cannon and 78 rounds of 0.5 inch ammunition.

January 1945 – No operational flying on 18 days of month – 3-4, 6-12, 15, 17-21, 25, 30-31 January – mainly due to adverse weather conditions. It was a cold and frosty month, with frequent snowfall and no thaw.

1 January 1945 – 41 Squadron was airborne at 08:35 for an armed reconnaissance of the Bonn-Koblenz area. Eleven aircraft in three sections took part, led by Sqn Ldr Benham in Red Section of three aircraft. However, soon after departure, Blue Section began to fall apart as three pilots – WOs Robert Fleming (RM765) and Viv Rossow (RM698), and Flt Lt Charles Samouelle (RM790) – all dropped out of the operation and returned to Ophoven with what is only described as 'mechanical trouble'.[29] The remaining pilot, Flt Lt 'Jack' Henry, then likely joined Benham's Red Section, thereby bringing it up to a full strength of four aircraft.

The remaining two sections, Red (Benham RM791, Reid RM794, Stowe RM797, Henry RM963) and Yellow (Spencer RM767, Stevenson RM759, Harding RM842, Gibbs RM789), subsequently enjoyed some success along the Rhine, north of Koblenz, where Flt Lt Harding and Fg Off Peter Gibbs damaged a three-ton transport, and Red Section attacked a railway siding, damaging 15 railway trucks between them. WO Ian Stevenson also claimed two MET shared damaged, though it is not clear with whom.

Happy with their success, they were on their return to base when a radio message was received from Control informing them that Ophoven was under attack. It was, however, just a minor part in a major Luftwaffe offensive.

Bodenplatte

At 09:15 on New Year's Day 1945, in support of their Ardennes Offensive, the Luftwaffe launched *Unternehmen Bodenplatte* [Operation 'Baseplate'], a large-scale, low-level, simultaneous fighter and fighter-bomber strike by 750-800 aircraft, which targeted Allied airfields throughout Belgium, the Netherlands and northern France. Their aim was to destroy as many aircraft on the ground as possible and weaken the Allied air striking capability.

Fg Off Harry Cook, Flt Lt 'Jack' Henry RNZAF and Sqn Ldr Doug Benham at Ophoven, January 1945. © Terry Spencer, via Cara and Raina Spencer

Although dozens of aircraft of JG11 were assigned to a direct attack on the USAAF airfield at Asch, causing wide-spread damage, Ophoven was left relatively unscathed. It is likely that the RAF had inadvertently outwitted the Luftwaffe when 125 Wing arrived from Brussels and Diest the previous day. Nevertheless, the Americans at Asch were quickly airborne and took on the Luftwaffe in the air, claiming no less than 28 of the 65 Me109s and FW190s that had participated in the attack.

As several of 41 Squadron's pilots were airborne on an armed reconnaissance at the time, they were absent during the attack on Ophoven and arrived back around an hour after it was all over. The only visible sign of the attack as they drew near was a large column of smoke rising from a burning fuel dump. The damage was in fact greater, but still comparatively small in relation to other airfields.

> *New Year's Day saw everyone up bright and early and 41 Squadron were away on an Armed Recce when the Hun turned up in some force and proceeded to strafe us and the American strip nearby [i.e. Asch]. Considering everything, his shooting was poor. 350 Squadron came off worse having had seven aircraft u/s but not all badly damaged. 130 had one damaged. Two airmen were wounded and a petrol dump was set on fire. The Wing cannot claim any Huns destroyed over base, but the Americans got quite a few. Just after the strafe, 610 were able to report one FW 190 destroyed by F/Lt Gaze – a good show. The Wing was able to continue work all day and 130, 610 and 41 were constantly in the air on Recces and Patrols, and some Met, Goods Trucks and a Signal Box were shot up by 41 Sqdn. Altogether we flew 39 sorties on December 31st and 81 on January 1st.*[30]

Although 83 Group as a whole reported 148 casualties, of which 21 were deaths, 41 Squadron had suffered no casualties or damage as a result of the morning's offensive by the Luftwaffe and was likely one of the few Allied squadrons across the entire Western Front that operated all day without any problem whatsoever.

The Allied air forces across the Low Countries suffered serious losses today and reported a total of 465 aircraft destroyed or seriously damaged on the ground. Although initially caught by surprise – as had indeed been the intention – the RAF and USAAF fought back and the Luftwaffe also lost a significant 277 aircraft on the operation. The losses from *Bodenplatte* on both sides equated to a ratio of almost 3:2, which were extremely poor odds for the Luftwaffe, considering they had begun the day with a distinct advantage.

It is believed 62 German aircraft were lost to Allied fighters across the front and a staggering 172 to anti-aircraft fire, this latter figure apparently a consequence of the fact that German Intelligence was not aware of the extent of Allied AA batteries in operation. It also apparent today that several

Luftwaffe aircraft fell victim to their own Flak, as German batteries had not been informed of the Luftwaffe's pending attack in the secrecy surrounding preparations for the air offensive.

During the afternoon of 1 January, 41 Squadron flew three patrols in sections of four to the St. Vith and Liege areas, but encountered no Luftwaffe activity. A railway siding was attacked near St. Vith and Flt Lt 'Jack' Henry (RM696) claimed a damaged truck in the same area, but all pilots returned to base without anything further to report. The last pilots were back on the ground at Ophoven at 16:40.

Separately, WO Peter Hale, who was one of the few men lucky enough to be selected to take leave at home over Christmas, was having an extremely difficult time getting back to the Squadron. He flew from Northolt to Evere in a Dakota on 30 December, but after five attempts to land in poor weather, the pilot gave up and flew all the way back to Northolt.

On New Year's Eve, another attempt was made, which was finally successful. Yet he was still had to get from Evere to Diest. He managed to get an Anson to fly him there during the afternoon, but found they'd gone, having missed them by only a few short hours. Informed they had moved to Ophoven, the Anson pilot agreed to fly him onwards, but they were unable to locate the airfield. Left little choice, they flew back to Evere, where Hale was compelled to stay the night. Undeterred, however, he found some friends and spent an enjoyable night in Brussels seeing in the new year.

The following morning, he was intent on getting to Ophoven as early as possible, but just after 09:00 *Bodenplatte* was launched and Me109s and FW190s arrived and strafed Evere. Continuing his run of bad luck, Hale's Anson was hit on the ground and his intended mode of transport destroyed. Once the commotion had died down again, he found he was left little choice but to start walking east hoping to hitch a ride at least part way to Ophoven.

He was in luck at last. Before long, Hale managed to hitch a ride with an Army truck all the way to Ophoven, where he arrived during the afternoon. Under normal circumstances, a direct transfer to Ophoven from Northolt would have only taken about two hours; it had taken poor Hale two full days!

Within 83 Group on 1 January 1945, in the wake of *Bodenplatte*, the following statistics were recorded[31]:

Wing	Sorties	E/A	MET	Locos	Trucks	Losses
39	23	3-0-3	-	-	-	-
121	54	-	2-0	6-9	55-158	-
122	115	10-1-4	0-2	11-17	0-9	1-1
124	30	0-0-1	-	3-1	0-12	-
125	70	1-0-0	0-2	-	-	-
126	141	24-3-7	-	1-1	0-1	3-2
127	48	5-2-0	2-1	0-1	-	1-1
143	34	5-0-2	3-5	-	-	4-4
Totals	515	48-6-17	7-10	21-29	55-180	9-8

Despite a major attack by the Luftwaffe, 125 Wing had remained virtually unscathed, and had a surprisingly quiet day in comparison to other Wings within the Group.

83 Group's airfields at Eindhoven and Evere were the hardest hit, with 71 aircraft destroyed or damaged at the former aerodrome, mostly from 438 and 439 (RCAF) Squadrons, which were lined up ready for take-off, and another 24 at the latter. Nonetheless, the Group's squadrons flew 547 sorties throughout the day, initially claiming 71 Luftwaffe aircraft (48-6-17), although it is believed today that the number is closer to a total of 45 aircraft destroyed, probable and damaged.

On days when the weather hindered flying during the Ardennes Offensive ('The Battle of the Bulge'), all the aircrew used to 'beat' for Germans left behind in the retreat. These images show the men preparing for and undertaking such a search.
© Terry Spencer, via Cara and Raina Spencer

The successes and failures of *Bodenplatte* have long been debated, but it should be noted that, despite their losses, the Allied air forces were able to recover much more rapidly from them than the Luftwaffe. It is felt, therefore, that the German Air Force was seriously weakened by the operation and some historians believe it effectively destroyed the Luftwaffe's fighter arm for good.

2 January 1945 – Five patrols were undertaken by A Flight in the vicinity of Ophoven from 08:40 in case the Luftwaffe returned, but all were uneventful. By the time the weather came down in the early afternoon, at least 17 sorties had been completed, and the last pilots were on the ground at 12:50.[32] The Wing as a whole logged 54 sorties – more than any other Wing within the Group – and claimed four MET destroyed and two MET and two railway trucks damaged, thereby becoming one of only two Wings that made any claims at all during the day. It stood in stark contrast to the previous day's excitement.

The poor weather and snow continued for another two days and it was not until 5 January that 41 Squadron was airborne on operations again. On 4 January, OC, A Flight, Flt Lt Terry Spencer, was promoted to Squadron Leader and posted to command 350 Squadron. Flt Lt Ross Harding was named as his successor and the Squadron threw them both a party to celebrate their respective promotions. Members of the Wing's squadrons also attended, as did Wg Cdr Keefer.

Spencer Departs

Few characters on the Squadron during World War II can be compared with Terry Spencer who was posted to 350 Squadron as its new Commanding Officer on 4 January 1945, replacing Sqn Ldr Leopold Collignon, who had recently been wounded on operations.

Spencer had been OC, A Flight, with 41 Squadron since the beginning of May 1944, and had seen the unit through D-Day operations and the V1 onslaught. He claimed no less than seven V1s destroyed, but an eighth is also recorded in his logbook that did not make it to the official records. One of these he succeeded in destroying by tipping it up with the wing of his aircraft, an event sketched into his logbook by fellow pilot and amateur artist, Flt Lt Tom Slack, who titled the drawing "Tip 'em Up Terry".

In early September 1944, Spencer had led a section of four pilots on an armed reconnaissance over Belgium where they encountered two of the Luftwaffe's highest-scoring Aces, Hptm Emil 'Bully' Lang, the Commanding Officer of II/JG26 (173 victories) and Lt. Alfred Gross (52 victories), in FW190s over Tirlemont. Though one of the section was killed, the two Aces were shot down, Lang killed and Gross so seriously wounded that he did not return to service before the end of the War [see Chapter 7].

In November, Spencer led the Squadron's advance party to Diest and arrived in Belgium almost a month ahead of the rest of the unit. He then returned to Lympne to brief the Squadron on conditions at their first Continental base of the War.

However, Spencer's most daring exploits were yet to unfold. On 26 February 1945, whilst OC of 350 Squadron, he was hit by Flak in the Rheine-Lingen area of Germany and captured. Just over a month later, he escaped from camp by bicycle, and subsequently motorcycle, with another ex-41 Squadron pilot, Sqn Ldr 'Jimmy' Thiele, in a Steve-McQueen-style getaway, in which the pair made it back to Allied lines.

Spencer returned to 350 Squadron, where he once again took over command between 2 and 19 April. On this latter date, however, he was shot down once again, this time over Wismar Bay. He succeeded in baling out and deploying his parachute at a height of just 30-40 feet, which he miraculously survived, only to be captured again. The successful jump has since been credited by the Guinness Book of Records as having been the lowest authenticated survived bale-out on record.

Spencer was injured and hospitalised, but liberated by advancing Allied armies approximately two weeks later. Not surprisingly, perhaps, Spencer was awarded an immediate DFC for his

Flt Lt Terry Spencer was promoted to Acting Squadron Leader and took over command of 350 (Belgian) Squadron on 4 January 1945. He became a freelance photographer after the War, who spent three months on tour with The Beatles in the 1960s. © Terry Spencer, via Cara and Raina Spencer

exploits. In 1947, he was also awarded the Territorial Efficiency Medal and the Belgian Croix de Guerre with Palm.[33]

WO John Chalmers, who at Spencer's departure was with 610 Squadron but would join 41 Squadron in March 1945, had the following recollections of Spencer.

> He was a brave man. One of that rare breed who seem to have no fear. You can imagine what an asset he would be in any squadron. And yet he looked so normal. None of the jutting jawed devil may care Hollywood image. An average sort of a man. Except he had this disregard for danger.[34]

5 January 1945 – Most of the Wing was airborne at 09:35 to escort six Boston and twelve Mitchell bombers of the U.S. 9th Air Force to the St. Vith area, approximately 93km south-southwest of Ophoven, where communications centres were to be bombed. 41, 130 and 610 Squadrons were involved in what constituted 41's first bomber escort since arriving on the Continent. However, 10/10ths cloud was found over the target area and the bombers returned home without dropping a single bomb. The Wing landed at Ophoven again at 10:45, where 41 Squadron found Fg Off Rupert Munson (RM863) awaiting them, having had to turn back with mechanical trouble after only five minutes in the air.

The weather had improved by lunchtime and the Wing was up again at 14:30 to repeat the morning's operation. On this occasion, conditions were ideal and the bombers were able to complete their task. The Luftwaffe did not interfere and the bombing was concentrated and accurate, although there was some heavy Flak to contend with. The Wing landed again, unscathed, just before 16:00 and this concluded the day's flying activity, although one Mitchell bomber followed them in, an engine having fallen victim to anti-aircraft fire. Despite the seriousness of the operation, however, the Wing still found humour in the antics of one bomber's crew.

> There was a good deal of R/T natter and someone in the bomber formation had left his transmitter on. We hope the bomber boy who was saying such nasty things about one of his engines got his aircraft home safely. What he wanted to do with it would not have helped much.[35]

6-12 January 1945 – No operational flying due to the cold biting wind and snowfall. Despite the inactivity in the air, however, there was much to do on the ground as fresh snowfall necessitated the clearing of the strip and de-icing of aircraft and machines.

It was not all work, though; on one morning a snowball fight was organised, which saw some enthusiastic pitched battles between the men. One of the Wing's pilots then found a snow sledge, which many men enjoyed rides on, and Wg Cdr Keefer and 130 Squadron's Sqn Ldr Phillip Tripe made some skis, upon which several men enjoyed being towed around the airfield behind a motorcar. Films were also shown in the evenings, which included the Hollywood fantasy romantic comedy *I Married a Witch*, starring Veronica Lake, and quizzes were held to occupy the men, covering questions on the British, U.S. and German air forces, and other military and general knowledge subjects.

During this time, Sqn Ldr Benham and Lord Gisborough (who spoke fluent French) arranged for 41 Squadron's aircrew to visit a nearby coalmine where the senior engineers had their own bathrooms, fitted with a bath and hot water. It was quite a treat for the men, who were able to enjoy soap and a soak in a hot bathtub for the first time in a long while.

13 January 1945 – The weather cleared at last around midday and, after a week on the ground, the Wing finally got airborne again. 41, 130, and 610 Squadrons' pilots were briefed at 12:45 for bomber escort duties, this time as area cover for U.S. 9th Air Force Mitchells targeting Stadtskull, east of Malmedy, and almost 80km south-southwest of Ophoven. 32 aircraft were airborne in total, eleven of which were from 41 Squadron.

The pilots took off at 13:45 in three sections, led by Flt Lt Ross Harding in his first operation since being appointed OC A Flight. There was no opposition from the Luftwaffe, and the bombers completed their mission unopposed. On completion of the operation, all three squadrons were released for freelance attacks on ground targets in the St. Vith-Houffalize area, and whilst 130 Squadron found a few targets of opportunity, 610 and 41 Squadrons returned having found nothing worthy of their attention. As the weather came down again soon after 41's pilots landed at 15:15, this constituted the day's only operational flying.

14 January 1945 – Despite the day's good weather, the Squadron's only operational flying was an armed reconnaissance to the Dorsel area from 14:10 by nine aircraft in three sections of three,

Fg Off Frank Hegarty served with 41 Squadron from 7 January 1945 to 6 August 1945, during which time he claimed one destroyed FW190, one destroyed Ju88, and one shared destroyed Me110. He remained with the RAF after the War, and was killed in a flying accident in early 1962. © 41 Squadron RAF

led by Flt Lt Harding. Fg Off Donald Tebbit (RM788) could not get off the ground at Ophoven owing to engine trouble, but the remaining eight pilots (Harding RM704, Moyle RM879, Balasse RM690, Reid RM796, Kelly RM698, Munson RM791, Stowe RM759, Hale RM790) continued on and located a number of ground targets near Pelm, just east of Gerolstein. These were duly attacked and claims included a diesel engine and six railway wagons damaged by Flt Lts Ross Harding and Bill Stowe, a tank and two 15cwt transports damaged by Flt Lt Daniel Reid and Flt Sgt 'Hugh' Kelly, and another two MET shared destroyed and nine shared damaged by the same quartet, ably assisted by WO Peter Hale and Flt Sgt 'Micky' Moyle.

The rest of the Wing was similarly occupied in the same general area, thereunder 350 Squadron making their initial operational flights today as a part of 125 Wing. All four squadrons returned safely, claiming a variety of ground targets during a total of 43 sorties.

Separately, the day also saw the departure of Australian Flt Lt 'Jack' Refshauge on the grounds of ill health – he had not flown an operational sortie since 18 December. Twenty-five-year-old Refshauge, who had joined the Squadron in mid-April 1944, had been suffering a recurrent respiratory tract infection and Allergic Rhinitis that had grounded him often since the onset of winter, and had also kept him from flying with his previous unit, 453 Squadron.

The Squadron's Medical Officer, Flt Lt Frederick 'Doc' Herman felt that his illness may clear up if he were posted to a warmer climate, and as Refshauge was eager to continue flying, Herman made a formal recommendation that exactly this be done. He felt Refshauge was a "good type and physically and mentally very suitable to continue on operational flying if he could serve where his Rhinitis would clear up"[36] and Sqn Ldr Benham concurred.

> *This Pilot is most keen to remain on operational duties. He is a first class officer, and a steady and satisfactory pilot…. It is requested that he be posted to a more satisfactory climate where his health would not impair his operational efficiency, when it is felt he would be an asset to any Squadron.*[37]

Refshauge's wish was granted and he was subsequently posted to an operational squadron in India, where he flew until the cessation of hostilities in the Far East.[38]

16 January 1945 – As poor weather prevented an earlier start to the day's flying, the first of the Squadron's aircraft to be airborne today were two pilots on a brief weather reconnaissance at 13:20. Following a report of favourable conditions, eleven aircraft undertook an armed reconnaissance to the area around Vogelsang Aerodrome, in Nordrhein-Westphalen, around 15km east of the Belgian border. 130, 350, and 610 Squadrons were also airborne on their own operations.

The RAF had bombed the 50,000-square-metre Wehrmacht training camp and barracks in December 1944, and as a result of this, and more particularly the launch of the Ardennes Offensive on 16 December, the Wehrmacht had abandoned the base, officially called *Ordensburg Vogelsang, but* left nearby Walberhof Airfield in operation. Their intention was to utilise the grass strip as a staging area for the evacuation of wounded from *Bodenplatte*. As the airfield was located at the entrance to the barracks, the Allies called it 'Vogelsang Aerodrome'.[39]

The Squadron was airborne at 15:05 as Yellow (Harding RM707, Cook RM790, Gibbs RM767, Coleman RM759), Red (Benham RM791, Miller RM680, Rossow RM788) and Blue Sections (Henry RM796, Munson RM698, Samouelle RM696, Fleming RM879), led by Sqn Ldr Benham. They headed southeast in the direction of the base, which lay approximately 80km away, but within about 20 minutes Flt Lt Ross Harding was told he was streaming glycol. He promptly pulled out of the patrol, handing over command of Yellow Section to Flt Lt 'Sammy' Samouelle, and landed safely back at base at 15:50. Just after he left, however, the Squadron came under accurate and heavy anti-aircraft fire just southeast of Aachen.

Plt Off Peter Gibbs, also in Yellow Section, was hit whilst attempting to attack a train. He was not hurt, but also pulled out and headed for base. On his way back, however, he was attacked by USAAF Thunderbolts, which abruptly withdrew when they realised their error.

Notwithstanding this, a short while later he was hit by Flak once again, which this time severed his rudder and elevator control cables, effectively making his aircraft impossible to control. He still remained airborne and unhurt, but there was little he could do to get his aircraft down safely. No matter what he tried, he could not point its nose toward Ophoven and gradually strayed off course in a general north-westerly direction, but too far west. However, his aircraft's performance began to deteriorate near Westerlo and, when it started into a spin he could not control, Gibbs realised it was time to bale out. Fortunately, by this time he was back over Allied lines.

Oblivious to Gibbs' problems, the remaining nine pilots continued on and claimed at least two MET destroyed in flames and seven damaged. Other sources suggest the afternoon's bag also included three damaged railway trucks and two ammunition dumps hit.[40] They returned at 16:15 to find Gibbs had not made it back.

However, news was soon received that he was safe, and he arrived back at Ophoven after dinner that same evening to tell his story. He had actually injured himself when he baled out, as he had clipped his back on the tailplane[41], and then landed in a cherry tree. He came down near Kaaibeekhoeve [Kaaibeek Farm] in Westerlo, in the Province of Antwerp, around 20km and a few flying minutes north of Diest. However, before being able to extricate himself and climb down, he was confronted by the farmer, who had armed himself with a pitchfork, and was obliged to first convince him that he was not a Luftwaffe pilot. Fortunately, Gibbs had studied French at Oxford before the War, and was soon able to persuade the farmer otherwise and get some help.

His aircraft crashed behind a row of houses in Polderstraat [Polder Street] and it was sheer luck that neither a house was damaged nor a person hurt. A pigeon house was, however, demolished that cost the lives of its inhabitants.

The 125 Wing ORB made light of the situation, which, considering Gibbs had been hit twice by Flak and attacked once by Thunderbolts, may well have had a fatal outcome. One of 130 Squadron's pilots, who had similarly made an unscheduled landing that day, was also parodied in the following day's ORB:

> We were glad to welcome back last night F/O Gibbs of 41 Sqdn and F/O Jones of 130 Sqdn. F/O Gibbs was hit by flak and made his way towards our lines with his engine playing all manner of tricks. Finally he was forced to the conclusion that it was time to leave, so over the side he went and landed on quite friendly territory – in fact near Diest. He was back in time for late dinner. Jones nearly took out an army jeep – with one of Monty's Liaison officers in it as he crossed a road whilst force landing – the 17th January is nearly all taken up with the adventures of these two, and other losses. Weather was very poor with snow being waist deep!![42]

21 January 1945 – Though there was no operational flying today due to the weather conditions, several pilots were airborne on formation practice and Flt Lt 'Jack' Henry undertook local flying and a gun test for 75 minutes. Whilst underway, he spotted a German staff car near Roermond and, unable to resist the opportunity offered him, strafed it and left it on fire. Fortunately, the occupants managed to clamber to safety in time. Flt Lt Harry Cook also shot up a gun post.

22 January 1945 – The first of the day's three operations consisted of a ten-aircraft armed reconnaissance to the Münster area, led by Sqn Ldr Benham, which was airborne at 09:05. It was a successful operation. Red Section (Benham RM791, Gibbs RM790, Coleman RM759, Fleming RM879) spotted a large transport and trailer south of Coesfeld, which was duly shot up. An Intelligence Report that day records they…

> …saw and attacked articulated closed wooden waggon size of Queen Mary and attacked 45 degrees head on – front end went up in flames. Strikes seen along body.[43]

Sqn Ldr Benham also set fire to a 15 cwt. truck on the same road. Near Borkan, Flt Lt 'Jack' Henry (RM796) sighted a concentration of rolling stock in the marshalling yards and damaged

Fg Off Peter Gibbs was hit by Flak, southeast of Aachen, on 16 January 1945. On his way home, he was attacked by USAAF Thunderbolts and hit by Flak a second time, the latter severing his rudder and elevator control cables. Now unable to steer toward Ophoven, he gradually strayed off course and finally baled out near Westerlo, Belgium, injuring his back in doing so. © Michael Gibbs

a locomotive and nine trucks. In the Coesfeld-Lotte area, the Squadron damaged three more transports, and possibly destroyed two more MET and damaged another five in other locations in the surrounding areas.

Considering the operation had been so successful even before reaching Münster, when intense heavy and light Flak greeted them between Coesfeld and Bocholt, Sqn Ldr Benham decided it was best they quit whilst still ahead and return to base. On their return journey, however, he started suffering engine trouble and called for emergency homing. He was directed to B.80 Volkel, in the south-eastern Netherlands, where he landed safely, whilst the rest of the Squadron continued to Ophoven and pancaked at 10:30.

The day's second operation was a scramble at 11:30 by Red and Yellow Sections, consisting of six aircraft, on the report of inbound enemy aircraft – a rare occurrence these days. However, nothing was seen, despite the pilots patrolling the base area for half an hour, and they landed again at 12:05.

The day's final operation was another armed reconnaissance of the Münster area by eight aircraft, from 13:50. Unfortunately, the weather had deteriorated from the morning's cloudless but hazy conditions and the pilots returned to Ophoven at 15:15, having not fired a shot.

Separately, Flt Lt Charles 'Sammy' Samouelle was posted to 130 Squadron this afternoon, taking over as OC A Flight, when his predecessor was promoted to command the Squadron on Sqn Ldr Tripe's posting home.[44]

23 January 1945 – It was an intense and deadly day for the entire Wing, in which 41 Squadron went head-to-head with the Luftwaffe for the first time in a long while. The Squadron flew a total of four armed reconnaissance operations (25 sorties) throughout the day, and returned home claiming a mixed bag of aerial victories and ground targets. However, they would also mourn the loss of one of their own.

A Bold Attack

In the first operation on 23 January 1945, seven pilots were airborne at 08:40 for an armed reconnaissance to the Münster area, led by Sqn Ldr Benham.[45]

The operation started innocuously enough, much the same as many others before it, with random attacks on ground targets of opportunity. Red Section (Benham RM791, Hegarty RM798, Stowe RM863, Hale RM790) attacked a stationary troop train in a cutting in a wood between Billerbeck and Havixbeck, just west of Münster. The four pilots made a head-on attack and left the locomotive on fire with steam issuing from it.

Blue Section (Henry RM696, Munson RM788, Balasse RM765) also found some targets of their own. Following the railway line towards Münster, looking out for more rolling stock, Flt Lt 'Jack' Henry came across and shot up a 'utility car' whilst Flt Lt 'Momo' Balasse shot up a horse-drawn transport.

However, shortly afterwards, as they moved around to the east of Hamm, WO Peter Hale spotted a squadron of long-nosed FW190D-9's on the deck heading southwest away from Münster, "and the chase started".[46] These proved to be no less than 21 FW190 fighter bombers from JG27 carrying 250lb bombs, flying just above ground level. They were protected by another 24 long-nosed FW190D-9 fighters flying top cover between 2,000 and 4,000 feet. This upper formation belonged to 1. Gruppe of Fürstenau-based JG26, which were on a mission to Mönchengladbach.

The odds were stacked markedly against 41 Squadron's seven pilots as they dropped their tanks and dived boldly upon them. The time was just on 09:30. The main body of the Luftwaffe formation turned towards the Ruhr, making for the Datteln and Waltrop balloon defences, curving to starboard at 360 mph. 41 Squadron followed them, gradually overhauling with 18lb boost. Then the sky erupted as Spitfires and Focke-Wulfs flew in every direction to elude one or get onto the tail of another.

Flt Lt 'Jack' Henry got in first with his wingman, Australian Fg Off Rupert Munson, taking on two of the FW190 fighters flying above the rest. One of the 190s broke away sharply, but Henry was able to stay on the tail of the other, spraying it with a long three-to-four-second burst of fire at approximately 400 yards. Henry recognised at least one hit on the aircraft, but saw his fire all around it and, as they were so low, even in the snow in front of it. Smoke also issued from the 190, but he could not definitely say whether it was from damage or boost. He later claimed it damaged.

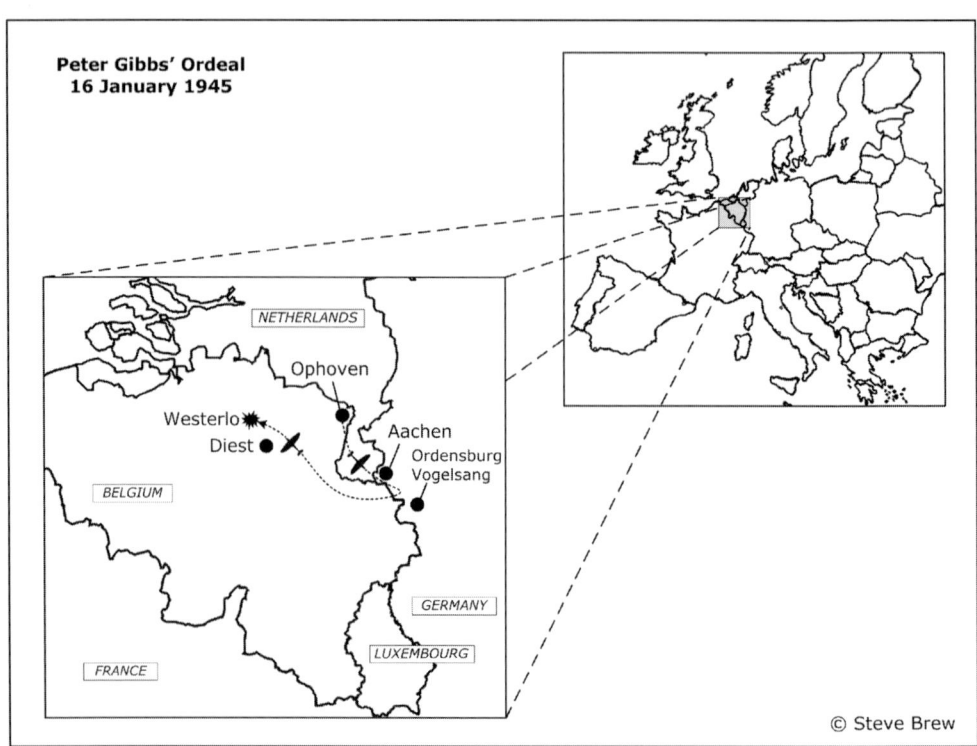

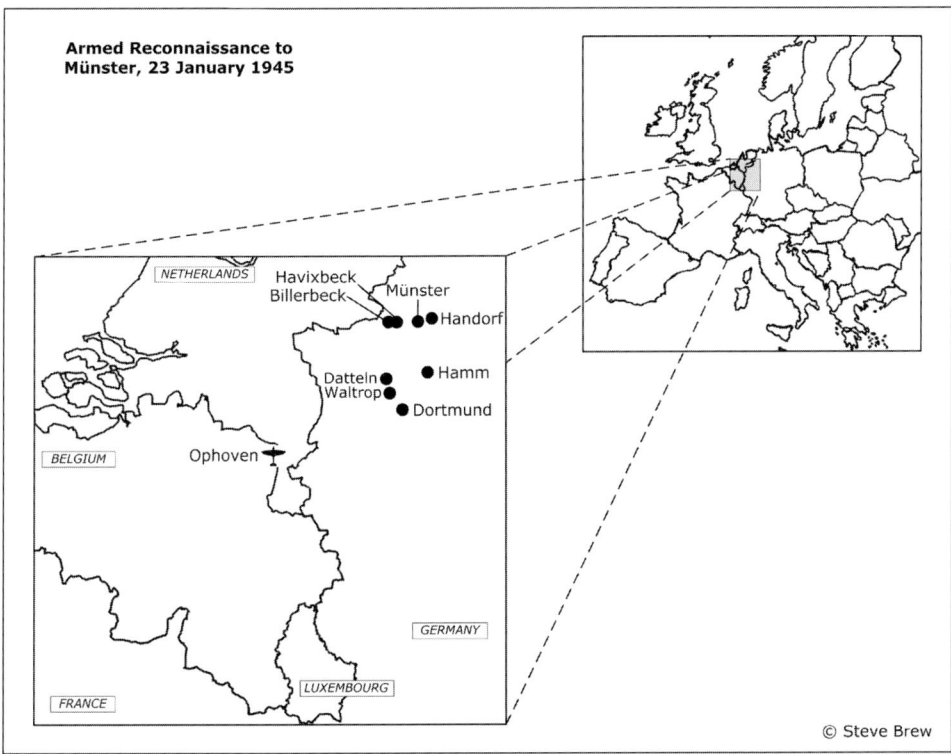

Meanwhile, Red Section had gone after the fighter bombers on the deck, whilst Blue 3, Belgian Flt Lt Maurice Balasse, remained above to cover them. Sqn Ldr Benham closed in on his own FW190, following it into a light turn to port, and opened up on it at a range of just 200 yards with half a ring deflection. The 190 then struck some trees, crashed and blew up.

Pulling out, Benham saw other pilots of the Squadron chasing their own aircraft. He checked his rear view mirror momentarily and suddenly realised he had a Focke-Wulf on his tail. Before he could react, however, he had taken a hit on his starboard wing, which struck the cannon ammunition tray, but he immediately took abrupt evasive action, and out-witted his opponent.

> *I pulled back and climbed vertically, turning to starboard. My No.2. (F/O. Hegarty) saw the FW 190 try to follow my manoeuvre but it flicked over and after stalling on its back, during which time the pilot baled out, the FW 190 spun in from 500 ft at A9038.*[47]

The pilot of this latter aircraft landed at Ostbevern at around 09:45 with serious head injuries.[48] Benham claimed both his FW190Ds destroyed, which constituted his sixth and seventh victories.

Now finding a Focke-Wulf on his own tail, Fg Off Francis Hegarty took wild evasive action, breaking "very sharply to port"[49], in fact so much so, that he was able to look back and see the 190 attempting the same manoeuvre. However, it flicked out of the turn instead, and spun straight into the ground from 500 feet and exploded at A9130. WO Peter Hale witnessed the combat and Hegarty claimed the FW190 destroyed. It was his first operational flight since joining the Squadron on 7 January and his first victory over all.

Whilst they were occupied, Canadian Flt Lt Bill Stowe chased another FW190 fighter bomber, which tried its best to elude him. However, Stowe was not going to give up easily and he chased his opponent a good five minutes long, heading southwards over several Ruhr Valley towns. At last, near Dortmund, he was able to close to 500 yards with 18lb boost in a curve to starboard and fired a one-second burst, thereby expending the last of his ammunition.

Belgian Flt Lt Maurice 'Momo' Balasse in the foreground with Fg Off Peter Graham to his rear. Balasse was shot down and killed over Handorf, Germany, by FW190s of JG26 during an armed reconnaissance to the Münster area on 23 January 1945.
© Ron Johnson, via Dan Johnson

However, his deflection shot was accurate and Stowe noticed strikes by the wing roots on both sides of the fuselage. Moreover, the 190 emitted "an increased amount of smoke," he felt, "above normal boost"[50], but as he was now out of ammunition, he felt it prudent to get back to base as quickly as possible. Leaving the FW190, Stowe made hurriedly for Ophoven where he claimed the FW190D damaged.

As the pilots began to arrive back at base, it soon became clear that 'Momo' Balasse was late. He was heard in combat during the mêlée, but had last been heard by Flt Lt Henry asking for a homing. He failed to return and was later confirmed killed.

The exact circumstances of Balasse's loss are unknown, although one report suggests he was hit by anti-aircraft fire from a Flak tower on the Dortmund-Ems Canal at Coerde, north-northeast of Münster. Eyewitnesses say that Balasse tried to climb but he lost control of his aircraft and came down just west of the Canal, on the edge of a wood on the land of farmer Anton Große-Kleimann.

Initially buried under a tree on Große-Kleimann's farm, Balasse was re-interred at No. 25 British Military Hospital Cemetery in Münster shortly after the war, but was moved to Reichswald Forest War Cemetery, in Kleve, close to the Dutch-German border, in July 1947. Re-interred yet again in April 1948, Balasse now rests in the Air Force Plot of Brussels Town Cemetery in Evere, Belgium.

He had joined 41 Squadron as a Flying Officer in November 1943, and became one of the Squadron's only two V1 Aces during Summer 1944, downing no less than seven-and-a-half flying bombs in the space of five weeks, and on one occasion shooting down two in a single day. In September 1944, Balasse took advantage of the Allied advance into Belgium and cheekily flew a private mission to Brussels to bring soap, food and other items to his family, seeing them for the first time since fleeing the country for England in April 1942. Promoted to Captain in the air echelon of the Belgian Army in November 1944, and to Flight Lieutenant in the RAFVR at the end of December, Balasse was 30 years old when he died, and the Squadron's second to last pilot to be killed in action before the cessation of hostilities.

41 Squadron's scrap with Jagdgeschwader 26 and 27 today constituted one of the first major air battles involving the RAF's Mk. XIV Spitfire. The Squadron's attack, though just seven Spitfires pitted against around 45 FW190D-9s, scattered JG26 and JG27, the former unit returning to Fürstenau at 10:00, just an hour after their departure, unable to fulfil their original mission. JG26 also suffered an additional loss to those inflicted by 41 Squadron; Lt Georg Kiefner of I./JG26 was hit by German Flak near Albachten and, although uninjured, was forced to abandon his aircraft.[51,52]

Victories, 23 January 1945	Dest.	Dam.	Location
Benham, Douglas I.	2 FW190D	-	Münster area, Germany
Hegarty, Francis M.	FW190D	-	Münster area, Germany
Henry, David J. V.	-	FW190D	Münster area, Germany
Stowe, William N.	-	FW190D	Dortmund, Germany

These aerial victories constituted the Squadron's first destroyed enemy aircraft since early September 1944, and its first damaged aircraft since late September 1943. They were also the first recorded by the Squadron on the Spitfire XIV.

However, this was only the day's first operation; another three were to follow. A second armed reconnaissance was airborne at 11:45, and consisted of four aircraft, designated Red Section (Harding RM863, Gray RM879, Gibbs RM788, Clanzy RM790), led by Flt Lt Ross Harding. The destination was the Münster area again, but as the weather had deteriorated, the four pilots were compelled to fly practically on the deck. Whilst it was dangerous to fly below the cloud base, it did offer good opportunities for locating ground targets, and it was not long before they discovered suitable quarry.

Harding, Fg Offs Eric Gray and Peter Gibbs, and WO Keith Clanzy made a concentrated attack on rolling stock on the single-track railway line south of Münster to Hamm. One locomotive and seven trucks were damaged, another two trucks set on fire, and two transports were also destroyed close to the line. They returned to Ophoven at 13:05.

The third operation was relatively unplanned and the result of advice received from the USAAF that the roads back into Germany from the St. Vith Salient were full of retreating German transport. Eight aircraft scrambled to the Blankenheim area at 14:20, led by Flt Lt 'Jack' Henry, but they found no sign of the reported traffic. Disappointed, they returned to base between 15:45 and 15:50.

The day's fourth and final armed reconnaissance was airborne at 16:25, consisting of six aircraft designated Yellow (Harding RM767, Hegarty RM790, Clanzy RM698) and Blue (Keefer (serial unknown), Gibbs RM879, Hale RM863) Sections, led by Wg Cdr George Keefer. They also headed for the Blankenheim area, but this time found ground targets plentiful.

Keefer and WO Keith Clanzy destroyed seven heavy transports between them, leaving two in flames, and Flt Lt Harding and Fg Off Francis Hegarty claimed another eight destroyed between them, leaving three in flames. WO Peter Hale attacked and damaged a truck, but Fg Off Peter Gibbs did not make any attack as his radio was malfunctioning. They all returned together at 17:15.

Altogether, 125 Wing flew 117 sorties on 23 January 1945, and they caused considerable damage. Their claims included three aircraft destroyed and two damaged, 12 MET destroyed and 150 damaged, one locomotive destroyed and seven damaged, two railway trucks destroyed and 22 damaged, and five horse-drawn transports, three tanks, two armoured vehicles, two tugs, and two barges damaged. It was quite a bag for one day's work.

However, it came at great cost. The nature of their targets was reflected in the damage inflicted upon the Wing's units. 41 Squadron's Flt Lt Maurice Balasse, 350 Squadron's Flt Sgt Bob Huens and 610 Squadron's WO George Tate were all hit by Flak and killed. 130 Squadron's Fg Off Bill Dobbs crash-landed his Flak-damaged aircraft at base, and Sqn Ldr Terry Spencer, also badly shot up by Flak, limped his aircraft safely back to base, where he fortunately made a good landing.

24 January 1945 – Good weather all day; nine sections of two carried out patrols over Nijmegen and Weert between 08:00 and 15:10, but all returned with nothing to report.

25 January 1945 – Although the weather was good around Ophoven today, it was considered unfavourable in forward areas, which restricted the Wing's operations. Although a small number of pilots from 130, 350, and 610 Squadrons were airborne, 41 undertook no operational flying at

all, but this allowed the men a good opportunity to prepare for a temporary move to B.80 Volkel in the Netherlands.

Today also marked the end of the German Ardennes Offensive. After 40 days of solid fighting, the Allied armies on the north and south of the Western Front finally met up again for the first time since the offensive was launched in mid-December.

26 January 1945 – The Squadron was ready to move today, but the weather at Volkel was considered too poor to land. As such, they remained in Ophoven another day and a single operational patrol of Weert was undertaken by Fg Off 'Ricky' Gray and Flt Sgt 'Hugh' Kelly between 12:25 and 14:25. They returned with nothing to report except for the weather being too unsuitable for flying.

27 January 1945 – Flt Lt Bill Stowe and WO Peter Hale flew the last patrol from Ophoven, a weather test between 09:30 and 09:55, which constituted the day's only operational flying. As weather prevented further flying, it was not until after lunch that the Squadron – eleven aircraft in all – was able to make their move north to Volkel, a transfer of around 30 minutes for the pilots. Apparently underwhelmed, the ORB records,

Today the Squadron left the gloomy environment of Y.32, with it's [sic] neighbouring slack [sic] heaps, and coal mines, for the frozen south of Holland.[53]

130, 350, and 610 Squadrons also moved north into the Netherlands during the afternoon, but their destination was B.78 Eindhoven. Whilst they remained with 125 Wing, 41 Squadron left the Wing temporarily to join 122 Wing. Rather more upbeat about the move, that Wing's history states,

…41 Squadron flew in with Spitfire XIV's, and remained with 122 for about six weeks, thus giving the Wing the rather unwieldy total of six Squadrons. 41 very quickly fell in with their new colleagues' pronounced views on German railways and achieved excellent results, although their rather limited range kept them out of the more fruitful areas.[54]

Upon 41 Squadron's arrival in Volkel, they found the Wing consisted of five Hawker Tempest Mk V units: 3, 56 (Punjab), 80, 274 and 486 (NZ) Squadrons, under the command of Gp Capt Patrick G. Jameson DSO DFC, whose Wing Commander Flying was Wg Cdr John B. Wray DFC.

The Tempest squadrons had moved to the Continent following Operation *Market Garden* and were well established at Volkel having now been based there since October 1944. They had achieved a respectable tally of victories, particularly during December, when 52 Luftwaffe aircraft were shot down and 89 trains destroyed, but at the cost of 20 of their own aircraft.

In January, the Tempests were allocated a major role in attacking ground targets to repel German ground forces involved in the Ardennes Offensive, but also took the lead in attacks on the Luftwaffe's growing jet fleet. Being unable to catch them, they instead developed a new tactic, in which they headed to the jets' bases and waited for them to return, finding them most vulnerable practically unarmed, at low speed and low altitude, preparing to land. The strategy enjoyed some success, until the Germans countered by installing Flak batteries for some distance along the aerodromes' flight paths.

Whilst the Tempests had recorded a substantial number of victories in January 1945, they came at a significant price. The Wing lost no less than 47 pilots during this first month of the year, which resulted in a decision at higher echelons to provide them their own high fighter cover. Herein lay the reason for 41 Squadron's move to Volkel.

However, as will be seen, this is not exactly what eventuated, as 41 Squadron generally continued to be allocated their own independent operations throughout the six weeks of January to March 1945 that they were attached to 122 Wing. It was the rare occasion that the Squadron provided top cover for a Wing operation, a fact that is all the more difficult to understand when one considers that the Wing's casualties continued to mount to such an extent that they were actually taken off ground attacks for a few weeks in March.

It would also prove an intense, and indeed expensive, period for 41 Squadron, both in men and machines, as the drive to the Rhine continued. Indeed, the 41 Squadron that re-joined 125 Wing in mid-March would be a very different one to that which arrived in Volkel today.

As an aside, however, as they settled in they found an old friend in the form of Sqn Ldr 'Jimmy' Thiele, who had been with 41 Squadron as a Flight Lieutenant from February to September 1944, and was now in command of 3 Squadron.

Volkel

B.80 Volkel, in the south-eastern Netherlands, just to the southeast of the town of Uden, was constructed by the Luftwaffe in 1940 as a night fighter airfield and named *Nachtlandeplatz Volkel*. It boasted a brick runway of 5,000 feet length.

By 1943, however, the airfield had taken on a more important role, was renamed *Fliegerhorst Volkel*, and became an operational base for the 5th Bomber Group [*5. Zerstörer Gruppe*], equipped with Ju88s, and the 3rd Group of the 7th Fighter Wing [*III./JG7*], equipped with Me262s.

Other units also utilised the airfield from time to time, such as an Arado Ar234 squadron during early September 1944, and a V1 unit that fired several flying bombs from here to targets in the United Kingdom. The RAF was aware of the Volkel's significance and, despite the presence of several Flak batteries, made several successful bombing attacks on the airfield, most extensively during Operation *Market Garden* in September 1944.

So great was the damage from Allied bombing during this period, that the Luftwaffe ceased operations from Volkel shortly thereafter, but destroyed what was left of the airfield's infrastructure and facilities before they did. However, the area was liberated a short time afterwards and the RAF made necessary repairs to bring Volkel back into operation. Its first occupants were the Tempests of 122 Wing, which arrived in October 1944.

Although the airfield was fully operational by the time of 41 Squadron's arrival in late January, it still lacked sufficient accommodation. This was provided in an old junior school house nearby which did not have any heating or hot water. As such, it proved very cold and uncomfortable, and newspapers became prized possessions, not for the reading, but for warmth they gave men on their cots at night. It was difficult to get hot water for a brew, and the cook house and mess were in a separate building, which meant venturing out into the cold to find some warmth!

The Squadron's WO Peter Hale recalls the airfield had solid runways and tracks, and that the aircraft stands were well dispersed. Although the airfield provided plenty of room for landing, the tracks did not, however, allow any room for weaving.

Local entertainment was generally lacking, despite the pilots once trying to hold a social with the locals; many men were disappointed when all the lasses arrived with chaperones! For occasions when leave time was too brief to allow a return home, the Squadron maintained an apartment in Brussels, where many of the men chose to take their days off instead.

28 January 1945 – The Squadron made its first flights from Volkel today, which consisted of six sections of two aircraft to the Nijmegen and Weert areas between 13:30 and 17:20. All patrols returned without incident, mainly due to the persistent 10/10ths cloud cover.

29 January 1945 – Due to weather conditions, flying only commenced at 10:45 when Red Section was airborne to patrol Nijmegen and Blue Section at 10:55 to patrol Weert. However both were recalled early to participate in an armed reconnaissance of the Gutersloh area and landed back at Volkel at 11:30.

Despite hurrying home, the operation they were called back for did not get off the deck until 15:00. Although it consisted of six pilots led by Flt Lt Ross Harding, it appears that only one of the pilots on the Nijmegen and Weert patrols was actually utilised.[55] The weather was poor with visibility down to 1,000 yards, even at ground level, but they found a few ground targets below the cloud base, and Harding (RM707), Plt Off Pat Coleman (RM707), Flt Lt Tommy Burne (RM688) and WO Ian Stevenson (RM789) claimed two three-ton trucks destroyed and one damaged between them. 'Steve' Stevenson also made his own attack on an anti-tank gun demonstration range, in which he damaged several guns, and shot up huts, a pylon and a telegraph pole.

30-31 January 1945 – No operational flying was undertaken today due to the cold, muddy and icy conditions, but two pilots joined the Squadron on 31 January. The first of these was Flt Lt Peter Cowell, who was returning to the unit for his second tour, having already spent 20 months with the Squadron between November 1942 and July 1944. He came from 83 GSU and brought with him 25-year-old Welshman Fg Off Clifford Mottershead, who was taking up his first operational posting since re-mustering as a pilot after 30 months as a Wireless Operator with 12 Group.

During the month of January 1945, 41 Squadron flew 195 operational sorties, totalling 247 hours and 15 minutes, and 14 non-operational sorties, totalling 9 hours and 30 minutes. The pilots expended 12,016 rounds of 20mm cannon and 19,277 rounds of 0.5 inch calibre ammunition.

February 1945 – No operational flying took place on twelve days during the month: 4-5, 7, 12, 15, 17-20, 23, and 26-27 February. Nonetheless, it would prove to be an extremely busy and eventful month.

1 February 1945 – Poor weather once again restricted flying for 122 Wing, and the day's operational flying for 41 Squadron consisted of a single armed reconnaissance to the Münster area at 15:30 by Blue Section (Henry RM696, Reid RM863, Kelly RM790). Stationary trains were sighted at Dülmen and Buldern, but these were not attacked as it was felt these were most likely Flak traps. The trio damaged a three-ton truck and trailer and returned to Volkel at 16:35, with nothing else to report.[56]

Meanwhile, WO Peter Hale and two further unnamed Sergeant Pilots flew back to Westhampnett in an Anson via Heesch, in the Netherlands, to retrieve three new RM series Spitfire XIVs. They returned with them on 3 February via Eindhoven.

A new NCO pilot also arrived on the Squadron today in the form of 22-year-old Flt Sgt L. Harry Smart. Smart had joined the RAFVR in the summer of 1941, and completed his flying training in the United States. He then returned to the United Kingdom and spent the next 15 months as a Tug Pilot at No. 3 Glider Training School at Stoke Orchard, before completing a course at 57 OTU in late 1944. Although he had logged a respectable 830 flying hours, he had flown none operationally; 41 Squadron was his first operational unit.

2 February 1945 – The morning's weather looked promising for operations but a gale started soon after midday, which put an end to flying. As such, the Squadron's only operation of the day was an armed reconnaissance by Red Section (Benham RM791, Tebbit RM819, Wilkinson RM707, Moyle RM790) to the Gutersloh-Paderborn area from 09:40, led by Sqn Ldr Benham. Flt Sgt 'Micky' Moyle and Fg Off 'Tebby' Tebbit both returned to base with R/T trouble, and the remaining pair, Sqn Ldr Benham and Fg Off Johnny Wilkinson, carried on alone "to uphold the honour of the Squadron"![57]

The pair enjoyed considerable success and returned to Volkel reporting having been active southeast of Münster, leaving two MET destroyed and in flames on the autobahn southeast of Beckum, a truck destroyed near Albersloh, two MET and an armoured car damaged between Sendenhorst and Wolbeck, and one MET destroyed and another damaged near Telgte, just northeast of Münster.[58]

Flt Lt Peter Cowell rejoined 41 Squadron for his second tour on 31 January 1945. He was promoted to OC B Flight on 26 March 1945 and remained with the unit until 31 March 1946. © Rossow family

3 February 1945 – Early morning mist cleared to sunny conditions, which resulted in a busy day of ground attacks and dodging Flak defences. Three armed reconnaissance operations were flown between 10:35 and 17:00, comprising of 23 sorties, and several ground victories were claimed. However, three aircraft were hit by Flak, four pilots returned suffering problems with their engines or R/T systems, and one pilot was wounded.

The first operation consisted of eight aircraft in Yellow (Harding RM797, Hegarty RM819, Stevenson RM789, Coleman RM863) and Red (Henry RM696, Kelly RM790, Burne RM698, Gray RM789) Sections, led by Flt Lt 'Jack' Henry, to a large triangular area formed by the towns of Osnabrück, Minden and Hamm. Many ground targets of opportunity were found by the pilots, but the German Flak defences were active and accurate.

Flt Lt Ross Harding damaged a locomotive near Rheine, followed later by an attack on another train defended by no less than three Flak wagons. These were formidable foes and it was not long before one of the Spitfires was struck. Flt Lt Tommy Burne took a hit in his wing from a 40mm shell but was himself not hurt. He pulled out of the operation and returned safely to Volkel, escorted by Flt Lt Harding.

Meanwhile, the remaining six pilots found numerous targets, thereunder two searchlights that they claimed destroyed and a searchlight post and lorries damaged south of Rheine by Plt Off Pat Coleman and WO Ian Stevenson. The pair then spotted two three-ton trucks hiding behind a house and proceeded to take them out, with the assistance of Fg Off Francis Hegarty; with many hits observed on both the trucks and the house. Flt Sgt 'Hugh' Kelly also destroyed a truck and damaged two more near Osnabrück.

However, Fg Off 'Ricky' Gray missed out on some of the action, returning 45 minutes early with technical trouble. The rest of the pilots returned to Volkel at 11:50.

The second armed reconnaissance was airborne at 13:35, with seven aircraft destined for the Münster-Gutersloh area, led by Flt Lt Daniel Reid. However, whilst still underway to the target area, Reid (RM790) started to have R/T trouble, and turned back, handing the reins to Fg Off Peter Gibbs, who was leading Red Section.

Red Section (Gibbs RM819, Cowell RM797, Moyle RM863), then proceeded to attack trains near Münster, claiming two locomotives damaged between them.[59] Blue Section (Wilkinson RM842, Gray RM696, Fleming RM789) found their own targets, with Fg Offs Johnny Wilkinson and 'Ricky' Gray sharing three damaged MET near Coesfeld, whilst Wilkinson also strafed some barges on a canal north of Münster.

However, they all had considerable accurate Flak to contend with, and two of the aircraft were hit. 'Micky' Moyle had the unenviable experience of having an AA shell pass through his cockpit a mere six inches from his head, and in another close shave, Plt Off Bob Fleming took a hit through his hood. The shell shattered the canopy, sending shards of Perspex flying, one of which cut his face. They were both extremely lucky escapes and, considering the speed at which the aircraft and projectiles were travelling, the pair likely came within hundredths of a second between life and death. Shaken, damaged, injured, but victorious, the six aircraft returned to base at 14:50.

Eight aircraft in two sections of four were airborne at 16:00 for the third and final operation of the day, which was an armed reconnaissance to an area bounded by Münster, Hamm and Paderborn. However, in a repetition of what was becoming all too common lately, two pilots were forced to pull out with technical problems within minutes of getting under way, and returned to base. Red Section's Fg Off Cliff Mottershead (RM842), who was on his first operational sortie with the Squadron, suffered R/T failure, whilst Yellow Section's WO 'Steve' Stevenson (RM819) was forced to return with engine trouble within just five minutes of taking off.

Two trains were soon seen near Hamm by the remaining six pilots, and Sqn Ldr Benham, leading Red Section (Benham RM791, Reid RM696, Woolley RM788), and Flt Lt Ross Harding, leading Yellow Section (Harding RM787, Hegarty RM790, Coleman RM600), led their respective sections down to make simultaneous attacks. A short while later, Harding also took on a train by himself that was "running hard for Ahlen"[60], and brought it to a halt. Other ground targets were found nearby and the pilots returned to Volkel at 17:00 claiming four locomotives, three MET and one railway wagon damaged.

6 February 1945 – Following two days of poor weather, Yellow Section of three aircraft was airborne at 08:10 today for an armed reconnaissance to Hamm. The weather was still less than ideal and 10/10ths cloud was found even at low altitudes. A few horse-drawn vehicles were seen in the Dorsten area but not attacked and the trio returned at 09:30 with nothing more to report.

A second armed reconnaissance was sent up at 11:05, heading for the Dümmer Lake area, led by Flt Lt Daniel Reid. Blue Section (Reid RM788, Gray RM799, Woolley RM885, Clanzy RM790) found and attacked two locomotives near Diepenau, about 27km southeast of Dümmer Lake, and returned to Volkel at 12:15, claiming them both damaged.

Separately, WO Keith Clanzy left on leave today, but was injured on his return to the unit, when he fell off the back of a truck, breaking his wrist and injuring his leg in the process. He was posted non-effective sick and is last mentioned on a mid-March nominal roll still with this status, but did not return to the Squadron upon his recovery.[61]

8 February 1945 – A busy day for 122 Wing, in which 101 sorties were flown, totalling over 140 hours. 41 Squadron was the first of the Wing's units airborne when five aircraft took off at 08:05 for an armed reconnaissance to the Münster area, led by Flt Lt 'Jack' Henry. Blue 3, Flt Lt Tommy Burne (RM719) returned within 20 minutes with hood problems, but as the weather conditions were so poor, the rest of the pilots returned at 09:00 with nothing to report.[62]

At 14:00, another seven aircraft were airborne for an armed reconnaissance to the Osnabrück-Dümmer Lake area, led by Flt Lt 'Jack' Henry. Plt Off Pat Coleman (RM680) returned early with a rough engine, accompanied by WO 'Steve' Stevenson (RM789), but when the remaining trio found low-lying 10/10ths cloud cover over the target area, they returned within the hour, claiming just a single locomotive damaged south of Rheine.

A final five aircraft were sent on an armed reconnaissance of the Rheine area at 16:30, led by Flt Lt Tommy Burne. Fg Off Johnny Wilkinson returned early with a rough engine and the remaining pilots landed after only 50 minutes in the air, with nothing to report.[63]

9 February 1945 – Poor weather in the morning prevented the Wing from "going over to annoy the Hun"[64] until after lunch, and in the end the Squadron only undertook a single operation all day. Yellow Section (Harding RM819, Smart RM797, Cowell RM863, Moyle RM680), led by Flt Lt Ross Harding, was airborne at 14:45 and headed for the Ahlen area, where they found numerous ground targets. They returned at 16:00 claiming four locomotives damaged – two on the Ahlen-Oelde line and two on the Beckum-Lippstadt line, plus one MET destroyed and another MET damaged on the autobahn north of Beckum.

As a result of the generally unfavourable weather, only two other squadrons within the Wing were airborne during the day, and in fact "had it not been for [the Wing's] distinguished lodgers, 41 Sqdn., the score sheet would have remained totally blank."[65]

10 February 1945 – Due to continuing adverse weather conditions, the day's operations did not commence until after lunch, and consisted of two separate armed reconnaissances of four aircraft to the Ahlen and Osnabrück-Dümmer Lake areas. However, being compelled to operate below a cloud base of just 1,000 feet, the German Flak batteries took full advantage of the opportunity offered them. Their fire was concentrated and accurate, and took its toll both on men and machines.

The first of these saw Yellow Section (Harding RM788, Tebbit RM819, Hegarty RM797, Stevenson RM863) airborne at 14:00, led by Flt Lt Ross Harding. Fg Off Donald Tebbit dropped out early with a rough engine, but the limited visibility restricted the hunt for ground targets by the remaining trio. They found some MET north of Hamm and left two destroyed and in flames, and one damaged.

Before long, they came across a train near Lippstadt Aerodrome and prepared to attack it. However, just as they were about to, concentrated light Flak opened up on them from surrounding fields and aerodrome defences. Flt Lt Harding's port wing was hit by a 40mm shell, which jammed the aileron and caused both his altimeter and air speed indicator to malfunction. He pulled out and returned gingerly to base, escorted by Fg Off Hegarty and WO Stevenson, with his aircraft threatening to stall at around 140 mph all the way home. Underway, Stevenson took the opportunity to strafe a work party near Coesfeld, damaging an excavator, and they landed back at Volkel at 15:05.

Flt Lt Henry is Captured

The second armed reconnaissance on 10 February 1945 was undertaken by Blue Section (Henry RM842, Munson RM680, Payne RM863, Gray RM799). Airborne at 16:25, their destination was the Osnabrück-Dümmer Lake area, led by Flt Lt 'Jack' Henry. The quartet spotted a train near Rheine and proceeded to attack the locomotive, but was met by accurate Flak. Flt Lt Henry was hit, and his cooling system damaged. Streaming glycol, it was not long before his engine seized and he was obliged to bale out. His aircraft crashed in a field southwest of Eschendorf Aerodrome, east of Rheine.

The remaining aircraft landed back at base at 17:00. Having come down well behind lines, it was no surprise when news was received that Henry had been captured. He was replaced as OC B Flight, that same day by Flt Lt Daniel Reid.[66] The following addendum was made in Henry's logbook,

> Blue section of [four] *aircraft attacked a locomotive in the vicinity of Dumner* [sic] *Lake. F/Lt Henry was the first to attack and was greeted by heavy Flak. He continued to attack the loco and was seen to damage it. As he pulled up white vapour streamed from the A/C and he said his A/C was hit. He turned towards home but his engine seized and he* force-landed *baled out in the vicinity of Rheine. He was last seen gliding down towards the clouds at a height of 3000 feet.*[67,68]

OC B Flight, Flt Lt 'Jack' Henry RNZAF served with 41 Squadron from 28 August 1944 to 10 February 1945 when he was shot down by Flak during an attack on a locomotive near Rheine, Germany, and captured.
© 41 Squadron RAF

A subsequent note, added by Henry after his repatriation, adds, "Taken P.O.W. after baling out. Escaped from forced march to Munich. Returned [to] England 19 April 1945."[69]

It proved to be an expensive day for the entire Wing, and Flt Lt Henry was not the only 122 Wing pilot lost on 10 February 1945. All six squadrons were airborne during the afternoon, and a total of 50 sorties were flown, but they lost four pilots for the score of two MET destroyed, and two MET, 23 locomotives, 11 wagons, 13 barges and two signal boxes damaged.

Following 41 Squadron's misfortune, 274 Squadron's Flt Lt John Woolfries was hit by Flak and force-landed in enemy-held territory. 3 Squadron then lost Plt Off Morris Rose who force-landed in the Paderborn area after suffering engine trouble and, soon after, ex-41 Squadron pilot 'Jimmy' Thiele, who was now commanding 3 Squadron, was also hit by Flak near Dorsten and forced to bale out.[70]

Sqn Ldr Thiele was attacking a train when he was hit. His aircraft (Tempest V, NV644) caught fire and he sustained burns to his eyes, face and wrists before he was able to bale out. He was captured and hospitalised for some weeks before he made good an escape with ex-41 Squadron pilot and Officer Commanding, 350 Squadron Sqn Ldr Terry Spencer on 31 March and returned to Allied lines by bicycle and motorcycle.

11 February 1945 – Three operations were flown today, the first of which was an armed reconnaissance by Yellow Section (Tebbit RM797, Coleman RM799, Cowell RM863, Wilkinson RM791, Rossow RM696) to the Münster area from 08:35, led by Fg Off Don Tebbit. WO Viv Rossow returned to base within 15 minutes with technical problems, leaving the other four pilots to continue the mission without him.

In due course, Yellow Section spotted several trains on the Münster-Gutersloh line and attacked three locomotives towing coal trucks, leaving them damaged. Fg Off 'Johnny' Wilkinson and Plt Off Pat Coleman also damaged eight railway trucks, and the quartet returned at 10:00 with nothing further to report.

The next operation was airborne at 11:00 on an armed reconnaissance to the Rheine-Dümmer Lake area, led by Flt Lt Daniel Reid. The five pilots, designated Blue Section (Reid RM696, Burne RM863, Rossow RM797, Munson RM879, Gray RM799), soon became four when Fg Off Rupert Munson pulled out and returned to base with technical trouble. However, there was little quarry for the remaining four pilots, but they did strafe and damage three tugs and a barge on the Mittelland Canal, just west of Bramsche, before returning to base at 12:20.

The day's third operation consisted of four aircraft, designated Yellow Section (Harding RM797, Smart RM863, Moyle RM696, Tebbit SM817), which were airborne at 13:50, led by Flt Lt Ross

Harding. Their target area was bounded by the towns of Münster, Gutersloh and Lippstadt, and included sweeps of both the Münster and Lippstadt Aerodromes.

Representative of the Luftwaffe's distinct lack of presence and almost complete Allied air superiority, both airfields were completely devoid of aircraft and provided the pilots not one single suitable target. Carrying on, however, Yellow Section discovered both road and rail targets, and returned at 15:10 claiming two locomotives damaged near Lippstadt, a three-ton lorry damaged near Warendorf, and two lorries destroyed and a lorry and trailer damaged near Beckum.

Though the weather came down again around 15:30 when drizzle deteriorated to snow, and stopped any further operations, the Wing had still managed a healthy total of 84 sorties during the day and varying claims on 39 locomotives, 67 railway trucks, 50 MET, five tugs, seven barges, a signal box, and one enemy aircraft destroyed. This effort elicited a congratulatory message from the AOC-in-C 2 TAF, AM Sir Arthur Coningham, to the AOC 83 Group, AVM Harry Broadhurst, praising their "magnificent work" and "great success at train busting".[71] It appears rolling stock was the main target for the whole Group that day.

Separately, 41 Squadron's Flt Lt Harry Cook was posted away today, recommended for rest as he was beginning to show the signs of fatigue. He had already completed two tours, and had now been with 41 Squadron for 14 months, having destroyed one V1 and numerous ground targets during that time. However, he had previously claimed two aircraft destroyed, four probable and four damaged during the Battle of Britain.[72]

13 February 1945 – Following a day of poor weather and no operational flying, the Squadron was up in force again today, with three operations airborne before midday and another in the early afternoon, totalling 19 sorties. It was another busy day of ground attacks and, for the first time in three weeks, the Luftwaffe was also encountered. However, things did not all go in the Squadron's favour.

The first two operations were airborne simultaneously at 08:40 on separate armed reconnaissances: A Flight's Red Section (Tebbit RM819, Coleman RM797, Cowell RM789, Wilkinson RM797)[73] to the Münster-Gutersloh area, led by Fg Off Don Tebbit, and B Flight's Blue Section (Reid RM885, Fleming RM863, Burne RM790, Munson NH712) to the Ahlen area led by Flt Lt Daniel Reid.

Although Plt Off Pat Coleman returned early with a broken gunsight, the remaining pilots had no trouble finding a good amount of suitable ground targets. In an area between the southeast of Münster and the southwest of Warendorf, Red Section damaged a yellow 30-seat Kraftpost bus, a three-ton transport, three large trucks, a 15cwt van, a saloon car and a barge. They also claimed a locomotive damaged north of Münster, and three barges strafed on the Dortmund-Ems Canal. Blue Section was similarly successfully, claiming three locomotives and one MET damaged at

Flt Lt Ross Harding showing 40mm Flak damage to the wing of his Spitfire XIV, RM788, sustained near Lippstadt Aerodrome on 10 February 1945. © Ross Harding, via Dan Johnson

An Me110 similar to this was shot down and destroyed by Flt Lt Ross Harding, Fg Off 'Ricky' Gray RAAF, and Fg Off Frank Hegarty south of Lippstadt, Germany, on 13 February 1945. However, return fire from the Messerschmitt's dorsal gunner also shot Harding down. © Deutsches Bundesarchiv Bild 101I-377-2801-013

Soest, southeast of Hamm, and another damaged that was attempting to hide under a bridge in the same area. They then came across approximately 40 trucks in a nearby cutting, which were strafed and twelve left "more or less severely damaged".[74] Both sections returned to Volkel at 10:10.

Another Flight Commander is Lost

The day's third operation was airborne at 11:25 to the Ahlen-Paderborn area, consisting of six aircraft in Yellow (Harding RM819, Hegarty RM863, Stevenson RM789) and Blue (Woolley RM791, Gray NH712, Payne RM790) Sections, led by Flt Lt Ross Harding.

Just after midday, WO 'Steve' Stevenson spotted some ground targets in the Oestereiden area, approximately 27km southwest of Paderborn, and dived down with Fg Off Eric Gray to attack them. The remaining four pilots covered them from above and orbited for a short time at 3,000 feet over an area approximately 16km south of Lippstadt.

The weather was not ideal and there was 7/10ths to 9/10ths cloud over the area. However, Fg Off Francis Hegarty suddenly noticed an Me110 appear out of the cloud cover from 2 o'clock, descending in a southerly direction straight towards them in a gentle turn to starboard. No doubt the Luftwaffe pilot was as surprised as they were and took immediate evasive action. Being in a perfect position for an attack, Eric Gray had only to climb slightly to get onto the Messerschmitt's tail. He explained later,

> *I had no reflector sight and so had to make a guess at deflection which was not very successful though I scored at least two strikes with .5 on* [the] *Port wing. I kept on firing but* [the] *E/A went into cloud. I passed over this cloud and did a 90° turn* [to the] *right to intercept the E/A when it flew out. When it did come out both engines were on fire and the crew of two baled out.*[75]

Hegarty watched Gray make his attack and observed strikes on the aircraft, which resulted in smoke issuing from its port engine. As Gray climbed up over the cloud cover, Flt Lt Harding followed the Me110 into the murk and pressed home his own attack at close range, achieving strikes with both cannon and machine gun fire. From behind him, Hegarty saw his attack cause part of the cockpit canopy to fly off.

As Harding pulled away, Hegarty moved in for his own attack, opening fire at a range of 250 feet and holding down the firing button on his control column for a full six seconds. He saw strikes on the aircraft's nose and watched as its starboard engine burst into flames.

Though only seconds had passed as Gray climbed over the cloud and encountered the aircraft on the other side, both Harding and Hegarty had been able to make solid attacks, which accounted for Gray's observation of both engines on fire. The Me110 then went down in flames, exploding on impact near the Lippstadt-Soest railway line just south of Benninghausen, and approximately 7.5 km southwest of Lippstadt. This was one of only three interceptions made by 83 Group today and the only aircraft shot down. The Group ORB was almost critical of the Me110's pilot, recording he "carelessly and fatally flew through an orbit by 41 Squadron over Lippstadt".[76]

However, in the brief but intense encounter, the Messerschmitt's dorsal gunner had managed to fire back and hit Harding's aircraft. With a thin stream of oil emitting from his punctured oil cooler, he turned west and pulled up into cloud cover. Ordering the Squadron to re-form, he reported a steadily rising oil temperature, and made a beeline for Allied lines. Soon afterwards, his transmissions ceased; he was last heard calling for homing. When the remaining five pilots ascended out of the cloud ceiling, Harding was nowhere to be seen. They landed back at Volkel at 12:45 to find he had not returned.[77]

It later transpired that Harding had force-landed at Werl, approximately 32km east-northeast of Dortmund, still a long way behind the front line, and was immediately captured. His internment constituted the second loss of a Flight Commander within three days, and he was replaced as OC A Flight, by Flt Lt Frank Woolley.[78] "We shall all miss such a grand Flight Commander & friend."[79]

The Me110, since identified as a G-4 of Dortmund-based 11/NJG1 (G9+FY, WNr. 730364), was claimed by Hegarty and Gray, who both confirmed Harding's participation in the shared victory.[80] WO Stevenson, who claimed one MET destroyed and two damaged, was close enough to observe Harding's attack, also confirmed that, "…F/Lt. Harding shared in the destruction of this Me.110 by getting strikes on the starboard engine and wing root."[81]

Two hours after their return, a fourth operation was airborne on an armed reconnaissance of the Ahlen-Paderborn and Gutersloh areas. It consisted of five aircraft, designated Yellow (Cowell RM690 & Moyle RM789) and Blue (Woolley SM817, Munson RM885, Moyle RM863) Sections, which were led by Flt Lt Frank Woolley. Within 25 minutes, however, Flt Sgt 'Micky' Moyle pulled out with technical trouble and returned to base, leaving the four pilots to continue without him.

There was a little excitement when an Me262 appeared, and Flt Lt Woolley gave chase in a westerly direction, towards Gutersloh. However, the aircraft easily out-paced him and disappeared into cloud cover at 3,000 feet. Giving up, the pilots re-formed and sought out some suitable

Flt Lt Ross Harding served with 41 Squadron from 5 July 1943 to 13 February 1945, and was OC A Flight from 4 January 1945. He was hit by return fire from the dorsal gunner of an Me110 south of Lippstadt on 13 February 1945 and captured. He retired from the RAF as an Air Vice Marshal in 1976. © 41 Squadron RAF

ground targets instead. It was not long before they found some MET, but there was little else going and they returned to base at 14:45, claiming one MET destroyed and two damaged.

14 February 1945 – The Squadron's operations were limited by inclement weather today, but a solid fight was still had soon after breakfast that became the Squadron's highest single daily aerial victory tally in almost three years.

At 07:45, Flt Lt Frank Woolley, on his first full day as OC A Flight, led seven aircraft, designated Blue (Woolley RM791, Gray RM885, Rossow RM696) and Yellow (Tebbit RM863, Wilkinson RM680, Stevenson RM789, Moyle RM799) Sections, on an armed reconnaissance of the Osnabrück area. As they approached Rheine Aerodrome from the north at an altitude of 3,000 feet, a dozen long-nosed FW190Ds were seen orbiting at 1,000 feet, as well as several Me262s which were in the process of taking off. The Focke-Wulfs belonged to their old foes, JG26, who were still forming up to cover thirteen Me262s, which belonged to I./KG51, on a bombing mission to attack Allied troop concentrations at Gennep, in the Netherlands, and Kleve, in Germany.

Although they realised they had been spotted when red Verey lights rose into the sky from the airfield's watch hut, and despite being outnumbered by over four to one, Blue Section dived straight into the swarm of milling aircraft, coming under intense light Flak as they did.

Woolley went after the FW190s, but his Australian counterparts, Fg Off 'Ricky' Gray (Blue 2) and WO Viv Rossow (Blue 4), opted instead for the low-flying, low-speed Me262s just becoming airborne. Woolley picked out a trio of FW190s and closed in for an attack. As he did, however, another FW190, which had slipped in behind him without being seen, opened up from approximately 400 yards.

With skill borne from several years' experience, Woolley banked hard and turned on the aircraft. Within a short time, the hunter became the hunted, and Woolley chased the FW190 back to Rheine Airfield. As they flew a circuit, intense light Flak opened up from the aerodrome and Woolley took a good hit in his tail from a 40mm shell which blew off half his rudder and caused a partial malfunction of the elevators.

Nonetheless, he continued his attack and fired three short bursts at the Focke-Wulf from a range of approximately 400 yards. He initially noticed no strikes, but then the aircraft made a sudden steep climb and two large objects fell from it, which he felt were the hood and pilot. Now overshooting the FW190, Woolley passed underneath it at an altitude of under 300 feet, and last saw the Focke-Wulf spiralling down from 500 feet. Believing it "quite probable that the e/a was hit by the flak,"[82] Woolley claimed the aircraft probable.

Rossow had quickly set his sights on an Me262 orbiting Rheine Aerodrome approximately 2,000 feet below him, but around 2,500 yards distant. He dived upon the Messerschmitt, opening fire from 400 yards at an angle of 30°, and closing to 250 yards at 10°, in a burst lasting approximately four seconds. He then felt his engine running rough and had some difficulty maintaining his aim, but considered this was likely a result of his high speed.[83] Nonetheless, he was able to recognise his fire strike the tail and wing roots. As the 262 was actually reducing speed in preparation for landing, Rossow's rate of closing was too fast and he overshot. However, now realising he was under attack, the Luftwaffe pilot suddenly opened up his throttle and pulled away.

Around this time, Gray dived into the mêlée, and was considering an attack on four FW190s to his starboard when an Me262 passed beneath him in the opposite direction. Executing a vertically-banked turn, he noticed Rossow chasing this same aircraft. Judging Rossow's distance to be approximately 500 yards behind the Me262, and assuming he was not closing on it, Gray continued his turning dive and came in approximately 300 yards behind the jet, immediately opening fire with cannon at an angle of about 15°. As he observed no hits, he fired another burst with greater deflection but to no avail. With the 262 now pulling away, Gray gave up on it.

During Gray's attack, Rossow caught him up and flew as his No. 2, slightly to starboard. Shortly after Gray ceased firing, Rossow saw the jet turn slightly to starboard and took a parting shot, opening fire at it at a long range of 700 yards. With the 262 now at full speed, the pair had no chance of hitting or catching it and finally conceded 'defeat'. The Me262 soon disappeared into cloud showing no sign of slowing.

Now taking stock of the situation, Gray was unable to locate Woolley, but called Rossow back and told him to form up on him. By this time, reports were being received from Yellow Section, which had remained above to cover them, that enemy aircraft had been seen several thousand feet higher. 486 (NZ) Squadron, also in the vicinity, were making similar warnings. Not wanting to be caught at such a low altitude, Gray and Rossow quickly climbed to 15,000 feet looking for them but "could not see any [aircraft] of any description".[84] As such, they dropped back to 6,000 feet and decided to head home to look for ground targets on the way.

The pair set a course of 270° and flew due west, but within about three minutes noticed an Me262 below them at 2,000 feet, heading in the opposite direction for Rheine. Unobserved, Gray pulled a hard vertical turn and dived upon the Messerschmitt, opening fire with his .5 inch calibre machine guns from 300 yards and closing to just 50. He immediately observed strikes at the rear of the cockpit and believed he may have hit the pilot, as the jet slowed dramatically. So quick was his rate of closing, that Gray had to pull up over it to avoid a collision. He looked back to see it out of control in a gradual dive.

Gray completed a climbing turn to 5,000 feet and looked for the jet again, but could find no further trace of it, not helped by the fact he was now looking into the sun. Deciding it was time to head home, Rossow and Gray formed up and set their course for Volkel anew. Underway, they took the opportunity offered them to attack and damage a locomotive.

Back at Rheine Aerodrome, Yellow Section had remained around 4,000 feet above the airfield to cover Blue Section. They had spotted no less than twelve more FW190s above them and to the east of the airfield, initially at 6,000 feet. These belonged to III/JG54, which were forming up to provide high cover for the Me262 mission. Though they had a disadvantage in altitude, Yellow Section soon gained numbers when they met 486 Squadron in the area, and climbed together to take on the Luftwaffe.

The 190s were orbiting to port and climbing, and were now followed on the same path by WO 'Steve' Stevenson (Yellow 3) and Flt Sgt 'Micky' Moyle (Yellow 4). However the Spitfire XIV's rate of climb was faster and the pair soon levelled out with the 190s at approximately 15,000 feet. Some FW190s were already orbiting at that altitude, or slightly higher, and spotted the pair coming up from behind. Four of these turned on Stevenson and Moyle from their port side and the air exploded in a frenzy of twisting and turning aircraft as each tried to get on the tail of the other.

Moyle's keen eye noticed one of the quartet lagging, and he managed to get behind it. Initially opening fire at 450 yards at 30°, he saw no strikes. However, he increased deflection to 1⅓ rings and, maintaining 30°, opened fire again. This time, he recognised strikes along the wing root, and continued firing until the FW190 burst into flames and spewed thick black smoke. The aircraft then flicked over and dived straight to earth in a spiral, still belching back smoke from the underside of the fuselage. He was able to watch it long enough to see it pass through low scattered cloud, followed by a large explosion as it hit the ground.

Meanwhile, Stevenson had also managed to get onto the tail of a Focke-Wulf and fired a good burst at it. His fire struck the engine cowling and wings, and the engine immediately emitted black oily smoke. The 190 flicked over, and he last saw it in a dive pouring black smoke, but could not watch it all the way down as another half-dozen enemy aircraft were still in the vicinity.

Before long, Stevenson gained the advantage on another 190 and fired. Once again, he saw his fire strike the target, but he was forced to break off when he spotted two fighters on his tail. Taking violent evasive action, he was able to shake them, and even got in a brief burst of fire at yet another FW190 before his ammunition ran out. At this juncture, he made a beeline for base.

Moyle had similar thoughts. Finding himself suddenly alone in the sky, as is the strange nature of aerial combat, Moyle called for homing but found his battery flat, which hindered his receipt of

WO 'Micky' Moyle RAAF in the cockpit. He claimed his first victory, a destroyed FW190 in the Rheine area, on 14 February 1945. © Rossow family

messages. Now very much on his own, he set his course to 260° and headed west towards Allied lines, as quickly as he could. He recognised and crossed the Maas River and soon spotted the Squadron's old airfield, Y.32 Ophoven, but landed RM799 just southeast at the USAAF airfield, Y.29 Asch.

Moyle later completed his flight to Volkel to find Blue and Yellow Sections had both arrived back at the airfield without further incident between 09:00 and 09:15. So much had happened, and yet the day had barely begun!

Moyle claimed his FW190 destroyed, Woolley his FW190 probably destroyed, Rossow and Gray each an Me262 damaged, and Stevenson one FW190 probable and a second damaged. However, when Fg Off Don Tebbit stepped forward to state he had seen one of Stevenson's aircraft in flames, in a steep turning dive from 15,000 feet, which gradually became vertical and disappeared into cloud at 1,500 feet, the Intelligence Officer, Lord Gisborough, made a formal request to have his probable victory raised to destroyed. Unfortunately, though, an assessment undertaken by 2 TAF in March 1945, likely made on the basis of the pilots' combat films, was not favourable. 'Steve' Stevenson's probable was not raised to destroyed, as it was felt that Don Tebbit's sighting could have equally applied to 'Micky' Moyle's FW190, but Woolley's claim of a probable was also disallowed, his FW190 downgraded to only damaged.[85]

However, it is said that fact is sometimes stranger than fiction, and this rings true on this occasion as contemporary analysis reveals that 41 Squadron and 2 TAF had both underestimated their victories on this date. The pilots had actually destroyed no less than four FW190Ds: three from III/JG54 and a fourth from I/JG26.[86]

As JG26 was flying low cover, the implication is that this was the aircraft dived upon and claimed as 'probable' by Woolley, and that rather than only being damaged, the FW190 was actually destroyed. Considering that JG54 was flying high cover, this would fit with Moyle's victory, and further imply that Stevenson's probable and damaged aircraft were also destroyed.[87]

The Luftwaffe's declared losses therefore fit neatly with 41 Squadron's claims, but unfortunately after their departure, and indeed despite these losses, fifty-three Me262s and their FW190 escort still managed to complete their operation and bomb their German and Dutch targets.

Victories, 14 February 1945	Dest.	Dam.	Location
Moyle, Crawford N.	FW190D	-	East of Rheine, Germany
Stevenson, Ian T.	2 FW190D	-	East of Rheine, Germany
Woolley, Frank G.	FW190D	-	Rheine Aerodrome, Germany
Gray, Eric	-	Me262	Rheine area, Germany
Rossow, Vivian J.	-	Me262	Rheine Aerodrome, Germany

During the rest of the day, the only further flying undertaken by the Squadron were two scrambles of each two pilots on reports of Me262s in the area, but these proved fruitless and the patrols landed again without anything to report.

WO Ian 'Steve' Stevenson shot claimed one probable and one damaged FW190 northeast of Münster on 14 February 1945. Contemporary research indicates both aircraft were in fact destroyed. © 41 Squadron RAF

On a separate note, today also marked 122 Wing's second birthday. Since D-Day, they had claimed 247½-15-146 aircraft, and destroyed or damaged a total of 1724 MET, 1625 railway trucks, 748 locomotives, and 481 tugs and barges, plus many more assorted targets along the way, thereunder a gas works, floating cranes, bridges, gun positions, marshalling yards, railway cuttings, ammunition dumps, flying bomb sites, radar sites and signal boxes. Though the newest member of the Wing, in their less than three weeks residence 41 Squadron had already added to this total 2-2-3 aircraft, at least 17 MET destroyed and 45 MET, 28 locomotives, eight barges and three railway trucks damaged.

16 February 1945 – A relatively quiet day upon which no flying was undertaken until the early afternoon, when the weather had improved sufficiently to allow the Wing to get airborne. Between 13:55 and 17:45, eight patrols of the Nijmegen and Venlo areas were undertaken by the Squadron, all of which were uneventful.

Apart from chasing countless odd Spits & Mustangs & all making our necks thoroughly sore, we had no joy at all & finished the day tired & somewhat disappointed.[88]

On 16 February 1945, 83 Group was spread over six airfields in Belgium and Holland, as shown in the below table.[89]

Airfield	Runway	Occupied by
B.56 Evere	3,600 ft. partially tracked	127 (RCAF) Wing
B.64 Diest	3,000 ft. untracked	409 & 410 RSUs
B.78 Eindhoven	5,000 ft. brick	39 (Recce), 125 & 143 (RCAF) Wings, 403 RSU, & 83 GCS
B.80 Volkel	5,000 ft. brick	121 & 122 Wings, 419 RSU
B.86 Helmond	5,000 ft. brick	124 Wing
B.88 Heesch	3,600 ft. PSP	126 (RCAF) Wing

WO Viv Rossow RAAF claimed a damaged Me262 at Rheine Aerodrome on 14 February 1945, but returned to base with what he thought was a rough engine. On landing, however, he found that his propeller had been hit by Flak. © 41 Squadron RAF

17-20 February 1945 – For four days in a row, weather kept the Squadron grounded and the days were instead taken up with watching combat films and playing sports. However, the Wing was pleasantly surprised by the arrival of the Duty Anson on 20 February, despite conditions, which brought in mail and a week's worth of newspapers.

25-year-old New Zealander, Flt Lt T. E. Lawrence – "not of Arabia," clarifies the ORB[90] – also joined 41 Squadron today from 145 Squadron, where he had flown Spitfire VIII's and IX's. Following his flying training, Tom Lawrence had undertaken all his operational flying in the North African and Mediterranean theatres with 229, 94, 93 and, most recently, 145 Squadron. This was his first Continental posting, which presented him an entirely different type of flying and fighting.

21 February 1945 – Following four days of poor weather that had kept the aircraft securely on the ground, the pilots were finally airborne again at 12:40 in Squadron strength, led by Sqn Ldr Benham. It was the first time in quite a while that the whole unit was up together, on this occasion flying an armed reconnaissance to Rheine, Bramsche and Twente Aerodromes, in Red (Benham RM791, Gray NH712, Coleman RM863, Cowell RM696), Blue (Reid RM885, Fleming RM879, Burne RM790, Rossow RM799) and Yellow (Woolley RM918, Hegarty RM797, Stevenson RM789, Hale RM680) Sections. To their disappointment, however, not a single 'real' aircraft was seen, though they "wasted bags of ammo on dummy A/C".[91]

However, some ground transport was spotted in the Lingen area, and two MET were destroyed and one MET, one horse-drawn vehicle, one locomotive and six railway trucks damaged.[92] The pilots attracted some light Flak and, after their return to Volkel at 14:15, Plt Off Pat Coleman found his jettison tank had been hit twice.

A second operation was airborne at 15:40, this time consisting of just four aircraft, designated Yellow Section (Stowe RM789, Moyle RM799, Tebbit RM680, Munson RM790) and led by Flt Lt Bill Stowe, to the Dümmer Lake area. Once again, no aircraft were seen, but ground targets of opportunity were, and one MET was destroyed and two MET and an oil truck damaged. They landed again at 17:00.

A third and final armed reconnaissance was up at 16:35, consisting of Sqn Ldr Benham, Flt Lt Daniel Reid and Plt Off Bob Fleming. However, the weather conditions proved unfavourable and the trio returned to Volkel 70 minutes later with nothing to report.

22 February 1945 – The Squadron conducted three fighter operations from Volkel today, totalling 23 sorties, the first of which was a sweep by eight aircraft to the Wesel and Ruhr areas at 10:25, led by

Flt Lt Frank Woolley. Although a large number of unidentified aircraft were seen in the distance, they dived away into haze and no contact was made. The pilots then returned to Volkel, landing at 11:25.

The second operation was a successful armed reconnaissance to the Dümmer Lake-Münster area at 13:10 by seven aircraft, designated Red (Benham RM791, Lawrence RN124, Burne RN123, Fleming RM879) and Blue (Reid RM885, Gray RM790, Munson RM696) Sections, and led by Sqn Ldr Benham. Three of these aircraft also ventured into the Bielefeld-Osnabrück area, but all seven pilots returned to base at 14:45 claiming between them two MET destroyed, and one locomotive, 21 covered railway trucks, an oil tanker and five MET damaged.

The day's third operation consisted of another eight aircraft in two sections of four aircraft, on an armed reconnaissance in the Gutersloh-Rheine and Soest-Paderborn areas from 16:00. Two locomotives and 14 MET were damaged, but whilst attempting to attack yet another locomotive, Fg Off Don Tebbit (RM789) was hit by Flak in his right-hand cooler. He tried to return to base, but his engine seized and he was forced to make an emergency landing whilst still east of Dülmen.[93] His wingman, WO Peter Hale, reported last seeing Tebbit set his aircraft on fire and run to hide in a ditch. The remaining seven pilots returned to Volkel at 17:25 and reported Tebbit's loss.[94]

Reflecting the changed attitude of the RAF, now safe in the knowledge it was nearing a victorious end to a long war, ORBs had begun to take on a more informal air. Once business-like and formal in their reporting of events, both the Squadron and 122 Wing ORBs were quite irreverently jovial about Tebbit's loss, the Wing ORB recording that Tebbit was "last seen walking casually away from his kite, which he had set on fire, stroking his moustache & muttering to himself…"![95] In a similar vein, the Squadron ORB noted that, "Despite his undoubted ability to carry on the war on his own, F/O Tebbit apparently succumbed to the enemy, and is believed to be a Prisoner of War…".[96,97]

24 February 1945 – The morning's operation was led by Flt Lt Peter Cowell for the first time. Seven aircraft were airborne at 09:55 for a fighter sweep to the Rheine-Münster area, but nothing of interest was seen and the pilots returned at 10:55.

The second operation was airborne at 13:25 to conduct an armed reconnaissance of the Minden-Rheine area. Yellow Section (Woolley RM918, Coleman RM707, Stevenson RM797, Smart RM799), led by Flt Lt Frank Woolley, found several ground targets south of Georgsdorf, just inside the German border and around 15km north of Nordhorn. They returned at 15:00 reporting having destroyed two MET, and damaging one MET and six barges. However, Plt Off Pat Coleman had found his guns would not function and could only watch.

The day's final operation, a sweep of the Rheine-Dümmer Lake-Münster areas led by Sqn Ldr Benham, consisted of eight aircraft in two sections of four, designated Red and Yellow. A Flak train was attacked and damaged by Yellow Section (Reid RM885, Fleming RM979, Burne RM790, Gray RM696), but unfortunately Flt Lt Tommy Burne was hit by concentrated Flak. Not only did his aircraft take a beating, but Burne himself sustained serious injuries to his chest and right arm, and his tin leg – the result of an encounter with the Japanese in Sumatra just over three years previous – was also damaged.

Burne immediately pulled up and reported his situation. He headed home to Volkel accompanied by Fg Off 'Ricky' Gray, but made a circuit before landing to allow another pilot to land first who had also reported he was wounded and had a damaged aircraft. When, at last, it became his turn to land, he made a textbook wheels-down landing, which is all the more remarkable when one considers the condition of RM790 was so poor that the Squadron felt at the time that it was only fit for salvage.

> *The last show was a sweep of eight aircraft led by the C.O. to the Rheine district. No contact could be made with the hun [sic], so before returning to base a locomotive was damaged. Unfortunately, this cost us one of our proudest possessions, as F/Lt. Tommy Burne was hit by flak & severely injured. In spite of multiple fractures to the right arm & a bad wound in the chest he brought his kite back to base & landed safely – wheels & all. […] Good show, Tommy, best of luck!*[98]

Flt Lt 'Tommy' Burne was hit by Flak and wounded in action in the Rheine-Münster area on 24 February 1945. He was hospitalised and did not return to the Squadron, but was awarded the DSO in May 1945 as, upon his return to base on 24 February, he had allowed another pilot in distress to land first despite his severe injuries. He retired from the RAF in 1970, his final role being ADC to HM the Queen. © 41 Squadron RAF

Burne was immediately evacuated to 50 Mobile Field Hospital, at St. Joseph's Hospital in Eindhoven and, following extended recuperation, did not return to the Squadron.[99] A telegram was sent to his parents, who were both doctors, to inform them he was wounded, but they were most concerned about the lack of detail provided them. Taking matters into her own hands, his mother wrote to Lord Gisborough on 2 March, seeking further information to put their minds to rest and to make sure their son's possessions were being taken care of.

> *I hope you will forgive me writing to you but I am nearly frantic about our son known to you, I think, as Tommy or "Tubby" Burne. We know he was dangerously wounded by Flak last Saturday, Feb 24th & that he is in No.50 Mobile Field Hospital & I have found out its whereabouts. We know it is chest (right side) & the official telegram said right arm – but there appears some doubt as to whether it is right hip too.*
>
> *Both his father & I are doctors & we naturally are terribly anxious to know the exact nature and condition of the multiple wounds – from a medical point of view. I was at the Casualty Department (P.4) R.A.F. yesterday and got not one scrap of further information.*
>
> *If you are allowed to tell me where & how it happened, I shall be grateful. I cannot imagine how he got back, or did he bale out; was it a crash landing? It is ghastly to think of his further sufferings. He was [illegible] months on the D.I. List in the Far East 3 years ago & has had a poor 3 years since compared with his normal life previously – But flying is his life and he wants to fly and be in the front line "with the boys" – so at least he's done what he most wished to do.*
>
> *As he appears to be still alive after 6 days, he must keep on hoping, but if his poor body is to be further mutilated, his life will be harder than ever. It tears one's heart strings. […]*
>
> *PS. I hope someone will salvage his possessions, the most important being his crutches (very special from S. Africa) & two prosthetic limbs (legs) and his Log[book]. In 1942 he lost everything & was evacuated from Sumatra with one shirt & a cigarette case.*[100]

Lord Gisborough's reply is unfortunately unknown. However, this is not the end of the story. As a result of the fact Burne allowed another pilot to land before him, despite his own injuries and poor condition, he was awarded the DSO – the Squadron's third and last of the War – on 29 May 1945. The citation reads,

> *This officer has displayed outstanding gallantry in air operations and throughout his example of devotion to duty has been unsurpassed. Whilst serving in the Far East theatre of war, Flight Lieutenant Burne was badly wounded. As a result his right leg was amputated below the knee. This in no way diminished his zeal for*

operational flying and, on his recovery, he became a fighter pilot. Since joining his present squadron he has participated in many sorties during which he has most effectively attacked numerous enemy locomotives, much mechanical transport and a number of barges. In February 1945, Flight Lieutenant Burne took part in an attack on an enemy target. Fierce anti-aircraft fire was encountered. Nevertheless, this pilot pressed home his attack from a low level. The aircraft was hit and Flight Lieutenant Burne was badly wounded in the chest and his right arm was rendered useless. Although in much physical distress, he flew the aircraft back to base where he gallantly allowed another pilot in trouble with a damaged aircraft to effect a landing first before coming down himself. This officer has set an example in keeping with the best traditions of the Royal Air Force.' [101, 102]

Returning now to 24 February 1945, the rest of the day's third operation was uneventful, except for large amounts of Flak, and the remaining seven pilots returned to Volkel at 17:30.

Separately, two new Flight Lieutenants joined the Squadron today from 83 GSU: 22-year-old Derek S. V. Rake[103] and 24-year-old New Zealander Roy R. G. Fisher.[104]

25 February 1945 – The day's first operation was airborne at 07:30, when Flt Lt Frank Woolley led eight pilots, designated Yellow and Blue Sections, on an armed reconnaissance of the Rheine-Dümmer Lake area.

A large number of enemy aircraft were seen above them near Gronau, close to the Dutch border, heading in the general direction of Wesel. At around the same time, Woolley (RM918), who was leading Yellow Section, started experiencing what the ORB only calls 'technical trouble', and pulled out of the operation. However, Blue Section, led by Flt Lt Daniel Reid (RM885), gave chase, but they were spotted as they climbed to intercept the enemy aircraft, and the Luftwaffe formation broke and scattered. Blue Section chased them eastwards all the way to the other side of Münster, but were unable to catch them and eventually gave up when the aircraft disappeared into the ground mist and poor light.

Reid reformed the section and returned to the Rheine area to re-join Yellow Section. On their way back, Reid's No. 2, Plt Off Bob Fleming, spotted a lone long-nosed FW190 flying below them. At the time, they were at 1,500 feet, and the 190 at 500 feet. Reid 'Tally-Hoed' and attacked the aircraft from its rear port quarter.

A short burst with both machine gun and cannon fire caused no visible effect, and the pilot took wild evasive action by diving to zero feet and weaving from side to side. However, Reid's speed was greater and he was able to close to 100 yards where he opened up again from dead astern. A burst of just one second resulted in a sudden explosion in the fuselage behind the cockpit and the entire tail came off the aircraft.

Derek Rake served with 41 Squadron as a Flight Lieutenant from 24 February 1945 to 4 August 1945. This portrait was commissioned whilst he was Station Commander at RAF Wyton between January 1967 and June 1969. © Gp Capt (ret) Derek S. V. Rake OBE AFC & Bar

The 190 fell to the ground approximately 2km east of Clausheide Airfield and was "completely destroyed by explosion and fire".[105] Blues 2 (Fleming RM979), 3 (Munson NH712), and 4 (Rossow RM696) witnessed the combat and attested to Reid's victory.[106] The Wing ORB recounted the story rather dramatically, recording that "F/Lt. Reid got his teeth into a lone Fw. 190 & shook it like a rat."[107]

Whilst all this was going on Flt Lt Woolley had returned to base, accompanied by Fg Off Johnny Wilkinson (RM680), but had left behind Yellow 3 and 4 (Stevenson RM797 & Coleman RM799). Now reunited with Blue Section, the six aircraft found and attacked a tug and three barges, which were claimed damaged. Coleman then started suffering R/T problems and he, too, headed home.

On the way back, carrying on the War by himself, Coleman strafed two huts, one of which exploded, which led him to believe it was being used to store ammunition. He also fired at dummy FW190s, destroyed one MET and damaged two more in a wood and, finally, jettisoned his 45-gallon drop tank onto a house near Lengerich, southwest of Osnabrück, which immediately caught fire. The remaining pilots were back on the ground at 09:00 after a very lively operation.

At 11:10, Sqn Ldr Benham led six aircraft on the day's second operation, an armed reconnaissance of the Rheine-Münster-Gutersloh areas, in three sections of two, designated Red, Yellow and Blue. Six MET were damaged in the region, but soon afterwards Fg Off 'Ricky' Gray (NH712) started experiencing 'technical trouble' with his aircraft. He returned early with Flt Lt Peter Cowell (RM979), leaving Red (Benham RM696, Hale RM680) and Yellow (Coleman RM707, Smart RM797) Sections to continue the patrol.

Although unable to find any further enemy targets, the quartet became a target themselves when a lone USAAF Mustang approached them near Rheine, and attempted to get behind them, into a stern attack position. The pilot's efforts were thankfully unsuccessful, and he was "finally scared away".[108] The Squadron landed again at 12:50.

The day's final operation was airborne at 14:40 in the form of three pilots designated Blue Section (Reid RM885, Gray RM916, Lawrence RM696), assigned to an armed reconnaissance of the Dülmen-Münster-Soest area. It was a relatively quiet patrol, the trio finding little ground activity, and they returned at 16:00 claiming four MET damaged in the Münster area.

28 February 1945 – The day consisted of only two operations, which were complete by lunch time. The first of these was airborne at 09:10, when eight aircraft were airborne to escort B-25 Mitchell bombers to the Geldern area, led by Sqn Ldr Benham. It was the first time in quite a while that the Squadron had been assigned to a bomber escort. However, 10/10ths cloud cover was found over the target area and no results of the bombing could be seen. Additionally, Sqn Ldr Benham (RM791) started experiencing R/T problems and returned early with his No. 2, Fg Off Francis Hegarty (RM799). the remaining pilots arrived back at 10:15.

The second operation was an armed reconnaissance to the Soest-Hamm-Münster area by eight aircraft at 11:20, led by Flt Lt Frank Woolley. Red (Woolley RM918, Rake RM759, Stevenson RM704, Hale RM799) and Blue (Cowell RN124, Mottershead NH712, Fleming RM879, Rossow RM696) Sections enjoyed a successful patrol and the pilots returned at 12:50 claiming one locomotive, ten trucks and three MET damaged in the Hamm-Münster area, and two barges damaged on the Twente Canal.

This was OC A Flight, Frank Woolley's last operation with 41 Squadron, as he was promoted to Acting Squadron Leader and posted to command 350 (Belgian) Squadron at Eindhoven during the afternoon. He was replacing another ex-41 Squadron OC, A Flight, Terry Spencer, who was hit by Flak during an armed reconnaissance on 26 February, had baled out and was captured.[109]

During the month of February 1945, 41 Squadron had flown a total of 209 sorties, totalling 258.34 operational hours of flying for the loss of three pilots. However, the Squadron also claimed

3-2-3 enemy aircraft[110], 24 MET and one armoured vehicle destroyed, and 41 railway trucks, 39 locomotives, 28 MET and 20 barges damaged.[111]

122 Wing as a whole flew 1,296 sorties during the month, totalling just over 1,848 operational hours, and made claims for 32-2-27 enemy aircraft, 106 MET, 42 railway trucks, three locomotives, and one armoured vehicle destroyed, and 613 railway trucks, 481 locomotives, 375 MET, 118 barges, two armoured vehicles and one horse-drawn vehicle damaged. However, pilot losses amounted to a massive 31 pilots – the equivalent of more than an entire Squadron.

It appears to be for this reason that the Wing was ordered to suspend all air-to-ground operations on 2 March. They were now to concentrate solely on aerial targets and this, in effect, ended 41 Squadron's reason for being posted to 122 Wing. Not surprisingly, therefore, another move would shortly be afoot.

1 March 1945 – The day's activity was limited to a single area cover operation for medium bombers attacking the Wesel-Maltern-Enschede area.[112] Eight aircraft were airborne at 16:30, led by Flt Lt Daniel Reid, for what transpired to be an uneventful mission, except for some technical trouble experienced by Fg Off Roy Fisher (RM879). He left for home slightly earlier than the other pilots, but only beat them back by about five minutes, putting down at Volkel at 17:50.

2 March 1945 – Though a cold and wintry day with frequent showers of sleet, it was a busy one for the Squadron. Between 07:05 and 14:55, 27 sorties were flown on 12 patrols in the Nijmegen and Venlo areas, and on Area Cover to 147 Lancasters bombing a synthetic oil plant near Dortmund. The Squadron also recorded what is believed to have been the RAF's first confirmed destruction of an Arado Ar234 jet today, but sadly another of the Squadron's pilots was killed during the morning. There is perhaps some consolation, in retrospect, that his death was the Squadron's last of the War.

41 Squadron was the first unit of the entire Group to make a claim against the Luftwaffe today and the event is recorded in the Group ORB Appendix thus:

> *41 Squadron drew the first blood of the day by destroying an Arado 234 at 0735 which was encountered at 10,000* [feet] *N.E. of WEERT. This aircraft fell near VENLO and is reported to be in a condition worth examining.*[113]

The Squadron Downs its First Jet

The first two patrols on 2 March 1945 were airborne simultaneously at 07:05, Blue Section (Reid RM885 & Kelly RN124) to the Nijmegen area, and Red Section (Stowe RM680 & Smart RM707) to the Venlo area. The latter two pilots' patrol was uneventful and they returned at 08:50 with nothing to report. The former pair, however, intercepted a jet near Nijmegen and made an attack.

The aircraft was one of 21 from Stab/KG76 and III. Gruppe KG76, which were airborne that morning to attack targets in the Maastricht-Aachen-Jülich area. They were escorted by 71 Me109Ks and 109Gs from JG27. The jets had already been spotted by pilots of 130 and 222 Squadrons. 130 Squadron's Fg Off Vic Murphy RAAF later recalled,

> *…I was leading a Section of Spitfires* [and] *noticed an oncoming dot ahead, approaching tremendously fast! Within seconds it passed approx 500' below me (our combined speed would have been 1,000 m.p.h.) I noticed German Air Force markings on a black fuselage. It was a twin engine jet!! I immediately radioed my location, the compass heading of the German plane and the height.*[114]

This information was relayed to Reid and Kelly by Control, when approximately 30 minutes into their patrol, and they immediately gave chase. Close to Nijmegen, they emerged from their cover between cloud layers and sighted an aircraft flying about a mile ahead of them at 9,000 feet.

OC B Flight, Flt Lt Danny Reid RAAF became the first RAF pilot to destroy an Arado Ar234, when he shot down Oblt Walter Sütterlin of 9./KG76, near Enschede, on 2 March 1945. He was awarded the DFC on 1 June 45. © Daniel Reid, via Garry Cooper

Finding themselves dead astern and 1,000 feet below its altitude, they were in a perfect position for an attack. At this time, Reid was only able to identify it as "jet propelled and not an Me.262 (or Meteor)".[115] Considering they may need some additional speed, Reid ordered Kelly to slow down and drop his jettison tank; his own speed was already too high to allow him to do so himself. Unseen, Flt Lt Reid closed on the aircraft and later reported,

> *The E/A turned slightly to Starboard and continued towards the North East, weaving slightly from time to time. I kept out of the enemy pilot's view by keeping under his tail-plane and slowly overhauled him at an I.A.S. of 340 m.p.h. at 8/9000 ft. [...] I closed to 100 yards or less, firing with .5 M.G. and cannon whilst still overtaking. I saw strikes on the Port wing, Port jet engine and fuselage. E/A immediately emitted dense clouds of brownish black smoke, possibly jet exhaust. I continued firing and saw flashes in the smoke, breaking away at extremely close range, and being hit in the Port radiator by debris. I next saw E/A going down in a wide spiral to Starboard with white smoke or vapour pouring from holes all along the Port wing, and dark smoke from the fuselage.*[116]

It was only now that Reid identified the jet as an Arado Ar234 *Blitz* [Lightning], basing his conclusion on "the long nose of the a/c and the straight tapered wings with rounded tips".[117] Just as he did so, a large piece of the aircraft – probably the canopy – suddenly detached itself and the pilot, 24-year-old Oblt. Walter Sütterlin of 9./KG76, baled out. He saw the parachute open and watched the jet crash and explode near Enschede, which was also witnessed by Flt Sgt Kelly. Sütterlin was uninjured.

Reid and Kelly returned to Volkel at 08:20, where Reid claimed one Ar234 destroyed. It was the Squadron's first confirmed destruction of a jet aircraft, and one of only three destroyed by the Squadron during the War. Moreover, notes Reid's *Pilot Service Record*, it was "believed to be the first of these A/c [sic] to [be] shot down and destroyed"[118] by the RAF. The Wing ORB recorded,

> *...Blue Section found a jet-propelled Arado 234 near Nijmegen, after playing hide & seek in the clouds & overhauled it during a long chase at 10,000 feet to past Enschede – Tempest boys please note – where it was shot down in flames by F/Lt. Reid. We think we'll chalk that one up, as it appears to be the first one of its kind to be destroyed.*[119]

Reid also noted a number of observations about this aircraft in an addendum to his Combat Report:

At all times this particular aircraft had its nose wheel lowered, which possibly assisted the Spitfire XIV to overtake it. The nosewheel [sic] was suspended by a single strut, with a single fork on the Port side of the wheel.

The fuselage, whilst in line astern, appeared to be circular in section.

The tailplane appeared rather small in relation to the wings, and was set rather high.

The mainplane was set high on the fuselage, with a thin section and moderate dihedral starting at the fuselage.

The jet engines appeared small in relation to the mainplane and were underslung [sic].

No trail was visible from the jet engines whilst E/A was being pursued, but immediately after being attacked it emmitted [sic] large clouds of brownish black smoke which appeared to come from the jets.

The upper surface of the fuselage and mainplanes was camouflaged brown and green.

I saw no identification markings on the aircraft and can definitely state that no black crosses were painted on the upper surface of the mainplane.[120]

However, whilst Reid may have been the first RAF pilot to down such an aircraft, he was *only just* the first. III Gruppe KG76 lost two aircraft this morning, the second falling to 222 Squadron's Flt Lt George Varley in Tempest V, EJ882. This Arado exploded in mid-air at Hammermühle, approximately 3km west of Recke, and its pilot, Lt. Eberhard Rögele, was killed.[121] 222 Squadron's WO Tom Hannam also claimed a third jet damaged.

Despite today's victories against Ar234s, these were not the first to fall into Allied hands. One such jet made a wheels-up landing in a field southeast of Jülich on the afternoon of 22 February and, although this area was still in German hands at the time, the ground was subsequently overrun by Allied ground forces. The aircraft was captured almost completely intact, with little damage, and brought back further behind Allied lines for a detailed examination, where its markings, FI+MT, revealed it belonged to 9./KG76 – the same Gruppe as those shot down by the RAF on 2 March. The pilot was Hptm. Josef Regler and the WkNr 140 173.

Flt Lt Danny Reid's own sketch of his Arado Ar234 victory on 2 March 1945. © Daniel Reid, via Garry Cooper

Intelligence at the time of the Arado's capture points to it having been attacked in the Aachen-Dülmen area by Lt. David Fox in a USAAF P-47 Thunderbolt of the 391st Squadron, 366th FG, XXIX TAC, at around 17:30 on 22 February during Operation *Clarion*. The Arado was hit in the starboard engine, which caught fire, and a piece of the aircraft was seen to fly off, assumed to have been the canopy. Although the fighter squadron initially thought they had been attacked by Me262s, the discovery of the Ar234 in the same area, the burnt-out starboard engine, and a canopy recovered some distance away, all pointed to the Arado being the jet damaged by Fox. It would appear, therefore, that although 41 Squadron's Flt Lt Daniel Reid was the first *RAF* pilot to shoot down an Ar234 twin jet aircraft, he was not the first Allied pilot to do so. This 'honour' fell instead to the USAAF's Lt. David Fox.

The Last Pilot to be Killed in Action

The day's third operation would be memorable for another reason.

Flt Lt Peter Cowell (RM696) and Fg Off Cliff Mottershead (RN123) were airborne at 09:05 as Black Section for an armed reconnaissance to Nijmegen. Unfortunately, little is known about the patrol except that the pair dived down to investigate some aircraft and became separated. When Cowell climbed again, Mottershead was nowhere to be seen. Cowell made brief radio contact with him, but he did not return to base, and Cowell landed alone at 10:55.

Initially only listed as missing, the Squadron hoped Mottershead had 'merely' been captured: "We hope we may see him again one day."[122] However, it was not to be, and he was later confirmed killed, thereby becoming the Squadron's final fatality of the War. He is believed to have been shot down by an Me109.[123]

25-year-old Mottershead, of Stockport, Cheshire, was initially buried in the temporary US Military Cemetery at Margraten in the Netherlands on 4 March 1945, implying he must have come down in Allied territory. However, the details are still somewhat unclear as Margraten lies approximately 113km south of Nijmegen – to where their reconnaissance was to take them – and 92km south of Volkel, where the Squadron was based. A few years after the War, his body was re-interred and he now lies in Maastricht General Cemetery, in Limburg.

The day's remaining armed reconnaissance flights were uneventful, as was an area cover patrol for Mitchell bombers attacking Geldern by a trio of pilots led by Flt Lt Bill Stowe. Any celebration of the Squadron's first victory against a Luftwaffe jet today was dampened by the loss of Cliff Mottershead. Though he had only been with the Squadron a little over a month – he had arrived with Flt Lt Peter Cowell on 31 January – "his loss was felt by everybody".[124]

3 March 1945 – Almost a repetition of 2 March, seven patrols in sections of two were flown in the Nijmegen and Venlo areas between 06:35 and 13:15. Unlike the previous day, however, all were uneventful.

At 14:50, an armed reconnaissance of the Wesel area was also mounted by Red (Reid RM791 & Rossow RN124), Yellow (Stowe RM797 & Wilkinson RM916) and Blue (Stevenson RM704 & Moyle RM799) Sections, led by Flt Lt Daniel Reid. Flt Sgt 'Micky' Moyle was forced to return early with 'technical trouble', but the remainder of the pilots had a successful trip during which they claimed nine MET destroyed and 24 damaged; it was an 'impressive' bag for five pilots.

WO 'Steve' Stevenson had a scare, however, when he lost three-quarters of a propeller blade to Flak. He returned 15 minutes early, at an altitude of only 5,000 feet, unable to fly any higher, accompanied by Flt Lt Reid. He later recorded later in his logbook, "Hit on prop, got back to base with 4 blades. A/C cat A.C".[125] The remaining three pilots landed at 15:50.

A final operation was airborne at 17:05, led by Sqn Ldr Benham, when five aircraft conducted an armed reconnaissance of the same area as the 14:50 operation. Red (Benham RM791 & Lawrence

Fg Off Clifford Mottershead served with 41 Squadron from 31 January 1945 to 2 March 1945, when he was shot down and killed in the Nijmegen area, thereby becoming the Squadron's final fatality of the War. © 41 Squadron RAF

RN124), Blue (Cowell RM707) and Yellow (Rake RM918 & Coleman RM797) Sections also found several ground targets of opportunity in the Wesel area and returned claiming three MET destroyed and 12 damaged. Plt Off Pat Coleman was forced to return early after he flew through a concentration of light Flak near Rheine and noticed he was losing petrol. It transpired that his jettison tank had been holed by 20mm Flak. The remaining pilots landed back at Volkel at 18:00.[126]

5 March 1945 – Following a day of inclement weather that had kept 122 Wing grounded, conditions cleared sufficiently for a Wing operation to be mounted in the afternoon, which was a sweep of aerodromes in the Rheine area. Nos. 3 and 274 (Tempest) Squadrons participated, accompanied by eight Spitfires from 41 Squadron to provide top cover, led by Sqn Ldr Benham. Red and Blue Sections, each of four aircraft, were airborne together at 16:05, but nothing was seen. Flt Lt Daniel Reid (RM916) departed for home early with engine trouble, and the rest of the pilots pancaked at 17:35.

News also arrived today that 41 Squadron was to fly home for two weeks' Armament Practice Camp in southern England. However, they also learned they would not be returning to 122 Wing but re-joining 125 Wing instead. Thus, the afternoon's combined sweep constituted the Squadron's last with the Wing.

> *Much against our will though, we must say goodbye to our friends of 122 Wing, our grief at the coming parting only softened by the thought of a fortnight in Merrie [sic] England. We have spent a very happy month at Volkel Spa & the help which every member of 122 – without exception – has given us on the working line has only been equalled by their friendliness in off-duty hours. On the operations side we must specially thank the G.C. & Wingco Brooker for giving us every assistance in getting on with the job – it has been a very fruitful month for us. But we can't in fairness mention names when saying "Thank you", for everyone has done their level best for us. So when you find yourselves near 125 Wing, drop in & ask for the dreaded 41, the pleasure will be all ours.*[127]

122 Wing reciprocated, bidding 41 Squadron a fond farewell, and recorded for posterity,

> *We are proud to have had this famous Squadron with us, even for so short a period, for although they have added considerably to our congestion & our headaches, they have also added notably to our score-sheet. […] We wish them continued success & a cheerful time wherever they may find themselves whether on the fair*

fields of England, the bombed fields of Germany, or the paddy fields of China. Nothing, we feel, can daunt them, after 38 days at the world-famous Volkel Spa.[128]

The Wing ORB records that between 28 January and 5 March 1945, 41 Squadron flew 296 sorties, totalling 372 hours, but lost four pilots. However, the Squadron also claimed 4-3-2 enemy aircraft, 32 MET destroyed, and 122 MET, 41 railway trucks, 39 locomotives and 20 barges damaged.[129]

7 March 1945 – After a day of packing and preparation, the Squadron flew to RAF Warmwell in Dorset in the afternoon, via a brief stop in Manston to refuel. The transfer to Manston took 50 minutes, and the remaining leg to Warmwell another 55.

There was one incident during the transfer, when Plt Off Pat Coleman landed at Warmwell. The tail wheel of RM707 became stuck in its retracted position on landing, and the rudder was smashed. It was an inglorious and perhaps embarrassing end to a return home that all the pilots were excited about.

Their departure from B.80 Volkel represented a defining moment in the Squadron's history. To any observer, the War was almost over; within just two months, Europe would once again be at peace for the first time since Hitler gained power in 1933. The brief pause in Warmwell paved the way for the Squadron's final advance into Germany and prepared it for a period almost as intensive as the Battle of Britain.

Between their arrival back on the Continent on 19 March and the cessation of hostilities on 8 May, the Squadron claimed no less than 33 aircraft destroyed, two probable, and four damaged in the air and 22 damaged on the ground. Their ground victories against hardware are countless. It was an exhausting period, which saw the departure of a number of pilots, the arrival of several more, a new Commanding Officer, two new bases, and new latest-series Spitfire XIVs with 'teardrop' hoods.

Despite the graciousness of the Squadron's parting words to 122 Wing, their six weeks in Volkel had been expensive for the unit, having lost one man killed in action (Mottershead), one wounded in action (Burne), three pilots, thereunder two Flight Commanders (Harding, Henry and Tebbit), shot down and captured, a third Flight Commander (Woolley) posted away on promotion, and two pilots posted on medical grounds (Clanzy and Cook).

Now, as the Squadron lifted off for Warmwell on 7 March, four more pilots left the unit: Flt Lt Harry Charnock DFC DFM[130] and Fg Off Peter Gibbs, who were both posted away on medical grounds, the latter pilot considered medically unfit to continue operational flying following his encounter with Flak in mid-January[131], and Fg Offs Rupert Munson RAAF[132] and 'Jimmy' Payne[133] whose tours had expired. Thus, within the short space of just one-and-a-half months at Volkel, practically half the Squadron's pilots had departed.

Of these latter four men, Peter Gibbs merits a particular mention for his post-War life and, oddly enough, also for his demise. A violinist of some note, he became a professional musician after he left the Air Force in August 1945. He initially formed his own string quartet but joined the Philharmonia Orchestra in 1954. Within two years, however, he had joined the London Symphony Orchestra and during this time became rather (in)famous for a dressing down he gave to one of the Century's most celebrated performing artists, Herbert von Karajan.

The Orchestra felt that von Karajan had been unprofessional when conducting smaller, 'less important' concerts during a tour of the United States in Winter 1956. He had often just bowed once and left the stage at the end of concerts, refusing to return for encores, despite the applause from the audience. The orchestra was slighted by this behaviour, and eventually had enough. The last straw came when von Karajan left the stage in Boston in January 1956 after the last note was played, neither waiting for applause nor calls for an encore. The orchestra, in which Gibbs was playing First Violin, was also upset by this apparent insult to both them and the audience, but turned up nonetheless on time for an early rehearsal the following morning. Von Karajan, however, came in late, much to the disgruntlement of the whole orchestra. When he finally arrived, Peter Gibbs, an impromptu, self-appointed spokesman, stood up and addressed him directly, demanding an apology. Some accounts of this event quote Gibbs as saying, "I did not spend four years of my life fighting bastards like you (or 'trying to shoot down Nazis like you') to be insulted before our own Allies as you did last evening."[134]

Von Karajan ignored him completely and continued conducting as if nothing had happened. That night, however, during a concert, von Karajan chose his moment and, during the interval, refused to go back on stage until a letter was signed stating that Gibbs be immediately sacked. The orchestra responded with a demand that von Karajan be sacked instead, but with the audience waiting for von Karajan and the orchestra to return to the stage, the orchestra's managers had little choice but to bow to the conductor's demand. Although Gibbs was never to play with the Philharmonia again after this incident, it is understood that von Karajan also never conducted the Philharmonia again either, and it is said that he vowed to never conduct an English orchestra again.

Despite this infamous outburst, Gibbs became leader of the BBC Scottish Symphony Orchestra in December 1960, before returning to the London Symphony Orchestra as its Deputy Leader in 1963. He then formed and ran a building company with a colleague, which occupied him between 1964 and 1975. However, after a few years' break, Gibbs started playing the violin professionally once again, performing as First Violin in the Covent Garden Royal Opera House Orchestra in London from 1969 to 1970, and as Joint Leader of the Royal Opera House Orchestra, from 1971 to 1972.

All this time, Gibbs also flew privately. He had joined the Surrey Flying Club in June 1957 – flying for the first time since the end of the War – and then flew more-or-less continuously until his death in December 1975. Gibbs bought himself a Tiger Moth and found great pleasure in peacetime flying. He also became known as a bit of a prankster with the orchestras he played in and is on record as having bombed the London Symphony Orchestra bus with bags of flour when they were touring Belgium in 1958!

However, flying was also what brought about Gibbs' premature death in December 1975. He took off for a brief flight in a Cessna from Glenforsa Airfield on the Isle of Mull in Scotland in the evening of Christmas Eve 1975, but failed to return. A search was mounted but no trace whatsoever could be found of him. Oddly, his body was found part way up Pennygown Hill, approximately one mile from Glenforsa Airfield, four months after his disappearance – *sans* aircraft – showing the signs of having lain there all that time. The original search for Gibbs had passed through the area at the time he had gone missing, but nothing had been seen. His body gave away no clues as to his cause of death.

Gibbs' missing Cessna eluded and bewildered officials and locals alike and his case soon became known as the 'Great Mull Air Mystery'.[135] It was not until September 1986 – almost 11 years after Gibbs' death – that his aircraft (Cessna F150H, G-AVTN) was located in the sea off Oban. The aircraft's remains also gave up no clue as to the reason it was there.

It can only be assumed today that Gibbs, for some reason, came down in the sea and that he had managed to free himself and swim ashore. It is thought he then tried to make his way back to the airfield, around a mile away, but, considering the time of year, location, and likely temperatures of both the water and air, probably succumbed to the effects of exposure.

Let us now return to March 1945.

Flt Lts Rake and Fisher had arrived on 24 February to bolster numbers, but there were no further new pilots until 41 Squadron arrived at Warmwell. The commencement of their course at Armament Practice Camp coincided with the disbandment of 610 Squadron, previously a fellow member of 125 Wing at Ophoven, whose course preceded that which 41 was about to commence. Formed in March 1936 as an Auxiliary Air Force squadron, their final record of aerial victories totalled 132 aircraft destroyed, 46½ probable, 53 damaged and 50 V1s destroyed.

Despite the "very much regretted"[136] demise of 610 Squadron just as the War was moving into its final phase, the distribution of the unit's pilots could hardly have been better for 125 Wing. Instead of being posted to unfamiliar units in different parts of the world, 610 Squadron's pilots were, on the whole, retained within the Wing, thereby providing 41, 130, and 350 Squadrons

From left to right, Fg Off 'Lew' Munson RAAF, Flt Lt Johnnie Wilkinson, Flt Sgt Harry Smart, Fg Off 'Wally' Jallands, WO Peter Hale, Plt Off Pat Coleman, WO Hugh Kelly, Flt Lt Derek Rake, and WO Ian Stevenson, early March 1945. © Rossow family

a number of experienced pilots who flew the same aircraft, were used to the theatre and style of operations, and many of whom already knew each other to some extent.

As such, whilst in Warmwell, 41 Squadron now received from 610 Squadron 25-year-old Flt Lt John B. 'Shep' Shepherd DFC, 22-year-old Flt Lt Raymond P. R. Finucane, 31-year-old Flt Lt Arnold W. Jolly, 21-year-old Norwegian 2 Lt Carl S. Bødtker and 24-year-old WO John A. Chalmers.

Shepherd had been with the [R]AuxAF since late 1937, having joined as an LAC, and had now been with 610 since May 1944, having been awarded a DFC in September 1942 and a Bar in August 1943, both with 118 Squadron. He took over command of 610 Squadron in late February 1945, by which time he had been credited with 6-2-4 (of which two destroyed aircraft were shared) plus 6½ destroyed V1s. On arrival at 41 Squadron, he immediately took over as OC A Flight. Although this was effectively a step backwards, by the end of March 1945 he would become 41 Squadron's next Commanding Officer.

Finucane, the younger brother of the famed late Wg Cdr Brendan E. F. 'Paddy' Finucane DSO DFC, had previously been a WAG with Bomber Command, but had re-mustered as a pilot in 1943. He had been with 610 Squadron since the beginning of January 1945. Jolly had only been with 610 since 10 February, but had several years' service behind him, including a tour of Malta. He left the Mediterranean with a respectable score of 2⅓-0-2, and had been awarded a Mention in Despatches in mid-1943. Bødtker had only been with 610 a few days, but had previously completed a 15-month tour with 332 (Norwegian) Squadron. He had logged over 1,000 flying hours, of which almost 200 were operational. Chalmers had been with 610 since Christmas Eve and was therefore quite up to date with all the 'gen'. He brought with him experience gained in Navy Cooperation during the Normandy Landings and a respectable list of ground targets in northern Germany.

41 Squadron also gained two further pilots whilst at Warmwell: 21-year-old Fg Off Walter J. Jallands and 24-year-old WO F. Victor Whale who were both posted to 41 from 83 GSU, on their first operational postings. These seven 'new' pilots replaced a number of those recently lost, but yet more pilots would join the unit in the near future.

Crossing the Rhine
8 March – 15 April 1945

9

APC Warmwell

Between 7 and 18 March 1945, the Squadron attended a dive-bombing course at 17 Armament Practice Camp at RAF Warmwell in Dorset. Arriving back in England on the afternoon of 7 March, for the first time in four months, the pilots were greeted by dull and windy weather.

The following day, as the course got underway, the weather had improved somewhat, but remained cloudy. Nonetheless, 25 pilots were able to undertake limited range estimation practice with their camera guns throughout the day. During the afternoon, 610 Squadron's Spitfire XIV's commenced their transfers back to the Continent to be issued to other squadrons.

Little information can be gleaned from available sources on the Squadron's course at Warmwell, although it is clear that weather disrupted the entire programme to some extent.

8 March — Range estimation practice and a camera gun exercise that was recalled early.

9 March — Weather fine and frosty; full flying programme of range estimation and line of flight practice, followed by low-level bombing and air-to-air firing.

10 March — Fine weather all day; the Squadron completed 66 details of air-to-air firing with the drogue and dive-bombing practice from 8,000 to 4,000 ft.

11 March — Thick mist in the morning prevented flying until 13:00, after which the course continued with air-to-air firing and gyro-sight practice.

12 March — Perfect weather and a full flying programme, including dive-bombing practice from 8,000 to 4,000 ft.

13 March — Fine clear day; the Squadron completed 52 details of air-to-air firing and dive-bombing.

14 March — As mist and low cloud prevented flying all day, the pilots watched instructional films instead.

15 March — As poor weather, mist and sea fog prevented flying all day, the pilots were given lectures and shown more instructional films instead.

16 March — Lingering inclement weather and poor visibility prevented flying until 13:00, when the programme resumed.

17 March — Fine and clear; limited flying details were completed in the morning, thereunder a gyro-gunsight exercise, followed by aircraft servicing in the afternoon in preparation for the Squadron's return to the Continent. The Squadron received its first 'teardrop hood' Mk. XIVs today to take back with them.

18 March   41 Squadron left for the Netherlands, flying directly from Warmwell to Eindhoven, without a refuelling stop, in a 100-minute transfer. They were followed over by their ground crew in 20 Dakota transports, and replaced the same day by 350 Squadron, who arrived with 15 Spitfires and 22 Dakotas full of ground crew.

The 41 Squadron ORB summarises the course, stating "excellent results were achieved [by the pilots], especially by S/Ldr D. I. Benham, D.F.C., A.F.C., F/Lt. W. N. Stowe, and W/O I. T. Stevenson".[1] All the men passed out with an average error of less than 50 yards, apparently the best results ever achieved at 17 APC.

However, their aircraft all suffered under the strain of dive bombing, which led the Squadron to the quick conclusion that they would not undertake bombing on active operations! The Spitfire XIV was clearly not built for such activity. Flt Lt Johnnie Wilkinson recalled that the Squadron practiced dive-bombing with small bombs attached under each wing. The pilots were ordered to approach from 12,000 feet, roll into a vertical dive, then pull up and release a bomb onto a target placed in the sea a few yards off the coast. Unfortunately, the exercise literally bent the wings of twelve Spitfires and, as a result, the remaining dive-bombing exercises were cancelled.[2]

Circumstantial evidence suggests that the damaged aircraft included at least RM879, RM885, RM916, and RM918. It therefore comes as no surprise that when 41 Squadron returned to the Continent, it did so with several new aircraft.

Eindhoven

Upon the Squadron's arrival back on the Continent from Warmwell on 18 March 1945, they did not return to Volkel and 122 (Tempest) Wing, but rather re-joined 125 Wing and were posted to B.78 Eindhoven instead, where they found their 'old friends' 130 Squadron; 350 Squadron were still a part of the Wing, but had already departed for their own sojourn at APC in Warmwell and 610 Squadron had just been disbanded. 125 Wing was happy to see them again, recording in their ORB, "Welcome to the Squadron after their long absence".[3]

Known 41 Squadron Spitfire XIV Serials and Codes September 1944–April 1945

MV249	EB-F	RB143	EB-T	RM770	EB-R	RM916	EB-N
MV254	EB-H	RB159	EB-W	RM788	EB-U	RM928	EB-U
MV255	EB-L	RM680	EB-B/F	RM789	EB-G	RM931	EB-M
MV257	EB-M	RM693	EB-S	RM790	EB-T/W	RN123	EB-P
MV260	EB-P	RM696	EB-W	RM791	EB-V	RN124	EB-T
MV264	EB-Q	RM698	EB-P	RM792	EB-B/G	RN198	EB-B
MV266	EB-J	RM699	EB-S	RM797	EB-E	RN208	EB-X
MV267	EB-G	RM701	EB-K	RM799	EB-J	SM817	EB-R
NH692	EB-T	RM704	EB-A	RM819	EB-B	SM820	EB-N
NH712	EB-R	RM707	EB-H	RM842	EB-N	SM823	EB-E
NH745	EB-V	RM759	EB-D	RM863	EB-L	SM825	EB-B
NH832	EB-V	RM765	EB-Y	RM879	EB-S	SM826	EB-B
NH915	EB-H	RM767	EB-B	RM915	EB-K	SM829	EB-B

© Steve Brew

WO Victor 'Vickie' Whale served with 41 Squadron from 7 March 1945 to 12 February 1946. Commissioned in the RAF in 1949, he retired as a Flight Lieutenant in 1961. © Rossow family

Situated approximately 8km west of the city, in the province of Noord-Brabant in the southern Netherlands, the airfield was taken over by the RAF after the city's liberation on 18 September 1944. Since that time, Eindhoven had become an important centre for the Royal Air Force, which was now home to 83 Group Headquarters. It was from here that stores, vehicles and ammunition were supplied to the Group's Wings. B.78 had become a large and well-established airfield, which 125 Wing shared with 143 (RCAF) Wing (438, 439 and 440 Squadrons), 403 Repair and Salvage Unit, 83 Group Communication Squadron, and 91 Forward Staging Post.

They were sustained by a complex array of support units. 125 and 143 Wings' aircraft were serviced by each squadron's own Servicing Echelon. 125 Wing drew their stores from 401 Air Stores Park, 143 Wing and 403 RSU drew theirs from 406 Air Stores Park, and 83 GCS theirs from 83 Group Rear Headquarters. 61 Wing Signals Section, 361 Air Liaison Section[4], and 2806 and 2876 Squadrons RAF Regiment were attached to 125 Wing, 59 Wing Signals Section, 12 (Canadian) Air Liaison Section and 2703, 2726, and 2781 Squadrons RAF Regiment to 143 Wing, and 2 Air Delivery Letter Service to 83 GCS. Each was also assigned several Mobile Signals Units.

A number of RAF units were based within in the town itself, the largest of these being 83 Group's Main Headquarters, which included an Air POW Intelligence Section and an Air Ministry Technical Intelligence Section.[5] All three were resident in the Dommelhuis Hotel. 401 Air Stores Park was based at 352 Boschdijk, 5137 (Bomb Disposal) Squadron at 14 Jacob Catslaan, 70 Mechanical Transport Light Repair Unit at 59 Bezemstraat, 71 Mechanical Transport Light Repair Unit at 347 Heezerweg, 13 Personnel Transit Centre at 2 Treurenburgstraat, 307 Mobile Signals Servicing Unit at 148 Tongelresestraat, and an RAF Police Unit at 11 Jan Smitzlaan. Headquarters 2 Company, 11 Air Formation Signals, was also based in Eindhoven, and many of the town-based units also had Mobile Signals Units attached to them. Additionally, 83 Group Headquarters also maintained two Telephone Operator Sections.

Meals were provided at the NAAFI/EFI at 15 Sint Trudostraat, which was manned by No. 206 Bulk Issue Stores, and a mobile canteen was also set up in a Cigar Factory in Dommelstraat, manned by 155 Mobile Canteen Depot. Significant medical facilities were also available in the town, thereunder 50 and 52 (RCAF) Mobile Field Hospitals, based in St. Joseph's Hospital in Veldhoven, and several dental units, thereunder 108 Mobile Dental Surgery for 125 Wing and

256 Mobile Dental Surgery (RCDC) for 143 Wing. 511G and 512G MSUs were attached to 50 and 52 MFH respectively.

In addition to these, other units were based in Eindhoven, which, although not actually a part of 83 Group, either drew their stores from 83 Group units, or relied on 83 Group for their day-to-day administration. These included 72 Wing's Northern Detachment and 123 AMES (mobile radar), 80 Wing's 80 MSU, 85 Group's 5357 Airfield Construction Wing (5022 and 5023 (General Trade) Squadrons) and 8 Concealment and Display Unit and, finally, a Netherlands Air Force Recruiting Centre.

125 Wing's dispersals areas at Eindhoven, Netherlands, in March 1945. © Gp Capt (ret) Derek S. V. Rake OBE AFC & Bar

Painting perhaps a clearer picture, 125 and 143 Wings and their supporting units at Eindhoven consisted of the following elements:[6]

B.78 Eindhoven		
Wings	125 Wing	143 Wing
Squadrons	41, 130 & 350 Squadrons	438, 439 & 440 Squadrons
Servicing Units	6041, 6132 & 6350 SEs	6438, 6439 & 6440 SEs
Air Liaison	361 ALS	12 (Canadian) ALS
Stores Supply	401 ASP	406 ASP
Hospital Units	50 MFH	52 (RCAF) MFH
Dental Units	108 MDS	256 MDS (RCDC)
RAF Regiment	2806 & 2876 Sqns.	2703, 2726, & 2781 Sqns.
Signals Units	61 Wing Signals Section, & 505C, 520G, 529J, 5001Q, 5251Q, & 5419J MSUs	59 Wing Signals Section, & 5021C, 5035J, 5037J, 5400G, & 5431Q MSUs

41 Squadron arrived at Eindhoven equipped with several new MV Series Spitfire XIVe's, some fitted with so-called 'teardrop' or 'bubble' hoods and reverting to unclipped wings. Several more MV Series aircraft also arrived over the ensuing days, along with a number of RN and SM Series Spitfire XIV's. These included:

Serial	Arrival	Serial	Arrival	Serial	Arrival
MV249	21 March 1945	MV262	21 March 1945	RN210	20 March 1945
MV254	20 March 1945	MV264	20 March 1945	SM817	26 March 1945
MV255	7 March 1945	MV266	20 March 1945	SM820	28 March 1945
MV257	9 March 1945	RN198	22 March 1945	SM826	26 March 1945
MV260	22 March 1945	RN208	23 March 1945	SM829	31 March 1945

Whilst it is not clear exactly which of these had teardrop hoods, 2 Lt Carl Bødtker's logbook reveals that at least MV264, MV266, and SM820 were fitted with such hoods and unclipped wings.[7]

No operational flying was undertaken by the Squadron on 18 March, as they were getting settled in to their new billets and base.

19 March 1945 – Still settling in to their new home, the only operational flying undertaken all day was by Red Section (Finucane RM931, Rake RM797) who escorted ACM Sir Arthur Tedder GCB, the AOC-in-C and Deputy Supreme Allied Commander of SHAEF, from Eindhoven. The pair was airborne at 11:15 and returned two hours later. During the afternoon, several pilots undertook practice flying with gyro-sights, and this concluded the day's flying.

Nominal Roll, March 1945

The following list has been extracted from an undated document, titled *Nominal Roll. 41 Squadron.*, held in 41 Squadron's Archives. It is assumed the Roll dates from between 19 and 21 March 1945, as this was the period that Flt Lt Raymond Finucane is believed to have been with the Squadron, and his name appears upon it. Pilots' names are listed in the order and general format they appear on the original document, although a few minor corrections have been made by the author.[8]

A Flight.

104443. Sqn Ldr D.I. Benham D.F.C., A.F.C.

B Flight.

A Flight	B Flight
104447. Flt Lt J. Shepherd DFC & Bar	A.401666. Flt Lt D. J. Reid
J.10643. Flt Lt W. N. Stowe	NZ.411494. Flt Lt T. E. Lawrence
124494. Flt Lt D. S. V. Rake	122410. Flt Lt R. P. R. Finucane
150189. Fg Off J. F. Wilkinson	116826. Flt Lt A. W. Jolly
164406. Fg Off F. M. Hegarty	1619. 2nd Lt. C. S. Bødtker (Norwegian)
190247. Plt Off P. T. Coleman	164846. Fg Off W. J. Jallands
1348985. WO I. T. Stevenson	A.414020. Fg Off E. Gray
1332528. WO P. H. Hale	NZ.412671 Fg Off R. R. G. Fisher
785066. WO J. A. Chalmers	190167. Plt Off R. Fleming
1338427. Flt Sgt L. H. Smart	A.414835. WO V. J. Rossow
A.437353. Flt Sgt C. N. Moyle	1318817. Flt Sgt H. F. Kelly
	1376359. WO F. V. Whale
	976899. WO T. K. Clanzy, N/E Sick

<u>Officers Ground Staff.</u>
139601. Flt Lt H. Anderson. Medical Officer
136130. Fg Off A. McAllister. Adjutant.

<u>Airmen Ground Staff.</u>
1197888. Sgt E. Fullam. Fitter 11E.
1629100. LAC J. S. Matcher. Clk./GD.
2225675. AC2 B. Roberts. Ach/GD. (Batman Officers Mess)
3216283. AC2 E. Weldon. Ach/GD. (Batman Officers Mess)

125 Wing pilots and airmen filling jerrycans by an RAF Bedford three-ton fuel tanker at Eindhoven, March 1945. Note the aircraft taxiing in, rear centre, and the dispersals area, rear left. © Gp Capt (ret) Derek S. V. Rake OBE AFC & Bar

A Taylorcraft Auster III (AOP) being refuelled from jerrycans at Eindhoven, March 1945. © Gp Capt (ret) Derek S. V. Rake OBE AFC & Bar

20 March 1945 – Twelve aircraft were airborne at 15:20 for a Wing operation with a like number of aircraft from 130 Squadron, led by Sqn Ldr Benham. Their goal was to sweep the Münster area, in particular seeking out enemy aircraft on the region's aerodromes. However, not a single one was seen and the Wing returned at 16:55.

At 17:00, another escort was provided to a VIP, on this occasion none other than MRAF Viscount Trenchard GCB GCVO DSO, who was travelling between Eindhoven and Volkel. The honour fell to Fg Off Jallands (RM915) and Plt Off Bob Fleming (RM696) who landed at Volkel with Trenchard at 17:15, waited on the ground for an hour, then escorted him back to Eindhoven again. They arrived back at the latter airfield at 18:30.

21 March 1945 – Fine weather marked the first day of spring. The morning's activity consisted of two medium bomber escorts. The first comprised eight aircraft to Coesfeld, led by Sqn Ldr Benham between 09:10 and 10:35. They were preceded by 130 Squadron performing a similar escorting to medium bombers to the same area. 41 Squadron's second escort, led by Flt Lt John Shepherd between 09:25 and 10:55, was also to Coesfeld, making it the third attack by bombers on Coesfeld within just two hours.

This latter escort, however, consisted of only four aircraft, thereby providing half of a composite escort squadron. The other half was provided by a quartet from 130 Squadron. Flt Sgt 'Micky' Moyle (RM915) returned 30 minutes early from the second escort with engine trouble, but otherwise both escorts were completely uneventful. However,

Today… was anything but a pleasant one for the Hun, for he was handed a shower of steel by the RAF. From early morning till last light, heavies and mediums pounded his lines of communications, his airfields and his fuel supplying depots. His transport and troops were strafed by fighter bombers and by rocket-firing Typhoons. 125 Wing was not heavily engaged but it fulfilled its commitments. 130 Sqdn were away first at 0830 to escort Mediums bombing Coesfeld and pilots were able to report concentrated bombing. Soon after 0900 hours 41 Sqdn sent off eight aircraft to escort a further bunch of Mediums on the same target and our pilots were able to report that the bomber boys were again "bang-on". Later still, a composite team of 41 and

Fg Off Rupert 'Lew' Munson RAAF left 41 Squadron on 14 March 1945 when his tour expired and he retired from the RAAF in 1977 as a Wing Commander in the Medical (Pharmaceutical) Branch. © Munson family

130 went with a third box again to Coesfeld and bombing was again reported to be good. The Hun flew no aircraft in opposition to these raids but at times the flak was intense and although our aircraft escaped, some of the Mediums were hit. Two Mitchells, a Lancaster and a Halifax landed at B.78.[9]

At 16:00, 41 Squadron was airborne once again, this time this time to participate in a Wing sweep of the Rheine-Münster area, led by Wg Cdr Keefer. The Squadron contributed nine aircraft, led by Sqn Ldr Benham, and 130 Squadron another twelve. However, no enemy aircraft or suitable ground targets were seen and the operation was uneventful. It was clear, though, that the 'final push' into Germany was about to begin as "the sky seemed full of American and British heavy and medium bombers, attacking targets across the Rheine [sic] in preparation for the crossings."[10] The Wing landed again just before 17:30, with nothing to report.

However, the day also saw two separate ground accidents with aircraft, which had dire results for the pilots. The first of these involved Flt Lt Ray Finucane, who taxied his aircraft too fast and then braked, which resulted in the airmen guiding his wing-tips being injured in falls. A harsh penalty awaited him. Barely a week with 41 Squadron, he was immediately taken off operations, then posted away.[11]

The second accident involved WO Peter Hale, who was blown off the runway at Eindhoven when he landed in a cross-wind and tipped one of the new aircraft, MV255, onto its nose. Hale recalls that this followed close on the tail of Finucane's accident and that Wing Commander Keefer felt he could not punish Finucane but not him. As such, Hale was also taken off operations and posted away temporarily to 83 GSU, in Dunsfold, Surrey, where he arrived on 23 March and remained until 16 April. On his return to the Continent, he was posted to 130 Squadron, now sharing a new base at Celle, Germany, with 41 and 350 Squadrons. However, when now Sqn Ldr John Shepherd realised the 'error', he formally requested Hale's return, and was successful. Hale was therefore back in the fold for the last intensive fight before the cessation of hostilities, where we shall next see him.

On 21 March 1945, 83 Group was spread over seven airfields in Belgium, Holland and Germany, as shown in the following table.[12]

Airfield	Runway	Occupied by
B.64 Diest	3,000 ft. untracked	409 & 410 RSUs & 653 AOP Squadron
B.78 Eindhoven	5,000 ft. brick	125 & 143 (RCAF) Wings, 403 RSU, & 83 GCS
B.80 Volkel	5,000 ft. brick	122 Wing & 419 RSU
B.86 Helmond	5,000 ft. brick	124 Wing
B.88 Heesch	3,600 ft. PSP	126 (RCAF) Wing
B.90 Petit Brogel	5,000 ft. PSP	39 (Recce) & 127 (RCAF) Wing
B.100 Goch	3,600 ft. PSP	121 Wing

22 March 1945 – Practically a repetition of the previous day, this one was entirely taken up with bomber escorts, and the Squadron was brought to readiness at 06:00 in preparation for the busy day that lay before them. As 350 Squadron was still at Warmwell, 41 and 130 Squadrons found themselves involved in four escorts each, with two of the four combined operations. 41 Squadron flew 21 sorties during the day and 130 another 24.

41 Squadron's first operation was airborne at 09:00, consisting of eight aircraft designated Red and Blue Sections, led by Sqn Ldr Benham, in which they escorted 69 B-26 Marauders of the 9th USAAF to Ahaus. As the visibility was very good, the results of the bombing could be seen by the pilots. It was very concentrated and accurate. As there was little Flak and the Luftwaffe did not attempt to hinder them, the two sections arrived back at Eindhoven at 10:30 without incident, although in the company of an unlucky Flak-damaged B-26, which made perfect landing at Eindhoven on one engine and with two wounded crew.

Ten minutes after Red and Blue Sections were airborne, Yellow Section of four aircraft took to the air with four aircraft from 130 Squadron, to form a composite escort squadron to 49 medium bombers of the 9th USAAF to Haltern, east-northeast of Wesel, led by Wg Cdr Keefer. They returned at 10:45, also with nothing to report.[13]

At 15:40, another eight aircraft were airborne, this time led by Flt Lt John Shepherd, to escort 100 Halifaxes and 12 Lancasters of 6 and 8 Groups, Bomber Command, to rail and canal targets and a fuel dump in the Dorsten area. The visibility had deteriorated since the morning and thick haze now blanketed the area up to 12,000 feet, created by the smoke rising from uncountable fires in umpteen cities and towns. The operation was uneventful for the Squadron except for the sighting of a single aircraft, possibly a jet, which dived through the bomber formation and was immediately lost in the haze. The Squadron did not give chase and returned to base at 17:25.

WO Keith Clanzy's service with 41 Squadron ended in mid-March 1945, when he broke his wrist and injured a leg in a fall from a truck on 18 February 1945. Discharged from the RAF later that year, he gained a BSc (Eng) from London University in 1948, and retired in 1979 as HM Principal Electrical Inspector of Mines and Quarries. © Keith Clanzy, via Patricia Clanzy-Hodge

Flt Lt Raymond Finucane, younger brother of the late famed Ace 'Paddy', served with 41 Squadron briefly from around 19 March 1945 until taken off flying duties on 21 March 1945 following a taxiing accident. He ended the War with 486 (NZ) Squadron and retired from the RAF in late 1962. © Ray Finucane, via Maurice Byrne

The day's last operation for the Squadron was little more than token support of a 130 Squadron escort of 74 8th USAAF B-17 Flying Fortresses to the military barracks at Dorsten, around 18km north of Gelsenkirchen. A single pilot was airborne at 15:55 to fly as Wg Cdr Keefer's No. 2, but his name is not recorded in the ORB. Another jet was seen, this time identified as an Ar234, but similarly to the previous sighting, also quickly disappeared into the smoke haze. The operation was otherwise uneventful and the pilots landed back at Eindhoven again at 17:30.

The pilots were awed by the continuous heavy pounding being delivered by the bombers. "Every town, small and large, in Western Germany seemed to have been well and truly pranged."[14]

23 March 1945 – The Wing was airborne at 09:25 on a sweep of the Rheine area, led by Wg Cdr Keefer, in which 12 aircraft from 41 Squadron participated. Reports were received of enemy aircraft attacking bombers over Wesel and the pilots hurried to the area, but nothing was seen. Blue Section's Fg Off Walter Jallands (RM759) and Flt Sgt Hugh Kelly (MV264) both landed at B.86 Helmond, 20km east of Eindhoven, short of fuel, but the remaining pilots returned to Eindhoven at 11.00. 130 Squadron also undertook a sweep of the Rheine area during the morning.

41 Squadron was up again at 13:30, once again led by Wg Cdr Keefer. On this occasion, seven aircraft designated Red and Yellow Sections flew an armed reconnaissance of a triangular area formed by the towns of Rheine, Osnabruck, and Münster. The operation should have consisted of eight aircraft, but Red Section's Flt Lt Bill Stowe (RM797) suffered engine failure prior to take-off and remained behind.

However, ground targets were difficult to find and when the Squadron returned at 14:55, their only claim was a single MET damaged near Rheine by Flt Lt Daniel Reid (MV264). It was, however, the unit's first claim against a ground target in almost three weeks.

For the day's last operation, another escort was on the cards. Seven aircraft were off the deck as Red and Yellow Sections at 16:40, led by Flt Lt Daniel Reid, ordered to escort a box of 9th USAAF B-26 Marauders to the communications centre at Ahaus. They returned at 18:25 after an uneventful mission, with nothing to report.

On landing, however, newcomer Flt Sgt William Pairman came down too hard and damaged MV266. It was his first operational flight with the Squadron, but this brought no sympathy. Suffering a similar fate to Raymond Finucane and Peter Hale, he was also immediately taken off operations, and subsequently posted away.[15]

In the late afternoon, the pilots of 41 and 130 Squadrons were briefed by the OC, 125 Wing, Gp Capt David Scott-Malden, and the AOC 83 Group, AVM Harry Broadhurst, on the "general plan for the crossing of the Rhine, and the particular sphere of operations allotted to the Wing."[16] "All the highly paid officials from the Group were there," records the 125 Wing ORB with wry humour, but then Flt Lt Derek Rake recalls it was quite a serious and sobering affair.

Flt Sgt William Pairman served briefly with 41 Squadron from 21 March 1945-22 April 1945. He was grounded after a heavy landing on 23 March 1945, but remained with the unit until posted to 130 Squadron on 22 April, where he saw out the War. © Andrew Pairman

We were told that the Luftwaffe would probably use their ME 262s to dive bomb our troops as they crossed the river in their landing craft and that they would come in at high level. Our task would be to stop them. One of the pilots on 41 Sqn politely asked the AOC 83 Gp. how we were going to do this since the 262s were at least 100 mph faster than our Spits. Air Vice-Marshal Broadhurst replied "Attack them head on and if necessary, fly into them"!!![17]

After the briefing, the Wing's pilots were "keyed up for the job and with dreams of Jet jobs coming up asking for trouble, both squadrons… retired early."[18]

The Battle of the Rhine

By the third week of March 1945, the Allied armies had advanced to the Rhine. Field-Marshal Sir Bernard Montgomery KCB DSO and his Generals were now preparing to launch Operation *Plunder*, which foresaw the first crossing of the Rhine between the towns of Rees and Rheinberg on 24 March 1945, by the British 2nd and U.S. 9th Armies.

The British 2nd Army, on the northern flank, consisted of the VIII, XII, and XXX Army Corps and, for the initial stages of the battle, the 2nd Canadian Corps and XVIII U.S. Airborne Corps. This latter unit comprised the 6th British and 17th U.S. Airborne Divisions. The British 2nd Army's total forces therefore included no less than four armoured divisions, two airborne divisions, eight infantry divisions, five independent armoured brigades, one Commando brigade and one independent infantry brigade. On the southern flank, the 9th U.S. Army consisted of the XIII, XVI, and XIX Army Corps, which were formed of three armoured and nine infantry divisions. The 79th Armored Division also supported the operation with its specialised armour and amphibious equipment and resources.

The 2nd Army's first major objective was to secure bridges at Emmerich, whilst the 9th Army was allocated the task of capturing the city of Wesel, considered to be an important communications centre. They were then expected to extend and establish a bridgehead east of the Rhine large enough to enable major forces to move in behind them, and then drive east and northeast.

However, the crossing was a daunting task; later, Monty would refer to the Rhine as "the greatest water obstacle in Western Europe".[19] On this part of the front, the river was 400-500 yards wide at low tide and 700-1,200 at high tide, flowing, on average, at about 3½ knots. Dykes controlled the course of the river, but these presented another formidable obstacle for the Allied armies, measuring approximately 18 metres wide at the base, and three to five metres high. Solid preparation for these obstacles and the crossing of so wide a river were crucial to Monty's strategy, as was keeping pace with the retreating Wehrmacht.

The offensive was preceded by massive daylight and night-time bombing of key targets along the front by medium and heavy bombers from both the RAF and USAAF, supported by 2 TAF to a depth of 50 miles beyond the Rhine, in which 125 Wing participated. Indeed, this is what had kept 41 and 130 Squadrons so busy the past few days.

At 15:30 on 23 March, Monty gave the official order to launch Operation *Varsity*, the airborne component of the main operation, *Plunder*. That evening, Gp Capt Scott-Malden gathered 125 Wing's pilots together to inform them that the Rhine crossings were about to commence.

In support of the briefing, a message was received from the AOC-in-C 2 TAF, Air Marshal Sir Arthur Coningham KCB DSO MC DFC AFC, addressed to all ranks within 2 TAF. It read:

> *Best wishes to you all for this last great battle and the advance to the East. In association with the great Air Forces now operating on Germany you have prepared the way for our Armies in a truly magnificent manner. Now comes the final flurry and I know you will do even better.*
>
> *I want you to go all out but be calm and efficient. Congratulations, warm thanks and again best wishes.*[20]

24 March 1945 – During the night of 23-24 March, the Rhine crossings commenced, and by dawn the assaulting divisions had traversed the river and successfully accomplished their initial objectives.

That morning, the XVIII U.S. Airborne Corps, consisting of the 6th British and 17th U.S. Airborne Divisions, were landed by glider and parachute on the eastern bank of the Rhine within range of supporting artillery on the western bank. They quickly made contact with the night's assaulting divisions, thus bolstering troop numbers and hindering any effective counter-attack, particularly on the 2nd Army's northern flank, where the German opposition was heaviest.

With the bridgehead now firmly established, the engineers moved up bridges and ferries, deploying craft that the Royal Navy had transported by road across Belgium, southern Holland and all the way to the Rhine. It now fell to the Allied air forces' fighters to give them air cover and keep the Wehrmacht at bay, so the crossings could continue unhindered.

It comes as no surprise, therefore, that 41 Squadron's day started early, and consisted of no less than five full operations. A day usually consisted of three, and possibly four operations, but five were flown today between 06:00 and 19:35. Forty-one sorties in a single day was a demanding and exhausting undertaking, as much for the pilots as for their indomitable ground crews.

The first operation was airborne at 06:00, when Wg Cdr Keefer (who flew a 41 Squadron aircraft) led nine aircraft on a fighter sweep of the bridgehead area. The two sections, designated Red and Blue, consisted of Wg Cdr Keefer RCAF (MV257), Flt Lt Bill Stowe RCAF (RM797), WO Ian Stevenson (RM792), and Flt Sgt 'Micky' Moyle RAAF (MV266) in the former section, and Flt Lt Daniel Reid RAAF (MV264), 2 Lt Carl Bødtker RNoAF (RM759), Fg Off Roy Fisher RNZAF (RN210), and WO Viv Rossow RAAF (RM928) in the latter. It was a suitably international operation.

Flt Lt Derek Rake (RM931) flew as spare man, attached to Red Section, but he turned back at the Rhine to accompany home Fg Off Fisher, who was having oxygen trouble. They landed at 06:35. Despite their high hopes, however, the sweep was uneventful and the pilots returned to Eindhoven between 07:30 and 07:35 with nothing to report.

Wg Cdr Keefer was up again at 08:50 to lead the Squadron on a fighter sweep covering the airborne landings behind Wesel. This operation consisted of eight aircraft, and nearly all the participants were senior Squadron officers; not a single NCO pilot took part. Red Section consisted of Wg Cdr Keefer, Flt Lts Rake and Shepherd and Fg Off Hegarty, and Blue Section of Sqn Ldr Benham, Flt Lts Cowell and Jolly, and Plt Off Fleming.

However, the operation was dogged with technical problems. Peter Cowell (MV264) suffered engine failure before getting airborne and could not take off, and was left behind. Then, part way into the operation, Plt Off Bob Fleming (RN210) started having trouble with his engine instruments and returned to base early, putting down at 09:35. This same aircraft had also created problems for Fg Off Roy Fisher on the morning's first operation.

There was a little excitement for the rest of the pilots when aircraft were spotted above them at 25,000 feet. The Squadron climbed to investigate, but it soon transpired they were USAAF P-38 Lightnings. Otherwise, they found no customers, and considered the Luftwaffe was "apparently not in a fighting mood".[21]

Whilst returning to base, Fg Off Hegarty (RN198) ran short of fuel and was compelled to land at Volkel at 10:00. The remaining five pilots landed back at base ten minutes later, with little to report.

The day's third operation was led by Sqn Ldr Benham, when nine aircraft were airborne as Red and Yellow Sections at 11:50 for a fighter sweep. Flt Lt Jolly, who was the spare man, returned at 12:15, and the remaining eight pilots landed between 13:10 and 13:25, once again, astoundingly, with nothing to report. Where was the Luftwaffe?!

Operation four was up at 14:55, led by Flt Lt Bill Stowe. On this occasion, seven aircraft were sent on a sweep to Herrenburg, south of Münster, to investigate what was only described as 'ground movement'. A thick haze covered the town, causing poor visibility that forced the pilots to orbit the area at just 2,000 feet to discover what had been reported. Flt Lt Derek Rake (RN198) dived down lower to get a closer look, but the area's Flak batteries opened up and he was hit in the port wing. He pulled up and away, and turned west for base.

Rake was shaken but not injured and kept control of his aircraft. He made a successful but very dicey landing at Volkel at 16:10, with neither flaps nor brakes. Despite this, reports the ORB, "nothing worth reporting was seen at Herrenburg"[22], and the rest of the Squadron put down at Eindhoven at 16:20.

The day's last operation was in the air at 17:55. Sqn Ldr Benham led nine aircraft, Red Section of four and Yellow Section of five, on a fighter sweep of the Bocholt area. Enemy ground movement had been reported, and "four Squadrons immediately converged on the place".[23] However, there was nothing to be seen, and whilst spare man, Fg Off Johnnie Wilkinson (MV264), was sent back at 18:15, another four aircraft were sent home to land before dark, landing at Eindhoven at 19:10. The remaining quartet joined them between 19:30 and 19:35. There was, once again, nothing to report.

The story was the same for the 130 Squadron; despite dozens of sorties being flown, "the gallant one hundred and twenty-fifth could not get any joy".[24] In fact, throughout the day, despite hundreds of aircraft from 2 TAF and other Air Forces providing fighter cover to the crossings and advance, barely 20 enemy aircraft were sighted across the entire front. This led 125 Wing to conclude,

> *The Hun either could not or would not play. His airfields have been pranged good and hard recently by bombers and with 83 Group sitting above his airfields most of the day waiting for him to come up he is rather between the devil and the deep blue sea.*[25]

This therefore left the Allied air forces to concentrate on their major objective – ground targets – instead, and impede any efforts by the Wehrmacht to move up troops and equipment to counter the Allied ground offensive. Indeed, by the end of the day, news was received by the Wing that the Rhine crossings were progressing according to plan and that the advancing Allied armies had managed to reach and link up with the airborne troops. The day could hardly have gone better.

In the middle of all the action today, a new pilot arrived on the Squadron in the form of 23-year-old Trinidadian Flt Lt Fernand Farfan, who would soon become known by the rather amusing nickname 'Fanny'.[26]

25 March 1945 – The second day of the Rhine crossings proved to be an intense one for 41 Squadron, upon which they claimed multiple ground victories during four separate operations, but this time they came at a price.

The first mission, an armed reconnaissance of the Rheine-Münster area, was airborne at 07:40, led by OC B Flight, Flt Lt Daniel Reid, and consisted of nine aircraft, designated Red and Yellow

Following service on Malta, in North Africa and in France, Trinidadian Flt Lt Fernand 'Fanny' Farfan served with 41 Squadron from 24 March 1945 to 25 September 1945. He retired from the RAF in April 1949. © Philip Farfan

Sections. Flt Lt Derek Rake (MV254), who was leading Yellow Section, returned within ten minutes with a rough engine. WO Ian Stevenson took over command of the section and the spare man, Fg Off Walter Jallands, moved from Red Section to Yellow to fill the gap. Over the target area, the sections split up, each seeking for their own targets of opportunity.

Red Section (Reid MV264, Hale RM931, Lawrence MV255, Fleming RN210) found and damaged an MET and strafed a supply dump near Dolmen, whilst Yellow Section (Stevenson RM915, Hegarty RM799, Smart MV260, Jallands RM745) destroyed an ammunition truck in a ball of flames and damaged two more MET southwest of Münster. The eight pilots landed back at Eindhoven at 09:20. Despite the seriousness of their task, it was still intertwined with some good humour, and the ORB reports that upon their return, "a meek voice was heard to say he thought he was firing at a lorry, but it was only a shadow…"![27]

Another armed reconnaissance to the same area was airborne at 10:45, which consisted of seven aircraft in two sections, designated Red (Shepherd RM931, Bødtker RM696, Moyle MV255, Stowe RM797) and Blue (Cowell MV264, Jolly RN210, Fisher RN208), led by Flt Lt John Shepherd. A successful operation, the pilots returned at 12:20 claiming no less than two MET destroyed and 12 barges, 10 railway trucks in a siding and two MET damaged in the area.

Just after lunch, at 13:45, Sqn Ldr Benham led nine pilots on the day's third armed reconnaissance of the Rheine-Münster area. The spare man, WO 'Vickie' Whale (RN210), returned at 14:05 with technical trouble, and the remaining eight pilots continued on, finding a landing strip near Nordhorn. Upon investigation, they observed no ground activity so continued to Bocholt, where they destroyed a motorcycle with a sidecar and a halftrack.

Flt Lt Daniel Reid (MV264) then led Blue Section on an attack on a large round storage tank in the centre of Bocholt. Assuming it was full of oil, he made his attack at an altitude of just 1,000 feet. However, it was actually a gasometer and immediately blew up in a ball of flames.

As he pulled sharply away, he came under intense accurate Flak from a nearby battery, which hit both his tail section and a wing. A 13mm shell also pierced the armour plating behind his cockpit and shrapnel entered his back.[28] It was time to call it a day anyway, and the Squadron now escorted Reid back home, who continued to maintain control of his aircraft, despite his injuries. However, instead of landing at Eindhoven, he put down early at Volkel. The rest of the pilots continued to base, where they landed at 15:15.

Reid was given initial treatment at Volkel, and then transported to 50 Mobile Field Hospital at Eindhoven where he was operated on. Within two days of the incident, his parents received the ever-feared knock on the door, when a telegram was delivered from the RAAF office in Collins Street, Melbourne. It read,

> *401666 FLIGHT LIEUTENANT D.J. REID INJURED STOP REGRET TO INFORM YOU THAT YOUR SON FLIGHT LIEUTENANT DANIEL JOSEPH REID WAS INJURED AND ADMITTED TO MOBILE FIELD HOSPITAL ON 25TH MARCH 1945 SUFFERING BULLET WOUND IN BACK RECEIVED AS RESULT AIR OPERATIONS STOP KNOWN DETAILS ARE HE WAS PILOT OF SPITFIRE AIRCRAFT WHICH WAS STRUCK BY TWO [ARMOUR] PIERCING BULLETS ONE OF WHICH INJURED HIS BACK STOP EXTENT OF INJURY NOT YET ADVISED BUT FURTHER INFORMATION IS ANTICIPATED WHICH WILL BE CONVEYED TO YOU IMMEDIATELY RECEIVED STOP DESIRE TO EXPRESS SYMPATHY IN YOUR ANXIETY.*[29]

Initially considered in a serious condition, he was found to have a piece of shrapnel embedded in the left lumbar region of his back, which was removed, and within a few days his condition was upgraded to satisfactory. Reid was evacuated to England and was still recuperating in hospital when the War in Europe came to an end. He did not return to the Squadron, and the unit had lost yet another Flight Commander.[30]

Returning now to 25 March, the day was not yet over and at 16:25, a fourth operation – yet another armed reconnaissance to the Rheine-Münster area – was led by Wg Cdr Keefer, consisting of eight aircraft. Flt Lt Peter Cowell (RM928) returned at 17:30 as he could not get any feed from his drop tank, and feared he had a fuel leak. The remaining six pilots (Keefer MV257, Bødtker RM759, Jolly RN208, Shepherd RM931, Moyle MV267, Stowe RM797, Stevenson MV254) continued on to claim three MET damaged in the Coesfeld area, but one aircraft was hit and damaged by Flak.[31] The damage did not hinder the aircraft's operation and all the pilots returned together at 17:55.

> *Light flak was odd. You would think a bullet would come towards you straight, but it actually has a sort of spiral flight. It also looks quite slow at first and then it suddenly zips past you very speedily. It was a touch sobering to realise there were six or more ordinary bullets which you could not see in between the tracers which you could. This at altitude, lower down it was a different matter.*
>
> *After our patrol was ended we were permitted, encouraged, to attack any targets we could find. Tanks naturally, trucks, cars, locomotives, barges. That was very satisfactory. We avoided and were advised to avoid German Airfields. They were very heavily defended and it was considered an unnecessary risk to take them on....*
>
> *Occasionally there would be a heavily armed locomotive, a trap. The sides of various carriages would drop down and there would be batteries of anti-aircraft guns all firing away. It wasn't common and once discovered word soon got around. Another problem to be avoided was an explosion caused during an attack where flying debris could cause difficulties.*[32]

26 March 1945 – An extremely busy day lay before the Squadron during which nine separate patrols (42 sorties) were flown east of the Rhine to cover the bridgeheads, along a line between Haldern and Herrenburg. Whilst they were generally uneventful, "at least they gave out pilots a good picture of the progress of our troops in the assault east of the Rheine [sic]".[33] These patrols consisted of the following operations:

Op.	Section	A/C	Led by	Timings
1	Red	6	Shepherd	05:55-07:35
2	Yellow	6	Cowell	07:40-09:20
3	Red	5	Shepherd	08:45-10:30

4	Yellow	6	Lawrence	10:45-12:35
5	Red	3	Rake	11:55-13:40
6	Yellow	4	Cowell	13:40-15:15
7	Red	4	Stowe	14:40-16:20
8	Yellow	4	Shepherd	16:40-17:50
9	Red	4	Cowell	17:40-19:30

The first, second, fourth, fifth, sixth, eighth and ninth patrols were uneventful. During the second, however, 2 Lt Carl Bødtker (MV255) suffered engine problems and returned early. He put down at Volkel at 08:30 but his engine failed on approach and he crash-landed, sustaining superficial injuries in the process. The aircraft was damaged to Cat E status and struck from charge on 4 May 1945.

On the third patrol, between 08:45 and 10:30, Flt Sgt 'Micky' Moyle (RM817) returned within ten minutes with engine trouble and WO John Chalmers (RN208), who was airborne late after suffering engine trouble on the ground, could not find and catch up with the rest of Red Section due to poor visibility and returned at 09:25. However, the remaining three pilots (Shepherd MV266, Stowe MV249, Stevenson RM915) found a few ground targets of opportunity in the Rhede area, just east of Bocholt, and returned claiming a Panzer IV medium tank and an armoured car damaged, and a despatch motorcycle destroyed.

The seventh patrol, airborne at 14:40, was in the most part uneventful except that Flt Lt Bill Stowe realised the tank he had attacked in the morning with Sqn Ldr Shepherd and WO Ian Stevenson had moved further down the road. He therefore led Red Section (Stowe MV254, Chalmers RM915, Lawrence RM696, Jallands RN210) down to attack it anew, and returned at 16:20 with nothing else to report.

Though otherwise uneventful, Fg Off Francis Hegarty (RM797) returned 25 minutes early from the day's second last patrol with engine trouble. It was the fourth such frustrating occurrence on a long and "very tiring day for the Squadron".[34]

Separately, Flt Lt Peter Cowell was appointed OC B Flight, to replace 'Denny' Reid, who was recuperating in hospital.

We have heard that F/Lt. D.J. Reid is progressing favourably, but will not be returning to the Squadron. We all sympathise with him in his misfortune and wish him the best of luck in whatever the future may have in store for him.[35]

22-year-old Peter Cowell, though a few years younger than Reid, was an appropriate replacement, and considered "a most personable man, very popular and respected".[36] He would hold the position for over a year.

27 March 1945 – As the morning mist did not fully lift all day, the only operation flown by the Squadron was a patrol between Winterswijk and Dorsten by six aircraft from 18:10, which was led by Flt Lt John Shepherd. Flt Sgt 'Micky' Moyle (RM799) landed at Volkel at 18:20 with engine trouble and WO Ian Stevenson (RM915) joined him there five minutes later with a broken connecting rod, which had broken through both sides of his engine. The patrol was otherwise uneventful, and the section landed again at 19:45.

During the day, 21-year-old Yorkshireman Flt Sgt Peter Scott joined the unit. Scott had joined the RAFVR almost three years previously and had completed EFTS, SFTS and OTU in Canada. He then returned to the United Kingdom where he attended 53 OTU at Kirton, prior to a posting to 83 GSU at Dunsfold. 41 Squadron was now his first operational posting.

In the evening, the Wing held a party in the Officers Mess in which dancing partners were provided by the available women's services or local Dutch ladies. The 83 Group band kept them entertained and a good time was had by all.

Having rejoined 41 Squadron for his second tour with the unit on 31 January 1945, Flt Lt Peter Cowell was promoted to OC B Flight on 26 March 1945, after the incumbent, Flt Lt Danny Reid RAAF was hit by Flak and seriously wounded. © Peter Cowell, via Dan Johnson

28 March 1945 – Within four days of the launch of Operation *Plunder*, the Allied bridgehead east of the Rhine was firmly established, and on 28 March the advance to the Elbe began. For 41 Squadron, the day consisted of three armed reconnaissances and a bomber escort in support of ground troops.

The first operation was airborne at 10:15, when Flt Lt Peter Cowell led eight aircraft on an armed reconnaissance of an area bounded by the towns of Enschede, Rheine, Osnabrück and Münster. Fg Off Roy Fisher (RM928) returned within 15 minutes with an unserviceable drop tank, but the remaining pilots (Cowell MV260, Kelly SM820, Whale RN210, and four others unidentified) found and attacked substantial concentrations of enemy formations on the roads. When they returned at 11:45, they claimed 12 MET, 25 trucks, 20 flat cars, one tug and nine barges damaged, one barge left in flames and an RDF aerial strafed.[37]

The second armed reconnaissance was airborne at 12:40, when Flt Lt Tom Lawrence led six aircraft to the same area. Having found a few ground targets of opportunity west of Osnabrück, Red Section moved around to the east of the town where they found more. Lawrence (MV260) had already commenced a dive on them when three long-nosed FW190D's passed below him in the opposite direction.

He made a tight diving turn to starboard, followed by his No. 2, Flt Lt Arnold Jolly (RN208), and informed the rest of the section. Jolly was left behind in the tight turn as Lawrence made a dash for the 190s, closing from an initial 1,000 yards to just 450. As he drew near, however, they emitted blue smoke, indicating he had been spotted and had just engaged emergency power to boost their speed. With his jettison tank still under his belly, and at a speed too great to release it, Lawrence was unable to gain on them any further and instead fired two bursts at the aircraft from this range. He noticed three shells from his cannon strike one of the aircraft on the first burst, but lost any residual advantage by the second, when one of his cannon failed to fire.

By this time, Lawrence was dangerously vulnerable, now flying alone and practically on the deck over Rheine Aerodrome. Finding himself suddenly coming under intense light Flak, and without ammunition for his own defence, he broke south and distanced himself from the area as quick as possible. The section returned at 14:10, claiming a total of five MET damaged, and Lawrence claimed his FW190 damaged.[38]

The day's third operation was an escort by eight aircraft of Mitchells to Malmedy-Königsfeld area at 15:20, led by Flt Lt Peter Cowell. Normally a fairly straightforward job, this escort almost failed completely.

Flt Sgt Peter Scott served with 41 Squadron from 27 March 1945 to 30 January 1946, during which time he claimed one shared destroyed and two damaged FW190s. © 41 Squadron RAF

Rendezvous was finally made over 10/10 cloud and after much milling round, the Bombers were separated and the Squadron finished up escorting one box of six.[39]

The bombing run went unchallenged and 41's pilots returned to Eindhoven at 17:00 with nothing else to report. It was quite an anti-climax to what transpired to be the Squadron's last bomber escort of the War and indeed the last of this nature in its history.[40]

The day's final operation, a third armed reconnaissance to the bridgehead, proved uneventful due to adverse weather conditions. Eight aircraft were airborne at 18:05, led by Flt Lt John Shepherd. When poor weather was encountered over the Rhine, the unit turned for home and put down again only 40 minutes after they had left, with nothing to report.

Separately, Gp Capt David Scott-Malden left 125 Wing today on a posting to Air Staff Plans 1 at the Air Ministry in London, and handed over command of the Wing to Gp Capt James Edgar 'Johnnie' Johnson DSO** DFC*, one of the RAF's highest-scoring Aces. Johnson had previously been Wing Commander Flying with 127 Wing and had just been promoted to Group Captain.

B.104 Damm

29 March 1945 – No operational flying was undertaken today due to the weather, but this allowed the Squadron to take a brief rest from flying and servicing aircraft. However, the Wing had received orders to relocate to a new airfield at Damm, which had been assigned the identifier 'B.104'. The location allocated was presently just a field around 14km east-north-east of Wesel, immediately behind the front line, at 51°40' N 6°46' E. It was planned to lay 3,600 feet of sheet metal tracking with sod taxi and dispersal areas.

The day was therefore spent packing and preparing for the move prompting the Wing ORB commented, "Yet another move in the offing but in view of the advance of our armies, who would grumble?"[41]

30 March 1945 – The weather having considerably improved, the move to Damm began early for the Wing's ground staff.

"A" Echelon moved off at 0730 hours on their trek across the Rhine. The crossed the Maas at Venlo and the Rhine at Xanten. After passing through Wesel which was still burning, they finally fetched up at B.104 (Damm) at 1530 hours, at the same time as 39 Recce Wing. Houses were commandeered and everyone in sight of being straight by nightfall. The strip is still under construction and it will certainly be a few days before it is suitable for the 'kites' to fly in.[42]

They were preceded by 6 Mobile Field Photographic Section and 'A' Echelon of 39 Recce Wing, which had headed out of B.90 Petit Brogel at 07:00, accompanied by an escort of RAF Regiment with Bofors anti-aircraft guns. They took the same route as 125 Wing's Echelon, entering Germany through Venlo and crossing the Rhine over the Bailey pontoon bridge at Xanten.

As they passed through Wesel, the city was in rubble and still burning six days after the battle for the town. They found the fields full of the signs of the Allied landings, with gliders abandoned everywhere, some fully intact and others just burnt-out frames.

The convoy arrived in Damm mid-afternoon, after a trip of 102 miles. It had taken an hour and 45 minutes to reach Xanten from Venlo, and another two just to get from the Rhine and through Wesel to Damm. 39 Recce Wing was clearly underwhelmed by what they found:

B.104 was a field – a field of mud and water, and vehicles were sinking to their hubs everywhere. […] Half of the Wing had completed this long awaited move in Germany but the first 'strip' was not up to expectations and we hoped we would not be here for long.[43]

However, once tent accommodation was set up, the men not on duty took advantage of being in Germany for the first time, and were busied "collecting souvenirs, German helmets, respirators, rifles, etc."[44]

Meanwhile, 125 Wing continued to operate out of Eindhoven and spent the day on a series of patrols. 41 Squadron certainly had a busy day; six patrols were flown between Ahaus and Dülmen, totalling 22 sorties, between 09:35 and 19:25.[45]

Most of these were uneventful, but on the second, which was off the deck at 10:45, Red Section (Shepherd MV266, Hegarty MV254, Farfan RM759, Chalmers MV267) claimed 24 MET and one 88mm gun damaged in the Dülmen area. On one of the later patrols, airborne at 12:50, Flt

One of the RAF's highest-scoring Aces, Gp Capt James E. 'Johnnie' Johnson DSO** DFC*, took over command of 125 Wing on 28 March 1945. © Terry Spencer, via Cara and Raina Spencer

Lt Bill Stowe (MV249) and Flt Sgt Harry Smart (RM759) also damaged one locomotive and ten railway trucks near Münster.

31 March 1945 – At Damm, 125 Wing's 'A' Echelon spent the day working hard on making the strip serviceable but soon realised it was not going to be as easy a job as initially envisaged. They reported it would be several days yet before the Wing's Spitfires would be able to fly in.

However, it had not taken the German military long to find out the site was being prepared as an airfield, and they were shelled today, but there were thankfully no casualties. Security was also tightened when German civilians living around the site were moved away and orders were given that servicemen were only allowed to leave the airfield site in groups of three or more, with loaded arms.

A farm was also commandeered today, with its entire livestock, and the men enjoyed roast pork and venison for dinner for the first time in a long while, immediately improving morale.

Back at B.78, the Wing's operations were hampered by poor weather and 41 Squadron's activity was confined to just two fighter sweeps all day, the first at 07:10 and the second at 17:30. The morning's operation comprised six aircraft designated Red Section and led by Wg Cdr Keefer. Flt Lt 'Fanny' Farfan (MV254) had some engine trouble, which forced him to return to base within the first half hour, and the rest of the pilots returned at 09:00 with nothing to report.

On the evening's operation, eight aircraft[46] designated Red and Yellow Sections headed for the Osnabrück-Dümmer Lake area, led by Flt Lt John Shepherd, with eight aircraft from 130 Squadron. The sweep was completely uneventful due to 10/10ths cloud cover over the target area, but the return journey proved more of a challenge. The Squadron faced a strong headwind all the way home, which slowed their pace. Five pilots were forced to land at Volkel, low on fuel, where they all stayed overnight. SM829, flown by Plt Off Pat Coleman, was damaged on landing here and he recorded in his logbook that day, "petrol consumption too high – crash landed at Volkel at dusk after gliding from the Rhine"[47], a distance of some 45km! Also short of fuel, WO Viv Rossow (RN208) landed at B.89 Mill, around 40km northeast of Eindhoven, and only the remaining two pilots landed at Eindhoven at 19:20.

41 Squadron had flown an intensive month in March 1945, despite ten days at Warmwell, logging no less than 309 operational sorties, totalling 447 hours and 15 minutes, and 24 non-operational sorties, totalling 14 hours and 45 minutes. The pilots expended 6,905 rounds of 20mm cannon ammunition and 8,392 rounds of 0.5 inch calibre.

1 April 1945 – Easter Sunday. No operational flying was undertaken all day, mainly a result of adverse weather conditions. It was but a brief lull before the storm of a month that would prove more intensive than any since the Battle of Britain.

Work continued at Damm throughout the day to make the strip serviceable, but the weather continued to work against them. However, a Wehrmacht storehouse was found and commandeered, which provided the men, amongst other niceties, jam and additional cooking utensils. The cooks laid on a fresh chicken dinner for the men.

2 April 1945 – As the previous day's poor weather persisted into the afternoon, the day's flying did not commence until 15:35, when a section of four aircraft led by Flt Lt Peter Cowell took off for a weather reconnaissance flight, searching for somewhere that offered the chance of action. They returned at 17:10 but on their return journey reported having found good weather around Lingen.

As a result, Flt Lt John Shepherd took up seven aircraft designated Red and Yellow Sections at 17:00, even before Cowell's quartet had landed, and headed for the Lingen-Osnabrück area. Yellow Section (Stowe RM797, Smith MV256, Hegarty RM792) had some luck, shooting up two MET at Bippen, but Red Section found nothing of note, and the seven aircraft returned at 18:25.

A third and last operation was up just ten minutes after Red and Yellow Sections' return, when

WO Ian Stevenson in the cockpit of his Spitfire XIV, EB-E, Spring 1945. © Neil Stevenson

Flt Lt Tom Lawrence led four aircraft on an armed reconnaissance of the same area. By this time, however, the weather had deteriorated again and they returned at 19:50 with nothing to report.

At Damm, 'A' Echelon battled on against the elements, contending with strong winds and frequent rainy spells. Even though work continued until 23:30, the outlook was bleak and the initial assumption of a few days' work to get the strip serviceable was now revised to no promised timeframe at all! There was some excitement during the early evening when a Luftwaffe jet appeared over the airfield site, which was greeted by the RAF Regiment's Bofors. No hit was registered and the aircraft soon flew off.

3 April 1945 – The past few days' bad weather lingered until after lunch, when it cleared sufficiently to allow a weather reconnaissance to be undertaken. At 13:00, Flt Lt Bill Stowe led four aircraft designated Yellow Section (Stowe RM797, Smith MV249, Rake MV254, Hegarty RM792) to the Quackenbrück area, around 45km north of Osnabrück, but sighted a convoy of approximately 35 vehicles on the road near Herzlake, still 24km west of their planned destination. These were attacked and the pilots claimed 12 destroyed and six damaged, assisted by one vehicle that destroyed several others when it exploded.

The quartet left the rest of the convoy to twelve aircraft from 130 Squadron that had since arrived on the scene, and landed back at Eindhoven at 14:35. The convoy had been decimated by the time the Wing had finished with them: 130 Squadron claimed another four MET destroyed and 15 damaged of their own, leaving no vehicle unscathed. No less than 16 MET had been destroyed and another 21 damaged.

At 14:20, before Stowe's section had returned, a second armed reconnaissance was airborne. Flt Lt Peter Cowell led eight aircraft to the Lingen area, but they soon found themselves flying through storms, heavy rain and hail. They were separated in the putrid weather and zero visibility and landed again individually or in pairs at 14:30, 14:45, and 15:25, with nothing to report but poor flying conditions.

The Squadron tried once again at 17:20, when Flt Lt John Shepherd led twelve aircraft on an armed reconnaissance. They crossed the Rhine, but were greeted by the same very poor weather, so gave up and returned home, setting down at Eindhoven at 18:10.

The continuing rainfall had resulted in boggy conditions at Damm, and the slow progress was beginning to frustrate 2 TAF's plans for 125 Wing's advance into Germany. During the day, Gp Capt 'Johnnie' Johnson therefore decided it was time to go and see the strip first hand. He recalled later,

> After swaying across the river on a very temporary wooden bridge, we drove through what remained of the little town of Wesel. Bomber Command had hammered this place a few hours before the assault and now it smouldered and stank in the warm sunshine. [...] The airfield, at a place called Damme [sic], was quite unsuitable; the ground being badly drained and water-logged. We could never operate our Spitfires from this site until it had thoroughly dried out, so I phoned the group commander and said it wasn't on.[48]

There it was; an executive decision to end the speculation. B.104 Damm was not to be, and the Wing's advance into Germany and across the Rhine was on hold for now. However, if they could not move to Damm, they needed to find another suitable base, close to the front, as soon as possible.

The decision could not have come sooner; the roads in the area were in an atrocious state and high winds and rain all day resulted in the mess tent being blown down during the afternoon. Fortunately, though, a new tent could be erected in its place in the early evening, in time for dinner.

'A' Echelon's work now ceased at Damm and they, and the other units there with them – 'A' Echelon of 39 (Recce) Wing, 3 AFAS, 6 (RCAF) MFPS, A Section of 426 RRU, and 2765, 2856, and 2876 Squadrons RAF Regiment – all waited for news on whether they would return to their respective airfields, or be sent elsewhere.

4 April 1945 – The weather cleared sufficiently at Eindhoven overnight to allow eleven aircraft up for a successful armed reconnaissance from 06:50. The sections split up and Red (Shepherd MV266, Chalmers MV249, Farfan RM797, Moyle RM931, Coleman RM915) headed for the Meppen area, whilst Blue Section, led by Flt Lt Peter Cowell made for the Lingen-Osnabrück area. A number of ground targets were found near Meppen, just 15km inside the German border, and around 18km north of Lingen, where a lorry, a staff car and a horse-drawn vehicle were damaged. Eight barges and two tugs were also damaged on nearby canals. Red Section landed again at 08:10 and Blue at 08:30.

The day's second and third operations were then not airborne until around eight hours later, when Flt Lt John Shepherd led four aircraft on an armed reconnaissance at 16:30, and Flt Lt Bill Stowe led a second quartet, airborne just ten minutes later. Shepherd's Red Section (Shepherd SM820, Kelly RN208, Jolly SM817, Whale RM928) enjoyed considerable success on the Dortmund-Ems Canal, where they claimed three tugs and eleven barges damaged, and also shot up a half-track near Nordhorn. They returned at 18:25, having been in the air for almost two hours.

Meanwhile, Stowe's Yellow Section (Stowe MV260, Smith MV267, Rake MV249, Hegarty RM915) were wreaking havoc of their own in the Nordhorn area and returned at 18:10 claiming one lorry and trailer destroyed, and three staff cars, a jeep, a motorcycle with sidecar, and two tugs damaged. This concluded the day's flying.

5 April 1945 – A busy day with five separate operations between 08:00 and 18:50, despite rain interrupting flying for a few hours.

The first two armed reconnaissances were airborne simultaneously at 08:00, when eleven aircraft focussed on the Meppen area. Flt Lt Peter Cowell led five aircraft designated Red Section (Cowell RN210, Scott SM820, Gray RM928, Jolly RM817, Whale RN208) to the north of the town whilst Flt Lt Bill Stowe took six aircraft designated Yellow Section (Stowe RM931, Smart RM915, Rake MV267, Smith RM759, Hegarty SM826, Wilkinson MV249) to the south of the town.

Red Section found several targets of opportunity and returned at 09:45 claiming eight barges, two MET and four half-tracks damaged near Wettrup. Yellow Section also enjoyed some success, claiming one MET destroyed and three damaged at Löningen and Lindern. However, they also came under attack by concentrated Flak at Meppen and Stowe's propeller was damaged. He was unhurt, but returned just ahead of the rest of the section. However, when they arrived back at Eindhoven few minutes later, Fg Off Roy Smith's engine cut on approach and he made a heavy, forced landing, which ended in a bomb crater just short of the strip. Thankfully, he was unhurt, but RM759 was considered to have sustained Cat. E damage.

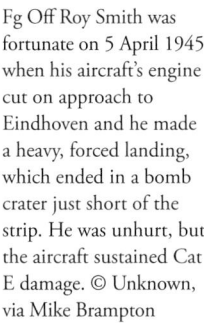

Fg Off Roy Smith was fortunate on 5 April 1945 when his aircraft's engine cut on approach to Eindhoven and he made a heavy, forced landing, which ended in a bomb crater just short of the strip. He was unhurt, but the aircraft sustained Cat E damage. © Unknown, via Mike Brampton

Rain then set in, which postponed further flying until just after midday, when Flt Lt John Shepherd (RM797) took up four pilots, despite the weather, for an armed reconnaissance of the Meppen-Quackenbrück area. Red and Blue Sections had no success whatsoever, and in fact it was "the enemy [that] did all the shooting"[49] instead: Shepherd's Spitfire was shaken by a close Flak burst and he found on his return at 13:20 that the machine had sustained damage in two places.

Flt Lt Stowe also led four aircraft on a weather reconnaissance at 16:05 and returned 40 minutes later with reports of very poor weather in the area they covered. Flt Lt Cowell also tried his luck at 18:00, when he led four aircraft on a patrol of the Rheine area. This operation was also thwarted by thunderstorms and, when they returned at 18:50, Plt Off Pat Coleman (RM915) reported that hail had broken his cine-camera and damaged the radiator grill. This concluded the day's flying.

During the day, the Squadron gained another new and very experienced pilot, when 25-year-old Australian Flt Lt F. A. O. 'Tony' Gaze DFC and Bar joined the Squadron from 83 GSU to take over command of A Flight.[50]

6 April 1945 – No operational flying all day due to unsuitable weather. However, news was received that the Wing would now remain in the Netherlands, but move north to B.106 Twente at first light the following morning instead.

By 12 April 1945, only No. 3 Aviation Fuel and Ammunition Section remained at Damm, in case of emergency landings by Allied aircraft, but they soon left and the proposed airfield site was abandoned, never to be used as a base by any Allied air force. Their parent unit, 407 AFAP, bemoaned the move,

> *The stocking of the site near WESEL had, as it turned out, been a waste of effort as the airfield was never used, and it became necessary to uplift all stocks again and push them forward to NIENBORG.*[51]

7 April 1945 – Flt Lt Tony Gaze got straight down to business and led Red Section of six aircraft on an armed reconnaissance at 09:05. Despite the improved weather, nothing was seen and it was felt that "the enemy [had] kept well under cover".[52] They returned at 10:20 with nothing to report.

Flt Lt Peter Cowell had taken up a second section of six aircraft at the same time as Gaze for an armed reconnaissance of the Meppen area. B Flight's Blue Section (Cowell MV260, Gray SM820, Lawrence NH832, Jolly SM817, Bødtker MV264, Whale RM697) enjoyed a little more success that Gaze's section, although two pilots, believed to have been 2 Lt Carl Bødtker and WO 'Vickie' Whale, returned around 30 minutes early with engine trouble. The rest of the section landed at 10:55 claiming three MET damaged.

This constituted the Squadron's, and indeed the Wing's, entire operational flying today, as the afternoon was spent moving to Twente. The Wing's 'A' Echelon arrived at their new base from Damm during the afternoon, following a journey of eight hours to cover a mere 55 miles, which is testament to the poor road conditions and heavy traffic.

Twente

Located just west of the German border, around 4km north of Enschede and 5km east of the town of Hengelo, at 52°16' N, 6° 53' E, Twente Aerodrome was a significant Luftwaffe base until early 1945. It had only been in Allied hands for a day at the time of the Wing's arrival, and this provided 41 Squadron the honour of being amongst the first Allied units to be based east of the Rhine.[53]

First impressions from Twente were encouraging. The Wing found the airfield and accommodation in good condition, with plenty of room for all and sufficient office furniture left behind. However, one surprise awaited them:

> *The wily Huns had placed 500 lb bombs in all the buildings but had omitted to explode them – a serious omission from their point of view.*[54]

These were soon cleared by the bomb disposal unit, but the main issue with the airfield were the three 5,100-foot strips, which were constructed of brick. They had been bombed by the Allied air forces on a number of occasions and, although they had been repaired, mismatching bricks had left the surfaces uneven and dangerous.

Fortunately, however, an area of grass lay on the airfield's eastern side, which was reasonably dry and of sufficient size to serve as a runway instead. Although it required constant maintenance, the grass strip proved successful and remained serviceable.

In the meantime, the airfield construction teams set about repairing two of the three runways, but they would not be completed until after the Wing's departure. A mobile flare path was also erected as a temporary measure, but in the end the permanent lighting was not repaired. The airfield otherwise had a good infrastructure, with brick taxi tracks and several small hangars on the airfield's eastern side. Water was available and accommodation provided in the barrack area. It was also well-connected, as the main road to Enschede led from the airfield's southeast corner, and a railway station was available nearby.

A camouflaged Flak tower at Twente in the Netherlands, to where 41 Squadron moved on 7 April 1945. © Gp Capt (ret) Derek S. V. Rake OBE AFC & Bar

125 Wing was not alone at Twente, as 124 Wing had also been moved forward with them. The Wings and their supporting units consisted of the following elements:[55]

B.106 Twente		
Wing	125 Wing	124 Wing
Squadrons	41, 130 and 350 Sqns	137, 181, 182 & 247 Sqns
Servicing Unit	6041, 6132 & 6350 SEs	6137, 6181, 6182 & 6247 SE
Repair & Salvage Units	409 RSU & Advanced Salvage Detachment (70 MTLRU)	
Refuelling & Rearming Unit	A Section, 426 RRU	
Stores Supply	401 ASP	406 ASP
Air Liaison Section	361 ALS	363 ALS
Hospital Unit	Advanced Surgical Detachment (50 MFH)	
Dental Units	108 MDS	117 MDS
RAF Regiment	2794 and 2876 Squadrons	
Bomb Disposal Unit	6225 BD Flight	
Signals Units	61 Wing Signals Section, and 5419J & 55064 CB MSUs	62 Wing Signals Section, and 5414J & 55063 CB MSUs

Benham Departs

As the Squadron moved to Twente, Sqn Ldr Benham left the Squadron, to be replaced by the present OC A Flight, Flt Lt John Shepherd. Douglas Benham had joined 41 Squadron in August 1944 on the recommendation of Commanding Officer of the Lympne Wing, Wg Cdr Colin Gray, who was asked to nominate a suitable Commanding Officer by 11 Group SASO, Air Cdre Cecil Bouchier [See also Chapter 6].

Tasked with cleaning up the Squadron and re-instilling discipline at a time when morale was low and discipline lax, Benham had successfully turned the Squadron around and had created a

Flt Lts Derek Rake and Bill Stowe RCAF relaxing between operations at Twente, early April 1945. The sign states in German, "Nur für Schwimmer" – Only for swimmers. © Gp Capt (ret) Derek S. V. Rake OBE AFC & Bar

coolly efficient and close-knit unit of men, with a respectable record. During Benham's tenure as Commanding Officer, three men had been killed in action, but none in flying accidents. Four had been shot down and captured, but only two had been wounded in action and five in flying accidents. However, during his watch, the Squadron's pilots had also claimed no less than 12 enemy aircraft destroyed and five damaged, and over 500 ground targets destroyed or damaged. It comes as no surprise, then, that he was awarded a Bar to his DFC, fittingly, on VE Day.

He was a popular Commanding Officer, and "everyone was sad to see him go".[56] His successor, John Shepherd, had joined the Squadron approximately one month prior to his promotion, but had been associated with 41 Squadron as a member of 125 Wing since January 1945. It was, perhaps, an odd time to be handing over, respectively taking over, command – with the Squadron in the thick of the final push towards Berlin, and only one month prior to the cessation of hostilities, as it was – and it was certainly a case of being 'thrown in the deep end' for Shepherd during the Squadron's most intensive period since the Battle of Britain, but he would rise to the challenge and become as respected as Benham.[57]

8 April 1945 – Operations got off to an early, albeit abortive, start from the new base. At 06:35, Flt Lt Tony Gaze led a section into the air, but within five minutes – and with only Flt Lts Derek Rake and Bill Stowe airborne beside himself – the mission was abandoned, as it was found that the cloud base had dropped to only 100 feet. However, the situation improved throughout the morning, and by the end of the day another five patrols (28 sorties) had been flown in the Nienburg area, which enjoyed some success against rolling stock.

Op.	Section	A/C	Led by	Timings
1	Red	6	Shepherd	11:30-13:15
2	Blue	6	Cowell	13:10-14:30
3	Red	4	Gaze	15:15-16:25
4	Blue	6	Jolly	16:30-18:20
5	Red	6	Gaze	18:10-19:45

On the first of these, Red Section (Shepherd MV266, Hegarty RM792, Stowe RM931, Smith RM696, Rake MV254, Smart SM817) spotted two locomotives pulling tankers, east of the Weser River. Shepherd split the Section and sent three pilots to attack one, led by Flt Lt Bill Stowe, whilst he took on the second with the remaining two pilots.

LEFT Sqn Ldr Doug Benham DFC AFC ended his tenure as OC 41 Squadron on 8 Aparil 1945, and was awarded a Bar to his DFC on 8 May 1945. He retired from the RAF on 30 December 1957, following 30 months as Wg Cdr Ops in Aden. © 41 Squadron RAF

RIGHT The Wings, Caterpillar Club badge and medals of Wg Cdr Douglas I. Benham. They include the Officer of the Order of the British Empire (Military), Distinguished Flying Cross with Bar, Air Force Cross, 1939-1945 Star, Air Crew Europe Star with France and Germany clasp, Africa Star with North Africa 1942-43 clasp, Defence Medal, War Medal 1939-1945, Coronation Medal 1953, and Air Efficiency Award. © Benham family

Stowe's section damaged the locomotive and six tankers, but they did not catch fire, so were likely empty. Shepherd's section, however, had more success and "within a very short space of time, the entire train was ablaze".[58] They claimed the locomotive, 12 tankers and two coaches destroyed.

During the afternoon, other sections – the ORB does not identify them – also claimed another locomotive and six trucks damaged. Entries on several *Pilot Service Records* suggest these may have been claimed on Blue Section's 16:30 patrol, thereunder one MET destroyed and another damaged in the Nienburg area by WO 'Vickie' Whale, and on Red Section's 18:10 patrol. This concluded another long day's flying.[59]

9 April 1945 – As a result of haze and low cloud, the day was relatively quiet for the Squadron and included only three operations, the first of which was not airborne until 15:40. At that time, Flt Lt Peter Cowell led Blue Section of six aircraft (Cowell MV260, Kelly NH832, Jolly SM817, Jallands SM826, Fisher SM820, Gray MV264) on a patrol between Meppen and Fürstenau. They returned at 17:25 claiming six MET damaged in the Meppen area.

The second operation saw Sqn Ldr Shepherd leading Red Section of six aircraft on a sweep of the Oldenburg-Emden area at 16:05, but they returned at 17:25 with nothing to report. The third and last operation, a sweep from Meppen to Bramsche at 19:00, was led by Flt Lt Gaze, and consisted of six aircraft designated Red Section. No suitable ground targets could be located, chiefly as a result of poor visibility, and although several aircraft had been seen, investigation revealed they were all friendly. The section returned at 20:45, having not fired a shot.

10 April 1945 – Owing to good weather, it was a busy day for the Wing, but although 84 sorties were flown, it was relatively uneventful. Patrols were undertaken by the Squadron to the Borstel-Dümmer Lake area at 09:10 led Flt Lt Tony Gaze, at 12:00 led by Flt Lt Tom Lawrence, and at 18:00 led by Flt Lt Arnold Jolly. All three returned with nothing to report.

At 15:55, however, Wg Cdr Keefer led Black Section of six aircraft (Keefer, Lawrence NH832, Kelly RN208, Gray MV264, Hegarty RM790, Chalmers RM696) on a successful freelance patrol to the Celle-Wietzenbruch area, the first time they had ventured so far north-east. Unbeknown to them at the time, however, they would soon be based in the region. Several ground targets were attacked, including two large lorries destroyed and four MET damaged in the Fassberg area, and five railway trucks set on fire and destroyed and ten more damaged on a siding in the Visselhövede-Soltau area. Although another locomotive was spotted, the section was out of ammunition by this time, so they left it alone and returned to base at 17:30.

A final operation was mounted at 18:40, when Sqn Ldr Shepherd led Red Section of five aircraft (Shepherd NH832, Smith MV254, Gaze RM792, Stowe SM823, Whale RM915) on a freelance patrol north of Nienburg. On the Bremen-Hamburg railway line, near Metzendorf, rolling stock was attacked and two locomotives and ten railway trucks were damaged. Although not mentioned in the ORB, WO Vic Whale's *Pilot Service Record* suggests that six MET were also damaged at Nienburg. There was brief excitement when an Ar234 was chased, but its superior speed enabled its escape and the section returned to Twente at 20:30.

Separately, two new pilots joined the Squadron today, 23-year-old Yorkshireman WO Peter Wheatley and 25-year-old Palestinian Flt Sgt Aharon Remez. Wheatley had joined the RAFVR in July 1941 and completed SFTS in Canada before returning to the United Kingdom to attend 57 OTU. Remez, who had been in the United States at the outbreak of War, joined the RAFVR in December 1942 and completed almost all his flying training in Canada, before travelling to the United Kingdom to attend 53 OTU. Though Wheatley had already logged 1,300 flying hours, and Remez 400, their postings to 41 Squadron constituted the first for both to an operational unit.

Despite joining the unit within a month of the end of the War, Remez was a man destined for great things. Within three years of joining 41 Squadron as an NCO pilot, he would become a Brigadier General and the Commanding Officer of the fledgling Israeli Air Force. WO John Chalmers remembers him with great admiration,

> *The most interesting pilot in the squadron was Aharon Remez. By a long way. An Israeli. He was better educated, more mature, more intelligent and certainly more interesting than the rest of us. Known as Ron or Rem. A delightful man. Looked like a pugilist. […] A great fellow… a lovely man.*[60]

11 April 1945 – It proved to be a long and busy day, with eight patrols (33 sorties) of the Bremen-Nienburg area flown by the Squadron, between 06:25 and 20:50. Upon the conclusion of each patrol, the sections were released to undertake freelance sweeps for ground targets of opportunity.

Flt Lt John Shepherd DFC* joined 41 Squadron as OC A Flight, on 7 March 1945, and was promoted to OC 41 Squadron on Sqn Ldr Douglas Benham's departure on 8 April 1945. He remained with the Squadron until 22 January 1946 when he was killed in a flying accident. © John McGill

Flt Lt Tony Gaze DFC* was posted to 41 Squadron on 5 April 1945, and was promoted to OC A Flight three days later on Flt Lt John Shepherd's succession to the command of 41 Squadron. He served with the Squadron until 1 May 1945, during which time he claimed one and one shared destroyed FW190s, one destroyed Ju52, and one shared destroyed Ar234; via John Foreman

It was a successful day, as far as attacks were concerned, and it marked the first time in two weeks that the Squadron claimed a victory against the Luftwaffe.

The first patrol was airborne at 06:25, when Flt Lt Peter Cowell led Blue Section of six aircraft. They returned at 08:20 claiming one MET and one horse-drawn vehicle damaged.

The second patrol, consisting of four aircraft led by Flt Lt Tony Gaze, was more successful. Airborne at 08:50, Red Section (Gaze SM823, Hegarty SM826, Coleman MV264, Wilkinson RM931) attacked rolling stock northeast of Bremen, on the Ottersburg-Sottrum and Mahndorf-Achim lines. On the former railway line, two locomotives were damaged and on the latter a third.

A short while later, whilst diving to attack a fourth locomotive west of Ottersburg, Flt Lt Gaze spotted a lone three-engined Ju52 transport aircraft flying east at an altitude of just 200 feet, approximately one mile south of the railway line. His own height at the time was only 500 feet as he was already in a dive on the locomotive. He took a quick parting shot at the locomotive, then pulled out and gave chase.

Gaze drew to within 300 yards of the Junkers before opening fire from astern at 30°, then kept his finger on the button he closed to just 50 yards. His shells struck the aircraft along the fuselage and hit the port engine, which immediately caught fire. He pulled up and out of the attack and looked back to see it turn hard to port and crash in flames in a ploughed field.

"Two men got out of the wreckage and ran away," reports the ORB, "while F/Lt Gaze gave it another burst to keep it burning."[61] Red 2, Fg Off Frank Hegarty, also strafed at the aircraft whilst on the ground, and the section returned to Twente at 10:20, where Gaze claimed it destroyed. He now had ten victories to his credit.

The six subsequent patrols of the Bremen-Nienburg area were mostly uneventful. These consisted of Blue Section of four aircraft at 10:20, led by Flt Lt Jolly; Red Section of four aircraft at 12:40, led by Flt Lt Stowe; Blue Section of four aircraft at 15:00, led by Flt Lt Cowell; Red Section of four aircraft at 16:50, led by Flt Lt Gaze; Blue Section of four aircraft at 18:25, led by 2 Lt Bødtker; and finally an undesignated trio consisting of Wg Cdr Keefer, Sqn Ldr Shepherd and Flt Lt Roy Fisher at 18:25.

During these patrols, an Ar234 and an Me262 were chased over Bremen, but without success, and a total of one MET was destroyed and six damaged.[62] Flt Sgt Remez and WO Wheatley also made their first operational flights during the afternoon and evening.

Separately, Sqn Ldr Terry Spencer returned to 350 Squadron to take over command of the unit today, following his capture, internment and subsequent escape from captivity. Sqn Ldr Frank Woolley, who had taken over 350 Squadron on Spencer's loss, was now posted to command 130 Squadron, when that unit's Commanding Officer, Sqn Ldr Martin Hume, was posted home, his tour expired. This resulted in the strange coincidence that the Wing's three squadrons – 41, 130 and 350 – were all commanded by present or past 41 Squadron officers.

THIS SPREAD AND FOLLOWING 3 PAGES
As 125 Wing advanced through the Netherlands and into Germany, the destruction wrought on the Luftwaffe by Allied air forces become more and more evident. © Gp Capt (ret) Derek S. V. Rake OBE AFC & Bar

Palestinian Flt Sgt (later WO) Aharon Remez served with 41 Squadron from 10 April 1945 to 31 March 1946. He became a Brigadier General and served as the first Commander of the Israeli Air Force from July 1948 to December 1950. Remez was also the Israeli Ambassador to the United Kingdom from May 1965 to July 1970. © John A. Chalmers

12 April 1945 – Another busy day, with seven operations (32 sorties) flown in the Delmenhorst-Verden and Bremen-Rethem areas between 08:20 and 21:05. These consisted of Red Section of four aircraft at 08:20, led by Flt Lt Gaze; Blue Section of four aircraft at 10:05, led by Flt Lt Jolly; Red Section of four aircraft at 12:15, led by Sqn Ldr Shepherd; Blue Section of four aircraft at 14:05, led by Flt Lt Cowell; Red Section of four aircraft at 16:15, led by Flt Lt Gaze; Blue Section of four aircraft at 17:25, led by Flt Lt Lawrence; and Red Section of two aircraft at 19:45, led by Flt Lt Cowell. Most of the patrols were uneventful, although the Squadron claimed one locomotive, two railway trucks and one MET damaged for the day.[63]

On the fifth patrol, however, the Squadron intercepted the Luftwaffe for the second time in just two days. At around 17:00, Flt Lt Tony Gaze was leading Red Section (Gaze SM823, Wilkinson SM826, Rake MV267, Chalmers RM915) on a patrol of the Delmenhorst-Verden area at 8,000 feet, when his No. 2, Flt Lt Johnnie Wilkinson, sighted an Arado 234 *Blitz* at the same altitude at nine o'clock, heading south, approximately five miles west of Bremen. Flt Lt Gaze dropped his 45-gallon jettison tank, and immediately gave chase.

The Ar234 must have seen Gaze coming, as the pilot made the fatal error of turning 180° to head north again. Gaze took the advantage and cut the corner, closing quickly to 800 yards where he opened fire and obtained immediate strikes on the jet's fuselage and starboard wing. He continued firing whilst closing further, striking the aircraft repeatedly and causing the starboard engine to catch fire. Gaze was within 100 yards of the aircraft by the time he was forced to break off the attack, when the Arado's pilot took wild evasive action and flicked over to avoid the stream of fire from the Spitfire's guns. The aircraft "spun violently down flicking one way and then another"[64] reported Gaze, until it disappeared into the haze at 1,000 feet.

Gaze left it to its fate but Red 3, Flt Lt Derek Rake, followed it down to confirm its destruction. He saw instead that the Arado recovered at barely 300 feet, on the south-eastern outskirts of Bremen, and closed in to finish it off himself. However, the Ar234 pilot cleverly manoeuvred his damaged aircraft over an aerodrome but Rake continued on through the light Flak that rose to meet him, and closed to 800 yards. At this distance, he opened fire and kept his finger on the firing button until the gap between them was just 100 yards.

Rake saw his fire strike the aircraft along the length of the fuselage and caused the port engine to catch fire. He recalls,

I was flying Spit XIV [EB-]G on that sortie and even now have it clearly in my mind that the gyro gunsight fitted in this aircraft helped me to open fire at the range and angle off so that my 1st burst hit the Arado's port engine and smoke came from it.[65]

Now fatally damaged, the pilot attempted to force-land his stricken machine in a field near Huchting, 5km southwest of Bremen. However, it blew up on impact and Gaze and Rake returned to Twente claiming the Ar234 shared destroyed. It was Gaze's eleventh victory and Rake's first.[66]

A Junkers Ju52/3m similar to this was shot down over Ottersburg, Germany, by Flt Lt Tony Gaze on 11 April 1945. © Unknown, author's collection

On 12 April 1945, 83 Group was spread over six airfields in Holland and Germany, as shown in the below table.[67]

Airfield	Occupied by	Squadrons
B.110 Achmer	121 & 143 (RCAF) Wing	175, 184 & 245 Sqns. (RAF) and 438, 439 & 440 Sqns. (RCAF)
B.114 Diepholz	Under Construction	N/A
B.100 Goch	127 (RCAF) Wing	403, 416, 421 & 443 Sqns. (RCAF)
B.88 Heesch	126 (RCAF) Wing	401, 402, 411 & 412 Sqns. (RCAF)
B.112 Hopsten	122 Wing & 83 GCS	3, 56, 80 & 486 (RNZAF) Sqns.
B.108 Rheine	39 (Recce) Wing	400, 414 & 430 Sqns. (RCAF)
B.106 Twente	124 and 125 Wings	137, 181, 182 & 247 Sqns., and 41, 130, 350 Sqns.

13 April 1945 – On this busy but relatively quiet day, six patrols (24 sorties) were undertaken in the Bremen-Rethem area between 10:30 and 20:05. These consisted of Blue Section of four aircraft at 10:30, led by Sqn Ldr Shepherd; Red Section of four aircraft at 12:40, led by Flt Lt Gaze; Blue Section of four aircraft at 14:30, led by Flt Lt Cowell; Red Section of four aircraft at 15:55, led by Flt Lt Gaze; Blue Section of four aircraft at 16:40, led by Flt Lt Lawrence; and Red Section of four aircraft at 18:30, led by Sqn Ldr Shepherd.

Most sorties were uneventful, with the exception of two MET damaged at Rottenburg by Flt Lts Tony Gaze (MV254) and Bill Stowe (RM915) on the 12:40 patrol, and a three-ton lorry destroyed at Bremen by Flt Lt Johnnie Wilkinson (MV249) on the 15:55 patrol, which "blew up with a large explosion".[68] In fact, these three ground victories were the only ones claimed by the entire Wing all day.

14 April 1945 – It was a much quieter day today, with just four patrols airborne in the Delmenhorst-Nienburg and Bremen areas, the first of which was not in the air until mid-afternoon. These consisted of Red Section of four aircraft at 15:45, led by Flt Lt Gaze; Blue Section of four aircraft

Escape kit photograph of Flt Lt Derek Rake, who claimed a shared destroyed Arado Ar234 with Flt Lt Tony Gaze on 12 April 1945. © 41 Squadron RAF

at 17:45, led by Flt Lt Roy Fisher; Red Section of four aircraft at 18:45, led by Sqn Ldr Shepherd; and Red Section of four aircraft at 19:30, led by Flt Lt Gaze. The first, second and last patrols were uneventful, but the third proved quite successful for Sqn Ldr Shepherd.

A Double Victory

On the day's third operation, Red Section (Shepherd SM825, Farfan RM792, Jolly SM817, Kelly RN210) was airborne at 18:45 for an armed reconnaissance of the Bremen area, but Flt Lt 'Fanny' Farfan was forced to return to base early with engine trouble. Shortly after Farfan's departure, however, Sqn Ldr Shepherd claimed an impressive, if somewhat unusual, double victory.

On their way home, the remaining trio passed over Nordholz Aerodrome at 7,000 feet just before 20:00, when two Luftwaffe aircraft were seen taking off in an unusual line astern fashion. Diving down for a closer look, Shepherd recognised them as an Me110 towing a rocket-powered Me163 *Komet* at an altitude of just 100 feet. It is believed to have been the first time the Squadron had encountered such an aircraft.

Labouring under the weight, the vulnerable Me110 was still at a relatively low speed, but Shepherd's was almost too great. Almost over-shooting, he fired a quick but accurate burst at the Me110 before pulling out his dive.

> *I was closing very rapidly but managed to get a short burst in, on the Me110, obtaining a strike on port engine and cockpit. The 110 went into a left hand diving turn, turning over onto its back, and crashed into a field, bursting into flames.*[69]

The *Komet*'s pilot released the tow line, but was unable to escape. The aircraft had neither the speed nor altitude to rescue itself, and made a wide, earthward dive to port, which ended when it hit the ground about three fields from where the Me110 had come down.[70] Shepherd returned to Twente with Jolly and Kelly at 20:25, where he claimed both aircraft destroyed. Shepherd is believed to have been the only RAF pilot to have destroyed an Me163 in the air, although it was not under its own rocket power at the time. Having not met the Luftwaffe for two weeks, the Squadron had now destroyed an average of one aircraft per day over the last four days; things were heating up again.

Separately, the Wing's next move was announced today; at last they would be moving into Germany. A reconnaissance party left Twente today bound for B.118 Celle in Lower Saxony.

Warrant Officers John Chalmers, 'Vickie' Whale, Hugh Kelly and Peter Hale, Celle or Kastrup, April-May 1945.
© Rossow family

Nominal Roll, April 1945

The following list has been extracted from an undated document, merely titled *Nominal Roll. 41 Squadron.*, held in 41 Squadron's Archives. The Roll must date from between 10 April 1945, when Flt Sgt Aharon Remez and WO Peter Wheatley joined the Squadron, and 17 April, when WO Peter Hale returned from his attachment to 83 GSU. Pilots' names are listed in the order they appear on the original document. Minor corrections have been made by the author.

104447	Sqn Ldr	J.B.	Shepherd	DFC & Bar
60096	Flt Lt	F.A.O.	Gaze	DFC & Bar
124530	Flt Lt	P.	Cowell	
J.1064	Flt Lt	W. M.	Stowe	
NZ411494	Flt Lt	T. E.	Lawrence	
124494	Flt Lt	D.S.V.	Rake	
116826	Flt Lt	A.W.	Jolly	
NZ412671	Flt Lt	R.R.G.	Fisher	
150189	Flt Lt	J.F.	Wilkinson	
164846	Fg Off	W.J.	Jallands	
A414020	Fg Off	E.	Gray	
157691	Fg Off	F.W.	Farfan	
164845	Fg Off	R.D.A.	Smith	
164406	Fg Off	F.M.	Hegarty	
190167	Plt Off	R.	Fleming	
190247	Plt Off	P.T.	Coleman	
1619	2 Lt	C.S.	Bødtker	

1348985	WO	I.T.	Stevenson	
1332528	WO	P.H.	Hale	(Attached GSU)
785066	WO	J.A.	Chalmers	
1376359	WO	F.V.	Whale	
A414835	WO	V.J.	Rossow	
1537032	WO	P.E.	Wheatley	
1318817	Flt Sgt	H.F.	Kelly	
1338427	Flt Sgt	L.H.	Smart	
A437353	Flt Sgt	C.N.	Moyle	
1001096	Flt Sgt	W.R.	Pairman	N/E (Awaiting posting)
605523	Flt Sgt	A.	Remez	
1624619	Sgt Plt	P.F.	Scott	

OFFICERS & AIRMEN GROUND STAFF

139601	Flt Lt	H.	Anderson	Medical Officer
136130	Fg Off	A.	McAllister	[Adjutant]
1197888	Sgt	E.	Fullam	Fitter IIE (Continuity NCO)
1629100	LAC	J.S.	Matcher	Clk./GD
2225675	AC2	B.	Roberts	Ach/GD (Batman)
3216283	AC2	E.	Weldon	Ach/FM (Batman)

A second document, from around the same period, allocates R/T Call Signs, similar to the list of late December 1944 [see chapter 8], but places pilots in their respective flights. It appears to date from slightly earlier than the above document as Flt Lt Tony Gaze's name appears on the document typewritten, but Remez and Wheatley handwritten, suggesting the original must have been originally compiled between 6 and 10 April 1945. Leaving away the call signs this time, as well as the ranks and initials to avoid repetition of the above, the Flight allocation is shown below, with pilots listed in the order the appear on the document. An asterisk (*) has been added to a few names by the author to indicate they were added to the type-written list by hand.

A Flight	B Flight
Gaze	Cowell
Stowe	Lawrence
Rake	Gray
Wilkinson	Fisher
Hegarty	Jallands
Smith	Fleming
Coleman	Rossow
Stevenson	Clanzy
Moyle	Whale
Smart	Kelly
Chalmers*	Bødtker*
Farfan*	Jolly*
Remez*	Scott*
	Wheatley*

41 Squadron Spitfire XIV, EB-R, taxiing, location unknown, early 1945. © Rossow family

15 April 1945 – Poor weather today restricted flying to a total of just five minutes by four aircraft. Flt Lt Tom Lawrence led Blue Section of four aircraft off the deck at 08:00 for a patrol to Bremen, but they returned just five minutes later, realising the weather was too poor to continue. This concluded the day's flying.

Following the Reconnaissance Party's departure for Celle the previous day, 'A' Echelon headed out at 07:30 this morning to join them.

> *The journey was uneventful but was even longer than expected owing to detours on account of demolished bridges over canals and railways. However the convoy arrived safe and sound at 1900 hours and to their delight found the airfield buildings undamaged although in a pretty poor mess after the army had systematically ransacked them. The area is well wooded and quite attractive.*[71]

Victory in their Sights

16 April – 31 May 1945

10

16 April 1945 – Improved weather brought increased activity by the Wing today and 41 Squadron completed five patrols to the Bremen-Rethem area between 07:45 and 17:30, totalling 19 sorties. The weather was still clearing as the first patrol took off and this caused them to be diverted to Nijmegen on their return. However, this proved disastrous for one of the pilots.

Red Section (Gaze SM823, Rake MV254, Farfan RN210, Chalmers RN208) was airborne at 07:45 for an uneventful patrol, but the weather affected their return to such an extent that their fuel ran too low to make it back to Twente. Flt Lts Tony Gaze and Derek Rake, and Fg Off 'Fanny' Farfan, all landed safely at Nijmegen at 10:05, but WO John Chalmers' fuel ran out short of the aerodrome and he force-landed his aircraft by the Arnhem-Emmerich railway line.[1] He recalled,

> *I was in a section of 4, led by Tony Gaze…. I was number 4 in the section and this meant I would use more fuel than the others, inevitably, because I was on the outside of all turns with a wider radius and more distance to catch up, using the finger four formation. Hence I was the first to call up to say I was running short of fuel. […] we were, not to put gloss on it, not entirely aware of our position. I eventually ran out of fuel, and made a forced landing. Not really my fault. One of the others in the section had his engine stop just after successfully landing.*
>
> *It was a misty morning, as I recall, and under these conditions visibility is quite good looking down. What I hadn't experienced up till then was that visibility at lower heights and seen almost horizontally is very different and very much reduced. So I had a problem finding the field I had picked out in the first place in which to land. The area I eventually found myself approaching was smaller than I would have wished for with a large embankment at the end. I finished up striking the embankment with some force and ended up straddling a railway track. I had no idea where I was in relation to the front line and hoped I wasn't in German occupied territory. Then a figure appeared and said "Ali?". I think that may have meant was I an ally. I said, "Deutsch?" He shook his head, to my relief and said "cigarette?". Ah, that universal word. An army jeep then arrived, took me off for breakfast and then back to the aerodrome.*[2]

Blue Section was next airborne at 09:45, led by Flt Lt Roy Fisher, Yellow Section at 11:45, led by Sqn Ldr Shepherd, Blue Section at 13:45, led by Flt Lt Arnold Jolly, and finally Red Section at 15:50, led by Flt Lt Tony Gaze. These were generally uneventful, although one MET was destroyed; it is not clear by whom. Meanwhile, over at Celle,

> *'A' Echelon spent the day feverishly setting up shop and cleaning out the buildings. The officers' mess is on the 'grand scale' and includes a swimming pool which at the moment is full of very dirty water.*[3]

Their work was quickly done and during the late afternoon 41, 130 and 350 Squadrons flew a 35-minute transfer to their new aerodrome, B.118, just southwest of the town of Celle, thereby becoming the first Allied air units to be based east of the Weser. Boasting a population of some 40,000 at the beginning of the War, foreign labourers and refugees from various parts of the crumbling Reich had swollen the populace by another 50%.

There was little time for many of 41 Squadron's men to settle in as four pilots were sent on patrol of the area from 18:50, led by Flt Lt Tom Lawrence. This appears to have been in response to two incidents during the day when enemy aircraft flew over the airfield and were engaged by Allied anti-aircraft fire. However, the patrol was uneventful and the quartet returned at 20:35 with nothing to report.

There was one final patrol before the end of this busy day, when Wg Cdr Keefer led a sweep of the Parchim-Schwerin area. On their return leg, they intercepted the Luftwaffe once again and, after a feisty little battle, came home victorious.

Black Section (Keefer MV257, Wilkinson MV249, Shepherd MV267, Rake RM696, Farfan RM792, Jolly RM915) took off at 19:50 and headed northeast for the Schwerin area. The outbound journey was uneventful, but at around 20:20 on their way back to Celle, whilst at 7,000 feet heading southwest towards Hagenow, Sqn Ldr Shepherd spotted three FW190s flying 3,000 feet below them, but ahead and to their starboard on a parallel course. Perfectly positioned, Shepherd notified Keefer and Black Section dived upon them.

However, the three Luftwaffe pilots saw them coming and broke formation, two to port and one to the deck. Shepherd, flying Black 3, went after the latter of these, and with his superior speed was soon in close enough range to open fire. He immediately saw strikes on the engine, which spewed thick black smoke, and stalled. Shepherd had to break away to avoid hitting him, but looked back to see the pilot bale out at about 500 feet. The FW190 fell to the ground and exploded and, unfortunately, the pilot fared no better when his parachute failed to open.

Simultaneously, Black 2, Flt Lt Johnnie Wilkinson, went after the pair that broke to port, and turned inside them. Choosing the starboard of the two aircraft, Wilkinson closed to 250 yards, where he opened up with a two-second burst whilst still in the turn. His fire immediately struck home and he recognised hits on the port side of both the engine and cockpit.

However, Wilkinson's speed was too great and he overshot, passing under the tail of the Focke-Wulf as it continued to turn away from him. He braked hard and straightened his turn to bring him directly behind the aircraft again. From this position, he opened fire anew, streaming a long, seven-second burst into the 190's engine and cockpit area. This had the desired effect and the aircraft started spewing oil, which quickly covered Wilkinson's windscreen.

Despite his limited visibility, he almost blindly fired at the aircraft a final time, and then watched it make "a gentle dive into a field between two woods… and burst into 200 yards of flame".[4] This constituted Wilkinson's first victory.

Black 1, Wg Cdr Keefer, had meanwhile gone after the last of the trio, but this pilot proved more difficult to catch. Though he had initially closed on the aircraft and seen his fire strike its mark, the FW190 continued on, cleverly flying through his own Flak over Hagenow Airfield for protection. Keefer followed the Luftwaffe pilot across the airfield once, but when he turned to go back through it a second time, Keefer decided to quit whilst he was ahead and broke off his attack.

The six pilots formed up again and headed back to Celle, where they landed at 20:55, Shepherd and Wilkinson claiming their FW190s destroyed, and Keefer his damaged. However, there was one final twist when Flt Lt Derek Rake formally reported seeing "3 separate explosions and fires on the ground… and concluded that all three aircraft had been destroyed."[5] Whether the third pilot was shot down by his own Flak over Hagenow Airfield or whether he was downed as a result of Wg Cdr Keefer's fire is pure speculation, but it should be noted that Keefer only claimed his FW190 damaged and there is no annotation on his Combat Report to suggest any change was made to his claim, or indeed any elevation sought at all.

A New Base in Germany

Celle Aerodrome was located in the state of Niedersachsen, just 35km northeast of Hanover, and only a few days previously had still been in enemy hands. Known locally as *Fliegerhorst* [Aerodrome] *Celle-Wietzenbruch*, it had been cleared by elements of the 15th Scottish Division on 12 April, and 125 Wing now became the first Allied unit to be based there.

The aerodrome was originally created in secrecy during Germany's military build-up of the 1930s. Ground was first broken in early 1933, and its real purpose disguised by the announcement of the building of an airfield for the 'German Air Sport Association'. Following intensive work to turn the boggy ground into a useable airstrip, it quickly became a flying school with the capacity for some 60 aircraft.

Flying began early in 1934 and by the end of the year four large hangars were also completed and brought into service. A fifth hangar complex, which included administrative offices, was finished a year later. The aerodrome soon became home to a so-called 'A School' that trained pilots on single-engined, two-seater monoplanes and biplanes up to 2,000kg, such as the Heinkel He45, He46, He72 *Kadett* and Focke-Wulf FW44 *Stieglitz*. The base accommodated approximately 100 students, 25 instructors, and a large number of technical and logistics personnel.

Allied aircraft, including Spitfires of 41 Squadron, parked on Celle Aerodrome, Germany, late April or early May 1945. © Gp Capt (ret) Derek S. V. Rake OBE AFC & Bar

In 1936, the school was expanded and became a 'B School' for single-engined aircraft above 2,000kg. It then became home to the high-winged Focke-Wulf FW56 *Stösser* trainer, and subsequently the Arado Ar96 trainer and the Junkers multi-purpose W33 and W34 monoplanes.

Celle was later re-classified and renamed *Flugzeugführerschule-C* (*FFS-C*) [Pilot School C], which trained pilots on single and multiple-engined aircraft over 2,500kg. Celle then began training pilots on Germany's largest military aircraft at the time, the Junkers Ju52 passenger aircraft and the Ju86, Dornier Do17 and Heinkel He111 bombers. So much for the German Air Sport Association! The school continued at Celle until late summer 1939, when it was moved to Leipzig.

After the commencement of the War, Celle was generally only used as a short-term home for various squadrons, such as *Stuka-Geschwader* [Dive-Bomber Wing] 77, which was stationed here during winter 1939-1940. Others just came for refresher courses. In the later War years, it was also often used as a refuelling and ammunition replenishment depot by fighters of German home defence squadrons.

The last unit to be stationed at Celle was *FFS-A52* which arrived on 20 January 1945 from Danzig, via a short stay in Halberstadt, and was disbanded in Celle on 15 March, almost four weeks before the town was occupied.

However, there were still approximately 100 ground personnel left at the airfield until just a day prior to its capture. They made no attempt to destroy its infrastructure before to their departure, and left behind a single Flight Sergeant as caretaker, who handed over the facility without a shot being fired when Allied troops arrived on 12 April.

Four days later, whilst the 15th Scottish Division were still in the thick of the battle for Uelzen, just 50km to the northeast, 41 Squadron touched down at Celle-Wietzenbruch Aerodrome, which was now designated 'B.118 Celle'. It was the unit's first base in Germany and was of great strategic importance. The Squadron's previous three bases had been in the Netherlands, which were initially located close enough to the targets they were sent to attack. However, the further east the front moved into Germany, the more serious became the issue of the Spitfire's range. 125 Wing's arrival at Celle now placed them just 225 kilometres by air due west of Berlin.

41 Squadron's WO Peter Hale recalls Celle was a large airfield with a fully surfaced runway. They were accommodated in very comfortable Luftwaffe quarters that were well furnished and undamaged, and included a 'nice NCO's mess' and good food. However, most of the base's mobile equipment was either destroyed by the retreating Luftwaffe or advancing British troops, including a cellar of wine that was completely destroyed. WO John Chalmers had similar recollections:

The aircrew rest area in a Nissen hut at Celle, Germany, April 1945. © Gp Capt (ret) Derek S. V. Rake OBE AFC & Bar

RAF Nissen huts amongst farm buildings at Celle, April 1945. © Gp Capt (ret) Derek S. V. Rake OBE AFC & Bar

Celle was an oddly shaped aerodrome. Very large dispersal area as I recall. Good runway. Excellent living conditions and facilities. The German Air Force looked after its own very well indeed. Many surprising details… there was a skittles alley in or next to the bar. Another feature which surprised and amused us was a facility for vomiting. A vomitarium! Where an over indulged drinker could relieve himself and make space for more to come. The crew accommodation likewise was very good indeed. You did get the feeling they were the elite. We enjoyed taking advantage.[6]

In his autobiography, Gp Capt 'Johnnie' Johnson also recalls the ample facilities, which included centrally heated messes, spacious workshops, a cinema, a swimming pool, and an Officers' Mess with a fine dining room and beer cellar with murals depicting the history of the Luftwaffe. He also remembers the vomiting basins referred to by John Chalmers, called *Brechbecken*, and explains they were located in the beer cellar's lavatories, made of porcelain with chrome grab handles on each side, and had extra-large drainage holes for obvious reasons!

The Wing and its supporting echelons settling in at Celle today consisted of the following units:[7]

B.118 Celle	
Wing	125 Wing
Squadrons	41, 130 and 350 Squadrons
Servicing Units	6041, 6132 & 6350 SEs
Repair & Salvage Unit	409 RSU (Detachment with 39 (Recce) Wing)
Refuelling & Rearming Unit	A Section, 426 RRU
Stores Supply	401 ASP
Air Liaison Unit	361 ALS
Medical Unit	B Flight, 1 CAEU (2 Group)
Dental Unit	108 MDS
RAF Regiment	2875 and 2876 Squadrons
Signals Units	61 Wing Signals Section, and 5419J & 55064 CB MSUs

During the 24 days that 41 Squadron called Celle home, it is believed that around ten other squadrons shared the airfield with them: 130, 137, 175, 245, 350, 414 Recce (RCAF), 438 (RCAF), 439 (RCAF), 440 (RCAF) and 486 (RNZAF). With so much traffic, one of the ground crews' and engineers' first jobs was to extend the runway by 300 metres with steel plating.

Now based in potentially hostile territory, however, the servicemen were wary of the residents and generally did not go off base or into the town, nor did they socialise with the locals. Nonetheless, when they found that Bergen-Belsen Concentration Camp was located nearby, a number of men took the opportunity to witness the atrocities with their own eyes.

Bergen-Belsen

Located approximately 20km north-northwest of Celle Aerodrome as the crow flies, the proximity of Bergen-Belsen led many airmen to visit the camp to see it for themselves. Not all men made the journey, but 350 Squadron actually took a day off from flying to go there. They were struck by the indescribable stench of the camp, which was noticeable down-wind from several kilometres away.

Initially built in 1940 as a Prisoner of War Camp for French and Belgian POWs, the camp was designated Stalag XI-C and intended to house no more than 600 men. Then, after the launch of Operation *Barbarossa*, the camp was transformed to house Russian prisoners instead. Between the arrival of the first Russians in summer 1941, and spring 1942, conditions in the camp deteriorated, primarily due to over-crowding and it is reported that up to 18,000 of these men died of hunger, disease and exposure to the elements.

In early 1943, Bergen-Belsen was taken over by the *SS-Totenkopfverband*, cleared of its Prisoners of War and transformed into what was designated an *Aufenthaltslager* [Detention Camp], intended to temporarily hold Jews who were to be exchanged for interned German civilians in other countries. In March 1944, an area of the camp was designated an *Erholungslager* [Recuperation Camp] to house prisoners from other camps who were considered too sick to work, but five

41 Squadron pilots, thereunder Fg Off Frank Hegarty, second from right facing the camera, survey the damage at Celle Aerodrome, April 1945. © Gp Capt (ret) Derek S. V. Rake OBE AFC & Bar

Flt Lt Peter Cowell standing in front of the remains of a Focke Wulf FW58 *Weihe* light transport aircraft at Celle in April 1945. © Cowell family

months later another change was made to the camp's role when 8,000 female prisoners were transferred to Bergen-Belsen from Auschwitz to provide labour for local factories.

By December 1944, Bergen-Belsen had transformed once again to become the final destination for prisoners when it became a fully functioning *Konzentrationslager* [or *KZ*; a Concentration Camp]. At the beginning of that month, Bergen-Belsen housed well over 15,000 inmates, composed of anti-Nazi Christians, Czechs, Gypsies, homosexuals, Jews, Poles and other political prisoners. Their numbers swelled further in the closing months of the War as prisoners were moved into Germany away from the advancing Allied armies.

Bergen-Belsen was not equipped with gas chambers, but it soon became a 'death camp' in every sense of the word. Over-crowding on such a scale, coupled with a lack of food, quickly resulted in appalling conditions that were particularly conducive to the quick spread of disease, and typhus soon becoming the prevalent illness.

During February 1945, when the camp population practically doubled from around 22,000 inmates to over 41,500, some 7,000 deaths were recorded. Though the population 'only' grew by another 1,500 people in March, the death rate more than doubled to over 18,000. Another 9,000 people are believed to have died between 1 and 15 April 1945 – the date upon which the camp was liberated – by which time it is thought to have held around 60,000 inmates. Today, it is estimated that well over 50,000 men, women and children died at Bergen-Belsen during its existence. One of the most well-known of these was Anne Frank.

When Allied troops liberated the camp, they found thousands of unburied bodies. 41 Squadron's Palestinian pilot, WO Aharon 'Rem' Remez had a particularly difficult time coming to terms with the atrocities suffered by 'his people'.

> *Rem changed considerably after we went into German territory. […] Rem visited this camp and others and became noticeably withdrawn. Little wonder! We guessed what he might have been doing but nothing was said. He was never quite the same afterwards.*[8]

In fact, Remez's son Gideon also recalls his father's stories of this period:

> He told me about the support and sympathy that he received from his comrades in the Squadron, who covered for him when he went to work among the Holocaust survivors in Germany and to assist their then-illegal immigration to Palestine.[9]

Shortly after his liberation from captivity, ex-Prisoner of War and 41 Squadron pilot WO Bill Brew also visited the camp and was equally horrified. He remembers having seen a camp guard, now himself a prisoner, spread-eagled on the ground, staked out before the camp gates, who was customarily spat on by all who passed as a sign of their absolute disgust.

The Wing's photographic section also paid a visit to the camp and obtained images, which were subsequently exhibited at Celle.[10] Voicing their own opinion on the matter, 350 Squadron recorded in their ORB that,

> Some pilots with the Medical Officer, the Adjutant and the Engineering Officer went to visit the camp of horrors and came back absolutely shocked. There was [sic] several women and children and men from our country in this camp and the Squadron knowing this fact took steps to help in the recovery of these dying people. Everybody gave something to help their countrymen, food, clothes, shoes and medical supplies.
> All of us especially those who saw it will remember and keep in our mind the savage and cruel side of the bestial as inhuman [sic] Germany.[11]

However, despite the generous assistance afforded the survivors by Remez, the pilots of 350 Squadron, and many, many others, the inmates were in such poor condition that another 14,000 people died after the liberation.

17 April 1945 – Operations started early on this busy day, when six aircraft were airborne at 05:45 for an armed reconnaissance of the Lübeck-Hamburg area, led by Flt Lt Tony Gaze. Red Section (Gaze MV254, Hegarty SM826, Farfan MV249, Jolly MV264, Bødtker RM928, Gray MV260) had a successful trip, initially finding a good concentration of rolling stock, from which they claimed three locomotives, ten railway trucks and five passenger coaches damaged.

Soon afterwards, Gaze spotted a lone Ju88 at between 2,000 and 3,000 feet near Lübeck Aerodrome and gave chase, closely followed by his No. 2, Fg Off Frank Hegarty. It may have become Gaze's next victory but, within a short burst of machine gun fire, his ammunition ran out, and he was forced to break off the attack. Hegarty broke with him but, whilst still in the circuit, spotted the aircraft again and dived upon it alone. Red Verey lights rose from the aerodrome to warn all and sundry of Hegarty's presence, but he ignored them, opening fire at 800 yards and keeping his finger on the firing button until his ammunition ran out. By this time, he had closed to just 400 yards.

Hegarty saw his fire strike the fuselage and port engine, and then watched as the Ju88 turned southwards at low altitude, streaming smoke from the engine. Accelerating, again, he pulled in alongside the aircraft to identify it, recognising it as a Ju88C, with a sky blue paint scheme and radar apparatus protruding from its nose.

The aircraft then made a forced landing in a field around two miles south of Lübeck Aerodrome and Hegarty flew over it to take some cine-gun film and provide evidence for his victory. At this time, he also saw two men scramble from the aircraft and take cover.

When Red Section returned at 07:30, every man was out of ammunition, and Hegarty claimed his Ju88 destroyed. However, considering the aircraft was "not badly damaged"[12], his claim was questioned. Not prepared to forfeit the victory, he returned to the area the following day and strafed the Junkers, thereby setting it on fire and sealing its fate. One Ju88 destroyed to Hegarty.

The day's second operation was an armed reconnaissance to the same area by Blue Section (Lawrence MV260, Jallands SM826, Fisher RN210, Coleman MV254) at 08:45, led by Flt Lt Tom Lawrence. They found a few ground targets of opportunity, claiming one locomotive and three MET damaged. At around 09:30, they came across a busy airstrip near Parchim, observing from 5,000 feet "several (8 plus) JU 188's dispersed about a wooded area away from an actual airfield".[13]

Plt Off Pat Coleman dived down and strafed the strip, gaining good strikes on one aircraft in particular. There was no explosion or fire, however, which led Coleman to believe it was not fuelled up at the time. When the section returned to Celle at 10:20, he claimed one Ju188 damaged on the ground.[14] Despite the countless ground targets the Squadron had claimed since 1939, this was only the second aircraft the unit had claimed damaged on the ground, and it was almost three years since the Squadron had made a similar claim.

Red Section (Shepherd MV254, Hegarty RN210, Farfan MV249, Moyle SM817) mounted the next armed reconnaissance, which was airborne at 11:50, led by Sqn Ldr Shepherd. Initially intending to head for the Lübeck-Hamburg area again, they were diverted to attack river traffic on the Elbe, where they found two tugs towing large barges. Both were strafed and one set on fire, which ran aground on a bend in the river near Bleckede. They landed again at 13:15, every aircraft out of ammunition.

Flt Lt Roy Fisher led the day's fourth armed reconnaissance back to the day's hunting ground around Lübeck and Hamburg. Blue Section (Fisher MV254, Jallands SM817, Kelly RM928, Scott MV249) was airborne at 15:15, and located good concentrations of MET. They returned at 16:50 claiming three railway trucks destroyed and one locomotive, 17 railway trucks and 2 MET damaged.

Flt Lt Tony Gaze was airborne again at 17:40, leading Red Section (Gaze MV267, Wilkinson SM826, Rake MV260, Chalmers RM792) on an armed reconnaissance of the same area. It was a long but successful operation, and they returned two hours later claiming six railway trucks and five MET destroyed, and one locomotive, 30 railway trucks and seven MET damaged, in addition to a factory being left in flames.

Though not mentioned on the Squadron's F540, the F541 suggests there was a further and final operation undertaken this evening from 19:10, when Blue Section of five aircraft was airborne on an armed reconnaissance led by Sqn Ldr Shepherd. They returned in less than an hour later, but their destination and activity is unknown.

Thus ended a very busy first full day for the Squadron operating from Celle. The Wing ORB recorded today,

> *It is already obvious that now we are well up we are going to be very busy here. A big effort was made to fly as many aircraft as often as possible and considerable success was achieved. [...] All the time, met [sic] was being clobbered good and hard. Everyone [is] working at full pressure and we shall be glad when 'B' party arrive to-morrow.*[15]

On 17 April 1945, 83 Group was spread over five airfields in Germany, as shown in the below table.[16]

Airfield	Occupied by	Squadrons
B.110 Achmer	121 & 143 (RCAF) Wing	175, 184 & 245 Sqns (RAF) and 438, 439 & 440 Sqns (RCAF)
B.118 Celle	125 Wing	41, 130, 350 Sqns
B.114 Diepholz	127 (RCAF) Wing	403, 416, 421 & 443 Sqns (RCAF)
B.112 Hopsten	122 & 124 Wings, and 83 GCS	3, 56, 80, 137, 486 (RNZAF), 181, 182 & 247 Sqns
B.116 Wunstorf	39 (Recce) & 126 (RCAF) Wings	400, 401, 402, 411, 412, 414 & 430 Sqns (RCAF)

18 April 1945 – A much later start to operations today, the first armed reconnaissance was airborne at 12:30, led by Sqn Ldr Shepherd. Six aircraft, designated Red Section (Shepherd SM823, Chalmers SM826, Moyle RM792, Rake MV254, Gray MV264, Bødtker NH692), headed for the Hamburg area and returned at 14:00 claiming two locomotives and one MET damaged.

Red Section (Gaze SM823, Hale MV260, Coleman RM915, Smith RM696, Farfan MV254, Hegarty NH692) was airborne again at 14:55, when Flt Lt Tony Gaze led the sextet on an armed reconnaissance to the same area. A little more successful than Sqn Ldr Shepherd's operation, when they returned they claimed three tugs, one paddle-steamer and another MET damaged south of Lübeck, and Plt Off Pat Coleman also damaged a Junkers Ju88 on the ground three miles east of Pötrau.

Whilst diving to attack a staff car at around 16:00, he spotted a dozen twin-engined aircraft dispersed under the cover of trees just west of a disused but undamaged airfield. He made a single sweep over the aircraft against considerable light Flak, but still managed to observe several strikes on a Ju88. Before their return, however, the pilots made a rather unusual sighting.

> *Whilst the aircraft were orbitting* [sic] *over the Autobahn between Lübeck and Hamburg, a flying bomb and an unidentified twin jet aircraft were sighted flying on a southerly course. They turned west, slightly above our aircraft which gave chase. The bomb, which appeared to have two shining metal balls suspended beneath the fuselage on metal rods, flew straight, climbing slightly. The jet, which had a twin tail, weaved gently maintaining formation with the bomb, about 300 yards from it in line-abreast. The nearest of our aircraft got within 1,500 yards of them but could not jettison it's* [sic] *tank.*[17]

During the chase, however, Fg Off Roy Smith was forced to pull out when a connecting rod broke through the piston head of his aircraft, and he returned to base immediately. He landed without further mishap and the rest of the section was not far behind him, putting down at 16:30.

An hour later, three aircraft were scrambled on the report of enemy aircraft over Celle at 10,000 feet. Red Section was airborne at 17:30 but could not make contact and returned at 18:35 with nothing to report.

A final armed reconnaissance took place at 19:00 when Sqn Ldr Shepherd took Black Section (Shepherd MV266, Gaze MN254, Wilkinson MV260, Farfan NH692, Moyle RM915, Gray MV264) back to the Hamburg-Lübeck area. It was a successful end to the day and they returned just before 21:00, claiming four locomotives, 13 covered railway trucks and five MET damaged.

Two Pilots Return from Captivity

With 125 Wing now based in Germany, it was clear that the War was entering its final phase. In addition to the obvious signs of Germany's weakening, however, there was another sign the end was near: large numbers of escaped Prisoners of War were finding their way to Celle.

> *We are getting hundreds of Allied and British prisoners who have escaped and are working their way here. Dakotas are using the strip to bring in petrol and are taking the ex-prisoners back. Camps are being established at Celle but we still get a number coming direct to Intelligence and of course we give them a lift. One interesting man was RAF prisoner No. 1, shot down in a Whitley on September 9th, 1939 over Potsdam.*[18]

In his autobiography, Gp Capt 'Johnnie' Johnson also recalled the myriad of escaped and liberated airmen finding their ways to Celle, remembering them arriving in appropriated motor vehicles, by horse and cart, and by foot. Although returning them to England was no issue on account of the available air transport, the abandoned jumble of vehicles left Celle Aerodrome looking like a 'second-hand junk-yard'.

Even two of 41 Squadron's own pilots arrived at Celle; they had been behind wire since late summer 1941. Shortly after the unit's arrival at Celle, two ragged, dirty and hungry characters without any form of identification appeared at the gate requesting entry, claiming they were ex-41 Squadron pilots.

Some of the Squadron's men were fetched, but nobody knew who they were. Not surprisingly, there was no-one left from 1941 who could vouch for them. As the pair still insisted they were telling the truth, the Intelligence Officer, Flt Lt Lord Gisborough, was summoned and after a long trawl though old records, it was established they were the Squadron's Australian Sergeant Pilots, now Warrant Officers, William 'Bill' Brew [the author's great uncle] and Alan Bull, who were both shot down over France in August 1941, and had been Prisoners of War ever since.

Although Brew and Bull were lost on separate operations, almost two weeks apart, they were both sent to the same initial POW Camp, Stalag III-E, in Kirchhain, Germany. From then on, the two men stuck together and had been moved with each other to four further camps by April 1945. In early May 1942, they were transferred to Stalag Luft III at Sagan [Żagań], in annexed Poland, in mid-July 1943 to Stalag Luft VI at Heydekrug, in Prussia [today Šilutė, Lithuania], in August 1944 to Stalag 357 at Thorn [Toruń], in annexed Poland, and finally, in September 1944, to Stalag 357 at Örbke in Germany. Örbke is located several kilometres northwest of Celle.

They had quite a story to tell. On 6 April 1945, as a part of the mass movements of Prisoners of War further eastwards into Germany, away from advancing troops, they were marched out of Örbke towards the Elbe. Brew described the poor state they were in:

As I fell back behind because of weakness – I was only 7 stone – I passed a dog whose paws were worn through, it was hobbling along and quite pitiful.[19]

A few days later, while the column sat in the road having a break, Brew motioned to Bull that they should roll into the ditch on the side of the road. The two men lay down, rolled themselves into the trench and hid. Nobody realised they were missing and, much to their thrill, in due course the column resumed the march and left without them.

When they felt it was safe, they ran off and hid in a nearby forest, where they spent the night. They were awoken next morning by the sound of trucks, and peered cautiously from behind bushes to see German Army trucks pulling up in front of a nearby disused factory. As they watched, a number of men and women climbed down from the back of the trucks and were marched inside. Minutes later, they heard the sound of machine gun fire and shortly afterwards the trucks drove off again. When all was quiet again, they approached the building and looked inside. To their shock, they saw dozens of bodies; everyone had been executed.

The pair immediately started moving west again, towards advancing Allied troops. A few days later, as they crossed a clearing in a forest, they heard gun fire and suddenly found themselves in the midst of a large group of retreating German Infantry. Exhausted and hungry, they expected to be recaptured.

Instead, the Wehrmacht troops went on past as a British tank appeared from the forest. The vehicle approached the pair and stopped. Two soldiers lay across its turret, one on each side and each with a machine gun. With their hands raised, the dishevelled men shouted their identification and asked for food. They were given some biscuits, a pudding, and an Iron Cross, and told to wait for the supply column, which was expected to be several hours away. Indeed, in time, more troops reached them, and they realised they really were free.

When they heard their old Squadron was now based nearby, they made their way to Celle. Although Brew was unable to pinpoint the exact date, it is believed they arrived there only a day or so after 41 Squadron's arrival, possibly around 18 April 1945.

On 22 April, still wearing the rags they had arrived in – they had nothing else to wear – Brew and Bull were flown to England in an aircraft full of former Prisoners of War. Upon arrival, each man was sprayed for lice. Brew also had severe Beriberi, which required intensive medical treatment. They showered and were issued with a set of new pyjamas and, as they had nothing else to wear, spent all day walking around in them.

The following morning, the pair was awoken early, issued rail tickets and instructed to report to 11 PRDC, which occupied both the Grand and Metropole Hotels in Brighton, Sussex. Brighton had been set up to receive the large numbers of ex-Prisoners of War, which were now being liberated in Germany by advancing Allied troops, and were flooding back into the United Kingdom for rehabilitation and debriefing.

Upon arrival, they were issued a new uniform and over the following weeks were questioned about their internment. Brew's records show he found the accommodation at the various POW camps very poor, recalling he had two blankets, no heating, very small cooking facilities, and often barely enough food to stay alive. As his boots were initially confiscated, he wore clogs for the first nine months of captivity before he finally obtained another pair of boots. There were scarce bathing and sanitary facilities and although there was no work, there were plenty of sports and good reading material available. However, as a result of poor sanitation, Brew reported he suffered stomach ailments in Stalag Luft III and VI and Stalag 357, and added that there was always a shortage of drugs, bandages and dental equipment.

News of Brew's liberation soon reached his parents in Sydney, when a telegram arrived at their door on 27 April 1945, announcing:

402220 W/O W. A. BREW SAFE STOP PLEASED TO INFORM YOU THAT YOUR SON WARRANT OFFICER WILLIAM AUBREY BREW HAS BEEN LIBERATED BY THE ALLIED ARMIES AND IS NOW SAFE IN THE UNITED KINGDOM STOP ANTICIPATE YOUR SON WILL COMMUNICATE WITH YOU DIRECT.[20]

However, it would still be several months before he and his family would be reunited.

In early August, Brew and Bull were advised they were to be repatriated to Australia, and on 7 August 1945 the pair embarked aboard the troopship HMAT *Orion*. They both believed they would be sent to the Pacific to fly against the Japanese, but had not reached the Panama Canal when news was received that the War came to an end. *Orion* arrived in Sydney on 9 September and Brew was demobilised by the end of November; Bull's return to civilian life followed in early January 1946.

19 April 1945 – The first armed reconnaissance was off the deck at 08:50, led by Flt Lt Tom Lawrence. Blue Section (Lawrence MV260, Wheatley RM693, Jolly SM826, Scott SM823, Fisher MV264, Jallands MV249) headed for the area between Salzwedel and Lübeck, where they located a concentration of MET and returned between 10:05 and 10:15 claiming two MET destroyed and three damaged near Lübeck.

The day's second operation was airborne at 11:00, when Flt Lt Derek Rake led Yellow Section (Rake MV266, Hegarty MV254, Coleman RM915, Smith RM931, Stevenson MV260, Wilkinson MV249) to the same area. Plt Off Pat Coleman returned early with R/T trouble, and the rest of the section landed at 12:30 without further mishap. Between them, they claimed two locomotives, ten railway trucks and ten MET damaged. A large warehouse, which the pilots believed contained military stores, was also strafed and left on fire.

At 15:00, a third armed reconnaissance was airborne and headed to the Hamburg area, led by Flt Lt Arnold Jolly. Blue Section (Jolly SM826, Remez MV254, Bødtker MV260, Scott MV249) located a concentration of MET in the Ludwigslust area and returned at 16:25 claiming four MET and one truck destroyed, and two MET and five trucks damaged.

A final operation was mounted at 19:10, when Sqn Ldr Shepherd let a sweep of ten aircraft to the Wismar-Neumünster area. They did not find any suitable targets and made no attacks, but the pilots did sight six submarines alongside a like number of supply ships in Neustadt Bay area from 6,000 feet at 19:45. They landed again at 20:50.

20 April 1945 – Today would prove to be one of 41 Squadron's most intensive days in some time, and one of the most successful of the War. In addition to a significant number of MET destroyed and damaged, the Squadron claimed no less than seven aircraft destroyed and one probable, for no loss of their own. The rest of the Wing also had a successful day. 130 Squadron claimed three destroyed, one probable and one damaged, and 350 added another five destroyed and one probable. The Wing's score for the day was a massive 15 destroyed, three probable and one damaged, for the loss of two pilots from 350 Squadron.

41 Squadron's first operation was in the air at 10:40 when six aircraft flew to the Wismar-Hamburg area, led by Sqn Ldr Shepherd. Red Section (Shepherd SM823, Chalmers RM931, Smith MV249, Bødtker MV260, Gray MV264, Scott RM928) returned at 12:25 claiming two MET destroyed and 11 MET, two locomotives and two covered railway trucks damaged.

At 11:50, the next section was off, led by Flt Lt Tom Lawrence. The four aircraft, designated Blue Section (Lawrence NH692, Wheatley RM915, Jolly SM817, Jallands RM792), headed for the Hamburg area, claiming one locomotive and ten covered railway trucks damaged near Lübeck, and a second locomotive and another eight covered railway trucks damaged north of Lake Schwerin, around 42km from the Baltic coast. They returned to Celle at 13:25.

Just after lunch, Flt Lt Gaze took up Red Section (Gaze SM823, Moyle MV249, Coleman MV267, Hegarty RM693) for an armed reconnaissance of the Lübeck-Wittenberg area. Airborne at 13:25, Plt Off Pat Coleman returned within ten minutes with an unserviceable aircraft, but the remaining three pilots had a successful operation. When they returned at 15:20, they claimed four MET damaged near Neukloster, one staff car destroyed and another damaged at Güstrow, and one lorry and two trailers destroyed, and one lorry and two trailers damaged south of Goldberg.

Before their return, Flt Lt Roy Fisher was airborne, leading Blue Section (Fisher MV264, Rossow NH692, Remez MV264, Stevenson RM915, Coleman MV254) on the day's fourth armed reconnaissance to the same general area. Airborne at 14:35, they found little MET, and could only claim two damaged. However at 15:05, WO Viv Rossow sighted a lone long-nosed FW190D, flying at 1,000 feet, in a northerly direction, just north of Neuruppin Aerodrome. The aircraft was 5,000 feet below them at 3 o'clock from their position.

Blue 3 and 4 (Remez and Stevenson) dived on the aircraft but overshot due to excessive speed, and were themselves attacked by the FW190. Coleman now made his own attack on the FW190 from above and behind. Using his gyro sight, he fired a short burst from 200 yards and 40° port astern. Coleman saw strikes and the 190 immediately broke hard to port to escape his fire.

Not shaken so easily, Coleman followed him around. Although he lost some distance in the turn, he soon closed again and made a second attack, firing a two-second burst from a distance of 300 yards dead astern. Coleman was now flying at just 1,000 feet. His fire struck home again and he later recalled,

I shot down a long-nosed FW 190 just north of Neuruppin aerodrome [sic]*, the pilot rolled on his back & baled out whilst I was firing, machine plunged into the Binenwalde lake* [sic] *& pilot landed amidst trees on lake's SE. verge.*[21]

When Blue Section returned at 16:25, Coleman claimed one FW190D destroyed.[22]

It appears a fifth armed reconnaissance was airborne at 16:05. It is not mentioned on the Squadron's F540, but Flt Lt Tom Lawrence is recorded on the F541 as having led Red Section of four aircraft (Lawrence, Wheatley, Jolly, Jallands) on an operation between 16:05 and 17:45. Though their destination was likely the same as the others today, neither this nor their successes are recorded.

Flt Lt Tony Gaze led the next armed reconnaissance, four aircraft designated Red Section (Gaze RM792, Hegarty RM915, Farfan MV249, Chalmers MV264), which were airborne at 18:10. Heading back to the same area, they found a convoy of ten vehicles heading south on the road from Grevesmühlen. These were duly attacked and seven were left destroyed and the remaining three damaged.

Fg Off Frank Hegarty was forced to head back to base at 19:20 when his engine started running rough and his propeller was damaged by a cannon fairing that blew off. Before the rest of the section returned at 20:00, they destroyed two more MET and damaged another two.

A Fine Evening's Work

At 19:00, Sqn Ldr Shepherd was airborne again, leading seven aircraft on a sweep of the Wittstock-Hagenow area. Yellow (Shepherd MV266, Wilkinson RM931, Stevenson RM928) and Blue (Fisher MV260, Scott SM817, Gray RM693, Rossow NH692) Sections initially headed east for half an hour, then turned north. A few minutes later, approximately half way between Oranienburg and Neuruppin at an altitude of 7,000 feet, Fg Off 'Ricky' Gray sighted eight to ten aircraft flying in the opposite direction 3,000 feet below them.

He notified Sqn Ldr Shepherd, who told him to take a look. Diving upon the aircraft with his No. 2, Gray soon recognised them as long-nosed FW190Ds. He pulled in behind the closest aircraft but was spotted and the enemy aircraft immediately broke formation and climbed to engage 41 Squadron. However, they suddenly had an apparent change of heart, and turned away again. Sqn Ldr Shepherd later reported that…

> …*on sighting us* [the enemy aircraft] *commenced a climbing turn towards us then apparently thought better of it, and the majority of them half rolled and aileron turned down to the deck. At no time did I see any of them make a serious effort to fight it out.*[23]

From this point on, the battle was all one-sided. Before his Focke-Wulf could escape, Fg Off Gray opened fire at 200 yards and closed to just 70. Black smoke immediately spewed from its engine, and the pilot made a hard aileron turn and dived for the deck. Gray commenced a dive after him but quickly realised there was no necessity. "He could not pull out of the dive and crashed in the woods."[24]

Immediately afterwards, Gray spotted a second FW190 nearby at 1,000 feet. Just as he was positioning himself onto the aircraft's tail, Gray realised he'd been spotted again. The pilot panicked and made a steep sudden turn to shake him. However, he went into a spin and crashed, despite the fact Gray had not fired a shot at it. The pilot managed to bale out and Gray saw him descending by parachute. The aircraft was last seen burning fiercely on the ground.[25]

The sky had by now exploded in frenzied dogfights as Spitfires chased Focke-Wulfs, each of the Allied pilots seeking out a suitable target. Sqn Ldr Shepherd latched onto the tail of one and opened fire from approximately 200 yards. His shells hit the cockpit and engine, and it immediately went down in flames.

WO 'Steve' Stevenson found his own 190, and opened fire at a range of 400 yards with a deflection of 45°. His aim was accurate and he saw immediate strikes on the fuselage and wing root. The Focke-Wulf pilot tightened his turn to avoid the fire, but Stevenson opened up again, his deflection now increased to 60°. This time, his fire struck the cockpit, fuselage and starboard wing root. This was too much for the aircraft, which then "went into a shallow starboard dive and exploded in a sheet of flame on hitting the ground".[26] The pilot did not bale out.

Flt Lt Johnnie Wilkinson was approached by another FW190, which pulled up in a starboard climbing turn towards him and started firing at him. However, the Luftwaffe pilot had not allowed enough deflection and his aim was wide of the mark. Wilkinson made a hard aileron turn to come around behind the 190, and as he did saw Sgt Plt Peter Scott attacking the same aircraft. Scott opened fire at 250 yards with 40° deflection and closed to just 25 yards before he ceased firing and overshot. Wilkinson saw Scott's fire strike the Focke-Wulf's engine, then closed in to 200 yards for his own attack. His three-second burst also hit the 190 and the aircraft burst into flames and dived straight into Teschendorf Wood where it blew up.

The sky was suddenly empty of enemy aircraft. Sqn Ldr Shepherd called up the pilots and reformed the Squadron. They had been out-numbered, seven Spitfire XIVs pitted against ten long-nosed Focke-Wulf 190Ds, and yet five enemy aircraft had been destroyed for no loss of their own. No-one had sustained any damage but Flt Lt Roy Fisher reported a rough engine and was sent home early, where he arrived without mishap at 20:10. The rest of Blue Section (Scott, Gray

& Rossow) formed up on Yellow Section and they continued north towards Wittstock, which they reached without seeing any more aircraft. They patrolled the area for a short while at low altitude but when they found nothing of interest, Sqn Ldr Shepherd decided to head home to Celle again via the Neuruppin area.

On approaching Neuruppin just after 20:00, activity was spotted around the aerodrome involving a number of enemy aircraft of varying types, at differing altitudes. WO Viv Rossow looked down to see an aircraft flying on a reciprocal course to his, approximately 5,000 feet below him. Blue Section was given the go-ahead and dived upon it. Before long, Rossow recognised it as a jet-powered Me262 *Schwalbe*.

Reluctant to use full throttle as his fuel was already low from the evening's activity, he fired a burst at the aircraft from 800 yards to force it to weave. Better than that, the Messerschmitt turned a full 90° to port. Though Rossow was initially unable to close to less than about 600 yards due to the jet's superior speed, this gave him a new opportunity and he fired again, this time eliciting thick black smoke from the aircraft. Rossow's immediate thought was that this was only the jet's boost, but his fire had hit its target and the 262 slowed considerably.

In time, he was able to overhaul it, but as they were now approaching Neuruppin Aerodrome at an altitude of just 500 feet, Rossow climbed away to starboard to avoid the inevitable Flak. However, he was able to watch the Me262 make a hard turn to port and crash-land on the airfield. He claimed the jet probably destroyed.[27]

Yellow Section had remained above Blue Section to provide them cover, but Flt Lt Johnnie Wilkinson spotted a short-nosed FW190 at the same altitude, off to port, flying in the opposite direction. They were spotted at the same time and the aircraft dived away, with several pilots giving chase. Flying on the port side of Yellow Section, Wilkinson was best positioned to make an attack, but Sqn Ldr Shepherd was also closing fast.

When the Focke-Wulf made a climbing turn to port, Wilkinson fired but did not allow for sufficient deflection and missed the aircraft. Seeing Wilkinson's original attack fail, Shepherd closed from below. Wilkinson soon positioned himself dead astern of the 190 and opened up again at 200 yards with a six-second burst. He saw strikes on the engine, which immediately caught fire, then saw the aircraft "suddenly burst into a mass of fire around the engine and cockpit".[28]

This appears to have been the result of Sqn Ldr Shepherd's fire, as he had also opened up from below Wilkinson at a range 200 yards and closing. The aircraft burst into flames, and both men recalled seeing the aircraft's port undercarriage wheel drop from its bay. Shepherd and Wilkinson broke off the attack and the 190 dived to the ground in Teschendorf Wood, around 12km north-northwest of Oranienburg Aerodrome and exploded. They claimed the aircraft shared destroyed.

On their return to Celle at 20:40, Blue and Yellow Sections claimed six FW190s destroyed and an Me262 probable. Every pilot made a claim, except for Flt Lt Roy Fisher, who had returned early with engine trouble. All the pilots had seen action and were dangerously low on fuel. Rossow put down with just three gallons of fuel left in his tank. It was, in the words of the 125 Wing ORB, "A fine evening's work."[29]

Victories, 20 April 1945	Dest.	Prob.	Location
Coleman, Patrick T.	FW190D	-	12km N. of Neuruppin Aerodrome
Gray, Eric	FW190D	-	Teschendorf
Gray, Eric	FW190D	-	Teschendorf
Rossow, Vivian J.	-	Me262	Neuruppin Aerodrome
Scott, Peter F.	FW190D	-	Kremmen Forest
Wilkinson, John F.	FW190D	-	Kremmen Forest
Shepherd, John B.	FW190D	-	Kremmen Forest

Shepherd, John B.	FW190D	-	Teschendorf Wood
Wilkinson, John F.		-	
Stevenson, Ian T.	FW190D	-	Teschendorf Wood

Not only was it a successful day for the Wing, but also for the entire Group, which claimed a "total score of 36-3-8 in the air and 2-0-1 [on the ground]… better than the Group has done since the profitable days of last autumn."[30] The tally was recorded as follows:[31]

Wing	Sorties	E/A32	MET	Locos	R/Trks	Tanks	Barges	Losses
121	64	-	12-9	0-1	8-7	0-1	-	-
122	65	2-0-0	21-35	0-5	3-15	-	-	-
124	80	2-0-1	38-6	1-0	11-6	3-2	-	1/1
125	86	14-3-2	17-47	0-12	8-15	-	0-1	2/2
126	120	20-0-6	7-30	0-9	1-20	-	0-2	4/2
127	113	-	5-15	0-2	0-10	-	-	-
143	52	-	1-0	0-1	12-17	-	-	-
39	60	-	-	-	-	-	-	-
Totals	640	38-3-9	101-142	1-30	43-90	3-3	0-3	7/5

21 April 1945 – Following the intensity of the previous day, today got off to a slow start due to inclement weather. Two sections of four aircraft designated Red and Blue patrolled the base area between 06:20 and shortly after 07:00, when they were recalled owing to the poor conditions, and all flying was then cancelled until the weather improved mid-afternoon. There was then only enough time left in the day to mount two operations.

The first of these was an armed reconnaissance to the Lübeck area by six aircraft, led by Flt Lt Tony Gaze. Red Section (Gaze MV267, Moyle RM931, Farfan RM792, Smith MV254, Wilkinson MV249, Smart SM826) was airborne at 16:10 and returned at 18:05, claiming four MET destroyed and five damaged, and two covered railway trucks damaged.

There were also two sightings of interest to report. The first of these was an Me262, which was seen flying in a south-south-westerly direction at 2,000 feet near Lübeck. The pilots fired at extreme range, but no strikes were seen. The second was a Flak trap, which was spotted near Ludwigslust. They described it as "a line of trucks with steam coming from one end"[33], and steered well clear of it.

The day's last operation was an armed reconnaissance by Blue Section (Jolly MV266, Remez RM915, Bødtker NH692, Scott RM928, Gray MV264, Rossow SM826) to the same area from 19:00, led by Flt Lt Arnold Jolly. Unfortunately, WO Viv Rossow experienced some technical trouble on the ground and got airborne late. He tried to catch up with the rest of the section, but to no avail. However, he had a little excitement when an Me262 crossed his path in almost the reciprocal direction and he opened fire at it at a range of just 200 feet. He saw no strikes, and returned to base at 20:10 to tell his story.

The remaining five pilots were a little more successful. They returned only 15 minutes after Rossow, claiming four covered railway trucks damaged near Hamburg, and reported having seen several Me262s on the ground at Perleberg Aerodrome. There is no indication of why these were not attacked.

The day was much the same for the rest of the Wing, as poor weather put paid to any large operations being mounted. Despite similar successes against MET and rolling stock by 130 and 350 Squadrons, "compared with the previous day's bag, nothing spectacular occurred".[34]

A Plane of Their Own

In his memoirs of this period, which are deposited with the Imperial War Museum, Flt Lt Johnnie Wilkinson relates a story, which does not appear to have been recorded anywhere else. He describes how, after their arrival in Celle, he found that the Luftwaffe had left a number of aircraft scattered around the airfield and in the surrounding forest. Some had been smashed with sledgehammers and others burned. However, using good pieces from a number of different aircraft, he, Flt Lt 'Fanny' Farfan, and 'Steve' Fisher[35] built their own composite aircraft, painted it yellow and added RAF roundels. The Engineering Officer was not particularly impressed with their efforts, he recalled, but they managed to get it to fly.

The aircraft they rebuilt they believed was a Bücker Bü181 *Bestmann*, a single-engined two-seat trainer, which a steel-ribbed frame around the cockpit, but was otherwise built of wood covered in fabric. It had a length of 7.85 metres (25.7 ft.) and a wingspan of 10.6 metres (34.7 ft.). Although its cruising speed was just 121 mph – almost a quarter of the Spitfire XIV's maximum speed (448 mph) – its top speed was only slightly greater, at 134 mph. Wilkinson states the aircraft remained with the Squadron during their subsequent moves.

22 April 1945 – Poor weather once again hampered 125 Wing's operations today, although several patrols to the Uelzen-Lüneburg area were undertaken during the day. For their part, 41 Squadron mounted 20 sorties to the area in five separate patrols between 11:50 and 21:10. The day's claims amounted to just two MET destroyed and two MET and a locomotive damaged. Although the ORB does not allocate the victories to any particular patrol, *Pilot Service Records* suggest that the locomotive was damaged on the day's second patrol by Yellow Section (Farfan MV249, Hegarty SM826, Stevenson RM915, Smith MV254) between 13:55 and 15:30, whilst the four MET were claimed by Yellow Section (Gaze MV249, Smart SM826, Moyle RM915, Hale MV254) on the 18:05 to 19:50 patrol. All other patrols were uneventful, except for reports of being fired upon by American Flak behind Allied lines.

Separately, the Wing ORB indicates that in the space of less than a week, Celle Aerodrome had become a very busy and comfortable base.

> *The airfield is now well organised with Dakotas coming in with petrol on a large scale and evacuating Allied ex-prisoners and wounded. [...] We are getting a cinema going on the camp and there is an excellent recreation room. Now that the army have moved out we should have quite adequate accommodation.*[36]

In fact, Celle would remain a significant Allied airfield for many years to come.

23 April 1945 – Weather still played havoc with flying plans and very little was achieved by the Wing during the morning. 41 Squadron was kept in readiness until 11:35 when four aircraft designated Yellow Section took off for a weather reconnaissance flight along the Elbe River, led by Flt Lt 'Fanny' Farfan. They returned 65 minutes later reporting the weather too poor for further flying. The Squadron then remained on the ground for the next six hours.

At 18:25, Flt Lt Tony Gaze decided to chance the weather and led six aircraft designated Red Section (Gaze SM823, Chalmers SM826, Coleman MV267, Jolly SM817, Gray RM915, Kelly RM696) on an armed reconnaissance of the Hamburg area. They had considerable success and, when they returned at 19:55, claimed no less than six MET destroyed and left in flames, and one locomotive, 30 covered railway trucks and 18 MET damaged.

As if this were not a big enough bag for one evening, the day's last operation would yield even greater results. At 19:20, prior to Red Section's return, Sqn Ldr Shepherd led Black Section (Shepherd MV264, Hegarty RM693, Hale MV249, Smith RM792, Stevenson SM817, Moyle RM928)[37] to the Parchim-Pritzwalk area for their own armed reconnaissance.

WO Peter Hale, flying as Black 3, spotted a convoy of over 100 MET heading south on the

Kyritz-Senzke-Nauen road, northwest of Berlin, being passed by a second, smaller convoy heading north. The two convoys stretched for miles and they were quite literally sitting ducks. They reported the location to the Wing, and a section from 350 Squadron (Bangerter RM618, Delorme RM869, Watkins NH689, van Eeckhoudt NH697) soon joined them over the area.

41 and 350 Squadrons made repeated attacks on the convoys, which were likely intended to aid the defence of Berlin, and they were decimated. "What a picnic!" recorded Hale later in his logbook. Whilst information on individual actions is limited, the Squadron ORB records that Sqn Ldr Shepherd hit a petrol tanker, which burst into flames, and a lorry, which blew up, sending smoke 3,000 feet into the air. This latter vehicle must have been carrying ammunition as the explosion destroyed several more MET around it and a nearby house. In fact, so great was the explosion, that Shepherd's aircraft was slightly damaged by debris. Black Section landed at Celle again at 20:40.

On their return, 41 Squadron claimed 34 MET destroyed and 26 damaged, whilst 350 Squadron claimed another three MET destroyed and 21 damaged. Between them, they had accounted for a massive 84 vehicles destroyed or damaged out of approximately 100. The haul included lorries, petrol tankers, staff cars, troop carriers and horse-drawn vehicles. Moderate light Flak was experienced, but had not caused the pilots any trouble. The 83 Group ORB hailed their successes as "the [Group's] two most successful shows of the day."[38]

Despite constraints on the day's operations as a result of the weather, the Squadron's bag just on the evening's two armed reconnaissances totalled a massive 40 MET destroyed, and 39 MET, 30 covered railway trucks and one locomotive damaged. It had been a disastrous and deadly day for the Wehrmacht and Reichsbahn in this sector.

24 April 1945 – Another intensive day that would be both significant and memorable for several reasons. During a Wing sweep in the morning, 41 Squadron was one of the units involved when the RAF met the Soviet Air Force [*Voenno-Vozdushnye Sily* (Military Air Forces) or *VVS*] for the first time in the air over Germany.

Later in the day, one of the Squadron's sections found and shot up 16 aircraft on the ground, and another considerable bag of ground targets was added to the Squadron's tally: six MET destroyed, and 72 MET, 11 railway trucks and five locomotives damaged. In the space of just two days, the Squadron accounted for the destruction or damage of over 200 road and rail targets.

Sadly, it was also a memorable day for an accident that left one man maimed for life. Two of the Squadron's pilots collided in their aircraft on the ground and were hospitalised, but one of them lost a leg. It was an unfortunate end to his flying career when victory was so close.

The first of the day's seven operations was airborne at 05:45, when Flt Lt 'Fanny' Farfan led Red Section (Farfan SM823, Gaze MV266, Chalmers MV249, Smith MV267) on a patrol of the Lauenburg-Uelzen area. They found and damaged a locomotive and three railway trucks, then spotted an Me262 heading southeast at 6,500 feet. Farfan gave chase but was unable to catch it and the section landed at 07:35.

Flt Lt Peter Cowell led the second operation, an armed reconnaissance to the Lübeck-Wismar-Parchim area at 06:45 by Blue Section (Cowell RM928, Kelly RM693, Bødtker SM817, Wheatley RM696, Fisher SM820, Remez RM915). They had little more luck than Red Section, and returned at 07:45 claiming one locomotive damaged east of Lübeck, and another two damaged southeast of the same town.

The next operation was a 34-aircraft-strong Wing sweep to the Rathenow area, west of Berlin, on reports of several Wings of Luftwaffe aircraft covering Wehrmacht ground movements in the area. It was a major operation, which included all three Squadrons and both the Group Captain and Wing Commander.

09:45 Wing Sweep, 24 April 1945	
Gp Capt 'Johnnie' Johnson	Leading 350 Squadron
Wg Cdr George Keefer	Leading 41 Squadron
41 Squadron	10 Spitfire XIVs (incl. Keefer)
130 Squadron	12 Spitfire XIVs
350 Squadron	12 Spitfire XIVs (incl. Johnson)

Airborne at 09:45, 41 Squadron's contingent consisted of Kudos Yellow Section of four aircraft (Shepherd MV266, Hegarty MV267, Gaze RB143, Hale RM792), and Kudos Red Section of six aircraft (Keefer MV257, Stevenson RM915, Gray RM693, Scott RB159, Bødtker SM817, Rossow SM820).

The Squadron's Flt Lt Bill Stowe had joined 130 Squadron as OC, B Flight, this very morning and therefore participated in the sweep with 130, which was otherwise led by two further ex-41 Squadron pilots, Commanding Officer Sqn Ldr Frank Woolley DFC, and OC, A Flight, Flt Lt Charles 'Sammy' Samouelle DFC*.[39] 350 Squadron was also headed by a new Commanding Officer on this operation, Sqn Ldr Harry Walmsley, who was on his first operation with the Squadron as its OC, having just been promoted to Squadron Leader to replace ex-41 Squadron pilot Sqn Ldr Terry Spencer, who had been shot down and captured again on 19 April.

> Soon after crossing the Elbe [41] Squadron sighted a very large number of single-engined aircraft and went to investigate them. They proved to be Russian aircraft engaged in ground attacks on Germans retreating from the North Eastern sector. […] This was the first contact to be made by British Fighters with Russian aircraft.[40]

It appeared that the earlier reports of enemy aircraft in the area were erroneous, and that they were Russian Yakovlev Yak-9 and Ilyushin Il-2 *Stormovik* fighters, and Petlyakov Pe2 bombers instead. WO Peter Hale recalls the Wing met the VVS in the Nauen-Rathenow area, about 37km west-northwest of the centre of Berlin, and approximately 190km east of Celle; "they were all over the sky with no obvious formation. They suddenly appeared in the sky like a swarm of bees."[41]

41 Squadron then proceeded to join the Russians in their ground attacks and damaged 38 MET of their own. Information on 130 and 350 Squadrons' participation is scant, with the former Squadron's ORB suggesting they saw no action at all, finding the sweep 'unproductive'. The 350 Squadron ORB records, "…we met for the first time Yaks and *Stormoviks* aeroplanes" [sic][42], but there is no mention of them being involved in the fight. As such, it appears that only 41 Squadron got in amongst the Russians and joined their attack on the retreating Wehrmacht.

Although nothing official is recorded – for obvious reasons – various stories have filtered through of 125 Wing pilots being fired upon by the Russians, having mistaken them for Luftwaffe aircraft, and indeed vice-versa. It is understood, therefore, that RAF operations over Berlin were banned after this encounter, to avoid misidentifications and friendly fire incidents. In fact, the Group ORB puts on a rather politically correct face to counter any suggestions of friendly fire incidents that day!

> There was a fair amount of enemy air activity today, but with the Russian bombline [sic] rapidly closing on our own it is difficult to ascertain whether we were dealing with enemy aircraft operating over our area or over the Russian front. Indeed, the important thing nowadays seems to be not so much to shoot down German aircraft as to avoid attacking Russian aircraft. It is understood that 125 Wing had numerous escapes today, firstly when they found 80 STORMOVIKS on the very boundary between our airforces [sic] and later when they met an unusual twin-engined bomber. Fortunately superior recognition triumphed over their natural desire to shoot down any aircraft not recognised as British or American, so that the Group's copy book remains so far unblotted.[43]

The choice of words is interesting not least because of the emphasis put on not attacking Russian aircraft – despite the fact Allied pilots suggest it was the Russians who were trigger happy – but also because of the use of the word 'nowadays': as far as can be determined, this was the first time RAF fighters had encountered VVS fighters over Europe. It is therefore difficult not to imagine that this paragraph was more politically motivated than just summarising the day's events.

Keefer's Red Section led the Wing back, putting down at Celle at 11:05, closely followed by 350 Squadron between 11:05 and 11:15, then Shepherd's Yellow Section at 11:20, and finally 130 Squadron, at 11:25. The 125 Wing ORB hailed the event as follows,

> *Well, the 125 Gold Medal Wing is in the news again. By virtue of the number of wireless sets now on the unit strength everyone will doubtless have heard on the 9 p.m. news that British fighters had met Russian fighters in an area unspecified west of Berlin and that the British fighters had flown with the 'Hammers and Sickles' for some time. This was on a sweep in grand style, the Group Captain leading 350 Sqdn, the Wing Commander leading 41 Sqdn and S/Ldr Woolley leading 130 Sqdn. Having shown off our aircraft to the Russians, the rest of the day was spent in hardwork* [sic] *– getting Huns while the stocks last.*[44]

So much excitement, and yet the day had hardly begun. The whole Wing would be up again during this intensive day, but on their own individual operations.

41 Squadron's fourth mission of the day was airborne at 12:30 when Yellow Section (Farfan SM817, Smith MV249, Coleman SM820, Smart RM696) was sent on an armed reconnaissance of the Pritzwalk-Ludwigslust area, led by Flt Lt 'Fanny' Farfan. They spotted a convoy of 20 MET near Perleberg and attacked them, claiming six destroyed, then flew northwest to the Lübeck area, and damaged a locomotive and eight wagons north of Bad Oldesloe.

Whilst landing back at Celle at 14:15, however, Flt Sgt Harry Smart and Fg Off Roy Smith collided and were both injured and admitted to hospital. Whilst Smith's wounds were minor, Smart was quite seriously hurt and suffered wounds to the head and legs. It was soon realised one of his legs could not be saved, and it was amputated. It was a severe blow for the 22-year-old.

It is believed that Smart's engine cut on the runway just after he landed, and that Smith, who was in the process of landing, and beyond the point of no return, hit him from behind. Strangely, despite the seriousness of the accident, it warrants no mention in the Squadron ORB. The 125 Wing ORB, however, records the following:

> *We had one piece of very bad luck, an accident on the runway when a section of 41 Sqdn were landing. This resulted in both pilots being taken to hospital. F/Sgt Smart with severe injuries and F/O Smith badly shaken. We hear the former has lost a leg and has head injuries. Everyone will wish him speedy recovery and every sympathy with his bad luck, and also to F/O Smith.*[45]

Plt Off Pat Coleman also noted in his logbook, "F/Sgt. Harry Smart seriously wounded, collision on landing." He later pencilled in, "leg amputated & head wound."[46] Little else is known about the accident.[47] Smith was back in action by the end of the month, and the 125 Wing ORB noted the following day, "We are glad to say that F/Sgt Smart of 41 Sqdn is making good progress although still seriously ill."[48] He was no doubt evacuated home shortly afterwards, and is believed to have died in July 1985.

Sixteen Claims on One Operation

At 14:55, Flt Lt Peter Cowell took up Blue Section (Cowell MV266, Kelly RM915, Fisher SM820, Jallands SM817) on an armed reconnaissance to the Lübeck-Wismar area. They found a concentration of MET near Lake Schwerin, and damaged four apiece, but then, on their way back to Celle, found 20 twin-float seaplanes on the shore of Lake Ratzeburg, around 44km west-

Flt Sgt Harry Smart served with 41 Squadron from 1 February 1945 to 24 April 1945, when he lost a leg in a flying accident at Celle. © 41 Squadron RAF

northwest of Schwerin. An understandable misidentification, the location was actually the shore of Küchensee [Küchen Lake], which adjoined its larger neighbour.

Whilst at an altitude of 4,500 feet, Flt Lt Roy Fisher called up Flt Lt Peter Cowell to report he had spotted around two dozen float planes parked around a bend in the eastern shore of the lake, which lay just south of the town of Ratzeburg.

Diving down for better identification, the section recognised them as single-engined, two-seater Arado Ar196 reconnaissance aircraft, which were conveniently lined up side-by-side along the beach. Sixteen were parked in a line out in the open, except for a reed-bed which offered meagre camouflage around them, with an additional four around a curve in the shoreline, which offered them some protection.[49]

To say the first sixteen were 'sitting ducks' would be so apt a statement that it comes as no surprise whatsoever that Cowell, Fisher, Jallands and Kelly flew neatly down the line and holed every single one of them. The latter four remained unscathed.

The attack appeared to have come as such a bolt from the blue for those on the ground that the Blue Section's initial strike drew no return fire and only minimal and ineffective Flak from the town of Ratzeburg. Noting that not a single one of the Ar196s had burst into flames, Cowell took the opportunity whilst the small window of time was open to him, and turned his section to make a second hasty, and hopefully definitive, attack. The four pilots flew down the line again and their cannon fire added to the damage done by their first strike.

A local boy who lived near the lake witnessed Blue Section's strike on the Arados, and recalled many years later,

> *I had just completed my daily newspaper round west of the lake on the main road to Mölln, high above its water level, at about 15:40 hours, when four Spitfires suddenly appeared above us at tree-top height, attacking those floatplanes with machine guns, damaging all 12 aircraft. [...] At the time I was completely taken by surprise and, as hot cartridge cases rained upon us, my first thoughts were that we might have become their target – with nowhere to hide. This fear quickly gave way to being impressed by the pilots' spectacular flying skills in their dive to the water-level below and subsequent steeply banked climb towards the south. After this encounter we did not hang around for long....*[50,51]

WO Hugh Kelly was one of four claimants of 16 damaged Arado Ar196s on Lake Ratzeburg on 24 April 1945.
© Cowell family

All sixteen aircraft had been hit numerous times, but would not explode. By now, however, the Flak from Ratzeburg had intensified and Cowell decided to leave the area as quickly as possible and head home, before any of the four was hit. They put down at Celle at 16:20.

Unable to witness their definitive destruction, the pilots had no choice but to only log the sixteen Arados as damaged ground targets, which Cowell, Fisher, Jallands and Kelly shared fairly and squarely between them, at four each. As the location of the final four Ar196s had made it impossible to attack them on the same dives as the first sixteen, they were spared. In his Combat Report, Cowell reasoned that the aircraft would not catch fire as they were "presumably not full of petrol"[52]; probably no surprise at this stage of the war, just two weeks from its end.

The long day was still not over, however, and Flt Lt Tony Gaze led Red Section (Gaze SM817, Chalmers RM928, Coleman MV267, Stevenson RM915) on the next armed reconnaissance, to the Parchim area at 17:20. They found little of interest, but returned at 18:25, claiming four damaged MET west of Lake Schaal and another two damaged east of Sternberg.

The day's final operation was airborne at 19:15, when Sqn Ldr Shepherd led six aircraft on an armed reconnaissance of the Lake Schwerin area. Blue Section (Shepherd MV266, Gaze MV267, Chalmers RM792, Lawrence SM817, Rossow RM928, Gray SM820) attacked a convoy on the road between Rhinow and Hohenhauen, and returned to Celle at 21:00 claiming 12 MET damaged.

It had been a long and tiring day for the ground crew as much as for the pilots. Flying had commenced before 06:00 and continued for over 15 hours. The Squadron had flown seven armed reconnaissances, totalling 37 sorties. The Wing's other Squadrons had also had an intensive day, with 130 Squadron flying 45 sorties and 350 another 42. The 125 Wing ORB summed the day up, "Altogether a very successful day and a record one for sorties flown."[53]

25 April 1945 – Operations began today at 07:50, when Flt Lt Peter Cowell led Blue Section (Cowell MV266, Kelly NH692, Lawrence SM817, Jallands RM792) on an armed reconnaissance of the Parchim-Wismar-Neumünster areas. It was a successful operation. On the railway line north of Lübeck, they came across a train and proceeded to attack it but soon realised it was a Flak trap and made a hasty exit! A short while later, they came across another train in the Bad Segeberg area and were able to damage the locomotive. What came next, however, was a little less expected.

Around 09:00, shortly after attacking the train, Blue Section was orbiting at 6,000 feet, preparing to make a course for Celle, when Cowell spotted two Me262s heading east just 500 feet above them, flying line abreast. Cowell made a sharp turn to give chase, and as they passed over him, he jettisoned his long range fuel tank to give him more speed.

By the time they realised Cowell was on their tails, they were already up to 2,000 yards ahead of him, but opened their throttles and dived to ground level. Cowell followed them down at 440 mph, and then levelled out behind them at 400 mph, closing slowly. Recognising they were heading for Lübeck, it was immediately obvious to Cowell that they intended to lead him over the Flak defences and he realised he had no chance of closing to a suitable range beforehand.

With experience gleaned from many hundreds of hours flying, he sensibly gave up and climbed back to 3,000 feet, the rest of the section following. However, assuming the danger had passed, the Luftwaffe pilots then made a fatal error. Cowell…

> …*observed the E/A making for the aerodrome south of LUBECK. The ME 262 on the starboard side did a turn to starboard and put his wheels and flaps down with the intention of doing a right hand circuit to land west to east. I was therefore able to cut him off and make a short head on attack. No results were observed. I then broke sharply to port and was able to make a 60° beam attack as he continued in his circuit. I observed strikes in the cockpit area and between the starboard nacelle and the fuselage, and a large sheet of flame issued from this point. The pilot of the E/A then landed his machine on the grass beside the runway where it slewed round to starboard and volumes of white smoke issued from it. The other machine landed on the runway in the opposite direction (W-E) and it appeared that either the starboard tyre burst, or the starboard leg collapsed for the aircraft slewed round off the runway on to the grass, dragging its starboard wing tip on the ground. Final results of the fire on the first ME 262 were not observed owing to intense light flak from the aerodrome defences.*[54]

Heading for home, Blue Section passed over Lake Ratzeburg, where they attacked four Ar196 float planes. Although the ORB does not elaborate, these were likely the four left unscathed by Cowell, Jallands and Kelly during the previous afternoon's armed reconnaissance in which 16 of these aircraft were damaged in the same location.

On this occasion, however, they were less fortunate and immediately met with intense Flak. Flt Sgt 'Hugh' Kelly's machine was hit and both his R/T and rudder were damaged. More damage was suspected when his oil temperature started to rise, so he put down early and without incident at B.152 Fassberg.

Cowell, Lawrence and Jallands continued to Celle, where they landed at 09:30 to report a very busy and successful trip. Blue Section made no claims for the Ar196s, but Cowell claimed the first Me262 probable and the second damaged; this was the last claim of the War to be made by the Squadron for a probably destroyed aircraft. The 125 Wing ORB made light of the Me262 pilots' confusion on being bounced by Cowell, jibing,

> *These two [aircraft] were found flying east to LUBECK and in their excitement tried to land in opposite directions. This is bound to add to the fun of the spectators but must frighten Flying Control to say the least.*[55]

At 08:55, over half an hour prior to Blue Section's return, Flt Lt Tony Gaze took up Red Section (Gaze MV267, Hale RB143, Farfan SM826, Stevenson RB159) for the day's second armed reconnaissance to the Parchim-Wismar-Neumünster area. WO Peter Hale was forced to return within 35 minutes with 'technical trouble', leaving Gaze, Flt Lt Farfan and WO Stevenson to continue on alone. However, this operation was a much quieter affair than the previous and they returned at 10:40 claiming three MET destroyed and seven damaged, thereunder a staff car, near Grevesmühlen.

Twenty minutes after Red Section's return, Sqn Ldr Shepherd took up Blue Section for an armed reconnaissance, but ran into bad weather and returned at 12:45 with nothing to report and no claims made.

125 Wing's 200th Hun

Flt Lt Gaze was up again after lunch on 25 April 1945, leading Red Section (Gaze SM823, Chalmers RM915, Coleman SM826, Hale RM928) on an armed reconnaissance to the Schwerin area. The section was airborne at 13:15 but as Gaze was compelled to return early with an unserviceable R/T system, the remaining three young pilots continued on by themselves, led by Plt Off Pat Coleman.

At 14:15, whilst flying at 4,000 feet, just below the 7/10ths cloud base, Coleman sighted an aircraft approximately 1,000 feet above them through breaks in the cloud. He climbed to investigate it, but was spotted and the aircraft dived away from him. Coleman lost contact briefly, but then it dropped below the cloud base about 10 miles west of Plau Lake, where Red 2 and 4 were waiting for it. Chalmers recognised the aircraft immediately as a Junkers Ju188 medium bomber and dived after it.[56]

Before long, Chalmers was on its tail, and opened fire at 600 yards, obtaining strikes on the fuselage, wings and cockpit area; then he hit the starboard engine, which immediately burst into flames. By now, Coleman had joined him, flying slightly behind him, and was able to see Chalmers' hits on the aircraft. He took some photos of the aircraft with his independent camera button, and continued to close range.

Straining under the damage, the Ju188 slowed considerably and Chalmers was forced to break off his attack at just 50 yards, now easily overhauling the Junkers. Taking the opportunity presented to him, Coleman slipped in behind it, and opened fire himself, scoring several strikes. He descended with the Ju188 to almost treetop height, then broke away to gain height again. Having circled around again, Chalmers pulled in behind the Junkers and made yet another attack.

The bomber crash-landed wheels-up in the middle of Rechlin Aerodrome. Both Chalmers and Coleman passed over the aircraft twice again to strafe it, and left it burning. The latter pilot recorded in his logbook,

> *Sighted a Ju.188 nr Plauer [sic] Lake, W/O Johnny Chalmers & I attacked it & forced it to crash land on Rechlin aerodrome wheels up and with its starboard engine on fire. We made two independent strafes on the E/A and left it afire.*[57]

During their strafing attacks, they also spotted other aircraft parked on the airfield and attacked these, too. Chalmers damaged an Fi156 Fieseler Storch and Coleman used up the remainder of his .5 calibre on an FW190 that was parked outside the watch tower on the north-western side of the aerodrome.

Coming under increasingly intense self-exploding and tracer Flak from the airfield, Coleman called up Chalmers and they climbed again to join WO Peter Hale, then reformed and headed for Celle, where they landed at 14:40. Coleman and Chalmers claimed a shared destroyed Ju188, plus a damaged Fieseler Storch on the ground by Chalmers and a damaged FW190 on the ground by Coleman. WO John Chalmers later recalled of this victory – his first – that there was, "certainly no feeling of triumph. Just a job completed".[58]

Also in the air at the time, Frank Woolley, now OC, 130 Squadron, shot down a Siebel Si204 transport aircraft at about the same time as Chalmers and Coleman brought down their Ju188. Between them, they had managed to down the Wing's 200th aircraft, but no-one could agree on who should be awarded the accolade.

> *Both these combats by 41 Sqdn and 130 Sqdn were at approximately 1400 hours and as that completes the destruction of our 200th Hun since the Wing was formed we can only award the honour jointly to S/Ldr Woolley, P/O Coleman and W/O Chalmers. Congratulations to all pilots past and present who have contributed to this by no means small total.*[59]

Either way, the honour of the Wing's 200th victory fell to past and present members of 41 Squadron.

However, the day was not yet over, and Flt Lt Peter Cowell took Blue Section (Cowell MV266, Jallands RM915, Fisher SM817, Remez SM826) on an armed reconnaissance of the Lübeck area at 16:10. They claimed two MET destroyed and ten damaged southeast of Lübeck and returned at 17:50.[60] A final patrol of the Lauenburg area was mounted by Red Section of four pilots at 19:25, led by Sqn Ldr Shepherd. However, it was uneventful, and the pilots returned at 21:15, thereby concluding another long day's flying.

Victories, 25 April 1945	Dest	Prob	Dam	Grnd	Location
Chalmers, John A.	Ju188	-	-	-	10m west of Plau Lake-Rechlin Aerodrome
Coleman, Patrick T.					
Cowell, Peter	-	Me262	Me262	-	Lübeck Aerodrome
Chalmers, John A.	-	-	-	Fi156	Ground, Rechlin A'drome
Coleman, Patrick T.	-	-	-	FW190	Ground, Rechlin A'drome

The Wing's other Squadrons, 130 and 350, also had a very successful day in the air, the former Squadron claiming 3-2-4 and the latter 2-0-1. Wg Cdr Keefer also claimed a FW190 destroyed for the Wing. Between Keefer and his three Squadrons, they had claimed all but two of the entire Group's aerial tally for the day.

The nature of the day's victories, and the range of aircraft falling to Group's pilots – a Fi156, FW190s, a Ju87 *Stuka*, a Ju188, Me109s, Me262s and an Si204 in the air (10-3-6), and a Do26 flying boat, a Fi156, an FW189 *Uhu*, FW190s, a He111, Ju87s, a Ju88, an Me109, and Me262s on the ground (7-0-25) – prompted the Group ORB to record,

A bewildering variety of aircraft were attacked today in the narrowing area of Germany between the Russian advance and our own. Only two sizeable formations were seen. A few of the other sightings, including the jets, were on recce, and the remainder were doubtless composed of various test, training and communication flights. The number and variety of these suggest that some airfields are still carrying on with their old routine, oblivious of the fact that they are now in the front line. An efficient and centralised control would not have allowed this state of affairs to continue, and it is indeed possible that this control no longer exists. [...]

A large number of aircraft were also attacked on the ground, and the chief lesson that emerges is that the jets are using LUBECK and HAGENOW, and the standard fighter HAGENOW, LUBECK, SCHWERIN, NEUSTADT, RECHLIM [sic] and LUDWIGSLUST. All airfields appear to be full of Aircraft, although it may be doubted if more than a small portion of these are fit for operations.[61]

The Group's total score of enemy aircraft as aerial and ground targets on 25 April 1945 amounted to the following:[62]

Wg	Do26	Fi156	FW189	FW190	He111	Ju87	Ju88	Ju188	Me109	Me262	Si204	Unid
122	-	-	-	-	-	-	-	-	1-0-0	1-0-0	-	0-0-1
124	-	-	-	-	-	-	-	-	-	-	-	0-0-3
125	-	0-0-1	-	6-0-4	-	0-1-0	-	1-0-0	1-0-1	0-2-1	1-0-0	-
127	0-0-1	-	1-0-0	3-0-3	1-0-0	0-0-6	1-0-1	-	-	0-0-3	-	0-0-5
Totals	0-0-1	0-0-1	1-0-0	9-0-7	1-0-0	0-1-6	1-0-1	1-0-0	2-0-1	1-2-4	1-0-0	0-0-9

26 April 1945 – Though a 'comparatively peaceful day', according to the 125 Wing ORB, 41 Squadron's day started early with two operations airborne before breakfast. Sqn Ldr Shepherd led the first, Blue Section of four aircraft, to the Pritzwalk-Wustrow area at 06:15, and Flt Lt Tony Gaze the second, Red Section of four aircraft, to the Parchim-Lübeck-Hagenow area at 06:20. Both were uneventful, and returned at 07:25 and 08:00 respectively.

At 10:45, Gaze was airborne again, leading Red Section (Gaze SM823, Wilkinson RB143, Hale RM792, Chalmers SM826) back to the Parchim-Lübeck-Hagenow area. This time they found scattered ground targets of opportunity and returned at 12:30 claiming two MET destroyed and five damaged.

Flt Lt Peter Cowell led the next armed reconnaissance, by Red Section again, to Lübeck at 14:05. They sighted an Ar234 jet over Lübeck Aerodrome at an altitude of 500 feet, but the pilot opened his throttle when he realised he had been seen and escaped due to his superior speed. "He got away by hedge hopping at full gallop and we had to give up the chase."[63] Red Section landed back at Celle, unable to make any claim for aerial or ground targets.

The day's fifth and last operation was airborne at 16:30, when Sqn Ldr Shepherd led Red Section of six aircraft on an armed reconnaissance of the Parchim-Wustrow area. It, too, was uneventful owing to heavy haze, which hindered their view of the ground, and the section returned at 18:25 with nothing to report.

The early end to the evening's operations allowed the whole Wing to enjoy a dining-in night in the Officers' Mess in honour of the success they had enjoyed since arriving in Celle.

> *…the Group Captain made a speech in which he honoured the success of the Wing during the last few weeks. Success such he said* [sic] *as he had never seen before during his long career in the Royal Air Force.*[64]

By 26 April, the units now based at Celle with 41 Squadron consisted of the following:[65]

B.118 Celle	
Squadrons	41, 130 and 350 Squadrons (125 Wing)
Servicing Unit	6041, 6132 and 6350 SEs
Repair & Salvage Unit	409 RSU (Detachment with 39 Wing)
Refuelling & Rearming Unit	Headquarters and A Section, 426 RRU
Forward Staging Post	91 FSP (46 Group)
Staging Post	19 SP (46 Group)
Air Liaison Unit	361 ALS
Stores Supply66	401, 404 and 406 (RCAF) ASPs
Hospital Unit	50 Mobile Field Hospital
Medical Unit	B Flight, 1 CAEU (2 Group)
Dental Unit	108 MDS
RAF Regiment	2875 and 2876 Squadrons
Signals Units	61 Wing Signals Section, and 511G (50 MFH), 591C (404 ASP), 5419J (125 Wg.), 5343D (91 FSP), 5348D (91 FSP), 5352P (91 FSP) & 55064 CB (125 Wg.) MSUs
Personnel Transit Centre	13 PTC

27 April 1945 – Despite the late previous night, the Wing was up early, commencing with a section of four pilots from 350 Squadron just before 06:00, who were up for an armed reconnaissance of the Ludwigslust area. The quartet (Orban NH654, Kicq SM814, Neulinger RB155, Gigot RM733) located a large convoy on the road between Kyritz and Perleberg, and radioed their find back to Celle. Within a short time, they were joined by sections from 41 and 130 Squadrons, the former sending up Red Section (Cowell MV266, Jallands RM693, Fisher SM820, Remez RM915) at 06:15 and the latter another four aircraft at 06:35.

The convoy was hit hard. 350 Squadron claimed it was "very successful in MET destroyed"[67], 41 Squadron claimed three destroyed, and 130 Squadron claimed seven destroyed and three damaged. The three sections were back on the ground soon after 07:30, reporting the convoy was "well alight".[68] A good team effort by all three of the Wing's squadrons.

Flt Sgt Peter Scott enjoying a quiet moment between operations. © Rossow family

It was a busy morning for Peter Cowell, who was potentially suffering less than other pilots following the previous night's revelry, as he was up again at 08:20 for his second armed reconnaissance in around two hours. On this occasion, he led Red Section (Cowell MV264, Scott RB159, Fisher SM823, Whale SM826) with fresh aircraft, but Flt Sgt Peter Scott was forced to come home early with radiator trouble. The remaining trio found another convoy, although the location is not recorded, and returned at 09:45, claiming two MET destroyed and five damaged, thereunder two staff cars.

Flt Lt Tony Gaze led the day's third operation, an armed reconnaissance to the Parchim area by Blue Section (Gaze SM817, Hale MV254, Wilkinson RB143, Stevenson RM915) at 09:25. Southeast of Goldberg, they found a two-mile-long convoy, which included at least two Panzer Mk. IV medium tanks and two tactical reconnaissance vehicles. The quartet returned at 11:20 claiming four MET destroyed and 13 damaged. This tally included at least one staff car destroyed, and two armoured vehicles, two horse-drawn vehicles, and a 3-ton truck damaged.

At 12:25, Flt Lt Tom Lawrence led Blue Section (Lawrence SM820, Hale SM826, Gray MV264, Jallands SM823) on an armed reconnaissance of the Lake Schwerin area. By now, the weather had started to deteriorate and targets began to become difficult to find. The section returned at 13:55 claiming just two MET damaged south of Lake Schwerin, and this concluded the day's flying.

However, the day ended on a sad note when news came through that 22-year-old Australian WO Alister Miller, who had served with 41 Squadron between October 1944 and January 1945, and had been transferred to 130 Squadron in February, had been lost, presumed dead on operations with 130 today.

A section of 130 Sqdn saw a Ju 188 while on an armed recce to the PARCHIM-WISMAR area. The e/a was at zero feet and after attacking some met [sic] the section attacked the e/a. W/O Miller is reported as having damaged it but unfortunately was himself shot down by return fire. He went straight in and it is feared there is little hope of his survival.[69]

A little more detail is offered by 130 Squadron's ORB, which explains "…our pilot was seen to crash and blow up. We are compelled to assume that W/O. Miller has been killed. The JU.188 was damaged."[70] Miller had indeed been killed, and was initially buried in Siggelkow Cemetery, falsely identified by locals as a Canadian pilot. He was correctly identified in 1947 and lies today in Berlin 1939-1945 War Cemetery.

LEFT Whilst at Celle in April 1945, Flt Lts Johnnie Wilkinson and 'Fanny' Farfan rebuilt a German Bücker Bü181 *Bestmann*, a single-engined two-seat trainer, from parts left behind at the airfield. They painted it yellow and applied RAF roundels for easy recognition. © Philip Farfan

RIGHT Another view of the Squadron's Bücker Bü181 *Bestmann*, bearing RAF roundels at Celle, April 1945. The man in cockpit is possibly Flt Lt 'Fanny' Farfan. © Gp Capt (ret) Derek S. V. Rake OBE AFC & Bar

28 April 1945 – The poor weather kept the Squadron on the ground for over 24 hours and it was not airborne on operations again until 17:10 today. At that time, Plt Off Pat Coleman led Pink Section (Coleman SM826, Chalmers MV264, Hale RM931, Moyle RM928) up on a weather reconnaissance.

On reporting the weather to be suitable for operations, he was permitted to undertake an armed reconnaissance of the Parchim-Lübeck area. Coleman attacked and destroyed a 15cwt truck near Mestlin but around 17:45, and whilst reforming the section at 2,000 feet, with the intention of heading further north, he sighted a green camouflaged He111 flying northeast at an altitude of 400 feet, just west of Goldberg.

Coleman immediately dived on the aircraft, ordering the rest of the section to follow him in. Coleman opened fire with a long burst at a range of 400 yards with 20° deflection, closing to 200 yards, and observed immediate strikes along the wings and fuselage. The rear gunner was firing back at him all the while, and Coleman broke away to port when his port aileron was hit.

His No. 2, WO John Chalmers, now commenced his own attack on the bomber, opening with a short burst at 600 yards. He closed to 400 yards and kept firing until he had closed to just 30. At the same time, WO Peter Hale dived on the bomber from 3,000 feet, opening fire at 400 yards with 30° deflection, closing to just 50 yards and reducing his deflection to just 5°. Their simultaneous attacks were devastating for the He111; its starboard engine caught fire, another fire started on the wing between the starboard engine and the fuselage, and pieces of the bomber started to detach themselves.

As Chalmers and Hale broke away, Flt Sgt 'Micky' Moyle moved in to finish the job, coming in from above with a 1½ second burst at 300 yards. His fire was accurate, too, striking the fuselage and port engine, which burst into flames. A short while later, the Heinkel crash-landed in flames near Niendorf.

The quartet returned to Celle at 18:20, claiming the bomber and one MET destroyed. Coleman found a round from the bomber's rear gunner had gone through an empty gun port on his port wing and exited through the aileron. He recorded in his logbook, "Section shared in destroying HE111. I blew up 15 cwt M/T. Area West of Goldberg. Rear gunner hit me in port wing."[71]

Just fifteen minutes after their return, Flt Lt Tom Lawrence led Red Section (Lawrence SM823, Gray RM693, Bødtker SM820, Scott RM915) on an armed reconnaissance of the Parchim-Lübeck area, the same region that Coleman's section had been sent to. It was a relatively quiet patrol and they returned at 20:05 claiming one MET damaged, believed to have been a horse-drawn vehicle, in the Schwerin area.

At 19:20, Flt Lt Tony Gaze was airborne to lead the day's final operation, an armed reconnaissance of the Schwerin area by Blue Section (Gaze SM826, Wilkinson MV254, Farfan SM817, Stevenson RM928). As they approached Schwerin at around 20:30, they sighted orbiting aircraft.

> *F/Lt Gaze and F/Lt Wilkinson encountered 10 plus FW 190's from 5,000 feet down to the deck over SCHWERIN airfield. The section was at 9,000 feet and the two went down, the remaining two remaining above. The e/a were bombed up and promptly jettisoned onto their own airfield and the town which could not have increased their popularity.*[72,73]

When the Focke-Wulfs dropped their bombs on the airfield and town, Gaze had a fleeting fear that he was diving on Typhoons. A moment later, however, he "identified them as definately [sic] FW 190's".[74]

Gaze and Flt Lt Johnnie Wilkinson dived to attack a pair of fighters that were climbing towards them, but Gaze found his gun-sight malfunctioning. This forced him to close to just 150 yards behind one of the short-nosed FW190s before opening fire, but as he did the aircraft half rolled and Gaze overshot. Wilkinson took his mark and followed the 190 down. His prey was not easily caught, but his perseverance paid off. It was, however, a tight scrape.

> *I throttled right back and went into fine pitch as I rolled over and followed [the] E/A, which pulled up in a steep port climbing turn leaving wing tip trails. I fired a 3 second burst at him in the turn, but with incorrect deflection. I still had too much speed and had to roll round his tail as he straightened up. E/A was still doing [a] gentle turn to port, when I fell in behind him again firing a two second burst from 250 yards, but missed. Opening up I closed to 50 yards, where I could see clearly that the E/A [still] had a bomb under the belly. I gave a two second burst, seeing strikes over the engine and cockpit. E/A immediately blew up and I ducked in my cockpit as I had to go through the wreckage. I felt the intense heat on my head and shoulders and everything was red. As I looked up, there was a bit of blazing wreckage falling into the buildings of SCHWERIN aerodrome and bits of flames trickling off[f] my wings. The engine was vibrating badly so I got an emergency homing. On returning I had to land fast as my A/C was wallowing. When I got out, one propeller blade tip was missing and most of the fabric on the elevators and rudders was burnt off. There were also little dents and holes all over the A/C.*[75]

Meanwhile, seeing that Wilkinson was on the tail of this aircraft, Gaze chased the second of the pair. The Focke-Wulf entered cloud and Gaze went in after it, but was buffeted by its slipstream and temporarily lost control of his Spitfire. He dropped through the cloud base as he regained

A Heinkel He111 similar to this was shared destroyed by Plt Off Pat Coleman and WOs John Chalmers and Peter Hale, and Flt Sgt 'Micky' Moyle RAAF west of Goldberg on 28 April 1945. © Deutsches Bundesarchiv Bild 101I-343-0694-21

WO Peter Hale served with 41 Squadron from 8 August 1944 to 21 March 1945, and from 17 April 1945 to 8 August 1945. Aside from scores of ground targets, he also shared the destruction of a Heinkel He111 with three other pilots on 28 April 1945. © 41 Squadron RAF

control, but found himself confronted with a dozen 190s. He pulled back up sharply into the cloud cover again.

A few moments later, Gaze exited the cloud in time to see an aircraft crash and explode near the marshalling yards just north of the aerodrome. Having already heard Wilkinson during this time report he had been hit, his first fear was that the downed aircraft was his No. 2. However, it was soon clear it was not.

Gaze and Wilkinson therefore assumed one of the Luftwaffe aircraft lost control and spun in. Considering they had not fired at it but that its loss must be attributed to their action, Gaze recorded on his Combat Report,

Blue 3 & 4 do not want to claim this [aircraft] so there is nothing left but for myself and Blue 2, F/LT Wilkinson to claim it shared. […] I reluctantly claim one unidentified E/A destroyed shared with F/LT Wilkinson.[76]

The rest of the section returned to Celle at 20:55 and this concluded the day's flying. For his part, Wilkinson claimed one short-nosed FW190 destroyed and the second aircraft, "unidentified undoubtedly F.W."[77], shared destroyed with Gaze. In its familiar, tongue-in-cheek fashion, the 125 Wing ORB quipped,

Neither pilot fired at it so the cause was probably stage fright. Neither wanted to claim it but we cannot destroy Huns even without ammo without chalking it up, so they are sharing it.[78]

Victories, 28 April 1945	Dest.	Location
Chalmers, John A.	He111	West of Goldberg-Niendorf
Coleman, Patrick T.		
Hale, Peter H.		
Moyle, Crawford N.		
Gaze, Frederick A. O.	FW190	Schwerin Aerodrome
Wilkinson, John F.		
Wilkinson, John F.	FW190	North of Schwerin Aerodrome

Separately, it was reported today that Celle's cinema had now been brought into operation for the men's entertainment, but the offices were still being cleaned out by local women under supervision. A Station football league was also being organised.

29 April 1945 – The Wing was off to an early start and 41 Squadron flew six operations today. However, their eagerness was in vain; the weather was poor with strong wind, and little of interest was seen all day, despite numerous patrols by the Wing over the Elbe bridgehead.

Op.	Section	A/C	Led by	Timings	Details
1	Blue	5	Shepherd	05:55-06:50	Patrol, Wittenburg-Ludwigslust line
2	Blue	4	Shepherd	10:45-12:10	Patrol, location not recorded
3	Red	4	Cowell	12:20-14:00	Patrol, Elbe Bridgehead
4	Blue	6	Gaze	14:10-16:00	Patrol, Elbe Bridgehead
5	Black	3	Coleman	15:45-17:30	Patrol, Elbe Bridgehead
6	Red	4	Gaze	19:10-21:05	Sweep, Elbe Bridgehead

41 Squadron sighted a trio FW190s near Lüneburg on the first of their bridgehead patrols, but two escaped into cloud cover and the third shot down by an unknown Spitfire. This was the only sighting of enemy aircraft by any of the Wing's squadrons all day.

> *The nearest approach to anything in the nature of 'spoil' was in the afternoon when a section of 41 Sqdn saw 3 FW 190's NNE of LUNEBERG, 2 of them were lost in cloud and the third was looking like a nice prize for our pilots when a rude Spitfire XVI intervened and shot the e/a down. So ended our excitement for the day.*[79]

The day's fifth patrol consisted of a composite operation of three aircraft from 41 Squadron (Coleman, Hale and Wheatley) and three from 350 Squadron (Delorme, Gigot, Boels). They experienced intense 30mm Flak but returned unscathed and with nothing else worthy of reporting.

WO John Chalmers served with 41 Squadron from 7 March 1945 to 25 October 1945, during which time he claimed two destroyed Fieseler Fi156 Storch, a shared destroyed Junkers Ju188, a shared destroyed Heinkel He111, and one Fieseler Storch damaged on the ground. © Rossow family

The only other incidents of note were that WO Peter Hale (RM928) returned within 15 minutes from the day's second operation with what is only referred to as 'technical trouble', and Flt Lt Peter Cowell (MV264) who suffered similar problems on the third operation, and returned to Celle within 40 minutes of take-off.

30 April 1945 – "What a day!" begins the day's entry in the Wing ORB. And indeed it was. 83 Group also reported an extremely busy and successful day over all, which saw 536 sorties flown for claims of no less than 38-1-24 aircraft, of which 3-0-16 were on the ground. The price was two pilots and three aircraft of their own.

> *Towards the end of the war [...] we had such complete control of the skies. I was almost sorry for a German who did get airborne. His chances of survival were very limited.*[80]

41 Squadron flew seven operations in the Wittenburg-Ludwigslust area between 06:05 and 21:15, totalling 32 sorties. 130 Squadron flew 30 sorties between 07:00 and 18:00 and 350 Squadron another 39 sorties between 06:40 and 21:20. However, the hard work brought its rewards and 41 Squadron ended the day with three aircraft destroyed, 350 Squadron with six destroyed and 130 Squadron with another ten, all for no loss.

402 (RCAF) Squadron from 126 Wing, another member of 83 Group flying Spitfire XIVs, claimed an additional six enemy aircraft destroyed and two damaged in the same general area as 125 Wing. It was a deadly day for the Luftwaffe in this sector, having sustained the loss of 25 aircraft – one Ju88, one Ju188, one Me109, one Siebel Si204, and 21 FW190s.

The day started for 41 Squadron at 06:05 when Flt Lt Tony Gaze took up Red Section on a patrol of the Schwerin area. Although the section made no claims on its return, it did report one significant piece of intelligence:

> *...F/Sgt. C.N. Moyle discovered an extremely well camouflaged air-strip on the edge of a wood, five miles south of Schweriner* [sic] *Lake. From this strip came most of the aircraft shot down by the Wing during the last few days of the war.*[81,82]

Moyle (NH832) estimated there were at least 30 FW190s and Me109s parked around the airfield, and from this point onwards, the Wing's patrols all "kept a special eye on this area".[83] It was not long before they were in action against these aircraft, and 350 Squadron, and 130 Squadron in particular, saw considerable action in the area.

However, despite the fact that 41 Squadron flew a further six patrols today, only two were fruitful. On one, Flt Lt Tony Gaze damaged two MET in a convoy of over 50 in the Schwerin area, but this action is not allocated to any particular operation in the ORB. In fact, it almost looked as if the Squadron would end the day without a single aerial victory, but on their last patrol, their luck changed. By that time, however, 130 and 350 Squadrons had already claimed all of their own victories for the day and were celebrating claims for a massive 16 aircraft destroyed.[84]

Op.	Section	A/C	Led by	Timings
1	Red	4	Gaze	06:05-07:35
2	Blue	4	Cowell	07:30-09:05
3	Red	4	Farfan	09:30-11:25
4	Blue	4	Lawrence	11:25-12:55
5	Red	5	Shepherd	14:10-16:00
6	Blue	6	Lawrence	17:05-18:40
7	Red	5	Shepherd	19:05-21:15

Flt Sgt Crawford 'Micky' Moyle RAAF shared the destruction of a Heinkel He111 with three other pilots on 28 April 1945. He was promoted to Warrant Officer the following day and commissioned in October 1945. © Rossow family

Red Section (Shepherd MV266, Gaze SM823, Chalmers RM931, Hale SM820, Smith RB143) was airborne at 19:05 for a patrol of the Elbe bridgehead near Lauenburg.[85] Around an hour and 15 minutes later, the section received a report from Ground Control of enemy aircraft approaching the bridges near Lauenburg from the northeast. Sqn Ldr Shepherd immediately spotted a lone FW190 and made quick work of it.

> *Just then our A.A. opened up and I saw an FW 190 bomber, slightly above and 12 o'clock, coming towards me. I pulled up and around on to his tail as he passed and gave him a short burst; he immediately caught fire and crashed in flames a few miles North of LAUENBURG.*[86]

Immediately afterwards, Flt Lt Tony Gaze spotted a second FW190 through a gap in the clouds north of Lauenburg, about 2,000 feet above him. He climbed towards it and, on reaching the cloud ceiling, fired a one-second burst at it. Realising he was under attack, the pilot jettisoned his bomb and dived for the cloud cover. Gaze fired another one-second burst before he could escape, and hit the short-nosed Focke-Wulf in several places. Pieces immediately broke off the aircraft and it caught fire behind the cockpit. The 190 continued its dive to the ground and exploded on impact near a village around three miles north of Lauenburg.[87]

By this time, Shepherd had returned to the bridgehead and reformed the section, where Gaze joined them within a few minutes, and they continued to patrol the area between two cloud layers at 6,000 feet. Anti-aircraft fire was seen again, indicating the presence of enemy fighters, and within moments a gaggle of eight Me109s were spotted. Messerschmitt 109s were a rare sight for the Squadron these days.

As Red Section approached in the turn, the 109s all jettisoned their bombs. Sqn Ldr Shepherd managed to single one out and gave chase. When Flt Lt Gaze tried to do the same, the remaining Messerschmitts formed a defensive circle – a tactic used since World War I – and he found himself under fire from the leading aircraft, just as he was about to open fire on the last. He was forced to break off his attack and the 109s quickly climbed into the cloud cover. Gaze gave chase once again, "but was not quick enough and they disappeared".[88]

Shepherd, meanwhile, was in hot pursuit of his own 109 and closed to 400 yards before opening fire. His aim was straight and he immediately obtained strikes, causing glycol to pour

During the last two weeks of April 1945, Flt Lt Johnnie Wilkinson claimed two destroyed FW190s, and three shared destroyed FW190s. © 41 Squadron RAF

from underneath it. The pilot immediately jettisoned his hood and made a controlled dive towards the ground. Shepherd fired three more bursts at the 109 to ensure it was finished and hit it on each occasion. Finally, the aircraft made a heavy crash-landing in a field a few miles northwest of Ratzeburg Lake. Shepherd passed over it again and fired yet another burst, this time setting the wreck on fire.

Red Section returned to Celle at 21:15, where Gaze claimed a short-nosed FW190 destroyed, and Shepherd one FW190 and one Me109 destroyed. So rare were combats with 109s these days, that this was the first destroyed by the Squadron since October 1943!

Although the news was yet to be announced, the greatest Allied victories in Germany today were the suicides of Adolf Hitler and Joseph Goebbels. The Third Reich was in tatters and the War was all but over. There were only a few days fight left in the Luftwaffe, Kriegsmarine and Wehrmacht, but they would be intensive, as last ditch battles were fought on many fronts, despite ammunition, fuel, equipment and manpower all being in short supply.

125 Wing had played a significant role in the Allied advance towards Berlin, and fought long and hard battles in this exhaustive last full month of World War II. The Wing flew approximately 1,800 sorties in April 1945 and made some respectable claims against hardware, as illustrated in the following table:[89]

Hardware, April 1945	Destroyed	Probable	Damaged
Aircraft (Air)	71	7	15
Aircraft (Ground)	22	-	21
MET	325	-	782
Tanks	-	-	3
Locomotives	2	-	128
Railway Trucks	53	-	465
Barges	3	-	53
Tugs	-	-	9

Victory in their Sights

In the space of eight days in late April/early May 1945, Flt Lt Peter Cowell, claimed two destroyed Focke-Wulf FW190s, and one probable and one damaged Messerschmitt Me262s in the air, and four damaged Arado Ar196s on the ground. © Cowell family

For their part, 41 Squadron had flown more operational sorties and hours during April 1945 than the Wing's other two squadrons, but despite this still expended over 20% less ammunition than them.

125 Wing Operational Sorties and Ammunition Expenditure, April 1945[90]						
Sqn	Sorties	FH	20mm	.303 cal.	.5 cal.	Total rounds
41	599	928.30	43,076	-	58,781	101,857
130	595	918.00	44,852	22,390	59,982	127,224
350	593	854.30	25,737	96,752	-	122,489
Totals	1,787	2,701	113,665	119,142	118,763	351,570

An Intensive Day

1 May 1945 – Another intensive day for the Squadron as the War reached its climax. By the time the last aircraft was back on the ground at Celle that evening, the Squadron's pilots had claimed no less than ten victories for no loss of their own.

Whilst Field Marshal Montgomery's forces fought their way across northern Germany towards Berlin, the Allied Air Forces continued to meet a defiant Luftwaffe in the skies above Germany, bravely defending the remnants of their homeland. Despite serious fuel shortages and overwhelming odds, they kept up sporadic but fierce opposition to the tsunami of forces conquering German territory from east and west, in a vain effort to repulse the inevitable fall of the Third Reich.

The first of the Squadron's several patrols today did not take off until 11:25 when Red Section (Cowell SM820, Jallands NH692, Bødtker NH832, Scott RM928, Remez MV264, Gray RM931) was sent on an uneventful bridgehead patrol, led by Flt Lt Peter Cowell. They found nothing of interest to report and, once relieved, moved on to the Schwerin area in search of targets of opportunity.

By around 13:00, Red Section had completed a sweep around Lake Schwerin, which has an overall length of around 21km and a maximum width of about 6km. Then they made an orbit of Schwerin Aerodrome at 4,000 feet, and had just done so when Red 4, Sgt Plt Peter Scott notified his colleagues he had just seen a single aircraft at ground level flying east, in the opposite direction to them. Scott and Red 3, 2 Lt Carl Bødtker, immediately broke formation and dived after it. Almost simultaneously, Red 5 and 6 – Flt Sgt Aharon 'Rem' Remez and Fg Off 'Ricky' Gray – sighted a second, and they, too, dived out of the formation and after their prey. Cowell and his No. 2, Fg Off Walter Jallands, stayed above to give them cover, and turned back over the lake and climbed through thick cumulous to 6,000 feet.

Although more aircraft may have been involved, it appears that at least some of the aircraft intercepted over Lake Schwerin by Red Section were six long-nosed FW190D-9s of JG51, the infamous *Mölders Geschwader*. The six aircraft had taken off from their base at Neu Redlin under the command of 13./JG51's 22-year-old Ace Fhj-Obfw Heinz Marquardt[91], to escort a formation of twelve FW190F-8 ground-attack aircraft to Berlin. It was intended to be their last operation before surrendering. Having completed the mission, they flew to Schwerin, and were just commencing their approach to the airfield at 13:00 when they were spotted by 41 Squadron's Red Section.

Sgt Plt Scott dived towards the aircraft he'd spotted but lost sight of it, and pulled back up to join 2 Lt Bødtker. As they regrouped, they spotted five more FW190s heading west at 6 o'clock at an altitude of 2,000 feet, and both turned hard to give chase. Bødtker closed in on one aircraft and opened fire at 600 yards. He kept his finger on the button for a good six to seven seconds whilst he closed his range to 200 yards. His fire was accurate and he observed pieces flying off the 190 just before it disappeared into a cloud. Losing sight of the aircraft momentarily, Bødtker dropped below the cloud cover to 1,000 feet and, in a turn to port looking for it, observed a FW190 hit the ground and explode south of Lake Schwerin, around half a mile ahead of where it had disappeared into the cloud.

Fg Off Gray and Flt Sgt Remez also lost the aircraft they had dived after, but Gray had seen Bødtker's combat and confirmed the victory. Peter Scott, meanwhile, had opened fire on the 190 flying to the port of the aircraft Bødtker had attacked, and also observed strikes. However, his target then climbed into cloud cover and he lost it. Pulling up to find it, he saw two FW190s heading north and chased them. Positioning himself behind the starboard of the pair, he opened fire. The 190 did not react, so Scott closed in to 300 yards as they both repeatedly disappeared into cloud and re-emerged, allowing Scott to fire only every few seconds, on each occasion they came out of the cloud cover. Once again, Scott saw strikes on this 190, but it soon disappeared completely into cloud and it, too, was lost.

Whilst this cat-and-mouse chase was going on, further above them Flt Lt Cowell had spotted two long-nosed FW190s flying east across the 61km^2 lake at zero feet. Unbeknown to him at the time, they were Fhj-Obfw Marquardt and his wingman, Iron Cross-decorated Fw Heinz Radlauer. He dived on the pair, utilising his advantages of surprise, height and speed, and ordered Jallands to cover him closely. Cowell was soon in a position to fire but was spotted and Marquardt banked to starboard and Radlauer to port. Jallands stayed with his No. 1, as Cowell broke after the starboard of the pair – Marquardt – and opened fire at 300 yards, immediately scoring strikes and causing the aircraft to spew black smoke and pull up almost vertically.

Cowell now closed to just 50 yards, firing hard, and struck the aircraft again around the cockpit and on the port wing. A moment later, the 190 stalled, flipped over, and fell straight into the southeast corner of Lake Schwerin. Marquardt was injured in the face and head, but managed to bale out in time, and landed, coincidentally, in the grounds of a nearby hospital.[92] Fw Radlauer had managed to escape in the direction of Flensburg just above the tree-tops, pursued part way by another Spitfire.

> *Against destiny we are all helpless. That was shown on 1st May when our Ofw. Marquardt – honoured and recognised by the whole Group as being one of our finest fighter pilots – was shot down by a Spitfire over Schwerin during the last mission of the war...*[93]

On 1 May 1945, Flt Lt Peter Cowell shot down JG51's Iron Cross-decorated Fw Heinz Radlauer in his Focke Wulf FW190D near Lake Schwerin, Germany. Many years later, Radlauer sent this photo of himself to Cowell. © Cowell family

Now seeking new prey, Cowell and Jallands soon found another FW190 orbiting to their north. Cowell closed to 300 yards before opening fire, and kept on firing while he reduced his range to just 50 yards. This resulted in a large piece of the port wing flying off, after which the pilot baled out. The aircraft hit the ground on the south-eastern lake shore.[94]

Satisfied with the job, Cowell called Red Section home, and they returned to Celle without loss at 13:25. Sgt Plt Scott claimed two FW190D damaged (the last damaged by the Squadron during the War), 2 Lt Bødtker claimed one FW190D destroyed and Cowell two FW190Ds destroyed.

Bødtker actually had a double celebration that day. Not only did he record his first, and indeed only, definitive victory of the War, but he was also promoted from Fenrik (2nd Lieutenant) to Løytnant (Lieutenant). In fact, within days, his victory today was to become an additional notable statistic: it was the final aerial victory of the war recorded by a Norwegian pilot.

In early 1995, almost fifty years after this clash, following some research into who had shot him down, Heinz Marquardt made contact with Peter Cowell, writing a simple but moving letter.

> *50 jear* [sic] *ago (1. Mai* [sic] *1945) I flew the last mission from the JG 51 (Mölders) in the II WW. I was shot down at 13^{00}h over the Schwerin Lake. But I baild* [sic] *out and survived. I flew the Longnose* [sic] *which pulled up vertically.*[95]

Peter Cowell promptly replied to Marquardt, apologising that he could only reply in English, but expressing both his 'surprise and delight' at hearing from him. He typed,

> *I have often thought of that day, 1st May 1945, and wondered what kind of people my two adversaries had been on that occasion. Little did I think that one of them was such an accomplished air ace as yourself with 121 victories in combat! What of the other one – who was he and did he survive also?*
>
> *It was unlucky for both of you that fate should have decreed that we met under such circumstances on that day. The day that was to have been your last mission of the war.*
>
> *I cannot apologise for destroying your FW 190 – that was an effect of the war and part of my duty as a Spitfire pilot in the R.A.F. I know that you would have had similar feelings had our positions been reversed and <u>you</u> had seen <u>me</u> first! I saw your colleague bale out of his aircraft but I did not see you do the same*

and it pleased me to learn that you had both parachuted to safety as it was so near the end of the war with Germany. I understand that you were wounded and ended up in hospital. I regret that and hope that your wounds were not too serious or long-lasting.

As it is nearly 50 years since our two countries were at war, and we are now partners together in Europe, it seems appropriate that we should forget our differences and learn from past mistakes on both sides in order that our children and grandchildren may continue to live in peace and happiness and not suffer the misery and heartache that war brings to all its participants.[96]

Cowell made it clear that Marquardt was welcome in his home if he was ever in England. The following month, in return, Cowell received an invitation from Generalleutnant Fritz Wenger to join Heinz Marquardt at a *Mölders-Vereinigung* [Mölders Association] reunion of past airmen of the *Mölders Geschwader* in Donau in May 1995.

Cowell replied he would be honoured to attend, and subsequently did so with his wife. They were treated as the guests of honour, and Cowell and Marquardt struck up a strong friendship that lasted the rest of their lives.

Returning now to 1 May 1945, two further patrols took place that afternoon, Red Section (Gaze, Smith, Hale, Chalmers) between 13:55 and 15:50, led by Flt Lt Tony Gaze, and Blue Section (Shepherd, Lawrence, Fisher, Rossow, Whale) between 16:10 and 17:45, led by Sqn Ldr Shepherd. Both returned without incident and Gaze's patrol constituted his final sortie with 41 Squadron. He was posted to 616 Squadron at B.109 Quackenbrück during the afternoon as OC, A Flight, flying the RAF's first jet aircraft, the Gloster Meteor F.3, as a part of 122 Wing.[97]

Flt Lt Fernand 'Fanny' Farfan took over as interim Flight Commander upon Gaze's departure, and led the next operation, at 18:25, when Red Section (Farfan SM817, Wilkinson SM820, Stevenson RM915, Coleman SM823) was airborne for a patrol around Lake Schwerin and Wittenberg. It was a long and tiring operation, in which they saw considerable action.

Approximately one hour into the flight, the pilots sighted a FW190 at their same altitude – 6,000 feet – when it suddenly appeared out of cloud cover over the bridges at Lauenburg. WO 'Steve' Stevenson approached the aircraft from 5 o'clock and opened up when he was within range. Realising he was under attack, the FW190 pilot half-rolled back into cloud cover in an effort to escape. Estimating where he would exit, Stevenson flew around to the other side of the cloud and engaged him when he exited.

On seeing Stevenson, the FW190 immediately dived back into the cloud cover and soon reappeared, much to everyone's surprise, between Red 1 and 2 – Flt Lts 'Fanny' Farfan and Johnnie Wilkinson! Ducking back into the cloud again, the pilot continued to try to out-manoeuvre Red Section with half rolls. Giving up on this tactic, the pilot dived for the deck, but Stevenson spotted him and dived after him. He closed to 600 yards and fired a short burst, which caused the pilot to weave to avoid becoming a static target. Stevenson then closed his range to just 300 yards and opened up again but this time observed strikes on the FW190.

However, the pilot and his aircraft were not done yet. Clearly an experienced flyer, the Luftwaffe pilot throttled back and forced Stevenson to overshoot him. Stevenson now became the hunted as the FW190 dropped in behind him, onto his tail. A feisty dogfight ensued for several minutes, during which Stevenson successfully deployed a similar tactic to the German pilot, by pulling up and executing a stall turn, which put him back onto the Focke-Wulf's tail.

Trying to evade Stevenson again, the pilot made a tight turn and dropped his bombs, but spun out, flicked over and went straight in, exploding on impact at the edge of a wood southwest of Wittenburg. One FW190 destroyed to Stevenson.

Around the time of Stevenson's victory, Plt Off Pat Coleman, flying Red 4, became separated from the rest of the section whilst identifying an aircraft. He therefore decided to "scout round Schwerin airfield before returning to base".[98] Climbing to 24,000 feet, he flew along the Baltic coast heading east, then turned south at Rostock before descending below the 1,000-foot-thick cloud base at 7,000 feet, then jettisoned his 45-gallon drop-tank and approached Lake Schwerin from the east. Descending to 6,000 feet, he spotted over nine FW190's "nipping in and out of the cloud above".[99]

Despite being out-numbered, he climbed to make an attack on the rear-most aircraft in the gaggle, hoping to duck back into cloud cover to make good his escape. However, he was soon spotted and, after much weaving in and out of the cloud, found two of the Focke-Wulfs on his tail, firing at him. Taking desperate evasive action, he made a climbing turn and proceeded to play "hide and seek with them in and out of cloud".[100] Finally succeeding in losing them, he dropped below the cloud base again and was pleased to find the sky clear, except for a single FW190 ahead of him.

> *I attacked this one using the gyro sight, he climbed and my gyro sight disappeared below my vision, however I continued to pull my nose straight through him whilst firing and observed strikes about the cockpit. The e/a went into a tight spiral towards the ground but I didn't attempt to follow up my attack until I saw it straighten out in an easterly course. I then pursued* [it] *closing rapidly* [and] *saw him jettison his hood, losing height all the time and finally bale out, I believe too low for his parachute to open fully. The e/a crashed in flames* [...] *S.W. of Plau.*[101]

Coleman climbed again to 200 feet above the cloud ceiling, and headed across the lake towards Schwerin. Once again, however, he came under attack from a FW190, but eluded him under the cover of cloud. Dropping down through the cloud base once again, he found he had not been followed and was alone again.

After a short while, Coleman spotted two more FW190s, this time flying northwards in close line abreast, just above wave height. Diving to their altitude, he swept in from behind and prepared to open fire. He clearly startled the two unsuspecting pilots, he later reported, as when still about 800 yards behind them, he saw "the left hand e/a turn sharply into the other. The two e/a interlocked and plunged into the northerly waters of the lake, the cause, presumably, panic."[102]

Coleman then returned to base, claiming three FW190s destroyed. Within minutes, he had become not just an Ace but also the Squadron's ninth-highest-scoring pilot of the entire War. He was only surpassed by the legendary pilots Lock, Webster, Bennions, Lovell, Mackenzie, Ryder, Shepherd and Boyle – all bar one from the Battle of Britain period. His three victories on 1 May were his final of the War and, in total, he was credited with 5¼ aircraft destroyed in the air and three damaged on the ground. His victories and bravery were recognised with the award of the DFC on 24 July 1945.

The remaining three pilots in the Section reported sighting eight seaplanes at Travemünde, a large naval vessel – a cruiser or a battleship – around 20 miles north of Wismar, and intensive shipping activity off Lübeck. None of these, however, were engaged.

The four pilots arrived back at Celle at 20:30 to find another patrol was still in the air on a sweep of the Schwerin area, led by Sqn Ldr John Shepherd. Having departed Celle at 19:30, it would be another 50 minutes before Blue Section (Shepherd MV266, Gray MV264, Cowell NH915, Jallands NH692, Bødtker RM928, Scott RB159) would touch down again.

Several individual FW190s were seen by Blue Section as they appeared out of cloud and disappeared back in again. Most of these were too far away to do anything about, although Flt Lt Peter Cowell and Fg Off Walter Jallands did chase after one of these to no avail. At around 20:20, however, Fg. Off Eric Gray spotted a pair of FW190's flying eastwards at 7,000 feet, near Lake Schwerin, and he and Sqn Ldr Shepherd gave chase.

> *Looking around to ensure that nothing was making a pass of us, I spotted a FW 190, about 1000 ft above and around on our tail. We broke around on this aircraft and quite a dogfight ensued amongst the three of us, the E/A pilot appeared to have lots of clues and made use of cloud cover as much as possible, this went on for 5 to 8 minutes...*[103]

Finally in a position to attack, Gray closed to 300 yards and opened fire, scoring strikes forward of the cockpit. The 190 immediately broke to starboard and dived back into cloud cover. Shepherd and Gray went in after it. Soon it emerged to Gray's port and he saw Shepherd firing on it and achieving strikes.

In wild evasive action, the aircraft broke again and the pair gave chase as it headed for the cover of another cloud. Gray closed to within 150 yards and opened fire again as it entered the cloud, holding his fire button for a full three seconds. Owing to the cloud cover, he did not see if his strikes hit home, however the 190 came out the other side streaming black smoke, then commenced a fast spin.

Gray followed it down a short while until he saw the pilot bale out. From above, he and Shepherd saw the aircraft finally hit the deck and explode a few miles east of Lake Schwerin. They shared the victory – a long-nosed FW190D – which was Shepherd's seventh and last of the War. Gray would also claim no more victories before the cessation of hostilities and finished the war with a score of two and two shared destroyed and one damaged.

Two of the section's pilots returned to Celle at 21:05 short of fuel, and the remaining four at 21:20. This concluded a very busy day's flying, in which eight aircraft were destroyed and two damaged for no loss.

Victories, 1 May 1945	Dest.	Dam.	Location
Bødtker, Carl S.	FW190D	-	South of Lake Schwerin
Coleman, Patrick T.	FW190	-	Southwest of Plau
Coleman, Patrick T.	2 FW190	-	Lake Schwerin
Cowell, Peter	2 FW190D	-	Lake Schwerin
Gray, Eric	FW190D	-	East of Lake Schwerin
Shepherd, John B.			
Scott, Peter F.	-	2 FW190D	Near Lake Schwerin
Stevenson, Ian T.	FW190	-	Southwest of Wittenberg

125 Wing's other two Squadrons also enjoyed some success in the Schwerin area that day. 130 Squadron damaged 20 MET between Schwerin and Sternberg, shot down an Me109 over Schwerin and damaged an He111 near Lübeck. Like 41 Squadron, 350 Squadron also encountered FW190s around Lake Schwerin – at least 20, they believed – and returned claiming four of them destroyed.

Not only was it a successful day for the Wing, but also for the entire Group. Between the eight Wings, 576 sorties were flown for claims of 19-1-13 aircraft and a massive 340-594 MET. The full tally was recorded as follows[104]:

Wing	Sorties	E/A105	MET	Locos	R/Trks	Tanks	Rly Cuts	Losses
121	45	-	45-78	-	8-8	0-2	-	-
122	91	3-0-0	93-223	0-3	7-9	-	-	1-1
124	71	-	128-174	2-0	11-8	1-4	-	-
125	78	13-0-3	3-33	-	-	-	-	-
126	94	0-0-2	-	-	-	-	-	2-2
127	147	3-1-8	71-86	-	-	-	-	-
143	24	-	-	0-4	1-4	-	3	-
39	26	-	-	-	-	-	-	1-1
Totals	576	19-1-13	340-594	2-7	27-29	1-6	3	4-4

2 May 1945 – It was another long day in which five bridgehead patrols were flown in the Lauenburg-Lüneburg area between 06:25 and 16:25, followed by two operations in the Oldenburg-Rendsburg area and Lübeck-Rendsburg area, respectively, between 17:45 and 21:15. These constituted a total of 28 sorties.

Op.	Section	A/C	Led by	Timings
1	Red	4	Farfan	06:25-07:20
2	Blue	4	Cowell	08:45-10:25
3	Red	4	Shepherd	10:45-12:40
4	Red	3 (4)	Jallands	13:10-14:45
5	Red	3	Farfan	15:15-16:45
6	Blue	4	Lawrence	17:45-19:25
7	Red	5	Shepherd	20:00-21:15

However, in contrast to the previous day, only one of these patrols saw any action, when Red Section (Shepherd MV266, Smith NH915, Coleman RM931, Chalmers RM915), encountered four Fieseler Fi156 Storche near Schwerin.

Constituting the third operation of the day, Red Section took to the air at 10:45 and conducted their assigned patrol of the bridgehead area. After completing the job uneventfully, the quartet were released and given permission by Kenway Control to make a sweep of the Lake Schwerin area. At 12:05, whilst flying over the lake at approximately 6,000 feet, Fg Off Roy Smith spotted a lone Fieseler Storch reconnaissance aircraft directly below their formation flying on the deck. Smith notified Sqn Ldr Shepherd and dived after it.

> ...I broke away and having done a loose spiral down to avoid building up too much speed I attacked from the rear and above giving a three second burst as I closed in I observed strikes on the aircraft which did a slow diving turn to port.[106]

Smith broke away and looked back to see the Storch had crashed near Schwerin and was on fire. He also claimed a second Storch damaged on the ground but there is no explanation of the circumstances in his Combat Report.

Around ten minutes after Smith had dived on his first Storch, WO John Chalmers made a similar sighting. Still with the rest of the formation at 6,000 feet, he spotted another lone Storch directly below them, this one flying northwards at an altitude of just 50 feet. He notified Sqn Ldr Shepherd and dived upon it. After verifying it was indeed an enemy aircraft, he opened fire with a two-second burst and scored immediate strikes on the cockpit and wing, which caused it to crash into a farm house near Lake Schwerin.

Within five minutes, he spotted another Storch also heading north at the same altitude. He notified Shepherd again and immediately went after this one, too. Closing in on the aircraft, he fired a four-second burst, which struck its target and the Storch burst into flames and crashed into a field in the same area.

Chalmers claimed both aircraft destroyed, and many years later had the following recollection of the event.

> I actually feel embarrassed about [them]. I mean, it wasn't a contest. Again, it was a job that needed to be done. But it gave me no satisfaction. It could just as well have been a locomotive or a truck. The only difficulty was that the closing speed was so fast it was not easy to actually hit the machines. If I recall, one of them crashed into a farm yard. Time changes your perspective of war. At the time they were the enemy and you had a job to do. Now many of my feelings are of regret. Had they been Focke-Wulf 190s, that would have been different. Of course as a pilot if one did kill someone one did not see the result, as a soldier might. It was rather remote.[107]

These were Chalmers' final victories of the War, having previously shared the destruction of two other aircraft in the air – half a Ju188 and a quarter of a He111 – and damaging a further aircraft – another Storch – on the ground, all during April 1945. Smith's two victories today constituted his full tally for the war: one destroyed in the air and one damaged on the ground.

A Junkers Ju188 similar to this was shot down by Flt Lt Derek Rake in the Norderstapel-Husum area on 3 May 1945, which constituted the Squadron's final victory against the Luftwaffe in its history. © Deutsches Bundesarchiv Bild 146-1989-039-18A

The only other events worthy of mention today were that Flt Lt Tom Lawrence, allocated as Red 3 on the fourth bridgehead patrol, suffered engine failure in RM928 and could not take off from Celle at 13:10, and that on the fifth bridgehead patrol, one MET was damaged. This ground victory was claimed by Red Section (Farfan MV266, Stevenson SM826, Moyle NH915), which was airborne at 15:15 and returned at 16:45.

130 and 350 Squadrons also enjoyed some success today. 130 Squadron destroyed four Bücker Bü131 *Jungmann* training aircraft near Lake Schwerin in the early morning. A few hours later, they also brought down an Me109 near Schwerin Aerodrome. For their part, 350 Squadron encountered a large stationary German convoy between Crivitz and Schwerin which was "duly clobbered… to the tune of 55 damaged".[108] Later in the day, a section of four pilots from 350 also claimed an Arado 234 jet destroyed.

There was, however, a loss reported by 125 Wing during the day. Former 41 Squadron pilot, Flt Lt Bill Stowe, who had left the unit in late April to become a Flight Commander with 130 Squadron was hit by debris from the explosion of one of his targets whilst attacking MET, and he was compelled to force-land his Spitfire XIV, SM833, behind Axis lines near Lake Schwerin. Stowe remained concealed from German forces and subsequently managed to walk back to Allied lines unaided.

As a whole, 83 Group flew 815 sorties today, claiming 41-1-16 aircraft in the air and on the ground, and 610-967 MET, 4-24 locomotives and 43-90 railway trucks, for the loss of four pilots and aircraft. The scale of these victories is staggering.

3 May 1945 – It was a relatively quiet day today, despite four operations being airborne between 05:55 and 16:20, but it was also the day upon which the Squadron claimed its final aerial victory of the War.

The first of operation was a sweep of the Lübeck area by Red Section, led by Flt Lt Tom Lawrence, which reported sighting over 200 MET concentrated northwest of Lübeck heading north on the Plön-Kiel road. They came under intense Flak around Plön but returned to Celle unscathed at 07:30 with nothing more to report.

The Final Victory

The day's second operation, an armed reconnaissance of the Lübeck area by Yellow Section (Rake NH915, Wilkinson SM820, Chalmers SM826, Hale RM963), took to the air at 08:05, led by Flt Lt Derek Rake. Approximately one hour into the patrol, Yellow 2, Flt Lt Johnnie Wilkinson, called up Rake and reported seeing MET on a road near Norderstapel. Rake dived down and strafed the road, flying northwards along the length of the vehicles, damaging at least one.

As he climbed again, he spotted a twin-engined Ju188 medium bomber, heading east around five miles away, at approximately 1,000 feet. Rake, then at an altitude of just 200 feet, called up the section and immediately gave chase. Realising he had been seen, the Ju188's pilot swung northwards and dived for the deck. The tactic did not help.

> *I fired several bursts from extreme range having recognised the E/A as a JU 188. I observed pieces fall off the wings and the E/A began to weave slightly. I came into line astern and the tail gunner commenced firing at me. By this time, I was catching up slightly and my next burst, at about 600 yards must have killed or disabled the tail gunner as he ceased firing. I closed range down to about 100 yards; the E/A's port engine caught fire and my aircraft was covered in oil. He made an effort to crash land but on hitting the ground his port wing came off and the rest of the E/A was burning. I circled to take a photo of the debris....*[109]

At this time, Rake found himself over Husum Aerodrome and saw FW190s, Ju87 Stukas and large transport aircraft dispersed around it. He took the opportunity to fire at one of these aircraft but saw no strikes. Flak from the airfield soon became too intense to continue his attack, and he was forced away.

Before the pilots returned to Celle, they also saw intensive shipping activity on both sides of the Peninsula. Wilkinson and Chalmers touched down at Celle again at 09:20, and Rake and Hale joined them 30 minutes later.

Rake's claim of one Ju188 destroyed constituted his first full victory, although he had previously shared a half-victory with Flt Lt Tony Gaze. More significantly, however, it was the Squadron's final aerial victory against the Luftwaffe in its history.

At 11:20, Blue Section (Cowell SM817, Jallands RM693, Fisher RM928, Whale NH692, Gray NH915, Wheatley RM931) was airborne on an armed reconnaissance of the Flensburg area, led by Flt Lt Peter Cowell. They found a good concentration of motorised transport heading north between Schleswig and Flensburg, and returned at 13:00 claiming four MET destroyed and another 24 damaged. They also reported seeing many aircraft on the ground at Flensburg Aerodrome, and the estuary full of shipping, and sighted three large flying boats, which they believed to have been six-engined BV222 *Vikings*, parked on the lake at Schleswig.

The day's fourth and last operation was an armed reconnaissance in the Flensburg area by Red Section at 15:25, led by Sqn Ldr Shepherd. However, the weather was not on their side, and they returned just under an hour later with nothing to report but bad conditions and poor visibility.

On the whole, 83 Group enjoyed considerable success again today, flying a massive 897 sorties. They claimed 51-0-26 aircraft in the air and on the ground, and 353-765 MET, 3-19 locomotives, 34-61 railway trucks and 14-101 shipping vessels, for the loss of seven pilots and nine aircraft.

Flt Lt Derek Rake poses for a shot in front of Spitfire XIV, NH915, EB-H, the aircraft he was flying when he shot down the Squadron's 200th and final Luftwaffe aircraft of the War, Celle, May 1945. © Gp Capt (ret) Derek S. V. Rake OBE AFC & Bar

Separately, Plt Off Pat Coleman was sent on a week's aircrew leave today, and thus missed the last days of the War. He flew to Croydon via Brussels in a four-hour transfer in a Dakota troop carrier, and returned to the Squadron on 11 May.

4 May 1945 – The day passed uneventfully, despite four patrols being undertaken in the Hamburg-Boizenburg area between 07:00 and 15:25.

> *Today, with poor weather and a battle ground nearly out of reach, we could hope for little spectacular. A strong cross wind developed in the afternoon and operations ended early.*[110]

Nonetheless, a total of sixteen sorties were flown by the Squadron, as follows:

Op.	Section	A/C	Led by	Timings
1	Red	4	Farfan	07:00-08:40
2	Blue	4	Fisher	09:25-11:05
3	Red	4	Rake	11:25-13:00
4	Red	4	Cowell	13:35-15:25

130 Squadron sent up four patrols of four aircraft between 06:20 and 14:15 to the same area as 41 Squadron, and 350 Squadron sent up five patrols of their own to the Hamburg area between 05:35 and 13:40. As a whole, the Wing flew 54 sorties, but all operations were uneventful. It was the same story across much of the front in this sector.

> *The G.A.F. on its last day in this part of the world, remained for the most part on the ground. Disorganisation and shortage of petrol prevented any final fireworks and the aircraft, which at one time had ranged at will over two continents, spent their last day packed into a tiny corner of the Reich, tamely awaiting the end.*[111]

The big event of the day, however, was the return of three of the Wing's pilots, the most astounding being that of Sqn Ldr Terry Spencer who had been shot down at low altitude on 19 April and captured for the second time in three months.

> *From the reports received at the time it seemed impossible that [Spencer] could be alive, but the impossible happened. He was shot out of his aircraft as it plunged towards the sea in WISMAR BAY and as his parachute opened, he hit the water. Having struck out for land he was surprised to find that he was only in four feet of water, so waded ashore in soft mud. Although badly burnt, bruised, and shaken he was forced to walk over a mile. He was eventually liberated and brought back home where he arrived this afternoon. F/Lt Stowe who landed in 'no man's land' got back to 142 Wing and an Auster brought him back to the Wing. F/Lt Smith of 350 Squadron who crash landed in enemy territory on the 20th April also came back today. He evaded for some days until hunger drove him to join a batch of American prisoners until he was liberated by the Americans.*[112]

That evening, a party was held in Spencer's honour, led by Wg Cdr Keefer. However, the day's biggest surprise was yet to be announced. The party,

> *...exploded in the most perfect and general drunkness [sic] when it was announced that the General Officer Commanding all the German forces in our sect[or] VON KLUGE has capitulated to the most Glorious 2nd Army to which we were proud to belong and support.*[113]

The War was finally coming to an end. Earlier that evening near Luneburg, Field Marshal Sir Bernard Montgomery, General Officer Commander in Chief of 21st Army Group, had co-signed the unconditional surrender of all German forces in north-western Germany, Holland and

Denmark. It pre-dated the general surrender[114], and would take effect the following morning at 08:00 on 5 May 1945. The document read,

Instrument of Surrender
of
All German armed forces in HOLLAND, in
northwest Germany including all islands,
and in DENMARK.

The German Command agrees to the surrender of all German armed forces in HOLLAND, in northwest GERMANY including the FRISIAN ISLANDS and HELIGOLAND and all other islands, in SCHLESWIG-HOLSTEIN, and in DENMARK, to the C.-in-C. 21 Army Group.
This to include all naval ships in these areas. [This line is handwritten]
These forces to lay down their arms and to surrender unconditionally.

All hostilities on land, on sea, or in the air by German forces in the above areas to cease at 0800 hrs. British Double Summer Time on Saturday 5 May 1945.

The German command to carry out at once, and without argument or comment, all further orders that will be issued by the Allied Powers on any subject.

Disobedience of orders, or failure to comply with them, will be regarded as a breach of these surrender terms and will be dealt with by the Allied Powers in accordance with the accepted laws and usages of war.

This instrument of surrender is independent of, without prejudice to, and will be superseded by any general instrument of surrender imposed by or on behalf of the Allied Powers and applicable to Germany and the German armed forces as a whole.

This instrument of surrender is written in English and in German.

The English version is the authentic text.

The decision of the Allied Powers will be final if any doubt or dispute arises as to the meaning or interpretation of the surrender terms.[115]

The surrender was signed by Field Marshal Montgomery for the Allies at 18:30 on 4 May 1945, and countersigned by Generaladmiral Hans-Georg von Friedeburg[116], General Eberhard Kinzel, Rear Admiral Gerhard Wagner, Oberst Fritz Poleck, and Major Hans Frieda.

5 May 1945 – The final day of the War in 125 Wing's sector started early but left just enough time for one final patrol by each of the squadrons. 130 Squadron was up first, sending three aircraft (Gibbins, Seymour and another unidentified pilot) to the Hamburg area between 05:45 and 07:10. 41 Squadron was airborne at 06:20 when Red Section (Farfan SM826, Rake NH915, Smith RM931, Cowell MV264, Jolly SM817, Fisher SM820) headed for the Hamburg-Lübeck area. They landed at 08:05 with nothing to report. Finally, three pilots from 350 Squadron (Featherstone, Watkins & Doncq), almost missing the opportunity for a final operation, took off at 07:45 – just 15 minutes before the surrender came into effect – and returned an hour later, with nothing to report. In their ORB, they recorded,

Ennoying [sic] *enough was the fact that the capitulation was to come into affect* [sic] *only today at 08.00 hrs. So we had to fly again and we did it but God only knows where we went. […] So when Kenway said*

> *"Ten to eight boys" and also when he says* [sic] *"Eight oclock* [sic] *boys you may go home", did they use A, B and C channels to be sure not to have ended the last patrol of the war in an improper place such as a wood or garden.*[117]

130 Squadron, however, saw some action on their patrol, being vectored onto a Siebel Si204 transport aircraft by Kenway Control at 06:30, with orders to escort it to an Allied airfield or force it down.

> *The aircraft was flying south near HAMBURG and on sighting our aircraft immediately turned north and started evasive action. As the war was still on, F/LT Gibbons* [sic] *and F/Sgt Seymour had no option but to shoot it down, and that was that. Shortly afterwards the section met 4 Fw 190's and they adopted the correct tactics by waggling their wings and dropping their under-cart. They were at zero feet and obviously very nervous. Our pilots, with visions of Lugers, tried to bring them to B.118 but as soon as the Huns saw a strip at B.152 they were not prepared to take further risks and promptly landed.*[118]

The Siebel caught fire during Gibbins and Seymour's attack and crashed west of Hamburg. Not only was this 125 Wing's final victory of World War II, but also that of 2 TAF.

For 125 Wing, the rest of the day was taken up with celebrations, but the 2nd Army still had much work to do, spending the day moving forward 'not to conquer but to occupy' the rest of the sector, taking thousands of prisoners as they did.

> *Prisoners taken by* [the] *2nd Army since the ELBE crossing are estimated at 400,000 plus. They i*[n]*clude such varied characters as William Joyce (Lord Haw-Haw) and Field Marshal MILCH, the creator, with GOERING, of the Air Force with which Germany entered the war, and up till recently the Inspector General of the LUFTWAFFE. Approximately 60 Generals and a whole string of high ranking officers from the OBERKOMMANDO DER LUFTWAFFE, are also among the total.*[119]

During the day, much to his bitter disappointment, WO Peter Hale was sent home on leave, spending a night in Brussels before continuing on to Croydon in Surrey. He returned on 14 May to find the Squadron had left Celle and was now based in Copenhagen.

Between 1 May 1945 and the cessation of hostilities on 5 May, 41 Squadron had flown 81 operational sorties, totalling 128 hours and 45 minutes, and four non-operational sorties, totalling four hours. The pilots expended 4,078 rounds of 20mm cannon and 5,200 rounds of 0.5 calibre ammunition.

A captured Siebel Si204 bearing RAF roundels at Celle, April 1945. One such aircraft was shot down by 130 Squadron west of Hamburg on 5 May 1945, becoming not only 125 Wing's last victory of the War, but also the last by 2TAF. © Gp Capt (ret) Derek S. V. Rake OBE AFC & Bar

125 Wing Scoreboard showing aircraft victories and ground targets for 130, 350 and 41 Squadrons, and total victories for the Wing, to 5 May 1945. © Gp Capt (ret) Derek S. V. Rake OBE AFC & Bar

83 Group, of which 41 Squadron had been a member since arriving on the Continent on 4 December 1944, recorded the following statistics during the eleven months since D-Day, 6 June 1944-5 May 1945:[120]

Sorties[121]	128,241
Losses – Aircraft	958
Losses – Pilots	711

Target	Dest.	Prob.	Dam.
Enemy Aircraft	1,263½	75	728
MET	9,723	-	17,470
Locomotives	719	-	2,505
Railway Trucks	3,868	-	9,943
Ships	45	-	292
Barges	292	-	995

83 Group also recorded the following aerial victories and losses between December 1944 and May 1945:[122]

	Victories against the Luftwaffe			Group Losses	
	Dest.	Prob.	Dam.	Aircraft	Pilots
Dec. 1944	91½	5	46	95	71
Jan. 1945	122	8	59	65	46
Feb. 1945	56	2	42	92	82
Mar. 1945	59	6	31	85	55
Apr. 1945	235	9	146	113	98
May 1945	131	2	71	19	16
Totals	694½	32	395	469	368

Flt Lt Derek Rake on the wing of his aircraft, Spitfire XIV, NH915, EB-H, at Celle, May 1945. © Gp Capt (ret) Derek S. V. Rake OBE AFC & Bar

6-8 May 1945 – The 41 Squadron ORB records simply, "Nil returns"[123] for this period, as the pilots remained on the ground until the general surrender was signed. Elsewhere in the Wing, however, much was going on.

On 6 May, 350 and 130 Squadrons, and 6132 Servicing Echelon were advised they would be posted to B.152 Fassberg to join 122 Wing. The latter two units' stays would, however, only be brief. After 130 Squadron relinquished their Spitfire XIVs and took over 411 (RCAF) Squadron's Mk. IXs on 7 May, both were to be transferred to Fighter Command and return to England on 10 May, to their new base at North Weald.

As such, it looked like 41 Squadron would remain the sole member of 125 Wing. Within a day, however, three new squadrons arrived at Celle: 137, 414 (Recce) and their old friends from 122 Wing, 486 RNZAF. This left the aerodrome, in the words of the 125 Wing ORB, "choc-a-block with aircraft".[124] The units then based at Celle with 41 Squadron consisted of the following:[125]

B.118 Celle	
Wing	125 Wing
Squadrons	41, 130, 137, 414 (RCAF) and 486 (RNZAF) Squadrons
Servicing Unit	6041, 6132, 6137, 6404 and 6486 SEs
Forward Staging Post	91 FSP (46 Group)
Staging Post	19 SP (46 Group)
Air Liaison Unit	361 ALS
Stores Supply[126]	401, 404 and 406 (RCAF) ASPs
Hospital Unit	50 Mobile Field Hospital
Medical Unit	B Flight, 1 CAEU (2 Group)
Dental Unit	108 MDS
Signals Units	61 Wing Signals Section, and 511G (50 MFH), 5419J (125 Wing), 5343D (91 FSP), 5348D (91 FSP), 5352P (91 FSP) & 55064 CB (125 Wing) MSUs
Personnel Transit Centre	13 PTC

The End Finally Arrives

At 15:00 on 8 May, everyone gathered around the radio to hear the Prime Minister, Winston Churchill, announce Germany's complete and unconditional surrender and the official declaration of peace in Europe. He paid tribute to those who had died in its achievement, but reminded them that total peace had not yet come to the world. Japan was yet to be defeated and this would still need a great effort to accomplish. His broadcast was followed in the evening by a message from the King, in which he thanked his people for their sacrifices over the past almost six years.

There was also some unexpected excitement during the evening when a lone Ju88 flew in from Norway and landed at Celle Aerodrome. Bringing the aircraft to a stop, the crew disembarked and surrendered. The rest of the night was taken up by surprisingly modest victory celebrations. It was hard to believe that it was finally over.

> *I still remember the strangeness of it all. Suddenly there seemed no meaning to our lives. It was all over. No more operations. No more briefings. No more dangers! Hostilities over. Finished. At first I didn't feel elated. Flattened rather. Then the reality dawned. The war was won. The killing stopped. It was only later that one realised one had survived and was thankful. […]*
>
> *…I [did not] realise the end of the war was imminent. It is perhaps strange to hear that, after all we were at the forefront but, looking back, it always surprises me that we knew so little of what was going on. There were no newspapers. We knew little of the "big picture". We lived in our own self-contained squadron world.… We lived in a sort of a news vacuum.*[127]

The Squadron Moves On

Soon after the cessation of hostilities on 5 May, it was announced that 125 Wing would move to B.160 Kastrup in Copenhagen, Denmark.[128] Then, on 7 May, 130 and 350 Squadrons were posted away with 6132 Servicing Echelon and the movement order was cancelled, much to everyone's disappointment. However, only a day later, with 137, 414 and 486 Squadrons now members of the Wing, it was announced that the move was on once again and should take place on 9 May, but without 414 Squadron. They would form a rather unwieldy composite wing of 41 (Spitfire), 137 (Typhoon) and 486 (Tempest) Squadrons.

On the morning of 9 May, 'A' Party left for Kastrup by air, followed by Dakota-loads of ground personnel. By lunchtime, they were all gone, except for the Wing's motor vehicles, which would follow up the rear by road, and a party of men who would remain in Celle a while longer as a rear element for administrative purposes. 41, 137 and 486 Squadrons flew up during the afternoon – a transfer of 70 minutes – leaving just 'B' Party with their vehicles, who left soon after. "So ends our operational activity at B.118 and we can justly look back on our record with pride."[129]

However, notice of the move was so short that it looked like the Wing would have to leave for Copenhagen without any medical facilities. 50 Mobile Field Hospital had been based in Celle with 125 Wing, but were already destined for B.152 Fassberg, so could not accompany them. A solution to the problem had to be found quickly.

> *Short notice was given of the move of the air party to Copenhagen, and it was fortunate that plans had already been made for a light surgical team from either M.F.H., and a light sick quarters from any wing, to be ready for a Wing moving into Berlin by air if the occasion arose. It was possible therefore at 2 hours' notice to include in the air party a surgical team from 50 M.F.H. and a small sick quarters party from 124 Wing under S/L. Taylor Brown. This party set up sick quarters with surgical facilities in the sick quarters at Copenhagen Kastrup.*[130]

The day also saw a few personnel movements for the Squadron, bidding farewell to both Flt Lt Roy Fisher[131], who was posted to 130 Squadron, and Lt. Carl Bødtker[132] who was posted back to the

Royal Norwegian Air Force. At the same time, Flt Lt Bill Stowe re-joined the Squadron from 130 Squadron, and brought with him Flt Lt John Lee DFC.[133]

Kastrup

Located 8km south of the centre of Copenhagen, and lying just five metres above sea level on the island of Amager, Kastrup Airport was opened in 1925 as a small grass strip that soon became one of the first civil airports in the world. In 1939, a large passenger terminal was opened that catered for 72,000 annual passengers, but the outbreak of War curtailed almost all pleasure and business travel.

When Germany occupied the country on 9 April 1940, the Luftwaffe took over the airfield and called it *Fliegerhorst Kastrup*. In summer 1941, they laid the airfield's first concrete runway, which measured 1,400 metres by 65 metres on completion. Very limited civilian traffic was able to operate throughout the War, although confined to the boundaries of the German Reich.

In April 1941, the Luftwaffe's *Blindflugschule 4* (*BFS 4*) [Instrument Flying School 4] moved in, using Kastrup as its main base, with satellite airfields at Kolberg, Neumünster, Pütnitz, Schwerin and Værløse. It was equipped with Ju86s and Ju88s. In October 1943, the school was re-classified and became *Flugzeugführerschule-B34* (*FFS-B34*) [Pilot School B34]. It continued in this capacity until October 1944, when pilot training ended, but it was not until early February 1945 that the school was formally disbanded.

During the German occupation, thousands of Danes fled Denmark for Sweden and the United Kingdom, but one escape involving Kastrup was particularly brash. A 21-year-old civilian aircraft mechanic named Per Hiul used to watch his German employers at the controls of their aircraft and, though he had never flown himself, decided this would be his means of escape. In July 1944, he successfully stole a He111 bomber from Kastrup and managed to take off and fly to Sweden. Once in Swedish airspace, however, anti-aircraft fire opened up from Helsingborg and he was hit. The aircraft crash-landed in a field, and although Hiul was hurt, he survived to tell the story.

By the time of the German surrender, more runways and taxiways had been built at Kastrup, and as the terminal had barely been used – and the airport had never suffered aerial bombardment – the infrastructure was still intact and in excellent condition when 125 Wing arrived. This left the aerodrome in the envious position of being one of the few unscathed in occupied Europe and therefore also one of the most modern.

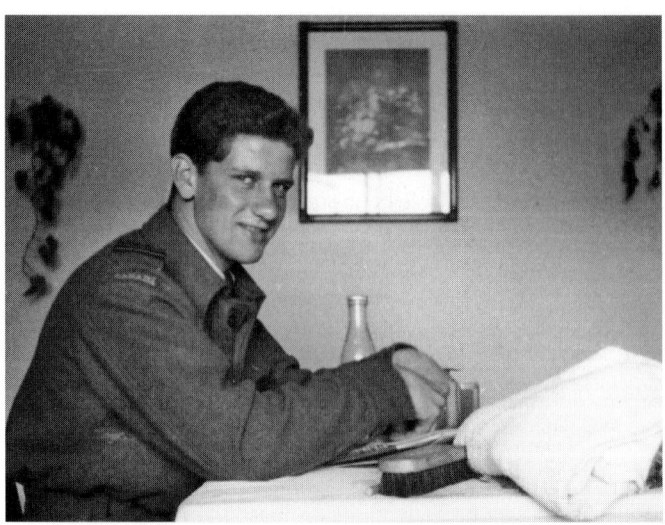

Following his posting to 130 Squadron as a Flight Commander on 24 April 1945, and subsequently coming down in Germany and walking back to Allied lines through No Man's Land, Flt Lt Bill Stowe was posted back to 41 Squadron on 9 May 1945. © Cowell family

41 Squadron at Kastrup, May 1945. On propeller: Fg Off Eric Gray RAAF and Plt Off Pat Coleman; on wing left to right: Flt Lt John Wilkinson, Flt Lt Arnold Jolly, WO Vivian Rossow RAAF, WO Ian Stevenson, WO Crawford Moyle RAAF, WO Peter Hale, WO Vic Whale, WO Aharon Remez (Palestine), WO Hugh Kelly, Flt Sgt Peter Scott, WO John Chalmers and WO Peter Wheatley; standing left to right: Fg Off Alexander McAllister (Adjutant), Fg Off Frank Hegarty, Fg Off Walter Jallands, Flt Lt Peter Cowell, Sqn Ldr John Shepherd DFC, Flt Lt Bill Stowe, Fg Off Roy Smith, Flt Lt John Lee DFC and Flt Lt Tom Lawrence RNZAF. © Neil Stevenson

From left to right, WO 'Vickie' Whale, WO 'Micky' Moyle RAAF, WO Viv Rossow RAAF, Flt Lt Bill Stowe RCAF, Sqn Ldr John Shepherd DFC*, WO Peter Hale, Fg Off 'Ricky' Gray RAAF, ca. May 1945. © Neil Stevenson

From left to right, Fg Off 'Ricky' Gray RAAF, WO Hugh Kelly, WO Ian Stevenson, WO Viv Rossow RAAF, chatting with an unknown pilot at Kastrup, May 1945. © Neil Stevenson

The first Allied forces to arrive in Copenhagen were the SHAEF Mission to Denmark, headed by Maj Gen Richard Dewing CB DSO MC, who landed at Kastrup in an air convoy of DC3 Dakotas on 6 May 1945, with orders to set up an interim government. 125 Wing arrived just three days later.

10 May 1945 – No flying was undertaken all day, whilst 41 Squadron settled itself into their comfortable new quarters at Kastrup. The Danes welcomed 125 Wing with open arms, the Wing ORB recording that day, "Already the people of COPENHAGEN are falling over themselves to invite us to their homes and it is obvious considerable stamina will be required to keep pace with them."[134]

The Squadron's WO John Chalmers remembered their arrival and his time in Copenhagen with great fondness, recalling…

…we all flew to Kastrup Aerodrome in Copenhagen to begin what was probably the best time of our lives, before or since. The welcome we got was truly wonderful. A huge fuss was made over us, which was rare indeed in life but very nice. In restaurants strangers would send over drinks, pay for our meals. We were spoiled and loved it. The food, too, after years of austerity all the things, simple things, we had missed were now readily available. And the Danes were just super. I have never lost my great fondness for the Danish people. It was a fabulous time.

One of our first jobs was to acquire some transport. We "obtained" a touring Mercedes Benz, a milk float (very handy for getting to and from dispersal), a small armoured vehicle (impressive but uncomfortable for picking up one's date), an American Ford and a monstrous NSU motorbike. […]

Petrol for all this transport? Not a problem. We had recourse to high grade aviation fuel from the tanks of German aircraft dotted around the place. The main difficulty was persuading someone it was his turn to suck on the rubber tube to start the flow. It was vile. We all took turns, carefully monitored by all the others.

The food, the parties, the friendly girls. Yes, undoubtedly, the time of our lives. We then found a stack of

German parachutes and were able to do deals with various ladies' clothing establishments who were interested in obtaining good quality silk. The proceeds enabled us to buy small radios which fitted nicely into a space behind the seats in the Spitfires. Those parachutes gave us a good standard of living.

[…] …the food was marvellous and things were available that we hadn't had for years and in some cases, ever. A particular favourite was Danish Blue Cheese and we had our own large round cheese ceremoniously paraded into the mess past the other squadrons' tables each night and reverently placed in front of the CO. This became tradition and even after we had left Copenhagen we used to fly the Auster back on a food mission on fairly regular occasions. The Blue Cheese was always top of the list. The Auster was booked out as a training exercise. There were always volunteers![135]

11 May 1945 – The great excitement of the day was a 50-minute escort provided by twelve aircraft at 17:40 to the AOCinC 2 TAF, Air Marshal Sir Arthur Coningham KCB DSO MC DFC AFC, who was leaving Copenhagen. Except for the transfer from Celle to Kastrup, this was the first proper flying the Squadron undertaken since the morning of 5 May. The pilots returned at 18:30.[136]

Plt Off Pat Coleman returned from leave today. Retracing his steps from Croydon to Celle in four-hour flight in a Dakota, he arrived to find the Squadron had moved to Kastrup. Boarding another Dakota the same day, he then flew to Copenhagen, which took another two hours.

12 May 1945 – More excitement this morning when Field Marshal Bernard 'Monty' Montgomery arrived at Kastrup at 11:30 and drove into Copenhagen to meet King Christian X, and was received by the Danish Prime Minister, Vilhelm Buhl. Monty departed Kastrup again that afternoon for which 41 Squadron provided an escort of six aircraft as far as Lübeck. Following a 55-minute flight, the pilots refuelled and arrived back at Kastrup at 20.15 after a faster 40-minute flight.[137]

Warrant Officers Peter Hale, Hugh Kelly, Aharon Remez (Palestine) and Viv Rossow RAAF, ca April 1945. © Rossow family

WO Viv Rossow tries out a captured German 20mm Flak gun, Celle or Kastrup, May 1945. © Rossow family

14 May 1945 – Squadron formation practice.

15 May 1945 – WO Peter Hale arrived in Kastrup from leave, via Celle, and found a single airman on duty. He was told that the entire Squadron was in Copenhagen celebrating and enjoying all the treats the city had to offer. Not surprisingly, he hurried to join them!

17 May 1945 – The only activity of the day was a Squadron formation drill practiced by 12 pilots between 11:00 and 11:55.

18 May 1945 – Demonstration formation flying and dummy air-ground attack practice.

19 May 1945 – Wing Formation practice during the afternoon in which 12 of the Squadron's pilots participated.

21 May 1945 – Several sections were airborne for practice flying between 10:55 and 15:55. WO Ian Stevenson had a minor incident during one of these sessions, when RM915 blew a hole in its cylinder head.

22 May 1945 – During the afternoon the Wing put on an air display before the Danish Commander in Chief, Lt Gen Ebbe Gørtz, and large crowds that had turned out for the display. Attacks were made on targets – German MET – lined up along the beach at the edge of the aerodrome by all three squadrons. 137 went in first firing rockets from their Typhoons, followed by 486 in their Tempests, and finally 41 in their Spitfires, making cannon and machine-gun attacks. Three Mosquitos led by AVM Basil Embry CB DSO AFC also performed aerobatics and re-enacted the attack on Gestapo headquarters in Copenhagen, in which Embry had personally participated. The crowds were "very evidently impressed"[138] by what they saw, recorded the ORB, and the show was considered a resounding success.

B Flight aircraft parked on the airfield at Kastrup in May 1945. In the foreground, Flt Lt Peter Cowell's EB-P for Peter (probably MV260), and behind it EB-L, EB-R, and EB-V. © Cowell family

Flt Lt Peter Cowell gazing skywards, watching aircraft over Kastrup airfield in May 1945. Note the aircraft in the background, which is identified by its code letters 'GCK' as the personal aircraft of Wg Cdr George C. Kiefer DSO DFC*, who was 125 Wing's Wing Commander Flying upon 41 Squadron's arrival on the Continent in December 1944. © Cowell family

WO Viv Rossow by 41 Squadron Spitfire XIV, EB-U (probably RM693), at Celle or Kastrup after the cessation of hostilities. © Rossow family

WO Ian 'Steve' Stevenson in front of his Spitfire XIV, RM915, EB-K, at Kastrup, May 1945.
© Neil Stevenson

23-31 May 1945 – There is little information available on the last week of May. Both the Squadron and Wing ORBs summarise the final week of the month in a single paragraph. The Squadron's ORB records that Flt Lts 'Fanny' Farfan and Johnnie Wilkinson, and WO 'Steve' Stevenson were chosen as an aerobatics team for displays, whilst on 25 May, Flt Lt Ross Harding made a brief visit to the Squadron, following three months as a Prisoner of War.

Plt Off Pat Coleman's and WO Viv Rossow's logbooks suggest that these days were generally spent by the pilots practicing formation aerobatics, but there were also two highlights for Coleman: On 23 May, he spent three hours as second pilot in a Siebel 204, and on 31 May he had the opportunity to fly a FW190 solo, spending an hour gaining 'experience on type'.

The 125 Wing ORB provides virtually no detail on this week, and sums up the period, "Nothing further to report. Hospitality on terrific scale continues...."[139] It is, however, known that the units based at Kastrup with 41 Squadron on 26 May consisted of the following:[140]

B.160 Kastrup	
Squadrons	41, 137, and 486 (RNZAF) Squadrons (125 Wing)[141]
Servicing Echelons	6041, 6137 and 6486 SEs
Refuelling & Rearming Unit	A Section, 426 RRU
Staging Post	123 SP (46 Group)
Air Liaison Unit	361 ALS
Stores Supply[142]	401 ASP
Hospital Unit	Surgical Team detachment from 52 (RCAF) MFH, and Sick Quarters Party detachment from 124 Wing
Dental Unit	108 MDS
RAF Regiment	2856 Squadron
Signals Units	61 Wing Signals Section, and 5419J (125 Wing), 5449W (B.160/2 TAF) & 55064 CB (125 Wing) MSUs

And so the month of May 1945 ended in much of an anti-climax after the intense beginning to the month, as the Squadron rapidly settled into a mundane peacetime tedium. WO John Chalmers remembered,

After the armistice life settled into a rather dull routine. We practiced formation flying, scrambles, aerobatics, gunnery and so on. One felt a bit pointless. Waiting to be demobbed, really.[143]

This unusual picture from above shows WO Viv Rossow RAAF in the cockpit of his Spitfire XIV.
© Rossow family

Nominal Roll, 31 May 1945

No official nominal roll exists for the pilots serving with 41 Squadron at the end of May 1945, but the following list has been compiled from various sources, and is believed to be accurate.

Sqn Ldr John B. Shepherd DFC
Flt Lt William N. Stowe RCAF (OC, A Flight)
Flt Lt Peter Cowell (OC, B Flight)
Flt Lt Fernand W. Farfan (Trinidad)
Flt Lt Arnold W. Jolly
Flt Lt Thomas E. Lawrence (RNZAF)
Flt Lt John Lee DFC
Flt Lt Derek S. V. Rake
Flt Lt John F. Wilkinson
Fg Off Eric Gray (RAAF)
Fg Off Francis M. Hegarty
Fg Off Walter J. Jallands
Fg Off Roy D. A. Smith
Plt Off Patrick T. Coleman
WO John A. Chalmers
WO Peter H. Hale
WO Crawford N. Moyle (RAAF)
WO Vivian J. Rossow (RAAF)
WO Ian T. Stevenson
WO Frederick V. Whale
WO Peter E. Wheatley
Flt Sgt Hubert F. Kelly
Flt Sgt Aharon Remez (Palestine)
Flt Sgt Peter F. Scott

A little more relaxed after the cessation of hostilities, WO Viv Rossow or WO 'Vickie' Whale stands before Spitfire XIV, EB-T (serial unknown), in just shorts! © Rossow family

ABOVE The cessation of hostilities provided the Squadron time to relax and muck around a bit. WO Viv Rossow RAAF, and possibly WO 'Micky' Moyle RAAF, carry WO 'Vickie' Whale parallel to the ground. © Rossow family

LEFT Clowning for the camera, WO John Chalmers curtsies. © Rossow family

A Few Statistics in Closing

Throughout the War, almost 325 men served as pilots on 41 Squadron. They claimed a total of 200 aircraft destroyed in the air and one on the ground, 61 aircraft probably destroyed in the air, 109 aircraft damaged in the air and 22 on the ground, and 53 V1 flying bombs destroyed (45 plus 8 shared) and one damaged. Additionally, there were countless ground targets destroyed and damaged; an accurate figure is impossible to determine.

The pilots had been awarded three DSOs, 16 DFCs, one DFM and one Mention in Despatches between 3 September 1939 and 8 May 1945, but another five DFCs were also awarded after the cessation of hostilities. These went to Sqn Ldr John Shepherd (2nd Bar), Flt Lts Peter Cowell and Daniel Reid, Fg Off Patrick Coleman, and WO Ian Stevenson, making a total of 21 DFCs for the Squadron's World War II service.

However, the unit also mourned 64 men (60 pilots and four ground crew) killed in action or in accidents, whilst at least 56 men (54 pilots and two ground crew) sustained wounds in action or injuries in accidents. Another 21 pilots came down in Axis territory and became Prisoners of War. These casualties represent approximately 18.3%, 16.5%, and 6.4%, respectively, of the total number of pilots who served on the Squadron between 1 September 1939 and 31 May 1945. These combined figures equate to a total casualty rate of a little over 41% amongst the Squadron's pilots.

Varying statistics exist for cost of the air war in both victories and losses. The British Government started releasing its first figures for the European and Middle East theatres in early May 1945, even before the cessation of hostilities, but these figures were generally too premature to be reliable.[144] Although completely accurate figures will likely never be available, and available totals therefore just estimates, a better picture has developed over the ensuing years, largely the result of painstaking efforts by military historians, researchers and authors, and through the release of documents previously closed under secrecy laws. As such, today's estimates of losses are closer to the following:

One man investigates the cockpit of a captured Arado Ar234, whilst one of the pilots is photographed in front of it, possibly at Celle or Kastrup, © Rossow family

WO Ian 'Steve' Stevenson with a captured FW190 at Kastrup, May 1945. © Neil Stevenson

RAF – Total aircraft losses in Europe and the Mediterranean (i.e. excluding the Pacific Theatre) are considered to be approximately 22,000, of which around 10,000 were fighters and 12,000 bombers. Aviation historian Chaz Bowyer estimated Fighter Command losses at 4,790 aircraft, 3,690 men killed, 1,215 men wounded and 601 Prisoners of War.

Luftwaffe – Figures were kept until early January 1945, after which reporting began to break down. Until this time, total losses from frontline units were considered to have been approximately 40,600 aircraft destroyed in combat and 10,450 as a result of accidents. Another 20,500 were damaged in combat and 15,150 damaged in accidents. In addition to these figures, total losses from flying schools and other non-frontline units, as a result of both combat and accidents, were believed to be about 12,400, whilst damaged aircraft were placed at just under 10,000. These figures exclude aircraft casualties between early January and early May 1945.[145] It is believed that approximately 2.5 million men served in the Luftwaffe, of which 432,706 were eventually listed as killed or missing in action. This equates to a casualty rate of 17.3%.

In many ways, Germany is still coming to terms with its role and actions in World War II. As recently as April 2009, for example, the *Süddeutsche Zeitung* interviewed the late, then 91-year-old, Luftwaffe Lieutenant General Günther Rall, who was one of the most successful Luftwaffe fighter pilots of World War II, having claimed some 275 victories. During the War, he was seen publicly as a national hero, but was privately a critic of the Hitler regime. Rall re-joined the Luftwaffe after the War and went on to become an Inspector of the Luftwaffe and finally an Air Attaché to NATO prior to his retirement.

The newspaper posed an interesting question, which was representative, perhaps, of present generations' sensitivities about the humanity and ethics of what the Luftwaffe – and, indeed, of the Third Reich as a whole – had inflicted upon the world. It was more of a statement provoking a response, than a proper question.

From left to right, WO Peter Hale, WO 'Vickie' Whale, WO Hugh Kelly, Fg Off 'Wally Jallands', WO 'Micky' Moyle RAAF, Flt Lt Bill Stowe RCAF, unknown with cigarette, Flt Lt Arnold Jolly, Flt Lt 'Fanny' Farfan. © Rossow family

The entertainment on the Continent was not always of a professional nature! The Squadron's pilots on stage during a concert after the cessation of hostilities. © Rossow family

WO Viv Rossow RAAF and Sgt Plt Aharon Remez (Palestine) at the Tivoli Gardens amusement park in Copenhagen with a Danish local and Danish airmen (note the Wings on their breasts). The lady in the middle and man first from the right are possibly Mr and Mrs Larsen. Mr Larson is wearing the armband of the Danish Resistance. © Rossow family

You fought during a time when one saw his opponent in another aircraft from close proximity and fired at him with machine guns. And in the process of achieving your 275 victories, you probably killed many men whose faces you could recognise.

Rall responded,

I understand your question. But we didn't think like that. It was war. No, we were proud of every aerial victory, and particularly happy that we weren't the one on the receiving end. Of course, these days, in quiet moments, I tell myself: You killed. To protect others and not to be killed yourself. But also: What for? The Third Reich had trained 30,000 fighter pilots. 10,000 survived the Second World War, not including Prisoners of War and those considered no longer fit for service. A third. That is the highest loss rate after the U-Boat crews. […] The War stole our youth.[146]

In closing, I would like to share the thoughts of some of the Squadron's pilots at the end of the War, such as then WO John Chalmers, who has generously shared with me so many of his memories of people, places and events for this History of 41 Squadron. Like Rall, he has also spent many years thinking about this period of his life and the experiences he made. Feeling a deserved pride in his participation in bringing a long and deadly war to a close, he recalled that,

41, at the time I was privileged to be a member, was first class both in terms of leadership… and personnel. […] I was lucky to have had so many marvellous comrades in my comparatively short time with the squadron. Even now I remember them well and with great fondness.

…it was the Airforce [sic] that was the making of me and an experience I wouldn't have missed. I am grateful to have had the experience. These sentiments are shared by so many of my colleagues.[147]

In a similar vein, Fg Off Ron Johnson remembered his time with 41 Squadron was…

…an experience I enjoyed very much. […] 41 Squadron was always a friendly unit with excellent relationships among the pilots and between the pilots and ground staff. We had good leaders at Wing, Squadron and Flight levels and this made for high standards of morale and performance.[148]

And, finally, Flt Lt Peter Cowell felt that,

The days in 41 I remember with the greatest affection for I met some of my best friends at that time and some wonderful characters. I am extremely proud to have had the good fortune to be a member of such an old and famous Squadron.[149]

Their statements capture sentiments that no doubt many members of 41 Squadron since 1945 can also identify with.

Thankfully, it would be another fifty years and two generations before the Squadron would once again be called upon to fire its weapons in anger in Europe.

I. The Pilots
August 1942-May 1945

This Appendix consists of short biographies of all the pilots who served with 41 Squadron between August 1942 and May 1945.

ADAMS, STANLEY BRUCE 'Bruce', R.133839/J.85677, RCAF; b Toronto, Ont, Can, 26 May 21; ed Nthn Vocational Sch, Toronto; enl in RCAF, Toronto, 19 Oct 41; 12 Equipment Depot, Oct 41; 3 ITS, Victoriaville Que, 28 Feb 42; LAC, 25 Apr 42; 17 EFTS (Finch & Moth), Stanley NS, 8 May 42; 4 EFTS (Finch & Moth), Windsor Mills Que, 5 Jun 42; 14 SFTS (Harv), Alymer Ont, 1 Aug 42; plt badge & Sgt Plt, 30 Nov 42; Y Depot, Halifax NS, 4 Dec 42; emb Halifax for UK, 24 Dec 42; poss 9 EFTS (Moth), Ansty, ca Jan-Mar 43; Manning Pool, Apr 43; Flt Sgt, 20 May 43; poss 17 (P)AFU (Hurr, Master I/II), Watton, Nflk, & subs Calverley, Chesh, Apr-Jun 43; Crse 51, 57 OTU (Spit), Eshott, NBL, Jul-14 Sep 43; 41 Sqn, 8 Oct-1 Dec 43; com Plt Off (J.85677), 30 Nov 43; RF/EF, attempted CL but stalled at 50-75 ft, spun in, crashed & severely inj in Spit XII, MB846, Tang, 1 Dec 43; repat to Can, 14 May 44; 1 Trng Cmd, 13 Jun 44; to RC, 3 Jan 45; rlsd 24 Apr 45; occ post-war, accountant in pte practice (FCA); d Toronto, 7 Jul 2002

ANDERSON, ROBERT EDMUND 'Andy', A.402337, RAAF; b New Farm, Bris QLD, 22 Oct 20; res Fairfield NSW, 1922-40; ed Fairfield PS & Parramatta Intermediate HS; occ Jnr Clerk NSW Public Svce, Works Depot, Bridge St, Syd, 1935; enl in RAAF, Syd, 9 Apr 40; entered RAAF as AC2 & to 2 ITS, Brdfld Pk NSW, 19 Aug 40; LAC, 16 Sep 40; Crse 4, 5 EFTS Narromine NSW (Moth), 19 Sep-8 Nov 40 (30.05 hrs dual & 25.40 hrs solo; 1st dual, 20 Sep 40; 1st solo, 30 Sep 40); 2 ED Brdfld Pk, 14 Nov 40; att RCAF, 28 Nov 40; to Vncvr per *Aorangi*, 28 Nov 40; layover, Auck NZ, 4-6 Dec 40; arr Vncvr Can, 23 Dec 40; 1 SFTS (Harv), Borden, Ont, 27 Dec 40-17 Mar 41; Sgt Plt, 17 Mar 41; 1 TED, Debert, Nova Scotia, 17 Mar 41; to Glasgow per *Georgic*, 6 Apr 41; disemb UK, 20 Apr 41; 13 Intake, 3 PDC, Uxb, England, 20 Apr 41; Crse 20, 57 OTU (Spit), Hwdn, Flint, 26 Apr-2 Jun 41; 58 OTU (Spit), Ggmth, Stirling, 2 Jun 41; A Flt, 457 (Aust) Sqn (Spit), Baginton, Warks, 14 Jul 41; 452 (Aust) Sqn (Spit), Kenley, 26 Sep 41; part of 1 Dest He114 (shared sqn claim), 13 Feb 42; leave, 16-23 Jan & 4-11 Feb 42; 55 OTU (Hurr), Usworth, Dur, 18 Feb-2 Sep 42; att FIC, 11 OTU, CFS Upavon (Master), 15 Mar-10 Apr 42; com Plt Off, 15 May 42 (gaz 9 Jun 42); leave, Lon, 2-9 Jun 42; 32 Sqn (Hurr II), WMalling, 7 Sep 42; marr Helen 'Maud' Elderfield (WAAF Driver), Edmonton, Lon, 28 Sep 42; 1 ED, W Kirby, Chesh, 2 Nov 42; emb for Gib w 32 Sqn per SS *Empire Foam*, 8 Nov 42; Fg Off, 15 Nov 42; arr Gib, 22 Nov 42; 32 Sqn (Hurr II), Maison Blanche, Algeria, att 323 Wg, 17 Dec 42; att HQ NW Africa Coastal Air Force, 16-22 Apr 43; 14 Sqn (Mstg), RAF Blida, Algeria, 16 Apr-18 Jun 43; Aircrew Pool, Algiers, 23 Jun 43; to UK per SS *Samaria*, 28 Jun 43; arr Liv, 24 Jul 43; NE sick, Abbey Lodge Sick Qtrs, RAF Depot Uxb, 26 Jul 43; 84 Grp Comms Flt, Gatwick, 2 Sep 43; att 1530 BAT Flt (Oxford), Wtrg, 12 Grp, 28-31 Dec 43; 31 Base, Stradishall, 1 Jan 44; 84 GSU (Mstg, Spit, Tmpst & Typhn), Aston Down, Gloucs, 1 Mar 44; Temp Flt Lt (WS), 18 Mar 44 (gaz 28 Jun 44); B Flt, 41 Sqn, 18 Mar-18 Dec 44 (192.55 FH, thereof 86.30 operational); att Air Show Unit, Thorney Is, Hants, 11-18 May 44; ½ Dest V1 w Flt Lt C. R. Birbeck, N of Maidstone, Kent, 22 Jun 44; ½ Dest V1 w WO A. S Appleton, 12m SE of Beachy Head, Ssx, 9 Jul 44; leave, 17-24 Jul 44; hit by AA over Münster, G., but NI, then stalled on landing at Diest & seriously inj face, 18 Dec 44; 85 GSU, 7 Jan 45; 9 PRC, 14 Jan 45; FI, 53 OTU (Spit), KiL, 31 Jan-12 May 45; att FI, CGS Catfoss (Spit), 14 Feb-28 Mar 45; 11 PDRC Bnmth, 16 May 45; disemb Syd, Aust, & to 2

PD, 7 Jul 45; 61 Refresher Crse, 5 SFTS Holding Pool, Uranquinty NSW, 16 Aug 45; 2 PD, Syd, 7 Sep 45; demob, 28 Sep 45; emp NSW Public Svce & res Fairfield NSW, 1946; Eng Crse, Syd Uni, 1946; res Haberfield NSW, 1947; grad BE (Civil), 1950; res Lismore NSW, 1951; res Moree NSW, 1953; res Strathfield NSW, 1954; res Adaminaby Dam Township, Eaglehawk NSW, & occ Resident Eng, Adaminaby Dam Project, Snowy Mountains Scheme, 1956; res Maroubra NSW, 1959; ret as Inspecting Eng, Water Supply, Jul 81; d Maroubra NSW, 10 Dec 84, aged 64; bur in Niche 67, Wall VXD, Pergola Fountain, RAAF Sect, Rookwood Cem, Syd NSW

APPLETON, ARTHUR STANLEY 'Archie' & 'Junior', 1576662, RAFVR; b Eastry, Kent, 19 Dec 21; occ student on enl in RAFVR, 11 Oct 41; Sgt Plt, 1942; 57 OTU (Spit), Eshott, NBL, 1942; 2 TEU (Spit), Ggmth, Stirling, 1943; WO, 1943; A Flt, 41 Sqn, 21 Mar-18 Dec 44; ½ Dest V1 w Flt Lt R. E Anderson, 12m SE of Beachy Head, Ssx, 7 Jul 44; 1 Dest V1, 20m S of Hastings, Ssx, 21 Jul 44; 1 Dest V1, 3m SE of Bexhill, Ssx, 23 Jul 44; SD/AA in Spit XIV, RM699, during attack on loco 10m NW of Münster, G., inj (cut leg when baling out) & captured at Rheine, G., 18 Dec 44; Stalag Luft VII, Bankau, 9-19 Jan 45; Stalag III-A, Luckenwalde, 25 Jan-10 May 45; res on repat, Shottenden, nr Canterbury, Kent

ATKINSON, THOMAS GUY, 1218340, RAFVR; b Runcorn, Chesh, 29 Jan 23; ed Northampton Sch; enl in RAFVR, Cardington, 2 Feb 41; 2 BFTS (Stearman, Vultee & Harv), Polaris Flt Academy, War Eagle Fld, Lanc CA, USA, 1941-42; Sgt Plt, 1942; 41 Sqn, 14 Jul-21 Oct 42; 1435 Sqn (Spit Vc), Luqa, 12 Dec 42; com Prob Plt Off (143721), 17 Feb 43; ½ Dest FW190, w Flt Sgt S. H. Benjamin, 2 Jul 43; 1 Dest Me109, 2 Jul 43; 1 Dam Me109, 10 Jul 43; posted to UK, tour exprd, 19 Jul 43 (ORB: "One who arrived as an N.C.O. and turned out to be a good officer and leader"); Fg Off (WS), 17 Aug 43; 56 (Punjab) Sqn (Typhn Ib), 1943; KIA in Typhn Ib, MM969, aged 21, 3 May 44; s of Edward W & Elizabeth A. Atkinson, of St Albans, Herts; bur Div 67, Row P, Grave 18, Ste Marie Cem, Le Havre

AUSTEN-SMITH, Roy David, *see SMITH, Roy David Austen*

BALASSE, MAURICE ARTHUR LEON 'Momo', 135893, RAFVR (Belgian); b R'jev, Russia, 27 Jun 14; Pilot Sch, Wevelghem, B., 7 May 34; Cpl Student Plt, 25 Oct 34; Elementary Brevet, 12 May 35; Mil Flg Brevet & to Sgt Plt, 31 Aug 35; 1/3/1 Regt Aé, Tirlemont, B., 1 Sep 35; Higher Mil Flg Brevet, 31 Aug 37; Sgt Plt 1st Class, 26 Sep 37; 3/3/3 Regt Aé, Brussels, 1 Jul 38; moved w 3 Regt into F., 13 May 40; rtnd to B., unemp in occ B., 20 Aug 40; left B. for Gib, via Paris, Dijon & Lyon, 28 Apr 42; crossed Pyrenees into Spain, 8 May 42; arrested Figueras, Spain, 9 May 42; imprisoned Barcelona, 5 Jul 42; imprisoned Miranda, 19 Aug 42; lib 26 Aug 42 & taken to Gib, arr 8 Sep 42; shipped to Eng & arr 6 Oct 42; com 2 Lt, AMB, 25 Dec 42; enl in RAFVR, 1 RC, Uxb, 31 Dec 42; com Prob Plt Off in RAF, 30 Dec 42; 1 RC, 31 Dec 42; Crse 42, 5 (P) AFU (Master I/II), Ternhill, Salop, 19 Jan-14 Mar 43; 61 OTU (Spit), Rednal, Salop, 19 Mar-22 May 43; 41 Sqn, 1-10 Jun 43; 349 (Belgian) Sqn (Spit Va), Coolham, Ssx, 11 Jun 43-25 Jul 43; admtd Ranceby Hosp, Sandford, Lincs, 25 Jul 43; Fg Off, 30 Jul 43; RAF Rehab Unit, 7 Aug 43; B Flt, 41 Sqn (again), 6 Nov 43; att 611 (W Lancs) Sqn, 6-23 Nov 43; 41 Sqn (again), 23 Nov 43-23 Jan 45; RF, baled out of Spit XII, MB842, over Channel, RR, 12 Jun 44; 1 Dest V1, 10m N of Hastings, Ssx, 23 Jun 44; 1 Dest V1, 4m N of Bexhill, Ssx, 3 Jul 44; ½ Dest V1 w Flt Sgt F. G. Woollard, 1m W of Lydd/N of Rye, Ssx, 4 Jul 44; ½ Dest V1 w Tmpst (other sqn), nr Lamberhurst, Kent, 19 Jul 44; ½ Dest V1 w Fg Off J. C. J. Payne, into Channel, 10m SE of Hastings, Ssx, 23 Jul 44; ½ Dest V1 w Mstg (other sqn), 5-8m S of Beachy Head, Ssx, 26 Jul 44; 1 Dest V1, 10-15m W of Le Touquet, F., & 1 Dest V1, 3m SE of Woodchurch, Kent, 29 Jul 44; flew personal trip to Brussels, B., to visit his family w soap, food & other articles in short supply, w Flt Lt D. J. V. Henry, 9 Sep 44; Capt, AMB, 26 Nov 44; Flt Lt, 30 Dec 44; SD/KIA in Spit XIV, RM765, over Handorf, G., by FW190Ds of JG26 during armed recce to Münster area, 23 Jan 45, aged 30; init bur under tree on farm of Anton Große-Kleimann, Handorf, 23 Jan 45; reint in 25 Brit Mil Hosp Cem, Münster, after War; reint in Reichswald Forest War Cem, Kleve, G., 8 Jul 47; reint in Brussels Town Cem, Evere, B., Air Force Plot II/4, 14 Apr 48

BANACH, WŁADISŁAW, P.1673, PAF/RAFVR (Polish); b Tarnowa, PL, 15 Jun 19; ed Krakow, PL; OCS of Avtn, PAF College, Dęblin, nr Warsaw, PL, 1938-39; evac PL to F with OCS Dęblin via Romania, 1939; evac F & cpltd flg trng in UK as Sgt Plt; com Plt Off, 1 Dec 41; 9 AGS, Llandwrog, 1942; Crse 23, 58 OTU (Spit), Ggmth, Stirling, 16 Jun-7 Sep 42; 317 (Wileński) Sqn (Spit Vb), Woodvale, 10 Sep 42; 41 Sqn, 27 Oct-9 Dec 42; 1 Off Sch, Uxb, 9 Dec 42-13 Apr 43; Fg Off, 1 Mar 43; 317 (Wileński) Sqn (again), 14 Apr-Dec 43; Flt Lt, 1 Dec 43; FI, 25 (P) EFTS, 5 Jan 44-EOW; KW, 1944

BEARD, ANTHONY WILLIAM, 1331949, RAFVR; b Wanstead, E Lon, 4 Dec 22; ed Friend's Sch, Saffron Walden; enl in RAFVR, Uxb, 21 Jan 41; 22 EFTS (Moth), Cambridge, 1941; 31 SFTS (Harv), Kingston, Ont, Can, 1941; Sgt Plt, 1942; Crse 7, 5 (P)AFU (Master I/II), Ternhill, Salop, 12 May 42; 52 OTU (Spit), Aston Down, Gloucs, 1942; 41 Sqn, FM 26 Aug-LM 24 Dec 42; d Penrith, Cumb, Sep 2003

BEDNARZ, JOZEF, 782356, PAF/RAFVR (Polish); b Rymacze, Wolyń Prov, PL, 13 Jun 20; ed Architecture Coll; 1st level avtn trng (prob gliders only), Avtn Sch, Świdnik, PL; evac to France & joined PAF, Lyon-Bron, 1939; evac to UK & joined RAFVR as Sgt Plt (P.782356), Blackpool, 1940; 15 EFTS, Carlisle, Cumb, 1941; 8 SFTS, Montrose, Scot, 1941; 58 OTU (Spit), Ggmth, Stirling, 17 Jun 42; 317 (Wileński) Sqn (Spit Vb), Woodvale, Lancs, 10 Sep 42; 403 (Wolf) Sqn (Spit Vb), Ctk, 26 Oct 42; 41 Sqn, 17 Dec 42-1 Feb 43; KIFA during low level flt over beach W of Pwllheli, Caern, Wales, in Spit Mk. Vb, X4279, 1 Feb 43, aged 22; bur Grave 620, Portmadoc Public Cem, Caern, Wales

BENHAM, DOUGLAS IAN 'Dougie', 104443, RAFVR; b Wimbledon, 30 Dec 17; ed Southend GS, Esx; joined RAFVR, Rcfd, Esx & to 34 E&RFTS Southend, as Sgt Plt u/t (745064), 16 Feb 38 (FF 4 Mar 39); Officer Cadet Trng, Bexhill, Sep 39; 10 (B) OTU (Whitley), Abingdon, Oxon, May 40; trans from BC to FC, & to ftr trng, 7 EFTS, Desford, Leics, Jul 40; plt badge, 17 Aug 40; C Flt, 8 SFTS (Master), Montrose, 3 Sep-Nov 40; NF trng, 54 OTU (Defiant), Church Fenton, Dec 40-Jan 41; 55 OTU (Hurr), Aston Down, Jan 41; A Flt, 607 Sqn (Hurr I), Macmerry & Drem, until 31 Aug 41; com Prob Plt Off (104443), 21 Aug 41; FI, 59 OTU (Hurr I & Master), Crosby-on-Eden, Cumb, 8 Sep 41-15 Apr 42; att No 6 FIC, CFS Upavon, Wilts, 20 Oct-5 Nov 41 (grad QFI); Actg Flt Lt & OC B Flt, 242 Sqn (Spit Vb), N Weald, 16 Apr 42; Fg Off (WS), 21 Jul 42; emb Greenock for N Africa w 242 Sqn per SS *Leinster*, arr Gib & flew to Maison Blanche, 322 Wg, 8 Nov 42; ½ Dest Ju88 but CD/SD from rtrn fire (windscreen & wg) in Spit Vb, 'V', & baled out, 9 Nov 42; ½ Dest S79, 16 Nov 42; 1 Dest FW190 & 1 Dam Me109, 26 Nov 42; 1 Dam Me109, 29 Nov 42; 1 Prob FW190, 4 Dec 42; 1 Dest FW190, 1 Dest Ju87, 2 Dam FW190s & 3 Dam Ju87s, 1 Jan 43; 1 Dest & 1 Prob Ju87, 2 Jan 43; 1 Prob Me109, 26 Feb 43; DFC (242 Sqn), 19 Mar 43; OC & CFI, Tactical OTU (Spit Vb), Kalaa Djerda, Tunisia, 15 Apr 43 (USAAF Kittyhawk plt conv to Spits); Temp AVM in order to act as Escort Off to 2 German Generals & Luft Ace Hans Möller (Staffelkapitan 1./JG53, 15 vics, SD 25 Mar 43), 28-29 May 43 (Algiers-Gib, DC-3, 28 May 43; Gib-Hendon, B-24, 29 May 43); FLS, Milfield NBL, 20 Jun-9 Jul 44; EF/WUL in FLS Spit Vb, EP276, Glentress, Peebles, 25 Jun 44; CFI, 61 OTU (Spit), Rednal, Salop, 9-26 Jul 44 (FF 10 Jul 44); Flt Lt (WS), 21 Jul 43; 504 Sqn (Spit Vb), Detling, 26 Jul-27 Aug 44; Actg Sqn Ldr & OC, 41 Sqn, 28 Aug 44-8 Apr 45; AFC (61 OTU), 1 Sep 44; 2 Dest FW190D, Münster-Waltrop, G., 23 Jan 45; leave, Apr-May 45; Bar to DFC, 8 May 45; OC, AMMRU (Science 3), Kingsway, Lon, May 45; app to perm com as Flt Lt, 1 Jul 46 (sen 1 Sep 45); Sqn Ldr, 1 Nov 47 (sen 1 Aug 47); OC, Gunnery Sqn, 203 AFS (Spit), Stradishall, Sflk, Apr-31

Aug 49; redes & trans to 226 ACU (Meteor & Vamp), Stradishall, & rmnd OC, 1 Sep 49; Actg Wg Cdr & Wg Cdr Trng, HQ FC, Stanmore, Nov 51; Wg Cdr Flying, RAF Tang (Meteor), 1 Sep 52; att Escort Off for Queen at RAF Coronation Review, Odiham, 15 Jul 53; Wg Cdr Ops, HQ BFA (subs BFAP), Aden, 12 Dec 54-Jun 57; OBE, 13 Jun 57; Wg Cdr Ops, RAF Box, Smrst, Jun-Dec 57; ret 30 Dec 57, rtng Wg Cdr; Chf Exec, ITWW, Pontcanna, Wales, Sep 1958-66 (att NBC, Rockefeller Cntr, NYC, Sep-Dec 58); Freeman, City of Lon, 1 Sep 64; Liveryman, WCW, Sep 64; consultant, Harlech TV, Pontcanna, 1968-70; occ builder & property letting, 1970-77; rtnd to Wales, 1978; d Manorbier, Wales, 28 Oct 09

BENJAMIN, SYDNEY HYMAN, 1272288, RAFVR; b Montagu Mansions, Lon, 10 Jul 22; ed St Pauls; enl in RAFVR, Uxb, 25 Nov 40; 5 ITW, Torquay, Cornwall, 1940-41; 2 BFTS (Stearman, Vultee & Harv), Polaris Flt Academy, Grand Central Air Terminal, Glendale, CA, & subs War Eagle Fld, Lanc, CA, USA, 1941; Sgt Plt, 1941; OTU, 1942; 41 Sqn, FM 5 Aug-27 Dec 42; emb for Malta, Jan 43; 1435 Sqn (Spit Vc), Malta, FM 2 Mar 43; Flt Sgt, 1943; ½ Dest FW190 w Plt Off T. G. Atkinson, 2 Jul 43; 1 Dest Me109, 2 Jul 43; SD/KIA in Spit IX, in engagement w 15 MC202s & 10 Me109s over front line area bet Syracuse & Augusta, Italy, whilst providing air support for invasion of Sicily, 12 Jul 43, aged 20; s of Samuel & Milly Benjamin, of Kingsway, Hove, Ssx; bur Grave II.A.4, Syracuse War Cem, Sicily, Italy

BIGGS, STANLEY JOHN, 1263193; RAFVR; b Paddington, Lon, 14 Apr 20; ed Claremont Ave Sch & Marylebone Day Coll; enl in RAFVR, Uxb, 22 Aug 40; 1 ITW, Babbacombe, 1940; 22 EFTS, Cambridge, 1940; 5 SFTS, Ternhill, 1941; Sgt Plt (1263193), 1941; 56 OTU (Hurr), Sutton Bridge, 1941; 257 Sqn (Hurr IIb), Coltishall, 15 Oct 41; 535 Sqn (Hurr IIc), High Ercall, 15 Sep 42-25 Jan 43 (dsbnd); Flt Sgt, 1942; Sup, RAF High Ercall, pending disposal, 25 Jan 43; 41 Sqn, 12 Feb-7 Jun 43; CL/NI in Spit XII, EN232 ('carelessness'), Friston, 28 May 1943; PDC, Blackpool, 9 Jun 43; emb Greenock per USS *Christobal*, 20 Jun 43; disemb Algiers, 27 Jun 43; by road to Tunis, then by DC-3 to Malta, arr 4 Jul 43; 229 Sqn (Spit Vc), Krendi, from AHQ Malta, w Flt Sgt W. G. Downing, 5 Jul 43-7 Jan 44; WO, 2 Aug 43; att 335 Wg, Catania, 26 Nov-4 Dec 43; LM on patrol in Hurr II, 30 Dec 43; KIFA in Spitfire Vc, JK889, 7 Jan 44, aged 23; s of Joseph & Maud Biggs of Kenton, Harrow, Mdx; bur Protestant Men's Sec, Plot F, Coll Grave 48, Capuccini Naval Cem, Malta

BIRBECK, CLIVE ROBERT 'Joe' & 'Jumbo', 108990, RAF; b Ceylon (Sri Lanka), 2 Sep (2 Apr 22 on PSR, poss also 7 Nov 23; known to have falsified DOB on entry); youngest s of Brig J. H. B. Birbeck; ed Bedford Sch; occ student & res Clapham, Bedford, on enl in RAF, Uxb, 10 Aug 40; LAC (1277445), 28 Oct 40; 4 ITW, Paignton, 28 Oct 40; flg trng, Carlisle & Kidlington; com Prob Plt Off (108990), 18 Oct 41; 53 OTU (Spit), Llandow, Glam, 1941; 610 (Cty of Chester) Sqn (Spit Vb), Leconfield, 9 Dec 41; MFSU, Speke, 2 Apr 42; Prob Fg Off (WS), 1 Oct 42; B Flt, 41 Sqn, 8 Feb 43-23 Jul 44; att 91 Sqn (Spit Vb), Hwkge, with Fg Off R. M. Hoare, 28 Mar-1 Apr 43; 1 Prob FW190, Somme Est, F., 27 Apr 43 (claimed as Dest, but reduced to Prob by FC, 3 May 43); 1 Dest FW190, Le Touquet-Beussent, F., 4 Sep 43; 1 Prob FW190, W of Évreux, F., 22 Sep 43; EF & baled out of Spit XII, EN608, 20-25m S of Ford, Ssx, after combat w FW190 on Ramrod 237, RR, 22 Sep 43; 1 Dam Me109G & 1 Dam FW190, bet Beauvais & Dieppe, F., 27 Sep 43; Flt Lt (WS), 18 Oct 43; ½ Dest V1 w Fg Off R. E. Anderson, N of Maidstone, Kent, 22 Jun 44; HQ ADGB, 23 Jul 44; Ftr Afltn duties on old Spit XIIs, FAU, AFDU, Wtrg w Flt Lt P. Cowell, 26 Jul 44; FIU, AFDU, Wtrg, 2 Aug 44; 501 Sqn (Tmpst V), Mstn, 11 Aug 44; 1 Dest V1, 12/13 Oct 44; 1 Dest V1, 25 Oct 44; 84 GSU (Mstg, Spit, Tmpst & Typhn), Thruxton, Hants, Dec 44; 127 Sqn (Spit IX/XVI), B.79 Woensdrecht, 6 Jan 45; SD/AA in Spit XVI, RK896, during attack on midget sub pens at Maasluis, NL, baled out & captured nr Overflakkee Is, NL, 17 Jan 45; Stalag XIIIB, Nuremburg, 2 Mar-4 Apr 45; Stalag VIIA, Moosburg, 19-29 Apr 45; res on repat, Clapham, nr Bedford; emgtd to Cape Town, SA, 1947; d 2002

BØDTKER, Carl Sejersted, 1619, RNoAF (Norwegian); b Oslo, 11 Jun 23; ed Oslo; enl in RNoAF, Toronto, Ont, Can, 20 Jul 41; flg trng in 'Little Norway', Toronto, 13 Jan-2 Apr 42; 32 SFTS (Harv), Moose Jaw, Sask, Can, 11 Apr-31 Jul 42; RNoAF Advanced Trng, Toronto, 20 Aug-20 Sep 42; Crse 32, 5 (P)AFU (Master I/II), Calverley & Ternhill, Salop, 22 Oct-14 Dec 42; Crse 43, 57 OTU (Spit), Eshott, NBL, 15 Dec 42-3 Mar 43 (grad above avge in flg & avge in gunnery); B Flt, 332 (Norwegian) Sqn (Spit IX), N Weald & Bognor Regis, 10 Mar 43-17 Jun 44; CD in Spit IX, BS255, AH-R, from Me109s during Circus 282 to Caen, F., 13 Apr 43; com 2 Lt (Fenrik), 1 Oct 43; FA, crashed on TO in Spit IX, MH854, AH-Y, 29 Mar 44; 1 Dest Me410 on grnd, Juvincourt, F., 11 Apr 44; 84 Grp (C) Sqn (Auster V & Anson), Whmpnt, Ssx, & Gilze Rijen, NL, 1 Jul 44-1 Feb 45; RF/CL & flipped over in Auster V, NJ691, nr Breda, NL, 21 Sep 44; 83 GSU (Spit XIV), Dnsfld, 9-21 Feb 45; B Flt, 610 (Cty of Chester) Sqn (Spit XIV), 17 APC, Warmwell, Dorset, 22 Feb-7 Mar 45 (dsbnd); B Flt, 41 Sqn, 7 Mar-9 May 45; Lt (Løytnant), 1 May 45; 1 Dest FW190, S of Schwerin A/D, 1 May 45 (final WWII aerial vic for a Norwegian pilot); rtnd to Norway, 11 May 45; 332 Sqn (Spit IX), Værnes, nr Trondheim, 17 Oct-15 Nov 45; emp at Thofte's Flyselskap A/S, 1947; Norwegian rep for French Jodel homebuilt aircraft, 1959; founded coy later re-named Caseb Aviation, rep several French aviation coys in Norway, incl Ecureil, Super Puma, ATR 42 & 72, Super Broussard, & later also armament coy Thales; d 28 May 87

BOYD, Robert James 'Bob', 126765, RAFVR; b Walsall, Staffs, 29 Sep 18; ed Wolverhampton GS; joined RAFVR, Birm, 26 Jun 39; 13 EFTS, White Waltham, Bucks, 1939; 7 SFTS (Master), Montrose, 1940; Sgt Plt (754178), 1940; 7 OTU (Spit), Hwdn, Flint, 1940; 234 (Madras Pres) Sqn (Spit I), St Eval, Sep 40; 609 (W Riding) Sqn (Spit I/IIa), Middle Wallop, 22 Nov 40; RF/FL Spit IIa, P8098, Ash, nr Mstn, 21 May 41; 1 Dest Me109F, 21 Jun 41; 1 Prob Me109F, 24 Jun 41; 1 Dest & 1 Dam Me109F, 11 Jul 41; SD/AA in Spit Vb, W3187, baled out off Calais, F., RR, 31 Jul 41 (Caterpillar Club); RF/FL Spit Vb, W3603, nr Sandwich, Kent, 7 Aug 41; 53 OTU (Spit), Llandow, Glam, Sep 41; 61 OTU (Spit), Heston, Mdx, Feb 42; com Prob Plt Off (126765), 19 Jun 42; B Flt, 41 Sqn, bef 2 Nov 42 (or 18 Nov 42)-6 Sep 43[1]; Prob Fg Off (WS), 19 Dec 42; KIA, poss hydraulic failure as result of AA nr Fauville-en-Caux, F., in Spit XII, MB796, on Ramrod S35 to Rouen-Sotteville Marshalling Yards, baled out but parachute caught on tailplane, 6 Sep 43, aged 24; s of Walter & Dora Boyd of Wolverhampton; bur Grave A.2, Grandcourt War Cem, Seine-Maritime, F.

BRADSHAW, John Tyron 'Jack', 605510, RAFVR/USAAF (American); b Morristown NJ, 5 Nov 21; ed Woodberry Forest Sch, VA, Academy of Aeronautics, & Princeton; tried to join USAAC & USN, 1941, but rejected due lack of 2 yrs coll; applied for RAFVR at Brit Embassy, Washington DC & acc, 1941; 3 BFTS (Stearman, Vultee & Harv), Miami OK, USA, Mar 42; plt badge & Sgt Plt, 18 Sep 42; 31 PD Moncton NB, Can, 23 Nov 42; emb for UK per *Queen Elizabeth*, 9 Nov 42; disemb UK, 22 Nov 42; 31 PRC, Harrogate, 22 Nov 42; 10 FIS (Moth), Woodley, Dec 42; requested assignment to ftrs; 5 (P)AFU (Master I/II), Ternhill, Salop, Jan 43; 61 OTU (Spit), Rednal, Salop, Feb 43; Flt Sgt, 1943; 3 TEU (Hurr & Typhn), Annan, Dumfries, Mar 44; Maintenance Test Plt, 3501 GSU (Spit XIV), Cranfield, Bucks, Apr 44; 26 Sqn (Mstg & Spit), Lee-on Solent, May 44 (anti-shipping patrols & sweeps over B. & NL); 1 Dam Ju88, 28 May 44; spotting G. positions for HM Ships *Rodney* & *Erebus*, Sword Beach, D-Day, 6 Jun 44; 41 Sqn, 18 Aug-1 Nov 44; marr Doreen Hornby of Yks, Sep 44; trans to USAAF, 1 Nov 44, by which time flown 76 missions & logged 1,572 FH on Hurr I & IIC, Spit I, II ,V, XII & XIV, Tmpst I & V, & Mstg I; 56 FG ('Zemke's Wolfpack'), 63 FS, USAAF (Thunderbolt & Mstg) in Europe until EOW (23 missions); in transit to Pacific aboard B-24 when 1st Atomic Bomb dropped on Hiroshima, 6 Aug 45; redirected to Bradley Fld, CT, USA, where orders cancelled, 7 Aug 45; demob Oct 45; occ ferrying A/C to S America after war; flew for Pan American Grace Airways (PANAGRA) & ret as Dir of Flt Safety, 1982; res in Dallas, TX, since 1966; life member of

Commemorative Air Force (Midland, TX), American Air Museum in Britain (IWM, Dxfd), Spit Society (Southampton), P-47 Thunderbolt Pilots Assoc (Ridgewood, NJ), & docent, Frontiers of Flight Museum (Dallas, TX)

BROWN, Walter Wilson, 1345121, RAFVR, b Tranent, Scot, 28 Sep 21; ed Preston Lodge Sch, Scot; enl in RAFVR, Edin, 20 Mar 41; flg trng in USA, 1941-42; Sgt Plt, 17 May 42; B Flt, 41 Sqn, 28 Dec 42-LM 6 Jan 43; Flt Sgt, 17 May 43; WO, 17 May 44; 130 (Punjab) Sqn (Spit Vb), ca Jun 44-6 Mar 45; com Prob Plt Off (177898), 9 May 44; Plt Off cnfmd & to Fg Off (WS), 9 Nov 44; BPC, 6 Mar 45; Flt Lt (WS), 9 May 46

BURNE, Thomas Roper 'Tommy' & 'Tubby', 33457, RAF; b Sngpr, 19 Feb 20; ed Marlborough; joined RAF & to RAFC Cranwell, 13 Jan 38; com Prob Plt Off (33457), & to 1 GR Sch, Thorney Is, 8 Oct 39; 206 Sqn (Anson & Hudson), Bircham Newton, 14 Jan 40; Fg Off, 8 Oct 40; 1 Dam ship, Dec 40; 53 Sqn (Hudson), St Eval, 4 Jul 41; Flt Lt (WS), 8 Oct 41; 62 Sqn (Blenheim), Sngpr, 19 Jan 42; WIA when Jap bomb hit wg of Hudson bomber from which he was alighting, Sumatra, 7 Feb 42; leg amputated & replaced with prosthesis, hosp & SL, 7 Feb 42-28 May 43; AFC & MiD, 11 Jun 42; Flt Lt, 8 Apr 43; SFTS, RAFC Cranwell, 29 May 43; Crse 36, 53 OTU (Spit), KiL, 14 Jul-27 Sep 43; 2 TEU (Spit), Ggmth, Stirling, 5 Oct 43; B Flt, 41 Sqn, 16 Dec 43-24 Feb 45; AA/WIA (chest & right arm) in Spit XIV, RM790, 24 Feb 45; 50 MFH, 24 Feb 45; DSO (41 Sqn), 29 May 45 (upon return to base, 24 Feb 45, despite severe inj, allowed another plt to land 1st); Sqn Ldr, 1 Aug 47; OC, 1 Sqn (Meteor), Tang, 15 Jul 47-3 Feb49 & 1 Oct 49-9 Jan 50; Wg Cdr, 1 Jul 51; AIB, ca 1950; Gp Capt, 1 Jan 58; app ADC to MH the Queen, 18 Sep 68; ret medically unfit, 27 Jan 70; d 27 Nov 81 [see also *Evening Standard*, 24 Mar 45]

CHALMERS, John Allan, 785066/201462, RAFVR; b Shanghai, China, 6 Jun 20; ed George Herriot's Sch, Edin, Scot; enl in RAFVR (785066), Sngpr, 23 Jul 41; 25 EFTS (Moth), Belvedere, Rhod, Feb 42 (FF 2 Mar 42); 20 SFTS (Harv), Cranborne, Rhod, 25 Feb-23 Oct 42; plt badge & Sgt Plt, 23 Oct 42; AFU, S Rhod, 1942; Nav Crse, 15 EFTS (Moth), Kingstown, Carlisle, Cumb, Mar 43 (FF 23 Mar 43); 11 AFU (Oxford), Shawbury, Apr 43 (FF 24 Apr 43); 7 AFU (Master II), Peterborough, Cambs, May 43 (FF 11 May 43); 58 OTU (Master I), Ggmth, Stirling, Jul 43 (FF 19 Jul 43); 2 TEU (Spit), Ggmth, Stirling, Oct 43 (FF 28 Oct 43); 63 (TacR) Sqn (Spit V), Lee-on-Solent, 8 Jun 44; rested, Ballyhalbert NI, 4 Jul-5 Aug 44; 1687 (Ftr Afltn) Flt, Ingham, Lincs, 7-28 Aug 44; 83 GSU (Spit XIV), Bognor Regis, Thorney Is & Tang, 29 Aug-23 Dec 44; 610 (Cty of Chester) Sqn (Spit XIV), Brussels, 24 Dec 44-7 Mar 45 (dsbnd); 41 Sqn, 7 Mar-25 Oct 45 (LF Tmpst II, 25 Oct 46); 1 Dam Fi156 on grnd, Rechlin A/D, G., 25 Apr 45; ½ Dest Ju188 w Plt Off P. T. Coleman, Rechlin A/D, G., 25 Apr 45; ¼ Dest He111 w Plt Off P. T. Coleman, WO P. H. Hale & Sgt Plt C. N. Moyle, W of Goldberg, G., 28 Apr 45; 2 Dest Fi156, Lake Schwerin area, G., 2 May 45; EF at 500 ft on TO, CL & inj ("crack to the head") in Spit XIV, RM931 (exploded & burnt out), 2m W of Vaerlöse Airfield, Denmark, 1 Jul 45; com Prob Plt Off (201462), 13 Oct 45 (FM in ORB, 25 Nov 45; gaz 11 Dec 45); Fg Off, 13 Apr 46; emb for Shanghai, 4 Dec 46; demob, 28 Jan 47; post-War occ airline plt; d Berkhamsted, Herts, 14 Jun 2011

CHAPMAN, Robert Hugh, 40510, RAF; b Hong Kong, 9 Feb 19; ed Highgate Sch; enl in RAF, Desford, & com Plt Off, 6 Dec 37; flg trng, Desford & Sealand; grntd SSC as Prob APO, 19 Feb 38; 32 Sqn (Gaunt & Hurr), Bgn Hill, 17 Sep 38; Plt Off, 6 Dec 38; Fg Off, 6 Jul 40; 102 MU, Khartoum, Sudan, until 7 May 41; 112 Sqn (Glad), Helwan, Egypt, 16 May 39-10 Sep 40; 250 (Sudan) Sqn (Tomahawk), Aqir, Palestine, 7 May 41; Flt Lt (WS), 6 Jul 41; FI, 57 OTU (Spit), 1943; Temp Sqn Ldr, 1 Jul 43; 64 Sqn (Spit Vb), Coltishall, 14 Dec 43; Actg Sqn Ldr & OC, 41 Sqn, 28 May-28 Aug 44; 1 Dest V1, 30m SE of Beachy Head, Ssx, 3 Jul 44; Sqn Ldr (WS), 10 Aug 45; app to com as Flt Lt in RAF GDB, on ext svce (4 yrs on AL), 18 Dec 45 (sen 1 Dec 42), rtng WTR; Sqn Ldr, 1 Aug 47; ret 18 Mar 58; d 1989

CHAPPELL, Charles Gordon, 40672; b Manch, 7 Sep 15; ed Manch GS; joined RAF, Lon, 7 Mar 38; EFTS, Brough; grntd SSC as Prob APO, 7 May 38; Plt Off, 7 Mar 39; 3 Obs Sch, until 6 Apr 40; 52 (B) Sqn (Battle & Anson), Upwood, 3 Sep 39-6 Apr 40; 5 OTU (Harv, Spit & Hurr), Aston Down, Gloucs, until 19 Aug 40; 65 (East India) Sqn (Spit I), Turnhouse, 19 Aug 40 (50 FH op flg); Fg Off, 3 Sep 40; 609 (W Riding) Sqn (Spit I), Middle Wallop, 9 Oct 40; IFA, Nov 40; FI at EFTS & SFTS, Nov 40; Flt Lt, 3 Sep 41; trans to Res & called up for svce, 7 Mar 42; 41 Sqn, FM 6 Sep 42-LM 27 Nov 42; OC, A Flt, 26 Sep-ca 27 Nov 42; Sup, 229 Sqn (Spit Vc), Krendi, Malta, 11 Jun 43; 185 Sqn (Spit Vc), Hal Far, Malta, FM 23 Jun-25 Aug 43; OC A Flt, 152 Sqn (Spit Vc), Lentini E Sicily, 30 Aug-27 Oct 43 (broke ankle in football match); Sqn Ldr, 1 Jan 44; rel Temp Sqn Ldr, & to Flt Lt (Subs) from Flt Lt (WS), 1 Nov 47 (sen 1 Dec 42); svce ext 5 yrs, RAFRO GDB, WEF 28 Oct 50; com rel in RAFRO GDB, rtng Sqn Ldr, on app to RAuxAF, 13 Apr 55; com Fg Off (5 yrs AL & 5 yrs Res) in Sec Br of recons RAuxAF, 13 Apr 55 (sen 19 Jan 55); Flt Lt, 1 Jan 56; trans to Gen List of RAuxAF, 2 Feb 58; svce ext 5 yrs, WEF 13 Apr 60; trans to Res, 1 Nov 63; com rel, 13 Apr 65

CHARNOCK, Harry Walpole, 147902, RAFVR; b Chorley, Lancs, 20 Jun 05; ed Harrow; RAFC, Cranwell, Jan 24-Dec 25; app to perm com as Plt Off on grad from Cranwell, 16 Dec 25; 32 Sqn (Grebe, Gamecock & Siskin), Kenley, 16 Dec 25; Fg Off, 16 Jun 27; fined £15 & £5 5s. costs for dangerous driving in Strand, Lon, against 1-way traffic & side-swiping bus w/o stopping, 4 Apr 29; 1 Sqn (Siskin IIIa), Tang, 18 Aug 30; cashiered by GCM for low flg, 12 Dec 30; joined RAFVR, Uxb, 5 Sep 39; Sgt Plt (901005), 1939; 64 Sqn (Spit I), Kenley, 20 Jun-6 Sep 40; CL nr Ternhill in Spit I, K9903, 6 Sep 40; 19 Sqn (Spit, I), Dxfd, 12 Sep 40-Dec 41; 1 Dest Me109E, 5 Nov 40; CL/TON in Spit II, P7430, Dxfd, 20 Feb 41; Flt Sgt, 1941; eng cowling blown off, FL/NI in Spit II, P7379, Dxfd, 28 Feb 41; 1 Dest Me109F, 21 Jul 41; 1 Dest Me109E, 7 Aug 41; DFM (19 Sqn), 7 Apr 42; WO, 1942; 72 Sqn (Spit Vb/IX), Bgn Hill (& subs Tunisia), 23 Jun 42-May 43; 1 Dest Me109E, 25 Nov 42; 1 Dest & 1 Prob Me109, 27 Nov 42; 1 Dest Me109, 4 Dec 42; 1 Dest Me109 & 1 Dest FW190, but himself SD/WIA (head & arm), CL in enemy territory, 18 Dec 42; com Prob Plt Off (147902), 12 Jan 43; DFC (72 Sqn), 26 Feb 43; evaded & rtnd to Allied lines & 72 Sqn, ca mid-Mar 43; rtnd to UK, 1943; Prob Fg Off (WS), 12 Jul 43; FI, 57 OTU (Spit), Eshott, NBL, Nov 43; FI, 61 OTU (Spit), Rednal, Salop, Jan 44; Sup, FDF, AFDU, Wtrg, 12 Jan 44; flg duties, 84 GSU (Mstg, Spit, Tmpst & Typhn), Aston Down, Gloucs, 8 Jul 44; 222 Sqn (Spit IXb), Funtington, 12 Jul 44; inj in MVA, Jul 44; 41 Sqn, FM 12 Sep 44-7 Mar 45 (medically unfit); Flt Lt (WS), 12 Jan 45; OL2 (Knight) & CdG (B) w Palm, 27 Jun 47; rel com in RAFVR, rtng Flt Lt, 31 Jan 49; com Fg Off in recons RAFVR, GDB, 31 Jan 49; ext svce by 3 yrs, 31 Jan 52; rel com, 31 Jan 55; d 24 May 74

CHATTIN, Peter Warren, 1239825, RAFVR; b Holly Hall, Dudley, Worcs, 1 Oct 20; ed Dudley GS, 1931-37; occ shop assist, Bon Marché, Gloucs, 1938-41; marr Irene Ramsey, 1940; joined RAFVR, 3 ACRC, St John's Wood, Lon, 11 Aug 41; 8 ITW, Newquay, Cornwall, 1941; 22 EFTS, Cambridge, 1941; ACDC, Heaton Pk, Manch, 1942; emb prob Gourock, Scot, for Can; 31 PD Moncton NB, Can, 1942; train to Ponca City, OK, USA & to Crse 5, 6 BFTS (Stearman, Vultee & Harv), Ponca City, 22 Jan-8 Aug 42; plt badge & to Sgt Plt, Aug 42; emb for UK, Y Depot, Halifax NS; 3 PRC, Bournemouth, Dorset, Oct 42; 1 GIS (Master II & Hotspur II), Thame, Bucks, 19 Nov-16 Dec 42 (7.30 FH dual, 7.55 FH solo, grad 60%); Flt Sgt, 1 Jun 43; Tug Plt, 1 Tug Flt, 3 GTS (Master II & Moth), Stoke Orchard & Northleach, Gloucs, 17 Dec 42-2 Aug 43 (8.30 FH dual, 184.15 FH solo); FA/NI, UCC, when misjudged height in Master II, DL538, Northleach, 17 Feb 43; FA/NI, WUL in Master II, EM346, Stoke Orchard, 1 Mar 43; FA/NI, HL, starboard UCC in Master II, DL456, Northleach, 14 May 43; Crse 37, 53 OTU (Spit I/II & Master I/III), KiL & Hibaldstow, Lincs, 3 Aug-26 Oct 43 (4.30 FH dual, 60.35 FH solo, 1.10 night FH, 10 hrs Link); 1 TEU (Hurr I/IV, Spit I, & Master I), Tealing & Kinnell, Scot, Nov 43-9 Jun 44 (140 FH day dual, 20 FH night dual, 385 day solo, 15 FH night solo, grad above avge); A Flt, 41 Sqn, 11 Jun-3 Sep 44 (1st op flt, 12 Jun 44, 72 FH & 1 hr Link); WO, 1 Jun 44; 1 Dest V1 in Spit XII, MB837, but CD (prop & wg) from explosion, Thames Est, 8 Jul 44; 1 Dest V1, 4m NW of Ashford, Kent, 12 Jul 44; 1 Dam FW190A (Uffz Hans-Joachim Borreck), Overhespen, B., but SD/KIA in Spit XII, EN622, by Lt Alfred Gross in FW190 of Stab II./JG26, Neerhespen, B., 3 Sep 44, aged 23; s of Thomas & Olive K. Chattin of Brierley Hill, Staffs, & husb of Irene E. Chattin; init bur Overhespen, map ref K101476, but reint in Grave III.C.13, Geel War Cem, Antwerp, B., 12 Jul 46

CLANZY, Thomas Keith 'Keith', 976899, RAFVR; b Bridgend, Glam, 19 Jan 19; ed Lewis Sch, Pengam & S Wales and Monmouthshire Sch of Mines; enl in RAFVR, 3 RC Padgate, 2 Jan-13 Feb 40; MAEE, Helensburgh, Scot, 13 Feb-9 May 40; 2 EWS, Yatesbury, 9 May-9 Oct 40; RAF Stn Pembroke Dock, 10 Oct 40-31 Jan 41; RAF Stn Carew Cheriton, Pembs, 31 Jan-18 Jul 41; RAF Stn Pembroke Dock (again), 18 Jul-2 Nov 41; ACRC Regent's Pk, 3 Nov-12 Dec 41; 2 ITW, Cambridge, 13 Dec 41-21 Mar 42; 22 EFTS, Cambridge, 21 Mar-28 Apr 42; ACDC Heaton Pk, 29 Apr-16 May 42; emb for Can, May 42; 31 PD Moncton NB, 26 May-16 Jun 42; Crse 9, 5 BFTS (Stearman, Vultee & Harv), Riddle McKay Aero Coll, Riddle Fld, Clewiston, FL, USA, 19 Jun 42-1 Jan 43; plt badge & to Sgt Plt, 1 Jan 43; 31 PD Moncton NB, 4-26 Jan 43; emb for UK, Jan 43; 7 PRC, Harrogate, 4 Feb-3 Mar 43; Whitley Bay, 3-31 Mar 43; 7 PRC, Harrogate, 31 Mar-17 Apr 43; 3 PRC, Bournemouth, 17 Apr-4 May 43; 7 (P)AFU, Peterborough, 4 May-22 Jun 43; Flt Sgt, ca Jun 43; 2 FIS, Montrose, Scot, 23 Jun-23 Aug 43; Crse 38, 53 OTU (Spit), KiL, 7 Sep-14 Dec 43 (poss retained as Staff Plt or FI until 11 Feb 44); WO, ca Jan 44; 1 TEU (Spit & Hurr), Tealing, Angus, 12 Feb-19 May 44; GSU, Cranfield, 20 May-20 Jun 44; 274 Sqn (Spit IX), Detling, 20 Jun-11 Aug 44; 83 GSU (Mstg, Spit & Typhn), Whmpnt, Ssx, 11 Aug-4 Nov 44; 41 Sqn, 6 Nov 44-LM mid-Mar 45 (1st op 8 Dec 44; last op, 6 Feb 45); to Diest via Tilbury & Ostend, 6-17 Nov 44; N/E Sick (fell off truck rtng from leave, broke wrist & inj leg), 18 Feb 45 but DNR; 11 PHU, Innsworth, 19 Feb 45; 4 RS, Madley, 24 Sep 45; BSc (Eng), London Uni, Aug 48; emp Tredegar Iron & Coal Coy, 1948-51; Mining Inspector, Min of Fuel & Power, 2 Nov 1951; Pres, AMEME, 1972-73; HM Principal Electrical Inspector of Mines & Quarries, Dept of Energy, 1973-79; occ, contract work for Ministry & UN; Hon Fellow, AMEME, Feb 83; ret to Easton, Sflk, 1986; d Ipswich, Sflk, 4 Sep 09

CLARK, Fraser Dudley, NZ.414590, RNZAF; b Wanganui, NZ, 30 Jun 22; ed Wanganui Tech Coll; occ clerical cadet, NZR, Wanganui; NZ Army, TF (WWCR), 18 mths; enl in RNZAF & to ITW, Levin, 16 Aug 41; 3 EFTS, Harewood, 27 Sep 41; 1st solo Flt, 8 Oct 41; 2 FTS, Woodbourne, 9 Nov 41; plt badge, 20 Dec 41; Sgt Plt, 31 Jan 42; att to RAF & emb for UK per *Akaroa*, 22 Feb 42; arr UK, 14 Apr 42; 3 PRC, Bnmth, Hants, 15 Apr 42; Crse 8, 5 (P)AFU (Master I/II), Ternhill, Salop, 19 May 42; 53 OTU (Spit), Llandow, Glam, 9 Jun 42; Staff Plt, 53 OTU, ca 10 Sep 42; 41 Sqn, 18 Oct 42-18 Feb 43 (11 ops); Air Firing Crse, Valley, 28 Nov-3 Dec 42; 485 (NZ) Sqn (Spit Vb), Whmpnt, 19 Feb 43 (62 ops); visited 41 Sqn at Hwkge in 485 Sqn Spit, 25 Apr 43; com Plt Off, 15 Jul 43; KIA in Spit IX, EN631, by FW190s E of Le Havre, during Ramrod 212, Part II, to Beaumont-le-Roger airfield, F., 22 Aug 43; s of George & Jessie A. Clark (nee Hamilton) of Te Puke & Wanganui, resp; bur Grave C.19, Pont-Audemer Communal Cem, Eure, F. [see also photograph in TWN, 27 Oct 43]

CLOUSTON, John Greville, NZ.40218 (prev A40218), RNZAF; b Wlngtn NZ, 8 Jan 19; ed Wlngtn Coll & Wlngtn Tech Coll; occ Clerk, Murray, Roberts & OC, Wlngtn; NZ Army TF, pre-1940 for 1½ yrs; applied unsuccessfully for RAF SSC, 1937; joined RNZAF as airman pilot u/t, ITW GTS Levin, 15 Jan 40; 1 EFTS (Moth), Taieri, 10 Feb 40; 1 SFTS (Avro & Gordon), Wigram, 9 Apr 40; plt badge, 10 Jun 40; Sgt Plt, 27 Jul 40; att RAF & emb Lyttelton for UK per *Akaroa*, 11 Aug 40; 1 Depot, Uxb, 30 Sep 40; 7 OTU (Master & Spit), Hwdn, Flint, ca 19 Oct 40 (redes 57 OTU, 1 Nov 40); 258 Sqn (Hurr), Drem, 2 Dec 40 (146 ops); com Plt Off (40218), 8

May 41; Actg Flt Lt, 12 Sep 41; 403 (Wolf) Sqn (Spit Vb), Debden, Esx, 12 Sep 41; 111 Sqn (Spit Vb), N Weald, Esx, 12 Nov 41 (8 ops); Fg Off, 12 Dec 41; 486 (NZ) Sqn (Hurr & Typhn), KiL, 8 Mar 42 (63 ops); att CGS, Sutton Bridge, Lincs, 19 Aug-ca 18 Sep 42; Flt Lt, 12 Dec 42; Instr, SGO, Bgn Hill, 19 Jan 43; Sup Sqn Ldr, 41 Sqn, 8 Nov 43-12 Jan 44 (11 ops); att FLS (Spit), Aston Down, Gloucs, 5 Dec 43-2 Jan 44 (7 ops); 165 (Ceylon) Sqn (Spit), Culmhead, 13 Jan 44 (55 ops); SD (AA or EA) on 330th op, S of Baud, F., in Spit IXb, MK589, while attacking Me110 during Rodeo to Brittany, baled out over Channel (3km W of Trégastel) & captured, 6 Jun 44; whilst being trnsprtd by road from Tours to POW camp w 6 POWs, truck was strafed by Allied ftrs & inj but later DOW, 21 Jun 44, aged 25; s of Allan W & Violet L. Clouston of Rotorua & husb of Joyce E Clouston of Karori, Wlngtn, NZ; orig bur Tours, but later reint in Plot L, Row D, Grave 20, Nantes (Pont-du-Cens) Communal Cem, Loire-Atlantique, F. [see also photos in TWN, 7 Aug 40, 17 Sep 41 & 31 Jan 45]

COATES, Herbert Percival, 1262926, RAFVR; b Montevideo, Uruguay, 8 Dec 19; ed Buenos Aires Coll; 3 hrs 27 mins civ flg, Uruguay, 1938; 20 hrs 21 mins, civ flg, Uruguay, 1939; 75 hrs 5 mins civ flg, Transporte de la Hoya Anterior, Uruguay, 1940; enl in RAFVR, Montevideo, Uruguay, 11 May 40; emb for UK, ca Jun 40; joined RAFVR, Uxb, 8 Aug 40; ITW, 22 Aug 40; LAC, 17 EFTS (Moth), Rutland, Mar 41 (1st dual, 25 Mar 41; 1st solo, 27 Mar 41); 32 SFTS (Harv), Moose Jaw, Sask, Can, 23 Jun 41 (1st dual, 27 Aug 41); plt badge & to Sgt Plt, 1941; Crse 29, 57 OTU (Spit), Hwdn, Flint, 11 Nov 41-5 Jan 42 (1st Spit solo, JZ-W, 27 Nov 41); 81 Sqn (Spit Vb), Turnhouse, Jan 42; 289 (AAC) Sqn (Lysander, Hudson, Hurr), Kirknewton, ca Mar-18 Aug 42 (FF 22 Mar 42); Flt Sgt, 1942; 222 Sqn (Spit Vb), Drem, 18 Aug 42 (FF ZD-Y, 26 Aug 42); 41 Sqn, 17 Feb-LM 4 Mar 43

COLEMAN, Patrick Tinsley, 1386814/190247, RAFVR; b St John's Wood, Lon, 7 Jul 22; ed Southend HS; occ Clerk, Bank of England, 1939-41; enl in RAFVR, Euston Hse, Lon, as AC2, 20 Mar 41; mob., 14 Jul 41; 4 ITW, Paignton, Jul 41; LAC plt u/t, 18 Sep 41; Sgt Plt u/t (1386814), BFTS (Stearman, Vultee & Harv), Maxwell Fld, AL, 16 Oct 41; plt badge & to Sgt Plt, 17 May 42; rtnd to UK, Jun 42; Crse 14, 5 (P)AFU (Master I/II), Ternhill, Salop, 30 Jun 42; 4 SS, Madley, 1943; Flt Sgt, 20 May 43; Crse 33, 53 OTU (Spit), Llandow, Glam, & KiL, 1 May-10 Jul 43; 83 Grp (C) Sqn (Anson, Auster III/IV, Hudson, Hurr II, Oxford, Proctor, Spit V), Redhill, Surrey, Jul 43-9 Apr 44; 1 TEU (Hurr II & Spit I), Tealing, Angus, 12 Apr-7 Jun 44 (Hurr 19.20 FH, Spit 21.0 FH); WO, 17 May 44; att F Flt (RP Hurr IV), RAF Kinnell, Scot, 28-31 May 44 (7.55 FH); A Flt, 41 Sqn, 7 Jun 44-6 Aug 45 (1st op flt, 13 Jun 44); FL at Lympne w CD from exploding V1, 7 Jul 44; leave, 1-9 Aug 44; 1 Dest FW190A-8 (52-vic Ace Lt Alfred Gross, WIA), Overhespen, B., 3 Sep 44; com Prob Plt Off (190247), 12 Dec 44; leave; 31 Dec 44-9 Jan 45; leave, 18-29 Mar 45; 1 Dam Ju188 on grnd, nr Parchim, G., 17 Apr 45; 1 Dam Ju88 on grnd, 3m E of Pötrau, G., 18 Apr 45; 1 Dest FW190, N of Neuruppin A/D, G., 20 Apr 45; ½ Dest Ju188 w J. A. Chalmers, Rechlin A/D, G., 25 Apr 45; ¼ Dest He111 w WO J. A. Chalmers, WO P. H. Hale & Sgt Plt C. N. Moyle, W of Goldberg, G., 28 Apr 45; 1 Dam FW190 on grnd, Rechlin, G., 25 Apr 45; 1 Dest FW190, SW of Plau, & 2 Dest FW190, Lake Schwerin, G., 1 May 45; Fg Off (WS), 12 Jun 45; DFC, 24 Jul 45; to Great Dunmow, UK, per TC Halifax (3 hrs 20 min), 8 Aug 45; TCAHC, Morecambe, Lancs, 8 Aug 45; att 44 Grp, Melton Mowbray, for ferry trng, 17 Aug-11 Sep 45; compassionate leave, Sep 45-Jan 46; recalled to AL w HQFC, 23 Feb 46; rlsd 6 Jul 46; emp Bank of England, 1946-52; rel com w RAFVR & app to com as Fg Off, RAF (5 yrs on AL), 16 Jan 52; Flt Lt, GDB, 21 Feb 56; trans to Sec Branch (Int) as Fg Off, 26 Nov 56 (sen 24 May 52); ext svce by 5 yrs, 16 Jan 57; Flt Lt, 24 May 58; ext svce as Flt Lt by 2 yrs, Sec Branch, 16 Jan 62; d 10 Aug 62

COLLIS, Ronald Thomas Harry, 111107, RAFVR; b Lon, 22 Jul 20; ed Wembley Cty Sch, Alperton Hall, Mdx; enl in RAFVR, Uxb, 18 Jun 40; 10 EFTS, Weston-super-Mare, Mar-May

41; 1 FIS, Luton, May-Jun 41; com Prob Plt Off (111107) [from Sgt Plt 1253309], 11 Jul 41; Fg Off (WS), 11 Jul 42; 7 (P)AFU (Hurr & Master), Peterborough, Cambs, May 43; 61 OTU (Spit), Rednal, Salop, Jul 43; Flt Lt (WS), 11 Jul 43; 41 Sqn, 15 Aug 43-18 Jun 44; 1 Dest FW190 N of Rouen, F., 20 Oct 43 (claimed Dest, only admitted Prob, but later elevated to Dest, evidence on PSR "raised to destroyed" & on DFC citation); att FLS, Aston Down, for Crse, 6-15 Jan 44; Adjt, ca 16 Jan 44-15 Jun 44; OC A Flt, 126 Sqn (Spit IX), Culmhead, Smrst, 19 Jun 44; SD/AA in Spit IXb, ML366, 5J-J, w of Cap de Carteret, baled out into sea, 8 Jul 44; RR by RN, 9 Jul 44; 1 Dest Me109, 24 Jul 44; att 1 FLS (Hurr, Spit & Typhn), Milfield NBL, for Crse, 8 Oct 44; DFC (126 Sqn), 11 May 45; MiD, 14 Jun 45; app to com as Flt Lt (4 yrs on AL), 1 Jan 47 (sen 1 Sep 45), gaz 27 May 47; trans, to Class C Res, 7 Sep 47, gaz 30 Sep 47; rel com in RAFVR on app to RN as Actg Instr Lt, 24 Aug 50; HMS *Daedalus*, RN Barracks, RNAS Lee-on-Solent, Hants, 5 Mar 51; Instr Lt, 28 Mar 51 (sen 27 Jun 44); Instr Lt Cdr., 27 Jun 52; HMS Peregrine, RNAS Ford, Ssx, 24 Apr 53; trans to Emergency List, 25 Aug 55; occ Atmospheric Physicist, Stanford Research Instr [later SRI Int], ca 1956-86; author, *Contending Fighters of World War II*, Trafford, 2003

COOK, ARTHUR CHARLES, 142068; b Lon, 13 Apr 17; ed St Olave's Sch, Lon; enl in RAFVR, Lon, 2 Feb 42; 28 EFTS; LAC (1257737), 1942; RAF Coll, Cranwell; com Prob Plt Off (142068), 15 Apr 43; 53 OTU, KiL, 1943; 41 Sqn, 20 Jul-30 Aug 43; IFA, RF/CL in Spit XII, MB862, Cat E, Tang, 30 Aug 43 (DNR); Prob Fg Off, 15 Oct 43; Actg Flt Lt, 1944; MiD, 1 Jan 45; trans to ASD Br, 12 Jul 45

COOK, HARRY, 126096, RAFVR; b Grimsby, 31 Aug 20; ed St James Coll, Grimsby; joined RAFVR, Grimsby, 18 Jun 39; flg trng, Grimsby, Hamble, Kinloss, & Cranfield; Sgt Plt (754199), 1940; 7 OTU (Spit), Hwdn, Flint, 1940; 266 (Rhod) Sqn (Spit I), Wtrg, Aug 40; 66 Sqn (Spit I), Gravesend, 14 Sep 40; ½ Dest He111, 15 Sep 40; 1 Dest Me109E, 24 Sep 40; 1 Dest & 1 Dam Me110, 27 Sep 40; 1 Dest Me109E, 30 Sep 40; 1 Dest Me109E, 27 Oct 40; 1 Dest Me109E, 26 Nov 40; CD/CL at Hnch, Esx, in Spit Ia, X4543, 13 Oct 40; CD to Spit I, X4599, 20 Oct 40; Flt Sgt, 1941; FI, 57 OTU (Spit), Hwdn, Flint, Feb-Sep 41; IFA in Dominie, in MAC w Master, Hwdn, 19 Jul 41; test plt, Sep 41-Aug 42; WO, 1942; com Prob Plt Off (126096), 18 Jun 42; 234 (Madras Pres) Sqn (Spit Vb), Portreath, Cornwall, 3 Sep 42; 26 (AC) Sqn (Spit), Gatwick, 5 Oct 42; Prob Fg Off (WS), 18 Dec 42; MSFU (Sea Hurr), Speke, 1942-43; Fg Off, 18 Jun 43; A Flt, 41 Sqn, 16 Dec 43-11 Feb 45; 1 Dest V1, mid-Channel, 9 Aug 44; Flt Lt (WS), 18 Jun 44; 9 PDC, 1 Wg, Feb 45; FI, 57 OTU (Spit), Eshott, NBL, 27 Mar 45; ferry duties, 229 Grp, TCAHC, Morecambe, Lancs, 30 May 45; demob, 1946

COOMBES, WILLIAM MICHAEL 'Bill', A.403800/O21987, RAAF; b Tenterfield NSW, 14 Feb 18; ed De La Salle Coll, Armidale NSW, 1928-30, & Glen Innes HS NSW, 1930-34; 33rd Btn Militia, 1935-36; occ Grocery Mgr; joined RAAF, 2 RC Syd & to Crse 12, 2 ITS, Brdfld Pk NSW, 3 Mar 41; LAC, 26 Apr 41; 4 EFTS, Mascot NSW, 29 May 41; 2 ED, Brdfld Pk, 24 Jul 41; att RCAF & emb Syd for Vncvr Can, via NZ & Fiji per MV *Awatea*, 8 Aug 41; disemb Vancouver & to 3 MD, Edmonton, Alta, Can, 29 Aug 41; Crse 38, 1 SFTS (Harv), Borden, Ont, Can, 11 Sep 41; plt badge & to Sgt Plt, 19 Dec 41; 1 Y Depot, Halifax NS, 21 Dec 41-7 Jan 42; ceased att to RCAF, 7 Jan 42, & att RAF, 8 Jan 42-6 Jan 43; emb Halifax for UK, 8 Jan 42; disemb UK, 19 Jan 42; 3 PRC, 20 Jan-15 Feb 42; 17 (P)AFU (Master), Watton, Nflk, 16 Feb-7 Apr 42; Crse 34, 57 OTU (Spit), Eshott, NBL, 7 Apr-9 Jun 42; 41 Sqn, 9 Jun-18 Sep 42 (91.40 FH, of which 31 Op FH/28 sorties); com Prob Plt Off, 29 Aug 42; 3 PRC, Wilmslow, 20 Sep-28 Oct 42; disemb Melb & to 1 PD, Melb, 7 Jan 43; 2 ED, Brdfld Pk, 24 Jan 43; Spit Refresher Crse, 2 OTU, Mildura VIC, 14 Jan 43; Fg Off & to 4 ED, Adelaide, 28 Feb 43; 55 OBU Pool, Birdum NT, 28 Feb 43 (arr 15 Mar 43); 452 (Aust) Sqn (Spit Vc/VIII), Strauss NT, Aust, 17 Mar 43-2 Feb 44 (204 FH); ½ Dest & ½ Prob Pete, Millingimbi NT, 10 Aug 43; 1 Dam Jap Ftr, Pioneer Creek NT, 7 Sep 43; Flt Lt, 28 Aug 43; 55 OBU, Birdum NT, 2 Feb 44; 2 ED Brdfld Pk, 16 Feb 44; marr Loyla

Nancye Sherborne, Concorde NSW, 14 Mar 44 (d 8 Feb 84); FI, 2 OTU (Wirraway), Mildura VIC, 3 Apr 44 (120 FH); FI, 8 OTU (Spit & Wirraway), Narrowmine NSW, 12 Jul 44-2 Jun 45 (173 FH); att Crse 10, 1 OTU FIC, CFS (Wirraway), Parkes NSW, 28 Jun-31 Jul 44 (34 FH); att No 54 Admin (ASD) Crse, Sch of Admin, Victor Hbr, S Aust, 22 Jan-26 Mar 45; att Spit Refresher Crse, 21 May 45; 2 RPP, Moratai, 16 Jun 45; Flt Cdr, 452 Sqn RAAF (Spit VIII), Tarakan, Borneo, 2 Aug 45 (5 sorties, 6.35 Op FH); 2 PD, Brdfld Pk, 24 Nov 45; Flt Cdr, 5 SFTS Flg Pool, Uranquinty NSW, 7 Jan 46; Adjt NSW Sqn ATC, Syd, 17 Jan 46; OC NSW Sqn ATC, 18 Aug 47; app to SSC with RAAF as Flt Lt (O21987), 23 Sep 48; Flt Cdr, 3 (TacR) Sqn RAAF (Auster, Mstg & Wirraway), Fairbairn ACT, 7 Mar 49 (160 FH); 9 Int Crse, SLAW, 15 Aug-23 Sep 49; att QLD Sqn ATC, 14 Nov-11 Dec 49; No 3 FIC, CFS, E Sale VIC, 9 Jan 50; Sqn Ldr, 1 Mar 50; FI, 1 FTS, Pt Cook VIC, 26 Jun 50; app to perm com as Sqn Ldr, 1 Sep 50; att VIC Sqn ATC, 24 Oct-13 Nov 50; CGI, 1 AFTS, Pt Cook, 20 Feb 51; att Base Sqn Richmond NSW, 26 Jan 53; Supry, Base Sqn Mamote, PNG, 13 Feb 53; OC, Base Sqn Mamote, PNG, 1 Mar 53-22 Nov 54; Coronation Medal, 2 Jun 53; att Base Sqn Laverton, 28 Nov-8 Dec 54; emb Melb for UK per RMS *Arcadia*, 9 Dec 54; Crse 45, RAFSC, Bracknell, 5 Jan 55 (grad psa); Wg Cdr, 1 Jul 55; SOT, RAAF Overseas HQ, Lon, 9 Jan 56; sailed UK to Aust per RMS *Strathmore*, disemb Melb, 29 Jan 57; Base Stn Laverton VIC, 29 Jan 57; OC, 1 AFTS, Pt Cook VIC, 4 Feb 57; att CFS for Vamp Conv Trng, 10-28 Feb 58; att CFS for Vamp Conv Trng, 28-30 Apr 58; Staff Duties, Dir of Est, Dept of Air, Melb, 18 Jan 60; Staff Duties, Dir of Est, Dept of Air, Cnbra, 17 Oct 60; Dept of Org, Dept of Air, 2 Jul 62; ORG1, Dept of Org, 17 Sep 62; att language sch, 9 Nov-4 Dec 64; AE, 28 Jan 65; Actg Gp Capt, 13 Mar 65-16 May 67; emb Syd, 13 Mar 65; disemb Sngpr, 25 Mar 65; Air Attaché, Saigon, Vietnam, 15 Apr 65-12 May 67; dep Vietnam by air, 13 May 67; arr Syd, 14 May 67; DGPP (Plans 2), Dept of Air, 15 May 67; ret Fairbairn ACT, 14 Feb 68, rtng Wg Cdr (hon Gp Capt); d ACT, 8 Feb 91

COPE, Arthur Reginald, A.409294, RAAF; b Glenferrie VIC, 15 Dec 20; ed Collingwood Tech Sch, 1932-34; Sgt, 57/60th Btn, Royal Aust Army Militia, Oct 37-Aug 41; occ cabinet maker & cycle assembler & res Thornbury VIC, on enl in RAAF, 1 RC, Melb, 16 Jul 41; AC2 on joining RAAF, 15 Aug 41; Crse 19, 4 ITS, Victor Hbr, 16 Aug 41; 5 days leave, 8-12 Nov 41; LAC, 3 EFTS, 13 Nov 41; Crse 19, 7 SFTS, Deniliquin, 8 Feb-28 May 42; plt badge, 3 Apr 42; Sgt Plt, 28 May 42; 1 ED, Ascot Vale, 29 May 42; 2 ED, Brdfld Pk NSW, 15 Jun 42; att RAF & emb Syd for UK, 2 Jul 42; arr UK & to 3 PRC, Bnmth, Hants, 18 Aug 42; 7 days leave, 24-30 Aug 42; 17 (P)AFU (Master), Watton, Nflk, 1 Sep 42; Crse 41, 57 OTU (Spit), Hwdn, Flint, 22 Sep-3 Nov 42; Crse 27, 58 OTU (Spit), Ggmth, Stirling, 3 Nov-15 Dec 42; 5 days leave, 17-21 Dec 42; B Flt, 41 Sqn, 22 Dec 42-30 Jan 43; 4 days emb leave, 14-17 Jan 43; 1 PDC, W Kirby, Chesh, 30 Jan 43; to North Africa, ferrying aircraft, Feb 43; MPD, took off from Gib in Spit Vc, JG747, for Maison Blanche, via refuelling stop at USAAF A/D at La Sénia [Es Sénia], Oran, Algeria, but failed to arrive, 9 Mar 43, aged 22 (assumed to have been tank trouble); s of Charles J. W & Vera Cope of Thornbury VIC, Aust; rmbd Panel 12, Col 2, Malta Mem

COWELL, Peter, 124530, RAFVR; b Loughton, Esx, 16 Jan 23; ed Watford GS; joined RAFVR, Uxb, Feb 41; 6-mth RAF Crse, Manch UAS, 1941; 5 BFTS (Stearman, Vultee & Harv), Riddle McKay Aero Coll, Riddle Fld, Clewiston, FL, USA, 1941-42; plt badge & to Sgt Plt (1334023), 1942; Prob Plt Off (124530), 19 Jun 42; rtnd to UK, Jun 42; 17 (P)AFU (Master), Watton, Nflk, Jul-Aug 42; Crse 40, 57 OTU (Spit), Hwdn, Flint, 1 Sep-3 Nov 42; A Flt, 41 Sqn, 17 Nov 42-23 Jul 44; Prob Fg Off (WS), 19 Dec 42; att 91 Sqn (Spit Vb), Hwkge, with Plt Off D. D. Davies for op trng, 24-27 Mar 43; 1 Dest FW190, nr Beaumont-le-Roger, F., 20 Oct 43; Adjt, 41 Sqn, 27 Oct 43-ca Jun 44; Flt Lt (WS), 19 Jun 44; HQ ADGB, 25 Jul 44; Ftr Afltn duties (Spit XII), FAU, AFDU, Wtrg, w Flt Lt C. R. Birbeck, 26 Jul-11 Dec 44; 7 days leave, 18 Aug 44; FA/NI, tail wheel knocked off by A/D lighting on landing, Spit Vb, AB169, 10 Sep 44; leave, 19 Oct 44; marr 21 Oct 44; 9 days leave, 21-30 Nov 44; 84 GSU, Aston Down, Gloucs, 1-11 Jan 45; 83 GSU

(Spit XIV), Dnsfld, 12-30 Jan 45; 41 Sqn (again), 31 Jan 45-31 Mar 46 (1st op flt, 16 Feb 45); OC B Flt, 26 Mar 45-31 Mar 46; 4 Dam Ar196 on Lake Ratzeburg, G., 24 Apr 45; 1 Prob & 1 Dam Me262, Lübeck A/D, G., 25 Apr 45; 2 Dest FW190Ds (Fhj-Obfw Heinz Marquardt & Fw Heinz Radlauer of JG51), Lake Schwerin, G., 1 May 45; DFC (41 Sqn), 24 Jul 45, in recognition 3 Dest, 1 Prob & 1 Dam A/C, 14 Dest & 191 Dam grnd targets (incl Ar196s of 24 Apr 45) w 41 Sqn; Sabre Eng Crse, UK, 20 Oct 45; EF on TO, NI, in Tmpst V, Lübeck, 12 Dec 45; MVA/NI, when Ford utility over-turned enroute to CPH for football match, 17 Dec 45; 26 Sqn (41 Sqn redes 26 Sqn), 31 Mar 46; to RAF Shawbury for 9 mth eng crse, 26 Apr 46; demob Jun 46; post-War occ, charter airline plt, & subs plt for BEA, 1950-69; d 9 May 03

CROSS, Peter David, 915594, RAFVR; b Hampstead, Lon, 17 Mar 20; enl in RAFVR, Uxb, 15 Feb 40; AFP trng, Craig Fld (Harv), Selma, AL, USA, 1940; BFTS (Stearman, Vultee & Harv), Cochran Fld, GA, USA, 1941-42; Sgt Plt (915594), 1942; 59 OTU (Hurr), Milfield, NBL, 1942; B Flt, 41 Sqn, 29 Jan-27 Feb 43; RAF Valley, Wales, 27 Feb 43; 198 Sqn (Typhn IB), 1944-45; com Prob Plt Off (197976), 12 May 45; Fg Off (WS), 12 Nov 45

CURTIS, Keith Roe 'Curt', J.22759, RCAF; b Toronto, Ont, Can, 21 Nov 22; ed Northern Vocational Sch, Toronto; enl in RCAF as Air Crew Cadet, Toronto Ont, 7 Jul 41; 1 Manning Pool, Montreal Que, 25 Jun-13 Aug 41; 3 ITS, Victoriaville Que, 15 Aug-25 Sep 41; 21 EFTS (Finch & Link Trainer), Miramichi Flg Sch, Chatham NB, 29 Sep-20 Nov 41; 9 SFTS (Harv & Link Trainer), Summerside PEI & Centralia Ont, 27 Nov 41-10 Apr 42; plt badge & Sgt Plt (R.112595), 10 Apr 42; Staff Plt, 1 Wireless Sch (Anson, Beechcraft, Moth & Norseman), St Hubert Que, 10 Apr-19 Dec 42; com Plt Off (J.22759), 19 Nov 42; 2 SFTS (Link Trainer), Uplands Ont, 31 Dec 42-22 Jan 43; Y Depot (Link Trainer), Halifax NS, 6-28 Feb 43; Camp Miles Standish, Taunton Mass USA, 1-7 Mar 43; emb for UK, 7 Mar 43; PDRC (Link Trainer), Bournemouth, Apr-May 43; 17 (P)AFU (Master II), Wrexham, 15 May-14 Jun 43; Crse 51, 57 OTU (Spit), Eshott NBL, 30 Jun-14 Sep 43; A Flt, 41 Sqn, 8 Oct 43-26 Aug 44; Fg Off, 19 Nov 43; 1 Dest V1, SSE of Tunbridge Wells, Kent, 20 Jun 44; 417 (City of Windsor) Sqn (Spit VIII), Perugia, Italy, 27 Aug 44; Flt Lt, 19 Nov 44; 3 PRC, Bournemouth, 27-30 May 45; dschgd Toronto Ont, 17 Oct 45; joined RAF as Sgt Plt (4015082), Ottawa, Can, 8 Oct 47; emb Halifax for UK per SS *Aquitania*, 10 Oct 47; disemb. Southampton, 16 Oct 47; RAF Burtonwood, 16-19 Oct 47; RAF S Cerney, 21 Oct 47; 1 (P) RFU, Moreton in the Marsh, 5 May 48; 595 Sqn (Spit XVI & Vamp I), Pembrey, 7 May 48; Flt Sgt, Aug 48; CFS South Cerney, 1 Sep 48; QFI, Little Rissington, 1 Nov 48; 3 FTS (Harv II), Feltwell, Nflk, 31 Mar 49-11 Jul 51; 102 FRS (Spit XXII), North Luffenham, 11 Jul-11 Oct 51; att 205 AFS (Meteor Conv), Middleton St George, 28 Aug-19 Sep 51; 206 AFS (Meteor), Oakington, Oxon, 11 Oct 51-9 Nov 52; 4 Home Ferry Unit, Hwdn, Flint, 12 Nov 52-1 Sep 53; com Plt Off (4015082), 19 Nov 53 (sen 18 Nov 53); 226 OCU (Meteor VIII), Stradishall, 14 Dec 53-26 Feb 54; plt & member of 'Black Knights' aerobatics team, 54 Sqn (Meteor & Hunter), Odiham, Hants, 1 Mar 54-3 Dec 56; Fg Off, 18 Nov 55; 45 Sqn (Venom), Butterworth, Malaya, 30 Jan-15 Nov 57; 60 Sqn (Venom) Tengah, Sngpr, 1 Nov 57-15 Oct 59; Flt Lt, 18 Nov 58; 242 OCU (Hastings), Dishforth, Co-Pilot, Feb-Jul 60 & Capt, Aug-Oct 60; 48 Sqn (Hastings), Changi, Sngpr, Nov 60-Apr 63; Air Traffic Control, Shawbury, Aug-Nov 63; Air Traffic Control, RAF St Mawgan, Nov 63-Sep 66; 511 Sqn (Britannia), Lyneham & Brize Norton, Apr 67-May 72; Sqn Ldr, 1 Jan 72; Britannia Simulator, Lyneham, May 72-May 75; ret (med unfit), 2 May 75, rtng Sqn Ldr; d Saltash, Cornwall, 22 Dec 08

DAVIDSON, John Sharpe, A.401775, RAAF; b Yarragon VIC, Aust, 3 Jan 22; ed Geelong Coll & Melb Uni VIC; enl in RAAF, Somers VIC, 29 Mar 41; AC2, 1 ITS, Somers VIC, 29 Mar 41; LAC, 1 ED, Ascot Vale, 24 May 41; att RAF & emb Syd for UK, 27 Jun 41; disemb UK, 31 Jul 41; emb UK for SA, 14 Aug 41; disemb Durban, SA, 31 Aug 41; ITW, S Rhod, 3 Sep 41; 26 EFTS (Moth), Guinea Fowl, S Rhod, 18 Sep 41; 3 days leave, 5-7 Nov 41; 22 SFTS (Harv),

Thornhill, S Rhod, 18 Nov 41; plt badge, 23 Dec 41; 3 days leave, 2-4 Jan 42; 7 days leave, 27 Feb-5 Mar 42; Sgt Plt, 28 Feb 42; 7 days leave, 7-13 Mar 42; 9 days leave, 21-29 Mar 42; att AFTC Pollsmoor, Rhod, 7-9 Apr 42; emb SA for UK, 9 Apr 41; disemb UK, 4 May 42; 3 PRC, Bnmth, Hants, 4 May 42; 17 (P)AFU (Master), Watton, Nflk, 26 May 42; reprimanded by DCM for refusing to carry out an order (to undertake instrument flg) on 11 Jun 42 & for making false statement (that he had carried out instrument flg), 30 Jul 42; 7 days PL, 7-13 Aug 42; 56 OTU (Hurr & Spit), Tealing, Angus, 15 Aug 42; Flt Sgt, 28 Aug 42; 285 (AA Co-Op & Target Towing) Sqn (Defiant), Honiley, Warks, 24 Oct 42 (FF, 2 Nov 42; LF, 21 Nov 42, total 40FH); 41 Sqn, 26 Nov 42-30 Jan 43 (FF 30 Nov 42, LF 13 Jan 43); 10 days PL, 31 Dec 42-9 Jan 43; 10 days emb leave, 14-23 Jan 43; 5 days emb leave, 25-29 Jan 43; 1 PDC, W Kirby, 30 Jan 43; 126 Sqn (Spit Vb/Vc/IX), Malta, Sicily & Italy, 13 Mar 43 (FF 14 Mar 43, LF 31 Mar 44); com Plt Off, 25 Jun 43; admtd SSQ Luqa, 10-13 Aug 43; Fg Off, 25 Dec 43; emb Italy w Sqn for UK, 1 Apr 44; 126 Sqn (Spit IX), Sawbridgeworth, May 44 (FF 10 May 44, LF 15 Aug 44); att RAF Stn Sawbridgeworth, 22 May 44; att RAF Stn Culmhead, 3 Jul 44; HQ ADGB, 19 Aug 44; AEAF Comms Sqn (Anson, Auster, DC-3, Hurr, Oxford, Spit), Heston, 11 Sep 44 (FF 11 Sep 44, redes SHAEF (RAF) Comms Sqn, 15 Oct 44, LF 8 Dec 44, total 70FH); 17 days leave, 20 Dec 44-5 Jan 45; 10 days leave, 3-12 Feb 45; 126 Sqn (Mstg III), Bentwaters, Sflk, 9 Feb 45 (FF 11 Feb 45, LF 25 Jun 45, total 80FH); marr Rosemary F. Davidson, High Halden, Kent, 16 Feb 45; 10 days leave, 17-27 Feb 45; 10 days leave, 1-10 May 45; 10 days leave, 6-15 Jun 45; Flt Lt, 25 Jun 45; ACHU, Cranfield, 3 Jul 45; 14 days leave, 5-18 Jul 45; 31 days leave, 19 Jul-18 Aug 45; 14 days leave, 31 Aug-13 Sep 45; 11 PDRC, 17 Sep 45; emb UK for Aust per *Sterling Castle*, 4 Oct 45; disemb Syd & to 2 PD, 4 Nov 45; 7 days leave, 5-11 Nov 45; 1 PD, 13 Dec 45; dschgd 19 Dec 45 with 30 days re-est leave & 68 days WL; MiD, 1 Jan 46

DAVIES, David Douglas 'Daibach', 122377, RAFVR; b Ammanford, Carm, Wales, 18 Aug 20; ed Aberystwyth Uni; enl in RAFVR, Weston-super-Mare, Jan 41; 3 BFTS (Stearman, Vultee & Harv), Miami OK, USA, 1941; Sgt Plt (1337830), 1941; com Prob Plt Off (122377), 14 Mar 42; 9 (P)AFU (Master I/III), Hullavington, 1942; 57 OTU (Spit), Hwdn, Flint, 1942; Prob Fg Off (WS), 1 Oct 42; B Flt, 41 Sqn, 18 Nov 42-LM 1 Aug 43; att 91 Sqn (Spit Vb), Hwkge, with Fg Off P. Cowell for op trng, 24-27 Mar 43; com rel due ill health, rtng Fg Off, 18 Feb 44

DOWNING, William George 'Bill', 649040, RAFVR; b Irthlingborough, Northants, 6 Mar 20; ed Downham Central Sch & Acton Tech Coll; occ Eng; joined RAFVR, Viceroy Hse, Lon, Jun 39; AC2, RAF W Drayton, 26 Jun 39; LAC, qual armourer, 1940; Cpl Armourer, 257 Sqn (Spit I), Hendon, May 40; 421 Flt (Hurr I) Gravesend, 8 Oct 40; acc for flg trng & to Crse 10, 6 ITW, Aberystwyth; PDC W. Kirby, 1941; 26 EFTS (Moth), Guinea Fowl, S Rhod, 1 Aug-12 Sep 41 (1st solo, 18 Aug 41); 22 SFTS (Harv), Thornhill, Rhod, 23 Sep 41-26 Feb 42; plt badge, 2 Jan 42; Sgt Plt (649040), Feb 42; 5 (P)AFU (Master I/II), Ternhill, Salop, 5-20 Jun 42; 61 OTU (Spit II), Rednal, Salop, 26 Jun-Nov 42 (1st solo on type, 27 Jun 42); att 61 OTU, Montford Bridge, 25 Aug-14 Sep 42; 41 Sqn (init as Staff Plt), 3 Nov 42-7 Jun 43 (LF 28 May 43; 197.5 FH); 7 days PL, 3 Dec 42; hosp 2 mths w fractured elbow, Dec 42; Flt Sgt, Feb 43; marr Joan Redley, 8 Jun 43; PDC, Blackpool, 9 Jun 43; emb Greenock per USS *Christobal*, 20 Jun 43; disemb Algiers, 27 Jun 43; by road to Tunis, then by DC-3 to Malta, arr 4 Jul 43; 229 Sqn (Spit Vc), Krendi, from AHQ Malta (ex-UK w Flt Sgt S. J. Biggs), 5-19 Jul 43; 1 Prob Me110, 12 Jul 43; 2 Dest Me110, but himself SD, last seen in dinghy 8m S of Riposto, Sicily, rescued by fisherman but captured, 19 Jul 43 [see also p. 44, 'Black Crosses off my Wingtip' by Sqn Ldr I. F. 'Hap' Kennedy, 1994 (2005) ISBN 0919431828]; Campo Concentramento P.G. 66, Capua, nr Naples, Italy, 19 Jul-Sep 43 (escaped twice but recaptured); Stalag XIII-C (POW No. 668), Hammelburg, G., Sep-Oct 43 (escaped once but recaptured); Stalag Luft VI, Heydekrug, E Prussia, 6 Oct 43-Jul 44; WO, Feb 44; Stalag 357, Thorn, Poland, Jul-Aug 44; Stalag 357 (Fallingbostel), Örbke, G., Aug 44-6 Apr 45; res on repat, Carshalton Beeches, Surrey; demob, 16 Oct 45; PC1, Northants Constabulary, Aug 45-Jan 51; Crse

82, FRS Finningley (Wlngtn T10), 6 Mar-18 Jun 51; No 22 Staff Plts Crse, CNCS Shawbury, 19 Jun-11 Sep 51; Staff Plt, 1 ANS (Anson & Wlngtn), Hullavington, 19 Sep-4 Feb 53; scndd to 5 ANS (Wlngtn), Lindholme, 27 Oct-3 Dec 51; 1 OCTU Spitalgate, 4 Feb-6 May 53; app to SSC as Plt Off (8 yrs on AL & 4 yrs in Res), 7 May 53 (649040, same as NCO No; sen 22 Feb 51); 242 OCU (Valetta), Dishforth, 12 May-20 Aug 53; 114 Sqn (Valetta), Fayid, Egypt, 22 Sep 53-24 Apr 55; Fg Off, 7 May 54; ADC to the AOC, HQ 205 Grp, MEAF, 24 Apr 55-4 Mar 56; Ops Northolt, 30 Apr-1 Jun 56; FI, 7 FTS (Vamp), Valley, 3-30 Jun 56; FIC, CFS, S Cerney, 17 Jul-25 Sep 56; CFS, Little Rissington, 2 Oct-12 Dec 56; Flt Lt, 7 Nov 56; JARIC (Radar-Photo), Medmenham & Brampton, 1 Jan 57-10 Apr 58; emb Southampton for NY per *Queen Mary*; Tech Instr, Sheppard AFB, Wichita Falls, Texas, 25 Apr 58-22 Jul 60; Flt Cdr, Met Comms Sqn, Dishforth, Yks, 30 Jul 60-15 May 62; HQ 23 Grp Comms Flt, 16 May 62-30 Sep 64; Nrthrn Comms Sqn, Topcliffe, 1 Oct 64-30 Jan 66; Sqn Ldr, 1 Jan 66; Valetta Conv Flt, Gaydon, 31 Jan 66; OC, Comms Sqn, Luqa, Malta, Apr 66-Jul 68; ret for RAF, 31 Jul 68; occ clerical pos, Northants Police, Wootton Hall, 1970-75; emp Ed Dept, Northants Cty Council, 1975-80; ret 1980; d 11 Feb 10

DUCHATEAU, Roger Alphonse Joseph 'Chat', 135896, RAFVR (Belgian); b Wonck (Liege), B., 1 Jun 14; admtd to Belg Royal Mil Academy (Ecole Militaire), 16 Nov 34; grad, 23 Nov 36; 11 Regt de Ligne, 26 Dec 36-26 Sep 38 (att Air Sch, 26 Dec 36-24 Jun 37, att 1 Regt Aé, 25 Jun 37-15 May 38, att Plt Sch, 16 May-26 Sep 38); Obs Brevet, 30 Oct 37; Flg Brevet, 14 Mar 39; 1 Regt Aé, 27 Sep 38-31 Mar 39 (att Plt Sch, 6 Oct 38-31 Mar 39); 2 Regt Aé, 1 Apr 39-20 Aug 40; 2/I/2°Aé, 10 May 40; unemp, 21 Aug 40-10 Feb 41 (moved into F. w his unit after B. was invaded, but rtnd to B. after F. capitulated); civil emp, 11 Feb 41-15 Jul 42; left B., 16 Jul 42, arr Gib, 16 Sep 42, arr UK, 28 Oct 42; Air Force Depot, 29 Oct-29 Dec 42; 1 RC, Uxb (joined RAFVR), 30 Dec 42-18 Jan 43; com Plt Off, 30 Dec 42; com Lt, AMB, 14 Jan 43; Crse 42, 5 (P)AFU (Master I/II), Ternhill, Salop, 19 Jan-15 Mar 43; 61 OTU (Spit), Rednal, Salop, 16 Mar-24 May 43; 41 Sqn, 25 May-9 Jun 43; 349 (Belgian) Sqn (Spit Vb), Kingscliffe, 10 Jun-2 Aug 43; Fg Off, 30 Jun 43; 41 Sqn (again), 3 Aug-24 Nov 43; Capt AMB, 16 Sep 43; att RAF Hawarden, Flint, 14-17 Nov 43; 350 (Belgian) Sqn (Spit Vb/c & XIV), 25 Nov 43-30 Mar 45; BTS, 31 Mar-22 Apr 45; att BAF, 23 Apr-5 Feb 46; 1 OATS, Digby, 6 Feb-4 Mar 46; att BAF, 5 Mar-30 Nov 46 (dschgd from RAF, 1 Oct 46, having flown 133 active missions (248 op FH) & crdtd w 13 locos. & 37 MET Dest or Dam); admin duties, 1 Dec 46-27 Apr 47; 160 Wg, 28 Apr-10 Oct 47; OC, 350 Sqn (Spit XIV), Beauvechain, B., 11 Oct 47-5 Aug 48; OC, 1 Wg, 6 Aug 48-14 Feb 50; awarded Belg COC, OOC, COL, COL2, Commemorative Medal, 1940-45 (w 2 crossed swords), MMC, 1940-45, & CdE; Min of Colonies, 15 Jul 50; ret 1 Oct 53; d Tenerife, Canary Is, Spain, 21 Jan 89

DUCKWORTH, Robert, 1425494, RAFVR; b Accrington, Lancs, 7 Feb 20; ed Preston RC Coll; enl in RAFVR, Cardington, 11 Feb 41; 2 BFTS (Stearman, Vultee & Harv), Polaris Flt Academy, War Eagle Fld, Lanc, CA, USA, 1941; Sgt Plt, 1942; 59 OTU (Hurr), Milfield, NBL, 1942; 41 Sqn, 19 Jan-ca Feb 43; 195 Sqn (Typhn), Woodvale, 1943; Flt Sgt, 1943; WIA or inj on active svce w LAC R. P. Collins, 8 Jul 43; DOW or DOI, 16 Oct 43, aged 23; s of William & Lillie Duckworth of Alvaston, Derby; bur St Michael Churchyard, Alvaston

EAST, Walter Raymond 'Wingco', 1330277, RAFVR; b Lewisham, Lon, 16 Mar 22; ed Roan Secondary Sch, Greenwich; enl in RAFVR, 24 May 41; 6 ITW, Aberystwyth, 1941; 2 EFTS, Staverton, nr Cheltenham, 1941; 8 SFTS, Montrose, Scot, 1941-42; Sgt Plt, 1942; 58 OTU (Spit), Ggmth, Stirling, 1942; 41 Sqn, 18 Jun 42-3 May 43; SD/KIA in Spit XII, EN612, off Dieppe by Lt Walter Radener of 4./JG26 during shipping recce to Dieppe, F., 3 May 43, aged 21; s of Philip W & Dorothy R. East of Lewisham, Lon; rmbd Panel 148, Runnymede Mem, Surrey

FARFAN [FARFAN de los GODOS], Fernand William 'Fanny', 157691, RAFVR (Trinidadian of Spanish descent); b Montserrat, Trinidad, 29 Aug 21; ed St Mary's Coll, Trinidad; joined

RAFVR, 2 Mar 41; 4 ITW, Paignton, 1941; 8 EFTS, Woodley, 1941; LAC (1386843), 3 Oct 41; 9 SFTS (Master & Hurr), Hullavington, 1941; Sgt Plt, 1942; 61 OTU (Spit), Heston, Mdx, 1942; 601 (Cty of Lon) Sqn (Spit Vb), Digby, 22 Mar 42; emb King George V Dock, Glasgow, for Luqa, Malta, per USS *Wasp* (Op 'Calendar'), 13 Apr 42; arr Malta & to 601 Sqn (Spit Vc), 20 Apr 42; 1 Prob 'Italian bomber', 10 May 42; left Malta, 28 Jun 42; W Desert, Jun-Aug 42; 1 Dam Me109G, Jul 42; 80 Sqn (Hurr II), Palestine & Egypt, 1 Oct 42; 123 (E India) Sqn (Glad II, Hurr IIc & Spit Vc), Doshen Tappeh, Tehran, Iran, 22 Oct 42; com Prob Plt Off (157691), 10 Mar 43; to Libya & Egypt w 123 Sqn, 2 Apr 43; SD/AA but evaded, during Op 'Thesis' over Crete, in Hurr IIc, KW964, 23 Jul 43; AHQ Air Def, E Med, 8 Sep 43; rtnd to 123 Sqn for visit, 17 Sep 42; Fg Off (WS), 10 Sep 43; to UK, HQ 11 Grp, 1943; FI, 57 OTU (Spit), Eshott, NBL, 8 Dec 43; 1 FLS (Hurr, Spit & Typhn), Milfield, NBL, 22 May 44; 83 GSU (Mstg, Spit & Typhn), Tang, Ssx, 14 Jun 44; 602 (City of Glasgow) Sqn (Spit IX & XVI), B.11 Longues, F., 17 Jul 44; 1 Dest FW190, 26 Aug 44; 1 Dest FW190, 20 Sep 44; Flt Lt (WS), 10 Mar 45; 41 Sqn, 24 Mar-25 Sep 45; Temp OC, A Flight, 2-9 May 45; 2 mths leave from 25 Sep 45, but DNR; home to Trinidad in DC-3, Oct 45; OL2 (Knight) w Palm & CdG (B) w Palm (601 Sqn), 27 Jun 47; Fg Off, 1 Nov 47 (sen 10 Sep 46); marr Nicole H. Despointes, 1947; sen of 10 Sep 46 incr to 10 Mar 44, WEF 3 Sep 48; rel WS rank of Flt Lt, 1 Jan 48 (gaz 3 Sep 48); rel com 27 Apr 49, rtng Flt Lt; d Trinidad, 26 May 98

FEARON, David Nigel, 41389, RAF; b Lon, 10 May 20; ed Cheltenham; joined RAF, Brough, 6 Oct 38; grntd SSC as Actg Prob Plt Off, 14 Dec 38; flg trng Brough & Little Rissington; Prob Plt Off, 10 Oct 39; Fg Off, 3 Sep 40; Flt Lt (WS), 3 Sep 41; 64 Sqn (Spit Vb), Ayr, 6 Apr 43; 41 Sqn, 20 May 43-LM 23 Apr 44; Temp Sqn Ldr, 1 Jul 44; grntd perm com as Flt Lt (4 yrs ext svce on AL), 8 Aug 46; Flt Lt, 25 Feb 47 (sen 1 Dec 42); Sqn Ldr, 1 Aug 47; marr Patricia W. Mortimore, ca 1948; app to perm com as Sqn Ldr, 6 Jan 49; Wg Cdr, 1 Jan 54; ret, 10 May 66

FEATHERSTONE, Allan, 52997, RAFVR; b 26 Jun 14; Sgt Plt (534567); com Prob Plt Off (52997), 2 Mar 43; Fg Off (WS), 2 Sep 43; 83 GSU (Mstg, Spit & Typhn), Bognor Regis, Ssx, 1944; 610 (Cty of Chester) Sqn (Spit XIV), B.56 Evere, 23 Dec 44; Flt Lt (WS), 2 Mar 45; 350 (Belgian) Sqn (Spit XIV), B.78 Eindhoven, 4 Apr-20 May 45; 41 Sqn, 20 May-30 Jul 45; SEAC Ferry Command, 30 Jul 45; Flt Lt, 2 Sep 46; trans to Tech Branch, 27 Oct 48; app to perm com as Flt Lt in Ftr Control Branch, 4 Apr 51; ret 26 Jun 63; d 2006

FINUCANE, Raymond Patrick Robert, 122410, RAFVR; b Rathmines, Dublin, 17 Mar 22; joined RAFVR, Yatesbury, Wilts, 1940; Sgt, WO/AG (1268623), 101 (B) Sqn (Wlngtn), 3 Grp, Oakington, 1941 (33 ops); com Prob Plt Off (122410), 1 May 42; Fg Off, 1 Nov 42; re-mustered as plt, 1943; Flt Lt, 1 May 44; 610 (Cty of Chester) Sqn (Spit XIV), Eindhoven, FM 5 Jan 45; 41 Sqn, FM 19 Mar-21 Mar 45 ('after prang'; 2 ops); TA in Spit XIV (serial NR), braked suddenly & inj two airmen at wingtips, imm taken off ops & posted, 21 Mar 45; 83 GSU (Spit XIV), Dnsfld, Mar 45; 486 (NZ) Sqn (Tmpst), Fassberg, G., 21 Apr-30 Jul 45; ferry duties, 151 RU, Luneburg, G., 1 Aug 45-26 Apr 46; Actg Off i/c Flg, 19 Mar 46; Stn Adjt, RAF Luneburg, 27 Apr 46; det to BAFO as unit rep at Victory Parade, Lon, 19 May 46; att Moral Leadership Crse, Gronau, G., 7 Oct 46; rlsd under Class A, 5 Nov 46; rel com in RAFVR, rtng Flt Lt, on app to com as Fg Off (5 yrs) in recons RAFVR ACB, 16 Feb 52; Flt Lt, ACB, 4 Nov 54; svce ext 5 yrs, WEF 16 Dec 57; rel com 16 Dec 62; emp, Aer Lingus, London, & subs in commercial publishing; d Liss, Surrey, 12 Feb 09

FISHER, Douglas Percy 'Jackie', 656212/169435, RAFVR; b Stoke on Trent, 24 Apr 18; ed Central Secondary Sch & HS of Commerce; enl in RAFVR, Stratford-on-Avon, 10 May 41; 10 ITW, Scarborough, 1941; 6 EFTS, Sywell, 1941; 34 SFTS (Harv), Medicine Hat, Alta, Can, 1941; Sgt Plt, 1942; 17 (P)AFU (Master), Watton, Nflk, 1942; 59 OTU (Hurr), Milfield, NBL,

1942; 535 Sqn (Hurr IIc), High Ercall, 16 Oct 42-25 Jan 43 (dsbnd); Sup, RAF High Ercall, pending disposal, 25 Jan 43; 41 Sqn, 12 Feb 43-LM 29 Sep 44 (6 wks absence, ill health, until 15 Jul 44); AA/WIA in Spit XII, EN231, & hosp 17 days, 18 Jul 43; 1 Dest Me109, Évreux, F., 20 Oct 43; com Prob Plt Off (169435), 6 Dec 43; 1 Dest V1, 50m SSW of Dngnss, 16 Jul 44; Fg Off (WS), 6 Jun 44; Flt Lt (WS), 6 Dec 45; com rel, rtng Flt Lt, on appt. to com as Fg Off with recons RAFVR GD, 16 Jun 48; permission to retain Flt Lt on 14 Sep 48 withdrawn, 5 Apr 49; rel com as Fg Off, 5 Apr 49; Master Plt (656212) [Hon RAF Com], 18 Oct 51

FISHER, Roy Robert George, NZ.412671 & 131376, RNZAF; b Pukerimu, Cambridge, NZ, 21 Oct 20; ed Leamington Primary & Hamilton Tech Coll; enl in RNZAF (412671) & to ITW, Levin, as LAC, 4 May 41; 2 EFTS, Bell Block, NZ, 14 Jun 41 (FF 16 Jun 41); emb to Can per *Awatea*, 14 Aug 41; disemb Vncvr Can, 29 Aug 41; 2 SFTS (Harv), Uplands, Ont, 2 Sep 41; Sgt Plt & plt badge, 21 Nov 41; 1Y Depot, 25 Nov 41; emb Can, 9 Dec 41; disemb, UK & to 3 PRC, Bnmth, Hants, 19 Dec 41; 9 (P)AFU (Master I/III), Hullavington, 5 Jan 42; 3 PRC, Bnmth, Hants, 2 Feb 42; 55 OTU (Hurr), Usworth, Dur, 24 Feb 42; 257 Sqn (Hurr II, Spit Vb), Honiley, 4 May 42; 232 Sqn (Spit Vb), Llanbedr, 15 May 42; 93 Sqn (Spit), Kingscliffe, 29 Sep 42; RAF Stn Wtrg, 21 Oct 42; arr Algiers w 93 Sqn, 13 Nov 42; arr Tunisia w 93 Sqn, 21 Nov 43; 1 Dam Ju87, 21 Nov 42; 1 Dam Me109F, 1 Dec 42; com Prob Plt Off (412671), 9 Jan 43; CL/IFA, 25 Feb 43; 2 Dam Me109G, Apr 43; arr Malta w 93 Sqn, 1 Jun 43; HQ MEC, 4 Jul 43; Temp Fg Off, 9 Jul 43; ½ Dest Ju88 w Fg Off S. Browne, 11 Jul 43; 1 Dam Ju87 in the air, & 1 Dest Mc202, ½ Dam Ju87 & ½ Dam Me109 on grnd, 13 Jul 43; OS tour exprd & rested HQ ME & 203 Grp, 19 Aug 43; Target Towing Flt, 13 AGS, Ballah, 1 Oct 43; Target Towing Flt, 77 OTU, Qastina, 17 Feb 44; 22 PTC, 3 Jun 44; , HQ MAAF, 7 Jun 44; MiD, 8 Jun 44; arr Italy & to 3 BPD, Naples, 13 Jun 44; 93 Sqn (again), Piombino, Italy, 17 Jul 44; EF & CL, Beaurepaire, nr Lyon, F., retrieved by US L-5 Sentinel 'Grasshopper' A/C & avoided capture, 30 Aug 44; 56 PTC, 14 Dec 44; dep Italy to UK, 20 Dec 44; Temp Flt Lt, 9 Jan 45; 83 GSU (Spit XIV), Dnsfld, 23 Jan 45; 41 Sqn, 24 Feb-9 May 45 (1st op flt, 28 Feb 45; 44 sorties over NL & G.); 4 Dam Ar196 on Lake Ratzeburg, G., 24 Apr 45; 130 (Punjab) Sqn (Spit XIV), B.152 Fassberg, 9 May 45; 12 (RNZAF) PDRC, 5 Jun 45; MiD, 14 Jun 45; disemb NZ & to 2 PD(T) Wlngtn, 4 Aug 45; ceased att to RAF, 16 Aug 45; rel com in RNZAF, 9 Nov 45; RNZAF Res, 12 Nov 45; trans to Gen Res (131376), 13 Jun 50; trans to Active Res (Nrthrn Res Wg), 20 Oct 50; trans back to Gen Res, 3 Nov 55; ret, 21 Oct 75; d Pukerimu, Cambridge, 22 Dec 88

FLEMING, Robert 'Bob', 656285/190167, RAFVR; b Newmains, Lanark, Scot, 16 Dec 18; ed Morningside PS & Newmains PS; joined RAFVR, ex-Army, Stratford-on-Avon, 10 May 41; 4 BFTS (Stearman, Vultee & Harv), Falcon Fld, Mesa, Ariz., USA, 1941; Flt Sgt, 1943; B Flt, 41 Sqn, 21 Jan 44-20 Apr 45; WO, 1944; Prob Plt Off (190167), 11 Dec 44; 9 PDC, 20 Apr-10 May 45; Sup FI, 57 OTU (Spit), Eshott, NBL, 10 May 45; SEAC Ferry Duties, 12 FU, Melton Mowbray, 30 May 45; Fg Off (WS), 11 Jun 45

GALITZINE, Prince Emanuel Vladimirovitch, 106181, RAF/RAFVR; b Kislovodsk, Russia, 28 May 18; orig Russian royalty (grt-grt gson of Catherine the Great) but emgtd to UK w family aboard RN ship from Crimea to Constantinople, then train to Paris, 1919; ed Königsberg Uni, E Prussia, & Lancing Coll, Lancing, W Ssx, & St Paul's; emp Prudential after ed; founded coy Curzon Films; naturalised w bros George & Nicholas & fthr Prince Vladimir, an Art Expert & Dealer of Chessington, Surrey, 3 Apr 33; grntd SSC in RAF as Prob APO (41395), 14 Dec 38; to Finland & joined FiAF to fight Soviets, Helsinki, Mar 40; flg trng, Parola, Finland; 39 Sqn FiAF (Fokker D.XXI), Mar 40-Feb 41; rtnd to Lon after mthr † in Blitz (Oct 40) & rejoined RAFVR as LAC (193113), Hullavington, Jul 41; com Prob Plt Off (106181), 13 Sep 41; 504 Sqn (Spit IIa/IIb/Vb), Ballyhalbert, NIre, 19 Nov 41; 222 Sqn (Spit Vb), N Weald, 12 Mar 42; 611 (W Lancs) Sqn (Spit IX), Drem, (18 sweeps, 2 Rhubarbs, Dieppe), ca Apr-Sep 42; 1 Dam FW190,

19 Aug 42; FL in Spit Vb, BL367, w glycol leak, 19 Aug 42; SS Flt (Spit VI/VII/IX), Northolt, (2 sweeps), Sep 42; 1 Dam Ju86R, 12 Sep 42; Fg Off (WS), 13 Sep 42; marr Gwendoline Rhodes, Dec 42; 124 (Baroda) Sqn (Spit Vb), N Weald, (1 sweep), O/F 26 Jan 43; 308 (Krakowski) Sqn, Ch. Fenton, (2 sweeps), ca Apr 43; 41 Sqn, 14 May-LM 24 Sep 43; Flt Lt (WS), 13 Sep 43; 1 Prob FW190, SW of Beauvais, F., 24 Sep 43; att BAT Course, Wtrng, 26-28 Sep 43 (recalled; crse not completed); 83 (Composite) Grp HQ & PA to AVM Sir W. Dickson, OC 83 Grp, Gatton Pk, Reigate, Dec 43; 72 Sqn (Spit IX), 324 Wing, Italy, Sep 44; post-War occ plt, Airline Svces of India & BEA; app to com as Flt Lt (106181) in RAuxAF (5 yrs on AL & 5 yrs in Res), 18 Feb 52 (sen 29 Nov 51); emp by A. V. Roe (Avro); trans to Res, 2 Oct 54; rel com, 18 Feb 62, emgtd to Peru, & Dir, Aero Condos aircraft coy, Peru, 1960s; rtnd to Lon, 1991; emp Air Foyle, 1991; d Lon, 23 Dec 02, aged 84; funeral, Russian Orthodox Cathedral, Lon, 2 Jan 03; see also combat reports, dating from Sep 42, in TNA AIR 50/396

GARRIE, THOMAS ADAMSON 'Tommy', 1348819, RAFVR; b Edin, Scot, 10 Sep 21; ed Bellevue Intnl Sch, Edin; joined RAFVR, ACRS, Lon, 18 Aug 41; 2 BFTS (Stearman, Vultee & Harv), Polaris Flt Academy, War Eagle Fld, Lancaster, CA, USA, 1942; Sgt Plt, 1942; Flt Sgt, 1943; 41 Sqn, 18 Sep 43-LM 18 Mar 44; occ post war, Post Office, Edin

GAZE, FREDERICK ANTHONY OWEN 'Tony', 60096, RAFVR; b Melb, Aust, 3 Feb 20; ed Geelong (CE) GS, Corio VIC; studied Natural Sciences, Queens' Coll, Cambridge Uni, 1938-39; enl in RAFVR, 6 Jan 40; LAC (911051), 1 ITW, Cambridge, 26 Jul 40; 7 EFTS, Desford, 26 Jul 40-3 Sep 40, 5 SFTS Sealand, 10 Sep 40; 5 SFTS, Ternhill, 3 Nov-31 Dec 40; com Prob Plt Off (60096), 15 Jan 41 (sen 9 Jan 41); 610 (Cty of Chester) Sqn (Spit IIa), Whmpnt, 10 Mar-18 Nov 41; 1 Dest & 1 Prob Me109E, 26 Jun 41; 1 Dam Me109E, 2 Jul 41; ½ Dest Me109E, 6 Jul 41; 1 Dest Me109F & 1 Dest Me109E, 10 Jul 41; 1 Prob Me109F, 17 Jul 41; DFC (610 Sqn), 5 Aug 41; FI, 57 OTU (Spit), Hwdn, Flint, 21 Nov 41-3 Jun 42 (OC B Flt, 57 OTU, 17 Mar-3 Jun 42); Plt Off cnfmd & to Fg Off, 15 Jan 42 (sen 9 Jan 42); att Merlin Eng Handling Crse, RR, Derby, 28 Apr 42; Flt Cdr, 616 (S Yks) Sqn (Spit VI), Kingscliffe, 3 Jun-31 Aug 42; 1 Prob FW190, 13 Jul 42; 1 Dest & 1 Dam FW190, 18 Jul 42; 1 Dest Do217, 19 Aug 42; OC, 64 Sqn (Spit IX), Hnch, 1 Sep-2 Nov 42; 1 Dam FW190, 6 Sep 42; 1 Dam FW190, 11 Oct 42; apparent scapegoat for failed Spit IX Wing op he led to cover B17 raid on Morlaix, F., in which all but 1 of 133 (Eagle) Sqn's aircraft were lost, 26 Sep 42; rtnd to 616 (S Yks) Sqn as Flt Cdr, 9 Nov 42-8 Jan 43; Flt Lt (WS), 15 Jan 43 (sen 9 Jan 43; gaz 11 May 43); 1st Bar to DFC (616 Sqn), 19 Jan 43; PR speech-maker for Dept PR3, Air Min, 20 Jan-23 May 43; SHQ Hnch, (Sup w 453, 222 & 129 Sqns.), Hnch, Esx, 24 May-24 Aug 43; att 268 (TacR) Sqn (Mstg & Typhn) as FI, Odiham, 20 Jun-9 Jul 43; 1 Dam FW190, 16 Aug 43; 1 Dest FW190, 17 Aug 43; 1 Prob Me109G, 19 Aug 43; OC A Flt, 66 Sqn (Spit Vb/c), Kenley, 26 Aug-4 Sep 43; 1 Dest FW190, 4 Sep 43; SD over Ault in Spit Vb, AR281, by Lt Gerhard Vogt in FW190 of II/JG26, 4 Sep 43; evaded capture & rtnd via Spain & Gib; arr UK & admtd to hosp for surgery to repair facial dam, 28 Oct 43; AFDU, Wtrg, 10 Feb 44; Ftr Afltn duties, 5 Grp, Bomber Cmd, Swinderby, 14 Feb 44; Flt Cdr, 610 (Cty of Chester) Sqn (Spit XIV), Friston, 22 Jul 44-4 Mar 45 (dsbnd); 1 Dest V1, 5 Aug 44; OC B Flt, 610 Sqn, 31 Dec 44-10 Mar 45; 1 Dest FW190D, 1 Jan 45; 1 Dest Me262, 14 Feb 45; 83 GSU (Spit XIV), Dnsfld, 11 Mar-4 Apr 45; 41 Sqn, 5 Apr-1 May 45; OC A Flt, 41 Sqn, 8 Apr-1 May 45; 1 Dest Ju52/3m, Ottersburg, G., 11 Apr 45; ½ Dest Ar234 w Flt Lt D. S. V. Rake, W of Bremen, G., 12 Apr 45; ½ Dest FW190D w Fg Off J. F. Wilkinson, Schwerin, G., 28 Apr 45; 1 Dest FW190D, N of Lauenberg, G., 30 Apr 45; OC A Flt, 616 (S Yks) Sqn (Meteor F3), B.109 Quackenbrück, 1 May 45; 2nd Bar to DFC (610 Sqn), 1 Jun 45; app OC when 616 (S Yks) Sqn dsbnd & formed nucleus of new 263 Sqn, 31 Aug 45; OC, Eng Sch, Rolls Royce, Derby, Dec 45; OC, 691 (Navy Co-Op) Sqn (Martinet, Oxford, Spit), Exeter, 10 May 46; CGI & OC Test Flt, 61 OTU (Spit), Keevil, 1 Sep 46; rel com as Flt Lt in RAFVR, 8 Mar 48, rtng Sqn Ldr; rtnd to Aust & emp on fthr's farm, then emp in Import-Export coy; com Fg Off, 21 Sqn RAAF (CAF,

Wirraway), Laverton, 23 Jan 49; rtnd to UK as racing drvr & exchange plt w 600 Sqn RAuxAF (Meteor F.4), Bgn Hill, 2 Jul 50 (exchange cxld due RAF wanting more flg than RAAF willing to pay); occ F2 racing drvr, 1951, & F1 racing drvr, 1952; occ racing drvr, sports cars & 'Formula Libre', until 1957; competitor, World Gliding Championships, Cologne, G., 1960; res Herts to 1976, then rtnd to Aust to farm; OAM (for svce to mtr racing), 26 Jan 06

GIBBS, NORMAN PETER 'Peter' & 'Gibby', 173284, RAFVR; b Swindon, 25 Dec 21; ed Swindon GS, grad 1939, & Corpus Christi Coll, Oxford (studied French), 1940-41; joined RAFVR, Oxford, Apr 41; emb for Can per TSS (HMT) *Pasteur*, ca 8 Sep 41 (arr 15 Sep 41); 4 BFTS (Stearman, Vultee & Harv), Falcon Fld, Mesa, Ariz., USA, Sep 41 (FF 30 Sep 41); Sgt Plt (1317449), May 42; 58 OTU (Master, Lysander & Spit), Balado Bridge, Kinross, 15 Jun 42-12 Apr 43 (1st solo on Spit, 11 Mar 43); IFA/MAC/CL in Lysander, 26 Oct 42; admtd RAF Hosp, Glen Eagle Hotel, 26 Oct 42-Jan 43; Crse 32, 53 OTU (Master/Spit), Llandow, Glam, & KiL, 13 Apr-22 Jun 43; emb for N Africa, per SS *Highland Princess*, Jul 43; No. 1 APD (Spit Vc/IXc), Maison Blanche, Algiers, 28 Jul-28 Sep 43; emb for UK per MS *Marnix van St Aldegonde*, Oct 43; 2 TEU, Balado Bridge, Kinross, 11 Nov-9 Dec 43; com Prob Plt Off (173284), 20 Jan 44; A Flt, 41 Sqn, 21 Jan 44-7 Mar 45; 1 Dest V1 (41 Sqn's 1st V1), N of Eastbourne, Ssx, 20 Jun 44; 1 Dest V1, off Beachy Head, Ssx, 21 Jun 44; 1 Dest V1, 8-10m S of Hastings, Ssx, 24 Jun 44; 1 Dest V1, 2m S of Eastbourne, Ssx, 8 Jul 44; Fg Off (WS), 20 Jul 44; AA, SE of Aachen, G., & baled out of Spit XIV, RM767, nr Westerlo, Prov of Antwerp, B., 16 Jan 45; dep 41 Sqn med unfit, 7 Mar 45; rel com, med unfit, 1 Aug 45, rtng Fg Off; post-War ed studied for B.Mus., St Edmunds Hall, Oxford Uni, 45; occ prof musician (violin); formed & played in 'Peter Gibbs String Quartet', 1949-53; violin, Philharmonia Orchestra, 1954-55; Surrey Flg Club (Moth), 27 Jun 57 (1st flg since War, then flew constantly until Dec 75) violin, LSO, 1957-59; Ldr, BBC SSO, 4 Dec 60-4 May 63; app to com as Fg Off (173284, 4 yrs svce) in RAFVR (TB), 25 Jun 62 (served on 6 & 12 Sqns (450 FH)); Dep Ldr, LSO, 1963-64; partner, Gibbs & Rae Builders, ca 1964-75; RAFVR svce extended by 4 yrs, 25 Jun 66; 1st violinist, Covent Garden Royal Opera Hse Orchestra, Lon, 1969-70; RAFVR svce extended by 4 yrs, 25 Jun 70; joint leader, Royal Opera Hse Orchestra, 1971-72; rel com in RAFVR, 15 May 71; KIFA in Cessna F150H, G-AVTN, Isle of Mull, Scot, 24 Dec 75 (body located on Pennygown Hill, 1m from Glenforsa Airfield, 4 mths later, A/C located in Sound of Mull, off Oban, Scot, Sep 86)

GILLITT, FRANK NORMAN 'Gilly', 108132, RAFVR; b Buenos Aires, Argentina, 3 Aug 19; ed Wellingborough Sch, Northants, 1931-36; emp Barclay's Bank, Lon; joined RAFVR, AC2 (1377726), 9 RC, Blackpool, 5 Sep 40; 1 RW, 23 Oct 40; 5 ITW, Torquay, 9 Nov 40; LAC, 4 Jan 41; 17 EFTS, Stanley (Windsor) NS, Can, Mar-Jun 41; 9 SFTS, Summerside PEI, Can, 21 Jun-1 Sep 41; plt badge & to Sgt Plt, 1 Sep 41; com Prob Plt Off (108132), 1 Sep 41; 3 PRC, 14 Sep 41; Crse 14, 58 OTU (Spit), Ggmth, Stirling, 28 Oct 41; WUL/NI in bad visibility in Spit I, X4817, Kilsyth, Scot, 3 Dec 41; 91 (Nigeria) Sqn (Spit Vb), Hwkge, 23 Dec 41-2 Oct 42; att No 2 SON for Nav Crse, 8-24 Jan 42; MVA & admtd Royal Victoria Hosp, Flkstn, 21 May 42; conf Plt Off & prmtd to Fg Off (WS), 1 Sep 42; 1 Prob Ju88, off Dover but CD/CL in Spit Vb, EN771, 26 Sep 42; Actg Flt Lt & OC A Flt, 41 Sqn, 2-22 Oct 42; KIFA in Spit Vb, BM573, flew into hill Tarren Hendre, nr Towyn, Merioneth, Wales, in bad weather w Fg Off R. Harrison & Fg Off T. R. Scott, 22 Oct 42, aged 23; s of Frank S & Phyllis I. Gillitt, & nephew of Margaret Gillitt, all of Wellingborough, Northants; bur Block S, Grave 47, Doddington Road Cem, Wellingborough

GLEN, ARTHUR ALLAN 'Pinkie', 998543 (NCO) & 115232 (Off), RAFVR; b Kingston upon Hull, E Yks, 2 May 18; ed Hymers Coll, Hull; occ Clerk, Davis & Thornton Solicitors & subs, Hull Food Control Comm, Guildhall, Hull; Air Obs, RAFVR, 25 May 40; AC2 plt u/t, 1 Jul 40; 4 ITW, Paignton, Devon, 15 Jul 40; 11 EFTS, Perth, 25 Aug 40 (1st dual, 26 Aug 40); 8 SFTS, Montrose, Scot, 5 Oct 40-14 Jan 41; plt badge & Sgt Plt (998543), 8 Jan 41; Crse 17, 57 OTU (Spit), Hwdn,

Flint, 17 Jan-10 Mar 41 (1st solo in Spit, 5 Feb 41); 41 Sqn, 11 Mar 41-3 May 42 (FF 13 Mar 41); ½ Dam He111 w Sgt Plt G. W. Swanwick, 10m N of Flamborough Hd, 10 Apr 41; day & NF trng cpltd, 25 Apr 41; marr Mercia Sumpton, 5 May 41; 1 Dest Me109F, Gravelines, F., 14 Aug 41; 7 days leave, 13 Oct 41; com Prob Plt Off (115232), 2 Jan 42; 2 Dest Me109E, off Fécamp, F., 14 Mar 42; cpltd 50 op sorties, 19 Apr 42; 1 Dam FW190, Marquise, F., 26 Apr 42 (orig claimed as Prob); cpltd tour (59 op sorties) & posted OS, 3 May 42; DFC (41 Sqn), 8 May 42 (gaz 29 May 42); to Malta per HMS *Eagle*; 1 of 8 Spits flown off *Eagle*, approx 50m from Algiers for Ta Kali & bounced by ca 12 Me109s off Pantellaria in Spit Vc, BR359, guns inop, but arr safely after 3½ hr flt, 3 Jun 42 & posted to 603 (City of Edin) Sqn; 2 Dam Me109s, Malta, 23 Jun 42; 1 Dest & 1 Dam Me109F & 1 Dam Z1007, Malta, 26 Jun 42; 2 Dest Ju88s, 1 Dest Me109F & ½ Dam Z1007, Malta, 6 Jul 42; sick, sand fly fever, Malta, ca Jul 42; inj by bomb blast on grnd, Jul 42; declared unfit for duty & removed from ops, LF in Malta 24 Jul 42; evac Malta to Gib, 1 Aug 42, dep Gib for Lisbon, 9 Aug 42, dep Lisbon for Foynes & Poole, 10 Aug 42, arr UK, 11 Aug 42; FI, 52 OTU (Spit), Aston Down, Gloucs, 3 Sep 42; hosp for 6 w§ks, poss Imperial Hotel, Torquay, Cornwall, 8 Sep 42; Fg Off, 1 Oct 42; Admin & light duties, A. V. Roe & Co Ltd, Oct 42; att 11 Grp for Sector Controller Crse, 5 Jan 43; Grnd Controller Trng, Tang, 20 Jan 43; GCI Controller, RAF Black Gang, IoW, 1 Jul 43; 41 Sqn (again), 20 Jul 43-26 May 44; att Crse, FLS (Spit Vb), Charmy Down, Smrst, & Aston Down, Gloucs, 5-19 Aug 43; Actg Flt Lt & OC B Flt, 5 Sep 43-26 Jan 44; 2 Dest FW190, N of Beauvais, F., 24 Sep 43; Bar to DFC (41 Sqn), 5 Nov 43; Flt Lt (WS), 2 Jan 44; Actg Sqn Ldr & OC, 41 Sqn, 26 Jan-26 May 44; att Grnd Attack Crse, 1 FLS (Spit, Hurr & Typhn), Milfield, NBL, 21 Feb-11 Mar 44; rel Actg Sqn Ldr & to 10 Grp HQ as Supry pending disposal, 26 May 44; 9 days PL, 29 May-6 Jun 44; Actg Sqn Ldr & Staff, 1 Sqn, FLS, Milfield, 6 Jun 44 (FF 10 Jun 44); att 56 PGIC, CGS Catfoss (Spit & Master), 6 Oct-5 Dec 44; DFTS, CFE, 16 Jan-9 Dec 45 (Milfield, 16 Jan-26 Oct 45, & W Raynham, 27 Oct-9 Dec 45); 100 PDC, Uxbridge, 10 Dec 45; A Class rel from RAFVR, 4 Feb 46; emp Central Manufacturing & Trading Coy (Dudley) Ltd, becoming Seles Dir, 1955-70; ret to Filey, Yks after heart attack, 1970; d 19 Dec 79

GOENS, RIJKLOF VAN 'Charlie', 124239, RAFVR (Dutch); b Bandoeng, Dutch E Indies (Indonesia), 25 Jul 14; ed Apeldoorn HS, NL, 1926-32; FI, Dutch Institute of Aircraft, Nationale Luchtvaart Sch (Nat Flt Sch), Feb 37; fled occupied NL for UK over 3 mths from Jan 42; joined RAFVR, 22 Jun 42; plt badge, 23 Jun 42; com Actg Plt Off, 7 Jul 42; 22 EFTS (Moth), Cambridge, 7 Jul 42; Fg Off, 7 Jan 43; RAFC Cranwell, 3 Feb 43; cnfmd in rank, 7 Jul 43; 61 OTU (Spit), Rednal, Salop, 13 Jul 43; 2 TEU (Spit), Ggmth, Stirling, Oct 43-Jan 44; B Flt, 41 Sqn, 19 Jan-17 Aug 44; det for Spit XII display purposes, 9-19 Mar 44 & 20 Mar-14 Apr 44; Flt Lt, 7 Jul 44; MPD in Spit XII, MB880, during Diver patrol, 17 Aug 44, aged 30, presumed ditched in Eng Channel, 10 mins after TO from Lympne, close to shore off Dover, poss result of Allied AA fire; s of Gustaaf H. and Willemine (Minie) M. H. M. d van Goens of Apeldoorn, NL; rmbd Panel 203, Runnymede Mem, Surrey

GOODALL, BERNARD BRYN, NZ.411981, RNZAF; b Nelson NZ, 1 Apr 19; ed Putaruru HS; occ dryerman, Whakatane Paper Mills, enl in RNZAF as airman plt u/t, ITW, Levin, 23 Mar 41; 3 EFTS, Harewood, NZ, 4 May 41; emb Auck for Halifax, Can, per *Dominion Monarch*, 22 Jul 41; arr Halifax & att RCAF, 16 Aug 41; 6 SFTS (Harv), Dunnville, Ont, 18 Aug 41; plt badge & Sgt Plt, 7 Nov 41; 1 Y Depot, Debert NS, 12 Nov 41; att RAF & emb for UK, 9 Dec 41; 3 PRC, Bnmth, Hants, 19 Dec 41; 58 OTU (Spit), Ggmth, Stirling, 10 Feb 42; 41 Sqn, 21 Apr-15 Aug 42 (225 FH, 41 ops, incl 12 convoy patrols, 2 sector recce sorties, 2 low-level attacks in F., a shipping recce and an ASR search); KIFA, flew into grnd at or nr Blounce Farm, ca 2½m SSW of RAF Odiham, Hants, whilst delivering Spit Vb, P8607, 'Palembang Oeloe II' to Tang, after collecting it from Debden, Esx, 15 Aug 42, aged 23; s of Kenneth B. & Caroline G. Goodall, née MacMahon, of Whakatane, Auck NZ; init bur Weston Patrick, later reint Grave 2.I.1, Brookwood Mil Cem, Woking, Surrey; see also photograph in TWN, 4 Nov 42

GRAHAM, PETER BARTLEMY, 1317590/161780, RAFVR; b Oxford, 11 Apr 23; ed Manor Hse, Horsham, Ssx, & St Edward's Sch, Oxford; occ schoolmaster on enl in RAF, Oxford, 23 Apr 41; 11 ITW, Scarborough, Yks, Aug 41; transit camp, RAF Padgate, nr Warrington, Lancs, Oct 41; emb Liv to Halifax NS per SS *Pasteur*, Oct 41; 31 PD, Moncton NB, Can, Oct 41; USAAF familiarisation, Gunter Fld, Montgomery, AL, Nov 41; AIA, Tuscaloosa, AL, (60 hrs on Stearman), Nov 41; ACBFS, Gunter Fld, Montgomery, AL, (70 hrs on Vultee), Feb 42; AFP trng, Craig Fld (Harv), Selma, AL, May 42; FA, ground looped Harv AT6, 18 May 42; Gunnery Sch, Eglin Fld, FL, Jun 42; USAAF Wings & RAF Wings, & prmtd to Sgt Plt (1317590), 1 Jul 42; 31 PD, Moncton NB, Jul 42; emb Halifax for Liv, Jul 42; 2 wks leave, Aug 42; 17 (P)AFU (Master II), Watton, Nflk, 24 Aug-21 Sep 42; Staff, 61 OTU (Lysander & Martinet), Rednal, Salop, for drogue towing duties, 22 Sep 42; X Sqn, 61 OTU (Spit), 26 Feb 43 (score 89%); FA/WUL in Spit I, 24 Apr 43; B Flt, 41 Sqn, 5 May 43-1 Sep 44; AA/WIA (right elbow) in Spit XII, EN238, nr St Valéry, F., 23 Jul 43; 17 days in St Richard's Hosp, Chichester, then 14 days SL; rtnd to 41 Sqn, 25 Aug 43; Flt Sgt, Oct 43; 1 Dam FW190, 15m NW of Beauvais, F., 27 Sep 43; com Prob Plt Off (161780), 29 Oct 43; 2 wks leave, Nov 43; 3 wks leave, Apr 44; Fg Off (WS), 29 Apr 44; att ACRC, Sheffield, ca 26 May-16 Jun 44; 1 Dest V1, 6m W of Hailsham, Ssx, 7 Jul 44 (orig claimed as ½); 1 wk leave, 5-12 Aug 44; 1 Dest V1, nr Wrotham, Kent, 16 Aug 44; 1 Dest V1, Denge Wood, Kent, 17 Aug 44; SD/AA in Spit XII, MB831, during attack on train-load of V2s nr Esquelbecq, F., & captured nr St Omer, 1 Sep 44; Dulag Luft, Oberursel, G., 7-15 Sep 44; Stalag Luft I, Barth, G., 18 Sep 44-1 May 45; repat from Barth, G., to Ford, Ssx, per USAAF B-17 Flying Fortress, 16 May 45; marr Sylvia Patteson, 26 May 45; Flt Lt (WS), 29 Oct 45; undergraduate, King's Coll, Cambridge, Jan 46; dschgd from RAFVR, Mar 46; occ Sch teacher, Haileybury & Imperial Service Coll, Hertford, Sep 48; com Fg Off (161780) in TB, RAFVR, 23 Dec 48; com rel, 1 Aug 50; ordained 24 May 53; d Buckland Newton, Dorset, 12 Oct 09

GRAY, ERIC 'Ricky', A.414020, RAAF; b Toowoomba QLD, Aust, 29 Nov 21; ed Newtown HS, Toowoomba; occ apprent letterpress operator, Harrison Printing Coy, Toowoomba; enl in RAAF, 3 RC, Bris, 20 Jul 41; AC2, 3 ITS, Sandgate QLD, 20 Jul 41; LAC, 31 Jan 42; 2 EFTS, Archerfield QLD, 4 Feb 42 (Moth, 61.5 FH); 5 EFTS, Narrowmine NSW, 12 Apr 42; 7 SFTS, Deniliquin NSW, 3 May 42 (Wirraway, 139 FH); plt badge, 23 Jun 42; Sgt Plt, 15 Oct 42; 3 ED, Sandgate QLD, 16-23 Oct 42; 2 ED, Brdfld Pk NSW, 30 Oct 42; att RAF & emb Syd for UK, 13 Dec 42; disemb UK, 3 Apr 43; 11 PDRC, 4 Apr 43; 7 days leave, 10-16 Apr 43; Flt Sgt, 15 Apr 43; 17 (P)AFU (Master), Watton, Nflk, 1 Jun 43 (Calverley from 22 Jun 43; 52.4 FH); Crse 53, 57 OTU (Spit), Eshott NBL, 10 Aug-2 Nov 43 (72.4 FH); 65 days pte leave, 2 Nov 43-5 Jan 44; Crse 12, Grnd Fighting Duties, GFS, RAF Boulmer, NBL, 7-28 Jan 44; 6 days leave, 29 Jan-3 Feb 44; op trng, 2 TEU (Spit), Ggmth, Stirling, 4 Feb 44 (42.4 FH); com Plt Off, 6 Apr 44; att AOC, 9 Grp HQ, 12-13 Apr 44; 3501 GSU (Spit XIV), Cranfield, Bucks, 19 May 44 (18.2 FH); B Flt, 41 Sqn, 21 Jul 44-3 Sep 45 (157 op FH); 1 Dest V1, 6m S of Hastings, Ssx, 26 Jul 44; 1 Dest V1, 7m off Flkstn, Kent, 20 Aug 44; Fg Off, 6 Oct 44; to Diest via Tilbury & Ostend, 6-17 Nov 44; att RAF Hereford, 83 Grp, for ACOS Crse, 13 Dec 44-10 Jan 45; ⅓ Dest Me110 (G9+FY of 11/NJG1) w Flt Lt R. P. Harding & Fg Off F. M. Hegarty, 10m S of Lippstadt, G., 13 Feb 45; 1 Dam Me262, W of Rheine, G., 14 Feb 45; 2 Dest FW190Ds, Teschendorf, G., 20 Apr 45; ½ Dest FW190D w Sqn Ldr J. B. Shepherd, E of Lake Schwerin, G., 1 May 45; Sup, Flg Control, 124 Wg, 3 Sep 45; 33 PDC, 16 Oct 45; 14 ACHU, Millom, Cumb, 22 Oct 45; 11 PDRC, 3 Nov 45; repat to Aust per *Stirling Castle*; disemb Melb VIC, & to 1 PD, 21 Feb 46; 3 PD, Redbank QLD, 3 Apr 45; dschgd from RAAF, 5 Apr 46; d Toowoomba QLD, 19 Apr 05

GRAY, JAMES ARTHUR BRYCE, 1127628, RAFVR; b Lon, 24 Aug 21; ed Queen's Pk Sch, Glasgow; joined RAFVR, 3 RC Padgate & to RW, Stratford on Avon, 3-17 May 41; 3 Sqn, ITW, Scarborough, 17 May-1 Jul 41; 31 EFTS (Moth), Calgary, Can, 30 Jul-27 Sep 41; 34 SFTS (Harv), Medicine Hat, Alta, 28 Sep-19 Dec 41; Sgt Plt, 19 Dec 41; 2 FIS (Oxford & Tutor), Montrose

& Dalcross, Scot, 21 Jan-23 Apr 42; 2 GTS (Hotspur), Weston-on-the-Green, 14 May-4 Jun 42; 102 GOTU (Hotspur), Kidlington, 13 Jun-30 Jul 42; 5 GTS (Hotspur), Kidlington & Shobdon, 31 Jul 42-5 Apr 43; Flt Sgt, 19 Dec 42; 61 OTU (Master & Spit I/II/V), Rednal, 7 Apr-21 Jun 43; 41 Sqn, 11 Jul-3 Oct 43; FTR, believed SD over Crèvecœur-le-Grand, F., in Spit XII, MB834, 3 Oct 43, aged 22; s of Frederick B. & Dorothy M. Gray of Glasgow; bur Plot 6, Row C, Grave 10, Abbeville Communal Cem Ext, Somme, F.

GREEN, Ronald Edward, 928607/121075, RAFVR; b Battlesbridge, Esx, 13 Feb 21; res Rochford, Esx; ed Southend Tech Coll; joined RAFVR, 4 Jun 40; 13 EFTS, White Waltham, Bucks, 1940; 5 SFTS Ternhill, 1940-41; Sgt Plt, 1941; Crse 2, 53 OTU (Spit), Heston, Mdx, 19 Apr-27 May 41; 122 (Bombay) Sqn (Spit I), Turnhouse, 27 May-24 Aug 41; 41 Sqn w Flt Sgt A. J. Watton, 28 Aug 41-14 Oct 42; 7 days leave, 13 Oct 41; Flt Sgt 1942; com Prob Plt Off (121075), 28 Apr 42; 1 Dest Me109F off B. coast, 12 Feb 42; 1 Dam FW190, Guînes, F., 3 May 42; Fg Off (WS), 28 Oct 42; 126 Sqn (Spit Vc), Malta, 1942; Actg Flt Lt, 1943; DFC, 31 Aug 43; Flt Lt (WS), 28 Apr 44; OC, 64 Sqn (Mstg III), Bentwaters, Mar 45; rel com in RAFVR as Flt Lt, rtng Sqn Ldr, on app to com as Fg Off in recons RAFVR, 31 May 49

GRIFFITH, Lyndon Poynton, NZ.40968, RNZAF; b Levin, NZ, 3 Mar 22; ed Horowhenua Coll; enl in RNZAF, 9 Apr 40; EFTS, Taieri, 6 May 40; 1 FTS, Wigram, 1 Jul 40; final flt in NZ before emb for UK, 18 Oct 40; Sgt Plt, 26 Oct 40; att RAF & emb for UK per *Rangitata*, 31 Oct 40 (see also photo of passing-out grp, 'The Weekly News', 6 Nov 40); 616 (S Yks) Sqn (Spit IIa), Tang, 6 Mar 41; 485 (NZ) Sqn (Spit I) O/F, Driffield, 15 Mar 41; 1 Dam Me109E, 16 Aug 41; SD/AA in Spit Vb, W3643, baled out 8m off F. coast, RR by ASR off Hythe, 29 Aug 41 (member of 'Caterpillar' and 'Goldfish' clubs); 1 Dam Me109E, 13 Oct 41; com Plt Off, 18 Nov 41; Flt Cdr, 122 (Bombay) Sqn (Spit Vb), Hornchurch, 10 May 42; 1 Prob FW190, 17 May 42; DFC, 5 Jun 42; 1 Dest FW190, 6 Jun 42; 1 Dest & 1 Dam FW190, 30 Jul 42; Fg Off, 10 Aug 42; 2 Dam Do217 & 1 Dam Ju88 (Op Jubilee), 19 Aug 42; 1 Dest FW190, 6 Dec 42; SGO, 9 Grp, 29 Dec 42-22 Apr 43; FC SAT, 22 Apr-10 Aug 43; 485 (NZ) Sqn (Spit IXb), Bgn Hill, 10 Aug-26 Oct 43; Flt Lt, 10 Aug 43; 41 Sqn, 2 Nov 43-26 Jan 44 (1st op, 5 Nov 43); 501 Sqn (Spit Vb), Hwkge, 28 Jan-11 Aug 44; 200th sweep over F., 29 May 44; 1 Prob Me109, 8 Jun 44; 274 Sqn (Tmpst V), Mstn, 12 Aug-26 Sep 44; 1 Dest V1, 16 Aug 44; 1 Dest V1 (but CD from explosion), 24 Aug 44; 1426 (EA) Flt, Dxfd, 26 Sep 44-1 Jan 45 (flew Mstg, Ju88 & Me109); 504 Sqn (Spit IX), Mstn & Hwkge, 5 Jan-2 Mar 45; Test Plt, 84 GSU (Mstg, Spit, Tmpst & Typhn), Aston Down, Gloucs, 13 Mar-15 Jul 45; trans to RNZAF RAFO as Flt Lt, 12 May 45; flew B-24, Meteor and FW190, Jun 45; app to SSC with RAF as Flt Lt (Nos. 501133/130556, 8 yrs on AL, 4 yrs in Res), 7 Mar 50 (sen 12 Mar 49); trans to Res as Flt Lt, 7 Oct 53; d Aust, 2003

HALE, Peter Harold, 1332528, RAFVR; b Harpenden, 28 Jul 22; ed St Clement Danes, Holborn Estate & Chichester HS; occ shop assist, WH Smith; enl in RAFVR, Uxb, 27 Jan 41; 1 ACRC Babbacombe, 12-28 Jun 41; 4 ITW, Paignton, 28 Jun-7 Sep 41; 21 EFTS, Booker, Bucks, 8 Sep-22 Nov 41; ACDC, Heaton Pk, Manch, 29 Nov-22 Dec 41; emb Clyde for Halifax, per HMT *Bergensfjord*, 23 Dec 41-1 Jan 42; 31 PD, Moncton NB, Can, 2-7 Jan 42; 41 SFTS, Weyburn, Sask, 11-14 Jan 42; Crse 36, 39 SFTS, Swift Current, Sask, 15 Jan-25 Apr 42; plt badge & Sgt Plt, 24 Apr 42; CFS, Trenton, Ont, 27 Apr-16 May 42; 31 BGS, Picton, Ont, 16 May-5 Oct 42; Staff Plt (conv), 31 SFTS, Kingston, Ont, 5 Oct 42-15 Jul 43; Crse 15, 1 OTU (Hurr), Bagotville, Que, 17 Jul-18 Sep 43; 31 PD, Moncton NB, 26 Sep-9 Oct 43; train to NYC, 9-10 Oct 43; emb NYC for Clyde per HMT *Queen Mary*, 10-16 Oct 43; PDC Harrogate (leave), 17 Oct-23 Nov 43; Flt Sgt, Nov 43 (sen 24 Apr 43); Crse 40, 53 OTU (Spit), KiL, 23 Nov 43-22 Feb 44; 4 TEU (Hurr), Annan, 23 Feb-2 Mar 44; 1 TEU (Spit), Tealing, Angus, 3 Mar-5 Jun 44; WO, 24 Apr 44; 83 GSU (Spit XIV), Redhill, 6-22 Jun 44; 3501 GSU (Spit XIV), Cranfield, Bucks, 23 Jun-6 Aug 44; 41 Sqn, 8 Aug 44-21 Mar 45; RR Eng Crse, Derby, 15-26 Sep 44; 10 days leave,

22-31 Dec 44; 7 days leave, 6-14 Feb 45; FA in Spit XIV, MV255, blown off runway into mud on landing in cross-wind & TON, 21 Mar 45; 83 GSU (Spit XIV), Dnsfld, 23 Mar-16 Apr 45; 130 (Punjab) Sqn (Spit XIV), Celle, G., 17 Apr 45; retrieved by Sqn Ldr J. B. Shepherd & rtnd to 41 Sqn, 17 Apr-8 Aug 45; ¼ Dest He111 w Plt Off P. T. Coleman, WO J. A. Chalmers & Sgt Plt C. N. Moyle, W of Goldberg, G., 28 Apr 45; 7 days leave, 5-14 May 45; TCAHC, Morecambe, Lancs, 11-17 Aug 45; 12 FU, Melton Mowbray, 17-30 Aug 45; TCAHC, Morecambe, Lancs, 1 Sep-8 Oct 45; 229 Grp Delhi, India, 18 Oct-3 Nov 45; 17 ACHU, RAF Pocklington, Full Sutton, Yks, 8 Nov 45-4 Jan 46 (incl 3 wks leave); SHQ, RAF Cranwell, 22 Jan-24 Jun 46; demob 100 PDC, Uxb, 24 Jun 46; emp WH Smith, Sep-Dec 46; Meteorological Off, Feb 47-Mar 82; ret Mar 82

HARDING, Ross Philip, 113876, RAFVR; b Fareham, Hants, 22 Jan 21; ed Bishops Wordsworth, Salisbury, & St Edmund Hall, Oxford Uni (Oxford UAS), 1939-41; occ student on enl in RAFVR, Oxford, 7 Mar 41; LAC (1315623), 1941; 16 EFTS, Derby, 1941; 6 SFTS, Little Rissington, 1941; com Prob Plt Off (113876), 3 Dec 41; Prob Fg Off (WS), 1 Jan 43; Crse 32, 53 OTU (Spit), Llandow & KiL, 13 Apr-22 Jun 43; A Flt, 41 Sqn, 5 Jul 43-13 Feb 45; Flt Lt (WS), 3 Mar 44; att OATS, RAFC Cranwell for JCC, 21 Mar-8 Apr 44; att FLS (Spit Va/b/c & Hurr IV), Milfield, NBL, 24 May-14 Jun 44; 1 Dest V1, NW of Rye, Ssx, 5 Jul 44; 1 Dest V1, Romney Marsh-N of Ivychurch, Kent, 15 Aug 44; 1 Dest V1, 1½m NE of Brenzett, Kent, but hit by Allied AA (Cat B) in Spit XII, MB854, & CL Romney-Brenzett, 17 Aug 44; Dep OC, A Flt, 28 Jul 44; CM hearing, Redhill, for charge under Section 39A(1)(e), but acquitted, 1 Sep 44; OC A Flt, 4 Jan 45-13 Feb 45; ⅓ Dest Me110 (G9+FY of 11/NJG1) w Fg Offs E. Gray & F. M. Hegarty, 10m S of Lippstadt, but SD by rear gunner in Spit XIV, RM819, & captured, Werl, G., 13 Feb 45; Dulag Luft, Oberursel, G., Feb-Mar 45; Stalag XIIID, Nuremburg, G., 7 Mar-4 Apr 45; Stalag VII-A, Moosburg, G., 19-29 Apr 45; res on repat, 'Chandos', Halse Rd., Salisbury, Wilts; MiD, 14 Jun 45; Flt Lt, 1 Sep 45; Actg Sqn Ldr, Jan 46; OC, 152 Sqn (Spit VIII/XIV), Tengah, Sngpr, Jan-10 Mar 46 (dsbnd); grntd perm com as Flt Lt in RAF, 12 Mar 47 (sen 1 Sep 45); Sqn Ldr, 1 Jul 50; att RAFSC, Andover, Jan 51; Staff, Assist CAS (Ops), 1952; OC, 96 Sqn (Meteor NF.11), Ahlhorn, G., 1955; Wg Cdr, 1 Jul 58; Dir Staff, RAFSC, Andover, 1958; OC, Oxford UAS, 29 Aug 60; Dep Chief, Brit Mil Mission, Berlin, 14 Dec 62; Gp Capt, 1 Jul 63; OC, RAF Valley & 4 FTS, 23 Jul 65; CBE, 1 Jan 68; Dir Staff (Air), JSSC, Latimer, Bucks, 19 Feb 68; Actg Air Cdre & Air Attaché, Moscow, 7 Aug 70-Oct 72; Air Cdre, 1 Jan 72; Dir of Pers Svce 1, 27 Nov 72-Jan 74; Actg AVM, 31 Jan 74; Senior RAF Instr, RCDS, Lon, 31 Jul 74-Jan 76; ret 7 Feb 76, rtng AVM; Head, Airwork Services Ltd, Oman, 1977-79; Chmn, MOD Selection Board, 1979-84; Spec Adviser, HCDC, 1984; d 29 Nov 98

HARRISON, Ronald, 119918, RAFVR; b Windsor, 8 Feb 20; ed Wycombe Tech Coll; joined RAFVR, Uxb, 5 Nov 41; 10 ITW, Scarborough, 1940; 31 EFTS (Moth), De Winton, Calgary, Can, 1941; 34 SFTS (Harv), Medicine Hat, Alta, 1941; Sgt Plt (1271060), 1941; com Prob Plt Off (119918), 19 Dec 41; 5 (P)AFU (Master I/II), Ternhill, Salop, 1942; 61 OTU (Spit), Rednal, Salop, 1942; 41 Sqn, 24 Jun-22 Oct 42; Fg Off (WS), 1 Oct 42; KIFA in Spit Vb, R7296, flew into hill Tarren Hendre, nr Towyn, Merioneth, Wales, in bad weather w Fg Off (Actg Flt Lt) F. N. Gillitt & Fg Off T. R. Scott, 22 Oct 42, aged 22; s of William & Catherine Harrison of Slough, Bucks; bur CE Plot, Grave 676, Stoke Road Cem, Slough

HAYWOOD, Douglas 'Haybag', 46222, RAF; b Lon, 9 Jun 13; ed Kilburn GS; enl in RAF, Perth, 24 Aug 36; 9 FTS, Thornaby, 1937; Sgt Plt (580296), 1937; 88 Sqn AASF (Battle), F., 1938-40; SD/baled out of Battle, nr Provence, by 3 Me109s, 13 Jun 40; rtnd to UK & rejoined Sqn in Belfast, 1940; 504 Sqn (Hurr I), Filton, 20 Sep 40-8 Aug 41; com Prob Plt Off (46222), 19 Jul 41; Fg Off (WS), 19 Jul 42; 41 Sqn, 18 Sep 42-27 Aug 43; AA/WIA (foot) in Spit XII, EN607, over Dieppe, F., FL Littlestone, nr New Romney & hosp, 27 Apr 43; Flt Lt, 19 Jul 43; SD/AA or

EF, baled out of Spit XII, EN611, 10m ENE of Hardelot on Ramrod S8 to Watten, F., 27 Aug 43; captured at Boulogne (POW 2367), 28 Aug 43; Stalag Luft III, Sagan, G., 10 Sep 43-27 Jan 45; Stalag III-A, Luckenwalde, G., 3 Feb-8 May 45 (lib by Russians, 27 Apr 45); res on repat, Dudden Hill Lane, Willesden, Lon, NW10; app to com as Flt Lt (4 yrs on AL), 17 Apr 47 (sen 1 Jan 43); ext svce to 8 yrs, 28 Aug 51 (WEF 17 Apr 47); rel com as Sqn Ldr, med unfit, 20 Jun 55

HEALE, NORMAN WINGFIELD 'Jeep', 1514861, RAFVR; b Burnham-on-Sea, Smrst, 31 Aug 22; ed Sherborne Sch; occ Student on enl in RAFVR, Padgate, 10 Sep 41; 6 ITW, Aberystwyth, 1941; 31 EFTS (Moth), De Winton, Calgary, Can, 1941; 32 SFTS (Harv), Moose Jaw, Sask, 1942; Sgt Plt, 1942; 1 OTU (Hurr), Bagotville, Que, 1942; 58 OTU (Spit), Ggmth, Stirling, 1943; 41 Sqn, 22 Mar-LM 17 May 43; OSR landing too fast in Spit XII, EN229, Hwkge, 17 May 43 ("carelessness"); A Flt, 130 (Punjab) Sqn (Spit Vb), WMalling, FM 14 Aug 43; com Prob Plt Off (177623), 9 May 44; MAC/RR in Spit Vb, W3128, w Flt Sgt G. M. Ferguson (†) in Spit Vb, AB208, 6m S of St Catherine's Pt., IoW, 17 Jun 44; Plt Off cnfmd & to Fg Off (WS), 9 Nov 44; CD (Allied AA) on sweep of Liege in Spit XIV, 22 Dec 44; SD/WIA in Spit XIV, RM914, by JG26 over Greven, G., during sweep nr Rheine & captured, 2 Mar 45; admtd Emsdetten Hosp, G., 3-6 Mar 45; Dulag Luft, Oberursel, G. 14 Mar 45; Dulag Luft, Wetzlar, G., 15 Mar-1 Apr 45; res on repat, Eton Coll, Windsor, Berks, May 45; Flt Lt (WS), 9 May 46; app to SSC as Fg Off in RAF GDB (6 yrs on AL), 14 Oct 47 (sen 9 May 45); Fg Off (subs), 1 Nov 47 (sen 9 May 45); Flt Lt (subs), 9 Nov 47; 72 Sqn (Vamp F1), Odiham, 1947; 54 Sqn (Vamp F1), Odiham, 1948; tour of USA & Can w 54 Sqn, 14 Jul 48; app to perm com as Flt Lt, 20 Sep 48 (gaz 19 Apr 49); KCVSA, 1 Jan 49; Sqn Ldr, 1 Jan 55; marr Inge Munch Hanson of CPH, Eridge Green, 11 Feb 58; Dept of Air Member for Supply & Admin, Dir of Movements, MOD, 1960; ret, 31 Aug 71

HEGARTY, FRANCIS MICHAEL 'Frank', 164406, RAFVR; b Lon, 9 Aug 24; ed St Joseph's Academy, Blackheath; enl Euston Hse, Lon, 15 Nov 42; LAC (1399019), 1942; 29 EFTS (Moth), Clyffe Pypard, Wilts, 4 Jun-8 Jul 43; 34 EFTS (Moth), Assiniboia, Sask, Can, 15 Jul-12 Nov, 43; 41 SFTS (Harv), Weyburn, Sask, 13 Nov 43-14 Jan 44; 37 SFTS (Harv), McCall Fld, Calgary, Alta, 15 Jan-9 Mar 44; com Prob Plt Off (164406), 10 Mar 44; 1 OTU (Hurr), Bagotville, Que, 25 Mar-17 Jun 44; att RCAF Greenwood, NS, 16-29 Jul 44; Fg Off, 10 Sep 44; Crse 50, 53 OTU (Spit), KiL, 12 Sep-20 Nov 44 (95%, 'excellent'); 41 Sqn, 7 Jan-6 Aug 45; 1 Dest FW190D, Münster-Waltrop, G., 23 Jan 45; ⅓ Dest Me110 (G9+FY of 11/NJG1) w Flt Lt R. P. Harding & Fg Off E. Gray, 10m S of Lippstadt, G., 13 Feb 45; 1 Dest Ju88, Lübeck A/D, G., 17 Apr 45; SEAC, 6 Aug 45; app to SSC as Flt Lt in RAF GDB (6 yrs on AL), 29 Sep 47 (sen 10 Sep 47); grntd perm com as Flt Lt, 10 Sep 48; AFC, 1 Jan 51; Bar to AFC, 10 Jun 54; Sqn Ldr, 1 Oct 54; Air Staff, HQ Brit Forces, AFAP, Aden, 10 Jan 60; Wg Cdr., 1 Jul 60; KIFA in Meteor T7, WF771, during asymmetric flt practice, RAF Flying College, Manby, 29 Jan 62

HENRY, DAVID JOHN VERDUN 'Jack', NZ.40229, RNZAF; b Invercargill, NZ, 5 Feb 16; ed HS & Tech Coll; occ clerk on enl in RNZAF, Invercargill, 14 Jan 40; flg trng, Levin, Wigram & Woodbourne; com Prob Plt Off (NZ.40229), 27 Jul 40; Plt Off cnfmd & Fg Off, 27 Jul 41; to UK, 13 Dec 41; Crse 15, 52 OTU (Spit), Aston Down, Gloucs, 20 Mar-12 May 42; 485 (NZ) Sqn (Spit Vb), Kenley, 12 May 42; Flt Lt, 27 Jul 42; Flt Cdr, 93 Sqn (Spit Vb/c), Wansford, 17 Oct 42; to N Africa, disemb Tunisia, 22 Nov 42; 1 Dest Ju87 on grnd, 1 Dec 42; 1 Dest & 1 Dam Me109, 18 Apr 43; 1 Dest Ju52/3m, 9 May 43; DFC, 25 May 43 (no citation); PD (pending posting), 1 Jun 43; MiD, 2 Jun 43; Instr, Parachute Flt, 28 Jun 43; PD, 10 Jul 43; CGS, Sutton Bridge, Lincs, Oct 43; RNZAF Liaison Off, Ottawa, Can, 12 Nov 43; rtnd to UK, Jul 44; Actg Sqn Ldr, 1 Apr 44; Sup, 130 (Punjab) Sqn (Spit XIV), Tang, 6-27 Aug 44; OC B Flt, 41 Sqn, 28 Aug 44-10 Feb 45 (1st op flt, 30 Aug 44); CL (blew tire) & IFA (lacerated forehead) in Spit XII, MB856, when landing nr Brussels, B., escorting Fg Off M. A. L. Balasse to visit family, 9 Sep 44; flew Brussels to Croydon as pax in DC-3 on leave, 3 Jan 45; rtnd to Brussels from Northolt as pax in DC-3; 13 Jan 45; 1 Dam FW190D, Münster-Waltrop, G., 23 Jan 45; SD/AA in Spit XIV, RM842, during attack on loco nr Rheine, G., FL SW of Eschendorf A/D (E of Rheine) & captured, 10 Feb 45; held at Eschendorf, 10-12 Feb 45; Dulag Luft, Oberursel, G. (5 days solitary confinement), 15-20 Feb 45; Rcvg Depot, Wetzlar, G., 20-23 Feb 45, Oflag XIII-A, Langwasser-Nuremberg, G., 23 Feb-4 Apr 45; escaped from Nuremberg area during forced march to Munich w 3 other Fg Offs & reached U.S. lines after 12 days walking, Apr 45; repat to UK, 19 Apr 45; EAF (Me109G & FW190), Tang, 12 May 45; Sqn Ldr, 28 Nov 45; dschgd, 28 Nov 45; joined RNZAF Res as Sqn Ldr (130327), 28 Nov 45-5 Feb 71; rel com 31 Jul 47; ret Feb 71; d after stroke, Invercargill, 7 Aug 84

HOARE, REGINALD MERRICK, 108809, RAFVR; b Manadon, nr Plymouth, Devon, 22 Jun 18; ed Sunningdale & Eton Coll; leg amputated & replaced with prosthesis; joined RAFVR, 1 RC, Babbacombe, 16 Feb 41; occ wine merchant; 5 ITW, Torquay, Cornwall, 1941; 1 EFTS (Moth), Hatfield, 1941; 9 SFTS (Master & Hurr), Hullavington, 1941; com Prob APO (108809), 11 Oct 41; 52 OTU (Spit), Aston Down, Gloucs, 1941-42; 41 Sqn, 22 Apr 42-1 Apr 43; Prob Fg Off (WS), 1 Oct 42; att 91 Sqn (Spit Vb), Hwkge, for op trng with Fg Off C. R. Birbeck, 26 Mar-1 Apr 43; SD/AA in 91 Sqn Spit Vb, BL423, in bad weather during a shipping recce, E of Nieuport, B., & captured at Ostend, 1 Apr 43 (A/C crashed at Leffinge, S of Ostend); Stalag Luft III (POW 978), Sagan, 14 Apr 43-12 Feb 45; Flt Lt (WS), 11 Oct 43; Stalag VIIID, Nuremburg, 18 Feb-2 Apr 45; Stalag VIIA, Moosburg, 6-29 Apr 45; res after repat, Lon SW1; emp in banking & restoration; marr Barbara J. Buckland, 1950 (d. 1984); marr Meriel C. Gold, 1984; d 2005

HOGARTH, RYCHERDE HENRY WILSHERE 'Dickie', 117493, RAFVR; b Oxford, 29 Oct 21; ed Cheltenham & Christ Church, Oxford; joined RAFVR, Cardington, 18 Oct 40; 7 ITW, Newquay, Devon, 1940; BFTS (Stearman, Vultee & Harv), Cochran Fld, GA, USA, 1940-41; AFP trng, Craig Fld (Harv AT6), Selma, AL, USA, 1941; Sgt Plt (1198361), 1941; com Prob Plt Off (117493), 7 Jan 42; 41 Sqn, 24 Jun 42-18 Jul 43; Prob Fg Off (WS), 1 Oct 42; 1 Dest Ju88D-1 (1st ever Spit XII vic), 2m off Ostend, B., 17 Apr 43; SD/KIA in Spit XII, EN235, nr Abbeville by JG2, on Ramrod 148 to Abbeville-Drucat A/D, F., 18 Jul 43, aged 21; s of Rev Dr. Oswald J. & Violet E Hogarth, nee Vereker, of Maritzburg, Natal, SA; init bur Notre Dame de la Chapelle Cem, Abbeville, on 24 Jul 43, reint Plot 6, Row C, Grave 7, Abbeville Communal Cem Ext, Somme

HOLLOW, ROBERT KEITH, A.408843, RAAF; b Rutherglen VIC, 10 Feb 14; ed to Intermediate Cert, Wangaratta HS VIC; occ Sch teacher, res Neilborough VIC; enl in RAAF, Melb, 20 Jun 41; joined RAAF, 18 Oct 40; AC2, 4 ITS, Victor Hbr, SA, Aust, 20 Jun 41; LAC, 16 Aug 41; 11 EFTS Benalla, 20 Aug-16 Sep 41; 2 ED, Brdfld Pk NSW, 17 Oct 41; marr Caroline E., 18 Oct 41; att to RCAF & emb Syd for SF USA, 13 Nov 41; disemb SF, 1 Dec 42; train to Toronto, Can; Crse 44, 1 SFTS (Harv), Camp Borden, Ont, 7 Dec 41; plt badge & com Plt Off, 27 Mar 42; 1 Y Depot, Halifax NS, 29 Mar 42; emb Halifax for UK, 1 May 42; disemb UK, 12 May 42; 3 PRC, Bnmth, Hants, 13 May 42; 7(P)AFU Peterborough, Cambs, 24 Jun 42; Crse 39, 57 OTU (Spit), Hwdn, Flint, 21 Jul-13 Oct 42; IFA, Hwdn, 21 Aug 42; Fg Off, 27 Sep 42; 41 Sqn, 25 Oct-28 Nov 42; att RAF Llanbedr, 28 Nov 42; att 452 (Aust) Sqn, 2 Dec 42; emb UK for Melb, 3 Dec 42; disemb Melb, 22 Feb 43; 2 ED, Brdfld Pk NSW, 22 Feb 43; Refresher Crse, 2 OTU Mildura, 12 Mar 43; 79 Sqn RAAF (Spit Vc), Wooloomanata VIC, 4 May 43; emb Bris for New Guinea by air via Townsville, 20 May 43; disemb back in Bris, 1 Dec 43; temp duty, 13 ARD, 8-18 Aug 43; 1 ED, 1 Dec 43; leave, 4-10 Dec 43; 23 Crse, Sch of AC, 12 Dec 43-15 Jan 44; RAAF HQ (Dept of Sigs), 17-18 Jan 44; leave, 19 Jan-1 Feb 44; temp duty, Bremer Bay (Air Ex observation), 26-29 Feb 44; Flt Lt, 27 Mar 44; temp duty, Air Supp Ex, 25-28 Apr 44; temp duty, Air Supp Ex, 24-25 May 44; 5 PD (NE), 28 May 44; 1 Mil Rehab Hosp (NE), 13 Aug-11 Sep 44; 6 RAAF Hosp (NE), 14 Nov-17 Dec 44; 1 PD (pending posting), 18 Dec 44; leave, 20 Dec 44-13 Jan 45; Instr, Aircrew

Sch, 6 Feb 45; 6 RAAF Hosp (NE), 10-16 Jun 45; leave, 14-20 Jul 45; 1 PD, 15 Aug 45; dschgd at own request to resume civ occ, 6 Oct 45; d Bendigo VIC, 24 Jan 06

HONE, DOUGLAS HAROLD, 80816, RAFVR; b Kensington, 30 Sep 17; ed Jesmond Coll & Wallington GS; joined RAFVR, Lon, 1938; flg trng, Gatwick, Cambridge, Grantham, Little Rissington, Kidlington; Sgt Plt (742620), 1939; com Prob Plt Off (80816), 9 Jun 40; 615 (Cty of Surrey) Sqn, 9 Jun 40-19 Jul 41; 2 Prob Me109E, 19 Jun 40; ¼ Dest He59 seaplane, 27 Jul 40; 1 Dest Do17, 29 Jul 40; FL Kenley in Hurr P3901 w CD (dashboard & wgs 'shot to hell') sustained in friendly fire incident w Hurr outside Deal, 14 Aug 40; FL in Hurr V7318 at Longfield, Gvsnd, w CD from Do17 rear-gunner over Thames Est, 24 Aug 40; 1 Prob Me109 but WIA (leg & thigh) & CL in Hurr V6564, Rochford A/D, w CD from Me109s over Thames Est, hosp Southend Hosp, 26 Aug 40; rtnd to 615 Sqn, Prestwick, Scot, 29 Sep 40; SD by JG51 during patrol & inj in CL in Hurr II, Z2698, Maidstone-Tenterden, hosp 2 wks, 26 Feb 41; rtnd to 615 Sqn, Kenley, 15 Mar 41; Fg Off (WS), 9 Jun 41; FI, 56 OTU, Sutton Bridge, 9 Jul 41; 41 Sqn, 23 May 42-30 Aug 43; Flt Lt (WS), 9 Jun 42; OC B Flt, 10 Jun 42-30 Aug 43; 10-day crse, 9 Nov 42; 1 Dam FW190, 2m W of Dieppe, F., 19 Aug 42 (grntd 8 Sep 42); att FLS, Charmy Down, Jul 43; 7 days leave, 16 Aug 43; 501 Sqn (Spit IX), Hwkge, FM 3 Sep-Dec 43; OC B Flt, 7 Oct 43; Ftr Controller, Jan 44; AE, 20 Sep 45; rlsd 1946; rel com in RAFVR, rtng Flt Lt, on app to com as Fg Off in recons RAFVR, ACB, 20 May 49; rel com in RAFVR, 3 Jul 50; app to perm com as Fg Off in RAF, FCB, & rel Flt Lt (WS), 3 Jul 50; Flt Lt, FCB, 7 Jun 51; trans to Supp List, conditions of svce as Flt Lt, 21 Aug 63; ext svce to 29 Sep 75, WEF 25 Dec 73; ret, 30 Sep 75, rtng Flt Lt

HOOD, PATRICK, 115166, RAFVR; b poss Lambeth, Lon, 1911; LAC (1293446), 1940; com Prob Plt Off (115166), 21 Nov 41; Prob Fg Off (WS), 1 Oct 42; 41 Sqn, FM 17 Oct 43-LM 10 Jan 44; Flt Lt (WS), 21 Nov 43

HOPE, ALAN, 1526844, RAFVR; b Warrington, Chesh, 4 Oct 22; joined RAFVR, 18 Apr 41; 17 EFTS, Peterborough, Oct-Nov 41; 3 BFTS (Stearman, Vultee & Harv), Miami OK, USA, Jan-Aug 42; Sgt Plt, 1942; Crse 29, 5 (P)AFU (Master I/II), Ternhill, Salop, 6 Oct 42; Crse 19 or 20, 2 FIS Montrose, Nov-Dec 42, & Watton, Jan-Feb 43; 58 OTU (Spit), Ggmth, Stirling, Feb-Apr 43; Flt Sgt, 1943; 41 Sqn, 6 May-LM 11 Nov 43; poss posted to Flg Trng Cmd, Nov 43; d 1971

HYDE, GEOFFREY COCKAYNE, 37403, RAF; b Ecclesall Bierlow, Yks, 1915; grntd SSC as Prob APO, 21 Oct 35; 11 FTS Wtrg, 2 Nov 35; Plt Off, 26 Aug 36; Fg Off, 26 Mar 38; Flt Lt, 26 Mar 40; Temp Sqn Ldr, 1 Jun 41; Test Plt, Castle Bromwich, 1941; op trng, 58 OTU (Spit), Ggmth, Stirling, 3 Feb 42; 65 (East India) Sqn (Spit Vb), Great Sampford, 21 Jun-9 Jul 42 (1 sweep); Sup Sqn Ldr, 64 Sqn (Spit IX), Hnch, 13 Jul 42; 41 Sqn, 28 Jul-19 Aug 42; AA/KIA in Spit Vb, BL777, during 13:00 mission of Battle of Dieppe (Op *Jubilee*), 19 Aug 42, aged 27; husb of Pamela H. Hyde of Elford, Staffs; bur Grave D.34, Dieppe Canadian War Cem, Hautot-sur-Mer, Seine-Maritime, F.

IMBERT, ANDRÉ, 791047/31114, FAFL/RAFVR (French); b Lédas, F., 4 May 20; ed France; civil brevet pilot, 1938; student, l'École d'Aviation d'Istres, 1939; 124 Air Btn, Cazaux, 1939; Ecole de Pilotage, Rayack, 1939; Syria, Apr 40; Palmyre, Syria, 1940; Haifa, Palestine, 1940; trans to RAF & app Sgt Plt (791047), Cairo, Egypt, 17 Aug 40; 4 SFTS, Habbaniyah, Iraq, 1940; 20 SFTS, S Rhod, 1941; 53 OTU (Spit), Llandow, Glam, Nov 41; Flt Sgt, 1941; 611 (W Lancs) Sqn (Spit Vb/IX), Drem, 17 Apr-26 Jul 42; OSR on FF in Spit IX, dam wg tip & prop, 26 Jul 42 (611 Sqn ORB: "extremely annoying" as 1st FA since Apr 42 & posted away "as a direct repercussion from his breaking a Spitfire on Sunday"); 41 Sqn, 31 Jul-LM 6 Sep 42; 1 Dam FW190, but also CD to own Spit Vb, EN836, off Dieppe, 19 Aug 42; 165 (Ceylon) Sqn (Spit Vb), Tang, FM (1st op) 12 Dec 42; com Sous-Lieutenant & Plt Off (31114), RAFVR, 1943; SD/KIA in Spit Vc,

EE603, SK-M, by FW190 (Hptm Karl Borris, Stab I./JG26), 1km E of Borssele, NL, Ramrod 154 to Ghent, B., 25 Jul 43 (165 Sqn ORB: "one of the Squadron's veterans, universally liked, loss is deeply felt"); init bur Oosterbegraafplaats Flushing (Vlissingen) Gen Cem, NL, but reint French Mil Cem, Kapelle, Zeeland, NL; posth awarded CdG (F) 39-45 & Médaille de la Résistance

INGHAM, BERNARD, 112519, RAFVR; b Bolton, Mar Qtr 1920; res The Riggs, Bolton Road, Bolton; joined RAFVR, Jul 35; flg trng Tunbridge & St Bees, Cumb; occ studying eng at LMS Works, Horwich, 1939; Sgt Plt (754889), Aug 39; 234 (Madras Pres) Sqn (Spit I), St Eval, FM 24 Nov 40; 72 Sqn (Spit Vb), Gravesend, 14 Jul 41; com Prob Plt Off (112519), 17 Nov 41; ⅓ Dest Me109E & ⅓ Dest FW190, 22 Nov 41; 1 Dest FW190, 12 Feb 42; Actg Flt Lt & Flt Cdr, 129 (Mysore) Sqn (Spit Vb), Whmpnt, 16 Feb 42; Fg Off, 15 May 42; DFC, 17 Jul 42; 1 Dest Do217 over Dieppe (Op *Jubilee*), 19 Aug 42; Actg Sqn Ldr & OC, 41 Sqn, 25 Jul-20 Nov 43; Wg Cdr Flying, Spitfire Wing, RAF Tangmere, 16 Nov 43; Flt Lt, ca 17 Nov 43 (poss not gaz); att FLS Milfield, early 44; Sqn Ldr (WS), 16 Feb 44; marr Joan M. Stringer, St Austell, Cornwall, Sep Qtr 44; rel com (med unfit), 1 Dec 45, rtng Wg Cdr; d of TB, 6 Aug 47, aged 27; s of Alfred J. & Marion Ingham, & husb of Joan M. Ingham of Llanelli, Carm, Wales; bur Grave 102, St Mary New Churchyard, Easebourne, Ssx

INNESS, RICHARD FREDERICK, 41292, RAFVR; b Calcutta, India, 4 Jan 18; ed Ardingly College, Ssx.; app to SSC as Prob APO (41292), 29 Oct 38; cnfmd as APO & to Plt Off, 29 Aug 39; 152 (Hyderabad) Sqn (Spit I), Acklgtn, 22 Feb 40-19 Feb 41; MAC/FL, 20 Apr 40; 1 Dam Me109, 25 Jul 40; 1 Dest Me110, 13 Aug 40; Fg Off, 3 Sep 40; ⅓ Dest Ju88, 26 Sep 40; 1 Dest Me109, 27 Sep 40; FI, 53 OTU (Spit), Heston, 20 Feb-9 Sep 41; Actg Flt Lt, 3 Aug 41; Flt Lt (WS), 3 Sep 41; 611 Sqn (Spit Vb), Hnch, 10 Sep 1941; trans to RAFO as Flt Lt, 29 Aug 42; arr RAF Hwkge, ex-Croydon, for duties as OC A Flt, 41 Sqn, 25 Apr 43; OC A Flt, 41 Sqn, 27-30 Apr 43 (no op flg); Sup, Bgn Hill, 1 May 43; OC, 130 (Punjab) Sqn (Spit Vb), Ctk, 1 Nov 43-Feb 44; OC, 222 Sqn (Spit IX), Acklgtn, Feb-Jun 44; Temp Sqn Ldr, 1 Jul 44; occ, 3rd Secretary, UK Embassy, Romania, 1947; occ, flt & Freight business, Camberley, Surrey, 1948-53; grntd ext svce of 3 yrs in RAFO GDB as Flt Lt, WEF 6 Apr 50 (Flt Lt (WS) converted to Flt Lt, WEF 1 Nov 47 (sen 1 Dec 42), on rel com as Temp Sqn Ldr, gaz 6 Apr 51); marr Rosemary Stevenson, 27 Aug 53; occ Freight Broker, 1955; d Camberley, Surrey, 2 Dec 08; bur Brookwood Cem

IRVINE, JOHN, 1564314, RAFVR; b Glasgow, Scot, 18 Feb 24; ed N Kelvinside HS; joined RAFVR, 11 Nov 41; EFTS, UK, 1942; SFTS, Calgary, Alta, Can, 1942; plt badge & to Sgt Plt, 1943; 1 OTU (Hurr), Bagotville, Que, Can, 1943; 667 (Target Towing) Sqn (Defiant), Gosport, 5 May-10 Jun 44; 3501 GSU (Spit XIV), Cranfield, Bucks, 11 Jun-23 Jul 44; 26 Sqn (Mstg & Spit), Lee-on-Solent, 23 Jul-17 Aug 44; 41 Sqn, 18 Aug-LM 23 Sep 44; Typhn Conv Crse, Aston Down, Sep 44; 84 GSU, Thruxton, Oct 44; 263 Sqn (Typhn Ib), B.70 Antwerp, 9 Nov 44; WO, 5 May 45; to Can, 1946, rejoined RAF, 1947 & served in Germany, Malaya & Aden; d 1995

JALLANDS, WALTER JOSEPH 'Wally', 164846, RAFVR; b Nottingham, 30 Sep 23; ed Henry Mellish HS, Notts; joined RAFVR, 3 ACRC, St John's Wood, Lon, 28 Sep 42; 11 EFTS (Finch), Cap-de-la-Madeleine (Trois-Rivières), Que, Can, 1943; LAC (1815860), 1943; 8 SFTS (Harv), Weyburn, Sask, 1943-44; com Prob Plt Off (164846), 7 Apr 44; 61 OTU (Spit), Rednal, Salop, 1944-45; Fg Off (WS), 7 Oct 44; 83 GSU (Spit XIV), Dnsfld, early 1945; 41 Sqn, 7 Mar-18 Dec 45; 4 Dam Ar196 on Lake Ratzeburg, G., 24 Apr 45; demob, Class B, 18 Dec 45

JOHNSON, RONALD, 129667, RAFVR; b Frosterley, Dur, 6 May 14; ed Walsingham GS, Dur, & Goldsmith's Coll, Uni of Lon; occ teacher, Banstead, Surrey, 1935-40; joined RAFVR, Uxb, & to grnd defence duties 24 Jul 40; ITW, Torquay, Devon, Sep-Dec 40; 22 EFTS (Moth), Cambridge, Dec 40-Jan 41; 31 SFTS (Battle), Kingston, Ont, Can, Feb-Jun 41; Sgt Plt (1258907), Jun 41;

Crse 6, 53 OTU (Spit), Llandow, Glam, 15 Jul-25 Aug 41; 64 Sqn (Spit Vb), Turnhouse, 23 Sep 41-May 42; Flt Sgt, 1942; FI, 55 OTU (Hurr), Annan, Dumfries, 28 May 42; FI, 57 OTU (Spit II & Master), Hwdn, Flint & Eshott, NBL, Jun 42-Feb 43; com Prob Plt Off (129667), 11 Jul 42; Fg Off (WS), 11 Jan 43; posted to Malta but posting cancelled, Feb 43; 41 Sqn, 24 Feb 43-28 Apr 44; 7 days leave, 20-27 Sep 43; scndd to Min of A/C Prod, & posted as Spit XI/XVI Prod Test Plt, Vickers Armstrong, Castle Bromwich, May 44; Flt Lt (WS), 11 Jul 44; test plt, evt Spit XXI development, S Marston, 1945; com rel due medical unfitness, 28 Oct 45, rtng Flt Lt; post-War occ, sch teacher, Banstead, Surrey, 1946-52; HS Headmaster, Mitcham, 1952-57; Headmaster, Fleetwood Secondary Sch, Chessington, 1957-64; Pres, Surrey Cty Teacher's Assoc, 1961; Headmaster, Horley Secondary Sch, 1964-70; Headmaster, Warblington Secondary Sch, 1970-74; ret, 1974; d 2003

JOLLY, ARNOLD WILLIAM, 116826, RAFVR; b Vncvr, Can, 31 Oct 13; ed Handsworth Tech Coll, Birm; joined RAFVR, Birm, Sep 39; LAC (937817), 7 EFTS, Desford, 11 Jun 40; 10 SFTS, Ternhill, 24 Jul 40; Sgt Plt, 1940; OTU, 1940; 257 Sqn (Hurr I), Coltishall, 1-16 Jan 41; 46 Sqn (Hurr I), Digby, 16 Jan-17 Feb 41; 615 (Cty of Surrey) Sqn (Hurr I/II), Kenley, 17 Feb-5 Apr 41; emb UK for Malta per HMS *Ark Royal*, Apr 41; 261 Sqn (Hurr I), Ta Kali, Malta, 27 Apr 41; ⅓ Dest Ju88, 5 May 41; 185 Sqn (Hurr I/IIa/IIc), Hal Far, Malta, 12 May 41-Mar 42; Temp Flt Sgt, 1941; att 46 Sqn, 4 Jun 41; 1 Dest & 1 Prob MC200, 27 Jun 41; 1 Dest MC200, 4 Jul 41; 1 Dam MC200, 29 Sep 41; CD from Me109Fs, 29 Dec 41; com Prob Plt Off (116826), 13 Jan 42; 1 Dam MC200, 24 Jan 42; Prob Fg Off (WS), 1 Oct 42; MiD, 2 Jun 43; 132 MU, Helwan, Egypt, 1943; EF/FL/IFA (legs), in Spit Vc, EE846, 5m E of Al Matariyah, Egypt, 10 Jun 43; evac to UK; Flt Lt (WS), 13 Jan 44; 83 GSU (Spit XIV), Dnsfld, 1944-9 Feb 45; 610 (Cty of Chester) Sqn (Spit XIV), Eindhoven, 14 Feb-4 Mar 45 (dsbnd); 17 APC Warmwell, Dorset, 22 Feb-7 Mar 45; 41 Sqn, 4 Mar-ca Aug 45; demob, Aug 45; rel com in RAFVR, rtng Flt Lt, on app to recons RAFVR, 2 Nov 48; app to com as Fg Off in recons RAFVR, 2 Nov 48; com rel as Fg Off, 2 Nov 53

KELLY, HUBERT FRANCIS 'Hugh', 1318817, RAFVR; b Lewisham, Lon, 10 Jul 23; ed William Ellis Sch & Highgate, Lon; joined RAFVR, Oxford, 16 May 41; 5 BFTS (Stearman, Vultee & Harv), Riddle McKay Aero Coll, Riddle Fld, Clewiston, FL, USA, 1941-42; Sgt Plt (1318817), 1942; 2 TEU (Spit), Ggmth, Stirling, 1 Feb 43; 17 (P)AFU (Master), Watton, Nflk, 1 Jun 43; 61 OTU (Spit), Rednal, Salop, 20 Aug 43; Flt Sgt, 1943; 274 Sqn, (Spit IX), WMalling, 30 Jul-11 Aug 44 (10 op FH); 83 GSU (Mstg, Spit & Typhn), Whmpnt, Ssx, 11 Aug-5 Nov 44; 41 Sqn, 6 Nov 44-31 Mar 46; WO, 1945; 4 Dam Ar196 on Lake Ratzeburg, G., 24 Apr 45; 7 days leave, 18-25 Sep 45; com Prob Plt Off (201428), 13 Oct 45; 26 Sqn (Spit XIV), 1 Apr 46; marr Danish national, 18 Aug 46 (met 12 May 45); d 17 Oct 03

KING, JEFFREY CECIL 'Argus', A.401823/O215028, RAAF; b St Arnaud VIC, Aust, 18 Mar 22; ed Geelong CE GS, Corio VIC, Feb 35-Dec 38; occ Bank Clerk, Nat Bank, Geelong, & res Geelong W, on enl in RAAF, 1RC, Melb VIC, 31 Mar 41; AC2, 1 ITS, Somers VIC, 31 Mar 41; LAC, 24 May 41; 10 EFTS, Temora NSW, 29 May 41; 2 ED, Brdfld Pk NSW, 24 Jul 41; att RCAF & emb Syd for Vncvr Can, via NZ & Fiji per MV *Awatea*, 8 Aug 41; 3 MD, Edmonton, Alta, Can, 29 Aug 41; Crse 38, 1 SFTS (Harv), Borden, Ont, Can, 11 Sep 41; plt badge & to Sgt Plt, 19 Dec 41; 1 Y Depot, Halifax NS, 21 Dec 41-7 Jan 42; ceased att to RCAF, 7 Jan 42 & att RAF, 8 Jan 42-6 Jan 43; emb Halifax for UK, 8 Jan 42; disemb UK, 19 Jan 42; 3 PRC, 20 Jan-15 Feb 42; 17 (P)AFU (Master), Watton, Nflk, 16 Feb-7 Apr 42; 6 days leave, 1-6 Apr 42; Crse 34, 57 OTU (Spit), Eshott, NBL, 7 Apr-9 Jun 42 (grad above avge); 41 Sqn, 9 Jun-18 Sep 42; 7 days PL, 13-19 Jul 42; 7 days PL, 26 Aug-1 Sep 42; 7 days PL, 11-17 Sep 42; 3 PRC, Wilmslow, 20-29 Sep 42; disemb Melb & to 1 ED, 16 Dec 42; No 1 Capstan (Spit Refresher) Crse, 2 OTU, Mildura VIC, 2-29 Jan 43; FA/NI Tocumwal, 6 Feb 43 ('carelessness', charged £10 towards costs); 55 OBU Pool, Birdum NT, 4 Mar 43; 452 (Aust) Sqn (Spit Vc/VIII), Strauss NT, Aust, 10 Mar

43-4 Jan 44; Flt Sgt, 1 Apr 43; 14 days leave, 12-25 Jun 43; com Plt Off, 1 Jul 43; 1 Prob Jap Ftr, Pioneer Creek NT, 7 Sep 43; 14 days leave, 24 Sep-8 Oct 43; IFA (burns) on TO, OSR & CL Spit A58-109 during test flt, belly tank burst into flames & A/C caught fire, Hughes Strip NT, & admtd SSQ, 11 Dec 43; Fg Off, 1 Jan 44; 55 OBU (RPP), Birdum NT, 5-6 Jan 44; 1 ED, 7-27 Feb 44; 1 AD, Laverton VIC, 28 Feb-26 Mar 44; No 4 Staff Nav (Ftr Plt) Crse, 3 AOS, Port Pirie, S Aust, 13 Mar-26 Jun 44; att 2 ITS for Lecture Technique Crse, 13-25 Mar 44; 4 days leave, 17-20 Jun 44; Staff Plt, AGS, W Sale VIC, 27 Jun-30 Jul 44; 14 days leave, 29 Jun-12 Jul 44; 36 EFI Crse, CFS, Parkes NSW, 31 Jul-6 Nov 44; 1 PD, 7 Nov 44-5 Jan 45; att 1 ITS for High Alt Crse, 21-28 Nov 44; 8 days leave, 23-30 Dec 44; marr Valda M., 28 Dec 44 (d Killarney Heights NSW, 6 Aug 84); No 39 FOT Crse, 8 OTU (Spit & Wirraway), Narrowmine NSW, 6 Jan-1 Mar 45; att 3 PD, 14-30 Mar 45; 3 RPP, Morotai, 15 Apr 45; 452 Sqn RAAF (Spit VIII), Morotai, Dutch E Indies, 16 Apr-19 Sep 45; Flt Lt, 1 Jul 45; 1 Dest Mitsubishi Dinah in Spit VIII, MD341, QY-V, Balikpapan, 25 Jul 45; 3 RPP, Morotai, 20 Sep 45; 1 PD, 24 Sep 45; att RAAF HQ for aptitude testing, 25 Sep 45; dschgd with 90 days leave, 16 Oct 45; post-War occ, Insurance Inspector; MiD (452 Sqn), 17 Feb 46 (or 25 Jun 46); app to com as Temp Flt Lt with CAF Res, 5 Jun 48; moved from Croydon VIC to Wagga NSW, Apr 49; Flt Lt, GD Plt, ACAF, 25 May 51; trans from ACAF to CAF Gen Res, 12 Feb 53; d Killarney Heights NSW, 26 Nov 74

KNIGHT, HAROLD CROSBIE, 80270, RAFVR (South African); b Cape Prov, SA, 1915; ed Queen's Coll, Queenstown, Cape Prov; joined RAFVR, Salisbury, Rhod, Mar 41; 22 FTS (Harv), Thornhill, S Rhod, Aug-Sep 41; Sgt Plt (778649), Aug 41; com Prob Plt Off (80270), 26 Aug 41; emb Capetown for St John NB per *Christiaan Huygens*, Sep 41; emb St John NB for UK, Nov 41; Crse 31, 57 OTU (Spit), Hwdn, 6 Jan-7 Apr 42; 41 Sqn w T. A. H. Slack, 14 Apr-21 Oct 42; Plt Off cnfmd & to Fg Off (WS), 26 Aug 42; 185 Sqn (Spit Vc), Hal Far, Malta, 27 Oct 42-LM 9 Jun 43; 1 Prob Me109, 24 Jan 43; Temp Flt Lt, ca Feb 43; Flt Lt (WS), 26 Aug 43; 137 Sqn (Typhn Ib), Mstn, FM 9 May 44; AA/KIA, nr Roulers in Typhn Ib, MN152 or JR433, crashed nr Maldegem, 21 May 44, aged 27; s of Reginald & Helena Knight of Queenstown; bur Grave 2440, Maldegem Communal Cem, Maldegem, Oost-Vlaanderen, B.

LANE, ROY 'Lulu', 41028, RAF; b Southsea, Hants, 12 Sep 19; ed King Edward VI GS; joined RAF & to 13 EFTS, White Waltham, Bucks, 27 Jun 38; grntd SSC as Prob APO, 20 Aug 38; 11 FTS, Shawbury, 1939; Plt Off, 27 Jun 39; 43 Sqn (Hurr I), Tang, Jun 40; 1 Dest Ju87, Aug 40; 1 Dam He111, Aug 40; 1 Dam Ju88, Aug 40; 1 Dam Ju87, Aug 40; SD/WIA (burns & shoulder), baled out after combat w He111s, inverted descent (only ankles in parachute harness) & lndd on shoulder, Bognor Regis, 26 Aug 40 (hosp 8 mths); Fg Off, 3 Dec 40; MSFU, Speke, 27 Jun 41-Mar 43 (convoy to Gib, Dec 41, & to Russia, May 42); Flt Lt (WS), 3 Dec 41; att 602 (City of Glasgow) Sqn (Spit Vb), Kenley, Feb 42; trans to RAFO as Flt Lt, 27 Jun 42; 41 Sqn, 6 Apr-LM 27 Sep 43; to Burma as Temp Sqn Ldr & poss ALO, late 1943; executed by Japs, Burma, 26 Apr 44, aged 24; s of Sidney & Edith Lane of Southampton; bur Grave 17.A.24, Taukkyan War Cem, Myanmar (Burma)

LAWRENCE, THOMAS EDWARD, NZ.411494, RNZAF; b Auck NZ, 16 Oct 19; ed Dargaville Dist HS, N Auck; joined RNZAF, plt u/t, Levin, 2 Mar 41; emb Auck for Can per *Awatea*, 18 Jun 41; flg trng NZ & Can; plt badge & to Sgt Plt, 25 Sep 41; com Plt Off, 25 Sep 41; 229 Sqn (Hurr IIc), LG.07 Gerwala, Nov 41; 94 Sqn (Hurr IIc), El Gamil, Jun 42; Fg Off, 25 Sep 42; 93 Sqn (Spit Vc/IX), 324 Wg, Souk-el-Kemis, Apr 43; 145 Sqn (Spit VIII/IX), Fano, Oct 44; Flt Lt, 25 Sep 43; 41 Sqn, 20 Feb-Aug 45; 1 Dam FW190D, Rheine A/D, G., 28 Mar 45; 9 PDC, Aug 45; to RNZAF Res as Flt Lt, 31 Jan 46; d 1986

LEE, JOHN, 133032, RAFVR; Sgt Plt (1377974), 1942; com Prob Plt Off, (133032), 6 Oct 42; 93 Sqn (Spit Vc), 324 Wg, Souk-el-Kemis, 1942-43; DFC (93 Sqn), 19 Mar 43; Prob Fg Off

(WS), 6 Apr 43; 610 (Cty of Chester) Sqn (Spit XIVe), Friston, 23 Jul 44; Flt Lt (WS), 6 Oct 44; hit by AA/FL/NI, Brussels, 9 Feb 45; 130 (Punjab) Sqn (Spit XIV), Eindhoven, 3 Mar 45; 41 Sqn, 9 May-4 Aug 45; Instr duties, SEAC Ferry Cmd, India, 5 Aug 45

LLOYD, JOHN MAXWELL WAUCHOPE 'Max', 1177131, RAFVR; b Birm, 21 May 20; ed King Edward GS, Camp Hill, Birm; joined RAFVR, 8 Aug 40; AC2 (1177131), 1 ITW, Cambridge, 12 Aug 40; 5 EFTS, Meir (Stoke on Trent), 22 Dec 40; 5 FTS Ternhill, 27 Apr 41; plt badge & to Sgt Plt, 1 Aug 41; 58 OTU (Spit), Ggmth, Stirling, 4 Aug 41; 124 (Baroda) Sqn (Spit I), Castletown, 16 Sep 41; 41 Sqn, 19 Sep-7 Oct 41; admtd Halton Hosp & posted NE sick, Tang, 7 Oct 41-15 Mar 42; att 57 OTU (Spit), Hwdn, Flint, for refresher crse, 16 Mar 42; 41 Sqn (again), FM 26 May-20 Aug 42; RAF Gib, 10 Sep-20 Oct 42; to Malta per B-24 (AL561) as pax, 20 Oct 42; 229 Sqn (Spit Vc), Krendi, Malta, 20 Oct 42 (1st op flt, 22 Oct 42); Flt Sgt, 1 Dec 42; com Prob Plt Off (139274), 31 Dec 42; 1 Dest S82, 19 Apr 43; 59 OTU, Milfield, NBL, 3 Jun 43; Prob Fg Off (WS), 19 Sep 43; CGS, Sutton Bridge, 21 Aug 43; X Sqn, 59 OTU, Brunton NBL, 18 Sep 43; 65 (E India) Sqn (Mstg III), Gravesend, 26 Jan 44-14 Apr 45; 2 Dam Me109s, 14 Jun 44; 1 Dest Me109, 27 Jun 44; 1 Dam Me109, 26 Sep 44; Flt Lt (WS), 31 Dec 44; DFC, 21 Mar 45; 1 Prob Me109, 5 Apr 45; 61 OTU, Rednal, 14 Apr 45; OC, A Flt, 61 OTU, 29 Sep 45; app to com as Fg Off in RAFVR, 27 May 47; 16 RFS, Burnaston, Derby, 26 Jul 47; Flt Lt, 1 Mar 51 (sen 27 Jan 49); ext svce for 3 yrs, 27 May 52; rel com, 27 May 55; post-War emp MOD, RAF Burghfield & subs Electro-mec Reading; d 21 Nov 87

LOWETH, RONALD ARTHUR, 125537, RAFVR; b Sutton Coldfield, Birm, 7 Apr 16; ed Bishop Vesey's GS, Sutton Coldfield; joined RAFVR, 17 May 40; flg trng USAAC, Emery Riddle Flg Sch (Stearman), Dorr Fld, Arcadia FL, & Craig Fld, Selma AL; Sgt Plt (1005150), 1942; com Prob Plt Off (125537), 20 May 42; Prob Fg Off (WS), 20 Nov 42; 56 OTU (Hurr & Spit), Tealing, Angus, 1943; 41 Sqn, 5 Jul 43-LM 10 Jan 44; Flt Lt (WS), 20 May 44; poss Test Plt, 1944-45

MACKENZIE, JOHN NOBLE 'Mac', 40547 (post-War 58282), RAF/RNZAF; b Goodwood, Otago, NZ, 11 Aug 14; gson of former PM Sir Thomas Mackenzie; ed Timaru & Otago Boys HS, Dunedin, NZ; occ farming partnership w fthr, Hillend, NZ; applied for RAF SSC, Apr 37; prov acc, Jul 37; to UK per RMS *Remuera*, 29 Oct-5 Dec 37; Init Trng, 7 E&RFTS (Moth), Desford, 6 Dec 37-21 Feb 38 (25 FH solo & 25.45 FH dual); grntd SSC as APO, 19 Feb 38; Off Crse, RAF Depot, Uxb, 21 Feb-9 Mar 38; Intermediate & Advanced Trng, 9 FTS (Audax, Fury & Hart), Hullavington, 9 Mar-24 Aug 38 (57.30 FH solo & 33.25 FH dual); Gunnery Crse, Acklgtn, NBL, 24 Aug-9 Sep 38; 41 Sqn, 17 Sep 38-15 Mar 41 (FF 28 Sep 38); Plt Off, 6 Dec 38; att Parachute Crse, Mstn, 4-11 Feb 39; 2 days leave, 9 Oct 39; 3 days leave, 17 Nov 39; TA in Spit I, K9890, when bump on runway caused flare to dislodge & puncture hole in fuselage, 24 Nov 39; 5 days leave, 8 Jan 40; NE Sick, SSQ, 27 Mar 40; FA/HL in Spit Ia, N3108, Ctk, 6 May 40; 4 days WL, 21 Jun 40; CD from Me109s over Dover & FL at Ringwould, nr Deal, in Spit I, N3112, 29 Jul 40; 1 Prob Ju88, Seaham Hbr, Dur, 15 Aug 40; Fg Off, 3 Sep 40; 1 Dest & 1 Prob Me109E over Thamesmouth-Canterbury, 6 Sep 40; 1 Dest Me109E, 9 Sep 40; 1 Dest He111, S of WMalling, 11 Sep 40; 1 Prob Do17, S of Lon, 15 Sep 40; CD from Me109Es over Dover & CL in Spit I, R6887, 17 Sep 40; 1D & 1 Dam Me109E, Eng Channel, 23 Sep 40; 1D Me109E, Eng Channel, 5 Oct 40; ½ Dam Do215 w Sqn Ldr D. O. Finlay (later dest by Plt Off J. G. Lecky), SE of Maidstone, 7 Oct 40; CD in Spit I, X4178, in combat w Do17 over Flkstn, 7 Oct 40; 2 Dam Me109E over Bgn Hill, resp SE of Dngnss, 25 Oct 40; RF & CL Spit II, P7442, W of Tandridge, Surrey, after combat w Me109s, 25 Oct 40; 1D Me109, Dngnss-Ashford, 30 Oct 40; DFC, gaz 15 Nov 40 (prsntd Mar 41); 1D Me109E, Outer Thames Est, 17 Nov 40; 1D Me109E of 3/JG51, Maidstone-Drundale, Kent, 27 Nov 40; 7 days leave, 9 Dec 40; Actg Flt Lt & OC A Flt, 41 Sqn, 16 Jan-15 Mar 41; FL Spit IIa, P7689, after becoming lost in poor weather & low vis, Bottisham, Cambs, 7 Feb 41; 485 (NZ) Sqn (Spit I) O/F, Driffield, w Plt Off E P

Wells, 15-29 Mar 41; Ftr Controllers Crse, Woodlands, 29 Mar-19 Apr 41, & Stanmore (Ayr), 19-28 Apr 41; Ftr Controller, Ctk, 28 Apr-11 Aug 41; Wilmslow, 11-15 Aug 41; to Freetown, Sierra Leone, per HMT *Strathmore*, 15-28 Aug 41; transit camp, Freetown, 28 Aug-2 Sep 41; to Takoradi, Gold Coast (Ghana) per SS *Mary Slessor*, 2-9 Sep 41; Flt Lt, 3 Sep 41; Takoradi, 9-12 Sep 41; to Hurghada, Egypt, in Hurr I, Z4932, 12-16 Sep 41, then to Cairo in Bombay A/C, 16 Sep 41; Houseboat SS *Egypt*, Cairo, 16-24 Sep 41; to Sngpr via Baghdad, Basra, Calcutta, Rangoon, Bangkok & Penang on Emp Flg Boat, 24-29 Sep 41; Flt Cdr, 488 (NZ) Sqn (Buffalo), Kallang, Sngpr, 29 Sep 41-7 Feb 42; Actg Sqn Ldr & CO, 488 Sqn, 23 Jan-23 Feb 42; evac to Java, per HMS *Danae*, 7-9 Feb 42 & to Tjilitan, Batavia (Java), 9-23 Feb 42; evac to Fremantle, Aust, per MV *Deucalion*, 23 Feb-2 Mar 42; Army Camp, Northam WA, 3-16 Mar 42; Northam to Adelaide SA by train, 16-19 Mar 42; Emb Depot, Adelaide, 19-24 Mar 42; to NZ per SS *Esperance Bay*, 24-31 Mar 42; OC, 14 Sqn RNZAF (Kittyhawk), O/F at Masterton, NZ, w ex-488 Pers, 25 Apr-1 Aug 42; marr Margaret Stevenson, Balclutha, 1942; OC, 11 (F) OTU, Ohakea, NZ, 1 Aug 42-17 Mar 43; emb Lyttelton NZ for UK per MV *Port Phillip*, 4 May 43-8 Jun 43; 1 PDC, Jun 43; RAF Eshott, NBL, 23 Jun 43; Crse, CGS Sutton Bridge, Lincs, 30 Jun-5 Aug 43; OC, G&B Sqn, 61 OTU (Spit), Rednal, Salop, 5 Aug 43-1 Feb 44; Sqn Ldr, 1 Jan 44; trans to RNZAF, Jan 44; Sup Sqn. Ldr, 41 Sqn, 1-9 Feb 44; Rednal, 9 Feb-2 Apr 44; OC, 64 Sqn (Spit Vb & IX), Coltishall, 2 Apr-31 Aug 44; rtnd to NZ via NY per *Queen Mary*, train to SF, & ship to Auck Sep-Dec 44; Corsair Conv Crse, RNZAF Ardmore, 18 Feb-22 Mar 45; FLS, Ohakea, Mar 45; rlsd from RNZAF at own request, Oct 45; rtnd to UK & app to com w RAF as Flt Lt (58282, 4 yrs on AL), 25 Jul 46; Air Min, 26 Jul-20 Nov 46; 1 Refresher Sch, Euston, 21 Nov-5 Dec 46; OC, AFDS (Meteor & Vamp), CFE, W Raynham, 5 Dec 46-Apr 48; Sqn Ldr, 1 Aug 47; Res Cmd Officer, Air Min, Apr 48-Jan 50; grntd perm com as Sqn Ldr, 30 Dec 48; leave, NZ, Jan-Aug 50; OC, ADW, SLAW, Old Sarum, Wilts, 20 Aug 50-20 Apr 53; 81 Grp, 20 Apr-21 Sep 53; AHQ Hong Kong, 22 Sep 53-23 Aug 55; HQ FEAF, Sngpr, 24 Aug-8 Dec 55; leave NZ, 8 Dec 55-5 Feb 56; to UK by air, 5-17 Feb 56; HQ TTC, Brampton, 19 Mar 56-12 Oct 57; ret, 18 Dec 57, rtng Sqn Ldr, & rtnd to NZ; occ Statistics Off, NZ Govt, Wlngtn, 1958; occ owner of car dealership, Balclutha, Otago, 1960; occ Dir, S Pacific Salmon Coy Ltd; d NZ, 28 Mar 93

MALONE, CHARLES JOHN 'Jack', J.29253, RCAF; b Lon, Ont, Can, 6 Mar 23; ed Sir Adam Beck Collegiate, Lon, Ont, 1936-40; Uni of Western Ont, Lon, Ont, 1940-41; AC2 (R.90398), RCAFSR, Lon, Ont, 8 Mar 41; 1 MD, Toronto, Ont, Mar 41; 1 BGS, Jarvis, Ont, Apr 41; LAC, 3 ITS, Victoriaville, Que, Jun 41; 17 EFTS (Finch), Stanley NS, Jul 41; 8 SFTS (Anson I), Moncton NB, Sep 41; plt badge & to Sgt Plt (R.90398), 5 Dec 41; 1 Y Depot, Halifax, NS, Dec 41; to UK per *Dominion Monarch*, Dec 41; arr Liv, UK, Jan 42; 3 PRC, Bnmth, Hants, Jan 42; Crse 3, 2 FIS, Montrose, Scot, Mar 42; FI, 7 (P)AFU (Master I & II), Peterborough, Cambs, Jun 42; Flt Sgt, Jun 42; 1 PDC, W Kirby, Chesh, Jul 42; Glasgow to Brooklyn, NY, per USAT *Thomas H. Barry*, Jul 42; 31 PD, Moncton NB, Can, Jul 42; FI, 32 SFTS (Harv), Moose Jaw, Sask, Aug 42; FI, 34 SFTS (Harv), Medicine Hat, Alta, Nov 42; FI, 13 SFTS (Harv), St Hubert, Que, Dec 42; WO2, Dec 42; 1 (F) OTU (Hurr), Bagotville, Que, May 43; com Plt Off (J.29253), 6 Aug 43; 1 Y Depot, Halifax, NS, Aug 43; NY to UK per HMS *Queen Mary*, Aug 43; arr Greenock, Scot, Sep 43; 3 PRC, Bnmth, Hants, Oct 43; Crse 57, 57 OTU (Spit), Eshott, 7 Dec 43-25 Jan 44 & Boulmer, NBL, 25 Jan-22 Feb 44; A Flt, 41 Sqn, 29 Feb-15 Aug 44 (total 123.10 FH); Fg Off, ca 6 Feb 44; hosp Eastbourne (tonsillitis), 13-20 Mar 44; SL, 21-29 Mar 44; RR Eng Handling Crse, Derby, 1-7 May 44; ½ Dest V1 W Flt Lt R. G. Kleimeyer (129 Sqn), 2m NW of Ashford, Kent, 15 Aug 44; 18 PDC, Lon, Aug 44; 3 PDC, Lyneham, Wilts, Aug 44; 28 PTC, Rear HQ DAF, Sienna, Italy, Aug 44; 417 (City of Windsor) Sqn (Spit VIII), 244 Wing RAF, DAF Italy, Aug 44; Actg Flt Lt and Flt Cdr, 10 Nov 44; rel Actg Flt Lt, Mar 45; 56 PTC, Portichi, Italy, Mar 45; HQ MEC RAF, Cairo, Egypt, Apr 45; Temp Flt Lt, May 45; 22 PTC, Aboukir, Egypt, May 45; MEC TC RAF, Cairo, Egypt, May 45; 3 PRC, Bnmth, Hants, May 45; Greenock, Scot, to Halifax, NS, per *Isle de France*, May 45; 1 RD RCAF, Lachine, Que, Jul 45; 4 RC RCAF, Toronto, Ont, Aug

45; hon dschgd & trans to RCAF Class E Res as Flt Lt, 17 Sep 45; trans to RCAF Class A Res, Sep 46; re-com in RCAF as Fg Off (33568), 10 Oct 50; FI Refresher Crse, CFS Trenton, Ont, Oct 50; FI (Res Support), 420 (F) Aux Sqn, Jan 51; Fire Power Display Team, Canadian Nat Exhibition, 17 Aug-6 Sep 51; Staff, 1 OTU, Chatham, NB, 19 Nov 51; Flt Lt, 1 Jul 53; SORP, ADC HQ, St Hubert, Que, Jan 54; F86 Sabre Crse, 1 OTU, Chatham, NB, Feb 58; pilot, 439 (F) Sqn RCAF (Sabre), Marville, F., Jun 58; CD, 1958; FI (WIF), 1 (F) Wing, Marville, F., Jan 59; Staff Officer, 1 ADHQ, Metz, F., Mar 59; awaiting Crse, RCAF Stn Centralia, Ont, Aug 62; 5 Supply Off Crse, 1 COS, Centralia, Ont, Dec 62; Warehousing Off & later Stock Control Off, RCAF Stn Downsview, Ont, Apr 63; Sqn Ldr, Feb 64; BLO, RCAF Stn Centralia, Ont, Jul 64; DC, RPD, CFB Clinton, Ont, Sep 66; Staff Off, CFHQ Ottawa, Ont, Jun 67; Maj, 1 Feb 68; Clasp to CD, 1968; NE, terminal leave, CFHQ, Ottawa, Ont, 1 Apr 68; hon dschgd, 26 Oct 68, rtng Maj

MATTHEW, IAN GEORGE STEWART, 114998, RAFVR; b Burton on Trent to Scot parents, 28 Aug 20; enl in RAFVR, Derby, app Sgt (745819), 22 Apr 39; 8 EFTS Reading, May 40; 5 SFTS Sealand, Jul 40; plt badge, 1 Jul 40; Crse 10, 7 OTU (Spit), Hwdn, Flint, 29 Sep 40; 611 (W Lancs) Sqn, Ternhill, 6 Nov 40; 66 Sqn (Spit IIa), Bgn Hill, 27 Nov 40; Temp Flt Sgt, 1 Jun 41; FI, 58 OTU (Spit), Ggmth, Stirling, 8 Jul 41-7 May 42; com Prob Plt Off (114998), 23 Dec 41; 91 (Nigeria) Sqn (Spit Vb), Hwkge, 28 May 42; Prob Fg Off (WS), 1 Oct 42; DFC, 27 Jul 43; 1 Dest FW190, 2 Sep 43; 1 Dest Me109, 23 Sep 43; Actg Sqn Ldr, 18 Nov 43; OC, 41 Sqn, 20 Nov 43-25 Jan 44; Flt Lt (WS), 18 Dec 43; Tactics Off, 12 Grp HQ, 1 Feb-17 Aug 44; OC, 33 Sqn (Spit IX & Tmpst V), Marville, F., Sep 44-Mar 45; 1 Dest Me109, 25 Feb 45; Student, Flg Control Sch, 23 Oct-8 Dec 45; Chief FC Off, RAF Gatow, Berlin, 24 Feb-19 Jun 46; ret 19 Sep 46, rtng Sqn Ldr; moved to Can, Jul 57

MAY, STANLEY HENRY (born SUFFOLK), A.412602, RAAF; b Syd, Aust, 9 Nov 21; ed Kurri Kurri HS; occ warehouse assist & Jun salesman, Newcastle NSW, res Belmont NSW on enl in RAAF, 2RC, Syd, 19 Jul 41; 1 ITS, Somers VIC, 19 Jul-10 Oct 41; LAC, 11 Oct 41; 11 EFTS, Benalla VIC, 15 Oct-10 Dec 41; 7 SFTS, Deniliquin, 14 Dec 41-30 Apr 42; plt badge, 7 Mar 42; 2 ED, Brdfld Pk NSW, 30 Mar 42; Sgt Plt, 30 Apr 42; att RAF & emb for UK, 16 Jun 42; arr UK & to 3 PRC, Bnmth, Hants, 25 Aug 42; 7 days leave, 2-8 Sep 42; Crse 25, 5 (P)AFU (Master I/II), Ternhill, Salop, 11 Sep-13 Oct 42; Crse 42, 57 OTU (Spit), Hwdn, Flint, & Eshott, NBL, 13 Oct 42; Flt Sgt, 30 Oct 42; 7 days leave, 7-13 Dec 42; B Flt, 41 Sqn, 2 Feb-19 Sep 43; 7 days leave, 9-15 Mar 43; 7 days leave, 20-26 May 43; 7 days leave, 17-23 Jul 43; SD/WIA (cannon shell splinters, left hand) during Ramrod 232 to Lille-Nord Airfield in Spit XII, MB800, bet Ypres and B. coast, by FW190 of JG26, 19 Sep 43 (aircraft located & excavated, 5 Jul 09); lndd on outskirts of Hoogstade, B., on Furnes-Ypres road & moved eastward along Yser River, then taken by locals to Oostvleteren & into hiding; NE/MIA, RAF Uxb, 19 Sep 43; evaded capture & rtnd to UK via France, Spain & Gib; WO, 30 Oct 43; crossed Spanish border, 31 Oct 43; San Sebastian, 1-4 Nov 43; to Madrid by MV, stayed in Brit Embassy, Madrid, 4-7 Nov 43; obtained civ clothing & cash from Mil Attaché in Madrid; crossed into Gib, 8 Nov 43; dep Gib, 10 Nov 43; arr Bristol, 11 Nov 43; 11 PRDC, Brighton, 17 Dec 43; emb UK, arr Aust & to 2 ED, 22 Jan 44; 1 ED, 5 Mar 44; 2 OTU, Mildura NSW, 19 Mar 44; 9 days leave, 4-12 May 44; 1 ED, 13 May 44; com Prob Plt Off, 1 Jun 44; 1 RPP for disposal, 5 Jun 44; 79 Sqn RAAF (Spit Vc/VIII), Los Negros, Admiralty Is, 15 Jun 44-11 Feb 45; 14 days leave, 18 Sep-1 Oct 44; Fg Off, 1 Dec 44; 2 PD, 12 Feb 45; marr Jean, 12 Feb 45; 42 days ops leave, 13 Feb-26 Mar 45; ferry plt, 2 AD, 16 Apr 45; 2 days leave, 30-31 May 45; 2 days leave, 2-3 Jul 45; 2 PD pending demob, 10 Jul 45; dschgd 27 Aug 45; post-War occ, jeweller; d Belmont NSW 28 Jul 02

McKELLAR, LESLIE DUNCAN, J.23539, RCAF; b Winnipeg, Man, Can, 22 Nov 19; ed Winnipeg, 11 yrs & business coll, 1 yr; enl in RCAF, Winnipeg, 5 Jun 41; 2 MD, Brandon, Man, 12 Jul 41; 15 SFTS (guard duty), Claresholm, Alta, 22 Jul 41; 4 ITS, Edmonton, Alta, 20 Aug 41;

LAC, 24 Sep 41; 5 EFTS (Moth), Lethbridge, Alta, 24 Sep 41; 12 SFTS (Anson), Brandon, Man, 22 Nov 41-13 Mar 42; plt badge & Sgt Plt, 13 Mar 42; Y Depot, Halifax, 14 Mar 42; OS posting cancelled, posted to 14 (F) Sqn, CWHE, Can, 3 Apr 42; Ottawa, 14 Aug 42; Flt Sgt, 13 Sep 42; com Plt Off (J.23539), 7 Nov 42; 3 BGS, 10 Nov 42; Fg Off, 7 May 43; 41 Sqn, 14 Jun-4 Aug 44; Flt Lt, 7 Nov 44; repat to Can, 5 Aug 45; 5 RC, 9 Aug 45; rlsd 18 Sep 45

MILLER, ALISTER DONALD 'Andy', A.418145, RAAF; b Armadale VIC, Aust, 30 Oct 22; ed Hampton HS VIC, Feb 35-Dec 39; ed Taylor's Coaching Coll, Melb, Feb-Dec 40; ed Eng Crse, Melb Uni, Mar-Nov 41; occ Supply Clerk, Air Board VIC Barracks, & res Hampton VIC, on enl in RAAF, 1 RC, Melb VIC, 25 Apr 42; AC2, 1 ITS, Somers VIC, 25 Apr 42; LAC, 18 Jul 42; Crse 27, 7 EFTS, Western Jct, 31 Jul 42; Crse 27, 7 SFTS, Deniliquin, 26 Oct 42; Sgt Plt, 11 Feb 43; 1 WAGS, Ballarat VIC, 22 Feb 43; reprimanded under AFA Sect 11 for performing acrobats in A3-71, 28 Jun 43; Flt Sgt, 11 Aug 43; 1 ED Ascot Vale, 7 Oct 43; 2 ED Brdfld Pk NSW, 26 Oct 43; emb Syd for UK, 4 Nov 43; disemb 10 Dec 43; 11 PDRC, 11 Dec 43; 7 days leave, 22-28 Dec 43; att 26 EFTS, 18 Feb-10 Mar 44; 7 (P)AFU (Hurr & Master), Peterborough, Cambs, 18 Apr 44; marr Doris M. Munn, Weston, Surrey, 3 Jun 44; Crse 48, 53 OTU (Spit), KiL, 4 Jul-5 Sep 44; WO, 11 Aug 44; 83 GSU (Mstg, Spit & Typhn), Bognor Regis & Whmpnt, Ssx, 7 Sep 44; 41 Sqn w Flt Sgt C. N. Moyle, 23 Oct 44-21 Jan 45; ACRC, Norton, Sheffield, 21 Jan-16 Feb 45 (71%); SSQ, 31 Jan-5 Feb 45; 130 (Punjab) Sqn (Spit XIV), B.78 Eindhoven NL, 2 Mar 45; AA/FL in Spit XIV, RN196, 8m inside G. lines nr Groenlo, NL, but ER, 1 Apr 45; 125 Wg HQ, 19-21 Apr 45; SD/KIA in Spit XIVb, NH691, during armed recce to Parchim, G., by rtrn fire from rear gunner of Ju188 at alt of just 20-50 ft, cart-wheeled & exploded on impact, E of Siggelkow, G., 27 Apr 45, aged 22; s of Donald J. & Mary T. Miller, & husb of Doris M. Miller of Esher, Surrey; init bur Siggelkow Cem, falsely ID'd as Can plt, but exhumed by 4 MREU & reint Grave 9.C.11., Berlin 39-45 War Cem, G., Sep 47; appears on Melb VIC, Roll of Hon

MOFFETT, HUBERT BRUCE 'Bruce', J.6368, RCAF; b Viceroy, Sask, Can, 9 Apr 16; ed Belcarres, & Comm HS, Regina, Sask; occ sen audit clerk, Rooke Thomas Chartered Accountants, 1935-40; joined RCAF, 2 ITS, Regina, Sask, 26 Oct 40; 13 EFTS, St Eugene, Ont, 20 Mar-2 May 41 (1st dual 20 Mar 41; 1st solo 10 Apr 41; 28.5 FH dual & 27.45 FH solo); 6 SFTS (Harv & Yale), Dunnville, Ont, 19 May-28 Jul 41 (grad above avge; 64.25 FH dual & 96 FH solo); com Plt Off (J.6368), 28 Jul 41; disemb UK, 15 Sep 41; 53 OTU (Spit), Llandow, Glam, 5 Oct-10 Nov 41 (grad avge); 416 (City of Oshawa) Sqn (Spit IIa/Vb) O/F, Peterhead, Scot, 10 Nov 41-28 Mar 42; Fg Off, ca 28 Jan 42; 7 days leave, 18 Nov 41; MSFU, Speke, 29 Mar 42-5 Apr 43 (detachment Gib, 31 Jul-20 Sep 42; detachment Algiers, 15 Jan-12 Feb 43); 41 Sqn, 7 Apr 43-26 Feb 44; Flt Lt, ca 28 Jul 43; OC A Flt, 91 (Nigeria) Sqn, 26 Feb-16 Aug 44; SD RAF's 1st V1 in daylight by ftr, 16 Jun 44; 1 Dest V1, 19 Jun 44; 1 Dest V1, 27 Jun 44; 1 Dest V1, 3 Jul 44; 1 Dest V1, 15 Jul 44; 1 Dest V1, 29 Jul 44; 1 Dest V1, 30 Jul 44; 1 Dest V1, 3 Aug 44; emb UK for Can, 20 Sep 44; 1 mth leave, Oct 44; dschgd from RCAF, Regina, Sask, 8 Mar 45; occ public accountant, 1945-51; rejoined RCAF as Fg Off (38891), Regina, Sask, 1 May 51; marr May P. Meikle, 21 Sep 51 (d 13 Jul 10); 1 (F) OTU, Chatham NB, Can, 15 Feb-28 May 54; 427 Sqn, 3 (F) Wing, Zweibrücken, G., 1954; Flt Lt, Instr Rating Crse, 2 FTS, Moose Jaw, 1958; CD, ca 1960; dschgd from RCAF, Moose Jaw, Sask, 7 Jul 61; occ hosp administrator, 1961, later Mayor of Baclarres, Sask; d Kelowna BC, 11 Jul 81

MONK, CLIFFORD GEORGE, 1332152, RAFVR; b Streatham, Lon, 10 Oct 22; ed Broadwater; joined RAFVR, Uxb, 21 Jan 41; 22 EFTS (Moth), Cambridge, 1941; 31 SFTS (Harv), Kingston, Ont, Can, 1941; Sgt Plt, 1941; 5 (P)AFU (Master I/II), Ternhill, Salop, 1942; 52 OTU (Spit), Aston Down, Gloucs, 1942; 41 Sqn, 25 Aug 42-ca late Jan 43; unkn postings on Malta & in ME, 1942-44; com Prob Plt Off (178312), 10 Jun 44; 247 Sqn (Typhn Ib), F., 1944; Plt Off cnfmd & to Fg Off (WS), 10 Dec 44; CD/AA in Typhn Ib, MP120, & FL 6m NW of Wesel, G., 24

Mar 45; inj in MVA & lost one lung, 8 May 45; DFC (247 Sqn), 2 Oct 45; trans to ASD, 6 Dec 45; MiD, 1 Jan 46; com rel, 19 Apr 46, rtng Fg Off; emgtd to Can, mid-1950s; d Sarnia, Ont, Can, 21 Oct 09

MOTTERSHEAD, Clifford Harper, 164378, RAFVR; b Sale, Chesh, 24 Oct 19; ed Colwyn Bay, Wales; LAC (997093) on joining RAFVR, Padgate, 14 May 40; Wireless Operator, 12 Grp FC, 2½ yrs, 1940-43; 11 EFTS (Moth), Perth, 1943; 31 EFTS (Cornell), De Winton, Alta, Can, 1943; 37 SFTS (Harv), Calgary, Alta, 1944; com Prob Plt Off (164378), 10 Mar 44; 1 OTU (Hurr), Bagotville, Que, 1944; 57 OTU (Spit), Eshott, NBL, 1944; Fg Off (WS), 10 Sep 44; 83 GSU (Spit XIV), Dnsfld, late 1944-30 Jan 45; 41 Sqn, 31 Jan-2 Mar 45 (1st op flt, 3 Feb 45); MIA, later confirmed SD/KIA in Spit XIV, RN123, Nijmegen area, NL, 2 Mar 45, aged 25; s of David & Francis Mottershead of Heaton Chapel, Stockport, Chesh; init bur Allied Plot F, Grave 38, Temp US Mil Cem, Margraten, NL, 4 Mar 45; reint 1947/48 to Row 4, Grave 164, Maastricht General Cem, Limburg, NL

MOYLE, Crawford Noal 'Micky', A.437353/O4971, RAAF; b Port Pirie, S Aust, 3 May 22; ed Norwood HS, 1936-37, & St Peter's Coll, Adelaide, S Aust, 1938-39; emp Clerk, Forwood Down & Coy, Adelaide, 1 Mar 40-1 Feb 42; emp Clerk, BHP, Whyalla, S Aust, 1 Feb-30 Sep 42; enl in RAAF, 5RC, Adelaide, 8 Oct 42; AC2, Crse 36, 4 ITS, Victor Hbr SA, 2 Jan-1 Apr 43; LAC, 27 Mar 43; Crse 35, 1 EFTS (Moth), Parafield, S Aust, 1 Apr-3 Jun 43; 2 ED, Brdfld Pk NSW, 3 Jun 43; att RCAF, 3 Jul 43-28 Apr 44; emb Bris for Can, 15 Jun 43; disemb Can & to 3 MD, Edmonton, Alta, 3 Jul 43; Crse 85, 14 SFTS (Harv), Aylmer, Ont, 10 Jul-29 Oct 43; plt badge & to Sgt Plt, 29 Oct 43; Crse 21, 1 OTU (Hurr), Bagotville, Que, 20 Nov 43-25 Feb 44; SSQ, 29 Nov-6 Dec 43; att Camp Borden, Ont, 10-24 Mar 44; att 8 OTU, Greenwood NS, 25 Mar-18 Apr 44; 1Y Depot, Lachine, Que, 19 Apr 44; Flt Sgt, 29 Apr 44; emb Can for UK, 29 Apr 44; disemb UK, 7 May 44; 11 PDRC, 11 May 44; Crse 48, 53 OTU (Spit), KiL, 4 Jul-5 Sep 44 (score 95% 'very good indeed'); 83 GSU (Spit IX/XIV), Thorney Is, Ssx, 7 Sep 44; 41 Sqn w WO A. D. Miller, 23 Oct 44-29 Oct 45 (200 Op FH); 1 Dest FW190D, E of Rheine, G., 14 Feb 45; ¼ Dest He111 w Plt Off P. T. Coleman, WO J. A. Chalmers, WO P. H. Hale, W of Goldberg, G., 28 Apr 45; WO, 29 Apr 45; 7 days leave, 18-25 Sep 45; com Plt Off (437353), 13 Oct 45; 14 ACHU, 30 Oct 45; emb Plymouth for Aust, 14 Mar 46; Fg Off, 13 Apr 46; disemb Syd & to 2 PD, Brdfld Pk NSW, 15 Apr 46; 4 PD, Springbank, S Aust, 23 May 46; dschgd, 6 Jun 46; post-War occ, Clerk, Dept of Works & Housing, Jul 48; marr Norma Walsh, 10 Mar 50; app for admission to RAAF Res (CAF), 18 Jan 51; com Fg Off (O4971) in RAAF (CAF) GD Branch & to 24 (City of Adelaide) Sqn (Mstg) RAAF (CAF), 28 Aug 51; re-app for 24 mths, 7 Sep 53; rlsd 7 Sep 55

MUNSON, Rupert William 'Lew', A.414065/O218089, RAAF; b Ingham QLD, 20 Feb 21; ed Ingham State Sch QLD, Jan 33-Feb 35; enl in RAAF, Townsville QLD, 13 Jan 41; joined RAAF, Cronulla NSW, 20 Jul 41; AC2, 3 ITS, Sandgate QLD, 21 Jul-13 Oct 41; LAC, 2 EFTS, Archerfield QLD, 16 Oct-10 Dec 41; Crse 18, 2 SFTS, Wagga (Forest Hill) NSW, 14 Dec 41-2 Apr 42; plt badge & to Sgt Plt, 1 Apr 42; 5 SFTS, Uranquinty NSW, 3 Apr 42; 3ED, Sandgate QLD, 20 May 42; 2ED, Brdfld Pk NSW, 15 Jun 42; emb Syd for UK, 2 Jul 42; arr UK, 17 Aug 42; 3 PRC, Bournemouth UK, 18 Aug 42; 17 (P)AFU (Master), Watton, Nflk, 1 Sep 42; 53 OTU (Spit), Llandow, Glam, 22 Sep-15 Dec 42; Flt Sgt, 30 Oct 42; 132 Sqn (Spit), Newchurch, Kent, 15 Dec 42-19 May 44; NE sick, RAF Martelsham, 23 Jan-18 Feb 43; com Plt Off, 28 Feb 43; SD/AA in Spit Vb, BL929, 10m NNW of Ostend, & rescued by ASR, 25 Jul 43; att RR for Crse, 19-22 Oct 43; att 3 GTS, 20-27 Mar 44; Fg Off, 28 Mar 44; marr Gertrude A. Hainen, UK, 20 Apr 44; Staff Plt, 53 OTU, KiL, 19 May-1 Dec 44; 41 Sqn, 1 Dec 44-14 Mar 45 (tour exp); FI, 53 OTU (Spit), KiL, 28 Apr-12 May 45; att Air Min & posted AIU, May-Nov 45; Flt Lt, 28 Sep 45; 11 PDRC pending repat, 3 Nov 45; 1 PD, Brdfld Pk NSW, 3 Jan 46; 3 PD, Redbank QLD, 17 Feb 46; demob, 20 Feb 46; post-War ed Ultimo Tech NSW, Feb-Dec 47, & Syd Uni NSW, Feb

48-Dec 50 (grad Ph.C); post-War occ, Pharmacist; cert of registration of Pharmacy Board NSW, 7 Aug 51; com Flt Lt (Pharmacist) (O218089) in Medical Branch RAAF, 3 Hosp, RAAF Richmond NSW, 2 Oct 56; 1 SD, Tottenham VIC, 20 Apr 59; BSLAV, Laverton VIC, 30 Nov 59; resigned com, 2 Dec 59; emp Kingsway Chemist, Accra, Ghana, Sep 60-Feb 64; app to 4-yr SSC as Prob Flt Lt in Medical (Pharmaceutical) Branch RAAF, 18 Feb 66; NSW Sqn ATC, Sydney NSW, 21 Feb 66; 3 Hosp, RAAF Richmond NSW, 30 Mar 66; Actg Sqn Ldr, 25 Mar 68; Flt Lt & to 4 Hosp, RAAF Butterworth, Malaysia, 27 Jan 69; Sqn Ldr, 1 Jan 70; emb Penang for Syd NSW, 25 Jan 71; HQ Southern Cmd, Melb VIC, 2 Feb 71; DEPAIR, Cnbra ACT, 10 Sep 71; 3 Hosp, RAAF Richmond NSW, 3 Feb 75; DEPAIR, Cnbra ACT, 16 Dec 75; Actg Wg Cdr, 17 Dec 75; Wg Cdr, 1 Jan 76; ret 23 Jun 77

NEIL, THOMAS FRANCIS, 'Ginger', 79168, RAFVR; b Bootle, Lancs, 14 Jul 20; ed Bootle Sch Liv, & Eccles Sch, Manch; joined RAFVR & to 17 E&RFTS, Barton, Manch, 17 Oct 38; mob, 2 Sep 39; 4 ITW, Bexhill, Nov 39; 8 FTS, Montrose, 1 Dec 39; Sgt (742234), May 40; 249 (Gold Coast) Sqn (Hurr I/II), Ch Fntn, 10 May 40; com Plt Off (79168), 12 May 40; 1 Dest Me109, 7 Sep 40; 1 Dest He111, 11 Sep 40; 2 Dest Me109Es & 1½ Dest Do17, 15 Sep 40; 1 Dam He111, 18 Sep 40; 1 Dest Me110, 1 Dest Ju88, ½ Prob Ju88 & 1 Prob Me110, 27 Sep 40; ⅓ Dest Do17, 6 Oct 40; DFC, 8 Oct 40; 1 Dest Me109E, 25 Oct 40; 1 Prob Do17, 27 Oct 40; ¼ Dest Ju88, 28 Oct 40; 2 Dest Me109Es & 1 Dest Ju87, 7 Nov 40; MAC/NI w Wg Cdr F. V. Beamish over Kent, baled out of Hurr I, V7676, GN-J, 7 Nov 40; Bar to DFC, 26 Nov 40; Flt Cdr, 13 Dec 40; Prob Fg Off (WS), 3 Mar 41; att 24 Sqn as OC, 1 ADF O/F, 22-28 Mar 41; Fg Off (WS), 12 May 41; to Ta Kali, Malta, w 249 Sqn, per HMS *Ark Royal*, arr 21 May 41; 1 Dest MC200, 12 Jun 41; left Malta for UK, via ME, SA, W Africa & Can, 26 Dec 41; arr Liv, UK, Mar 42; Tactics Off, 81 Grp, Mar-Jun 42; Flt Lt (WS), 3 Mar 42; CFI, 56 OTU (Hurr & Spit), Tealing, Angus, Jun-Sep 42; Actg Sqn Ldr & OC, 41 Sqn, 3 Sep 42-25 Jul 43; FI, 53 OTU (Spit), KiL, 25 Jul 43; FLO, 100th Ftr Wg, 9th USAAF, Jan 44; poss 1st English plt to land on French soil after D-Day, Jun 44; Instr, SLAW, Old Sarum, Jan 45; 1 IAF Sqn (Hurr), Indian Wg, Burma, Mar 45; Instr, SLAW (again), Old Sarum, Apr-Dec 45; Crses 4 & 5, Emp Test Plts Crse (flg captured G. A/C), Cranfield, Jan 46-Jun 47; app to com as Flt Lt, 4 yrs ext svce, 16 May 46; grntd perm com as Flt Lt, 1 Jul 46 (sen 1 Sep 45); RAF Farn, 1947; RAF Boscombe Down, 1947-50; high alt pressure suit exp, Wright-Patterson AFB, Dayton, Ohio, 1948; Bronze Star (USA), 2 Aug 49; Staff Off, HQFC, 1950-51; Sqn Ldr, 1 Jan 51; att RAFSC, Bracknell, 1952; OC, 208 Sqn (Meteor), Fayid, Egypt, 1952-56; AFC, 2 Jan 56; Wg Cdr, 1 Jan 57; Wg Cdr Ops, Metropolitan Sector, 1957-58; RAFFC, Manby, 1958; Sec to Chrmn of BJSM, Brit Embassy, Washington DC, 4 Feb 59; MOD, 1962-64; ret 1964, rtng Wg Cdr; Director, Brit consultancy coy, Boston, Mass, 1965-67; Dir, Shoe Industry, 1967-1980s; Sec, Chamber of Comm, 1980s; ret 1980s

NEWMAN, BENJAMIN BERNARD 'Barney', A.405875, RAAF; b Ayr QLD, Aust, 12 Sep 18; ed Ayr State Sch, Ayr HS, St Joseph's Coll, Mudgee, & Uni of Qld; Lance Sgt (Q15676), 9 Btn CMF, Apr 37-Sep 40; Cypher Sgt, Aust Int Corps, att 7 Inf Brig CMF, Feb-Jun 41; occ student, Uni of Qld, on joining RAAF, 3 RC, Bris, 21 Jun 41; AC2 (405875), 3 ITS, Sandgate QLD, 21 Jun 41; LAC, 16 Aug 41; 2 EFTS, Archerfield QLD, 20 Aug 41; 2 ED Brdfld Pk NSW, 17 Oct 41; att RCAF, 17 Nov 41; emb Syd, 18 Nov 41; disemb SF USA, 1 Dec 41; 1 SFTS (Harv), Camp Borden, Ont, Can, 7 Dec 41; 14 days C/B for being in possession of aircraft photos contrary to regs, 22 Feb 42; plt badge & com Prob Plt Off, 27 Mar 42; 1 Y Depot Halifax, NS, 29 Mar 42; emb Halifax for UK, 1 May 42; disemb UK, 12 May 42; Crse 12, 5 (P)AFU (Master I/II), Ternhill, Salop, 23 Jun 42; 61 OTU (Spit), Rednal & Montford Bridge, Salop, 14 Jul 42; Fg Off (WS), 27 Sep 42; 41 Sqn, 12 Oct 42-25 Oct 43; 1 Prob Me109G (claimed as Dam but raised to Prob), Bernay-Évreux, F., 16 Sep 43; 1 Prob FW190 (claimed as Dam but raised to Prob), Beauvais, F., 24 Sep 43; 1 Dest Me109G, nr Beaumont-le-Roger, F., 20 Oct 43; 11 PDRC, 25 Oct 43; transit to Aust, disemb Bris, 1 Jan 44; 3 ED, 1-22 Jan 44; 14 Spit Refresher Crse, 2 OTU, 13

Feb 44; Flt Lt (WS), 27 Mar 44; 1 PD, 10 May 44; 79 Sqn RAAF (Spit VIII), 13 May 44; FTR/ KIFA in Spit VIII, MT900, A58-654, when port wing broke off at cannon whilst attacking huts at low altitude in Toe Toeli area of Halmahera Is in Molucca Is Grp, 2 Aug 45, aged 26 (79 Sqn's last WWII casualty); s of Benjamin & Helena I. Newman of Ayr QLD; remains not found until after war & bur Grave 28.D.1, Ambon War Cem, Indonesia, 25 Oct 45; see also AWM images 119865 & PO2482.006 (bro 404733 Fg Off J. R. Newman KIA 30 Sep 43)

ODDY, Clifford 'Cliff', 1218157, RAFVR; b Leeds, Yks, 2 Aug 22; ed W Leeds HS; joined RAFVR, 1 Feb 41; flg trng Arnold Scheme, USA, 1941-43; plt badge & to Sgt Plt, 1942; 610 (Cty of Chester) Sqn (Spit Vb), Bolt Head, FM 14 Oct 43-LM 16 Jan 44 (20 op FH); 1 TEU (Spit & Hurr), Tealing, Angus, Jan-7 Jun 44; Flt Sgt, 1943; B Flt, 41 Sqn, 8 Jun-17 Jul 44; KIFA in Moth II, DV575, in MAC w Flt Sgt R. L. Short (†), in Spit XII, MB877, 17 Jul 44, aged 21; s of Clifford & Catherine Oddy of Armley, Leeds, & husb of Elsie Oddy of Headingley, Leeds; bur Section G, Grave 1219, Armley Cem, Leeds, Yks

OXENHAM, Russel Edwin George, 1317677, RAFVR; b Plymouth, Devon, 1922; occ Editorial Staff, Western Evening Herald; Sgt Plt, 1942; 41 Sqn, FM 26 Aug-24 Sep 42; KIFA in Spit Vb, AD574, wg tip hit water & A/C crashed into sea in low level dive during trng ex, Dundrum Bay, 1¼m off Newcastle, Cty Down, NIre, 24 Sep 42, aged 20; s of Edwin & Olive Oxenham of Mutley, Plymouth; bur Section C, General Grave 9740, Plymouth Efford Cem, Devon

PAIRMAN, William Robert, 1001096, RAFVR; b Biggar, Lanark, Scot, 19 Oct 20; joined RAFVR, 3 RC Padgate, 28 May 40; RAF Blackpool, 27 Aug 40-7 Jan 41; 4 AOS, W Freugh, Scot, 21 Jan 41-8 Jan 42; 3 ACRC, Regent's Pk, Lon, 9-27 Jan 42; 17 ITW, Scarborough, Yks, 28 Jan-28 May 42; 15 EFTS, Carlisle, Cumb, 29 May-19 Jun 42; ACDC, Heaton Park, Manch, 26 Jun-28 Aug 42; emb for Can, 20 Aug 42; 31 PD, Moncton NB, Can, 28 Aug-22 Sep 42; 32 EFTS (Stearman & Moth), Bowden, Alta, 26 Sep 42-8 Jan 43; 37 SFTS (Harv), Calgary, Alta, 9 Jan-30 May 43; plt badge & to Sgt Plt ca 30 May 43; 31 PD, Moncton NB, 5-26 Jun 43; emb for UK, 26 Jun 43; 7 PRC, Harrogate, Yks, 26 Jul-1 Aug 43; 14 (P) AFU, Fraserburgh, Scot, 2 Aug-1 Sep 43; 14 (P) AFU, Banff, Scot, 9 Sep 43-8 Jan 44; 12 RS (Anson & Oxford), St Athans, Glam, & 10 RS (Anson), Carew Cheriton, Pembs, Wales, 12 Jan-2 Aug 44; Flt Sgt, ca 30 May 44; 1 PDC, W Kirby, Chesh, 11-20 Aug 44; emb for Cairo, 21 Aug 44; 5 MEARC, Heliopolis, Egypt, 8-21 Sep 44; 71 OTU (Harv, Hurr IIc, Spit Vb/c), Ismailia, Egypt, 21 Sep-21 Dec 44; 22 PTC, Almaza, Egypt, Dec 44; Cairo-Benghazi-Bari-Naples by DC-3 as pax, 7 Jan 45; 56 PTC Naples, Italy, 10 Jan 45; Naples-Marseilles-St Mawgan by B-24 as pax, 14 Jan 45; 1 PDC, W Kirby, Chesh, 15 Jan 45; 7 PRC, Harrogate, Yks, 16 Jan 45; leave, 17-28 Jan 45; 83 GSU (Spit XIV), Whmpnt & Dnsfld, 29 Jan-20 Mar 45 (1st solo on type, 30 Jan 45); A Flt, 41 Sqn, 21 Mar-22 Apr 45 (1st op flt, 23 Mar 45); FA/HL/NI in Spit XIV, MV266, 23 Mar 45; 130 (Punjab) Sqn (Spit XIV), Celle, G., 22-30 Apr 45; Celle-Croydon-Celle for leave, 1 May-11 Jun 45; WO, ca 30 May 45; 83 GCS, Schleswig, G., 11 Jun 45-4 Mar 46; demob RAF Uxb, 8 Mar 46; emgtd to Can, Sep 46; emgtd to USA, Nov 46; rtnd to UK, Nov 48; emgtd to Aust, Jan 50; post-War occ crop dusting plt in Ecuador, Costa Rica, Can & Jamaica; emgtd to Jamaica, late 1960s; d 20 Jan 10

PARRY, Hugh Lawrence, 89399, RAFVR; b Dartford, Kent, 29 Oct 15; ed Dartford GS; emp by Henry H. Prall, Chartered Surveyor, Dartford, 1932-36; emgtd to Johannesburg, SA, Sep 36; occ surveyor, West Springs Mine, Anglo-American Coy of SA, Jan 37; occ surveyor, Rhod Broken Hill Development Coy, N Rhod (Zambia), Sep 37; emp by Mufulira Copper Mines (MCM), 1 Aug 38; rtnd to UK to join RAF, 24 Sep 39; res Dartford, Kent, on enl in RAFVR, Uxb, 2 Dec 39; AC2 (908532), Uxb, 5 Dec 39; 3 ITW, Hastings, Jan 40; Grnd Def, RAF Turnhouse, Edin, May 40; LAC, plt u/t, 1 EFTS (Moth), Hatfield, 1 Jul 40; Pre-Ftr Crse, 10 EFTS (Moth),

Yatesbury, Jul-Aug 40; LAC, 15 SFTS (Harv), Kidlington, Oxford, 31 Aug 40 (1st solo, 10 Sep 40); 55 OTU (Spit & Hurr), Aston Down, Gloucs, 5 Dec 40; com Prob Plt Off (89399), 30 Dec 40 (sen 1 Dec 40); 260 Sqn (Hurr), Skitten, 20 Feb 41; 266 (Rhod) Sqn (Spit), Wtrg, Stamford, Lincs, 29 Apr 41; 1 Dest Me109, 12 Sep 41; Actg Flt Lt & OC B Flt, 13 Nov 41; Fg Off (WS), 30 Dec 41 (sen 1 Dec 41); OC B Flt, 601 (Cty of Lon) Sqn (Spit Vb), Digby, 27 Mar 42; emb King George V Dock, Glasgow, w 601 Sqn for Luqa, Malta, per USS *Wasp* (Op 'Calendar'), 13 Apr 42; arr Malta, 20 Apr 42 (Spit Vc); rtnd to UK for rest, 4 Jul 42 (arr Whitchurch on B-24 from Gib); 3 wks leave, 6-27 Jul 42; Test Plt, Vickers Armstrong Ltd (Supermarine) (Spit VII, VIII, XI, XII, XIV, XX & XXI), Southampton, 28 Jul 42; Flt Lt (WS), 30 Dec 42 (sen 1 Dec 42); Sup Flt Lt, 41 Sqn, 25 Mar-30 Apr 43; OC A Flt, 1 May-24 Sep 43; SD/WIA (shrapnel, right shoulder) nr Crillon, F., in Spit XII, MB802, during Ramrod 243 to Beauvais A/D by plt of JG2 Richthofen (prob Fw Siegfried Lemke of 1./JG2), 24 Sep 43; evaded immed capture & walked 4 days in direction of Vernon, F.; arr at farm 10-12km SW of Vernon, & hidden, 28 Sep 43; moved to Évreux, ca early Oct 43 & stayed ca 3 mths; taken to Paris, 11 Jan 44; betrayed & arrested by Gestapo, 7 Feb 44; interrogation in Gestapo HQ, Paris, 7-9 Feb 44; Fresnes Prison, Paris, 9-21 Feb 44; Dulag Luft (POW 3535), Oberursel, G., 22-28 Feb 44; Stalag Luft III, Sagan, G., 2 Mar 44-28 Jan 45; evac camp, 28 Jan 45 & marched to Bad Muskau, then Spremberg, & entrained for Marlag-Milag Nord, nr Bremen, 3 Feb-10 Apr 45; evac camp mid-Apr 45, marched to Hamburg, then Trenthorst Farm, Lübeck; lib late Apr 45; rtnd to N Rhod, res Mufulira, Jul 45; occ surveyor, MCM, Dec 45; Assist Chief Surveyor, 1947; marr Dale Ellis, a survey draughtswoman w MCM, 13 Sep 47; Chief Surveyor of 3 mines in RST Grp at Chibuluma, Chambishi & Kalengwa, 1952-68; left Rhod, & rtnd to Durban, SA, 1968; occ surveyor, Durban Corp City Eng Dept, 1970-83; ret & rtnd to UK, 1983 [See also IWM Interview, ID No 8985/7]

PAYNE, JIM CHARLES JOE 'Jimmy', 1331403/170730, RAFVR; b Edmonton, Mdx, 28 Jan 21; ed Regent Street Polytechnic; enl in RAFVR, 2 Jan 41; joined RAFVR, Babbacombe, 31 May 41; flg trng, Class 42C, Arnold Scheme, USAAF, USA, Aug 41-Mar 43, grad Sgt Plt (1331403), Mar 42; Crse 32, 53 OTU (Spit), Llandow, Glam, & KiL, 13 Apr-22 Jun 43; Flt Sgt, 1943; B Flt, 41 Sqn, 5 Jul 43-7 Mar 45; 7 days leave, 21-27 Aug 43; att 1530 BAT Flt, Wtrng, 17-21 Oct 43; com Prob Plt Off (170730), 1 Jan 44; 1 Dest V1, SW of Rye, Ssx, 23 Jun 44; Fg Off (WS), 1 Jul 44; 1 Dest V1, N of Hastings, Ssx, 13 Jul 44; ½ Dest V1 w Fg Off M. A. L. Balasse, 5m SE of Rye, Ssx, 23 Jul 44; Test Plt, RSU, Mingaladon, Burma, Jul 45; Flt Lt (WS), 1 Jan 46; dschgd early Summer 46; d Oct 08

POLAK, JERZY, P.1802, PAF/RAFVR (Polish); b PL, 20 Sep 18; OCS of Avtn, PAF College, Dęblin, nr Warsaw, 1938-39; evac PL to France with OCS Dęblin via Romanian border, 1939; evac France for UK, arr 27 Jun 40; cpltd flg trng in UK, incl refresher Crse at Old Sarum, as Sgt Plt, 1940; Staff Plt, 2 SS, Yatesbury, Wilts, Dec 41; 58 OTU (Spit), Ggmth, Stirling, 27 Dec 41-2 Mar 42; 308 (Krakowski) Sqn (Spit IIa), Woodvale, 9-20 Mar 42; com Plt Off, 19 Mar 42; 306 (Toruński) Sqn (Spit Vb), Churchstanton, Smrst, 29 Mar-18 Dec 42; att Crse, Off Sch, Cosford, 11 Nov 42; B Flt, 41 Sqn, 19 Dec 42-29 Apr 43; Fg Off, 1 Mar 43; 315 (Dębliński) Sqn (Spit IX/Mstg III), Northolt, 29 Apr 43-30 Dec 44; Flt Lt, 1 Mar 44; ⅓ Dest Ar96, 25 May 44; 2 Dest Me109Fs, 24 Jun 44; ¼ Dest V1, 28 Aug 44; KW, 1st Bar to KW & 2nd Bar to KW, 1944; rested, Polish Depot, Blackpool, 2 Jan 45; FI, 61 OTU (Spit), Rednal, Salop, 10 Feb 45; RAF Hwdn, Flint, 16 Jun 45; FI, 58 OTU (Spit), Ggmth, Stirling, 16-30 Jun 45; 309 (Ziemia Czerwienska) Sqn (Mstg III), Andrews Fld, Esx, 1 Jul 45-late 46; Flt Cdr, 309 Sqn, 17 Sep 45; rmnd in UK after war

POYNTON, THOMAS REX 'Rex', 86361, RAFVR (S. African); b Eshowe, Zululand, 22 Mar 20; ed Michaelhouse, Balgowan, Natal; joined RAFVR, Bristol, 16 Aug 39; flg trng, 39 E&RFTS, 3 ITW, 1 EFTS, 11 FTS, 7 BGS, 2 CFS, 12 EFTS, 5 FIS, 1939-40; Sgt Plt (754967), Sep 40; com

Prob Plt Off (86361), 28 Sep 40; FI, 14 EFTS & 19 EFTS, 1940-42; CM at Elmdon under Sect 40 & sen as Plt Off reduced to 22 Sep 41, WEF 19 Dec 41; Crse 14, 52 OTU (Spit), Aston Down, Gloucs, 10 Feb-13 Apr 42; 41 Sqn, 16 Apr 42-23 Apr 43; EF/FL Spit Vb, W3843, Thorney Is, 31 May 42; 1 Dest FW190, mid-Channel off Selsey, 10 Jun 42; Prob Fg Off (WS), 22 Sep 42; Actg Flt Lt & OC A Flt, ca 28 Nov 42-23 Apr 43; SD/KIA in Spit XII, EN601, poss by Obfw Paul Fritsch in FW190 of 5/JG26, N of Dieppe, F., 23 Apr 43, aged 23, dived into Channel & not recovered; s of Thomas & Gladys Poynton of Eshowe, Zululand; rmbd Panel 120, Runnymede Mem, Surrey

PRICKETT, LESLIE ALFRED, 1051809/139811; b Stockport, Chesh, 22 Apr 22; ed Worksop Coll, Notts; occ solicitors clerk & res Hazel Grove, Chesh, on joining RAFVR, Padgate, 4 Jun 40; flg trng USAAC flg Sch, USA, 1940-41; Sgt Plt (1051809), 1941; Crse 35, 57 OTU (Spit), Hwdn, Flint, 28 Apr-30 Jun 42; 41 Sqn, 2 Jul 42-27 Aug 43; RF/CL in Spit Vb, R7336, Gunter's Farm, nr Sandwich, Mstn, 25 Jul 42; ¼ Dam Ju88D w Sgt Plt K. G. Warren & 2 plts from 315 (Dębliński) Sqn, 20m SSE of Dublin, Éire, 14 Aug 42; com Prob Plt Off (139811), 16 Jan 43; Fg Off (WS), 16 Jul 43; EF/FL in Spit XII, EN236, 60-70m S of St Omer during Ramrod S8 to Watten & lndd in fld nr Campagne-lès-Boulonnais, F., 27 Aug 43; taken by locals to Riotte & remained 28 Aug-4 Sep 43; by car to Renty, 4 Sep 43 (stayed ca 6 wks); to Auxi-le-Chateau, ca late Oct 43 (stayed 3 days); truck to Amiens, then train to Paris, ca late Oct 43; captured by Gestapo whilst awaiting pick-up at Place de Patin, Paris, for next move, 17 Dec 43; Fresnes Prison, Paris, 17-28 Dec 43; Dulag Luft, Oberursel (POW 3273), 29 Dec 43-9 Jan 44; Stalag Luft III (Belaria), Sagan, G., 10 Jan 44-27 Jan 45 ('chief utensil maker' of plates, pots, etc., from cocoa cans); Flt Lt (WS), 16 Jan 45; Oflag III-A, Luckenwalde, G., Feb-4 May 45 (lib by Russians, 27 Apr 45); res on repat, Hazel Grove, Chesh; rel com in RAFVR, rtng WTR, on app to RAuxAF, 3 Feb 47; trans to Sec Branch, RAuxAF, as Fg Off, rtng existing rank & sen, 19 Sep 49; No 139811 changed to 91244, 22 Nov 49; Flt Lt, 14 Sep 51; ext svce by 5 yrs, WEF 3 Feb 52; trans to RAuxAFRO as Flt Lt, 2 Feb 58

QUINE, ROBERT, A.405878, RAAF; b Bris QLD, Aust, 6 Oct 22; ed Norman Pk State Sch, Oct 33-Dec 35, & CE GS, Bris, Jan 36-Dec 37; occ Warehouse Assist, 'Optical Products', res Norman Pk, Bris, on enl in RAAF, 27 Nov 40; joined RAAF as AC2, 3 RC, Bris & to Crse 16, 3 ITS, Sandgate QLD, 21 Jun 41; LAC, 16 Aug 41; 3 days leave, 17-20 Aug 41; 2 EFTS, Archerfield QLD, 20 Aug 41 (66.05 FH); 2ED Brdfld Pk NSW, 17 Oct 41; att RCAF & emb for Can, 13 Nov 41; disemb Vncvr 1 Dec 41; 3 SFTS (Anson), Currie Airfield, Calgary, 4 Dec 41 (120.25 FH); plt badge & to Sgt Plt, 27 Mar 42; 1Y Depot, Halifax, 29 Mar 42; att RAF & emb Halifax for UK, 1 May 42; disemb UK & to 3 PRC, Bath Hotel, Bnmth, Hants, 12 May 42; Crse 12, 5 (P)AFU (Master I/II), Ternhill, Salop, 23 Jun 42; 61 OTU (Spit), Rednal, Salop, 14 Jul 42; Flt Sgt, 27 Sep 42; 41 Sqn, 6 Oct 42-29 Jan 43; 7 days PL, 7-13 Oct 42; Air Firing Crse, RAF Valley, 28 Nov-3 Dec 42; 10 days PL, 30 Dec 42-8 Jan 43; 4 days emb leave, 14-17 Jan 43; 1 PDC, W Kirby, 30 Jan 43; BPD, Gib, 21 Mar 43; WO, 1 Apr 43; 325 Wg MAAF, 8 Apr 43; 322 Wing MAAF, 20 Apr 43; 324 Wing MAAF, 28 Apr 43; 152 Sqn (Spit Vc), Souk-el-Khemis, Tunisia, 29 Apr 43; FTR/KIA air ops in Comiso Airfield-Gela Reg, Sicily, in Spit Vc, JK511, 12 Jul 43; s of late Arthur H. Quine & of Louisa Quine of Norman Pk QLD; rmbd Panel 11, Column 2, Malta Mem; also appears on [Anglican] CE GS War Mem, Oaklands Pde, E Bris QLD

RAKE, DEREK SHANNON VAUGHAN, 124494, RAFVR; b Alderholt, Dorset, 26 May 22; ed Wimbourne GS, Dorset, 1940, & Southampton Uni Coll, 1941; Southampton UAS, Sep 40-Sep 41; enl in RAFVR, Oxford, 10 Apr 41; LAC (1321395), Sep 41; emb Liv for Halifax NS per SS *Tamaroa*; PDC, Moncton NB; train to Ponca City, OK, USA; Crse 4, 6 BFTS (Stearman, Vultee & Harv), Ponca City, 4 Dec 41-20 Jun 42 (above avge); plt badge & Sgt Plt, 18 Jun 42; com Prob Plt Off (124494), 19 Jun 42; scndd to USAAF for FIC, CFS, Maxwell Fld, Montgomery AL, 17 Jul-15 Aug 42; USAAF Wings & FI Status, 15 Aug 42; FI, ACBFS (Vultee), Gunter Fld,

Montgomery, 18 Aug 42-20 Apr 43 (USAAF Instrument Rating & AA Cat); Prob Fg Off (WS), 19 Dec 42; rtnd to UK, May 43; ACHU, Harrogate, May-Dec 43; 7 (P)AFU (Hurr & Master II), RAF Westwood, Peterborough, Cambs, Jan-Apr 44 (above avge); Crse 45, 53 OTU (Spit I/II), KiL, 4 Apr-12 Jun 44; 3 TEU (Hurr), Annan, Dumfries, 15-16 Jun 44; Flt Lt (WS), 19 Jun 44; AFDU (Spit II/Va), Milfield, NBL, 22-26 Jun 44; 32 Sqn (Spit Vc), Balkan Air Force, Canne, Italy, 18 Aug 44-6 Jan 45; SD/AA/WIA (left arm & right hand), FL behind Axis lines in Spit Vc, ER637, Pristina, Yug, 18 Nov 44; evaded, taken care of by locals in Skopje who hid him & fetched a doctor, then helped him rtn to 32 Sqn, 30 Nov 44; to UK, via Naples, 6 Jan 45; 83 GSU (Spit XIV), Dnsfld, 10-24 Feb 45; 41 Sqn, 24 Feb-4 Aug 45 (1st op flt, 28 Feb 45); ½ Dest Ar234 w Flt Lt F. A. O. Gaze, W of Bremen, G., 12 Apr 45; 1 Dest Ju188 (41 Sqn's 200th & last EA destroyed in WWII), 3 May 45; att FLS (Mstg IV, Spit IX/XII & FW190), Tang, Ssx, 8 May-7 Jul 45 (rtnd to 41 Sqn, 24 Jul 45); Instr duties, SEAAF, India, 5 Aug-8 Sep 45; TWDU (Beau X, Mosq VI, Mstg IV, Spit XIV, Thunderbolt), Amarda Road, India, 9 Sep-19 Nov 45; 22 APC (Harv II, Spit VIII/XIV, Thunderbolt II), Ranchi, India, 28 Nov 45-16 Mar 46; ext svce as Fg Off, rtng WTR (4 yrs on AL), 28 Feb 46; FI for conv to Spits, 20 Sqn (Harv, Hurr & Spit XIV), Mhawbi & Mingaladon, Burma, 23 Mar-14 Apr 46; Flt Cdr, 20 Sqn (Spit XIV & Tmpst II/V), Agra, India, 14 Apr-31 May 46 (delivered important despatches from HE The Viceroy of India to Reg Governors); rtnd to UK by sea; Flt Lt (WS) to Flt Lt, 1 Jul 46 (sen 19 Dec 45); 74 Sqn (Meteor III), Horsham St Faith, Nflk, 16 Sep 46-31 Jan 47; FIC, CFS (Harv II), Little Rissington, 4 Mar-13 Jun 47 (grad Cat C); FI, 20 SFTS (Harv II & Moth), S Cerney, 30 Jun 47-27 Sep 49 (redes 2 FTS); Cat B FI, 10 Oct 47; app to perm com as Flt Lt, 7 Aug 48; Cat A2 FI, 3 Nov 48; to FEAF, HKG, to form HKAAF (Auster V, Harv & Spit XVIII), incl Ftr Sqn, FCU & Admin Unit, late 1949 (redes RHKAAF); Sqn Ldr, 1 Jan 51; AFC, 7 Jun 51; RAFSC, Bracknell, 8 Nov 51 (grad psa, Dec 52); Org 3 (Wks Svcs), HQCC (Anson, Chipmunk & DC-3), Northwood, Herts, Jan 53-6 Oct 55 (127 FH); OBE, 9 Jun 55; Crse 80, AWJR (Meteor VII/VIII), Manby, Lincs, 27 Oct-29 Dec 55; Green Instrument Rating, 22 Dec 55; Crse 7, RAFFC (Cnbra, Hunter IV, Lincoln, Meteor VII/VIII & Valetta), Manby, Lincs, Jan-Jun 56 (grad pfc); Flt Cdr, 88 (Night Intruder) Sqn (Cnbra B(I)8), Wildenrath, G., Jun-Jul 56; Wg Cdr, 1 Jan 57; Dep Chief SHAPE Ops Centre, ASOD, SHAPE, Rocquencourt, Paris, Jul 56-Jun 58; att Jet Refresher IRT (Vamp T.11), Worksop, Notts, Jan-Feb 58; 231 OCU (Cnbra), Bassingbourn, Cambs, 19 Jun-6 Jul 58; OC, 192 (ELINT) Sqn (Comet C2(RC) & Cnbra B6(RC)), CSE, Watton, Nflk, 7 Jul 58-5 Sep 60 (redes 51 Sqn, 21 Aug 58); Bar to AFC, 11 Jun 60 (rec for DSO on completion of 50 AMOs but awarded AFC); assessed as exceptional Long Range Recce plt & awarded Master Green Instrument Rating; Ops Recce 3, Air Min (DDO Recce), Sep 60-Mar 64; SASO, CRE, Brampton, Mar 64-Nov 66; Gp Capt, 1 Jul 64; Cnbra Refresher Crse, 231 OCU, Bassingbourn, 7-18 Nov 66 (Instrument Rating renewed); conv to Victor B.2, Wtrg, 2-16 Jan 67; Stn Cdr, RAF Wyton (UK Recce Force base), Cambs, 27 Jan 67-27 Jun 69; NDCC, Kingston, Ont, Sep 69-Jul 70 (grad ndc); Gp Capt Org, HQTC, Brampton, Aug 70-Feb 72; DDO Recce, MOD (Air), Feb 72-Jul 74; SOA, HQ 11 Grp, Bentley Priory, Jul 74-Mar 76; ret, 26 Mar 76

REFSHAUGE, JOHN GEORGE HAMILTON 'Jack' & 'Ref', A.409447, RAAF; b Sandringham VIC, Aust, 28 Apr 19; ed Caulfield GS, E St Kilda VIC, 1929-38 (Sch Capt, 1938); Melb Uni Rifles (V66216), Jan 39-Aug 41; Pte, 13 Feb 39; Cpl, 1 Jul 40; LSgt, 25 Feb 41; occ 1st yr Med Student at Melb Uni & res Hawthorn VIC, on enl in RAAF, 1 RC, Melb, 1 Jul 41; joined RAAF, 15 Aug 41; AC2, 1 ITS, Somers VIC, 15 Aug-7 Nov 41; admtd 2 RAAF Hosp, 13 Sep-3 Oct 41; 11 days SL, 4-15 Oct 41; LAC, 8 Nov 41; Crse 19, 11 EFTS (Moth), Benalla, 12 Nov 41-4 Feb 42; 2 ED, Brdfld Pk NSW, 5 Feb 42; Crse 20, 2 SFTS (Wirraway), Wagga (Forest Hill) NSW, 8-23 Mar 42, & subs (on closure of 2 SFTS) 5 SFTS (Moth & Wirraway), Uranquinty NSW, 23 Mar-23 Jul 42 (Intermediate, 8 Mar-4 Jun 42 & Advanced, 5 Jun-23 Jul 42); admtd 1 RAAF Hosp, Wagga NSW, 10-13 Jun 42; plt badge, 22 Jul 42; com Prob Plt Off, 23 Jul 42; 1 ED, 24 Jul 42; att RAF & emb Syd for UK, 24 Aug 42; att RAF ME, 3-19 Oct 42; disemb UK, 17 Nov 42; 14 days SL,

19 Dec 42-1 Jan 43; 3 PRC, Bnmth, Hants, 2 Jan 43; 14 days leave, 6-19 Jan 43; cnfmd in rank & prmtd to Fg Off, 23 Jan 43; 7 days leave, 25-31 Jan 43; att ATA, White Waltham, Bucks, 5 Feb 43; Crse 46, 5 (P)AFU (Master I/II), Ternhill, Salop, 2-30 Mar 43; pupil, 59 OTU (Hurr & Typhn), Milfield, NBL, 30 Mar-9 Jun 43; 6 days leave, 12-17 May 43; 7 days leave, 9-15 Jun 43; Staff Plt, Bomber Def Trng, 1685 BDTF, 93 (B) Grp, RAF Ossington, 22 Jun 43-16 Jan 44; att AFDU, Wtrg, 5 Jul 43; 7 days leave, 11-17 Aug 43; 10 days leave, 12-21 Dec 43; 453 (Aust) Sqn (Spit IX), Detling, 17 Jan-28 Feb 44 (no flg due illness); temp duty, 16 APC, Hutton-Cranswick, 26-31 Jan 44; 10 days SL, 29 Jan 44; Refresher Crse, 13 OTU (Spit I/II), Bicester, Oxon, 25 Mar-13 Apr 44; A Flt, 41 Sqn, 14 Apr 44-14 Jan 45; 7 days leave, 6-12 May 44; SD/AA (poss from US Merchant Navy) & WIA (bullets left hand & left leg), baled out of Spit XII, MB794, nr Cherbourg, F., 9 Jun 44; RR & admtd to US Army 94th GH, Falfield, Gloucs, 9 Jun-4 Jul 44; trans to RAFH, Wroughton, Wilts, 5-7 Jul 44; admtd RAF Rehab Unit, Loughborough, Leics, 8-16 Jul 44; SL, 17 Jul-18 Aug 44; Temp Flt Lt, 23 Jul 44; 10 days SL, SHQ Tang, 19 Aug-9 Sep 44; rtnd to 41 Sqn 10 Sep 44-14 Jan 45; to Diest via Tilbury & Ostend, 6-17 Nov 44; att 83 GSU (Spit XIV), Dnsfld, 14 Jan-1 Feb 45; BPC, 1 Feb 45; 1 CMB, Lon, 5 Feb 45; 7 days leave, 28 Feb-6 Mar 45; 13 days leave, 7-19 Mar 45; 2 PDC, 20 Mar 45; HQ ACSEA, 25 Mar 45; 132 Sqn (Spit XIV), Madura, India, 21 May 45; RAF Bhopal, India, 28 Jun 45; emb for Aust 29 Aug 45; disemb Adelaide & to 1 PD, Melb, 25 Oct 45; annual leave, 25-31 Oct 45; 30 days disemb leave, 1-30 Nov 45; dschgd Aust w 82 days pay in lieu of leave, 19 Jan 46; grad MBBS, Melb Uni, 23 Oct 51; enl in Royal Aust Army (VX700272), 28 Mar 52; dschgd from Army, 1 May 52; app to com as Flt Lt in Medical Br of RAAF Reserve, 21 Oct 52; occ ENT Surgeon, Melb; OBE (C), for svce to sports medicine, 3 Jun 78; Hon Fellow, RACGP, 11 Oct 84; AM for svce to sports medicine, 6 Jun 87; d 26 Nov 99 (younger bro of Maj Gen Sir William D. Refshauge KTB AC CBE ED MiD*** MBBS FRCOG FRACS FRACP FRACMA FRACOG, 1913-2009)

REID, DANIEL JOSEPH, A.401666, RAAF; b Yarraville VIC, Aust, 28 Apr 20; ed Christian Bros Coll, Melb; occ storeman & traveller w L. E. Wade Pty Ltd, & law student on enl in RAAF, 1 RC, Melb VIC, 1 Jun 40; joined RAAF, 28 Mar 41; AC2, Crse 13, 1 ITS, Somers VIC, 29 Mar-23 May 41; LAC, 24 May 41; 10 EFTS (Moth), Temora NSW, 28 May-23 Jul 41 (52 FH); 2 ED Brdfld Pk, 24 Jul 41; att RCAF & to Vncvr Can, per TSS *Awatea*, 8-29 Aug 41; disemb Vncvr 29 Aug 41; 3 MD, Edmonton, Alta, 30 Aug-10 Sep 41; 1 SFTS (Harv), Camp Borden & Edenvale, Ont, 13 Sep-19 Dec 41 (92 FH); plt badge & to Sgt Plt, 19 Dec 41; com Prob Plt Off, 19 Dec 41; Y Depot, Halifax, NS, 20 Dec 41-8 Jan 42; att RAF, 6 Jan 42; emb for UK per SS *Bayano*, 8 Jan 42; disemb UK, 21 Jan 42; 3 PRC, Bnmth, Hants, 22 Jan-17 Feb 42; 41 OTU, Old Sarum, Wilts, 17 Feb-14 Mar 42; Crse 4, 5 (P)AFU (Master I/II), Ternhill, Salop, 17 Mar-22 Apr 42; 61 OTU (Spit), Rednal, Salop, 23 Apr-2 Jun 42, & Montford Bridge, 2-22 Jun 42 (total 50 FH); Cinegun Assessment Crse, AFDU Dxfd, 27 Jun-1 Jul 42; Parachute Packing Crse, 12 STT, Melksham, 15-22 Jul 42; appt. cnfmd & prmtd to Plt Off, 19 Jun 42; 453 (Aust) Sqn (Spit Vb), Drem, Scot, 22 Jun-22 Nov 42 (FF 26 Jun 42, LF 17 Nov 42, 21 ops, 85 FH); FA/HL in Spit Vb during NFE, Hnch, 16 Nov 42; 1 PDC, W Kirby, Chesh, 22-23 Nov 42; emb UK for Gib per SS *Llanstephan Castle*, 25 Nov 42; RAF Gib, 3-10 Dec 42; RAF Maison Blanche, Algeria, 11-17 Dec 42; B Flt, 152 Sqn (Spit Vc), Souk el Arba, Tunisia, 17 Dec 42-20 Feb 43 (FF 19 Dec 42, LF 18 Feb 43, 32 ops, 50 FH); Fg Off, 19 Dec 42; att 325 Wg, 15 Jan-4 Feb 43; admtd 19 CCS, Souk el Arba, BPD, 20-23 Feb 43; admtd 72 GH, Souk Ahras, 24-27 Feb 43; admtd 96 GH, Maison Carree, Algiers, 28 Feb-13 Mar 43; evac to UK per HMHS *Oxfordshire*, 13 Mar 43; admtd Ronkswood Hosp, Worcs w pleural effusion [collapsed lung], 23 Mar-20 May 43; admtd RAFH Pontypridd, Glam, 21 May-27 Jul 43; RAF MRU, 28 Jul 43; MRU, Loughborough, 3 Sep 43-11 Jan 44; att Bristol Aero Eng Sch, 11-24 Oct 43; att Rotol Prop Sch, 25 Oct-8 Nov 43; att RR Aero Eng Sch, 9 Nov-13 Dec 43; att AV Roe Airframes Sch, 14 Dec 43-4 Jan 44; Temp Flt Lt, 19 Dec 43; RAF Uxb, 5-21 Jan 44; 61 OTU (Spit), Rednal, Salop, 22 Jan-19 Apr 44 (40 FH); 2 days leave, 1-2 Apr 44; 13 OTU (Spit), Bicester, Oxon, 20 Apr-2 Aug 44 (85 FH); att

CGS Catfoss (Spit) for 40 PGIC, 18 May-21 Jun 44 (51 FH); 41 Sqn, 3 Aug 44-25 Mar 45 (FF 5 Aug 44, LF 25 Mar 45, 94 ops, 160 FH); ½ Dest V1 w Flt Lt L. A. Wood (274 Sqn), 10m NW of Ashford, Kent, 23 Aug 44; 8 days leave, 27 Aug-3 Sep 44; 9 days leave, 17-25 Jan 45; OC B Flt, 10 Feb-25 Mar 45; 1 Dest FW190D-9 (White 17, 5./JG26, Lt Josef Bott WIA), 2km E of Clausheide Airfield, G., 25 Feb 45; 1 Dest Arado Ar234B (Oblt Walter Sütterlin of 9./KG76), nr Enschede, NL, 2 Mar 45; hit by AA/WIA (back) while attacking a gasometer in Spit XIV, MV264, Bocholt, G., 25 Mar 45; admtd 50 MFH, Eindhoven, 25 Mar 45; evac to UK & posted 1 PHU, 29 Mar 45; admtd RAF GH, Ely, Cambs, 30 Mar 45; admtd RAFH Church Village, Pontypridd, Glam, 17 Apr 45; DFC (41 Sqn), 1 Jun 45; 10 days SL, 21-30 Jun 45; 11 PDRC, Charmy Down, 24 Oct 45-21 Jan 46; emb UK to Aust per HMS *Indomitable*, 3 Apr 46; disemb Fremantle, 3 May 46; 5PD, 16 May 46; dschgd at 1 PHU, 29 Aug 46; 1 PD, 14 Jun 46; rlsd 29 Aug 46; post-war occ law student; joined Franciscan Order of Friars Minor, 18 Feb 51; ordained Rev Father Urban Reid, 28 Jul 57; plt, Mgr & administrator, Franair, Franciscan Mission Air Svce, Aitape, PNG, 1961-66; parish priest & subs Vicar-Gen of Diocese of Aitape, 1966-92; d of cancer, Melb VIC, 1 May 93, aged 72

REMEZ, AHARON 'Rem'/'Remy', 605523, RAFVR; b Tel Aviv, Palestine, 8 May 19; ed HS, Palestine; joined Haganah (paramilitary defence force), 1936; Emissary, Habonim Youth Movement, USA, 1939-42; flg trng nr Cream Ridge Farm, NJ, 1942; joined RAFVR, Moncton, NB, Can, 17 Dec 42; 3 ITS, Victoriaville, Que, 1943; 11 EFTS (Finch), Cap-de-la-Madeleine (Trois-Rivières), Que, 1943; plt badge & to Sgt Plt, 1943; 1 OTU (Hurr), Bagotville, Que, 1943; 53 OTU (Spit), KiL, 1944-45; Flt Sgt, 1944; 41 Sqn, 10 Apr 45-31 Mar 46; WO, 1945; FA in Spit XIV, MV264, touched wg on grnd & turned over, logbook endorsed 'carelessness', Utersen, G., 28 Jul 45; 7 days leave, 18-25 Sep 45; 26 Sqn (41 redes 26 Sqn), 1 Apr-6 Aug 46; assisted w org of immigration of remaining European Jewry, 1945-46; rtnd to Palestine, Aug 46; Kibbutz Kfar Blum, Upper Galilee, 1946-47; Chief of Ops, Haganah Air Service, 10 Nov 47; Brig Gen[2], founder & 1st CO of Israeli Air Force, Jul 48-Dec 50; rel com & ret, Dec 50; Head of Purchasing Delegation, Israeli MOD mission to US, 1951-53; Israeli Def Minister's Aide for Avtn, 1953-54; Member of Board, Solel Boneh construction coy, 1954-59; Member, Worker's Party of Eretz Yisrael, 3rd Knesset (House Comm & Foreign Affairs & Defense Comm), 15 Aug 55-19 Dec 59; Admin Dir, Weizman Institute, 1959-60; Dir, Dept for Intl Co-op, Foreign Affairs Min, 1960-65; Israeli Ambassador to UK, 18 May 65-Jul 70; Dir Gen, Israeli Ports Authority, 1970-77; Chrmn, Israeli Avtn Authority, 1977-81; d 3 Apr 94, aged 74

ROBERTS, PETER HUGH PERCY, 1211364, RAFVR; b Gillingham, Dorset, 20 Aug 22; ed Gillingham GS; joined RAFVR, Cardington, 29 Nov 40; 22 EFTS (Moth), Cambridge, 1941; 31 SFTS (Harv), Kingston, Ont, Can, 1941; plt badge & to Sgt Plt, 1941; 5 (P)AFU (Master I/II), Ternhill, Salop, 1941-42; 52 OTU (Spit), Aston Down, Gloucs, 1942; 41 Sqn, 25 Aug-LM 15 Dec 42; Flt Sgt, 1942; 7 days PL, 3 Dec 42; 185 Sqn (Spit Vc), Hal Far, Malta, FM 2 Mar-ca 28 Jul 43; com Prob Plt Off (169717), 28 Nov 43; Fg Off (WS), 28 May 44; Flt Lt (WS), 28 Nov 45; 1 PDC, 1946; 130 (Punjab) Sqn (Spit IX), Mstn, 1 Apr 46; Flt Cdr, 165 (Ceylon) Sqn (Spit IX), Dxfd, 23 May-1 Sep 46 (redes 66 Sqn); app to SSC as Flt Lt in RAF GDB (6 yrs on AL), 15 Oct 47 (sen 28 May 47); app to perm com as Flt Lt, 4 Oct 48; KCVSA, 1 Jan 52; OC, 185 Sqn (Vamp V), Hal Far, Malta, Sep 52-1 May 53 (dsbnd); Sqn Ldr, 1 Oct 54; ret 21 Nov 60

ROBERTSON, COLIN STUART 'Robbie', A.421627, RAAF; b Ashfield NSW, 7 Mar 18; occ clerk 'manufacturers rep' on enl in RAAF, 2RC, Woolloomooloo NSW, 28 Feb 42; AC2, Crse 26, 2 ITS, 28 Feb 42; LAC, 20 Jun 42; 8 EFTS, Narrandera, 25 Jun 42; 2 ED, Brdfld Pk NSW, 17 Sep 42; att RCAF & emb for Can, 6 Oct 42; disemb Can & to 2 MD, Brandon, Man, 24 Oct 42; 14 SFTS (Harv), Alymer, Ont, 21 Nov 42-19 Mar 43; plt badge & Sgt Plt, 19 Mar 43; 1 Y Depot, Halifax NS, 30 Mar 43; att 31 RAF Depot, Moncton, NB, 20 Apr-16 May 43; att RAF &

emb Halifax for UK, 16 May 43; disemb, UK & to 11 PDRC, 24 May 43; 17 (P)AFU (Master), Wrexham, 22 Jun 43; Merlin Eng Handling Crse, RR, Derby, 25 Jul 43; Crse 38, 53 OTU (Spit), KiL, 7 Sep-14 Dec 43; Flt Sgt, 19 Sep 43; 1 TEU (Spit & Hurr), Tealing, Angus, 10 Feb 44; IFA nr Tealing, 19 Mar 44; admtd SSQ, 19-21 Mar 44; 41 Sqn, 8 Jun-22 Aug 44; 1 Dest V1, 6m N of Pevensey, Ssx, 26 Jun 44; 1 Dest V1, mid-Channel, 27 Jul 44; 83 GSU (Mstg, Spit & Typhn), Bognor Regis, Ssx, 22 Aug 44; WO, 19 Sep 44; 453 (Aust) Sqn (Spit IXb/XVI), Coltishall, 6 Oct 44; com Plt Off, 7 Nov 44; 7 days leave, 15-21 Nov 44; admtd SSQ, 3-6 Dec 44; admtd SSQ, 16-18 Dec 44; 10 days leave, 4-13 Jan 45; 7 days leave, 15-21 Feb 45; 7 days leave, 11-17 Apr 45; Fg Off, 7 May 45; 7 days leave, 4-10 Jun 45; 11 PDRC, 17 Oct 45; emb UK for Aust, 28 Oct 45; disemb Syd & to 2 PD, 28 Nov 45; 7 days leave, 28 Nov-6 Dec 45; paid 82 days in lieu of leave (7 days RL, 45 days WL, 30 days re-est), dschgd, 11 Feb 46

ROBINSON, KENNETH BASIL 'Robbie', 1126985/139816, RAFVR; b Killiney, Dublin, Eire, 14 Apr 22; ed Portora Royal Sch, Enniskillen, NIre; enl in RAFVR, Belfast NI, 27 Jun 40; joined RAFVR, Stratford-on-Avon, 1940; 10 ITW, Scarborough, 1940; 1 EFTS, Hatfield, 1941; 5 SFTS, Ternhill, 1941; Sgt Plt (1126985), 1941; 4 SFTS, Cambridge, 1942; Crse 35, 57 OTU (Spit), Hwdn, Flint, 28 Apr-30 Jun 42; 41 Sqn, 1 Jul-21 Oct 42; com Prob Plt Off (139816), 16 Jan 43; Fg Off (WS), 16 Jul 43; 41 Sqn (again), 17 Jan-7 Jun 44; KAS, SD/AA (radiator) & baled out of Spit XII, MB881, SE of Sark, 7 Jun 44; ASR aircraft made 17 attempts to rescue, but by 18th & successful attempt, was dead, lost to either drowning or hypothermia, aged 22; s of Ernest & Lilian Robinson of Monkstown, Cty Dublin, Eire; bur Sect R.1., Grave 9, Buckland Monachorum Cem, Devon

ROGOWSKI, JAN ALEKSANDER, P.781018, PAF/RAFVR (Polish); b Budzanów, nr Trembowla, PL, 3 Jan 20; ed Coll, 4 yrs; joined PAF, Lwów, PL [today Lviv, Ukraine], 8 Nov 39; joined RAFVR, Mstn, 1 Feb 40; 15 EFTS, Carlisle, Cumberland, 1941; 8 SFTS, Montrose, Scot, 1941; Sgt Plt, 1941; 58 OTU (Spit), Ggmth, Stirling, 14 Apr 42; 306 (Toruński) Sqn (Spit Vb), Northolt, 17 Jun 42; 403 (Wolf) Sqn (Spit Vb), Ctk, 30 Oct 42; Flt Sgt, 1942; 306 (Toruński) Sqn (again) (Spit IX), Ctk, 20-27 Dec 42; 41 Sqn, 28 Dec 42-14 Apr 43; 315 (Dębliński) Sqn (Spit IX), Northolt, 14 Apr-28 May 43; SD/KIA by Me109 over Bergues, F., in Spit IX, BR624, PK-P, during Circus 305, 28 May 43; bur Grave C 2, Pihen-les-Guines Cem, Calais, F.

ROSSOW, VIVIAN JAMES 'Bill', A.414835, RAAF; b Nanango QLD, Aust, 26 Sep 18; ed Buckland State Sch, Nanango, & Scott's Coll, Melb VIC (by correspondence); Trooper & Hotchkiss Machine Gunner, 2 LH Regt (Q3286), Mar 39-8 Nov 41; occ dairy farmer & res Aspley, Bris, on enl in RAAF, 3 RC, Bris, 9 Nov 41; AC2, 3 ITS, Sandgate QLD, 9 Nov 41; LAC, 28 Feb 42; Crse 23, 2 EFTS (Moth & Link Trainer), Archerfield QLD, 2 Apr 42; Crse 24, 7 EFTS, Western Jct TAS, 26 Apr 42; Crse 25, 5 SFTS (Wirraway), Uranquinty NSW, 10 Aug-17 Dec 42; plt badge, 14 Dec 42; Sgt Plt, 17 Dec 42; 3 ED, Sandgate QLD, 18 Dec 42; 1 ED, Ascot Vale, 10 Jan 43; att RAF & emb Melb for SF USA, 15 Jan 43; subs train to Boston & 6 wks at Camp Miles Standish, awaiting passage to UK; disemb UK & to 11 PDRC, Bnmth, 17 Mar 43; 7 days leave, 1-7 Apr 43; att 8 Corps Guards Armoured Div (Grenadier Guards), 23 Apr-5 May 43; 17 (P)AFU (Anson & Master), Wrexham, Wales, 25 May 43; Drogue Towing duties, 61 OTU (Martinet), Rednal & Oswestry, Salop, 4 Aug-7 Nov 43; Flt Sgt, 1 Nov 43; Crse 56, 57 OTU (Spit I/II & Master), Eshott, NBL, 9 Nov 43-1 Feb 44; 8 days leave, 26 Jan-2 Feb 44; GFS (Spit I), RAF Boulmer, NBL, 3-25 Feb 44; 10 days leave, 26 Feb-6 Mar 44; 1 TEU (Spit V & Hurr II/IV), Kinnell, Scot, 7 Mar 44 (55.4 FH, grad 'Exceptional'); Staff, 3501 GSU (Spit V/IX/XIV), Cranfield, 19 May 44; SSQ, 22 Jun-5 Jul 44; att Gyro Gunsight Crse, 17 APC (Spit IX), Southend, 21-31 Jul 44; 41 Sqn, 9 Aug 44-19 Jul 45; 1 Dest V1, 5m WNW of Ashford, Kent, 16 Aug 44; 1 Dam V1, W of Gris Nez, F., 23 Aug 44; SSQ Lympne, 28-29 Sep 44; WO, 1 Nov 44; 1 Dam Me262, but CD/AA (prop) in Spit XIV, RM696, Rheine A/D, G., 14 Feb 45; marr Margaret Usher, N Castletown,

Dur, 7 Apr 45; 1 Prob Me262, Neuruppin A/D, G., 20 Apr 45; Sup, BPC, 19 Jul 45, 1 Wg, 9 PDC, UK, 20 Jul 45; 16 ACHU, UK, 10 Aug 45; 11 PDRC, Bournemouth, 24 Sep 45; emb UK for Syd, Aust, Oct 45; disemb Syd & to 2 PD, 28 Nov 45; dschgd 3 PD & paid £52/5/6 in lieu of 82 days RL, WL & re-est leave, & £12/6/- subsistence allowance, 17 Jan 46; post-War emp, Telecom, ret 1976; 6 mths hols in UK, 1977-78; 9 mths hols in UK, 1982; d Bris QLD, 23 Nov 93; bur Portion 18N, Grave 44, Pinaroo Lawn Cem, Bridgeman Downs QLD

ROWE, Malcolm P., 926918, RAFVR; b Holmes Chapel, Chesh, 26 Jan 20; ed Sale HS & Manch Arts Coll; joined RAFVR, Uxb, 23 May 40; 26 EFTS, Guinea Fowl, S Rhod, 1940; 22 SFTS, Thornhill, Rhod, 1941; Sgt Plt, 1941; Crse 9, 5 (P)AFU (Master II/II), Ternhill, Salop, 2 Jun 42; 61 OTU (Spit), Rednal, Salop, 1942; 41 Sqn, 3 Nov 42-27 Apr 43 (A Flt, 3 Nov 42-26 Feb 43; B Flt 27 Feb-27 Apr 43); Flt Sgt, 1942; sent on emb leave, 27 Apr 43

SABOURIN, Jack Andrew, 115037, RAFVR; b Lon, 23 Aug 16; ed Regent Street Polytechnic; joined RAFVR, Uxb, 28 Aug 39; 13 EFTS, White Waltham, Bucks, 1939; 7 SFTS (Master), Montrose, 1940; Sgt Plt (900114), 1940; 258 Sqn (Hurr I), Acklgtn, 21 Jan-26 Feb 41; 615 (Cty of Surrey) Sqn (Hurr IIa/b), Kenley, 27 Feb-21 Dec 41; MSFU (Sea Hurr), Speke, 22 Dec 41; com Prob Plt Off (115037), 23 Dec 41; Prob Fg Off (WS), 1 Oct 42; 610 (Cty of Chester) Sqn (Spit Vb), Whmpnt, 18 Apr-7 May 43; 501 Sqn (Spit Vb), Friston, 8 May-1 Aug 43; CACU (Anson, Hurr, Master & Spit), Detling, Kent, 2 Aug-11 Oct 43 (dsbnd); 41 Sqn, FM 28 Oct 43-LM 26 Jan 44; Flt Lt (WS), 23 Dec 43; app to SSC as Flt Lt (8 yrs AL & 4 yrs Res), 19 Jul 49 (sen 23 Dec 47); app to perm com as Flt Lt, 1 Oct 50; trans to FCB as Flt Lt, 27 Mar 51 (sen 23 Jun 50); Sqn Ldr, GDB, 1 Jul 58; ret 3 Sep 66, rtng Sqn Ldr

SAMOUELLE, Charles James 'Sammy', 113341, RAFVR; b Islington, N Lon, 2 Feb 20; ed Acland Central Sch, Lon; occ Bell Hop, Savoy Hotel, 1936; joined RAFVR, Euston, 8 Aug 40; 4 ITW, Paignton, 1940; 6 EFTS, Brooklands Avtn, Sywell, Jan-Mar 41; 32 SFTS (Harv), Moose Jaw, Sask, Can, Apr-Jun 41; Sgt Plt (1375201), Jun 41; 53 OTU (Spit), Llandow, Glam, Aug-Sep 41; 92 (E India) Sqn (Spit Vb), Bgn Hill, 10 Sep 41-31 Jan 43; com Prob Plt Off (113341), 25 Nov 41; to ME w 92 Sqn via TC Almaza, 1 Jan 42 (arr Mar 42); temp att 80 Sqn, Jul 42; 1 Dest Me109F, 17 Jul 42; 2 Dam Ju87s, 27 Jul 42; Actg Flt Lt & OC A Flt, 4 Aug 42; 1 Dam Me109, 16 Aug 42; 1 Dest & 1 Prob Me109F, but SD/FL/NI in Spit Vc, BR523, 19 Aug 42; 1 Prob Me109, 23 Aug 42; 4 Dam Me109s, 1 Sep 42; 1 Dam Me109, 3 Sep 42; 1 Dest Me109, 29 Sep 42; Prob Fg Off (WS), 1 Oct 42; 1 Dest Me109F, 7 Oct 42; 1 Dest & 1 Prob Me109, 9 Oct 42; 1 Dest Me109, 29 Oct 42; 1 Dest Me109, 2 Nov 42; 1 Dam Me109, 9 Nov 42; 1 Dest Me109F, 7 Jan 43; ½ Dest MC202, 11 Jan 43; 1 Prob Me109, 13 Jan 43; 1 Dest Ju87D, 21 Jan 43; 'from Sgt to Flt Cdr in 12 months', on dep from 92 Sqn, 31 Jan 43; to UK via Heliopolis by air, 1 Feb 43; DFC, 5 Feb 43; Bar to DFC, 23 Feb 43; Air Min, Mar 43; Public Relations duties, visiting & giving talks at factories, Jun 43; OC, 2 Sqn, 53 OTU (Spit), Hibaldstow, Sep 43-Aug 44; Flt Lt (WS), 25 Nov 43; Refresher Crse, 53 OTU (Spit), Llandow, Glam, 5 Sep 44; 41 Sqn, 3 Oct 44-22 Jan 45; OC A Flt, 130 (Punjab) Sqn (Spit XIV), Ophoven, 22 Jan 45; 1 Dest & 1 Dam FW190, 2 Mar 45; 2 Dam Me109 on grnd, 19 Mar 45; 1 Dest Fi156 on grnd, 18 Apr 45; 1 Dest Me109G, 20 Apr 45; 1 Dest & 1 Dam FW190, 24 Apr 45; PR duties, Air Min, & scndd to NSC, Aug 45-Apr 46; demob, 1946; dep to Dist Commissioner, NSC, SE Reg, May 46; rejoined RAF on trans to ACB as Temp Flt Lt, 18 Aug 47 (sen 8 Apr 45); ATC Crse, Aug 47; Senior Controller, RAF Hendon, Sep 47; Flt Lt 1 Nov 47 (sen 1 Sep 45); app to SSC as Flt Lt (6 yrs AL & 4 yrs Res), 2 Nov 48 (sen 16 Jul 46); 99 Sqn (York), Berlin, 1948; app to perm com as Flt Lt, 6 Apr 49; FIC, CFS, Nov 49; Flt Cdr, 3 FTS (Harvard), Feltwell, May 50; CGC, 14 FTS, Holme-on-Spalding Moor, Apr-Dec 52; OC, 21 SAFS (Meteor), Finningley, Dec 52-Feb 53; Work Study Crse, COA, Cranfield, Mar 53-Jun 54; Sqn Ldr, 1 Jan 54; Work Study Off, Air Min, Jul 54-Jun 56; Work Study Off, 2 TAF, G., Jun 56-Sep 58; CFS, Little Rissington, Oct-Nov 58; 6 FTS Ternhill, Nov 58-Apr 59; Wg Cdr

Flying, Bruggen, 1959; Wg Cdr & Wg Cdr Flying, RAF Oakington, Cambs, 1 Jul 60; Wg Cdr Flying Trng, Dishforth; OC, JSWS, Old Sarum & High Wycombe; OBE, 1 Jan 71; ret 2 Feb 75, rtng Wg Cdr; occ trng staff, Brit Steel & ret after acc, 1980; d Bucks, Mar 97

SCHOU, Kenneth Victor James, NZ.412744, RNZAF; b Dannevirke, NZ, 17 May 14; ed Dannevirke N Sch & Dannevirke HS, 1919-28; marr Doreen Alice Findlay Stark, 1 Jun 40; occ Hairdresser on enl in RNZAF, Levin, 4 May 41; 2 EFTS, New Plymouth, NZ, 14 Jun-26 Jul 41 (grad 70%); emb Auck for Vncvr, Can, per MV *Awatea*, 14 Aug 41; disemb Vncvr & att RCAF, 29 Aug 41; 2 SFTS, Can, 2 Sep 41; plt badge & to Sgt Plt, 21 Nov 41; 1 Y Depot, Halifax NS, 26 Nov 41; emb Halifax for UK, 9 Dec 41; disemb UK & to 3 PRC, Bournemouth, 19 Dec 41; 58 OTU, Ggmth, Scot, 10 Feb 42; 41 Sqn, 21 Apr-30 Sep 42; Flt Sgt, 1942; com Plt Off, 28 Aug 42; RAF Stn Llanbedr, 21 Oct 42; RAF Gib, 21 Oct 42; 1435 Sqn (Spit Vc), Malta, 25 Oct 42-LM 1 May 43; Fg Off, 28 Feb 43; to UK, May 43; 1 PDC, 24 May 43; Comms Flt, Newtownards, NIre, 22 Jun 43; to ME & rtn, Sep 43; RAF Long Kesh, Lisburn, NIre, 25 Mar 44; HQ, RAF NIre, 1 May 44; Flt Lt, 28 Aug 44; 12 (RNZAF) PDRC, 6 Nov 44; emb UK per MV *Remeura* on repat to NZ, 12 Dec 44; att to RAF CXLD 1 Feb 45; disemb NZ, 18 Feb 45; NE Pool, Accommodation Camp, 19 Feb 45; trans to Reserve A1, 28 May 45; joined Gen Res (133284), 27 Sep 50; svce ext 4 yrs, to 26 Sep 58; svce ext 4 yrs, to 26 Sep 62; ret, 17 May 64; res on ret, Dowding St, Hamilton; post-War occ, clerk, State Advances Corp, Hamilton, 1950-58; d., Hamilton, NZ, 22 Mar 94

SCOON, Jellicoe Esslemonte Norbert Cecil, 1803977, RAFVR; b Trinidad, 14 Nov 20; ed Brit W Indies; joined RAFVR, Euston, 13 Mar 42; ITW & EFTS, UK, 1942; Sgt Plt (1803977), 1942; 1 SFTS (Oxford), Cranwell, Lincs, 1942; 53 OTU (Spit), Llandow, Glam, 1942-43; 41 Sqn, Mar-Apr 43; Flt Sgt, 1943; WO, 1944; 198 Sqn (Typhn), 1943; com Plt Off (196215), 28 Mar 45; EF & WUL in Typhn IB, PD466, TP-S, S of Eimke, G., after attack on shipping, 3 May 45; Fg Off (WS), 28 Sep 45

SCOTT, Peter F. 'Scotty', 1624619, RAFVR; b Hull, Yks, 2 Sep 23; ed Beverley GS, Yks; joined RAFVR, Hull, 10 Mar 42; 11 EFTS (Finch), Cap-de-la-Madeleine (Trois-Rivières), Que, Can, 1942; 8 SFTS (Harv & Anson), Weyburn, Sask, 1942-43; Sgt Plt (1624619), 1943; 1 OTU (Hurr), Bagotville, Que, 1943; 53 OTU (Spit), KiL, 1944 ('good', 90%); Flt Sgt, 1944; 83 GSU (Spit XIV), Dnsfld, 1944-45; 41 Sqn, 27 Mar 45-30 Jan 46; ½ Dest FW190 w Flt Lt J. F. Wilkinson, Teschendorf Wood, G., 20 Apr 45; 2 Dam FW190Ds, nr Lake Schwerin, G., 1 May 45; rlsd under 'Class B', 30 Jan 46; d ca 2007

SCOTT, Thomas Roland, 115515, RAFVR; b Berne, Switz, 13 Oct 22; ed Eton Coll; joined RAFVR, Oxford, 17 Dec 40; 2 BFTS (Stearman, Vultee & Harv), Polaris Flt Academy, Grand Central Air Terminal, Glendale, CA, & subs War Eagle Fld, Lancaster, CA, USA, 1941; Sgt Plt (1313069), 1941; com Prob Plt Off (115515), 6 Dec 41; 61 OTU (Spit), Rednal, 1942; Prob Fg Off (WS), 1 Oct 42; 41 Sqn, 21 Jul-22 Oct 42; KIFA in Spit Vb, BL518, flew into hill Tarren Hendre, nr Towyn, Merioneth, Wales, in bad weather w Fg Off (Actg Flt Lt) F. N. Gillitt & Fg Off R. Harrison, 22 Oct 42, aged 20, s of Oswald, DSO, & Hermione Scott of Winchester; bur Grave 602, Portmadoc [Porthmadog] Public Cem, Caern, Wales

SHEA, David John, J.22158, RCAF; b Hamilton, Ont, Can, 3 Jul 23; ed Cathedral RC HS, Hamilton, 1939-40; emp Firestone Tire Coy (Machine Shop), 1940; att Galt A/C Sch, 1940; occ airframe fitter, White Aircraft Coy, 29 Jan-22 Dec 41; joined RCAF, Hamilton, & to 1 MD, Toronto, Ont, 14 Jan 42; 1 BGS, Jarvis, Ont, 15 Feb 42; 6 ITS, Toronto, 12 Apr-18 Jul 42; LAC (R.145923), 5 Jun 42; 10 EFTS (Moth), Mount Hope, Ont, 19 Jul-12 Sep 42 (30 FH day dual, 32.35 FH day solo plus & 2.30 FH night dual); 6 SFTS (Harv), Dunnville, Ont, 13 Sep 42-13 Jan 43 (57.05 FH day dual, 77.40 FH day solo, 6.15 FH night dual & 9.55 FH night solo); plt badge

& com Plt Off (J.22158), 30 Dec 42; Y Depot, Halifax, 14 Jan 43; to UK, 2 Feb 43; arr UK, 13 Feb 43; att 50 Grp (6 EFTS), 14 Apr 43; 7 (P)AFU (Hurr & Master), Peterborough, Cambs, 11 May 43; 58 OTU (Spit), Ggmth, Stirling, 22 Jun-30 Sep 43; Fg Off, ca 30 Jun 43; att 3 PRC, Bnmth, Hants, pending posting, 30 Sep-31 Dec 43; 2 TEU (Spit), Ggmth, Stirling, 31 Dec 43; 41 Sqn, 19 Jan-13 Mar 44; KIFA landing in high winds, Lympne in Spit XII, EN237, 13 Mar 44, aged 20; s of John & Kathleen Shea of Hamilton, Ont, Can; bur Grave 44.I.10, Brookwood Mil Cem, Surrey

SHEPHERD, John Bean 'Shep', 104447, RAFVR; b Edin, Scot, 20 Jul 19; ed Edin; 603 (City of Edin) Sqn, Turnhouse, 3 Jul 37-20 Oct 39; LAC (803581), AuxAF, Nov 37; re-mustered to plt u/t & to 11 E&RFTS, Perth, Scot, 21 Oct 39; Sgt Plt, 1940; 65 Sqn (Spit I), Turnhouse, 2-4 Sep 40; 234 (Madras Pres) Sqn (Spit I), Middle Wallop, 5 Sep 40-LM 16 Jan 42; ⅓Dam Ju88, 23 Mar 41; ½ Dest Me109, 17 Jun 41; 1 Prob Ju88, 12 Aug 41; com Prob Plt Off (104447), 21 Aug 41; 1 Dest & 1 Dam Me109F, 15 Oct 41; Actg Flt Lt, 15 Nov 41; Prob Fg Off (WS), 8 Feb 42; Test Plt, Vickers Armstrong (Supermarine), Weybridge, ca Feb-Aug 42; Flt Cdr, 118 Sqn (Spit Vb), Ibsley, 12 Aug 42-10 Oct 43; ¼ Dest Do217, 19 Aug 42 (Op Jubilee); Fg Off, 21 Aug 42; DFC (118 Sqn), 22 Sep 42; Flt Lt (WS), 8 Feb 43; 1½ Dest Me109, 18 Jul 43; 1 Dam Me109F, 25 Jul 43; 1 Prob Me109G, 2 Aug 43; 1st Bar to DFC (118 Sqn), 27 Aug 43; HQFC, Oct 43; OC, FAU, AFDU, Wtrg, 4 Nov 43-17 May 44; 610 (Cty of Chester) Sqn (Spit XIV), Bolt Hd, 18 May 44-4 Mar 45 (dsbnd); 1 Dest V1, 20 Jun 44; ½ Dest V1, 22 Jun 44; 1 Dest V1, 7 Jul 44; 1 Dest V1, 9 Jul 44; 1 Dest V1, 12 Jul 44; 1 Dest V1, 29 Jul 44; ½ Dest V1, 4 Aug 44; OC, 610 (Cty of Chester) Sqn (Spit XIV), 28 Feb-4 Mar 45; att 17 APC Warmwell, Dorset, 22 Feb-7 Mar 45; OC A Flt, 41 Sqn, 7 Mar-7 Apr 45; OC, 41 Sqn, 8 Apr 45-22 Jan 46; 1 Dest Me110 & 1 Dest Me163 Komet (former towing latter), Nordholz A/D, G., 14 Apr 45; 1 Dest FW190, Hagenow, G., 16 Apr 45; 1 Dest FW190D, Kremmen Forest, G., 20 Apr 45; ½ Dest FW190D, w Fg Off J. F. Wilkinson, nr Neuruppin, G., 20 Apr 45; 1 Dest FW190D, N of Lauenburg, G., & 1 Dest Me109, NW of Lake Ratzeburg, G., 30 Apr 45; ½ Dest FW190D w Fg Off E. Gray, E of Lake Schwerin, G., 1 May 45; admtd hosp, Schleswig, 21 Jul-3 Aug 45; 2nd Bar to DFC (41 Sqn), 14 Sep 45; KIFA (neck broken), EF at 200 ft & CL in anti-tank ditch in Tmpst V, NV640, Wunstorf, 22 Jan 46, aged 26; funeral held Lübeck, 25 Jan 46; s of William & Rosetta Shepherd of Edin; bur Grave 5A, G9, Hamburg Cem, Hamburg, G.

SHORT, Roger Lee 'Roy' & 'Shorty', 1333690, RAFVR; b Sunderland, Dur, 28 Oct 21; ed Lymington Elem Sch; joined RAFVR, Uxb, 17 Feb 41; flg trng USAAC/USAAF, AL & GA, USA, 1941-42; plt badge & to Sgt Plt (1333690), 1942; (P)AFU, 1942-43; Crse 37, 53 OTU (Spit), KiL, 3 Aug-26 Oct 43, Flt Sgt, 1943; 1 TEU (Spit & Hurr), Tealing, Angus, ca 10 Feb 44; A Flt, 41 Sqn, 8 Jun-17 Jul 44; ½ Dest V1, Ashford, 25 Jun 44; KIFA in Spit XII, MB877, in MAC w Flt Sgt C. Oddy (†) in Moth II, DV575, 17 Jul 44, aged 22; s of Henry & Elizabeth Short, & husb of Dorothy E. Short of S Ruislip, Mdx; bur Plot O, Grave 80, Hwkge Cem, Kent

SLACK, Thomas Adams Hume, 112428, RAFVR; b Micheldever, nr Winchester, Hants, 29 Apr 16; ed Uppington, Salop; occ Foreign Rep, Brit-American Tobacco Coy, Sngpr, on enl in RAFVR, Sngpr, 19 Oct 40; GFTS, Kallang, Sngpr, 19 Oct 40; 4 FTS (Hart & Audax), Habbaniyah, Iraq, Jan-May 41; Sgt Plt (785032), Aug 41; 22 FTS (Harv), Thornhill, S Rhod, Aug-Sep 41; com Plt Off (112428), 16 Sep 41; emb Capetown for St John NB per *Christiaan Huygens*, Sep 41; emb St John NB for UK, Nov 41; Crse 31, 57 OTU (Spit), Hwdn, 6 Jan-7 Apr 42; 41 Sqn w H. C. Knight, 14 Apr 42-23 Aug 44; cartoonist of some talent who drew caricatures of many 41 Sqn pilots; Fg Off (WS), 16 Sep 42; FL Crse, FLS, RAF Chedworth, Jan 43; SD/WIA (knee) in Spit XII, EN233, by JG2, baled out & lndd Foucaucourt-Hors-Nesle, 15m SW of Abbeville, F., 18 Jul 43; evaded capture & rtnd to UK via France, Spain & Gib; emb Seville for Gib per SS *Borgholm*, 20 Aug 43; dep Gib, 23 Aug 43; arr Bristol, 24 Aug 43; interviewed by MI9 re evasion, 24 Aug 43; Flt Lt (WS), 16 Sep 43;

rtnd to 41 Sqn, ca 24 Sep 43 (1st non-op flt, 27 Sep 43; 1st op 3 Oct 43); sent on lecture tour of RAF stations, 4 Oct-18 Dec 43; OC B Flt, 27 Jan-23 Aug 44; 1 Dest V1, Dngnss-Isle of Oxney, Kent, 4 Aug 44; EF (fuel cock) in Spit XII, EN226, FL N of Hesdin, F., on Rodeo 392 & captured, 23 Aug 44; Dulag Luft (POW 7747), Oberursel, G., 26 Aug 44; Stalag Luft III, 3 Sep 44-27 Jan 45; Stalag III-A, Luckenwalde, G., 5 Feb-20 May 45; lib by Russians, 25 Apr 45, but not rlsd until Russian-Allied POW exchange over Elbe, 20 May 45; repat to UK, 23 May 45; res on repat, Micheldever, Hants; post-War emp Imperial Tobacco OC, Sngpr; d Aug 94

SMART, LIONEL HARRY 'Harry', 1338427, RAFVR; b Chorley Wood, Herts, 9 Nov 22; ed Brookshill Cty Sch, Mdx; joined RAFVR, Weston-super-Mare, 1 Jun 41; 6 ITW, Aberystwyth, 1941; Crse 43B, USAAF, AL, USA, 1942; Sgt Plt, 1942; 5 GTS, Shobdon, Hereford, 1942-43; Tug Plt, 3 GTS, Stoke Orchard & Northleach, Gloucs, 30 Jun 43-18 Sep 44; FA/UCC in Master II, DL456, Stoke Orchard, 26 Jul 43 (logbook endorsed); FA/NI, retracted UC too soon after TO, Master II, DL397, Stoke Orchard, 22 Nov 43; att RAF Pershore for decompression tests, 29 Nov 43; FA/OSR in Master II, DL520, Bibury, Gloucs, 24 Dec 43; att 5 (P)AFU (Master I/II), Ternhill, Salop, for refresher Crse, 12 Jan-10 Feb 44; FA/NI in Master II, DL456, bounced on landing & broke tail wheel structure, Stoke Orchard, 17 Apr 44; interviewed at HQ, 23 Grp, re application for com, 1 Aug 44 (unsuccessful); FA/NI in Master II, DL448, due to uneven surface of strip, Stoke Orchard, 15 Aug 44; Flt Sgt, 1944; Crse 68, 57 OTU (Spit), Eshott NBL, 19 Sep-5 Dec 44; 41 Sqn, 1 Feb-24 Apr 45; EF/COG/IFA (leg & head) w Fg Off R. D. A. Smith (in Spit XIV, MV249 or RB143), on landing Spit XIV, RM696, after armed recce to Pritzwalk-Ludwigslust area, G., & admtd hosp, 24 Apr 45 (leg amputated, DNR); d 2 Jul 85

SMITH, DONALD HAMILTON, A.407256, RAAF; b Victor Hbr, S Aust, 18 Aug 15; ed Victor Hbr & Scotch Coll Adelaide; occ farmer on enl in RAAF, 5 RC Adelaide, 17 Aug 40; AC2, 1 ITS, Somers VIC, 18 Aug-11 Oct 40; LAC, 3 EFTS, Essendon VIC, 17 Oct-15 Dec 40; Crse 5, 2 SFTS, Wagga (Forest Hill) NSW, 16 Dec 40-6 Apr 41; plt badge, 3 Apr 41; com Plt Off, 8 Apr 41; 4 ED, Adelaide, 15 Apr 41; att RAF & emb Syd for UK, 27 May 41; disemb UK & to 60 OTU (Defiant), Macmerry, E Lothian, 10 Sep 41; Fg Off, 8 Oct 41; 15 SFTS (Harv), Kidlington, 1 Nov 41; FIS, CFS Upavon, 14 Nov-4 Dec 41; 452 (Aust) Sqn (Spit Vb), Andreas IoM, 2 Apr 42; arr Malta per HMS *Eagle*, 3 Jun 42; 126 Sqn (Spit Vc), Luqa, 3 Jun-3 Aug 42; ⅓ Dest Cant Z1007, 6 Jul 42; 1 Dest Me109F, 8 Jul 42; 1 Dest Ju88 & 1 Prob Me109F, 10 Jul 42; 1 Dest Ju88 but WIA (ankle) & FL Spit Vc, BP992, Malta, 14 Jul 42; admtd St Patricks Hosp, Malta, 14 Jul 42; evac to UK & posted NE to 1 Depot, Uxb, Aug 42; admtd RAFH, Halton, 11 Aug 42 (& subs Torquay & Wroughton Hosps); admtd Loughborough Hosp, 24 Mar-12 Apr 43; Flt Lt, 8 Apr 43; refresher, 53 OTU (Spit), Llandow, 27 Apr 43; 7 days PL, 18-26 May 43; marr 20 May 43; 41 Sqn, 23 May 43-2 May 44; 1 Dam FW190, 10m S of Beachy Hd, Ssx, 4 Jun 43; 7 days leave, 6-12 Jul 43; 7 days leave, 18-24 Aug 43; 1 Dest FW190, W of Évreux, F., 22 Sep 43; OC, A Flt, 41 Sqn, 25 Sep 43-2 May 44; att Crse 12, FC Sch of Tactics, FLS Aston Down (Spit V), 18 Oct-7 Nov 43; 9 days leave, 11-19 Nov 43; 7 days leave, 1-7 Feb 44; 7 days leave, 22-28 Mar 44; Medal for Valour (USSR), 11 Apr 44; Actg Sqn Ldr & OC, 453 (Aust) Sqn (Spit IX), 125 Airfield, Ford, 2 May-27 Sep 44; 4 days leave, 21-24 May 44; 1 Dam Me109, 16 Jun 44; Sqn Ldr, 1 Jul 44; 1 Dest Me109 & 1 Dam FW190, 9 Jul 44; 7 days leave, 15-21 Aug 44; 1 Prob Me109, 26 Aug 44; DFC, 19 Sep 44; HQ ADGB, 28 Sep 44; 21 days SL, 28 Nov-18 Dec 44; Wg Cdr & OC, 11 PDRC, Charmy Down, 15 Jan 45; att RAF Balderton as member of GCM, 20-21 Feb 45; 9 days leave, 14-22 Mar 45; 11 days leave, 20-30 Aug 45; emb UK for Aust, 25 Sep 45; disemb Melb & to 1 PD, 17 Oct 45; paid 68 days WL, 30 days disemb leave & 7 days RL in lieu of time; 4 PD, Adelaide, 26 Nov 45; dschgd, 4 Dec 45

SMITH, JOHN BRITTAIN, 111494, RAFVR; b Leigh, Lancs, 8 Mar 21; ed St Paul's Sch, Monton, Lancs; joined RAFVR, Padgate, 3 Jan 41; flg trng 10 EFTS, Perth, CFS, Peterborough, 1941;

Sgt Plt (1035360), 1941; com Prob Plt Off (111494), 20 Sep 41; 52 OTU (Spit), Aston Down, Gloucs, 1942; Fg Off (WS), 20 Sep 42; FI, 29 EFTS, 1942; 41 Sqn, 9 Sep-LM 25 Nov 43; Flt Lt (WS), 20 Sep 43

SMITH, Roy David Austen, 164845, RAFVR; b Melb VIC, Aust, 28 Jun 24; ed Hurstpierpoint Coll, Hassocks, Ssx; joined RAFVR, 5 Sep 42; LAC (1808356), 11 EFTS (Finch), Cap-de-la-Madeleine (Trois-Rivières), Que, Can, 1943; 8 SFTS (Harv & Anson), Weyburn, Sask, 1943; Sgt Plt (1624619), 1943; 1 OTU (Hurr), Bagotville, Que, 1943-44; com Prob Plt Off (164845), 7 Apr 44; 53 OTU (Spit), KiL, 1944 ('very good', 89%); Fg Off (WS), 7 Oct 44; 41 Sqn, 27 Mar 45-31 Mar 46; COG/IFA w Flt Sgt L. H. Smart (in Spit XIV, RM696), on landing Spit XIV, MV249 (or RB143), after armed recce to Pritzwalk-Ludwigslust area, G., & admtd hosp, 24 Apr 45; 1 Dest Fi156 in air & 1 Dam Fi156 on grnd, Schwerin area, G., 2 May 45; 26 Sqn (Spit XIV), 1 Apr 46; app to com as Fg Off on ext svce (4 yrs on AL), 15 Aug 46; Flt Lt, 7 Oct 47; app to perm com as Flt Lt, 15 Jan 48; 60 Sqn (Spit FR.18), Sembawang, Sngpr, 49; Flt Cdr, 33 Sqn (Tmpst II), Kuala Lumpur, Malaysia, May 50; DFC (Malaya), 6 Mar 53; Staff, RAF College Cranwell, 1953; Sqn Ldr, 1 Oct 54; Flt Cdr, 73 Sqn (Venom & Cnbra), Akrotiri, Cyprus, 1956; Wg Cdr, 1 Jul 60; Air Staff, Air Min, 1960; OC, 57 Sqn (Victor), Honington, 24 Jul 64; Gp Capt, 1 Jul 66; Air Staff, HQ 2 TAF, 1966; OC, RAF Wattisham, 1968; Air Cdre, 1 Jan 70 (changed name to hyphenated Austen-Smith bet Gp Capt & Air Cdre, ca 1966-70); Dir of Pers (Air), 26 Mar 70-Jan 72; Actg AVM, Special Duty, Air Staff, MOD, 14 Feb 72; AOC & Cmdt, RAFC Cranwell, 23 Sep 72-18 Jul 75; AVM, 1 Jan 73; CB, 14 Jun 75; SASO, NEAF, 8 Nov 75; OC, BFC, Air Cmdr, Cyprus, & Administrator, Sovereign Base Areas, Akrotiri & Dhekelia, Cyprus, 1 Apr 76-27 Apr 78; Def Attaché, Head of Brit Def Staff, BJSM, Washington DC, 4 Aug-31 Oct 1978; KBE, 16 Jun 79; AM, 1 Jul 79; ret, 1 Nov 81; Gentleman Usher to HM the Queen, 2 Nov 82-24 Jul 94; CVO, 31 Dec 93; Extra Gentleman Usher to HM the Queen, 28 Jun 94

SOLAK, Jerzy Jakub 'George', 76766, PAF/RAFVR (Polish); b Przecław, Krakow, PL, 22 Aug 10; res Lwów, Poland [today Lviv, Ukraine], 1920s; ed Gen Cert of Ed & grad Lwów Polytechnik, Ukraine; joined PAF, 1930; grad SPRL, Dęblin, PL, 1935; Light Bomber Sqn (Breguet XIX & Potez XXV), 69 (AC) Sqn (Lublin R-XIII), & Ftr Sqn (PZL. P7), 6 Air Regt, Lwów, 1935-39; drafted into 6 Air Regt, Aug 39; arranged evac for himself & grp of 6 Air Regt students via Romania to F., Sep 39; arr UK, Jan 40; joined RAFVR, Eastchurch, 8 Feb 40; 7 OTU, Hwdn, Flint, 1940; 151 Sqn (Hurr I), Stapleford, 28 Aug 40; 249 (Gold Coast) Sqn (Hurr I), N Weald, 27 Sep 40; 317 (Wileński) Sqn (Hurr I), Acklgtn, 26 Feb 41; com Plt Off, 20 Mar 41; Fg Off, 20 Sep 41; KW, 30 Oct 41; B Flt, 164 Sqn (Spit Va), Skeabrae, 9 Jun 42; 609 (W Riding) Sqn (Typhn Ia/b), Dxfd, 8 Aug 42; Test Plt, AFDU, Dxfd, 3 Nov 42; 41 Sqn, 9 Apr-12 Oct 43; 1 Dest FW190, 3-5m S of Eastbourne, Ssx, 4 Jun 43; Flt Lt, 1 Sep 43; PLO, HQFC, 12 Oct 43; 1st & 2nd Bars to KW, 20 Oct 43; 492 FS, 48 FG, 9 USAAF, Blackpool, 4 Jun 44; SD/AA/WIA (legs & hands) over Basse-Normandy in P-47 Thunderbolt, 42-26334, F4-V, & captured, 10 Aug 44; A/C crashed at Landisacq, nr Tinchebray, F., (rediscovered, 2004); escaped & rtnd to 48 FG, 20 Aug 44; HQ PAF, 18 Dec 44; Polish Depot, Blackpool, 24 Apr 45; 9 PDC, 29 May 45; 84 Grp USAAF, 7 Jun 45; SKVM, 26 Jun 45; HQ, 84 Grp USAAF, 12 Aug 45; RAF Coltishall, 6 May 46; emgtd to USA, 1948; occ eng & architect; d 5 Mar 02, aged 92

SPENCER, Terence 'Terry', 47269, RAFVR; b Bedford, 8 Mar 18; ed Southwood Hse, Cheltenham Coll, 1932-36, & studied eng, Birm Uni, 1936-Sep 39; Cpl, Warks Yeo, 1937; com 2 Lt (109268), RE, 20 Dec 39 (Regular Army Emergency Com); occ foundry eng, res IoW, on trans to RAFVR, 10 Oct 41; com Prob Plt Off (47269) & to 19 EFTS, Sealand, 11 Oct-28 Nov 41; B Flt, 28 EFTS (Moth), Wolverhampton, 29 Nov 41-28 Apr 42 (1st dual 4 Dec 41, 1st solo, 22 Dec 41; grad above avge); FL in MOTH, T6689, Cosford, 19 Feb 42; C Flt, 1 SFTS (Master II & Oxford I/II), Cranwell, 29 Apr-31 Aug 42 (grad above avge); C Flt, 41 OTU (Harv,

Magister & Mstg), Old Sarum, 1 Sep-3 Nov 42; Fg Off (WS), 1 Oct 42; A Flt, 26 Sqn (Mstg & Tomahawk), Gatwick, 4 Nov 42-1 Feb 44 (1st op flt, 23 Nov 42); att 1 Sch of Air Nav (Anson), Cranage, Chesh, 1-12 Dec 42 (4.00 FH); CD from FW190s over Channel, 22 Jan 43; CL/NI Tomahawk, AK125, AC burnt out, Detling, 27 Jan 43; NE sick, admtd 14 RC GH, 17 May-4 Jun 43; admtd Horton EMS, Epsom, 5-11 Jun 43; OC, A Flt, 26 Sqn, 10 Jun 43-1 Feb 44; admtd RAF Hosp Halton, 12-16 Jun 43; att A Flt Detachment, 26 Sqn (Mstg, Oxford & Spit Vb), Ballyhalbert, NIre, 23 Aug-4 Nov 43 & 16 Nov-5 Dec 43; Flt Lt (WS), 11 Oct 43; att Ftr Ldr Crse, FLS (Spit Vb), Aston Down, Gloucs, 5-31 Dec 43; Flt Cdr, 165 (Ceylon) Sqn (Spit IX & Oxford), Culmhead, 2 Feb-1 May 44; WUL/NI in Spit IX, SK-G, 22 Feb 44; OC A Flt, 41 Sqn, 2 May 44-3 Jan 45; 1 Dest V1, 10-15m NNE of Hastings, Ssx, 23 Jun 44; 1 Dest V1, High Halden, Kent, 25 Jun 44; 1 Dest V1 by tipping it up w own wg, 5m N of Hastings, Ssx, 9 Aug 44; EF/CL/NI in orchard on landing at Lympne during flt in 33 Sqn Spit IXa, 5R-Z, 20 Aug 44; 1 Dest V1, 2m NNW of Appledore, Kent, 19 Aug 44; 1 Dest V1, 2m S of Mersham, Kent, 23 Aug 44; 1 Dest V1, nr Harrietsham, Kent, 23 Aug 44; 1 Dest V1, 15m N of Rye, Ssx, 27 Aug 44; hit by AA/FL Spit XII, MB882, Lympne, 26 Aug 44; 1 Dest FW190A-5 (173-vic Ace Hptm Emil 'Bully' Lang, of Stab II./JG26 †), Overhespen, B., 3 Sep 44; to Diest via Tilbury & Ostend, 6-17 Nov 44; Actg Sqn Ldr & OC, 350 (Belgian) Sqn, Ophoven, 4 Jan-26 Feb 45 (1st op flt, 13 Jan 45); AA/FDF, during armed recce in Spit XIV, RM739, baled out in Rheine-Lingen area, inj when left hip hit tailplane, captured & admtd Mil Hosp Burgsteinfurt, G., 26 Feb-7 Mar 45; solitary confinement, Rheine A/D, G., 8-11 Mar 45; to Frankfurt by train, 11-13 Mar 45; Dulag Luft, Oberursel, G., 14 Mar 45; Rcvg Depot, Wetzlar, G., 16-31 Mar 45; escaped w ex-41 Sqn pilot, Sqn Ldr K. F. Thiele, when main gate of camp was left open & reached Allied lines by bicycle & subs motorcycle, 31 Mar 45; repat to Croydon, Surrey, by DC-3, 3 Apr 45; rtnd to Brussels-Evere from Croydon per DC-3, 10 Apr 45; rtnd to 350 Sqn (B.106 Twente) as OC, 11-19 Apr 45 (1st op flt, 12 Apr 45); 1 Dest Ju88 on grnd, Lauenburg, G., 19 Apr 45; hit by rocket fire in Spit XIV, SM814 (stbd wg blown off & second hit in fuselage which blew up), whilst strafing trawler in Wismar Bay, G., blown out of AC at 50ft & WIA, parachute opened & survived to be captured again, 19 Apr 45 (since crdtd in Guinness Book of Records as having made lowest authenticated bale-out on record); Luft Hosp, Wismar, G., 20 Apr-1 May 45; Luft Lazarett, Scharbeutz, G., 1-3 May 45; lib by 7 Armoured Div, 3 May 45; driven to Celle, 4 May 45; admtd 50 MFH, Celle, 4-7 May 45; to UK per DC-3, 7 May 45; admtd burns unit, RAF Hosp Cosford, 8-31 May 45; 106 PRC, Cosford, 1-26 Jun 45; DFC (350 Sqn), 22 Jun 45; 125 Wg, Husum, G., 27 Jun-16 Jul 45; 616 (S Yks) Sqn (Meteor III), Lübeck, G., 17 Jul-13 Aug 45 (FF exp on type, 20 Jul 45); 124 Wg (Anson, Spit XIV & Tmpst V), Lübeck, G., 14 Aug-23 Oct 45; 80 Sqn (Tmpst V & Fieseler Storch), Sylt, G., 24 Oct-28 Nov 45; 124 Wg, 30 Nov-17 Dec 45; rtnd to UK, 13 Dec 45 (LF in RAF in Mosq, 15 Dec 45); demob w 68 days paid leave, 17 Dec 45; emp Percival A/C Coy Ltd, Luton, 1 Mar-27 Apr 46; flew Proctor V, ZS-ATZ, to SA, 5-22 Mar 46; occ, personal plt (Proctor V) for Ben du Preez, MD of Kimlite Industries Ltd (IDB), JNB, SA, 2 May-4 Nov 46; CdG (B) w Palm 40, 24 Jan 47; occ plt, W Kimberly Diamond Corp (Piper Cub & Proctor V), JNB, SA, 8 Mar-30 Jun 47; occ plt, African-Italian Financial & Industrial Corp Ltd (Auster, Fairchild & Proctor), JNB, SA, 1 Jul 47-6 Oct 48; rtnd to UK 26 Jul 47 & marr actress Lesley Brook, 19 Aug 47 (res Shanklin, IoW); TEM, 28 Nov 47; emgtd to SA, Jul 48, & started aerial-photography coy 'Skyfotos', Oct 48; occ freelance photographer for LIFE mag, Sep 52-Sep 72; rtnd to UK, 1961; occ freelance photographer for PEOPLE mag, 1972-92; author of *It was Thirty Years Ago Today* (Bloomsbury, 1994) & *Living Dangerously* (Percival, 2002); d Odiham, Hants, 8 Feb 09

SPURR, LAWRENCE ESMOND 'Larry', R.176504, RCAF; b Middleton, NS, Can, 15 Jun 23; ed MacDonald HS, Middleton; enl in RCAF, Annapolis Royal, NS, 22 Jun 42; joined RCAF, Halifax NS, 7 Jul 42; 6 ITS, Toronto, Ont, Jan-Feb 43; 12 EFTS (Finch), Goderich, Ont, Mar-Apr 43; 6 SFTS (Harv), Dunnville, Ont, May-Aug 43; Sgt Plt, 1943; 1 OTU (Hurr), Bagotville, Que, 1943; 61 OTU (Spit), Rednal, Salop, 1943; 3 TEU (Hurr & Typhn), Annan, Dumfries, 1944;

Flt Sgt, 1944; 41 Sqn, 14 Jun-4 Aug 44; GSU, 5-22 Aug 44; com Plt Off (J.91114), Aug 44; 416 (City of Oshawa) Sqn (Spit IX), Illiers l'Évêque, F., 23 Aug 44; one of five 416 Sqn pilots SD (in Spit XVI, SM335) by U.S. AA, 24 Dec 44 (1 killed, 1 evaded, & 3 others, incl Spurr (NI), rtnd safely); ½ Dam Me262, 25 Feb 45; Fg Off, Mar 45; ½ Dest Do217, 3 May 45; rec for CdG (B), but not awarded; MiD, 1 Jan 4 War, Mar-Aug 52; 1 Dest MiG-15, 14 Jul 52; US DFC, 1952; rlsd from RCAF, Dec 70; d in MVA, 6; rmnd in RCAF after War; scndd to USAF & posted to 25 FS (Sabre), 51 FIW, USAF, Korean Jan 73, aged 49

STEPHENS, Ronald Vincent, A.420631, RAAF; b Batemans Bay NSW, Aust, 12 Mar 21; ed Stanmore Commercial Coll; commercial traveller on enl in RAAF, 2RC, Syd, 8 Nov 41; AC2, Crse 22, 2 ITS, 8 Nov 41-27 Feb 42; LAC, 28 Feb 42; 6 days leave, 22-28 Apr 42; Crse 24, 8 EFTS Narrandera NSW, 30 Apr-24 Jun 42; Crse 25, 5 SFTS Uranquinty NSW, 10 Aug-14 Dec 42; plt badge, 14 Dec 42; Sgt Plt, 17 Dec 42; 2 ED, Brdfld Pk NSW, 18 Dec 42; 1 ED, Ascot Vale VIC, 9 Jan 43; att RAF & emb Melb for UK, 17 Jan 43; disemb UK & to 11 PDRC, Bnmth, 17 Mar 43; 7 days PL, 1-7 Apr 43; 21 Regt, 23 Apr-5 May 43; 17 (P)AFU (Master), Calverley, Chesh, 25 May 43; Flt Sgt, 17 Jun 43; Crse 53, 57 OTU (Spit), Eshott NBL, 10 Aug-2 Nov 43; 7 days PL, 2-8 Nov 43; 7 days leave, 9-15 Nov 43; 7 days leave, 16-22 Nov 43; 7 days leave, 23-29 Nov 43; 7 days leave, 30 Nov-6 Dec 43; 7 days leave, 7-13 Dec 43; 7 days leave, 14-20 Dec 43; 7 days leave, 21-27 Dec 43; 7 days leave, 28 Dec 43-3 Jan 44; 2 days leave, 4-5 Jan 44; Crse 12, Grnd Fighting, GFS Boulmer, 7-28 Jan 44; 6 days leave, 29 Jan-3 Feb 44; 2 TEU, Ggmth, Stirling, 4 Feb-20 Mar 44; B Flt, 41 Sqn, 21 Mar-8 May 44; att RAF Stn Exeter, 8-19 May 44; 165 (Ceylon) Sqn (Spit IX & Mstg III), Predannack, 19 May 44; WO, 17 Jun 44; com Plt Off, 7 Aug 44; 9 days leave, 29 Sep-7 Oct 44; 7 days leave, 23-29 Nov 44; 9 days leave, 31 Jan-8 Feb 45; Fg Off, 8 Feb 45; 9 days leave, 29 Mar-6 Apr 45; 2 days leave, 13-14 May 45; ACHU Cranfield, 9 Jul 45; 14 days leave, 19 Jul-1 Aug 45; 11 PDRC, Bnmth, 18 Aug 45; disemb Aust & to 2 PD, 5 Oct 45; 7 days leave, 6-13 Oct 45; att 2 RC, 9 Nov 45; dschgd w 7 days RL, 38 WL, & 38 re-est leave, 29 Nov 45; MiD, 1 Jan 46; d Lake Cathie NSW, 24 Aug 04

STEPP, Malta Leon Jr., 67579/O-885155, RAFVR/USAAF (American); b San Jose, CA, USA, 30 Oct 19; ed San Mateo Jr. Coll & San Jose State Coll, CA, USA; joined RAFVR, Halifax NS, Can, 30 Apr 40; flg trng Spartan SOA, Tulsa, OK, USA, 1940-41; com Prob Plt Off (67579), 1941; 56 OTU (Hurr), Sutton Bridge, Lincs, 1941; 124 (Baroda) Sqn (Spit I), Castletown, IoM, 16-18 Jul 41; 121 (Eagle) Sqn (Hurr I/IIb, Spit IIa/Vb), KiL, 18 Jul 41-23 May 42; Fg Off, 1942; Actg Flt Lt & OC A Flt, 41 Sqn, 23 May-26 Sep 42; 1 Dam FW190, Dieppe, F., 19 Aug 42; trans to USAAF as Capt, 26 Sep 42; 121 (Eagle) Sqn/335th Squadron USAAF (P-47 Thunderbolt), 4 FG/8 AF, Rochford, 26 Sep 42; 336th Sqn (P-47 Thunderbolt), Debden, 1943; visited 41 Sqn at Hwkge to show newest U.S. A/C (P-47 Thunderbolt), 26 Apr 43; 1 Dam FW190, 14 May 43; FI, 2906 Obs Grp USAAF (OTU), Atcham, Shrops, 1943; KIFA in P-47 Thunderbolt 42-7872 at Cats Tor, Chesh, whilst on trng flt from Atcham, 30 Sep 43; init bur UK, but reint Sect B, Site 741-L, Golden Gate Nat Cem, CA, 21 Jan 49

STEVENSON, Ian Turnbull 'Steve', 1348985, RAFVR; b Glasgow, Scot, 2 May 22; ed Auchterarder PS & Morrison's Academy, Crieff, Perth, Scot; joined RAFVR, Edin, 1 May 41; ACRC London, 15 Dec 41-3 Jan 42; ACDW, Brighton, 3-31 Jan 42; 4 ITW, Paignton, 4 Feb-28 Apr 42; 15 EFTS, Carlisle, 29 Apr-19 May 42; PDC, Manch, 27 May-1 Jun 42; 31 PD, Moncton NB, Can, 11 Jun-6 Jul 42; ACRC, Turner Fld, GA, USA, 8 Jul-7 Aug 42; Darr Aero Tech Flg Sch, Albany GA, 7 Aug-10 Oct 42; ACBFS (Vultee), Gunter Fld, Montgomery, AL, USA, 10 Oct-18 Dec 42; Sgt Plt, 1942; AFP trng, Craig Fld (Harv), Selma, AL, 18 Dec 42-27 Feb 43; 31 PD, Moncton NB, 2-8 Mar 43; 7 PRC, Harrogate, 17 Mar-1 Jun 43; att RAF Whitley Bay, 14-19 May 43; 17 (P)AFU (Master), Bodney, 1-28 Jun 43, & Calverley, 28 Jun-6 Jul 43; 58 OTU (Spit), Ggmth, Stirling, 13 Jul-6 Sep 43, & Balado Bridge, 6 Sep-4 Oct 43; Flt Sgt, 1943; 2 CTW, Balado

Bridge, 20 Oct-15 Nov 43; 2 TEU (Spit), Ggmth, Stirling, 15 Nov-15 Dec 43; A Flt, 41 Sqn, 21 Dec 43-6 Aug 45; ½ Dest V1 w Flt Lt L. Majewski (316 Sqn), Eastbourne, Ssx, 7 Jul 44; 1 Dest V1, SE of Dngnss, Kent, 20 Jul 44; WO, 1944; 1 Dest V1, 6m NE of Maidstone, Kent, 5 Aug 44; flew last op sortie in 41 Sqn Spit XII, MB858, w Fg Off D. F. J. Tebbit in MB850, 12 Sep 44; 2 Dest FW190D, NE of Münster, G., 14 Feb 45 (orig grntd 1 Prob & 1 Dam); 1 Dest FW190, Teschendorf Wood, G., 20 Apr 45; 1 Dest FW190, SW of Wittenberg, G., 1 May 45; DFC, 24 Jul 45; TCAHC, Morecambe, Lancs, 13-17 Aug 45; 12 FU, Melton Mowbray, 17-30 Aug 45; TCAHC, Morecambe, Lancs, 1-6 Sep 45; 229 Grp Delhi, India, 18 Oct-3 Nov 45; 17 ACHU, RAF Pocklington, Full Sutton, Yks, 4-7 Jan 46; RAF Ctk, Yks, 7-9 Jan 46; RAF Pocklington, 9-10 Jan 46; RAF Valley, Ang, 21 Jan-7 Feb 46; RAF Kirkham, Lancs, 7 Feb-7 Mar 46; post-War occ in rubber plantations, Malaya; drafted into Federation of Malaya Auxiliary Police as Hon Inspector during Malayan Emergency, 1948-60; CPM, 1 Jun 53; d Perth, Scot, 10 Feb 03

STILL, JAMES WEBSTER, 655535, RAFVR; b Edin, Scot, 14 Sep 20; ed Boroughmuir HS, Scot; enl in RAFVR on trans from RCOS, 12 Apr 41; EFTS, Reading, 1941; SFTS, Ternhill, 1941; Sgt Plt (655535), 1941; Crse 32, 53 OTU (Spit), Llandow, Glam, & KiL, 13 Apr-22 Jun 43; Flt Sgt, 1942; 41 Sqn, 5 Jul 43-LM 10 Jan 44; WO, 1943; com Prob Plt Off (161079), 30 Oct 43; poss posted to Flying Trng Cmd, Jan 44; Fg Off (WS), 30 Apr 44; FI, 57 OTU (Spit), Eshott, NBL, 1944; 1 Sqn (Spit IX), Detling, 19 Sep 44; MiD, 14 Jun 45; Flt Lt (WS), 30 Oct 45; rel com in RAFVR, rtng Flt Lt, on app to com as Fg Off in RAuxAF, 20 Aug 50 (sen 20 Aug 50); Flt Lt, 8 Oct 52; trans to RAuxAFRO, 20 Aug 55; rel com 20 Aug 60

STONIER, JACK, 610635; b Wigan, Lancs, 20 Nov 20; ed Newton GS; joined RAF, 6 Apr 38; flg trng USA; Sgt Plt, 1942; 41 Sqn, 14 Jul 42-27 Apr 43 (sent on emb leave); Flt Sgt, 1943; com Prob Plt Off (53631), 28 Sep 43; Plt Off cnfmd & to Fg Off (WS), 28 Mar 44; 1565 (Met) Flt, RAF ME, Nicosia, Cyprus, Oct 44; AFC (1565 Flt), 14 Jun 45; Flt Lt (WS), 28 Sep 45; Flt Lt, 1 Nov 47 (sen 28 Mar 47); app to SSC as Flt Lt, 16 Jun 48 (sen 28 Mar 47); ret 16 Jun 55

STOWE, WILLIAM NORTH 'Bill', J.10643, RCAF; b Edmonton, Alta, 2 Nov 22; ed Toronto, Ont; COTC, ex-RRCA, on enl in RCAF (R.105314), Toronto, 28 May 41; 1 MD, Toronto, May-Jun 41; Guard Duties, 3 BGS, Picton, Ont, Jun-Aug 41; 5 ITS, Belleville, Ont, Aug-Sep 41; 1 EFTS, Malton, Ont, Sep-Nov 41; 2 SFTS (Harv), Uplands, Ont, Nov 41-Feb 42; com Plt Off (J.10643), Mar 42; 118 Sqn RCAF (Kittyhawk), Dartmouth, NS (& subs Annette Is, Alaska), 18 Mar 42-1 Aug 43; Fg Off, Sep 42; to UK per SS *Queen Mary*, Oct 43; arr UK, 16 Oct 43; Crse 57, 57 OTU (Spit), Eshott, 7 Dec 43-25 Jan 44 & Boulmer, NBL, 25 Jan-22 Feb 44; A Flt, 41 Sqn, 24 Feb 44-24 Apr 45; Flt Lt, Mar 44; 1 Dam FW190D, Dortmund, G., 23 Jan 45; OC B Flt, 130 (Punjab) Sqn (Spit XIV), Celle, G., 24 Apr 45; 1 Dest FW190 & ½ Dest Me109, 24 Apr 45; 1 Prob Me262, 25 Apr 45; 1½ Dest FW190, 30 Apr 45; FL Spit XIV, SM833, behind Axis lines nr Lake Schwerin, G., after CD from explosion resulting from attack on MET, 2 May 45; walked back to Allied lines thru NML; OC A Flt, 41 Sqn, 9 May-20 Jun 45; 412 (Falcon) Sqn (Spit XIV), Fassberg, 20 Jun 45; DFC (130 Sqn), 24 Jul 45 (received 28 Jun 49); 430 (City of Sudbury) Ftr Recce Sqn (Spit XIV), 7 Aug 45; rtnd to UK, Aug 45; repat to Can & demob, Sep 45; joined post-War RCAF Auxiliary (120663) & to 400 (City of Toronto) Sqn (Vamp III), Downsview, 28 Jun 48-Apr 54; Flt Cdr, 1951; Wg Cdr, 1 Jun 52; OC, 400 Sqn, Sep 52; RCAF Res (Chipmunk), Regina, Sask, Jul 55-Jan 57; Eng Off, 400 Sqn (Expeditor), Malton, Ont, Mar 58; emp as eng, Rybka, Smith & Ginsler Ltd, 1958; Pres, Rybka, Smith & Ginsler, 1978-84; d 28 Oct 05

TEBBIT, DONALD FRANK JELLICOE 'Tebby', 156650, RAFVR; b Ipswich, Sflk, 23 Jul 14; ed Queen Elizabeth's Sch, Ipswich; occ Retail Dist Mgr on enl in RAFVR, 3 Aug 39; 4 EFTS, Brough, 1940; 9 SFTS (Master & Hurr), Hullavington, 1940; Sgt Plt (951767) 1940; 56 OTU (Hurr), Sutton Bridge, Lincs, 1940-41; 263 Sqn (Wlwnd I), Exeter, 17 Feb-13 Aug 41; att 286

AAC Sqn (Defiant, Hurr, Master & Oxford), Zeals, Aug 41-6 Oct 42; WO, 1 Aug 42; B Flt, 263 Sqn (Wlwnd I/Typhn Ib), Warmwell, 7 Oct 42-20 Jan 44; com Prob Plt Off (156650), 14 Aug 43; Fg Off (WS), 14 Feb 44; 3 mths leave, May-Jul 44; A Flt, 41 Sqn, 23 Jul 44-22 Feb 45; flew last op sortie by 41 Sqn Spit XII, in MB850, w Flt Sgt I. T. Stevenson in MB858, 12 Sep 44; IFA (facial burns & lacerations), EF on TO, retracted UC to stop A/C but 90-gallon jettison tank caught fire, 5 Oct 44; admtd E Grinstead for burns treatment; SD/AA/FL during attack on train in Spit XIV, RM789, W of Coesfeld/E of Dülmen, G., & captured, 22 Feb 45; Dulag Luft, Oberursel, G., 24 Feb-2 Mar 45; Rcvg Depot, Wetzlar, G., 2-3 Mar 45; Oflag XIII-A, Nuremburg, G., 5-30 Mar 45; Stalag VII-A, Moosburg, G., 30 Mar-29 Apr 45; MiD, 14 Jun 45; rtnd to 41 Sqn for visit, 14 Jul 45; res on repat, Sandhurst Ave, Ipswich, Sflk; Flt Lt (WS), 14 Aug 45; Flt Lt, 25 Apr 47 (sen 14 Feb 47); app to perm com as Flt Lt, 28 Apr 49; trans to FC Branch, 24 Sep 50 (sen 14 Aug 49); Sqn Ldr, 1 Jul 55; ret 23 Apr 65, rtng Wg Cdr

THIELE, KEITH FREDERICK, 'Jimmy', NZ.404966, RNZAF; b Christchurch, NZ, 25 Feb 21; ed Christchurch Boys' HS; occ journalist Star-Sun & res in Christchurch, on enl in RNZAF, Levin, 1 Dec 40; LAC (404966), 3 EFTS (Moth), Harwood, 20 Jan-28 Feb 41 (1st solo, 29 Jan 41); Int Crse, 2 FTS (Oxford), Woodbourne, Blenheim, 3 Mar-14 Apr 41 (20 FH dual & 25 FH solo); plt badge, 14 Apr 41; Advanced Crse, 2 FTS (Oxford), Woodbourne, 15 Apr-22 May 41 (13 FH dual & 33 FH solo); com Prob Plt Off (404966), 24 May 41; emb leave, 25 May 41; emb NZ for Montreal & to 1 MD, Toronto, Ont, Can, 18 Jun 41; emb Montreal for UK, 19 Jul 41; disemb UK & to 3 PRC, Bnmth, Hants, 31 Jul 41; 22 OTU (Wlngtn), Wellesbourne, 3 Aug-2 Oct 41; 405 (Vncvr) Sqn (Wlngtn & subs Halifax), Pocklington, 15 Oct 41 (1st op, 31 Oct 41); Actg Sqn Ldr, 9 May 42; att Halifax Conv Crse, 1652 CU, Marston Moor, 18 Apr-18 May 42; Fg Off, 24 May 42; Flt Lt, 9 Aug 42; DFC (405 Sqn), 11 Aug 42; att Crse 3, 1501 BAT Flt, Abingdon, Berks, 17-22 Aug 42; att 10 OTU (Whitley V), Abingdon, 15-18 Sep 42; 3 FIS, ECFS Hullavington, 19 Sep-11 Oct 42; rvtd to Flt Lt & to 1661 Lanc Conv Flt, Waddington, 1-24 Dec 42; B Flt, 467 (Aust) Sqn (Lanc), Bottesford, Notts, 24 Dec 42-12 May 43 (tour exp); C Flt Cdr & Actg Sqn Ldr, 30 Mar 43; CD/AA (both starboard engines u/s, plt's Perspex windscreen & m/u turret blown in, multiple shrapnel holes in skin) in Lanc III, LM310, after bombing sortie to Duisburg, WUL/NI, Coltishall, 03:55, 13 May 43; DSO (467 Sqn), 14 May 43; 1st Bar to DFC (467 Sqn), 28 May 43; 24 Sqn (DC-3, Hudson, Wlngtn a.o.), Hendon, 9 Jun 43; HQ, 45 (AF) Grp, 10 Jul 43; Ferry Plt, 45 (AF) Grp (Anson, DC-3, Hudson, Mariner, Lanc, Liberator, Ventura), Dorval, Can, Jul-Sep 43; conv to ftr plt, Crse 57, 57 OTU (Spit), Eshott, 7 Dec 43-25 Jan 44 & Boulmer, NBL, 25 Jan-22 Feb 44; B Flt, 41 Sqn, 24 Feb-18 Aug 44; 1 Dest V1, Channel off Cliff End, Ssx, 14 Jul 44; conv crse to Tmpst & Typhn, 2 GSU, Swanton Morley, 18 Aug 44; 83 GSU (Mstg, Spit & Typhn), Bognor Regis, Ssx, 6-24 Sep 44, Thorney Is, 24 Sep-13 Oct 44; 486 (NZ) Sqn (Tmpst V), Volkel, NL, 13 Oct-12 Dec 44; Flt Cdr, 3 Sqn (Tmpst V), Volkel, NL, 14 Dec 44; 1 Dest Me109, 24 Dec 44; OC, 3 Sqn, 26 Dec 44; 1 Dest Me109, 29 Dec 44; 2x½ Dest FW190s & 1½ Dest Ju52/3m's on grnd, 14 Jan 45; AA/SD/FDF/WIA (burns to eyes, face & wrists) in Tmpst I, NV644, during attack on train N of Dortmund, baled out E of Dorsten & captured, 10 Feb 45; held at Dortmund A/D, 12-17 Feb 45; Dulag Luft, Oberursel, G., 18-22 Feb 45; hosp for inj, Hohemark, 22 Feb-6 Mar 45; Rcvg Depot, Wetzlar, G., 6-31 Mar 45; escaped w another ex-41 Sqn pilot, Sqn Ldr T. Spencer, when main gate of camp was left open & reached Allied lines by bicycle & subs motorcycle, 31 Mar 45; rtnd to 3 Sqn, 2 Apr 45 (LF 4 Apr 45); 2nd Bar to DFC, 8 May 45; rtnd to NZ Sep 45; Actg Sqn Ldr & OC, Auck Wg, Air Trng Grp, 2 Oct 45; Wigram, 17 Dec 45; No 3 Refresher Crse (Harv, Hudson, Oxford), CFS, Wigram, 4 Feb 46; rvtd to Flt Lt, 2 May 46; rel com, & dschgd in UK, 5 Dec 46; emp as plt with LAMS Ltd, Stansted UK, flying ex-RAF Halifaxes worldwide, 1946-48; stuck in Aust when coy went into liquidation, Mar 48; emp as plt with QANTAS, 1948-64; built & operated Marina at The Spit, Sydney NSW, 1964-74; sailed, 1974-78; hobby yachtsman

THOMAS, John Islwyn, 1576607, RAFVR; b Merthyr Tydfil, Glam, 5 Nov 20; ed Lewis' Sch, Pengam, & Goldsmith's Coll; occ Sch Master on joining RAFVR, Birm, Jul 40; 5 BFTS (Stearman, Vultee & Harv), Riddle McKay Aero Coll, Riddle Fld, Clewiston, FL, USA, 1940-41; Sgt Plt (1576607); OTU, 1942; 41 Sqn, 16 Nov 42-24 Apr 43; FA/CL during NFE, Llanbedr, 23 Jan 43; KIFA in Spit XII, EN610, EF (broken oil pipe) in tight turn in preparation for landing, CL nr White Horse Inn, Canterbury Road, Hwkge, Kent, on rtn from a shipping recce, 24 Apr 43, aged 22; s of late John B. & late Jessie M. Thomas; bur Grave 190, Hengoed Welsh Baptist Chapelyard, Glam, Wales

UNDERWOOD, Bernard Walter 'Barney', 925018, RAFVR; b Bury St Edmonds, Sflk, 29 Feb 20; occ Clerk, Cty Accountant, W Sflk Cty Council; learnt to fly w Civ Air Guard, grad Jun 39; joined RAFVR, 1940; 22 EFTS (Moth), Cambridge, 16 Nov 40; 33 SFTS (Anson), Carberry, Man, Can, 2 Feb 41; Sgt Plt, May 41; 61 OTU (Spit), Heston, Mdx, 10 Jul-15 Aug 41; WUL (could not lower UC) in Spit I, N3281, Heston, 21 Jul 41; 19 Sqn (Spit IIa), Coltishall, Nflk, 31 Aug-15 Oct 41; 41 Sqn, 23 Oct-19 Nov 41; 2 days leave, 16 Nov 41; NE sick, RAF Tang, 19 Nov 41 (op on sinuses, temp restriction to 10,000 ft); rested, 58 OTU (Spit), Ggmth, Stirling, 31 Mar-4 Jul 42; Flt Sgt, 1942; 41 Sqn (again), ca 12 Aug-1 Oct 42; NE sick (sinuses), Oct 42-Feb 43; refresher Crse, 5 (P)AFU (Master I/II), Ternhill, 26 Feb-8 May 43; Temp WO, 1943; com Prob Plt Off (183184), 2 Aug 44; ferry plt, SAC, 748 Sqn FAA, Seafire Pool, RNAS Dale, Pembroke (& subs RNAS Stretton, Lancs), Nov 44; Plt Off cnfmd & to Fg Off (WS), 2 Feb 45; demob, 13 Mar 46; emp post-War w W Sflk Cty Council; rel com in RAFVR, rtng Fg Off, on app to com as Fg Off (5 yrs), in ACB of recons RAFVR, 24 Oct 52; svce ext 5 yrs, 24 Oct 57; joined friend to run fruit importing coy, Kent, 1958; Flt Lt, GDB (Photographic Interpretation), 19 Feb 59; rel com in GDB, 24 Oct 62, rtng Flt Lt; retired 1986; d 14 Feb 11

VAN GOENS, Rijklof, see GOENS, Rijklof van

VANN, William H., 1123162, RAFVR; b Ashton-under-Lyne, Lancs, 29 Nov 21; ed Stamford HS, Lincs; joined RAFVR, Padgate, 10 Oct 40; 5 ITW, Torquay, Jan-Jun 41; 8 EFTS, Woodley, Jun-Aug 41; 8 SFTS, Montrose, Scot, Sep 41-Apr 42; Sgt Plt (1123162), 1942; 59 OTU (Hurr), Crosby-on-Eden, Cumb, May-Jun 42; 243 Sqn (Spit Vb/VI), Ouston, 24 Jun 42-14 Mar 43 (1st op, 31 Jul 42); to N Africa, arr Philippeville [Skikda], Algeria, 7 Dec 43; ACTC, Algiers, 14 Mar 43; Flt Sgt, 1943; 41 Sqn, 21 Jul-LM 24 Dec 43; 1 Dam FW190, W of Évreux, F., 22 Sep 43; WO, 1 May 44-Jul 47

VINE, Edward Ernest, 1114209, RAFVR; b Liv, Lancs, 7 Jun 21; occ invoice clerk; ed Liv Institute HS; joined RAFVR, Padgate, 28 Aug 40; USAAC, Lakeland FL, 1941; ACBFS (Vultee), Gunter Fld, Montgomery, AL, 1941-42; Sgt Plt (1114209), 1942; AFP trng, Craig Fld (Harv), Selma, AL, USA, 1942; 41 Sqn late Jul-LM 4 Nov 42; emb UK for Malta, Dec 42; 1435 Sqn (Spit Vc), Luqa, Malta, 17 Jan 43; SD/WIA by Me109, 6m S of Comiso, Italy, 3 Mar 43 [see also pp. 19-24, 'Black Crosses off my Wingtip' by Sqn Ldr I. F. 'Hap' Kennedy, 1994 (2005) ISBN 0919431828]; rescued & captured (POW 83765) & hosp, Sicily, 3-28 Mar 43; hosp Freising, G., 1-30 Apr 43; Stalag VII-A, Moosburg, G., 30 Apr-16 Jun 43; escaped May 43, but captured 5 days later nr Munich; Stalag Luft I, Barth, G., 19 Jun-7 Nov 43; Stalag Luft VI, Heydekrug, E Prussia, 7 Nov 43-15 Jul 44; Stalag Luft IV, Gross Tychow, G. (Tychowo, PL), 19 Jul 44-6 Feb 45; forced march to Hannover; address on repat, Meols, Chesh

WAGNER, Herbert Appleton 'Wag', 130242, RAFVR (American); b Garrison, Maryland, USA, 10 Nov 20; ed St Paul's Sch, Princeton Uni, Johns Hopkins Uni, 1940-41; occ insurance off on enl in RAFVR, RAF Delegation, Washington DC, Oct 41; 2 BFTS (Stearman, Vultee & Harv), Polaris Flt Academy, War Eagle Fld, Lanc CA, USA, Jan-Jul 42; plt badge & com Prob Plt

Off (130242), Aug 42; emb NYC for Glasgow per HMTS *Queen Mary*, Sep 42; 53 OTU (Spit I/II), Rhoose, Glam, Sep 42; Staff Plt, 53 OTU, Nov 42-Apr 43; IFA, baled out of Spit IIa, P7822, after MAC, flown into by student plt assumed dazzled by sunlight (Fg Off R. A. H. Nelson †) in Spit I, X4067, during fmtn flg practice over Bristol Channel, 1m S of RAF St Athan, Glam, 15 Feb 43; Fg Off, Feb 43; 41 Sqn, 2 May 43-2 Jun 44; leave, 20-27 Sep 43; SD/AA, Brehon Is, Guernsey, in Spit XII, MB843, during shipping recce, baled out at 3,000 ft & captured (POW 4711), 2 Jun 44; init held in Chartres, F.; Dulag Luft, Oberursel, G., Jun 44; Stalag Luft I, Barth, G., 24 Jul 44-1 May 45; Flt Lt, Aug 44; com resigned, 30 Oct 45, rtng Flt Lt; post-War occ, ran own companies, incl Blakeslee-Lane Inc, specialising in corporate buyouts; d Owings Mills, Maryland, USA, 26 Nov 05

WALL, Peter R., 1387647, RAFVR; b Croydon, Surrey, 11 May 21; joined RAFVR, ACRC Lords Cricket Grnd, 1941; ITW, Clare Coll, Cambridge, 1941; BFTS, FLA, GA & AL, USA, 1941-42 (200 FH); Sgt Plt & Flt Sgt (1387647), 1942; 17 (P)AFU (Master), Bodney, Nflk, 1942; Drogue Towing duties, 61 OTU (Lysander & Martinet), Rednal & W Felton, 1942-43; op trng, OTU, 1943; 41 Sqn, 5 May 43-LM 4 Dec 43; FA in Spit XII, MB844 (Cat B), lndd w/o flaps & struck Fg Off J. A. Sabourin in Spit XII, EN603 (Cat E), 4 Dec 43; posted to Flg Trng Cmd as Inst (Oxford), Dec 43; Instr, 3 (P)AFU, Southrop, Gloucs, 1944; Instr, 3 FIS (Master & Oxford), Lulsgate Bottom, Bristol, 1944; Instr, 18 (P)AFU (Harv), Church Lawford, 1945; post-War occ Home Office; ret May 81; OBE, Nov 81; d 2003

WARE, James Philip 'Jimmy', A.420311, RAAF; b Epping NSW, Aust, 4 Feb 21; ed Teralba PS & Newcastle Jun Boys HS; res Narrabeen NSW & occ stone quarryman & timber cutter on enl in RAAF, Syd, 11 Oct 41; AC2, Crse 22, 2 ITS Brdfld Pk NSW, 11 Oct 41; LAC, 28 Feb 42; Crse 24, 8 EFTS (Wirraway), Narrandera NSW, 30 Apr 42; admtd Narrandera Dist Hosp, 29 Jul-1 Aug 42; Crse 25, 5 SFTS Uranquinty NSW, 10 Aug 42; plt badge, 15 Oct 42; Sgt Plt, 17 Dec 42; high alt flg crse, Melb, 28-31 Dec 42; 2 OTU Mildura NSW, 3 Jan 43; 1 ED Ascot Vale VIC, 6 Jan 43; 2 ED Brdfld Pk NSW, 13 Jan 43; 1 ED Ascot Vale VIC, 24 Feb 43; emb Melb for UK, 6 Mar 43; disemb UK, 17 Apr 43; 11 PDRC, Bnmth, 18 Apr 43; att Whitley Bay, 12 May-2 Jun 43; Flt Sgt, 17 Jun 43; 17 (P)AFU (Master), Calverley, 29 Jun 43; admonished for interfering w fmtn of A/C to which he did not belong, 27 Jul 43; 58 OTU (Spit), Ggmth, Stirling, 7 Sep 43; 53 OTU (Spit), KiL, 5 Oct 43; 1 TEU (Spit & Hurr), Tealing, Angus, 10 Feb 44; SR for damaging AM property (pushed a panel out of a hut door) & ordered pay cost of damage of 15/9, 21 Feb 44; att RAF Boulmer, 13 Mar-3 Apr 44; refresher Crse, ACRS, Sheffield, 15 Apr-9 May 44; B Flt, 41 Sqn, 8 Jun-1 Nov 44 (50 sorties, incl 39 anti-Diver); WO, 17 Jun 44; 1 Dest V1, N of Hollingbourne, Kent, 18 Aug 44; 10 days leave, 11-20 Sep 44; SR & grndd by GCM (21 Nov-7 Dec 44) for striking 2 grnd staff of Stn Flt & 2784 RAF Regt, Lympne, 21 Oct 44 (found guilty on 1st charge but not 2nd); att RAF Stn Hwkge, 2 Nov 44-1 Feb 45; 9 days leave, 22-30 Jan 45; 451 (Aust) Sqn (Spit XVI), Hwkge, 2 Feb 45 (last op flt, 22 Mar 45, LF 24 Mar 45); complained of headaches after flg & requested max of 1 flt per day, but grndd, 24 Mar 45; marr Alice, 26 Mar 45; posted RAF Coltishall, 6 Apr 45; 11 PDRC, 9 May 45; demoted to AC1 Gen Hand & plt badge withdrawn as "unsuitable aircrew" & "lacking in moral fibre" (NAA Personnel File, A9301, 5528423), 11 Jul 45; admtd RAFH Halton, 15-19 Aug 45; 2 PD, 19 Oct 45 (forfeited £4 for loss of equipment); 7 days SL, 24-30 Nov 45; dschgd 'services no longer required w disciplinary effect', no leave or payment in lieu granted, 22 Jan 46; total flg w RAAF/RAF 60 sorties, incl 39 anti-Diver sorties, 11 armed recces, 4 sweeps, 3 shipping recces & 3 bomber escorts, 76.05 FH); fought dschgd w support of MP W. C. Wentworth, & case subs reviewed by Air Board, which deleted 'w disciplinary effect', 10 Feb 55; post-War occ, surf lifesaver, Syd NSW; d Syd, 16 May 2002, bur Palmdale NSW

WARREN, Kenneth George, 1203923, RAFVR; b Hampton in Arden, nr Birm, 18 Jan 20; ed King Edward GS & Coll of Art, Birm; joined RAF, Cardington, 27 Jul 40; 5 ITW, Torquay,

Cornwall, Aug-Nov 40; 2 BFTS (Stearman, Vultee & Harv), Polaris Flt Academy, Grand Central Air Terminal, Glendale, CA, & subs War Eagle Fld, Lanc, CA, USA (90 FH), 1941-42; USAAF badge & RAF plt badge, 1942; Crse 14, 53 OTU (Spit), Llandow, Glam, Wales, grad 17 Mar 42 (7 FH); 41 Sqn, 1 Apr-2 Sep 42; ¼ Dam Ju88D w Sgt Plt L. A. Prickett & 2 plts from 315 (Dębliński) Sqn, 20m SSE of Dublin, Éire, 14 Aug 42; emb for Takoradi, Ghana, Sep 42; 5-day, 3,600m ferry flt of 6 Spit Vb's led by 1 Beau from Takoradi to Abu Sueir, Egypt, Nov 42; 92 (E India) Sqn (Spit Vb/c), Medenine, Tunisia, 4 Mar 43; WO, Sep 43; com Prob Plt Off (174221), 15 Jan 44; Fg Off (WS), 15 Jul 44; Flt Lt (WS), 15 Jan 46; HQ 244 Wg, Treviso, Italy, 1947; emgtd to Can, 1954; occ chief designer, JB Parkind architects, Toronto; d 28 Dec 09

WEEDS, Brian Morrell, NZ.413525, RNZAF; b Invercargill, NZ, 15 Apr 22; enl in RNZAF, LAC Airman Pilot, 15 Jun 41; 1 ITW, Levin, 15 Jun-25 Jul 41; 1 EFTS, Taieri, 26 Jul-5 Sep 41; emb Auck for SF USA (via Fiji, Pago Pago, Honolulu & San Diego), per SS *Monterey*, 22 Sep 41; arr SF USA & att RCAF, 7 Oct 41; to Brandon, Man, Can, via Vncvr by train; 12 SFTS, Brandon, Man, 9 Oct 41-12 Feb 42; plt badge & to Sgt Plt; 16 Jan 42; 1Y Depot, Halifax NS, 25 Feb-1 Mar 42; emb for UK, 1 Mar 42; arr in UK, 9 Mar 42; PRC, Bournemouth, 10 Mar-18 Apr 42; PRC, Harrogate, 19-27 Apr 42; 11 AFU, Shawbury, 28 Apr-6 Jun 42; att 1524 BAT Flt, Newton, 17-24 May 42; 1521 BAT Flt, Stradishall, 7-13 Jun 42; 13 OTU (Spit & Mosq), Bicester, Oxon, 16 Jun-7 Sep 42; 487 (Light Bomber) Sqn RNZAF (Ventura), Feltwell & Methwold, 18 Sep 42-5 Jun 43; att 1508 BAT Flt, Horsham, 22-25 Nov 42; Flt Sgt, 1 May 43; ACRC Eastchurch, 6 Jun-12 Jul 43; Crse 67, 5 (P)AFU (Master), Ternhill, Tatenhill & Chetwynd, 13 Jul-26 Dec 43; 61 OTU (Spit), Rednal & Montford Bridge, Salop, 27 Dec 43-18 Mar 44; 3 TEU (Hurr & Typhn), Annan, Dumfries, 13 Apr-8 May 44; WO, 1 May 44; 587 AAC Sqn (Henley III, Hurr II/IV, Martinet I, Oxford I/III), Culmhead, 9 May-2 Jun 44; 3 TEU (Hurr & Typhn), Annan, Dumfries, 3-10 Jun 44; 3501 GSU (Spit XIV), Cranfield, Bucks, 11 Jun-23 Jul 44; 26 Sqn (Mstg & Spit), Lee-on-Solent, 23 Jul-17 Aug 44; 41 Sqn, 18 Aug-9 Oct 44 (9 hrs 45 mins on Spit XII); IFA (right knee & forehead) stalled on landing, CL Spit XII, MB862, Lympne, 11 Sep 44; hosp in SSQ, Lympne, 11-12 Sep 44; PDC Brighton, 10 Oct-1 Nov 44; to NZ, 2 Nov 44-1 Jan 45; dschgd, 14 Apr 45; emp Cable Price Steel; ret 1982; d Invercargill, NZ, 13 Feb 98

WELSH, Terence Deane, 42033, RAF; b Staines, Mdx, 28 Jan 15; joined RAF, Brough, 4 Feb 39; 4 EFTS, Brough, 1939; grntd SSC as Prob APO, 29 Apr 39; 12 FTS, Grantham, 1939; 264 Sqn (Defiant I) O/F, Sutton Bridge, 4 Nov 39-27 May 41; Prob Plt Off, 6 Nov 39; Plt Off, 6 Mar 40 (sen adjusted to 6 Feb 40, WEF 12 Jul 40); att Nav Crse, St Athan, Glam, 5-10 May 40; ⅓ Dest He111, 27 May 40; 1 Dest Me109E, 1 Dest Me110 & 2 Dest Ju87s, 29 May 40; 1 Dest Ju88 & 1 Dam Me109E, 24 Aug 40; Fg Off (WS), 6 Feb 41; DFC, 11 Feb 41; 1 Dest He111, Beachy Hd, 12/13 Mar 41; OC A Flt, 125 Sqn (Defiant I/II) O/F, Colerne, 28 May-12 Nov 41; FI, 60 OTU (Blenheim & Defiant), High Ercall, ca 13 Nov 41; 277 (ASR) Sqn (Defiant), Hwkge, ca Jan-Jul 42; Flt Lt (WS), 6 Feb 42; 1 Sqn (Hurr I/IIb & Typhn Ib), Acklgtn, 23 Jul (arr 30 Jul) 42; att BAT Crse, 1529 Flt, Wtrng, 9-16 Aug 42; 41 Sqn, FM 5 Nov-LM 20 Dec 43; trans to ASD Branch, 27 Mar 45; dschgd, 5 May 54; d 1980

WHALE, Frederick Victor 'Vickie', 1376359, RAFVR; b Lon, 14 Apr 20; ed Enfield Tech Coll; joined Euston Hse, Lon, 23 Aug 40; 9 RC, Blackpool, Lancs, Aug-Oct 40; RAF Drem, Oct 40-Jan 41; 10 (Sigs) RC, Blackpool, Jan-Mar 41; RAF Middleton-St. George, Dur, Mar-May 41; RAF Leconfield, Yks, May-Jun 41; 4 ITW, Paignton, Jun-Sep 41; 15 EFTS, Carlisle, Cumb, Sep-Dec 41; 32 SFTS (Harv), Bowden, Alta, Can, Jan-Feb 42 & Moose Jaw, Sask, Feb-Jun 42; 31 BGS, Picton, Ont, Jun-Sep 42; 41 SFTS, Weyburn, Sask, Sep 42; 31 SFTS, Kingston, Ont, Oct 42-12 Mar 43; 31 PD, Moncton NB, 15-27 Mar 43; 7 PRC, Harrogate, 4-23 Apr 43; RAF Whitley Bay, 28 Apr-31 May 43; 7 (P)AFU, Wrexham, 1 Jun-8 Aug 43; 56 OTU, Tealing, 10 Aug-3 Oct 43; 56 OTU, Milfield, 4 Oct-23 Nov 43; RAF Brunton (det to Army), 23 Nov-23

Dec 43; 1 TEU (Spit & Hurr), Tealing, Angus, 28 Jan-4 Mar 44; RAF Kinnell, 4-27 Mar 44; RAF Tealing, 27 Mar-3 Apr 44; 3 TEU (Hurr & Typhn), Annan, Dumfries, 4 Apr-30 May 44; 83 GSU (Spit XIV), Redhill, 1 Jun-Jul 44; WO, 1944; 83 GSU, Bognor Regis, Thorney Is, Whmpnt & Dnsfld, Jul 44-Jan 45; 41 Sqn, 7 Mar 45-12 Feb 46; RF/FL in Russian zone nr Rostock in Tmpst V w Fg Off G. S. West-Jones, 6 Dec 45, rtnd 14 Dec 45; 9 MFH, 12 Feb 46; sent home to hosp for pleurisy, admtd RAFH Wroughton; 22 Feb 46; demob, Mar 46; grntd SSC as Plt Off (1376359, 8 yrs on AL & 4 yrs, in Res), Cardington, 14 Apr 49 (sen 28 Feb 49); OCTU, Spital Gate, Mar-Apr 49; 1 (P)RFU, Finningly, May-Jun 49; RAF Benson, Jun 49; 237 OCU, Leuchars, Jul-Sep 49; 541 Sqn, Benson, Sep 49-Nov 52; Fg Off, 14 Apr 50; Flt Lt, 14 Oct 52; RAF Ahlhorn, G, Nov 52; ext svce on AL ext to 9 yrs from 28 Feb 49 (gaz 27 Jul 56); trans to RAFO as Flt Lt, 28 Feb 58; rel com, 28 Feb 61, rtng Flt Lt; d 19 Aug 2000

WHEATLEY, Peter Etherington, 1537032, RAFVR; b Hull, Yks, 13 Feb 22; ed Hull GS & Manch Uni (member, Manch UAS); joined RAFVR, Padgate, 16 Jul 41; 16 EFTS, Derby, 1941; 33 SFTS (Anson), Carberry, Man, Can, 1942; Sgt Plt, 1942; Flt Sgt, 1943; 57 OTU (Spit), Eshott, NBL, 1945; WO, 1944; 41 Sqn, 10 Apr 45-7 Jan 46; EF/FL/IFA (burns), Lübeck, in Tmpst V, 18 Oct 45; to 2 FIS, Yatesbury, 7 Jan 46; d Hull, Dec 89

WHITE, Frederick Cheslyn, A.403614, RAAF; b Ashfield NSW, Aust, 19 Mar 16; ed Parramatta HS; occ Carpenter's Assist (apprent 1938-40) & res Lidcombe NSW, on enl, 2RC, Syd, 3 Feb 41; AC2, 3 Feb 41; Crse 11, 8 EFTS (Moth), Narrandera NSW, 3 Apr 41; LAC, 2 ITS, 29 Mar 41; 2ED, Brdfld Pk NSW, 29 May 41; att RCAF & emb Syd for Can, 13 Jun 41; Crse 11, 2 SFTS (Harv), Uplands, Ottawa, Ont, 3 Jul 41; forfeited 1 day pay for AWOL, 26-27 Jun 41; plt badge & Sgt Plt, 25 Sep 41; 1Y Depot, Halifax, 27 Sep-6 Oct 41; att RAF & emb Halifax for UK, 7 Oct 41; disemb UK & to 3 PRC, Bournemouth, Hants, 19 Oct 41; 9 SFTS (Master & Hurr), Hullavington, 4 Nov 41; Crse 13, 52 OTU (Spit), Aston Down, Gloucs, 29 Dec 41-10 Mar 42; 452 (Aust) Sqn (Spit Vb), Andreas, IOM, 10 Mar 42; admtd Mil Hosp, Douglas, IOM, 29 Mar 42; admtd Mil Hosp, Preston, 29 Mar-10 Apr 42; NE sick, RAF Andreas, IOM, 20 May 42; admtd Mil Hosp, Preston, 5 Aug 42; 41 Sqn, 2 Sep-15 Oct 42 (2 sorties, 33.15 FH); admtd Moreton Hall Hosp, Chester, 3 Sep 42; 6 days op leave, 14 Sep 42; 9 PDC, 16-22 Oct 42 (emb for Aust); disemb Melb, detached RAF & to 1 ED, 7 Jan 43; 2 ED, 21 Jan 43; 2 OTU (Wirraway & Spit), Mildura NSW, 27 Jan 43; Flt Sgt, 1 Feb 43; att 4 ED, 22 Feb 43 (1 day); att 1 ED, 24 Feb 43 (1 day); 55 PD, Darwin, 28 Feb 43; 457 (Aust) Sqn (Spit Vc), Livingstone NT, 8 Mar 43 (11 sorties, 88.45 FH); NI in Spit Vc, BR568, in COG with Spit Vc, BS171, after landing on FF w 457 (Aust) Sqn, Livingstone, 19 Mar 43; reprimanded under Sect 39, forfeited £5 pay, 23 Mar 43; 14 days ops leave, 18 Sep-6 Oct 43; app for com declined, 17 Nov 43; 55 RPP, 18 Nov 43; 2ED, 29 Nov 43; disemb leave, 30 Nov-14 Dec 43; test & ferry plt, 2AP (Anson, Auster, Boomerang, D.H.12, Kittyhawk, Moth, Mstg, Oxford, Ryan, Seafire, Shrike, Spit, Vengeance, Vultee, Wirraway), Amberley QLD (subs Bankstown, Oakey & Richmond), 15 Dec 43 (575 FH); 2 days leave, 19-20 Jan 44; WO, 1 Feb 44; 2 days leave, 22-23 Feb 44; 7 days leave, 19-25 Jun 44; 5 days leave, 22-27 Aug 44; 10 days leave, 3-12 Oct 44; com Plt Off, 1 Nov 44; att 6AD, 18 Dec 44-11 Mar 45; 9 days leave, 29 Jan-6 Feb 45; att 3AD, 12 Mar 45; Fg Off 1 May 45; 10 days leave, 24 Dec 45; 3 (C) Unit, 11 Jan 46; 2 PD, 6 May-4 Aug 46; demob & rlsd from RAAF, 8 Aug 46; post-War occ, builder; d Mona Vale NSW, 28 Apr 91

WILKINSON, John Francis 'Johnnie', 150189, RAFVR; b Northampton, 1 Feb 23; ed Christs Hospital, Horsham, Ssx; joined RAFVR, Birm, 17 Dec 41; 2 ITW, Cambridge, 1942; LAC (1581574), 5 BFTS (Stearman, Vultee & Harv), Riddle McKay Aero Coll, Riddle Fld, Clewiston, FL, USA, 1942-43; com Prob Plt Off (150189), 20 Feb 43; 57 OTU (Spit), Eshott, NBL, 1943; 2 TEU (Spit), Ggmth, Stirling, 1943-44; Fg Off (WS), 20 Aug 43; 3501 GSU (Spit XIV), Cranfield, Bucks, 20 May 44; A Flt, 41 Sqn, 21 Jul 44-30 Dec 45; ½ Dest V1 w Flt Sgt Jakub Bargielowski

(315 Sqn), E of Ashford, Kent, 11 Aug 44; Flt Lt (WS), 20 Feb 45; 1 Dest FW190, Hagenow, G., 16 Apr 45; ½ Dest FW190 w Sqn Ldr J. B. Shepherd, nr Neuruppin, G., 20 Apr 45; ½ Dest FW190 w Sgt Plt P. F. Scott, Teschendorf Wood, G., 20 Apr 45; 1 Dest FW190, Schwerin, G., 28 Apr 45; ½ Dest FW190 w Flt Lt F. A. O. Gaze, Schwerin, G., 28 Apr 45; 2 FIS, 30 Dec 45; FI, after War [see also private papers, 38pp & photographs, IWM, ID 12780 03/32/1]

WILSON, GEORGE S., 1007094, Trinidadian; b St James, Trinidad, 13 May 22; ed Queen's Royal Coll & Strathallan Sch, Scot; joined RAFVR, Padgate, 22 Jul 40; 22 EFTS (Moth), Cambridge, 1940; 11 SFTS (Harv), Yorkton, Sask, Can, 1941; Sgt Plt (1007094), 1941; Flt Sgt, 1942; 53 OTU, Stormy Down, Glam, 1942-43; EF/WUL in Spit K9801, 6 Feb 1943; 41 Sqn, 11 Mar-LM 20 May 43; WO, 1943

WOOD, ROBERT LESLIE 'Woody', 119101, RAFVR; b Gorleston-on-Sea, Nflk, 25 May 22; ed Great Yarmouth GS; joined RAFVR, Norwich, 1 Jan 41; flg trng, Terrell, TX, 1941; Sgt Plt (1331378), 1942; com Prob Plt Off, 24 Jan 42; B Flt, 41 Sqn, 14 Jul-21 Oct 42; Prob Fg Off (WS), 1 Oct 42; 1435 Sqn (Spit Vc), Luqa, FM 19 Nov 42; 609 (W Riding) Sqn (Typhn 1B), Mstn, 11 Nov 43; Flt Lt (WS), 24 Jan 44; AA/KIA in Typhn 1b, MN544, during attack on radar stn. nr Fécamp, F., & crashed into Hse, 11 May 44, aged 21; s of Herbert L. & Ivy E Wood of Great Dunmow, Esx; rmbd Panel 204, Runnymede Mem

WOOLLARD, FREDERICK GILBERT 'Freddie', 1312058, RAFVR; b Newtown, Berkley, Gloucs, 20 Dec 20; ed Dursley HS; joined RAFVR, Uxb, 16 Nov 40; 7 ITW, Newquay, 1940; 18 EFTS, Fairoaks, 1941; 9 SFTS (Master & Hurr), Hullavington, 1941; Sgt Plt, 1941; 59 OTU (Hurr), Crosby-on-Eden, Cumb, 1941-42; B Flt, 33 Sqn (Hurr IIb/c), Sidi Haneish, Libya, 28 Mar 42 (22.5 FH); CD (oil tank) from Me109, FL Hagiag el Baheira, ESE of Tobruk, 20 Apr 42; SD/WIA in Hurr IIc, 3 Jul 42 (DNR); staff, 61 OTU (Spit), Rednal, Salop, 1943; Flt Sgt, 1943; FA/WUL in Spit IIa, P7447, 21 Sep 43; 2 TEU (Spit), Ggmth, Stirling, 1943; B Flt, 41 Sqn, 18 Dec 43-18 Jul 44, ½ Dest V1 with Fg Off M. A. L. Balasse, 1m W of Lydd/N of Rye, Ssx, 4 Jul 44; CL/IFA (face), HL at Lympne in Spit XII, MB841, 18 Jul 44; admtd E Grinstead Hosp for plastic surgery on nose (became one of Dr. Sir Archibald McIndoe's 'Guinea Pigs')

WOOLLEY, FRANK GEOFFREY, 105174, RAFVR; b Derby, 1 Jun 22; ed ISC, Maidenhead; joined RAFVR, LAC (785004), Sngpr, 17 Jul 40; 4 AACU, Aug 40; 4 SFTS, Habbaniyah, Iraq, Sep 40-Mar 41; com Prob Plt Off (105174), 29 Mar 41; 244 Sqn (Vincent), Shaibah, Iraq, 29 Mar 41-Apr 42; DFC (244 Sqn), 15 Jul 41; SD/WIA in error by 261 Sqn Hurr, S Iran, 26 Aug 41; Plt Off cnfmd & to Fg Off (WS), 29 Mar 42; to SA, Apr 42; to UK, Sep 42; Crse 42, 57 OTU (Spit), Hwdn, 13 Oct 42; 132 Sqn (Spit Vb), Martlesham Hth, 25 Jan-31 Oct 43; Flt Lt (WS), 29 Mar 43; OC B Flt, 602 (City of Glasgow) Sqn (Spit IX), Detling, 1 Nov 43-7 Jul 44 (tour exprd); 1 Dam FW190D, 2 Jul 44; FLS, HQ ADGB, Aston Down, Gloucs, Jul-Oct 44; CFE, Wtrg, Oct-Dec 44; 83 GSU (Mstg, Spit & Typhn), Dnsfld, Dec 44-12 Jan 45; 41 Sqn, 29 Jan-28 Feb 45 (1st op flt, 6 Feb 45); OC A Flt, 13 Feb-28 Feb 45; 1 Dest FW190D (orig claimed PD, reduced to Dam, but actually Dest) but CD/AA (tail, elevators & rudder) in Spit XIV, RM791, Rheine A/D, G., 14 Feb 45; OC, 350 (Belgian) Sqn (Spit XIV), Eindhoven, 1 Mar-10 Apr 45; 1 Dest FW190D, 13 Mar 45; OC, 130 (Punjab) Sqn (Spit XIV), Twente NL, 10 Apr 45-23 Jul 46; 1 Dest Me108, 22 Apr 45; 1 Dest Si204, 25 Apr 45; 1 Dest FW190A, 28 Apr 45; Bar to DFC (130 Sqn), 24 Jul 45; grntd perm com as Flt Lt, 1 Jul 46 (sen 1 Sep 45, gaz 29 Apr 47); HQ 11 Grp, 23 Jul 46; grntd ext svce as Flt Lt (4 yrs on AL), 15 Aug 46; 54 Sqn (Vamp), Odiham, Dec 47-Feb 49; KCVSA, 1 Jan 49; EFS, Hullavington, Feb 49-Apr 51; Sqn Ldr, 1 Jul 49; Air Min, Jul 49; dep Dir of Org (P), Air Min, Oct 51; student, Staff Coll, Bracknell, Jan 53; 209 AFS, Dec 53; Wg Cdr Flg, 123 Wg, Wunstorf, G., Feb 54-Aug 56; Wg Cdr, 1 Jan 56; AFC, 31 May 56; Instr, Staff Coll, Bracknell, Sep 56-Jul 59; Flg Coll (Cnbra), Manby, Jul 59; EF on TO/KIFA in Cnbra

B.2, WH699, 2m WSW of Strubby, Lincs, 28 Nov 59 (Sqn Ldr P. M. Walker & Wg Cdr C. E. Ness survived)

ZIMEK, JAN JÓZEF, P.780963, RAFVR (Polish); b S Poland, 20 Nov 18; occ law student; poss in PAF Res, 1939; arr UK, Jan 40; 58 OTU (Spit), Ggmth, Stirling, 25 Mar 42; 315 (Dębliński) Sqn (Spit Vb), Woodvale, 26 May 42; 317 (Wileński) Sqn (Spit Vb), Woodvale, 5 Sep 42; 41 Sqn, 26-31 Oct 42; FTR/RF/CL/IFA (forehead & arms), Wells, nr Oulart, Cty Wexford, Eire, in Spit Vb, BM533, after becoming lost during offensive patrol w Sgt Plt P. H. P. Roberts, 31 Oct 42; briefly admtd hosp then interned Curragh Camp, Kildare, Eire, Nov 42; serious inj in incident w G. internees whilst on parole & admtd Sir Patrick Dun's Hosp, Dublin, late May 43; regained consciousness, 26 Jun 43; rlsd & rtnd to UK, 6 Jul 43; admtd Halton Hosp, Chesh, 10 Jul 43; subs movements unkn; d Workington, Cumb, as 'Janus Jozef Zimek', 4 Dec 86

Name	1942					1943												1944												1945				
	A	S	O	N	D	J	F	M	A	M	J	J	A	S	O	N	D	J	F	M	A	M	J	J	A	S	O	N	D	J	F	M	A	M
Officers Commanding																																		
HYDE, Geoffrey Cockayne	K																																	
NEIL, Thomas Francis																																		
INGHAM, Bernard																																		
MATTHEW, Ian George Stewart																																		
GLEN, Arthur Allan																																		
CHAPMAN, Robert Hugh																																		
BENHAM, Douglas Ian																																		
SHEPHERD, John Bean																																		
Officer & NCO Pilots																																		
GOODALL, Bernard Bryn	K																																	
LLOYD, John Maxwell Wauchope																																		
COOMBES, William Michael																																		
IMBERT, André																																		
KING, Jeffrey Cecil																																		
OXENHAM, Russel Edwin George		K																																
SCHOU, Kenneth Victor James																																		
STEPP, Malta Leon Jr.																																		
WARREN, Kenneth George																																		
ATKINSON, Thomas Guy																																		
GREEN, Ronald Edward			K																															
HARRISON, Ronald																																		
KNIGHT, Harold Crosbie																																		
ROBINSON, Kenneth Basil			K																															
SCOTT, Thomas Roland																																		
WOOD, Robert Leslie																																		
UNDERWOOD, Bernard Walter																																		
VINE, Edward Ernest																																		
BEARD, Anthony William																																		

I. The Pilots

Name	1942					1943												1944												1945				
	A	S	O	N	D	J	F	M	A	M	J	J	A	S	O	N	D	J	F	M	A	M	J	J	A	S	O	N	D	J	F	M	A	M
BENJAMIN, Sydney Hyman																																		
ROBERTS, Peter Hugh Percy																																		
MONK, Clifford George																																		
HOARE, Reginald Merrick									P																									
POYNTON, Thomas Rex									K																									
STONIER, Jack																																		
EAST, Walter Raymond										K																								
HOGARTH, Rycherde Henry Wilshere												K																						
HONE, Douglas Harold																																		
PRICKETT, Leslie Alfred													P																					
SLACK, Thomas Adams Hume													E											P										
WHITE, Frederick Cheslyn																																		
CHAPPELL, Charles Gordon																																		
HAYWOOD, Douglas														P																				
GILLITT, Frank Norman			K																															
ZIMEK, Jan Józef			I																															
HOLLOW, Robert Keith																																		
BANACH, Władisław																																		
QUINE, Robert																																		
CLARK, Fraser Dudley																																		
NEWMAN, Benjamin Bernard																																		
DAVIDSON, John Sharpe																																		
THOMAS, John Islwyn								K																										
ROWE, Malcolm P.																																		
DOWNING, William George																																		
DAVIES, David Douglas																																		
BOYD, Robert James														K																				
COWELL, Peter																																		
BROWN, Walter Wilson																																		
COPE, Arthur Reginald							K																											

Name	1942					1943												1944												1945				
	A	S	O	N	D	J	F	M	A	M	J	J	A	S	O	N	D	J	F	M	A	M	J	J	A	S	O	N	D	J	F	M	A	M
BEDNARZ, Jozef							K																											
POLAK, Jerzy																																		
ROGOWSKI, Jan Aleksander																																		
CROSS, Peter David																																		
DUCKWORTH, Robert																																		
COATES, Herbert Percival																																		
BIGGS, Stanley John																																		
MAY, Stanley Henry														E																				
JOHNSON, Ronald																																		
BIRBECK, Clive Robert																																		
FISHER, Douglas Percy																																		
SCOON, Jellicoe Esslemonte N. C.																																		
WILSON, George S.																																		
HEALE, Norman Wingfield																																		
PARRY, Hugh Lawrence														P																				
INNESS, Richard Frederick																																		
LANE, Roy																																		
SOLAK, Jerzy Jakub																																		
MOFFETT, Hubert Bruce																																		
DUCHATEAU, Roger Alphonse Joseph																																		
GALITZINE, Emanuel Vladimirowitch																																		
HOPE, Alan																																		
WALL, Peter R.																																		
FEARON, David Nigel																																		
SMITH, Donald Hamilton																																		
WAGNER, Herbert Appleton																						P												
GRAHAM, Peter Bartlemy																								P										
BALASSE, Maurice Arthur Leon																																		
COOK, Arthur Charles																																		
GRAY, James Arthur Bryce													K																					

I. The Pilots

Name	1942				1943												1944												1945				
	A	S	O	N	D	J	F	M	A	M	J	J	A	S	O	N	D	J	F	M	A	M	J	J	A	S	O	N	D	J	F	M	A	M
VANN, William H.																																		
GLEN, Arthur Allan						▓	▓																											
LOWETH, Ronald Arthur						▓	▓																											
STILL, James Webster						▓	▓																											
HARDING, Ross Philip						▓	▓	▓	▓	▓	▓	▓	▓	▓	▓	▓	▓	▓	▓	▓	▓	▓	▓	▓	▓	▓	▓	▓	▓		P			
PAYNE, Jim Charles Joe						▓	▓	▓	▓	▓	▓	▓	▓	▓	▓	▓	▓	▓	▓	▓	▓	▓	▓	▓	▓	▓	▓	▓	▓			▓		
DUCHATEAU, Roger Alphonse Joseph														▓	▓	▓	▓																	
COLLIS, Ronald Thomas Harry														▓	▓	▓	▓	▓	▓	▓	▓	▓	▓	▓										
SMITH, John Brittain						▓	▓																											
GARRIE, Thomas Adamson									▓	▓																								
ADAMS, Stanley Bruce						▓	▓																											
SABOURIN, Jack Andrew						▓	▓																											
HOOD, Patrick						▓	▓																											
CURTIS, Keith Roe											▓	▓	▓	▓	▓																			
WELSH, Terence Deane						▓	▓																											
CLOUSTON, John Greville						▓	▓																											
GRIFFITH, Lyndon Poynton						▓	▓																											
BALASSE, Maurice Arthur Leon											▓	▓	▓	▓	▓	▓	▓	K																
WOOLLARD, Frederick Gilbert													▓	▓	▓	▓	▓	▓	▓	▓	▓	▓	▓	▓	▓	▓	▓	▓	▓					
BURNE, Thomas Roper																																		
COOK, Harry																																		
STEVENSON, Ian Turnbull																																		
SHEA, David John																					K													
ROBINSON, Kenneth Basil																							K											
GOENS, Rijklof van																									K									
GIBBS, Norman Peter																																		
FLEMING, Robert																						▓	▓	▓	▓	▓	▓	▓	▓			▓	▓	
MACKENZIE, John Noble																																		
MALONE, Charles John																					▓	▓	▓	▓	▓	▓	▓	▓	▓					
THIELE, Keith Frederick																																		

Name	1942				1943												1944												1945				
	A	S	O	N	D	J	F	M	A	M	J	J	A	S	O	N	D	J	F	M	A	M	J	J	A	S	O	N	D	J	F	M	A	M
STOWE, William North																			░	░	░	░	░	░	░	░	░	░	░	░	░	░	░	░
STEPHENS, Ronald Vincent																			░	░	░	░	░											
ANDERSON, Robert Edmund																			░	░	░	░	░	░										
APPLETON, Arthur Stanley																				░	░	░	░					P						
REFSHAUGE, John George Hamilton																							░	░										
SPENCER, Terence																								░										
ODDY, Clifford																								K										
SHORT, Roger Lee																								K										
McKELLAR, Leslie Duncan																																		
ROBERTSON, Colin Stuart																																		
SPURR, Lawrence Esmond																																		
CHATTIN, Peter Warren																									K									
WARE, James Philip																																		
COLEMAN, Patrick Tinsley																								░	░	░	░	░						
TEBBIT, Donald Frank Jellicoe																								░	░	░	░	░		P				
GRAY, Eric																								░	░	░	░	░						
WILKINSON, John Francis																								░	░	░	░	░						
IRVINE, John																								░	░	░	░							
WEEDS, Brian Morrell																									░	░	░	░						
BRADSHAW, John Tyron																										░	░	░						
HENRY, David John Verdun																											░	░		P				
REID, Daniel Joseph																												░	░	░	░	░	░	░
HALE, Peter Harold																												░	░	░	░	░	░	░
ROSSOW, Vivian James																												░	░	░	░	░	░	░
CHARNOCK, Harry Walpole		░																										░	░	░	░	░	░	░
SAMOUELLE, Charles James		░																										░	░	░	░	░	░	░
MILLER, Alister Donald																												░	░	░	░	░	░	░
MOYLE, Crawford Noal																												░	░	░	░	░	░	░
CLANZY, Thomas Keith 'Keith'																												░	░	░	░	░	░	░
KELLY, Hubert Francis																												░	░	░	░	░	░	░

I. The Pilots

Name	1942					1943												1944												1945				
	A	S	O	N	D	J	F	M	A	M	J	J	A	S	O	N	D	J	F	M	A	M	J	J	A	S	O	N	D	J	F	M	A	M
MUNSON, Rupert William																																		
WOOLLEY, Frank Geoffrey																																		
MOTTERSHEAD, Clifford Harper																																K		
HEGARTY, Francis Michael																																		
COWELL, Peter																																		
SMART, Lionel Harry																																		
FISHER, Roy Robert George																																		
LAWRENCE, Thomas Edward																																		
RAKE, Derek Shannon Vaughan																																		
FINUCANE, Raymond Patrick Robert																																		
PAIRMAN, William Robert																																		
SHEPHERD, John Bean																																		
BODTKER, Carl Sejersted																																		
CHALMERS, John Allan																																		
FARFAN, Fernand William																																		
JALLANDS, Walter Joseph																																		
JOLLY, Arnold William																																		
SCOTT, Peter F.																																		
SMITH, Roy David Austen																																		
WHALE, Frederick Victor																																		
GAZE, Frederick Anthony Owen																																		
REMEZ, Aharon																																		
WHEATLEY, Peter Etherington																																		
FEATHERSTONE, Allan																																		
LEE, John																																		

E = Evaded
I = Interned
K = Killed
P = POW

© Steve Brew

II. Officers Commanding
August 1942-May 1945

This Appendix lists 41 Squadron's Officers Commanding between August 1942 and May 1945. In some cases, men arrived on the Squadron as Supernumeraries or served as Flight Commanders prior to the below dates, but only took over command on the dates indicated.

No.	Name	From	To
10	Hyde, Geoffrey Cockayne†	28 July 1942	19 August 1942
-	Hone, Douglas Harold[1]	19 August 1942	3 September 1942
11	Neil, Thomas Francis	3 September 1942	25 July 1943
12	Ingham, Bernard	25 July 1943	20 November 1943
13	Matthew, Ian George Stewart	20 November 1943	26 January 1944
14	Glen, Arthur Allan	26 January 1944	28 May 1944
15	Chapman, Robert Hugh	28 May 1944	28 August 1944
16	Benham, Douglas Ian	28 August 1944	8 April 1945
17	Shepherd, John Bean†	8 April 1945	22 January 1946

The symbol '†' indicates a death in office.

III. FLIGHT COMMANDERS
August 1942-May 1945

This Appendix lists 41 Squadron's Flight Commanders from August 1942 to May 1945. In some cases, men arrived on the Squadron earlier, but only took over as Flight Commander on the dates shown below.

A FLIGHT

No.	Name	From	To
10	Stepp, Malta L.	23 May 1942	26 September 1942
11	Chappell, Charles G.	26 September 1942	27 November 1942
12	Poynton, T. Rex†	28 November 1942	23 April 1943
13	Innes, Richard F.	27 April 1943	30 April 1943
14	Parry, Hugh L.	1 May 1943	24 September 1943
15	Smith, Donald H.	25 September 1943	1 May 1944
16	Spencer, Terence	2 May 1944	4 January 1945
17	Harding, Ross P.	4 January 1945	13 February 1945
18	Woolley, Frank F.	13 February 1945	27 February 1945
19	Shepherd, John B.	7 March 1945	7 April 1945
20	Gaze, Frederick A. O.	8 April 1945	1 May 1945
21	Farfan, Fernand W.	1 May 1945	9 May 1945
22	Stowe, William N.	9 May 1945	20 June 1945

B FLIGHT

No.	Name	From	To
8	Hone, Douglas H.	10 June 1942	30 August 1943
9	Glen, Arthur A.	5 September 1943	26 January 1944
10	Slack, Thomas A. H.	27 January 1944	23 August 1944
11	Henry, David V. J.	28 August 1944	10 February 1945
12	Reid, Daniel J.	10 February 1945	26 March 1945
13	Cowell, Peter	26 March 1945	31 March 1946

The symbol '†' indicates a death in office.

IV. GROUND STAFF
August 1942-May 1945

This Appendix consists of short biographies of key members of 41 Squadron's Ground Staff between August 1942 and May 1945.

INTELLIGENCE OFFICER

CHALONER, THOMAS WESTON PEEL LONG, The Rt Hon Lord Gisborough, 2nd Baron Gisborough of Cleveland, Yks, JP, 'Gizzie', 73814, RAFVR; b Sedgehill, Yks, 6 May 89, 2nd s of 1st Baron Gisborough, Col Richard G. W. & Margaret B. Chaloner; ed Eton, Radley & Trinity Coll, Cambridge; 2 Lt, 4 Btn, APWO Yks Regt, 20 Jul 09; emp by Vickers, ca 1912; scndd to RFC as Lt & Equip Off (442), 5 Jun 15; Hon Capt, 10 Aug 15 (gaz 30 May 16); CFS, Upavon, 15 Sep 15; Fg Off, 23 Oct 15; Hounslow Hosp, 23 Oct-21 Dec 15; 17 Sqn (BE2c), Egypt, Dec 15-Feb 16; 33 Sqn (BE2c), Coal Aston, Mar 16; 13 Sqn (BE2c), Savy, F., 18 May 16; SD/NI in BE2c, 2763, at Croix, on a mission to bomb St Quentin Railway Stn, F., 1 Jul 16; init held in St Quentin Civ Prison, then moved to Krefeld, Rheinland, G; escaped May 18 & interned in NL, 16 May 18; repat to UK, 22 Jan 19; leave until 26 Mar 19; FIS, Upavon, 10 Apr 19; 38 TDS, Tadcaster, 2 May 19; trans to UL, 13 May 19; restored to Est on ceasing to be emp, 25 Aug 20; rel com in RAF on app to TF, 21 Sep 20, rtng Capt; Temp Capt, 4 Btn, Green Howards, 10 Apr 21; marr Esther I. M. Hall (1901-72), 7 Nov 23; dt Angela M., b 1925; Maj, 4 Btn, Green Howards, 16 Feb 26; TD, 4 Feb 27; s Thomas R. J. L., b 1927; rel com, 28 Feb 30, rtng Maj; succ as 2nd Baron Gisborough, 23 Jan 38 (older bro & successor, Richard G. H., KAS in WWI)[1]; com Prob Plt Off in ASD Branch, 1 Aug 39; Ops Duties, SHQ Ctk, 28 Aug 39; Fg Off, 1 Oct 39, wef 4 Sep 39; Actg Flt Lt, 1 Oct 39, wef 5 Sep 39; rel Actg Flt Lt, 21 Nov 39; Int Duties, Ctk satellite airfield Thornaby, 23 Feb 40; Int Off, 41 Sqn, 6 May 40-19 Jun 45; 2 wks leave, Oct-Nov 40; Temp Flt Lt, 1 Dec 41; rlsd Jun 45; later involved in public works in Yks, served on Bench & Chrmn of Cleveland Conservative Assoc; inj in hand tractor acc on Guisborough Estate, DOI a week later, 11 Feb 51

GISBOROUGH, Lord, *see CHALONER, Thomas Weston Peel Long*

ADJUTANTS

COLLIS, RONALD THOMAS HARRY, 111107, RAFVR; b Lon, 22 Jul 20; ed Wembley Cty Sch, Alperton Hall, Mdx; enl in RAFVR, Uxb, 18 Jun 40; 10 EFTS, Weston-super-Mare, Mar-May 41; 1 FIS, Luton, May-Jun 41; com Prob Plt Off (111107) [from Sgt Plt 1253309], 11 Jul 41; Fg Off (WS), 11 Jul 42; 7 (P)AFU (Hurr & Master), Peterborough, Cambs, May 43; 61 OTU (Spit), Rednal, Salop, Jul 43; Flt Lt (WS), 11 Jul 43; 41 Sqn, 15 Aug 43-18 Jun 44; 1 Dest FW190 N of Rouen, F., 20 Oct 43 (claimed Dest, only admitted Prob, but later elevated to Dest, evidence on PSR "raised to destroyed" & on DFC citation); att FLS, Aston Down, for Crse, 6-15 Jan 44; Adjt, ca 16 Jan 44-15 June 44 (see also Appendix I, The Pilots)

McALLISTER, ALEXANDER 'Mac', 136130; LAC, Balloon Br (873883); com Prob APO, 31 Dec 42; trans to ASD Br, 24 Feb 43; Prob Plt Off, 25 Feb 43; Prob Fg Off (WS), 25 Aug 43; Adjt, 41 Sqn, ca Jun 44-6 Aug 45 (demob)

SMITH, HARRY W., Fg Off, RAFVR; Adjt, 41 Sqn, at least 31 Jul 42-ca early 44; 7 days leave plus 48-hr pass, 30 Apr 43[2]

MEDICAL OFFICERS

ANDERSON, HAZLEY, MRCS LRCP, RAFVR, 139601; b Aston, Warks, 1917; com Fg Off in Medical Br, 18 Mar 43; Flt Lt (WS), 18 Mar 44; MO, 610 Sqn, 1944; MO, 41 Sqn, ca Jan-May 45

ARMIN, RICHARD HAYWARD, MB ChB MRCS LRCP, RAFVR, 100464; b Devizes, Wilts, 1915; com Fg Off in Medical Br, 24 Jun 41; Flt Lt (WS), 24 Jun 42; MO, 41 Sqn, at least 27 Jul 42-30 Apr 43; 17 ITW, Scarborough, 1 May 43; Consultant Psychiatrist & Dep Physician Supt, Mendip Hosp, Wells, Somerset, 1954; d Burnham-on-Sea, Somerset, 8 Dec 09

BURNETT, WALTER 'Jock', MB ChB, RAFVR, 134326; com Fg Off in Medical Br, 10 Dec 42; MO, 41 Sqn, 1 May 43-at least 29 May 44; Flt Lt (WS), 10 Dec 43

HERMAN, FREDERICK GUSTAV, MRCS LRCP, RAFVR 140841; b NY, USA, 17 Sep 11; emgtd to UK with family, 1925; ed Bradfield & Fitzwilliam Coll, Cambridge; clinical trng, Charing Cross Hosp, grad 1942; com Fg Off in Medical Br, 1943; MO, 41 Sqn, ca Jun 44-at least Jan 45; Flt Lt, 1945; post-War postgrad trng in pathology, Charing Cross & Epsom Dist Hosps; Staff (latterly Consultant Pathologist), Queen Mary's Hosp, Sidcup, 1952-retirement; rel com, rtng Flt Lt (WS), 17 Sep 56; d USA, 11 Jul 87

ENGINEERING OFFICERS

NORMAN, RICHARD HUBERT 'Monty', 48386, RAF; Sgt (566311); com Prob APO in Tech Br, 29 Apr 42 (sen 31 Dec 41); Prob Plt Off, 27 May 42 (sen 29 Jan 42); Prob Fg Off (WS), 27 Nov 42; Eng Off, 41 Sqn, ca Jul 43-ca Jun 44; Actg Flt Lt, ca 31 Dec 43; Eng Off, 6488 SE, ca Jul 44; MBE, 1 Jan 45

WHIPP, ROGER HENRY 'Whippy', 46361, RAF; b 12 Oct 07; Sgt & Flt Sgt (365022); com Prob APO in Tech Br, 15 Aug 41 (sen 14 Jul 41); Prob Plt Off, 14 Nov 41; Eng Off, 41 Sqn, ca 21 Aug-18 Oct 42; Prob Fg Off (WS), 1 Oct 42; Eng Off, 72 Sqn (Spit Vb), Ouston NBL, 18-31 Oct 42; Sup, RAF Ouston (not fit for OS svce), 31 Oct-1 Dec 42; Eng Off, 41 Sqn (again), 2 Dec 42-ca Jul 43; Temp Flt Lt, 1 Jul 44; Flt Lt (WS), 1 Jan 46; app to perm com as Flt Lt in Tech Br, 1 Jul 46 (sen 1 Sep 45); Sqn Ldr, 1 Jan 49; Wg Cdr, 1 Jan 55; OBE (M), 12 Jan 58; ret 12 Oct 59

V. CASUALTIES, ACCIDENTS AND INCIDENTS
August 1942-May 1945

This Appendix is a chronological list of 41 Squadron's casualties, accidents and incidents to men and machines between August 1942 and May 1945.

This is believed to be as thorough a list as is possible today, and draws on data in ORBs and Appendices at Squadron, Wing, Sector and Group levels, Air Ministry Accident Investigation Branch reports, AM1180 Flying Accident Cards, pilots' logbooks, diaries, personal accounts, and other sources.

Date	Pilot Name	Mk[1]	Serial	Cas[2]	Details[3]
14AUG42	Prickett, Leslie A.	Vb	AR331	NI	CD radiator, 20m SSE Dublin
15AUG42	Goodall, Bernard B.	Vb	P8607	KFA	2½m SSW of Odiham, Hants
19AUG42	Hyde, Geoffrey C.	Vb	BL777	KIA	AA, Dieppe, F.
19AUG42	Imbert, André	Vb	EN836	NI	CD, Dieppe, F.
19AUG42	6 unknown A/C (NR)	Vb	NR	NI	AA, Dieppe, F.
19AUG42	Benjamin, Sydney H.	Vb	EN836	NI	WUL/UC failure, Hamble
27AUG42	Hoare, Reginald M.	Vb	W3457	NI	OSR/WUL, Brize Norton, Ox
23SEP42	Chappell, Charles C.	Vb	NR	NI	'Hood trouble', RTB
24SEP42	Oxenham, Russel E. G.	Vb	AD574	KFA	Wing hit sea, Dundrum Bay
27SEP42	Scott, Thomas R.	Vb	NR	NI	FA, hit tree, Eglinton
22OCT42	Chappell, Charles C.	Vb	NR	NI	Internal glycol leak, RTB
22OCT42	Gillitt, Frank N.	Vb	BM573	KFA	Hilltop, Tarrenhendre, Mer
22OCT42	Harrison, Ronald	Vb	R7296	KFA	Hilltop, Tarrenhendre, Mer
22OCT42	Scott, Thomas R.	Vb	BL518	KFA	Hilltop, Tarrenhendre, Mer
26OCT42	Monk, Clifford G.	Vb	R6919	IFA	EF/CL, Penrhos; SOC
31OCT42	Zimek, Jan J.	Vb	BM533	NI	FTR/RF/CL, Oulart, Éire
02NOV42	Chappell, Charles G.	Vb	BL850	NI	WUL on NFE, Llanbedr, Mer
17NOV42	Quine, Robert	Vb	AD536	NI	OSR, NFE, Llanbedr, Mer
21DEC42	Davies, David D.	Vb	NR	NI	Weather, overnight at Valley
21DEC42	Hone, Douglas H.	Vb	NR	NI	Weather, overnight at Valley
03JAN43	Boyd, Robert J.	III	Master	NI	Starter failure, o'nite Atcham
14JAN43	Polak, Jerzy	Vb	NR	NI	EF, RTB, Llanbedr, Mer
17JAN43	Thomas, John I.	Vb	NR	NI	RF, landed nr Valley, Ang
21JAN43	Thomas, John I.	Vb	NR	NI	Glycol leak, RTB, Llanbedr
23JAN43	Thomas, John I.	Vb	EB-M	NI	FA/CL, NFE, Llanbedr, Mer
27JAN43	Haywood, Douglas	I	Mrtnet	NI	Wheels bogged, Llanbedr
01FEB43	Bednarz, Josef	Vb	X4279	KFA	FA, W of Pwllheli, Caern
04FEB43	Cowell, Peter	Vb	EB-K	NI	Tyre burst whilst taxiing
04FEB43	Haywood, Douglas	Vb	NR	NI	Bird strike, RTB, Llanbedr
28FEB43	Rowe, Malcolm P.	Vb	BL299	IFA	EF/FL, nr Whitchurch Hth

Date	Pilot Name	Mk[1]	Serial	Cas[2]	Details[3]
09MAR43	Cope, Arthur R.[4]	Vc	JG747	MPD	Med, u/w to La Sénia, Algeria
01APR43	Hoare, Reginald M.[5]	Vb	BL423	POW	AA, Ostend, B.
17APR43	Birbeck, Clive R.	XII	EN604	NI	AA, 6m N. of Dieppe, F.
17APR43	Hogarth, Rycherde HW	XII	EN235	NI	CD starboard wg, Ostend, B.
19APR43	Solak, Jerzy J.	Vb	BL406	NI	COG Cat B, N Weald, Esx
19APR43	Haywood, Douglas	XII	NR	NI	WUL, Hawkinge, Kent
23APR43	Newman, Benjamin B.	XII	EN236	NI	AA Cat. A, Ostend, B.
23APR43	Poynton, T. Rex	XII	EN601	KIA	SD off Dieppe, F.
24APR43	Newman, Benjamin B.	XII	EN236	NI	AA Cat. A, Ostend, B.
24APR43	Thomas, John I.	XII	EN610	KFA	EF in tight turn, CL, Hwkge
26APR43	Solak, Jerzy J.	XII	EN603	NI	'Engine trouble', RTB
27APR43	Birbeck, Clive R.	XII	EN608	NI	CD W of Somme Estuary, F.
27APR43	Haywood, Douglas	XII	EN607	WIA	CD off F., FL Littlestone, K.
29APR43	Davies, David D.	XII	EN611	NI	AA Ostend, B.
02MAY43	Wilson, George S.	XII	EN612	NI	Flaps u/s, landed Mstn, Kent
03MAY43	East, Walter R.	XII	EN612	KIA	SD off Dieppe, F.
12MAY43	Fisher, Douglas P.	XII	EN238	NI	'Engine trouble', RTB
14MAY43	Hope, Alan	XII	NR	NI	U/C problems, Hwkge, Kent
14MAY43	Parry, Hugh L.	XII	MB802	NI	Radio u/s, RTB
14MAY43	Prickett, Leslie A.	XII	MB802	NI	U/C problems, Hwkge, Kent
14MAY43	Wilson, George S.	XII	EN609	NI	'Engine trouble', RTB
17MAY43	Heale, Norman W.	XII	EN239	NI	OSR, Hwkge, Kent
17MAY43	Murrin, Wilfred F.[6]	NA	NA	KAS	Bicycle accident, Flkstn, K.
20MAY43	Galitzine, Emanuel V.	XII	EN604	NI	'R/T u/s', but continued op
28MAY43	Biggs, Stanley J.	XII	EN232	NI	CL, Friston, Ssx
04JUN43	Smith, Donald H.	XII	EN602	NI	'R/T u/s', Eastbourne, Ssx
07JUN43	Moffett, H. Bruce	XII	EN611	NI	'Weather u/s', landed Redhill
11JUN43	Lane, Roy	XII	EN603	NI	TA, Friston, Ssx
12JUN43	Smith, Donald H.	XII	EN609	NI	Weather u/s, landed Ford, Ssx
12JUN43	Prickett, Leslie A.	XII	MB800	NI	Weather u/s, landed Ford, Ssx
12JUN43	Lane, Roy	XII	EN233	NI	Weather u/s, lndd Tangmere
12JUN43	Wall, Peter R.	XII	EN226	NI	Weather u/s, lndd Tangmere
13JUN43	Lane, Roy	XII	EN233	NI	'R/T u/s', RTB
20JUN43	Moffett, H. Bruce	XII	EN611	NI	Loose hood, RTB
29JUN43	Wagner, Herbert A.	XII	NR	NI	JTF, RTB
01JUL43	Parry, Hugh L.	XII	MB802	NI	AA, Abbeville/Drucat A/D, F
01JUL43	Hone, Douglas H.	XII	EN234	NI	Hit wireless mast on TO
02JUL43	Neil, Thomas F.	XII	EN237	NI	'Engine trouble', RTB
04JUL43	Boyd, Robert J.	XII	MB796	NI	'Flap trouble', lndd Tangmere
07JUL43	Slack, Thomas A. H.	XII	EN226	NI	EF delayed TO, RTB
08JUL43	Slack, Thomas A. H.	XII	NR	NI	MAC w drogue towing wire
09JUL43	Newman, Benjamin B.	XII	EN236	NI	JTF, RTB
17JUL43	Galitzine, Emanuel V.	XII	EN266	NI	'R/T u/s', but continued op

Date	Pilot Name	Mk[1]	Serial	Cas[2]	Details[3]
17JUL43	Slack, Thomas A. H.	XII	MB802	NI	JTF, RTB
17JUL43	Graham, Peter B.	XII	EN231	NI	'Engine trouble', RTB
18JUL43	Fisher, Douglas P.	XII	EN231	NI	CD & R/T u/s, nr Poix, F.
18JUL43	Hogarth, Rycherde HW	XII	EN235	KIA	SD, nr Abbeville, F.
18JUL43	Moffett, H. Bruce	XII	EN611	NI	RF, landed Friston, Ssx
18JUL43	Neil, Thomas F.	XII	EN237	NI	'Jettison tank trouble', RTB
18JUL43	Slack, Thomas A. H.	XII	EN233	WIA	SD/ER Foucaucourt, F.
18JUL43	Wall, Peter	XII	EN603	NI	RTB to accompany T. F. Neil
23JUL43	Graham, Peter B.	XII	EN238	WIA	AA, St. Valéry-en-Caux, F.
27JUL43	Glen, Arthur A.	XII	MB846	NI	JTF, would not jettison, RTB
29JUL43	Wall, Peter	XII	MB800	NI	'Jettison tank trouble', RTB
31JUL43	Davies, David D.	XII	MB829	NI	RF, landed Friston, Ssx
31JUL43	May, Stanley H.	XII	EN611	NI	RF, landed Friston, Ssx
01AUG43	Johnson, Ronald	XII	MB801	NI	R/T trouble, RTB
01AUG43	Fearon, David N.	XII	MB847	NI	Rtnd. early with R. Johnson
04AUG43	Wall, Peter	XII	MB800	NI	Jettison tank empty, RTB
08AUG43	Wagner, Herbert A.	XII	EN609	NI	Jettison tank fell off, RTB
09AUG43	Cowell, Peter	XII	MB834	NI	JTF, would not jettison, RTB
09AUG43	Newman, Benjamin B.	XII	EN236	NI	JTF, would not jettison, RTB
09AUG43	Cook, Arthur C.	XII	EN226	NI	RF, landed Hwkge, Kent
09AUG43	Payne, Jim C. J.	XII	EN608	NI	Landed Hwkge due weather
11AUG43	May, Stanley H.	XII	EN611	NI	CD, bullet in engine, Dieppe
12AUG43	Ingham, Bernard	XII	EN237	NI	Unable to lock hood, RTB
12AUG43	Smith, Donald H.	XII	MB845	NI	JTF, would not jettison, RTB
12AUG43	Smith, Donald H.	XII	MB845	NI	JTF, would not jettison again
12AUG43	Fisher, Douglas P.	XII	MB829	NI	R/T trouble, RTB
16AUG43	Haywood, Douglas	XII	EN602	NI	UC u/s, WUL Tangmere, Ssx
16AUG43	Moffett, H. Bruce	XII	EN608	NI	DNTO, puncture, Whmpnt
17AUG43	Payne, Jim C. J.	XII	EN234	NI	JTF, would not jettison, RTB
18AUG43	Johnson, Ronald	XII	MB801	NI	Bird strike, mirror & spinner
18AUG43	Still, James W.	XII	EN226	NI	HL, broke oleo leg, Hwkge
19AUG43	Johnson, Ronald[7]	XII	MB801	NI	R/T & flap indicator u/s, RTB
19AUG43	Payne, Jim C. J.	XII	EN231	NI	RF, landed Ford, Ssx
23AUG43	Prickett, Leslie A.	XII	MB862	NI	Oxygen failure, RTB
27AUG43	Graham, Peter B.	XII	MB829	NI	RF, landed Ford, Ssx
27AUG43	Haywood, Douglas	XII	EN236	POW	SD/EF, 10m ENE Hardelot, F
27AUG43	Hone, Douglas H.	XII	MB796	NI	JTF, would not jettison, RTB
27AUG43	Loweth, Ronald A.	XII	MB846	NI	RF, landed Hawkinge, Kent
27AUG43	Prickett, Leslie A.	XII	EN611	POW	EF, 60-70m S. of St. Omer, F.
27AUG43	Still, James W.	XII	EN609	NI	RF, landed Ford, Ssx
28AUG43	Hope, Alan	XII	MB844	NI	RF, landed Manston, Kent
28AUG43	Ingham, Bernard	XII	MB845	NI	RF, landed Ipswich, Sflk
28AUG43	Johnson, Ronald	XII	MB829	NI	'Tank trouble', Woensdrecht

V. Casualties, Accidents and Incidents

Date	Pilot Name	Mk[1]	Serial	Cas[2]	Details[3]
28AUG43	Newman, Benjamin B.	XII	MB800	NI	RF, landed Manston, Kent
28AUG43	Parry, Hugh L.	XII	MB802	NI	RF, landed Manston, Kent
28AUG43	Wagner, Herbert A.	XII	EN609	NI	RF, landed Manston, Kent
28AUG43	Wall, Peter R.	XII	MB838	NI	RF, landed Manston, Kent
30AUG43	Cook, Arthur C.	XII	MB862	IFA	RF/USR/CL, Tangmere, Ssx
30AUG43	Loweth, Ronald A.	XII	EN234	NI	'Tank trouble', RTB
30AUG43	Payne, Jim C. J.	XII	MB804	NI	Air pressure rgltr valve u/s
31AUG43	Birbeck, Clive R.	XII	EN234	NI	JTF, would not jettison, RTB
31AUG43	Fearon, David N.	XII	MB834	NI	RF, landed Friston, Ssx
31AUG43	Graham, Peter B.	XII	MB829	NI	RF, landed Friston, Ssx
31AUG43	[Illegible]	XII	MB802	NI	'Fuel failure', RTB
31AUG43	Harding, Ross P.	XII	MB829	NI	RF, landed Tangmere, Ssx
31AUG43	Still, James W.	XII	MB801	NI	JTF, would not jettison, RTB
31AUG43	Wall, Peter R.	XII	MB845	NI	RF, landed Friston, Ssx
02SEP43	Harding, Ross P.	XII	EN608	NI	JTF, would not jettison, RTB
04SEP43	Birbeck, Clive R.	XII	EN608	NI	RF, landed Shoreham, Ssx
04SEP43	Fisher, Douglas P.	XII	MB829	NI	JTF, RTB
04SEP43	Graham, Peter B.	XII	MB829	NI	Damaged radiator, lndd Ford
04SEP43	Ingham, Bernard	XII	MB838	NI	Oxygen leak, lndd Tangmere
04SEP43	Johnson, Ronald	XII	EN608	NI	JTF, would not jettison
04SEP43	Loweth, Ronald A.	XII	MB837	NI	'Tank trouble', RTB
04SEP43	Solak, Jerzy J.	XII	EN609	NI	RF, landed Friston, Ssx
06SEP43	Boyd, Robert J.	XII	MB796	KIA	AA, Normandy, F.
08SEP43	Collis, Ronald T. H.	XII	RM797	NI	Tyre burst on TO, Tangmere
08SEP43	Hope, Alan	XII	MB838	NI	RF, landed Friston, Ssx
08SEP43	May, Stanley H.	XII	EN231	NI	RF, landed Ford, Ssx
08SEP43	Still, James W.	XII	EN609	NI	RF, landed Friston, Ssx
08SEP43	Wall, Peter R.	XII	MB846	NI	RTB early, reason NR (JTF?)
11SEP43	Lane, Roy	XII	MB844	NI	R/T trouble, RTB
11SEP43	Parry, Hugh L.	XII	MB802	NI	RTB early, reason NR
11SEP43	Payne, Jim C. J.	XII	MB804	NI	Fuel cock leaking, RTB
13SEP43	Cowell, Peter	XII	MB834	NI	Hit twice by AA, Bmnt-Le R.
15SEP43	Glen, Arthur A.	XII	MB846	NI	EF, lndd Manston, Kent
15SEP43	Graham, Peter B.	XII	MB829	NI	Lndd Manston without flaps
19SEP43	May, Stanley H.	XII	MB800	ER	SD, bet Ypres & Dunkirk
21SEP43	Vann, William H.	XII	EN231	NI	RF, landed, Friston, Ssx
22SEP43	Birbeck, Clive R.	XII	EN608	RR	EF ditched 20-25m S of Ford
23SEP43	Glen, Arthur A.	XII	MB846	NI	Engine loose, RTB
24SEP43	Glen, Arthur A.	XII	MB801	NI	'R/T u/s'
24SEP43	Graham, Peter B.	XII	EN231	NI	Jet tank fell off in dive
24SEP43	Harding, Ross P.[8]	XII	MB837	NI	'Engine trouble', RTB
24SEP43	Parry, Hugh L.	XII	MB802	WIA	SD/POW, Poix-Beauvais area
25SEP43	Glen, Arthur A.	XII	MB801	NI	Rudder jammed, RTB

Date	Pilot Name	Mk[1]	Serial	Cas[2]	Details[3]
27SEP43	Birbeck, Clive R.	XII	EN608	NI	RF, landed Friston, Ssx
27SEP43	Fearon, David N.	XII	EN234	NI	RF, landed Friston, Ssx
27SEP43	Graham, Peter B.	XII	MB798	NI	RF, landed Friston, Ssx
27SEP43	Gray, James A. B.	XII	EN237	NI	RF, landed Lympne, Kent
27SEP43	Harries, Raymond H.	XII	MB836	NI	RF, landed Friston, Ssx
27SEP43	Hope, Alan	XII	MB838	NI	RF, landed Friston, Ssx
27SEP43	Lane, Roy	XII	MB844	NI	RF, landed Lympne, Kent
27SEP43	Moffett, H. Bruce	XII	MB837	NI	RF, landed Friston, Ssx
27SEP43	Newman, Bernard B.	XII	MB857	NI	RF, landed Friston, Ssx
27SEP43	Smith, Donald H.	XII	MB845	NI	RF, landed Friston, Ssx
27SEP43	Vann, William H.	XII	EN231	NI	RF, landed Friston, Ssx
27SEP43	Wall, Peter R.	XII	EN237	NI	RF, landed Friston, Ssx
02OCT43	Still, James W.	XII	EN237	NI	RF, landed Friston, Ssx
03OCT43	Gray, James A. B.	XII	MB834	KIA	SD, Crèvecœur, F.
03OCT43	Johnson, Ronald	XII	MB846	NI	Flat tyre, Westhampnett, Ssx
03OCT43	Johnson, Ronald	XII	MB801	NI	Oil filter cap blew off on TO
03OCT43	Johnson, Ronald	XII	MB801	NI	EF, engine cutting, RTB
03OCT43	Payne, Jim C. J.	XII	MB797	NI	JTF, RTB
03OCT43	Smith, Donald H.	XII	MB845	NI	JTF, RTB
03OCT43	Still, James W.	XII	MB837	NI	JTF, RTB
03OCT43	Vann, William H.	XII	MB798	NI	Flight cancelled, Manston, K.
03OCT43	Wagner, Herbert A.	XII	MB850	NI	Got lost & returned alone
13OCT43	Still, James W.[9]	XII	MB838	NI	AA in wing, Cabourg, F.
15OCT43	Payne, Jim C. J.	XII	MB804	NI	Landed without flaps
20OCT43	Birbeck, Clive R.	XII	EN605	NI	AA, Le Havre, F.
20OCT43	Collis, Ronald T. H.	XII	MB850	NI	SF in dive, N of Rouen, F.
20OCT43	Cowell, Peter	XII	MB795	NI	CD, Beaumont-le-Roger, F.
20OCT43	Fisher, Douglas P.	XII	MB804	NI	AA, port aileron, Seine Est
20OCT43	Graham, Peter B.	XII	MB798	NI	Accompanied C. R. Birbeck
20OCT43	Newman, Benjamin B.	XII	MB858	NI	CD, Beaumont-le-Roger, F.
20OCT43	Harding, Ross P.	XII	EN231	NI	RF, landed Friston, Ssx
20OCT43	Still, James W.	XII	MB838	NI	RF, landed Friston, Ssx
22OCT43	Birbeck, Clive R.	XII	EN605	NI	'Petrol trouble', RTB
22OCT43	Harding, Ross P.	XII	EN603	NI	'Hood u/s', RTB
25OCT43	Glen, Arthur A.	XII	MB837	NI	'R/T trouble', RTB
26OCT43	Birbeck, Clive R.	XII	EN605	NI	AA in tail, Dieppe area, F.
04NOV43	Johnson, Ronald	XII	MB801	NI	AA rudder & tail, Hardelot, F
05NOV43	Moffett, H. Bruce	XII	MB858	NI	'R/T u/s', RTB
05NOV43	Smith, John B.	XII	EN603	NI	'R/T u/s', RTB
08NOV43	Hope, Alan	XII	MB830	NI	'Electric system u/s', RTB
08NOV43	Unnamed Pilot (NR)	XII	NR	NI	Slight CD/AA, F.
11NOV43	Payne, Jim C. J.	XII	MB797	NI	Landed without flaps, Tang
11NOV43	Sabourin, Jack A.	XII	EN237	NI	'R/T u/s', RTB

V. Casualties, Accidents and Incidents

Date	Pilot Name	Mk[1]	Serial	Cas[2]	Details[3]
15NOV43	Wagner, Herbert A.	XII	MB838	NI	EF on TO, cart-whld, Tang
18NOV43	Curtis, Keith R.	XII	EN237	NI	'Petrol trouble', RTB
20NOV43	Unnamed Pilot (NR)	XII	MB801	NI	FA, Cat. E, no details avail
20NOV43	Smith, Donald H.	XII	MB845	NI	JTF, RTB
23NOV43	Adams, S. Bruce	XII	MB798	NI	JTF, RTB
23NOV43	11 Pilots	XII	11 A/C	NI	Landed Hwkge to refuel
25NOV43	Clouston, John G.	XII	MB794	NI	JTF, RTB
26NOV43	Wagner, Herbert A.	XII	EN603	NI	'Engine trouble', RTB
29NOV43	Johnson, Ronald	XII	MB837	NI	Engine hit by .303 round
29NOV43	Adams, S. Bruce	XII	MB846	NI	'Engine trouble', late take off
01DEC43	Adams, S. Bruce	XII	MB846	IFA	RF/EF/CL, Tangmere, Ssx
01DEC43	Clouston, John G.	XII	EN237	NI	'Hood u/s', RTB
01DEC43	Curtis, Keith R.	XII	EN603	NI	'R/T u/s', RTB
01DEC43	Glen, Arthur A.	XII	MB837	NI	DNTO, reason NR
01DEC43	Payne, Jim C. J.	XII	MB804	NI	RF, landed Hawkinge, Kent
01DEC43	Smith, Donald H.	XII	MB845	NI	JTF, RTB
01DEC43	Welsh, Terence D.	XII	MB844	NI	'Engine trouble', RTB
02DEC43	Collis, Ronald T. H.[10]	XII	MB795	NI	'u/s engine', RTB
02DEC43	Graham, Peter B.	XII	EN605	NI	'R/T u/s', RTB
04DEC43	Payne, Jim C. J.	XII	MB804	NI	Bird strike in radiator
05DEC43	Welsh, Terence D.	XII	MB840	NI	JTF, RTB
05DEC43	Glen, Arthur A.	XII	MB847	NI	JTF, RTB
05DEC43	Graham, Peter B.	XII	MB798	NI	RF, landed Friston, Ssx
13DEC43	Collis, Ronald T. H.	XII	MB795	NI	RF, landed Ford, Ssx
13DEC43	Sabourin, Jack A.	XII	EN237	NI	RF, landed Lympne, Kent
21DEC43	Wagner, Herbert A.	XII	MB795	NI	Lndd with 1 flap, Ford, Ssx
22DEC43	Birbeck, Clive R.	XII	EN605	NI	'Engine trouble', lndd Hwkge
22DEC43	Hood, Patrick	XII	MB847	NI	Escrtd Birbeck, lndd Hwkge
22DEC43	Johnson, Ronald	XII	MB880	NI	Escrtd Birbeck, lndd Hwkge
22DEC43	Payne, Jim C. J.	XII	EN231	NI	Escrtd Birbeck, lndd Hwkge
23DEC43	Graham, Peter B.	XII	MB798	NI	Engine surging & cutting
30DEC43	Graham, Peter B.	XII	MB847	NI	DNTO, prob EF, Tangmere
30DEC43	Payne, Jim C. J.	XII	MB797	NI	R/T u/s, RTB
31DEC43	Balasse, Maurice A. L.	XII	MB797	NI	R/T u/s, RTB
31DEC43	Glen, Arthur A.	XII	MB881	NI	R/T u/s, RTB
02JAN44	9 A/C, Pilots Unknown	XII	NR	NI	RF, landed Friston, Ssx
04JAN44	Collis, Ronald T. H.	XII	MB858	NI	JTF, RTB
04JAN44	Graham, Peter B.	XII	MB798	NI	Fuel leak, landed Friston, Ssx
05JAN44	4 A/C, Pilots Unknown	XII	NR	NI	CNTO, reason(s) NR
05JAN44	1 A/C, Pilot Unknown	XII	NR	NI	RF?, landed Friston, Ssx
07JAN44	Curtis, Keith R.	XII	EN237	NI	Hood u/s, RTB
07JAN44	Glen, Arthur A.	XII	MB881	NI	JTF, RTB
08JAN44	Curtis, Keith R.	XII	EN237	NI	RF, landed Friston, Ssx

Date	Pilot Name	Mk[1]	Serial	Cas[2]	Details[3]
09JAN44	Harding, Ross P.	XII	MB794	NI	Lost, lndd Portsmouth Airport
14JAN44	Harding, Ross P.	XII	MB794	NI	'Hood u/s', RTB
21JAN44	Cook, Harry	XII	MB795	NI	Charged A/C too late
21JAN44	Harding, Ross P.	XII	EN237	NI	JTF, RTB
23JAN44	Harding, Ross P.	XII	MB794	NI	JTF, RTB
25JAN44	Cook, Harry	XII	MB862	NI	Instruments u/s, RTB
26JAN44	Graham, Peter B.	XII	MB798	NI	'R/T trouble'
28JAN44	Birbeck, Clive R.	XII	EN605	NI	High radiator temp, RTB
28JAN44	Graham, Peter B.	XII	MB798	NI	Escorted C. R. Birbeck home
29JAN44	Graham, Peter B.	XII	MB847	NI	RF, landed Friston, Ssx
03FEB44	Payne, Jim C. J.	XII	MB804	NI	COG with 91 Sqn A/C
06FEB44	Glen, Arthur A.	XII	MB881	NI	A/C would not start, DNTO
06FEB44	Fisher, Douglas P.	XII	MB794	NI	'Engine trouble', RTB
14FEB44	Cowell, Peter	XII	NR	NI	Reflector sight bracket u/s
14FEB44	Johnson, Ronald	XII	MB880	NI	Engine cut on TO, Southend
20FEB44	Pilot unknown, NR	II	T/Moth	NI	Crashed on TO, Southend
22FEB44	Shea, David J.	XII	NR	NI	'Starting trouble, DNTO
22FEB44	Shea, David J.	XII	NR	NI	Poor weather, lndd Ford, Ssx
25FEB44	Birbeck, Clive R.	XII	MB881	NI	'Engine trouble', lndd Friston
29FEB44	Wagner, Herbert A.	XII	MB843	NI	A/C hit by small calibre bullet
02MAR44	Cook, Harry	XII	MB845	NI	'Engine trouble', RTB
04MAR44	Birbeck, Clive R.	XII	MB830	NI	RF, landed Friston, Ssx
05MAR44	Collis, Ronald T. H.	XII	MB863	NI	'Engine trouble', RTB
05MAR44	Cowell, Peter	XII	MB795	NI	'Engine trouble', RTB
05MAR44	Robinson, Kenneth B.	XII	MB840	NI	Escorted P. Cowell
05MAR44	Remaining 9 Pilots	XII	9 A/C	NI	Bad weather, lndd WMalling
06MAR44	Wagner, Herbert A.	XII	MB843	NI	Unwell, could not fly, WMlg
13MAR44	Cook, Harry	XII	MB862	NI	Poor weather, lndd Lympne
13MAR44	Harding, Ross P.	XII	MB794	NI	'R/T duff', RTB
13MAR44	Shea, David J.	XII	EN237	KFA	EF/CL, Lympne, Kent
13MAR44	Wagner, Herbert A.	XII	NR	NI	TON, Friston, Ssx
16MAR44	Woollard, Frederick G.	XII	MB798	NI	'Engine trouble', RTB
18MAR44	Fearon, David N.	XII	MB847	NI	Poor weather, lndd Lympne
18MAR44	Slack, Thomas A. H.	XII	MB830	NI	Poor weather, lndd Lympne
18MAR44	Thiele, Keith F.	XII	MB837	NI	Poor weather, lndd Lympne
18MAR44	Woollard, Frederick G	XII	MB798	NI	Poor weather, lndd Lympne
25MAR44	Cowell, Peter[11]	XII	MB882	NI	Hit water, broke prop blades
25MAR44	Gibbs, N. Peter	XII	MB845	NI	RTB, accompanied P. Cowell
28MAR44	Curtis, Keith R.	XII	MB845	NI	Engine trouble?, RTB early
01APR44	Cook, Harry	XII	MB862	NI	'Mechanical trouble', RTB
01APR44	Malone, C. John	XII	MB794	NI	Escorted H. Cook
09APR44	Fearon, David N.	XII	MB847	NI	'Engine u/s', RTB
12APR44	Balasse, Maurice A. L.	XII	MB842	NI	RF, landed Manston, Kent

V. Casualties, Accidents and Incidents

Date	Pilot Name	Mk[1]	Serial	Cas[2]	Details[3]
12APR44	Birbeck, Clive R.	XII	EN605	NI	RF, landed Manston, Kent
21APR44	Birbeck, Clive R.	XII	EN605	NI	EF, DNTO, Friston, Ssx
29APR44	Collis, Ronald T. H.[12]	XII	MB882	NI	Starting trouble, delayed TO
29APR44	Harding, Ross P.[12]	XII	MB794	NI	Starting trouble, delayed TO
29APR44	Refshauge, John G. H.[13]	XII	MB794	NI	'Rough engine', RTB
29APR44	Wagner, Herbert A.[13]	XII	MB795	NI	'Rough engine', RTB
30APR44	Cowell, Peter	XII	MB795	NI	'Engine trouble', RTB
02MAY44	Graham, Peter B.	XII	MB798	NI	'Engine, R/T & compass u/s'
03MAY44	Graham, Peter B.	XII	MB829	NI	TA, TON, Ramsbury, Wilts
08MAY44	Fisher, Douglas P.[14]	XII	MB847	NI	'Engine trouble', RTB
08MAY44	Payne, Jim C. J.[14]	XII	MB804	NI	'Engine trouble', RTB
09MAY44	Unknown (NR)	XII	NR	NI	IFF malfunctioning, RTB
10MAY44	Unknown (NR)	XII	NR	NI	Oleo leg broke off on landing
16MAY44	Cook, Harry[15]	XII	NR	NI	'Engine trouble', RTB
16MAY44	Stevenson, Ian T.[15]	XII	NR	NI	'Engine trouble', RTB
22MAY44	Woollard, Frederick G[16]	XII	MB858	NI	Skidded, oleo leg collapsed
28MAY44	Cowell, Peter	XII	EN224	NI	JTF, RTB, Bolt Head
01JUN44	Gibbs, N. Peter	XII	EN224	NI	AA tail fin, Guernsey
02JUN44	Collis, Ronald T. H.	XII	MB837	NI	Aircraft u/s, RTB
02JUN44	Gibbs, N. Peter	XII	MB837	NI	JTF, RTB
02JUN44	Wagner, Herbert A.	XII	MB843	POW	AA radiator, Guernsey
03JUN44	Collis, Ronald T. H.	XII	MB845	NI	AA fuselage, Brittany/Grnsy
07JUN44	Collis, Ronald T. H.	XII	EN224	NI	AA tail, Guernsey
07JUN44	Cowell, Peter	XII	EN620	NI	AA wings, Guernsey
07JUN44	Robinson, Kenneth B.	XII	MB881	KAS	AA radiator, N of Guernsey
09JUN44	Refshauge, John G. H.	XII	MB794	WIA	SD/AA, Cherbourg, F.
12JUN44	Balasse, Maurice A. L.	XII	MB842	NI	RF Channel, RR by ASR
12JUN44	Gibbs, N. Peter	XII	MB845	IFA	RF/CL, Bolt Head, Devon
18JUN44	Slack, Thomas A. H.	XII	MB876	NI	AA/EF, ditched, RR by ASR
18JUN44	Ware, James P.	XII	EN231	NI	RF & ditched, RR by ASR
20JUN44	Harding, Ross P.	XII	EN229	NI	RF/CL, Redhill, Ssx
20JUN44	Gibbs, N. Peter	XII	MB875	NI	RF?, lndd Horne, Surrey
21JUN44	Stowe, William N.	XII	EN229	NI	Tail wheel fell off on TO
23JUN44	Balasse, Maurice A. L.	XII	MB830	IFA	RF/CL, W of Farleigh, Kent
23JUN44	Coleman, Patrick T.	XII	EN620	NI	RF, lndd Woodchurch, Kent
24JUN44	Harding, Ross P.	XII	EN602	NI	EF/FL, Friston, Ssx
27JUN44	Gibbs, N. Peter	XII	EN620	NI	CL, Whmpnt, Ssx
27JUN44	Robertson, Colin S.	XII	EN221	IFA	CL/COG w EN224, Whmpnt
27JUN44	No Pilot [Stationary]	XII	EN224	NA	COG with EN221, Whmpnt
05JUL44	Harding, Ross P.	XII	EN602	NI	'Gunsight u/s'
07JUL44	Coleman, Patrick T.	XII	EN228	NI	CD exploding V1, Lympne
08JUL44	Chattin, Peter W.	XII	MB837	NI	CD exploding V1, Thms Est
11JUL44	Graham, Peter B.	XII	MB798	NI	'Engine & airframe u/s'

Date	Pilot Name	Mk[1]	Serial	Cas[2]	Details[3]
17JUL44	Oddy, Clifford[17]	II	T/Moth	KFA	MAC, Lympne, Kent
17JUL44	Short, Roger[17]	XII	MB877	KFA	MAC, Lympne, Kent
18JUL44	Woollard, Frederick G.	XII	MB841	IFA	HL/CL, Lympne, Kent
21JUL44	Payne, Jim C. J.	XII	MB861	NI	WUL, COG with MB840
21JUL44	No Pilot [Stationary]	XII	MB840	NA	COG with MB861, Lympne
22JUL44	Coleman, Patrick T.	XII	MB862	NI	'R/T u/s', Lympne, Kent
03AUG44	Chattin, Peter W.	XII	MB795	NI	EF 8,000 ft., landed Brenzett
03AUG44	McKellar, Leslie D.	XII	MB850	NI	Landed Brenzett, reason NR
03AUG44	Tebbit, Donald F. J.	XII	MB795	NI	Landed Brenzett, reason NR
05AUG44	Stevenson, Ian T.	XII	MB795	NI	Cannon jammed, Brede, Ssx
12AUG44	Chattin, Peter W.	XII	EN609	NI	Burst tyre on lndng, Lympne
17AUG44	Harding, Ross P.	XII	MB854	NI	EF/CL Brookland, Kent
17AUG44	Goens, Rijklof van	XII	MB880	MPD	FTR, Allied AA, Kent
20AUG44	Spencer, Terence[18]	IX	5R-Z	NI	EF/CL, orchard nr Lympne
22AUG44	Graham, Peter B.	XII	MB831	NI	R/T u/s, Lympne, Kent
23AUG44	Slack, Thomas A. H.	XII	EN226	POW	EF/FL, Hesdin, F.
25AUG44	Chapman, Robert H.	XII	EN227	NI	JTF?, RTB within 10 mins
25AUG44	Weeds, Brian M.	XII	MB875	NI	EF on TO, o/turned, Lympne
26AUG44	Chattin, Peter W.	XII	MB878	NI	AA, N of St. Omer, F.
26AUG44	Harding, Ross P.	XII	EN602	NI	JTF?, RTB within 10 mins
26AUG44	Stevenson, Ian T.	XII	EN229	NI	AA wing, N of St. Omer, F.
26AUG44	Reid, Daniel J.	XII	EN238	NI	JTF?, RTB within 10 mins
26AUG44	Spencer, Terence	XII	MB882	NI	AA hood, N of St. Omer, F.
30AUG44	2 A/C, Pilots Unknown	XII	NR	NI	CD/AA, E of Roulers, B.
30AUG44	Stowe, William N.	XII	MB862	NI	CD/AA, E of Roulers, B.
01SEP44	Balasse, Maurice A. L.	XII	EN609	NI	Delayed TO, Lympne, Kent
01SEP44	Chattin, Peter W.	XII	EN622	NI	Delayed TO, Lympne, Kent
01SEP44	Chattin, Peter W.	XII	MB850	NI	RF, lndd Manston after dark
01SEP44	Coleman, Patrick T.	XII	EN238	NI	'Dud jet tank', Lympne, Kent
01SEP44	Coleman, Patrick T.	XII	MB857	NI	RF, lndd Manston after dark
01SEP44	Fisher, Douglas P.	XII	EN615	NI	Delayed TO, Lympne, Kent
01SEP44	Graham, Peter B.	XII	MB831	POW	AA Esquelbecq-St. Omer, F.
01SEP44	Gray, Eric	XII	EN228	NI	Delayed TO, Lympne, Kent
01SEP44	Henry, David J. V.	XII	MB856	NI	Delayed TO, Lympne, Kent
01SEP44	Spencer, Terence	XII	MB882	NI	AA tail, N of St. Omer, F.
01SEP44	Spencer, Terence	XII	MB882	NI	RF, lndd Manston after dark
01SEP44	Stowe, William N.	XII	MB862	NI	RF, lndd Manston after dark
03SEP44	Pilot unknown, NR	XII	NR	NI	Fire while refuelling, Lympne
03SEP44	Chattin, Peter W.	XII	EN622	KIA	SD Neerhespen, B.
03SEP44	Spencer, Terence	XII	MB882	NI	CD starboard wg, Tirlemont
09SEP44	Henry, David J. V.	XII	MB856	IFA	CL burst tyre, Brussels, B.
11SEP44	Weeds, Brian M.	XII	MB862	IFA	FA/CL, Lympne, Kent
12SEP44	Pilot unknown, NR	XII	NR	NI	Carburettor trouble, Katwijk

V. Casualties, Accidents and Incidents

Date	Pilot Name	Mk[1]	Serial	Cas[2]	Details[3]
12SEP44	Entire Squadron	XII	NR	NI	RF, landed Bradwell Bay
14SEP44	Tebbit, Donald F. J.	XIV	RM767	NI	JTF?, RTB within 10 mins
14SEP44	Tebbit, Donald F. J.	XIV	RM698	NI	'Oxygen deficiency', RTB
14SEP44	Fleming, Robert	XIV	NR	NI	Weather u/s, landed Manston
14SEP44	Rossow, Vivian J.	XIV	NR	NI	Weather u/s, landed Manston
17SEP44	Stowe, William N.	XIV	RM797	NI	EF, lndd Manston, Kent
19SEP44	Entire Squadron	XIV	12 A/C	NI	Weather u/s, landed Manston
23SEP44	Gibbs, N. Peter	XIV	RM789	NI	Mechanical trouble, RTB
27SEP44	Fisher, Douglas P.	XIV	RM796	NI	Accompanied J. P. Ware
27SEP44	Hale, Peter H.	XIV	NR	NI	Accompanied D. F. J. Tebbit
27SEP44	Spencer, Terence	XIV	NR	NI	R/T u/s, Rotterdam NL
27SEP44	Tebbit, Donald F. J.	XIV	NR	NI	Engine trouble, RTB
27SEP44	Ware, James P.	XIV	RM788	NI	Fire & smoke from eng, RTB
29SEP44	Hale, Peter H.	XIV	RM789	NI	Engine trouble, RTB
29SEP44	Entire Sqn. (excl. Hale)	XIV	11 A/C	NI	Weather u/s, landed Manston
05OCT44	Gibbs, N. Peter	XIV	RM797	NI	EF, Eindhoven, RTB
05OCT44	Tebbit, Donald F. J.	XIV	RM793	IFA	EF on TO/CL Lympne, Kent
05OCT44	No Pilot [Stationary]	XIV	RM705	NA	Run into by J. P. Ware
05OCT44	Ware, James P.	XIV	RM788	NI	TA/COG/DNTO, Lympne, K
05OCT44	Wilkinson, John F.	XIV	RM769	NI	'R/T failure', RTB
06OCT44	Appleton, Arthur S.	XIV	RM699	NI	Oxygen leak, RTB
06OCT44	Harding, Ross P.	XIV	RM707	NI	RF, overnight in Antwerp, B.
06OCT44	Stowe, William N.	XIV	RM769	NI	RF, overnight in Antwerp, B.
06NOV44	Anderson, Robert E.	XIV	RM698	NI	A/C u/s, delayed TO, Lympne
06NOV44	Hale, Peter H.	XIV	RM704	NI	A/C u/s, landed Manston, K.
09NOV44	Charnock, Harry W.	XIV	RM767	NI	CD/AA, Wanne-Eickel, G.
09NOV44	Hale, Peter H.	XIV	RM797	NI	A/C u/s, landed Manston, K.
16NOV44	Wilkinson, John F.[19]	XIV	RM765	NI	EF/RF, landed Ghent, B.
16NOV44	Miller, Alister D.[19]	XIV	RM793	NI	Lndd Ghent w J.F. Wilkinson
21NOV44	Moyle, Crawford N.	XIV	RM707	NI	EF, landed Manston, Kent
26NOV44	Wilkinson, John F.	XIV	RM793	NI	EF, landed Manston, Kent
30NOV44	Appleton, Arthur S.	XIV	RM699	NI	EF, landed Manston, Kent
30NOV44	Charnock, Harry W.	XIV	RM789	NI	EF, landed Manston, Kent
05DEC44	Cook, Harry	XIV	NR	NI	EF, CNTO, Evere, B.
08DEC44	Rossow, Vivian J.	XIV	RM699	NI	'Oxygen trouble', RTB
17DEC44	Moyle, Crawford N.	XIV	RM680	NI	'Mechanical trouble', RTB
18DEC44	Anderson, Robert E.	XIV	RM770	NI	AA NE Münster, G.
18DEC44	Anderson, Robert E.	XIV	RM769	IFA	EF/CL Diest, B.
18DEC44	Appleton, Arthur S.	XIV	RM699	IOA	AA NE Münster, G., POW
18DEC44	Hale, Peter H.	XIV	RM790	NI	'Oxygen trouble', RTB
18DEC44	Henry, David J. V.	XIV	RM710	NI	'Mechanical trouble', RTB
18DEC44	Rossow, Vivian J.	XIV	RM788	NI	Damaged whilst lndg, Diest
22DEC44	Coleman, Patrick T.	XIV	RM759	NI	ASI u/s, assisted lndg, Eindh.

Date	Pilot Name	Mk[1]	Serial	Cas[2]	Details[3]
22DEC44	Gibbs, N. Peter	XIV	RM789	NI	Weather u/s, lndd Eindhoven
22DEC44	Harding, Ross P.	XIV	RM701	NI	Weather u/s, lndd Eindhoven
22DEC44	Henry, David J. V.	XIV	RM710	NI	Weather u/s, lndd Eindhoven
22DEC44	Spencer, Terence	XIV	RM767	NI	Assisted PTC to land, Eind
22DEC44	Stevenson, Ian T.	XIV	RM863	NI	Weather u/s, lndd Eindhoven
23DEC44	Entire Squadron	XIV	12 A/C	NI	Weather u/s, lndd Eindhoven
26DEC44	Charnock, Harry W.	XIV	RM680	NI	'Mechanical trouble', RTB
26DEC44	Henry, David J. V.	XIV	RM698	NI	AA in tail, Malmedy area, B
26DEC44	Samouelle, Charles J.	XIV	RM696	NI	'Mechanical trouble', RTB
31DEC44	Henry, David J. V.[20]	XIV	RM842	NI	'UC trouble', WUL, Diest, B.
01JAN45	Fleming, Robert	XIV	RM765	NI	'Mechanical trouble', RTB
01JAN45	Rossow, Vivian J.	XIV	RM698	NI	'Mechanical trouble', RTB
01JAN45	Samouelle, Charles J.	XIV	RM790	NI	'Mechanical trouble', RTB
05JAN45	Munson, Rupert W.	XIV	RM863	NI	'Mechanical trouble', RTB
14JAN45	Tebbit, Donald F. J.	XIV	RM788	NI	EF, CNTO, Diest, B.
16JAN45	Gibbs, N. Peter	XIV	RM767	IOA	AA SE of Aachen, G., RR
16JAN45	Harding, Ross P.	XIV	RM707	NI	Streaming glycol, RTB
22JAN45	Benham, Douglas I.	XIV	RM791	NI	'Eng trouble', landed Volkel
23JAN45	Balasse, Maurice A. L.	XIV	RM765	KIA	AA, Coerde, NE Münster, G.
23JAN45	Benham, Douglas I.	XIV	RM791	NI	CD wg, Münster-Waltrop, G.
23JAN45	Gibbs, N. Peter	XIV	RM879	NI	'Radio u/s', Blankenheim, G.
02FEB45	Moyle, Crawford N.	XIV	RM790	NI	'R/T trouble', RTB
02FEB45	Tebbit, Donald F. J.	XIV	RM819	NI	'R/T trouble', RTB
03FEB45	Burne, Thomas R.	XIV	RM698	NI	AA in wing, nr Rheine, G.
03FEB45	Fleming, Robert	XIV	RM789	WIA	AA thru hood, Münster, G.
03FEB45	Gray, Eric	XIV	RM789	NI	'Technical trouble', RTB
03FEB45	Mottershead, Clifford H	XIV	RM842	NI	'R/T failure', RTB
03FEB45	Moyle, Crawford N.	XIV	RM863	NI	AA 6" behind head, Münster
03FEB45	Reid, Daniel J.	XIV	RM790	NI	'R/T trouble', RTB
03FEB45	Stevenson, Ian T.	XIV	RM819	NI	'Engine trouble', RTB
08FEB45	Burne, Thomas R.?[21]	XIV	RM719	NI	'Technical trouble', RTB
08FEB45	Coleman, Patrick T.	XIV	RM680	NI	'Rough engine', RTB
08FEB45	Wilkinson, John F.?[22]	XIV	NR	NI	'Rough engine', RTB
10FEB45	Harding, Ross P.	XIV	RM788	NI	AA in wg, nr Lippstadt, G.
10FEB45	Henry, David J. V.	XIV	RM842	POW	AA/FL, E of Rheine, G.
10FEB45	Tebbit, Donald F. J.	XIV	RM819	NI	'Rough engine', RTB
11FEB45	Munson, Rupert W.	XIV	RM879	NI	'Technical trouble', RTB
11FEB45	Rossow, Vivian J.	XIV	RM696	NI	'Technical trouble', RTB
13FEB45	Coleman, Patrick T.	XIV	RM797	NI	'Gunsight broken', RTB
13FEB45	Harding, Ross P.	XIV	RM819	POW	SD, SW of Lippstadt, G.
13FEB45	Moyle, Crawford N.	XIV	RM789	NI	'Technical trouble', RTB
14FEB45	Woolley, Frank G.	XIV	RM791	NI	AA tail unit, Rheine A/D, G.
14FEB45	Rossow, Vivian J.	XIV	RM696	NI	AA propeller, Rheine A/D, G.

V. Casualties, Accidents and Incidents

Date	Pilot Name	Mk[1]	Serial	Cas[2]	Details[3]
14FEB45	Moyle, Crawford N.	XIV	RM799	NI	Flat battery, landed Y29 Asch
18FEB45	Clanzy, T. Keith	NA	NA	IOA	MVA, broke wrist, DNR
21FEB45	Coleman, Patrick T.	XIV	RM863	NI	AA jettison tank, Lingen, G.
22FEB45	Tebbit, Donald F. J.	XIV	RM789	POW	AA/CL, E of Dülmen, G.
24FEB45	Burne, Thomas R.	XIV	RM790	WIA	AA, Rheine-Münster area, G.
24FEB45	Coleman, Patrick T.	XIV	RM707	NI	Guns u/s, Georgsdorf, G.
25FEB45	Coleman, Patrick T.	XIV	RM799	NI	'R/T trouble', RTB
25FEB45	Gray, Eric	XIV	NH712	NI	'Technical trouble', RTB
25FEB45	Woolley, Frank G.	XIV	RM918	NI	'Technical trouble', RTB
28FEB45	Benham, Douglas I.	XIV	RM791	NI	'R/T trouble', RTB
01MAR45	Fisher, Roy R. G.	XIV	RM879	NI	'Technical trouble', RTB
02MAR45	Mottershead, Clifford H	XIV	RN123	KIA	SD, nr Nijmegen, NL
03MAR45	Coleman, Patrick T.	XIV	RM797	NI	AA, jettison tank, Rheine, G.
03MAR45	Moyle, Crawford N.	XIV	RM799	NI	'Technical trouble', RTB
03MAR45	Stevenson, Ian T.	XIV	RM704	NI	AA propeller blade, Wesel G.
05MAR45	Reid, Daniel J.	XIV	RM916	NI	'Engine trouble', RTB
07MAR45	Coleman, Patrick T.	XIV	RM707	NI	Rudder broken, Warmwell
13MAR45	Unknown (NR)	XIV	RM879	NI	Cat AC, Warmwell, Dorset
13MAR45	Unknown (NR)	XIV	RM885	NI	Cat AC, Warmwell, Dorset
13MAR45	Unknown (NR)	XIV	RM916	NI	Cat AC, Warmwell, Dorset
13MAR45	Unknown (NR)	XIV	RM918	NI	Cat AC, Warmwell, Dorset
21MAR45	Finucane, Raymond PR	XIV	NR	NI	TA, injured airmen, Eindhvn
21MAR45	Hale, Peter H.	XIV	MV255	NI	TON on landing, Eindhoven
21MAR45	Moyle, Crawford N.	XIV	RM915	NI	'Engine trouble', RTB
23MAR45	Jallands, Walter J.	XIV	RM759	NI	RF, landed B.86 Helmond NL
23MAR45	Kelly, Hubert F.	XIV	MV264	NI	RF, landed B.86 Helmond NL
23MAR45	Pairman, William R.	XIV	MV266	NI	HL, Eindhoven, NL
23MAR45	Stowe, William N.	XIV	RM797	NI	EF, CNTO, Eindhoven, NL
24MAR45	Cowell, Peter	XIV	MV264	NI	EF, CNTO, Eindhoven, NL
24MAR45	Fisher, Roy R. G.	XIV	RN210	NI	'Oxygen trouble', RTB
24MAR45	Fleming, Robert	XIV	RN210	NI	'U/S eng instruments', RTB
24MAR45	Hegarty, Francis M.	XIV	RN198	NI	RF, landed Volkel NL
24MAR45	Rake, Derek S. V.	XIV	RN198	NI	AA port wg, Herrenburg, G.
25MAR45	Cowell, Peter	XIV	RM928	NI	No feed from jettison tank, RTB
25MAR45	Rake, Derek S. V.	XIV	MV254	NI	'Engine trouble', RTB
25MAR45	Reid, Daniel J.	XIV	MV264	WIA	AA wing & tail, Bocholt, G.
25MAR45	Un-named pilot (NR)	XIV	NR	NI	AA, Rheine-Münster area, G.
25MAR45	Whale, Frederick V.	XIV	RN210	NI	'Technical trouble', RTB
26MAR45	Bødtker, Carl S.	XIV	MV255	IFA	EF/CL, Volkel, NL
26MAR45	Chalmers, John A.	XIV	RN208	NI	'Engine trouble', RTB
26MAR45	Hegarty, Francis M.	XIV	RM797	NI	'Engine trouble', RTB
26MAR45	Moyle, Crawford N.	XIV	RM817	NI	'Engine trouble', RTB
27MAR45	Moyle, Crawford N.	XIV	RM799	NI	'Engine trouble', landed B.20

Date	Pilot Name	Mk[1]	Serial	Cas[2]	Details[3]
27MAR45	Stevenson, Ian T.	XIV	RM915	NI	Broken rod, landed B.20
28MAR45	Fisher, Roy R. G.	XIV	RM928	NI	'U/S drop tank', RTB
31MAR45	Farfan, Fernand W.	XIV	MV254	NI	'Technical trouble', RTB
31MAR45	4 A/C, Pilots unknown	XIV	5 A/C	NI	RF, landed Volkel, NL
31MAR45	Coleman, Patrick T.	XIV	SM829	NI	RF/CL, Volkel, NL
31MAR45	Rossow, Vivian J.	XIV	RN208	NI	RF, landed B.89 Mill, NL
05APR45	Shepherd, John B.	XIV	RM797	NI	AA Meppen-Quackenbrück, G
05APR45	Smith, Roy D. A.	XIV	RM759	NI	EF/CL/USR, Eindhoven NL
05APR45	Coleman, Patrick T.	XIV	RM915	NI	Hail damage, camera & grill
05APR45	Stowe, William N.	XIV	RM931	NI	AA Propeller, Meppen, G.
07APR45	Bødtker, Carl S.	XIV	MV264	NI	'Engine trouble', RTB
07APR45	Whale, Frederick V.	XIV	RM697	NI	'Engine trouble', RTB
14APR45	Farfan, Fernand W.	XIV	RM792	NI	'Engine trouble', RTB
16APR45	Chalmers, John A.	XIV	RN208	NI	RF/CL Nijmegen, NL
18APR45	Smith, Roy D. A.	XIV	RM696	NI	Rod thru piston head, RTB
19APR45	Coleman, Patrick T.	XIV	RM915	NI	'R/T trouble', RTB
20APR45	Coleman, Patrick T.	XIV	MV267	NI	Aircraft unserviceable, RTB
20APR45	Fisher, Roy R. G.	XIV	MV260	NI	'Rough engine', RTB
20APR45	Hegarty, Francis M.	XIV	RM915	NI	'Rough engine' & prop. dam.
21APR45	Rossow, Vivian J.	XIV	SM826	NI	'Technical trouble', TO late
23APR45	Shepherd, John B.	XIV	MV264	NI	CD from explosion, Rathenow
24APR45	Smith Roy D. A.[23]	XIV	MV249	IFA	COG with RM696, Celle, G.
24APR45	Smart, Lionel H.	XIV	RM696	IFA	COG with MV249, Celle, G.
25APR45	Gaze, Frederick A. O.	XIV	SM823	NI	'Unserviceable R/T', RTB
25APR45	Hale, Peter H.	XIV	RB143	NI	'Technical trouble', RTB
25APR45	Kelly, Hubert F.	XIV	NH692	NI	AA R/T & rudder, Ratzeburg
27APR45	Scott, Peter F.	XIV	RB159	NI	Damaged radiator, RTB
28APR45	Coleman, Patrick T.	XIV	SM826	NI	CD port wg, nr Niendorf, G.
28APR45	Gaze, Frederick A. O.	XIV	SM826	NI	Gun sight u/s, Schwerin A/D
28APR45	Wilkinson, John F.	XIV	MV254	NI	CD, explosion, Schwerin A/D
29APR45	Hale, Peter H.	XIV	RM928	NI	'Technical trouble', RTB
29APR45	Cowell, Peter	XIV	MV264	NI	'Technical trouble', RTB
02MAY45	Lawrence, Thomas E.	XIV	RM928	NI	EF, CNTO, Celle, G.
03MAY45	Chalmers, John A.	XIV	RN208	NI	Non-Op, RF/CL nr Celle, G.
21MAY45	Stevenson, Ian T.[24]	XIV	RM915	NI	Hole in cylinder head, CPH
24MAY45	Stevenson, Ian T.[24]	XIV	RB159	NI	Oil leak, Copenhagen, Denmk

VI. Roll of Honour
August 1942-May 1945

This Appendix lists the names of the 23 men who died or were killed during their service with 41 Squadron between August 1942 and May 1945. A total of 64 men appear on the unit's World War II Roll of Honour.

Pilot	Rank	Age	Date	Details
Balasse, Maurice Arthur Leon	Flt Lt	30	23JAN45	KIA
Bednarz, Jozef	Sgt Plt	22	01FEB43	KFA
Boyd, Robert James	Fg Off	24	06SEP43	KIA
Chattin, Peter Warren	WO	23	03SEP44	KIA
Cope, Arthur Reginald[1]	Sgt Plt	22	09MAR43	MPD
East, Walter Raymond	Sgt Plt	21	03MAY43	KIA
Gillitt, Frank Norman	Flt Lt	23	22OCT42	KFA
Goens, Ryklof van	Flt Lt	30	17AUG44	MPD
Goodall, Bernard Bryn	Sgt Plt	23	15AUG42	KFA
Gray, James Arthur Bryce	Sgt Plt	22	03OCT43	KIA
Harrison, Ronald	Fg Off	22	22OCT42	KFA
Hogarth, Rycherde Henry Wilshere	Fg Off	21	18JUL43	KIA
Hyde, Geoffrey Cockayne	Sqn Ldr	27	19AUG42	KIA
Mottershead, Clifford Harper	Fg Off	25	02MAR45	KIA
Murrin, Wilfred Francis[2]	Cpl	23	18MAY43	KAS
Oddy, Clifford	Sgt Plt	21	17JUL44	KFA
Oxenham, Russel Edwin George	Sgt Plt	20	24SEP42	KFA
Poynton, Thomas Rex	Flt Lt	23	23APR43	KIA
Robinson, Kenneth Basil	Fg Off	22	07JUN44	KAS
Scott, Thomas Roland	Fg Off	20	22OCT42	KFA
Shea, David John	Fg Off	20	13MAR44	KFA
Short, Roger Lee	Sgt Plt	21	17JUL44	KFA
Thomas, John Islwyn	Sgt Plt	23	24APR43	KFA

VII. Prisoners of War
August 1942-May 1945

This Appendix shows the names, dates and places of capture and Camps of the eleven pilots who became Prisoners of War whilst serving with 41 Squadron between August 1942 and May 1945. Men who served with 41 Squadron but became Prisoners of War whilst with subsequent squadrons are not listed.

Name	Capture Date	Place of Capture	Camps
Hoare, Reginald M.[1]	01APR43	Ostend, Belgium	Stalag Luft III, Sagan, Germany (Żagań, Poland), Apr 1943-Feb 1945; Stalag VIII-D, Nuremberg (Nürnberg), Germany, Feb-Apr 1945; Stalag VII-A, Moosburg, Germany, Apr 1945
Haywood, Douglas	27AUG43	Boulogne, France	Stalag Luft III, Sagan, Germany (Żagań, Poland), Sep 1943-Jan 1945; Stalag III-A, Luckenwalde, Germany, Feb-May 1945
Prickett, Leslie A.[2]	17DEC43	Paris, France	Fresnes Prison, Paris, France, Dec 1943; Stalag Luft III, Sagan, Germany (Żagań, Poland), Jan 1944-Jan 1945; Oflag III-A, Luckenwalde, Germany, Feb-May 1945
Parry, Hugh L.[3]	07FEB44	Paris, France	Fresnes Prison, Paris, France, Feb 1944; Stalag Luft III, Sagan, Germany (Żagań, Poland), Mar 1944-Jan 1945; Marlag & Milag Nord, Westertimke, Germany, Feb-Apr 1945
Wagner, Herbert A.	02JUN44	Guernsey, Channel Islands	Stalag Luft I, Barth, Germany, Jul 1944-May 1945
Slack, Thomas A. H.	23AUG44	Hesdin, France	Stalag Luft III, Sagan, Germany (Żagań, Poland), Sep 1944-Jan 1945; Stalag III-A, Luckenwalde, Germany, Feb-May 1945
Graham, Peter B.	01SEP44	Near St. Omer, France	Stalag Luft I, Barth, Germany, Sep 1944-May 1945
Appleton, Arthur S.	18DEC44	Rheine, Germany	Stalag Luft VII, Bankau, Germany (Bąków, Poland), Jan 1945; Stalag III-A, Luckenwalde, Germany, Jan-May 1945
Henry, David J. V.	10FEB45	East of Rheine, Germany	Oflag XIII-A, Nürnberg-Langwasser, Germany, Feb-Apr 1945
Harding, Ross P.	13FEB45	Werl, Germany	Stalag XIII-D, Nürnberg-Langwasser, Germany, Mar-Apr 1945; Stalag VII-A, Moosburg, Germany, Apr 1945
Tebbit, Donald F. J.	22FEB45	West of Coesfeld, Germany	Oflag XIII-A, Nürnberg-Langwasser, Germany, Mar 1945; Stalag VII-A, Moosburg, Germany, Mar-Apr 1945

VIII. Aerial Victories
August 1942–May 1945

During World War II, 41 Squadron was credited with destroying 200 aircraft in the air and one on the ground, probably destroying 61 aircraft in the air, damaging 109 aircraft in the air and 22 on the ground, and destroying 53 (45 plus 8 shared) V1 flying bombs and damaging one. This appendix lists the Squadron's victories for the period August 1942 to May 1945. Consolidated entries, such as those of 13 February 1945, indicate the individual victory was shared by more than one pilot.

DESTROYED AIRCRAFT (AIR TO AIR)

Date	Pilot	Aircraft	Location[1]	CR[2]
17APR43	Hogarth, Rycherde H. W.	Ju88D-1	2m off Ostend, B.	255
04JUN43	Solak, Jerzy J.	FW190	3-5m S of Eastbourne, Ssx	379
04SEP43	Birbeck, Clive R.	FW190	Le Touquet-Beussent, F.	107
22SEP43	Smith, Donald H.	FW190	W of Évreux, F.	378
24SEP43	Glen, Arthur A.	2 FW190	N of Beauvais, F.	233
20OCT43	Collis, Ronald T. H.[3]	FW190	N of Rouen, F.	157
20OCT43	Cowell, Peter	FW190	Nr Beaumont-le-Roger, F.	165
20OCT43	Fisher, Douglas P.[4]	Me109	Évreux, F.	212
20OCT43	Newman, Benjamin B.	Me109G	Nr Beaumont-le-Roger, F.	324
03SEP44	Spencer, Terence	FW190A-5	Overhespen, B.	SA
03SEP44	Coleman, Patrick T.	FW190A-8	Overhespen, B.	SA
23JAN45	Benham, Douglas I.	2 FW190D	Münster-Waltrop, G.	67
23JAN45	Hegarty, Francis M.	FW190D	Münster-Waltrop, G.	250
13FEB45	Gray, Eric	Me110G	10m S of Lippstadt, G.	240
13FEB45	Harding, Ross P.	Me110G	10m S of Lippstadt, G.	240
13FEB45	Hegarty, Francis M.	Me110G	10m S of Lippstadt, G.	240
14FEB45	Moyle, Crawford N.	FW190D	E of Rheine, G.	494
14FEB45	Stevenson, Ian T.[5,6]	2 FW190D	NE of Münster, G.	494
14FEB45	Woolley, Frank G.[7]	FW190D	Rheine Aerodrome, G.	496
25FEB45	Reid, Daniel J.	FW190D-9	2km E of Clausheide, G.	352
02MAR45	Reid, Daniel J.	Ar234	Nr Enschede, NL	176
11APR45	Gaze, Frederick A. O.	Ju52/3m	Ottersburg, G.	224
12APR45	Gaze, Frederick A. O.	Ar234	W of Bremen, G.	171
12APR45	Rake, Derek S. V.	Ar234	W of Bremen, G.	175
14APR45	Shepherd, John B.	Me110	Nordholz A/D, G.	364
14APR45	Shepherd, John B.	Me163	Nordholz A/D, G.	364
16APR45	Shepherd, John B.	FW190	Hagenow, G.	365

Date	Pilot	Aircraft	Location[1]	CR[2]
16APR45	Wilkinson, John F.	FW190	Hagenow, G.	481
17APR45	Hegarty, Francis M.	Ju88C	Lübeck A/D, G.	252
20APR45	Coleman, Patrick T.	FW190D	N of Neuruppin A/D, G.	152
20APR45	Gray, Eric[8]	2 FW190D	Teschendorf, G.	241
20APR45	Scott, Peter F.	FW190D	Teschendorf Wood, G.	362
	Wilkinson, John F.			483
20APR45	Shepherd, John B.	FW190D	Kremmen Forest, G.	366
20APR45	Shepherd, John B.	FW190D	Nr Neuruppin, G.	366
	Wilkinson, John F.			483
20APR45	Stevenson, Ian T.	FW190D	Teschendorf Wood, G.	390
25APR45	Chalmers, John A.	Ju188	Rechlin A/D, G.	143
	Coleman, Patrick T.			153
28APR45	Chalmers, John A.	He111	W of Goldberg, G.	155
	Coleman, Patrick T.			
	Hale, Peter H.			
	Moyle, Crawford N.			
28APR45	Gaze, Frederick A. O.	FW190D	N of Schwerin A/D, G.	225
	Wilkinson, John F.			484
28APR45	Wilkinson, John F.	FW190D	Schwerin A/D, G.	484
30APR45	Gaze, Frederick A. O.	FW190D	N of Lauenberg, G.	226
30APR45	Shepherd, John B.	FW190	N of Lauenberg, G.	367
		Me109	NW of Lake Ratzeburg, G.	
01MAY45	Bødtker, Carl S.	FW190D	S of Schwerin A/D, G.	111
01MAY45	Coleman, Patrick T.[9]	FW190	SW of Plau, G.	156
		2 FW190	Lake Schwerin, G.	
01MAY45	Cowell, Peter	2 FW190D	Lake Schwerin, G.	169
01MAY45	Gray, Eric	FW190D	E of Lake Schwerin, G.	242
	Shepherd, John B.			368
01MAY45	Stevenson, Ian T.	FW190	SW of Wittenberg, G.	392
02MAY45	Chalmers, John A.	2 Fi156	Lake Schwerin area, G.	145
02MAY45	Smith, Roy D. A.	Fi156	Schwerin area, G.	34
03MAY45	Rake, Derek S. V.	Ju188	Norderstapel-Husum, G.	350

PROBABLY DESTROYED AIRCRAFT

Date	Pilot	Aircraft	Location	CR[2]
27APR43	Birbeck, Clive R.[10]	FW190	Somme Estuary, F.	103
16SEP43	Newman, Benjamin B.[11]	Me109G	Bernay-Évreux, F.	321
22SEP43	Birbeck, Clive R.[12]	FW190	W of Évreux, F.	109
24SEP43	Galitzine, Emanuel V.	FW190	SW of Beauvais, F.	217
24SEP43	Newman, Benjamin B.[13]	FW190	Beauvais, F.	323
20APR45	Rossow, Vivian J.	Me262	Neuruppin A/D, G.	357
25APR45	Cowell, Peter	Me262	Lübeck A/D, G.	168

DAMAGED AIRCRAFT (AIR TO AIR)

Date	Pilot	Aircraft	Location	CR²
14AUG42	Prickett, Leslie A.[14]	Ju88D	20m SSE of Dublin, Éire	SA
	Warren, Kenneth G.[14]			SA
	Miksa, Wlodzimierz[14]		NW of Barrow, Lancs	SA
	Malec, Jerzy[14]			SA
19AUG42	Hone, Douglas H.[15]	FW190	2m W of Dieppe, F.	SA
19AUG42	Imbert, André	FW190	Off Dieppe, F.	267
19AUG42	Stepp, Malta L.	FW190	Dieppe, F.	387
04JUN43	Smith, Donald H.	FW190	10m S of Beachy Hd, Ssx	377
22SEP43	Vann, William. H.	Me109G	W of Évreux, F.	407
27SEP43	Birbeck, Clive R.	Me109G	Bet Beauvais & Dieppe, F.	108
		FW190		
27SEP43	Graham, Peter B.	FW190	15m NW of Beauvais, F.	234
03SEP44	Chattin, Peter W.	FW190A	Overhespen, B.	SA
23JAN45	Henry, David J. V.	FW190D	Münster-Waltrop, G.	253
23JAN45	Stowe, William N.	FW190D	Dortmund, G.	393
14FEB45	Gray, Eric	Me262	W of Rheine, G.	496
14FEB45	Rossow, Vivian J.	Me262	Rheine A/D, G.	356
28MAR45	Lawrence, Thomas E.	FW190D	Rheine A/D, G.	270
16APR45	Keefer, George C.[16]	FW190	Hagenow A/D, G.	116
25APR45	Cowell, Peter	Me262	Lübeck A/D, G.	168
01MAY45	Scott, Peter F.	2 FW190D	Nr Lake Schwerin, G.	363

DAMAGED AIRCRAFT (AIR TO GROUND)

Date	Pilot	Aircraft	Location	CR²
17APR45	Coleman, Patrick T.	Ju188	Ground, nr Parchim, G.	150
18APR45	Coleman, Patrick T.	Ju88	Ground, 3m E of Pötrau, G.	151
24APR45	Cowell, Peter	16 x Ar196	Shore, Ratzeburg Lake, G.	167
	Fisher, Roy R. G.			
	Jallands, Walter J.			
	Kelly, Hubert F.			
25APR45	Chalmers, John A.	Fi156	Ground, Rechlin A/D, G.	143
25APR45	Coleman, Patrick T.	FW190	Ground, Rechlin A/D, G.	153
02MAY45	Smith, Roy D. A.	Fi156	Ground, Schwerin area, G.	34

DESTROYED V1 FLYING BOMBS[17]

Date	Pilot	Location	CR[2]
20JUN44	Gibbs, N. Peter	N of Eastbourne, Ssx	502
20JUN44	Curtis, Keith R.	SSE of Tunbridge Wells, Kent	502
21JUN44	Gibbs, N. Peter	Off Beachy Head, Ssx	227
22JUN44	Anderson, Robert E. Birbeck, Clive R.	N of Maidstone, Kent	500
22JUN44	Robertson, Colin S.[18]	6m N of Pevensey, Ssx	500
23JUN44	Balasse, Maurice A. L.	10m N of Hastings, Ssx	505
23JUN44	Payne, Jim C. J.	SW of Rye, Ssx	505
23JUN44	Slack, Thomas A. H. Tempests, other sqns	Hastings, Ssx	505
23JUN44	Spencer, Terence	10-15m NNE of Hastings, Ssx	381
24JUN44	Gibbs, N. Peter	8-10m S of Hastings, Ssx	228
25JUN44	Short, Roger L.[19] 2 Spitfires, other sqn	Ashford, Kent	504
25JUN44	Spencer, Terence	High Halden, Kent	504
03JUL44	Balasse, Maurice A. L.	4m N of Bexhill, Ssx	48
03JUL44	Chapman, Robert H.	30m SE of Beachy Head, Ssx	146
04JUL44	Balasse, Maurice A. L. Woollard, Frederick G.	1m W of Lydd/N of Rye, Ssx	SA
05JUL44	Harding, Ross P.*	NW of Rye, Ssx	245
07JUL44	Graham, Peter B.[20]	6m W of Hailsham, Ssx	503
07JUL44	Stevenson, Ian T.[21] Majewski, Longin[21]	Eastbourne, Ssx	503
08JUL44	Chattin, Peter W.	Thames Estuaary	501
08JUL44	Gibbs, N. Peter	2m S of Eastbourne, Ssx	501
09JUL44	Anderson, Robert E. Appleton, Arthur S.	12m SE of Beachy Head, Ssx	497
12JUL44	Chattin, Peter W.	4m NW of Ashford, Kent	147
13JUL44	Payne, Jim C. J.	N of Hastings, Ssx	339
14JUL44	Thiele, Keith F.	Channel off Cliff End, Ssx	SA
16JUL44	Fisher, Douglas P.	50m SSW of Dungeness, Kent	204
19JUL44	Balasse, Maurice A. L. Tempest, other squadron	Nr Lamberhurst, Kent	49
20JUL44	Stevenson, Ian T.	SE of Dungeness, Kent	388
21JUL44	Appleton, Arthur S.	20m S of Hastings, Ssx	498
23JUL44	Balasse, Maurice A. L. Payne, Jim C. J.	10m SE of Hastings, Ssx	499
23JUL44	Appleton, Arthur S.	8m S of Bexhill, Ssx	499
26JUL44	Gray, Eric	6m S of Hastings, Ssx	238
26JUL44	Balasse, Maurice A. L. Mustang, other squadron	5-8m S of Beachy Head, Ssx	51

Date	Pilot	Location	CR²
27JUL44	Robertson, Colin S.	Mid-Channel	353
29JUL44	Balasse, Maurice A. L.[#]	10-15m W of Le Touquet, F.	52
29JUL44	Balasse, Maurice A. L.	3m SE of Woodchurch, Kent	53
04AUG44	Slack, Thomas A. H.	Dngnss-Isle of Oxney	376
05AUG44	Stevenson, Ian T.[*]	Brede, Ssx	389
09AUG44	Spencer, Terence[*]	5m N of Hastings, Ssx	382
09AUG44	Cook, Harry	Mid-Channel	158
11AUG44	Wilkinson, John F.[22] Bargielowski, Jakub[22]	E of Ashford, Kent	480
15AUG44	Malone, Charles J.[22] Kleimeyer, Robert G.[23]	2m NW of Ashford, Kent	303
15AUG44	Harding, Ross P.	Romney Marsh-N of Ivychurch, Kent	246
16AUG44	Rossow, Vivian J.	5m WNW of Ashford, Kent	355
16AUG44	Graham, Peter B.[24]	Nr Wrotham, Kent	235
17AUG44	Harding, Ross P.	1½m NE of Brenzett, Kent	247
17AUG44	Graham, Peter B.	Denge Wood, Kent	236
18AUG44	Ware, James P.	N of Hollingbourne, Kent	429
19AUG44	Spencer, Terence	2m NNW of Appledore, Kent	383
20AUG44	Gray, Eric	7m off Folkestone, Kent	239
23AUG44	Spencer, Terence	2m S of Mersham, Kent	384
23AUG44	Spencer, Terence	Nr Harrietsham, Kent	385
23AUG44	Reid, Daniel J.[25] Wood, Leonard A.[25]	10m NW of Ashford, Kent	351
27AUG44	Spencer, Terence	15m N of Rye, Ssx	386

DAMAGED V1 FLYING BOMBS

Date	Pilot	Location	CR²
23AUG44	Rossow, Vivian J.	W of Gris Nez, F.	StO

IX. Ground Victories
August 1942-May 1945

There has never been any definitive record of 41 Squadron's World War II ground victories against hardware other than enemy aircraft. The below list, the first of its type, has been compiled by extracting data from the Squadron's ORB, Station and Wing ORBs, Combat Reports, Intelligence Reports, *Pilot Service Records*, pilots' logbooks, and other sources.

The greatest issue in reconciling claims of ground targets was attempting to separate repetition and error from fact, particularly as many claims were shared. It proved extremely difficult to correlate victories shared between pilots, as some pilots indicated particular claims were shared, whilst other pilots who claimed the same victories did not. It was also often unclear during which operation claims were made on any given day or even with whom pilots shared their claims, particularly during the intensive period between January and May 1945.

As such, any record of ground victories is likely to be erroneous to some extent. Although every effort has been made to achieve the most accurate record possible, this data should be treated as a guide only, with the understanding that whilst some victories may not be recorded, others may be duplicated.

Date	Object Claimed	Area
19AUG42	1 gun post damaged	Dieppe, F.
17APR43	1x 400-ton ship shot up & damaged, Cat C	6m N of Dieppe, F.
21APR43	1x 300-ton motor barge shot up	5m S of Boulogne, F.
23JUL43	Hutted camp shot up	Épreville, F.
05AUG43	1 locomotive damaged	Vassonville, F.
05AUG43	1 blue motor car damaged	6m S of Dieppe, F.
08AUG43	Several goods wagons damaged	Southeast of Caen, F.
09AUG43	1 locomotive damaged	1m S of Dieppe, F.
09AUG43	1 large blue staff car destroyed	¼m E of Le Bourg, F.
11AUG43	2 locomotives damaged, Cat B	Crosville & St. Aubin, S of Dieppe, F.
13OCT43	4 locomotives & numerous goods wagons damaged	Falaise-Trouville-sur-Mer area, F.
26OCT43	3 locomotives & wagons damaged	Ouville, Crosville & Vassonville, F.
08MAY44	1 light Flak post shot up	Dinan-Dinard Aerodrome, F.
11MAY44	1 large staff car shot up, into ditch	Plougonver, F.
11MAY44	1x 3-ton truck damaged	Guingamp, F.
11MAY44	1x 3-ton truck damaged	Plouaret, F.
11MAY44	8 camouflaged HDVs destroyed	S of St.-Michel-en-Grève, F.
14MAY44	1 MET ('technical lorry') damaged	St. Méen-le-Grande, F.
14MAY44	1 camouflaged motor car shot up, into ditch	Bet St Méen-le-Grande & Broons, F.
28MAY44	4 motor cars damaged	Road bet Bourbriac & Morlaix, F.
28MAY44	1 locomotive damaged	Nr Yffiniac, F.
29MAY44	40 goods trucks damaged	La Haye-du-Puits, F.
29MAY44	4 locomotives damaged	Lessay area, F.

31MAY44	Dispersal huts shot up	Vannes, F.
31MAY44	1 lorry destroyed	Kerlin Bastard, F.
31MAY44	1 locomotive & goods wagons damaged	Carhaix area, F.
31MAY44	1 locomotive destroyed	Landévant, F.
31MAY44	1x 400-ton merchant ship damaged	Blavet River bet Hennebont & Lorient, F.
01JUN44	Flak post shot up	Guernsey, Channel Islands
01JUN44	3 locomotives damaged Cat B	St. Brieuc-Yffiniac-Lamballe area, F.
07JUN44	1 camouflaged lorry damaged	Nr St. Brieuc, F.
07JUN44	1 large camouflaged MT tanker w 2 turrets damaged	Nr Guingamp, F.
07JUN44	1 lorry damaged	Nr Morlaix, F.
07JUN44	1 locomotive, 16 goods wagons damaged	Railway line E of Morlaix, F.
07JUN44	1 large lorry damaged	S of Morlaix, F.
10JUN44	Fishing boats damaged	Sark Harbour, Channel Islands
12JUN44	1 armoured car with 2 guns damaged	S of Guingamp, F.
12JUN44	2 cars set on fire	Nr St. Gilles-Pligeaux, F.
12JUN44	1 encampment shot up	N of Corlay, F.
12JUN44	4 large motor lorries w camouflage netting & 1 large vehicle carrying wireless aerials damaged	Bet Loudéac & St Méen-le-Grande, F.
12JUN44	1 locomotive destroyed and 4 railway carriages damaged	Nr Broons, F.
12JUN44	4 lorries & 1 balloon damaged	Nr Loudéac, F.
16JUN44	Gun positions shot up	Lannion A/D, F.
16JUN44	Radar station shot up	Lannion, F.
16JUN44	1 staff car & 1 lorry shot up	Lamballe-St Brieuc area, F.
17JUN44	1 camouflaged lorry shot up	Nr Plancoët, F.
17JUN44	1 large camouflaged wagon shot up	Bet Plestin-les-Grèves & Noyal, F.
17JUN44	1x 2-ton truck damaged	Bet Lamballe and Plancoët, F.
17JUN44	24 railway trucks damaged in a Station	E of Plancoët, F.
17JUN44	1 staff car strafed & set on fire	S of Plancoët, F.
17JUN44	1x 15 cwt truck damaged	S of Dinan, F.
17JUN44	1 lorry damaged	Bet Pleudihen-sur-Rance & Combourg, F.
26AUG44	6 barges damaged	Canal, N of Ypres, B.
26AUG44	1 barge damaged	Junction of 2 canals, 8m S of Bergues, F.
30AUG44	1 locomotive damaged	Thourout, B.
30AUG44	3 covered railway wagons in flames & 24 damaged	Roulers, B.
30AUG44	5 barges damaged	N of Roulers, B.
30AUG44	2 tugs towing 3 barges each, damaged	E of Roulers, B.
30AUG44	3 large covered technical lorries damaged	SE of Roulers, B.
30AUG44	2x 8-ton Reichsbahn lorries & trailers destroyed in flames, 2 railway wagons destroyed, and 13 railway wagons (2 smoking), 7 lorries, 1 staff car, and 1 light anti-tank gun & carrier damaged	Bet Roulers & Courtrai, B.
31AUG44	1 locomotive damaged, Cat B	St Omer, F.
31AUG44	1 locomotive damaged, Cat B	Lille area, F.

31AUG44	1x 5-ton covered lorry in flames, and 3x 3-ton lorries, 1 car & 1 barge damaged	Armentières, F.
31AUG44	10 railway trucks damaged	Dixmude, B.
31AUG44	6 lorries damaged	Menin, Roulers & Poperinghe, B.
31AUG44	9 covered railway wagons damaged	Roulers, Menin & Dixmude, B.
01SEP44	1 railway wagon destroyed (flames), & 1 locomotive & 12 wagons damaged	Railway sidings, W of Menin, B.
01SEP44	4 open railway wagons & 2 passenger coaches damaged	Menin Station, B.
01SEP44	1 lorry destroyed and 2 damaged	Menin area, B.
01SEP44	1 locomotive damaged	Thielt-Deinze railway line, B.
01SEP44	2 lorries damaged, Cat B	Cassel, F.
01SEP44	1x 80-foot barge damaged	Canal N of Ypres, B.
01SEP44	1 locomotive damaged, Cat B	Nr Esquelbecq, F.
01SEP44	4 barges damaged	S of St Omer, F.
01SEP44	1 locomotive of a goods train damaged, Cat B	Armentières, F.
01SEP44	6 locomotives Cat B and 6 railway wagons damaged	S of Ypres, B.
01SEP44	3 ammunition trucks destroyed (blew up)	SW of Ypres, B.
03SEP44	20 closed railway wagons damaged	Proven, NW of Poperinghe, B.
03SEP44	3 barges damaged	N of Ypres, B.
12SEP44	V2 site strafed (6 concrete huts, 1 tunnel w 2 entrances, 1 derrick, 2 railway lines, & new excavations)	2½ km N of Katwijk, NL
16SEP44	1x 32-seat charabanc transporter in flames	Warmond, N of Leiden, NL
18SEP44	1 flak barge destroyed	S of Bruinisse, Schouwen Island, NL
18SEP44	C-47 Dakota (force-landed & captured USAAF aircraft)	Nr Haamstede, Schouwen Island, NL
18SEP44	1 gun post damaged	W coast of Schouwen Island, NL
18DEC44	8 locomotives damaged	S, SW & NE of Münster, G.
18DEC44	Hutted camp shot up, and 4 armoured cars, 1 lorry & 1 motorcar damaged	30m W of Coesfeld, G.
01JAN45	1x 3-ton transport and 15 railway trucks damaged	Bonn-Koblenz, G.
01JAN45	1 MET and 1 signal box damaged	Unknown, NR
01JAN45	2 MET damaged	S. Ruhr, G.
01JAN45	1 truck and a railway siding damaged	St. Vith area, B.
14JAN45	2 MET destroyed, and 1 tank, 2x 15 cwt transports, 9 MET, 1 diesel engine & 6 railway wagons damaged	Nr Pelm, G.
16JAN45	2 MET destroyed, 7 MET & 3 railways trucks damaged, & 2 ammunition dumps hit	SE of Aachen-Vogelsang A/D area, G.
21JAN45	1 German staff car strafed and left on fire	Unknown, NR
22JAN45	2 MET destroyed and 5 MET damaged	Coesfeld area, G.
22JAN45	3 transports damaged	Coesfeld-Lotte area, G.
22JAN45	1 locomotive & 9 trucks damaged	Nr Borken, G.
22JAN45	1 large transport and trailer & 1x 15 cwt truck destroyed	S of Coesfeld, G.
23JAN45	1 locomotive damaged	Bet Billerbeck & Havixbeck, G.
23JAN45	1 utility car & 1 HDV shot up	Münster area, G.
23JAN45	2 transports destroyed, 2 railway trucks set on fire, and 1 locomotive & 7 railway trucks damaged	Münster-Hamm, G.
23JAN45	15 heavy transports destroyed (5 in flames) & 1 truck damaged	Blankenheim area, G.

Date	Description	Location
29JAN45	2x 3-ton trucks destroyed & 1 damaged, 7 anti-tank guns damaged & huts shot up	Gutersloh area, G.
01FEB45	1 truck and trailer damaged	Münster-Dülmen, G.
02FEB45	1 lorry & 1 MET destroyed, 2 MET in flames, 3 MET & 1 armoured car damaged	Albersloh, SE of Beckum, nr Sendenhorst & Wolbeck, nr Telgte, G.
03FEB45	2 searchlights destroyed, 1 locomotive, 1 train w 3 flak wagons 2 searchlight posts, 2 lorries, 2x 3-ton trucks & a house damaged	Rheine-Osnabrück area, G.
03FEB45	2 locomotives & barges damaged	Münster area, G.
03FEB45	3 MET damaged	Coesfeld, G.
03FEB45	1 truck destroyed & 2 trucks damaged	Nr Osnabrück, G.
03FEB45	4 locomotives, 4 MET & 1 railway wagon damaged	Münster-Hamm-Paderborn area, G.
06FEB45	2 locomotives damaged	Nr Diepenau, G.
08FEB45	1 locomotive damaged	S of Rheine, G.
09FEB45	1 MET destroyed and 1 MET damaged	N of Beckum, G.
09FEB45	4 locomotives damaged	Ahlen-Oelde & Beckum-Lippstadt lines, G
10FEB45	Poss 1 locomotive damaged	Nr Rheine, G.
10FEB45	2 MET destroyed, 1 MET damaged	N of Hamm, G.
10FEB45	1 excavator damaged	Nr Coesfeld, G.
11FEB45	3 locomotives & 8 railway trucks damaged	Münster-Gutersloh line, G.
11FEB45	3 tugs and 1 barge damaged	Ems-Weser Canal, W of Bramsche, G.
11FEB45	2 locomotives damaged	Nr Lippstadt, G.
11FEB45	1x 3-ton lorry damaged	Nr Warendorf, G.
11FEB45	2 lorries destroyed and 1 lorry & trailer damaged	Nr Beckum, G.
13FEB45	1x 30-seat bus, 1x 3-ton transport, 3 large trucks, 1x 15 cwt van, 1 saloon car & 1 barge damaged	SE of Münster, G.
13FEB45	1 locomotive damaged & 3 barges strafed	N of Münster, G.
13FEB45	4 locomotives, 1 MET & 12 trucks damaged	Soest-Ahlen area, G.
13FEB45	1 MET destroyed & 2 MET damaged	Nr Ostereiden, G.
13FEB45	1 MET destroyed and 2 MET damaged	Ahlen-Paderborn area, G.
14FEB45	1 locomotive damaged	Rheine area, G.
21FEB45	2 MET destroyed, 1 MET, 1 HDV, 1 locomotive & 6 railway trucks damaged	Lingen area, G.
21FEB45	1 MET destroyed, 2 MET & 1 oil truck damaged	Dümmer Lake, G.
22FEB45	2 MET destroyed, & 1 locomotive, 21 covered railway trucks, 1 oil tanker & 5 MET damaged	Dümmer Lake-Münster & Bielefeld-Osnabrück areas, G.
22FEB45	2 locomotives & 14 MET damaged	Gutersloh-Rheine & Soest-Paderborn areas, G.
24FEB45	2 MET destroyed, 1 MET and 6 barges damaged	S of Georgsdorf, G.
24FEB45	1 locomotive damaged	Rheine-Münster area, G.
25FEB45	1 ammunition hut & 1 MET destroyed, 1 tug, 3 barges, 1 hut & 2 MET damaged	Rheine-Dümmer Lake area, G.
25FEB45	1 house destroyed	Nr Lengerich, G.
25FEB45	6 MET damaged	Rheine-Münster-Gutersloh area, G.
25FEB45	4 MET damaged	Münster area, G.
28FEB45	1 locomotive, 2 barges, 10 trucks & 3 MET damaged	Hamm-Münster area, G.

03MAR45	9 MET destroyed & 24 damaged	Wesel area, G.
03MAR45	3 MET destroyed & 12 damaged	Wesel area, G.
23MAR45	1 MET damaged	Nr Rheine. G.
25MAR45	1 MET damaged & a supply dump strafed	Nr Dolmen, G.
25MAR45	1 ammunition truck destroyed & 2 MET damaged	SW of Münster, G.
25MAR45	2 MET destroyed & 12 barges, 10 railway trucks & 2 MET damaged	Rheine-Münster area, G.
25MAR45	1 gasometer, 1 motorcycle with sidecar & 1 halftrack destroyed	Bocholt, G.
25MAR45	3 MET damaged	Coesfeld-Rheine-Münster area, G.
26MAR45	1 despatch motorcycle destroyed & 1 Mk. IV tank & 1 armoured car damaged	Nr Rhede, G.
28MAR45	11 MET, 6 HDTs, 25 trucks, 20 flat cars, 1 tug and nine barges damaged, 1 barge left in flames & 1 RDF antennae strafed.[1]	Enschede-Rheine-Osnabrück-Münster area, G.
30MAR45	24 MET & 1x 88mm gun damaged	Dülmen area, G.
30MAR45	1 locomotive & 10 railway trucks damaged	Münster area, G.
02APR45	2 MET damaged	Bippen, G.
03APR45	12 MET destroyed and 6 damaged	Herzlake, G.
04APR45	8 barges, 2 tugs, 1 lorry, 1 staff car & 1 HDV damaged	Meppen area, G.
04APR45	3 tugs & 11 barges damaged	Ems-Dortmund Canal, G.
04APR45	1 lorry & trailer destroyed, & 3 staff cars, 1 jeep, 1 motorcycle with sidecar, 1 half-track & 2 tugs damaged	Nr Nordhorn, G.
05APR45	8 barges, 4 half-tracks & 2 MET damaged	Nr Wettrup, G.
05APR45	1 MET destroyed & 3 damaged	Löningen and Lindern, G.
07APR45	3 MET damaged	Meppen area, G.
08APR45	1 locomotive, 12 tankers, 2 passenger coaches & 1 MET destroyed, & 2 locomotives, 6 tankers, 6 trucks & 1 MET damaged	Nienburg area, G.
09APR45	6 MET damaged	Meppen area, G.
10APR45	2 large lorries destroyed & 4 MET damaged	Fassberg area, G.
10APR45	5 railway trucks destroyed & 10 damaged	Visselhövede-Soltau area, G.
10APR45	2 locomotives and 10 railway trucks damaged	Bremen-Hamburg line, nr Metzendorf, G.
11APR45	1 MET & 1 HDV damaged	Bremen-Nienburg area, G.
11APR45	3 locomotives damaged	Ottersburg-Sottrum & Mahndorf-Achim lines, G.
11APR45	1 MET destroyed and 2 MET damaged	Verden, G.
11APR45	4 MET damaged	Bremen area, G.
12APR45	1 locomotive, 2 wagons & 1 MET damaged	Bremen area, G.
13APR45	2 MET damaged	Rottenberg, G.
13APR45	1x 3-ton lorry destroyed	Bremen, G.
16APR45	1 MET destroyed	Bremen-Rethem area, G.
17APR45	3 railway trucks destroyed, 6 locomotives, 27 railway trucks, 5 passenger coaches & 5 MET damaged	Lübeck-Hamburg area, G.
17APR45	1 tug destroyed & 1 tug damaged	Elbe River, nr Bleckede, G.
18APR45	2 locomotives & 1 MET damaged	Hamburg area, G.
18APR45	3 tugs, 1 paddle-steamer & 1 MET damaged	S of Lübeck. G.

18APR45	4 locomotives, 13 covered railway trucks & 5 MET damaged	Hamburg-Lübeck area, G.
19APR45	2 MET destroyed, 1 warehouse set on fire, & 2 locomotives, 10 railway trucks & 13 MET damaged	Nr Lübeck, G.
19APR45	4 MET and 1 truck destroyed, and 2 MET and 5 trucks damaged	Ludwigslust area, G.
20APR45	2 MET destroyed, & 11 MET, 2 locomotives & 2 covered railway trucks damaged	Wismar-Hamburg area, G.
20APR45	1 locomotive & 10 covered railway trucks damaged	Nr Lübeck, G.
20APR45	1 locomotive & 8 covered railway trucks damaged	N of Lake Schwerin, G.
20APR45	4 MET damaged	Nr Neukloster, G.
20APR45	1 staff car destroyed & 1 staff car damaged	Güstrow, G.
20APR45	1 lorry & 2 trailers destroyed, & 1 lorry and 2 trailers damaged	S of Goldberg, G.
20APR45	2 MET destroyed & 4 MET damaged	Lübeck area, G.
20APR45	7 MET destroyed & 3 MET damaged	Outside Grevesmühlen, G.
21APR45	4 MET destroyed, & 5 MET & 2 covered railway trucks damaged	Lübeck area, G.
21APR45	4 railway trucks damaged	Hamburg, G.
22APR45	2 MET destroyed, & 2 MET & 1 locomotive damaged	Uelzen-Luneburg area, G.
23APR45	6 MET destroyed in flames, & 1 locomotive, 30 covered railway trucks & 18 MET damaged	Hamburg area, G.
23APR45	34 MET destroyed and 26 damaged	Kyritz-Senzke-Nauen road, G.
24APR45	1 locomotive & 3 railway trucks damaged	Lauenburg-Uelzen area, G.
24APR45	1 locomotive damaged	E of Lübeck, G.
24APR45	2 locomotives damaged	SE of Lübeck, G.
24APR45	38 MET damaged	W of Rathenow, G.
24APR45	1 locomotive & 8 railway trucks damaged	N of Bad Oldesloe, G.
24APR45	6 MET destroyed	Nr Perleberg, G.
24APR45	16 MET damaged	Nr Lake Schwerin, G.
24APR45	4 MET damaged	W of Lake Schaal, G.
24APR45	2 MET damaged	E of Sternberg, G.
24APR45	12 MET damaged	Bet Rhinow & Hohennauen, G.
25APR45	1 locomotive damaged	Bad Segeberg, G.
25APR45	3 MET destroyed & 7 damaged	Nr Grevesmühlen, G.
25APR45	2 MET destroyed & 10 damaged	SE of Lübeck, G.
26APR45	2 MET destroyed & 5 MET damaged	Parchim-Lübeck-Hagenow area, G.
27APR45	3 MET destroyed	Kyritz-Perleberg road, G.
27APR45	2 MET destroyed & 5 MET damaged	NR, Germany
27APR45	4 MET (incl 1 staff car) destroyed & 13 MET (incl 2 AFVs, 1x 3-ton truck, & 2 HDVs) damaged	SE of Goldberg, G.
27APR45	2 MET damaged	S of Lake Schwerin, G.
28APR45	1x 15 cwt truck destroyed	Mestlin, G.
28APR45	1 MET (poss HDV) damaged	Schwerin area, G.
30APR45	2 MET damaged	Schwerin area, G.
02MAY45	1 AFV damaged	Bridgehead, Nr Lauenburg, G.
03MAY45	1 MET damaged	Norderstapel, G.
03MAY45	4 MET destroyed & 24 MET damaged	S of Flensburg, G.

X. Decorations
August 1942-September 1945

The decorations listed in this appendix are those awarded to pilots of 41 Squadron, for their service with this unit between August 1942-September 1945. Decorations awarded for service with other squadrons or units are not shown.

Decoration   **Distinguished Service Order (DSO)**
Description   Established in 1886 to reward officers of all services for meritorious or distinguished service in war. Since 1917, awarded for gallantry in action. The order is generally awarded to officers in command, although awards to lower officer ranks could be made for a high degree of gallantry just short of deserving the Victoria Cross.
Recipient   Burne, Thomas Roper, 29 May 1945

Decoration   **Distinguished Flying Cross (DFC)**
Description   Established in 1918 to reward Air Force officers and warrant officers for acts of valour, courage or devotion to duty performed whilst flying in active operations against the enemy. A straight silver bar with an eagle in the centre was awarded for a further act, which would have earned the order in the first place.
Recipients   Glen, Arthur Allan, 5 November 1943 (Bar)
Benham, Douglas Ian, 8 May 1945 (Bar)
Reid, Daniel Joseph, 1 June 1945
Coleman, Patrick Tinsley, 24 July 1945
Cowell, Peter, 24 July 1945
Stevenson, Ian Turnbull, 24 July 1945
Shepherd, John Bean, 14 September 1945 (2nd Bar)

XI. Aircraft in Service
August 1942-May 1945

This appendix lists the aircraft flown by 41 Squadron between August 1942 and May 1945. As aircraft were usually phased in over a period of days or weeks, the dates shown below indicate when the first of each aircraft type was delivered to the unit.

MAIN EQUIPMENT

Type	First Date of Issue
Supermarine Spitfire Mk Va	28 July 1941
Supermarine Spitfire Mk Vb	28 July 1941
Supermarine Spitfire Mk XII	24 February 1943
Supermarine Spitfire Mk XIV	12 September 1944

KNOWN HACKS

Dates indicate periods when these aircraft are known to have been in service with 41 Squadron.

- Miles M25 Martinet, M14 Magister & M9 Master III, August 1942-February 1943
- de Havilland DH.82 Tiger Moth, 674, August 1942-April 1943
- Supermarine Spitfire Vb, P8799, EB-L, April-July 1943[1]
- de Havilland DH.82A Tiger Moth II, DE374, May 1943-June 1944
- de Havilland DH.82A Tiger Moth II, DE575, July 1944[2]
- de Havilland DH.82A Tiger Moth II, T6034, September 1944

XII. Base Locations
August 1942-May 1945

Base	County/Country	Arrival	Group
Debden	Essex	8 July 1942	11
Longtown[1]	Cumberland	4 August 1942	13
Llanbedr	Merioneth	9 August 1942	9
Tangmere[2]	Sussex	16 August 1942	11
Llanbedr	Merioneth	20 August 1942	9
Eglinton[3]	Londonderry	22 September 1942	13
Llanbedr	Merioneth	30 September 1942	9
Tangmere[4]	Sussex	8 October 1942	11
Llanbedr[5]	Merioneth	11 October 1942	9
High Ercall	Salop	25 February 1943	9
Hawkinge[6]	Kent	13 April 1943	11
Biggin Hill	Kent	21 May 1943	11
Friston	Sussex	28 May 1943	11
Westhampnett[7]	Sussex	21 June 1943	11
Tangmere[8]	Sussex	4 October 1943	11
Southend[9]	Essex	7 February 1944	11
Tangmere	Sussex	20 February 1944	11
Friston	Sussex	11 March 1944	11
Bolt Head	Devon	29 April 1944	10
Fairwood Common[10]	Glamorgan	16 May 1944	10
Bolt Head	Devon	24 May 1944	10
West Malling	Kent	19 June 1944	11
Tangmere[11]	Sussex	26 June 1944	11
Westhampnett	Sussex	27 June 1944	11
Friston	Sussex	2 July 1944	11
Lympne	Kent	11 July 1944	11
B.56 Evere[12]	Belgium	4 December 1944	83
B.64 Diest/Schaffen[13]	Belgium	5 December 1944	83
Y.32 Ophoven[14]	Belgium	31 December 1944	83
B.80 Volkel	Netherlands	27 January 1945	83
Warmwell[15]	Dorset	7 March 1945	10
B.78 Eindhoven	Netherlands	18 March 1945	83
B.106 Twente	Netherlands	7 April 1945	83
B.118 Celle	Germany	16 April 1945	83
B.160 Kastrup	Denmark	9 May 1945	83

XIII. Extant Combat Films
August 1942–May 1945

This Appendix shows the Combat Films for 41 Squadron known to be still in existence for the period August 1942-May 1945, which are held by the Imperial War Museum in London. All films are Black & White and silent. Note that the names in the 'Pilot' column have been amended by the author from what appears in the catalogue to reflect pilots' correct names. Films should therefore be sought according to their Catalogue and Film Numbers.

Date	Pilot	Time	Target	Format	Catalogue No	Film No
04JUN43	Smith, Donald H.	11:30	FW190s	16mm	CGE 834-1330	1185
04JUN43	Solak, Jerzy J.	11:30	FW190	16mm	CGE 834-1330	1184
09JUN43	Johnson, Ronald	11:30	Do217	16mm	CGE 834-1330	1214
16SEP43	Newman, Benjamin B.	18:20	Me109	16mm	CGE 2763-3119	2818
22SEP43	Smith, Donald H.	17:00	FW190	16mm	CGE 2763-3119	2945
24SEP43	Galitzine, Emanuel V.	16:30	FW190	16mm	CGE 2763-3119	3032
24SEP43	Glen, Arthur A.	16:30	FW190	16mm	CGE 2763-3119	3033
24SEP43	Newman, Benjamin B.	16:30	FW190	16mm	CGE 2763-3119	3031
27SEP43	Birbeck, Clive R.	11:30	FW190	16mm	CGE 2763-3119	3096
27SEP43	Fearon, David N.	11:30	Me109	16mm	CGE 2763-3119	3099
27SEP43	Graham, Peter B.	11:30	FW190	16mm	CGE 2763-3119	3097
13OCT43	Still, James W.	15:00	Locomotives	16mm	CGE 3120-3442	3357
13OCT43	Wagner, Herbert A.	15:00	Locomotives	16mm	CGE 3120-3442	3358
20OCT43	Collis, Ronald T. H.	10:10	Me109	16mm	CGE 3120-3442	3434
20OCT43	Cowell, Peter	10:10	FW190	16mm	CGE 3120-3442	3432
20OCT43	Newman, Benjamin B.	10:10	Me109	16mm	CGE 3120-3442	3433
23JUL44	Appleton, Arthur S.	NR	Flying bombs	16mm	CGE 7804-8329	8053
23JUL44	Balasse, Maurice A. L.	11:00	Flying bombs	16mm	CGE 7804-8329	8052
09AUG44	Spencer, Terence	06:40	Flying Bomb	16mm	CGE 8805-9265	8954
11AUG44	Wilkinson, John F.	14:20	Flying Bomb	16mm	CGE 8805-9265	9066
15AUG44	Harding, Ross P.	08:45	Flying Bomb	16mm	CGE 8805-9265	9234
16AUG44	Rossow, Vivian J.	16:30	Flying Bomb	16mm	CGE 8805-9265	9235
28AUG44	Balasse, Maurice A. L.	21:30	Flying Bomb	16mm	CGE 8805-9265	9626
01SEP44	Harding, Ross P.	20:30	Ground Targets	16mm Neg	CGE 10003-10186	10058
03SEP44	Burne, Thomas R.	12:15	Ground Targets	16mm Neg	CGE 10003-10186	10060
03SEP44	Henry, David J. V.	12:15	Ground Targets	16mm Neg	CGE 10003-10186	10063
03SEP44	Reid, Daniel J.	12:15	Ground Targets	16mm Neg	CGE 10003-10186	10062
03SEP44	Rossow, Vivian J.	12:15	Ground Targets	16mm Neg	CGE 10003-10186	10061
03SEP44	Coleman, Patrick T.	14:00	FW190	16mm Neg	CGE 10003-10186	10136
03SEP44	Stowe, William N.	14:00	Enemy Aircraft	16mm Neg	CGE 10003-10186	10135
12SEP44	Stevenson, Ian T.	12:00	Ground Targets	16mm	CGE 10187-10483	10362

Date	Pilot	Time	Target	Format	Catalogue No	Film No
25MAR45	Cowell, Peter	17:00	Ground Target	16mm Neg	CGB 6971-7282	7132
25MAR45	Stowe, William N.	17:00	Ground Target	16mm Neg	CGB 6971-7282	7133
26MAR45	Chalmers, John A.	15:00	Ground Target Train	16mm Neg	CGB 7283-7608	7320
26MAR45	Shepherd, John B.	15:00	Ground Target	16mm Neg	CGB 6971-7282	7135
26MAR45	Stowe, William N.	15:00	Ground Target	16mm Neg	CGB 7283-7608	7319
26MAR45	Stowe, William N.	15:00	Ground Target	16mm Neg	CGB 6971-7282	7134
28MAR45	Hegarty, Francis M.	11:00	Ground Target & Barges	16mm Neg	CGB 7283-7608	7593
28MAR45	Kelly, Hubert F.	11:00	Ground Target	16mm Neg	CGB 7283-7608	7595
28MAR45	Smart, Lionel H.	11:00	Ground Target & Barges	16mm Neg	CGB 7283-7608	7594
28MAR45	Whale, Frederick V.	11:15	Ground Target & Barges	16mm Neg	CGB 7283-7608	7596
28MAR45	Fleming, Robert	13:25	Ground Target	16mm Neg	CGB 7283-7608	7599
28MAR45	Lawrence, Thomas E.	13:25	Ground Target & FW190s	16mm Neg	CGB 7283-7608	7597
28MAR45	Moyle, Crawford N.	13:25	Ground Target	16mm Neg	CGB 7283-7608	7598
28MAR45	Stevenson, Ian T.	13:25	Ground Target	16mm Neg	CGB 7283-7608	7600
30MAR45	Farfan, Fernand W.	11:00	Ground Target	16mm Neg	CGB 7609-7952	7918
30MAR45	Hegarty, Francis M.	11:00	Ground Target	16mm Neg	CGB 7609-7952	7920
30MAR45	Shepherd, John B.	11:00	Ground Target	16mm Neg	CGB 7609-7952	7917
30MAR45	Coleman, Patrick T.	13:30	Ground Target	16mm Neg	CGB 7609-7952	7922
30MAR45	Smart, Lionel H.	13:30	Ground Target	16mm Neg	CGB 7609-7952	7921
02APR45	Lawrence, Thomas E.	18:15	Ground Targets	16mm Neg	CGB 7954-8233	8203
02APR45	Hegarty, Francis M.	19:15	Ground Target	16mm Neg	CGB 7954-8233	8202
03APR45	Hegarty, Francis M.	14:00	Ground Targets & Barges	16mm Neg	CGB 8234-8526	8402
03APR45	Rake, Derek S. V.	14:00	Ground Targets & Barges	16mm Neg	CGB 8234-8526	8404
03APR45	Smith, Roy D. A.	14:00	Ground Targets & Barges	16mm Neg	CGB 8234-8526	8403
03APR45	Stowe, William N.	15:00	Ground Targets & Barges	16mm Neg	CGB 8234-8526	8405
04APR45	Chalmers, John A.	07:40	Barges & Tugs	16mm Neg	CGB 8234-8526	8410
04APR45	Coleman, Patrick T.	07:40	Barges & Tugs	16mm Neg	CGB 8234-8526	8414
04APR45	Farfan, Fernand W.	07:40	Barges & Tugs	16mm Neg	CGB 8234-8526	8413
04APR45	Gray, Eric	07:40	Ground Target	16mm Neg	CGB 8234-8526	8409
04APR45	Hale, Peter H.	07:40	Ground Targets & Barges	16mm Neg	CGB 8234-8526	8406
04APR45	Kelly, Hubert F.	07:40	Ground Target	16mm Neg	CGB 8234-8526	8412
04APR45	Moyle, Crawford N.	07:40	Barges & Tugs	16mm Neg	CGB 8234-8526	8407
04APR45	Shepherd, John B.	07:40	Ground Target	16mm Neg	CGB 8234-8526	8411
04APR45	Kelly, Hubert F.	15:45	Barges	16mm Neg	CGB 8234-8526	8502
04APR45	Rake, Derek S. V.	15:45	Barges & Ground Target	16mm Neg	CGB 8234-8526	8494
04APR45	Shepherd, John B.	15:45	Barges	16mm Neg	CGB 8234-8526	8492
04APR45	Whale, Frederick V.	15:45	Barges & Ground Target	16mm Neg	CGB 8234-8526	8493
04APR45	Smith, Roy D. A.	17:15	Ground Target	16mm Neg	CGB 8234-8526	8495
04APR45	Stowe, William N.	17:15	Barge Ground Target	16mm Neg	CGB 8234-8526	8496
05APR45	Wilkinson, John F.	08:45	Ground Target	16mm Neg	CGB 8234-8526	8497
05APR45	Hegarty, Francis M.	09:00	Ground Target	16mm Neg	CGB 8234-8526	8500
05APR45	Rake, Derek S. V.	09:00	Ground Target	16mm Neg	CGB 8234-8526	8499
05APR45	Smart, Lionel H.	09:00	Ground Target	16mm Neg	CGB 8234-8526	8501

Date	Pilot	Time	Target	Format	Catalogue No	Film No
05APR45	Stowe, William N.	09:00	Barge Ground Target	16mm Neg	CGB 8234-8526	8498
08APR45	Hegarty, Francis M.	12:45	Ground Targets	16mm	CGB 9376-9670	9486
08APR45	Shepherd, John B.	12:45	Ground Targets	16mm	CGB 9376-9670	9489
08APR45	Smart, Lionel H.	12:45	Ground Targets	16mm	CGB 9376-9670	9487
08APR45	Smith, Roy D. A.	12:45	Ground Targets	16mm	CGB 9376-9670	9484
08APR45	Stowe, William N.	12:45	Ground Targets	16mm	CGB 9376-9670	9485
08APR45	Bødtker, Carl S.	18:00	Ground Targets	16mm	CGB 9376-9670	9491
08APR45	Fisher, Roy R. G.	18:00	Ground Targets	16mm	CGB 9376-9670	9493
08APR45	Scott, Peter F.	18:00	Ground Targets	16mm	CGB 9376-9670	9490
08APR45	Whale, Frederick V.	18:00	Ground Targets	16mm	CGB 9376-9670	9492
08APR45	Chalmers, John A.	19:00	Ground Targets	16mm	CGB 9376-9670	9496
08APR45	Gaze, Frederick A. O.	19:00	Ground Targets	16mm	CGB 9376-9670	9497
08APR45	Smith, Roy D. A.	19:00	Ground Targets	16mm	CGB 9376-9670	9494
08APR45	Stowe, William N.	19:00	Ground Targets	16mm	CGB 9376-9670	9495
09APR45	Cowell, Peter	17:00	Ground Targets	16mm	CGB 9376-9670	9499
09APR45	Kelly, Hubert F.	17:00	Ground Targets	16mm	CGB 9376-9670	9498
11APR45	Coleman, Patrick T.	09:30	Ground Targets	16mm	CGB 9376-9670	9501
11APR45	Wilkinson, John F.	09:30	Ground Targets	16mm	CGB 9376-9670	9500
11APR45	Gaze, Frederick A. O.	10:00	Ground Targets & Ju52	16mm	CGB 9376-9670	9502
11APR45	Chalmers, John A.	13:30	Ground Targets	16mm	CGB 9376-9670	9621
11APR45	Chalmers, John A.	18:15	Ar234	16mm	CGB 9376-9670	9623
11APR45	Gaze, Frederick A. O.	18:15	Ar234	16mm	CGB 9376-9670	9625
11APR45	Wilkinson, John F.	18:15	Ar234	16mm	CGB 9376-9670	9622
12APR45	Gaze, Frederick A. O.	09:45	Ground Targets	16mm	CGB 9376-9670	9626
12APR45	Farfan, Fernand W.	09:45	Ground Targets	16mm	CGB 9376-9670	9627
12APR45	Gaze, Frederick A. O.	17:00	Ar234	16mm	CGB 9376-9670	9630
12APR45	Rake, Derek S. V.	17:00	Ar234	16mm	CGB 9376-9670	9629
12APR45	Wilkinson, John F.	17:00	Ar234	16mm	CGB 9376-9670	9628
22APR45	Farfan, Fernand W.	17:30	Ground Target	16mm Neg	CGB 12192-12489	12249
22APR45	Hegarty, Francis M.	17:30	Ground Target	16mm Neg	CGB 12192-12489	12250
23APR45	Fisher, Roy R. G.	07:15	Ground Target	16mm Neg	CGB 12192-12489	12289
23APR45	Coleman, Patrick T.	19:00	Ground Target Vehicle	16mm Neg	CGB 12192-12489	12279
23APR45	Gaze, Frederick A. O.	19:00	Ground Target	16mm Neg	CGB 12192-12489	12278
23APR45	Chalmers, John A.	19:15	Ground Target Vehicle	16mm Neg	CGB 12192-12489	12280
23APR45	Gray, Eric	19:15	Ground Targets, Train & Vehicle	16mm Neg	CGB 12192-12489	12281
24APR45	Stevenson, Ian T.	10:30	Ground Targets	16mm	CGB 12490-12756	12593
24APR45	Scott, Peter F.	10:45	Ground Targets	16mm	CGB 12490-12756	12596
24APR45	Hale, Peter H.	11:00	Ground Targets	16mm	CGB 12490-12756	12597
24APR45	Coleman, Patrick T.	13:00	Ground Targets	16mm	CGB 12490-12756	12600
24APR45	Smart, Lionel H.	13:00	Ground Targets	16mm	CGB 12490-12756	12599
24APR45	Smith, Roy D. A.	13:00	Ground Targets	16mm	CGB 12490-12756	12598
24APR45	Cowell, Peter	15:45	Ground Targets	16mm	CGB 12490-12756	12602
24APR45	Fisher, Roy R. G.	15:45	Ground Targets	16mm	CGB 12490-12756	12601

Date	Pilot	Time	Target	Format	Catalogue No	Film No
24APR45	Kelly, Hubert F.	15:45	Ground Targets	16mm	CGB 12490-12756	12603
24APR45	Jallands, Walter J.	16:00	Ground Targets	16mm	CGB 12490-12756	12604
24APR45	Chalmers, John A.	18:15	Ground Targets	16mm	CGB 12490-12756	12605
24APR45	Coleman, Patrick T.	18:30	Ground Targets	16mm	CGB 12490-12756	12606
24APR45	Gaze, Frederick A. O.	18:30	Ground Targets	16mm	CGB 12490-12756	12607
25APR45	Cowell, Peter	08:00	Ground Targets & Me 262s	16mm	CGB 12490-12756	12612
25APR45	Gray, Eric	09:00	Ground Targets	16mm	CGB 12490-12756	12613
25APR45	Jallands, Walter J.	09:00	Ground Targets	16mm	CGB 12490-12756	12614
25APR45	Gaze, Frederick A. O.	10:00	Ground Targets	16mm	CGB 12490-12756	12616
25APR45	Stevenson, Ian T.	10:00	Ground Targets	16mm	CGB 12490-12756	12615

XIV. INDEX TO TNA COMBAT REPORTS
September 1939-May 1945

This Appendix contains a full index of all of 41 Squadron's Combat Reports held in The National Archives in TNA AIR 50/18 and AIR 50/443, and in the ORB Appendices in TNA AIR 27/427, 27/428, 27/429, and 27/431, listed in numerical order.

Many of those included in the Appendices are duplicates of those in AIR 50/18, but some are not, and can only be found there. Nonetheless, there are still significant gaps and over fifty victories have no corresponding Combat Report available in the National Archives.[1]

AIR 50/18 COMBAT REPORTS

This file includes Combat Reports for 17 October 1939-3 May 1945.

CR	Pilot	Date	Claim[2]	Location[3]
1	Intelligence Report	15AUG40	Multiple	Durham area
2	Intelligence Report	15AUG40	-	Page 2 of CR 1
3	Intelligence Report	15AUG40	-	Page 3 of CR 1
4	Intelligence Report	15AUG40	-	Page 4 of CR 1
5	Intelligence Report	15AUG40	-	Page 5 of CR 1
6	Intelligence Report	15AUG40	-	Page 6 of CR 1
7	Intelligence Report	15AUG40	-	Page 7 of CR 1
8	Intelligence Report	15AUG40	-	Page 8 of CR 1
9	Intelligence Report	15AUG40	-	Page 9 of CR 1
10	Intelligence Report	15AUG40	-	Page 10 of CR 1
11	Adams, Dennis A.	01OCT40	Me109E	Epsom, Surrey
12	Adams, Dennis A.	01OCT40	-	Page 2 of CR 11
13	Adams, Dennis A.	27OCT40	Me109E	Off Folkestone, Kent
14	Adams, Dennis A.	27OCT40	-	Page 2 of CR 13
15	Adams, Dennis A.	30OCT40	Me109E	SW of Maidstone, Kent
16	Adams, Dennis A.	30OCT40	-	Page 2 of CR 15
17	Aldous, Eric S.	18SEP40	Me109E	N of Dover, Kent
18	Aldous, Eric S.	18SEP40	-	Page 2 of CR 17
19	Aldridge, Frederick J.	17OCT40	Me109E	10m S of Chatham, Kent
20	Aldridge, Frederick J.	17OCT40	-	Page 2 of CR 19
21	Aldridge, Frederick J.	25OCT40	Me109E	Nr Maidstone, Kent
22	Aldridge, Frederick J.	25OCT40	-	Page 2 of CR 21
23	Aldridge, Frederick J.	30OCT40	Me109E	W of Ashford, Kent
24	Aldridge, Frederick J.	30OCT40	-	Page 2 of CR 23
25	Aldridge, Frederick J.	17NOV40	Me109E	Off Felixstowe, Esx
26	Aldridge, Frederick J.	17NOV40	-	Page 2 of CR 25

CR	Pilot	Date	Claim[2]	Location[3]
27	Allen, John J.	14MAR42	Me109F	Nr Fécamp, F.
28	Allen, John J.	27MAY42	FW190F	Dieppe-Fécamp, F.
29	Allen, John J.	27MAY42	Me109F	E of Bembridge, Hants
30	Allen, John J.	27MAY42	-	Page 2 of CR 29
31	Allison, Jack W.	08JUL40	Ju88	SE Scarborough, Yks
32	Angus, Robert A.	30OCT40	Me109	Tonbridge-Ashford, Kent
33	Angus, Robert A.	30OCT40	-	Page 2 of CR 32
34	Smith, Roy D. A.	02MAY45	Fi156	Schwerin, G.
			Fi156	Ground Schwerin, G.
35	Babbage, Cyril F.	14AUG41	Me109	Gravelines, F.
36	Babbage, Cyril F.[4]	18SEP41	Crts Hawk	1m N of Ostend, B.
37	Babbage, Cyril F.	18SEP41	-	Page 2 of CR 36
38	Bache, Leslie L.	20SEP41	Me109E	Doudeville-St. Valéry, F.
39	Bache, Leslie L.	20SEP41	-	Page 2 of CR 38
40	Baker, Henry C.	15SEP40	2 He111	Southend, Esx
41	Baker, Henry C.	15SEP40	-	Page 2 of CR 40
42	Baker, Henry C.	30SEP40	Me109	10m SW of Dungeness
43	Baker, Henry C.	30SEP40	-	Page 2 of CR 42
44	Baker, Aubrey C.	20OCT40	Me109	Orpington, Kent
45	Baker, Aubrey C.	20OCT40	-	Page 2 of CR 44
46	Baker, Aubrey C.[17]	10JAN41	Me109	Off Cap Gris Nez, F.
47	Baker, Aubrey C.	10JAN41	-	Page 2 of CR 46
48	Balasse, Maurice A. L.	03JUL44	V1	4m N of Bexhill, Ssx
49	Balasse, Maurice A. L.	19JUL44	V1	Dungeness, Kent
50	Blank Aircraft Accident Report		-	-
51	Balasse, Maurice A. L.	26JUL44	V1	5-8m S of Beachy Head, Ssx
52	Balasse, Maurice A. L.	29JUL44	V1	10-15m W of Le Touquet, F.
53	Balasse, Maurice A. L.	29JUL44	V1	3m SE of Woodchurch, Kent
54	Bamberger, Cyril S.	23SEP40	Me109	NR, 25,000 ft.
55	Bamberger, Cyril S.	23SEP40	-	Page 2 of CR 54
56	Bamberger, Cyril S.	27SEP40	Me109	Dover, Kent
57	Bamberger, Cyril S.	27SEP40	-	Page 2 of CR 56
58	Bamberger, Cyril S.	05OCT40	Me109	Canterbury, Kent
59	Bamberger, Cyril S.	05OCT40	-	Page 2 of CR 58
60	Beardsley, Robert A.	18SEP40	2 Me109	Isle of Sheppey, Kent
61	Beardsley, Robert A.	18SEP40	-	Page 2 of CR 60
62	Beardsley, Robert A.	30SEP40	Me109E	3m S of Dungeness, Kent
			Do215	
63	Beardsley, Robert A.	30SEP40	-	Page 2 of CR 62
64	Beardsley, Robert A.	25OCT40	-	Page 2 of CR 66
65	Beardsley, Robert A.	18AUG41	Me109F	St. Omer-Calais, F.
			Me109F	Gravelines, F.
66	Beardsley, Robert A.	25OCT40	2 Me109E	Nr Dungeness, Kent

CR	Pilot	Date	Claim[2]	Location[3]
67	Benham, Douglas I.	23JAN45	2 FW190	Münster-Waltrop, G.
68	Benham, Douglas I.	23JAN45	-	Page 2 of CR 67
69	Bennions, George H.	28JUL40	Me109E	Dover, Kent-Calais, F.
70	Bennions, George H.	28JUL40	-	Page 2 of CR 69
71	Bennions, George H.	29JUL40	Me109E	Dover area, Kent
72	Bennions, George H.	29JUL40	-	Page 2 of CR 71
73	Bennions, George H.	15AUG40	Me110 / He111	Seaham Harbour, Dur
74	Bennions, George H.	15AUG40	-	Page 2 of CR 73
75	Bennions, George H.	05SEP40	-	Page 2 of CR 76
76	Bennions, George H.	05SEP40	Me109	S of Gravesend, Kent
77	Bennions, George H.	05SEP40	Ju88 / Ju88	Sheppey, Kent / Isle of Sheppey, Kent
78	Bennions, George H.	05SEP40	-	Page 2 of CR 77
79	Bennions, George H.	06SEP40	2 Me109	E of Eastchurch, Kent
80	Bennions, George H.	06SEP40	-	Page 2 of CR 79
81	Bennions, George H.	11SEP40	Me110	Maidstone, Kent
82	Bennions, George H.	11SEP40	-	Page 2 of CR 81
83	Bennions, George H.	15SEP40	Me109	Ashford, Kent
84	Bennions, George H.	15SEP40	-	Page 2 of CR 83
85	Bennions, George H.	15SEP40	Do17	East London-south coast
86	Bennions, George H.	15SEP40	-	Page 2 of CR 85
87	Bennions, George H.	17SEP40	Me109	Maidstone, Kent
88	Bennions, George H.	17SEP40	-	Page 2 of CR 87
89	Bennions, George H.	18SEP40	Me109	Maidstone, Kent
90	Bennions, George H.	18SEP40	-	Page 2 of CR 89
91	Bennions, George H.	18SEP40	3 Me109	W of Gravesend, Kent
92	Bennions, George H.	18SEP40	-	Page 2 of CR 91
93	Bennions, George H.	23SEP40	Me109	Dover, Kent
94	Bennions, George H.	23SEP40	-	Page 2 of 93
95	Bennions, George H.	28SEP40	Me109 / Me109	Canterbury, Kent / Newhaven, Ssx
96	Bennions, George H.	28SEP40	-	Page 2 of 95
97	Bennions, George H.	01OCT40	Me109	Henfield, Ssx
98	Beurling, George F.	03MAY42	FW190	2-3m off Gris Nez, F.
99	Bennions, George H.	01OCT40	-	Addendum to CR 97
100	Bennions, George H.	01OCT40	-	Page 2 of Addendum to CR 97
101	Blatchford, H. Peter / Harris, Albert	17OCT39	He111	20m E of Whitby, Yks
102	Blatchford, H. Peter	17OCT40	-	Page 2 of CR 101
103	Birbeck, Clive R.	27APR43	FW190	Somme Estuary, F.
104	Birbeck, Clive R.	11AUG43	½ Loco.	S of Dieppe, F.

CR	Pilot	Date	Claim[2]	Location[3]
105	Birbeck, Clive R.	04SEP43	FW190	Le Touquet, F.
106	Birbeck, Clive R.	04SEP43	-	Page 2 of CR 105
107	Birbeck, Clive R.[5]	04SEP43	-	Le Touquet-Beussent, F.
108	Birbeck, Clive R.	27SEP43	FW190	Beauvais-Dieppe, F.
			Me109	
109	Birbeck, Clive R.	22SEP43	FW190	W of Évreux, F.
110	Birbeck, Clive R.	26OCT43	3 Locos.	Dieppe-Clères, F.
	Fearon, David N.			
111	Bødtker, Carl S.	01MAY45	FW190	S of Schwerin Lake, G.
112	Boret, Robert J.	15AUG40	Ju88	S of Newcastle, NBL
113	Boret, Robert J.	05OCT40	Me109	Dover area, Kent
114	Boyle, John G.	05OCT40	-	Page 2 of CR 113
115	Boyle, John G.	11AUG40	Ju88	Helmsley, Yks
116	Keefer, George C.[6]	16APR45	FW190	Hagenow, G.
117	Boyle, John G.	05SEP40	Me109	Maidstone, Kent
118	Boyle, John G.	05SEP40	-	Page 2 of CR 117
119	Boyle, John G.	15SEP40	Me109	E of London
			Do17	Isle of Sheppey, Kent
120	Boyle, John G.	15SEP40	-	Page 2 of 119
121	Boyle, John G.	17SEP40	2 Me109	Dover-Channel Area
122	Boyle, John G.	17SEP40	-	Page 2 of CR 121
123	Brew, William A.	18AUG41	Me109	Béthune, F.
124	Brew, William A.	21AUG41	Me109	Hesdin, F.
125	Brown, M. Peter	30SEP40	Do17	Off Dungeness, Kent
126	Brown, M. Peter	30SEP40	-	Page 2 of CR 125
127	Brown, M. Peter	20OCT40	Me109E	NW of West Malling, Kent
128	Brown, M. Peter	20OCT40	-	Page 2 of CR 127
129	Brown, M. Peter	25OCT40	Me109E	Ashford-Rye, Ssx
130	Brown, M. Peter	25OCT40	-	Page 2 of CR 129
131	Buchanan, George A.[7]	18SEP41	Hs123	Ostend, B.
132	Buchanan, George A.	18SEP41	-	Page 2 of CR 131
133	Bush, Charles R.	22AUG41	Me109	20m NE of Le Havre, F.
134	Bush, Charles R.[7]	18SEP41	Hs123	Ostend, B.
135	Bush, Charles R.	21SEP41	Me109	Near Béthune, F.
136	Bush, Charles R.	21SEP41	-	Page 2 of CR 135
137	Cambridge, Roy F.	14MAR42	Me109	NE of Fécamp, F.
138	Cambridge, Roy F.	14MAR42	-	Page 2 of CR 137
139	Carr-Lewty, Robert A.	29JUL40	Me109	Dover area, Kent
140	Carr-Lewty, Robert A.	29JUL40	-	Page 2 of CR 139
141	Carr-Lewty, Robert A.	05SEP40	Me109	Maidstone, Kent
142	Carr-Lewty, Robert A.	05SEP40	-	Page 2 of CR 141
143	Chalmers, John A.	25APR45	Ju188	10m W of Plau Lake, G.
			Fi156	Ground, Plau Lake, G.

CR	Pilot	Date	Claim[2]	Location[3]
144	Chalmers, John A.	25APR45	-	Copy of CR 143
145	Chalmers, John A.	02MAY45	2 Fi156	Schwerin Lake area, G.
146	Chapman, Robert H.	03JUL44	V1	30m SE of Beachy Hd., Kent
147	Chattin, Peter W.	12JUL44	V1	4m NW of Ashford, Kent
148	Coker, Frank A.	14MAR42	Me109	8-10m NE of Étretat, F.
149	Coker, Frank A.	14MAR42	-	Page 2 of CR 148
150	Coleman, Patrick T.	17APR45	Ju188	Ground, Segeberg, G.
151	Coleman, Patrick T.	18APR45	Ju188	Ground, E of Pötrau, G.
152	Coleman, Patrick T.	20APR45	FW190	N of Neuruppin, G.
153	Coleman, Patrick T.	25APR45	Ju188	10m W Plau Lake, G.
153	Coleman, Patrick T.	25APR45	FW190	Ground, Rechlin, G.
154	Coleman, Patrick T.	25APR45	-	Copy of CR 153
155	Chalmers, John A.; Coleman, Patrick T.; Hale, Peter H.; Moyle, Crawford N.	28APR45	He111	W of Goldberg, G.
156	Coleman, Patrick T.	01MAY45	3 FW190	SW of Plau, G.
157	Collis, Ronald T. H.	20OCT43	Me109	North of Rouen, F.
158	Cook, Harry	09AUG44	V1	Mid-Channel, off Dieppe, F.
159	Cory, Guy W.	07SEP40	Me109	E of Maidstone, Kent
159	Cory, Guy W.	07SEP40	Do215	E of Maidstone, Kent
160	Cory, Guy W.	07SEP40	-	Page 2 of CR 159
161	Cory, Guy W.	23SEP40	Me109E	Dover, Kent
162	Cory, Guy W.	23SEP40	-	Page 2 of CR 161
163	Cory, Guy W.	25OCT40	2 Me109E	SE of Dungeness, Kent
164	Cory, Guy W.	25OCT40	-	Page 2 of CR 163
165	Cowell, Peter	20OCT43	FW190	Beaumont-le-Roger, F.
166	Cowell, Peter	20OCT43	-	Carbon copy of CR 165
167	Cowell, Peter; Fisher, Roy R. G.; Jallands, Walter J.; Kelly, Hubert F.	24APR45	16 Ar196	Shore, Ratzeburg Lake, G.
168	Cowell, Peter	25APR45	2 Me262	S of Lübeck, G.
169	Cowell, Peter	01MAY45	2 FW190	Schwerin Lake, G.
170	Darling, Edward V.	11AUG40	Ju88	Helmsley, Yks
171	Gaze, Frederick A. O.	12APR45	Ar234	W of Bremen, G.
172	Lovell, Anthony D. J.	08JUL40	Ju88	SE of Scarborough, Yks
173	Lovell, Anthony D. J.	08JUL40	-	Page 2 of CR 172
174	Lovell, Anthony D. J.	15AUG40	2 Me110	Barnard Castle, Dur
175	Rake, Derrick S. V.	12APR45	Ar234	W of Bremen, G.
176	Reid, Daniel J.	02MAR45	Ar234	Nr Enschede, NL
177	Reid, Daniel J.	02MAR45	-	Page 2 of CR 172
178	Intelligence Report[8]	11AUG40	Ju88	Thirsk, Yks

CR	Pilot	Date	Claim[2]	Location[3]
179	Intelligence Report	11AUG40	-	Page 2 of CR 178
180	Intelligence Report	11AUG40	-	Page 3 of CR 178
181	Darling, Edward V.	06SEP40	Me109	Thames Estuary
182	Darling, Edward V.	06SEP40	-	Page 2 of CR 181
183	Darling, Edward V.	15SEP40	Do215	5m off Dover, Kent
184	Darling, Edward V.	15SEP40	-	Page 2 of CR 183
185	Darling, Edward V.	15SEP40	He111	6m E of Hornchurch, Esx
186	Darling, Edward V.	15SEP40	-	Page 2 of CR 185
187	Darling, Edward V.	18SEP40	Me109	5m W of Dover, Kent
188	Darling, Edward V.	18SEP40	-	Page 2 of CR 187
189	Darling, Edward V.	18SEP40	Ju88	Chatham, Kent
190	Darling, Edward V.	18SEP40	-	Page 2 of CR 189
191	Darling, Edward V.	23SEP40	Me109	Dover, Kent
192	Darling, Edward V.	23SEP40	-	Page 2 of CR 191
193	Darling, Edward V.	27NOV40	Me109	Nr Tonbridge, Kent
194	Darling, Edward V.	27NOV40	-	Page 2 of CR 193
195	Fee, John C.	04MAY42	Me109	Le Havre, F.
196	Fee, John C.	04MAY42	-	Page 2 of CR 195
197	Fee, John C.	21MAY42	2 Ships	Seine Estuary, F.
198	Fee, John C.	21MAY42	-	Page 2 of CR 197
199	Finlay, Donald O.	01OCT40	Me109	Epsom, Surrey
200	Finlay, Donald O.	01OCT40	-	Page 2 of CR 199
201	Finlay, Donald O.	07OCT40	Do215	SE Maidstone, Kent
	Lecky, John G.			2m into English Channel
202	Lecky, John G.	07OCT40	-	Page 2 of CR 201
203	Finlay, Donald O.	09OCT40	Me109	Maidstone, Kent
204	Fisher, Douglas P.	15JUL44	V1	50m SSW Dungeness, Kent
205	Finlay, Donald O.	09OCT40	-	Page 2 of CR 203
206	Finlay, Donald O.	20OCT40	Me109	Nr Biggin Hill, London
207	Finlay, Donald O.	20OCT40	-	Page 2 of CR 206
208	Finlay, Donald O.	23NOV40	Me109	Ivychurch, Kent
209	Finlay, Donald O.	23NOV40	-	Page 2 of CR 208
210	Finlay, Donald O.	27NOV40	Me109	5-8m SW Dungeness, Kent
211	Finlay, Donald O.	27NOV40	-	Page 2 of CR 210
212	Fisher, Douglas P.	20OCT43	Me109	Évreux, F.
213	Fisher, Douglas P.	20OCT43	-	Page 2 of CR 212
214	Ford, Roy C.	15AUG40	No Claim	Seaham Harbour, Dur
215	Ford, Roy C.	05SEP40	Me109	Sheppey, Kent
216	Ford, Roy C.	05SEP40	-	Page 2 of CR 215
217	Galitzine, Emanuel V.	24SEP43	FW190	SW Beauvais, F.
218	Gaunce, Lionel M.	21AUG41	Me109	Hesdin, F.
219	Gaunce, Lionel M.	27AUG41	Me109	St. Omer, F.
220	Gaunce, Lionel M.	28AUG41	Me109	Le Havre, F.

CR	Pilot	Date	Claim[2]	Location[3]
221	Gaunce, Lionel M.	28AUG41	-	Page 2 of CR 220
222	Gaunce, Lionel M.	17SEP41	Me109F	S of Boulogne, F.
223	Gaunce, Lionel M.	17SEP41	-	Page 2 of CR 222
224	Gaze, Frederick A. O.	11APR45	Ju52	Ottersburg, G.
225	Gaze, Frederick A. O.	28APR45	FW190	Schwerin, G.
226	Gaze, Frederick A. O.	30APR45	FW190	N of Lauenberg, G.
227	Gibbs, N. Peter	21JUN44	V1	Off Beachy Head, Ssx
228	Gibbs, N. Peter	24JUN44	V1	8m S of Hastings, Ssx
229	Glen, Arthur A.	14AUG41	Me109	Pas de Calais, F.
230	Glen, Arthur A.	09DEC41	Distillery	Ypreville, F.
231	Glen, Arthur A.	14MAR42	2 Me109	Off Fécamp, F.
232	Glen, Arthur A.	14MAR42	-	Page 2 of CR 231
233	Glen, Arthur A.	24SEP43	2 FW190	N of Beauvais, F.
234	Graham, Peter B.	27SEP43	FW190	15m NW Beauvais, F.
235	Graham, Peter B.	16AUG44	V1	Nr Waltham, Kent
236	Graham, Peter B.	17AUG44	V1	Denge Wood, Kent
237	Gray, Colin F.	22AUG41	Me109	20m NE of Le Havre, F.
238	Gray, Eric	26JUL44	V1	Boulogne, F.
239	Gray, Eric	20AUG44	V1	7m off Folkestone, Kent
240	Gray, Eric / Harding, Ross P. / Hegarty, Francis M.	13FEB45	Me110	10m S of Lippstadt, G.
241	Gray, Eric	20APR45	2 FW190	Teschendorf, G.
242	Gray, Eric	01MAY45	FW190	E of Schwerin Lake, G.
243	Green, Ronald E.	03MAY42	FW190	Guînes, F.
244	Green, Ronald E.	03MAY42	-	Page 2 of CR 243
245	Harding, Ross P.	05JUL44	V1	NW of Rye, Ssx
246	Harding, Ross P.	15AUG44	V1	Romney Marsh, Kent
247	Harding, Ross P.	17AUG44	V1	1m NE of Brenzett, Kent
248	Healy, Terence W. R.	05OCT40	Me109	N of Biggin Hill, Kent
249	Healy, Terence W. R.	05OCT40	-	Page 2 of CR 248
250	Hegarty, Francis M.	23JAN45	FW190	Münster-Waltrop, G.
251	Hegarty, Francis M.	23JAN45	-	Page 2 of CR 250
252	Hegarty, Francis M.	17APR45	Ju88	Lübeck Aerodrome, G.
253	Henry, David J. V.	23JAN45	FW190	Münster-Waltrop, G.
254	Henry, David J. V.	23JAN45	-	Page 2 of CR 253
255	Hogarth, Rycherde H.	17APR43	Ju88	2m off Ostend, B.
256	Hood, Hilary R. L.	29JUL40	Me109 / Ju87	Dover area, Kent
257	Hood, Hilary R. L.	29JUL40	-	Page 2 of CR 256
258	Hood, Hilary R. L.	05SEP40	Do17	S of Gravesend, Kent
259	Hood, Hilary R. L.	05SEP40	-	Page 2 of CR 258
260	Howitt, Isaac E.	11SEP40	No Claim	Dungeness, Kent

CR	Pilot	Date	Claim[2]	Location[3]
261	Howitt, Isaac E.	11SEP40	-	Page 2 of CR 260
262	Howitt, Isaac E.	11SEP40	-	Page 3 of CR 260
263	Hugo, Petrus H.	14MAR42	Me109	8m N of Fécamp, F.
264	Hugo, Petrus H.	14MAR42	-	Page 2 of CR 263
265	Hunt, Leonard	14JUL41	No Claim	40m E of Teesmouth, Dur
266	Hunt, Leonard	14JUL41	-	Page 2 of CR 265
267	Imbert, André	19AUG42	FW190	Off Dieppe, F.
268	Langley, Gerald A.	11SEP40	Ju88	15m SE of London
269	Langley, Gerald A.	11SEP40	-	Page 2 of CR 268
270	Lawrence, Thomas E.	28MAR45	FW190	Rheine area, G.
271	Lovell, Anthony D. J.	06SEP40	Me109	15m N of Manston, Kent
272	Lovell, Anthony D. J.	06SEP40	-	Page 2 of CR 271
273	Lovell, Anthony D. J.	15SEP40	Me109	SE of Canterbury, Kent
274	Lovell, Anthony D. J.	15SEP40	-	Page 2 of CR 273
275	Lovell, Anthony D. J.	15SEP40	Me109E	3m SW of Hornchurch, Esx
276	Lovell, Anthony D. J.	15SEP40	-	Page 2 of CR 275
277	Lovell, Anthony D. J.	30SEP40	Do215	10m S of Hastings, Kent
278	Lovell, Anthony D. J.	30SEP40	-	Page 2 of CR 277
279	Lovell, Anthony D. J.	01OCT40	Me109E	S of Canterbury, Kent
280	Lovell, Anthony D. J.	01OCT40	-	Page 2 of CR 279
281	Lovell, Anthony D. J.	20OCT40	Me109E	Near Biggin Hill, SE London
282	Lovell, Anthony D. J.	20OCT40	-	Page 2 of CR 281
283	Lovell, Anthony D. J.	30OCT40	Me109E	SW of Maidstone, Kent
284	Lovell, Anthony D. J.	30OCT40	-	Page 2 of CR 283
285	Lovell, Anthony D. J.	17NOV40	Me109E	7m N of Herne Bay, Kent
286	Lovell, Anthony D. J.	17NOV40	-	Page 2 of CR 285
287	Lovell, Anthony D. J.	27NOV40	Me109E	Nr Tonbridge, Kent
288	Lovell, Anthony D. J.	27NOV40	-	Page 2 of CR 287
289	Lovell, Anthony D.J.[15]	22JAN41	He111	SW of Clacton, Esx
290	Lovell, Anthony D.J.	22JAN41	-	Page 2 of CR 189
291	Lovell, Anthony D.J.[18]	30MAR41	Ju88	Ouston, Dur
292	Lovell, Anthony D. J.	30MAR41	-	Page 2 of CR 291
293	Intelligence Report[9]	30MAR41	Ju88	Ouston, Dur
294	McAdam, John	07SEP40	2 Do17 Me109E	½m E of St. Paul's
295	McAdam, John	07SEP40	-	Page 2 of CR 294
296	McAdam, John	07SEP40	-	Page 3 of CR 294
297	McAdam, John	09SEP40	Me109E	Ashford, Kent
298	McAdam, John	09SEP40	-	Page 2 of CR 297
299	McAdam, John	27NOV40	Me109E	Nr Tonbridge, Kent
300	McAdam, John	27NOV40	-	Page 2 of CR 299
301	McAdam, John	25OCT40	-	Page 2 of CR 302
302	McAdam, John	25OCT40	Me109E	Biggin Hill-Dungeness, Kent

CR	Pilot	Date	Claim[2]	Location[3]
303	Malone, Charles J.	14AUG44	V1	2m NW of Ashford, Kent
304	Marples, Roy	12AUG41	Me109F	St Valéry, F.
305	Marples, Roy	21AUG41	Me109F	Nr, Fruges, F.
306	Marples, Roy[10] Ranger, Geoffrey H. Whiteford, Cyril J. L.	18SEP41	Ju52	Off Ostend, B.
307	May, Stanley H.[11]	11AUG43	1½ Locos.	S of Dieppe, F.
308	Meagher, Patrick E.	09MAY41	Ju88	Whitby, Yks
309	Meagher, Patrick E.	09MAY41	-	Page 2 of CR 308
310	Middlemiss, Robert G.	10APR42	FW190	Off Hardelot, F.
311	Mileham, Denys E.	05OCT40	2 Me109	NW of Folkestone, Kent
312	Mileham, Denys E.	05OCT40	-	Page 2 of CR 311
313	Mileham, Denys E.	17NOV40	Me109	Thames Estuary
314	Mileham, Denys E.	17NOV40	-	Page 2 of CR 313
315	Mitchell, Herbert R.	07AUG41	Me109	Béthune, F.
316	Morrogh-Ryan, Oliver	15AUG40	Ju88	Seaham Harbour, Dur
317	Morrogh-Ryan, Oliver	05SEP40	Me109	Isle of Sheppey, Kent
318	Morrogh-Ryan, Oliver	05SEP40	-	Page 2 of CR 317
319	Scott, William J. M.	29JUL40	No Claim	Dover, Kent
320	Scott, William J. M.	29JUL40	-	Page 2 of CR 319
321	Newman, Benjamin B.	16SEP43	Me109	Bernay-Évreux, F.
322	Newman, Benjamin B.	16SEP43	-	Page 2 of CR 321
323	Newman, Benjamin B.	24SEP43	FW190	Beauvais, F.
324	Newman, Benjamin B.	20OCT43	Me109	Beaumont-le-Roger, F.
325	Norwell, John K.	17SEP40	Me109	10m W of Manston, Kent
326	Norwell, John K.	17SEP40	-	Page 2 of CR 325
327	Norwell, John K.	17SEP40	2 Me109	S of Chatham, Kent
328	Norwell, John K.	17SEP40	-	Page 2 of CR 327
329	Norwell, John K.	27SEP40	Me109	5m S of Faversham, Kent
330	Norwell, John K.	27SEP40	-	Page 2 of CR 329
331	Palmer, Wilfred	18AUG41	Me109	Lille, F.
332	Palmer, Wilfred	21AUG41	Me109	Near Fruges, F.
333	Palmer, Wilfred	27AUG41	2 Me109	St. Omer-Gravelines, F.
334	Palmer, Wilfred	27AUG41	-	Page 2 of CR 333
335	Palmer, Wilfred	18SEP41	2 Me109F	Dixmude, B.-Boulogne, F.
336	Palmer, Wilfred	18SEP41	-	Page 2 of CR 335
337	Palmer, Wilfred	10APR42	2 FW190	4m off Boulogne, F.
338	Palmer, Wilfred	10APR42	-	Page 2 of CR 337
339	Payne, Jim J. C.	13JUL44	V1	15m S of Hastings, Ssx
340	Pinny, John A. H.	10APR42	FW190	4m off Boulogne, F.
341	Poynton, T. Rex	10JUN42	FW190	Mid-Channel
342	Poynton, T. Rex	10JUN42	-	Page 2 of CR 341
343	Ranger, Geoffrey H.	11JUL41	He111	W of Scarborough, Yks

CR	Pilot	Date	Claim[2]	Location[3]
344	Ranger, Geoffrey H.	11JUL41	-	Page 2 of CR 343
345	Ranger, Geoffrey H.	18AUG41	Me109	Armentières, F.
346	Ranger, Geoffrey H.[10]	18SEP41	Ju52	Off Ostend, B.
347	Ranger, Geoffrey H.	18SEP41	-	Page 2 of CR 346
348	Ranger, Geoffrey H.	21SEP41	Me109	10m NW Gosnay, F.
349	Ranger, Geoffrey H.	21SEP41	-	Page 2 of CR 348
350	Rake, Derrick S. V.	03MAY45	Ju188	Norderstapel-Husum, G.
351	Reid, Daniel J.	23JUL44	V1	10m NW of Ashford, Kent
352	Reid, Daniel J.	25FEB45	FW190	Rheine, G.
353	Robertson, Colin S.	27JUL44	V1	Mid-Channel
354	Robertson, Colin S.	27JUL44	-	Page 2 of CR 353
355	Rossow, Vivian J.	16AUG44	V1	5m WNW of Ashford, Kent
356	Rossow, Vivian J.	14FEB45	Me262	Rheine area, G.
357	Rossow, Vivian J.	20APR45	Me262	SE Neuruppin, G.
358	Scott, William J. M.	06SEP40	Me109	Thames Estuary
359	Scott, William J. M.	06SEP40	-	Page 2 of CR 358
360	Scott, William J. M.	07SEP40	Me109	Dover, Kent
361	Scott, William J. M.	07SEP40	-	Page 2 of CR 360
362	Scott, Peter F.	20APR45	FW190	Kremmen Forest, G.
363	Scott, Peter F.	01MAY45	2 FW190	Nr Schwerin Lake, G.
364	Shepherd, John B.	14APR45	Me110 / Me163	Nordholz, G.
365	Shepherd, John B.	16APR45	FW190	Hagenow, G.
366	Shepherd, John B.	20APR45	2 FW190	Kremmen Forest, G.
367	Shepherd, John B.	30APR45	FW190 / Me109	Lauenberg, G.
368	Shepherd, John B.	01MAY45	FW190	Schwerin Lake, G.
369	Shepherd, John B.	01MAY45	-	Copy of CR 368
370	Shipman, Edward A.	17OCT39	He111	20m E of Whitby, Yks
371	Shipman, Edward A.	17OCT39	-	Page 2 of CR 370
372	Shipman, Edward A.	28JUL40	No Claim	Dover, Kent, & SE Coast
373	Shipman, Edward A.	28JUL40	-	Page 2 of CR 372
374	Shipman, Edward A.	15AUG40	Me110	West of Durham
375	Shipman, Edward A.	21AUG40	He111	15m E Flamborough Hd., Yks
376	Slack, Thomas A. H.	04AUG44	V1	Dungeness-Isle of Oxney
377	Smith, Donald H.	04JUN43	FW190	Eastbourne, Ssx
378	Smith, Donald H.	22SEP43	FW190	W of Évreux, F.
379	Solak, Jerzy J.	04JUN43	FW190	3m S of Eastbourne, Ssx
380	Spencer, Terence	23JUN44	V1	10-15m NNE Hastings, Ssx
381	Spencer, Terence	23JUN44	-	Page 2 of CR 380
382	Spencer, Terence	09AUG44	V1	5m N of Hastings, Ssx
383	Spencer, Terence	19AUG44	V1	2m NNW Appledore, Kent

CR	Pilot	Date	Claim[2]	Location[3]
384	Spencer, Terence	23AUG44	V1	2m N of Mersham, Kent
385	Spencer, Terence	23AUG44	V1	Nr Harrietsham, Kent
386	Spencer, Terence	27AUG44	V1	15m N of Rye, Ssx
387	Stepp, Malta L.	19AUG42	FW190	Dieppe, F.
388	Stevenson, Ian T.	20JUL44	V1	SE of Dungeness, Kent
389	Stevenson, Ian T.	05AUG44	V1	6m NE of Maidstone, Kent
390	Stevenson, Ian T.	20APR45	FW190	Teschendorf Wood, G.
391	Stevenson, Ian T.	20APR45	-	Copy of CR 390
392	Stevenson, Ian T.	01MAY45	FW190	Wittenberg, G.
393	Stowe, William N.	23JAN45	FW190	Münster-Waltrop, G.
394	Stowe, William N.	23JAN45	-	Page 2 of CR 393
395	Swanwick, George W.	18SEP41	Me109E	Off Ostend, B.
396	Swanwick, George W.	18SEP41	-	Page 2 of CR 395
397	Usmar, Frank	15AUG40	He111	Durham area
398	Usmar, Frank	15AUG40	-	Diagram to CR 397
399	Usmar, Frank	No Date	No Claim	Dngnss.-Romney Msh., Kent
400	Valiquet, Charles N.	18AUG41	Me109	Lille, F.
401	Valiquet, Charles N.	31AUG41	Me109	Le Trait, F.
402	Valiquet, Charles N.	31AUG41	-	Page 2 of CR 401
403	Valiquet, Charles N. / Glen, Arthur A.	09DEC41	Distillery	Page 2 of CR 404
404	Valiquet, Charles N. / Glen, Arthur A.	09DEC41	Distillery	Ypreville, F.
405	Arkel, Jan van	03MAY42	FW190	Cap Blanc Nez, F.
406	Arkel, Jan van	04MAY42	FW190 / Me109	Le Havre, F. / NE of Le Havre, F.
407	Vann, William H.	22SEP43	Me109	W of Évreux, F.
408	Vykoukal, Karel J.	04MAY42	FW190	Le Havre, F.
409	Vykoukal, Karel J.	04MAY42	-	Page 2 of CR 408
410	Wainwright, Derek W.	27MAY42	Me109	W of Selsey, Ssx
411	Walker, James R.	07OCT40	Me109	Kent Coast
412	Walker, James R.	07OCT40	-	Page 2 of CR 411
413	Walker, James R.	09OCT40	Me109	5-10m off French coast
414	Walker, James R.	09OCT40	-	Page 2 of CR 413
415	Wallens, Ronald W.	28JUL40	No Claim	Dover, Kent
416	Wallens, Ronald W.	28JUL40	-	Page 2 of CR 415
417	Wallens, Ronald W.	08AUG40	3 Me109	Bet. Manston & Calais
418	Wallens, Ronald W.	08AUG40	-	Page 2 of CR 417
419	Webster, J. Terence	08AUG40	4 Me109	Bet. Manston & Calais
420	Webster, J. Terence	08AUG40	-	Page 2 of CR 419
421	Wallens, Ronald W.	11AUG40	Ju88	Thirsk, Yks
422	Wallens, Ronald W.	11AUG40	-	Page 2 of CR 421
423	Blank Combat Report	No Date	-	-

CR	Pilot	Date	Claim[2]	Location[3]
424	Wallens, Ronald W.	15AUG40	Me110	Durham area
425	Wallens, Ronald W.	05SEP40	Me109	S of Gravesend-Channel
			Do17	
426	Wallens, Ronald W.	05SEP40	-	Page 2 of CR 425
427	Wallens, Ronald W.	05SEP40	Me109	10m SE of Dover, Kent
428	Wallens, Ronald W.	05SEP40	-	Page 2 of CR 427
429	Ware, James P.	18AUG44	V1	N of Hollingbourne, Kent
430	Swanwick, George W.	13OCT41	Me109	10m off Boulogne, F.
431	Webster, J. Terence	17DEC39	He115	5m SE of Whitby, Yks
432	Webster, J. Terence	17DEC39	-	Page 2 of CR 431
433	Webster, J. Terence	17DEC39	-	Page 3 of CR 431
434	Webster, J. Terence	17DEC39	-	Page 4 of CR 431
435	Webster, J. Terence	17DEC39	-	Page 5 of CR 431
436	Webster, J. Terence	17DEC39	-	Page 6 of CR 431
437	Webster, J. Terence	17DEC39	-	Page 7 of CR 431
438	Webster, J. Terence	17DEC39	-	Page 8 of CR 431
439	Webster, J. Terence	09FEB40	No Claim	Anson off Whitby, Yks
440	Webster, J. Terence	01MAR40	No Claim	20m ENE Hartlepool, Dur
441	Webster, J. Terence	19JUN40	He111	Teesmouth, Dur
442	Webster, J. Terence	19JUN40	-	Page 2 of CR 441
443	Webster, J. Terence	19JUN40	-	Copy of CR 441
444	Webster, J. Terence	19JUN40	-	Copy of CR 442
445	Webster, J. Terence	19JUN40	-	Page 3 of CR 441
446	Webster, J. Terence	19JUN40	-	Page 4 of CR 441
447	Webster, J. Terence	27JUL40	Me109	5m off Dover, Kent
448	Webster, J. Terence	27JUL40	-	Page 2 of CR 447
449	Webster, J. Terence[12]	28JUL40	Me109	Dover area, Kent
			He113	
450	Webster, J. Terence	28JUL40	-	Page 2 of CR 449
451	Webster, J. Terence	29JUL40	Me109	Dover area, Kent
			Ju87	
452	Webster, J. Terence	29JUL40	-	Page 2 of CR 451
453	Webster, J. Terence	05AUG40	He111	Off Dover, Kent
454	Webster, J. Terence	05AUG40	-	Page 2 of CR 453
455	Webster, J. Terence[13]	05SEP40	He113	Gravesend-Ashford, Kent
			Me109E	
456	Webster, J. Terence	05SEP40	-	Page 2 of CR 455
457	Wells, Edward P.	17OCT40	Me109E	Off Kent coast
458	Wells, Edward P.	17OCT40	-	Page 2 of CR 457
459	Wells, Edward P.	25OCT40	Me109E	Biggin Hill, Kent
460	Wells, Edward P.	25OCT40	-	Page 2 of CR 459
461	Wells, Edward P.	25OCT40	Me109E	SE of Dungeness, Kent
462	Wells, Edward P.	25OCT40	-	Page 2 of CR 461

CR	Pilot	Date	Claim[2]	Location[3]
463	Wells, Edward P.	02NOV40	Me109E	N of Dungeness, Kent
464	Wells, Edward P.	02NOV40	-	Page 2 of CR 463
465	Wells, Edward P.[14]	11NOV40	CR42	E of Orford Ness, Sflk
466	Wells, Edward P.	11NOV40	-	Page 2 of CR 465
467	Wells, Edward P.	11NOV40	Hs126	5m NE of Gris Nez, F.
468	Wells, Edward P.	11NOV40	-	Page 2 of CR 467
469	Wells, Edward P.	27NOV40	Me109	Chatham-Dover, Kent
470	Wells, Edward P.	27NOV40	-	Page 2 of CR 469
471	Wells, Edward P.[15]	22JAN41	He111	SW of Clacton, Esx
472	Wells, Edward P.	22JAN41	-	Page 2 of CR 471
473	Intelligence Report[15]	22JAN41	He111	SW of Clacton, Esx
474	Intelligence Report	22JAN41	-	Page 2 of CR 473
475	Whiteford, Cyril J. L.	18SEP41	Me109	Ostend, B.
476	Whiteford, Cyril J. L.	18SEP41	-	Page 2 of CR 475
477	Whiteford, Cyril J. L.	21SEP41	Me109	5m NW of St. Omer, F.
478	Whiteford, Cyril J. L.	21SEP41	-	Page 2 of CR 477
479	Whiteford, Cyril J. L.	13OCT41	Me109	Arques, F.
480	Wilkinson, John F.	11AUG44	V1	Lympne-Ashford, Kent
481	Wilkinson, John F.	16APR45	FW190	Hagenow, G.
482	Wilkinson, John F.	16APR45	-	Copy of CR 481
483	Wilkinson, John F.	20APR45	2 FW190	Kremmen Forest, G.
484	Wilkinson, John F.	28APR45	2 FW190	Schwerin, G.
485	Williams, Marx G.	24JUL41	Ju88	50m E of Teesmouth, Dur
486	Williams, Marx G.	24JUL41	-	Page 2 of CR 485
487	Williams, Marx G.	12AUG41	Me109F	10m NE of St Valéry, F.
488	Wilson, William R.	03MAY42	FW190	Calais, F.
489	Wilson, William R.	03MAY42	-	Page 2 of CR 488
490	Winskill, Archie L.	14AUG41	Me109F	Lille-St. Omer, F.
491	Winskill, Archie L.	14AUG41	-	Page 2 of CR 490
492	Wright, William A.	10JUN42	No Claim	12m S of St. Catherine's Pt
493	Wright, William A.	10JUN42	-	Page 2 of CR 492
494	Moyle, Crawford N.	14FEB45	FW190	E of Rheine, G.
494	Stevenson, Ian T.	14FEB45	2 FW190	E of Rheine, G.
495	Stevenson, Ian T.	14FEB45	-	Page 2 of CR 495
496	Gray, Eric	14FEB45	Me262	W of Rheine, G.
496	Woolley, Frank	14FEB45	FW190	Rheine Aerodrome, G.
497	Anderson, Robert E.	09JUL44	V1	12m SE Beachy Head, Ssx
497	Appleton, Archie S.	09JUL44	V1	12m SE Beachy Head, Ssx
498	Appleton, Archie S.	21JUL44	V1	20m S of Hastings, Ssx
499	Appleton, Archie S.	23JUL44	V1	3m SE of Bexhill, Ssx
499	Balasse, Maurice A. L.	23JUL44	V1	5m SE of Rye, Ssx
499	Payne, Jim J. C.	23JUL44	V1	5m SE of Rye, Ssx

CR	Pilot	Date	Claim[2]	Location[3]
500	Anderson, Robert E.	22JUN44	V1	N of Maidstone, Kent
	Birbeck, Clive R.			
	Robertson, Colin S.	22JUN44	V1	6m N of Pevensey, Ssx
501	Chattin, Peter W.	08JUL44	V1	Thames Estuary
	Gibbs, N. Peter		V1	2m E of Eastbourne, Ssx
502	Curtis, Keith R.	20JUN44	V1	SSE Tunbridge Wells, Kent
	Gibbs, N. Peter		V1	N of Eastbourne, Ssx
503	Graham, Peter B.	07JUL44	V1	6m W of Hailsham, Ssx
	Stevenson, Ian T.		V1	Eastbourne, Ssx
504	Short, Roger L.	25JUN44	V1	Ashford, Kent
	Spencer, Terence		V1	Hastings, Ssx
505	Balasse, Maurice A. L.	23JUN44	V1	10m N of Hastings, Ssx
	Payne, Jim C. J.		V1	SW of Rye, Ssx
	Slack, Thomas A. H.		V1	Hastings, Ssx
506	Intelligence Report	05SEP40	Multiple	Maidstone, Kent
507	Intelligence Report[16]	06SEP40	Ju88	Hornchurch-Calais
508	Intelligence Report	20OCT40	Multiple	Biggin Hill area, Kent
509	Intelligence Report[14]	11NOV40	CR42	E of Orford Ness, Sflk
510	Intelligence Report[17]	10JAN41	Me109	Wissant, F.
511	Intelligence Report	10JAN41	-	Page 2 of CR510
512	Intelligence Report[18]	30MAR41	Ju88	Ouston, Dur
513	Does not exist	-	-	-
514	Lock, Eric S.	05SEP40	Me109	Isle of Sheppey, Kent
			2 He111	
515	Lock, Eric S.	05SEP40	-	Page 2 of CR 514
516	Lock, Eric S.	05OCT40	2 Me109	W. Malling-Ashford, Kent
517	Lock, Eric S.	05OCT40	-	Page 2 of CR 516
518	Lock, Eric S.[16]	06SEP40	Ju88	20m behind Calais, F.
519	Lock, Eric S.	06SEP40	-	Page 2 of CR 518
520	Lock, Eric S.	11SEP40	Ju88	17m S of Maidstone, Kent
			Me110	25m SSE of Maidstone, Kent
521	Lock, Eric S.	11SEP40	-	Page 2 of CR 520
522	Lock, Eric S.	14SEP40	2 Me109	Dungeness-Ramsgate, Kent
523	Lock, Eric S.	14SEP40	-	Page 2 of CR 522
524	Lock, Eric S.	15SEP40	Me109	E of London
			Do17	Shoeburyness, Esx
525	Lock, Eric S.	15SEP40	-	Page 2 of CR 524
526	Lock, Eric S.	18SEP40	Me109	East Kent
527	Lock, Eric S.	18SEP40	-	Page 2 of CR 528
528	Lock, Eric S.	18SEP40	2 Me109	Maidstone & Kent
529	Lock, Eric S.	18SEP40	-	Page 2 of CR 526
530	Lock, Eric S.[19]	20SEP40	He113	Channel, off Dover
			Hs126	Channel, off Boulogne, F.

CR	Pilot	Date	Claim[2]	Location[3]
531	Lock, Eric S.	20SEP40	-	Page 2 of CR 530
532	Lock, Eric S.	05OCT40	Me109E	S of Dungeness, Kent
533	Lock, Eric S.	05OCT40	-	Page 2 of CR 532
534	Lock, Eric S.	09OCT40	Me109E	10m off Dover, Kent
534	Lock, Eric S.	09OCT40	2 Me109E	Channel, S. Dungeness, Kent
535	Lock, Eric S.	17NOV40	-	Page 2 of CR 542
536	Lock, Eric S.	11OCT40	Me109E	5m off Dungeness, Kent
537	Lock, Eric S.	11OCT40	-	Page 2 of CR 536
538	Lock, Eric S.	20OCT40	Me109E	N of Biggin Hill, London
539	Lock, Eric S.	09OCT40	-	Page 2 of CR 534
540	Lock, Eric S.	25OCT40	Me109E	SE of Biggin Hill, London
541	Lock, Eric S.	20OCT40	-	Page 2 of CR 538
542	Lock, Eric S.	17NOV40	2 Me109E	N Thames Estuary-Channel
543	Lock, Eric S.	17NOV40	-	Page 2 of CR 542
544	Mackenzie, John N.	15AUG40	Ju88	Seaham Harbour, Dur
545	Mackenzie, John N.	06SEP40	2 Me109E	Thamesmouth-Canterbury
546	Mackenzie, John N.	06SEP40	-	Page 2 of CR 545
547	Mackenzie, John N.	11SEP40	He111	S of W. Malling, Kent
548	Mackenzie, John N.	11SEP40	-	Page 2 of CR 547
549	Mackenzie, John N.	15SEP40	Do17	S of London
550	Mackenzie, John N.	23SEP40	-	Page 2 of CR 550A
550A	Mackenzie, John N.	23SEP40	Me109E	English Channel
551	Mackenzie, John N.	15SEP40	-	Page 2 of CR 549
552	Mackenzie, John N.	05OCT40	Me109E	English Channel
553	Mackenzie, John N.	05OCT40	-	Page 2 of CR 552
554	Mackenzie, John N.	07OCT40	Do215	SE of Maidstone, Kent
555	Mackenzie, John N.	25OCT40	Me109E	Biggin Hill area, London
556	Mackenzie, John N.	07OCT40	-	Page 2 of CR 554
557	Mackenzie, John N.	25OCT40	-	Page 2 of CR 555
558	Mackenzie, John N.	25OCT40	Me109E	SE of Dungeness, Kent
559	Mackenzie, John N.	25OCT40	-	Page 2 of CR 558
560	Mackenzie, John N.	30OCT40	Me109E	Dungeness-Ashford, Kent
561	Mackenzie, John N.	30OCT40	-	Page 2 of CR 560
562	Mackenzie, John N.	17NOV40	Me109E	Outer Estuary
563	Mackenzie, John N.	17NOV40	-	Page 2 of CR 562
564	Mackenzie, John N.	27NOV40	Me109E	Nr Tonbridge, Kent
565	Mackenzie, John N.	27NOV40	-	Page 2 of CR 564
566	Ryder, E. Norman	03APR40	He111	Off Whitby, Yks
567	Ryder, E. Norman	03APR40	-	Page 2 of CR 566
568	Ryder, E. Norman	03APR40	-	Page 3 of CR 566
569	Ryder, E. Norman	03APR40	-	Page 4 of CR 566
570	Ryder, E. Norman	03APR40	-	Page 5 of CR 566
571	Ryder, E. Norman	03APR40	-	Page 6 of CR 566

CR	Pilot	Date	Claim[2]	Location[3]
572	Ryder, E. Norman	03APR40	-	Page 7 of CR 566
573	Ryder, E. Norman	03APR40	-	Page 8 of CR 566
574	Ryder, E. Norman	03APR40	-	Page 9 of CR 566
575	Ryder, E. Norman	03APR40	-	Page 10 of CR 566
576	Ryder, E. Norman	03APR40	-	Page 11 of CR 566
577	Ryder, E. Norman	03APR40	-	Page 12 of CR 566
578	Ryder, E. Norman	03APR40	-	Page 13 of CR 566
579	Ryder, E. Norman	03APR40	-	Page 14 of CR 566
580	Ryder, E. Norman	15AUG40	Ju88	6m NW Seaham Hbr., Dur
581	Ryder, E. Norman	05SEP40	Me109	Maidstone area, Kent
582	Ryder, E. Norman	05SEP40	-	Page 2 of CR 581
583	Ryder, E. Norman	05SEP40	Me109	Isle of Sheppey, Kent
584	Ryder, E. Norman	05SEP40	-	Page 2 of CR 583
584A	Ryder, E. Norman	06SEP40	Me109E	Eastchurch, Kent
585	Ryder, E. Norman	06SEP40	-	Page 2 of CR 584A
586	Ryder, E. Norman	07SEP40	Me109E Do17	10m S of Whitstable, Kent
587	Ryder, E. Norman	07SEP40	-	Page 2 of CR 586
588	Ryder, E. Norman	10SEP40	Ju88	15m SE Hornchurch, Esx
589	Ryder, E. Norman	10SEP40	-	Page 2 of CR 588
590	Ryder, E. Norman	15SEP40	Do17	Isle of Sheppey, Kent
591	Intelligence Report	07SEP40	Multiple	Home base-Dover, Kent
592	Ryder, E. Norman	15SEP40	-	Page 2 of CR 590
593	Ryder, E. Norman	25OCT40	Me109E	North of Maidstone, Kent
594	Ryder, E. Norman	25OCT40	-	Page 2 of CR 593
595	Ryder, E. Norman	30OCT40	Me109E	S of Maidstone, Kent
596	Ryder, E. Norman	30OCT40	-	Page 2 of CR 595
597	Ryder, E. Norman	27NOV40	Me109E	Maidstone, Kent
598	Ryder, E. Norman	27NOV40	-	Page 2 of CR 597
599	Ryder, E. Norman	03APR40	-	Page 15 of CR 566
600	Ryder, E. Norman	03APR40	-	Page 16 of CR 566
601	Ryder, E. Norman	03APR40	-	Page 17 of CR 566
602	Ryder, E. Norman	03APR40	-	Page 18 of CR 566
603	Ryder, E. Norman	03APR40	-	Page 19 of CR 566

TNA AIR 27/427, ORB APPENDICES SEPTEMBER 1939-APRIL 1940

This file includes Combat Reports for 17 October and 18 December 1939. Those marked with an asterisk are *not* included in AIR 50/18, above.

CR	Pilot	Date	Claim[2]	Location[3]
35	Shipman, Edward A.	17OCT39	He111	20m E of Whitby, Yks
36	Shipman, Edward A.	17OCT39	-	Page 2 of CR 35
37	Shipman, Edward A.*	17OCT39	-	Page 3 of CR 35
98	Webster, J. Terence*	17DEC39	He115	5m SE of Whitby, Yks
99	Webster, J. Terence*	17DEC39	-	Page 2 of CR 98

TNA AIR 27/428, ORB APPENDICES MAY-DECEMBER 1940

This file includes Combat Reports for 25 October-17 November 1940. Those marked with an asterisk are *not* included in AIR 50/18, above.

CR	Pilot	Date	Claim[2]	Location[3]
192	Aldridge, Frederick J.	25OCT40	Me109E	Nr Maidstone, Kent
193	Aldridge, Frederick J.	25OCT40	-	Page 2 of CR 192
194	Beardsley, Robert A.	25OCT40	2 Me109E	Nr Dungeness, Kent
195	Beardsley, Robert A.*	25OCT40	-	Page 2 of CR 194
196	Brown, M. Peter	25OCT40	Me109E	Ashford, Kent-Rye, Ssx
197	Brown, M. Peter	25OCT40	-	Page 2 of CR 196
198	Cory, Guy W.	25OCT40	2 Me109E	SE of Dungeness, Kent
199	Cory, Guy W.	25OCT40	-	Page 2 of CR 198
200	Healy, Terence W. R.*	25OCT40	Me109E	Nr Biggin Hill, Kent
201	Healy, Terence W. R.*	25OCT40	-	Page 2 of CR 200
202	Lock, Eric S.	25OCT40	Me109E	SE of Biggin Hill, London
203	Lock, Eric S.*	25OCT40	-	Page 2 of CR 202
204	McAdam, John	25OCT40	Me109E	Biggin Hill-Dungeness
205	McAdam, John*	25OCT40	-	Page 2 of CR 204
206	Mackenzie, John N.	25OCT40	Me109E	Biggin Hill area, London
207	Mackenzie, John N.	25OCT40	-	Page 2 of CR 206
208	Mackenzie, John N.	25OCT40	Me109E	SE of Dungeness, Kent
209	Mackenzie, John N.	25OCT40	-	Page 2 of CR 208
210	Ryder, E. Norman	25OCT40	Me109E	North of Maidstone, Kent
211	Ryder, E. Norman	25OCT40	-	Page 2 of CR 210
212	Wells, Edward P.	25OCT40	Me109E	SE of Dungeness, Kent
213	Wells, Edward P.	25OCT40	-	Page 2 of CR 212
214	Wells, Edward P.	25OCT40	Me109E	Biggin Hill, Kent
215	Wells, Edward P.	25OCT40	-	Page 2 of CR 214
216	Adams, Dennis A.	30OCT40	Me109E	SW of Maidstone, Kent
217	Adams, Dennis A.	30OCT40	-	Page 2 of CR 216

CR	Pilot	Date	Claim²	Location³
218	Aldridge, Frederick J.	30OCT40	Me109E	W of Ashford, Kent
219	Aldridge, Frederick J.	30OCT40	-	Page 2 of CR 218
220	Angus, Robert A.	30OCT40	Me109E	Tonbridge-Ashford, Kent
221	Angus, Robert A.	30OCT40	-	Page 2 of CR 220
222	Lovell, Anthony D. J.	30OCT40	Me109E	SW of Maidstone, Kent
223	Lovell, Anthony D. J.	30OCT40	-	Page 2 of CR 222
224	Mackenzie, John N.	30OCT40	Me109E	Dungeness-Ashford, Kent
225	Mackenzie, John N.	30OCT40	-	Page 2 of CR 224
226	Ryder, E. Norman	30OCT40	Me109E	S of Maidstone, Kent
227	Ryder, E. Norman	30OCT40	-	Page 2 of CR 226
228	Wells, Edward P.	02NOV40	Me109E	N of Dungeness, Kent
229	Wells, Edward P.	02NOV40	-	Page 2 of CR 228
230	Wells, Edward P.	11NOV40	Hs126	5m NE of Griz Nez, F.
231	Wells, Edward P.	11NOV40	-	Page 2 of CR 230
232	Wells, Edward P.	11NOV40	CR42	E of Orford Ness, Sflk
233	Wells, Edward P.	11NOV40	-	Page 2 of CR 232
234	Aldridge, Frederick J.	17NOV40	Me109E	Off Felixstowe, Esx
235	Aldridge, Frederick J.	17NOV40	-	Page 2 of CR 234
236	Lock, Eric S.	17NOV40	2 Me109E	N. Thames Estuary-Channel
237	Lock, Eric S.	17NOV40	-	Page 3 of CR 236
238	Lovell, Anthony D. J.	17NOV40	Me109E	7m N of Herne Bay, Kent
239	Lovell, Anthony D. J.	17NOV40	-	Page 2 of CR 238
240	Mackenzie, John N.	17NOV40	Me109E	Outer Estuary
241	Mackenzie, John N.	17NOV40	-	Page 2 of CR 240
242	Mileham, Denys E.	17NOV40	Me109	Thames Estuary
243	Mileham, Denys E.	17NOV40	-	Page 2 of CR 242
244	Lock, Eric S.	17NOV40	-	Page 2 of CR 236

TNA AIR 27/429, ORB APPENDICES JANUARY-DECEMBER 1941

This file includes Combat Reports for 12 August-20 September 1941. Those marked with an asterisk are *not* included in AIR 50/18, above. Note that several folios have information on their reverse sides that have not been given a page number. e.g. CR246 is a two-page document.

CR	Pilot	Date	Claim²	Location³
213	Marples, Roy	12AUG41	Me109F	St Valéry, F.
214	Williams, Marx G.	12AUG41	Me109F	10m NE of St Valéry, F.
246	Gaunce, Lionel M.	17SEP41	Me109F	S of Boulogne, F.
247	Swanwick, George W.	18SEP41	Me109E	Off Ostend, B.
248	Buchanan, George A.	18SEP41	Hs1234	Ostend, B.
249	Bush, Charles R.	18SEP41	Hs1234	Ostend, B.
250	Palmer, Wilfred	18SEP41	2 Me109F	Dixmude, B.-Boulogne, F.
251	Palmer, Wilfred	18SEP41	-	Page 2 of CR 250

CR	Pilot	Date	Claim[2]	Location[3]
252	Babbage, Cyril F.[4]	18SEP41	Hawk	1m N of Ostend, B.
253	Ranger, Geoffrey H.[10]	18SEP41	Ju52	Off Ostend, B.
254	Whiteford, Cyril J.L.[10]	18SEP41	Ju52	Off Ostend, B.
255	Bache, Leslie L.	20SEP41	Me109E	Doudeville-St Valéry, F.
256	Woodhouse, Henry*[20]	20SEP41	Me109E	Doudeville-St Valéry, F.

TNA AIR 27/431, ORB APPENDICES APRIL 1944-MAY 1945

This file includes Daily Squadron Intelligence Reports for April 1944 to May 1945. Some of these mention victories by specific pilots, and sometimes go into more detail than the ORB's F540/541. They are not Combat Reports as such, but may be an additional source of information.

Dates	Pages
April 1944	6-41
April-May 1945	46-59
June 1944	64-74
July 1944	78-106
August 1944	111-145
September 1944	153-181
October 1944	185-201
November 1944	206-224
December 1944	229-240
January-April 1945	245-305

TNA AIR 50/443, 146 WING, TANGMERE COMBAT REPORTS, JULY 1943-MAY 1944

This file includes Combat Reports for 41, 91, 118, 193, 257, 402 & 416 Squadrons for the period July 1943-May 1944. The Combat Reports within the file that are annotated '41 Squadron' relate to Wg. Cdr. Raymond H. Harries' victories whilst leading the Spitfire XII Wing and flying with 41 Squadron on operations from Westhampnett and Tangmere during September and October 1943.

CR	Pilot	Date	Claim[2]	Location[3]
2	Harries, Raymond H.	22SEP43	2 FW190	Just S of Évreux, F.
3	Harries, Raymond H.	22SEP43	-	Page 2 of CR 2
4	Harries, Raymond H.	27SEP43	Me109G	10m N of Beauvais, F.
5	Harries, Raymond H.	20OCT43	2 Me109G	N of Évreux & Rouen area, F.
5A	Harries, Raymond H.	20OCT43	-	Page 2 of CR 5

Styles and Terminology

ALPHABETICAL ORDER
Names are generally listed in strict alphabetical order. Thus MALONE, for example, appears after MACKENZIE, but before McKELLAR. Foreign surnames including 'van' appear in order of suffix, not prefix, and as such VAN GOENS is listed under GOENS, van.

ENGLISH COUNTIES
In all cases, English counties named in this work follow the county designations that existed at the time of an event, and will therefore not necessarily correlate with those amalgamated, re-named, reorganised or abolished after 1974.

DATES
Dates are always shown in the format 'Day Month Year', either written in full (e.g. 1 August 1942) or abbreviated to DDMMMYY (e.g. 01AUG42) or D Mmm YY (e.g. 1 Aug 42), unless they appear in another format in a quote. In such cases, they are cited verbatim.

LANGUAGE
In most cases, foreign language words and names have been used in their original forms and have not been anglicised. Diacritics, most commonly umlauts in German (ä, ö, ü) and accents in French (e.g. à, é, ô), but also other foreign language symbols (e.g. ç, ě, ę, ń, ø, ó, ř), are used where they appear in names, or are considered suitable in the context of the dialogue.

MAPS
Maps used in this book have been created by the author for illustrative purposes only, and may not necessarily be to scale. Please consult official maps for proper detail.

MEASUREMENTS
As Imperial measurements were used in the British Commonwealth and United States throughout the period covered by this work (1942-45), they have been purposely used in the text, particularly in references to distance in the United Kingdom. Metric measurements are, however, used where they were already in use in a particular location at the time, e.g. Germany, and in cases where it was felt a comparison of imperial and metric measurements was suitable.

THE NATIONAL ARCHIVES
In April 2003, the Public Record Office (PRO) was amalgamated with the Historical Manuscripts Commission (HMC) to become 'The National Archives' ('TNA'). As such, although the Archives is still often referred to as the Public Record Office, and indeed more so by its abbreviation 'PRO', the Archives is referred to throughout this work by its new name and abbreviation 'TNA'.

TIMES
All times used in the text are shown in military-style 24-hour time, but without the use of 'hours' or 'hrs', e.g. 15:00, unless they appear in another format in a quote. In such cases, they are cited verbatim. To convert a certain time to p.m., deduct 12 hours from any time between 13:00 and 24:00. e.g. 15:00 minus 12 hours = 3.00 p.m.

Glossary of Terms

AM1180	Air Ministry Form 1180, Flying Accident Card, filled in for each flying accident suffered by an aircraft. It usually provided detail on pilot, cause and circumstances. At the time of writing, they are held by the RAF Museum at Hendon in London.
Big Ben	Code word for operations pertaining to V2 rocket manufacture, assembly and launch sites.
beat-up	Flying at low level, e.g. over an aerodrome or column of men. The former is usually associated with showing-off and resulted in disciplinary action; the latter flown to create fear and confusion into an enemy column, and could be included in an attack with live ammunition. Those practiced by 41 Squadron in Llanbedr in 1942 were practice attacks, without ammunition on Army columns during Army co-operation exercises.
Cine-gun camera	A small camera which filmed the view through the gun sight when the guns were fired. The films were used for instructional purposes and to verify a pilot's success against his opponent.
Circus	Co-ordinated bomber or fighter-bomber attacks on specific targets with fighter support.
Crossbow	A top-level code name for airborne operations against the German long-range weapons programmes (V1s, V2s & V3s, etc.), aka 'Crossbow targets'.
Dorsal	Gun position on the top of an aircraft's fuselage, usually facing to the rear, for example on the He111 and B-17 Flying Fortress.
E-Boat	*Kriegsmarine* motor torpedo boat, called an *S-Boot* [*Schnell-Boot* ≈ Fast Boat] by the Germans, and E-Boat by the Allies, likely meaning 'Enemy Boat', to differentiate it from Allied motor torpedo boats ('MTB's).
F540	Form 540, Squadron (or other unit) Operations Record Book (diary of events).
F541	Form 541, Squadron Operations Record Book Appendix (detail of work carried out, listing aircraft, pilots and sortie timings).
Flak	*Flugabwehrkanone* (anti-aircraft cannon).
Geschwader	A Luftwaffe unit, not quite as large as an RAF Group, but larger than a Wing, with three *Gruppen* of three *Staffeln*, each *Staffel* consisting of around 12 aircraft.
Gruppe	A Luftwaffe unit, roughly equivalent to an RAF Wing.
Hack	Usually a biplane or ex-service (retired) aircraft used to run non-operational squadron errands, pick up pilots, practice instrument flying, etc.
Jim Crow	Coastal patrols of France and Belgium, tasked with reporting weather conditions and enemy shipping movements.
Kriegsmarine	German Navy.
line abreast	Aircraft flying in a straight line on either side of a Flight Commander or Section Leader.
line astern	Aircraft flying one behind the other in a straight line, often used in attacks, when each aircraft followed the one in front to attack a target and took his turn firing after the aircraft in front broke away; also known as a No. 1 Attack.
Luftwaffe	German Air Force.

Noball	Code word for operations pertaining to V1 flying bomb manufacture, assembly and launch sites.
Oboe	A blind bombing targeting system using radio transponders and receivers to pinpoint targets, usually deployed by de Havilland Mosquito 'Pathfinders' leading the way, ahead of bombers.
ORB	Operations Record Book; see also *F540* and *F541*
Pancake	To land, also a radio code word used to ask for permission to, or order aircraft to land.
Pilot Service Record	A set of unofficial records of most pilots who served with 41 Squadron during World War II, held in the Squadron's Archives. The records were commenced at the time a man joined the Squadron and were often updated with victories and other details throughout his tenure.
port	Left or left-hand side.
R-Boat	*Kriegsmarine* minesweeper [*Räumboot* ≈ Clearance Vessel], used for a variety of purposes including ASR, coastal patrol, convoy escort, mine-laying and minesweeping.
Ramrod	A daylight bomber raid on a strategic target in enemy territory, escorted by fighters for protection.
Ranger	A roving ground attack, usually a deep penetration flight into a specified enemy-held area, to engage targets of opportunity.
Rhubarb	Low level ranging patrol over enemy territory seeking ground targets of opportunity, often using cloudy conditions as cover, to provide the element of surprise.
Rodeo	A fighter operation over enemy territory.
Roadstead	A fighter operation mounted against enemy shipping.
Scramble	To take off with all possible haste, to intercept an unknown aircraft plot, or an enemy aircraft, raid or formation.
Section 40	A clause within court martial law under which a person was charged. Section 40 covered actions that prejudiced 'good order and military discipline'.
Staffel	A Luftwaffe unit, roughly equivalent to an RAF Squadron.
starboard	Right or right-hand side.
Sweep	An offensive mission over enemy territory with the intention of attacking targets of opportunity or dominating airspace.
Tally Ho	A pilot's radio code word indicating he had the target in sight and was taking over the interception and attack from Control at this point.
Ventral	Gun position underneath an aircraft's fuselage, usually facing to the rear, for example on the He111 and B-17 Flying Fortress.
Wehrmacht	German Army.
Window	Code name for pieces of aluminium foil dropped by RAF bombers to jam German radar, first used during raids on Hamburg in July 1943 (American 'Chaff'; German 'Düppel').
ZZ Landing	An abbreviation for 'Zero/Zero', i.e. zero cloud base and zero visibility (cloud base or fog on the deck). A ZZ landing was a method to assist the pilot to land in bad visibility, using a series of radio bearings, before radar and other more sophisticated radio aids were available to pilots. In modern passenger aircraft, this is a computerised procedure that is often taken care of by the 'auto-pilot'. The method used in World War II was fairly simple to understand but extremely difficult to put into practice and master.

RAF AND LUFTWAFFE EQUIVALENT RANKS

British Rank	Abbreviation	German Rank	Abbreviation
No equivalent rank	-	Reichsmarschall	RM
Marshal of the RAF	MRAF	Generalfeldmarschall	Gen Feldm
Air Chief Marshal	ACM	Generaloberst	Gen Ob
Air Marshal	AM	General	Gen
Air Vice-Marshal	AVM	Generalleutnant	Gen Lt
Air Commodore	Air Cdre	Generalmajor	Gen Maj
Group Captain	Gp Capt	Oberst	Obst
Wing Commander	Wg Cdr	Oberstleutnant	Obstlt
Squadron Leader	Sqn Ldr	Major	Maj
Flight Lieutenant	Flt Lt	Hauptmann	Hptm
Flying Officer	Fg Off	Oberleutnant	Oblt
Pilot Officer	Plt Off	Leutnant	Lt
[Officer Cadet]	No Eq. Rank	Fähnrich	Fahnr
Warrant Officer	WO	Stabsfeldwebel	Stabsfw
[Flt Sgt Officer Cadet]	No Eq. Rank	Fahnenjunker-Oberfeldwebel	Fhj-Obfw
Flight Sergeant	Flt Sgt	Oberfeldwebel	Obfw
Sergeant Pilot	Sgt Plt	Feldwebel	Fw
Corporal	Cpl	Unteroffizier	Uffz
Leading Aircraftman	LAC	Obergefreiter	Ogfr
Aircraftman 1st Class	AC1	Gefreiter	Gefr
Aircraftman 2nd Class	AC2	Flieger	Flg

Abbreviations

The following abbreviations and symbols have been used in the text.

†	Killed, died, or since passed away		Section
*	Indicates a Bar to a decoration	AFB	Air Force Base (USA)
2 Lt	2nd Lieutenant	AFC	Air Force Cross
a.o.	and others / amongst others	AFDE	Air Fighting Development Establishment
AA	anti-aircraft cannon/fire (aka 'Flak')		
AAC	Anti-Aircraft Co-Operation	AFDS	Air Fighting Development Squadron
AACU	Anti-Aircraft Co-Operation Unit	AFDU	Air Fighting Development Unit
AAP	Aircraft Acceptance Park	AFI	Air Firing Instructor or Advanced Flying Instructor
AASF	Advanced Air Striking Force		
A/C	Aircraft / aircraft	afltn	affiliation
AC	Army Cooperation	AFM	Air Force Medal
AC1	Aircraftman 1st Class	AFS	Advanced Flying School
AC2	Aircraftman 2nd Class	AFSEA	Air Forces, Southeast Asia
ACAF	Active Citizens Air Force (Aust)	AFT	Advanced Fighter Training
ACB	Aircraft Control Branch	AFTS	Advanced Flying Training School
ACBFS	Air Corps Basic Flying School (USA)	AFU	Advanced Flying Unit
acc	accident / accepted	AFV	Armoured Fighting Vehicle
ACDC	Air Crew Despatch Centre	AG	Air Gunner / Air Gunnery
ACDW	Air Crew Despatch Wing	AGS	Air Gunnery School
ACHS	Air Crew Holding Station	AHQ	Air Headquarters
ACHU	Aircrew Holding Unit	AIA	Alabama Institute of Aeronautics (civil primary flying school)
ACinC	Air Commander-in-Chief		
Acklgtn	Acklington, Northumberland	AIB	Accident Investigation Branch
ACOS	Air Crew Officers School	Air Cdre	Air Commodore
ACRC	Aircrew Reception Centre, or Aircrew Refresher Course	Air Min	Air Ministry
		AIU	Accident Investigation Unit
ACS	Assistant Chief of Staff	AL	active list, or State of Alabama, USA
ACSEA	Air Command South East Asia	ALG	Advanced Landing Ground
ACT	Australian Capital Territory	ALO	Air Liaison Officer
ACTC	Aircrew Transit Camp	ALS	Air Liaison Section
Actg	Acting (rank)	Alt/alt	altitude
ACU	Aircraft Conversion Unit	Alta	Province of Alberta, Canada
A/D	Aerodrome	AM	Air Marshal, or Air Ministry, or Member of the Order of Australia Medal
ADC	Air Defence Command, or Aide de Camp		
ADF	Aircraft Delivery Flight	AMB	Aviation Militaire Belge (predecessor to Belgian Air Force)
ADGB	Air Defence Great Britain		
ADHQ	Air Defence Headquarters	AMEME	Association of Mechanical, Electrical & Mining Engineers (UK)
Adjt	Adjutant		
Admin	Administration	AMES	Air Ministry Experimental Station (often a mobile radar station)
admtd	admitted (e.g. to hospital)		
ADU	Aircraft Delivery Unit	AMMRU	Air Ministry Manpower Research Unit
Aé	Aéronautique		
AE	Air Efficiency Award	AMO	Air Ministry Order, or Air Ministry Operation
AEAF	Allied Expeditionary Air Force		
AF	Atlantic Ferry, e.g. 45 AF Grp.	Ang	Anglesey, Wales
AFAP	Air Forces Arabian Peninsula, or Aviation Fuel and Ammunition Park	ANS	Air Navigation School
		AO	Armament Officer
AFAS	Aviation Fuel and Ammunition	AOA	Air Officer i/c Administration

Abbreviations

AOC	Air Officer Commanding	B-24	American heavy bomber, Consolidated B-24 'Liberator'
AOC in C	Air Officer Commanding in Chief		
AONS	Air Observers Navigation School	B-25	American medium bomber, North American Aviation B-25 'Mitchell'
AOP	Air Observation Post		
AOS	Air Observer School	B-26	American medium bomber, Martin B-26 'Marauder'
AP	Armour Piercing ammunition		
APC	Armament Practice Camp	BAF	Blind Approach Flight, or Belgian Air Force
APO	Acting Pilot Officer, or Army Post Office		
		BAFO	British Air Forces of Occupation
App	Appendix	BAS	Blind Approach School
app	appointed / appointment	BAT	Beam Approach Training
Apprent/apprent	Apprentice/apprentice	BC	Bomber Command, or British Columbia, Canada
approx	approximately		
APS	Air Pilotage School	BDTF	Bomber (Defence) Training Flight
APWO	Alexandra, Princess of Wales' Own	BEA	British European Airways
Ar196	German Arado 196 reconnaissance seaplane	Beau	Bristol Beaufighter
		bef	before
Ar234	German Arado 234 jet-powered bomber	BEF	British Expeditionary Force
		Belg	Belgium / Belgian
ARD	Airframe Repair Depot	Berks	County of Berkshire, England
arr	arrived	bet	between
arr	arrived / arrival	BFA	British Forces Aden
ASB	Aircraft Safety Branch	BFAP	British Forces Arabian Peninsula
ASD	Administrative & Special Duties Branch	BFC	British Forces, Cyprus
		BFTS	British Flying Training School (USA)
ASI	Air Speed Indicator	BG	Bomb Group (USAAF)
ASO	Air Staff Officer	Bgn Hill	Biggin Hill, SE London
ASOC	Air Staff Officer in Charge	BGS	Bombing and Gunnery School
ASOD	Air & Special Operations Division	Birm	Birmingham, Warwickshire
ASP	Air Stores Park	BJSM	British Joint Services Mission (USA)
ASR	Air-Sea Rescue	BLO	Base Logistics Officer
Assist	Assistant	Bnmth	Bournemouth, Hampshire
Assoc	Association	BOAC	British Overseas Airways Corporation
AST	Air Service Training		
ATA	Air Transport Auxiliary	BPC	Base Personnel Centre
ATS	Armament Training School	BPD	Base Personnel Depot
att	attached to (unit), or attended (e.g. course)	BR	Bomber Reconnaissance, e.g. 5 Bomber Reconnaissance Squadron RCAF appears as '5 (BR) Sqn.'
Auck	Auckland, New Zealand		
Aust	Australia	Br	Branch (generally of the RAF)
Aux	Auxiliary	Brdfld Pk	Bradfield Park, NSW, Australia
AuxAF	Auxiliary Air Force	Brig	Brigade / Brigadier
avge	average	Brig Gen	Brigadier General
AVM	Air Vice Marshal	Bris	Brisbane QLD, Australia
Avtn / avtn	Aviation / aviation	Brit	British
AWJR	All Weather Jet Refresher	bro(s)	brother(s)
AWM	Australian War Memorial	BS	Bombardment Squadron (USAAF)
AWO	[Aircraft] Awaiting Write-Off	Btn	Battalion
AWOL	Absent/Absence without Leave	Bucks	County of Buckinghamshire, England
AZ	State of Arizona, USA		
B	Bomber, e.g. 27 Bomber Squadron appears as '27 (B) Sqn.'	bur	buried
		BWI	British West Indies
b	born	C	Coastal
B.	Belgium / Belgian	C&C Airways	Cairo to Capetown Airways
B.Mus.	Bachelor of Music	C/B	Confined to Barracks
B.VI.Z .303	Batch Mark 6 incendiary .303 ammunition	ca	circa
		CA	State of California, USA
B-7	American light bomber, Douglas B-7 'Boston' (aka A-20 'Havoc')	CACU	Coast Artillery Co-Operation Unit
		Caern	Caernarvonshire, Wales
B-17	American heavy bomber, Boeing B-17 'Flying Fortress'	CAF	Canadian Armed Forces / Citizens Air Force (Aust.)

CAM	Catapult Aircraft Merchantman	CMB	Central Medical Board, London
Cambs	County of Cambridgeshire, England	Cmd	Command / commanded
Can	Canada	Cmdr	Commander
Capt	Captain	Cmdt	Commandant
Carm	Carmarthenshire, Wales	CME	Central Medical Establishment
CAS	Chief of Air Staff	CMG	Companion, Most Distinguished Order of St Michael and St George
Cat A	Category A damage to aircraft, could be repaired on site	Cmn	Common
Cat AC	Repair beyond on-site capability, but can be undertaken on site by another unit or contractor	Cnbra	Canberra ACT, Australia
		CNCS	Central Navigation & Control School
		cnfmd	confirmed (e.g. in rank)
Cat B	Category B damage to aircraft, repairable at an MU or contractor off site	CNTO	Could not take off
		CO	State of Colorado, USA
		COA	College of Aeronautics
Cat C	Category C damage to aircraft, only repairable to ground instructional airframe status	COC	Belgian Chevalier (Knight) of the Order of the Crown
		COE	Court of Enquiry
		COG	collision on ground
Cat E	Category E damage to aircraft, irreparable and struck off charge	COL	Belgian Chevalier (Knight) of the Order of Leopold
CB	Companion, The Most Honourable Order of the Bath	Col	Colonel
		COL2	Belgian Chevalier (Knight) of the Order of Leopold II
CBE	Commander, The Most Excellent Order of the British Empire		
		Coll/coll	College, college, or collective
CCS	Casualty Clearing Station	com	commission or commissioned
CD	Combat Damage (shot up, damaged, but able to land again at base)	Comm	Committee
		Comms	Communications
CdC	Croix de Chevalier (France)	Conv/conv	conversion/converted
CdE	Croix des Evades (Belgium)	Co-op	Co-operation
CdG	Croix de Guerre [Belgian or French awards indicated by '(B)' or '(F)']	Corp	Corporation
		CoS	Chief of Staff or 'completion of service'
Cdr	Commander		
CE	Church of England	COTC	Canadian Officer Training Corps
Cem	Cemetery	Coy	Company
CENTO	Central Treaty Organisation	CPH	Copenhagen, Denmark
Cert	Certificate	Cpl	Corporal
CFB	Canadian Forces Base	cpltd	completed
CFD	Canadian Forces Decoration (usually designated 'CD')	CPM	Colonial Police Medal
		CR	Combat Report
CFE	Central Fighter Establishment	CR42	Italian biplane fighter, Fiat CR.42 'Falco'
CFEO	Chief Flying Examining Officer		
CFHQ	Canadian Forces Headquarters	crdtd	credited
CFI	Chief Flying Instructor	CRE	Central Reconnaissance Establishment
CFS	Central Flying School		
CGC	Chief Ground Controller	Crse/crse	Course/course
CGH	Canadian General Hospital	crt-whld	cart-wheeled
CGI	Chief Ground Instructor	CSE	Central Signals Establishment
CGM	Conspicuous Gallantry Medal	CSO	Commissioned Signals Officer
CGS	Central Gunnery School	Ctk	Catterick, Yorkshire
Ch Fntn	Church Fenton, Yorkshire	CTW	Combat Training Wing
Chesh	County of Cheshire, England	Cty	County
Chf Exec	Chief Executive	CU	[Aircraft] Conversion Unit
Chf Tech	Chief Technician	Cumb	County of Cumberland, England
Chmn	Chairman	CVO	Commander of the Royal Victorian Order
CHWE	Canadian Home War Establishment		
CIC	Centre d'Instruction de Chasse [aka. Centre d'Instruction des Pilotes de Chasse] (Fighter Training Unit)	cwt.	centum weight (or hundred weight)
		CXLD/cxld	cancelled
		d	died
CinC	Commander in Chief	D.I. List	Dangerously Injured List
civ	civil / civilian	DAF	Desert Air Force
CL	crash-landing or crash-landed	Dam	damaged
CM	court-martial / court-martialled		

DC	District of Columbia	EFS	Empire Flying School
DC-3	American transport aircraft, Douglas DC-3 Dakota	EFTS	Empire Flyer Training Scheme / Elementary Flying Training School
DCM	District Court Martial	ELINT	ELectronic Signals INTelligence
DDO	Deputy Director of Operations	emb	embarked
DDOP	Deputy Director of Plans	emgtd	emigrated
DDOR	Deputy Director of Operational Requirements	Emp	Empire
		emp	employed / employer / employment
Def	Defence	EMS	Emergency Medical Services
demob	demobilised	Eng	Engine / Engineer / Engineering
dep	departed	enl	enlisted / enlistment
Dep	Deputy	ENSA	Entertainments National Service Association
DEPAIR	Department of the Air		
Dept	Department	EO	Equipment Officer
Derby	County of Derbyshire, England	ER	Evaded capture and returned to UK or, if POW, escaped and returned
Dest	destroyed or destruction		
det	detached	Est	Establishment or Estuary
DFC	Distinguished Flying Cross	Esx	County of Essex, England
DFM	Distinguished Flying Medal	ETPS	Empire Test Pilots' School
DFTS	Day Fighter Training Squadron	evac	evacuated
DGPP	Director-General, Policy and Planning	EWS	Electrical and Wireless School
		Ex/ex	exercise
Dir	Director / Directorate	exp	experiment(s)
disemb	disembarked	exprd	expired
Dist	District	Ext	Extension
Div	Division	ext svce	extended service
DLI	Durham Light Infantry	F	Fighter, e.g. 29 Fighter Squadron appears as '29 (F) Sqdn.'
DNE	Does not exist		
Dngnss	Dungeness, Kent	F.	France
DNR	Did not return	FA	Flying accident (take-off, landing, flying, engine failure, not combat-related)
Dnsfld	Dunsfold, Surrey		
DNTO	Did not take off		
Do17	German Dornier 17 light bomber	FAA	Fleet Air Arm
Do215	German Dornier 215 light bomber and reconnaissance aircraft	FAFL	Forces Aériennes Françaises Libres (Free French Air Force)
DOB	Date of birth	Farn	Farnborough, Hants
DOI	Died later of injuries sustained in an accident (not combat related)	FAU	Fighter Affiliation Unit
		FC	Fighter Command, or Fighter Control
DOW	Died later of wounds sustained in combat		
		FCA	Fellow of the Institute of Chartered Accountants
drvr	driver		
dsbnd	disbanded	FCB	Fighter Control Branch
dschgd	discharged	FCU	Fighter Control Unit
DSO	Distinguished Service Order	FDF	fire during flight, or Flying Development Flight
dt	daughter		
DTT	Director of Technical Training	FEAF	Far East Air Force
Dulag Luft	Durchgangslager Luftwaffe (Air Force POW Transit Camp)	FF	Fleet Fighter, or first flight
		FG	Fighter Group (USAAF)
Dumfries	Dumfriesshire, Scotland	Fg Off	Flying Officer
Dur	County of Durham, England	FH	flying hours
Dxfd	Duxford, Cambridge	FI	Flying Instructor
E	East	Fi103	German flying bomb Fieseler 103, more commonly known as the 'V1'
E&RFTS	Elementary & Reserve Flying Training School		
		Fi156	German reconnaissance aircraft Fieseler 156 'Storch'
EA or E/A	enemy aircraft		
EAF	Enemy Aircraft Flight, Tangmere	FiAF	Finnish Air Force
ECFS	Empire Central Flying School	FIC	Flying Instructor's Course
ed	educated	FIS	Flying Instructor's School
Edin	Edinburgh, Scotland	FIW	Fighter Interception Wing
EF	engine failure	FL	forced-landing or force-landed, or State of Florida, USA
EFI	Elementary Flying Instructor		

Fld / fld	Field / field	gson	grandson
Flg / flg	Flying / flying	GSU	Group Support Unit
Flint	County of Flintshire, Wales	GTS	Glider Training School
Flkstn	Folkestone, Kent	Gvsnd	Gravesend, Kent
FLO	Flying Liaison Officer	Hants	County of Hampshire, England
FLS	Fighter Leaders' School	Harv	North American Aviation AT6 Harvard
Flt Cdr	Flight Commander		
Flt Lt	Flight Lieutenant	Hbr	Harbour
Flt Sgt	Flight Sergeant	HCDC	House of Commons Defence Committee, London
Flt/flt	Flight / flight		
FM	first mentioned	Hd	Head
fmtn	formation	HD	Home Defence
FOCU	Fighter Operational Conversion Unit	HDT	Horse-drawn transport
FOT	Fighter Operational Training	HDV	Horse-drawn vehicle
FRS	Flying Refresher School	HE/I	High Explosive/Incendiary ammunition
FS	Fighter Squadron (USAAF)		
FSP	Forward Staging Post	He111	German Heinkel 111 bomber
ft	foot / feet	He113	A non-existent German fighter aircraft created for propaganda purposes, often misidentified for the Me109
FTC	Flying Training Command		
FTR	failed to return		
Ftr(s)/ftr(s)	Fighter(s) / fighter(s)		
FTS	Flying Training School	He115	German Heinkel 115 seaplane reconnaissance aircraft & torpedo bomber
FU	Ferry Unit		
FW	Fighter Wing (USAAF)		
FW190	German Focke-Wulf 190 fighter	Herts	Hertfordshire, England
FW200	German Focke-Wulf 200 'Condor' long-range reconnaissance aircraft and bomber	HKAAF	Hong Kong Auxiliary Air Force
		HKG	Hong Kong
		HL	heavy landing
G.	German / Germany	HM	His/Her Majesty('s)
GA	State of Georgia, USA	HMAT	His Majesty's Australian Troopship
GAPAN	Guild of Air Pilots and Air Navigators	HMHS	His Majesty's Hospital Ship
		HMS	His Majesty's Ship
Gaunt	Gloster Gauntlet biplane fighter	HMTS	His Majesty's Troopship
gaz	gazetted	Hnch	Hornchurch, Essex
GCM	General Court Martial	Hon	Honourable, Honorary or Honour
GCS	Group Communication Squadron	Hosp/hosp	Hospital / hospitalised
GCU	Group Communication Unit	hp	horse power
GDB	General Duties Branch	HQ	headquarters
Gen	General	HQAFNE	Headquarters, Allied Forces Northern Europe
GFS	Ground Fighting School		
GFTS	Government Flying Training School	HQCA	Headquarters Coastal Area
Ggmth	Grangemouth, Stirling, Scotland	HQCC	Headquarters Coastal Command
GH	General Hospital	HQFC	Headquarters Fighter Command
GI	Gunnery Instructor	HQTC	Headquarters Training Command
Gib	Gibraltar	hr / hrs	hour / hours
GIC	Gunnery Instructors Course	HRH	His Royal Highness
GIS	Glider Instructors School	HS	High School
Glad	Gloster Gladiator biplane fighter	Hs123	German Henschel 123 biplane dive-bomber
Glam	County of Glamorganshire, Wales		
Gloucs	County of Gloucestershire, England	Hs126	German Henschel 126 reconnaissance aircraft
GOTU	(Glider) Operational Training Unit		
GP	General Purpose	Hse	House
Gp Capt	Group Captain	HSL	High Speed Launch
GR	General Reconnaissance	Hth	Heath
grad	graduated or graduation	Hurr	British Hawker Hurricane fighter
Grnd/grnd	Ground / ground	husb	husband
grndd	grounded	Hwdn	Hawarden, Flintshire, Wales
grntd	granted	Hwkge	Hawkinge, Kent
Grp	Group	IAF	Indian Air Force
grt	great or gross register tons	IAS	Indicated Air Speed
GS	Grammar School	IC or i/c	in charge

IDB	illicit diamond buying	KIFA	Killed in flying accident
IFA	injured in flying accident	KiL	Kirton-in-Lindsey, Lincolnshire
IFF	Identification, Friend or Foe	km	kilometre/s
IFTS	Initial Flying Training School	kmph	kilometres per hour
imm	immediately	KR	King's Regulations
incl	including	KTS	Composite Training School (RCAF)
incr	increased	KW	Krzyz Walecznych (Polish Cross of Valour)
Inf	Infantry		
init	initially	LA	Louisiana, USA
inj	injured / injuries	LAC	Leading Aircraftman
Inst/inst	Instructor / instruction	LAMS	London Aero & Motor Services
Int	Intelligence	Lanark	Lanarkshire, Scotland
Intl	International	Lanc	British Avro Lancaster bomber
IoM	Isle of Man	Lancs	Lancashire, England
IoW	Isle of Wight	lb.	pound/s (weight)
IRT	Instrument Rating Test	LCpl	Lance Corporal
Is	Island	LD	Long Delay
ISC	Imperial Service College	Leics	County of Leicestershire, England
ITW	Initial Training Wing	LF	last flight
ITWW	Independent Television Wales and West	LFS	Lancaster Finishing School
		LG	London Gazette
Jap	Japanese	LH	Light Horse
JAPS	Joint Administrative Planning Staff	lib	liberated
JARIC	Joint Air Reconnaissance Intelligence Centre	Lincs	County of Lincolnshire, England
		Liv	Liverpool, Lancashire
JCC	Junior Commanders Course	LM	last mentioned
Jct	Junction	LMS	London, Midland and Scottish Railway
JG	Jagdgeschwader, roughly translated to Fighter Wing		
		lndd	landed
JNB	Johannesburg, South Africa	loco	locomotive
J. P.	Jet Propelled (Bomb), i.e. V1	LoH	Legion of Honour (France)
JP	Justice of the Peace	LoM	Legion of Merit (USA)
JPS	Joint Planning Staff	Lon	London
JSSC	Joint Services Staff College, Latimer, Bucks	Lon	London
		LRCP	Licentiate of the Royal College of Physicians
JSWS	Joint Services Warfare School		
JTF	Jettison tank failure	LSgt	Lance Sergeant
Ju188	German Junkers 188 medium bomber	LSO	London Symphony Orchestra
		Lt	Lieutenant
Ju34	German Junkers 34 passenger and transport aircraft	Luft	Luftwaffe
		m	mile(s)
Ju52	German Junkers 52 transport aircraft 'Tante Ju'	MAAF	Mediterranean Allied Air Force
		MAC	Martin's Air Charter (today Martinair)
Ju87	German Junkers 87 'Stuka' dive-bomber		
		MAEE	Marine Aircraft Experimental Establishment
Ju88	German Junkers 88 bomber & reconnaissance aircraft		
		mag	magazine
K.	County of Kent, England	Mag	Miles M14 Magister
KAS	killed on active service	Maj	Major
KBE	Knight Commander, The Most Excellent Order of the British Empire	Maj Gen	Major General
		Man	Province of Manitoba, Canada
		Manch	Manchester, Lancashire (arch.)
KCB	Knight Commander, The Most Honourable Order of the Bath	marr	married
		Mass	Massachusetts, USA
KCVSA	King's Commendation for Valuable Service in the Air	max	maximum
		MBBS	Bachelor of Medicine and Surgery
KFA	Killed in flying accident	MBE	Member, The Most Excellent Order of the British Empire
KG	Kampfgeschwader, roughly translated to Bomber Wing		
		MC	Military Cross
kg	kilogram/s	MCM	Mhangura Copper Mines Ltd.
KIA	Killed in action	MCRU	Mobile Control Reporting Unit

MD	Manning Depot	Nav	Navigation
MDS	Mobile Dental Surgery	NB	New Brunswick, Province of Canada
Mdx	County of Middlesex, England	NBL	County of Northumberland, England
ME	Middle East		
Me109	German Messerschmitt 109 fighter (Also referred to as Bf109)	NCO	Non-commissioned Officer
		NCR	No combat report available for clarification
Me110	German Messerschmitt 110 fighter-bomber (Also referred to as Bf110)	ndc	'Passed National Defence College'
Me163	German Messerschmitt 163 'Komet' rocket-powered fighter	NDCC	National Defence College of Canada
		NDEA	Not due to enemy action
Me210	German Messerschmitt 210 'Hornisse' heavy fighter & ground attack aircraft	NE	non-effective, or Northeast
		NEAF	Near East Air Force
		NF	Newfoundland, Canada, or Night Fighter
Me262	German Messerschmitt 262 'Schwalbe' jet-powered fighter	NFE	night-flying exercise
MEAF	Middle Eastern Air Force	Nflk	County of Norfolk, England
MEARC	Middle East Aircrew Reception Centre	NI	not injured
		NIre	Northern Ireland
MEC	Middle East Command	NJG	Nachtjagdgeschwader (Luftwaffe Night Fighter Wing)
Mech	Mechanic / Mechanical / Mechanised		
Med	Mediterranean	NL	The Netherlands (Holland)
Melb	Melbourne VIC, Australia	No	Number
Mem	Memorial	Notts	County of Nottinghamshire, England
Mer	Merionethshire, Wales		
MET	mechanised/motorised enemy transport	nr	near
		NR	Not recorded data is not recorded in source documentation
Met	Meteorological		
MFH	Mobile Field Hospital	NS	Nova Scotia, Canada
MFPS	Mobile Field Photographic Section	NSC	National Savings Committee
MG	machine gun	NSW	State of New South Wales, Australia
Mg Dir	Managing Director	NW	Northwest
Mgr	Manager	NY	State of New York, USA
MIA	missing in action	NYC	New York City
MiD	Mention in Despatches	NYR	Not Yet Returned
Mil	Military	NZ	New Zealand
min/mins	minute / minutes	NZFPM	New Zealand Fighter Pilots Museum, Wanaka, NZ
Mk.	Mark, i.e. Version		
MO	Medical Officer	NZR	New Zealand Railways
MoD	Ministry of Defence	OAM	Medal of the Order of Australia
Mosq	De Havilland Mosquito	OATS	Officers Advanced Training School
MPD	Missing, presumed dead	OBE (C)	Officer, The Most Excellent Order of the British Empire (Civil Division)
mph	miles per hour		
MRAF	Marshal of the Air Force	OBE (M)	Officer, The Most Excellent Order of the British Empire (Military Division)
MREU	Missing Research and Enquiry Unit		
MRU	Medical Rehabilitation Unit		
MSFU	Merchant Ship Fighter Unit	obit	obituary
Mstg	North American P-51 Mustang long-range fighter-bomber	Obs	Observer
		OBU	Operational Base Unit
Mstn	Manston, Kent	OC	Officer Commanding
MT	motorised transport	occ	occupation
MTB	motorised torpedo boat	OCS	Officer Cadet School
mths	months	OCTU	Officer Cadet Training Unit
Mtnet	Miles M25 Martinet	OCU	Operational Conversion Unit
MU	Maintenance Unit	O/F	on formation
MV	Motor vehicle	Off	Office or Officer
MVA	Motor vehicle accident	OK	State of Oklahoma, USA
N	North	OL2	Belgian Order of Leopold II
NA	Not applicable	Ont	Ontario, Canada
NAA	National Archives of Australia	OOC	Belgian Officer of the Order of the Crown
NAAFI	Navy, Army, Air Force Institute		
Nat	National	op	operational

ops	operations	pte	private
ORB	Operations Record Book	PZL. P7	Polish fighter aircraft, 1933-1939
Org/org	Organisation / organisation	QCVSA	Queen's Commendation for Valuable Service in the Air
orig	originally		
OS	overseas	QFI	Qualified Flying Instructor
OSR	overshot runway (on landing)	QLD	State of Queensland, Australia
OTU	Operational Training Unit	qual	qualified or qualification
Oxon	County of Oxfordshire, England	Que	Province of Quebec, Canada
(P)	(Pilots), e.g. (P)AFU (see AFU)	RAAF	Royal Australian Air Force
P-38	USAAF fighter, Lockheed P-38 'Lightning'	RACGP	Royal Australian College of General Practitioners
P-47	USAAF fighter, Republic P-47 'Thunderbolt'	RAF	Royal Air Force
		RAFC	Royal Air Force College
P-51	long range USAAF fighter, North American Aviation P-51 'Mustang'	RAFCC	Royal Air Force Cadet College
		RAFFC	Royal Air Force Flying College
PA	Personal Assistant	RAFH	Royal Air Force Hospital
PAF	Polish Air Force	RAFO	Reserve of Air Force Officers
pax	passenger	RAFR	Royal Air Force Regiment
PD	Personnel Depot	RAFSC	Royal Air Force Staff College
PD(T)	Port Depot (Transit)	RAFVR	Royal Air Force Volunteer Reserve
PDC	Personnel Despatch Centre	RAuxAF	Royal Auxiliary Air Force
PDRC	Personnel Despatch and Reception Centre	RAuxAFRO	Royal Auxiliary Air Force Reserve of Officers
PEI	Prince Edward Island, Province of Canada	RC	Recruiting Centre, Release Centre, Roman Catholic, or Red Cross
Pembs	Pembrokeshire, Wales	RCAF	Royal Canadian Air Force
perm com	permanent commission	RCAFSR	Royal Canadian Air Force Special Reserve
Pers	Personnel		
pfc	'Passed Flying College'	RCDS	Royal College of Defence Studies, London
PFF	Pathfinder Force		
PGIC	Pilot Gunnery Instructors Course	Rcfd	Rochford, Kent
Ph.C	Pharmaceutical Chemistry degree	Rcvg	Receiving
PHU	Personnel Holding Unit	RDF	Radio Direction Finding
Pk	Park	reatt	reattached
PL	privilege leave	rec	recommended
PLO	Polish Liaison Officer	recce	reconnaissance
Plt Off	Pilot Officer	recons	reconstituted
Plt(s) / plt(s)	Pilot(s) / pilot(s)	redes	re-designated
PM	Prime Minister	re-est	re-establishment
PNG	Papua New Guinea	ref	reference
poss	possible / possibly	Reg/reg	Region(al)/region(al)
POW	Prisoner of War	regs	regulations
PR	Public Relations or Photographic Reconnaissance	Regt	Regiment
		Rehab	Rehabilitation
PRC	Personnel Receiving Centre	reint	reinterred
Pres	President	rel com	relinquished commission
prmtd	promoted / promotion	Rep/rep	representative / represented
Prob	probationary (rank) or Probable / Probably Destroyed (aircraft)	repat	repatriated / repatriation
		Res	Reserve
Prod	Production	res	residence or residing
prof	professional	resp	respectively
prop	propeller	ret	retired or retirement
Prot	Protestant	Rev	Reverend
Prov/prov	Province or provisionally	RF	Ran out of fuel or short on fuel
prsntd	presented	RFC	Royal Flying Corps
PS	Public School	RFU	Refresher Flying Unit
psa	'Passed Staff College Air Force'	RHKAAF	Royal Hong Kong Auxiliary Air Force
PSP	Perforated (or Pierced) Steel Planking		
PSR	Pilot Service Record (see also Glossary)	Rhod	Rhodesia
		RL	recreational leave
PTC	Personnel Transit Centre	rlsd	released

rmbd	remembered	Sgt Plt	Sergeant Pilot
rmnd	remained	SHAEF	Supreme Headquarters Allied Expeditionary Force
RN	Royal Navy		
RNAS	Royal Navy Air Service	SHAPE	Supreme Headquarters Allied Powers Europe
RNLAF	Royal Netherlands Air Force		
RNLI	Royal National Lifeboat Institution	SHQ	Station Headquarters
RNoAF	Royal Norwegian Air Force	Shrops	County of Shropshire, England
RNZAF	Royal New Zealand Air Force	Sigs	signals
ROS	Repaired on Site	SKVM	Srebrny Krzyż Virtuti Militari (Polish Silver Cross of Virtuti Militari)
RP	Rocket Projectile		
RPAH	Royal Prince Alfred Hospital	SL	Sick Leave
RPP	Reserve Personnel Pool	SLAW	School of Land/Air Warfare, Old Sarum, Wilts
RR	Rescued and returned to Squadron (e.g. baled out into Channel, picked up by ASR), or Rolls-Royce		
		Smrst	County of Somerset, England
		Sngpr	Singapore
RRCA	Royal Regiment of Canadian Artillery	SOA	Senior Officer i/c Administration
		SOC	(aircraft) struck off charge
RS	Radio School	SOE	Special Operations Executive
RSU	Repair and Salvage Unit	SON	School of Navigation
R/T	Radio Telephone / Radio Telephony	SORP	Staff Officer Reserve Personnel
Rt Hon	Right Honourable	SOT	Staff Officer Training
RTB	Pilot returned to base early	SP	Staging Post
rtn	return	Spec	Special / Specialist
rtnd	returned	Spit	Supermarine Spitfire
rtng	returning, or retaining the rank of…	SPRL	Szkoła Podchorążych Rezerwy Lotnictwa (Polish Air Force Reserve Cadet School), Dęblin, Poland
rtrvd	retrieved		
RU	Repair Unit		
rvtd	reverted	Sqn / sqn	Squadron / squadron
RW	Receiving Wing	Sqn Ldr	Squadron Leader
R-XIII	Lublin R-XIII, Polish army cooperation aircraft, 1932-1939	SR	Severe Reprimand/Severely Reprimanded
s	son	SS	Signals School
S	South	SS Flt	Special Service Flight
S Aust	State of South Australia	SSC	Short Service Commission
SA	South Africa, or Squadron Archive (41 Squadron's own Archive)	SSO	Scottish Symphony Orchestra
		SSQ	Station Sick Quarters
SAC	School of Air Combat	Ssx	County of Sussex, England
SALO	Senior Air Liaison Officer	St/Ste	Saint
Salop	County of Shropshire, England	Staffs	County of Staffordshire, England
SAO	Senior Air Officer	Stalag Luft	Stammlager Luftwaffe, POW Camp for Allied Air Force NCOs and ORs
SAP/I	Semi-Armour Piercing/Incendiary ammunition		
		stbd	starboard
SAS	School of Air Support	Stirling	Stirlingshire, Scotland
Sask	Province of Saskatchewan, Canada	Stn	Station
SASO	Senior Air Staff Officer	Stn Cdr	Station Commander
SAT	School of Air Tactics	StO	Station ORB
Sch	School	STSO	Senior Technical Staff Officer
scndd	seconded	STT	School of Technical Training
Scot	Scotland / Scottish	subs	subsequent / subsequently / substantive (rank)
SD	Shot down or Stores Depot		
SE	Southeast, or Servicing Echelon	succ	succeeded
SEAAF	South East Asia Air Forces	Sup	Supernumerary
Sec	Secretary / Secretarial	Supp/supp	Support / support
Sect	Section	Svce/Svcs	Service(s)
sen	seniority	SW	Southwest
SF	Structural failure (of aircraft) or San Francisco, California, USA	Switz	Switzerland
		Syd	Sydney NSW, Australia
		TA	Taxiing accident (before leaving the ground, not combat-related) or Territorial Army
Sflk	County of Suffolk, England		
SFTS	Service Flying Training School		
SGO	Sector Gunnery Officer		
Sgt	Sergeant	TacR	Tactical Reconnaissance

Abbreviations

TAF	Tactical Air Force	V1	German flying bomb, 'Vergeltungswaffe' (Vengeance Weapon) 1, officially Fieseler Fi103
Tang	Tangmere		
TAS	State of Tasmania, Australia		
TB	Training Branch	V2	German rocket, 'Vergeltungswaffe' (Vengeance Weapon) 2, officially *Aggregat* A-4
TC	Transit Centre		
TCAHC	Transport Command Aircrew Holding Centre		
		Vamp	de Havilland DH.100 Vampire fighter
TCS	Troop Carrier Group (USAAF)		
TCS	Troop Carrier Squadron (USAAF)	VIC	State of Victoria, Australia
TD	Training Depot Squadron	vic / vics	victory / victories
Tech	Technical	vis	visibility
TED	Troop Embarkation Depot	Vncvr	City of Vancouver BC, Canada
TEM	Territorial Efficiency Medal	W	West
Temp	Temporary (rank)	w	with
temp	temporary / temporarily	w/o	without
TEU	Tactical Exercise Unit	WA	State of Western Australia
TF	Territorial Forces	WAAF	Women's Auxiliary Air Force
Tmpst	Hawker Tempest fighter	WAGS	Wireless Air Gunners School
TNA	The National Archives, formerly the Public Record Office (PRO)	Warks	County of Warwickshire, England
		WCW	Worshipful Company of Wheelwrights
TO	Take-off / took off		
TON	Tipped (aircraft) on nose	WD	Western Desert
TOT	Time over target	WDAF	Western Desert Air Force
trans	transfer / transferred	WEF	with effect from
Trng / trng	Training / training	Wg / wg	Wing / wing
TTC	Technical Training Command	Wg Cdr	Wing Commander
TV	Hawker Tempest Mk. V	Wg Ldr	Wing Leader
TWDU	Tactical Weapons Development Unit	Whmpnt	Westhampnett
TWN	The Weekly News [NZ newspaper]	WIA	Wounded in action
TX	State of Texas, USA	WIF	Wing Instrument Flight
Typhn	British Hawker Typhoon fighter-bomber	Wilts	County of Wiltshire, England
		WkNr	Werknummer (Works Number: Luftwaffe aircraft serial)
UAS	University Air Squadron		
UC	undercarriage	wks	weeks
UCC	undercarriage collapse(d)	WL	War Leave
UK	United Kingdom	Wlngtn	Wellington, New Zealand
UL	Unemployed List	Wlwnd	British Westland Whirlwind heavy fighter-bomber
UN	United Nations		
unemp	unemployed	WMalling	West Malling, Kent
Uni	University	WO	Warrant Officer
unkn	unknown	WO/AG	Wireless Operator/Air Gunner
U/S	unserviceable	WO1	Warrant Officer 1st Class
US/U.S.	United States	WO2	Warrant Officer 2nd Class
USAAC	United States Army Air Corps (2 Jul 1926-20 Jun 1941)	Worcs	County of Worcestershire, England
		WS	war substantive (rank)
USAAF	United States Army Air Force (20 Jun 1941-18 Sep 1947)	WTR	wartime rank
		Wtrg	Wittering, Northamptonshire
USAASC	United States Army Air Support Command	WUL	wheels-up (belly) landing
		WWI	World War 1
USAF	United States Air Force (18 Sep 1947-present)	WWII	World War 2
		Yeo	Yeomanry
USAT	United States Army Transport	Yks	County of Yorkshire, England
USN	United States Navy	yr/yrs	year / years
u/t	under training	Yug	Yugoslavia
u/w	underway	Z1007	Italian medium bomber, Cant Z.1007 'Alcione'
Uxb	Uxbridge, Middlesex		

Further Reading

Those wishing to further their research in a particular direction may wish to consult the following records and publications.

NATIONAL ARCHIVES, KEW, SURREY

TNA AIR 27/425	ORB, 1 January 1941–31 December 1943
TNA AIR 27/426	ORB, 1 January 1944–31 May 1945
TNA AIR 27/430	ORB Appendices, January–December 1943[1]
TNA AIR 27/431	ORB Appendices, April 1944–April 1945[2]
TNA AIR 50/18	41 Squadron Combat Reports, October 1939–May 1945
TNA AIR 50/443	146 Wing, Tangmere, Combat Reports: 41, 91, 118, 193, 257, 402 and 416 Squadrons, July 1943–May 1944

PUBLICATIONS BY OR ABOUT 41 SQUADRON PILOTS

Almost Unknown; The Story of Squadron Leader Tony Gaze OAM DFC**, Australian Spitfire ace and racing driver, Stewart Wilson, 2009, Chevron Publishing Group, ISBN 9780980591217

Contending Fighters of World War II, Ron Collis, 2003, Trafford Publishing, ISBN 9781553954996

From the Cockpit: Spitfire, Wg. Cdr. T. F. Neil DFC* AFC AE, 1990, Specialty Press, ISBN 0711019185

Griffon Spitfire Aces, Osprey Aircraft of the Aces No. 81, Andrew Thomas, 2008, Osprey Publishing Ltd., ISBN 9781846032981

Happy is the Day; A Spitfire Pilot's Story, Tom Slack, 1987, United Writers Publications, ISBN 185200004X

Living Dangerously, Terence & Lesley Spencer and Sandy Gall, Percival Press, 2002, ISBN 0954286200 (Updated and re-published 2012)

Skypilot; Memoirs from Take-Off to Landing, Peter Graham, 2001, Pentland Books, ISBN 1858219094

NOTES TO TEXT

1 OPERATION *JUBILEE*; 1 – 22 AUGUST 1942

1. 41 Squadron ORB, 6 August 1942, TNA AIR 27/425.
2. Ibid., 9 August 1942.
3. Tom Slack in his autobiography, *Happy is the Day; A Spitfire Pilot's Story*; 1987, United Writers Publications; reproduced with the Publisher's permission.
4. 1456 Flight was re-designated 535 Squadron on 2 September 1942.
5. The F540 of the Squadron ORB on 14 August 1942 erroneously fails to mention the interception by two pilots of a Junkers Ju88 off Dublin, whilst the F541 lists the sorties but records them as having occurred on 13 August.
6. This Luftwaffe unit is 1. Fernaufklärungsstaffel/Aufklärungsgruppe 123 [No. 1 Long Range Reconnaissance Squadron/Reconnaissance Group 123], which belonged to Luftflotte 3 [3rd Air Fleet] (France/Belgium). Reconnaissance aircraft of Aufklärungsgruppe 123 were frequent visitors to the skies over England and this was in fact not the first time that 41 Squadron had encountered a Ju88 of this unit. On 30 March 1941, for example, a Ju88A of 1.(F)/123 was shot down by the Squadron's Flt Lt Anthony D. J. Lovell over Middlesbrough, Yorkshire.
7. The distance from Barrow-in-Furness to Dublin is approximately 120 miles. Considering the Ju88D's maximum speed was 300-350 mph, it would have taken 20-25 minutes for the aircraft to have covered this distance at full throttle, implying that it must have left the Barrow-in-Furness area by 12:20 at the latest. As such, the timings around Malec's, and particularly Miksa's, sorties are a little confusing, as Miksa is recorded as having landed back at RAF Woodvale at approximately the same time as 41 Squadron was making their interception of the Ju88 just northeast of Dublin. An Intelligence Report held with 315 (Polish) Squadron's Combat Reports in TNA AIR 50/125 states that Miksa broke off his attack when the Ju88 entered Barrow-in-Furness's balloon barrage area, and was vectored back to Woodvale. However, Miksa only had a third of the distance to cover between Barrow and Woodvale than the Ju88D had between Barrow and Dublin, when the two aircrafts' maximum speeds were roughly similar. Either Miksa landed back at Woodvale earlier than 12:40 or, if he did indeed land at Woodvale at 12:40, then this would suggest that despite the statement that he broke off his attack at Barrow-in-Furness, he must have followed the Ju88 out again as it headed southwest towards Dublin, before returning to Woodvale.
8. No. 9 Group Intelligence Report, *Combats Within The Group, 14th August, 1942. Llanbedr.*, 41 Squadron Archives.
9. The Coastwatching Service was set up by the Irish Government in 1939. Eighty-three Look-Out Posts ringed the Irish coast between 1939 and 1945, manned by nine personnel each, working in three 8-hour shifts, with orders to report and log every incident they observed. Each post was equipped with binoculars, a telescope, silhouettes of ships and aircraft, a logbook, telephone, fixed compass card, Admiralty charts, visual signals apparatus and a bicycle [see also articles by Maj Gen James Quinn in the Irish Defence Journal 'An Cosantóir' in April 1983 and January 1988]. The Daily Report Summaries from the Look-Out Posts are held today in the Defence Forces Military Archives, Cathal Brugha Barracks, Rathmines, Dublin 6, Ireland.
10. Original hand-written Combat Report for Sgt Plt Leslie A. Prickett, 14 August 1942, 41 Squadron Archives.
11. *The Greatest Air Battle; Dieppe, 19th August 1942*, Norman Franks, 1997, Grub Street.
12. Sgt Plt Bernard Goodall enlisted in the RNZAF in March 1941, and completed EFTS in New Zealand before sailing to Canada for his SFTS course. Graduating with his Wings, he was then shipped to the United Kingdom to undertake OTU, and upon completion of this course was posted to 41 Squadron on 21 April 1942. By the time of his death on 15 August 1942, he had gathered considerable experience during 41 operational flights, which had included convoy patrols, sector reconnaissance flights, low-level attacks in France, shipping reconnaissance flights and Air-Sea Rescue searches. Goodall was initially buried in the village of Weston Patrick, around two miles northwest of where he was killed, but later reinterred at Brookwood Military Cemetery in Woking, Surrey. A plaque commemorating his name was erected in Weston Patrick churchyard cemetery in March 1994.
13. Summary report for Operation *Jubilee*, titled *BATTLE OF DIEPPE Secret. Operation Jubilee* [sic]. *Wednesday 19 th* [sic] *August 1942.*, 41 Squadron Archives.
14. Ibid. The author of the document is not identified but is likely to have been the Intelligence Officer, Lord Gisborough.
15. The F540 on 18 August 1942 states the pilots took off at 14:30, whereas the F541 states 14:10.
16. The F540 on 18 August 1942 states the area patrolled was "St. Catherines", whereas the F541 states it was "Selsey".
17. 41 Squadron ORB, 19 August 1942, TNA AIR 27/425.
18. Intelligence Report titled *Preliminary and Composite Report No. 2* to 11 Group Air Intelligence from RAF Tangmere, dated 19 August 1942, 41 Squadron Archives.

19. These sorties are not mentioned on the Squadron ORB's F540 on 19 August 1942, but are listed on the F541 with timings of 08:30-09:55, erroneously mirroring those of Atkinson and Lloyd's earlier ASR sorties.
20. The 41 Squadron ORB on 19 August 1942 states there were eight Hurricane bombers on the operation, but 175 Squadron's own ORB that day states there were actually ten.
21. The Squadron had only eleven aircraft involved in their second mission over Dieppe on 19 August 1942, with four aircraft each in Red and Blue Sections, but only three in Yellow Section.
22. *Report by the Air Force Commander on the combined operation against Dieppe – 19 August 1942*, 11 Group ORB Appendix, TNA AIR 25/204.
23. *Intelligence Form F. Intelligence Escort and Combat Report No 7, 41 Squadron Tangmere (Llanbedr)*, original telex dated 19 August 1942, 41 Squadron Archives.
24. Summary report for Operation *Jubilee* titled *BATTLE OF DIEPPE Secret. Operation Jubillee* [sic]. *Wednesday 19 th* [sic] *August 1942.*, 41 Squadron Archives.
25. 175 Squadron ORB, 19 August 1942, TNA AIR 27/1110.
26. The first of 412 (Canadian) Squadron's losses had its entire tail section blown off. The aircraft spun in over land and its pilot, Plt Off John Brookhouse, was killed. The second was hit in the engine, causing a glycol leak which compelled its pilot, Flt Sgt William Aldcorn, to bale out into the Channel 15 miles off Beachy Head when the engine seized on the way home. He was picked up by a motor launch 40 minutes later.
27. 41 Squadron ORB, 19 August 1942, TNA AIR 27/425.
28. Ibid.
29. *Pilot Service Record* for Flt Lt Malta L. Stepp, 41 Squadron Archives.
30. 41 Squadron ORB, 19 August 1942, TNA AIR 27/425.
31. Combat Report for Sgt Plt André Imbert, No. 267, 19 August 1942, TNA AIR 50/18.
32. An original document showing Flt Lt Douglas Hone's Combat Film Assessment for 19 August 1942 is held in 41 Squadron's Archives. Unfortunately, the Combat Film itself does not appear to have survived.
33. No title, original telex from 41 Squadron Intelligence to 11 Group Intelligence, with copies to RAF Tangmere, RAF Valley and 9 Group, dated 9 September 1942, 41 Squadron Archives.
34. Combat Report for Flt Lt Douglas H. Hone, dated 9 September 1942, 41 Squadron Archives.
35. Ibid.
36. *Pilot Service Record* for Flt Lt Douglas H. Hone, 41 Squadron Archives.
37. 41 Squadron ORB, 19 August 1942, TNA AIR 27/425.
38. Summary report for Operation *Jubilee* titled *BATTLE OF DIEPPE Secret. Operation Jubillee* [sic]. *Wednesday 19 th* [sic] *August 1942.*, 41 Squadron Archives.
39. 253 Squadron's Flt Lt John Ellacombe landed in the Channel about 500 yards offshore, close to two of the last boats to leave Dieppe and was rescued.
40. *Intelligence Form F. Intelligence Escort Report No 8. 41 Squadron Tangmere (Llanbedr)*, original telex dated 19 August 1942, 41 Squadron Archives.
41. Summary report for Operation *Jubilee* titled *BATTLE OF DIEPPE Secret. Operation Jubillee* [sic]. *Wednesday 19 th* [sic] *August 1942.*, 41 Squadron Archives.
42. Intelligence Report titled *Preliminary and Composite Report No. 5* to 11 Group Air Intelligence from RAF Tangmere, dated 19 August 1942, 41 Squadron Archives.
43. 41 Squadron ORB, 19 August 1942, TNA AIR 27/425.
44. *Pilot Service Record* for Sqn Ldr Geoffrey C. Hyde, 41 Squadron Archives.
45. Summary report for Operation *Jubilee* titled *BATTLE OF DIEPPE Secret. Operation Jubillee* [sic]. *Wednesday 19 th* [sic] *August 1942.*, 41 Squadron Archives.
46. RAF Llanbedr ORB, 19 August 1942, TNA AIR 28/494.
47. The Squadron's F540 makes no mention of the 16:00 patrol and even suggests that the previous patrol was the last of the day. This patrol is, however, mentioned on the F541 and in an Intelligence Report in 41 Squadron's Archives.
48. This Spitfire Vb serial, BL513, is possibly erroneous and is more likely to have been BL518.
49. The Imperial War Museum in London holds a silent Black and White 35mm film of 41 Squadron's activity during Operation *Jubilee*, made by an RAF Film Production Unit. Film ARY 17-7, titled *RAF OPERATIONS IN SUPPORT OF THE DIEPPE RAID*, and filmed between 18 and 19 August 1942, it shows, "General scenes of operations in support of the Dieppe Raid. The first part of this reel shows Bostons, possibly of 88 Squadron being prepared for action. At the end Spitfires of 41 Squadron are worked on by their ground crews and are seen taking off [….] Good scenes of ground crews bombing up and working on aircraft".
50. These figures, recorded by the Tangmere Wing immediately following Operation *Jubilee*, are for illustration only and likely differ somewhat today, with the availability of a range of declassified records.
51. Although clearly written on 19 August 1942, the message took a few days to move down through the chain of command and reach the Squadron.
52. *LBR GPI NR GPI 40/21 NOT WT PASS TO 41 SQDN*, undated but stamped telex 'R.A.F. LLANBEDR 21 AUG 1942' and 'No 41 SQUADRON 22 AUG 1942 ROYAL AIR FORCE'. The reverse side of the document is signed by the participating pilots, 41 Squadron Archives.

53. Posted to RAF Gibraltar in early September 1942, Sgt Plt Max Lloyd was flown to Malta on 20 October, where he joined 229 Squadron at Krendi. Initially promoted to Flight Sergeant at the beginning of December, he was commissioned on the last day of the year. Lloyd claimed a destroyed Italian aircraft in April 1943, and at the conclusion of his six-month tour returned to the United Kingdom, where he was rested as a flying instructor with 59 OTU. In late January 1944, by now a Flying Officer, Lloyd returned to operations with 65 Squadron, and remained with this unit until mid-April 1945. He enjoyed considerable success with 65 Squadron, claiming one destroyed, one probable and three damaged enemy aircraft, and was awarded the DFC in March 1945. Rested as a flying instructor with 61 OTU at the end of his tour, Lloyd ended the War as Flight Lieutenant, but was appointed to a commission as a Flying Officer with the RAFVR in May 1947. Promoted to Flight Lieutenant in March 1951, he retired from the Air Force in May 1955 and was subsequently employed by the Ministry of Defence for some years. He passed away in November 1987.

2 LLANBEDR; 23 AUGUST 1942 – 24 FEBRUARY 1943

1. This is believed to have been 1st Officer Louise Shuurman of No. 15 ATA Pool, Hamble, an all-female ferry pool. The daughter of the Dutch Consul General in New Orleans, USA, Shuurman arrived in the United Kingdom in March 1942 and served with the ATA until the end of the War.
2. The Link Trainer was one of the earliest forms of flight simulator, which was named for its inventor, American aviation pioneer Edwin Link. His simulators were used widely as a blind flying training aid during World War II. Mounted upon a universal joint on a turntable, a series of vacuum-operated bellows, manipulated by valves attached to a pilot's controls, permitted limited banking, pitches, and yaws.
3. There are several discrepancies between the 41 Squadron ORB's F540 and F541 on 2 September 1942. The first of these is that the F540 makes no mention of the 11:45 scramble, although it is recorded on the F541 and, secondly, the F540 notes a return time of the 15:25 patrol of the Irish coast, whereas the F541 records a return at 15:35. In addition to the timing difference, the F540 records that only Coombes and Stepp participated in the mission to Ireland, but F541 entries show that Sgt Plts Atkinson and Imbert also participated.
4. Commissioned in January 1944, Sgt Plt Kenneth Warren spent the rest of the War in the Mediterranean, and was active during the invasion of Italy. He was promoted to Flight Lieutenant in January 1946 and released in 1947. According to his family, he was also awarded the DFC and AFC and attained the rank of Wing Commander by the time of his release. His logbook, donated to a church in England, could not be located for this publication. After graduating from the Royal College of Art, Warren emigrated to Canada in 1954, where sadly his medals were stolen. He passed away on 28 December 2009 after leading an enriched life as an industrial designer, college instructor and watercolourist, particularly of aviation art.
5. 41 Squadron ORB, 4 September 1942, TNA AIR 27/425.
6. 1 (C) OTU ORB, 6 September 1942, TNA AIR 29/707.
7. The following day, Penrith Police reported that the aircraft had been located, burnt out on the side of Wildboar Scar, above Crowdundle Beck near Appleby-in-Westmorland. It had apparently flown into the side of the hill in bad weather. The crew, Plt Off Paul Bourke (pilot), Sgt John Bumpstead (nav), and Sgts Leslie Griffin, Robert Band, and Ronald Hewett (WO/AGs), of No. 32 Course's 2 Squadron, were all killed.
8. RAF Llanbedr ORB, 6 September 1942, TNA AIR 28/494.
9. This may have been Convoy OS.40, which departed Liverpool for Freetown on 9 September 1942.
10. Plt Off William Coombes and Sgt Plt Jeffrey King left the Squadron on a posting home to 452 Squadron RAAF, based at Richmond in NSW. The Squadron had returned to Australia from the United Kingdom in June 1942 to defend the country against Japanese attacks on its northern coast. The two men had been together since SFTS in Borden in late 1941. Having also attended a course together at the Pilots' Advanced Flying Unit at RAF Watton in early 1942, and subsequently OTU at Eshott in spring, they were posted together as NCO pilots to 41 Squadron on 9 June 1942. Coombes and King had experienced the intensity of the Squadron's summer, defending the southern English coast against the Luftwaffe's tip-and-run raids, and participated in the aerial support of the Canadian landings at Dieppe in August. With this invaluable experience under their belts, they were now sent home to join 452 Squadron and to face an altogether different enemy – the Imperial Japanese Army Air Force and Navy Air Service. Coombes was commissioned before their departure and left 41 Squadron as a Pilot Officer. By the time they arrived on 452 Squadron in mid-March 1943, now based at Strauss in the Northern Territory, he had been promoted to Flying Officer. King was commissioned with 452 Squadron at the beginning of July 1943. Both men were destined to survive the war, although King was lucky to survive a flying accident in December 1943. Unable to take off from Hughes Strip, in the Northern Territory, his Spitfire overshot the end of the runway and ripped open its belly tank. The aircraft exploded into flames and burnt out. King was able to escape, but sustained burns which hospitalised him for some time. King was demobilised in October 1945, by then a Flight Lieutenant, but Coombes remained in the RAAF and retired as a Wing Commander in early 1968.
11. RAF Llanbedr ORB, 20 September 1942, TNA AIR 28/494.
12. RAF Eglinton, located eight miles (13km) east-north-east of a village of the same name, was opened as a part of 13 Group in April 1941. In 1943, the airfield was converted to the Fleet Air Arm base, HMS *Gannet*, to provide

air cover for the North Atlantic convoys. After its closure in 1966, the site was used briefly for commercial flying, though predominantly by the Eglinton Flying Club. In the late 1970s, the land was purchased by Derry City Council and redeveloped over the subsequent 15 years to become today's City of Derry Airport.

13. 41 Squadron ORB, 22 September 1942, TNA AIR 27/425. Note that whilst this is the entry for 22 September 1942, it was clearly written at least eight days later, at it refers to the Squadron's move back to Llanbedr on 30 September. It is also interesting to note that these dates generally do not agree with others recorded in this work, most notably those listed in Appendix XII (Base Locations), which follow the dates upon which the pilots arrived in the various locations, usually ahead of the ground crews and clerical staff. It would appear, therefore, that the dates listed in this quote from the ORB roughly follow the dates upon which the ground staff arrived at the various locations.
14. 41 Squadron ORB, 23 September 1942, TNA AIR 27/425.
15. Ibid., 24 September 1942.
16. The body of 20-year-old Sgt Plt Russel E. G. Oxenham, who is believed to have joined the Squadron during the last week of August, was recovered from his aircraft and sent home, and was buried in Plymouth Efford Cemetery in Devon.
17. 41 Squadron's ORB's F540 and F541 on 25 September 1942 contradict each other on the timings of this event as the former report states Green section was airborne at 17:10 (but does not list a return time), whilst the latter report states the scramble took place between 15:35 and 16:15. The Eglinton ORB, on the other hand, records no timings, but calls it Raid X, and states that it 'faded' before an interception could be made.
18. *Squadron Diary, 41 Squadron, "B" Flight*, dated 20 Sep 1942-1 Mar 1943, entry for 26 September 1942, 41 Squadron Archives.
19. 41 Squadron ORB, 26 September 1942, TNA AIR 27/425.
20. *Squadron Diary, 41 Squadron, "B" Flight*, dated 20 Sep 1942-1 Mar 1943, entry for 27 September 1942, 41 Squadron Archives.
21. 41 Squadron ORB, 27 September 1942, TNA AIR 27/425.
22. The 41 Squadron ORB does not record the aircraft serial or provide any more detailed information.
23. 41 Squadron ORB, 29 and 30 September 1942, TNA AIR 27/425.
24. *Squadron Diary, 41 Squadron, "B" Flight*, dated 20 Sep 1942-1 Mar 1943, entry for 9 October 1942, 41 Squadron Archives.
25. 41 Squadron ORB, 15 October 1942, TNA AIR 27/425.
26. Fg Off Harold Knight was posted to 185 Squadron at Hal Far, flying Spitfire Vc's. He was flown to Malta and took up his posting within a week of leaving 41 Squadron. Having claimed a probable Me109 in late January 1943, he was promoted to Flight Lieutenant seven months later. By May 1944, Knight was back in Europe, flying Typhoon Ib's with Manston based 137 Squadron. He was hit by Flak near Roulers [Roeselare], Belgium, on 21 May 1944 and crashed outside Maldegem, Belgium. The aircraft exploded on impact and Knight was killed instantly. He is buried today in Maldegem Communal Cemetery in Oost-Vlaanderen, Belgium.

    Plt Off Robert Wood and Sgt Plt Thomas Atkinson were both posted to 1435 Squadron at Luqa, flying Spitfire Vc's, where the Commanding Officer was ex-41 Squadron Flight Commander, Sqn Ldr Tony Lovell DSO DFC*. It is understood that Wood arrived ca mid-November 1942 (he is first mentioned in the ORB on 19 November), when he was promoted to Flying Officer. Atkinson joined the Squadron on 12 December 1942, and was commissioned with 1435 Squadron in mid-February 1943. Wood was posted home a year later and joined 609 Squadron at Lympne flying Typhoons on 11 November 1943. Promoted to Flight Lieutenant in late January 1944, he was hit by Flak during an attack on a radar station near Fécamp, France, on 11 May 1944, and crashed into a house, killing him instantly. He is remembered today on the Runnymede Memorial

    Atkinson enjoyed some success in the air, claiming an Me109 destroyed and an FW190 shared destroyed with another ex-41 Squadron pilot, Flt Sgt Sydney Benjamin on 2 July 1943. The pair had known each other from their 41 Squadron days in Llanbedr and Benjamin had been similarly posted from there to Malta, arriving on 1435 Squadron in spring 1943. Eight days after these victories, Atkinson claimed another Me109 damaged. On 19 July 1943, he was posted home, tour expired, praised by the 1435 Squadron ORB as "One who arrived as an N.C.O. and turned out to be a good officer and leader" [TNA AIR 27/2342, 19 July 1943]. Within a month of his departure, he was promoted to Flying Officer and posted to 56 Squadron, based in southern England, flying Typhoons. On 3 May 1944, he was killed in action over France, aged 21, and is buried today in Ste. Marie Cemetery, Le Havre.
27. The Squadron ORB's F541 on 22 October 1942 shows Flt Lt Douglas Hone and Fg Off Rycherde Hogarth's time in the air as 11:50-13:15, whereas the F540 states it was 09:20-09:55.
28. *Squadron Diary, 41 Squadron, "B" Flight*, dated 20 Sep 1942-1 Mar 1943, entry for 22 October 1942, 41 Squadron Archives.
29. OD stands for 'Other Denomination'. During the War, a Staff Chaplain served the same purpose as a Principal Chaplain does in the RAF today. Appleyard, a Congregationalist who served in the RAF from 1929-1957, was the Principal Chaplain for the RAF's Presbyterian, Methodist and United Board of the Chaplaincy Branch (PMUB). The Congregationalists were part of the PMUB, and had a significant representation within the branch during the War. The PMUB was replaced in the post-War RAF by the 'Church of Scotland and Free Churches' (CSFC).
30. There are some inconsistencies between various reports about the actual location of the accident site. The Squadron

ORB, for example, states the location was "9 miles from Towyn" and the Llanbedr Station ORB states, "6 miles South East of Towyn". However, the actual location was on Tarrenhendre, six miles northeast of Towyn, which lies within today's Snowdonia National Park, in the post-1974 Welsh county of Gwynedd.

31. The 41 Squadron ORB states Plt Off Thomas R. Scott's funeral was held on 26 October 1942, but the Llanbedr Station ORB states it was held on 27 October.
32. RAF Llanbedr ORB, 27 October 1942, TNA AIR 28/494.
33. 41 Squadron ORB, 26 October 1942, TNA AIR 27/425.
34. *Pilot Service Record* for Plt Off Thomas R. Scott, 41 Squadron Archives.
35. 41 Squadron ORB, 30 November 1942, TNA AIR 27/425.
36. AM1180 Flying Accident Card for Sgt Plt Clifford C. Monk, Spitfire Vb, R6919, 26 October 1942, RAF Museum, Hendon.
37. The pilots are not named in the ORB but circumstantial evidence suggests these may have been Polish Plt Off Wladislaw Banach and Sgt Plt Jan Zimek.
38. The 41 Squadron ORB's F541 states on 31 October 1942 that the scramble took place between 16:15 and 17:40, but the F540 states they took off at 14:00. The AM1180 Flying Accident Card puts the time of Zimek's crash-landing in Eire at 19:00, suggesting that the 16:15 take-off time is more likely.
39. *Pilot Service Record* for Sgt Plt Jan Zimek, 41 Squadron Archives.
40. AM1180 Flying Accident Card for Sgt Plt Jan Zimek, Spitfire Vb, BM533, 31 October 1942, RAF Museum, Hendon.
41. Ibid.
42. It is not clear why Zimek was taken to the local Post Office to have his injury attended to on 31 October 1942. This statement is made in a document from G2 Dublin to G2 Curragh, referenced 'G2/X/1089' and titled, *Forced landing of British aircraft at Wells, Oulart, Co. Wexford, 31/10/1942*, which is held in the Defence Forces Military Archives, Cathal Brugha Barracks, Rathmines, Dublin 6, Ireland.
43. 'A.I.' is Airborne Interception Radar and 'c.m. type A.S.V.' refers to Air-to-Surface Vessel radars operating with wavelengths measured in centimetres or less. Wavelength is inversely proportional to frequency so the higher the operating frequency the smaller (shorter) the wavelength.
44. *No. 9 Group Standing Operational Instruction No. 71(A), Destruction of Aircraft Forced to Land in Enemy or Neutral Territory*, Appendix D to 9 Group ORB, dated 12 September 1942, TNA AIR 25/179.
45. This refers to an attempted mass break-out from the camp by 33 Allied airmen on 9 February 1942, which was put down with what was felt to be excessive force that landed several men in hospital for treatment. For further information, see the chapter 'The Big Punch-Up', pp. 126-136, in Dwyer's *Guests of the State*, Brandon, 1994.
46. Undated draft letter, *R.A.F. Personnel Interned in Eire*, TNA AIR 10/1021.
47. *Guests of the State; The story of Allied and Axis servicemen interned in Ireland during World War II*, T. Ryle Dwyer, 1994, Brandon.
48. Both Allied and German internees were permitted a very liberal amount of parole for weekends, race meetings, and dances in local towns on a parole that required renewal in person on a daily basis. In fact, between December 1942 and May 1943, they were even allowed to leave The Curragh on parole overnight until 08:00 the next morning, when their parole was renewed. This meant that the men were generally free to do what they wanted and "seek their own diversions", as one record puts it.
49. *Forces Repatriated from Eire*, 1940-1945, TNA WO 208/3347.
50. Zimek's reproach was actually a clever quip and a double-edged sword. On the one hand he was rebuking Kerniewski for fraternising with Krupp, but on the other hand was criticising Krupp by suggesting that Kerniewski, as a member of the 'Herrenvolk', i.e. 'Master Race', was 'lowering himself' to Krupp's level.
51. *Forces Repatriated from Eire*, 1940-1945, TNA WO 208/3347.
52. Ibid.
53. Ibid.
54. Ibid.
55. Ibid.
56. Ibid.
57. RAF Valley ORB, monthly summary for November 1942, TNA AIR 28/874.
58. It is not clear on which date Plt Off Robert J. Boyd joined 41 Squadron. The B Flight Diary, an informal record of the Flight's activity in 41 Squadron's Archives, states that he took his first flight with the Squadron, in EB-U, on 2 November 1942, implying he had probably been with the unit a few days already. However, after his death on 6 September 1943, the Squadron ORB states that he joined the unit on 18 November 1942.
59. The Squadron ORB on 2 November 1942 states the time of Chappell's flying accident was 19:45, but the AM Form 1180 Flying Accident Card for the incident cites the time as 19:22.
60. *Squadron Diary, 41 Squadron, "B" Flight*, dated 20 Sep 1942-1 Mar 1943, entry for 15 November 1942, 41 Squadron Archives.
61. 41 Squadron ORB, 20 November 1942, TNA AIR 27/425.
62. *Squadron Diary, 41 Squadron, "B" Flight*, dated 20 Sep 1942-1 Mar 1943, entry for 20 November 1942, 41 Squadron Archives.

63. Ibid., entry for 21 November 1942.
64. The original "Pip-squeak" set used by the RAF was known as the Master Contactor, and was fitted in most Fighter Command aircraft, including the Spitfire, Hurricane, Gladiator, Defiant, and Blenheim, during 1940-41. The Contactor was basically a clockwork mechanism in a small wooden box, approximately 6-7 inches square, which was located out of sight behind the pilot's seat. It was connected to the TR.9 R/T set (and later to the VHF versions) by a cable which included an on/off switch accessible to the pilot. This mechanism was synchronised with the exact time being used by the relevant local Sector organisation, so that all formations in the air would be in harmony. In essence, a Ground Station would request 'Pip' and the pilot would operate a switch on the box and answer 'Squeak' to do so. This would produce an extra pulse on the RDF display alongside the otherwise anonymous transmission from the aircraft, and thus identify it. As the clockwork was running continuously, a pilot could activate the circuit at will, which was a usually done by the leader of each formation. The purpose of the Contactor was that the clockwork would automatically permit the transmission of a fairly high 'squeak' on a given frequency for 14 seconds of each minute. Because the timing of the transmission of each formation was on a different section of the clock, up to four formations could be simultaneously transmitting their individual signal without interfering with another, providing a two-second 'silence' between transmissions from four individual formation leaders. These transmissions (or squeaks) were picked up by very directional, manually operated aerials at strategically located positions in each sector, and at least three of the bearings thus obtained were passed by permanently open phone lines to 'Triangulation Stations' where approximate positions were established. This information was then passed through Filter Rooms to Operations Room. As positions were being generated every minute, the work of manually obtaining simultaneous bearings for four formations was quite laborious. However, this was necessary as early radar struggled to provide useful information over land, and therefore this system was relied upon to provide the location of each individual RAF fighter formation in a sector minute-by-minute. On the downside, though, positions presented in the Operations Room generally lagged behind a formation's true position by several minutes. This tool was used in unison with approximate positions for enemy formations, provided by the Royal Observer Corps, which had been previously identified by radar over France, the English Channel, or the North Sea, as the case may be. Although this sounds very rudimentary, it did work, and this is how the Battle of Britain was fought and won. 'Pip-squeak' provided the location of RAF formations, the Royal Observer Corps provided those of Luftwaffe formations, and the Operations Rooms the interception bearings for British fighters scrambled to meet them. Radar only gave preliminary information on the approach of Luftwaffe formations, to which were allocated 'Raid Numbers' and the Operations Room then had to bring together all the information provided by the radar Filter Rooms, and Royal Observer Corps to give the RAF the information they needed to intercept incoming enemy formations. Later Contactors had a miniature clock face showing when a Pip-Squeak transmission would cut in. The original 'Pip-squeak' set was superseded in 1943 by the first proper IFF system, known as IFF Mk. I. However, a later version, the Mk. III, was considered the first truly successful IFF set, and was adopted universally by all Allied forces in the lead-up to D-Day. Source: Chapters 1 ('The Biggin Hill Experiment'), 2 ('The Application of Radar'), 3 ('The Battle of Britain'), and 5 ('Early Development and I.F.F. Mark I'), RAF Signals, Volume 5, 'Fighter Control & Interception', issued by the Air Ministry (AHB) 1952, a.k.a. CD [Confidential Document] 1116, security classification downgraded to unclassified in March 1975 and renamed AP 1116, via David Duxbury.
65. 41 Squadron ORB, 25 November 1942, TNA AIR 27/425. As an aside, it should be noted that 41 Squadron had known Sqn Ldr Bullimore some years. The unit had already crossed paths with him when he was posted to RAF Catterick for Operations Room duties as a Pilot Officer in early September 1939, whilst 41 Squadron was based there. By late January 1940, now a Flying Officer, but Acting Flight Lieutenant, Bullimore was appointed to the rank of Acting Squadron Leader when he took up the post of Squadron Leader Operations. As such, 41 Squadron and Bullimore would have dealt with each other on a daily basis during this period.
66. 41 Squadron ORB, 25 November 1942, TNA AIR 27/425.
67. *Squadron Diary, 41 Squadron, "B" Flight*, dated 20 Sep 1942-1 Mar 1943, entry for 26 November 1942, 41 Squadron Archives.
68. Fg Off Robert Hollow was attached to 452 Squadron on 2 December 1942 and embarked for Australia a day later. After his arrival, he attended a refresher course before being posted to 79 Squadron RAAF in New Guinea in May 1943. Returning to Australia in December 1943, Hollow attended a course at the School of Army Cooperation ahead of several short postings and a few extended periods of illness and hospitalisation. He ended the War as a flying instructor and was discharged at his own request to resume his civil occupation in October 1945. He passed away in January 2006.
69. There are a few ambiguities in the ORB today. The F541 also lists a short patrol undertaken by Fg Off Rex Poynton (W3378) and Sgt Plt Malcolm Rowe (AR393) as Red Section between 13:00 and 13:25, but the F540 does not mention it. Conversely, Flt Lt Douglas Hone and Fg Off Douglas Haywood's patrol to Dublin is mentioned on the F540, but is not recorded on the F541.
70. It is not clear who the writer of this paragraph in the ORB on 30 November 1942 was, though clearly a gifted English speaker. However, as the Adjutant, Intelligence Officer and Flight Commanders are named and praised in the text, it can be assumed they were not the authors. The only person not mentioned is the CO, Sqn Ldr Tom Neil, so it may well have been him. This was not usually the case, but the clear effort to boost morale, coupled with what appears to be a subtle hint to decision-makers further up the food chain, may well suggest that this is a correct assumption.

71. The claim of 11 pilots being posted away on 20 September 1942 cannot be substantiated; it does not appear to be supported by the available facts.
72. 41 Squadron ORB, 30 November 1942, TNA AIR 27/425.
73. *Squadron Diary, 41 Squadron, "B" Flight*, dated 20 Sep 1942-1 Mar 1943, entry for 2 December 1942, 41 Squadron Archives.
74. 41 Squadron ORB, 16 December 1942, TNA AIR 27/425.
75. Ibid.
76. RAF Llanbedr ORB, 17 December 1942, TNA AIR 28/494.
77. The entry in the B Flight Diary on 21 December 1942 states there were six pilots involved in the formation flying exercise, but the Squadron ORB states that nine pilots took off. It is not clear whether B Flight's Diary implies this was just the number of pilots participating from B Flight, or if this was the total number of pilots involved in the exercise. The ORB actually reports that all nine pilots were ordered to return after 20 minutes, whereas the B Flight Diary indicates that two pilots landed at Valley and stayed overnight. If there were in fact nine pilots involved, and we know four returned to Llanbedr and two landed in Valley, the movements of the remaining three aircraft remains unknown.
78. *Squadron Diary, 41 Squadron, "B" Flight*, dated 20 Sep 1942-1 Mar 1943, entry for 22 December 1942, 41 Squadron Archives.
79. RAF Llanbedr ORB, 24 December 1942, TNA AIR 28/494.
80. 41 Squadron ORB, 24 December 1942, TNA AIR 27/425.
81. RAF Llanbedr ORB, 25 December 1942, TNA AIR 28/494.
82. 41 Squadron ORB, 25 December 1942, TNA AIR 27/425.
83. Miscellaneous undated notes inside the back cover of the B Flight Diary hint at who the "sprinkling of Squadron Men" may have been in the Station Concert Party. The notes are not completely legible, but list men's names against instruments. It states Cook – Trombone, Clement – accordion, Scott – Trumpet, Sailor – piano, Welch – guitar, Rowe – drums, Hone – saxophone. As an aside, the Station ORB records that the party went on until 23:59, whereas the Squadron ORB states festivities went on until 01:00!
84. RAF Llanbedr ORB, 26 December 1942, TNA AIR 28/494.
85. Ibid.
86. *Squadron Diary, 41 Squadron, "B" Flight*, dated 20 Sep 1942-1 Mar 1943, entry for 27 December 1942, 41 Squadron Archives.
87. Sgt Plt Sydney Benjamin embarked for Malta in early 1943 and was posted to 1435 Squadron, where he is first mentioned in Squadron records on 2 March 1943. On 2 July, he claimed one destroyed Me109, and a half share in the destruction of a FW190 with another ex-41 Squadron pilot, Plt Off Thomas Atkinson, but just ten days later he was shot down and killed in an engagement with MC202s and Me109s over the front line area between Syracuse and Augusta, Italy, whilst providing air support for the invasion of Sicily. Aged just 20 at the time, he was buried in Syracuse War Cemetery.
88. Intelligence Report titled, *Composite Rhubarb Report. No. 41 Squadron. Westhampnett, 22nd December, 1942. (Received from Tangmere)*, 41 Squadron Archives.
89. Ibid.
90. RAF Llanbedr ORB, 31 December 1942, TNA AIR 28/494.
91. 41 Squadron ORB, 31 December 1942, TNA AIR 27/425.
92. RAF Valley ORB, summary for January 1943, TNA AIR 28/874.
93. 41 Squadron ORB, 7 January 1943, TNA AIR 27/425.
94. Combat Report titled 'EXERCISE Practice Interception – Valley Sector', 14 January 1943, 41 Squadron Archives.
95. Ibid.
96. 41 Squadron ORB, 15 January 1943, TNA AIR 27/425.
97. RAF Llanbedr ORB, 15 January 1943, TNA AIR 28/494.
98. *Squadron Diary, 41 Squadron, "B" Flight*, dated 20 Sep 1942-1 Mar 1943, entry for 15 January 1943, 41 Squadron Archives.
99. *Squadron Diary, 41 Squadron, "B" Flight*, dated 20 Sep 1942-1 Mar 1943, entry for 24 January 1943, 41 Squadron Archives.
100. Ibid., entry for 27 January 1943.
101. The names of the pilots and serials of the aircraft involved in the ASR patrol for the Skua on 29 January 1943 are not recorded on the Squadron's F541.
102. Having left 41 Squadron on a posting to North Africa, 22-year-old Sgt Plt Arthur R. Cope RAAF was lost whilst ferrying Spitfire Vc, JG747, from Gibraltar to Maison Blanche, via a refuelling stop at the USAAF airfield at La Sénia, Algeria, on 9 March 1943. Cope was the last pilot to take off from Gibraltar at 10:30 in a formation of six aircraft, but the cause of his loss remains uncertain. Pilots flying in the same formation reported there was no radio communication from him indicating he was in any trouble; they simply noticed he was no longer with them. This occurred shortly after the pilots changed over from their auxiliary fuel tanks to their main tanks. Whilst noting that the actual cause of his loss could not be established with certainty, the official finding assumed that Cope

103. Flt Sgt (retrospectively promoted to WO) Robert Quine was flying as Red 4 in Spitfire Vc, JK511, as one of eight aircraft from 152 Squadron, which were detailed to cover the Sicilian beaches on 12 July 1943. When attacked by enemy aircraft, the formation broke into sections of two, and individual combats ensued. At their conclusion, the formation leader ordered the pilots to form up again, at an altitude of 7,000 feet over Gela, however no reply was received from Quine. He was posted missing and, in March 1944, formally presumed to have died on 12 July 1943, aged 20. Like Sgt Plt Arthur Cope, he is also remembered on the Malta Memorial.
104. *Squadron Diary, 41 Squadron, "B" Flight*, dated 20 Sep 1942-1 Mar 1943, entry for 31 January 1943, 41 Squadron Archives.
105. Ibid.
106. 41 Squadron ORB, 1 February 1943, TNA AIR 27/425.
107. RAF Llanbedr ORB, 3 February 1943, TNA AIR 28/494.
108. The 41 Squadron ORB on 4 February 1943 erroneously states the search was conducted in Cornwall Bay, but the search location was actually Cardigan Bay.
109. The Wellington's three crew – Sgt Plt Francis Ayley (RAF), Fg Off Raymond Hann (RCAF), and Sgt. Peeti Karena (RNZAF) – were never found, and their status remains 'missing, presumed dead'. They are remembered today on the Runnymede Memorial.
110. 41 Squadron ORB, 4 February 1943, TNA AIR 27/425.
111. Intelligence Report, *GPI LBR NRLBR6/4 NOTWT*, dated 4 February 1943, 41 Squadron Archives. It appears the letter K on the typewriter was playing up as it was over-typing each preceding letter.
112. Intelligence Report, *GPI LBR NRLBR1/6 NOTWT*, dated 6 February 1943, 41 Squadron Archives. It appears the letter K on the typewriter had not yet been repaired!
113. RAF Llanbedr ORB, 7 February 1943, TNA AIR 28/494. Note also the similarities between this day's Army cooperation exercise and the previous day's, including the congratulatory message from an Army Officer. It is believed they were nonetheless separate exercises, despite the fact that an Intelligence Report only exists for 6 February, and an Army cooperation exercise is only mentioned in the Squadron ORB on 7 February, as the Sections, locations and timings are all different.
114. 41 Squadron ORB, 8 February 1943, TNA AIR 27/425.
115. *Pilot Service Record* for Fg Off Clive R. Birbeck, 41 Squadron Archives.
116. *Squadron Diary, 41 Squadron, "B" Flight*, dated 20 Sep 1942-1 Mar 1943, entry for 11 February 1943, 41 Squadron Archives.
117. The Squadron ORB and B Flight Diary contradict each other on some details of the Squadron scramble practiced on 11 February 1943. The ORB states the scramble took place at 15:11 and that all aircraft were in the air within four minutes, whereas the B Flight Diary states ten aircraft (six from B Flight and four from A Flight) were airborne within 2½ minutes and returned at 14:45. Unfortunately, being non-operational sorties, the pilots, aircraft serials, and take-off and landing times are not recorded on the F541, so this source does not assist with clarity.
118. The 41 Squadron ORB on 13 February 1943 records the timings as airborne at 11:35, back on the ground at 12:25 and 50 minutes in the air, whereas the Llanbedr Station ORB lists the timings as 11:37 and 12:35, respectively.
119. The B Flight Diary states that the 24 hours 35 minutes flying time logged by B Flight's pilots on 16 February 1943 also included five hours' night flying, whereas the ORB states the five hours were in addition.
120. *Squadron Diary, 41 Squadron, "B" Flight*, dated 20 Sep 1942-1 Mar 1943, entry for 16 February 1943, 41 Squadron Archives.
121. The ORB's F540 on 16 February 1943 records the time Fg Off Peter Cowell and Sgt Plt Douglas Fisher returned as 12:47, but the F541 states their was return at 12:35. The Llanbedr Station ORB further muddies the water, stating the pilots returned at 12:30.
122. By the time of his posting to 485 (NZ) Squadron in February 1943, Sgt Plt Fraser Clark RNZAF had completed eleven operational sorties with 41 Squadron. He was commissioned in mid-July 1943, but killed just five weeks later during Ramrod 212, an escort of thirty-six Marauders to Beaumont-le-Roger Airfield on 22 August 1943. 485 Squadron was flying as High Cover on the operation with 341 Squadron, but soon after crossing the French coast at 20,000 feet, they encountered a substantial force of FW190s approaching head-on at the same altitude. They were estimated to have numbered approximately twice their own combined strength, but an additional 15-20 enemy aircraft dived upon them from above soon afterwards and a ferocious fight ensued, in which the Wing was split up. In the subsequent chaos, 485 Squadron lost four pilots, but claimed one FW190 of its own, whilst 341 Squadron claimed two more. Of 485 Squadron's four casualties, one was captured, a second baled out into the Channel and was rescued by ASR, a third baled out and evaded capture, but Clark, flying EN631, was killed in action.
123. Although documented in the RAF Valley ORB, the date of this exercise is not recorded, and it is not mentioned at all in the Squadron or Llanbedr Station ORBs. In fact, the only mention of any shipping-related activity this month

in the Squadron ORB is on 18 February 1943. The author therefore assumes the exercise most likely took place on this date.
124. Contradicting the Squadron ORB on 19 February 1943, the Llanbedr ORB states they were only required to orbit base at 10,000 feet, and makes no mention of Exeter, although the two documents do agree on the timings.
125. 41 Squadron ORB, 19 February 1943, TNA AIR 27/425.
126. RAF Llanbedr ORB, 22 February 1943, TNA AIR 28/494.

3 GRIFFON POWER; 25 FEBRUARY – 20 JUNE 1943

1. 41 Squadron ORB, 25 February 1943, TNA AIR 27/425.
2. RAF Llanbedr ORB, 25 February 1943, TNA AIR 28/494.
3. The 41 Squadron ORB states 'Talwyn' or 'Tarwyn' Bach (difficult to read). However, this is a misspelling of the location, Talwrn Bach (pronounced 'Talurn Bark', in Welsh). In English, the location is called Talwrn (or Llanbedr) Halt. It is believed the railway station closed as am official station in the mid-1930s, but was still occasionally utilised for military movements during World War II, such as in this case with 41 Squadron's ground crew. Although unstaffed, the station is still in use today as a part of the Cambrian Coast Railway. However, trains only stop on request.
4. 41 Squadron ORB, 25 February 1943, TNA AIR 27/425.
5. Source: *Spitfire*, Stewart Wilson, 1999, Aerospace Publications, ISBN 1875671455.
6. 41 Squadron ORB, 4 April 1943, TNA AIR 27/425.
7. Ibid.
8. 41 Squadron ORB, 26 February 1943, TNA AIR 27/425.
9. Unfortunately, little more is known of Sgt Plt Peter Cross. It is, however, understood he was commissioned on 12 May 1945 and also served with 198 Squadron.
10. 41 Squadron ORB, 28 February 1943, TNA AIR 27/425.
11. RAF Atcham ORB, 28 February 1943, TNA AIR 28/39.
12. *Squadron Diary, 41 Squadron, "B" Flight*, dated 20 Sep 1942-1 Mar 1943, entry for 28 February 1943, 41 Squadron Archives.
13. Ibid.
14. There is a slight contradiction in the 41 Squadron ORB in March 1943, as the entry for 6 March states that five Spitfire Mk. XIIs had been delivered to the unit to date, whereas the entry for 12 March states that Squadron strength now stood at three Mk. XIIs and two Mk. Vs.
15. 91 Squadron ORB, 28 March 1943, TNA AIR 27/740.
16. Fg Off Peter Cowell and Plt Off David Davies' return from Hawkinge is recorded in the Squadron ORB on 29 March 1943, but their departure for Hawkinge is not. However, Cowell's flying logbook shows he and Davies flew operational patrols with 91 Squadron on 24, 25, 26 and 27 March 1943. Flt Lt Douglas Hone later stated that pilots were attached to 91 Squadron at Hawkinge to "familiarise themselves with shipping reconnaissance work" (Correspondence from Flt Lt Douglas Hone AE to Dan Johnson, 15 January 1984). This appears similar to the experience gained at Westhampnett over Christmas and New Year 1942-1943. How many other pilots besides Fg Offs Birbeck, Cowell and Hoare, and Plt Off Davies, if any, were attached to Hawkinge during this time is unknown.
17. 41 Squadron ORB, 31 March 1943, TNA AIR 27/425.
18. Ibid., 1 April 1943.
19. Ibid., 8 May 1943.
20. Letter, handwritten, untitled and unreferenced, from Mrs. Una Hoare to Flt Lt Lord Gisborough, dated 22 May 1943, 41 Squadron Archives.
21. *War Office: Directorate of Military Intelligence: Liberated Prisoner of War Interrogation Questionnaires*, 1945-1946, Questionnaire for Fg Off Reginald Hoare, TNA WO344/146/1.
22. Hoare's aircraft, BL423, lay buried at Leffinge until it was discovered by the Belgian Aviation History Association Archaeology Team (BAHAAT) approximately 60 years later. In mid-August 2003, a team arrived on the site after digging in various locations in a one-acre field for almost an entire day. The smell of aviation fuel indicated to the team that they had at last found the aircraft, but the Spitfire's remains lay at a depth of approximately three metres. Eyewitnesses recalled that the aircraft had gone in almost vertically at high speed, the wings had folded back on impact, and the momentum had carried the fuselage deep underground. Employing a crane, the team were able to extract several large pieces of the aircraft, including the engine, with the serial plate perfectly legible after cleaning. As the aircraft had been buried for so long in the muddy clay of the field, with no oxygen, the metal and aluminium had been preserved as if it were new; there was no corrosion on any of the airframe. Some of the parts recovered include the tail wheel unit, with air still in the tyre, the radio and oxygen bottles, throttle and cockpit instruments, gun-sight, rudder pedal and armour-plating, two 20mm Hispano cannon and thee Browning .303 machine guns. The parts are now on display in BAHAAT's museum. For more information, see http://users.telenet.be/airwareurope/en/start_e.htm (rtrvd Jul 2010).
23. Correspondence from Fg Off Ronald Johnson to Dan Johnson, 15 November 1983; reproduced with Dan's kind permission.

24. 41 Squadron ORB, 4 April 1943, TNA AIR 27/425.
25. Correspondence with Flt Lt Hugh L. Parry, May 2005.
26. Flt Lt Hugh Parry enlisted at Uxbridge in early December 1939. Completing ITW at Hastings, EFTS at Hatfield and Yatesbury, and SFTS at Kidlington, he was commissioned in December 1940 and subsequently completed OTU at Aston Down. His first operational posting was to 260 Squadron at Skitten in late February 1941, followed only two months later by a move to 266 (Rhodesia) Squadron at Wittering, where he claimed his first victory in mid-September. In March 1942, Parry was posted to 601 Squadron as a Flight Commander and sailed with the unit to Malta aboard USS *Wasp* less than three weeks later. On completion of his tour in July 1942, Parry returned to the United Kingdom for leave and was subsequently posted to Supermarine as a Test Pilot, where he flew several prototypes, thereunder the Spitfire XII.
27. Flt Lt Roy Lane had joined the RAF fifteen months prior to the War and was granted a Short Service Commission in August 1938. He was posted to 43 Squadron at Tangmere in June 1940, and claimed four quick victories in August, during the early stages of the Battle of Britain. Unfortunately, however, Lane's run of successes was only short-lived as he was shot down by return fire from a He111 and baled out over Bognor Regis on 26 August 1940. He suffered burns and a serious shoulder injury after an inverted decent in his parachute, in which only his ankles were in the parachute harness. As a result, he spent the following eight months in hospital and was out of action until well into 1941. In late June 1941, now a Flying Officer, Lane joined the Merchant Ship Fighter Unit in Speke soon after its formation, and escorted convoys to Gibraltar and Russia. The intention was to fly ship-borne Sea Hurricanes from catapults mounted on CAM ships in the event of the Luftwaffe menacing the convoy. In February 1942, Lane was briefly attached to 602 Squadron at Kenley, but left the MFSU in April 1943 on posting to 41 Squadron.
28. Flt Lt. Jerzy Jakub 'George' Solak was born on 22 August 1910 and educated at the Lwów Polytech. He joined the Polish Air Force in 1930 and graduated from the Polish Air Force Reserve Cadet School in Dęblin, in 1935, subsequently being posted to the Polish Light Bomber Squadron. At the outbreak of War, Solak was drafted into the 6th Air Regiment, but evacuated from the country in September 1939, taking a route to the United Kingdom via Romania and France. He arrived in the United Kingdom in January 1940 and joined the RAFVR the following month, after which he was posted to 7 OTU at Hawarden. There followed postings to 151 Squadron in August and 249 Squadron in September 1940, as an NCO pilot, before moving to 317 (Polish) Squadron in February 1941. Solak remained with this unit until June 1942, during which time he was commissioned and promoted to Flying Officer. In June 1942, he was posted to 164 Squadron and just two months later to 609 Squadron, where he was promoted to Flight Lieutenant. In November 1942, he joined the AFDU at Duxford as a Test Pilot, remaining with this unit until his posting to 41 Squadron on 9 April 1943.
29. 41 Squadron ORB, 12 April 1943, TNA AIR 27/425.
30. *No. 41 Squadron & 3016 Echelon Movement Order*, drafted by Squadron Adjutant Fg Off Harry W. Smith, undated, but relating to the Squadron's move from RAF High Ercall to RAF Hawkinge on 12 April 1943, 41 Squadron Archives.
31. Correspondence with Flt Lt Hugh L. Parry, May 2005.
32. *The GEN*, undated hand-written document written by Fg Off Thomas Slack, ca. April 1943; 41 Squadron Archives.
33. Correspondence from Flt Lt Douglas Hone AE to Dan Johnson, 15 January 1984; reproduced with Dan's kind permission.
34. 41 Squadron ORB, 12 April 1943, TNA AIR 27/425.
35. *AI/821 16/APR. HAWKINGE COMPOSITE JIM CROW REPORT 16/APR/43.*, Intelligence Report for 06:25-07:20 patrol by Fg Off Douglas Haywood, 16 April 1943, 41 Squadron Archives.
36. Fg Off Rycherde Hogarth's starboard cannon jammed after three rounds, as a result of the links, thus limiting his available ammunition.
37. This aircraft was Ju88D-1, Wknr 430646, of the long distance reconnaissance unit 3./(F)122. The crew survived, but the Observer, Oblt Herbert Schulz, and gunner, Uffz Hans Weidemüller, were wounded.
38. 41 Squadron ORB, 17 April 1943, TNA AIR 27/425.
39. Fg Off Clive Birbeck's starboard cannon breech block did not lock, thereby reducing his fire power.
40. 41 Squadron ORB, 17 April 1943, TNA AIR 27/425.
41. The information in this table has been extracted and transcribed from a handwritten document titled *Ammunition Expenditure Report (Combat)* for 17 April 1943 [erroneously dated 18 April 1943], 41 Squadron Archives.
42. The Whitney Straight involved in this collision is believed to have been ES922 (ex G-AERS) of the Northolt Station Flight, which was damaged to Cat. B status on this date and struck off charge on 31 May 1943.
43. 41 Squadron ORB, 19 April 1943, TNA AIR 27/425.
44. Unfortunately, the serial of the Spitfire XII involved in this accident on 19 April 1943 does not appear to have been recorded in available documentation.
45. 41 Squadron ORB, 20 April 1943, TNA AIR 27/425.
46. RAF Hawkinge ORB, 21 April 1943, TNA AIR 28/345.
47. 41 Squadron ORB, 22 April 1943, TNA AIR 27/425.
48. Ibid, 23 April 1943.
49. The Squadron ORB's F540 states that Sgt Plts Douglas Fisher and John Thomas' take-off time was 11:25, but the

F541 states it was 11:15. Alternatively, the Air Accident Report states that their flight duration was 35 minutes, whilst the F541 states that their landing/crash time was 11:55.
50. The RAF Hawkinge ORB on 24 April 1943 states the location was "just off the main Folkestone road".
51. RAF Hawkinge ORB, 24 April 1943, TNA AIR 28/345.
52. *Air Ministry and Successors: Civil Aviation Accident Reports (C, W, and S Reports) and Technical Memoranda*, accident investigation report for Spitfire XII, EN610, dated 4 June 1943, TNA AVIA 5/22/W1521.
53. That is, concerning the overheard German radio message.
54. Note that there is no Point 1, only the preceding paragraph and the below Points 2 and 3.
55. *Combat: 41 Squadron – 27.4.43. F/O. Birbeck.*, memo from Headquarters, 11 Group, to RAF Station Hawkinge, referenced *11G/810/Int.*, dated 3 May 1943, 41 Squadron Archives.
56. 41 Squadron ORB, 27 April 1943, TNA AIR 27/425.
57. 'Wings for Victory' Week was a Government-sponsored appeal in May 1943 to raise money from the general public towards the War effort by buying War Bonds, Savings Bonds, Defence Bonds and Savings Certificates, and coincided with a week of parades, talks, exhibitions and air shows. During the War, there were similar appeals titled 'Warship Week', 'Spitfire Week', 'War Weapons Week' and 'Tanks for Attack Week'. The purpose of all these campaigns was to finance the building of ships, tanks and aircraft that would then 'belong' to the particular locality where the funding had been derived. Each County was set a target for the amount they should raise, and districts within them were set individual targets to make up the County's total. Commemorative plaques were subsequently awarded by the War Ministry to recognise achievement. The Borough of Lydd's goal was the cost of two Spitfires, totalling £10,000.
58. Letter to Flt Lt Hugh Parry from the Mayor of Lydd, Alderman Gordon T. Paine, dated 28 April 1943, Appendix C (Folio 94) to 41 Squadron ORB, TNA AIR 27/430.
59. 41 Squadron ORB, 28 April 1943, TNA AIR 27/425.
60. Ibid., 28 April 1943.
61. Ibid., 29 April 1943.
62. Fg Off Jerzy Polak, remained with 315 Squadron until 30 December 1944, during which time he was promoted to Flight Lieutenant and credited with 2⅓ destroyed enemy aircraft and a ¼ share in a V1. During 1944, he was also awarded the Polish Cross of Valour [Krzyz Walecznych] and two Bars, rested initially at the Polish Depot at Blackpool, and subsequently as a Flying Instructor at 61 OTU until the cessation of hostilities. In July 1945, Polak returned to operations with 309 Polish Squadron and remained with this unit until late 1946 when he was demobbed. He settled in the United Kingdom and did not return to live in his native Poland.
63. 41 Squadron ORB, 29 April 1943, TNA AIR 27/425.
64. RAF Hawkinge ORB, 29 April 1943, TNA AIR 28/345.
65. Ibid., 1 May 1943.
66. 41 Squadron ORB, 2 May 1943, TNA AIR 27/425.
67. Intelligence Report from RAF Hawkinge to 11 Group, 09:43 on 3 May 1943, 41 Squadron Archives.
68. 41 Squadron ORB, 3 May 1943, TNA AIR 27/425.
69. Ibid., 11 May 1943.
70. Ibid., 12 May 1943.
71. Ibid.
72. As Sgt Plt Alan Hope was on a non-operational flight, the serial of the aircraft he was flying is not recorded in the ORB. 'Spitfire; The History' (Morgan and Shacklady) does however, have an entry for EN228 showing a Cat. B flying accident on this date, so it may well have been this aircraft.
73. Correspondence with Flt Lt Hugh L. Parry, May 2005.
74. 41 Squadron ORB, 14 May 1943, TNA AIR 27/425.
75. Ibid., 15 May 1943.
76. Ibid., 16 May 1943.
77. Ibid.
78. 41 Squadron ORB, 17 May 1943, TNA AIR 27/425.
79. AM1180 Flying Accident Card for Sgt Plt Norman W. Heale, Spitfire XII, EN229, 17 May 1943, RAF Museum, Hendon.
80. 41 Squadron ORB, 17 May 1943, TNA AIR 27/425.
81. Ibid., 18 May 1943.
82. Body of a letter from Mrs. B. L. M. Murrin to Fg Off H. W. Smith, dated 7 July 1943; 41 Squadron Archives.
83. 41 Squadron ORB, 20 May 1943, TNA AIR 27/425.
84. 41 Squadron returned to RAF Biggin Hill in late March 1951 and remained there until the end of January 1958, when the base was closed by the RAF for good. The unit thus became the last RAF squadron ever to call Biggin Hill home.
85. 41 Squadron ORB, 23 May 1943, TNA AIR 27/425.
86. Correspondence with Flt Lt Hugh L. Parry, May 2005.
87. Peter Graham in his autobiography, *Skypilot; Memoirs from Take-Off to Landing*, 2001, Pentland Books, ISBN 1858219094; reproduced with his permission.

88. Having enlisted in the RAAF in Adelaide in August 1940, Flt Lt Donald Hamilton Smith attended ITS, EFTS and SFTS in Australia, gaining his Wings and a commission prior to embarkation for the United Kingdom in late May 1941. Smith was posted to OTU in Scotland in September 1941 and promoted to Flying Officer before being sent to 15 SFTS as a Flying Instructor in November. This unit was re-designated 15 (P)AFU the following March, while he was still there. Smith's first operational posting came in early April 1942, when he joined 452 (Australian) Squadron, then based at Andreas on the Isle of Man. His posting only lasted two months, as he was sent to Malta aboard HMS *Eagle* in early June 1942 and posted to 126 Squadron on arrival. In the thick of the action over Malta at the time, Smith made some quick successes, claiming a shared destroyed Cant Z1007 on 6 July, a destroyed Me109F on 8 July, a destroyed Ju88 and a probable Me109F on 10 July, and finally a destroyed Ju88 on 14 July. In this latter action, however, he was wounded in action and force-landed his Spitfire, resulting in admission to hospital and subsequent evacuation to the United Kingdom. In April 1943, Smith was promoted to Flight Lieutenant, discharged from hospital, and sent to 53 OTU for a refresher course, in preparation for his return to service. In mid-May 1943, he was granted a week's leave, during which time he married, and was sent to 41 Squadron on 23 May on his first posting since being wounded in Malta the previous July.
89. Having been with the Belgian Air Force since late 1934, Fg Off Roger Alphonse Joseph Duchateau had considerably more experience than almost every other pilot on 41 Squadron at the time. He had fought in the brief defence of Belgium in May 1940, and initially moved into France with his unit, but when that country was also conquered, he returned home unemployed. Remaining in Belgium as a civilian for the ensuing two years, he fled the country in July 1942 and made his way to England via France and Gibraltar. After his arrival in October 1942, Duchateau joined the RAFVR and was immediately commissioned, subsequently undertaking courses at AFU and OTU in early 1943, which he completed on 24 May. He was posted to 41 Squadron a day later, on his first operational posting since arriving in the United Kingdom. Although his stay would be brief, Duchateau would later return to 41 Squadron on a second posting later in the year.
90. 41 Squadron ORB, 26 May 1943, TNA AIR 27/425.
91. Ibid., 27 May 1943.
92. Flt Sgt Stanley J. Biggs was posted to Malta with Flt Sgt William G. Downing on 7 June 1943, embarking for the Mediterranean from Greenock two weeks later. The pair arrived in Malta on 4 July, whereupon they were posted to 229 Squadron at Krendi, flying Spitfire Vc's. Promoted to Warrant Officer in early August, Biggs was killed in a flying accident on 7 January 1944, aged 23, and is buried today in Capuccini Naval Cemetery on Malta.
93. RAF Friston ORB, 28 May 1943, TNA AIR 28/286.
94. Peter Graham in his autobiography, *Skypilot; Memoirs from Take-Off to Landing*, 2001, Pentland Books, ISBN 1858219094; reproduced with his permission.
95. Correspondence with Flt Lt Hugh L. Parry, May 2005.
96. 41 Squadron ORB, 31 May 1943, TNA AIR 27/425.
97. Ibid., 1 June 1943.
98. Similar to his compatriot Fg Off Roger Duchateau, who had joined 41 Squadron a week before him, Plt Off Maurice Arthur Leon Balasse had also joined the Belgian Air Force in 1934 and fought in the brief defence of Belgium in May 1940. Initially retreating into France with his unit, he also returned home unemployed when that country was conquered. He fled Belgium in late April 1942 and travelled to Gibraltar via Paris, Dijon, and Lyon, and crossed the Pyrenees into Spain on 8 May 1942. Arrested by Spanish authorities the following day, Balasse remained imprisoned in Spain until late August, when he was liberated and escorted to Gibraltar. However, he did not reach England until early October, and did not join the RAFVR until the last day of the year. Balasse was immediately commissioned and, between January and May 1943, attended courses at AFU and OTU. He was posted to 41 Squadron on 1 June 1943 on his first operational posting since arriving in the United Kingdom. Although his stay would only last ten days, he would return to 41 Squadron again later in the year.
99. 41 Squadron ORB, 2 June 1943, TNA AIR 27/425.
100. Ibid., 3 June 1943.
101. Ibid.
102. The 41 Squadron ORB on 4 June 1943 states that Fg Off Solak and Flt Lt Donald Smith saw 18 FW190s, whereas the 11 Group ORB states there were 16 aircraft.
103. Fg Off Jerzy J. Solak's Combat Report, No. 379, 4 June 1943, TNA AIR 50/18.
104. Ibid.
105. Ibid.
106. Flt Lt Donald H. Smith's Combat Report, No. 377, 4 June 1943, TNA AIR 50/18.
107. Fg Off Jerzy J. Solak's Combat Report, No. 379, 4 June 1943, TNA AIR 50/18.
108. Flt Lt Donald H. Smith's Combat Report, No. 377, 4 June 1943, TNA AIR 50/18.
109. Ibid.
110. The details provided in this table are those recorded in Flt Lt Donald Smith and Fg Off Jerzy Solak's Combat Reports for 4 June 1943. It should be noted, however, that combat films for this engagement do in fact still exist, and are held today by the Imperial War Museum in Catalogue No. CGE 834-1330, Film Nos. 1184 and 1185.
111. Aviation historian and author Chris Goss states (Dec. 2010) that his research indicates that only one fighter bomber was lost to IV/SKG 10 in this engagement, and that this was to Flak.

112. 41 Squadron ORB, 4 June 1943, TNA AIR 27/425.
113. Ibid.
114. 41 Squadron ORB, 5 June 1943, TNA AIR 27/425.
115. Ibid.
116. 41 Squadron ORB, 7 June 1943, TNA AIR 27/425.
117. The combat film for Fg Off Ronald Johnson's engagement with this Do217 on 9 June 1943 is held today by the Imperial War Museum in Catalogue No. CGE 834-1330, Film No. 1214.
118. Correspondence from Ronald Johnson to Dan Johnson, 23 November 1982; reproduced with Dan's kind permission.
119. Ibid.
120. 41 Squadron ORB, 11 June 1943, TNA AIR 27/425.
121. Ibid., 13 June 1943.
122. Ibid., 14 June 1943.
123. Ibid., 15 June 1943.
124. Ibid., 17 June 1943.
125. Ibid.
126. Ibid.
127. 41 Squadron was based at Merston from 28 July-16 December 1941, at Westhampnett from 16 December 1941-1 April 1942, and at Merston again from 1 April-15 June 1942. Both airfields were satellites of Sector Station, RAF Tangmere, in the Tangmere Wing.
128. 41 Squadron ORB, 20 June 1943, TNA AIR 27/425.
129. Ibid.
130. The *Queen Mary* low loader was a transport vehicle built to 1938 Air Ministry specifications, which was designed to transport aircraft fuselages with their wings removed. They measured approximately 40 feet in length and had a low floor with a ground clearance of just 12 inches.

4 THE SPITFIRE XII WING; 21 JUNE 1943 – 29 FEBRUARY 1944

1. Sommerfeld track was named after Kurt Sommerfeld, an Austrian engineer who adapted a 1920s British idea of using wire-netting to improve a muddy grass surface. Full-scale trials carried out by the Royal Engineers in early 1941 proved sufficiently encouraging to justify its mass production, and it was first used operationally in the North African campaign. The track consisted of wire mesh of 12 or 13 gauge with ⅜ inch (9.5mm) steel bearing rods threaded through transversely at 8 inch (200mm) intervals. Rolls measuring 10 feet 7 inches (3.25 metres) in width and 25 yards (23 metres) in length were linked together with 1½ x ⅜ inch (38mm x 9.5mm) flat steel bars, 5 yards (4.5m) in length, which were passed through loops at the end of the rods. Joints between sections were connected with metal buckles wound around the first and last bearing rods of each section. It was light, easily laid, and very practical not only for muddy runways, but also for beach surfaces in landing operations.
2. Peter Graham in his autobiography, *Skypilot; Memoirs from Take-Off to Landing*, 2001, Pentland Books, ISBN 1858219094; reproduced with his permission.
3. Interview with Flt Lt Hugh L. Parry, May 2005.
4. 41 Squadron ORB, 23 June 1943, TNA AIR 27/425.
5. Entry for 26 June 1943 in the logbook of Flt Lt Douglas Hone, via Dan Johnson.
6. The bomber force consisted of B-17 Flying Fortresses of the U.S. 8th Air Force's 91st, 92nd, 303rd, 305th, 306th, 351st, 379th, 381st, and 384th Bomb Groups.
7. B-17 Flying Fortress 42-30048 was subsequently salvaged by Luftwaffe, repaired and put into service with KG200 as A3+CE.
8. Source of USAAF data: *AchtungBABY*, http://achtungbaby.home.insightbb.com/ramrod_iii.htm (rtrvd May 2011).
9. The Luftwaffe claimed two Spitfires, nine Thunderbolts and six Flying Fortresses destroyed during Ramrod 108, whereas actual Allied losses were one Spitfire, five Thunderbolts and five Flying Fortresses. Conversely, Allied claims totalled two FW190s and one Me109 destroyed, two FW190s and one Me109 probably destroyed, and one of each damaged, whereas Luftwaffe declared losses were one Me109, which was Lt. Walter Rentsch of 2./JG2 in Me109G-3, Wk. Nr. 16271, Blue 10. Of the bomber crews, five men were killed in action, 13 evaded, and 32 became Prisoners of War. Five fighter pilots were also killed and one evaded (Sources: 11 Group ORB Appendix and *AchtungBABY*, http://achtungbaby.home.insightbb.com/ramrod_iii.htm, rtrvd May 2011.).
10. Entry for 28 June 1943 in the logbook of Fg Off Prince Emanuel Galitzine, via Dan Johnson.
11. As this was a non-operational sortie, the serial is not recorded in the 41 Squadron ORB on 29 June 1943. The incident is only recorded in Plt Off Herbert Wagner's logbook (via Dan Johnson).
12. Entry for 29 June 1943 in the logbook of Flt Lt Douglas H. Hone, via Dan Johnson.
13. Entry for 29 June 1943 in the logbook of Fg Off Prince Emanuel V. Galitzine, via Dan Johnson.
14. 41 Squadron ORB, 30 June 1943, TNA AIR 27/425.
15. Correspondence with Flt Lt Hugh Parry, May 2005.
16. 41 Squadron ORB, 1 July 1943, TNA AIR 27/425.

17. Ibid., 4 July 1943.
18. The 41 Squadron ORB on 4 July 1943 states they sighted 15 to 25 FW190s, whereas the 11 Group ORB Appendix states the number was 25 to 30.
19. 41 Squadron ORB, 4 July 1943, TNA AIR 27/425.
20. Ibid., 7 July 1943.
21. Ibid., 13 July 1943.
22. Ibid., 14 July 1943.
23. A copy of the article and photograph are pasted into the 41 Squadron ORB on 14 July 1943, but the newspaper and edition from which it was sourced are unknown.
24. Entry for 14 July 1943 in the logbook of Fg Off Ronald Johnson, via Dan Johnson.
25. This appears to be Captain (later Colonel) Carroll D. 'Dale' Briscoe (1921-2009) of the 306th Bomber Group, who served with the USAAF from 1941 to 1970.
26. Signal to Officers Commanding Biggin Hill, North Weald, Northolt, Tangmere, Kenley and Hornchurch from Headquarters 11 Group, relaying the signal to all concerned from General Anderson Commanding 8th U.S. Bomber Command, dated 15 July 1943, for distribution to Wing Commander Flying, and 41 and 91 Squadrons, stamped *No 41 SQUADRON 17 JUL 1943 ROYAL AIR FORCE*, 41 Squadron ORB, 15 July 1943, TNA AIR 27/425.
27. Entry for 15 July 1943 in the logbook of Prince Emanuel Galitzine, via Dan Johnson.
28. 41 Squadron ORB, 15 July 1943, TNA AIR 27/425.
29. The 11 Group ORB Appendix for June-September 1943, held in TNA AIR 25/206, does not contain the usual summary for Ramrod 144 on 16 July 1943. As such, the information within this table has been extracted from a weekly summary, which does not include the same amount of detail otherwise provided in this work.
30. 41 Squadron ORB, 16 July 1943, TNA AIR 27/425.
31. Ibid.
32. Ibid., 17 July 1943.
33. Ibid., 18 July 1943.
34. An Intelligence Report for the action on 18 July 1943 held in 41 Squadron's Archives, *41 Squadron. Tangmere Wing. Westhampnett. 18.7.43*, states the number of aircraft were 15-18 Me109G and two FW190s, whereas the Squadron ORB and 11 Group ORB Appendix both state there were 25-30 Me109s and "a few FW 190s".
35. The 41 Squadron ORB's F541 on 18 July 1943 states that Sqn Ldr Neil and Sgt Plt Peter Wall returned at 18:55, which is more-or-less the same time as the rest of the Squadron. However, the F540 indicates that the pair returned early when Neil developed trouble with his jettison tank and did not participate in the combats. The F541 entry is therefore erroneous and, as such, I have entered 'Unknown' for both men in the 'Time Down' column.
36. 41 Squadron ORB, 18 July 1943, TNA AIR 27/425.
37. Ibid.
38. Intelligence Report, *41 Squadron. Tangmere Wing. Westhampnett. 18.7.43*, 41 Squadron Archives.
39. Ibid.
40. 41 Squadron ORB, 18 July 1943, TNA AIR 27/425.
41. Correspondence from Ronald Johnson to Dan Johnson, 23 November 1982; reproduced with Dan's kind permission.
42. Source: Handwritten note, *Brief Report of Combat Ammunition Expenditure*, written by Flt Sgt G. Harris and addressed to the Squadron's Intelligence Officer, 18 July 1943, 41 Squadron Archives.
43. Tom Slack in his autobiography, *Happy is the Day; A Spitfire Pilot's Story*, 1987, United Writers Publications; reproduced with the Publisher's permission.
44. *Escape/Evasion Reports: Code M19/SPG*, Fg Off Thomas A. H. Slack, TNA WO 208/3314/1366.
45. Correspondence with Flt Lt Hugh L. Parry, May 2005.
46. Correspondence from Flt Lt Tom Slack to Dan Johnson, 20 February 1984; reproduced with Dan's kind permission.
47. For more information on Fg Off Thomas Slack's evasion, see Chapters 6, 7 and 8 of his autobiography, *Happy is the Day; A Spitfire Pilot's Story*, Tom Slack, 1987, United Writers Publications, ISBN 185200004X. His own sketch of his parachute descent on 18 July 1943 adorns the cover.
48. When asked about the origin of the nickname 'Pinkie', Sqn Ldr Glen's son Ian responded "I cannot give you a definitive answer but I think it is because my Dad was fair-skinned. This meant that he didn't tan when under the sun but turned a shade of pink. In his logbook, the Commander of 603 Sqdn. signed off his spell in Malta with the words "Bloody sorry to lose you Pinkie – short but sweet". It could well have been Malta where the name originated." [Correspondence with Ian Glen, February 2007]
49. Peter Graham in his autobiography, *Skypilot; Memoirs from Take-Off to Landing*, 2001, Pentland Books, ISBN 1858219094; reproduced with his permission.
50. Entry for 23 July 1943 in the logbook of Sgt Plt Peter Graham, via Dan Johnson.
51. 41 Squadron ORB, 23 July 1943, TNA AIR 27/425.
52. 88 Sqn. Boston IIIA, BZ399, was shot down by Hptm Hans Naumann of 6./JG26. The four crew, Fg Off J. B. Wilson RNZAF, Plt Off W. T. MacDonald, Flt Lt F. J. G. Partridge (Squadron Gunnery Officer), and Flt Sgt Thomas T. H. Hunt (RAF film crew), were captured. Naumann is reputed to have drunk a glass of Cognac with the four men, before they were sent into captivity.

53. 41 Squadron ORB, 26 July 1943, TNA AIR 27/425.
54. There is a slight anomaly between sources as the RAF Tangmere ORB states that 41 Squadron also participated in Exercise 'Eric' today, an interception of friendly bombers, but Forms 540 and 541 of 41 Squadron's ORB make no mention of it.
55. 41 Squadron ORB, 27 July 1943, TNA AIR 27/425.
56. Ibid., 29 July 1943.
57. Ibid.
58. The 41 Squadron ORB on 30 July 1943 place the location the Wing crossed in at "just west of Dieppe", whereas the 11 Group ORB Appendix states the bombers and escort Wings crossed in five miles east of St. Valéry.
59. 41 Squadron ORB, 30 July 1943, TNA AIR 27/425.
60. Ibid., 31 July 1943.
61. Fg Off David Davies and Flt Sgt Stanley May departed Friston again by air at 13:40 and reached Westhampnett at 13:55.
62. Unfortunately, very little detail is available on Ramrod 181 as the usual summary for the operation is missing from the 11 Group ORB Appendix at the National Archives in TNA AIR 25/206. The details below are therefore extracted from a month-end summary in the same file, and from details provided in 41 Squadron's ORB.
63. Entry for 31 July 1943 in the logbook of Fg Off Ronald Johnson; via Dan Johnson.
64. 41 Squadron ORB, 31 July 1943, TNA AIR 27/425.
65. The source of this nominal roll is the Squadron ORB of 31 July 1943. It lists all names with initials only, and forenames have been added by the author.
66. Entry for 4 August 1943 in the logbook of Plt Off Ross Harding; via Dan Johnson.
67. 41 Squadron ORB, 4 August 1943, TNA AIR 27/425.
68. Ibid., 5 August 1943.
69. Combat Report for Fg Off Clive R. Birbeck, 5 August 1943, 41 Squadron Archives.
70. 41 Squadron ORB, 5 August 1943, TNA AIR 27/425.
71. Ibid., 6 August 1943.
72. Ibid., 8 August 1943.
73. Ibid., 9 August 1943.
74. RAF Tangmere ORB, 9 August 1943, TNA AIR 28/815.
75. Typewritten document titled *RAMROD 191*, 9 August 1943, 41 Squadron Archives. This data has been laid out as close to the original format as possible.
76. RAF Tangmere ORB, 11 August 1943, TNA AIR 28/815.
77. Entry for 11 August 1943 in the logbook of Fg Off Ross P. Harding; via Dan Johnson.
78. This weather reconnaissance on 11 August 1943 is only recorded on the Squadron ORB's F541, and is not mentioned on the ORB's F540 or in the RAF Tangmere ORB.
79. 41 Squadron ORB, 11 August 1943, TNA AIR 27/425.
80. The Squadron ORB's F541 records the second pilot as Fg Off Benjamin Newman, whereas the F540 states the second pilot was Sgt Plt Alan Hope.
81. 41 Squadron ORB, 11 August 1943, TNA AIR 27/425.
82. As the exercise was non-operational by its very nature, the participants and their serials are not recorded on the Squadron ORB's F541 on 12 August 1943.
83. There are a few ambiguities in the Squadron ORB on 15 August 1943. First, the entry on the F540 for 14 August appears to have been merged with that of 15 August, and there is no separate entry for the latter date. Additionally, the F540 states that "visibility was so poor that they returned to base", whereas the F541 states "the weather over the target area was too clear for an attack to be made".
84. 41 Squadron ORB, 16 August 1943, TNA AIR 27/425.
85. Although established as an airfield during World War I and used by the RAF, Bryas Sud [Brias], appears to have only been used by the Luftwaffe during World War II. A grass airfield, located a couple of miles northeast of St. Pol-sur-Ternoise in the Pas-de-Calais Department, it was used by Jagdgeschwader 2 (JG2) in 1941, and the tactical reconnaissance unit 5(F)./123 was formed there in January 1943. It is understood to have comprised a few hangars constructed by the Luftwaffe and a bunker for the Fighter Controller [Jafü/Jagdführer].
86. 41 Squadron ORB, 17 August 1943, TNA AIR 27/425.
87. Ibid.
88. Ibid., 18 August 1943.
89. Entry for 18 August 1943 in the logbook of Fg Off Ronald Johnson; via Dan Johnson.
90. It is not clear why Flt Sgt James Still was landing at Hawkinge on 18 August 1943, just 15 minutes after the 41 Squadron ORB's F541 records him landing at Westhampnett on return from Ramrod 208.
91. 11 Group ORB Appendix, 19 August 1943, TNA AIR 25/206.
92. The Koolhoven F.K.58 was a single-engined fighter built under licence in the Netherlands for the French Air Force [Armée de l'Air], and were in service from January 1939 to May 1940. As only about 18 were ever built, and as it is believed that all airframes surviving after the Battle of France were scrapped during the German occupation, it is doubtful whether they were the fighters seen by the Northolt Wing on 19 August 1943.

93. The Squadron ORB's F541 on 19 August 1943 states that Fg Off Ronald Johnson's "tank would not jettison", but Johnson contradicts this in his logbook, recording instead, "R.T. & Flap indicator u/s…".[Entry of 19 August 1943 in the logbook of Fg Off Ronald Johnson; via Dan Johnson]
94. The 41 Squadron ORB on 19 August 1943 states the cloud cover was 10/10ths cloud at 6,000-7,000 feet whereas the 11 Group ORB Appendix states the cloud cover was 9/10ths-10/10ths at 3,000 feet.
95. 11 Group ORB Appendix, 19 August 1943, TNA AIR 25/206.
96. Entry for 19 August 1943 in the logbook of Flt Sgt Jim C. J. Payne; via Dan Johnson.
97. 41 Squadron ORB, 19 August 1943, TNA AIR 27/425.
98. Ibid., 20 August 1943.
99. The 41 Squadron ORB states that the target of the Ramrod was Abbeville Aerodrome, whereas the 11 Group ORB Appendix states it was Abbeville Marshalling Yards. It is understood that the latter of these is correct.
100. 11 Group ORB Appendix, 20 August 1943, TNA AIR 25/206.
101. 41 Squadron ORB, 20 August 1943, TNA AIR 27/425.
102. Ibid., 21 August 1943.
103. Ibid., 22 August 1943.
104. Entry for 22 August 1943 in the logbook of Fg Off Herbert A. Wagner; via Dan Johnson.
105. The 41 Squadron ORB on 24 August 1943 states that the Spitfire XII Wing acted as "escort cover to bombers going to Bernay airfield [sic]", however the 11 Group ORB makes it clear that no bombers were involved in Part IV of Ramrod 215, and no further mention of bombers is made in the text of the Squadron ORB. As such, and in view of the Spitfire XII Wing's activity in the broader context of Group operations, it is believed that the Squadron ORB entry is incorrect and that the Wing acted independently as a fighter sweep only.
106. The RAF Tangmere ORB (TNA AIR 28/815) names this operation on 25 August 1943 as Ramrod 15A. However, this is erroneous as it is both out of number sequence and omits the Operation 'Starkey' 'S' prefix. 41 Squadron's ORB does not name the operation, but the 11 Group ORB Appendix (TNA AIR 25/206) indicates the operation was Ramrod S.2.
107. The 11 Group ORB Appendix for June-September 1943, held in TNA AIR 25/206, does not contain the usual summary for Ramrod S.2 of 25 August 1943. As such, the information within this table has been extracted from a weekly summary, which does not include the same amount of detail otherwise provided in this work.
108. The summary for Ramrod S.5 on 26 August 1943 is included in the 11 Group ORB Appendix for June-September 1943 (TNA AIR 25/206), but lacks the usual detail on participating squadrons, and only names the Wings. As such, the information within this table does not include the same amount of detail otherwise provided in this work.
109. There is a slight contradiction between the 41 Squadron ORB and 11 Group ORB Appendix on 27 August 1943, as the Squadron F541 states the pilots were airborne from Westhampnett at 08:40, whereas the 11 Group ORB Appendix states 08:40 was the rendezvous time at Selsey.
110. The Tangmere Wing ORB on 27 August 1943 even suggests the target was "ammunition dumps at Worton [sic], North of St. Omer".
111. No contemporary work provides a cause for Fg Off Douglas Haywood's loss. His POW Repatriation Questionnaire does not state what happened, rather only that he was not wounded.
112. 41 Squadron ORB, 27 August 1943, TNA AIR 27/425.
113. Liberation Report for Flt Lt Leslie Prickett, MI9, 7 Nov 1945, *Liberation Reports*, TNA WO 208/3340/1561.
114. 41 Squadron ORB, 27 August 1943, TNA AIR 27/425.
115. Ibid.
116. Correspondence from Flt Lt Douglas Hone AE to Dan Johnson, 15 January 1984; reproduced with Dan's kind permission.
117. 41 Squadron ORB, 28 August 1943, TNA AIR 27/425.
118. Ibid., 29 August 1943.
119. The pilot, Plt Off Clarence O. Motheral RCAF and navigator-bombardier Plt Off William J. Dumsdory RCAF, both baled out, evaded capture and returned to the United Kingdom. Flt Sgt Victor E. Scuse and Sgt Eifion Lewis were both killed.
120. 41 Squadron ORB, 31 August 1943, TNA AIR 27/425.
121. The Squadron ORB on 31 August 1943 lists all names with initials only. Forenames have been added by the author.
122. 41 Squadron ORB, 2 September 1943, TNA AIR 27/425.
123. Entry for 2 September 1943 in the logbook of Fg Off Prince Emanuel Galitzine, via Dan Johnson.
124. 41 Squadron ORB, 2 September 1943, TNA AIR 27/425.
125. Ibid.
126. Ibid., 3 September 1943.
127. The pilot lost by 131 Squadron was O-660240 Lt Franklin David Burt USAAF, of the 12th Reconnaissance Squadron, 67th Reconnaissance Group, who was attached to 131 Squadron RAF to gain operational experience. Burt's body was not recovered and he is remembered today on the Tablets of the Missing at the Cambridge American Cemetery and Memorial, Madingley, Cambridgeshire.
128. The 41 Squadron ORB on 4 September 1943 contains two ambiguities. The F541 states the pilots took off for the day's second Ramrod at 17:50, whereas the F540 states the time was 17:50 in the third [time] column, and 17:30

in the fourth [summary of events] column. Additionally, the F540 states the target was St. Pol Airfield, whereas the 91 Squadron ORB, RAF Tangmere ORB, 11 Group ORB and 11 Group ORB Appendix all indicate that the target was actually St. Pol Marshalling Yards.
129. 41 Squadron ORB, 4 September 1943, TNA AIR 27/425.
130. Ibid.
131. Peter Graham in his autobiography, *Skypilot; Memoirs from Take-Off to Landing*, 2001, Pentland Books, ISBN 1858219094; reproduced with his permission.
132. The National Archives holds two reports for Fg Off Birbeck's action on 4 September 1943 in TNA AIR 50/18, one being his own personal Combat Report, No. 107, and the other an Intelligence Report providing more detail than his Combat Report, Nos. 105-106.
133. Combat Report for Fg Off Clive R. Birbeck, No. 105, 4 September 1943, TNA AIR 50/18.
134. Unfortunately, little detail is available on Part IV as the page covering this part of the Ramrod is missing from the 11 Group ORB Appendix (AIR 25/206) at the National Archives. As such, I have been unable to establish the squadrons comprising the escort for the 36 Marauders that bombed Hazebrouck Marshalling Yards, and only a summary of Operation 'Starkey' provides a brief synopsis of the results.
135. 11 Group ORB Appendix, 5 September 1943, TNA AIR 25/206.
136. *Intelligence Form "F"*, handwritten report on the loss of Fg Off Robert J. Boyd, 6 September 1943, 41 Squadron Archives.
137. Kigass was a priming pump used to prime Griffon engines, which was mounted in the lower right hand side of the cockpit.
138. 41 Squadron ORB, 6 September 1943, TNA AIR 27/425.
139. Excerpt from a letter to Fg Off Robert J. Boyd's father, Mr Walter Boyd, from Fg Off Harry Smith, 41 Squadron's Adjutant, dated 7 September 1943. Reproduced with the kind permission of Steve Bracey.
140. 41 Squadron ORB, 6 September 1943, TNA AIR 27/425.
141. 41 Squadron's ORB for 7 September 1943 is unclear as to the destination of today's operation. The F540 only states, "a target in occupied France", and the F541 erroneously states, "to St Mayo marshalling yards". However, the RAF Tangmere ORB (albeit incorrectly in the entry for 6 September 1943, instead of 7 September) and the 11 Group ORB Appendix both clarify that the Spitfire XII Wing participated in Part III of Ramrod S.38, in which the target was St. Omer Marshalling Yards.
142. 41 Squadron ORB, 7 September 1943, TNA AIR 27/425.
143. Ibid., 8 September 1943.
144. Ibid.
145. Ibid.
146. Ibid.
147. Ibid.
148. Ibid., 9 September 1943.
149. Flt Sgt Jim C. J. Payne's early return from Ramrod 216 on 11 September 1943 is only recorded in his logbook and is not mentioned in the Squadron ORB.
150. Entry for 13 September 1943 in the logbook of Fg Off Peter Cowell, 13 September 1943; via Dan Johnson.
151. 41 Squadron ORB, 13 September 1943, TNA AIR 27/425.
152. 41 Squadron's ORB's F540 appears to be missing the entry for 14 September 1943. Although the date itself is missing, the details of Ramrod 218 are erroneously included in the entry for 13 September at 16:55. The F541 entries are, however, included as normal.
153. 11 Group ORB Appendix, 15 September 1943, TNA AIR 25/206.
154. 41 Squadron ORB, 15 September 1943, TNA AIR 27/425.
155. Entry for 15 September 1943 in the logbook of Flt Lt Arthur A. Glen; via his son Mike.
156. 11 Group ORB Appendix, 15 September 1943, TNA AIR 25/206.
157. Source: Untitled document outlining orders for the Spitfire XII Wing's participation in Ramrod 223 on 16 September 1943, 41 Squadron Archives. The table is laid out as close to the original format as possible.
158. *Intelligence Form 'F' Ramrod 223 Part I Tangmere Spitfire XII Wing. Westhampnett.*, Intelligence Report for 16 September 1943, 41 Squadron Archives.
159. 41 Squadron ORB, 16 September 1943, TNA AIR 27/425.
160. Combat Report for Fg Off Benjamin B. Newman, No. 321, TNA AIR 50/18.
161. Ibid.
162. 41 Squadron ORB, 16 September 1943, TNA AIR 27/425.
163. 11 Group ORB Appendix, 18 September 1943, TNA AIR 25/206.
164. *TANG/176 19 SEPT.*, Intelligence Report from RAF Tangmere to 11 Group, 19 September 1943, 41 Squadron Archives.
165. *Ramrod 232 I, Intelligence Form "F"*, Intelligence Report for the Westhampnett Wing, 19 September 1943, 41 Squadron Archives.
166. Entry for 19 September 1943 in the logbook of Fg Off Herbert A. Wagner, via Dan Johnson.

167. In achieving his victory, Wg Cdr Raymond Harries had expended 208 rounds of cannon and 552 rounds of machine gun ammunition. 91 Squadron's Flt Lt John Doll had expended 116 rounds of cannon and 480 rounds of machine gun to achieve his own two victories.
168. *Ramrod 232 I, Intelligence Form "F"*, Intelligence Report for the Westhampnett Wing, 19 September 1943, 41 Squadron Archives.
169. Another Intelligence Report in 41 Squadron's Archives, *TANG/176 19 SEPT.* (Intelligence Report from RAF Tangmere to 11 Group, 19 September 1943), states he "was seen to peel off for no apparent reason".
170. A letter from Sqn Ldr Bernard Ingham and a memo from Flt Lt Arthur Glen, both of which are held in Flt Sgt Stanley May's Casualty File [NAA *Correspondence files, multiple number (Melbourne) series (Primary numbers 1-323)*, Series A705, Barcode 1073726.], state that they believed that May's R/T system had malfunctioned, which explained why no-one heard anything from him and why he did not respond to calls by Glen to rejoin the Squadron. May makes no mention of his R/T malfunctioning in any of his reports from the time, but aviation researcher Dan Johnson met May at a 1986 Squadron reunion, at which time he told Johnson that this was indeed the case [Correspondence with Dan Johnson, April 2010].
171. 11 Group ORB Appendix, 19 September 1943, TNA AIR 25/206.
172. Entry for 19 September 1943 in the logbook of Flt Sgt Jim C. J. Payne, via Dan Johnson.
173. Letter from Sqn Ldr Bernard Ingham to Flt Sgt Stanley May's mother, dated 21 September 1943, held in May's RAAF Casualty File, NAA *Correspondence files, multiple number (Melbourne) series (Primary numbers 1-323)*, Series A705, Barcode 1073726.
174. Flt Sgt Stanley H. May's aircraft was excavated in July 2009 by Belgian aircraft archaeologists, Dirk Decuypere and Wim Huyghe, the former of whom wrote to the author, "We did find much less than we had expected but we still found sufficient evidence that we dug on the crash-site of Stan May's Spitfire.... [...] Stan May was right when he wrote in his evasion report… that when he returned to his aircraft and saw it inverted half sunk in the soil. We surmise a lot had been removed by the Germans and maybe also by civilians later so that we did not find the mass of wreckage that we had found in all our previous excavations. Apart from several fragments from the motor (on one fragment we can read 'Griffon'), we recovered one of the 20mm cannons and quite some smaller parts that once they are cleaned will reveal other details."[E-mail correspondence with Dirk Decuypere, July 2009.]
175. Evasion Report for Flt Sgt Stanley H. May, *Escape/Evasion Reports: Code MI9/SPG*, 11 November 1943, TNA WO 208/3316/1546.
176. NAA *Correspondence files, multiple number (Melbourne) series (Primary numbers 1-323)*, Series A705, Barcode 1073726.
177. After returning to the United Kingdom, now WO Stanley May was interrogated by Intelligence Officers, and did not return to 41 Squadron. As was generally the case in such situations (41 Squadron's Tom Slack being a notable exception), May was removed from the Theatre and sent to the Pacific. He arrived in Australia on 22 January 1944, and was posted to OTU in Mildura, likely for a refresher course, in March. May was commissioned on 1 June 1944 and posted to 79 Squadron RAAF at Los Negros, in the Admiralty Islands, two weeks later. He was promoted to Flying Officer in December 1944 and remained with 79 Squadron, flying Spitfires in the southwest Pacific, until mid-February 1945. Returning to Australia, he was given 42 days leave and then spent a short period as a ferry pilot before his discharge and demobilisation in late August 1945. After the War, May opened a jewellers business, which is still in the family, and passed away in July 2002.
178. The Squadron ORB's F540 on 19 September 1943 provides information on the morning's Ramrod 232, but makes no mention of the afternoon's Ramrod 233. However, the F541 lists ten pilots participating in the operation between 17:00 and 18:10, and the RAF Tangmere ORB and 11 Group ORB Appendix also confirm the Squadron's participation in Ramrod 233.
179. Jerzy Józef Krzysztofiński remained in the United Kingdom after the War, was granted British citizenship in 1950 and adopted the English name George Kingsley.
180. The crew of Mitchell II, FL683, that was shot down at Hesdin on 21 September 1943 were Fg Off Arthur G. G. Atkins (Pilot), Fg Off Samuel A. R. Tanner (Navigator), Flt Sgt Allan R. Breakspear (Aimer) and Sgt Kenneth S. H. Lawson (AG). All are buried in Noyellette Communal Cemetery, 13km west of Arras, Pas-de-Calais, and are the only Commonwealth War Graves Commission burials in this cemetery.
181. 11 Group ORB Appendix, 21 September 1943, TNA AIR 25/206.
182. Ibid., 22 September 1943.
183. The 41 Squadron ORB on 22 September 1943 clarifies that "five or 6 F.W. 190s" were seen below, whereas Wg Cdr Raymond Harries, in Part IV, Combat Cuts for September 1943 in the 11 Group ORB Appendix merely states he saw, "several E/A" approach.
184. Wg Cdr Raymond Harries Combat Report, summarised, in Part IV, Combat Cuts, for September 1943, 11 Group ORB Appendix, TNA AIR 25/206.
185. Combat Report for Fg Off Clive R Birbeck, No. 109, TNA AIR 27/425.
186. Fg Off Clive R. Birbeck initially claimed this 22 September 1943 victory as one FW190 destroyed but a hand-written annotation on his Combat Report (No. 109, TNA AIR 27/425) indicates it was only "admitted probably destroyed". However, Birbeck's *Pilot Service Record*, 41 Squadron's own internal record of each pilots' service, suggests

it may indeed have finally been accepted as destroyed, as it is shown as such on his service sheet and carried through on this record until his departure from the Squadron in July 1944. In this work, however, only the 'official' record, his Combat Report, has been followed, and he is thus shown here as achieving a probable victory, not a definitive victory.
187. Combat Report for Sgt Plt William H. Vann, No. 407, 22 September 1943, TNA AIR 50/18.
188. Combat Report for Flt Lt Donald H. Smith, No. 378, 22 September 1943, TNA AIR 50/18.
189. There is also an anomaly in the 41 Squadron ORB on 22 September 1943 as the F540 states that "in the general mix up, F/O B.B. Newman attacked and probably destroyed an FW 190. ---- confirmed by S/Ldr. Kynaston of 91 Squadron". The F541 also states, "F/O Newman 1 PROBABLE" but fails to mention Flt Lt Donald Smith's victory. However, Newman was not a participant in the Ramrod, and there is no mention of Newman in other documents such as the RAF Tangmere ORB, the 11 Group ORB, and the 11 Group ORB Appendix, all of which list the victory claims made by pilots involved in the operation. Additionally, no Combat Report exists for Newman, who is otherwise known to have claimed victories on 16 September, 24 September, and 20 October 1943.
190. 41 Squadron ORB, 22 September 1943, TNA AIR 27/425.
191. Fg Off Clive Birbeck lists his location on his Air/Sea Rescue Questionnaire as "25 miles S. of Ford"; the Squadron ORB on 22 September 1943 states his position was "about 20 miles South of Ford"; and the 11 Group ORB Appendix states his location was "15-20 miles SE. Selsey". All of these locations are, however, more-or-less the same.
192. 11 Group ORB Appendix, 23 September 1943, TNA AIR 25/206.
193. 41 Squadron ORB, 23 September 1943, TNA AIR 27/425.
194. Ibid.
195. Entry for 23 September 1943 in the logbook of Flt Lt Arthur A. Glen; via Mike Glen and reproduced with his permission.
196. 41 Squadron ORB, 23 September 1943, TNA AIR 27/425.
197. Ibid., 24 September 1943.
198. 11 Group ORB Appendix, 24 September 1943, TNA AIR 25/206.
199. 41 Squadron ORB, 24 September 1943, TNA AIR 27/425.
200. Ibid.
201. Whilst the 41 Squadron ORB on 24 September 1943 states that command of the Wing was handed over to Flt Lt 'Pinkie' Glen, in reviewing the events of this day with Hugh Parry in 2011, he recalled that command was actually handed over to him.
202. Fg Off Ross Harding returned from Ramrod 243 on 24 September 1943, recording the reason in his logbook was "engine trouble", and lists his aircraft's serial as MB837. This contradicts the Squadron ORB for this operation, which not only does not mention his return but also shows him flying MB839. *Spitfire; The History* (Morgan & Shacklady, 1999) indicates that MB839 transferred to 91 Squadron on 11 June 1943, whereas MB837 served on 41 Squadron from around August 1943 through to at least July 1944. This therefore suggests that the serial Harding recorded in his logbook, MB837, is in fact correct, and that it is the ORB that is erroneous.
203. 41 Squadron ORB, 24 September 1943, TNA AIR 27/425.
204. The 41 Squadron ORB for 24 September 1943 and the Westhampnett Wing's Intelligence Report for the Ramrod both state that ten FW190s dived past 41 and 91 Squadrons, whereas the 11 Group ORB Appendix for the operation states they were 15 Me109s.
205. Combat Report for Flt Lt Arthur A. Glen, No. 233, 24 September 1943, TNA AIR 50/18.
206. 41 Squadron ORB, 24 September 1943, TNA AIR 27/425.
207. Combat Report for Fg Off Prince Emanuel V. Galitzine, No. 217, 24 September 1943, TNA AIR 50/18.
208. Combat Report for Fg Off Benjamin B. Newman, No. 323, 24 September 1943, TNA AIR 50/18.
209. Ibid.
210. *Intelligence Form 'F' Tangmere Sector, Ramrod 243 Part I* [sic], 24 September 1943, 41 Squadron Archives.
211. Combat Report for Sqn Ldr Norman A. Kynaston, 91 Squadron, No. 50, 24 September 1943, TNA AIR 50/39.
212. Combat Report for Flt Lt John C. S. Doll, 91 Squadron, No. 23, 24 September 1943, TNA AIR 50/39.
213. Ibid.
214. Flt Lt Glen's, and Fg Offs Galitzine and Newman's combat films are all held today in the Imperial War Museum. See Appendix XIII (Extant Combat Films) for further information.
215. 41 Squadron ORB, 24 September 1943, TNA AIR 27/425.
216. *Intelligence Form 'F' Tangmere Sector, Ramrod 243 Part I* [sic], 24 September 1943, 41 Squadron Archives.
217. http://www.nzfpm.org.nz/article.asp?id=stenborg (rtrvd Aug 2011).
218. Entry for 24 September 1943 in the logbook of Fg Off Prince Emanuel V. Galitzine; via Dan Johnson.
219. Entry for 24 September 1943 in the logbook of Flt Lt Arthur A Glen; reproduced with the permission of his son Mike.
220. Citation for the award of a Bar to the DFC for Flt Lt Arthur A. Glen, 2 November 1943, London Gazette Issue 36235. This information is licensed under the terms of the Open Government Licence (http://www.nationalarchives.gov.uk/doc/open-government-licence/).
221. Correspondence from Ronald Johnson to Dan Johnson, 23 November 1982; reproduced with Dan's kind permission.

222. Correspondence with Flt Lt Hugh L. Parry, May 2005.
223. This was 1st Lt. Paul Pascal of Philadelphia, who was the navigator of USAAF B-17F Flying Fortress 42-5865 'Janie' (100th Bomber Group, 351st Bomber Squadron) which crashed at Bailleul, about 7 km west of St. André-de-l'Eure on 3 September 1943.
224. Missing notice for Flt Lt Hugh L. Parry, *The Times*, edition of 3 December 1943.
225. Interview with Flt Lt Hugh L. Parry, November 2008.
226. During a trip to France with his wife in June 1952, Hugh Parry went to look for Jeanette Huet in Avenue President Wilson. They were informed that she had moved but the people they spoke to knew where she was and they were able to meet again in a tearful and happy reunion and shared stories. Jeanette explained she had been taken out to be shot three times, and on the last occasion was only saved by the intervention of the Swiss Ambassador, who said to the Germans, in essence, "You've lost the War. We know who is in the prison and will know who is missing, if anyone is shot. We also know who you are and will therefore make sure you are held accountable. Jeanette believed this is what had saved her.
227. Correspondence with Flt Lt Hugh L. Parry, May 2005.
228. Liberation Report for Flt Lt Hugh L. Parry, *Liberation reports*, TNA WO 208/3339/1057.
229. Sqn Ldr Roger J. Bushell led the escape from the tunnel 'Harry' in the 'Great Escape' from Stalag Luft III on 24-25 March 1944, but was arrested the following day trying to board a train at Saarbrücken railway station. He was one of the fifty men executed by the Gestapo on 29 March 1944. Awarded a posthumous Mention in Despatches for his services as a Prisoner of War in June 1946, he is buried today in the Old Garrison Cemetery in Poznań, Poland.
230. Correspondence with Flt Lt Hugh L. Parry, May 2005.
231. Flt Lt Hugh Parry returned to Rhodesia in July 1945, where he was employed as a surveyor by Mufulira Cooper Mines. By 1947, he had become Assistant Chief Surveyor and married the same year. Between 1952 and 1968, Parry was Chief Surveyor for the Chibuluma, Chambishi & Kalengwa Mines, after which he left Rhodesia and moved to South Africa, employed as a surveyor with the Durban Corporation City Engineering Department for the ensuing 13 years. He retired in 1983 and returned to the United Kingdom, and was still residing in Wiltshire at the time of writing.
232. Prince Emanuel V. Galitzine was employed as a civil aviation pilot until 1952, when he joined the Royal Auxiliary Air Force as a Flight Lieutenant for five years on the active list and five years in reserve. Only two-and-a-half years later, however, he found employment with Avro and was transferred to the Reserve, but did not actually relinquish his commission until February 1962. At this time, he emigrated to Peru to found Aero Condos Aircraft Company, trading in aircraft parts. Galitzine returned to the United Kingdom in 1991, where he was briefly employed by Air Foyle. He died in London in December 2002, aged 84.
233. RAF Tangmere ORB, 26 September 1943, TNA AIR 28/815.
234. Sgt Plt Peter Graham's Combat Report on 27 September 1943 (No. 234, TNA AIR 50/18) states it was a group of "15 mixed enemy aircraft", presumably Me109s and FW190s, whereas 41 Squadron's ORB states they were "a bunch of ME. 109Gs".
235. 41 Squadron ORB, TNA AIR 27/425, 27 September 1943.
236. Combat Report for Sgt Plt Peter B. Graham, No. 234, 27 September 1932, TNA AIR 50/18.
237. Fg Off Clive Birbeck's and Sgt Plt Peter Graham's combat films are all held today in the Imperial War Museum. See Appendix XIII (Extant Combat Films) for further information.
238. *Pilot Service Record* for Sgt Plt Peter B. Graham, 41 Squadron Archives.
239. Wg Cdr Raymond H. Harries in *Combat Cuts* for 27 September 1943, 11 Group ORB Appendix, TNA AIR 25/206.
240. Flt Lt David Fearon's combat film has survived and is held in the Imperial War Museum. See Appendix XIII (Extant Combat Films).
241. Flt Lt Richard Easby's Combat Report states that Fg Off Albert O'Shaughnessy's Me109 burst into flames whereas O'Shaughnessy's Combat Report states the Me109 blew up in mid-air.
242. 11 Group ORB Appendix, 27 September 1943, TNA AIR 25/206.
243. 41 Squadron ORB, TNA AIR 27/425, 27 September 1943.
244. 11 Group ORB, 27 September 1943, TNA AIR 25/194.
245. 41 Squadron ORB, entry for 28-30 September 1943, TNA AIR 27/425.
246. Ibid.
247. *Sector Intelligence Office, R.A.F. Tangmere, Daily Intelligence Sheet Vol. 3 No. 269. Part I*, 28 September 1943, 41 Squadron Archives.
248. The 11 Group ORB on 30 September 1943 contradicts this statement slightly, stating that as top-scorer in 11 Group that month, 91 Squadron had actually claimed 18 enemy aircraft destroyed, two more than referred to in Sir Archibald Sinclair's congratulatory message.
249. 41 Squadron ORB, entry for 28-30 September 1943, TNA AIR 27/425.
250. Ibid.
251. 41 Squadron ORB, 3 October 1943, TNA AIR 27/425. The ORB does not provide any information on the reason for the cancellation of Flt Sgt William H. Vann's flight, which is an unusual term to use in any case, but it may have

been that engine trouble had hindered his participation. Additionally, the Squadron F541 indicates that he landed at Manston in MB798 but his flight was cancelled on MB797. That said, the F541 also indicates that Flt Sgt Jim Payne arrived at, and departed from, Manston in MB797 at the same time, so it is likely that Vann's aircraft was MB798 on both occasions, and that the listing of MB797 is erroneous.

252. Two of the crew of 88 Squadron Boston BZ316, Sgt G. G. K. Gray and Sgt Addison, survived and were rescued by 277 (ASR) Squadron Walrus W3097, but Sgt Ronald G. Bickel was killed. Similarly, two of the crew of BZ322, Flt Sgt W. D. D. Davies and Sgt J. Batson, survived and were rescued by 277 (ASR) Squadron Walrus HD908, but Fg Off Robert Christie was killed.
253. 342 Squadron Boston BZ319 crashed into the Seine River near the Pont de Tolbiac bridge in Paris and the crew were killed. Lt Yves F. Lamy (pilot), Adjt Louis Balchen (navigator), and Sgts Jacques Jouniaux (gunner) and Robert Rousserie (WO/AG) are remembered today on a plaque on the bridge. Two of the crew of BZ388, Lt Jean Barlier (alias of Jean-Annet d'Astier de la Vigerie), and Sgt Jean Godin, were captured, but Lt Yves Lucchesi and Sgt Guy Marulli de Barletta both evaded.
254. These were 88 Squadron Boston II's BZ316 and BZ322, and the crew killed were Sgt Ronald G. Bickel of the former aircraft and Fg. Off Robert Christie of the latter.
255. 41 Squadron ORB, 3 October 1943, TNA AIR 27/425.
256. Entry for 3 October 1943 in the logbook of Fg Off Ronald Johnson; via Dan Johnson.
257. *Pilot Service Record* for Flt Sgt James A. B. Gray, 41 Squadron Archives.
258. 41 Squadron ORB, 3 October 1943, TNA AIR 27/425.
259. Entry for 3 October 1943 in the logbook of Fg Off Ronald Johnson; via Dan Johnson.
260. *TANG/267 3/OCT*, Intelligence Report for Ramrod 259 from RAF Tangmere to 11 Group, 3 October 1943, 41 Squadron Archives.
261. 41 Squadron ORB, 4 October 1943, TNA AIR 27/425.
262. Ibid.
263. RAF Tangmere ORB, 4 October 1943, TNA AIR 28/815.
264. 11 Group ORB Appendix, 9 October 1943, TNA AIR 25/207.
265. Entry for 9 October 1943 in the logbook of Fg Off Peter Cowell; via Dan Johnson.
266. Correspondence from Ronald Johnson to Dan Johnson, 26 September 1984; reproduced with Dan's kind permission.
267. The 41 Squadron ORB on 13 October 1943 states that the wing of Fg Off Herbert Wagner's aircraft was damaged by Flak. However, this statement appears to be erroneous, as Wagner's flying logbook and both his and WO James W. Still's Combat Reports state that it was Still's wing (MB838) that was hit by Flak.
268. Combat Report for WO James W. Still, 13 October 1943, 41 Squadron Archives.
269. Both combat films still exist, and are held today in the collections of the Imperial War Museum. See Appendix XIII (Extant Combat Films) for details.
270. Entry for 14 October 1943 in the logbook of Flt Lt Donald H. Smith; via Dan Johnson.
271. 41 Squadron ORB, 14 October 1943, TNA AIR 27/425.
272. This aircraft was likely RAF Bassingbourn (Station 121) based B-17 Flying Fortress, 42-29741, 'Corn State Terror', of 91st Bomber Group, 324th Bomber Squadron.
273. Flt Lt Donald H. Smith and Flt Sgt Alan Hope are listed on the Squadron ORB's F541 on 15 October 1943 as having made a flight between 17:50 and 18:40 to guide in a lost bomber, but this is an erroneous entry that mirrors the previous afternoon's flight by the same two men with the same aircraft and timings, in which they unsuccessfully sought to locate a Flying Fortress 40 miles south of Selsey Bill. See 14 October 1943.
274. 41 Squadron ORB, 15 October 1943, TNA AIR 27/425.
275. Entry for 15 October 1943 in the logbook of Fg Off Herbert A. Wagner; via Dan Johnson.
276. *TANG/312 17/OCT*, Intelligence Report from RAF Tangmere to 11 Group, 17 October 1943, 41 Squadron Archives.
277. 41 Squadron's Blue, Green and Black Sections are referred to in the Squadron's F540 and in an Intelligence Report on 17 October 1943, but the pilots and aircraft serials are erroneously omitted from the F541.
278. B Flight's patrol between 12:15 and 13:20 is not mentioned on either the F540 or the F541 of the Squadron's ORB on 17 October 1943. The only reference appears to be on an Intelligence Report, *TANG/318 17/OCT EXERCISE PIRATE*, dated 17 October 1943, in 41 Squadron's Archives.
279. 41 Squadron ORB, 20 October 1943, TNA AIR 27/425.
280. *Rodeo 263, Intelligence Form "F", Tangmere Wing*, 20 October 1943, 41 Squadron Archives. The original quote actually states "vector 100° flat out", but analysis other information provided in the Intelligence Report, particularly the fact the Wing turned northeast but did not find the aircraft, suggests that 100° is a typing error and that the vector would have actually been 010° (north-northeast).
281. Ibid.
282. 91 Squadron ORB, 20 October 1943, TNA AIR 27/740.
283. Combat Report for Wg Cdr Raymond H. Harries, No. 5, 20 October 1943, TNA AIR 50/443.
284. Combat Report for Sqn Ldr Norman A. Kynaston, 91 Squadron, No. 51, 20 October 1943, TNA AIR 50/39.
285. *Rodeo 263, Intelligence Form "F", Tangmere Wing*, 20 October 1943, 41 Squadron Archives.

286. Combat Report for Flt Lt John C. S. Doll, 91 Squadron, No. 25, 20 October 1943, TNA AIR 50/39.
287. Ibid.
288. Combat Report for Flt Sgt Raymond S. Nash, 91 Squadron, No.20, 20 October 1943, TNA AIR 50/39.
289. Combat Report for Fg Off Benjamin B. Newman, No. 324, 20 October 1943, TNA AIR 50/18.
290. Ibid.
291. Entry for 20 October 1943 in the logbook of Fg Off Peter Cowell; via Dan Johnson.
292. Correspondence from Flt Lt Peter Cowell to Dan Johnson, 24 April 1984; reproduced with Dan's kind permission.
293. Combat Report for Fg Off Ronald T. H. Collis, No. 157, 20 October 1943, TNA AIR 50/18.
294. *Rodeo 263, Intelligence Form "F", Tangmere Wing*, 20 October 1943, 41 Squadron Archives.
295. Ibid.
296. Entry for 20 October 1943 in logbook of Fg Off Ronald T. H. Collis, via Dan Johnson.
297. Combat Report for Fg Off Ronald T. H. Collis, No. 157, 20 October 1943, TNA AIR 50/18.
298. *Assessment of Combat Claims*, Ref. *11G/810/Int.*, from Headquarters 11 Group to RAF Station Tangmere, 20 December 1943, 41 Squadron Archives.
299. The document includes a Point 2 in the body of the text, but does not include a Point 1. The quoted paragraphs reflect the entire content of the body of the document.
300. *Pilot Service Record* for Flt. Sgt. Douglas P. Fisher, 41 Squadron Archives.
301. Combat Report for Flt Sgt Douglas P. Fisher, No. 212, 20 October 1943, TNA AIR 50/18.
302. Ibid.
303. Ibid.
304. Ibid.
305. Correspondence from Ronald Johnson to Dan Johnson, 20 January 1983; reproduced with Dan's kind permission.
306. 41 Squadron ORB, 20 October 1943, TNA AIR 27/425.
307. Fg Offs Collis, Cowell and Newman's combat films for 20 October 1943 have survived and are held in the collections of the Imperial War Museum. See Appendix XIII (Extant Combat Films) for further information. No Combat Reports for 91 Squadron appear to have survived for this day.
308. 41 Squadron ORB, 20 October 1943, TNA AIR 27/425.
309. Appendix to 41 Squadron ORB, 20 October 1943, TNA AIR 27/430.
310. Saunders' telegram fails to mention Flt Sgt Douglas Fisher's victory, bringing the total to ten, which is understandable as it was not claimed until September 1944.
311. 41 Squadron ORB, 23 October 1943, TNA AIR 27/425.
312. Letter from Director-General of Organisation, Air Ministry, AVM George C. Pirie, to the AOC-in-C, Headquarters Fighter Command, AM Sir Trafford Leigh-Mallory, *Allied Expeditionary Air Force: Re-equipment of Squadrons 1943-1944*, 18 October 1943, TNA AIR 37/475.
313. Memo from SASO, Headquarters Fighter Command, via Ops. 1, Wg Cdr Kenneth Holden, *Allied Expeditionary Air Force: Re-equipment of Squadrons 1943-1944*, 23 October 1943, TNA AIR 37/475.
314. Telex from Air Ministry to Headquarters Fighter Command, *Allied Expeditionary Air Force: Re-equipment of Squadrons 1943-1944*, 26 October 1943, TNA AIR 37/475.
315. *TANG/375 24/10*, Intelligence Report for Ramrod 283 from RAF Tangmere to 11 Group, 24 October 1943, 41 Squadron Archives.
316. 41 Squadron ORB, 28 October 1943, TNA AIR 27/425.
317. Ibid.
318. 41 Squadron ORB, 2 November 1943, TNA AIR 27/425.
319. Ibid., 4 November 1943.
320. Marauder 41-18075 was captained by H. M. Price USAAF (MACR 1216), and Marauder 41-31889 was captained by R. Williamson USAAF (MACR 1047).
321. 41 Squadron ORB, 5 November 1943, TNA AIR 27/425.
322. This is the first mention of Flt Lt Terence Deane Welsh in the ORB, and it is assumed he joined the Squadron a few days prior to this date. The 28-year-old had joined the RAF in early 1939 and been posted to his first operational unit, 264 Squadron, as a Pilot Officer on Probation in early November 1939. Welsh claimed several victories during summer 1940 and was awarded a DFC in February 1941, by which time he had been promoted to Flying Officer. He was posted to 125 Squadron as a Flight Commander in May 1941, and rested later that year as a flying instructor before being posted to 277 (ASR) Squadron, where he remained until July 1942. At this time, he was posted to 1 Squadron at Acklington, and served with this unit until late 1943 when he was posted to 41 Squadron.
323. The Squadron ORB's F540 on 6 November 1943 erroneously states that no operational flying was carried out on this date "owing to unsuitable weather", however the ORB's F541, the RAF Tangmere ORB, and an Intelligence Report within 41 Squadron's Archives, all state that the Squadron was airborne on an ASR patrol.
324. Although parachutes were seen to open by other bombers and escorting fighters, the entire crew were killed and are buried today in the Calais Canadian War Cemetery in Leubringhen, France. The crew were A.413145 Flt Sgt Keith M. Smith RAAF (pilot), R.121885 WO2 Carl M. Berg RCAF (Navigator), R.122979 WO2 John H. Cowieson RCAF (WO/AG), R.145806 WO2 Joseph A. Grenier RCAF (AG).

325. It has not been possible to identify the 41 Squadron aircraft hit by Flak during Ramrod 300 on 8 November 1943, or its pilot, as the serial is not recorded in the Squadron, Station and Group ORBs, or in an Intelligence Report for the operation.
326. Research suggests that whilst the Allies became aware of the site, they did not know its full extent or appreciate its potential. As such, despite the bombing on 11 November 1943, the site remained in operation and went on to house V1 flying bomb production facilities in addition to the V2 operations. The site was captured in early July 1944, within a month of D-Day, and subsequently visited by both General Eisenhower and Winston Churchill, who were reportedly astonished by the magnitude and scope of the facility. See also: http://www.atlantikwall.org.uk/new_page_61.htm (rtrvd May 2011).
327. 41 Squadron ORB, 11 November 1943, TNA AIR 27/425.
328. Entry for 12 November 1943 in the logbook of Flt Sgt Jim C. J. Payne, via Dan Johnson.
329. This incident is not mentioned in the Squadron ORB on 15 November 1943, but Fg Off Herbert Wagner records in his flying logbook, "Engine quit on take-off, cartweeled [sic] off end of runway"; via Dan Johnson.
330. The RAF Tangmere ORB states that 41 Squadron was airborne on three weather reconnaissances on 18 November 1943, but the Squadron ORB's F540 and F541 both only record one.
331. 41 Squadron ORB, 18 November 1943, TNA AIR 27/425.
332. This aircraft was 10 Squadron Halifax II, HX181, ZA-K, and the crew were Flt Sgts Benjamin Holdsworth and John Harper (RAAF), and Sgts Raymond J. H. Steel, Clive Telfer, Albert J. Oudinot, Robert V. Downs, and Charles E. Smith.
333. Four of these Typhoons belonged to 197 Squadron and two to 486 (NZ) Squadron. The ownership of the Spitfires is unclear.
334. Correspondence with Sqn Ldr Ian Matthew, January 2005.
335. Entry for 23 November 1943 in the logbook of Fg Off Ronald Johnson, via Dan Johnson.
336. Entry for 23 November 1943 in the logbook of Flt Sgt Jim C. J. Payne, via Dan Johnson.
337. The crew of 226 Squadron Mitchell II, FL196, MQ-J, killed on 25 November 1943 were Flt Sgts Henry F. Bovingon and Wilfred M. Thomas, and Sgts James R. G. Blamey and Alan W. Brown.
338. 11 Group ORB Appendix, 25 November 1943, TNA AIR 25/207.
339. 41 Squadron ORB, 25 November 1943, TNA AIR 27/425.
340. 11 Group ORB Appendix, 25 November 1943, TNA AIR 25/207.
341. *Tangmere Composite Ramrod 336 Report 26/11/43*, Intelligence Report for Ramrod 336, 26 November 1943, 41 Squadron Archives.
342. 41 Squadron ORB, 29 November 1943, TNA AIR 27/425.
343. Entry for 29 November 1943 in the logbook of Fg Off Ronald Johnson, via Dan Johnson.
344. 41 Squadron ORB, 29 November 1943, TNA AIR 27/425.
345. 11 Group ORB Appendix, 1 December 1943, TNA AIR 25/207.
346. Plt Off Bruce Adams was posted to No. 1 Training Command in Canada in June 1944, and was discharged in April 1945. He became an accountant in private practise and died in Toronto in July 2002.
347. The Squadron ORB on 2 December 1943 states that Flt Lt Ronald Collis returned early as a result of jettison tank trouble, but Collis wrote in his own logbook that the reason was engine trouble.
348. The RAF Tangmere ORB and an Intelligence Report in 41 Squadron's Archives both indicate that a bombing run was also made by Tangmere based 197 and 486 (NZ) Squadrons. However, as these two squadrons are not mentioned in 10 Group's Operational Report for Ramrod 111, it is not clear how they fitted into the operation.
349. 22-year-old Flt Sgt Peter Wall had joined 41 Squadron exactly seven months prior to his flying accident on 4 December 1943. He was posted to Flying Training Command later that month and in 1944 held two postings in this Command, the first at No. 3 (Pilots) Advanced Flying Unit at Southrop, and the second at No. 3 Flying Instructors School at Lulsgate Bottom. In 1945, he was posted as an instructor to No. 18 (Pilots) Advanced Flying Unit at Church Lawford, where he saw out the War. In civilian life, Wall worked for the Home Office and was awarded an OBE for his services in November 1981. He died in 2003.
350. 'Crossbow' was a top-level code name for all airborne operations against the German long-range weapons programmes.
351. 41 Squadron ORB, 5 December 1943, TNA AIR 27/425.
352. The 41 Squadron ORB's F541 records that Flt Sgts Douglas Fisher and William Vann were airborne from 08:00 to 10:05, but this length of flight was impossible at the time without refuelling. The F540, however, whilst omitting a landing time, does state that the two pilots took off at 08:50, which would be a more realistic flying time if the pilots did indeed land at 10:05.
353. Having joined the RAF at Cranwell in January 1938, Flt Lt Thomas Burne was commissioned in October 1939 and posted to his first operational unit, Coastal Command's 206 Squadron at Bircham Newton, in January 1940. This was followed by a posting to 53 Squadron in July 1941 as a Flying Officer. Shipped out to the Far East Theatre as a Flight Lieutenant in January 1942 to join 62 Squadron at Singapore, Burne was seriously injured when a Japanese bomb hit the wing of a Hudson bomber from which he was alighting less than three weeks later. This resulted in the amputation of one of his legs and his repatriation to the United Kingdom where he was fitted with a prosthetic leg.

He remained on sick leave and in recuperation until May 1943, and during this time was awarded an AFC and a Mention in Dispatches. Finally becoming fit enough to fly again, Burne was granted a transfer to fighters, and was sent to SFTS at the end of May 1943, followed by OTU in July and finally TEU in early October. He joined 41 Squadron on 16 December 1943 as his first operational posting since February 1942 and his first as a fighter pilot. However, the Squadron was gaining a very experienced pilot who had already logged 1,385 flying hours, of which 800 were operational with Coastal Command.

354. Having joined the RAFVR in June 1939, Fg Off Harry Cook had undertaken his entire flying training in the United Kingdom and was a Sergeant Pilot with 266 Squadron, and subsequently 66 Squadron, during the Battle of Britain. He claimed several victories during the Battle, and was rested from February to September 1941 as a flying instructor with 57 OTU. Following this posting, Cook became a test pilot, during which time he was commissioned, and was posted back to operations with 234 Squadron at Portreath in September 1942. One month later, however, he moved to 26 Squadron, and before the year was out had joined the MSFU at Speke. Following a period of rest on the conclusion of his second tour, Cook was posted to 41 Squadron on 16 December 1943 to commence his third, having logged 900 flying hours, of which 150 were operational, with claims of two destroyed, four probable and four damaged enemy aircraft.

355. Flt Sgt Frederick Woollard had joined the RAFVR in November 1940 and undertook his flying training in the United Kingdom. His first operational posting came in late March 1942, when he was sent to Libya to join 33 Squadron. Woollard gained significant battle experience in North Africa, being shot up by an Me109 near Tobruk in April 1942 and shot down and wounded in action at the beginning of July. Repatriated to the United Kingdom as a result of the latter incident, Woollard spent some time recovering from his wounds before being posted as staff to 61 OTU at Rednal. In preparation for his return to operations, he was posted to TEU in late 1943 and was then sent to 41 Squadron on 18 December 1943, with 320 flying hours in his logbook, of which 22 hours and 30 minutes were operational on Hurricanes with 33 Squadron in Libya.

356. 41 Squadron ORB, 20 December 1943, TNA AIR 27/425.
357. Le Mesnil-Allard was a site located at 49°50'35" N 1°35'52" E, approximately 0.5km west of the village of Le Mesnil-Allard, 2.5km northeast of Aubermesnil-aux-Érables, and 28km southeast of Le Tréport in Haute-Normandie.
358. 41 Squadron ORB, 22 December 1943, TNA AIR 27/425.
359. Ibid., 24 December 1943.
360. Ibid., 30 December 1943.
361. Entry for 30 December 1943 in the logbook of Flt Lt Thomas A. H. Slack; via Dan Johnson.
362. Recollections of Fg Of Keith R. Curtis, via his daughter Karen Neale, June 2003.
363. RAF Tangmere ORB, 31 December 1943, TNA AIR 28/815.
364. 41 Squadron ORB, 31 December 1943, TNA AIR 27/425.
365. Intelligence Report, *TANGMERE COMPOSITE REPORT – RAMROD 412 – 2nd Jan.1944.*, 41 Squadron Archives.
366. Entry for 2 January 1944 in the logbook of Fg Off Herbert A. Wagner; via Dan Johnson.
367. Both the RAF Tangmere ORB and an Intelligence Report for the operation on 3 January 1944 use this term without further explanation of its meaning or the patrols' intent.
368. The crew of 21 Squadron Mosquito VI, HX954, Flt Lt Francis O. J. Pearce (pilot) and Fg Off Francis H. Greenaway (navigator), were captured, whilst the crew of Mosquito VI, LR331, Flt Sgt Hugh Baird RNZAF (pilot) and Fg Off John F. Parker RCAF (navigator), were both killed.
369. Intelligence Report *TANGMERE COMPOSITE RAMROD 418 REPORT 4 JAN 44.*, 41 Squadron Archives.
370. 'Longuemont' was a site located at 50°01'00" N 1°42'08" E on what is today land containing a number of farmhouses at Tours-en-Vimeu, Picardie. The farms are located on a road named 'La Grande Rue Longuemort', which may suggest that 'Longuemont' is actually a misspelling or misinterpretation of 'Longuemort'. The site lies approximately 2.5km southeast of the centre of Tours-en-Vimeu, 1.5km southwest of the village of Grébault-Mesnil, and 2km north of Martainneville, Picardie.
371. Entry for 5 January 1944 in the logbook of Plt Off Jim C. J. Payne; via Dan Johnson.
372. The 41 Squadron ORB does not record the pilots or serials of the four aircraft that did not get airborne for Rodeo 275 on 5 January 1944, and does not document any evidence of issues. The only indicator that this was not planned is the comment in Plt Off Jim C. J. Payne's logbook.
373. *COMPOSITE REPORT – TANGMERE SPITFIRE XII WING. RAMROD No. 428 – 6th January, 1943* [sic], 41 Squadron Archives.
374. Fg Off Heninger's Spitfire XII, EN223, was excavated in early September 2011 and filmed by the BBC as a part of their documentary series, "Dig WW2" with Dan Snow, first screened in winter 2011-2012. The excavation of the engine identified Heninger's loss not a result of enemy attack, but rather con-rod failure.
375. These three sites were located just southeast and south-southeast of Cherbourg, La Glacerie approximately 4.5km from Cherbourg, 'La Sorellerie I' just under 7km from Cherbourg at 49°35'10" N 01°33'53" W, and 'La Sorellerie II' less than 1.5km further south at 49°34'25" N 01°33'35" W.
376. This Noball site was located in Bois de Pottier [Pottier Wood] at 50°29'50" N 01°56'45" E, almost 22km east of Étaples.
377. Petit Bois Tillencourt was a construction works and ski site located at 50°10'12" N 1°59'05" E, approximately half a kilometre southwest of Yvrencheux, 13.5km northeast of Abbeville, and 38km southeast of Berck-sur-Mer.

378. Entry for 14 January 1944 in the logbook of Plt Off Peter B Graham, via Dan Johnson.
379. The 11 Group ORB Appendix does not record the Squadrons or Wings tasked with providing the First and Second Fighter Sweeps of Ramrod 456 on 14 January 1944; the page that would have been expected to contain that data is blank.
380. Intelligence Report, *TANG/59 14/JAN ADDITION TO COMPOSITE REPORT TANG/55*, 14 January 1944, 41 Squadron Archives.
381. 'Le Grismont' was a site located in a wood at 50°39'00" N 02°17'35" E, 11km south of St. Omer, 7km west of Aire-sur-la-Lys, and 3km northeast of Thérouanne, Pas-de-Calais.
382. 'Bois d'Enfer' was a site located in woods at 50°38'30" N 02°13'15" E, approximately 2.5km west-northwest of Thérouanne, 0.5km north-northeast of Upen d'Aval, and 1.5km south of Herbelles, Pas-de-Calais.
383. Intelligence Report *TANG/67 21st. Jan COMPOSITE REPORT TANGMERE SPITFIRE XII WING RAMROD No. 470 (21/1/44)*, 41 Squadron Archives.
384. Marauder 41-31618 of 386th Bomb Group, 555th Bombardment Squadron, is believed to have fallen victim to Fw Gerd Wiegand 4./JG26.
385. Correspondence from Flt Lt Peter Cowell to Dan Johnson, 24 April 1984; reproduced with Dan's kind permission.
386. 'Heudiere' was located at 49°43'15" N 0°55'00" E, between the villages of Le Mesnil-Rury and Le Torp-Mesnil, 26km southwest of Dieppe and 22km southeast of St. Valéry.
387. 'Bois Megle' was located in a wood at 49°29'20" N 0°57'22" E, 11.5km northwest of Rouen and 61km due east of Le Havre.
388. The crew of 487 (NZ) Squadron Mosquito VI, HX951, which were killed on 31 January 1944, were Flt Sgt Arthur Settle and Fg Off Marshall L. Jones RCAF.
389. It is apparent from 41 Squadron ORB F541 entries that several other patrols were flown by the Squadron during the afternoon of 31 January 1944. However, anomalies in the timings and details leave it unclear as to who flew when and why. For example, Flt Lt Tom Slack and Flt Sgt Jim Payne are shown as flying a search for 91 Squadron aircraft between 13:20 and 14:15 – before the aircraft collided and went missing! Two sections are also shown flying patrols of the Isle of Wight between 13:00 and 14:25, and between 13:55 and 14:45. As none of these patrols are mentioned in the ORB's F540, their exact nature remains unclear.
390. Entry for 31 January 1944 in the logbook of Flt Sgt Jim C. J. Payne; via Dan Johnson.
391. The pilots, serials and squadron/s of these two aircraft are not identified.
392. Entry for 3 February 1944 in the logbook of Plt Off Jim C. J. Payne, via Dan Johnson.
393. 'Beaulieu Ferme' was located in a wood at 49°52'10" N 1°39'45" E, 29km southwest of Abbeville, 42km east-southeast of Dieppe, and 1km northeast of Campneuseville.
394. The RAF Tangmere ORB on 4 February 1944 erroneously reports that 41 and 91 Squadrons provided a fighter sweep for Ramrod 513 during the afternoon. However, the 11 Group ORB Appendix, and Intelligence Reports for the Spitfire XII Wing held in 41 Squadron's Archives, show that both the Wing's morning and afternoon operations were named 'Ramrod 508'. Ramrod 513 also took place, but it involved Bomphoons, RP Typhoons and RP Hurricanes in attacks on Noball sites from 16:30, however without any fighter cover.
395. *Tangmere Composite Report – Ramrod 508 – 4th February, 1944*, 41 Squadron Archives.
396. Although Sqn Ldr John N. Mackenzie's posting to 41 Squadron between 1 and 9 February 1944 is evidenced by entries in his own logbook, and a single entry in the 41 Squadron ORB's F541 on 5 February 1944, the reason for the posting is unknown. Entries in his logbook suggest that his arrival on 41 Squadron marked the commencement of his third tour, but it may also have simply been that he was filling time and gaining a refresher on operations before being posted to command 64 Squadron, which role he fulfilled from the beginning of April 1944.
397. RAF Tangmere ORB, 5 February 1944, TNA AIR 28/815.
398. 41 Squadron ORB, 5 February 1944, TNA AIR 27/426.
399. Ibid., 6 February 1944.
400. The Noball site 'Bois Coquerel' is correctly Bois de Coquerel [Coquerel Wood] and is located at 50°00'50" N 01°50'05" E, just east-southeast of the village of Limeux, and around 10km south of Abbeville, in the Somme Department.
401. 41 Squadron ORB, 7 February 1944, TNA AIR 27/426.
402. The 41 Squadron ORB on 9 February 1944 states that the pilots undertook 30 air firing sorties, whereas the 17 APC ORB indicates there were only 25.
403. 41 Squadron ORB, 10 February 1944, TNA AIR 27/426.
404. Entry for 11 February 1944 in the logbook of Fg Off Peter Cowell, via Dan Johnson.
405. The 41 Squadron ORB on 12 February 1944 states that the pilots undertook eight air firing sorties, whereas the 17 APC ORB indicates there were only three.
406. The 41 Squadron ORB on 13 February 1944 states that the pilots undertook 35 air firing sorties, whereas the 17 APC ORB indicates there were 32.
407. Entry for 13 February 1944 in the logbook of Fg Off Peter Cowell, via Dan Johnson.
408. The 41 Squadron ORB on 14 February 1944 states that the pilots undertook 25 air firing sorties and 'several cine-gun exercises', whereas the 17 APC ORB only records 24 air firing sorties.

409. Entry for 14 February 1944 in the logbook of Fg Off Peter Cowell, via Dan Johnson.
410. 41 Squadron's ORB on 15 February 1944 states that 19 air firing sorties and 12 cine-gun sorties were carried out, but the 17 APC ORB states only that 17 air firing sorties were undertaken.
411. 41 Squadron ORB, 17 February 1944, TNA AIR 27/426.
412. Ibid., 18 February 1944.
413. Ibid.
414. This flying accident on 20 February 1944 is not mentioned in 41 Squadron's ORB, and is only mentioned in the RAF Southend ORB (AIR 28/692). However, there is no indication whatsoever of whom the pilot and passenger were; the only mention of them is that they were not injured.
415. 41 Squadron ORB, 20 February 1944, TNA AIR 27/426.
416. Ibid., 22 February 1944.
417. The Squadron ORB's F541 on 22 February 1944 does not list any of the Squadron's flights for the day, and states only 'No flying'. Strictly speaking, the Squadron *did* fly – to Manston and back – but as these were non-operational flights, the ORB does not record any pilots or serials, and therefore also does not record the serial of Fg Off David Shea's aircraft that would not start at Friston.
418. 'Bois Rempre' was a wood located at 50°32'00" N 01°53'50" E, approximately 18.5km east-northeast of Étaples.
419. *Tangmere Composite Report – Ramrod 587 – 24th February, 1944.*, 41 Squadron Archives.
420. 41 Squadron ORB, 24 February 1944, TNA AIR 27/426.
421. The Squadron ORB's F541 on 24 February 1944 is missing the list of pilots and serials involved in Ramrod 587, and erroneously states instead, 'No flying'.
422. 41 Squadron ORB, 25 February 1944, TNA AIR 27/426.
423. 11 Group ORB Appendix, 25 February by 1944, TNA AIR 25/208.
424. Entry for 25 February 1944 in the logbook of Plt Off Jim C. J. Payne, via Dan Johnson.
425. Entry for 25 February 1944 in the logbook of Plt Off Peter B. Graham, via Dan Johnson.
426. 41 Squadron ORB, 25 February 1944, TNA AIR 27/426.
427. Flt Lt H. Bruce Moffett returned to Canada in late September 1944 and was discharged from the RCAF in March 1945. He was subsequently employed as a public accountant, but rejoined the RCAF as a Flying Officer in May 1951. During the ensuing ten years, Moffett served as a flying instructor and flew with 427 Squadron, based in Zweibrücken, Germany. Following his discharge from the RCAF in July 1961, he was employed as a hospital administrator and subsequently served as the Mayor of Baclarres, Saskatchewan. He died in Kelowna, British Columbia, on 11 July 1981.
428. The 41 Squadron ORB's F541 on 28 February 1944 states the pilots were airborne at 13:35, whereas the F540 and an Intelligence Report for the day both state the take-off time was 12:35.
429. 41 Squadron ORB, 28 February 1944, TNA AIR 27/426.
430. The 41 Squadron ORB's F540 on 28 February 1944 states that 41 Squadron escorted the second and third boxes, whereas an Intelligence Report for the day, *Tangmere Composite Ramrod 597 Report 28/FEB/44*, states that 41 Squadron escorted the first and second boxes.
431. 41 Squadron ORB, 28 February 1944, TNA AIR 27/426.
432. The crew of 464 Squadron Mosquito VI, LR389, Fg Off Cyril Timson (pilot) and Sgt Philip H. Edwards (navigator), are buried in Grandcourt War Cemetery, Haute-Normandie, whilst the crew of 21 Squadron Mosquito VI, LR403, Fg Off Robert W. Offler RCAF (pilot) and Fg Off Anthony C. J. Mango (navigator), have not been found and are remembered today on the Runnymede Memorial in Surrey.

5 PREPARING FOR *OVERLORD*; 1 MARCH – 19 JUNE 1944

1. Intelligence Report, *TANG/166 2/3/44*, 2 March 1944, 41 Squadron Archives.
2. 342 Squadron Boston IIIA, BZ308, OA-V, had taken off from Hartfordbridge to participate in Ramrod 613 on 2 March 1944. The aircraft was hit by Flak and crashed in Bois de la Justice at approximately 18:02. The pilot, Sgt Pierre Desprès FAFL (30781) and Air Gunner, Adj-chef François Baleste FAFL (31440), were both killed and initially buried in a nearby field ('Pâture Bonnier') as 1745 'Sgt Desprest' and 5076 'Adj Nastivell'. They were exhumed in 1947, positively identified, and subsequently re-interred, Desprès at Tourlaville, Manche, and Baleste at St.Pol-sur-Ternoise. The second Air Gunner, Adj Jean Vergerio FAFL (31053) was wounded and admitted to the German Hospital Calmette in Lille. However, he died of his wounds on 14 March 1944 and was buried at Lille. He, too, was subsequently reinterred, and lies today in Joeuf, Meurthe-et-Moselle. The fourth member of the crew, Sgt G. Liniéres FAFL (3095) was unhurt and spent the rest of the War as a POW. With thanks to Henk Welting for this information.
3. Intelligence Report, *TANG/169 2/3/44*, 2 March 1944, 41 Squadron Archives.
4. 41 Squadron ORB, 2 March 1944, TNA AIR 27/426.
5. Ibid.
6. Ibid., 3 March 1944.
7. Ibid.

8. The location of "Malines Marshalling Yards" is in the Dutch-speaking town Mechelen, in the province of Antwerp, Belgium, approximately 25km north of Brussels. It is called *Malines* in French, but usually called *Mechlin* in English.
9. 41 Squadron ORB, 4 March 1944, TNA AIR 27/426.
10. Ibid., 5 March 1944.
11. With thanks to Peter Gibbs' son, Michael, for sharing his father's memories, February 2011.
12. 41 Squadron ORB, 10 March 1944, TNA AIR 27/426.
13. Ibid., 11 March 1944.
14. Peter Graham in his autobiography, *Skypilot; Memoirs from Take-Off to Landing*, 2001, Pentland Books, ISBN 1858219094; reproduced with his permission.
15. 41 Squadron ORB, 12 March 1944, TNA AIR 27/426.
16. The serial of Fg Off Herbert Wagner's aircraft on 13 March 1944 is not recorded in ORB's F541.
17. *AI/74 13 MAR Composite Air/Sea Rescue Patrol Report* from RAF Lympne to 11 Group, 13 March 1944, 41 Squadron Archives.
18. The investigation based this conclusion on the fact that Fg Off Harry Cook had nothing left in his jettison tank, but still had 35 gallons of fuel remaining in his main tank.
19. Second World War Service Files: Canadian Armed Forces War Dead, Shea, David John, RG 24, Box 28631, Library and Archives Canada, 395 Wellington St., Ottawa, Ontario, Canada, K1A 0N4.
20. 41 Squadron ORB, 13 March 1944, TNA AIR 27/426.
21. Ibid.
22. The Squadron ORB's F540 on 14 March 1944 records that the section scrambled to intercept the Mosquito was Red Section, but the F541 erroneously omits the usual list of pilots' names and aircraft serials. It summaries both 14 and 15 March instead as "No operational flying on these dates".
23. *FRI/108 16/3/44 Composite ASR Patrol Report*, from RAF Friston to 11 Group, 16 March 1944, 41 Squadron Archives.
24. Ibid.
25. 41 Squadron ORB, 16 March 1944, TNA AIR 27/426.
26. Entry for 16 March 1944 in the logbook of Fg Off Herbert A. Wagner; via Dan Johnson.
27. The 41 Squadron ORB on 16 March 1944 states that the downed pilot was a Canadian of 401 Squadron. However, evidence suggests this was more likely Fg Off T. M. Saunderson of 412 (RCAF) Squadron who was flying Spitfire IX, MJ149, when he suffered engine trouble over the Somme Estuary and ditched. He originally came ashore, but German troops would not come down to the beach to retrieve him as it was mined. As such, Saunderson got back in his dinghy and paddled out again, eventually being rescued a few hundred yards off the coast an ASR Sea Otter. The Sea Otter was JM796, and the pilot Flt Lt (then Plt Off) Tom Fletcher DFC DFM* of 277 (ASR) Squadron, who was the most decorated ASR pilot in the RAF and was once recommended for the Victoria Cross. This particular rescue was mentioned in Fletcher's Obituary in *The Telegraph* on 31 March 2010. The other two members of the Sea Otter's crew were Fg Off Leonard R. Healey DFM (awarded a DFC in August 1944) and Flt Sgt T. Gregory. As this crew's rescue occurred between 14:30 and 16:55, it is most likely that this was indeed the air-sea rescue that 41 Squadron covered on 16 March 1944. As an aside, a History of 412 Squadron [http://www.manitobamilitaryaviationmuseum.com/PDF/412Squadron.pdf, rtrvd Mar 2011] states that the 'unknown pilot' referred to in 41 Squadron's Intelligence Report was J.14013 Flt Lt Donald C. Laubman (awarded two DFCs in late 1944) of 412 Squadron.
28. The Squadron ORB's F540 on 19 March 1944 states that the quartet took off from Lympne at 14:45 and landed at Friston at 17:10, but does not explain what they were doing in the meantime. That said, the time '14.45' is likely erroneous as the Spitfire XII could not stay airborne almost 2½ hours, even with auxiliary tanks, without refuelling. The F541 provides no assistance as the flights were non-operational and such flights are not normally listed on the F541 anyway. As such, it is more likely that the take-off time from Lympne should read 16:45.
29. The 41 Squadron ORB's F540 on 19 March 1944 contains the details recorded in this paragraph, but the F541 omits the usual list of aircraft serials it would record for operational flights. The F541 states erroneously instead "No operational flying this day".
30. 41 Squadron ORB (F541), 20 March 1944, TNA AIR 27/426.
31. 41 Squadron ORB, 21 March 1944, TNA AIR 27/426.
32. Ibid.
33. The Squadron ORB's F540 on 25 March 1944 states that Plt Off Peter Graham and Fg Off Maurice Balasse's destination was Dieppe, whereas the F541 states it was Cherbourg.
34. Correspondence from Flt Lt Peter Cowell to Dan Johnson, 24 April 1984; reproduced with Dan's kind permission.
35. 41 Squadron ORB, 25 March 1944, TNA AIR 27/426.
36. Entry for 25 March 1944 in logbook of Fg Off Herbert A. Wagner; via Dan Johnson.
37. This ASR patrol is not mentioned on the Squadron ORB's F540 on 25 March 1944, but it is listed on the F541, and recorded in an Intelligence Report for the operation, held in 41 Squadron's Archives.
38. *FRI/123 26/3, Friston Composite A/S/R Patrol Report*, addressed to 11 Group, copy to Biggin Hill, 26 March 1944, 41 Squadron Archives.

39. 41 Squadron ORB, 26 March 1944, TNA AIR 27/426.
40. *FRI/124 26/3, Friston Composite A/S/R Patrol Report*, addressed to 11 Group, copy to Biggin Hill, 26 March 1944, 41 Squadron Archives.
41. The wreckage the pilots sighted was possibly from Lancaster ND440 of 97 Squadron RAF. The aircraft was hit by Flak during an attack on Berlin during the night of 24/25 March and finally forced to ditch in the Channel between Calais and Cap Gris Nez. The Flight Engineer was killed, but the remaining crew were picked up by the Germans and become Prisoners of War. It is possible that the wreckage floated this distance in the 24 hours since the aircraft came down.
42. *FRI/125 26th March*, Intelligence Report to 11 Group, copy Biggin Hill, 26 March 1944, 41 Squadron Archives.
43. The Squadron ORB on 28 March 1944 states they crossed in over Lion-sur-Mer, but an Intelligence Report for the same operation states they came in over Cabourg, approximately 9 miles / 14.5km further east.
44. The Squadron ORB on 28 March 1944 states they orbited Conches at 8,000 feet, but an Intelligence Report for the same operation states they orbited at 6,000 feet.
45. The Squadron ORB's F540 on 31 March 1944 states there were three ASR patrols, but the F541 and an Intelligence Report both list four pilots and aircraft in two sections.
46. *FRI/131 1/4 Friston Composite A/S/R Report 1/4/44*, 1 April 1944, 41 Squadron Archives.
47. The Squadron ORB on 1 April 1944 does not state whose aircraft had developed engine trouble, but the F541 lists Fg Off Harry Cook as flying Spitfire XII, MB862, as Red 1, and Fg Off John Malone MB794, as Red 2, and adds, "Air Sea Rescue. Returned owing to mechanical trouble". However, a separate hand-written Intelligence Report held in 41 Squadron's archives states "Mechanical trouble on leaders a/c", which implies it was Cook's aircraft, MB862, with the problem.
48. Although the 41 Squadron ORB and Intelligence Reports for 1 April 1944 clearly discuss a search two for [Republic P-47] Thunderbolt pilots, there are no matching losses on this date for the 8th or 9th US Air Forces. There were, however, two P-51 Mustang losses that day from the 362nd FS, 357th FG, in which O-728720 Capt Davis T. Perron in P-51B 43-6792 and O-745519 1st Lt Elmer D. Rydberg in P-51B 43-6629 lost their lives. Searches were also made for the pair by other units on 2 April 1944 in an area bordered by Dover, Boulogne, Dieppe and Beachy Head.
49. 41 Squadron ORB, 6 April 1944, TNA AIR 27/426.
50. Ibid.
51. RAF Friston ORB, 8 April 1944, TNA AIR 28/286.
52. 41 Squadron ORB, 11 April 1944, TNA AIR 27/426.
53. Recommendation for the Russian Medal for Valour, A.407256 Donald Hamilton Smith RAAF, TNA AIR 2/4798, with thanks to Hugh Halliday and Tom Thorne.
54. Particular thanks to Hugh Halliday for assistance with the interpretation of the award.
55. The Squadron ORB on 12 April 1944 states that Flt Lt Keith Thiele and Flt Sgt Robert Fleming found "a cloudless sky and perfect visibility", but the weather conditions quoted in the text have been extracted from an Intelligence Report for the reconnaissance [41 Squadron Archives], which contradict the ORB and suggest the conditions were far from cloudless.
56. *Opflash No. 4 for 12th April*, 12 April 1944, 41 Squadron Archives.
57. This was 107173 Fg Off Bertrand John Henry Daventry, who was a pre-War newspaper photographer.
58. Close observation of Fg Off B. J. Daventry's most famous photograph, of a formation of seven of 41 Squadron's Spitfire XIIs, reveals that one of the aircraft is actually out of formation, and only a part of the fourth aircraft appears behind the third, MB794, EB-H. Versions of this photograph have since been produced where the fourth aircraft has been airbrushed out of the picture to 'clean it up'. It is assumed that the pilot of MB882, EB-B, in the photograph is Flt Lt Don Smith as it was his regular aircraft, but it is not known who was flying the other aircraft. Strangely, the event is not mentioned in the Squadron ORB, but several pilots have pasted the pictures into their logbooks, presumably having cut them out of newspapers or magazines.
59. *Opflash No 4 for 12th April 1944*, 12 April 1944, 41 Squadron Archives.
60. On 17 April 1944, the 41 Squadron ORB states, "F/O REFSHAUGE joined the Squadron and was assigned to 'A' Flight". However, it is unclear whether this is a late entry in the ORB (as often happened), or whether he was posted to 41 Squadron on 14 April 1944 and actually arrived on 17 April. Both Refshauge's RAAF personnel file [*RAAF Officers Personnel files, 1921-1948*, Series A9300, Barcode 5251127, NAA] and *Pilot Service Record* [41 Squadron Archives] indicate that his tenure with 41 Squadron commenced on 14 April 1944.
61. The 11 Group ORB Appendix does not identify the Spitfire squadrons from 134 Airfield that were involved in Ramrod 742 on 18 April 1944.
62. The 11 Group ORB Appendix does not identify the Spitfire squadrons involved in the fighter umbrella over the target area in Ramrod 742 on 18 April 1944.
63. Entry for 18 April 1944 in the flying logbook of Flt Lt Robert E. Anderson; reproduced with the permission of Doug Fishburn.
64. 41 Squadron ORB, 19 April 1944, TNA AIR 27/426.
65. A Squadron Intelligence Report and the 11 Group ORB Appendix on 20 April 1944 both contradict the Squadron ORB, which indicates the skies were clear over the target area. The presumption that the Squadron ORB is erroneous

is supported by the fact that the bombers all aborted the mission on account of the "target being obscured by cloud" (11 Group Appendix, Ramrod 756, 20 April 1944, TNA AIR 25/209).
66. The 41 Squadron ORB's F541 on 20 April 1944 only lists eight pilots and serials participating in Ramrod 760, and the F540 does not state a number. However, an Intelligence Report for the operation in 41 Squadron's Archives (*OPFLASH NO. FRI/2 FOR 20 APL*) and the 11 Group Appendix (TNA AIR 25/209) both indicate that 12 aircraft from 41 Squadron participated.
67. Entry for 20 April 1944 in Fg Off Herbert A. Wagner's flying logbook; via Dan Johnson.
68. The RAF called the Douglas DB-7 light bomber the Boston. However, when used as a night-fighter by the RAF, the variant was called the Havoc. This latter name was adopted by the USAAF when the DB-7 went into service with the US as the Douglas A-20 attack bomber.
69. *OPFLASH NO. FRI/2 FOR 20 APL*, Intelligence Report for Ramrod 760, from Biggin Hill to 11 Group, 20 April 1944, 41 Squadron Archives.
70. Ibid.
71. 41 Squadron ORB, 21 April 1944, TNA AIR 27/426.
72. *OPFLASH NO. 4 FOR 21 APRIL 1944*, Intelligence Report from Friston to Biggin Hill, 20 April 1944, 41 Squadron Archives.
73. 41 Squadron ORB, 22 April 1944, TNA AIR 27/426.
74. Ibid., 23 April 1944.
75. Ibid., 24 April 1944.
76. Both quotes are from *OPFLASH NO. 2 FOR 25TH APRIL*, Intelligence Report form Friston to Biggin Hill, 25 April 1944, 41 Squadron Archives.
77. An analysis of aircraft losses on 25 April 1944 has narrowed possibilities but failed to definitively identify the aircraft that plunged into the sea, causing the splash that Plt Offs Douglas Fisher and Peter Graham observed. Bomber Command activity during this period was confined to night-time operations, thereby ruling out an RAF aircraft of this Command being lost at this time of the day. Training Command lost two Wellingtons from separate OTUs on Operation *Sweepstake*, but these are also believed to have been lost during the night. Coastal Command lost an Anson today, but at approximately 14:40 off Tuskar Rock, Wexford, in the mouth of the Irish Sea, thereby making it too late and too far away. There appear to be no matching losses among those of the US 8th Air Force, which was operating in the Vitry-le-François area of France, but the 9th Air Force lost one Marauder and two Mustangs. The former aircraft crashed at Blosseville, France, but both Mustangs came down in Germany, ruling all three out as possible candidates. 2 TAF lost three Mosquitos on this day, one at 01:00, one at 14:50, which appears to be too late, and one at 19:08. Fighter Command also recorded two losses today, both from 441 Squadron, following combat with FW190s near Lâon. One aircraft came down in France, whilst the other is still missing. The pilot, Fg Off Richard H. Sparling, who was flying Spitfire IX, MK394, may have come down in the Channel, and could be a possible candidate. He is remembered today on the Runnymede Memorial.
78. 41 Squadron ORB, 26 April 1944, TNA AIR 27/426.
79. Ibid.
80. *OPFLASH NO. 3 FOR 26TH APRIL*, Intelligence Report from Friston to Biggin Hill, 26 April 1944, 41 Squadron Archives.
81. 41 Squadron ORB, 26 April 1944, TNA AIR 27/426.
82. *OPFLASH NO 6 27 APRIL 1944*, Intelligence Report from RAF Friston to 11 Group, copy Biggin Hill, 27 April 1944, 41 Squadron Archives.
83. 41 Squadron ORB, 27 April 1944, TNA AIR 27/426.
84. Ibid.
85. Mantes-Gassicourt was formed in 1930 through the merging of the communes of Mantes and Gassicourt, but was renamed Mantes-la-Jolie, as it is known today, in 1953.
86. This location appears to be Bois de Coquerel [Coquerel Wood], in the village of Limeux, 10km south of Abbeville.
87. 41 Squadron ORB, 28 April 1944, TNA AIR 27/426.
88. Ibid., 29 April 1944.
89. Ibid.
90. In this incident on 29 April 1944, it is believed that only one of the two pilots – Flt Lt Collis *or* Flt Lt Harding – suffered what the ORB's F540 only describes as 'starting trouble', but it does not identify which one.
91. In this incident on 29 April 1944, it is believed that only one of the two pilots – Fg Off Refshauge *or* Fg Off Wagner – suffered what the ORB's F540 describes only as 'a rough engine', but it does not identify which one. Considering the fact that MB794 was involved both in the day's 17:45 scramble, in which an aircraft suffered starting trouble, and in this 20:45 scramble, in which an aircraft had a rough engine, circumstantial evidence may suggest that MB794 was the problem in both cases.
92. There is a slight discrepancy in the Squadron ORB on 29 April 1944, as the F540 states that Fg Offs Refshauge and Wagner landed again at 21:05, whereas the F541 states they landed at 21:45. However, the fact that the F540 states they "landed straight away" as a result of a rough engine suggests that 21:05 is more likely the correct time. Moreover, 21:45 is the time of return of the day's final third and final scramble, so it is likely the time was erroneously written in both entries.

93. Sommerfeld track was named after Kurt Sommerfeld, an Austrian engineer who adapted a 1920s British idea of using wire-netting to improve a muddy grass surface. Full-scale trials carried out by the Royal Engineers early in 1941 proved sufficiently encouraging to justify its mass production, and it was first used operationally in the North African campaign. The track consisted of wire mesh of 12 or 13 gauge with ⅜ inch (9.5mm) steel bearing rods threaded through transversely at 8 inch (200mm) intervals. Rolls measuring 10 feet 7 inches (3.25 metres) in width and 25 yards (23 metres) in length were linked together with 1½ x ⅜ inch (38mm x 9.5mm) flat steel bars, 5 yards (4.5m) in length, which were passed through loops at the end of the rods. Joints between sections were connected with metal buckles wound around the first and last bearing rods of each section. It was light, easily laid, and very practical not only for muddy runways, but also for beach surfaces in landing operations.
94. Peter Graham in his autobiography, *Skypilot; Memoirs from Take-Off to Landing*, 2001, Pentland Books, ISBN 1858219094; reproduced with his permission.
95. The 16:40 scramble by Flt Lt Thomas Burne and WO Arthur Appleton on 30 April 1944 is recorded on the Squadron ORB's F540 but not on the F541. As such their aircraft serials are unknown. Previously that afternoon, they had flown a patrol together in MB881 and MB829, so they may have used these aircraft again on this scramble, as they do not appear to have been flown by any other pilots listed on the F541 during the day.
96. 41 Squadron ORB, 30 April 1944, TNA AIR 27/426.
97. The details around Fg Off Peter Graham's early return to base on 2 May 1944 do not appear in the ORB; they are only recorded in his logbook. In this document, he recorded, "Returned to land through 10/10 low cloud at 100 feet with engine, R/T & compass U/S".
98. The 10 Group and RAF Bolt Head ORBs both record the shipping that was observed by the four pilots on their St. Malo patrol on 2 May 1944, but these statements are contradicted by the Squadron ORB, which states the patrol was "entirely uneventful, no ships being found and no opposition being encountered".
99. *Confidential Report (Officers)*, contained in the personnel file of Flt Lt Donald H. Smith, *RAAF Officers Personnel files, 1921-1948*, Series A9300, Barcode 5256138, NAA.
100. Correspondence from Flt Sgt John Irvine to Dan Johnson, dated 28 September 1982; reproduced with the kind permission of Dan Johnson (Irvine joined the Squadron in July 1944).
101. 41 Squadron ORB, 3 May 1944, TNA AIR 27/426.
102. Peter Graham in his autobiography, *Skypilot; Memoirs from Take-Off to Landing*, 2001, Pentland Books, ISBN 1858219094; reproduced with his permission.
103. 10 Group ORB Appendix, summary for May 1944, TNA AIR 25/188.
104. There are some contradictions in the reporting of the Squadron's activity on 5 May 1944. The Squadron ORB's F541 records five Convoy Patrols, whereas the F540 states "The usual patrols were carried out all day SOUTH of PORTLAND [ORB's capitals] and 5 practice flights were also flown. Weather was much improved and we were beginning to hope we might do something offensive". Alternatively, the RAF Bolt Head ORB states that 41 Squadron flew two convoy patrols in the morning "but deteriorating weather conditions stopped flying soon after mid-day".
105. The Squadron ORB's F541 on 6 May 1944 states that the take-off time was 06:50, whereas the F540 states both 06:40 and 06:50. The 10 Group ORB records the take-off time as 06:50, but the RAF Bolt Head ORB does not record any times at all.
106. As 'Lake Morbihan' does not exist, it is possible any of the surrounding lakes was meant. However, it may be that the Gulf of Morbihan [Golfe du Morbihan] was the location. This is more plausible when one considers the Breton name for the gulf, *Ar Mor Bihan*, means 'little sea'. It is a natural harbour, lying south of Vannes, approximately 5km wide and 21km long, with a 1km wide opening to the Atlantic Ocean on its western side.
107. The Squadron ORB's F540 on 7 May 1944 states that Flt Lt Terence Spencer participated in this ASR patrol, but the F541 fails to list him. However, Spencer's own logbook confirms he was a participant.
108. Available information does not identify which of the two aircraft had engine trouble on 8 May 1944, but both Plt Offs Douglas Fisher and Jim Payne returned to base as a result.
109. This patrol appears on the Squadron ORB's F540 on 8 May 1944, but is not listed on the F541. The location of the patrol is also not recorded, and the operation is not mentioned at all in the RAF Bolt Head ORB.
110. 41 Squadron ORB, 8 May 1944, TNA AIR 27/426.
111. Dinard-Pleurtuit Airfield is today's St. Malo Airport, which is located 5km south-southwest of Dinard, Brittany.
112. Entry for 8 May 1944 in the flying Logbook of then Fg Off Peter Cowell, via Don Johnson.
113. 41 Squadron ORB, 8 May 1944, TNA AIR 27/426.
114. This statement in the Squadron ORB on 9 May 1944 contradicts the 10 Group ORB on the same date which states "The second recco to Morlaix and Abervrach [sic] saw nothing", whilst the Bolt Head ORB makes no mention of the two shipping reconnaissances whatsoever.
115. Entry for 9 May 1944 in the logbook of Flt Lt Terence Spencer; copyright Terry Spencer, via Cara and Raina Spencer.
116. This aircraft was Seafire F.III, LR862, of 894 Squadron, and its pilot, Lt. P. A. Meakin, was captured.
117. 41 Squadron ORB, 9 May 1944, TNA AIR 27/426.
118. Neither the pilot nor the serial of the aircraft that lost its oleo leg on 10 May 1944 are recorded in the Squadron ORB, as it was a non-operational flight. The only details are recorded in the RAF Bolt Head ORB. However, the aircraft in question was likely Spitfire XII, EN605.

119. The Squadron ORB's F541 records five operational sorties on 10 May 1944, as a part of a Ranger operation to St. Brieuc and Morlaix. This is, however, an erroneous entry as the sorties were a part of the following day's 10 Group Rodeo 134. See 11 May 1944 for details.
120. 41 Squadron ORB, 11 May 1944, TNA AIR 27/426.
121. Entry for 11 May 1944 in the logbook of Plt Off Jim C. J. Payne, via Dan Johnson.
122. Ibid., 12 May 1944.
123. There is a slight contradiction between sources in the number of aircraft involved in this hostile raid on 12 May 1944. The Squadron and RAF Bolt Head ORBs both state there were three aircraft, whereas the 10 Group ORB states there were only two.
124. 41 Squadron ORB, 12 May 1944, TNA AIR 27/426.
125. There are slight contradictions in the timings of this scramble on 12 May 1944. The Squadron ORB's F540 records 09:10-09:55, whereas the F541 records 09:20-09:55. Whilst the RAF Bolt Head ORB mentions the operation, it does not record timings, and the 10 Group ORB states 09:13-10:15.
126. 10 Group ORB, 12 May 1944, TNA AIR 25/183.
127. Entry for 12 May 1944 in the logbook of Fg Off Herbert A. Wagner, via Dan Johnson.
128. This was Temp Lt Anthony D. Hawkins-King RNVR, who was flying Seafire F.III, LR837. He was awarded a posthumous Mention in Despatches on 23 May 1944, and is remembered today on the Lee-on-Solvent Memorial, in Hampshire.
129. Entry for 13 May 1944 in the logbook of Flt Lt Terence Spencer; copyright Terry Spencer, via Cara and Raina Spencer.
130. The Squadron ORB's F540 and 10 Group ORB on 14 May 1944 both state that seven pilots participated in the Rodeo, but the Squadron ORB's F541 and the RAF Bolt Head ORB both state that eight pilots participated. It is therefore not clear which source is correct, and there is no indication of who, if anyone, may have not taken off or returned early.
131. Combat Report for Fg Off William N. Stowe, 14 May 1944, 41 Squadron Archives.
132. Entry for 14 May 1944 in the logbook of Flt Lt Terence Spencer; copyright Terry Spencer, via Cara and Raina Spencer.
133. There is a contradiction in the Squadron ORB on 15 May 1944, as the F540 states "there were no operational sorties during the day", whereas the F541 lists four scrambles. Moreover, the RAF Bolt Head ORB states the Squadron undertook "uneventful sorties" during the day, and Flt Lt Terry Spencer recorded his participation in a scramble in his logbook.
134. It is understood that only one of the two pilots – Fg Off Harry Cook *or* Flt Sgt Ian Stevenson – suffered what the ORB's F540 on 16 May 1944 describes only as 'engine trouble', but it does not identify which one. These facts are recorded on the F540, but the F541 fails to list the serials of the aircraft, even though it was an operational scramble. However, as a result of the problem, both pilots returned to base early, instead of conducting a routine patrol as was intended.
135. 41 Squadron ORB, 16 May 1944, TNA AIR 27/426.
136. RAF Fairwood Common was decommissioned by the RAF in 1946, and sold for commercial development in 1956. The airfield is the site of today's Swansea Airport.
137. The numbers and types of sorties listed here reflect those provided in the 11 APC ORB (TNA AIR 29/704), and differ from those in the 41 Squadron ORB, which states there were 24 sorties of air-to-air firing and 16 of air-to-ground firing.
138. As all the flying between 17 and 24 May 1944 was non-operational, no pilots, aircraft serials or timings are recorded on the Squadron ORB's F541.
139. The numbers and types of sorties listed here reflect those provided in the 11 APC ORB (TNA AIR 29/704), whereas 41 Squadron's ORB merely states a total of 95 were sorties flown today.
140. The numbers and types of sorties listed here reflect those provided in the 11 APC ORB (TNA AIR 29/704); 41 Squadron's ORB merely states there were a total of 55 sorties flown today.
141. The numbers and types of sorties listed here reflect those provided in the 11 APC ORB (TNA AIR 29/704); 41 Squadron's ORB merely states there were a total of 73 sorties flown today.
142. The numbers and types of sorties listed here reflect those provided in the 11 APC ORB (TNA AIR 29/704); 41 Squadron's ORB merely states there were a total of 80 sorties flown today.
143. The numbers and types of sorties listed here reflect those provided in the 11 APC ORB (TNA AIR 29/704), and differ from those in the 41 Squadron ORB, which states there were 32 sorties of air-to-air firing and 25 of dive bombing.
144. For further detail, see the RAF Fairwood Common ORB (TNA AIR 28/263) and 10 Group ORB Appendix (TNA AIR 25/188).
145. The numbers and types of sorties listed here reflect those provided in the 11 APC ORB (TNA AIR 29/704), and differ from those in the 41 Squadron ORB, which states there were 45 sorties of air-to-air firing and 35 of low-level bombing.
146. Source: 11 APC ORB, *REPORT ON COURSE NO. 17*, 24 May 1944, TNA AIR 29/704.
147. Fairwood Common ORB, TNA AIR 28/263, 24 May 1944.

148. 11 APC ORB, 24 May 1944, TNA AIR 29/704.
149. 41 Squadron ORB, 26 May 1944, TNA AIR 27/426.
150. Citation for Actg Flt Lt Arthur A. Glen's Bar to his DFC, 2 November 1943, *The London Gazette*, No. 36235. This information is licensed under the terms of the Open Government Licence (http://www.nationalarchives.gov.uk/doc/open-government-licence).
151. Correspondence from Flt Lt Ronald T. H. Collis to Dan Johnson, 2 November 1989; reproduced with Dan's kind permission.
152. Correspondence from Flt Lt Peter Cowell to Dan Johnson, 24 April 1984; reproduced with Dan's kind permission.
153. Entries from the personal diary of Flt Lt Terry Spencer, reproduced with his permission, copyright Terry Spencer, via Cara and Raina Spencer.
154. This latter scramble is mentioned on the Squadron ORB's F540 on 27 May 1944 but is not listed on the F541.
155. This scramble is listed on the Squadron ORB's F541 on 27 May 1944, but not mentioned on the F540. However, the details are included in the 10 Group ORB. The Bolt Head ORB makes no mention of the Squadron's activities whatsoever, and the day is summed up in three words, "Nothing to report".
156. The Squadron ORB's F540 on 28 May 1944 states that the morning's shipping reconnaissance was undertaken by Flt Lt Thomas Slack and Flt Sgt Robert Fleming. However, the F541 lists Flt Lt Terry Spencer and Fg Off Charles J. Malone instead. It is believed that Spencer's is the correct entry as it is substantiated by entries in his own logbook that day, which show a shipping reconnaissance to St. Peter Port, St. Malo, and Lézardrieux with light Flak.
157. Entry for 28 May 1944 in the logbook of Fg Off Peter Cowell, via Dan Johnson.
158. The Squadron ORB's F541 on 28 May 1944 states that Fg Off Peter Cowell returned "owing to mechanical trouble", but Cowell confirms in his logbook that the issue was that his jet tank would not feed fuel to his aircraft's engine.
159. This patrol is mentioned on the Squadron ORB's F540 on 29 May 1944, and in both the RAF Bolt Head and 10 Group ORBs. However, the sorties are not listed on the Squadron's F541, and there is no indication of who the participating pilots were.
160. 41 Squadron ORB, 29 May 1944, TNA AIR 27/426.
161. Entry for 29 May 1944 in the logbook of Flt Lt Terence Spencer; copyright Terry Spencer, via Cara and Raina Spencer.
162. These shipping reconnaissances are mentioned on the Squadron ORB's F540 on 30 May 1944, but are not listed on the F541. Timings and more detailed information are provided in the 10 Group ORB and some detail is also available in the RAF Bolt Head ORB, but there is no record of the four pilots who participated in them, except that Flt Lt Terry Spencer's logbook indicates he was amongst them.
163. 41 Squadron ORB, 1 June 1944, TNA AIR 27/426.
164. There are slight discrepancies between the Squadron ORB on 1 June 1944, and the RAF Bolt Head and 10 Group ORBs. The Squadron ORB indicates that Fg Off Kenneth Robinson and Plt Off Peter Gibbs attacked and damaged three trains in the Yffiniac area to Category B status, whereas both the Bolt Head and 10 Group ORBs state that the pair attacked four trains between St. Brieuc and Lamballe, resulting in three locomotives being claimed damaged to Cat. B status.
165. The Squadron ORB's F541 on 1 June 1944 states that both sections landed at the conclusion of their patrols at 09:30, whereas the RAF Bolt Head ORB states both sections landed at 09:45, and the 10 Group ORB states that the former section landed at 09:30 and the latter at 09:45.
166. There are a number of inconsistencies in regard to this operation in the Squadron ORB on 2 June 1944. First, the F540 states that this shipping reconnaissance was flown by Flt Lt Thomas Slack and Fg Off Robert Anderson, who landed again at 16:25, whereas the F541 lists Flt Lts Ronald Collis and William Stowe instead. In addition, the RAF Bolt Head ORB provides a combination of the two entries, stating that the pilots were actually Flt Lts Ronald Collis and Fg Off Robert Anderson. That said, it appears that the true participants were indeed Collis and Stowe, as both pilots have entries in their logbooks indicating they made a five-minute flight, followed by a 75-minute shipping reconnaissance to Sept-Îles, Morlaix, Lannilis and L'Aber-Wrac'h. As no other Squadron operations to this area are recorded on 2 June 1944, it is reasonably safe to assume that they were the participants, and not Slack and/or Anderson. The erroneous Slack and Anderson entry appears to be a duplication of an afternoon ASR patrol they made that day, also as Black Section, in which they returned after 16:00. According to the F541, it was both pilots' only operational flight that day.
167. 41 Squadron ORB, 2 June 1944, TNA AIR 27/426.
168. The reason a Walrus was not deployed earlier in the day is not clear, but it was probably the result of another ASR search underway 15 miles off Portland between 05:45 and 16:40 today for a missing bomber. This search consumed the services of two Spitfires, one Warwick and three Walruses from 276 Squadron, and two Walruses and two Spitfires from 11 Group.
169. RAF Bolt Head ORB, 2 June 1944, TNA AIR 28/89.
170. Entry for 2 June 1944 in the logbook of Fg Off Peter Cowell, via Dan Johnson.
171. Fg Off Herbert Wagner was promoted to Flight Lieutenant whilst in captivity, and liberated by Russian troops on 1 May 1945. He resigned his commission at the end of October that year and returned to the United States where he was latterly president of a company specialising in corporate buyouts. He passed away in November 2005.

172. Correspondence with Fg Off Herbert Wagner, September 2005.
173. 41 Squadron ORB, 2 June 1944, TNA AIR 27/426.
174. The details of the Squadron's first two patrols on 3 June 1944 have been extracted from meagre details in the Squadron and RAF Bolt Head ORBs, and somewhat more detail in the 10 Group ORB. However, the participants are not recorded on the Squadron ORB's F541, which in fact fails to list any operational sorties prior to 18:20. That said, Flt Lts William Stowe and Ronald Collis' logbooks suggest they were both involved. Stowe's logbook shows a shipping reconnaissance to Guernsey of 70 minutes' duration, whilst Collis' shows a shipping reconnaissance of the same duration to St. Peter Port, St. Malo and L'Aber Vrac'h. Whether these were the same patrol or whether one flew in each cannot be established. As an aside, Collis' logbook also records, "Hit in fuselage slightly", presumably by Flak, although the location is not recorded. He states he was flying EB-G at the time, which is believed to have been MB845, the same aircraft he had flown the previous late afternoon, searching for signs of submarines on Guernsey with Flt Lt Terry Spencer.
175. The 41 Squadron ORB on 3 June 1944 contains conflicting statements as the F540 says Red Section was airborne at 18:50, whereas the F541 states they took off at 18:30.
176. 41 Squadron ORB, 4 June 1944, TNA AIR 27/426.
177. RAF Bolt Head ORB, 5 June 1944, TNA AIR 28/89.
178. The invasion stripes applied to the Squadron's aircraft on 5 June 1944 consisted of five alternating 18-inch-wide stripes – white-black-white-black-white – painted 6 inches (15cm) inboard of the roundels on each wing, and 18 inches (46cm) forward of the tailplane at the rear of the fuselage. The application of these stripes today is not mentioned in the ORB, and only receives a mention in Plt Off Jim C. J. Payne's logbook (via Dan Johnson), where he noted today, "All A/C painted with Black & White Recognition Stripes".
179. Entry for 5 June 1944 in the logbook of Flt Lt Terry Spencer, copyright Terry Spencer, via Cara and Raina Spencer.
180. Operation *Overlord* was the over all codename for the Allied invasion of Europe in France, which ran from 6 June 1944 until the River Seine was crossed on 19 August. The assault itself was an operation of its own, codenamed *Neptune*, which began on 6 June 1944 and ended on 30 June, by which time the beachhead was firmly in Allied hands.
181. Source of statistics: D-Day Museum, Portsmouth, United Kingdom, http://www.ddaymuseum.co.uk (rtrvd Apr 2011).
182. *Order of the Day*, statement issued to the soldiers, sailors and airmen of the Allied Expeditionary Force by General Dwight D. Eisenhower on 6 June 1944. This text has been extracted from an original document, glued into the logbook of Flt Lt Terry Spencer on the double page covering 29 May-6 June 1944; copyright ownership unknown, believed public to be domain.
183. *Communique Number 1*, General Dwight D. Eisenhower, 6 June 1944; copyright ownership unknown, believed public to be domain.
184. Extract from Prime Minister Winston Churchill's speech, *War Situation; Liberation of Rome: Landings in France*, to the House of Commons, 6 June 1944, House of Commons Hansard, Parliamentary Archives, HC Deb 06 June 1944 vol 400 cc1207-11. This information is licensed under the terms of the Open Parliament Licence.
185. 41 Squadron ORB, 6 June 1944, TNA AIR 27/426.
186. The Squadron's F540 on 6 June 1944 states that Flt Lt Clive Birbeck and WO Arthur Appleton commenced the day with a convoy patrol at 10:25, but the F541 makes no mention of them, and lists Plt Off Jim Payne and Flt Sgt Frederick Woollard as the pilots on this patrol.
187. The Squadron ORB's F540 on 6 June 1944 also states that Flt Lt Clive Birbeck and Fg Off Robert Anderson were scrambled during this period, taking off at 11:35 and landing again at 13:05 "having seen nothing". However, the F541 does not list the scramble, pilots or serials. Alternatively, the F541 lists a Rodeo flown by Flt Lts Tom Slack and Keith Thiele between 11:55 and 13:35, but no destination is listed, and the F540 contains no mention of the patrol at all. Evidence in the RAF Bolt Head ORB, however, suggests the patrol was more likely a shipping reconnaissance ("4 Spitfires XII of 41 Sqdn did a shipping reconnaissance"), which pairs them up with Fg Off Maurice Balasse and Sqn Ldr Chapman.
188. Entry for 6 June 1944 in the logbook of Flt Lt Terry Spencer, copyright Terry Spencer, via Cara and Raina Spencer.
189. 10 Group ORB, 6 June 1944, TNA AIR 25/183.
190. The identity of these vessels is unclear. The Royal Navy's 10th Destroyer Flotilla is, however, known to have been in the area as it participated in the *Battle of Ushant* soon after 01:00 on 9 June 1944, when its eight destroyers clashed with the remaining four destroyers of the Kriegsmarine's 8th Destroyer Flotilla 30 miles east-northeast of Île de Batz, Brittany. This battle was still two days away at the time of the sighting tonight by Flt Lt Clive Birbeck and Flt Sgt Frederick Woollard, but whilst the identity of the minesweepers is unknown, the Allied destroyers they saw may have been from the 10th Destroyer Flotilla. A search of the Flotilla's ships' logs should reveal if they were indeed the vessels in question, but lies out of the scope of this work.
191. Source of statistics: D-Day Museum, Portsmouth, United Kingdom, http://www.ddaymuseum.co.uk (rtrvd 11 April 2011).
192. The 41 Squadron ORB's F540 on 7 June 1944 states that Sqn Ldr Robert Chapman and Flt Lt Terry Spencer participated in this shipping reconnaissance, but the F541 lists Fg Off Keith Curtis.
193. The 41 Squadron ORB's F540 on 7 June 1944 names the two participating sections as Red and Black, but the F541 lists them as White and Blue. However, Fg Off Peter Cowell records in his logbook that he was flying Red 1 and Fg

Off Robinson Red 2, which makes sense as the two pilots were from A Flight. It is, however, possible that the other section, which consisted of B Flight pilots led by Flt Lt Thomas Slack, was either Black or Blue Section.

194. The Squadron ORB's F541 on 7 June 1944 states that Blue Section's return time was 09:40. This is not 100% correct as Flt Lt Ronald Collis records in his logbook that the operation was of one hour and 50 minutes duration, implying he returned at 10:30. Whilst Fg Off Peter Cowell and Flt Lt William Stowe escorted the Walrus back to base and landed at 09:40, Collis stayed on to drop Fg Off Robinson his dinghy and orbit him until relieved. See also Point 196, below.
195. 10 Group ORB, 7 June 1944, TNA AIR TNA AIR 25/183.
196. According to the Squadron ORB on 7 June 1944, "it was over 30 minutes before F/Lt Collis could drop his own dinghy" to Fg Off Robinson, but the F541 indicates (i) that Robinson baled out at 09:10 (the 10 Group ORB states 09:15) and (ii) that the rest of the section (including Collis) landed again at 09:40. This would place Collis back in Bolt Head 30 minutes after Robinson had baled out, that is, at the same time as he is reported to have been dropping his dinghy to Robinson. Collis' logbook appears to clarify the situation, as it states he was in the air one hour and 50 minutes, which suggests his return time was actually 10:30, not 09:40. As an aside, the logbooks of other two pilots in the section, Flt Lt William Stowe and Fg Off Peter Cowell, both confirm their flying times were both of one hour duration, which correlates with the timings in the F541.
197. The 10 Group ORB on 7 June 1944 states that Fg Off Robinson actually died on board the launch.
198. Entry for 7 June 1944 in the logbook of Fg Off Peter Cowell, via Dan Johnson.
199. Entry for 7 June 1944 in the logbook of Flt Lt Ronald T. H. Collis, via Dan Johnson.
200. Entry for 7 June 1944 in the logbook of Flt Lt William N. Stowe, via Dan Johnson.
201. Entry for 7 June 1944 in the logbook of Flt Lt Terry Spencer, copyright Terry Spencer, via Cara and Raina Spencer.
202. Correspondence with Flt Lt Ronald T. H. Collis, September 2003.
203. Sqn Ldr Keith F. 'Jimmy' Thiele DSO DFC**, undated and unpublished autobiography, 41 Squadron Archives.
204. *Pilot Service Record* for Fg Off Kenneth B. Robinson, 41 Squadron Archives.
205. The Squadron ORB's F541 records two ASR patrols during the morning, the first 09:35-11:10 by Flt Lt Robert Anderson and WO Arthur Appleton as Green Section, and the second 10:40-12:00 by Flt Sgts Frederick Woollard and Robert Fleming as Black Section. It appears that one of these sections was deployed on the rescue operation for Fg Off Kenneth Robinson, and the other on the search for the Coastal Command dinghy. Unfortunately, here is no indication of which section was deployed on which operation.
206. The Squadron ORB's F540 on 7 June 1944 states that this section was airborne between 14:00 and 15:30, whereas the F541 states they were airborne between 17:55 and 18:45. A Combat Report for the operation in 41 Squadron's Archives states that the attacks were delivered around 19:00, suggesting that the earlier timings are completely erroneous, whilst the return time of the latter is probably also inaccurate. The 10 Group ORB records their departure as 17:59 and their return as 19:49, which is circumstantially more likely to be correct.
207. The 10 Group ORB indicates the bomber in question was a Liberator, however contemporary research suggests it was actually B-17 Flying Fortress 42-97238 'Our Captain' of the 381st Bomber Group. They had been on a bombing mission to Kerlin Bastard Airfield, but had taken a hit by Flak that was so serious they were unable to make it back to the United Kingdom and forced to ditch in the Channel.
208. 41 Squadron ORB, 8 June 1944, TNA AIR 27/426.
209. Entry for 8 June 1944 in the logbook of Plt Off Jim C. J. Payne, via Dan Johnson.
210. Entry for 7-8 June 1944 in the personal diary of Flt Sgt Patrick Coleman; reproduced with the kind permission of the Coleman family via Mike Brampton.
211. The 10 Group ORB on 9 June 1944 states that 41 Squadron had fourteen aircraft on the sweep, but both the Squadron and RAF Bolt Head ORBs state there were twelve.
212. Entry for 9 June 1944 in the logbook of Fg Off Peter Cowell, via Dan Johnson.
213. Entry for 9 June 1944 in the logbook of Flt Lt Terry Spencer; copyright Terry Spencer, via Cara and Raina Spencer.
214. Telex message from OC Bolt Head to RAAF Overseas Headquarters, Kingsway, London, dated 10 June 1944, personnel file of JGH Refshauge, NAA.
215. Telex message from Sqn Ldr Chapman, Bolt Head, to RAAF Overseas Headquarters, Kodak House, London WC2, dated 13 June 1944, personnel file of JGH Refshauge, NAA.
216. RAAF Casualty File for Fg Off John G. H. Refshauge, *Correspondence files, multiple number (Melbourne) series (Primary numbers 1-323)*, Series A705, Barcode 1078012, NAA.
217. Correspondence with Sqn Ldr (then Fg Off) Keith R. Curtis, via his daughter Karen Neale, June 2003.
218. Correspondence from Flt Lt Tom Slack to Dan Johnson, 20 February 1984; reproduced with Dan's kind permission.
219. The Squadron ORB on 10 June 1944 states the attack was on vessels in Sark Harbour, whereas the RAF Bolt Head ORB states the attack was on vessels in a bay on the north-eastern coast of Sark, and the 10 Group ORB states the attack was on vessels southeast of Sark.
220. 41 Squadron ORB, 10 June 1944, TNA AIR 27/426.
221. Ibid., 12 June 1944.
222. The 41 Squadron ORB's F540 on 13 June 1944 indicates that a shipping reconnaissance was flown between 04:00 and 05:20, however the F541 shows that the first flight of the day was between 14:00 and 15:20, suggesting a

transcription error. Evidence in both the RAF Bolt Head and 10 Group ORBs confirm that the Squadron was not airborne on this date until 14:00.
223. The Squadron ORB's F540 on 15 June 1944 states that eight of the Squadron's pilots flew this operation, as do the RAF Bolt Head and 10 Group ORBs, however the Squadron F541 only lists seven pilots and aircraft serials – Spencer, Stevenson, Cook, Malone, van Goens, Anderson and Fleming.
224. 41 Squadron ORB, 15 June 1944, TNA AIR 27/426.
225. 10 Group ORB, 17 June 1944, TNA AIR 25/183.
226. Entry for 17 June 1944 in the logbook of Flt Lt William Stowe, via Dan Johnson.
227. Tom Slack in his autobiography, *Happy is the Day; A Spitfire Pilot's Story*, 1987, United Writers Publications; reproduced with the Publisher's permission.
228. Entry for 18 June 1944 in the logbook of Flt Sgt James Ware, via Dan Johnson.
229. Correspondence from Flt Lt Tom Slack to Dan Johnson, 8 March 1983; reproduced with Dan's kind permission.
230. Trafford Publishing, ISBN 9781553954996, January 2003.

6 REPELLING THE V1; 19 JUNE – 27 AUGUST 1944

1. Extract from Prime Minister Winston Churchill's speech, *War and International Situation*, to the House of Commons, 22 February 1944, House of Commons Hansard, Parliamentary Archives, 22 February 1944 vol 397 cc683-684. This information is licensed under the terms of the Open Parliament Licence.
2. Excerpt from correspondence with WO John Chalmers, then of 610 Squadron, who joined 41 Squadron in March 1945; September 2009.
3. Recollections of the V1 by Fg Off Peter Graham in his autobiography *Skypilot; Memoirs from Take-Off to Landing*, 2001, Pentland Books; reproduced with his kind permission.
4. RAF West Malling ORB, 19 June 1944, TNA AIR 28/907.
5. Recollections of the V1 by Fg Off Peter Graham in his autobiography *Skypilot; Memoirs from Take-Off to Landing*, 2001, Pentland Books; reproduced with his kind permission.
6. Between 20 June and 28 August 1944, the period during Summer 1944 in which 41 Squadron was deployed on anti-Diver patrols, the author has included at the beginning of each day's entries the weather and daytime Diver activity recorded by 11 Group in their ORB (TNA AIR 25/195). The Diver information usually consists of the volume of V1s that (i) were plotted by the Group, (ii) made landfall, (iii) were shot down by fighters, (iv) were shot down by anti-aircraft defences, and (v) were brought down by the balloon barrage, to put 41 Squadron's activity into some context. Please note, however, that this information is only correct for the day period (05:30-23:30), and that Divers plotted in the night period (23:30-05:30) were recorded separately in the ORB. As 41 Squadron's aircraft were day fighters, and the pilots did not fly operationally after dark, night-time Diver activity has been excluded from this work due to its irrelevance to the Squadron's operations. It should also be noted that during this period, to extend the hours of daylight, Britain operated on Double British Summer Time (DBST), which meant that British time was equal to German time on the Continent.
7. 41 Squadron ORB, 20 June 1944, TNA AIR 27/426.
8. The 41 Squadron ORB for June 1944 (TNA AIR 27/426) is somewhat confusing, as there is one F540 for 19-28 June, and a second F540, almost verbatim but not quite, for 20-30 June 1944. The quote in Note 7, above, has been excerpted from the latter sheet.
9. The Squadron ORB's F541 for 20 June 1944 shows 46 sorties making up 23 patrols and as such it is impossible to match the F541 with the statement on the F540 that there were "thirteen unsuccessful patrols".
10. Note that the Squadron ORB's F541 on 20 June 1944 states that Yellow Section was airborne at 19:00, but that Plt Off Peter Gibbs landed again at 19:40 and Fg Off Peter Cowell landed at 20:05. However, Gibbs' Combat Report (No. 502, TNA AIR 50/18) states that he was airborne at 19:20, intercepted the V1 at 19:55 and landed again at 20:00. There is no indication which of these accounts is correct, but the timings in the text have been extracted from Gibbs' Combat Report.
11. Entry for 20 June 1944 in Plt Off N. Peter Gibbs logbook.
12. Correspondence with Sqn Ldr (then Fg Off) Keith R. Curtis, via his daughter Karen Neale, August 2005.
13. Entry for 20 June 1944 in the logbook of Flt Lt Terence Spencer; copyright Terry Spencer, via Cara and Raina Spencer.
14. Entry for 20 June 1944 in the logbook of Flt Lt Ross P. Harding; Spitfire Society.
15. The Squadron ORB's F540 states there was one successful patrol and 19 unsuccessful. However, the F541 only lists 16 patrols in total.
16. Entry for 21 June 1944 in then Fg Off Peter Cowell's logbook, via Dan Johnson.
17. Undated and unpublished anecdotal autobiography of Sqn Ldr Keith F. 'Jimmy' Thiele, 41 Squadron Archives.
18. The Squadron F541 on 22 June 1944 lists 24 patrols (48 sorties). However, the F540 states that on top of Flt Sgt Colin Robertson's, and Flt Lt Clive Birbeck's and Fg Off Robert Anderson's successful patrols, there were "ten more unsuccessful patrols during the remainder of the day". This statement therefore appears to be erroneous, as simple deduction suggests there were 22 more unsuccessful patrols, not ten.

19. *Pilot Service Record* for Flt Sgt Colin S. Robertson, 41 Squadron Archives.
20. Entry for 22 June 1944 in the logbook of Flt Lt Terence Spencer; copyright Terry Spencer, via Cara and Raina Spencer.
21. These Tempests may have included 3 Squadron's Flt Lt Remy van Lierde and 486 Squadron's Plt Off Raymond J. Danzey, both of whom claimed a shared V1 in the Hastings area at 04:59. No other claims on this date appear to fit the time and location.
22. Entry for 23 June 1944 in the logbook of Plt Off Jim C. J. Payne; Spitfire Society.
23. Entry for 23 June 1944 in the logbook of Flt Lt William N. Stowe; Spitfire Society.
24. Combat Report for Flt Lt Terry Spencer, 23 June 1944, No. 381, TNA AIR 50/18.
25. Flt Lt Terry Spencer submitted two Combat Reports for this action on 23 June 1944. These can be found in folios 380 and 381 in TNA AIR 50/18. Although most details are similar, the latter of the two, No. 381, offers more information on Spencer's attack, although the former mentions that the two Tempests that cut in also opened fire, which the latter does not.
26. Entry for 23 June 1944 in the logbook of Flt Lt Terence Spencer; copyright Terry Spencer, via Cara and Raina Spencer.
27. 41 Squadron ORB, 23 June 1944, TNA AIR 27/426.
28. The Squadron ORB's F540 on 24 June 1944 states there were 19 patrols, but the F541 actually lists 20, the additional anti-Diver patrol being a single aircraft patrol by Plt Off Peter Gibbs in MB875 between 16:00 and 17:00.
29. The location where the V1 was brought down differs slightly between reports. The Squadron ORB on 24 June 1944 states it was "about 8 miles South of Hastings"; Gibbs' logbook records "sea about 10 mls. South of Hastings", and Gibbs' Combat Report (No. 228, TNA AIR 50/18) states just "Hastings".
30. Entry for 24 June 1944 in the logbook of Flt Lt Ross P. Harding; Spitfire Society.
31. Source: RAF West Malling ORB, 24 June 1944, TNA AIR 28/907.
32. The Squadron ORB's F540 on 25 June 1944 states that besides Flt Lt Terry Spencer and Flt Sgt Roger Short's successful patrol between 22:45 and 23:35, "22 other patrols were flown throughout the day". However, the F541 only lists a total of 21 patrols.
33. Flt Lt Terry Spencer's Combat Report (No. 504, TNA AIR 50/18) states that the location his V1 came down was "Fixed at Hulden R.3756", but no such location exists. However, the coordinate – wR3756 on the British Cassini Grid – shows the location was High Halden, Kent.
34. 41 Squadron ORB, 25 June 1944, TNA AIR 27/426.
35. There is a slight ambiguity in the day's reports with regard to Flt Sgt Roger Short V1 claim on 25 June 1944. As quoted in the text, the Squadron ORB states Short claimed a half share, but his Combat Report (No. 504, TNA AIR 50/18) states the victory was "shared with 2 Spitfires", which implies a third share. The RAF West Malling ORB (TNA AIR 28/907) does not assist in clarifying the situation as it only states "1 Diver (shared) destroyed by F/Sgt Short".
36. Confusingly, the Squadron ORB's F540 on 27 June 1944 states that the unit flew 13 unsuccessful anti-Diver patrols throughout the day, whereas the F541 lists 19 patrols (38 sorties) and the Tangmere Station ORB states they flew 28 sorties.
37. 41 Squadron ORB, 27 June 1944, TNA AIR 27/426.
38. Ibid., 28 June 1944.
39. Ibid.
40. The identity of the pilot who wrote this is known to the author but withheld for reasons of privacy. It has, however, been reproduced with his permission.
41. 41 Squadron ORB, 1 July 1944, TNA AIR 27/426.
42. Ibid., 2 July 1944.
43. Entry in WO Patrick Coleman's personal diary for July 1944; reproduced with the kind permission of the Coleman family via Mike Brampton.
44. The Squadron ORB's F541 on 3 July 1944 states that Blue Section landed again at 06:35, but Fg Off Maurice Balasse's Combat Report (No. 48, TNA AIR 50/18) states his attack was made at 06:35 and that he landed back at Friston at 06:42.
45. 41 Squadron ORB, 3 July 1944, TNA AIR 27/426.
46. Unfortunately, details of Sqn Ldr Robert Chapman's victory are a little convoluted. The Squadron ORB's F540 on 3 July 1944 records that "during the second of these [patrols] S/Ldr Chapman destroyed one Jet Propelled Bomb…". However, the F541 that day states that the second patrol consisted of Flt Lt Thomas Slack in MB238 [sic] and Flt Sgt James Ware in EN226, who were airborne as Green Section at 07:05 and returned at 07:35; Chapman is not mentioned at all. The timings and details used in the text have therefore been extracted from Chapman's Combat Report (No. 146, TNA AIR 50/18). The entry on the F540, the existence of the Combat Report, and mention of Chapman's victory in the ORB's Appendix (TNA AIR 27/431) all prove the combat took place, and therefore suggest that the F541 is the erroneous document.
47. The Squadron ORB's F540 on 4 July 1944 states that 11 patrols took place today, but the F541 appears to list 15, along with pilots' names, aircraft serials, departure times and return times. Three, however, are crossed out with

dashes, thus '- – – -', suggesting they may have been non-operational flights instead, that were erroneously included on the F541. This still leaves 12 operational patrols on the F541 versus the 11 stated on the F540.
48. The Squadron ORB's F540 on 4 July 1944 states that the victory occurred on the day's second anti-Diver patrol, but the F541 indicates it was, in fact, the third.
49. Combat Report for Fg Off Maurice Balasse and Flt Sgt Frederick Woollard, 4 July 1944, 41 Squadron Archives.
50. Correspondence with then Sqn Ldr (then Fg Off) Keith R. Curtis, via his daughter Karen Neale, August 2005.
51. 41 Squadron ORB, 6 July 1944, TNA AIR 27/426.
52. There are two slight discrepancies in the Squadron ORB on 6 July 1944. The F540 states flying commenced at 07:55 and that 17 patrols were undertaken, but the F541 shows the first patrol airborne at 07:25 and lists 18 patrols.
53. Tom Slack in his autobiography, *Happy is the Day; A Spitfire Pilot's Story*; 1987, United Writers Publications; reproduced with the Publisher's permission.
54. There are two slight discrepancies in the Squadron ORB on 7 July 1944. The F540 states that 16 patrols were undertaken (Fg Off Peter Graham's and "15 other patrols") and that flying ceased at 23:00, but the F541 lists only 13 patrols shows the last landing at 23:30.
55. Combat Report for Fg Off Peter B. Graham, No. 503, 7 July 1944, TNA AIR 50/18.
56. *Pilot Service Record* for Fg Off Peter B. Graham, 41 Squadron Archives.
57. The 41 Squadron ORB on 7 July 1944 states that Fg Off Peter Graham's V1 was brought down ten miles west of Hailsham, Sussex, but Graham's Combat Report for the action states that it came down eight miles northeast of Lewes. Considering the V1 came in over Friston and was intercepted six miles east of Hailsham on a course of 320°, it is more likely that it was brought down northeast of Lewes rather than further west of Hailsham.
58. In his Combat Report on 7 July 1944 (No. 503, TNA AIR 50/18), WO Ian Stevenson erroneously identifies the aircraft that overshot him as a Tempest. However, 316 (Polish) Squadron was flying Mustang III's at this time.
59. Combat Report for Flt Sgt Peter W. Chattin, No. 501, 8 July 1944, TNA AIR 50/18.
60. Entry for 8 July 1944 in the logbook of Flt Sgt Peter W. Chattin; reproduced with the kind permission of his son Mike.
61. 41 Squadron ORB, 8 July 1944, TNA AIR 27/426.
62. Ibid.
63. *Skypilot; Memoirs from Take-Off to Landing*, Peter Graham, 2001, Pentland Books; reproduced with his kind permission.
64. Flt Lt Robert Anderson and WO Arthur Appleton recorded the location of the interception of their V1 on 9 July 1944 on their combined Combat Report (No. 497, TNA AIR 50/18) as 12 miles southeast of Beachy Head, Sussex, but did not record the location the V1 was actually brought down, as was generally the practice.
65. 41 Squadron ORB, 9 July 1944, TNA AIR 27/426.
66. The five moves referred to in the Squadron ORB on 9 July 1944 were from Bolt Head to West Malling on 19 June 1944, to Tangmere on 26 June 1944, to Westhampnett on 27 June 1944, to Friston on 2 July 1944, and now to Lympne on 11 July 1944.
67. 41 Squadron ORB, 10 July 1944, TNA AIR 27/426.
68. Entry in WO Patrick Coleman's personal diary for July 1944; reproduced with the kind permission of the Coleman family via Mike Brampton.
69. 41 Squadron ORB, 11 July 1944, TNA AIR 27/426.
70. Lympne is pronounced 'Lim'.
71. *Skypilot; Memoirs from Take-Off to Landing*, Peter Graham, 2001, Pentland Books; reproduced with his kind permission.
72. These details on the Officers' Mess were provided in Flt Lt John Wilkinson's anecdotal autobiography, *Wilkinson J F Flight Lieutenant, My Experiences in World War II as a Royal Air Force Fighter Pilot*, undated, IWM, ID No. 03/32/1.
73. Tom Slack in his autobiography, *Happy is the Day; A Spitfire Pilot's Story*; 1987, United Writers Publications; reproduced with the Publisher's permission.
74. Combat Report for Fg Off Jim C. J. Payne, 41 Squadron Archives.
75. Entry for 13 July 1944 in the logbook of Fg Off Jim C. J. Payne; Spitfire Society.
76. The Squadron ORB's F541 on 14 July 1944 lists the pair in this order, suggesting that Fg Off Jim C. J. Payne was No. 1, leading the section. However, as Flt Lt Keith F. Thiele held the higher rank and it was he who made the attack on the V1, it is most likely that Thiele was Black 1, leading the section, and not Payne.
77. *Opflash No. 4 for 14.7.44*, 41 Squadron Archives.
78. The Squadron ORB's F540 on 16 July 1944 states that 15 patrols were carried out during the day, but the F541 only lists 14.
79. Combat Report for Fg Off Douglas P. Fisher, No. 204, 16 July 1944, TNA AIR 50/18.
80. Strangely, despite the seriousness of the accident – the Squadron's deadliest since September 1942 – it is not mentioned in the Squadron's ORB on 17 July 1944. The only hint is that Flt Sgts Ian Stevenson and Roger Short are shown on the F541 as having taken of at 15:55, with Oddy's sortie ending at 16:00 and Stevenson's at 16:10, which would account for Stevenson doing a circuit and landing again. Most information on the accident is revealed on the Air Accident Cards, AM Forms 1180, for Spitfire MB877 and Tiger Moth DE575, dated 17 July 1944, which are held at the Royal Air Force Museum, Department of Research and Information Services, Grahame Park Way, Hendon, NW9 5LL.

81. Entry for 17 July 1944 in the logbook of Flt Lt Terence Spencer; copyright Terry Spencer, via Cara and Raina Spencer.
82. Ibid., 22 July 1944.
83. Entry in WO Patrick Coleman's personal diary for 19 July 1944; reproduced with the kind permission of the Coleman family via Mike Brampton.
84. Air Accident Cards, AM Forms 1180, for Spitfire MB877 and Tiger Moth DE575, 17 July 1944, Royal Air Force Museum, Hendon.
85. Flt Sgt Clifford Oddy was the husband of Elsie Oddy of Headingley, Leeds, and the son of Clifford and Catherine Oddy of Armley, Leeds. He was buried in Leeds Armley Cemetery in Yorkshire. Flt Sgt Roger L. Short was the husband of Dorothy Short of South Ruislip, Middlesex, and the son of Henry and Elizabeth Short. He was buried in Hawkinge Cemetery, Kent.
86. 41 Squadron ORB, 18 July 1944, TNA AIR 27/426.
87. Ibid.
88. The Squadron ORB's F540 on 19 July 1944 states that the V1 fell to Fg Off Maurice Balasse on the day's "fourth patrol which took off at 08.30", however, the F541 shows the patrol that took off at 08:30 involving Balasse was actually the day's second operational patrol. This may indicate two other non-operational patrols took place prior to Balasse's, or may simply be erroneous. It should also be noted, however, that this particular patrol operated from Newchurch, rather than Lympne. Flt Lt Keith F. Thiele flew the first anti-Diver patrol of the day with Balasse as Blue Section at 05:00 and, whilst not recorded, they may have landed at Newchurch on their return at 06:05. This may explain why the pair started the 08:30 patrol from Newchurch and used the same aircraft and section designation as on their first patrol.
89. The 41 Squadron ORB's F540 states that 22 patrols were undertaken on 20 July 1944 "with one recco this [sic] was in [sic] the second patrol of the day". However, the F541 only lists 21 patrols and all of these are designated anti-Diver patrols.
90. 41 Squadron ORB, 20 July 1944, TNA AIR 27/426.
91. Entry for 21 July 1944 in the logbook of Plt Off Jim C. J. Payne; Spitfire Society.
92. Excerpt from correspondence with WO John A. Chalmers, January 2009.
93. 41 Squadron ORB, 22 July 1944, TNA AIR 27/426.
94. Fg Off Jim C. J. Payne's logbook [Spitfire Society] records, "Intercepted and closed to 200 yards on Diver – gave 4x2 seconds bursts hitting jet on port wing – slowed it down – F/O Balasse my No. 2 finished it off. Claimed ½ Diver destroyed south of Hastings."
95. The time that Fg Off Peter Graham and WO Arthur Appleton were airborne as Black Section on 23 July 1944 is not 100% clear. The Squadron ORB's F540 states they were airborne at 14:30 to relieve Fg Offs Jim Payne and Maurice Balasse, but the F541 is illegible, with the second digit overtyped and showing 1X:45, the overtyped numbers appearing to be a 4 and a 5, implying 14:45 or 15:45. If they were relieving Payne and Balasse, 14:45 would make more sense, although this contradicts the time given on the F540 (14:30). To add to the confusion, however, the Combat Report for Appleton's V1 on this patrol states he was airborne at 13:45, intercepted the V1 at 14:45 and returned at 15:35. Although technically possible, it is unlikely that Appleton was airborne from 13:45 until 15:35 when anti-Diver patrols usually only took approximately 75-90 minutes. Therefore, considering the F540's statement that "…soon after reaching the patrol line [Graham and Appleton] were vectored onto another bomb…", it is most likely that the pair were airborne at 14:30, intercepted the V1 at 14:45, and returned to Lympne at 15:35. These are the timings used by the author in the text.
96. Combat Report for WO Arthur S. Appleton, No. 499, 23 July 1944, TNA AIR 50/18.
97. Flt Lt Peter Cowell remained with FAU for a few months, then transferred for a short time to 83 GSU at Dunsfold before being posted back to 41 Squadron for a second tour on 31 January 1945. Flt Lt Clive Birbeck only remained with FAU a short while, before being transferred to the Fighter Interception Unit, similarly based at Wittering. On 11 August, however, Birbeck and five other pilots were posted from the FIU to 501 Squadron at Manston when a number of men were transferred away from 501 Squadron unit to form the nucleus of 274 Squadron, reforming at the same airfield. Birbeck achieved two night victories over V1s in October 1944, and in December was sent to 84 GSU at Thruxton. Returning to operations again in early January 1945, he was posted to 127 Squadron, then based at B.79 Woensdrecht in the Netherlands. However, his tenure was extremely brief as he was shot down by Flak during an attack on the midget submarine pens at Maasluis only 11 days later and captured. Birbeck spent two months at Stalag XIIIB at Nuremburg before force-marching to Stalag VIIA at Moosburg, where he was liberated by advancing Allied troops on 29 April 1945.
98. 41 Squadron ORB, 24 July 1944, TNA AIR 27/426.
99. 11 Group ORB, 27 July 1944, TNA AIR 25/195.
100. The Squadron ORB's F540 on 27 July 1944 states that nine patrols were carried out, but the F541 only lists eight. However, the RAF Lympne ORB also states that 18 aircraft from 41 Squadron were airborne on anti-Diver patrols, which suggests that nine patrols is likely to be the correct number.
101. The 41 Squadron ORB's F540 states on 28 July 1944 that 21 patrols were undertaken, but the F541 only lists 20. Alternatively, the RAF Lympne ORB states that 41 Squadron sent up 44 aircraft (22 patrols) on this date.

102. Entry in WO Patrick Coleman's personal diary for the period 24 July-1 August 1944; reproduced with the kind permission of the Coleman family via Mike Brampton.
103. The 41 Squadron ORB's F540 states on 29 July 1944 that six patrols were undertaken, and the RAF Lympne ORB states the Squadron had 12 aircraft in the air on anti-Diver patrols, which amounts to the same thing. However, the Squadron's ORB's F541 actually lists the serials, names and timings of 14 aircraft (seven patrols) on this date.
104. The location of Fg Off Maurice Balasse's V1 interception on his 18:00 anti-Diver patrol on 29 July 1944 differs slightly between sources. His Combat Report [No. 52, TNA AIR 50/18] states "10/15 miles from Le Touquet" at 2,500 feet; the Squadron ORB states "3000 feet off Le Touquet"; Balasse's *Pilot Service Record* [41 Squadron Archives] states "2,500 ft 12 miles from Le Touquet"; and the RAF Lympne ORB states "12 miles from Le Touquet" without an altitude.
105. This account of Fg Off Maurice Balasse's first V1 victory on 29 July 1944 has been compiled using several sources. His Combat Report [No. 52, TNA AIR 50/18] barely suggests the V1 was knocked off course by his slip-stream, whereas the RAF Lympne ORB clearly states the V1 "appeared to become caught in the Spitfires [sic] slip-stream". The Squadron ORB suggests Balasse "…misjudged his approach and narrowly missed a collision as he passed under the bomb", but makes no reference to him passing out. It is finally Balasse's *Pilot Service Record* [41 Squadron Archives], however, which reveals "Dived in front of flying Bomb. Blacked out & recovering [sic]. P.O. [sic] Payne confirms Bomb into sea as a result of Balasse's slip stream…".
106. 41 Squadron ORB, 29 July 1944, TNA AIR 27/426.
107. Being a non-operational flight, the serial of Fg Off Maurice Balasse's Spitfire XII on his 21:25 air test is not recorded on the Squadron ORB's F541 on 29 July 1944.
108. Fg Off Maurice Balasse's Combat Report [No. 53, TNA AIR 50/18], his *Pilot Service Record* [41 Squadron Archives], and the RAF Lympne ORB all state the V1 was destroyed three miles southeast of Woodchurch, whereas the Squadron ORB on 29 July 1944 states the location was "…about a mile South East of Wood Church".
109. 41 Squadron ORB, 29 July 1944, TNA AIR 27/426.
110. The RAF Lympne ORB on 30 July 1944 states that 41 Squadron sent up 46 aircraft (i.e. 23 patrols) on anti-diver patrols, thereby contradicting 41 Squadron's ORB, which lists 20 patrols (40 aircraft) were airborne on anti-Diver operations.
111. The Squadron ORB's F540 states that 15 patrols were carried out on 31 July 1944, but the F541 only lists nine patrols (18 aircraft and their pilots). However, the RAF Lympne ORB corroborates the Squadron's F540, stating that 18 aircraft from 41 Squadron carried out anti-Diver patrols.
112. 41 Squadron ORB, 1 August 1944, TNA AIR 27/426.
113. Extract from Prime Minister Winston Churchill's speech, *War Situation*, to the House of Commons, 2 August 1944, House of Commons Hansard, Parliamentary Archives, HC Deb 02 August 1944 vol 402 cc1475-1476. This information is licensed under the terms of the Open Parliament Licence.
114. The Squadron ORB's F540 states that the Squadron undertook 20 anti-Diver patrols on 3 August 1944, but the F541 only lists 19. Of no assistance, the RAF Lympne ORB states the Squadron sent up 44 aircraft (22 patrols) on anti-Diver operations.
115. The 41 Squadron ORB's F540 on 4 August 1944 states "twenty one patrols were carried out" but the F541 only lists 17 patrols and 34 pilots and serials. The RAF Lympne ORB states that 41 Squadron had 33 aircraft airborne, which is closer to the F541. As such, 17 patrols has been used in the text.
116. Flt Sgt Lawrence E. 'Larry' Spurr, was posted to 416 (City of Oshawa) Squadron at B.2 Bazenville, France, flying Spitfire IXs, as a freshly commissioned Pilot Officer on 23 August 1944. On Christmas Eve, he was involved in a disastrous operation when he was one of five 416 Squadron pilots shot down by U.S. anti-aircraft fire over France. One pilot was killed, one evaded and three others, including Spurr returned safely. He remained in the RCAF after the War and was awarded a Mention in Despatches in January 1946. Spurr flew Sabres for the USAAF during the Korean War and was awarded a United States DFC, before being released from the RCAF in December 1970. Sadly, he was killed in a motor vehicle accident a little over two years later.
117. 41 Squadron ORB, 6 August 1944, TNA AIR 27/426.
118. Ibid., 7 August 1944.
119. Ibid., 8 August 1944.
120. Ibid., 9 August 1944.
121. Combat Report for Fg Off Harry Cook, 9 August 1944, No. 158, TNA AIR 50/18.
122. Despite the fact Fg Offs Jim Payne and Maurice Balasse identified the bomber in their report (*Lympne Opflash No. 463*, 9 August 1944, 41 Squadron Archives) as a Lancaster, analysis of bomber operations and losses against this date and timeframe suggests the bomber in question was in fact Halifax III, MZ363, of 427 Squadron, which had taken off from RAF Leeming at 19:00. They were a part of a formation of 58 Halifaxes and 20 Mosquitos sent to bomb Noball targets at La Neuville. MZ363 was the operation's only loss. Although Payne and Balasse reported seeing five parachutes, none of the crew of seven survived. Four of the men are buried on French soil and the remaining three are commemorated on the Runnymede Memorial in Surrey. The crew were Fg Offs G. P. Wyse RCAF (pilot) and J. S. Beresford RCAF (co-pilot), Plt Off J. J. Ringer RCAF (Navigator), and WO2 R. S. Ferguson RCAF, and Sgts R. G. Grout RCAF, S. J. Levesque RCAF, and A. MacKay (Air Gunners).
123. 41 Squadron ORB, 10 August 1944, TNA AIR 27/426.

124. The 41 Squadron ORB's F540 states that 15 patrols were undertaken on 11 August 1944, but the F541 only lists 14 operational patrols. Alternatively, the RAF Lympne ORB states the Squadron had 27 aircraft in the air on anti-Diver operations, which would also indicate that 14 patrols (likely 13 x 2 aircraft and 1 x 1 aircraft) were undertaken.
125. 315 Squadron's Flt Sgt Jakub Bargielowski was flying Mustang III, FX878 on this sortie on 11 August 1944.
126. 130 Squadron ORB, entries for 5-10 August 1944, TNA AIR 27/938.
127. 41 Squadron ORB, 12 August 1944, TNA AIR 27/426.
128. Ibid., 13 August 1944.
129. Ibid., 14 August 1944.
130. 11 Group ORB, 14 August 1944, TNA AIR 25/195.
131. 130 Squadron ORB, 15 August 1944, TNA AIR 27/938.
132. Combat Report for Fg Off Charles J. 'Jack' Malone, No. 303, 14/15 August 1944, TNA AIR 50/18.
133. There are some contradictions between sources concerning the date of Fg Off C. J. 'Jack' Malone's victory. Malone's Combat Report (No. 303, TNA AIR 50/18) bears the date 14 August 1944, and the victory is also reported in the Lympne Station ORB on this date. However, 41 Squadron's ORB reports the victory on 15 August and the timings and details on Malone's Combat Report (White Section, up at 08:00, down at 09:35), though dated 14 August, tally with the ORB's F541 entries on 15 August. Moreover, according to the F541, Malone did not fly operationally at all on 14 August, and no such patrol took place between 08:00 and 09:35. Most importantly, however, Malone's entries in his logbook support the F541, indicating that he did not fly operationally on 14 August, and that the sortie and victory in question in fact occurred on 15 August 1944.
134. Fg Off Charles J. 'Jack' Malone was posted to 417 (City of Windsor) Squadron in Italy flying Spitfire VIIIs in August 1944 and was promoted to Flight Commander in early November. Following a period with Middle East Command in Egypt in early 1945, he returned to Canada in May and was demobilised in September that year. Malone was re-commissioned in the RCAF in October 1950 and served with 420 Squadron, 1 OTU and 439 Squadron, the latter of which was based in France, equipped with the F86 Sabre. In February 1964, following a five-year tenure with Air Defence Headquarters in Metz, Malone was promoted to Squadron Leader and posted home to Canada where he spent his remaining four years with the RCAF in ground staff roles. He was promoted to Major in February 1968 and retired in October that year, retaining his rank.
135. The available documentation does not explain why Flt Sgt Vivian Rossow made the attack, as Fg Off Rijklof van Goens – flying as Blue 1 – would usually have taken the lead.
136. 41 Squadron ORB, 16 August 1944, TNA AIR 27/426.
137. The ORB makes no mention of Fg Off Peter Graham damaging a V1 on 16 August 1944, and the only evidence appears in his logbook. Although there is no 'official' evidence available, this may have constituted the Squadron's first such victory.
138. The 41 Squadron ORB on 17 August 1944 states the cloud cover was 7/10ths at 800 and 3,000 feet, whereas Flt Lt Ross Harding states on his Combat Report (No. 247, TNA AIR 50/18) that day that there was 9/10ths cloud cover at 500 and 3,000 feet.
139. Flt Lt Ross Harding's Combat Report (No. 247, TNA AIR 50/18) states that the victory was confirmed by 1497923 Sgt Moorhouse of No. 7 Searchlight Battery, Royal Artillery, based at Hamstreet, Kent, around half way between Brenzett and Ashford.
140. Excerpt from a letter from AVM (then Flt Lt) Ross Harding to Dan Johnson, dated 3 December 1986.
141. 11 Group ORB, 17 August 1944, TNA AIR 25/195.
142. Fg Off Peter Graham in correspondence with Rob Philips, 13 November 2003 and 6 January 2004; reproduced with Rob Philips' permission.
143. Fg Off Peter Graham in a letter to Rob Philips, dated 26 November 2003; reproduced with Rob Philips' permission.
144. 41 Squadron ORB, 17 August 1944, TNA AIR 27/426.
145. Entry for 17 August 1944 in the flying logbook of Fg Off Peter Graham; reproduced with his permission. The ORB makes no mention of Graham damaging a V1 on 17 August 1944, and the only evidence appears in his logbook. Although there is no 'official' evidence available, this may have constituted the Squadron's second such victory.
146. The Squadron ORB's F540 on 18 August 1944 states that the unit flew 15 anti-Diver patrols, but the F541 only lists 14. The RAF Lympne Station ORB also states that 41 Squadron made 28 sorties, which equates to 14 patrols.
147. Flt Lt Keith F. 'Jimmy' Thiele was posted to 486 (NZ) Squadron at Volkel on 13 October 1944, and then to 3 Squadron as a Flight Commander on 14 December. He was promoted to become the Squadron's Commanding Officer on 26 December 1944, but was shot down by Flak during attack on train north of Dortmund on 10 February 1945 and suffered burns to his eyes, face and wrists before he could bale out to safety. On landing, Thiele was captured and initially held at Dortmund Aerodrome for a few days, before being sent to Dulag Luft. He was admitted to hospital for his wounds at Hohemark from 22 February-6 March 1945 and on his release was sent to the Receiving Depot at Wetzlar, where he was reunited with Flt Lt Terry Spencer. On 31 March 1945, Thiele and Spencer escaped in Steve-McQueen-style on bicycles and subsequently motorcycles when the main gate of the camp was left open, and successfully reached Allied lines. Thiele returned to 3 Squadron briefly but made his last flight with the Squadron on 4 April 1945. He was awarded a second Bar to his DFC for his exploits on 8 May 1945 and returned to New Zealand at the end of September. On 2 October, Thiele became Officer Commanding of

the Auckland Wing Air Training Group, with the rank of Acting Squadron Leader, and attended a refresher course at CFS Wigram from 4 February 1946. His rank reverted to Flight Lieutenant on 2 May 1946 and he resigned his commission in the RNZAF seven months later. In civil life, Thiele initially became a charter pilot for LAMS Ltd., flying ex-RAF Halifaxes around the world, until the company went into liquidation in March 1948. He then joined QANTAS, where he remained until 1964, after which he built and operated Marina in Sydney until 1974. He then sailed for four years, spent a brief time as an avocado farmer in Queensland, and went sailing again for several more years, living on his yacht and having, in his own words, 'no fixed abode', and only a post office box in Sydney's northern beaches to reach him through. This was the case until at least 1984, but he subsequently moved to Bundaberg, Queensland, where he was still living at the time of writing.

148. Flt Sgt John Tyron Bradshaw had joined the RAFVR at the British Embassy in Washington DC in 1941 and trained at BFTS in Oklahoma, where he was awarded his Wings in September 1942. He shipped to England two months later and was sent to Flying Instructors School. Unhappy with his posting, however, he requested reassignment to fighters and spent the next 17 months at AFU, OTU, TEU, and GSU, before being posted to his first operational unit, 26 Squadron, at Lee-on Solent in May 1944. Here, he was involved in anti-shipping patrols, sweeps over Belgium and the Netherlands, and spotting German positions for the Royal Navy at Sword Beach during D-Day. He also recorded his first victory, a damaged Ju88, in late May.

149. WO Brian Morrell Weeds enlisted in the RNZAF in June 1941 and attended ITW and EFTS in New Zealand prior to shipping to Canada in October to complete SFTS. Awarded his Wings in January 1942, Weeds arrived in the United Kingdom in early March and was posted to 11 AFU in April. Following two brief attachments to BAT Flights, he sent to 13 OTU at Bicester, which he graduated in early September 1942. At this time, Weeds was posted to his first operational unit, 487 (RNZAF) Light Bomber Squadron, at Feltwell. Weeds remained with the unit until June 1943, during which time he was promoted to Flight Sergeant. Likely a result of applying for a transfer from bombers to fighters, he was then posted to AFU in July 1943, followed by OTU in December 1943 and TEU in April 1944, prior to being posted to 587 Anti-Aircraft Cooperation Squadron at Culmhead as a Warrant Officer in early May 1944. His tenure was only brief, however, as were ensuing postings to TEU, GSU and 26 Squadron, all completed within the space of just ten weeks.

150. Sgt Plt John Irvine joined the RAFVR in November 1941 and completed both SFTS and OTU in Canada, and returned to the United Kingdom with his Wings in spring 1944. In May that year, he was posted to his first operational unit, 667 Squadron, at Gosport, employed in target towing. A month later, Irvine was posted to GSU, arriving on the same day as Brian Weeds, and was subsequently posted with him to 26 Squadron on 23 July.

151. The Squadron ORB's F540 on 19 August 1944 states that the unit flew 18 anti-Diver patrols, but the F541 only lists 17, one of which consisted of only one aircraft, therefore equating to 33 sorties. However, the timings of the single aircraft patrol (Flt Lt Ross Harding, Red Section, EN227, 13:30-14:25) suggests he may have only been a replacement for Flt Sgt Ian Stevenson (Red 1, MB882, 13:00-13:15), who landed within 15 minutes, presumably with engine problems. During this time, Red 2, WO Peter Hale (EN229, 13:00-14:35), remained in the air and may have been joined by Harding. The RAF Lympne Station ORB does not help at all, recording that 41 Squadron flew 29 sorties, which equates to 15 patrols.

152. Combat Report for Flt Lt Terence Spencer, No. 383, 19 August 1944, TNA AIR 50/18.

153. 41 Squadron ORB, 19 August 1944, TNA AIR 27/426.

154. Entry in Plt Off Patrick Coleman's logbook for 19 August 1944; reproduced with the kind permission of the Coleman family via Mike Brampton. The ORB makes no mention of Coleman damaging a V1 on 19 August 1944, and the only evidence appears in his logbook. Although there is no 'official' evidence available, this may have constituted the Squadron's third such victory.

155. The 41 Squadron ORB states Flt Lt Terry Spencer was test flying a Spitfire XII during his flying accident on 20 August 1944, but Spencer's logbook records the aircraft was a Spitfire IXa, 5R-Z, which indicates it was an aircraft of 33 Squadron, which operated Spitfire IXs out of Tangmere at the time. Spencer also made several flights on another of this Squadron's aircraft, 5R-E, during August 1944, and it appears other 41 Squadron pilots on did the same, gaining experience on the type. For example, Fg Off Donald Tebbit's logbook shows that he flew 5R-E on 3 and 4 August 1944, and 5R-X on 5 and 6 August. Later that month, Tebbit has recorded flights on another squadron's Spitfire IXs.

156. 41 Squadron ORB, 20 August 1944, TNA AIR 27/426.

157. Ibid., 21 August 1944.

158. As Fg Off John F. Wilkinson had only made a single combat claim since joining the Squadron on 21 July 1944, this film is likely to have been his shared destroyed V1 with Flt Sgt Jakub Bargielowski of 315 Squadron, four miles east of Ashford, Kent, on 11 August 1944. This film is still in existence and is held by the Imperial War Museum. See also Appendix XIII (Extant Combat Films).

159. The Lympne Station ORB states that 130 Squadron had 10 aircraft airborne on anti-Diver patrols on 22 August 1944, but this is believed to be erroneous as 130 Squadron's ORB (TNA AIR 27/938) on this date states that "Bad weather persisted during the day and no patrols were possible".

160. Following approximately six weeks with 83 GSU, Flt Sgt Colin Robertson was posted to 453 (Australian) Squadron at Coltishall, Norfolk, as a Warrant Officer in early October 1944. He was commissioned a month later, and

remained with this unit until October 1945, when he was repatriated to Australia as a Flying Officer. Extended leave was granted on his arrival home and he was discharged from the RAAF in February 1946.

161. The Squadron ORB's F541 on 23 August 1944 states that Red Section was airborne at 08:20, but the F540 and Flt Lt Terence Spencer's two Combat Reports for the patrol record the take-off time as 08:05. In fact, 08:20 was the time that Spencer intercepted his first V1, so this is likely to have caused the confusion.
162. The Squadron ORB erroneously states that Flt Lt Terry Spencer's victories on 23 August 1944 were the Squadron's 80th and 81st. As the analysis of 41 Squadron's V1 victories in this work clearly shows that they were the 50th and 51st, it is likely that the this error came about through a transcription from handwriting.
163. 41 Squadron ORB, 23 August 1944, TNA AIR 27/426.
164. WO Patrick Coleman's logbook states on 23 August 1944, "SWEEP – Pas-de-Calais to find JU188's in Amiens area" (Coleman family via Mike Brampton), but this is not mentioned elsewhere.
165. According to an Intelligence Report for the day (*Ref. 41S/S.233/Air, OpRep A. No. 145 for 24 hours ending Sunset. 23.8.44* [41 Squadron Archives]), the operation should have included 12 aircraft, but only 11 participated. The identity of the twelfth pilot and the reason for the failure to participate are not recorded.
166. 41 Squadron ORB, 23 August 1944, TNA AIR 27/426.
167. Tom Slack in his autobiography, *Happy is the Day; A Spitfire Pilot's Story*; 1987, United Writers Publications; reproduced with the Publisher's permission.
168. Ibid.
169. This statement by Flt Lt Tom Slack's interrogator was, in fact, correct. His parents posted a message in the Missing section of *The Times* on 23 July 1943 (pg. 1; Issue 49605; col A) after his first loss (See Chapter 4) stating, "SLACK – Missing from air operations, F/O. TOM A. H. SLACK, R.A.F., son of Tom A. Slack, Rose Cottage, Micheldever." He may, however, have been assisted by another piece of intelligence, as Slack had left his Mae West at the scene of his first descent on 18 July 1943, which he later learned had been seized by the Wehrmacht. In his Escape and Evasion Report, Slack wrote, "I heard later that the troops arrived just after I had left, and secured both my mae west [sic] and my parachute".[See *Escape/Evasion Reports: Code MI9/SPG*, Fg Off Thomas A. H. Slack, TNA WO 208/3314/1366.] Had Slack penned his name and/or number on his Mae West, as many pilots did, this may have provided his interrogator with another piece of evidence.
170. Flt Lt Tom Slack initially returned home to Micheldever, Hampshire, and is then believed to have spent some time back in the Far East, where he had grown up. Unfortunately, nothing is known of his subsequent life but that he retired to Mousehole, Cornwall, where he wrote his autobiography, *Happy is the Day; A Spitfire Pilot's Story*, in 1987 (United Writers Publications, ISBN 185200004X). He passed away in August 1994.
171. Flt Sgt Vivian Rossow's damaged V1 on 23 August 1944 is the only such victory by the Squadron recorded in an official document, in this case the RAF Lympne Station ORB, whereas the other three claimed by the pilots – by Fg Off Peter Graham on 17 and 18 August 1944, and by Plt Off Patrick Coleman on 19 August 1944 – only appear in their personal logbooks, and are therefore 'unofficial'.
172. The pilot who shared Flt Lt Daniel Reid's V1 victory on 23 August 1944 was Flt Lt Leonard Wood of 274 Squadron, who was flying Tempest V, EJ646.
173. The 41 Squadron ORB's F540 states that a total of ten anti-Diver patrols were undertaken on 24 August 1944, but the F541 only lists nine. The RAF Lympne Station ORB records that 17 aircraft from the Squadron were airborne on anti-Diver operations, which may also suggest that nine patrols were undertaken.
174. 41 Squadron ORB, 24 August 1944, TNA AIR 27/426.
175. Correspondence from WO Brian Weeds to Dan Johnson, dated 24 May 1984; reproduced with Dan's kind permission.
176. 41 Squadron ORB, 26 August 1944, TNA AIR 27/426.
177. *Op. Rep. No. 146 for 24 hours ending sunset. 26.8.44.*, 41 Squadron Archives.
178. 130 Squadron ORB, 26 August 1944, TNA AIR 27/938.
179. This was WO Peter Chattin's first sweep over the Continent, however he had previously participated in anti-Diver patrols.
180. Entry in WO Patrick Coleman's personal diary for the period 26 August 1944; reproduced with the kind permission of the Coleman family via Mike Brampton.
181. 41 Squadron ORB, 27 August 1944, TNA AIR 27/426.
182. Ibid.
183. Although their frequency decreased as time passed, V1s continued to be fired into the United Kingdom, and to targets on the Continent, until the end of March 1945, when all the launch sites were finally over-run. However, 41 Squadron was no longer involved in anti-Diver defence after August 1944. Almost 30,000 V1 flying bombs were produced, of which 9,250 were fired at England between June 1944 and March 1945. Of these, around 2,400 came down in London killing about 6,200 people, seriously injuring another 18,000, and destroying or damaging over one million homes and buildings. Of all the V1s fired at England, it is believed that about 2,000 were shot down by fighters, about 2,000 destroyed by anti-aircraft fire, and almost 300 brought down by barrage balloons. This is a remarkable feat considering that, when the V1 onslaught began, the only effective defence was interception by a select number of high performance fighter aircraft, in particular the Hawker Tempest. Even late Mark Spitfires, such as the Spitfire XII with which 41 Squadron was equipped, were too slow to catch a V1 and therefore patrolled at altitudes well above the V1's

usual ceiling to enable them to swoop on them from above, with the additional speed gained in a dive. Anti-aircraft gunners also found the relatively small, but fast-moving targets difficult to hit. Initially, it took them an average of 2,500 anti-aircraft shells to bring down a single V1. The British also tried to bring V1s down with barrage balloons, but once the Germans wised up to this and attached balloon cable cutters to the leading edges, their effectiveness fell markedly. By mid-August 1944, however, the threat was almost completely overcome following the introduction of two new and effective electronic aids for anti-aircraft guns, which had been conceived and developed in the United States. The first of these was radar-based automatic gun-laying and the second the proximity fuse. Although the technology was not perfect, it reduced the average number of shells required to bring down a V1 from around 2,500 to just 100. By the third week of August 1944, the guns were bringing down around 60% of all the V1s entering the gun belt; in the last week of the month it had increased to almost 75%. This success rate therefore freed up aircraft, such as 41 Squadron's Spitfire XIIs, to be better deployed on the growing front on the Continent.

184. 41 Squadron ORB, 27 August 1944, TNA AIR 27/426.
185. 130 Squadron ORB, 27 August 1944, TNA AIR 27/938.
186. The 11 Group ORB Appendix for Ramrod 1238 on 27 August 1944 (TNA AIR 25/213) indicates that twelve of 41 Squadron's Spitfires participated in the escort to Marquise/Mimoyecques but 41 Squadron's Intelligence Report for the day (Ref: 41S/S.233/Air., Oprep A. No. 147. for 24 hours ending Sunset. 27.8.44., 41 Squadron Archives) and ORB's F541 both state that 'eight out of eight' Spitfires participated.
187. 41 Squadron ORB, 27 August 1944, TNA AIR 27/426.
188. Flt Lt Keith Curtis remained in the United Kingdom after the War and joined the RAF as a Sergeant Pilot in October 1947. Following refresher flying courses, Curtis was posted to 595 Squadron at Pembrey in May 1948, initially flying Spitfire XVIs, but later Vampires. He then qualified as a Flying Instructor and spent a number of postings in this role before he was commissioned in November 1953. Converting to Meteors, Curtis returned to operational flying in March 1954 when he joined 54 Squadron at Odiham, and subsequently became a member of the RAF aerobatic team, the 'Black Knights'. Promoted to Flying Officer in November 1955, he was sent to Malaya in February 1957, serving with 45 Squadron at Butterworth until posted to 60 Squadron at Tengah in Singapore nine months later. Curtis was promoted to Flight Lieutenant in November 1958, finally reaching his wartime rank again 13 years after relinquishing it. Curtis returned to the United Kingdom in November 1959 to convert to Hastings troop and freight aircraft, but was back in Singapore a year later on a posting to 48 Squadron at Changi, flying this type. Returning to the United Kingdom definitively in April 1963, Curtis took up postings in Air Traffic Control, where he remained until September 1966. At this time, he joined 511 Squadron at Lyneham, flying Britannias and was promoted to Squadron Leader whilst with this unit, in January 1972. In May 1972, Curtis was posted to the Britannia Simulator at Lyneham, and retired three years later, retaining his rank. He died at Saltash, Cornwall, in December 2008.
189. Correspondence between Dan Johnson and Sqn Ldr (retd.) Robert H. Chapman, 1989.
190. Entry for 28 August 1944 in the logbook of Flt Lt Terry Spencer; copyright Terry Spencer, via Cara and Raina Spencer.
191. Sqn Ldr Douglas Ian 'Dougie' Benham was born in Wimbledon in December 1917 and joined the RAFVR as a Sergeant Pilot under training in February 1938. In September 1939, he commenced Officer Cadet training and was posted to 10 Bomber Squadron at Abingdon on graduation in May 1940. However, he sought and obtained a transfer to Fighter Command just two months later, following the losses wrought at Dunkirk. His fighter Wings were awarded in mid-August 1940, but despite the Battle of Britain raging in England's south, he was sent to 8 SFTS, 54 OTU and 55 OTU before being posted to his first operational unit, 607 Squadron, flying Hurricanes, in early 1941. Benham was commissioned in August 1941 and was sent to 59 OTU at Crosby-on-Eden two weeks later as a Flying Instructor, where he remained until April 1942. During this period, he attended a Flying Instructors Course at CFS Upavon, and graduated as a QFI. Benham returned to operations as Acting Flight Lieutenant and OC, B Flight, with 242 Squadron in mid-April 1942. Following his promotion to Flying Officer, he sailed with the unit for North Africa, arriving at Maison Blanche in November 1942 where they became a part of 322 Wing. Only a day later, Benham claimed his first victory, a half share in a Junkers Ju88, but was also hit by return fire and forced to bale out of his own aircraft. A series of victories then followed in quick succession, including five damaged aircraft in a single day, and he was awarded the DFC in March 1943. In April 1943, exactly a year after joining 242 Squadron, he was posted to the Tactical OTU at Kalaa Djerda, Tunisia, as its Commanding Officer and Chief Flying Instructor. The main role of the OTU was to convert USAAF Kittyhawk pilots to Spitfires. Benham was posted back to the United Kingdom in June 1944, where he attended FLS at Milfield, before being posted to 61 OTU at Rednal as CFI. During this time he was promoted to Flight Lieutenant and, on 26 July 1944, posted to 504 Squadron at Detling. His tenure was only brief, however, as Wg Cdr Colin Gray asked him to take over as Commanding Officer of 41 Squadron, which he did on 27 August 1944.
192. Sqn Ldr Robert H. Chapman was promoted to Squadron Leader (WS) on 10 August 1945, then in mid-December 1945 appointed to a commission on extended service as a Flight Lieutenant in the RAF General Duties Branch, with a seniority of 1 December 1942, but retaining his wartime rank. Though little is known of Chapman's subsequent postings, it is known that he was promoted to substantive Squadron Leader on 1 August 1947, retired from the RAF on 18 March 1958, and died in 1989.

7 BIG BEN, *MARKET GARDEN* & THE OIL CAMPAIGN; 28 AUGUST – 3 DECEMBER 1944

1. 41 Squadron ORB, 28 August 1944, TNA AIR 27/426.
2. The RAF Lympne ORB on 28 August 1944 states that four aircraft from 41 Squadron undertook anti-Diver patrols today, whereas the Squadron ORB's F540 does not mention them at all. The only mention of anti-Diver patrols is on the Squadron's F541, which lists a brief patrol being undertaken by Yellow Section (Flt Lt Terry Spencer and Flt Sgt Ian Stevenson) between 16:50 and 17:05. Considering the RAF Lympne ORB entry, it may therefore have been that the 15:40 scramble by Red Section (Flt Lt William Stowe and Flt Sgt Peter Chattin) was the result of an incoming V1, and was thus recorded on the Lympne ORB as an anti-Diver patrol. Note also that the F541 shows Spencer and Stevenson taking off at 16:50 and returning only 15 minutes later. Anti-Diver patrols usually lasted over an hour, but as the Squadron was briefed at 17:30 for a Ramrod in which Spencer participated, it appears they were called back early.
3. Flt Lt Terry Spencer later recalled that he had shot down an eighth V1 on 28 August 1944, following his seventh on 27 August, but this victory is not mentioned in the Squadron or Station ORBs, Combat Reports, the day's Intelligence Report, or any other documentation available today. When queried on the victory, Terry himself could not recall the location and had not recorded any detail in his logbook or diary. As such, the author has only recognised in this work the Squadron's official tally of 53 V1s (45 + 8 shared) destroyed.
4. The 41 Squadron ORB on 28 August 1944 refers to the target as an oil refinery, an Intelligence Report for the day calls their destination 'oil targets', and the 11 Group ORB and Appendices refer to the target as 'Fuel Dumps'.
5. The USAAF Chronology (http://paul.rutgers.edu/~mcgrew/wwii/USAAF/html/Aug.44.html, accessed January 2009) names the fuel and ammunition targets more precisely as Barisis-aux-Bois (south of St. Quentin) and Doullens, an ammunition dump at Querrieu (northeast of Amiens), and an ammunition and fuel dump at Forêt de Laigue (northeast of Compiègne).
6. This data has been extracted from the 11 Group ORB Appendix for 28 August 1944 (*NO.11 GROUP OPERATIONAL ACTIVITY SYNOPSIS, Dawn 28/8/44 to dawn 29/8/44*), TNA AIR 25/213, with slight amendments made where appropriate.
7. The 11 Group ORB Appendix for 28 August 1944 states that 12 aircraft of 41 Squadron participated in Ramrod 1243, but the 41 Squadron ORB only lists ten pilots. As such, the number of 41 Squadron pilots in the text has been reduced to ten. The 130 Squadron ORB provides no information on the number of pilots participating from that Squadron, so we only have the numbers provided in the 11 Group ORB Appendix (listed here) to rely on.
8. The 41 Squadron ORB on 28 August 1944 states that 'no serious opposition' was met, but does not elaborate on what this means. However, it may account for the fact that the pilots fired off 790 rounds of 20mm ammunition during the Ramrod [Intelligence Report for 28 August 1944, *Ref. 41S/S.233/Air., Oprep A. No. 150 for 24 hours ending Sunset. 28.8.44*, 41 Squadron Archives]. Unfortunately, the Squadron's Intelligence Report also does not explain further, and no Combat Reports exist for any combats or attacks that may have taken place.
9. 41 Squadron ORB, 28 August 1944, TNA AIR 27/426.
10. Having joined the RNZAF in January 1940, Flt Lt David J. V. Henry was commissioned on completion of his flying training and promoted to Flying Officer prior to shipping to the United Kingdom in December 1941. Following OTU at Aston Down, he was posted to his first operational unit, 485 (RNZAF) Squadron, in May 1942. Henry was promoted to Flight Lieutenant two months later and posted to 93 Squadron as a Flight Commander in October, travelling with them to North Africa the following month. Awarded the DFC in May 1943 and a Mention in Despatches in June, Henry returned to the United Kingdom on the completion of his tour of duty and was briefly posted to CGS at Sutton Bridge in October 1943. The following month, he flew to Ottawa, Canada, to take up the post of RNZAF Liaison Officer, and remained there until July 1944, when he returned to the United Kingdom once again. On 6 August, Henry returned to operations as a Supernumerary with 130 (Punjab) Squadron at Tangmere, his arrival coinciding with the unit's upgrade from Spitfire Vbs to XIVs. On 28 August, having spent just three weeks with 130 Squadron, Henry transferred to 41 Squadron – both units now based together at Lympne – where he became OC, B Flight.
11. 41 Squadron ORB, 29 August 1944, TNA AIR 27/426.
12. The data in this table has been extracted from the 11 Group ORB Appendix for 30 August 1944 (*NO.11 GROUP OPERATIONAL ACTIVITY SYNOPSIS, Dawn 30/8/44 to dawn 31/8/44*), TNA AIR 25/213, but slight amendments have been made by the author where appropriate.
13. 41 Squadron ORB, 30 August 1944, TNA AIR 27/426.
14. This list of ground victories is taken from 41 Squadron's Intelligence Report for 30 August 1944 [*Ref. 41S/S.233/Air., Oprep A. No. 151 for 24 hours ending Sunset. 30.8.44*, 41 Squadron Archives] but the 11 Group ORB Appendix [*NO.11 GROUP OPERATIONAL ACTIVITY SYNOPSIS, Dawn 30/8/44 to dawn 31/8/44*], TNA AIR 25/213] states the bag was Marshalling yards at Roulers shot up, 20 railway wagons damaged, one locomotive Cat. B, three railway wagons destroyed, six MET lorries, one anti-tank gun and one MET carrier damaged.
15. 41 Squadron ORB, 30 August 1944, TNA AIR 27/426.
16. The Squadron's Intelligence Report for 30 August 1944 [*Ref. 41S/S.233/Air., Oprep A. No. 151 for 24 hours ending Sunset. 30.8.44*, 41 Squadron Archives], the RAF Lympne Station ORB, and the 11 Group ORB Appendix [*NO.11*

GROUP OPERATIONAL ACTIVITY SYNOPSIS, Dawn 30/8/44 to dawn 31/8/44, TNA AIR 25/213] all state that ten pilots from 41 Squadron participated in the second sweep. However, the Squadron ORB's F541 lists eleven pilots and aircraft, which are shown in the table.

17. 41 Squadron ORB, 30 August 1944, TNA AIR 27/426.
18. This list of ground victories is taken from 41 Squadron's Intelligence Report for 30 August 1944 [*Ref. 41S/S.233/Air.*, *Oprep A. No. 151 for 24 hours ending Sunset. 30.8.44*, 41 Squadron Archives] but the 11 Group ORB Appendix [*NO.11 GROUP OPERATIONAL ACTIVITY SYNOPSIS, Dawn 30/8/44 to dawn 31/8/44*), TNA AIR 25/213] states the bag was strikes on 11 barges and two tugs towing three barges east of Roulers, two railway wagons destroyed and two damaged, one lorry destroyed and one damaged, two 8-ton Reichsbahn lorries and trailers destroyed, three MET damaged, two heavy AFVs damaged and one staff car damaged.
19. Although the 41 Squadron ORB on 30 August 1944 does not identify the aircraft that were damaged by Flak, *Spitfire; The History* (Eric B. Morgan and Edward Shacklady, 1987-2000, Key Books) suggests that one of the aircraft was Spitfire XII, MB862, which sustained Cat. AC damage. The ORB identifies this aircraft as that of Flt Lt William Stowe.
20. The 11 Group ORB Appendix [*NO.11 GROUP OPERATIONAL ACTIVITY SYNOPSIS, Dawn 31/8/44 to dawn 1/9/44*), TNA AIR 25/213] on 31 August 1944 states that 41 Squadron returned from their armed reconnaissance at 15:33; the Squadron's Intelligence Report for the day [*Ref. 41S/S.233/Air.*, *Oprep A. No. 152 for 24 hours ending Sunset. 31.8.44*, 41 Squadron Archives] states that the Squadron returned at 15:53, and the Squadron ORB's F540 and F541 both state that the return time was 16:05.
21. The 11 Group ORB, the RAF Lympne Station ORB and the Squadron's Intelligence Report for 31 August 1944 all state that 12 pilots from 41 Squadron participated in this armed reconnaissance, but the Squadron ORB's F541 only lists 11 pilots and their aircraft (four pilots in Yellow and Blue Sections, but only three in Red Section). Conveniently however, the Squadron's Intelligence Report, in an exception to the general rule, lists the names of all participating pilots, and this shows that Lympne's Wing Commander Flying, Wg Cdr Colin Gray was the twelfth man, flying with Balasse, Rossow and Irvine. The author has therefore added Wg Cdr Gray to the below table, which is otherwise extracted from the Squadron ORB's F541. As there is no indication of which aircraft was flown by Gray, however, the serial column indicates 'NR', i.e. not recorded.
22. This list is a conglomeration of two separate lists of claims by 41 Squadron for this armed reconnaissance on 31 August 1944. One appears on 41 Squadron's Intelligence Report for the day [*Ref. 41S/S.233/Air.*, *Oprep A. No. 152 for 24 hours ending Sunset. 31.8.44*, 41 Squadron Archives] and the other in the 11 Group ORB Appendix [*NO.11 GROUP OPERATIONAL ACTIVITY SYNOPSIS, Dawn 31/8/44 to dawn 1/9/44*), TNA AIR 25/213], which illustrate the difficulty of obtaining an accurate picture of events. 41 Squadron's list states, "1 Loco damaged Cat.B. [no location mentioned], 9 Covered R.R. Wagons [no indication of destroyed or damaged] at Roulers, Menin and Diximude [sic], 10 R.R. Trucks [no indication of destroyed or damaged] at Diximude [sic]. 10 Lorries damaged, one in flames. Menin, Roulers & Armentietieries [sic] 1 Motor Car [no location mentioned; no indication of destroyed or damaged] 1 Barge damaged. Place unknown." The 11 Group list states, "1 stationary loco (Steam up) Cat. B in LILLE area. Strikes on 10 stationary R/R waggons containing scrap metal near ROULERS and on 1 barge near ARMENTIERES. 6 lorries in MENIN area, 1 car and 3 3-ton covered lorries in ARMENTIERES area, 1 lorry in POPERINGHE area all damaged. One 5-ton covered lorry (flamer) near ARMENTIERES." Alternatively, the 41 Squadron ORB simply lists the day's claims as, "1 Loco damaged – 9 covered R.R. wagons – 10 R.R. trucks – 10 lorries, 1 barge – 1 motor Car – all damaged" without any indication of locations.
23. 130 Squadron ORB, 31 August 1944, TNA AIR 27/938.
24. See House of Commons Hansard, HC Deb 10 November 1944 vol 404 cc1653-4, http://hansard.millbanksystems.com/commons/1944/nov/10/german-long-range-rockets (rtrvd Mar 2010).
25. It is difficult to establish the exact nature of the operations undertaken by 41 Squadron on 1 September 1944, as the Squadron ORB states that all three patrols were armed reconnaissances, but only mentions that the second was intended to search for V2 sites. However, whilst the Lympne ORB makes no mention of their nature at all, the 11 Group ORB Appendix indicates that two major Group operations were undertaken today, in which armed reconnaissances were flown. In the first of these, 114 *armed Crossbow reconnaissance* sorties were undertaken between 06:50 and 21:20 in the Lumbres-St. Omer-Bethune-Hesdin area and, in the second, 213 *armed reconnaissance* sorties were undertaken between 09:59 and 21:23 in the Ghent-Aulnoye-Calais area. The tables in the 11 Group ORB Appendix are also not completely clear on which squadrons participated in which of the two operations. However, despite the fact that 41 Squadron's first patrol was to Ghent (a destination in the latter operation), they were airborne at 06:50 when the Crossbow reconnaissances began, which was well before the 09:59 commencement of the Ghent-Aulnoye-Calais operations. Based on timings alone, this implies that the first operation was likely a Crossbow operation, which is supported by the 11 Group ORB Appendix that shows the first two patrols listed in the table on a page titled "CROSSBOW Armed Recces". The third operation is listed on a page titled "Armed Recces" but annotated "Big Ben area", so it, too, was likely amongst the day's Crossbow operations, rather than the 09:59-21:23 Ghent-Aulnoye-Calais operations.
26. 41 Squadron ORB, 1 September 1944, TNA AIR 27/426.
27. *Skypilot; Memoirs from Take-Off to Landing*, Peter Graham. 2001, Pentland Books, and reproduced with his kind permission.

28. Ibid.
29. Fg Off Peter Graham states in his autobiography that "one of my captors marched me to the nearby village of Esquelbecq" (*Skypilot; Memoirs from Take-Off to Landing*, Peter Graham, 2001, Pentland Books). However, if the train that he and Fg Off Balasse attacked was on the Thielt-Deinze railway line in Belgium, as was reported by Balasse, then Graham would actually have had to have flown in a westerly or more south-westerly direction to have come down near Esquelbecq, rather than northwest to the nearest coast.
30. "Extract from German Instructions on dealing with P/W, 28.8.44", *Dulag Luft and other interrogation reports: information obtained by Germans from British Prisoners of War*, 1944-1945, TNA AIR 40/2318.
31. After baling out of MB831 on 1 September 1944, Fg Off Peter Graham landed safely but was immediately captured near St. Omer. He was sent to Dulag Luft on 7 September and remained there for interrogation until 15 September. He was transferred to Stalag Luft I at Barth, Germany, on 18 September where he was reunited with 41 Squadron's Fg Off Herb Wagner, who had been shot down on 2 June 1944; they remained close friends for the rest of their lives. Graham was held at Stalag Luft I until his liberation on 1 May 1945, when he was repatriated home. He married his sweetheart less than four weeks later and was accepted as an undergraduate at King's College in January 1946, prior to his discharge from the RAFVR in March. By September 1948, Graham had become a teacher at Hailbury and the Imperial Service College in Hertford, but rejoined the RAFVR as a Flying Officer in the Training Branch just two months later. He only remained in the service for 20 months, and then went to theological college, after which he was ordained in May 1953. Peter died at home in Buckland Newton, Dorset in October 2009.
32. Telex to HQ 11 Group and 41 Squadron from Air Ministry Kingsway, dated 18 November 1944, and stamped *R.A.F. STATION LYMPNE 28NOV1944 SIGNAL OFFICE*, original document held in 41 Squadron's Archives.
33. 41 Squadron ORB, 1 September 1944, TNA AIR 27/426.
34. Intelligence Report, *Oprep A. No. 154 for 24 hours ending Sunset. 1.9.44, Ref:- 41S/S.233/Air.*, 1 September 1944, 41 Squadron Archives.
35. The 127 Squadron pilots involved in the collision on landing at Lympne on 1 September 1944 were 21-year-old Flt Sgt Roy M. Housden, who was killed, and Flt Lt Douglas J. McNally, who was injured.
36. Entry in WO Patrick Coleman's personal diary for 1 September 1944; reproduced with the kind permission of the Coleman family via Mike Brampton.
37. There is a possible anomaly in the Squadron ORB's reporting of the pilots returning to Lympne on 2 September 1944, after being stranded at Manston on the evening of 1 September 1944. The F540 on 2 September states that WO Peter Hale returned to Lympne from Manston with Flt Lts Terry Spencer and Bill Stowe, and WOs Peter Chattin and Patrick Coleman. However, the F541 on 1 September does not show WO Peter Hale participating in the previous evening's armed reconnaissance, although it is possible he was also stranded at Manston after a non-operational sortie.
38. *Oprep A. No. 156 for 24 hours ending Sunset. 3.9.44*, 41 Squadron ORB Appendix, TNA AIR 27/431. There is no indication of which aircraft was ablaze and why.
39. Calais was not liberated until 29 September 1944.
40. *Oprep A. No. 156 for 24 hours ending Sunset. 3.9.44*, 41 Squadron ORB Appendix, TNA AIR 27/431.
41. 41 Squadron ORB, 3 September 1944, TNA AIR 27/426.
42. The Squadron ORB's F541 on 3 September 1944 refers to the two sections as Red and Blue, whereas all other documents, including the F540 and Combat Reports, refer to Spencer's quartet as Black Section. WO Pat Coleman's Diary also refers to the other section as White.
43. Flt Lt Terry Spencer states in his Combat Report [41 Squadron Archives] that he sighted two FW190s, which is repeated in the 11 Group ORB Appendix [Part V, Combat Cuts, TNA AIR 25/214], however it was actually a *Kette* of three.
44. Combat Report for Flt Lt Terry Spencer, original hand-written document dated 3 September 1944; 41 Squadron's Archives.
45. *Oprep A. No. 156 for 24 hours ending Sunset. 3.9.44*, 41 Squadron ORB Appendix, TNA AIR 27/431.
46. *INTELLIGENCE FORM F. 3.9.44., BIGGIN HILL SECTOR – RAF LYMPNE*, original carbon copy, signed by 41 Squadron's Intelligence Officer, Flt Lt Lord Gisborough; 41 Squadron Archives.
47. Entry in WO Patrick Coleman's personal diary for 3 September 1944; reproduced with the kind permission of the Coleman family via Mike Brampton.
48. Combat Report for WO Patrick Coleman, original hand-written document dated 3 September 1944; 41 Squadron Archives.
49. *INTELLIGENCE FORM F. 3.9.44., BIGGIN HILL SECTOR – RAF LYMPNE*, original carbon copy; 41 Squadron Archives.
50. *Oprep A. No. 156 for 24 hours ending Sunset. 3.9.44*, 41 Squadron ORB Appendix, TNA AIR 27/431.
51. Various sources disagree on whether this victory over Gross' FW190 on 3 September 1944 was attributable to WO Pat Coleman alone, or whether he shared it with Flt Lt William Stowe. The Squadron ORB states that two FW190s were destroyed, but does not say by whom; the Squadron ORB Appendix states that one FW190 was destroyed by Flt Lt Terry Spencer, and the other by Stowe, Coleman and WO Peter Chattin; the RAF Lympne ORB states the second FW190 was destroyed by Coleman; and the Biggin Hill Sector Intelligence Report and 11 Group ORB

Appendix both state that the second FW190 was shared by Coleman and Stowe. However, Coleman's Combat Report for the day shows he claimed one FW190 destroyed, whereas Stowe's shows no claim [both Combat Reports are the original hand-written versions, which are held in 41 Squadron's Archives and are not available in the files of TNA]. Moreover, Coleman records in his personal diary, "Bill Stowe confirms my victory – the squadron's 159th destroyed in this war" [reproduced with the kind permission of the Coleman family via Mike Brampton], whilst Spencer recorded in his logbook, "1 Fw 190 Destroyed. W/O Coleman got another…"[copyright Terry Spencer]. Spencer also states in his autobiography *Living Dangerously* (Percival, 2002, ISBN 0954286200) that Coleman shot down Gross. These comments all suggest that Coleman was the sole claimant for Gross' FW190.

52. See *The JG 26 War Diary, Volume Two 1943-1945*, Chapter 7, *Defense of the German Border, September – December 1944*, Donald Caldwell, 1998, Grub Street.
53. Entry in the logbook of WO Peter Chattin for 3 September 1944, reproduced with the kind permission of his son, Mike.
54. Entry in WO Patrick Coleman's personal diary for 3 September 1944; reproduced with the kind permission of the Coleman family via Mike Brampton.
55. 11 Group ORB Appendix, TNA AIR 25/214.
56. Entry in WO Patrick Coleman's personal diary for 3 September 1944; reproduced with the kind permission of the Coleman family via Mike Brampton.
57. 41 Squadron ORB, 5 September 1944, TNA AIR 27/426.
58. Ibid., 8 September 1944.
59. Ibid., 9 September 1944.
60. Excerpt from correspondence with John T. 'Jack' Bradshaw, May 2005.
61. 130 Squadron ORB, 10 September 1944, TNA AIR 27/938.
62. Siebel ferries were originally built as landing craft for the intended 1940 invasion of England, but these were later dispersed and used for a number of practical jobs throughout the German forces. Built in small yards in Belgium, France, Germany and the Netherlands, the craft consisted of twin steel hulls in catamaran style, 20 feet apart, which provided for a shallow draft. They were powered by two engines and designed to carry 60-80 tons of equipment on western European estuaries to supplement port facilities and coastal batteries. The craft were generally armed with light machine guns or a 37mm gun, but variants were also built as anti-aircraft or artillery platforms fitted with 88mm guns, as evacuation/hospital ferries, and also as repair ferries.
63. WO Brian Weeds was posted to PDC Brighton on 10 October 1944, and embarked for home on 2 November. He arrived in New Zealand on 1 January 1945 and was discharged from the RNZAF on 14 April. He died in Invercargill in February 1998.
64. 11 Group ORB Appendix (*NO.11 GROUP OPERATIONAL ACTIVITY SYNOPSIS, Dawn 11/9/44 to dawn 12/9/44*), 11 September 1944, TNA AIR 25/214.
65. 41 Squadron ORB, 11 September 1944, TNA AIR 27/426.
66. 11 Group ORB Appendix (*NO.11 GROUP OPERATIONAL ACTIVITY SYNOPSIS, Dawn 11/9/44 to dawn 12/9/44*), 11 September 1944, TNA AIR 25/214.
67. The coordinates and locations listed here are those given on documentation at the time (*NO.11 GROUP OPERATIONAL ACTIVITY SYNOPSIS, Dawn 11/9/44 to dawn 12/9/44*, 11 September 1944, TNA AIR 25/214), and relate to the Nord de Guerre Grid. Next to these, I have listed in brackets the equivalent longitude and latitude.
68. The Squadron ORB's F541 on 12 September 1944 omits the usual list of pilots and aircraft serials, however an Intelligence Report in 41 Squadron's Archives (*REF. 11G/S. 500/63/1. 12TH SEPTEMBER 1944. RAMROD NO. 1275.*) has a list of six pilots names upon it in handwriting, which implies these were the pilots in question. They are Flt Lt Terry Spencer, Fg Off Donald Tebbit, WO Patrick Coleman, and Flt Sgts John Bradshaw, John Irvine and Ian Stevenson. Supporting this, WO Coleman's logbook [courtesy of the Coleman family via Mike Brampton] confirms he was one of the participants: "0745 V2 Site shot up". Nonetheless, there is no list of the serials of the aircraft flown by them.
69. The aircraft serial and pilot reporting carburettor trouble on 12 September 1944 are not identified in the Squadron ORB. However, the Squadron's Intelligence Report for the operation (*Oprep A. 165 for 24 hours ending Sunset. 12.9.44. Ref : 41S/S.233/Air.*, 41 Squadron Archives) adds that all the pilots "Landed back at Bradwell Bay for petrol".
70. Little information is available on these Flying Fortress escorts on 12 September 1944, but 11 Group ORB Appendices from previous days show similar patrols being undertaken by Fortresses with continuous escorts provided by other squadrons. The patrols appear to have been a readiness state in case of V2 launches, so that the launch sites could be bombed immediately. The details provided in the Squadron ORB on 12 September are also contradictory as the F540 states ten pilots participated – five from each Flight – but the F541 states that 11 pilots participated in the escorts, in pairs and trios. The RAF Lympne ORB concurs with the F541, but the day's Intelligence Report (*Oprep A. 165 for 24 hours ending Sunset. 12.9.44. Ref : 41S/S.233/Air.*, 41 Squadron Archives) states instead that initially three and subsequently seven pilots (a total of ten) participated in two separate escort operations.
71. Fg Off Harry W. Charnock had originally been commissioned in the RAF on graduation from Cranwell in late 1925. He then led a colourful career, initially being fined for driving down the Strand against one-way traffic and

side-swiping a bus without stopping in April 1929. Although his RAF career survived this initial transgression, a low flying incident with 1 Squadron was too much, and he was cashiered by General Court Marshal in December 1930, thereby ending his career just five years into his permanent commission. The outbreak of War, however, offered Charnock a new opportunity to fly, and he was forgiven and re-accepted into the RAF in September 1939, though from the bottom, without a commission. He saw service through much of the Battle of Britain and enjoyed an exemplary career, which saw three victories and the award of a DFM by April 1942. A further six victories followed in the Middle East during the second half of 1942, which resulted both in his being commissioned and the award of a DFC in January and February 1943, respectively. In fact, Charnock was shot down wounded behind enemy lines on 18 December 1942, but evaded and returned to Allied lines in mid-March 1943; his commissioning and DFC were both awarded in his absence. Following recuperation, he was repatriated to the United Kingdom and promoted to Flying Officer in July that year. Charnock was rested in instructor roles at 57 and 61 OTUs between November 1943 and January 1944, then spent six months with the Flying Development Flight at Wittering, finally returning to operations with 222 Squadron on 12 July 1944. His tenure was, however, quite brief as he was injured in a motor vehicle accident later that same month. Upon recuperation, instead of returning to 222 Squadron, he was sent to 41, having practically not flown operationally for well over a year.
72. 41 Squadron ORB, 12 September 1944, TNA AIR 27/426.
73. Source: Spitfire, Stewart Wilson, 1999, Aerospace Publications, ISBN 1875671455.
74. All aircraft shown in the table as having arrived on 12 September 1944 are actually shown in *Spitfire; The History* (Eric B. Morgan and Edward Shacklady, 1987-2000, Key Books) as having been delivered on 15 September. However, the aircraft must have arrived earlier than 15 September because the 41 Squadron ORB shows the aircraft been flown between 12 and 15 September.
75. The Squadron ORB is not clear on Fg Off Donald Tebbit's aircraft issues on 14 September 1944. The F540 only records his flight with Flt Sgt Ian Stevenson as an escort to a Flying Fortress ending within 15 minutes as a result of what it calls an 'oxygen deficiency' in RM698. However, the F541 records a second, previous, operational flight alone in RM767 between 14:20 and 14:30, also titled 'Escort to Fortress' but with no explanation given for his early return. As the Fortress escorts usually consisted of sections of two pilots, it is possible that the second pilot's name – likely Stevenson – has been erroneously omitted. As there were no other operational flights by the Squadron recorded today, it is most probable that the mission was therefore never fulfilled.
76. 41 Squadron ORB, 15 September 1944, TNA AIR 27/426.
77. These Nord de Guerre map references are listed in the 11 Group ORB Appendix (*NO.11 GROUP OPERATIONAL ACTIVITY SYNOPSIS, Dawn 14/9/44 to dawn 15/9/44*, 14 September 1944, TNA AIR 25/214). However, considering all the pinpoints bar the last one (qD1435) are in the Wassenaar area, it is possible the last reference is erroneous, i.e. possibly missing two digits.
78. Unfortunately, the Squadron ORB's F541 on 16 September 1944 only lists six of the eleven participating pilots on this armed reconnaissance. As such, Flt Lt Ross Harding's aircraft serial is unknown. The pilots listed are Sqn Ldr Douglas Benham, Flt Lts Robert Anderson, David Henry, and Daniel Reid, Fg Off Maurice Balasse, and WO Arthur Appleton.
79. See *Casualty Services, Air Raid Casualties, Statistics*, TNA HO 186/2232.
80. 130 Squadron ORB, TNA AIR 27/938, 17 September 1944.
81. The Squadron ORB's F541 on 17 September 1944 only records the names and aircraft serials of eight pilots, whereas an Intelligence Report for the day (*Oprep A. No. 170 for 24 hours ending Sunset. 17.9.44, Ref : 41S/S.233/Air*, 41 Squadron Archives) and the 11 Group ORB Appendix (*NO.11 GROUP OPERATIONAL ACTIVITY SYNOPSIS, Dawn 17/9/44 to dawn 18/9/44*, TNA AIR 25/214) both state that 12 pilots participated. The Squadron F540 does not assist as it only discusses 'the Squadron' participating in activity without providing numbers.
82. 41 Squadron ORB, 17 September 1944, TNA AIR 27/426.
83. 11 Group ORB Appendix (*NO.11 GROUP OPERATIONAL ACTIVITY SYNOPSIS, Dawn 17/9/44 to dawn 18/9/44*), 17 September 1944, TNA AIR 25/214.
84. 11 Group ORB Appendix (*NO.11 GROUP OPERATIONAL ACTIVITY SYNOPSIS, Dawn 18/9/44 to dawn 19/9/44*), 18 September 1944, TNA AIR 25/214.
85. The 41 Squadron ORB's F540 on 18 September 1944 states that Flt Lt Terry Spencer "split the Squadron up into two sixes", but as there were only eleven pilots on the operation, this statement is obviously erroneous. However, the F541 suggests that the pilots were split into eight and three, as Red and Yellow Sections (eight pilots) are shown to have returned at 17:15, whereas Blue Section (three pilots) returned at 16:30.
86. 41 Squadron ORB, 18 September 1944, TNA AIR 27/426.
87. Although five C-47 Dakotas are recorded to have been lost on this date, the most likely of these to have been the aircraft destroyed by 41 Squadron was C-47A, 42-93098 (c/n. 12972), of the USAAF's 439th TCG, 94th TCS, which force-landed on Haamstede Aerodrome. It is believed the aircraft was piloted by Major Joseph A. Beck II (O-402363), the unit's Commanding Officer, who was captured.
88. 41 Squadron ORB, 18 September 1944, TNA AIR 27/426.
89. Ibid., 19 September 1944.
90. 130 Squadron ORB, 19 September 1944, TNA AIR 27/938.

91. 41 Squadron ORB, 19 September 1944, TNA AIR 27/426.
92. The 41 Squadron ORB's F540 on 20 September 1944 states the pilots of Blue Section returned at 18:15, whereas the F541 states they returned at 18:00.
93. 41 Squadron ORB, 20 September 1944, TNA AIR 27/426.
94. Ibid., 22 September 1944.
95. Ibid., 26 September 1944.
96. Ibid.
97. Unfortunately, the 41 Squadron ORB's F541 on 27 September 1944 lists the names and serials of only six of the twelve pilots participating in Rodeo 404. These are Flt Lts David Henry and Daniel Reid, Fg Offs Douglas Fisher and Jim Payne, and WOs Arthur Appleton and James Ware. We are only informed about Flt Lt Terry Spencer, Fg Off Donald Tebbit and WO Peter Hale's participation in the F540, but the names of the remaining three pilots are unknown.
98. 41 Squadron ORB, 29 September 1944, TNA AIR 27/426.
99. The 41 Squadron ORB's F540 on 29 September 1944 states that the Squadron landed at Manston at 10:05, whereas the F541 states the time was 10:00.
100. 41 Squadron ORB, 29 September 1944, TNA AIR 27/426.
101. The synthetic oil plant at Bottrop had previously been bombed on 20 July and 27 September 1944, whilst the synthetic oil plant at Sterkrade had previously suffered attacks on the night of 18/19 August and on 27 September 1944. Both targets would receive at least another six visits from Bomber Command and/or the USAAF prior to the cessation of hostilities.
102. The 11 Group ORB and its Appendix (TNA AIR 25/195 and 214, respectively) state that 200 Halifaxes and Lancasters bombed Bottrop and Sterkrade on 30 September 1944, but the Bomber Command Campaign Diary for September 1944 (rtrvd Feb 2010) states: "139 aircraft – 108 Halifaxes, 21 Lancasters, 10 Mosquitos – of 4 and 8 Groups attempted to attack the oil plant at Sterkrade but the target was cloud-covered. Only 24 aircraft attacked the main target; other aircraft bombed the general town area of Sterkrade. 136 aircraft – 101 Halifaxes, 25 Lancasters, 10 Mosquitos – of 6 and 8 Groups encountered similar conditions at Bottrop. Only 1 aircraft attempted to bomb the oil plant; the remainder of the force bombed the estimated positions of various Ruhr cities. No aircraft lost.". This information suggests that a far greater number of bombers and Mosquitos may have participated in the operation than stated by 11 Group.
103. The 41 Squadron ORB's F540 on 30 September 1944 states that 41 Squadron was airborne at 11:20 and landed again at 13:15, whereas the F541 states these timings were 11:55 and 12:10, respectively, which are clearly erroneous. Moreover, the 11 Group ORB's Appendix (*NO.11 GROUP OPERATIONAL ACTIVITY SYNOPSIS, Dawn 30/9/44 to dawn 1/10/44*), TNA AIR 25/214.) states that the Wing was airborne at 11:15 and landed at 13:30, which suggests that the timings on the F540 are more likely correct.
104. The bomber lost on Ramrod 1302 was Halifax VII, LW197, OW-S, of Linton-on-Ouse-based 426 Squadron, which was hit by Flak and crashed at 13:15 at Buschhausen in the northern outskirts of Oberhausen. Five of the crew were killed (Fg Off T. Frederickson RCAF, Sgt J. Sullivan, Flt Sgt I. T. Pelechaty RCAF, Flt Sgt G. E. Ryan RCAF, and Sgt V. A. McPhee RCAF) and are buried today in the Reichswald Forest War Cemetery. The remaining two members of the crew (Flt Sgt D. E. Turnquist RCAF and Fg Off A. N. Nicholson RCAF) both became Prisoners of War.
105. 41 Squadron ORB, 30 September 1944, TNA AIR 27/426.
106. RAF Lympne ORB, 1 October 1944, TNA AIR 28/509.
107. Ibid., 2 October 1944.
108. 41 Squadron ORB, 2 October 1944, TNA AIR 27/426.
109. 11 Group ORB Appendix, (*NO.11 GROUP OPERATIONAL ACTIVITY SYNOPSIS, Dawn 2/10/44 to dawn 3/10/44*), 2 October 1944, TNA AIR 25/215.
110. Flt Lt Charles J. Samouelle had joined the RAFVR in August 1940, and completed ITW and EFTS in the United Kingdom before undertaking SFTS in Canada. Returning to the United Kingdom, Samouelle completed OTU in Glamorgan, after which he was posted to his first operational unit, 92 Squadron, at Biggin Hill in early September 1941. He was commissioned in November 1941, and remained with 92 Squadron when they shipped to the Middle East in January 1942. It was here that Samouelle achieved his first aerial victories and displayed his leadership abilities, which resulted in him being promoted to Acting Flight Lieutenant and OC, A Flight, in August 1942, just eleven months after joining the Squadron as an NCO pilot. Promotion to Flying Officer followed in October 1942, and by the time of his departure at the end of January 1943 had achieved 7-4-6 aerial victories. In the month he returned to the United Kingdom, February 1943, Samouelle was awarded both a DFC and a Bar, and was rested in ground duties until September 1944, when he undertook a refresher course at 53 OTU. He was now joining 41 Squadron directly from that course.
111. Air Cdre Cecil Bouchier served with 41 Squadron as a Flight Lieutenant, and as OC, B Flight, from 1926 to 1929.
112. This is a reference to 41 Squadron's pending move to the Continent, which was notified on 1 October 1944, but subsequently delayed until 4 December 1944.
113. 41 Squadron was based at Hornchurch from 28 May-8 June 1940, 26 July-8 August 1940, and 3 September 1940-23 February 1941, whilst Air Cdre Bouchier was Station Commander at RAF Hornchurch from December 1938 to December 1940.

114. Body of a letter to Sqn Ldr Douglas I. Benham DFC AFC from Air Cdre Cecil Bouchier CBE DFC, dated 4 October 1944, from the collection of Wg Cdr Benham OBE DFC AFC, and reproduced with his kind permission.
115. 41 Squadron ORB, 5 October 1944, TNA AIR 27/426.
116. Ibid.
117. Research of German sources, such as *Gelsenkirchener Geschichten* (http://www.gelsenkirchener-geschichten.de/, rtrvd Feb 2010), indicate that locals and historians are unclear as to what the RAF referred to as the 'Nordstern Synthetic Oil Plant'. It appears, from damage done on this operation that the targets were likely the Nordstern and Scholven Collieries, which provided coal for the Gelsenberg and Scholven hydrogenation plants, or the hydrogenation plants themselves (although these never bore the name 'Nordstern'), in the north-western Gelsenkirchen districts of Horst and Scholven. The bombing also hit the nearby borough of Buer.
118. Additionally, 635 Squadron Lancaster III, ND453, was hit by Flak over Gelsenkirchen but managed to make it back across the Channel. However, it overshot the runway and crashed at Shottisham, four miles southeast of Woodbridge, Suffolk. The Wireless Operator was killed and both Air Gunners injured.
119. There is a slight contradiction between accounts concerning the location that the Lympne Wing rendezvoused with the bombers on Ramrod 1318 on 6 October 1944. The 41 Squadron ORB states that rendezvous was made prior to making landfall, whereas the 610 Squadron ORB states it was over Bergen op Zoom, east of Walcheren Island. It could, however, be that 41 Squadron was leading the Wing and met the bombers off the coast first, and that 610 Squadron was behind 41 Squadron, and that by the time they caught up with the bombers, they had already reached Bergen op Zoom.
120. 41 Squadron ORB, 5 October 1944, TNA AIR 27/426.
121. German sources indicate that, in the Gelsenkirchen attack, bombs hit Horst and Scholven as planned, but also did damage to the district of Buer, which lay between them.
122. 41 Squadron ORB, 5 October 1944, TNA AIR 27/426.
123. See also the report titled, "River Waal Line; Enemy's Plans for a Counter-Blow" in *The Times*, edition of 7 Oct 1944 (Issue 49971, page 4, column B) which explains the situation in more detail.
124. Additionally, 460 Squadron Lancaster III, PB254, was hit by incendiaries over Emmerich, causing a fire onboard. Three crew baled out but the pilot was able to limp back across the Channel and subsequently crash-landed at Hawkinge.
125. 350 Squadron's pilots should have numbered 12, and included Sqn Ldr Michel Donnet and Fg Off Robert Vanderveken, but both their aircraft failed to start.
126. 11 Group ORB Appendix, (*NO.11 GROUP OPERATIONAL ACTIVITY SYNOPSIS, Dawn 7/10/44 to dawn 8/10/44*), 7 October 1944, TNA AIR 25/215.
127. Source: *Bildersammlung zur Zerstörung der Stadt Kleve im Zweiten Weltkrieg*, http://www.heimat-kleve.de/impressionen_II/zerstoerung/zerstoerung.htm (rtrvd Feb 2010).
128. Bomber Command Campaign Diary for 14 October 1944, http://www.raf.mod.uk/bombercommand/oct44.html (rtrvd Feb 2010).
129. *Bomber Boys: Fighting Back 1940-1945*, Patrick Bishop, Harper Press, 2007, ISBN 9780007189861.
130. 12 Sqn. Lancaster I, ME788, was not lost as a result of enemy action, rather it ditched between Mablethorpe and Grimsby at 07:10 on the outbound leg.
131. This figure was established by Duisburg's Air Defence Police [Luftschutzpolizei].
132. Source: Stadtmuseum Duisberg, *Bomben auf Duisberg; Der Luftkrieg und die Stadt 1940 – 1960*, http://www.stadtmuseum-duisburg.de/austellung/download/Bombenkrieg4.pdf (rtrvd Feb 2010).
133. Source: RP Online, *Trümmerwüste Duisburg*, Peter Korte, http://www.rp-online.de/niederrheinnord/duisburg/nachrichten/duisburg/Truemmerwueste-Duisburg_aid_597984.html (rtrvd Feb 2010).
134. 41 Squadron ORB, entry for 18-22 October 1944, TNA AIR 27/426.
135. Ibid.
136. This refers to the period between 29 April and 19 June 1944, when 41 Squadron was based at Bolt Head, Devon, with 610 Squadron.
137. 610 Squadron ORB, 21 October 1944, TNA AIR 27/2108.
138. WO James P. Ware was posted to RAF Hawkinge on 2 November, where he was charged with two counts of striking fellow servicemen (Cpl G. E. Shaw of RAF Lympne's Station Flight and LAC E. H. Webber of 2847 Squadron RAF Regiment) by General Court Martial on 21 November 1944. Although the second count was dismissed, Ware was severely reprimanded for the first count, and did not return to 41 Squadron; his whereabouts and occupation are unknown until he was posted to 451 (Australian) Squadron at Hawkinge on 2 February 1945. Ware had begun to complain of headaches after being struck during the brawl he was involved in on 21 October 1944, and these reportedly resurfaced when he recommenced flying with 451 Squadron for the first time since the brawl. He complained about them after his first operational flight with this unit, and returned early from the second, demanding that he be made to fly no more than one operation per day. At this point, however, he was taken off flying altogether and sent for medical examinations to identify the problem. However, Ware's RAAF personnel file (*RAAF Personnel files of Non-Commissioned Officers (NCOs) and other ranks, 1921-1948*, Series A9301, Barcode 5528423, NAA) indicates that doctors could not find any evidence of, or reason for, the headaches he was reporting. Subsequent reports reveal that doctors and 451 Squadron's Commanding Officer began to suspect that the headaches

may have been invented and that Ware simply no longer wished to fly. One document suggests that Ware's case was beginning to look like other known cases of aches and pains reported by airmen who no longer wished to serve and the suggestion was made to the AOC 12 Group, AVM John W. Baker CB MC DFC, that Ware was likely "lacking in moral fibre" (*RAAF Personnel files of Non-Commissioned Officers (NCOs) and other ranks, 1921-1948*, Series A9301, Barcode 5528423, NAA). Baker concurred. In the meantime, Ware had been posted to RAF Coltishall on 6 April 1945, then to 11 PDRC for repatriation on 9 May. Whilst there, the decision on his fate came through and on 19 June, he was reduced in rank to AC1 General Hand, effective 19 July, and his flying badge was withdrawn. He arrived back in Australia on 19 October 1945, and was discharged from the RAAF on 22 January 1946, his "services no longer required with disciplinary effect" (*RAAF Personnel files of Non-Commissioned Officers (NCOs) and other ranks, 1921-1948*, Series A9301, Barcode 5528423, NAA). Ware fought this ruling with the support of MP William C. Wentworth, and in February 1955 the Air Board reviewed his case. However, he gained little. His service record maintained his discharge as it stood, but the court removed the words 'with disciplinary effect'.

139. WO Alister Miller enlisted in the RAAF in Melbourne in April 1942 and completed his entire flying training in Australia, earning his Wings in February 1943. Arriving in the United Kingdom in December 1943, Miller attended EFTS and AFU, and married in June 1944, prior to being posted to 53 OTU at Kirton in July. He was promoted to Warrant Officer in August 1944 and posted to 83 GSU at Bognor Regis in early September.

140. Flt Sgt Crawford Moyle enlisted in the RAAF in Adelaide in early January 1943, and attended EFTS in Australia prior to shipping to Canada, where he completed SFTS, earned his Wings, and was posted to OTU. He travelled to the United Kingdom in June 1944 and was posted to 53 OTU at Kirton, followed by 83 GSU at Bognor Regis in early September.

141. 610 Squadron ORB, 24 October 1944, TNA AIR 27/2108.

142. Bomber Command Campaign Diary for 25 October 1944, http://www.raf.mod.uk/bombercommand/oct44.html (rtrvd Feb 2010).

143. 610 Squadron ORB, 26 October 1944, TNA AIR 27/2108.

144. 11 Group ORB Appendix, (*NO.11 GROUP OPERATIONAL ACTIVITY SYNOPSIS, Dawn 28/10/44 to dawn 29/10/44*), 28 October 1944, TNA AIR 25/215.

145. Entry in Flt Lt Robert E. Anderson's logbook on 28 October 1944, reproduced with the kind permission of Doug Fishburn.

146. RAF Battle Honours, http://www.raf.mod.uk/history_old/sqn_hons_ww2_3.html. See also 41 Squadron's Battle Honours, http://www.raf.mod.uk/organisation/41squadron.cfm (both rtrvd Feb 2010).

147. 10 Sqn. Halifax III, MZ576, was not lost as a result of enemy action, rather it ditched off Immingham after a loss of engines on the outbound leg. The crew were rescued by HMS *Middleton*.

148. 26-year-old Canadian Sqn Ldr George St. C. B. Reid was killed on his return from Ramrod 1350 on 28 October 1944 when he flew into thick cloud at an altitude of just 200 feet and is thought to have suffered instrument failure. He was believed to have been buried in Slipje, near Ostend [Oostende], but the surprise discovery of his remains still in his aircraft in Maldegem, Belgium, during its excavation in 1996, proved that the man buried in Slipje had been falsely identified. Reid was subsequently buried in the Canadian military cemetery in Adegem, Belgium, on 6 September 1996. See also *Spitfire pilot laid to rest at last*, The Independent, 8 Sep 1996, http://www.independent.co.uk/news/spitfire-pilot-laid-to-rest-at-last-1362308.html (rtrvd Feb 2010).

149. Source: *Bombenkrieg in Rheinland, Köln Nippes im Luftkrieg 1944*, Teil 2, http://www.bunkerarchaeologie.de/index.php?module=Pagesetter&func=viewpub&tid=9&pid=10 (rtrvd Feb 2010).

150. Flt Sgt John T. 'Jack' Bradshaw was subsequently sent to the Pacific to fight against the Japanese, but was still in transit when the first Atomic Bomb was dropped on Hiroshima. The aircraft was redirected to Bradley Field in the United States, where his orders were cancelled, and he was demobbed three months later. Bradshaw was initially occupied after the War ferrying aircraft to South America, but was then employed by Pan American Grace Airways (PANAGRA) until his retirement in 1982.

151. Research of German sources such as *Gelsenkirchener Geschichten* (http://www.gelsenkirchener-geschichten.de/, rtrvd Feb 2010), indicate that that locals and historians are unclear as to what the RAF referred to as the 'Nordstern Synthetic Oil Plant'. It appears, from damage done on this operation that the targets were likely the Nordstern and Scholven Collieries, which provided coal for the Gelsenberg and Scholven hydrogenation plants, or the hydrogenation plants themselves (although these never bore the name 'Nordstern'), in the western and north-western Gelsenkirchen districts of Scholven and Horst. These were put out of action and closed after the raid, but the bombing also hit the boroughs of Schalke and the old town area, in the city's north, and Bulmke and Hüllen, to the city's south.

152. 41 Squadron ORB, 6 November 1944, TNA AIR 27/426.

153. WO Keith Clanzy's daughter states that on his return from training in the United States, the RAF wanted him to become a flying instructor. However, as he wanted to go into active duty he gently messed up his night landings on a regular basis, until they gave up. His flying apparently improved vastly once he got posted to an active squadron!

154. 41 Squadron ORB, 7 November 1944, TNA AIR 27/426.

155. Wanne-Eickel was incorporated into the nearby city of Herne in 1975, by which name it is generally known today.

156. The 41 Squadron ORB does not actually state how many aircraft participated in Ramrod 1363 on 9 November 1944, and the F541 only lists six aircraft serials and pilots. However, the RAF Lympne ORB states that "14 A/C. of

610 Squadron, 11 A/C. of 41 Squadron and 12 A/C of 350 Squadron" participated in Ramrod 1363, although it is not clear whether the eleven aircraft from 41 Squadron include WO Peter Hale in RM797, who turned back shortly after take-off, or whether eleven were left after his departure.

157. 41 Squadron ORB, 9 November 1944, TNA AIR 27/426.
158. 610 Squadron ORB, 9 November 1944, TNA AIR 27/2108.
159. 11 Group ORB Appendix, 9 November 1944 (*NO.11 GROUP OPERATIONAL ACTIVITY SYNOPSIS, Dawn 9/11/44 to dawn 10/11/44*), TNA AIR 25/216.
160. 41 Squadron ORB, 16 November 1944, TNA AIR 27/426.
161. The RAF Lympne ORB on 16 November 1944 states that Fg Off John F. Wilkinson landed in the Ghent area short of fuel on account of engine trouble, accompanied by WO Alister D. Miller. The 11 Group ORB Appendix (*NO.11 GROUP OPERATIONAL ACTIVITY SYNOPSIS, Dawn 16/11/44 to dawn 17/11/44*), TNA AIR 25/216), which lists all of Ramrod 1372's aircraft and personnel casualties makes no mention of the landing, even though it mentions a similar incident with 350 Squadron. The 41 Squadron ORB's F540 also makes no mention of the pair landing in Belgium, but the F541 simply lists Miller and Flt Lt Ross P. Harding (RM767) – not Wilkinson – as "Landed at Antwerp" – not Ghent – at 15:40.
162. 125 Wing ORB, 19 Nov 1944, TNA AIR 26/185.
163. The 11 Group ORB Appendix (*NO.11 GROUP OPERATIONAL ACTIVITY SYNOPSIS, Dawn 21/11/44 to dawn 22/11/44*), TNA AIR 25/216), indicates that one pilot of 41 Squadron returned early with mechanical problems and a second as escort ("1 (41) mech. 1 (41) escort") but neither are identified. The 41 Squadron ORB's F541 only shows Flt Sgt Crawford Moyle landing at Manston at 14:25, but makes no mention of an escort or who the second pilot may have been.
164. The 11 Group ORB Appendix (*NO.11 GROUP OPERATIONAL ACTIVITY SYNOPSIS, Dawn 26/11/44 to dawn 27/11/44*), TNA AIR 25/216), records that two of 41 Squadron's pilots landed at Manston with mechanical problems ("41 2 mech landed Manston"), but does not identify them. The 41 Squadron ORB's F540 makes no mention of any pilots landing at Manston, but the F541 shows that Fg Off John F. Wilkinson did so, without any explanation. It does not, however, identify the second pilot.
165. 41 Squadron ORB, 26 November 1944, TNA AIR 27/426.
166. Research of German sources, such as *Schwere Luftangriffe auf Osterfeld im 2. Weltkrieg* (http://www.osterfeld-westfalen.de/krieg.html, rtrvd Feb 2010), indicate that the above-ground machinery and facilities at Osterfeld Colliery were severely damaged in the attack, the works railway between Emscher Railway Station and the Osterfeld Colliery cut (although repaired by 3 December 1944), the nearby Osterfeld Coking Plant damaged, and parts of the town of Osterfeld destroyed. Additionally, a Russian Prisoner of War Camp housing mine labourers was almost completely destroyed, killing 170 men.
167. 125 Wing ORB, 1 December 1944, TNA AIR 26/185.
168. 610 Squadron ORB, 2 December 1944, TNA AIR 27/2108.
169. Ibid., 3 December 1944.
170. The 350 Squadron ORB's F540 on 3 December 1944 (TNA AIR 27/1746) suggests the reason the Squadron landed at Evere was twofold: "The Squadron gets posted to BRUSSELS and *thus* remains in Evere after landing there *because* of bad weather" [author's italics]. However, it should be noted that there are some ambiguities in the Squadron's moves during this period, as the F540 states that twelve pilots participated in Ramrod 1390, whereas the F541 only lists ten. Moreover, whilst an overnight stay at Evere is suggested by an entry in the F540 the following day, showing that Sqn Ldr Collignon flew from B.56 to Lympne and back, entries for Fg Off Pacco and Flt Sgt Laloux that day show them flying Manston to Lympne, despite the F540 on 3 December showing them as having been amongst the pilots remaining in Evere. Additionally, the F540 on 6 December 1944 shows Fg Off Vanderveken arriving in B.56 from Lympne, even though he, too, was one of the pilots participating in Ramrod 1390 and remaining in Evere. Clearly, many of the pilots' flights were not recorded in the ORB, which makes it difficult to plot this Squadron's move from Lympne during early December 1944.

8 CONTINENTAL OPERATIONS; 4 DECEMBER 1944 – 7 MARCH 1945

1. 41 Squadron ORB, 4 December 1944, TNA AIR 27/426.
2. Strictly speaking, 41 Squadron had arrived at Schaffen Aerodrome, not Diest. Schaffen is the name of the airfield and surrounding village, whereas Diest is the nearby town where they were billeted. However, the airfield was known to the men as Diest, and was always referred to in the ORB as Diest, rather than Schaffen. As such, the airfield is referred to as Diest throughout by the author.
3. 41 Squadron ORB, 7 December 1944, TNA AIR 27/426.
4. The Squadron's F540 on 6 December 1944 indicates there was no flying, but the F541 shows seven pilots undertook reconnaissance sorties during the afternoon.
5. 125 Wing ORB, 6 December 1944, TNA AIR 26/185.
6. Source: *NO. 83 GROUP AIRFIELD CONSTRUCTION AND OCCUPATION PROGRAMME. (as at 6th December, 1944.)*, 83 (Composite) Group ORB Appendix, TNA AIR 25/706.

Notes to Text

7. 41 Squadron ORB, 7 December 1944, TNA AIR 27/426.
8. The aircraft and pilots involved in the two 'prangs' referred to in the ORB on 7 December 1944 are not recorded.
9. Entry in Flt Lt Robert E. Anderson's logbook on 8 December 1944, reproduced with the kind permission of Doug Fishburn.
10. The Messerschmitt Me262 *Schwalbe* (Swallow) was the world's first jet fighter, with an over-all length of 10.6 metres, a wingspan of 12.6 metres, a height of 3.5 metres and a crew of one. Its maximum speed was 900 kmph, and armaments consisted of two to four 30mm cannon, or twenty-four 55mm rockets, or two 250kg bombs (one version was also able to carry two 500kg bombs). The Me262 first flew under jet power in July 1942, but was not introduced for training until Spring 1944. Although the first victory was claimed in July 1944 (against an RAF Mosquito), full operational missions were not undertaken until the following month. However, after the Commanding Officer of the only unit then equipped with them was shot down and killed in November 1944, the jets were withdrawn from service to revise current combat techniques and devise and practice new procedures. As such, it is surprising that Flt Lts Robert Anderson and John Refshauge saw three Me262s at all during December; it would have been a rare sight indeed. It should be noted, though, that as they were seen over Dutch territory then held by the Germans, their sorties were most likely non-operational training flights. In January 1945, JG7 was formed as a jet fighter unit, and KG54 as a fighter-bomber unit, specialising in a ground attack role. However, neither of these units were fully operational until around the end of January-beginning of February.
11. WO Arthur S. Appleton was kept at Dulag Luft over Christmas and New Year, where he received treatment to his leg. On completion of his interrogation and recuperation, he was sent to Stalag Luft VII, at Bankau, on 9 January 1945, but transferred to Stalag III-A, Luckenwalde a few days later (the dates on his ex-POW Questionnaire [TNA WO 344/8/2] are ambiguous), where he remained until 10 May 1945. Upon repatriation, he resided at Shottenden, outside Canterbury, Kent.
12. 41 Squadron ORB, 18 December 1944, TNA AIR 27/426.
13. Upon recuperation, Flt Lt Robert E. Anderson was taken off operations and fulfilled flying instructor posts at 53 OTU at Kirton-in-Lindsey, and CGS at Catfoss, until the cessation of hostilities. He was repatriated to Australia soon afterwards, arriving in Sydney in early July, and was demobbed in late September 1945. Having secured a position in the NSW Public Service, Anderson attended Sydney University from 1946 and graduated with a BE (Civil) in 1950. In subsequent years, he lived in different areas of the State of NSW, employed on various public works projects, thereunder as Resident Engineer on the Adaminaby Dam, which formed a part of the Snowy Mountains Hydro-Electric Scheme. Anderson continued working until the early 1980s, but died in Sydney in December 1984, almost 40 years to the day since his flying accident, aged just 64.
14. The Squadron ORB's F540 on 19 December 1944 states that no operational flying took place, but the F541 and 125 Wing ORB both record that patrols were undertaken by 41 Squadron during the day.
15. 41 Squadron ORB, 23 December 1944, TNA AIR 27/426.
16. The timings of the patrol are recorded on *Opflash 125/24/2* [41 Squadron Archives] as 13:15-14:55, but this does not correlate with any of the sorties recorded on the Squadron ORB's F541 on 24 December 1944, so may have been an additional patrol. Unfortunately, the Opflash does not identify the section or the pilots, so the participants remain unknown.
17. Similar to the previously mentioned patrol, the timings of this one (15:30-16:15), recorded on *Opflash 125/24/6* [41 Squadron Archives], also do not correlate with the timings on the F541 on 24 December 1944, nor is the pilot named.
18. *Opflash 125/24/6*, 24 December 1944, 41 Squadron Archives.
19. Neerpelt is approximately 15 miles south of Eindhoven, just inside the Belgian border. It has proven impossible to identify what these objects might have been as they do not appear to have been similar to the forms of Window known at this time.
20. Once again, the details appearing in the Opflash (*Opflash 125/24/7*, six Spitfire XIV, 15:30-16:40) do not match the timings recorded on the Squadron's F541 on 24 December 1944.
21. *Opflash 125/24/7*, 24 December 1944, 41 Squadron Archives.
22. On this occasion, the sheets of paper were most likely sheets of foil Window. An attack by 327 bombers and 11 Mosquitoes on the airfields at Lohausen and Mülheim [today Düsseldorf and Essen Airports] took place on 24 December 1944, which may have had a flight path close to the area 41 Squadron was patrolling, and would account for Window being used. Some of these were formed into v-shapes for stability, which might explain the impression they were conical or small parachutes.
23. 41 Squadron ORB, 24 December 1944, TNA AIR 27/426.
24. Ibid., 25 December 1944.
25. Flt Lt David J. V. Henry's logbook indicates he did not arrive at Asch/Ophoven until the conclusion of his second patrol on 31 December 1944.
26. There is some confusion about the location of the new base, probably as the Squadron ORB states on 31 December 1944, "Y.32. Asch". However, Y.32 was actually the number for Ophoven Aerodrome. In fact, subsequent ORB entries begin to 'distance' themselves from Asch, stating "Y.32 Near Asch", but continue to use the number Y.32. Asch was numbered Y.29, and was an American airfield, located approximately 8.5km south-southwest of Ophoven,

from which Mustangs of the 352nd Fighter Group (8th Air Force) and Thunderbolts of the 366th Fighter Group (9th Air Force) operated. Royal Air Force units, namely 41, 130, 350, and 610 Squadrons, were based at nearby Y.32 Ophoven, a fact confirmed by many sources, thereunder the 125 Wing ORB.

27. 125 Wing ORB, 31 December 1944, TNA AIR 26/185.
28. *MEDICAL HISTORY OF THE WAR. Medical Extract for the month of December, 1944, Ref: 83G/1519/5/Med.*, 11 January 1945, 83 (Composite) Group ORB, TNA AIR 25/706.
29. The Squadron ORB on 1 January 1945 is ambiguous as it states that WO Vivian Rossow returned early with mechanical problems, but shows his return time in line with the pilots that completed the armed reconnaissance to Koblenz. Additionally, although not mentioned in the ORB, Rossow's *Pilot Service Record* shows a ground victory by him on this date, in which he claimed one MET and a signal box damaged. It should also be noted, however, that Rossow participated in another patrol that afternoon and as no location of these ground victories is recorded the victories may have been on the afternoon patrol instead.
30. 125 Wing ORB, 1 January 1945, TNA AIR 26/185.
31. Source: *NO. 83 GROUP INTELLIGENCE SUMMARY NO. 196, Up to 2359 hours, 1st January, PART 1*, 1 January 1945, 83 (Composite) Group ORB Appendix, TNA AIR 25/706. Note that the number of sorties flown by 125 Wing appearing in the 83 Group table differ to the number quoted in the 125 Wing ORB (70 vs. 81). The reason for this disparity is unknown but the higher total may take non-operational sorties into account.
32. The Squadron ORB's F540 for 2 January 1945 states eight patrols took place today, but the F541 only lists five. The entries from the F541 have been used in the text.
33. Sqn Ldr Terry Spencer was demobbed mid-December 1945 and headed to South Africa in Spring 1946, taking three weeks to fly himself there in a single-engined Percival Proctor. He was employed there as the personal pilot of Ben du Preez, Managing Director of Kimlite Industries, which was a cover for illicit diamond buying. Spencer returned to the United Kingdom where he married the actress Lesley Brook (who starred in at least 24 films between 1937 and 1948) in August 1947 and resided for a time on the Isle of Wight, before returning to South Africa in July 1948. On this occasion, he launched a new career by founding the aerial-photography company 'Skyfotos' in October that same year. The company enjoyed some success, but he was to become a more successful freelance photographer for LIFE magazine, for whom he worked between September 1952 and September 1972. During his time with LIFE, he covered several conflicts, including Biafra, Congo, and the Vietnam War, and spent three months on tour with a then little-known band called *The Beatles*. When LIFE folded in 1972, Spencer moved to People magazine, where he spent the ensuing 20 years. He authored and published two books, the first a renowned coffee table picture book about The Beatles (*It was Thirty Years Ago Today*, Bloomsbury, 1994, ISBN 0747516871), and the second an autobiography (*Living Dangerously*, Percival, 2002, ISBN 0954286200), which he co-authored with his wife. Ever prepared to answer researchers' queries about his life and exploits, including those of this author, Terry Spencer always responded with an apparent untiring energy and enthusiasm, attached to the world via e-mail until after his 90th birthday. Following his death in Odiham, Hampshire, on 8 February 2009, *The Times* published a glowing obituary of a man who was a real-life adventurer, and whose life and exploits were the very stuff of 'Boys Own' magazines.
34. Excerpt from correspondence with WO John A. Chalmers, June 2009.
35. 125 Wing ORB, 5 January 1945, TNA AIR 26/185.
36. Flt Lt Frederick G. Herman's formal recommendation in Flt Lt John G. H. Refshauge's personnel file, *RAAF Officers Personnel files, 1921-1948*, Series A9300, Barcode 5251127, NAA.
37. Sqn Ldr Benham's formal recommendation in Flt Lt John G. H. Refshauge's personnel file, *RAAF Officers Personnel files, 1921-1948*, Series A9300, Barcode 5251127, NAA.
38. Flt Lt John Refshauge was posted back to the United Kingdom on 14 January 1945 and taken on strength at 83 GSU at Dunsfold in Surrey. Following some leave, he was posted to India in late March and joined 132 Squadron at Madura. He remained in India until August, when he was repatriated to Australia and subsequently demobbed. Having broken off his first year of medicine at Melbourne University when he joined the RAAF in July 1941, Refshauge resumed to his course in 1946 and graduated MBBS in October 1951. He rejoined the RAAF in October 1952 as a Flight Lieutenant in the Medical Branch of the Reserve and served several years before leaving to specialise in Sports Medicine. In recognition of his work in this latter field, Refshauge was awarded the OBE in June 1978 and the AM in June 1987. He died in 1999.
39. Vogelsang and its airfield were captured by the 1st Battalion, 47th Regiment, 9th US Infantry Division, almost without opposition on 4 February 1945. The British military initially occupied the barracks in 1946 and used it as a training camp, but it was taken over by the Belgian military in 1950. The Belgians rebuilt the barracks, and other parts of the complex that were destroyed during the War, and subsequently used it as their own military training centre. Whilst under their control, the barracks were also used to train NATO troops and some Bundeswehr units. The base was handed back to the German government in December 2005 and it was subsequently released to the public and incorporated into the Eifel National Park.
40. The two destroyed and seven damaged MET on 16 January 1945 are recorded in the Squadron ORB, but the 125 Wing ORB states they also damaged three rail trucks. For the same operation, Flt Lt David J. V. Henry claims in his flying logbook one truck damaged and two ammunition dumps hit, and WO Vivian J. Rossow claims one MET destroyed and one damaged on his *Pilot Service Record*. This example illustrates the difficulty of reconciling claims

of ground targets and the impossible task of separating repetition, overlap and error from fact, particularly as many claims were shared. As such, despite efforts, any record of ground targets is bound to contain some margin of error.

41. Plt Off N. Peter Gibbs believed this injury resulted in him suffering a slipped disc around ten years later and subsequently spending six months on his back.
42. 125 Wing ORB, 17 January 1945, TNA AIR 26/185.
43. *Addition to Opflash No.125/22/18*, dated 22 January 1945, 41 Squadron Archives. The reference to the *Queen Mary* refers not to the troopship of this name, but rather to a trailer used by the RAF for hauling aircraft fuselages. The three-ton low loading trailer was designed to Air Ministry specifications and measured 40 feet in length. It was called the *Queen Mary* because it was the longest vehicle on the road at the time.
44. Flt Lt Charles J. Samouelle remained in the RAF after the cessation of hostilities, was awarded the OBE in the 1971 New Year's Honours List, and retired from the RAF in February 1975, retaining Wing Commander. Note that whilst the 41 Squadron ORB makes no announcement of Samouelle's departure, the 130 Squadron ORB records his arrival and take-over of A Flight on 22 January 1945. Confusingly, however, at the end of January 1945, the 130 Squadron ORB also summarises the month's personnel movements, erroneously stating that Samouelle was posted to the unit on 11 January. A review of 41 Squadron's F541 for the month of January 1945 reveals that Samouelle continued flying operationally with 41 Squadron up to and including 22 January and, as such, it is clear that the compiler of the 130 Squadron ORB erroneously typed two 1's (11), instead of two 2's (22) when adding the date of Samouelle's arrival on 130 Squadron.
45. The Squadron ORB's F540 on 23 January 1945 states there were eight aircraft involved in the 08:40-09:55 armed reconnaissance, but the F541 only records the names of seven. However, an original intelligence report for the day, Oprep 23, *41S/S.233/Air*, which is held in 41 Squadron's archives, clearly states the operation only involved seven pilots and aircraft.
46. 41 Squadron ORB, 23 January 1945, TNA AIR 27/426.
47. Combat Report for Sqn Ldr Douglas I. Benham, No. 67, 23 January 1945, TNA AIR 50/18.
48. The pilot of Sqn Ldr Benham's second victory on 23 January 1945 was Lt. Xaver Ellenrieder of IV./JG26 (Blue 6, WNr. 211006), who landed in his parachute at Ostbevern at around 09:45 with serious head injuries. Whilst Benham's Combat Report states that Ellenrieder spun in from 500 feet, author Donald Caldwell suggests in his *JG26 War Diary* that the altitude was actually 500 *metres*, i.e. 1,800 feet. After recovering from his wounds, Ellenrieder took over command of I./JG26 and ended the War as an Ace with 12 victories.
49. Combat Report for Fg Off Francis M. Hegarty, No. 250, 23 January 1945, TNA AIR 50/18.
50. Combat Report for Flt Lt William N. Stowe, No. 393, 23 January 1945, TNA AIR 50/18.
51. Contemporary research suggests that the two other pilots brought down by Benham and Hegarty on 23 January 1945 were Uffz. Walter Planz of I./JG26 (White 11, WNr. 210153), who crashed at Albachten, west of Münster, at 09:30, and Lt. Hans-Helmuth Cordt of IV./JG26 (Blue 16, WNr. 400605), who came down near Leeden-Tecklenburg at around the same time. Both pilots were killed, but it has proven impossible to definitively match the victors to their specific victories.
52. There is an inconsistency between the locations 41 Squadron felt the aircraft came down on 23 January 1945, and the locations indicated in contemporary writings, such as those of Donald Caldwell in his *JG26 War Diary*. Sqn Ldr Douglas Benham's first victory, at A9543, corresponds to 51° 38' 26" N, 7° 35' 34" E, which appears to be in a field located approximately 17km northeast of the centre of Dortmund. His second victory, at A9038, corresponds to 51° 41' 08" N, 7° 39' 54" E, which appears to be in a small wood around 7km northeast of the location he declared in his first victory, and around 24km northeast of the centre of Dortmund. Fg Off Francis Hegarty's victory, at A9130, corresponds to 51° 34' 07" N, 7° 36' 27" E, which appears to be at Methler, approximately 11km northeast of the centre of Dortmund. This location is also about 8km south of Benham's second victory. However, considering that Planz crashed at Albachten (about 8km southwest of the centre of Münster), Ellenrieder at Ostbevern (16km northeast of Münster), and Cordt near Leeden-Tecklenburg (about 33km northeast of the centre of Münster), it is apparent that 41 Squadron was operating several kilometres further north than they thought. Moreover, the fact that Balasse came down 3km northeast of the centre of Münster would lend weight to this theory. In view of the speeds 41 Squadron's pilots would have been flying, their unfamiliarity with the area, and an obvious inability to stop and verify locations, this inaccuracy is perhaps not surprising.
53. 41 Squadron ORB, 27 January 1945, TNA AIR 27/426.
54. *The History of 122 Wing, 83 Group, Second Tactical Air Force*, 1945.
55. There are a few discrepancies in the 41 Squadron ORB on 29 January 1945. The F540 states there were six pilots involved in the 15:00-16:05 armed reconnaissance to Gutersloh, but the F541 only records five names and five aircraft serials. Moreover, of the aircraft recorded, one serial is erroneous as Flt Lt Ross Harding and WO Patrick Coleman are both listed as having flown RM707. However, Coleman's flying logbook shows he was flying EB-H on this date, which was the code lettering for RM707. This would therefore indicate that if Coleman was flying this aircraft, Harding's serial on the F541 on this date is the incorrect one.
56. The ORB on 1 February 1945 states no other targets were found besides the Flak trains, but Flt Lt David J. V. Henry recorded in his logbook that they damaged a truck and trailer. Flt Sgt Hubert F. Kelly also has these same victories recorded on his *Pilot Service Record*, and the 122 Wing ORB confirms a victory against MET.

57. 41 Squadron ORB, 2 February 1945, TNA AIR 27/426.
58. There was possibly one more MET destroyed and another damaged, as the Squadron ORB on 2 February 1945 states the "final bag was 5 destroyed and 5 damaged", but only four of each are actually recorded in the text of the ORB. Confusingly, Fg Off John Wilkinson's *Pilot Service Record* records three and five.
59. Under normal circumstances, as he held a higher rank, Flt Lt Peter Cowell would have led the Section on 3 February 1945 rather than Fg Off Peter Gibbs. However, this sortie constituted Cowell's first operational flight – and indeed his first over Germany – since his return to the Squadron for his second tour of duty on 31 January.
60. 41 Squadron ORB, 3 February 1945, TNA AIR 27/426.
61. WO Keith Clanzy was offered a commission in the RAF at the end of the War but instead returned to South Wales to complete the obligations of his apprenticeship with the Tredegar Iron and Coal Company Limited (later becoming the National Coal Board). He studied all aspects of Colliery Engineering at the South Wales and Monmouthshire School of Mines, Treforest, and gained his Higher Grade Diploma in August 1947. Clanzy went on to gain his BSc (Eng) from London University in August 1948 and worked for the Tredegar Iron and Coal Company for the next three years before moving to London in 1951 to take up a position as Mining Inspector with the Ministry of Fuel and Power. Later that year, he was elected Associate Member Group C of the Institute of Mining Engineers, advancing to Group A in April 1959. He led a distinguished career, helping to revolutionise the entire concept of mining safety in the United Kingdom and internationally. An active member of the Association of Mechanical, Electrical and Mining Engineers (AMEME), Clanzy served as their President from 1972 to 1973. He retired as HM Principal Inspector of Mines in 1979 but continued to do Contract work for a number of years both for the Ministry and the United Nations, and AMEME made him an Honorary Fellow of the Association in February 1983. In the Spring of 1986 he moved to the village of Easton in Suffolk where he remained active in village life until his death on 4 September 2009.
62. There is a discrepancy in the details provided on the 09:00 mission in the Squadron ORB on 8 February 1945. The F540 states "W/O R. Fleming [note the incorrect rank; he was now commissioned] returned early with a u/s hood", whilst the F541 makes no mention of Fleming and instead lists Flt Lt Thomas R. Burne returning in RM719 twenty minutes into the armed reconnaissance with "technical trouble". It is therefore also possible that either man could have flown this sortie, but it should be noted that Fleming is not shown on the F541 at all flying operationally between 3 and 13 February 1945. Considering the cuts to the face that Fleming sustained in operations on 3 February, it is likely that Fleming was not flying, and that is was Burne instead.
63. There is a discrepancy in the details provided on the 16:30 mission in 41 Squadron ORB on 8 February 1945. The F540 states that five pilots were involved in the 16:30 armed reconnaissance to the Rheine area and that Fg Off John Wilkinson returned early with a "rough engine". However, the F541 states the armed reconnaissance was to the Münster-Hamm area and does not record Wilkinson's participation. Five pilots are listed – Flt Lt Thomas Burne, WO Viv Rossow, Flt Lt Frank Woolley, Flt Sgt Harry Smart, and Flt Lt Peter Cowell – but Wilkinson is not amongst them. In fact, he is not shown on the F541 as having flown all day. It may therefore have been one of these five pilots instead, who returned with the rough engine. As such, the serial of the aircraft in question is also unclear.
64. 122 Wing ORB, 9 February 1945, TNA AIR 26/181.
65. Ibid.
66. Flt Lt David Henry was held at Eschendorf until 12 February, then transferred to Dulag Luft, where he was held for five days in solitary confinement. On 20 February, he was transferred to Wetzlar and on 23 February to Oflag XIII, at Langwasser, outside Nuremberg, where he remained until 4 April. During a forced march away from advancing Allied troops, Henry escaped with three RNZAF Flying Officers and reached Allied lines by foot. He was repatriated to the United Kingdom on 19 April and, following recuperation and leave, was posted to the Enemy Aircraft Flight at Tangmere, where he made flights in both the Me109 and FW190. Henry was promoted to Squadron Leader on 28 November 1945, but discharged from the RNZAF on the same day, upon being commissioned with the same rank in the RNZAF Reserve. He remained with the Air Force until February 1971 and died in Invercargill, New Zealand, in August 1984.
67. Entry for 10 February 1945 in the flying logbook of Flt Lt David J. V. Henry.
68. Note that this comment, added to Flt Lt David Henry's logbook on 10 February 1945, states that the locomotive was damaged, whereas the Squadron ORB and an Intelligence Report for this date state that the pilots made no claims. Further, the statement also claims that Flt Lt Henry baled out, whereas the Squadron ORB and an Intelligence Report for this date both state he made a forced landing, and crash-landed, respectively. It is not clear who wrote the original statement, but it appears to have been Henry himself who crossed out 'force landed' and replaced it with 'baled out' after his repatriation. The next statement in Henry's logbook (see subsequent text), which he added himself, certainly suggests this was the case.
69. Undated entry in the flying logbook of Flt Lt David J. V. Henry.
70. 274 Squadron's 129720 Flt Lt John W. Woolfries (Tempest V, EJ751) was captured and spent the remaining months of the War as a PoW. 3 Squadron's 189177 Plt Off Morris J. A. Rose (Tempest V, NV656) evaded capture and returned to Allied lines.
71. *NO. 83 GROUP INTELLIGENCE SUMMARY NO 239. Up to 2359 hours 13th February. PART II.*, 13 February 1945, 83 (Composite) Group ORB Appendix, TNA AIR 25/706.

72. Flt Lt Harry Cook returned to the United Kingdom where he was rested, initially as a Flying Instructor at 57 OTU and, from the end of May 1945, as a ferry pilot with 229 Group Transport Command. He was demobilised in 1946 and his subsequent movements are unknown.
73. Plt Off Patrick Coleman and Fg Off John Wilkinson are both shown on the Squadron's F541 on 13 February 1945 as having flown RM797 on this operation. However, evidence from Coleman's logbook states he was flying EB-E that day, which is known to have been RM797's code lettering. This suggests it was Coleman who was flying RM797, and that the entry for Wilkinson is erroneous.
74. 41 Squadron ORB, 13 February 1945, TNA AIR 27/426.
75. Statement made by Fg Off Eric Gray on a combined Combat Report for Flt Lt Ross Harding (in absentia), Fg Offs Eric Gray and Francis Hegarty, and WO Ian Stevenson, 13 February 1945, 41 Squadron Archives.
76. *NO. 83 GROUP INTELLIGENCE SUMMARY NO 239. Up to 2359 hours 13th February. PART 1.*, 13 February 1945, 83 (Composite) Group ORB Appendix, TNA AIR 25/706.
77. The other two pilots on the 11:25 operation on 13 February 1945, who are not mentioned in the text, were Flt Lt Frank Woolley (RM791) and Fg Off Jim Payne (RM790).
78. Flt Lt Ross Harding was held at Dulag Luft until 7 March 1945, when he was sent to Stalag XIIID at Nuremburg. It is believed he was then force-marched over 125km southeast with other POWs to Stalag VII-A at Moosburg, where he was held between 19 and 29 April, then liberated and repatriated to England. Harding remained in the Air Force after the cessation of hostilities in Europe, was awarded a Mention in Despatches in June 1945 and promoted to Flight Lieutenant on 1 September. In January 1946, he was promoted to Squadron Leader and posted to Singapore, where he took over command of 152 Squadron. However, his tenure was only brief as the unit was disbanded just two months later. Harding was granted a permanent commission as a Flight Lieutenant in March 1947 and promoted to Squadron Leader in July 1950. He attended the RAF Staff College at Andover in 1951 and was then posted as staff to the office of the Assistant Chief of Air Staff (Operations). From 1955, Harding commanded 96 Squadron at Ahlhorn, Germany, flying Meteor NF.II's until his promotion to Wing Commander in July 1958. At this time, he was posted back to the RAF Staff College at Andover as staff where he spent two years, before taking command of the Oxford University Air Squadron, in August 1960. In December 1962, Harding returned to Germany, where he held the office of Deputy Chief of the British Military Mission to Berlin, and was promoted to Group Captain in that role the following July. Returning to the United Kingdom two years later, he took command of RAF Valley and 4 FTS, and was awarded the CBE for his services in January 1968. A month later, Harding was appointed Director of Staff (Air) at the Joint Services Staff College at Latimer, in Buckinghamshire, where he remained until August 1970. At this juncture, Gp Capt Harding was promoted to Acting Air Commodore and posted to Moscow as Air Attaché. His promotion to full Air Commodore followed in January 1972, as did a posting to the Directorate of Personnel in November that same year. Promoted to Acting Air Vice-Marshal at the end of January 1974, he was posted to the Royal College of Defence Studies in London as Senior Air Force Director of Staff six months later. Harding retired from the RAF in early February 1976, retaining Air Vice-Marshal, and in civilian life remained linked to aviation, initially as Head of Airwork Services Ltd. in Oman from 1977 to 1979, then as Chairman of the Ministry of Defence Selection Board for the ensuing five years. In 1984, he was briefly a Special Adviser to the House of Commons Defence Committee in London, but then definitively retired. He died in November 1998.
79. 122 Wing ORB, 13 February 1945, TNA AIR 26/181.
80. The crew of the Me110 shot down by 41 Squadron on 13 February 1945 were 21-year-old Uffz. Gerhard Bauer, who was the pilot, 24-year-old Uffz. Rudolf Serafin, the mechanic, and Uffz. Hans Mayer, the wireless operator. Bauer, born on 22 August 1924, and Serafin, born on 1 February 1921, were both killed and are buried today in Lippstadt War Cemetery. Mayer baled out wounded and survived the incident.
81. Statement by WO Ian Stevenson on a combined Combat Report for Flt Lt Ross Harding (in absentia), Fg Offs Eric Gray and Francis Hegarty, and WO Ian Stevenson, 13 February 1945, 41 Squadron Archives.
82. Statement by Flt Lt Frank G. Woolley on a combined Combat Report for Woolley and Fg Off Eric Gray, No. 496, 14 February 1945, TNA AIR 50/18.
83. Although WO Vivian Rossow only states in his Combat Report that his engine was running rough, the Squadron ORB on 14 February 1945 indicates the propeller of his aircraft, RM696, had actually been hit by Flak. This is quite likely to have given Rossow the impression his engine was running rough.
84. Statement by Fg Off Eric Gray on a combined Combat Report for Gray and Flt Lt Frank G. Woolley, No. 496, 14 February 1945, TNA AIR 50/18.
85. Flt Lt Frank Woolley's *Pilot Service Record* shows his victory over a FW190 on 14 February 1945 as probable. However, the word 'PROBABLE' has been crossed out and 'DAMAGED' inserted instead, along with the comment, "See letter of 6.3.45 in Sqdn File Assessments". Fortunately, this latter document has survived and, like Woolley's *Pilot Service Record*, is also held in 41 Squadron's Archives. It is a typed, half-page document addressed to 'C.O., No. 41 Squadron' from 'S.I.O., No.122 Wing', dated 6 March 1945, and referenced *122W/52/2/Int.*
86. The Luftwaffe pilots shot down by 41 Squadron on 14 February 1945 were Uffz. Oskar Seidenfuss (White 11, WNr. 211010) and Ogfr. Rudolf Zogbaum (White 3, WNr. 210973), both of 9/JG54, who were killed in action, and Uffz. Wilhelm Düsing of 2/JG26 (Black 12, WNr. 400238), and Uffz. Helmut Brisch of 10/JG54 (Black 6) who both baled out injured. Uffz. Seidenfuss was born in Wehlingen, Germany, on 13 August 1924, and is buried today

in Georgsmarienhütte Forest Cemetery, Kloster Oesede. Ogfr. Zogbaum was born in Magdeburg, Germany, on 9 April 1924, and is buried today in Sassenburg War Cemetery. Uffz. Düsing returned to service with 2/JG26 but was shot down again on 19 March 1945 by a USAAF P-51 Mustang of 479th FG. He baled out but sustained severe head injuries on landing, which ended his flying career.

87. I./KG51 records five Me262 casualties on 14 February 1945. Two of these were recorded near Flugplatz Mülheim (Mulheim Aerodrome), one at Emmerich and two where the locations are unnamed. The victories at Mülheim are too far to the southwest to be relevant, but Emmerich lies more-or-less on the flight path back to Volkel, so may be relevant to Fg Off Eric Gray's claim. The remaining two unnamed locations, however, provide too little detail to allow any definitive conclusions to be made on 41 Squadron's remaining Me262 claim.
88. 122 Wing ORB, 16 February 1945, TNA AIR 26/181.
89. Source: *NO. 83 GROUP AIRFIELD CONSTRUCTION AND OCCUPATION PROGRAMME. (as at 16th February, 1945.)*, 83 (Composite) Group ORB Appendix, TNA AIR 25/706.
90. 41 Squadron ORB, 26 March 1945, TNA AIR 27/426.
91. Entry in Plt Off Patrick Coleman's Logbook for 21 February 1945; reproduced with the kind permission of the Coleman family via Mike Brampton.
92. Although not mentioned in the ORB on 21 February 1945, Plt Off Patrick Coleman's *Pilot Service Record* suggests that he also damaged two dummy Me110s on this patrol.
93. On his Liberated Prisoner of War Interrogation Questionnaire (TNA WO 344/8/314/1), Fg Off Donald Tebbit names the place he came down on 22 February 1945 as "W[est] of Koesfeld" [sic].
94. There are several discrepancies in the Squadron ORB on 22 February 1945. The main issue is that the F540 states that seven aircraft participated in the day's second operation and eight in the third. However, the F541 only lists a total of 11 pilots for the two operations, instead of 15. It is apparent that three pilots from the second operation are missing, and the F540 suggests that Flt Lt William Stowe was one of them. Additionally, the F541 states that WO F. V. Whale saw Fg Off Tebbit set his aircraft alight and run to a ditch. However, Whale did not join the Squadron until 7 March – approximately two weeks after this event – which perhaps attests to how long after these events the ORB was actually written, and may well explain the errors in 22 February's entries. That said, Whale does not appear on the F541, whereas WO Peter Hale does, and Hale also confirmed to the author that it was indeed he who made this report.
95. 122 Wing ORB, 22 February 1945, TNA AIR 26/181.
96. 41 Squadron ORB, 22 February 1945, TNA AIR 27/426.
97. Fg Off Donald Tebbit was captured on 22 February 1945 and spent approximately one week at Dulag Luft before passing through the Receiving Depot at Wetzlar, and arriving in Oflag XIII-A, outside Nuremburg, on 5 March. He remained there until the end of the month when he was transferred to Stalag VII-A at Moosburg, where he was when liberated on 29 April 1945. Tebbit returned home to Ipswich for recuperation and was awarded a Mention in Despatches in mid-June. He remained in the RAF and in mid-July was able to wrangle a visit to 41 Squadron, by then based in Lübeck, Germany. Little is known of Tebbit's post-War deployments, but he was promoted to Flight Lieutenant (WS) in August 1945, then to substantive Flight Lieutenant in late April 1947 with a seniority of 14 February 1947. In April 1949, he was granted a permanent commission as Flight Lieutenant, and transferred to the Flying Control Branch 18 months later with the same rank, but a seniority of 14 August 1949. A promotion to Squadron Leader followed at the beginning of July 1955, and he retired three months short of his 51st birthday on 23 April 1965, retaining Wing Commander.
98. 122 Wing ORB, 24 February 1945, TNA AIR 26/181.
99. Despite his injuries, Flt Lt Thomas Burne remained in the RAF. Unfortunately, little is known of postings between 1945 and 1968, but it is known that he was promoted to Squadron Leader in August 1947, to Wing Commander in July 1951, and to Group Captain in January 1958. He is believed to have spent some time in the Air Investigation Branch in the 1950s but in September 1968 was appointed Aide de Camp to Her Majesty The Queen. He retired medically unfit in late January 1970 and died in late November 1981.
100. Excerpt from an original hand-written letter to 41 Squadron's Intelligence Officer, Flt Lt Lord Gisborough, from Mrs. C. V. Burne, the mother of Flt Lt Thomas Burne, dated 2 March 1945, 41 Squadron Archives.
101. Citation for Flt Lt Thomas R. Burne's DSO, Fourth Supplement to The London Gazette of 25 May 1945, dated 29 May 1945, Issue No. 37099. This information is licensed under the terms of the Open Government Licence (http://www.nationalarchives.gov.uk/doc/open-government-licence).
102. Entries in the 122 Wing and 41 Squadron ORBs on 24 February 1945 give no indication of who the other pilot was, who landed ahead of Flt Lt Burne.
103. Flt Lt Derek Shannon Vaughan Rake joined the RAFVR in April 1941 and undertook his flying training at 6 BFTS in Ponca City, Oklahoma, after which he was awarded his Wings and commissioned in June 1942. He was kept in the United States for the next nine months as a flying instructor, and returned to the United Kingdom as a Flying Officer in May 1943. Following courses at AFU, OTU, and TEU, and a promotion to Flight Lieutenant, Rake was posted to his first operational unit, 32 Squadron, on 18 August 1944. A part of the Balkan Air Force, based in Canne, Italy, the unit was equipped with Spitfire Vc's. Rake was active with this Squadron until 18 November 1944, when he was hit by Flak and wounded in his left arm and right hand, and made a forced landing behind Axis lines near Pristina, Yugoslavia. Rake managed to evade German forces and was hidden and taken care of by locals

in Skopje who fetched a doctor for his wounds, then helped him to return to his unit twelve days later. He was then evacuated home via Naples on 6 January 1945, and posted to 83 GSU on 10 February, following leave and recuperation. 41 Squadron became his second operational unit on 24 February 1945.

104. Flt Lt Roy Robert George Fisher joined the RNZAF in May 1941 and undertook his initial training in New Zealand. He was shipped to Canada in August 1941, where he completed SFTS and was awarded his Wings in late November. Arriving in the United Kingdom a few weeks later, Fisher attended AFU and OTU prior to being posted to his first operational unit, 257 Squadron, then based at Honiley, at the beginning of May 1942. Within two weeks, Fisher was on the move again, this time to 232 Squadron at Atcham, then to 93 Squadron at Kingscliffe in late September. When 93 Squadron was shipped to Tunisia in November, Fisher went with them, and it was here that he claimed his first victories, a damaged Ju87 in late November and a damaged Me109F in early December. Fisher was commissioned in January 1943, claimed two damaged Me109G's in April 1943, and moved to Malta with the Squadron at the beginning of June. A promotion to Flying Officer came in early July, which was immediately followed by several more victories – a shared destroyed Ju88 on 12 July, and a damaged Ju87 in the air, and a destroyed Mc202, a shared damaged Ju87 and a shared damaged Me109 on the ground, all on the same day, on 13 July. When his tour expired on 19 August 1943, he was rested initially on the staff of RAF Ballah, then RAF Qastina, before returning to 93 Squadron on 17 July, now based at Piombino, Italy. During this time, he was also Mentioned in Despatches. 93 Squadron moved to Corsica and subsequently to southern France, where Fisher suffered engine failure and crashed his aircraft at Beaurepaire, near Lyon, on 30 August. However, he avoided capture when he was rescued in a USAAF L-5 Sentinel 'Grasshopper' light aircraft, and continued to fly with 93 Squadron for another four months. Fisher was repatriated to the United Kingdom on 20 December 1944 and promoted to Flight Lieutenant in early January 1945. He was posted to 83 GSU on 23 January and to 41 Squadron with Flt Lt Derek Rake on 24 February 1945.
105. Combat Report for Flt Lt Daniel J. Reid, 25 February 1945, 41 Squadron Archives.
106. The aircraft was FW190D-9, White 17, of 5./JG26, flown by Lt. Josef Bott. Miraculously, Bott actually survived the incident, though seriously wounded, and was admitted to Nordhorn Hospital.
107. 122 Wing ORB, 25 February 1945, TNA AIR 26/181.
108. 41 Squadron ORB, 25 February 1945, TNA AIR 27/426.
109. Flt Lt Frank Woolley only remained Commanding Officer of 350 Squadron approximately six weeks, as Sqn Ldr Terry Spencer escaped captivity and returned to 350 Squadron to take over command again on 11 April. At this time, Woolley was posted to command 130 Squadron, where he was destined to remain until Summer 1946. He enjoyed considerable success with 130 Squadron, personally claiming another three victories before the cessation of hostilities, which resulted in him being awarded a Bar to his DFC in July 1945. He remained in the RAF after the War, and was awarded a Kings Commendation for Valuable Services in the Air on the 1949 New Year's Honours List. By January 1956, Woolley had been promoted to Wing Commander and was a awarded the AFC at the end of May of the same year. Unfortunately, however, his flying career was cut short on 28 November 1959 when he was killed in a flying accident in a Canberra B2 bomber during a flying course at RAF Manby.
110. This victory score for February 1945 reflects the claims recorded at that time in the 122 Wing ORB and does not take into account the confirmed victories of 14 February that we know about today, which imply a total of 6-0-2.
111. Source: 122 Wing ORB, 28 February 1945, TNA AIR 26/181.
112. The 122 Wing ORB appears to contradict the 41 Squadron ORB on 1 March 1945, stating that the Squadron provided area cover for Typhoons operating in the Emmerich-Wesel-Dorsten area, and makes no mention of bombers.
113. *NO. 83 GROUP INTELLIGENCE SUMMARY NO. 256, Up to 2359 hours, 2nd March, PART 1*, 2 March 1945, 83 (Composite) Group ORB Appendix, TNA AIR 25/707.
114. Extract from the diary of 409642 Fg Off Victor E. Murphy RAAF of 130 Squadron, 2 March 1945; reproduced with the kind permission of his son, Victor Murphy.
115. Flt Lt Daniel J. Reid's Combat Report, No. 176, 2 March 1945, TNA AIR 50/18.
116. Ibid.
117. Ibid.
118. Flt Lt Daniel J. Reid's *Pilot Service Record*, 41 Squadron Archives.
119. 122 Wing ORB, 2 March 1945, TNA AIR 26/181.
120. NOTES ON ENEMY AIRCRAFT (ARADO 234), Combat Report No. 177, addendum to Flt Lt Daniel J. Reid's Combat Report, No. 176, 2 March 1945, TNA AIR 50/18.
121. Lt. Eberhard Rögele was born in Ochsenhausen, Baden-Württemberg, Germany, on 15 February 1924, and died 2 March 1945, aged 21, in 9./KG76 Arado 234, WNr. 140178, F1+QT. He is buried in Ochsenhausen Cemetery, Biberach, Germany.
122. 41 Squadron ORB, 2 March 1945, TNA AIR 27/426.
123. The 83 Group ORB on 2 March 1945 (*NO. 83 GROUP INTELLIGENCE SUMMARY NO. 256, Up to 2359 hours, 2nd March, PART 1*, 2 March 1945, 83 (Composite) Group ORB Appendix, TNA AIR 25/707) suggests Fg Off Clifford Mottershead was lost 'cause unknown', but listed him under a heading 'Casualties – Not due to Enemy action'. However, contemporary research suggests he was likely shot down by an Me109.

124. 41 Squadron ORB, 2 March 1945, TNA AIR 27/426.
125. Entry in the logbook of WO Ian T. Stevenson on 3 March 1945; reproduced with the kind permission of Neil Stevenson.
126. There are a few discrepancies in the ORB concerning the 17:05 armed reconnaissance on 3 March 1945, as only five pilots and serials are listed on the F541, whereas the F540 states the remaining five aircraft returned to base at 18:00 after Plt Off Pat Coleman's early departure as a result of a petrol leak. Additionally, the F540 states that Coleman suffered his petrol leak after he and WO Ian Stevenson flew through light Flak. However, according to the F541, Stevenson was not a participant in this operation. As Flt Lt Derek Rake was the other half of (Coleman's) Yellow section, it was most likely Rake, rather than Stevenson, that flew through Flak with Coleman. On the other hand, this may also be a hint as to the cause of Stevenson's propeller blade loss on the 14:50 operation, where the details may have become confused with those of the 17:05 operation.
127. 41 Squadron's farewell to 122 Wing as recorded in the 122 Wing ORB, 5 March 1945, TNA AIR 26/181.
128. 122 Wing's farewell to 41 Squadron as recorded in the 122 Wing ORB, 6 March 1945, TNA AIR 26/181.
129. The victory score recorded in this statement for aircraft between 28 January and 5 March 1945 reflects the claims recorded at that time in the 122 Wing ORB and does not take into account the confirmed victories of 14 February that we know about today.
130. Despite being considered medically unfit, Flt Lt Harry Charnock remained in the RAFVR another ten years, relinquishing his commission in January 1955. In 1947, he was awarded the Belgian Knight of the Order of Leopold II and Croix de Guerre with Palm. He died in May 1974.
131. The Squadron ORB's F541 reveals that Fg Off Peter Gibbs had not flown operationally since 3 February, and several Intelligence Reports in 41 Squadron's archives are signed by him, which suggest he was employed in ground duties during this time.
132. Fg Off Rupert W. Munson, of Ingham in northern Queensland had joined 41 Squadron at the beginning of December 1944 and had therefore only been with the unit a little over three months when his tour expired. After leave, he spent two weeks at 53 OTU before being attached to the Ministry of Transport and posted to their Air Investigation Unit, where he remained until posting to 11 PDRC pending repatriation in November 1945. Munson embarked for Australia on 3 January 1946 and was demobbed in late February. Following his release, Munson went to university and graduated in 1950 with a degree in Pharmaceutical Chemistry. Initially working as a Pharmacist, he rejoined the RAAF in October 1956, entering the Medical Branch at RAAF Richmond. Munson left again a little over three years later and travelled to Ghana, where he was employed as a Pharmacist in Accra for almost 3½ years. In February 1966, he rejoined the RAAF anew, appointed to a four-year Short Service Commission as a Flight Lieutenant in the Medical Branch and was initially posted to No. 3 Hospital at RAAF Richmond. Munson spent two years at RAAF Butterworth in Malaysia between January 1969 and January 1971 and was promoted to Squadron Leader whilst there. Postings to HQ Southern Command in Melbourne, to the Department of the Air in Canberra, to RAAF Richmond and back to Canberra again followed over the ensuing four years, and he was promoted to Wing Commander in January 1976. Munson retired in June 1977 and, at the time of writing (Nov 2011) was living in New South Wales.
133. Fg Off Jim C. J. Payne was one of the Squadron's longest serving pilots of World War II, having joined the unit as a Flight Sergeant from OTU in July 1943. He was commissioned in January 1944, and was promoted to Flying Officer six months later. On his departure from 41 Squadron, he was sent to Burma where he served as a Test Pilot with the Repair and Salvage Unit at Mingaladon from July 1945. Promoted to Flight Lieutenant on 1 January 1946, he returned home a few months later and discharged from the RAFVR in early Summer 1946. He died in October 2008.
134. *Raymond Leppard on Music: An Anthology of Critical and Personal Writings*, Raymond Leppard & Thomas P. Lewis, 1993, Pro/Am Music Resources, ISBN 0912483962 & 9780912483962. See also http://www.petercarter.net/blog/cp9.html (rtrvd Feb 2011).
135. For further information, see http://www.independent.co.uk/news/uk/this-britain/the-riddle-of-the-lost-flight-570326.html and http://mysite.wanadoo-members.co.uk/paysage/mullair.html
136. 125 Wing ORB, 3 March 1945, TNA AIR 26/185.

9 CROSSING THE RHINE; 8 MARCH – 15 APRIL 1945

1. 41 Squadron ORB, entry for 7-18 March 1945, TNA AIR 27/426.
2. *Wilkinson J F Flight Lieutenant, My Experiences in World War II as a Royal Air Force Fighter Pilot*, undated, Imperial War Museum, ID No. 03/32/1.
3. 125 Wing ORB, 18 March 1945, TNA AIR 26/185.
4. The Air Liaison Section was manned by Air Liaison officers from the Allied armies, who acted as the interface between the RAF and ground forces.
5. The Air Prisoner of War Intelligence Section actively sought out and interviewed Luftwaffe Prisoners of War and the Air Ministry Technical Intelligence Section examined enemy aircraft that fell into Allied hands.
6. Source: *LOCATION STATEMENT. (as at 0900-hours 15th March, '45)*, 83 (Composite) Group ORB Appendix, TNA AIR 25/707.

7. Some sources suggest that, of the MV-serialed Spitfire XIV's from MV258 onwards, even serials were fitted with the 'teardrop' (or 'bubble') hood, and odd serials retained the standard hood. This is believed to have come about as the aircraft were built in the same factory on parallel assembly lines, with the standard-hooded Spitfires on one, and the teardrop hoods on the other.
8. There is a slight ambiguity on the Nominal Roll of mid-March 1945 as the line for Raymond Finucane states, "124530. F/LT. R.P. Finucane". This service number is actually Flt Lt Peter Cowell's; Finucane's is 122410. Moreover, Cowell is missing from the Nominal Roll, but was on the Squadron at the time, so should have been included on the list.
9. 125 Wing ORB, 21 March 1945, TNA AIR 26/185.
10. 41 Squadron ORB, 21 March 1945, TNA AIR 27/426.
11. Flt Lt Raymond Finucane was posted to 486 (NZ) Squadron at Fassberg, flying Tempests on 21 April 1945. He remained with the unit until the end of July, when he was posted to 151 Repair Unit at Luneberg for ferry duties. In April 1946, Finucane became Station Adjutant at RAF Luneburg, but was released under Class A in early November. He rejoined the reconstituted RAFVR in February 1952, and relinquished his commission in December 1962.
12. Source: *NO. 83 GROUP AIRFIELD CONSTRUCTION AND OCCUPATION PROGRAMME. (as at 21st March, 1945.)*, 83 (Composite) Group ORB Appendix, TNA AIR 25/707.
13. The 41 Squadron ORB's F540 on 22 March 1945 indicates that four aircraft participated in the 09:10 bomber escort led by Wg Cdr George Keefer. However the F541 only lists three pilots: Stowe, Wilkinson and Smart, which may imply that Keefer was the fourth pilot.
14. 41 Squadron ORB, 21 March 1945, TNA AIR 27/426.
15. Though grounded, Flt Sgt William Pairman remained with 41 Squadron until late April 1945, appearing on a nominal roll as "N/E (Awaiting posting)" mid-month. He was posted to 130 Squadron on 22 April, but posted home for leave only days later, on 1 May. Whilst on leave he was promoted to Warrant Officer and posted to 83 GCS at Schleswig on 11 June. He remained here until 4 March 1946, when he flew home to be demobbed at Uxbridge four days later. Pairman emigrated to Canada in September 1946, but moved to the United States only two months later. In November 1948, he returned to the United Kingdom, but was on the move again in January 1950, when he emigrated to Australia. Pairman was later employed as a crop dusting pilot in Ecuador, Costa Rica, and finally Jamaica, where he settled in the late 1960s. He died in Jamaica in January 2010.
16. 130 Squadron ORB, 23 March 1945, TNA AIR 27/938.
17. Excerpt from correspondence with Gp Capt (ret) Derek S. V. Rake OBE AFC, January 2009.
18. 125 Wing ORB, 24 March 1945, TNA AIR 26/185.
19. No. 37711, Supplement to The London Gazette, 3 September 1946, *Operations in North-West Europe from 6th June, 1944, to 5th May, 1945*; War Office despatch submitted to the Secretary of State for War on 1 June 1946 by Field Marshal The Viscount Montgomery of Alamein, GCB DSO.
20. Undated, unreferenced and untitled typed communiqué *HQ: Second TAF Main… From AOC INC.* [sic] [AM Sir Arthur Coningham KCB DSO MC DFC AFC] *To all ranks Second T.A.F.*, dating from ca. 23 March 1945, 41 Squadron Archives.
21. 41 Squadron ORB, 24 March 1945, TNA AIR 27/426.
22. Ibid.
23. Ibid.
24. 125 Wing ORB, 24 March 1945, TNA AIR 26/185.
25. Ibid.
26. A Trinidadian of Spanish decent, Flt Lt Farfan, whose full name was Fernand William Farfan de los Godos, had travelled to the United Kingdom to join the RAFVR in March 1941, and had since served with 601 Squadron in Malta, 80 Squadron in Egypt, and 123 Squadron in Iran, Libya and Egypt, during which time he had claimed one probable Italian bomber and one damaged Me109. He was commissioned in March 1943, and shot down over Crete in July, but evaded and returned to Allied lines. At this time, he was posted back to the United Kingdom for rest. Following a six-month tenure as a Flying Instructor at 57 OTU, he attended a course at Fighter Leaders' School and spent a month with 83 GSU, before going back onto operations with a posting to Normandy with 602 Squadron in July 1944. He claimed a destroyed FW190 in September, and was promoted to Flight Lieutenant on 10 March 1945, just two weeks prior to his posting to 41 Squadron.
27. 41 Squadron ORB, 25 March 1945, TNA AIR 27/426.
28. The Squadron ORB on 25 March 1945 states that Flt Lt Daniel Reid was wounded in the back and legs. However, his RAAF personnel file, held in the Australian National Archives (*RAAF Officers Personnel files, 1921-1948*, Series A9300, Barcode 5255899), states on several occasions that Reid was injured in the back by shrapnel and does not mention his legs at all.
29. RAAF Casualty File for Flt Lt Daniel J. Reid, *Correspondence files, multiple number (Melbourne) series (Primary numbers 1-323)*, Series A705, Barcode 1055431, NAA.
30. Flt Lt Daniel Reid was evacuated to England on 27 March 1945, and was in hospital until at least June 1945, when he was allocated light ground duties for three months. At the beginning of June, he was awarded the Distinguished Flying Cross and in late October posted to 11 Personnel Despatch and Reception Centre at Charmy Down. Reid

was repatriated to Australia in early April 1946 and arrived in Fremantle a month later, then returned to Melbourne and was released from the RAAF at the end of August 1945. Initially studying law, he joined the Franciscan Order of Friars Minor in early 1951 and was ordained the Rev. Father Urban Reid in July 1957. He subsequently spent 31 years in New Guinea, initially as a pilot, manager and administrator of Franair, the Franciscan Mission Air Service in Aitape, from 1961-1966, and subsequently as a parish priest and then Vicar-General of the Diocese of Aitape, from 1966-1992. He passed away in Melbourne in May 1993, aged 72.

31. The serial and pilot of the aircraft hit by Flak on the 16:25 armed reconnaissance on 25 March 1945 are not identified in the ORB.
32. Excerpt from correspondence with WO John A. Chalmers, June 2009.
33. 41 Squadron ORB, 26 March 1945, TNA AIR 27/426.
34. Ibid.
35. Ibid.
36. Excerpt from correspondence with WO John A. Chalmers, November 2008.
37. The Squadron ORB's F540 on 28 March 1945 states that eight aircraft participated in the 10:45 armed reconnaissance, but the F541 only lists four pilots and their serials. Additionally, a separate Intelligence Report (*Oprep. A. No. 87 for 24 hours ending sunset 28.3.45*, Ref. *41S./S.233/Air.* [41 Squadron Archives]) suggests the 12 MET included six horse-drawn transports.
38. The Squadron ORB's F540 on 28 March 1945 states that six aircraft participated in the 12:40 armed reconnaissance, but the F541 only lists three pilots and their serials. The third pilot identified on the F541 is Plt Off Robert Fleming, who was flying RM928. Additionally, the ground victories claimed by the Squadron today, which are recorded in the text, are those gleaned from unit's ORB. However, entries on a number of *Pilot Service Records* suggest the tally that day may have been far greater and included, in addition to those already listed, one armoured vehicle destroyed and four MET, one horse-drawn vehicle and 45 railway trucks damaged in the Münster area, and another armoured vehicle and trailer destroyed, one three-ton truck, one tug, eight MET, two horse-drawn vehicles and 30 trucks damaged, without any indication of the location(s).
39. 41 Squadron ORB, 26 March 1945, TNA AIR 27/426.
40. There is an ambiguity with entries concerning the bomber escort in the Squadron's ORB on 28 March 1945. Neither the USAAF nor Bomber Command operated in the Malmedy-Königsfeld area on this date. The 8th USAAF attacked industrial targets at Berlin and Hannover and the 9th USAAF attacked Neuenheerse and Erbach oil depots. 2 TAF's 2 Bomber Group also attacked marshalling yards at Attendorn (22 Mitchells and Bostons), Engelskirchen (36 Mitchells and Bostons) and Olpe (43 Mitchells and Bostons). However, these targets are up to 150km northeast of Malmedy. Whilst the target of the Mitchell bombers mentioned in 41 Squadron's ORB is not clear, it is felt it was most likely one of the of 2 TAF targets, particularly as the USAAF targets are too far away, and therefore considered too great a margin of error to be realistic. The 2 TAF targets also possibly make more sense from Eindhoven than Malmedy.
41. 125 Wing ORB, 29 March 1945, TNA AIR 26/185.
42. Ibid., 30 March 1945.
43. 39 (Reconnaissance) Wing RCAF ORB, 30 March 1945, TNA AIR 26/61.
44. 6 MFPS ORB, 30 March 1945, TNA AIR 29/543.
45. There are discrepancies in different reports of the Squadron's activity on 30 March 1945. The Squadron ORB's F540 and an Intelligence Report (*Oprep. A. No. 88 for 24 hours ending sunset 30.3.45*, Ref. *41S/S.233/Air.* [41 Squadron Archives]) both state the unit flew six patrols totalling 22 sorties. However the ORB's F541 actually lists seven patrols, totalling 25 sorties. These were airborne at 09:35 (6 aircraft), 10:45 (4 aircraft), 11:50 (3 aircraft), 12:50 (2 aircraft), 14:40 (4 aircraft), 15:55 (2 aircraft), and 17:30 (4 aircraft).
46. 41 Squadron's ORB F540 on 31 March 1945 states that nine aircraft were involved, but the F541 only lists eight pilots' names.
47. Entry in Plt Off Patrick Coleman's Logbook for 21 February 1945; reproduced with the kind permission of the Coleman family via Mike Brampton.
48. Gp Capt J. E. 'Johnnie' Johnson in his autobiography *Wing Leader*; (1956, Chatto and Windus). It should also be noted that the 125 Wing ORB (TNA AIR 26/185) on 2 April 1945 states that Gp Capt Johnson flew to the airfield, "The C.O. flew in, probably the first Spitfire to land – voluntarily – east of the Rhine."
49. 41 Squadron ORB, 5 April 1945, TNA AIR 27/426.
50. Australian Flt Lt Frederick Anthony Owen 'Tony' Gaze DFC*, whose father Irvine had been a member of Sir Ernest Shackleton's Antarctic exploration party in 1915-1917, was in the United Kingdom studying at Cambridge at the outbreak of War and enlisted in the RAFVR in January 1940. He was commissioned at the conclusion of his flying training and posted to his first operational unit, 610 Squadron, in March 1941. Clearly a talented young pilot, his several successes in the air had won him the DFC within five months of joining them. Following his promotion to Flying Officer, Gaze was rested for approximately six months as a Flying Instructor at 57 OTU, before returning to operations as a Flight Commander with 616 Squadron. A handful of victories followed in quick succession, and in September 1941, despite still being a Flying Officer, he took over command of 64 Squadron. The victories continued to rise, but his flying career was almost ended by a failed escort operation he led later that same month. Gaze had led a Wing escort to B-17 Flying Fortresses to Morlaix, France, during which all but one of 133 (Eagle) Squadron's

aircraft were lost. He was held accountable – some say he was made the scapegoat – and subsequently stripped of his command. He returned to 616 Squadron as a Flight Commander in November 1942, but was nonetheless promoted to Flight Lieutenant and awarded a Bar to his DFC in January 1943. Following a five-month rest in an administrative job with the Air Ministry, Gaze spent Summer 1943 attached to several squadrons at Hornchurch and Odiham where he claimed another four victories, but was shot down and wounded over France in September. He managed to evade and escaped over the Pyrenees to Gibraltar, from where he was returned to England in late October and underwent surgery to repair facial damage. Following extended rest, Gaze was posted to 610 Squadron in late July 1944, joining fellow Flight Lieutenant, John Shepherd. He claimed a V1 in August, and famously shot down a FW190 during *Bodenplatte*, thereby becoming the only 125 Wing pilot to have inflicted any damage on the Luftwaffe during the attack. Gaze had been promoted to OC, B Flight, only the day before and remained with the Squadron until its disbanding in March 1945, finally claiming an Me262 destroyed on 14 February. Whilst several pilots were posted to other 125 Wing squadrons, Gaze was posted back to the United Kingdom for a brief rest and spent almost a month at 83 GSU at Dunsfold, Surrey. It was from this unit that he was now posted to 41 Squadron and take over command of A Flight from his old friend John Shepherd, who was about to be promoted to the Squadron's Commanding Officer.

51. 407 AFAP ORB, AIR 29/822.
52. 41 Squadron ORB, 7 April 1945, TNA AIR 27/426.
53. B.106 Twente Aerodrome is now the site of Enschede Airport Twente. Though a civil airport with no scheduled flights at the time of writing, Twente (Enschede) housed units of the Royal Netherlands Air Force until 2007.
54. 125 Wing ORB, 7 April 1945, TNA AIR 26/185.
55. Source: *LOCATION STATEMENT. (as at 0900-hours 12th April, '45)*, 83 (Composite) Group ORB Appendix, TNA AIR 25/707.
56. 41 Squadron ORB, 8 April 1945, TNA AIR 27/426.
57. Flt Lt (Actg Sqn Ldr) Douglas Benham DFC AFC immediately went on leave, but was posted as Officer Commanding of the Air Ministry Manpower Research Unit, in Kingsway, London, in May 1945. He remained in the RAF after the cessation of hostilities and was promoted to Squadron Leader in August 1947. In April 1949, Benham took command of the Gunnery Squadron at 203 Advanced Flying School, flying the Spitfire, at Stradishall, Suffolk. This unit disbanded on 31 August 1949 and reformed as 226 Aircraft Conversion Unit the following day, which was equipped with the Meteor and Vampire. In November 1951, Benham took up a new posting as Wing Commander Training at Headquarters, Fighter Command, in Stanmore, but was posted to RAF Tangmere ten months later as Wing Commander Flying. Benham was honoured to be chosen as Escort Officer for Her Majesty the Queen at the RAF Coronation Review at Odiham in July 1953, and he was posted to Aden as Wing Commander Operations, HQ BFA, on 12 December 1954. His services were recognised in June 1957 when he was awarded an OBE, and he retired at the end of that year, on his 40th birthday, retaining Wing Commander. The following year, he joined Independent Television Wales and West (ITWW), then in its infancy, as its first Chief Executive, where he remained 18 years. During this time, he was made a Freeman of the City of London in September 1964, and became a Liveryman with the Worshipful Company of Wheelwrights that same month. Following two years of employment as a Consultant with Harlech TV, Benham spent several years working as a property developer and in property letting, before retiring to Wales in the late 1970s.
58. 41 Squadron ORB, 8 April 1945, TNA AIR 27/426.
59. The *Pilot Service Records* [41 Squadron Archives] showing claims against rolling stock on 8 April 1945 include Flt Lts Arnold Jolly and Roy Fisher, 2 Lt Carl Bødtker, WO Frederick Whale and Sgt Plt Peter Scott of Blue Section at 16:30, and Flt Lt Tony Gaze, Plt Off Pat Coleman and WO John Chalmers of Red Section at 18:10.
60. Excerpt from correspondence with WO John A. Chalmers, December 2008.
61. 41 Squadron ORB, 11 April 1945, TNA AIR 27/426.
62. Although the Squadron ORB on 11 April 1945 does not allocate the ground victories to any specific sections, entries on *Pilot Service Records* suggest that one MET was destroyed and three damaged in the Verden-Nienburg area by Red Section (Stowe SM823, Rake MV266, Farfan RM792, Chalmers SM817) on the 12:40 patrol, and that possibly two more were damaged in the Bremen area by Blue Section (Cowell MV260, Wheatley RM928, Kelly MV267, Scott RM696) on the 15:00 patrol.
63. Although the Squadron ORB on 12 April 1945 does not allocate these ground victories to any specific sections, entries on *Pilot Service Records* suggest that the locomotive and two trucks were damaged in the Bremen area by Red Section (Gaze RB143, Rake MV254, Stowe NH832, Farfan SM826) on the 08:20 patrol, and one MET damaged in the same area by Sgt Plt Peter Scott (RM928) of Blue Section on the 10:05 patrol.
64. Combat Report for Flt Lt F. A. O. 'Tony' Gaze, No. 171, 12 April 1945, TNA AIR 50/18.
65. Excerpt from correspondence with Gp Capt (ret) Derek S. V. Rake OBE AFC, January 2009.
66. The Ar234 claimed by Flt Lts Tony Gaze and Derek Rake on 12 April 1945 was an Ar234B-2b, flown by 23-year-old Oblt Bruno Radau of 1.(F)/123. Radau survived the incident, but struck his head on the instrument panel and lost consciousness.
67. Source: *LOCATION STATEMENT. (as at 0900-hours 12th April, '45)*, 83 (Composite) Group ORB Appendix, TNA AIR 25/707.
68. 41 Squadron ORB, 13 April 1945, TNA AIR 27/426.

69. Combat Report for Sqn Ldr John B. Shepherd, No. 364, 14 April 1945, TNA AIR 50/18.
70. The Me110 is believed to have been an Me110G-4 of 7./NJG3, whose pilot, 20-year-old Lt Wolfgang Gareis, was towing the Me163 to its new base at Husum. Gareis was seriously injured and died on 19 April 1945. Two other crew-members survived the incident. Gareis was born on 13 September 1924 and is buried today in Row 1, Grave 19, of Pfaffenhofen War Cemetery. The Me163 was piloted by seven victory Ace, 26-year-old Fw Werner Nelte of 1./JG400, who was killed. Nelte was born on 10 August 1918 and is buried in Grave 123 of Cuxhaven-Brockeswalde War Cemetery.
71. 125 Wing ORB, 15 April 1945, TNA AIR 26/185.

10 VICTORY IN THEIR SIGHTS; 16 APRIL – 31 MAY 1945

1. The location of WO John Chalmers' forced landing on 16 April 1945 is in the present-day Zevenaar area. A note in his logbook states, "8 miles North East of Arnhem, 9 miles from the front line."
2. Excerpt from correspondence with WO John A. Chalmers, November 2008.
3. 125 Wing ORB, 16 April 1945, TNA AIR 26/185.
4. Combat Report for Flt Lt John F. Wilkinson, No. 481, 16 April 1945, TNA AIR 50/18.
5. Typed annotation, signed by Flt Lt Derek Rake on the bottom of Sqn Ldr John B. Shepherd's Combat Report, No. 365, 16 April 1945, TNA AIR 50/18.
6. Excerpt from correspondence with WO John A. Chalmers, June 2009.
7. Source: *LOCATION STATEMENT. (as at 0900-hours 17th April, '45)*, 83 (Composite) Group ORB Appendix, TNA AIR 25/707.
8. Excerpt from correspondence with WO John A. Chalmers, January 2009.
9. Excerpt from correspondence with WO Aharon Remez's son Gideon, June 2008.
10. 125 Wing ORB, 28 April 1945, TNA AIR 26/185. The whereabouts of these photographs today is unknown.
11. 350 Squadron ORB, entry for 9-31 May 1945, TNA AIR 27/1746.
12. 41 Squadron ORB, 17 April 1945, TNA AIR 27/426.
13. Combat Report for Plt Off Patrick T. Coleman, No. 150, 17 April 1945, TNA AIR 50/18.
14. 41 Squadron's ORB suggests the aircraft damaged by Plt Off Patrick Coleman on 17 April 1945 was a Ju88, and the 125 Wing ORB repeats this. However, Coleman's Combat Report (No. 150, TNA AIR 50/18) states three times that the aircraft he damaged was actually a Junkers Ju188.
15. 125 Wing ORB, 17 April 1945, TNA AIR 26/185.
16. Source: *LOCATION STATEMENT. (as at 0900-hours 17th April, '45)*, 83 (Composite) Group ORB Appendix, TNA AIR 25/707.
17. 41 Squadron ORB, 18 April 1945, TNA AIR 27/426.
18. 125 Wing ORB, 18 April 1945, TNA AIR 26/185.
19. Statement by WO William A. Brew, December 2004.
20. RAAF Casualty File for WO William A. Brew, *Correspondence files, multiple number (Melbourne) series (Primary numbers 1-323)*, Series A705, Barcode 1064848, NAA.
21. Entry in the logbook of Plt Off Patrick T. Coleman, 20 April 1945; reproduced with the kind permission of the Coleman family via Mike Brampton.
22. The location where this FW190 came down on 20 April 1945 is believed to be on the south-eastern shore of 22-metre-deep Kalksee [Kalk Lake], approximately 12km north of Neuruppin Aerodrome, which is surrounded by the Binenwalde Forest. Binenwalde is a village on the north-eastern edge of the lake.
23. Combat Report for Sqn Ldr John B. Shepherd, No. 366, 20 April 1945, TNA AIR 50/18.
24. Combat Report for Fg Off Eric Gray, No. 241, TNA AIR 50/18.
25. Fg Off Eric Gray did not see what happened to this aircraft. His Combat Report for 20 April 1945 (No. 241, TNA AIR 50/18) states he saw a parachute within seconds of the aircraft going into a spin and then saw an aircraft burning on the ground. He was initially hesitant to claim it destroyed pending Flt Lt Roy Fisher's statement on the combat, as he felt the FW190 may also have been attacked by him. However, when Fisher entered no claim for the aircraft, Gray consequently claimed it for himself, explaining at the end of his Combat Report that it "spun, burst in flames and the pilot baled out as the result of my attack although I did not fire. I now claim two F.W. 190's Destroyed". Nonetheless, the Squadron ORB on 20 April 1945 states that Fisher destroyed a FW190; this statement is clearly erroneous.
26. Combat Report for WO Ian T. Stevenson, No. 390, 20 April 1945, TNA AIR 50/18.
27. Contemporary research suggests that WO Viv Rossow's opponent on 20 April 1945 was Obfw Hermann Buchner of III/JG7, a 58-victory Ace and Knights Cross holder. It is believed he was landing an Me262A-1b at Rotenburg Aerodrome following combat with P-51 Mustangs over Steinhuder Lake when attacked by an Allied fighter. However, whilst the circumstances are similar, both Rotenburg and Steinhuder Lake lie approximately 230km (145 miles) west of Neuruppin, which is too great a distance and too large a margin of error. As such, I am unsure whether Rossow's Me262 was in fact Obfw Hermann Buchner.
28. Combat Report for Flt Lt John F. Wilkinson, No. 483, 20 April 1945, TNA AIR 50/18.

29. 125 Wing ORB, 20 April 1945, TNA AIR 26/185.
30. *NO. 83 GROUP INTELLIGENCE SUMMARY NO. 305, Up to 2359 hours, 20th April, PART 1*, 20 April 1945, 83 (Composite) Group ORB Appendix, TNA AIR 25/707.
31. Source: *NO. 83 GROUP INTELLIGENCE SUMMARY NO. 305, Up to 2359 hours, 20th April, PART 1*, 20 April 1945, 83 (Composite) Group ORB Appendix, TNA AIR 25/707.
32. The totals for enemy aircraft in the table on 20 April 1945 include ground victories.
33. 41 Squadron ORB, 21 April 1945, TNA AIR 27/426.
34. 125 Wing ORB, 21 April 1945, TNA AIR 26/185.
35. The identity of 'Steve Fisher' is not clear. There was a WO Ian 'Steve' Stevenson and a Flt Lt Roy Fisher with the Squadron at the time, and the OC, 6041 Servicing Echelon, was one Fg Off 'Steve' Stephenson. However, whether Wilkinson is referring to one of these men, or one of the ground crew, is unclear.
36. 125 Wing ORB, 22 April 1945, TNA AIR 26/185.
37. Note that SM817 is allocated to both Flt Lt Arnold Jolly on the 18:25-19:55 operation and to WO Ian Stevenson on the 19:20-20:40 operation on 23 April 1945. As Jolly did not return to Celle before Stevenson's departure that evening, one of the two serials is obviously erroneous. WO Stevenson's logbook indicates he was flying EB-R today, which is believed to have been the lettering for SM817. If this was the case, it would suggest that Flt Lt Jolly's serial is the erroneous one. The serials are, however, recorded in the text as they appear on the Squadron's F541.
38. *NO. 83 GROUP INTELLIGENCE SUMMARY NO. 308, Up to 2359 hours, 23rd April, PART 1*, 23 April 1945, 83 (Composite) Group ORB Appendix, TNA AIR 25/707.
39. Flt Lt William N. Stowe had some immediate success with 130 Squadron, claiming a shared destroyed Me109 and an individual destroyed FW190 the same afternoon he joined the unit. However, he force-landed his aircraft behind enemy lines near Lake Schwerin on 2 May 1945 after it suffered damaged from an explosion caused by his own attack on MET. He walked back to Allied lines through No Man's Land and reached Celle again on 9 May. At this time, he was posted back to 41 Squadron as OC, A Flight.
40. 41 Squadron ORB, 24 April 1945, TNA AIR 27/426.
41. Interview with WO Peter Hale, April 2009.
42. 350 Squadron ORB, 24 April 1945, TNA AIR 27/1746.
43. *NO. 83 GROUP INTELLIGENCE SUMMARY NO. 309, Up to 2359 hours, 24th April, PART 1*, 24 April 1945, 83 (Composite) Group ORB Appendix, TNA AIR 25/707.
44. 125 Wing ORB, 24 April 1945, TNA AIR 26/185.
45. Ibid.
46. Entry in the logbook of Plt Off Patrick T. Coleman, 24 April 1945; reproduced with the kind permission of the Coleman family via Mike Brampton.
47. There is also some doubt as to the aircraft Fg Off Roy D. A. Smith was flying on the 12:30 armed reconnaissance on 24 April 1945. The Squadron ORB's F541 records it as Spitfire XIV, RB143, but this aircraft is listed on the F541 as having flown on subsequent days. However, MV249 is recorded in *Spitfire; The History* as having been damaged on this date and subsequently stuck off charge, which suggests Smith was most likely flying MV249 rather than RB143.
48. 125 Wing ORB, 25 April 1945, TNA AIR 26/185.
49. Research undertaken by then Ratzeburg resident, James Schauer, suggests these Ar196s came from a number of sources. Around a dozen Arados were parked up permanently in the tall reed bed in early 1942, following Allied bombing raids on Lübeck, Hamburg and Cologne, the barely successful 'Channel Dash' and a decline in German ship-borne aircraft operations. These 12 aircraft were later joined by others, which suggests there may well have been around 20 aircraft parked up at the time they were spotted by 41 Squadron on 24 April 1945. Schauer's research reveals that, "…several of [the] Ar 196 aircraft near Ratzeburg showed considerable signs of corrosion, presumably following exposure to sea water. Also, all had their tanks drained of fuel and guns removed; they were not in any way provided with netting, thus relying entirely on natural reed growth for the most basic in 'camouflage'. Interestingly, while providing 'interesting' targets for several Allied units including 41 Sqn, not one of these attacked the regional hydro power station close to the southern-most aircraft which would have presented far more effective target. Similarly, although several attacks were affected by the mobile anti-aircraft batteries protecting the trains loaded with rocket fuel and components at the railway station, these too would have provided a much bigger 'bang'…" [Correspondence between James Schauer and the author, November 2009].
50. Excerpt from *The Destruction of Blohm & Voss BV 238 Prototype, Then the World's largest Aircraft, The Canadian Story*, James A. Schauer, Flt Lt RAF (Retd), January 2009, and reproduced with his permission.
51. James Schauer recalls that twelve Arados were damaged by 41 Squadron on 24 April 1945, whereas 41 Squadron reported sixteen out of twenty were damaged. Only an hour after 41 Squadron's attack, however, sixteen Tempests of 33 and 222 Squadrons also attacked these same aircraft, which the 33 Squadron ORB described as "a line of 9+ Arados". They claimed nine damaged and one destroyed (as it collapsed), but lost Fg Off Wilson of 222 Squadron to Flak in the process.
52. Combat Report for Flt Lt Peter Cowell, No. 167, 24 April 1945, TNA AIR 50/18.
53. 125 Wing ORB, 24 April 1945, TNA AIR 26/185.
54. Combat Report for Flt Lt Peter Cowell, No. 168, 25 April 1945, TNA AIR 50/18.

55. 125 Wing ORB, 25 April 1945, TNA AIR 26/185.
56. 41 Squadron's ORB on 25 April 1945 identifies this aircraft as a Junkers Ju88, but both WO John Chalmers' and Plt Off Patrick Coleman's Combat Reports for the action (CRs 143 and 153, respectively, TNA AIR 50/18) and 125 Wing's ORB for this date all confirm that the aircraft was in fact a Junkers Ju188.
57. Entry in the logbook of Plt Off Patrick T. Coleman, 25 April 1945; reproduced with the kind permission of the Coleman family via Mike Brampton.
58. Excerpt from correspondence with WO John A. Chalmers, June 2009.
59. 125 Wing ORB, 25 April 1945, TNA AIR 26/185.
60. The Squadron ORB's F540 on 25 April 1945 states Blue Section returned at 17:00, whereas the F541 states their return was at 17:50.
61. *NO. 83 GROUP INTELLIGENCE SUMMARY NO. 310, Up to 2359 hours, 25th April, PART 1*, 25 April 1945, 83 (Composite) Group ORB Appendix, TNA AIR 25/707.
62. Source: *NO. 83 GROUP INTELLIGENCE SUMMARY NO. 310, Up to 2359 hours, 25th April, PART 1*, 25 April 1945, 83 (Composite) Group ORB Appendix, TNA AIR 25/707. Note that the totals for enemy aircraft in the table on 25 April 1945 include ground victories.
63. 125 Wing ORB, 26 April 1945, TNA AIR 26/185.
64. 350 Squadron ORB, 26 April 1945, TNA AIR 27/1746.
65. Source: *LOCATION STATEMENT. (as at 0900-hours 26th April, 1945)*, 83 (Composite) Group ORB Appendix, TNA AIR 25/707.
66. 125 Wing drew their stores from 401 ASP, which was based at B.116 Wunstorf; 409 RSU, 91 FSP, 19 SP and the two RAF Regiment squadrons drew theirs from 404 ASP, which was based at B.118 Celle; 50 MFH and 426 RRU drew theirs from 406 (RCAF) ASP, which was based at B.150 Hustedt.
67. 350 Squadron ORB, 27 April 1945, TNA AIR 27/1746.
68. 125 Wing ORB, 27 April 1945, TNA AIR 26/185.
69. Ibid.
70. 130 Squadron ORB, 27 April 1945, TNA AIR 27/938.
71. Entry in the flying logbook of Plt Off Patrick T. Coleman for 28 April 1945; reproduced with the kind permission of the Coleman family via Mike Brampton.
72. 125 Wing ORB, 28 April 1945, TNA AIR 26/185.
73. Flt Lt F. A. O. 'Tony' Gaze's and Flt Lt John F. Wilkinson's Combat Reports for 28 April 1945 (Nos. 225 and 484 respectively; TNA AIR 50/18) both slightly contradict the 125 Wing ORB as they state their own initial altitude was 8,000 feet and, on first sighting them, the Focke-Wulfs' altitudes ranged from 3,000 feet down to the deck.
74. Combat Report for Flt Lt F. A. O. 'Tony' Gaze, No. 225, 28 April 1945, TNA AIR 50/18.
75. Combat Report for Flt Lt John F. Wilkinson, No. 484, 28 April 1945, TNA AIR 50/18.
76. Combat Report for Flt Lt F. A. O. Tony Gaze, No. 225, 28 April 1945, TNA AIR 50/18.
77. Combat Report for Flt Lt John F. Wilkinson, No. 484, 28 April 1945, TNA AIR 50/18.
78. 125 Wing ORB, 28 April 1945, TNA AIR 26/185.
79. Ibid, 29 April 1945. Note that the 41 Squadron ORB slightly contradicts this statement, recording instead that it was a Spitfire XIV – not a Mk. XVI – that was involved. It is mostly likely that the 125 Wing entry is erroneous and that XIV has simply been mistyped as XVI.
80. Excerpt from correspondence with John A. Chalmers, November 2008.
81. 41 Squadron ORB, 30 April 1945, TNA AIR 27/426.
82. The 125 Wing ORB on 30 April 1945 contradicts the 41 Squadron ORB by stating that the strip was 11 miles south-southeast of Schwerin.
83. 125 Wing ORB, 30 April 1945, TNA AIR 26/185.
84. 130 Squadron's victories on 30 April 1945 included three FW190s at Banzkow at 09:45, five FW190s in the Lake Schwerin area at 11:25, one FW190 at Winsen at 13:50, and one Si204 over Lake Schwerin at 17:30. 350 Squadron's claims for six FW190s were all made in the Lake Schwerin area between 10:45 and 11:00. As an aside, 402 (RCAF) Squadron's claims were four FW190s and one Ju188 destroyed and two FW190s damaged at Schwerin on their 10:30-12:20 patrol, and a Ju88 destroyed at Kalkhorst on their 14:37-16:12 patrol.
85. Although not particularly significant in the scheme of things, it should perhaps be noted that there are numerous discrepancies in various documents concerning 41 Squadron's final patrol on 30 April 1945. The Squadron's F541, the 125 Wing ORB, and Flt Lt F. A. O. 'Tony' Gaze's Combat Report all state that Red Section was airborne at 19:05; the Squadron's F540 records 19:10 and Sqn Ldr John Shepherd's Combat Report states 19:11. 125 Wing's ORB states the patrol consisted of six aircraft, the Squadron's ORB (both the F540 and F541) state it consisted of five aircraft, and Flt Lt Tony Gaze's Combat Report states he was leading just four; there is nothing to indicate a pilot or pilots could not take off, or returned early. Sqn Ldr John Shepherd states he was flying as No. 3, whereas the Squadron ORB's F541 states he was 'No. 1 leading'. Flt Lt Tony Gaze's Combat Report indicates he was leading the section, which agrees with the Squadron ORB's F540. Further, Sqn Ldr Shepherd's Combat Report states he was on an Elbe bridgehead patrol, whereas the 125 Wing ORB states Red Section was sent to the Weser bridgehead. Confusing, to say the least!
86. Combat Report for Sqn Ldr John B. Shepherd, No. 367, 30 April 1945, TNA AIR 50/18.

87. The location recorded by Flt Lt Tony Gaze in his Combat Report on 30 April 1945 suggests the FW190 would have come down within an area roughly bounded by the villages Krüzen, Juliusburg, Lütau and Basedow.
88. Combat Report for Flt Lt F. A. O. 'Tony' Gaze, No. 226, 30 April 1945, TNA AIR 50/18.
89. Source: 125 Wing ORB, 30 April 1945, TNA AIR 26/185.
90. The data in this table is extracted from *SHAEF (MAIN AND REAR): Summary of effort: 2 TAF Groups Nos. 2, 83, 84, 85 monthly statistical record*, TNA AIR 37/1068. Note that the total number of sorties flown by 41, 130 and 350 Squadrons during April 1945 (1,787) differs slightly to the total given in the 125 Wing ORB (1,885). The Wing's greater total may be put down to non-operational hours being included and/or those flown by Gp Capt Johnson and Wg Cdr Keefer. It is also known that 41 Squadron flew an additional 40 non-operational sorties, totalling 19 hours and 15 minutes.
91. FjObfw Heinz 'Negus' Marquardt was an Ace with 121 aerial victories, plus 16 unconfirmed, from 320 combat missions, most of which had been achieved on the Eastern Front. Marquardt had been with 13./JG51 since 1 April 1945 and during the ensuing month claimed 23 victories, thereunder his hundredth on 14 April. He was awarded the Deutsches Kreuz in Gold on 10 September 1944, following his sixtieth victory, and the Ritterkreuz on 18 November 1944, following his eighty-ninth.
92. Obfw Heinz Marquardt received immediate medical attention and was still hospitalised when Germany capitulated less than a week later. Then transferred to a hospital at Göppingen, 35km east of Stuttgart, he was discharged 23 August 1945 and remained in Germany as a Prisoner of War. Marquardt travelled to Switzerland in 1947, where he became a flying instructor, but returned to Germany and joined the Bundesluftwaffe on its formation in 1956. Initially commissioned Leutnant, he attained the rank of Oberstleutnant prior to his retirement in September 1973. For the ensuing ten years, he was employed by the German charter airline Condor, before definitively retiring to Frankfurt.
93. Excerpt from a letter from Heinz Marquardt to Peter Cowell, dated January 1995, a copy of which is held in 41 Squadron's Archives, and may be a translated extract from the War Diary of IV./JG 51.
94. This may have been 15-victory Ace Fw Heinz Radlauer of 15/JG51, who baled out unhurt during this clash. Peter Cowell later met Heinz Radlauer, when the latter visited Shoreham Aircraft Museum in 2001.
95. Body of a letter from Heinz Marquardt to Peter Cowell, dated January 1995, a copy of which is held in 41 Squadron's Archives.
96. Body of a letter from Peter Cowell to Heinz Marquardt, dated February 1995, a copy of which is held in 41 Squadron's Archives.
97. Flt Lt F. A. O. 'Tony' Gaze was awarded a second Bar to his DFC on 1 June 1945, and appointed Commanding Officer when 616 Squadron disbanded and formed the nucleus of a new 263 Squadron on 31 August 1945. Within four months, however, he was appointed Officer Commanding of the Engineering School at Rolls-Royce in Derby. In May 1946, he was posted to 691 (Navy Co-Operation) Squadron in Exeter as Commanding Officer, but four months later became Chief Ground Instructor and OC Test Flight at 61 OTU at Keevil. Gaze resigned his commission as Flight Lieutenant in the RAF in March 1948, retaining Squadron Leader, and returned to Australia, where he was employed on his father's farm. After spending a short period with an Import-Export company, Gaze joined the RAAF, and was commissioned a Flying Officer. He was posted to 21 Squadron RAAF at Laverton in January 1949 where he flew the Wirraway, but returned to the United Kingdom as a racing driver and exchange pilot with 600 Squadron RAuxAF in July 1950, flying the Meteor F.4 out of Biggin Hill. Disappointingly for Gaze, the exchange was cancelled after only a short period as the RAF wanted Gaze to undertake more flying than the RAAF was willing to pay for, understood to have been around £250 per hour. Having had a love of fast cars for many years, by 1951 Gaze had become a Formula 2 racing driver and shortly afterwards moved into Formula 1 and 'Formula Libre', where he raced until 1957. In 1960, Gaze competed in the World Gliding Championships in Cologne, and resided in Hertfordshire until 1976, when he returned to Australia to farm. In January 2006, he was awarded an OAM for his service to motor racing, and resides at the time of writing in Victoria, Australia. A building at Goodwood Aerodrome and Racecourse (previously Westhampnett Aerodrome) in West Sussex is named after Gaze, and he named his own farm 'Goodwood'.
98. Combat Report for Plt Off Patrick T. Coleman, No. 156, 1 May 1945, TNA 50/18.
99. Ibid.
100. 41 Squadron ORB, TNA AIR 27/426, 1 May 1945.
101. Combat Report for Plt Off Patrick T. Coleman, No. 156, 1 May 1945, TNA 50/18.
102. Ibid.
103. Combat Report for Sqn Ldr John B. Shepherd, No. 368, TNA AIR 50/18.
104. Source: *NO. 83 GROUP INTELLIGENCE SUMMARY NO. 316, Up to 2359 hours, 1st May, PART 1*, 1 May 1945, 83 (Composite) Group ORB Appendix, TNA AIR 25/707.
105. The totals for enemy aircraft in the table on 1 May 1945 include ground victories.
106. Combat Report for Fg Off Roy D. A. Smith, No. 34, TNA AIR 50/18.
107. Excerpt from correspondence with John A. Chalmers, June 2009.
108. 125 Wing ORB, 2 May 1945, TNA AIR 26/185.
109. Combat Report for Flt Lt Derek S. V. Rake, No. 350, 3 May 1945, TNA AIR 50/18.

110. 125 Wing ORB, 4 May 1945, TNA AIR 26/185.
111. *NO. 83 GROUP INTELLIGENCE SUMMARY NO. 319, Up to 2359 hours, May 4th, PART 1*, 4 May 1945, 83 (Composite) Group ORB Appendix, TNA AIR 25/707.
112. 125 Wing ORB, 4 May 1945, TNA AIR 26/185.
113. 350 Squadron ORB, 4 May 1945, TNA AIR 27/1746.
114. This first Instrument of Surrender to Field Marshal Bernard Montgomery by all German forces in north-western Germany, Holland and Denmark was superseded by the Rheims Instrument of Surrender of 7 May 1945 and the Berlin Instrument of Surrender of 8 May 1945.
115. Instrument of Surrender, 4 May 1945, IWM.
116. The main signatory, General Admiral Hans-Georg von Friedeburg, had succeeded Grand Admiral Karl Dönitz as Commander-in-Chief of the Kriegsmarine when Dönitz became Reichspräsident following Hitler's suicide. In early May 1945, Dönitz ordered von Friedeburg to negotiate a truce with the Allied forces in the west, but Montgomery informed him that nothing was negotiable and only an unconditional surrender would be acceptable. Seeing no other option, von Friedeburg signed this Instrument of Surrender on 4 May. He was also in attendance, representing the Kriegsmarine, when the General Instrument of Surrender was signed Colonel-General Alfred Jodl in Rheims, France, two days later, and signed the third and final Instrument of Surrender in the presence of the Russians in Berlin on 8 May 1945, once again on behalf of the Kriegsmarine. He committed suicide only two weeks later, on 23 May 1945.
117. 350 Squadron ORB, 5 May 1945, TNA AIR 27/1746.
118. 125 Wing ORB, 5 May 1945, TNA AIR 26/185.
119. *NO. 83 GROUP INTELLIGENCE SUMMARY NO. 320, Up to 2359 hours, 5ht May, PART 1*, 5 May 1945, 83 (Composite) Group ORB Appendix, TNA AIR 25/707.
120. Source: Campaign Statistics, 83 (Composite) Group ORB Appendix, TNA AIR 25/707.
121. During the time 41 Squadron was with 83 Group (from 4 December 1944), the following numbers of sorties were flown by the Group: December 1944 – 7,474 sorties, January 1945 – 5,819 sorties, February 1945 – 8,162 sorties, March 1945 – 12,356 sorties, April 1945 – 14,119, and May 1945 – 2,882 sorties, making a total of 50,812 in this period.
122. Source: Campaign Statistics, 83 (Composite) Group ORB Appendix, TNA AIR 25/707.
123. 41 Squadron ORB, entry for 6 and 7 May 1945, TNA AIR 27/426.
124. 125 Wing ORB, 7 May 1945, TNA AIR 26/185.
125. Source: *LOCATION STATEMENT. (as at 0900-hours 8th May, 1945)*, 83 (Composite) Group ORB Appendix, TNA AIR 25/707.
126. 125 Wing drew their stores from 401 ASP, which was based at B.116 Wunstorf; 91 FSP and 19 SP drew theirs from 404 ASP, which was based at B.156 Luneberg; 50 MFH drew theirs from 406 (RCAF) ASP, which was based at B.150 Hustedt; 1 CAEU drew their stores from 125 Wing.
127. Excerpts from correspondence with WO John A. Chalmers, June 2009.
128. The Aerodrome is the site of today's Copenhagen Airport, Kastrup (CPH).
129. 125 Wing ORB, 9 May 1945, TNA AIR 26/185.
130. *MEDICAL HISTORY OF THE WAR. Medical Extract for May, 1945, Ref: 83G/S.3003/Med.*, 14 June 1945, 83 (Composite) Group ORB Appendix, TNA AIR 25/706.
131. On 5 June, soon after 130 Squadron was posted back to England, Flt Lt Roy R. G. Fisher was posted 12 (RNZAF) PDRC in preparation for repatriation to New Zealand. On 14 June, he was awarded a Mention in Despatches, and sailed for New Zealand shortly afterwards. Fisher disembarked in Wellington on 4 August and ceased his attachment to the RAF twelve days later. He relinquished his commission in the RNZAF on 9 November, and joined the RNZAF Reserve three days later. Fisher remained in the Reserve until his retirement in October 1975 and died at Pukerimu, New Zealand, in December 1988, aged 68.
132. 2 Lt Carl Bødtker returned to Norway on 11 May 1945, and served with 332 Squadron at Værnes until late in the year. He remained in the aviation industry in some capacity for the rest of his life, which included employment with Thofte's Flyselskap, and as the Norwegian sales representative for the French homebuilt aircraft company, Jodel. He later founded a company called Caseb Aviation, and represented several French aviation companies in Norway, thereunder Ecureil, Super Puma, ATR, Super Broussard, and the armaments sector of Thales. He died in May 1987.
133. Flt Lt John Lee had been commissioned in the RAFVR in October 1942 whilst with 93 Squadron, and was awarded the DFC in March 1943. He was posted to 610 Squadron as a Flying Officer in July 1944 and remained with the unit until its disbanding in March 1945, at which time he was posted to 130 Squadron. Lee ended the War with this squadron and was posted to 41 Squadron on 130's move from Celle to Fassberg.
134. 125 Wing ORB, 10 May 1945, TNA AIR 26/185.
135. Excerpts from correspondence with WO John A. Chalmers, June 2009.
136. As the Squadron ORB's F541 only recorded operational flying, there is no further information on individual sorties after 5 May 1945. As such, there is no indication of which pilots participated in the escort to Air Marshal Coningham on 11 May 1945. However, WO Ian Stevenson's and Vivian Rossow's logbooks reveal that they were amongst them.
137. The Squadron ORB's F541 does not record the names of the six pilots involved the escort of Fld Mshl Montgomery on 12 May 1945, but Plt Off Pat Coleman's logbook reveals he was one of them.

138. 41 Squadron ORB, 22 May 1945, TNA AIR 27/426.
139. 125 Wing ORB, entry for 23-31 May 1945, TNA AIR 26/185.
140. Source: *LOCATION STATEMENT. (as at 0900-hours 26th May, 1945)*, 83 (Composite) Group ORB Appendix, TNA AIR 25/707.
141. A rear party from 125 Wing was still in B.152 Fassberg at this time.
142. 125 Wing and 2856 Squadron RAF Regiment drew their stores from 401 ASP, which was based at B.152 Fassberg, and 123 SP drew their stores from 125 Wing.
143. Excerpt from correspondence with WO John A. Chalmers, June 2009.
144. See, for example, *The Times* editions of 2 May, 16 June, and 31 October 1945. The 2 May 1945 release stated that the RAF's toll on Axis air forces from 3 September 1939 to 28 April 1945 by home-based commands was 7,911 aircraft, whilst RAF losses were 11,449. These figures included 6,977 claims against the Luftwaffe by Fighter Command for the loss of 2,998 fighters. On 16 June 1945, updated figures not previously released 'for security reasons' stated total RAF losses were in fact 16,385 aircraft, an almost 50% increase on the early May figures, which included 3,558 from Fighter Command and 2,115 from 2 TAF. On 31 October, new figures were published showing that the RAF lost 79,281 men and the USAAF another 79,265 in bombing raids on Germany. At the peak of the air offensive on the Western Front, the report continued, 28,000 aircraft were in service, manned and maintained by 1.3 million men, but the RAF lost an estimated 22,000 aircraft (ca. 33% higher than the previous figure) and USAAF 18,000.
145. It should be noted that a simple addition of these figures to achieve an over all figure is not possible as some aircraft were damaged several times before they were definitively struck from charge. With thanks to Andreas Brekken for his assistance with these figures.
146. Excerpt from Über Helden ['About Heroes'], an interview with Lieutenant General Günther Rall by J. Käppner and K. Kister, *Süddeutsche Zeitung*, 5 April 2009. Reproduced with the permission of the Süddeutsche Zeitung and translated by the author. Rall died on 4 October 2009. http://www.sueddeutsche.de/politik/interview-mit-guenther-rall-ueber-helden-1.408068 (rtrvd Mar 2012).
147. Excerpts from correspondence with WO John A. Chalmers, November and December 2008.
148. Correspondence from Fg Off Ronald Johnson to Dan Johnson, 23 November 1982; reproduced with Dan's kind permission.
149. Correspondence from Flt Lt Peter Cowell to Dan Johnson, 20 February 1984; reproduced with Dan's kind permission.

APPENDIX I – THE PILOTS

1. It is not clear on which date Plt Off Robert J. Boyd joined 41 Squadron. The B Flight Diary, an informal record of the Flight's activity in 41 Squadron's Archives, states that he took his first flight with the Squadron, in EB-U, on 2 November 1942, implying he had probably been with the unit a few days already. However, after his death on 6 September 1943, the Squadron ORB states that he joined the unit on 18 November 1942.
2. Aharon Remez wanted the Israeli Air Force to be a separate service under an arrangement similar to today's US Joint Chiefs of Staff, but the Military and Ben-Gurion preferred a unified command, which prevailed. This disagreement was a part of a larger dispute that led to Remez's eventual resignation from office. At the time, however, Remez held the rank of 'Aluf Avir', which roughly translates to 'Brigadier General of the Air Force'. As the Israeli Defence Forces grew, a new rank was created under Aluf and the designation Aluf Avir was abolished. As such, subsequent Israeli Air Force commanders were ranked only as Aluf, similar to commanders of the Israeli ground forces, and is now equivalent to the rank of Major General. It is for this reason that contemporary works generally refer to Remez as Major General, rather than Brigadier General. Nonetheless, after his retirement, he was addressed in English as 'Brigadier General'.

APPENDIX II – OFFICERS COMMANDING

1. Flt Lt Douglas Hone only commanded the Squadron in a caretaker role between the loss of Sqn Ldr Geoffrey Hyde and the arrival of Sqn Ldr Thomas Neil; he was not actually posted to the position. It should be said that other Flight Commanders, such as Flt Lt Donald Smith in February-March 1944, also acted as Squadron Commander in absence of the Commanding Officer, but in such cases, there was a Squadron Leader in command of the unit at the time, and they were only away on leave, on courses, or at conferences, and as such have not been included in this list. Flt Lt Hone has been consciously included as there was no other Commanding Officer during this period, and he filled the role until the next Squadron Leader arrived.

APPENDIX IV – GROUND STAFF

1. Captain Richard Godolphin Hume Chaloner, 3rd Battalion, Wiltshire Regiment, attached to 20 POW Company, and first son of the first Baron Gisborough, Richard Godolphin Walmesley & Margaret Chaloner, died of accidental injuries in France on 3 April 1917, aged 33, and is buried in Calais Southern Cemetery. According to the family,

'Huie', as he was called, was killed by a British soldier when he returned to camp during a storm. The sentry at the gate challenged the approaching figure, but it is assumed Chaloner did not hear him as he failed to identify himself. Fearing the worst, the sentry fired a shot and Chaloner was mortally wounded. Thus, the Baron's second son, Thomas Weston Peel Long Chaloner, who served as 41 Squadron's Intelligence Officer throughout World War II, became the 2nd Baron Gisborough on the death of his father, on 23 January 1938.

2. Despite in-depth research, it proved impossible by the time this work went to print to positively identify Fg Off Harry W. Smith. He held the rank of Flying Officer (according to the ORB), at least 31 July 1942 to 7 September 1943, but it is known that a minimum of three Harry W. or Harold W. Smiths of Officer rank served in the RAF during World War II. These held the Services Numbers 51173, 78016 and 105591, but I was unable to establish which of these, if any, was 41 Squadron's Adjutant. Smith filled the role definitely between 31 July 1942 and 27 October 1943, but possibly earlier than July 1942 and later than October 1943.

APPENDIX V – CASUALTIES, ACCIDENTS AND INCIDENTS

1. As 41 Squadron flew Spitfires for the duration of World War II, nearly all references made to aircraft marks (i.e. versions) in this appendix relate to this aircraft type.
2. Casualty type. For an explanation of abbreviations used, please see the Abbreviations appendix.
3. Details of Casualty. For an explanation of abbreviations used, please see the Abbreviations appendix.
4. Sgt Plt Arthur R. Cope had left 41 Squadron on posting to North Africa and was lost whilst ferrying Spitfire Vc, JG747, from Gibraltar to Maison Blanche, via a refuelling stop at the USAAF airfield at La Sénia, Algeria, on 9 March 1943. The cause of his loss remains uncertain, as other pilots accompanying him reported there was no radio communication from Cope indicating he was in any trouble; they simply noticed he was no longer with them. An official enquiry assumed that Cope's loss was likely a result of a failure to switch from the auxiliary to the main fuel tank, but makes no judgement on whether the cause was human error or mechanical failure. Even though Cope had been posted away from 41 Squadron by this time, he was still underway to his posting and had not yet joined his new unit. As such, he is still listed as a member of 41 Squadron in official records.
5. 41 Squadron's Fg Off Reginald M. Hoare was attached to 91 Squadron at Hawkinge for a few days from 26 March 1943, with fellow pilot Fg Off Clive R. Birbeck. On 1 April 1943, whilst flying a dawn shipping reconnaissance patrol with 91 Squadron's Fg Off Barrass J. Todd, they entered heavy rain and low cloud, and Hoare was not seen or heard from again. Hoare had been hit by Flak and baled out, and was captured near Ostend. His aircraft came down at Leffinge, due south of the town. Birbeck returned to 41 Squadron on 3 April, but Hoare spent the remainder of the war behind wire.
6. 549592 Corporal Wilfred Francis Murrin, a member of the Squadron's ground crew, died on 18 May 1943, aged 23. He was cycling downhill near Folkestone on 17 May 1943, when his dynamo jammed the front wheel. He fell, fractured his skull, and died the following day.
7. The Squadron ORB's F541 on 19 August 1944 states that Fg Off Ronald Johnson's "tank would not jettison", but Johnson contradicts this in his logbook, recording instead, "R.T. & Flap indicator u/s…".
8. Fg Off Ross Harding returned from the Squadron's escort of Marauders to Beauvais on 24 September 1943, recording the reason in his logbook was "engine trouble". He records his aircraft's serial as MB837. This contradicts the Squadron ORB on this operation, which not only does not mention his return but also shows Harding flying MB839. Referring to Spitfire; The History (Morgan & Shacklady, 1999), MB839 transferred to 91 Squadron on 11 June 1943, whereas MB837 served on 41 Squadron from around August 1943 through to at least July 1944. This therefore suggests that the serial Harding recorded in his logbook, MB837, is in fact correct, and that it is the ORB that is erroneous.
9. The 41 Squadron ORB on 13 October 1943 states that Fg Off Herbert Wagner's aircraft wing was damaged by Flak. However, this statement is erroneous, as both Wagner's flying logbook and WO James Still's Combat Report state that it was Still's aircraft that was hit by Flak.
10. Flt Lt Ronald T. Collis states in his logbook on 2 December 1943 that he returned to base owing to engine trouble ("Ret'd u/s Engine"), but the Squadron ORB's F541 states he returned to base "owing to drop tank being u/s".
11. This incident involving Fg Off Peter Cowell in MB882 on 25 March 1944 is only recorded in the ORB as him having returned to base within 15 minutes of take-off, without any reason given. The details were, however, provided by Cowell himself, and are recorded in his flying logbook.
12. In this incident on 29 April 1944, only one of the two pilots – Flt Lt Collis *or* Flt Lt Harding – is believed to have suffered what the ORB's F540 only describes as 'starting trouble', but it does not identify which one. However, as a result, both pilots were delayed in becoming airborne.
13. In this incident on 29 April 1944, only one of the two pilots – Fg Off Refshauge *or* Fg Off Wagner – is believed to have suffered what the ORB's F540 describes only as 'a rough engine', but it does not identify which one. However, as a result, both pilots returned to base early.
14. In this incident on 8 May 1944, only one of the two pilots – Plt Off Fisher *or* Plt Off Payne – suffered what the ORB's F540 describes only as 'engine trouble', but does not identify which one. However, as a result, both pilots returned to base early.

15. In this incident on 16 May 1944, it is understood that only one of the two pilots – Fg Off Cook *or* Flt Sgt Stevenson – suffered what the ORB's F540 describes only as 'engine trouble', but it does not identify which one. These facts are recorded on the F540, but the F541 fails to list the serials of the aircraft, even though it was an operational scramble. However, as a result of the problem, both pilots returned to base early, instead of continuing on to conduct a routine patrol as was intended.
16. This accident is not recorded in the Squadron ORB, but the Fairwood Common ORB (TNA AIR 28/263), where 41 Squadron was based 16-24 May for air-firing practice, records that this aircraft crashed on landing at 14:40, that the starboard oleo leg collapsed, and starboard mainplain oleo leg, rudder and propeller were damaged, but it does not name the pilot. However, in its monthly summary of flying accidents, the 10 Group ORB Appendix (TNA AIR 25/188) names Flt Sgt Frederick Woollard as the pilot and explains that the rudder bar jammed on landing, forcing the aircraft to skid and the oleo leg to collapse.
17. The deaths of Sgt Plt Clifford Oddy and Flt Sgt Roger Short on 17 July 1944 occurred in a mid-air collision with each other. Oddy was flying a Tiger Moth II, DE575, and Short Spitfire XII, MB877.
18. Flt Lt Terry Spencer was flying a 33 Squadron Spitfire IXa, with the code lettering 5R-Z at the time of this accident on 20 August 1944. The aircraft was likely MH790.
19. The RAF Lympne ORB on 16 November 1944 states that Fg Off John F. Wilkinson (RM765) landed in the Ghent area short of fuel on account of engine trouble during Ramrod 1372, accompanied by WO Alister D. Miller (RM793). The 41 Squadron ORB's F540 makes no mention of the pair landing in Belgium, but the F541 simply lists Miller and Flt Lt Ross P. Harding (RM767) – not Wilkinson – as "Landed at Antwerp" (not Ghent) at 15:40.
20. The 41 Squadron ORB on 31 December 1944 records the serial of the aircraft that Flt Lt David Henry belly-landed in that day as RM842. However, other sources suggest that this aircraft was not received by 41 Squadron until 18 January 1944, almost three weeks later. This was also the aircraft and serial that Flt Lt Henry was flying when he was shot down and captured on 10 February 1945. There appears to be no other immediately obvious candidate for the aircraft flown by Henry during his 31 December 1944 belly-landing and, as such, the aircraft involved in this incident remains in question.
21. There is a discrepancy in the details provided on the 09:00 mission in the Squadron ORB on 8 February 1945. The F540 states "W/O R. Fleming [incorrect rank; he was now commissioned] returned early with a u/s hood", whilst the F541 makes no mention of Fleming at all and lists Flt Lt Thomas R. Burne in RM719 instead returning 20 minutes into the armed reconnaissance with "technical trouble". It is therefore possible that either pilot flew this sortie, but it should be noted that Fleming is not shown on the F541 at all flying operationally between 3 and 13 February 1945.
22. There is a discrepancy in the details provided on the 16:30 mission in Squadron ORB on 8 February 1945. The F540 states that five pilots were involved in the armed reconnaissance and that Fg Off John F. Wilkinson returned early with a "rough engine". However, the F541 does not record Wilkinson's participation. Five pilots are listed – Flt Lt Thomas Burne, WO Vivian Rossow, Flt Lt Frank Woolley, Flt Sgt Harry Smart and Flt Lt Peter Cowell – but Wilkinson is not amongst them. In fact, he is not shown on the F541 as having flown all day. It may therefore have been one of these five pilots who returned with the rough engine instead and, as such, the serial of the aircraft in question is also unclear.
23. There is some doubt as to the aircraft Fg Off Roy D. A. Smith was flying on the 12:30 armed reconnaissance on 24 April 1945. The Squadron ORB's F541 records it as Spitfire XIV, RB143, but this aircraft is listed on the F541 as having flown on subsequent days. However, MV249 is recorded in *Spitfire; The History* as having been damaged on this date and subsequently stuck off charge, which suggests Smith was most likely flying MV249 rather than RB143.
24. As all flights made by 41 Squadron's pilots after the cessation of hostilities on 8 May 1945 were considered non-operational, the ORB stopped recording flights, pilots and serials on the F541. These two incidents are recorded in WO Ian T. Stevenson's logbook, but only by the code letters 'EB-K' and 'EB-W'. It is believed, however, that the serials were RM915 and RB159, respectively, as these aircraft bore these letters during April 1945 and were still with the Squadron in early May.

APPENDIX VI – ROLL OF HONOUR

1. Sgt Plt Arthur R. Cope had left 41 Squadron on posting to North Africa and was lost whilst ferrying Spitfire Vc, JG747, from Gibraltar to Maison Blanche, via a refuelling stop at the USAAF airfield at La Sénia, Algeria, on 9 March 1943. Even though Cope had been posted away from 41 Squadron by this time, he was still underway to his posting and had not yet joined his new unit. As such, he is still listed as a member of 41 Squadron in official records.
2. 549592 Cpl. Wilfred Francis Murrin, a member of 41 Squadron's ground crew, died on 18 May 1943, aged 23. He was cycling downhill near Folkestone on 17 May 1943, when his dynamo jammed the front wheel. He fell, fractured his skull, and died the following day. He was the husband of Beatrice L. M. Murrin, of Crediton Bow, and is buried in Bow (Nymet Tracey) St. Bartholomew Churchyard Extension, Devon, in Row 2, Grave 14.

APPENDIX VII – PRISONERS OF WAR

1. Fg Off Reginald M. Hoare was attached to 91 Squadron at Hawkinge for a few days from 26 March 1943. On 1 April 1943, he was hit by Flak over the Belgian coast during a shipping reconnaissance flight, baled out and was captured.
2. Fg Off Leslie A. Prickett force-landed with engine failure 60-70 miles south of St. Omer on 27 August 1943. He evaded capture until 17 December 1943, when he was betrayed by a double agent and arrested. He spent two weeks in Fresnes Prison, after which he was sent to Stalag Luft III.
3. Flt Lt Hugh L. Parry was shot down at Beauvais, France, on 24 September 1943 but avoided capture until 7 February 1944, when he was betrayed and arrested. He spent two weeks in Fresnes Prison in Paris, after which he was sent to Stalag Luft III.

APPENDIX VIII – AERIAL VICTORIES

1. There may be an element of discrepancy in the Location between the location of an interception, the location the attack took place, and the location an aircraft or V1 flying bomb was brought down. This list is provided as a guide only and Combat Reports should be reviewed for accuracy.
2. This column refers to the number of the Combat Report pertaining to each claim, as they appear on microfilm at the National Archives in TNA AIR 50/18. They are generally sorted and numbered in alphabetical order of a pilot's surname, rather than chronologically. As a result, for example, the Squadron's first confirmed victory is recorded on a Combat Report numbered 370, as 'Shipman' appears towards the end of the alphabet. Where Combat Reports are of more than one page in length, only the number of the first page is shown. If Combat Reports could not be located in AIR 50/18, claims shown in this Appendix have been substantiated through entries in the Squadron's ORB and Appendices, in Station ORBs, in pilots' Flying Logbooks, or from the original, sometimes hand-written, Combat Reports held in 41 Squadron's own Archive collection. The most significant of these is the latter resource as a large number of the Combat Reports held in the Squadron's Archives cannot be found amongst those in the National Archives' collection and, as such, fill many of the gaps in TNA AIR 50/18 and in the Combat Reports found in the ORB's Appendices (TNA AIR 27/427-429). However, it is important to note that in contrast to the National Archives' collection, 41 Squadron's own collection is kept in chronological order and is <u>unnumbered</u>. It is for this reason that where a Combat Report from the Squadron's Archives has been utilised in this Appendix, it is only denoted by the letters 'SA' ['Squadron Archives'] and not by a Combat Report number.
3. This FW190 was originally claimed by Fg Off Ronald T. H. Collis on 20 October 1943 as destroyed. However, it was initially only admitted as probable, but a letter from HQ 11 Group (11G/810/Int), dated 20 December 1943, lifted it to destroyed after all.
4. The Me109 claimed by Plt Off Douglas Fisher on 20 October 1943 crashed into the ground whilst he was pursuing it, and was therefore claimed destroyed.
5. WO Ian T. Stevenson originally claimed this FW190 on 14 February 1945 as damaged, but it was upgraded to probable on the evidence of Fg Off Donald F. J. Tebbit, who saw the aircraft in flames, in a vertical dive from 15,000 to 1,500 feet, which was the ceiling of the cloud base. However, contemporary research confirms that this aircraft was actually destroyed. JG54 and JG26 lost four aircraft in combats with 41 Squadron around Rheine Aerodrome on this date.
6. WO Ian T. Stevenson originally claimed this FW190 on 14 February 1945 as damaged, but contemporary research confirms that this aircraft was actually destroyed. JG54 and JG26 lost four aircraft in combats with 41 Squadron around Rheine Aerodrome on this date.
7. Flt Lt Frank G. Woolley originally claimed this FW190D at Rheine Aerodrome on 14 February 1945 as probably destroyed. However it was disallowed and reduced to damaged. This is recorded on his *Pilot Service Record* where *PROBABLE* was written, but crossed out and replaced with *DAMAGED* and the comment, *See letter of 6.3.45 in Sqdn File Assessments*. [Ref. *Pilot Service Record*, 41 Squadron Archives]. However, despite this reduction, contemporary research confirms that this aircraft was actually destroyed. JG54 and JG26 lost four aircraft in combats with 41 Squadron around Rheine Aerodrome on this date.
8. This second FW190D claimed destroyed at Teschendorf by Fg Off Eric Gray on 20 April 1945 spun in and crashed during his combat with it, despite the fact he did not fire, and was therefore awarded destroyed.
9. These two FW190s claimed destroyed by Plt Off Patrick Coleman 1 May 1945 collided with each other. According to Coleman's Combat Report (CR 156), he swept in from behind the two aircraft, which were flying side-by-side, and surprised them. As a result of what Coleman felt was panic, one pilot suddenly turned towards the other, instead of breaking away, and collided with the FW190 flying beside him. Both fell to the ground and were destroyed.
10. Fg Off Clive R. Birbeck originally claimed this FW190 over the Somme Estuary on 27 April 1943 as destroyed, but it was only admitted as probable.
11. There is an element of contradiction in available resources concerning Fg Off Benjamin B. Newman's victory on 16 September 1943. Both Newman's Combat Report (CR 321) and the Squadron ORB state he damaged an Me109G between Bernay and Évreux, which was upgraded to probably destroyed. However, Newman's *Pilot Service Record*

states that the victory was actually over an FW190. As the ORB indicates that 41 and 91 Squadrons encountered both types of aircraft during their Ramrod to Beaumont-le-Roger that day, it is impossible to say conclusively which type of aircraft Newman's adversary was flying.
12. Fg Off Clive R. Birbeck originally claimed this FW190 west of Évreux on 22 September 1943 as destroyed, but was only admitted as probable.
13. Flt Lt Benjamin B. Newman originally claimed this FW190 over Beauvais 24 September 1943 as damaged, but it was upgraded to probable
14. This victory, a damaged Ju88D on 14 August 1942, was shared between four pilots: two from 41 Squadron, Sgt Plts Kenneth G. Warren and Leslie A. Prickett south-southeast of Dublin, and two from 315 (Polish) Squadron, Flt Lt Wlodzimierz Miksa and Sgt Plt Jerzy Malec, who had damaged it previously, northwest of Barrow.
15. This victory is neither recorded in the Squadron ORB nor in any contemporary works as Flt Lt Douglas H. Hone's claim of this FW190 damaged over Dieppe on 19 August 1942, during Operation *Jubilee*, was not submitted until 8 September 1942. The reason for this postponement lay in subsequent analysis of cine camera film from the day's operations. Realising his failure to claim a legitimate victory, he belatedly submitted a claim and was granted a FW190 damaged. His *Pilot Service Record* states, ...Cine Film showed hits with cannon shell on Port Tail Plane with cockpit in direct line beyond. Claimed as F.W. 190 Damaged 8.9.42. [Ref. *Pilot Service Record*, 41 Squadron Archives]
16. This claim of a damaged FW190 in Combat Report 116, on 16 April 1945, went to Wg Cdr George C. Keefer DSO DFC, Wing Commander Flying of 125 Wing, who was leading Black Section of six aircraft on a 41 Squadron operation, flying a 41 Squadron aircraft, MV257.
17. V1 victories marked with an asterisk (*) indicate those achieved by pilots tipping up the wing of the V1 with the wingtip of their own aircraft, whilst the victory marked with a hash (#) indicates a V1 destroyed by the turbulence from a pilot's jet-stream.
18. Flt Sgt Colin Robertson's destruction of a V1 six miles north of Pevensey on 22 June 1944 (CR 500) was originally declared shared with a Tempest from another squadron. However, Robertson's *Pilot Service Record* states, *1 Flying Bomb Destroyed confirmed over Tempest claim by A.O.C.* [Ref. *Pilot Service Record*, 41 Squadron Archives]. It should be noted, however, that Robertson's *Pilot Service Record* erroneously states the date was 26 June 1944, although this could have been the date the claim was granted.
19. When Flt Sgt Roger Short shot down this V1 on 25 June 1944 with two Spitfires from another squadron, it was claimed as a half victory, not a third.
20. Plt Off Peter B. Graham originally claimed this V1 on 7 July 1944 as a half shared victory with a Tempest from another squadron. However, this was upgraded to a full individual victory when the Tempest pilot made no claim of his own.
21. Flt Sgt Ian T. Stevenson shared this V1 victory over Eastbourne, Sussex, on 7 July 1944 with Flt Lt Longin Majewski of 316 Squadron, who was flying Mustang III, FB351.
22. Fg Off John F. Wilkinson shared this V1 victory between Lympne and Ashford, Kent, on 11 August 1944 with Flt Sgt J. Bargielowski of 315 Squadron, who was flying Mustang III, FX878.
23. Fg Off Charles J. Malone shared this V1 victory two miles northwest of Ashford, Kent, on 15 August 1944 with Flt Lt Robert G. Kleimeyer of 129 Squadron (ex-41 Squadron, 1942), who was flying Mustang III, FB137.
24. Plt Off Peter B. Graham stated that he originally only claimed this V1 on 16 August 1944 as probably destroyed. This is because, despite the fact he had shot off the V1's starboard wing and had seen it in a spin towards the ground, he could not witness its final destruction as he had entered the balloon barrage, and was forced to cease his pursuit and pull up. The victory was, however, later confirmed.
25. Flt Lt Daniel J. Reid shared this V1 victory northwest of Ashford on 23 August 1944 with Flt Lt Leonard A. Wood of 274 Squadron, who was flying Tempest V, EJ646.

APPENDIX IX – GROUND VICTORIES

1. This summary of the ground victories claimed on 28 March 1945 has been compiled from entries in the Squadron ORB. However, a number of *Pilot Service Records* suggest the tally that day was far greater and included in addition to those listed one armoured vehicle destroyed and four MET, one horse-drawn vehicle and 45 railway trucks damaged in the Münster area, and another armoured vehicle and trailer destroyed, one three-ton truck, one tug, eight MET, two horse-drawn vehicles and 30 trucks damaged, without any indication of the location(s) thereof.

APPENDIX XI – AIRCRAFT IN SERVICE

1. Spitfire Vb, P8799, was received on 24 April 1943 and transferred to 501 Squadron on 7 July 1943. In correspondence with Dan Johnson, dated 26 September 1984, then Fg Off Ronald Johnson (no relation) refers to this aircraft as EB-L, which he flew on 22 May and 4 June 1943.
2. Tiger Moth II, DE575, was flown by Sgt Plt Clifford Oddy on 17 July 1944, when he crossed the flight path of Sgt Plt Roger Short taking off in Spitfire XII, MB877, killing both men.

APPENDIX XII – BASE LOCATIONS

1. The Squadron was posted to RAF Longtown for Exercise *Dryshod*. The Squadron should have flown up to Longtown on 2 August 1942, but the move was hampered by poor weather and they did not arrive until 4 August. The pilots flew to their new base, RAF Llanbedr, on 9 August and the ground crews departed from Longtown by ground transport on 10 August, and arrived in Llanbedr on 11 August.
2. The move to RAF Tangmere took place specifically for the Squadron's participation in Operation *Jubilee*, the Allied attack on Dieppe, which took place on 19 August 1942.
3. For Exercise *Punch*, which ran from 23-29 September 1942.
4. For Exercise *Aflame*, which only ran from 8-10 October 1942, as the Squadron arrived late and the exercise was prematurely cancelled, in both cases due to bad weather.
5. Several sections were attached to RAF Westhampnett from 13 December 1942 to 13 January 1943 during this period for operational training.
6. The main party moved to RAF Hawkinge on 12 April 1943, but the pilots and aircraft arrived on 13 April.
7. During the Squadron's stay at RAF Westhampnett between 21 June and 4 October 1943, several operations were flown from other Stations. These included a Rhubarb from Manston on 28 August, a fighter sweep from Manston on 30 August, convoy patrols from Lympne on 2 September, a Ramrod from Bradwell Bay on 5 September, Ramrods from Lympne and Hawkinge on 8 September, a Ramrod from Manston on 15 September, Ramrods from Manston and West Malling on 19 September, and two Ramrods from Manston on 3 October.
8. During the Squadron's stay at RAF Tangmere between 4 October 1943 and 11 March 1944, several operations were flown from other Stations. These included a Ramrod from Hawkinge and back to Manston on 9 October, two Ramrods from Manston on 10 November 1943, a Ramrod from Hawkinge on 26 November, a Ramrod from Manston on 4 December 1943, a Ramrod from Bradwell Bay on 13 December 1943, a Ramrod from Friston on 21 February 1944, and a Ramrod from Hawkinge on 25 February 1944.
9. For an air firing course at 17 Armament Practice Camp, based at RAF Southend.
10. For an air-to-air firing and air-to-ground bombing course at 11 Armament Practice Camp, based at RAF Fairwood Common.
11. The Squadron's operations from RAF Tangmere on 26 June 1944 only consisted of three anti-Diver patrols (six sorties), before moving on to Westhampnett the following morning, by which time the ground crews had arrived from West Malling.
12. B.56 Evere can barely be considered a base. When the Squadron flew to the Continent on 4 December 1944, they only landed at Evere as they were concerned about the condition of the strip at B.64 Diest. The pilots then travelled to Diest by road, where they stayed overnight, and returned to Evere the following morning to pick up their aircraft and fly them back to Diest, where they remained more or less until the end of the year.
13. Owing to bad weather and "impossible landing conditions" at B.64 Diest on 23 December 1944, the pilots could not return to the airfield and were instead re-directed to B.78 Eindhoven. They stayed overnight and operated temporarily from Eindhoven on 24 December, but returned to Diest that evening.
14. There is some confusion about whether 41 Squadron was based at Asch or Ophoven during this period. This probably stems from an entry in the Squadron ORB on 31 December 1944, which states, "Y.32. Asch", however Y.32 was actually the number for Ophoven. In fact, subsequent ORB entries began to distance themselves from Asch, stating "Y.32 Near Asch", though all entries still state Y.32. Asch's number was Y.29 and was an American aerodrome from which fighters of the U.S. 352nd and 366th Fighter Groups operated. Royal Air Force units – namely 41, 130, 350 and 610 Squadrons – were based at nearby Y.32 Ophoven, a fact confirmed by many sources, thereunder the 125 Wing ORB.
15. For an air-to-air and ground firing course at 17 Armament Practice Camp, based at RAF Warmwell.

APPENDIX XIV – INDEX TO TNA COMBAT REPORTS

1. As the Combat Reports held in TNA AIR 50/18 are numbered in alphabetical rather than chronological order, it was felt prudent to keep the index as a complete list, rather than breaking it up and only including those pertaining to the period August 1942 to May 1945. Such a breakdown would make little sense and result in a haphazard and incomplete list with missing numbers, which would defeat its purpose. Likewise, whilst the Combat Reports held within the Appendices of ORBs *are* in chronological order, and *could* be separated and included with the pending volume covering September 1939-July 1942, it also was felt it would make more sense to keep everything together and maintain a single full record of all Combat Reports available at the National Archives in the same place. As such, this Appendix covers the entire period from September 1939 to May 1945.
2. As a point of reference only, the 'Claim' column in this Appendix indicates the aircraft or object claimed in the Combat Report, but not whether it was claimed destroyed, probably destroyed or damaged; misidentifications of aircraft have also not been corrected.
3. In the 'Location' column in this Appendix, errors or inaccuracies have generally not been corrected, but counties or countries have been added, as appropriate, to assist with identification.
4. The Curtiss Hawk claimed by Plt Off Cyril F. Babbage in Combat Report 36 of TNA AIR 50/18 and folio 252

of TNA AIR 27/429 on 18 September 1941 was actually a FW190. This is believed to have been the RAF's first sighting – and therefore an understandable misidentification – of the Luftwaffe's new Focke-Wulf FW190A-1 fighter.
5. Combat Report 107 relates to the victory against a FW190 claimed by Fg Off Clive R. Birbeck on 4 September 1943, which is claimed in CRs 105-106.
6. This claim of a damaged FW190 in Combat Report 116, on 16 April 1945, went to Wg Cdr George C. Keefer DSO DFC, Wing Commander Flying of 125 Wing, who was flying with 41 Squadron on this operation and flew a 41 Squadron aircraft, MV257.
7. This destruction of a Henschel Hs123 on 18 September 1941, shared by Plt Off George Buchanan (CRs 131-132) and Flt Lt Charles Bush (CR 134), was a misidentification of a Gotha 145.
8. Combat Reports 178-180 are an Intelligence Report relating to the Ju88 claimed by Fg Off John G. Boyle (CR 115), Sgt Plt Edward V. Darling (CR 170), and Fg Off Ronald W. Wallens (CRs 421-22) on 11 August 1940.
9. Combat Report 293 is an Intelligence Report relating to Flt Lt Anthony D. J. Lovell's victory against a Ju88 by on 30 March 1941, which is claimed in CRs 291-292.
10. The Ju52 claimed by Flt Lt Roy Marples, Plt Off Geoffrey Ranger and Sgt Plt Cyril Whiteford in Combat Reports 306 and 346 of TNA AIR 50/18, and folios 253 and 254 of TNA AIR 27/429, on 18 September 1941 was a misidentification of a Junkers Ju34.
11. Combat Report 307 for Flt Sgt Stanley H. May is incorrectly dated 12 August 1943. It should read 11 August 1943, as it relates to an action that took place on this latter date. See also Combat Report 104 of 11 August 1943 for Fg Off Clive R. Birbeck.
12. The claim of an He113 by Flt Lt J. Terence Webster on 28 July 1940 in Combat Report 449 is believed to have actually been an Me109E.
13. The claim of an He113 by Flt Lt J. Terence Webster on 5 September 1940 in Combat Report 455 is believed to have actually been an Me109E.
14. Combat Report 509 is an Intelligence Report relating to Plt Off Edward P. Wells' victory against a CR42 on 11 November 1940, which is claimed in CRs 465-466.
15. Combat Reports 473-474 are an Intelligence Report relating to Flt Lt Anthony D. J. Lovell and Plt Off Edward P. Wells' victory over a He111 on 22 January 1941, which is also claimed in CRs 289-290 and 471-472.
16. Combat Report 507 is an Intelligence Report relating to Plt Off Eric S. Lock's victory against a Ju88 on 6 September 1940, which is claimed in CRs 518-519.
17. Combat Reports 510-511 are an Intelligence Report relating to Sgt. Aubrey C. Baker's victory against an Me109 on 10 January 1941, which is claimed in CRs 46-47
18. Combat Report 512 is an Intelligence Report relating to Flt Lt Anthony D. J. Lovell's victory against a Ju88 on 30 March 1941, which is claimed in CRs 291-292 (See also Combat Report 293).
19. The claim of an He113 by Plt Off Eric Lock on 20 September 1940 in Combat Report 530 is believed to have actually been an Me109E.
20. Wing Commander Henry de Clifford Anthony Woodhouse DFC, was the Tangmere Wing Commander Flying, having recently replaced Douglas Bader who had baled out and was captured on 9 August 1941. His destruction of an Me109E over Doudeville, near St. Valery, France, on 20 September 1941 (CR 256, TNA AIR 27/429, Appendices January-December 1941) was shared with 41 Squadron's Flt Lt Leslie L. Bache.

FURTHER READING

1. There are no Appendices to the Squadron ORB for January-December 1942 or January-April 1944.
2. Includes Combat Reports and Squadron Intelligence Reports for June-September 1944.

BIBLIOGRAPHY

ARCHIVAL RECORDS

The National Archives, Kew

2ND TACTICAL AIR FORCE: *Airfields: maps*, TNA AIR 37/400
Alphabetical list of British and Dominion Air Force PoWs in Germany and German occupied territories, March 1945, TNA AIR 20/2336
Air Ministry and Successors: Civil Aviation Accident Reports (C, W, and S Reports) and Technical Memoranda; TNA AVIA 5/22/W1521 (Thomas)
Air Ministry: Combat Reports, Second World War, Fighter Command:
No.41 Squadron, TNA AIR 50/18 [Combat Reports]
No.91 Squadron, TNA AIR 50/39 [Combat Reports]
Air Ministry: Combat Reports, Second World War, Fighter Wings:
133 (Polish) Wing: 129, 306, 309 & 315 Squadrons, TNA AIR 50/436
146 Wing, Tangmere: 41, 91, 118, 193, 257, 402 & 416 Squadrons, TNA AIR 50/443
150 Wing, Newchurch: 3, 65, 122 & 316 (Polish) Squadrons, TNA AIR 50/444
Allied Expeditionary Air Force: Re-equipment of Squadrons 1943-1944, TNA AIR 37/475
Dulag Luft and other interrogation reports: information obtained by Germans from British Prisoners of War, 1944-1945, TNA AIR 40/2318
Escape Reports, TNA WO 208/3352, pieces 2430 (Thiele) & 2432 (Spencer)
Escape/Evasion Reports: Code MI9/SPG, TNA WO 208, pieces 3314/1366 (Slack), 3315/1502 (Gaze) & 3316/1546 (May)
Forces Repatriated from Eire, 1940-1945, TNA WO 208/3347
Ill-Treatment of Allied Nationals and Prisoners of War at Gestapo Headquarters, Avenue Foch, Paris, in 1943 and 1944, TNA WO 311/933
Judge Advocate General's Office, Royal Air Force Courts Martial Registers, General Courts Martial, Home, 13 Jun 18-20 Dec 60, TNA AIR 21/3
Judge Advocate General's Office, Royal Air Force Courts Martial Registers, District Courts Martial, Home, 1 Apr 38-2 Nov 42, TNA AIR 21/4B
Liberation reports, TNA WO 208, pieces 3339/1057 (Parry) & 3340/1561 (Prickett)
Mission No. 87: Watten, site in course of construction for aeronautical facilities, 27 Aug., Aug-Sep 43 (VIII Fighter Command Narrative for 27 Aug 43), TNA AIR 40/436
Noball Target List, Mar 1944, TNA AIR 40/1674
Officers reports: pages 539-1169 containing report numbers 101-445, Committee of the Treatment of Prisoners of War, Vol. 2, TNA WO 161/96 (Chaloner)
Officers' Service Records, Department of the Master-General of Personnel, Air Ministry, 1918-1919, TNA AIR 76/81 (Chaloner)
Operations Record Books for the following Squadrons:-
  41 Squadron RAF, TNA AIR 27 pieces 425 (1 Jan 41-31 Dec 43), 426 (1 Jan 44-31 May 45), 430 (App Jan-Dec 43) & 431 (App Apr 44-Apr 45)
  Other Squadrons, TNA AIR 27, pieces 5 (1 Sqn), 32 & 34-35 (3 Sqn), 113 (8 Sqn), 164 (12 Sqn), 252-253 (19 Sqn), 287 (23 Sqn), 292 (24 Sqn), 306 (25 Sqn), 2405 (26 Sqn), 341 (29 Sqn), 363 (32 Sqn), 368 & 370 (33 Sqn), 440-442 (43 Sqn), 501 (52 Sqn), 511-512 (54 Sqn), 589-590 (64 Sqn), 592 & 594 (65 Sqn), 598 (66 Sqn), 623-625 (72 Sqn), 629 & 631 (73 Sqn), 641-643 (74 Sqn), 664-665 (79 Sqn), 670 (80 Sqn), 678 (81 Sqn), 738 & 740-741 (91 Sqn), 744 (92 Sqn), 764 (96 Sqn), 850 (108 Sqn), 867-868 (111 Sqn), 872-873 (112 Sqn), 882 (114 Sqn), 907 (118 Sqn), 914 (121 Sqn), 915 (122 Sqn), 917 (123 Sqn), 919 (124 Sqn), 922 (125 Sqn), 929 (127 Sqn), 934 (129 Sqn), 937-938 (130 Sqn), 954 (137 Sqn), 969 (141 Sqn), 985-986 (145 Sqn), 989 (146 Sqn), 1110 (175 Sqn), 1025 (152 Sqn), 1029 (153 Sqn), 1085 (164 Sqn), 1087 (165 Sqn), 1140 (185 Sqn), 1315 (213 Sqn), 1360 (219 Sqn), 1371 (222 Sqn), 1418-1420 (229 Sqn), 1428 (232 Sqn), 1439 (234 Sqn), 1453 (238 Sqn), 1471 (242 Sqn), 1474 (243 Sqn), 1487 (247 Sqn), 1498 (249 Sqn), 1501 (250 Sqn), 1519 (255 Sqn), 1537 (260 Sqn), 1547-1548 (263 Sqn), 1553 (264 Sqn), 1558-1559 (266 Sqn), 1589 (274 Sqn), 1601-1602 (277 Sqn), 1621 (286 Sqn), 1625 (289 Sqn), 1626 (290 Sqn), 1678 (308 Sqn), 1706 (317 Sqn), 1746 (350 Sqn), 1802 (410 Sqn), 1805 (412 Sqn), 1816 (416 Sqn), 1820 (418 Sqn), 1892 (452 Sqn), 1893 (453 Sqn), 1930 (467 Sqn), 1933 (485 Sqn), 1934 (486 Sqn), 1963-1964 (504 Sqn), 1950-1952 (501 Sqn), 2004 (535

Sqn), 2074-2078 (602 Sqn), 2079 (603 Sqn), 2102 (609 Sqn), 2106-2108 (610 Sqn), 2109-2110 (611 Sqn), 2123 (615 Sqn), 2126-2127 (616 Sqn), 2132 (615 Sqn), 2342-2343 (1435 Sqn), 2819 (192 Sqn) & 2868 (51 Sqn)

Operations Record Books for the following Flying Training Schools:-
TNA AIR 29, pieces 550 (2 FTS, Brize Norton), 553 (3 FTS, Grantham), 554 (4 FTS, Abu Sueir, Egypt), 556 (5 SFTS, Sealand), 558 (6 SFTS, Little Rissington), 560 (11 FTS, Shawbury), 567 (7 FTS, Peterborough), 604 (Central Flying School [CFS], Upavon), 617 (6 EFTS, Sywell & 7 EFTS, Desford), 630 (2 FIS, Montrose)

Operations Record Books for the following Operational Training Units:-
TNA AIR 29, pieces 681 (52 & 53 OTU), 682 (55 OTU), 683 (7 OTU, subs. 57 OTU), 684 (58 & 59 OTU), 685 (61 OTU), 686 (71 OTU) & 707 (1 (C) OTU)

Operations Record Books for the following RAF Stations:-
TNA AIR 28, pieces 39 (Atcham), 62 (Brussels/Evere), 64 (Biggin Hill), 89 (Bolt Head), 168 (Coltishall), 188 (Debden), 193 (Detling), 201 (Digby), 251 (Eglinton), 263 (Fairwood Common), 286 (Friston), 345 (Hawkinge), 346 (High Ercall), 419 (Kenley), 494 (Llanbedr), 509 (Lympne), 601 (Northolt), 603 (North Weald), 692 (Southend), 815 (Tangmere), 874 (Valley), 888 (Warmwell), 907 (West Malling), & 1929 (Wyton)

Operations Record Books for the following Wings:-
39 Reconnaissance Wing RCAF, AIR 26/61
122 Wing RAF, TNA AIR 26/181
125 Wing RAF, TNA AIR 26/185

Operations Record Books for the following Groups:-
9 Group RAF, TNA AIR 25 pieces 177 (Sep 40-Sep 44) & 179 (App Jan-Dec 42)
10 Group RAF, TNA AIR 25 pieces 183 (Jan 44-May 45), 187 (App Jan-Apr 1944), and 188 (App May-Jun 44)
11 Group RAF, TNA AIR 25 pieces 194 (Jan 42-Dec 43), 195 (Jan-Dec 44), 204 (App Jul-Dec 42), 205 (App Jan-May 43), 206 (App Jun-Sep 43), 207 (App Oct-Dec 43), 208 (App Jan-Mar 44), 209 (App Apr 44), 211 (App Jun 44), 212 (App Jul 44), 213 (App Aug 44), 214 (App Sep 44), 215 (App Oct 44), & 216 (App Nov 44)
83 (Composite) Group, TNA AIR 25 pieces 698 (Apr 1943-Feb 1946), 706 (App Dec 44-Feb 45) & 707 (App Mar-May 45)

Operations Record Books for the following miscellaneous units:-
1 ADF, Hendon & Croydon, TNA AIR 29/890
1 TEU, Tealing, TNA AIR 29/683
3 GTS, Stoke Orchard & Northleach, TNA AIR 29/525
6 Mobile Field Photographic Section, TNA AIR 29/543
11 APC, Fairwood Common, TNA AIR 29/704
17 APC, Southend, TNA AIR 29/704
151 Repair Unit, Luneburg, TNA AIR 29/825
407 Aviation Fuel & Ammunition Park, TNA AIR 29/822
Air Fighting Development Unit (AFDU), TNA AIR 29/770A
R.A.F. Personnel Interned in Eire, 1940-1945, TNA AIR 20/1021
R.A.F. Pilot's Flying Log Books:
Sgt. H. P. Coates, Uruguayan Civil Pilot's Personal Flying Log Book showing civil flying in Uruguay, 1938-40, R.A.F. training in Britain and Canada and fighter operations, 1942, Dec 38-Sep 42, TNA AIR 4/15
SHAEF (MAIN AND REAR): Summary of effort: 2 TAF Groups Nos. 2, 83, 84, 85 monthly statistical record, 1944-1945, TNA AIR 37/1068
Stalag 357, Fallingbostel: nominal roll, casualties, reports etc., Nov 43-Jul 45, TNA AIR 40/277
Summary of Sorties, Aug 40-Sep 42, TNA AIR 16/1037
War Office: Directorate of Military Intelligence: Liberated Prisoner of War Interrogation Questionnaires, 1945-1946, TNA WO 344, pieces 8/2 (Appleton AS), 29/1 (Birbeck), 95/1 (Downing), 123/1 (Graham PB), 132/2 (Harding), 139/2 (Haywood), 140/1 (Heale), 141/2 (Henry), 146/1 (Hoare), 244/2 (Parry), 259 (Prickett), 290/2 (Slack), 298/2 (Spencer), 314/1 (Tebbit), 328/2 (Vine) & 329/1 (Wagner)

41 Squadron Archives

41st Squadron of the Line, nominal roll compiled by Sqn Intelligence Officer, Flt Lt Lord Gisborough, for Sector Intelligence Officer, RAF Tangmere, Ref. 'TS/62/Int.', dated 28 Jun 43
Ammunition Expenditure Report (Combat), handwritten and unreferenced document for 17 Apr 1943 [dated 18 Apr 1943]
Ammunition Expenditure in Combat, handwritten and unreferenced document for 21 Apr 1943 [dated 22 Apr 1943]
Assessment by 2 TAF of 41 Squadron's combat claims of 23 Jan and 14 Feb 45, untitled, but referenced '122W/52/2/Int.' and dated 6 Mar 45.
Assessment of Combat Claims, Ref. *11G/810/Int.*, 20 Dec 43, memo regarding Flt Lt R. T. H. Collis' claim of a FW190 on 20 Oct 43
Combat: 41 Squadron – 27.4.43. F/O. Birbeck., memo from Headquarters, 11 Group, to RAF Station Hawkinge, referenced *11G/810/Int.* and dated 3 May 43.

Combat Reports, original documents, unnumbered & un-indexed, for 14 Aug 42 (Prickett & Warren), 19 Aug 42 (Hone, Imbert, Stepp), 17 Apr 43 (Birbeck & Hogarth), 27 Apr 43 (Birbeck), 23 Jul 43 (Birbeck & Graham) 5 Aug 43 (Birbeck & Harding), 22 Sep 43 (Vann), 13 Oct 43 (Still & Wagner), 14 May 44 (Stowe), 7 Jun 44 (Balasse, Fleming, Slack & Thiele), 4 Jul 44 (Balasse & Woollard), 13 Jul 44 (Payne), 14 Jul 44 (Thiele), 23 Jul 44 (Balasse & Payne), 29 Jul 44 (Balasse x 2), 3 Sep 44 (Coleman, Spencer & Stowe), 18 Dec 44 (Appleton), 13 Feb 45 (Gray, Hegarty & Harding [in absentia]), 14 Feb 45 (Gray, Moyle, Rossow, Stevenson & Woolley) & 25 Feb 45 (Reid)

HQ: Second TAF Main... From AOC INC. [sic] [AM Sir Arthur Coningham KCB DSO MC DFC AFC] *To all ranks Second T.A.F.*, undated, unreferenced and untitled typed communiqué dating from ca. 23 March 45.

Intelligence Reports, original documents, unnumbered & un-indexed, for 14, 17-19 & 28 Aug 42; 22 Dec 42; 9 & 14 Jan 43; 4, 6 & 8 Feb 43; 1, 16, 17, 21 & 27 Apr 1943; 3 May 43; 18 & 23 Jul 43; 8 & 9 Aug 43; 6, 16, 18, 19, 22, 24, 27 & 28 Sep 43; 3, 8, 9, 13, 14, 17, 18, 20, & 22-26 Oct 43; 3-8, 10, 11, 15, 19, 20, 23-26 & 29 Nov 43; 1, 2, 4, 5, 13, 20 & 31 Dec 43; 2-8, 10, 14, 20, 21, 23-26, 28, 29 & 31 Jan 44; 3, 4, 6, 21, 24, 25, 28 & 29 Feb 44; 1-5, 13, 16, 20 & 25-31 Mar 44; 1, 8, 12, 15, 18-23 & 25-27 Apr 44; 9, 17, 23, 26-28 & 30-31 Aug 44; 1, 3, 12, 16-20, 23 & 26-27 Sep 44; 18, 24 & 25 Dec 44; 14-16 & 21-23 Jan 45; 3, 10-11, 13 & 25 Feb 45; 1 & 24-31 Mar 45

LBR GPI NR GPI 40/21 NOT WT; PASS TO 41 SQDN, original telex, undated but stamped 'R.A.F. LLANBEDR 21 AUG 1942' and 'No 41 SQUADRON 22 AUG 1942 ROYAL AIR FORCE'

Letter, handwritten, untitled and unreferenced, from Mrs Una Hoare to Flt Lt Lord Gisborough, dated 22 May 1943

No. 41 Squadron & 3016 Echelon Movement Order, drafted by Squadron Adjutant Fg Off H. W. Smith, undated, but relating to the Squadron's move from RAF High Ercall to RAF Hawkinge on 12 Apr 43

Nominal Roll. 41. Squadron., undated (ca. 19-21 Mar 45)

Nominal Roll. 41. Squadron., undated (ca. 10-17 Apr 45)

Nominal Roll. No. 41 Squadron, dated 18 Mar 44

Nominal Roll of Flying Personnel, undated (ca. 11-14 Jun 44)

Nominal Roll Officers and Airmen 41 Squadron Tangmere 2.3.44, Ref. *41S/521/P.2*.

Nominal Roll Officers and Aircrew 41 Squadron Bolt Head, undated (ca. 29 Apr-8 May 44)

Pilot Service Records, original documents, unreferenced & un-indexed, dating 1942-1945, for Adams SB, Anderson, Appleton AS, Atkinson, Balasse, Banach, Beard, Bednarz, Benham, Benjamin, Biggs, Birbeck, Bødtker, Boyd, Bradshaw, Brown WW, Burne, Cambridge, Chalmers, Chapman RH, Chappell, Charnock, Chattin, Clanzy, Clark, Coates, Coleman, Collis, Cook AC, Cook H, Coombes, Cope, Cowell, Cross, Curtis, Davidson, Davies, Downing, Duchateau, Duckworth, East, Farfan, Fearon, Fisher DP, Fisher RRG, Fleming R, Galitzine, Garrie, Gaze, Gibbs, Gillitt, Glen, Goens van, Goodall, Graham, Gray E, Gray JAB, Green, Griffith, Hale, Harding, Harrison, Haywood, Heale, Hegarty, Henry, Hoare, Hogarth, Hollow, Hone, Hope, Hyde, Imbert, Irvine, Jallands, Jarred, Johnson, Jolly, Kelly, King, Knight, Lane, Lawrence, Lloyd JMW, Loweth, Malone, May, McKellar, Miller, Moffett, Monk, Mottershead, Moyle, Munson, Neil, Newman, Oddy, Parry, Payne, Polak, Poynton, Prickett, Quine, Rake, Refshauge, Reid, Remez. Roberts, Robertson, Robinson, Rogowski, Rossow, Rowe, Sabourin, Samouelle, Schou, Scoon, Scott PF, Scott TR, Shea, Shepherd, Short, Slack, Smart, Smith DH, Smith JB, Smith RDA, Solak, Spencer, Spurr, Stephens, Stepp, Stevenson, Still, Stonier, Stowe, Tebbit, Thiele, Thomas JI, Vann, Vine, Wagner, Ware, Warren, Welsh, Whale, Wheatley, White, Wilkinson, Wilson GS, Wood, Woollard, Woolley & Zimek

Pilots with more than Twelve Confirmed Victories Obtained while Serving with Fighter Command (including B.A.F.F. and A.A.S.F.) up to 31st January, 1943, Ref. I.B.313

R/T Call Signs, undated (ca. 18 Dec 1944-4 Jan 45)

Squadron Diary, 41 Squadron, "B" Flight, dated 20 Sep 42-1 Mar 43

Thiele, Keith Frederick, Squadron Leader, undated and unpublished anecdotal autobiography sent by Thiele to 41 Squadron

Other Repositories

Air Force Museum of New Zealand, 45 Harvard Ave, Wigram 8042 (Private Bag 4739, Christchurch 8140), New Zealand.
  Pilots Flying Logbook, Sqn Ldr Keith F. Thiele (copy), Accession No. 1987/143

Centre de Documentation Historique des Forces Armées [Centre for Historical Documentation of the Armed Forces], Quartier Reine Elisabeth, Rue d'Evere 1, 1140 Evere, Belgium
  Services effectués comme officier [Officer's Service Record] for Roger Duchateau

Imperial War Museum, Lambeth Road, London, United Kingdom, SE1 6HZ.
  Parry, Hugh Lawrence, IWM Interview, Sep 1985, ID No. 8985/7
  Wilkinson J F Flight Lieutenant, My Experiences in World War II as a Royal Air Force Fighter Pilot, undated, ID No. 03/32/1

Library & Archives Canada, 395 Wellington Street, Ottawa, Ontario, Canada, K1A 0N4
  Second World War Service Files: Canadian Armed Forces War Dead, Shea, David John, RG 24, Box 28931

National Archives of Australia, PO Box 7425, Canberra BC, ACT 2610, Australia.
  Army Militia service records, attestation documents (Form A7), alphabetical series, Series B4747, Barcode 9310329 (Refshauge)
  Correspondence files, multiple number (Melbourne) series (Primary numbers 1-323) [RAAF Casualty Files], Series A705, Barcodes 1055013 (Hollow), 105543 (Reid), 1064848 (Brew), 1065454 (Cope), 1073726 (May), 1074277 (Miller),

1077540 (Quine) & 1078012 (Refshauge)

RAAF Officers Personnel files, 1921-1948, Series A9300, Barcodes 5244887 (Robertson CS), 5251127 (Refshauge), 5251414 (Newman), 5253015 (Stephens), 5255899 (Reid), 5256138 (Smith), 5260094 (White), 5261426 (May), 5371472 (Gray), 5379869 (Davidson), 5379922 (Anderson) & 5382249 (Hollow)

RAAF Personnel files of Non-Commissioned Officers (NCOs) and other ranks, 1921-1948, Series A9301, Barcodes 5522658 (White), 5523391 (Rossow), 5527802 (Cope), 5528423 (Ware), 5531415 (Miller) & 5540571 (Quine)

RAAF Personnel Files – All Ranks [WWII pilots with Post-War Service], Series A12372, Barcodes 12759789 (Coombes), 30702261 (King), 30702791 (Munson) & 30705216 (Moyle)

New Zealand Defence Force Archives, Trentham Military Camp, Private Bag 905, Upper Hutt 5140, New Zealand.
RNZAF Service Record for NZ.412744 Schou, Kenneth Victor James

RAF Disclosures Section, Trenchard Hall, RAF Cranwell, Sleaford, Lincs., NG34 8HB.
RAF Service Record of 108132 Gillitt, Frank Norman, RAFVR

Royal Air Force Museum, Grahame Park Way, Hendon, United Kingdom, NW9 5LL.
Flying Accident Cards, Air Ministry Form 1180, for 19 Aug 42 (Benjamin), 27 Aug 42 (Hoare), 24 Sep 42 (Oxenham), 26 Oct 42 (Monk), 31 Oct 42 (Zimek), 2 Nov 42 (Chappell), 13 Nov 42 (Quine), 13 May 43 (Heale), 28 May 43 (Biggs), 18 Aug 43 (Still), 1 Dec 43 (Adams SB), 17 Jul 44 (Oddy & Short), 1 Jul 45 (Chalmers) & 28 Jul 45 (Remez)
Pilot's flying log book of Flt. Lt. N. P. Gibbs, 1941-1975, 30 Sep 41-22 Oct 75, MF10005/6

LOGBOOKS, UNPUBLISHED RECORDS AND PERSONAL ACCOUNTS

Adams, John, interview (DVD) with Adams, S. Bruce, *1990s Home video interview: S. Bruce Adams re 41 Squadron at Tangmere*, March 1990
Anderson, Robert E., flying logbook
Benham, Douglas I., flying logbook, personal accounts & correspondence
Birbeck, Clive R., interview, via Dan Johnson
Chalmers, John A., personal accounts
Chattin, Peter W., flying logbook
Clanzy, T. Keith, flying logbook and obituary
Coleman, Patrick T., flying logbook, personal diary, Officer's Pay & Allowances Book
Collis, Ronald T. H., flying logbook, via Dan Johnson
Cowell, Peter, flying logbook, via Dan Johnson
Curtis, Keith R., flying logbook and personal accounts
Downing, William G., memoirs *Just for Fun* and *Chapter Two* (undated), & flying logbook
Fishburn, Doug, *Robert Edmund Anderson (RAAF 402337) in World War II*, 2005
Galitzine, Prince Emanuel V., flying logbook, via Dan Johnson
Gaze, F. A. O. 'Tony', personal accounts
Gibbs, N. Peter, flying logbook, via Dan Johnson
Glen, Arthur A., flying logbook
Graham, Peter B., personal accounts, & flying logbook, via Dan Johnson
Gray, James A. B., flying logbook
Griffith, Lyndon P., flying logbook
Hale, Peter H., flying logbook & personal accounts
Harding, Ross P., flying logbook, via Dan Johnson
Henry, David V. J., flying logbook
Hone, Douglas H., flying logbook, via Dan Johnson
Johnson, Dan, private collection of letters and personal papers dated 1982-1989, from Collis, Cowell, Galitzine, Gisborough, Graham, Harding, Henry, Hone, Irvine, Johnson, Maunder, Moffett, Newman, Refshauge, Rossow, DH Smith, Slack, Solak, Spencer, Stowe, Tebbit, Thiele, Wagner & Weeds
Johnson, Ronald, flying logbook, via Dan Johnson
Lloyd, J. Max W., flying logbook
Malone, C. J. 'Jack', flying logbook & personal accounts
Pairman, William R., flying logbook
Parry, Hugh L., personal accounts
Payne, Jim C. J., flying logbook, via Dan Johnson
Philips, Rob, *Rijklof van Goens*, May 1994
Rake, Derek S. V., personal accounts
Reid, Daniel J., flying logbook, via Dan Johnson
Rossow, Vivian J., flying logbook
Schauer, James A., Flt Lt (Ret) RAF, *The Destruction of Blohm & Voss BV 238 Prototype, Then the World's largest Aircraft, The Canadian Story*, January 2009
Slack, Thomas A. H., flying logbook, via Dan Johnson

Smets, Henri J. L. (350 Sqn), flying logbook, via Serge Bonge
Smith, Donald H., flying logbook, via Dan Johnson
Spencer, Terence, flying logbook & personal accounts
Stevenson, Ian T., flying logbook
Stowe, William N., flying logbook, via Dan Johnson
Tebbit, Donald F. J., flying logbook, via Dan Johnson
Wagner, Herbert A., personal accounts, & interview & flying logbook, via Dan Johnson
Ware, James P., flying logbook, via Dan Johnson
Whale, F. Victor, flying logbook

PERIODICALS

British Medical Journal, BMJ Publishing Group Ltd, BMA House, Tavistock Square, London WC1H 9JP, United Kingdom, http://www.bmj.com
The Daily Telegraph, Telegraph Group Ltd, 1 Canada Square, Canary Wharf, London E14 5DT, http://www.telegraph.co.uk/, editions of 9 Jan 03 (obit Galitzine)
The Globe and Mail, 444 Front Street West, Toronto, Ontario, M5V 2S9 Canada, http://www.globeandmail.com, various editions 1939-1947
The Hamilton Spectator, 44 Frid Street, Hamilton, Ontario, Canada, L8N 3G3, http://www.hamiltonspectator.com, various editions 1939-1949
The News Shopper, Mega House, Crest View Drive, Petts Wood BR5 1BT, United Kingdom, http://www.newsshopper.co.uk, 12 Jul 01 edition, 'Old Adversaries Reunite 56 Years Later'
The Sydney Morning Herald, John Fairfax Pty. Ltd, GPO Box 506, Sydney NSW 2001, Australia, http://www.smh.com.au, editions of 1940-1945
The Times, Times Newspapers Ltd, 3 Thomas More Square, London E98 1XY, many editions 1918-2009, incl 3 Dec 43 (missing notice, Parry), & 3 Feb, 2 Mar & 12 Mar 51 (death & obit, Lord Gisborough) and 9 Feb 09 (obit Spencer)

PUBLISHED WORKS

Aces High, A Tribute to the Most Notable Fighter Pilots of the British and Commonwealth Forces in WWII; Christopher Shores & Clive Williams, 1994, Grub Street, ISBN 1898697000
Aces High, A Further Tribute to the Most Notable Fighter Pilots of the British and Commonwealth Air Forces in WWII (Volume 2); Christopher Shores, 1999, Grub Street, ISBN 1898697000
Almost Unknown; The Story of Squadron Leader Tony Gaze OAM DFC**, Australian Spitfire ace and racing driver, Stewart Wilson, 2009, Chevron Publishing Group, ISBN 9780980591217
Australia in the War of 1939-45, Series 3 (Air) Vol III, Air War Against Germany and Italy 1939-43, John Herington, 1954, AWM, Canberra
Aviateurs de la Liberté; Mémorial des Forces Aériennes Françaises Libres, Col. Henri Lafont, Service Historique de l'Armée de l'Air, ISBN 2-904521-46-1
British Gallantry Awards, 1855-2000, Peter Duckers, 2001, Shire Publications, ISBN 0747805164
By Such Deeds; Honours and Awards in the Royal New Zealand Air Force, 1923-1999, Group Captain Colin M. Hanson, OBE, RNZAF (Rtd.), 2001, Volplane Press, ISBN 0473073013
Cassell's Chronology of World History; Dates, Events and Ideas that Made History, Hywel Williams, 2005, Weidenfeld & Nicolson, ISBN 0304357308
Chronology of the War at Sea, 1939-1945, Derek Masters (orig. in German as *Chronik des Seekrieges, 1939-1945*, Jurgen Rohwer & Gerhard Hümmelchen), Ian Allan, 1972, ISBN 0711002770
Diver! Diver! Diver!, RAF and American Fighter Pilots Battle the V-1 Assault over South-East England 1944-45, Brian Cull with Bruce Lander, 2008, Grub Street, ISBN 190494339X
The Fight for the Skies: Allied Fighter Aircraft in Europe and North Africa, 1939-1945, Roger A. Freeman, 1999, Sterling Publishing, ISBN 1854094130
The Fighter Aces of the RAF, 1939-1945, E. C. R. Baker, 1962, William Kimber, ASIN B0000CLIP8
Fighter Command War Diaries, July 1943 – June 1944, John Foreman, 2003, Crecy Publishing, ISBN 1871187435
Fighter Squadrons of the RAF and their Aircraft, John Rawlings, 1993 (revised edition), Crecy Publishing, ISBN 0947554246
For Your Tomorrow; A record of New Zealanders who have died while serving with the RNZAF and Allied Air Services since 1915, Vol. 1: Fates 1915-1942 (1998, ISBN 0473052741), Vol. 2: Fates 1943-1998 (1999, ISBN 0473063115) & Vol. 3; Biographies & Appendices (2008, ISBN 9780473128289) Errol W. Martyn, Volplane Press
From the Cockpit; Spitfire, Wg. Cdr. T. F. Neil DFC* AFC AE, 1990, Specialty Press, ISBN 0711019185
Griffon Spitfire Aces, Osprey Aircraft of the Aces No. 81, Andrew Thomas, 2008, Osprey Publishing Ltd, ISBN 9781846032981
Guests of the State; The story of Allied and Axis servicemen interned in Ireland during World War II, T. Ryle Dwyer, 1994, Brandon Book Publishers Ltd, ISBN 0863221823

Happy is the Day; A Spitfire Pilot's Story; Tom Slack, 1987, United Writers Publications, ISBN 185200004X

Hatching an Air Force; 2 SFTS, 5 SFTS, 1 BFTS, Uranquinty and Wagga Wagga, Peter Ibsley, 2002, Banner Books, ISBN 1875593241

The History of 122 Wing, 83 Group, Second Tactical Air Force, published Copenhagen, 1945; a semi-official history of the wing, attributed to no author, but including a foreword by CO Gp Capt 'Pat' Jameson

The JG 26 War Diary, Volume Two 1943-1945, Donald Caldwell, 1998, Grub Street, ISBN 1898697868

The Last Escape; The untold story of Allied prisoners of war in Germany 1944-45, John Nichol & Tony Rennell, 2002, Penguin Books, ISBN 041400388X

Malta; Blitzed But Not Beaten, Philip Vella, 1991, Progress Press Co Ltd, ISBN 9990930074

McIndoe's Army, The injured airmen who faced the world, Peter Williams & Ted Harrison, 1979, Pelham Books Ltd, ISBN 0720711916

Navy List, editions of 1951-1955, TNA library 359.3 ADH

RAF Fighter Command Victory Claims of World War Two, Part Two, 1 January 1941-30 June 1943, John Foreman, 2005, Red Kite, ISBN 0954620151

The Royal Air Force List, His/Her Majesty's Stationary Office, London, Crown copyright, editions of 1920-1960

The Royal Air Force Retired List, 1973, Her Majesty's Stationary Office, London, 1973, Crown copyright, SBN 117715840

Royal Air Force Bomber Command Losses of the Second World War, Vols. 1942 (1998, ISBN 090459789X), 1943 (2004, ISBN 0904597903), 1944 (1997, ISBN 0904597911) & 1945 (2004, ISBN 090459792X), W. R. Chorley, Midland Counties Publications

Royal Air Force Fighter Command Losses of the Second World War, Vol. 2, 1942-1943 (1998, ISBN 1857800753) & Vol. 3, 1944-1945 (2000, ISBN 1857800931), Norman L. R. Franks, Midland Publishing

Runways to Victory; Belgian Airfields and Allied Tactical Fighter Operations 1944-1945, Peter Celis, 2003, Marhav Publications, ISBN 9080563927

A Short Historical Account of No. 83 Group During the Period 1st April, 1943 to the End of the War in Europe, Sqn. Ldr. D. R. Morgan BA, 1957

Skypilot; Memoirs from Take-Off to Landing, Peter Graham, 2001, Pentland Books, ISBN 1858219094

Spitfire, Stewart Wilson, 1999, Aerospace Publications, ISBN 1875671455.

Spitfire; The History, Eric B. Morgan and Edward Shacklady, 1987-2000, Key Books, ISBN 0946219486

Sussex Airfields of the Second World War, Robin J. Brooks, 1993-2002, Countryside Books, ISBN 1853062596

Those Other Eagles; A Tribute to the British, Commonwealth and Free European Fighter Pilots who Claimed Between Two and Four Victories in Aerial Combat, 1939 – 1982, Christopher Shores, 2004, Grub Street, ISBN 1904010881

V-1 Flying Bomb 1942-1952; Hitler's infamous 'doodlebug'; New Vanguard series No. 106, Steven J. Zaloga, 2005, Osprey Publishing Ltd, ISBN 1841767913

Wing Leader, Gp Capt J. E. 'Johnnie' Johnson, 1956, Chatto & Windus

OFFICIAL BODIES AND WEBSITES

350 (Belgian) Squadron – Royal Air Force, Serge Bonge, http://www.350sqn.be/ (rtrvd Mar 12)

The A-4/V-2 Resource Site, http://www.v2rocket.com/start/deployment/watten.html (rtrvd Mar 10)

Aircrew Remembrance Society, http://www.aircrewremembrancesociety.com (rtrvd Mar 12)

Air Force Association of Canada, Honours & Awards Database, http://airforce.ca/honours-awards/search-awards-database/ (rtrvd Mar 12)

Air Historical Branch, Building 824, RAF Northolt, West End Road, Ruislip, Middlesex, HA4 6NG, UK, http://www.raf.mod.uk/ahb/ (rtrvd Mar 12)

Air of Authority; A History of RAF Organisation, Malcolm B. Barrass 2001-2012, http://www.rafweb.org (rtrvd Mar 12)

Australian War Memorial, GPO Box 345, Canberra ACT 2601, Australia, http://www.awm.gov.au (rtrvd Mar 12)

Belgian Aviation History Association Archaeology Team, Cynrik De Decker, http://users.telenet.be/airwareurope/home.html (rtrvd Jan 11)

Bomber Command Campaign Diary, http://www.raf.mod.uk/bombercommand/aug44.html, sep44.html, oct44.html, & nov44.html (rtrvd Mar 10)

Combat Chronology of the US Army Air Forces, Dec 1941-Sep 1945, Charles McGrew, http://paul.rutgers.edu/~mcgrew/wwii/usaf/html/index.html (rtrvd Jan 11)

The Commonwealth War Graves Commission, 2 Marlow Road, Maidenhead, Berkshire SL6 7DX, United Kingdom, http://www.cwgc.org/ (rtrvd Mar 12)

Democracy at War: Canadian Newspapers and the Second World War, Canadian War Museum, General Motors Court, 330 Sussex Drive, Ottawa, Ont., Canada, K1A 0M8, http://www.warmuseum.ca/cwm/exhibitions/newspapers/intro_e.shtml (rtrvd Mar 12)

Flight magazine (Flightglobal Archive), Reed Business Information, Quadrant House, Sutton, Surrey, UK, SM2 5AS, various editions of 1920-1950, http://www.flightglobal.com/pdfarchive/index.html (rtrvd Mar 12)

Gelsenkirchener Geschichten, Die interaktive Spurensammlung Gelsenkirchener Geschichte – Soziokulturelles von Gestern und Heute, http://www.gelsenkirchener-geschichten.de/ (rtrvd Feb 09)

Hansard 1803-2005, House of Commons Hansard, Parliamentary Archives, http://hansard.millbanksystems.com/sittings/1940s (rtrvd Mar 12)

Imperial War Museum, Lambeth Road, London SE1 6HZ, http://www.iwm.org.uk/ (rtrvd Jan 11), incl. 'The V Weapons Campaign Against Britain, 1944-1945', Terry Charman, Historian, Research & Information Dept., http://london.iwm.org.uk/upload/package/4/dday/pdfs/VWeaponsCampaign.pdf (rtrvd Jan 10)

King's College London, Liddell Hart Centre for Military Archives, Strand, London, UK, WC2R 2LS, Survey of the Papers of Senior UK Defence Personnel, 1900-1975, http://www.kcl.ac.uk/library/archivespec/collections/LHCMA.aspx (rtrvd Mar 12)

The Knesset; The Israeli Parliament, http://www.knesset.gov.il/main/eng/home.asp (rtrvd Jan 11)

The London Gazette, PO Box 7923, London SW8 5WF, United Kingdom, editions of 1930-1975 (Of particular note: No. 37711, Supplement to The London Gazette, 3 Sep 1946, *Operations in North-West Europe from 6th June, 1944, to 5th May, 1945*; War Office despatch submitted to the Secretary of State for War by Field Marshal The Viscount Montgomery of Alamein, GCB DSO, 1 Jun 1946.), http://www.london-gazette.co.uk/search (rtrvd Jan 11)

The Luftwaffe, 1933-1945, Michael Holm, 1997-2011, http://www.ww2.dk/ (rtrvd Jan 11)

National Air Force Museum of Canada, PO Box 1000, Station Forces, Astra, Ont., Canada, K0K 3W0, http://www.airforcemuseum.ca/ (rtrvd Jan 11)

New Zealand Fighter Pilots Museum, State Highway 6, Wanaka, New Zealand, http://www.nzfpm.co.nz/ (rtrvd Jan 11)

Peak District Air Accident Research Website, Alan L. Clark, 2000-2011, http://www.peakdistrictaircrashes.co.uk/ (rtrvd Mar 12)

Polish Air Force 1940-1947 Operations Record Books, http://orb.polishaf.pl (rtrvd Jul 11)

Polish Squadrons Remembered, http://www.polishsquadronsremembered.com (rtrvd Jul 11)

RAF Commands; a history of the squadrons and associated units forming RAF Commands during the period September 1939 to August 1945, website and forum, and its contributors; Ross McNeill, 1999-2011, http://www.rafcommands.com/ & http://www.rafcommands.com/forum/index.php (rtrvd Nov 11)

The Royal Air Force, History Section, http://www.raf.mod.uk/history/ (rtrvd Jan 11)

Schwere Luftangriffe auf Osterfeld im 2. Weltkrieg, Josef Kortz, http://www.osterfeld-westfalen.de/krieg.html (rtrvd Feb 09)

The Spitfire Society, PO Box 202, Biggin Hill, Westerham, TN16 9DA, England, http://www.spitfiresociety.demon.co.uk/ (rtrvd Jan 11)

Stadtmuseum Duisberg, *Bomben auf Duisberg; Der Luftkrieg und die Stadt 1940 – 1960*, http://www.stadtmuseum-duisburg.de/austellung/download/Bombenkrieg4.pdf (rtrvd Feb 2010)

USAAS-USAAC-USAAF Aircraft Serial Numbers – 1908 to Present, http://www.joebaugher.com/usaf_serials/usafserials.html (rtrvd Sep 11)

Volksbund Deutsche Kriegsgräberfürsorge e. V. [German War Graves Commission], Bundesgeschäftsstelle, Werner-Hilpert-Strasse 2, 34112 Kassel, Germany, http://www.volksbund.de/kurzprofil/homepage_en.asp (rtrvd Jan 11)

The World War Two Nominal Roll, Department of Veterans' Affairs, PO Box 9998, Canberra ACT 2601, Australia, http://www.ww2roll.gov.au/ (rtrvd Jan 11)